D1146319

C003296267

Portsmouth
CITY COUNCIL
LIBRARY SERVICE

FOR USE
IN THE
REFERENCE
LIBRARY
ONLY

PORTSMOUTH

WITHDRAWN

CLASS NO.
TITLE NO.

0660007614

STORE

CL-5

DA

KILOMETRES
500   0   500

300

5047 km
3138 mi

ST. JOHN'S

EL-PORT
SQUES

EY

2422 km
505 mi

QUEBEC

FREDERICTON   HALIFAX

TRANS - CANADA   HIGHWAY

OTTAWA 190 km
118 mi   MONTRÉAL

TORONTO

ALERT

HAMPSHIRE COUNTY LIBRARY

REFERENCE BOOK

IS BOOK IS NO
THE L   JT
SSION

Canada Year Book 1976-77

Special Edition

An annual review
of economic, social and political
developments in Canada

Published by authority of the
Minister of Industry, Trade and Commerce

© Minister of Supply and Services Canada 1977

Available by mail from

Publications Distribution
Statistics Canada
Ottawa, Canada K1A 0T6

Printing and Publishing
Supply and Services Canada
Ottawa, Canada K1A 0S9

or through your bookseller

Catalogue No. CS11-202/1977

ISBN 0-660-00761-4

Price, Canada: $12.50
Other countries: $15.00
Price subject to change without notice

Typesetting: Southam Business Publications Limited, Contract OKP 6-1910
Printing: Librairie Beauchemin Limitée, Contract O2KT 6-8176A

HAMPSHIRE COUNTY LIBRARY

5052298

Preface

This special edition of the *Canada Year Book* should stand as a landmark in statistical records for it is a bridge between the old and new systems of measurement. All data in imperial units are repeated in metric and all imperial tables are followed by equivalent metric tables in colour for immediate identification.

It is planned that future editions will carry metric measurements only for many sectors of the economy. In other areas, both imperial and metric will be continued until conversion is complete.

The *Canada Year Book 1976-77* covers as much information as is usually contained in two separate editions. Since the series began in 1905, such double-year volumes have been produced periodically to provide continuity of reporting. An earlier series was published between 1885 and 1904, based on the first *Year-Book and Almanac of British North America for 1867*.

The latest information available at time of preparation is given. More than 600 tables, meticulously compiled from hundreds of official sources, provide details along with data from recent years. In every chapter, sources are listed. The appendices, going beyond statistics, give useful information about federal government departments and agencies, a summary of legislation of a two-year period, a chronology of significant events, Canadian honours, Canada's diplomatic and consular service, and books about Canada. The introductory article on Canada's conversion to the metric system was authorized by Metric Commission Canada.

This book could not have been compiled without the assistance and specialized knowledge of hundreds of experts outside of as well as within Statistics Canada. We gratefully acknowledge their contribution.

Peter Kirkham
Chief Statistician of Canada
Ottawa, December 1977

Produced by the Canada Year Book Section
Information Services, Statistics Canada
Assistant Director – Publishing: Tom Mitchell

Editor: Borgny Eileraas Pearson
French editor and technical adviser: Frances L. O'Malley
Production supervisor and editor of tables: Ella Blair
Editorial assistants: J.H. Johnstone, Diane Basso,
                    Denis Schuthe, Susan Aldridge
Production liaison: Alice Guay
Production assistants: Patricia Harris, Audrey Miles,
                    Louise Cojbasic, Helen Wieland
Book design: Sarah Gould
Cover and jacket design: John MacCraken
Chart preparation: Charles Gravel, Gérard Montplaisir,
                    Danielle Baum
End leaf maps: Department of Energy, Mines and Resources
Metric Coordinator for Statistics Canada: Jack MacKinnon
Verification of metric conversions: Alma Brown, Constance Blakey

Contents

Canada converts to the metric system

Canada has made significant progress along the road to conversion to the metric system. Although use of that system has been legal in Canada since 1871, long-standing identification with the measuring system of Great Britain tended to confine use of metric units to the scientific area only. The impetus to give primacy to metric measurement began with the publication by the Government of Canada of the *White paper on metric conversion in Canada* in January 1970. Metric Commission Canada, which was set up in 1971 as a result of that white paper, estimated that Canada's conversion would be substantially completed by the end of 1980, and would be marked by a voluntary and cooperative endeavour. By handling conversion on a voluntary basis and spreading it over several years, the commission hoped to keep costs to a minimum by linking changes to normal replacement of machinery and supplies.

In 1974 the National Program of Guideline Dates for Metric Conversion was approved and four distinct phases for conversion set out. Phase One (investigation) was virtually completed in 1975. Eleven steering committees and about 60 sector committees by that time were deciding on policies, objectives and strategies for metric conversion in almost every sector of the economy. Planning, the second phase, progressed during 1975-76, with some sectors entering the third phase, scheduling. The final phase, actual implementation of metric measurement in the various fields of the economy, was already partly under way in a few sectors such as Health and Welfare, Meteorology, Food and Beverages. With implementation expected to peak in 1978, the end of 1980 has been forecast as the guideline date when the economy will be working substantially in metric units.

On a day-to-day basis, Canadians have gradually become exposed to the widening use of metric terms. On April 1, 1975 the daily public weather reports and forecasts announced temperatures in degrees Celsius (the name of the Swedish astronomer who devised the system in 1742). On September 1, 1975 precipitation was measured in millimetres (mm) for rainfall and centimeters (cm) for snowfall. On April 1, 1976 the Atmospheric Environment Service began giving wind speeds in kilometres per hour (km/h), atmospheric pressure in kilopascals (kPa) and distances in kilometres (km).

Since October 1, 1975 water flow, usage and related data have been given in metric units on the St. Lawrence Seaway; the Canadian St. Lawrence Seaway Authority and the United States Seaway Development Corporation are cooperating to ensure that conversion may proceed smoothly.

An increasing number of commercial household products became available in metric dimensions during 1975 and 1976. Canada's sugar refining companies now mark their product in metric-sized packages (1 kg, 2 kg, 4 kg, 10 kg and 40 kg). Clinical thermometers changed over to Celsius in 1975, with normal body temperature of 37°C indicated on the stem. After December 1977 all "new" wine will be bottled in metric sizes. Metric cooking measures standards published by the Canadian Government Specifications Board call for three liquid measures, three dry and five small spoon-type measures; all have been produced and are available in retail outlets.

Why Canada is going metric

In a world which is now 99% on the metric system or in the process of actively converting, the potential benefits of the system to Canada amply justify conversion. These derive principally from the inherent simplicity of teaching and understanding the system with its inevitable and far-reaching effects on trade and commerce.

As to simplicity, everything in the metric system is in multiples or divisions of 10. In the imperial or customary system, the numerical progressions used to create multiples or subdivisions of units are complex. A yard is multiplied by 1,760 to make a mile; it is divided by three to make a foot, further divided by 12 to make an inch which in turn is divided into halves, quarters, eighths and sixteenths. The ounce is achieved by dividing the pound by 16; a division of the ounce by a further 16 produces the dram which, when divided by $27^{11}/_{32}$ results in the grain. The multiple of the bushel, the dry barrel, is gained by multiplying by $3^{9}/_{32}$. The bushel's subdivision, the peck, is made by dividing by four. The peck divided by eight makes a dry quart and that divided by two gives a dry pint. In the 10-based system, on the other hand, multiplication by 10 produces multiples and division by 10 subdivisions. Fractions are replaced by decimals. A single progression is learned for all units of length, capacity and mass.

Education in relation to conversion to the metric system involves two prime audiences: the general public and the student in the educational system. For the former, a continuing and ambitious information program is being carried out by MCC. With regard to the latter (a provincial responsibility), governments have been training teachers and adapting curricula accordingly. The process began with the teaching of the metric system as the predominant method in Grades 1, 2 and 3 in British Columbia in September 1973; it should be completed in all provinces and territories by the 1979-80 school year. Thus the burden of learning by rote an illogical and complex system of weights and measures is being progressively lifted from the shoulders of school children, with significant saving of time.

Many professional associations require use of metric measurement in their technical publications, and in scientific work outside universities there is consistent use of metric units. Support of conversion has been voiced by such groups as the Canadian Pharmaceutical Association, the Canadian Council of Professional Engineers, the Chemical Institute of Canada and the Engineering Institute of Canada.

It is in the area of trade and commerce that the most marked benefits may be expected to accrue in the longer term. The United States and Canada remain one another's best customer, and the United States has been going metric for several years. Conversion in the Commonwealth and Japan involves many Canadian customers, and the countries of the European Common Market are long-standing users of the metric system. Future trade with the developing nations, virtually all of which have adopted the metric system, may prove of significance. Because a trading nation must be alert to the measurement and standards system of the buyer, the overwhelming world movement to the metric system is an unanswerable argument for Canadian conversion.

History of measurement and the metric system

There is general agreement that the first quantity measured must have been length, and that the first linear units were based on parts of the human body. The thickness of a finger is known to be the origin of the digit, a unit of ¾ inch that probably came from the Sumerians but whose first known use was by the ancient Egyptians. It lingers today in rural areas of Great Britain, their metrication notwithstanding. The measure of a man's thumb is the origin of the inch as is his foot that of the foot. In ancient Egypt, among other early civilizations, the cubit was the distance from the tip of the middle finger, when the hand was outstretched, to the elbow (the hieroglyph for a cubit is a forearm). The hand (4 inches) is still the unit used to measure the height of horses. The pace was about equal to the distance covered by an adult male in a long step, and the fathom was the distance covered by the outstretched arms, from the finger tips of one hand to those of the other.

It is likely that volume was the second quantity that primitive man undertook to measure. This was probably effected at first by using any convenient receptacle — cupped hands, shells, gourds, the skulls of large animals, pottery. The measuring of weight (more properly "mass" because weight is the measure of attraction between two objects controlled by gravitational force) was a more complex process and no doubt ranged over the millennia from the hefting of an object in one hand against stones in the other to the more sophisticated balance scale. This form of measure among ancient peoples appears to have been largely restricted to precious metals and gems while in most commercial dealings either capacity measures were used or items simply counted, as they often are today.

By cultural diffusion over thousands of years the variants of many measuring systems, used by great trading states, passed from Mesopotamia and Egypt to Greece and in turn to Rome. South European adoption saw changes in the names of units, but little change in values. Rome made few innovations but nonetheless influenced the development of the traditional system in several ways. For example, through trade and conquest the Roman Empire imposed a fairly uniform system of measurement throughout the known world, although local systems were honoured in many cases. It adopted a duodecimal system (one based on divisions and multiples of 12) which still exists in the 12 ounces in a troy pound and 12 inches in a foot. Much nomenclature in the traditional system derives from Latin. The abbreviation for pound, lb., comes from libra, the same word in Latin, and the libra and the pes (the Roman foot) were divided into unciae, or 12 parts. From unciae derive the inch and ounce, as does the mile from a thousand paces (a pace equalling five Roman feet or two strides).

After the fall of the Roman Empire a multiplicity of measuring systems were current among the tribes and localities of Europe. The resulting confusion was assisted by the advent of the Dark Ages, the subsequent feudal system, and the widespread introduction of Arabic numerals to Europe after the 10th century. Feudal barons decreed measurement standards in their own territories and the often conflicting edicts or monarchs compounded the chaos. The crude systems of the Middle Ages prevailed without much question until the 16th and early 17th centuries, when scientists began to think of regularization. Science could not progress without an exact, uniform and invariable system of weights and measures. At the end of the 18th century, scientists created the metric system.

Origin of the system is generally credited to Gabriel Mouton, a vicar in Lyons, France. In 1670 he devised a decimal system of weights and measures based on many of the same principles as the metric system.

Subsequently, committees of the Academy of Science in Paris developed the system more than a century later, at the instigation of Charles Maurice de Talleyrand-Périgord. In April 1790 he proposed to the revolutionary National Assembly that the system of weights and measures be reviewed, with a new length unit to be adopted, based on some unchanging standard in nature. It was decided in March 1791 to measure the length of the quadrant which lies on the Paris meridian and let one 10 millionth of this distance equal the basic unit of length for the new system. Units of mass and volume to follow would also be based in some way on this primary measure. It was not until 1793 that a name was picked for the new unit. It was called the metre, from the Greek word metron, which simply meant "a measure".

It was decided that the metre should be based on multiples of 10. It was further decided that all multiples of the metre would contain the word "metre" in them with a short prefix. All units smaller, submultiples, would use Latin words or roots as prefixes and all larger units would use Greek prefixes. For most uses, the metre needed to be split or expanded into only six other units describing length. Thus multiples between related units ceased to be a confusion of 2s, 3s, 4s, 12s and 16s, among many others, but just simple powers of 10.

From January 1, 1840 the metric system became mandatory in France. The more general acceptance in Europe was gradual, but the London Exposition of 1851 marked something of a turning point. Here businessmen, manufacturers and merchants mingled with scientists, statesmen and economists and a new impetus was afforded the metric principle. Unofficial international committees were formed to consider the subject of weights and measures. In 1870 the French government invited other nations to a conference and 15 nations attended, including Great

Britain and the United States. This conference led to the signing in 1875 of the Treaty of the Metre, a treaty under which an International Bureau of Weights and Measures was established. France ceded Le Pavillon de Breteuil, a former royal estate, to the bureau and declared the land, still the world centre of metrology, to be international territory. The treaty also established an international conference of a diplomatic nature with the designation General Conference on Weights and Measures which was to meet nominally every six years. Between meetings of the conference the general supervision of the International Bureau was to be in the hands of an international committee.

The first task of the International Bureau of Weights and Measures was the construction of new standards for the metre and kilogram. Standards were to be constructed for distribution to the nations supporting the bureau in addition to the national standards to be kept in France, and the task was a large one. At the first General Conference on Weights and Measures held in 1889, the work of the International Bureau in constructing and comparing the standards was approved, new definitions of the metre and kilogram in forms of the new standards were adopted and the distribution of international standards to the interested governments was authorized. The prototype of the metre was made of a platinum alloy with 10% iridium; the length of the metre bar when it was at $0°C$ was chosen as the international standard. Two things disturbed scientists, however, about using a prototype for a standard. One was that some unchangeable standard in nature was preferable and the other was that the prototype might be destroyed. A search was made for some unchangeable standard in nature which was exactly the same size as the metre prototype. In 1927, on advice from the Nobel prize-winning American physicist Albert Abraham Michelson, the metre was redefined as being a length equal to "1 553 164.13 wave lengths of red light emitted by a cadmium vapour lamp excited under certain specified conditions". This was a provisional definition and later the metre was redefined as "1 650 763.73 wave lengths of the orange-red line of krypton 86". This definition of the standard metre is the most precise so far, based on a fact of nature that will always be the same. It was adopted in 1960 at the eleventh meeting of the General Conference on Weights and Measures.

Recent movement to the metric system

The movement to adopt a standard metric system has become world-wide in scope. It is virtually universal, now encompassing over 99% of the world's population. Within the English-speaking world, Great Britain opted in May 1965 for a gradual adoption of metric units, spurred by the industrial sector of the economy. A target of 1975 was set for complete conversion, although that has since been postponed. Australia passed a Metric Conversion Act in June 1970, stating as its object the progressive introduction of the metric system of measurement of physical quantities with a target date for completion of 1979. New Zealand established a Metric Advisory Board in 1969 and in April 1970 the government announced approval in principle of conversion over a seven-year period, giving as a target date the end of 1976. Both states are now about 75% converted. South Africa commenced its program in 1966 and 10 years later it was substantially completed. Canada has benefited from the experience of these countries.

The fact that the United States officially adopted the metric system in December 1975 is a point of high interest to Canada in view of the massive two-way trade between the two countries. Two systems of weights and measures exist side by side in the US today with roughly equal but separate legislative sanction. Throughout US history the customary system (inherited from, but now different from, the British imperial system) has been customarily used. A plethora of federal and state legislation has given it standing, through implication, as the primary weights and measures system of the United States. However, the metric system is the only one that has ever received specific legislative sanction by Congress (known as the "Law of 1866"). Over the last 100 years the metric system has seen slow, steadily increasing use and today is of importance nearly equal to the customary system.

On February 10, 1964 the National Bureau of Standards of the United States issued the following statement: "Henceforth it shall be the policy of the National Bureau of Standards to use the units of the International System (SI), as adopted by the Eleventh General Conference on Weights and Measures (October 1960), except when the use of these units would obviously impair communication or reduce the usefulness of a report". SI is the abbreviation of Système International, the internationally recognized term used in reference to the metric system. On July 2, 1971 following the report of a metric conversion study committee, the US commerce secretary recommended gradual changeover during a 10-year period at the end of which the United States would be predominantly, but not exclusively, on the metric system.

Already the United States is moving quickly in some influential sectors. For example, 50% of all components in General Motors automobiles are now in metric dimensions. The Ford plant in Lima, Ohio, has been producing all-metric engines since 1973, and the essentially all-metric General Motors Chevette is now on the market. Chrysler intends to launch an all-metric sub-compact in 1977, and newsprint, 80% of which the US imports from Canada, will be in metric measure within two years.

The President of the United States signed the Metric Conversion Act on December 23, 1975 formalizing the US government's involvement in bringing about a smoother transition to the use of the metric system in America. It outlined the general duties and responsibilities of the United States Metric Board which was to coordinate and synchronize increasing use of metric measurement in the various sectors of the economy.

Background to metric conversion in Canada

Canada's long interest in the metric system began in 1870. In that year, Parliament appointed a committee to inquire into the United Kingdom's progress in establishing a uniform international system of decimal measures, weights and coins, and to report on how such a system might be applied in Canada.

The committee reported in part to the House of Commons: "In contemplation of the early adoption of the metric system, and with a view that the youth of the country be made acquainted with it, your Committee would call the attention of the House to the propriety of suggesting to the Government the importance of causing this system to be taught in all schools over which they have control directly or indirectly. It is simple, easily learned, and not readily forgotten; and young men instructed in it will thus acquire additional facility in understanding the trade with countries where this system prevails exclusively."

Following the committee's recommendations, Parliament passed an act in 1871 whose object was "to render permissive the use of the Metric or of the decimal system of Weights and Measures." This event was recorded in *The Canada Year Book 1872-73:* "The measure found very strenuous and earnest advocacy in the House of Commons and its success not only in Great Britain but throughout the civilized world is only a question of time." This was followed in 1873 by the Weights and Measures Act legalizing the use of the metric system in commerce and trade.

Despite this encouraging beginning, Canada did not advance very far toward metric until almost 100 years later. It kept a foot in both the metric and inch-pound camps, however, which was in itself something of a feat. For example, in 1907 Canada became the first country of the British Empire after Great Britain to sign the Treaty of the Metre, and Canada has participated ever since in the activities of the International Bureau of Weights and Measures. By 1913, all precise measuring instruments were being verified in terms of the metre. In 1951, Parliament passed the Length and Mass Units Act which defined the yard as a fraction of the international metre and the pound as a fraction of the international kilogram. At the same time, it passed a new Weights and Measures Act which provided for the standards of measure and weight to be calibrated and certified in accordance with the provisions of the Length and Mass Units Act. About the same time, the Electrical and Photometric Units Act defined the units of electrical measure and the units of photometric measure. However, the legalization of the metric system did not lead to its extensive use in industry or trade. Metric units had been used to some extent in the photographic, optical, sports, electrical and pharmaceutical fields for many years.

The question of metric conversion for Canada came increasingly to the fore in the late 1960s after the British decision in 1965 to abandon the imperial system in favour of the metric. Representations had been pressed upon the government, in varying degrees of urgency, from such widely diverse segments of the nation as the Consumers' Association of Canada, the Canadian Home and School and Parent-Teacher Federation, the Agricultural Institute of Canada, the Canadian Chamber of Commerce, the Canadian Teachers' Federation, the Canadian Pharmaceutical Association, the Canadian Council of Professional Engineers, the Chemical Institute of Canada, the Engineering Institute of Canada, the Canadian Hospital Association and the Canadian Construction Association. These concerned and broadly representative groups of citizens had realized the logic of conversion in an almost totally metric world. They had become convinced of the practical benefits to be derived from this system in competitive world markets.

Consequently an Interdepartmental Committee on the International System of Units was established in January 1968 by the government to study the matter. By its terms of reference it was to organize studies with regard to the applicability of SI in Canada, examine and report on any apparent need for action by government to assist in the adoption of SI, consider the adequacy of communication and information in the public and private sectors on all aspects of the subject, and encourage liaison and coordination of activities in the field of conversion within existing departments and agencies. The committee possessed information on the experience of other countries that were in the process of metric conversion as well as a report of studies undertaken by the Canadian Standards Association. Although it held no public hearings, it made an in-depth study of the present and proposed use of the metric system and considered the views and resolutions of professional, industrial and consumer organizations. It also examined the implications of metric conversion for the consumer, for education and for industry and trade.

White paper on metric conversion

The committee's report in mid-1969 led to the tabling in the House of Commons of the white paper on metric conversion on January 16, 1970 urging conversion to the metric system.

In it the government accepted its leadership responsibility in planning for the processes of change. Realizing the need for a transitional period, the government would propose arrangements for the division of responsibilities in the public and private sectors for studies, planning, consultation and organization of a coordinated approach. The process of change would be initiated within departments of the government itself. Public education as to the objectives and timing of conversion would be an endeavour of prime importance. Liaison with provincial and territorial governments would be initiated and maintained.

In order to initiate metric conversion in Canada the principal actions proposed were the establishment of a full-time metric commission to advise upon and coordinate overall planning and the assignment of responsibility to the projected Standards Council of Canada to develop standards for conversion in industry.

Establishment of Metric Commission Canada

To implement the policy set out in the white paper, the Metric Commission was created by order-in-council in June 1971 for the purpose of advising the Minister of Industry, Trade and Commerce on plans for conversion. To this end the commission initiated studies relating to the implications for the Canadian economy; prepared, in wide consultation, an overall program for conversion; and disseminated information concerning conversion. The commission was to advise the minister on the need for legislation or any other action that might be required to facilitate conversion and to make such reports on its activities as the minister might require. In July 1971 the first full-time chairman of the Metric Commission was appointed. He began to organize a group of part-time metric commissioners who would represent Canadians in all regions and cover a cross-section of the economy, and called the Metric Commission's first meeting on January 19, 1972.

The implementation of metric conversion requires that standards be available in metric SI terms to support that conversion. Standards set out the requirements for products, materials, devices, processes and services, to ensure uniformity and the safety of their users. Consequently, standards are one of the fundamental tools through which metric conversion will be achieved.

Standards in use in Canada may be categorized according to the level at which they are approved. These levels are: the company, the industry, and the standard-writing organization, as well as the national and international levels. The Standards Council of Canada is responsible for providing the required coordination for the conversion of standards within Canada. That council is also the Canadian member of the International Organization for Standardization and sponsors the Canadian membership on the International Electrotechnical Commission. These latter organizations, with headquarters in Geneva, represent national member organizations in countries containing four fifths of the world's population.

Effects of conversion on everyday life

In supermarkets, the use of metric designations on packages of food has already become familiar to shoppers. The effects of conversion will eventually pervade the lives of all Canadians though change to metric standards and language may have little or no effect on some products. These include those that are designated by numbered sizes (such as women's dresses) that are not the actual dimensions.

Long after the metric system has come into full use, thousands of homes will contain unconverted hardware items. People will not discard bathroom scales until they are no longer working. Kitchen stoves with thermometers in Celsius will make their due appearance but the old stove may be good for another 10 or 15 years. A change to the metric system will have no apparent effect on such domestic items as toasters, mixers, oil burners, electric motors, garden tools, lawn-mowers and many others for which dimensions are inconsequential. Eventually a new lawn-mower will cut a 48-cm swath instead of a 19-inch one, but to the user the two will be the same.

In sports, reaction to conversion may be varied. All international competition in swimming, track and field is in metric terms. In most court and playing-field sports adaptation will probably be the permanent response, keeping the same dimensions expressed in metric language. Significant changes to a baseball diamond would be unlikely because of the effect on the game. Distance between bases will remain the same though that distance may be described as 27.43 m instead of 90 feet. The same is true of basketball, tennis and squash. Football would present little difficulty since the field is almost exactly 100 m (metres) long.

In the important realm of transportation, highway speed limits are among the first obvious conversions. Adjustments are made to the nearest round figure. For example, 50 miles an hour converts closely to 80 km/h. September 1977 was the month chosen for Canadian speed limits to be posted in kilometres per hour (km/h) instead of miles per hour. As far as railroad lines are concerned there would be no question of tearing up track and replacing it with the metric-gauge track of Europe: two different gauges of track in a system would require two different sets of wheels and axles for every locomotive and car, and this would be both impossible and useless. Inevitably unusual and unthought of problems arise for solution. The British Metrication Board was posed the question of what to do about mileposts (used to pin-point accidents and repairs) situated along rail track. Relocation by kilometre would require 60% more posts so the mileposts were renamed; for example Milepost 42 is now simply Marker 42.

While almost every corner of life will be affected by metric conversion, there will still be some untranslatable expressions that have entered the language too deeply to be affected. Pound-cake, for example, will undoubtedly retain its name; those who are given the proverbial inch may continue to take a mile; however, the western "ten-gallon hat" is already being described as a 45 litre hat in cartoons.

Information program of Metric Commission Canada

The primary role of Metric Commission Canada is to prepare and coordinate an overall metric conversion program within the Canadian economy. Its information resposibilities are to furnish, publish and disseminate information on the plans for and progress of metric conversion.

During 1975-76 the commission's information program was expanded to make Canadians aware of the four-phase program of guideline dates for metric conversion; to generate a national climate of receptivity and acceptance of the metric system; to ensure that Canadians understand metric measurements; and to inform the appropriate audiences of coming events in the conversion plans that are established by the sector committees.

The inauguration of Celsius in weather reports in April 1975 occasioned a record number of public inquiries in the preceding month, and less than 1% of the letters received were critical. Inquiries handled by the Metric Commission for the year exceeded 120,000, 60% in English and 40% in French. When rainfall was expressed in millimetres (mm) and snowfall in centimetres (cm) after September 1, 1975 there was not any increase in inquiries.

A stylized M and maple leaf symbolizes metric conversion in Canada. Properly applied by organizations in all sectors of the economy, it identifies metric materials, supplies, publications and products. The growing use of this symbol will mark Canada's adoption of the simplest, most advanced and universal metric measurement system — the International System of Units (SI).

Relative weights and measures: Canadian imperial, United States and metric SI

The following are conversion factors for units in this edition of the *Canada Year Book* and some of the others in common use. For a fuller listing, readers are referred to *Canadian Metric Practice Guide,* published by the Canadian Standards Association, 178 Rexdale Blvd., Rexdale, Ont., M9W 1R3. In metric SI, spaces are used instead of commas to separate groups of three digits; a space is optional with a four-digit number. In all Statistics Canada publications, a period is used as a decimal marker.

Area
1 square mile = 2.589 988 km^2 (square kilometres)
1 acre = 4 046.856 m^2 (square metres) = 0.404 685 6 ha (hectare)

Length
1 inch = 0.025 4 m (metres)
1 foot = 0.304 8 m
1 statute mile = 5,280 feet = 1.609 344 km
1 nautical mile = 6,080 feet = 1.852 km
1 yard = 0.914 4 m

Volume and capacity
1 board foot (fbm) = 2.359 737 dm^3 (cubic decimetres)
1 cubic foot = 28.316 85 dm^3
1 bushel = 36.368 72 dm^3
1 gallon = 160 fluid ounces = 4.546 090 dm^3 (cubic decimetres or litres)
1 quart = 40 fluid ounces = 1.136 522 dm^3
1 pint = 20 fluid ounces = 0.568 261 dm^3
1 US gallon = 128 fluid ounces = 3.785 412 dm^3
1 US quart = 32 fluid ounces = 0.946 353 dm^3
1 US pint = 16 fluid ounces = 0.473 176 dm^3
1 imperial proof gallon = 1.36 US proof gallons
1 barrel (petroleum or other liquid) = 34.9723 Canadian gallons = 42 US
    gallons = 0.158 987 3 m^3
1 registered ton = 100 cubic feet* = 2.831 685 m^3

Mass (weight)
1 ounce (avoirdupois) = 0.91146 ounce troy (oz t) = 28.349 523 g (grams)
1 ounce (troy or apothecary) = 31.103 476 8 g
1 pound (avoirdupois) = 0.453 592 37 kg (kilograms)
1 ton (short) = 2,000 pounds = 907.184 74 kg
1 ton (long) = 2,240 pounds = 1 016.046 908 8 kg
1 registered ton (see Volume and capacity above)

Length and mass
1 ton mile = 1.459 997 t.km (metric tonne kilometres)

Temperature
Fahrenheit temperature = 1.8 (Celsius temperature) +32
Celsius temperature = 5/9 (Fahrenheit temperature −32)

The following weights and measures are used in connection with the principal field crops and fruits.

Crops (1 000 kg = 1 tonne)	Pounds per bushel	Kilograms per bushel
Wheat, potatoes and peas	60	27.215 8
Oats	34	15.422 3
Barley and buckwheat	48	21.772 7
Rye, flaxseed and corn	56	25.401 4
Rapeseed, mustard seed, pears, plums, cherries, peaches and apricots	50	22.679 9
Sunflower seed	24	10.886 3
Apples	42	19.050 8

Miscellaneous
1 quart of strawberries or raspberries = 1.50 pounds (0.680 39 kg) in BC
                                        = 1.25 pounds (0.566 99 kg) in all other provinces
It takes 2.3 bu (62.596 3 kg) of wheat to produce 100 lb. (45.359 2 ĸg) of flour.

*Gross registered tonnage of a ship, as used by *Lloyd's Register of Shipping,* is a measurement of the total capacity of the ship and is not a measure of weight. Net registered tonnage equals gross registered tonnage minus space used for accommodation, machinery, engine area and fuel storage, and so states the cargo carrying ability of the ship.

Physiography

Chapter 1

Physiography   Chapter 1

In this chapter, metric figures for text and tables are conversions rather than official metric designations. Nautical miles are used at sea, for ocean transportation and air navigation, and statute miles for coastline and inland measurements. Use of the nautical mile, equal to one minute of latitude, will be continued internationally and will be extended to the Great Lakes shipping system; the exception will be in measurements less than a nautical mile, when metres will be used.

Geography   1.1

Canada, occupying the northern half of North America with the exception of Alaska and Greenland, is the largest country in the Western Hemisphere and second largest in the world. The lands within its 3,851,809 sq miles (9 976 139 km²) of territory are extremely diverse, ranging from almost semi-tropical areas of the Great Lakes peninsula and the southwest Pacific Coast, wide fertile prairies and great areas of mountains, rocks and lakes to seemingly endless stretches of northern wilderness and arctic tundra. The southernmost point is Middle Island in Lake Erie, at 41°41′N. In a straight line 2,875 miles (4 627 km) northward, past the treeline and far into the Arctic, is Cape Columbia on Ellesmere Island, Canada's northernmost point, at 83°07′N. From east to west at the widest point, the straight-line distance is 3,223 miles (5 187 km) — from Cape Spear, Nfld., at 52°37′W, to Mount St. Elias, YT, at 141°W.

Canada is at the crossroads of contact with principal powers and some of the most populous areas of the world. In the south, it borders on the United States for 3,986.8 miles (6 416 km). In the north, the Arctic archipelago penetrates far into the polar basin, making Canada neighbour to northern Europe and the Union of Soviet Socialist Republics. In the east, Labrador and the island of Newfoundland command the shortest crossings of the north Atlantic Ocean and link Canada geographically with Britain and France. In the west, the broad arc of land between Vancouver in southern British Columbia and Whitehorse in Yukon Territory provides departure points for crossings of the north Pacific Ocean between continental North America and the Far East. The length of the Yukon–British Columbia border adjoining Alaska is 1,539.8 miles (2 478 km).

In size, Canada's 3,851,809 sq miles (9 976 139 km²) may be compared with the area of the USSR at 8,649,539 sq miles (22 402 202 km²), China (including Taiwan) at 3,705,408 sq miles (9 596 962 km²), and Brazil at 3,286,488 sq miles (8 511 964 km²). It is more than 40 times the size of Britain and 18 times the size of France. This immense area, which seems to afford extensive scope for settlement, imposes its own limitations. Much of the land is mountainous and rocky or under an arctic climate. Probably not more than one third of the total is developed; less than 8% is occupied farm land and 27% productive forests. The population, at 22,992,604 on June 1, 1976, may be compared with 214,529,000 for the United States (1976) and with 107,145,000 for Brazil (1975), according to official estimates published by the United Nations.

Politically, Canada is divided into 10 provinces and two territories. Each province is sovereign in its own sphere and administers its own natural resources. The resources (except for game) of the Yukon Territory and Northwest Territories, because of their remoteness, their great extent and meagre and scattered populations, are administered by the federal government. The approximate land and freshwater areas of the provinces and territories are given in Table 1.1.

There is no permanent settlement in approximately 89% of Canada. Only the smallest province, Prince Edward Island, is completely occupied. Large parts of the interior of Nova Scotia, New Brunswick and the Gaspé Peninsula are vacant. On the island of Newfoundland in a broken fringe around the coast and on the shores of the St. Lawrence River below Quebec City there are only narrow bands of settlement.

About 57.8% of Canada's population lives between the American border and a 650-mile (1 046 km) east-west line from Quebec City to Sault Ste Marie. The eight largest cities in this block (Montreal, Toronto, Hamilton, Ottawa, London, Windsor, Quebec City, Kitchener) account for more than one third of the Canadian population.

The largest tract of continuous settlement is in the Prairie provinces, with a southern margin along the American border of some 900 miles (1 448 km). At its easternmost reach in Manitoba the northern margin of continuous settlement is about 100 miles (161 km) north of the international boundary; in the west, the northern margin reaches the 55th parallel, about 400 miles (644 km) north of the boundary. This block occupies about 6.2% of the area of Canada and contains four cities (Edmonton, Calgary, Winnipeg, Regina). North of this block, the Peace River district, astride the Alberta–British Columbia border, is an agricultural area which reaches the 57th parallel.

There is continuity of settlement throughout the southern half of British Columbia in narrow interconnecting strips following mountain valleys and coastal plains. British Columbia's greater population density, however, is in the Lower Fraser Valley, principally in the Vancouver metropolitan area.

North of the areas already described there are a number of disjunct settlements, the most notable in regard to size being in Ontario and Quebec between the 47th and 50th parallels. From east to west these are: the Lac St-Jean Lowland some 100 miles (161 km) north of Quebec City, the Clay Belts astride the Ontario–Quebec border, the Lakehead, and the Dryden and Fort Frances areas in Ontario near the Manitoba boundary. Outside these urban-rural blocks there are numerous settlements related to mining, forest industries, transportation, administration, defence, hunting, and fishing but with little or no agricultural base.

The geographical knowledge of Canada is reasonably complete considering its size and large areas of difficult access. The whole country has been surveyed and mapped. Comparisons of different features and areas can be made, as all map sheets of a series are drawn to the same specifications, and vertical air photographs showing still more details of the terrain are available for the whole country, varying in scale from about one inch to the mile (2.5 cm to the km) in the Arctic to four inches to the mile (10.2 cm to the km) or larger in settled areas. (See sub-section 1.1.5 Surveying and mapping.)

The Canadian Permanent Committee on Geographical Names, administered by the Department of Energy, Mines and Resources, deals with all questions of geographical nomenclature affecting Canada and undertakes research and investigation into the origin and usage of geographical names. The committee is composed of representatives of the federal mapping agencies and other federal agencies concerned with nomenclature and one appointed by each province.

1.1.1   Mountains and other heights

The great Cordilleran mountain system is Canada's most impressive physical feature. Many peaks in the various ranges embodied in the Canadian Cordillera are over 15,000 ft (over 4 500 m) in height, and a total of approximately 580 sq miles (1 502 km²) of territory lies above the 10,000-ft (3 048 m) mark. Mount Logan in the St. Elias Mountains of the Yukon Territory, which rises 19,524 ft (5 951 m) above sea level, is the highest point in Canada.

The highest points in each province are: Newfoundland, 5,232 ft (1 595 m); Prince Edward Island, 465 ft (142 m); Nova Scotia, 1,747 ft (532 m); New Brunswick, 2,690 ft (820 m); Quebec, 5,210 ft (1 588 m); Ontario, 2,275 ft (693 m); Manitoba, 2,729 ft (832 m); Saskatchewan, 4,567 ft (1 392 m);

Alberta, 12,294 ft (3 747 m); British Columbia, 15,300 ft (4 663 m); Yukon
Territory, 19,524 ft (5 951 m); and the Northwest Territories, 9,062 ft (2 762 m).

Rossland, BC, has the highest elevation, 3,465 ft (1 056 m), of any city in
Canada and Banff, Alta., is the highest hamlet at 4,580 ft (1 396 m). Chilco Lake,
with an area of 75 sq miles (194 km²), is the highest major lake at 3,842 ft
(1 171 m). Heights of the more important Canadian mountains and other
elevations are given in Table 1.2.

Inland waters   1.1.2

Water is the most basic of man's resources; without it, no living thing can survive.
Abundant water supplies have been essential to the development of Canada's
fisheries and wildlife resources, hydro-electric power, agriculture, recreational
activities, navigation, domestic water supply and industrial production.

The source of water supply is precipitation, which varies widely in quantity
over Canada. Each year 8,000,000 million tons (7 254 478 million t) of water fall
on Canada in the form of rain and snow. Much of it is evaporated, some is stored
temporarily in lakes, groundwater reservoirs and glaciers, and a large amount
drains as surface runoff following streams and rivers to the oceans. In areas that
have little precipitation, water is a treasured commodity. The opposite extreme
causes floods, erosion and other problems. In most of Canada there is ample
precipitation averaging about 30 to 36 inches (76 cm to 91 cm) annually in many
regions. The greatest demand for water occurs in the hot weather of summer;
prolonged dry spells may mean water shortage at that time.

It has been estimated that 292,000 sq miles (756 276 km²) or 7.6% of
Canada's total area is covered by lakes (Table 1.1). This water surface area is one
of the dominant features of the Canadian environment. Lake storage is
valuable — it represents water that can be drawn upon in time of drought to be
replaced in time of plenty. Lakes are natural regulators of river flow; they smooth
out the peak flows during flood periods and sustain stream flow during dry
seasons. There are probably more lakes in Canada than in any other country.
Among the largest bodies of fresh water in the world is the five-lake system of the
Great Lakes with an area of almost 100,000 sq miles (258 999 km²); 37% is in
Canada and 63% in the United States (Table 1.3). These lakes are sufficiently
large to have measurable, although very slight, tides. Other large lakes in Canada
are Great Bear Lake, Great Slave Lake and Lake Winnipeg, with areas ranging
from 9,200 to 12,100 sq miles (23 828 to 31 339 km²). Countless smaller lakes are
scattered throughout the country, particularly in the Canadian Shield. For
example, in the region southeast of Lake Winnipeg there are some 3,000 lakes in
an area of 6,090 sq miles (15 773 km²); and to the southeast of Reindeer Lake in
Saskatchewan there are some 7,500 lakes in an area of 5,300 sq miles (13 727
km²). The size and elevation of Canada's lakes over 150 sq miles (388 km²) in
area are listed in Table 1.4.

Groundwater is another important source of freshwater supply for
communities, industries and irrigators. It contributes about 10% of the water
supplied by municipal water systems in Canada. Although the quantities involved
are much smaller than those from rivers and lakes, many communities and some
industries are completely dependent on groundwater supplies. In some areas,
particularly the prairies, groundwater is the principal source of flow in some
streams during extended periods of dry weather.

The volume of water stored as snow and ice in the glaciers of North America
is many times greater than that stored in all the lakes, rivers and reservoirs. Most
of this is permanently frozen in the polar ice caps and is inaccessible, but the polar
ice masses have a strong indirect influence on the hydrologic cycle through their
effect on weather patterns. In the temperate regions, however, the alpine glaciers
exert a direct influence on the hydrologic cycle as water from melting glaciers
frequently sustains stream flow during dry seasons. It has been estimated that in
the hot summer months, glaciers may contribute up to 25% of the flow in the
Saskatchewan and Athabasca rivers. About 94,400 sq miles (244 495 km²) or 75%

of the glaciated areas of Canada are in the Arctic islands and 31,300 sq miles (81 067 km²) or 25% on the mainland. Of the latter figure some 23,500 sq miles (60 865 km²) are in the Pacific drainage basin and 6,300 sq miles (16 317 km²) in the Yukon drainage basin. The remaining 1,500 sq miles (3 885 km²) are shared among the Arctic, Great Slave, Saskatchewan–Nelson and Labrador drainage basins. Altogether, the number of glaciers in Canada is estimated at 75,000.

In Canada 90% of the water used comes from streams and other surface sources such as lakes and man-made reservoirs. The combined mean annual flow of all streams in Canada has been estimated to be 3.5 million cu ft per second (99.1 million dm³/s), equivalent to about 60% of Canada's mean annual precipitation. This represents about 9% of the total flow of all the rivers of the world.

It is understandable that Canada's history of settlement and industrial development has been influenced by its great rivers. From the earliest times, settlements have centred around water supplies. In the early days, water for transportation took priority. Canada's first industry, the fur trade, flourished because of the ready access to the interior provided by the St. Lawrence River, the Great Lakes and many other large and small waterways. The plentiful water supplies of the fertile plains of southern Ontario and Quebec attracted an industrious farming people. The river-borne transportation of lumber and later the power of water-driven turbines were vital factors in building the country's industrial base. Today more than ever water is a key to Canada's development, supplying renewable energy required for industrial growth, providing easy and cheap transport for raw materials and playing a vital part in their processing.

Water problems in Canada are associated with storage, distribution and pollution. Current demands for greater and more diversified water use are complicated by a need to reverse the trend toward deterioration in water quality resulting from urbanization, industrialization and agricultural developments. The allied topics of pollution and water quality are matters of major concern since they have a direct bearing on Canada's national well-being and economic growth.

The international boundary line between Canada and the United States, including Alaska, is 5,525 miles (8 892 km) long. Of this total, 3,146 miles (5 063 km) lie along or across water bodies. The economic importance of boundary water basins to both countries is indisputable. The natural resources of the boundary basins and the transportation and hydro-electric power resources of the waterways in these basins have helped foster concentration of population and industrial development in Canada along a broad band bordering the 49th parallel.

The approximate population in some selected boundary basins is summarized in the following table. (The Canadian statistics are compiled from census divisions that approximate the basin boundary; the US statistics were published in 1974, prepared jointly by the US Departments of Commerce and Agriculture for the US Water Resources Council. Both give 1971 figures.)

	Canada	United States
Saint John–St. Croix	450,000	125,000
Chaudière	215,000	395,000
St. François	295,000	20,000
Richelieu–Lake Champlain	325,000	335,000
Lake Ontario–Upper St. Lawrence	4,430,000	4,115,000
Lake Erie–Lake St. Clair	1,580,000	9,780,000
Lake Huron–Lake Michigan	690,000	14,900,000
Lake Superior	265,000	535,000
Lake of the Woods–Rainy River	80,000	20,000
Red River	715,000	545,000
Souris River	100,000	110,000
Missouri–Milk	200,000	225,000
Pend d'Oreille–Kootenay	86,000	225,000
Columbia River	190,000	195,000
Lower Mainland	1,490,000	1,190,000
Alaska Panhandle and Yukon	80,000	315,000

With so many common watersheds, it is not surprising that late in the 19th century a good many water problems were emerging along the Canada–US frontier. After extensive bilateral discussions, the Boundary Waters Treaty was signed in 1909. This treaty set out clear limitations of the freedom with which one country could act if such action might affect the other country. Under the treaty, the International Joint Commission was created to deal with problems that could arise along the boundary. Over the years the commission has dealt with problems in international basins extending from the Pacific to the Atlantic Ocean, ranging from small streams to the mighty St. Lawrence River where average flow, at the International Power Project at Cornwall, Ontario, is approximately 245,000 cu ft per second (6 937 628 dm³/s). More recently, the International Joint Commission was given primary responsibility for overseeing implementation of the Canada–US Agreement on Great Lakes Water Quality, with the goals of improving water quality in those areas of the Great Lakes suffering from pollution and ensuring that Great Lakes water quality will be protected in the future.

Table 1.5 lists the principal rivers of Canada and their tributaries. The tributaries and sub-tributaries are indicated by indention of names; thus, the Ottawa and other rivers are shown as tributary to the St. Lawrence, and the Gatineau and other rivers as tributary to the Ottawa.

The accompanying map shows the major drainage basins of Canada. Probably the most important is the Atlantic drainage basin, being dominated by the Great Lakes–St. Lawrence system which drains an area of approximately 678,000 sq miles (1 756 012 km²) and forms an unequalled navigable inland waterway through a region rich in natural and industrial resources. From the head of Lake Superior to Belle Isle at the entrance of the Gulf of St. Lawrence the distance is 2,280 miles (3 669 km). The entire drainage area north of the St. Lawrence and the Great Lakes is occupied by the southern fringe of the Canadian Shield, a rugged, rocky plateau with many tributary rivers. These rivers, as well as the St. Lawrence itself, provide much of the electric power necessary to operate the industries of the area. South of the St. Lawrence, the smaller rivers are important locally. The Saint John, for instance, drains a fertile area and provides most of New Brunswick's hydro power.

The Hudson Bay drainage basin is the largest in area and its main river is the Nelson. The Winnipeg River, a tributary of the Nelson, is completely developed for hydro-electric power but development of the Nelson itself is just beginning. The Saskatchewan River, tributary to the Nelson, drains the great agricultural region of the mid-west and is an important source of water for irrigation and hydro-electric power.

The Arctic drainage basin is dominated by the Mackenzie, one of the world's longest rivers. It flows 2,635 miles (4 241 km) from the head of the Finlay River to the Arctic Ocean and drains an area of approximately 700,000 sq miles (1 812 992 km²) in the three westernmost provinces and the two territories. Except for a 16-mile (26 km) portage in Alberta, barge navigation is possible from Waterways on the Athabasca River to the mouth of the Mackenzie, a distance of 1,700 miles (2 736 km).

The rivers of the Pacific basin rise in the mountains of the Cordilleran Region and flow to the Pacific Ocean over tortuous, precipitous courses, through steep canyons and over innumerable falls and rapids. They provide power for large hydro-electric developments and in season swarm with salmon returning inland to their spawning grounds. The Fraser River rises in the Rocky Mountains and, toward its mouth, flows through a rich agricultural area. The Columbia is an international river which has a total fall of 2,650 ft (808 m) during its course and has thus a tremendous power potential. Although a considerable part of the United States potential has been developed, the Canadian portion of the basin remained relatively untouched until recent years when three large reservoirs were constructed in Canada under the terms of the Columbia River Treaty. These reservoirs make it possible for British Columbia to develop up to 4 000 MW of hydro-electric generating capacity in the Columbia basin in Canada. The Yukon

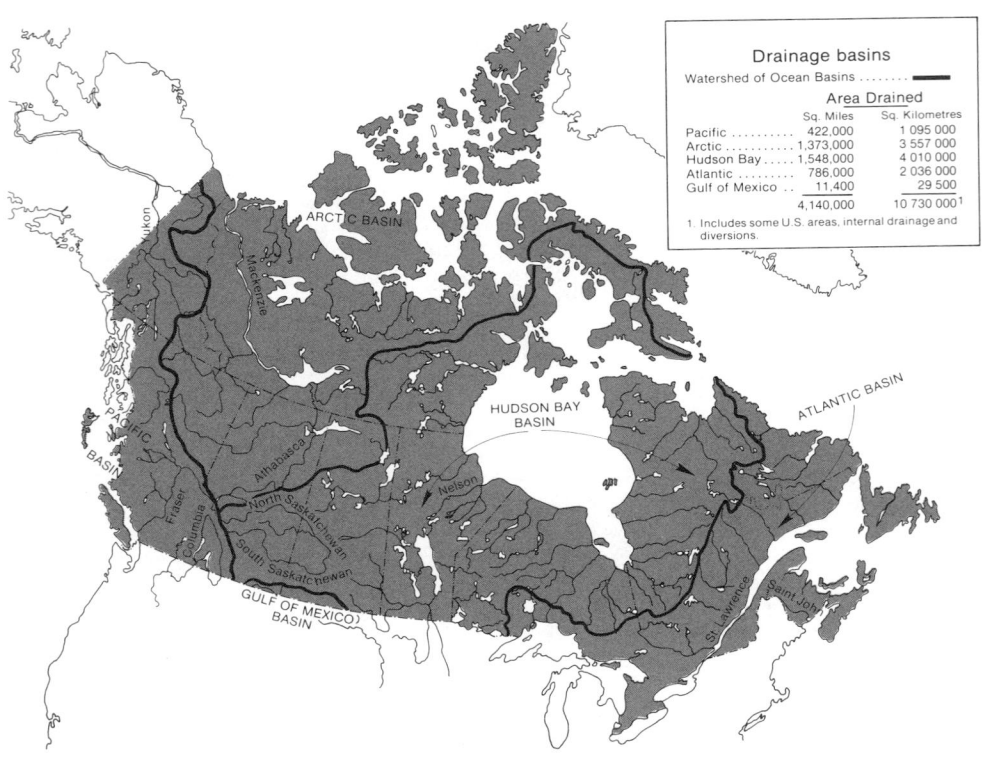

River, also an international river and the largest on the Pacific slope, is as yet of relatively little economic importance.

Utilization of inland water. Over 43% of all water withdrawn in Canada (excluding withdrawals associated with hydro projects) is for one end use, condenser cooling in steam-electric plants. About 99% of this water is returned for reuse. Municipal water use, including small industrial processors served by the municipal systems of Canada, accounts for some 10.5% of current water withdrawals. On average, approximately 75% of the water pumped into the system is discharged as storm and sanitary sewage containing waste materials.

Other industrial users, manufacturing and mining firms, account for 38% of the total withdrawals of water and about 10% of that intake is consumed or lost. Discharged water is frequently returned to source in a highly polluted condition and may be unfit for most uses downstream. Canadian agriculture depends largely upon plentiful supplies of water from melting snow and rainfall. In many regions of Canada, however, such natural sources of water are inadequate. Agriculture requires 7.7% of the nation's total withdrawals annually for irrigation, stock-watering and rural domestic use.

Hydro-electric power generation utilizes the kinetic energy of falling water to produce electricity. Except for evaporation losses from the surface of reservoirs, the water is not consumed or changed in any way. However, flooding of land for storage and interference with natural flow may cause serious adverse effects.

Although navigation along the natural waterways opened up the country to settlement and economic development, water transport is no longer the principal mode of transportation. It is competing with railways, pipelines, aircraft and motor carriers. Water still provides the most economical means of transporting bulky raw materials of Canada's export trade such as wheat, pulp and paper, lumber and minerals. This is especially true in the Great Lakes–St. Lawrence and the Mackenzie River regions.

Water-oriented recreational activities which Canadians enjoy during their leisure take many forms, including swimming, boating, sightseeing, fishing, hunting, and water skiing. Although the provincial and federal governments produce data on different dimensions of recreation, coordinated information on the role of water in outdoor recreation is not yet available on a countrywide basis. It is known, however, that the magnitude of water-oriented recreation is large and is continuing to grow as more leisure time becomes available.

Fish and wildlife resources from river and lake systems make a vital contribution to the economy of Canada. Apart from being a recreational area for sport-fishing and hunting, the inland waters also support important commercial fisheries. Fish and wildlife require water of high quality. When water systems are put to multiple-purpose use, it is imperative to ensure that pollution does not destroy these resources. Within government agencies, shifts in emphasis have led to increased work on water pollution problems. Universities are also developing programs in the direction of environment-related water research.

Coastal waters
1.1.3

The coastline of Canada, measuring over 150,000 statute miles (241 402 km), is one of the world's longest. It comprises the following measurements — Mainland: Atlantic 9,843 miles (15 841 km); Pacific 4,363 miles (7 022 km); Hudson Strait 2,643 miles (4 253 km); Hudson Bay 7,623 miles (12 268 km); Arctic 11,884 miles (19 125 km); total 36,356 miles (58 509 km). Islands: Atlantic 18,176 miles (29 251 km); Pacific 11,622 miles (18 704 km); Hudson Strait 5,340 miles (8 594 km); Hudson Bay 9,181 miles (14 775 km); Northwest Territories south of Arctic Circle 13,800 miles (22 209 km); Arctic 57,014 miles (91 755 km); total 115,133 miles (185 289 km).

To describe Canada's coastal waters would require the resources of oceanography, marine biology and meteorology. However, basic to any study of the oceanic-continental margin is the physical relief of the sea floor; the information presented here is restricted to this with a few salient features of the Atlantic, Pacific and Arctic marginal seas surrounding Canada.

Atlantic. Along this coastal area, the sea has inundated valleys and lower parts of the Appalachian Mountains and of the Canadian Shield. The submerged continental shelf effecting the transition from continental to oceanic conditions is distinguished by great width and diversity of relief. From the coast of Nova Scotia its width varies from 60 to 100 nautical miles (111 to 185 km), from Newfoundland 100 to 280 miles (185 to 519 km) at the entrance of Hudson Strait, and northward it merges with that of the Arctic Ocean. The outer edge varies in depth from 100 to 200 fathoms (183 to 366 m) before the shelf gives way to the declivity leading to abyssal depths. The overall gradient of the Atlantic continental shelf is slight but the whole area is studded with shoals, plateaus, banks, ridges and islands and the coasts of Nova Scotia and Newfoundland are rugged and fringed with islets and shoals. Off Nova Scotia, the 40-fathom (73 m) line lies at an average of 12 miles (22 km) from the shore and constitutes the danger line for coastal shipping. The whole floor of the marginal sea appears to be traversed by channels and gullies cutting well into the shelf.

The topography of much of the Atlantic marginal sea floor was shaped by processes of glacial erosion and deposition. Large areas, however, undergo constant change due to continuous marine deposition of materials eroded by rivers, wave action, wind and ice.

Hudson Bay and Hudson Strait bite deeply into the continent. Hudson Bay is an inland sea 317,501 sq statute miles (822 324 km²) in area having an average depth of about 70 fathoms (128 m); the greatest charted depth in the centre of the Bay is 141 fathoms (258 m). Hudson Strait separates Baffin Island from the continental coast and connects Hudson Bay with the Atlantic Ocean. It is 430 miles (796 km) long and from 37 to 120 miles (69 to 222 km) wide; its greatest charted depth of 481 fathoms (880 m) is close inside the Atlantic entrance. Great irregularities of the sea floor are indicated but, except in inshore waters, few navigational hazards have been located.

Pacific. The marginal sea of the Pacific differs strikingly from the other marine zones of Canada. The hydrography of British Columbia is characterized by bold, abrupt relief — a repetition of the mountainous landscape. Numerous inlets penetrate the mountainous coasts for distances of 50 to 75 miles (93 to 139 km). They are usually a nautical mile or two (2 to 4 km) in width and of considerable depth, with steep canyon-like sides. From the islet-strewn coast, the continental shelf extends from 50 to 100 sea miles (93 to 185 km) to its oceanward limit at depths of about 200 fathoms (366 m). The sea floor drops rapidly to the Pacific deeps, parts of the western slopes of Vancouver Island and the Queen Charlotte Islands lying only four miles (7 km) and one mile (2 km), respectively, from the edge of the declivity. These detached land masses are the dominant features of the Pacific marginal sea. In a region so irregular in hydrographic relief, shoals and pinnacle rocks are numerous, necessitating cautious navigation.

Arctic. The submerged plateau extending from the northern coast of North America is a major part of the great continental shelf surrounding the Arctic Ocean, on which lie all the Arctic islands of Canada, Greenland, and most of the Arctic islands of Europe and Asia. This shelf is most uniformly developed north of Siberia where it is about 500 miles (926 km) wide; north of North America it surrounds the western islands of the archipelago and extends 50 to 300 miles (93 to 556 km) seaward from the outermost islands.

The floor of the submerged part of this continental margin is nearly flat to gently undulating, with isolated rises or hollows. Most of it has an average slope seaward of about one half a degree, with an abrupt break at the outer edge to the continental slope whose declivity is commonly six degrees or more. From the Alaskan border eastward to the mouth of the Mackenzie River the shelf is shallow and continuous with the coastal plain on the mainland; its outer edge lies at a depth of about 35 fathoms (64 m) and about 40 miles (74 km) offshore. This shelf is continuous with that north of Alaska and Siberia. Near the western edge of the Mackenzie River delta, it is indented by a deep valley, the Herschel Sea Canyon, whose head comes within 15 miles (28 km) of the coast. Between Herschel Sea Canyon and Amundsen Gulf, the typical features of the continental shelf are replaced by the submerged portion of the Mackenzie River delta, which forms a great pock-marked undersea plain, most of it less than 30 fathoms (55 m) deep, up to 75 miles (139 km) wide and 250 miles (463 km) long.

North and east of the submerged portion of the Mackenzie River delta, the continental shelf is more deeply submerged than that off the mainland and Alaska. Its gently undulating surface is, for the most part, 200 fathoms (366 m) or more below sea level, and most of the well-defined continental shoulder is over 300 fathoms (549 m) deep, giving way to the smooth continental slope which extends without significant interruption to the abyssal Canada Basin at about 2,000 fathoms (3 658 m). The deeply submerged continental shelf extends along the entire west coast of the Canadian Arctic archipelago from Banks Island to Greenland. All of the major channels between the islands — Amundsen Gulf, M'Clure Strait, Prince Gustav Adolf Sea, Peary Channel, Sverdrup Channel and Nansen Sound — have flattish floors at about the same depth as the shelf and appear to enter it "at grade", although there are a few local irregularities that may be the result of glacial action. No deep indentations or canyons are known to cut the continental slope or continental shelf off the archipelago, except one sinuous canyon that heads off Robeson Channel at the northeastern end, close to Greenland. Submerged sides of the channels of the archipelago, and slopes from the islands' western shores to the inner edge of the deeply submerged shelf, are marked in many places by a series of steps or terraces.

The continental shelf bordering the Arctic Ocean, the adjacent mainland particularly near the Mackenzie River delta, and the islands of the archipelago have been subjected to intensive scientific study and mineral resource exploration during the past 20 years. Coordinated programs of research and surveys have studied bedrock geology, development of the terrain, sediments on the sea floor and the nature and history of ice caps. Gravity, seismic, aeromagnetic, geomagnetic and geothermal investigations have obtained information on physical characteristics of the rocks beneath the surface, and the nature and stability of the crust underlying the islands, the continental shelf and the continental slope. A complementary program of geodetic, topographic and hydrographic surveys has provided background maps and charts, and information about both terrestrial and marine physiography. Also there have been less intensive but relevant studies of the biology of the Arctic lands and oceans. As a result a great deal of reliable scientific information is now available for an area about which very little was known 25 years ago.

Islands   1.1.4

The largest islands of Canada are in the North, all in an arctic climate. The northern group extends from the islands in James Bay to Ellesmere Island which reaches 83°07′N. Those in the District of Franklin, north of the mainland of Canada, are generally referred to as the Canadian Arctic archipelago; those in the extreme north — lying north of the M'Clure Strait–Viscount Melville Sound–Barrow Strait–Lancaster Sound water passage — are known as the Queen Elizabeth Islands.

On the west coast, Vancouver Island and the Queen Charlotte Islands are the largest and most important but the coastal waters are studded with many small rocky islands.

The largest islands off the east coast are the island of Newfoundland (part of the province of Newfoundland), the province of Prince Edward Island, Cape Breton Island (part of Nova Scotia), Grand Manan and Campobello islands (parts of New Brunswick) and Anticosti Island and the Magdalen group (parts of Quebec).

Notable islands of the inland waters include Manitoulin Island 1,068 sq miles (2 766 km²) in area, lying in Lake Huron, the so-called Thirty Thousand Islands of Georgian Bay and the Thousand Islands in the outlet from Lake Ontario into the St. Lawrence River.

The areas of principal islands by region are given in Table 1.6.

Surveying and mapping   1.1.5

The needs for maps and surveys of Canada are met mainly by the Department of Energy, Mines and Resources which compiles topographical, geological and aeromagnetic maps, aeronautical charts and specialized maps showing electoral district boundaries, land use and other features. Some types of maps and surveys are also produced by provincial and private agencies. In the field of geodesy, the Geodetic Survey maintains a network of horizontal and vertical control points across Canada. The Topographical Survey has completed the mapping of Canada at the scale of four miles to one inch (6.4 km/2.5 cm). All settled areas and regions of northern development have been mapped at a scale of one and a quarter inches to one mile (3.1 cm/km). There are 800 maps available on a relatively large scale covering all major cities and their suburbs. Photomaps, made possible by advances in air photography and photogrammetry, are also available. The Legal Surveys Division is responsible for the technical management of legal surveys of land under federal jurisdiction, such as the northern territories, national parks and Indian reserves. It also executes such surveys on behalf of administering departments, collaborates in the demarcation of provincial boundaries, prepares descriptions of electoral districts and generally provides land-surveying services to other departments.

The Surveys and Mapping Branch is Canada's major agency for preparing aeronautical charts of airports, airways and radio and other aids for air navigation. As a service to map-makers, prospectors, engineers, foresters, and town planners, the department maintains a National Air Photo Library in Ottawa containing all air photographs taken by or for the federal government. The library is responsible for storage, documentation and handling of airborne remote-sensing photography and Earth Resources Technology Satellite imagery. Geological surveys provide an inventory of the potential resources of Canada, and aid in the discovery of mineral deposits, and in other aspects of the national economy influenced by geological factors. Large reconnaissance projects are mounted in northern regions, and detailed investigations in the southern areas. Geological maps are published separately or as part of scientific papers. Geophysical surveys result in maps showing such features as variations in terrestrial magnetism, gravity and seismology. The Geological Survey outlines local magnetic variations indicating mineral deposits, while the Earth Physics Branch maps the earth's total magnetic field. Seismic observatories throughout Canada compile and update earthquake zoning maps of Canada. A gravity map of Canada is also available.

1.2   Geology

Canada is composed of some 17 geological provinces that may be grouped under four main categories — continental shelf, platform, orogen and shield. The geologically youngest provinces, the Atlantic, Pacific and Arctic continental shelves are made up of little-deformed sediments and volcanics, mainly of Mesozoic and Cenozoic age, which are still accumulating along the margins of the present continental mass. The St. Lawrence, Interior, Arctic and Hudson platforms are formed of thick flat-lying Phanerozoic strata covering large parts of the crystalline basement rocks of the continental interior, the extension of the Canadian Shield. The Appalachian, Cordilleran and Innuitian orogens are mountain belts of deformed and metamorphosed sedimentary and volcanic rocks mainly Phanerozoic and Proterozoic in age, intruded by granitic plutons. They were produced during the various Phanerozoic orogenies 50 to 500 million years ago. Of the seven provinces comprising the Precambrian Canadian Shield, the Grenville, Churchill, Southern and Bear embrace the orogenic belts produced during the Proterozoic orogenies, 900 to 1,800 million years ago. The remaining three, the Superior, Slave and Nutak provinces, were deformed during the Archean Eon, and include the oldest continental crust known in Canada, 2,500 to 3,000 million years old. The Precambrian orogenic belts have many features in common with those of Phanerozoic age but are so deeply eroded that the mountainous parts have been reduced to plains or lowlands and in many places the basement crystalline rocks upon which the sediments and volcanics initially accumulated are now exposed.

The land and freshwater area of Canada is 3,852,000 sq miles (9 976 634 km²), but unique among the nations of the world, Canada also includes within the confines of this area some 858,000 sq miles (2 222 210 km²) of marine waters. The rocks beneath have geological features akin to the adjacent regions on-shore. In addition, the submarine area of the bordering continental shelves is about 523,000 sq miles (1 354 564 km²) and of the continental slopes, 563,000 sq miles (1 458 163 km²). Altogether, this embraces 5,526,000 sq miles (14 312 274 km²), about 3% of the surface of the globe.

For an account of Canada's geology see the *Canada Year Book 1973* pp 8-14.

Geological provinces

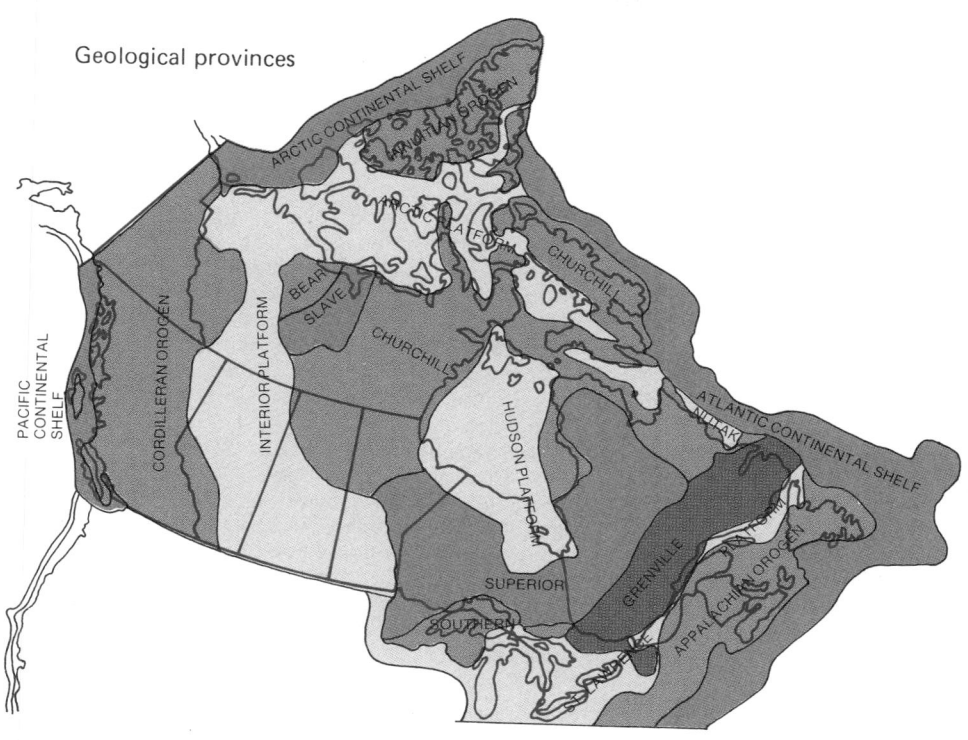

Climate and time zones   1.3

Climate   1.3.1

Climate depends primarily on radiative exchanges between the sun, the
atmosphere and the surface of the earth. In addition, the regional climates of
Canada are controlled by the geography of North America and by the general
movement of air from west to east across the continent. The climate of the Pacific
Coast is cool and fairly dry in summer but mild, cloudy and wet in winter. Interior
British Columbia has climates varying more with altitude than latitude: wet
windward mountain slopes with heavy snows in winter; dry "rainshadow"
valleys, very hot in summer; and high plateaus with marked day to night
temperature contrasts. A vast area of interior Canada, from the Rocky Mountains
to the Great Lakes, has a continental-type climate — bitterly cold winters, short
but warm summers and scanty precipitation. The southern portions of Ontario
and Quebec have a humid climate with cold winters, hot summers and generally
ample precipitation throughout the year. The four Atlantic provinces have a
humid continental-type climate although in the immediate coastal areas there is a
marked maritime effect. On the northern islands, along the Arctic Coast and
around Hudson Bay arctic conditions persist, with long frigid winters and only a
few months each year with temperatures averaging above freezing. The
precipitation is light in the tundra area north of the treeline. Between the arctic
and southern climates a vast band of Boreal Canada has a transitional type climate
with bitter long winters but appreciable summer periods. Precipitation is light in
the west, but heavier falls occur in the Ungava Peninsula.

Climatic data. Temperature and precipitation data for typical stations in various districts are shown in Table 1.7. Additional data from hundreds of stations and reports concerning the climates of Canada and the regions are available from the Atmospheric Environment Service, Department of Fisheries and the Environment. Definitions, methods of observation, the instrumentation used and other information are included in the department's publications.

1.3.2   Standard time and time zones

The rotation of the earth on its axis was once considered uniform and the unit of time, the second, was defined as 1/86400 of the mean solar day. Improvements in clocks and in methods of making astronomical observations demonstrated conclusively that there are irregularities in earth rotation too large to be neglected. In 1956 the International Committee on Weights and Measures defined the second in terms of the annual motion of the earth about the sun, called ephemeris time. In 1957 the first cesium atomic clock was calibrated with respect to ephemeris time; in 1967 the cesium second was adopted as the international standard. The second now is defined as the duration of 9,192,631,770 periods of the radiation corresponding to a transition of the cesium atom.

Based on atomic clocks, Canada's time is established by the National Research Council with a precision of one ten-millionth of a second per day, and coordination with other countries is maintained to the same precision through the Bureau international de l'Heure in Paris. Irregularities in the rotation of the earth give rise to a difference between mean solar time and atomic time, and a leap second is introduced to ensure that this difference, called DUT1, does not exceed 0.8 seconds. At present DUT1 is decreasing by about one twelfth of a second per month, and positive leap seconds were necessary on June 30, 1972 and on December 31, 1972, 1973, 1974 and 1975.

A continuous broadcast of Canadian time is made on station CHU, Ottawa (3330 kHz, 7335 kHz, 14670 kHz), with a bilingual voice announcement each minute, and with a split pulse code to give the value of DUT1. Once a day the time signals are broadcast across Canada on the CBC networks.

Standard Time, adopted at a World Conference at Washington, DC in 1884, sets the number of time zones in the world at 24, each zone ideally extending over one twenty-fourth of the surface of the earth and including all the territory between two meridians 15° of longitude apart. In practice, the zone boundaries are quite irregular for geographic and political reasons. Universal Time (UT) is the time of the zone centred on the zero meridian through Greenwich. Each of the other time zones is a definite number of hours ahead of or behind UT to a total of 12 hours, at which limit the international date-line runs roughly north-south through the mid-Pacific.

Canada has six time zones. The most easterly, Newfoundland Standard Time, is three hours and 30 minutes behind UT, and the most westerly, Pacific Standard Time, is eight hours behind UT. In between, from east to west, the remaining zones are called Atlantic, Eastern, Central and Mountain. On October 28, 1973, the nine hour Western Yukon Time Zone was eliminated by order of the Yukon Territorial Council, placing the entire Yukon eight hours behind UT.

Legal authority for the time zones. Time in Canada has been considered a matter of provincial rather than federal jurisdiction. Each of the provinces and territories has enacted laws governing the standard time to be used within its boundaries. These laws determine the location of the time zone boundaries. Lines of communication, however, have sometimes caused communities near the boundary of a time zone to adopt the time of the adjacent zone, and in most cases these changes are acknowledged by amendments to provincial legislation. During the two World Wars, there were federal enactments concerning time but these were of temporary duration. In 1941 the time determined at the Dominion Observatory was designated as official time for Dominion official purposes. On April 1, 1970, this became the responsibility of the National Research Council.

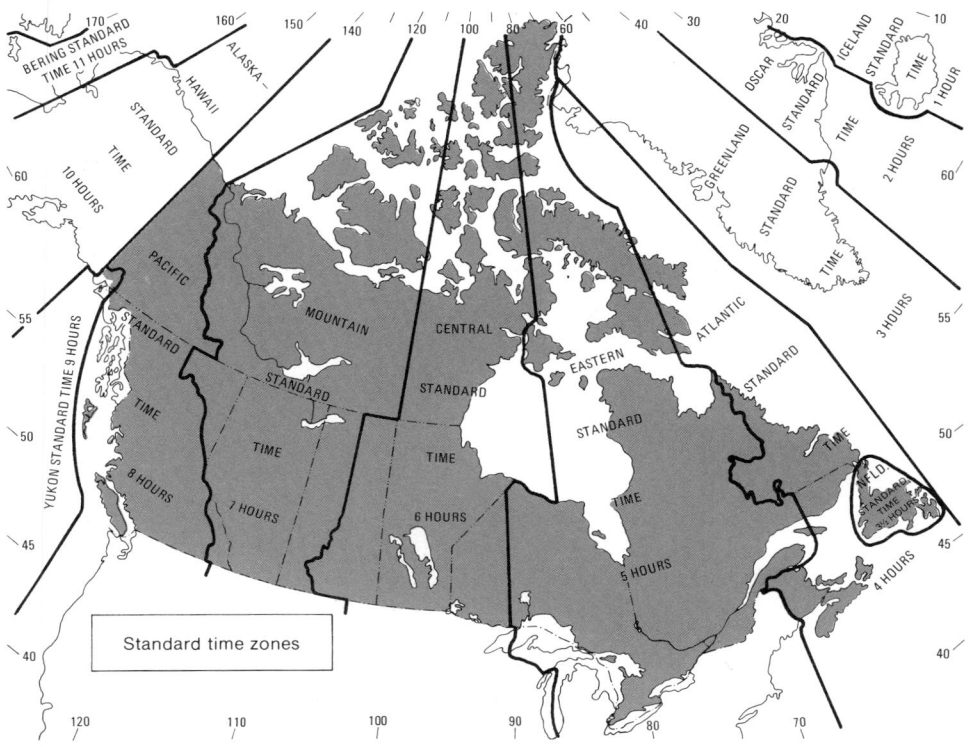

Standard time zones

Daylight saving time. Although daylight saving time had been urged in many quarters before World War I, its first use in Canada came as a federal war measure in 1918. Today most provinces have legislation controlling the provincial or municipal adoption (or rejection) of daylight saving time; in the other provinces the authority is left to the municipalities. By general agreement, daylight saving time, where it is observed, is in force for six months from the last Sunday in April until the last Sunday in October.

Public land   1.4

The total area of Canada and areas of the individual provinces and territories are classified by tenure in Table 1.8. All lands, with the exception of those privately owned or in process of alienation, are Crown lands under the jurisdiction of either the federal or the provincial governments.

Federal public land. Public lands under the administration of the federal government comprise lands in the Northwest Territories including the Arctic archipelago and the islands in Hudson Strait, Hudson Bay, James Bay and Ungava Bay, lands in the Yukon Territory, ordnance and admiralty lands, national parks and national historic parks and sites, forest experiment stations, experimental farms, Indian reserves and, in general, all public lands held by the several departments of the federal government for various purposes connected with federal administration. These lands are administered under the Territorial Lands Act (RSC 1970, c.T-6) and the Public Lands Grants Act (RSC 1970, c.P-29).

The largest areas under federal jurisdiction are in the Northwest Territories and the Yukon Territory where only 93 sq miles (241 km²) of a total area of

1,511,979 sq miles (3 916 007 km²) are privately owned and 1,485.6 sq miles (3 847.7 km²) are under the administration of the territorial governments.

Provincial and territorial public land. Public lands of Nova Scotia, New Brunswick, Quebec, Ontario and British Columbia (except the "railway belt" and Peace River block) have been administered since Confederation by the provincial governments. In 1930, the federal government transferred the unalienated portions of the natural resources of Manitoba, Saskatchewan and Alberta and of sections of British Columbia to the respective governments, and all unalienated lands in Newfoundland, except those administered by the federal government, became provincial public lands under the Terms of Union on March 31, 1949. All land in Prince Edward Island has been alienated except 133 sq miles (344 km²) under federal or provincial administration.

The transfer by the federal government of land within and immediately surrounding established communities in the Northwest Territories and the Yukon Territory to the respective territorial governments began in September 1970 when four such transfers were completed, three in the Northwest Territories and one in the Yukon, for a total of 665 sq miles (1 722 km²). Since then 15 transfers were completed in the following areas: Yukon Territory: Faro 91 sq miles (236 km²), Beaver Creek 2 sq miles (5 km²), Mayo 4 sq miles (10 km²), Teslin 1 sq mile (2.6 km²), Carmacks 12 sq miles (31 km²), Destruction Bay 2 sq miles (5 km²), Carcross 9.6 sq miles (24.9 km²), Watson Lake 2 sq miles (5 km²), Northwest Territories: Frobisher Bay 51 sq miles (132 km²), Aklavik 8 sq miles (21 km²), Fort Simpson 140 sq miles (363 km²), Fort Smith 22 sq miles (57 km²), Fort Providence 81 sq miles (210 km²), Hay River–Enterprise 142 sq miles (368 km²), Norman Wells 175 sq miles (453 km²), Fort McPherson 31 sq miles (80 km²), Fort Franklin 25 sq miles (65 km²), Fort Good Hope 22 sq miles (57 km²).

1.4.1   Federal parks

Parks Canada, a program of the Department of Indian Affairs and Northern Development, includes National Parks, National Historic Parks and Sites, historic waterways, wild rivers and byways. Parks Canada has its headquarters in Ottawa but operational responsibility rests with five regional offices: the Atlantic regional office in Halifax, the Quebec regional office in Quebec City, the Ontario regional office in Cornwall, the Prairie regional office in Winnipeg and the Western regional office in Calgary.

National historic parks and sites. The National Historic Parks and Sites of Canada commemorate persons, places and events of major significance in the historical development of Canada. The Dominion Forest Reserves and Parks Act in 1911 created in the Department of the Interior a Dominion Parks Board to administer national and historic parks. In 1917, Fort Anne at Annapolis Royal, NS was declared Canada's first National Park of historic significance.

A seven-member Historic Sites and Monuments Board of Canada was formed to advise the minister on sites of national historical interest. The board met for the first time at Ottawa on October 28, 1919. The second National Historic Park was established in 1927 and by 1950 there were nine, receiving over 150,000 visitors annually.

The National Parks Act of 1930 provided that the Governor in Council may set apart any land as a National Historic Park to commemorate an historic event, or preserve any historic landmark or any object of historic, prehistoric or scientific interest of national importance. The Historic Sites and Monuments Act of 1953 provided the statutory base for the operation of the Historic Sites and Monuments Board and defined the role of the board as adviser to the minister. Further legislation was enacted in 1955 and 1959 to amend and broaden the scope of the original act. The Canadian Historic Sites Division, now the National Historic Parks and Sites Branch, was created in the Department of Northern Affairs and National Resources in 1955 to develop, interpret, operate and maintain historic parks and sites and to act as secretariat for the board.

A policy statement in 1968 specified that for commemoration, a site or structure must be closely associated with a person, place or event of national historical importance, or it must illustrate the cultural, social, political, economic or military patterns of history or of a prehistoric people or archaeological discovery, or be valuable as an example of architecture. The statement included guidelines for the provision of visitor services, interpretative programs and information to the public. Standards were established for the preservation, restoration and reconstruction of structures which stressed authenticity in the materials used and in the furnishings and artifacts. The policy recognized the need for a comprehensive program to give full thematic and geographical representation and to establish a long-range planning program.

The Historic Sites and Monuments Act provides for a board of 15 members: two representatives each from Ontario and Quebec and one from each of the eight other provinces appointed by the Governor in Council, the Dominion Archivist, one representative from the National Museums of Canada and one from the Department of Indian Affairs and Northern Development as ex officio members. Proposed amendments to the act would provide for inclusion of members to represent the Yukon and Northwest Territories. The members are generally historians of distinction. The board may recommend that sites, buildings and other structures of national importance be developed as National Historic Parks or Historic Sites or that commemoration be carried out by the erection of plaques of the Historic Sites and Monuments Board of Canada, or in exceptional circumstances, of distinctive monuments. Suggestions for the establishment of historic sites and parks come from many sources — the general public, members of Parliament, historical societies and other groups, department staff and board members themselves. Before a site is referred to the board for consideration, a background paper is prepared by the National Historic Parks and Sites Branch research staff. The board then determines the significance of the site and makes its recommendation, favourable or unfavourable, to the minister. After approval has been granted to a project, a development plan is prepared.

Since its establishment, the National Historic Parks and Sites Branch has been instrumental in the creation of some 80 national historic parks and major sites, over 53 operational, and in the commemoration with plaques of over 650 persons and events of national (as opposed to local or regional) significance. Negotiations are being conducted with certain provinces for the acquisition of other sites. The department has entered into 40 cost-sharing agreements with provincial and municipal governments and with incorporated non-profit societies for the acquisition and restoration of architecturally or historically significant buildings and structures on the understanding that the other party will pay the balance of the acquisition and restoration costs and will maintain the buildings in perpetuity. A number of monuments which commemorate people and events significant in the nation's history are maintained by the National Historic Parks and Sites Branch.

Full details on location and characteristics of national historic parks and sites may be obtained from the Department of Indian Affairs and Northern Development.

Another branch undertaking is the Canadian Inventory of Historic Building, begun in 1970 — a computerized program to survey, analyze and categorize old buildings in Canada. So far the exteriors of more than 165,000 buildings have been surveyed and almost all have been indexed; interiors of approximately 1,800 of these structures have been surveyed by the CIHB.

A step toward the preservation of the nation's historic resources was the establishment in 1972 of Heritage Canada, an independent corporation concerned with the conservation of buildings, sites and natural and scenic areas. It received an initial federal capital endowment of $12 million and the interest on this fund is used to further its work. Heritage Canada enlists the support of the general public and of foundations and corporations; membership is open to anyone.

National parks. Canada's National Parks system, encompassing more than 50,000 sq miles (129 499 km²), is the largest and most rapidly expanding in the world. It has grown from the federal government's efforts, with cooperation of provincial and territorial governments, to preserve natural areas of outstanding scenic and biological interest for the benefit of the public.

The national park concept, which began with Yellowstone National Park in the United States in 1872, was soon applied in Canada. In 1885 the Canadian government reserved from private ownership the mineral hot springs of Sulphur Mountain in what is now Banff National Park. Two years later this 10-sq mile (26 km²) reserve was extended to 260 sq miles (673 km²) and named Rocky Mountain Park, the first federal park in Canada. Two land reserves in southern British Columbia — Yoho and Glacier — were made by the federal government in 1886, a reserve of 54 sq miles (140 km²) in the Waterton Lakes area of southern Alberta in 1895, and an area of 5,000 sq miles (12 950 km²) around Jasper, Alta. in 1907. These four reserves in the western mountain ranges, together with Rocky Mountain Park, formed the nucleus of the national park system after the Dominion Forest Reserves and Parks Act was passed in May 1911. A National Parks Branch was created that year to protect, administer and develop the parks.

By 1930, nine more national parks had been established. Three in Ontario consisted of federally owned Crown land or land held in trust for Indians: St. Lawrence Islands National Park, Point Pelee National Park and Georgian Bay Islands National Park. Prince Albert National Park in Saskatchewan and Riding Mountain National Park in Manitoba were former federal forest reserves. Elk Island National Park near Edmonton was established as a preserve for buffalo and Wood Buffalo National Park, a 17,300-sq mile (44 807 km²) area straddling the Alberta–Northwest Territories border, as a refuge for the largest surviving herd of buffalo in North America. In British Columbia two scenic areas were preserved — Mount Revelstoke National Park and Kootenay National Park.

Between 1930 and 1973 the following new parks were added: Northwest Territories: Nahanni and Auyuittuq (Baffin Island); Yukon Territory: Kluane; British Columbia: Pacific Rim; Ontario: Pukaskwa; Quebec: La Mauricie and Forillon; New Brunswick: Kouchibouguac and Fundy; Nova Scotia: Cape Breton Highlands and Kejimkujik; Prince Edward Island: Prince Edward Island National Park; Newfoundland: Terra Nova and Gros Morne.

For parks in the Yukon Territory and Northwest Territories, lands have been reserved from all alternative disposition by Orders in Council and proclamation. Within provinces, land is acquired by the province acting within a federal-provincial agreement to establish a national park. These lands are or will be transferred to Canada and the establishment of the park is formalized by Parliament.

In 1971, *The national parks system planning manual* was published, in recognition that new and comprehensive measures are needed to preserve Canada's natural heritage. With a view to protecting not only unique and outstanding areas of the Canadian land and sea-scapes but also those representative of its physical, biological, and oceanographic characteristics, 48 distinctive natural regions were identified for which natural history themes have been defined.

A detailed list of national parks was included in the 1972 and 1973 editions of the *Canada Year Book,* and a location map and details of these parks are available in *Canada's national parks* published by the Department of Indian Affairs and Northern Development.

National marine parks. Canada is bounded by three oceans and has the largest volume of fresh water in the world. The national parks system will be extended to include representations of the Pacific, Arctic and Atlantic coasts and inland waters, with identification of the Marine Natural Regions and Marine Natural History Themes.

National landmarks. Preservation of specific natural wonders, such as the Chub crater in northern Quebec, the frozen pingoes of the Arctic, semi-desert and eroded hills of the Prairies and mountain caves and sea-scapes, would allow on-site interpretation of Canada's natural evolution.

Agreements for Recreation and Conservation (ARC). Canadians have become increasingly concerned about their heritage and governments at all levels have been acting to protect and preserve it before it is too late. To provide Canadians new opportunities to appreciate their natural, cultural and historical heritage, Parks Canada created a new program — Agreements for Recreation and Conservation — with two principal elements: waterways and land-based byways. The waterways and byways to be developed through the ARC program will be mutually agreed upon by provincial and federal governments.

Waterways are differentiated into historic waterways and wild rivers. Canada's rivers, lakes, coastal waters, and canals were important in the history of Canada, and the ARC program plans to develop a system of historic waterways offering a diversity of recreational opportunities. For example, canal systems such as the Trent–Severn and Rideau (in Ontario) provide for water and shoreland recreational activities as well as giving insight into Canada's historical and cultural heritage. The second type of waterway, wild rivers, is an integral part of Canada's natural heritage. Some of these waterways have historical value, but their main attractiveness lies in their beauty and untamed nature.

Byways will provide trails for hiking, horseback riding, bicycling or scenic roadways for leisure motoring. Trails for non-motorized vehicles will be established for their scenic and historic interest. Motor trails will introduce a new concept of automobile travel, inviting motorists to leave the super highways and take leisurely drives through scenic countryside. Parkways will also provide access to recreational areas, campgrounds, picnic sites, hiking and nature trails, and where possible will link important parks and historic sites.

Wild rivers. Many undeveloped Canadian rivers, some with historic appeal, have been surveyed as potential wilderness routes.

Gatineau Park. In addition to the national parks a 138-sq-mile (357 km²) recreation area known as Gatineau Park north of Ottawa and Hull is being developed by the federal government as part of the National Capital Region under the National Capital Commission. It is a wilderness area of great potential, extending northward from Hull for 35 miles (56 km). With 25 miles (40 km) of parkway, magnificent lookouts, lakes, fishing streams, beaches, picnic areas, camping sites, skiing and walking trails it is one of the finest recreation areas in Canada, enjoyed by nearly 1.8 million visitors each year. A master plan for further development is under way.

Provincial parks

1.4.2

All provincial governments have established parks within their boundaries. Some are wilderness areas set aside so that portions of the country might be retained in their natural state. Most of them, however, are smaller areas of exceptional scenic interest, easily accessible and equipped or slated for future development as recreational parks with camping and picnic facilities.

Newfoundland. Altogether, 3,099 sq miles (8 026 km²) of wilderness, reservation, parklands and public beaches are administered by provincial government agencies. Of this land, 2,788 sq miles (7 221 km²) are contained within two wilderness areas and seven seabird sanctuaries administered by the Wildlife Division of the Department of Tourism. The remaining 311 sq miles (806 km²) are under the jurisdiction of the Provincial Parks Division of the Department of Tourism. Of that area, 73 sq miles (189 km²) are in 47 developed provincial parks, 2.5 sq miles (6.5 km²) in protected public beaches and fishery access roads and 235 sq miles (609 km²) in 15 provincial park reserves. Operation of these parks is directed toward preservation of the natural environment; most of them are located in wilderness areas, developed only for picnicking and camping. Regulations prohibit hunting and other types of resource exploitation; sports fishing, however, is encouraged. There is a continuing upward trend in the number of park users, both in day-use and overnight areas.

Prince Edward Island. Under the Prince Edward Island provincial park system 39 areas comprise five classes of parks: nature preserves, natural environment parks, recreation parks, wayside/beach access, and historic parks. The parks system enhances the scenic drives which loop the coastal areas of the province.

Green Park, an historic park in a natural setting at the junction of the Bedford and Trout rivers, incorporates a shipbuilding centre consisting of the original home of James Yeo (a shipbuilder of the mid-1800s) an interpretative centre and a shipbuilding site. Strathgartney Park, a 40-acre (16 ha) area on the Trans-Canada Highway between Charlottetown and Borden is a picnic site and campground with hardwood groves, fresh spring water and a view over the West River. Lord Selkirk Park, an area of 30 acres (12 ha) of historic interest, at Eldon, contains an old French cemetery and marks the spot where Lord Selkirk landed. Brudenell River Park and Golf Course, comprising 1,285 acres (520 ha) at Roseneath, has a considerable area of woodland and runs to the shore of the Brudenell River. Jacques Cartier Park, an area of 23 acres (9 ha) at Kildare Beach near Alberton, is the historic place where Jacques Cartier first landed on Prince Edward Island. Cabot Park at Malpeque, named in honour of John Cabot, is a 300-acre (121 ha) area with sandy beaches and a museum. Several small parks have been developed or are under development. A fee of $5.00 tax included is charged for serviced tent and trailer sites and $3.75 tax included for unserviced sites. The parks are maintained by the Department of Tourism, Parks and Conservation.

Nova Scotia. The provincial park system, administered by the Department of Lands and Forests, Parks and Recreation Division, consists of 19 overnight campground parks, 52 day-use picnic park and roadside rest sites and 20 day-use beach parks with a total area of 10,962 acres (4 436 ha). In addition, 100 sites containing about 13,168 acres (5 329 ha) are held in reserve for future development. Overnight camping parks which are easily accessible from main arterial routes, usually contain a day-use picnic ground. The number of campsites in these parks varies from 12 to 165 with camp park size ranging between 29 and 1,667 acres (12-675 ha). Basic facilities include potable water, vault toilets, picnic tables, and trailer dumping stations; serviced campsites are not available for trailers. Picnic parks are roadside day-use rest areas located at 20- to 40-mile (32-64 km) intervals along major highways (other than on the controlled access routes). These parks range in size from less than one acre (0.4 ha) to more than 290 acres (117 ha) with basic facilities similar to those in campground parks. Day-use beach parks serve as recreational areas provided with picnic tables, potable water, vault toilets or flush toilets and change houses. The overnight camping fee is $4.00 per party per night with no charges in any park for day-use entry. Provincial parks supply a little less than 10% of the total number of campsites in Nova Scotia.

New Brunswick. The New Brunswick provincial park system, administered by the Department of Tourism, includes 23 recreational parks ranging in size from 25 to 1,400 acres (10-567 ha), 21 rest areas, seven campground parks, seven beach parks, a marine park and a resource park. Most are in rural areas throughout the province, adjacent to or easily accessible from main trunk roads. All contain tables, some form of toilet facility and a potable water supply; more elaborate facilities are available in the larger parks. A vehicle fee is charged at some parks and a daily camping fee of $3.00 to $4.00 is in effect at 25 of the larger parks, subject to change without notice. The department also maintains a wildlife park at Woolastook near Fredericton. In 1975 over 3.5 million persons visited the provincial parks. Several parks have organized activity programs and supervised swimming with life-guards. Mactaquac, near Fredericton, one of two year-round parks, boasts a championship 18-hole, 7,030-yd (6 428 m) golf course and two marinas. Both Mactaquac and New River Beach parks, between St. Stephen and Saint John, have interpretative programs with naturalists on staff. During the winter there are facilities for snowmobiling, cross-country skiing, snowshoeing, tobogganing, skating, sleigh rides and camping. Sugarloaf, near Campbellton, the other year-round park, features an alpine ski hill with three lifts, cross-country skiing, skating, snowmobiling, tobogganing and tennis. Campobello Provincial Park on Campobello Island has a 9-hole, 3,290-yd (3 008 m) golf course and lodge. In the past few years services on the 54,000 acres (21 853 ha) of parkland in New Brunswick have been expanded and improved.

Quebec. The provincial Parks Branch administers Quebec's parks and reserves with a view to preserving the natural environment for the enjoyment of future generations while allowing adequate facilities for today's population to make full use of the educational and recreational pursuits made possible by nature's bounty. During 1975-76 the Operations Division of the Parks Branch was responsible for 47 parks and 43 reserves, including 22 salmon streams totalling 300 miles (483 km) in length, and 60 campgrounds with more than 6,700 campsites.

The first park (Mont-Tremblant) was established in 1894. It covers 990 sq miles (2 564 km²) in area and is located north of Montreal. Five years later Laurentides Provincial Park was established north of Quebec City. It covers an area of some 2,690 sq miles (6 967 km²). New parks and reserves are being added year by year. The most recent additions were St. Bruno in 1975 and Kanogami and Frontenac parks in 1976.

More than a score of activities are carried out in the parks and reserves. They are important to tourism in terms of the number of visitors attracted from within and outside the province. In 1975-76 an unprecedented total of more than 5.5 million visits was recorded compared with nearly 4.0 million in 1974-75. The increases were most noticeable in the following activities: hiking, 164,000 persons; swimming, 176,000; canoeing, 44,000. Snowshoeing, cross-country and downhill skiing drew more than 1,050,000 visitors compared with some 720,000 in 1974-75.

Moose hunting by Quebec residents is permitted in Mont-Tremblant and Laurentides parks and in the La Vérendrye, Haute-Mauricie, Mastigouche, Saint-Maurice, Portneuf, Matane and Dunière reserves. Deer hunting is allowed in the Rimouski and Île d'Anticosti reserves. Small game hunting is also permitted in certain areas. Trout fishing, as well as fishing for other species, is carried out in about 20 parks and reserves. The Parks Branch also operates one salmon stream in the Quebec district, 10 in Gaspé–Lower St. Lawrence district, two in the North Shore district and nine on the Île d'Anticosti reserve.

In most parks and reserves, accommodation suited to the activity is available. During the summer season, the Parks Branch can also accommodate about 2,100 persons a night, in addition to the campgrounds.

Ontario. There are 122 provincial parks available for public use in Ontario and several new parks are being developed; 111 other areas, comprising 1,974 sq miles (5 089 km²), are held in reserve for future development. The total area of the Ontario provincial park system is about 18,692 sq miles (48 412 km²). The parklands are administered by the Parks Division of the Ministry of Natural Resources. The seven largest parks — Polar Bear, Algonquin, Quetico, Lake Superior, Missinaibi, Killarney and Sibley — have a combined area of about 15,076 sq miles (39 047 km²). Polar Bear Park is the largest, occupying 9,300 sq miles (24 087 km²) of Hudson Bay Lowland bordering Hudson Bay and James Bay and containing boreal forest, tundra and arctic flora and fauna. Algonquin Park covers 2,910 sq miles (7 537 km²), has 17 picnic and camping areas accessible by car and offers fine canoeing opportunities.

Under the Wilderness Areas Act of 1959, 40 wilderness areas have been established, varying in size, character and significance according to their historic, scientific, aesthetic or cultural values. In 1967 a policy of park classification and parkland zoning, to achieve a balanced park system and to provide a framework for effective development and management, defined five park classes — primitive, natural environment, wild river, nature reserve and recreation. Some areas once protected under the Wilderness Areas Act for their scientific value are being changed in law to be protected as nature reserves under the Provincial Parks Act. There are now seven nature reserves, four of them previously under the Wilderness Areas Act; all contain natural features and phenomena that are either unique or typical of the primitive or contemporary landscapes which form the ecological mosaic of Ontario. By the end of 1975, there were also five wild river parks: Mississagi, Chapleau–Nemegosenda, Lady Evelyn, Mattawa and Winisk.

To meet pressures for recreational space Ontario created the North Georgian Bay Recreational Reserve covering 4,500 sq miles (11 655 km²) between Algoma and Parry Sound on the north shore of Georgian Bay. It includes the channel between Manitoulin Island and the mainland, the 30,000 islands, the route of the voyageurs by way of French River, the remaining shoreline of Lake Nipissing and the La Cloche Mountains.

The number of park visitors increases year by year; in 1975 there were over 11 million including 1.6 million campers using more than 20,000 campsites. The charge for vehicles is $1.50 a day or $15 a year, and the camping charge $3.50 a night including vehicle. Picnic tables, fireplaces, fuelwood, tested drinking water and washrooms are provided at supervised tent and trailer campgrounds and most parks have trailer sanitation stations. Interpretative and naturalist programs are being expanded and museums, outdoor exhibits, conducted trips, illustrated talks and labelled nature trails are available in many parks.

Manitoba. The provincial parks system of Manitoba, administered by the Parks Branch of the Department of Tourism, Recreation and Cultural Affairs, consists of 12 major classifications. Provincial Natural Parks are relatively spacious land and water areas usually perpetuating one or more of the unique or representative environments of the province and providing recreational facilities which enable visitors to experience the naturalness of the park. Provincial Wilderness Parks are areas of limited development to maintain and preserve unique features or situations. Provincial Recreation Parks are spacious areas readily accessible for all-purpose recreational use. Provincial Recreational Trailways, Parkways and Waterways are routes of travel significant in the history and development of the province, and provide opportunities for camping, picnicking and interpretation. Provincial Heritage Parks were established for their human history and unique natural value or quality in illustrating or interpreting the provincial heritage, and not for their recreational potential. Provincial Wayside Parks are close to highways to serve transient users. Marine Parks are near waterways and provide facilities for recreational boating as well as fishing. Access Sites provide basic facilities for boating to permit access to fishing waters. Seasonal Dwelling Sites make space available for building summer homes. Information centres near highways provide regional interest and provincial travel information.

There are 10 provincial parks in Manitoba. Asessippi Provincial Park covers nine sq miles (23 km²) of scenic river valley and rolling hills behind the Shellmouth Dam at the junction of the Shell and Assiniboine rivers. Birds Hill Provincial Park is a 13-sq-mile (34 km²) multi-purpose park offering an 80-acre (32 ha) man-made lake within easy reach of Winnipeg. Clearwater Provincial Park, located 20 miles (32 km) north of The Pas, covers 230 sq miles (596 km²). Duck Mountain Provincial Park comprises 492 sq miles (1 274 km²) of rolling land and 73 lakes northwest of Dauphin. Grass River Provincial Park near Cranberry Portage comprises 230 sq miles (596 km²) of virtually roadless, rugged terrain that challenges veteran outdoorsmen. Grand Beach Provincial Park 60 miles (97 km) north of Winnipeg on the east shore of Lake Winnipeg is a 14-sq-mile (36 km²) park fronted by three miles (5 km) of broad white sand beach. Hecla Provincial Park covers 332 sq miles (860 km²) and is the most recent addition to the park system; it includes the Lake Winnipeg islands of Hecla, Black, Deer and several smaller islands; Grindstone Point, adjacent to the park on the mainland, is a recreation area; Hecla village is an historic Icelandic fishing site. Spruce Woods Provincial Park 30 miles (48 km) east of Brandon has an area of 90 sq miles (233 km²). Turtle Mountain Provincial Park covers 73 sq miles (189 km²) along the international border in the southwest corner of the province. Whiteshell Provincial Park, with an area of more than 1,056 sq miles (2 735 km²) of rugged Precambrian country, is Manitoba's largest provincial park.

Manitoba provincial parks cover a total area of about 3,385 sq miles (8 767 km²). There are also 43 provincial recreation areas, 10 provincial forest reserves, 90 provincial wayside parks, 45 historical sites and two provincial heritage parks. The parks system contains more than 60 campgrounds with over 5,000 campsites, many hunting and fishing lodges, motels, hotels and cabins, over 25 hiking trails, 15 snowmobile trails, and 18 canoe routes.

The number of park visitors was estimated at over 4 million for the year ended March 31, 1976. The admission fee to Manitoba's provincial parks is $1 a day or $5.50 for the season.

Saskatchewan. Saskatchewan's 17 provincial parks, comprising 1,880 sq miles (4 869 km²) of recreation land, range from forested parklands in the prairies and valley parks in the Qu'Appelle Valley to rugged northland settings. Each park offers camping, picnicking, boating and swimming facilities and a variety of recreational activities. Several operate a supervised recreation program for all ages — arts and crafts, hikes along nature trails, social functions and numerous team sports. Moose Mountain has a split-fieldstone chalet and modern cabin accommodation. Cabin facilities are available at Cypress Hills, Duck Mountain and Greenwater Lake parks. Golf courses are found at Cypress Hills, Greenwater Lake, Moose Mountain, Duck Mountain, Meadow Lake, Battlefords and Pike Lake parks. Lodgepole pine and white spruce in Cypress Hills Park provides cover for elk, deer, beaver, sharp-tailed grouse; antelope range on the plains nearby. In Duck Mountain, Moose Mountain and Greenwater Lake parks there are moose, elk, bear, deer and beaver, several varieties of grouse and many species of waterfowl and smaller land birds. Pike, pickerel and perch abound in almost all park lakes; brook, lake and rainbow trout are found in northern waters and brook and brown trout in the Cypress Hills area. Canoe routes and commercially operated fishing and hunting camps are features of three semi-wilderness parks — La Ronge, Nipawin and Meadow Lake. Roadside camp and picnic grounds, and four official campgrounds and several other camping areas are available along the province's 406-mile (653 km) stretch of Trans-Canada Highway, along the Yellowhead Route and Highways 5 and 14. Saskatchewan also operates 86 regional parks designed primarily for local patrons but attracting large numbers of tourists. Danielson Park has a modern visitors' centre with cafeteria and interpretative displays. Wildcat Hill is a 40,000-acre (16 187 ha) wilderness area in east-central Saskatchewan. Marked sites of historic interest total 143 and include the Wood Mountain NWMP Post, Last Mountain House, Touchwood Hills, Cannington Manor, Steele Narrows, Fort Carlton and Cumberland House historic parks. Winter recreation facilities include ski resorts at White Track in Buffalo Pound Provincial Park and at Mount Blackstrap in the Blackstrap Recreation Area, ski slopes in Duck Mountain Provincial Park and several of the regional parks and cross-country ski and snowmobile trails.

Alberta has 51 provincial parks containing 355.5 sq miles (921 km²); 49 of these, with a total area of approximately 216 sq miles (559 km²), are in use and continuing development. Kananaskis Provincial Park, with an area of 132 sq miles (342 km²), the largest, is in the southwest part of the province. Others are: Aspen Beach, Beauvais Lake, Big Hill Springs, Big Knife, Bow Valley, Bragg Creek, Calling Lake, Chain Lakes, Crimson Lake, Cross Lake, Cypress Hills, Dillberry Lake, Dinosaur, Dry Island Buffalo Jump, Garner Lake, Gooseberry Lake, Gregoire Lake, Hasse Lake, Jarvis Bay, Kinbrook Island, Lac Cardinal, Lesser

Slave Lake, Little Bow, Little Fish Lake, Long Lake, Ma-Me-O Beach, Miquelon Lake, Moonshine Lake, Moose Lake, O'Brien, Park Lake, Pembina River, Pigeon Lake, Police Outpost, Red Lodge, Rochon Sands, Saskatoon Island, Sir Winston Churchill, Taber, Thunder Lake, The Vermilion, Tillebrook Trans-Canada Campsite, Wabamun Lake, William A. Switzer (formerly Entrance), Williamson, Willow Creek, Winagami Lake, Woolford, Writing-on-Stone and Young's Point. These parks, generally provided with picnic, camping and playground facilities, are maintained by the Department of Recreation, Parks and Wildlife, Provincial Parks Division, primarily for the recreation and enjoyment of residents and visitors. There is a park within easy reach of almost every town in Alberta and over 4 million tourists and vacationers visit the parks annually.

Four areas have been set aside to protect the natural environment for present and future generations. Willmore Wilderness Park, 1,774.8 sq miles (4 596.7 km²) adjoins Jasper National Park in the north and extends along the British Columbia border. Siffleur Wilderness Area, 159.1 sq miles (412.1 km²), White Goat Wilderness Area, 171.7 sq miles (444.6 km²) and Ghost River Wilderness Area, 59.1 sq miles (153.1 km²) all are on the east side of Jasper and Banff national parks.

Complementing the wilderness areas are six natural areas established in representative zones of Alberta: Kootenay Plains, 8,320 acres (3 367 ha); Foothills, 160 acres (65 ha); Parkland, 159.6 acres (64.6 ha); Brown-Lowrey, 686.5 acres (277.8 ha); Red Rock Coulee, 801 acres (324 ha) and Plateau Mountain, 320 acres (129 ha).

British Columbia. There are 322 (175 developed) provincial parks in British Columbia, with a total area of about 10,287,023 acres (4 163 010 ha). Class A parks are intended to preserve outstanding natural, scenic and historic features for public recreation; they have a high degree of legislative protection against exploitation and alienation. Class B parks, also primarily for the protection of natural attractions, may permit other resource use if it does not unduly impair recreational values. Class C parks are intended primarily for local residents and are usually managed by local park boards. Nature Conservancy Areas in any park are fully protected from resource development and are dedicated to a variety of recreational uses. There are also 20 Recreation Areas encompassing a total area of 562,592 acres (227 673 ha) and one wilderness conservancy, Purcell, of 325,000 acres (131 523 ha) administered by the Parks Branch. There are immense wilderness areas such as Tweedsmuir Park and Wells Gray Park and outstanding scenic and mountain parks such as Garibaldi, Mount Robson, Manning, Bowron Lake, Mount Edziza, Atlin, Kwadacha Wilderness, Tatlatui and Mount Assiniboine. The formal gardens of Peace Arch Park are a monument to the goodwill between Canada and the United States. Vancouver Island is the site of Strathcona, first (1911) and at 561,453 acres (227 212 ha) one of the largest parks in the system, and a number of smaller parks. The restored gold town of Barkerville became the first provincial historic park; Fort Steele in the East Kootenay area is also being restored to preserve another of British Columbia's pioneer settlements. Eighteen marine parks with mooring facilities and campgrounds have been developed on mainland inlets and coastal islands.

The popularity of British Columbia's parks with their integrated campgrounds and picnic areas is attested to by the fact that over 550,000 camper party nights and 7,000,000 day visits were recorded during 1975.

1.4.3   The National Capital Region

Canada's Capital lies on the south shore of the Ottawa River below the Chaudière Falls and just above the confluence of the Rideau and Gatineau rivers. It was called "Ottawa" for Outaouac or Outaouais, the name of an Indian tribe from Lake Huron which traded with the French in the 17th century.

The United Province of Canada, following its formation in 1841, shuttled its capital between Kingston, Toronto, Montreal and Quebec and was trying to agree on a permanent site. At the end of 1857 Queen Victoria settled the dispute by choosing Ottawa and in 1866 the government of the Province of Canada moved to Ottawa. The next year the first Parliament of the new Dominion of Canada met in an incomplete Parliament Building on the former Barrack Hill.

During most of the next decade Ottawa grew and the government expanded. By the end of the century, Ottawa was a flourishing industrial centre with a population of 59,000. However, little effort had been made to preserve or enhance its natural beauty until the Ottawa Improvement Commission was formed in 1899. Several studies and plans for the improvement of the National Capital were considered but these were deferred because of World War I and for other reasons. Fire destroyed the Parliament Building in 1916 and left standing only the Library which now forms part of the building of neo-Gothic architecture which replaced it. The beautification of the Capital was continued by the Ottawa Improvement Commission until 1927 when it was replaced by the Federal District Commission. The first major step in the redevelopment of the National Capital took place in 1951 with the tabling of a comprehensive master plan for the National Capital Region, the "Gréber Plan". The National Capital Commission was formed in 1959 to carry out its recommendations.

Ottawa today, with a population of some 304,462, and the city of Hull on the north side of the Ottawa River, with a population of about 61,039, comprise the core of the National Capital Region, an area of about 1,800 sq miles (4 662 km²) in Ontario and Quebec. In lineal distance, the nearest extremity of the region to Parliament Hill is 18 miles (29 km) and the farthest is 35 miles (56 km). Within that area there are 57 municipalities and a total population of about 693,288. Industrial development in the region is limited, a large proportion of the work force being employed by or associated with the federal government.

Although the terms of reference of the National Capital Commission are "to prepare plans for and assist in the development, conservation and improvement of the National Capital Region in order that the nature and character of the seat of the Government of Canada may be in accordance with its national significance", the commission does not have jurisdictional authority over any of the municipal or regional authorities or the two provincial governments concerned. Most matters affecting the municipalities — such as planning, zoning, land use, building density, public transit, parking and construction of streets, arterial roads and highways — are within their sole jurisdiction, subject only to provincial government approval, so that the National Capital Commission in its development efforts depends essentially upon the cooperation of each municipality and provincial government.

In recent years, the efforts of the commission have focused on the development of a unified and lively core for the Capital. At a constitutional conference in Ottawa in 1969, the federal and provincial first ministers declared "the cities of Ottawa and Hull and their surrounding areas" to be the Canadian Capital Region. Almost immediately, work began to remove the longstanding economic disparity between Hull and Ottawa; 59 acres (24 ha) were acquired in Hull for a federal building program to house various government departments. These include 44 acres (18 ha) acquired in 1972 from the E.B. Eddy Company. In 1973 work was completed on the new Portage Bridge linking Ottawa and Hull and the new Airport Parkway from the airport to downtown Ottawa–Hull was opened.

The recreational amenities of the region have been developed for people to use and enjoy. In addition to scenic driveways, parks and playgrounds, the Rideau Canal provides a five-mile (8 km) ice skating surface in winter and boating in summer. Maple sugar shanties, large garden allotments and 50 miles (80 km) of bicycle paths winding past waterways and through pleasant wooded areas have also been developed. Public concerts in the parks, walking tours, attractive pedestrian malls and museums are there for the participation of all Canadians and their visitors.

1.5   The environment

The Department of the Environment was created in June 1971 to spearhead the attack on pollution and ensure the management and development of Canada's renewable natural resources. It has the responsibility to initiate government-wide programs and to coordinate efforts related to environmental protection. It also provides specialist advisory services to other departments in the formulation of programs and in the development of regulations under Federal Acts assigned to other ministers.

The Environmental Protection Service of the department is responsible for developing and enforcing environmental protection regulations and other instruments used in implementing federal laws relating to the environment. It also serves as an information source for other federal departments.

The water pollution control program's main objectives are: the reduction of existing pollution and the prevention of new problems; achievement of regional water quality objectives; and the development of new technologies to solve water pollution control problems more economically. Water pollution control regulations and guidelines are being developed for all major industrial sectors. Regulations already exist governing the pulp and paper industry, mercury from the chlor-alkali industry and the petroleum refinery industry. These regulations, promulgated under the Fisheries Act, restrict the amount of effluents an industry can discharge into waters inhabited by aquatic life. Other programs include water pollution surveys in shellfish growing areas; phosphorus concentration control regulations; analytical and advisory services to other federal departments and agencies; inventories of water pollution problems in Canada and annual assessments of pollution control costs and studies on the treatment of municipal and industrial waste waters.

The broad objectives of the air pollution control program are to preserve, restore, or enhance the quality of the ambient air in Canada. Programs include: collection and evaluation of information regarding air pollution sources in Canada; development of abatement and compliance programs for stationary and mobile air pollution sources; preparation of regulations controlling the amount of lead in leaded gases and defining the limits of lead and phosphorus in "unleaded" grades of gasoline as well as regulations defining national emission standards for secondary lead smelters; maintenance of a mobile motor vehicle emission testing facility and promulgation of national air quality objectives.

The Environmental Conservation Directorate is developing and implementing programs designed to protect and conserve the environment. The environmental emergency program involves activities associated with environmental threats, such as oil spills. The program examines the national state of preparedness to cope with such accidents, and coordinates the development of improved preparedness. It also acts as the focal point through which the expertise and resources of the department can deal with an environmental accident.

The environmental contaminants program involves protection from the adverse effects of identifiable substances produced by industrial activities. This program is responsible for the management of hazardous materials, and development of codes of good practice and guidelines for the identification, transportation, storage and disposal of environmentally hazardous materials. Two acts developed under this program are: the Environmental Contaminants Act, by which the federal government may provide for the control of chemicals that may be disseminated in the environment, are persistent and are harmful to human health or the environment; the Ocean Dumping Control Act, by which deliberate dumping of certain substances from ships, aircraft and platforms at sea is subject to a permit issued by the Environmental Protection Service. The solid waste management program's objectives are to reduce the impact on the environment and increase resource recovery and energy conservation from solid wastes.

The federal activities environmental protection program deals with facilities and activities of all federal government agencies and Crown corporations, concerning both land installations and vessels. These include treatment and disposal of waste water, solid waste management, air pollution, noise pollution and other operations which threaten environmental quality. This program has the responsibility for a national approach to the management of noise and for the development and implementation of ecological protection regulations, guidelines and codes; analysis and appraisal of ecological impact studies; implementation of control measures; and enforcement and surveillance activities.

The federal government is committed to cleaning up pollution problems at federal facilities within a reasonable time. Clean-up projects have dealt with water, air, noise, dust and solid waste pollution problems at airports, government offices, laboratories, grain elevators, defence bases, parks, ships and harbours.

Federal legislation   1.5.1

A large number of statutes are concerned with renewable resources and environmental quality management. Major pieces of legislation for which the Department of the Environment (since September 1976 known as the Department of Fisheries and the Environment) is responsible include the following: The Fisheries Act (RSC 1970, c.F-14, amended 1970); The Canada Water Act (and phosphate regulations) (RSC 1970, c.5 1st Supp.); The Migratory Birds Convention Act (RSC 1970, c.M-12); The International River Improvements Act (RSC 1970, c.I-22); The Game Export Act (RSC 1970, c.G-1); The Fisheries Development Act (and the Fish-Chilling Assistance Regulations) (RSC 1970, c.F-21, amended 1973 and 1974); The Clean Air Act (and Lead Free Gasoline Regulations) (SC 1970-71-72, c.47); The Forestry Development and Research Act (RSC 1970, c.F-30); Canada Wildlife Act (SC 1973, c.21); Weather Modification Information Act (SC 1970-71-72, c.59); and Fish Inspection Act (RSC 1970, c.F-12); Environmental Contaminants Act (SC 1973-74, c.55); Ocean Dumping Control Act (SC 1973-74, c.72).

An Interdepartmental Committee on the Environment was established in 1973. This committee, with representation at the deputy minister level, is the primary forum for interdepartmental consultation on environmental and related resource issues and assists the Department of Fisheries and the Environment in coordinating the development and implementation of Canada's environmental policies and programs.

Federal-provincial programs   1.5.2

Jurisdiction over renewable resources and environmental matters is shared by the federal and provincial governments. In some areas, such as fisheries, legislative jurisdiction rests with the federal government, although management and administrative responsibilities have been delegated to certain provinces; in other areas, such as forest resources, the legislative jurisdiction rests with the provinces.

In order to develop further cooperative action, the Department of Fisheries and the Environment has initiated discussions with the provinces toward concluding Federal-Provincial Accords for the Protection and Enhancement of Environmental Quality. These accords are viewed as "umbrella" agreements under which subsidiary agreements covering specific aspects of environmental action may be signed.

There is a wide range of federal-provincial programs and activities in the environmental and renewable resource field and examples of some of the current ones follow.

Assessments of the potential environmental impact of major projects, in which the federal government has an interest, are being carried out by federal departments in cooperation with provincial and territorial governments. Procedures have been issued which ensure that environmental matters are taken into account. This process will provide for consultation and cooperation with the provinces and territories in assessments of projects of mutual concern.

The National Air Pollution Surveillance Network established under the authority of the Clean Air Act consists, with certain exceptions, of monitoring stations operated by provincial governments using equipment loaned by the federal government.

The management of Canada's water resources requires continuing institutional arrangements within which all jurisdictions and expertise can be brought together for joint goal setting, planning and operation. Federal-provincial agreements under the authority of the Canada Water Act provide for water basin management programs and include agreements for joint study of water management in specific geographical areas. Also arrangements may be made with individual provinces to coordinate federal and provincial water quality monitoring programs and to exchange data.

Many other formal and informal federal-provincial programs are related to specific aspects of renewable resources and the environment such as fisheries, forest and wildlife management, hydrometric data gathering, flood damage assistance and flood control, forest pest control and weather forecasting. Specific non-recurring joint programs are developed from time to time. An example is the Canada/Ontario study to survey Great Lakes shoreline damage resulting from recent high water levels and to provide the basis for recommendations on long-term remedial and protective measures.

1.5.3 International programs

Canada is involved in two distinct types of multilateral programs — those which are primarily environmental and those which are primarily resource conservation and management. Most of the latter focus on the aquatic environment. For example, Canada is a member of the International Council for Exploration of the Sea. This 17-member body encourages and coordinates studies of the marine environment with particular reference to the living resources of the sea, primarily in the North Sea and North Atlantic. Canada is also a member of 10 international fisheries commissions established under formal conventions. These commissions assume responsibility for the investigation of specific living marine resources in defined areas, in order to further rationalize development and conservation of fisheries of common concern to member states.

Canada is participating in the International Hydrological Program set up under UNESCO to facilitate a better scientific understanding of hydrological phenomena, and was chairman of the intergovernmental council for IHP during the biennium 1975-77. Canada is also participating in the Operational Hydrological Program set up under World Meteorological Organization auspices to facilitate a better understanding of operational methods in hydrology. These two international programs are closely coordinated.

Canada played an active role in preparing for the UN Water Conference in Argentina in March 1977, a high level policy conference focussing on coordinated water management at the national level.

Canada has also been active in the Intergovernmental Maritime Consultative Organization (IMCO), one of the specialized agencies of the United Nations, particularly on the Marine Environment Protection Committee. In October 1973, IMCO sponsored an international conference on marine pollution which drafted an international agreement regulating the intentional and negligent discharges of oil and other harmful substances by ships and other equipment operating in the marine environment. The International Convention on Dumping of Wastes at Sea, formulated in accordance with a recommendation of the Stockholm UN Conference and concluded and opened for signature on December 29, 1972, has been signed and ratified by Canada. Canada has been an active member in the consultative meetings concerning that convention.

Because Canada has an extensive coastline and continental shelf, it was deeply involved in preparations for the Third United Nations Conference on the Law of the Sea. The procedural session opened in New York in December 1973 and substantive sessions took place in Caracas (Summer 1974), Geneva (Spring 1975), and New York (Spring 1976 and August 1976). Among the issues dealt with at the conference were sovereign rights over the resources of the continental shelf, rights concerning the management and conservation of living resources in coastal waters, rights of coastal states to take measures to protect their marine environment, rights to control scientific research within zones of maritime jurisdiction, and rights of all states to the disposition of the riches of the seabed beyond national jurisdiction for the benefit of all mankind.

Among broad-spectrum multilateral environmental organizations, the United Nations Environment Program (UNEP) involves the largest cross-section of developed and developing countries with economies ranging from centrally-planned to free-enterprise. This program, formed as a result of the Stockholm United Nations Conference on the Human Environment in 1972, has headquarters in Nairobi, Kenya. Canada is a member of the Governing Council, has participated in the development of its program, and has contributed to the UN Environment Fund. The fourth session of the Governing Council was held in Nairobi in April 1976 and priority programs approved included: human settlements and habitat; human health and well-being; natural disasters; environment and development; environmental management; social outer limits; oceans and marine living resources; water and desertification; terrestrial ecosystems; socio-economic impact of environmental measures; energy; and the Earthwatch program. Nationally, work continued on a coordinated federal-provincial response to the Stockholm Action Plan. A substantive result of this domestic activity was the publication of a report prepared by a federal-provincial task force on a Canadian action plan, *Canada's environment — a framework for action.*

Canada also played an active and visible role in three major UN-sponsored conferences, the World Population Conference, Bucharest, August 1974, the World Food Conference, Rome, November 1974, and Habitat: UN Conference on Human Settlements, Vancouver, June 1976.

In 1973 Canada became a full member of the Economic Commission for Europe, one of five regional economic commissions within the UN system. Environmental-related activities are undertaken by a large number of the commission's principal subsidiary bodies, with a coordinating responsibility assigned to Senior Advisers on Environmental Problems. Canada participated in a number of activities and played a prominent role in the fourth session of the Senior Advisers on Environmental Problems, held in Geneva in February 1976. Canada indicated particular interest in priority setting and resource allocation in areas of common interest to a number of international organizations such as transboundary air pollution and non-waste technology.

Canada has also continued to participate in the UNESCO program on Man and the Biosphere (MAB) — an internationally coordinated interdisciplinary research program focusing on conservation of the resources of the biosphere. As a member of the International Coordinating Council, Canada has been influential in building social science concerns into the development of proposals. Canada has continued to provide experts to participate in international meetings to further develop specific proposals. Nationally, work on three sub-program areas, urbanization, agricultural and forestry practices and coastal ecosystems has progressed to the stage of publishing provisional research frameworks and work is well advanced on the fourth, Science for the North. Now that the infrastructure of the Canadian program is in place, more emphasis is being placed on the selection of research projects and programs consistent with international and Canadian MAB criteria and on the service Canada/MAB can provide in areas related to environmental management.

In 1970, the Organization for Economic Cooperation and Development established an Environment Committee to promote understanding and international agreement on the assessment of environmental problems, particularly as they affect economic and social development, and proposed solutions. Canada has participated actively in the work of this committee and its various sector and advisory groups. Late in 1974, the first Environment Committee meeting at the ministerial level was held to review progress. Recommendations on future work endorsed at that time are being implemented, subject to amendment reflecting changing conditions such as those flowing from the economic problems of the mid-70s.

Canada is also a member of the North Atlantic Treaty Organization's Committee on the Challenges of Modern Society. The work of this body is conducted through a series of pilot projects on specific problems. Member countries participate only in those problems of special interest to them. Canada was the lead country in a pilot project on inland water pollution, completed in 1974, and also of another completed project on coastal water pollution. Canada is participating in pilot projects on waste water treatment, advanced health care, energy conservation, disposal of hazardous wastes and air pollution assessment. In late 1975, the committee accepted Canada's offer to lead a new project on nutrition and health.

Many international organizations are monitoring programs and Canada has continued to participate in these collaborative efforts. For example, Canada is a member of the World Weather Watch, and has now established nine of a planned 11-station network for monitoring air pollution in non-urban areas. In addition, and in cooperation with some provinces, Canada is providing air quality data for Canadian cities as part of a World Health Organization program. Canada also contributed to the program of the Integrated Global Ocean Station System (IGOSS), the Global Investigation of the Pollution of the Marine Environment (GIPME) of the Intergovernmental Oceanographic Commission (IOC), participated in the Group of Experts on the Scientific Aspects of Marine Pollution (GESAMP), and cooperated in the continuing development of the Global Environmental Monitoring System, an integral part of the Earthwatch program.

Sources

1.1 Geography Division, Surveys and Mapping Branch, Department of Energy, Mines and Resources; population of Canada, the 1976 Census of Canada; population of the United States and Brazil from *Population and vital statistics report, data available as of 1 April 1976, United Nations, New York, 1976* and areas of the USSR, China and Brazil from the United Nations *Statistical year book — 1971.*
1.1.1 Topographical Survey Directorate, Surveys and Mapping Branch, Department of Energy, Mines and Resources.
1.1.2 - 1.1.3 Information Services Directorate, Department of Fisheries and the Environment.
1.1.4 - 1.1.5 Geography Division, Department of Energy, Mines and Resources.
1.2 Geological Survey of Canada, Department of Energy, Mines and Resources.
1.3.1 Information Services Directorate, Department of Fisheries and the Environment.
1.3.2 Division of Physics, National Research Council.
1.4 - 1.4.1 Canada Year Book Section, Information Division, Statistics Canada; Information Services, Department of Indian Affairs and Northern Development; except Gatineau Park supplied by the National Capital Commission.
1.4.2 Supplied by the respective provincial government departments.
1.4.3 National Capital Commission.
1.5 Information Services Directorate, Department of Fisheries and the Environment.

Tables

Tables

..	not available	e	estimate
...	not appropriate or not applicable	p	preliminary
—	nil or zero	r	revised
--	too small to be expressed		certain tables may not add due to rounding

1.1 Approximate land and freshwater areas, by province

Province or territory	Land sq miles	Freshwater sq miles	Total sq miles	Percentage of total area
Newfoundland	143,045	13,140	156,185	4.1
Island of Newfoundland	41,164	2,195	43,359	1.1
Labrador	101,881	10,945	112,826	3.0
Prince Edward Island	2,184	—	2,184	0.1
Nova Scotia	20,402	1,023	21,425	0.6
New Brunswick	27,835	519	28,354	0.7
Quebec	523,860	71,000	594,860	15.4
Ontario	344,092	68,490	412,582	10.7
Manitoba	211,775	39,225	251,000	6.5
Saskatchewan	220,182	31,518	251,700	6.5
Alberta	248,800	6,485	255,285	6.6
British Columbia	359,279	6,976	366,255	9.5
Yukon Territory	205,346	1,730	207,076	5.4
Northwest Territories	1,253,438	51,465	1,304,903	33.9
Franklin	541,753	7,500	549,253	14.3
Keewatin	218,460	9,700	228,160	5.9
Mackenzie	493,225	34,265	527,490	13.7
Canada	3,560,238	291,571	3,851,809	100.0

1.2 Principal heights in each province

Province and height	Elevation ft	Province and height	Elevation ft
NEWFOUNDLAND		QUEBEC (concluded)	
Long Range Mountains		Rond Summit (Sutton Mountains)	3,175
Lewis Hills	2,672	Mount Bayfield	2,925
Gros Morne	2,644	Mount Orford	2,875
Table Mountain (St. Barbe District)	2,375	Hereford Mountain	2,775
Mount St. Gregory	2,251	Barn Mountain	2,775
Gros Paté	2,152	Le Pinacle Mountain	2,325
Blue Mountain	2,128	The Laurentians	
Blue Hills of Couteau		Mont Tremblant	3,175
Peter Snout	1,625	Mont Sainte-Anne	2,625
Central Highlands		Mont Sir Wilfrid	2,569
Main Topsail	1,822	Monteregian Hills	
Mizzen Topsail	1,761	Brome Mountain	1,750
Torngat Mountains		Shefford Mountain	1,700
Unnamed peak (58°57′ 63°47′)	5,232	Mont Saint-Hilaire	1,350
Cirque Mountain	5,144	Yamaska Mountain	1,350
Mount Cladonia	4,766	Rougemont	1,300
Mount Eliot	4,553		
Mount Tetragona	4,450	ONTARIO	
Quartzite Mountain	3,890	Highest point, Timiskaming District	
Blow-Me-Down Mountain	3,880	(47°20′ 80°44′)	2,275
Kaumajet Mountains		Ogidaki Mountain	2,183
Bishops Mitre	3,650	Batchawana Mountain	2,142
Finger Hill	3,390	Tip Top Mountain	2,099
		Niagara Escarpment	
PRINCE EDWARD ISLAND		Blue Mountains	1,775
		Osler Bluff	1,725
Highest point on the Island, Queens County (46°20′ 63°27′)	465	Caledon Mountain	1,400
		High Hill	1,163
NOVA SCOTIA		Mount Nemo	1,000
Highest point, Cape Breton (46°42′ 60°36′)	1,747	MANITOBA	
Franey Mountain	1,405	Baldy Mountain	2,729
Nuttby Mountain (Cobequid)	1,204	Porcupine Hills	2,700
Dalhousie Mountain (Cobequid)	1,115	Riding Mountain	2,000
NEW BRUNSWICK		SASKATCHEWAN	
Mount Carleton	2,690	Cypress Hills	4,567
Moose Mountain	1,325	Wood Mountain	3,325
		Vermilion Hills	2,575
QUEBEC		ALBERTA	
Mont D'Iberville (Torngat Mountains)	5,210	Mount Columbia	12,294
Appalachian Mountains		The Twins	12,250
Mont Jacques-Cartier (Shickshock Mountains)	4,160	Mount Alberta	11,874
Mount Richardson	3,887	Mount Assiniboine	11,870
Mount Albert District		Mount Forbes	11,852
Albert Sud Summit	3,775	Mount Temple	11,626
Mount Logan	3,725	Mount Lyell	11,550
Mont Mégantic	3,625	Mount Hungabee	11,550
Albert Nord Summit	3,554	Snow Dome	11,550
Matawees Mountain	3,525	Mount Kitchener	11,500

1.1   Approximate land and freshwater areas, by province   M

Province or territory	Land km²	Freshwater km²	Total km²	Percentage of total area
Newfoundland	370 485	34 032	404 517	4.1
Island of Newfoundland	*106 614*	*5 685*	*112 299*	*1.1*
Labrador	*263 871*	*28 347*	*292 218*	*3.0*
Prince Edward Island	5 657	—	5 657	0.1
Nova Scotia	52 841	2 650	55 491	0.6
New Brunswick	72 092	1 344	73 436	0.7
Quebec	1 356 791	183 889	1 540 680	15.4
Ontario	891 194	177 388	1 068 582	10.7
Manitoba	548 495	101 592	650 087	6.5
Saskatchewan	570 269	81 631	651 900	6.5
Alberta	644 389	16 796	661 185	6.6
British Columbia	930 528	18 068	948 596	9.5
Yukon Territory	531 844	4 481	536 325	5.4
Northwest Territories	3 246 390	133 294	3 379 684	33.9
Franklin	*1 403 134*	*19 425*	*1 422 559*	*14.3*
Keewatin	*565 809*	*25 123*	*590 932*	*5.9*
Mackenzie	*1 277 447*	*88 746*	*1 366 193*	*13.7*
Canada	9 220 975	755 165	9 976 140	100.0

1.2   Principal heights in each province   M

Province and height	Elevation m	Province and height	Elevation m
NEWFOUNDLAND		Rond Summit (Sutton Mountains)	968
Long Range Mountains		Mount Bayfield	892
Lewis Hills	814	Mount Orford	876
Gros Morne	806	Hereford Mountain	846
Table Mountain (St. Barbe District)	724	Barn Mountain	846
Mount St. Gregory	686	Le Pinacle Mountain	709
Gros Paté	656	The Laurentians	
Blue Mountain	649	Mont Tremblant	968
Blue Hills of Couteau		Mont Sainte-Anne	800
Peter Snout	495	Mont Sir Wilfrid	783
Central Highlands		Monteregian Hills	
Main Topsail	555	Brome Mountain	533
Mizzen Topsail	537	Shefford Mountain	518
Torngat Mountains		Mont Saint-Hilaire	411
Unnamed peak (58°57′ 63°47′)	*1 595*	Yamaska Mountain	411
Cirque Mountain	1 568	Rougemont	396
Mount Cladonia	1 453		
Mount Eliot	1 388	**ONTARIO**	
Mount Tetragona	1 356	Highest point, Timiskaming District	
Quartzite Mountain	1 186	(47°20′ 80°44′)	*693*
Blow-Me-Down Mountain	1 183	Ogidaki Mountain	665
Kaumajet Mountains		Batchawana Mountain	653
Bishops Mitre	1 113	Tip Top Mountain	640
Finger Hill	1 033	Niagara Escarpment	
		Blue Mountains	541
PRINCE EDWARD ISLAND		Osler Bluff	526
Highest point on the Island, Queens		Caledon Mountain	427
County (46°20′ 63°27′)	*142*	High Hill	354
		Mount Nemo	305
NOVA SCOTIA			
Highest point, Cape Breton (46°42′ 60°36′)	*532*	**MANITOBA**	
Franey Mountain	428	Baldy Mountain	*832*
Nuttby Mountain (Cobequid)	367	Porcupine Hills	823
Dalhousie Mountain (Cobequid)	340	Riding Mountain	610
NEW BRUNSWICK		**SASKATCHEWAN**	
Mount Carleton	*820*	Cypress Hills	*1 392*
Moose Mountain	404	Wood Mountain	1 013
		Vermilion Hills	785
QUEBEC			
Mont D'Iberville (Torngat Mountains)	*1 588*	**ALBERTA**	
Appalachian Mountains		Mount Columbia	*3 747*
Mont Jacques-Cartier (Shickshock		The Twins	3 734
Mountains)	1 268	Mount Alberta	3 619
Mount Richardson	1 185	Mount Assiniboine	3 618
Mount Albert District		Mount Forbes	3 612
Albert Sud Summit	1 151	Mount Temple	3 544
Mount Logan	1 135	Mount Lyell	3 520
Mont Mégantic	1 105	Mount Hungabee	3 520
Albert Nord Summit	1 083	Snow Dome	3 520
Matawees Mountain	1 074	Mount Kitchener	3 505

1.2   Principal heights in each province (concluded)

Province and height	Elevation ft	Province and height	Elevation ft
ALBERTA (concluded)		**BRITISH COLUMBIA** (concluded)	
Mount Athabasca	11,452	Mount Sir Alexander	10,740
Mount King Edward	11,400	Fresnoy Mountain	10,730
Mount Brazeau	11,386	Mount Gordon	10,550
Mount Victoria	11,365	Mount Stephen	10,495
Stutfield Peak	11,320	Cathedral Mountain	10,464
Mount Joffre	11,316	Odaray Mountain	10,350
Deltaform Mountain	11,235	The President	10,297
Mount Lefroy	11,230	Mount Laussedat	10,035
Mount Alexandra	11,214		
Mount Sir Douglas	11,174	**YUKON TERRITORY**	
Mount Woolley	11,170	St. Elias Mountains	
Lunette Peak	11,150	Mount Logan	19,524ʳ
Mount Hector	11,148	Mount St. Elias	18,008
Diadem Peak	11,060	Mount Lucania	17,147
Mount Edith Cavell	11,033	King Peak	16,971
Mount Fryatt	11,026	Mount Steele	16,644
Mount Chown	10,930	Mount Wood	15,885
Mount Wilson	10,700	Mount Vancouver	15,700
Clearwater Mountain	10,420	Mount Hubbard	15,015
Mount Coleman	10,286	Mount Walsh	14,780
Eiffel Peak	10,101	Mount Alverstone	14,565
Pinnacle Mountain	10,062	McArthur Peak	14,253
		Mount Augusta	14,070
BRITISH COLUMBIA		Mount Kennedy	13,905
Vancouver Island Ranges		Mount Strickland	13,818
Golden Hinde	7,219	Mount Newton	13,811
Mount Albert Edward	6,828	Mount Cook	13,760
Mount Arrowsmith	5,962	Mount Craig	13,250
Coast Mountains		Mount Malaspina	12,750
Mount Waddington	13,104	Mount Badham	12,625
St. Elias Mountains		Mount Seattle	10,082
Fairweather Mountain	15,300		
Mount Root	12,860	**NORTHWEST TERRITORIES**	
Monashee Mountains		Arctic Islands	
Mount Begbie	8,963	Baffin	
Storm Hill	5,300	Penny Ice Cap	6,750
Selkirk Mountains		Mount Thule	5,614
Mount Sir Sandford	11,555	Cockscomb Mountain	5,330
Mount Dawson	11,123	Barnes Ice Cap	3,685
Adamant Mountain	11,009	Knife Edge Mountain	2,493
Grand Mountain	10,842	Banks	
Iconoclast Mountain	10,666	Durham Heights	2,400
Rogers Peak	10,546	Devon	
Purcell Mountains		Ice Cap	6,300
Mount Farnham	11,343	Ellesmere	
Mount Karnak	11,100	Barbeau Peak, highest point in	
Columbia (Cariboo) Mountains		Arctic Islands	8,584
Sir Wilfrid Laurier	11,300	Commonwealth Mountain	7,250
Rocky Mountains		Mount Jeffers	6,250
Mount Robson	12,972	Mount Wood	4,750
Mount Clemenceau	12,001	Mount Cheops	4,750
Mount Goodsir	11,750	Victoria	
Mount Bryce	11,507	Shaler Mountains	2,150
The Helmet	11,250	Mount Bumpus	1,650
Resplendent Mountain	11,240	Mainland	
Mount King George	11,226	Mount Sir James MacBrien	9,062
Whitehorn Mountain	11,139	Franklin Mountains	
Mount Huber	11,051	Cap Mountain	5,175
Mount Freshfield	10,945	Mount Clark	4,798
Mount Mummery	10,918	Pointed Mountain	4,610
Mount Vaux	10,891	Nahanni Butte	4,579
Mount Ball	10,865	Richardson Mountains	
Bush Mountain	10,850	Mount Goodenough	3,219
Mount Geikie	10,843		

1.3   Elevations, areas and depths of the Great Lakes

Lake	Elevation[1] ft	Length miles	Breadth miles	Maximum depth ft	Total area sq miles	Area on Canadian side of boundary sq miles
Superior	600	350	160	1,330	31,700	11,100
Michigan	579	307	118	923	22,300	—
Huron	579	206	183	750	23,000	13,900
St. Clair	573	26	24	21	430	268
Erie	570	241	57	210	9,910	4,930
Ontario	245	193	53	802	7,340	3,880

[1]Long-term mean, 1860-1972; International Great Lakes Datum, 1955.

1.2 Principal heights in each province (concluded)   M

Province and height	Elevation m	Province and height	Elevation m
ALBERTA (concluded)		**BRITISH COLUMBIA** (concluded)	
Mount Athabasca	3 491	Mount Sir Alexander	3 274
Mount King Edward	3 475	Fresnoy Mountain	3 271
Mount Brazeau	3 470	Mount Gordon	3 216
Mount Victoria	3 464	Mount Stephen	3 199
Stutfield Peak	3 450	Cathedral Mountain	3 189
Mount Joffre	3 449	Odaray Mountain	3 155
Deltaform Mountain	3 424	The President	3 139
Mount Lefroy	3 423	Mount Laussedat	3 059
Mount Alexandra	3 418		
Mount Sir Douglas	3 406	**YUKON TERRITORY**	
Mount Woolley	3 405	St. Elias Mountains	
Lunette Peak	3 399	Mount Logan	*5 951*
Mount Hector	3 398	Mount St. Elias	5 489
Diadem Peak	3 371	Mount Lucania	5 226
Mount Edith Cavell	3 363	King Peak	5 173
Mount Fryatt	3 361	Mount Steele	5 073
Mount Chown	3 331	Mount Wood	4 842
Mount Wilson	3 261	Mount Vancouver	4 785
Clearwater Mountain	3 176	Mount Hubbard	4 577
Mount Coleman	3 135	Mount Walsh	4 505
Eiffel Peak	3 079	Mount Alverstone	4 439
Pinnacle Mountain	3 067	McArthur Peak	4 344
		Mount Augusta	4 289
BRITISH COLUMBIA		Mount Kennedy	4 238
Vancouver Island Ranges		Mount Strickland	4 212
Golden Hinde	2 200	Mount Newton	4 210
Mount Albert Edward	2 081	Mount Cook	4 194
Mount Arrowsmith	1 817	Mount Craig	4 039
Coast Mountains		Mount Malaspina	3 886
Mount Waddington	3 994	Mount Badham	3 848
St. Elias Mountains		Mount Seattle	3 073
Fairweather Mountain	*4 663*		
Mount Root	3 920	**NORTHWEST TERRITORIES**	
Monashee Mountains		Arctic Islands	
Mount Begbie	2 732	Baffin	
Storm Hill	1 615	Penny Ice Cap	2 057
Selkirk Mountains		Mount Thule	1 711
Mount Sir Sandford	3 522	Cockscomb Mountain	1 625
Mount Dawson	3 390	Barnes Ice Cap	1 123
Adamant Mountain	3 356	Knife Edge Mountain	760
Grand Mountain	3 305	Banks	
Iconoclast Mountain	3 251	Durham Heights	732
Rogers Peak	3 214	Devon	
Purcell Mountains		Ice Cap	1 920
Mount Farnham	3 457	Ellesmere	
Mount Karnak	3 383	Barbeau Peak, highest point in	
Columbia (Cariboo) Mountains		Arctic Islands	2 616
Sir Wilfrid Laurier	3 444	Commonwealth Mountain	2 210
Rocky Mountains		Mount Jeffers	1 905
Mount Robson	3 954	Mount Wood	1 448
Mount Clemenceau	3 658	Mount Cheops	1 448
Mount Goodsir	3 581	Victoria	
Mount Bryce	3 507	Shaler Mountains	655
The Helmet	3 429	Mount Bumpus	503
Resplendent Mountain	3 426	Mainland	
Mount King George	3 422	Mount Sir James MacBrien	*2 762*
Whitehorn Mountain	3 395	Franklin Mountains	
Mount Huber	3 368	Cap Mountain	1 577
Mount Freshfield	3 336	Mount Clark	1 462
Mount Mummery	3 328	Pointed Mountain	1 405
Mount Vaux	3 320	Nahanni Butte	1 396
Mount Ball	3 312	Richardson Mountains	
Bush Mountain	3 307	Mount Goodenough	981
Mount Geikie	3 305		

1.3 Elevations, areas and depths of the Great Lakes   M

Lake	Elevation[1] m	Length km	Breadth km	Maximum depth m	Total area km²	Area on Canadian side of boundary km²
Superior	183	563	257	405	82 103	28 749
Michigan	176	494	190	281	57 757	—
Huron	176	332	295	229	59 570	36 001
St. Clair	175	42	39	6	1 114	694
Erie	174	388	92	64	25 667	12 769
Ontario	75	311	85	244	19 011	10 049

[1]Long-term mean, 1860-1972; International Great Lakes Datum, 1955.

1.4   Elevations and areas of principal lakes[1] (exceeding 150 sq miles), by province

Province and lake	Elevation ft	Area sq miles	Province and lake	Elevation ft	Area sq miles
NEWFOUNDLAND AND LABRADOR			**SASKATCHEWAN** (concluded)		
			Montreal	1,608	176
Ashuanipi	1,735	231	Peter Pond	1,382	300
Atikoniak	1,700	167	Pinehouse	1,262	156
Grand	284	208	Primrose	1,964	173
Joseph	1,700	174	Reindeer[2]	1,106	2,568
Melville	tidal	1,185	Scott	1,458	152
Michikamau	1,510	784	Tazin	1,130	151
Lobstick	1,500	197	Wollaston	1,306	1,035
Ossokmanuan Reservoir	1,570	322			
Smallwood Reservoir	1,545	2,500e	**ALBERTA**		
			Bistcho	1,812	165
NOVA SCOTIA			Claire	700	555
			Lesser Slave	1,892	451
Bras d'Or	tidal	424			
			BRITISH COLUMBIA		
QUEBEC			Atlin[2]	2,190	299
Albanel	1,276	172	Babine	2,332	191
Bienville	1,400	482	Kootenay	1,745	157
Cabonga Reservoir	1,185	262	Ootsa	2,800	156
Dozois Reservoir	1,135	156	Williston	2,180	680
Eau Claire	790	534			
Evans	792	211	**YUKON TERRITORY**		
Gouin Reservoir	1,325	606	Kluane	2,563	158
Kaniapiskau	1,850	182			
Leaf	tidal	175	**NORTHWEST TERRITORIES**		
Lower Seal	860	223			
Manouane	1,620	226	Aberdeen	261	425
Minto	550	294	Amadjuak	370	1,203
Mistassini	1,220	902	Angikuni	842	197
Payne	425	206	Artillery	1,196	213
Pipmuacan	1,300	378	Aubry	845	151
Saint-Jean	321	387	Aylmer	1,230	327
Sakami	640	229	Baker	8	729
			Bluenose	1,828	155
ONTARIO			Buffalo	870	237
Abitibi[2]	868	360	Clinton Colden	1,230	284
Big Trout	698	255	Colville	805	176
Lake of the Woods[2] (total			Contwoyto	1,460	370
1,679) Canadian part 1,216	1,060	1,216	De Gras	1,365	244
Nipigon	855	1,872	Des Bois	975	181
Nipissing	644	321	Dubawnt	774	1,480
Rainy (total 360)			Ennadai	1,020	263
Canadian part 286	1,108	286	Eskimo North	1	324
St. Joseph	1,218	190	Eskimo South	5	243
Sandy	906	203	Faber	699	170
Seul	1,170	640	Ferguson	35	227
Simcoe	718	287	Garry	487	377
Trout (English River)	1,294	160	Great Bear	512	12,096
			Great Slave	513	11,031
MANITOBA			Hall	21	190
Cedar	830	522	Hazen	520	209
Cross	679	292	Hottah	592	354
Dauphin	853	201	Kamilukuak	874	245
Gods	585	444	Kaminak	173	232
Granville	848	189	Kaminuriak	302	212
Island	744	472	Kasba	1,102	518
Manitoba	813	1,799	Keller	810	152
Molson	724	154	La Martre	870	686
Moose	838	528	Mac Alpine	578	173
Oxford	612	155	Mackay	1,415	410
Playgreen	711	254	Mallery	520	185
Sipiwesk	601	176	Netilling	95	2,140
Southern Indian	835	868	Netsilik	26	151
Winnipeg	713	9,417	Nonacho	1,045	303
Winnipegosis	830	2,075	Nueltin[2]	911	880
			Point	1,229	271
SASKATCHEWAN			Princess Mary	380	202
Amisk	964	166	Selwyn[2]	1,306	277
Athabasca[2]	700	3 064	Snowbird	1,177	195
Black	922	179	South Henik	604	198
Churchill	1,382	216	Takiyuak	1,250	417
Cree	1,597	554	Tathlina	920	221
Deschambault	1,063	209	Tebesjuak	480	222
Doré	1,506	248	Tehek	437	186
Frobisher	1,381	199	Trout	1,650	195
Île à la Crosse	1,380	151	Tulemalu	916	258
La Ronge	1,193	546	Wholdaia	1,195	262
			Yathkyed	461	559

Areas given are for mean water levels. All elevations are in feet above mean sea level.
[1]Excludes Great Lakes, see Table 1.3.
[2]Spans provincial or territorial boundary. Listed under province or territory containing larger portion. Area given is total area.

1.4   Elevations and areas of principal lakes[1] (exceeding 388 km²), by province   M

Province and lake	Elevation m	Area km²	Province and lake	Elevation m	Area km²
NEWFOUNDLAND AND LABRADOR			**SASKATCHEWAN** (concluded)		
Ashuanipi	529	598	Montreal	490	456
Atikoniak	518	433	Peter Pond	421	777
Grand	87	539	Pinehouse	385	404
Joseph	518	451	Primrose	599	448
Melville	tidal	3 069	Reindeer[2]	337	6 651
Michikamau	460	2 031	Scott	444	394
Lobstick	457	510	Tazin	344	391
Ossokmanuan Reservoir	479	834	Wollaston	398	2 681
Smallwood Reservoir	471	6 475			
			ALBERTA		
NOVA SCOTIA			Bistcho	552	427
			Claire	213	1 437
Bras d'Or	tidal	1 098	Lesser Slave	577	1 168
QUEBEC			**BRITISH COLUMBIA**		
Albanel	389	445	Atlin[2]	668	774
Bienville	427	1 248	Babine	711	495
Cabonga Reservoir	361	679	Kootenay	532	407
Dozois Reservoir	346	404	Ootsa	853	404
Eau Claire	241	1 383	Williston	664	1 761
Evans	241	546			
Gouin Reservoir	404	1 570	**YUKON TERRITORY**		
Kaniapiskau	564	471	Kluane	781	409
Leaf	tidal	453			
Lower Seal	262	578	**NORTHWEST TERRITORIES**		
Manouane	494	585	Aberdeen	80	1 101
Minto	168	761	Amadjuak	113	3 116
Mistassini	372	2 336	Angikuni	257	510
Payne	130	534	Artillery	365	552
Pipmuacan	396	979	Aubry	258	391
Saint-Jean	98	1 002	Aylmer	375	847
Sakami	195	593	Baker	2	1 888
			Bluenose	557	401
ONTARIO			Buffalo	265	614
Abitibi[2]	265	932	Clinton Colden	375	736
Big Trout	213	660	Colville	245	456
Lake of the Woods[2] (total			Contwoyto	445	958
4 349) Canadian part 3 149	323	3 149	De Gras	416	632
Nipigon	261	4 848	Des Bois	297	469
Nipissing	196	831	Dubawnt	236	3 833
Rainy (total 932)			Ennadai	311	681
Canadian part 741	338	741	Eskimo North	0.3	839
St. Joseph	371	492	Eskimo South	2	629
Sandy	276	526	Faber	213	440
Seul	357	1 658	Ferguson	11	588
Simcoe	219	743	Garry	148	976
Trout (English River)	394	414	Great Bear	156	31 328
			Great Slave	156	28 570
MANITOBA			Hall	6	492
Cedar	253	1 352	Hazen	158	541
Cross	207	756	Hottah	180	917
Dauphin	260	521	Kamilukuak	266	635
Gods	178	1 150	Kaminak	53	601
Granville	258	490	Kaminuriak	92	549
Island	227	1 222	Kasba	336	1 342
Manitoba	248	4 659	Keller	247	394
Molson	221	399	La Martre	265	1 777
Moose	255	1 368	Mac Alpine	176	448
Oxford	187	401	Mackay	431	1 062
Playgreen	217	658	Mallery	158	479
Sipiwesk	183	456	Netilling	29	5 543
Southern Indian	255	2 248	Netsilik	8	391
Winnipeg	217	24 390	Nonacho	319	785
Winnipegosis	253	5 374	Nueltin[2]	278	2 279
			Point	375	702
SASKATCHEWAN			Princess Mary	116	523
Amisk	294	430	Selwyn[2]	398	717
Athabasca[2]	213	7 936	Snowbird	359	505
Black	281	464	South Henik	184	513
Churchill	421	559	Takiyuak	381	1 080
Cree	487	1 435	Tathlina	280	572
Deschambault	324	541	Tebesjuak	146	575
Doré	459	642	Tehek	133	482
Frobisher	421	515	Trout	503	505
Ile à la Crosse	421	391	Tulemalu	279	668
La Ronge	364	1 414	Wholdaia	364	679
			Yathkyed	141	1 448

Areas given are for mean water levels. All elevations are in metres above mean sea level.
[1]Excludes Great Lakes, see Table 1.3.
[2]Spans provincial or territorial boundary. Listed under province or territory containing larger portion. Area given is total area.

1.5   Lengths of principal rivers and their tributaries

Drainage basin and river	Length miles	Drainage basin and river	Length miles
FLOWING INTO THE PACIFIC OCEAN		FLOWING INTO HUDSON BAY AND HUDSON STRAIT (concluded)	
Yukon (mouth to head of Nisutlin)	1,979	Koksoak (to head of Caniapiscau)	543
(International Boundary to head of		Nottaway (via Bell to head of Mégiscane)	482
Nisutlin)	714	Rupert (to head of Témiscamie)	474
Porcupine	448	Eastmain	470
Stewart	400	Attawapiskat (to head of Bow Lake)	465
Pelly	378	Kazan (to head of Ennadai Lake)	455
Teslin	244	Grande rivière de la Baleine (Great Whale)	450
Columbia (mouth to head of Columbia Lake)	1,243	George	350
(International Boundary to head of		Moose (to head of Mattagami)	340
Columbia Lake)	498	Abitibi (to head of Louis Lake)	340
Kootenay	485	Mattagami (to head of Minisinakwa Lake)	275
Elk (to head of Elk Lake)	137	Missinaibi	265
St. Mary	73	Harricana	331
Slocan (to head of Slocan Lake)	60	Hayes	300
Kettle (to head of Holmes Lake)	209	Aux Feuilles (Leaf)	298
Okanagan (to head of Okanagan Lake)	195	Winisk	295
Similkameen	156	Broadback	280
Canoe	105	A la Baleine (Whale)	266
Spillimacheen	52	de Povungnituk	242
Kicking Horse (to head of Wapta Lake)	52	Innuksuac	239
Illecillewaet	48	Petite rivière de la Baleine (Little Whale River)	236
Fraser	850	Arnaud	234
Thompson (to head of North Thompson)	304	Nastapoca	224
North Thompson	210	Kogaluc	189
South Thompson (to head of Shuswap)	206		
Shuswap	115	FLOWING INTO THE ATLANTIC OCEAN	
Nechako (to head of Eutsuk Lake)	287	St. Lawrence River	1,900
Stuart (to head of Driftwood)	258	Lake Superior	
Chilcotin	146	Nipigon (to head of Ombabika)	130
West Road	141	Magpie (to head of Merekeme Lake)	71
Quesnel (to head of Mitchell Lake)	126	Lake Huron	
Lillooet	110	Spanish	210
Bridge	88	French (to head of Sturgeon)	180
Skeena	360	Mississagi	165
Bulkley (to head of Maxam Creek)	160	Saugeen	100
Stikine	335	Lake St. Clair	
Nass	236	Thames	163
Homathko	85	Lake Erie	
		Grand	165
FLOWING INTO THE ARCTIC OCEAN		Lake Ontario	
Mackenzie (to head of Finlay)	2,635	Trent (to head of Irondale)	250
Peace (to head of Finlay)	1,195	Moira	77
Smoky	306	Ottawa River	790
Finlay	250	Gatineau	240
Parsnip	145	du Lièvre	205
Athabasca	765	Madawaska (to head of Madawaska Lake)	143
Pembina	340	Coulonge	135
Liard	693	Petawawa (to head of Butt Lake)	116
South Nahanni	350	Rouge	115
Fort Nelson (to head of Sikanni Chief)	321	Mississippi (to head of Mazinaw Lake)	105
Petitot	251	South Nation	100
Hay	436	Rideau	91
Peel (mouth of west channel to head of Ogilvie)	425	Dumoine	80
Arctic Red	310	du Nord	70
Slave (from Peace River to Great Slave Lake)	258	de la Petite Nation	60
Fond du Lac (to outlet of Wollaston Lake)	172	Saguenay (to head of Péribonca)	434
Back (to outlet of Muskox Lake)	605	Péribonca	280
Coppermine	525	Mistassini	185
Anderson	430	Ashuapmuchuan	165
Horton	384	Saint-Maurice	350
		Matawin	100
FLOWING INTO HUDSON BAY AND HUDSON STRAIT		Manicouagan (to head of Mouchalagane)	348
		aux Outardes	310
Nelson (to head of Bow)	1,600	Romaine	308
(to outlet of Lake Winnipeg)	400	Betsiamites (to head of Kanouanis)	276
Saskatchewan (to head of Bow)	1,205	Moisie	255
South Saskatchewan (to head of Bow)	865	Bersimis	240
Red Deer	450	St-François	174
Bow	365	St-Augustin	145
Oldman	225	Chaudière	120
North Saskatchewan	800	Richelieu (to mouth of Lake Champlain)	106
Battle (to head of Pigeon Lake)	354	Churchill (to head of Ashuanipi)	532
Red (to head of Sheyenne)	545	Saint John	418
Assiniboine	665	Tobique (to outlet of Nictau Lake)	92
Winnipeg (to head of Firesteel)	505	du Petit-Mécatina	340
English	382	Natashquan	255
Fairford (to head of Manitoba Red Deer)	425	Exploits	153
Churchill (to head of Churchill Lake)	1,000	Eagle	145
Beaver (to outlet of Beaver Lake)	305	Miramichi	135
Severn (to head of Black Birch)	610	Gander (to head of Northwest Gander River)	109
Albany (to head of Cat)	610	Nepisiguit (to outlet of Nepisiguit Lake)	75
Thelon	562	St. Mary's (to head of North Nelson)	59
Dubawnt	523	Mersey (to outlet of 11 Mile Lake)	58
La Grande-Rivière (Fort George River)	555	Bay du Nord	41
		Pipers Hole	23

1.5 Lengths of principal rivers and their tributaries   M

Drainage basin and river	Length km	Drainage basin and river	Length km
FLOWING INTO THE PACIFIC OCEAN		**FLOWING INTO HUDSON BAY AND HUDSON STRAIT** (concluded)	
Yukon (mouth to head of Nisutlin)	3 185	Koksoak (to head of Caniapiscau)	874
(International Boundary to head of		Nottaway (via Bell to head of Mégiscane)	776
Nisutlin)	1 149	Rupert (to head of Témiscamie)	763
Porcupine	721	Eastmain	756
Stewart	644	Attawapiskat (to head of Bow Lake)	748
Pelly	608	Kazan (to head of Ennadai Lake)	732
Teslin	393	Grande rivière de la Baleine (Great Whale)	724
Columbia (mouth to head of Columbia Lake)	2 000	George	563
(International Boundary to head of		Moose (to head of Mattagami)	547
Columbia Lake)	801	Abitibi (to head of Louis Lake)	547
Kootenay	781	Mattagami (to head of Minisinakwa Lake)	443
Elk (to head of Elk Lake)	220	Missinaibi	426
St. Mary	117	Harricana	533
Slocan (to head of Slocan Lake)	97	Hayes	483
Kettle (to head of Holmes Lake)	336	Aux Feuilles (Leaf)	480
Okanagan (to head of Okanagan Lake)	314	Winisk	475
Similkameen	251	Broadback	451
Canoe	169	A la Baleine (Whale)	428
Spillimacheen	84	de Povungnituk	389
Kicking Horse (to head of Wapta Lake)	84	Innuksuac	385
Illecillewaet	77	Petite rivière de la Baleine (Little Whale River)	380
Fraser	1 368	Arnaud	377
Thompson (to head of North Thompson)	489	Nastapoca	360
North Thompson	338	Kogaluc	304
South Thompson (to head of Shuswap)	332		
Shuswap	185	**FLOWING INTO THE ATLANTIC OCEAN**	
Nechako (to head of Eutsuk Lake)	462	St. Lawrence River	3 058
Stuart (to head of Driftwood)	415	Lake Superior	
Chilcotin	235	Nipigon (to head of Ombabika)	209
West Road	227	Magpie (to head of Merekeme Lake)	114
Quesnel (to head of Mitchell Lake)	203	Lake Huron	
Lillooet	177	Spanish	338
Bridge	142	French (to head of Sturgeon)	290
Skeena	579	Mississagi	266
Bulkley (to head of Maxam Creek)	257	Saugeen	161
Stikine	539	Lake St. Clair	
Nass	380	Thames	262
Homathko	137	Lake Erie	
		Grand	266
FLOWING INTO THE ARCTIC OCEAN		Lake Ontario	
Mackenzie (to head of Finlay)	4 241	Trent (to head of Irondale)	402
Peace (to head of Finlay)	1 923	Moira	124
Smoky	492	Ottawa River	1 271
Finlay	402	Gatineau	386
Parsnip	233	du Lièvre	330
Athabasca	1 231	Madawaska (to head of Madawaska Lake)	230
Pembina	547	Coulonge	217
Liard	1 115	Petawawa (to head of Butt Lake)	187
South Nahanni	563	Rouge	185
Fort Nelson (to head of Sikanni Chief)	517	Mississippi (to head of Mazinaw Lake)	169
Petitot	404	South Nation	161
Hay	702	Rideau	146
Peel (mouth of west channel to head of Ogilvie)	684	Dumoine	129
Arctic Red	499	du Nord	113
Slave (from Peace River to Great Slave Lake)	415	de la Petite Nation	97
Fond du Lac (to outlet of Wollaston Lake)	277	Saguenay (to head of Péribonca)	698
Back (to outlet of Muskox Lake)	974	Péribonca	451
Coppermine	845	Mistassini	298
Anderson	692	Ashuapmuchuan	266
Horton	618	Saint-Maurice	563
		Matawin	161
		Manicouagan (to head of Mouchalagane)	560
FLOWING INTO HUDSON BAY AND HUDSON STRAIT		aux Outardes	499
		Romaine	496
Nelson (to head of Bow)	2 575	Betsiamites (to head of Kanouanis)	444
(to outlet of Lake Winnipeg)	644	Moisie	410
Saskatchewan (to head of Bow)	1 939	Bersimis	386
South Saskatchewan (to head of Bow)	1 392	St-François	280
Red Deer	724	St-Augustin	233
Bow	587	Chaudière	193
Oldman	362	Richelieu (to mouth of Lake Champlain)	171
North Saskatchewan	1 287	Churchill (to head of Ashuanipi)	856
Battle (to head of Pigeon Lake)	570	Saint John	673
Red (to head of Sheyenne)	877	Tobique (to outlet of Nictau Lake)	148
Assiniboine	1 070	du Petit-Mécatina	547
Winnipeg (to head of Firesteel)	813	Natashquan	410
English	615	Exploits	246
Fairford (to head of Manitoba Red Deer)	684	Eagle	233
Churchill (to head of Churchill Lake)	1 609	Miramichi	217
Beaver (to outlet of Beaver Lake)	491	Gander (to head of Northwest Gander River)	175
Severn (to head of Black Birch)	982	Nepisiguit (to outlet of Nepisiguit Lake)	121
Albany (to head of Cat)	982	St. Mary's (to head of North Nelson)	95
Thelon	904	Mersey (to outlet of 11 Mile Lake)	93
Dubawnt	842	Bay du Nord	66
La Grande-Rivière (Fort George River)	893	Pipers Hole	37

1.6   Areas of major islands, by region

Region and island	Area sq miles	Region and island	Area sq miles
Baffin Island	195,928	HUDSON BAY AND HUDSON STRAIT	
QUEEN ELIZABETH ISLANDS		Southampton	15,913
		Coats	2,123
Ellesmere	75,767	Mansel	1,228
Devon	21,331	Akimiski	1,159
Axel Heiberg	16,671	Flaherty	612
Melville	16,274	Nottingham	530
Bathurst	6,194	Resolution	392
Prince Patrick	6,119	Vansittart	385
Ellef Ringnes	4,361	Akpatok	349
Cornwallis	2,701	Salisbury	311
Amund Ringnes	2,029	Big	310
Mackenzie King	1,949	White	305
Borden	1,079	Loks Land	162
Cornwall	872		
Eglinton	595		
Graham	532	PACIFIC COAST	
Lougheed	505	Vancouver	12,079
Byam Martin	444	Graham	2,456
Île Vanier	435	Moresby	1,007
Cameron	409	Princess Royal	869
Meighen	369	Pitt	531
Brock	295	Banks	382
King Christian	249	King	312
North Kent	228	Porcher	201
Emerald	212	Nootka	197
Alexander	187	Aristazabal	162
Massey	167	Gilford	148
Little Cornwallis	159	Hawkesbury	141
		Hunter	140
ARCTIC ISLANDS SOUTH OF QUEEN ELIZABETH ISLANDS		Calvert	127
		Texada	116
Victoria	83,896	Swindle	110
Banks	27,038	McCauley	106
Prince of Wales	12,872	Louise	106
Somerset	9,570	Quadra	104
King William	5,062		
Bylot	4,273		
Prince Charles	3,676	ATLANTIC COAST	
Stefansson	1,723	Newfoundland and Labrador	
Richards	836	Newfoundland (main island)	42,031
Air Force	664	South Aulatsivik	176
Wales	439	Killinek	104
Rowley	421	Fogo	98
Russell	363	Random	96
Jens Munk	355	New World	73
Langley and Ellice	301	Tunungayualok	72
Bray	266	West Okak	69
Foley	246	Paul	69
Royal Geographical Society Islands	235	Gulf of St. Lawrence	
Sillem	186	Cape Breton	3,981
Matty	184	Anticosti	3,066
Spicer Islands	177	Prince Edward	2,184
Koch	177	Boularderie	74
Jenny Lind	162	Shippegan	58
Prescott	159	Bay of Fundy	
Crown Prince Frederick	155	Grand Manan	53

1.7   Temperature and precipitation data for typical stations in various districts

District and station	Temperatures (Celsius)						Precipitation		
	Mean Jan.	Mean July	Highest on record	Lowest on record	Av. dates of freezing temperatures (0°C or lower)		Total (all forms) mm	Snowfall cm	Av. number of days (all forms)
					Last in spring	First in autumn			
NEWFOUNDLAND									
Island									
Belle Isle	-9.6	9.4	22.8	-35.0	June 21	Sept. 26	893.1	240.0	149
Gander A	-6.1	16.5	35.6	-31.1	June 4	Oct. 5	1 078.2	354.8	204
St. Andrew's	-3.6	15.0	27.2	-23.9	June 3	Sept. 24	1 112.3	196.3	176
St. John's A	-3.8	15.3	30.6	-23.3	June 3	Oct. 12	1 511.5	363.7	210
Labrador									
Cartwright	-13.1	12.9	36.1	-37.8	June 20	Sept. 9	946.4	433.8	179
Goose A	-16.3	15.8	37.8	-39.4	June 6	Sept. 17	876.8	409.2	176
MARITIME PROVINCES									
Prince Edward Island									
Charlottetown A	-6.7	18.4	34.4	-27.8	May 17	Oct. 15	1 127.8	305.1	169
Nova Scotia									
Annapolis Royal	-3.9	18.3	32.8	-27.2	May 19	Oct. 2	1 204.5	218.2	149
Halifax	-3.2	18.3	34.4	-25.0	May 1	Nov. 1	1 318.8	210.8	152
Sydney A	-4.4	17.9	35.0	-25.6	May 23	Oct. 16	1 340.9	288.0	179
Yarmouth A	-2.7	16.4	30.0	-21.0	May 2	Oct. 24	1 283.2	204.5	157

1.6   Areas of major islands, by region   M

Region and island	Area km²	Region and island	Area km²
Baffin Island	507 451		
QUEEN ELIZABETH ISLANDS		HUDSON BAY AND HUDSON STRAIT	
Ellesmere	196 236	Southampton	41 214
Devon	55 247	Coats	5 499
Axel Heiberg	43 178	Mansel	3 181
Melville	42 149	Akimiski	3 002
Bathurst	16 042	Flaherty	1 585
Prince Patrick	15 848	Nottingham	1 373
Ellef Ringnes	11 295	Resolution	1 015
Cornwallis	6 996	Vansittart	997
Amund Ringnes	5 255	Akpatok	904
Mackenzie King	5 048	Salisbury	805
Borden	2 795	Big	803
Cornwall	2 258	White	790
Eglinton	1 541	Loks Land	420
Graham	1 378		
Lougheed	1 308	PACIFIC COAST	
Byam Martin	1 150	Vancouver	31 284
Ile Vanier	1 127	Graham	6 361
Cameron	1 059	Moresby	2 608
Meighen	956	Princess Royal	2 251
Brock	764	Pitt	1 375
King Christian	645	Banks	989
North Kent	591	King	808
Emerald	549	Porcher	521
Alexander	484	Nootka	510
Massey	433	Aristazabal	420
Little Cornwallis	412	Gilford	383
		Hawkesbury	365
ARCTIC ISLANDS SOUTH OF		Hunter	363
QUEEN ELIZABETH ISLANDS		Calvert	329
Victoria	217 290	Texada	300
Banks	70 028	Swindle	285
Prince of Wales	33 338	McCauley	275
Somerset	24 786	Louise	275
King William	13 111	Quadra	269
Bylot	11 067		
Prince Charles	9 521	ATLANTIC COAST	
Stefansson	4 463	Newfoundland and Labrador	
Richards	2 165	Newfoundland (main island)	108 860
Air Force	1 720	South Aulatsivik	456
Wales	1 137	Killinek	269
Rowley	1 090	Fogo	254
Russell	940	Random	249
Jens Munk	919	New World	189
Langley and Ellice	780	Tunungayualok	186
Bray	689	West Okak	179
Foley	637	Paul	179
Royal Geographical Society Islands	609	Gulf of St. Lawrence	
Sillem	482	Cape Breton	10 311
Matty	477	Anticosti	7 941
Spicer Islands	458	Prince Edward	5 657
Koch	458	Boularderie	192
Jenny Lind	420	Shippegan	150
Prescott	412	Bay of Fundy	
Crown Prince Frederick	401	Grand Manan	137

1.7   Temperature and precipitation data for typical stations in various districts (continued)

District and station	Temperatures (Celsius)				Av. dates of freezing temperatures (0°C or lower)		Precipitation		
	Mean Jan.	Mean July	Highest on record	Lowest on record	Last in spring	First in autumn	Total (all forms) mm	Snowfall cm	Av. number of days (all forms)
MARITIME PROVINCES									
(concluded)									
New Brunswick									
Chatham A	-9.3	19.2	37.8	-35.0	May 22	Sept. 21	1 051.2	309.4	152
Grand Falls	-11.9	18.3	36.7	-43.3	May 24	Sept. 21	1 021.6	265.2	105
Moncton A	-7.9	18.6	37.2	-32.2	May 23	Sept. 23	1 099.3	313.7	156
Saint John A	-7.1	17.1	34.4	-36.7	May 18	Oct. 2	1 400.3	204.7	149
QUEBEC									
Northern									
Fort Chimo A	-23.4	11.4	32.2	-46.7	June 27	Aug. 30	483.8	236.7	155
Inoucdjouac (Port Harrison)	-24.7	8.9	30.0	-46.1	July 1	Sept. 4	355.6	122.9	133
Nitchequon	-22.9	13.6	32.2	-49.4	June 13	Sept. 13	764.5	284.7	192
Schefferville A	-22.7	12.6	31.7	-50.6	June 18	Aug. 31	722.5	335.5	188
Southern									
Bagotville A	-15.7	17.8	36.1	-43.3	May 26	Sept. 18	936.6	341.6	177
Montreal McGill	-8.9	21.6	36.1	-33.9	Apr. 22	Oct. 23	999.0	243.1	164
Pointe au Père	-10.9	15.4	32.2	-36.1	May 19	Sept. 28	848.6	285.8	135
Quebec A	-11.6	19.2	35.6	-36.1	May 18	Sept. 28	1 088.4	326.6	164
Sept-Iles A	-13.9	15.1	32.2	-43.3	May 30	Sept. 17	1 090.3	423.2	146
Sherbrooke	-9.6	20.1	36.7	-41.1	May 12	Sept. 27	972.6	244.6	170

1.7 Temperature and precipitation data for typical stations in various districts (concluded)

District and station	Mean Jan.	Mean July	Highest on record	Lowest on record	Last in spring	First in autumn	Total (all forms) mm	Snowfall cm	Av. number of days (all forms)
ONTARIO									
Northern									
Kapuskasing A	-18.2	17.0	36.7	-44.4	June 13	Sept. 5	871.5	321.8	186
Sioux Lookout A	-18.7	18.4	36.1	-46.1	May 29	Sept. 20	741.5	236.7	165
Thunder Bay A	-14.8	17.5	37.2	-41.1	May 31	Sept. 10	738.5	222.0	141
Trout Lake	-24.1	15.9	35.6	-47.8	June 11	Sept. 16	597.3	212.3	158
Southern									
London A	-6.0	20.5	36.7	-31.7	May 9	Oct. 6	924.5	201.2	165
Ottawa A	-10.9	20.7	37.8	-36.1	May 11	Oct. 1	850.9	215.6	152
Parry Sound	-9.5	19.3	37.8	-41.1	May 14	Oct. 2	1 020.1	296.7	158
Toronto	-4.4	21.8	40.6	-32.8	Apr. 20	Oct. 30	789.9	141.0	134
Windsor A	-4.3	22.3	38.3	-26.1	Apr. 29	Oct. 20	836.1	103.6	137
PRAIRIE PROVINCES									
Manitoba									
Churchill A	-27.6	12.0	33.9	-45.0	June 22	Sept. 12	396.6	183.9	141
The Pas A	-22.4	17.9	36.7	-49.4	May 28	Sept. 20	449.7	157.2	128
Winnipeg A	-18.3	19.7	40.6	-45.0	May 25	Sept. 21	535.2	131.3	121
Saskatchewan									
Regina A	-17.3	18.9	43.3	-50.0	May 27	Sept. 12	397.9	114.8	114
Saskatoon A	-18.7	18.8	40.0	-47.8	May 27	Sept. 15	352.6	112.5	103
Swift Current A	-13.9	18.7	38.9	-42.8	May 28	Sept. 19	389.9	123.7	112
Alberta									
Beaverlodge CDA	-14.9	15.6	36.7	-47.8	May 22	Sept. 7	454.7	183.6	129
Calgary A	-10.9	16.5	36.1	-45.0	May 28	Sept. 12	437.1	153.9	113
Edmonton Ind. A	-14.7	17.5	34.4	-48.3	May 14	Sept. 19	446.5	132.1	121
Medicine Hat A	-12.1	20.2	42.2	-46.1	May 17	Sept. 20	347.8	121.7	89
BRITISH COLUMBIA									
Pacific Coast and Coastal Valleys									
Estevan Point	4.5	13.8	28.9	-13.9	Apr. 5	Nov. 18	3 027.9	34.3	203
Langara	2.5	12.4	25.6	-14.4	Apr. 3	Nov. 26	1 675.6	61.2	248
Prince Rupert	1.8	13.6	32.2	-21.1	Apr. 19	Nov. 5	2 414.5	113.0	227
Vancouver A	2.4	17.4	33.3	-17.8	Mar. 31	Oct. 30	1 068.1	52.3	161
Victoria									
Gonzale Hts	4.1	15.7	35.0	-15.6	Feb. 28	Dec. 9	657.1	32.8	142
Southern Interior									
Glacier	-11.3	14.4	36.7	-35.6	June 12	Sept. 6	1 492.8	969.5	192
Kamloops A	-6.0	20.9	40.6	-37.2	May 5	Sept. 28	260.6	77.0	90
Penticton A	-2.9	20.1	40.6	-27.2	May 10	Oct. 1	296.2	69.1	100
Princeton A	-8.1	17.6	41.7	-42.8	June 3	Sept. 12	359.1	157.0	115
Central Interior									
Barkerville	-9.8	12.3	35.6	-46.7	June 29	Aug. 18	1 148.8	581.4	185
McBride	-9.1	15.9	37.8	-46.7	June 9	Sept. 1	524.5	197.4	128
Prince George A	-11.8	14.9	34.4	-50.0	June 10	Aug. 28	620.7	233.4	162
Smithers A	-10.6	14.6	34.4	-43.9	June 10	Sept. 1	512.2	197.4	158
Northern Interior									
Atlin	-16.6	12.6	30.6	-50.0	June 5	Aug. 28	283.2	121.4	86
Dease Lake	-19.3	12.6	33.9	-51.1	June 29	Aug. 13	394.5	186.7	143
Fort Nelson A	-23.2	16.7	36.7	-51.7	May 24	Sept. 5	446.4	191.5	130
Fort St. John A	-17.2	15.9	33.3	-47.2	May 20	Sept. 9	449.8	206.2	128
Smith River A	-24.5	14.1	33.3	-58.9	June 21	Aug. 11	465.3	211.6	148
YUKON TERRITORY									
Dawson	-28.6	15.5	35.0	-58.3	May 26	Aug. 27	325.5	136.4	120
Snag A	-28.2	13.9	31.7	-62.8	June 18	Aug. 9	359.7	140.5	118
Watson Lake A	-25.3	14.9	33.9	-58.9	May 30	Sept. 3	432.3	227.3	153
Whitehorse A	-18.9	14.1	34.4	-52.2	June 5	Sept. 1	260.3	127.8	118
NORTHWEST TERRITORIES									
Mackenzie Basin									
Fort Good Hope	-31.0	15.9	34.4	-55.6	June 3	Aug. 19	283.7	124.0	101
Fort Simpson A	-27.6	16.1	35.0	-53.3	May 31	Aug. 29	343.2	137.9	126
Hay River A	-25.5	15.6	35.6	-48.3	June 6	Sept. 11	339.8	165.1	109
Barrens									
Baker Lake	-33.6	10.7	30.6	-50.6	June 25	Aug. 31	213.0	88.9	96
Chesterfield	-31.8	8.7	30.6	-51.1	June 29	Sept. 6	263.5	112.8	98
Coppermine	-29.4	9.3	32.2	-50.0	June 27	Aug. 21	216.3	101.9	110
Arctic Archipelago									
Clyde	-26.9	4.6	22.2	-45.6	July 13	July 18	206.3	152.9	94
Eureka	-36.6	5.5	19.4	-53.9	June 27	Aug. 5	58.4	38.4	52
Frobisher Bay A	-26.2	7.9	24.4	-45.6	June 30	Aug. 29	415.2	246.9	135
Mould Bay	-33.8	3.7	16.1	-53.9	July 12	July 19	86.4	59.9	73
Resolute A	-32.6	4.3	18.3	-52.2	July 10	July 20	136.4	78.7	94

A = Airport, Ind. A = Industrial Airport.
CDA = Canada Department of Agriculture.

1.8   Total area classified by tenure, 1975 (sq miles)

Item	Province or territory						
	Nfld.	PEI	NS	NB	Que.	Ont.	Man.
Federal Crown lands other than national parks, Indian reserves and forest experiment stations	170	6	70	575	500[1]	447	100
National parks	903	8	514	167	305	742	1,150
Indian reserves	–	3	44	65	1,574[2]	2,588	920
Federal forest experiment stations	–	–	–	35	11	40	–
Privately owned land or land in process of alienation from the Crown	6,853	1,904	14,444	15,349	43,500	45,955	53,280
Provincial or territorial lands other than provincial parks and provincial forests	147,831	168	1,221	11,002	467,492	344,118	186,735[3]
Provincial parks	311	17	34	83	75,000	18,692	3,390
Provincial forests	117	78	5,098	1,078	6,478	–	5,425
Total area	156,185	2,184	21,425	28,354	594,860	412,582	251,000
	Sask.	Alta.	BC	YT	NWT		Canada
Federal Crown lands other than national parks, Indian reserves and forest experiment stations	2,105	1,177	349	198,145	1,287,251		1,490,895
National parks	1,496	20,692[4]	1,811	8,500	16,450[5]		52,738
Indian reserves	2,196	2,549	1,309	2	52		11,302
Federal forest experiment stations	–	23	–	–	–		109
Privately owned land or land in process of alienation from the Crown	95,503	77,663	21,139	65	28		375,683
Provincial or territorial lands other than provincial parks and provincial forests	13,790	–	208,329	364	1,122		1,382,172
Provincial parks	1,857	2,537	16,073	–	–		117,994
Provincial forests	134,753	150,644[6]	117,245	–	–		420,916
Total area	251,700	255,285	366,255	207,076	1,304,903		3,851,809

[1]Includes Gatineau Park (137.5 sq miles) and Quebec Battlefields Park (0.36 sq mile) which are under federal jurisdiction but are not technically national parks.
[2]Includes increase awarded by the James Bay Agreement.
[3]Includes 2,220 sq miles under lease.
[4]Includes that part of Wood Buffalo Park in Alberta (13,840 sq miles).
[5]Includes that part of Wood Buffalo Park in Northwest Territories (3,460 sq miles).
[6]Includes some privately owned land and other provincial lands.

1.8   Total area classified by tenure, 1975 (km²)   M

Item	Province or territory						
	Nfld.	PEI	NS	NB	Que.	Ont.	Man.
Federal Crown lands other than national parks, Indian reserves and forest experiment stations	440	16	181	1 489	1 295[1]	1 158	259
National parks	2 339	21	1 331	433	790	1 922	2 978
Indian reserves	–	8	114	168	4 077[2]	6 703	2 383
Federal forest experiment stations	–	–	–	91	28	103	–
Privately owned land or land in process of alienation from the Crown	17 749	4 931	37 410	39 754	112 664	119 023	137 995
Provincial or territorial lands other than provincial parks and provincial forests	382 881	435	3 162	28 495	1 210 799	891 261	483 641[3]
Provincial parks	805	44	88	215	194 249	48 412	8 780
Provincial forests	303	202	13 204	2 792	16 778	–	14 051
Total area	404 517	5 657	55 490	73 437	1 540 680	1 068 582	650 087
	Sask.	Alta.	BC	YT	NWT		Canada
Federal Crown lands other than national parks, Indian reserves and forest experiment stations	5 452	3 048	904	513 193	3 333 965		3 861 400
National parks	3 875	53 592[4]	4 690	22 015	42 605[5]		136 591
Indian reserves	5 687	6 602	3 390	5	135		29 272
Federal forest experiment stations	–	60	–	–	–		282
Privately owned land or land in process of alienation from the Crown	247 352	201 146	54 750	168	72		973 014
Provincial or territorial lands other than provincial parks and provincial forests	35 716	–	539 570	943	2 906		3 579 809
Provincial parks	4 810	6 571	41 629	–	–		305 603
Provincial forests	349 009	390 166[6]	303 663	–	–		1 090 167
Total area	651 900	661 185	948 596	536 324	3 379 683		9 976 139

[1]Includes Gatineau Park (356.1 km²) and Quebec Battlefields Park (0.93 km²) which are under federal jurisdiction but are not technically national parks.
[2]Includes increase awarded by the James Bay Agreement.
[3]Includes 5 750 km² under lease.
[4]Includes that part of Wood Buffalo Park in Alberta (35 845 km²).
[5]Includes that part of Wood Buffalo Park in Northwest Territories (8 961 km²).
[6]Includes some privately owned land and other provincial lands.

Sources

1.1, 1.2, 1.6 Topographical Survey Directorate, Surveys and Mapping Branch, Department of Energy, Mines and Resources.
1.3, 1.4 *Inventory of Canadian freshwater lakes,* Inland Waters Directorate, Water Resources Branch, Department of Fisheries and the Environment.
1.5, 1.7 Information Services Directorate, Department of Fisheries and the Environment.
1.8 Property Services Branch, Department of Public Works; Parks Canada, Department of Indian Affairs and Northern Development; Canadian Forestry Service, Department of Fisheries and the Environment; and respective provincial government departments.

The constitution and the legal system

Chapter 2

Tables

The constitution and
the legal system

Chapter 2

As the society of a country becomes more highly developed, the body of law, in response to the changing needs of its citizens, becomes more complex. This chapter outlines some of the features of the Canadian legal system, particularly those which have a federal concern. The Canadian constitution, the major written parts of which are contained in the British North America Act, is considered in some detail, as is the distribution of legislative power between the federal and provincial governments. There are also short notes on the Canadian legal system, the development of Canadian criminal law, the courts and the judiciary, the legal profession and the federal legal aid scheme. There is a description of the organization and work of the federal Department of Justice. Information concerning the enforcement of the criminal law and on correctional institutions is set out in the concluding sections.

The constitution

2.1

The Canadian federal state of 10 provinces and two territories had its foundation in an act of the British Parliament, the British North America Act, 1867, which was fashioned for the most part from the Seventy-two Resolutions drafted by the Fathers of Confederation at Quebec in 1864. The BNA Act provided for the federal union of the three British North American Provinces — Canada (Ontario and Quebec), Nova Scotia and New Brunswick — into one Dominion under the name Canada. The country that was brought into existence on proclamation of the BNA Act on July 1, 1867 consisted of only four of its present provinces, Ontario, Quebec, New Brunswick and Nova Scotia. However, Section 146 of the act made provision for the possible future entry into Confederation of the colonies or provinces of Newfoundland, Prince Edward Island and British Columbia, and of Rupert's Land and the North-Western Territory, a vast expanse then held by the Hudson's Bay Company. In 1870, the company surrendered its territories to the British Crown which transferred them at once to Canada. In exchange it received a cash payment from the Canadian government of £300,000, one twentieth of the lands in the southern part, "the fertile belt", of the territory, and designated blocks of land around its trading posts. From this new territory was carved the province of Manitoba in 1870, much smaller at its inception than at present, and later, in 1905, the provinces of Saskatchewan and Alberta. British Columbia entered Confederation in 1871 on the condition that a railway linking it with eastern Canada be commenced within two years. Despite the original provision in the BNA Act for their entry into Canada, it was not until 1873 that Prince Edward Island entered the union, and much later, 1949, that Newfoundland joined (see Table 2.1).

Although the BNA Act of 1867 and its amendments contain a substantial portion of Canada's constitution, it is not a comprehensive constitutional document. There are unwritten and equally important parts such as common law, convention and usage which were transplanted from Great Britain over 200 years ago and which are basic to the Canadian style of democratic government. Among these are the principles governing the Cabinet system of responsible government with the close relationship between executive and legislative branches.

The constitution of Canada, in its broadest sense, also includes other Imperial statutes (Statute of Westminster — 1931) and Imperial Orders in Council (those admitting various provinces and territories to the federation); statutes of the Parliament of Canada pertaining to such matters as succession to the throne, the royal style and title, the Governor General, the Senate, the House of Commons, the creation of courts, the franchise and elections, as well as judicial decisions that interpret the BNA Act and other statutes of a constitutional nature. Moreover, the constitutions of the provinces of Canada form part of the overall Canadian constitution, and provincial acts which are of a fundamental constitutional nature similar to those listed above are also part of the constitution. The same can be said of both federal and provincial Orders in Council that are of a similar fundamental nature.

Although the essential principles of Cabinet government are based on custom or constitutional usage, the federal structure of Canadian government rests on the explicit written provisions of the BNA Act. Apart from the creation of the federal union, the dominant feature of the act was the distribution of powers between the central or federal government and the component provincial governments. The primary purpose was to grant to the Parliament of Canada legislative jurisdiction over all subjects of general or common interest, while giving to the provincial legislatures jurisdiction over all matters of local or particular interest.

Unlike the written constitutions of many nations, the BNA Act lacks comprehensive "bill of rights" clauses, although it does accord specific although limited constitutional protection to the use of the English and French languages (Sect. 133) and special safeguards with respect to sectarian or denominational schools. Freedom of speech, freedom of assembly, freedom of religion, freedom of the press, trial by jury and similar liberties enjoyed by the individual citizen are not recorded in the BNA Act but rather depended on the statute law and the common law inheritance until these rights were confirmed, as far as federal law is concerned, by the passage of a Canadian Bill of Rights — An Act for the Recognition and Protection of Human Rights and Fundamental Freedoms (SC 1960, c.44) assented to August 10, 1960.

The right to use either the English or the French language in the House of Commons, the Senate, the legislature of Quebec and the federal and Quebec courts is constitutionally guaranteed by Section 133 of the BNA Act. The use of the English and French languages in the administration of the Government of Canada and its Crown corporations is dealt with in the Official Languages Act (RSC 1970, c.O-2). That act provides that government notices to the public, certain orders and regulations, and final decisions of federal courts are to be made or issued in both languages and that, in the National Capital Region and in federal bilingual districts, government services are to be available in both languages. The Commissioner of Official Languages for Canada is responsible for ensuring compliance with this act.

2.1.1 Amendment of the constitution

No provision was made in the BNA Act of 1867 for its amendment by any legislative body in Canada but both the Parliament of Canada and the provincial legislatures were given legislative jurisdiction with respect to certain matters relating to government. Thus, for example, the Parliament of Canada was given jurisdiction with respect to the establishment of electoral districts and election laws and the privileges and immunities of members of the Senate and House of Commons. Each provincial legislature was empowered to amend the constitution of its province except as regards the office of Lieutenant Governor. Amendments to the BNA Act have been made by the British Parliament on 14 occasions since 1867. By an amendment to the BNA Act passed in 1949, the authority of the Parliament of Canada to legislate with respect to constitutional matters was considerably enlarged and it may now amend the constitution of Canada except as regards the legislative authority of the provinces, the rights and privileges of provincial legislatures or governments, schools, the use of English or French and the provision that no House of Commons shall continue for more than five years other than in time of real or apprehended war, invasion or insurrection.

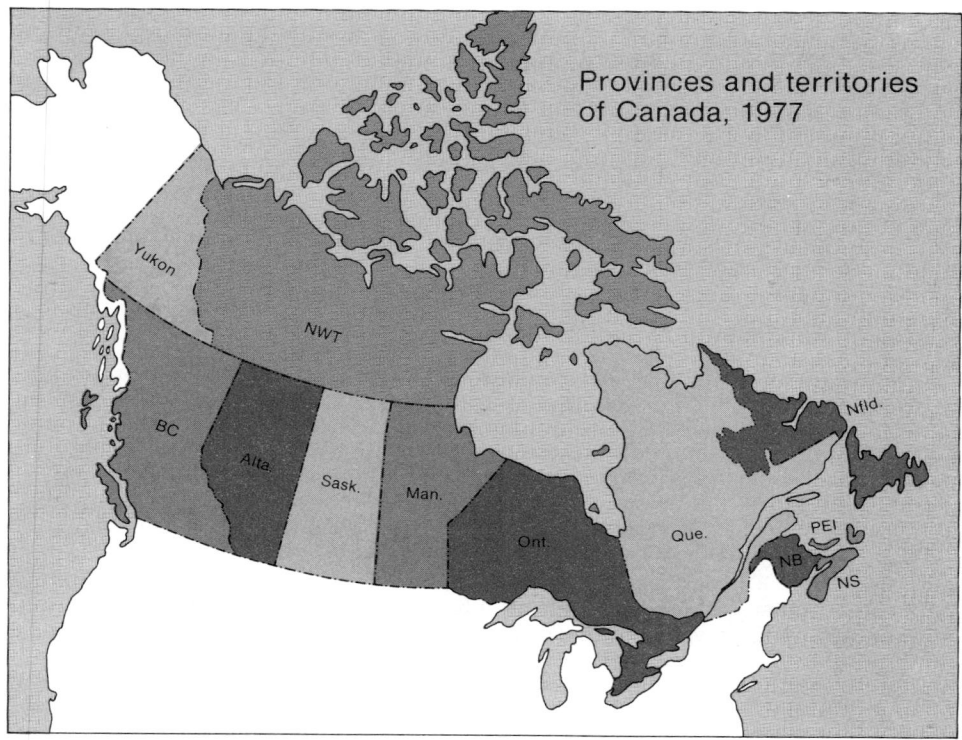

Provinces and territories of Canada, 1977

The search for a satisfactory procedure for amending the constitution in Canada which satisfies the need to safeguard basic provincial and minority rights and yet possesses sufficient flexibility to ensure that the constitution can be altered to meet changing circumstances has been the subject of repeated consideration in the Parliament of Canada as well as in a series of federal-provincial conferences and meetings held in 1927, 1935-36, 1950 and 1960-61. In October 1964 the text of a draft bill "to provide for the amendment in Canada of the Constitution of Canada", which embodied an amending procedure or formula, recommended by a conference of Attorneys General, was unanimously accepted by a conference of the Prime Minister and the Premiers. However, Quebec subsequently withdrew its approval of the formula and it was never adopted.

Between February 1968 and June 1971, eight federal-provincial conferences were held to study the drafting of a new constitution. A committee was established to provide assistance in the study of constitutional questions. The provincial governments, with one exception, and the federal government submitted proposals for a new constitution. The discussions culminated in the drafting of the Canadian Constitutional Charter, 1971, which set out specific constitutional reforms, including a revised amendment procedure. The charter was considered at the Constitutional Conference in Victoria, BC in June 1971, but was not accepted.

Treaty-making powers   2.1.2

The federal government has primary responsibility for the conduct of external affairs. The policy in discharging this responsibility is to promote the interest of the entire country and of all Canadians.

In matters of specific concern to the provinces, it is Canadian government policy to assist them in achieving their particular aspirations and goals, as illustrated by the "entente" signed by Quebec and France in the field of education in February 1965. Provincial and federal authorities cooperated in a procedure that enabled Quebec, within the framework of the constitution and national policy, to participate in international arrangements. Once it is determined that what a province wishes to achieve in the field of provincial jurisdiction falls within the framework of Canadian foreign policy, the provinces may discuss arrangements with the authorities of the country concerned. For a formal international agreement the federal signature of treaties and conduct of overall foreign policy must come into operation.

2.2   Distribution of federal and provincial powers

Since the purpose of the BNA Act was to create a federal system of government, important provisions of that document deal with the division of powers between the federal and provincial governments. Each level of government is virtually sovereign with respect to the powers it exercises. While the federal government under the British North America Act has the power to disallow provincial legislation, this power has not been exercised in recent years. Hence, provincial governments are as sovereign as the federal government when acting within its sphere of power.

The primary scheme of the distribution of powers was to grant to the federal government jurisdiction over all subjects of general or national concern while giving to provincial legislatures jurisdiction over all matters of a local nature. Section 91 of the BNA Act lists federal powers. It gives the Parliament of Canada a general power to "make laws for the peace, order and good government of Canada" and gives a list of classes of subjects over which Parliament has exclusive authority which illustrate but do not restrict the general power. The list contains 31 classes of federal powers such as regulation of trade and commerce, defence, currency, raising money by any mode or system of taxation, postal services, navigation and shipping, weights and measures and criminal law. Section 92 assigns to the provinces the power to legislate regarding direct taxation within the province, the management and sale of public lands and timber belonging to the province, municipal institutions, laws relating to property and civil rights and all matters of a merely local or private nature. (For details see *Canada Year Book 1973* pp 71-73.) Section 95 of the BNA Act gave the federal government and the provinces concurrent powers over agriculture and immigration but federal law prevails in cases where the laws of both levels of government are in conflict. Similar concurrent powers exist in respect of old age pensions and supplementary benefits, including survivors and disability benefits, but no federal legislation affects the operation of provincial laws in this field if a conflict occurs with provincial legislation.

The drafters of the BNA Act in 1867 probably thought that such a division of powers was so definite and precise that no future difficulties would arise in deciding what subjects were under federal legislative control and what subjects were under provincial legislative control. However, the powers enumerated in Sections 91 and 92 are not mutually exclusive and sometimes overlap. As a result, the interpretation to be placed on the division of powers between the federal and provincial governments has given rise to innumerable legal disputes, parliamentary discussions, royal commission inquiries and federal-provincial conferences. Often, however, the division of powers has remained unclear.

Difficulty in interpreting the division of powers has also arisen as a result of new social, technological and political conditions that were unforeseen at the time of Confederation. Social welfare legislation, such as unemployment insurance, and legislation concerning modern communication facilities were not contemplated by the drafters of the BNA Act. Nevertheless, power to legislate on these subjects had to be assigned either to the federal or provincial governments by reference to the BNA Act. Canada's emergence into the international community as a completely independent nation, which also was not foreseen in 1867, required an allocation of responsibility for new concepts such as aviation, broadcasting and citizenship between the two levels of government or in some cases to one or another government.

One significant outcome of the allocation of powers under the BNA Act has been that the expenditures of the provincial governments have often outstripped their tax resources. In 1867, the provinces were assigned responsibility for social services such as hospitals and schools as well as for municipal institutions. At that time this did not involve major expenditure of public funds. However, changing demands of society and the entry of government into the field of social welfare led to the expenditure of large sums. The provinces have power to levy direct taxation within the province for provincial purposes while the federal government has a broader authority to levy taxes by "any means of taxation". The federal government has therefore substantial tax resources. While the provinces have responsibility for many costly public institutions they often do not have the necessary financial resources. In order to redress this, numerous federal-provincial tax-sharing agreements and shared-cost programs have been entered into by the federal and provincial governments. Such agreements were not, of course, anticipated by the original drafters of the BNA Act. Nevertheless these agreements have resulted in new constitutional arrangements and techniques for dealing with federal-provincial economic relations and have come to be known collectively as "cooperative federalism".

The legal system   2.3

Common law and Quebec civil law   2.3.1
The legal system in the provinces and territories derives from the common law system of England with the exception of Quebec, where the system has been influenced by the legal developments of France. Quebec has its own Civil Code and Code of Civil Procedure. However, in the field of public law the principles of common law apply. Over the years, both Canadian common law and Quebec civil law have developed unique characteristics. The body of law changes as society changes. In many of the provinces there are now law reform commissions which have been charged with the function of inquiring into matters relating to the reform of the law having regard to both the statute law and the common law. A general revision of the Civil Code is taking place in Quebec under the auspices of the Civil Code Revision Office. At the federal level there is the Law Reform Commission of Canada whose purpose is "to study and keep under review on a continuing basis the statutes and other laws comprising the law of Canada with a view to making recommendations for their improvement, modernization and reform".

Criminal law   2.3.2
Criminal law is that branch or division of law which treats of crimes and their punishment. A crime may be described as an act against society, as distinct from a dispute between individuals. It has been defined as any act done in violation of those duties which an individual owes to the community and for the breach of which the law has provided that the offender shall make restitution to the public.

The criminal law of Canada has as its foundation the criminal law of England built up through the ages and consisting first of customs and usages and later expanded by principles enunciated by generations of judges. There is no statutory declaration of the introduction of English criminal law into those parts of Canada that are now New Brunswick, Nova Scotia and Prince Edward Island. Its introduction there depends upon a principle of the common law itself by which

English law was declared to be in force in uninhabited territory discovered and planted by British subjects, except in so far as local conditions made it inapplicable. The same may be said of Newfoundland although the colony dealt with the subject in a statute of 1837. In Quebec, its reception depends upon the Royal Proclamation of 1763 and the Quebec Act of 1774. In each of the other provinces and in the Yukon Territory and Northwest Territories, the matter has been dealt with by statute.

The criminal law systems of the provinces as they exist today are based on the British North America Act of 1867. Section 91 of the act provides that "The exclusive legislative authority of the Parliament of Canada extends to ... the criminal law, except the constitution of courts of criminal jurisdiction but including the procedure in criminal matters". By Section 92(14), the legislature of the province exclusively may make laws in relation to "the Administration of Justice in the Province, including the Constitution, Maintenance, and Organization of Provincial Courts, both of Civil and Criminal Jurisdiction and including Procedure in Civil Matters in those Courts". The Parliament of Canada may, however (Sect. 101), establish any additional courts for the better administration of the laws of Canada. It should be noted that the Statute of Westminster, 1931 effected important changes, particularly by abrogating in part the Colonial Laws Validity Act, 1865 (Br.) and confirming the right of a Dominion to make laws having extraterritorial operation.

At the time of Confederation each of the colonies affected had its own body of statutes relating to the criminal law. In 1869, in an endeavour to assimilate them into a uniform system applicable throughout Canada, Parliament passed a series of acts, some of which dealt with specific offences and others with procedure. Most notable of the latter was the Criminal Procedure Act, but other acts provided for the speedy trial or summary trial of indictable offences, the powers and jurisdiction of justices of the peace in summary conviction matters and otherwise, and the procedure in respect of juvenile offenders.

Codification of the criminal law through a criminal code bill founded on the English draft code of 1878, Stephen's *Digest of criminal law,* Burbidge's *Digest of the Canadian criminal law,* and the relevant Canadian statutes was brought about by the Minister of Justice, Sir John Thompson, in 1892. This bill became the Criminal Code of Canada and came into force on July 1, 1893. It must be remembered, however, that the criminal code was not exhaustive of the criminal law. It was still necessary to refer to English law in certain matters of procedure and it was still possible to prosecute for offences at common law. Moreover, Parliament has declared offences under certain other acts, e.g. the Narcotic Control Act, to be criminal offences.

An examination and study of the criminal code was authorized by Order in Council dated February 3, 1949, and the commission which had been assigned the task of revising the code presented its report with a draft bill in February 1952. After coming before successive sessions of Parliament it was finally enacted on June 15, 1954 and the new Criminal Code (RSC 1970, c.C-34) came into effect on April 1, 1955. Since the new code came into force a number of important amendments have been made. These include an amendment in 1956 providing that motions for leave to appeal to the Supreme Court of Canada in criminal cases should be heard by a quorum of at least five judges of that court instead of by a single judge; amendments effected in 1959, providing a statutory extension of the definition of "obscenity" and making provision for seizure and condemnation of offending material without a charge necessarily being laid against any person; amendments dealing with genocide and public incitement of hatred; extensive amendments relating to the allowing of time for payment of fines; amendments dealing with offences committed in aircraft in flight over the high seas; important and extensive amendments relating to the invasion of privacy and interception of communications; and an amendment forbidding the publication in a newspaper or broadcast of a report that any admission or confession tendered in evidence at a preliminary inquiry or a report of the nature of such admission or confession unless the accused has been discharged or, if the accused has been committed for trial, the trial has ended. (In 1969 a new amendment laid down that the accused may apply to the magistrate or justice holding a preliminary inquiry for an order forbidding publication of any of the evidence until the accused has been discharged or the trial itself has ended.)

In 1960 (SC 1960, c.44) Parliament enacted what is known as the Canadian Bill of Rights. Although the act sets out further details, its general scope appears in Section 1, which reads as follows: "It is hereby recognized and declared that in Canada there have existed and shall continue to exist without discrimination by reason of race, national origin, colour, religion or sex, the following human rights and fundamental freedoms, namely, (a) the right of the individual to life, liberty, security of the person and enjoyment of property, and the right not to be deprived thereof except by due process of law; (b) the right of the individual to equality before the law and the protection of the law; (c) freedom of religion; (d) freedom of speech; (e) freedom of assembly and association; and (f) freedom of the press."

In 1961 the offence of murder was divided into capital and non-capital, the death penalty was abolished in relation to the offence of non-capital murder, and the term "criminal sexual psychopath" was dropped and the term "dangerous sexual offender" substituted; in 1965 provision was made for the right to appeal in habeas corpus proceedings.

The concept of "non-capital murder" was introduced into Canadian criminal law in 1961. At that time, capital murder was defined to include, for example, planned and deliberate murder, murder in the course of certain violent acts and murder of peace officers and prison officers. Life imprisonment was substituted for the death penalty in cases where the accused was convicted of non-capital murder.

In 1966 the House of Commons, in a free vote, rejected a bill under which the death penalty for murder would have been completely abolished. In 1967, an act was passed under which the definition of capital murder was restricted to the murder of police officers or prison officers. This act was brought into force on December 29, 1967, and continued in force for five years. It was replaced by a new act, brought into force on January 1, 1974, which retained the 1967 restrictive definition of capital murder ("murder punishable by death") for a period of four years to end on December 31, 1977. In 1976 Parliament eliminated the death penalty for piracy, treason and murder, although the penalty still exists for certain offences under the National Defence Act. Convicted murderers are now to be sentenced to life imprisonment, and must serve at least 15 years in prison before becoming eligible for parole.

Some very comprehensive amendments to the criminal code are contained in the Criminal Law Amendment Act which was assented to on June 27, 1969 and, with certain exceptions, came into force on August 26, 1969. Among the changes were amendments relating to gaming and lotteries, "drinking and driving", homosexual acts and therapeutic abortion. It also affected the law relating to the publication of evidence, as mentioned above, as well as the law relating to the issue of fitness to stand trial on the grounds of insanity.

In 1971 Parliament passed the Bail Reform Act which changed the criminal code by restricting police power of arrest for minor offences and requiring the police, as a general rule, to release persons arrested for minor or less serious offences as soon as possible. In addition, a justice is required to issue a summons unless the public interest requires a warrant of arrest. Save in very exceptional cases "cash bail" was abolished and, as a general rule, a person charged with an offence will be released simply on his written undertaking to attend court.

In 1972 the Criminal Law Amendment Act introduced a wide variety of reforms. Rules regarding jury duty were changed and men and women were made equally eligible and responsible to serve. The possibility of more flexible and appropriate law enforcement was enhanced by providing that individuals accused of certain kinds of crimes, such as obstructing the police, could be tried either by summary conviction or indictment. New offences were created with regard to hijacking and endangering the safety of aircraft, to soliciting for the purpose of prostitution by either male or female and to disturbing the peace of an apartment building. The offences of vagrancy and attempted suicide were abolished. Important changes were introduced with respect to sentencing — maximum sentences were increased for certain crimes connected with the administration of justice, whipping was abolished, and provision was made to permit a judge not to sentence an accused found guilty if the public interest would not be served by sentencing him. Provision was made to permit jail sentences under 90 days to be served at night and on weekends so that the individual might continue to earn a living and support his family. Where an accused is found guilty of certain minor offences, the court, where it feels it is in the best interests of the accused and is not contrary to the public interest, may order that the accused be discharged either absolutely or upon conditions prescribed in a probation order. Speaking generally, a discharged accused is deemed not to have been convicted. However, should an accused conditionally discharged subsequently be convicted of an offence, the court may revoke the discharge and convict him of the offence to which the discharge relates.

In 1974 the Protection of Privacy Act amended the criminal code by creating an offence where a person listens to, records or acquires a private communication. Provision is made for peace or public officers obtaining authorization from a judge to intercept such communications, for the manner in which the person whose private communication is being lawfully intercepted is to be informed of this fact, and for the way in which such intercepted communications may be used in evidence.

In 1976 further extensive amendments were made to the criminal code covering the protection of diplomats, the testing of drivers suspected of being impaired, the theft or use of stolen credit cards and the right of an accused to be released on bail pending trial. Provisions regarding evidence in cases of rape and other sexual offences were revised.

2.4   Courts and the judiciary

2.4.1   The federal judiciary
The Parliament of Canada is empowered by Section 101 of the British North America Act from time to time to provide for the constitution, maintenance and organization of a general Court of Appeal for Canada and for the establishment of any additional courts for the better administration of the laws of Canada. Under this provision, Parliament has established the Supreme Court of Canada, the Federal Court of Canada and certain specialized courts.

Supreme Court of Canada. This court, first established in 1875 and now governed by the Supreme Court Act (RSC 1970, c.S-19), consists of a chief justice, who is called the Chief Justice of Canada, and eight puisne judges. The Chief Justice and the puisne judges are appointed by the Governor in Council and hold office during good behaviour but are removable by the Governor General on address of the Senate and the House of Commons. They cease to hold office on attaining the age of 75 years. The court sits at Ottawa and exercises general appellate jurisdiction throughout Canada in civil and criminal cases. The court is also required to consider and advise on questions referred to it by the Governor in Council and it may also advise the Senate or the House of Commons on private bills referred to the court under any rules or orders of the Senate or of the House of Commons.

Appeals may be brought from any final judgment of the highest court of final resort in a province by obtaining leave to do so from that court or from the Supreme Court itself. The Supreme Court may grant leave to appeal from any judgment whether final or not, and as well there is provision for *per saltum* appeals whereby the highest court of final resort in a province may grant leave on a question of law alone from a final judgment of some other court in that province. Appeals in respect of indictable offences are regulated by the criminal code. Appeals from federal courts are regulated by the statute establishing such courts. The judgment of the Supreme Court of Canada in all cases is final and conclusive.

Chief Justice and Judges of the Supreme Court of Canada as at January 1, 1977

Chief Justice of Canada, Rt. Hon. Bora Laskin *(appointed December 27, 1973, first appointed a Judge of the Supreme Court, March 23, 1970)*
Hon. Mr. Justice Ronald Martland *(appointed January 15, 1958)*
Hon. Mr. Justice Wilfrid Judson *(appointed February 5, 1958)*
Hon. Mr. Justice Roland Almon Ritchie *(appointed May 5, 1959)*
Hon. Mr. Justice Wishart Flett Spence *(appointed May 30, 1963)*
Hon. Mr. Justice Louis-Philippe Pigeon *(appointed September 21, 1967)*
Hon. Mr. Justice Robert George Brian Dickson *(appointed March 26, 1973)*
Hon. Mr. Justice Joseph Philemon Jean Marie Beetz *(appointed January 1, 1974)*
Hon. Mr. Justice Roland Chamilly Louis-Philippe de Grandpré *(appointed January 1, 1974).*

Federal Court of Canada. The Federal Court of Canada was constituted by an act of the Parliament of Canada under Section 101 of the British North America Act, 1867, which, after authorizing the creation of the Supreme Court of Canada, confers on the Parliament of Canada authority to constitute other courts for the better administration of the laws of Canada. The Federal Court of Canada is a court of law, equity and admiralty and it is a superior court of record having civil and criminal jurisdiction (Sect. 3 of the act). The Exchequer Court of Canada, (established in 1875), was replaced in December 1970 by the Federal Court of Canada (SC 1970-71, c.1).

The court has two divisions called the Federal Court — Appeal Division, and the Federal Court — Trial Division. The Appeal Division may be called the Court of Appeal or Federal Court of Appeal (Sect. 4 of the act). The Court of Appeal consists of the Chief Justice of the Federal Court of Canada and five other judges. The Trial Division consists of the Associate Chief Justice of the Federal Court of Canada and nine other judges. Every judge is an ex officio member of the division of which he is not a regular member (Sect. 5). In addition to the establishment of full-time judges, an added capacity to cope with the purely judicial work of the court is provided by the authority to invite retired federally appointed judges to act as deputy judges of the court (Sect. 10). This authority extends also to federally appointed judges who are still in office, but only with the consent of the appropriate Chief Justice or Attorney General. Former district judges in Admiralty are also deputy judges of the court and their services can be utilized on a limited basis (Sect. 60(3)).

Provision is also made in the act for quasi-judicial officers called prothonotaries (Sect. 12). Their duties are defined by the rules and may be of a judicial nature (Sect. 46(1)(h)). In addition to being taxing-masters, they can, subject to supervision by the court, deal with interlocutory work, and even take trials in minor matters as the Associate Chief Justice may find expedient in order to ensure the expeditious dispatch of the court's business.

While all the full-time judges must reside in or near the National Capital Region (Sect. 7), each division of the court can sit any place in Canada and the place and time of the sittings must be arranged to suit the convenience of the litigants (Sects. 15 and 16). In addition, there is authority in the statute (Sect. 7(2)) for a rota of judges to provide for a continuity of judicial availability in any place where the volume of work, or other circumstances, makes such an arrangement expedient.

Judges of the Federal Court of Canada as at January 1, 1977

Chief Justice, Hon. Wilbur Roy Jackett *(appointed June 1, 1971)*
Associate Chief Justice, Hon. Arthur Louis Thurlow *(appointed to Court of Appeal, June 1, 1971; appointed Associate Chief Justice, December 4, 1975)*
Court of Appeal Judges: Hon. Louis Pratte *(appointed to Trial Division, June 10, 1971; appointed to Court of Appeal, March 5, 1973)*, Hon. Darrel Verner Heald *(appointed to Trial Division, July 9, 1971; appointed to Court of Appeal, December 4, 1975)*, Hon. John J. Urie *(appointed June 8, 1973)*, Hon. William F. Ryan *(appointed April 11, 1974)*, Hon. Gerald Eric Le Dain *(appointed September 1, 1975)*
Trial Division Judges: Hon. Angus Alexander Cattanach *(appointed June 1, 1971)*, Hon. Hugh Francis Gibson *(appointed June 1, 1971)*, Hon. Allison Arthur Mariotti Walsh *(appointed June 1, 1971)*, Hon. Frank U. Collier *(appointed September 16, 1971)*, Hon. George A. Addy *(appointed September 17, 1973)*, Hon. Patrick M. Mahoney PC *(appointed September 17, 1973)*, Hon. Raymond G. Decary *(appointed September 17, 1973)*, Hon. Jean-Eudes Dubé PC *(appointed April 24, 1975)*, Hon. Louis Marceau *(appointed December 23, 1975)*
Deputy Judges of the Federal Court (Section 60(3), Federal Court Act): Hon. Robert S. Furlong, Hon. Dalton C. Wells.

Miscellaneous courts. The Railway Act, 1903 (RSC 1970, c.R-2) established the Board of Railway Commissioners for Canada as a court of record; by the Transport Act, 1938 (RSC 1970, c.T-14) the name was changed to the Board of Transport Commissioners for Canada, and by the National Transportation Act, 1967 (RSC 1970, c.N-17) to the *Canadian Transport Commission*. This court exercises jurisdiction with respect to transport matters under the Railway Act, the Aeronautics Act, the Transport Act and the National Transportation Act, and with respect to telegraph and telephone matters under the Railway Act. The Governor in Council is given jurisdiction to vary or rescind any order of the commission and an appeal lies from the commission to the Supreme Court of Canada on a question of jurisdiction or of law.

By virtue of Section 91(21) of the British North America Act, 1867, Parliament has exclusive legislative jurisdiction in relation to bankruptcy and insolvency. By the Bankruptcy Act (RSC 1970, c.B-3) the superior courts of the provinces are constituted *bankruptcy courts;* original jurisdiction is conferred upon the trial courts and appellate jurisdiction is conferred upon the appeal courts of the provinces.

The Tax Review Board, created in 1949 as the Income Tax Appeal Board and later changed to the Tax Appeal Board, now operates under the Tax Review Board Act 1970 (SC 1970-71, c.11). The board is a court of record and has jurisdiction to hear appeals by taxpayers against their assessment under the Income Tax Act and also appeals under the Estate Tax Act, the Old Age Security Act and certain sections of the Canada Pension Plan. An appeal lies from the board to the Federal Court of Canada and a further appeal from that court to the Supreme Court of Canada.

The Court Martial Appeal Court was established in 1959 by an amendment to the National Defence Act (RSC 1970, c.N-4). The judges of the court are not fewer than four judges of the Federal Court of Canada designated by the Governor in Council and such additional judges of a superior court of criminal jurisdiction as are appointed by the Governor in Council. The Governor in Council designates one of the judges to be president of the court. The court hears appeals from courts martial respecting the legality of a finding of guilty on any charge and the legality of a sentence passed by a court martial. An appeal lies from the Court Martial Appeal Court to the Supreme Court of Canada on a question of law only.

The Immigration Appeal Board was established in 1967 by the Immigration Appeal Board Act (RSC 1970, c.I-3). The board is a court of record, with a broad discretionary jurisdiction with respect to temporary or permanent admission of individuals into Canada, and to hear appeals from decisions or orders under the Immigration Act. The establishing act provides for the operation of the board and in particular for the legal and administrative processes involved in appeals by individuals against deportation, detention and the refusal of admission of sponsored relatives ordered under the provisions of the Immigration Act or Regulations. An appeal lies to the Federal Court of Canada and, on leave, to the Supreme Court of Canada.

The provincial judiciary   2.4.2

Certain provisions of the British North America Act govern to some extent the provincial judiciary. Under Section 92(14) the legislature of each province exclusively may make laws in relation to the administration of justice in the province including the constitution, maintenance and organization of provincial courts of both civil and criminal jurisdiction. Section 96 provides that the Governor General shall appoint the judges of the superior, district and county courts in each province, except those of the courts of probate in Nova Scotia and New Brunswick.

The territorial judiciary   2.4.3

In 1971 amendments [now cited as RSC 1970, c.48 (1st Supp.)] to the Yukon Act and the Northwest Territories Act were proclaimed in force, simultaneously with certain ordinances of the Yukon Territory and the Northwest Territories, allowing the territorial governments to assume responsibility for the administration of justice other than the conduct of criminal prosecutions.

In the Yukon Territory, provision was made for a Territorial (now Supreme) Court, a Magistrate's Court, justices of the peace and a Court of Appeal. The Supreme Court consists of a single judge of superior court rank and the Magistrate's Court. Both are located in Whitehorse, although from time to time Magistrate's Court sittings are held in other communities. There are 32 justices of the peace, appointed by the Commissioner, located at 15 points in the Territory. The Judge of the Supreme Court of the Northwest Territories is ex officio Judge in the Yukon Territory and vice versa. The Court of Appeal consists of the Chief Justices of British Columbia, the Justices of Appeal of British Columbia and the Judge of the Supreme Court of the Northwest Territories.

The court system in the Northwest Territories consists of a superior court called the Supreme Court of the Northwest Territories, presided over by one judge located in Yellowknife. The Court of Appeal of the Territories consists of the Justices of Appeal of Alberta and the judges of the Yukon Territory and Northwest Territories Supreme Courts. There are also two full-time magistrates appointed by the Commissioner who have jurisdiction similar to provincial judges; a number of justices of the peace, also appointed by the Commissioner, serve in widely scattered settlements in the Territories.

Salaries, allowances and pensions of judges   2.4.4

Section 100 of the British North America Act provides that the "Salaries, Allowances, and Pensions of the Judges of the Superior, District, and County Courts (except the Courts of Probate in Nova Scotia and New Brunswick) and of the Admiralty Courts in Cases where the Judges thereof are for the Time being paid by Salary, shall be fixed and provided by the Parliament of Canada". These are provided under the Judges Act (RSC 1970, c.J-1 as amended by SC 1970-71, c.55, SC 1973-74, c.17, SC 1974-75, c.48).

The salary of the Chief Justice of Canada is $65,000 per annum and those of the puisne judges of the Supreme Court of Canada, $60,000. The salaries of the Chief Justice and the Associate Chief Justice of the Federal Court of Canada are $55,000 per annum and of the other judges of the Federal Court, $50,000.

All Chief Justices of provincial superior courts, the Senior Associate Chief Justice and the Associate Chief Justice of the Superior Court of Quebec receive annual salaries of $55,000; the puisne judges of these courts and the judges of the two territorial courts receive $50,000 per annum. Where judicial offices are created for supernumerary judges, the incumbents will receive the salary of a puisne judge. Supernumerary judges are those judges of a superior court of a province who have given up their regular judicial duties to hold themselves available to perform such special judicial duties as may be assigned to them from time to time by the Chief Justice or Associate Chief Justice of the court of which they are a member. The chief judges of county and district courts receive salaries of $48,000 per annum and the remaining judges and junior judges of all county and district courts, $43,000 per annum.

Every judge who is in receipt of a salary under the Judges Act is paid an additional salary of $3,000 per annum as compensation for any extra-judicial services that he may be called upon to perform by the Government of Canada or the government of a province, and for the incidental expenditures that the fit and proper execution of his office as judge may require. In the case of each judge of the Federal Court of Canada and of the territorial courts of the Yukon Territory and the Northwest Territories an additional allowance of $3,000 per annum is paid as compensation for special incidental expenditures inherent in the exercise of his office as judge.

The Judges Act provides that a judge of a superior or county court who, for the purpose of performing any function or duty as such judge, attends at any place other than that at which or in the immediate vicinity of which he is by law obliged to reside, is entitled to be paid, as a travelling allowance, his moving or transportation expenses and reasonable travelling and other expenses incurred by him in so attending. If a judge uses his personal automobile because of the lack of good public transportation facilities, he is paid a travel allowance.

2.5 Legal services

2.5.1 The legal profession

The adjective "fused" is sometimes used to describe the legal profession in common law Canada since practising lawyers are both called as barristers and admitted as solicitors. Admission to practise is a provincial matter. Statutes setting out the powers and responsibilities of the provincial organizations are: (Alberta) The Legal Profession Act RSA 1970, c.203 as am.; (British Columbia) The Legal Professions Act RSBC 1960, c.214 as am.; (Manitoba) The Law Society Act RSM 1970, c.L-100; (New Brunswick) The Barristers' Society Act, 1973, SNB 1973, c.80; (Newfoundland) The Law Society Act RSN 1970, c.201 as am.; (Nova Scotia) Barristers and Solicitors Act RSNS 1967, c.18 as am.; (Ontario) The Law Society Act RSO 1970, c.238; (Prince Edward Island) The Legal Profession Act RSPEI 1951, c.84 as am.; (Saskatchewan) The Legal Profession Act RSS 1965, c.301 as am.; (Northwest Territories) The Legal Profession Ordinance RONWT 1956, c.57 as am.; (Yukon) The Legal Profession Ordinance ROY 1971, c.L-4 as am. In Quebec the legal profession is divided into the separate branches of advocate and notary and their statutes are the Bar Act, SQ 1966/67, c.77 as am. and the Notarial Act, SQ 1968, c.70.

2.5.2 Legal aid

For many years the provision of legal services to persons unable to afford the fees normally charged by a lawyer was viewed as a responsibility to be assumed by individual lawyers on a voluntary basis as a form of charity. In more recent times all provincial governments have moved to establish publicly funded legal aid programs under which persons of limited means are able to obtain the services of a lawyer in a number of criminal and civil matters at either no cost or modest cost to themselves depending upon the client's financial circumstances. The lawyers who act for clients in matters covered by a provincial legal aid program are then paid by the government, usually at a reduced rate, on a fee for services basis or by salary depending upon the type of legal aid program operated in the province. The provincial legal aid programs vary considerably in terms of formalities, scope of coverage and methods of providing the legal services. Some are established by legislative enactment while others exist and operate by way of informal agreements between the provincial government and the law society. Some programs provide for fairly comprehensive coverage in both criminal and civil matters while others at present encompass only criminal offences. Again, some plans operate on a fee for services basis whereas others rely partially or mainly on the services of state salaried lawyers. In some provinces a mixed system is in operation.

In 1971 the federal government entered the field and concluded an agreement with the government of the Northwest Territories for sharing the costs of providing legal aid in both criminal and civil matters for persons in the Territories financially unable to retain the services of a lawyer. This comprehensive legal aid program was implemented on August 17, 1971. In the Yukon Territory the legal aid program is a service operated by the territorial bar with the government paying the fees to lawyers who act for legal aid clients charged with criminal offences.

In August 1972, the federal government announced that it was prepared to enter into agreements with the provincial governments under which federal funds would be paid to the provinces to assist them in developing or expanding their legal aid programs in matters related to criminal law. Agreements have since been concluded with all the provincial governments. Amendments to these agreements provided that the federal government would contribute the lesser of 75 cents per capita of the provincial population or 90% of the program expenditures toward the costs of providing lawyers' services to eligible persons subject to criminal charges or proceedings under federal laws. These federal-provincial agreements enable the provincial governments to determine the method or methods by which legal services will be provided to persons who qualify for assistance, but in cases where an individual is charged with a criminal offence carrying a penalty of mandatory life imprisonment that person is entitled to retain a lawyer of his or her own choice. The agreements also ensure that a person otherwise eligible to receive legal aid will not be disqualified as a recipient only because he or she is not a resident of the province in which the criminal proceedings take place.

The federal Department of Justice   2.6

The Department of Justice of the Government of Canada is divided, for administrative and functional purposes, into a number of service areas. Lawyers working for the department may be assigned to sections, or work on such matters as jurimetrics or the federal court reports in Headquarters Legal Services, or as legal advisers to other government departments or agencies as part of Departmental Legal Services, or to offices in Vancouver, Edmonton, Saskatoon, Winnipeg, Toronto, Montreal and Halifax as part of Regional Legal Services. The sections within Headquarters Legal Services, each headed by a director, are described below.

Advisory and Research Services. This section is responsible for research and preparing legal opinions requested by the Government of Canada and its various departments and agencies.

Civil Law. This section conducts litigation and provides legal advice for the government on all matters of a non-criminal nature arising in the province of Quebec.

Civil Litigation. The lawyers in this section are responsible for the conduct of the non-criminal litigation involving the Government of Canada originating in those provinces where the common law prevails. This litigation includes customs and excise tax matters, expropriation cases, disputes over contracts, accident claims, suits for defamation and claims for breach of copyright.

Constitutional, Administrative and International Law. This section is responsible for coordinating and providing legal advice in the general fields of constitutional and administrative law within the Government of Canada and its various departments and agencies. It is concerned with long-term policy in constitutional affairs and with problems of federal-provincial relations. The section also deals with work in the areas of public and private international law. Canada became a member of The Hague Conference on Private International Law in 1968 and the department is responsible for Canadian participation in the conference. This section coordinates Canadian activities in relation to the conference, which meets every other year, and it has a similar role with regard to Unidroit, the International Institute for the Unification of Private Law. In both public and private international law this section has a particular interest in matters concerning the countries of the British Commonwealth.

Criminal Law. The lawyers in this section participate in criminal litigation in every jurisdiction. They work in cooperation with members of the department's six regional offices in the prosecution of violations of federal statutes and regulations and are involved in the extradition of persons to and from Canada. An additional and very important function is the work on criminal law amendment which involves considering and assessing the suggestions for the amendment of the criminal code and certain other statutes received from many sources. The section advises the Minister of Justice with respect to these recommendations.

Legislation. The work of this section is concerned with the preparation of legislation from the time a topic is given approval in principle by Cabinet until the resulting enactment receives Royal Assent. The periodic revisions of the *Statutes of Canada* are also compiled here as are the office consolidations of certain acts which are prepared in the periods between major revisions.

Policy Planning. This section is responsible for developing legal initiatives and responses to emerging social problems. It is concerned, in cooperation with other departments and levels of government, with assessing recommendations for changes in the law proposed by the Law Reform Commission of Canada and other groups.

Privy Council. This section is responsible for the examination of what is sometimes called subordinate legislation. From time to time Parliament delegates certain legislative functions to other bodies and officials and it is the responsibility of this section to consult with the Clerk of the Privy Council in order to maintain general supervision over the legislative product resulting from this delegation and to consider whether it is within the authority conferred by Parliament (see Statutory Instruments Act, 1970-71, c.38). The section is asked to assume responsibility for the actual drafting of certain subordinate legislation. Lawyers in this section also act as legal advisers to the Clerk of the Privy Council and his staff.

Programs and Law Information Development. This section is intended to develop and administer programs of a service, research or informational nature with respect to such matters, for example, as legal aid, compensation for victims of crimes, native courtworkers and law for the layman.

Property and Commercial Law. This section handles all the work involved when land is required for public purposes and also deals with contracts between the government and private businesses.

Tax Litigation. The lawyers in this section represent the Crown in all aspects of most federal tax litigation. The section has also an advisory function on tax matters with the Department of National Revenue.

A booklet entitled *Department of Justice,* describing in detail the work of the sections, is available free upon request. It was written for recruitment purposes in 1972 and much of the information in it is still current.

Police forces   2.7

Organization of police forces   2.7.1

The police forces of Canada are organized in three groups: (1) the federal force, which is the Royal Canadian Mounted Police; (2) provincial police forces — Ontario and Quebec have their own provincial police forces but all other provinces engage the services of the Royal Canadian Mounted Police to perform parallel functions within their borders; and (3) municipal police forces — most urban centres of reasonable size maintain their own police forces or engage the services of the provincial police, under contract, to attend to police matters. In addition, the Canadian National Railways, the Canadian Pacific Railway Company and the National Harbours Board have their own police forces.

The Royal Canadian Mounted Police. The Royal Canadian Mounted Police is a civil force maintained by the federal government. It was established in 1873 as the North-West Mounted Police for service in what was then the North-Western Territory and, in recognition of its services, was granted the prefix "Royal" by King Edward VII in 1904. Its sphere of operations was expanded in 1918 to include all of Canada west of Port Arthur and Fort William (now Thunder Bay). In 1920 it absorbed the Dominion Police, its headquarters was transferred from Regina to Ottawa and its title was changed to Royal Canadian Mounted Police.

The force now operates under authority of the Royal Canadian Mounted Police Act (RSC 1970, c.R-9). It is responsible to the Solicitor General of Canada and is controlled and managed by a Commissioner who holds the rank and status of a deputy minister and is empowered under the act to appoint members to be peace officers in all provinces and territories of Canada.

The administration of justice within the provinces, including the enforcement of the Criminal Code of Canada, is part of the power and duty delegated to the provincial governments. All provinces, except Ontario and Quebec, have entered into contracts with the Royal Canadian Mounted Police to enforce criminal and provincial laws, under the direction of the respective attorneys general. In addition, in these eight provinces, the force is under agreement to provide police services to 177 municipalities, thereby assuming the enforcement responsibility of municipal as well as criminal and provincial laws within these communities. The Yukon Territory and Northwest Territories are policed exclusively by the Royal Canadian Mounted Police and therefore criminal offences, federal statutes and all ordinances of the territories fall within the ambit of force responsibility. The force maintains liaison officers in London, Paris, Bonn, Rome, Hong Kong and Washington and represents Canada in the International Criminal Police Organization, which has its headquarters in Paris.

The 13 operational divisions, alphabetically designated, make up the strength of the force across Canada; they comprise 42 subdivisions which include 708 detachments. "Headquarters" Division, as well as the Office of the Commissioner, is located at Ottawa. Divisional headquarters, for the most part, are located in the provincial or territorial capitals, except for "C" Division which is in Montreal and "A" Division which is in Ottawa. "N" Division in Ottawa and "Depot" Division in Regina are training divisions.

A teletype system links the widespread divisional headquarters with the administrative centre at Ottawa and a network of fixed and mobile radio units operates within the provinces. The focal point of the criminal investigation work of the force is the Directorate of Laboratories and Identification; its services, together with those of divisional and subdivisional units and of six crime detection laboratories, are available to police forces throughout Canada.

The Canadian Police Information Centre at RCMP Headquarters, a duplexed computer system, is staffed and operated by the force. Law enforcement agencies throughout Canada have access via a series of remote terminals to information on stolen vehicles, licences, wanted persons and stolen property.

The RCMP operates the Canadian Police College at which force members and selected representatives of other Canadian and foreign police forces may study the latest advances in the fields of crime prevention and detection.

As of January 1, 1976 the force had a total strength of 17,560 including regular members, special constables, civilian members and public service employees.

Ontario Provincial Police. The Ontario Provincial Police, a Crown force, is the third largest deployed force on the North American continent, having a total authorized strength of more than 5,000 (1976) uniformed and civilian personnel.

The OPP is administered from general headquarters at Toronto by the Commissioner, under the Ministry of the Solicitor General. Other senior executive officers include two deputy commissioners and six assistant commissioners. The force has two principal sides — Operations and Services — each of which is administered by a deputy commissioner. In turn, six divisions at the next level — Field, Traffic, Management, Staff Services, Special Services, and Staff Development — are administered by their respective assistant commissioners. Specialized branches under Special Services include Auto Theft, Criminal Investigation, Anti-rackets, Security, Intelligence, and Special Investigations.

For policing and administration purposes, the province is divided geographically into 17 districts. In the field, there are 189 detachments controlled through 17 district headquarters located at Chatham, London, Burlington, Niagara Falls, Downsview, Mount Forest, Barrie, Peterborough, Belleville, Perth, Long Sault, North Bay, Sudbury, Sault Ste Marie, South Porcupine, Thunder Bay and Kenora; 14 municipalities are policed under special contract.

Under provisions of the Ontario Police Act, the force is responsible for: (1) enforcing federal and provincial statutes in those areas that are not required to maintain their own police departments; (2) maintaining a traffic patrol on the more than 10,000 miles (16 093 km) of King's Highways and 65,000 miles (104 607 km) of secondary county and township roads; (3) enforcing the Liquor Licence Act and the Liquor Control Act for Ontario; (4) maintaining a Criminal Investigation Branch and other specialized branches to assist all other forces in the investigation of major crimes; and (5) assisting other forces by providing additional manpower in the event of emergencies.

Under the Staff Services Division, the Central Records and Communications Branch offers 24-hour seven-day-week service to all police departments in Ontario on such matters as criminal and fingerprint records. The branch also serves as the Ontario Police Force's Driver Suspension Control Centre.

The OPP operates one of the largest frequency-modulation radio networks in the world, with 113 fixed radio stations and more than 1,696 radio-equipped mobile units including motorcycles, boats, helicopters and fixed-wing aircraft. It also operates the Ontario Provincial Police telecommunications network connecting all 17 districts as well as other police departments on a local, national and international basis. Extensions to routine police service are provided by identification, canine, SCUBA, marine-bush rescue units, and aircraft, strategically located throughout the province and available to other law-enforcement agencies upon request.

The year 1974 saw the first recruitment of women in the force's 66-year history. Recruitment of both men and women will permit qualified young persons to make a career in a long-established police force. Officers from inspector up to and including the rank of Commissioner receive the Queen's Commission in the same manner as members of Canada's Armed Forces.

Quebec Police Force. Under the authority of the Attorney General, the Quebec Police Force is responsible for maintaining peace, order and public safety throughout the province, and for prevention and investigation of criminal offences and violations of provincial law. The force is under the command of a director general who is assisted by five assistant directors general and a director of personnel and communications. The force, with general headquarters in

Montreal, is divided into six services: planning, personnel and communications, administration, operations, technical, and special services (intelligence and security).

For police purposes, the province is divided into eight districts each under the command of a Chief Inspector or an Inspector. *Bas St-Laurent* District, including the sections of Chandler, Rimouski and Baie-Comeau, has 19 detachments; *Saguenay–Lac St-Jean,* six detachments; *Quebec,* including the sections of Québec-Nord, Québec-Sud and Rivière-du-Loup, 23 detachments; *La Mauricie,* nine detachments; *L'Estrie,* six detachments; *Montreal,* including the sections of Joliette, Montreal, Saint-Jean, and Arctic Quebec, 28 detachments; *Outaouais* and *Nord-Ouest,* eight detachments each. Strength of the Quebec Police Force at the end of 1975 was 4,108 officers, non-commissioned officers and constables and 968 civilian employees.

Municipal police forces. Provincial legislation makes it mandatory for cities and towns to furnish adequate municipal policing for the maintenance of law and order in their communities. Also, all villages and townships or parts of townships having a population density and a real property assessment sufficient to warrant maintenance of a police force, and having been so designated by Order in Council, are responsible for adequate policing of their municipalities.

Uniform crime reporting   2.7.2

The present method of reporting police statistics (police administration, crime and traffic enforcement statistics), known as the Uniform Crime Reporting Program, was started on January 1, 1962. The program was developed by the (then) Dominion Bureau of Statistics in cooperation with the Canadian Association of Chiefs of Police Committee on Uniform Crime Reporting.

As shown in Table 2.2, police personnel in Canada numbered 58,103 at the end of 1974, including 48,051 sworn-in police officers, 9,478 other full-time employees serving as clerks, technicians, artisans, commissionaires, guards, special constables, etc. and 574 cadets. The ratio of police personnel per 1,000 population was 2.5 and the ratio of police was 2.1. Provincial and territorial ratios for police personnel ranged from 1.5 to 5.1 per 1,000 persons and for police only from 1.4 to 4.4. Total municipal police personnel numbered 32,845 made up of 30,415 members of municipal forces; 2,380 Royal Canadian Mounted Police and 50 Ontario Provincial Police under municipal contracts.

Six policemen were killed by criminal action during 1974 and seven policemen lost their lives accidentally while on duty. Police transport facilities at the end of the year included 11,004 automobiles, 828 motorcycles, 970 other motor vehicles, 419 boats, 27 aircraft, 230 horses and 252 service dogs.

Table 2.3 shows the number of crimes dealt with by the police in 1974 including offences under the criminal code, federal statutes, provincial statutes and municipal by-laws other than traffic; offences cleared by charge and otherwise; and the number of adults and juveniles charged. Offences reported or known to police which investigation proved unfounded are not shown but numbered 118,984 including 93,996 under criminal code classifications; 13,969 under federal statutes; 7,772 under provincial statutes; and 3,247 under municipal by-laws.

During 1974, police reported 109,098 offences against the person including 545 murders, 521 attempted murders, 11,111 rape and other sexual offences, and 96,864 offences of wounding and other assaults (not indecent). All offences against the person resulted in the charging of 37,237 persons, 1,991 of them juveniles. During the year there were 963,748 cases of robbery, breaking and entering, theft, fraud and other offences against property resulting in 180,477 persons charged, 46,082 of them juvenile males and 6,245 juvenile females. There were 3,249 cases of prostitution, 3,264 gaming and betting, 10,812 offensive weapons and 366,714 other criminal code offences. In addition to 44,394 offences under various federal statutes, there were 53,030 under the

Narcotic Control Act and 5,555 under the controlled and restricted drug parts of the Food and Drugs Act. These two classifications resulted in the charging of 50,530 persons including 2,507 juvenile males and 390 juvenile females.

Provincial and territorial fire marshals and commissioners reported 6,636 suspected or known incendiary offences of which 803 were proven unfounded after investigation; 1,125 cases were cleared by charge and 871 cleared otherwise. Charges were laid against 809 adults and 460 juveniles.

There were 80,339 motor vehicles stolen (an estimated 790.9 per 100,000 registered vehicles); 68,820 or 85.7% of these vehicles were recovered. Police were asked to locate 24,621 missing adults and 60,192 missing juveniles of whom 23,488 adults and 58,999 juveniles were located. Police reported investigating death by drowning of 1,274 persons.

During 1974, police departments reported 239,737 (192,914 in 1973) criminal code traffic offences resulting in 174,559 (139,063) persons charged, 5,867 (4,527) of them females. Total traffic charges under other federal statutes numbered 10,395 (8,734); 2,269,590 provincial statutes (other than the three selected offences almost identical to those under the criminal code that are shown separately in Table 2.4) (1,962,416 in 1973) and 318,690 (401,833) municipal by-laws excluding parking. Parking violations numbered 6,545,172 (5,140,216).

There were 729,442 (668,001) traffic accidents reported of which 5,326 (5,342) involved fatalities, 152,938 (149,852) resulted in injuries and 571,177 (512,807) involved property damage over $200 ($100 in Quebec). There were 6,659 (6,437) persons killed in traffic accidents including 5,152 (4,891) drivers and passengers, 1,207 (1,233) pedestrians, 216 (223) cyclists and 84 (90) others. Persons injured numbered 223,192 (219,438).

2.8   Crime and delinquency

2.8.1   Adult offenders and convictions

Offences may be classified under two headings, "indictable offences" and "offences punishable on summary conviction". Indictable offences are grouped in two main categories: offences that violate the criminal code and offences against federal statutes. These include the more serious crimes. Offences punishable on summary conviction — those not expressly made indictable — include offences against the criminal code, federal statutes, provincial statutes and municipal by-laws. Increases in the total number of summary conviction offences do not measure adequately the increase in the seriousness of crime. Many summary conviction offences amount to mere disturbances of the peace, minor upsets to public safety, health and comfort such as parking violations, intoxication and practising trades without licence. Nevertheless, summary conviction offences may include more serious charges such as assault and contribution to juvenile delinquency.

Adults convicted of indictable offences. Statistics are available for persons convicted of indictable offences. Thus it is possible to determine the population engaged in prohibited activities and to help in the treatment of anti-social behaviour in terms of subject-centred action. In the present counting system, although individuals may be charged with more than one offence, only one offence is tabulated for each person and is selected according to the following criteria: (1) if the person were tried on several charges, the offence is that for which proceedings were carried to the farthest stage — conviction and sentence; (2) if there were several convictions, the offence is that for which the heaviest punishment was awarded; (3) if the final result of proceedings on two or more charges were the same, the offence is the more serious one, as measured by the maximum penalty allowed by the law; and (4) if a person were prosecuted for one offence and convicted of another, e.g. charged with murder and convicted of manslaughter, the offence is the one for which the person was convicted.

In 1972 there were 55,541 adults charged with 95,131 indictable offences of whom 45,614 were found guilty of 77,650 offences (see Table 2.5). All data for 1971 and 1972 exclude returns for Quebec and Alberta. It should be noted that figures given in Tables 2.5 - 2.8 and 2.11 are based on information received through the provincial judicial systems and consequently cannot be compared with data reported by police under the Uniform Crime Reporting Program (Tables 2.2 - 2.4) which include these two provinces.

Table 2.6 classifies indictable offences by type of offence for 1971 and 1972. Class I covers offences against the person and in 1972, 4,693 males and 316 females were convicted in this category, mostly for assaults of various kinds. Classes II to IV deal with offences against property. Thefts predominate among the offences in these classes, and breaking and entering, extortion and robbery — serious crimes which involve acts of violence — are the next most numerous. Class V deals with offences relating to currency and Class VI with miscellaneous offences; among the latter, the most numerous convictions are for offences connected with gaming, betting and lotteries. In 1972 there were 2,753 men and 281 women convicted under federal statutes of whom 2,249 men and 228 women were offenders under the Narcotic Control Act.

The number of female offenders convicted of indictable offences decreased from 7,735 in 1971 to 7,283 in 1972 with Ontario and Newfoundland accounting for the difference. The ratio of female offenders to total persons convicted decreased from 13.9% in 1971 to 13.3% in 1972 for Newfoundland and from 17.2% in 1971 to 16.4% in 1972 for Ontario. Table 2.7 summarizes the most serious court sentences given for indictable offences and Table 2.8 shows the method of trial and disposition of cases.

Two kinds of sentences — probation and commitment to an institution — maintain, for a certain period of time, a relationship between the person dealt with by the court and the legal institutions of a community. There are several types of institutions to which a person can be committed, such as penitentiaries, reformatories, jails and industrial farms. Theoretically, every institution has a specific purpose which is supposed to be taken into account when arriving at a legal decision. In practice, however, the availability of an institution in a given community is a factor in determining the decision rendered by the court.

Convictions for summary conviction offences. Offences punishable on summary conviction under the criminal code or under the provincial summary conviction acts as the case may be are triable by magistrates and justices of the peace. Data relating to these offences are based on convictions; no information is available on either the number of persons involved in these offences or the number of charges (see Table 2.9).

Appeals. Appeal is an important safeguard in Canada's legal system. The conviction or the sentence pronounced by a judge of a first instance court may be appealed on the grounds that the verdict was unreasonable, that there was a wrong decision on some question of law or that there was a miscarriage of justice. In 1972 there were 3,123 appeals in indictable cases disposed of by the courts, of which 290 were Crown appeals and 2,833 appeals of the accused. Of the Crown appeals, 76 were from acquittal and 214 from sentence. Appeals in summary conviction cases disposed of by the courts numbered 2,388 in 1972. Of these, 610 were appeals of the informant and 1,778 appeals of the accused. The informant appeals comprised 497 from acquittal and 113 from sentence, and appeals of the accused comprised 1,389 from conviction and 389 from sentence.

Juvenile delinquents   2.8.2

Juvenile delinquent, as defined in the Juvenile Delinquents Act, means any child who violates any provision of the criminal code or of any federal or provincial statute, or of any by-law or ordinance of any municipality, or who is guilty of sexual immorality or any similar form of vice, or who is liable by reason of any other act to be committed to an industrial school, or juvenile reformatory under the provision of any federal or provincial statute. The commission by a child of any of these acts constitutes an offence known as a delinquency. The upper age limit of children brought before the juvenile courts in the provinces varies. The Juvenile Delinquents Act defines a child as meaning any boy or girl apparently or actually under the age of 16 years, or such other age as may be directed in any province. In Prince Edward Island, Nova Scotia, New Brunswick, Ontario and Saskatchewan under 16 is the official age; in Alberta under 16 for boys and under 18 for girls; in Newfoundland under 17; in Quebec, Manitoba and British Columbia under 18 years. Up to 1967, it was the practice of Statistics Canada to publish information about juvenile delinquents 16 years of age and over separate from that of juveniles under 16 years of age. From 1967 on, the figures include all those considered as juveniles by the respective provinces, regardless of the differing upper age limits.

Included in the statistics of juvenile delinquents (Tables 2.10 - 2.12) are cases (alleged as well as adjudged) which were brought before the courts and dealt with formally. A case was counted separately each time a child appeared before the court for a new delinquency or delinquencies. In instances where multiple delinquencies were dealt with at one court appearance, only one delinquency — the most serious — was selected for tabulation. Delinquencies reported as informal cases by the courts were not included nor were cases of children presenting conduct problems which were not brought to court or which were dealt with by the police, social agencies, schools or youth-serving agencies. Thus, community facilities for dealing with children's problems may have an influence on the number of cases referred to court and, therefore, an effect on the statistics of juvenile delinquents.

2.9   Correctional institutions

Correctional institutions may be classified under three headings: (1) training schools — operated by the provinces or private organizations under provincial charter for juvenile offenders serving indefinite terms up to the legal age for children in the particular province; (2) provincial adult institutions; and (3) penitentiaries — operated for adult offenders by the federal government in which sentences of over two years are served.

2.9.1   Institutions and training schools

There is a limited amount of statistical information available with respect to correctional institutions. "In-custody" figures shown in Table 2.13 for penitentiaries refer only to those persons under sentence, but the figures for admissions include those received from courts as well as by transfer from other penitentiaries and by cancellation of paroles. Figures for releases include expiry of sentences, transfers between penitentiaries, releases on parole, deaths, pardons and releases on court order. In-custody figures for provincial and county institutions may include, in addition to those serving sentences, persons awaiting trial, on remand for sentence or psychiatric examination, awaiting appeal or deportation, any others not yet serving sentence and, for training school population, juveniles on placement.

Population figures in Table 2.13 are for a given day of the year. These figures represent, in effect, a yearly census of correctional institutions and, as such, are not necessarily indicative of the daily average population count. For instance, if an abnormal number of commitments is made to a certain institution on or just prior to the end of the year, the result will be an unrepresentative population total for the institution in that year.

With this limitation in mind, certain changes in the total populations of the various correctional institutions may be noted. The population in penitentiaries decreased in 1974 after increasing in the previous years. The population in provincial adult institutions increased after having decreased in the previous years. The population in training schools decreased in 1974 after having increased in 1973.

Table 2.14 shows the number of admissions to penitentiaries by offence for the years 1972 to 1974 and the percentage of total admissions accounted for by each offence type. Admissions are classified by major offence, determined as described above (Section 2.8.1). From the table it can be seen that the various offence categories have each accounted for a fairly stable percentage of the total admissions to penitentiaries over this three-year period. Certain variations are, however, evident.

Admissions for rape increased over the three-year period both in number and as a percentage of total admissions. Assault admissions also increased steadily. In contrast, admissions for prison breach declined. Admissions under the Narcotic Control Act and for parole violation decreased in 1974 after having increased in the previous year. The largest offence categories were consistently robbery and breaking and entering, accounting together for over one third of the total admissions in each year.

Canadian Penitentiary Service   2.9.2

The Canadian Penitentiary Service operates under the Penitentiary Act (RSC 1970, c.P-6) and is under the jurisdiction of the Solicitor General of Canada. It is responsible for all federal penitentiaries and for the care and training of persons committed to those institutions. The Commissioner of Penitentiaries, under the direction of the Solicitor General, is responsible for control and management of the service, and related matters.

Headquarters of the Penitentiary Service is in Ottawa. Regional directorates are located in Vancouver, BC; Kingston, Ont.; Ville de Laval, Que.; Saskatoon, Sask.; and Moncton, NB. Five correctional staff colleges, at Kingston, Ville de Laval, New Westminster, Edmonton and Moncton, train service recruits and supply refresher courses for senior penitentiary officers. Conferences for CPS and special groups are also held at the colleges.

In the year ended December 31, 1975, the federal penitentiary system controlled 54 institutions: 14 maximum, 14 medium, and 26 minimum security institutions. Total inmate population was 8,580, of whom 139 were female offenders; 41% (including females) were in maximum security; 46% in medium security, and 13% in minimum security institutions. New, smaller institutions are being designed to provide more rehabilitation facilities for inmates, with indoor and outdoor recreation. Plans to phase out old institutions are being worked out.

After sentence by the court, prisoners are received by CPS in a reception centre, a maximum security institution where security and training classification is carried out. Based on diagnostic results, each inmate is placed in an institution that provides the best training program and degree of security required. Minimum stay at the centre is usually six weeks. Maximum security institutions include psychiatric centres, which operate as a medical service within CPS. Institutions classified as maximum are located at Dorchester, NB; Ste-Anne-des-Plaines and Ville de Laval, Que.; Kingston and Bath, Ont.; Stony Mountain, Man.; Prince Albert, Sask.; Abbotsford and New Westminster, BC.

Inmates transferred from maximum to medium and minimum security institutions usually have greater opportunity to take part in training programs but must first establish suitability as a lower security risk. Medium security units are located at: Springhill, NS; Cowansville and Ville de Laval, Que.; Campbellford, Kingston and Joyceville, Ont.; Drumheller and Innisfail, Alta.; Agassiz, Abbotsford, Mission City and William Head, BC.

Minimum security institutions including Community Correctional Centres, forestry camps and farms, are located at: Dorchester, Saint John and Blackville, NB; Halifax and Apple River, NS; Ville de Laval and Ste-Anne-des-Plaines, Que.; Kingston, Gravenhurst, Petawawa, Toronto and Bath, Ont.; Stony

Mountain and Winnipeg, Man.; Prince Albert and Regina, Sask.; Edmonton and Calgary, Alta.; Victoria, Agassiz, Vancouver and Mission City, BC. Community Correctional Centres are located in urban communities across Canada offering parolees contact with potential employers and access to communities as a rehabilitative measure. Some inmates sentenced to federal penitentiary terms in Newfoundland are held in the provincial centre at St. John's, Nfld., under provisions of Section 14, Penitentiary Act. Contracts whereby services are exchanged between the federal government and some provinces provide for inmate transfers with full-cost recovery.

Opportunities for upgrading and extending educational levels are provided in the institutions and through day parole or temporary absence passes to the outside community. Classes are full- and part-time. Correspondence courses are also offered at elementary, secondary and university levels. More than 100 trade courses geared to 15 different occupations are available in the major institutions. In 1975, approximately 3,000 trainees were awarded diplomas or apprenticeship credits. Most institutional chapels have multi-purpose programs where religious instruction is given and other programmed activities are available. Community participation in the programs is encouraged.

In the temporary absence program 48,642 permits were granted in 1975 to 29,087 individuals and 18,536 groups; 214 inmates failed to return. Temporary absence is granted for periods up to three days by heads of institutions, and 15 days by the Commissioner of Penitentiaries for humanitarian, rehabilitative, and medical reasons. Evening and weekend activities involving the outside community continued. Twenty-one citizen participation committees comprising 210 citizens operated in the institutions. More than 4,000 citizen volunteers were involved in inmate programs in the institutions and outside; these included ex-inmates. Community-based programs, such as Alcoholics Anonymous, drama, music instruction, public speaking, lectures, films, recreation, discussion groups led by private agencies, professionals, voluntary citizens, and community groups all have a part in the inmate's life. Trade schools within the institutions provide training in 25 occupations including woodwork, metal, textiles, printing, automotive repair, painting and finishing, masonry, stationary engineering, agriculture, food preparation and housekeeping.

Medical treatment for the mentally ill is given at three psychiatric centres; in Abbotsford, BC; Kingston, Ont.; and Ville de Laval, Que. A staff of specialists is available in each centre full- or part-time. Within each institution medical facilities provide hospital and out-patient treatment. Inmates requiring surgery are transported to nearby community or armed forces hospitals. Physicians, nurses, psychiatrists, psychologists, and dentists provide daily health facilities for all inmates.

2.9.3   The parole system

Parole is a conditional release of selected prison inmates at the optimum time, once they are lawfully eligible, to help them reintegrate into the community. The National Parole Board has jurisdiction for parole over any adult inmate committed to a federal prison who has been convicted of an offence under any federal statute. The board also has parole jurisdiction for inmates serving definite sentences in provincial institutions where the inmate is sentenced under a federal statute.

The board has no jurisdiction over a child under the Juvenile Delinquents Act or an inmate serving a sentence for a breach of a provincial statute, such as a liquor control act. Moreover, the board does not review a conviction or the length of a sentence; this is the function of the court. Additionally, parole is not granted as leniency nor as a pardon.

The parole system offers a means of rehabilitation while protecting society. Indeed, the board is as concerned with the protection of society as with the reformation of the offender and thus supervision is as much a part of the parole system as guidance. All parolees are under supervision subject to certain restrictions and conditions.

The National Parole Board is composed of 19 members, including a chairman and vice-chairman, who are appointed by Order in Council. Its headquarters is in Ottawa and there are regional boards in each of five geographic regions of Canada, in Vancouver, Saskatoon, Kingston, Montreal and Moncton.

The board grants two types of parole: full and day parole. Full parole is a full-time release that may continue until the end of the sentence, including remission periods. Offenders who are serving two years or more are generally in federal institutions under federal jurisdiction; the others are in provincial institutions. Federal inmates serving definite term, non-life, sentences become eligible for parole consideration after serving one third of the sentence or after seven years, whichever comes first; in any case, all must serve a minimum of nine months. If parole is not granted at the first review the board must continue to look at the case at least once every two years. Eligibility for anyone declared to be an habitual criminal or dangerous sexual offender is calculated differently. Inmates in provincial institutions serving sentences under federal law may also be paroled by the board. Eligibility comes after one third of the sentence is served. However, British Columbia and Ontario have their own parole boards and in those provinces an inmate may be serving a definite or fixed term plus an indeterminate term. The National Parole Board may grant parole during the definite term, the provincial board during the indeterminate term. The board has the authority to grant an earlier release in exceptional circumstances where it believes the case is deserving and the best interest of the community and inmate will be served.

Anyone sentenced to preventive detention as an habitual criminal or dangerous sexual offender has his case reviewed at least once a year under the criminal code to see if he should be granted parole. However, few such inmates are released before 10 years have been served. An offender sentenced to life as a maximum sentence for a crime other than murder becomes eligible for parole after serving seven years.

Inmates sentenced to life for murder before July 26, 1976 may become eligible after a minimum of 10 years. For those sentenced to life terms after January 1974, the eligibility date may depend on the jury's recommendation and the judge's pronouncement of the earliest possible date for eligibility. This may be set at any time between 10 and 20 years. Inmates sentenced on or after July 26, 1976, have different periods to serve before eligibility.

Since July 1976, offenders sentenced to life imprisonment for first degree murder are not eligible for parole consideration before they have served 25 years. First degree murder covers all planned and deliberate murders; contracted murders; murder of police officers, prison employees, or others authorized to work in a prison; and murder while committing or attempting to commit rape, indecent assault on a male or female, kidnapping and forcible confinement, or hijacking. Anyone who commits a second murder, no matter of what nature, is considered to have committed a first degree murder.

Any other murder is second degree murder and the mandatory period to be served before parole eligibility is between 10 and 25 years, as indicated by the sentencing judge, after the view of the convicting jury has been sought. A person convicted of second degree murder and sentenced to serve more than the minimum 10 years, before becoming eligible for parole, may appeal this additional period of ineligibility to the court of appeal.

Anyone convicted of first degree murder who has served 15 years of the 25 year mandatory period before parole eligibility or anyone convicted of second degree murder, whose mandatory term exceeds 15 years, and who has served 15 years of the sentence, may apply for a judicial review by a superior court judge and a jury to reduce the remaining period of ineligibility and to be declared eligible for parole.

Day parole may be granted before full parole for up to four months for education or training not available in the institution and the inmate will return to the institution or to a special centre from time to time during the duration of that parole. Except for someone serving a life sentence, eligibility for day parole comes after an inmate has served either six months or one half of the time before he is eligible for full parole, whichever time is closer to the date for full parole eligibility. Subject to this, a day parole program may begin two years before the full parole eligibility date for anyone except a lifer who may be granted it three years before that date.

Another type of release, mandatory supervision, is administered by the board. Anyone released from a federal institution 60 days or more before the end of his sentence, because of statutory and earned remission of the sentence, is subject to supervision for the full period of the remission. The release conditions are the same as those for parole.

If the inmate violates the conditions of his release — parole, or mandatory supervision — or commits a further offence or misbehaves in any manner, the board may suspend and then revoke the release, returning him to the institution to serve the part of his sentence that was outstanding at the time his release was granted. Because of a court decision, day paroles are no longer revoked and the board is preparing a new system to differentiate between terminations for violations and terminations when a project prematurely ends. If the person on any release commits an indictable offence for which he might be sentenced to two years or more, his parole is automatically forfeited and he is returned to the institution to serve the unexpired balance of his sentence plus any new term to which he is sentenced for the new offence.

Eligibility for an inmate who forfeits his parole by being convicted of an indictable offence, for which he might be sentenced to two years or more, comes either after he serves one half of his new term, which is made up of the remainder of his sentence plus any new sentence, or after he serves seven years, whichever comes first.

The decision of the board about any one inmate is based on reports it receives from the police, from the trial judge or magistrate, and from various people at the institution who deal with him. Reports may also be obtained from a psychologist or a psychiatrist. Normally, a community investigation is made to secure as much information as possible about his family and background, his work record, and his position in the community. These reports help the board to assess the likelihood that the offender can lead a law-abiding life.

When all the reports are received and the community investigation completed, they are analyzed and presented to the board for consideration. Parole for inmates in provincial institutions is granted or refused on the basis of these reports and investigations. For the inmate in a federal institution there is one more step before the board makes its decision. He is interviewed by a panel of two or more board members before his parole eligibility date to clarify or amplify his reasons for requesting parole and any aspects of his case that may have come to light through report and investigation.

All members have an equal vote on cases and there is a system of voting that states the minimum number of votes needed to grant parole in certain types of cases. Except for those specific instances, two votes are sufficient to grant or refuse full parole and one vote for a decision on day parole.

In federal cases the first voting is made by members of the regional board located in the same region as the inmate. If the regional members fail to reach agreement or if more than two votes are required, the case is sent to Ottawa for additional votes. When the case is of a type normally calling for more than two votes, one, three, or five additional board members in Ottawa will study the case, after the study and recommendation is made by the regional members. Cases of manslaughter, rape, drug trafficking, and armed robbery require more than two votes. If the inmate was sentenced as an habitual criminal or a dangerous sexual offender, or is serving life, the case is also reviewed in Ottawa. In cases of provincial inmates the vote is made by members at headquarters.

A parolee is under the care of a supervisor in one of the district offices of the National Parole Service, an after-care agency worker, or a probation officer.

In 1975 the board granted 2,552 full paroles. This number together with those already on parole meant that there were 6,457 inmates at liberty in Canada for part or all of the year. Similarly, with the granting of 2,106 day paroles there were 2,874 inmates on day parole during the year, and with 2,439 inmates released on mandatory supervision there were 4,048 offenders at liberty for part or all of the year. During the same year there were 281 revocations of full parole and 341 of mandatory supervision. Some 2,204 day paroles were either terminated or completed during the same period. In 1975 there were 483 forfeitures of full paroles, 62 of day paroles, and 642 of mandatory supervision releases.

Significant changes to the board's operations were proposed under the Peace and Security legislation introduced in Parliament in 1976. Part of the proposals, contained in Bill C-84, became law July 26, 1976, affecting the eligibility of inmates sentenced to life for murder, on or after that date. Some of the other changes proposed in Bill C-83 would mean the expansion of the board from 19 to 26 members to permit a more extensive review of cases, the transfer of responsibility for temporary absences without escort from penitentiaries to the board, the participation by community representatives in the parole decision process for those convicted of murder or serving indeterminate sentences, and the introduction of more procedural safeguards for parole applicants. Additionally, the National Parole Service would join with the Canadian Penitentiary Service to form a federal corrections agency.

Through the Parole Act the National Parole Board is involved in the pardon granting process under the Royal Prerogative of Mercy when asked to do so by the Solicitor General of Canada. This concerns free pardons, ordinary pardons, and remissions of fines, forfeitures or penalties. Under the Criminal Records Act (RSC 1970, c.12 1st Supp.) the board also has specific responsibility for investigations and recommendations concerning pardons of people who were convicted and subsequently rehabilitated. Under that act a pardon may be granted two years after the end of a sentence for a summary offence or five years after a sentence for an indictable offence.

Sources
2.1 - 2.6 Advisory and Research Services, Department of Justice.
2.7 Judicial Division, Institutional and Public Finance Statistics Branch, Statistics Canada; Royal Canadian Mounted Police; Ontario Provincial Police; Quebec Police Force.
2.8 - 2.9.1 Judicial Division, Institutional and Public Finance Statistics Branch, Statistics Canada.
2.9.2 Canadian Penitentiary Service.
2.9.3 National Parole Board.

Tables

. .	not available	e	estimate
. . .	not appropriate or not applicable	p	preliminary
—	nil or zero	r	revised
- -	too small to be expressed		certain tables may not add due to rounding

2.1 Provinces and territories of Canada, dates of admission to Confederation, legislative processes by which admission was effected, present area and seat of government

Province, territory or district	Date of admission or creation	Legislative process	Present area sq miles	Seat of provincial or territorial government
Ontario[1]	July 1, 1867	Act of Imperial Parliament — The British North America Act, 1867 (Br. Stat. 1867, c. 3) and Imperial Order in Council, May 22, 1867	412,582	Toronto
Quebec[2]	July 1, 1867		594,860	Quebec
Nova Scotia	July 1, 1867		21,425	Halifax
New Brunswick	July 1, 1867		28,354	Fredericton
Manitoba[3]	July 15, 1870	Manitoba Act, 1870 (SC 1870, c. 3) and Imperial Order in Council, June 23, 1870	251,000	Winnipeg
British Columbia	July 20, 1871	Imperial Order in Council, May 16, 1871	366,255	Victoria
Prince Edward Island	July 1, 1873	Imperial Order in Council, June 26, 1873	2,184	Charlottetown
Saskatchewan[4]	Sept. 1, 1905	Saskatchewan Act, 1905 (SC 1905, c. 42)	251,700	Regina
Alberta[4]	Sept. 1, 1905	Alberta Act, 1905 (SC 1905, c. 3)	255,285	Edmonton
Newfoundland	Mar. 31, 1949	The British North America Act, 1949 (Br. Stat. 1949, c. 22)	156,185	St. John's
Northwest Territories[5]	July 15, 1870	Act of Imperial Parliament — Rupert's Land Act, 1868 (Br. Stat. 1868, c. 105) and Imperial Order in Council, June 23, 1870	1,304,903	
Mackenzie[6]	Jan. 1, 1920		527,490	Yellowknife
Keewatin[6]	Jan. 1, 1920	Order in Council, Mar. 16, 1918	228,160	
Franklin[6]	Jan. 1, 1920		549,253	
Yukon Territory[7]	June 13, 1898	Yukon Territory Act, 1898 (SC 1898, c. 6)	207,076	Whitehorse
Canada			3,851,809	

[1]The area of Ontario was extended by the Ontario Boundaries Extension Act, 1912 (SC 1912, c. 40).

[2]Extended by Quebec Boundaries Extension Act, 1912 (SC 1912, c. 45).

[3]Extended by the Extension of Boundaries Act of Manitoba, 1881 and the Manitoba Boundaries Extension Act, 1912 (SC 1912, c. 32).

[4]Saskatchewan and Alberta created as provinces in 1905 from the area formerly comprised in the provisional districts of Assiniboia, Athabaska, Alberta and Saskatchewan established May 17, 1882 by minute of Canadian Privy Council concurred in by Dominion Parliament and Order in Council, Oct. 2, 1895.

[5]By an Imperial Order in Council passed on June 23, 1870 pursuant to the Rupert's Land Act, 1868 (Br. Stat. 1868, c. 105), the former territories of the Hudson's Bay Company known as Rupert's Land and the North-Western Territory were transferred to Canada effective July 15, 1870. These territories were designated as the North-West Territories by the Act of SC 1869, c. 3, and as the Northwest Territories by RSC 1906, c. 62. By Imperial Order in Council of July 31, 1880 (effective Sept. 1, 1880), all British territories and possessions in North America not already included within Canada and all islands adjacent thereto (with the exception of the Colony of Newfoundland and its dependencies) were annexed to Canada and these additional territories were formally included in the North-West Territories by SC 1905, c. 27. The province of Manitoba was formed out of a portion of the territories by the Manitoba Act, 1870 (SC 1870, c. 3) and a further portion was added to Manitoba in 1881 by SC 1881, c. 14. The provinces of Alberta and Saskatchewan were formed out of portions of the territories in 1905 and in 1912 other portions were added to Manitoba, Ontario and Quebec.

[6]By SC 1876, c. 21, a separate district to be known as the District of Keewatin was established and provision was made for the local government thereof. The Act was expressed to come into force by proclamation. It provided that portions of the District might be re-annexed to the North-West Territories by proclamation; in 1886 a portion of the District of Keewatin was re-annexed and in 1905 the entire Keewatin District was re-annexed. The Act of 1876 was never proclaimed. By Order in Council of May 8, 1882 the provisional districts of Assiniboia, Saskatchewan, Alberta and Athabaska were created for the convenience of settlers and for postal purposes. By Order in Council of Oct. 2, 1895 the further provisional districts of Ungava, Franklin, Mackenzie and Yukon were created. The boundaries of these provisional districts were re-defined by Order in Council of Dec. 18, 1897. Subsequently the Yukon Territory was formed, the provinces of Alberta and Saskatchewan were created and other portions of the territories were annexed to Quebec, Ontario and Manitoba. By Order in Council dated Mar. 16, 1918 (effective Jan. 1, 1920) the remaining portions of the Northwest Territories were divided into three provisional districts known as Mackenzie, Keewatin and Franklin.

[7]The provisional district of Yukon established in 1895 was created a judicial district of the North-West Territories by proclamation issued pursuant to Sect. 51 of the North-West Territories Act (RSC 1886, c. 50) on Aug. 16, 1897 and, by the Yukon Territory Act (SC 1898, c. 6), was declared to be a separate territory.

2.2 Police personnel, actual strength, 1973 and 1974

Force	1973				1974			
	Police	Cadets	Other full-time employees	Total	Police	Cadets	Other full-time employees	Total
Royal Canadian Mounted Police	11,987	—	3,861	15,848	12,971	—	3,411	16,382
Ontario Provincial Police	3,766	24	1,196	4,986	3,860	32	1,219	5,111
Quebec Police Force	3,995	9	862	4,866	4,013	5	932	4,950
Municipal Police (excl. RCMP and OPP contracts)	25,000	530	3,549	29,079	26,156	537	3,722	30,415
Canadian National Railways Police	502	—	28	530	496	—	29	525
Canadian Pacific Railway Company Police	329	—	91	420	324	—	92	416
National Harbours Board Police	230	—	64	294	231	—	73	304
Total	45,809	563	9,651	56,023	48,051	574	9,478	58,103

2.1   Provinces and territories of Canada, dates of admission to Confederation, legislative processes by which admission was effected, present area and seat of government   **M**

Province, territory or district	Date of admission or creation	Legislative process	Present area km²	Seat of provincial or territorial government
Ontario[1]	July 1, 1867	Act of Imperial Parliament — The British North America Act, 1867 (Br. Stat. 1867, c. 3) and Imperial Order in Council, May 22, 1867	1 068 582	Toronto
Quebec[2]	July 1, 1867		1 540 680	Quebec
Nova Scotia	July 1, 1867		55 491	Halifax
New Brunswick	July 1, 1867		73 437	Fredericton
Manitoba[3]	July 15, 1870	Manitoba Act, 1870 (SC 1870, c. 3) and Imperial Order in Council, June 23, 1870	650 087	Winnipeg
British Columbia	July 20, 1871	Imperial Order in Council, May 16, 1871	948 596	Victoria
Prince Edward Island	July 1, 1873	Imperial Order in Council, June 26, 1873	5 657	Charlottetown
Saskatchewan[4]	Sept. 1, 1905	Saskatchewan Act, 1905 (SC 1905, c. 42)	651 900	Regina
Alberta[4]	Sept. 1, 1905	Alberta Act, 1905 (SC 1905, c. 3)	661 185	Edmonton
Newfoundland	Mar. 31, 1949	The British North America Act, 1949 (Br. Stat. 1949, c. 22)	404 517	St. John's
Northwest Territories[5]	July 15, 1870	Act of Imperial Parliament — Rupert's Land Act, 1868 (Br. Stat. 1868, c. 105) and Imperial Order in Council, June 23, 1870	3 379 683	
Mackenzie[6]	Jan. 1, 1920	Order in Council, Mar. 16, 1918	1 366 193	Yellowknife
Keewatin[6]	Jan. 1, 1920		590 931	
Franklin[6]	Jan. 1, 1920		1 422 559	
Yukon Territory[7]	June 13, 1898	Yukon Territory Act, 1898 (SC 1898, c. 6)	536 324	Whitehorse
Canada			9 976 139	

[1] The area of Ontario was extended by the Ontario Boundaries Extension Act, 1912 (SC 1912, c. 40).

[2] Extended by Quebec Boundaries Extension Act, 1912 (SC 1912, c. 45).

[3] Extended by the Extension of Boundaries Act of Manitoba, 1881 and the Manitoba Boundaries Extension Act, 1912 (SC 1912, c. 32).

[4] Saskatchewan and Alberta created as provinces in 1905 from the area formerly comprised in the provisional districts of Assiniboia, Athabaska, Alberta and Saskatchewan established May 17, 1882 by minute of Canadian Privy Council concurred in by Dominion Parliament and Order in Council, Oct. 2, 1895.

[5] By an Imperial Order in Council passed on June 23, 1870 pursuant to the Rupert's Land Act, 1868 (Br. Stat. 1868, c. 105), the former territories of the Hudson's Bay Company known as Rupert's Land and the North-Western Territory were transferred to Canada effective July 15, 1870. These territories were designated as the North-West Territories by the Act of SC 1869, c. 3, and as the Northwest Territories by RSC 1906, c. 62. By Imperial Order in Council of July 31, 1880 (effective Sept. 1, 1880), all British territories and possessions in North America not already included within Canada and all islands adjacent thereto (with the exception of the Colony of Newfoundland and its dependencies) were annexed to Canada and these additional territories were formally included in the North-West Territories by SC 1905, c. 27. The province of Manitoba was formed out of a portion of the territories by the Manitoba Act, 1870 (SC 1870, c. 3) and a further portion was added to Manitoba in 1881 by SC 1881, c. 14. The provinces of Alberta and Saskatchewan were formed out of portions of the territories in 1905 and in 1912 other portions were added to Manitoba, Ontario and Quebec.

[6] By SC 1876, c. 21, a separate district to be known as the District of Keewatin was established and provision was made for the local government thereof. The Act was expressed to come into force by proclamation. It provided that portions of the District might be re-annexed to the North-West Territories by proclamation; in 1886 a portion of the District of Keewatin was re-annexed and in 1905 the entire Keewatin District was re-annexed. The Act of 1876 was never proclaimed. By Order in Council of May 8, 1882 the provisional districts of Assiniboia, Saskatchewan, Alberta and Athabaska were created for the convenience of settlers and for postal purposes. By Order in Council of Oct. 2, 1895 the further provisional districts of Ungava, Franklin, Mackenzie and Yukon were created. The boundaries of these provisional districts were re-defined by Order in Council of Dec. 18, 1897. Subsequently the Yukon Territory was formed, the provinces of Alberta and Saskatchewan were created and other portions of the territories were annexed to Quebec, Ontario and Manitoba. By Order in Council dated Mar. 16, 1918 (effective Jan. 1, 1920) the remaining portions of the Northwest Territories were divided into three provisional districts known as Mackenzie, Keewatin and Franklin.

[7] The provisional district of Yukon established in 1895 was created a judicial district of the North-West Territories by proclamation issued pursuant to Sect. 51 of the North-West Territories Act (RSC 1886, c. 50) on Aug. 16, 1897 and, by the Yukon Territory Act (SC 1898, c. 6), was declared to be a separate territory.

2.3   Crime statistics, by type of offence, 1973 and 1974 (based on Uniform Crime Reporting Program)

Year and offence	Actual offences[1]	Offences cleared		Persons charged			
		By charge	Other-wise	Adults		Juveniles	
				Male	Female	Male	Female
1973							
Criminal code	1,298,551	289,776	181,703	206,388	32,716	51,324	6,981
Murder, capital and non-capital	474	346	58	333	49	23	—
Attempted murder	483	394	26	351	39	10	2
Manslaughter	66	59	1	56	8	1	—
Rape	1,593	675	348	852	2	62	1
Other sexual offences	10,401	3,689	2,049	3,222	32	334	27
Wounding	1,882	1,061	428	776	194	95	16
Assaults (not indecent)	89,695	29,637	44,081	27,799	2,450	1,315	269
Robbery	13,166	3,777	611	3,923	285	903	92
Breaking and entering	198,040	33,132	14,267	22,141	865	16,793	802
Theft, motor vehicle	71,591	13,212	5,389	9,605	326	5,801	233
Theft over $200	63,382	7,031	4,101	6,173	607	1,718	97
Theft $200 or under	414,573	58,744	42,542	32,844	13,434	14,679	3,970
Having stolen goods	13,791	12,148	1,056	7,590	790	1,731	198
Fraud	71,771	34,768	9,534	14,747	3,348	534	148
Prostitution	3,573	3,436	56	676	2,748	18	57
Gaming and betting	3,009	2,578	254	2,936	229	12	4
Offensive weapons	8,949	6,340	1,373	5,237	269	353	32
Other criminal code[1]	332,112	78,749	55,529	67,127	7,041	6,942	1,033
Federal statutes[2]	42,786	29,474	7,255	19,086	1,158	655	469
Narcotic Control Act	46,451	37,196	3,627	34,220	4,578	1,917	304
Controlled drugs under the Food and Drugs Act	6,321	4,418	836	3,941	654	195	67
Provincial statutes[1]	339,119	243,652	85,566	216,162	14,999	6,957	4,001
Municipal by-laws[1]	75,907	37,395	24,523	31,646	4,341	1,016	99
1974							
Criminal code	1,456,881	305,264	196,933	215,261	35,066	56,209	7,555
Murder, capital and non-capital	545	414	52	370	62	34	—
Attempted murder	521	396	23	357	40	22	2
Manslaughter	53	54	1	46	11	3	—
Rape	1,823	803	321	918	3	84	11
Other sexual offences	9,288	1,027	483	1,082	13	66	14
Wounding	2,114	1,109	471	862	163	98	26
Assaults (not indecent)	94,750	31,175	44,986	28,782	2,537	1,331	300
Robbery	16,955	4,532	662	4,674	302	1,063	113
Breaking and entering	233,362	37,702	15,798	25,978	923	18,351	905
Theft, motor vehicle	83,309	15,150	6,015	11,091	368	7,087	283
Theft over $200	79,745	7,701	4,522	6,548	808	2,064	152
Theft $200 or under	459,192	62,352	46,509	34,657	15,277	15,058	4,397
Having stolen goods	15,312	13,546	1,281	8,144	928	1,787	220
Fraud	75,873	36,090	10,293	14,641	3,811	672	175
Prostitution	3,249	3,168	47	630	2,382	13	40
Gaming and betting	3,264	2,956	172	2,992	178	15	1
Offensive weapons	10,812	7,164	2,047	5,950	328	397	20
Other criminal code[1]	366,714	79,925	63,250	67,539	6,932	8,064	896
Federal statutes[2]	44,394	30,861	9,480	19,171	1,526	1,159	524
Narcotic Control Act	53,030	42,497	5,109	39,544	4,332	2,268	347
Controlled drugs under the Food and Drugs Act	5,555	3,800	665	3,278	479	239	43
Provincial statutes[1]	368,716	265,468	90,187	240,509	15,856	7,339	3,726
Municipal by-laws[1]	81,306	30,840	29,138	25,585	3,295	1,255	171

[1]Except traffic.
[2]Except traffic, Narcotic Control Act and Food and Drugs Act.

2.4   Traffic enforcement statistics, by type of offence, 1974 (based on Uniform Crime Reporting Program)

Offence	Actual offences	Offences cleared		Persons charged	
		By charge	Otherwise	Male	Female
Criminal code	239,737	177,837	12,136	168,692	5,867
Criminal negligence					
Causing death	234	239	2	233	6
Causing bodily harm	105	97	2	79	1
Operating motor vehicle	716	650	13	572	17
Failing to stop or remain at scene of accident	70,635	12,350	9,165	10,938	850
Dangerous driving	6,547	6,153	211	5,728	125
Failure or refusal to provide breath sample	12,909	13,035	82	12,533	378
Driving while impaired	132,691	129,651	2,385	123,964	4,280
Driving while disqualified	15,900	15,662	276	14,645	210
Federal statutes (except parking)	..	..	..	10,395	
Provincial statutes (except parking)	..	..	..	2,269,590	
Municipal by-laws (except parking)	..	..	..	318,690	

2.4   Traffic enforcement statistics, by type of offence, 1974 (based on Uniform Crime Reporting Program) (concluded)

Offence	Actual offences	Offences cleared		Persons charged	
		By charge	Otherwise	Male	Female
Provincial statutes[1]	*113,402*	*68,212*	*13,065*	*62,323*	*5,540*
Failing to stop or remain at scene of accident	35,261	9,805	3,234	8,731	711
Dangerous driving	72,750	56,007	9,784	51,258	4,792
Driving while disqualified	5,391	2,400	47	2,334	37

[1]Provincial traffic offences almost identical to those under the criminal code.

2.5   Persons charged and persons convicted of indictable offences, with ratio per 100,000 population 16 years of age and over, by province and total, 1971 and 1972

Province or territory	Persons charged		Persons convicted				Persons convicted per 100,000 population 16 years of age and over	
	1971 No.	1972 No.	1971 No.	%	1972 No.	%	1971 No.	1972 No.
Newfoundland	1,163	946	1,127	97.0	877	92.7	355	269
Prince Edward Island	55	14	47	85.5	13	92.9	64	17
Nova Scotia	2,549	2,541	2,303	94.3	2,260	88.9	444	417
New Brunswick	2,343	1,985	2,233	95.3	1,803	90.3	538	422
Ontario	29,382	29,634	25,888	88.1	23,985	80.9	478	437
Manitoba	3,198	4,588	2,719	85.0	3,416	74.5	399	495
Saskatchewan	3,910	3,933	3,729	95.4	3,541	90.0	595	565
British Columbia	11,045	11,426	9,424	85.3	9,309	81.5	612	585
Yukon Territory and Northwest Territories	453	474	404	89.2	410	86.5	1,347	1,277
Total[1]	54,098	55,541	47,874	88.5	45,614	82.1	498	466

[1]Excludes Quebec and Alberta.

2.6   Persons charged and convicted of indictable offences, by class of offence, 1971 and 1972

Class of offence	1971			1972		
	Persons charged	Persons convicted		Persons charged	Persons convicted	
		Male	Female		Male	Female
Criminal code						
Class I. Offences against the person	7,213	5,429	344	6,526	4,693	316
Class II. Offences against property with violence	8,399	7,488	196	7,740	6,665	162
Class III. Offences against property without violence	29,432	20,231	6,470	29,483	18,719	5,900
Class IV. Malicious offences against property	1,574	1,296	84	1,711	1,310	102
Class V. Forgery and other offences relating to currency	1,328	986	244	1,273	903	236
Class VI. Other offences	3,784	2,943	242	4,356	3,288	286
Total, criminal code	51,730	38,373	7,580	51,089	35,578	7,002
Federal statutes	2,368	1,766	155	4,452	2,753	281
Total[1]	54,098	40,139	7,735	55,541	38,331	7,283

[1]Excludes Quebec and Alberta.

2.7 First court sentences given for indictable offences, by province, 1971 and 1972

Year and sentence	Nfld.	PEI	NS	NB	Ont.	Man.	Sask.	BC	YT and NWT	Canada[1]
1971										
Option of fine	446	19	901	719	9,065	605	994	2,802	83	15,634
Jail										
Under one year	214	6	519	534	5,315	624	1,094	3,011	147	11,464
One year and over	56	1	33	123	944	219	203	579	31	2,189
Reformatory and training school	—	—	8	7	1,430	—	—	1	—	1,446
Penitentiary										
Under two years	—	—	2	10	44	—	9	21	—	86
Two years and under five	30	8	199	85	627	139	89	296	5	1,478
Five years and under ten	1	1	10	10	159	23	13	81	2	300
Ten years and under fourteen	—	—	7	—	31	8	1	29	—	76
Fourteen years and over	—	—	—	—	13	—	—	9	—	22
Life	2	—	2	—	8	3	1	12	—	28
Preventive	—	—	—	—	1	—	—	1	—	2
Death	—	—	—	—	—	—	—	—	—	—
Suspended sentence without probation	10	4	62	217	1,747	640	445	233	12	3,370
Suspended sentence with probation	368	8	560	528	6,504	458	880	2,349	124	11,779
Total	1,127	47	2,303	2,233	25,888	2,719	3,729	9,424	404	47,874
1972										
Option of fine	324	—	877	573	8,573	837	817	3,067	94	15,162
Jail										
Under one year	176	5	501	451	5,147	694	981	2,794	138	10,887
One year and over	35	—	34	101	949	228	193	546	43	2,129
Reformatory and training school	—	—	2	1	1,038	—	—	—	—	1,041
Penitentiary										
Under two years	2	—	2	1	8	2	—	4	—	19
Two years and under five	21	1	149	91	526	159	80	253	8	1,288
Five years and under ten	2	—	12	13	150	27	16	93	2	315
Ten years and under fourteen	—	—	7	2	30	7	2	35	—	83
Fourteen years and over	—	—	—	3	2	6	—	10	—	21
Life	2	—	7	—	29	3	6	21	—	68
Preventive	—	—	—	—	1	—	—	3	—	4
Death	—	—	—	—	—	—	—	1	—	1
Suspended sentence without probation	19	—	40	249	1,428	793	519	387	14	3,449
Suspended sentence with probation	296	7	629	318	6,104	660	927	2,095	111	11,147
Total	877	13	2,260	1,803	23,985	3,416	3,541	9,309	410	45,614

¹Excludes Quebec and Alberta.

2.8 Method of trial of persons charged with indictable offences, showing disposition of cases, by province and total, 1972

Year and method of trial	Nfld.	PEI	NS	NB	Ont.	Man.	Sask.	BC	YT and NWT	Canada[1]
By judge and jury										
Convicted	8	—	40	14	477	50	57	154	20	820
Acquitted	4	—	12	1	219	10	15	76	1	338
Detained because of insanity	—	—	2	—	12	—	2	5	—	21
Disagreement of jury	—	—	—	—	4	—	—	—	—	4
Stay of proceedings	—	—	—	2	6	15	4	27	3	57
No bill	1	—	—	—	32	—	—	—	—	33
Conditional discharge	—	—	—	—	4	—	—	—	—	4
Absolute discharge	—	—	—	—	—	—	—	2	—	2
By a judge without jury										
Convicted	2	8	147	38	872	120	273	209	9	1,678
Acquitted	—	1	56	—	296	24	62	61	3	503
Detained because of insanity	—	—	1	—	2	—	—	1	—	4
Disagreement of jury	—	—	—	—	—	—	—	—	—	—
Stay of proceedings	—	—	—	1	1	16	40	21	1	80
No bill	—	—	—	—	1	—	—	—	—	1
Conditional discharge	—	—	2	—	33	2	—	1	—	38
Absolute discharge	—	—	—	1	7	1	1	2	—	12

2.8   Method of trial of persons charged with indictable offences, showing disposition of cases, by province and total, 1972 (concluded)

Year and method of trial	Nfld.	PEI	NS	NB	Ont.	Man.	Sask.	BC	YT and NWT	Canada¹
By a magistrate with consent										
Convicted	521	5	1,020	830	11,824	1,772	1,540	4,650	223	22,385
Acquitted	13	—	82	59	1,500	66	55	465	6	2,246
Detained because of insanity	—	—	—	3	2	—	1	6	—	12
Disagreement of jury	—	—	—	—	1	—	—	—	—	1
Stay of proceedings	—	—	—	2	24	413	15	559	27	1,040
No bill	—	—	—	—	5	—	—	1	—	6
Conditional discharge	13	—	10	5	464	68	23	56	2	641
Absolute discharge	—	—	9	5	546	32	9	22	—	623
By a magistrate, absolute jurisdiction										
Convicted	346	—	1,053	921	10,812	1,474	1,671	4,296	158	20,731
Acquitted	13	—	74	58	1,582	76	101	386	4	2,294
Detained because of insanity	—	—	—	—	—	1	—	—	—	1
Disagreement of jury	—	—	—	—	—	—	—	—	—	
Stay of proceedings	—	—	—	1	2	196	5	248	13	465
No bill	—	—	—	—	—	—	—	—	—	
Conditional discharge	21	—	14	25	598	138	38	126	4	964
Absolute discharge	4	—	19	19	308	114	21	52	—	537
Total, persons charged	946	14	2,541	1,985	29,634	4,588	3,933	11,426	474	55,541
Total, persons convicted	877	13	2,260	1,803	23,985	3,416	3,541	9,309	410	45,614

¹Excludes Quebec and Alberta.

2.9   Convictions for summary conviction offences¹, by type, 1971 and 1972

Type of offence	1971	1972
CRIMINAL CODE	*104,458*	*104,825*
Attempts, conspiracies, accessories, counselling	169	134
Attempt to commit suicide	84	21
Bawdy house	132	126
Causing disturbance by being drunk	2,670	1,724
Common assault	8,176	7,965
Communicating venereal disease	25	28
Contempt of court	47	32
Corrupting morals	215	253
Cruelty to animals	87	48
Damage not exceeding $50 and other interference with property	3,291	3,113
Disorderly conduct	9,860	8,705
Duty of persons to provide necessaries	136	74
Duty to safeguard dangerous places	14	2
Fraudulently obtaining food or lodging	974	715
Fraudulently obtaining transportation	122	154
Gaming, betting, lotteries	467	556
Intimidation	111	151
Killing or injuring bird or animal other than cattle	42	46
Motor vehicle		
Criminal negligence in operation	412	252
Dangerous driving	1,991	2,035
Dangerous operation of vessel, etc.	101	135
Driving while impaired	27,762	25,392
Driving while disqualified	5,039	5,640
Driving with more than 80 mg in blood	24,734	27,502
Failing to stop at scene of accident	3,119	3,346
Failure or refusal to provide breath sample	4,089	5,801
Motor vehicle equipped with smoke screen	42	70
Taking motor vehicle without consent	1,580	1,506
Offensive weapons	1,119	1,202
Personating peace officer	31	101
Recognizance, breach of	2,964	2,938
Vagrancy	3,281	883
Other criminal code	4,572	4,175
FEDERAL STATUTES	*30,712*	*28,849*
Customs	102	63
Excise	783	421
Fisheries	793	952
Food and drugs	1,906	2,932
Harbour board and merchant seamen's	236	193
Immigration	440	352
Income tax	7,366	8,957
Indian		
Intoxication	111	201
Other	447	236
Juvenile delinqents		
Adults who contribute to delinquency	579	474
Inducing child to leave home, etc.	16	20
Sexual immorality	1,274	142

2.9   Convictions for summary conviction offences[1], by type, 1971 and 1972 (concluded)

Type of offence	1971	1972
FEDERAL STATUTES (concluded)		
Lord's day	336	343
National defence	186	255
Railway	1,076	562
Unemployment insurance	2,607	1,805
Weights and measures	95	248
Other federal statutes	12,359	10,693
PROVINCIAL STATUTES	*1,186,021*	*1,281,582*
Children of unmarried parents	1,732	1,104
Deserted wives and children's maintenance	9,626	10,762
Game and fisheries	6,715	7,026
Highway traffic		
Driving without due care and attention	39,537	49,027
Other traffic	965,337	1,046,581
Liquor control	139,676	125,862
Master and servant	466	435
Medical, dentistry and pharmacy	38	62
Mental diseases	137	120
Prairie and forest fire prevention	67	48
Protection of children	4,241	4,989
Public health	526	523
School laws	295	209
Other provincial statutes	17,628	34,834
MUNICIPAL BY-LAWS	*117,947*	*102,206*
Intoxication	2,403	522
Traffic	86,992	75,088
Other	28,552	26,596
Total convictions	1,439,138	1,517,462

[1]Excludes Quebec, Alberta and Yukon Territory.

2.10   Juvenile delinquents, by group of offence, and ratio per 100,000 juvenile population, 1971-73[1]

Group of offence		1971	1972	1973
Delinquencies against the person	No.	1,723	1,726	1,963
	Ratio	38	38	43
Delinquencies against property with violence	No.	8,790	9,064	9,335
	Ratio	192	199	205
Delinquencies against property without violence	No.	15,093	15,116	15,298
	Ratio	330	331	335
Wilful and forbidden acts in respect of certain property	No.	2,112	2,640	2,668
	Ratio	46	58	58
Forgery and delinquencies relating to currency	No.	136	174	156
	Ratio	3	4	3
Other delinquencies	No.	10,944	13,463	14,731
	Ratio	239	295	323
Total	No.	38,798	42,183	44,151
	Ratio	848	924	968

[1]Canada total juvenile population figure in 1971 was 4,576,700, 4,564,000 in 1972, and 4,562,000 in 1973.

2.11   Juvenile delinquents classified by type of delinquency and percentage distribution, 1971-73

Delinquency		1971	1972	1973
Manslaughter and murder and causing death by criminal negligence	No.	24	21	25
	%	0.06	0.05	0.06
Murder, attempt	No.	11	8	5
	%	0.03	0.02	0.01
Common assault	No.	771	747	862
	%	1.99	1.77	1.95
Other delinquencies against the person	No.	315	313	404
	%	0.81	0.74	0.92
Breaking and entering a place	No.	8,407	8,694	8,905
	%	21.67	20.61	20.17
Robbery and extortion	No.	383	370	430
	%	0.99	0.88	0.97

2.11   Juvenile delinquents classified by type of delinquency and percentage distribution, 1971-73 (concluded)

Delinquency		1971	1972	1973
Theft and having in possession[1]	No.	13,159	13,033	12,984
	%	33.92	30.90	29.41
False pretences and fraud and corruption	No.	219	213	302
	%	0.57	0.51	0.68
Arson and other fires[2]	No.	194	222	244
	%	0.50	0.53	0.55
Other interference with property	No.	2,295	4,053	4,182
	%	5.92	9.61	9.47
Incorrigibility and vagrancy	No.	1,431	657	444
	%	3.69	1.56	1.01
Immorality	No.	409	390	320
	%	1.06	0.92	0.72
Theft, auto	No.	1,126	1,246	1,437
	%	2.90	2.95	3.26
Various other delinquencies	No.	10,054	12,216	13,607
	%	25.89	28.95	30.82
Total	No.	38,798	42,183	44,151
	%	100.00	100.00	100.00

[1]Includes having in possession, theft, theft from mail, theft of bicycle.
[2]Includes false alarm of fire.

2.12   Disposition of delinquents, by type of sentence and percentage distribution, 1971-73

Type of sentence		1971	1972	1973
Reprimanded	No.	524	791	1,076
	%	1.35	1.88	2.44
Probation[1]	No.	12,422	12,053	11,990
	%	32.02	28.57	27.16
Fined or made restitution	No.	4,318	5,220	6,237
	%	11.13	12.37	14.13
Detained indefinitely	No.	207	129	77
	%	0.53	0.31	0.17
Sent to training school	No.	1,641	1,190	1,108
	%	4.23	2.82	2.51
Final disposition suspended	No.	5,897	7,179	7,763
	%	15.20	17.02	17.58
Mental hospital	No.	14	35	20
	%	0.04	0.08	0.04
Other	No.	13,775	15,586	15,880
	%	35.50	36.95	35.97
Total dispositions	No.	38,798	42,183	44,151
	%	100.00	100.00	100.00

[1]Includes probation of court and probation of parents.

2.13   Population in penitentiaries, in provincial adult institutions and in training schools, years ended Dec. 31, 1972-74

Type of institution	In custody at beginning of year	Movement in	Movement out	In custody at end of year	% change
1972					
Penitentiaries	7,483	12,115	11,345	8,253	+10.3
Provincial adult institutions	10,682	124,974	125,650	10,006	-6.3
Training schools	1,959	11,923	12,005	1,877	-4.2
For boys	1,308	7,744	7,783	1,269	-3.0
For girls	651	4,179	4,222	608	-6.6
1973					
Penitentiaries	8,253	12,778	11,920	9,111	+10.4
Provincial adult institutions	10,006	163,035	163,239	9,802	-2.0
Training schools[1]	1,877	12,602	12,426	2,053	+9.4
For boys	1,184	7,607	7,532	1,259	+6.3
For girls	608	4,146	4,097	657	+8.1
1974					
Penitentiaries	9,111	13,792	14,404	8,499	-6.7
Provincial adult institutions	9,728	156,182	155,923	9,987	+2.7
Training schools[1]	2,053	13,320	13,452	1,921	-6.4
For boys	1,259	7,462	7,579	1,142	-9.3
For girls	657	4,659	4,699	617	-6.1

[1]Totals include two co-educational schools not included in the figures broken down by sex.

2.14   Penitentiary admissions, by offence, 1972-74

Offence	1972		1973		1974	
	No.	% of total	No.	% of total	No.	% of total
Homicide	260	6.1	248	5.7	235	6.5
Rape	91	2.2	118	2.7	152	4.2
Other sexual offences	108	2.6	82	1.9	94	2.6
Wounding	51	1.2	68	1.6	53	1.5
Assault	97	2.3	120	2.8	117	3.3
Robbery	699	16.5	707	16.4	646	17.9
Breaking and entering	860	20.3	840	19.4	700	19.4
Prison breach	161	3.8	44	1.0	27	0.8
Theft	361	8.5	349	8.1	303	8.4
Having stolen goods	201	4.7	204	4.7	117	3.3
Fraud	307	7.3	263	6.1	233	6.5
Prostitution and procuring	—	—	4	0.1	1	- -
Offensive weapons	66	1.6	51	1.2	57	1.6
Habitual criminal	10	0.2	7	0.2	—	—
Dangerous sexual offender	3	0.1	1	- -	1	- -
Motor vehicle	14	0.3	22	0.5	16	0.4
Other criminal code	179	4.2	200	4.6	124	3.4
Narcotic Control Act	325	7.7	484	11.2	393	10.9
Parole violators	412	9.7	465	10.8	327	9.1
Other federal statutes	27	0.6	42	1.0	6	0.2
Total	4,232	99.9	4,319	100.0	3,602	100.0

Sources

2.1 Legal Research and Planning Section, Legal Branch, Department of Justice.
2.2 - 2.14 Judicial Division, Institutional and Public Finance Statistics Branch, Statistics Canada.

Government

Chapter 3

Government

Organization of the federal government

In most countries, the legal framework within which political processes take place is provided through a constitution. The written constitution of Canada is embodied in the British North America Acts. The first of these acts, passed by the British Parliament in 1867, not only established the institutions through which legislative, executive and judicial powers are exercised in Canada but also established a federal form of government. A central government — the federal government — has legislative jurisdiction primarily over matters of national concern and over those matters not otherwise assigned to the provinces. The 10 provincial governments are assigned specific areas of legislative jurisdiction, including municipal institutions.

In Canada there is a fusion of the executive and legislative powers. Formal executive power is vested in the Queen, whose authority is delegated to the Governor General, her representative. Legislative power is vested in the Parliament of Canada which consists of the Queen, an appointed upper house called the Senate and a lower house called the House of Commons, elected by universal adult suffrage. The independence of the judiciary is safeguarded through the constitutional provision that superior court judges are appointed by the Governor in Council (i.e. by the Governor General on advice of the Cabinet) and that they hold office during good behaviour and cannot be removed unless both Houses of Parliament, the Cabinet and the Governor General agree.

In the Canadian system, where the executive is part of Parliament, democratic principles could not be adhered to without the constitutional convention that the government is responsible to the House of Commons. When the government loses the confidence of the House of Commons, it must resign or the Prime Minister must request the Governor General to dissolve Parliament and call a general election. Although there are conventions that help in deciding when the government has lost the confidence of the House, all doubt is removed when the government is defeated on a motion on which it had explicitly staked its life or when a motion of non-confidence in the government is passed. If the government resigns, the Governor General can call on the Leader of the Opposition (who is usually the leader of the political party that has the second largest number of seats in the House of Commons) to form a new government. If a government that has lost the confidence of the House of Commons and is granted a dissolution is defeated in the ensuing general election and if no clear majority is elected, the government has two choices — it can remain in office and seek the confidence of the House of Commons when it meets or it can resign at once. If it resigns, the Governor General will normally ask the leader of another party, usually the one that has won the most seats, to form a new government. The primary responsibility of the Governor General in either circumstance is to provide the nation with a government capable of carrying on with the support of the House of Commons.

The Prime Minister and his Cabinet, who with one or two exceptions are members of the House of Commons, are, formally speaking, the Queen's advisers. In fact there are virtually no significant actions that can be taken by the Queen or her representative in Canada, the Governor General, without the advice of the Cabinet. The Prime Minister and his Cabinet determine executive policies and are responsible for them to the House of Commons. The Queen and the Governor General have the traditional rights to be consulted, to encourage and to warn the government.

The demands of Canadian citizens are directed primarily to members of Parliament, directly to Cabinet Ministers or indirectly to Cabinet Ministers through the public service. These demands may originate from individuals, political parties or pressure groups; members of Parliament, Cabinet Ministers and public servants may take the initiative in suggesting the adoption of policies and programs in the public interest. Although the roles performed by Parliament, the public service and the Cabinet cannot be defined with absolute precision, the following description deals with the most obvious and primary roles of each in the Canadian political system.

The determination of public policy rests with the Cabinet but begins generally with the formulation of policy by the individual ministers. Working in cooperation with public servants, a minister formulates policy proposals for consideration by his colleagues in the Cabinet. The Cabinet studies the policies submitted and chooses those it wishes to implement. The Cabinet may itself formulate policies, but it may also decide to select a policy from among the alternatives submitted. A Cabinet committee system that operates on a functional basis and, more especially, the Cabinet Committee on Priorities and Planning enhances the capacity of Cabinet in its primary role of policy determination and priority setting.

In conformity with the principle of the rule of law, all executive acts must be authorized by law, and laws are enacted by Parliament. Executive acts may be carried out under a statute which specifies how a policy is to be implemented, or under a statute which authorizes the Governor in Council to undertake specific acts. Much of the activity of the public service is authorized through the yearly enactment of Appropriation Acts approving the expenditure of public funds for specific purposes. Apart from its concern with the appropriation of funds, Parliament is concerned with the discussion and authorization of policy submitted for its approval by the government. The approval of policies is accomplished mainly through the enactment of legislation. To enable the House of Commons to perform this role more efficiently numerous changes in the rules of procedure were adopted in January 1969, and are now included in the Standing Orders of the House of Commons.

The most significant feature of these processes is that Cabinet Ministers, who constitute the government, have seats in Parliament and thus share in the exercise of the legislative power. In fact, the majority of legislation enacted by Parliament is submitted by the government; the British North America Act provides that all financial measures must originate in the House of Commons.

The role of the judiciary is to apply the laws enacted by Parliament. In the Canadian government, Parliament is supreme. This means, among other things, that the judiciary must apply the law as Parliament has enacted it and cannot declare laws to be unconstitutional if they are within the legislative jurisdiction of Parliament or of the legislature that enacted them.

The administration of legislation and of the government's policies is carried out through a public service comprising employees organized as of 1976 in 25 departments of government and a large number of special boards, commissions and Crown corporations or other agencies. Legislation and tradition have combined to develop a non-partisan public service, whose employees' tenure is unaffected by changes in government. The only direct contact between public servants and Parliament occurs when they are called to appear as witnesses before parliamentary committees; public servants do not, by convention, express opinions on public policy but usually appear as experts and to explain existing policy. Public servants who head agencies such as the Public Service Commission, the Office of the Auditor General, the Office of the Commissioner of Official Languages, the Library of Parliament or the Office of the Chief Electoral Officer are responsible directly to Parliament. They are not subject to direction by the government on matters of policy and may appear before parliamentary committees to explain the policies of their agencies.

The growth in number, variety and complexity of the demands placed on the government requires it not only to adjust its policies but to make significant changes in the organization of the public service so that required policies can be implemented. Major reorganization of the public service was authorized by the passage of a series of Government Organization Acts in 1966, 1969 and 1970.

The Executive   3.1.1

The Crown. The British North America (BNA) Act of 1867 (Sect. 9) provides that "the Executive Government and authority of and over Canada is ... vested in the Queen". The functions of the Crown (that is, the formal executive represented by the Queen), which are substantially the same as those of the Crown in relation to the British government, are discharged in Canada by the Governor General.

The Sovereign. Since Confederation Canada has had six sovereigns: Victoria, Edward VII, George V, Edward VIII, George VI and Elizabeth II. The present sovereign is not only Queen of Canada but of other countries in the Commonwealth. Her Majesty's title for Canada was approved by Parliament and established by a Royal proclamation on May 28, 1953: Elizabeth the Second, by the Grace of God of the United Kingdom, Canada and Her other Realms and Territories Queen, Head of the Commonwealth, Defender of the Faith.

From time to time the Queen personally discharges the functions of the Crown in respect of Canada, such as the appointment of the Governor General, which Her Majesty does on the recommendation of the Prime Minister of Canada. During a Royal visit, the Queen may participate in ceremonies that are normally carried out in her name by the Governor General, such as the opening and dissolution of Parliament, the assent to bills passed by the House of Commons and the Senate, and the granting of a general amnesty.

The Governor General is the representative of the Crown in Canada. The Right Honourable Jules Léger, the 21st Governor General since Confederation, was appointed by Queen Elizabeth on October 5, 1973 and took office on January 14, 1974. Constitutionally, the Queen of Canada is the Canadian head of state but the Governor General fulfils her role on her behalf. The letters patent revised and re-issued under the Great Seal of Canada on October 1, 1947 authorized the Governor General "to exercise on the advice of his Canadian ministers, all Her Majesty's powers and authorities in respect of Canada".

Following are the Governors General of Canada since Confederation, with dates of appointment:

The Viscount Monck of Ballytrammon, June 1, 1867
The Baron Lisgar of Lisgar and Bailieborough, December 29, 1868
The Earl of Dufferin, May 22, 1872
The Marquis of Lorne, October 5, 1878
The Marquis of Lansdowne, August 18, 1883
The Baron Stanley of Preston, May 1, 1888
The Earl of Aberdeen, May 22, 1893
The Earl of Minto, July 30, 1898
The Earl Grey, September 26, 1904
Field Marshal HRH The Duke of Connaught, March 21, 1911
The Duke of Devonshire, August 19, 1916
General The Baron Byng of Vimy, August 2, 1921
The Viscount Willingdon of Ratton, August 5, 1926
The Earl of Bessborough, February 9, 1931
The Baron Tweedsmuir of Elsfield, August 10, 1935
Major General The Earl of Athlone, April 3, 1940
Field Marshal The Viscount Alexander of Tunis, March 21, 1946
The Right Honourable Vincent Massey, January 24, 1952
General The Right Honourable Georges P. Vanier, August 1, 1959
The Right Honourable Roland Michener, March 29, 1967
The Right Honourable Jules Léger, October 5, 1973.

One of the most important responsibilities of the Governor General is to ensure that the country always has a government. If the office of the Prime Minister becomes vacant because of death, resignation or defeat of the government in the House of Commons, the Governor General must see that the office of the Prime Minister is filled and that a new government is formed.

As the representative of the Queen, the Governor General summons, prorogues and dissolves Parliament on the advice of the Prime Minister. He signs Orders in Council, commissions and many other state documents, and gives his assent to bills that have been passed in both Houses of Parliament and which thereby become acts of Parliament with the force of law (unless Parliament prescribes specifically otherwise). Like the Queen, in virtually all cases constitutional convention binds him to carry out these duties in accordance with the advice of his responsible ministers. Should he not wish to accept their advice, and should they maintain that advice, his only alternative is to replace the existing government with a new government. This alternative could be exercised only if, at the same time, the principle of responsible government could be upheld. This means that the Governor General's discretion in choosing another government is strictly limited to a situation in which a person other than the existing Prime Minister could command the confidence of the House of Commons.

Canadian honours system. An exclusively Canadian honours system was introduced in 1967 with the establishment of the Order of Canada. The honours system was enlarged in 1972 with the addition of the Order of Military Merit and three decorations to be awarded in recognition of acts of bravery. A complete description of these awards and a list of the recipients during 1975 and 1976 are given in Appendix 4.

The Privy Council. The BNA Act of 1867 (Sect. 11) provides for "a council to aid and advise in the Government of Canada, to be styled the Queen's Privy Council for Canada...". The Council that in fact advises the Queen's representative, the Governor General, is the Committee of the Privy Council whose membership is identical to that of Cabinet.

Membership in the Privy Council is for life and includes Cabinet Ministers of the government of the day, former Cabinet Ministers, various members of the Royal Family, past and present Commonwealth Prime Ministers, Premiers of provinces, former Speakers of the Senate and the House of Commons of Canada and a few other distinguished persons. It is a condition of office that all ministers must first be sworn of the Privy Council. A member of the Privy Council of Canada is styled "Honourable" and may use the initials PC after his name. A member of the Privy Council of Britain is styled "Right Honourable". The Governor General, the Chief Justice of Canada and the Prime Minister of Canada automatically assume the title "Right Honourable" when they take office.

The Privy Council as a whole has met on only a few ceremonial occasions; its constitutional responsibilities to advise the Crown on matters respecting the Government of Canada are discharged exclusively by the Committee of the Privy Council, which is composed of those members of the Privy Council currently holding ministerial office. The legal instruments through which executive authority is exercised are called Orders in Council. The Committee of the Privy Council makes a submission to the Governor General for his approval which he is obliged to give in almost all circumstances; with this approval, the submission becomes an Order in Council. Meetings of the Committee of the Privy Council or a sub-committee of this committee are held without formal ceremony.

The office of the President of the Privy Council was formerly occupied, more often than not, by the Prime Minister but from time to time, especially in recent years, it has been occupied by another minister. On July 5, 1968, the Prime Minister explained that the incumbent of the office of President of the Privy Council would also be the Government Leader in the House of Commons, with the broad responsibility of directing House business, including supervision of the government's replies to questions in the House and of parliamentary returns in general, and a special responsibility of ensuring that Parliament, through its operations and organization of business, can effectively discharge its vital role in the Canadian political process under the increasing pressure of modern government.

The following, with the dates when they were sworn in, were members of the Queen's Privy Council for Canada in January 1977:

Hon. William Earl Rowe, August 30, 1935
Hon. Joseph Thorarinn Thorson, June 11, 1941
Hon. Lionel Chevrier, April 18, 1945
Hon. Paul Joseph James Martin, April 18, 1945
Hon. Douglas Charles Abbott, April 18, 1945
Hon. Milton Fowler Gregg, September 2, 1947
Hon. Stuart Sinclair Garson, November 15, 1948
Hon. Hugues Lapointe, August 25, 1949
Hon. Gabriel-Édouard Rinfret, August 25, 1949
Hon. Walter Edward Harris, January 18, 1950
Hon. James Sinclair, October 15, 1952
Hon. William Ross Macdonald, May 12, 1953
Hon. John Whitney Pickersgill, June 12, 1953
Hon. Jean Lesage, September 17, 1953
Hon. George Carlyle Marler, July 1, 1954
Hon. Paul Theodore Hellyer, April 26, 1957
Rt. Hon. John George Diefenbaker, June 21, 1957
Hon. Howard Charles Green, June 21, 1957
Hon. Donald Methuen Fleming, June 21, 1957
Hon. George Hees, June 21, 1957
Hon. Léon Balcer, June 21, 1957
Hon. George Randolph Pearkes, June 21, 1957
Hon. Gordon Churchill, June 21, 1957
Hon. Edmund Davie Fulton, June 21, 1957
Hon. Douglas Scott Harkness, June 21, 1957
Hon. Ellen Louks Fairclough, June 21, 1957
Hon. John Angus MacLean, June 21, 1957
Hon. Michael Starr, June 21, 1957
Hon. William McLean Hamilton, June 21, 1957
Hon. William Joseph Browne, June 21, 1957
Hon. Jay Waldo Monteith, August 22, 1957
Hon. Francis Alvin George Hamilton, August 22, 1957
HRH The Prince Philip, Duke of Edinburgh, October 14, 1957
Hon. Henri Courtemanche, May 12, 1958
Hon. David James Walker, August 20, 1959
Hon. Joseph-Pierre-Albert Sévigny, August 20, 1959
Hon. Hugh John Flemming, October 11, 1960
Hon. Noël Dorion, October 11, 1960
Hon. Walter Dinsdale, October 11, 1960

Hon. Jacques Flynn, December 28, 1961
Hon. Paul Martineau, August 9, 1962
Hon. Richard Albert Bell, August 9, 1962
Rt. Hon. Roland Michener, October 15, 1962
Hon. Marcel-Joseph-Aimé Lambert, February 12, 1963
Hon. Théogène Ricard, March 18, 1963
Hon. Frank Charles McGee, March 18, 1963
Hon. Martial Asselin, March 18, 1963
Hon. Walter Lockhart Gordon, April 22, 1963
Hon. Mitchell William Sharp, April 22, 1963
Hon. Azellus Denis, April 22, 1963
Hon. George James McIlraith, April 22, 1963
Hon. William Moore Benidickson, April 22, 1963
Hon. Maurice Lamontagne, April 22, 1963
Hon. Lucien Cardin, April 22, 1963
Hon. Allan Joseph MacEachen, April 22, 1963
Hon. Jean-Paul Deschatelets, April 22, 1963
Hon. Hédard Robichaud, April 22, 1963
Hon. John Watson MacNaught, April 22, 1963
Hon. Roger Teillet, April 22, 1963
Hon. Judy V. LaMarsh, April 22, 1963
Hon. Charles Mills Drury, April 22, 1963
Hon. John Robert Nicholson, April 22, 1963
Hon. Harry Hays, April 22, 1963
Hon. John Joseph Connolly, February 3, 1964
Hon. Maurice Sauvé, February 3, 1964
Hon. Yvon Dupuis, February 3, 1964
Hon. George Stanley White, June 25, 1964
Hon. Edgar John Benson, June 29, 1964
Hon. Léo Alphonse Joseph Cadieux, February 15, 1965
Hon. Lawrence T. Pennell, July 7, 1965
Hon. Jean-Luc Pepin, July 7, 1965
Hon. Alan Aylesworth Macnaughton, October 25, 1965
Hon. Jean Marchand, December 18, 1965
Hon. John James Greene, December 18, 1965
Hon. Joseph Julien Jean-Pierre Côté, December 18, 1965
Hon. John Napier Turner, December 18, 1965
Hon. Maurice Bourget, February 22, 1966
Rt. Hon. Pierre Elliott Trudeau, April 4, 1967
Hon. Joseph-Jacques-Jean Chrétien, April 4, 1967
Hon. Pauline Vanier, April 11, 1967

Hon. John Parmenter Robarts, July 5, 1967
Hon. Louis-J. Robichaud, July 5, 1967
Hon. Dufferin Roblin, July 5, 1967
Hon. William Andrew Cecil Bennett, July 5, 1967
Hon. Alexander B. Campbell, July 5, 1967
Hon. Ernest Charles Manning, July 5, 1967
Hon. Joseph Robert Smallwood, July 5, 1967
Hon. Robert L. Stanfield, July 7, 1967
Rt. Hon. John Robert Cartwright, September 4, 1967
Hon. Charles Ronald McKay Granger, September 25, 1967
Hon. Bryce Stuart Mackasey, February 9, 1968
Hon. Donald Stovel Macdonald, April 20, 1968
Hon. John Carr Munro, April 20, 1968
Hon. Gérard Pelletier, April 20, 1968
Hon. Jack Davis, April 26, 1968
Hon. Horace Andrew Olson, July 6, 1968
Hon. Jean-Eudes Dubé, July 6, 1968
Hon. Stanley Ronald Basford, July 6, 1968
Hon. Donald Campbell Jamieson, July 6, 1968
Hon. Eric William Kierans, July 6, 1968
Hon. Robert Knight Andras, July 6, 1968
Hon. James Armstrong Richardson, July 6, 1968
Hon. Otto Emil Lang, July 6, 1968
Hon. Sydney John Smith, October 10, 1968
Hon. Herbert Eser Gray, October 20, 1969
Hon. Robert Douglas George Stanbury, October 20, 1969
Rt. Hon. Joseph Honoré Gérald Fauteux, March 23, 1970
Hon. Jean-Pierre Goyer, December 22, 1970
Hon. Alastair William Gillespie, August 11, 1971

Hon. Martin Patrick O'Connell, August 11, 1971
Hon. Patrick Morgan Mahoney, January 21, 1972
Hon. Stanley Haidasz, November 27, 1972
Hon. Eugene F. Whelan, November 27, 1972
Hon. Warren Allmand, November 27, 1972
Hon. J. Hugh Faulkner, November 27, 1972
Hon. André Ouellet, November 27, 1972
Hon. Daniel J. MacDonald, November 27, 1972
Hon. Marc Lalonde, November 27, 1972
Hon. Jeanne Sauvé, November 27, 1972
Rt. Hon. Bora Laskin, January 7, 1974
Hon. Lucien Lamoureux, August 8, 1974
Hon. Raymond Joseph Perrault, August 8, 1974
Hon. Barnett Jerome Danson, August 8, 1974
Hon. J. Judd Buchanan, August 8, 1974
Hon. Roméo LeBlanc, August 8, 1974
Hon. Muriel McQueen Fergusson, November 7, 1974
Hon. Pierre Juneau, August 29, 1975
Hon. Marcel Lessard, September 26, 1975
Hon. Jack Sydney George Cullen, September 26, 1975
Hon. Leonard Stephen Marchand, September 15, 1976
Hon. John Roberts, September 15, 1976
Hon. Monique Bégin, September 15, 1976
Hon. Jean-Jacques Blais, September 15, 1976
Hon. Francis Fox, September 15, 1976
Hon. Anthony Chisholm Abbott, September 15, 1976
Hon. Iona Campagnolo, September 15, 1976
Hon. Joseph-Philippe Guay, November 3, 1976.

The Prime Minister is the leader of the political party requested by the Governor General to form the government, which almost always means that he is the leader of the party with the strongest representation in the House of Commons. His position is one of exceptional authority stemming in part from the success of the party at an election. The Prime Minister chooses his Cabinet. When a member of Cabinet resigns, the remainder of the Cabinet is undisturbed; when the Prime Minister vacates his office, this act normally carries with it the resignation of all those in the Cabinet.

Part of the authority of the Prime Minister lies in his prerogative to recommend the dissolution of Parliament. This prerogative, which in most circumstances permits him to precipitate an election, is a source of considerable power both in his dealings with his colleagues and with the opposition parties in the House of Commons. The Prime Minister is also responsible for the organization of the Cabinet and its committees; for the organization and functions of his own office, as well as the Privy Council and Federal-Provincial Relations offices; and for the allocation of responsibilities between ministers.

Another source of the Prime Minister's authority derives from the appointments which he recommends including Privy Councillors, Cabinet Ministers, Lieutenant Governors of the provinces, provincial administrators,

Speakers of the Senate, Chief Justices of all courts, Senators and certain senior executives of the public service. The Prime Minister also recommends the appointment of a new Governor General to the Sovereign, although this normally follows consultation with his Cabinet.

Following are the Prime Ministers since Confederation, with dates of administrations:

Rt. Hon. Sir John Alexander Macdonald, July 1, 1867 — November 5, 1873
Hon. Alexander Mackenzie, November 7, 1873 — October 16, 1878
Rt. Hon. Sir John Alexander Macdonald, October 17, 1878 — June 6, 1891
Hon. Sir John Joseph Caldwell Abbott, June 16, 1891 — November 24, 1892
Rt. Hon. Sir John Sparrow David Thompson, December 5, 1892 — December 12, 1894
Hon. Sir Mackenzie Bowell, December 21, 1894 — April 27, 1896
Rt. Hon. Sir Charles Tupper, May 1, 1896 — July 8, 1896
Rt. Hon. Sir Wilfrid Laurier, July 11, 1896 — October 6, 1911
Rt. Hon. Sir Robert Laird Borden, October 10, 1911 — October 12, 1917 (Conservative Administration)
Rt. Hon. Sir Robert Laird Borden, October 12, 1917 — July 10, 1920 (Unionist Administration)
Rt. Hon. Arthur Meighen, July 10, 1920 — December 29, 1921 (Unionist — National Liberal and Conservative Party)
Rt. Hon. William Lyon Mackenzie King, December 29, 1921 — June 28, 1926
Rt. Hon. Arthur Meighen, June 29, 1926 — September 25, 1926
Rt. Hon. William Lyon Mackenzie King, September 25, 1926 — August 6, 1930
Rt. Hon. Richard Bedford Bennett, August 7, 1930 — October 23, 1935
Rt. Hon. William Lyon Mackenzie King, October 23, 1935 — November 15, 1948
Rt. Hon. Louis Stephen St-Laurent, November 15, 1948 — June 21, 1957
Rt. Hon. John George Diefenbaker, June 21, 1957 — April 22, 1963
Rt. Hon. Lester Bowles Pearson, April 22, 1963 — April 20, 1968
Rt. Hon. Pierre Elliott Trudeau, April 20, 1968 — . . . .

The Cabinet. The Cabinet's primary responsibility in the Canadian political system is to determine priorities among the demands expressed by the people and to define policies to meet those demands. The Cabinet is a committee of ministers chosen by the Prime Minister, generally from among members of the House of Commons, although one or two Cabinet Ministers are usually chosen from the Senate including the Leader of the Government in the Senate. It is unusual for a senator to head a department of government because the constitution provides that measures for appropriating public funds or imposing taxes must originate in the House of Commons. If a senator headed a department, another minister in the House of Commons would have to speak on his behalf in respect of its affairs.

In January 1977, the following were members of the 20th Ministry according to precedence:

Prime Minister, Rt. Hon. Pierre Elliott Trudeau
President of the Queen's Privy Council for Canada, Hon. Allan Joseph MacEachen
Minister of Industry, Trade and Commerce, Hon. Jean Chrétien
Minister of Finance, Hon. Donald Stovel Macdonald
Minister of Labour, Hon. John Carr Munro
Minister of Justice and Attorney General of Canada, Hon. Stanley Ronald Basford
Secretary of State for External Affairs, Hon. Donald Campbell Jamieson
President of the Treasury Board, Hon. Robert Knight Andras
Minister of Transport, Hon. Otto Emil Lang
Minister of Supply and Services, Hon. Jean-Pierre Goyer
Minister of Energy, Mines and Resources, Hon. Alastair William Gillespie
Minister of Agriculture, Hon. Eugene Francis Whelan
Minister of Indian Affairs and Northern Development, Hon. W. Warren Allmand
Minister of State for Science and Technology, Hon. James Hugh Faulkner
Minister of State for Urban Affairs, Hon. André Ouellet
Minister of Veterans Affairs, Hon. Daniel Joseph MacDonald
Minister of National Health and Welfare, Hon. Marc Lalonde

Minister of Communications, Hon. Jeanne Sauvé
Leader of the Government in the Senate, Hon. Raymond Joseph Perrault
Minister of National Defence, Hon. Barnett Jerome Danson
Minister of Public Works, Hon. J. Judd Buchanan
Minister of Fisheries and the Environment, Hon. Roméo LeBlanc
Minister of Regional Economic Expansion, Hon. Marcel Lessard
Minister of Manpower and Immigration, Hon. Jack Sydney George Cullen
Minister of State (Small Business), Hon. Leonard Stephen Marchand
Secretary of State of Canada, Hon. John Roberts
Minister of National Revenue, Hon. Monique Bégin
Postmaster General, Hon. Jean-Jacques Blais
Solicitor General of Canada, Hon. Francis Fox
Minister of Consumer and Corporate Affairs, Hon. Anthony Chisholm Abbott
Minister of State (Fitness and Amateur Sport), Hon. Iona Campagnolo
Minister without Portfolio, Hon. Joseph-Philippe Guay.

Each Cabinet Minister usually assumes responsibility for one of the departments of government, although a minister may hold more than one portfolio at the same time or he may hold one or more portfolios and one or more acting portfolios. A Minister without portfolio may be invited to join the Cabinet because the Prime Minister wishes to have him or her in the Cabinet without the heavy duties of running a department, or to provide a suitable balance of regional representation, or for such other reason as the Prime Minister sees fit. Because of the cultural and geographical diversity in Canada, it is necessary for the Prime Minister to give close attention to the representational aspect of his Cabinet.

With the enactment of the Ministries and Ministers of State Act (Government Organization Act, 1970), five categories of Ministers of the Crown may be identified: departmental ministers, ministers with special parliamentary responsibilities, ministers without portfolio, and two types of ministers of state. Ministers of state "for designated purposes" may head a "Ministry of State" created by proclamation. They are charged with responsibilities for developing new and comprehensive policies in areas where there is particular urgency and importance and have a mandate effectively determined by the Governor in Council. They may have powers, duties and functions and exercise supervision and control of elements of the public service, and may seek parliamentary appropriations independently of any minister to cover the cost of their staff and operations. Other ministers of state, usually "undesignated", may be appointed to assist a departmental minister in the discharge of his responsibilities. They may have statutory powers, duties and functions and are limited in number by the appropriations that Parliament is willing to pass. They receive the same salary as a minister without portfolio, as provided for in the estimates of the minister with whom they are associated. All ministers are appointed on the advice of the Prime Minister by Commissions of Office issued by the Governor General under the Great Seal of Canada, to serve at pleasure, and to be accountable to Parliament as members of the government and for any responsibility that might be assigned to them by law or otherwise.

In Canada, almost all executive acts of the government are carried out in the name of the Governor in Council. The Committee of the Privy Council makes submissions to the Governor General for his approval, and he is bound by the constitution in nearly all circumstances to accept them. About 3,326 such Orders in Council were enacted in 1976 compared with 3,417 in 1975. Although some were fairly routine and did not require much discussion in Cabinet, others were of major significance and required extensive deliberation, sometimes covering months of meetings of officials, Cabinet committees, and the full Cabinet.

Hundreds of other policy issues must also be resolved as Cabinet must consider and approve the policy underlying each piece of proposed legislation. After it is drafted proposed legislation must be examined in detail. Recently, between 40 and 60 bills have been considered by Cabinet during the course of a parliamentary session. Proposals for sweeping reform of large areas of government organization or administration and policy to be adopted in fundamental constitutional changes or at a major international conference are among the issues which, on occasion, demand this extensive and detailed consideration.

The Cabinet committee system. The nature and volume of policy issues to be decided on by Cabinet do not lend themselves to discussion by 25 or 30 ministers. The first Cabinet committee system was established after the outbreak of World War II. Since then, growing demands on the executive have further stimulated the delegation of some Cabinet functions to its committees.

Cabinet committees tend to have a membership of fewer than 10 ministers, providing a forum capable of ensuring thorough study of policy proposals. The membership of Cabinet committees is confidential and the same rules of secrecy that apply to the deliberations of Cabinet apply to those of Cabinet committees. Otherwise, these committees might develop an importance and authority of their own which would be inconsistent with the principle of the collective responsibility of ministers. The Prime Minister determines the establishment of Cabinet committees, their membership, and terms of reference. Ministers may invite one or two officials to act as advisers during Cabinet committee meetings. The secretariats of the Cabinet committees are provided by the Privy Council Office and the Secretary of a Cabinet committee is usually also an Assistant Secretary to the Cabinet. Treasury Board, which is a Cabinet committee — or more precisely a sub-committee of the Committee of the Privy Council — is the only exception; it has its own secretariat headed by a secretary who has the status of a deputy minister.

Under the direction of the Prime Minister, the Secretary to the Cabinet prepares agenda and refers memoranda to Cabinet to the appropriate committee for study and report to the full Cabinet. Except where the Prime Minister instructs otherwise, all memoranda to Cabinet are submitted over the signature of the minister concerned.

The terms of reference of Cabinet committees cover virtually the total area of government responsibility. All memoranda to Cabinet are first considered by a Cabinet committee, except when they are of exceptional urgency or when the Prime Minister directs otherwise, in which case an item may be considered immediately by the full Cabinet.

In 1976 there were four coordinating committees: Priorities and Planning; Legislation and House Planning; Federal-Provincial Relations; and the Treasury Board and five subject-matter committees: Economic Policy; External Policy and Defence; Social Policy; Science, Culture and Information; and Government Operations. These committees meet regularly.

In addition there were four special and ad hoc committees of the Cabinet that met as required: the Cabinet committees on the Public Service, Security and Intelligence, Labour Relations and the Special Committee of Council which considers all submissions to the Governor in Council on behalf of the Committee of the Privy Council. The accompanying chart indicates the relationship of these committees to the Cabinet process.

Evidence of the utility of the Cabinet committee system is the growing reliance that has been placed on it since World War II. The following is a brief outline of the involvement of Cabinet and Cabinet committees in respect of a piece of legislation that the government ultimately introduces in the House of Commons or the Senate.

On the initiative of a minister a policy proposal is prepared, the implementation of which will require new legislation or the amendment of existing legislation. The proposal is addressed formally to Cabinet, but is considered first by the appropriate subject-matter committee. If approval is given, the proposal goes forward for confirmation or further consideration by Cabinet. If Cabinet confirms the committee's decision or makes a revision, the Department of Justice is instructed by the minister who made the proposal to prepare a draft

The Cabinet committee system

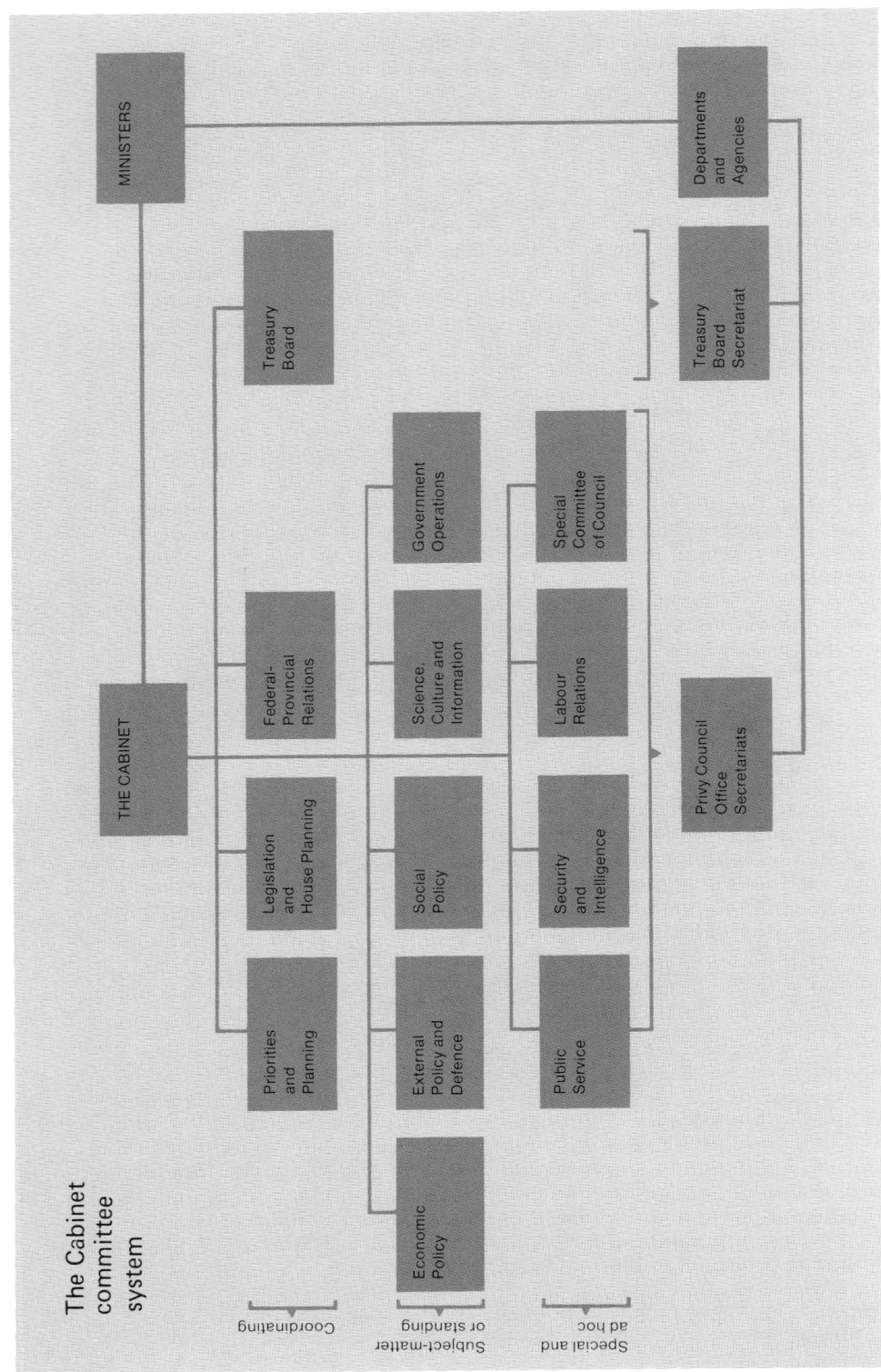

bill expressing in legal terms the intent of the policy proposal. If the draft bill meets with the minister's approval, he submits it to the Cabinet Committee on Legislation and House Planning and it is examined from a legal rather than a policy point of view. If this committee agrees that the bill is acceptable in all respects and could be introduced in Parliament, it so reports to Cabinet and Cabinet decides whether to confirm the committee's decision. If confirmation is given, the Prime Minister initials the bill and it is then introduced either in the Senate or the House of Commons, depending on constitutional and political considerations.

The order and manner in which a bill is considered in Parliament is the responsibility of the President of the Privy Council and House Leader who negotiates these matters with his counterparts in the opposition parties. If a bill is to be introduced in the Senate, the House Leader will discuss questions such as timing and tactics with the Leader of the Government in the Senate, who in turn will negotiate consideration of the bill with his counterpart in the Senate.

The Privy Council Office is a secretariat providing staff support to the Committee of the Privy Council and to the Cabinet. For the purposes of the Financial Administration Act it is considered a department of government. The Privy Council Office provides secretariats to serve the Cabinet, the Committee of the Privy Council and their various sub-committees except the Cabinet Committee on Federal-Provincial Relations, which is served by the Federal-Provincial Relations Office. Since the Prime Minister is, in effect, chairman of the Cabinet, he is the minister responsible for the Privy Council Office. The work of the Privy Council Office is directed by a public servant known as the Clerk of the Privy Council and Secretary to the Cabinet. He is the senior member of the public service of Canada.

Parliamentary secretaries. The Parliamentary Secretaries Act of June 1959 provided for the appointment of 16 parliamentary secretaries from among the members of the House of Commons to assist ministers in the performance of their duties. That act was amended by the Government Organization Act, 1970, which allows the number of parliamentary secretaries to equal the number of ministers who hold offices listed in Section 4 of the Salaries Act (i.e. ministers with departmental responsibilities, the Prime Minister, the Leader of the Government in the Senate and the President of the Privy Council). A parliamentary secretary works under the direction of his minister and has no legal authority in respect of the department with which he is associated, nor is he given acting responsibility or any of the powers, duties and functions of a minister in the event of his minister's absence or incapacity. Parliamentary secretaries are appointed by the Prime Minister and hold office for 12 months.

The Legislature   3.1.2

As previously stated, the federal legislative authority is vested in the Parliament of Canada — the Queen, the Senate, and the House of Commons. Bills may originate in either the Senate or the House, subject to the provisions of Section 53 of the British North America (BNA) Act, 1867, which provides that bills for the appropriation of any part of the public revenue or the imposition of any tax or impost shall originate in the House of Commons. Bills must pass both Houses and receive Royal Assent before becoming law. In practice, most public bills originate in the House of Commons although, at the request of the government, more have recently been introduced in the Senate in order that bills may be dealt with there while the Commons is engaged in other matters such as the debate on the Speech from the Throne. Private bills usually originate in the Senate. The Senate may delay, amend or even refuse to pass bills sent to it from the Commons, but differences are usually settled without serious conflict.

Section 91 of the BNA Acts, 1867 to 1964, assigns to the Parliament of Canada legislative authority in very clearly specified areas. These are discussed in detail in Chapter 2.

Under Section 95, the Parliament of Canada may make laws in relation to agriculture and immigration concurrently with provincial legislatures although federal legislation is paramount in the event of conflict. An amendment to the BNA Act in 1951 (Br. Stat. 1950-51, c.32) authorized the Parliament of Canada to make laws in relation to old age pensions in Canada subject to the proviso that no such law should affect the operation of any provincial laws in relation to old age pensions. By the BNA Act, 1964 this amendment was extended to permit the payment of supplementary benefits, including survivors and disability benefits irrespective of age, under a contributory pension plan.

The passage of legislation. If a bill is introduced and approved in the House of Commons, it is then introduced in the Senate and follows a similar procedure. If a bill is first introduced in the Senate, the reverse procedure is followed. There are three types of bills: public bills introduced by the government; public bills introduced by private members of Parliament; and private bills introduced by private members of Parliament. Each type is treated in a slightly different manner, and there are even differences in procedure when the House deals with government bills introduced pursuant to "supply" and "ways and means" motions on the one hand, and other government bills on the other. The following outline describes the procedure for a government bill introduced in the House of Commons.

The sponsoring minister gives notice that he intends to introduce a bill on a given subject. Not less than 48 hours later he moves for leave to introduce the bill and that the bill be given first reading. This is granted automatically because this first step does not imply approval of any sort. It is only after first reading that the bill is ordered printed for distribution to the members.

At a later sitting the minister moves that the bill be given second reading and that it be referred to an appropriate committee of the House of Commons. A favourable vote on the motion for second reading represents approval of the bill in principle so there is often an extensive debate, which, according to the procedures of the House of Commons, must be confined to the principle of the bill. The debate culminates in a vote which, if favourable, results in the bill being referred to the appropriate committee of the House, where it is given clause-by-clause consideration.

At the committee stage, expert witnesses and interested parties may be invited to give testimony pertaining to the bill, and the proceedings may cover many weeks.

The House committee prepares and submits a report to the House of Commons which must decide whether to accept the report, including any amendments that the committee has made to the bill. At the report stage any member may, on giving 24 hours notice, move an amendment to the bill. All such amendments are debated and are usually put to a vote. Following that, a motion "that the bill be concurred in" or "that the bill, as amended, be concurred in", is put to the vote.

After this report stage, the minister moves that the bill be given third reading and passage. Debate of this motion is limited to whether the bill should be given third reading. Amendments are permitted at this stage but they must be of a general nature, similar to those allowed on second reading. If the vote is favourable, the bill is introduced in the Senate where it goes through a somewhat similar though not identical process, since each House has its own rules of procedure. The bill is then presented to the Governor General for Royal Assent and signature. Depending on the provisions in the bill itself it may come into force when it is signed by the Governor General, on an appointed day, or when it is officially proclaimed.

Duration and sessions of Parliaments. The length and sessions of the first to the 12th Parliaments, covering the period from Confederation to 1917, are given in the *1940 Canada Year Book* p 46; of the 13th to the 17th Parliaments in the 1945 edition, p 53; of the 18th and 19th Parliaments in the 1957-58 edition, p 46;

Passage of legislation

Policy proposal requiring legislation (submitted to Cabinet by a Minister)

Consideration of policy proposal in a subject – matter committee and decision or recommendation

Cabinet confirmation of committee decision

Responsible Minister issues drafting instructions for legislation to Department of Justice

Cabinet confirmation of committee decision and Prime Minister's signature

Consideration of draft Bill by Cabinet Committee on Legislation and House Planning

Draft Bill prepared by Department of Justice and approved by responsible Minister

The Cabinet process

Parliament First Reading in either Senate or House of Commons[1] (reading of title and brief explanation of Bill)

Parliament Second Reading in same House of Parliament (debate and vote on principle of Bill)

Consideration by appropriate Parliamentary committee (clause by clause examination of Bill)

Introduction of Bill into other House of Parliament and repetition of the process

Parliament Third Reading and vote

Parliament Report Stage and vote on any amendments prepared by committee

The legislative process

The Governor General in presence of Senate and House of Commons assents to Bill and signs it into law

1. All money Bills must be introduced in the House of Commons.

of the 20th to the 23rd Parliaments in the 1965 edition, p 65; of the 24th to the 26th Parliaments in the 1975 edition, p 132; and of the 27th to the 30th Parliaments in this edition, Table 3.1.

The Senate has grown from an original membership of 72 at Confederation, through the addition of members to represent new provinces and the general increase in population, to a total of 104 members; the latest change in representation was made on June 19, 1975 when an act of Parliament (SC 1974-75-76, c.53) amended the Canadian Constitution to entitle the Yukon Territory and the Northwest Territories to be represented by one senator each. The growth of representation in the Senate is summarized in Table 3.2.

Senators are appointed by the Governor General by instrument under the Great Seal of Canada. By constitutional usage the actual power of nominating senators resides in the Prime Minister whose advice the Governor General accepts in this regard. Until the passage of "An Act to make provision for the retirement of members of the Senate" (SC 1965, c.4), assented to on June 2, 1965, senators were appointed for life; that act set 75 years as the age at which any person appointed to the Senate after the coming into force of the act would cease to hold his place in the Senate.

In each of the four main areas of Canada (Ontario, Quebec, Atlantic provinces and western provinces) except Quebec, senators represent the whole of the province for which they are appointed; in Quebec, one senator is appointed for each of the 24 electoral divisions of what was formerly Lower Canada. The deliberations of the Senate are presided over by a Speaker appointed by the Governor in Council (in effect by the government) and government business in the Senate is sponsored by the Government Leader in the Senate.

The Senate retains its traditional role in respect of legislation originating in the House of Commons, namely, to take a "sober second look" at such legislation and amend it if necessary; such amendments are often concurred in by the House of Commons. If representatives of the two Houses cannot resolve disagreements arising from Senate amendments, the legislation cannot be further considered.

The Senate provides a national forum for the discussion of public issues and the airing of grievances from any part of Canada. Through its own committees and its participation in joint committees of both Houses the Senate is particularly active in making studies in depth on matters of public concern.

Since 1971, Senate committees have been performing a new function, that of studying the subject-matter of government bills, including "money bills", in advance of their formal introduction in the Senate. Under this procedure, amendments to a bill suggested by a Senate committee are often accepted by the government and by the House of Commons before the bill itself actually reaches the Senate.

In January 1977 the representation in the Senate was as follows:

Newfoundland
Eric Cook
Chesley William Carter
James Duggan
William John Petten
Frederick William Rowe

Prince Edward Island
Florence Elsie Inman
Orville Howard Phillips
M. Lorne Bonnell
2 vacancies

Nova Scotia
Donald Smith
Harold Connolly
John Michael Macdonald
Margaret Norrie

Henry D. Hicks
Bernard Alasdair Graham
Augustus Irvine Barrow
Ernest George Cottreau
George Isaac Smith
1 vacancy

New Brunswick
George Percival Burchill
Fred A. McGrand
Edgar Fournier
Charles Robert McElman
Hervé J. Michaud
Michel Fournier
Louis-J. Robichaud
Daniel Riley
2 vacancies

Quebec
Sarto Fournier
Hartland de Montarville Molson
Josie Alice Dinan Quart
Louis Philippe Beaubien
Jacques Flynn
Maurice Bourget
Azellus Denis
Jean-Paul Deschatelets
Alan Aylesworth Macnaughton
J.G. Léopold Langlois
Paul Desruisseaux
Maurice Lamontagne
Raymond Eudes
Louis de Gonzague Giguère
Paul C. Lafond
H. Carl Goldenberg
Renaude Lapointe
Martial Asselin
Jean-Pierre Côté
Maurice Riel
Jean Marchand
John Ewasew
Pietro Rizzuto
1 vacancy

Ontario
Salter Adrian Hayden
Norman McLeod Paterson
John J. Connolly
David A. Croll
Joseph A. Sullivan
Lionel Choquette
Allister Grosart
David James Walker
Rhéal Belisle
Daniel Aiken Lang
William Moore Benidickson
Douglas Keith Davey

Andrew Ernest Thompson
Keith Laird
Richard James Stanbury
Eugene A. Forsey
George James McIlraith
John James Greene
Joan Neiman
John Morrow Godfrey
4 vacancies

Manitoba
J. Campbell Haig
Paul Yuzyk
Douglas Donald Everett
Gildas L. Molgat
William C. McNamara
1 vacancy

Saskatchewan
Alexander Hamilton McDonald
Hazen Robert Argue
Herbert Orville Sparrow
Sidney L. Buckwold
David Gordon Steuart
1 vacancy

Alberta
Donald Cameron
Earl Adam Hastings
Harry William Hays
Ernest C. Manning
2 vacancies

British Columbia
Ann Elizabeth Haddon Bell
Edward M. Lawson
George Clifford van Roggen
Guy Williams
Raymond Joseph Perrault
Jack Austin.

The House of Commons. Following the 1971 Census the number of members in the House of Commons was determined by the Representation Commissioner in accordance with Section 51 of the British North America Act, with the total representation at 264.

The readjustment of the federal electoral districts was carried out during 1972 and 1973 in accordance with the Electoral Boundaries Readjustment Act. The last of 10 reports was submitted to the House of Commons early in July 1973. After debate it was agreed to suspend the readjustment until January 1, 1975. To this effect, Bill C-208 "Electoral Boundaries Readjustment Suspension Act" was given Royal Assent on July 27, 1973.

On December 20, 1974 Royal Assent was given to the Representation Act, 1974 which removed the temporary suspension of the Electoral Boundaries Readjustment Act and provided for representation in the House of Commons under a revised formula awarding each province the following number of members: Ontario 95, Quebec 75, Nova Scotia 11, New Brunswick 10, Manitoba 14, British Columbia 28, Prince Edward Island four, Saskatchewan 14, Alberta 21, Newfoundland seven, the Northwest Territories two and the Yukon Territory one. The revised number of members in the House of Commons, following the next general election, would be 282.

The number of representatives of each province elected at each of the 30 general elections since Confederation is given in Table 3.3. Historical data concerning representation may be found in the *Canada Year Book 1973.*

Salaries, allowances and pensions. Members of the Senate and House of Commons receive sessional allowances of $24,000 per annum. For each session of Parliament, they may also be paid such travelling expenses between their place of residence or constituency and Ottawa as may be required for the performance of their duties. A senator receives an annual expense allowance of $5,300 and a member of the House of Commons receives an expense allowance of $10,600 to $14,475 dependent upon the electoral district represented; neither is subject to income tax and is payable monthly. Members of the House of Commons may receive up to $7,900 annually for the payment of staff in their constituency, and up to $2,400 annually for rental of premises in their constituency. In addition to the sessional allowance, the member of the Senate occupying the recognized position as Leader of the Government in the Senate is paid an annual allowance of $20,000 and the member of the Senate occupying the recognized position as Opposition Leader in the Senate is paid an annual allowance of $8,000; but if the Leader of the Government is in receipt of a salary under the Salaries Act the annual allowance is not paid. The remuneration of the Prime Minister is $33,300 a year and of a Cabinet Minister and the Leader of the Opposition in the House of Commons $20,000 a year in addition to the sessional and expense allowances each receives as a member of Parliament. The Chief Government Whip, the Chief Opposition Whip, the Opposition House Leader and the leader of a party having a recognized membership of 12 or more in the House of Commons, other than the Prime Minister and the Leader of the Opposition, each receives an annual allowance of $5,300 in addition to the sessional allowance. In addition to sessional and expense allowances, the Speaker of the Senate receives a salary of $12,000 per annum, the Speaker of the House of Commons, $20,000 per annum and the Deputy Speaker of the House of Commons, $8,000 per annum. The Speakers of the Senate and of the House of Commons are also each entitled to $3,000 and the Deputy Speaker of the House of Commons to $1,500, in lieu of residence; these allowances are not taxable. The Deputy Chairman of Committees receives an annual allowance of $5,300. Parliamentary secretaries to Ministers of the Crown receive an annual allowance of $5,300, in addition to their sessional and expense allowances. Motor vehicle allowances of $2,000 are paid to Ministers of the Crown and to the Leader of the Opposition in the House of Commons, and motor vehicle allowances of $1,000 are paid to the Speakers of the Senate and of the House of Commons; these allowances are not taxable.

A member of Parliament contributes, by reservation, 7.5% of his sessional indemnity toward his retirement allowance, which is based on the average of the sessional indemnity received over the best consecutive six years of his pensionable service accumulated as follows: 3.5% of this six-year average for each of the first 10 years of pensionable service; 3% of this average for each of the next 10 years; 2% of this average for each of the next five years; and 2% of this average for each of the years of pensionable service earned by his contributions from salary for extra duties performed as a minister, etc.; subject to an overall maximum of 75% of that best six-year average. The member holding the office of Prime Minister contributes by reservation from the salary payable to him under the Salaries Act, an amount equal to 6% of that salary to the Consolidated Revenue Fund. Survivors' benefits are as follows: 60% of the member's pension entitlement to the widow or widower; if there is a surviving parent, 10% of the member's pension entitlement for each child up to three; and if there is no surviving parent, 20% of the member's pension entitlement for each child up to four. A member who was a member on March 31, 1970 had a year in which to elect to come under the plan described here or to remain under a previous plan, described in the *1969 Canada Year Book* p 75.

An act to make provision for the retirement of members of the Senate (SC

1965, c.4) entitles a senator appointed after June 2, 1965 to become a contributor under the provisions of the Members of Parliament Retiring Allowances Act. Senators appointed prior to that date and who have not attained the age of 75 years, who elect under the provisions of this act, are also entitled to become contributors. Under the provisions of the Retirement Act, as amended, a senator contributes, by reservation, 6% of $24,000. A senator appointed before June 2, 1965 who (a) within one year of attaining the age of 75 years resigns his place in the Senate, or (b) resigns due to some permanent infirmity disabling him from performing his duties in the Senate, may be granted an annuity equal to $16,000. The widow of a person granted such an annuity may receive an annuity equal to three fifths of the annuity to the ex-member of the Senate.

Every former Prime Minister who held office for four years will receive from the Consolidated Revenue Fund an allowance of two thirds of the annual salary provided for Prime Ministers under the Salaries Act, the allowance to commence when a Prime Minister ceases to hold that or any other office in Parliament, or attains the age of 65 years, whichever is the later, and to continue during his lifetime. The widow of a Prime Minister will receive an annual payment of one half of the allowance that was being paid or that would have been paid in the event that he died before receiving the allowance, such allowance to commence immediately after the death of her husband and to continue during her natural life or until her remarriage.

None of these allowances is payable while the recipient remains a senator or a member of the House of Commons.

The federal franchise. The present federal franchise laws are contained in the Canada Elections Act (RSC 1970, c.14, 1st Supp.) as amended by the Election Expenses Act (SC 1973-74, c.51). Generally, the franchise is conferred upon all Canadian citizens who have attained the age of 18 years and are ordinarily resident in the electoral district on the date fixed for the beginning of the enumeration at the election. Persons denied the right to vote are: the Chief Electoral Officer and the Assistant Chief Electoral Officer; judges appointed by the Governor in Council; the returning officer for each electoral district; persons undergoing punishment as inmates of any penal institution; persons restrained of their liberty of movement or deprived of the management of their property by reason of mental disease; and persons disqualified under any law relating to the disqualification of electors for corrupt or illegal practices.

The Special Voting Rules set out in Schedule II to the Canada Elections Act prescribe voting procedures for members of the Canadian Forces, for members of the federal public service posted abroad, and also for veterans in receipt of treatment or domiciliary care in certain institutions.

Electoral districts, voters on list, votes polled and names and addresses of members of the House of Commons elected at the 30th general election, July 8, 1974 are given in Table 3.4. Table 3.5 indicates voters on the lists and votes polled at federal general elections in 1965, 1968, 1972 and 1974.

The Judiciary   3.1.3

The Parliament of Canada is empowered by Section 101 of the British North America Act to provide for the constitution, maintenance and organization of a general Court of Appeal for Canada and for the establishment of any additional courts for the better administration of the laws of Canada. Under this provision Parliament has established the Supreme Court of Canada, the Federal Court of Canada and certain miscellaneous courts. A detailed discussion of the judiciary and legal system of Canada is presented in Chapter 2.

3.2   Federal government administration

3.2.1   Financial administration and control

The financial affairs of the Government of Canada are administered and controlled under the basic principle that no tax shall be imposed and no money spent without the authority of Parliament and that expenditures shall be made only for the purposes authorized by Parliament. The most important constitutional provisions relating to Parliament's control of finances are contained in the British North America (BNA) Act which provides that all federal taxing and appropriating measures must originate in the House of Commons. The government is responsible for introducing all money bills. Financial control is exercised through a budgetary system based on the principle that all the financial needs of the government for each fiscal year should be considered at one time so that both the current and prospective conditions of the public treasury may be clearly evident.

Estimates and appropriations. Coordination of the estimates process is carried out by Treasury Board. The board is a separate department of government, its minister having the designation of President of the Treasury Board. Under the Financial Administration Act, the board may act for the Privy Council in all matters relating to financial management (including estimates, expenditures, financial commitments, establishments, revenues and accounts), personnel management and general administrative policy in the public service.

Under present practice departments submit forecasts of their requirements about 12 months before the beginning of a new fiscal year. Forecasts of what they will require in each of the coming three years to maintain the current levels of service in each program are termed "A Budgets". At the same time departments submit forecasts of requirements for new activities or expansion in existing activities, referred to as "B Budgets". These proposals are reviewed by Treasury Board in the light of expenditure guidelines approved by the Cabinet which express the government's priorities. The Treasury Board Secretariat prepares recommendations for the budgetary and non-budgetary allocations to each program for Treasury Board and Cabinet review. In August of the year preceding the fiscal year, departments are advised of the allocations approved by Cabinet. Departments then develop detailed estimates of their resource requirements for the new year against these approved allocations. These estimates are submitted at the end of October. Following review by Treasury Board and approval by Cabinet they are tabled in Parliament in February.

Main Estimates and Supplementary Estimates are referred to committees of the House of Commons. The timing of such referrals, the timing of committee reports and all other matters having to do with the business of supply in the House of Commons are regulated by the Standing Orders of the House (March 1975). The Standing Orders call for the referral of the new year Main Estimates to standing committees of the House by March 1 of the expiring fiscal year and they must report back to the House not later than May 31 in the new fiscal year. Supplementary Estimates are referred immediately after they are tabled to the Standing Committees, and dates by which reports must be made are stipulated.

Section 58 of the Standing Orders establishes three supply periods ending not later than December 10, March 26 and June 30. The first supplementary estimates for a year are usually dealt with in the December 10 period and the final supplementary estimates in the March 26 period. In addition, interim supply (consisting of 3/12ths for all voted items in Main Estimates and extra 12ths for some voted items) is dealt with in the March 26 period. In the June 30 period, the House is asked to provide full supply on Main Estimates. In each supply period a number of days are allotted to the business of supply. Opposition motions have precedence over all government supply motions on allotted days and opportunities to put forward motions of non-confidence in the government are provided. On the last allotted day in each period, normally at 15 minutes before the ordinary time of adjournment, the Speaker interrupts the proceedings in progress and puts every question necessary to dispose of any business relating to supply. No debate may take place after the Speaker has acted in this way and the Appropriation Acts then before the House must be voted on. These Appropriation Acts authorize payments out of the Consolidated Revenue Fund of the amounts included in the estimates, whether main or supplementary, subject to the conditions stated in them.

In addition, there are a number of items, such as interest on the public debt and family allowances, authorized under other statutes. Although it is not necessary for Parliament to approve these items annually, they are included in the Main Estimates for purposes of information. Provision also exists for the expenditure of public money when Parliament is not in session or in emergencies where no parliamentary appropriation is available. Under the Financial Administration Act, the Governor in Council, on the report of the President of the Treasury Board that there is no appropriation for the expenditure and on the report of the appropriate minister that the expenditure is urgently required, may order a special warrant issued authorizing disbursement of the amount required. Such warrants must be published in the *Canada Gazette* within 30 days of issue and reported to Parliament within 15 days of the next session of Parliament.

Disbursements are also made for purposes not reflected in the budgetary accounts but recorded in the government's statement of assets and liabilities, such as loans to and investments in Crown corporations, loans to international organizations and to national, provincial and municipal governments, and loans to veterans. There are also disbursements in connection with deposit and trust accounts and annuity, insurance and pension accounts which the government holds or administers, including the Canada Pension Plan fund and the Unemployment Insurance Account which are operated as separate entities. These are excluded from the calculation of the annual budgetary surplus or deficit.

The budget. The Minister of Finance usually presents his annual budget speech in the House of Commons some time after the Main Estimates have been introduced. The budget speech reviews the state of the national economy and the financial operations of the government for the previous fiscal year and gives a forecast of the probable financial requirements for the year ahead, taking into account the Main Estimates and making allowances for Supplementary Estimates. At the close of his address, the minister tables the formal notices of ways and means motions for any changes in the existing tax rates or rules and customs tariff which, in accordance with parliamentary procedure, must precede the introduction of any money bills. These resolutions give notice of the amendments which the government intends to ask Parliament to make in the taxation statutes. However if a change is proposed in a commodity tax, such as a sales tax or excise duty on a particular item, it is usually effective immediately; the legislation, when passed, is retroactive to the date of the speech.

The budget speech is delivered in support of a motion that the House approves in general a budgetary policy of the government; debate on this motion may take up six sitting days, but once it is passed the way is clear for consideration of the budget resolutions. When these have been approved by the committee, a report to this effect is made to the House, and the tax bills are introduced and dealt with in the same manner as all other government financial legislation.

Revenues and expenditures. Administrative procedures governing revenues and expenditures are, for the most part, contained in the Financial Administration Act.

With respect to revenues, the basic requirement is that all public money shall be paid into the Consolidated Revenue Fund, which is the aggregate of all public money on deposit to the credit of the Receiver General. The Minister of Supply and Services is the Receiver General for Canada. Treasury Board has prescribed detailed regulations governing the receipt and deposit of such money. The Bank of Canada and the chartered banks are the custodians of public money. Balances are apportioned among the various chartered banks according to a percentage allocation established by agreement among all the banks and communicated to the Department of Finance by the Canadian Bankers' Association. The daily operating account is maintained with the Bank of Canada and the division of funds between it and the chartered banks takes into account the immediate cash requirements of the government and consideration of monetary policy. The Minister of Finance may purchase and hold securities of, or guaranteed by, Canada and pay for them out of the Consolidated Revenue Fund or may sell such securities and pay the proceeds into the fund. Thus, if cash balances in the fund exceed immediate requirements they may be invested in interest-earning assets. In addition, the Minister of Finance has established a purchase fund to assist in the orderly retirement of the public debt.

Treasury Board exercises central control over the budgets of departments and over financial administrative matters generally, principally during the annual consideration of departmental long-range plans and of the estimates. The board also has the right to maintain continuous control over certain types of expenditure to ensure that activities and commitments for the future are held within approved policies, and that the government is informed of and approves any major development of policy or significant transaction that might give rise to public or parliamentary criticism.

To ensure enforcement of the expenditure decisions of Parliament, the government and ministers, the Financial Administration Act provides that no payment shall be made out of the Consolidated Revenue Fund without the authority of Parliament and no charge shall be made against an appropriation except on the requisition of the appropriate minister or a person authorized by him in writing. These requisitions, which must meet certain standards prescribed by Treasury Board regulation, are presented to the Receiver General, who makes the payment.

At the beginning of each fiscal year, or whenever Treasury Board may direct, each department submits a division into allotments of each vote included in its estimates. Once approved these allotments cannot be varied or amended without the consent of the board; expenditures charged to appropriations are limited to such allotments. To avoid over-expenditures, commitments due to be paid within a fiscal year are recorded and controlled by the departments concerned. Commitments made under contract that will fall due in succeeding years are recorded since the government must be prepared in the future to ask Parliament for appropriations to cover them. Any unexpended amounts in the annual appropriations lapse at the end of the fiscal year, but for 30 days subsequent to March 31 payments may be made and charged to the previous year's appropriations for work performed, goods received or services rendered prior to the end of that fiscal year.

Under the Financial Administration Act, every payment against an appropriation is made by the Receiver General by cheque or other instrument. After presentation for payment, the cheques or instruments are cleared daily by the chartered banks through the Bank of Canada to the Cheque Redemption Control Division of the Receiver General; the banks are then reimbursed through a cheque drawn on the Receiver General's account with the Bank of Canada.

Public debt. In addition to collecting and disbursing public money, the government receives and pays out substantial sums in connection with its public debt operations. The Minister of Finance is authorized to borrow money by the issue and sale of securities at whatever rate of interest and under whatever terms and conditions the Governor in Council approves. Although new borrowings require specific authority of Parliament, the Financial Administration Act authorizes the Governor in Council to approve borrowings as required to redeem maturing or called securities. To ensure that the Consolidated Revenue Fund will be sufficient to meet lawfully authorized disbursements, he may also approve the temporary borrowing of such sums as are necessary for periods not exceeding six months. The Bank of Canada acts as the fiscal agent of the government in the management of the public debt.

Accounts and financial statements. Under the Financial Administration Act, Treasury Board may prescribe the manner and form in which the accounts of Canada and the accounts of individual departments shall be kept. Annually, on or before December 31 or, if Parliament is not then sitting, within any of the first 15 days after Parliament resumes, the *Public accounts,* prepared by the Receiver General, is laid before the House of Commons by the Minister of Finance. The *Public accounts* contains a survey of the financial transactions of the fiscal year ended the previous March 31 and statements of revenues and expenditures, assets and direct and contingent liabilities, together with other accounts and information required to show the financial position of Canada. The statement of assets and liabilities is designed to disclose the net debt, which is determined by offsetting against the gross liabilities only those assets regarded as readily realizable or interest- or revenue-producing. Fixed capital assets, such as government buildings and public works, are charged to budgetary expenditures at the time of acquisition or construction and are shown on the statement of assets and liabilities at a nominal value of $1. Monthly financial statements are also published in the *Canada Gazette.*

The Auditor General. The government's accounts are subject to an independent examination by the Auditor General who is an officer of Parliament. With respect to expenditures, this examination is a post-audit to report whether the accounts have been properly kept, the money spent for the purposes for which it was appropriated by Parliament and expenditures made as authorized; any audit before payment is the responsibility of the requisitioning department or agency. With respect to revenues, the Auditor General must ascertain that all public money is fully accounted for and that the rules and procedures applied ensure an effective check on the assessment, collection and proper allocation of the revenue. With respect to public property, he must satisfy himself that essential records are maintained and that the rules and procedures applied are sufficient to safeguard and control it. The Auditor General reports the results of his examination to the House of Commons, calling attention to any case which he considers should be brought to the notice of the House. He also reports to ministers, the Treasury Board or the government any matter which in his opinion calls for attention so that remedial action may be taken promptly. It is the usual practice to refer the *Public accounts* and the *Auditor General's report* to the House of Commons Standing Committee on Public Accounts, which may review them and report the findings and recommendations to the House of Commons.

Government employment   3.2.2

Treasury Board (a statutory committee of Cabinet) has overall responsibility for personnel management in the federal public service. It is responsible for development and application of personnel policies, systems and methods to ensure that the human resources needed to carry out programs effectively are obtained at competitive prices and used efficiently with due regard for the individual and collective rights of employees.

Under provisions of the amended Financial Administration Act and the Public Service Staff Relations Act, both proclaimed on March 13, 1967, Treasury Board is responsible for the development of policy guidelines, regulations, standards and programs in the areas of classification and pay, conditions of employment, collective bargaining and staff relations, official languages, human resources training, development and utilization, pensions, insurance and other employee benefits and allowances, and other personnel management matters affecting the public service. Treasury Board is responsible for making recommendations on organization development, human resources planning, the determination and evaluation of training needs and education programs, and standards governing health and safety. It advises departments and agencies on the design and implementation of systems to improve personnel management.

Responsibility for classification and the administration of salaries has, with a few exceptions, been delegated to departments, subject to a monitoring process. Benefit programs and allowance policies approved by the board are designed to give maximum responsibility for administration to departments.

Under the system of collective bargaining established by the Public Service Staff Relations Act, Treasury Board is the employer for all employees in the public service, except for certain separate employers such as the National Research Council and the National Film Board. The board negotiates collective agreements with the unions representing 80 bargaining units and advises departments on their administration. Consultations are held with representatives of bargaining agents, directly or through the National Joint Council, on matters which are not subject to bargaining or which have wide application in the public service. The board determines terms and conditions of employment of employees excluded from collective bargaining, and develops policy guidelines and standards to govern physical working conditions and occupational health and safety. It determines the employer's position on grievances referred to adjudication, and advises or assists departmental management regarding discipline and grievance cases. The board presents the position of the employer in applications for certification by employee organizations and in hearings before the Public Service Staff Relations Board on applications for the exclusion of employees from bargaining units.

The board develops policy guidelines, coordinates the administration and recommends periodic revision of pension, insurance and related programs for the public service and negotiates reciprocal pension transfer agreements with other public and private employers. It also studies and proposes means of ensuring compatibility between public service employee benefits and social security programs such as medicare and the Canada and Quebec Pension Plans.

Public Service Commission. The Public Service Employment Act, which became effective on March 13, 1967, continues the status of the Public Service Commission as an independent agency responsible to Parliament. The commission has the exclusive right and authority to make appointments to and from within the public service. The commission is also empowered to operate staff development and training programs, to assist deputy heads in carrying out training and development and in 1972 was charged with investigations into cases of alleged discrimination on grounds of sex, race, national origin, colour or religion in the application and operation of the Public Service Employment Act. Age and marital status were added to these grounds by amendment to the Public Service Employment Act in 1975.

It may establish boards to render decisions on appeals against appointments made from within the public service and against release or demotion for incompetence or incapacity, to make recommendations on the revocation of appointments improperly made under delegated authority and to render decisions on allegations of political partisanship.

The commission grants or withholds approval of applications for leave of absence from public servants who wish to be candidates in federal, provincial or territorial elections and conducts investigations into allegations of improper political activities on the part of public servants.

The act authorizes the commission to delegate to deputy heads any of its powers, except those relating to appeals and inquiries. The commission has delegated powers to make appointments in the Operational and Administrative Support categories; employing departments are required to use the Canada Manpower Centres as their recruitment agency for appointments from outside the public service. Delegations of appointing authority in the Administrative and Foreign Service, Technical, and Scientific and Professional categories have been made under conditions which retain the commission's authority as the central recruitment agency for the public service of Canada with a few exceptions, i.e.

those cases where a department is virtually the sole employer of a particular occupational specialty. The commission ensures that appointments made under delegated authority comply with the law and with commission policies.

The Public Service Commission performs its role as guardian of the merit principle to ensure that high standards are maintained in the service, consistent with adequate representation of the two official language groups, a bilingual capability to the extent prescribed by the government, equal employment and career development opportunities irrespective of sex, race, national origin, colour or religion, and encouragement of opportunities for disadvantaged people.

Every citizen may apply for positions. Competitive examinations are announced through the news media and posters displayed on public notice boards of major post offices, Canada Manpower Centres, Public Service Commission offices and elsewhere.

The commission's major task — staffing the public service according to merit — is done on an occupational basis. The classification system divides the service into six broad occupational categories which are further divided into groups of occupationally similar jobs. For each major category or group there is a program of recruitment, selection and placement. Comprehensive manpower planning, developed in cooperation with Treasury Board and employing departments, has been introduced for several occupational groups. Continuous recruitment techniques, utilizing candidate inventories, have been developed and are used when appropriate. Appointments are made from within the service except where the commission believes it is in the best interests of the service to do otherwise. Appointments from within are made either through a formal competition or from an employee inventory. "Data STREAM", the commission's computerized manpower inventory, is the primary employee inventory for the Executive, Scientific and Professional, Technical and the Administrative and Foreign Service categories. Under the Public Service Employment Act, public servants who are candidates in a competition open to all or part of the service may appeal the selections to the Public Service Commission.

When a promotion is made without competition, those who would have been eligible to apply if a competition had been held may appeal. Public servants may also appeal the decision of a deputy head to recommend release or demotion because of incompetence or incapacity.

Consistent with the emphasis on managerial development and continuing education, the Public Service Commission offers interdepartmental courses in government administration, occupational training and management improvement. The commission acts as the consultant and adviser to deputy heads, and training and development facilities are made available to train employees for specific occupations or for promotion in administrative and managerial ranks.

In order that departments may perform their functions effectively and serve the public in accordance with the Official Languages Act, the commission ensures that employees appointed are qualified to meet the linguistic requirements of positions and, in situations where they do not qualify, that incumbents or winners of competitions for bilingual positions receive continuous training in their second official language for up to 52 weeks. Part-time language training is also available to other public servants.

The commission exercises specific responsibilities in language training, research and the development of selection standards with regard to the linguistic requirements of positions and groups of positions within the federal public service. It must establish the method of assessing language knowledge and it must also establish the degree of language knowledge or proficiency possessed by candidates for positions.

The formulation of appropriate selection standards is to be determined in accordance with the decisions of the individual deputy heads with respect to the linguistic requirements of positions and groups of positions.

3.2.3   Native peoples

3.2.3.1   Indians

The federal Department of Indian Affairs and Northern Development is responsible for meeting statutory obligations toward the Indian people registered under the Indian Act and for programs approved specifically for them.

The department's Local Government Branch assists with the physical development of Indian communities which involves planning, housing, water, sanitation, electricity and the construction and maintenance of roads on reserves. Indian participation in these activities as well as in services such as school maintenance, fire and police protection and local government is increasing as the concept of band management is extended. In 1975-76, $52.4 million was provided for capital investments in community improvements, and $9.0 million for operating expenditures. On May 25, 1976 the Joint Work Group on Housing, comprised of departmental officials and National Indian Brotherhood representatives, presented its Technical Report to the Minister of IAND. The department undertook preparation of a Treasury Board submission and consultation with CMHC, Manpower and Immigration, and DREE to obtain the necessary approvals.

The role of the federal government in programs for Indian people is changing from direct program management at the local level to an advisory and consultative capacity as the Indian people assume responsibility for managing their own affairs. Emphasis is placed on the definition of needs and priorities with the department and Indian bands working jointly, and on the development of close consultation in both policy and administrative matters.

Under agreements with the federal government, provincial Indian associations receive funds to administer community development programs planned jointly with government officials, but administered by the associations themselves. These programs are intended to help Indian people to improve social, economic and cultural conditions in their communities.

Since the first such agreement was concluded with the Manitoba Indian Brotherhood in 1969, others have been entered into with Indian associations in Nova Scotia, New Brunswick, Ontario, Saskatchewan, British Columbia, the Yukon Territory and the Northwest Territories. In 1975-76 these associations handled over $5.4 million in community development funds.

The Indian-Eskimo Economic Development Branch, to raise the economic status and increase the independence of individuals and bands, assists in the creation of business and employment opportunities in service and secondary industries and in resource utilization and land development, including the development of mineral resources on Indian reserves. Many programs are conducted in cooperation with other federal departments, provincial governments and private organizations. Assistance is in the form of loans, grants and contributions, loan guarantees, technical and management advice, and specialized training. The loans are provided from the Indian Economic Development Fund, capitalized at $70 million for the five years ended March 31, 1976. During 1974 a new guaranteed loan fund of $30 million was established. In addition the Indian Economic Development Fund has appropriated $27 million during the past six years in grants and contributions to encourage economic activity through the provision of basic infrastructure and professional and technical services. For the fiscal year ended March 31, 1976, the fund provided $46.3 million in loans, guarantees, grants and contributions.

The Lands and Membership Branch is responsible for ensuring that treaty obligations with respect to lands and memberships are met and that statutory responsibilities under the Indian Act with respect to membership and the administration and management of Indian lands are fulfilled. The branch also assists bands in obtaining maximum benefits from mineral resources on their own reserves.

Since 1969 the government has provided financial assistance to Indian and Inuit people to conduct research to support their claims to traditional interests in lands, and their rights under treaty or the Indian Act. The government has recognized that its lawful obligations to Indian people must be met, and has agreed to undertake negotiations with Indian and Inuit people. Claims may be based on traditional use and occupancy of land in areas where the Indian interest has not been extinguished by treaty or superseded by law (comprehensive claims), or they may be based on interpretation of treaties and legislation, or the administration of assets (specific claims).

In 1974 the department established the Office of Native Claims to act as the government's representative in negotiating claims settlements, to advise on policies relating to the development of claims and to coordinate the government's response to claim proposals.

Progress has been made toward settlement of claims based on traditional use and occupancy of land. The first settlement of such a claim was reached in November 1975 with the signing of the James Bay Agreement between the Cree and Inuit people of northern Quebec and the federal and Quebec governments. Negotiations were launched with the Indians of the Yukon Territory. Discussions also took place with the Nishga Indians of British Columbia. The Inuit of the Northwest Territories presented their claim proposal in February 1976. In addition, the Indians and Métis of the Northwest Territories indicated that they would submit a comprehensive claim in November 1976.

By June 1976, six specific claims which had been submitted to the department for negotiation were settled; 15 were not approved for negotiation, five were under negotiation, three were awaiting court decisions, 10 were under review or awaiting band action, and remedial measures were recommended for seven claims.

The Policy Planning and Research Branch conducts projects for the Indian and Eskimo Affairs Program, and coordinates similar projects of other branches. The branch is responsible for legislative planning, for formulating broad socio-economic policies, and for consulting on major policy issues with organizations that represent Canadian Indians. The Research Division conducts a small research program directly related to major policy issues and contracts with other agencies to carry out related work. It provides research services to the Indian and Eskimo Affairs Program and to other agencies conducting studies on Indian rights and treaties. This division also administers a program to finance the research, development and negotiation of Indian claims, under which $2.7 million is being allocated in the form of contributions and loans to claimants in the fiscal year 1976-77.

Inuit   3.2.3.2

Canada's 18,000 Inuit or Eskimo people, most of whom live in the Northwest Territories, Arctic Quebec and northern Labrador, are the concern of the federal Department of Indian Affairs and Northern Development, the government of the Northwest Territories and provincial governments.

From 1966 to 1975 the Northern Rental Housing Program provided 1,505 three-bedroom houses for the Inuit people. On April 1, 1975 the Northwest Territories Housing Corporation became responsible for Inuit housing, and new accommodation since then has been supplied under National Housing Act building programs.

Counselling units are maintained in Ottawa and Winnipeg for Inuit students attending various high school, technical school, college and university programs in southern Canada and a program has been instituted to enable parents to come south to visit their children.

The Department of National Defence offers employment at its station at Alert to civilian Inuit. A Student Centre for Inuit was established in Ottawa during

1974 and an Inuit Orientation Centre was planned for 1976. Inuit are involved in a departmental On-the-Job Training program to place them in middle management positions related to resource development and the environment. A special unit has been established in the North by the Public Service Commission to improve employment and career possibilities for northern native people.

The Inuit Tapirisat of Canada (Eskimo Brotherhood) was founded in 1971 with financial assistance from the Department of the Secretary of State. Affiliated with Inuit Tapirisat are the Committee of Original Peoples Entitlement (COPE), serving native people in the Mackenzie Delta and the Western Arctic, the Labrador Inuit Association (LIA), serving Inuit residents of Labrador, and the Northern Quebec Inuit Association (NQIA) for those Inuit living in Nouveau-Québec. Other regional associations in the Northwest Territories have been established by Inuit Tapirisat in the Central Arctic, Baffin and Keewatin regions to facilitate local participation in domestic affairs.

Of major significance for the Inuit is the enormous task which the Tapirisat undertook to prepare a presentation on their land claims to the Government of Canada. In early 1976 the organization presented the government *Nunavut,* a proposal for land claims settlement. In the preparation of this document, the Inuit Tapirisat of Canada engaged in considerable land claim research. Among the research documentation was the Inuit Land Use and Occupancy Study, an environmental, geographical and historical work which the government has agreed to publish.

Similar studies were undertaken by the Indian Brotherhood and the Métis Association in the Mackenzie region of the Northwest Territories, and by the Labrador Inuit Association. Northern native associations were provided financial assistance to enable them to participate in matters relating to northern development, such as the Mackenzie Valley Pipeline Enquiry.

Additional programs included the Inuit Language Commission, established to make recommendations regarding the revision and standardization of Inuktitut (the Eskimo language) orthographies; the publication of a layman's guide to Canadian law entitled *Inuit and the Law;* legal services centres in Frobisher Bay, NWT and Happy Valley, Labrador, to provide counsel and guidance for the Inuit; the support of an Inuit film-making society in Frobisher Bay formed to produce native language programs for broadcast on the CBC Northern Service television; and the development of a syllabic character typewriter element to meet the increasing need for written material in Inuktitut.

The work of Inuit artists and craftsmen is promoted by preparing interpretive exhibits for circulation to museums, universities and other institutions in Canada and abroad. Artists are protected against copyright infringement and competitive mass reproductions through a program of information to artists and the public, promotion of the use of the "Canada Eskimo Art" trademark and support of legal action where infringements occur. Information on art and culture is conveyed to the public through booklets, articles and lectures at art galleries.

The Inuit Cultural Institute based at Eskimo Point, NWT is a focal point for Inuit cultural concerns and programs related to traditional and present-day Inuit life. The institute also administers and oversees the work of the Inuit Language Commission.

As a result of the search for oil, gas and minerals in the Arctic, many Inuit are finding employment in petroleum and related industries. The petroleum industry reports for the 1974/1975 seasons that 761 northern residents accepted employment. Studies have been undertaken with a view to increasing native involvement in the mining industry which is showing an overall decline. However, many Inuit still live by their traditional skills of hunting, trapping and fishing. One of the most successful enterprises is the production and sale of Inuit artwork — stone, bone and ivory sculpture and graphics. The industry is expanding and cooperatives are run by the Inuit.

Departments, boards, commissions and corporations

In Canada the work of government is conducted by federal departments, special boards, commissions and Crown corporations. During the past quarter-century this last type of organization, the Crown corporation, has been used frequently for administering and managing many public services in which business enterprise and public accountability must be combined. The historical evolution of Crown corporations is described in the *1972 Canada Year Book* p 153. Part VIII of the Financial Administration Act (RSC 1970, c.F-10) provides a uniform system of financial and budgetary control and of accounting, auditing and reporting for Crown corporations. In addition, that legislation defines a Crown corporation as a corporation that is ultimately accountable, through a minister, to Parliament for the conduct of its affairs and establishes three classes of corporation — departmental, agency and proprietary.

Departmental corporations. A departmental corporation is defined as a Crown corporation that is a servant or agent of Her Majesty in right of Canada and is responsible for administrative, supervisory or regulatory services of a governmental nature. The following corporations are classified as departmental corporations in Schedule B to the Financial Administration Act:

Agricultural Stabilization Board
Atomic Energy Control Board
Director of Soldier Settlement
The Director, The Veterans' Land Act
Economic Council of Canada
Fisheries Prices Support Board
Medical Research Council
Municipal Development and Loan Board
National Museums of Canada
National Research Council
Science Council of Canada
Unemployment Insurance Commission.

Agency corporations. An agency corporation is defined as a Crown corporation that is an agent of Her Majesty in right of Canada and is responsible for the management of trading or service operations on a quasi-commercial basis or for the management of procurement, construction or disposal activities on behalf of Her Majesty in right of Canada. The following corporations are classified as agency corporations in Schedule C to the Financial Administration Act:

Atomic Energy of Canada Limited
Canadian Arsenals Limited
Canadian Commercial Corporation
Canadian Dairy Commission
Canadian Film Development Corporation
Canadian Livestock Feed Board
Canadian National (West Indies) Steamships Limited
Canadian Patents and Development Limited
Canadian Saltfish Corporation
Crown Assets Disposal Corporation
Defence Construction (1951) Limited
Loto Canada
National Battlefields Commission
National Capital Commission
National Harbours Board
Northern Canada Power Commission
Royal Canadian Mint
Uranium Canada Limited.

Proprietary corporations. A proprietary corporation is defined as a Crown corporation that is responsible for the management of lending or financial operations, or for the management of commercial or industrial operations involving the production of or dealing in goods and the supplying of services to the public, and is ordinarily required to conduct its operations without parliamentary appropriations. The following corporations are classified as proprietary corporations in Schedule D to the act:

Air Canada
Canada Deposit Insurance Corporation
Canadian Broadcasting Corporation
Cape Breton Development Corporation
Central Mortgage and Housing Corporation
Eldorado Aviation Limited
Eldorado Nuclear Limited
Export Development Corporation
Farm Credit Corporation
Federal Business Development Bank
Federal Mortgage Exchange Corporation
Freshwater Fish Marketing Corporation
National Railways, as defined in the Canadian National–Canadian Pacific Act
Northern Transportation Company Limited
Petro-Canada
Pilotage Authorities
   Atlantic Pilotage Authority
   Great Lakes Pilotage Authority
   Laurentian Pilotage Authority
   Pacific Pilotage Authority
St. Lawrence Seaway Authority
Seaway International Bridge Corporation Limited (formerly Cornwall International Bridge
   Company Limited)
Teleglobe Canada.

Departmental corporations are governed by the provisions of the Financial Administration Act that are applicable to departments generally. Agency and proprietary corporations are subject to the provisions of the Crown corporations part of the act; if there is any inconsistency between its provisions and those of any other act applicable to a corporation, the latter prevail. The same part provides for control and regulation of corporation budgets and bank accounts, turning over surplus money to the Receiver General, providing loans for limited working-capital purposes, awarding contracts and establishing reserves, keeping and auditing accounts, and preparing financial statements and reports for submission to Parliament through the appropriate minister.

A further form of control is exercised by Parliament through the power to vote financial assistance to a corporation, which may secure financing through parliamentary grants, loans or advances, by the issue of capital stock to the government, or by borrowings from the private sector of the general public, sometimes with a government guarantee. Several corporations finance all or a portion of their requirements from their own resources or earnings.

Before 1952 Crown corporations did not pay corporate income taxes. However, the Income Tax Act was amended, effective January 1, 1952, to make proprietary Crown corporations subject to the Income Tax Act in the same manner as any privately owned corporation; it is now possible to make a more realistic comparison of the financial statements of these Crown companies with those of private industry, and thus assess the relative efficiency of their operations. Crown corporations also pay provincial retail sales taxes, gasoline or motor vehicle fuel taxes and motor vehicle fees subject to the terms of the Crown Corporations (Provincial Taxes and Fees) Act of 1964.

Unclassified corporations. The following Crown corporations are not classified in the Financial Administration Act but are governed by their own acts of incorporation: the Bank of Canada, the Canada Council, the Canadian National Railways Securities Trust, the Canadian Wheat Board, and the National Arts Centre Corporation. The only provision of the Financial Administration Act to which they are subject is that governing the appointment of auditors, although the Governor in Council has the power in some instances to add an unclassified corporation to one of the schedules to the Financial Administration Act.

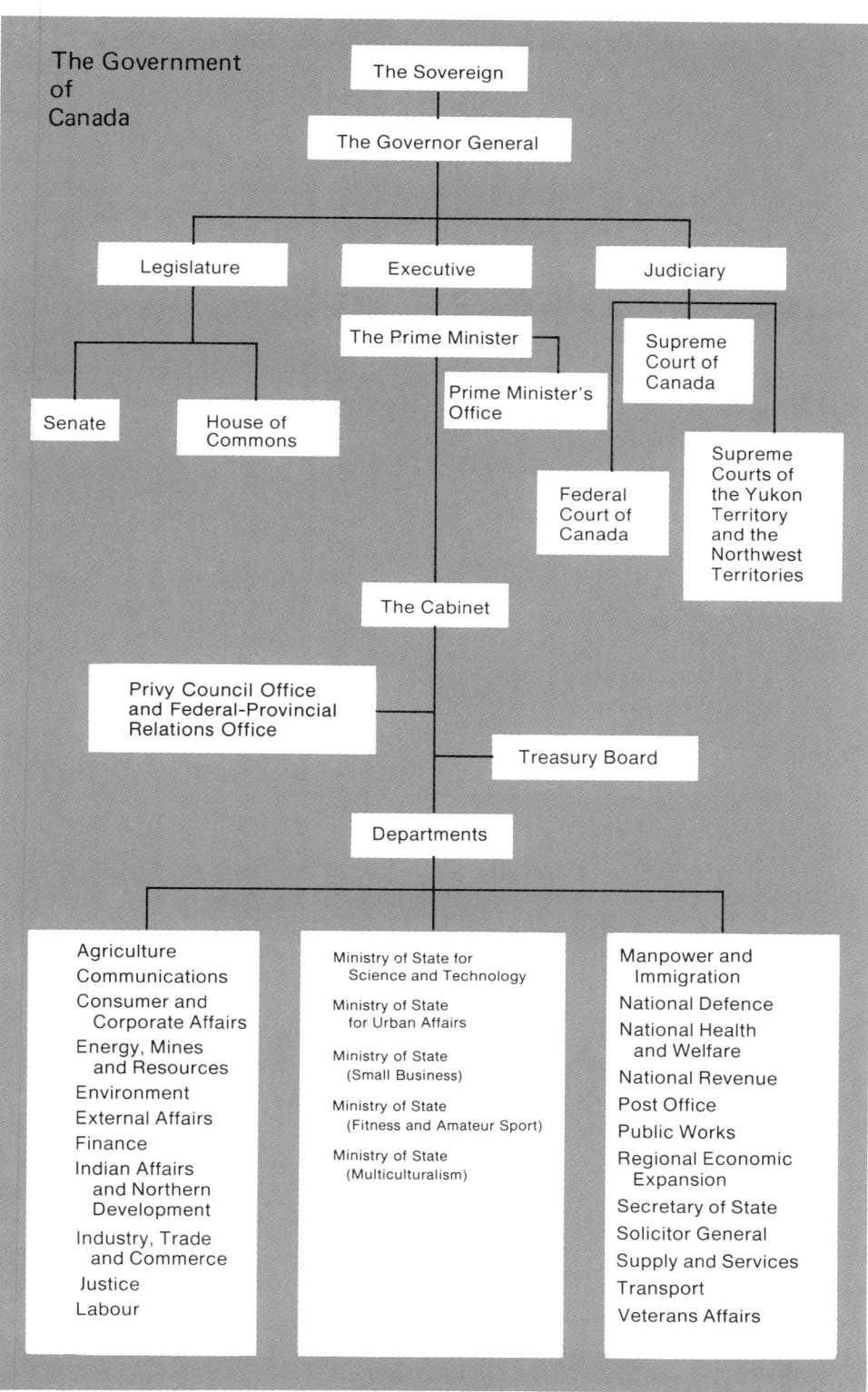

The Government of Canada

The Sovereign

The Governor General

Legislature — Executive — Judiciary

The Prime Minister

Prime Minister's Office

Senate   House of Commons

Supreme Court of Canada

Federal Court of Canada

Supreme Courts of the Yukon Territory and the Northwest Territories

The Cabinet

Privy Council Office and Federal-Provincial Relations Office

Treasury Board

Departments

Agriculture
Communications
Consumer and Corporate Affairs
Energy, Mines and Resources
Environment
External Affairs
Finance
Indian Affairs and Northern Development
Industry, Trade and Commerce
Justice
Labour

Ministry of State for Science and Technology
Ministry of State for Urban Affairs
Ministry of State (Small Business)
Ministry of State (Fitness and Amateur Sport)
Ministry of State (Multiculturalism)

Manpower and Immigration
National Defence
National Health and Welfare
National Revenue
Post Office
Public Works
Regional Economic Expansion
Secretary of State
Solicitor General
Supply and Services
Transport
Veterans Affairs

Other corporations. The government has participated in the establishment of some corporations that are not subject to the provisions of the Financial Administration Act and do not report to Parliament. The Canada Development Corporation, Telesat Canada and Panarctic Oils Ltd. are corporations of this type.

An alphabetical list of federal ministers and the departments and other agencies for which they report to Parliament follows (as in effect in January 1977). Brief descriptions of the functions of many of these government organizations and related agencies will be found in Appendix 1. The accompanying organization chart illustrates the federal structure to the departmental level.

Minister of Agriculture
Department of Agriculture
Agricultural Products Board
Agricultural Stabilization Board
Canadian Dairy Commission
Canadian Grain Commission
Canadian Livestock Feed Board
Crop Insurance Administration
Farm Credit Corporation
National Farm Products Marketing Council

Minister of Communications
Department of Communications
Canadian Radio-television and
    Telecommunications Commission
Teleglobe Canada

Minister of Consumer and Corporate Affairs
Department of Consumer and Corporate
    Affairs
Anti-Inflation Board
Canadian Consumer Council
Copyright Appeal Board
Patent Appeal Board
Restrictive Trade Practices Commission

Minister of Energy, Mines and Resources
Department of Energy, Mines and
    Resources
Atomic Energy Control Board
Atomic Energy of Canada Limited
Board of Examiners for Dominion Land
    Surveyors
Canadian Permanent Committee on
    Geographical Names
Columbia River Treaty Permanent
    Engineering Board
Eldorado Aviation Limited
Eldorado Nuclear Limited
Energy Supplies Allocation Board
Interprovincial and Territorial Boundary
    Commissions
National Energy Board
Oils and Gas Committee
Petro-Canada
Uranium Canada Limited

Secretary of State for External Affairs
Department of External Affairs
Canadian International Development
    Agency

Foreign Claims Commission
International Boundary Commission
International Development Research
    Centre
International Joint Commission
Roosevelt Campobello International Park
    Commission

Minister of Finance
Department of Finance
Anti-dumping Tribunal
Bank of Canada
Canada Deposit Insurance Corporation
Department of Insurance
Tariff Board

Minister of Fisheries and the Environment
Department of the Environment
Canadian Saltfish Corporation
Environmental Assessment Panel
Fisheries Prices Support Board
Fisheries Research Board of Canada
Freshwater Fish Marketing Corporation
International Fisheries Commissions

*Minister of Indian Affairs and Northern
    Development*
Department of Indian Affairs and Northern
    Development
Government of the Northwest Territories
Government of the Yukon Territory
Historic Sites and Monuments Board of
    Canada
National Battlefields Commission
Northern Canada Power Commission
Northwest Territories Water Board
Oil and Gas Committee
Yukon Territory Water Board

Minister of Industry, Trade and Commerce
Department of Industry, Trade and
    Commerce
Export Development Corporation
Federal Business Development Bank
Foreign Investment Review Agency
General Adjustment Assistance Board
Loto Canada
Machinery and Equipment Advisory Board
Metric Commission Canada
National Design Council

Standards Council of Canada
Statistics Canada
Textile and Clothing Board
Minister of State (Small Business)

Minister of Justice and Attorney General of
   Canada
Department of Justice
Anti-Inflation Appeal Tribunal
Law Reform Commission
Tax Review Board

Minister of Labour
Department of Labour
Canada Labour Relations Board
Merchant Seamen Compensation Board

Minister of Manpower and Immigration
Department of Manpower and Immigration
Canada Manpower and Immigration
   Council
Immigration Appeal Board
Unemployment Insurance Commission

Minister of National Defence
Department of National Defence
Defence Construction (1951) Limited
Defence Research Board
National Emergency Planning
   Establishment

Minister of National Health and Welfare
Department of National Health and Welfare
Advisory Council on the Status of Women
Medical Research Council
National Advisory Council on Fitness and
   Amateur Sport
National Council of Welfare
Office of the Coordinator, Status of Women
Pension Appeals Board
Minister of State (Fitness and Amateur Sport)

Minister of National Revenue
Department of National Revenue (Customs
   and Excise)
Department of National Revenue
   (Taxation)
Office of the Administrator, Anti-Inflation
   Act

Postmaster General
Post Office Department

Minister of Public Works
Department of Public Works

Minister of Regional Economic Expansion
Department of Regional Economic
   Expansion
Atlantic Development Council

Canadian Council on Rural Development
Cape Breton Development Corporation
Prairie Farm Rehabilitation Administration
Regional Development Incentives Board

Minister of State for Science and Technology
Ministry of State for Science and
   Technology
Canadian Patents and Development
   Limited
National Research Council of Canada
Science Council of Canada

Secretary of State of Canada
Department of the Secretary of State
Canada Council
Canadian Broadcasting Corporation
Canadian Film Development Corporation
National Arts Centre Corporation
National Film Board
National Library of Canada
National Museums of Canada
Public Archives of Canada

Solicitor General
Department of the Solicitor General
Canadian Penitentiary Service
National Parole Board
Royal Canadian Mounted Police
Correctional Investigator

Minister of Supply and Services
Department of Supply and Services
Canadian Arsenals Limited
Canadian Commercial Corporation
Canadian Government Specifications Board
Crown Assets Disposal Corporation
Royal Canadian Mint
Office of the Custodian of Enemy Property

Minister of Transport
Department of Transport
Air Canada
Canadian National Railways
Canadian Transport Commission
Canadian Wheat Board
Maritime Pollution Claims Fund
National Harbours Board
Northern Transportation Company Limited
Pilotage Authorities
   Atlantic Pilotage Authority
   Great Lakes Pilotage Authority, Limited
   Laurentian Pilotage Authority
   Pacific Pilotage Authority
St. Lawrence Seaway Authority
Seaway International Bridge Corporation
   Limited

President of Treasury Board
Treasury Board Secretariat

Minister of State for Urban Affairs
Ministry of State for Urban Affairs
Central Mortgage and Housing Corporation
National Capital Commission

Minister of Veterans Affairs
Department of Veterans Affairs
Army Benevolent Fund Board
Bureau of Pensions Advocates
Canadian Pension Commission
Pension Review Board
War Veterans Allowance Board

3.2.5   Federal Identity Program

The use of identifying titles as alternatives to the statute names of departments in this edition of the *Canada Year Book*, e.g. Labour Canada as well as the Department of Labour, is consistent with the policy of the Federal Identity Program. This program resulted from a conclusion of the 1969 Task Force on Government Information: visual communications of the Government of Canada were in urgent need of improvement. The heart of FIP is the consistent application of specific identifying symbols by all departments, agencies and other services of the Government of Canada. These symbols, organized into systematic format with distinctive typography and colour for each application, form the visual identity of the government.

Policy direction for the program emanates from the Cabinet Committee on Science, Culture and Information. Details of the program and the task of coordinating their implementation are the responsibility of the Treasury Board Secretariat's Administrative Standards Division. Treasury Board has set up an advisory committee to provide advice on the management of the program.

The departments, agencies and other government organizations to which the program applies are required not only to implement it, but to assist with its further development through active participation. These bodies are now in the process of adopting identifying titles where appropriate. These titles, such as Revenue Canada for Department of National Revenue and Health and Welfare Canada for Department of National Health and Welfare, will not replace the formal names which may be required for contracts, federal-provincial agreements and other legal applications. However, on such documents, the title shall appear as the principal identifying device.

3.3   Provincial and territorial governments

3.3.1   Provincial governments

In each of the provinces, the Queen is represented by a Lieutenant Governor appointed by the Governor General in Council. The Lieutenant Governor acts on the advice and with the assistance of his Ministry or Executive Council which is responsible to the legislature and resigns office under circumstances similar to those described concerning the federal government.

The legislature of each province is unicameral, consisting of the Lieutenant Governor and a Legislative Assembly. The Legislative Assembly is elected by the people for a statutory term of five years but may be dissolved within that period by the Lieutenant Governor on the advice of the Premier of the province.

Sections 92, 93 and 95 of the British North America Act, 1867 (Br. Stat. 1867, c.3 and amendments) assign legislative authority in certain areas to the provincial governments (see Chapter 2).

Details regarding qualifications and disqualifications of the franchise are contained in the Elections Act of each province. In general, every person at a specified age who is a Canadian citizen or (in certain provinces) other British subject, who complies with certain residence requirements in the province and the electoral district of polling and who falls under no statutory disqualifications, is entitled to vote. Voting privileges are given to persons in Prince Edward Island, New Brunswick, Quebec, Ontario, Manitoba, Saskatchewan and Alberta at the age of 18 and in Newfoundland, Nova Scotia and British Columbia at 19 years.

Newfoundland   3.3.1.1

The government of Newfoundland has a Lieutenant Governor, an Executive Council and a House of Assembly made up of 51 members elected for a term not to exceed five years. On July 4, 1974 the Honourable Gordon A. Winter became the Lieutenant Governor. The 37th Legislature in the history of Newfoundland and the ninth since Confederation, elected September 16, 1975, comprised 30 Progressive Conservatives, 16 Liberals, four members of the Liberal Reform party and one Independent Liberal.

The Premier receives a salary of $21,280 and Cabinet Ministers $13,440 per annum, plus a car allowance of $3,000, sessional indemnity of $8,960 and a travelling expense allowance of $4,480. Each member of the House of Assembly receives a sessional indemnity of $8,960 plus a travelling and expense allowance of $4,480. The Leader of the Opposition receives an additional allowance of $13,440.

The Executive Council of Newfoundland in January 1977

Premier, Hon. F.D. Moores

President of the Council, Hon. Dr. T.C. Farrell

Minister of Justice and Minister responsible for Intergovernmental Affairs, Hon. T. Alex Hickman

Minister of Finance and President of the Treasury Board, Hon. C.W. Doody

Minister of Education, Hon. Wallace House

Minister of Transportation and Communications, Hon. James Morgan

Minister of Social Services, Hon. R.C. Brett

Minister of Health and Minister of Rehabilitation and Recreation, Hon. Dr. Harold Collins

Minister of Industrial Development and Rural Development, Hon. John Lundrigan

Minister of Municipal Affairs and Housing, Hon. J.W. Dinn

Minister of Public Works and Services and Minister of Manpower and Industrial Relations, Hon. Joseph G. Rousseau

Minister of Consumer Affairs and Environment, Hon. A.J. Murphy

Minister of Fisheries, Hon. Walter Carter

Minister of Tourism, Hon. T.V. Hickey

Minister of Mines and Energy, Hon. A.B. Peckford

Minister of Forestry and Agriculture, Hon. Edward Maynard.

Prince Edward Island   3.3.1.2

The government of Prince Edward Island consists of a Lieutenant Governor, an Executive Council and a Legislative Assembly. The Honourable Gordon L. Bennett was appointed Lieutenant Governor effective October 24, 1974. The Legislative Assembly has 32 members from 16 electoral districts who may serve for a statutory term not exceeding five years. Each district elects two representatives to the Legislature. The 53rd Assembly elected April 29, 1974 consisted of 26 Liberals and six Progressive Conservatives; as at October 1, 1976 party standings had changed to 23 Liberals and five Progressive Conservatives with four seats vacant.

A member of the Assembly receives $7,000 per annum and an additional $3,500 tax-free for travelling and other expenses incurred in attending sessions and representing his district. In addition the Premier receives a salary of $24,000, a Cabinet Minister $14,500 and a Minister without portfolio $14,500. The Speaker of the Assembly is paid an additional indemnity of $2,000 and his tax-free allowance is $1,000; higher sessional indemnities and allowances are also available to the Deputy Speaker in the amounts of $1,000 and $500, respectively, and to the Leader of the Opposition in the amount of $10,000. All indemnities and allowances accrue from the date of election to the legislature and are paid monthly. No sessional indemnity or expenses are paid for any special session of the Legislature.

The Executive Council of Prince Edward Island in January 1977

Premier, President of the Executive Council, Minister of Justice, Attorney and Advocate General, and Minister responsible for Cultural Affairs, Hon. Alexander B. Campbell

Minister of Development and Minister of Industry and Commerce, Hon. John H. Maloney

Minister of Public Works and Minister of Highways, Hon. Bruce L. Stewart

Provincial Secretary, Hon. Arthur J. MacDonald

Minister of Education and Minister of Finance, Hon. W. Bennett Campbell

Minister of Municipal Affairs, Minister of Tourism, Parks and Conservation and Minister of the Environment, Hon. Gilbert Clements

Minister of Health and Minister of Social Services, Hon. Catherine Callbeck

Minister of Fisheries and Minister of Labour, Hon. George Henderson

Minister of Agriculture and Forestry, Hon. A.E. Ings

Minister without Portfolio (and responsible for the PEI Housing Corporation), Hon. George Proud.

3.3.1.3   Nova Scotia

The government of Nova Scotia consists of a Lieutenant Governor, an Executive Council and a House of Assembly. The Honourable Clarence L. Gosse became Lieutenant Governor on October 1, 1973. The Legislature has 46 members elected for a maximum term of five years. On April 2, 1974, 31 Liberals, 12 Progressive Conservatives and three New Democrats were elected to the province's 51st Legislature and 28th since Confederation.

Each member of the House of Assembly is paid an annual indemnity of $9,600 and an annual expense allowance of $4,800. In addition to the amounts to which they are entitled under the House of Assembly Act, the Premier of the province receives an annual salary of $25,000, all other Cabinet members $21,000 or such lesser salary as the Governor in Council may determine, the Leader of the Opposition $21,000, the Speaker $11,000, the Deputy Speaker $3,500, and any member occupying the recognized position of leader of a recognized party other than the Premier and Leader of the Opposition $6,000.

The Executive Council of Nova Scotia in January 1977

Premier and President of the Executive Council, Hon. Gerald A. Regan

Deputy Premier and Minister of Finance, Hon. Peter Nicholson

Minister of Recreation, Hon. A. Garnet Brown

Attorney General and Minister in charge of administration of the Human Rights Act, Hon. Leonard L. Pace

Minister of Public Works and Minister in charge of administration of the Liquor Control Act, Hon. Benoit Comeau

Minister of Mines and Minister in charge of the Nova Scotia Energy Council, Hon. J. William Gillis

Minister of Public Health, Minister in charge of administration of the Drug Dependency Act and Registrar General, Hon. Maynard C. MacAskill

Minister of Highways, Hon. J. Fraser Mooney

Minister of Municipal Affairs, Hon. Glen M. Bagnell

Minister of Tourism, Hon. Maurice E. DeLory

Minister of Agriculture and Chairman of the Treasury Board, Hon. John Hawkins

Minister of Development and Minister in charge of administration of the Civil Service Act, the Civil Service Joint Council Act and the Research Foundation Corporation Act, Hon. Alexander M. Cameron

Provincial Secretary and Minister in charge of administration of the Communications and Information Act, Hon. Harold M. Huskilson

Minister of Fisheries, Hon. Daniel S. Reid

Minister of Labour and Minister in charge of administration of the Housing Development Act, Hon. Walter R. Fitzgerald

Minister of Social Services and Minister responsible for Status of Women, Hon. William M. MacEachern

Minister of Education, Hon. George M. Mitchell

Minister of Lands and Forests, Minister of the Environment and Minister in charge of administration of the EMO (NS) Act and Regulations, Hon. Vincent J. MacLean

Minister of Consumer Affairs and Minister in charge of administration of the Residential Tenancies Act, Hon. Guy A.C. Brown.

3.3.1.4   New Brunswick

The government of New Brunswick has a Lieutenant Governor, an Executive Council and a Legislative Assembly. The Honourable H.J. Robichaud was sworn in October 8, 1971, as Lieutenant Governor. The Legislature elected November 18, 1974, the 48th in New Brunswick's history and 21st since Confederation, had

58 members, including 33 Progressive Conservatives and 25 Liberals, elected for a statutory term not to exceed five years.

The Premier receives $25,000 per annum in addition to the salary for any other portfolio he may hold. Each Cabinet Minister is paid $16,000; each member of the Legislative Assembly receives $8,000 and a $2,500 allowance for expenses. The Leader of the Opposition receives an additional $16,000. The Speaker and Deputy Speaker are paid $5,000 and $2,500, respectively, in addition to the regular indemnity.

The Executive Council of New Brunswick in January 1977

Premier, Hon. Richard Hatfield

Provincial Secretary and Minister of Justice, Hon. Paul S. Creaghan

Chairman of the New Brunswick Electric Power Commission, Hon. G.W.N. Cockburn

Minister of Finance, Hon. Lawrence Garvie

Chairman of Treasury Board, Hon. Jean Maurice Simard

Minister of Fisheries, Hon. Omer Léger

Minister of Supply and Services, Hon. Harold Fanjoy

Minister of Transportation, Hon. Wilfred Bishop

Minister of Natural Resources, Hon. Roland Boudreau

Minister of Agriculture and Rural Development, Hon. Malcolm MacLeod

Minister of Health, Hon. Brenda Robertson

Minister of Social Services, Hon. Leslie Hull

Minister of Labour and Manpower, Hon. Rodman E. Logan

Minister of Education, Hon. Charles Gallagher

Minister of Municipal Affairs, Hon. Horace B. Smith

Minister of Commerce and Development, Hon. Gerald S. Merrithew

Minister of Youth, Recreation and Cultural Resources, Hon. Jean-Pierre Ouellet

Minister of Tourism and Environment, Hon. Fernand Dubé.

Quebec

3.3.1.5

In Quebec, legislative and executive powers are vested in the National Assembly and the Executive Council. As the representative of the Crown, the Lieutenant Governor, the Honourable Hugues Lapointe, plays a role in the functioning of both branches.

The National Assembly consists of 110 members elected for a maximum term of five years. Party standings in January 1977, following the general election of November 15, 1976, were as follows: Parti Québécois 71, Liberals 26, Union nationale 11, Ralliement des créditistes, one, and Independent, one.

All members receive an annual indemnity of $24,500 and a tax-free representation allowance of $7,000. In addition, the Executive Council Act and the Legislative Assembly Act provide for additional taxable allowances for the Prime Minister ($36,750), ministers ($26,950), ministers without portfolio ($24,500), the Speaker of the National Assembly ($26,950), deputy speakers ($12,250), parliamentary assistants ($7,350), the Leader of the official Opposition ($26,950), leaders of other recognized parties ($11,025), the House Leader of the official Opposition ($11,025), house leaders of other recognized parties ($9,080), Chief Government Whip ($11,025), Chief Whip of the official Opposition ($7,350), whips of other recognized parties and deputy whips ($6,125) and the chairmen of elected commissions ($3,675). Internal regulations also provide for allowances for specified travelling by a member, for maintaining an office in his constituency and for a second residence in Quebec in cases where the member represents a riding outside the capital area.

Members of the Executive Council of Quebec in January 1977

Prime Minister, Hon. René Lévesque

Vice-Prime Minister and Minister of Education, Hon. Jacques-Yvan Morin

House Leader and Minister of State for Parliamentary Reform, Hon. Robert Burns

Minister of Intergovernmental Affairs, Hon. Claude Morin

Minister of Finance and Revenue Minister, Hon. Jacques Parizeau

Minister of State for Cultural Development, Hon. Camille Laurin

Minister of State for Social Development, Hon. Pierre Marois

Minister of State for Economic Development, Hon. Bernard Landry

Minister of State for Planning, Hon. Jacques
  Léonard
Minister of Justice, Hon. Marc-André
  Bédard
Minister of Transport, Public Works and
  Supply, Hon. Lucien Lessard
Minister responsible for the Environment,
  Hon. Marcel Léger
Minister responsible for Youth, Sports and
  Leisure, Hon. Claude Charron
Minister responsible for Energy, Hon. Guy
  Joron
Minister of Consumer Affairs, Hon. Lise
  Payette
Minister of Agriculture, Hon. Jean Garon
Minister of Social Affairs, Hon. Denis
  Lazure

Minister of Municipal Affairs, Hon. Guy
  Tardif
Minister of Labour and Manpower and
  Minister of Immigration, Hon. Jacques
  Couture
Minister of Cultural Affairs and Minister of
  Communications, Hon. Louis O'Neill
Minister of Natural Resources and Minister
  of Lands and Forests, Hon. Yves Bérubé
Minister of Industry and Commerce, Hon.
  Rodrigue Tremblay
Minister of Tourism, Fish and Game, Hon.
  Yves Duhaime
Public Service Minister and Vice-President
  of the Treasury Board, Hon. Denis De
  Belleval.

3.3.1.6 Ontario

The government of Ontario consists of a Lieutenant Governor, an Executive Council and a Legislative Assembly. In April 1974 the Honourable Pauline McGibbon took office as Lieutenant Governor. The Legislative Assembly is composed of 125 members elected for a statutory term not to exceed five years. At the general election September 18, 1975, 51 Progressive Conservatives, 38 New Democrats and 36 Liberals were elected to the province's 30th Legislature.

In addition to the regular ministries are the following provincial agencies: the Niagara Parks Commission, the Ontario Municipal Board, Ontario Hydro, the St. Lawrence Development Commission, the Ontario Northland Transportation Commission, the Liquor Control Board and the Liquor Licence Board.

Under the provisions of the Legislative Assembly Act (RSO 1970, c.240 as amended) each member of the Assembly is paid an annual indemnity of $15,000 and an expense allowance of $7,500. In addition, the Speaker receives a special annual indemnity of $9,000, the Chairman of the Committee of the Whole House $5,000 and the Leader of the Opposition a salary of $18,000. Each member of the Cabinet having charge of a ministry receives the ordinary indemnity as a member of the Legislature in addition to his salary as a Minister of the Crown. The salary provided in the Executive Council Act for the Premier is $25,000 and for a Cabinet Minister having charge of a ministry $18,000. The Leader of the Opposition receives a representation allowance of $3,000 per annum. Each Minister without portfolio receives an annual salary of $7,500.

The Executive Council of Ontario in January 1977

Premier and President of the Council, Hon.
  William G. Davis
Minister of Housing, Hon. John Rhodes
Provincial Secretary for Resources
  Development, Hon. Donald R. Irvine
Attorney General, Hon. Roy McMurtry
Minister of Revenue, Hon. Arthur K. Meen
Minister of Agriculture and Food, Hon.
  William Newman
Minister of the Environment, Hon. George
  A. Kerr
Minister of Community and Social Services,
  Hon. James Taylor
Provincial Secretary for Justice and Solicitor
  General, Hon. John P. MacBeth
Minister of Education, Hon. Thomas L.
  Wells
Minister of Labour, Hon. Bette Stephenson

Treasurer of Ontario and Minister of
  Economics and Intergovernmental
  Affairs, Hon. W. Darcy McKeough
Minister of Correctional Services, Hon.
  John Smith
Minister of Transportation and
  Communications, Hon. James Snow
Minister of Natural Resources, Hon. Leo
  Bernier
Chairman of the Management Board of
  Cabinet, Hon. James Auld
Minister of Government Services, Hon.
  Margaret Scrivener
Minister of Health, Hon. Frank S. Miller
Minister of Consumer and Commercial
  Relations, Hon. Sidney B. Handleman
Minister of Colleges and Universities, Hon.
  Harry Parrott

Provincial Secretary for Social
Development, Hon. Margaret Birch
Minister of Industry and Tourism, Hon.
Claude Bennett
Minister of Energy, Hon. Dennis R.
Timbrell

Minister of Culture and Recreation, Hon.
Robert S. Welch
Chairman of the Cabinet and Minister
without portfolio, Hon. René Brunelle
Minister without portfolio, Hon. L.C.
Henderson.

Manitoba   3.3.1.7

In addition to a Lieutenant Governor, Manitoba has an Executive Council
composed of 17 members and a Legislative Assembly of 57 members elected for a
maximum term of five years. The Honourable Francis L. Jobin became
Lieutenant Governor on March 15, 1976. In the general election June 28, 1973,
31 New Democrats, 21 Progressive Conservatives and five Liberals were elected
to the 30th Legislature. After two by-elections in June 1975, the NDP held 31
seats, Progressive Conservatives 22, and Liberals three. One seat was vacant.

The Premier of the province is paid a salary of $16,600 a year and each of the
other members of the Cabinet $15,600. Members of the Legislature are each paid
a sessional indemnity of $11,568 and a tax-free expense allowance of $5,784 for
the fiscal year ended March 31, 1977. Each member attending the session receives
an additional allowance of $900 for expenses incidental to the discharge of his
duties as member. The Leader of the Opposition is paid $15,600. The Speaker of
the Legislative Assembly receives an additional indemnity of $5,000 and
expenses not exceeding $1,000 in aggregate. The Deputy Speaker receives an
additional indemnity of $2,500 and expenses not exceeding $500 in aggregate.
Members required to live away from home receive a per diem allowance of $25
from the opening of the session to prorogation excepting days during an
adjournment of the Assembly for a period of four or more continuous days.

The Executive Council of Manitoba in January 1977

Premier, President of the Council, Minister
responsible for the Manitoba Hydro Act,
and Minister of Dominion-Provincial
Relations, Hon. Edward Schreyer
Minister of Labour, Minister charged with
the administration of the Civil Service
Superannuation Act and the Public
Servants Insurance Act, Hon. A.R.
Paulley
Minister of Mines, Resources and
Environmental Management and
Minister responsible for the Manitoba
Development Corporation Act, Hon.
Sidney Green
Minister of Agriculture, Hon. Samuel
Uskiw
Minister of Finance and Minister of Urban
Affairs, Hon. Saul A. Miller
Minister of Consumer and Corporate
Affairs, Minister of Cooperative
Development and Minister responsible
for the Manitoba Telephone System and
Communications, Hon. René Toupin
Minister of Industry and Commerce and
Minister responsible for the Manitoba
Housing and Renewal Corporation, Hon.
Leonard Evans
Minister of Highways and Minister
responsible for the Manitoba Public
Insurance Corporation, Hon. Peter
Burtniak

Attorney General, Keeper of the Great Seal
and Minister responsible for the
administration of the Liquor Control Act,
Hon. Howard Pawley
Minister of Continuing Education, Minister
of Manpower and Minister of Tourism,
Recreation and Cultural Affairs, Hon.
Ben Hanuschak
Minister of Public Works, Hon. Russell
Doern
Minister of Health and Social Development
and Minister responsible for Manitoba
Lotteries Act, Hon. L.L. Desjardins
Minister of Northern Affairs, Hon. Ronald
McBryde
Minister of Education and Chairman of
Management Committee of Cabinet,
Hon. Ian Turnbull
Minister of Municipal Affairs and Minister
responsible for the Civil Service Act,
Hon. Billie Uruski
Minister responsible for Corrections and
Rehabilitative Services, Hon. Joseph R.
Boyce
Minister of Renewable Resources and
Transportation Services, Hon. Harvey
Bostrom.

3.3.1.8   Saskatchewan

The government of Saskatchewan consists of a Lieutenant Governor, an Executive Council and a Legislative Assembly. On March 3, 1976 the Honourable George Porteous became Lieutenant Governor. The statutory number of members of the Legislative Assembly is 61, elected for a maximum term of five years. As a result of the general election June 11, 1975, 39 New Democrats, 15 Liberals and seven Progressive Conservatives were elected to form Saskatchewan's 18th Legislature.

The Premier receives $21,380 and each Cabinet Minister $16,200 annually in addition to a sessional indemnity and allowance. The Leader of the Opposition receives $16,200 plus an office allowance of $35,000 per annum. The leader of a third party receives $8,100 plus an office allowance of $17,500 per annum, the Speaker $6,050 and the Deputy Speaker $3,630.

Each member of the Legislature is paid an annual indemnity of $7,260, an expense allowance of $6,480 and a sessional allowance of $3,025. Each of the members for the two northernmost constituencies of Athabasca and Cumberland receives an $8,260 annual indemnity and a $6,730 expense allowance. Government and Opposition Whips are paid an annual allowance of $1,210 each and legislative secretaries an annual allowance of $3,000 each. The third party whip is paid an annual allowance of $605.

The Executive Council of Saskatchewan in January 1977

Premier and President of the Council, Hon. A.E. Blakeney
Attorney General, Hon. R.J. Romanow
Minister of Industry and Commerce, Hon. N. Vickar
Minister of Finance, Hon. W.E. Smishek
Minister of Labour, Hon. G.T. Snyder
Minister of Government Services and Minister of Cooperation and Cooperative Development, Hon. E.B. Shillington
Minister of Northern Saskatchewan, Hon. G.R. Bowerman
Minister of the Environment and Minister of Telephones, Hon. N.E. Byers
Minister of Continuing Education and Minister in charge of the Saskatchewan Transportation Company, Hon. D.L. Faris

Minister of Municipal Affairs, Hon. G.S. MacMurchy
Minister of Highways and Transportation, Hon. E. Kramer
Provincial Secretary, Hon. E.L. Cowley
Minister of Culture and Youth and Minister of Education, Hon. E.L. Tchorzewski
Minister of Consumer Affairs, Hon. E.C. Whelan
Minister of Health, Hon. W.A. Robbins
Minister of Mineral Resources, Hon. J.R. Messer
Minister of Agriculture, Hon. Edgar E. Kaeding
Minister of Tourism and Renewable Resources, Hon. A.S. Matsalla
Minister of Social Services, Hon. H.H. Rolfes.

3.3.1.9   Alberta

In addition to the Lieutenant Governor (since April 1974 the Honourable Ralph Steinhauer) the government of Alberta is composed of an Executive Council and a Legislative Assembly of 75 members elected for a maximum of five years. On March 26, 1975, 69 Progressive Conservatives, four members of the Social Credit party, one of the New Democratic Party and one Independent-Social Credit member were elected to form the 18th Legislature.

Each member of the Legislative Assembly receives a sessional indemnity of $10,790, a $5,395 expense allowance and $40 for each day during the session when the member is necessarily absent from his ordinary place of residence. In addition to the indemnity and expense allowance, the Speaker receives a salary of $9,592 and the Deputy Speaker $5,995. The salary of the Leader of the Opposition, in addition to the indemnity and expense allowance, is $26,378. The Speaker, Deputy Speaker and Leader of the Opposition also receive $40 for each day during the session when they are necessarily absent from their ordinary place of residence. In addition to the sessional indemnity and allowance the Premier receives $32,373, other Ministers $26,378 and Ministers without portfolio $19,184.

The Executive Council of Alberta in January 1977

Premier and President of the Executive Council, Hon. Peter Lougheed

Deputy Premier and Minister of Transportation, Hon. Hugh M. Horner

Minister of Energy and Natural Resources, Hon. Donald R. Getty

Minister of Federal and Intergovernmental Affairs and Government House Leader, Hon. Louis D. Hyndman

Minister of Hospitals and Medical Care, Hon. Gordon T.W. Miniely

Provincial Treasurer, Hon. C. Mervin Leitch

Minister of Labour, Hon. Neil S. Crawford

Minister of Advanced Education and Manpower, Hon. Bert Hohol

Minister of Housing and Public Works, Hon. William J. Yurko

Minister of Environment, Hon. David J. Russell

Attorney General, Hon. James L. Foster

Solicitor General, Hon. Roy A. Farran

Minister of Utilities and Telephones, Hon. Allan A. Warrack

Minister of Government Services, also responsible for Culture, Hon. Horst A. Schmid

Minister of Social Services and Community Health, Hon. Helen Hunley

Minister of Business Development and Tourism, Hon. Robert W. Dowling

Minister of Recreation, Parks and Wildlife, Hon. J.A. Adair

Minister of Municipal Affairs, Hon. Dick Johnston

Minister of Consumer and Corporate Affairs, Hon. Graham Harle

Minister of Agriculture, Hon. Marvin Moore

Minister of Education, Hon. Julian Koziac

Minister without portfolio (Native Affairs), Hon. Robert Bogle

Minister without portfolio, Hon. Stu McCrae

Associate Minister for Energy and Natural Resources in charge of Public Lands and Minister without portfolio, Hon. Dallas Schmidt.

British Columbia

3.3.1.10

The government of British Columbia consists of a Lieutenant Governor, an Executive Council and a Legislative Assembly. On March 19, 1973 the Honourable Walter Stewart Owen took office as the Lieutenant Governor. The Legislative Assembly has 55 members who are elected for a term not to exceed five years. As a result of the December 11, 1975 election, 34 Social Credit members, 19 New Democrats, one Liberal and one Progressive Conservative were elected to the Assembly.

Each member of the Executive Council and the Legislative Assembly receives an annual allowance of $16,000 and an annual expense allowance of $8,000. In addition, the Premier is paid an annual salary of $28,000, each Cabinet Minister (with portfolio) $24,000 and each member of the Executive Council without portfolio $21,000. The Leader of the Opposition and the Speaker receive special expense allowances of $19,000; the Deputy Speaker and the Leader of a recognized political party, $8,500. These salaries and expense allowances were reduced by 10% for the period April 1, 1976 to March 31, 1977.

The Executive Council of British Columbia in January 1977

Premier, President of the Council, Hon. William R. Bennett

Provincial Secretary, Deputy Premier and Minister of Travel Industry, Hon. Grace M. McCarthy

Minister of Finance, Hon. Evan Wolfe

Attorney General, Hon. Garde B. Gardom

Minister of Health, Hon. Robert H. McClelland

Minister of Human Resources, Hon. William N. Vander Zalm

Minister of Agriculture, Hon. James J. Hewitt

Minister of Economic Development, Hon. Donald M. Phillips

Minister of Labour, Hon. L. Allan Williams

Minister of Mines and Petroleum Resources, Hon. James R. Chabot

Minister of Forests, Hon. Thomas M. Waterland

Minister of Municipal Affairs and Housing, Hon. Hugh A. Curtis

Minister of Education, Hon. Pat L. McGeer

Minister of Environment, Hon. James A. Nielsen

Minister of Consumer and Corporate Affairs, Hon. Kenneth Rafe Mair

Minister of Energy, Transport and Communication, Hon. John (Jack) Davis

Minister of Highways and Public Works, Hon. Alex V. Fraser

Minister of Recreation and Conservation, Hon. Robert Samuel Bawlf.

3.3.2   Territorial governments

3.3.2.1   Yukon Territory

The constitution for the government of the Yukon Territory is based on two federal statutes: the Yukon Act (RSC 1970, c.Y-2) and the Government Organization Act (SC 1966, c.25). The Yukon Act provides for a Commissioner as head of government and for a legislative body called the Yukon Legislative Council. Under the Government Organization Act, the Minister of Indian Affairs and Northern Development is responsible (with the Governor in Council) for directing the Commissioner in the administration of the territory.

The executive level of the Yukon government consists of the Commissioner and Executive Committee. The Office of the Commissioner incorporates several functions: head of the territorial government and senior representative of the Department of Indian Affairs and Northern Development in the Yukon Territory. In addition, the Commissioner performs duties similar to those of a Lieutenant Governor in relation to the Legislature.

In administering the territorial government the Commissioner is assisted by the Executive Committee, which is modelled on a cabinet structure. The committee is composed of the Commissioner, as chairman, with two Assistant Commissioners and three Councillors as members. Each of the members is assigned portfolios by the chairman.

The territorial government forgoes its taxing authority on private and corporate incomes and collection of corporate taxes and succession duties in deference to annual federal-territorial financial agreements. Under these agreements the federal government contributes the funds necessary to cover the deficit arising from the forecast of revenues available to the territory and the forecast cost of services to be provided.

Administration. The territorial public service, comprising approximately 1,200 employees, is organized into 11 conventional administrative departments and a number of special service departments. Whitehorse is the administrative centre of the government. A few departments have necessary regional postings and territorial agents represent the government in outlying communities.

Health services and land are administered jointly by the territorial and federal governments. Health services are administered and operated by the Yukon Hospital Insurance/Health Care Insurance Services Department in conjunction with the Department of National Health and Welfare. The program will eventually be transferred to the territorial department.

Certain areas have been designated to the Commissioner for administration under the Territory's Lands Ordinance. The remaining land is under the jurisdiction of the Department of Indian Affairs and Northern Development.

In addition to these shared responsibilities, the federal government, through the Department of Indian Affairs and Northern Development, retains control of the natural resources of the Yukon, except game. Local administration is carried out by federal public servants.

Legislature. The Yukon Act delineates the jurisdiction of the Council. It is like those of provincial assemblies with two exceptions: matters touching on natural resources, except legislation concerning the preservation of game, are reserved to the federal government, and budgetary matters are reserved to the Commissioner. Council is called into session and prorogued by the Commissioner.

Legislative authority for the Yukon is vested in the Commissioner in Council. All bills must be approved by Council and be assented to by the Commissioner before becoming law. As in other jurisdictions, the Governor in Council may disallow any ordinance within one year. Ordinances are printed on a sessional basis and consolidated annually.

Amendments to the Yukon Act passed by Parliament in 1974 provided for an immediate expansion of the membership of Council from seven to 12 and for future expansion to 20 members. Members are elected for a four-year term of office. The Council nominates three of its members to the Executive Committee who will each administer one of the following portfolios: Education, Local Government, and Health, Welfare and Rehabilitation.

The Council meets at least twice a year usually in the territorial capital, Whitehorse. A daily record of Council sessions is published under the authority of the Speaker and the Queen's Printer.

Commissioner, Council and Council staff of the Yukon Territory in January 1977

Commissioner, A.M. Pearson

Assistant Commissioner (Executive), P.J. Gillespie

Assistant Commissioner (Administrative), M.E. Miller

Clerk of Council, L.J. Adams

Legal Adviser to the Commissioner and Council, P. O'Donoghue

Executive Committee: A.M. Pearson, chairman; P.J. Gillespie, M.E. Miller, F. Whyard, D. Lang, J.K. McKinnon, members; L.J. Adams, secretary

Members of Council: A. Berger, B. Fleming, J. Hibberd, D. Lang, E. Millard, S. McCall, W. Lengerke, D. Taylor, F. Whyard, G. McIntyre, J.K. McKinnon, H. Watson.

Northwest Territories   3.3.2.2

The Northwest Territories Act (RSC 1970, c.N-22) provides for an executive, legislative and judicial structure. The Commissioner is the chief executive officer, appointed by the federal government and responsible for the administration of the Northwest Territories under the direction of the Minister of Indian Affairs and Northern Development. In practice, all major policy decisions are taken on the advice of the Council of the Northwest Territories. The Commissioner can spend funds only to the extent voted by Council and all new revenue measures are subject to Council approval. Normally the Commissioner obtains federal approval of proposed legislation and budgetary measures before submitting them to Council.

The Council of the Northwest Territories consists of 15 elected members and has a life of four years. It meets at least twice a year, usually for three weeks at a January session and two weeks at a spring session, but more often if required. A Clerk of Council and a legal adviser provide the main administrative assistance. Debates are recorded verbatim.

The Northwest Territories Act gives the Territorial Council authority to legislate in most areas of government activity except for natural resources other than game; these are reserved to the federal government. Legislation must receive three readings and have the assent of the Commissioner. The federal government may disallow any ordinance within one year. The Commissioner proposes most legislation but private members' bills are allowed, except for money matters, which are the prerogative of the Commissioner. Besides draft legislation, the Council gives considerable time to policy papers in which the Commissioner seeks advice or authority to take a particular course of action.

Parliament approved significant legislation in 1974 for the political development of the Northwest Territories. Amendments to the Northwest Territories Act increased the number of elected members of the Territorial Council from 10 to 15 and eliminated appointed members. Elections were held in March 1975 for the first entirely elected Council. The new Council selects its speaker from among its members; previously the Commissioner was the presiding officer. Council also nominates two other members to the Executive Committee along with the Commissioner, who is chairman, the Deputy Commissioner and an Assistant Commissioner. This committee advises the Commissioner on broad policy matters and acts as a consultative body for him.

The Minister of Justice is the Attorney General of the Northwest Territories under the Criminal Code of Canada, with responsibility for criminal but not for civil matters or the constitution or organization of the courts (see Chapter 2). Law enforcement is provided by the Royal Canadian Mounted Police.

Administration. In 1963 a full-time Commissioner was appointed and charged with building up a territorial administration located initially in Ottawa. In September 1967 the Commissioner and about 50 staff members moved to Yellowknife and assumed responsibility for the game management service, municipal affairs, the issuing of all licences, tax collection and the operation of the liquor system (already staffed by territorial contract employees). Operational responsibility for other government services was transferred from federal to territorial control in the Mackenzie District on April 1, 1969, and in the Eastern Arctic on April 1, 1970. The territorial government is structured to carry out its administration through five program and six service departments, each under the direction of a senior public servant reporting to one member of the Executive. The field staff is organized into four regions with regional directors at Fort Smith, Inuvik and Frobisher Bay and a district director at Rankin Inlet.

Continuing federal responsibility. The Government Organization Act charges the Minister of Indian Affairs and Northern Development with responsibility for the development of the North and for the general coordination of federal activities in the area. Other federal government agencies, such as the Northern Health Service of the Department of National Health and Welfare and the Royal Canadian Mounted Police, are responsible for health and police services with the territorial government sharing their costs. The Ministry of Transport operates mainline airports throughout the North; the Canadian Broadcasting Corporation provides special shortwave northern broadcasts and maintains local stations in the territories. Federal cost-shared national assistance programs, within the competence of the territorial government, are available to it on the same conditions as they are to the provinces.

Extensive financial assistance is given to the territorial government under special federal-territorial agreements, which usually cover a period of five years. These agreements allocate the financial responsibility of each government for the provision of services in the territories and fix the amount of the federal financial payments to the territorial government for the life of the agreement.

Commissioner, Council and Council staff of the Northwest Territories in January 1977

Commissioner, S.M. Hodgson
Deputy Commissioner, J.H. Parker
Clerk of the Council, W.H. Remnant
Legal Adviser, Ms. P.Flieger
Members of the Council: Bill Lyall, Ipeelee Kilabuk, Mark Evaluarjuk, Don M.

Stewart, Ludy Pudluk, Tom Butters, Peter Ernerk, William Lafferty, Arnold McCallum, Bryan Pearson, John Steen, Dave Nickerson, Peter Fraser, Richard Whitford.

3.4   Royal Commissions and Commissions of Inquiry

3.4.1   Federal commissions

Royal Commissions, now generally called Commissions of Inquiry, established up to April 30, 1975 under Part I of the Inquiries Act are given in previous editions of the *Canada Year Book* beginning with the 1940 edition. The following list presents the federal commissions established between that date and June 28, 1976, and the name of the chief commissioner or chairman.

Financial Claims Commission, Hon. Thane A. Campbell
Bilingual Districts Advisory Board, Paul Fox
Inquiry into Rail Needs of Manitoba, Saskatchewan and Alberta, Emmett Hall
Inquiry into Costs and Revenue of Grain (Rail) Traffic, Carl M. Snavely
Commission of Inquiry into Financial Controls of Air Canada, Hon. Mr. Justice W.Z. Estey
Inquiry into Crash of Lockheed Aircraft near Rea Point, NWT, Judge W.A. Stevenson
Commission of Inquiry into Bilingual Air Traffic Services in Quebec, Co-Commissioners: Hon. Mr. Justice W.R. Sinclair, Hon. Mr. Justice Julien Chouinard, Hon. Mr. Justice D.V. Heald
Correctional Investigator, Penitentiary Problems, Miss Inger Hansen
Royal Commission on Financial Management and Accountability, Allen T. Lambert.

Provincial commissions   3.4.2

The following list presents provincial commissions established between January 1975 and October 1976, the name of the chief commissioner or chairman, and the date each was established:

Prince Edward Island
Georgetown Shipyard Commission of Inquiry, Hon. Frederic A. Large, September 15, 1975
To inquire into matters pertaining to the Queens County Jail, Alan K. Scales QC, November 30, 1975.

Nova Scotia
Rent Review Commission, Kenneth M. Mounce, November 1975.

Quebec
To inquire into non-discrimination in fringe benefits, Roland Boutin, January 1975
To inquire into rehabilitation of children and adolescents in training schools, Manuel G. Batshaw, February 1, 1975
To inquire into health conditions in the asbestos industry, René Beaudry, June 18, 1975
To inquire into mercury in Quebec, André Barbeau, November 21, 1975
To inquire into haemodynamics and heart surgery, Maurice McGregor, December 12, 1975
To inquire into the operation of lotteries and race courses in Quebec, Jacques Gilbert, January 28, 1976.

Ontario
To inquire into the long range planning of Ontario's electrical power needs, Dr. Arthur Porter, March 12, 1975
To study the possible harm to the public interest of the increasing exploitation of violence in the communications industry, Hon. Judy LaMarsh, May 7, 1975
To inquire into the pricing of petroleum products, Claude Malcolm Isbister, July 16, 1975
To inquire into all structural and procedural aspects of the management of Algoma University College, John W. Whiteside QC, March 10, 1976.

British Columbia
To inquire into all ramifications of the implementation of an assessment system based on actual value and to review all aspects of real property taxation procedures, Robert McMath, April 24, 1975
To examine the overall administrative, operational, and financial processes utilized in the operation of Vancouver Community College Technical and Vocational Institute, Dr. George Suart, May 15, 1975
To inquire into and formulate recommendations upon all matters relating to disposition of rights by the Crown to harvest timber and to occupy forested land in British Columbia, Dr. Peter Pearse, June 12, 1975
To inquire into the redefinition of electoral districts in order to give proper and effective representation of people in all parts of the province in the Legislative Assembly, Hon. T.G. Norris QC, July 21, 1975
To inquire into the education of practical nurses and related hospital personnel, Dr. Noel A. Hall, December 1, 1975.

Local government   3.5

Local government in Canada comprises all government entities created by the provinces and territories to provide services that can be more effectively discharged through local control. Broadly speaking, local government services are identified in terms of seven main functions: protection, transportation, environmental health, environmental development, recreation, community services and education. In addition local government may operate, through the medium of government enterprises, such facilities as public transit and the supply of electricity and gas. Education is normally administered separately from the other local functions.

Under the British North America Act local government was made a responsibility of the provincial legislatures, a responsibility extended to the territories when their governments were constituted in the present forms. The unit of local government, apart from the school board, is usually the municipality which is incorporated as a city, town, village, township or other designation. The powers and responsibilities of municipalities are delegated to them by statutes passed by their respective provincial or territorial legislatures.

An increasing number of special agencies or joint boards and commissions have been created to provide certain services for groups of municipalities. Local government revenue has been supplemented by provincial grants, either made unconditionally or for specific purposes. Certain functions traditionally assigned to local government have been assumed in whole or in part by the provinces. Besides encouraging the amalgamation of small units, the provinces have established new levels of local government to provide services which can be better discharged at a regional level. "Second-tier" local governments now cover the whole of British Columbia and are planned for all of Ontario, where several now exist, and for Quebec, where three have been established. In Manitoba the Metropolitan Corporation of Greater Winnipeg and its constituent municipalities were amalgamated into a single city on January 1, 1972.

The major local revenue source available to local government is the taxation of real property, supplemented by taxation of personal property, businesses and amusements. Revenue is also derived from licences, permits, rents, concessions, franchises, fines and surplus funds from municipal enterprises.

Since a description of all forms of local government would be too complex for easy comprehension, the following paragraphs outline only municipal organization in each province and in the territories as at January 1, 1975. Table 3.6 gives the total number of each type of municipality in each province and territory.

Newfoundland has 285 incorporated areas: two cities, 106 towns, 11 rural districts, 41 local improvement districts, 124 local government communities and one metropolitan area. Towns and rural districts have elected councils and local improvement districts have appointed trustees. Local government communities in smaller settlements have limited powers and functions. The St. John's Metropolitan Area covers the area adjoining and surrounding the city of St. John's and the town of Mount Pearl and is similar in organization to a local improvement district. There are no rural municipalities in the usual sense. Only about 0.2% of the total area is municipally organized.

Prince Edward Island has one city, eight towns and 26 villages. There is no municipal organization for the remainder of the province, but it is divided into three counties and subdivided into school sections with elected school boards.

Nova Scotia is divided into 18 counties; 12 constitute separate municipalities and the remaining six are each divided into two districts or municipalities, making a total of 24 rural municipalities. Under the jurisdiction of these municipalities are 25 incorporated villages that provide limited services. Three cities and 38 towns, although located within counties or districts, are entirely independent of them except as to joint expenditures. There is no part of the province that is not municipally organized.

New Brunswick municipal organization includes six cities, 20 towns and 85 villages. The remainder of the province is not municipally organized and is administered by the provincial government. There are 213 unincorporated local service districts which are not municipal organizations but were established to provide services of a municipal nature.

Quebec. The more densely settled areas comprising about one third of the province are municipally organized; the remainder is governed by the province as "territories". The organized area is divided into 72 municipal counties, administered by a county corporation. Cities and towns are excluded from the county system for political and administrative purposes except for certain joint expenditures. The remaining municipal corporations and the unorganized territory within counties fall under the county system. Counties have no direct powers of taxation; funds to finance services in their jurisdiction are provided by their component municipalities. On January 1, 1975, there were 1,573 municipalities comprising 68 cities, 208 towns, 266 villages, 486 parishes, 152 townships, 13 united townships and 380 municipal organizations without designation. Major municipal consolidations began in 1965 with the fusion of the 14 municipalities on Île Jésus into the new city of Laval. In 1970, the Montreal and Quebec Urban Communities and the Outaouais Regional Community were established with integration of services to be staged gradually.

Ontario. In Ontario, slightly more than 10% of the area includes 95% of the total population and is municipally organized; the remainder is under direct provincial administration. The settled section is divided into one metropolitan municipality, 10 regional municipalities, one district municipality and 27 counties. There are 39 cities, five separated towns, five boroughs, 137 towns, 121 villages, 473 townships and 13 improvement districts. The Municipality of Metropolitan Toronto, in existence since January 1954, encompasses one city and five boroughs and is responsible for assessments, police, water supply, sewerage, metropolitan road systems, and planning. The regional municipalities of Durham, Halton, Hamilton–Wentworth, Niagara, Ottawa–Carleton, Peel, Sudbury, Waterloo and York have replaced county administrations and assumed certain responsibilities over all municipalities within their boundaries. The District Municipality of Muskoka was incorporated in January 1971 to assume responsibilities, similar to those of the regional municipalities, over the reorganized municipalities of the former district of Muskoka. This form of regional government is contemplated in other areas. Each county, although an incorporated municipality, comprises the towns (with the exception of six separated towns), villages and townships within it. Some municipalities are located outside the counties in areas called districts. These districts in western and northern Ontario are not municipal entities.

Manitoba has five cities, 33 towns, 40 villages and 105 rural municipalities. There are 19 local government districts each with a resident administrator to carry out the functions of a municipal council. The unorganized areas are the direct responsibility of the provincial government.

Saskatchewan has 11 cities, 131 towns, 350 villages and 292 rural municipalities. The area so organized consists of most of the southern part of the province, the remainder of this portion being administered by the province through 10 unincorporated local improvement districts. The northern part is sparsely populated and some municipal services are provided by the province through the operation of the Northern Administration District.

Alberta has nine cities, 103 towns, 167 villages, 18 municipal districts and 30 counties. The counties administer schools in addition to municipal services. There are 22 improvement districts and three special areas administered by the Special Areas Board.

British Columbia. In 1967, the government of British Columbia instituted regional government. By January 1972, 28 regional districts had been established. These regional districts are assuming responsibility for certain services from municipalities within their boundaries as well as providing services to previously unorganized areas. There are 32 cities, 11 towns, 58 villages and 37 districts. Districts are mostly rural although some adjacent to the principal cities of Vancouver and Victoria are largely urban in character. Unincorporated local districts have been set up to provide certain municipal services.

Yukon Territory and Northwest Territories. In the Yukon Territory, there are two cities, one town and five local improvement districts; the Northwest Territories includes one city, three towns, three hamlets and seven local improvement districts. The local improvement districts in the Yukon and the hamlets in the Northwest Territories, although incorporated, are developmental forms of local government.

3.6   External relations

3.6.1   Canada's international status

The growth of Canada's international status is reflected in the development of the Department of External Affairs. Until the 20th century Canadian negotiations with foreign countries were conducted through the British Foreign Office and dealings with other parts of the Empire through the Colonial Office; Canadian interests abroad were handled by British diplomatic and consular authorities and all Canadian communications to other governments went through the Governor General. The gradual recognition of Canadian autonomy in international affairs and increased Canadian responsibilities abroad made expansion of services and representation after 1920 not only inevitable but imperative. British diplomatic and consular authorities could no longer conveniently look after all Canadian interests. An important step in the evolution of the Department of External Affairs as the foreign service arm of the Canadian government resulted from an agreement reached at the 1926 Imperial Conference which changed the Governor General's role from that of representative of the British government to that of personal representative of the Sovereign. Britain, no longer officially represented, appointed a High Commissioner to Canada in 1928; after July 1, 1927 correspondence from foreign governments, including that from the Dominions Office in London, was directed to the Secretary of State for External Affairs (a portfolio held by the Prime Minister until 1946) instead of to the Governor General.

In the 1920s and 1930s Canada established diplomatic relations with Australia, Belgium, France, Ireland, Japan, the Netherlands, New Zealand, South Africa and the United States and during the 1940s, with the wartime governments of Belgium, Czechoslovakia, Greece, the Netherlands, Norway, Poland, Yugoslavia functioning in London or Cairo; and with the Argentine Republic, Brazil, Chile, China, Cuba, Denmark, Mexico, Newfoundland, Peru, Finland, Iceland, Italy, Sweden, Switzerland, Turkey, Uruguay and the USSR. High Commissioners were accredited to India, Pakistan, Ceylon (now Sri Lanka), Bangladesh, Papua New Guinea and Seychelles as they became independent and joined the Commonwealth.

Similarly in the 1960s, Canada developed its diplomatic relations in the French-speaking world, particularly with the newly independent francophone states of Africa. Relying on a system of multiple accreditation, Canada now has ambassadorial links with all of the 21 francophone African countries. Diplomatic relations were established with the Holy See in 1969 and with the People's Republic of China in 1970. Since then Canada has added new missions in Africa, Asia and the Middle East. Today, Canada maintains formal diplomatic relations with all countries in Latin America and the Middle East and has diplomatic, consular or trade representation in some 140 countries.

Membership in international organizations has entailed establishment of a Permanent Canadian Delegation to the United Nations in New York in 1948 and a Canadian office at the organization's European headquarters in Geneva in 1949. These Permanent Missions have since been expanded to include UN agencies in Paris and Vienna. Canada was one of the founding members of the North Atlantic Treaty Organization (NATO) in 1949 and when the NATO Permanent Council was established in 1952 a Canadian Permanent Delegation was set up in Paris (transferred to Brussels in 1967). Canada maintains a permanent delegation to the Organization for Economic Cooperation and Development in Paris, and the Mission of Canada to the European Communities in Brussels is responsible for Canada's relations with the European Economic Community, the European Atomic Energy Community and the European Coal and Steel Community. Canada also maintains a permanent observer mission to the Organization of American States in Washington, DC. In addition, officials of the Department of External Affairs represent Canada at many international conferences.

Diplomatic and/or consular representation   3.6.1.1

The addresses of Canadian representatives abroad and representatives of other countries in Canada may be found in Appendix 5.

Federal-provincial aspects of Canada's international relations   3.6.1.2

As a result of the growing international dimension of provincial interests abroad, a Federal-Provincial Coordination Division was established in 1967 in the Department of External Affairs. The purpose of this division was to maintain liaison with the provinces to facilitate their legitimate international activities in a manner that would meet provincial objectives, yet be consistent with a unified Canadian foreign policy.

The federal government's position on provincial international relations was outlined in the 1968 White Paper *Federalism and international relations,* which emphasizes that Canada's foreign relations must serve and reflect the interests of all provinces as well as those of its two major linguistic communities. The federal government's international policies include recognition of legitimate provincial interests beyond national borders, and continued promotion of national unity through adequate projection internationally of Canada's bilingual character.

Provincial participation at international conferences and in the work of international organizations is assured by including provincial officials on Canadian delegations, and by canvassing provincial governments for their views on the positions and attitudes which Canada might adopt on the subjects treated by these organizations. These include areas of particular interest to the provinces such as human and civil rights, education, health, agriculture, labour and environment.

Other aspects of Canada's international relations of particular interest to the provinces include the promotion of trade, investment, industrial development, immigration, tourism, cultural exchanges, environmental questions, science and technology, bilateral and multilateral agreements, and assistance to developing countries. In matters of aid, the federal government encourages a detailed federal-provincial consultation to ensure that specific projects are coordinated within the framework of Canada's aid contributions. The promotional activities of the provinces coupled with their increased interests in international activities have led to a greatly increased number of provincial visits abroad. The federal government, through the Department of External Affairs and its embassies and high commissions, assists provincial officials by making arrangements and appropriate appointments for their visits abroad and in coordinating visits of foreign personalities to provincial capitals.

Treaty-making powers. Once it has been determined that what a province seeks to achieve through agreements, in fields of provincial jurisdiction, falls within the framework of Canadian foreign policy, provision is made for direct provincial participation in negotiating with the authorities of the foreign country. When these arrangements are to be incorporated in an international agreement having legal effect, however, this can be achieved only through the exercise of the federal power to conclude treaties.

International activities   3.6.2

Canada and the Commonwealth   3.6.2.1

Originally a tightly knit coalition of five members, the Commonwealth has evolved into an international association of 36 sovereign states embracing approximately one quarter of the earth's land surface and population, the latter characterized by a diversity of races, colours, creeds and languages. Comprising both developed and developing countries, and governments committed to various international organizations, the Commonwealth represents a unique association whose members are bound by shared political and social values, similar attitudes and institutions, a similar political and historical experience, and a common language. The interests of its members extend to all continents.

Commonwealth members (with the year when membership was proclaimed in parentheses if post-1931) are as follows: Australia, Britain, Canada, New Zealand, The Bahamas (1973), Bangladesh (1972), Barbados (1966), Botswana (1966), Cyprus (1961), Fiji (1970), Gambia (1965), Ghana (1957), Grenada (1974), Guyana (1966), India (1947), Jamaica (1962), Kenya (1963), Lesotho (1966), Malawi (1964), Malaysia (1963), Malta (1964), Mauritius (1968), Nauru (Special Member), Nigeria (1960), Papua New Guinea (1975), Seychelles (1976), Sierra Leone (1961), Singapore (1965), Sri Lanka (Ceylon) (1948), Swaziland (1968), Tanzania (1964), Tonga (1970), Trinidad and Tobago (1962), Uganda (1962), Western Samoa (1970) and Zambia (1964). Nauru has special membership in the Commonwealth with all the advantages of membership except attendance at Heads of Government meetings. Through their association with Britain, which has retained responsibility for foreign affairs and defence, the five West Indies Associated States of Antigua, Dominica, St. Kitts–Nevis–Anguilla, St. Lucia and St. Vincent are also associated with the Commonwealth, as are the British dependencies and the external territories of Australia and New Zealand in the Caribbean, the Atlantic and the Pacific.

Membership in the Commonwealth is an important aspect of Canadian foreign policy. Canada has consistently supported its expansion and development as a vigorous and effective association working for international peace and progress. Canadian objectives have remained constant: to strengthen the association, to encourage more active participation in it by members, and to assist its development as a vehicle for practical cooperation. The organization has no binding rules, and decisions are by consensus rather than formal vote.

The Commonwealth Secretariat in Marlborough House, London, organizes and services official Commonwealth conferences, facilitates the exchange of information between member countries and collates their views. Canada's assessment to the 1976-77 budget of the Secretariat was 19% of the total, or approximately $607,800. In 1976 Canada contributed over $9 million to various Commonwealth institutions and programs, with particular emphasis on the Commonwealth Fund for Technical Cooperation, the Commonwealth Youth Program and the Commonwealth Foundation.

An important duty of the Secretariat is the organization of Commonwealth Heads of Government meetings such as the one held in Kingston, Jamaica in April-May 1975 and the next in London in mid-1977. Of more than 50 Commonwealth conferences held in 1976, some 20 were in the non-governmental sector, such as the Commonwealth Parliamentary Conference in Mauritius and the Dalhousie Conference on the Commonwealth and Non-Governmental Bodies. Major governmental meetings included the Commonwealth Senior Officials Meeting in Canberra, Commonwealth Finance Ministers Meeting in Hong Kong, the Commonwealth Youth Council Meeting in Malta, and the Commonwealth Science Council Meeting, in Colombo.

3.6.2.2   Canada and "la Francophonie"

The term "la Francophonie" generally describes countries that are wholly or partly French-speaking — i.e. the French-speaking community. This term has also been used to designate a movement aimed at providing the French-speaking world with an organized framework and functional structures.

To demonstrate abroad the bilingual aspect of Canadian society, the federal government fosters the strengthening of ties with francophone countries. In the last few years relations with French-speaking countries of Europe have been considerably expanded and diversified, complemented by the establishment of ties with the French-speaking countries of the Third World. Development aid remains an important activity.

Canada also participates in multilateral organizations such as the Agency for Cultural and Technical Cooperation, of which it is a founding member. At the agency's fourth general conference in Mauritius in November 1975 it was agreed in principle to create a multilateral mechanism to collect voluntary contributions for furthering development of Third World member-countries, which comprise the majority of members, by means of economic, social and cultural cooperation.

Also adopted were the principle of regrouping the agency's programs around three main cores — development, education and scientific and technical cooperation — and the promotion of national cultures and languages. The conference noted the Canadian proposal to entertain a symposium of directors-general of broadcasting agencies of francophone countries in the spring of 1977. The First International Francophone Youth Festival, which Canada hosted in Quebec City in 1974 in cooperation with the government of Quebec, would be followed by a second festival at Libreville, Gabon in 1977.

Canada is a member of the Conference of Ministers of Education of French-speaking Countries; at the annual session in February 1976 in N'Djamena, Quebec's Minister of Education headed the Canadian delegation. Canada also participated in the Conference of Ministers of Youth and Sports of French-speaking Countries in Paris during August 1976 with the Canadian delegation headed by the minister responsible for the Quebec High Commission for Youth, Recreation and Sport.

The federal government is not alone in its efforts to draw francophone countries closer. On the bilateral level, the provinces take part in joint commissions and in the implementation of Canadian government aid programs. On the multilateral level, New Brunswick, Ontario, Manitoba and Quebec participate in some of the agency's activities. The federal and Quebec governments have agreed on an arrangement under which the latter has a more distinct status within the agency's institutions, activities and programs.

Various private French-language associations also work to develop relations between their members around the world. The agency has stimulated their activities and led to the creation of a number of new organizations. The Canadian government supports several that are either Canadian or have significant Canadian participation.

Canada and the United Nations   3.6.2.3

Since the inception of the United Nations, support for the UN system has been an integral part of Canadian foreign policy. Canada has played a significant role in General Assembly matters and is a member of a number of subsidiary or ad hoc bodies of the General Assembly including the Special Committee on Peacekeeping Operations, the Conference of the Committee on Disarmament, the Committee on the Peaceful Uses of Outer Space, the United Nations Scientific Committee on the Effects of Atomic Radiation, the Committee on Contributions and the Board of Auditors. At the beginning of 1977, the General Assembly had 147 members and was close to achieving universal membership.

Canada served on the Security Council for three terms (1948-49, 1958-59 and 1967-68) and was elected at the 31st Assembly to assume a seat again for the biennium 1977-78. Seats on the council are allocated among regions and Canada will represent the "Western European and others" group, along with the Federal Republic of Germany which is to serve on the council for the first time.

On the 12 occasions that UN troops have been dispatched to deal with threats to peace and security, Canada has actively participated. In 1976 Canada had over 1,500 persons involved in UN peacekeeping, the largest commitment being to the United Nations Emergency Force (UNEF) in the Sinai, where over 850 specialists of the Canadian Armed Forces were employed in logistics support for the UNEF. A similar role was being performed by 150 Canadian personnel in the United Nations Disengagement Observer Force (UNDOF) in the Golan Heights area. In Cyprus Canada provided infantry personnel to patrol and monitor the existing arrangements between the disputants.

Canada contributed over $6 million to peacekeeping in 1975 under the UN's collective scale of assessments. At the same time, Canada actively sought equitable reimbursement arrangements for countries which were participants in

UN peacekeeping forces. Standard scales of reimbursement for each of the troop-contributing countries have been adopted for UNEF/UNDOF. This is a significant advance over previous peacekeeping operations where the reimbursement scales for participating countries were often uneven.

Canada has also served at regular intervals on the third principle organ of the UN, the Economic and Social Council, and in 1975 began a further three-year term. Generally, two sessions of the council are held annually, one in New York to discuss social and humanitarian questions, and one in Geneva to examine economic questions including, for example, food problems and international cooperation. The Economic and Social Council is also charged with coordinating the work of some 167 subsidiary bodies of the UN system. Some examples of those on which Canada is represented are: the Governing Council of the UN Environment Program (UNEP), the Commission on Narcotic Drugs and the Committee on Science and Technology for Development.

In recent years the UN has devoted a greater proportion of its time to human rights, and a number of new declarations, conventions and covenants have been promulgated. In 1976 four international human rights instruments came into force: the International Covenant on Economic, Social and Cultural Rights; the International Covenant on Civil and Political Rights; the latter's related Optional Protocol; and the International Convention on the Suppression and Punishment of the Crime of Apartheid. Canada has encouraged the preparation of such international instruments and has stressed the importance of building better mechanisms for the effective enforcement of standards. To emphasize Canada's commitment, special importance has been placed on securing membership on UN human rights bodies. A Canadian currently serves on the Commission on Human Rights and the UN Human Rights Committee.

Canada's support of United Nations human rights activities has recently been qualified in the aftermath of General Assembly Resolution 3379 (XXX) of November 1975, which defined Zionism as a form of racism and racial discrimination. Because of Canada's opposition to this resolution, no decision has been taken on whether to attend the 1978 Conference on the Decade for Action to Combat Racism and Racial Discrimination. Canada will not attend unless Resolution 3379 is revoked or neutralized, or unless all discussion of Zionism is ruled to be out of order.

Canada is the ninth largest contributor to the UN itself, and in 1976 was assessed 3.18% of the regular budget or in dollar terms nearly $10 million (Table 3.7). Canada also makes voluntary contributions to regular and special UN programs of the United Nations Development Program, the United Nations Commissioner for Refugees, the United Nations Children's Fund, the United Nations Relief and Works Agency for Palestine Refugees, the World Food Program, the United Nations Institute for Training and Research, the United Nations Education and Training Plan for Southern Africa, the United Nations Fund for Population Activities, the Committee on Racial Discrimination, the Trust Fund for South Africa and the Fund for Drug Abuse Control. The United Nations Development Program is the largest of these, and has a team leadership function in coordinating development activities in the UN system. Canada's voluntary donations in both cash and commodities to various UN programs totalled approximately $140 million in the 1975-76 fiscal year.

Specialized agencies. Canada is a member of all 14 specialized agencies of the UN, and is the host country of one, the International Civil Aviation Organization. Canada maintains permanent missions to the UN Headquarters in both New York and Geneva, and has accredited representatives to agencies located in Paris (UNESCO), Rome (FAO) and Vienna (IAEA). The contributions of these agencies has been one of the greatest strengths of the UN system.

The World Bank Group, consisting of the International Bank for Reconstruction and Development (IBRD) or World Bank, the International Finance Corporation and the International Development Association, is by far the largest of the multilateral aid-giving institutions. A brief summary of the agencies follows:

The International Labour Organization (ILO), originally established with the League of Nations in 1919, became a specialized agency of the UN in 1946. It brings together representatives of governments, employers and workers from 126 (1975) member states in an attempt to promote social justice by improving living and working conditions in all parts of the world. Canada has been a member of the ILO from its inception and as a leading industrial state has been assigned one of the 10 non-elective seats on the governing body.

The Food and Agriculture Organization (FAO), established in 1945, is one of the largest of the specialized agencies, with 136 members. Raising the nutrition levels and living standards of its member countries and improving production and distribution techniques for food, agriculture, fishery and forest products are two of its objectives. The FAO Secretariat provides advisory services, collects and publishes agricultural and fisheries statistics, and organizes international conferences and meetings of experts.

FAO has headquarters in Rome and regional offices in Washington, Bangkok, Rio de Janeiro, Santiago and Cairo. Canada participates in FAO functions and is a member of the FAO Council, the Committee on Commodity Problems, the Committee on Fisheries, the Consultative Sub-Committee on Surplus Disposals, the FAO Group on Grains, the North American Forestry Commission and other FAO bodies. The Joint FAO-WHO Food Standards Program, controlled by the Codex Alimentarius Commission, is administered by an executive committee of which Canada is a member.

The World Food Program was established under the joint auspices of the FAO and the UN to provide food aid on a multilateral basis for emergency relief, including the feeding of children, and to promote economic and social development. Its approved target for pledges for 1976-77 was $750 million. Between January 1963 and the end of 1974, Canada pledged $132 million to the program and was ranked as its second largest supporter; the 1975-76 regular plus supplementary pledges totalled approximately $100 million, making Canada the program's largest contributor. For 1977-78 Canada pledged $100 million and gave a supplementary pledge of grain amounting to $45-50 million, depending upon the price.

The World Health Organization (WHO), with 145 members and two associate members, is a directing and coordinating authority on international health matters. The objective is "the attainment by all peoples of the highest possible level of health"; WHO provides advisory and technical services from its Geneva headquarters to help countries develop and improve their national health services. At the 28th World Health Assembly in Geneva in May 1975, Canada was elected to the WHO Executive Board for a three-year term.

The United Nations Educational, Scientific and Cultural Organization (UNESCO) was established in 1946 "to contribute to peace and security by promoting collaboration among the nations through education, science and culture in order to further universal respect for justice, for the rule of law, for human rights and fundamental freedoms". Its headquarters is in Paris and membership is 135 states and three associate members.

UNESCO has three main components — the General Conference which is the policy-making body, the Executive Board and the Secretariat. Representatives from member states make up the General Conference which meets every two years. The 18th Session of the General Conference in Paris in 1974 approved a budget of approximately US$170 million for 1975-76, giving priority to the educational needs of the developing countries and to science activities, particularly the application of science to development; the Canadian assessment rate is 2.91%.

The International Civil Aviation Organization (ICAO), with headquarters in Montreal, was established in 1947 to promote the safe, orderly and economic development of international civil aviation. It has a membership of 129 (1975). Canada has been a member of the 30-nation council, the governing body of ICAO since its inception as a state of chief importance in air transport.

The International Telecommunication Union (ITU), founded to oversee application of the International Telegraph Convention of 1865 and the International Radio Telegraph Convention of 1906, is concerned with international cooperation for the improvement and use of telecommunications for the benefit of the general public; it has 143 member countries and one associate member. Canada is represented on the 36-member Administrative Council, the executive organ of the ITU.

The World Intellectual Property Organization (WIPO) came into force in January 1974 to protect intellectual property (e.g. patents, copyright) and to ensure administrative cooperation among the unions previously established for these purposes, the Paris and Berne Unions. In May 1975 memberships in the three organizations were 60, 81 and 64 respectively. Canada is a member of all three.

The World Meteorological Organization (WMO), a specialized agency of the UN since 1951, has evolved from the International Meteorological Organization founded in 1878; in 1975 WMO had 143 members. One of its major programs is the "World Weather Watch" for developing an improved world-wide meteorological system and environment. Canada was elected to the Organization's Executive Committee at the seventh WMO Congress in 1975.

The Inter-Governmental Maritime Consultative Organization (IMCO) was established in 1959 to promote international cooperation on technical shipping problems and the adoption of the highest standards of safety and navigation; its membership in 1975 was 88. IMCO exercises bureau functions for International Conventions of Safety of Life at Sea, Prevention of Pollution of the Sea by Oil, and Facilitation of International Maritime Traffic. At the ninth Assembly in 1975, Canada was re-elected to the Council of IMCO for a two-year term and continued to hold a seat on the Maritime Safety Committee.

The Universal Postal Union (UPU), one of the oldest and largest of the specialized agencies, was founded in Berne in 1874 with the principal aim of improving postal services throughout the world and promoting international collaboration. It has 154 members. The Universal Postal Congress meets every five years to review the Universal Postal Convention and its subsidiary instruments. In the interim, UPU activities are carried on by an executive council, a consultative committee on postal studies and an international bureau. Canada was elected to the executive council in 1974 during the 17th Congress in Lausanne.

The International Monetary Fund (IMF), created by the Bretton Woods Conference in 1944 and established in 1945, was designed to facilitate the expansion of world trade and payments as a means of raising world standards of living and of fostering economic development. It promotes stability and order with respect to exchange rates, and provides financial mechanisms for balance of payments assistance to enable member countries to correct temporary imbalances with a minimum of disturbance to the international monetary system. The original membership of 45 countries has grown to 128, of which about 100 are classified as developing.

Canada's participation in the International Monetary Fund is authorized under the Bretton Woods Agreement Act of 1945. The Canadian quota and subscription is SDR1,100 million; however, with a quota increase agreed to in January 1976, this would increase to SDR1,357 million. The SDR (Special Drawing Rights) has been defined as being equal in value to a fixed basket of 16 currencies, one of which is the Canadian dollar. Fund holdings of Canadian dollars as of December 31, 1975 amounted to the equivalent of SDR793.4 million or 72.1% of the Canadian quota. The reserve position of Canada in the IMF at the end of 1975 amounted to SDR553.6 million of which SDR246.9 million represented loans by Canada to the Oil Facility. The Oil Facility assists member countries in financing deficits arising from increases in the costs of imports of petroleum products.

The International Bank for Reconstruction and Development (World Bank), also originated in the Bretton Woods Conference of 1944. Its early loans were made to assist in the postwar reconstruction of Europe but it has played an increasingly important role in providing financial assistance and economic advice to the less-developed countries. It has become the world's largest multilateral source of development finance. By December 31, 1975 the World Bank had made loans totalling US$29 billion to 68 of its 127 member countries in Central and South America, the Caribbean, Oceania, Asia, Africa and Southern Europe.

Most World Bank loans are made to finance infrastructure projects (roads, rails, ports and electricity generation and transmission) which provide the framework basic to a country's economy but which generally do not attract private investors. Increasingly, however, more emphasis has been given to other sectors such as agriculture, rural development, telecommunications, education, water supply and sewage.

Canada's subscription to the World Bank is the equivalent of $1,136.1 million in current US dollars out of a total for all countries of US$30,821 million. Only 10% of each subscription is paid in, however, with the balance remaining as a guarantee against which the bank is able to sell its own bonds in world capital markets.

The International Development Association (IDA) was established as an affiliate of the IBRD in 1960. Its resources come mainly from governments in the form of interest-free advances, enabling it to make loans on very soft terms (0% and 50 years repayment). IDA lends to its member countries whose per capita income is less than $375 a year.

Since IDA cannot borrow from world capital markets, its loanable resources have been derived largely from budgetary allocations from its member governments, principally the developed-country, or Part I, members. Total resources made available or committed to IDA from the beginning of its operations to the end of 1975 were approximately $11.5 billion, and as a Part I member, Canada had paid in $502.9 million to IDA.

The International Finance Corporation (IFC), established in 1956 as an affiliate of the IBRD assists less-developed member countries to promote the growth of the private sector of their economies. IFC provides risk capital for productive private enterprises in association with private investors and management, encourages the development of local capital markets, and stimulates the international flow of private capital. IFC makes investments in the form of share subscriptions and long-term loans, carries out stand-by and underwriting arrangements and provides financial and technical assistance to privately controlled development finance companies. Of IFC's total subscribed capital of US$107 million, Canada provided US$3.6 million. In addition to its subscribed capital, IFC is able to finance its activities through loans from its parent institution, the World Bank. Total investment and underwriting commitments by IFC to December 31, 1975 amounted to US$1,331 million in 57 countries. Commitments made during 1975 were US$196 million.

The International Atomic Energy Agency (IAEA) was created in 1957 as an autonomous international organization under the aegis of the UN which has empowered it to try to accelerate and enlarge the contribution of atomic energy to peace, health and prosperity throughout the world. At the end of 1975, membership consisted of 106 states. Because Canada has been designated as one of the members most advanced in nuclear technology, including the production of source materials, a Canadian representative has served on the Board of Governors since the agency's inception.

Conferences and symposia, dissemination of information and provision of technical assistance are among the methods adopted to carry out the IAEA's functions. With the rapid expansion in the use of nuclear power, much activity is devoted to this field as well as to the use of isotopes in agriculture and medicine. Another significant role relates to the development and application of safeguards to ensure that nuclear materials supplied for peaceful purposes are not diverted to military uses. Under terms of the Treaty for the Non-Proliferation of Nuclear Weapons, each non-nuclear weapons state adhering to the treaty was to conclude an agreement with the IAEA providing for safeguards on its entire nuclear program. The IAEA also imposes safeguards pursuant to agreements relating to individual nuclear facilities. Agency inspectors have carried out safeguard inspections in Canada and in more than 60 other countries.

World conferences. In 1976 the UN continued sponsoring world conferences of both on-going and special nature. In the former category, for example, the series of meetings on the Law of the Sea continued, with Canada taking active part as a major coastal state. Of the latter type, the International Labour Organization convened the World Conference on Employment, Income Distribution, Social Progress and the International Division of Labour to promote better understanding of the nature and magnitude of employment problems.

At the fourth UN Conference on Trade and Development (UNCTAD) in Nairobi, Kenya from May 5-31, 1976, 13 resolutions were adopted covering a wide range of issues, such as the establishment of an integrated program for commodities, international assistance measures, and the transfer of technology. Thus UNCTAD IV marked an important step in the continuing dialogue between developing and developed countries.

In 1976 Canada hosted Habitat, the United Nations Conference on Human Settlements, the largest conference ever held under UN auspices. Two significant features were the extensive use of audio-visual material submitted by 123 countries, and a simultaneous non-governmental forum, which helped focus world attention on such basic issues as the control and value of land, the conservation of resources, the environment, the rights of indigenous peoples, the status of women and the need for public participation in the planning and development of settlements. The success of the conference will be measured in the long term by the extent to which it provides guidance and assistance to governments in dealing with the problems of human settlements. In the short term, the immediate importance of the conference was to provide an international meeting for discussion of human settlements and how governments and international organizations might deal with them.

3.6.2.4   Canada and the Conference of the Committee on Disarmament

Canada is an active member of the Conference of the Committee on Disarmament (CCD), a 31-nation negotiating body. This committee, with the United States and the Soviet Union as co-chairmen, represents in microcosm the world-wide concern with the arms race. The CCD is seeking a comprehensive prohibition of nuclear weapons testing including underground tests, a ban on the development, production and stockpiling of chemical weapons and a prohibition of modification of the environment for military or other hostile purposes.

3.6.2.5   Canada and Mutual Balanced Force Reductions in Central Europe

Canada continues to participate in the Conference on the Mutual Reduction of Forces and Armaments and Associated Measures in Central Europe, which opened officially in Vienna in October 1973.

Canada, NATO and NORAD

NATO. Canada was one of the founding members of the North Atlantic Treaty Organization (NATO) in 1949. Successive Canadian governments reaffirmed the conviction that Canada's security remained linked to that of Europe — probably still the most sensitive point in the East-West balance of power.

Following an extensive defence structure review by the government the Minister of National Defence in November 1975 announced the government's intention to purchase major new items of equipment for the Canadian Armed Forces. Counter to the general NATO trend the minister announced a considerable increase in the Canadian defence budget over the next five years, with emphasis on capital acquisitions. Following these decisions it was announced that Canada would purchase 18 Aurora long-range patrol aircraft to replace the obsolete Argus and would equip the Canadian Forces in Europe with Leopard 1 main battle tanks, subject to a satisfactory contract being concluded with the manufacturer.

At the Conference on Security and Cooperation in Europe (CSCE) in Helsinki, August 1975, members of NATO agreed to notify each other of major military manoeuvres in Central Europe in which they are participating. In the autumn of 1975 Canada issued notification of two manoeuvres in the Federal Republic of Germany in which Canadian troops took part. Since then other countries have also issued announcements. Provision was also made for the voluntary invitation of observers to manoeuvres. NATO supports this provision fully, and observers were invited to one of the autumn manoeuvres. Observers came from all the CSCE countries except those of the Warsaw Pact.

Canada also participates in the Mutual and Balanced Force Reductions (MBFR) negotiations in Vienna. Negotiations are generally recognized as being difficult because they touch on vital security interests of both NATO and the Warsaw Pact. It was hoped that a new NATO proposal to include the consideration of some of its nuclear weapons in the negotiations would break a two-year deadlock. Similarly, it was hoped that a way would be found around the deadlock in the Strategic Arms Limitations Talks (SALT) between the US and the USSR.

A number of unresolved problems remain a source of continuing concern to the NATO Alliance. All NATO members continued to experience, in varying degrees, the impact of inflation, energy disruption and the after effects of a severe recession. Many of the Allies shared the problem of maintaining an adequate level of defence capability in the face of serious strains on their economies. One positive factor was a growing readiness of NATO Alliance members, including Canada, to seek economies by increasing specialization in the development, production and acquisition of military equipment to avoid costly duplication.

In the pursuit of Canadian foreign policy objectives, such as the diversification of international economic relations, including the negotiation of a Framework Agreement for Commercial and Economic Cooperation with the European Communities, Canadian membership in NATO plays an important role. NATO is a unique forum for the exchange of views among its members through its regular organs and through such related bodies as the North Atlantic Assembly and the Atlantic Council of Canada. Membership in NATO motivates Canada to participate actively in European affairs, and thus contributes to the development of Canada's political, economic and scientific-technological relations with Europe.

NORAD. In continuing its cooperation with the United States in North American defence, Canada seeks to make an effective contribution to the maintenance of a stable strategic balance between the super-powers. This contributes to Canada's overriding defence objective of preventing nuclear war. In the context of North American defence, the government advocates participating in surveillance and warning systems, in anti-submarine defence and in measures designed to protect the retaliatory capacity of the US.

In air defence, this cooperation was reaffirmed in May 1975 when Canada agreed to renew the North American Air Defence Command (NORAD)

Agreement for five years. The government concluded that it was in Canada's interest to continue to cooperate with the United States on questions of North American defence, both as a means of dealing with mutual security problems and as a contribution to the general security of the NATO area. It was also concluded that, although it was substantially diminished, there continued to be a bomber threat to North America that required some defence and that this could most efficiently and economically be provided through a continuation of the air-defence arrangement that had been worked out by the two governments through NORAD.

The Canadian and US governments were both developing national civil-military surveillance and control systems of their respective airspaces, and it was concluded that these new arrangements would be enhanced by a continuation of NORAD. To further the effectiveness of the new national systems, the two governments agreed to redefine NORAD's regional boundaries. For Canada this would have the practical effect in future of all operations in Canadian airspace being controlled from centres in Canada by Canadians.

One of the principle consultative mechanisms for Canada–US defence cooperation is the Permanent Joint Board on Defence (PJBD). Through its regular meetings during 1975, the board provided a forum for the discussion of such issues as the dispersal of US aircraft to Canadian bases in times of crisis, the renewal of the NORAD Agreement, the renewal of an agreement to operate jointly a torpedo-testing range at Nanoose Bay, BC, and the possible industrial development of surplus lands at the US-leased naval station at Argentia, Nfld. The board also provided an opportunity to both countries to exchange views on various aspects of their mutual defence policies.

As a continuing function, the department coordinates Canadian cooperation with the US in various research activities.

3.6.2.7   Canada and the United States

There is no more important external relationship for Canada than that with the United States. As a result of geography and economic and social patterns, the two countries frequently meet to discuss various aspects of governmental policies and programs. In addition to informal consultations, there are official and technical committees in which Canadian and US officials discuss bilateral matters ranging from economic questions to defence to transboundary environmental matters. For example, the International Joint Commission, an independent agency, was jointly established by the US and Canada to deal with regulation of flows of boundary waters and the abatement of transboundary air and water pollution. Canada and the US have a long history of defence cooperation through the Permanent Joint Board on Defence and through NATO.

Canada and the US also work together on international questions in multilateral organizations such as the UN, the OECD, GATT, the IMF and others in which both countries are active members.

In trade, each is the other's best customer, and in 1975 two-way trade between the two countries was approximately $45 billion. Canada sells to the United States about 65% of all exports and buys from the US about 20% of all US exports.

Demographic and economic patterns make for a somewhat asymmetric relationship between Canada and the US that poses a challenge for Canada. In pursuit of Canadian goals, however, it is fundamental to Canadian foreign policy that Canada continue to maintain sound mutually beneficial relations with the US.

3.6.2.8   Canada and the Commonwealth Caribbean

Canada has long enjoyed close relations with the countries of the Commonwealth Caribbean. The current phase began with the Commonwealth Caribbean–Canada Conference of 1966, followed by a special Canadian Mission to the area in 1970. In April 1975 the Prime Minister visited Trinidad and Tobago, Barbados and Guyana, then went to the Commonwealth Heads of Government Meeting in Kingston, Jamaica.

In 1975 Canadian investment in the region was estimated at approximately $400 million; Canadian imports from the region totalled $184.5 million while exports were valued at $378.4 million. Canadian bilateral development assistance to the Caribbean, begun in 1958, has averaged approximately $20.0 million a year in loans and grants in recent years. It has been concentrated in the sectors of education, air transport, water supply and agriculture. Funds have also been made available on a multilateral basis through various organizations including the United Nations and the Caribbean Development Bank.

More than 3,000 Canadians are permanent residents in the region and over 200,000 visit the islands annually. There are Canadian High Commissions in Jamaica, Trinidad and Tobago, Guyana, and Barbados, and these four countries and Grenada maintain High Commissions in Ottawa. There is also a Commissioner for the Eastern Caribbean in Montreal who represents the five West Indies Associated States (Antigua, Dominica, St. Kitts–Nevis–Anguilla, St. Lucia and St. Vincent) and Montserrat.

Canada and Latin America 3.6.2.9

Canada maintains diplomatic relations with all Latin American countries through 13 resident missions and dual or multiple accreditation from those missions. In addition, Canada is associated with the Inter-American System through a Permanent Observer Mission to the Organization of American States in Washington and membership or observer status in many Inter-American institutions.

During 1975 Canadian trade with Latin America declined slightly in comparison with rapid growth in the preceding year. The decline was caused principally by economic difficulties experienced by the region because of inflation and, in many countries, the increase in the cost of oil and drops in prices of major export commodities. Canadian imports from Latin America during 1975 amounted to $1,649 million ($1,829 million in 1974) while Canadian exports to the area amounted to $1,257 million ($1,259 million in 1974). Canadian sales in Latin America in 1975 were nevertheless double those in the Middle East. Canada's trade deficit declined from $570 million in 1974 to $392 million in 1975.

In March 1975 the Minister of Industry, Trade and Commerce led a trade mission to Cuba and Venezuela. Early in the year the Minister President of the National Bank of Cuba paid an official visit to Canada and in September the Deputy Prime Minister of Cuba took part in the initial meeting of the Canada–Cuba Joint Committee on Economic and Trade Relations when a bilateral air agreement was signed.

The growth of Canadian relations with Latin America has led to contacts and exchanges in many other fields. The Minister of National Health and Welfare visited Cuba and concluded an understanding for exchanges in the nursing and hospital fields. There was an exchange of Olympic training teams between Canada and Cuba. The Prime Minister visited Mexico, Cuba and Venezuela at the beginning of 1976.

In 1975, the Canadian International Development Agency (CIDA) provided $17 million to Latin American countries, mostly in technical assistance, and committed about $3 million in matching grants to non-governmental organizations. Canada provided funds for multilateral assistance programs to the Inter-American Development Bank (IDB) and to various specialized technical organizations, including $7.5 million allocated to the preparation of development projects.

At the multilateral level, Canada is also an active member of many Inter-American organizations, namely: the Pan American Institute of Geography and History (PAIGH), the Pan American Health Organization (PAHO), the Inter-American Institute for Agricultural Sciences (IAIAS), the Inter-American Statistical Institute (IASI), the Inter-American Centre for Tax Administrators (IACTA), the Centre for Latin American Monetary Studies (CEMLA), the Postal Union of the Americas and Spain (PUAS). Canada supports various technical and professional Inter-American organizations. In May 1975, Canada hosted annual meetings of the IAIAS, of the Commission of Geography of the PAIGH and of the Inter-American Centre for Tax Administrators.

3.6.2.10   Canada and Europe, the Middle East, Africa, and the Far East

Canada and Europe. Canada's relations with Western Europe have developed steadily. These countries have long been major political, cultural and economic partners of Canada and as a result of Western Europe's growing prosperity and vitality are likely to assume even greater importance. Canada maintains close bilateral relations with Western European countries, and has resident diplomatic missions in almost all of them. Along with a number of Western European nations, Canada is an active member of NATO, OECD and also wider international associations such as GATT, the Economic Commission for Europe of the United Nations and the European Regional Group of UNESCO.

Formal negotiations for a contractual link between Canada and the European Communities were begun in March 1976 and led on July 6, 1976 to the signature of a framework agreement for commercial and economic cooperation. This will provide a focus for cooperation between Canada and the European Communities which should lead to increased trade and investment opportunities for both sides.

Canada and the Eastern European states have in recent years increased trade, scientific and technological cooperation as well as cultural exchanges. Canada participated in the Conference on Security and Cooperation in Europe, which opened in Helsinki in July 1973 and culminated in the signing of the Helsinki Final Act by the 35 participants on August 1, 1975, which opened the door to agreement to establish diplomatic relations with the German Democratic Republic.

A new era in Canadian-Soviet relations, based on a more candid and friendly atmosphere and on the principle of mutual benefit, was opened in 1971 with the Protocol on Consultations, the Agreement on Cooperation in the Industrial Application of Science and Technology, and the General Exchanges Agreement, which provide for regular and long-term cooperation between Canada and the USSR. Canada has also been pursuing improved and mutually beneficial relations with other Eastern European countries and now has resident diplomatic missions in Moscow, Prague, Warsaw, Belgrade, Budapest and Bucharest and maintains diplomatic relations with Bulgaria through a non-resident ambassador.

Canada and the Middle East. Canada has consistently attempted to follow a policy of balance and objectivity between the parties to the Arab-Israeli dispute. Over the years, Canada has supported the efforts of the UN Relief and Works Agency (UNRWA) to alleviate the plight of Palestine refugees and has contributed to the maintenance of the cease-fire that followed the war of October 1973 by providing troops to serve with UN peacekeeping forces.

Many of the major oil-exporting countries of the Middle East have put their increased revenues to use by expanding their developmental projects. In addition, some have sought to employ a part of their surpluses in assisting other countries that lack such valuable resources. These countries are becoming more aware of Canada's potential as a reliable supplier not only of the traditional but also of the more sophisticated goods and services they require. In 1975 Canadian exports to the Middle East increased by some 70% for a total value of $420 million, while the value of Canada's imports from this region, mainly of oil, rose by about 64%, to reach $2,140 million.

Canada and Africa. Direct relations were established with former British colonies in Africa as they became independent members of the Commonwealth. Increasing contacts and diplomatic relations with the newly independent French-speaking African states soon followed. Canada now maintains diplomatic relations with almost all the independent African states and through resident Canadian missions in 15 countries. The development of bilateral diplomatic and commercial relations has been accompanied by a significant and growing program of Canadian development assistance to Africa. This program directed $212 million in bilateral assistance to the African continent in 1975-76 and approximately the same amount in 1976-77.

Canada and the Asian and Pacific Region. The countries of Asia and the Western Pacific include some of the more highly industrialized in the world as well as some of the poorest. Canada is expanding its trade and economic relations with the former group and is providing development assistance to the latter. Consistent with the government's policy of diversifying foreign relations, considerable effort has been made to expand and strengthen relations, in particular with Japan, but also with Australia, New Zealand, China and Indonesia.

The importance of Asia as a trading area is evident from the emergence of Japan by 1973 as Canada's second largest bilateral trading partner, immediately behind the US, with two-way trade amounting to more than $3.3 billion in 1975. Relations between the two governments, between the two business communities, and on a people-to-people level continued to grow. Similar links were forged between Canada and Indonesia, and other member states of the Association of South East Asian Nations (ASEAN) as meetings between government representatives, businessmen and travel by the general public increased during 1975.

Canada's interest in cooperation and development is promoted through participation in the Colombo Plan, Canada's official observer status with the Economic and Social Commission for Asia and the Pacific, and active membership in the Asian Development Bank. This is particularly evident in the Indian sub-continent. Since development assistance was first given under the Colombo Plan in 1951, Canada had disbursed approximately $2.3 billion in the region. During 1975, for example, India, Pakistan, and Bangladesh were respectively the first, second and third largest net recipients of Canadian aid.

A part of this relationship, the partnership developed since 1956 with India and Pakistan in the field of peaceful uses of nuclear energy, became highly controversial when India exploded a nuclear device in May 1974 using plutonium derived from one of the Canadian donated installations. In Canada's view, the test had a seriously destablizing effect on international efforts to limit and control the proliferation of nuclear-explosive technology. Canada's reaction to the event was to suspend nuclear cooperation and place under review certain other aspects of its aid program that might contribute indirectly to India's nuclear effort. Protracted bilateral discussions on the implications of the explosion were unable to resolve differences in the nuclear policies of the two countries, resulting in a decision by the Canadian government in May 1976 to terminate its program of nuclear cooperation with India, although the Canadian government remains prepared to pursue common objectives with India in other fields of mutual interest. Talks with Pakistan, aimed similarly at upgrading safeguards governing Canadian nuclear facilities in that country, continued.

For more than a quarter century parts of Asia have been centres of tension and conflict. Canada participated in various international efforts to restore peace in Kashmir, Korea and Indonesia. From 1954 to 1973 Canada was a member of the two International Control Commissions that were called upon to supervise the application of various international agreements on Indochina. As hostilities drew to a close in early 1975, Canada set up a special humanitarian aid program to Indochina at a cost of $16.75 million, enabling supplies of food and medicine to be distributed to the areas most seriously affected by the long war. The Canadian program was administered locally by international organizations such as UNICEF, UNHCR and the Red Cross. Canada maintains diplomatic relations with Viet-Nam and Laos but not with Cambodia.

Relations between Canada and the People's Republic of China continued to develop and two-way Sino-Canadian trade reached $420 million in 1975. Several scientific and commercial missions were exchanged. In April 1975, a Canadian landscape painting exhibition was held in Peking and Shanghai, the first exhibition of Western painting in China since the Cultural Revolution began.

Canada and the Asian Development Bank. Canada is a member of the Asian Development Bank, established in 1966 with Articles of Agreement patterned broadly after those of the World Bank and other international financial institutions. The balance of the bank's subscribed capital stock (as at December 31, 1975) is US$3,201.5 million, of which $1,055.6 million belongs to the paid-in portion and the balance remains as a callable guarantee against which the bank may sell its bonds on world capital markets. Asian regional countries, including Japan, Australia and New Zealand, have subscribed US$2,314.9 million and non-regional countries have subscribed the remaining US$886.6 million. Canada's paid-in portion totalled US$24.1 million, and a special increase for Canada of a further $156.3 million ($150.0 million of which will be paid in) was approved.

An Asian Development Fund provides assistance to developing member countries on concessional terms. Canada's contribution to this fund was US$10 million, and as part of the fund's replenishment Canada pledged a further $76.4 million over three years. Canada had previously contributed US$25 million to the Asian Development Bank's former Multi-purpose Special Fund.

3.6.2.11   Canada and the OECD

The Organization for Economic Cooperation and Development (OECD) was established in Paris in September 1961 as successor to the Organization for European Economic Cooperation (OEEC) founded in 1948 by the countries of Western Europe to facilitate reconstruction of their war-shattered economies and to administer the Marshall Plan. With the establishment of the OECD, Canada and the United States and later Japan (May 1964), Australia (June 1971) and New Zealand (May 1973) joined with the countries of Western Europe to form a major intergovernmental forum for consultation and cooperation among the advanced industrialized nations in virtually every major field of economic activity. At present 24 countries are full members while Yugoslavia has a special status entitling it to participate in certain activities.

The aim of the OECD is to facilitate the formulation of policy approaches which are conducive to stability, balanced economic growth and social progress of both member and non-member countries. The organization provides an instrument for assembling and examining knowledge relevant to policy-making and also a forum, meeting the year round, for the exchange and analysis of ideas and experiences from all member countries.

The organization plays a significant role in harmonizing international economic and financial policy and is the main area where industrialized nations hold consultations on questions of development assistance. The original focus on more traditional economic, trade and development matters has altered and new activities have been undertaken in agriculture, the environment, industry, science and technology, international investment and multinational enterprises, social affairs, manpower and education. The International Energy Agency (IEA) established within the framework of the OECD in November 1974, plays an important role in four main areas: emergency oil sharing, consultations on the oil market, promotion of the accelerated development of new sources of energy, and relations between oil consuming and oil producing countries. Another agency of the OECD, the Nuclear Energy Agency has been involved in the coordination and exchange of views of the technical aspects of nuclear power. This broader orientation places increasing emphasis on the qualitative, as well as the quantitative, aspects of economic growth in the world.

The OECD brings together government officials, representatives of private business, labour unions, universities and other non-governmental bodies at the international level. Within Canada, the Canadian Business and Industry Advisory Committee, comprising representatives of the Canadian Chamber of Commerce and the Canadian Manufacturers' Association was established in 1962 to ensure input from the business community. Arrangements also exist for consultation with Canadian labour organizations, universities and other non-governmental bodies. Representatives of provincial governments attend OECD meetings when subjects of particular interest to the provinces are being discussed.

Canadian development assistance programs

3.6.2.12

The Canadian International Development Agency (CIDA) is responsible for the operation and administration of Canada's international development assistance programs. In 1975-76 Canada disbursed $903.5 million for foreign aid, an increase of $159.8 million over the previous year. Of that amount $318.6 million was disbursed to multilateral assistance programs and $525.7 million to bilateral assistance programs. The remaining funds were divided among non-governmental organizations working in international development, international emergency relief programs, the International Development Research Centre, incentives to Canadian private investment in developing countries and the CIDA scholarship fund for Canadians taking postgraduate degrees in international development and related fields.

CIDA's multilateral assistance programs are directed toward the United Nations and its affiliated organizations, the World Bank Group, the regional development banks and several regional institutions.

CIDA's bilateral development program is divided into three types of aid — technical assistance, economic assistance and international food aid — and into five regional programs. During 1975, 3,734 students and trainees from developing countries studied in Canada under CIDA's technical assistance program and 963 Canadian advisers and educators worked overseas. Under a unique feature of Canada's technical training program more than 600 students and trainees studied in developing countries other than their own.

Canadian bilateral economic assistance is divided almost evenly between grants and loans. Most loans are extended for 50 years and are interest free, with no repayment required for the first 10 years. Disbursements for bilateral food programs totalled $119.3 million in 1975-76.

Canada's role in the Colombo Plan, a program initiated by Commonwealth governments in 1951 (and subsequently joined by other governments) to administer aid to South and Southeast Asia, is the largest and oldest of the regional bilateral aid programs administered by CIDA. It received $244 million from CIDA in 1974-75 and $258 million in 1975-76. However, because of the size of the Asian population it has much less impact than aid from Canada has in such areas as the Caribbean or parts of Africa.

Since 1951 Canada has provided more than $2.2 billion in bilateral aid, most of it directed to Bangladesh, India, Indonesia, Pakistan and Sri Lanka. In recent years Canada's program in this area has changed considerably. Capital assistance, in the form of loans and grants, is now provided for specific economic sectors given priority by the recipient countries in fields such as communications, transportation, electric power development, agriculture, fisheries, mining, lumbering, medicine and public health.

CIDA's programs in francophone Africa, which includes the eight least developed nations of the world, were initially concentrated on technical assistance projects particularly in education and health. Since 1970, however, Canada has broadened the scope of its assistance and increased its support in the area from $29.7 million to $105.0 million in 1975-76. Canada has become increasingly involved in the economic development of the region through projects that combine capital and technical assistance, and which accord with the priorities of the countries concerned.

The Special Commonwealth Africa Assistance Plan resulted from discussions at the 1960 Commonwealth Prime Ministers' meeting. Canadian assistance to Commonwealth Africa has grown from an initial provision for technical and educational assistance to include a variety of capital projects and pre-investment surveys. Undertakings in energy, transportation, communications, agriculture and economic planning in eastern and southern Africa have balanced an original focus on west Africa. Between 1960 and March 1976, Canada contributed $457 million to bilateral development programs in the region. In 1975-76 the expenditures for Commonwealth Africa totalled $108.3 million, for projects ranging from mining to beekeeping.

Canadian economic and technical assistance to the Commonwealth Caribbean began in 1958. Since then the region has received more Canadian aid per capita than any other area of the world. Canada's bilateral allocations, amounting to more than $160 million since 1964 including $21.9 million in 1975-76, have contributed to construction projects, transportation surveys, water systems, medical assistance, support for the University of the West Indies and other development projects.

In 1971 CIDA began a bilateral technical assistance program concentrating on agriculture, forestry, fisheries, education and community development. In 1974-75 a bilateral loan program was introduced; in 1975-76 disbursements in Latin America were $27.0 million.

CIDA is also involved with non-governmental aid organizations and business and industry. In the 1968-69 fiscal year $4 million was disbursed to help voluntary agencies increase their contribution to international development. This figure had risen to $32 million by 1975-76. It has been estimated that the total value of private assistance to developing nations from Canadian organizations is about $59 million annually.

CIDA has become involved in the private sector of developing countries' economies and in expanding suitable Canadian enterprises overseas. The organization works with Canadian business, the Department of Industry, Trade and Commerce, international finance corporations, development banks, and overseas corporations to identify and help finance worthwhile investment opportunities in all types of secondary industry in the developing world.

The International Development Research Centre (IDRC) is an international organization supported financially by Canada. Established in 1970 to initiate and encourage research focused on the problems of the world's developing regions, it fosters cooperation between developing nations as well as between the developed and the developing world. In its role as coordinator of international development research, it helps developing regions to build up research capabilities, innovative skills and institutions required to solve their own problems. The centre offers research awards to PhD candidates and mid-career professionals who are Canadian citizens or landed immigrants with three years' residence.

IDRC's chairman, vice-chairman and nine of the other 19 governors are Canadian citizens. There is a strong international element. In 1976 six governors were from developing nations (Jamaica, Mexico, Ethiopia, Zaïre, Iran and Indonesia) and one from each of Britain, France, the United States and Australia. Professional staff included citizens of 14 countries.

Operations are conducted under five programs: Agriculture, Food and Nutrition Sciences; Information Sciences; Population and Health Sciences; Social Sciences and Human Resources; and Publications. As at June 30, 1976 IDRC had approved 375 projects worth $69.8 million involving grantees in 75 countries. Most of the research activities and related seminars were conducted in developing countries by their research organizations. The Canadian government's contribution to IDRC was $27 million in 1975-76 and $29.7 million in 1976-77.

3.7   Defence

3.7.1   The Department of National Defence

The Department of National Defence was created by the National Defence Act, 1922, which established one civil department of government in place of the previous Departments of Militia and Defence, Naval Service and the Air Board. The department now operates under authority of RSC 1970, c.N-4.

The Minister of National Defence has the control and management of the Canadian Forces, the Defence Research Board and all matters relating to national defence establishments. He is responsible for presenting to Cabinet matters of major defence policy for which Cabinet direction is required. He is also responsible for the National Emergency Planning Establishment which replaced the Emergency Measures Organization on April 1, 1974. The minister continues to be responsible for certain civil emergency powers, duties and functions as outlined in Order in Council PC 1965-1041 dated June 8, 1965, as amended.

The Chief of the Defence Staff is the senior military adviser to the minister and is charged with the control and administration of the Canadian Forces. He is responsible for the effective conduct of military operations and the readiness of the Canadian Forces to meet the commitments assigned to the department.

The Defence Research Board is responsible for advising the minister on scientific matters relating to defence and for evaluating the contribution of science and technology to defence.

The Minister of National Defence is responsible for administering the following laws which relate to the Department of National Defence: National Defence Act (RSC 1970, c.N-4), Defence Services Pension Continuation Act (RSC 1970, c.D-3), Canadian Forces Superannuation Act (RSC 1970, c.C-9) and Visiting Forces Act (RSC 1970, c.V-6).

Liaison in other countries. The Chief of the Defence Staff, the Canadian military representative to the North Atlantic Treaty Organization, is responsible for advice on all NATO military matters and acts as a military adviser to the government and to Canadian delegations to NATO. For purposes of liaison and international cooperation in defence, Canada also maintains: the Canadian Defence Liaison Staff London, the Canadian Defence Liaison Staff Washington, two logistic liaison units in the United States, a Canadian member of the NATO Military Committee in Permanent Session in Brussels, a Military Adviser to the Canadian Permanent Representative to the North Atlantic Council and also a Canadian National Military Representative to Supreme Headquarters Allied Powers Europe (SHAPE), and Canadian Forces Attachés in various countries throughout the world. In addition, a number of defence matters of concern to both Canada and the United States are considered by the Permanent Joint Board on Defence, which provides advice on such matters to the respective governments.

The command structure of the Canadian Forces   3.7.2

The Canadian Forces are organized on a functional basis to reflect the major commitments assigned by the government. All forces devoted to a primary mission are grouped under a single commander. Specifically, the Canadian Forces are formed into National Defence Headquarters and five major commands reporting to the Chief of the Defence Staff.

Mobile Command   3.7.2.1

The role of Mobile Command is to provide military units suitably trained and equipped for the protection of Canadian territory, to maintain operational readiness of combat formations in Canada required for overseas commitments, and to support United Nations or other peacekeeping operations.

The forces assigned include: three airportable combat groups in Canada, the Canadian Airborne Regiment, the Canadian Contingent of the United Nations Force in Cyprus, the Canadian Contingent of the United Nations Middle East, and one combat training centre.

The Militia is assigned its traditional role as a sub-component in support of the Regular Force. Under the present organization, units of the Militia have been placed under either the Commander, Mobile Command or Canadian Forces Communication Command.

Mobile Command exercises command and control of 99 Militia Combat Units plus administrative and service units through five Militia Area Headquarters and 21 Militia Districts located as follows: Esquimalt, Vancouver and Victoria; Edmonton, Southern Alberta, Saskatchewan and Winnipeg; Hamilton, London, North Bay, Ottawa, Toronto and Windsor; Montreal and Quebec; and West Nova Scotia, Cape Breton, West New Brunswick, East New Brunswick, Prince Edward Island and Newfoundland. Mobile Command Militia is charged with providing trained individuals for augmentation and reinforcement of the Regular Force, providing trained sub-units to support the field force for the defence of Canada and the maintenance of internal security, providing trained personnel for the augmentation of the civil emergency operations organization, and forming the base on which the Regular Force could be expanded for service in an emergency.

3.7.2.2   Maritime Command

All Canadian Maritime Forces are under the command of the Commander, Maritime Command, whose headquarters is in Halifax. The Deputy Commander is the Commander, Maritime Forces Pacific with headquarters in Esquimalt. The role of Maritime Command is to defend Canadian interests from assault by sea, to support measures to protect Canadian sovereignty, to support Canadian military operations as required and to conduct search and rescue operations within the Atlantic and Pacific Search and Rescue Areas (roughly the Atlantic provinces and British Columbia).

As at December 1975, the following vessels were in service in Maritime Command: 20 Destroyer Escorts/Destroyer Escorts Helicopter Equipped including four new Iroquois Class Helicopter Destroyers, three Operational Support Ships, three Oberon Class Submarines, six Bay Class Coastal Patrol Vessels (employed as training vessels), and two Escort Repair Vessels (retained in service as alongside workshops and temporary accommodation vessels).

The Naval Reserve is an essential component of Maritime Command. Its primary function is to provide trained personnel to augment the fleet in emergencies. Another essential role is to provide and maintain naval control of shipping in time of emergency or war to meet national and NATO requirements. There are 16 naval reserve units in major Canadian cities.

3.7.2.3   Air Command

With the formation of Air Command on September 2, 1975 overall responsibility for Canada's military air forces was again vested in one senior commander to provide greater flexibility in the employment of air power as well as to increase operational effectiveness, safety and economy.

The command's principal function is to provide operationally-ready regular and reserve air forces to meet Canada's national, continental and international commitments, and to carry out regional commitments within the Prairie Region — Saskatchewan, Alberta and Manitoba.

Air Command, with headquarters at Winnipeg, consists of four operational groups: Air Defence Group, Air Transport Group, Maritime Air Group, and 10 Tactical Air Group. Air Command also exercises command and control over the air training schools and the reserve.

Air Defence Group (ADG), with headquarters at North Bay, Ont., is responsible for maintaining sovereignty of Canada's airspace. In addition, the group provides Canada's contribution to NORAD, the joint Canada–US North American Air Defence Command.

It has command of three all-weather fighter squadrons, a training squadron, two transcontinental radar lines, a satellite tracking unit and an electronic warfare squadron.

Air Transport Group. The Air Transport Group provides airlift resources to enable the Canadian Forces to meet their commitments. It also undertakes national and international tasks as directed by the government. The group provides search and rescue service for downed aircraft and coordinates marine search and rescue operations. Heavy transport resources consist of 24 C-130 Hercules aircraft and five Boeing 707 aircraft. A squadron at Ottawa provides medium-range passenger transport with seven Cosmopolitan and seven Falcon aircraft.

Transport and rescue squadrons at Comox, BC, Edmonton, Alta., Trenton, Ont., and Summerside, PEI, are equipped with Buffalo and Twin Otter fixed-wing aircraft, and some with Labrador and Voyageur helicopters. Rescue Coordination centres at Trenton, Ont., and Edmonton coordinate search and rescue activities. They work closely with Maritime Command in Victoria and Halifax.

Air Movements units at Ottawa, Trenton, Edmonton and Lahr, Federal Republic of Germany, with detachments at Comox and Vancouver, BC, Winnipeg, Man., and Greenwood and Shearwater, NS provide passenger and cargo-processing services.

In 1975 strategic and tactical airlift by 10 Tactical Air Group aircraft enabled other elements of the forces to participate in a wide range of activities embracing national sovereignty, North American defence, NATO, humanitarian missions and contributions to hemispheric security.

About half of the group's flying is devoted to joint exercises with Mobile Command and other Canadian Forces Commands, often in conjunction with NATO allies. The remainder is used to support Canadian Forces Europe, isolated bases in northern Canada, Canadian military and civil missions abroad, and DND and other government agencies in Canada.

Maritime Air Group (MAG) was created on September 2, 1975 as a component of Air Command. The group is responsible for management of all air resources engaged in maritime patrol, maritime surveillance and anti-submarine warfare.

The commander of Maritime Air Group, while responsible to the commander of Air Command, is under the operational control of the commander of Maritime Command while carrying out surveillance roles. A close working relationship between Maritime Command and Maritime Air Group enables them to utilize a common operations centre.

The group conducts surveillance flights over Canada's coastal waters and the Arctic archipelago. It also provides anti-submarine air forces as part of Canada's contribution to NATO.

Air Reserves. The Air Reserve is organized into four Air Reserve Wing Headquarters at Montreal, Toronto, Winnipeg and Edmonton and six flying squadrons of six DHC Otter aircraft each, at Montreal (two), Toronto (two), Winnipeg (one) and Edmonton (one). The Air Reserve is required to provide light tactical air transport support to the Regular Force and in particular to Mobile Command ground forces. Air Reserve tasks include logistic airlift, air evacuation of patients, aerial surveillance and photography, and communications and liaison.

The Canadian Forces Training System (CFTS) 3.7.2.4

The CFTS was created on September 2, 1975 with the formation of Air Command and the realignment of the Canadian Forces command structure. With headquarters at CFB Trenton, Ont., it plans and conducts all recruit, trades, specialist and officer classification training common to more than one command.

The commander of Canadian Forces Training System also assumes regional commitments in Central Region (the province of Ontario), including responsibility for planning and implementing aid to the civil power, assistance to civil authorities and other federal departments, liaison with the provincial government and its agencies, and provision of support services to selected units of other commands.

Information on recruit and trades training, training for officers, flying training, the three Canadian military colleges, the cadet movement and other related programs is included in Chapter 7, Education, Training and Cultural Activities.

3.7.2.5   The Canadian Forces Communication Command (CFCC)

The CFCC maintains strategic communications for the Canadian Forces and, in emergencies, for the federal and provincial governments. The command also provides points for interconnecting strategic and tactical networks. CFCC also operates the major DND automatic data processing centres.

The 12 Canadian Forces Communication Command Militia Units are centred in: Vancouver, Edmonton and Calgary; Regina and Winnipeg; Toronto and Ottawa; Montreal and Quebec; and Saint John, Halifax and Charlottetown. Their tasks collectively include the augmentation of Canadian Forces Communication Command in an emergency, the provision of communications support to Mobile Command Militia in emergency operations (peace), the provision of instructors for the training of Mobile Command unit signalers, and the provision of communications support for control of Mobile Command Militia tactical exercises.

Canadian Forces Europe. The Canadian Forces allocated to support NATO in Europe consist of land and air elements. The land element is No. 4 Canadian Mechanized Brigade Group operationally responsible to the Central Army Group. The air element, No. 1 Canadian Air Group, consisting of three CF-104 Starfighter squadrons, is operationally assigned to No. 4 Allied Tactical Air Force. These elements are located in the Baden-Baden area of the Federal Republic of Germany and are supported administratively by CFB Europe at Lahr.

Administration of military bases in Canada. Staffs and services required below Command Headquarters level to administer and support units based in a particular locality have been organized on Canadian Forces bases. Each base has been allocated to a functional commander to whom the base commander reports.

Function/regional organization. Functional commanders have been assigned a regional as well as a functional responsibility for representation to provincial governments, aid to the civil power, emergency and survival operations, administration of cadets, and provision of regional support services for all units in the region.

Canada has been divided into six regions with five of them assigned to functional commanders as follows: Atlantic (Newfoundland, Nova Scotia, Prince Edward Island, New Brunswick) — Maritime Command; Eastern (Quebec) — Mobile Command; Central (Ontario) — Canadian Forces Training System; Prairie (Manitoba, Saskatchewan, Alberta) — Air Command; and Pacific (British Columbia) — Maritime Forces Pacific. One region, comprising the Yukon Territory and Northwest Territories, has been assigned to Commander Northern Region with headquarters in Yellowknife, NWT who also exercises a coordinating function for all military activities in the region.

3.7.3   Operations in 1975-76

Maritime air, surface and sub-surface forces participated in NATO exercises in the North Atlantic and in combined exercises with forces from New Zealand, Australia, Britain and the United States on both the Pacific and Atlantic coasts. Training exercises were conducted in the Bermuda, Caribbean and Southern California areas to maintain the Maritime Forces at an operational level. An exercise was also held in the Arctic to assess capabilities in northern waters.

Argus aircraft from both east and west coast squadrons maintained daily long-range patrols and surveillance of adjacent ocean areas and in the Arctic; many hours were also flown on search and rescue missions. Shore-based Tracker aircraft flew similar missions, concentrating on coastal patrols, fisheries protection and pollution prevention.

In fulfilment of obligations under NATO, Canada continued to provide ground and air forces for the defence of Western Europe as outlined in Section 3.6.2.6 Canada, NATO and NORAD.

To exercise Canadian sovereignty and to familiarize troops with the problems of living, moving and fighting in the North, exercise New Viking continued to be Mobile Command's most important northern exercise. From advanced bases in Churchill and Resolute Bay forces were deployed to forward patrol bases in all parts of the Canadian Arctic archipelago.

The Canadian Airborne Regiment, the command's quick reaction force for both defence of Canada and international peacekeeping operations, exercised in the Arctic and participated in exercises overseas.

The Canadian Forces continued to provide support for United Nations operations as described in Section 3.6.2.3 Canada and the United Nations.

National Emergency Planning Establishment   3.7.4

The Canada Emergency Measures Organization was created to coordinate the civil aspects of defence policy delegated to federal departments and agencies to meet the threat of nuclear war on Canada. In late 1973 certain changes were made to ensure an effective response to any emergency. The Canada Emergency Measures Organization was re-named the National Emergency Planning Establishment effective April 1, 1974. The new organization works under the direction of the Privy Council Office with its main function to mitigate the effects of disasters in Canada. It will continue to have regional offices in each provincial capital to ensure continuing support for provincial authorities in the development of mutual emergency capabilities.

Sources
3.1 Government Organization Division, Privy Council Office; Clerk of the Senate; House of Commons Division, Department of Supply and Services; Office of the Chief Electoral Officer.
3.2.1 Secretary of the Treasury Board.
3.2.2 Secretary of the Treasury Board; Public Relations Division, Public Service Commission.
3.2.3 Deputy Minister, Department of Indian Affairs and Northern Development.
3.2.4 Government Organization Division, Privy Council Office; Organization Division, Planning Branch, Treasury Board; *Canada Year Book* staff.
3.2.5 Communications Division, Treasury Board.
3.3 Supplied by the respective provincial and territorial governments.
3.4.1 Privy Council Office.
3.4.2 Supplied by the respective provincial governments.
3.5 Public Finance Division, Institutional and Public Finance Statistics Branch, Statistics Canada.
3.6 Information Division, Department of External Affairs; Information Division, Canadian International Development Agency; International Development Research Centre.
3.7 Directorate of Parliamentary Affairs, Department of National Defence.

Tables

Tables

..	not available	e estimate
...	not appropriate or not applicable	p preliminary
—	nil or zero	r revised
- -	too small to be expressed	certain tables may not add due to rounding

3.1 Duration and sessions of Parliaments, 1966-76

Order of Parliament	Session	Date of opening	Date of prorogation	Days of session	Sitting days of House of Commons	Date of election, writs returnable, dissolution, and length of Parliament[1,2]
27th Parliament	1st	Jan. 18, 1966	May 8, 1967	476[6]	250	Nov. 8, 1965[3]
	2nd	May 8, 1967	Apr. 23, 1968	352[7]	155	Dec. 9, 1965[4]
						Apr. 23, 1968[5]
						2 yr, 4 m, 15 d
28th Parliament	1st	Sept. 12, 1968	Oct. 22, 1969	386[8]	199	June 25, 1968[3]
	2nd	Oct. 23, 1969	Oct. 7, 1970	349[9]	155	July 25, 1968[4]
	3rd	Oct. 8, 1970	Feb. 16, 1972	497[10]	244	Sept. 1, 1972[5]
	4th	Feb. 17, 1972	Sept. 1, 1972	197[11]	91	4 yr, 1 m, 8 d
29th Parliament	1st	Jan. 4, 1973	Feb. 26, 1974	418[12]	206	Oct. 30, 1972[3]
	2nd	Feb. 27, 1974	May 8, 1974	71	50	Nov. 20, 1972[4]
						May 9, 1974[5]
						1 yr, 5 m, 20 d
30th Parliament	1st	Sept. 30, 1974	Oct. 12, 1976	743[13]	343	July 8, 1974[3]
	2nd	Oct. 12, 1976				July 30, 1974[4]

[1]The ordinary legal limit of duration for each Parliament is five years.
[2]Duration of Parliament in years, months and days. The life of a Parliament is counted from the date of return of election writs to the date of dissolution, both days inclusive (BNA Act, Sect. 50).
[3]Date of general election.
[4]Writs returnable.
[5]Dissolution of Parliament.
[6]Includes Easter adjournment from Apr. 6, 1966 to Apr. 19, 1966; two summer adjournments from July 14, 1966 to Aug. 29, 1966 and Sept. 9, 1966 to Oct. 5, 1966; Christmas adjournment from Dec. 21, 1966 to Jan. 9, 1967 and Easter adjournment from Mar. 22, 1967 to Apr. 3, 1967.
[7]Includes summer adjournment from July 7, 1967 to Sept. 25, 1967; Christmas adjournment from Dec. 21, 1967 to Jan. 22, 1968; and Easter (Liberal Convention) Mar. 28, 1968 to Apr. 23, 1968.
[8]Includes Christmas adjournment from Dec. 20, 1968 to Jan. 14, 1969; Easter adjournment from Apr. 2, 1969 to Apr. 14, 1969; and summer adjournment from July 25, 1969 to Oct. 22, 1969.
[9]Includes Christmas adjournment from Dec. 19, 1969 to Jan. 12, 1970; Easter adjournment from Mar. 25, 1970 to Apr. 6, 1970; and summer adjournment from June 26, 1970 to Oct. 5, 1970.
[10]Includes Christmas adjournment from Dec. 18, 1970 to Jan. 11, 1971; Easter adjournment from Apr. 7, 1971 to Apr. 19, 1971; summer adjournment from June 30, 1971 to Sept. 7, 1971; Christmas adjournments from Dec. 23, 1971 to Dec. 28, 1971; and Dec. 31, 1971 to Jan. 12, 1972.
[11]Includes Easter adjournment from Mar. 29, 1972 to Apr. 13, 1972; and summer adjournment from July 7, 1972 to Aug. 31, 1972.
[12]Includes Easter adjournment from Apr. 19, 1973 to May 6, 1973; summer adjournments from July 27, 1973 to Aug. 30, 1973 and Sept. 21, 1973 to Oct. 15, 1973; Christmas adjournments from Dec. 22, 1973 to Jan. 2, 1974 and Jan. 14, 1974 to Feb. 26, 1974.
[13]Includes Christmas adjournment from Dec. 20, 1974 to Jan. 22, 1975; Easter adjournment from Mar. 27, 1975 to Apr. 7, 1975; summer adjournment from July 31, 1975 to Oct. 13, 1975; Christmas adjournment from Dec. 20, 1975 to Jan. 26, 1976; Easter adjournment from Apr. 14, 1976 to Apr. 26, 1976; and summer adjournment from July 16, 1976 to Oct. 12, 1976.

3.2 Representation in the Senate since Confederation, 1867

Province or territory	1867	1870	1871	1873	1882	1887	1892	1903	1905	1915-1948	1949-1974	1975
Ontario	24	24	24	24	24	24	24	24	24	24	24	24
Quebec	24	24	24	24	24	24	24	24	24	24	24	24
Atlantic provinces	24	24	24	24	24	24	24	24	24	24	30	30
Nova Scotia	12	12	12	10	10	10	10	10	10	10	10	10
New Brunswick	12	12	12	10	10	10	10	10	10	10	10	10
Prince Edward Island	...	...	...	4	4	4	4	4	4	4	4	4
Newfoundland	...	...	...	...	...	...	...	...	...	...	6	6
Western provinces	...	2	5	5	6	8	9	11	15	24	24	24
Manitoba	...	2	2	2	3	3	4	4	4	6	6	6
British Columbia	...	...	3	3	3	3	3	3	3	6	6	6
Saskatchewan	...	...	...	...	...	2	2	4	4	6	6	6
Alberta									4	6	6	6
Territories	...	...	...	...	...	...	...	...	...	...	...	2
Yukon Territory	...	...	...	...	...	...	...	...	...	...	...	1
Northwest Territories	...	...	...	...	...	...	...	...	...	...	...	1
Total	72	74	77	77	78	80	81	83	87	96	102	104

3.3 Representation in the House of Commons, as at federal general elections 1867-1974

Province or territory	1867	1872	1874 1878	1882	1887 1891	1896 1900	1904	1908 1911	1917 1921	1925 1926 1930	1935 1940 1945	1949	1953 1957 1958 1962 1963 1965	1968 1972 1974
Ontario	82	88	88	92	92	92	86	86	82	82	82	83	85	88
Quebec	65	65	65	65	65	65	65	65	65	65	65	73	75	74
Nova Scotia	19	21	21	21	21	20	18	18	16	14	12	13	12	11
New Brunswick	15	16	16	16	16	14	13	13	11	11	10	10	10	10
Manitoba	...	4	4	5	5	7	10	10	15	17	17	16	14	13
British Columbia	...	6	6	6	6	6	7	7	13	14	16	18	22	23
Prince Edward Island	...	...	6	6	6	5	4	4	4	4	4	4	4	4
Saskatchewan	...	...	...	...	4	4	10	10	16	21	21	20	17	13
Alberta								7	12	16	17	17	17	19
Yukon Territory	...	...	...	...	...	...	1	1	1	1	1	1	1	1
Mackenzie River NWT[1]													1	1
Newfoundland	...	...	...	...	...	...	...	...	...	...	...	7	7	7
Total	181	200	206	211	215	213	214	221	235	245	245	262	265	264

[1]Electoral district of Northwest Territories in 1963, 1965, 1968, 1972 and 1974.

3.4 Electoral districts, voters on the list, votes polled and names and addresses of members of the House of Commons as elected at the thirtieth general election, July 8, 1974

Province and electoral district	Population, Census 1971	Voters on list	Total votes polled (incl. rejections)	Votes polled by member	Name of member	Postal address	Party affiliation[1]
NEWFOUNDLAND (7 members)							
Bonavista—Trinity—Conception	69,543	44,012	26,839	13,258	D. Rooney	Lower Island Cove	Lib.
Burin—Burgeo	54,044	31,149	16,698	13,550	Hon. D.C. Jamieson	Swift Current	Lib.
Gander—Twillingate	71,480	40,875	23,035	12,721	G.S. Baker	Gander	Lib.
Grand Falls—White Bay—Labrador	75,106	41,250	23,290	12,689	B.Rompkey	Grand Falls	Lib.
Humber—St. George's—St. Barbe	82,263	44,731	28,104	16,500	J. Marshall	Corner Brook	PC
St. John's East	87,477	52,148	30,371	16,941	J.A. McGrath	Portugal Cove	PC
St. John's West	82,191	50,205	27,197	14,550	W. Carter	St. John's	PC
PRINCE EDWARD ISLAND (4 members)							
Cardigan	23,363	15,212	13,043	6,958	Hon. D.J. MacDonald	Bothwell	Lib.
Egmont	30,629	18,583	14,581	7,583	D. MacDonald	Alberton	PC
Hillsborough	35,639	25,322	19,801	9,917	H. Macquarrie	Victoria	PC
Malpeque	22,010	13,952	11,224	5,649	Hon. J.A. MacLean	Belle River	PC

3.4   Electoral districts, voters on the list, votes polled and names and addresses of members of the House of Commons as elected at the thirtieth general election, July 8, 1974 (continued)

Province and electoral district	Population, Census 1971	Voters on list	Total votes polled (incl. rejections)	Votes polled by member	Name of member	Postal address	Party affiliation[1]
NOVA SCOTIA (11 members)							
Annapolis Valley	74,123	48,463	36,702	19,174	P. Nowlan	Wolfville	PC
Cape Breton—East Richmond	64,371	40,428	31,923	14,192	A. Hogan	Glace Bay	NDP
Cape Breton Highlands—Canso	62,550	41,476	32,406	17,977	Hon. A.J. MacEachen	Inverness	Lib.
Cape Breton—The Sydneys	68,135	43,553	32,682	14,371	R. Muir	Sydney Mines	PC
Central Nova	62,726	42,956	32,532	17,459	E.M. MacKay	Lorne	PC
Cumberland—Colchester North	65,899	46,059	34,388	18,078	R.C. Coates	Amherst	PC
Dartmouth—Halifax East	98,399	61,917	43,030	22,090	M. Forrestall	Dartmouth	PC
Halifax	64,523	42,970	30,339	14,865	Hon. R.L. Stanfield[2]	Ottawa	PC
Halifax—East Hants	100,637	70,222	50,199	25,563	B. McCleave	Halifax	PC
South Shore	65,420	46,174	33,660	18,206	L.R. Crouse	Lunenburg	PC
South Western Nova	62,177	40,549	30,969	15,067	C. Campbell	Yarmouth	Lib.
NEW BRUNSWICK (10 members)							
Carleton—Charlotte	59,244	38,195	24,541	12,315	F.A. McCain	Florenceville	PC
Fundy—Royal	70,316	48,459	31,594	13,631	G. Fairweather	Rothesay	PC
Gloucester	63,556	39,011	28,598	16,031	H. Breau	Tracadie	Lib.
Madawaska—Victoria	54,772	33,187	22,395	14,310	E. Corbin	Edmundston	Lib.
Moncton	80,188	56,121	45,433	20,671	L. Jones	Moncton	Ind.
Northumberland—Miramichi	54,094	32,320	24,186	12,648	M. Dionne	Millerton	Lib.
Restigouche	52,485	31,208	22,709	12,492	Hon. J.-E. Dubé	Campbellton	Lib.
Saint John—Lancaster	68,460	42,945	28,024	12,860	M. Landers	Saint John	Lib.
Westmorland—Kent	51,856	34,805	26,686	16,340	R.-A. LeBlanc	Memramcook	Lib.
York—Sunbury	79,586	50,267	35,326	17,673	J.R. Howie	Fredericton	PC
QUEBEC (74 members)							
Abitibi	58,427	38,197	22,758	12,425	G. Laprise	LaSarre	SC
Argenteuil—Deux-Montagnes	80,574	54,218	39,071	20,414	F. Fox	St-Eustache	Lib.
Beauce	69,984	46,155	33,221	13,855	Y. Caron	St-Georges-Ouest	Lib.
Beauharnois—Salaberry	73,396	48,313	33,864	16,828	G. Laniel	Valleyfield	Lib.
Bellechasse	64,675	42,225	27,641	12,550	A. Lambert	Berthier-sur-Mer	SC
Berthier	62,521	42,574	29,050	15,266	A. Yanakis	St-Gabriel-de-Brandon	Lib.
Bonaventure-Îles-de-la-Madeleine	55,004	33,376	21,867	12,977	A. Béchard	Carleton	Lib.
Brome—Missisquoi	76,787	51,019	38,680	19,490	H. Grafftey	Knowlton	PC
Chambly	120,337	82,787	56,583	30,099	B. Loiselle	Beloeil	Lib.
Champlain	62,068	41,017	30,332	14,466	R. Matte	St-Marc-des-Carrières	SC
Charlevoix	59,686	39,016	25,595	10,372	C. Lapointe	Tadoussac	Lib.
Chicoutimi	82,658	51,405	35,405	17,096	P. Langlois	Chicoutimi	Lib.
Compton	62,197	39,068	27,198	11,474	C. Tessier	Lac-Mégantic	Lib.
Drummond	75,533	49,826	38,606	15,561	Y. Pinard	Drummondville	Lib.
Frontenac	67,991	42,338	29,817	14,236	L. Corriveau	Thetford Mines	Lib.
Gaspé	56,280	34,679	21,436	12,213	J.-A. Cyr	Chandler	Lib.
Gatineau	81,320	53,833	33,404	19,513	G. Clermont	Thurso	Lib.
Hull	93,804	61,475	38,837	26,872	G. Isabelle	Lucerne	Lib.
Joliette	83,417	57,126	42,603	21,935	R. LaSalle	Crabtree	PC
Kamouraska	63,228	39,885	23,805	11,664	C.-E. Dionne	St-Pascal	SC
Labelle	82,228	55,680	39,534	16,224	M. Dupras	St-Jérôme	Lib.
Lac-Saint-Jean	56,862	33,618	24,483	11,162	M. Lessard	Alma	Lib.
Langelier	58,559	36,584	22,463	13,616	Hon. J. Marchand	Quebec	Lib.
Lapointe	72,451	44,318	28,634	16,617	G. Marceau	Jonquière	Lib.
Laprairie	131,675	89,276	60,419	35,276	I. Watson	Laprairie	Lib
Lévis	80,037	56,925	38,538	20,348	R. Guay	Lauzon	Lib.
Longueuil	112,703	79,375	50,876	24,500	J. Olivier	Longueuil	Lib.
Lotbinière	70,964	46,948	36,505	21,448	A. Fortin	Victoriaville	SC
Louis-Hébert	106,928	74,430	51,825	32,441	Albanie Morin	Sillery	Lib.
Manicouagan	80,461	57,879	25,945	16,229	G. Blouin	Sept-Îles	Lib.
Matane	48,373	29,449	17,133	11,194	P. De Bané	Matane	Lib.
Montmorency	116,204	79,714	54,754	27,082	L. Duclos	Ste-Foy	Lib.
Pontiac	59,956	37,761	23,249	12,642	T. Lefebvre	Davidson	Lib.
Portneuf	116,079	80,495	55,065	25,630	P. Bussières	Charlesbourg	Lib.
Québec-Est	81,782	52,449	34,032	19,019	G. Duquet	Quebec	Lib.
Richelieu	77,197	53,200	38,334	20,801	F. Côté	Ste-Brigitte-des-Saults	Lib.
Richmond	62,741	38,576	28,305	11,825	L. Beaudoin	Bromptonville	SC
Rimouski	69,276	44,692	31,515	15,085	E. Allard	Rimouski	SC
Rivière-du-Loup—Témiscouata	59,816	37,302	25,714	11,071	R. Gendron	Rivière-du-Loup	Lib.
Roberval	53,671	33,606	23,464	12,877	C.-A. Gauthier	Mistassini	SC
Saint-Hyacinthe	82,540	56,801	43,602	21,453	C. Wagner	Saint-Hyacinthe	PC
Saint-Jean	83,274	54,334	37,571	18,798	W.B. Smith	Hemmingford	Lib.

3.4   Electoral districts, voters on the list, votes polled and names and addresses of members of the House of Commons as elected at the thirtieth general election, July 8, 1974 (continued)

Province and electoral district	Popu- lation, Census 1971	Voters on list	Total votes polled (incl. rejec- tions)	Votes polled by member	Name of member	Postal address	Party affili- ation[1]
QUEBEC (concluded)							
Saint-Maurice	71,147	47,117	33,009	20,468	Hon. J. Chrétien	Shawinigan	Lib.
Shefford	79,083	51,856	38,397	15,572	G. Rondeau	Granby	SC
Sherbrooke	97,550	66,005	44,944	23,903	Irénée Pelletier	Sherbrooke	Lib.
Témiscamingue	54,545	32,226	22,911	14,026	R. Caouette[2]	Rouyn	SC
Terrebonne	122,332	83,020	55,124	28,651	J.-R. Comtois	Repentigny	Lib.
Trois-Rivières métropolitain	95,389	64,050	42,278	24,335	C.-G. Lajoie	Cap-de-la-Madeleine	Lib.
Villeneuve	58,859	38,259	24,695	10,452	A. Caouette	Val-d'Or	SC
Island of Montreal and Île-Jésus							
Ahuntsic	90,537	56,170	39,547	24,041	Hon. Jeanne Sauvé	Montreal	Lib.
Dollard	123,429	79,270	57,138	37,200	Hon. J.-P. Goyer	St-Laurent	Lib.
Duvernay	112,102	69,264	47,526	25,674	Y. Demers	Ville-de-Laval	Lib.
Gamelin	92,533	57,861	37,993	20,625	A. Portelance	Montreal	Lib.
Hochelaga	65,390	38,884	22,991	10,561	Hon. G. Pelletier	Westmount	Lib.
Lachine-Lakeshore	92,202	57,365	42,591	22,068	R. Blaker	Pointe-Claire	Lib.
Lafontaine	70,166	42,952	25,890	11,429	C.A. Lachance	Montreal	Lib.
LaSalle—Émard—Côte Saint-Paul	116,235	72,724	47,179	28,146	J. Campbell	LaSalle	Lib.
Laurier	67,023	31,634	18,573	10,085	F.-E. Leblanc	Montreal	Lib.
Laval	115,908	71,697	48,729	29,715	M. Roy	Laval-des-Rapides	Lib.
Maisonneuve—Rosemont	74,499	44,444	27,576	13,817	S. Joyal	Montreal	Lib.
Mercier	118,807	74,272	44,505	22,545	P. Boulanger	Pointe-aux-Trembles	Lib.
Montréal—Bourassa	124,746	78,559	48,646	26,550	J.-L. Trudel	Montreal	Lib.
Mount Royal	90,844	59,202	43,525	32,166	Rt. Hon. P.-E. Trudeau[2]	Ottawa	Lib.
Notre-Dame-de-Grâce	77,052	45,939	33,177	20,151	Hon. W. Allmand	Montreal	Lib.
Outremont	75,621	44,931	30,725	20,400	Hon. M. Lalonde	Montreal	Lib.
Papineau	73,439	41,921	25,583	14,532	Hon. A. Ouellet	Montreal	Lib.
Saint-Denis	77,362	36,737	25,640	15,310	M. Prud'homme	Montreal	Lib.
Saint-Henri	57,162	29,790	17,664	8,813	G. Loiselle	Montreal	Lib.
Saint-Jacques	53,179	24,845	14,740	7,709	J. Guilbault	Montreal	Lib.
Sainte-Marie	58,381	34,418	20,595	8,300	R. Dupont	Longueuil	Lib.
Saint-Michel	138,109	81,077	49,012	29,822	Monique Bégin	Saint Léonard	Lib.
Vaudreuil	112,103	71,417	51,630	29,685	H.T. Herbert	Hudson	Lib.
Verdun	74,718	47,567	31,286	17,633	Hon. B. Mackasey	Verdun	Lib.
Westmount	83,645	51,592	37,127	20,816	Hon. C.M. Drury	Ste-Cécile-de-Masham	Lib.
ONTARIO (88 members)							
Algoma	52,746	30,937	21,927	11,360	M. Foster	Desbarats	Lib.
Brant	97,549	62,333	46,444	19,453	D. Blackburn	Brantford	NDP
Bruce—Gray	63,308	46,111	36,225	17,158	C. Douglas	Wingham	Lib.
Cochrane	54,786	31,793	21,073	11,379	R.W. Stewart	Moonbeam	Lib.
Elgin	66,608	43,088	33,799	15,851	J. Wise	St. Thomas	PC
Essex—Windsor	94,846	60,901	44,305	24,357	Hon. E.F. Whelan	Amherstburg	Lib.
Fort William	60,207	38,892	28,336	13,789	P. McRae	Thunder Bay "F"	Lib.
Frontenac—Lennox and Addington	61,668	40,801	29,329	14,102	D. Alkenbrack	Napanee	PC
Glengarry—Prescott—Russell	62,599	41,302	30,714	18,478	D. Éthier	Dalkeith	Lib.
Grenville—Carleton	119,408	79,873	62,620	33,946	W. Baker	Ottawa	PC
Grey—Simcoe	67,997	47,652	34,454	15,917	G. Mitges	Owen Sound	PC
Halton	105,801	68,063	52,145	23,520	F. Philbrook	Oakville	Lib.
Halton—Wentworth	124,390	82,370	61,964	26,798	B. Kempling	Dundas	PC
Hamilton East	74,709	39,992	28,356	15,298	Hon. J.C. Munro	Hamilton	Lib.
Hamilton Mountain	106,266	67,718	50,965	22,217	G. MacFarlane	Hamilton	Lib.
Hamilton—Wentworth	99,169	67,067	48,002	18,874	S. O'Sullivan	Hamilton	PC
Hamilton West	81,664	49,060	34,372	15,421	L.M. Alexander	Hamilton	PC
Hastings	64,328	42,657	31,076	14,893	J. Ellis	Belleville	PC
Huron—Middlesex	58,515	38,560	29,122	17,185	R.E. McKinley	Zurich	PC
Kenora—Rainy River	54,853	33,993	23,197	10,317	J.M. Reid	Kenora	Lib.
Kent—Essex	85,580	53,937	36,198	17,800	B. Daudlin	Leamington	Lib.
Kingston and The Islands	82,907	53,642	38,820	17,844	Flora MacDonald	Kingston	PC
Kitchener	106,127	66,445	48,427	21,091	P. Flynn	Kitchener	Lib.
Lambton—Kent	67,892	43,021	29,687	14,315	J.R. Holmes	Wallaceburg	PC
Lanark—Renfrew—Carleton	63,818	43,953	34,816	18,242	P. Dick	Kanata	PC
Leeds	66,263	43,597	33,375	17,724	T. Cossitt	Brockville	PC
Lincoln	84,935	52,148	39,087	17,499	B. Andres	Niagara-on-the-Lake	Lib.
London East	89,221	53,199	36,788	18,429	C.R. Turner	London	Lib.
London West	106,317	76,796	57,593	32,188	J. Buchanan	London	Lib.
Middlesex—London—Lambton	92,814	58,435	44,306	20,703	L. Condon	Strathroy	Lib.
Mississauga	172,532	118,909	87,492	38,517	T. Abbott	Oakville	Lib.
Niagara Falls	89,537	55,345	39,004	20,618	R. Young	Niagara Falls	Lib.
Nickel Belt	85,577	46,001	35,587	17,668	J. Rodriguez	Capreol	NDP
Nipissing	67,312	41,154	30,743	16,549	J.-J. Blais	North Bay	Lib.
Norfolk—Haldimand	74,568	47,842	37,046	17,867	W. Knowles	Langton	PC
Northumberland—Durham	73,705	50,584	38,965	16,824	A. Lawrence	Janetville	PC
Ontario	87,842	54,783	42,440	20,096	N.A. Cafik	Pickering	Lib.
Oshawa—Whitby	111,361	72,407	51,661	25,013	E. Broadbent[2]	Oshawa	NDP
Ottawa—Carleton	130,906	93,141	72,344	38,465	Hon. J. Turner	Ottawa	Lib.

3.4   Electoral districts, voters on the list, votes polled and names and addresses of members of the House of Commons as elected at the thirtieth general election, July 8, 1974 (continued)

Province and electoral district	Population, Census 1971	Voters on list	Total votes polled (incl. rejections)	Votes polled by member	Name of member	Postal address	Party affiliation[1]
ONTARIO (concluded)							
Ottawa Centre	70,584	46,561	35,640	15,308	H. Poulin	Ottawa	Lib.
Ottawa—Vanier	71,277	45,372	32,365	21,773	J.-R. Gauthier	Ottawa	Lib.
Ottawa West	98,956	68,085	52,907	23,604	L. Francis	Ottawa	Lib.
Oxford	80,336	51,752	40,937	18,934	B. Halliday	Tavistock	PC
Parry Sound—Muskoka	62,162	43,279	31,807	14,030	S. Darling	Burks Falls	PC
Peel—Dufferin— Simcoe	119,885	79,104	58,927	27,298	R. Milne	Brampton	Lib.
Perth—Wilmot	72,996	48,075	35,226	17,636	B. Jarvis	Stratford	PC
Peterborough	85,064	58,250	45,235	23,865	Hon. J.H. Faulkner	Lakefield	Lib.
Port Arthur	57,456	36,647	26,756	14,523	Hon. R.K. Andras	Thunder Bay	Lib.
Prince Edward— Hastings	74,856	48,835	35,844	19,219	Hon. G. Hees	Cobourg	PC
Renfrew North— Nipissing East	61,707	35,060	26,701	14,613	L.D. Hopkins	Petawawa	Lib.
Sarnia—Lambton	83,631	51,728	36,917	20,661	J. Cullen	Sarnia	Lib.
Sault Ste Marie	81,002	47,643	37,898	19,050	C. Symes	Sault Ste Marie	NDP
St. Catharines	101,418	68,509	49,011	22,526	G. Parent	St. Catharines	Lib.
Simcoe North	93,655	64,616	47,326	18,857	P.B. Rynard	Orillia	PC
Stormont—Dundas	72,052	46,332	34,669	18,047	E. Lumley	Cornwall	Lib.
Sudbury	94,624	57,344	44,579	23,374	J. Jerome[3]	Sudbury	Lib.
Thunder Bay	53,214	32,842	21,029	11,435	K. Penner	Dryden	Lib.
Timiskaming	49,870	30,205	22,061	10,263	A. Peters	New Liskeard	NDP
Timmins	53,616	33,297	25,379	12,904	J. Roy	Timmins	Lib.
Victoria—Haliburton	60,996	44,758	32,932	17,570	W.C. Scott	Kinmount	PC
Waterloo—Cambridge	120,719	81,248	61,466	25,479	M. Saltsman	Cambridge	NDP
Welland	82,860	53,088	37,845	21,228	V. Railton	Port Colborne	Lib.
Wellington	75,989	50,983	39,421	18,139	F. Maine	Guelph	Lib.
Wellington—Grey— Dufferin—Waterloo	73,846	48,948	34,125	17,253	P. Beatty	Fergus	PC
Windsor—Walkerville	87,514	52,447	40,099	18,977	M. MacGuigan	Windsor	Lib.
Windsor West	90,466	51,150	35,056	19,474	Hon. H. Gray	Windsor	Lib.
York North	125,296	87,554	68,819	34,179	B.J. Danson	Willowdale	Lib.
York—Simcoe	99,624	67,128	50,331	23,591	S. Stevens	King City	PC
Metropolitan Toronto							
Broadview	78,601	35,119	23,754	9,392	J. Gilbert	Toronto	NDP
Davenport	84,780	27,622	20,851	12,294	C.L. Caccia	Toronto	Lib.
Don Valley	104,606	71,345	57,702	29,180	J. Gillies	Ottawa	PC
Eglinton	78,314	52,008	41,133	19,951	Hon. M. Sharp	Ottawa	Lib.
Etobicoke	135,971	92,769	73,969	37,847	Hon. A. Gillespie	Toronto	Lib.
Greenwood	80,797	43,720	31,992	11,038	A.F. Brewin	Toronto	NDP
High Park—Humber Valley	86,050	53,016	40,997	17,389	O. Jelinek	Toronto	PC
Parkdale	82,207	36,612	25,307	13,134	Hon. S. Haidasz	Toronto	Lib.
Rosedale	81,265	47,645	35,723	17,227	Hon. D.S. Macdonald	Toronto	Lib.
St. Paul's	72,174	46,761	35,561	16,100	J. Roberts	Toronto	Lib.
Scarborough East	149,514	89,142	65,578	30,586	M. O'Connell	Scarborough	Lib.
Scarborough West	87,383	51,012	37,691	13,702	A. Martin	Scarborough	Lib.
Spadina	75,487	24,711	17,506	9,393	P. Stollery	Toronto	Lib.
Toronto—Lakeshore	77,227	46,537	35,713	14,241	K. Robinson	Toronto	Lib.
Trinity	81,073	27,364	20,395	10,683	A. Nicholson	Toronto	Lib.
York Centre	160,051	88,379	64,350	31,792	B. Kaplan	Toronto	Lib.
York East	102,910	65,188	48,709	20,682	D. Collenette	Toronto	Lib.
York—Scarborough	193,156	124,638	98,594	47,450	Hon. R. Stanbury	Don Mills	Lib.
York South	85,768	38,715	29,191	12,473	U. Appolloni	Toronto	Lib.
York West	139,650	72,177	53,391	28,075	J. Fleming	Weston	Lib.
MANITOBA (13 members)							
Brandon—Souris	62,547	41,314	28,856	16,624	Hon. W.G. Dinsdale	Brandon	PC
Churchill	77,507	45,107	27,476	11,415	C. Smith	Thompson	PC
Dauphin	54,110	34,440	24,611	11,439	G. Ritchie	Dauphin	PC
Lisgar	56,974	35,657	23,375	16,478	J.B. Murta	Graysville	PC
Marquette	54,070	33,253	23,885	16,033	C. Stewart	Minnedosa	PC
Portage	51,951	31,138	21,731	11,829	P.P. Masniuk	Inwood	PC
Provencher	62,089	37,738	24,590	13,405	J. Epp	Steinbach	PC
St. Boniface	103,943	69,572	51,522	21,812	J.-P. Guay	St. Boniface	Lib.
Selkirk	98,106	66,551	50,643	22,441	D. Whiteway	Winnipeg	PC
Winnipeg North	83,845	54,039	37,006	15,026	D. Orlikow	Winnipeg	NDP
Winnipeg North Centre	73,559	43,086	27,160	12,023	S.H. Knowles	Winnipeg	NDP
Winnipeg South	94,743	65,017	50,888	23,297	Hon. J. Richardson	Winnipeg	Lib.
Winnipeg South Centre	114,803	76,499	56,688	32,277	D. McKenzie	Winnipeg	PC
SASKATCHEWAN (13 members)							
Assiniboia	57,131	33,321	26,852	9,986	R. Goodale	Wilcox	Lib.
Battleford—Kindersley	66,855	38,453	29,201	10,751	C. McIsaac	North Battleford	Lib.
Mackenzie	47,919	29,049	20,600	8,292	S.J. Korchinski	Rama	PC
Meadow Lake	50,391	28,281	19,363	7,419	B. Cadieu	Spiritwood	PC
Moose Jaw	61,810	37,703	28,282	11,678	D. Neil	Moose Jaw	PC
Prince Albert	72,195	44,292	30,167	17,787	Rt. Hon. J.G. Diefenbaker	Prince Albert	PC
Qu'Appelle—Moose Mountain	64,000	37,174	27,813	13,124	Hon. A. Hamilton	Estevan	PC

3.4   Electoral districts, voters on the list, votes polled and names and addresses of members of the House of Commons as elected at the thirtieth general election, July 8, 1974 (concluded)

Province and electoral district	Population, Census 1971	Voters on list	Total votes polled (incl. rejections)	Votes polled by member	Name of member	Postal address	Party affiliation[1]
SASKATCHEWAN (concluded)							
Regina East	89,048	56,872	40,883	15,030	J. Balfour	Regina	PC
Regina—Lake Centre	97,537	64,657	47,449	16,874	L. Benjamin	Regina	NDP
Saskatoon—Biggar	87,303	56,160	37,781	14,296	R. Hnatyshyn	Saskatoon	PC
Saskatoon—Humboldt	102,185	63,682	47,362	23,242	Hon. O.E. Lang	Saskatoon	Lib.
Swift Current— Maple Creek	60,972	36,309	27,360	11,336	F. Hamilton	Swift Current	PC
Yorkton—Melville	68,896	43,363	32,155	14,586	L. Nystrom	Yorkton	NDP
ALBERTA (19 members)							
Athabasca	67,746	36,601	20,887	13,157	P. Yewchuk	Lac La Biche	PC
Battle River	59,545	35,138	24,770	16,819	A. Malone	Rosalind	PC
Calgary Centre	87,346	56,802	37,834	23,810	H. Andre	Calgary	PC
Calgary North	118,118	67,720	46,796	30,102	E. Woolliams	Calgary	PC
Calgary South	133,796	86,392	61,108	41,530	P. Bawden	Calgary	PC
Crowfoot	55,672	34,635	23,956	18,048	J. Horner	Pollockville	PC
Edmonton Centre	94,410	55,929	33,576	18,165	S.E. Paproski	Edmonton	PC
Edmonton East	105,904	57,434	35,444	18,293	W.M. Skoreyko	Sherwood Park	PC
Edmonton—Strathcona	109,725	69,820	47,278	25,808	D. Roche	Edmonton	PC
Edmonton West	126,765	86,100	57,430	29,990	Hon. M. Lambert	Edmonton	PC
Lethbridge	75,795	47,857	32,545	20,602	K. Hurlburt	Fort Macleod	PC
Medicine Hat	62,697	39,647	28,391	15,525	B. Hargrave	Walsh	PC
Palliser	100,115	72,591	49,750	34,184	S. Schumacher	Drumheller	PC
Peace River	62,413	36,588	23,430	14,153	G. Baldwin	West Peace River	PC
Pembina	94,678	61,731	44,161	19,172	P. Elzinga	Sherwood Park	PC
Red Deer	78,792	48,123	33,438	22,251	T.G. Towers	Red Deer	PC
Rocky Mountain	63,834	40,711	26,322	16,042	J. Clark	Edson	PC
Vegreville	58,986	35,509	25,537	18,328	D. Mazankowski	Vegreville	PC
Wetaskiwin	71,537	46,718	31,996	21,341	S. Schellenberger	Spruce Grove	PC
BRITISH COLUMBIA (23 members)							
Burnaby—Richmond— Delta	123,381	82,889	62,180	34,013	J. Reynolds	Delta	PC
Burnaby—Seymour	103,410	66,348	49,521	18,058	M. Raines	Burnaby	Lib.
Capilano	103,918	66,491	52,838	25,797	R. Huntington	West Vancouver	PC
Coast Chilcotin	67,858	43,695	29,423	10,336	J. Pearsall	Powell River	Lib.
Comox—Alberni	89,644	56,598	38,158	13,594	H. Anderson	Port Alberni	Lib.
Esquimalt—Saanich	105,411	74,919	55,299	27,571	D. Munro	Victoria	PC
Fraser Valley East	85,401	55,196	40,656	18,780	A.B. Patterson	Abbotsford	PC
Fraser Valley West	117,467	77,253	55,522	22,925	R. Wenman	Surrey	PC
Kamloops—Cariboo	104,739	68,925	49,196	20,474	L.S. Marchand	Kamloops	Lib.
Kootenay West	67,513	42,245	30,373	12,575	B. Brisco	Trail	PC
Nanaimo—Cowichan— The Islands	97,106	68,325	50,125	20,434	T.C. Douglas	Nanaimo	NDP
New Westminster	106,331	66,956	47,000	15,397	S.M. Leggatt	Port Coquitlam	NDP
Okanagan Boundary	101,304	74,876	53,665	23,044	G.H. Whittaker	Kelowna	PC
Okanagan—Kootenay	92,717	61,905	43,269	17,164	H. Johnston	Salmon Arm	PC
Prince George— Peace River	108,022	60,773	40,186	18,769	F. Oberle	Chetwynd	PC
Skeena	87,917	43,901	30,498	12,218	I. Campagnolo	Prince Rupert	Lib.
Surrey—White Rock	104,072	68,892	49,472	21,540	B. Friesen	White Rock	PC
Vancouver Centre	91,473	67,222	45,929	19,064	Hon. R. Basford	Vancouver	Lib.
Vancouver East	85,071	41,537	26,710	9,671	A. Lee	Vancouver	Lib.
Vancouver Kingsway	85,005	46,322	32,268	12,002	S. Holt	Vancouver	Lib.
Vancouver Quadra	79,949	49,692	39,277	18,892	B. Clarke	Vancouver	PC
Vancouver South	88,701	57,141	44,078	23,247	J.A. Fraser	Vancouver	PC
Victoria	88,211	64,965	48,576	26,771	A.B. McKinnon	Victoria	PC
YUKON TERRITORY (1 member)							
Yukon	18,388	12,312	8,354	3,913	E. Nielsen	Whitehorse	PC
NORTHWEST TERRITORIES (1 member)							
Northwest Territories	34,807	21,299	13,008	5,410	W. Firth	Yellowknife	NDP

[1] Party standings as a result of the general election, July 8, 1974: Liberal 141, Progressive Conservative 95, New Democratic 16, Social Credit 11, Independent 1.
[2] Leader of a political party.
[3] Speaker of the House of Commons.

3.5 Voters on the lists and votes polled at the federal general elections of 1965, 1968, 1972 and 1974

Province or territory	Voters and votes polled			
	Voters on the lists			
	1965	1968	1972	1974
Newfoundland	226,082	237,594	289,294	304,370
Prince Edward Island	56,484	58,216	68,992	73,069
Nova Scotia	401,521	412,791	492,001	524,767
New Brunswick	304,734	317,912	387,136	406,518
Quebec	2,933,031	3,083,260	3,693,918	3,849,009
Ontario	3,609,895	3,846,064	4,601,282	4,803,822
Manitoba	517,928	531,563	610,568	633,411
Saskatchewan	508,733	517,598	558,876	569,316
Alberta	725,447	774,565	955,531	1,016,046
British Columbia	972,063	1,059,959	1,312,832	1,407,066
Yukon Territory[3]	6,660	7,559	10,857	12,312
Northwest Territories[4]	12,326	13,807	19,491	21,299
Total	10,274,904	10,860,888	13,000,778	13,621,005
	Votes polled			
	1965	1968	1972	1974
Newfoundland	148,392	161,570	182,482	175,534
Prince Edward Island	72,006[1]	51,225	59,078	58,649
Nova Scotia	420,146[2]	339,600	391,590	388,830
New Brunswick	244,184	254,716	298,164	289,492
Quebec	2,073,314	2,229,345	2,790,172	2,592,679
Ontario	2,770,222	2,973,745	3,650,542	3,582,489
Manitoba	382,362	403,272	453,642	448,431
Saskatchewan	404,631	416,793	442,246	415,268
Alberta	534,870	567,416	722,338	684,649
British Columbia	731,438	804,108	961,441	1,014,219
Yukon Territory[3]	5,760	6,563	8,638	8,354
Northwest Territories[4]	9,403	9,563	14,328	13,008
Total	7,796,728	8,217,916	9,974,661	9,671,602

[1]Each voter in the double-member constituency of Queens County, PEI had two votes; in 1963, 26,472 voters on the list cast 42,703 votes; in 1965, 26,250 voters on the list cast 44,895 votes.
[2]Each voter in the double-member constituency of Halifax, NS had two votes; in 1963, 122,846 voters on the list cast 183,402 votes; in 1965, 124,633 voters on the list cast 184,153 votes.
[3]Electoral district of Yukon.
[4]Electoral district of Northwest Territories.

3.6 Number of municipalities classified by type and size group, by province, as at Jan. 1, 1975

Type and size group	Nfld.	PEI	NS	NB	Que.	Ont.	Man.	Sask.	Alta.	BC	YT	NWT	Canada
TYPE													
Regional municipalities	—	—	—	—	75	39	—	—	—	28	—	—	142
Metropolitan and regional municipalities[1]	—	—	—	—	3	12	—	—	—	—	—	—	15
Counties and regional districts	—	—	—	—	72	27	—	—	—	28	—	—	127
Unitary municipalities	119	35	65	111	1,573	780	183	784	327	138	3	7	4,125
Cities[2]	2	1	3	6	68	44	5	11	9	32	2	1	184
Towns	117[3]	8	38	20	208	142	33	131	103	11	1	3	815
Villages	—	26	—	85	266	121	40	350	167	58	—	3	1,116
Rural municipalities[4]	—	—	24	—	1,031	473	105	292	48	37	—	—	2,010
Quasi-municipalities[5]	166	—	—	—	—	13	19	10	22	—	5	7	242
Total	285	35	65	111	1,648	832	202	794	349	166	8	14	4,509
POPULATION SIZE GROUP (1971 Census)													
Unitary municipalities													
Over 100,000	—	—	1	—	3	14	1	2	2	2	—	—	25
50,000-99,999	1	—	2	1	10	13	—	—	—	6	—	—	33
10,000-49,999	1	1	16	6	70	66	3	5	12	29	1	—	210
Under 10,000	117	34	46	104	1,490	687	179	777	313	101	2	7	3,857
Total	119	35	65	111	1,573	780	183	784	327	138	3	7	4,125

[1]Includes urban communities in Quebec; and Metropolitan Toronto, regional municipalities and the district municipality in Ontario.
[2]Includes the five boroughs of Metropolitan Toronto.
[3]Includes 11 rural districts.
[4]Includes municipalities in Nova Scotia; parishes, townships, united townships and municipalities in Quebec; townships in Ontario; rural municipalities in Manitoba and Saskatchewan; municipal districts and counties in Alberta; and districts in British Columbia.
[5]Includes local government communities, local improvement districts and the metropolitan area in Newfoundland; improvement districts in Ontario and Alberta; local government districts in Manitoba; local improvement districts in Saskatchewan and the Yukon Territory; and hamlets in the Northwest Territories.

3.7   Canadian financial contributions to the United Nations, years ended Mar. 31, 1975 and 1976 with totals for 1945-76 (thousand dollars Canadian)

Agency	1975	1976	Total 1945-76
UN regular budget	8,838	9,856	91,857
Peacekeeping			
UNEF I	- -	—	5,910
ONUC	- -	—	9,187
UNFICYP	3,362	1,930	26,321
UN Special Account	—	4,620	8,927
UNEF II	2,803	—	3,757
Social and economic programs			
UNDP	22,200	24,500	161,071
Special Fund	—	—	21,378
EPTA	—	—	26,376
UNHCR	550	600[1]	39,332
UNICEF	2,500	3,500	33,875
UNRWA	1,150	1,350	32,753
UNITAR	60	60	660
UNETPSA	175	175	649
WFP	3,739	10,000	141,252
UNFPA	2,500	3,500	13,052
UN Fund for Congo	—	—	4,489
Committee on Elimination of Racial Discrimination	2	3	13
Trust Fund for South Africa	10	10	60
UN Fund for Drug Abuse Control	200	200	950
UN Voluntary Fund for Environment	—	—	16,215
Miscellaneous	—	—	1,004
Specialized agencies, IAEA and GATT			
ILO	1,497	2,761	19,567
FAO	2,141	3,321	25,678
WHO	1,395	3,761	33,234
UNESCO	2,453	2,491	22,617
ICAO	424	443	6,599
IMCO	27	42	294
ITU	503	690	4,791
WMO	178	243	1,390
UPU	132	130	1,006
IAEA regular and operational budgets	881	1,155	7,220
GATT	557	651	3,898
WIPO	117	141	258
Miscellaneous	—	—	92
UN Association in Canada	35	35	470
Total	58,429r	76,168	766,202

[1]Does not include a special contribution of $500,000 for former Portuguese Territories in Africa.

Sources

3.1 Committees Branch, House of Commons.
3.2 Clerk of the Senate.
3.3 Office of the Representation Commissioner.
3.4 - 3.5 Office of the Chief Electoral Officer.
3.6 Public Finance Division, Institutional and Public Finance Statistics Branch, Statistics Canada.
3.7 Information Division, Department of External Affairs.

Demography

Chapter 4

Tables

Demography　　　　　　　　　　　　　　　　Chapter 4

Population growth　　　　　　　　　　　　　　　4.1

The most fundamental fact about a population is its rate of growth which affects almost every aspect of the national life. The opening up of a new continent and the gradual evolution of an industrial and urban economy form the historical background for population growth in Canada. Several demographic elements have combined to produce this growth: births, deaths, immigration and emigration, which are the processes, or components, of population change.

The early period　　　　　　　　　　　　　　　4.1.1

The growth of Canada's population today is the culmination of a trend which began early in the 17th century with the arrival of the first French settlers. From this beginning, the population of the area now known as Canada (excluding Newfoundland) grew from a handful of colonists and an unknown number of native Indians and Eskimos in 1611 to about 2.4 million in 1851 and 3.7 million at the first Census of Canada in 1871. Rough estimates suggest there were about 136,000 Indians in 1851.

Growth rates in the early settlement years were irregular. The immigrant population grew rapidly while the native population remained almost stationary or declined as a result of attrition from warfare and disease. Between 1681, when the number of settlers passed the 10,000 mark, and 1851 the average annual growth rate of the non-native population in each decade varied between 1.6% and 4.5%; the average annual growth rate for the whole period was 3.2%. The small size of the initial population and the continuous expansion into empty lands were contributing factors in the rapid growth rates in the early periods.

The decade 1851-61 was one of surging growth, second only to the growth rate in the first decade of the present century (Table 4.1). The average annual growth rate during this period was 2.9%, with about 23% of the population increase due to net migration; over 350,000 immigrants arrived and there was very little emigration. A long period of slow growth followed and lasted until the beginning of the 20th century. Between 1861 and 1901 the average growth rate was closer to 1%, matched only by the rate during the depression period of the 1930s. This slow growth toward the end of the last century was due to heavy emigration resulting in a net migration loss (Table 4.2). Emigrants included elements of both the Canadian and foreign-born populations. While many immigrants continued to come to Canada during this period a large number of them re-emigrated to the United States where prospective settlers found more favourable economic and climatic conditions. The westward movement in the United States attracted not only settlers from many parts of that country, but from Canada as well.

Recent trends　　　　　　　　　　　　　　　4.1.2

The beginning of the present century witnessed a flood of immigrants which helped to raise the growth rate to 3.0% per annum during 1901-11, the highest rate since 1851. Over 1.5 million immigrants entered Canada in this decade, as many as had arrived during the previous 40 years. Over 44% of the total population increase during this period was due to migration gain.

Following this phenomenal increase, the intercensal rate of increase dropped during each successive decade until it reached a low of 10.9% during 1931-41 when reduced birth rates during the economic depression seriously affected population growth; immigration was negligible, and there was a net migration loss of about 92,000 persons.

After 1941, the population again registered an accelerated growth, reaching a near-record rate of expansion of 30.2% in 1951-61, nearly three times the rate of increase in 1931-41. Part of the increase after 1941 was accounted for by the addition of Newfoundland in 1949 but the surge in birth rates (commonly referred to as the "baby boom") and the upswing in immigration during the immediate postwar years were the main factors.

After 1956 a steady decline in population growth occurred, reaching a rate of 1.5% per annum in 1966-71. This gradual fall in the growth rate — the lowest except the depression decade — has evoked special interest mainly because it occurred after the peak of 3.3% in 1956-57 and at a time when the economic outlook was favourable for high growth rates. The annual growth rate in 1973-74 was estimated to be about 1.6%. In absolute numbers, between 1966 and 1971 the population increased by 1,553,000, or 310,000 a year, which was about 25% lower than the increase during 1951-56.

4.1.3   Future prospects

The dominant component of population growth in Canada since 1851 has been natural increase. This trend is likely to continue with a modest contribution from migration. Of the two components of natural increase (births minus deaths), the birth rate will continue to be the dynamic and crucial factor of growth. Moreover, fluctuations in birth rates can create major economic and social problems as society adjusts itself to the effects of such fluctuations. For example, although the postwar "baby boom" is long past, society is now feeling the impact of this generation on the labour market and other aspects of the national economy. Similarly, problems associated with the sharp drop in the birth rate since 1957 are being felt, for example, by school systems as fewer children enter school.

Because of the importance of the fertility factor, the tempo of future growth depends mainly on whether the total fertility rate of 2.19 births (1971), which is close to the "replacement level" of 2.13 births under existing mortality conditions, will remain constant, fall or rise. A fertility rate close to the replacement level does not mean that Canada will soon reach zero population growth. Calculations show that even if immigration ceased, and the average fertility rate were only 2.13, the population would continue to grow until about the year 2040, when birth and death rates would each stabilize at about 13 per 1,000 population. This long delay in achieving zero growth may be attributed to the current high percentage of young people who are moving into the child-bearing age groups.

Table 4.3 summarizes for Canada as a whole the results of population projections for Canada and the provinces prepared under different assumptions of fertility and migration. For a full account of the methodology and results of these projections, see *Population projections for Canada and the provinces, 1972-2001,* Statistics Canada Catalogue No. 91-514.

Projection A uses the highest fertility assumption of 2.60 children by 1985, and a net migration gain of 100,000 a year, with a total population increase from 21.6 million in 1971 to 27.8 million in 1986 and 34.6 million by 2001. On the other hand, Projection C is a low projection based on an assumed fertility rate of 1.80 by 1985, and a net migration gain of 60,000 a year. This projection yields a total population of 25.4 million by 1986 and 28.4 million by 2001.

These projections indicate that after a short phase of increase in the population growth rate (i.e. between 1976 and 1986), the rate will gradually decline toward the end of the century to about 1.3% per annum according to Projection A, and to 0.6% under Projection C. The slowdown in population growth and fertility rates will cause some aging of Canada's population. With an upward shift in the age structure, there will be a steady decline in the child-dependency ratio and an increase in the old age dependency ratio.

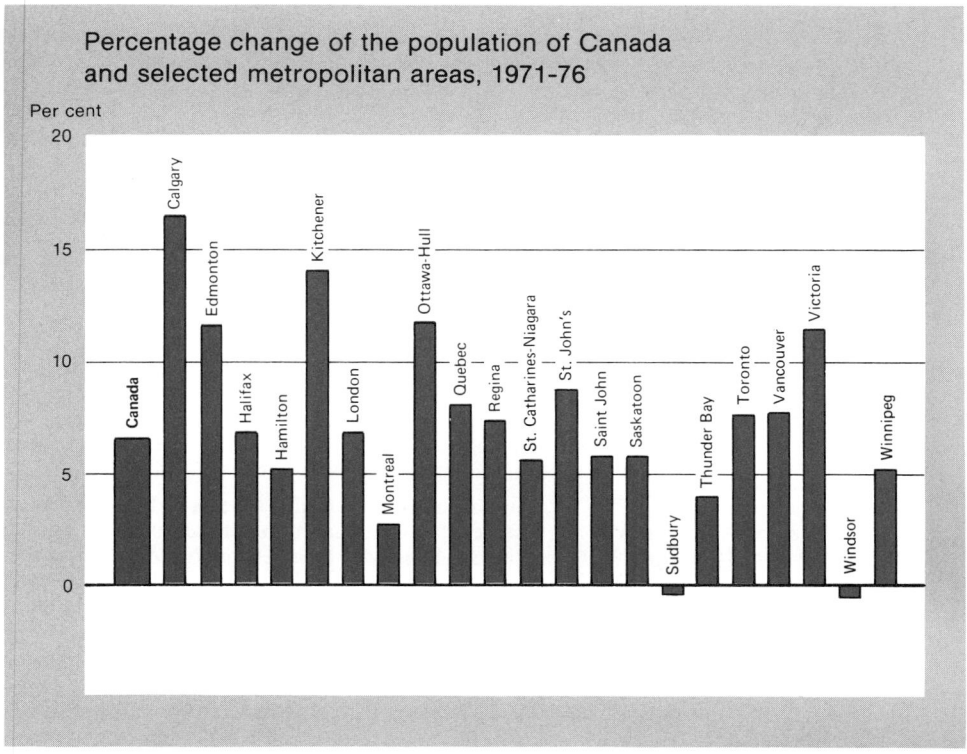

Percentage change of the population of Canada and selected metropolitan areas, 1971-76

Population distribution   4.2

Decennial and quinquennial censuses of Canada make possible periodic assessments of the nation's human resources. They provide data on the distribution of population for many types of geographical, political, and statistical entities. Used as benchmarks, the census counts enable annual estimates to be made for some of the larger areas (e.g. provinces, counties, metropolitan areas). A small selection of these data is presented in this section, embodying results of the 1971 Census, estimates to 1975 where applicable and the earliest published data from the 1976 Census.

The 1976 Census. Canada took its third quinquennial census on June 1, 1976. The aim of this census was to keep statistical information abreast of the demographic and socio-economic factors that form the foundation for decision making in both the private and public sectors. The census is a principal source of information for measuring social and economic progress, and for detecting those needs which necessitate the development and implementation of policies and programs such as regional development, health and welfare programs, education facilities, immigration, low income housing and transportation networks.

Questions of the 1976 Census covered age, sex, marital status, relationship to head of household, and mother tongue (the language first learned and still understood). These were asked of every person whose usual place of residence on June 1, 1976 was in Canada. In addition there were questions on type and tenure of housing of Canadian households. Sampling was also used in the 1976 Census. Persons 15 years of age and over of every third private household provided answers for school attendance, level of schooling, labour force activity and migration (place of residence five years ago).

The population of Canada at June 1, 1976 was 22,992,604, an increase of 6.6% or 1,424,693 from the previous census in 1971. The provinces of Alberta and British Columbia recorded the largest growth rates at 12.9% each. Ontario's growth was next in line at 7.3%. (Table 4.4)

The Calgary census metropolitan area (CMA) showed the greatest increase at 16.5% with Kitchener census metropolitan area following at 14.1%. The Toronto CMA became the largest in Canada, with a population of 2,803,101, some 7.7% more than in 1971, while Montreal CMA was very close behind at 2,802,485, showing a growth of 2.7% since 1971. (Table 4.9)

4.2.1   Provincial and sub-provincial areas

The basic legal reason for decennial censuses is to enable a redistribution of seats in the House of Commons. Under the terms of the Electoral Boundaries Readjustment Act, the census must provide population counts by electoral districts. Those from the 1971 Census are shown in Chapter 3, Table 3.4, according to the electoral district boundaries established by the 1966 Representation Order (i.e. the redistribution following the 1961 Census).

Provincial trends, 1951-71. Ontario, British Columbia, Alberta and the Northwest Territories had growth rates higher than national figures in all five-year periods between 1951 and 1971 (see Table 4.4). However, a decline in the rate of growth occurred in all provinces as birth rates began to fall in the mid-1950s. The most spectacular change took place in Quebec where the rate of growth declined by about 70% between 1951-56 and 1966-71 (i.e. from 14.1% to 4.3%). The growth rate in Quebec in 1966-71 was less than half of the rate during the preceding five-year period.

The lowest rates for 1966-71 were in the Atlantic provinces, Quebec, Manitoba and Saskatchewan. Saskatchewan registered a decline while British Columbia had the highest growth rate (16.6%) followed by Alberta and Ontario. The uneven rates of increase imply that net migration reinforced the natural growth of population in Ontario, Alberta and British Columbia and depressed it in all others (see Table 4.5).

Provincial estimates, 1975. In addition to the five-year census, estimates are constructed for the total population of Canada and for each province on both an annual and quarterly basis. The estimates of population begin with the preceding census counts, the births of each year are added and the deaths subtracted; immigrants are added and an estimate of emigrants subtracted. Family allowance statistics showing the number of migrant families by province are used in estimating interprovincial shifts in population. Finally, the next census serves as a basis for revision of all annual estimates of each intercensal period.

Table 4.6 shows the revised annual population estimates by province for the years 1967 to 1970, and the provisional estimates for 1973, 1974 and 1975. Included in the table are the actual enumerated counts for the two "benchmark" census years of 1966 and 1971. The estimate for Canada of 22,800,000 population at June 1, 1975 is the result of adding 344,000 births and 213,000 immigrants to the previous 1973 estimate of 22,095,000 and then subtracting 167,000 deaths and a residual of 36,000 representing mainly emigrants.

Cities, towns and villages. As at June 1, 1971, some 65.4% of Canada's population lived in 2,120 centres classified as incorporated cities, towns and villages. These are grouped into 13 broad size categories in Table 4.7. Only two cities within whose incorporated boundaries had a population over 500,000 (Montreal and Toronto), representing a combined 8.9% of the total population. At the other end of the scale, 1,093 or one half of all incorporated cities, towns and villages had less than 1,000 population, but together they accounted for only 2.1% of Canada's population.

Canadian cities and towns having a population of over 50,000 in 1971 are listed in Table 4.8 together with figures for 1961 and 1966. The date of incorporation to their present status of a city or town is indicated also.

Metropolitan areas. For census purposes a metropolitan area represents the main labour market of a continuous built-up area having a population of 100,000 or more. The growth of 22 census metropolitan areas over the period 1951-71 appears in Table 4.9. Populations of these areas in earlier censuses were adjusted to conform to the boundaries delineated for the 1971 Census. The 1976 Census population figures have been added, based on 1976 census metropolitan areas.

The proportion of Canada's population in the major metropolitan centres increased steadily and over one half (55.1%) resided in the 22 metropolitan areas as defined for the 1971 Census. Calgary showed the highest rate of growth in the period 1966-71 at 22.1%, followed by Edmonton at 16.5%. The greatest gains in numbers were registered by Toronto at 338,000 and by Montreal at 172,000. Vancouver became Canada's third urban agglomeration to pass the "over-a-million" population mark.

Because of the growing interest in the expanding metropolitan areas a series of intercensal estimates was begun in 1957. As in preparation of intercensal population estimates for provinces, the births in the metropolitan areas were added to the census population and deaths subtracted. Immigrants reporting these metropolitan areas as places of destination were added and allowances made for losses by emigration. Also, the net in-movement by internal migration was calculated from family allowances and other data.

Population density   4.2.2

At six persons a sq mile ($2.3/km^2$) in 1971, Canada's crude or average population density still ranks among the lowest in the world. Table 4.10 shows that if the Yukon Territory and Northwest Territories were omitted from this calculation, there would be 10 persons a sq mile ($3.9/km^2$) in 1971 compared to eight ($3.1/km^2$) in 1961 and six ($2.3/km^2$) in 1951. However, such average density figures over all types of land terrain and open spaces in the country or in individual provinces obscure the high urban densities which can reach close to 20,000 persons a sq mile ($7\,722/km^2$) as in the overall figure for the cities of Montreal and Toronto. Moreover, the highest provincial densities are not necessarily found among the provinces with the largest populations. For example, the highest average density of any province is that of Prince Edward Island (51 persons a sq mile) ($19.7/km^2$), which has the smallest population and represents an anomaly resulting from its very limited land area rather than from heavy concentrations of population. In contrast, the far more populous province of British Columbia, with its vast mountainous regions and areas of sparse population, has an average density of only six persons a sq mile ($2.3/km^2$).

Urban and rural   4.2.3

The urban population was defined in the 1971 Census as all persons living in incorporated cities, towns and villages with a population of 1,000 and over, as well as in unincorporated places of 1,000 and over having a population density of at least 1,000 a sq mile ($386/km^2$). Also considered as urban were the built-up fringes of these cities, towns and villages if they met the same criteria of population and density. All the remaining population was classified as rural.

Over three quarters (76.1%) of Canada's population lived in an urban environment, with the degree of urbanization ranging from 38.3% in Prince Edward Island to 82.4% in Ontario. In comparison with the national average, only Ontario and Quebec were more highly urbanized. (Table 4.11)

The rural population, 23.9% of the Canadian total in 1971, is classified in Table 4.11 as non-farm or farm. The rural farm population was defined for census purposes as persons living in rural areas on an agricultural holding of one or more acres (at least 0.4 hectares) with sales of agricultural products amounting to $50 or more in the previous year. The rural non-farm category in 1971 accounted for 17.3% of the population, compared to 6.6% for the rural farm segment.

4.3   Demographic and social characteristics

4.3.1   Sex, age and marital status

Age, sex and marital status represent the most fundamental variables of vital trends: births, deaths, marriages, and dissolutions of marriages. Social and economic factors, by their effects on vital events and migration, also influence these characteristics. An unbroken series of census data is available as far back as the first Census of Canada in 1871; only recent trends are summarized here.

Sex ratios. The relatively short demographic history of Canada has been characterized by an excess of males until recent years. Over the past century the sex ratio (i.e. number of males per 100 females) reached a peak of 113 in 1911 following a decade of heavy immigration in which males have traditionally predominated. By 1971 the sex ratio had almost evened out at 100.2 with only 22,425 more males than females in a total population of over 21.5 million (Table 4.12). In the older settled provinces the sex ratio has varied between Nova Scotia's 104 in 1911, and Quebec's and Ontario's 1971 ratio of 99. In the western provinces, which were being rapidly settled early in this century, the sex ratio has ranged between Alberta's 1911 high of 149 and Manitoba's 1971 figure of 100.

Age structure. Age composition is a reflection of past trends in vital rates and immigration. Lower birth rates of the 1961-71 period compared to those of the 1950s had a tremendous impact on the population under 15 years of age in 1971. This group decreased by 211,000 or 3.2% between 1966 and 1971 compared with a gain of 399,800 or 6.4% in the 1961-66 period. The proportion of this age group in the total population fell from 34.0% in 1961 to 29.5% in 1971 (Table 4.13).

The population of working age (generally regarded as 15-64 years) increased substantially, with a gain in excess of 1,559,000 or 13.1% in the 1966-71 period. This group comprised 62.3% of the total population in 1971 compared with 59.4% in 1966 and 58.4% in 1961. Of the total 1961-71 increase, 49.8% of the gain occurred in the 15-24 age group. This young adult group in 1971 was, of course, the cohort of children born in the high-birth-rate years following World War II. The proportion of persons 65 years of age and over was approximately the same (roughly 8%) in 1971 as in 1961 and 1966.

Estimates of the population by age group and sex are shown in Table 4.14 for Canada and the provinces as at June 1, 1975. These estimates are subject to revision when data from the 1976 Census become available.

Marital status. Analyses of trends and size of the single, married, widowed and divorced segments of the population are most revealing when observed in relation to their distributions at different age levels and by sex. Table 4.15 shows these three demographic characteristics in relationship to each other, based on the 1971 Census. The figures show such imbalances as the far greater numbers of single males than single females at younger age levels and the reverse for widows as compared to widowers in older age groups. These conditions result from generally earlier ages of marriage for females, the longer life expectancy of females and the greater tendency for widowers to remarry.

Among recent trends is the steady decrease, since 1951, in the number of married females in the child-bearing ages in relation to the total married women of all ages. This is possibly one contributing factor in the sharply declining birth rates. In 1971, 59.7% of all married females were in the age group 15-44, compared to 61.2% in 1966, 62.9% in 1961, and 64.0% in 1951.

One striking change revealed by the 1971 Census was the large increase in the number of divorced persons, reflecting in part relaxations in the divorce laws.

Divorced persons of all ages in 1971 increased to almost three times the size of the 1966 figure (from 64,776 to 175,115). The age group 15-24 showed the greatest relative increase, but the actual numbers were small compared to most older groups. However, the total number of divorced persons represented fewer than 1% of Canada's population in 1971. (See also Section 4.8.2.)

Language   4.3.2

In the 1971 Census, three questions were asked on the languages of the Canadian people. Two represented the more traditional census inquiries: one on mother tongue (the language first spoken in childhood and still understood) and the other on official language (the ability to speak English, French, or both languages). The third question concerned the language most often spoken at home.

Mother tongue. Summary figures on mother tongue in Table 4.16 show the principal languages reported in the 1971 Census with comparative figures for 1961. The proportion of the Canadian population reporting English mother tongue increased from 58.5% in 1961 to 60.2% in 1971, while those reporting French declined from 28.1% to 26.9%. Italian, Greek, Chinese, and Portuguese showed significant advances, while Ukrainian, German, Netherlands, Polish and Yiddish were among those registering declines.

Table 4.17 shows the number and proportion of the population reporting English or French as their mother tongue, by province. The relative gains in English mother tongue over the 1961-71 period occurred mostly in the western provinces at the expense of others such as Ukrainian, German and Polish, as descendants of earlier immigrants reported English as their mother tongue to a greater extent than in previous decades.

Official language. Table 4.18 shows 1971 Census figures on the population reporting the ability to speak one or both of Canada's two official languages, with comparative data for 1961. In 1971 a total of 67.1% were able to speak English only, 18.0% French only, and 13.4% were bilingual. These ratios represent a slight increase in the proportion able to speak both English and French over 1961, when the percentage was 12.2.

Language spoken in the home. This new inquiry was introduced in the 1971 Census on the recommendation of the Royal Commission on Bilingualism and Biculturalism and other groups. It added insight into the languages of Canada since some persons, particularly immigrants, did not indicate either of the two official languages as the one they spoke most often in their homes. Conversely, many with a non-English mother tongue no longer used their mother tongue. Table 4.16 indicates that 67.0% of the population spoke English most often in their homes, whereas only 60.2% reported English as their mother tongue.

Ethnicity, religion, birthplace   4.3.3

Because of the varied nature of Canada's population, the measurements provided by decennial censuses on such subjects as ethnic and religious composition are of widespread interest and in continuous demand. Tables 4.19 to 4.21 show summary figures from the 1971 Census, with comparative data for earlier years.

Ethnic groups. The ethnic composition of Canada has changed considerably because of many factors, including differences in the flow and source of immigrants. Trends in recent years have been characterized by a decline in the proportions of British Isles groups and a corresponding increase in European ethnic groups other than French. For example, the former groups had dropped from 57.0% of the total population in 1901 to 44.6% by 1971, whereas other European groups rose from 8.5% to 23.0%. The French ethnic group remained relatively stable, starting at 30.7% in 1901, and moving irregularly lower to 28.7% by 1971. Table 4.19 provides 1971 figures for the larger ethnic groups, together with data from 1951 and 1961.

Religious denominations. Census figures do not measure church membership or the degree of affiliation with a particular religious body. Respondents were asked "What is your religion?" and to enter a specific religious denomination, sect or community, with the opportunity to report "no religion" if so desired. As shown in Table 4.20, three out of every four persons in Canada in 1971 reported one of the three numerically largest denominations — Roman Catholic, United Church or Anglican. Largest relative gains since 1961 occurred in such groups as Jehovah's Witnesses and Pentecostal. None of the major denominations registered numerical declines in the 1961-71 period, but the Anglican, Baptist, Lutheran, Presbyterian and United Church groups were among those showing percentage losses relative to the total population.

Country of birth. The proportion of the population born outside Canada ranged from a high of 22% throughout the period 1911-31, following heavy waves of immigration, to a low of 15% in 1951 following a period of lower immigration and rising birth rates. Persons born in the United Kingdom comprised over 11% of the population in 1911 and 1921, but this declined gradually to 4.3% by 1971 in the face of the rising proportions of Canadian-born and immigration from other European countries. Persons born in the latter countries rose from 5.6% of Canada's population in 1911 to 7.8% in 1971 (Table 4.21).

4.3.4   The native peoples

Many centuries before the first European settlers arrived on what is now Canadian soil, this vast country had received immigrants in the prehistoric period. Present-day Inuit (Eskimos) and Indians are the descendants of these early settlers but as a result of heavy immigration by other groups they now represent less than 2% of Canada's population. Administration relating to the affairs of the Indian and Inuit peoples is described in Chapter 3. Demographic data on their numbers and locations, from the 1971 Census of Canada summary figures, show a total of 295,215 native Indian people and 17,550 Inuit. The former figure includes both registered or status Indians and non-status.

From a later source, there were 282,762 persons registered as status Indians by the Department of Indian Affairs and Northern Development as of December 31, 1975. These are persons who are entitled to be so registered in accordance with the terms of the Indian Act. They comprise 566 bands who occupy or have access to some 2,216 reserves having a combined area of about 6.2 million acres (2.5 million ha). Membership of these bands is distributed among the provinces and territories as shown in Table 4.22. The 29 Indian bands in the Yukon Territory and Northwest Territories are located in seven reserves and in 46 settlements that have not been formally designated as reserves. There are presently no Indian bands in Newfoundland.

About two thirds of Canada's roughly 18,000 Inuit reported in the 1971 Census live in communities in the Northwest Territories (11,400), and the remainder mainly in Arctic Quebec (3,800), Labrador (1,000), and Northern Ontario (800). As in the rest of Canada, the Inuit birth rate has been declining, but at a faster rate and from a much higher level. By 1971 the birth rate for the Inuit population in the Northwest Territories had decreased to about 38 per 1,000 as compared with the Canadian average of 17 per 1,000.

4.4   Households and families

4.4.1   Household size and type

A household, as defined in the census, consists of a person or a group of persons occupying one dwelling, usually a family with or without lodgers or employees. However, it may consist of a group of unrelated persons, of two or more families sharing a dwelling, or of one person living alone. The statistics presented in this section pertain to private households only. Collective households such as hotels, motels, institutions of various types (usually considered to contain 10 or more persons unrelated to the household head) have been excluded.

The number of private households in Canada increased to 6 million in 1971 from 4.5 million a decade earlier, a gain of almost one third. The population rate of increase was considerably lower at 18%. This difference reflects the marked rise in the number of households of only one or two persons. Table 4.23 shows that the rate of growth in the number of households was not uniform across the country. During the 1961-71 period, urban areas experienced 44.6% growth compared to only 1.9% for rural areas. Growth rates ranged from 9.1% in Saskatchewan to 45.4% in British Columbia and 60.2% in the Yukon Territory and Northwest Territories. Quebec, Ontario and Alberta had growth rates higher than the national average.

Households by size. Table 4.23 also shows the average size of households by province for 1961, 1966 and 1971. In the 1971 Census, the average Canadian household had 3.5 persons as compared to 3.7 in 1966 and 3.9 in 1961. In all these censuses, the average number of persons per household was highest in Newfoundland. While the decline in the average size of households during 1961-66 was attributable to mainly two provinces, New Brunswick and Quebec, a further drop in the average size during 1966-71 was realized in all provinces. The average household size in rural areas was 3.9 persons, compared to 3.4 persons in urban areas.

Households by type. All private-type households are divided for census purposes into two basic categories: family households and non-family households. Table 4.24 shows the distribution on this basis for 1961, 1966 and 1971.

Family households increased in number from 3.9 million in 1961 to almost 4.4 million in 1966 and to 4.9 million in 1971, but dropped proportionately from 86.7% in 1961 to 84.5% in 1966 and to 81.7% in 1971. The proportion consisting of two or more families dropped from 3.7% in 1961 to 2.0% in 1971, indicating a decrease in over-crowding in households. Non-family households, on the other hand, increased in number and in proportion to the total number of households; this is mainly attributable to the increase in the proportion of one-person households from 9.3% in 1961 to 11.4% in 1966 and 13.4% in 1971. Thus, new family formation alone was not responsible for the overall increase in the number of households; some family persons and families who previously shared accommodation now maintained their own households.

The distribution of households by type varied significantly with the sex of the head. Only 35.6% (354,565) of the 997,240 households with female heads were family households, compared to 90.8% (4,578,885) for the 5,044,065 households with male heads. Almost half (49.1%, or 489,865) of all female-head households consisted of women living alone. The corresponding figure for households with male heads was only 6.4% (321,970).

Households by age and marital status of head. The upward trend in households headed by persons under 25 years of age is indicated in Table 4.25. Although total households increased by 16.6% between 1966 and 1971, the number of households with heads under 25 years of age grew by 54.0%, reaching 414,470 in 1971 from 269,065 in 1966. By province, this group increased by as much as 72.6% in Manitoba and 63.0% in Newfoundland. Quebec registered the largest growth in households with heads 70 years of age and over, increasing 17.5% to 125,095 in 1971 compared to 106,459 in 1966. Nationally, however, the proportion of households with heads 70 and over declined to 10.3% from 10.7%.

Growth in the number of households analyzed by marital status of head may be seen in Table 4.26. The most significant increase during the 1961-71 period was recorded by households with divorced heads, at 316.9%; the proportion of households with divorced heads more than tripled from 0.6% in 1961 to 1.9% in 1971. At 92.2%, the increase in households with single never-married heads was the next highest. The rate of increase over the decade was 36.4% for households with widowed heads and 25.6% for households with married heads (including separated).

4.4.2   Family size and composition

A family, as defined in the Canadian census, consists of a husband and wife with or without unmarried children, or a parent with one or more unmarried children, living together in the same dwelling. Adopted children and stepchildren have the same status as own children.

The number of families in Canada increased to 5.0 million in 1971 from 4.1 million in 1961, a gain of approximately one fourth over the decade. Following the patterns of provincial population growth, and reflecting the factors of migration, the largest rate of increase occurred in British Columbia (35.4% in the 1961-71 period), followed by Alberta (25.0%), and Ontario (24.5%).

Families by size. The number and average size of families are given in Table 4.27 by province for 1961, 1966 and 1971. Although the average size remained the same at 3.9 persons between 1961 and 1966, it dropped to 3.7 persons between 1966 and 1971, reflecting declining birth rates. Quebec, New Brunswick and Newfoundland had the largest reductions in average family size, decreasing from 4.2 persons in 1961 to 3.9 in 1971 for Quebec, from 4.3 to 4.0 for New Brunswick, and 4.7 to 4.4 for Newfoundland.

Families maintaining own households. In families "maintaining their own households" the head of the family is also the head of the household. Families not maintaining their own households fall into two census sub-categories: families related to the head of the household, and non-related lodging families. The few who do not fit these sub-categories are mostly families of employees living in their employer's household.

Table 4.28 shows that 96.6% of Canadian families in 1971 maintained their own households, an increase both in number and in proportion to the total number of families. The majority remaining were related families, mostly small in size, usually two persons (e.g. the daughter and son-in-law of the household head) with the head of the family under 25 years of age. Lodging families, although increasing slightly in number, constituted a low proportion of 0.8%.

Husband-wife families. For the analysis of family data, a subdivision into husband-wife families and one-parent families in Table 4.29 shows the distribution by age of family head. One-parent families are further classified into those with male and female heads. In husband-wife families, for statistical tabulating purposes the husband was considered the head of the family in 1971 and earlier censuses.

Between 1966 and 1971 the proportion of husband-wife families dropped slightly, but in actual number they increased, remaining a predominant proportion (90.6%) of total Canadian families. Most one-parent families were headed by females; these families increased both in number and proportion from 6.6% in 1961 to 7.5% in 1971. This reflects an increase in "broken" families in Canada because the proportion of females heading such families increased in the age groups 25-34 and 35-44, the ages at which most divorces were granted.

Families by mother tongue of head. For census purposes, mother tongue is defined as "the first language learned that is still understood". The proportion of family heads reporting English, French, or other mother tongue in the 1971 Census showed a pattern fairly similar to that for the population as a whole. (Table 4.30) For example, 60.2% of the Canadian population reported English as the mother tongue, as compared with 57.3% of all family heads. The corresponding proportions for French mother tongue were 26.9% and 25.6%. However, mother tongues other than English or French were reported by only 13.0% of the total population, but by 17.2% of all family heads.

Children in families. There were 8.8 million children in families in 1971. These were children never married and under 25 years of age who were living with their parents or guardians at the time of the census. They are classified in Table 4.31 into selected age groups which roughly correspond to pre-school-age (under six years), elementary school age (6-14), the secondary school level (15-18), and college or working age (19-24).

Declining birth rates were reflected dramatically in the proportionate increases of children in families during the 1966-71 period. The 19-24 age group in families increased by 20.1% over the five years, the 15-18 group by 16.9%, the 6-14 group by only 5.8%, while those under six years declined by as much as 16.2%. Children in families for all age groups increased from 7.8 million in 1961 to 8.8 million in 1971, but the average number of children per family declined from 1.9 to 1.7.

The vital components of population change   4.5

Vital statistics are an indispensable key to the interpretation of population change. They provide a measure of the pace of increase by natural means (births minus deaths) and the rate at which women marry and reproduce. These vital processes are reflected in statistics from the records of births, deaths, marriages and divorces registered in the provinces and territories of Canada.

History of vital statistics   4.5.1

An historical summary of vital statistics data for Canada and the provinces back to 1921 is contained in *Vital statistics, Preliminary annual report* (Statistics Canada Catalogue No. 84-201). Some rough estimates of birth, natural increase, and death rates back to the mid-1800s by 10-year periods are given in Sections 4.6.1, 4.6.3 and 4.7.1, which follow.

Summary of principal data   4.5.2

Table 4.32 provides a summary of the principal vital statistics for 1971, 1972, 1973 and 1974 for Canada, the provinces and territories, with comparative figures by five-year periods back to 1951-55. Table 4.33 shows similar data for urban centres of 50,000 population and over for 1974 with comparative averages for 1961-65 and 1966-70. More detailed information on vital statistics, including analyses of recent trends, is published annually in the Statistics Canada reports *Vital statistics, volume I, births* (Catalogue No. 84-204), *Vital statistics, volume II, marriages and divorces* (Catalogue No. 84-205), *Vital statistics, volume III, deaths* (Catalogue No. 84-206) and *Causes of death, provinces by sex and Canada by sex and age* (Catalogue No. 84-203). Certain unpublished data are available on request.

Fertility   4.6

Of all the demographic factors which produce population change (fertility, mortality, nuptiality, immigration, emigration), none exerts greater influence than the rate of reproduction or fertility. By comparison, the nation's death and immigration rates could be considered far more stable and it is the birth and fertility rates that may well continue to be the dominant factor in the foreseeable future in shaping the demographic structure of Canada (see Section 4.1).

Births   4.6.1

No accurate figures on Canadian crude birth rates are available prior to 1921, when the annual collection of official national figures was initiated. However, the following rough estimates of the average annual crude rates of live births (i.e. per 1,000 total population) for each 10-year intercensal period between 1851 and 1921 may be inferred from studies of early Canadian census data: 1851-61, 45; 1861-71, 40; 1871-81, 37; 1881-91, 34; 1891-1901, 30; 1901-11, 31; 1911-21, 29.

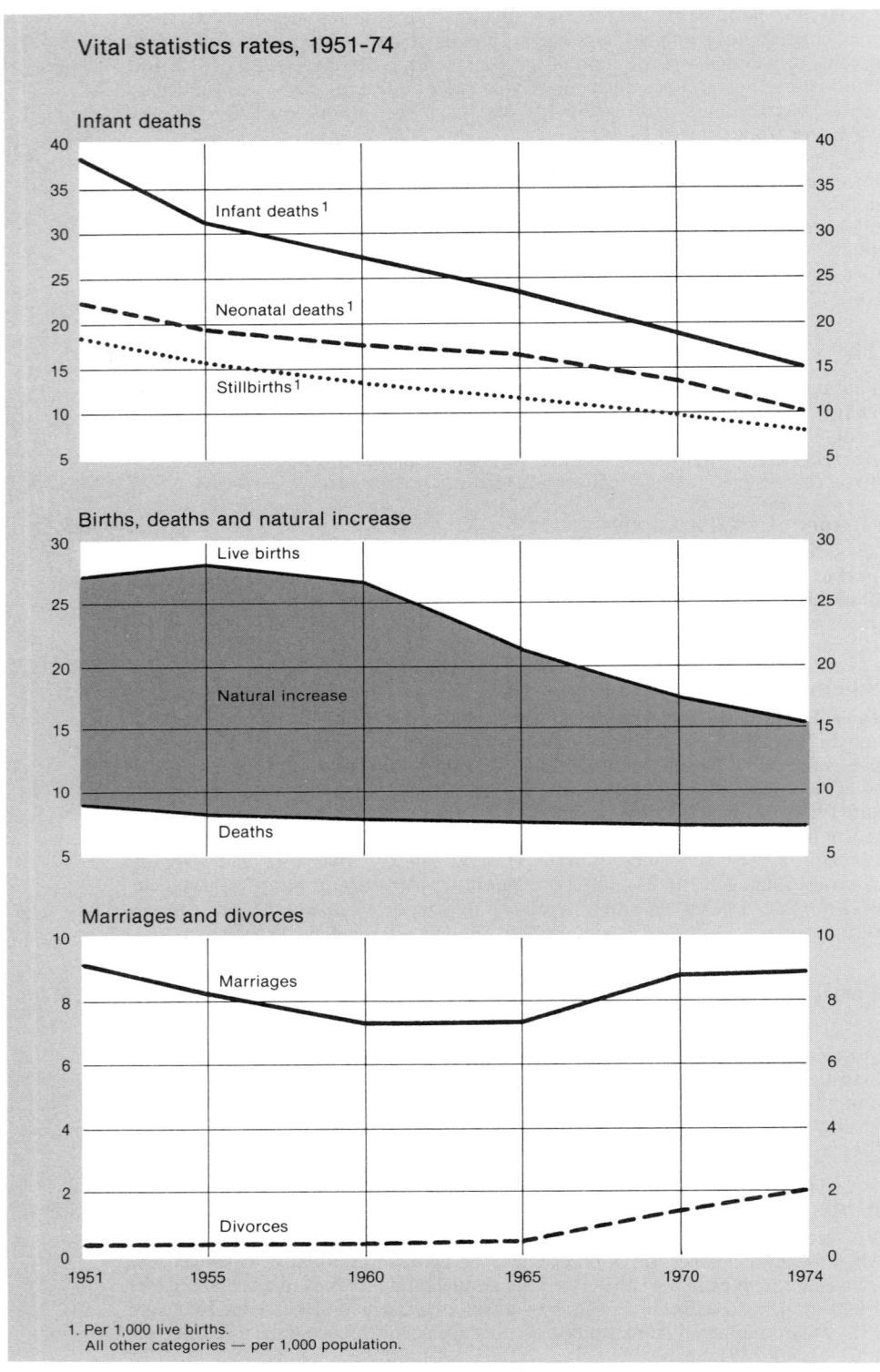

Vital statistics rates, 1951-74

Infant deaths

Infant deaths [1]

Neonatal deaths [1]

Stillbirths [1]

Births, deaths and natural increase

Live births

Natural increase

Deaths

Marriages and divorces

Marriages

Divorces

1. Per 1,000 live births.
   All other categories — per 1,000 population.

The general trend in the national crude birth rate since 1951 is shown in Table 4.32. The annual rates declined steadily from 29.3 in 1921 to a record low of 20.1 in 1937, recovered sharply in the late 1930s and rose during World War II to 24.3 in 1945. Following the war the birth rate rose to a high of 28.9 in 1947. Between 1948 and 1959 it remained remarkably stable at between 27.1 and 28.5, but has since declined dramatically to a record low of 15.4 by 1974.

The rates for most provinces followed trends similar to the national trend with some regional differences. All provinces had record high rates immediately following World War II, but during the 1951-55 period average birth rates in Ontario and the western provinces were higher than during 1946-50 and those for Quebec and the Maritime provinces were lower. In fact, Ontario, Alberta and British Columbia had record high crude birth rates during the 1956-60 period. By 1973 all provinces had record low rates. In 1974 a slight improvement in birth rate was observed in some of the provinces due mainly to the favourable age structure.

Since these crude birth rates are based on the total population they do not reflect the true fertility of the women of reproductive ages in the different provinces. A more accurate measure of the true birth rate is one based on the number of women between the ages of 15 and 45. (Table 4.38; Section 4.6.2)

Sex of live births. The number of males to every 1,000 females born in Canada has averaged around 1,057 since the middle 1930s. Provincial sex ratios vary more widely because of the relatively fewer number of births involved — the smaller the total number of births, the greater the chance of wide sex-ratio variations from year to year. In 1974, 1,058 male infants were born in Canada for every 1,000 females.

Age of mothers. The distribution of infants born alive in 1974 by age of the mother is given in Table 4.34. It shows that 68.8% of the live births in 1974 to all mothers were among 20-29-year-olds, another 14.4% to 30-34-year-olds, and only about 11.5% of births were to mothers under 20.

Order of birth. Table 4.34 also shows the order of birth of all live-born infants in 1974 according to the age of the mother. As would be expected, 31,715 or four out of every five of the 38,314 infants born to mothers 15-19 years of age were the first live-born child, whereas slightly less than half (45%) of the children born to mothers of 20-24 years were their second or later live-born child. In 1974, 312 infants were born to mothers who had not yet reached their 15th birthday.

Table 4.35 summarizes the pattern of family formation since 1951 and shows that the percentages of first and second children have been increasing in recent years. This has been accompanied generally by a reduction in the proportion of third and higher birth orders.

Stillbirths. The 2,766 stillbirths of at least 28 weeks gestation that were delivered in 1974 represented a ratio of about eight for every 1,000 foetuses born alive. As is evident from Table 4.36, the stillbirth ratio, decreasing steadily, has been cut by more than half over the past quarter-century. Ratios in some provinces have been reduced more than in others.

Table 4.37 illustrates that the risk of having a stillborn child increases with the age of the mother. Although stillbirth rates for mothers of all ages have been declining, they continue to be much higher for older than for younger mothers.

Fertility rates   4.6.2

The sex and age composition of a population is a fundamental factor affecting its birth rates. Since almost all children are born to women between the ages of 15 and 45, variations in the proportion of women of these ages to the total population will cause variations in the crude birth rate of different countries, or of different regions, even though the actual rates of reproduction or fertility of the women are identical. It is therefore conventional practice to calculate age-specific fertility rates, i.e. the number of infants born annually to every 1,000 women in each of the reproductive age groups.

As might be expected, Table 4.38 indicates that women in their 20s are the most reproductive. On the average, for every 1,000 women between the ages of 20 and 24, there were 113 infants born during 1974. Expressed another way, about one woman out of eight in that age group gave birth to a live-born infant. For the fourth consecutive year, women in the age group 25-29 had a higher rate (131) than those in their early 20s.

Another measure of fertility is the gross reproduction rate, shown in Table 4.38 to indicate the average number of female children born to each woman living through the child-bearing ages. In other words, the gross reproduction rate represents the average number of females that would be born to each woman who lived to age 50 if the fertility rate of the given year remained unchanged during the whole of her child-bearing period. A rate of 1.000 indicates that, on the basis of current fertility and without making any allowance for mortality among mothers during their child-bearing years, the present generation of child-bearing women would exactly maintain itself.

Canada has always had one of the highest gross reproduction rates among the industrialized countries of the world. Even at low birth rates in the 1930s the rate varied between 1.300 and 1.500 and since World War II has ranged from 1.640 in 1946 to a high of 1.915 in 1959. However, since 1963 the national gross reproduction rate dropped sharply from 1.788 to 0.911 in 1974 — appreciably below the replacement level of 1.000 for the first time in Canada's history. Among the provinces, Quebec, British Columbia and Ontario had the lowest gross reproduction rates in 1974, all below the replacement level.

4.6.3   Natural increase

The excess of births over deaths, or "natural increase", has been the main factor in the growth of Canada's population. Some idea of the rate of natural increase back to the mid-1800s may be obtained from the estimates of births and deaths (see Sections 4.6.1 and 4.7.1) which produce the following natural increase rates (per 1,000 population): 1851-61, 23; 1861-71, 19; 1871-81, 18; 1881-91, 16; 1891-1901, 14; 1901-11, 18; 1911-21, 16.

During the 1920s and early 1930s the birth rate declined much more rapidly than the death rate and the natural increase rate dropped to a record low of 9.7 in 1937. Higher birth rates during and after World War II and a continued declining death rate caused the natural increase rate to rise steadily from 10.9 in 1939 to a record 20.3 in 1954. After that there was a steady drop due to declining birth rates and the natural increase rate fell below 10 for the first time in 1971 at 9.5. It dropped still further to 8.0 in 1974. Table 4.32 gives average rates of natural increase in the provinces for five-year periods 1951-70 and for individual years 1971, 1972, 1973 and 1974.

4.7   Mortality

The Canadian crude death rate is one of the lowest in the world (7.4 per 1,000 population in 1974). After a continuous gradual decline over the past century, the rate appears to have levelled off since about 1967. In the opinion of demographers, further reductions in the crude death rate are likely to be small, and to affect primarily persons in the older age groups.

4.7.1   General mortality

No official crude death rates (i.e. rates per 1,000 total population) are available prior to 1921. However, studies of the early Canadian censuses resulted in the following estimated annual crude rates: 1851-61, 22; 1861-71, 21; 1871-81, 19; 1881-91, 18; 1891-1901, 16; 1901-11, 13; 1911-21, 13.

Typical of pioneer populations, Canada had high death rates in the mid-1800s with the crude death rate estimated as between 22 and 25. It is assumed that while mortality was high at all ages, the rate among infants, children and young adults must have been particularly high. Even in 1921 the Canadian infant mortality rate was 102.1 per 1,000 live births. With increasing urbanization and improved sanitation and medical services, the crude death rate dropped by 50% from 22 to 11 between 1851 and 1930. It continued to decline to a low of 7.3 in 1970 and 1971, rising slightly to 7.4 in 1973 and 1974.

Table 4.32 shows the trends in crude death rates since 1951 in the provinces and territories. The low rate shown for Newfoundland is mainly due to the high proportion of young people, and the relatively high rates for Saskatchewan, Manitoba and British Columbia to the high proportion of elderly people there.

Table 4.33 shows the numbers of deaths in urban centres of 50,000 population and over in 1974, and the average deaths a year for the periods 1961-65 and 1966-70.

Age and sex distribution of deaths. Since 1921 the mortality trend at all ages has been downward. However, the principal factor in lowering the general death rate has been the reduction in the mortality of infants and children. Between 1951 and 1974, death rates for infants and for children under five years of age dropped by about 60% (Table 4.39). Rates for the five-to-14 group also declined steeply. However, rates for boys and young men from 15 to 24 were actually higher than in 1951. Death rates for males over 25 were appreciably lower in 1974 than in 1951, except for men of 65-74 years, for whom there was little change. Rates for females of all ages declined substantially between 1951 and 1974.

As shown in Table 4.40 males under 40 accounted for 18.1% of all male deaths in 1961 but for only 13.6% in 1971; in 1961, 16.4% of all female deaths were of persons under 40, but only 10.7% in 1971.

Sharp reductions in male infant and child mortality, and substantial declines in the female rates for all younger age groups, have tended to raise the average age at death. Over 1961-71 the average for males rose 3.6 years from 59.7 to 63.3, while that for females advanced 5.1 years, from 63.1 to 68.2. The male median age at death rose only slightly, from 67.9 to 68.5, but the gain for females was 2.5 years, from 72.2 to 74.7. Thus half the females who died in 1971 were more than 74.7 years old.

Causes of death. Table 4.41 presents details of the 1974 Canadian deaths and death rates based on 50 causes as given in the International Abbreviated List (International Classification of Diseases, 8th Revision). Of the 166,794 deaths in 1974, 82,141 or over 49% were due to cardiovascular diseases, i.e. to ailments of the heart and circulatory system. Cancer accounted for 33,751, or 20.2%, accidents for 12,945 or 7.8%, and respiratory ailments for 10,911 or 6.5%. Combined, these four causes were responsible for 139,748 deaths, or 83.8% of the total.

The proportion of older people in the population has been rising in recent years. Consequently, cancer and cardiovascular diseases account for a larger proportion of all deaths than formerly. On the other hand, deaths of infants, children and young adults from such diseases as pneumonia and tuberculosis have sharply declined.

Table 4.42 shows that the leading causes of infant mortality are radically different from the main causes of death at later periods. Accidents are the primary cause of death for males between one and 44 years of age. The majority of deaths among older males are due either to cardiovascular diseases or to cancer.

Accidents are also the primary cause of mortality among girls, with cancer being the leading cause of death of young and middle-aged women. Cardiovascular diseases and cancer are the leading causes of death for elderly women.

Infant mortality   4.7.2

Table 4.43 shows that mortality rates for both male and female infants (under one year of age) have been reduced by more than 60% since 1951. For example, if the 1951 death rate had remained unchanged until 1974, there would have been

13,307 infant deaths in that year, as against the observed 5,192. The improvement is due to many factors including better prenatal and postnatal care, improved sanitation, the use of antibiotics and higher living standards. In recent years, also, older women (a high-risk group) have been having fewer babies.

The 1974 provincial mortality rates for infants of both sexes ranged from 13.4 for Ontario to 20.7 in Saskatchewan, with the rates for the Northwest Territories being substantially higher. The national death rate for all infants was 15.0, the lowest on record, with most of the provinces recording the lowest infant mortality rates in history. (Table 4.43)

Male infant mortality in Canada in recent years was 20-25% higher than the corresponding female mortality. Of 1,000 infant boys born alive in Canada during 1974, 16.6 failed to reach their first birthday, whereas for every 1,000 infant girls born alive there were only 13.4 fatalities by the end of the first year. Thus, while about 1,058 males are born for every 1,000 females, the higher male infant mortality reduces the excess to some extent during the first year.

Ages of infant deaths. Table 4.44 shows that 3,506 or nearly 68% of the 5,192 infants who died during 1974 within a year of their birth died during the first four weeks of life, the "neonatal" period; 2,033 or about 58% of these neonatal deaths occurred during the first day of life and 3,069 or 87.5% during the first week. Deaths in the neonatal period are caused mainly by conditions associated with pregnancy, difficult labour or congenital malformations. As in the case of the infant mortality rate, the Canadian neonatal death rate dropped by over half since 1951, from 22.6 to 10.1 in 1974, with substantial improvements in all the provinces (see Table 4.43).

Causes of infant deaths. Of the 5,192 infants dying in 1974, 2,451 or over 47% died of "perinatal" conditions of early infancy. There were 1,064 deaths from anoxia or hypoxia (absence or deficiency of oxygen), and 498 due to immaturity of the foetus. In the "perinatal" mortality group, 219 deaths were ascribed to conditions of the placenta or umbilical cord. Congenital malformations accounted for 1,204 deaths. Of the 420 deaths from respiratory diseases, 282 were due to pneumonia. Suffocation by food and other objects caused 151 infant deaths in 1974. Of the 175 infant deaths from infective and parasitic diseases 87 were due to intestinal infections (see also Table 4.42).

4.7.3   Life expectancy

Life tables are measures of life expectancy compiled from the death rates prevailing over a period. They assume that a given cohort of people (usually 100,000) are born simultaneously in a particular year and continue to be subject all their lives to the death rates prevailing in that year, or perhaps to the average death rates for a three-year period centred around that year. The "expected" deaths in the cohort are calculated (in the case of a "complete" life table) for the first year of life, second year of life, etc., and the diminishing cohort is "followed" for 100 or more years until it has been virtually eliminated. Life expectancy at birth is calculated for the entire cohort and, subsequently, remaining life expectancy is calculated for the survivors at one year, two years, etc. It should be noted that the assumptions of such a life table are never fulfilled in practice and that the hypothetical cohorts in life tables do not represent any actual population. Usually, the persons in an actual cohort born in the life-table year will have a higher life expectancy than those in the life-table cohort because during their lifetimes public health conditions will presumably constantly improve and standards of medical care will also presumably advance.

Seven official sets of life tables were published, based on deaths in the three-year period around each of the censuses of 1931, 1941, 1951, 1956, 1961, 1966 and 1971. The Canadian life table values for the 1971 period are given for selected ages in Table 4.45. This table shows that at 1970-72 mortality rates 2,002 of

100,000 males born would have died in their first year with 97,998 surviving to one year of age, that 126 more would have died in their second year with 97,872 reaching their second birthday and so on, with 191 survivors at 100 years of age. The "probability of dying" column represents the ratio between the population at each age and the number of "expected" deaths in the coming year. The "expectation of life" column shows the number of remaining years of life expected at each age, given the 1970-72 mortality rates.

Male probabilities of dying were higher than the corresponding female probabilities at all ages. Mortality rates and the probabilities of dying were lowest at the age of about 10 for both sexes. Then male probabilities rose rapidly, reflecting accidents to teen-age boys; the female probabilities rose more gradually. Male mortality was fairly constant from the age of 20 to the late 30s, and then increased steadily with advancing age. Female mortality rose slowly between 10 and 25 years, then more rapidly. About 11,200 of the male cohort would have died by age 50 as compared with roughly 6,600 of the female cohort, and 58,575 males would reach age 70 as compared with 75,995 females.

Life expectancy values over the 1951-71 period are shown in Table 4.46. By 1971, Canadian life expectancy at birth had reached an all-time high of 69.3 years for males and nearly 76.4 years for females. These figures are roughly comparable to the expectancies of other countries with highly developed programs of medical care. Because infant mortality is still quite substantial, life expectancies for male and female infants one year old were only slightly higher than expectancies at birth. Male expectancy at age 20 was 51.7 years, or 6.5 years below the corresponding female expectancy of 58.2. At age 40, the comparative expectancies were 33.2 for men and 39.0 for women. By age 65, the male expectancy had dropped to 13.7 years, with the female expectancy being about 3.8 years higher, at 17.5 years.

Table 4.47 shows the life expectancies for five Canadian regions for 1951 and 1961, and expectancies by province for 1966 and 1971. The steady widening of the gap between male and female expectancies, evident at the national level, seemed to be continuing in every province to judge from the 1966 and 1971 figures. For the periods around the 1956 and 1961 censuses, the Prairie region showed the highest life expectancies, both male and female. Throughout the 1951-61 interval, Quebec life expectancies were the lowest, although they showed marked improvement over the decade.

In both the 1966 and 1971 periods, Saskatchewan life expectancies at birth were the highest for males and females alike, and Quebec expectancies, although increasing, were still the lowest. In 1971, the Saskatchewan male expectancy at birth (71.1 years) was 2.8 years above the corresponding Quebec expectancy of 68.3. For female expectancies at birth, Saskatchewan set an all-time record of 77.6, about 2.3 years above the corresponding Quebec expectancy of 75.3. All the 1971 life expectancies in the four western provinces were above the national average. Ontario male rates at the younger ages were around the Canadian average, dropping slightly below for older men. Ontario female expectancies were fractionally above the national level.

In the Atlantic provinces, 1971 life expectancies for the very young did not differ greatly from the national average except in Nova Scotia for both males and females, which were somewhat below it, and Prince Edward Island females which were above it. This was also true for the expectancies at 20 years of age. The male expectancies at 40 were around the Canadian figure with Prince Edward Island a little higher and Nova Scotia slightly lower. Prince Edward Island showed the female expectancy at 40, a year above the national average, while Newfoundland and Nova Scotia were slightly below it. The Prince Edward Island expectancies at age 65 were above the Canadian level with the male expectancies at 65 for the other Atlantic provinces clustered around it. The Newfoundland female expectancy at 65 was somewhat below the Canadian level.

4.8   Nuptiality

This section includes statistics on marriages and marriage rates and also on dissolutions of marriages. In the *Canada Year Book 1973* pp 201-204, expanded coverage of the latter topic focussed attention on dramatic increases in the number of divorces resulting from changes in 1968 to Canada's divorce laws.

4.8.1   Marriages

In 1974, there were 198,824 marriages solemnized in Canada. The rate of marriage was 8.9 per 1,000 population, down from 9.0 in 1973, reversing an upward trend which began in the early 1960s. There were similar slight declines in most provinces. In 1974, Alberta recorded 9.7 marriages per 1,000 population, the highest of any province. (Table 4.32)

Birthplace of brides and grooms. For Canada as a whole in 1973, Table 4.48 shows that 73.1% of the brides and 68.5% of the grooms were married in the province in which they were born; 11.7% of brides and 13.7% of grooms were married in a province other than that of their birth. Persons born outside Canada constituted 15.2% of the brides and 17.8% of the grooms. There were significant variations in these percentages among the various provinces. In terms of marrying persons born outside Canada, Ontario and British Columbia are both relatively high.

Proportionately more brides tend to marry in the province of their birth than do grooms. Further, the proportions of both brides and grooms marrying in the region of their birth are lowest in the territories, British Columbia, Alberta, Manitoba and Ontario. These are the regions which have generally been subject to the largest net inflows of population in recent years.

Age and marital status. Table 4.49 shows that in 1974 the great majority of brides and grooms reported their previous marital status as single, with divorced and widowed following in that order. A total of 172,107 or over 86.6% of all brides in 1974, and 85.8% of all grooms, had previously never been married. The proportion of brides marrying in 1974 who were previously divorced was about 9.6%, and widowed, 3.8%.

In 1974 the median age at marriage — the age above and below which half the marriages occurred — was 23.5 for bachelors and 21.3 for spinsters. In terms of averages, bachelors averaged 24.7 years of age, and spinsters 22.4.

Religious denomination. Some indication of the influence that religion has in selecting marriage partners is shown in Table 4.50. For example, about 51% of all marriages in 1974 in Canada (excluding Quebec) were between persons of the same religious denomination. This percentage would have been significantly higher if it had been possible to include marriages contracted in the province of Quebec. Percentages were higher for such denominations as Jewish and Roman Catholic and lower for others: Anglican, Baptist, Presbyterian and United Church.

4.8.2   Divorces

The number of decrees absolute granted in Canada has risen sharply as a result of the 1968 changes in divorce legislation. For Canada as a whole the number of divorces rose to over 36,704 in 1973 as compared to an average of about 11,000 divorces over the three-year period 1966-68. Data for 1974 indicate a further increase to 45,019 decrees absolute granted in Canada. In 1974 Alberta recorded a divorce rate of 288.6 per 100,000 population, and British Columbia 285.6, the highest rates among the provinces. By comparison, Newfoundland and Prince Edward Island recorded the lowest rates, at 55.5 and 82.3. (Table 4.32)

Sex of petitioners. Table 4.51 shows that almost twice as many divorces were granted in 1974 to female petitioners (29,691), as to males (15,328). This represents a ratio of 52 divorces to male petitioners for every 100 to females. Among the provinces, Alberta showed the lowest ratio of male petitioners (38 to every 100 female) while British Columbia had the highest (60).

Grounds for divorce. A cause for divorce can be mentioned singly in a decree or in combination with others. Table 4.52 indicates that in 1974 "separation for not less than 3 years" was the most frequent cause of divorce, accounting for 33.8% of all causes reported. This was followed by adultery (29.4%), mental cruelty (16.2%), and physical cruelty (13.8%).

Dependent children. Of the 45,019 divorces granted in 1974, 41.3% involved no dependent children. Table 4.53 shows increases in the proportion of divorces involving dependent children from 55.4% in 1971 to 58.7% in 1974. Almost two out of every five of the latter cases involved one child only, and almost one third of them involved two children.

Duration of marriage. The duration of marriage in 15.5% of the divorces in Canada in 1974 was less than five years, and in 43.7% of the cases it was less than 10 years. The short-term trend over four years indicates a relative shortening of the average marriage period before divorce. Table 4.54 shows that in 1971 only 14.4% of the divorces involved marriages of less than five years duration and 39.6% to those of less than 10 years. The median duration of marriage for 1971 divorces was 12.6 years, as compared to 11.7 in 1974.

Marital status. More than nine out of every 10 persons divorced in 1974 were single at the time of their marriage, i.e. representing a first divorce. Slightly over 5% of the divorces were to persons who were divorced at the time of their last marriage, and a little less than 2% to those who were widowed. (Table 4.55)

Migration   4.9

Sections 4.5 to 4.8 were concerned with the vital components of population change (fertility, mortality, nuptiality). In addition to these factors, the flows of population across national borders (immigration and emigration) also affect the country's growth and demographic structure. This section provides data on the numbers and characteristics of immigrants entering Canada (Tables 4.56 to 4.62), as well as estimates of the numbers of emigrants leaving (Table 4.63). The relative influence of net migration (the excess of immigrants over emigrants) compared to natural increase (the excess of births over deaths) in past growth rates of Canada over the period 1851-1971 is shown in Table 4.2.

On the subject of internal migration within Canada, some estimates of total net migration by province in the 1961-71 period are given in Table 4.5. Demographic studies resulting from the 1971 Census will provide detailed analyses of the most recent trends on internal migration within Canada as did the monographs from the 1961 Census. Brief summary data from the 1971 Census are provided in Tables 4.64 to 4.66.

Immigration   4.9.1

There are three principal objectives of Canada's immigration policy: to stimulate economic growth and encourage social and cultural development; to encourage family reunion; and to alleviate the plight of refugees through humanitarian programs. Immigration law, regulations and practice are designed to protect Canadian national security, public health and economic and social welfare by excluding people whose presence in Canada would endanger these interests.

The Immigration Regulations describe the standards immigrants must meet to qualify for admission. Since 1967 Canada's immigration policies have been based on non-discrimination and universality. Considered are such things as the applicant's occupational skills, training, ability and personal initiative.

On January 1, 1973 the Minister of Manpower and Immigration introduced regulations designed to control the employment and long-term visits of non-immigrants, and since November 5, 1972 persons seeking permanent residence in Canada have been required to apply at an immigration office outside Canada.

Non-immigrants wishing to remain in Canada longer than 30 days must register with an immigration office, and any violation of the regulations constitutes an offence under the Immigration Act.

On August 15, 1973 legislation was enacted to allow those who did not have landed immigrant status in Canada to regularize their position, to reduce the backlog of cases before the Immigration Appeal Board and to modify the appeals system for the future. By the deadline on October 15, 1973 a total of 49,900 persons had registered under the program.

In February 1974, the Immigration Regulations were amended to relate the entry of immigrants more closely to the needs of Canada's economy. Immigrants had to possess abilities for which there was a demand in Canada, or the applicant had to have a firm job offer from a Canadian employer. Sponsored dependents were not affected. The amended regulations also eased the entry of adopted children or half-sisters/brothers. In October 1974 further changes were introduced with regard to acceptability of applicants able to give evidence of pre-arranged employment that could not be filled by a Canadian resident, or who would go to areas in Canada where their skills were in persistent shortage.

Canada's tradition of resettling refugees has been manifested in recent years by emergency programs, the latest having been the Vietnamese refugee movement of 1975. By August 31, 1976, over 6,000 refugees from South East Asia had been brought to Canada. Also expanded was the Chilean refugee program under which 5,000 Chilean refugees were accepted for resettlement in Canada, with special consideration of Chilean refugees in Argentina.

In September 1973 the Minister of Manpower and Immigration announced the government's intention to create a new long-term basis for Canada's immigration and population policy. The goal would be to create new immigration legislation that would serve the future needs of Canada as well as those of the present, to define objectives as to pace of population growth and its settlement, and to determine the kind of social and cultural environment wanted by Canadians. Throughout 1974 a special task force was involved with writing a Green Paper designed to outline options in the field of immigration and the consequences of each. It was tabled in Parliament in February 1975 and a Special Joint Committee of the Senate and House of Commons was convened to conduct public consultations. The report of the Special Joint Committee, arrived at after extensive hearings in centres throughout the country, was presented to Parliament in November 1975.

On November 22, 1976 a new Immigration bill was introduced in the House of Commons, reflecting the results of the previous three years' effort. The bill affirmed fundamental objectives of Canadian immigration law: family reunification, non-discrimination, concern for refugees and the promotion of Canada's economic, social, demographic and cultural goals.

There are Manpower and Immigration offices in more than 60 cities throughout the world, and examination of immigrants and visitors is carried out at more than 500 ports of entry on Canadian coasts, at points along the international boundary and at certain airports and inland offices.

The extent of immigration to Canada in any period is affected both by domestic conditions and by conditions abroad. A review of these factors, together with an analysis of trends, may be found in the *1972 Canada Year Book* pp 222-225. The numbers of immigrant arrivals for each year over the period 1949-75 are shown in Table 4.56 of the present edition.

Origin of immigrants. In 1975 Canada received 187,881 immigrants from various countries of origin, a decrease of 30,584 or 14% from the 1974 total of 218,465. Tables 4.57 and 4.58, showing the country of last permanent residence and of citizenship of immigrants, respectively, indicate that by world area the continents of Europe, Asia, North and Central America, Africa and Australasia contributed a lower proportion of the total immigration in 1975 than in the previous year. On the other hand, there was an increased percentage from South America.

The United Kingdom was the largest source area for immigrants with 34,978 in 1975, followed by the United States with 20,155.

Destination of immigrants. Upon arrival in Canada, immigrants are asked to state their intended destinations. According to these records, Ontario absorbed by far the highest proportion of arrivals during 1975 — 52.5% of both the males and the females. British Columbia was the second most-favoured province of destination, receiving 15.1% of the males and 16.1% of the females, followed by Quebec with 15.6% of the males and 14.3% of the females. The proportions intending to settle in the Prairie provinces were 14.3% for males and 13.6% for females, and in the Atlantic provinces, 3.0% for both males and females. The provincial distribution as shown in Table 4.59 for 1975 and 1974 has changed little from year to year over the past two decades.

Sex, age and marital status. The sex distribution of immigrants for 1970-75 is shown in Table 4.60. In the period 1973-75 adult males constituted 36.8% of the immigrants, adult females 36.4%, and children under 18 years of age the remaining 26.8%. The number of female immigrants coming into Canada was higher than the number of male immigrants in every year from 1957 to 1964; since then, with the exception of 1969, 1971, 1972 and 1975 the trend has been in favour of males. There was an excess of 5,336 males over females in 1973 and 3,779 in 1974. In 1975, females exceeded males by 2,515. Single males as shown in Table 4.61 surpassed single females by 8,225 in 1975, but in all ever-married categories women outnumbered men: married females exceeded married males by 5,665; there were 5,591 widows compared to 925 widowers; divorcees outnumbered divorced men by 352; and there were 501 separated females, compared to 392 males. Of the total immigration for 1975, persons under 15 years of age totalled 27.2% and of those over 14 years, 24.4% were single, 43.5% married, and 4.9% were widowed, divorced or separated.

Intended occupations. Some 81,189 persons were added to the labour force in 1975 compared with 106,083 in 1974. The remainder, those not destined to the labour force were largely dependents of immigrants or close relatives sponsored by individuals in Canada. Persons employed in the product, fabricating and assembling occupations represented the largest occupational group with 11,936 workers. Other major groups were professional and technical with 8,928, service with 7,082 and construction with 5,893.

Emigration

4.9.2

Emigration from Canada tends to offset to some extent present and past immigration activities. The major outward movement has been to the United States, both of native-born Canadians and of Europeans who originally migrated to Canada, and has attained considerable proportions at certain periods. No Canadian statistics on emigration are available but Table 4.63 gives figures taken from the annual reports of the Immigration and Naturalization Service of the United States Department of Justice. These figures show the numbers of persons entering the United States from Canada during the years ended June 30, 1966-75 with the expressed intention of establishing permanent residence. They do not include persons travelling for pleasure, even for extended periods of time, holders of border-crossing cards (normally issued to persons living in border areas but working in the United States) or casual tourist crossings in these same areas.

Of the 7,654 Canadian-born persons entering the United States in the year ended June 30, 1974 with the intention of remaining permanently, 3,360 were males and 4,294 females. Approximately one fifth, or 1,563, of the native-born emigrants were males in the productive age group, 20-59 years. By occupation, the largest group of the total of 7,654 native-born persons was the professional or technical group which numbered 904; clerical and kindred workers numbered 383; and craftsmen and kindred workers numbered 307. On the other hand 5,057 persons, or 66.1% of the total, were classed as housewives, children and others with no reported occupation. Altogether, 42.2% of the total were persons under 20 years of age.

Of the 12,301 persons entering the United States from Canada claiming Canada as country of last permanent residence — which includes native-born persons and those born in other countries who have resided in Canada — the Immigration and Naturalization Service of the United States Department of Justice lists 1,970 as professional, technical and kindred workers; 709 as craftsmen, foremen and kindred workers; and 616 as clerical and kindred workers. Housewives, children and others not in the labour force amounted to 6,803 or 55.3% of the total.

4.9.3   Internal migration

As people move from one place of residence to another within the nation's borders, they set up varying patterns of migration which differ in intensity and directional flow. These internal movements have marked effects on regional economies, and they exert an influence on future population growth.

Migration by province of birth. Census figures on birthplace (province of birth) shed some light on internal migration flows, by comparing the numbers of persons born in a given province with their province of present residence. Such figures give no indication of the periodicity of the migrating process, and they apply only to the Canadian-born population presently living in a given province, but they do reflect something of the accumulated results of the major patterns of interprovincial movement of native-born persons over the years.

Data from the 1971 Census in Table 4.64 show that Ontario, Alberta and British Columbia have been net gainers of Canadian-born migrants from other provinces, while the remaining provinces have been net losers. Newfoundland and Quebec showed the fewest numbers of their 1971 population as having been born in another province (3.3% and 4.6%, respectively), while British Columbia showed the highest (37.4%). These percentages reflect low rates of Canadian-born in-migrants to the former two provinces, and a high rate to the latter one. Saskatchewan-born persons were the most likely to be found living in a province other than that of their birth (40.0%), while Quebec-born and Ontario-born persons were the least likely (6.1% and 7.4%, respectively). This reflects a high rate of out-migration of native-born persons from the former province, and low rates from the latter two.

Migration by residence five years ago. Useful estimates on internal migration result from including questions in national censuses to determine the place of residence of each person at the date of the census five years earlier. From a comparison with their present residence, it is possible to estimate the size, directional flows and characteristics of the migrating population. Such questions were included in both the 1961 and 1971 censuses of Canada. Migration trends as revealed by the 1961 Census were issued in monographs (see Catalogue Nos. 99-548 and 99-557) and other studies (see Catalogue No. 99-513). A few basic summary results of the 1971 Census, which included questions on place of residence five years earlier at June 1, 1966, are presented in Tables 4.65 and 4.66.

The migration status of the population in 1971 in terms of residence in 1966 is summarized in Table 4.65. It shows that almost one half (47.4%) of Canada's population five years of age and over in 1971 were living in a different home than five years earlier. A total of 23.5% had moved within the same municipality, while 23.9% had moved from one municipality to another. The latter group consisted of 14.0% who were movers within the same province, 4.3% from one province to another, and 4.2% from outside Canada. Ontario was the most-favoured province of destination for in-migrants from other provinces and from outside Canada. A total of 40.6% of all 1966-71 interprovincial migrants and immigrants from abroad were living in Ontario in 1971. British Columbia was next, receiving 18.4% of these migrants, followed by Quebec (12.9%) and Alberta (11.2%).

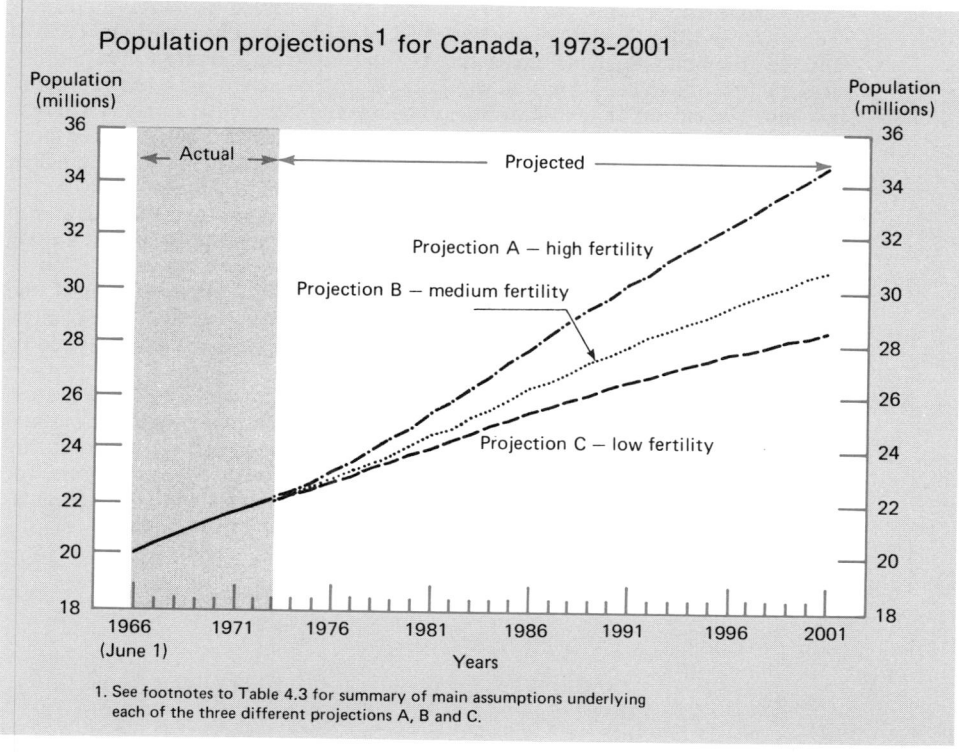

Population projections[1] for Canada, 1973-2001

Population (millions)

1. See footnotes to Table 4.3 for summary of main assumptions underlying each of the three different projections A, B and C.

Migration by type of locality. Table 4.66 compares the type of locality of residence on June 1, 1966 and June 1, 1971 for migrants who had moved from one municipality to another. Metropolitan areas constituted the favourite destination, as well as being the major locality of origin. A total of 58.0% of all migrants moved to a municipality within a metropolitan area. Immigrants from outside Canada showed the greatest propensity to locate in a metropolitan area, and this was the destination of 80.9% of their numbers. By locality of origin, 44.6% of the 1966-71 migrants residing in metropolitan areas in 1971 were also living in a metropolitan area in 1966 (i.e. in a different municipality of the same or other metropolitan area), 15.2% were from other urban localities, 9.7% from rural areas, and 24.3% were from outside Canada.

Only about 217,000 or 4.6% of all 1966-71 migrants had been living in predominantly farm localities in 1966 before moving. However, this figure represented over 10% of the total farm population. One third (32.8%) from farm localities were living in metropolitan areas in 1971, over one half (54.2%) in other urban or rural non-farm localities, and only 13.0% in predominantly farm areas. The decline in the rural farm population of all ages (i.e. the total population living on farms in all rural localities) was from 1.9 million in 1966 to 1.4 million in 1971 (see Section 4.2.3 and Table 4.11).

Citizenship   4.9.4

Citizenship statistics. Citizenship certificates are "issued" for various reasons to persons who are already Canadian citizens; certificates are "granted" to those who become Canadian citizens by the grant of such certificates. In 1975, 142,278 certificates were issued and 140,688 granted.

New Citizenship Act. Bill C-20, the Citizenship Act received Royal Assent on July 16, 1976, and the legislation was expected to come into effect early in 1977. It replaced the first Canadian Citizenship Act, in force from January 1, 1947, which was the first one to be introduced within the Commonwealth. By it the concept of a "Canadian citizen" had first come into being, and it provided a means whereby non-Canadian British subjects and aliens permanently residing in Canada or those who might subsequently immigrate to Canada could apply for Canadian citizenship. During the years it had been amended some 60 times.

The new legislation was designed to be more equitable than the old, and to meet the modern conditions that prevail in Canadian society. It covers, among other things, questions of the right to citizenship, the loss and resumption of citizenship, the issuance of certificates of citizenship, offences against the Citizenship Act, the status of persons in Canada and the triability at law of non-citizens as if they were Canadian citizens. The Citizenship Act is administered by the Department of the Secretary of State.

Specifically, it shortens the length of residence in Canada prior to application for citizenship from five to three years, and introduces a more equitable method of calculating residence. It removes various discriminatory provisions, ensuring that men and women will be treated equally. It reduces the age of majority for purposes of citizenship from 21 to 18, and gives the same status to all applicants, eliminating the preferential status formerly accorded to British subjects.

Sources

4.1 Population Estimates and Projections Division, Content and Analysis Branch, Census and Household Surveys Field, Statistics Canada. The early growth of Canada's population is analyzed in more detail in Vol. I of the 1931 Census; other accounts of growth prior to the present century are contained in: Vol. I, 1941; Vol. X, 1951; Bulletin 7.1-1 (Catalogue No. 99-511), 1961; and Bulletin 5.1-1 (Catalogue No. 99-701), 1971. More detailed accounts of recent population growth are available in the *Canada Year Book,* 1969 edition pp 153-165, 1970-71 edition pp 210-220, and in above census reports 99-511 and 99-701.

4.2 - 4.3.3 Census Characteristics Division, Content and Analysis Branch, Census and Household Surveys Field, Statistics Canada; except 1973 population estimates for provinces, metropolitan areas, and age groups provided by Population Estimates and Projections Division of Census and Household Surveys Field.

4.3.4 Program Statistics Division, Program Analysis and Management Services Branch, Department of Indian Affairs and Northern Development.

4.4 Census Characteristics Division, Content and Analysis Branch, Census and Household Surveys Field, Statistics Canada.

4.5 - 4.8 Health Division, Institutional and Public Finance Statistics Branch, Institutions and Agriculture Statistics Field, Statistics Canada.

4.9.1 Canada Immigration Division, Department of Manpower and Immigration.

4.9.2 Population Estimates and Projections Division, Content and Analysis Branch, Census and Household Surveys Field, Statistics Canada.

4.9.3 Census Characteristics Division, Census and Household Surveys Field, Statistics Canada.

4.9.4 Citizenship Registration Branch, Department of the Secretary of State.

Tables

..   not available
...   not appropriate or not applicable
—   nil or zero
--   too small to be expressed

e   estimate
p   preliminary
r   revised
certain tables may not add due to rounding

All figures of the 1971 Census in Tables 4.11 to 4.13, 4.15 to 4.21, and 4.23 to 4.31, have been subjected to a confidentiality procedure to prevent the possibility of associating small figures with an identifiable individual. The particular technique used is known as "random rounding". Under this method, all last or "unit" digits in a table (including all totals) are randomly rounded (either up or down) to "0" or "5". This technique provides the strongest possible protection against direct, residual, or negative disclosures without adding any significant error to the census data. However, since totals are independently rounded they do not necessarily equal the sum of individual rounded figures in distributions. Also, minor differences can be expected for corresponding totals and cell values in various census tabulations.

4.1   Growth of the population of Canada, 1851-1971

Census year	Population No.	Increase during intercensal period No.	%	Average annual rate of population growth %
1851	2,436,297			
1861	3,229,633	793,336	32.6	2.9
1871	3,689,257	459,624	14.2	1.3
1881	4,324,810	635,553	17.2	1.6
1891	4,833,239	508,429	11.8	1.1
1901	5,371,315	538,076	11.1	1.1
1911	7,206,643	1,835,328	34.2	3.0
1921	8,787,949	1,581,306	21.9	2.0
1931	10,376,786	1,588,837	18.1	1.7
1941	11,506,655	1,129,869	10.9	1.0
1951[1]	14,009,429	2,502,774	21.8	1.7
1961	18,238,247	4,228,818	30.2	2.7
1971	21,568,311	3,330,064	18.3	1.7

[1]Newfoundland included for the first time. Excluding Newfoundland the increase would have been 2,141,358 or 18.6%.

4.2   Growth components of Canada's population, 1851-1971

Period	Total population growth '000	Births '000	Deaths '000	Natural increase '000	Ratio of natural increase to total growth %	Immi-gration '000	Emi-gration '000	Net mi-gration '000	Ratio of net mi-gration to total growth %
1851-1861	793	1,281	670	611	77.0	352	170	182	23.0
1861-1871	460	1,370	760	610	132.6	260	410	-150	-32.6
1871-1881	636	1,480	790	690	108.5	350	404	-54	-8.5
1881-1891	508	1,524	870	654	128.7	680	826	-146	-28.7
1891-1901	538	1,548	880	668	124.2	250	380	-130	-24.2
1901-1911	1,835	1,925	900	1,025	55.9	1,550	740	810	44.1
1911-1921	1,581	2,340	1,070	1,270	80.3	1,400	1,089	311	19.7
1921-1931	1,589	2,420	1,060	1,360	85.5	1,200	970	230	14.5
1931-1941	1,130	2,294	1,072	1,222	108.1	149	241	-92	-8.1
1941-1951[1]	2,503	3,212	1,220	1,992	92.3	548	382	166	7.7
1951-1961	4,228	4,468	1,320	3,148	74.5	1,543	463	1,080	25.5
1961-1971	3,330	4,105	1,497	2,608	78.3	1,429	707	722	21.7

[1]Includes Newfoundland in 1951 but not in 1941.

4.3   Projected population of Canada up to 2001

Year	Population as at June 1 '000	Annual rate of population growth %	Distribution by age 0-19 %	20-44 %	45-64 %	65+ %
Projection A[1]						
1971	21,568.3	...	39.4	33.9	18.6	8.1
1976	23,086.1	1.4	36.1	36.4	18.9	8.6
1981	25,311.5	1.8	34.3	38.6	18.1	9.0
1986	27,810.9	1.9	33.9	39.6	17.2	9.3
1991	30,177.6	1.6	34.9	38.1	17.2	9.8
1996	32,347.1	1.4	35.6	36.2	18.3	9.9
2001	34,611.4	1.3	34.6	35.4	20.2	9.8
Projection B[2]						
1971	21,568.3	...	39.4	33.9	18.6	8.1
1976	22,846.3	1.2	35.9	36.4	19.1	8.6
1981	24,472.5	1.4	33.2	38.9	18.6	9.3
1986	26,258.6	1.4	31.6	40.5	18.1	9.8
1991	27,902.1	1.2	31.8	39.6	18.2	10.4
1996	29,317.0	1.0	31.8	37.7	19.7	10.8
2001	30,655.5	0.9	30.8	36.4	21.9	10.9

4.3   Projected population of Canada up to 2001 (concluded)

Year	Population as at June 1 '000	Annual rate of population growth %	Distribution by age 0-19 %	20-44 %	45-64 %	65+ %
Projection C[3]						
1971	21,568.3	...	39.4	33.9	18.6	8.1
1976	22,772.4	1.1	35.7	36.5	19.1	8.7
1981	24,041.4	1.1	32.0	39.6	19.0	9.4
1986	25,382.9	1.1	29.3	41.9	18.7	10.1
1991	26,591.4	0.9	28.4	41.5	19.1	11.0
1996	27,569.7	0.7	27.8	39.8	20.9	11.5
2001	28,369.7	0.6	26.7	37.9	23.6	11.8

The above figures represent new series of projections replacing those in the *1974 Canada Year Book* (see text in Section 4.1.3).
[1]Projection A assumptions: total fertility will change from 2.19 children in 1971 to 2.60 by 1985 and then remain constant through 2001; net migration gain of 100,000 per year; and expectation of life at birth will increase gradually to 70.2 years for males and 78.4 for females by 1986 and then remain constant through 2001.
[2]Projection B assumptions: total fertility will change to 2.20 children by 1985 and then remain constant through 2001; net migration gain of 60,000 per year; and mortality same as Projection A.
[3]Projection C assumptions: total fertility will change to 1.80 children by 1985 and then remain constant through 2001; net migration is same as Projection B; and mortality is same as Projection A.

4.4   Population and percentage change of population, by province, 1951-76

Province or territory	Population and percentage change					
	Population					
	1951	1956	1961	1966	1971	1976
Newfoundland	361,416	415,074	457,853	493,396	522,104	557,725
Prince Edward Island	98,429	99,285	104,629	108,535	111,641	118,229
Nova Scotia	642,584	694,717	737,007	756,039	788,960	828,571
New Brunswick	515,697	554,616	597,936	616,788	634,557	677,250
Quebec	4,055,681	4,628,378	5,259,211	5,780,845	6,027,764	6,234,445
Ontario	4,597,542	5,404,933	6,236,092	6,960,870	7,703,106	8,264,465
Manitoba	776,541	850,040	921,686	963,066	988,247	1,021,506
Saskatchewan	831,728	880,665	925,181	955,344	926,242	921,323
Alberta	939,501	1,123,116	1,331,944	1,463,203	1,627,874	1,838,037
British Columbia	1,165,210	1,398,464	1,629,082	1,873,674	2,184,621	2,466,608
Yukon Territory	9,096	12,190	14,628	14,382	18,388	21,836
Northwest Territories	16,004	19,313	22,998	28,738	34,807	42,609
Canada	14,009,429	16,080,791	18,238,247	20,014,880	21,568,311	22,992,604
	Percentage change					
	1951-56	1956-61	1961-66	1966-71		1971-76
Newfoundland	14.8	10.3	7.8	5.8		6.8
Prince Edward Island	0.9	5.4	3.7	2.9		5.9
Nova Scotia	8.1	6.1	2.6	4.4		5.0
New Brunswick	7.5	7.8	3.2	2.9		6.7
Quebec	14.1	13.6	9.9	4.3		3.4
Ontario	17.6	15.4	11.6	10.7		7.3
Manitoba	9.5	8.4	4.5	2.6		3.4
Saskatchewan	5.9	5.1	3.3	-3.0		-0.5
Alberta	19.5	18.6	9.9	11.2		12.9
British Columbia	20.0	16.5	15.0	16.6		12.9
Yukon Territory	34.0	20.0	-1.7	27.8		18.8
Northwest Territories	20.7	19.1	25.0	21.1		22.4
Canada	14.8	13.4	9.7	7.8		6.6

4.5   Components of population change, by province, 1961-66 and 1966-71

Province or territory	Total population change		Natural increase		Net migration	
	1961-66	1966-71	1961-66	1966-71	1961-66	1966-71
Newfoundland	35,543	28,708	59,577	49,096	-24,034	-20,388
Prince Edward Island	3,906	3,106	8,506	5,207	-4,600	-2,101
Nova Scotia	19,032	32,921	59,526	37,418	-40,494	-4,497
New Brunswick	18,852	17,769	53,229	35,233	-34,377	-17,464
Quebec	521,634	246,919	457,717	288,727	63,917	-41,808
Ontario	724,778	742,236	487,852	373,072	236,926	369,164
Manitoba	41,380	25,181	70,340	49,260	-28,960	-24,079
Saskatchewan	30,163	-29,102	75,691	50,867	-45,528	-79,969
Alberta	131,259	164,671	134,607	105,293	-3,348	59,378
British Columbia	244,592	310,947	104,103	88,494	140,489	222,453
Yukon Territory and Northwest Territories	5,494	10,075	6,745	6,720	-1,251	3,355
Canada	1,776,633	1,553,431	1,517,893	1,089,387	258,740	464,044

4.6   Annual estimates of population, by province, as at June 1, 1966-75 (thousands)

Province or territory	Census 1966	Estimates 1967-70				Census 1971	Estimates 1973-75		
		1967	1968	1969	1970		1973	1974	1975
Nfld.	493	499	506	514	517	522	541	542	549
PEI	109	109	110	111	110	112	115	117	119
NS	756	760	767	775	782	789	805	813	822
NB	617	620	625	628	627	635	652	662	675
Que.	5,781	5,864	5,928	5,985	6,013	6,028	6,081	6,134	6,188
Ont.	6,961	7,127	7,262	7,385	7,551	7,703	7,939	8,094	8,226
Man.	963	963	971	979	983	988	998	1,011	1,019
Sask.	955	957	960	958	941	926	908	907	918
Alta.	1,463	1,490	1,524	1,559	1,595	1,628	1,683	1,714	1,768
BC	1,874	1,945	2,003	2,060	2,128	2,185	2,315	2,395	2,457
YT	14	15	15	16	17	18	20	19	21
NWT	29	29	30	31	33	35	38	38	38
Canada	20,015	20,378	20,701	21,001	21,297	21,568	22,095	22,446	22,800

4.7   Populations of incorporated cities, towns and villages classified by size group, 1961, 1966 and 1971

Size group	1961			1966			1971		
	Incorporated centres	Population	% of total population	Incorporated centres	Population	% of total population	Incorporated centres	Population	% of total population
Over 500,000	2	1,863,469	10.2	2	1,886,839	9.4	2	1,927,138	8.9
Between									
400,000 and 500,000	—	—	—	1	410,375	2.1	3	1,267,727	5.9
300,000 and 400,000	1	384,522	2.1	2	707,500	3.5	2	611,514	2.8
200,000 and 300,000	5	1,338,294	7.3	3	845,867	4.2	4	900,778	4.2
100,000 and 200,000	4	568,056	3.1	6	997,051	5.0	8	1,060,048	4.9
50,000 and 100,000	17	1,134,214	6.2	26	1,740,446	8.7	26	1,870,435	8.7
25,000 and 50,000	41	1,431,909	7.9	43	1,438,388	7.2	49	1,633,969	7.6
15,000 and 25,000	43	862,101	4.7	52	1,019,205	5.1	59	1,150,768	5.3
10,000 and 15,000	61	743,474	4.1	65	781,611	3.9	55	675,748	3.1
5,000 and 10,000	132	932,936	5.1	125	898,136	4.5	144	1,028,412	4.8
3,000 and 5,000	151	579,201	3.2	165	637,117	3.2	173	670,537	3.1
1,000 and 3,000	465	793,465	4.4	471	818,003	4.1	502	866,086	4.0
Under 1,000	1,039	437,207	2.4	1,057	445,246	2.2	1,093	451,810	2.1
Total	1,961	11,068,848	60.7	2,018	12,625,784	63.1	2,120	14,114,970	65.4

4.8   Population of incorporated cities and towns of 50,000 and over, 1961, 1966 and 1971

Incorporated city or town	Year of incorporation	1961	1966	1971
Brantford, Ont.	1877	55,201	59,854 *	64,421
Burlington, Ont.	1915	47,008	65,941 *	87,023
Calgary, Alta.	1893	249,641	330,575 *	403,319 *
Dartmouth, NS	1961	46,966	58,745	64,770
Edmonton, Alta.	1904	281,027	376,925 *	438,152 *
Guelph, Ont.	1879	39,838	51,377 *	60,087 *
Halifax, NS	1841	92,511	86,792	122,035 *
Hamilton, Ont.	1846	273,991	298,121 *	309,173
Hull, Que.	1875	56,929	60,176 *	63,580 *
Kingston, Ont.	1846	53,526	59,004	59,047 *
Kitchener, Ont.	1912	74,485	93,255 *	111,804 *
LaSalle, Que.	1958	30,904	48,322	72,912
Laval, Que.	1965	124,741	196,088	228,010
London, Ont.	1855	169,569	194,416	223,222 *
Longueuil, Que.	1920	24,131	25,593	97,590 *
Mississauga, Ont.	1968	62,616	93,492 *	156,070 *
Montreal, Que.	1832	1,191,062	1,222,255 *	1,214,352 *
Montreal N., Que.	1959	48,433	67,806	89,139 *
Niagara Falls, Ont.	1903	22,351	56,891 *	67,163 *
Oakville, Ont.	1857	10,366	52,793 *	61,483 *
Oshawa, Ont.	1924	62,415	78,082	91,587
Ottawa, Ont.	1854	268,206	290,741	302,341
Peterborough, Ont.	1905	47,185	56,177 *	58,111 *
Quebec, Que.	1832	171,979	166,984	186,088 *
Regina, Sask.	1903	112,141	131,127 *	139,469 *
Saint John, NB	1785	55,153	51,567	89,039 *
St. Catharines, Ont.	1876	84,472	97,101	109,722 *
Ste-Foy, Que.	1955	29,716	48,298 *	68,385 *
St. James-Assiniboia, Man.	1969	44,434	59,255	71,431
St. John's, Nfld.	1888	63,633	79,884 *	88,102 *
St-Laurent, Que.	1955	49,805	59,479 *	62,955 *
St-Léonard, Que.	1963	4,893	25,328 *	52,040 *
Sarnia, Ont.	1914	50,976	54,552	57,644
Saskatoon, Sask.	1906	95,526	115,892 *	126,449 *
Sault Ste Marie, Ont.	1912	43,088	74,594 *	80,332
Sherbrooke, Que.	1875	66,554	75,690	80,711
Sudbury, Ont.	1930	80,120	84,888 *	90,535
Thunder Bay, Ont.	1970	98,671	104,539	108,411

4.8   Population of incorporated cities and towns of 50,000 and over, 1961, 1966 and 1971 (concluded)

Incorporated city or town	Year of incor- poration	1961	1966	1971
Toronto, Ont.	1834	672,407	664,584	712,786 *
Trois-Rivières, Que.	1857	53,477	57,540 *	55,869
Vancouver, BC	1886	384,522	410,375	426,256
Verdun, Que.	1912	78,317	76,832	74,718
Victoria, BC	1862	54,941	57,453	61,761
Windsor, Ont.	1892	114,367	192,544 *	203,300 *
Winnipeg, Man.	1873	265,429	257,005 *	246,246

*Indicates a boundary change since the preceding census. Population totals in these cases are based on a different area, i.e. the boundaries at that particular census year.

4.9   Population of census metropolitan areas (based on 1971 boundaries) 1951-71, and 1976

Census metropolitan area	1951	1956	1961	1966	1971	1976[1]
Calgary	142,315	201,022	279,062	330,575	403,319	469,917
Chicoutimi-Jonquière	91,161	110,317	127,616	132,954	133,703	128,643
Edmonton	193,622	275,182	359,821	425,370	495,702	554,228
Halifax	138,427	170,481	193,353	209,901	222,637	267,991
Hamilton	281,901	341,513	401,071	457,410	498,523	529,371
Kitchener	107,474	128,722	154,864	192,275	226,846	272,158
London	167,724	196,338	226,669	253,701	286,011	270,383
Montreal	1,539,308	1,830,232	2,215,627	2,570,982	2,743,208	2,802,485
Ottawa-Hull	311,587	367,756	457,038	528,774	602,510	693,288
Quebec	289,294	328,405	379,067	436,918	480,502	542,158
Regina	72,731	91,215	113,749	132,432	140,734	151,191
Saint John, NB	80,689	88,375	98,083	104,195	106,744	112,974
St. Catharines-Niagara	189,046	233,034	257,796	285,453	303,429	301,921
St. John's, Nfld.	80,869	92,565	106,666	117,533	131,814	143,390
Saskatoon	55,679	72,930	95,564	115,900	126,449	133,750
Sudbury	80,543	107,889	127,446	136,739	155,424	157,030
Thunder Bay	73,713	87,624	102,085	108,035	112,093	119,253
Toronto	1,261,861	1,571,952	1,919,409	2,289,900	2,628,043	2,803,101
Vancouver	586,172	694,425	826,798	933,091	1,082,352	1,166,348
Victoria	114,859	136,127	155,763	175,262	195,800	218,250
Windsor	182,619	208,456	217,215	238,323	258,643	247,582
Winnipeg	357,229	412,741	476,543	508,759	540,262	578,217

[1]Based on 1976 Census Metropolitan area.

4.10   Land area and density of population, by province, 1951-71

Province or territory	Land area sq miles	Population per sq mile				
		1951	1956	1961	1966	1971
Newfoundland	143,045	2.53	2.90	3.20	3.45	3.65
Prince Edward Island	2,184	45.07	45.46	47.91	49.70	51.11
Nova Scotia	20,402	31.50	34.05	36.12	37.06	38.67
New Brunswick	27,835	18.53	19.93	21.48	22.16	22.80
Quebec	523,860	7.74	8.84	10.04	11.04	11.50
Ontario	344,092	13.36	15.71	18.12	20.23	22.39
Manitoba	211,775	3.67	4.01	4.35	4.55	4.66
Saskatchewan	220,182	3.78	4.00	4.20	4.34	4.21
Alberta	248,800	3.78	4.51	5.35	5.88	6.54
British Columbia	359,279	3.24	3.89	4.53	5.22	6.08
Canada (excl. the territories)	2,101,454	6.65	7.64	8.66	9.50	10.24
Yukon Territory	205,346	0.04	0.06	0.07	0.07	0.09
Northwest Territories	1,253,438	0.01	0.02	0.02	0.02	0.03
Canada	3,560,238	3.93	4.52	5.12	5.62	6.06

4.10   Land area and density of population, by province, 1951-71   **M**

Province or territory	Land area km²	Population per km²				
		1951	1956	1961	1966	1971
Newfoundland	370 485	0.98	1.12	1.24	1.33	1.41
Prince Edward Island	5 657	17.40	17.55	18.50	19.19	19.73
Nova Scotia	52 841	12.16	13.15	13.95	14.31	14.93
New Brunswick	72 092	7.15	7.70	8.29	8.56	8.80
Quebec	1 356 791	2.99	3.41	3.88	4.26	4.44
Ontario	891 194	5.16	6.07	7.00	7.81	8.64
Manitoba	548 495	1.42	1.55	1.68	1.76	1.80
Saskatchewan	570 269	1.46	1.54	1.62	1.68	1.63
Alberta	644 389	1.46	1.74	2.07	2.27	2.53
British Columbia	930 528	1.25	1.50	1.75	2.02	2.35
Canada (excl. the territories)	5 442 741	2.57	2.95	3.34	3.67	3.95
Yukon Territory	531 844	0.02	0.02	0.03	0.03	0.03
Northwest Territories	3 246 389	- -	0.01	0.01	0.01	0.01
Canada	9 220 974	1.52	1.75	1.98	2.17	2.34

4.11   Number and percentage of the population classified as urban, and rural by non-farm and farm, by province, 1971

Province or territory	Urban		Rural						Total population
			Non-farm		Farm		Total		
	No.	%	No.	%	No.	%	No.	%	No.
Newfoundland	298,800	57.2	218,775	41.9	4,525	0.9	223,305	42.8	522,105
Prince Edward Island	42,780	38.3	47,725	42.7	21,130	18.9	68,860	61.7	111,640
Nova Scotia	447,400	56.7	315,290	40.0	26,270	3.3	341,555	43.3	788,960
New Brunswick	361,145	56.9	247,845	39.1	25,565	4.0	273,410	43.1	634,555
Quebec	4,861,240	80.6	861,215	14.3	305,300	5.1	1,166,520	19.4	6,027,765
Ontario	6,343,630	82.4	995,840	12.9	363,640	4.7	1,359,475	17.6	7,703,105
Manitoba	686,445	69.5	171,390	17.3	130,410	13.2	301,800	30.5	988,245
Saskatchewan	490,630	53.0	202,280	21.8	233,335	25.2	435,610	47.0	926,240
Alberta	1,196,250	73.5	195,590	12.0	236,025	14.5	431,620	26.5	1,627,875
British Columbia	1,654,405	75.7	456,700	20.9	73,520	3.4	530,215	24.3	2,184,620
Yukon Territory	11,215	61.0	7,120	38.7	55	0.3	7,170	39.0	18,390
Northwest Territories	16,830	48.4	17,955	51.6	25	0.1	17,980	51.7	34,805
Canada	16,410,785	76.1	3,737,730	17.3	1,419,795	6.6	5,157,525	23.9	21,568,310

4.12   Sex distribution of the population, by province, 1971 and sex ratios, 1961, 1966 and 1971

Province or territory	Population, 1971		Males to 100 females		
	Male	Female	1961	1966	1971
Newfoundland	266,110	256,000	105	104	104
Prince Edward Island	56,225	55,415	104	103	101
Nova Scotia	396,470	392,495	103	101	101
New Brunswick	319,420	315,135	102	101	101
Quebec	2,994,550	3,033,215	100	100	99
Ontario	3,840,910	3,862,200	101	100	99
Manitoba	494,610	493,635	103	101	100
Saskatchewan	470,720	455,515	108	105	103
Alberta	827,785	800,090	107	104	103
British Columbia	1,100,375	1,084,250	104	103	101
Yukon Territory	9,920	8,470	127	119	117
Northwest Territories	18,280	16,530	126	118	111
Canada	10,795,370	10,772,945	102	101	100

4.13   Age distribution of the population, 1961, 1966 and 1971

Age group	Number			Percentage		
	1961	1966	1971	1961	1966	1971
0- 4 years	2,256,401	2,197,387	1,816,155	12.4	11.0	8.4
5- 9 "	2,079,522	2,300,857	2,254,005	11.4	11.5	10.4
10-14 "	1,855,999	2,093,513	2,310,740	10.2	10.5	10.7
15-19 "	1,432,559	1,837,725	2,114,345	7.9	9.2	9.8
20-24 "	1,183,646	1,461,298	1,889,400	6.5	7.3	8.8
25-29 "	1,209,297	1,241,794	1,584,125	6.6	6.2	7.3
30-34 "	1,271,810	1,241,697	1,305,425	7.0	6.2	6.1
35-39 "	1,270,924	1,286,144	1,263,870	7.0	6.4	5.9
40-44 "	1,118,961	1,257,028	1,262,530	6.1	6.3	5.9
45-49 "	1,015,316	1,089,915	1,239,040	5.6	5.4	5.7
50-54 "	863,188	988,264	1,052,540	4.7	4.9	4.9
55-59 "	705,835	816,300	954,725	3.9	4.1	4.4
60-64 "	583,635	663,410	777,020	3.2	3.3	3.6
65-69 "	487,102	531,709	619,960	2.7	2.7	2.9
70-74 "	402,175	427,207	457,380	2.2	2.1	2.1
75-79 "	274,237	300,365	325,510	1.5	1.5	1.5
80-84 "	146,817	177,319	204,170	0.8	0.9	0.9
85-89 "	60,784	76,790	100,010	0.3	0.4	0.5
90 years and over	20,039	26,158	37,380	0.1	0.1	0.2
Total	18,238,247	20,014,880	21,568,310	100.0	100.0	100.0

4.14   Estimated population by age group and sex, by province, as at June 1, 1975[1] (thousands)

Province or territory	Age group and sex							
	0-4 years		5-9 years		10-14 years		15-19 years	
	Male	Female	Male	Female	Male	Female	Male	Female
Newfoundland	30.8	29.1	31.8	30.6	34.0	32.7	32.3	31.2
Prince Edward Island	5.2	4.8	5.4	5.3	6.8	6.4	6.5	6.3
Nova Scotia	34.7	33.0	36.9	35.2	44.5	42.6	43.7	41.5
New Brunswick	30.2	28.9	31.4	29.9	38.0	36.1	38.2	36.2
Quebec	216.7	204.9	256.4	245.5	332.3	317.1	337.0	324.8
Ontario	325.1	307.8	346.1	330.3	420.7	400.4	403.6	387.4
Manitoba	43.7	41.3	43.4	42.0	51.7	49.5	50.6	48.7
Saskatchewan	37.1	35.6	39.1	37.5	49.8	47.8	50.6	48.8
Alberta	78.3	74.1	81.6	78.3	97.0	93.2	93.8	88.6
British Columbia	94.3	90.0	101.2	97.6	121.0	115.0	119.3	114.7
Yukon Territory	1.2	1.1	1.1	1.1	1.2	1.1	1.0	0.9
Northwest Territories	2.9	2.7	2.7	2.5	2.7	2.4	1.8	1.7
Canada	900.2	853.4	977.3	935.7	1,199.9	1,144.5	1,178.5	1,131.0
	20-24 years		25-34 years		35-44 years		45-54 years	
	Male	Female	Male	Female	Male	Female	Male	Female
Newfoundland	28.2	27.3	36.9	36.4	25.9	24.0	23.2	21.4
Prince Edward Island	5.6	5.6	7.8	7.9	5.9	5.5	5.3	5.3
Nova Scotia	40.0	38.2	59.8	57.9	42.1	41.1	39.4	40.8
New Brunswick	34.6	33.8	48.9	46.5	32.7	32.4	31.1	32.1
Quebec	304.8	301.6	499.4	499.8	360.3	358.3	327.4	341.1
Ontario	368.7	366.7	652.0	642.8	492.2	471.0	462.4	465.8
Manitoba	47.2	46.8	74.8	72.9	52.7	50.6	52.0	54.6
Saskatchewan	44.8	42.7	54.5	53.0	44.6	43.3	49.2	48.7
Alberta	82.3	80.6	137.5	136.2	104.8	97.2	91.6	88.4
British Columbia	109.7	107.3	198.0	191.2	148.7	135.4	134.2	133.6
Yukon Territory	0.8	0.9	2.2	2.0	1.6	1.1	1.0	0.8
Northwest Territories	1.5	1.5	3.3	3.0	2.2	1.8	1.4	1.1
Canada	1,068.3	1,053.1	1,775.3	1,749.7	1,313.5	1,261.9	1,218.2	1,233.8
	55-64 years		65-69 years		70+ years		All ages	
	Male	Female	Male	Female	Male	Female	Male	Female
Newfoundland	20.2	18.3	6.4	6.1	10.1	12.4	279.8	269.5
Prince Edward Island	5.0	5.2	2.0	2.0	3.9	5.2	59.4	59.5
Nova Scotia	35.6	37.1	13.3	13.6	21.4	29.7	411.4	410.7
New Brunswick	26.8	27.5	10.0	10.5	16.8	22.5	338.7	336.4
Quebec	234.3	257.3	82.6	97.7	116.6	172.0	3,067.8	3,120.1
Ontario	327.7	345.6	116.0	133.4	180.7	279.2	4,095.2	4,130.4
Manitoba	45.2	47.6	17.0	18.4	29.6	38.0	507.9	510.4
Saskatchewan	44.7	44.8	17.0	16.7	32.4	35.2	463.8	454.1
Alberta	64.9	65.9	23.5	23.5	41.1	45.6	896.4	871.6
British Columbia	103.2	111.6	38.5	40.8	66.2	85.6	1,234.3	1,222.8
Yukon Territory	0.6	0.5	0.2	0.1	0.1	- -	11.0	9.6
Northwest Territories	0.9	0.6	0.3	0.2	0.2	0.2	19.9	17.7
Canada	909.0	962.0	326.7	362.9	519.1	725.8	11,385.9	11,413.7

[1]Totals do not necessarily add, due to rounding.

4.15   Marital status of the population 15 years and over, by age group and sex, 1971

Age group	Sex	Single[1]	Married	Widowed	Divorced	Total
15-24 years	M	1,693,645	317,350	2,705	2,515	2,016,205
	F	1,374,290	603,585	3,945	5,730	1,987,540
	T	3,067,935	920,930	6,640	8,245	4,003,745
25-34 years	M	293,005	1,149,810	3,415	15,355	1,461,585
	F	179,150	1,214,385	9,450	24,975	1,427,960
	T	472,155	2,364,195	12,865	40,340	2,889,545
35-44 years	M	126,565	1,132,775	6,990	19,490	1,285,815
	F	88,225	1,099,585	26,605	26,160	1,240,580
	T	214,790	2,232,360	33,595	45,650	2,526,400
45-54 years	M	100,980	997,320	16,280	17,740	1,132,315
	F	84,990	973,660	77,965	22,650	1,159,265
	T	185,970	1,970,980	94,235	40,395	2,291,575
55-64 years	M	80,565	729,935	31,510	12,095	854,105
	F	83,640	620,580	159,310	14,105	877,630
	T	164,195	1,350,515	190,815	26,200	1,731,740

4.15   Marital status of the population 15 years and over, by age group and sex, 1971 (concluded)

Age group	Sex	Single[1]	Married	Widowed	Divorced	Total
65-69 years	M	31,915	238,045	22,710	3,380	296,050
	F	34,595	178,810	106,945	3,560	323,910
	T	66,515	416,855	129,660	6,940	619,955
70 years and over	M	50,980	323,525	107,525	3,780	485,810
	F	68,145	198,245	368,680	3,570	638,640
	T	119,125	521,765	476,200	7,350	1,124,445
Total	M	2,377,645	4,888,760	191,125	74,355	7,531,890
	F	1,913,025	4,888,845	752,895	100,760	7,655,525
	T	4,290,675	9,777,605	944,025	175,115	15,187,415

[1]The total number of single persons of all ages (including those under 15) amounted to 10,671,575, comprising 5,641,130 males and 5,030,445 females.

4.16   Population by mother tongue, 1961 and 1971, and language most often spoken in the home, 1971

Language	Mother tongue				Language most often spoken in the home	
	1961		1971		1971	
	No.	%	No.	%	No.	%
English	10,660,534	58.45	12,973,810	60.15	14,446,235	66.97
French	5,123,151	28.09	5,793,650	26.86	5,546,025	25.71
Italian	339,626	1.86	538,360	2.50	425,235	1.97
German	563,713	3.09	561,085	2.60	213,350	0.99
Ukrainian	361,496	1.98	309,855	1.44	144,760	0.67
Indian and Eskimo	166,531	0.91	179,820	0.83	137,285	0.64
Greek	40,455	0.22	104,455	0.48	86,830	0.40
Chinese	49,099	0.27	94,855	0.44	77,890	0.36
Portuguese	18,213	0.10	86,925	0.40	74,765	0.35
Polish	161,720	0.89	134,780	0.62	70,960	0.33
Magyar (Hungarian)	85,939	0.47	86,835	0.40	50,670	0.23
Netherlands	170,177	0.93	144,925	0.67	36,170	0.17
Croatian, Serbian, etc.	28,866	0.16	74,190	0.34	29,310	0.13
Yiddish	82,448	0.45	49,890	0.23	26,330	0.12
Czech and Slovak	51,423	0.28	45,150	0.21	24,555	0.11
Indo-Pakistani	4,505	0.02	32,555	0.15	23,110	0.11
Finnish	44,785	0.25	36,725	0.17	18,280	0.08
Spanish	6,720	0.04	23,815	0.11	17,710	0.08
Arabic (incl. Syrian)	12,999	0.07	28,550	0.13	15,260	0.07
Russian	42,903	0.24	31,745	0.15	12,590	0.06
Japanese	17,856	0.10	16,890	0.08	10,500	0.05
Estonian	13,830	0.08	14,520	0.07	10,110	0.05
Lithuanian	14,997	0.08	14,725	0.07	9,985	0.05
Lettish	14,062	0.08	14,140	0.07	9,250	0.04
Danish	35,035	0.19	27,395	0.13	4,690	0.02
Romanian	10,165	0.06	11,300	0.05	4,455	0.02
Flemish	14,304	0.08	14,240	0.07	3,190	0.01
Swedish	32,632	0.18	21,680	0.10	2,210	0.01
Norwegian	40,054	0.22	27,405	0.13	2,160	0.01
Gaelic	7,533	0.04	21,200	0.10	1,175	--
Icelandic	8,993	0.05	7,860	0.04	995	--
Welsh	3,040	0.02	3,160	0.01	370	--
Other	10,443	0.06	41,830	0.19	31,900	0.15
Total	18,238,247	100.00	21,568,310	100.00	21,568,310	100.00

4.17   Numerical and percentage distribution of English, French, and other mother tongues, by province, 1961 and 1971

Province or territory		1961				1971			
		English	French	Other	Total	English	French	Other	Total
Nfld.	No.	451,530	3,150	3,173	457,853	514,515	3,640	3,950	522,105
	%	98.6	0.7	0.7	100.0	98.5	0.7	0.8	100.0
PEI	No.	95,564	7,958	1,107	104,629	103,100	7,365	1,180	111,640
	%	91.3	7.6	1.1	100.0	92.4	6.6	1.1	100.0
NS	No.	680,233	39,568	17,206	737,007	733,555	39,335	16,075	788,960
	%	92.3	5.4	2.3	100.0	93.0	5.0	2.0	100.0
NB	No.	378,633	210,530	8,773	597,936	410,400	215,725	8,430	634,560
	%	63.3	35.2	1.5	100.0	64.7	34.0	1.3	100.0
Que.	No.	697,402	4,269,689	292,120	5,259,211	789,185	4,867,250	371,325	6,027,760
	%	13.3	81.2	5.6	100.0	13.1	80.7	6.2	100.0
Ont.	No.	4,834,623	425,302	976,167	6,236,092	5,971,570	482,040	1,249,495	7,703,105
	%	77.5	6.8	15.7	100.0	77.5	6.3	16.2	100.0
Man.	No.	584,526	60,899	276,261	921,686	662,720	60,545	264,980	988,245
	%	63.4	6.6	30.0	100.0	67.1	6.1	26.8	100.0

4.17   Numerical and percentage distribution of English, French, and other mother tongues, by province, 1961 and 1971 (concluded)

Province or territory		1961				1971			
		English	French	Other	Total	English	French	Other	Total
Sask.	No.	638,156	36,163	250,862	925,181	685,915	31,605	208,720	926,245
	%	69.0	3.9	27.1	100.0	74.1	3.4	22.5	100.0
Alta.	No.	962,319	42,276	327,349	1,331,944	1,263,935	46,500	317,440	1,627,875
	%	72.2	3.2	24.6	100.0	77.6	2.9	19.5	100.0
BC	No.	1,318,498	26,179	284,405	1,629,082	1,807,255	38,035	339,335	2,184,620
	%	80.9	1.6	17.5	100.0	82.7	1.7	15.5	100.0
YT	No.	10,869	443	3,316	14,628	15,345	450	2,595	18,385
	%	74.3	3.0	22.7	100.0	83.5	2.4	14.1	100.0
NWT	No.	8,181	994	13,823	22,998	16,305	1,160	17,335	34,810
	%	35.6	4.3	60.1	100.0	46.8	3.3	49.8	100.0
Canada	No.	10,660,534	5,123,151	2,454,562	18,238,247	12,973,810	5,793,650	2,800,850	21,568,310
	%	58.5	28.1	13.5	100.0	60.2	26.9	13.0	100.0

4.18   Numerical and percentage distribution of the population speaking one or both of the official languages, by province, 1961 and 1971

Year and province or territory	English only		French only		English and French		Neither English nor French	
	No.	%	No.	%	No.	%	No.	%
1961								
Newfoundland	450,945	98.5	522	0.1	5,299	1.2	1,087	0.2
Prince Edward Island	95,296	91.1	1,219	1.2	7,938	7.6	176	0.2
Nova Scotia	684,805	92.9	5,938	0.8	44,987	6.1	1,277	0.2
New Brunswick	370,922	62.0	112,054	18.7	113,495	19.0	1,465	0.2
Quebec	608,635	11.6	3,254,850	61.9	1,338,878	25.5	56,848	1.1
Ontario	5,548,766	89.0	95,236	1.5	493,270	7.9	98,820	1.6
Manitoba	825,955	89.6	7,954	0.9	68,368	7.4	19,409	2.1
Saskatchewan	865,821	93.6	3,853	0.4	42,074	4.5	13,433	1.5
Alberta	1,253,824	94.1	5,534	0.4	56,920	4.3	15,666	1.2
British Columbia	1,552,560	95.3	2,559	0.2	57,504	3.5	16,459	1.0
Yukon Territory	13,679	93.5	38	0.3	825	5.6	86	0.6
Northwest Territories	13,554	58.9	109	0.5	1,614	7.0	7,721	33.6
Canada	12,284,762	67.4	3,489,866	19.1	2,231,172	12.2	232,447	1.3
1971								
Newfoundland	511,620	98.0	510	0.1	9,350	1.8	625	0.1
Prince Edward Island	101,820	91.2	680	0.6	9,110	8.2	30	- -
Nova Scotia	730,700	92.6	4,185	0.5	53,035	6.7	1,035	0.1
New Brunswick	396,855	62.5	100,985	15.9	136,115	21.5	600	0.1
Quebec	632,515	10.5	3,668,020	60.9	1,663,790	27.6	63,445	1.1
Ontario	6,724,100	87.3	92,840	1.2	716,065	9.3	170,090	2.2
Manitoba	881,715	89.2	5,020	0.5	80,935	8.2	20,585	2.1
Saskatchewan	867,315	93.6	1,825	0.2	45,985	5.0	11,110	1.2
Alberta	1,525,575	93.7	3,310	0.2	81,000	5.0	17,990	1.1
British Columbia	2,054,690	94.1	1,775	0.1	101,435	4.6	26,725	1.2
Yukon Territory	17,130	93.2	5	- -	1,210	6.6	35	0.2
Northwest Territories	25,500	73.3	100	0.3	2,120	6.1	7,085	20.4
Canada	14,469,540	67.1	3,879,255	18.0	2,900,155	13.4	319,360	1.5

4.19   Population by ethnic group, 1951, 1961 and 1971

Ethnic group	1951		1961		1971	
	No.	%	No.	%	No.	%
British Isles	6,709,685	47.9	7,996,669	43.8		
English	3,630,344	25.9	4,195,175	23.0		
Irish	1,439,635	10.3	1,753,351	9.6		
Scottish	1,547,470	11.0	1,902,302	10.4	9,624,115	44.6
Welsh and other	92,236	0.7	145,841	0.8		
French	4,319,167	30.8	5,540,346	30.4	6,180,120	28.7
Other European	2,553,722	18.2	4,116,849	22.6	4,959,680	23.0
Austrian	32,231	0.2	106,535	0.6	42,120	0.2
Belgian	35,148	0.2	61,382	0.3	51,135	0.2
Czech and Slovak	63,959	0.5	73,061	0.4	81,870	0.4
Danish	42,671	0.3	85,473	0.5	75,725	0.4
Finnish	43,745	0.3	59,436	0.3	59,215	0.3
German	619,995	4.4	1,049,599	5.8	1,317,200	6.1
Greek	13,966	0.1	56,475	0.3	124,475	0.6
Hungarian	60,460	0.4	126,220	0.7	131,890	0.6
Icelandic	23,307	0.2	30,623	0.2	27,905	0.1
Italian	152,245	1.1	450,351	2.5	730,820	3.4
Jewish	181,670	1.3	173,344	1.0	296,945	1.4
Lithuanian	16,224	0.1	27,629	0.2	24,535	0.1
Netherlands	264,267	1.9	429,679	2.4	425,945	2.0

4.19   Population by ethnic group, 1951, 1961 and 1971 (concluded)

Ethnic group	1951 No.	1951 %	1961 No.	1961 %	1971 No.	1971 %
Other European (concluded)						
Norwegian	119,266	0.8	148,681	0.8	179,290	0.8
Polish	219,845	1.6	323,517	1.8	316,425	1.5
Portuguese	..	..	..	..	96,875	0.4
Romanian	23,601	0.2	43,805	0.2	27,375	0.1
Russian	91,279	0.7	119,168	0.7	64,475	0.3
Spanish	..	..	..	..	27,515	0.1
Swedish	97,780	0.7	121,757	0.6	101,870	0.5
Ukrainian	395,043	2.8	473,337	2.6	580,660	2.7
Yugoslavic	21,404	0.2	68,587	0.4	104,950	0.5
Other	35,616	0.2	88,190	0.5	70,460	0.3
Asiatic	72,827	0.5	121,753	0.7	285,540	1.3
Chinese	32,528	0.2	58,197	0.3	118,815	0.6
Japanese	21,663	0.2	29,157	0.2	37,260	0.2
Other	18,636	0.1	34,399	0.2	129,460	0.6
Other	354,028	2.5	462,630	2.5	518,850	2.4
Eskimo	9,733	0.1	11,835	0.1	17,550	0.1
Native Indian	155,874	1.1	208,286	1.1	295,215	1.4
Negro	18,020	0.1	32,127	0.2	34,445	0.2
West Indian	..	..	..	..	28,025	0.1
Other and not stated	170,401	1.2	210,382	1.2	143,620	0.7
Total	14,009,429	100.0	18,238,247	100.0	21,568,310	100.0

4.20   Principal religious denominations of the population, 1951, 1961 and 1971

Religious denomination	1951 No.	1951 %	1961 No.	1961 %	1971 No.	1971 %
Adventist	21,398	0.2	25,999	0.1	28,590	0.1
Anglican Church of Canada	2,060,720	14.7	2,409,068	13.2	2,543,180	11.8
Baptist	519,585	3.7	593,553	3.3	667,245	3.1
Christian Reformed	..	..	62,257	0.3	83,390	0.4
Greek Orthodox	172,271	1.2	239,766	1.3	316,605	1.5
Jehovah's Witnesses	34,596	0.2	68,018	0.4	174,810	0.8
Jewish	204,836	1.5	254,368	1.4	276,025	1.3
Lutheran	444,923	3.2	662,744	3.6	715,740	3.3
Mennonite [1]	125,938	0.9	152,452	0.8	181,800	0.8
Mormon	32,888	0.2	50,016	0.3	66,635	0.3
Pentecostal	95,131	0.7	143,877	0.8	220,390	1.0
Presbyterian	781,747	5.6	818,558	4.5	872,335	4.0
Roman Catholic	6,069,496	43.3	8,342,826	45.7	9,974,895	46.2
Salvation Army	70,275	0.5	92,054	0.5	119,665	0.6
Ukrainian (Greek) Catholic [2]	191,051	1.4	189,653	1.0	227,730	1.1
United Church of Canada	2,867,271	20.5	3,664,008	20.1	3,768,800	17.5
Other	317,303	2.2	469,030	2.6	1,330,480	6.2
Total	14,009,429	100.0	18,238,247	100.0	21,568,310	100.0

[1]Includes "Hutterites".
[2]Includes "Other Greek Catholic".

4.21   Country of birth of the population, 1951, 1961 and 1971

Country of birth	1951 No.	1951 %	1961 No.	1961 %	1971[1] No.	1971[1] %
Canada[1]	11,949,518	85.3	15,393,984	84.4	18,272,780	84.7
United Kingdom	912,482	6.5	969,715	5.3	933,040	4.3
Other Commonwealth countries	20,567	0.1	47,887	0.3	170,100	0.8
United States	282,010	2.0	283,908	1.6	309,640	1.4
European countries	801,618	5.7	1,468,058	8.0	1,684,510	7.8
Germany	42,693	0.3	189,131	1.0	211,060	1.0
Italy	57,789	0.4	258,071	1.4	385,755	1.8
Netherlands	41,457	0.3	135,033	0.7	133,525	0.6
Poland	164,474	1.2	171,467	0.9	160,040	0.7
USSR	188,292	1.3	186,653	1.0	160,120	0.7
Other	306,913	2.2	527,703	2.9	634,010	2.9
Asiatic countries	37,145	0.3	57,761	0.3	119,425	0.6
Other	6,089	- -	16,934	0.1	78,800	0.4
Total	14,009,429	100.0	18,238,247	100.0	21,568,310	100.0

[1]For figures on province of birth, see Table 4.64.

4.22   Indian bands and registered population, by province and type of residence, Dec. 31, 1974 and 1975

Province or territory	Number of bands	Registered band membership			
		On reserves	Off reserves	Crown land	Total[1]
1974					
Prince Edward Island	2	302	151	—	453
Nova Scotia	12	3,709	1,414	27	5,150
New Brunswick	15	3,688	1,184	12	4,884
Quebec	39	17,973	6,771	5,276	30,020
Ontario	112	35,820	19,979	4,777	60,576
Manitoba	55	28,320	9,222	2,704	40,246
Saskatchewan	68	28,160	11,447	1,379	40,986
Alberta	41	24,720	5,989	1,872	32,581
British Columbia	193	33,702	17,481	622	51,805
Yukon Territory	13	56	365	2,282	2,703
Northwest Territories	16	7	534	6,491	7,032
Canada, 1974	566	176,457	74,537	25,442	276,436
1975					
Prince Edward Island	2	293	160	8	461
Nova Scotia	12	3,757	1,465	30	5,252
New Brunswick	15	3,738	1,226	28	4,992
Quebec	39	19,929	5,480	5,233	30,642
Ontario	112	36,317	20,226	5,078	61,621
Manitoba	55	28,270	9,836	3,081	41,187
Saskatchewan	68	28,513	12,442	1,465	42,420
Alberta	41	24,637	7,010	1,904	33,551
British Columbia	193	33,145	18,536	1,043	52,724
Yukon Territory	13	7	422	2,299	2,728
Northwest Territories	16	229	423	6,532	7,184
Canada, 1975	566	178,835	77,226	26,701	282,762

[1]Bands whose members were known to reside in more than one province or territory were allocated to that province or territory in which the majority was known to reside.

4.23   Households and average persons per household, by province, 1961, 1966 and 1971

Province or territory	Households				Average persons per household		
	1961	1966	1971	% increase 1961-71	1961	1966	1971
Newfoundland	87,940	96,632	110,475	25.6	5.0	5.0	4.6
Prince Edward Island	23,942	25,360	27,895	16.5	4.2	4.2	3.9
Nova Scotia	175,341	185,245	208,425	18.9	4.0	4.0	3.7
New Brunswick	132,715	141,761	158,100	19.1	4.4	4.2	3.9
Quebec	1,191,469	1,389,115	1,605,750	34.8	4.2	4.0	3.7
Ontario	1,640,881	1,876,545	2,228,160	35.8	3.7	3.6	3.4
Manitoba	239,754	259,280	288,720	20.4	3.7	3.6	3.3
Saskatchewan	245,424	260,822	267,845	9.1	3.6	3.6	3.4
Alberta	349,816	393,707	464,945	32.9	3.7	3.6	3.4
British Columbia	459,534	543,075	668,305	45.4	3.4	3.3	3.2
Yukon Territory and Northwest Territories	7,920	8,931	12,685	60.2	4.2	4.3	4.0
Canada	4,554,736	5,180,473	6,041,305	32.6	3.9	3.7	3.5
Urban	3,280,682	3,941,459	4,743,280	44.6	3.7	3.6	3.4
Rural	1,274,054	1,239,014	1,298,025	1.9	4.2	4.1	3.9

4.24   Households by type, 1961, 1966 and 1971

Type of household	Number			Percentage		
	1961	1966	1971	1961	1966	1971
Family households	3,948,935	4,376,409	4,933,450	86.7	84.5	81.7
One-family households	3,780,992	4,246,753	4,812,360	83.0	82.0	79.7
Family of household head	3,734,581	4,209,549	4,773,900	82.0	81.3	79.0
Without additional persons	3,262,610	3,754,530	4,285,960	71.6	72.5	70.9
With additional persons	471,971	455,019	487,935	10.4	8.8	8.1
Family other than that of household head	46,411	37,204	38,465	1.0	0.7	0.6
Two-or-more family households	167,943	129,656	121,085	3.7	2.5	2.0
Including family of household head	165,703	128,325	120,000	3.6	2.5	2.0
With no family of household head	2,240	1,331	1,090	- -	- -	- -
Non-family households	605,801	804,064	1,107,855	13.3	15.5	18.3
One person only	424,750	589,571	811,835	9.3	11.4	13.4
Two or more persons	181,051	214,493	296,020	4.0	4.1	4.9
Total households	4,554,736	5,180,473	6,041,300	100.0	100.0	100.0

4.25   Households by age and sex of head, 1961, 1966 and 1971

Age and sex of head	Number			Percentage		
	1961	1966	1971	1961	1966	1971
Under 25 years	179,725	269,065	414,470	3.9	5.2	6.9
Male	159,420	227,040	334,750	3.5	4.4	5.5
Female	20,305	42,025	79,720	0.4	0.8	1.3
25-34 years	938,389	1,014,676	1,265,290	20.6	19.6	20.9
Male	894,796	954,508	1,154,085	19.6	18.4	19.1
Female	43,593	60,168	111,205	1.0	1.2	1.8
35-44 years	1,072,159	1,190,133	1,252,500	23.5	23.0	20.7
Male	1,001,147	1,102,647	1,142,540	22.0	21.3	18.9
Female	71,012	87,486	109,960	1.6	1.7	1.8
45-54 years	936,625	1,052,705	1,173,055	20.6	20.3	19.4
Male	833,040	928,751	1,022,330	18.3	17.9	16.9
Female	103,585	123,954	150,725	2.3	2.4	2.5
55-64 years	681,014	803,338	955,995	15.0	15.5	15.8
Male	558,443	655,003	764,230	12.3	12.6	12.6
Female	122,571	148,335	191,765	2.7	2.9	3.2
65-69 years	266,099	298,002	358,775	5.8	5.8	5.9
Male	198,175	215,140	256,305	4.4	4.2	4.2
Female	67,924	82,862	102,475	1.5	1.6	1.7
70 years and over	480,725	552,554	621,220	10.6	10.7	10.3
Male	317,902	346,991	369,825	7.0	6.7	6.1
Female	162,823	205,563	251,395	3.6	4.0	4.2
Total household heads	4,554,736	5,180,473	6,041,300	100.0	100.0	100.0
Male	3,962,923	4,430,080	5,044,065	87.0	85.5	83.5
Female	591,813	750,393	997,240	13.0	14.5	16.5

4.26   Households by marital status of head, 1961, 1966 and 1971

Marital status of head	Number			Percentage			Percentage increase		
	1961	1966	1971	1961	1966	1971	1961-66	1966-71	1961-71
Married[1]	3,778,473	4,196,595	4,745,795	83.0	81.0	78.6	11.1	13.1	25.6
Widowed	461,486	553,119	629,670	10.1	10.7	10.4	19.9	13.8	36.4
Divorced	27,027	40,263	112,665	0.6	0.8	1.9	49.0	179.8	316.9
Single, never married	287,750	390,496	553,170	6.3	7.5	9.2	35.7	41.7	92.2
Total households	4,554,736	5,180,473	6,041,300	100.0	100.0	100.0	13.7	16.6	32.6

[1]Includes household heads who are married but separated.

4.27   Families and persons per family, by province, 1961, 1966 and 1971

Province or territory	Families			Average persons per family		
	1961	1966	1971	1961	1966	1971
Newfoundland	89,267	97,011	108,135	4.7	4.6	4.4
Prince Edward Island	21,969	22,728	24,260	4.2	4.2	4.0
Nova Scotia	161,894	166,237	180,720	4.0	4.0	3.8
New Brunswick	124,653	129,307	140,430	4.3	4.3	4.0
Quebec	1,103,822	1,229,301	1,357,185	4.2	4.2	3.9
Ontario	1,511,478	1,657,933	1,881,840	3.6	3.7	3.6
Manitoba	215,831	222,735	236,000	3.7	3.8	3.6
Saskatchewan	211,776	216,674	215,760	3.8	3.9	3.7
Alberta	305,671	331,158	382,110	3.8	3.9	3.7
British Columbia	394,023	445,297	533,625	3.6	3.6	3.5
Yukon Territory and Northwest Territories	7,060	7,885	10,620	4.3	4.5	4.3
Canada	4,147,444	4,526,266	5,070,680	3.9	3.9	3.7

4.28   Families by type, 1961, 1966 and 1971

Type of family	Number			Percentage		
	1961	1966	1971	1961	1966	1971
Maintaining own household	3,911,529	4,345,718	4,898,290	94.3	96.0	96.6
Not maintaining own household	235,915	180,548	172,390	5.7	4.0	3.4
Related	157,120	134,854	126,775	3.8	3.0	2.5
Not related	78,795	45,694	45,615	1.9	1.0	0.9
Lodging	72,416	38,583	40,705	1.7	0.8	0.8
Other	6,379	7,111	4,910	0.2	0.2	0.1
Total families	4,147,444	4,526,266	5,070,680	100.0	100.0	100.0

4.29   Husband-wife families and one-parent families by age of head, 1961, 1966 and 1971

Age of head	1961 No.	1961 %	1966 No.	1966 %	1971 No.	1971 %
Husband-wife families	3,800,026	91.6	4,154,381	91.8	4,591,935	90.6
Under 25 years	174,574	4.2	214,742	4.7	292,885	5.8
25-34 years	920,871	22.2	945,374	20.9	1,087,900	21.5
35-44 years	989,141	23.8	1,069,471	23.6	1,072,485	21.2
45-54 years	792,269	19.1	874,492	19.3	940,320	18.5
55-64 years	505,109	12.2	593,864	13.1	684,335	13.5
65 years and over	418,062	10.1	456,438	10.1	514,015	10.1
One-parent families	347,418	8.4	371,885	8.2	478,745	9.4
Male	75,203	1.8	71,502	1.6	100,680	2.0
Under 25 years	1,510	- -	2,407	0.1	4,225	0.1
25-34 years	6,551	0.2	5,559	0.1	16,535	0.3
35-44 years	11,684	0.3	12,176	0.3	22,215	0.4
45-54 years	15,671	0.4	15,918	0.4	22,525	0.4
55-64 years	13,522	0.3	13,313	0.3	16,375	0.3
65 years and over	26,265	0.6	22,129	0.5	18,805	0.4
Female	272,215	6.6	300,383	6.6	378,065	7.5
Under 25 years	10,993	0.3	12,542	0.3	25,295	0.5
25-34 years	30,662	0.7	36,327	0.8	66,665	1.3
35-44 years	52,498	1.3	59,515	1.3	78,350	1.5
45-54 years	59,539	1.4	68,592	1.5	85,165	1.7
55-64 years	46,578	1.1	50,480	1.1	59,505	1.2
65 years and over	71,945	1.7	72,927	1.6	63,090	1.2
Total family heads	4,147,444	100.0	4,526,266	100.0	5,070,680	100.0

4.30   Families by mother tongue of head, by province, 1971

Province or territory	Total family heads	Mother tongue of family head English No.	English %	French No.	French %	Other No.	Other %
Newfoundland	108,135	106,125	98.1	970	0.9	1,040	1.0
Prince Edward Island	24,260	22,230	91.6	1,665	6.9	365	1.5
Nova Scotia	180,720	165,320	91.5	10,520	5.8	4,880	2.7
New Brunswick	140,435	93,355	66.5	44,780	31.9	2,300	1.6
Quebec	1,357,185	180,890	13.3	1,070,380	78.9	105,910	7.8
Ontario	1,881,835	1,368,260	72.7	120,255	6.4	393,315	20.9
Manitoba	235,995	142,665	60.5	14,905	6.3	78,425	33.2
Saskatchewan	215,760	139,605	64.7	8,365	3.9	67,785	31.4
Alberta	382,115	266,850	69.8	12,340	3.2	102,925	26.9
British Columbia	533,630	412,035	77.2	11,500	2.2	110,095	20.6
Yukon Territory and Northwest Territories	10,615	5,995	56.5	430	4.0	4,200	39.6
Canada	5,070,680	2,903,325	57.3	1,296,105	25.6	871,250	17.2

4.31   Children living at home by age group and province, 1971[1]

Province or territory	Under 6 years	6-14 years	15-18 years	19-24 years	Total children living at home
Newfoundland	74,245	117,845	44,255	23,050	259,400
Prince Edward Island	12,070	22,615	8,830	5,465	48,980
Nova Scotia	84,055	152,460	59,725	34,940	331,180
New Brunswick	69,660	129,785	52,565	31,655	283,670
Quebec	586,750	1,164,895	471,580	355,760	2,578,985
Ontario	771,305	1,409,820	532,285	328,480	3,041,890
Manitoba	102,575	179,925	70,815	39,610	392,920
Saskatchewan	95,755	180,540	72,325	31,220	379,840
Alberta	181,755	326,320	118,485	53,460	680,015
British Columbia	209,750	391,140	147,065	78,495	826,445
Yukon Territory and Northwest Territories	8,860	11,925	2,985	1,500	25,265
Canada	2,196,780	4,087,270	1,580,910	983,635	8,848,595

[1]Figures in this table are slightly different from those published in the *1973 Canada Year Book*. This is due to the fact that only preliminary data were available at that time.

4.32 Summary of principal vital statistics, by province, 1951-74

Province or territory and year	Live births No.	Rate[2]	Deaths No.	Rate[2]	Natural increase[1] No.	Rate[2]	Marriages No.	Rate[2]	Divorces No.	Rate[3]
NEWFOUNDLAND										
Av. 1951-55	13,101	34.1	2,926	7.6	10,175	26.5	2,836	7.4	5	1.3
`` 1956-60	14,934	34.6	3,114	7.2	11,820	27.4	3,032	7.0	5	1.2
`` 1961-65	15,104	31.8	3,142	6.6	11,962	25.2	3,331	7.0	5	1.0
`` 1966-70	13,057	25.8	3,122	6.2	9,935	19.6	4,147	8.2	56	11.1
1971	12,767	24.5	3,199	6.1	9,568	18.4	4,685	9.0	150	28.7
1972	12,898	24.2	3,349	6.3	9,549	17.9	5,106	9.6	177	33.3
1973	11,906	22.0	3,405	6.3	8,501	15.7	5,048	9.3	224	41.4
1974	10,236	18.9	3,286	6.1	6,950	12.8	4,276	7.9	301	55.5
PRINCE EDWARD ISLAND										
Av. 1951-55	2,720	27.2	923	9.2	1,797	18.0	623	6.2	10	9.8
`` 1956-60	2,674	26.6	953	9.5	1,721	17.1	645	6.4	4	3.9
`` 1961-65	2,767	25.7	1,006	9.3	1,761	16.4	672	6.2	8	7.8
`` 1966-70	2,063	18.9	1,020	9.4	1,044	9.6	817	7.5	45	41.3
1971	2,103	18.8	1,007	9.0	1,096	9.8	961	8.6	61	54.7
1972	2,010	17.8	1,052	9.3	958	8.5	1,013	9.0	65	57.5
1973	1,886	16.4	1,020	8.9	866	7.5	1,014	8.8	54	47.0
1974	1,939	16.6	1,088	9.3	851	7.3	990	8.5	96	82.3
NOVA SCOTIA										
Av. 1951-55	18,246	27.5	5,802	8.8	12,444	18.7	5,283	8.0	212	32.0
`` 1956-60	19,097	26.9	6,062	8.5	13,035	18.4	5,289	7.4	227	32.0
`` 1961-65	18,526	24.7	6,312	8.4	12,214	16.3	5,313	7.1	277	36.9
`` 1966-70	14,217	18.7	6,622	8.7	7,594	10.0	6,335	8.3	573	75.4
1971	14,250	18.1	6,682	8.5	7,568	9.6	6,883	8.7	721	91.4
1972	13,536	17.0	6,904	8.7	6,632	8.3	7,291	9.2	927	116.7
1973	13,289	16.5	6,928	8.6	6,361	7.9	7,273	9.0	1,249	155.2
1974	12,941	15.9	6,899	8.5	6,042	7.4	7,112	8.7	1,591	195.6
NEW BRUNSWICK										
Av. 1951-55	16,496	31.0	4,576	8.6	11,920	22.4	4,306	8.1	167	31.4
`` 1956-60	16,567	29.0	4,640	8.1	11,927	20.9	4,357	7.6	194	34.0
`` 1961-65	15,668	25.8	4,749	7.8	10,919	18.0	4,531	7.5	199	32.7
`` 1966-70	11,984	19.3	4,873	7.8	7,112	11.4	5,481	8.8	267	42.9
1971	12,187	19.2	4,943	7.8	7,244	11.4	6,149	9.7	482	76.0
1972	11,806	18.4	4,982	7.8	6,824	10.6	6,455	10.0	466	72.5
1973	11,425	17.5	5,084	7.8	6,341	9.7	6,357	9.8	574	88.0
1974	11,444	17.3	5,205	7.9	6,239	9.4	6,108	9.2	755	114.1
QUEBEC										
Av. 1951-55	128,523	30.0	34,269	8.0	94,254	22.0	35,584	8.3	327	7.6
`` 1956-60	139,844	28.6	35,714	7.3	104,130	21.3	36,798	7.5	403	8.2
`` 1961-65	131,453	24.0	37,698	6.9	93,755	17.1	38,126	7.0	380	6.9
`` 1966-70	99,068	16.8	39,475	6.7	59,592	10.1	46,768	7.9	2,018	34.1
1971	89,210	14.8	40,738	6.8	48,472	8.0	49,695	8.2	5,201	86.3
1972	83,603	13.8	42,311	7.0	41,292	6.8	53,830	8.9	6,421	106.1
1973	84,057	13.8	42,666	7.0	41,391	6.8	51,943	8.5	8,091	133.1
1974	85,627	14.0	42,767	7.0	42,860	7.0	51,532	8.4	12,272	200.1
ONTARIO										
Av. 1951-55	128,861	26.1	44,715	9.0	84,146	17.1	45,213	9.1	2,430	49.2
`` 1956-60	152,688	26.4	49,431	8.5	103,257	17.9	46,482	8.0	2,801	48.4
`` 1961-65	152,629	23.5	52,664	8.1	99,965	15.4	46,794	7.2	3,342	51.3
`` 1966-70	130,166	17.8	55,415	7.6	74,751	10.2	62,216	8.5	7,452	102.1
1971	130,395	16.9	56,623	7.4	73,772	9.5	69,590	9.0	12,205	158.4
1972	125,060	16.0	58,905	7.5	66,155	8.5	72,278	9.2	13,183	168.5
1973	123,776	15.6	59,876	7.5	63,900	8.0	72,371	9.1	13,781	173.6
1974	124,229	15.3	60,556	7.5	63,673	7.9	72,716	9.0	15,277	188.7
MANITOBA										
Av. 1951-55	21,321	26.4	6,775	8.4	14,546	18.0	7,104	8.8	356	44.1
`` 1956-60	22,408	25.6	7,293	8.3	15,115	17.3	6,600	7.5	315	35.9
`` 1961-65	22,137	23.4	7,637	8.1	14,500	15.3	6,674	7.1	376	39.7
`` 1966-70	17,734	18.3	7,868	8.1	9,865	10.2	8,283	8.5	805	82.9
1971	18,031	18.2	8,025	8.1	10,006	10.1	9,127	9.2	1,383	140.0
1972	17,398	17.6	8,225	8.3	9,173	9.3	9,181	9.3	1,413	142.5
1973	16,964	17.0	8,196	8.2	8,768	8.8	9,196	9.2	1,620	162.3
1974	17,311	17.1	8,430	8.3	8,881	8.8	9,231	9.1	1,796	177.6
SASKATCHEWAN										
Av. 1951-55	23,554	27.5	6,547	7.6	17,007	19.9	6,876	8.0	231	26.9
`` 1956-60	24,046	26.9	6,753	7.5	17,293	19.4	6,395	7.1	247	27.6
`` 1961-65	22,811	24.4	7,268	7.8	15,543	16.6	6,316	6.7	298	31.8
`` 1966-70	17,852	18.7	7,466	7.8	10,386	10.9	7,460	7.8	566	59.3
1971	16,054	17.3	7,413	8.0	8,641	9.3	7,813	8.4	815	88.0
1972	15,473	16.9	7,590	8.3	7,883	8.6	7,877	8.6	826	90.1
1973	14,806	16.3	7,646	8.4	7,160	7.9	7,847	8.6	887	97.7
1974	15,118	16.7	7,814	8.6	7,304	8.1	7,988	8.8	1,039	114.6
ALBERTA										
Av. 1951-55	31,087	30.6	7,527	7.4	23,560	23.2	9,750	9.6	612	60.4
`` 1956-60	36,920	30.6	8,329	6.9	28,591	23.7	10,230	8.5	788	65.1
`` 1961-65	37,004	26.5	9,317	6.7	27,687	19.8	10,581	7.6	1,226	87.5
`` 1966-70	30,851	20.2	9,839	6.4	21,012	13.8	13,711	9.0	2,481	162.4

4.32   Summary of principal vital statistics, by province, 1951-74 (concluded)

Province or territory and year	Live births No.	Rate²	Deaths No.	Rate²	Natural increase¹ No.	Rate²	Marriages No.	Rate²	Divorces No.	Rate³
ALBERTA (concluded)										
1971	30,545	18.8	10,525	6.5	20,020	12.3	15,614	9.6	3,656	224.6
1972	29,282	17.7	10,699	6.5	18,583	11.2	16,345	9.9	3,767	227.8
1973	29,288	17.4	10,763	6.4	18,525	11.0	16,280	9.7	4,435	263.5
1974	29,813	17.4	11,252	6.6	18,561	10.8	16,691	9.7	4,947	288.6
BRITISH COLUMBIA										
Av. 1951-55	31,347	25.1	12,233	9.8	19,114	15.3	11,131	8.9	1,461	116.9
" 1956-60	38,930	25.7	13,980	9.2	24,950	16.5	11,955	7.9	1,514	100.0
" 1961-65	36,753	21.5	15,236	8.9	21,517	12.6	11,927	7.0	1,592	93.1
" 1966-70	34,266	17.1	16,737	8.3	17,529	8.7	17,186	8.6	3,272	163.1
1971	34,852	16.0	17,783	8.1	17,069	7.9	20,389	9.3	4,926	225.5
1972	34,563	15.4	18,021	8.0	16,542	7.4	20,659	9.2	5,036	224.1
1973	34,352	14.8	18,095	7.8	16,257	7.0	21,303	9.2	5,687	245.7
1974	35,450	14.8	19,177	8.0	16,273	6.8	21,734	9.1	6,840	285.6
YUKON TERRITORY										
Av. 1951-55	413	43.0	90	9.4	323	33.6	94	9.8		
" 1956-60	505	39.4	91	7.1	414	32.3	109	8.5		
" 1961-65	509	34.9	87	6.0	422	28.9	107	7.3	17	118.0
" 1966-70	407	27.1	89	5.9	319	21.3	153	10.2	31	206.7
1971	506	27.5	104	5.7	402	21.8	166	9.0	47	255.6
1972	451	23.9	103	5.5	348	18.4	181	9.5	47	248.7
1973	420	21.3	111	5.6	309	15.7	206	10.3	60	300.0
1974	495	25.5	114	5.9	381	19.6	190	9.8	46	237.1
NORTHWEST TERRITORIES										
Av. 1951-55	666	40.1	284	17.1	382	23.0	115	6.9		
" 1956-60	943	46.7	310	15.3	633	31.4	155	7.7	1	
" 1961-65	1,174	45.9	250	9.8	924	36.1	154	6.0	3	11.5
" 1966-70	1,244	41.5	229	7.6	1,015	33.8	212	7.1	13	43.3
1971	1,287	37.0	230	6.6	1,057	30.4	252	7.2	25	71.8
1972	1,239	34.4	272	7.6	967	26.8	254	7.1	36	100.0
1973	1,204	31.9	249	6.6	955	25.3	226	5.9	42	110.5
1974	1,042	27.8	206	5.5	836	22.3	256	6.8	59	157.3
CANADA										
Av. 1951-55	416,334	28.0	126,666	8.5	289,668	19.5	128,915	8.7	5,811	39.1
" 1956-60	469,555	27.6	136,669	8.0	332,886	19.6	132,047	7.8	6,498	38.2
" 1961-65	456,534	24.1	145,368	7.7	311,166	16.4	134,524	7.1	7,723	40.7
" 1966-70	372,909	18.0	152,755	7.4	220,154	10.6	172,769	8.3	17,579	84.8
1971	362,187	16.8	157,272	7.3	204,915	9.5	191,324	8.9	29,672	137.6
1972	347,319	15.9	162,413	7.4	184,906	8.5	200,470	9.2	32,364	148.3
1973	343,373	15.5	164,039	7.4	179,334	8.1	199,064	9.0	36,704	166.1
1974	345,645	15.4	166,794	7.4	178,851	8.0	198,824	8.9	45,019	200.6

¹Excess births over deaths.
²Per 1,000 population.
³Per 100,000 population.

4.33   Summary of principal vital statistics for cities, towns and other municipal subdivisions¹ of 50,000 population and over², 1974 with averages for 1961-65 and 1966-70

Province and urban centre	Live births Av. 1961-65	Av. 1966-70	1974	Deaths Av. 1961-65	Av. 1966-70	1974	Marriages³ Av. 1961-65	Av. 1966-70	1974
NEWFOUNDLAND									
*St. John's, c	1,966	1,812	1,569	542	608	711	736	932	954
PRINCE EDWARD ISLAND									
Charlottetown, c⁴	417	307	287	232	246	263	157	157	223
NOVA SCOTIA									
Dartmouth, c	1,700	1,409	1,270	230	261	298	287	379	459
*Halifax, c	2,109	1,791	1,741	736	855	963	1,047	1,281	1,534
NEW BRUNSWICK									
*Saint John, c	1,743	1,598	1,475	690	766	836	607	728	896
QUEBEC									
*Hull, c	1,640	1,289	1,087	419	423	433	430	520	637
LaSalle, c	1,062	1,371	1,191	210	295	418	128	222	321
Laval, c	3,939	3,372	2,938	669	902	1,191	599	968	1,170
*Longueuil, c	639	1,674	1,956	225	442	561	185	567	655
*Montreal, c	28,576	20,066	12,211	10,309	10,462	10,415	10,548	11,766	11,300
*Montreal North, c	1,453	1,490	1,540	343	382	463	215	386	448
*Quebec, c	3,601	2,672	2,292	1,612	1,587	1,681	1,536	1,683	1,975
*Ste-Foy, c	1,038	1,098	876	158	190	232	130	389	492
*St-Laurent, t	1,059	948	710	272	352	414	287	401	415
*St-Léonard, c	316	834	1,074	45	124	246	22	170	234
Sherbrooke, c	1,812	1,505	1,256	590	592	606	572	698	806
*Trois-Rivières, c	1,384	947	633	438	433	466	447	475	556
Verdun, c	1,547	1,119	746	606	665	784	528	636	601

4.33 Summary of principal vital statistics for cities, towns and other municipal subdivisions[1] of 50,000 population and over[2], 1974 with averages for 1961-65 and 1966-70 (concluded)

Province and urban centre	Live births Av. 1961-65	Live births Av. 1966-70	Live births 1974	Deaths Av. 1961-65	Deaths Av. 1966-70	Deaths 1974	Marriages[3] Av. 1961-65	Marriages[3] Av. 1966-70	Marriages[3] 1974
ONTARIO									
*Brantford, c	1,191	1,045	1,054	550	622	600	489	612	729
*Burlington, t	1,203	1,347	1,525	274	324	429	246	415	570
*Etobicoke, b	5,117	4,081	3,414	1,311	1,502	1,913	881	1,215	1,769
*Guelph, c	1,010	996	1,044	364	405	457	352	509	587
*Hamilton, c	6,467	5,475	4,642	2,447	2,495	2,554	2,351	2,946	2,962
*Kingston, c	1,363	1,126	835	481	523	555	527	718	788
*Kitchener, c	2,081	2,131	2,249	564	670	826	655	1,009	1,084
*London, c	4,129	3,752	3,606	1,482	1,576	1,686	1,387	1,914	2,168
*Mississauga, t	1,697	2,402	4,272	344	458	797	287	511	1,559
*Niagara Falls, c	1,151	1,030	877	441	456	565	416	549	661
*Oakville, c	905	913	1,033	186	227	312	223	450	535
Oshawa, c	1,769	1,686	1,727	459	509	641	545	691	883
Ottawa, c	6,034	4,745	3,694	2,271	2,443	2,612	2,209	3,051	3,490
*Peterborough, c	1,035	890	803	442	489	557	384	571	677
*St. Catharines, c	1,910	1,764	1,669	696	791	902	666	909	1,117
Sarnia, c	1,220	1,034	881	358	399	413	373	537	591
*Sault Ste Marie, c	1,439	1,512	1,228	385	487	519	488	645	803
Scarborough, b	6,419	5,150	5,369	1,237	1,546	2,070	962	1,765	2,218
*Sudbury, c	2,353	1,881	1,620	525	560	639	706	928	1,105
Thunder Bay, c	1,998	1,682	1,707	835	909	1,080	745	951	1,078
*Toronto, c	15,362	13,680	10,258	7,354	6,737	6,332	10,293	13,413	14,166
*Windsor, c	2,498	3,654	3,150	1,274	1,708	1,711	1,217	1,907	2,072
*York, b	3,497	3,101	2,557	1,022	1,009	1,005	488	523	521
*York, E., b	1,852	1,693	1,724	853	865	1,025	184	185	315
York, N., b	7,967	8,547	8,312	1,551	2,134	2,958	943	1,617	2,174
MANITOBA									
*Winnipeg, c	5,788	4,631	8,846	2,672	2,708	4,571	2,620	3,180	5,445
SASKATCHEWAN									
*Regina, c	3,265	2,840	2,681	820	928	1,073	1,004	1,263	1,421
*Saskatoon, c	2,770	2,676	2,283	769	911	1,073	923	1,281	1,351
ALBERTA									
*Calgary, c	8,083	7,503	7,349	2,002	2,238	2,567	2,410	3,483	4,654
*Edmonton, c	9,704	8,776	7,325	2,014	2,224	2,736	3,209	4,428	4,854
BRITISH COLUMBIA									
*Burnaby, dm	2,057	1,837	1,626	769	857	964	530	798	805
Coquitlam, dm	745	793	763	147	181	264	105	175	233
*North Vancouver, dm	864	797	812	228	233	281	140	251	340
Richmond, twp	1,093	898	721	231	265	205	171	291	470
Saanich, dm	1,042	827	747	416	485	510	199	334	415
Surrey, dm	1,761	1,577	1,810	550	637	740	288	451	654
Vancouver, c	6,743	6,317	4,888	4,758	4,928	5,049	3,881	5,044	4,860
Victoria, c	972	804	699	898	1,001	1,151	671	925	1,221

[1]Figures for certain subdivisions may not be comparable for the periods shown because of changes in area boundaries, particularly for those indicated by an asterisk: c=city, t=town, b=borough, dm-district municipality and twp=township.
[2]As at the date of the 1971 Census.
[3]By place of occurrence.
[4]Population fewer than 50,000 at date of 1971 Census but included as the largest urban centre in Prince Edward Island.

4.34 Number of live-born children in order of live births, by age of mother, 1974[1]

Order of birth of child	Under 15	15-19	20-24	25-29	30-34	35-39	40-44	45 and over	Age not stated	All ages	% of total
1st child	309	31,715	61,262	42,035	9,617	1,878	356	15	246	147,433	44.0
2nd	3	5,963	38,345	47,825	16,219	3,073	398	15	18	111,859	33.4
3rd	—	566	9,272	20,194	11,845	3,011	462	26	6	45,382	13.5
4th	—	58	1,943	6,128	5,723	2,211	482	21	4	16,570	5.0
5th	—	3	454	1,842	2,329	1,424	409	21	2	6,484	1.9
6th	—	—	96	719	1,078	891	306	25	—	3,115	0.9
7th	—	—	20	302	586	584	227	26	1	1,746	0.5
8th	—	—	5	119	352	350	180	20	1	1,027	0.3
9th	—	—	3	38	187	260	125	11	—	624	0.2
10th	—	—	1	17	126	166	111	12	—	433	0.1
11th	—	—	1	4	49	120	92	7	—	273	0.1
12th	—	—	—	—	16	88	68	4	—	176	0.1
13th	—	—	—	2	8	38	50	3	—	101	··
14th	—	—	—	—	5	17	30	8	1	61	··
15th	—	—	—	—	—	17	13	5	—	35	··
16th	—	—	—	—	—	2	13	3	—	18	··
17th	—	—	—	—	—	—	5	3	—	8	··

4.34 Number of live-born children in order of live births, by age of mother, 1974[1] (concluded)

Order of birth of child	Age of mother									All ages	% of total
	Under 15	15-19	20-24	25-29	30-34	35-39	40-44	45 and over	Age not stated		
18th	—	—	—	—	—	—	3	—	—	3	--
19th	—	—	—	—	—	1	—	1	—	2	--
20th and over	—	—	—	—	—	1	—	—	—	1	--
Not stated	—	9	7	13	2	1	3	—	23	58	--
Total	312	38,314	111,409	119,238	48,142	14,133	3,333	226	302	335,409	100.0
% of total	0.1	11.4	33.2	35.5	14.4	4.2	1.0	0.1	0.1	100.0	...

[1]Excludes Newfoundland.

4.35 Percentage distribution of total live births, by order of birth, 1951-74[1]

Year	1st child	2nd child	3rd child	4th and later children	Total
1951	28.3	25.4	17.2	29.1	100.0
1956	26.7	24.0	17.8	31.5	100.0
1961	25.9	23.2	18.0	32.9	100.0
1966	33.1	24.8	16.2	25.9	100.0
1967	36.0	25.7	15.4	22.9	100.0
1968	37.8	26.7	15.1	20.3	100.0
1969	38.5	27.5	15.2	18.8	100.0
1970	39.9	28.0	15.2	16.9	100.0
1971	40.6	29.3	14.9	15.2	100.0
1972	41.9	30.9	14.3	12.9	100.0
1973	43.3	32.3	13.7	10.7	100.0
1974	44.0	33.4	13.5	9.1	100.0

[1]Excludes Newfoundland.

4.36 Stillbirths and ratio per 1,000 live births, by province, 1951-74

Year	Nfld.	PEI	NS	NB	Que.	Ont.	Man.	Sask.	Alta.	BC	YT	NWT	Canada
Number (28 weeks or more gestation)													
Av. 1951-55	222	52	337	291	2,705	2,017	336	313	425	374	6	11	7,088
" 1956-60	274	46	304	267	2,446	1,992	301	262	388	418	5	12	6,714
" 1961-65	261	47	256	220	1,727	1,818	278	242	358	370	5	19	5,600
" 1966-70	171	28	181	158	1,074	1,402	195	174	278	311	4	20	3,996
1971	158	23	139	138	807	1,221	164	159	254	310	6	17	3,396
1972	121	22	124	137	685	1,159	173	140	229	238	6	12	3,046
1973	151	15	119	132	658	1,034	151	144	206	243	3	10	2,866
1974	127	20	123	125	629	1,019	128	132	188	252	7	16	2,766
Ratio													
Av. 1951-55	17.0	19.0	18.4	17.7	21.0	15.6	15.7	13.3	13.7	11.9	14.1	16.5	17.0
" 1956-60	18.3	17.1	15.9	16.1	17.5	13.0	13.4	10.9	10.5	10.7	10.7	12.3	14.3
" 1961-65	17.3	17.1	13.8	14.0	13.1	11.9	12.5	10.6	9.7	10.1	9.0	16.0	12.3
" 1966-70	13.0	13.5	12.7	13.1	10.8	10.7	10.9	9.7	9.0	9.0	9.8	16.0	10.7
1971	12.4	10.9	9.8	11.3	9.0	9.4	9.1	9.9	8.3	8.9	11.9	13.2	9.4
1972	9.4	10.9	9.2	11.6	8.2	9.3	9.9	9.0	7.8	6.9	13.3	9.7	8.8
1973	12.7	8.0	9.0	11.6	7.8	8.4	8.9	9.7	7.0	7.1	7.1	8.3	8.3
1974	12.4	10.3	9.5	10.9	7.3	8.2	7.4	8.7	6.3	7.1	14.1	15.4	8.0

4.37 Stillbirths and ratio per 1,000 live births, by age of mother, 1974[1]

Age group of mother	Live births	Stillbirths	Stillbirth ratio per 1,000 live births
Under 20 years	38,626	316	8.2
20-24 years	111,409	757	6.8
25-29 "	119,238	836	7.0
30-34 "	48,142	402	8.4
35-39 "	14,133	232	16.4
40-44 "	3,333	81	24.3
45 years and over	226	10	44.2
Age not stated	302	5	16.6
Total, all ages	335,409	2,639	7.9

[1]Excludes Newfoundland.

4.38   Age-specific fertility rate and gross reproduction rate per 1,000 women, 1926-74[1]

Year and province or territory	Age group							Total fertility rate	Gross reproduction rate
	15-19	20-24	25-29	30-34	35-39	40-44	45-49		
Canada									
1926	29.0	139.9	177.4	153.8	114.6	50.7	6.0	3,357	1.628
1931	29.9	137.1	175.1	145.3	103.1	44.0	5.5	3,200	1.555
1936	25.7	112.1	144.3	126.5	90.0	36.3	4.4	2,696	1.310
1941	30.7	138.4	159.8	122.3	80.0	31.6	3.7	2,832	1.377
1946	36.5	169.6	191.4	146.0	93.1	34.5	3.8	3,374	1.640
1951	48.1	188.7	198.8	144.5	86.5	30.9	3.1	3,503	1.701
1956	55.9	222.2	220.1	150.3	89.6	30.8	2.9	3,858	1.874
1961	58.2	233.6	219.2	144.9	81.1	28.5	2.4	3,840	1.868
1966	48.2	169.1	163.5	103.3	57.5	19.1	1.7	2,812	1.369
1971	40.1	134.4	142.0	77.3	33.6	9.4	0.6	2,187	1.060
1972	38.5	119.8	137.1	72.1	28.9	7.8	0.6	2,024	0.982
1973	37.2	117.7	131.6	67.1	25.7	6.4	0.4	1,931	0.937
1974	35.3	113.1	131.1	66.6	23.0	5.5	0.4	1,875	0.911
1974									
Prince Edward Island	48.7	124.3	145.9	79.7	33.9	10.8	0.4	2,219	1.048
Nova Scotia	54.3	124.6	128.2	61.4	25.0	6.3	0.5	2,002	0.968
New Brunswick	53.8	132.6	140.0	66.1	26.0	8.0	0.6	2,136	1.054
Quebec	16.6	91.1	126.6	67.5	23.6	5.6	0.4	1,657	0.806
Ontario	38.3	114.6	129.4	66.9	22.5	4.8	0.3	1,884	0.915
Manitoba	52.5	127.9	145.8	74.7	27.3	7.2	0.4	2,179	1.046
Saskatchewan	51.0	139.2	165.7	80.6	30.4	9.5	0.6	2,385	1.170
Alberta	47.7	140.4	142.2	64.3	21.8	5.2	0.4	2,110	1.033
British Columbia	40.2	120.3	122.7	58.4	18.0	3.9	0.2	1,819	0.884
Yukon Territory	102.5	252.9	162.0	71.3	24.0	6.0	2.5	3,106	1.475
Northwest Territories	127.6	235.3	155.3	100.0	47.0	26.3	3.3	3,474	1.633

[1]Excludes Newfoundland.

4.39   Percentage change in death rate for each age group, by sex, 1951-74

Age group	Male	Female	Age group	Male	Female
Under 1 year	-61.1	-60.6	50-54 years	-11.5	-27.7
1- 4 years	-57.1	-61.1	55-59 "	-9.9	-30.4
5- 9 "	-50.0	-57.1	60-64 "	-7.3	-29.8
10-14 "	-37.5	-40.0	65-69 "	-0.6	-30.5
15-19 "	+21.4	-33.3	70-74 "	-2.6	-32.5
20-24 "	+5.3	-40.0	75-79 "	-10.6	-36.3
25-29 "	-11.1	-45.5	80-84 "	-10.3	-32.6
30-34 "	-28.6	-46.7	85 years and over	-77.7	-26.3
35-39 "	-8.0	-40.0			
40-44 "	-10.3	-36.7	All ages	-14.9	-19.2
45-49 "	-9.4	-28.9			

4.40   Numerical and percentage distribution of deaths by age group and sex, 1961, 1966 and 1971

Age group	Distribution									% change in death rate 1961-71
	1961			1966			1971			
	No.	%	Rate[1]	No.	%	Rate[1]	No.	%	Rate[1]	
Male										
Under 1 year	7,447	9.0	30.5	5,138	5.8	25.8	3,712	4.1	19.9	-34.8
1- 4 years	1,154	1.4	1.3	988	1.1	1.1	679	0.7	0.9	-30.8
5- 9 "	672	0.8	0.6	669	0.8	0.6	641	0.7	0.6	—
10-14 "	527	0.6	0.6	620	0.7	0.6	589	0.6	0.5	-16.7
15-19 "	840	1.0	1.2	1,212	1.4	1.3	1,489	1.6	1.4	+16.7
20-24 "	969	1.2	1.7	1,324	1.5	1.8	1,697	1.9	1.8	+5.9
25-29 "	895	1.1	1.5	980	1.1	1.6	1,176	1.3	1.5	—
30-34 "	1,041	1.3	1.6	1,054	1.2	1.7	1,090	1.2	1.6	—
35-39 "	1,422	1.7	2.3	1,456	1.7	2.2	1,416	1.5	2.2	-4.3
40-44 "	1,916	2.3	3.4	2,146	2.4	3.4	2,310	2.5	3.6	+5.9
45-49 "	2,993	3.6	5.8	3,111	3.5	5.7	3,523	3.8	5.7	-1.7
50-54 "	4,242	5.1	9.6	4,855	5.5	9.7	4,839	5.3	9.3	-3.1
55-59 "	5,494	6.6	15.2	6,352	7.2	15.4	6,887	7.5	14.6	-3.9
60-64 "	7,028	8.5	24.0	7,911	9.0	24.0	8,755	9.5	22.9	-4.6
65-69 "	8,545	10.3	35.7	9,226	10.5	36.2	10,279	11.2	34.7	-2.8
70-74 "	10,582	12.8	54.0	10,549	12.0	53.1	10,663	11.6	51.9	-3.9
75-79 "	10,970	13.3	81.8	11,102	12.6	79.9	11,058	12.1	79.0	-3.4
80-84 "	8,635	10.4	125.1	10,006	11.4	124.0	10,182	11.1	118.8	-5.0
85 years and over	7,337	8.9	208.9	9,214	10.5	213.4	10,838	11.8	198.5	-5.0
Total, all ages	82,709	100.0	9.0	87,913	100.0	8.7	91,823	100.0	8.5	-5.6

4.40 Numerical and percentage distribution of deaths by age group and sex, 1961, 1966 and 1971 (concluded)

Age group	Distribution									% change in death rate 1961-71
	1961			1966			1971			
	No.	%	Rate¹	No.	%	Rate¹	No.	%	Rate¹	
Female										
Under 1 year	5,493	9.4	23.7	3,822	6.2	20.2	2,644	4.0	15.1	-36.3
1- 4 years	844	1.4	1.0	775	1.3	0.9	551	0.8	0.8	-20.0
5- 9 "	405	0.7	0.4	480	0.8	0.4	424	0.7	0.4	—
10-14 "	278	0.5	0.3	318	0.5	0.3	365	0.6	0.3	—
15-19 "	322	0.6	0.5	467	0.8	0.5	579	0.9	0.6	+20.0
20-24 "	342	0.6	0.6	403	0.7	0.5	559	0.9	0.6	—
25-29 "	418	0.7	0.7	384	0.6	0.6	485	0.7	0.6	-14.3
30-34 "	562	1.0	0.9	564	0.9	0.9	565	0.9	0.9	—
35-39 "	880	1.5	1.4	845	1.4	1.3	815	1.2	1.3	-7.1
40-44 "	1,099	1.9	2.0	1,293	2.1	2.0	1,290	2.0	2.1	+5.0
45-49 "	1,617	2.8	3.2	1,823	2.9	3.3	1,901	2.9	3.0	-6.2
50-54 "	2,237	3.8	5.3	2,434	3.9	5.0	2,480	3.8	4.6	-13.2
55-59 "	2,749	4.7	8.0	3,115	5.0	7.7	3,477	5.3	7.2	-10.0
60-64 "	3,725	6.4	12.8	4,064	6.6	12.2	4,345	6.6	11.0	-14.1
65-69 "	5,304	9.1	21.4	5,393	8.7	19.5	5,614	8.6	17.3	-19.2
70-74 "	7,058	12.1	34.2	7,063	11.4	30.9	7,138	10.9	28.3	-17.3
75-79 "	8,290	14.2	59.2	8,695	14.0	53.9	8,930	13.6	48.1	-18.7
80-84 "	7,871	13.5	101.2	9,048	14.6	93.6	9,763	14.9	82.4	-18.6
85 years and over	8,782	15.1	192.2	10,964	17.7	183.4	13,524	20.7	163.3	-15.0
Total, all ages	58,276	100.0	6.5	61,950	100.0	6.2	65,449	100.0	6.1	-6.2

	1961		1966		1971	
	Male	Female	Male	Female	Male	Female
Average age at death	59.7	63.1	62.0	65.9	63.3	68.2
Median age at death²	67.9	72.2	68.4	73.5	68.5	74.7

¹Per 1,000 population per age group.
²The age above and below which half of the total number of annual deaths occurred.

4.41 Deaths and rate per 100,000 population according to the International Abbreviated List of 50 Causes, 1974

Abbreviated "B" List No.	Detailed List No.	Cause (eighth revision)	Deaths	Rate per 100,000 population
1	000	Cholera	—	—
2	001	Typhoid fever	2	- -
3	004,006	Bacillary dysentery and amoebiasis	4	- -
4	008,009	Enteritis and other diarrhoeal diseases	269	1.2
5	010-012	Tuberculosis of respiratory system	223	1.0
6	013-019	Other tuberculosis, including late effects	107	0.5
7	020	Plague	—	—
8	032	Diphtheria	5	- -
9	033	Whooping cough	2	- -
10	034	Streptococcal sore throat and scarlet fever	2	- -
11	036	Meningococcal infection	55	0.2
12	040-043	Acute poliomyelitis	1	- -
13	050	Smallpox	—	—
14	055	Measles	20	0.1
15	080-083	Typhus and other rickettsioses	—	—
16	084	Malaria	—	—
17	090-097	Syphilis and its sequelae	20	0.1
18	Remainder of 000-136	All other infective and parasitic diseases	409	1.8
19	140-209	Malignant neoplasms, including neoplasms of lymphatic and haematopoietic tissue	33,751	150.4
20	210-239	Benign neoplasms and neoplasms of unspecified nature	314	1.4
21	250	Diabetes mellitus	3,164	14.1
22	260-269	Avitaminoses and other nutritional deficiency	169	0.8
23	280-285	Anaemias	322	1.4
24	320	Meningitis	99	0.4
25	390-392	Active rheumatic fever	21	0.1
26	393-398	Chronic rheumatic heart disease	1,166	5.2
27	400-404	Hypertensive disease	1,507	6.7
28	410-414	Ischaemic heart disease	51,817	230.8
29	420-429	Other forms of heart disease	4,155	18.5
30	430-438	Cerebrovascular disease	16,481	73.4
31	470-474	Influenza	441	2.0
32	480-486	Pneumonia	5,207	23.2
33	490-493	Bronchitis, emphysema and asthma	3,074	13.7
34	531-533	Peptic ulcer	790	3.5
35	540-543	Appendicitis	83	0.4
36	550-553, 560	Intestinal obstruction and hernia	653	2.9
37	571	Cirrhosis of liver	2,618	11.7
38	580-584	Nephritis and nephrosis	561	2.5

4.41   Deaths and rate per 100,000 population according to the International Abbreviated List of 50 Causes, 1974 (concluded)

Abbre-viated "B" List No.	Detailed List No.	Cause (eighth revision)	Deaths	Rate per 100,000 population
39	600	Hyperplasia of prostate	167	1.5[1]
40	640-645	Abortion	3	0.9[2]
41 {	630-639 650-678	Other complications of pregnancy, childbirth and the puerperium	32	9.3[2]
42	740-759	Congenital anomalies	1,718	7.7
43 {	764-768 772, 776	Birth injury, difficult labour and other anoxic and hypoxic conditions	1,244	5.5
44 {	760-763, 769-771 773-775, 777-779	Other causes of perinatal mortality	1,207	5.4
45	780-796	Symptoms and ill-defined conditions	1,592	7.1
46	Remainder of 240-738	All other diseases	16,458	73.3
47	E810-E823	Motor vehicle accidents	6,325	28.2
48 {	E800-E807 E825-E949	All other accidents	6,620	29.5
49	E950-E959	Suicide and self-inflicted injuries	2,902	12.9
50	E960-E999	All other external causes	1,014	4.5
		All causes	166,794	743.1

[1]Per 100,000 males.
[2]Less than 0.1 per 100,000 live births.

4.42   Leading causes of death, by sex at various age groups, 1974

Cause	Male No.	Rate[1]	Cause	Female No.	Rate[1]
Under 1 year			**Under 1 year**		
Congenital anomalies	647	364.1	Congenital anomalies	557	331.5
Anoxia and hypoxia	636	357.9	Anoxia and hypoxia	428	254.8
Immaturity	258	145.2	Immaturity	240	142.9
Pneumonia	170	95.7	Pneumonia	112	66.7
Accidents	124	69.8	Accidents	101	60.1
1-4 years			**1-4 years**		
Accidents	296	40.7	Accidents	183	26.4
Congenital anomalies	163	22.4	Congenital anomalies	134	19.4
Cancer	47	6.5	Cancer	46	6.6
Pneumonia	36	4.9	Pneumonia	31	4.5
Enteritis and other diarrhoel diseases	11	1.5	Enteritis and other diarrhoel diseases	7	1.0
5-19 years			**5-19 years**		
Accidents	2,109	62.4	Accidents	760	23.5
Cancer	241	7.1	Cancer	154	4.8
Suicide	222	6.6	Congenital anomalies	119	3.7
Congenital anomalies	129	3.8	Suicide	40	1.2
Cardiovascular diseases	66	2.0	Cardiovascular diseases	36	1.1
20-44 years			**20-44 years**		
Accidents	3,568	88.8	Cancer	995	25.3
Cardiovascular diseases	1,315	32.7	Accidents	810	20.6
Suicide	1,066	26.5	Cardiovascular diseases	524	13.3
Cancer	920	22.9	Suicide	378	9.6
Cirrhosis of liver	251	6.2	Cirrhosis of liver	120	3.1
45-64 years			**45-64 years**		
Cardiovascular diseases	12,161	581.6	Cancer	5,409	251.1
Cancer	6,174	295.3	Cardiovascular diseases	4,333	201.1
Accidents	1,784	85.3	Accidents	630	29.2
Cirrhosis of liver	1,059	50.6	Cirrhosis of liver	426	19.8
Suicide	581	27.8	Suicide	300	13.9
65 years and over			**65 years and over**		
Cardiovascular diseases	32,697	3,956.1	Cardiovascular diseases	30,966	2,930.7
Cancer	11,264	1,362.9	Cancer	8,485	803.0
Pneumonia	2,220	268.6	Pneumonia	1,882	178.1
Bronchitis, emphysema and asthma	1,817	219.8	Accidents	1,220	115.5
Accidents	1,360	164.5	Bronchitis, emphysema and asthma	422	39.9
All ages			**All ages**		
Cardiovascular diseases	46,258	412.4	Cardiovascular diseases	35,883	319.5
Cancer	18,655	166.3	Cancer	15,096	134.4
Accidents	9,241	82.4	Accidents	3,704	33.0
Pneumonia	2,904	25.9	Pneumonia	2,303	20.5
Bronchitis, emphysema and asthma	2,460	21.9	Diabetes mellitus	1,829	16.3

[1]Under one year rates are per 100,000 live births; all other age group rates are per 100,000 population.

4.43   Infant deaths and stillbirths, by province and sex, 1951-74

Province or territory and year	Infant deaths (<1 yr)			Neonatal deaths (<28 days)					Post-neo-natal deaths (28 days to 1 yr)	Still-births (28+ weeks gesta-tion)	Perinatal deaths (Stillbirths plus deaths <7 days)[1]
	Male	Female	Total	Male	Female	Total	<7 days	7-27 days			
NEWFOUNDLAND											
Number											
1951	361	276	637	176	112	288	209	79	349	189	398
1961	335	253	588	197	128	325	269	56	263	281	550
1971	173	120	293	123	84	207	175	32	86	158	333
1973	135	95	230	98	66	164	140	24	66	151	291
1974	108	73	181	70	48	118	101	17	63	127	228
Rate[1]											
1951	60.3	48.0	54.3	29.4	19.5	24.5	17.8	6.7	29.8	16.1	33.4
1961	41.7	33.5	37.7	24.5	16.9	20.8	17.3	3.6	16.9	18.0	34.7
1971	26.3	19.4	22.9	18.7	13.5	16.2	13.7	2.5	6.7	12.4	25.8
1973	22.1	16.4	19.3	16.0	11.4	13.8	11.8	2.0	5.5	12.7	24.1
1974	20.2	15.0	17.7	13.1	9.8	11.5	9.9	1.7	6.2	12.4	22.0
PRINCE EDWARD ISLAND											
Number											
1951	60	30	90	29	17	46	33	13	44	56	89
1961	55	38	93	29	25	54	47	7	39	46	93
1971	29	17	46	24	13	37	34	3	9	23	57
1973	18	12	30	16	3	19	15	4	11	15	30
1974	21	13	34	18	12	30	29	1	4	20	49
Rate[1]											
1951	43.7	23.5	33.9	21.1	13.3	17.4	12.4	4.9	16.5	21.1	32.9
1961	37.4	27.8	32.8	19.7	18.3	19.0	16.6	2.5	13.8	16.2	32.2
1971	26.1	17.1	21.9	21.6	13.1	17.6	16.2	1.4	4.3	10.9	26.8
1973	17.9	13.6	15.9	15.9	3.4	10.1	8.0	2.1	5.8	8.0	15.8
1974	20.5	14.2	17.5	17.6	13.1	15.5	15.0	0.5	2.1	10.3	24.9
NOVA SCOTIA											
Number											
1951	344	250	594	218	134	352	298	54	242	319	617
1961	309	229	538	187	140	327	280	47	211	300	580
1971	160	105	265	108	72	180	148	32	85	139	287
1973	113	93	206	78	57	135	107	28	71	119	226
1974	98	87	185	59	56	115	94	21	70	123	217
Rate[1]											
1951	38.9	30.2	34.7	24.7	16.2	20.6	17.4	3.2	14.1	18.6	35.4
1961	31.0	24.3	27.8	18.8	14.9	16.9	14.4	2.4	10.9	15.5	29.5
1971	21.8	15.2	18.6	14.7	10.4	12.6	10.4	2.2	6.0	9.8	19.9
1973	16.6	14.3	15.5	11.5	8.8	10.2	8.1	2.1	6.0	9.8	19.9
1973	16.6	14.3	15.5	11.5	8.8	10.2	8.1	2.1	5.3	9.0	16.9
1974	14.7	13.9	14.3	8.8	8.9	8.9	7.3	1.6	5.4	9.5	16.6
NEW BRUNSWICK											
Number											
1951	472	363	835	241	199	440	334	106	395	293	627
1961	248	186	434	145	105	250	217	33	184	222	439
1971	130	74	204	97	48	145	135	10	59	138	273
1973	105	68	173	75	47	122	113	9	59	132	245
1974	93	80	173	65	57	122	114	8	51	125	239
Rate[1]											
1951	57.6	46.0	51.9	29.4	25.2	27.4	20.8	6.6	24.5	18.2	38.3
1961	29.1	23.0	26.2	17.0	13.0	15.1	13.1	2.0	11.1	13.4	26.1
1971	20.7	12.5	16.7	15.5	8.1	11.9	11.1	0.8	4.8	11.3	22.2
1973	17.9	12.2	15.1	12.8	8.4	10.7	9.9	0.8	4.5	11.6	21.2
1974	16.0	14.2	15.1	11.2	10.1	10.7	10.0	0.7	4.5	10.9	20.6
QUEBEC											
Number											
1951	3,335	2,486	5,821	1,864	1,311	3,175	2,398	777	2,646	2,768	5,166
1961	2,464	1,855	4,319	1,666	1,189	2,855	2,489	366	1,464	1,929	4,418
1971	948	692	1,640	690	500	1,190	1,059	131	450	807	1,866
1973	795	583	1,378	570	425	995	874	121	383	658	1,532
1974	733	558	1,291	531	393	924	811	113	367	629	1,440
Rate[1]											
1951	53.7	42.3	48.1	30.0	22.3	26.3	19.8	6.4	21.8	22.9	41.8
1961	34.7	28.0	31.5	23.5	18.0	20.8	18.1	2.7	10.7	14.1	31.8
1971	20.6	16.0	18.4	15.0	11.6	13.3	11.9	1.5	5.0	9.0	20.7
1973	18.3	14.4	16.4	13.1	10.5	11.8	10.4	1.4	4.6	7.8	18.1
1974	16.7	13.4	15.1	12.1	9.4	10.8	9.5	1.3	4.3	7.3	16.7
ONTARIO											
Number											
1951	2,010	1,535	3,545	1,389	1,040	2,429	2,033	396	1,116	1,975	4,008
1961	2,090	1,536	3,626	1,507	1,120	2,627	2,378	249	999	1,870	4,248
1971	1,146	844	1,990	821	603	1,424	1,255	169	566	1,221	2,476
1973	979	761	1,740	693	545	1,238	1,093	145	502	1,034	2,127
1974	915	751	1,666	621	542	1,163	1,020	143	503	1,019	2,039
Rate[1]											
1951	33.9	27.6	30.9	23.5	18.7	21.2	17.7	3.4	9.7	17.2	34.3
1961	25.9	20.0	23.0	18.7	14.6	16.7	15.1	1.6	6.3	11.9	26.6
1971	17.1	13.3	15.3	12.2	9.5	10.9	9.6	1.3	4.3	9.4	18.8
1973	15.4	12.7	14.1	10.9	9.1	10.0	8.8	1.2	4.1	8.4	17.0
1974	14.3	12.4	13.4	9.7	9.0	9.4	8.2	1.2	4.0	8.2	16.2

4.43   Infant deaths and stillbirths, by province and sex, 1951-74 (continued)

Province or territory and year	Infant deaths (<1 yr)			Neonatal deaths (<28 days)					Post-neonatal deaths (28 days to 1 yr)	Stillbirths (28+ weeks gesta-tion)	Perinatal deaths (Stillbirths plus deaths <7 days)[1]
	Male	Female	Total	Male	Female	Total	<7 days	7-27 days			
MANITOBA											
Number											
1951	369	289	658	209	169	378	301	77	280	340	641
1961	341	247	588	211	169	380	336	44	208	301	637
1971	184	132	316	117	87	204	177	27	112	164	341
1973	164	114	278	105	64	169	145	24	109	151	296
1974	152	120	272	97	79	176	146	30	96	128	274
Rate[1]											
1951	35.6	30.2	33.0	20.1	17.7	19.0	15.1	3.9	14.0	17.0	31.6
1961	28.6	21.7	25.2	17.7	14.9	16.3	14.4	1.9	8.9	12.9	27.0
1971	20.0	15.0	17.5	12.7	9.9	11.3	9.8	1.5	6.2	9.1	18.7
1973	18.7	13.9	16.4	12.0	7.8	10.0	8.5	1.4	6.4	8.9	17.3
1974	16.9	14.4	15.7	10.8	9.5	10.2	8.4	1.7	5.5	7.4	15.7
SASKATCHEWAN											
Number											
1951	353	323	676	226	175	401	338	63	275	303	641
1961	373	245	618	244	151	395	334	61	223	266	600
1971	189	136	325	132	90	222	199	23	103	159	358
1973	161	100	261	112	68	180	156	24	81	144	300
1974	181	132	313	112	79	191	172	19	122	132	304
Rate[1]											
1951	31.8	30.4	31.1	20.3	16.5	18.5	15.6	2.9	12.6	13.9	29.1
1961	30.3	21.0	25.8	19.8	12.9	16.5	13.9	2.5	9.3	11.1	24.7
1971	23.2	17.2	20.2	16.2	11.4	13.8	12.4	1.4	6.4	9.9	22.1
1973	21.3	13.8	17.6	14.8	9.4	12.2	10.5	1.6	5.5	9.7	20.1
1974	23.5	17.8	20.7	14.5	10.7	12.6	11.4	1.3	8.1	8.7	19.9
ALBERTA											
Number											
1951	531	358	889	345	212	557	462	95	332	402	864
1961	612	432	1,044	418	289	707	629	78	337	372	1,001
1971	325	223	548	226	162	388	334	54	160	254	588
1973	242	174	416	153	113	266	227	39	150	206	433
1974	264	185	449	157	121	278	234	44	171	188	422
Rate[1]											
1951	38.6	27.0	32.9	25.1	16.0	20.6	17.1	3.5	12.3	14.9	31.5
1961	30.8	22.7	26.8	21.0	15.2	18.2	16.2	2.0	8.6	9.6	25.5
1971	20.5	15.2	17.9	14.3	11.0	12.7	10.9	1.8	5.2	8.3	19.1
1973	16.1	12.2	14.2	10.2	7.9	9.1	7.8	1.3	5.1	7.0	14.7
1974	17.4	12.7	15.1	10.3	8.3	9.3	7.8	1.5	5.7	6.3	14.0
BRITISH COLUMBIA											
Number											
1951	487	352	839	299	214	513	435	78	326	365	800
1961	534	411	945	331	264	595	515	80	350	412	927
1971	381	272	653	271	188	459	417	42	194	310	727
1973	319	256	575	211	169	380	333	47	195	243	576
1974	349	223	572	226	138	364	325	39	208	252	577
Rate[1]											
1951	33.8	25.8	29.9	20.7	15.7	18.3	15.5	2.8	11.6	13.0	28.1
1961	27.1	21.8	24.5	16.8	14.0	15.4	13.3	2.1	9.1	10.7	23.8
1971	21.2	16.1	18.7	15.1	11.2	13.2	12.0	1.2	5.6	8.9	20.7
1973	18.1	15.3	16.7	12.0	10.1	11.1	9.7	1.4	5.7	7.1	16.6
1974	19.1	12.9	16.1	12.4	8.0	10.3	9.2	1.1	5.9	7.1	16.1
YUKON TERRITORY											
Number											
1951	10	9	19	4	2	6			13	2	8
1961	13	10	23	6	4	10	7	3	13	4	11
1971	8	5	13	3	3	6	4	2	7	6	10
1973	4	3	7	2	2	4	2	2	3	3	5
1974	7	5	12	3	2	5	4	1	7	7	11
Rate[1]											
1951	57.8	53.3	55.6	23.1	11.8	17.5			38.1	5.8	23.3
1961	45.8	36.5	41.2	21.1	14.6	17.9	12.5	5.4	23.3	7.2	19.6
1971	29.0	21.7	25.7	10.9	13.0	11.9	7.9	4.0	13.8	11.9	19.5
1973	19.2	14.2	16.7	9.6	9.4	9.5	4.8	4.8	7.1	7.1	11.8
1974	26.9	21.3	24.2	11.5	8.5	10.1	8.1	2.0	14.1	14.1	21.8
NORTHWEST TERRITORIES											
Number											
1951	43	27	70	20	14	34			36	11	26
1961	73	51	124	25	14	39	22	17	85	16	38
1971	39	24	63	51	12	23	19	4	40	17	36
1973	34	11	45	15	5	20	16	4	25	10	26
1974	25	19	44	14	6	20	19	1	24	16	35
Rate[1]											
1951	135.6	81.3	107.9	63.1	42.2	52.4			55.5	16.9	39.4
1961	128.1	93.2	111.0	43.9	25.6	34.9	19.7	15.2	76.1	14.3	33.5
1971	58.8	38.4	49.0	16.6	19.2	17.9	14.8	3.1	31.1	13.2	27.6
1973	52.8	19.6	37.4	23.3	8.9	16.6	13.3	3.3	20.8	8.3	21.4
1974	45.3	38.8	42.2	25.4	12.2	19.2	18.2	1.0	23.0	15.4	33.0

4.43   Infant deaths and stillbirths, by province and sex, 1951-74 (concluded)

Province or territory and year	Infant deaths (<1 yr)			Neonatal deaths (<28 days)			<7 days	7-27 days	Post-neo-natal deaths (28 days to 1 yr)	Still-births (28+ weeks gesta-tion)	Perinatal deaths (Stillbirths plus deaths <7 days)[1]
	Male	Female	Total	Male	Female	Total					
CANADA											
Number											
1951	8,375	6,298	14,673	5,020	3,599	8,619	6,862	1,757	6,054	7,023	13,885
1961	7,447	5,493	12,940	4,966	3,598	8,564	7,523	1,041	4,376	6,019	13,542
1971	3,712	2,644	6,356	2,623	1,862	4,485	3,956	529	1,871	3,396	7,352
1973	3,069	2,270	5,339	2,128	1,564	3,692	3,221	471	1,647	2,866	6,087
1974	2,946	2,246	5,192	1,973	1,533	3,506	3,069	437	1,686	2,766	5,835
Rate[1]											
1951	42.7	34.0	38.5	25.6	19.4	22.6	18.0	4.6	15.9	18.4	35.8
1961	30.5	23.7	27.2	20.3	15.6	18.0	15.8	2.2	9.2	12.7	28.1
1971	19.9	15.1	17.5	14.1	10.6	12.4	10.9	1.5	5.2	9.4	20.1
1973	17.4	13.6	15.5	12.0	9.4	10.8	9.4	1.4	4.8	8.3	17.6
1974	16.6	13.4	15.0	11.1	9.1	10.1	8.9	1.3	4.9	8.0	16.7

[1]Perinatal rates per 1,000 live- and still-born infants; all other rates per 1,000 live births.

4.44   Infant deaths, by age, 1974

Time of death	Deaths		Cumulative deaths		Time of death	Deaths		Cumulative deaths	
	No.	%	No.	%		No.	%	No.	%
1st day	2,033	39.2	2,033	39.2	1st month	3,506	67.5	3,506	67.5
2nd "	376	7.2	2,409	46.4	2nd "	410	7.9	3,916	75.4
3rd "	302	5.8	2,711	52.2	3rd "	329	6.3	4,245	81.8
4th "	147	2.8	2,858	55.0	4th "	280	5.4	4,525	87.2
5th "	95	1.8	2,953	56.9	5th "	153	2.9	4,678	90.1
6th "	73	1.4	3,026	58.3	6th "	129	2.5	4,807	92.6
7th "	43	0.8	3,069	59.1	7th "	88	1.7	4,895	94.3
					8th "	83	1.6	4,978	95.9
1st week	3,069	59.1	3,069	59.1	9th "	60	1.2	5,038	97.0
2nd "	209	4.0	3,278	63.1	10th "	63	1.2	5,101	98.2
3rd "	131	2.5	3,409	65.7	11th "	50	1.0	5,151	99.2
4th "	97	1.9	3,506	67.5	12th "	41	0.8	5,192	100.0

4.45   Canadian life table, 1971

Age	Male				Female			
	Number living at each age	Number dying between each age and the next	Prob-ability of dying before reaching next birthday	Expec-tation of life yr	Number living at each age	Number dying between each age and the next	Prob-ability of dying before reaching next birthday	Expec-tation of life yr
At birth	100,000		.02002	69.34	100,000		.01544	76.36
		2,002				1,544		
1 year	97,998		.00128	69.76	98,456		.00115	76.56
		126				113		
2 years	97,872		.00094	68.85	98,343		.00073	75.64
		92				72		
3 "	97,780		.00084	67.91	98,271		.00061	74.70
		83				60		
4 "	97,697		.00071	66.97	98,211		.00057	73.74
		69				56		
5 "	97,628		.00061	66.02	98,155		.00050	72.79
		232				179		
10 "	97,396		.00039	61.17	97,976		.00028	67.91
		267				157		
15 "	97,129		.00106	56.33	97,819		.00046	63.02
		682				262		
20 "	96,447		.00178	51.71	97,557		.00057	58.18
		872				279		
25 "	95,575		.00164	47.16	97,278		.00060	53.34
		730				315		
30 "	94,845		.00152	42.50	96,963		.00077	48.51
		773				433		
35 "	94,072		.00188	37.83	96,530		.00112	43.71
		1,037				644		
40 "	93,035		.00291	33.22	95,886		.00173	38.99
		1,645				988		

4.45 Canadian life table, 1971 (concluded)

Age	Male				Female			
	Number living at each age	Number dying between each age and the next	Probability of dying before reaching next birthday	Expectation of life yr	Number living at each age	Number dying between each age and the next	Probability of dying before reaching next birthday	Expectation of life yr
45 years	91,390		.00464	28.77	94,898		.00260	34.37
		2,569				1,465		
50 ''	88,821		.00761	24.52	93,433		.00403	29.86
		4,060				2,236		
55 ''	84,761		.01213	20.57	91,197		.00618	25.53
		6,042				3,301		
60 ''	78,719		.01918	16.95	87,896		.00931	21.39
		8,675				4,804		
65 ''	70,044		.02961	13.72	83,092		.01449	17.47
		11,469				7,097		
70 ''	58,575		.04436	10.90	75,995		.02337	13.85
		13,787				10,371		
75 ''	44,788		.06552	8.47	65,624		.03876	10.63
		14,812				14,387		
80 ''	29,976		.09701	6.41	51,237		.06514	7.88
		13,644				17,609		
85 ''	16,332		.14355	4.74	33,628		.10766	5.67
		9,841				17,008		
90 ''	6,491		.20977	3.43	16,620		.17137	3.99
		4,891				11,358		
95 ''	1,600		.30027	2.45	5,262		.26132	2.76
		1,409				4,427		
100 ''	191		.41969	1.71	835		.38255	1.89

4.46 Expectation of life, 1951, 1961, 1966 and 1971 (years)

Age	1951		1961		1966		1971	
	Male	Female	Male	Female	Male	Female	Male	Female
At birth	66.33	70.83	68.35	74.17	68.75	75.18	69.34	76.36
1 year	68.33	72.33	69.50	74.98	69.53	75.71	69.76	76.56
2 years	67.56	71.55	68.63	74.11	68.64	74.81	68.85	75.64
3 ''	66.68	70.66	67.71	73.18	67.71	73.88	67.91	74.70
4 ''	65.79	69.74	66.78	72.23	66.77	72.93	66.97	73.74
5 ''	64.86	68.80	65.83	71.27	65.82	71.97	66.02	72.79
10 ''	60.15	64.02	61.02	66.41	61.00	67.12	61.17	67.91
15 ''	55.39	59.19	56.20	61.51	56.16	62.22	56.33	63.02
20 ''	50.76	54.41	51.51	56.65	51.50	57.37	51.71	58.18
25 ''	46.20	49.67	46.91	51.80	46.94	52.52	47.16	53.34
30 ''	41.60	44.94	42.24	46.98	42.29	47.68	42.50	48.51
35 ''	37.00	40.24	37.56	42.18	37.62	42.88	37.83	43.71
40 ''	32.45	35.63	32.96	37.45	33.01	38.15	33.22	38.99
45 ''	28.05	31.14	28.49	32.82	28.55	33.51	28.77	34.37
50 ''	23.88	26.80	24.25	28.33	24.31	29.02	24.52	29.86
55 ''	20.02	22.61	20.30	24.01	20.38	24.70	20.57	25.53
60 ''	16.49	18.64	16.73	19.90	16.81	20.58	16.95	21.39
65 ''	13.31	14.97	13.53	16.07	13.63	16.71	13.72	17.47
70 ''	10.41	11.62	10.67	12.58	10.83	13.14	10.90	13.85
75 ''	7.89	8.73	8.21	9.48	8.37	9.94	8.47	10.63
80 ''	5.84	6.38	6.14	6.90	6.36	7.26	6.41	7.88
85 ''	4.27	4.57	4.46	4.89	4.79	5.16	4.74	5.67
90 ''	3.10	3.24	3.16	3.39	3.60	3.60	3.43	3.99
95 ''	2.24	2.27	2.20	2.32	2.71	2.48	2.45	2.76
100 ''	1.60	1.59	1.49	1.56	2.04	1.69	1.71	1.89

4.47 Expectation of life at selected ages, by region or province, 1951, 1961, 1966 and 1971 (years)

Region or province and age	1951		1961		1966		1971	
	Male	Female	Male	Female	Male	Female	Male	Female
ATLANTIC PROVINCES								
At birth	66.57	70.50	68.58	73.92	..	..	..	..
1 year	69.08	72.41	70.06	75.10	..	..	..	..
20 years	51.59	54.52	52.17	56.82	..	..	..	..
40 ''	33.48	35.99	33.76	37.70	..	..	..	..
65 ''	13.90	15.42	14.16	16.35	..	..	..	..
NEWFOUNDLAND								
At birth	..	..	..	..	68.94	74.43	69.28	75.72
1 year	..	..	..	..	70.22	75.41	69.99	76.22
20 years	..	..	..	..	52.27	57.08	51.90	57.86
40 ''	..	..	..	..	33.78	37.83	33.22	38.58
65 ''	..	..	..	..	14.31	16.22	13.52	16.91

4.47   Expectation of life at selected ages, by region or province, 1951, 1961, 1966 and 1971 (years) (concluded)

Region or province and age	1951		1961		1966		1971	
	Male	Female	Male	Female	Male	Female	Male	Female
PRINCE EDWARD ISLAND								
At birth	..	..	..	..	68.32	75.51	69.30	77.35
1 year	..	..	..	..	69.43	76.22	70.10	77.64
20 years	..	..	..	..	51.56	57.88	52.04	59.36
40 "	..	..	..	..	33.49	38.77	33.83	39.96
65 "	..	..	..	..	14.43	17.57	14.40	18.41
NOVA SCOTIA								
At birth	..	..	..	..	68.34	74.80	68.66	75.97
1 year	..	..	..	..	69.16	75.43	69.05	76.13
20 years	..	..	..	..	51.32	57.16	51.02	57.77
40 "	..	..	..	..	32.99	37.96	32.80	38.50
65 "	..	..	..	..	13.80	16.75	13.58	17.14
NEW BRUNSWICK								
At birth	..	..	..	..	68.53	75.26	69.07	76.41
1 year	..	..	..	..	69.30	75.97	69.49	76.61
20 years	..	..	..	..	51.58	57.79	51.59	58.36
40 "	..	..	..	..	33.35	38.53	33.23	39.15
65 "	..	..	..	..	14.01	17.04	13.78	17.56
QUEBEC								
At birth	64.42	68.58	67.28	72.77	67.88	73.91	68.28	75.25
1 year	67.19	70.71	68.71	73.80	68.77	74.57	68.74	75.52
20 years	49.76	52.92	50.82	55.54	50.81	56.25	50.74	57.18
40 "	31.54	34.36	32.29	36.38	32.33	37.05	32.30	38.02
65 "	12.81	14.17	13.16	15.27	13.24	15.79	13.08	16.62
ONTARIO								
At birth	66.87	71.85	68.32	74.40	68.71	75.53	69.55	76.76
1 year	68.34	72.91	69.14	74.95	69.29	75.87	69.82	76.81
20 years	50.58	54.76	51.03	56.53	51.14	57.45	51.63	58.35
40 "	32.03	35.75	32.35	37.27	32.44	38.17	32.91	39.08
65 "	13.07	14.92	13.05	15.90	13.10	16.72	13.37	17.57
PRAIRIE PROVINCES								
At birth	68.36	72.28	69.79	75.66	..	..	..	..
1 year	69.90	73.43	70.96	76.40	..	..	..	..
20 years	52.24	55.53	52.90	58.08	..	..	..	..
40 "	33.86	36.63	34.37	38.83	..	..	..	..
65 "	13.88	15.51	14.22	17.00	..	..	..	..
MANITOBA								
At birth	..	..	..	..	69.80	76.11	70.16	76.93
1 year	..	..	..	..	70.54	76.57	70.60	77.21
20 years	..	..	..	..	52.48	58.25	52.67	58.88
40 "	..	..	..	..	34.11	39.10	34.18	39.66
65 "	..	..	..	..	14.18	17.42	14.32	18.02
SASKATCHEWAN								
At birth	..	..	..	..	70.45	76.45	71.05	77.59
1 year	..	..	..	..	71.49	77.06	71.76	77.98
20 years	..	..	..	..	53.50	58.80	53.82	59.62
40 "	..	..	..	..	35.22	39.61	35.59	40.51
65 "	..	..	..	..	15.00	17.59	15.44	18.54
ALBERTA								
At birth	..	..	..	..	70.10	76.24	70.42	77.30
1 year	..	..	..	..	70.82	76.72	70.90	77.52
20 years	..	..	..	..	52.70	58.30	52.94	59.17
40 "	..	..	..	..	34.36	39.09	34.60	40.06
65 "	..	..	..	..	14.46	17.34	14.64	18.24
BRITISH COLUMBIA								
At birth	66.73	72.37	68.94	75.42	69.21	75.84	69.85	76.69
1 year	67.97	73.32	69.83	76.00	69.94	76.33	70.26	76.85
20 years	˙50.41	55.51	51.85	57.61	51.91	58.01	52.29	58.53
40 "	32.45	36.72	33.56	38.46	33.70	38.93	34.10	39.49
65 "	13.50	15.86	13.98	16.94	14.20	17.41	14.50	18.00

4.48 Marriages and rate per 1,000 population, by province, with percentage distribution of bridegrooms and brides by birthplace, 1951, 1961, 1971 and 1973

Province or territory	Year	Total marriages	Rate per 1,000 population	Born in province where married		Born in other provinces		Born outside Canada	
				Grooms %	Brides %	Grooms %	Brides %	Grooms %	Brides %
Newfoundland	1951	2,517	7.0	85.2	96.7	2.4	1.9	12.4	1.4
	1961	3,306	7.2	88.0	97.2	3.8	1.6	8.2	1.2
	1971	4,685	9.0	91.6	95.3	4.2	3.3	4.2	1.4
	1973	5,048	9.3	91.3	95.4	5.2	3.1	3.5	1.5
Prince Edward Island	1951	583	5.9	82.3	91.1	12.9	6.0	4.8	2.9
	1961	624	6.0	81.7	89.6	15.4	7.2	2.9	3.2
	1971	961	8.6	78.9	88.1	17.4	9.5	3.7	2.4
	1973	1,014	8.8	80.2	88.2	16.3	9.7	3.5	2.1
Nova Scotia	1951	5,094	7.9	78.2	86.7	15.9	9.0	6.0	4.3
	1961	5,292	7.2	75.2	87.8	18.8	8.8	6.0	3.4
	1971	6,883	8.7	77.9	85.6	16.2	10.9	5.9	3.5
	1973	7,273	9.0	78.0	84.7	16.6	11.6	5.4	3.7
New Brunswick	1951	4,386	8.5	80.0	86.9	10.1	6.7	9.8	6.4
	1961	4,504	7.5	75.4	86.3	14.9	7.9	9.7	5.8
	1971	6,149	9.7	77.9	86.2	14.8	9.5	7.2	4.3
	1973	6,357	9.8	80.3	86.6	14.2	10.3	5.5	3.1
Quebec	1951	35,704	8.8	86.7	89.5	6.1	5.5	7.2	5.0
	1961	35,943	6.8	83.6	87.4	5.7	4.8	10.7	7.8
	1971	49,695	8.2	84.2	88.1	5.2	4.3	10.7	7.6
	1973	51,943	8.5	85.2	88.5	3.7	2.9	11.1	8.6
Ontario	1951	45,198	9.8	65.9	72.4	14.6	12.2	19.5	15.4
	1961	44,434	7.1	61.5	67.2	12.9	11.0	25.6	21.8
	1971	69,590	9.0	60.1	66.1	12.7	11.2	27.2	22.7
	1973	72,371	9.1	62.0	67.3	11.6	10.4	26.4	22.3
Manitoba	1951	7,366	9.5	67.9	75.1	15.4	13.3	16.8	11.6
	1961	6,512	7.1	66.6	74.5	18.5	14.5	14.8	11.0
	1971	9,127	9.2	67.1	75.2	17.7	13.8	15.1	11.0
	1973	9,196	9.2	68.3	74.8	17.0	14.1	14.7	11.1
Saskatchewan	1951	6,805	8.2	78.3	86.4	10.7	6.4	11.1	7.2
	1961	6,149	6.6	79.3	85.8	11.9	8.7	8.8	5.5
	1971	7,813	8.4	78.9	85.3	14.4	10.1	6.6	4.6
	1973	7,847	8.6	79.3	86.9	14.6	9.2	6.1	3.9
Alberta	1951	9,305	9.9	56.0	67.4	25.7	19.6	18.3	13.0
	1961	10,474	7.9	54.4	62.3	25.8	21.8	19.8	15.9
	1971	15,614	9.6	54.8	62.0	28.5	24.4	16.6	13.5
	1973	16,280	9.7	55.7	62.5	28.4	25.0	15.9	12.5
British Columbia	1951	11,272	9.7	35.5	41.6	43.1	43.0	21.3	15.5
	1961	10,964	6.7	36.4	45.9	35.9	32.4	27.7	21.8
	1971	20,389	9.3	43.1	50.5	32.1	29.3	24.9	20.3
	1973	21,303	9.2	43.7	50.5	32.4	29.3	23.9	20.2
Yukon Territory	1961	128	8.8	12.5	24.2	63.3	52.3	24.2	23.4
	1971	166	9.0	10.2	20.5	67.5	59.0	22.3	20.5
	1973	206	10.3	10.7	17.5	67.5	63.6	21.8	18.9
Northwest Territories	1961	145	6.3	54.5	61.4	35.9	31.7	9.7	6.9
	1971	252	7.2	41.3	55.6	43.3	33.3	15.5	11.1
	1973	226	5.9	29.2	45.6	58.0	42.9	12.8	11.5
Canada	1951[1]	128,230	9.2	70.5	76.5	15.1	12.8	14.5	10.6
	1961	128,475	7.0	67.9	74.2	14.3	11.7	17.9	14.1
	1971	191,324	8.9	67.2	73.2	14.5	12.3	18.3	14.5
	1973	199,064	9.0	68.5	73.1	13.7	11.7	17.8	15.2

[1]Excludes the Yukon Territory and Northwest Territories.

4.49 Brides and bridegrooms, by age and marital status, 1974

Age group	Brides							
	Number				Percentage			
	Spinsters	Widows	Divorced	Total	Spinsters	Widows	Divorced	Total
Under 15 years	105	—	—	105	0.1	—	—	0.1
15-19 "	53,510	15	71	53,596	31.1	0.2	0.4	27.0
20-24 "	87,610	209	2,277	90,096	50.9	2.7	11.9	45.1
25-29 "	20,403	350	5,235	25,988	11.9	4.6	27.4	13.1
30-34 "	4,717	416	3,697	8,830	2.7	5.4	19.4	4.4
35-39 "	1,776	453	2,485	4,714	1.0	5.9	13.0	2.4
40-44 "	847	575	1,874	3,296	0.5	7.5	9.8	1.7
45-49 "	605	876	1,536	3,017	0.4	11.4	8.1	1.5
50-54 "	402	1,118	979	2,499	0.2	14.6	5.1	1.3
55-59 "	245	1,053	451	1,749	0.1	13.8	2.4	0.9
60-64 "	176	1,041	201	1,418	0.1	13.6	1.1	0.7
65 years and over	134	1,465	110	1,709	0.1	19.2	0.6	0.9
Total, stated ages	170,530	7,571	18,916	197,017	99.1	98.9	99.2	99.1
Age not stated	1,577	82	148	1,807	0.9	1.1	0.8	0.9
Total, all ages	172,107	7,653	19,064	198,824	100.0	100.0	100.0	100.0
Average age yr	22.4	52.7	35.0	24.7	...	...	...	...

4.49   Brides and bridegrooms, by age and marital status, 1974 (concluded)

Age group	Bridegrooms							
	Number				Percentage			
	Bachelors	Widowers	Divorced	Total	Bachelors	Widowers	Divorced	Total
Under 15 years	—	—	—	—	—	—	—	—
15-19 "	15,598	2	7	15,607	9.1	- -	- -	7.8
20-24 "	95,562	46	800	96,408	56.1	0.7	3.8	48.5
25-29 "	40,831	157	4,339	45,327	23.9	2.3	20.4	22.8
30-34 "	9,639	222	4,668	14,529	5.6	3.2	21.8	7.3
35-39 "	3,158	257	3,364	6,779	1.9	3.8	15.8	3.4
40-44 "	1,684	417	2,687	4,788	1.0	6.1	12.6	2.4
45-49 "	1,014	593	2,099	3,706	0.6	8.7	9.9	1.9
50-54 "	667	800	1,478	2,945	0.4	11.7	6.9	1.5
55-59 "	409	940	843	2,192	0.2	13.7	4.0	1.1
60-64 "	270	1,052	524	1,846	0.2	15.4	2.5	0.9
65 years and over	235	2,314	340	2,889	0.1	33.7	1.6	1.5
Total, stated ages	169,067	6,800	21,149	197,016	99.1	99.3	99.3	99.1
Age not stated	1,611	51	146	1,808	0.9	0.7	0.7	0.9
Total, all ages	170,678	6,851	21,295	198,824	100.0	100.0	100.0	100.0
Average age yr	24.7	58.3	38.4	27.4	...	...	...	...

4.50   Marriages by religious denominations of brides and bridegrooms, 1974

Denomination of bridegroom	Denomination of bride										Total marriages	Percentage of grooms
	Angli-can	Bap-tist	East-ern Orth-odox	Jewish	Lu-ther-an	Pres-by-terian	Roman Catho-lic[1]	United Church	Other sects	Not stated		
Anglican	7,504	701	126	38	603	810	4,731	4,680	1,569	24	20,786	14.1
Baptist	710	2,222	18	6	124	200	992	1,050	581	6	5,909	4.0
Eastern Orthodox	174	37	1,232	4	67	35	436	274	230	1	2,490	1.7
Jewish	66	2	5	1,069	8	14	107	54	84	1	1,410	1.0
Lutheran	622	144	64	6	1,388	192	1,138	1,137	567	5	5,263	3.6
Presbyterian	932	179	28	8	180	1,485	1,205	1,231	385	4	5,637	3.8
Roman Catholic[1]	4,589	914	320	75	1,087	1,066	26,919	6,044	3,650	61	44,725	30.3
United Church	4,247	932	195	33	1,034	1,082	6,143	15,249	2,070	36	31,021	21.1
Other sects	2,061	643	180	89	725	531	4,399	2,865	18,020	26	29,539	20.1
Not stated	53	13	3	1	24	5	100	63	39	211	512	0.3
Total	20,958	5,787	2,171	1,329	5,240	5,420	46,170	32,647	27,195	375	147,292[2]	100.0
Percentage of brides	14.2	3.9	1.5	0.9	3.6	3.7	31.3	22.1	18.5	0.3	100.0	51.1[3]

[1]Includes Greek Catholic.
[2]Excludes 51,532 marriages in the province of Quebec.
[3]Percentage of marriages between persons of the same religious denomination.

4.51   Divorces[1] granted to male and female petitioners, by province, 1971-74

Province or territory	1971		1972		1973		1974	
	Male	Female	Male	Female	Male	Female	Male	Female
Newfoundland	62	88	61	116	84	140	90	211
Prince Edward Island	10	51	23	42	20	34	36	60
Nova Scotia	277	444	325	602	429	820	517	1,074
New Brunswick	183	299	182	284	189	385	295	460
Quebec	2,250	2,951	2,504	3,917	3,055	5,036	3,723	8,549
Ontario	4,559	7,646	4,823	8,360	5,087	8,694	5,747	9,530
Manitoba	503	880	489	924	535	1,085	594	1,202
Saskatchewan	300	515	296	530	298	589	369	670
Alberta	974	2,682	1,057	2,710	1,178	3,257	1,368	3,579
British Columbia	1,757	3,169	1,879	3,157	2,177	3,510	2,554	4,286
Yukon Territory	23	24	18	29	24	36	14	32
Northwest Territories	9	16	13	23	13	29	21	38
Canada	10,907	18,765	11,670	20,694	13,089	23,615	15,328	29,691

[1]Only those filed under the new divorce laws of July 2, 1968.

4.52 Alleged grounds for divorce[1] by type of offence, 1971-74

Alleged grounds	1971		1972		1973		1974	
	No.	%	No.	%	No.	%	No.	%
Marital offence								
Adultery	11,261	28.5	12,645	29.6	14,853	30.3	17,806	29.4
Physical cruelty	5,102	12.9	5,579	13.0	6,598	13.5	8,340	13.8
Mental cruelty	5,677	14.4	6,308	14.7	7,734	15.8	9,774	16.2
Other	176	0.4	152	0.4	142	0.3	174	0.3
Total	22,216	56.2	24,684	57.7	29,327	59.9	36,094	59.7
Marriage breakdown by reason of:								
Addiction to alcohol	856	2.2	859	2.0	1,032	2.1	1,607	2.7
Separation for not less than 3 years	13,874	35.1	14,803	34.6	16,197	33.1	20,415	33.8
Desertion by petitioner for not less than 5 years	1,988	5.0	1,919	4.5	1,806	3.7	1,778	2.9
Other	588	1.5	504	1.2	583	1.2	535	0.9
Total	17,306	43.8	18,085	42.3	19,618	40.1	24,335	40.3
Total, alleged grounds[2]	39,522	100.0	42,769	100.0	48,945	100.0	60,429	100.0

[1]See footnote to Table 4.51.
[2]Totals are higher than the numbers of divorces because some divorce decrees involve more than one alleged ground.

4.53 Divorces[1] by number of dependent children, 1971-74

Number of children	1971		1972		1973		1974	
	No.	%	No.	%	No.	%	No.	%
0	13,241	44.6	14,305	44.2	15,890	43.3	18,588	41.3
1	6,189	20.9	7,078	21.9	8,209	22.4	10,277	22.8
2	5,430	18.3	5,956	18.4	6,842	18.6	8,817	19.6
3	2,825	9.5	2,963	9.2	3,384	9.2	4,349	9.7
4	1,250	4.2	1,294	3.9	1,520	4.2	1,850	4.1
5 and more	737	2.5	768	2.4	859	2.3	1,138	2.5
Total, divorces	29,672	100.0	32,364	100.0	36,704	100.0	45,019	100.0
Average number of children	1.17	...	1.15	...	1.16	...	1.22	...

[1]See footnote to Table 4.51.

4.54 Divorces[1] by duration of marriage, 1971-74

Duration of marriage	1971		1972		1973		1974	
	No.	%	No.	%	No.	%	No.	%
Less than 1 year	75	0.3	84	0.3	99	0.3	105	0.2
1 year	472	1.6	524	1.6	645	1.8	716	1.6
2 years	931	3.1	1,022	3.2	1,165	3.2	1,457	3.2
3 "	1,258	4.2	1,465	4.5	1,712	4.7	2,019	4.5
4 "	1,638	5.5	1,948	6.0	2,152	5.9	2,794	6.2
Total, 1-4 years	4,299	14.4	4,959	15.3	5,674	15.6	6,986	15.5
5 years	1,687	5.7	2,020	6.2	2,403	6.5	2,797	6.3
6 "	1,586	5.3	1,924	5.9	2,237	6.1	2,730	6.1
7 "	1,468	4.9	1,717	5.3	2,146	5.8	2,674	5.9
8 "	1,471	5.0	1,523	4.7	1,900	5.2	2,356	5.2
9 "	1,270	4.3	1,465	4.5	1,664	4.5	2,129	4.7
Total, 5-9 years	7,482	25.2	8,649	26.7	10,350	28.1	12,686	28.2
10-14 years	5,631	18.9	5,905	18.2	6,490	17.7	8,164	18.1
15-19 "	4,290	14.5	4,442	13.7	4,930	13.4	5,923	13.2
20-24 "	3,438	11.6	3,518	10.9	3,896	10.6	4,755	10.6
25-29 "	2,307	7.8	2,445	7.6	2,734	7.4	3,263	7.3
30 years and over	2,123	7.2	2,323	7.2	2,502	6.8	3,034	6.7
Not stated	27	0.1	39	0.1	29	0.1	103	0.2
Total, divorces	29,672	100.0	32,364	100.0	36,704	100.0	45,019	100.0
Median duration of marriage	12.6	...	12.1	...	11.8	...	11.7	...

[1]See footnote to Table 4.51.

4.55 Divorces[1] by marital status of husband and wife at time of marriage, 1971-74

Marital status	1971		1972		1973		1974	
	No.	%	No.	%	No.	%	No.	%
Husband								
Single	27,525	92.8	30,151	93.2	34,205	93.2	42,120	93.6
Widowed	482	1.6	470	1.4	522	1.4	624	1.4
Divorced	1,662	5.6	1,739	5.4	1,973	5.4	2,268	5.0
Not stated	3	- -	4	- -	4	- -	7	- -
Total	29,672	100.0	32,364	100.0	36,704	100.0	45,019	100.0
Wife								
Single	27,236	91.8	29,914	92.4	33,972	92.6	41,799	92.9
Widowed	712	2.4	727	2.3	734	2.0	866	1.9
Divorced	1,723	5.8	1,722	5.3	1,997	5.4	2,349	5.2
Not stated	1	- -	1	- -	1	- -	5	- -

[1]See footnote to Table 4.51.

4.56 Immigrant arrivals, 1949-75

Year	Arrivals	Year	Arrivals	Year	Arrivals
1949	95,217	1958	124,851	1967	222,876
1950	73,912	1959	106,928	1968	183,974
1951	194,391	1960	104,111	1969	161,531
1952	164,498	1961	71,689	1970	147,713
1953	168,868	1962	74,586	1971	121,900
1954	154,227	1963	93,151	1972	122,006
1955	109,946	1964	112,606	1973	184,200
1956	164,857	1965	146,758	1974	218,465
1957	282,164	1966	194,743	1975	187,881

4.57 Immigrant arrivals, by country of last permanent residence, 1974 and 1975

Country of last permanent residence	1974	1975	Country of last permanent residence	1974	1975
Europe	88,694	72,898	Turkey	431	320
Austria	780	724	USSR	602	278
Belgium	613	656	Yugoslavia	3,200	2,932
British Isles	38,456	34,978	Other Europe	299	392
England	28,828	27,761	Africa	10,450	9,867
Northern Ireland	2,391	1,977	Egypt, Republic of	928	892
Scotland	6,259	4,182	Ghana	242	274
Wales	931	1,031	Kenya	2,394	2,477
Lesser Isles	47	27	Morocco	786	545
Czechoslovakia	77	107	Nigeria	332	263
Denmark	573	580	South Africa, Republic of	1,157	1,567
Finland	320	256	Tanzania	2,024	2,188
France	4,232	3,891	Uganda	423	112
Germany, Federal Republic of	3,619	3,469	Zambia	213	188
Greece	5,632	4,062	Other Africa	1,951	1,361
Hungary	383	301	Australasia	2,594	2,174
Ireland, Republic of	1,292	1,098	Australia	2,022	1,654
Italy	5,226	5,078	New Zealand	540	509
Malta	693	408	Other Australasia	32	11
Netherlands	2,103	1,448			
Norway	229	187	Asia	50,566	47,382
Poland	945	809	Bangladesh	158	104
Portugal	16,333	8,547	China	379	903
Spain	727	697	Cyprus	677	1,021
Sweden	593	408	Hong Kong	12,704	11,132
Switzerland	1,336	1,272	India	12,868	10,144

4.57   Immigrant arrivals, by country of last permanent residence, 1974 and 1975 (concluded)

Country of last permanent residence	1974	1975	Country of last permanent residence	1974	1975
Asia (concluded)			St. Kitts, Nevis	118	105
Indonesia	213	188	St. Vincent	487	350
Iran	243	205	Trinidad and Tobago	4,802	3,817
Iraq	81	41	United States	26,541	20,155
Israel	1,090	1,527	Other North and Central		
Japan	859	635	America	1,315	1,115
Jordan	254	216			
Korea, South	2,843	4,316	South America	*12,528*	*13,270*
Lebanon	1,762	1,506	Argentina	1,593	1,567
Malaysia	605	461	Bolivia	38	65
Pakistan	2,315	2,165	Brazil	560	531
Philippines	9,564	7,364	Chile	1,884	2,297
Singapore	405	442	Colombia	1,037	1,046
Sri Lanka	527	369	Ecuador	1,841	1,698
Syria	314	246	French Guiana	5	1
Taiwan	1,382	1,131	Guyana	4,030	4,394
Viet-Nam, South	373	2,269	Paraguay	250	252
Other Asia	950	997	Peru	418	494
North and Central America	*51,817*	*39,638*	Surinam	18	74
Antigua	202	145	Uruguay	659	661
Bahamas	129	169	Venezuela	195	190
Barbados	790	782	Oceania	*1,816*	*2,652*
Bermuda	215	173	Fiji	1,530	2,323
Grenada	399	340	Mauritius	247	253
Haiti	4,857	3,431	Other Oceania	39	76
Jamaica	11,286	8,211	Total, all countries	218,465	187,881
Mexico	676	845			

4.58   Immigrant arrivals, by country of citizenship, 1974 and 1975

Country of citizenship	1974	1975	Country of citizenship	1974	1975
Australia	1,621	1,358	New Zealand	568	457
Austria	366	291	Norway	211	188
Belgium	354	332	Pakistan	2,627	2,520
Britain and colonies	48,023	40,495	Philippines	9,704	7,576
Central America	571	556	Poland	1,074	935
China	3,635	1,166	Portugal	17,609	9,530
Czechoslovakia	148	161	South Africa	952	1,272
Denmark	536	494	South America	11,970	12,790
Egypt	995	954	Spain	717	646
Finland	363	301	Sri Lanka	659	536
France	3,048	3,196	Sweden	497	395
Germany, Federal Republic of	2,654	2,387	Switzerland	1,003	902
Greece	5,702	4,032	Trinidad and Tobago	4,872	3,936
Haiti	5,035	3,533	Turkey	480	383
Hungary	482	432	Union of Soviet Socialist		
India	14,264	11,600	Republics	252	230
Ireland, Republic of	1,652	1,495	United States	25,121	18,912
Israel	1,082	1,668	Yugoslavia	4,061	3,676
Italy	5,820	4,940	Other African	6,471	5,861
Jamaica	11,471	8,519	Other Asian	8,851	10,786
Japan	810	587	Other European	889	757
Lebanon	1,530	1,227	Stateless	3,724	8,643
Mexico	629	776	Other	2,534	4,357
Morrocco	828	625			
Netherlands	2,000	1,468	Total	218,465	187,881

4.59   Intended province of destination of male and female immigrants, 1974 and 1975

Province or territory	1974			1975		
	Male	Female	Total	Male	Female	Total
Newfoundland	506	530	1,036	606	500	1,106
Prince Edward Island	138	173	311	118	117	235
Nova Scotia	1,314	1,287	2,601	1,071	1,053	2,124
New Brunswick	1,129	1,078	2,207	1,044	1,049	2,093
Quebec	17,512	15,946	33,458	14,441	13,601	28,042
Ontario	60,622	59,493	120,115	48,021	50,450	98,471
Manitoba	3,545	3,878	7,423	3,560	3,574	7,134
Saskatchewan	1,157	1,087	2,244	1,360	1,477	2,837
Alberta	7,347	6,942	14,289	8,349	7,928	16,277
British Columbia	17,690	16,791	34,481	13,970	15,302	29,272
Yukon Territory and Northwest Territories	162	138	300	143	147	290
Canada	111,122	107,343	218,465	92,683	95,198	187,881

4.60   Sex distribution of immigrants, 1971-75

Year	Male	Female	Total
1971	60,444	61,456	121,900
1972	60,070	61,936	122,006
1973	94,768	89,432	184,200
1974	111,122	107,343	218,465
1975	92,683	95,198	187,881

4.61   Marital status of immigrant arrivals, by sex and age group, 1974 and 1975

Sex and age group	Single		Married		Widowed		Divorced		Separated		Total	
	1974	1975	1974	1975	1974	1975	1974	1975	1974	1975	1974	1975
Male												
0- 4 years	9,528	8,523	—	—	—	—	—	—	—	—	9,528	8,523
5- 9 ,,	10,620	9,907	—	—	—	—	—	—	—	—	10,620	9,907
10-14 ,,	7,802	7,748	—	—	—	—	—	—	—	—	7,802	7,748
15-19 ,,	7,194	6,570	54	88	—	—	—	—	—	1	7,248	6,659
20-24 ,,	13,279	8,691	3,681	3,210	4	—	28	14	36	11	17,028	11,926
25-29 ,,	10,832	7,564	10,730	9,280	13	7	196	118	143	92	21,914	17,061
30-34 ,,	3,302	2,287	9,715	8,099	20	9	222	209	142	76	13,401	10,680
35-39 ,,	1,070	740	7,008	5,896	18	12	201	142	88	69	8,385	6,859
40-44 ,,	452	267	4,113	3,293	20	18	117	114	83	36	4,785	3,728
45-49 ,,	178	117	2,707	2,008	30	24	85	64	55	34	3,055	2,247
50-54 ,,	91	66	1,819	1,393	34	42	59	52	33	31	2,036	1,584
55-59 ,,	50	31	1,181	898	67	70	32	21	20	6	1,350	1,026
60-64 ,,	47	32	1,453	1,762	110	175	27	15	11	13	1,648	1,997
65-69 ,,	38	23	998	1,175	130	187	18	17	7	13	1,191	1,415
70 years +	38	35	762	883	295	381	21	14	15	10	1,131	1,323
Total, male	64,521	52,601	44,221	37,985	741	925	1,006	780	633	392	111,122	92,683
Female												
0- 4 years	8,978	8,102	—	—	—	—	—	—	—	—	8,978	8,102
5- 9 ,,	9,800	9,362	—	5	—	—	—	—	—	—	9,800	9,362
10-14 ,,	7,359	7,475	4	5	—	—	—	—	—	—	7,363	7,480
15-19 ,,	6,839	6,137	1,604	1,721	—	—	2	1	5	1	8,450	7,860
20-24 ,,	9,713	6,523	9,671	9,030	9	8	57	51	68	30	19,518	15,642
25-29 ,,	6,135	4,197	12,331	11,303	31	24	234	187	150	68	18,881	15,779
30-34 ,,	2,047	1,260	8,176	7,416	55	35	239	203	120	63	10,637	8,977
35-39 ,,	920	437	5,091	4,449	84	49	198	146	104	38	6,397	5,119
40-44 ,,	450	216	2,996	2,600	139	131	135	111	75	49	3,795	3,107
45-49 ,,	284	138	2,168	1,818	250	327	125	88	88	36	2,915	2,407
50-54 ,,	195	115	1,690	1,564	513	597	122	86	86	52	2,606	2,414
55-59 ,,	149	82	1,257	1,368	695	842	65	74	70	34	2,236	2,400
60-64 ,,	147	107	1,116	1,317	842	1,054	62	87	59	61	2,226	2,626
65-69 ,,	106	102	622	663	806	912	36	53	41	47	1,611	1,777
70 years +	231	123	373	395	1,264	1,561	38	45	24	22	1,930	2,146
Total, female	53,353	44,376	47,099	43,649	4,688	5,540	1,313	1,132	890	501	107,343	95,198

4.62   Intended occupations of immigrants, 1973-75

Intended occupation	1973r	1974	1975
WORKERS			
Managerial and administrative	*5,993*	*6,445*	*5,763*
Government administrators	75	70	65
Managerial (owners, managers, officials)	4,361	4,752	4,102
Other	1,557	1,623	1,596
Professional and technical			
Natural sciences, engineering and mathematics	*7,358*	*8,705*	*8,928*
Physical sciences			
Chemists	408	329	245
Geologists and related	168	145	102
Physicists	130	119	95
Other	600	491	384
Life sciences			
Agriculturists and related scientists	95	115	119
Biologists and related scientists	318	307	262
Other	53	86	86
Architects and engineers			
Architects	111	175	218
Engineers			
Chemical	217	233	207
Civil	401	509	530
Electrical	439	522	517
Industrial	186	157	129
Mechanical	452	427	379
Metallurgical	40	26	18
Mining	35	46	42
Petroleum	31	23	25
Aerospace	56	30	28
Nuclear	3	10	9
Other	113	75	81

4.62 Intended occupations of immigrants, 1973-75 (continued)

Intended occupation	1973r	1974	1975
WORKERS (continued)			
Architecture and engineering			
Surveyors	149	118	112
Draughtsmen	1,000	1,551	2,005
Other	1,495	2,171	2,444
Mathematics, statistics, and systems analysis			
Mathematicians, statisticians and actuaries	170	141	110
Systems analysts	686	897	781
Other	2	2	–
Social sciences	1,395	1,290	1,075
Economists	301	241	244
Sociologists and anthropologists	76	51	32
Psychologists	157	139	90
Other	185	146	122
Social work			
Social workers	320	294	222
Other	59	130	112
Law and jurisprudence	131	140	124
Library, museum and archival sciences			
Librarians and archivists	139	125	113
Other	27	24	16
Religion	521	504	409
Teaching	3,483	3,289	2,613
University	1,337	1,100	766
Elementary and secondary	1,513	1,543	1,290
Other	633	646	557
Medicine and health	5,281	6,349	5,604
Health diagnosing and treating			
Physicians and surgeons	1,153	1,081	806
Dentists	70	83	83
Veterinarians	77	64	69
Osteopaths and chiropractors	10	8	8
Other	10	11	16
Nursing and therapy			
Supervisors of nurses	19	11	9
Graduate nurses (except supervisors)	1,389	1,702	1,839
Physiotherapists	281	331	334
Other	1,117	1,745	1,392
Other medicine and health			
Pharmacists	88	65	75
Optometrists	8	7	7
Other	1,059	1,241	966
Artistic, literary and performing arts	1,492	1,462	1,192
Advertising and illustrating artists	116	124	100
Fine and commercial art and photography	576	591	492
Performing and audiovisual arts	477	451	344
Writers and editors, publication	199	187	133
Writers and editors, radio, television, theatre and motion pictures	19	31	17
Other	105	78	106
Sport and recreation	130	135	116
Clerical and related	13,451	15,660	11,803
Stenographic and typing	5,125	6,251	4,340
Bookkeeping and accounting	3,352	3,356	2,618
Office machine and electronic data-processing equipment operators	709	731	600
Material recording, scheduling and distributing	720	895	532
Library, file and correspondence clerks	261	224	187
Reception, information, mail and message distribution	421	524	430
Other	2,863	3,679	3,096
Sales	4,017	4,119	3,294
Commodities	3,363	3,450	2,779
Services	534	566	435
Other	120	103	80
Services	10,277	10,604	7,082
Protective	271	386	388
Food and beverage preparation	3,447	4,053	3,034
Lodging and other accommodation	414	408	187
Personal	4,819	3,761	2,322
Apparel and furnishings	143	289	130
Other	1,183	1,707	1,021
Farming, horticultural and animal-husbandry	3,079	2,637	1,511
Farmers	127	98	53
Farm management	94	74	44
Other	2,858	2,465	1,414
Fishing, hunting and trapping	64	50	27
Forestry and logging	157	243	144
Mining and quarrying, including oil and gas field	163	233	178

4.62 Intended occupations of immigrants, 1973-75 (concluded)

Intended occupation	1973r	1974	1975
WORKERS (concluded)			
Processing	*2,190*	*3,075*	*1,689*
Mineral ore treating	78	92	58
Metal processing	273	444	257
Clay, glass and stone processing	130	132	60
Chemicals, petroleum, rubber and plastic processing	54	94	73
Food and beverage processing	980	997	629
Wood processing (except paper pulp)	172	507	121
Pulp and paper making	27	41	23
Textile processing	443	716	443
Other	33	52	25
Machining and related	*5,457*	*7,603*	*5,178*
Metal machining	1,676	3,403	2,354
Metal shaping (except machining)	3,481	3,844	2,598
Wood machining	137	135	99
Clay, glass and stone machining	70	65	39
Other	93	156	88
Product fabricating, assembling and repairing	*13,427*	*15,466*	*11,936*
Metal products	194	410	285
Electrical and electronic equipment	1,414	1,539	1,566
Wood products	665	760	497
Textile, fur and leather products	5,746	5,658	3,721
Rubber, plastic and related products	161	209	171
Other, including mechanics and repairmen (n.e.c.)	5,247	6,890	5,696
Construction	*7,053*	*8,476*	*5,893*
Excavating, grading and paving	256	406	241
Electrical power linemen	31	35	52
Electricians and repairmen	774	820	648
Wire communications and electric power lighting equipment, installing and repairing	147	246	317
Carpenters	1,836	1,872	1,167
Brick and stone masons and tile setters	1,054	914	658
Concrete finishing	134	162	98
Plasterers	124	144	84
Painters and paperhangers	615	618	412
Roofing and waterproofing	32	57	36
Pipefitting and plumbing	452	494	383
Structural-metal erectors	42	65	64
Glaziers	20	25	35
Other	1,536	2,618	1,698
Transport equipment operating	*1,065*	*1,315*	*1,055*
Air	97	117	131
Railway	18	14	11
Water	134	167	168
Motor	813	1,012	742
Other	3	5	3
Material-handling and related (n.e.c.)	*727*	*1,119*	*694*
Other crafts and equipment operating	*599*	*668*	*489*
Printing and related	455	514	373
Stationary engine and utilities equipment operating	68	80	46
Electronic and related communications equipment operating	42	45	31
Other	34	29	39
Not stated and unknown	*4,849*	*6,636*	*4,516*
Total, workers	92,228	106,083	81,189
NON-WORKERS			
Spouses	27,530	32,470	30,175
Children	44,149	61,008	56,722
Other	20,293	18,904	19,795
Total, non-workers	91,972	112,382	106,692
Total, immigrants	184,200	218,465	187,881

4.63 Canadian-born persons entering the United States from Canada and elsewhere, and total persons entering the United States from Canada, years ended June 30, 1966-75[1]

Year	Entering US from Canada		Canadian-born entering US from elsewhere	Year	Entering US from Canada		Canadian-born entering US from elsewhere
	Canadian-born	Total			Canadian-born	Total	
1966	27,707	37,273	651	1971	12,847	22,709	281
1967	22,729	34,768	713	1972	10,543	18,596	233
1968	27,189	41,716	473	1973	8,680	14,800	271
1969	18,196	29,303	386	1974	7,297	12,301	357
1970	13,466	26,850	338	1975	6,969	11,215	339

[1]Includes only persons who have declared their intention of remaining permanently in the US when applying for a visa.

4.64 Internal migration of Canadian-born population, by province of birth and by province of residence, 1971 (thousands)

Province or territory of birth	Province or territory of residence, 1971											Total (place of birth)
	Nfld.	PEI	NS	NB	Que.	Ont.	Man.	Sask.	Alta.	BC	YT and NWT	
Newfoundland	496	1	17	4	7	60	2	1	2	5	- -	594
Prince Edward Island	- -	95	7	5	3	20	1	1	3	3	- -	139
Nova Scotia	4	4	661	26	21	116	5	3	12	21	- -	874
New Brunswick	2	3	20	539	49	81	3	2	7	12	- -	718
Quebec	3	1	10	16	5,303	252	9	6	18	31	1	5,650
Ontario	5	3	24	15	137	5,210	40	27	60	107	2	5,630
Manitoba	- -	- -	3	2	14	91	702	36	53	107	2	1,011
Saskatchewan	- -	- -	3	1	8	81	53	710	145	178	3	1,183
Alberta	- -	- -	3	2	7	43	13	20	1,003	162	6	1,260
British Columbia	- -	- -	3	1	7	39	8	9	41	1,056	5	1,170
Yukon Territory and Northwest Territories	- -	- -	- -	- -	2	4	1	1	3	4	28	43
Total (place of residence)	513	108	752	611	5,559	5,996	837	815	1,346	1,688	48	18,273

4.65 Population 5 years and over, by migration status for the period 1966-71, by province, 1971

Migration status (based on residence as at June 1, 1966)	Province of residence as at June 1, 1971									
	Nfld.		PEI		NS		NB		Que.	
	'000	%	'000	%	'000	%	'000	%	'000	%
Non-migrants	380	82.7	81	80.7	575	80.6	468	81.5	4,417	79.7
Non-movers[1]	303	65.9	67	66.5	435	61.0	355	61.9	3,063	55.3
Movers within same municipality	77	16.8	14	14.2	140	19.6	113	19.6	1,354	24.4
Migrants[2]	79	17.3	20	19.3	138	19.4	106	18.5	1,125	20.3
Within same province	56	12.1	8	8.2	69	9.7	53	9.2	836	15.1
From different province	13	3.0	9	8.4	46	6.5	37	6.4	78	1.4
From outside Canada	4	0.9	2	1.5	13	1.8	9	1.6	138	2.5
Province of residence in 1966 not stated	6	1.3	1	1.3	10	1.4	7	1.3	73	1.3
Total[3]	459	100.0	101	100.0	713	100.0	574	100.0	5,542	100.0

Migration status	Ont.		Man.		Sask.		Alta.		BC		YT and NWT		Canada	
	'000	%	'000	%	'000	%	'000	%	'000	%	'000	%	'000	%
Non-migrants	5,291	75.0	702	78.0	670	79.1	1,073	72.8	1,313	65.5	27	58.8	14,996	76.1
Non-movers[1]	3,579	50.7	488	54.2	499	58.9	715	48.5	857	42.7	11	24.2	10,371	52.6
Movers within same municipality	1,712	24.3	214	23.8	171	20.2	358	24.3	456	22.8	16	34.6	4,625	23.5
Migrants[2]	1,765	25.0	198	22.0	177	20.9	401	27.2	693	34.5	19	41.2	4,721	23.9
Within same province	995	14.1	98	10.9	119	14.0	190	12.9	340	16.9	2	5.0	2,766	14.0
From different province	241	3.4	57	6.3	36	4.3	128	8.6	194	9.7	12	26.8	852	4.3
From outside Canada	439	6.2	32	3.5	12	1.4	60	4.1	115	5.7	2	4.0	824	4.2
Province of residence in 1966 not stated	90	1.3	12	1.3	10	1.2	23	1.6	44	2.2	3	5.4	279	1.4
Total[3]	7,055	100.0	900	100.0	846	100.0	1,474	100.0	2,006	100.0	46	100.0	19,717	100.0

[1]Persons living in same dwelling as at June 1, 1966 and June 1, 1971.
[2]Persons whose residence as at June 1, 1971 was in a different municipality than as at June 1, 1966.
[3]Excludes persons in the Armed Forces or in other government service, stationed outside Canada.

4.66   Migrant[1] population 5 years and over, by type and locality of residence in 1966 and 1971

Locality of residence in 1966	Locality of residence in 1971				Total migrants (by residence in 1966)
	Census metropolitan areas[2]	Other urban localities	Rural localities[3]		
			Predominantly non-farm	Predominantly farm	
	Number (thousands)				
Census metropolitan areas[2]	1,220	297	202	64	1,783
Other urban localities	417	347	197	61	1,023
Rural localities[3]					
Predominantly non-farm	196	201	125	38	560
Predominantly farm	71	82	35	28	217
Outside of Canada	666	99	47	12	824
Residence in 1966 not stated	168	81	51	15	315
Total migrants (by residence in 1971)	2,738	1,107	657	218	4,720
	Percentage distribution (residence in 1966)				
Census metropolitan areas[2]	44.6	26.8	30.7	29.3	37.8
Other urban localities	15.2	31.4	30.0	28.1	21.7
Rural localities[3]					
Predominantly non-farm	7.1	18.1	19.1	17.3	11.9
Predominantly farm	2.6	7.6	5.3	12.9	4.6
Outside of Canada	24.3	8.9	7.1	5.4	17.4
Residence in 1966 not stated	6.1	7.3	7.8	6.9	6.7
Total migrants (by residence in 1971)	100.0	100.0	100.0	100.0	100.0
	Percentage distribution (residence in 1971)				
Census metropolitan areas[2]	68.4	16.6	11.3	3.6	100.0
Other urban localities	40.8	34.0	19.3	6.0	100.0
Rural localities[3]					
Predominantly non-farm	35.0	35.9	22.4	6.8	100.0
Predominantly farm	32.8	38.1	16.1	13.0	100.0
Outside of Canada	80.9	12.0	5.7	1.4	100.0
Residence in 1966 not stated	53.3	25.6	16.3	4.8	100.0
Total migrants (by residence in 1971)	58.0	23.5	13.9	4.6	100.0

[1]See footnote 2, Table 4.65.
[2]As defined for the 1971 Census (see text in Section 4.2.1).
[3]Rural figures exclude a very small part of the rural population living within the fringe boundaries of census metropolitan areas. Predominantly farm localities are those municipalities in which the majority of the population live on farms (as defined in the 1971 Census of Agriculture). The converse is true of predominantly non-farm localities.

Sources

4.1 - 4.3, 4.63 Population Estimates and Projections Division, Content and Analysis Branch, Census and Household Surveys Field, Statistics Canada.

4.4 - 4.21, 4.23 - 4.31, 4.64 - 4.66 Characteristics Division, Content and Analysis Branch, Census and Household Surveys Field, Statistics Canada.

4.22 Program Statistics Division, Indian and Eskimo Affairs Program, Department of Indian Affairs and Northern Development.

4.32 - 4.55 Health Division, Institutional and Public Finance Statistics Branch, Institutions and Agriculture Statistics Field, Statistics Canada.

4.56 - 4.62 Canada Immigration Division, Department of Manpower and Immigration.

Health

Chapter 5

Health

Chapter 5

Federal health services

Under the British North America Act, responsibility for administration of health services is the direct concern of provincial governments, with municipalities sometimes exercising considerable influence over matters delegated to them by provincial legislatures. Although patterns of health services in the provinces are similar, their organization, system of financing, and administration vary.

On the national level, the Department of National Health and Welfare is the chief federal agency responsible for the promotion, preservation, and restoration of the health of Canadians, and for social security and social welfare, in conjunction with other federal agencies and provincial and local services. The health side of the department is organized into five branches.

The Health Protection Branch provides services to protect the public from health hazards of all types. It is composed of eight organizational units: Foods, Drugs, Environmental Health, Non-medical Use of Drugs, Laboratory Centre for Disease Control, Field Operations, Planning and Evaluation, and Administration.

The Health Programs Branch administers federal aspects of Canada's two major health programs, hospital and medical insurance; supports health-care-delivery-system and resource development; undertakes health promotion; and both supports and conducts research. This branch is made up of the following units: Policy Development and Coordination, Health Insurance and Resources, Research Programs, Health Standards, Health Consultants and Finance and Management Services.

The Medical Services Branch has direct responsibility for the health care and public health services of Indians and Inuit and of all residents of the Yukon Territory and Northwest Territories, as well as for quarantine and immigration medical services, public service health, a national prosthetics service, and civil aviation medicine.

The Fitness and Amateur Sport Branch encourages, promotes, and develops fitness and amateur sport by enhancing the competitive excellence of Canada's athletes and by encouraging participation in activities oriented to fitness and recreation.

The Long Range Health Planning Branch is concerned with assessing the orientation of health services and the organization of resources.

Other federal agencies carry out specialized health functions; for example, Statistics Canada is responsible for gathering vital and other health statistics, the Department of Veterans Affairs administers hospitals and health services for war veterans, and the Canada Department of Agriculture has certain responsibilities connected with health aspects of food production.

Health care

Public medical care. The Medical Care Act was passed by Parliament in December 1966 and federal contributions to participating provinces became payable from July 1, 1968. As at April 1, 1972 all provinces and territories had entered the federal program. Under the act, federal government contributions to the provinces are based on half of the per capita cost of the insured services of the national program furnished under the plans of all provinces, excluding administration, multiplied by the number of insured persons in each province. The minimum criteria to be met are described in the following paragraphs.

Comprehensive coverage must be provided for all medically required services rendered by a physician or surgeon. There can be no dollar limit or exclusion except on the ground that the service was not medically required. The federal program includes not only those services that have been traditionally covered as benefits to a greater or lesser extent by the health insurance industry, but also those preventive and curative services that have been traditionally covered through the public sector in each province, such as medical care of patients in mental and tuberculosis hospitals and services of a preventive nature provided to individuals by physicians in public health agencies.

The plan must be universally available to all eligible residents and cover at least 95% of the total eligible provincial population (in fact the plans cover over 99% of those eligible). A "uniform terms and conditions" clause is intended to ensure that all residents have access to coverage and to prevent discrimination in premiums on account of previous health, age, non-membership in a group, or other considerations. If a premium system of financing is selected, subsidization in whole or in part for low-income groups is permitted. It has been left to the individual province to determine whether its residents should be insured on a voluntary or compulsory basis. Utilization charges at the time of service are not precluded by the federal legislation if they do not impede, either by their amount or by the manner of their application, reasonable access to necessary medical care, particularly for low-income groups. The plan must provide portability of benefit coverage when the insured resident is temporarily absent from the province and when moving residence to another participating province. The provincial medical care insurance plan must be administered on a non-profit basis by a public authority that is accountable to the provincial government for its financial transactions. It is permissible for provinces to assign certain administrative functions to private agencies.

These criteria leave substantial flexibility with each province to determine its own administrative arrangements for the operation of its medical care insurance plan and to choose the way in which it will be financed, i.e. through premiums, sales tax, other provincial revenues, or by a combination of methods. Federal contributions to the provinces under this program totalled $763 million in the fiscal year 1974-75.

Provincial programs providing health care services (apart from those already insured under the Medical Care Act) for welfare recipients establishing eligibility on the basis of financial need are supported financially by the federal program known as the Canada Assistance Plan. This program provides for federal payment of half the cost of personal health care services, as well as welfare services. The provinces are free to make available a wide range of health care benefits.

Hospital insurance. Provincial hospital insurance programs, operating in all provinces and territories since 1961, cover 99% of the population of Canada. Under the Hospital Insurance and Diagnostic Services Act of 1957, the federal government shares with the provinces the cost of providing specified hospital services to patients insured by these programs. Specifically excluded are tuberculosis hospitals and sanatoria, hospitals or institutions for the mentally ill, and institutions providing custodial care. The methods of administering and financing the program in each province and the provision of services above the stipulated minimum required by the act are left to the province.

Insured in-patient services must include accommodation, meals, necessary nursing service, diagnostic procedures, most pharmaceuticals, the use of operating rooms, case rooms, anaesthesia facilities, and radiotherapy and physiotherapy if available. Similar out-patient services may be included in provincial plans and authorized for contribution under the act. All provinces include a fairly comprehensive range of out-patient services. The Government of Canada contributes to each province out of the Consolidated Revenue Fund the sum of 25% of the per capita cost of in-patient services in Canada and 25% of the per capita cost of in-patient services in the province, multiplied by the average number of insured persons in that province. Thus, the total contribution is about 50% of the sharable cost for all Canada, but the proportion of federal support is higher in provinces where the per capita cost is below the national average and lower in the other provinces. Contributions for insured out-patient services in each province are paid in the same proportion as the contributions to the cost for in-patients.

Under the Established Programs (Interim Arrangements) Act, a province could, prior to October 31, 1965, have contracted out of various federal-provincial programs, including hospital insurance, and on January 1, 1965, Quebec did so. Accordingly, the federal contribution to the Quebec hospital insurance program is made through tax abatement and not under the Hospital Insurance Act. Federal payments to the provinces (including Quebec) under this program for the fiscal year 1974-75 amounted to $1,828 million.

Health resources fund. The Health Resources Fund Act of 1966 provided a fund of $500 million over a 15-year period (1966-80) for financial assistance in the planning, acquisition, construction, renovation, and equipping of health training and research facilities. Up to 50% of eligible costs of approved projects are supported by federal contributions. Of the total amount, $400 million is allocated to provinces on a per capita basis, $25 million is further allocated to the Atlantic provinces for joint projects, and $75 million for support of health training and research projects of national significance.

Professional training grant. The program includes the administration of the Professional Training Grant, which provides assistance to the provinces in an extended program for the training of health and hospital personnel.

Community health. The federal community health program is aimed at promoting lifestyles that will improve personal health, and at developing comprehensive community health services readily accessible to all Canadians. The Health Promotion Division of the Health Consultants Directorate develops health-promotion and education services as essential components of community health services, seeks to increase public awareness of health responsibilities, and works with health agencies to improve personal health.

The Community Health Division of the directorate is concerned with consulting, planning, developing, and evaluating community health services and centres. The main thrust is to promote community health services as identified in the Castonguay-Nepveu Report, the Manitoba White Paper, the Hastings Report, and others; to facilitate coordination of community health-services planning; and to encourage shifts in emphasis from institutional care to ambulatory care, and from curative services to health-promotional and preventive services.

Health services for specific groups. Through its Medical Services Branch, the Department of National Health and Welfare provides or arranges for several types of medical and health service for persons whose care is by custom or legislation a federal responsibility.

Indians, as residents of a province or territory, are entitled to the benefits of medical care and hospital insurance. These insured benefits are supplemented by Medical Services, which assists Indian bands in arranging for transportation and in obtaining drugs and prostheses. Emphasis is placed on a comprehensive public health program which provides dental care for children, immunization, school health services, health education, and prenatal, postnatal and well-baby clinics. Through direct financial assistance to organizations of native peoples, support is given to Indian programs directed toward improving the quality of life by means of adult education, family planning, accident prevention, venereal disease control programs, and the suppression of alcoholism and drug abuse. Since Indians comprise only 1% of the Canadian population and are distributed widely throughout Canada, a network of specially designed health facilities has been constructed in almost 200 communities that would otherwise lack health facilities. Approximately 51 of these are nursing stations, 100 are health centres, 46 are out-patient clinics, and nine are hospitals.

Increasing numbers of Indians are being trained and employed in the public health and medical care programs to facilitate understanding and health activities in local communities.

With the exception of insured hospital and medical care programs, administered by the Yukon and Northwest Territories governments, the Department of National Health and Welfare manages health services for all residents of the two northern territories. These comprise all normal health department activities including a comprehensive public health program, special arrangements to facilitate inter-station communication, and the transportation of patients from isolated communities to referral medical centres. Several university groups have interests in delineated zones for providing, on a rotation basis, medical personnel and students. Their activities are supported financially through government contracts and medical care insurance. Departmental facilities include four hospitals, two nursing stations, five health stations, and 10 health centres in the Yukon Territory and four hospitals, 39 nursing stations, seven health stations and seven health centres in the Northwest Territories.

Under the Quarantine Act, all vessels, aircraft, and other conveyances and their crews and passengers arriving in Canada from foreign countries are subject to inspection by quarantine officers to detect and correct conditions that could lead to the entry into Canada of such diseases as smallpox, cholera, plague, and yellow fever. Fully organized quarantine stations are located at all major seaports and airports. The branch is responsible for enforcing standards of hygiene on federal property including ports and terminals, interprovincial means of transport, and Canadian ships and aircraft.

Under the Department of National Health and Welfare Act and the Immigration Act, the Medical Services Branch determines in Canada and other countries the health status of all persons referred to them by the Department of Manpower and Immigration for Canadian immigration purposes and, additionally, provides or arranges health care services for certain persons after arrival in Canada, including immigrants who become ill en route to their destination or while seeking employment.

The Medical Services Branch is responsible for a comprehensive occupational health program for federal employees throughout the country and abroad. This service includes health counselling, surveillance of the occupational and working environment, pre-employment, periodic and special examinations, first aid and emergency treatment, and a wide range of advisory services and special health programs.

The department provides an advisory service to the Ministry of Transport concerning the health and safety of all those involved in Canadian civil aviation. Regional and headquarters aviation medical officers review all medical examinations, participate in aviation safety programs, and assist in air accident investigations. Close liaison with authorities responsible for foreign aviation medicine is maintained as standards are usually based upon international agreements.

Prosthetic Services make available high quality services in prosthetic and orthotic rehabilitation under the terms of agreements with most provinces and with the Department of Veterans Affairs, and provide a national focal point for related expertise.

Medical Services physicians provide an assessment and advisory service to the Unemployment Insurance Commission in relation to claims for benefits under the Sickness and Maternity Benefit Plan. The Canada Pension Plan maintains its own disability assessment service.

Emergency Health Services prepares plans to ensure that the health component of the department is able to continue operating in the event or threat of nuclear attack and to advise, assist and stimulate provincial and municipal health departments in planning for both peacetime and wartime emergencies.

Health protection   5.1.2

The Health Protection Branch is responsible for developing an integrated program to protect the public against unsafe foods, drugs, cosmetics, and medical and radiation emitting devices; harmful microbial agents and technological and social environments deleterious to health; environmental pollutants and contaminants of all kinds; and fraudulent drugs and devices.

The branch contains six operational directorates — Foods, Drugs, Environmental Health, Laboratory Centre for Disease Control, Non-medical Use of Drugs, and Field Operations. It is responsible for enforcing the Food and Drugs Act and Regulations, the Narcotic Control Act and Regulations, the Proprietary or Patent Medicine Act, and the Radiation Emitting Devices Act and Regulations.

Food. Standards of safety and purity are developed through laboratory research and maintained by means of a regular and widespread inspection program. The inspection of food-manufacturing establishments plays a major role in the production of clean, wholesome foods containing ingredients that meet recognized standards. Changing food technology requires the development of methods of laboratory analysis to ensure the safety of new types of ingredients and packaging materials. The Food and Drug Regulations list chemical additives that may be used in foods, the amounts that may be added to each food, and the underlying reason. Information on new additives must be submitted for careful review before they are included in the permitted list. Considerable emphasis is placed on studies to ensure that the levels of pesticide residues in foods do not constitute a health hazard. The effect of new packaging and processing techniques on the bacteria associated with food spoilage is also of special concern.

Human nutrition. Following the Nutrition Canada survey in 1972, steps have been taken to increase the fortification of food with vitamins and minerals. Revised dietary standards have been published and a new Canada Guide appeared in 1977, together with other material informing the public about good nutrition and stressing its importance in the prevention of disease.

Drugs. The Health Protection Branch regulates the manufacture and distribution of drugs in Canada. The conditions under which drugs are to be manufactured are described in the Manufacturing Facilities and Control Regulations. They relate to facilities, employment of qualified personnel, quality control procedures, maintenance of records, and a suitable system to enable a complete and rapid recall of any batch of drugs from the market. Pharmaceutical plants are regularly visited by inspectors to ensure that the drugs produced meet the quality standards required for sale in Canada.

When a new drug with unknown properties is to be placed on the market, the manufacturer is required by law to provide specified information, including a quantitative list of all ingredients, evidence of safety and effectiveness, the formulation of dosage forms and reports of any adverse effects. This information is studied carefully to ensure that the drug is safe and effective for the purposes claimed. Even after a new drug is on the market, its sale can be banned by the Health Protection Branch if the Drug-Adverse-Reaction Reporting Program indicates that the drug is unsafe and injurious. Plants manufacturing biological products such as serums and vaccines must be licensed according to specifications of the Food and Drug Act and Regulations, whether they are located in Canada or abroad.

Another major activity of the branch is the Quality Assessment of Drugs program to enable the public to purchase high quality drugs at a reasonable price. This program includes integrated action involving inspection of manufacturing facilities, assessment of claims and clinical equivalency and quality of competing brands, and provision of information to provincial governments, professionals, and the general public.

Non-medical use of drugs. Objectives of the Non-medical Use of Drugs Directorate may be described under four main headings: prevention, to develop and stimulate programs intended to prevent mood-altering drugs being used in ways that may result in physical, mental and social health problems; treatment, to stimulate development of effective means of dealing with the immediate physical and mental problems caused by the use of mood-altering drugs; rehabilitation, to stimulate development of effective means of restoring casualties of mood-altering drugs to health; and education, to develop and promote information and education programs aimed at preventing drug abuse and at persuading smokers to stop and young persons not to start.

Environmental health. The Environmental Health Directorate is responsible for studying the adverse effects on human health of the chemical and physical environment, and for ensuring the safety, effectiveness, and non-fraudulent nature of medical devices. The directorate is responsible for developing health hazard assessments for the work and home environments, household products, and air and water criteria. Research on radiation hazards is conducted and environmental and occupational exposures are monitored. The directorate is responsible for the enforcement of the Radiation Emitting Devices Act and that portion of the Food and Drugs Act dealing with medical devices and radioactive pharmaceuticals. Additionally, the directorate jointly administers the Hazardous Products Act with the Department of Consumer and Corporate Affairs.

Disease control. The Laboratory Centre for Disease Control Directorate is involved in the development and implementation of improved laboratory diagnostic procedures and other measures to combat communicable disease agents. Activities entail developing methods for detecting and preventing disease, producing and distributing standardized diagnostic reagents to federal, provincial and other health organizations, and providing a national reference service for identification of disease-producing bacteria, viruses and parasites.

The directorate maintains surveillance of birth defects, poisonings, and adverse drug reactions. Epidemiological research is carried out on both communicable and non-communicable diseases. A program is also under way to assess the effect of social and environmental change on health including the calculation of risk factors due to lifestyle.

5.1.3   Research, planning, standards and consultation

Medical research. Most federal grants supporting health science research in universities and hospitals are channelled through the Medical Research Council, which reports to Parliament through the Minister of National Health and Welfare.

Health statistics and economics. Health statistics are collected by the Health Division, Statistics Canada, as well as by various units in the Department of National Health and Welfare, with coordination by an interdepartmental committee. Plans are under way for a jointly operated continuing Canada Health Survey based on household interviews and limited physical measurements.

Statistics Canada has established collection systems for data on vital statistics, special diseases, health manpower, and hospital and institutional care. Units in the Health Protection Branch of National Health and Welfare are concerned with data on health products, health hazards, and certain disease areas. In the Health Programs Branch, the Health Economics and Statistics Division operates a medical care data bank, and integrates health statistical data from various sources. The division undertakes socio-economic research in a variety of fields including medical and hospital care, community health, health expenditures and resources, and other matters relating to health costs and utilization. These studies support departmental health planning, as well as the production of publications designed to increase public understanding of the organization, cost and performance of Canada's health services and resources.

Health planning. The Long Range Health Planning Branch is responsible for continuously assessing the overall orientation of health services and the organization of resources and factors influencing the health of Canadians. The branch also collaborates with other branches of the department in developing proposals for implementing the general program. The branch has specialists in the following fields: medicine, pharmacy, epidemiology, economics, sociology, demography, political science, statistics and administration.

Standards and consultation. The Department of National Health and Welfare extends technical advisory services to provincial agencies, universities, and other organizations for the development of health programs, health manpower, and health research. Consultative services are available through the various administrative units of the department.

Coordination and promotion of health standards development is now centred in the Health Standards and Consultants Directorate of the Health Programs Branch. The Institutional Services Division of the Health Consultants Directorate provides an information and consultation service on design and plant operation. Other technical advice is available through programs directly operated by the department for health protection including the safety of foods, drugs, and health appliances, environmental health, the Laboratory Centre for Disease Control, and other specialized areas.

International health services   5.1.4

Through the Department of National Health and Welfare, Canada participates in the activities of the Pan American Health Organization, the World Health Organization, other United Nations specialized agencies, and other intergovernmental organizations whose programs have a substantial health component. Similarly, the department takes part in bilateral exchanges with countries that have scientific, technological, or cultural arrangements with Canada. Canadian participation in such multilateral and bilateral activities is coordinated primarily by the International Health Services Directorate, which is also responsible for the administration of WHO/PAHO Fellowship Programs.

In addition, each year, Canadian experts in public health and in the health sciences undertake specific assignments abroad, as special advisers or consultants, at the request of the World Health Organization, the Pan American Health Organization, or one of the other agencies.

The department is responsible for the enforcement of regulations governing the handling and shipping of shellfish under the International Shellfish Agreement between Canada and the United States. Other responsibilities include the custody and distribution of biological, vitamin, and hormone standards for WHO and certain duties in connection with the Single Convention on Narcotic Drugs, 1961.

Fitness and amateur sport   5.1.5

Canada's Fitness and Amateur Sport Program seeks to improve the fitness level of Canadians and to encourage their participation in physical recreation and amateur sport. Established in 1961 by an act of Parliament, the program in the 1975-76 fiscal year had approximately $21 million allocated toward this objective. The program, administered by the Fitness and Amateur Sport Branch of the Department of National Health and Welfare, included four divisions: Sport Canada; Recreation Canada; Program Operations and Administration; and Planning, Research and Evaluation. Activities were grouped under four broad program areas: promotion and communications, resource development, training, and competitions.

Promotion and communications. Production and distribution of brochures and films, setting up displays, and staging conferences were a regular part of the branch's effort. The Sport Demonstration Tour, support for ParticipAction, and an effort in employee-fitness programs sought to increase public awareness of the need to be fit and the enjoyment to be found in physical recreation and sports.

Resource development. The development of resources for sport and recreation, particularly human resources, is a mainstay of the program. Sport Canada and

Recreation Canada provide contributions to national sport and recreation associations for administration and leadership training. Many administrative services are available from the National Centre for Sport and Recreation, which is supported by the program. Recreation Canada makes special contributions to Indian and Métis organizations.

Training. Game Plan, a major cooperative effort involving the federal government, the provinces, and the Canadian Olympic Association is designed to provide additional support for training and competitive experience that Canadian athletes require for elite international competition. Sport Canada is heavily involved with Game Plan in addition to its own support program for Olympic and non-Olympic sports. Grants-in-aid provide special assistance to many Canadian athletes in educational programs, while the Canada Fitness Award is a popular motivational project designed for the 7-17 age group.

Competitions. Support is available for competitions at the developmental and elite levels. This support includes payment of the travel costs of athletes, coaches and officials to national championships. A major part of the support for the Canada Games and Arctic Games comes from the branch. Sport Canada also provides contributions for the travel costs of athletes to some major international competitions, including world championships, Pan-American, British Commonwealth and Olympic Games.

National Advisory Council on Fitness and Amateur Sport. This autonomous body, created by the 1961 Fitness and Amateur Sport Act, advises the Minister of National Health and Welfare on matters relating to fitness and amateur sport.

5.1.6 Federal-provincial cooperation

Since the federal and provincial governments share responsibility for dealing with health matters in Canada, a formal structure has been established for federal-provincial collaboration and cooperation. The following are its elements: Conference of Ministers of Health; Conference of Deputy Ministers of Health; Federal-Provincial Advisory Committees on Community Health, Health Insurance, Health Manpower, and Health Standards. The four advisory committees facilitate the work of the ministers and deputy ministers, and assist them in achieving their objectives, in identifying major issues, and in solving problems. They may set up groups to deal with particular subjects requiring more detailed study.

The Conferences of Ministers and of Deputy Ministers of Health involve matters relating to the promotion, protection, maintenance, and restoration of the health of the people of Canada. Normally, the Conference of Ministers meets annually, and the Conference of Deputy Ministers meets twice a year, to discuss various problems relating to provision and financing of health services in Canada.

5.2   Provincial and local health services

The responsibility for regulation of health care, operation of health insurance programs and direct provision of some specialized services rests with the provincial governments; some health responsibilities are delegated to local authorities. Although each of the provinces assigns primary responsibility for health to one department the distribution of function varies from one province to another. In Alberta, Manitoba and Quebec, health and social services are combined within the same department. Other provinces maintain liaison between departments responsible for these related services.

In a number of provinces, health insurance plans and some specialized programs are administered by semi-autonomous boards or commissions. Some report directly to a minister of health; others are under the jurisdiction of a deputy minister. In New Brunswick and Ontario health insurance programs are operated directly by the health departments.

In each province, both institutional and ambulatory care for tuberculosis and mental illness is provided by an agency of the department responsible for health, with increasing attention directed to preventive services. Programs related to other particular health problems such as cancer, alcoholism and drug addiction, venereal diseases and dental conditions have been developed by government agencies, often in cooperation with voluntary associations. A number of provincial programs serve specific population groups such as mothers and children, the aged, the needy, and those requiring rehabilitation.

Environmental health responsibilities, involving education, inspection, and enforcement of standards, are frequently shared by health departments and other agencies.

Public health or community health units are among the most decentralized. Some are responsible for local health education, school health and organized home care. Although local and regional involvement in health services has been concentrated in hospital planning and some public health aspects, several provinces have inaugurated district and regional boards.

Hospital and institutional care   5.2.1

Apart from care in mental hospitals and tuberculosis sanatoria, virtually all care provided in other (general and allied special) hospitals is covered by provincial hospital insurance plans through agreements made under the Hospital Insurance and Diagnostic Services Act, 1957. Newfoundland, Saskatchewan, Alberta and British Columbia operated hospital insurance plans prior to the proclamation of the federal act and these provinces with Manitoba entered federal-provincial agreements on July 1, 1958, the earliest possible date under the act. Prince Edward Island, Nova Scotia, New Brunswick and Ontario followed in 1959, the territories in 1960, and Quebec in 1961. Effective January 1, 1965 Quebec elected to accept cost-sharing tax abatements in lieu of hospital insurance payments under the Established Programs (Interim Arrangements) Act.

Plans are administered by provincial departments of health, or of social affairs in some provinces, and by separate commissions in others. In some provinces, hospital insurance and medical care insurance are combined under one administration.

Coverage is automatic or compulsory in most provinces for all residents; in Ontario some persons are eligible to remain outside the plan; in Alberta a resident who elects to remain outside the medical care plan must also opt out of the hospitalization plan.

Provincial plans insure all approved available in-patient services at the standard ward level as indicated in the federal act and agreements. In view of the federal requirement, all provinces guaranteed to provide these services upon entering into agreements and there has since been virtually no change in the range of insured in-patient services.

Out-patient services have remained an option of the province. In the initial years of operation under the act many provincial plans provided only limited out-patient services. With a continuous improvement in coverage through the years, all provinces now provide a fairly comprehensive range of insured out-patient services.

All plans pay for insured in-patient services in other provinces at their prevailing rates, but approval of the administering commission is required by Nova Scotia and Prince Edward Island except for emergency care. For in-patient services outside Canada, limits on rates and the volume of services apply in most provinces. Payments for out-of-province insured out-patient services are generally limited by the rates payable within the province with restrictions on service volumes. Nova Scotia makes no payment for out-patient care outside the province.

Provinces finance their portion of the cost of sharable hospital care through a variety of methods including general revenue, premiums, sales (hospital) tax, and in some instances a combination of these sources.

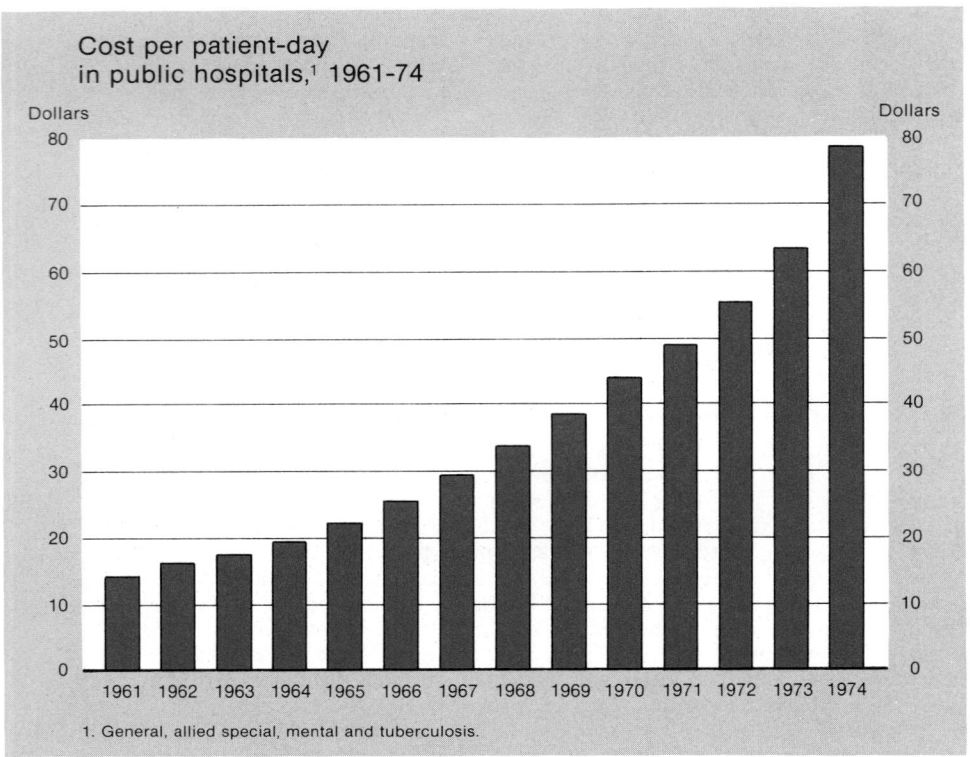

Cost per patient-day
in public hospitals,[1] 1961-74

1. General, allied special, mental and tuberculosis.

Ontario charges a monthly premium of $16 for single persons and $32 for families for both hospital and medical care. The Ontario plan requires compulsory payroll deductions in employee groups consisting of 15 or more persons. For other residents coverage is voluntary. This is the only semi-voluntary plan. In Alberta the joint premium charge for medical care and hospital insurance is $6.40 a month for single persons and $12.80 for families. Premium assistance is available in both Ontario and Alberta for certain residents with limited incomes, and premium exemption is provided for residents over 65 years of age.

Quebec, Alberta, British Columbia and the Northwest Territories levy authorized charges directly to patients for insured services. In Quebec, all in-patients in hospital centres for prolonged care as well as those in prolonged-care hospital centres for short-stay are charged $6 a day with the exception of patients with limited resources and children under 18 years. In Alberta in-patients of general hospitals, other than newborn infants, are charged $5 for the first day of care, while patients receiving auxiliary (chronic) hospital care are charged $4 a day commencing with the 121st day of care. In British Columbia, in-patients (excluding newborn) pay $4 a day and in the Northwest Territories, $1.50.

In addition to emergency services for out-patients, most hospitals provide some ambulatory care, normally including radiology, laboratory and other diagnostic services. In larger hospitals, special ambulatory care units may be established for a wide range of conditions. Certain hospitals provide day and/or night care programs and hospital-based home care programs. In provinces where provincially operated ambulance services are not available, ambulance services may be hospital based.

Non-hospital institutional care is provided by a variety of facilities including nursing homes, homes for the aged, homes for unmarried mothers, child care institutions, hostels and senior citizens' lodges. Insurance coverage does not extend to these institutions except in Ontario, Manitoba and Alberta, but persons requiring care are eligible to apply for aid through the Canada Assistance Plan.

Ontario provides extended health (nursing home) care benefits under its health insurance plan. Manitoba has a personal care home program covering extended treatment, personal care and hostel care, and Alberta has an insured nursing home program. Daily authorized charges to the patient applicable to these programs are: Ontario $7.90, Manitoba $5.75, Alberta $4.00.

Some provincial insurance plans provide other services not eligible for cost-sharing under the federal act including home renal dialysis and home hyperalimentation equipment, supplies and medication, essential ambulance services at modest cost, and occupational and speech therapy in non-hospital facilities in Ontario; physiotherapy services in non-hospital facilities and services in community health and social centres in Saskatchewan; care in senior citizens' lodges at modest cost in Alberta; and equipment, supplies and medication for home renal dialysis in British Columbia.

Hospital statistics. Canadian hospitals are categorized for statistical purposes according to type of ownership: public, proprietary or federal; and type of service: general, allied special (extended care, rehabilitation, maternity, communicable diseases, pediatric, orthopaedic, neurological, cancer, nursing stations, outpost hospitals, etc.), mental or tuberculosis. General hospitals, which account for the largest proportion of beds, are divided into teaching (full and partial teaching) and non-teaching (with and without long-term units), which are further subdivided into varying bed-size groups based on rated bed capacity.

Data pertaining to the number of hospitals in operation (Table 5.3), their classification and rated bed capacity (Table 5.4), were available as at January 1, 1976 but 1974 data were the latest available for all other tables in this section.

Table 5.3 shows that the number and bed capacity of hospitals operating in Canada have remained relatively stable in recent years. Table 5.4 gives the number and bed capacity of public, proprietary and federal hospitals operating in Canada in 1975 and 1976 classified by province and by type of service. In 1976 public hospitals accounted for 94.9% of total rated bed capacity of all hospitals followed by federal hospitals (2.9%) and proprietary hospitals (2.2%). Corresponding 1975 and 1974 respective percentages (94.2%, 3.3%, 2.5%; and 93.5%, 3.8%, 2.7%) show a trend toward a higher proportion of public hospitals and a lower proportion of proprietary and federal hospitals. The proportion of rated beds in general and allied special hospitals as a group has been increasing in recent years while the proportion in mental hospitals and tuberculosis sanatoria on the whole has decreased. In 1976 general hospitals accounted for 64.8% of total rated beds as compared to 63.6% in 1975 and 62.6% in 1974 (5.5 beds per 1,000 population in 1976). Provincially, Saskatchewan had the highest ratio of general hospital beds per 1,000 population, i.e. 7.5 in 1976 and 1974 and 7.4 in 1975, while Quebec reported the lowest ratio with 4.6 beds per 1,000 population from 1974 to 1976. The rated bed capacity of mental hospitals declined from 22.3% of total rated beds in 1974 (1.9 per 1,000 population) to 21.0% in 1975 (1.8 per 1,000 population) and to 18.6% in 1976 (1.6 per 1,000 population); allied special hospitals increased from 14.5% in 1974 (1.4 per 1,000 population) to 15.1% in 1975 (1.4 per 1,000 population) and to 16.5% in 1976 (1.4 per 1,000 population); rated beds in tuberculosis sanatoria constituted 0.2% in 1976 (0.02 per 1,000 population) declining from 0.3% in 1975 (0.02 per 1,000 population) and 0.6% in 1974 (0.05 per 1,000 population). Rated beds per 1,000 population for all hospitals as a group declined from 8.8 in 1974 to 8.7 in 1975 and 8.6 in 1976.

Total adult and child admissions to all Canadian hospitals increased by 1.7% between 1972 and 1973 reaching in excess of 3.8 million or 172.5 patient admissions per 1,000 population. Between 1973 and 1974, the number of admissions increased by 35,500, or 0.9%, bringing the number of admissions per 1,000 population to 171.5. A study of Table 5.5 reveals that admissions to public general hospitals increased by 2.3% from 1972 to reach nearly 3.5 million in 1973, and another 1.5% increase between 1973 and 1974 brought the number to over 3.5 million; the number of patient admissions increased to 157.6 per 1,000 population in 1973 and remained at that figure in 1974.

Admissions to public mental hospitals totalled approximately 57,200 in 1973, an increase from 1972 of 3.3%, and from 1973 to 1974 decreased by 2.5% to 55,800; the rate per 1,000 population increased from 2.5 in 1972 to 2.6 in 1973 and decreased again to 2.5 in 1974. Over the same period, admissions to public tuberculosis sanatoria dropped by 26.0% to 2,278 in 1973 and again by 46.5% to 1,219 in 1974, the rate per 1,000 population remaining at 0.1 from 1972 to 1974. The average daily population in all Canadian hospitals decreased by 1.3% in 1973 and by 2.0% in 1974. Public general hospitals made up more than one half (56.7%) of the 1974 average daily population compared with 53.9% in 1973 and 52.9% in 1972. Public mental hospitals, second largest, accounted for 25.7% of the 1974 average daily population as against 27.7% in 1973 and 28.6% in 1972.

The average length of stay of adults and children in public general hospitals decreased from 9.7 days in 1972 to 9.4 days in 1973, and then increased again slightly to 9.5 days in 1974 (Table 5.6). Average length of stay was significantly correlated to bed capacity in general hospitals, in 1973 rising from 6.7 days in the 1- to 24-bed group of non-teaching general hospitals to 11.1 days in full-teaching general hospitals in the 1-499-bed group, and in 1974 rising from 6.9 days to 11.8 days in these hospital groups, a reflection of the fact that larger hospitals tend to provide more diversified and complex services. Provincially, average length of stay for public general hospitals as a group ranged in 1973 from 8.3 days in Prince Edward Island to 10.2 days in Quebec and in Nova Scotia, and in 1974 from 7.8 days in Prince Edward Island to 10.5 days in Quebec. Within the allied special group of hospitals there was considerable variation in the average length of stay, extending in 1974 from 8.5 days (8.1 in 1973) for pediatric hospitals to 10.0 days (9.7 in 1973) for the "other" group (maternity, neurological, orthopaedic, cancer hospitals, etc.) and then climbing sharply to 41.8 days (41.6 in 1973) for the convalescent/rehabilitation hospitals and to 218.2 days (211.7 in 1973) for chronic/extended care hospitals. Average length of stay for public general and allied special hospitals as a whole declined from 11.1 days in 1972 to 10.8 days in 1973, and then increased to 11.0 days in 1974.

Table 5.7 shows that there were almost 330,000 full-time employees (excluding paid medical staff in general and allied special hospitals) in the Canadian hospital industry as a whole in 1974, an increase of 6,400 full-time personnel from 1973 and of 6,600 from 1972. General hospitals as a group employed 192.0 full-time personnel per 100 rated beds in 1974, not much change from the group ratios of 191.7 and 192.6 recorded in 1973 and 1972, respectively. Provincially, this ratio varied from 140.0 in Saskatchewan to 242.0 in Newfoundland in 1974 and from 140.3 to 229.2 in these provinces in 1973. Taken as a group, general and allied special hospitals reported a ratio of 180.0 full-time personnel per 100 rated beds in 1974 compared to 178.9 in 1973 and 179.3 in 1972. In mental hospitals there were 97.3 full-time personnel per 100 rated beds in 1974, up from the 91.1 reported in 1973 and the 86.2 reported in 1972, while in tuberculosis sanatoria this ratio was 143.1 in 1974 as compared to 101.4 in 1973 and 100.5 in 1972.

Table 5.8 displays the revenues and expenditures of operating public general hospitals for the reporting years 1973 and 1974. From 1972 to 1973, revenues for these hospitals increased by 13.0% to $2,710.2 million, and from 1973 to 1974 increased by 23.9% to $3,359.1 million. Expenditures in 1974 were $3,409.4 million, representing a 23.8% increase from the 1973 figure of $2,753.7 million, which was a 12.8% increase from 1972. Salaries and wages accounted for 69.9% of expenditures in 1974 and 69.5% in 1973, while medical and surgical supplies accounted for 3.2% in 1974 and 3.3% in 1973, and drugs for 2.4% in 1974 and 2.7% in 1973.

Table 5.9 shows that cost per patient-day was highest for pediatric hospitals ($180.86 in 1974 and $151.43 in 1973), followed by the "other" hospitals group, which includes orthopaedic, maternity, neurological and cancer hospitals, ($164.94 in 1974 and $126.77 in 1973), and general hospitals ($99.68 in 1974 and $82.66 in 1973). Among the provinces, cost per patient-day in general hospitals ranged from $65.31 in Prince Edward Island to $122.41 in Quebec in 1974, and from $55.19 to $101.12 in the same provinces in 1973.

In-patients. Canadian hospital in-patient statistics for institutions exclusive of mental hospitals and tuberculosis sanatoria are available for most years from 1960 to date. Data are presented by age, sex and diagnostic classification. Similar information on patients treated in mental hospitals and tuberculosis sanatoria were available for some time before that year. Since 1968, statistics on primary surgical operations have been presented as counts of cases separated from hospital, the length of stay attributable to these cases, and appropriate rates. The classification systems currently used are the Canadian Diagnostic List and the International Classification of Diseases, Adapted — eighth revision.

It is recognized that the value of these data is limited in estimating total morbidity since many conditions do not require hospital in-patient treatment. However, the diagnostic standards of hospital-originated records are high, and the more serious and severe cases and conditions are likely to be hospitalized.

Tables 5.10 and 5.11 give hospital separation data by groups of diagnoses. Tables 5.12 and 5.13 show statistics concerning primary operations. In 1973, 3.7 million cases were discharged or died in hospital and 1.9 million primary operations were performed; expressed as rates, these represent 16,749 separations per 100,000 population and 8,465 operations per 100,000 population. It should be noted that these statistics present a count of events, i.e. separations or operations, not persons.

Medical care   5.2.2

Before the establishment of government-administered medical insurance, voluntary prepayment arrangements to cover the cost of physicians' services had developed in both public and private sectors. By the end of 1968, basic medical or surgical coverage, or both, were being provided to about 17.2 million Canadians, 82% of the population. Voluntary plans in the private sector covered about 10.9 million, or 52%, and public plans covered 6.3 million, or 30%. By early 1972 all 10 provinces and the two territories had met the criteria stipulated under the Medical Care Act as conditions for federal cost-sharing, and virtually the entire eligible population was insured for all required medical services plus a limited range of oral surgery. Members of the Canadian Armed Forces, the Royal Canadian Mounted Police, and inmates of federal penitentiaries whose medical care requirements are met under alternative provisions are excluded. Services by physicians that are not medically required (e.g. examinations for life insurance), services covered under other legislation (e.g. immunizations where available through organized public health services), and services to treat work-related conditions already covered by workmen's compensation legislation are not covered.

The federal government contributes, overall, half of the cost of insured services. The proportion varies somewhat from province to province, depending upon actual provincial cost levels. In 1974-75 the proportions ranged from 44.3% in British Columbia to 78.5% in Newfoundland, and in 1975-76 from 40.8% in British Columbia to 75.6% in Newfoundland.

Seven of the 12 provincial or territorial medical plans finance their share of the cost from general revenues only and in those plans there is virtually no direct cost to families, apart from additional billing that doctors may impose. Three provinces and the Yukon Territory levy premiums to help finance their share, and one employs a payroll tax. In their plans, premiums are paid by the government for welfare recipients and, in some cases, for residents 65 years and over, and various devices are used to keep the financial burden low for families who are just above the poverty line and so are not entitled to welfare assistance.

Each plan is described briefly in the paragraphs that follow, with the date indicating the order of its entry into the national program. Although most doctors are paid on a fee-for-service basis, alternative or additional arrangements include salary, sessional payments, contract service, capitation, and incentive pay. All provinces permit specialists to extra-bill for non-referred care if the specialist rate is higher than the rate the plan will pay for such service.

Saskatchewan (July 1962). The Saskatchewan program requires enrolment of the entire eligible population. Since January 1, 1974, when premiums were discontinued, the provincial share of the cost has been financed entirely from general revenues. The Medical Care Insurance Commission (MCIC), the principal administering agency, pays doctors for most of the services provided under the plan. About 42,000 residents obtain their insured service under terms and conditions identical to those of the MCIC but through a separate administering agency, the Swift Current Health Region. The provincial authority also arranges for payment for physicians' services in mental and tuberculosis institutions and for cancer control.

Benefits include home, office, and hospital visits, surgery, obstetrics, psychiatric care outside mental hospitals, anaesthesia, laboratory and radiological services, preventive medicine, refractions by optometrists, chiropractic services, and referred services by dentists for care of cleft palate and for orthodontic oral surgery. There are no waiting periods for eligibility and no exclusions for age or pre-existing conditions.

The MCIC pays for approved services by physicians on the basis of 100% of the negotiated payment schedule and in accordance with its assessment rules. The fees in this negotiated schedule are about 85% of those in the provincial medical association's own current fee schedule, which is used primarily for billing visitors and other non-insured patients. Participating chiropractors are paid under a formula combining contracted payments for radiography plus fee-for-service payments for visits, the payments being progressively discounted as volume per chiropractor increases.

A physician may choose among five ways to receive payment. First, the physician may receive payment directly from the MCIC as payment in full. Second, patient and physician may enrol voluntarily with an "approved health agency" that serves as intermediary, with respect to payment, between the public authority and the physician; here also, the physician receives the negotiated tariff. Third, a physician may be paid through clinics financed by per capita contributions from the provincial authority. Fourth, a physician may submit his account directly to the patient, who pays him either before or after seeking reimbursement from the public authority; the physician may bill the patient directly for an amount over and above what the public authority has paid. Fifth, physicians and patients may if they choose make private financing arrangements. No physician is compelled to confine himself to one or another mode of payment.

British Columbia (July 1968). The plan is governed by a public commission, originally with jurisdiction over "licensed carriers" — non-profit agencies charged with responsibility for day-to-day management of the separate components of the program. These carriers are being phased out in favour of centralized administration. In addition to physicians' services and 'a limited range of in-hospital oral surgery, the benefits include refractions by optometrists, some orthoptic services, limited physiotherapy, special nursing, chiropractic, naturopathy, and orthodontic services for cleft palate and harelip.

Participation in the program is voluntary. Premiums are $7.50 a month for a single person, $15 a month for a two-person family, and $18.75 a month for a family of three or more persons. For eligible residents (they must have resided in the province the preceding 12 consecutive months), the government offers subsidies totalling 90% of the premium for persons with no taxable income and 50% of the premium for persons with taxable income from $1 to $1,000.

Arrangements for payment to physicians are similar to those in Saskatchewan, except that the plan's payment-schedule is about 100% of the fee-schedule of the provincial medical association. A physician either bills the patient for services rendered, or accepts payment directly from the public authority. In the former case, the physician must notify the patient in writing, before rendering a service, that he is a non-participating physician and the patient must agree in writing that he is prepared to pay more than the amount of reimbursement that he may receive from the public authority. In the latter case, the physician may also charge a fee in excess of the tariff, provided the patient has been duly notified and agrees in writing to the extra charge, and provided the amount of the extra charge is made known to the public authority.

Newfoundland (April 1969). The plan covers all required medical services by doctors and a limited range of in-hospital oral surgery. Refractions by optometrists are not covered. All eligible residents are covered and there are no premiums, the provincial portion of costs for insured services being met from general revenues.

A physician must formally select, and use exclusively, one of the modes of payment available. A participating physician must accept the plan payment as payment in full. A non-participating physician may impose additional charges, provided that he informs the beneficiary that he is not a participating physician, reserving the right to charge in excess of the amount payable by the plan.

For several years, many doctors in Newfoundland contracted with the provincial government and with certain voluntary agencies to receive salaries for providing medical service in outlying areas. These arrangements were continued after 1969.

Nova Scotia (April 1969). All eligible residents are covered. Registration is required but there are no premiums, the entire provincial share of the cost being obtained from general revenues. The insured services include all necessary medical procedures, plus a limited range of oral-surgery procedures in hospitals. Refractions by optometrists are also covered.

Physicians must choose either to participate, accepting all payments directly from the plan, or not to participate. In either case, physicians may extra-bill, but they must obtain written consent from the patient before rendering the service, and the amount of the extra charge has to be made known to the commission.

The Nova Scotia plan is administered by a non-profit carrier designated by the public authority as its sole agent with respect to fee-for-service accounts. This agency carries out all functions relating to eligibility-checking and the processing and payment of claims, subject to review and audit by the public authority.

Manitoba (April 1969). Registration is compulsory for all eligible residents. Premiums were discontinued on July 1, 1973, and the provincial share of the cost is now financed entirely from general revenues. The insured benefits cover all medically-required services provided by medical practitioners and limited in-hospital dental surgery. Also included, with limitations, are refractions by optometrists and the services of chiropractors.

Physicians may choose to participate in the plan, and to accept all payments from public authority, or they may elect to receive payments direct from all their patients. In the former case, the amount received must be accepted as payment in full. A non-participating physician must give a patient reasonable notice if he intends to extra-bill. Payment is also made for prosthetic devices and certain limb and spinal orthotic devices and services that are medically required, contact lenses following surgery for congenital cataract, and artificial eyes.

Alberta (July 1969). Administration is by a Health Care Insurance Commission. A combined annual premium of $76.80 for single persons and $153.60 for families covers both medical and hospital insurance. Subsidies reduce the premiums to zero for single persons and families with no taxable income in the previous year; to $39.60 for single persons whose taxable income does not exceed $500; and to $79.20 for families whose combined taxable income does not exceed $1,000. Premium payments are waived if either the head of the household or that person's spouse is 65 years of age or over.

Registration and the payment of applicable premiums are compulsory. Failure to comply makes residents liable to a waiting period of three months following registration before becoming eligible for insured services.

In addition to the benefits of physicians' services and a limited range of oral surgery, with costs shared by the federal government, the Alberta program includes refractions by optometrists, services and appliances provided by a podiatrist, a limited range of osteopathic services, certain additional dental services and chiropractic services.

Residents objecting in principle to claiming benefits under the combined hospital and medical program can choose to remain outside the program (i.e. to opt out) and not be liable for premium payment. They are at liberty to obtain private insurance coverage for hospital and related care, but interpretations under the federal Medical Care Act prevent private carriers from offering insurance for physicians' services.

The plan also offers subscribers the option of purchasing insurance for additional health services (again, with subsidy provisions) from the voluntary Alberta Blue Cross agency. The optional membership offers coverage for hospital-differential charges for semi-private and private-ward care, ambulance services, drugs, appliances, home-nursing care, naturopathic services, clinical psychological services, and dental care needed because of accidental injury.

Doctors may elect to bill patients for fees beyond those paid by the plan. In such cases, doctors are required to notify patients beforehand, and must indicate to patients the total amount and also the amount that will be paid by the plan.

Ontario (October 1969). Enrolment is compulsory for employee groups of 15 or more persons and provision is made for the creation of compulsory groups in the case of five to 14 employees. The insured benefits cover all required services of medical practitioners and, in specified hospital settings, of oral surgeons, refractions by optometrists, a portion of out-of-hospital physiotherapy cost, ambulance cost, and, with limitations, certain paramedical services offered by chiropractors, osteopaths, and podiatrists.

Doctors may choose from two modes of receiving payment for insured services. Those billing directly to the medical plan are paid directly by the plan for the service rendered, and cannot bill the patient for the balance. Doctors electing to bill patients directly cannot be paid by the plan. Patients must pay the doctor the amount billed and can recover from the plan 90% of the fee for the service.

The levy for the combined hospital-medical premium is $192 a year for single persons and $384 for couples and families. Premiums are waived for welfare recipients and for all residents 65 years of age or over. Single persons and families with no or very low taxable income in the current year are eligible for 100% premium-subsidy assistance. A single person with taxable income between $1,534 and $2,000 or a couple or family with taxable income between $2,000 and $3,000 can qualify for 50% assistance.

Quebec (November 1970). Registration of all eligible residents is compulsory and the benefits include all required medical services of physicians, refractions by optometrists, and a limited range of dental services. The medical services, provided mostly by doctors engaged in private fee practice, are paid for on the basis of claims submitted.

Doctors who participate receive their entire remuneration, directly or indirectly, from the provincial agency, the Quebec Health Insurance Board, in accordance with a negotiated schedule of benefit payments for each service provided, and they cannot extra-bill. They may choose to be paid directly by the board, or indirectly by the patient, who is in turn reimbursed by the board.

Doctors who choose not to participate must collect all fees (except for emergency care) from the patient, who cannot, unlike in other provinces, seek reimbursement from the provincial agency. He must pay the entire amount.

Part of the provincial share of costs is financed by a tax on wage and salary earnings. Each taxpayer whose net income in a year equals or exceeds $5,957 if married, or $3,931 if single, contributes 1.5% of such income, up to a maximum contribution of $235 for employees who get at least three quarters of their income from wages and salaries and $375 for others. Employers also contribute 1.5% of their entire payroll. Persons who have earnings below the income thresholds and all welfare recipients are covered without payment of the tax on earnings.

Prince Edward Island (December 1970). Benefits are comparable to those in other provinces. Registration is required but is not a condition of eligibility. The provincial share of costs is met from general revenue. A doctor who decides to collect directly from his patient can extra-bill, but only up to the amount listed for the service in the medical association fee-schedule and only after obtaining the patient's written consent and notifying the provincial agency of the amount. A doctor who bills the provincial agency directly must accept its payment as payment in full unless he has obtained the patient's written consent.

New Brunswick (January 1971). Registration by the family head is required, although it is not an eligibility requirement. Doctors must indicate whether or not they intend to participate in the plan; if they so decide, they are obliged to accept the plan payment as payment in full. Those doctors who elect to deal directly with particular patients may extra-bill. The New Brunswick plan is generally comprehensive, including limited oral surgery in hospital.

The Northwest Territories (April 1971). Doctors who elect to submit accounts to the territorial insurance agency must accept as payment in full from the agency the amounts set forth in its benefit schedule. Those who choose to collect directly from patients must, initially, give notice to the agency that they are not participating, and must inform the patients beforehand of their intention. Refractions by optometrists are not covered. The territorial share of costs is met entirely from general revenues.

Because of isolated conditions in this far northern area, it is common, as in the outport areas of Newfoundland, for many doctors to work as salaried employees of third-party institutions and agencies.

The Yukon Territory (April 1972). The plan employs premium levies to finance its share of total costs. Registration is required, but coverage for insured services is not contingent on premium payment. Premiums are $57 a year for single persons, $111 for couples, and $132 for families of three or more. Employers are required to deduct the premiums from the wages or salaries of employees and remit the amounts deducted to the plan. Sharing of the cost of premiums under collective-bargaining agreements is permissible.

Premium assistance is available for low-income families. Individuals and families with no taxable income in the previous year are eligible to have the entire premium paid on their behalf. Half the premium is paid for single persons with taxable income of $500 or less, for couples with combined taxable income of $1,000 or less, and for families of three or more with combined taxable income of $1,300 or less. The federal government assumes responsibility for premium payments on behalf of native peoples.

Claims for payment may be made by a doctor either to the plan directly or to the patient. When a patient is billed directly, he must be supplied with an itemized account that can be used when seeking reimbursement from the plan. A doctor who elects to bill his patients can make any mutually satisfactory arrangement for remuneration, providing this is done prior to rendering service; otherwise he must accept what the plan pays as payment in full.

5.2.3   Special programs for welfare recipients

All provinces pay all or part of the cost of additional services required by residents in financial need under their social assistance programs. These costs are shared 50-50 by the federal government under the terms of the Canada Assistance Plan Act. The range of benefits varies from province to province, but may include such services as eyeglasses, prosthetic appliances, dental services, prescribed drugs, home care services, and nursing home care. Usually, if the benefit is universally available to insured residents under another program, this portion would not be administered under welfare auspices. The principal benefits are described in more detail below.

Physicians' services. The provincial medical care insurance plans cover provincial welfare recipients, without premium payments in provinces levying premiums. The rates of payment to their physicians are identical to those that apply to the general population. Benefits, usually a little broader, also include such otherwise uninsured items as travelling allowance and telephoned advice, the cost of these additional items being generally shared under the Canada Assistance Plan. Extra-billing by physicians is usually waived.

Hospital care. Every provincial hospital care insurance program covers welfare-allowance recipients without their payment of premiums or authorized charges.

Prescribed-drug benefits. In British Columbia, Alberta, Saskatchewan, Manitoba, New Brunswick, Quebec and Newfoundland, virtually all provincial public-assistance recipients are included in programs that provide prescribed drugs. In Alberta, recipients may purchase drugs and other benefits through the optional health plan at subsidized rates. The drug benefits in most provinces include practically every prescription drug and some unprescribed medications. Rates of payment to pharmacies and dispensing physicians are negotiated by provincial governments. In Saskatchewan, British Columbia and New Brunswick, certain beneficiaries may be obliged to pay a portion of the cost.

The government of Nova Scotia subsidizes recipients of local welfare allowances who purchase drugs provided under municipally-operated programs, and pays the full cost of drugs in certain cases of special need. Ontario paid 80% of municipal costs up to June 1976, and 100% thereafter. As already noted, Ontario also provides patients of nursing homes and persons receiving assistance under the government's province-wide family benefits program with free prescription drugs from a formulary of 1,200 items.

Dental care benefits. Dental benefit plans are operated for selected recipients of welfare in most provinces. In British Columbia, public-assistance recipients can qualify through special means tests for enrolment; a separate program is operated for the children, under 13 years of age, of all welfare recipients. The Ontario program provides dental benefits to persons in receipt of mothers' allowances and dependent fathers' allowances and their children under the age of 18; provincial assistance is also available for essential dental services for others, at municipal discretion. All provincial public-assistance recipients qualify for dental benefits under schemes operated in Alberta and Saskatchewan, and for selected categories of recipients in Manitoba.

Benefits under these dental plans typically exclude certain specified services and require prior authorization for some services. In the three most western provinces, posterior bridgework and prophylaxis are excluded. Prior authorization is required in British Columbia and Saskatchewan for dentures, relines, gold inlays, orthodontia, and periodontia. Payments to dentists are at negotiated fixed rates under each of these plans. Provision of dentures is subject to a co-charge of approximately 50% in Alberta and Saskatchewan.

Optical care benefits. Health benefit schemes for welfare recipients include certain optical care services and eyeglasses in the four western provinces. With the nation-wide implementation of public medical care insurance programs, refractions performed by physicians became general benefits under most schemes, and in a number of provinces refractions by optometrists as well. The optometric benefit is cost-shared when the beneficiary is eligible under the Canada Assistance Plan. Frames, lenses and fittings continue to be benefits of the provincial health benefit schemes in the western provinces. Certain restrictions typically govern the amount that will be paid for frames embellished for cosmetic purposes.

Non-physician benefits   5.2.4

Provinces also operate programs that provide personal health service benefits beyond those of the federal-provincial cost-shared hospital and medical programs.

Dental care. Seven provinces provide some insured dental care. The Newfoundland dental plan covers children to 10 years of age. In Prince Edward Island, children born in 1965 or after are eligible, and in Nova Scotia, those born in 1967 or later. The Quebec program covers children up to 10 years of age and, for all residents, oral surgery services provided by dentists in a university establishment determined by regulations. Saskatchewan operates a dental plan for children born from 1967 to 1971, and provides coverage for all residents for referred orthodontic services for abnormalities and particularly for care of cleft palate. Alberta provides a comprehensive range of dental goods and services, without direct charge at time of service, to all households (head, spouse and dependents) with a member 65 years of age or over. British Columbia covers orthodontic care of cleft lip and/or palate for residents under 21 years of age, where the service arises from plastic repair by a medical practitioner.

Prescribed drugs. Eight provinces have insurance programs for prescribed drugs. The Nova Scotia program provides all residents 65 years of age and over with prescription and certain other drugs, and prescribed ostomy equipment. New Brunswick entitles its residents 65 years of age and over to obtain without charge medically necessary drugs listed in a formulary, and provides a special drug-benefit entitlement for patients with cystic fibrosis. Quebec residents who receive any amount of guaranteed monthly income supplement added to their old age security pension also obtain specified insured drugs at no direct cost at time of service. Ontario provides drug benefits to residents eligible for federal and provincial income supplements or family benefits and to residents of nursing homes and homes for special care; the benefits are for drugs on an approved list of therapeutic products that can be prescribed by dentists or medical practitioners. The Manitoba plan for all residents covers 80% of the cost of certain drugs in excess of $50 a year per family. The $50 deductible is waived for welfare recipients and for others entitled to drugs under any other program. Saskatchewan has a program for all residents that covers the material-cost of prescribed drugs, with the patient paying a nominal negotiated prescribing fee. The province also meets the full cost of prescribed drugs, to a limit of $1,000 a year per patient, required by any resident with chronic end-stage kidney disease who is receiving kidney dialysis or transplant. Alberta makes available to all residents at a reduced premium the prescribed drugs and other benefits of its Blue Cross sponsored optional services program. All residents who are medically insured may purchase drugs for a co-insurance charge of 20%, after paying a deductible of $15 (for the entire benefit package). The premium and the $15 deductible are waived for persons aged 65 or over and their families. The British Columbia plan pays 50% of the cost of prescriptions in excess of $3 for persons in the highest bracket of medicare-premium assistance, and for all persons 65 years and over (exempt from the $3 charge). Most provinces also supply through health department auspices certain drugs that are important in the treatment of diseases with high drug-therapy costs, such as venereal disease, rheumatic fever, tuberculosis, or cystic fibrosis.

Optical care. Nova Scotia, Quebec, Ontario, Manitoba, Saskatchewan, Alberta, and British Columbia cover for all insured residents the cost of visual assessments of the eye performed by optometrists. Most provinces impose frequency limits for the insured service. Manitoba and Quebec cover the fitting of contact lenses in certain cases and Quebec also covers such additional services as tests for colour-blindness. Alberta provides a comprehensive range of prescribed goods and services for persons 65 years and over and their families.

Paramedical services. Chiropractic services are covered for all insured residents in Ontario, Saskatchewan, Alberta and, excluding X-rays, in British Columbia and Manitoba. Outside Saskatchewan there are limits on the number of services and their cost. Osteopathic services are provided on the same basis as physicians' services in Alberta and British Columbia; they are also a benefit in Ontario, with limitations as to amount. Podiatric services (chiropody) are a benefit in Ontario, Alberta and British Columbia, with limitations as to amount. British Columbia also provides limited amounts of orthoptic treatment and of the services of naturopaths and of visiting and special nurses. Physiotherapy in home and office is insured in Ontario and British Columbia under medical insurance auspices but the benefit is limited to what is provided under hospital insurance auspices in other provinces.

Other services. Alberta provides Blue Cross non-group membership at no cost to registered residents 65 years and over and their dependents, and at reduced rates to other residents unable to obtain similar coverage through their employment. The benefits include, in addition to the prescribed drugs, hospital differential charges for preferred accommodation, ambulance services, appliances, home-nursing care, naturopathic services, clinical psychological services, and dental care needed because of accident or injury, at subsidized rates of $27 a year for a single subscriber and $54 for a family. The premiums are even lower for those with limited income. Alberta residents aged 65 or over and their families are also eligible for hearing aids, approved surgical and medical equipment, supplies, and appliances. Under a special program Saskatchewan residents may purchase hearing aids and accessories at cost, and may obtain without charge hearing evaluations and hearing-aid fitting and repair; Saskatchewan residents may also borrow without charge wheelchairs, walkers, respiratory equipment and commodes. In Manitoba, extra benefits include limb prosthetic devices and services and, with prior approval of the insurance commission, prescribed limb and spinal orthotic devices and services. Quebec insures prosthetic, orthotic, and orthopaedic services and appliances.

5.2.5   Mental health and illness

Among provincially operated health services, mental health activities represent one of the largest administrative areas in expenditure and employees. In 1973, mental institutions reported operating expenditures of $524 million, while their personnel numbered 53,000; corresponding figures for 1974 were $593 million and 52,814.

No adequate measure of mental disorders exists, but in 1975 there were 132,001 admissions to psychiatric in-patient facilities, an increase of 4% over the previous year. Separations increased by 4% to 134,129 in 1975. The year-end census of patients on books totalled 53,279, a decrease of 3% from the previous year. Table 5.18 contains information on patient movement in the various types of psychiatric facilities. Beyond these hospitals and clinics, however, are many other cases.

At the end of 1975, 228 separate in-patient facilities and 140 psychiatric units in hospitals were caring for the mentally ill; most separate facilities are operated by the provinces. The majority of hospitalized patients reside in the 44 public mental hospitals. Most mental hospitals have undergone successive additions to their original structures and many have pioneered new treatments for mental illness. Several provinces are arranging for boarding-home care with the federal government sharing the cost of maintaining needy patients in such homes under the Canada Assistance Plan. In every province at least 88% (nationally, 96%) of the revenue of reporting mental institutions in 1973 was provided by the provincial government or the provincial insurance plan.

Community mental health facilities are being extended beyond mental institutions to provide greater continuity of care, deal with incipient breakdown, and rehabilitate patients in the community. Psychiatric units in general hospitals contribute by integrating psychiatry with other medical care and making it available to patients in their own community. In 1975, the 140 psychiatric units, which had 4,507 patients as the year closed, admitted 48% of the total admissions to all kinds of mental institutions. In-patient services in psychiatric units are benefits under all provincial hospital insurance plans. Some provinces have small regional psychiatric hospitals to facilitate patient access to treatment and the complete integration of medical services. Day-care centres, allowing patients to be in hospital during the day and at home at night, have been organized across the country. Community mental health clinics, some provincially operated, others municipally, and psychiatric out-patient services are open in all provinces.

Specialized rehabilitation services assist former patients to function more adequately and are operated by mental hospitals and community agencies. They include sheltered workshops that pay for work and provide training, and halfway houses in which patients can live and continue to receive treatment while becoming settled in a job.

Facilities for mentally retarded persons include day training schools or classes, summer camps and sheltered workshops as well as residential care in institutions. These facilities provide for social, academic, and vocational training. Manual skills are taught in the training-school workshops and some people are placed in jobs in the community.

Emotionally disturbed children presenting personality or behaviour disorders are treated at hospital units, community clinics, child guidance clinics, and other out-patient facilities.

Alcoholism is a disease afflicting at least 2% of adult Canadians. It is treated in hospitals, out-patient clinics, hostels, long-term residences or farms, and special facilities for the alcoholic offender. Official and voluntary agencies carry out public education, treatment, rehabilitation and research. Among these agencies are Alcoholics Anonymous, the Alcoholism and Drug Addiction Research Foundation of Ontario, the Alcoholism Foundation of British Columbia, l'Office de la Prévention et du Traitement de l'Alcoolisme et des autres Toxicomanies in Quebec, the Alcoholism Foundation of Manitoba and the Nova Scotia Alcoholism Research Foundation. Community treatment programs for narcotic addicts have been established under the aegis of the Narcotic Addiction Foundation of British Columbia and the Ontario Alcoholism and Drug Addiction Research Foundation, supported primarily by provincial funds.

Specific diseases or disabilities   5.2.6

Heart disease. The death toll from heart disease in Canada in 1974 was 58,175, amounting to 259 deaths for each 100,000 persons. The male rate was higher than the female (308 against 210). Among men aged 45 to 64 years heart disease accounted for 40% of all deaths, and the single diagnostic class Ischemic Heart Disease (in which the heart muscle has its own blood supply restricted) killed 9,443 of the 25,308 men in this age group who died in 1974. In 1973, heart disease required 4,129,000 days of care in general and allied special hospitals.

The Canadian Heart Foundation, inaugurated in 1955, had by mid-1975 devoted $41.2 million to cardiovascular research in the universities and hospitals of Canada; its 1974-75 budget alone provided $5.9 million. The Medical Research Council spent $4.5 million on cardiovascular research in 1974-75.

Cancer. As the second leading cause of death in Canada, cancer accounts for about one of every five deaths, most of them occurring in the middle and later years of life. The death rate from cancer increased slightly, from 149.7 per

100,000 population in 1973 to 150.4 in 1974. That for females rose from 132.8 in 1973 to 134.4 in 1974, and for males decreased from 166.5 in 1973 to 166.3 in 1974.

Statistics Canada started a national cancer incidence reporting system on January 1, 1969 in cooperation with the National Cancer Institute and the nine existing provincial tumour registries; a registry has not yet been organized in Ontario. Participating provinces send a simple notification card with basic patient and diagnostic information for each new primary site of malignant neoplasm discovered. Data for 1973 are given in Tables 5.14 and 5.15.

Special provincial agencies for cancer control, usually in the health department or a separate cancer institute, carry out cancer detection and treatment, public education, professional training, and research in cooperation with local public health services, physicians and the voluntary Canadian Cancer Society branches. Although the provisions are not uniform, cancer programs in all provinces provide a range of free diagnostic and treatment services to both out-patients and in-patients. Hospital insurance benefits for cancer patients include diagnostic radiology, laboratory tests and radiotherapy. The cancer control programs in Saskatchewan and New Brunswick also pay for medical and surgical services; in most provinces these costs are covered under the public medical care insurance schemes.

Tuberculosis and respiratory diseases. Tuberculosis statistics reported by Statistics Canada for 1974 show reductions, in most cases, from the 1973 figures; new active cases totalled 3,354, or 14.9 per 100,000 population, and reactivated cases numbered 416, or 1.9 per 100,000. There were 330 deaths from tuberculosis or 1.5 per 100,000, compared with 408 deaths in 1973. Altogether, Canadians reported to be under treatment for tuberculosis in 1974 numbered 7,380 while an additional 13,910 susceptible persons received prophylactic drugs as a preventive measure. (Table 5.16)

Provincial health departments, assisted by voluntary agencies, conduct anti-tuberculosis case-finding programs through community tuberculin-testing and X-ray surveys with special attention to high-risk groups, routine hospital admission X-rays and follow-up of arrested cases. However, practising physicians detect the greatest number of new cases.

BCG vaccine, estimated to be effective for 80% of those vaccinated, is used in most provinces to protect high-risk groups. Quebec and Newfoundland routinely immunize children and in the Yukon Territory, BCG is routinely administered to all newborn. Treatment, including hospital care, drugs and rehabilitation services, is free in all provinces. Chemotherapy has shortened hospital stay and facilitated out-patient or domiciliary care.

Venereal diseases. Public health authorities estimate that the real incidence of venereal diseases may be three to four times the number of cases actually reported. The 1974 figure of 3,782 cases of syphilis or 16.8 per 100,000 population was almost unchanged from the 1973 figure of 3,766, which was 17.0 per 100,000 population. The total figure for gonorrhea cases in 1974 was 47,680 or 212.4 per 100,000, a marked increase over the 205.2 rate for 1973. Factors affecting this rise in incidence can be attributed to a supposed increase in sexual permissiveness, promiscuity and homosexuality, availability of the contraceptive pill, increased population mobility, change in social values, lack of case-reporting, and ignorance about venereal disease.

Provincial health departments have expanded public venereal disease clinics, which provide free diagnostic and treatment services at convenient hours. In some areas these departments pay private physicians to give free treatment to indigents. In addition, the provinces supply free drugs to physicians for treating private cases. Local departments of health or district health units carry out case-finding, follow-up of contacts, and health education programs, assisted by provincial directors of venereal disease control.

Therapeutic abortions. The 10 provinces and the two territories reported 48,198 therapeutic abortions performed during the 12-month period January to December 1974. This was 4,953 cases more than the 43,245 therapeutic abortions reported during the same 12-month period of 1973. Of these 48,198 cases, 48,136 cases (99.9%) were residents of Canada. In terms of rate per 100 live births, the 48,136 therapeutic abortions for Canadian residents amounted to 13.9% of live births for 1974 as against the therapeutic abortion rate of 12.6 per live births for 1973. (Table 5.17)

During 1975, for the first time during the period 1970-75, there was a decrease in the abortion rate. According to data published in December 1976 in the Statistics Canada publication *Therapeutic abortions, Canada, 1975 — advance information* (Catalogue No. 82-211) the 10 provinces and two territories reported that the hospitals under their jurisdictions performed 49,390 therapeutic abortions during the 12-month period January to December 1975. Canadian residents accounted for 49,311 or 99.8% of the total abortions performed. Although this was an increase of 1,175 over the previous year, the increase in the number of live births meant that the abortion rate declined from 13.9% in 1974 to 13.6% in 1975.

Notifiable diseases. The notifiable diseases most predominant in 1974 were venereal diseases (51,479), streptococcal sore throat and scarlet fever (20,274), infectious and serum hepatitis (5,746), and tuberculosis (3,354). Table 5.24 shows the number of notifiable diseases by province in that year.

Other diseases or disabilities. Many services for persons with chronic disabilities, such as heart disease, arthritis, diabetes, visual and auditory impairments, and for paraplegics, have been initiated by voluntary agencies assisted by federal and provincial funds. Today, treatment for specific conditions is available at hospital out-patient clinics and in-patient or day centres, at separate clinics and rehabilitation centres, and under home care programs.

Most large general hospitals conduct out-patient clinics for various diseases and disabilities including arthritis and rheumatism, diabetes, glaucoma, speech and hearing defects, heart diseases, and orthopaedic and neurological conditions.

Rehabilitation and home care. Rehabilitation services are provided by a wide range of public and voluntary agencies. Federal responsibility includes care of disabled veterans and handicapped native peoples. The Prosthetic Services Directorate of the Department of National Health and Welfare manufactures a number of prosthetic and orthotic appliances and provides fitting services in some larger cities. Physical medicine and rehabilitation services are based in several types of institution, including hospitals, separate in-patient facilities, workmen's compensation board centres, and out-patient centres for children. Financing is from various federal, provincial, and voluntary agency sources. Every province includes some institution-based services under hospital and medical care insurance. Two provinces have recently extended this coverage to include the supply and fitting of certain prosthetic and orthotic devices. Vocational rehabilitation for the disabled is also a joint federal-provincial activity.

Home care in Canada has developed in a variety of ways. Provincial home care programs characterize the numerous approaches and organizational structures that exist in Canada today. Some programs are oriented to specific disease categories; some are attached to specific hospitals or community centres, while others are seen as integral parts of comprehensive health-care-delivery-systems. The range of services delivered by the home care programs varies from nursing services alone to a complete array of health and social services. Some programs concentrate on patients requiring short-term active treatment, while others treat convalescent or chronic patients. Some have as specific objectives the reduction of institutional costs and length of stay, and others aim for continuity of care and provision of coordinated health care services to patients for whom home care is the most appropriate level of care.

Most home care programs are characterized by two features: centralization of control of the services within the program, and coordination of services to meet the changing needs of the patient. In some provinces, the departments of health play an active role in the financing and administration of home care programs, while in other provinces, local agencies, municipalities, and hospitals assume major responsibility for home care.

Special schools or classes for various groups of handicapped children are usually operated by school boards whereas most of the schools for the deaf and for the blind are residential schools operated by provincial governments.

5.2.7   Public health

Provincial and local structure. Provincial health departments, in cooperation with the regional and local health authorities, administer such services as environmental sanitation, communicable disease control, maternal and child health, school health, nutrition, dental health, occupational health, public health laboratories and vital statistics. Most provinces have delegated certain health responsibilities to health units in rural regions and to municipal health departments in urban centres. Several provinces also provide services directly to their thinly populated northern parts. Certain regulatory and preventive services, including case-findings, screening, diagnosis and referral, health education, personal health care, and supervision in certain areas of treatment services conducted through clinics and home visits, have continued to be the responsibility of local health authorities.

As metropolitan areas and population densities have increased, effective administration has required a broader geographical base. Some smaller local health services are provided or supervised by a regional health unit, or a regional structure intermediate between provincial departments and local health units provides technical advice. Some urban boards of health in metropolitan areas have been amalgamated to increase their effectiveness.

Maternal and child health. All provincial health departments have established maternal and child health consultant services that cooperate with the public health nursing services. The maternal and child health services also undertake studies in maternal and child care, including hospital care, and assist in the training of nursing personnel. At the local level, public health nurses provide preventive services to mothers, the newborn, and children through clinics, home and hospital visits, and school health services.

Nutrition and health education. Provincial health departments and some municipal or regional health departments employ consultants in nutrition to extend technical guidance and education to health and welfare agencies, schools, nursing homes, various community service agencies and other institutions and hospitals. They also provide diet counselling to selected patient groups such as diabetics, and conduct nutritional surveys and other research. Most provincial health departments have a division or unit of health education under a full-time professional health educator to promote public knowledge of health needs and measures. These divisions provide educational materials to other divisions of the health department, local health authorities, schools, voluntary associations, and the public. Many educational activities are directed to accident prevention and to changing habits harmful to health, such as cigarette smoking and the excessive use of alcohol and other drugs. All health workers carry out health education as part of their normal activities.

Dental health. Although public dental health programs at the provincial level have been largely preventive, increasing emphasis is now being given to dental treatment services. Dental clinics conducted by local health services are generally restricted to pre-school and younger school-age groups. A number of provinces send dental teams to remote areas lacking such services. All provinces have dental care schemes of varying coverage for welfare recipients. Other dental health programs are directed to the training of dentists, dental hygienists, dental nurses, dental therapists and dental assistants, the conducting of dental surveys, and extension of water fluoridation.

Communicable disease control. The larger provincial health departments have separate divisions of communicable disease control headed by full-time epidemiologists; in others this function is combined with one or more community health services. Local health authorities organize public clinics for immunization against diphtheria, tetanus, poliomyelitis, whooping cough, smallpox and measles. They also engage in case-finding and diagnostic services in cooperation with public health laboratories and private physicians. Special services for tuberculosis and venereal disease have already been described.

Public health laboratories. All provinces maintain a central public health laboratory and most have branch laboratories to assist local health agencies and the medical profession in the protection of community health and the control of infectious diseases. Public health bacteriology (testing of milk, water and food), diagnostic bacteriology, and pathology are the principal functions of the laboratory service, with medical testing for physicians and hospitals steadily increasing.

Emergency health services

5.2.8

The Emergency Health Services Division, established in 1959 within the federal Department of National Health and Welfare, encourages the provinces, with the support of an advisory committee, to develop their own emergency health services divisions. These are organized under a provincial director who is generally assisted by a health supplies officer and a nursing consultant. Federal Emergency Health Services are represented in the provinces by the Regional Director of the Medical Services Branch.

Provincial emergency health services ensure that vital health functions are maintained during or reorganized after an emergency or disaster. They assist local planners in establishing emergency medical units, train health professionals and the general public in emergency health procedures, and place emergency medical units from the national stockpile at strategic locations.

Health personnel

5.3

As of December 31, 1974 there were 37,297 active civilian physicians in Canada including interns and residents (Table 5.1). Well over one third, 14,125, were located in Ontario. Ontario and Quebec had the most favourable population-to-physician ratios at 578 and 581, respectively, compared with the national 608.

Province-to-province comparisons of ratios that include all physicians are to some extent distorted because of the differing proportions of interns and residents to other physicians in each province. If the intern-resident category is excluded, the most favourable ratio, 646, was in British Columbia, compared with the national figure of 728. Ontario, at 685, was the only other province with a population-to-physician ratio below the national average.

Table 5.1 also shows trends since 1965 in numbers and ratios for all active civilian physicians combined and for physicians excluding interns and residents. In each case the figures include physicians engaged in such activities as administration, teaching and research within the medical field, as well as those in the clinical practice of medicine.

Nurses. The nursing group makes up the largest single component of health manpower occupations, approximately 45% of the total. Other professions within this group include psychiatric nurses, nursing assistants and orderlies.

Registered nurses. Data on registered nurses are collected annually from the registrar of the provincial licensing/registration authority. The figures for registered nurses for 1974 appear in Table 5.20.

Hospital nursing salaries. Salaries of nurses in public general hospitals were 15.9% higher in 1974 than in 1972. For general duty registered nurses employed in public general hospitals, the average annual salary varied from $8,843 for those classified as graduate nurses only, to $10,844 for those with master's degrees in nursing (Table 5.19). Among graduate nurses without additional qualifications, mean salaries varied from $7,935 for general duty nurses (not registered) to $12,716 for nursing directors. As a rule, general duty registered nurses without additional qualifications, employed in public convalescent/rehabilitation hospitals, earned more than their counterparts in other types of hospitals.

Public health nursing salaries. Salaries of public health nurses varied according to education (Table 5.21). Directors with public health certificates were highest paid, with an average salary of $19,117, while staff nurses (registered nurses) were lowest paid, averaging $10,051.

Physiotherapists. Data on physiotherapists were collected in 1974 and 1975 as part of the health manpower statistical series. The figures shown in Table 5.22 pertain to qualified physiotherapists who are members of either the Canadian Physiotherapy Association or one of the provincial associations.

Radiological technicians. Statistics on radiological technicians were collected in 1973 and 1974 as part of the health manpower statistical series. Data shown in Table 5.23 relate to radiological technicians who are members of the Canadian Society of Radiological Technicians.

5.4   Government expenditure

During the six-year period 1968-73, collective federal, provincial and local governments' expenditure on health more than doubled; expanding from $2,665.2 million to $6,069.4 million. When adjusted for population growth, per capita expenditure on health was over twice as much in 1973 as in 1968, namely $270 compared with $127. The weight of all levels of government expenditure on health, net of intergovernment transfers, in relation to total government expenditure, was also slightly greater in 1973 than in 1968, being 12.9% and 10.8% respectively. When only the year to year trend is considered, all governments' collective expenditure on health increased by $591.4 million between 1972 and 1973, compared with an increase of $635.3 million between 1971 and 1972.

On the other hand, consolidated provincial-municipal expenditure on health, including outlays financed through federal government transfer payments, experienced a growth comparable to that described above. However, health expenditure is relatively more important in total provincial-municipal expenditure than is the case when all three levels of government are considered; for instance, in 1973, it was 20.8% at the provincial-municipal level, compared with 12.9% for all levels of government as an entity. Table 5.2 gives the relevant statistics.

Sources

5.1 - 5.3 Health Economics and Statistics, Health Programs Branch, Department of National Health and Welfare; Health Division, Institutional and Public Finance Statistics Branch, Statistics Canada.

5.4 Public Finance Division, Institutional and Public Finance Statistics Branch, Statistics Canada.

Tables

Tables

..	not available	e	estimate
...	not appropriate or not applicable	p	preliminary
—	nil or zero	r	revised
- -	too small to be expressed		certain tables may not add due to rounding

5.1 Physicians and population per physician, 1965-74, and by province, 1974

Year and province or territory	Active civilian physicians			
	Including interns and residents[1]		Excluding interns and residents[1]	
	Number	Population per physician[2]	Number	Population per physician[2]
1965 (Dec. 31)	25,481	779	20,792	955
1966 ``	26,528	763	21,615	936
1967 ``	27,544	747	22,472	916
1968 ``	28,209	740	22,969	909
1969 ``	29,659	714	24,430r	867
1970 ``	31,166	689	25,657	837
1971 ``	32,942	659	27,439	792
1972r ``	34,508	637	28,606	769
1973r ``	35,923	621	29,944	745
1974 ``	37,297	608	31,108	728
1974 (Dec. 31)				
Newfoundland	660	827	545	1,002
Prince Edward Island	114	1,035	112	1,054
Nova Scotia	1,320	620	1,039	787
New Brunswick	726	923	667	1,004
Quebec	10,603	581	8,317	741
Ontario	14,125	578	11,923	685
Manitoba	1,629	622	1,353	749
Saskatchewan	1,251	729	1,082	843
Alberta	2,662	656	2,234	782
British Columbia	4,151	588	3,780	646
Yukon Territory	23	870	23	870
Northwest Territories	33	1,121	33	1,121
Canada	37,297	608	31,108	728

[1]Based on data in *List catalogue*, Canadian Mailings Limited, for 1965 to 1967, and data supplied by Sales Management Systems Limited, for 1968 to 1974. Estimated number of interns and residents for 1965 to 1968 (and for 1971 in the case of one province) based on Statistics Canada data as well as Sales Management Systems. The 1973 data on the number of physicians were supplemented by specific information on interns and residents from 6 provinces and from 10 provinces for 1974.
[2]Based on Statistics Canada estimates of the population as of Jan. 1 of the following year.

5.2 Total, per capita and percentage distribution of consolidated government expenditure on health, fiscal years ended nearest to Dec. 31, 1968-73

Year	All levels of government[1]	Provincial-local government[2]
Total expenditure *(million dollars)*		
1968	2,665.2	2,593.5
1969	3,440.1	3,332.2
1970	4,224.0	4,106.7
1971	4,842.7	4,709.2
1972	5,478.0	5,326.1
1973[3]	6,069.4	5,902.7
Per capita expenditure *(dollars)*		
1968	127	123
1969	162	156
1970	196	190
1971	222	216
1972	248	241
1973[3]	270	263
Percentage of health expenditure to total consolidated government expenditure		
1968	10.8	17.5
1969	12.3	19.5
1970	13.4	20.8
1971	13.4	20.8
1972	13.4	21.3
1973[3]	12.9	20.8

[1]Excludes all intergovernment transactions.
[2]Excludes transactions occurring between provincial and local governments, but not between the latter and the federal government.
[3]More detailed information is available in Statistics Canada publication *Consolidated government finance*, (Cat. No. 68-202).

5.3   Number and bed capacity of operating public, proprietary and federal hospitals as at Jan. 1, 1974-76

Type	1974		1975		1976	
	Hospitals	Beds	Hospitals	Beds	Hospitals	Beds
General	903	124,949	899	126,419	923	127,884
Allied special	356	28,991	356	30,115	347	32,480
Mental	125	44,607	122	41,821	127	36,652
Tuberculosis	12	1,174	7	542	7	418
Total	1,396	199,721	1,384	198,897	1,404	197,434

5.4   Number and bed capacity of operating public, proprietary and federal hospitals, by province and type, as at Jan. 1, 1975 and 1976

Province or territory and category	Type of hospital								
1975	General			Allied special			Total, general and allied special		
	Hos-pitals	Beds	Beds per 1,000 popula-tion[1]	Hos-pitals	Beds	Beds per 1,000 popula-tion[1]	Hos-pitals	Beds	Beds per 1,000 popula-tion[1]
Newfoundland									
Public	33	2,638	4.8	14	507	0.9	47	3,145	5.7
Proprietary	—	—	—	—	—	—	—	—	—
Federal	—	—	—	—	—	—	—	—	—
Prince Edward Island									
Public	8	715	6.0	1	30	0.3	9	745	6.3
Proprietary	—	—	—	—	—	—	—	—	—
Federal	—	—	—	—	—	—	—	—	—
Nova Scotia									
Public	43	4,360	5.3	4	559	0.7	47	4,919	6.0
Proprietary	—	—	—	—	—	—	—	—	—
Federal	2	522	0.6	—	—	—	2	522	0.6
New Brunswick									
Public	37	4,375	6.5	1	20	- -	38	4,395	6.5
Proprietary	—	—	—	—	—	—	—	—	—
Federal	—	—	—	—	—	—	—	—	—
Quebec									
Public	125	27,977	4.5	62	10,097	1.6	187	38,074	6.2
Proprietary	2	193	- -	42	2,429	0.4	44	2,622	0.4
Federal	2	520	0.1	8	1,161	0.2	10	1,681	0.3
Ontario									
Public	190	42,483	5.2	43	6,829	0.8	233	49,312	6.0
Proprietary	6	148	- -	48	1,164	0.1	54	1,312	0.2
Federal	5	1,780	0.2	8	32	- -	13	1,812	0.2
Manitoba									
Public	79	6,146	6.0	2	409	0.4	81	6,555	6.4
Proprietary	—	—	—	1	40	- -	1	40	- -
Federal	3	664	0.7	13	47	- -	16	711	0.7
Saskatchewan									
Public	132	6,801	7.4	‣ 10	1,051	1.1	142	7,852	8.6
Proprietary	—	—	—	—	—	—	—	—	—
Federal	2	106	0.1	1	4	- -	3	110	0.1
Alberta									
Public	118	10,806	6.1	29	3,345	1.9	147	14,151	8.0
Proprietary	—	—	—	—	—	—	—	—	—
Federal	5	894	0.5	3	10	- -	8	904	0.5
British Columbia									
Public	92	14,448	5.9	25	2,218	0.9	117	16,666	6.8
Proprietary	2	16	- -	—	—	—	2	16	- -
Federal	2	351	0.1	—	—	—	2	351	0.1
Yukon Territory									
Public	—	—	—	1	4	0.2	1	4	0.2
Federal	3	142	6.8	3	12	0.6	6	154	7.3
Northwest Territories									
Public	5	204	5.4	—	—	—	5	204	5.4
Proprietary	—	—	—	—	—	—	—	—	—
Federal	3	130	3.4	37	147	3.9	40	277	7.3
Canada									
Public	862	120,953	5.3	192	25,069	1.1	1,054	146,022	6.4
Proprietary	10	357	- -	91	3,633	0.2	101	3,990	0.2
Federal	27	5,109	0.2	73	1,413	0.1	100	6,522	0.3

5.4   Number and bed capacity of operating public, proprietary and federal hospitals, by province and type, as at Jan. 1, 1975 and 1976 (continued)

Province or territory and category	Type of hospital								
1975	Mental			Tuberculosis			Total, all hospitals		
	Hos-pitals	Beds	Beds per 1,000 popula-tion[1]	Hos-pitals	Beds	Beds per 1,000 popula-tion[1]	Hos-pitals	Beds	Beds per 1,000 popula-tion[1]
Newfoundland									
Public	1	450	0.8	—	—	—	48	3,595	6.5
Proprietary	—	—	—	—	—	—	—	—	—
Federal	—	—	—	—	—	—	—	—	—
Prince Edward Island									
Public	2	296	2.5	1	30	0.3	12	1,071	9.0
Proprietary	—	—	—	—	—	—	—	—	—
Federal	—	—	—	—	—	—	—	—	—
Nova Scotia									
Public	5	1,647	2.0	2	217	0.3	54	6,783	8.3
Proprietary	—	—	—	—	—	—	—	—	—
Federal	—	—	—	—	—	—	2	522	0.6
New Brunswick									
Public	3	1,440	2.1	—	—	—	41	5,835	8.6
Proprietary	—	—	—	—	—	—	—	—	—
Federal	—	—	—	—	—	—	—	—	—
Quebec									
Public	26	8,558	1.4	—	—	—	213	46,632	7.5
Proprietary	1	60	- -	—	—	—	45	2,682	0.4
Federal	—	—	—	—	—	—	10	1,681	0.3
Ontario[2]									
Public	43	15,023	1.8	—	—	—	276	64,335	7.8
Proprietary	11	920	0.1	—	—	—	65	2,232	0.3
Federal	—	—	—	—	—	—	13	1,812	0.2
Manitoba									
Public	8	2,297	2.3	—	—	—	89	8,852	8.7
Proprietary	—	—	—	—	—	—	1	40	- -
Federal	—	—	—	—	—	—	16	711	0.7
Saskatchewan									
Public	4	1,818	2.0	1	92	0.1	147	9,762	10.6
Proprietary	—	—	—	—	—	—	—	—	—
Federal	—	—	—	—	—	—	3	110	0.1
Alberta									
Public	10	4,522	2.6	1	55	- -	158	18,728	10.6
Proprietary	—	—	—	—	—	—	—	—	—
Federal	—	—	—	—	—	—	8	904	0.5
British Columbia									
Public	7	4,720	1.9	2	148	0.1	126	21,534	8.8
Proprietary	1	70	- -	—	—	—	3	86	- -
Federal	—	—	—	—	—	—	2	351	0.1
Yukon Territory									
Public	—	—	—	—	—	—	1	4	0.2
Federal	—	—	—	—	—	—	6	154	7.3
Northwest Territories									
Public	—	—	—	—	—	—	5	204	5.4
Proprietary	—	—	—	—	—	—	—	—	—
Federal	—	—	—	—	—	—	40	277	7.3
Canada									
Public	109	40,771	1.8	7	542	- -	1,170	187,335	8.2
Proprietary	13	1,050	- -	—	—	—	114	5,040	0.2
Federal	—	—	—	—	—	—	100	6,522	0.3
1976	General			Allied special			Total, general and allied special		
	Hos-pitals	Beds	Beds per 1,000 popula-tion[3]	Hos-pitals	Beds	Beds per 1,000 popula-tion[3]	Hos-pitals	Beds	Beds per 1,000 popula-tion[3]
Newfoundland									
Public	33	2,670	4.8	14	506	0.9	47	3,176	5.7
Proprietary	—	—	—	—	—	—	—	—	—
Federal	—	—	—	—	—	—	—	—	—
Prince Edward Island									
Public	8	662	5.5	1	28	0.2	9	690	5.8
Proprietary	—	—	—	—	—	—	—	—	—
Federal	1	14	0.1	—	—	—	1	14	0.1
Nova Scotia									
Public	43	4,238	5.1	4	527	0.6	47	4,765	5.7
Proprietary	—	—	—	—	—	—	—	—	—
Federal	5	542	0.7	—	—	—	5	542	0.7
New Brunswick									
Public	37	4,409	6.4	1	20	- -	38	4,429	6.4
Proprietary	—	—	—	—	—	—	—	—	—
Federal	1	10	- -	—	—	—	1	10	- -

5.4   Number and bed capacity of operating public, proprietary and federal hospitals, by province and type, as at Jan 1, 1975 and 1976 (continued)

Province or territory and category	Type of hospital								
1976 (concluded)	General			Allied special			Total, general and applied special		
	Hos-pitals	Beds	Beds per 1,000 popula-tion[3]	Hos-pitals	Beds	Beds per 1,000 popula-tion[3]	Hos-pitals	Beds	Beds per 1,000 popula-tion[3]
Quebec									
Public	127	28,039	4.5	65	12,897	2.1	192	40,936	6.6
Proprietary	3	226	- -	41	2,365	0.4	44	2,591	0.4
Federal	4	441	0.1	8	937	0.2	12	1,378	0.2
Ontario									
Public	190	44,220	5.3	43	7,087	0.9	233	51,307	6.2
Proprietary	7	183	- -	40	1,041	0.1	47	1,224	0.1
Federal	10	1,695	0.2	8	32	- -	18	1,727	0.2
Manitoba									
Public	77	6,110	5.9	2	409	0.4	79	6,519	6.3
Proprietary	—	—	—	1	25	- -	1	25	- -
Federal	7	502	0.5	15	51	- -	22	553	0.5
Saskatchewan									
Public	132	6,820	7.3	5	1,001	1.1	137	7,821	8.4
Proprietary	—	—		—	—		—	—	
Federal	3	116	0.1	1	4	- -	4	120	0.1
Alberta									
Public	118	10,814	5.9	29	3,314	1.8	147	14,128	7.7
Proprietary	—	—	—	—	—	—	—	—	—
Federal	8	887	0.5	3	6	- -	11	893	0.5
British Columbia									
Public	92	14,729	5.9	23	2,055	0.8	115	16,784	6.7
Proprietary	2	16	- -	—	—	—	2	16	- -
Federal	5	103	- -	—	—	—	5	103	- -
Yukon Territory									
Proprietary	—	—	—	1	4	0.2	1	4	0.2
Federal	3	142	6.8	3	12	0.6	6	154	7.3
Northwest Territories									
Public	4	166	4.4	—	—	—	4	166	4.4
Proprietary	—	—	—	—	—	—			
Federal	3	130	3.4	39	159	4.2	42	289	7.6
Canada									
Public	861	122,877	5.3	187	27,844	1.2	1,048	150,721	6.5
Proprietary	12	425	- -	83	3,435	0.1	95	3,860	0.2
Federal	50	4,582	0.2	77	1,201	0.1	127	5,783	0.3

1976	Mental			Tuberculosis			Total, all hospitals		
	Hos-pitals	Beds	Beds per 1,000 popula-tion[3]	Hos-pitals	Beds	Beds per 1,000 popula-tion[3]	Hos-pitals	Beds	Beds per 1,000 popula-tion[3]
Newfoundland									
Public	1	450	0.8	—	—	—	48	3,626	6.5
Proprietary	—	—	—	—	—	—	—	—	—
Federal	—	—	—	—	—	—	—	—	—
Prince Edward Island									
Public	2	296	2.5	1	20	0.2	12	1,006	8.4
Proprietary	—	—	—	—	—	—	—	—	—
Federal	—	—	—	—	—	—	1	14	0.1
Nova Scotia									
Public	5	1,701	2.0	2	117	0.1	54	6,583	7.9
Proprietary	—	—	—	—	—	—	—	—	—
Federal	—	—	—	—	—	—	5	542	0.7
New Brunswick									
Public	3	1,440	2.1	—	—	—	41	5,869	8.5
Proprietary	—	—	—	—	—	—	—	—	—
Federal	—	—	—	—	—	—	1	10	- -
Quebec									
Public	24	5,173	0.8	—	—	—	216	46,109	7.4
Proprietary	1	60	- -	—	—	—	45	2,651	0.4
Federal	—	—	—	—	—	—	12	1,378	0.2
Ontario[2]									
Public	54	14,136	1.7	—	—	—	287	65,443	7.9
Proprietary	6	445	0.1	—	—	—	53	1,669	0.2
Federal	—	—	—	—	—	—	18	1,727	0.2
Manitoba									
Public	8	1,988	1.9	—	—	—	87	8,507	8.3
Proprietary	—	—	—	—	—	—	1	25	- -
Federal	—	—	—	—	—	—	22	553	0.5
Saskatchewan									
Public	4	1,799	1.9	1	78	0.1	142	9,698	10.4
Proprietary	—	—	—	—	—	—	—	—	—
Federal	—	—	—	—	—	—	4	120	0.1

5.4   Number and bed capacity of operating public, proprietary and federal hospitals, by province and type, as at Jan. 1, 1975 and 1976 (concluded)

Province or territory and category	Type of hospital								
1976 (concluded)	Mental			Tuberculosis			Total, all hospitals		
	Hos-pitals	Beds	Beds per 1,000 popula-tion[1]	Hos-pitals	Beds	Beds per 1,000 popula-tion[1]	Hos-pitals	Beds	Beds per 1,000 popula-tion[1]
Alberta									
Public	10	4,393	2.4	1	55	- -	158	18,576	10.2
Proprietary	—	—	—	—	—	—	—	—	—
Federal	—	—	—	—	—	—	11	893	0.5
British Columbia									
Public	9	4,771	1.9	2	148	0.1	126	21,703	8.7
Proprietary	—	—	—	—	—	—	2	16	- -
Federal	—	—	—	—	—	—	5	103	- -
Yukon Territory									
Proprietary	—	—	—	—	—	—	1	4	0.2
Federal	—	—	—	—	—	—	6	154	7.3
Northwest Territories									
Public	—	—	—	—	—	—	4	166	4.4
Proprietary	—	—	—	—	—	—	—	—	—
Federal	—	—	—	—	—	—	42	289	7.6
Canada									
Public	120	36,147	1.6	7	418	- -	1,175	187,286	8.1
Proprietary	7	505	- -	—	—	—	102	4,365	0.2
Federal	—	—	—	—	—	—	127	5,783	0.3

[1]Based on estimated population as at June 1, 1974.
[2]Tuberculosis sanatoria included under allied special.
[3]Based on estimated population as at June 1, 1976.

5.5   Movement of patients[1] and patient-days in reporting public, proprietary and federal hospitals, 1973 and 1974

Type of service and item	1973	1974	Type of service and item	1973	1974
PUBLIC HOSPITALS			**PROPRIETARY HOSPITALS**		
General			General		
Beds set up at Dec. 31	116,959	120,436	Beds set up at Dec. 31	434	357
Admissions	3,482,712	3,536,435	Admissions	15,371	12,856
Per 1,000 population	157.6	157.6	Per 1,000 population	0.7	0.6
Patient-days	33,281,898	34,263,829	Patient-days	130,375	104,706
Per 1,000 population	1,506.3	1,526.5	Per 1,000 population	5.9	4.7
Av. daily no. of patients	91,183.3	93,873.5	Av. daily no. of patients	357.2	286.9
Per 1,000 population	4.1	4.2	Per 1,000 population	- -	- -
Percentage occupancy[2]	77.1	76.2	Percentage occupancy[2]	81.7	79.5
Allied special			Allied special		
Beds set up at Dec. 31	23,401	23,506	Beds set up at Dec. 31	3,587	3,389
Admissions	176,413	170,651	Admissions	12,223	12,543
Per 1,000 population	8.0	7.6	Per 1,000 population	0.6	0.6
Patient-days	7,475,557	7,494,675	Patient-days	1,236,332	1,170,624
Per 1,000 population	338.3	333.9	Per 1,000 population	56.0	52.2
Av. daily no. of patients	20,481.0	20,533.4	Av. daily no. of patients	3,387.2	3,207.2
Per 1,000 population	0.9	0.9	Per 1,000 population	0.2	0.1
Percentage occupancy[2]	86.1	85.9	Percentage occupancy[2]	93.6	92.4
Mental			Mental		
Beds set up at Dec. 31	50,639	46,658	Beds set up at Dec. 31	992	997
Admissions	57,214	55,778	Admissions	3,751	4,124
Per 1,000 population	2.6	2.5	Per 1,000 population	0.2	0.2
Patient-days	17,118,841	15,547,115	Patient-days	351,381	351,422
Per 1,000 population	774.8	692.6	Per 1,000 population	15.9	15.7
Av. daily no. of patients	46,900.9	42,594.8	Av. daily no. of patients	962.7	962.8
Per 1,000 population	2.1	1.9	Per 1,000 population	- -	- -
Percentage occupancy[2]	90.8	90.1	Percentage occupancy[2]	96.5	96.1
Tuberculosis					
Beds set up at Dec. 31	869	415	**FEDERAL HOSPITALS**		
Admissions	2,278	1,219	General		
Per 1,000 population	0.1	0.1	Beds set up at Dec. 31	5,546	4,113
Patient-days	237,065	113,410	Admissions	54,381	46,140
Per 1,000 population	10.7	5.1	Per 1,000 population	2.5	2.1
Av. daily no. of patients	649.5	310.7	Patient-days	1,504,650	1,055,444
Per 1,000 population	- -	- -	Per 1,000 population	68.1	47.0
Percentage occupancy[2]	65.1	71.3	Av. daily no. of patients	4,122.3	2,891.6

5.5 Movement of patients¹ and patient-days in reporting public, proprietary and federal hospitals, 1973 and 1974 (concluded)

Type of service and item	1973	1974	Type of service and item	1973	1974
FEDERAL HOSPITALS (concluded)			Patient-days	365,450	360,302
Per 1,000 population	0.2	0.1	Per 1,000 population	16.5	16.1
Percentage occupancy²	68.6	63.2	Av. daily no. of patients	1,001.2	987.1
Allied special			Per 1,000 population	- -	- -
Beds set up at Dec. 31	1,328	1,307	Percentage occupancy²	71.8	72.1
Admissions	3,586	3,664			
Per 1,000 population	0.2	0.2			

¹Patients refer to adults and children. All ratios are based on population estimates as at June 1 of the year concerned.
²Based on rated bed capacity.

5.6 Average length of stay of adults and children in public general and allied special hospitals, by province, 1973 and 1974 (days)

Type of hospital	Nfld.	PEI	NS	NB	Que.	Ont.	Man.	Sask.	Alta.	BC	Canada¹
1973											
General											
Non-teaching with no long-term units											
1 - 24 beds	5.08	7.50	7.10	7.80	6.60	7.18	7.23	6.73	7.41	5.39	6.66
25 - 49 "	6.19	8.54	7.57	7.69	7.50	7.49	7.76	6.92	6.81	6.69	7.06
50 - 99 "	5.67	7.17	8.68	7.80	8.07	7.84	6.55	8.02	7.52	7.51	7.69
100 - 199 "	8.16	8.56	10.45	8.80	7.97	7.84	9.27	8.77	7.41	8.19	8.29
200+ "	8.79	9.73	10.06	7.90	9.49	8.31	8.90	11.59	7.96	7.56	8.66
Non-teaching with long-term units											
1 - 99 beds	16.37	—	—	—	12.71	10.31	8.01	5.91	13.51	8.94	10.08
100 - 199 "	—	7.58	—	—	9.41	9.23	8.51	—	10.39	9.43
200+ "	—	—	—	21.65	12.48	9.92	—	12.62	—	10.86	10.42
Total, non-teaching	7.16	8.32	9.37	8.39	9.18	8.96	7.87	7.70	7.41	9.09	8.70
Teaching, full											
1 - 499 beds	15.59	—	10.87	—	11.73	9.54	—	—	—	—	11.14
500+ "	—	—	13.71	—	11.97	10.57	10.54	12.73	9.94	10.05	10.86
Teaching, partial											
1 - 499 beds	10.89	—	—	—	9.56	13.91	9.08	10.74	—	8.97	9.92
500+ "	—	—	—	13.52	11.82	9.57	—	9.94	9.08	10.10	10.63
Total, general	9.24	8.32	10.15	9.41	10.15	9.39	8.79	8.81	8.55	9.31	9.41
Pediatric	10.93	—	8.12	—	7.88	7.95	—	—	9.41	6.01	8.13
Convalescent/ rehabilitation	45.34	27.59	24.83	61.38	51.63	32.63	—	—	43.80	46.07	41.63
Chronic/extended care	243.18	—	—	—	234.21	179.78	108.30	127.58	333.74	497.31	211.65
Other	4.24	—	6.84	—	12.11	9.40	—	1.57	7.82	7.45	9.70
All public general and allied special hospitals	9.68	8.52	10.03	9.46	12.28	10.64	9.82	9.62	11.25	10.05	10.79
1974											
General											
Non-teaching with no long-term units											
1 - 24 beds	4.53	6.83	7.23	7.19	7.24	7.97	7.22	6.72	7.97	5.56	6.85
25 - 49 "	6.76	7.11	7.43	7.73	8.00	7.29	8.08	6.88	6.71	6.87	7.11
50 - 99 "	5.50	6.66	8.64	7.70	8.19	7.89	7.51	8.43	7.23	7.24	7.70
100 - 199 "	7.61	8.36	10.47	8.74	7.93	7.72	7.19	8.32	7.93	7.43	8.18
200+ "	8.94	9.19	9.59	9.18	9.57	8.31	9.00	13.17	8.03	7.47	8.74
Non-teaching with long-term units											
1 - 99 beds	14.55	—	—	—	11.31	10.00	8.86	7.20	6.76	9.11	9.89
100 - 199 "	—	7.06	—	—	9.16	9.44	7.65	10.99	—	9.96	9.37
200+ "	—	—	—	22.33	13.19	9.71	14.80	14.63	—	10.71	10.44
Total, non-teaching	7.55	7.83	9.34	8.84	9.47	8.93	8.52	7.85	7.31	9.08	8.80
Teaching, full											
1 - 499 beds	15.33	—	11.06	—	13.05	9.75	—	—	—	—	11.80
500+ "	—	—	13.73	—	12.42	10.23	10.80	12.35	9.77	9.96	10.81

5.6   Average length of stay of adults and children in public general and allied special hospitals, by province, 1973 and 1974 (days) (concluded)

Type of hospital	Nfld.	PEI	NS	NB	Que.	Ont.	Man.	Sask.	Alta.	BC	Canada[1]
1974 (concluded)											
Teaching, partial											
1 - 499 beds	10.57	—	—	—	9.46	15.02	—	10.38	—	8.87	9.72
500+ ``	—	—	—	13.91	12.18	9.30	—	12.91	8.44	9.87	11.01
Total, general	9.88	7.83	10.17	9.84	10.47	9.29	9.22	9.29	8.41	9.27	9.50
Pediatric	9.76	—	8.15	—	8.58	8.49	—	—	10.42	5.15	8.52
Convalescent/ rehabilitation	38.52	31.09	24.27	62.40	44.70	33.51	—	—	42.30	59.17	41.75
Chronic/extended care	272.25	—	—	—	186.65	181.65	178.03	581.26	376.50	533.83	218.19
Other	4.33	—	6.68	—	17.80	9.60	1.75	—	7.21	6.77	9.98
All public general and allied special hospitals	10.20	8.05	10.06	9.89	12.91	10.50	9.97	10.02	11.38	10.09	10.95

[1]Includes the Yukon Territory and Northwest Territories.

5.7   Full-time personnel employed in reporting public, proprietary and federal hospitals, by province, 1973 and 1974

Province or territory	General[1]		General and allied special[1]		Mental		Tuberculosis	
	Number	Per 100 rated beds	Number	Per 100 rated beds	Number	Per 100 rated beds	Number	Per 100 rated beds
1973								
Newfoundland	6,036	229.2	6,754	215.2	620	137.8	—	—
Prince Edward Island	1,220	169.2	1,265	168.4	264	88.9	23	153.3
Nova Scotia	9,104	188.4	10,172	189.7	1,545	89.6	311	227.0
New Brunswick	8,425	192.4	8,463	192.4	1,201	87.7	—	—
Quebec	64,482	224.8	80,456	193.6	12,815	73.6	357	70.1
Ontario	86,135	195.0	96,648	186.1	19,893	115.2	—	—
Manitoba	12,516	200.3	13,573	192.2	2,278	99.7	—	—
Saskatchewan	9,365	140.3	10,270	133.2	1,353	74.5	141	97.9
Alberta	19,346	163.5	22,644	148.8	3,694	80.7	—	—
British Columbia	21,860	155.8	23,759	150.2	4,288	78.8	179	93.2
Yukon Territory	176	120.5	187	119.9	—	—	—	—
Northwest Territories	281	133.8	425	114.6	—	—	—	—
Canada	238,946	191.7	274,616	178.9	47,951	91.1	1,011	101.4
1974								
Newfoundland	6,383	242.0	7,189	228.7	645	143.3	—	—
Prince Edward Island	1,189	164.0	1,235	164.4	280	94.6	25	166.7
Nova Scotia	9,585	201.6	10,695	202.4	1,565	91.5	295	228.7
New Brunswick	8,272	191.1	8,307	191.1	1,264	92.3	—	—
Quebec	67,253	224.3	83,329	195.2	11,719	74.8	—	—
Ontario	87,041	191.0	98,265	182.8	19,938	125.7	—	—
Manitoba	13,380	198.9	14,103	195.3	2,456	107.7	—	—
Saskatchewan	9,900	140.0	10,494	133.9	1,176	89.3	134	93.1
Alberta	20,122	171.4	23,429	155.0	3,721	84.5	—	—
British Columbia	22,572	157.7	24,763	152.1	4,221	87.1	170	114.9
Yukon Territory	182	122.1	196	123.3	—	—	—	—
Northwest Territories	216	143.0	333	118.9	—	—	—	—
Canada	246,095	192.0	282,338	180.0	46,985	97.3	624	143.1

[1]Includes all medical interns and residents, other instructors, school staff and students of formally organized educational programs. Excludes all other medical staff.

5.8   Revenue and expenditure of operating public general hospitals, by province, 1973 and 1974

Year and province or territory	Operating hospitals	Total revenue $'000	Expenditure				
			Gross salaries and wages[1] %	Medical and surgical supplies %	Drugs %	Supplies and other expenses %	Total $'000
1973							
Newfoundland	33	54,598	63.6	3.4	3.3	29.7	57,644
Prince Edward Island	8	10,303	66.1	3.5	3.3	27.1	10,468
Nova Scotia	43	89,412	64.2	3.6	3.0	29.3	89,534
New Brunswick	37	84,747	66.8	3.8	2.5	26.9	86,370
Quebec	127	757,135	71.3	3.3	2.6	22.7	768,554
Ontario	189	1,038,328	68.7	3.2	2.6	25.5	1,046,298
Manitoba	79	124,280	67.0	3.5	3.1	26.5	124,280
Saskatchewan	131	104,694	70.8	3.2	3.1	27.0	107,405

5.8   Revenue and expenditure of operating public general hospitals, by province, 1973 and 1974 (concluded)

Year and province or territory	Operating hospitals	Total revenue $'000	Expenditure				
			Gross salaries and wages[1] %	Medical and surgical supplies %	Drugs %	Supplies and other expenses %	Total $'000
1973 (concluded)							
Alberta	118	191,819	69.5	3.1	2.9	24.6	199,116
British Columbia	92	252,279	73.8	3.4	2.5	20.3	261,249
Yukon Territory	—	—	—	—	—	—	—
Northwest Territories	4	2,650	65.8	3.6	2.1	28.5	2,810
Canada	861	2,710,245	69.5	3.3	2.7	24.5	2,753,728
1974							
Newfoundland	33	69,913	63.8	3.3	3.0	30.0	73,041
Prince Edward Island	8	12,089	66.4	3.9	3.3	26.4	12,358
Nova Scotia	43	107,916	64.0	3.8	2.9	29.3	108,012
New Brunswick	37	100,488	65.2	3.9	2.4	28.6	102,022
Quebec	127	954,722	70.9	3.2	2.3	23.6	967,190
Ontario	190	1,266,263	69.8	3.2	2.4	24.6	1,272,525
Manitoba	79	148,996	66.5	3.4	2.8	27.3	149,002
Saskatchewan	131	130,635	68.0	3.2	2.7	26.0	134,175
Alberta	117	225,231	69.0	3.2	2.7	25.2	238,366
British Columbia	92	339,999	75.0	3.2	2.2	19.6	349,643
Yukon Territory	—	—	—	—	—	—	—
Northwest Territories	3	2,834	64.1	3.2	2.5	30.2	3,085
Canada	860	3,359,086	69.9	3.2	2.4	24.4	3,409,419

[1]Includes medical staff remuneration.

5.9   Patient-day revenue[1] and expenditure ratios of reporting public hospitals, by province and type of hospital, 1973 and 1974 (dollars)

Year, province and type of hospital	Revenue		Expenditure				
	Gross income from in-patient services	Total	Gross salaries and wages[2]	Medical and surgical supplies	Drugs	Supplies and other expenses	Total
1973							
NEWFOUNDLAND							
General	63.81	76.90	51.66	2.75	2.70	24.09	81.19
Allied special							
Pediatric	74.41	87.32	59.07	3.77	2.38	25.90	91.13
Convalescent/rehabilitation	56.11	64.37	47.06	0.90	0.39	17.87	66.22
Chronic/extended care	15.90	16.97	15.07	0.13	0.13	3.32	18.65
PRINCE EDWARD ISLAND							
General	45.89	54.32	36.50	1.91	1.81	14.97	55.19
Allied special							
Convalescent/rehabilitation	41.35	52.05	41.02	0.28	0.53	10.22	52.05
Mental	13.10	13.24	12.69	0.12	0.40	5.11	18.32
Tuberculosis	32.69	33.95	25.93	0.51	0.52	6.99	33.95
NOVA SCOTIA							
General	59.82	74.97	48.18	2.68	2.24	21.97	75.07
Allied special							
Pediatric	98.82	114.27	72.66	4.33	1.78	38.13	116.90
Convalescent/rehabilitation	39.09	49.38	34.60	0.67	0.70	13.05	49.02
Other	81.95	90.44	58.78	2.37	1.58	27.26	89.99
Mental	29.74	31.71	23.92	0.13	0.50	7.44	31.99
Tuberculosis	64.19	72.51	56.89	0.78	2.15	12.69	72.51
NEW BRUNSWICK							
General	55.20	67.56	46.02	2.59	1.71	18.54	68.85
Allied special							
Convalescent/rehabilitation	45.67	51.75	38.53	0.65	0.43	13.08	52.70
Mental	21.94	22.26	17.38	0.09	0.29	4.50	22.26
QUEBEC							
General	90.30	99.52	72.22	3.34	2.67	22.89	101.12
Allied special							
Pediatric	131.42	152.34	113.47	4.28	2.87	35.89	156.50
Convalescent/rehabilitation	39.08	44.16	31.52	0.66	0.47	11.85	44.50
Chronic/extended care	29.67	32.74	24.73	0.35	0.55	7.22	32.85
Other	105.70	115.46	85.06	3.15	2.39	24.90	115.50
Mental	25.48	26.39	19.37	0.08	0.40	6.62	26.47
Tuberculosis	39.85	40.55	30.71	0.22	2.11	9.62	42.66

5.9   Patient-day revenue[1] and expenditure ratios of reporting public hospitals, by province and type of hospital, 1973 and 1974 (dollars) (continued)

Year, province and type of hospital	Revenue		Expenditure				
	Gross in-come from in-patient services	Total	Gross salaries and wages[2]	Medical and surgical supplies	Drugs	Supplies and other expenses	Total
1973 (concluded)							
ONTARIO							
General	71.13	85.29	59.05	2.75	2.21	21.93	85.95
Allied special							
Pediatric	131.00	172.90	117.98	4.30	7.63	52.29	182.20
Convalescent/rehabilitation	46.39	54.80	35.76	0.45	0.51	18.39	55.11
Chronic/extended care	32.02	34.73	25.17	0.38	0.53	8.36	34.45
Other	107.47	164.36	108.98	2.34	5.62	55.82	172.76
Mental	41.70	42.44	34.79	0.07	0.34	6.83	42.03
MANITOBA							
General	68.01	78.03	52.26	2.70	2.39	20.68	78.03
Allied special							
Chronic/extended care	35.84	37.60	29.02	0.47	0.84	7.27	37.60
Mental	27.45 ~	27.76	22.27	0.09	0.51	4.95	27.82
SASKATCHEWAN							
General	48.55	56.78	38.89	1.86	1.78	15.68	58.22
Allied special							
Chronic/extended care	42.45	47.68	35.64	1.42	0.40	12.64	50.10
Mental	20.35	20.62	17.05	0.09	0.35	3.81	21.30
Tuberculosis	30.26	30.91	22.45	0.20	0.62	7.35	30.62
ALBERTA							
General	57.91	66.96	48.32	2.16	1.98	17.06	69.52
Allied special							
Pediatric	79.37	97.96	70.36	1.12	0.96	20.75	93.20
Convalescent/rehabilitation	57.11	73.59	50.22	0.47	0.41	20.91	72.00
Chronic/extended care	21.27	22.63	15.93	1.42	0.38	7.57	24.12
Other	60.95	127.27	96.56	1.92	4.73	27.12	130.32
Mental	21.93	22.15	16.35	0.06	0.25	5.49	22.15
Tuberculosis	..	..	..	..	..	..	..
BRITISH COLUMBIA							
General	59.51	65.85	50.29	2.30	1.72	13.87	68.19
Allied special							
Pediatric	80.83	118.44	101.12	2.02	1.87	32.35	137.35
Convalescent/rehabilitation	31.72	35.97	28.60	0.42	0.37	7.39	36.78
Chronic/extended care	23.09	24.21	24.46	0.24	0.38	6.36	31.44
Other	71.15	123.17	93.47	1.96	3.59	27.38	126.37
Mental	27.84	27.96	22.09	0.29	0.35	5.22	27.96
Tuberculosis	59.03	59.03	40.52	0.34	3.22	14.95	59.03
NORTHWEST TERRITORIES							
General	60.07	67.40	47.02	2.58	1.52	20.34	71.46
CANADA							
General	70.30	81.33	57.46	2.72	2.21	20.27	82.66
Allied special							
Pediatric	118.98	145.70	103.36	4.07	4.15	39.85	151.43
Convalescent/rehabilitation	41.38	48.69	34.51	0.53	0.45	13.40	48.90
Chronic/extended care	29.07	31.66	23.71	0.36	0.47	7.68	32.27
Other	96.19	124.63	89.74	2.70	3.28	31.05	126.77
Mental	30.31	30.99	24.27	0.10	0.37	6.22	30.95
Tuberculosis	45.35	47.38	35.29	0.35	1.91	10.52	48.07
1974							
NEWFOUNDLAND							
General	78.94	93.52	62.29	3.25	2.88	29.29	97.71
Allied special							
Pediatric	90.61	104.55	68.91	4.13	2.54	32.90	108.48
Convalescent/rehabilitation	76.97	98.51	63.89	0.99	0.44	26.48	91.80
Chronic/extended care	19.03	23.57	19.37	0.14	0.15	5.98	25.65
PRINCE EDWARD ISLAND							
General	54.37	63.89	43.37	2.56	2.13	17.25	65.31
Allied special							
Convalescent/rehabilitation	48.34	61.21	47.84	0.20	0.51	13.84	62.38
Mental	17.91	17.91	13.98	0.12	0.39	5.74	20.22
Tuberculosis	33.30	34.59	27.18	0.44	0.59	6.38	34.59

5.9   Patient-day revenue[1] and expenditure ratios of reporting public hospitals, by province and type of hospital, 1973 and 1974 (dollars) (continued)

Year, province and type of hospital	Revenue		Expenditure				
	Gross income from in-patient services	Total	Gross salaries and wages[2]	Medical and surgical supplies	Drugs	Supplies and other expenses	Total
1974 (continued)							
NOVA SCOTIA							
General	71.93	89.63	57.39	3.42	2.58	26.32	89.71
Allied special							
Pediatric	114.78	133.71	83.85	4.80	2.26	45.00	135.91
Convalescent/rehabilitation	46.86	55.77	38.47	0.79	0.68	15.49	55.43
Other	100.14	112.41	73.48	3.38	1.97	32.94	111.78
Mental	35.50	38.12	28.40	0.11	0.49	9.30	38.31
Tuberculosis	64.80	74.61	66.48	0.58	2.46	17.54	87.06
NEW BRUNSWICK							
General	66.84	81.69	54.05	3.23	1.96	23.69	82.93
Allied special							
Convalescent/rehabilitation	52.38	59.29	43.36	0.68	0.48	16.01	60.53
Mental	27.17	27.44	21.16	0.10	0.34	5.85	27.44
QUEBEC							
General	109.95	120.84	86.75	3.89	2.86	28.91	122.41
Allied special							
Pediatric	164.07	187.02	136.21	5.23	3.63	43.31	188.37
Convalescent/rehabilitation	53.37	68.14	47.29	1.10	0.52	18.59	67.50
Chronic/extended care	36.98	41.42	30.11	0.41	0.57	9.85	40.94
Other	139.82	155.34	108.69	5.25	2.70	36.36	153.00
Mental	31.65	32.84	23.45	0.08	0.44	9.02	32.99
ONTARIO							
General	84.89	101.86	71.52	3.26	2.43	25.16	102.37
Allied special							
Pediatric	159.81	207.70	138.54	5.46	8.45	58.45	210.90
Convalescent/rehabilitation	58.64	69.24	45.65	0.50	0.54	22.69	69.38
Chronic/extended care	39.14	42.51	30.90	0.44	0.59	10.12	42.05
Other	134.95	197.01	133.00	2.76	6.24	64.15	206.16
Mental	50.56	51.89	40.87	0.10	0.38	10.43	51.78
MANITOBA							
General	79.76	92.13	61.35	3.10	2.53	25.14	92.13
Allied special							
Chronic/extended care	46.11	49.09	38.61	0.44	1.22	8.82	49.09
Mental	31.53	31.90	25.48	0.07	0.57	5.93	32.05
SASKATCHEWAN							
General	59.54	69.23	48.38	2.31	1.90	18.50	71.09
Mental	27.97	28.39	23.49	0.14	0.46	4.30	28.39
Tuberculosis	42.10	43.05	33.00	0.25	0.90	10.09	44.24
ALBERTA							
General	67.28	77.91	56.84	2.64	2.19	20.79	82.46
Allied special							
Pediatric	101.65	135.50	109.92	1.56	1.11	36.69	149.28
Convalescent/rehabilitation	63.32	82.17	58.10	0.53	0.40	25.26	84.29
Chronic/extended care	23.89	26.07	18.59	0.23	0.39	9.06	28.27
Other	75.07	160.69	115.55	2.44	7.50	35.87	161.36
Mental	27.37	27.59	20.67	0.09	0.25	6.37	27.37
Tuberculosis	..	..	..	..	..	..	..
BRITISH COLUMBIA							
General	74.63	83.14	64.09	2.78	1.93	16.75	85.55
Allied special							
Pediatric	113.13	166.59	138.92	2.62	2.12	40.83	184.49
Convalescent/rehabilitation	42.59	48.17	38.95	0.57	0.29	10.15	49.96
Chronic/extended care	27.60	28.99	27.78	0.26	0.30	8.09	36.43
Other	91.71	157.48	123.23	2.45	4.26	32.08	162.02
Mental[e]	35.54	35.72	28.31	0.37	0.45	6.59	35.72
Tuberculosis	44.26	44.26	52.60	0.73	2.35	17.95	73.63
NORTHWEST TERRITORIES							
General	81.11	91.17	63.62	3.13	2.49	30.00	99.24

5.9   Patient-day revenue[1] and expenditure ratios of reporting public hospitals, by province and type of hospital, 1973 and 1974 (dollars) (concluded)

Year, province and type of hospital	Revenue		Expenditure				
	Gross income from in-patient services	Total	Gross salaries and wages[2]	Medical and surgical supplies	Drugs	Supplies and other expenses	Total
1974 (concluded)							
CANADA							
General	84.90	98.21	69.68	3.24	2.42	24.34	99.68
Allied special							
Pediatric	147.25	177.72	123.96	4.96	4.82	47.12	180.86
Convalescent/rehabilitation	52.78	64.49	45.91	0.75	0.46	17.92	65.03
Chronic/extended care	34.76	38.46	28.35	0.38	0.54	9.65	38.92
Other	120.65	163.16	114.71	3.77	4.31	42.15	164.94
Mental[e]	37.60	38.58	29.51	0.12	0.41	8.57	38.61
Tuberculosis	49.01	52.38	48.72	0.49	1.77	14.36	65.34

[1] Adults and children.
[2] Includes medical staff remuneration.

5.10   Hospital separations, separations and days per 100,000 population, and average days of stay, by diagnostic category, 1973[1]

Diagnostic category[2]	Separations	Separations per 100,000 population	Days per 100,000 population	Average days of stay
Infective and parasitic diseases	109,290	496	4,645	9.4
Neoplasms	208,912	947	15,920	16.8
Endocrine, nutritional, and metabolic diseases	73,899	335	5,833	17.4
Diseases of the blood and blood-forming organs	26,400	120	1,322	11.0
Mental disorders	148,566	674	11,671	17.3
Diseases of the nervous system and sense organs	155,060	703	12,192	17.3
Diseases of the circulatory system	365,357	1,657	38,633	23.3
Diseases of the respiratory system	470,106	2,132	15,265	7.2
Diseases of the digestive system	447,856	2,031	19,047	9.4
Diseases of the genito-urinary system	350,154	1,588	11,872	7.5
Complications of pregnancy, childbirth and the puerperium	490,342	4,444	23,954	5.4
Diseases of the skin and subcutaneous tissue	64,099	291	2,640	9.1
Diseases of the musculoskeletal system and connective tissue	159,730	724	10,486	14.5
Congenital anomalies	43,310	196	2,272	11.6
Symptoms and ill-defined conditions	139,597	633	4,299	6.8
Accidents, poisonings, and violence (nature of injury)	347,512	1,576	17,205	10.9
Supplementary classifications	93,362	423	3,311	7.8
All causes	3,693,552	16,749	188,598	11.3

[1] Excludes newborn and data for the Yukon Territory and Northwest Territories.
[2] Major groupings of the International Classification of Diseases, Adapted — 8th Revision. More detailed information is available in Statistics Canada publication *Hospital morbidity* (Cat. No. 82-206) and *Hospital morbidity — Canadian diagnostic list* (Cat. No. 82-209).

5.11   Hospital separations per 100,000 population, by diagnostic category and age group, 1973[1]

Diagnostic category[2]	Under 15	15-24	25-44	45-64	65+	Total
Infective and parasitic diseases	1,023	309	233	259	500	496
Neoplasms	119	272	768	1,891	3,686	947
Endocrine, nutritional, and metabolic diseases	189	146	220	534	1,159	335
Diseases of the blood and blood-forming organs	181	69	47	84	335	120
Mental disorders	105	577	994	1,116	805	674
Diseases of the nervous system and sense organs	760	320	444	834	1,891	703
Diseases of the circulatory system	51	163	818	3,235	9,484	1,657
Diseases of the respiratory system	4,250	1,154	802	1,321	3,206	2,132
Diseases of the digestive system	903	1,511	2,053	3,263	4,142	2,031
Diseases of the genito-urinary system	504	1,114	2,180	2,422	2,579	1,588
Complications of pregnancy, childbirth and the puerperium	33	11,319	9,045	48	—	4,444
Diseases of the skin and subcutaneous tissue	302	328	245	264	370	291
Diseases of the musculoskeletal system and connective tissue	179	478	799	1,330	1,516	724
Congenital anomalies	451	145	96	72	52	196
Symptoms and ill-defined conditions	553	479	566	772	1,144	633
Accidents, poisonings, and violence (nature of injury)	1,253	1,956	1,396	1,442	2,659	1,576
Supplementary classifications	51	205	1,157	214	365	423
All causes	10,891	14,821	17,286	19,077	33,892	16,749

[1] Excludes newborn and data for the Yukon Territory and Northwest Territories.
[2] See footnote to Table 5.10.

5.12 Separated cases and operations in general and allied special hospitals, by age group, 1973[1]

Item		Under 15	15-24	25-44	45-64	65+	Total
All separated cases							
Cases	*No.*	672,416	618,017	987,000	794,344	621,775	3,693,552
Days in hospital	''	4,299,073	3,922,050	7,579,546	10,317,827	15,471,734	41,590,230
Av. days per case	''	6.4	6.3	7.7	13.0	24.9	11.3
Separated cases undergoing surgery							
Cases (primary operations)	*No.*	270,505	358,440	622,347	406,524	208,842	1,866,658
Days in hospital	''	1,357,090	2,197,256	4,397,820	4,642,148	3,845,146	16,439,460
Av. days per case	''	5.0	6.1	7.1	11.4	18.4	8.8
Rate per 100,000 population							
All separated cases		10,891	14,821	17,286	19,077	33,892	16,749
All operated cases		4,381	8,596	10,899	9,763	11,384	8,465
Days of all separated cases		69,632	94,056	132,744	247,792	843,330	188,598
Days of all operated cases		21,981	52,693	77,021	111,486	209,590	74,548
Population[2]		6,174,000	4,169,900	5,709,900	4,163,900	1,834,600	22,052,300

[1]Excludes newborn and data for the Yukon Territory and Northwest Territories.
[2]Estimate of Aug. 1, 1973, exclusive of the Yukon Territory and Northwest Territories.

5.13 Primary operations in general and allied special hospitals, by age group and by sex, 1973[1]

Operation		Under 15	15-24	25-44	45-64	65+	Total
Neurosurgery	M	1,574	1,459	3,045	4,272	1,721	12,071
	F	1,145	781	2,363	3,613	1,337	9,239
Ophthalmology	M	6,982	2,227	3,112	6,259	8,733	27,313
	F	6,269	1,929	2,666	6,273	12,936	30,073
Otorhinolaryngology	M	62,455	17,471	16,699	8,526	2,431	107,582
	F	57,117	21,470	14,238	6,747	1,687	101,259
Thyroid, parathyroid and adrenals	M	279	200	391	420	99	1,389
	F	311	519	1,585	1,845	438	4,698
Vascular and cardiac surgery	M	1,841	1,027	4,214	12,224	5,546	24,852
	F	1,536	1,170	10,000	11,479	3,818	28,003
Thoracic surgery	M	452	804	1,041	2,393	1,512	6,202
	F	323	298	697	1,211	878	3,407
Abdominal surgery	M	22,404	13,945	28,156	41,717	21,576	127,798
	F	11,187	19,785	38,755	40,340	18,677	128,744
Proctological surgery	M	631	4,204	10,443	7,544	2,400	25,222
	F	421	3,950	7,175	5,736	2,063	19,345
Urological surgery	M	15,815	5,353	10,977	18,682	26,578	77,405
	F	3,194	1,590	4,998	6,397	3,799	19,978
Breast surgery	M	111	234	218	315	224	1,102
	F	118	2,203	7,144	7,849	2,836	20,150
Gynecological surgery	F	630	28,635	171,371	61,804	8,984	271,424
Obstetrical procedures	F	654	133,193	142,417	638	—	276,902
Orthopaedic surgery	M	17,275	26,688	32,834	25,609	9,443	111,849
	F	12,561	12,949	18,013	24,732	18,620	86,875
Plastic surgery	M	8,824	9,113	8,697	6,816	3,342	36,792
	F	6,864	6,559	8,654	6,732	3,618	32,427
Oral and maxillofacial surgery	M	1,267	2,160	2,248	1,335	490	7,500
	F	1,038	1,139	1,331	1,020	462	4,990
Dental surgery	M	4,685	6,834	6,733	4,174	1,037	23,463
	F	5,287	8,980	7,398	3,941	881	26,487
Biopsy	M	983	912	2,408	5,407	4,605	14,315
	F	725	2,023	6,111	6,620	3,370	18,849
Diagnostic endoscopy	M	2,689	1,624	5,313	11,527	10,159	31,312
	F	3,082	3,109	6,976	7,678	5,699	26,544
Diagnostic radiography	M	2,048	2,020	6,203	9,848	4,964	25,083
	F	2,329	2,708	6,190	6,883	3,809	21,919
Radiotherapy and related therapies	M	159	102	300	696	492	1,749
	F	115	73	580	1,805	971	3,544
Physical medicine and rehabilitation	M	1,358	738	1,411	2,327	2,422	8,256
	F	983	675	1,497	2,231	3,067	8,453
Other non-surgical procedures	M	1,621	4,040	9,320	12,606	2,143	29,730
	F	1,144	3,545	8,424	8,251	972	22,336
Other surgical and non-surgical procedures	M	5	—	—	—	1	6
	F	14	2	1	2	2	21
All operations	M	153,458	101,155	153,763	182,697	109,918	700,991
	F	117,047	257,285	468,584	223,827	98,924	1,165,667
	T	270,505	358,440	622,347	406,524	208,842	1,866,658

[1]Excludes newborn and data for the Yukon Territory and Northwest Territories.

5.14   Malignant neoplasms and rate per 100,000 population, 1973

Province or territory of residence	Number of cases			Rate per 100,000 population		
	New primary sites	Deaths[1]	Hospital morbidity separations	New primary sites	Deaths	Hospital morbidity separations
Newfoundland	1,267	636	2,267	234.3	117.6	419.2
Prince Edward Island	403	193	635	350.7	168.0	552.7
Nova Scotia	2,259	1,372	5,291	280.7	170.5	657.4
New Brunswick	2,113	943	3,694	324.1	144.7	566.7
Quebec	16,927	9,141	28,343	278.3	150.3	466.1
Ontario	..	11,951	53,469	..	150.5	673.5
Manitoba	3,468	1,667	6,594	347.6	167.1	660.9
Saskatchewan	3,813	1,546	6,663	419.9	170.2	721.7
Alberta	4,823	1,998	9,653	286.5	118.7	573.4
British Columbia	9,446	3,578	15,350	408.0	154.6	663.1
Yukon Territory	34	15	..	172.6	76.1	..
Northwest Territories	98	29	..	259.3	76.7	..
Canada	44,651	33,069	131,959	315.4	147.9	598.4

[1]Includes only the deaths where underlying cause was stated to be due to malignant neoplasms.

5.15   Malignant neoplasms by A List Diagnosis and rate per 100,000 population, 1973

A List Diagnosis	Cases[1]	Rate per 100,000 population[1]	Deaths	Rate per 100,000 population	Hospital separations[2]	Rate per 100,000 population[2]
A45 Malignant neoplasm of buccal cavity and pharynx	1,387	9.8	722	3.3	3,325	15.1
A46 Malignant neoplasm of esophagus	343	2.4	580	2.6	1,504	6.8
A47 Malignant neoplasm of stomach	1,651	11.7	2,465	11.2	4,900	22.2
A48 Malignant neoplasm of intestine except rectum	3,357	23.8	3,844	17.4	10,116	45.9
A49 Malignant neoplasm of rectum and rectosigmoid junction	1,754	12.4	1,341	6.1	5,295	24.0
A50 Malignant neoplasm of larynx	450	3.2	310	1.4	1,795	8.1
A51 Malignant neoplasm of trachea, bronchus, and lung	3,847	27.3	6,144	27.8	14,489	65.7
A52 Malignant neoplasm of bone	135	1.0	172	0.8	1,108	5.0
A53 Malignant neoplasm of skin	8,439	59.9	367	1.7	3,994	18.1
A54 Malignant neoplasm of breast	5,084	36.1	3,046	13.8	14,937	67.7
A55 Malignant neoplasm of cervix uteri	878	12.5	546	4.9	5,140	23.3
A56 Other malignant neoplasm of uterus	1,255	17.8	465	4.2	4,165	18.9
A57 Malignant neoplasm of prostate	2,695	38.2	1,700	15.4	8,957	40.6
A58 Malignant neoplasm of other and unspecified sites	7,896	56.0	8,256	37.4	34,109	154.7
A59 Leukemia	960	6.8	1,370	6.2	6,699	30.4
A60 Other neoplasms of lymphatic and haematopoietic tissue	1,645	11.7	1,741	7.9	11,426	51.8
Total	41,776	296.3	33,069	149.7	131,959	598.4

[1]Excludes Ontario, the Yukon Territory and Northwest Territories.
[2]Excludes the Yukon Territory and Northwest Territories.

5.16   Summary statistics on the incidence of tuberculosis, 1974

Province or territory, age group and origin	Notifications		Patients under treatment at Dec. 31			Persons receiving preventive out-pa- tient drug treatment Dec. 31	Deaths
	New active cases	React- ivated cases	In- patients	Out- patients on drug treatment	Total		
PROVINCE OR TERRITORY	*Number*						
Newfoundland	145	21	31	323	354	134	6
Prince Edward Island	13	4	11	25	36	77	—
Nova Scotia	87	12	73	247	320	408	7
New Brunswick	85	15	27	240	267	231	6
Quebec	934	100	377	1,539	1,916	2,459	158
Ontario	979	123	302	1,701	2,003	6,061	78
Manitoba	261	31	51	485	536	986	20
Saskatchewan	148	19	46	272	318	253	11
Alberta	249	25	98	533	631	1,329	12
British Columbia	395	50	77	758	835	788	26
Yukon Territory	6	1	3	11	14	101	—
Northwest Territories	52	15	17	133	150	1,083	6
Canada	3,354	416	1,113	6,267	7,380	13,910	330

5.16   Summary statistics on the incidence of tuberculosis, 1974 (concluded)

Province or territory, age group and origin	Notifications		Patients under treatment at Dec. 31			Persons receiving preventive out-pa-tient drug treatment Dec. 31	Deaths
	New active cases	React-ivated cases	In-patients	Out-patients on drug treatment	Total		
PROVINCE OR TERRITORY	*Rate per 100,000 population*						
Newfoundland	26.7	3.9	5.7	59.2	64.8	24.5	1.1
Prince Edward Island	11.1	3.4	9.3	21.2	30.5	65.3	—
Nova Scotia	10.7	1.5	8.9	30.2	39.1	49.9	0.9
New Brunswick	12.8	2.3	4.0	35.8	39.9	34.5	0.9
Quebec	15.2	1.6	6.1	25.0	31.1	39.9	2.6
Ontario	12.1	1.5	3.7	20.8	24.5	74.2	1.0
Manitoba	25.8	3.1	5.0	47.8	52.9	97.2	2.0
Saskatchewan	16.3	2.1	5.0	29.8	34.9	27.7	1.2
Alberta	14.5	1.5	5.6	30.5	36.1	76.1	0.7
British Columbia	16.5	2.1	3.2	31.1	34.2	32.3	1.1
Yukon Territory	30.9	5.2	15.0	55.0	70.0	505.0	—
Northwest Territories	138.7	40.0	45.9	359.5	405.4	2,972.0	16.0
Canada	14.9	1.9	4.9	27.7	32.6	61.4	1.5
AGE GROUP	*Number*						
0 - 14	323	1	76	567	643	2,620	4
15 - 24	414	13	66	697	763	3,077	4
25 - 44	1,027	110	227	1,958	2,185	3,773	34
45 - 64	931	190	405	1,996	2,401	3,354	110
65 and over	659	102	339	1,049	1,388	1,086	178
Not stated	—	—	—	—	—	—	—
Total	3,354	416	1,113	6,267	7,380	13,910	330
	Rate per 100,000 population						
0 - 14	5.3	- -	1.2	9.2	10.4	42.6	0.1
15 - 24	9.6	0.3	1.5	16.0	17.5	70.7	0.1
25 - 44	17.4	1.9	3.8	32.8	36.6	63.2	0.7
45 - 64	21.9	4.5	9.5	46.6	56.0	78.3	2.6
65 and over	35.0	5.4	17.8	55.2	73.0	57.1	9.5
Total	14.9	1.9	4.9	27.7	32.6	61.4	1.5
ORIGIN[1]	*Number*						
Indian	480	84	142	897	1,039	1,490	. .
Inuit	39	13	13	120	133	760	. .
Other	2,835	319	958	5,250	6,208	11,660	. .
Total	3,354	416	1,113	6,267	7,380	13,910	. .
	Percentage distribution						
Indian	14	20	13	14	14	11	. .
Inuit	1	3	1	2	2	5	. .
Other	85	77	86	84	84	84	. .
Total	100	100	100	100	100	100	. .

[1]This classification is shown to point up the high incidence of tuberculosis among the native population; Indians constituted 1.1% of the total population in 1961 and Inuit 0.1%.

5.17   Total therapeutic abortions[1] and abortion rate per 100 live births, by province, 1973-75

Province or territory	Number of therapeutic abortions			Rate per 100 live births		
	1973	1974	1975	1973	1974	1975
Newfoundland	193	184	176	1.6	1.8	1.6
Prince Edward Island	41	50	77	2.2	2.6	3.8
Nova Scotia	932	1,062	1,017	7.0	8.2	7.1
New Brunswick	341	440	379	3.0	3.8	3.1
Quebec	3,141	4,453	5,579	3.7	5.2	6.5
Ontario	22,603	24,795	24,921	18.3	20.0	19.5
Manitoba	1,259	1,411	1,298	7.4	8.2	7.2
Saskatchewan	1,219	1,176	1,282	8.2	7.8	8.1
Alberta	4,047	4,391	4,333	13.8	14.7	12.9
British Columbia	9,176	10,024	10,076	26.7	28.3	26.1
Yukon Territory	76	63	77	18.1	12.7	14.9
Northwest Territories	51	75	95	4.2	7.2	8.7
Residence not reported	122	12	1	. . .	. . .	. . .
Canada	43,201	48,136	49,311	12.6	13.9	13.6

[1]In addition 44 abortions were performed on non-residents in 1973, 62 in 1974 and 79 in 1975.

5.18   Psychiatric in-patient movement, by type of institution and sex, 1975P

Type of institution	Reporting institutions	Admissions[1]		Separations[2]		Patients on books, Dec. 31, 1975[3]	
		Male	Female	Male	Female	Male	Female
Public mental hospital	44	21,184	13,893	22,229	14,622	13,569	10,074
Institution for the mentally retarded	87	2,805	1,923	3,041	2,188	11,365	8,533
Public psychiatric unit	133	25,037	37,825	24,956	37,653	1,530	2,173
Federal psychiatric unit	7	898	69	940	65	789	15
Psychiatric hospital	14	8,027	7,764	8,088	7,774	842	839
Aged and senile home	5	105	75	128	99	530	479
Hospital for addicts	20	8,122	1,721	8,092	1,752	369	58
Treatment centre for emotionally disturbed children	56	1,469	882	1,435	847	1,290	631
Epilepsy hospital	2	116	86	131	89	131	62
All institutions	368	67,763	64,238	69,040	65,089	30,415	22,864

[1]Includes first admissions, readmissions and transfers-in.
[2]Includes discharges, deaths and transfers-out.
[3]Includes in addition to patients actually in residence those absent on probationary leave, boarding in approved homes, or otherwise absent from the institutions but not officially separated.

5.19   Average annual salaries[1] of nursing personnel in public hospitals, by academic qualifications, employment category and type of hospital, 1974

Category	Average salary $
ACADEMIC QUALIFICATIONS[2]	
Graduate nurse only	8,843
Clinical postgraduate training	9,613
University diploma — one year	9,666
Bachelor's degree in nursing	9,400
Master's degree in nursing	10,844
EMPLOYMENT CATEGORY[3]	
Nursing director	12,716
Director nursing education	12,419
Associate or assistant director nursing education	11,939
Nursing supervisor	11,433
Head nurse	10,689
Assistant head nurse	9,528
Teacher	10,211
General duty	
Registered	8,848
Not registered	7,935
TYPE OF PUBLIC HOSPITAL[4]	
General	8,843
Chronic/extended care	9,243
Mental	8,728
Tuberculosis	7,861
Children's	8,416
Convalescent/rehabilitation	9,579
Other	9,024

[1]Excludes shift differential pay.
[2]General-duty (registered) nurse — public general hospitals.
[3]Graduate nurse without additional qualifications — public general hospitals.
[4]General-duty (registered) nurse without additional qualifications.

5.20   Registered nurses by employment status and province of employment or residence[1], 1974

Province or territory of employment or residence	Employment status		Not employed in nursing	Total
	Employed in nursing			
	Full-time	Part-time		
Newfoundland	1,825	413	182	2,420
Prince Edward Island	511	187	154	852
Nova Scotia	3,814	933	678	5,425
New Brunswick	2,497	926	1,093	4,516
Quebec	25,506	7,523	7,594	40,623
Ontario	34,850	13,384	25,557	73,791
Manitoba	4,098	1,550	1,095	6,743
Saskatchewan	3,873	1,754	979	6,606
Alberta	6,990	2,606	2,441	12,037
British Columbia	8,338	3,591	3,185	15,114
Yukon Territory and Northwest Territories	268	38	97	403
Canada	92,570	32,905	43,055	168,530

[1]Location of residence is used for those nurses who are not employed.

5.21   Average annual salaries of public health nurses, by academic qualifications, employment category and type of agency, 1975

Category	Average salary $
ACADEMIC QUALIFICATIONS[1]	
Registered nurse only	12,350
Registered nurse with public health certificate	13,715
Baccalaureate degree in nursing only	12,903
Baccalaureate degree and public health certificate	13,491
Baccalaureate degree major in public health	13,582
Master's degree in nursing only	13,310
Master's degree and public health certificate	—
Master's degree major in public health	15,026
EMPLOYMENT CATEGORY[2]	
Director	19,117
Assistant director (services)	17,105
Assistant director (education)	[3]
Consultant (generalized)	[3]
Consultant (specialized)	15,137
Supervisor	16,142
Assistant supervisor	15,435
Staff nurse (public health)	13,715
Staff nurse (registered nurse)	10,051
TYPE OF AGENCY[4]	
Department of National Health and Welfare	14,956
Department of National Defence	19,810
Provincial departments of health	13,780
Local/municipal/city departments of health	13,667
Local/county/regional departments of health	13,424
Other public health agencies	13,349

[1]Staff nurse (public health).
[2]Registered nurse with public health certificate.
[3]Confidential — fewer than 3 individuals.
[4]Staff nurse (public health) — registered nurse with public health certificate.

5.22   Physiotherapists by employment status and province of residence, 1974 and 1975

Province of residence	Employment status		Employed in other than physiotherapy	Not employed	Not stated	Total
	Employed in physiotherapy					
	Self-employed	Salaried				
1974						
Newfoundland	—	37	—	1	—	38
Prince Edward Island	—	18	—	1	—	19
Nova Scotia	3	74	—	5	—	82
New Brunswick	—	36	—	4	—	40
Quebec	40	544	11	117	9	721
Ontario	79	1,424	18	111	203	1,835
Manitoba	7	174	3	21	2	207
Saskatchewan	5	121	1	14	1	142
Alberta	14	303	11	65	2	395
British Columbia[1]	34	415	7	63	10	529
Not stated	—	—	—	—	3	3
Canada	182	3,146	51	402	230	4,011
1975						
Newfoundland	—	49	1	1	6	57
Prince Edward Island	1	12	—	2	—	15
Nova Scotia	3	108	1	8	3	123
New Brunswick	—	52	—	3	—	55
Quebec	54	616	16	129	65	880
Ontario	106	1,805	38	209	66	2,224
Manitoba	7	151	3	29	12	202
Saskatchewan	5	109	6	18	14	152
Alberta	16	315	9	76	38	454
British Columbia[1]	57	529	7	45	7	645
Not stated	—	—	—	—	—	—
Canada	249	3,746	81	520	211	4,807

[1]Includes the Yukon Territory and Northwest Territories.

5.23   Radiological technicians by employment status and province of residence, 1973 and 1974

Province or territory of residence	Employment status				
	Medical or health field	Other than medical or health field	Not employed	Not stated	Total
1973					
Newfoundland	109	5	15	1	130
Prince Edward Island	14	2	9	—	25
Nova Scotia	244	15	56	3	318
New Brunswick	132	4	39	1	176
Quebec	1,522	21	254	18	1,815
Ontario	1,827	70	469	17	2,383
Manitoba	317	9	109	—	435
Saskatchewan	219	1	77	2	299
Alberta	485	19	210	8	722
British Columbia	488	19	170	5	682
Yukon Territory and Northwest Territories	7	—	6	2	15
Canada	5,364	165	1,414	57	7,000
1974					
Newfoundland	125	2	21	1	149
Prince Edward Island	19	2	8	—	29
Nova Scotia	256	7	57	8	328
New Brunswick	158	7	52	—	217
Quebec	1,591	33	271	45	1,940
Ontario	2,008	67	556	33	2,664
Manitoba	365	8	109	2	484
Saskatchewan	214	4	93	7	318
Alberta	541	17	227	15	800
British Columbia	588	23	188	12	811
Yukon Territory and Northwest Territories	8	2	6	—	16
Canada	5,873	172	1,588	123	7,756

5.24 Reported cases of selected notifiable diseases and rate per 100,000 population, by province, 1974

International List No.	Disease	Nfld.	PEI	NS	NB	Que.	Ont.	Man.	Sask.	Alta.	BC	YT	NWT	Canada
		Number of cases												
009.1	Diarrhoea of the newborn, epidemic	–	11	1	–	65	–	1	–	6	–	–	1	85
032	Diphtheria	7	–	–	–	12	20	15	1	47	69	–	2	173
004	Dysentery, bacillary	201	5	2	58	196	486	648	73	386	203	–	97	2,355
062.1	Encephalitis, western equine	–	–	–	–	–	–	–	–	–	–	–	–	–
	Food poisoning, bacterial	3	1	21	1	335	–	3	6	6	2	–	3	381
005.0	Staphylococcal	3	1	21	1	333	–	3	6	6	2	–	3	371
005.1	Botulism	–	–	–	–	2	–	–	–	–	–	–	–	10
070	Hepatitis, infectious (including serum hepatitis)	23	106	62	27	326	890	806	459	995	1,392	27	633	5,746
	Hepatitis, infectious	22	106	52	25	264	779	742	443	946	1,381	24	630	5,414
999.2	Hepatitis, serum	1	–	10	2	62	111	64	16	49	11	3	3	332
055	Measles	53	–	1,107	99	920	4,333	222	1,107	3,443	573	14	114	11,985
	Meningitis, aseptic, due to enteroviruses	8	12	–	2	53	–	22	7	8	12	–	3	127
045.0	Coxsackie virus	–	7	–	–	22	–	2	1	–	–	–	–	32
045.1	ECHO virus	–	–	–	–	4	–	2	1	–	–	–	–	7
045.9	Not specified	8	5	–	2	27	–	18	5	8	12	–	3	88
036	Meningococcal infections	43	3	10	9	56	128	17	33	14	43	1	8	365
056	Rubella (German measles)	176	–	680	33	2,177	2,600	537	118	1,001	342	16	52	7,732
	Salmonella infections, other	154	21	102	24	1,483	1,108	97	278	307	302	6	28	3,910
003.0	With food as vehicle	–	9	31	1	640	–	3	1	25	–	–	–	710
003.9	Without mention of food as vehicle	154	12	71	23	843	1,108	94	277	282	302	6	28	3,200
034	Streptococcal sore throat and scarlet fever	53	5,621	1,966	70	700	3,448	1,003	529	5,104	789	79	912	20,274
010,011,012-019	Tuberculosis	145	13	87	85	934	979	261	148	249	395	6	52	3,354
	Typhoid and paratyphoid fever	9	–	2	8	57	90	4	7	4	6	–	1	188
001	Typhoid	–	–	–	5	37	64	1	7	4	3	–	1	122
002	Paratyphoid	9	–	2	3	20	26	3	–	–	3	–	–	66
	Venereal diseases	585	62	1,267	411	4,048	17,782	3,761	3,478	8,157[a]	9,633[P]	301	1,994	51,479
098	Gonococcal infections	575	55	1,178	396	3,383	15,614	3,577	3,370	8,036	9,207	299	1,990	47,680
090-097	Syphilis	10	7	89	15	665	2,162	184	101	121	422	2	4	3,782
099.0,099.1,099.2	Other	–	–	–	–	–	6	–	7	–	4	–	–	17
033	Whooping cough	62	46	117	10	332	798	20	62	63	66	–	3	1,579

5.24 Reported cases of selected notifiable diseases and rate per 100,000 population, by province, 1974 (concluded)

International List No.	Disease	Nfld.	PEI	NS	NB	Que.	Ont.	Man.	Sask.	Alta.	BC	YT	NWT	Canada
		Rate per 100,000 population												
009.1	Diarrhoea of the newborn, epidemic	–	–	0.1	–	1.1	[1]	0.1	–	0.4	–	–	2.7	0.6
032	Diphtheria	1.3	9.4	–	–	0.2	0.2	1.5	0.1	2.7	2.9	–	5.3	0.8
004	Dysentery, bacillary	37.1	–	0.2	8.8	3.2	6.0	64.1	8.0	22.5	8.5	–	258.7	10.5
062.1	Encephalitis, western equine	–	4.3	–	–	–	–	–	–	–	–	–	–	–
	Food poisoning, bacterial													
005.0	Staphylococcal	0.6	0.9	2.6	0.2	5.5	–	0.3	0.7	0.4	0.1	–	8.0	1.7
005.1	Botulism	0.6	0.9	2.6	0.2	5.4	[1]	0.3	0.7	0.4	–	–	–	2.6
070	Hepatitis, infectious (including serum hepatitis)	4.2	90.8	7.6	4.1	5.3	11.0	79.7	50.6	58.1	58.1	139.2	1,688.0	25.6
	Hepatitis, infectious	4.1	90.8	6.4	3.8	4.3	9.6	73.4	48.8	55.2	57.7	123.7	1,680.0	24.1
999.2	Hepatitis, serum	0.2	–	1.2	0.3	1.0	1.4	6.3	1.8	2.9	0.5	15.5	8.0	1.5
055	Measles	9.8	–	136.1	15.0	15.0	53.5	22.0	122.1	200.9	23.9	72.2	304.0	53.7
	Meningitis, aseptic, due to enteroviruses	1.5	10.3	–	0.3	0.9	[1]	2.2	0.8	0.5	0.5	–	8.0	0.9
045.0	Coxsackie virus	–	6.0	–	–	0.4	[1]	0.2	0.1	–	–	–	–	0.2
045.1	ECHO virus	–	–	–	–	0.1	[1]	0.2	0.1	0.5	0.5	–	–	–
045.9	Not specified	1.5	4.3	–	0.3	0.4	[1]	1.8	0.6	0.8	–	–	8.0	0.6
036	Meningococcal infections	7.9	2.6	1.2	1.4	0.9	1.6	1.7	3.6	–	1.8	5.2	21.3	1.6
056	Rubella (German measles)	32.4	–	83.6	5.0	35.5	32.1	53.1	13.0	58.4	14.3	82.5	138.7	34.6
	Salmonella infections, other	28.4	18.0	12.5	3.6	24.2	13.7	9.6	30.7	17.9	12.6	30.9	74.7	17.4
003.0	With food as vehicle	–	7.7	3.8	0.2	10.4	[1]	0.3	0.1	1.5	–	–	–	4.9
003.9	Without mention of food as vehicle	28.4	10.3	8.7	3.5	13.7	13.7	9.3	30.5	16.5	12.6	30.9	74.7	14.3
034	Streptococcal sore throat and scarlet fever	9.8	4,816.6	241.8	10.6	11.4	42.6	99.2	58.3	297.8	32.9	407.2	2,432.0	90.3
010,011, 012-019	Tuberculosis	26.7	11.1	10.7	12.8	15.2	12.1	25.8	16.3	14.5	16.5	30.9	138.7	14.9
	Typhoid and paratyphoid fever	1.7	–	0.2	1.2	0.9	1.1	0.4	0.8	0.2	0.3	–	2.7	0.8
001	Typhoid	–	–	–	0.8	0.6	0.8	0.1	0.8	0.2	0.1	–	–	0.5
002	Paratyphoid	1.7	–	0.2	0.5	0.3	0.3	0.3	–	–	0.1	–	2.7	0.3
	Venereal diseases	107.8	53.1	155.8	62.1	66.0	219.7	372.0	383.5	475.9[2]	402.2p	1,551.5	5,317.3	229.3
098	Gonococcal infections	106.0	47.1	144.9	59.8	55.1	192.9	353.8	371.6	468.9	384.4	1,541.2	5,306.7	212.4
090-097	Syphilis	1.8	6.0	10.9	2.3	10.8	26.7	18.2	11.1	7.1	17.6	10.3	10.7	16.8
099.0,099.1, 099.2	Other	–	[1]	–	–	–	0.1	–	0.8	–	0.2	–	–	0.1
033	Whooping cough	11.4	39.4	14.4	1.5	5.4	9.9	2.0	6.8	3.7	2.8	–	8.0	7.0

[1]Not reportable.
[2]Excludes 15 cases of syphilis, type undetermined.

Sources
5.1 Health Economics and Statistics, Health Programs Branch, Department of National Health and Welfare.
5.2 Public Finance Division, Institutional and Public Finance Statistics Branch, Statistics Canada.
5.3 - 5.24 Health Division, Institutional and Public Finance Statistics Branch, Statistics Canada.

Incomes and social security

Chapter 6

Tables

Incomes and social security

Chapter 6

Family incomes
6.1

Income distributions for families and individuals in Canada have been available since the first Survey of Consumer Finances was conducted in the spring of 1952. In the early years of the survey, the sample was restricted to non-farm families with the sample size ranging between 5,000 and 10,000 families. Because of this limited sample size, the amount of statistically reliable data which could be tabulated was severely restricted. Regional distributions could not be further broken down to give provincial distributions, and different personal or labour force characteristics could not be simultaneously cross-tabulated.

In 1966, coverage was extended to the farm population. Today the only individuals still excluded from the survey are residents of the Yukon Territory and Northwest Territories, persons living in institutions, on Indian reserves and in military camps. The survey was carried out every two years from 1966 until 1972 when it became annual. The sample gradually increased to 26,000 families in 1974 and now fluctuates between a large sample every second year and a small sample (12,000 or so) in the intervening years. Provincial distributions are still released only from the larger surveys. However, a much wider variety of tabulations is now published due to the advent of the computer and the increased scope of the survey. In addition, special tabulations can usually be provided on request. For a more detailed description of the survey and a much wider variety of tabulations than shown here, consult the annual report *Income distributions by size in Canada,* Statistics Canada Catalogue No. 13-207.

In addition to this main series of reports, a new annual series entitled *Income after tax, distributions by size in Canada* (Statistics Canada Catalogue No. 13-210) became available in 1971 and other reports have also been published on special topics related to the Survey of Consumer Finances (e.g. low income families in Canada, earnings and work experience, and assets and debts of families).

Family and income concepts
6.1.1

Terms such as "family", "unattached individuals", and "income" can be subject to varied definition and are defined here as meant in the annual Survey of Consumer Finances.

Family. A family is defined as a group of individuals sharing a common dwelling unit and related by blood, marriage or adoption. This is often referred to as the "economic family" concept and is broader as a definition than that employed by most demographic studies and the census where a family is restricted to a married couple with or without unmarried children or a parent with unmarried children. Under the survey definition all relatives in a household, regardless of the degree of relationship, constitute a family. This definition differs also from the "spending unit" concept of a family used in Family Expenditure Surveys described in Section 6.2.

Unattached individual. An unattached individual is a person living alone or rooming in a household where he is not related to any other household member. The incomes of unattached individuals are quite different from those of families, particularly as a large portion of them are young entrants to the labour force or elderly persons living on pensions. Tabulations on unattached individuals are not included here but can be found in *Income distributions by size in Canada,* Statistics Canada Catalogue No. 13-207.

Income. Survey estimates relate to money income received from all sources before payment of taxes and such deductions as pension contributions, insurance premiums, etc. This income may be composed of: wages and salaries; net income of the self-employed (e.g. partners in unincorporated businesses, professional practitioners and farmers); investment income (e.g. interest, dividends, and rents); transfer payments (e.g. old age pensions, family allowances); and other money income (e.g. retirement pensions, alimony). Thus the concept of income is similar to personal income in the national accounts except that, first, it covers only private households in the 10 provinces and not the non-commercial institutions such as churches and charitable organizations and, second, the survey estimates do not include imputed income such as the value of farm products produced and consumed on the farm. On the other hand, the survey income concept is broader than the income defined for the calculation of income tax since it includes such non-taxable money income as the guaranteed income supplement, pensions to the blind, etc.

6.1.2 Income trends, 1951-74

Tables 6.1 to 6.3 provide an indication of how family incomes changed over a period of years. The sample coverage changed in 1966 to include farm families, but this change does not seriously affect the comparability of the data with earlier years. The first part of Table 6.1 indicates that the average income (in current dollars) in all regions quadrupled from 1951 to 1974. The rate of increase in average income accelerated dramatically during this time. From 1951 to 1961 the average incomes of the five regions rose by between 48% (in the Prairies and BC) and 65% (in the Atlantic provinces). During the 1961-71 period the regional increases ranged from 87% to 104%. From 1971 to 1974 averages rose almost as much as between 1951 and 1961, from 39% to 59%. These changes, however, do not reflect the decrease in the purchasing power of the dollar. The second part of Table 6.1 does take this into account and gives the average incomes in constant 1971 dollars. Averages in all regions have still at least doubled in constant dollar terms since 1951.

Table 6.2 indicates that although the rates of increase in the various regions differed, the relative positions remained fairly constant. Table 6.3 shows how the actual income distribution for all Canada has shifted from 1965 to 1974.

6.1.3 Major sources of income

The percentage distribution of families by major source of income within quintiles is shown in Table 6.8 for 1951-74. For this type of analysis families are arranged in an ascending order by size of income and divided into five equal groups or quintiles. The characteristics (e.g. major source of income) are then tabulated for each quintile.

Table 6.8 shows that in the lowest quintile 48% of families had their major source of income from wages and salaries in 1951. This dropped to 34% in 1974. Meanwhile the percentage of families in the lowest quintile with major source government transfers rose from 27% in 1951 to 47% in 1974. In the highest quintile, wages and salaries remained the major source for 86% to 90% of families from 1951 to 1974.

6.1.4 Regional income distributions

Although the average family income for all of Canada was $14,833 in 1974, the average for the different regions ranged from a low of $11,647 in the Atlantic provinces to a high of $16,144 in Ontario. Only 10.6% of Canadian families received income of less than $5,000 while 41.6% received $15,000 or more. In Ontario and British Columbia the situation was the most favourable with only 8% having less than $5,000 and almost 50% over $15,000. In the Atlantic provinces, on the other hand, 16% of families were in the lower income bracket and only 24% in the higher. (Table 6.4)

Income distributions by family characteristics   6.1.5

Income distributions are influenced by a variety of personal and labour force characteristics of the family and its head. These include such characteristics of the head as sex, age, employment status, occupation, immigration status and education. Family characteristics used for classifying incomes include tenure (whether owner or renter), size of family, number of children, number and combination of income recipients, and labour force participation of wife. While only three summary classifications of family income are presented here relating to age and sex of head, education of head and income recipients, data on all other variables may be found in the annual report *Income distributions by size in Canada,* Statistics Canada Catalogue No. 13-207.

Incomes by age and sex of family head. Table 6.5 shows that the average income of families headed by males ($15,448) was almost twice that of families headed by females ($8,229) in 1974. For the younger age groups, in fact, the male-headed average was more than twice the female-headed one. The position of the 65 year and over female-headed families was greatly improved, however, and their average income of $9,635 was almost the same as the male-headed average of $9,968. Explaining this difference in income is the fact that many of the families headed by females are also single-parent families where the woman may find it difficult to obtain or hold a steady job due to the presence of young children in the family, or because many women still work in lower-paying occupations such as clerical, stenographic or sales.

For both male- and female-headed families the average incomes increase with age to reach a peak: for males at age 45-54 and for females at age 55-64.

Incomes by education of family head. Education of the family head is another factor which greatly affects the family income. Table 6.6 shows that the average income of families whose head had a university degree was nearly two and a half times that of families whose head had four years of schooling or less, and 65% higher than families whose head had attended but not completed high school. While 37% of families whose head had not completed high school had incomes of $15,000 or more in 1974, 74% of families whose head had a university degree were in that same income group and 30% had incomes of $25,000 or more. The difference in income between families whose head had only completed high school and families whose head had taken non-university post-secondary courses was minimal.

Incomes by combination of income recipients. The number and combination of family members receiving income will obviously affect the income of the family. In Table 6.7 families are first divided into two groups: (a) husband-wife families and (b) all other families. This latter group includes single-parent families as well as groups of relatives living together but not in a parent-child relationship, e.g. brothers and sisters. As expected, the average income of husband-wife families with at least three income recipients (head, wife and other relative) was much higher ($19,902) than the average for families with only the head as income recipient ($12,611). The same situation occurs for other families where the average with at least two recipients was $11,234 compared with $5,669 when the head was the only recipient.

Family spending   6.2

Household surveys of family expenditure provide information on consumer spending that can be related to family characteristics such as geographic location, family size and income level. In general, the survey program has consisted of two phases: the collection, by means of monthly record-keeping surveys throughout the reference year, of detailed information on family food expenditures; and the collection of information by annual recall of all family expenditure, income and changes in assets and liabilities. The record-keeping phase was not featured in all the survey programs, particularly in the more recent surveys.

A primary use of such surveys is to provide information for constructing, reviewing and revising the weights of the consumer price index (see Chapter 21). Initially these small-scale sample expenditure surveys carried out in selected Canadian urban centres since 1953 were designed to follow changes in the patterns of a well-defined group of middle-income urban families known as the "target group" of the consumer price index. In recent years the demand for expenditure statistics to serve other needs of government, business, welfare organizations and academic research has resulted in a widening in the scope and size of the surveys. This culminated in the expansion of the biennial program for 1969 to provide a large-scale national survey for the first time since 1948-49 covering both urban and rural households in the 10 provinces.

The most recent survey, the eleventh in the series, was carried out in February and March 1975 and refers to the calendar year 1974 (to be published as *Urban family expenditure, 1974*). In order to produce data for individual cities, the main sample was concentrated in 14 major urban centres, with no restrictions imposed on family composition or income. For the 1974 survey the usable sample of 6,630 spending units was distributed in the cities of St. John's, Halifax, Saint John, Montreal, Quebec, Ottawa, Toronto, Thunder Bay, Winnipeg, Regina, Saskatoon, Calgary, Edmonton and Vancouver.

6.2.1   Family (spending unit) concept

The definition of a family or spending unit used in the family expenditure surveys is not the same as that of the census, or the "economic family" concept used in the Surveys of Consumer Finances (see Section 6.1.1). The family or spending unit is defined as a group of persons dependent on a common or pooled income for the major items of expense and living in the same dwelling or one financially independent individual living alone. Never-married sons or daughters living with their parents are considered as part of their parents' spending unit. In the great majority of cases the members of spending units of two or more are related by blood, marriage or adoption, and are thus consistent with the "economic family" definition employed in surveys of family income, i.e. "a group of individuals sharing a common dwelling unit and related by blood, marriage or adoption". However, it should be noted that according to the "economic family" definition, unrelated persons living in the same household would be counted as unattached individuals. Under the definitions in the expenditure survey, it is possible for two or more unrelated persons to comprise one family or spending unit.

6.2.2   Family expenditure patterns

In addition to trend comparisons it is useful to classify the expenditure patterns of families by a number of related variables (e.g. family income, size of family, age of family head, and so on) to determine the influence and effects of these various factors on family spending habits. Such classifications will be available in the report *Urban family expenditure, 1974*. This section provides a brief trend comparison of expenditure patterns for 1969-74 and a classification of family expenditures in 1974 by income quintiles, income being the most influential of all factors bearing on most items of family spending.

Expenditure trends, 1969-74. While the average net income of survey families of two or more persons in 14 Canadian cities rose from $10,243 in 1969 to $16,147 in 1974, Table 6.9 indicates that there were few significant shifts in the overall expenditure patterns of these families during this period. The one possible exception arises from the increase in average incomes which resulted in personal income taxes forming 18.6% of total family expenditure in 1974 as compared to 15.2% in 1969. Food (17.2% in 1974), shelter (14.5%), clothing (7.2%), travel

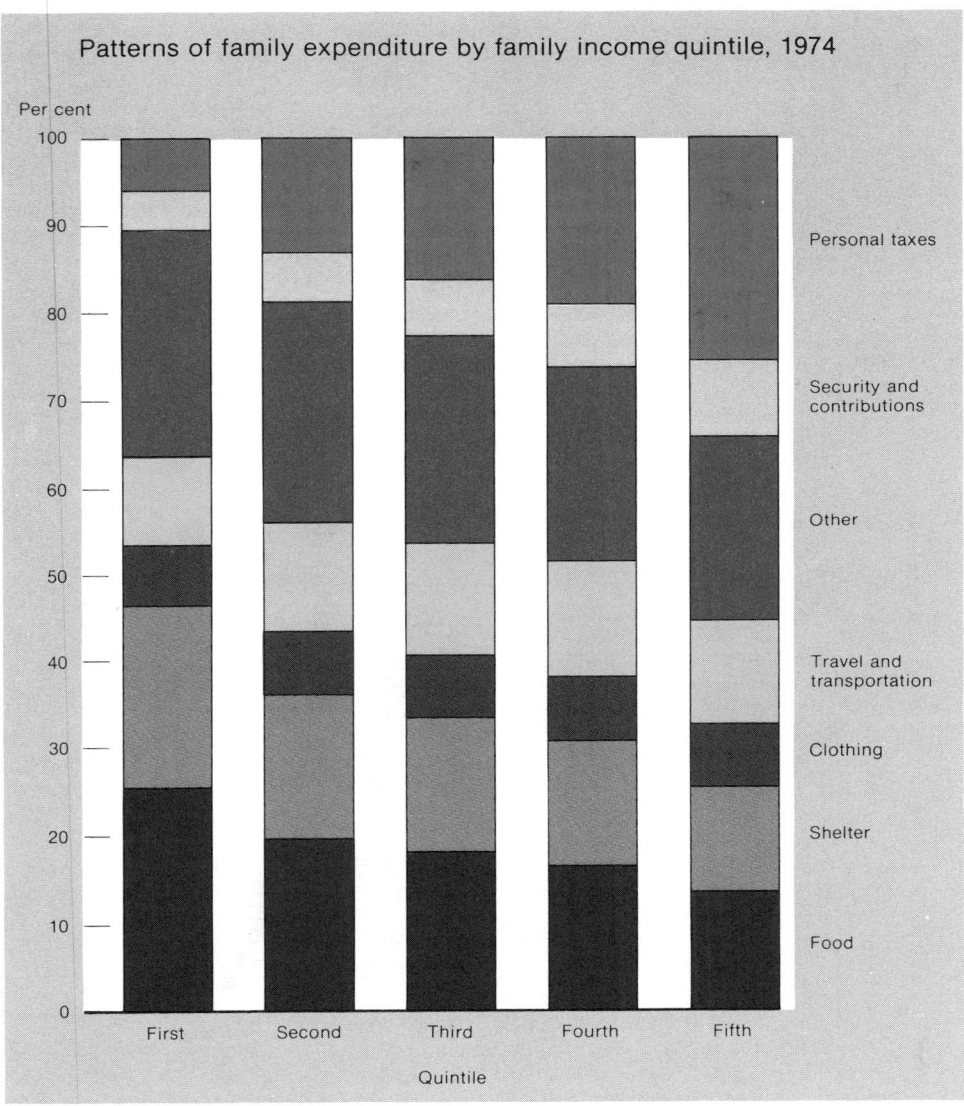

Patterns of family expenditure by family income quintile, 1974

and transportation (12.4%) and most other major items of expenditure were all within 1% of the proportions which they consumed of the family budget in the earlier 1969 survey year.

Expenditure patterns by family income quintile, 1974. Table 6.10 shows the expenditure patterns in 1974 of survey families of two or more persons arranged by income quintiles (families ranked in ascending order of income size and then divided into five equal groups). For example, the average net income before taxes of the 20% of all families comprising the lowest quintile was $6,187 as compared to an average of $29,676 for the 20% of families forming the highest quintile.

As might be expected the percentages of total expenditure on specific items in the family budget showed some significant differences throughout the five income quintiles. The 20% of families in the lowest group spent on the average 46.4% of their total expenditures on food and shelter alone. The proportion ranged downward to only 25.5% for the 20% of families in the highest group. Another offsetting difference was the amount for personal taxes which represented only 6.0% of total expenditures for families in the lowest group compared with 25.5% for those in the highest quintile. Evidence of the better financial position of families in the higher quintiles, despite their much larger tax expenditures, can be seen from the net change in assets and liabilities for 1974 which ranged from an average decrease of $403 for families in the lowest quintile group to an increase of $3,351 for those in the highest group. Other interesting differences in the characteristics of families from the low- to high-income ranges as shown in Table 6.10 were the following percentages: home-owners, from 34.4% of families to 79.7%; car or truck ownership, from 47.3% to 93.9%; and wife employed full-time in the labour force, from 2.9% to 34.7%. It should be noted also that the successive income classes are not homogeneous with respect to family size or number of full-time earners; average family size rose from 2.66 persons in the lowest class to 4.03 persons in the highest, and the number of full-time earners from 0.33 to 1.52 persons.

6.3   Social security programs

A wide range of income security and social service programs is provided by the federal, provincial and local governments. The publicly funded and administered programs are complemented by the activities of voluntary agencies.

Federal agencies in this field include the Department of Veterans Affairs which administers veterans allowances and welfare and treatment services for veterans and, where necessary, their dependents; the Department of Indian Affairs and Northern Development which administers a number of welfare programs for native people; the Department of Manpower and Immigration which administers training, relocation and employment opportunity programs; the Unemployment Insurance Commission, responsible for the administration of the Unemployment Insurance program; and the Department of National Health and Welfare. The NHW department administers the Canada Pension Plan, the Old Age Security pension, the Guaranteed Income Supplement and Spouse's Allowance, Family Allowances and the Canada Assistance Plan. The last program provides for federal sharing in certain costs of the provision by provinces and municipalities of social assistance and welfare services including institutional care.

The provinces, with the assistance of the municipalities in some, administer programs providing social assistance, social welfare services and programs of institutional care. The province of Quebec is responsible for the administration of the Quebec Pension Plan, a program comparable to the Canada Pension Plan, and Quebec and Prince Edward Island have supplementary programs of Family Allowances. Several provinces have programs providing supplementary cash assistance to elderly persons.

The National Council of Welfare is a citizens advisory body to the Minister of National Health and Welfare. Its 21 members include past and present welfare recipients and other low-income citizens, as well as social workers and others involved in the social welfare field. The purpose of the council is to provide the minister with an independent source of advice reflective of the concerns and experience of low-income Canadians and those who work with the poor.

Types of programs. Income security programs provide direct cash payments to eligible recipients. They include: income insurance schemes such as the Canada Pension Plan and Quebec Pension Plan, Workmen's Compensation and Unemployment Insurance; income support measures such as the Old Age Security Pension, the Guaranteed Income Supplement and Spouse's Allowance, Family Allowances programs and social assistance provided by the provincial and municipal programs.

Social services programs provide some services to anyone who applies (crisis intervention services, information and referral services and family planning services) and other specific services to designated groups. These last include preventive, protective and supportive services to children, rehabilitation services to disabled persons, social integration services to persons who are, or are at risk of being, socially isolated from community life, residential services to those needing care in an institutional setting, and supportive services to the elderly. They also include community development services and community oriented preventive services to specified communities.

Income security programs of NHW   6.4

Family Allowances: the federal program   6.4.1

The Family Allowances Act, 1973, which came into effect on January 1, 1974, replaced the former Family Allowances Act of 1944 and the Youth Allowances Act, 1964. Section 6.7 describes Supplementary Family Allowances programs in Quebec and PEI.

Under the act of 1973, Family Allowances are payable monthly on behalf of a dependent child under 18 years of age who is resident in Canada and is maintained by a Canadian citizen or landed immigrant resident in Canada or a non-immigrant admitted to Canada under specific conditions.

The allowance may be paid when the child or parent is absent from Canada in prescribed circumstances. The allowance is normally paid to the mother of the child. Family Allowances are taxable and must be included as income by the person who claims the child as a dependent.

Monthly, non-taxable Special Allowances are payable on behalf of a child under the age of 18 who is in the care of, and maintained by, a government, a government agency, or an approved private institution. Although normally paid to the institution which has care of the child, Special Allowances may be paid to the child's foster parent at the request of the institution.

The legislation provides for Family Allowances and Special Allowances to be increased at the beginning of each year if the consumer price index for Canada increases. In 1974, the monthly allowances stood at $20, in 1975 at $22.08. In 1976, however, indexation was suspended as a result of the federal government's expenditure restraint program. Consequently, the federal rates paid in 1976 were the same as those paid in 1975.

The act permits a provincial legislature to specify the Family Allowance rates to be paid to families resident in the province provided that: the rates are based only on the age of the child, the number of children in the family, or both; no monthly rate is less than 60% of the current federal monthly rate; and the total amount of Family Allowances paid in the province is, as far as practicable, the same as if the federal rates had been paid. Only Quebec and Alberta have specified their own rates. Provinces do not have the power to specify the Special Allowance rate.

Family Allowances rates paid in Quebec monthly during 1975 and 1976 under the federal Family Allowances program were as follows:

Per family	Federal rate 1975 and 1976
1st child	$13.25
2nd child	19.87
3rd child	32.84
Each additional child	36.16

An additional $5.52 is also paid on behalf of each child 12 years and over.

Alberta specified the 1974 rates in an Order in Council, dated December 19, 1973 which were subsequently incorporated in the Social Development

Amendment Act, 1974. The rates for 1975 are specified in the Social Development Amendment Act, 1975 (No. 1) and those for 1976 in the Social Development Amendment Act, 1975 (No. 2) c. 79. With indexation suspension, however, the rates actually paid were the same as those paid in 1975.

Monthly Family Allowances paid in Alberta, 1975, 1976:

Age of child	1975 and 1976
0- 6 years	$16.40
7-11 years	20.80
12-15 years	27.30
16-17 years	30.60

6.4.2 Canada Pension Plan

The Canada Pension Plan (CPP) is a compulsory, contributory, earnings-related pension plan that covers most employed members of the labour force between the ages of 18 and 70. The law was proclaimed in force on May 5, 1965, the collection of contributions started in January 1966, and the first benefits, retirement pensions, were paid in January 1967. With the exception of Quebec where the Quebec Pension Plan is in effect, the plan covers all of Canada. The Quebec and Canada pension plans have established administrative arrangements to deal with dual contributors so that pension credits under either plan are automatically taken into account for purposes of the other plan when a person moves from an area covered by one plan to that covered by the other (i.e. in or out of Quebec).

Contributions amounting to 1.8% of pensionable earnings falling within the range of $800 to $8,300 (1976) are made by employees, which are matched by the employer. Self-employed persons contribute 3.6% on the same range of earnings. The following types of benefits are payable.

Retirement pensions amount to 25% of a contributor's updated pensionable earnings averaged over the number of years contributions were required. Because the minimum period for averaging earnings is 120 months and applicants for pensions within the first 10 years could not contribute for 120 months, partial pensions were payable during this 10-year transitional period.

Although a retirement pension is payable on application as early as age 65, persons between the ages of 65 and 69 who are employed can postpone their applications and continue to contribute to the plan in order to increase their future benefits. Once benefits are being paid, however, contributions cannot be continued.

Disability pensions are paid on application to contributors who, having contributed for at least five whole or part calendar years in the last 10-year period, have been determined to be suffering from a severe and prolonged mental or physical disability. This pension, which begins four months after the month the person became disabled, consists of a fixed monthly amount ($41.44 in 1976) and 75% of the contributor's retirement pension calculated as though the contributor had reached the age of 65 when the disability pension commenced.

Children of persons receiving disability pensions receive benefits at the same monthly rate and under the same conditions of eligibility as those that apply to orphans (see below).

Survivors pensions are paid on application to the surviving spouse and orphans of a person who has contributed to the plan for at least one third of the calendar years for which he or she could have contributed. The full survivor's benefit is payable to a disabled spouse, a spouse with dependent children, and a spouse 45 years of age or older. A partial survivor's pension is payable to a spouse between the ages of 35 and 45. The full survivor's pension for a spouse under the age of 65 includes a flat rate component ($41.44 in 1976) and 37.5% of the contributor's actual retirement pension or imputed pension if the contributor was not in receipt of a pension at the time of death. When such a spouse reaches the age of 65, and becomes eligible for the Old Age Security pension, the surviving spouse's pension changes to 60% of the deceased contributor's actual or imputed retirement pension.

Orphans benefits are paid on behalf of a deceased contributor's unmarried, dependent children up to the age of 18, or 25 if the orphan continues to attend school or university full-time. The rate for each of the first four children equals the flat rate component of the survivor's pension, ($41.44 in 1976). For additional children, the rate for each one is one half this amount. However, each child receives the same amount, since the total orphans benefits for a family are divided equally among the children. An orphan may receive a benefit in respect of only one deceased contributor.

Death benefits. A lump-sum death benefit, equal to six times a contributor's monthly retirement pension, up to a maximum of 10% of that year's maximum pensionable earnings ($830 in 1976), is paid to the estate of a deceased contributor who has contributed to the plan for at least one third of the calendar years for which he or she could have contributed.

Between 1966 and 1973, the annual cost of living increase paid to CPP beneficiaries was limited to 2% a year. Since the beginning of 1974, however, this ceiling has been removed and all benefits are adjusted annually to reflect full cost of living increases.

Amendments to the Canada Pension Plan, effective January 1975, provided for: equal treatment for male and female contributors and beneficiaries; removal of the retirement and earnings test for persons aged 65 and over; fixing the rate of increase of the year's maximum pensionable earnings, i.e. it is to be increased each year by 12.5% until it is equal to the average annual wages and salaries of the industrial composite in Canada (for 1976 the maximum was $8,300); changing the basic exemption level of pensionable earnings from 12% to 10%; self-employed members of the labour force who are members of a prescribed religious sect to be exempted from contributions (and benefits) by filing their intentions with the Department of National Revenue; and a series of technical changes designed to improve the administration of the plan, and further elaborating on the rights and procedures of appeal.

Excess funds collected by the plan are lent to a province under a formula based on the ratio of contributions from that province to total contributions. Any funds not borrowed by the provinces are invested in federal securities.

An advisory committee, representing employers, employees, self-employed persons and the public, regularly reviews the operation of the plan, the state of the investment fund and the adequacy of coverage and benefits, and reports to the Minister of National Health and Welfare. The Canada Pension Plan authorizes reciprocal agreements to be made with other countries to achieve portability of pensions.

OAS, GIS and Spouse's Allowance   6.4.3

Under the Old Age Security Act of 1951 and its subsequent amendments, an OAS pension is payable to a person aged 65 and over provided the person has resided in Canada for 10 years immediately preceding the approval of an application for the pension. Any gaps in the 10-year period may be offset if the applicant has been present in Canada prior to that 10-year period and after the age of 18 for periods of time equal to three times the length of the gaps. In this case, the applicant must also have resided in Canada for at least one year immediately preceding the date on which his application for pension may be approved. The pension is also payable to persons aged 65 or over with 40 years of residence in Canada since age 18, no matter where they may live. Once the pension has been approved, a pensioner may leave Canada and continue to receive payments with the following proviso: if he has lived in Canada for 20 years since his 18th birthday, payment outside Canada may continue indefinitely; if not, payment is continued for six months

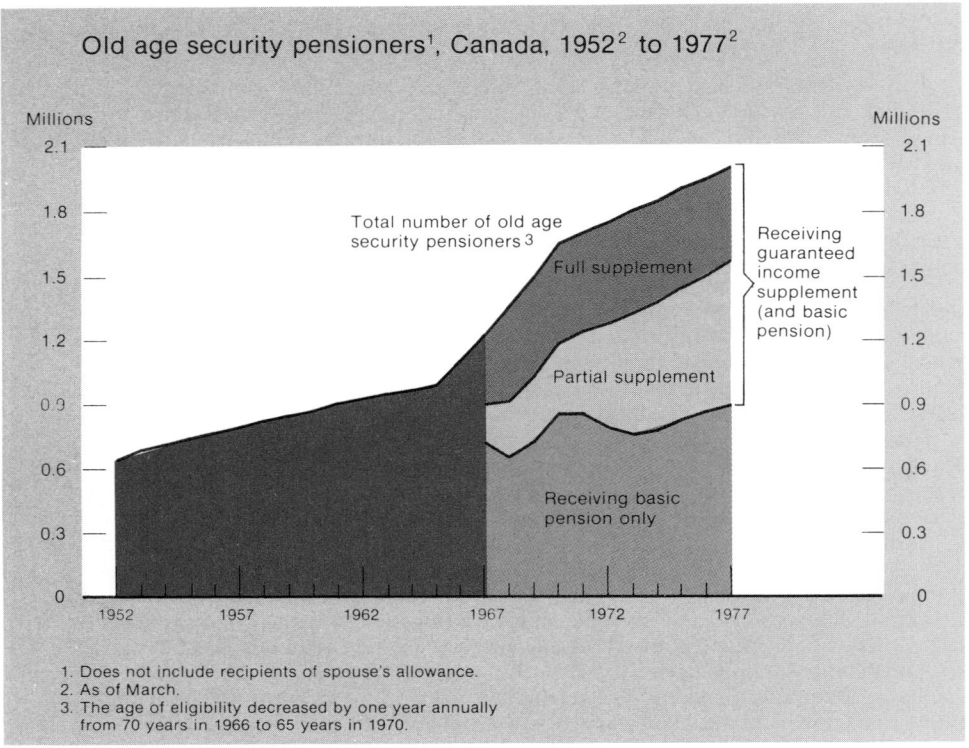

Old age security pensioners[1], Canada, 1952[2] to 1977[2]

1. Does not include recipients of spouse's allowance.
2. As of March.
3. The age of eligibility decreased by one year annually
   from 70 years in 1966 to 65 years in 1970.

after the month of departure and is then suspended, to be resumed only in the month in which he returns to Canada.

A 1966 amendment to the OAS Act provided for the payment of the Guaranteed Income Supplement (GIS). Recipients of the OAS pension with no other income may receive the maximum monthly supplement; those with other income may receive a partial supplement. The maximum GIS is reduced by $1 a month for every $2 a month of income over and above the Old Age Security pension and any supplement that may have been received. Income for this purpose is the same as that computed in accordance with the Income Tax Act. In the case of a married couple, each is considered to have one half of their combined income. Where one spouse does not receive the Old Age Security pension or a Spouse's Allowance, six times the amount of the monthly OAS pension of the current quarter is deducted from one half of the combined income in calculating the income of the pensioner for purposes of determining the amount of the supplement.

In June 1975 a further amendment to the Old Age Security Act introduced a Spouse's Allowance (SA), designed to provide relief in situations where two persons would otherwise have to live on the pension of one. The SA program went into effect on October 1, 1975. The spouse of an OAS pensioner is eligible for SA if that spouse is between 60 and 64 years of age and meets the same residence requirements as those stipulated for OAS. As of October 1, 1976 Spouse's Allowance is payable, upon application, if the annual combined income of the couple is less than $6,432 (excluding the OAS pension, the GIS and the Spouse's Allowance). The maximum amount is reduced by $3 for every $4 of the combined monthly income of the couple until the OAS equivalent portion is eliminated; the GIS equivalent is then reduced by $1 for every $4 of combined income. In October 1976 the OAS stood at $139.39. For a single pensioner, or a married one whose spouse was not in receipt of OAS or SA, the maximum monthly GIS on the above date stood at $97.76. For a married pensioner whose spouse was also in receipt of the OAS or SA, the maximum monthly GIS stood at $86.81. The maximum Spouse's Allowance was $226.20 ($139.39 OAS equivalent plus $86.81 GIS equivalent). OAS and maximum GIS and SA are adjusted every January, April, July and October to reflect the increase in the consumer price index.

The Old Age Security program is administered by the Department of National Health and Welfare through regional offices located in each provincial capital at which applications for pension are received. The regional office in Edmonton administers the program for residents of the Yukon Territory and the Northwest Territories.

Social services programs of NHW   6.5

National welfare grants   6.5.1
The National Welfare Grants program was established in 1962 to help develop and strengthen welfare services in Canada. Project grants are made to provincial and municipal welfare departments, non-governmental welfare agencies, citizens' organizations and universities. Fellowships are provided to individuals seeking advanced training in the social welfare field. The variety of provisions within the program, with its associated consultative services, allows it to operate as a flexible instrument in the development of welfare services and to give major emphasis to experimental activities. The allotment for the year ended March 31, 1976 was $3,729,100.

A wide range of demonstration, research and social development projects are eligible for grants, as are developmental projects related to welfare manpower. Fellowships are available for study at Canadian and foreign universities.

Expenditures under the National Welfare Grants program for the year ended March 31, 1975 totalled $3,999,802. A sum of $2,012,550 was expended on demonstration projects; $800,017 on research projects; $407,883 on manpower utilization and development, including demonstration, curriculum review in schools of social work and fellowships; $551,277 on general national welfare agency projects; $228,075 on special welfare projects including provincially administered bursary and staff development programs.

New Horizons Program   6.5.2
The New Horizons Program for retired Canadians was announced by the Minister of National Health and Welfare in July 1972. In January 1975, the Cabinet agreed to recommend that New Horizons be given continuing program status and that yearly contributions in grants be increased by $4 million, bringing the total annual amount for all costs to $14 million.

Primarily, the program was designed to alleviate the loneliness and sense of isolation which characterize the lives of many older people by offering them the opportunity to participate more actively in the life of the community. Grants are made available to groups of retired Canadians, consisting generally of no less than 10 members, for the purpose of planning and operating projects in which their talent and skills are utilized for their own betterment, that of other older persons, or of the community. Projects must be non-profit in nature. New Horizons is not an employment program in the sense that no money is allowed for salaries to the participants. Projects may be funded for up to 18 months. There is no fixed limit to the amount of a grant.

Projects funded include physical recreation; crafts and hobbies; historical, cultural and educational programs; social services; information services; and activity centres. As of June 22, 1976, 5,862 projects involving over 990,538 people had been awarded $34,200,011.

6.5.3   Family planning

The Family Planning Division of the Department of National Health and Welfare was formed in January 1972 to provide a centre of responsibility for the federal family planning program. Its objective is to ensure, in cooperation with the provinces and territories, the accessibility and availability of family planning services to all Canadians who want them. This is achieved by informing Canadians about the purpose and methods of family planning, promoting the training of health and welfare professionals and other staff involved in family planning services, and aiding family planning programs operating under public or voluntary auspices through federal grants-in-aid and joint federal-provincial programs.

The division's major program activities include consultation, information, training and the family planning grants. Consultation is provided to a broad range of government and non-government organizations. Information on family planning, sex education and family life education is distributed free of charge. Canadian material on these subjects is currently being developed. To the extent feasible, the division's consultants assist in training professional health, welfare and educational staff and others working in the area of family planning.

Since the inception of the Family Planning Grants program in April 1972, a total of $5.8 million has been provided for the support of innovative family planning services, demonstration, training and research projects and for university fellowships. Grant recipients have included provincial and municipal government departments, national and local voluntary family planning agencies, native community organizations and universities.

6.5.4   Emergency Welfare Services

The function of the Emergency Welfare Services Division of the Department of National Health and Welfare is to develop and maintain community capability to provide the basic survival and emergency social services in any emergency in Canada. This consists primarily of five emergency services — lodging, feeding, clothing, registration and inquiry, and personal services.

A program has been developed so that, in a national emergency, the division can coordinate the efforts of welfare departments at all levels of government, organizations, private social agencies, professional groups and volunteers to assist in recovery from a given situation and promote rehabilitation.

6.5.5   The Adoption Desk

The Adoption Desk was established in the Department of National Health and Welfare in 1975 to provide a coordinating and facilitating service to the provinces in the areas of international and interprovincial adoption placement. The interprovincial registry has been fully operational since October 1975 and has been instrumental in arranging a significant number of interprovincial adoption placements. The Adoption Desk has also coordinated a number of international adoption placements.

6.5.6   National Day Care Information Centre

This centre was established in the Department of National Health and Welfare in 1972 as a clearing house for information on day care. The centre has developed a series of pamphlets, a bibliography and a quarterly newsletter and makes an annual survey of day care services in Canada.

6.5.7   Rehabilitation services

The purpose of the Resource Centre of the Social Services Programs Branch is to compile and disseminate information related to rehabilitation of the physically, mentally or socially handicapped. The centre has published a bibliography on rehabilitation of the handicapped, a layman's guide to some of the literature and a bibliography on social service aspects of rehabilitation.

International welfare 6.5.8

Canada is actively involved in the social development activities of the United Nations, particularly with the executive board of UNICEF and the Organization for Economic Cooperation and Development on the development of social indicators, income transfer policy and the role of women in the economy.

Federal and provincial departments and agencies participate in the work of several international voluntary organizations. These include the International Council on Social Welfare, International Social Services and the International Union of Family Organizations.

Program information is exchanged on social affairs with UN agencies, the Council of Europe, the Organization of Economic Cooperation and Development, the Overseas Development Institute and social affairs departments in other countries.

Canadian officials engaged in social security participate in the International Social Security Association and the social security program of the International Labour Organization. For some years, Canada has had observer status at meetings of the Inter-American Conference on Social Security. Informal discussions on the possibility of bilateral agreements in social security have been held with the United Kingdom, Italy and the United States. The Department of National Health and Welfare arranges for the training in Canada of UN Fellowship recipients, foreign students and government officials when recommended by their governments.

Federal-provincial cost-sharing programs 6.6

Canada Assistance Plan 6.6.1

The Canada Assistance Plan, 1966, was designed in consultation with the provinces as a comprehensive public assistance measure for supporting the integration and improvement of provincial and municipal assistance programs and encouraging the development and extension of welfare services which would lessen, remove or prevent the causes and effects of poverty, child neglect or dependence on public assistance. Under agreements with the provinces and territories, the federal government contributes 50% of sharable costs of provincial and municipal expenditures for public assistance and welfare services. Through the plan, Canada also shares in the cost of work activity projects designed to improve the employability of persons who have unusual difficulty in finding or retaining jobs or in undertaking job training.

The only eligibility requirement specified under the Canada Assistance Plan for individuals or families applying for assistance under provincial programs is that of need, *regardless of its cause,* and determined through an assessment of budgetary requirements as well as of income and resources. A province must not require previous residence to be a condition of eligibility for assistance. Rates of assistance and eligibility requirements are set by the province so that they may be adjusted to local conditions and the needs of special groups. The provinces are required to establish procedures which enable applicants and recipients to appeal decisions relating to the provision of assistance.

Assistance includes any form of aid to, or on behalf of, persons in need for the purpose of providing basic requirements such as food, shelter, clothing, fuel, household and personal necessities; special items necessary for the safety, well-being, or rehabilitation of a person in need; non-insured health care services; and maintenance in a home for special care such as a home for the aged, a nursing home or a child care institution.

Welfare services, which include counselling and assessment, casework, rehabilitation services, community development and day care, homemaker and adoption services, are provided to persons in need or to persons who are likely to become in need if they do not receive these services. The federal government shares in administration costs of assistance and welfare services programs, such as salaries and employee benefits, and in the costs of related staff training, research and consulting services. These may be provided by provincial or municipal governments or by provincially approved non-profit agencies.

Federal payments under the Canada Assistance Plan amounted to $1.4 billion in the fiscal year 1975-76. This figure includes payments made to Quebec through the Department of Finance under the terms of the Established Programs (Interim Arrangements) Act.

6.6.2   Allowances for the blind and disabled

Under the Blind Persons Act, 1951, and the Disabled Persons Act, 1954, the federal government shares in the cost to the provinces of providing assistance to blind and disabled persons, aged 18 and over, who meet certain income and residence requirements. However, most provinces have now ceased to accept applications for these allowances since, under the Canada Assistance Plan, provinces can provide a more comprehensive assistance program to all persons in need, without categorizing them according to the cause, such as blindness or disability.

6.6.3   Vocational rehabilitation

Under the provisions of the Vocational Rehabilitation of Disabled Persons (VRDP) Act, the federal government contributes 50% of the costs incurred by a province in providing a comprehensive program for the vocational rehabilitation of physically and mentally disabled persons. A comprehensive program includes such services as medical, social and vocational assessment, counselling, restoration and placement services, the provision of prostheses, training, maintenance allowances and the provision of tools, books and other equipment. These services are provided directly by the provincial government or purchased from voluntary agencies. The disabled client participates in setting an employment objective for himself and in designing an appropriate program of services. His vocational goal may be employment in the competitive labour market, a profession, homemaking, farm work, sheltered employment or homebound work of a remunerative nature. Sharable costs also include the salary and necessary travelling costs of staff whose duties are directly related to this program and other administrative expenses necessary for the coordination and delivery of services to the disabled. Other rehabilitation services provided by agencies and voluntary organizations may be funded by a province and are eligible for 50% reimbursement from the federal government under the Canada Assistance Plan. All provinces and territories, except Quebec, participate in the VRDP program.

During the fiscal year 1975-76 the federal government contributed $16,513,878 to the provinces under the act and 48,747 clients received services.

6.7   Provincial income security programs

6.7.1   Social assistance

All provinces make legislative provision for assistance to persons in need and their dependents. Need is determined by the budget deficit method whereby the needs of the applicant and dependents are calculated according to a prescribed schedule or budget for items of basic need (food, clothing, personal and household needs). Assistance for shelter and utilities is paid according to actual costs, sometimes within stated maxima. The amount of the allowance is the difference between "need", so calculated, and the resources available to the applicant to meet that need. The maximum amount of monthly assistance paid toward items of basic need is subject to any ceilings which may be imposed by provincial legislation.

In addition to allowances to cover items of basic need, all provinces make provision for such special items as rehabilitation services, expenses incidental to education or to obtaining employment, counselling, homemaker services and institutional care. All provinces permit certain income or earnings exemptions and, under special circumstances, some provinces provide assistance to fully employed persons.

The provincial departments of welfare set rates of assistance and conditions of eligibility; they have regulatory and supervisory powers over municipal administration of assistance, and require certain standards as a condition of provincial aid. Municipal residence may determine the financially responsible authority within a province. The provincial authority takes responsibility for aid to persons residing outside municipal boundaries and for those who lack municipal residence.

The administration of assistance varies. In Nova Scotia, Ontario, Manitoba and Alberta, allowances to persons with long-term need, such as needy mothers with dependent children, disabled persons and the aged, are administered by the province, with other allowances administered by the municipalities. In Newfoundland, Prince Edward Island and New Brunswick, all assistance is administered by the provincial authority. In Quebec, the province administers assistance through regional and local offices except in Montreal where the municipality administers assistance on behalf of the province. In Saskatchewan, social assistance is administered by the province except in two municipalities. In British Columbia, social allowances are administered through regional and district offices of the provincial government and, in some municipalities, by municipal departments of welfare.

In the seven provinces where the municipalities have some administrative responsibility, the proportion of municipal costs borne by the province varies from 40% to 100% of assistance paid.

Quebec Pension Plan   6.7.2

The Quebec Pension Plan (QPP) was established in 1965 and is comparable to the Canada Pension Plan. Although the Canada and Quebec plans were introduced at the same time and are closely coordinated, a series of amendments to both plans have effected the following differences: the QPP continues to require that a person between the ages of 65 and 70 be retired from regular employment before a retirement pension is paid and that post-retirement earnings from any employment (beyond a certain limit) may reduce the monthly retirement pension; the QPP's survivors' and disability benefits flat rate component is $106.26 compared to $41.44 under the CPP (in January 1976); since January 1976, the QPP's orphans' and children's benefits have been fixed at $29.00 a month whereas those of the CPP are increased annually in accordance with the increases in the cost of living.

In 1975, 214,998 beneficiaries received close to $184 million in benefits.

Supplementary Family Allowance programs   6.7.3

Quebec has a provincial program embodied in the Quebec Family Allowances Plan of 1973. Certain criteria of eligibility under this plan differ somewhat from those of the federal program. In 1976 the province paid $3.68 for the first child in a family, $4.91 for the second, $6.14 for the third, and $7.36 for each additional child.

Prince Edward Island passed a Family Allowances Act in 1973. Under this act, the province pays $10 a month on behalf of the fifth and each subsequent child in a family in addition to the federal payment of $22.08. The provincial supplement is included in the monthly federal cheque.

Provincial income supplementation programs   6.7.4

Several provinces administer programs designed to supplement existing programs for certain groups such as the elderly and the disabled.

In Nova Scotia, under the Special Social Assistance Program, residents who are in receipt of the federal Guaranteed Income Supplement (GIS) may be eligible to receive annually a non-taxable lump sum which is scaled to the amount of GIS received. Maximum payments (i.e. for a person receiving the full GIS payment) are $110 annually per person.

In July 1974, Ontario introduced the Guaranteed Annual Income System (GAINS) to ensure a basic income for qualifying residents 65 years of age or older. The income guaranteed is adjusted periodically and as of July 1976 was $272.07 a month.

In Manitoba, the Manitoba Supplement for the Elderly, established in 1974 under The Social Services Administration Act, is designed to supplement the income of pensioners who are recipients of the federal GIS and of 60 to 64 year old spouses of pensioners. The supplement is paid quarterly and is reduced according to any outside income received by the pensioner. As of April 1976 single, widowed and divorced pensioners were guaranteed a monthly income of $238.24 and married couples with both spouses over 65, or where one spouse is a pensioner and the other between 60 and 64 years of age, were guaranteed $456.42 a month.

By regulations made under the Saskatchewan Assistance Act of 1975, the Saskatchewan income plan was established to provide senior citizens benefits to pensioners in receipt of the federal GIS. The program is income tested and maximum benefits are $240 a year or $20 a month for a single person or for a person in receipt of GIS whose spouse is not in receipt of OAS/GIS, and $216 a year or $18 a month for each of a married couple, both in receipt of OAS/GIS.

In 1975, an amendment to the Senior Citizens Benefits Act in Alberta permitted the implementation of a guaranteed income program for senior citizens in receipt of the federal GIS. Benefits payable under this program (known as the Alberta Assured Income Plan) range between $10.00 and $45.01 a month for a person who is single, widowed, divorced or a married person whose spouse is not a pensioner. For a married couple (both receiving OAS/GIS), the payments range between $10.00 and $47.20 a month each.

Under the Guaranteed Available Income for Need Act (GAIN), British Columbia provides a guaranteed minimum income to individuals aged 60 and over and handicapped persons aged 18 to 59 inclusive. To be eligible for GAIN benefits, an applicant must meet prescribed age, residence, assets and income qualifications. Effective July 1976 the guaranteed minimum monthly income under the GAIN program for persons in receipt of OAS/GIS or Spouse's Allowance was $272.07 (single) and $544.14 (married) where both were eligible; the guaranteed minimum monthly income for persons aged 60 to 64 not in receipt of OAS/GIS/SA benefits and for handicapped persons was $265 (single) and $530 (married) where both were eligible.

6.8   Provincial social services programs

6.8.1   Services for children

All provinces and territories have legislation governing basic child welfare services which include the protection and care of children, adoption services, services to unmarried parents and, in most provinces, services designed to prevent child neglect or need for protection. A number of provinces also offer help to families in emergency situations; this is provided for a limited time by agreement with the parents, and may take the form of special services to the child in his own home or a temporary foster home.

These services are administered by the provincial departments of social services through a division of child welfare. Direct services are provided through regional or local offices of the department or by provincially approved agencies. In some provinces these include children's aid societies.

Protection services include supervision of a child in his own home when there is some element of identifiable neglect or need for protection. When it seems necessary for the protection of the child to remove him from home, the child welfare authority may take the child to a place of safety, but he must be brought before a court within a specified time. A child found to be neglected or in need of protection as defined in provincial law may be committed either temporarily or permanently to the care and custody of the provincial child welfare authority. Temporary commitment is for a limited time, after which the case is reviewed by the court. Permanent committal has the effect of transferring guardianship rights to the child welfare authority. Care is provided according to the needs of the child in a foster boarding home, group home or in a specialized institution.

The child welfare authority arranges adoption placements where this appears appropriate. Children eligible for adoption placement are those legally free for adoption, that is, those in the permanent care and custody of the child welfare authority and those whose parents have formally relinquished them for the purpose of adoption. Adoptions, including those arranged privately, number about 20,000 annually.

Costs of maintenance of children in the care of the provincial authority or a provincially approved agency and of certain welfare services are sharable with the federal government under the Canada Assistance Plan.

Day care services are offered under a variety of auspices. Centres sponsored by public authority comprise approximately 8.0%, those sponsored by community boards 39.0%, parent cooperatives 9.0% and commercially sponsored centres 45.0%. In the past five years there has been a pronounced trend toward family day care. In 1975 there were approximately 70,000 day care spaces in Canada. In most provinces grants are available for the construction or renovation of facilities. Subsidies for day care services for the children of low-income families are provided by the provincial or municipal authority and are sharable under the Canada Assistance Plan.

Programs for the aged   6.8.2

Programs and services offered to the aged vary from province to province. Although by no means organized in all areas, such services as visiting nurse, homemaker, counselling, information and referral, meals-on-wheels, friendly visiting and housing registries have been established under public and voluntary auspices. Low-rental housing projects have been built in many communities; clubs and centres to provide recreation and social activities have been developed. Some provinces offer annual shelter assistance grants to senior citizens who are either tenants or home owners while others offer free prescription drugs.

In all provinces, homes for the aged and infirm are provided under provincial, municipal or voluntary auspices. These homes are required to meet standards set out in provincial legislation relating to homes for the aged, welfare institutions or public health. Homes for the aged, regardless of auspices, are usually inspected and in some provinces must be licensed.

Small proprietary boarding homes for the care of well elderly persons are found in some provinces. Those who suffer from long-term illnesses may be cared for in chronic or convalescent hospitals, private or public nursing homes and some homes for the aged. Costs of care in the chronic or convalescent hospitals are paid through the provincial hospital plans. In the case of needy persons in the so-called homes for special care, maintenance costs are shared on a federal-provincial basis under the Canada Assistance Plan. "Homes for special care" include homes for the aged, hostels, lodges and nursing homes. Various terms are used in the different provinces and within provinces.

In varying degrees, all provinces make capital grants toward the construction or renovation of homes for the aged by municipalities or voluntary organizations and, generally speaking, such homes are exempt from municipal taxation.

6.8.3   Vocational rehabilitation of disabled persons

All provinces and territories except Quebec have specific programs for the provision of vocational rehabilitation services for physically or mentally disabled persons for which costs are shared with the federal government. These services are provided to enable the individual to become capable of pursuing a substantially gainful occupation. The services are coordinated and administered by provincial departments but may be provided either directly by central or regional provincial offices or purchased from voluntary organizations. Vocational rehabilitation services include medical, social and vocational assessment to determine the individual's residual capacities. A suitable vocational plan is determined jointly by the individual and counselling staff.

Prosthetic and orthotic appliances, wheelchairs and other mobility aids are provided so that the individual may participate in a vocational training program or undertake employment. Other remedial and restorative treatment is provided as necessary. Any vocational training is made available in regular municipal or provincial vocational schools, private trade schools or business colleges, special training centres such as rehabilitation workshops, universities, or through training on the job in business or industry. The provision of all equipment necessary for training is also covered, as well as any travel cost. Maintenance allowances are usually provided for the individuals and their dependents while participating in the program. Where employment placement outside the competitive labour market is indicated, such placement is arranged by the province. Provincial authorities also assist in regular employment placement when special problems arise and their help is required.

In Quebec, assistance of various types and rehabilitation services for disabled persons are provided through a variety of departments and agencies. Because Quebec does not participate in the particular cost-sharing program with the federal government for the provision of all these services, the province would receive some cost-shared benefits for persons in need under the Canada Assistance Plan while other costs are borne fully by the province.

6.9   Programs for Indians

As with other Canadians, Indians are entitled to the benefits of universal federal welfare schemes such as Family Allowances, Old Age Security pensions, and the Guaranteed Income Supplement. Subject to the standard qualifying conditions, Indians also receive Canada or Quebec Pension Plan payments, Unemployment Insurance, Workmen's Compensation, and veterans benefits.

However, the extent to which provincial welfare benefits and services are available to Indians living on reserves and Crown land varies according to province. Similarly, the acceptance of financial responsibility for welfare assistance to Indians who do not live on reserves can vary. Most provinces seek recovery of the costs of assistance and services which are provided to such Indians if they have not acquired residence off a reserve in accordance with provincial requirements.

Federal-provincial arrangements. A number of individual arrangements have been worked out between the federal government and authorities at other levels. Under a 1965 agreement with Ontario, all provincial welfare programs are available to Indians living there, either on or off reserves. In Quebec, the federal government has contracts with eight private social agencies to furnish welfare service to Indians in their geographic jurisdictions. An agreement in 1973 between the federal and Alberta governments and the Blackfoot band permits the band to administer two programs offered by the province's Department of Health and Social Development to band members on the reserve. Similar agreements continue to be developed through federal-provincial negotiation and consultation with representatives of bands and associations. There are also the social assistance and other programs of the Department of Indian Affairs and Northern Development which are aimed directly at assisting the Indian people.

Role of Indian and Northern Affairs. The department seeks to attain four main objectives in the operation of welfare programs: to ensure that services available are comparable to those available to other Canadians in the province where they live; to increase Indian participation in the design and operation of social service programs; to strengthen family life and facilitate increased independence; and to facilitate the provision of social services by other government and private agencies to Indian people in their jurisdictions who request such service.

The department's social assistance program provides basic household essentials (food, clothing, shelter, fuel) to the needy. Scales of assistance and eligibility conditions are comparable to those of other residents of the provinces. Administration of this plan, as with other social services, is handled by departmental employees on some reserves, by employees of the band council on others.

Indian residents are subject to the child welfare legislation of the province in which they live. The aim of the federal department's child care program is to ensure the welfare of neglected, dependent, or delinquent Indian children living on reserves. In conformity with federal-provincial child welfare agreements, the department finances maintenance and protection services to Indian children in the Yukon, Manitoba, Nova Scotia and British Columbia. In provinces where child care services are provided on a voluntary basis, the department pays administrative costs and per diem rates for Indian children receiving care from foster homes or other agencies.

The department furnishes maintenance and care in homes for the aged and in other institutions for physically and socially handicapped adults. Indian recipients of benefits such as Old Age Security or the Guaranteed Income Supplement in amounts insufficient to meet their basic needs may get additional assistance from the department.

With departmental financial support, a growing number of bands are now administering their own day care centres and senior citizens' homes. The department also operates a rehabilitation program designed to prevent the development of social problems. It attempts to reduce the effects of physical disabilities and emotional difficulties.

The Work Opportunity Program was established in 1971 to give jobs to physically able social assistance recipients. Funds which would otherwise be spent on direct financial aid are used to provide native communities with facilities such as roads, and services such as day care, that they may lack. Each project is financed by a reallocation of social assistance funds amounting to the equivalent of what the participants would have been given had they remained in receipt of social assistance, plus funds from other sources (regional appropriations, provincial revenues, band revenues).

The program is an example of the transfer of social service administration from the government to the native people. Approval is granted only to projects that are planned, designed, and operated by band councils or groups empowered by them. Bands are expected to contribute to the cost of projects in accordance with a schedule worked out on the basis of the band's annual revenue. Project approval is also contingent on employment of those without jobs who are receiving or are likely to need social assistance. Bands operating projects are expected to pay reasonable wages and to meet other employer requirements such as coverage for Unemployment Insurance and Workmen's Compensation.

Veterans programs   6.10

The Department of Veterans Affairs administers most of the legislation known collectively as the Veterans Charter and also provides administrative facilities for the Canadian Pension Commission and the Commonwealth War Graves Commission. Rights of applicants and recipients under the War Veterans Allowance Act and Part XI of the Civilian War Pensions and Allowances Act are protected by the appeal and review functions of the War Veterans Allowance Board.

The principal benefits now available to veterans are medical treatment for those eligible, land settlement and home construction assistance, education assistance for the children of the war dead, general counselling services, disability and dependents pensions and war veterans allowances. The department may also extend assistance to or on behalf of modest-income veterans on a supplementary basis to that provided under the National Housing Act.

The work of the department, except the administration of the Veterans' Land Act, is carried out through 18 district offices and four sub-district offices in Canada; the benefits of the Veterans' Land Act are administered through five regional offices and 16 district offices across Canada.

6.10.1 Pensions and allowances

6.10.1.1 Disability and dependents pensions

Canadian Pension Commission. The Canadian Pension Commission administers the Pension Act (RSC 1970, c.P-7) and Parts I to X of the Civilian War Pensions and Allowances Act (RSC 1970, c.C-20). Members are appointed by the Governor in Council who may also impose upon the commission duties in respect of any other grants made under any statute other than the Pension Act. It reports to Parliament through the Minister of Veterans Affairs. The commission has district offices in principal cities across Canada.

The Pension Act. The evolution of Canada's pension legislation can be traced through statistical presentations in earlier editions of the *Canada Year Book*. The Pension Act was the subject of major modifications in 1971 and details of the principal changes are described in the *1972 Canada Year Book*.

The Pension Act provides for payment of pensions in respect of disability or death resulting from injury incurred during or attributable to service with the Canadian Forces in time of war or peace. Provision is also made for supplementing, up to Canadian rates, awards of pension to or in respect of Canadians for disability or death suffered as a result of service in the British or Allied Forces during World War I or World War II or payment of pension at Canadian rates in cases where no pension has been awarded by the government of the country concerned.

In 1972 a Joint Study Group composed of representatives of veterans organizations, the Canadian Pension Commission and the Department of Veterans Affairs was formed to study the basic rate of pension payable under Schedules A and B of the Pension Act, to delineate the problem related to the establishment and periodic adjustment of an equitable basic rate and to recommend solutions. As a result the rate of pension was established as the earning power of an unskilled labourer in the public service based on the average of an established composite group of five public service classifications. In July 1973 the acceptance of this basis brought about a 24% increase in pensions. This was followed by further increases of 6.7% in January 1974, 10.1% in January 1975, and 11.3% in January 1976, based on increases in the consumer price index for the 12-month periods ended September 30. Thus the basic monthly pension for a single pensioner suffering 100% disability rose to $512.54 with an additional pension of $128.14 for a wife, $66.69 for the first child, $48.64 for a second child and $38.44 for the third and each subsequent child. Pension awards to widows were increased to $384.41 and additional payments for orphan children or dependent brothers or sisters at the following rates: $133.36 for one, $230.65 for two and $62.74 for a third or subsequent child or dependent brother or sister.

War Veterans Allowances and Civilian War Allowances   6.10.1.2

War Veterans Allowance Board. The War Veterans Allowance Board is a quasi-judicial body consisting of eight members appointed by the Governor in Council. It acts as an appeal court for an applicant or recipient aggrieved by a decision of a district authority and may, on its own motion, review and alter or reverse any adjudication of a district authority. The board is responsible for advising the minister with respect to regulations concerning the acts.

War Veterans Allowance District Authorities. In 1950, 18 district authorities were established in the regional districts of the Department of Veterans Affairs and granted full power to adjudicate on all matters arising under the War Veterans Allowance Act. In 1960, a separate authority — the Foreign Countries District Authority — was established to look after recipients living outside Canada. The members of a district authority are employees of the Department of Veterans Affairs appointed by the minister with the approval of the Governor in Council.

War Veterans Allowances. The War Veterans Allowance Act provides an allowance to otherwise qualified war veterans who, because of age or incapacity, are no longer able to derive their maintenance from employment and to ensure that their income does not fall below a specified level. Widows, widowers and orphans of qualified veterans are eligible for benefits. Since its inception in 1930, the act has been amended on numerous occasions to meet additional needs of veterans and their dependents.

With effect from October 1, 1973, the WVA/CWA income levels were escalated by 5.3% and the rates by similar dollar amounts. The income levels are increased quarterly thereafter in accordance with the increase in the cost-of-living, except that orphans' income levels will continue to be adjusted annually.

As of April 1974, the rates for orphans were increased to $125 a month for each orphan, less any amount payable under the Family Allowances Act, 1973, for that orphan. The income level was increased to $135.95. Effective January 1, 1976, and on January 1 of each succeeding year, the income level would be increased in accordance with the rise in the cost-of-living.

Since April 1, 1974, the allowance paid on behalf of a child of a widow, widower or unmarried veteran ("married" rate) or an allowance paid to an orphan is continued to age 25 as long as the child or orphan continues his education. The former legislation required payment of the "married" rate of orphan's allowance to cease at age 21; otherwise, the allowance paid on behalf of the child is discontinued at age 17.

With effect from October 1, 1974, the legislation provides for the payment of an additional $50 a month ($58.56 as of July 1, 1976), less family allowances in pay under the Family Allowances Act, 1973, for each dependent child of a widow, widower or unmarried veteran after the first one and for each dependent child of all other recipients.

As of June 30, 1976 a total of 85,132 persons were receiving War Veterans Allowances: 48,702 veterans, 35,753 widows or widowers and 677 orphans. The monthly liability as of June 30, 1976 was estimated at $14.2 million.

Civilian War Pensions and Allowances. Part XI of the Civilian War Pensions and Allowances Act makes available to certain groups of civilians and their widows, widowers and orphans, benefits similar to those available to veterans under the War Veterans Allowance Act. These groups, which performed meritorious service in World War I and World War II, include: Canadian merchant seamen of both wars; non-Canadians who served in Canadian merchant ships in either war; Canadian voluntary aid detachments of World War I; and Canadian firefighters, Canadian welfare workers, Canadian transatlantic aircrew and the Newfoundland Overseas Forestry Unit of World War II.

As of June 30, 1976 a total of 4,048 civilians, including 995 widows or widowers and 14 orphans, were receiving these allowances. Total monthly cost was estimated at $800,000.

6.10.1.3   Bureau of Pensions Advocates

The Bureau of Pensions Advocates was established under the Minister of Veterans Affairs by the amendments to the Pension Act, 1971 (SC 1970-71, c.31), effective March 30, 1971. It succeeds the Veterans Bureau which had been in operation since 1930. The bureau is not part of the Department of Veterans Affairs but provides an independent professional legal aid service to applicants for awards under the Pension Act. The Chief Pensions Advocate is the chief executive officer and is assisted by pensions advocates, all of whom are lawyers, located at the bureau's head office in Ottawa and in district offices in major centres across Canada. Pensions advocates represent applicants as counsel at Entitlement Board and Pension Review Board hearings and provide a general counselling service to applicants relative to their claims under the Pension Act. No charge is made for the services of the bureau.

During the fiscal years 1974-75 and 1975-76, the Bureau of Pensions Advocates submitted 9,941 and 11,010 claims respectively to the Canadian Pension Commission, Entitlement Boards of the commission and the Pension Review Board. Of the 11,383 and 10,108 decisions rendered by these adjudicating bodies on bureau claims during the same periods of time, 35% and 29% were wholly or partially granted.

6.10.2   Social and health services for veterans

6.10.2.1   Veterans services

Welfare services for veterans and, where appropriate, their dependents, are provided by the Veterans Services Branch. These include the administration of assigned statutes; the conducting of field work and reporting for other branches of the department, the Canadian Pension Commission, the War Veterans Allowance Board and Services Benevolent Funds; and the provision of counselling services including referral to other public or private agencies and veterans organizations.

Assistance Fund. Recipients of benefits under the War Veterans Allowance Act and Part XI of the Civilian War Pensions and Allowances Act living in Canada may be given help from the Assistance Fund if their total income is lower than the permitted maximum. Assistance may take the form of a monthly supplement based on shelter, fuel, food, clothing, personal care and specified health costs or of a single award to meet an unusual or emergency need. The number of persons assisted in the year ended March 31, 1976 was 26,233, the number in receipt of monthly supplements at the end of 1976 was 22,297 and fund expenditures from April 1, 1975 to March 31, 1976, amounted to $10.9 million. Comparable statistics for one year earlier, in each case, are 25,074 persons assisted, 21,211 in receipt of monthly supplements and $10.75 million in fund expenditures.

Education assistance to children. The Children of War Dead (Education Assistance) Act provides help in the form of allowances and the payment of fees for the post-secondary education of children of persons whose deaths have been attributed to military service. Assistance is restricted to children registered in educational institutions in Canada that require secondary school graduation, matriculation or equivalent standing for admission, including, in addition to universities and colleges, such facilities as hospital schools of teaching and institutes of technology. From its inception in July 1953 to March 31, 1976, expenditures totalled $15.1 million of which $8.6 million was spent in allowances and $6.5 million in fees. By the end of March 1976, training had been approved for 7,155 children of Canada's war dead; of these, 3,313 had successfully completed training; 811 students in university and non-university courses were receiving assistance.

Veterans insurance. Under the terms of the Returned Soldiers Insurance Act (SC 1920, c.54 as amended), any veteran of World War I became eligible to contract for life insurance with the federal government for a maximum of $5,000. No policies have been issued under this act since August 31, 1933. During the eight years in which the act was open, 48,319 policies with a face value of $109.3 million were issued. On December 31, 1975, 2,446 policies with a value of $5.4 million were still in force.

The Veterans Insurance Act (RSC 1970, c.V-3) made life insurance up to a maximum of $10,000 available to veterans of World War II on their discharge as well as to widows of those who died during that war. The Veterans Benefit Act of 1954 extended this eligibility to veterans with active service in Korea. The period of eligibility to apply for this insurance ended October 31, 1968. By that date 56,148 policies amounting to $185.1 million had been issued and, of these, 18,805 policies with a value of $59.9 million were still in force on December 31, 1975.

Social and counselling services. Counsellors at district offices work closely with other branches of the department, with other public and private agencies and organizations in assisting veterans and their dependents to deal with problems of social adjustment, particularly those associated with physical disabilities or the disabilities associated with increasing age. A program of university, vocational, technical and home training with allowances is provided for disabled pensioned veterans and vocational rehabilitation is also promoted by training assistance. Sheltered workshops at Toronto and Montreal and home assembly work in other centres produce poppies and memorial wreaths associated with Remembrance Day observances.

Services benevolent funds. Veterans and their dependents receive considerable assistance through various services benevolent funds. All of these organizations work closely together and in cooperation with the Department of Veterans Affairs and veterans organizations. In addition to providing cash grants or loans, all organizations for serving or ex-service personnel carry out increasingly heavy counselling work, particularly in the field of debt consolidation and management.

The oldest of the services funds, the Royal Canadian Navy Benevolent Fund, was incorporated in 1942 and derived its original capital from undistributed prize monies accrued during World War I. In the year ended March 31, 1976, it approved 670 applications for loans or grants totalling $235,000; in the previous year 518 applications were approved for $140,319. The Royal Canadian Air Force Benevolent Fund was established in 1944 using assets from disbanded units of the Commonwealth Air Training Plan. Loans or grants totalling $269,541 were made in 905 cases during the year ended December 31, 1975. The Army Benevolent Fund was set up by Act of Parliament in 1947 and is administered by a board appointed by the Governor in Council. It is the only one of the funds required to report annually to Parliament (through the Minister of Veterans Affairs). Capital for this fund was derived from army canteen and mess funds accumulated during World War II. No provision was made in its charter for loan assistance and its operations extend only to persons who were on active service in the Canadian Army during World War II and their dependents. During the year ended March 31, 1976, 3,434 cases received $362,105 in grants under its Veterans Welfare Program. This was a reduction from the year ended March 31, 1975 when 3,510 received $417,157.

In 1950 the Canadian Army Welfare Fund was incorporated to make assistance available to personnel (and their dependents) enlisting in the army after World War II, who were thus ineligible for help under the three existing funds. While addressing itself primarily to the small-loan field for serving personnel, an amount of $100,000 is set aside annually for distress grants. Following unification of the forces, and because of a variety of legal complications precluding amalgamation of the existing funds, a fifth, the Canadian Forces Personnel Assistance Fund, was incorporated. Its primary role is in the field of small low-cost loans for serving personnel enlisting after February 1968. The grant and financial distress loan aspects of this program are expected to take on increasing importance in time. Administration of the two last-named funds is carried out on contract through the office of the Army Benevolent Fund Board.

6.10.2.2 Treatment services

The Treatment Services Branch of the Department of Veterans Affairs provides medical and dental services for entitled veterans throughout Canada as well as for members of the Armed Forces, the Royal Canadian Mounted Police and wards of other governments or departments at the request and expense of the authorities concerned. Prosthetic services are provided to entitled veterans by the Department of National Health and Welfare but are paid for by the Department of Veterans Affairs (DVA).

The branch provides examination and treatment for pensionable disabilities and provides treatment to war veterans allowance recipients (but not to their dependents) and veterans whose service and financial circumstances render them eligible for free treatment or at a cost adjusted to their ability to pay. If a bed is available, any veteran may receive treatment in a departmental hospital on a guarantee of payment of the cost of hospitalization. The pensioner receives treatment for his pensionable disabilities regardless of his place of residence but service to other veterans is available in Canada only. Subject to the approval of the department, an eligible veteran may also obtain treatment at the expense of the department in an outside hospital from a doctor of his choice. Domiciliary care may be provided to eligible veterans in departmental facilities where the need for active or chronic treatment is sufficiently light, provided that excess beds are available.

Under the federal-provincial hospital insurance program, DVA hospitals are recognized for the provision of insured services to veterans. Where treatment is given for a non-pensioned condition at a DVA hospital to a veteran, or elsewhere to a veteran eligible under the veterans treatment regulations, the hospitalization is an insured service under the federal-provincial hospital insurance program and his medical care is an insured service under the federal-provincial medical care insurance program. The department pays premiums where required on behalf of veterans who are eligible for war veterans allowances.

Hospital facilities. Treatment is provided in six active treatment hospitals located at Halifax, NS; Montreal and Sainte-Anne-de-Bellevue, Que.; London, Ont.; Winnipeg, Man.; and Calgary, Alta.; and in three domiciliary care homes at Ottawa, Ont., Saskatoon, Sask. and Edmonton, Alta. The number of beds set up in these institutions at December 31, 1975 was 3,880. In Ottawa both acute and chronic cases requiring definitive treatment are admitted to the National Defence Medical Centre. A veterans pavilion of 82 beds is located at St. John's General Hospital, St. John's, Nfld., 1,200 beds are available at Sunnybrook Hospital in Toronto, 150 beds at the Centre Hospitalier de l'Université Laval in Quebec and 200 beds at West Saint John Community Hospital in Saint John, NB, for the priority use of veterans, as well as some 766 beds in community hospitals located in St. John's, Nfld., Charlottetown, PEI, Kingston and Thunder Bay, Ont., Regina and Saskatoon, Sask. and Edmonton, Alta.

6.10.3 Land settlement and house construction

Because of the postwar rehabilitation nature and purpose of the legislation, March 31, 1975 was the final date for veterans of World War II or the Korean Special Force to apply for establishment under the various settlement plans of the Veterans' Land Act. Veterans who still had subsisting VLA contracts could apply for additional loans within the financial ceilings of the act to purchase land or effect improvements to their properties, up to March 31, 1977.

From enactment in 1942, loan and grant funds totalling more than $1.3 billion were expended in the establishment of approximately 140,000 veterans. Of these, almost 32,000 were settled as full-time farmers, over 95,000 as small holders, 1,420 whose principal occupation was commercial fishing, 5,841 as Crown land settlers, nearly 1,800 Indian veterans on reserve lands, and over 4,300 veterans who acted as their own contractors in building homes on city-sized lots. On March 31, 1976, nearly 57,000 veterans still had subsisting VLA contracts representing a remaining principal indebtedness of approximately $538 million.

The Veterans' Land Administration also has operational responsibility for the Special Housing Assistance Program; in 1975 the Department of Veterans Affairs was authorized to extend it on behalf of modest-income veterans. Financial assistance up to $600 annually may be provided to veterans, in addition to that available to them under the Assisted Home Ownership Program of the National Housing Act, for the purpose of reducing the proportion of their income required for principal, interest and taxes to a level they can afford. During 1975-76, assistance was approved on behalf of 96 veterans representing $47,200 in annual grants.

The Special Housing Assistance Program also provides authority to extend financial assistance to non-profit corporations who obtain loans under Section 15.1 of the National Housing Act for the development of low-rental projects intended primarily but not necessarily exclusively for housing veterans. In addition to the benefits available from Central Mortgage and Housing Corporation, the Department of Veterans Affairs may make a grant equal to 10% of the capital cost of such a project as determined by CMHC. During 1975-76, grants totalling approximately $363,000 were approved for three such projects involving 185 units.

Commonwealth War Graves Commission   6.10.4

The current charters of the Commonwealth War Graves Commission consist of two documents — the Original Charter of Incorporation dated May 21, 1917, and the new Supplemental Charter dated June 8, 1964. Under these charters the commission is entrusted with the marking and maintenance in perpetuity of the graves of those of the British Empire and Commonwealth Armed Forces who lost their lives between August 4, 1914, and August 31, 1921, and between September 3, 1939, and December 31, 1947, and with the erection of memorials to commemorate those with no known grave.

The Canadian High Commissioner in London, England, is the official commission member for Canada and the Minister of Veterans Affairs is the agent of the commission in Canada. The office of the Secretary General of the Canadian agency is in the Veterans Affairs Building, Ottawa.

Sources
6.1 - 6.2 Consumer Income and Expenditure Division, Census and Household Surveys Branch, Statistics Canada.
6.3 - 6.8 Program Information and Documentation Division, Policy and Program Development and Coordination Branch, Welfare, Department of National Health and Welfare.
6.9 Deputy Minister, Department of Indian Affairs and Northern Development.
6.10 Public Relations, Department of Veterans Affairs.

Tables

..	not available	e	estimate
...	not appropriate or not applicable	p	preliminary
—	nil or zero	r	revised
--	too small to be expressed		certain tables may not add due to rounding

6.1 Average income of families in current and constant dollars by region, selected years, 1951-74

Region	1951	1961	1967	1971	1973	1974
	Current dollars					
Atlantic provinces	2,515	4,156	5,767	7,936	9,965	11,647
Quebec	3,523	5,294	7,404	9,919	12,024	13,742
Ontario	3,903	5,773	8,438	11,483	13,912	16,144
Prairie provinces	3,261	4,836	6,908	9,309	11,760	14,755
British Columbia	3,669	5,491	7,829	11,212	13,942	15,620
Canada	3,535	5,317	7,602	10,368	12,716	14,833
	Constant (1971) dollars					
Atlantic provinces	3,810	5,544	6,667	7,936	8,839	9,318
Quebec	5,337	7,062	8,559	9,919	10,665	10,994
Ontario	5,913	7,701	9,754	11,483	12,340	12,915
Prairie provinces	4,940	6,451	7,986	9,309	10,431	11,804
British Columbia	5,559	7,325	9,050	11,212	12,367	12,496
Canada	5,356	7,093	8,788	10,368	11,279	11,866

6.2 Average income of families in each region as a percentage of the average for Canada, selected years 1965-74

Region	1965	1967	1969	1972	1973	1974
Atlantic provinces	79.3	75.9	76.0	80.9	78.4	78.5
Quebec	95.8	97.4	96.9	95.9	94.6	92.6
Ontario	109.9	111.0	110.8	110.0	109.4	108.8
Prairie provinces	93.0	90.9	91.0	92.7	92.5	99.5
British Columbia	104.6	103.0	103.3	101.3	109.6	105.3
Canada	100.0	100.0	100.0	100.0	100.0	100.0

6.3 Percentage distribution of families in constant (1971) dollars, showing average and median incomes, selected years, 1965-74

Income group in constant (1971) dollars	1965	1967	1969	1971	1973	1974
Under $3,000	12.1	9.9	9.6	9.0	6.5	5.6
$ 3,000 - $ 4,999	14.9	13.5	13.0	11.5	10.3	9.7
5,000 - 6,999	19.5	17.6	14.6	12.2	10.8	10.2
7,000 - 9,999	26.4	26.9	25.2	22.0	20.8	18.5
10,000 - 11,999	10.9	12.0	13.0	14.0	13.4	14.3
12,000 - 14,999	8.6	10.2	11.5	14.2	15.5	17.0
15,000 - 19,999	4.6	6.4	8.1	10.9	14.0	14.9
20,000 and over	2.7	3.5	4.9	6.2	8.6	9.8
Total	100.0	100.0	100.0	100.0	100.0	100.0
Average income $	8,127	8,788	9,490	10,368	11,279	11,866
Median income $	7,320	7,906	8,465	9,347	10,217	10,827

Median income refers to the middle or central value when incomes are ranged in order of magnitude. Median income is lower than average income in these tables since it is not as affected by a few abnormally large values in the distribution.

6.4   Percentage distribution of families by income group, by region, 1974

Income group		Atlantic provinces	Quebec	Ontario	Prairie provinces	British Columbia	Canada
Under $2,000		1.9	1.6	1.4	2.2	1.9	1.7
$ 2,000 - $ 2,999		2.9	2.3	1.3	1.9	1.3	1.8
3,000 - 3,999		4.7	3.4	2.2	3.2	1.3	2.8
4,000 - 4,999		6.7	4.8	3.1	5.9	3.3	4.3
5,000 - 5,999		5.7	3.9	2.6	4.6	4.8	3.8
6,000 - 6,999		5.3	4.0	3.1	3.4	3.2	3.6
7,000 - 7,999		5.9	5.4	3.5	3.3	3.0	4.1
8,000 - 8,999		6.4	4.9	3.4	5.5	4.0	4.5
9,000 - 9,999		6.6	4.9	4.2	4.8	4.5	4.7
10,000 - 11,999		12.7	10.9	9.2	9.3	8.8	10.0
12,000 - 14,999		17.3	19.0	16.1	16.2	17.1	17.0
15,000 - 24,999		19.5	26.9	38.2	29.1	35.6	31.8
25,000 and over		4.5	7.9	11.7	10.5	11.1	9.8
Total		100.0	100.0	100.0	100.0	100.0	100.0
Average income	$	11,647	13,742	16,144	14,755	15,620	14,833
Median income	$	10,612	12,571	14,980	13,010	14,414	13,516
Sample size	No.	2,100	1,854	2,777	1,931	975	9,637

6.5   Percentage distribution of families by income group, age and sex of head, 1974

Income group		Age group						
		Under 25	25-34	35-44	45-54	55-64	65 and over	Total
Families with male heads								
Under $2,000		1.7	1.4	0.8	0.6	2.4	0.9	1.2
$ 2,000 - $ 2,999		1.9	0.5	0.6	0.3	2.2	5.2	1.4
3,000 - 3,999		1.4	0.8	0.8	1.3	2.6	6.2	1.9
4,000 - 4,999		3.2	1.6	0.9	2.1	3.4	16.4	3.7
5,000 - 5,999		4.1	1.8	1.8	1.6	3.2	13.2	3.5
6,000 - 6,999		5.8	2.4	1.5	2.2	3.2	8.3	3.2
7,000 - 7,999		8.5	3.7	2.4	2.4	4.1	7.5	3.9
8,000 - 8,999		7.5	4.5	3.4	3.6	4.4	5.4	4.3
9,000 - 9,999		6.7	5.3	3.6	4.2	5.4	4.4	4.7
10,000 - 11,999		18.1	11.9	9.6	8.1	9.6	7.5	10.1
12,000 - 14,999		20.0	23.6	20.5	15.1	13.6	8.9	17.8
15,000 - 24,999		19.8	36.6	40.9	40.1	33.5	11.4	33.8
25,000 and over		1.1	5.8	13.4	18.3	12.6	4.7	10.6
Total		100.0	100.0	100.0	100.0	100.0	100.0	100.0
Average income	$	11,466	14,828	17,353	18,483	15,641	9,968	15,448
Median income	$	11,059	14,088	15,672	16,638	14,177	6,969	14,070
Sample size	No.	518	2,193	1,879	1,678	1,341	1,210	8,819
Families with female heads								
Under $2,000		13.9		4.2	6.0	3.2	1.9	6.9
$ 2,000 - $ 2,999		6.2		5.9	5.7	8.5	6.4	6.3
3,000 - 3,999		18.7		12.9	14.0	8.5	6.5	13.0
4,000 - 4,999		14.6		9.7	6.3	9.3	15.8	11.3
5,000 - 5,999		8.6		8.5	5.2	3.2	8.9	7.2
6,000 - 6,999		9.5		9.0	6.1	6.3	7.6	7.8
7,000 - 7,999		6.9		4.5	5.6	6.8	7.1	6.3
8,000 - 8,999		5.2		7.1	7.5	4.6	5.9	6.0
9,000 - 9,999		2.0		4.7	7.5	8.3	3.3	4.8
10,000 - 11,999		5.0		12.7	8.6	8.0	8.7	8.3
12,000 - 14,999		5.3		12.6	13.0	11.8	9.9	9.9
15,000 - 24,999		3.2		8.3	14.6	17.6	13.9	10.4
25,000 and over		0.7		—	—	3.9	4.0	1.7
Total		100.0		100.0	100.0	100.0	100.0	100.0
Average income	$	5,960		8,071	8,827	9,978	9,635	8,229
Median income	$	4,770		6,982	8,144	8,925	7,402	6,679
Sample size	No.	218		146	163	123	159	818
All families								
Under $2,000		3.4	2.2	1.1	1.1	2.5	1.1	1.7
$ 2,000 - $ 2,999		2.3	0.9	1.0	0.7	2.7	5.3	1.8
3,000 - 3,999		3.7	2.0	1.7	2.4	3.1	6.3	2.8
4,000 - 4,999		4.6	2.5	1.5	2.4	3.9	16.2	4.3
5,000 - 5,999		4.4	2.3	2.3	1.9	3.2	12.6	3.8
6,000 - 6,999		5.7	3.1	2.0	2.5	3.5	8.2	3.6
7,000 - 7,999		7.9	4.0	2.5	2.7	4.3	7.5	4.1
8,000 - 8,999		7.3	4.6	3.6	4.0	4.4	5.5	4.5
9,000 - 9,999		6.4	5.0	3.7	4.4	5.7	4.3	4.7
10,000 - 11,999		16.6	11.4	9.8	8.1	9.4	7.5	10.0
12,000 - 14,999		18.7	22.2	19.9	14.9	13.4	9.0	17.0
15,000 - 24,999		18.0	34.3	38.5	37.9	32.2	11.6	31.8
25,000 and over		1.0	5.4	12.4	16.7	11.9	4.8	9.8
Total		100.0	100.0	100.0	100.0	100.0	100.0	100.0
Average income	$	10,816	14,223	16,651	17,663	15,141	9,971	14,833
Median income	$	10,564	13,661	15,141	15,966	13,663	7,028	13,516
Sample size	No.	583	2,347	2,026	1,841	1,466	1,374	9,637

6.6   Percentage distribution of families by income group and education of head, 1974

Income group	Elementary schooling		Secondary schooling		Post-secondary (non-university)		University	
	0-4 years	5-8 years	Some	Completed	Some	Completed	Some	Degree
Under $2,000	1.7	1.9	1.9	1.5	0.6	1.1	1.9	1.2
$ 2,000 - $ 2,999	5.8	3.1	1.5	1.0	1.7	0.7	0.1	0.2
3,000 - 3,999	8.0	4.3	3.0	1.2	1.5	1.5	1.0	0.1
4,000 - 4,999	15.0	7.0	3.3	2.4	1.1	2.3	1.4	0.8
5,000 - 5,999	8.2	5.8	3.8	1.7	3.3	2.5	2.1	1.3
6,000 - 6,999	6.5	5.3	3.8	2.2	2.1	1.9	2.4	1.1
7,000 - 7,999	5.3	5.6	4.2	3.4	4.0	3.7	2.7	1.5
8,000 - 8,999	5.1	6.1	4.9	3.8	3.6	3.0	2.7	2.0
9,000 - 9,999	5.2	5.2	5.5	3.7	6.3	4.5	3.7	2.3
10,000 - 11,999	9.0	11.2	10.9	10.7	9.7	10.1	6.4	4.1
12,000 - 14,999	8.9	15.7	20.0	18.3	22.9	18.4	16.4	11.4
15,000 - 24,999	17.9	22.8	30.6	34.9	33.2	39.3	42.3	43.5
25,000 and over	3.5	6.1	6.7	10.1	10.2	11.1	16.9	30.5
Total	100.0	100.0	100.0	100.0	100.0	100.0	100.0	100.0
Average income $	9,822	12,534	13,886	16,070	16,727	15,869	17,905	22,899
Median income $	7,893	11,092	13,077	15,013	14,071	15,059	17,093	20,141
Sample size No.	630	2,514	2,760	1,527	255	700	524	727

6.7   Percentage distribution of families[1] by income group, family type, and combination of income recipients, Canada, 1974

Income group	Income recipient[2]				
	Husband-wife families			All other families	
	Head only	Head and wife only	Head, wife, and other family members[3]	Head only	Head and other family members[3]
Under $2,000	2.3	0.4	0.2	13.3	1.1
$ 2,000 - $ 2,999	2.3	1.1	0.4	10.0	3.3
3,000 - 3,999	2.9	1.9	0.2	20.9	6.0
4,000 - 4,999	4.1	5.0	0.7	12.9	8.7
5,000 - 5,999	4.3	4.2	0.8	8.3	6.0
6,000 - 6,999	4.7	3.0	1.5	9.6	6.6
7,000 - 7,999	5.4	3.8	2.2	5.4	6.7
8,000 - 8,999	6.8	3.8	2.5	4.4	6.2
9,000 - 9,999	6.5	4.4	3.3	2.1	6.6
10,000 - 11,999	14.7	10.0	5.4	5.5	9.9
12,000 - 14,999	18.4	19.1	15.1	4.5	14.6
15,000 - 24,999	22.7	35.5	44.9	1.4	20.2
25,000 and over	4.9	7.6	22.7	1.6	4.0
Total	100.0	100.0	100.0	100.0	100.0
Average income $	12,611	15,031	19,902	5,669	11,234
Median income $	11,384	13,968	18,347	4,449	9,823
Sample size No.	2,496	3,895	2,162	379	642

[1]Excludes 12,000 families who received no cash income in 1974 (see footnote 2 to Table 6.8).
[2]Data not shown for income recipient group "Other than head only" due to the small number of cases in the sample.
[3]"Other family members" refers to any income of children or other relatives.

6.8   Percentage distribution of families by major source of income within income quintiles, selected years, 1951-74

Major source of income within quintiles[1]	1951	1961	1965	1967	1971	1973	1974
Lowest quintile							
No income[2]	2.0	2.4	0.8	1.6	1.6	1.1	1.1
Wages and salaries	48.2	46.3	39.9	36.3	33.6	35.5	33.7
Net income from self-employment	10.5	9.1	18.1	19.2	11.8	10.6	10.4
Transfer payments	26.6	34.6	34.6	35.9	46.2	45.5	46.9
Investment income	7.0	3.4	3.4	3.0	3.3	3.2	3.3
Miscellaneous income	5.7	4.2	3.2	4.1	3.4	4.0	4.6
Second-lowest quintile							
Wages and salaries	85.5	83.5	80.0	80.8	81.0	80.8	82.1
Net income from self-employment	10.7	11.6	13.0	10.0	7.6	7.9	7.6
Transfer payments	1.1	1.8	4.1	4.1	4.9	5.5	5.0
Investment income	1.7	1.0	1.3	2.1	2.6	2.8	2.5
Miscellaneous income	1.0	2.0	1.7	3.0	3.9	3.0	2.8

6.8   Percentage distribution of families by major source of income within income quintiles, selected years, 1951-74 (concluded)

Major source of income within quintiles[1]	1951	1961	1965	1967	1971	1973	1974
Middle quintile							
Wages and salaries	91.8	91.3	88.9	92.0	93.1	91.3	90.9
Net income from self-employment	7.2	7.0	8.9	6.0	3.9	5.2	5.6
Transfer payments	0.3	0.3	0.4	0.7	0.3	1.1	1.0
Investment income	0.5	1.0	0.9	0.7	1.3	1.1	1.4
Miscellaneous income	0.2	0.5	0.8	0.7	1.4	1.3	1.0
Second-highest quintile							
Wages and salaries	92.4	92.1	90.8	93.8	94.7	93.9	92.6
Net income from self-employment	6.9	6.2	7.5	4.5	2.8	3.9	5.1
Transfer payments	- -	0.1	0.3	0.3	0.2	0.3	- -
Investment income	0.5	1.2	0.7	0.8	1.4	1.3	1.4
Miscellaneous income	0.3	0.5	0.7	0.6	0.9	0.7	0.8
Highest quintile							
Wages and salaries	85.9	86.8	86.7	89.1	91.2	90.0	86.9
Net income from self-employment	11.6	10.9	11.1	8.9	5.6	7.8	10.8
Transfer payments	- -	- -	- -	- -	0.1	- -	- -
Investment income	2.1	1.7	1.7	1.8	2.1	1.8	1.9
Miscellaneous income	0.4	0.6	0.6	0.2	0.9	0.3	0.5
All families							
No income[2]	0.4	0.5	1.1	0.3	0.3	0.2	0.2
Wages and salaries	80.8	80.0	73.6	78.4	78.7	78.3	77.2
Net income from self-employment	9.4	9.0	10.4	9.7	6.3	7.1	7.9
Transfer payments	5.6	7.3	10.7	8.2	10.3	10.5	10.6
Investment income	2.3	1.7	2.4	1.7	2.2	2.0	2.1
Miscellaneous income	1.5	1.6	1.8	1.7	2.1	1.9	1.9
Total	100.0	100.0	100.0	100.0	100.0	100.0	100.0

[1]Families are arranged in ascending order of size of total income and then divided into five equal groups, or quintiles.
[2]These are families who either immigrated in the survey year so that they had no income from Canadian sources in the previous year or are new families who had no income of their own in the previous year.

6.9   Patterns of expenditure for families of two or more persons, based on surveys of 14 Canadian cities, 1969 and 1974

Item		1969	1974	Item	1969	1974
Family characteristics				Percentage of total expenditure (concluded)		
Average				Household operation	4.0	3.7
Family size	No.	3.7	3.4	Furnishings and equipment	4.6	5.0
Children under 5	"	0.4	0.3	Household appliances	1.1	1.1
Children 5-15	"	0.9	0.8	Other	3.5	3.9
Adults 16-17	"	0.1	0.2	Clothing	8.2	7.2
Adults 18-64	"	2.1	2.1	Personal care	2.1	1.7
Adults 65 and over	"	0.2	0.2	Medical and health care	3.2	2.1
Full-time earners	"	1.0	1.0	Smoking and alcoholic beverages	3.6	3.3
Age of head	yr	44.2	43.7	Travel and transportation	12.3	12.4
Net income before taxes	$	10,243	16,147	Automobile (and truck)	9.8	9.8
Other money receipts	$	226	383	Purchase	4.5	4.7
Net change in assets and liabilities	$	297	863	Operation	5.3	5.1
Percentage				Other	2.5	2.6
Home-owners		56.1	57.7	Recreation	3.5	3.8
Car or truck owners		78.0	79.6	Reading	0.6	0.6
Wife employed full-time		15.4	20.0	Education	1.0	0.8
				Miscellaneous expenses	1.4	2.1
Average total expenditure	$	10,269	15,583	Total current consumption	77.6	74.4
Percentage of total expenditure				Personal taxes	15.2	18.6
Food		17.7	17.2	Security	4.8	5.1
Shelter		15.4	14.5	Gifts and contributions	2.4	1.9
Rented living quarters		5.5	4.6	Total expenditure	100.0	100.0
Owned living quarters		6.5	6.8			
Other housing		0.8	0.7			
Water and fuel		2.6	2.4			

6.10   Patterns of expenditure for families of two or more persons, by family income quintiles[1], based on survey of 14 Canadian cities, 1974

Item		Lowest quintile	Second-lowest quintile	Middle quintile	Second-highest quintile	Highest quintile
Family characteristics						
Average						
Family size	No.	2.7	3.3	3.5	3.7	4.0
Children under 5	"	0.3	0.4	0.4	0.3	0.2
Children 5-15	"	0.5	0.7	0.9	1.0	0.9
Adults 16-17	"	0.1	0.1	0.1	0.2	0.3
Adults 18-64	"	1.4	2.0	2.1	2.3	2.7
Adults 65 and over	"	0.5	0.2	0.1	0.1	0.1
Full-time earners	"	0.3	0.8	1.2	1.3	1.5
Age of head	yr	49.9	42.0	40.1	41.4	45.2
Net income before taxes	$	6,187	11,079	14,809	18,982	29,676
Other money receipts	$	299	271	342	394	608
Net change in assets and liabilities	$	-403	-280	502	1,144	3,351
Percentage						
Home-owners		34.4	46.6	58.1	69.6	79.7
Car or truck owners		47.3	77.8	88.4	90.7	93.9
Wife employed full-time		2.9	9.7	21.8	30.7	34.7
Average total expenditure	$	6,979	11,767	14,673	17,981	26,515
Percentage of total expenditure						
Food		25.5	19.9	18.1	16.6	13.7
Shelter		20.9	16.3	15.2	14.2	11.8
Rented living quarters		12.1	7.3	5.2	3.4	1.8
Owned living quarters		4.6	5.8	6.9	8.0	7.0
Other housing		0.4	0.5	0.5	0.6	1.1
Water and fuel		3.8	2.7	2.5	2.3	2.0
Household operation		5.0	4.2	3.8	3.5	3.3
Furnishings and equipment		5.0	5.4	5.3	5.0	4.7
Household appliances		1.4	1.1	1.3	1.1	0.9
Other		3.6	4.2	3.9	3.9	3.8
Clothing		6.9	7.2	7.3	7.3	7.2
Personal care		2.1	1.9	1.8	1.7	1.5
Medical and health care		2.6	2.4	2.2	2.0	1.8
Smoking and alcoholic beverages		4.0	3.8	3.6	3.1	2.9
Travel and transportation		10.5	12.8	13.0	13.4	11.9
Automobile (and truck)		7.8	10.5	10.8	10.7	8.8
Purchase		3.4	4.9	5.1	5.5	4.2
Operation		4.5	5.6	5.8	5.3	4.6
Other		2.6	2.3	2.2	2.6	3.0
Recreation		3.5	3.5	3.9	3.8	3.9
Reading		0.7	0.6	0.6	0.5	0.5
Education		0.9	0.7	0.6	0.7	1.0
Miscellaneous expenses		1.9	2.4	2.2	2.1	1.9
Total current consumption		89.6	81.1	77.5	73.9	66.0
Personal taxes		6.0	13.0	16.1	19.0	25.5
Security		2.6	3.9	4.6	5.4	6.4
Gifts and contributions		1.8	1.9	1.8	1.7	2.1
Total expenditure		100.0	100.0	100.0	100.0	100.0

[1]Weighted survey records of families are arranged in ascending order by size of total income and divided into five equal groups, or quintiles. Thus, each group, or quintile, represents a weighted 20% of families.

6.11   Canada Pension Plan, number of recipients in March 1975 and 1976 and net benefits paid by province, fiscal years ended 1975 and 1976

Province or territory	Recipients in March		Net benefits paid during fiscal year	
	1975	1976	1975 $'000	1976 $'000
Newfoundland	13,445	16,929	7,815	11,517
Prince Edward Island	4,545	5,753	2,326	3,500
Nova Scotia	36,621	45,273	22,735	33,394
New Brunswick	24,201	30,063	14,028	20,627
Quebec[1]	2,758	3,157	1,970	2,548
Ontario	323,878	398,257	210,308	313,811
Manitoba	43,194	52,285	25,153	38,209
Saskatchewan	36,910	44,877	19,689	29,417
Alberta	55,954	68,385	32,554	49,275
British Columbia	92,058	112,351	56,322	84,891
Yukon Territory	379	491	262	390
Northwest Territories	301	354	192	257
Canada[2]	634,244	778,175	393,353	587,834

[1]Excludes recipients of benefits under the Quebec Pension Plan; benefits are paid to residents of Quebec where total or partial contributions were made to the Canada Pension Plan.
[2]Includes 2,518 recipients of death benefits in 1975, and 3,285 in 1976. Death benefits are lump sum payments made to the estate.

6.12   Old Age Security (OAS), Guaranteed Income Supplement (GIS), Spouse's Allowance (SA), number of recipients in March 1975 and 1976 and net benefits paid, by province, fiscal years ended Mar. 31, 1975 and 1976

Province or territory	Recipients in March				Net benefits paid during fiscal year			
	OAS only	OAS and GIS	Spouse's Allowance[1]	Total recipients	OAS only $'000	GIS only $'000	Spouse's Allowance[1] $'000	Total $'000
Nfld.								
1975	6,222	29,266	—	35,488	48,306	24,761	—	73,067
1976	6,778	29,713	2,379	36,491	55,470	28,048	1,719	85,237
PEI								
1975	3,255	9,773	—	13,028	17,938	7,998	—	25,936
1976	3,363	9,874	666	13,237	19,879	9,073	529	29,480
NS								
1975	25,768	52,112	—	77,880	106,378	41,952	—	148,330
1976	26,562	52,839	3,473	79,401	120,928	46,629	2,640	170,197
NB								
1975	19,419	39,617	—	59,036	81,686	31,180	—	112,865
1976	20,696	39,647	2,086	60,343	91,782	35,304	1,682	128,767
Que.								
1975	176,629	289,114	—	465,743	630,827	233,086	—	863,914
1976	181,036	296,977	15,905	478,013	727,954	261,998	10,480	1,000,433
Ont.								
1975	361,792	340,869	—	702,661	958,094	248,668	—	1,206,762
1976	378,677	338,404	12,434	717,081	1,087,498	275,027	6,768	1,369,293
Man.								
1975	41,400	62,160	—	103,560	141,724	47,526	—	189,251
1976	43,066	61,950	3,745	105,016	159,905	51,823	2,463	214,191
Sask.								
1975	41,837	58,421	—	100,258	137,010	46,054	—	183,064
1976	44,395	57,128	3,415	101,523	154,703	48,394	2,316	205,413
Alta.								
1975	53,391	76,719	—	130,110	175,915	60,924	—	236,839
1976	56,514	76,460	3,968	132,974	202,982	64,525	2,376	269,883
BC								
1975	103,123	123,269	—	226,392	307,630	93,688	—	401,319
1976	108,618	122,999	6,103	231,617	351,963	101,451	3,982	457,395
YT								
1975	230	311	—	541	744	296	—	1,040
1976	247	314	3	561	887	311	2	1,199
NWT								
1975	207	775	—	982	1,471	617	—	2,089
1976	223	808	17	1,031	1,613	831	14	2,457
Canada								
1975	833,273	1,082,406	—	1,915,679	2,607,724	836,750	—	3,444,474
1976	870,175	1,087,113	54,194	1,957,288	2,975,562	923,413	34,970	3,933,945

[1]Spouse's allowance became payable in October 1975.

6.13   Family Allowances, number of children and accounts paid in March 1975 and 1976, and net benefits paid, by province, for the fiscal years ended Mar. 31, 1975 and 1976

Province or territory and year	Recipients as of March				Net benefits paid during fiscal year $'000
	Accounts			Children	
	Regular	Agency[1]	Foster		
Newfoundland					
1975	87,682	875	345	226,492	55,970
1976	90,302	939	273	225,904	60,222
Prince Edward Island					
1975	16,864	292	12	41,424	10,196
1976	17,200	125	118	41,107	10,967
Nova Scotia					
1975	122,703	2,659	17	277,678	68,828
1976	124,913	2,636	19	275,667	73,595
New Brunswick					
1975	101,025	902	1,074	237,343	58,755
1976	104,439	1,077	837	237,802	63,312
Quebec					
1975	924,412	14,378	332	1,987,845	496,632
1976	941,688	12,268	78	1,962,614	528,177
Ontario					
1975	1,228,565	12,675	21	2,566,805	637,404
1976	1,247,017	12,278	19	2,557,238	685,781

6.13 Family Allowances, number of children and accounts paid in March 1975 and 1976, and net benefits paid, by province, for the fiscal years ended Mar. 31, 1975 and 1976 (concluded)

Province or territory and year	Recipients as of March			Children	Net benefits paid during fiscal year $'000
	Accounts				
	Regular	Agency[1]	Foster		
Manitoba					
1975	146,926	3,047	205	327,376	81,332
1976	148,991	3,250	193	325,853	87,064
Saskatchewan					
1975	131,279	2,246	224	307,026	76,165
1976	134,335	2,166	321	306,707	81,641
Alberta					
1975	270,577	2,363	1,275	600,512	148,094
1976	280,815	2,943	968	608,729	160,732
British Columbia					
1975	355,557	6,058	556	745,344	184,145
1976	361,927	5,936	491	743,018	198,706
Yukon Territory					
1975	3,389	147	—	7,759	1,899
1976	3,490	157	—	7,757	2,108
Northwest Territories					
1975	6,927	203	36	18,878	4,663
1976	7,279	231	27	19,488	5,208
Canada					
1975	3,395,906	45,845	4,097	7,344,482	1,824,082
1976	3,462,396	44,006	3,344	7,311,884	1,957,513

[1]Each account consists of one child.

6.14 Pensions in force under the Pension Act as at Mar. 31, 1975 and 1976

Service	Disability		Dependent		Total	
	Pensions No.	Liability $	Pensions No.	Liability $	Pensions No.	Liability $
1975						
World War I	14,121	33,041,481	11,182	45,095,008	25,303	78,136,489
World War II	98,052	185,567,492	15,325	55,943,554	113,377	241,511,046
Special Force	2,070	3,621,994	164	571,566	2,234	4,193,560
Regular Force	3,877	5,610,151	686	3,081,932	4,563	8,692,083
Total	118,120	227,841,118	27,357	104,692,060	145,477	332,533,178
1976						
World War I	12,404	32,173,808	10,695	48,023,015	23,099	80,196,823
World War II	96,776	203,857,818	15,317	63,129,460	112,093	266,987,278
Special Force	2,084	4,097,845	161	647,244	2,245	4,745,089
Regular Force	4,106	6,544,077	711	3,541,925	4,817	10,086,002
Total	115,370	246,673,548	26,884	115,341,644	142,254	362,015,192

Sources

6.1 - 6.10 Consumer Income and Expenditure Division, Census and Household Surveys Field, Statistics Canada.
6.11 - 6.13 Welfare Information Systems, Welfare, Department of National Health and Welfare.
6.14 Public Relations, Department of Veterans Affairs.

Education, training and cultural activities

Chapter 7

Tables

Education, training and cultural activities

Chapter 7

Full-time enrolment in educational institutions in Canada in 1975-76 showed an increase in universities and in non-university post-secondary courses of 27,350 students, with a combined total of 584,441 compared with 557,191 in 1974-75. At the elementary-secondary level, enrolment in 1975-76 decreased by 41,445 to a total of 5.59 million students from 5.63 million the previous year; this continued a downward trend that began in 1971-72 after a high enrolment of 5.83 million in 1970-71.

Costs of education continued to rise, increasing from a preliminary total of $11,002.7 million for Canada in 1974-75 to an estimated $12,964.2 million in 1975-76. These preliminary figures and estimates are not final, however. For this edition of the *Canada Year Book*, 1974 was the latest year for which final data were available.

The cost of education in Canada for 1973-74 has been established at $9,635.2 million. This amount represents a per capita expenditure of $436 or of $1,038 per member of the labour force. By comparison, the cost of education 10 years earlier was $134 per capita of the population or $377 per member of the labour force. Following a rapid growth in the 1960s, total enrolment reached a peak in 1971-72. Declining by more than 1% from the previous year, the full-time enrolment at all levels was 6.44 million for 1973-74.

Changes in education

7.1

Across Canada, the necessity of assuring equality of opportunity and of providing diversified programs in the last 20 years led education planners to offer a wide choice of courses at all levels of education. At the secondary level courses now include fine arts, music, drama, urban planning and social geography. Community colleges and vocational institutions provide a widening range of advanced technological and paraprofessional courses. Universities offer varied interdisciplinary programs at all levels and some have instituted programs of Canadian studies.

At the post-secondary non-university level, several new structures have evolved. The most innovative type of institution that emerged across the country in the 1960s was the community college. In Quebec there are now about 36 colleges of this type: they are known as collèges d'enseignement général et professionnel and are commonly referred to as CEGEPs. There are also about 20 private colleges in the province. In Ontario, colleges of applied arts and technology (which incorporated the former institutes of technology and the provincial vocational centres and are known as CAATs) were set up in 1967 in 20 regions. This upsurge in the establishment of additional post-secondary vocational and technological institutions has occurred all across Canada to meet the labour market's increasing need for qualified technicians.

Another significant change in education was the greater accessibility of programs to students regardless of sex. Females, who constituted about 39% of the full-time post-secondary enrolment in 1971-72, accounted for 41% of this enrolment in 1973-74. They increasingly selected, and were selected for, certain post-secondary courses which previously had shown almost total male enrolments.

One of the notable increases in teaching facilities was in the area of library service. School libraries provide up-to-date reference books on all subjects in the school curricula and have assumed increasing importance as resource centres for audio-visual aids such as projectors, films, filmstrips, maps, tapes and records.

Efforts were being made to overcome the financial barriers to continuing education. Investigation by demographers and sociologists confirmed that financial constraints were denying advanced education to many Canadians. Consequently, various methods were tried to lighten the financial burden on the individual and to equalize the rapidly increasing load being carried by the taxpayer. The federal government assumed an increasingly prominent role, particularly in the retraining program of the Department of Manpower and Immigration which involves adult technical and vocational training, as well as in post-secondary and university education.

7.1.1   Federal responsibility

In Canada the organization and administration of public education is exercised by the provincial and territorial governments. The federal government is directly concerned only with schools for Indian children which are administered by the Education Branch of the federal Department of Indian Affairs and Northern Development, with schools for children of servicemen operated in Europe by the Department of National Defence, and with schools for inmates of federal penitentiaries. The federal government finances retraining of adults, provides financial support to the provinces amounting to at least 50% of operating costs of post-secondary education, participates to a considerable extent in informal education, and makes grants-in-aid for research personnel and equipment in universities. More detailed information on federal responsibility for education is given in Sections 7.3.3 and 7.4.

7.1.2   Provincial responsibility

Each of the 10 provinces and the two territories has the authority and responsibility for its own education system. As a consequence, organization, policies and practices differ from one to the other. Each has a department of education or of education and youth, headed by a minister who is a member of the Cabinet in the case of the provinces or responsible to the Council in the case of the territories; Ontario has, in addition, a Ministry of Colleges and Universities, Manitoba a Department of Colleges and Universities Affairs and Alberta a Department of Advanced Education. Each provincial department is administered by a deputy minister who is a professional educationist and a public servant. He advises the minister, supervises the department and gives a measure of permanency to its education policy and, in general, carries out that policy and is responsible for the enforcement of the Public School Act. The department of education usually also includes a chief inspector of schools and a staff of local inspectors, as well as directors or supervisors of curricula, technical education, teacher training, home economics, guidance, physical education, audio-visual education, correspondence instruction, adult education, other specialized sections according to the needs of the particular province, and technical personnel and clerks.

Other provincial departments having some responsibility for operating school programs include departments of labour which operate apprenticeship programs, agriculture departments which operate agriculture schools, departments of attorney general or of welfare which operate reform schools, and departments of lands and forests which operate forest ranger schools.

Each department of education has undertaken to provide inspection services to ensure maintenance of standards, teacher certification, courses of study and lists of prescribed or approved textbooks, financial assistance to local authorities in the construction and operation of schools and guidance regulations for trustees and teachers. In return, each department requires regular reports from the schools. When first introduced, government grants to schools were based on such factors as number of teachers, enrolment, days in session and attendance. Later, special grants were introduced in most provinces to meet a variety of expenditures, such as construction of a first school, organization of special classes, transportation of pupils, school lunches and other contingencies. A number of provinces made provision for equalization grants and now most of them have a foundation program of one kind or another.

The departments of education have expanded their services in the fields of health, audio-visual aids, art, music, agriculture, sociology, special education, correspondence courses and pre-vocational and trade courses. At the same time there has been an increasing delegation of authority to local boards and school staffs. One illustration is a reduction in the number of departmental (external) year-end examinations. Few provinces now provide for more than one or two such examinations — at the end of the final and, in some cases, at the end of the second-to-last year of the secondary school course. Another example is the increasing use of lists of approved textbooks from which local authorities may make their own choice, instead of lists of prescribed texts. Courses of study are now seldom planned by only one or two experts in the department; instead, they result from conferences and workshops including active teachers and other interested individuals or bodies. In most provinces "curriculum development" is considered to be a continuous procedure.

Elementary and secondary schools   7.1.2.1

In all provinces schools are established and operated by local education authorities functioning under the terms of a Public School Act and held responsible to the provincial government and resident ratepayers for the actual operation of the local schools. Through the delegation of authority, education has become a provincial-local partnership with the degree of decentralization reviewed intermittently.

Elementary and secondary schools may be classified as publicly controlled or private. The publicly controlled schools, sometimes referred to as "public" schools (including separate schools), encompass those that operate under the provincial school system with locally appointed or elected school boards. Private schools generally either provide a similar curriculum to that of publicly controlled schools or concentrate on business, commercial, trade, technical and correspondence courses, or provide a combination of such courses.

In recent years, school units have been consolidated and consequently enlarged in all provinces. With the growth of cities and towns and of educational facilities and requirements, the small local school board became inadequate as an administrative structure. While some of the original school boards remained as units, urban or regional school boards were created, having the responsibility for both elementary and secondary schools and for providing the necessary staff, buildings, equipment and transportation.

Community colleges   7.1.2.2

Although there are some privately operated colleges, the provinces are partially or totally responsible for coordinating, regulating and financing community colleges and related institutions. Some provincial governments completely finance these colleges while others do so in part. Similarly, the degree of local autonomy given the colleges varies by province.

Since 1960 Alberta, British Columbia, Ontario and Quebec have established new community college structures. In Alberta, the provincial agency is the Alberta College Commission composed of nine members, all appointed by the government. In British Columbia, an advisory board — the Academic Board — serves both universities and colleges and consists of nine members, six appointed by the universities and three by the provincial government. In Ontario, the administration of community colleges is carried out by the Ministry of Colleges and Universities. In Quebec, the Department of Education is responsible for many agency functions. The composition of governing boards varies by province; for example, in Quebec, it consists of 19 members including representatives from the university, the principal and academic dean, students and parents of students.

Universities   7.1.3

There are distinctive differences in Canadian systems of higher education. The universities and colleges long ago established by the French were based on the culture of Old France and were administered by Roman Catholic groups, either religious or secular. These French-language institutions still retain their traditional characteristics but conform almost entirely to the North American system of administration. The largest group of universities and colleges in Canada is administered by English-speaking staff and offers instruction in English. Apart from those founded and still administered by various Protestant religious groups, these institutions are mainly non-denominational, having been established through private subscription or by the provincial government concerned.

Civil legislation regarding the establishment of new institutions or changes in existing ones is usually enacted by provincial legislatures, except for federal military colleges and a few institutions originally established by Act of Parliament. Once an institution is legally chartered, control is vested in its governing body, the membership of which is indicated in the charter. The line of authority runs from the board of governors through the president (or rector) to the senate and deans and the faculty as a whole. The composition of the board of governors varies according to the type of institution. Provincial universities normally have government representation; church-related institutions have clergymen. Nearly all boards have either direct representation from the business community, alumni associations and other organizations, or are advised by these groups through advisory boards or committees. A recent phenomenon has been the inclusion of students on administrative bodies. The size of the board varies from a very few to over 60. It has ultimate control of the university and normally reserves to itself complete financial powers, including the appointment of the president and most other staff. On occasion there is faculty representation on the board and recently there have been attempts on the part of faculty groups of many institutions to obtain greater representation on the boards of governors. Responsibility for academic affairs is usually delegated to the senate. Composed mainly of faculty members, although there may also be alumni and representatives of non-academic groups included, the board is responsible for admission, courses, discipline and the awarding of degrees.

7.2   Levels of education

7.2.1   Pre-grade 1, elementary and secondary education

Pre-grade 1 enrolment in schools is neither compulsory nor universal throughout Canada, although kindergartens for five-year-olds are part of the elementary school system in large urban centres in most provinces. Recently, an increasing number of kindergartens are accepting four-year-olds. There are also some kindergartens which are run by private individuals and which accept children of three to five years of age.

The plan of eight grades elementary and four grades secondary education leading from grade 1 to university was for many years the basic plan for organizing the curriculum and schools other than those under the jurisdiction of the Catholic school boards of Quebec. This plan, although still followed in some school jurisdictions, has been modified from time to time in all provinces, cities or groups of schools. There are a number of variants to be found in Canada at present: the addition of one or even two years of secondary schooling; the introduction of junior high schools, changing the organization to a 6-3-3 or 6-3-4 plan; or the combining of the first six years of elementary school into two units, each designed to reach specified goals during the three-year period. In the recently established community colleges, the last one or two years of high school and the first one or two years of college are offered.

At the secondary level, three programs can generally be distinguished — the university entrance course, the general course for those wishing to complete an academic type of program before entering employment, and vocational courses for those wishing to enter skilled trades or pursue further training in the technological fields. However, in recent years changes in the curricula have allowed the student greater flexibility in program selection.

Secondary schools were at one time predominantly academic and prepared their pupils for entry into university. Until recently, vocational schools were to be found only in the large cities, although schools in some of the smaller centres did provide a few commercial and technical subjects as options in the academic curriculum. Today, in addition to the vocational schools and the regular secondary schools providing commercial courses, there are increasing numbers of composite and regional high schools offering regular academic subjects and vocational training in such courses as home economics, agriculture, shop-work and commercial subjects. Occupational or pre-employment classes, set up as part of the total program in regular vocational schools, require from one to three years or even four years for completion, and are terminal in nature. In addition to this type of course, some schools offer special, ungraded one- or two-year vocational programs to students who have completed the final years of high school. Some secondary schools also provide occupational programs for students who have shown no particular aptitude for an academic education or for training in a particular trade. These students learn no specific trade until perhaps their third year of studies.

Special education   7.2.2

There is increasing interest in the education of exceptional children. For gifted children, innovative, enriched and accelerated programs are being developed at both the elementary and secondary levels. New types of special classes are sometimes started by parents of children with a common disability, who band together to provide help and show the need for such service, which may then be taken over by public bodies. Progress in providing such education varies from province to province and is most commonly found in city school systems. There are six schools for the blind, 21 schools for the deaf, and a number of training schools for mental defectives. Special classes are conducted in tuberculosis sanatoria, mental hospitals and reformatories.

Trade and technical education   7.2.3

Increasing use of automated processes in business and industry is resulting in a shrinking market for unskilled and semi-skilled workers. Early school dropouts are finding it more difficult to get suitable employment and many are trying to acquire in their adult years the general education or training in the skilled trades that they missed in their youth. Persons still in the regular school system are tending to remain longer and go farther in the system, partly because of the changing attitudes of society toward education and partly for economic reasons.

To meet this growing demand for better educational facilities, educators are striving to provide comprehensive programs at all levels to satisfy the needs not only of the university-bound but also of the great majority who require adequate preparation for early entry into the labour force. It is now accepted that vocational education for adults as well as for youths is a public responsibility that must be made available, as needed, throughout the person's working life. Education of this nature is of national concern and has a direct impact on material prosperity, the economy and the standard of living.

The pattern of vocational education in Canada varies from province to province and there are variations within the provinces. However, there are three basic types of institutes offering vocational education: secondary schools, trade and occupational training schools and post-secondary institutes of technology. Many municipal school boards provide vocational courses as part of the regular secondary school program in technical or composite-type schools. Students in these schools get some general vocational training or training in certain specific fields, such as typing or auto mechanics, along with instruction in general academic or cultural subjects.

Trade and occupational training schools, on the other hand, are open only to those who have passed the provincial school-leaving age and have left the regular school system. These schools offer specialized training and their purpose is to develop competent people for a variety of occupations. Courses at the trade level do not usually require high school graduation; the grade level demanded varies according to province or trade from grade 8 to grade 12.

The third type, the institutes of technology, operate at a higher level of training. Enrolment in these institutions requires high school graduation or at least high school standing in such relevant subjects as mathematics and the sciences. The section on community colleges and related institutions provides more detail.

In addition to the vocational education and training provided by these three types of publicly operated schools, many private business colleges and trade schools

Sources of funds and expenditures for education, Canada, 1976-77
Millions of dollars

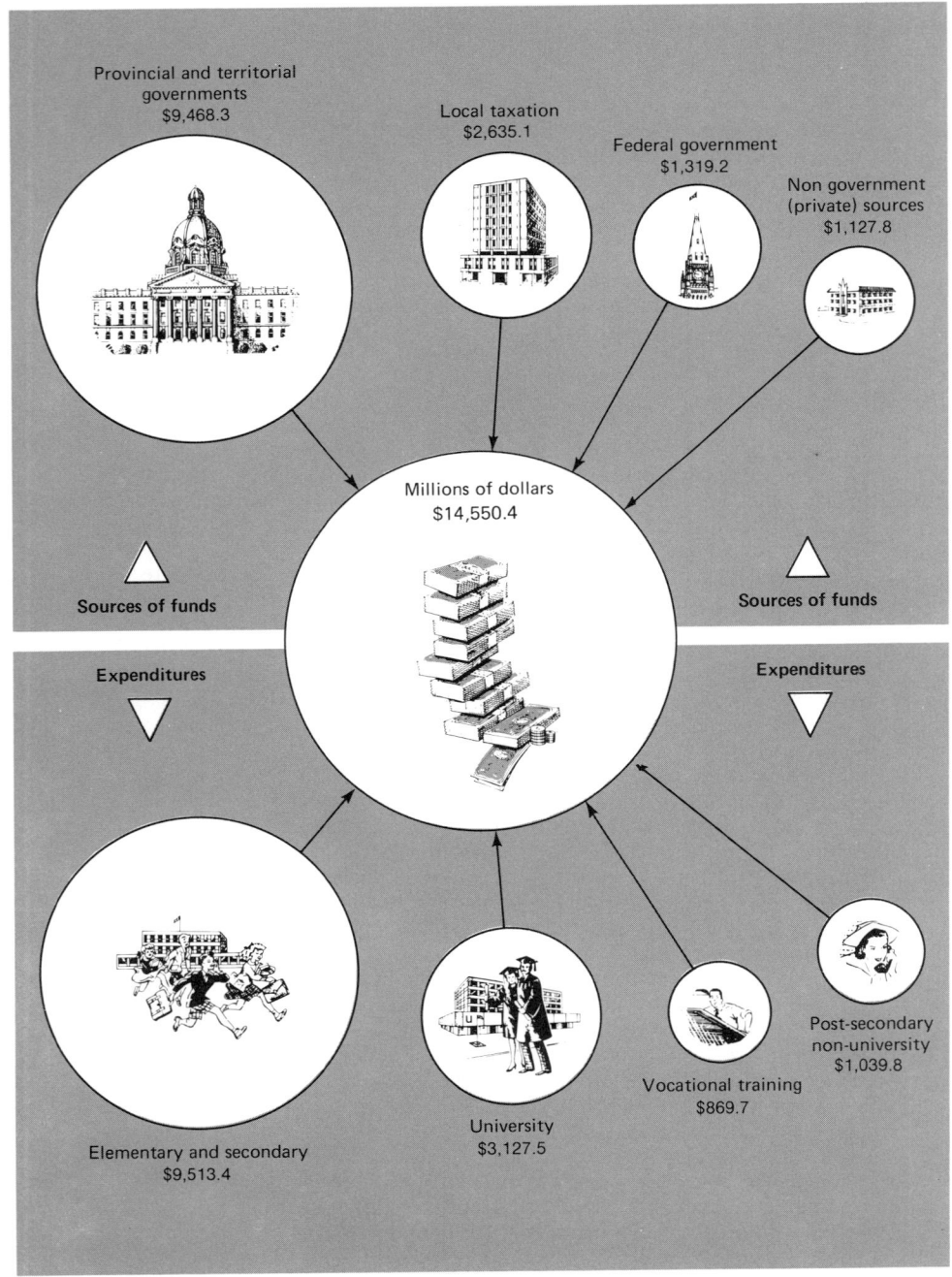

Provincial and territorial governments
$9,468.3

Local taxation
$2,635.1

Federal government
$1,319.2

Non government (private) sources
$1,127.8

Millions of dollars
$14,550.4

Sources of funds

Sources of funds

Expenditures

Expenditures

Elementary and secondary
$9,513.4

University
$3,127.5

Vocational training
$869.7

Post-secondary non-university
$1,039.8

offer a wide variety of business, trade and technical courses, some through correspondence. Vocational education is also carried out under a system of apprenticeship
training. Such training is given mainly on the job, with classes taken at the trade
schools either during the evening or full-time during the day for periods ranging
from three to 10 weeks a year.

Post-secondary non-university education   7.2.4

Community colleges and related institutions   7.2.4.1

Community colleges and related institutions provide post-secondary education in
various programs that enable students to proceed to university with credit of up to
three years of university study, or undertake technical/vocational training in programs of up to four years' duration, leading to the occupational level of the skilled
technologist.

Entry requirements involve secondary school graduation but in some institutions a "mature student" status is used to enable promising but otherwise ineligible
students to enter. Qualifying programs are also offered to help students overcome
academic deficiencies.

Programs offered in the technical/vocational sphere are widely diversified and
reflect the manpower requirements of the college region. Other programs offered are:
business administration, applied arts, health sciences and a wide variety of technologies such as architectural, mechanical, electrical, chemical and resource. Many of
these colleges offer credit and non-credit programs in continuing education.

There were 141 institutions offering college-level programs in Canada in
1973-74: 11 in the Atlantic provinces, 68 in Quebec including 36 CEGEPs
(collèges d'enseignement général et professionnel), 29 in Ontario, 21 of which
were CAATs (colleges of applied arts and technology), 21 in the Prairie provinces
and 12 in British Columbia.

Nursing education   7.2.4.2

Traditionally, nurses' (RN) diploma courses have been conducted in hospital
schools. In 1964 Ryerson Institute of Technology became the first non-hospital institution in Canada to provide nurses' diploma training. Since then, the trend has
been to transfer most diploma programs of nursing, which prepare graduates for
registration as RNs from hospital schools to community colleges. Hospital schools no
longer exist in Quebec, Ontario or Saskatchewan. In the other western provinces,
although most training in 1973-74 took place in hospital schools, nursing diploma
programs were also available in community colleges. Only in the Atlantic provinces
was training carried out exclusively in hospital schools. In many instances the transfer
of diploma programs to community colleges has reduced the duration of training
from three years to two. In Quebec the program still requires three years.

Schools of nursing are also located in universities where students work toward a
bachelor of science in nursing or an equivalent degree. These students, on graduation, are also eligible for registration but have an added advantage in entering teaching or administrative posts.

Teacher training   7.2.4.3

Until recently only teachers at the secondary level were required to have university
degrees. Teachers for the elementary schools were trained in teachers' colleges (or
normal schools). Over the past few years, however, requirement for all public school
teachers in Canada to have university degrees has been introduced. At present, the
requirement is almost universal.

In all provinces except Nova Scotia, New Brunswick, Quebec and Ontario, all
teacher training in 1973-74 was conducted at the university level where three or
four different courses leading to a degree were provided; about three quarters of
the time was devoted to academic courses in arts and science and the remainder to
professional courses. Teachers' colleges still existed in these four provinces but

were generally disappearing as independent institutions except in Nova Scotia where there was no plan to integrate its one teachers' college with the university; in New Brunswick, two teachers' colleges were operating. Five universities also offered degree programs in education. The pattern in Quebec was for students to complete the two-year academic program in a CEGEP and then continue their teacher training at university. Sixteen écoles normales have been absorbed by other institutions since 1969-70 and only two were still in operation. In Ontario only four teachers' colleges remained.

7.2.5 University education

A university may be defined as an institution of post-secondary education, professional training and research which has degree granting powers. The number of such institutions has risen to over 60 in the 1970s. In addition, there is a significant number of colleges affiliated with universities.

The largest group of universities provides instruction in English, although there are a number of French degree-granting institutions. In addition, there are a few bilingual institutions; the largest are the University of Ottawa and Laurentian University in Sudbury. Institutions range in size from those with full-time enrolments of less than 1,000 students and one faculty, to universities with more than 10,000 students with numerous faculties offering a wide range of programs.

Depending on the province, a student must have a junior or senior matriculation certificate in order to gain admission to courses leading to a first degree. Many universities now require that first students also write specified aptitude tests. The length of programs varies from three to four years for a pass bachelor's degree to five years or longer for a professional degree in medicine, theology, architecture and law. The master's degree program requires one or more years of study and intensive research after completion of the bachelor's degree. The doctorate normally requires at least two additional years beyond the second degree.

7.2.6 Continuing education

Continuing education, sometimes referred to as adult education, has become an important part of the education system. Diversified programs of study for adults through correspondence and extension courses are offered by school boards, provincial government schools, private trade schools and business colleges, business and professional associations, community colleges and related institutions, and universities. As a result, men and women who find it impractical or impossible to attend full-time or regular classes because of business and family responsibilities, illness or inaccessibility of schools are able to pursue accreditation at diverse educational levels or to advance their personal interests. Correspondence course study provides instruction to children and adults confined to home or hospital and to inmates of Canadian correctional institutions.

School boards, universities and community or regional colleges offer courses leading to formal accreditation as well as courses reflecting individual and community interests. Surveys of school boards and universities indicate that some 636,000 adults are enrolled in formal high school and university level courses on a part-time basis. In addition, more than 713,000 adults participate in a host of non-credit courses and related activities.

7.3 Provincial and territorial education systems

7.3.1 Education in the provinces

In most of the provinces, changes have occurred in the organizational structure of elementary and secondary education in recent years. These and specific changes in tertiary education, teacher training and nursing education are outlined in this section.

Newfoundland. Until recently, the system of education in Newfoundland, originally established in 1874, was strictly denominational. As a result of the recommendations of a provincial Royal Commission on Education and Youth set up in 1964, consolidation of the school systems of the major Protestant denominations has taken place but the Roman Catholic, Pentecostal and Seventh Day Adventist denominations still operate their own schools. Further reorganization occurred in 1969 when schools operated by 300 denominational boards in the province were regrouped into 35 districts. The Pentecostal Assemblies and the Seventh Day Adventists each operate one "school district" which, in theory if not in practice, embraces the whole province. The largest single denomination in the province, the Roman Catholic, continues to operate its own system but the number of its boards has been reduced from over 100 to 12.

Pre-grade 1 enrolment in Newfoundland is not compulsory but, with the construction of larger and more centralized elementary schools, most five-year-olds are attending kindergarten classes. The number of children in nursery schools and kindergartens run by private individuals remains quite small.

There are two major patterns of school organization: elementary schools (kindergarten and grades 1-6) with central high schools (grades 7-11), and elementary schools (kindergarten and grades 1-8) with regional high schools (grades 9-11). There are a few junior high schools (grades 7-9) and 11 district vocational schools. No vocational instruction, except for commercial courses, is given in the secondary schools.

Tertiary education includes both university and post-secondary non-university programs. Memorial University in Newfoundland offers degree courses in arts and sciences, commerce and business administration, education, engineering and applied sciences, and certificate courses in public administration and banking. Post-secondary non-university education is offered at the College of Trades and Technology and the College of Fisheries, Navigation, Marine Engineering and Electronics. Nurses' (RN) diploma courses are conducted exclusively in hospital schools.

Prince Edward Island. During the 1960s, Prince Edward Island moved from small education units to consolidation. In July 1972, a major reorganization of the provincial school administration changed the system formerly organized along county lines to one of five administrative units.

Kindergarten classes are not part of the publicly controlled school system; however, nurseries and kindergartens operated by private individuals provide some pre-grade 1 classes although the enrolment is still quite small in relation to the four- and five-year-old population.

The major pattern of school organization until junior matriculation is: elementary school (grades 1-6), junior high school (grades 7-9) and senior high school (grades 10-12); an additional pattern consists of elementary school (grades 1-8) and high school (grades 9-12). Prince Edward Island is working toward a system that will eliminate grade promotion in favour of subject promotion, using a credit system. About 3% of the elementary and secondary pupils currently receive their education in French, and French is taught as a second language in all other schools.

The province is served by a network of 15 regional high schools offering academic programs from grades 9-12 and a one- or two-year business education course. Two vocational high schools provide a variety of four-year trade courses — a one-year orientation program followed by three years of training in a specific trade concomitant with academic instruction in language, mathematics and science.

The Prince Edward Island School of Nursing is the only establishment offering a nursing diploma leading to professional registration (RN). In 1969 — the University of Prince Edward Island replaced the former Prince of Wales College and St. Dunstan's University, and Holland College was opened to offer post-secondary vocational training.

Nova Scotia. In Nova Scotia, the Educational Assistance Act and certain amendments to the Education Act, both passed by the provincial legislature in 1968, allowed for the creation of amalgamated school boards. Three amalgamated boards began operation in 1970-71. In addition, there are other boards designated as rural, urban and regional.

Nova Scotia has almost 100% of its five-year-old population in "primary" year in the publicly controlled schools; perhaps as a consequence, enrolment in private nurseries has increased only slightly in recent years.

The predominant grade organization in this province is: elementary school (primary and grades 1-6), junior high school (grades 7-9) and senior high school (grades 10-12). There are a few variations in this basic school pattern, such as primary to grade 6 and grades 7-12, or primary to grade 9 and grades 10-12. In 1969, a modified junior high school program was authorized which gives students of average or above-average standing extra instruction in one or more subjects. High school graduation is at either the grade 11 (junior matriculation) or the grade 12 (senior matriculation) level, although enrolment in the latter is not universal in this province. As a result of revisions in the school system since 1966, 13 regional vocational schools replaced the county vocational schools. Students now attend regional vocational schools for occupational training since the secondary schools provide only business and commercial programs.

In 1969, authority was given for the award of high school equivalency diplomas to adults who had not completed high school but had improved their educational standing through job experience or informal training. This diploma is awarded on the basis of a series of tests, developed and validated over a 25-year period by the Commission on Accreditation of the American Council on Education; Nova Scotia was the first Canadian province permitted to use these tests.

Nova Scotia has two institutes of technology offering trade-level and post-secondary vocational courses, an agricultural college providing post-secondary terminal and university transfer programs, a land survey institute and a nautical institute. All nursing training leading to the RN diploma is carried out in hospital schools. Several universities and colleges offer degree programs in many disciplines. Teacher training is given in one teachers' college and degree programs are offered in five universities — Acadia, Dalhousie, Mount Saint Vincent, St. Francis Xavier and Saint Mary's.

New Brunswick. There are 33 school districts in the province combined into seven regions, each administered by a regional superintendent. Instruction is available in both English and French; 34% of the student population at the elementary and secondary level take their instruction in the French language.

Pre-grade 1 classes are not offered in the publicly controlled school system, except in unusual or experimental circumstances. Enrolment in private nurseries and kindergartens is low in proportion to the number of five-year-olds in the province.

The province has a 12-year system of public education leading to junior matriculation. The most common patterns of school organization are: elementary school (grades 1-6), junior high school (grades 7-9) and senior high school (grades 10-12); and elementary school (grades 1-6) and high school (grades 7-12). Vocational courses are taught within the framework of the secondary school system and are taken concomitantly with academic instruction.

The New Brunswick Institute of Technology in Moncton and the Saint John Institute of Technology offer post-secondary vocational and technical programs. Teachers' colleges have been integrated with the university system. In addition to six hospital schools, the Saint John School of Nursing offers training leading to the RN diploma. Four universities offer a variety of degree programs.

Quebec. In 1964, the Quebec government, acting on recommendations of the provincial Royal Commission on Education (1961-64), passed legislation (under Bill 60) establishing a new administrative structure for the school system; the Department of Education replaced the former Departments of Youth and of Public Instruction. In addition to the Minister and Deputy Minister, the structure of the ministry included two Associate Deputy Ministers — one for the Catholic sector and one for the non-Catholic sector. This change of system required large increases in education expenditures to finance the building of new schools and to acquire additional teaching personnel and materials. Sixty-four regional school boards (55 Catholic and nine Protestant) were created with which 175 local school boards are affiliated.

Kindergartens admitting five-year-olds are now part of the school system. Elementary education, intended for pupils aged six to 11 is given in publicly controlled schools operated under the direction of local school boards. Since the autumn of 1968, pupils are enrolled in the first grade only if they have reached the age of six by October 1. The new system calls for six years of elementary school, five years of secondary school and a collegial level to be taken in post-secondary non-university institutions. Another emerging trend is a composite course with graduated options and promotion by subject matter.

The federal Department of Indian Affairs and Northern Development assumes full responsibility for the education of Inuit children living in northern Quebec, and uses the curriculum established by the Department of Education of Quebec.

Collèges d'enseignement général et professionnel (CEGEPs), inaugurated at the beginning of the 1967-68 school year, replaced many of the former classical colleges, normal schools, schools of nursing and technical institutes. These colleges, currently numbering about 35, admit students graduating from grade 11 and offer three-year terminal technical programs and two-year academic programs which are prerequisite for university entrance. Private or classical colleges offer the equivalent of the two-year university transfer program offered in the CEGEP, at the end of which successful students receive a diplôme d'études collégiales. Students may, however, continue at these establishments and work toward a degree granted by the university to which the college is affiliated.

There are at present four English-language CEGEPs in operation. In addition, interim arrangements provided for the equivalent two-year CEGEP program at McGill and Concordia universities. Nursing diploma (RN) programs are now carried out exclusively in the CEGEPs. Teacher training is given in the universities after completion of the academic program in the CEGEPs. There are several universities and colleges located in Quebec that offer a wide variety of degree, diploma and certificate programs.

Ontario. Under amendments to the Ontario School Act, county districts replaced former individual units that were administered by three-member boards of trustees. The larger cities, such as Toronto and Ottawa, are excluded and operate their own school systems. Roman Catholic schools are given a choice. In most of Ontario the separate administration of elementary and secondary schools has been abolished and these schools are now administered by the same board. With each county administered by one board, there has been a drastic reduction from thousands of districts to less than 200. An amendment to the act in 1969 provided for schools for trainable retarded children to be established under the jurisdiction of a special divisional board of education.

Ontario has a 13-grade system (senior matriculation) with provision for kindergarten and pre-school enrolment. The predominant pattern of school organization consists of elementary school (kindergarten and grades 1-8) and secondary school (grades 9-13). A variation in this organization is the 6-3-4 pattern: elementary school (kindergarten and grades 1-6), junior high school (grades 7-9) and senior high school (grades 10-13).

A "credit system" covers the former grades 9-12 leading to the secondary school graduation diploma. This provides more flexible schedule patterns with a view to greater freedom of student choice within an expanding range of subjects, even to the creation of individual timetables for students. A credit is given for a course successfully completed, normally after 110 to 120 hours of scheduled time. The diploma (grade 12 standing) is awarded after attaining a minimum of 27 credits.

High schools offer double-option trade courses in science, technology and trades programs, and double-option business courses in business and commerce programs. There is a two- or three-year occupational program to which some students may voluntarily return for a fourth year. There are also special one-year commercial and technical programs that follow grade 11 or 12.

In 1967 former institutes of technology and provincial vocational centres were incorporated into colleges of applied arts and technology known as CAATs. These colleges were set up in 20 regions to serve the communities at both the post-secondary and the occupational levels. While the CAATs were not designed to accommodate prospective university transfer students, the universities do accept first-class graduates from the two- or three-year post-secondary programs into the first- and second-year degree courses, respectively. On October 1, 1971 these institutions became the responsibility of the newly formed Department of Colleges and Universities. Four teachers' colleges existed in Ontario in 1973-74 but these would be integrated with the university system. There are over 20 universities and colleges in Ontario offering a wide program of courses leading to degrees, diplomas and certificates.

Manitoba. Over 90% of public school enrolment comes under the administration of 48 unitary division boards responsible for all public elementary and secondary education within their jurisdictions. Some schools in remote areas and other special schools are not included in these 48 unitary division boards.

Public kindergarten classes are available in most elementary schools. Enrolment has almost tripled in the past 10 years as these facilities have been expanded and the number of children in private nurseries and kindergartens has consequently declined.

There are two major patterns of school organization in the 12-grade system to senior matriculation: elementary (kindergarten and grades 1-8) and high school (grades 9-12); or elementary (kindergarten and grades 1-6), junior high school (grades 7-9) and senior high school (grades 10-12). Increased emphasis has been placed on open-area classrooms, higher qualifications for teachers, and improved curricula. Other innovations include: more meaningful curricula for Indian and Métis children now incorporated into regular elementary and secondary classes; emphasis on health programs in relation to alcohol and narcotics; audio-lingual programs in French and German at grade 10 level; and emphasis on continuous testing to replace formal examinations and on the concept of "independent study" for students in some secondary schools. Final examinations are set and marked under the auspices of the High School Examination Board of Manitoba. Entrance to university requires board standing in at least three subjects with school standing acceptable in two other subjects.

Vocational students may take either a pre-employment commercial or industrial program. Successful completion entitles them to an "academic transcript". Alternatively, students may complete the university entrance program and continue for an additional year in a special commercial program, or those following the industrial program may spend half their time in the university entrance program. There is also an occupational entrance program commencing at grade 7 and continuing until grade 10 or 11, during which period students receive part of their training on the job in business or industry.

The Manitoba Institute of Technology and Applied Arts, in Winnipeg and vocational centres at Brandon and The Pas, designated as community colleges in 1969, were renamed Red River Community College, Assiniboine Community College and Keewatin Community College, respectively. These institutions offer both post-secondary terminal career programs and vocational courses at the trades level. Although no provision is made for university-transfer programs, graduates from the career programs have, in special circumstances, been granted credits applicable to a university program. Training for nurses qualifying them for the RN diploma is provided at Red River College as well as at five hospital schools.

Teacher training is offered only at the university level. Seven colleges and universities have degree-granting programs. The largest — the University of Manitoba — offers courses in arts and sciences, law, medicine, education, applied sciences, architecture and many other fields.

Saskatchewan. Many schools in the larger centres offer kindergarten classes, although elsewhere in the province such classes are not normally available. The proportion of five-year-olds attending pre-grade 1 classes in the publicly controlled school system increased from about 27% in 1971-72 to 34% in 1973-74.

The traditional 12 elementary-secondary grades were replaced by four divisions, each consisting of three years of school for a student making normal progress. In

Divisions I and II, the principle of non-grading, involving continuous progress and flexible promotion, has been adopted. Division III programs have been planned to meet the special needs of pupils in the 13- to 15-year-old age group faced with the problems of emerging adolescence. Division IV is undergoing major changes in the scope of courses offered and in the content and methods used within particular subject areas. Amendments to the Saskatchewan School Act allow for exclusion from the regular system of children mentally deficient and incapable of learning. Educable handicapped children attend special classes in regular schools; blind and deaf children between seven and 16 years of age are educated in special schools.

Vocational subjects may be taken in general, industrial arts, commercial or special terminal programs, but none of these qualify the student for university entrance. Vocational courses in high schools were set up to provide a closer liaison between those schools and the technical institutes. Most vocational students in grade 9, apart from those in the commercial course, take five shops not associated with any one specific trade; similarly, students in grade 10 may take two shops. Five institutes and colleges offer vocational courses only at both post-secondary and trades levels. They have taken over the total responsibility for the nurses' (RN) diploma program.

The University of Saskatchewan and University of Regina both offer many degree programs.

Alberta. Education is under constant review by the province's Commission on Educational Planning, charged with the broad task of predicting what Alberta society will be like educationally, socially and economically during the last decades of the 20th century. Innovations in the elementary-secondary level include: extensive experimentation in programs carried out at the local school level; the use of French as the language of instruction during 50% of the school day in grades 3-12 in certain schools; construction of modern buildings incorporating the latest design in instructional facilities; movement toward the semester system and other methods of dividing the school year; and implementation of school television projects. The province is organized into divisions for purposes of education and each division is administered by its own school board.

Kindergarten classes are not part of the provincial school system although some school boards, particularly those in the cities, do provide such classes. In addition, about 20% of five-year-old children are enrolled in privately operated nursery schools and kindergartens.

The two predominant patterns of school organization are: elementary school (grades 1-6), junior high school (grades 7-9) and senior high school (grades 10-12); or elementary school (grades 1-8) and high school (grades 9-12). Alberta operates its secondary schools on the composite or comprehensive principle. Most of the wide range of vocational programs are offered in grades 10-12. In grade 12, some of the vocational courses lead to the granting of 15-20 credits; 100 credits are required for an Alberta High School Diploma.

In the fall of 1971, a new Department of Advanced Education was formed, separate from the Department of Education. This department was responsible for universities, public colleges, institutes of technology and the agricultural and vocational colleges formerly under the jurisdiction of the Department of Agriculture. Vocational programs at the post-secondary level are now offered through the community college system.

Nurses' (RN) diploma programs are given at both hospital schools and four community colleges: Lethbridge, Medicine Hat, Mount Royal and Red Deer.

One large university, the University of Alberta, offers a variety of courses including fine and applied arts, arts and science, medicine, dentistry, pharmacy, nursing, household science, engineering and applied science, agriculture, library science, law and education. The province also has two other universities — the University of Calgary and the University of Lethbridge. The Collège universitaire Saint-Jean offers a bilingual program toward the BA, BEd, and BSc degrees. A number of affiliated colleges offer up to two years of university level education.

British Columbia. British Columbia's former 13-year system of education, culminating in senior matriculation, has been replaced with a 12-year system. The predominant pattern of school organization consists of elementary school (grades 1-6), junior high school (grades 7-9) and senior high school (grades 10-12). Five of the six programs offered in grades 11 and 12 are vocationally oriented — commercial, industrial, community services including home economics (not specifically labour-force-oriented), visual and performing arts, and vocational. There are a substantial number of pupils enrolled in special classes, such as those for educable retarded, blind or deaf children. In most school districts, the less severely handicapped receive special instruction in regular schools and the more severely handicapped are taught in special schools under government or private operation.

Ten community colleges and the British Columbia Institute of Technology have been established since 1965. The colleges, operated by consortiums of school boards, enable residents of a particular geographic area to take the junior years of university or a post-secondary terminal vocational course. Vancouver City College is operated by the Vancouver School Board, and the British Columbia Institute of Technology, which offers post-secondary career programs only, is operated by the provincial Department of Education. Trinity Western College is a church-related institution which provides the first two years of university. Columbia College, a private non-denominational institution in Vancouver, offers a terminal career course in fashion design and transfer programs recognized by the University of British Columbia.

In addition to the hospital schools of nursing, the British Columbia Institute of Technology, Selkirk College and Vancouver City College offer the nurses' (RN) program and Vancouver City College provides specific training in psychiatric nursing.

The largest degree-granting institution — the University of British Columbia — has faculties of architecture, law, medicine, applied science, education, arts and science and others. A major development for the 1970s, based on the report of the Commission on the Future of the Faculty of Education, was the revision of the academic program and administrative structure of this university's Faculty of Education. Among the 85 recommendations are such innovations as the adoption of a single five-year Bachelor of Education program, introduction of the "teaching associate" idea, a new Master of Pedagogy degree, and student participation in decision-making at the operational level. There are two smaller universities, Victoria and Simon Fraser, and a number of small colleges, most of them church-related.

7.3.2   School systems in the territories

Yukon Territory. The school system is administered by the Yukon Department of Education and operated through a superintendent and staff at Whitehorse, appointed by the territorial government and responsible to the Commissioner of the Territory.

Northwest Territories. The Northwest Territories school system, in the districts of Mackenzie, Franklin and Keewatin, is operated by the Department of Education of the territorial government. An education curriculum has been developed relevant to the cultural heritage of Inuit, Indian and Métis students, who make up the majority of pupils in the schools. The department, with the assistance of the Department of Indian Affairs and Northern Development, is initiating the collection of stories and legends of the Dogrib people and a Dogrib grammar and a dictionary are being produced.

7.3.3   Education of Indians and Inuit

Indians. The number of Indian students enrolled in pre-vocational courses, in universities and in teacher training increased substantially in the early 1970s. Indian history, traditions and languages are now included in curricula, and native culture is stressed through language, visual aids, tapes and printed matter as well as Indian dances and arts.

Federal financial assistance for Indian students attending non-federal schools varies from payment of tuition fees and provision of school buses, many of them

operated by band councils or Indian contractors, to full maintenance either in boarding homes or student residences, which during the year accommodated 11,000 Indian students unable to attend local schools because of isolation or other reasons. There are federal schools for Indians in all provinces except Newfoundland.

Inuit (Eskimos). Inuit students attend schools in the Northwest Territories, Northern Arctic Quebec and in Labrador. The schools in the Northwest Territories are the responsibility of the government of the Northwest Territories. The Inuit schools in Arctic Quebec are the responsibility of the Department of Indian and Northern Affairs. The Inuit schools in Labrador are the responsibility of the province of Newfoundland. The Eskimo language (Inuktitut) is being used as a language of instruction in most Inuit communities in the lower grades. Inuit students attend post secondary and vocational programs in various locations in southern Canada.

Vocational education programs, including apprenticeship, are designed to train people for either wage employment or self-employment in specific occupations. Apprenticeship continues to be the most effective program for the development of trades people; manual skills are learned on the job where close watch is kept to assure that the apprentice is receiving work experiences in all available trades practice. In addition, each indentured apprentice receives six to eight weeks of full-time trade theory training in an in-school situation during each year of his apprenticeship. The government of the Northwest Territories has an adult vocational training centre at Fort Smith, NWT. Special programs for Inuit are available through the Department of Indian and Northern Affairs On-the-job Training Program and through the Public Service Commission, Northern Careers Program.

The Indian and Inuit Graduate Register published by the Department of Indian and Northern Affairs is a cumulative listing of Canadian Indian and Inuit graduates of universities, teachers' colleges and schools of nursing. The 1976 edition lists 905 graduates reported up to July 1976 including 47 from the Atlantic provinces, 143 from Quebec and 383 from Ontario. Graduates from the other provinces included: Manitoba, 98, Saskatchewan, 93, Alberta, 40 and British Columbia, 75, and from the Northwest Territories, 26.

It will be some time before an extensive university program is offered in the North. The University of Saskatchewan now offers courses in its research centre at Rankin Inlet, and the University of Alberta has expanded its program in the Mackenzie area, offering courses at Fort Smith, Yellowknife and Inuvik.

Financing education   7.4

Of the total expenditures on education across Canada amounting to $9,635.2 million in 1973-74, local governments contributed 20.1%, provincial governments 60.7%, the federal government 10.2% and the remaining 9.0% originated from fees and other sources (11.9% of the provincial share comes from federal transfers for post-secondary education and for minority language programs).

Local and provincial share   7.4.1

The magnitude of the elementary-secondary sector of education is most clearly evident when expressed in dollars. In 1973-74, total expenditures at this level were $6,312.9 million, or about 65% of all education expenditures in Canada.

The actual operation of public elementary and secondary schools is in the hands of the local elected or appointed school boards which determine the budgets and therefore the amount of taxes required for school purposes. In most cases, these taxes are levied and collected for the boards by the municipalities; however, in those areas where there is no municipal organization the school boards have the power to levy and collect taxes for school purposes. The municipal share of the cost of elementary and secondary education has declined in recent years. It represented 31.7% in 1971-72, 31.5% in 1972-73 and 30.5% in 1973-74. During the same period, provincial contributions rose from $3.2 billion to $3.8 billion. The contribution of these two levels of government differs from province to province, each provincial authority deciding on the magnitude of the municipal responsibility. In New Brunswick, the provincial government took full control of public elementary and secondary education. Consequently, the revenue used for public education is derived almost entirely from provincial taxes (real property and sales taxes). Financial arrangements in Prince Edward Island are similar.

7.4.2   Federal contributions

In 1973-74, federal government expenditures on education amounted to $985 million excluding monies transferred to provinces under the terms of the Federal-Provincial Fiscal Arrangements Act; of this, some $280 million was spent at the university level, and expenditures on non-university post-secondary education, including vocational training, amounted to $525 million. Finally, direct expenditures by the federal government on elementary-secondary education and teacher training accounted for $180 million.

Some 66 federal government departments and agencies contribute to education in one way or another. The federal government has no responsibility for the organization and administration of education but it does have a vital interest in the availability of education, the skills of the population and the extent of scientific research carried on in Canada, realizing the effect of these on the national economy and on individual and social development.

During the past few years, federal support to education has undergone significant change. As a result of the federal-provincial conference of October 1966, the federal government undertook to provide increased support to education. Recognizing that education is a provincial responsibility, it decided to discontinue payment of operating grants directly to universities and to expand its support beyond university education. It included in its program all, or almost all, post-secondary education, i.e. the educational institutions and courses requiring for admission at least junior matriculation, or its equivalent, in each province. The provinces were offered the choice of either a federal per capita grant of $15 based on population or 50% of operating costs of post-secondary education, whichever was greater. Implementing this proposal, Parliament passed the Federal-Provincial Fiscal Arrangements Act in March 1967. This act authorized the transfer of specific percentages of federal revenue plus required cash from the federal treasury to the provinces for a five-year period commencing with the 1967-68 fiscal year and renewed in 1972.

The financial resources transferred to the provinces were $422 million in 1967-68, $528 million in 1968-69, $654 million in 1969-70, $843 million in 1970-71, $985 million in 1971-72, and $1,058 million in 1972-73. The amount to be transferred to the provinces in 1973-74 was $1,143 million.

Adult Occupational Training Act. The federal government, through the Department of Manpower and Immigration, provides occupational training to adults who are or plan to be members of the labour force. If, in the opinion of a manpower counsellor at a Canada Manpower Centre, it is in the best interest of the individual and of the economy for an adult to undertake training or retraining, the person may be placed in a training place purchased by the federal government from a public or private training institution or from industry. The program also provides for payment of allowances to persons whose training programs have been arranged by a manpower counsellor. Payments range between $45.00 and $147.00 a week, depending on the individual's economic responsibilities.

Canada Student Loans Act. Full-time students may borrow up to $1,800 annually to a total of $9,800. Loans are interest-free while the student is enrolled and for six months thereafter. Provision is made for the total amount allocated to this program to be increased year by year in proportion to the increase in enrolment in post-secondary institutions. The purpose of the loan plan is to assist those students who, for financial reasons, would otherwise be prevented from acquiring a post-secondary education or would not be able to devote full time to their studies. These loans may be made only on the basis of certificates of eligibility issued by the participating province. There is no upper or lower age limit for eligibility. Funds authorized by certificates of eligibility are issued by the chartered banks, the federal government guaranteeing the loans and paying the interest while the student is attending college. All provinces except Quebec participate; Quebec offers its own student assistance program for the benefit of residents of that province.

The act provides for basic allocations for each province and also for supplementary allocations to compensate for differences in relative demand between provinces, based on provincial population in the 18-24-year age group. The basic allocations for the year 1974-75 for participating provinces totalled $97.6 million with authority for discretionary allocations up to $41.1 million, making a total maximum of $137.1 million authorized under the act. Loans actually authorized amounted to $118.2 million. In addition, federal payments to lending institutions in respect of interest on outstanding loans and other operational expenses amounted to $31.5 million.

Health Resources Fund Act. In 1966, the federal government inaugurated a program of massive financial support to the provinces to provide facilities for training professional personnel in health services. The Health Resources Fund Act (RSC 1970, c.H-4), administered by the Department of National Health and Welfare, authorized the establishment of a fund to assist financially in the planning, acquisition, construction, renovation and equipping of health training facilities, defined to mean any school, hospital or other institution for the training of persons in the health professions or associated occupations, or for conducting research in the health field; residential accommodation was excluded. The fund was established in the amount of $500 million, to be applied to costs incurred between January 1, 1966 and December 31, 1980; of that amount, $400 million is available to the provinces on a per capita basis, $25 million is available to the four Atlantic provinces for joint projects, and $75 million remains to be allocated by the Governor in Council. Contributions are payable to the provinces in amounts of up to 50% of the cost of projects approved by the Minister's Advisory Committee as part of a five-year plan for the development of health training facilities in a province.

During the first five years of operation of this program, 1966-67 to 1970-71, the federal government paid $143.2 million to the provincial treasuries in respect of approved projects. Projects financed included training facilities in universities or institutions connected with, or operated by, schools of medicine, schools of nursing, including new regional schools of nursing in Ontario, and schools for nursing assistants, as well as facilities for vocational types of training at the higher educational levels.

Canada Council. Through the Canada Council, the federal government in 1957 provided an amount of $100 million, half of which was to be distributed among the universities for specified building and equipment purposes, similar to the distribution of grants. Interest from the remaining $50 million was to be used to assist in the development of the arts, humanities and social sciences, mainly through scholarships (see Section 7.9.1).

Other contributions are more indirect and include scholarships, research grants and reports or services of value to the schools. Research grants are made by the National Research Council, the Defence Research Board, the Department of National Health and Welfare, the Department of Manpower and Immigration and other agencies. Some departments — Agriculture and National Health and Welfare, among others — provide materials and publications of value in the school programs; and the National Museums of Canada, the National Gallery, the National Film Board and the Canadian Broadcasting Corporation contribute directly or indirectly to various school programs.

More directly, the federal government is responsible for the education of Indians, members of the Armed Services and their dependents, and in-service training for permanent personnel and inmates of federal penitentiaries. It also assists in citizenship training and other out-of-school informal education activities.

External education assistance. The Canadian International Development Agency is responsible for the operation and administration of the technical assistance program

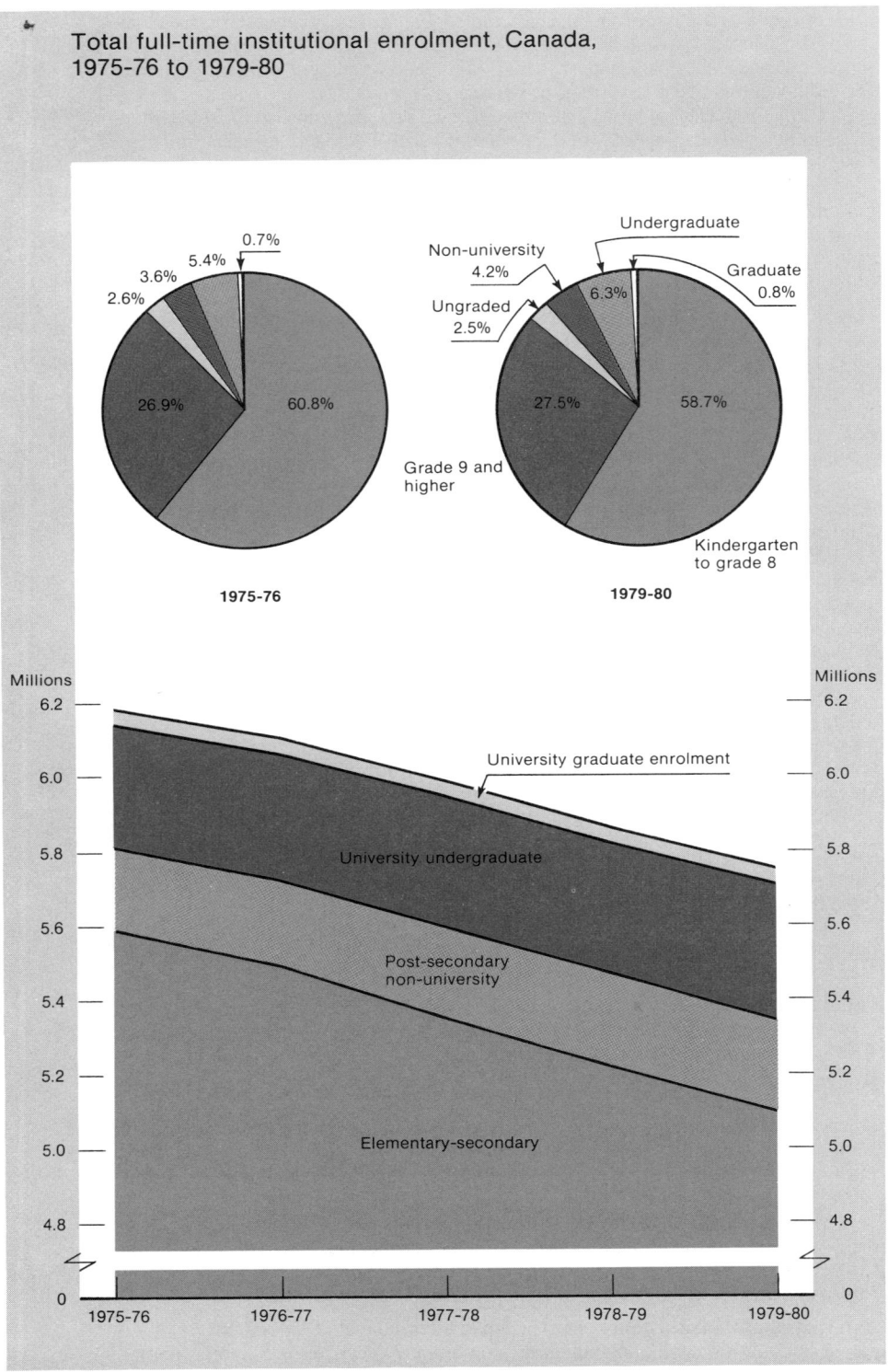

Total full-time institutional enrolment, Canada,
1975-76 to 1979-80

offered by the Canadian government to developing countries. The International Development Research Centre, Canadian-financed but international in character, supports and assists research into the economic and social problems faced by developing countries. The activities of both organizations are described in Chapter 3.

Statistics of education   7.5

Tables 7.1 to 7.10 trace a statistical image of education at all levels for each of the provinces from 1970 to 1974. Enrolment is shown in Tables 7.1, 7.4 and 7.5. Teacher characteristics are outlined in Tables 7.2, 7.3 and 7.4. Financial data are given in Tables 7.9 and 7.10.

Full-time enrolment in Canadian educational institutions increased by 25% from 1963-64 to 1973-74. Before 1970-71 there was a regular annual increase of about 200,000, but in 1971-72 the overall number fell for the first time. This decline has been evident at the elementary-secondary level since the 1970-71 peak year, particularly in the public school system which from 1971-72 to 1972-73 showed a decline of 1.2% and from 1972-73 to 1973-74 a further decline of 1.7%.

The secondary schools, on the other hand, in 1973-74 showed an increase of about 2.5% over the previous year. Nevertheless, the trend in recent years has been a reduction in the total number of students entering the school system. In 1966-67, there were 516,800 Grade 1 pupils; by 1973-74, the number had fallen to 395,300. This drop was mainly the result of the decline in births which began in the 1960s and is expected to continue until around 1980.

Full-time post-secondary enrolment rose from 220,200 in 1963-64 to 533,200, an increase of almost 150%. This increase took place in both university and non-university categories although in later years growth was faster in the non-university sector. Non-university enrolment in 1973-74 (201,100) was more than three times what it had been 10 years earlier (62,200). Enrolment in universities more than doubled during the same period (from 158,000 to 332,100).

The upward trend in earlier years of the popularity of continuing education is still going on and increases in registrations for both credit and non-credit courses were registered in 1973-74. Non-credit courses, accounting for 54% of all registrations, have increased everywhere except in Newfoundland. More than half of these courses were offered by school boards while the universities accounted for over a quarter. Of the 890,000 credit course registrations, 42% was in universities.

On a national basis in 1973-74, 92 of every 1,000 persons 15 and older not attending school on a regular basis were registered in continuing education courses.

Training for the Armed Forces   7.6

The training system   7.6.1

All recruit and most basic and advanced trades training in support of the Canadian Armed Forces takes place at various schools under the supervision of The Canadian Forces Training System. Maritime Command, Mobile Command and Air Command maintain functional control of trades and operational training for their personnel.

The Combat Arms School of the Combat Training Centre, CFB Gagetown, NB, conducts training for officers and men of the armoured, artillery and infantry units of the Regular and Reserve Forces, ranging from basic trades to advanced courses. Similar courses for French-speaking personnel are given at the Combat Arms School Detachment, CFB Valcartier, Que. Training for field engineers and construction trades is given at CFB Chilliwack, BC.

Recruit training takes place at CFB Cornwallis, NS, for English-speaking recruits and at CFB Saint-Jean, Que., for French-speaking recruits. Basic technical training in French is given also at CFB Saint-Jean, Que. and an expanding trades-training program in that language is given at most bases and schools.

Saint-Jean is also the site of the English-French Language School, although the official languages are taught on a limited scale at selected Canadian Forces Bases, and in civilian centres under the auspices of the Public Service Commission. Instruction in other languages is given at the Canadian Forces Foreign Language School in Vanier, Ont.

Support trades training is conducted at the School of Administration and Logistics, CFB Borden, Ont. Electronics training is conducted at the School of Communications and Electronic Engineering at CFB Kingston, Ont., and aerospace training at the School of Aerospace and Ordnance Engineering at CFB Borden. Training for various other technical specialties is conducted at a number of bases across Canada. Two Fleet Schools, one at CFB Esquimalt, BC and the other at CFB Halifax, NS, provide basic and advanced Maritime trades training and have training facilities for the operational warships on the east and west coasts.

Flying training to "wings" standard is based in the Prairie provinces, pilot selection and basic helicopter flying training at Portage la Prairie, Man., basic fixed-wing flying training at Moose Jaw, Sask., and advanced flying training at CFB Cold Lake, Alta. Air Navigator and Observer training is conducted at the Air Navigation School at CFB Winnipeg, Man. The operational command maintains operational flying training units and technical training units to give training on handling equipment to tradesmen and specialist officers.

7.6.2   Canadian military colleges

The three Canadian military colleges are the Royal Military College of Canada, founded at Kingston, Ont., in 1876; Royal Roads Military College, established in 1941 near Victoria, BC; and Collège militaire royal de Saint-Jean, established at Saint-Jean, Que., in 1952, primarily to meet the needs of French-speaking officer cadets. In 1959 the Ontario Legislature granted the Royal Military College a charter empowering it to grant degrees. In 1972 the Department of National Defence concluded an agreement which permits graduates of Collège militaire royal de Saint-Jean to be granted Université de Sherbrooke degrees. In 1967, the Canadian Services Colleges, as they were then known, were re-designated the Canadian Military Colleges.

The role of the colleges is to educate and train officer cadets and commissioned officers for a career in the Canadian Forces. Courses are designed to develop character and to provide a balanced liberal, scientific and military education leading to degrees in arts, science and engineering. The Royal Military College of Canada accepts senior matriculants and offers a four-year course. Royal Roads Military College accepts senior matriculants who, on successful completion of the second year, go to Collège militaire royal de Saint-Jean or to the Royal Military College of Canada for their third and fourth years. Collège militaire royal de Saint-Jean accepts junior and senior matriculants to pursue a five- or four-year program; the final two years in some disciplines are completed at the Royal Military College.

At the 1975 convocation ceremonies, 238 students received their bachelor's degrees and were commissioned in their chosen fields. In June 1975, Royal Roads Military College was awarded a degree-granting charter by the province of British Columbia and in September 1975 the third year of a degree program in ocean physics was started. In addition to the baccalaureate given at the three military colleges, the Royal Military College offers serving officers a graduate study program leading to master's degrees in arts, science and engineering.

In 1976, the Royal Military College celebrated its Centennial and a number of special events were planned to mark the occasion. These included the presentation of a new Queen's colour on Parliament Hill in May, a special graduation ceremony June 1 in Kingston, the issue of a commemorative stamp by the Post Office in June, and a special convocation to award an honorary degree to the Governor General.

Professional development system   7.6.3
A new four-level system of staff and defence courses for Canadian Armed Forces officers is being offered.

The Junior Staff Course, given at the Canadian Forces Staff School, Toronto, Ont., is a 10-week course conducted four times a year for junior captains selected from all officer classifications. Its aim is to prepare junior officers to perform staff functions of a general nature and to provide the foundation for their subsequent professional development. The course includes studies in staff duties, the communication process, service knowledge, leadership and management, professionalism and current affairs.

The Junior Command and Staff Course (Land) is a 16-week course given twice a year at the Canadian Land Forces Command and Staff College, Kingston, Ont. This course is designed to meet the need for performance-oriented command and staff training for selected junior officers employed in land force operations.

The Command and Staff Course is a 44-week course given at the Canadian Forces Staff College, Toronto, Ont., which is intended to develop selected officers for senior command and staff appointments. In broad terms the curriculum includes military studies, executive development studies, and national and international studies. The student body normally consists of Canadian Forces majors from all classifications and a limited number of foreign officers.

The National Defence College Course, Kingston, Ont., is a 47-week course for senior military officers and civilian officials of government departments and the private sector. It enables course members to study aspects of national and international affairs which affect Canada's defence. Lecturers are chosen from leaders in various fields in Canada and other countries. Field study trips in Canada and abroad familiarize students with conditions which affect Canada.

University of Manitoba program. The Department of National Defence has an agreement with the University of Manitoba to allow Armed Forces personnel and their dependents to work toward university degrees. This special program was developed because of the recognition of difficulties encountered by service personnel and their dependents in pursuing studies toward a university degree. Frequent transfers and non-acceptance by some universities of other universities' credits have led some service people to the accumulation of far more credits than were actually required for a degree. Under this program, servicemen and dependents can achieve credits with the University of Manitoba, and complete studies elsewhere, with the University of Manitoba granting the degree.

The cadet movement   7.6.4
Three civilian agencies sponsor the cadet movement in Canada. The Air Cadet League of Canada, the Army Cadet League and the Navy League of Canada promote the Royal Canadian Air Cadets, the Royal Canadian Army Cadets and the Royal Canadian Sea Cadet Corps for boys between the ages of 13 and 18. In addition the Navy League has two other organizations, the Navy League Cadets for boys ages 11 to 13 and the Wrenette Corps for girls. The Department of National Defence supports these leagues in their objectives of developing good citizenship, leadership and physical fitness among the youth of this country. The department provides a number of summer camps across the country, and sponsors exchange programs between provinces, and with the United States, Britain, and several European countries.

Military assistance programs   7.6.5
Canada assists many Commonwealth and non-NATO countries by sending military training teams to those countries or by training a small number of military personnel in Canada. Training teams are sent to countries such as Ghana and Tanzania. Training in Canada is offered to developing countries such as Cameroon, Jamaica, Kenya, Malaysia, Nigeria, Singapore and Zambia.

Canada provides training facilities for some NATO countries on a cost-recovery basis according to the provisions of the Visiting Forces and the NATO Status of

Forces Agreement. Under the terms of a 10-year agreement signed in 1971 British military forces train in Canada. A similar agreement was also signed with the Federal Republic of Germany. Training areas remain under Canadian command and control and all costs are paid by the two countries concerned.

Pilots from NATO countries have trained at Canadian defence establishments for many years. In recent years pilots from Denmark, Germany, Norway and the Netherlands have benefited from the program. Canada continues to tutor NATO pilots from the Netherlands under an agreement which is to continue until July 1981.

7.7 Cultural activities

7.7.1 Education in the arts

There has been considerable expansion of education opportunities in the arts in Canada in the past few years. Courses of artistic content have increased to some extent in the universities but the main growth has taken place in the newly established community colleges of Ontario and the collèges d'enseignement général et professionnel (CEGEPs) of Quebec. These colleges offer both a transfer diploma which allows the student to continue his studies at university, and a vocational diploma with which the student may seek employment.

Fine arts (architecture, painting and drawing, commercial and decorative arts, graphics, ceramics and sculpture) appears as an elective subject of the faculty of arts in a number of universities, where it may be taken as one of five, six or more subjects for a year or two. A number of universities offer a Bachelor of Arts degree with a major in fine arts. Others offer a Bachelor of Fine Arts degree. It is also possible to complete a master's degree and doctorate in fine arts in some Canadian universities. There are many colleges and schools of art with varying academic requirements for admission. These offer diploma or certificate courses and are concerned largely with the technical development of the artist. Courses vary in length with the requirements of the individual student but may extend over as many as four years. In some schools fine crafts as well as fine arts are taught. Summer schools of art are sponsored by some institutions, by universities and by various independent groups.

Degree courses in music, the most widespread of the performing arts, are offered at a number of Canadian universities. Opera may be studied at the Royal Conservatory Opera School of the University of Toronto where advanced students work in close collaboration with the Canadian Opera Company, and also at the Conservatoire de Musique et l'Art Dramatique in Montreal and Quebec City and at the Banff School of Fine Arts (summer). Degree courses in drama are given at several universities. The National Theatre School of Canada in Montreal offers complete practical training in English or French for talented students, in a three-year acting course and two years for technical and production studies. The National Ballet School at Toronto is the only residential ballet school in Canada. Professional instruction is also offered by Les Grands Ballets Canadiens, Montreal, and the Royal Winnipeg Ballet. Instruction in drama, ballet, opera, creative writing and fine arts is given in summer school courses at the Banff School of Fine Arts, affiliated with the University of Calgary.

7.7.2 Performing arts

In recent years, grants have been made available to performing arts groups from both the public and private sectors to help finance their productions. Ticket sales and funds from backers scarcely meet half the expenses incurred by such groups.

Statistics Canada carries out an annual survey of a number of performing arts groups receiving grants from the Canada Council. Data on performances, audiences and finances are gathered at the end of the groups' fiscal year. Art forms surveyed include theatre (29 companies), music (13), dance (5) and opera (4).

During 1974 these 51 groups gave a total of 10,730 performances, attended by audiences of 5.7 million people. Total grants received amounted to almost $19 million. Altogether, grants represented between 45% and 55% of total revenues. More precisely, grants accounted for 47% of all revenue for theatrical groups and 46% of total revenue for an opera company; music and dance received 52% and 53% respectively of their income from grants. In descending order of importance, the principal contributors were the federal government, provincial governments, private enterprise and municipal authorities. Other income came mainly from ticket sales, backers, television, recordings or films, program sales, interest or short-term investments and self-operated restaurants and bars.

On the expenditure side, personnel costs accounted for 60% to 65% of the total budget for theatre, dance or opera companies. This percentage rose to 80% for music groups. Publicity accounted for expenditures of 7% to 10% of total expenses, and administration from 3% to 5%. Other production costs, such as expenditures on sets, costumes, props, technical equipment and printing of tickets accounted for 11% of expenditures for theatre, 4% for music, 21% for dance and 25% for opera. Finally, rental of halls made up 5% to 9% of total expenses.

Table 7.11 gives average grants, revenues and expenditures by type of company and by spectator for 1974. Without financial help from both the public and private sectors, average deficits would have reached $268,862 for theatre groups, $477,092 for musical organizations, $725,734 for dance groups and $554,951 for opera. Amounts of grants, income and expenditures per spectator were highest for opera, due in part to the fact that an opera company drew an average of 72,599 spectators for the 1974 season while theatre groups performed before audiences averaging 92,654; music, 144,998 and dance, 177,723.

Other data show that the federal government contributed, per spectator, an average of $1.58 for theatrical performances, $1.39 for music, $1.88 for dance and $2.87 for opera.

Compared with 1973, percentage increases in grants to opera, theatre, music and dance were of the order of 6%, 15%, 25% and 33%. Revenue increased by 14% for theatre, 24% for music and 4% for dance groups over the same period. Expenses increased by 15% for theatre, 18% for music and 7% for dance. Opera revenues decreased by 4% and expenditures by 3%.

Art galleries   7.7.3

Public art galleries and art museums in the principal cities perform valuable educational services. Children's Saturday classes, conducted tours for school pupils and adults, radio talks, lectures and concerts are features of the programs of the various galleries. Many of these institutions supply travelling exhibitions for their surrounding areas or range even farther afield. Several organizations such as the Maritime Art Association, the Atlantic Provinces Art Circuit, the Western Canada Art Circuit, the Art Institute of Ontario, the Art Gallery of Ontario and the Fédération des centres culturels du Québec have been founded to carry out this sort of travelling program on a regional basis. On a smaller scale, art circuits are organized to serve certain areas such as those around St. John's, Nfld., Charlottetown, PEI, Trois-Rivières and Hull, Que., and Winnipeg, Man. The National Gallery of Canada conducts a nation-wide program of this nature and is one of the largest art circulating agencies in North America. Several galleries maintain an art rental service. Table 7.15 gives the number of art galleries and museums and their location by region.

Museums   7.7.4

The museums of Canada, as elsewhere, range from small collections of locally-gathered historical artifacts and objects to large government-operated institutions which collect, classify and display such objects as may be useful to the study and teaching of natural history, human history, science and technology, with special but not exclusive reference to Canada. Many of these larger museums, especially the components of the National Museums of Canada and the Royal Ontario Museum, have a long, distinguished heritage in research and publication of scholarly works and are important educational and cultural centres. They offer many educational services to the public through exhibits, guided tours, lectures and scientific and popular publications.

Direct work with schools may involve holding classes in the museum or arranging visits of museum lecturers, with exhibits, to the schools. More informal are guided tours for visiting school classes, loans of specimens, slides, filmstrips or motion picture films to schools, and training student-teachers in the educational use of the museum. For children, a number of museums have special programs not directly associated with school work including Saturday lectures and film showings, activity groups, nature clubs and field excursions. At the higher educational level, museum field parties provide research training to university students in many disciplines and museum staffs act as professional consultants, answer a host of inquiries on scientific and technical subjects, and serve as consultants or advisers to foreign scholars and institutions.

For adults, museums offer lectures, film shows and guided tours, the latter usually available throughout the year. Staff members may give lectures to service clubs, church groups, parent-teacher associations and hobby clubs. The latter, such as naturalists' groups, mineral clubs and astronomy societies, may be allowed to use the museum as their headquarters. Travelling exhibits are prepared for showing at local fairs, historical celebrations and conventions. Some Canadian museums have conducted regular radio or television programs and others have made occasional contributions. Some historical museums stage annual events during which the arts, crafts or industries represented by the exhibits are demonstrated to the public.

7.8   National Museums of Canada

The National Museums of Canada, a Crown corporation within the federal government, is responsible for the administration of the four National Museums in Ottawa: the National Gallery of Canada, the National Museum of Man, the National Museum of Natural Sciences, and the National Museum of Science and Technology. In 1972, the corporation was charged with the implementation and administration of the National Museum Policy. The objectives of this policy are to give the Canadian public easier access to the objects and collections that form the Canadian cultural heritage, and to preserve them for future generations. The National Museum Policy involves large and small museums in all regions of the country. Smaller institutions are encouraged to improve the abilities of their professional staff and improve the museum facilities so they can better preserve and display their artifacts. Larger institutions are encouraged to develop advisory services for smaller institutions, to help them improve the quality of their exhibitions and loans for people in more remote areas of the country.

Four major programs implemented under the National Museum Policy include the National Inventory of Collections, the Museumobiles, the Canadian Conservation Institute and the Museum Assistance Programs. The National Inventory of Collections is compiling a computerized inventory of the art and artifacts across Canada that compose the national cultural heritage. The Museumobile Program provides a number of mobile museum units that can be transported to rural and remote regions of the country not now served by museological institutions. The Canadian Conservation Institute will ultimately provide five well equipped laboratories across the country to help museums and art galleries preserve and conserve their collections. The Museum Assistance Programs provide financial and other assistance to museological institutions for projects that train and develop museum staff, improve facilities, support education and extension programs within museums and other projects, such as travelling exhibitions, that increase public viewing of the collections. The budget for these major programs was $15.4 million in 1975-76.

The Board of Trustees of the National Museums of Canada has created a Consultive Committee on National Museum Policy to oversee the development and implementation of the policy and programs under the National Museum Policy. This committee is composed of people from all regions of the country, who are representative of museum users.

The National Gallery of Canada 7.8.1

The beginnings of the National Gallery of Canada are associated with the founding of the Royal Canadian Academy of Arts in 1880. The Marquis of Lorne, then Governor General, had recommended and assisted in the founding of the Academy and among the tasks he assigned to that institution was the establishment of a National Gallery at the seat of government. Until 1907 the National Gallery was under the direct control of a Minister of the Crown but in that year, in response to public demand, an advisory arts council consisting of three persons outside government was appointed by the government to administer grants to the National Gallery. Three years later, the first professional curator was appointed.

In 1913, the National Gallery was incorporated by Act of Parliament and placed under the administration of a board of trustees appointed by the Governor General in Council; its function was to encourage public interest in the arts and to promote the interests of art throughout the country. Under this management, the gallery increased its collections and developed into an internationally recognized art institution. Today, a board of trustees reporting to the Secretary of State administers all the National Museums of Canada, including the National Gallery, under the National Museums Act (RSC 1970, c.N-12).

The gallery's collections have been built up along international lines and give the people of Canada an indication of the origins from which their own traditions are developing. The collection of Canadian art, the most extensive and important in existence, is continually being augmented. Over 60% of all acquisitions since 1966 have been Canadian. There are now more than 13,000 works of art in the collections, excluding photographs. Included are many Old Masters, 12 having been acquired from the famous Liechtenstein collection. The Massey collection was presented to the gallery during 1946-50 by the Massey Foundation. The Vincent Massey Bequest of 100 works was received in 1968. In 1974 an important gift of drawings was donated by Mrs. Samuel Bronfman of Montreal in memory of her husband. There is a growing collection of contemporary art, prints and drawings, and diploma works of the Royal Canadian Academy. The gallery's collection of photographs, built up since 1967, contains 6,000 works. The services of the gallery include the operation of a reference library open to the public containing more than 50,000 volumes and periodicals on the history of art and other related subjects.

A program of exhibitions, lectures, films and guided tours is maintained for visitors to the gallery in Ottawa. The interests of the country as a whole are served by circulating exhibitions, lecture tours, publications, reproductions and films prepared by the National Gallery staff. Promotion of and information on art films are handled by the Canadian Centre for Films on Art, and their distribution by the Canadian Film Institute. The gallery promotes interest in Canadian art abroad by participating in international exhibitions such as the Biennials of Venice and Paris, and by preparing major exhibitions of Canadian art for showing in other countries in collaboration with the Department of External Affairs. It also brings important exhibitions from abroad for showing in Canada.

Major exhibitions in Ottawa in 1975-76 included works of the American sculptor Donald Judd; High Victorian Design; photographs from the collection; Some Canadian Women Artists; recent acquisitions of European prints; El Dorado: The Gold of Ancient Columbia; and the Age of Louis XV.

The major acquisition of the year was a 16th century Italian painting, *The Madonna with Saints Sebastian and Roche* by Lorenzo Lotto. The National Gallery also purchased its first surrealist painting by Salvador Dali called *Gala and The Angelus of Millet*.

Important gifts received during the year included a marble *Bust of General James Wolfe* by Joseph Wilton, donated by the Earl of Rosebery; a Ming bowl donated anonymously; an album of photographs of the American Civil War donated by Phyllis Lambert; and *Homage to the Square: Stepped Foliage* by Joseph Albers, donated by Ronald Longstaffe.

7.8.2   The National Museum of Natural Sciences

This museum has seven divisions: Botany, Invertebrate Zoology, Vertebrate Zoology, Mineral Sciences, Palaeontology, Interpretation and Extension, and the Canadian Aquatic Identification Centre. Thousands of specimens, originating from field trips, purchases, donations and exchanges, are added annually to the reference collections. The National Herbarium contains more than 357,000 vascular plants, 126,000 mosses and liverworts, 45,000 lichens and 14,000 algae. The zoological collection includes about 2,500,000 molluscs, 635,000 crustaceans, 662,000 other invertebrates, 214,000 fishes, 70,000 reptiles and amphibians, 62,500 birds and 41,000 mammals.

Only part of the National Mineral Collection, containing approximately 16,000 catalogued specimens of gems and minerals, is displayed in the museum. Tens of thousands of specimens of minerals, rocks and ores from many regions of the world are contained in other collections of display and study materials. During 1975 almost 70 major research projects were undertaken by museum staff members or associated scientists from universities and other outside organizations. The museum provided financial assistance, facilities and field work for several National Research Council post-doctoral fellows, and collaborated with the National Parks Service in botanical and zoological surveys. The museum's High Arctic Research Program was in turn supported by the Department of Energy, Mines and Resources through the Polar Continental Shelf Project.

The Vertebrate Palaeontology Collection contains more than 12,600 fossils, which includes rare dinosaur specimens. Research was conducted on reptilian diversity and environments before extinction of the dinosaurs, the Pleistocene fauna of Saskatchewan and the unglaciated region of the Yukon Territory, and fossilized pollen and spores.

The Canadian Aquatic Identification Centre (CAIC) sorts and identifies zooplankton, fish larvae and eggs, phytoplankton and other marine life. CAIC, with some 500 species in its reference collection, serves researchers, management, and survey and environmental agencies throughout Canada. Another unit, the Zooarchaeological Identification Centre, identifies and interprets animal remains found in archaeological investigations. This service studies both natural history and human history, and can identify the species of an animal from a fragment of bone.

In the renovated Victoria Memorial Museum Building, shared by the National Museum of Natural Sciences and the National Museum of Man, two floors were opened to the public in October 1974. They featured audio-visual presentations, visitor-operated displays, drawings, models and specimens from the museum collections in four permanent exhibit halls, given to geology, palaeontology and zoology.

A gallery entitled The Earth presents an explanation of the tectonic plate theory and shows how natural forces shaped and continue to shape the world. In Life Through the Ages, drawings and specimens of early Canadian plants and animals show how some species adapted to change, whereas others died. The most impressive of these specimens are the dinosaurs of western Canada's Cretaceous Period. The Birds in Canada exhibit features life-like dioramas of Atlantic, Pacific, and Arctic birds. Mammals in Canada presents dioramas of present-day Canadian mammals in authentic settings.

The museum's newest exhibit hall, Animal Life, completed in October 1976, shows Canadian animals through a 500 million-year period to the present. In addition, a visitor may be guided through the story of man's effort to understand the origin and diversity of animal life, to decipher its cryptic genetic codes, and to unravel the evolutionary process which relates all animals of the world to each other. A Special Exhibits Hall displays temporary and travelling exhibits from the museum and other sources.

Public lectures, film presentations and special interpretative programs prepared by the Interpretation and Extension Division are popular with school classes and the general public. In addition, the division prepares publications, provides educational materials for loans to schools and conducts a program of travelling exhibits.

The National Museum of Man   7.8.3

Through its six divisions — Archaeological Survey of Canada, Canadian Ethnology Service, Canadian Centre for Folk Culture Studies, Canadian War Museum, History and Communications — the National Museum of Man conducts research in Canadian studies, collects and preserves artifacts of material culture and extends the museum's programs across Canada through exhibits and educational loans.

The Canadian Centre for Folk Cultural Studies is both a research institute and a repository of the largest archive in Canada of folk culture materials. The Canadian War Museum houses an extensive collection of the memorabilia of Canada's military past ranging from military art and medals to tanks and bayonets from all wars involving Canadian participants. The Archaeological Survey of Canada has undertaken more than 360 research and salvage projects in Canadian prehistory in the past 13 years, including 10 in 1975, which have dramatically altered the knowledge of Canada's past. The Canadian Ethnology Service collects and analyzes information pertinent to the traditional cultures of Canadian Indians, Inuit and Métis through ethnographic research and artifact acquisition and disseminates information through publications and exhibits. Research in Canadian history is conducted by the History Division which has acquired for preservation over 30,000 items of period furnishings and Canadiana. The Communications Division conducts an extension program to provide access to the museum's collection across Canada and to ensure museum service at the community level. Its responsibilities include travelling exhibitions, 10 of which were circulated in 1975-76, and educational loans including kits of museum materials. Exhibitions depict Canada's ethnic cultures, folk toys, Inuit history and art, Quebec furniture, and the Athapaskan Indians. Catalogues and monographs are part of the museum's diverse program of national and international travelling exhibitions, films and television programs.

The National Museum of Science and Technology   7.8.4

The newest of the four national museums, the National Museum of Science and Technology, opened in November 1967. This museum challenges visitors to climb, push, pull or just view its definitive collections. Thousands of others annually visit the National Aeronautical Collection at Rockcliffe Airport.

The exhibit pavilions contain examples from the history of ground transportation such as sleighs, streetcars, steam locomotives and antique cars, to aviation and space, beginning with Canada's first powered heavier-than-air flight. Trains have figured prominently both as acquisitions and in programs. Steam train excursions, operated in collaboration with the National Capital Commission, are popular summer events. There are also "seeing puzzles", experiments and skill-trying tests in the physics hall; the history of agriculture to present-day techniques; marine transport; meteorology; time pieces; a model workshop and astronomy.

In the National Aeronautical Collection over 90 aircraft illustrate the progress of aviation from primitive to present times and the importance of the flying machine in the development of Canada. Included is one of the world's largest collections of aircraft engines.

Educational programs are developed and conducted by a staff of tour guides on general or special topics for all age groups. The museum's observatory houses Canada's largest refracting telescope which is used for evening educational programs. The museum's 10,000-volume library places special emphasis on a retrospective collection of Canadian aviation. The museum participates in the creation of distinct exhibits for tour throughout Canada. There are also exchanges of artifacts with museums abroad.

7.9   Assistance to the arts

7.9.1   The Canada Council

The Canada Council was created in 1957 by an Act of Parliament, to "foster and promote the study and enjoyment of, and the production of works in the arts, humanities and social sciences". It carries out its task mainly through a broad program of fellowships and grants of various types. It also shares responsibility for Canada's cultural relations with other countries in cooperation with the Department of External Affairs. The council meets at least three times a year and is made up of a chairman, a vice-chairman and 19 members, appointed by the Governor in Council.

Within the limits of the Canada Council Act, the council enjoys a large measure of autonomy, setting its own policies and developing and carrying out its own programs in consultation with the academic and artistic community. The council reports to Parliament through the Secretary of State and also appears before the Standing Committee on Broadcasting, Film and Assistance to the Arts.

The council's income is derived from three sources: an annual grant of the Canadian government which amounted to $54.7 million for the year ended March 31, 1976 ($40.9 million, 1975); the Endowment Fund established by Parliament when it created the council, which yields over $5 million annually; and private funds willed or donated and used in accordance with the wishes of the donors.

Assistance to the humanities and social sciences accounted for $25.3 million in 1975-76, as compared with $22.3 million in 1974-75 (further references to 1974-75 are in parantheses). In support of research training, the council awarded 100 special MA scholarships totalling $650,000 ($573,000) and 1,387 (1,534) doctoral fellowships totalling $8.8 million ($8.7 million); for research work, 346 leave fellowships (390, includes post-doctoral fellowships) totalling $3.8 million ($3.5 million) and 681 (789) research grants to individuals, totalling $5.7 million ($5.4 million); 61 general research grants to universities, totalling $635,000 ($289,000); and a total of $2.7 million ($2.9 million) in assistance to learned meetings, special grants and studies, attendance of Canadian scholars at international conferences and publication of learned journals and scholarly manuscripts.

In the arts, the Canada Council spent $30.4 million ($21.9 million) of which $3.5 million ($2.5 million) was used to finance some 946 (820) grants to individuals in various art forms; $26.0 million ($18.9 million) was applied to grants to organizations, including $6.3 million ($5.5 million) for music and opera; $7.1 million ($5 million) for theatre, $4.3 million ($2.5 million) for dance, $3.4 million ($2.4 million) for visual arts and in 1975-76 only, photography, including $750,000 ($800,000) for the Art Bank, $4.5 million ($2.8 million) for writing and publication and $1.1 million for film and video ($1 million in 1974-75 included photography and cinema). Of the total arts budget, $1.2 million ($809,000) went to the council's Touring Office, created in 1973 to promote and stimulate the touring of the performing arts in Canada.

Through the Explorations Program, the council spent $1.2 million to assist projects on Canada's cultural and historical heritage and innovative projects which explore new forms of expression and creativity in the arts, humanities and social sciences.

The Canada Council administers, on behalf of the Canadian government, several programs of cultural and academic exchanges with Argentina, Belgium, Brazil, China, Federal Republic of Germany, Finland, France, Italy, the Netherlands, Switzerland, the United Kingdom, the USSR and the countries of continental Latin America. Under these programs, fellowships and scholarships are awarded to foreign nationals for study in Canada; Canadian cultural institutions receive grants to bring distinguished university professors, scholars and artists to Canada; and Canadian academics receive grants to lecture or conduct research abroad. Expenditures for cultural exchange programs totalled $950,000 in 1975-76 ($926,000 in 1974-75).

The Canada Council also administers the funds of the Canadian Cultural Institute in Rome, created in 1967 by an agreement between Canada and Italy. The institute's income is used to provide a small number of fellowships for Canadian artists and scholars wishing to work or study in Italy. The Killam Scholarships of the Canada Council were inaugurated in 1967 with funds from the I.W. Killam estate to help support scholars of exceptional ability engaged in research projects of far-reaching significance. In 1975-76, there were 45 awards made under this program, totalling $1.1 million, and the previous year, 40 awards totalling $889,000.

Under its power to "make awards to persons in Canada for outstanding accomplishments in the arts, humanities or social sciences", the Canada Council annually awards three $20,000 Molson prizes from a fund created by the Molson Foundation. The Governor General's Literary Awards, financed by the council, are awarded annually to six Canadian writers. In addition, the council awards annually two translation prizes to the year's best English and French translations of Canadian works and two children's literature prizes to the year's best English and French books for young people.

The Canada Council Act provides for certain functions in relation to the United Nations Educational Scientific and Cultural Organization. It has accordingly established a National Commission for UNESCO and provides its secretariat and budget. As an agent of the council, the Canadian Commission for UNESCO coordinates UNESCO program activities abroad and administers a modest program in furtherance of UNESCO objectives.

The National Arts Centre (NAC)   7.9.2

Parliament passed the National Arts Centre Act in 1966, creating a corporation to operate and maintain the centre, to develop the performing arts in the National Capital area, and to assist the Canada Council in the development of the performing arts elsewhere in Canada. The building itself, designed by Montreal architect Fred Lebensold, was opened to the public on May 31, 1969. It stands on Confederation Square in the heart of Ottawa, and is in the form of a series of hexagonal halls built on landscaped terraces along the Rideau Canal.

The NAC has three main halls. The Opera, with 2,300 seats, was designed primarily for opera and ballet, with a full-size orchestra pit and the most advanced sound, lighting and other technical equipment available. Its stage is one of the largest in the world, measuring 189 by 110 feet (58 by 34 m), and the Opera's facilities can handle the most complicated changes required by the largest touring companies. The 950-seat Theatre is ideal for Greek, Elizabethan or contemporary plays, and its stage can easily be adjusted from the conventional rectangular style to the thrust stage style used for Shakespearean drama. Like the Opera, it is fully equipped for television, simultaneous translation and film projection, and its technical facilities are among the best available. The Studio is a hexagonal room which can seat up to 350 persons in a variety of seating plans. It is used for theatre productions, conferences and cabarets.

Other NAC facilities include: the Salon, a small hall seating up to 150 persons and used for chamber concerts, poetry readings, and receptions; a 900-car indoor garage; Le Restaurant, a first class restaurant and bar; Le Café, a smaller restaurant which, in the summer months, overflows on to the sidewalks along the Rideau Canal; and several large rehearsal halls. The building is richly ornamented with works of art. Its foyers are used for exhibits, and public tours of the building are offered daily. On the terraces outside, the NAC plays host to art fairs, craft markets and summertime band concerts.

Under conductor and Music Director Mario Bernardi, the 46-member National Arts Centre Orchestra performs some 40 concerts a year in the centre and many more each year on tours in Canada and abroad. Music programming includes about 70 concerts a year, featuring distinguished soloists and guest orchestras from Canada and around the world.

The Theatre Department functions in both official languages. It offers two subscription series a year, one of English-language and one of French-language plays, and also non-series productions. There are more than 400 performances of live theatre a year at the centre. Some of the plays are produced by the Theatre

Department and others represent Canada's regional theatre or come from outside the country. It presents productions of several Canadian companies, among them the Manitoba Theatre Centre, the Playhouse Theatre Company, the Shaw Festival, the Stratford National Theatre, Le Théâtre du Nouveau Monde and Le Théâtre du Rideau Vert.

The Theatre Department also forms small companies which tour central Canada, performing in high schools and elsewhere, and offering professional theatre to communities which would not otherwise have the opportunity to enjoy it. Workshops for students and teachers are among the other services offered by the Theatre Department.

The Dance and Variety Department brings in some 100 different shows a year, including ballet, musical shows and comedy. The NAC is the only centre in Canada where every Canadian dance company of importance appears on a regular basis, and dance and variety programming has offered a showcase for performers from every part of the country. Each year during July, a festival of mainly musical entertainment is presented, centred around the NAC's own opera productions. Altogether, there are about 1,000 performances annually in the NAC, entertaining audiences of almost 800,000 people.

7.9.3   Provincial assistance to the arts

All provinces except Prince Edward Island give some form of financial assistance to artists (writers, poets, painters and sculptors), cultural organizations or community councils.

Newfoundland. The Cultural Affairs Division of the Department of Tourism contributes to the upkeep of cultural centres in the province and provides grants and awards to individuals or groups native to or touring the province for performances. Grants and awards enable local theatrical groups to produce and perform in centres around the province. For 1976 the provincial government budgeted $60,000 (including Cultural Olympic Projects) for these grants and a further $270,000 to enable locally, nationally and internationally known companies and groups to perform in the province at centres which normally would be unable to hire them. These funds also enable centres such as the Marine Museum in St. John's to purchase works to be exhibited.

Nova Scotia. In 1973, the Nova Scotia Department of Recreation was given the legislative mandate to be responsible for cultural development, covering a broad range of activities consisting of music, theatre, crafts, multiculturalism, festivals, arts councils, dance, visual arts, writing, film, and photography, the Art Bank of Nova Scotia and the newly developing Art Gallery of Nova Scotia. The department supports eight cultural federations which act as service agencies for arts and cultural programs throughout the province.

In the year ended March 31, 1975, grants to major cultural institutions included a grant of $25,000 to the Neptune Theatre Foundation; $25,000 to the Atlantic Symphony Orchestra; and $120,000 to the Art Gallery of Nova Scotia. For the following year, the cultural component of the department had a budget of $729,000 with a projected budget of $844,000 for the year ended March 1977.

In addition, a number of smaller grants were made available to community-based programs in the performing, visual and literary arts. The Nova Scotia Department of Tourism contributed $129,000 to cultural events and festivals in local promotion grants.

The Fine Arts and Handcrafts section of the Adult Education program of the Department of Education, with a budget of $186,597, provided leadership training courses and small grants to various cultural organizations. The Nova Scotia museum section of the Cultural Services Program of the department, with a budget of $1,482,575, disbursed grants to local museums and historical societies. Other major cultural expenditures included $2,137,942 for the Nova Scotia Provincial Library which serves communities with both permanent and mobile library facilities, and

$215,000 for the operations of the Provincial Archives, a contribution toward the preservation of the province's cultural heritage.

New Brunswick provides assistance to Le Centre de Promotion et de Diffusion de la Culture, a Moncton-based agency which coordinates Acadian cultural activities — choirs, theatre, and individual artist presentations. Assistance is also given to the provincial competitive Festival of Music, folk song and band festivals, dance troupes, Arts Councils, Provincial Youth Orchestra, Atlantic Symphony, Theatre New Brunswick, various choral and drama groups, art associations, arts councils and writers. In addition, the province assists in sponsoring tours by individual performing artists within and outside the province.

Quebec. The Department of Cultural Affairs was established on March 24, 1961 by an act of the provincial legislature. The department was charged with the administration of cultural organizations or institutions such as libraries, museums, archives and conservatories. It is also responsible for artistic, literary and scientific competitions and for the Cultural Properties Commission, private museums, the Museum of Contemporary Art, the Montreal Museum of Fine Arts, the Place des Arts and the Grand Théâtre of Quebec.

The Literary Affairs Branch of the department implements legislation on literary matters and books, including public libraries and library buildings, literary and scientific competitions, publishing insurance, the National Library of Quebec, and Orders in Council dealing with publishing and book distribution. During 1973-74 the Library Service of the branch distributed $2.2 million and 114 libraries and the Literary Affairs and Books Service made grants to associations and publishers of $190,200.

Many research projects are carried out for the Department of Cultural Affairs by its research service and private enterprise. Among recent results are the Miville-Deschenes report on the theatre in Quebec and the Jeannote report on music, opera and dance. Other research projects relating to an inventory of cultural goods and historic sites are under consideration. The general Secretariat of the department through its program "Aide à la création et à la recherche" supports artists, writers and researchers whose works contribute to the cultural and artistic growth of Quebec.

Theatre in Quebec has grown at a great rate; actors and acting troupes have multiplied. Montreal remains the heart of the theatrical movement, but elsewhere (the Eastern Townships, the Lac-Saint-Jean region and the lower St. Lawrence region) new centres of creativity have been formed. In the CEGEPs (Lionel Groulx in Sainte-Thérèse) and at universities (Université du Québec in Montreal) theatre is taught as a regular course. The government subsidizes permanent theatre companies and indirectly, through programs such as Perspectives-Jeunesse, non-permanent acting troupes.

The youth element in Quebec music is reflected by the fact that 78% of 'author-lyricists' have less than 12 years' experience. These artists often fill the dual role of composer-singer of their works. Nearly two thirds of male singers and about 25% of female singers have also written some literary works.

The Department of Cultural Affairs has established conservatories of music to serve in Montreal, Quebec, Trois-Rivières, Hull, Chicoutimi, Val d'Or and Rimouski. Summer music camps complement the training and studies of these conservatories. Prominent among these is the Centre d'arts d'Orford with others being the music camps of Lac-Saint-Jean, Lanaudière, des Jeunes violonistes, Cammac, Asbestos, Saint-Alexandre and Accord Parfait. The department, by means of financial aid, maintains these camps to serve all regions of Quebec.

In the last few years, dance has taken on great importance in the fields of education, leisure time and the theatre. Although les Grands Ballets Canadiens has as its main objective the promotion of ballet, it is also responsible for two institutions of learning: l'Académie des Grands Ballets Canadiens and l'École supérieure de la danse.

Métiers d'Art du Quebec inc. is the association of Quebec craftsmen which promotes the professional, economical and social interests of its members.

Ontario. The new Ministry of Culture and Recreation officially began operating in April 1975. Through its Arts Division, the ministry has allocated the following amounts to major provincial agencies and institutions in 1976-77 (allocations for 1975-76 following): the Ontario Arts Council, $10.5 million ($9.5 million), the Royal Ontario Museum, $6.9 million ($6.5 million), the McMichael Canadian Collection of Art, $556,500 ($580,000), the Art Gallery of Ontario, approximately $3.6 million ($3.4 million), the Royal Botannical Gardens, $598,000 ($560,000), CJRT-FM Corporations, $588,000 ($640,000), the Ontario Educational Communications Authority, $11.3 million ($12.7 million), the Ontario Science Centre, $5.9 million ($6.0 million).

In addition, the ministry provided $770,000 in 1976-77 for OUTREACH programs including Festival Ontario ($605,000 in 1975-76) and in 1976-77, $1.5 million was allocated for Olympic oriented programs through Wintario ($120,000 for pre-production costs of Ontario's Cultural Olympics celebration in 1975-76). During 1976-77, the Wintario Lottery made substantially more funding available to support cultural and recreational activities in the province.

The prime objectives of the Ontario Arts program are the encouragement of the pursuit of excellence in the arts and the promotion of wider participation in and enjoyment of arts activities by the citizens of Ontario. Other divisions in the Ministry of Culture and Recreation are the Heritage Conservation Division, the Sports and Fitness Division and the Citizenship and Multicultural Division. The ministry has six regional offices with a network of field staff which provide consulting services to communities and local groups. Other ministries involved in cultural programming are Agriculture and Food, Education, Natural Resources, Industry and Tourism, and Treasury, Economics and Intergovernmental Affairs.

The Province of Ontario Council for the Arts, an agency of the new ministry, was established by legislation in 1963 to promote the study, enjoyment and production of works in the arts. It provides financial assistance to performing and creative arts groups and individuals; advises and consults with members of the arts community; and develops projects aimed at promoting and expanding the arts and the public interest in them throughout the province. The council also collaborates with other agencies and levels of government in encouraging support for the arts. The Arts Council contributes to such organizations as the National Ballet of Canada, the Toronto Symphony Orchestra, the Toronto Arts Foundation, the Canadian Opera Company, the Stratford Shakespearean Festival and the Shaw Festival.

Manitoba. The Manitoba Arts Council was formed by legislation passed in 1965 providing for a chairman, vice-chairman and 10 members appointed by the Lieutenant Governor in Council, with the objective of promoting the study, enjoyment, production and performance of works in the arts by assisting and cooperating with those organizations involved in cultural development, providing for grants, scholarships or loans to Manitobans for study or research in the arts and making awards to citizens of Manitoba for outstanding accomplishment in the arts. Working on a budget of $481,500, the Manitoba Arts Council in the year ended March 31, 1976, made grants to 31 organizations including $65,000 to the Manitoba Theatre Centre, $40,000 to Rainbow Stage, $95,000 to the Royal Winnipeg Ballet, and $72,000 to the Winnipeg Symphony Orchestra. The Manitoba Arts Council's awards program provided assistance to individual Manitoba artists.

Saskatchewan. The Saskatchewan Arts Board was established in 1949 to make available to the people of Saskatchewan opportunities to engage in any of the following activities: drama, the visual arts, music, literature, handicrafts and other arts, to provide for the training of lecturers and instructors, to assist students ordinarily resident in Saskatchewan to pursue their studies in the arts, and to cooperate with organizations having similar objectives.

The Saskatchewan Arts Board, funded by the provincial government but functioning independently, is composed of not less than seven nor more than 15 volunteer members appointed annually by the Lieutenant Governor in Council. These

members are from all parts of the province but represent no specific areas or any specific discipline in the arts. The work of the board is carried out by a staff of three consultants and three office personnel under an executive director. Experts in various fields of the arts are engaged for specific projects.

Handicraft, visual and performing arts programs have been expanded to the point where some have reached the professional level. Workshops, lectures and seminars at an advanced level have been sponsored by the board, and considerable assistance has been given to local arts and crafts organizations in sponsoring similar projects at a local level. In most cases, the board prefers to assist established organizations in carrying out their own programs and to support the emerging professional.

The Saskatchewan School of the Arts, operated annually by the Saskatchewan Arts Board at Echo Valley Centre near Fort Qu'Appelle, offers one- to four-week courses during spring, summer and fall in band, orchestra, stage band, choral singing, piping and drumming, highland and national dancing, ballet, painting, pottery, acting, creative writing and weaving, with instruction by qualified teachers.

For several years an annual month-long Saskatchewan Festival of the Arts focused attention on the arts in communities throughout the province by presenting top-calibre artistic performances and exhibitions. This festival has been replaced by similar programs planned by individual communities to meet their specific needs, assisted by the Organization of Saskatchewan Arts Councils, a provincial body funded in part by the Saskatchewan Arts Board.

The board provides financial assistance to individual provincial artists to help them further their artistic training, or to establish themselves professionally. Emphasis is placed on assisting those in undergraduate studies or those striving to achieve professionalism.

The total budget of the Saskatchewan Arts Board in 1975 was $718,420. Assistance to organizations included a direct grant to Globe Theatre of $60,000 plus $23,269 in deficit protection to schools engaging Globe's School Company, $2,000 to the Kinsmen International Band Festival, $5,000 to the Mendel Art Gallery, $6,000 to the Norman Mackenzie Art Gallery, $3,500 to the Organization of Saskatchewan Arts Councils, $10,000 to Persephone Theatre, $3,000 to Photographers' Gallery, $3,000 to Regina Modern Dance Workshop, $47,500 to the Regina Symphony, $15,000 to the Saskatchewan Dance Theatre, $1,000 to the Saskatchewan Junior Concert Society, $6,160 to the Saskatchewan Music Educators' Association, $24,200 to the Saskatchewan Music Festival Association, $2,000 to the Saskatchewan Region D.D.F., $1,700 to the Saskatchewan Society for Education Through Art, $7,000 to the Saskatchewan Writers' Guild, $47,500 to the Saskatoon Symphony, $2,000 to the Shoestring Gallery, $2,000 to the Society for the Promotion of Art History Publications (RACAR), and $4,000 to the Yorkton International Film Festival. Four film-makers received assistance grants totalling $7,500, enabling them to continue work on individual film projects.

The Saskatchewan Arts Board may also provide, upon approval of a request, funds for workshops, consultants, aid for exhibitions, conferences, operating expenses of arts organizations, and special arts projects. In these areas the board expended in 1975: administration grants for 12 arts councils, $3,600; community galleries, $3,100; literary services including script reading, poets in the classroom, and duplication of original playscripts, $2,376; performing arts subsidies, providing deficit protection on professional performances in smaller communities, $7,022; visual arts subsidies to individuals and organizations for travel, materials, workshops and special projects, $13,956; art exhibitions, $2,100; consultants and conferences, $862; and assistance to 73 artists, $40,000. In 1975, the board's assistance to provincial arts groups and organizations totalled more than $325,312.

Alberta. The Department of Culture had its first full year of operation in 1975-76. It was one of two departments created when the former Department of Culture, Youth and Recreation was divided; the other is the Department of Recreation, Parks and Wildlife. The two divisions of the Department of Culture are Historic Resources and Cultural Development; the latter is responsible for encouraging cultural development in Alberta. Branches of the Cultural Development Division are responsible for performing arts, visual arts, film and literary arts, library services, cultural facilities, cultural heritage, Jubilee auditoriums and the censorship board.

The division's programs are intended to give the public opportunities to witness the best in performing arts tours and art exhibitions and to conduct training courses at regular intervals for a variety of leaders, particularly teachers, librarians, and music directors. Workshops and conferences are held to train people in all aspects of theatre. Awards to individuals wishing to further their training in some form of the arts amount to over $250,000 annually. The Alberta Art Foundation, established in 1972, has been allocated $50,000 annually for the purchase of Alberta arts and crafts. The budget for the year ended March 31, 1976 was in excess of $5 million.

A grants for libraries program provides for a system of central, regional, municipal and community libraries. Grants are provided to advance creative writing through professional training and writers workshops. Competitions are sponsored for new novelists, best published non-fiction work and best regional history.

The Southern Alberta Jubilee Auditorium at Calgary and Northern Alberta Jubilee Auditorium at Edmonton are identical multi-purpose facilities each containing a 2,762-seat theatre, four meeting rooms and exhibit area. In April 1975 a major $200 million program was launched by the departments of Alberta Culture and Recreation, Parks and Wildlife to develop cultural recreation facilities in Alberta communities over a 10-year period.

The Cultural Heritage Branch provides grants to ethno-cultural groups; the division assisted in the establishment of a Cultural Heritage Council. Under the Language Support Program financial help is available to ethno-cultural schools operated outside regular school hours.

The Alberta Film Censorship Board, attached to the division for administrative purposes, issues permits for all films approved for exhibition in Alberta.

British Columbia. The British Columbia Cultural Fund was set up by statute in 1967. That act set aside $5 million in an endowment fund, the interest from which was to be spent to stimulate the cultural development of the people of the province. In September 1967 an advisory committee was established to receive applications for cultural grants and to report their recommendations to the Department of Finance for the necessary funds. The amount of the endowment was raised to $10 million in 1969, to $15 million in 1972, and to $20 million in 1974. Proceeds from the Western Canada Lottery Foundation are used, in part, to support cultural activities.

An advisory body to the fund, the British Columbia Arts Board, was appointed in November 1974 to make recommendations to the Provincial Secretary on the allocation of cultural grants from the British Columbia Cultural Fund.

Up to December 31, 1975, grants totalling almost $7.1 million had been awarded by the fund to support cultural activities throughout the province. The fund also provides a small degree of financial support to the National Theatre School, the National Youth Orchestra, and the Canadian Music Centre.

Grants totalling $1.8 million were made in the fiscal year 1974-75, of which about 70% went to major non-profit organizations such as symphony, drama and opera societies. About 15% of the grants in each year went to Community Arts Councils and the remainder to art acquisitions, scholarships, seminars and miscellaneous grants.

7.10   Federal film agencies

7.10.1   National Film Board

The National Film Board, an agency of the federal government, was established by Act of Parliament in 1939 and reconstituted by the National Film Act in 1950 "to initiate and promote the production and distribution of films in the national interest". The board's films are produced in Canada's two official languages and have made a considerable contribution to the country's culture and to the national identity. In addition to 35 mm and 16 mm films, the board produces and distributes other visual aids material — filmstrips, 8 mm loop films, slide sets, overhead projectuals, multi-media kits and photo stories.

The growing sophistication of film audiences and the increasing importance of film as a means of communication are reflected in the nature of the films produced — features, documentaries, informational films, films for the specific needs of government departments, and films designed for particular social purposes. The board strives to serve as innovator of new cinema techniques, as well as a recorder of the nation's day-to-day evolution. Thus, new needs and greater public sensitivity have encouraged the board's film-makers to explore new film styles and to experiment in new areas of film production, and there have been corresponding new departures in the distribution and use of films as more people turn to films as a matter of course for information and assistance in many activities.

In Canada, the board's productions are distributed through community outlets, schools and universities, television stations, theatres and commercial sales. In all these areas annual figures show a steady and, in some instances, a marked increase. A large part of the 16 mm community film audience is reached through film libraries, film councils and special-interest groups. The growing demand for films can be attributed to the wide range of subject matter available; the board's catalogue lists 60 main and sub-categories. During 1975-76, community film distribution through 27 NFB libraries alone in Canada rose to a new high of 427,000 bookings. Aside from the board's own film libraries, many public and school libraries across Canada distribute its films. New releases are shown regularly over English- and French-language television networks in Canada and in theatres across the country.

NFB film distribution outside Canada also continued to increase and, for the second consecutive year, the total world audience for NFB productions exceeded one billion. Film distribution outside of Canada is handled by the board's offices in New York, London, Paris, Tokyo and Sydney. As well, distribution is effected by 92 Post Film Libraries operated jointly with the Department of External Affairs. For greater international distribution, many of the NFB films are versioned in several foreign languages. The film board, in cooperation with the Canadian Government Office of Tourism, distributes films supporting the travel industry to audiences throughout the world. NFB films are presented at many of the world's international film festivals with an annual average of 75 awards returning to Canada.

For the United States Bicentennial in 1976 the board's Still Photography Division published a special book of photographs concentrating on the Canada–US border. After "Between Friends/Entre Amis" was presented by Prime Minister Trudeau to President Ford as Canada's official gift to the US, copies were distributed to libraries, educational institutions and government and civic leaders in both Canada and the United States and the book has since been on sale to the public in both countries.

A significant film board project was launched in 1976 when the NFB was named the organization responsible for the official film of the XXI Olympiad. As many as 30 film crews and over 160 accredited individuals covered the two-week summer event in Montreal to produce this film, which was released in May 1977.

The NFB adopted a five-year plan of action to renew and re-establish the board as the central energizing force in Canadian film. A key development has been an integrated regional production program with production offices established in Vancouver, Winnipeg, Toronto, Moncton and Halifax in order to bring total film services closer to more Canadians.

Canadian Film Development Corporation   7.10.2

The Canadian Film Development Corporation was established in March 1967 to promote the development of a feature film industry in Canada, and in so doing it cooperates with federal and provincial departments and agencies with similar interests. It invests in Canadian productions in return for a share of the profits, makes loans to producers and assists financially in the promotion, marketing and distribution of feature films.

The corporation assisted in the production of 18 feature films during 1975-76, one of the lowest years on record. To maintain even this figure, it had to increase its financial contribution significantly. The drop in the number of films produced occurred almost entirely on the French side: from 14 in 1974-75 to seven. English-language features dropped by one, to 11 as opposed to 12 in 1974-75.

The corporation's revenues dropped slightly from $864,011 in 1974-75 to $833,998. The main sources were foreign sales of *Kamouraska, Death Weekend, Black Christmas* and *The Apprenticeship of Duddy Kravitz*. Some revenue was also derived from Canadian theatrical releases.

In a total of 75 projects including the 18 features the corporation invested $3.832 million in 1975-76, up $300,000 from the previous year. The amount contributed by the private sector — production houses, private investors, distribution companies and theatre chains, plus the writers, directors and producers who contributed part of their salaries — provided another $2.098 million. This figure represents a significant drop from the $4.536 million derived from these sources in 1974-75 and the amounts contributed by private investors outside the industry remained low at $688,000.

The total cost of the feature films funded by the CFDC in 1975-76 was $5.9 million. This figure was down $2.2 million from the $8.1 million invested in 1974-75. For the first time since its inception in 1968, the corporation's share of production costs exceeded the contribution of the private sector (64.62% to 35.38%).

The productions provided 75 assignments for Canadian writers, directors, producers and production managers, 1,070 roles for performers and employment for 308 technicians in the Canadian film industry. Laboratories earned $800,000 and equipment rental companies some $300,000.

A pattern discernible over the past few years, in which French-language films provided a reasonable if not complete return on investments through Quebec cinemas, suffered a setback. Receipts from the province did not live up to expectations. In the rest of Canada, box-office returns increased. An agreement reached between the corporation and the two major theatre chains, Famous Players Limited and Odeon Theatres (Canada) Limited, provides for four weeks of screening time for Canadian films in each of their theatres. Along with the quota agreements, Famous Players Limited committed $1 million to investment in Canadian films for 1976-77, and Odeon Theatres (Canada) Limited would spend $500,000 to the same end.

On the international scene, Canadian films won more awards in 1975-76 than in any other single year. The most prestigious prize was won at the Cannes Festival where Michel Brault shared the best director award for *Les Ordres*. This marked the first time a Canadian feature film had ever won a major award at Cannes. *Lies My Father Told Me* won the Golden Globe Award in the US as best foreign film of the year, the Christopher Award from the US Catholic Assembly for "dedication to the human spirit", and the Golden Venus Award as best feature film of the Virgin Islands Film Festival and was an Academy Award nomination for Best Screenplay category. *The Man Who Skied Down Everest* won an Academy Award for best feature length documentary of the year. *Eliza's Horoscope* won a gold medal and Special Jury Award at the Virgin Islands Film Festival.

To summarize briefly some of the other major awards: *The Apprenticeship of Duddy Kravitz:* nominated for best screen adaptation at the Academy of Motion Picture Arts & Sciences, Hollywood; *Les Ordres:* awarded the Victor-Morin Prize by the St. Jean Baptiste Society. Grand prix de l'Organisation Catholique Internationale du Cinéma, Italie; *Shivers:* Grand Prize of the 8th International Festival of Fantastic and Horror Films in Sitges, Spain.

French production. In 1975-76 the corporation participated in the production of seven feature films in the French language. The combined budgets of the seven films amounted to $1,896,554, the corporation's share amounting to $1,228,700.

The corporation also invested in nine script assistance projects, in the dubbing costs of four films and in nine promotional projects. In total the CFDC participated financially in 29 French productions. During 1975-76, 71 proposals were submitted to the corporation of which 41 were accepted, 27 rejected, and three withdrawn.

In seven years the corporation invested in 48 major productions in the French language, all films with costs in excess of $200,000. On the other hand, 16% of the total funding was allocated to the development of new talent through the financing of 23 features budgeted below $200,000.

A special investment program, designed to stimulate the growth of French-language features, has permitted eight first-feature directors to develop their craft. In 1975-76, one feature film was produced under this program, and a second was expected to enter production, chosen from seven applications. To keep pace with inflation, the maximum budget for films submitted was increased from $125,000 to $135,000, the corporation's share of costs remaining at 60%.

Scriptwriting program. The mosaic of CFDC services to the film industry was enriched with the addition of the Screenplay Development Program. This encourages experienced screenwriters or those working in related fields such as theatre or television to develop original screenplay ideas suitable for feature film production. The French-language arm of the program received 31 requests for financing, of which 23 were accepted. The corporation's commitment in the nine projects already signed totalled $54,500. A dialogue has been initiated with writers. This includes an enlarged script evaluation service, and a series of meetings in the course of script preparation.

English production. Eleven new English-language features were produced in 1975-76 with corporation assistance, 10 in Ontario and one in British Columbia. The cumulative cost of the 11 features was nearly $4.3 million. Of this, the corporation's share was approximately $1.7 million or nearly 39%. Investment from industry sources such as laboratories, distributors and exhibitors increased considerably over previous years, reaching a total of $1.09 million. For the second successive year, the response of private capital did not meet expectations, reaching only approximately $683,000.

The lowest budgeted film was produced for $283,260, the highest for $1.1 million, the average cost per film being $605,543. In addition, 26 pre-production projects were partially funded to the extent of $193,335. Lastly, $80,290 was invested in five projects previously supported by the CFDC. In total 48 English-language projects received corporation support. Under the Special Investment Program, from 21 applications received, five films by first-feature directors were selected for corporation support, four in Ontario and one in British Columbia.

English Screenplay Development Program. In its inaugural year this program received approximately 60 applications and invested $128,108 in 21 projects. Screenwriters' fees for these projects amounted to $77,170, while $30,250 was applied to securing options; the remaining funds covered such miscellaneous expenses as typing, duplication and producers' fees.

At the request of a group of writers, the corporation appointed an experienced producer and script editor to the newly created position of English script consultant, charged with the task of providing detailed, constructive feedback to writers supported by the program. Thus in September 1975 the screenwriters' workshop program began. The Ontario Arts Council provided 20% of the requisite financing in exchange for permitting screenwriters to attend the workshop. One of the corporation's main objectives is the combination of creative freedom with commercial potential.

Co-production agreements. No film industry can stand alone, international cooperation being the essence of creative and commercial growth. In September 1975 the Secretary of State signed a significant accord regarding co-productions by Canada and the UK; the first film to be produced, entitled *Find The Lady,* was partially funded by the CFDC. The Joint Commission authorized by the Film Relations Agreement between Canada and France met in Paris in November 1975 and endorsed a policy of producing bigger budget films, aimed at wider distribution in foreign markets. In

February 1976, the Secretary of State entrusted to the CFDC the responsibility for administering the existing co-production agreements with France, Italy and the UK. To further enhance co-production possibilities for Canadian directors, both French and English, the corporation proposed to negotiate an agreement between Canada and the Federal Republic of Germany.

Distribution. In 1975-76, 20 films were released in Canada with CFDC support, 11 in English and nine in French. Domestic box-office receipts amounted to $3.3 million. The 11 English-language films had total box-office receipts in Canada of over $2 million. Of these films, those with the highest receipts were: *Lies My Father Told Me* $600,000, *Recommendation For Mercy* $600,000, *It Seemed Like A Good Idea At The Time* $400,000, and *Shivers* (formerly *The Parasite Murders*) $259,000.

The international prestige and acclaim accorded to Quebec feature films has yet to be translated into wide European distribution. Their increasing visibility at film festivals, however, pays tribute to the readiness of the Quebec film industry to take its place among the masters of French-language cinema.

English-language films have succeeded in penetrating the European market in ever-increasing numbers and have continued to dominate foreign sales.

With the cooperation of the various agencies attached to the Secretary of State, new points of access to the foreign film market have been developed for Canadian films, both French and English. A Canadian Cinema Week was staged in the USSR in which seven features were presented in Moscow, Riga and Leningrad. The priority targets for 1976-77 were the Milan Fair, Japan and the UK.

Television. It was a rewarding year for Canadian films on domestic televison networks. The CBC French-language network (Radio-Canada) purchased a package of 20 films, most to be dubbed from English to French. The CBC English network presented only three Canadian films during the year, but was expected to purchase a large number of films for telecast in the new season. Global television showed 25 Canadian films, some repeatedly, for a cumulative total of 41 showings.

Radio-Canada presented 53 French-language Canadian features in 1975-76. Of these, 25 were CFDC funded. This represents a strengthening of Radio-Canada's commitment to domestic cinema, an increase of 13 over the number used in 1974-75. Radio-Québec telecast four Canadian feature films, two produced with the aid of the CFDC.

Return on investment. The first few years of the CFDC's existence were focused almost entirely on strengthening the production arm of the Canadian film industry. For more than a year, however, the corporation's energies have been turned increasingly toward the problems of effective marketing, promotion and distribution of more than 150 films, representing an investment of $15 million.

At the end of the fiscal year, 167 feature films financed by the corporation were in release, 20 more than at the same time the previous year. On March 31, 1976 the corporation had realized $3,541,457 from the sums invested since its inception.

7.11   Public archives and library services

7.11.1   The Public Archives of Canada

The Public Archives, established in 1872, operates under the direction of the Dominion Archivist by authority of the Public Archives Act. It serves a dual role. As a research institution, it is responsible for acquiring all nationally significant documents relating to the development of Canada, and for providing research services and facilities to make this material available to the public. As part of the government administration, it has broad responsibility in the promotion of efficiency and economy in management of government records.

The Archives Branch comprises eight divisions. The Manuscript Division contains manuscript collections, including private papers of statesmen and other distinguished citizens, records of cultural and commercial societies, and copies of records relating to Canada and now held in France, England and other countries. The holdings of the Public Records Division consist of selected records of all departments and agencies of the Government of Canada. The Picture Division has charge of documentary paintings, water colours, engravings, heraldry and medals. The Photography Division is responsible for the national collection of historical photographs. The National Film Archives has an extensive collection of films and sound recordings. The Map Division has custody of thousands of maps and plans pertaining to the discovery, exploration and settlement of this country and its topography, as well as a large collection of current topographical maps of foreign countries. The Library contains more than 80,000 volumes on Canadian history, including numerous pamphlets, periodicals and government publications. The Machine-Readable Archives Division holds selected automated public records and machine-readable archives of permanent value from the private sector.

Although documents in the Public Archives of Canada may not be taken out on loan, they may be consulted in the building, and a 24-hour-a-day service is provided for accredited research workers. Reproductions of available material may be obtained for a moderate fee and many documents on microfilm may be obtained on interlibrary loan. A diffusion program to make archival material more available to the public includes deposits of microfilm in provincial archives, travelling exhibitions, sets of slides and microfiche and popular publications.

The Records Management Branch assists departments and agencies in setting up and operating their records management programs. Its service includes recommendations and advice on scheduling and disposal of records. At the Ottawa, Toronto, Montreal, Vancouver, Winnipeg and Halifax records centres, it provides storage, reference service and planned and economical disposal of dormant records. Other regional centres are being established in major cities across Canada.

The Administration and Technical Services Branch, in addition to an extensive conservation and restoration program, provides a technical and advisory service on microfilming to government departments and agencies. Microfilm work is done for departments at cost. It also provides a full range of services to the National Library.

Branch offices of the Public Archives are located in London, England and Paris, France. The Public Archives also administers Laurier House in Ottawa as an historical museum.

The National Library of Canada   7.11.2

The National Library was formally established on January 1, 1953 by Act of Parliament. On the same date it absorbed the Canadian Bibliographic Centre which had been engaged in preliminary work and planning since 1950. The library is now governed by the National Library Act, 1969 which broadened the powers of the National Librarian and established a National Library Advisory Board consisting of 15 members. Under the act, the National Librarian has responsibility for making the facilities of the library available to the government and people of Canada and for coordinating federal government library services. He also administers the Legal Deposit regulations, which require two copies of current Canada publications to be deposited with the library.

The library's collection consists of more than 720,000 volumes of monographs, supplemented by microcopies of about 700,000 additional titles and over 9 000 metres of periodicals. Newspaper files formerly in several locations have been brought together and now form the largest collection of Canadian newspapers in Canada. The library has important holdings of Canadian, foreign, and international official publications, and an extensive collection of Canadian music scores, recordings, and manuscripts.

The library compiles and publishes the national bibliography, *Canadiana*, which is available in tape and printed editions; the possibility of a microfilm edition is being investigated. *Canadiana* lists new publications relating to Canada, and includes bibliographic descriptions of Canadian trade publications, official publications of the federal government and the 10 provinces, theses, films and phonograph records produced in Canada, works by Canadians and material on Canada published abroad. More than 30,000 titles were included in 1974, slightly fewer in 1975. Retrospective bibliographies are planned or in progress.

The National Library maintains the Canadian Union Catalogue, which provides a key to the main library resources of the country. This catalogue lists about 4 million volumes in about 340 government, university, public and special libraries in all provinces. New accessions are reported regularly; these numbered over 1.4 million cards in 1975-76. The Public Service Branch uses this catalogue to help it meet the requests sent in by Canadian libraries for location of materials. During the year ended March 31, 1976, the branch was asked to locate nearly 149,000 titles; it found about 78% of them to be held in Canadian libraries. Automation of the Union Catalogue is now under study.

The National Library provides for Canadian subscribers a computerized literature search in the fields of the social and behavioural sciences and the humanities. This encompasses both a current awareness service and retrospective bibliographies prepared from various machine-readable data bases. In early 1974 the library began publishing a series of periodicals lists which would complement the computerized search service by providing library locations for journals indexed in specific data bases. These specialized lists will eventually be consolidated to form a full-scale union list of social science and humanities serials.

In addition, the National Library offers reference service on these subjects, and consultative services in such fields as library automation, Canadian library developments and rare books. It is developing a children's literature consultant service and a library service for the visually and physically handicapped. It provides to provincial library agencies loan collections of books in languages other than English and French, and assists Canadian libraries to develop their collections by redistributing library materials through the Canadian Book Exchange Centre. It also plays an active coordinating role in attempts to develop national library and information networks, and is contributing to international efforts at universal bibliographic control.

A list of books about Canada, prepared by the National Library, is published in Appendix 6.

7.11.3 Public libraries

Public libraries in Canada are organized under provincial legislation which specifies the method of establishment, the services to be provided and the means of support. Municipalities may organize and maintain public libraries or join together to form regional libraries according to provincial legislation. Provincial public library agencies advise local and regional libraries and distribute grants.

Table 7.12 gives summary statistics on nearly 700 public libraries providing over 2,000 service points. Book circulation was 101.0 million or 4.5 per capita in 1974. The operating payments of all public libraries amounted to $107.9 million or $4.81 per capita compared with $4.02 in 1973. The full-time staff numbered 5,735 in 1974.

7.12 Book publishing

Books hold a prominent place in the realm of communication. They are a major tool in education and as a means of spreading knowledge are both the keeper and the messenger of a culture. Book importing and production in Canada in 1974 are summarized in the following paragraphs.

Book imports. Calculations based on figures received from Customs sources show that Canada imported books and pamphlets valued at $170 million in 1974. These books came mainly from the United States, 76%, with 10.5% from France, 8.3% from the United Kingdom, 1.1% from Italy, 1.0% from Belgium–Luxembourg and the remaining 3.1% from about 20 other countries.

Canadian publishing. In 1974, Canadian publishers issued 3,519 new titles and reprinted 2,241 others. Sales resulting from this production were estimated at some

$145 million, of which $22 million was attributable to exports. Within the framework of the cultural statistics program of Statistics Canada, considerable information has been gathered from which the following highlights have been extracted.

For analytical purposes, publishing has been divided into three commercial categories: school textbooks, commercial books, and multi-volume reference books. In the first category, 646 new titles were issued and 1,387 others were reprinted. Sales of new titles reached some 1.5 million copies and those of reprints reached 10 million. Of all textbooks published in Canada, some are adaptations of books from other countries, others are translations and a third group is Canadian in origin. English-language textbooks make up 85% of the 412 adaptations and these account for 40% of sales. French-language textbooks represent 109 of the 117 translations and account for over 25% of all copies of French texts sold by Canadian publishers. In addition, 60 adaptations are included in the French-language textbook group.

In the commercial book category, publishers reported sales of some 90 million copies. Nearly 72.4 million was among the 1,110 mass circulation paperback titles including nearly 71.4 million copies in English and 980,000 copies in French. Commercial books made up nearly 80% of all titles published in 1974 but less than 40% of the reprints.

Without distinction as to category, the number of copies sold by title of books published in 1974 could be broken down by subject matter as follows: literature, 47,800 copies; general, 19,000; recreation and hobbies, 7,400; philosophy and psychology, 6,500; geography and travel, 5,700 and household science, 5,000. Of 18 remaining topics, each title sold fewer than 5,000 copies on the average, with educational science in last place (except for military arts and national defence, which was represented by a single title) with an average sale of 825 copies for each of the 76 titles issued.

Though more books are imported than produced in Canada, production is substantial, particularly in the realm of paperbacks. It is noteworthy that new or reprint titles are issued in considerable numbers covering almost all fields. On the average, Canadian books are sold at the rate of 3,000 copies per title in the year of publication. Tables 7.13 and 7.14 give further details on book publishing in Canada in 1974.

Sources

7.1 - 7.5 Education, Science and Culture Division, Institutional and Public Finance Statistics Branch, Statistics Canada; Territorial and Social Development Branch, Department of Indian Affairs and Northern Development; Manpower Training Branch, Department of Manpower and Immigration.

7.6 Information Services, National Museums of Canada.

7.7 Education, Science and Culture Division, Institutional and Public Finance Statistics Branch, Statistics Canada.

7.8 Information Services, National Museums of Canada.

7.9.1 Information Services, The Canada Council.

7.9.2 Communications Department, National Arts Centre.

7.9.3 Newfoundland Information Service, Nova Scotia Department of Recreation, New Brunswick Information Service, Annuaire du Québec, Ontario Ministry of Culture and Recreation, The Manitoba Arts Council, Saskatchewan Arts Board, Alberta Culture, Deputy Provincial Secretary of British Columbia.

7.10.1 Information and Promotion Division, National Film Board.

7.10.2 Canadian Film Development Corporation.

7.11.1 Office of the Dominion Archivist, Public Archives of Canada.

7.11.2 Public Services Branch, National Library of Canada.

7.11.3 - 7.12 Education, Science and Culture Division, Institutional and Public Finance Statistics Branch, Statistics Canada.

Tables

.. not available	e estimate
... not appropriate or not applicable	p preliminary
— nil or zero	r revised
-- too small to be expressed	certain tables may not add due to rounding

7.1 Enrolment in elementary and secondary schools, by type of institution and by province, years ended 1970-74

Type of institution	Province or territory						
	Nfld.	PEI	NS	NB	Que.	Ont.	Man.
Public							
1970	160,097	29,553	213,131	173,808	1,581,020	1,986,796	245,564
1971	160,915	30,622	214,897	175,912	1,588,788	2,022,401	246,946
1972	162,818	30,570	214,780	175,997	1,577,079P	2,031,360	244,452
1973	161,723	29,340	211,262	173,851	1,526,586P	2,028,114	238,861
1974	159,831	29,056	207,651	170,179	1,464,599P	2,008,610	234,620
Private[1]							
1970	553	70	2,125	353	67,326	43,007	8,178
1971	722	29	1,649	463	62,492	44,116	8,284
1972	746	—	1,405	398	60,640	43,949	7,438
1973	843	—	1,394	636	67,903	44,826	7,224
1974	872	—	1,286	467	74,092	47,500	6,912
Federal[2]							
1970	—	65	506	620	4,402	6,605	5,938
1971	—	71	524	615	4,350	6,671	5,914
1972	—	66	565	671	4,658	7,157	6,064
1973	—	65	624	704	4,016	7,106	6,376
1974	—	53	645	728	5,059	7,149	6,830
Schools for the blind and the deaf							
1970	132	15	443	—	1,320	1,434	183
1971	144	12	450	—	1,281	1,427	168
1972	145	12	457	—	1,240	1,485	147
1973	134	10	488	—	1,059	1,416	173
1974	138	8	472	—	981	1,283	167
Total							
1970	160,782	29,703	216,205	174,781	1,654,068	2,037,842	259,863
1971	161,781	30,734	217,520	176,990	1,656,911	2,074,615	261,312
1972	163,709	30,648	217,207	177,066	1,643,617	2,083,951	258,101
1973	162,700	29,415	213,768	175,191	1,599,564	2,081,462	252,634
1974	160,841	29,117	210,054	171,374	1,544,731	2,064,542	248,529

	Sask.	Alta.	BC	YT	NWT	Canada
Public						
1970	249,915	413,719	513,150	4,090	8,192	5,579,035
1971	247,332	425,987	518,043	4,634	10,006	5,646,483
1972	243,579	427,968	524,305	4,806	11,209	5,648,923
1973	234,152	425,251	537,067	4,749	11,369	5,582,325
1974	223,798	419,737	549,019	4,957	12,627	5,484,684
Private[1]						
1970	1,854	5,342	22,359	—	—	151,167
1971	1,552	5,688	21,319	—	—	146,314
1972	1,710	5,439	21,777	—	—	143,502
1973	1,268	5,403	22,061	—	—	151,558
1974	1,309	5,367	21,421	—	—	159,226
Federal[2]						
1970	3,430	3,553	3,491	—	—	36,526[3]
1971	3,354	3,564	3,360	—	—	34,290[3]
1972	3,358	3,595	3,108	—	—	33,811[3]
1973	4,465	3,409	3,036	—	—	34,390[3]
1974	5,290	3,661	3,083	—	—	37,064[3]
Schools for the blind and the deaf						
1970	169	124	302	—	—	4,122
1971	164	135	285	—	—	4,066
1972	175	148	283	—	—	4,092
1973	178	152	277	—	—	3,887
1974	159	159	257	—	—	3,624
Total						
1970	255,368	422,738	539,302	4,090	8,192	5,770,850[3]
1971	252,402	435,374	543,007	4,634	10,006	5,831,153[3]
1972	248,822	437,150	549,473	4,806	11,209	5,830,328[3]
1973	240,063	434,215	562,441	4,749	11,369	5,772,160[3]
1974	230,556	428,924	573,780	4,957	12,627	5,684,598[3]

[1]Private kindergartens and nursery schools not included.
[2]Provincial figures are for federal schools for Indians and Inuit.
[3]Canada total also includes Department of National Defence schools overseas.

7.2   Teaching staff in elementary and secondary schools, by type of institution and by province, years ended 1970-74

Type of institution	Province or territory						
	Nfld.	PEI	NS	NB	Que.	Ont.	Man.
Public[1]							
1970	6,315	1,486	9,443	7,822	77,418	89,929	11,194
1971	6,437	1,606	9,999	7,897	77,978	93,000	11,534
1972	6,648	1,639	9,869	7,956	78,000e	92,488	11,731
1973	6,895	1,459	10,020	7,961	77,100e	96,221	11,398
1974	7,072	1,450e	10,280	7,805	74,700e	93,153	11,446
Private							
1970	59	6	159	40	4,396	3,316	532
1971	61	4	159	57	3,622	3,552	563
1972	66	—	141	50	3,500e	3,658	464
1973	68	—	130	53	3,670e	3,844	416
1974	75	—	131	35	3,900e	4,062	468
Federal[1,2]							
1970	—	4	24	26	188	278	240
1971	—	4	25	25	172	263	241
1972	—	4	26	27	205	302	247
1973	—	3	27	33	220	322	262
1974	—	3	30	39	235e	323	252
Schools for the blind and the deaf							
1970	21	3	87	—	221	258	29
1971	22	5	93	—	270	276	26
1972	22	5	97	—	278	294	27
1973	21	2	106	—	264	297	27
1974	21	4	112	—	209	266	30
Total							
1970	6,395	1,499	9,713	7,888	82,223	93,781	11,995
1971	6,520	1,619	10,276	7,979	82,042	97,091	12,364
1972	6,736	1,648	10,133	8,033	81,983	96,742	12,469
1973	6,984	1,464	10,283	8,047	81,254	100,684	12,103
1974	7,168	1,457	10,553	7,879	79,044	97,804	12,196

	Sask.	Alta.	BC	YT	NWT	Canada
Public[1]						
1970	11,553	19,821	20,815	219	516	256,531
1971	10,977	20,358	21,575	223	518	262,102
1972	10,716	20,521	22,112	247	587	262,514
1973	10,744	20,268	21,744	258	612	264,680
1974	10,924	20,370	23,247	223	627	261,297
Private						
1970	141	317	1,260	—	—	10,226
1971	113	340	1,250	—	—	9,721
1972	127	311	1,305	—	—	9,622
1973	92	314	1,354	—	—	9,941
1974	99	330	1,323	—	—	10,423
Federal[1,2]						
1970	174	174	159	—	—	1,768[3]
1971	170	165	149	—	—	1,569[3]
1972	165	171	145	—	—	1,594[3]
1973	216	185	137	—	—	1,683[3]
1974	210	157	73	—	—	1,633[3]
Schools for the blind and the deaf						
1970	27	24	49	—	—	719
1971	28	24	50	—	—	794
1972	29	28	52	—	—	832
1973	29	21	50	—	—	817
1974	28	29	52	—	—	751
Total						
1970	11,895	20,336	22,283	219	516	269,244[3]
1971	11,288	20,887	23,024	223	518	274,186[3]
1972	11,037	21,031	23,614	247	587	274,562[3]
1973	11,081	20,788	23,285	258	612	277,121[3]
1974	11,261	20,886	24,695	223	627	274,104[3]

[1]Includes full-time staff only.
[2]Provincial figures are for federal schools for Indians and Inuit.
[3]Canada total also includes Department of National Defence schools overseas.

7.3   Teachers[1] in elementary and secondary schools (median salary, years of experience and percentage holding a degree) by level[2] and by province, years ended 1973 and 1974

Teaching level		Nfld. 1973	Nfld. 1974	PEI 1973	PEI 1974	NS 1973	NS 1974	NB 1973	NB 1974
Elementary									
Median salary	$	6,976	8,092	6,712	..	7,937	8,774	7,131	7,999
Median experience	yr	6.0	6.0	9.1	..	8.0	8.0	8.2	9.0
Degree holders	%	34.9	41.9	25.3	..	35.3	38.3	35.1	40.8
Secondary									
Median salary	$	8,836	10,293	8,805	..	9,611	10,851	8,681	9,735
Median experience	yr	5.0	6.0	6.0	..	6.0	7.0	6.0	8.0
Degree holders	%	74.5	79.6	69.0	..	73.8	75.2	70.9	72.8

Teaching level		Ont. 1973	Ont. 1974	Man. 1973	Man. 1974	Sask. 1973	Sask. 1974	Alta. 1973	Alta. 1974
Elementary									
Median salary	$	8,774	9,704	8,030	8,898	8,371	9,022	9,704	10,758
Median experience	yr	6.0	7.0	6.0	7.0	8.0	9.0	8.0	8.0
Degree holders	%	27.5	35.6	37.8	45.3	29.4	37.1	57.6	64.4
Secondary									
Median salary	$	12,711	13,734	11,223	12,370	11,502	12,556	11,781	12,680
Median experience	yr	7.0	7.0	7.0	7.0	8.0	9.0	7.0	8.0
Degree holders	%	80.5	83.4	83.6	85.3	80.9	84.1	86.7	89.7

Teaching level		BC 1973	BC 1974	YT 1973	YT 1974	NWT 1973	NWT 1974	Canada[3] 1973	Canada[3] 1974
Elementary									
Median salary	$	9,735	10,696	12,525	13,889	12,044	12,959	8,712	9,704
Median experience	yr	7.6	7.1	6.6	7.0	6.0	6.0	7.0	7.0
Degree holders	%	45.4	51.5	60.6	64.1	44.8	50.1	[4]	[4]
Secondary									
Median salary	$	12,153	13,207	14,540	16,400	14,555	15,873	11,905	12,990
Median experience	yr	8.0	8.0	7.5	8.0	6.0	6.0	7.0	7.7
Degree holders	%	83.2	87.0	88.6	92.9	89.7	75.0	[4]	[4]

[1] In public schools only.
[2] Staff teaching both elementary and secondary grades classified as teaching at the secondary level.
[3] Information for Quebec not available.
[4] Breakdown by level not available; the percentage of degree holders in both elementary and secondary schools combined was 51.5 in 1972-73 and 56.9 in 1973-74.

7.4   Full-time enrolment at the post-secondary non-university level, and educational staff, by province, 1972-73 and 1973-74

Item	Nfld. 1972-73	Nfld. 1973-74	PEI 1972-73	PEI 1973-74	NS 1972-73	NS 1973-74	NB 1972-73	NB 1973-74
Full-time enrolment								
In educational institutions								
Post-secondary non-university level								
Community colleges								
Career programs	820	928	313	676	985	1,072	796	612
Transfer programs	—	—	—	—	130	167	—	—
Hospital schools of nursing	671	710	177	184	814	759	761	624
Teachers' colleges	—	—	—	—	548	511	412	—
Trades-level schools								
Public schools								
Pre-employment courses	3,455	4,066	825	650	6,386	6,580	2,525	2,716
Apprenticeship courses[1]	210	67	189	224	2,126	2,486	1,044	1,171
Academic upgrading courses[2]	2,272	2,240	—	722	3,083	2,135	1,340	1,638
Private schools	128	..	34	..	1,378	..	674	..
In industrial setting								
Registered apprentices	2,235	2,824	245	377	4,363	4,549	4,709	5,030
Publicly supported training-in-industry	1,398	678	228	97	1,306	2,106	1,568	1,763
Publicly supported training-on-the-job	1,742	1,278	978	454	3,499	2,120	2,738	1,873
Vocational rehabilitation programs for disabled	89	70	94	60	70	82	12	24
Full-time educational staff								
Community colleges	158	145	44	37	129	123	144	126
Hospital schools of nursing[p]	61	65	19	21	102	100	85	80
Teachers' colleges	—	—	—	—	60	56[p]	66	—
Public trades-level schools	378	340	96	94	538	520	294	324
Private trade schools	3	..	1	..	41	..	15	..

7.4   Full-time enrolment at the post-secondary non-university level, and educational staff, by province, 1972-73 and 1973-74 (concluded)

Item	Que. 1972-73	Que. 1973-74	Ont. 1972-73	Ont. 1973-74	Man. 1972-73	Man. 1973-74	Sask. 1972-73	Sask. 1973-74
Full-time enrolment								
In educational institutions								
Post-secondary non-university level								
Community colleges								
Career programs	44,700	47,502	42,367	54,606	2,387	1,774	2,241	2,475
Transfer programs	55,314	59,946	—	—	—	—	48	48
Hospital schools of nursing	—	—	8,072	—	983	905	172	—
Teachers' colleges	213	161	2,082	793	—	—	—	—
Trades-level schools								
Public schools								
Pre-employment courses	8,500³,e	10,000³,e	26,145	25,047	2,060	5,000e	3,209	4,007
Apprenticeship courses¹	2,700e	3,000e	10,500e	11,000e	906	1,500e	1,322	1,399
Academic upgrading courses²	..	..	27,604	31,938	..	1,728	3,290	2,867
Private schools	..	..	7,660	..	1,019	..	1,392	..
In industrial setting								
Registered apprentices	10,819	10,500e	26,178	28,883	3,079	3,387	3,238	3,450
Publicly supported training-in-industry	5,669⁴	6,544⁴	62,651	53,052	1,023	902	189	653
Publicly supported training-on-the-job	17,842	5,625	25,150	4,497	2,518	691	2,498	824
Vocational rehabilitation programs for disabled	...	...	2,063	1,436	850	650	277	364
Full-time educational staff								
Community colleges	7,480e	8,015e	3,354	4,246	255	181	211	226
Hospital schools of nursingP	—	—	1,006	—	125	120	20	—
Teachers' colleges	20	15P	187	100P	—	—	—	—
Public trades-level schools	..	..	1,374	1,502	258	197	244	194
Private trade schools	..	..	282	..	41	..	53	..

Item	Alta. 1972-73	Alta. 1973-74	BC 1972-73	BC 1973-74	YT 1972-73	YT 1973-74	NWT 1972-73	NWT 1973-74	Canada 1972-73	Canada 1973-74
Full-time enrolment										
In educational institutions										
Post-secondary non-university level										
Community colleges										
Career programs	9,347	9,637	6,064	6,429	—	—	—	—	110,020	125,711
Transfer programs	2,347	2,613	5,380	5,749	—	—	—	—	63,219	68,523
Hospital schools of nursing	1,636	1,111	1,174	1,120	—	—	—	—	14,460	5,413
Teachers' colleges	—	—	—	—	—	—	—	—	3,255	1,465
Trades-level schools										
Public schools										
Pre-employment courses	4,885	5,160	13,902	15,722	408	500	237	312	72,537	79,760
Apprenticeship courses¹	8,000e	8,500e	5,796	6,994	10	—	6	81	32,809	36,422
Academic upgrading courses²	3,111	4,254	4,127	5,623	159	98	383	118	..	..
Private schools	1,303	..	2,729	..	—	..	—	..	16,317⁵	..
In industrial setting										
Registered apprentices	12,348	13,099	12,309	14,707	35	39	224	280	79,782	87,125
Publicly supported training-in-industry	1,836	1,714	3,607	2,660	102	128	85	40	79,662⁴	70,337⁴
Publicly supported training-on-the-job	3,819	1,135	4,677	2,053	93	39	203	87	65,757	20,676
Vocational rehabilitation programs for disabled	276	545	572	468	1	23	7	7	4,311	3,729
Full-time educational staff										
Community colleges	981	966	1,064	1,024	—	—	—	—	13,820	15,089
Hospital schools of nursingP	176	140	100	88	—	—	—	—	1,694	614
Teachers' colleges	—	—	—	—	—	—	—	—	333	171P
Public trades-levels schools	402	414	264	307	..	..	..	..	..	..
Private trade schools	55	..	49	..	—	..	—	..	540⁵	..

¹Includes some part-time and correspondence students; these are also included in "Registered apprentices".
²Includes training in a second language.
³Excludes an estimated 20,000 skill-upgrading courses.
⁴Employees trained under Quebec program not included; data not available.
⁵Excludes Quebec where an insufficient number of schools responded.

7.5   Full- and part-time enrolment in universities, by level and province, years ended 1973 and 1974

Province and year		Undergraduate[1]		Graduate[2]		Non-university[3]	
		Full-time	Part-time	Full-time	Part-time	Full-time	Part-time
Newfoundland	1973	6,950	3,244	359	234	—	—
	1974	6,085	3,470	333	349	—	—
Prince Edward Island	1973	1,580	919	—	—	1	—
	1974	1,409	1,056	—	—	—	—
Nova Scotia	1973	14,934	3,172	1,162	390	—	—
	1974	15,204	3,884	1,158	480	—	—
New Brunswick	1973	9,659	4,679	570	154	—	—
	1974	9,871	4,921	505	212	99	1
Quebec	1973	48,224	40,953	9,603	6,997	8,417	5,262
	1974	53,950	37,233	9,175	8,160	4,751	5,821
Ontario	1973	117,181	51,816	16,495	9,208	1,519	20
	1974	123,552	55,649	16,966	10,130	1,035	161
Manitoba	1973	15,608	7,544	1,355	851	60	88
	1974	15,661	8,511	1,363	1,139	1	3
Saskatchewan	1973	12,389	3,352	696	584	295	573
	1974	12,695	4,376	629	610	209	539
Alberta	1973	24,257	6,328	3,507	1,638	—	208
	1974	25,605	5,951	3,178	1,626	247	309
British Columbia	1973	23,368	3,966	3,760	425	455	376
	1974	24,490	5,356	3,594	804	359	413
Total	1973	274,150	125,973	37,507	20,481	10,747	6,527
	1974	288,522	130,407	36,901	23,510	6,701	7,247

[1]Bachelors and first professional degrees, diplomas and certificates, auditors, special students, etc.
[2]Masters, doctorates, diplomas and certificates, interns and residents, qualifying and special students, etc.
[3]Diplomas, certificates, etc.

7.6   Graduate-level degrees awarded by Canadian universities, by field of study, region and percentage distribution by sex, 1972-73 and 1973-74P

Degree and field of study	Region and year					
	Atlantic provinces		Quebec		Ontario	
	1972-73	1973-74	1972-73	1973-74	1972-73	1973-74
Master						
Education	134	146	434	428	918	949
Fine and applied arts	—	—	24	27	46	55
Humanities	157	123	449	453	1,405	1,151
Social sciences	168	179	738	759	1,896	2,029
Agriculture and biological sciences	26	45	93	86	153	170
Engineering and applied sciences	58	44	214	216	499	466
Health professions	14	4	127	117	118	86
Mathematics and physical sciences	70	69	193	171	415	375
Total	627	610	2,272	2,257	5,450	5,281
Doctorate						
Education	—	—	5	8	48	38
Fine and applied arts	—	—	—	—	5	4
Humanities	8	10	52	38	131	173
Social sciences	2	3	63	74	151	177
Agriculture and biological sciences	15	18	34	29	89	93
Engineering and applied sciences	3	13	48	64	165	166
Health professions	5	3	71	60	61	56
Mathematics and physical sciences	36	26	102	83	260	227
Total	69	73	375	356	910	934

7.6 Graduate-level degrees awarded by Canadian universities, by field of study, region and percentage distribution by sex, 1972-73 and 1973P (concluded)

Degree and field of study	Region and year							
	Western provinces		Canada					
	1972-73	1973-74	1972-73			1973-74		
				M %	F %		M %	F %
Master								
Education	466	469	1,952	64	36	1,992	70	30
Fine and applied arts	25	38	95	57	43	120	53	47
Humanities	260	269	2,271	60	40	1,996	56	44
Social sciences	781	662	3,583	78	22	3,629	77	23
Agriculture and biological sciences	201	150	473	75	25	451	74	26
Engineering and applied sciences	240	202	1,011	98	2	928	98	2
Health professions	61	55	320	57	43	262	56	44
Mathematics and physical sciences	247	203	925	87	13	818	85	15
Total	2,281	2,048	10,630	73	27	10,196	73	27
Doctorate								
Education	69	82	122	81	19	128	87	13
Fine and applied arts	—	—	5	100	—	4	100	—
Humanities	37	43	228	80	20	264	75	25
Social sciences	74	71	290	82	18	325	78	22
Agriculture and biological sciences	112	107	250	88	12	247	89	11
Engineering and applied sciences	83	58	299	97	3	301	99	1
Health professions	41	34	178	82	18	153	86	14
Mathematics and physical sciences	159	138	557	96	4	474	94	6
Total	575	533	1,929	89	11	1,896	88	12

7.7 Diplomas and certificates awarded by Canadian universities, by level and field of study, region and percentage distribution by sex, 1972-73 and 1973-74P

Level and field of study	Region and year					
	Atlantic provinces		Quebec		Ontario	
	1972-73	1973-74	1972-73	1973-74	1972-73	1973-74
Undergraduate						
Education	68	64	1,697	1,875	1,259	506
Fine and applied arts	7	11	291	330	119	45
Humanities	2	5	112	127	262	255
Social sciences	109	134	456	614	678	340
Agriculture and biological sciences	—	1	35	16	126	42
Engineering and applied sciences	80	72	—	—	376	141
Health professions	103	187	102	227	322	229
Mathematics and physical sciences	1	3	20	22	63	57
Total	370	477	2,713	3,211	3,205	1,615
Graduate						
Education	38	68	26	116	30	—
Fine and applied arts	—	—	—	1	5	10
Humanities	—	—	5	1	14	55
Social sciences	3	6	137	101	95	166
Agriculture and biological sciences	—	—	3	—	3	15
Engineering and applied sciences	—	—	14	11	—	—
Health professions	—	—	78	59	107	113
Mathematics and physical sciences	—	—	3	—	—	—
Total	41	74	266	289	254	359

	Western provinces		Canada					
	1972-73	1973-74	1972-73			1973-74		
				M %	F %		M %	F %
Undergraduate								
Education	1,764	1,637	4,788	45	55	4,082	46	54
Fine and applied arts	25	16	442	25	75	402	22	78
Humanities	73	94	449	37	63	481	36	64
Social sciences	212	93	1,455	70	30	1,181	72	28
Agriculture and biological sciences	170	100	331	85	15	159	75	25
Engineering and applied sciences	—	—	456	99	1	213	97	3
Health professions	356	313	883	9	91	956	7	93
Mathematics and physical sciences	57	17	141	73	27	99	79	21
Total	2,657	2,270	8,945	49	51	7,573	46	54

7.7   Diplomas and certificates awarded by Canadian universities, by level and field of study, region and percentage distribution by sex, 1972-73 and 1973-74P (concluded)

Level and field of study	Region and year							
	Western provinces		Canada					
	1972-73	1973-74	1972-73			1973-74		
				M %	F %		M %	F %
Graduate								
Education	290	342	384	65	35	526	64	36
Fine and applied arts	—	—	5	40	60	11	27	73
Humanities	20	1	39	51	49	57	63	37
Social sciences	—	1	235	87	13	274	75	25
Agriculture and biological sciences	4	6	10	90	10	21	95	5
Engineering and applied sciences	8	8	22	96	4	19	100	—
Health professions	4	3	189	71	29	175	53	47
Mathematics and physical sciences	9	2	12	83	17	2	50	50
Total	335	363	896	72	28	1,085	66	34

7.8   Participation in continuing education courses per 1,000 population[1] by type of institution and by province, 1970-71 to 1973-74

Province or territory and year		School boards, departments of education		Department of education correspondence courses		Community colleges		Universities		Total
		Part-time credit	Non-credit	Part-time credit	Non-credit	Part-time credit	Non-credit	Part-time credit	Non-credit	
Newfoundland	1970-71	7.6	2.8	—	—	..	..	21.9	1.1	..
	1971-72	11.8	10.3	—	—	16.0	8.7	22.5	6.7	75.9
	1972-73	7.1	9.4	—	—	15.8	7.1	21.5	7.6	68.5
	1973-74	7.6	7.5	—	—	24.9	7.9	21.0	8.0	76.9
Prince Edward Island	1970-71	15.8	29.2	0.6	—	..	..	31.8	3.7	..
	1971-72	14.8	38.1	0.6	—	19.9	5.0	36.8	4.9	120.1
	1972-73	9.9	43.3	—	—	15.9	3.9	33.9	2.8	109.7
	1973-74	9.5	51.0	—	—	11.8	5.2	35.1	2.0	114.6
Nova Scotia	1970-71	9.9	21.3	1.3	—	..	..	17.1	6.0	..
	1971-72	6.6	21.0	1.6	—	8.6	0.3	16.1	6.4	60.6
	1972-73	6.6	25.3	1.8	—	6.5	1.3	16.9	7.9	66.3
	1973-74	8.3	29.2	2.2	—	5.6	1.6	18.5	11.5	77.0
New Brunswick	1970-71	7.3	15.8	2.1	—	..	..	24.8	5.7	..
	1971-72	5.3	15.2	1.5	—	3.4	—	24.1	5.0	54.4
	1972-73	4.4	16.2	1.2	—	3.7	—	22.5	7.3	55.3
	1973-74	3.0	19.5	1.0	—	6.3	0.1	22.6	7.3	59.9
Quebec	1970-71	28.4	13.7	1.4	—	—	4.7	25.5	6.0	79.7
	1971-72	26.7	17.6	0.7	—	—	5.6	23.7	5.5	79.9
	1972-73	26.0	17.4	0.5	0.5	—	6.0	21.7	7.2	79.3
	1973-74	22.1	18.8	0.4	0.6	—	5.4	18.7	10.2	76.1
Ontario	1970-71	7.9	18.8	10.5	—	..	..	21.9	8.8	..
	1971-72	6.3	21.5	10.2	—	9.5	7.1	22.7	7.4	84.9
	1972-73	4.2	25.3	9.4	—	12.0	8.4	23.5	8.3	91.0
	1973-74	4.4	24.9	8.8	—	12.5	11.3	24.0	12.2	98.3
Manitoba	1970-71	2.9	12.5	2.2	—	..	..	27.3	8.5	..
	1971-72	3.5	13.2	2.1	—	5.7	8.1	26.6	7.8	67.0
	1972-73	2.9	13.9	2.5	—	3.6	11.3	25.8	8.8	68.9
	1973-74	1.3	15.5	2.3	—	3.0	12.5	27.2	12.7	74.5
Saskatchewan	1970-71	4.6	10.6	3.9	—	..	..	17.2	10.7	..
	1971-72	3.5	10.6	4.9	—	8.3	2.1	21.0	13.1	63.5
	1972-73	3.8	11.9	2.9	—	6.6	2.4	20.2	17.6	65.5
	1973-74	2.4	9.8	2.2	- -	5.1	1.9	20.4	23.2	65.1
Alberta	1970-71	3.4	19.8	10.5	—	..	..	15.9	28.1	..
	1971-72	3.0	16.7	6.4	—	12.4	11.7	15.4	39.0	104.6
	1972-73	3.2	22.7	5.4	0.2	6.2	16.1	16.0	37.8	107.5
	1973-74	5.4	23.2	4.9	0.4	8.4	12.4	14.5	41.1	110.3
British Columbia	1970-71	12.1	70.6	5.6	2.3	..	..	10.4	12.6	..
	1971-72	6.0	66.1	4.8	2.0	18.1	10.5	7.7	17.0	132.2
	1972-73	5.5	62.0	4.4	1.2	16.7	20.4	7.5	18.6	136.3
	1973-74	6.0	56.6	3.3	1.4	17.5	23.2	8.1	18.2	134.3
Yukon and Northwest Territories	1970-71	3.5	21.9	—	—	..	..	—	—	..
	1971-72	0.3	24.9	—	—	36.4	..	—	—	61.5
	1972-73	7.2	27.7	—	—	17.6	—	—	—	52.5
	1973-74	7.9	57.8	—	—	15.5	10.4	—	—	91.6
Canada	1970-71	13.5	22.0	5.9	0.2	..	..	21.2	9.5	..
	1971-72	11.6	23.6	5.3	0.2	7.8	6.8	20.8	10.3	86.5
	1972-73	10.4	25.3	4.7	0.3	7.8	8.9	20.4	11.6	89.5
	1973-74	9.5	25.4	4.3	0.3	8.4	10.0	19.8	14.6	92.4

[1]Out-of-school population 15 years of age and over as of June 1 of years ended 1971-74.

7.9   Expenditures on education by level of study, and by province, 1971-72 to 1973-74 (million dollars)

Year and level of study	Province or region						
	Nfld.	PEI	NS	NB	Que.	Ont.	Man.
1971-72							
Elementary and secondary	92.2	20.8	144.8	132.9	1,619.7	2,045.2	229.8
Post-secondary							
Non-university	5.7	1.8	9.2	6.3	179.0	216.8	9.0
University	37.2	7.8	81.6	41.3	358.4	807.9	82.9
Vocational and							
occupational training	23.1	5.4	32.6	20.2	145.4	165.7	23.3
Total	158.1	35.9	268.2	200.7	2,302.5	3,235.6	345.0
1972-73							
Elementary and secondary	102.8	24.2	161.2	128.9	1,594.9	2,175.4	240.7
Post-secondary							
Non-university	5.5	1.9	8.7	6.4	216.0	219.3	9.0
University	44.1	9.1	69.0	44.2	385.5	786.5	93.8
Vocational and							
occupational training	26.7	5.6	32.7	23.1	157.7	177.5	25.0
Total	179.1	40.7	271.5	202.6	2,354.2	3,358.7	368.6
1973-74							
Elementary and secondary	138.1	29.6	180.2	139.6	1,915.2	2,317.4	272.9
Post-secondary							
Non-university	6.7	2.1	10.2	5.4	290.9	221.6	7.6
University	45.8	9.7	73.3	49.0	440.6	861.6	101.6
Vocational and							
occupational training	25.9	6.6	36.4	23.0	177.8	164.6	27.1
Total	216.6	47.9	300.0	217.1	2,824.5	3,565.2	409.2

	Sask.	Alta.	BC	YT	NWT	Overseas and undistributed	Total
1971-72							
Elementary and secondary	194.7	405.7	449.7	6.6	23.9	23.3	5,389.2
Post-secondary							
Non-university	6.8	50.8	34.6	- -	- -	10.0	530.0
University	69.5	185.0	163.5	0.1	- -	29.2	1,864.5
Vocational and							
occupational training	26.6	45.7	54.4	1.5	3.7	18.3	565.9
Total	297.6	687.1	702.2	8.2	27.6	80.8	8,349.7
1972-73							
Elementary and secondary	205.8	439.6	493.8	10.6	26.0	21.2	5,625.0
Post-secondary							
Non-university	8.5	50.5	36.7	- -	- -	10.4	573.0
University	68.6	175.9	157.1	0.1	- -	33.9	1,867.8
Vocational and							
occupational training	26.4	48.2	51.7	1.5	3.8	23.4	603.4
Total	309.4	714.2	739.4	12.2	29.9	88.8	8,669.2
1973-74							
Elementary and secondary	231.2	477.1	559.4	9.3	25.5	17.4	6,312.9
Post-secondary							
Non-university	9.3	46.4	44.1	- -	- -	12.0	656.5
University	74.2	165.0	170.9	0.2	- -	38.0	2,029.9
Vocational and							
occupational training	29.0	51.7	62.2	2.0	4.5	25.0	635.9
Total	343.8	740.2	836.7	11.5	30.0	92.4	9,635.2

7.10   Sources of funds for education at all levels, for years ended 1970-74 (million dollars)

Year	Sources of funds					
	Government			Fees	Other sources	Total
	Federal	Provincial[1]	Municipal			
1969-70	756.5	3,656.0	1,626.0	269.7	315.8	6,624.0
1970-71	930.1	4,316.0	1,719.4	320.5	390.1	7,676.0
1971-72	924.0	4,966.7	1,713.6	386.8	358.6	8,349.7
1972-73	943.8	5,257.0	1,777.3	414.4	276.6	8,669.2
1973-74	984.8	5,847.2	1,940.0	436.6	426.6	9,635.2

[1]Includes federal transfers to provinces for post-secondary education and for the minority language program, in the following amounts: $654,000 in 1969-70; $843,100 in 1970-71; $985,000 in 1971-72; $1,057,900 in 1972-73 and $1,143,200 in 1973-74.

7.11   Average grants, revenues and expenditures of the performing arts by company, spectator and by discipline, 1974

Discipline	By company			By spectator		
	Grants $	Revenues[1] $	Expenditures $	Grants $	Revenues[1] $	Expenditures $
Theatre	263,328	558,832	564,186	2.84	6.03	6.09
Music	486,338	931,668	922,422	3.35	6.43	6.36
Dance	635,249	1,209,771	1,300,256	3.57	6.81	7.32
Opera	446,025	965,594	1,074,520	6.14	13.30	14.80

[1]Includes average grants.

7.12   Summary statistics of public libraries, 1974 with totals for 1972 and 1973

Province or territory	Population '000	Libraries reporting	Bookstock[1]	Circulation	Total operating expenditure $'000	Full-time positions filled
Newfoundland	542	3	606,612	1,863,408	1,555,671	91
Prince Edward Island	117	1	148,252	410,534	385,400	32
Nova Scotia	813	11	815,822	2,854,287	2,305,740	165
New Brunswick	662	6	685,733	1,968,160	1,825,411	159
Quebec	6,134	96	4,927,896	11,051,535	10,385,561	571
Ontario	8,094	328	16,364,056	49,736,227	61,618,671	3,054
Manitoba	1,011	28	1,234,311	3,962,364	3,405,516	177
Saskatchewan	907	10	1,444,934	4,642,777	5,095,692	303
Alberta	1,714	144	2,639,848	8,088,489	7,158,807	428
British Columbia	2,395	67	3,771,159	16,241,310	13,491,946	726
Yukon Territory	19	1	90,000	125,831	479,150	21
Northwest Territories	38	1	64,229	87,134	205,669	8
Canada[2] 1974	22,446	696	32,792,852	101,032,056	107,913,234	5,735
1973	22,095	780	31,281,900	99,333,866	88,801	5,501
1972	21,820	746	29,450,861	95,657,130	78,040	5,181

[1]Books and other materials catalogued as books; does not include periodical and newspaper titles.
[2]Includes all full-time positions with the exception of those in libraries in population centres under 10,000 in Ontario where data are only available for professional positions.

7.13   Titles published and reprinted, by language and commercial category, 1974

Item	Commercial category						
	Multi-volume reference	Textbook					Total
		Kinder-garten to grade 3	Grades 4-6	Grades 7-9	Grades 10-13	Post-secondary	
Titles published							
English	69	82	69	62	107	145	465
French	8	13	55	10	36	55	169
Other	8	—	2	1	4	5	12
Total	85	95	126	73	147	205	646
Titles reprinted							
English	15	206	216	211	294	115	1,042
French	2	56	61	55	80	78	330
Other	—	—	—	1	7	7	15
Total	17	262	277	267	381	200	1,387

Item	Trade book				Total	Total, textbooks and trade books
	Schol-arly	Chil-dren's	Adult fiction	Adult non-fiction		
Titles published						
English	363	68	1,141	650	2,222	2,756
French	138	15	100	248	501	678
Other	29	2	10	24	65	85
Total	530	85	1,251	922	2,788	3,519
Titles reprinted						
English	129	33	122	288	572	1,629
French	34	16	53	154	257	589
Other	3	1	—	4	8	23
Total	166	50	175	446	837	2,241

7.14   Titles published and reprinted and copies sold, by language, according to UNESCO classification, 1974

UNESCO classification	Titles					
	English		French		Other	
	Published	Copies sold	Published	Copies sold	Published	Copies sold
General	136	3,424,875	67	553,377	7	3,455
Philosophy, psychology	27	249,511	22	79,819	2	500
Religion, theology	21	131,915	41	42,710	7	5,417
Sociology, statistics	33	152,301	11	7,735	3	4,799
Political science, economics	78	155,513	12	12,582	2	4,321
Law, public administration	147	222,753	23	23,321	4	1,473
Military science, national defence	1	294	—	—	—	—
Science of education	54	27,206	20	35,501	2	205
Political-economic aspects of trade	4	6,572	3	1,800	3	407
Ethnography, social anthropology	33	43,469	9	7,158	1	50
Linguistics, philology	80	330,215	44	112,398	6	22,847
Mathematics, accounting	94	438,348	37	41,771	—	—
Natural science	72	233,025	29	27,300	1	98
Medical science	18	32,229	16	20,083	2	2,740
Engineering, technology	42	62,506	36	20,904	1	1,932
Agriculture, stockbreeding	7	14,855	3	8,844	1	22
Domestic science, hotel management	22	98,606	6	42,526	—	—
Business management	51	99,567	24	15,432	—	—
Town planning, fine arts	45	56,754	8	6,986	5	4,620
Entertainment, hobbies	73	623,191	18	48,930	—	—
Literary history and criticism	30	32,677	10	5,106	4	2,021
Literature	1,265	66,807,050	126	136,830	10	13,610
Geography, travel	47	310,841	8	11,461	2	2,810
History, biography	210	666,576	52	80,956	9	4,359
Non-specified	166	35,893	53	35	13	1,034
Total	2,756	74,256,742	678	1,343,565	85	76,720
	English		French		Other	
	Reprinted	Copies sold	Reprinted	Copies sold	Reprinted	Copies sold
General	40	234,018	15	239,048	4	2,682
Philosophy, psychology	12	30,268	21	74,399	—	—
Religion, theology	28	260,280	28	102,850	—	—
Sociology, statistics	18	38,314	6	16,521	—	—
Political science, economics	64	159,534	2	1,751	—	—
Law, public administration	65	165,236	13	21,425	—	—
Military science, national defence	—		—	—	—	—
Science of education	60	549,324	44	210,278	—	—
Political-economic aspects of trade	7	4,586	—	—	—	—
Ethnography, social anthropology	20	21,284	1	2,249	—	—
Linguistics, philology	308	3,195,153	105	1,030,021	11	29,939
Mathematics, accounting	98	883,922	46	415,033	—	—
Natural science	66	470,188	30	62,291	—	—
Medical science	21	285,823	34	118,283	—	—
Engineering, technology	58	159,780	41	39,060	—	—
Agriculture, stockbreeding	6	43,750	2	9,001	—	—
Domestic science, hotel management	23	93,622	30	159,721	—	—
Business management	99	557,700	33	110,276	4	13,173
Town planning, fine arts	21	20,009	1	5,993	—	—
Entertainment, hobbies	25	198,746	32	151,754	—	—
Literary history and criticism	14	20,616	3	364	—	—
Literature	335	2,267,024	69	170,352	2	2,018
Geography, travel	69	498,918	13	58,953	1	678
History, biography	138	402,058	12	33,422	—	—
Non-specified	34	27,000	8	—	1	—
Total	1,629	10,587,153	589	3,033,045	23	48,490

7.15   Characteristics of large cultural institutions[1] by region and type, 1974

| Region | Type of museum | | Science | | | | | | | |
	Art museum or gallery	Restoration[2]	Natural and technology[3]	Living[4]	History	General[5]	Complex[6]	Archives	Other	Total
Atlantic provinces	2	5	1	—	1	3	2	2	4	20
Quebec	3	1	1	8	3	1	—	1	—	18
Ontario	7	10	1	6	1	3	2	2	2	34
Prairie provinces	3	3	1	3	—	1	5	—	1	17
British Columbia	2	5	—	7	—	1	1	2	—	18
Canada	17	24	4	24	5	9	10	7	7	107

[1] Expenditures over $100,000.
[2] Includes historic buildings and restorations, pioneer villages, restored fortifications, etc.
[3] Includes natural science museums, science and technology museums, planetaria and observatories.
[4] Includes aquaria, botanical gardens, arboretums, conservatories, zoos and wildlife refuges.
[5] Includes more than one category of collection, e.g. archaeology, entomology, ethnology.
[6] Two or more institutions operating on the same site, e.g. a planetarium and an art museum.

7.16   Bachelors' and first professional degrees awarded by Canadian universities, by field of study, province, and percentage by sex, 1972-73 and 1973-74[p]

Field of study	Nfld. 1972-73	Nfld. 1973-74	PEI 1972-73	PEI 1973-74	NS 1972-73	NS 1973-74	NB 1972-73	NB 1973-74	Que. 1972-73	Que. 1973-74	Ont. 1972-73	Ont. 1973-74
Agriculture	—	—	—	—	—	—	—	—	87	127	198	168
Architecture	—	—	—	—	19	11	—	—	112	144	84	168
Arts	385	454	137	145	1,353	1,295	1,127	1,042	3,391	4,076	15,776	17,190
Commerce and business administration	51	66	48	45	428	470	184	250	1,296	1,721	1,009	1,253
Dentistry	—	—	—	—	24	30	—	—	122	126	160	182
Education	689	744	90	108	719	790	909	818	3,788	3,020	2,833	2,852
Engineering	—	78	—	—	135	123	143	166	1,166	870	1,757	1,863
Environmental studies	—	—	—	—	—	4	—	—	—	17	183	211
Fine and applied arts	—	—	—	—	67	39	7	7	132	244	88	88
Forestry	—	—	—	—	—	—	45	41	—	—	65	70
Household science	—	—	—	—	131	138	18	32	58	80	168	260
Journalism	—	—	—	—	—	—	—	—	49	66	81	106
Law	—	—	—	—	115	143	58	60	735	795	874	934
Library science	64	95	—	—	—	—	—	—	—	—	30	—
Medicine	—	—	—	—	91	177	—	—	458	762	476	538
Music	27	18	2	6	2	6	25	24	119	102	182	209
Nursing	—	—	—	—	67	133	76	84	261	183	442	403
Optometry	—	—	—	—	—	—	—	—	38	30	41	57
Pharmacy	—	—	—	—	49	39	—	—	115	129	126	148
Physical and health education	33	34	—	—	62	67	124	121	235	216	607	716
Rehabilitation medicine	—	—	—	—	—	—	—	—	155	253	35	120

7.16 Bachelors' and first professional degrees awarded by Canadian universities, by field of study, province, and percentage by sex, 1972-73 and 1973-74P (concluded)

Panel 1 — Provinces Nfld. to Ont.

Field of study	Nfld. 1972-73	Nfld. 1973-74	PEI 1972-73	PEI 1973-74	NS 1972-73	NS 1973-74	NB 1972-73	NB 1973-74	Que. 1972-73	Que. 1973-74	Ont. 1972-73	Ont. 1973-74	M%	F%
Religion and theology	—	—	—	—	4	9	—	—	199	156	194	70	86	14
Science	167	177	72	51	609	649	196	239	1,525	2,148	3,889	3,967	90	10
Social work	17	18	—	—	—	—	16	12	218	158	120	195	51	49
Veterinary medicine	—	—	—	—	—	—	—	—	42	47	82	79	—	—
Other	—	—	—	—	—	—	—	—	—	—	217	66	—	—
Total	1,433	1,684	349	355	3,875	4,123	2,928	2,896	14,301	15,470	29,717	31,886	58	42

Panel 2 — Provinces Man. to BC and Canada

Field of study	Man. 1972-73	Man. 1973-74	Sask. 1972-73	Sask. 1973-74	Alta. 1972-73	Alta. 1973-74	BC 1972-73	BC 1973-74	Canada 1972-73	Canada 1973-74	M%	F%
Agriculture	84	81	69	70	75	88	59	65	572	599	84	16
Architecture	6	—	—	—	—	—	22	25	243	348	92	8
Arts	1,744	1,640	745	671	1,211	1,193	1,906	1,880	27,775	29,586	44	56
Commerce and business administration	151	173	210	235	368	343	220	254	3,965	4,810	84	16
Dentistry	27	30	10	9	37	52	34	36	414	465	92	8
Education	686	784	873	826	2,092	2,244	1,065	1,020	13,744	13,206	45	55
Engineering	192	165	162	192	391	384	237	216	4,183	4,057	99	1
Environmental studies	37	48	—	—	—	—	—	—	220	280	86	14
Fine and applied arts	72	73	17	9	60	66	51	61	494	560	43	57
Forestry	—	—	—	—	—	32	43	66	153	209	95	5
Household science	81	104	44	52	17	66	59	84	576	816	2	98
Journalism	—	—	—	—	—	—	—	—	130	172	57	43
Law	98	99	64	85	124	145	200	182	2,268	2,443	83	17
Library science	—	—	—	—	56	67	10	4	96	71	15	85
Medicine	99	88	26	42	200	234	64	59	1,478	1,995	79	21
Music	24	20	9	11	30	36	55	71	448	485	38	62
Nursing	75	50	96	73	108	147	63	70	1,215	1,161	2	98
Optometry	—	—	—	—	—	—	—	—	79	87	86	14
Pharmacy	46	36	71	68	72	83	70	88	549	591	50	50
Physical and health education	102	74	47	37	185	205	146	124	1,541	1,594	60	40
Rehabilitation medicine	17	18	—	3	24	35	41	33	272	462	9	91
Religion and theology	44	40	10	18	40	18	17	13	508	324	86	14
Science	590	583	274	297	794	895	746	803	8,862	9,809	74	26
Social work	113	80	—	—	—	94	—	—	484	557	30	70
Veterinary medicine	—	—	52	56	—	—	—	—	176	182	89	11
Other	—	31	18	—	16	—	—	26	251	123	39	61
Total	4,288	4,217	2,797	2,754	5,900	6,427	5,108	5,180	70,696	74,992	60	40

7.17   Number and median salaries of full-time teachers in universities by rank, highest degree and region, 1971-72 to 1973-74

Degree, region and year	Professors		Associate professors		Assistant professors		Rank next below assistant professor		Other		All ranks	
	Number	Median salary $	Number	Median salary $	Number	Median salary $	Number	Median salary $	Number	Median salary $	Number	Median salary $
Highest degree												
Doctorate												
1971-72	3,693	22,700	4,736	16,750	4,677	13,400	208	11,250	378	14,300	13,692	16,300
1972-73	3,976	22,850	5,138	17,500	4,657	14,000	219	11,750	328	13,500	14,318	17,150
1973-74	4,576	25,150	6,100	18,400	4,694	14,700	193	12,000	424	14,725	15,987	18,300
Master												
1971-72	735	22,300	1,424	16,600	3,178	12,950	1,703	10,700	541	11,200	7,581	13,100
1972-73	790	23,400	1,485	17,300	3,244	13,600	1,600	11,000	409	11,250	7,528	13,950
1973-74	847	24,700	1,643	18,300	3,181	14,450	1,522	11,750	491	13,200	7,684	15,000
Professional degree												
1971-72	293	27,500	261	20,500	404	17,000	95	13,000	84	14,475	1,137	20,000
1972-73	328	28,350	333	21,550	441	17,650	133	15,450	37	9,600	1,272	20,700
1973-74	428	30,275	424	22,000	516	18,175	120	15,000	41	10,200	1,529	21,800
Bachelor												
1971-72	266	22,450	378	17,200	748	13,500	718	10,150	371	10,000	2,481	12,850
1972-73	237	23,500	359	17,900	737	13,900	682	10,800	288	10,200	2,303	13,400
1973-74	221	24,450	340	18,550	639	14,500	596	11,500	272	11,000	2,068	14,250
Other												
1971-72	46	20,650	82	16,325	175	12,900	139	10,300	125	10,000	567	12,400
1972-73	56	22,900	92	16,725	159	13,400	113	11,000	81	11,300	501	13,650
1973-74	63	24,000	114	17,950	167	14,400	116	11,875	71	12,100	531	15,000
Region												
Atlantic provinces												
1971-72	412	21,000	584	16,000	1,126	12,550	524	10,000	81	8,700	2,727	13,400
1972-73	466	22,000	657	16,900	1,167	13,250	511	10,700	71	9,750	2,872	14,250
1973-74	527	23,000	773	17,500	1,330	14,000	469	11,300	92	10,325	3,191	15,200
Quebec												
1971-72	912	21,200	1,455	16,150	2,012	13,000	758	10,400	400	13,300	5,537	14,500
1972-73	986	22,500	1,583	17,050	2,261	13,550	691	10,750	178	14,150	5,699	15,350
1973-74	1,090	23,900	1,850	18,150	2,082	14,300	626	11,650	403	15,500	6,051	16,600
Ontario												
1971-72	2,214	23,900	2,716	17,450	3,458	13,850	1,130	11,250	436	12,300	9,954	16,000
1972-73	2,385	24,900	2,961	18,100	3,420	14,350	1,156	11,650	350	11,900	10,272	16,750
1973-74	2,715	26,000	3,415	18,800	3,386	15,000	1,054	12,175	340	12,475	10,910	17,875
Western provinces												
1971-72	1,495	23,200	2,126	16,700	2,586	13,200	451	10,000	582	10,900	7,240	15,050
1972-73	1,550	24,300	2,206	17,600	2,390	14,000	389	10,950	544	11,300	7,079	16,150
1973-74	1,803	25,800	2,583	18,700	2,399	15,000	398	11,500	464	12,000	7,647	17,700
Canada												
1971-72	5,033	22,800	6,881	16,800	9,182	13,300	2,863	10,600	1,499	10,900	25,458	15,050
1972-73	5,387	23,950	7,407	17,550	9,238	13,900	2,747	11,050	1,143	11,900	25,922	16,000
1973-74	6,135	25,200	8,621	18,500	9,197	14,700	2,547	11,800	1,299	13,000	27,799	17,150

7.18   Students[1] in continuing education courses by type of institution and by province, 1970-71 to 1973-74

Province or territory and year	School boards, departments of education		Department of education correspondence courses		Community colleges[2]		Universities		Total
	Part-time credit	Non-credit	Part-time credit	Non-credit	Part-time credit	Non-credit	Part-time credit	Non-credit	
Newfoundland									
1970-71	2,123	799	—	—	4,628	2,506	6,155	308	21,993
1971-72	3,433	2,978	—	—	4,705	2,120	6,503	1,945	20,374
1972-73	2,107	2,784	—	—	7,505	2,386	6,387	2,271	23,192
1973-74	2,292	2,259	—	—			6,327	2,423	
Prince Edward Island									
1970-71	1,026	1,901	38	—	1,323	332	2,069	243	7,992
1971-72	984	2,536	43	—	1,086	269	2,449	325	7,506
1972-73	677	2,966	—	—	826	365	2,319	189	8,053
1973-74	670	3,582	—	—			2,471	139	
Nova Scotia									
1970-71	4,634	10,026	631	—	4,099	138	8,016	2,820	28,967
1971-72	3,149	10,053	753	—	3,174	619	7,696	3,079	32,407
1972-73	3,245	12,361	875	—	2,821	818	8,280	3,853	38,480
1973-74	4,164	14,580	1,104	—			9,252	5,741	
New Brunswick									
1970-71	2,695	5,797	759	—	1,266	—	9,113	2,078	20,417
1971-72	1,980	5,702	553	—	1,446	—	9,052	1,864	21,331
1972-73	1,683	6,245	452	—	2,504	—	8,682	2,823	23,722
1973-74	1,208	7,721	402	—		20	8,963	2,904	
Quebec									
1970-71	104,446	50,285	5,299	—	—	17,316	93,731	22,024	293,101
1971-72	100,227	65,955	2,787	—	—	21,124	88,883	20,457	299,433
1972-73	99,456	66,668	1,777	1,961	—	23,018	82,818	27,428	303,126
1973-74	86,290	73,466	1,624	2,236	—	21,048	73,256	40,033	297,953
Ontario									
1970-71	37,692	89,433	50,198	—	46,541	34,883	104,376	41,780	414,367
1971-72	30,801	105,034	49,901	—	60,061	41,905	111,077	36,130	455,603
1972-73	21,211	126,575	47,110	—	64,666	58,480	117,402	41,339	506,370
1973-74	22,480	128,428	45,433	—			123,815	63,068	
Manitoba									
1970-71	1,795	7,651	1,347	—	3,545	4,990	16,675	5,189	41,342
1971-72	2,145	8,119	1,282	—	2,249	7,112	16,448	4,813	43,170
1972-73	1,802	8,744	1,561	—	1,930	8,014	16,179	5,523	47,688
1973-74	822	9,932	1,495	—			17,389	8,106	
Saskatchewan									
1970-71	2,555	5,886	2,166	—	4,652	1,186	9,609	5,953	35,453
1971-72	1,971	5,893	2,738	—	3,704	1,327	11,720	7,293	36,651
1972-73	2,136	6,685	1,617	—	2,867	1,103	11,319	9,863	36,842
1973-74	1,380	5,531	1,259	6			11,550	13,146	
Alberta									
1970-71	3,295	19,004	10,060	—	12,225	11,498	15,205	26,964	103,021
1971-72	2,915	16,466	6,347	—	6,236	16,321	15,204	38,366	108,908
1972-73	3,237	22,968	5,453	229	8,814	12,895	16,179	38,285	115,158
1973-74	5,586	24,227	5,160	421			15,159	42,896	
British Columbia									
1970-71	16,813	97,771	7,689	3,232	26,013	15,059	14,412	17,488	190,054
1971-72	8,666	94,973	6,942	2,923	24,958	30,437	11,028	24,450	203,787
1972-73	8,256	92,725	6,575	1,822	27,237	36,159	11,226	27,788	209,516
1973-74	9,314	88,345	5,125	2,215			12,634	28,487	

7.18   Students¹ in continuing education courses by type of institution and by province, 1970-71 to 1973-74 (concluded)

Province or territory and year	School boards, departments of education		Department of education correspondence courses		Community colleges²		Universities		Total
	Part-time credit	Non-credit	Part-time credit	Non-credit	Part-time credit	Non-credit	Part-time credit	Non-credit	
Yukon Territory and Northwest Territories									
1970-71	101	625	—	—			—	—	
1971-72	9	738	—	—	1,078	...	—	—	1,825
1972-73	221	851	—	—	542	...	—	—	1,614
1973-74	242	1,771	—	—	476	318	—	—	2,807
Canada									
1970-71	177,175	289,178	78,187	3,232			279,361	124,847	
1971-72	156,280	318,448	71,346	2,922	105,370	91,716	280,060	138,722	1,164,864
1972-73	144,031	349,572	65,420	4,012	108,161	123,128	280,791	159,362	1,234,477
1973-74	134,448	359,842	61,602	4,878	119,646	141,605	280,816	206,944	1,309,781

¹Number of individuals enrolled in school board credit courses and non-credit programs for all institutions are estimates based on course registrations.
²Includes institutes of technology, community colleges, colleges of applied arts and technology, trade and vocational schools, and colleges d'enseignement général et professionnel (CEGEPs) of Quebec.

7.19   Registrations in continuing education courses by type of institution and by province, 1970-71 to 1973-74

Province or territory and year	School boards, departments of education		Department of education correspondence courses		Community colleges¹		Universities		Total
	Part-time credit	Non-credit	Part-time credit	Non-credit	Part-time credit	Non-credit	Part-time credit	Non-credit	
Newfoundland									
1970-71	6,518	1,199	—	—			8,186	505	
1971-72	8,014	4,467	—	—	6,155	3,333	8,649	2,586	33,204
1972-73	6,282	4,176	—	—	6,257	2,819	8,495	3,021	31,050
1973-74	6,876	3,389	—	—	9,982	3,173	8,415	3,223	35,058
Prince Edward Island									
1970-71	3,605	2,852	38	—			2,752	323	
1971-72	3,770	3,803	43	—	1,760	442	3,257	432	13,507
1972-73	2,708	4,449	—	—	1,444	358	3,084	251	12,294
1973-74	2,680	5,373	—	—	1,099	485	3,286	185	13,108
Nova Scotia									
1970-71	9,267	15,039	1,027	—			10,661	3,751	
1971-72	6,299	15,080	1,063	—	5,452	183	10,236	4,095	42,408
1972-73	6,489	18,542	1,310	—	4,221	823	11,012	5,125	47,522
1973-74	8,328	21,870	1,684	—	3,752	1,088	12,305	7,636	56,663
New Brunswick									
1970-71	5,390	8,696	878	—			12,120	2,764	
1971-72	3,958	8,554	1,575	—	1,684	—	12,039	2,479	30,289
1972-73	3,366	9,366	1,220	—	1,923	—	11,547	3,754	31,176
1973-74	2,416	11,581	1,003	—	3,330	27	11,920	3,862	34,139
Quebec									
1970-71	203,206	84,478	7,948	—	—	23,030	124,662	29,292	472,616
1971-72	185,841	108,827	4,181	—	—	28,095	118,215	27,208	472,367
1972-73	175,535	135,952	2,665	2,942	—	30,614	110,148	36,479	494,335
1973-74	156,306	139,063	3,436	3,433	—	27,994	97,429	53,244	480,905

7.19   Registrations in continuing education courses by type of institution and by province, 1970-71 to 1973-74 (concluded)

Province or territory and year	School boards, departments of education		Department of education correspondence courses		Community colleges		Universities		Total
	Part-time credit	Non-credit	Part-time credit	Non-credit	Part-time credit	Non-credit	Part-time credit	Non-credit	
Ontario									
1970-71	75,384	134,149	75,296	—			138,820	55,567	
1971-72	61,601	157,551	85,989	—	61,899	46,394	147,732	48,052	609,218
1972-73	42,422	189,862	71,428	—	79,881	55,733	156,145	54,981	650,452
1973-74	44,959	192,642	77,237	—	86,006	77,778	164,674	83,880	727,176
Manitoba									
1970-71	3,589	11,476	1,820	—			22,178	6,901	
1971-72	4,289	12,179	2,043	—	4,715	6,636	21,876	6,402	58,140
1972-73	3,603	13,116	2,654	—	2,991	9,459	21,518	7,345	60,686
1973-74	1,644	14,898	1,854	—	2,567	10,659	23,127	10,781	65,530
Saskatchewan									
1970-71	5,110	8,829	3,147	—			12,780	7,918	
1971-72	3,943	8,839	4,242	—	6,187	1,578	15,588	9,701	50,078
1972-73	4,272	10,027	2,506	—	4,926	1,765	15,054	13,118	51,668
1973-74	2,760	8,297	1,825	9	3,813	1,467	15,362	17,484	51,017
Alberta									
1970-71	6,589	28,506	13,591	—			20,223	35,862	
1971-72	5,829	24,699	11,810	—	16,259	15,292	20,221	51,027	145,137
1972-73	6,472	34,453	7,907	332	8,294	21,707	21,518	50,919	151,602
1973-74	11,172	36,341	7,688	612	11,723	17,150	20,164	57,052	161,902
British Columbia									
1970-71	33,625	146,657	9,596	4,033			19,168	23,259	
1971-72	17,331	142,460	8,664	3,647	34,597	20,039	14,667	32,518	273,913
1972-73	16,512	139,088	8,123	2,250	33,194	40,481	14,931	36,958	291,537
1973-74	18,627	132,518	6,355	2,747	36,225	48,091	16,803	37,888	299,254
Yukon Territory and Northwest Territories									
1970-71	201	938	—	—			—	—	
1971-72	17	1,109	—	—	1,434	⋮	—	—	2,560
1972-73	440	1,277	—	—	721	—	—	—	2,438
1973-74	484	2,656	—	—	633	423	—	—	4,196
Canada									
1970-71	352,484	442,819	113,341	4,033			371,550	166,142	
1971-72	300,892	487,568	119,610	3,647	140,142	121,982	372,480	184,500	1,730,821
1972-73	268,101	560,308	97,813	5,524	143,852	163,759	373,452	211,951	1,824,760
1973-74	256,252	568,628	101,082	6,801	159,130	188,335	373,485	275,235	1,928,948

7.20   Registrations in formal non-credit courses by course, field of study and by province, 1973-74

Province and type of course	Primary industries	Natural sciences	Business and management	Education	Engineering and applied sciences	Fine and applied arts	Health sciences	Household sciences	Humanities	Mathematics and computer science	Social sciences	Transportation and communication	Trade and technical	Special programs for the handicapped	Unclassified	Total
NEWFOUNDLAND																
Professional development																
Extension diploma	—	—	443	118	—	34	55	—	42	107	245	—	—	—	—	1,044
Association diploma	—	—	117	—	—	—	—	—	—	—	12	—	—	—	—	129
No diploma	159	—	187	—	20	60	581	—	—	—	—	156	1,981	—	—	3,144
General interest	51	—	138	7	—	4,018	79	195	746	27	111	—	96	—	—	5,468
Total	210	—	885	125	20	4,112	715	195	788	134	368	156	2,077	—	—	9,785
PRINCE EDWARD ISLAND																
Professional development																
Extension diploma	—	—	—	—	—	—	—	—	—	—	—	—	—	—	—	—
Association diploma	—	—	—	—	—	—	—	—	—	—	—	—	—	—	—	—
No diploma	—	—	121	83	16	100	10	—	21	36	—	—	102	7	769	1,265
General interest	—	—	—	—	—	3,157	—	—	—	—	643	156	—	—	822	4,778
Total	—	—	121	83	16	3,257	10	—	21	36	643	156	102	7	1,591	6,043
NOVA SCOTIA																
Professional development																
Extension diploma	—	—	172	20	—	—	—	—	62	—	—	—	—	—	—	254
Association diploma	—	—	304	—	—	2	—	—	7	—	19	—	—	—	—	332
No diploma	423	48	1,023	217	78	268	3,222	593	153	886	644	—	389	—	—	7,944
General interest	54	31	984	67	64	11,051	341	5,642	1,797	437	295	485	805	—	11	22,064
Total	477	79	2,483	304	142	11,321	3,563	6,235	2,019	1,323	958	485	1,194	—	11	30,594
NEW BRUNSWICK																
Professional development																
Extension diploma	—	—	—	—	—	—	—	—	3	—	—	—	—	—	—	3
Association diploma	—	—	110	—	26	—	—	—	42	35	—	—	—	—	—	213
No diploma	20	—	2,469	12	259	899	123	3,656	55	—	129	175	1,179	—	—	8,976
General interest	21	85	121	5	45	3,593	—	327	1,285	—	274	424	68	—	30	6,278
Total	41	85	2,700	17	330	4,492	123	3,983	1,385	35	403	599	1,247	—	30	15,470
QUEBEC																
Professional development																
Extension diploma	—	—	15,103	20	—	19	491	69	4,318	3,153	3,847	—	669	—	—	27,689
Association diploma	—	—	5,611	—	127	—	—	—	209	873	561	—	—	—	35	7,416
No diploma	685	990	17,188	660	935	1,682	5,235	433	1,381	1,789	6,866	68	3,723	21	47	41,703
General interest	78	17	7,986	34	—	43,097	—	74,570	4,066	157	1,582	—	3,727	—	11,612	146,926
Total	763	1,007	45,888	714	1,062	44,798	5,726	75,072	9,974	5,972	12,856	68	8,119	21	11,694	223,734

7.20 Registrations in formal non-credit courses by course, field of study and by province, 1973-74 (continued)

Province and type of course	Primary industries	Natural sciences	Business and management	Education	Engineering and applied sciences	Fine and applied arts	Health sciences	Household sciences	Humanities	Mathematics and computer science	Social sciences	Transportation and communication	Trade and technical	Special programs for the handicapped	Unclassified	Total
ONTARIO																
Professional development																
Extension diploma	2,232	474	4,931	19	1,564	432	647	34	1,142	2,055	2,221	—	288	—	—	16,039
Association diploma	—	186	9,939	77	156	13	817	—	1,685	1,611	3,143	113	28	—	—	17,768
No diploma	2,324	573	22,622	1,171	387	1,817	11,993	1,135	3,984	1,939	4,545	197	4,059	—	195	56,941
General interest	2,390	994	9,496	1,204	1,063	116,490	1,303	37,946	36,074	676	11,435	14,227	21,777	67	8,410	263,552
Total	6,946	2,227	46,988	2,471	3,170	118,752	14,760	39,115	42,885	6,281	21,344	14,537	26,152	67	8,605	354,300
MANITOBA																
Professional development																
Extension diploma	—	—	—	—	—	—	—	—	—	—	69	—	—	—	—	69
Association diploma	—	—	1,366	—	37	—	—	8	121	69	277	—	31	—	—	1,909
No diploma	475	101	2,656	94	575	99	2,033	648	360	275	2,225	353	2,135	81	251	12,361
General interest	267	98	722	125	100	10,455	36	3,269	2,152	96	1,340	1,162	2,076	—	101	21,999
Total	742	199	4,744	219	712	10,554	2,069	3,925	2,633	440	3,911	1,515	4,242	81	352	36,338
SASKATCHEWAN																
Professional development																
Extension diploma	—	—	186	—	—	—	52	—	—	—	—	—	—	—	—	238
Association diploma	—	—	518	—	—	—	—	—	—	23	92	—	46	—	—	679
No diploma	6,398	18	1,019	85	46	38	5,293	278	473	56	376	61	707	—	200	15,048
General interest	253	39	740	—	39	4,801	188	2,476	1,088	49	772	199	637	—	11	11,292
Total	6,651	57	2,463	85	85	4,839	5,533	2,754	1,561	128	1,240	260	1,390	—	211	27,257
ALBERTA																
Professional development																
Extension diploma	—	—	2,146	—	—	336	54	—	173	122	679	—	—	—	—	3,510
Association diploma	—	—	2,412	—	245	—	1,472	—	331	720	751	—	14	—	—	5,945
No diploma	1,368	2,042	9,530	2,744	940	405	2,387	566	735	825	4,151	206	955	20	223	27,097
General interest	1,014	1,026	1,656	1,107	276	38,611	985	7,583	9,767	464	5,556	1,076	5,051	—	431	74,603
Total	2,382	3,068	15,744	3,851	1,461	39,352	4,898	8,149	11,006	2,131	11,137	1,282	6,020	20	654	111,155
BRITISH COLUMBIA																
Professional development																
Extension diploma	—	—	218	370	—	—	—	—	323	44	1,014	—	—	—	—	1,969
Association diploma	—	—	4,542	—	54	—	—	—	34	402	902	—	27	—	—	5,961
No diploma	4,159	853	12,777	3,241	2,146	2,224	4,647	259	3,376	2,182	6,368	405	19,747	150	130	62,664
General interest	1,086	1,347	735	889	210	68,704	209	24,133	17,050	102	6,859	10,611	1,452	—	17,263	150,650
Total	5,245	2,200	18,272	4,500	2,410	70,928	4,856	24,392	20,783	2,730	15,143	11,016	21,226	150	17,393	221,244

7.20 Registrations in formal non-credit courses by course, field of study and by province, 1973-74 (concluded)

Province and type of course	Primary industries	Natural sciences	Business and management	Education	Engineering and applied sciences	Fine and applied arts	Health sciences	Household sciences	Humanities	Mathematics and computer science	Social sciences	Transportation and communication	Trade and technical	Special programs for the handicapped	Unclassified	Total
YUKON TERRITORY AND NORTHWEST TERRITORIES																
Professional development																
Extension diploma	—	—	—	—	—	—	—	—	—	—	—	—	—	—	—	—
Association diploma	—	—	—	—	—	—	—	—	—	—	—	—	—	—	—	—
No diploma	—	—	133	15	—	15	83	7	27	—	—	—	131	—	45	456
General interest	—	35	152	—	17	976	323	430	250	—	84	11	345	—	—	2,623
Total	—	35	285	15	17	991	406	437	277	—	84	11	476	—	45	3,079
CANADA																
Professional development																
Extension diploma	2,232	474	23,199	547	1,628	821	1,299	103	6,063	5,481	8,006	—	957	—	—	50,810
Association diploma	—	186	24,870	77	581	15	2,289	8	2,429	3,733	5,774	86	146	—	35	40,229
No diploma	15,941	4,625	69,725	8,312	5,417	7,607	35,589	7,575	10,565	7,988	25,162	1,621	35,108	279	1,860	237,374
General interest	5,214	4,064	22,730	3,438	1,814	304,953	3,464	156,179	74,268	2,008	28,981	28,351	36,034	67	38,691	710,256
Total	23,387	9,349	140,524	12,374	9,440	313,396	42,641	163,865	93,325	19,210	67,923	30,058	72,245	346	40,586	1,038,669

Sources

7.1 – 7.20 Education, Science and Culture Division, Institutional and Public Finance Statistics Branch, Statistics Canada.

Labour

Chapter 8

Labour

Chapter 8

In 1976, substantial revisions went into effect in the Labour Force Survey, conducted monthly by Statistics Canada in order to indicate trends in the employment, unemployment and non-labour force situation in Canada. A general description of these changes, as well as data and summary statistics collected in both the Labour Force Survey and the decennial census are included in this chapter. There is also a review of the federal government departments concerned with employment regulations, programs and services, and such related subjects as labour legislation, compensation, pension plans, labour unions, wages and collective agreements.

In 1975 there were approximately 10,060,000 people in the civilian labour force in Canada, according to the Labour Force Survey Division (Table 8.1). Of that number, an estimated 9,363,000 persons were employed; 697,000 or 6.9% were unemployed. The proportion of the female population in the labour force increased from 38.3% in 1970 to 44.2% in 1975 (Table 8.2). It was anticipated that International Women's Year, observed in 1975, would result in a greater representation of women in the labour force in the remainder of the decade. Of approximately 7,162,000 males over 15 years of age in the population in 1970, 77.8% were in the labour force; in 1975 the participation rate was 78.4% of 8,111,000.

The government in relation to labour   8.1

Labour Canada   8.1.1

The Canada Department of Labour, now known as Labour Canada in accordance with the Federal Identity Program, was established by the Department of Labour Act (RSC 1970, c.L-2). Under this act, the Minister of Labour's responsibilities include: collecting, digesting and publishing in suitable form statistical and other information relating to the conditions of labour; instituting and conducting inquiries into important industrial questions upon which adequate information may not at present be available; issuing at least once a month *The Labour Gazette* and *La Gazette du Travail* which contain information regarding conditions of the labour market and kindred subjects.

The Minister of Labour is responsible for the Canada Labour Code, which has been in effect since July 1971 and consists of the following parts: Part I — Fair Employment Practices; Part III — Labour Standards; Part IV — Safety of Employees; and Part V — Industrial Relations. The Minister of Labour is responsible also for the administration of the Fair Wages and Hours of Labour Act, the Government Employees Compensation Act, and the Merchant Seamen Compensation Act. The Minister of Labour reports to Parliament on behalf of the Canada Labour Relations Board and the Merchant Seamen Compensation Board.

The industrial relations legislation now administered by Labour Canada applies to employers, employees and trade unions within federal jurisdiction. The department is responsible for conciliation procedures in industrial disputes, investigating complaints of unfair labour practices, refusals to bargain and violations of legislation; processing union applications for certification and decertification and conducting representation votes. It determines wage rates and hours of work as far as federal government contracts for construction or supplies are concerned, and promotes improved industrial relations through joint union-management consultation and by preventive mediation through industrial relations consultants. The department is responsible also for administering assistance granted under the Automotive Manufacturing Assistance Regulations and the Adjustment Assistance Benefits Program for displaced workers in the textile and clothing, and the footwear and tanning industries.

Reorganization of the department began in 1974-75. Its newly defined role is to promote and protect the rights of the parties involved in the world of work, a working environment conducive to physical and social well-being, and a fair return for efforts in the workplace; and in all cases to ensure equitable access to employment opportunities.

Reorganization included decentralization into five regions, with headquarters in Vancouver, Winnipeg, Toronto, Montreal and Moncton.

The department maintains records of labour legislation in the provinces and in other countries and provides liaison between the International Labour Organization and the federal and provincial governments.

8.1.2 Department of Manpower and Immigration

The Department of Manpower and Immigration recruits and develops manpower resources in line with the needs of the economy. The prime goal of Canada's manpower policy is to contribute to the country's economic and social goals by making the best use of its work force.

The department's domestic field activities are carried out in five regions through more than 450 Canada Manpower Centres and 95 Immigration Centres. Regional directors-general are responsible for both manpower and immigration activities in the field.

Broad objectives of the department in Canada are: to provide an effective employment service for both workers and employers through strategically located Canada Manpower Centres; to help workers attain their full potential through counselling or referral to skill-development and upgrading programs; to assist employers in recruiting skilled workers, and facilitate long-range manpower planning by providing up-to-date occupational and labour market information; to help labour and management adapt to technological change by assisting them to cooperate in manpower adjustment programs; to provide reception, settlement and job placement services for immigrants; to process documents for international travellers and enforce the Immigration Act and Regulations.

In the fiscal year ended March 31, 1976 Canada Manpower Centres assisted more than 851,183 persons, excluding casual workers, in finding continuing employment, and referred an additional 213,184 to full- or part-time courses under the Canada Manpower Training Program. In addition, 46,472 workers and trainees were granted moving and transportation assistance under the Canada Manpower Mobility Program.

The Manpower Division administers employment programs and services through Canada Manpower Centres. The Employer Services Branch deals with the demand side of the labour market, providing guidelines in the development and utilization of employment services for employers and specialized information on industrial needs. The branch directs the operations of the Canada Manpower Consultative Service which assists industries undergoing manpower dislocation as a result of technological change. It also administers the Canada Manpower Mobility Program to facilitate the movement of workers to areas of job opportunity. The Manpower Utilization Branch is concerned with the supply side of the labour market. It formulates policies and guidelines for employment counselling and aptitude and achievement tests used by Canada Manpower Centre counsellors. The branch also administers programs to assist new members of the labour force and students seeking summer employment. The Manpower Training Branch directs programs to help improve the qualifications of under-employed, unemployed or disadvantaged adult workers. Training courses are purchased from provincial or private schools or through contracts with employers and participants receive wage reimbursement or training allowances. The Special Programs Branch coordinates the application of all manpower programs and services to the needs of disadvantaged unemployed persons in the labour force.

In 1975-76 the federal government continued its programs to alleviate seasonal unemployment through the Local Initiatives Program, the Local Employment Assistance Program and Opportunities for Youth. The Job Creation Branch, established in 1973 as a permanent branch within the Manpower Division, directs the activities of these decentralized programs which are organized at regional, provincial and local levels. In the fiscal year ended March 31, 1976, LIP created more than 40,500 jobs through some 5,700 community oriented and managed projects. Opportunities for Youth created about 29,000 jobs in the summer of 1975, but this program was discontinued in 1976.

The Local Employment Assistance Program, intended to assist severely disadvantaged groups, funds projects on a longer-term basis than LIP and OFY. The number of projects in operation at March 31, 1976 was 108 employing 1,687 persons.

Community Employment Strategy, introduced by the minister in November 1974 completed its first year of a developmental phase. Discussions and studies that originated as part of the Federal-Provincial Social Security Review were undertaken and 11 provinces and territories began implementation of the program. The goal of Community Employment is to provide satisfactory work opportunities for people who experience regular unemployment and who depend on government support (or transfer payments) for some or all of their income. Existing programs and job opportunities are used wherever possible to utilize community initiative and resources, creating a sense of community involvement and responsibility.

The Manpower Delivery System provides three levels of service to people looking for employment. The first level consists of a Job Information Centre where job vacancies are displayed enabling clients to decide themselves which jobs they think they can fill. In addition, an Employment Opportunity Library at the centre contains information about the department's programs and the services of other departments and agencies. The second level of service is directed at people who are basically employable but who could benefit from counselling, from courses provided through the Canada Manpower Training Program or from assistance in finding and moving to jobs in other areas through the Canada Manpower Mobility Program. The third level is designed for clients who require concentrated counselling. Counsellors may use outside agencies for special assistance in helping these people to become employable. They are then referred to a job or may make selections from a "job bank".

The Immigration Division is responsible for the selection and reception of people coming to Canada who will be able to establish themselves economically, culturally and socially. They include people whose skills are required by the Canadian economy, relatives of Canadian residents, and refugees and non-immigrants entering on a short-term basis. The department is also responsible for enforcement and control measures to prevent the immigration of undesirable persons.

Since January 1973, all non-immigrants entering Canada to take temporary work must have an employment visa. Visitors are not permitted to come to Canada to look for work. This regulation protects the Canadian labour force against the unwarranted use of foreign labour.

To obtain an employment visa, the person concerned must have pre-arranged employment and certification by a Canada Manpower Centre that no Canadian citizen or landed immigrant is available for that job. Arrangements must be made at a Canadian immigration office in the person's own country.

The Strategic Planning and Research Division collects and analyzes information on national, regional and local labour market conditions in order to give direction to the department's policies and programs. In addition, it carries out research programs in support of its own and other divisions' activities and develops career and occupational counselling and training materials.

8.1.3   Federal and provincial labour legislation

8.1.3.1   Jurisdictions

The Canada Labour Code (RSC 1970, c.L-1) applies only to federal undertakings and any other operations that Parliament declares are for the general advantage of Canada or two or more of its provinces. The code consolidated previous legislation regulating employment practices and labour standards in the federal jurisdiction.

Because it imposes conditions on the rights of the employer and employee to enter into a contract of employment, labour legislation is, generally speaking, law in relation to civil rights, and provincial legislatures are authorized to make laws in relation both to local works and to property and civil rights. Power to enact labour legislation has therefore become largely a provincial prerogative, under which a large body of legislation has been enacted affecting working hours, minimum wages, the physical conditions of workplaces, apprenticeship and training, wage payment and wage collection, labour-management relations and workmen's compensation.

8.1.3.2   Federal labour legislation

Industrial relations. The Mediation and Conciliation Branch of the Department of Labour administers the provisions of Part V of the Canada Labour Code (Industrial Relations) relating to the application of formal conciliation procedures (i.e. the appointment of conciliation officers, conciliation commissioners and the establishment of conciliation boards). The branch also provides mediation services to parties in post-conciliation negotiations, including strike and lockout situations. If a dispute or difference between any employer and employees exists in an industry, the Minister of Labour may refer the matter to an Industrial Inquiry Commission for investigation. On behalf of the minister, the branch administers the code's provisions relating to certain types of complaints which must receive ministerial consent before they can be referred to the Canada Labour Relations Board. Other violations of the code referring ministerial consent to prosecution are also handled by the branch.

When requested, the minister may appoint single arbitrators or arbitration board chairmen if parties or nominees are unable to agree on the selection.

The Canada Labour Relations Board administers provisions contained in Part V of the Canada Labour Code governing the acquisition and termination of bargaining rights; successor rights and obligations; the disposition of applications relating to technological change, and to illegal strikes and lockouts; complaints of unfair practices; and granting of access to employers' premises.

Fair employment practices. Part I of the Canada Labour Code (Fair Employment Practices) prohibits discrimination in employment on the grounds of race, colour, religion or national origin in any federal work, undertaking or business. It covers discrimination by employers, by trade unions in regard to membership or employment, by employers who use employment agencies that discriminate, and in the use of any form of application for employment, advertisement, written or oral inquiry that expresses directly or indirectly any limitation, specification or preference as to race, colour, religion or national origin.

Labour standards. Part III of the Canada Labour Code (Labour Standards) provides minimum standards of employment applicable to employers and employees in industries that are under the legislative authority of the Parliament of Canada.

The code sets both standard and maximum hours of work. The overtime rate (one and a half times the regular rate) must be paid after eight hours in a day and 40 hours in a week, to a maximum of 48 hours in a week. Hours may be averaged when an employee's schedule of hours varies from day to day or week to week because of the nature of the work. If the Minister of Labour is satisfied that exceptional circumstances justify the additional hours, he may issue a permit allowing an employee to exceed the maximum hours. The Governor in Council may make regulations varying the standard and maximum hours for classes of employees in any specified industrial establishment where the code standards would be unduly prejudicial to the interest of the employees or seriously detrimental to the operation of the establishment. An inquiry must be held before such regulations may be made.

The minimum wage is $2.90 an hour for all persons 17 years of age or over and $2.65 an hour for persons under 17 as of April 1, 1976. The Governor in Council may issue orders from time to time increasing the minimum rate.

Employees are entitled to a two-week vacation with pay each year and a holiday with pay on each of the eight general holidays, or substitutes for them.

An employer must give advance notice to the Minister of Labour and the union, with a copy to the Department of Manpower and Immigration, when dismissing 50 or more employees during a four-week period. The length of notice varies according to the number of employees being dismissed: 50-100 employees, eight weeks; 101-300 employees, 12 weeks; more than 300 employees, 16 weeks. In addition, the employer and the trade union must provide the Department of Manpower and Immigration with whatever information it requests to assist the employees. The requirement to give notice may be waived for an industrial establishment or a specified class of employees by an order of the Minister of Labour, subject to any terms or conditions that he may determine.

Under the code's provisions respecting individual dismissals, every employee with three months service (except a manager, superintendent or member of a profession) is entitled to two weeks notice of termination of his employment. In lieu of such notice, he is entitled to two weeks wages at his regular rate for his regular hours of work. In addition, an employee who has completed five consecutive years of continuous employment is entitled to severance pay based on two days wages at the regular rate for the regular hours of work, for each year of employment up to a maximum of 40 days wages. However, the employer is not required to give severance pay to an employee who is dismissed for just cause or to a person who, on termination of employment, is entitled to a retirement pension.

The maternity protection provisions grant 17 weeks of maternity leave — 11 weeks before and six weeks after childbirth — and ensure job security to women absent from work because of pregnancy. To be eligible for maternity leave, a woman must have been continuously employed by her employer for 12 months. The code provides for voluntary prenatal leave up to 11 weeks before the anticipated date of delivery, and this period extends to the actual date of confinement.

The code prohibits an employer from paying men and women employees at different rates if they work in the same establishment at equally demanding jobs under the same or similar conditions. It also prohibits an employer from dismissing, laying off or suspending an employee solely because of garnishment.

Fair wages policy. Wages and hours on government construction contracts are regulated by the Fair Wages and Hours of Labour Act and Regulations. The rates are never less than the minimum hourly rate prescribed by Part III (Labour Standards) of the Canada Labour Code. Wages and hours of work on contracts for equipment and supplies are regulated by Order in Council.

Safety of employees. Part IV of the Canada Labour Code (Safety of Employees) incorporates the Canada Labour (Safety) Code of 1968, which was the first general safety legislation passed by the Parliament of Canada. To ensure safe working conditions for all employees in industries and undertakings under federal jurisdiction, Part IV provides for all the elements of a complete industrial safety program; obliges employers and employees to perform their duties in a safe manner and authorizes the making of regulations for dealing with occupational safety problems; complements other federal laws and provincial legislation;

authorizes advisory committees and special task forces to assist in developing the program under continuous consultation among federal and provincial government departments, industry and organized labour; and provides for research into causes and prevention of accidents and for an extended safety education program. Employees of the public service of Canada, although not covered by Part IV of the Canada Labour Code, are given equivalent protection under standards, issued by Treasury Board, complementary to the safety and health regulations of Part IV of the code. Regional safety officers and federally authorized provincial inspectors enforce the safety regulations.

As of January 31, 1975, regulations were in force governing coal mine safety, elevating devices, first aid, machine-guarding, noise control, hand tools, fire safety, temporary work structures, confined spaces, lighting, boilers and pressure vessels, building safety, dangerous substances, electrical safety, materials handling, protective clothing and equipment, sanitation, hours of service in the motor transport industry, and accident investigation and reporting.

8.1.3.3 Provincial labour legislation

Industrial relations. All provinces have legislation similar in principle to Part V of the Canada Labour Code, designed to establish harmonious relations between employers and employees and to facilitate the settlement of industrial disputes. These laws guarantee freedom of association and the right to organize, establish machinery (labour relations boards or other administrative systems) for the certification of a trade union as the exclusive bargaining agent of an appropriate unit of employees, and require an employer to bargain with the certified trade union representing his employees.

Alberta, Ontario, New Brunswick, Nova Scotia, Prince Edward Island and Newfoundland have special provisions in their general labour relations legislation dealing with accreditation of employers' organizations in the construction industry. In British Columbia accreditation provisions are not limited to the construction industry. Under every jurisdiction the legislation requires that the parties comply with conciliation or mediation procedures before a strike or lockout may legally take place. Every collective agreement must provide for the final settlement of disputes arising out of interpretation or application of the agreement without stoppage of work. Strikes and lockouts are prohibited during the term of a collective agreement. Unfair labour practices are prohibited under every legislation. In some provinces labour relations for "special groups" namely teachers, municipal and provincial police personnel, municipal firemen, hospital workers, civil servants and employees of Crown corporations are regulated by special legislation.

Employment standards. Most provincial and territorial jurisdictions have legislated some or all of the recognized basic standards, such as: annual vacations with pay, statutory holidays, hours of work and overtime rates, maternity protection, minimum wage rates and termination of employment.

Hours of work. In Alberta and British Columbia hours are limited to eight a day and 44 a week, and in Ontario to eight a day and 48 a week. One and a half times the regular rate is to be paid after eight and 44 hours in Alberta and after eight and 40 in British Columbia. The Ontario Act requires, with some exceptions, that one and a half times the regular rate be paid for work done, beyond 44 hours. The Manitoba and Saskatchewan acts do not limit daily and weekly hours but require the payment of one and a half times the regular rate if work is continued after eight and 40 hours; this provision applies to shop employees in Newfoundland where the rate for other employees is effective after 44 hours. In Nova Scotia, Newfoundland and Prince Edward Island one and a half times the regular rate must be paid after 48 hours in a week, in Quebec after 45 hours and in New Brunswick after 44 hours. One and a half times the regular rate is to be paid after standard hours of eight a day and 44 a week in the Northwest Territories and eight

a day and 40 a week in the Yukon Territory. Some exceptions are provided for in all acts. No general standard of hours of work are in effect in New Brunswick or Newfoundland.

Minimum wages. All jurisdictions have enacted minimum wage legislation to ensure adequate living standards for workers. These laws vest authority in a minimum-wage-fixing board or the Lieutenant Governor in Council to establish minimum wages for employees. Minimum wage orders are reviewed fairly frequently. In most provinces minimum wage orders now cover practically all employment. Domestic service in private homes is excluded in all provinces except Prince Edward Island. In Newfoundland, an employer may not pay less than $30 a week for domestic service. Farm labour is also excluded except in Newfoundland, but in several provinces people employed in farm-related occupations are covered. In Ontario and Nova Scotia this exclusion is limited to farming proper, although certain farm-related occupations are covered. Fruit, vegetable and tobacco harvesters are covered by the minimum wage in Ontario. Minimum wage rates apply in Manitoba to those employed in selling horticultural or market garden products grown by another person, in Saskatchewan to those in egg hatcheries, greenhouses, nurseries and brush-clearing operations, and in Alberta and Prince Edward Island to farm workers employed in commercial undertakings. Minimum wage rates set by the orders apply throughout the province and are the same for both sexes.

In the Northwest Territories and the Yukon, Labour Standards Regulations were issued under the Labour Standards Ordinance. Both ordinances require the payment of a minimum rate of wages to employees who are 17 and over.

Where employees are paid on a basis other than time, or on a combined basis of time and some other basis, they are required to receive the equivalent of the minimum wage. Provision is made in the legislation of almost all jurisdictions for the employment of handicapped workers at rates below the established minimum, usually under a system of individual permits. In all jurisdictions except New Brunswick, Newfoundland, Saskatchewan and the Yukon Territory, the orders set special minimum rates for young workers.

As of August 1, 1976, the minimum hourly wage rates for experienced adult workers were as follows: Newfoundland $2.50, Prince Edward Island $2.50, Nova Scotia $2.50, New Brunswick $2.55, Quebec $2.87, Ontario $2.65, Manitoba $2.60, Saskatchewan $2.80, Alberta $2.75, British Columbia $3.00, Northwest Territories $3.00 and Yukon Territory $3.00.

Regulation of wages and hours in certain industries. In five provinces, the general orders are supplemented by special orders, applying to a particular industry, occupation or class of workers and in some cases taking into account a special skill. British Columbia, which originally had a separate minimum wage order for each industry or occupation, has been consolidating its orders. Twelve special orders still remain; the minimum rates set by these orders are the same as the rate set in the general order. Quebec has three industry orders, governing the retail food trade, sawmills and forest operations. Formerly there were eight special orders. The rates set by all three special orders are lower than the general rates.

The other three provinces set only a few special rates. Nova Scotia has established rates for employees in beauty parlours and province-wide rates for logging and forest operations and for road building and heavy construction. In New Brunswick special rates have been set for construction, mining and primary transportation and for logging, forest and sawmill operations. In Alberta a weekly rate has been set for commercial agents and sales people. In Ontario special rates contained within the general regulation apply to the construction and ambulance service industries.

Under the Quebec Collective Agreement Decrees Act, certain terms of a collective agreement, including those dealing with hours and wages, may be made binding on all employers and employees in the industry concerned in a defined area, provided the parties to the agreement represent a sufficient proportion of the industry. The standards made binding under this procedure are contained in a decree, which has the force of law. Approximately 94 decrees applying to the garment trades, barbering and hairdressing, commercial establishments, garage and service stations, and other industries and services are in effect; a number of them apply throughout the province. Working conditions in the construction industry are governed by decrees under a separate act — the Construction Industry Labour Relations Act, 1968.

The Construction Industry Wages Act in Manitoba, which applies to both private and public construction work, provides for setting minimum wage rates and maximum hours of work at regular rates for employees in the construction industry, on the recommendation of a board equally representative of employers and employees, with a member of the public as chairman. Under this act annual schedules set the regular work week and hourly wage rates for various classifications of workers in the heavy construction industry, in the Greater Winnipeg building construction industry, in rural building construction and on major building projects.

Annual vacations and public holidays. All jurisdictions have annual vacations legislation applicable to most industries. The general standard is two weeks. In Manitoba workers are entitled to three weeks after five years of service, and in Saskatchewan three weeks after one year and four weeks after 13 years (with a gradual reduction to result in four weeks after 10 years as of July 1, 1978). Several jurisdictions, including the federal, Alberta, British Columbia, Manitoba, New Brunswick, Nova Scotia, Ontario, Saskatchewan, the Yukon Territory and the Northwest Territories have enacted legislation of general application dealing with public holidays. The number of holidays varies from six to nine and the provisions for payment also vary.

Vacation pay equals 4% of annual earnings in British Columbia, Newfoundland, Nova Scotia, Prince Edward Island, New Brunswick, the Yukon Territory, the Northwest Territories, Quebec and Ontario (2% in the first year); in Manitoba and Alberta, regular pay; and in Saskatchewan 3/52nds of annual earnings. The federal rate is 4%.

Termination of employment. As in the federal jurisdiction, eight provinces have legislation requiring an employer to give notice to the individual worker whose employment is to be terminated. In Saskatchewan and Prince Edward Island an employer must give an individual employee one week's written notice of termination; in Manitoba and Newfoundland, one regular pay period. In Alberta, Nova Scotia and Ontario the length of notice varies with the period of employment. In Ontario and Nova Scotia: three months to two years, one week; two to five years, two weeks; five to 10 years, four weeks; 10 years or more, eight weeks. Nova Scotia is similar to Ontario except that an employee with at least 10 years' service may not be discharged without just cause. In Alberta: three months but less than two years, seven days; two years or more, 14 days. Quebec requires the employer of a domestic, a servant, journeyman or labourer to give one week's notice of termination if the employee is hired by the week, two weeks' notice if hired by the month and a month's notice if hired by the year. Alberta, Manitoba, Newfoundland, Nova Scotia, Prince Edward Island and Quebec require an employee to give similar notice before quitting his job.

As in the federal jurisdiction, four provinces require an employer to give advance notice of a planned termination of employment or lay-off of a group of employees. The Manitoba and Ontario group notice requirements apply when an employer plans to terminate the employment of 50 or more persons within four weeks or less. The length of notice is related to the number of workers involved. In Manitoba the requirements are: 50-100 employees, 8 weeks; 101-300, 12 weeks; over 300, 16 weeks. In Ontario: 50-199, 8 weeks; 200-499, 12 weeks; 500 or more, 16 weeks. The Nova Scotia and Quebec group notice requirements apply when an employer contemplates the dismissal of 10 or more employees within a period of two months. Again, the length of notice required varies with the number of workers involved: 10-100, two months; 101-300, three months; 301 and over, four months.

Maternity protection. Several provinces have legislation to ensure the health and job security of women workers before and after childbirth. The British Columbia and New Brunswick acts provide for six weeks' leave before childbirth and six weeks after; the Manitoba and Nova Scotia acts allow 11 weeks before and six after. Ontario provides for a minimum of 17 weeks' leave. In Saskatchewan, the act provides for 12 weeks before and six weeks after. The postnatal leave is compulsory, unless a medical doctor authorizes an earlier return to work. In all jurisdictions, the right to maternity leave is supplemented by a guarantee that an employee will not lose her employment because of absence on maternity leave.

Human rights. Laws to ensure fair employment practices have been enacted throughout Canada. These include employment and employment-related subjects such as membership in trade unions. All provinces have augmented this legislation to form a human rights code. Most of these codes cover general matters, employment and employment-related subjects, and occupancy and property matters.

Most jurisdictions prohibit discrimination on grounds of race, religion, national origin, colour, sex, age and marital status. In selected cases the prohibited grounds include political beliefs, ethnic origin, physical handicap, creed and source of income.

Equal pay provisions are in force everywhere in Canada. Criteria for determining the meaning of equal work vary from one act to another. Methods of enforcement also vary.

Apprenticeship. All provinces have apprenticeship laws providing for an organized procedure of on-the-job training and school instruction in designated skilled trades, and statutory provision is made in most provinces for issuing qualification certificates, on application, to qualified tradesmen in certain trades. In some provinces legislation is in effect making it mandatory for certain classes of tradesmen to hold a certificate of competency.

Accident prevention. In Canada the provincial legislatures have the power to enact laws and regulations concerning the protection of workers against industrial accidents or diseases. Legal standards designed to ensure the safety, health and welfare of persons employed in industrial and commercial establishments, in mines and quarries and in other work places exist in all provinces. The authorities responsible for the administration of such standards are, in the main, the departments of labour, health and mines, and the workmen's compensation boards.

General safety laws and regulations cover a great part of all employment in the country except agriculture, mining and domestic service. They deal with most aspects of industrial safety and health in the working environment. Safeguards for the protection of workers are established with respect to such matters as sanitation, heating, lighting, ventilation and the guarding of dangerous machinery.

Other safety laws and regulations are of a more specific application. They are concerned with hazardous equipment and installations such as boilers and pressure vessels, electrical installations, elevating devices and gas and oil burning equipment. Others are directed toward hazardous industries such as mining, construction, excavation and logging.

Safety inspection is provided for in all provinces. An inspector is authorized to give directions for the carrying out of any matter regulated by the legislation. Penalties exist where an employer contravenes any provision of an occupational safety act or regulation or where he fails or neglects to comply with a direction made by a safety inspector.

Workmen's compensation. In Canada, workmen's compensation laws are within the competence of the provincial legislatures and are applicable to the majority of employers in each province. In all provinces compensation is provided for workers in most types of industries, for personal injuries sustained in the course of employment unless the disablement is for less than a stated number of days or where the injury is attributable solely to the worker's serious and wilful misconduct and does not result in death or serious disablement. Compensation is also payable for specified industrial diseases.

Each workmen's compensation act provides for an accident fund administered by a workmen's compensation board to which employers are required to contribute and from which compensation and medical benefits are paid. The acts thus provide for a system of compulsory collective liability, relieving employers of individual responsibility for accident costs. The assessment rate for each class of industry is fixed by the board according to the hazards of the class.

A worker entitled to receive compensation under a workmen's compensation act has no right of action against his employer for injury from an accident occurring in the course of employment or for an industrial disease.

Various types of benefits are provided for a worker protected by workmen's compensation legislation. Benefits for disability are based on a percentage of average weekly earnings subject to an annual ceiling. Persons having a permanent or temporary total disability are presumed not to be able to work at all and receive 75% of their average weekly earnings for as long as the disability lasts. Partial disablement entitles a worker to a proportionate compensation. Medical and hospital benefits are provided without limitation regardless of a waiting period.

One of the primary objectives of the compensation process in Canada is the rehabilitation of the injured worker. The boards may adopt any means considered expedient to aid in getting workers back to work and in lessening any handicap.

When a worker dies from an industrial accident or disease, the dependents are entitled to a monthly payment fixed by legislation. However, for recent cases in Alberta and Manitoba, the widow receives the permanent total disability pension the deceased worker would have been entitled to, if he had lived. This is also true for a widow with two or more children in British Columbia. In all provinces payments are made in respect of children. In Ontario and Quebec such payments may continue for as long as the child is pursuing his studies.

8.2   The labour force

8.2.1   Labour force (monthly surveys)

Since 1946, statistics relating to employment and unemployment at the national level, and since 1966 at the provincial level, have been provided through the Labour Force Survey. From 1945 until 1952, the survey was conducted quarterly and since November 1952, it has been carried out monthly. In January 1976, after three years of developmental work, substantial revisions to the survey were introduced to enhance the quality of the data and increase the range of data collected, particularly information relating to the dynamics of the labour market.

The sample used in the survey was designed to represent all persons in the population 15 years of age and over residing in Canada with the exception of the following: residents of the Yukon and Northwest Territories, persons living on Indian reserves, inmates of institutions and full-time members of the Armed Forces. Interviews are carried out in approximately 55,000 households chosen by area sampling methods across the country. (Until March 1977 the sample size had been fixed at approximately 30,000 households.) The estimates of employment, unemployment and non-labour force activity generated from the survey refer to a specific week each month, normally the week containing the 15th day.

The labour force is composed of that portion of the civilian non-institutional population 15 years of age and over who, during the reference week, were employed or unemployed.

Employment by industrial group, 1965 and 1975

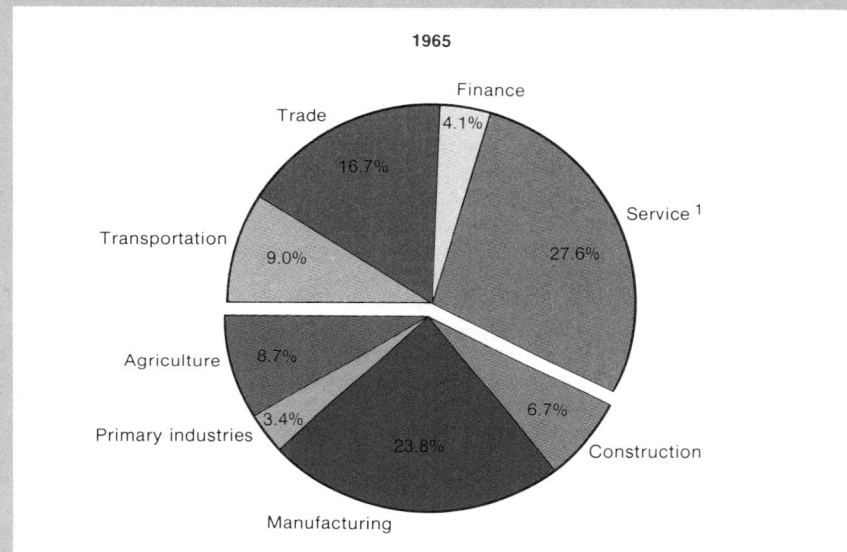

1965

- Finance 4.1%
- Trade 16.7%
- Service [1] 27.6%
- Transportation 9.0%
- Agriculture 8.7%
- Primary industries 3.4%
- Manufacturing 23.8%
- Construction 6.7%

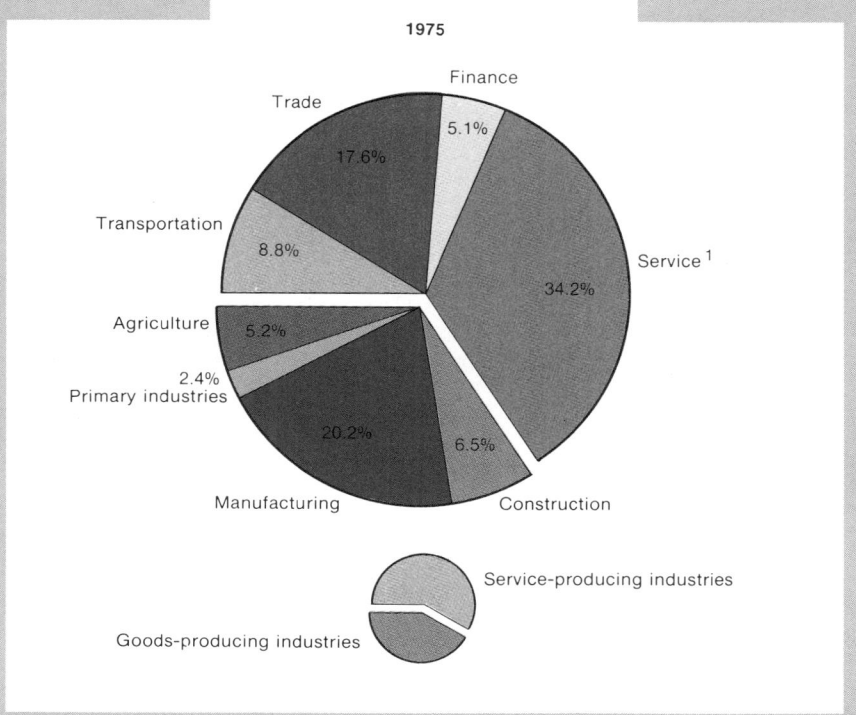

1975

- Finance 5.1%
- Trade 17.6%
- Service [1] 34.2%
- Transportation 8.8%
- Agriculture 5.2%
- Primary industries 2.4%
- Manufacturing 20.2%
- Construction 6.5%

- Service-producing industries
- Goods-producing industries

1. Includes public administration.

The employed include all persons who, during the reference week, did any work for pay or profit; that is, paid work in an employer-employee relationship or self-employment. Also included is unpaid family work which contributed directly to the operation of a farm, business or professional practice owned or operated by a related member of the household. The employed also include persons who had jobs but were not at work due to illness or disability, personal or family responsibilities, bad weather, labour dispute or other reason.

The unemployed are those who, during the reference week, were without work, had actively looked for work in the past four weeks and were available for work; had not actively looked for work in the past four weeks but had been on lay-off (with the expectation of returning to work) for 26 weeks or less and were available for work; or had a new job to start in four weeks or less and were available for work. Persons not in the labour force are those who are neither employed nor unemployed.

Because they are based on a sample of households, estimates derived from the labour force survey are subject to sampling error. In the design and processing of the survey, extensive efforts are made to minimize the sampling error; in general, the error, expressed as a percentage of the estimate, tends to decrease as the size of the estimate increases.

As noted, the substantial revisions were introduced into the Labour Force Survey in January 1976. These revisions included the introduction of an entirely new and expanded questionnaire, the adjustment of some definitions, a revision of the sample frame, a re-benchmarking of the population totals used to weight the sample and the adoption of new methods of transmitting and processing the survey information. This revised survey was run in parallel with the former survey throughout 1975 and, as expected, some of the estimates from the two surveys differed significantly. However, by using the relationships in the estimates from the two surveys for 1975, the estimates from the former survey have been revised for the period 1970 to 1974 allowing for the production of a consistent time series from 1970 to the present.

In the period 1970-75, the total Canadian labour force increased by 1.7 million persons or 19.8%. This was composed of an increase of 31% in the number of women in the labour force and an increase in the number of men of only 14%. These increases reflected corresponding increases in the participation rates (the labour force as a percentage of the corresponding population aged 15 and over) for women from 38.3% in 1970 to 44.2% in 1975 and for men from 77.8% to 78.4%.

The increase in the proportion of men in the labour force was generated by the increase in the participation rate of young males (age 15-24) from 62.5% to 69.0% which more than offset the slight decline for older males (25 and over) from 83.4% to 81.9%. In the case of women, both age groups increased their participation although the rise was more pronounced among those aged 15-24.

The total number of persons employed in Canada rose by 1.4 million or 18.2% over the 1970-75 period. Although employment rose in all provinces the increases were not uniform, ranging from 12.0% in Saskatchewan to 25.3% in British Columbia. Other increases were 17.8% in Newfoundland, 22.9% in Prince Edward Island, 15.2% in Nova Scotia, 19.3% in New Brunswick, 15.2% in Quebec, 19.0% in Ontario, 13.2% in Manitoba, and 22.9% in Alberta.

Unemployment as a percentage of the labour force varied from 5.4% in 1974 to 6.9% in 1975 with an average over the entire 1970-75 period of 6.0%. Throughout those years women had higher unemployment rates than men and young persons (age 15-24) had considerably higher rates than persons age 25 and over.

8.2.2   Labour force (1971 Census)

At each decennial census of Canada, questions are asked of persons 15 years of age and over relating to their employment status and present work activities. The census questions have the advantage of securing far more detailed information on the occupational and industrial structure and on other characteristics of the labour force than the regular monthly surveys in terms of both geographical areas and classifications. Summary tabulations from the 1971 Census are presented in Tables 8.6 - 8.11, 8.31 and 8.32. Further information is available in the many census reports issued on these and other aspects of Canada's labour force (see 1971 Census Publications, Statistics Canada Catalogue Nos. 94-701 to 94-789).

Because of differences in coverage, methodology and reference period, data from the census are in some ways not comparable with those collected by the monthly labour force survey. Of particular importance among these differences are those of coverage and actual questions asked, even though the fundamental concepts are the same. As stated in the preceding section, the small labour force survey sample (about 30,000 households) included persons 14 years and over but excluded the Yukon Territory and Northwest Territories, Indian reserves, members of the Armed Forces, overseas households and inmates of institutions. The 1971 Census questions were asked of all persons 15 years and over in a 33⅓% sample of households (about 2 million).

Foreign-born persons in the labour force. The labour force at the June 1, 1971 Census included all persons 15 years and over who, during the week preceding the enumeration, worked for pay or profit, did unpaid work in a family farm or business, looked for work, were on temporary lay-off or had jobs from which they were temporarily absent because of illness, vacation or strike. Results from the 1971 Census indicate that immigrants constituted 20% of the labour force. Tables 8.6 and 8.7 present data on the number of immigrants by country of origin and region of Canadian residence in 1971 and by age, sex and period of immigration to Canada. According to these figures, more than four fifths of the immigrants in the labour force came from Europe and one quarter from Britain. Over half the immigrants are concentrated in Ontario where they form more than a quarter of the labour force, as they do in British Columbia, while they make up less than 5% of the labour force in the Atlantic provinces. Table 8.7 indicates that immigrants tend to be older than the native-born, with only 15% under the age of 25 compared with 26%, and are to be found mainly in the 25-54 age range (29%). The proportion of immigrant workers aged 65 and over is more than twice that of native-born workers.

Class of worker. In connection with the questions on occupation and industry, the respondent was asked to report whether he was mainly working for wages and salary or was self-employed or was working without pay in a family business or farm. Table 8.8 provides 1961 and 1971 data for individuals in the experienced labour force, which for 1971 is defined as the total labour force minus persons looking for work, who last worked prior to January 1, 1970 or who never worked. For 1961 persons who never worked were excluded but persons looking for work but who had not worked since January 1, 1960 were included. The figures are not strictly comparable because of these differences in definition and because the question was asked in greater detail in 1971, in an attempt to isolate individuals such as executives with large shares in incorporated businesses who tend to report themselves as self-employed rather than as paid workers. It is uncertain how many of these individuals counted themselves as self-employed in 1961. However, even assuming that all of them did and adjusting the 1971 figures accordingly (to yield a count of 799,555, not shown in the table), the self-employed experienced at least a 15% decline in absolute terms since 1961, dropping from 14.5% of the labour force to 9%. On the other hand, paid workers increased from 83% to 87%, while the proportion of unpaid family workers rose slightly from 2.5% to almost 3.3%. The increase in this group is attributable to the more than twofold rise in the number of women in this category. However, response and processing errors inflated the 1971 count of unpaid female family workers by about 25% and the true increase was therefore less than twofold.

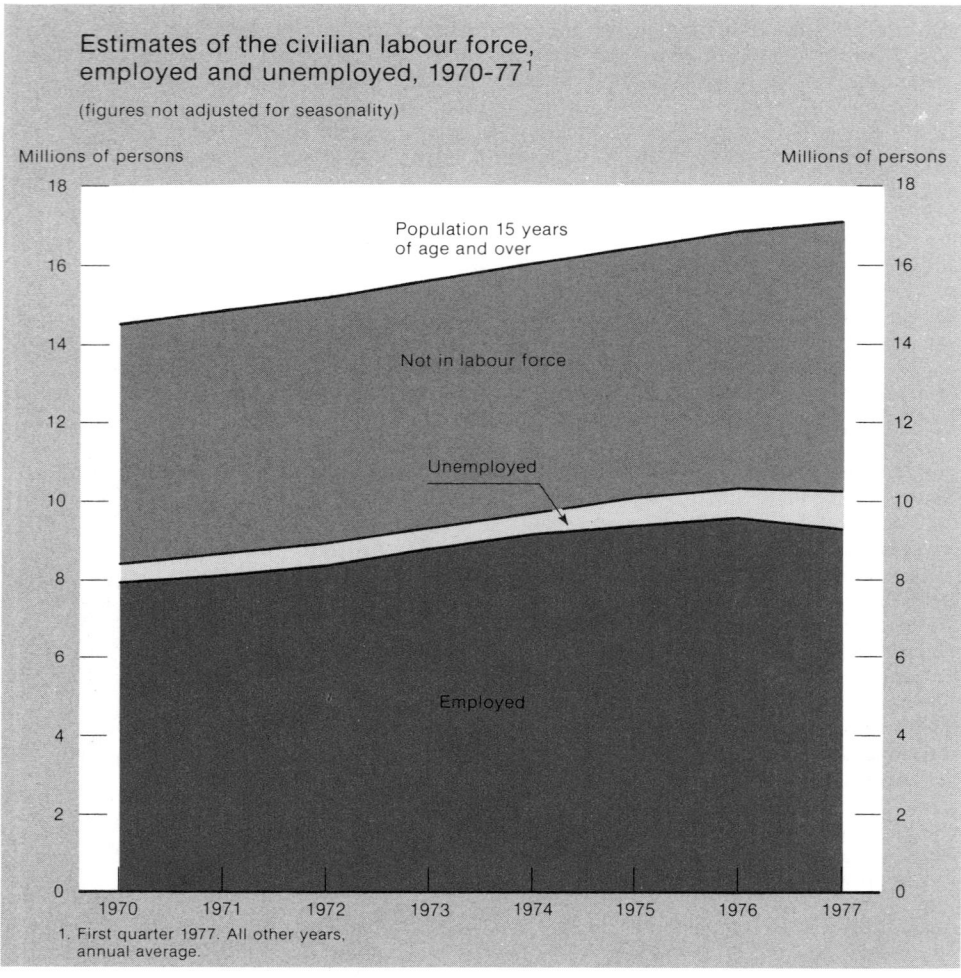

Estimates of the civilian labour force, employed and unemployed, 1970-77[1]

(figures not adjusted for seasonality)

1. First quarter 1977. All other years, annual average.

Persons who worked during 1970. In addition to information on the total (or current) labour force the 1971 Census also provided data on weeks worked during 1970, whether full-time or part-time, as well as average employment income received (Table 8.31). Respondents were asked to report 1970 income under 10 headings, covering income from employment, from government transfer payments and from other sources. Employment income was reported under three headings: income from wages, salaries, tips and commissions, net income from business or professional practice and net farm income. In the table, average employment income is computed only for those persons who, having worked in 1970, actually received payment for such work during the calendar year 1970. Unpaid family workers, persons who worked for payment in kind only and persons who may have worked during the Christmas season but who were not paid until 1971 are excluded.

The figures in Table 8.31 indicate that, while most individuals worked full-time (82%) during 1970, a larger proportion of females (29%) than males (11.6%) worked part-time. On the other hand, only 68.6% worked full-year (40-52 weeks) while 63% worked both full-time and full-year.

Males had higher average employment income than females, double that of females in 1970. Even for part-time work, in which females outnumbered males, male employment income was more than 50% higher. For full-time work, both male and female full-year (40-52 weeks) average employment income ($8,046 and $4,749, respectively) was more than double part-year (1-39 weeks) average employment income ($3,369 and $1,922, respectively), with the increase for females slightly higher. Nonetheless, full-year full-time male employment income was about 69% higher than that for females. It should be recalled in connection with these differences that the occupational distribution of males differs considerably from that of females.

Labour force by industry. In the 1971 Census respondents were asked for the name of their employer and the type of business, industry or service the firm was engaged in. For those self-employed, the name of the firm and type of activity were requested. Because a revised industrial classification was used (see *Standard industrial classification manual,* Catalogue No. 12-501) special tabulations had to be made in order to compare 1971 data with 1961. Government-owned and operated establishments primarily engaged in activities assigned to other industries, such as transportation, communication (including the post office), liquor sales, health and educational services, were classified to those industries rather than to Public Administration. The "Public Administration and Defence" division covers establishments primarily engaged in activities such as enacting legislation administering justice, collecting revenue and defence.

Table 8.9 shows the number of people 15 years of age and over in the labour force by sex and major industrial group for 1961 and 1971. Two significant changes are dramatically illustrated: the rapid growth of the tertiary or service sector of the economy and the increased participation of women in the labour force. From 1961 to 1971 the labour force in the primary industrial sector decreased by 174,335 or 20%, whereas the tertiary sector rose by 1,398,091 persons or 39%; the secondary sector, manufacturing and construction, increased by 22% over the decade. The number of women in the labour force rose from 1,766,332 in 1961 to 2,961,210 in 1971 with increases in all sectors but most particularly in the service sector (71%).

Table 8.10 shows the provincial distribution of the main industrial sectors. The number of people in the labour force in the primary industries declined in all provinces except British Columbia (where it rose 24%), and most particularly in Quebec (−39%); even in Saskatchewan, where the primary industries still account for 32% of the labour force, the decrease was 13%. In contrast to Saskatchewan, only 6% of Ontario's labour force is classified as being in the primary sector.

The secondary sector accounted for 29% of Canada's labour force in 1961 and 28% in 1971, when most provinces had between 18% and 25% of their labour force employed in this sector. In Quebec and Ontario 32% and 33%, respectively, were employed in manufacturing and construction, but in Saskatchewan the proportion was only 11%.

Growth in the tertiary or service sector has already been mentioned. Provincially, while both the number and proportion rose in all provinces after 1961, Prince Edward Island in 1971 had 61% of its labour force devoted to service industries compared to 50% in 1961. Quebec too altered its proportion considerably from 54% to 62%. In their overall labour force breakdowns, Nova Scotia with 68% and British Columbia with 67% led the country with over two thirds of their labour force in the service sector.

Occupation by sex. "Occupation" at the time of the 1971 Census was determined by three questions summarizing the kind of work performed by the respondent during the week prior to the census. Persons who were not employed during that week were asked to provide similar information on the work performed over the longest period of employment since January 1, 1970. The classification of occupations is based on the Canadian Classification and Dictionary of

Occupations of 1971 (see *Occupational classification manual,* Census of Canada 1971, Volume I, Catalogue No. 12-536).

The information shown in Table 8.11 has considerable social interest as it indicates careers followed by men and women with university degrees in 1970. The 'top 20' occupations account for 56% of the men and 65% of the women who had degrees and who worked. Although these data pertain to the labour force at the beginning of the decade, they do stress some facts, the most notable being that over 37% of all women with university degrees (who worked in 1970) were in teaching occupations, while among males with degrees, 18% were in teaching occupations. However, overall the male graduates worked in a far greater variety of occupations than women graduates.

It is expected that by 1980 the number of females with degrees who work will have risen dramatically. In 1970, the participation rate for all men was 76.4% while for all women it was only 35.5%. In 1976 these rates were 77.8% and 45.2% respectively, showing a continuation of the rising female participation evident over the years since World War II.

Following the activities of International Women's Year in 1975 and the overall change in social climate toward women and their careers, it will be interesting to see how much this pattern changes by the end of the decade.

8.3   Employment statistics

8.3.1   Employment, earnings and hours

Monthly records of employment have been collected from larger business establishments since 1921. The surveys currently conducted by Statistics Canada collect data on payrolls, per capita wages and salaries, hours of work, hourly and weekly wages and the number of salaried and wage-earning employees with their weekly salaries. Employment indexes are based on 1961=100; the data are compiled on the 1960 Standard Industrial Classification.

The survey covers all industries except agriculture, fishing and trapping, education and related services, health and welfare services, religious organizations, public administration and defence and private households.

The monthly employment statistics relate to the number of employees drawing pay in the last pay period in the month. Data are requested for all classes of employees except homeworkers and casual employees working less than one day in the pay period. Owners and firm members are also excluded. The respondents report the gross wages and salaries paid in the last pay period in the month, before deductions are made. The reported payrolls represent gross remuneration and paid absences in the period specified, including salaries, commissions, piece-work and time-work payments, and such items as shift premiums and regularly paid production, incentive and cost-of-living bonuses. The statistics on hours relate to the regular and overtime hours worked by those wage-earners for whom records of hours are maintained, and to hours credited to wage-earners absent on paid leave during the reported period. If the reported period exceeds one week, the payroll and hours data are reduced to weekly equivalents.

Employment. Table 8.13 indicates that, over the 1971-75 period, the industrial composite index of employment for Canada rose by 11.0%. Among the industry divisions showing gains over this period, services led with a 30.0% advance, followed by finance, insurance and real estate (21.9%), trade (21.0%), transportation, communications and other utilities (11.7%), manufacturing (2.9%) and construction (2.8%). Declines occurred in forestry (10.8%) and mining (1.0%) during the same period. Compared with 1974, the industrial composite index for 1975 decreased by 1.2%.

Annual average index numbers of employment for the years 1971-75 are shown by industrial division and group in Table 8.13, by province and by month for 1974 and 1975 in Table 8.14 and by metropolitan area and by month for 1974 and 1975 in Table 8.15.

Weekly earnings. Average weekly earnings have increased substantially in the years for which current payroll statistics have been collected, rising from $23.44 in 1939 to $102.83 in 1967 and $203.34 in 1975. The upward movement gained momentum beginning in 1946 and average annual increases for the 1946-52 period were more than double those for the 1939-45 period. After 1952 the rate of increase, in percentage terms, fell somewhat, particularly during the 1959-62 period. In the recent period, gains have been 11.0% in 1974 and 14.2% in 1975. Annual index numbers of employment and average weekly earnings for 1973-75 are presented by industry, province and urban area in Table 8.16. Table 8.17 shows annual average weekly earnings by industrial division for the years 1971-75 and monthly averages for 1974 and 1975.

Hours and earnings of hourly-rated wage-earners. The monthly survey of employment, payrolls and man-hours covers statistics of hours of work and paid absence of those wage-earners for whom records of hours are maintained, together with the corresponding totals of gross wages paid; these wage-earners are mainly hourly-rated production workers. Information on hours is frequently not kept by employers for ancillary workers nor, in many industries and establishments, for any wage-earners. Salaried employees are excluded by definition from the series. As a result of these exclusions, data are available for fewer industries and workers than are covered in the employment and average weekly earnings statistics.

During the period 1969-75 average weekly hours declined while average hourly earnings rose substantially. For the most part, upward wage-rate revisions in all industries were responsible for the increases. Technological changes, which in many cases involve the employment of more highly skilled workers at the expense of those in the lower-paid occupations, also contributed to the advance of average hourly earnings. As indicated in Table 8.18 from 1970 to 1975 average hourly earnings rose by 78.9% in construction, by 78.5% in mining and by 68.1% in manufacturing. During the same period, average weekly hours declined by 0.5% in construction, 2.5% in mining and 2.8% in manufacturing. Comparing 1975 to 1974 average hourly earnings increased by 18.4% in mining, by 17.1% in construction and by 15.8% in manufacturing; weekly hours decreased by 1.0% in mining, by 0.8% in manufacturing and by 0.3% in construction. Table 8.19 presents average weekly hours and hourly earnings in specified industries and selected urban areas for 1973-75.

Estimates of labour income   8.3.2

Labour income, as shown in Table 8.20, is defined as the compensation paid to employees for services rendered comprising wages and salaries and supplementary labour income. It includes all such payments made to residents of Canada (Canadians employed by the federal government abroad are considered to be residents of Canada) except those made to the Canadian Armed Forces. Remuneration to the latter fits the definition of labour income but is excluded here as it is treated as a separate item in the national income accounts.

Wages and salaries include directors' fees, bonuses, commissions, taxable allowances and benefits. A gross concept has been adopted and wages and salaries are measured before deductions. Supplementary labour income, which is defined as payments made by employers for the future benefit of employees, is composed of employers' contributions to employee welfare and pension funds including the Canada and Quebec Pension Plans, workmen's compensation funds and unemployment insurance.

Estimates of labour income based on the 1948 Standard Industrial Classification (SIC) have been published for 1926-69; those based on the 1960 SIC were originally published in 1969 for the period 1951-68 and then projected to the end of 1971. The entire series 1951-71 has been revised, carried back to 1947 and projected to 1975.

8.3.3   Employer labour costs

The labour costs survey, instituted in 1967, is designed to measure the content of total employee compensation. The results are of value in collective bargaining, in improving estimates of labour income and in developing better productivity measures. The survey also provides cost data for the various items studied in the Canada Department of Labour's survey of working conditions. In addition, all levels of government use the data in developing labour policy.

Since 1967 yearly labour cost surveys have covered one or more major industry divisions. Starting with 1976 labour cost surveys will cover all industries on a biennial basis. This change in the labour cost program will enable Statistics Canada to determine trends over a period of time.

The results of the 1975 survey of labour costs in the Statistics Canada Industry Group "Services to Business Management" (*Standard industrial classification manual*, revised 1970, Statistics Canada Catalogue No. 12-501) are shown in Table 8.33. This table shows that total compensation in 1975 amounted to $11,242 for each employee of which $10,615 represented salaries, wages and other direct payments and the remaining $627 represented employer payments to employee welfare and benefit plans.

Average costs per employee are derived from total employment. Information obtained in this survey shows that part-time and casual employment in Standard Industrial Classification 851, Employment Agencies and Personnel Suppliers, and in Standard Industrial Classification 855, Security and Investigation Services, represented 90% and 34% of the total employment in these two activities, respectively. Consequently, the average employer costs for the full year for the industry group as a whole are biased downwards. With these two activities removed, the average total compensation amounted to $12,877 of which $12,142 represented direct payments and $735 represented employer payments to welfare and benefit plans.

8.3.4   Wage rates, salaries and working conditions

Statistics on occupational wage and salary rates by industry and locality, with standard weekly hours of labour, are compiled by the Canada Department of Labour and published in an annual series of community reports *Wage rates, salaries and hours of labour.* The statistics are based on an annual survey covering some 32,000 establishments in most industries and apply to the last normal pay period preceding October 1. Average wage and salary rates, number of employees, 1st and 9th deciles, 1st and 3rd quartiles and medians are shown for a number of office and service occupations, maintenance trades, labourers and specific industry occupations. Information on concepts and methods of developing these statistics is given in the report.

Table 8.34 presents average wage and salary data for 12 Canadian cities on October 1, 1974 and October 1, 1975. Hourly and weekly rates of pay are listed for 23 occupations in the construction and manufacturing industries; salaries are specified for men and for women engaged in several office occupations.

Table 8.21 gives summary data on working conditions of office and non-office employees in manufacturing industries and in all industries for the years 1974-75. The percentages in this table denote the proportions that office and non-office employees in establishments reporting specific items bear to the total number of all such employees in all establishments replying to the survey; they are not necessarily the proportions of employees actually covered by the various items tabulated.

Pension plans   8.4

According to a survey of pension plans conducted by Statistics Canada at the beginning of 1974, the sharply increasing growth rate that characterized occupational pension plans in Canada over the 1950s and early 1960s reached its peak by mid-1960 and by the early 1970s levelled off and fell back somewhat. Pension plans which had grown to 8,920 in number by 1960 increased over 50% by 1965 to 13,660 plans; by 1970, the growth rate dropped sharply to 18% when plans numbered 16,137. Growth then ceased entirely with plans dropping to 15,853 representing a decline of under 2% by the beginning of 1974. Over these same periods the growth rate of plan membership also levelled off, although in actual numbers, participation continued to rise sharply. Membership, which in 1960 totalled 1.8 million workers, increased to 2.3 million by 1965, 2.8 million by 1970 and to a record level of over 3.4 million by 1974.

Pension plans were in operation in virtually all industrial sectors, but the degree of coverage varied widely from industry to industry. The most comprehensive coverage was in public administration and defence, where almost all the 830,700 employees at all government levels, the Armed Forces and the RCMP participated in a plan. Two out of three paid workers in mining and nearly 45% in manufacturing were covered. In transportation and communication, with some of the oldest and largest plans in the country such as those in the railway, telephone and trucking companies, almost half of the paid workers (364,000) had post-retirement protection. Of the employees working in finance, insurance and real estate about 43% were covered; approximately one in four workers in community, business and personal services — which includes hospitals, religious and welfare organizations and professional agencies, etc. — participated in occupational pension programs. Construction, with 235,000 plan members, had 44% of all workers covered by plans and trade, both retail and wholesale, with 196,200 participants, provided coverage for another 14% of workers in Canada.

Of the 15,853 pension plans in Canada at the beginning of 1974, 11,242 were funded by insurance companies, but these accounted for less than 15% of the members or 462,000 out of 3.4 million. Plans with the largest coverage were those designed for government employees; employee contributions are paid into government consolidated revenue funds which are not held in the form of cash or invested securities. Although only 21 in number, these plans applied to a total of 666,000 public servants including those covered by the federal superannuation plan, the Armed Forces, the RCMP and public servants in five provinces.

Aside from these public service plans, the larger plans tended to use either personal or corporate trustees as funding agencies. Although only one quarter of all occupational plans were trusteed, they covered more than 60% of the members — some 2.17 million out of the total of 3.42 million persons.

Total contributions paid by and on behalf of the 3.42 million members in 1974 amounted to over $2.99 billion with more than $1.64 billion paid into trusteed funds. With an annual cash inflow of this magnitude, trusteed pension funds have become one of the largest single pools of money in the country, growing at a rate of 10% to 12% annually, with the book value of assets accumulated reaching a record total of $18.28 billion by the end of 1974. Because the growth of these funds is so rapid and the total accumulated so large, they are surveyed annually by Statistics Canada; the results are published in *Trusteed pension plans, financial statistics* (Catalogue No. 74-201). A summary tabulation of the key financial data related to these funds is presented in Table 8.22.

The Canada and Quebec Pension Plans are discussed in Chapter 6.

Federal government annuities. The Government Annuities Act, which came into force on September 1, 1908 authorized the sale of annuities. The object was to assist Canadians to provide for their later years. The Annuities Act was one of the first significant pieces of social legislation in Canada. However, by the 1960s newer forms of legislation such as the Canada Pension Plan and the Old Age

Security covered the public more effectively than government annuities. Accordingly, by Cabinet directive, at the close of 1967 the sales force was disbanded and active sales promotion of annuities ceased.

During the years, inflationary pressures and rising interest rates had placed annuitants at a distinct disadvantage. The interest rate on government annuities ranged from 3% to 5¼% with the average rate about 4%.

The Government Annuities Improvement Act became law on December 20, 1975. By it the rate of interest on annuity contracts was raised to 7% and a further percentage adjustment was provided for when the annuity came under payment; greater flexibility was provided in annuities administration; and the sale of annuity contracts was formally terminated. This program comes under the administration of the Unemployment Insurance Commission.

8.5   Unemployment insurance

Unemployment insurance has been part of Canada's social and economic life since the Unemployment Insurance Act was passed in 1940. Since that time various amendments have brought new categories of workers into the plan and contributions and benefit rates have been raised periodically to meet changing economic conditions. However, until recently, the basic structure of the plan remained unaltered.

In 1968, when Parliament approved upward revisions of both contributions and benefit rates and broadened the scope of coverage, the Unemployment Insurance Commission was instructed to investigate the program and to recommend appropriate changes in philosophy and structure. The Unemployment Insurance Act, 1971, effective June 27, 1971, was the result of this study; its basic objectives were to provide assistance to cope with interrupted earnings resulting from unemployment, including unemployment from illness, and to cooperate with other agencies engaged in social development.

The 1971 act extended coverage to all regular members of the labour force (effective January 2, 1972) for whom there existed an employer-employee relationship. The only non-insurable employees were those who earned less than 20% of the maximum weekly insurable earnings or less than 20 times the provincial hourly minimum wage, whichever was less. Coverage, contributions and benefit entitlement ceased at age 70.

Employers and employees would absorb the cost of initial benefits and administration with the employer rate at 1.4 times the employee rate. The government share was confined to the cost of extended benefits and the excess cost of initial benefits resulting from a national unemployment rate greater than 4%. In 1975 the rate of employee contributions was $1.40 per $100 of insurable earnings with a maximum of $2.59 a week. The Department of National Revenue, Taxation collects the contributions.

Under the program, the duration of benefit was not determined solely by how long a person had worked. A claimant could draw benefits for a maximum of 51 weeks depending on his employment history and prevailing economic conditions, providing he had contributed for at least eight weeks in the last 52 and was available, capable and searching for work. Persons with 20 or more weeks of insured earnings (a "major labour force attachment") were eligible for a wider range of benefit that included a pre-payment of three weeks of regular benefit for work-shortage lay-offs, benefit payments when the interruption in earnings was caused by illness or pregnancy, and three weeks retirement benefit for older workers.

Sickness benefit was available for a maximum of 15 weeks for persons with a major labour force attachment whose earnings were interrupted by illness, injury or quarantine (excluding workmen's compensation). If a person was taken ill while on regular claim, sickness benefit was available but the combined duration of benefits during the initial benefit period could not exceed 15 weeks.

Maternity benefit was available for eight weeks before confinement, the week of confinement and six weeks after, to women who had had a major labour force attachment. They must also have been part of the labour force at least 10 of the 20 weeks prior to the 30th week before the expected date of confinement.

Retirement benefit, available for three weeks, was paid in a lump sum to claimants with a major labour force attachment who were 65-70 years of age and who had signified they had left the labour force by applying for the Canada Pension Plan or the Quebec Pension Plan, and to persons over 70. The benefit was paid without a waiting period and without regard to earnings or availability.

The benefit rate for all claims was two thirds of average insured earnings in the qualifying period to a weekly maximum of $123 and a minimum of $20 in 1975. For claimants with dependents and whose average qualifying earnings were equal to or less than one third of the maximum weekly insurable earnings, the benefit rate was 75%. During later stages of benefit all claimants with dependents drew benefit at 75% of qualifying earnings subject to the $123 maximum. The maximum insurable earnings and, therefore, the maximum benefit were subject to annual adjustment based on an index calculated from earnings of Canadian employees.

Income from employment in excess of 25% of the benefit rate was deducted. In the case of sickness and maternity, proceeds of wage-loss policies were deducted after the waiting period. All work-related income was deducted both during the waiting period and after the waiting period had been served.

The statistics in Table 8.23 summarize the Unemployment Insurance Commission's activities in the years 1971-75. Figures prior to July 1971 are affected by the Unemployment Insurance Act of 1955, which is described in the *Canada Year Book 1973* p 352.

To assess the impact of changing economic conditions on the insurance program, current operational data, such as claims filed and processed and payments made, are collected and published monthly by Statistics Canada. Current claims and payment data are useful for administrative purposes and are also a source of information to the public regarding financial and other aspects of the program. In addition to the monthly data on the operation of the Unemployment Insurance Act, detailed data on persons employed in insurable employment and benefit periods established and terminated are compiled annually and published in *Benefit periods established and terminated under the Unemployment Insurance Act* (Catalogue No. 73-201).

Employment injuries and workmen's compensation   8.6

Fatal employment injuries. Data on fatal employment injuries compiled by the Canada Department of Labour are collected from provincial workmen's compensation boards. On the average annually in the period 1965-74, 1,194 industrial workers sustained fatal injuries. Collisions, derailments or wrecks caused 279 deaths; being struck by an object, 263; falls and slips, 230; being caught in, on or between objects or vehicles, etc., 121; contacts with toxic materials or industrial diseases, 110; conflagrations, exposure to temperature extremes and explosions, 64; and the remaining 127 resulted from miscellaneous accidents. Table 8.24 presents statistics on fatal employment injuries in 11 industries for the years 1973-75. Employment injuries, extent of disability and amount of compensation paid are reported by province for the years 1974 and 1975 in Table 8.25. In 1974, 1,047,029 injuries resulted in $538 million in compensation compared with 985,677 injuries and $426 million in compensation in 1973. Preliminary figures for 1975 show 1,006,263 injuries resulted in $684 million in compensation.

8.7 Organized labour

8.7.1 Union membership

At January 1, 1975 labour unions reported a total of 2.9 million members in Canada, an increase of 5.5% over 1974 (Table 8.26). Union members made up 36.8% of non-agricultural paid workers and 29.7% of the total civilian labour force in 1975. Membership, by type of union and affiliation, is presented in Table 8.27. Canadian Labour Congress (CLC) affiliates, with 2 million members in 1975, accounted for 71.1% of total union membership in Canada, compared with 71.7% in 1974. Of the total in CLC affiliates in 1975, 1.2 million members belonged to unions that were also affiliated with the American Federation of Labor and Congress of Industrial Organizations (AFL–CIO) in the United States; membership of unions affiliated with the CLC but not holding affiliation with the AFL–CIO totalled 803,513 or 28.0% of the total. Federations affiliated with the Quebec-based Confederation of National Trade Unions (CNTU) had 173,610 members or 6.0% of total union membership in Canada; the Canadian Council of Unions (CCU) represented 20,358 members or 0.7%; another 1.4% of the total was reported by the Centrale des syndicats démocratiques with 40,027 members; and the remaining 20.8% belonged to various unaffiliated international and national unions and independent local organizations.

International unions with headquarters in the United States accounted for 51.4% of the 1975 membership, compared with 53.2% in 1974; national and regional unions, which charter locals in Canada only, made up 46.1% (43.6% in 1974). Independent local organizations and local unions chartered by the CLC and the CNTU accounted for the remaining 2.5%.

In 1975, 24 unions reported membership of 30,000 or more. Fourteen unions reported 50,000 or more members, accounting for 46.0% of the total membership. The 14 listed with their affiliation, ranked as follows in 1975 (1974 rank in parentheses):

1 (2) Canadian Union of Public Employees (CLC), 198,872
2 (1) United Steelworkers of America (AFL–CIO/CLC), 186,996
3 (3) Public Service Alliance of Canada (CLC), 135,998
4 (4) International Union, United Automobile, Aerospace and Agricultural Implement Workers of America (CLC), 117,486
5 (6) United Brotherhood of Carpenters and Joiners of America (AFL–CIO/CLC), 89,010
6 (5) Quebec Teachers' Corporation (Ind.), 84,905
7 (7) International Brotherhood of Teamsters, Chauffeurs, Warehousemen and Helpers of America (Ind.), 75,638
8 (8) International Brotherhood of Electrical Workers (AFL–CIO/CLC), 63,463
9 (11) Social Affairs Federation (CNTU), 61,130
10 (13) International Association of Machinists and Aerospace Workers (AFL–CIO/CLC), 57,209
11 (10) International Woodworkers of America (AFL–CIO/CLC), 56,000
12 (not included) Canadian Paperworkers Union (CLC), 56,000
13 (not included) Civil Service Association of Ontario (CLC) 55,448
14 (14) Canadian Food and Allied Workers, District 15 Council (AFL–CIO/CLC), 50,000.

8.7.2 Wages and collective agreements

The Canada Department of Labour publishes wage settlement data for collective agreements on a quarterly basis. The agreements covered are limited to negotiating units of 500 or more employees in all industries except construction. The base rate for a negotiating unit is defined as the lowest rate of pay, expressed in hourly terms, for the lowest paid classification used for qualified workers in the bargaining unit. In most cases the base rate represents pay for an unskilled or semi-skilled classification of workers. However, this is not so in contracts covering only skilled and/or professional workers. The wage data, therefore, are not necessarily representative of the average increases enjoyed by the workers in the negotiating unit as a whole. Nevertheless, the data on numbers of agreements and workers refer to all occupational groups in the negotiating unit.

Wage-rate data given in Tables 8.28 and 8.29 indicate that approximately 1.8 million workers were covered by 884 collective agreements at December 31, 1975. The average base rate rose 52.3 cents, or 12.8% during the 12-month period ended December 31, 1975, compared with an increase of 48.8 cents or 13.6% during the preceding 12-month period. On a year-over-year basis the consumer price index rose by 9.5% during the 12-month period ended December 31, 1975, and by 12.5% during the preceding 12-month period. When the wage increases are deflated by the consumer price index increase, the average base rate increased in real terms by 2.9% in 1975 and by 1.0% in 1974.

Additional data are available from the Canada Department of Labour on wage settlements during quarterly periods, including number of agreements settled, number of employees covered and duration of contracts. The agreements covered are again limited to negotiating units of 500 or more employees in all industries except construction. Details are not given here but, for 1975 as a whole, 402 contracts, affecting the wage rates of about 738,555 workers, were settled. On the average the 402 settlements provided an annual percentage increase in base rate equal to 16.8% compound over the term of the contracts. The comparable percentage for 1974 was 14.3% compound.

During 1975 settlements of one-year duration produced increases averaging 20.4%, those of two-year duration 21.7% and 11.4% for the first and second years, respectively; and those of three-year duration, 17.2%, 8.9% and 4.0% for the first, second and third years of the contract. These increases compare with those of 1974 as follows: one-year agreements, average increases of 16.1%; two-year agreements, average increases of 17.6% and 10.7%; and three-year agreements, average increases of 14.2%, 7.3% and 6.2% for the first, second and third years, respectively, of the contract.

A further breakdown reveals that of the 402 settlements during 1975, 135 agreements covering 261,160 employees were settled with a Cost of Living Allowance incorporated in the agreement. The 135 settlements produced increases, prior to the calculation of COLA, of 14.2% over the life of the agreement, whereas the 267 agreements (477,395 employees) without a COLA clause produced increases of 18.1%.

Strikes and lockouts   8.8

Statistical information on strikes and lockouts in Canada is compiled by the Labour Data Branch of the Canada Department of Labour on the basis of reports from Canada Manpower Centres and provincial departments of labour. Table 8.30 presents a breakdown by industry of strikes and lockouts in 1974 involving three or more workers and continuing for 10 or more man-days. The 1,216 work stoppages reported involved 592,220 workers and 9.2 million man-days.

The developments leading to work stoppages are often too complex to make it practicable to distinguish statistically between strikes on the one hand and lockouts on the other. Similarly, no distinction is made between legal and illegal strikes. The number of workers involved includes all workers reported on strike or locked out, whether or not they all belonged to the unions directly involved in the disputes leading to work stoppages. Workers indirectly affected, such as those laid off as a result of a work stoppage, are not included. Duration of strikes and lockouts in terms of man-days is calculated by multiplying the number of workers involved in each work stoppage by the number of working days the stoppage was in progress. The data on duration of work stoppages in man-days are provided to facilitate comparison of work stoppages in terms of a common denominator. They are not intended as a measure of the loss of productive time to the economy.

8.9   The Anti-Inflation Board

On October 14, 1975 the anti-inflation program went into effect. Prior to that time, wage and salary increases were being negotiated or established in the expectation that the rate of inflation was likely to continue or increase. Reports of large increases being demanded or obtained by various employee groups encouraged others to seek similar increases. The situation threatened to worsen as groups of employees coming off two- or three-year collective agreements attempted to catch up with others who had received large increases.

In this environment, the purpose of the compensation part of the anti-inflation program was to slow down gradually the rate of increase in labour costs while the restraints on prices and profits reduced the rate of increase in the cost of living.

Guidelines were introduced which employers and employees were encouraged to follow in arriving at wage or salary settlements. While all Canadians were expected to observe these guidelines voluntarily, large and strategic groups were required by law to comply, so that those who complied voluntarily would not then find themselves falling behind the larger or more powerful groups.

8.9.1   Compensation regulations

The aim of the regulations was to ensure that compensation for a group would not increase at a percentage rate higher than an allowable arithmetic guideline unless special circumstances justified a larger increase. These arithmetic guidelines were the sum of three elements: a basic protection factor set at 8% in the first program year, 6% in the second and 4% in the third; a national productivity factor of 2%; and an experience adjustment factor which could vary between plus and minus 2% a year, depending on a group's experience relative to the rise in the consumer price index (CPI) over the past two or three years. If, in any program year, the increase in the CPI exceeded the basic protection factor, the percentage allowed for the basic protection factor in the subsequent year would be increased by the amount of the difference.

Lower-paid employees were permitted increases beyond the arithmetic guidelines to an amount of $600 a year, or to raise their wage to $3.50 an hour. Groups at higher compensation levels were restricted to a maximum average increase of $2,400.

The regulations applied to employee groups rather than individuals. Employee groups were: bargaining units; groups established by the employer for purposes of determining salaries or wages; and the executives of each organization. Separate guidelines were calculated for each employee group and were applied to the total compensation of that group. Values of benefits such as vacations, statutory holidays and incentive plans were included in the compensation package subject to the guidelines.

The board could exercise discretion in granting increases beyond the arithmetic guidelines. Special consideration could be given to groups covered by compensation plans that were entered into prior to January 2, 1974 and expired prior to October 14, 1975, and groups whose wages had historically been closely related to those of other groups.

The guidelines also provided for certain types of payment to be excluded when calculating compensation increases. The calculations of these exclusions were straightforward, although in many cases they required board consideration. They included such things as the elimination of pay differentials based on sex, and payments made in order to overcome difficulties in recruiting and retaining staff.

8.9.2   Coverage and compliance

The anti-inflation guidelines applied to everyone, and all Canadians were expected to comply with them. Certain major groups were required by law to do so including: firms with 500 or more employees in Canada including associated firms, firms in the construction industry with 20 or more employees in Canada, and professionals. Firms considered to be of strategic importance to the anti-inflation program, and those involved in association bargaining could also be made subject to mandatory guidelines, as could employees of controlled firms and those of federal government departments, agencies and corporations, and of provincial and municipal governments and their agencies.

Initially it was expected that some 1,500 companies would be subject to enforcement. As legislation was implemented, and as provinces joined the federal program, the number of organizations which were subject to the regulations became known with greater precision. In the first year of controls the number of organizations monitored by the board were as follows: public sector 7,600, private sector (more than 500 employees) 7,230, construction (20 to 499 employees) 2,700, and professional firms 45,000.

Compensation plans covering 16,412 groups (2.4 million employees) were submitted to the Anti-Inflation Board between October 14, 1975 and September 7, 1976. This was about half of the estimated 5 million employees required by law to comply with the guidelines.

Approximately 59% or 9,643 of the compensation plans received by the board were at or below the arithmetic guidelines. The remaining 7,031 compensation plans covering more than 1.3 million employees contained increases beyond the arithmetic guidelines and therefore required a decision by the board. The board ruled on 2,696 of these cases covering 676,507 employees as of September 24, 1976. Each organization subject to the regulations had to define a separate executive group, and many of these groups were limited by the $2,400 compensation ceiling. Over 80% complied with the $2,400 limit.

Sources

8.1.1 Public Relations Branch, Canada Department of Labour.
8.1.2 Information Service, Department of Manpower and Immigration.
8.1.3 Public Relations Branch, Canada Department of Labour.
8.2.1 Labour Force Survey Division, Census and Household Surveys Field, Statistics Canada.
8.2.2 Census Characteristics Division, Census and Household Surveys Field, Statistics Canada.
8.3.1 - 8.3.3 Labour Division, General Statistics Branch, Statistics Canada.
8.3.4 Public Relations Branch, Canada Department of Labour.
8.4 - 8.5 Labour Division, General Statistics Branch, Statistics Canada.
8.6 - 8.8 Public Relations Branch, Canada Department of Labour.
8.9 Editing Services, Communications, Anti-Inflation Board.

Tables

Tables

..	not available	e	estimate
...	not appropriate or not applicable	p	preliminary
—	nil or zero	r	revised
- -	too small to be expressed		certain tables may not add due to rounding

It should be noted that figures shown for the latest year are subject to revision, and that some figures for earlier years have been revised.

8.1 Estimates of the civilian labour force and its main components, annual averages 1970-75

Year	Civilian population (15 years of age and over) '000	Civilian labour force (15 years of age and over)			Persons not in the labour force (15 years of age and over) '000	Participation rate %	Unemployment rate %
		Employed '000	Unemployed '000	Total labour force '000			
1970	14,528	7,919	480	8,399	6,129	57.8	5.7
1971	14,878	8,107	538	8,644	6,234	58.1	6.2
1972	15,227	8,363	557	8,920	6,307	58.6	6.2
1973	15,608	8,802	520	9,322	6,286	59.7	5.6
1974	16,039	9,185	521	9,706	6,334	60.5	5.4
1975	16,470	9,363	697	10,060	6,410	61.1	6.9

8.2 Distribution of population in the labour force and non-labour force categories, by age and sex, 1970-75

Sex, age and year	Population '000	Labour force			Not in labour force '000	Participation rate %	Unemployment rate %
		Employed '000	Unemployed '000	Total '000			
Male							
1970	7,162	5,260	315	5,575	1,587	77.8	5.7
1971	7,332	5,332	340	5,672	1,660	77.4	6.0
1972	7,501	5,476	340	5,816	1,685	77.5	5.8
1973	7,687	5,711	299	6,009	1,678	78.2	5.0
1974	7,901	5,919	298	6,217	1,684	78.7	4.8
1975	8,111	5,966	397	6,363	1,748	78.4	6.2
15-24 years							
1970	1,905	1,057	134	1,191	714	62.5	11.3
1971	1,967	1,084	149	1,233	734	62.7	12.1
1972	2,016	1,142	155	1,297	719	64.3	12.0
1973	2,071	1,243	139	1,382	688	66.7	10.1
1974	2,134	1,330	142	1,473	661	69.0	9.6
1975	2,194	1,325	190	1,515	680	69.0	12.6
25 + years							
1970	5,257	4,203	181	4,384	873	83.4	4.1
1971	5,365	4,247	191	4,439	926	82.7	4.3
1972	5,485	4,334	186	4,519	966	82.4	4.1
1973	5,617	4,467	160	4,627	990	82.4	3.5
1974	5,767	4,588	156	4,744	1,022	82.3	3.3
1975	5,916	4,641	206	4,848	1,069	81.9	4.3
Female							
1970	7,366	2,660	165	2,824	4,542	38.3	5.8
1971	7,546	2,775	197	2,972	4,574	39.4	6.6
1972	7,726	2,887	217	3,104	4,622	40.2	7.0
1973	7,921	3,091	221	3,313	4,608	41.8	6.7
1974	8,139	3,266	222	3,489	4,650	42.9	6.4
1975	8,359	3,397	301	3,697	4,662	44.2	8.1
15-24 years							
1970	1,901	860	81	941	961	49.5	8.6
1971	1,963	899	98	997	965	50.8	9.8
1972	1,999	936	99	1,035	964	51.8	9.6
1973	2,045	1,006	102	1,108	937	54.2	9.2
1974	2,102	1,071	106	1,177	925	56.0	9.0
1975	2,157	1,086	140	1,226	930	56.9	11.5
25 + years							
1970	5,465	1,800	84	1,884	3,581	34.5	4.5
1971	5,584	1,876	99	1,975	3,609	35.4	5.0
1972	5,727	1,951	117	2,068	3,659	36.1	5.7
1973	5,876	2,085	119	2,204	3,671	37.5	5.4
1974	6,037	2,195	117	2,312	3,725	38.3	5.1
1975	6,202	2,311	160	2,471	3,731	39.8	6.5

8.3   Employment, unemployment and unemployment rates, by province, 1970-75

Year	Province				
	Nfld.	PEI	NS	NB	Que.
Employment *('000)*					
1970	129	35	256	192	2,129
1971	135	38	257	198	2,176
1972	141	37	261	206	2,208
1973	153	40	276	217	2,338
1974	149	41	294	226	2,415
1975	152	43	295	229	2,452
Unemployment *('000)*					
1970	10		15	13	160
1971	13		19	13	171
1972	14	¹	20	16	178
1973	17		20	18	170
1974	23		22	19	171
1975	25		25	25	216
Unemployment rates *(%)*					
1970	7.2		5.5	6.3	7.0
1971	8.8		6.9	6.2	7.3
1972	9.0	¹	7.1	7.2	7.5
1973	10.0		6.8	7.7	6.8
1974	13.4		7.0	7.8	6.6
1975	14.2		7.8	9.9	8.1
	Ont.	Man.	Sask.	Alta.	BC
Employment *('000)*					
1970	3,037	371	333	633	805
1971	3,114	379	334	643	835
1972	3,248	387	338	668	869
1973	3,400	403	347	702	928
1974	3,550	421	357	747	987
1975	3,613	420	373	778	1,009
Unemployment *('000)*					
1970	140	21	18	34	67
1971	178	23	14	39	65
1972	172	22	18	40	74
1973	153	20	14	39	67
1974	165	16	12	27	65
1975	244	20	11	33	94
Unemployment rates *(%)*					
1970	4.4	5.4	5.1	5.1	7.7
1971	5.4	5.7	4.0	5.7	7.2
1972	5.0	5.4	5.1	5.6	7.9
1973	4.3	4.7	3.9	5.3	6.7
1974	4.4	3.7	3.3	3.5	6.2
1975	6.3	4.6	2.9	4.1	8.5

¹Prior to April 1976, unemployment figures for Prince Edward Island were not published due to high sampling error.

8.4   Employees by industrial group, 1975¹

Industrial group (1970 Standard Industrial Classification)	Estimates '000
Agriculture	486
Other primary industries	222
Manufacturing	1,890
Construction	610
Trade	1,649
Transportation, communication and other utilities	820
Finance, insurance and real estate	478
Service	2,537
Public administration	670
All industries	9,363

¹Comparable data for previous years not available.

8.5   Employees by occupation, 1974 and 1975

Occupation (1971 Census classification)	Estimates in thousands	
	1974	1975
Managerial, administrative	538	614
Natural sciences, engineering and mathematics	287	312
Social sciences	106	111
Religion	27	26
Teaching	395	420
Medicine and health	395	427
Art, literature and recreation	106	115
Clerical	1,534	1,640
Sales	986	1,039
Service	1,105	1,138
Farming, horticulture and animal husbandry	495	504
Fishing, hunting and trapping	25	20
Forestry and logging	65	49
Mining and quarrying	52	53
Processing	414	362
Machining	271	252
Product fabricating, assembling and repairing	900	872
Construction trades	660	652
Transport equipment operation	392	389
Materials handling	257	242
Other crafts and equipment operation	126	127
All occupations	9,137	9,363

8.6   Persons 15 years of age and over in the total labour force, by country of birth and region of residence, 1971

Country of birth	Canada[1]	Atlantic provinces	Quebec	Ontario	Prairie provinces	British Columbia
Total labour force	8,813,340	715,040	2,242,840	3,410,830	1,495,330	930,030
Born in Canada	7,049,575	682,545	1,989,720	2,430,865	1,241,715	688,765
Born outside Canada	1,763,770	32,495	253,115	979,960	253,610	241,265
US	124,405	7,575	18,020	45,390	30,460	22,590
Europe	1,429,985	21,130	194,180	830,880	199,030	182,160
Western Europe	*280,010*	*3,905*	*42,465*	*142,290*	*48,965*	*41,680*
Austria and Germany	144,730	1,450	13,355	75,920	29,170	24,400
Netherlands	85,774	1,875	2,795	52,020	15,515	13,425
France	26,405	315	18,895	4,415	1,510	1,200
Other Western Europe	23,100	265	7,425	9,935	2,770	2,655
Northern Europe	*513,355*	*14,055*	*33,595*	*298,545*	*72,415*	*93,450*
United Kingdom	450,850	12,835	30,185	268,380	60,270	78,110
Republic of Ireland	20,890	525	1,665	12,840	3,060	2,725
Scandinavia[2]	30,275	645	1,275	9,475	8,480	10,265
Finland	11,345	50	465	7,850	610	2,345
Southern Europe	*387,270*	*1,685*	*82,870*	*256,540*	*21,270*	*24,595*
Italy	234,360	710	53,150	156,485	10,755	13,120
Greece	50,995	530	17,315	29,145	2,015	1,965
Yugoslavia	48,805	120	3,210	35,190	5,130	5,035
Portugal	40,400	220	6,345	27,085	2,885	3,855
Other Southern Europe	12,710	100	2,850	8,640	485	620
Eastern Europe	*249,350*	*1,485*	*35,250*	*133,510*	*56,380*	*22,430*
Poland	87,835	555	12,510	46,420	22,035	6,230
USSR	78,605	355	8,305	41,605	20,850	7,440
Hungary	42,875	280	7,065	24,210	6,490	4,730
Czechoslovakia	25,345	230	3,270	14,370	4,515	2,900
Other Eastern Europe	14,690	65	4,095	6,900	2,495	1,135
Asia	97,700	2,450	14,080	43,935	13,815	23,285
Other	111,680	1,340	26,830	59,755	10,310	13,230

[1]Includes Yukon Territory and Northwest Territories.
[2]Includes Denmark, Iceland, Norway and Sweden.

8.7   Persons 15 years of age and over in the labour force, by period of immigration, sex and age group, 1971

Sex and period of immigration	Age group							
	15-19	20-24	25-34	35-44	45-54	55-64	65+	All ages
Both sexes	884,440	1,408,365	1,992,020	1,739,085	1,539,035	986,340	264,050	8,813,345
Born in Canada	809,770	1,215,735	1,582,555	1,325,140	1,193,100	754,850	168,425	7,049,575
Born outside Canada	74,675	192,635	409,465	413,945	345,930	231,505	95,625	1,763,770
Immigrated before 1946	—	—	10,805	31,550	87,180	125,135	77,835	332,505
Immigrated 1946-50	—	16,335	32,010	33,105	65,060	31,255	5,115	182,895
Immigrated 1951-60	41,410	79,970	120,920	230,530	148,575	58,035	8,865	688,305
Immigrated 1961-71	33,265	96,330	245,730	118,760	45,110	17,065	3,810	560,070
Male	500,910	816,010	1,355,925	1,194,705	1,023,715	684,280	184,700	5,760,245
Born in Canada	460,640	707,680	1,088,695	912,485	798,445	519,130	114,330	4,601,400
Born outside Canada	40,275	108,330	267,230	282,220	225,270	165,160	70,370	1,158,845
Immigrated before 1946	—	—	6,455	19,885	54,500	88,550	58,055	227,445
Immigrated 1946-50	—	9,615	21,740	22,055	40,100	22,975	3,675	120,170
Immigrated 1951-60	22,620	46,285	82,040	161,675	102,055	42,325	6,215	463,215
Immigrated 1961-71	17,655	52,430	156,995	78,605	28,605	11,300	2,430	348,020
Female	383,530	592,355	636,095	544,380	515,320	302,060	79,350	3,053,100
Born in Canada	349,130	508,055	493,860	412,655	394,655	235,720	54,095	2,448,175
Born outside Canada	34,400	84,305	142,235	131,725	120,660	66,345	25,255	604,925
Immigrated before 1946	—	—	4,350	11,665	32,680	36,585	19,780	105,060
Immigrated 1946-50	—	6,720	10,270	11,050	24,960	8,280	1,440	62,725
Immigrated 1951-60	18,790	33,685	38,880	68,855	46,520	15,710	2,650	225,090
Immigrated 1961-71	15,610	43,900	88,735	40,155	16,505	5,765	1,380	212,050

8.8   Persons 15 years of age and over in the labour force[1], by class of worker and sex, 1961 and 1971

Class of worker	1961			1971		
	Total	Male	Female	Total	Male	Female
Wage-earners	5,366,977	3,781,520	1,585,457	7,674,525	5,005,385	2,669,140
Paid workers	..	..	..	7,543,815	4,888,690	2,655,130
Self-employed in incorporated companies	..	..	..	130,705	116,695	14,010
Self-employed in unincorporated companies	940,488	846,467	94,021	668,850	586,130	82,720
Unpaid family workers	164,385	77,531	86,854	283,550	74,205	209,350
Total	6,471,850	4,705,518	1,766,332	8,626,925	5,665,715	2,961,210

[1]Includes the experienced labour force which is defined as the total labour force minus persons looking for work, who last worked prior to Jan. 1, 1970 or who never worked. For 1961, persons who never worked were excluded but persons looking for work who had not worked since Jan. 1, 1960 were included.

8.9   Labour force[1] 15 years of age and over, by major industrial group and sex, 1961 and 1971

Sector and industrial group[2]	1961		1971	
	Male	Female	Male	Female
Primary or extractive				
Agriculture	554,713	78,612	369,630	111,565
Forestry	106,387	2,193	71,025	3,355
Fishing and trapping	35,748	515	24,540	900
Mines, quarries and oil wells	112,254	3,963	129,675	9,360
Secondary or manufacturing				
Manufacturing	1,098,691	300,328	1,302,635	404,695
Construction	427,679	10,875	511,940	26,280
Tertiary or service				
Transportation, communication and other utilities	527,071	83,160	564,885	114,025
Trade	694,211	303,125	803,100	466,190
Finance, insurance and real estate	124,310	104,595	173,825	184,235
Community, business and personal service	518,515	750,332	865,345	1,176,045
Public administration and defence	389,360	86,620	468,420	163,320
Industry unspecified	116,579	42,014	380,700	301,240
Total	4,705,518	1,766,332	5,665,715	2,961,210

[1]Includes the experienced labour force which is defined as the total labour force minus persons looking for work, who last worked prior to Jan. 1, 1970 or who never worked. For 1961, persons who never worked were excluded but persons looking for work who had not worked since Jan. 1, 1960 were included.
[2]Data based on 1971 Standard Industrial Classification.

8.10   Labour force 15 years of age and over, by industrial sector and province, 1961 and 1971

Province	Primary		Secondary		Tertiary	
	1961	1971	1961	1971	1961	1971
Newfoundland	21,134	15,440	21,719	33,140	65,969	86,320
Prince Edward Island	11,386	8,130	5,242	7,020	16,790	24,010
Nova Scotia	33,689	21,980	49,693	62,790	149,301	181,165
New Brunswick	28,124	19,095	39,487	51,795	106,903	135,045
Quebec	199,943	122,110	593,646	621,435	923,263	1,218,450
Ontario	228,011	180,350	796,964	1,025,115	1,316,337	1,909,780
Manitoba	67,148	55,925	76,698	79,265	200,174	249,585
Saskatchewan	125,102	109,235	32,520	37,830	160,459	198,140
Alberta	120,187	115,575	79,817	114,850	278,396	400,625
British Columbia	55,891	69,285	149,818	210,830	355,172	558,305
Canada[1]	894,385	720,050	1,837,573	2,245,550	3,581,299	4,979,390

[1] Includes Yukon Territory and Northwest Territories.

8.11   Principal occupation unit groups, males and females with university degrees, who worked in 1970[1]

Rank	Male			Female		
	Occupation unit group	No.	% who worked in 1970	Occupation unit group	No.	% who worked in 1970
1	Secondary school teachers	46,455	10.08	Secondary school teachers	31,530	19.42
2	Physicians and surgeons	25,515	5.54	Elementary and kindergarten teachers	19,080	11.75
3	University teachers	20,655	4.48	Nurses, graduate except supervisors	6,655	4.10
4	Accountants, auditors and other financial officers	18,850	4.09	University teachers	4,855	2.99
5	Administrators in teaching and related fields	18,105	3.93	Secretaries and stenographers	4,745	2.92
6	Lawyers and notaries	14,880	3.23	Library and file clerks	4,250	2.62
7	Civil engineers	14,030	3.04	Social workers	3,880	2.39
8	Ministers of religion	12,045	2.61	Administrators in teaching and related fields	3,205	1.97
9	General managers and other senior officials	11,845	2.57	Post-secondary school teachers	2,990	1.85
10	Elementary and kindergarten teachers	10,170	2.21	Elementary and secondary school teaching and related occupations	2,955	1.82
11	Supervisors: sales occupations commodities	9,075	1.97	Physicians and surgeons	2,845	1.75
12	Electrical engineers	8,800	1.91	Librarians and archivists	2,705	1.67
13	Occupations related to management and administration	8,680	1.88	Bookkeepers and accounting clerks	2,345	1.44
14	Systems analysts, computer programmers and related groups	6,755	1.47	General office clerks	2,250	1.39
15	Mechanical engineers	6,310	1.37	Fine arts school teachers	2,075	1.28
16	Dentists	6,200	1.34	Sales clerks, commodities	2,005	1.23
17	Pharmacists	5,340	1.16	Medical laboratory technologists and technicians	1,980	1.22
18	Personnel and related officers	4,925	1.07	Occupations in welfare and community services	1,920	1.18
19	Government administrators	4,780	1.04	Typists and clerk-typists	1,705	1.05
20	Post-secondary school teachers	4,580	1.00	Dietitians and nutritionists	1,700	1.05
	All other occupations	202,695	44.00	All other occupations	56,660	34.90
	Total	460,690	100.00	Total	162,335	100.00

[1] 1971 Census of Canada, Income of individuals, Employment income by sex, occupation and schooling for Canada, Catalogue 94-768, Vol. III – Part 6 (Bulletin 3.6-10) May 1975.

8.12   Annual average index numbers[1] of employment, by industrial division, 1970-75, and monthly indexes 1974 and 1975

Year and month	Forestry	Mining (incl. milling)	Manufacturing	Construction	Transportation, communication and other utilities	Trade	Finance, insurance and real estate	Service[2]	Industrial composite
Averages									
1970	84.2	115.7	122.8	113.9	112.6	139.3	143.6	178.5	127.1
1971P	79.4	114.9	121.6	115.5	114.6	140.3	145.9	186.5	127.8
1972P	76.3	110.4	123.7	109.7	116.0	146.2	148.7	193.5	129.9
1973P	86.4	111.4	129.9	109.9	118.0	155.3	157.1	206.1	135.9
1974P	87.4	115.5	133.8	117.1	124.6	165.7	167.3	224.0	142.8
1975P	76.0	114.1	126.3	117.1	125.8	168.5	175.0	232.0	141.1

8.12　Annual average index numbers[1] of employment, by industrial division, 1970-75, and monthly indexes 1974 and 1975 (concluded)

Year and month	Forestry	Mining (incl. milling)	Manu-factur-ing	Con-struc-tion	Trans-portation, commu-nication and other utilities	Trade	Finance, insur-ance and real estate	Service[2]	Indus-trial com-posite
1974P									
January	80.6	111.4	131.2	99.1	119.5	160.9	162.6	210.4	137.5
February	78.2	113.0	131.1	99.6	119.3	159.4	163.0	212.1	137.3
March	72.3	113.6	132.3	101.6	119.9	160.5	163.7	215.4	138.4
April	65.5	110.3	133.2	105.9	121.1	162.3	164.4	218.2	139.5
May	80.3	114.4	135.6	114.3	125.1	164.5	167.2	226.6	143.3
June	82.3	120.4	138.0	123.0	128.4	166.3	168.4	233.8	146.5
July	102.1	120.8	135.7	129.9	129.2	162.9	170.2	232.3	146.0
August	105.1	118.7	136.4	133.8	126.4	163.1	169.0	232.9	146.0
September	102.4	116.0	135.9	133.7	126.8	168.1	168.3	229.5	146.3
October	100.5	115.7	134.9	132.3	127.6	171.4	169.4	229.7	146.5
November	94.9	116.7	132.5	124.7	127.0	173.7	170.4	227.0	145.1
December	84.3	115.4	128.4	106.8	125.0	175.2	170.8	220.3	141.4
1975P									
January	77.2	114.9	125.2	101.2	124.3	166.7	170.3	218.8	138.0
February	73.0	115.1	124.7	101.0	123.7	163.4	170.5	220.0	137.0
March	66.8	113.1	125.5	101.9	124.8	163.4	172.2	219.2	137.5
April	58.9	111.1	125.6	107.6	125.1	166.8	171.5	224.5	138.7
May	77.4	113.7	128.1	119.1	129.3	168.5	174.9	234.0	142.7
June	96.0	115.8	130.3	122.7	131.8	168.6	176.1	241.3	145.4
July	88.4	117.3	126.3	126.8	131.8	165.2	177.9	240.9	143.4
August	87.6	112.6	127.7	131.6	129.6	165.3	176.5	243.7	143.8
September	79.8	110.1	126.5	132.6	128.6	168.5	177.6	239.7	143.3
October	79.5	113.3	127.0	130.7	118.2	173.3	177.1	237.0	142.2
November	68.6	116.3	125.8	122.9	116.3	175.4	177.5	233.5	140.9
December	58.6	116.1	123.3	107.5	125.1	177.0	177.5	230.9	140.3

[1]Indexes are calculated as at the last pay period of each month (1961 = 100).
[2]Consists mainly of hotels, restaurants, laundries, dry-cleaning establishments and recreational and business services.

8.13　Annual average index numbers[1] of employment, by industrial division and group, 1971-75

Industry	1971P	1972P	1973P	1974P	1975P
FORESTRY	79.4	76.3	86.4	87.4	76.0
MINING (incl. milling)	114.8	110.4	111.4	115.5	114.1
Metals	106.1	100.7	102.9	107.6	109 1
Gold	40.6	35.4	34.9	34.6	35.5
Copper-gold-silver	123.5	142.0	140.1	147.4	144.7
Iron	132.5	124.7	152.6	168.9	175.5
Mineral fuels	112.7	115.1	115.8	120.5	126.6
Coal	77.9	78.7	75.3	76.6	87.0
Crude petroleum and natural gas	146.8	151.1	155.7	164.0	165.7
Non-metals (except fuels)	133.6	131.5	130.2	140.2	117.6
Asbestos	120.5	117.2	114.0	117.3	83.9
MANUFACTURING	121.6	123.7	129.9	133.8	126.3
Durable goods	131.4	134.9	144.1	149.4	139.8
Non-durable goods	113.7	114.7	118.4	121.1	115.5
Foods and beverages	108.6	107.9	110.2	110.9	107.5
Slaughtering and meat processing	105.8	104.8	104.2	107.5	106.6
Dairy products	100.2	98.1	96.8	94.4	91.0
Fish products	134.3	137.9	149.8	147.2	129.8
Fish and vegetable processing	112.5	110.4	116.1	117.1	112.7
Grain mill products	105.6	102.8	103.0	109.7	110.6
Biscuits	100.4	101.7	102.5	100.0	98.4
Bakeries	91.1	88.7	88.1	85.3	84.7
Confectionery	101.9	96.4	96.2	94.8	87.3
Soft drinks	115.3	110.3	113.0	115.3	118.0
Distilleries	113.4	117.8	119.3	116.7	115.8
Breweries	105.0	104.6	112.3	115.9	117.1
Tobacco processing and products	94.6	92.8	92.1	91.2	85.3
Rubber products	111.7	118.4	125.5	120.8	123.0
Leather products	91.5	89.1	91.5	91.5	87.4
Shoes (except rubber)	87.6	81.7	82.2	81.8	78.4
Luggage, handbags and small leather goods	111.1	119.0	130.8	132.4	123.2
Textile products	114.8	122.3	127.8	126.2	112.3
Cotton yarn and cloth	76.5	75.1	73.7	72.3	60.2
Woollen yarn and cloth	83.7	87.3	94.1	88.9	76.6
Synthetic textiles	122.8	128.6	130.7	128.9	110.8
Knitting mills	112.2	116.4	118.7	116.8	114.0
Hosiery	95.6	92.5	87.2	83.6	68.8
Other knitting mills	122.2	131.0	137.7	136.8	140.6

8.13 Annual average index numbers[1] of employment, by industrial division and group, 1971-75 (continued)

Industry	1971P	1972P	1973P	1974P	1975P
MANUFACTURING (concluded)					
Clothing	108.9	110.4	114.4	113.1	110.7
Men's clothing	119.7	124.1	128.1	128.2	123.9
Women's clothing	112.0	113.6	119.2	116.2	115.6
Wood products	115.9	121.3	132.7	132.4	117.2
Saw, shingle and planing mills	117.3	123.0	137.1	135.4	113.1
Furniture and fixtures	129.6	139.3	150.7	157.1	138.5
Household furniture	132.1	146.5	159.6	166.7	144.3
Paper and allied industries	119.4	119.6	121.7	133.0	117.2
Pulp and paper mills	115.4	114.9	115.5	127.1	108.1
Printing, publishing and allied industries	113.4	111.9	115.8	120.8	122.4
Commercial printing	116.1	114.4	121.4	128.8	128.9
Printing and publishing	108.4	106.3	104.6	108.0	109.4
Primary metal industries	128.9	127.5	132.4	138.3	135.0
Iron and steel mills	137.0	139.0	145.2	152.7	149.9
Iron foundries	130.0	136.0	144.6	155.1	142.4
Smelting and refining	118.9	109.0	112.8	115.9	116.0
Metal fabricating industries	130.9	133.3	141.8	148.4	139.1
Fabricated structural metals	112.4	98.3	103.5	113.1	118.6
Ornamental and architectural metals	121.4	123.2	142.5	149.1	131.1
Metal stamping, pressing and coating	138.5	147.7	151.8	155.2	140.7
Wire and wire products	133.7	136.7	147.9	152.0	137.6
Hardware, tools and cutlery	156.8	167.5	183.5	192.0	174.7
Heating equipment	96.7	98.6	101.5	105.3	99.0
Miscellaneous metal fabricating	127.9	134.1	145.2	152.2	136.4
Machinery (except electrical)	143.6	146.2	161.0	174.3	171.6
Agricultural implements	86.6	105.8	133.9	152.4	162.2
Miscellaneous machinery and equipment	146.0	148.5	167.6	185.4	178.5
Office and store machinery	210.8	190.7	158.1	141.6	150.3
Transportation equipment	144.3	152.5	163.7	161.2	151.1
Aircraft and parts	80.5	77.9	82.0	74.9	67.6
Motor vehicles	186.8	197.2	220.1	218.9	200.3
Assembling	175.9	180.0	194.2	202.2	186.7
Parts and accessories	184.7	194.2	218.1	205.4	184.2
Shipbuilding and repairing	93.3	113.0	106.6	100.9	111.4
Electrical products	134.1	135.8	142.6	154.2	140.0
Major appliances (incl. non-electrical)	103.1	113.3	120.6	120.8	100.1
Household radios and televisions	121.4	144.6	157.3	162.3	120.6
Communications equipment	155.8	143.3	155.1	169.5	147.7
Non-metallic mineral products	113.6	117.9	126.3	132.4	126.5
Concrete products	135.9	133.9	144.1	158.2	145.6
Clay products	100.3	93.1	99.9	103.0	97.1
Glass and glass products	118.8	125.9	137.2	138.3	129.3
Petroleum and coal products	105.6	105.9	105.7	113.5	115.0
Petroleum refineries	91.9	89.8	90.2	100.2	100.3
Chemicals and chemical products	116.3	114.3	117.8	123.7	124.6
Pharmaceuticals and medicines	148.6	154.2	164.2	170.3	164.5
Paints and varnishes	108.3	105.6	110.5	114.6	112.7
Soap and cleaning compounds	96.0	94.8	97.9	105.6	108.8
Industrial chemicals	112.5	105.8	104.5	109.9	114.9
Miscellaneous manufacturing industries	151.9	157.7	170.6	176.0	160.9
CONSTRUCTION	115.5	109.7	109.9	117.1	117.1
Building	125.2	115.4	117.1	124.7	121.5
General contractors	104.1	93.2	94.4	99.9	94.2
Special trade contractors	147.7	138.7	140.9	150.8	150.3
Engineering	98.8	99.0	97.7	104.1	109.7
Highways, bridges and streets	82.0	81.1	81.3	83.2	83.6
Other engineering	120.3	121.5	118.3	130.4	142.5
TRANSPORTATION, COMMUNICATION AND OTHER UTILITIES	114.6	116.0	118.0	124.6	125.8
Transportation	107.4	108.5	108.1	114.1	114.1
Air transport and services	158.2	166.8	180.7	206.0	213.1
Water transport and services	99.4	95.3	95.3	95.4	91.1
Railway transport	83.9	84.1	72.6	87.6	84.9
Truck transport	137.1	134.6	141.1	149.3	141.5
Bus transport, interurban and rural	135.7	141.8	147.0	156.8	161.7
Urban transit	114.1	116.4	124.2	132.8	143.8
Highway and bridge maintenance	116.0	121.1	116.0	114.4	119.7
Storage	110.1	111.6	112.4	111.4	112.2
Grain elevators	103.5	102.9	99.3	96.2	100.6
Other storage and warehousing	127.8	135.0	148.4	153.6	144.9
Communication	130.4	134.6	141.0	151.7	151.7
Radio and television broadcasting	136.4	138.8	143.6	153.0	162.9
Telephone	125.7	129.2	135.6	147.7	150.9
Telegraph and cable	78.7	77.8	72.6	76.6	78.4
Post office	153.1	160.7	171.5	182.3	171.2
ELECTRIC POWER, GAS AND WATER	124.4	122.5	128.9	133.2	141.3
Electric power	128.9	125.5	132.7	137.8	147.7
Gas distribution	102.9	109.3	113.5	113.8	124.1
TRADE	140.3	146.2	155.3	165.7	168.5
Wholesale	132.8	135.1	143.8	154.6	157.1
Retail	144.3	152.2	161.5	171.7	174.6
Food stores	144.1	151.7	157.1	164.1	170.8
Department stores	139.9	149.2	157.9	167.4	165.1
Variety stores	132.2	138.4	146.6	153.0	147.7
Automotive product stores	155.7	159.6	172.5	184.9	191.1

8.13   Annual average index numbers[1] of employment, by industrial division and group, 1971-75 (concluded)

Industry	1971P	1972P	1973P	1974P	1975P
FINANCE, INSURANCE AND REAL ESTATE	145.9	148.7	157.1	167.3	175.0
Financial institutions	148.5	155.9	168.7	180.7	189.9
Insurance and real estate	141.5	139.0	141.2	149.1	154.8
Insurance carriers	126.8	121.3	116.6	119.0	120.6
SERVICE	186.4	193.5	206.1	224.0	232.0
Recreational services	167.9	174.8	186.2	197.8	204.6
Business services	207.8	220.5	234.9	271.2	286.2
Personal services	167.9	172.8	182.5	194.8	202.1
Miscellaneous services	233.3	239.2	256.5	273.9	277.0
Industrial composite	127.8	129.9	135.9	142.8	141.1

[1]Indexes refer to the last week of each month (1961 = 100).

8.14   Annual average index numbers[1] of employment for industrial composite, by province, 1971-75, and monthly indexes 1974 and 1975

Year and month	Nfld.	PEI	NS	NB	Que.	Ont.	Man.	Sask.	Alta.	BC	Canada
Averages											
1971P	125.9	139.4	113.7	122.8	118.7	132.1	117.2	114.4	139.6	144.5	127.8
1972P	126.5	140.6	116.7	122.7	120.1	134.2	117.6	116.8	143.6	148.4	129.9
1973P	131.3	144.4	123.0	126.8	124.6	141.2	119.9	120.3	150.8	157.4	135.9
1974P	139.5	152.0	130.2	134.4	129.9	147.5	128.4	130.0	163.1	167.2	142.8
1975P	135.5	149.9	128.9	136.1	128.5	144.2	130.1	137.0	169.6	161.3	141.1
1974P											
January	131.5	132.5	123.0	123.9	125.3	143.4	121.7	120.8	152.7	160.9	137.5
February	126.4	133.4	124.6	124.1	125.0	142.8	121.6	122.5	154.6	162.2	137.3
March	125.8	135.5	125.5	124.3	125.5	143.6	122.7	122.6	156.5	166.2	138.4
April	127.8	140.5	126.7	123.6	126.3	145.0	124.7	123.4	157.4	167.4	139.5
May	136.5	155.2	131.4	132.6	130.4	148.1	129.3	129.0	162.2	168.7	143.3
June	149.9	170.0	134.6	142.9	133.9	151.5	131.5	134.1	167.0	165.2	146.5
July	151.7	175.8	134.9	145.2	131.7	149.6	131.8	136.4	169.6	172.1	146.0
August	147.0	172.2	135.8	144.9	132.9	148.9	132.4	135.9	169.4	172.9	146.0
September	149.8	162.6	133.6	141.8	133.3	150.2	131.7	135.1	167.8	171.2	146.3
October	146.4	158.1	132.4	139.7	133.9	151.0	131.5	134.8	168.5	169.1	146.5
November	144.7	149.5	132.0	137.7	132.2	149.5	132.0	134.8	166.9	167.4	145.1
December	136.7	139.0	127.6	131.5	127.8	146.4	129.6	132.3	164.3	163.0	141.4
1975P											
January	126.4	132.1	124.6	127.1	125.5	142.6	127.3	129.2	160.5	158.9	138.0
February	124.8	128.8	123.2	125.1	124.8	141.5	127.0	128.1	160.6	158.0	137.0
March	126.1	128.7	124.4	125.3	124.5	141.8	126.9	129.2	160.9	161.8	137.5
April	128.3	134.5	126.4	127.5	124.5	143.2	127.8	131.6	162.2	164.3	138.7
May	131.6	159.0	133.1	137.8	129.3	145.8	130.6	137.7	168.3	168.7	142.7
June	140.9	170.8	133.0	145.4	132.3	147.8	133.2	141.4	173.1	169.7	145.4
July	145.5	169.6	133.9	147.5	130.6	145.7	133.1	144.4	174.9	158.9	143.4
August	145.7	171.5	132.6	149.0	131.1	146.5	133.3	143.4	176.3	157.7	143.8
September	149.6	163.1	129.0	148.3	132.6	145.8	133.8	141.6	176.0	151.9	143.3
October	147.4	156.9	131.5	138.1	130.4	143.7	131.1	138.0	174.5	162.1	142.2
November	135.0	143.9	129.1	133.7	128.4	143.3	129.3	139.3	173.4	161.6	140.9
December	124.7	140.3	126.4	128.4	127.8	143.2	127.6	140.0	174.5	161.9	140.3

[1]Indexes refer to the last week of each month (1961 = 100).

8.15   Annual average index numbers[1] of employment for industrial composite, by metropolitan area, 1971-75, and monthly indexes 1974 and 1975

Year and month	Montreal	Quebec	Toronto	Ottawa-Hull	Hamilton	Windsor	Winnipeg	Vancouver
Averages								
1971P	120.2	129.8	135.5	143.1	123.6	150.0	120.1	144.9
1972P	120.9	132.1	139.0	146.8	123.9	153.4	120.2	149.8
1973P	126.0	134.4	147.2	156.9	129.8	160.4	123.0	157.6
1974P	130.9	137.4	154.5	168.5	136.5	159.8	130.0	169.1
1975P	130.8	137.2	152.4	167.1	134.1	148.1	132.4	166.4
1974P								
January	128.4	134.2	150.6	161.2	131.3	161.9	124.0	163.1
February	127.2	134.3	150.1	161.7	131.9	158.6	123.5	164.1
March	128.2	133.0	151.9	161.0	131.4	154.0	124.6	168.2
April	129.3	133.7	152.8	163.0	132.5	156.2	126.6	169.2
May	132.1	137.8	154.9	168.2	137.0	159.2	131.0	166.9
June	133.8	139.5	158.1	172.5	140.6	162.8	132.8	167.1
July	130.3	138.6	155.3	171.1	139.4	158.2	131.8	171.2
August	131.3	141.6	152.8	173.8	139.6	162.2	132.3	172.5
September	132.8	141.4	156.5	174.1	138.5	164.8	132.3	172.8
October	134.1	140.5	158.9	173.6	139.5	163.2	133.5	172.5
November	133.3	139.4	157.4	172.6	139.3	159.7	135.0	172.7
December	129.6	135.2	154.2	169.5	137.0	156.4	132.0	168.8

8.15   Annual average index numbers[1] of employment for industrial composite, by metropolitan area, 1971-75, and monthly indexes 1974 and 1975 (concluded)

1975P								
January	128.8	132.1	152.1	165.9	134.1	141.8	130.3	164.6
February	128.3	132.2	150.8	165.3	132.4	144.6	129.8	163.6
March	128.2	132.6	150.4	163.0	132.3	143.5	130.5	166.6
April	128.7	133.0	151.2	165.4	133.9	147.7	131.0	169.1
May	132.0	137.9	153.6	170.7	135.3	148.9	132.5	171.4
June	133.7	142.1	155.1	171.5	136.5	150.1	134.4	170.7
July	130.5	140.5	152.7	169.6	135.2	151.1	133.5	168.0
August	130.5	142.8	152.8	170.7	134.6	151.4	133.7	167.7
September	134.2	143.7	153.6	169.0	133.7	153.6	135.9	160.0
October	132.7	137.6	151.8	164.3	133.4	148.5	133.4	164.3
November	131.0	136.1	151.6	162.7	133.8	146.6	132.3	164.4
December	131.5	135.8	152.6	167.4	133.5	149.3	131.4	166.3

[1]Indexes refer to the last week of each month (1961 = 100).

8.16   Annual index numbers of employment and average weekly earnings, by industry, province and urban area, 1973-75

Industry, province and urban area	Employment (1961 = 100)			Average weekly wages and salaries (dollars)		
	1973P	1974P	1975P	1973P	1974P	1975P
INDUSTRY						
Forestry	86.4	87.4	76.0	197.04	219.64	249.58
Mining (incl. milling)	111.4	115.5	114.4	211.42	238.97	280.44
Manufacturing	129.9	133.8	126.3	167.48	185.62	213.43
Durable goods[1]	144.1	149.4	139.8	180.41	198.39	227.11
Non-durable goods[1]	118.4	121.1	115.5	154.71	172.86	199.98
Construction	109.9	117.1	117.1	225.45	250.30	290.95
Transportation, communication and other utilities	118.0	124.6	125.8	181.89	204.39	233.98
Trade	155.3	165.7	168.5	126.49	139.92	159.06
Finance, insurance and real estate	157.1	167.3	175.0	154.54	172.25	193.12
Service	206.1	224.0	232.0	114.53	126.08	143.69
Industrial composite	135.9	142.8	141.1	160.46	178.09	203.34
PROVINCE (industrial composite)						
Newfoundland	131.3	139.5	135.5	149.09	168.48	196.44
Prince Edward Island	144.4	152.0	149.9	111.17	126.92	149.84
Nova Scotia	123.0	130.2	128.9	134.44	149.98	172.40
New Brunswick	126.8	134.4	136.1	133.97	154.58	182.40
Quebec	124.6	129.9	128.5	154.30	172.89	199.22
Ontario	141.2	147.5	144.2	165.61	181.43	204.85
Manitoba	119.9	128.4	130.1	144.76	162.71	186.01
Saskatchewan	120.3	130.0	137.0	142.28	160.99	188.31
Alberta	150.8	163.1	169.6	161.12	178.72	207.38
British Columbia	157.4	167.2	161.3	178.22	200.55	230.01
URBAN AREA (industrial composite)						
Corner Brook, Nfld.	101.9	110.1	104.9	158.84	177.17	189.69
St. John's, Nfld.	166.2	171.7	165.0	138.63	150.10	175.17
Halifax, NS	133.3	146.3	146.7	135.78	148.56	171.23
Sydney, NS	97.6	97.9	92.1	145.05	167.27	196.37
Moncton, NB	148.5	152.7	153.1	126.19	143.72	166.04
Saint John, NB	119.3	129.6	135.3	140.83	162.92	192.38
Chicoutimi, Que.	111.0	119.3	116.2	177.40	199.87	226.83
Drummondville, Que.	135.0	139.1	130.1	124.59	138.67	159.34
Granby, Que.	120.8	110.5	113.9	124.52	139.26	162.09
Montreal, Que.	126.0	130.9	130.8	157.11	174.54	201.49
Ottawa, Ont.-Hull, Que.	156.9	168.5	167.1	151.23	165.13	186.03
Quebec, Que.	134.4	137.4	137.2	142.39	158.52	179.82
Rouyn-Noranda, Que.	98.6	107.8	101.0	154.44	182.99	221.52
Saint-Hyacinthe, Que.	132.6	123.6	118.4	118.69	133.92	157.16
Saint-Jean, Que.	150.6	151.3	138.0	132.18	148.35	170.62
Saint-Jérôme, Que.	151.8	149.3	136.1	133.21	150.10	176.70
Shawinigan, Que.	87.7	89.7	81.6	159.50	181.53	203.87
Sherbrooke, Que.	116.9	126.1	125.0	132.43	147.41	169.33
Sorel, Que.	172.7	184.0	186.7	175.36	197.97	228.30
Thetford Mines, Que.	126.0	126.7	79.2	158.90	174.40	196.18
Trois-Rivières, Que.	115.9	126.7	118.3	148.10	167.13	192.91
Valleyfield, Que.	137.0	142.7	139.1	157.97	179.99	203.80
Barrie, Ont.	209.1	222.7	219.2	148.22	155.96	175.46
Belleville, Ont.	134.4	142.7	137.5	139.12	151.03	171.09
Brampton, Ont.	332.1	360.1	353.2	170.50	186.95	211.71
Brantford, Ont.	143.7	152.4	153.2	154.54	170.50	195.25
Brockville, Ont.	134.4	141.2	133.7	152.45	168.30	192.46
Chatham, Ont.	178.5	184.5	179.1	177.37	185.32	208.19
Cornwall, Ont.	135.5	140.9	118.6	150.02	167.90	188.30
Guelph, Ont.	145.8	155.5	156.4	148.87	163.01	186.32

8.16   Annual index numbers of employment and average weekly earnings, by industry, province and urban area, 1973-75 (concluded)

Industry, province and urban area	Employment (1961 = 100)			Average weekly wages and salaries (dollars)		
	1973P	1974P	1975P	1973P	1974P	1975P
URBAN AREA (industrial composite) (concluded)						
Hamilton, Ont.	129.8	136.5	134.1	170.85	186.42	211.42
Kingston, Ont.	130.0	138.0	138.3	152.94	169.44	190.52
Kitchener, Ont.²	173.2	181.0	170.0	146.84	158.87	180.42
London, Ont.	132.4	138.5	132.9	154.86	171.57	193.92
Midland, Ont.	217.5	220.5	180.5	128.82	142.46	165.69
Niagara Falls, Ont.	120.8	125.7	125.7	150.75	161.15	179.39
North Bay, Ont.	122.2	134.1	132.6	159.98	178.71	198.35
Orillia, Ont.	151.9	161.5	154.9	127.72	137.65	163.66
Oshawa, Ont.	148.7	149.2	140.5	195.67	211.56	229.69
Owen Sound, Ont.	160.5	165.1	156.9	137.16	151.49	175.17
Pembroke, Ont.	108.6	119.7	111.0	121.66	134.09	158.41
Peterborough, Ont.	135.5	140.8	147.6	168.11	183.61	205.08
Port Hope, Ont.	176.9	189.3	180.5	159.47	172.54	199.22
St. Catharines, Ont.	146.1	145.6	136.1	180.83	196.10	216.46
St. Thomas, Ont.	226.7	225.5	197.3	181.41	194.12	204.09
Sarnia, Ont.	135.3	144.2	146.2	203.08	220.37	248.68
Sault Ste Marie, Ont.	126.9	136.0	137.2	185.24	204.14	223.10
Stratford, Ont.	184.6	187.7	173.3	136.49	149.66	172.07
Sudbury, Ont.	108.0	109.2	113.9	187.05	199.44	231.39
Thunder Bay, Ont.	137.9	145.6	138.9	158.70	178.31	203.29
Timmins, Ont.	80.3	82.2	87.1	158.01	182.42	214.54
Toronto, Ont.	147.2	154.5	152.4	166.81	182.36	206.08
Welland, Ont.	107.1	112.2	107.1	186.75	203.70	224.44
Windsor, Ont.	160.4	159.8	148.1	201.17	210.97	229.37
Woodstock, Ont.	166.4	152.5	133.4	153.46	163.65	182.64
Brandon, Man.	133.5	145.5	146.5	119.16	131.61	154.02
Winnipeg, Man.	123.0	130.0	132.4	136.89	150.81	172.86
Moose Jaw, Sask.	79.5	83.8	89.5	119.89	133.37	158.89
Prince Albert, Sask.	137.9	145.9	135.3	147.07	169.74	187.21
Regina, Sask.	131.3	141.2	152.9	139.30	156.57	184.39
Saskatoon, Sask.	139.7	152.8	158.2	132.65	147.32	171.61
Calgary, Alta.	163.0	179.7	189.6	159.47	175.66	203.18
Edmonton, Alta.	160.7	172.9	180.1	153.08	171.30	197.41
Lethbridge, Alta.	155.9	162.7	165.6	131.75	145.77	173.12
Medicine Hat, Alta.	112.8	122.8	143.4	140.69	153.98	209.29
Red Deer, Alta.	203.1	220.1	235.4	133.19	147.55	167.88
Kamloops, BC	294.8	314.4	301.0	162.11	180.67	203.86
Prince George, BC	279.2	302.3	274.4	181.82	205.66	233.32
Vancouver, BC	157.6	169.1	166.4	174.47	194.41	224.06
Victoria, BC	144.5	151.8	149.9	148.75	167.38	193.92

¹Durable goods manufacturing includes wood products, furniture and fixtures, primary metal industries, metal fabricating industries, machinery (except electrical), transportation equipment, electrical products and non-metallic mineral products; non-durable goods manufacturing includes all other manufacturing industries.
²Kitchener, Cambridge and Waterloo.

8.17   Annual average weekly earnings, by industrial division, 1971-75, and monthly averages 1974 and 1975 (dollars)

Year and month	Forestry	Mining (incl. milling)	Manufacturing	Construction	Transportation, communication and other utilities	Trade	Finance, insurance and real estate	Service¹	Industrial composite
Averages									
1971P	155.53	177.00	143.99	188.26	154.14	108.45	129.59	98.57	137.64
1972P	172.92	190.29	156.10	209.90	167.94	117.58	140.79	107.32	149.22
1973P	197.04	211.42	167.48	225.45	181.89	126.49	154.54	114.53	160.46
1974P	219.64	238.97	185.62	250.30	204.39	139.92	172.25	126.08	178.09
1975P	249.58	280.44	213.43	290.95	233.98	159.06	193.12	143.69	203.34
1974P									
January	204.70	225.36	175.77	233.27	195.10	129.79	164.19	119.18	167.72
February	217.94	226.44	176.38	236.42	196.16	131.58	166.79	118.80	169.06
March	222.42	229.45	178.72	239.22	197.76	133.34	169.73	119.59	171.07
April	217.80	229.79	179.96	240.62	199.40	135.64	171.49	121.51	172.56
May	217.67	233.96	181.67	247.39	203.84	138.18	172.10	123.55	175.41
June	201.20	233.54	182.55	249.53	200.95	141.72	172.11	125.97	176.40
July	218.39	234.63	184.94	254.81	205.66	144.52	174.04	129.13	180.07
August	223.95	240.44	187.60	258.06	206.74	143.97	174.09	129.92	181.73
September	229.86	245.54	192.61	268.64	208.62	143.22	172.90	129.38	184.34
October	240.59	252.72	196.84	270.92	211.22	144.29	174.21	131.25	187.10
November	240.26	258.24	197.76	266.43	212.14	146.02	175.94	132.52	187.65
December	200.85	257.52	192.61	238.28	215.12	146.78	179.46	132.49	183.91

8.17   Annual average weekly earnings, by industrial division, 1971-75, and monthly averages 1974 and 1975 (dollars) (concluded)

Year and month	For- estry	Mining (incl. milling)	Manu- factur- ing	Con- struc- tion	Trans- portation, communi- cation and other utilities	Trade	Finance, insur- ance and real estate	Service[1]	Indus- trial com- posite
1975P									
January	245.16	263.29	202.66	267.48	222.10	148.18	185.53	136.09	192.08
February	251.78	265.63	204.91	271.53	224.22	150.73	185.67	136.42	194.18
March	264.37	273.47	205.79	265.78	224.25	153.17	188.88	138.98	195.60
April	266.79	272.25	209.68	280.08	227.33	153.91	189.71	139.48	197.44
May	255.62	273.13	210.77	284.18	228.42	157.36	191.65	140.79	200.44
June	255.46	273.61	212.47	288.72	230.80	161.53	193.39	143.25	203.13
July	229.37	278.24	212.75	295.79	234.59	164.11	195.25	146.41	205.25
August	242.44	281.64	213.98	303.55	235.67	163.22	193.85	147.27	206.38
September	241.01	289.31	218.59	314.13	237.72	162.02	195.17	146.19	208.83
October	263.05	296.32	222.80	321.57	248.02	163.37	197.80	148.41	212.94
November	265.77	299.15	224.48	318.51	249.75	162.90	198.56	149.59	213.34
December	214.18	299.20	222.30	280.03	244.89	168.09	201.96	151.42	210.43

[1]Mainly hotels, restaurants, laundries, dry-cleaning establishments and recreational and business services.

8.18   Annual average weekly hours and hourly earnings of hourly rated wage-earners in specified industries, 1970-75, and monthly averages 1974 and 1975

Year and month	All manufactures		Mining (incl. milling)		Construction	
	Average weekly hours	Average hourly earnings $	Average weekly hours	Average hourly earnings $	Average weekly hours	Average hourly earnings $
Averages						
1970	39.7	3.01	41.0	3.71	39.2	4.21
1971P	39.7	3.28	40.4	4.04	39.2	4.75
1972P	40.0	3.54	40.3	4.34	40.1	5.15
1973P	39.6	3.85	40.9	4.82	39.5	5.66
1974P	38.9	4.37	40.4	5.50	39.1	6.43
1975P	38.6	5.06	40.0	6.51	39.0	7.53
1974P						
January	39.5	4.08	41.3	5.09	38.3	6.09
February	39.4	4.09	41.1	5.14	38.5	6.15
March	39.5	4.15	40.7	5.26	38.8	6.19
April	39.2	4.21	40.2	5.28	38.3	6.29
May	39.0	4.27	40.5	5.39	39.1	6.35
June	39.0	4.30	39.9	5.45	40.3	6.21
July	38.4	4.39	39.4	5.52	40.6	6.32
August	38.7	4.44	39.8	5.60	40.3	6.45
September	39.1	4.54	40.2	5.65	40.9	6.65
October	39.2	4.64	40.8	5.79	40.5	6.77
November	39.0	4.66	41.2	5.88	38.9	6.90
December	36.8	4.71	39.8	5.98	34.4	6.75
1975P						
January	38.7	4.77	40.6	5.99	38.0	7.04
February	38.7	4.83	40.8	6.02	38.3	7.12
March	38.3	4.91	40.6	6.27	36.8	7.18
April	38.8	4.96	40.0	6.25	39.0	7.24
May	38.6	5.01	39.6	6.38	39.3	7.29
June	38.5	5.07	39.2	6.44	39.8	7.33
July	38.1	5.07	39.3	6.57	40.5	7.43
August	38.4	5.07	39.4	6.63	40.3	7.67
September	39.0	5.14	39.7	6.78	40.7	7.89
October	39.1	5.24	40.5	6.88	40.9	8.04
November	39.0	5.28	40.6	6.95	39.8	8.19
December	37.7	5.34	40.1	7.01	35.1	7.88

8.19 Average weekly hours and hourly earnings of hourly rated wage-earners in specified industries and selected urban areas, 1973-75

Industry, province and urban area	Average weekly hours			Average hourly earnings ($)		
	1973P	1974P	1975P	1973P	1974P	1975P
INDUSTRY						
Mining (incl. milling)	40.9	40.4	40.0	4.82	5.50	6.51
Metal mining	39.6	39.4	39.4	4.94	5.65	6.60
Coal mining	40.7	39.8	38.2	4.45	5.25	6.38
Manufacturing	39.6	38.9	38.6	3.85	4.37	5.06
Durable goods[1]	40.3	39.5	39.1	4.17	4.69	5.41
Non-durable goods[1]	39.0	38.3	38.0	3.52	4.03	4.68
Construction	39.5	39.1	39.0	5.66	6.43	7.53
Building	37.9	37.5	37.4	5.88	6.63	7.68
Engineering	42.7	42.3	42.0	5.32	6.05	7.26
Other						
Urban transit	41.9	41.6	40.5	4.61	5.21	6.01
Highway and bridge maintenance	41.2	40.8	41.0	3.62	4.06	4.78
Hotels, restaurants and taverns	29.9	28.4	27.5	2.30	2.65	3.08
Laundries, cleaners and pressers	36.0	34.7	34.5	2.26	2.60	3.03
PROVINCE						
Manufacturing						
Newfoundland	41.1	38.4	37.8	3.29	4.17	4.81
Nova Scotia	39.1	38.2	38.5	3.30	3.87	4.57
New Brunswick	39.3	38.2	38.2	3.23	3.88	4.65
Quebec	40.1	39.6	39.1	3.35	3.87	4.56
Ontario	40.0	39.2	38.9	4.06	4.54	5.18
Manitoba	38.5	37.6	37.3	3.45	3.95	4.62
Saskatchewan	38.6	37.8	37.0	3.94	4.49	5.39
Alberta	38.5	37.4	37.4	4.11	4.66	5.53
British Columbia	37.3	36.4	36.1	4.91	5.66	6.55
SELECTED URBAN AREA						
Manufacturing						
Montreal	39.6	39.1	38.8	3.40	3.89	4.58
Toronto	40.1	39.3	38.9	3.84	4.31	4.94
Hamilton	39.4	38.8	38.7	4.50	4.95	5.68
Windsor	42.6	40.9	40.6	5.18	5.64	6.23
Winnipeg	38.5	37.5	37.2	3.40	3.87	4.54
Vancouver	37.0	36.0	35.7	4.80	5.43	6.37

[1]Durable goods manufacturing includes wood products, furniture and fixtures, primary metal industries, metal fabricating industries, machinery (except electrical), transportation equipment, electrical products and non-metallic mineral products; non-durable goods manufacturing includes all other manufacturing industries.

8.20 Wages and salaries, by industry and supplementary labour income, 1970-75, and by month 1974 and 1975 (million dollars)

Year and month	Industry						
	Agriculture	Forestry	Mining	Manufacturing	Construction	Transportation, communication and other utilities	Trade
Annual							
1970	368	491	1,155	11,589	3,436	4,881	6,054
1971r	389	552	1,240	12,293	4,215	5,191	6,562
1972P	407	586	1,292	13,581	4,581	5,718	7,414
1973P	490	739	1,504	15,416	5,571	6,457	8,462
1974P	546	883	1,823	17,757	6,594	7,703	9,986
1975P	662	875	2,121	19,257	7,846	8,664	11,579
1974P							
January	27.1	60.2	135.8	1,365.3	428.6	580.1	749.3
February	27.4	62.8	138.0	1,367.1	437.3	583.7	752.6
March	31.0	60.0	142.3	1,399.4	452.1	594.6	768.1
April	36.7	54.0	139.1	1,422.5	473.3	605.5	790.7
May	44.5	65.8	146.1	1,462.0	524.9	643.4	815.7
June	53.7	69.8	154.3	1,501.1	556.8	649.9	845.9
July	63.3	74.9	157.7	1,492.0	612.5	666.2	844.3
August	71.3	88.9	157.8	1,523.1	639.3	659.2	842.6
September	63.3	89.8	156.8	1,565.4	664.7	660.3	864.0
October	51.3	92.0	162.0	1,571.1	671.2	671.2	887.4
November	41.3	87.5	166.7	1,560.5	622.9	669.7	901.2
December	34.7	77.2	166.9	1,527.3	510.2	719.5	924.4

8.20   Wages and salaries, by industry and supplementary labour income, 1970-75, and by month 1974 and 1975 (million dollars) (concluded)

Year and month	Industry						
	Agriculture	Forestry	Mining	Manufacturing	Construction	Transportation, communication and other utilities	Trade
1975P							
January	31.6	70.9	166.5	1,518.0	509.7	677.8	888.0
February	32.0	68.6	167.4	1,514.5	518.5	677.0	883.9
March	36.4	69.0	171.4	1,544.0	534.6	694.0	902.3
April	43.3	61.5	166.2	1,553.7	585.2	695.7	925.0
May	52.9	75.2	176.8	1,606.1	655.2	722.0	954.2
June	64.2	93.0	178.3	1,646.1	674.0	745.0	980.7
July	76.4	84.7	175.2	1,610.6	721.9	765.3	975.3
August	87.0	80.1	178.0	1,622.7	757.3	757.9	969.3
September	78.1	75.6	175.2	1,648.2	777.0	742.0	982.2
October	64.0	77.2	182.5	1,665.5	780.5	738.2	1,014.8
November	52.1	70.4	191.7	1,670.3	718.3	704.8	1,031.0
December	44.1	48.3	191.5	1,656.8	613.4	744.3	1,072.5

	Finance, insurance and real estate	Service	Public administration and defence[1]	Total wages and salaries[2]	Supplementary labour income	Total labour income
Annual						
1970	2,384	10,389	3,407	44,203	2,503	46,706
1971r	2,579	11,576	3,944	48,591	2,938	51,528
1972P	3,037	12,903	4,493	54,070	3,500	57,570
1973P	3,720	14,636	5,071	62,145	4,213	66,358
1974P	4,421	17,265	6,153	73,200	5,320	78,521
1975P	5,155	20,372	7,428	84,021	6,565	90,587
1974P						
January	340.7	1,329.6	445.9	5,464.7	435.6	5,900.3
February	347.6	1,343.4	459.2	5,521.0	437.3	5,958.2
March	355.8	1,358.3	472.2	5,638.0	444.2	6,082.2
April	361.5	1,372.2	468.4	5,727.3	442.4	6,169.7
May	369.4	1,398.2	509.9	5,985.6	454.2	6,439.8
June	372.2	1,429.2	521.1	6,162.5	462.5	6,625.0
July	380.0	1,329.6	548.8	6,180.9	445.1	6,626.0
August	377.0	1,380.2	532.2	6,283.2	439.5	6,722.6
September	372.0	1,591.3	540.7	6,575.3	452.4	7,027.8
October	376.4	1,525.0	534.7	6,546.8	439.3	6,986.1
November	381.4	1,540.0	544.9	6,518.9	433.9	6,952.8
December	387.1	1,667.6	575.2	6,596.2	433.7	7,029.9
1975P						
January	401.2	1,577.7	558.3	6,403.0	547.6	6,950.6
February	402.6	1,589.9	560.5	6,416.7	545.1	6,961.8
March	414.2	1,610.6	570.1	6,550.7	552.3	7,103.1
April	414.8	1,637.7	569.6	6,655.5	550.0	7,205.5
May	425.0	1,685.6	605.1	6,964.0	564.2	7,528.2
June	433.0	1,709.0	640.4	7,171.2	577.4	7,748.6
July	441.8	1,706.4	666.8	7,232.9	558.5	7,791.4
August	434.8	1,562.9	640.8	7,097.2	536.0	7,633.2
September	440.2	1,873.4	654.3	7,452.9	551.6	8,004.5
October	445.5	1,803.8	627.1	7,403.4	535.7	7,939.1
November	446.3	1,805.1	646.9	7,341.0	527.1	7,868.0
December	455.3	1,810.3	688.7	7,332.7	519.6	7,852.3

Table based on the 1960 Standard Industrial Classification. Figure not adjusted for seasonality.
[1] Excludes military pay and allowances.
[2] Includes fishing and trapping.

8.21   Summary of selected working conditions of non-office and office employees in manufacturing and all industries, 1974 and 1975

Item		1974 Manufacturing industries	1974 All industries	1975 Manufacturing industries	1975 All industries
		Coverage			
NON-OFFICE EMPLOYEES					
Reporting establishments	No.	7,019	23,814	6,302	21,971
Employees	,,	860,626	2,203,775	776,924	2,151,622
OFFICE EMPLOYEES					
Reporting establishments	No.	6,985	18,902	6,245	17,281
Employees	,,	276,937	1,143,080	258,701	1,165,679
		Percentage of non-office employees			
STANDARD WEEKLY HOURS					
35 hours or less		2	2	3	3
Over 35 and under 37½ hours		1	3	2	4
37½ hours		3	10	3	9
Over 37½ and under 40 hours		1	4	1	6
40 hours		80	67	80	65
Over 40 and under 44 hours		5	4	5	3
44 hours and over		7	6	6	5
VACATIONS WITH PAY					
One week		52	42	44	35
Two weeks		97	87	97	81
After: 1 year or less		92	85	94	79
2 years		4	3	1	1
3 years or more		—	—	—	1
Three weeks		90	88	93	89
After: 1 year or less		2	11	2	17
2 years		1	3	1	4
3 years		8	8	10	10
4 years		3	9	3	6
5 years		39	31	45	34
6-9 years		26	18	22	11
10 years		9	6	8	5
15 years		1	1	1	1
Four weeks		78	79	82	83
After: 9 years or less		2	8	3	12
10 years		9	13	11	16
11-14 years		9	10	13	18
15 years		38	27	37	28
16-19 years		12	10	10	5
20 years		8	9	7	4
21 years or more		2	1	1	1
Five weeks		51	49	56	55
After: 24 years or less		26	23	31	31
25 years		22	20	23	17
30 years		2	6	—	5
Six weeks		16	11	20	18
After: 24 years or less		1	2	2	4
25 years		1	2	2	2
30 years		7	4	7	6
31 years or more		1	1	1	—
Paid holidays (statutory, public, etc.)					
8 days or less		12	13	11	11
9 days		23	16	18	13
10 days		34	40	31	34
11 days		15	19	22	26
12 days or more		14	11	17	14
		Percentage of office employees			
STANDARD WEEKLY HOURS					
Under 35 hours		1	6	1	6
35 hours		21	20	22	23
Over 35 and under 37½ hours		10	14	11	12
37½ hours		43	44	40	43
Over 37½ and under 40 hours		4	2	4	1
40 hours		20	13	21	12
Over 40 hours		1	1	1	1
VACATIONS WITH PAY					
One week		63	48	55	41
Two weeks		97	75	95	74
After: 1 year or less		95	74	94	73
2 years		1	1	1	—
3 years or more		—	—	1	—

8.21   Summary of selected working conditions of non-office and office employees in manufacturing and all industries, 1974 and 1975 (concluded)

Item	1974		1975	
	Manu-facturing industries	All industries	Manu-facturing industries	All industries
	Percentage of office employees (concluded)			
Three weeks	96	97	97	97
After: 1 year or less	4	27	6	28
2 years	1	7	2	8
3 years	11	11	12	11
4 years	3	3	3	5
5 years	43	33	47	35
6-9 years	25	12	21	6
10 years	8	4	6	3
Four weeks	88	90	90	92
After: 9 years or less	2	3	4	6
10 years	16	17	18	22
11-14 years	8	8	12	14
15 years	41	43	40	43
16-19 years	12	13	9	3
20 years or more	8	5	7	4
Five weeks	61	55	65	59
After: 24 years or less	31	18	38	29
25 years	26	22	24	15
30 years	2	14	—	14
Six weeks	14	8	19	13
After: 24 years or less	1	1	2	1
25 years	2	2	3	3
30 years	7	3	9	5
31 years or more	2	1	2	1
Paid holidays (statutory, public, etc.)				
8 days or less	9	6	6	5
9 days	20	14	17	12
10 days	36	39	32	35
11 days	21	30	28	33
12 days	5	3	6	5
13 days or more	8	8	10	9

8.22   Trusteed pension funds, income, expenditures and assets, 1972-74

Item	1972	1973	1974
TRUST ARRANGEMENTS	No.	No.	No.
(a) Corporate trustees	2,857	2,952	2,821
(b) Individual trustees	813	789	736
(c) Combinations of (a) and (b)	80	90	95
(d) Pension fund societies	28	28	28
Total trusteed funds	3,778	3,859	3,680
INCOME	$'000,000	$'000,000	$'000,000
Total contributions	1,469	1,763	2,128
Employer	944	1,168	1,417
Employee	525	595	711
Investment income	736	883	1,164
Net profit on sale of securities	117	114	49
Other	18	20	20
Total income	2,340	2,780	3,361
EXPENDITURES			
Pension payments out of funds	557	640	754
Cost of pension purchased	17	50	26
Cash withdrawals	160	202	201
Administration costs	18	20	22
Net loss on sale of securities	38	39	99
Other expenditures	13	6	68
Total expenditures	803	957	1,170
ASSETS (book value)			
Investment in pooled funds	978	1,063	1,196
Investment in mutual funds	55	49	41
Investment in segregated funds of insurance companies		146	200
Bonds	6,982	7,704	8,537
Bonds of or guaranteed by Government of Canada	393	356	366
Bonds of or guaranteed by provincial governments	3,707	4,132	4,550
Bonds of Canadian municipal governments, school boards, etc.	736	761	797
Other Canadian	2,132	2,432	2,813
Non-Canadian	14	23	11

8.22   Trusteed pension funds, income, expenditures and assets, 1972-74 (concluded)

Item	1972	1973	1974
ASSETS (book value) (concluded)			
Stocks	3,901	4,421	4,773
Canadian, common	3,200	3,717	4,069
Canadian, preferred	92	93	96
Non-Canadian, common	603	599	601
Non-Canadian, preferred	6	12	7
Mortgages	1,296	1,551	1,936
Insured residential (NHA)	760	898	1,072
Conventional	536	653	864
Real estate and lease-backs	46	51	53
Miscellaneous			
Cash on hand and in chartered banks	163	161	302
Guaranteed investment certificates	95	164	126
Short-term investments	261	554	755
Accrued interest and dividends receivable	125	143	169
Accounts receivable	145	162	194
Other assets	3	2	2
Total assets	14,050	16,171	18,284

8.23   Unemployment insurance statistics, 1971-75, and by month 1975

Year, month and end of period	Activity				
	Insured population[1] '000	Claims data ('000)		Benefits data	
		Claimants for UIC benefits (end of period)[1,2]	Initial and renewal claims received	Number of weeks '000	Average weekly payment $
1971	5,439	604	2,371	22,634	39.44
1972	7,845	804	2,470	30,462	61.79
1973	8,264	828	2,238	29,537	68.45
1974	8,617	828	2,410	28,461	74.89
1975	8,951	1,049	2,857	37,327	84.64
1975					
January	8,677	1,134	356	3,725	82.54
February	8,735	1,214	219	3,425	84.11
March	8,760	1,221	191	3,540	84.41
April	8,749	1,186	230	4,241	84.31
May	8,976	1,106	197	3,257	83.64
June	9,179	1,007	194	2,887	83.00
July	9,337	979	241	3,094	82.77
August	9,295	948	175	2,581	83.74
September	8,914	908	215	2,775	85.23
October	8,940	895	245	2,250	86.60
November	8,926	925	259	2,384	88.01
December	8,924	1,066	335	3,167	89.00

	Benefits data (concluded)					
	Benefits paid ($'000)					
	Regular	Sickness	Maternity	Retirement	Fishing	Total[3]
1971	- -	- -	- -	- -	- -	890,594
1972	1,764,031	58,854	36,431	2,440	20,403	1,871,802
1973	1,850,930	80,179	66,750	3,691	20,297	2,004,212
1974	1,924,543	98,321	81,708	4,164	22,675	2,119,213
1975	2,907,716	110,990	102,161	5,836	23,622	3,144,022
1975						
January	281,638	10,600	8,777	578	5,839	306,501
February	265,303	8,866	7,134	456	6,359	287,320
March	276,475	9,327	7,475	394	5,196	297,749
April	333,123	10,556	9,295	468	4,146	356,337
May	252,995	9,416	8,458	436	1,108	270,654
June	221,378	9,039	8,708	411	76	238,318
July	234,747	9,828	9,570	560	24	254,646
August	198,822	8,180	7,912	470	12	214,770
September	216,459	9,295	9,119	540	18	234,826
October	175,444	8,644	8,533	501	17	193,326
November	191,367	8,264	7,973	493	16	209,183
December	259,964	8,974	9,207	527	810	280,391

[1]Annual figures are annual averages.
[2]Persons who have applied for or are in receipt of unemployment insurance benefits at end of month.
[3]Figures are adjusted for cancellation of warrants and collection of overpayments; prior to July 1971, total includes ordinary, seasonal and fishing benefits.

8.24   Fatal employment injuries[1], by industry, 1973-75

Industry	Number			Percentage of total		
	1973	1974	1975	1973	1974	1975
Agriculture	25	36	12	2.0	2.5	1.2
Forestry	94	85	69	7.7	5.8	6.6
Fishing and trapping	15	11	19	1.2	0.8	1.8
Mining, quarrying and oil wells	166	204	149	13.5	13.9	14.3
Manufacturing	234	303	202	19.1	20.7	19.3
Construction	201	250	197	16.4	17.1	18.9
Transportation, communication and other utilities	241	257	174	19.6	17.5	16.7
Trade	78	128	60	6.4	8.7	5.7
Finance, insurance and real estate	6	6	3	0.5	0.4	0.3
Service	78	118	73	6.4	8.0	7.0
Public administration	89	67	86	7.2	4.6	8.2
Total	1,227	1,465	1,044	100.0	100.0	100.0

[1]The Canada Department of Labour compiles statistics of all fatal industrial accidents; Workmen's Compensation Board statistics (Table 8.25) include only those accidents covered by legislation.

8.25   Compensation claims for employment injuries and payments made, 1974 and 1975

Year and province	Compensation claims					Workmen's Compensation Board payments[2] $
	Medical aid only[1]	Non-fatal disabling injury	Fatal injury	Total disabling injury	Total injuries	
1974						
Newfoundland	6,999	7,309	22	7,331	14,330	6,722,355
Prince Edward Island	1,489	1,496	6	1,502	2,991	1,132,975
Nova Scotia	19,543	13,125	50	13,175	32,718	16,167,296
New Brunswick	17,883	9,663	29	9,692	27,575	9,541,135
Quebec	140,307	139,125	207	139,332	279,639	137,209,350
Ontario	246,429	180,575	676	181,251	427,680	210,506,646
Manitoba	16,371	19,255	42	19,297	35,668	13,591,608
Saskatchewan	15,186	13,308	53	13,361	28,547	16,204,393
Alberta	50,386	32,542	141	32,683	83,069	43,489,082
British Columbia	58,688	55,921	203	56,124	114,812	82,969,010
Total, 1974	573,281	472,319	1,429	473,748	1,047,029	537,533,850
1975P						
Newfoundland	5,700	6,260	39	6,299	11,999	6,303,306
Prince Edward Island	1,360	1,353	2	1,355	2,715	1,078,373
Nova Scotia	17,937	11,116	21	11,137	29,074	18,111,101
New Brunswick	18,381	8,576	48	8,624	27,005	10,541,259
Quebec	136,505	147,202	148	147,350	283,855	184,359,281
Ontario	220,149	166,876	639	167,515	387,664	274,477,000
Manitoba	17,693	18,440	41	18,481	36,174	15,907,022
Saskatchewan	15,432	14,145	45	14,190	29,622	18,642,462
Alberta	52,036	34,205	124	34,329	86,365	44,759,782
British Columbia	57,326	54,284	180	54,464	111,790	110,225,871
Total, 1975P	542,519	462,457	1,287	463,744	1,006,263	684,405,457

[1]Injuries requiring medical treatment but not causing disability for a sufficient period to qualify for compensation; the period varies among provinces.
[2]Includes, except where noted otherwise, payments to compensate loss of earnings, medical aid payments, cost of rehabilitation and hospitalization (not including capital expenditures) and pensions paid (not pensions awarded) for temporary and permanent disabilities; the Quebec compensation figure includes pensions awarded as well as pensions paid.

8.26   Union membership in Canada, 1955-75 (thousands)

Year	Members	Year	Members	Year	Members
1955	1,268	1962	1,423	1969	2,075
1956	1,352	1963	1,449	1970	2,173
1957	1,386	1964	1,493	1971	2,211
1958	1,454	1965	1,589	1972	2,371
1959	1,459	1966	1,736	1973	2,610
1960	1,459	1967	1,921	1974	2,726
1961	1,447	1968	2,010	1975	2,875

8.27   Union membership, by type of union and affiliation, as at January 1975

Type and affiliation	Unions No.	Membership No.	%
International unions	94	1,478,583	51.4
AFL-CIO/CLC	78	1,239,971	43.1
CLC only	5	153,023	5.3
AFL-CIO only	4	626	[1]
Unaffiliated unions	7	84,963	3.0
National unions	98	1,324,076	46.1
CLC	30	630,993	22.0
CNTU	9	173,053	6.0
CSD	3	27,763	1.0
CCU	9	20,358	0.7
Unaffiliated unions	47	471,909	16.4
Directly chartered local unions	244	32,566	1.1
CLC	110	19,497	0.7
CNTU	3	557	[1]
CSO	131	12,512	0.4
Independent local organizations	135	40,239	1.4
Total	571	2,875,464	100.0

[1] Less than 0.1%.

8.28   Employees covered by all collective agreements[1] for negotiating units covering 500 or more employees in all industries other than construction, as at Dec. 31, 1974 and 1975.

Region or province	Manufacturing industries Durable goods	Non-durable goods	Total manufacturing	Non-manufacturing industries except construction	All industries except construction
1974					
Atlantic	7,520	7,270	14,790	88,590	103,380
Newfoundland	—	3,050	3,050	20,840	23,890
Prince Edward Island	—	—	—	4,430	4,430
Nova Scotia	6,720	2,270	8,990	31,685	40,675
New Brunswick	800	1,950	2,750	31,635	34,385
Quebec	43,345	71,965	115,310	316,975	432,285
Ontario	130,100	59,060	189,160	196,205	385,365
Prairies	4,450	3,965	8,415	162,240	170,655
Manitoba	3,375	2,100	5,475	44,720	50,195
Saskatchewan	550	—	550	39,140	39,690
Alberta	525	1,865	2,390	78,380	80,770
British Columbia	55,625	14,965	70,610	117,950	188,560
Other[2]	33,960	21,275	55,235	394,195	449,430
Canada	275,020	178,500	453,520	1,276,155	1,729,675
1975P					
Atlantic	7,000	7,320	14,320	99,225	113,545
Newfoundland	—	3,050	3,050	28,495	31,545
Prince Edward Island	—	—	—	4,730	4,730
Nova Scotia	6,200	1,770	7,970	33,145	41,115
New Brunswick	800	2,500	3,300	32,855	36,155
Quebec	46,955	73,060	120,015	320,030	440,045
Ontario	150,135	55,980	206,115	224,145	430,260
Prairies	5,780	3,935	9,715	176,655	186,370
Manitoba	3,475	2,100	5,575	45,785	51,360
Saskatchewan	560	—	560	43,070	43,630
Alberta	1,745	1,835	3,580	87,800	91,380
British Columbia	46,845	15,460	62,305	138,250	200,555
Other[2]	7,705	26,675	29,380	421,510	450,890
Canada	264,420	177,435	441,850	1,379,815	1,821,665

[1] All agreements in force, irrespective of the year of settlement. There were 842 agreements covering 1.7 million employees as at Dec. 31, 1974 and 884 covering 1.8 million as at Dec. 31, 1975.
[2] Agreements pertaining to workers located in more than one province and in the Yukon Territory and Northwest Territories.

8.29   Year-over-year percentage and cents-per-hour increases in base rates under major collective agreement, by month, 1974 and 1975

Month	Collective agreement[1]					
	Manufacturing					
	Durable goods		Non-durable goods		Total manufacturing	
	%	¢	%	¢	%	¢
1974						
January	8.8	31.5	8.5	26.8	8.8	29.7
February	9.2	33.0	9.6	30.2	9.4	32.0
March	9.7	34.8	9.6	30.4	9.7	33.1
April	10.2	37.0	10.0	31.9	10.2	34.9
May	10.0	36.5	11.6	37.3	10.6	36.7
June	8.6	32.0	12.0	38.7	9.9	34.6
July	8.5	31.6	13.1	42.9	10.2	36.0
August	10.5	39.5	13.4	44.0	11.6	41.2
September	10.5	40.1	13.5	44.5	11.6	41.7
October	10.9	41.6	13.4	44.4	11.8	42.6
November	11.6	44.3	13.0	43.7	12.1	43.9
December	10.2	39.6	13.8	46.6	11.5	42.2
1975P						
January	10.5	40.9	14.0	47.9	11.8	43.6
February	10.1	39.5	12.9	44.6	11.1	41.4
March	9.9	39.3	12.9	44.9	11.1	41.4
April	9.5	38.0	13.0	45.8	10.8	41.0
May	9.7	39.0	12.6	45.2	10.8	41.3
June	10.1	40.7	12.4	44.7	11.0	42.1
July	9.9	40.1	10.7	39.4	10.2	39.6
August	9.0	37.2	11.9	44.4	10.1	39.9
September	8.7	36.6	11.7	43.7	9.9	39.4
October	8.7	36.7	11.3	42.5	9.7	39.0
November	10.6	45.1	10.6	40.4	10.6	43.1
December	10.4	44.5	10.1	38.7	10.3	42.1

Month	Commercial industries except construction		Non-commercial industries[2]		All industries except construction	
	%	¢	%	¢	%	¢
1974						
January	11.3	37.5	11.3	22.2	9.2	31.1
February	11.8	39.4	11.8	25.4	10.0	33.6
March	11.7	39.4	11.7	26.5	10.0	34.0
April	12.6	42.7	12.6	33.9	11.4	39.0
May	13.0	44.1	13.0	35.8	11.8	40.5
June	12.5	42.9	12.5	36.8	11.7	40.2
July	13.0	45.0	13.0	40.1	12.3	42.9
August	13.9	48.6	13.9	40.5	12.8	45.0
September	14.4	50.4	14.4	42.8	13.3	47.0
October	14.7	52.0	14.7	45.1	13.8	48.9
November	14.9	52.8	14.9	45.2	13.8	49.3
December	14.5	52.2	14.5	45.1	13.6	48.8
1975P						
January	13.9	51.5	13.9	53.8	14.2	52.3
February	13.3	49.8	13.3	51.5	13.6	50.3
March	13.5	50.5	13.5	52.5	13.7	51.2
April	13.1	49.9	13.1	51.0	13.2	50.2
May	13.2	50.8	13.2	49.9	13.1	50.2
June	14.1	54.5	14.1	52.3	13.9	53.4
July	13.6	53.4	13.6	46.0	12.7	49.9
August	13.0	51.6	13.0	49.5	12.7	50.5
September	12.7	50.8	12.7	50.4	12.6	50.5
October	12.4	50.2	12.4	51.7	12.6	50.8
November	12.9	52.6	12.9	51.6	12.8	52.0
December	12.7	52.4	12.7	52.4	12.8	52.3

[1]Based on all major collective agreements covering 500 or more employees in force except those in the construction industry. Data refer to rates actually paid in the month specified; no adjustments have been made for retroactive wage increases.
[2]This category consists of public administration and defence; education and related institutions; hospitals; welfare organizations; religious organizations; private households; miscellaneous services; highway and bridge maintenance; water system and other utilities.

8.30   Strikes and lockouts, by industry, 1974 with totals for 1970-74

Industry	Strikes and lockouts beginning during year	Strikes and lockouts in existence during year		
		Strikes and lockouts	Workers involved	Duration in man-days
Agriculture	1	1	503	2,450
Forestry	16	16	16,065	204,770
Fishing and trapping	6	7	5,114	102,220
Mines	60	61	30,735	515,250
Metal	33	34	19,942	314,760
Mineral fuels	12	12	6,080	178,790
Non-metal	11	11	1,926	6,890
Quarries	4	4	2,787	14,810
Incidental services	—	—	—	—

8.30   Strikes and lockouts, by industry, 1974 with totals for 1970-74 (concluded)

Industry	Strikes and lockouts beginning during year	Strikes and lockouts in existence during year		
		Strikes and lockouts	Workers involved	Duration in man-days
Manufacturing	656	685	232,436	4,814,560
Food and beverages	86	89	21,721	462,520
Tobacco products	—	—	—	—
Rubber	37	41	13,099	665,610
Leather	3	3	370	4,470
Textiles	29	29	6,603	101,600
Knitting mills	1	1	330	48,510
Clothing	8	8	10,784	77,070
Wood	42	45	20,339	296,730
Furniture and fixtures	16	17	1,911	56,360
Paper	57	58	29,483	235,650
Printing and publishing	26	28	3,068	24,700
Primary metals	51	52	23,025	491,850
Metal fabricating	73	76	12,290	251,880
Machinery	34	36	11,657	162,110
Transportation equipment	68	72	41,427	1,096,720
Electrical products	43	45	17,139	425,610
Non-metallic mineral products	43	45	10,978	205,320
Petroleum and coal products	4	4	1,271	4,470
Chemical products	26	26	5,002	139,310
Miscellaneous	9	10	1,939	64,070
Construction	70	72	154,856	2,409,980
Transportation and utilities	125	127	73,352	700,020
Transportation	77	77	33,047	325,300
Storage	3	3	684	26,520
Communication	31	33	36,854	333,360
Power, gas and water	14	14	2,767	14,840
Trade	72	77	9,634	118,970
Finance	6	6	107	2,010
Financial institutions	4	4	75	1,450
Insurance and real estate	2	2	32	560
Service	99	104	32,619	272,060
Education	39	39	13,926	153,330
Health and welfare	30	31	16,420	66,170
Religious organizations	—	—	—	—
Recreational services	3	3	188	6,790
Services to business	6	7	602	10,250
Personal services	5	5	261	9,190
Accommodation and food services	6	7	716	6,140
Miscellaneous services	10	12	506	20,190
Public administration	59	60	36,799	112,830
Federal administration	—	—	—	—
Provincial administration	6	6	23,530	32,880
Local administration	53	54	13,269	79,950
Other government offices	—	—	—	—
Total 1974	1,170	1,216	592,220	9,255,120
1973	677	724	348,470	5,776,080
1972	556	598	706,474	7,753,530
1971	547	569	239,631	2,866,590
1970	503	542	261,706	6,539,560

8.31   Persons 15 years of age and over, who worked full-time and part-time in 1970, by weeks worked, showing average employment income, 1971

Weeks worked		Worked			Worked full-time			Worked part-time		
		Total	Male	Female	Total	Male	Female	Total	Male	Female
Total	No.	9,586,280	6,093,085	3,493,190	7,870,030	5,388,080	2,481,950	1,716,250	705,005	1,011,240
With income	"	9,272,760	6,023,320	3,249,440	7,675,010	5,346,325	2,328,685	1,597,750	676,995	920,755
Average employment income	$	5,392	6,574	3,199	6,125	7,111	3,864	1,867	2,341	1,518
1-13 weeks	No.	1,036,620	492,740	543,880	529,015	282,645	246,375	507,600	210,100	297,505
With income	"	987,195	474,280	512,910	508,460	274,465	234,000	478,730	199,820	278,915
Average employment income	$	998	1,328	692	1,248	1,591	845	732	967	565
14-26 weeks	No.	993,325	519,485	473,835	629,050	357,645	271,400	364,275	161,840	202,435
With income	"	956,780	509,350	447,435	611,010	352,280	258,735	345,770	157,070	188,700
Average employment income	$	2,155	2,650	1,592	2,514	2,973	1,889	1,520	1,925	1,184
27-39 weeks	No.	971,820	572,635	399,185	694,065	446,070	247,995	277,755	126,565	151,190
With income	"	943,055	566,465	376,590	678,695	442,425	236,265	264,360	124,040	140,325
Average employment income	$	3,646	4,395	2,521	4,174	4,788	3,026	2,291	2,992	1,672
1-39 weeks	No.	3,001,765	1,584,860	1,416,900	1,852,130	1,086,360	765,770	1,149,630	498,505	651,130
With income	"	2,887,025	1,550,095	1,336,935	1,798,170	1,069,175	728,995	1,088,860	480,920	607,935
Average employment income	$	2,246	2,883	1,508	2,783	3,369	1,922	1,361	1,802	1,013
40-48 weeks	No.	1,300,650	818,640	482,015	1,084,575	740,560	344,015	216,080	78,075	138,000
With income	"	1,259,985	811,810	448,175	1,059,215	736,045	323,165	200,765	75,765	125,010
Average employment income	$	5,700	6,849	3,619	6,205	7,162	4,026	3,037	3,810	2,568
49-52 weeks	No.	5,283,865	3,689,585	1,594,285	4,933,330	3,561,155	1,372,175	350,540	128,430	222,110
With income	"	5,125,755	3,661,420	1,464,330	4,817,630	3,541,100	1,276,525	308,125	120,315	187,810
Average employment income	$	7,087	8,076	4,614	7,356	8,230	4,932	2,892	3,571	2,458
40-52 weeks	No.	6,584,515	4,508,225	2,076,300	6,017,905	4,301,715	1,716,190	566,620	206,505	360,110
With income	"	6,385,740	4,473,225	1,912,505	5,876,845	4,277,155	1,599,690	508,895	196,080	312,820
Average employment income	$	6,813	7,853	4,381	7,149	8,046	4,749	2,949	3,663	2,502

8.32   Labour force[1] 15 years of age and over, by occupation group, sex and education, 1971 Census

Occupation group	Total	Less than grade 9	Grades 9 to 11	Grades 12 and 13	University		Non-university post-secondary education		Vocational training	
					Without degree	With degree	None	Post-secondary education	None	Vocational training
Male										
All occupations	5,665,715	1,745,825	1,935,760	1,103,450	434,570	446,110	4,864,235	801,480	4,645,905	1,019,810
Managerial, administrative	313,935	19,695	68,090	90,345	51,920	83,880	237,625	76,310	251,485	62,445
Natural sciences, engineering and mathematics	217,025	8,900	33,540	62,740	36,775	75,070	152,205	64,815	155,800	61,225
Social sciences	49,525	1,310	4,620	6,195	5,930	31,465	40,600	8,925	44,245	5,280
Religion	19,885	1,305	1,380	1,865	2,885	12,445	14,105	5,780	17,305	2,575
Teaching	138,170	1,650	7,440	14,510	26,895	87,665	98,070	40,100	116,670	21,500
Medicine and health	83,865	6,740	15,155	10,830	7,935	43,200	68,420	15,445	67,490	16,380
Art, literature and recreation	58,585	6,315	16,625	17,970	10,265	7,410	43,975	14,610	44,220	14,365
Clerical	433,380	63,415	163,920	132,610	53,930	19,505	362,105	71,280	371,475	61,905
Sales	567,985	99,755	221,315	159,900	60,835	26,180	484,710	83,275	478,580	89,400
Service	521,935	181,470	204,565	93,720	31,270	10,910	462,040	59,895	425,330	96,605
Farming, horticulture and animal husbandry	405,305	195,890	138,290	48,150	18,220	4,755	382,930	22,375	376,460	28,840
Fishing, hunting and trapping	26,660	18,055	6,810	1,175	480	135	25,675	980	24,805	1,855
Forestry and logging	65,850	37,365	18,805	6,170	2,775	735	61,905	3,950	59,390	6,455
Mining and quarrying	58,785	26,230	21,420	6,905	3,315	910	54,590	4,195	52,835	5,950
Processing	275,180	118,885	99,440	38,825	13,355	4,675	251,715	23,460	240,910	34,265
Machining	227,260	85,495	92,025	40,480	7,815	1,445	185,300	41,960	148,680	78,580
Product fabricating, assembling and repairing	484,145	175,590	197,290	87,655	19,335	4,275	395,190	88,955	327,035	157,110
Construction trades	563,435	253,675	193,420	85,800	25,045	5,495	483,145	80,295	422,595	140,845
Transport equipment operation	330,245	145,990	129,625	38,740	13,035	2,845	307,140	23,100	294,250	35,990
Materials handling	165,385	66,065	63,170	25,265	9,105	1,780	154,495	10,885	151,175	14,210
Other crafts and equipment operation	95,300	23,715	42,895	22,170	4,970	1,550	76,460	18,840	62,130	33,170
Occupations, n.e.c.	145,900	59,310	47,575	22,525	11,125	5,365	131,955	13,950	128,560	17,345
Occupation not reported	417,995	149,000	148,340	88,905	17,335	14,415	389,895	28,100	384,485	33,515
Female										
All occupations	2,961,210	614,410	1,089,485	861,030	250,245	146,045	2,376,865	584,345	2,504,705	456,505
Managerial, administrative	58,310	3,325	17,740	21,190	7,605	8,445	41,035	17,270	45,890	12,420
Natural sciences, engineering and mathematics	17,110	680	2,745	5,090	3,285	5,310	12,770	4,335	13,285	3,820
Social sciences	29,530	1,165	4,470	7,070	4,860	11,960	21,415	8,115	24,415	5,115
Religion	3,705	745	1,105	790	390	675	2,635	1,075	3,020	685
Teaching	211,120	2,650	21,655	61,580	66,140	59,100	116,745	94,380	181,590	29,530
Medicine and health	242,690	19,420	72,095	101,195	32,070	17,910	111,410	131,275	150,900	91,785
Art, literature and recreation	21,895	1,460	5,885	7,275	3,905	3,370	16,230	5,660	17,250	4,645
Clerical	940,180	55,065	385,680	407,595	70,520	21,325	738,015	202,165	767,745	172,435
Sales	247,760	49,190	116,915	62,085	15,815	3,750	220,415	27,345	221,755	26,010
Service	447,985	171,555	187,295	65,295	19,865	3,975	409,605	38,380	392,050	55,935
Farming, horticulture and animal husbandry	106,845	47,885	38,010	16,750	3,635	570	99,105	7,745	100,155	6,695
Fishing, hunting and trapping	525	280	175	60	5	–	495	30	480	45
Forestry and logging	1,410	605	515	140	140	15	1,365	50	1,335	75
Mining and quarrying	380	140	155	45	35		360	25	330	55
Processing	59,560	31,765	21,445	4,720	1,400	240	57,085	2,480	56,460	3,105
Machining	13,675	5,840	5,920	1,510	350	45	12,845	835	12,590	1,090
Product fabricating, assembling and repairing	150,210	83,010	52,185	11,830	2,705	475	142,945	7,260	139,060	11,150
Construction trades	5,130	1,970	1,985	845	250	80	4,600	530	4,330	800
Transport equipment operation	8,190	2,405	3,865	1,465	390	70	7,475	715	7,360	830
Materials handling	40,450	17,545	17,090	4,325	1,280	210	38,615	1,840	38,310	2,140
Other crafts and equipment operation	13,540	3,830	6,215	2,675	630	185	12,040	1,505	11,620	1,920
Occupations, n.e.c.	21,730	9,000	7,405	2,680	1,270	1,375	20,135	1,595	20,225	1,505
Occupation not reported	319,270	104,870	118,930	74,815	13,700	6,950	289,530	29,745	294,545	24,730

n.e.c. = not elsewhere classified.
[1]Excludes persons looking for work, who last worked prior to Jan. 1, 1970 or who never worked.

8.33   Estimated composition of total employee compensation per employee[1] for services to business management in Canada, 1975 (dollars)

Compensation payments	Services to business management	Employment agencies and personnel suppliers[2]	Computer services	Security and investigation services[3]	Offices of accountants	Advertising services	Offices of architects	Engineering and scientific services	Offices of lawyers and notaries	Offices of management and business consultants	Miscellaneous services to business management
Direct payments to employees											
Pay for time worked											
Basic pay for regular work	8,823	3,798	12,053	4,788	10,165	10,904	11,793	11,904	9,272	9,808	6,839
Overtime, including premium pay	306	45	468	420	204	48	424	455	89	504	187
Commissions and other pay for time worked	215	47	998	11	14	277	65	73	87	150	337
Total	*9,342*	*3,890*	*13,519*	*5,220*	*10,382*	*11,229*	*12,283*	*12,433*	*9,448*	*10,463*	*7,364*
Pay for time not worked											
Paid holidays	359	120	542	146	445	423	501	500	399	393	267
Vacation pay	486	171	840	216	589	553	588	650	545	506	349
Sick leave	81	5	43	5	120	72	163	153	115	112	55
Personal and other leave	14	–	4	1	36	10	20	24	21	6	10
Total	*940*	*297*	*1,430*	*368*	*1,190*	*1,058*	*1,270*	*1,327*	*1,080*	*1,017*	*681*
Miscellaneous direct payments											
Non production bonus	208	8	7	14	164	278	455	463	215	190	152
Separation pay	18	3	32	18	6	41	35	22	24	29	13
Taxable benefits	97	9	249	35	57	126	60	112	54	58	105
Total (includes unspecified payments)	*333*	*20*	*316*	*80*	*227*	*464*	*552*	*612*	*297*	*278*	*273*
Gross payroll (total direct payments)	10,615	4,206	15,265	5,668	11,799	12,751	14,105	14,372	10,825	11,757	8,317
Employer contributions to employee welfare and benefit plans											
Workmen's compensation	48	37	75	40	12	14	25	71	2	39	43
Unemployment insurance	138	68	181	100	157	156	178	172	159	160	110
Canada or Quebec Pension Plan	102	56	123	84	122	114	122	121	119	117	85
Private pension plans	228	17	565	19	73	268	75	377	50	114	196
Life and health insurance plans[4]	106	12	183	29	125	134	192	149	117	159	83
Total (includes payments to other plans)	*627*	*191*	*1,132*	*273*	*488*	*687*	*593*	*903*	*449*	*589*	*525*
Total, employee compensation	11,242	4,397	16,397	5,941	12,287	13,438	14,698	15,275	11,274	12,346	8,842

Table based on the 1970 Standard Industrial Classification.
[1]All employees - regular full-time, part-time and casual.
[2]Ninety per cent of employees in this activity are part-time and casual employees.
[3]Thirty-four per cent of employees in this activity are part-time and casual employees.
[4]Includes provincial medicare, provided employer payments are not taxable benefits.

8.34 Average wage and salary rates for selected occupations in certain cities across Canada, Oct. 1, 1974 and 1975

Industry and occupation	Halifax–Dartmouth, NS 1974	1975	Saint John, NB 1974	1975	Sherbrooke, Que. 1974	1975	Montreal, Que. 1974	1975	Toronto, Ont. 1974	1975	Hamilton, Ont. 1974	1975
	$ an hr	$ an hr	$ an hr	$ an hr	$ an hr	$ an hr	$ an hr	$ an hr	$ an hr	$ an hr	$ an hr	$ an hr
ALL INDUSTRIES[1]												
General labourer, male	3.55	4.32	3.83	4.52	3.61	4.04	3.73	4.34	3.94	4.53	4.09	4.96
CONSTRUCTION (building and structures only)												
Bricklayer and mason	6.35	6.85	6.35	6.90	6.52	7.07	6.52	7.07	8.08	8.54	8.59	8.99
Bulldozer engineer	5.81	6.31			6.08	6.63	6.08	6.63	8.78,8.25	8.70,10.42	8.78,8.48	9.22,10.42
Carpenter	5.35,5.72	5.90,6.97	5.91	6.55	6.30	6.85	6.30	6.85	6.50	7.83,9.30	8.14	8.70
Cement finisher	5.85	6.35	5.72	6.47	6.05	6.60	6.05	6.60	7.27	7.87	7.10	7.65
Crane engineer	6.53	7.08			6.41	6.96	6.41	6.96	9.54,8.85	9.30,10.87	9.54,8.98	10.87,9.72
Electrician	5.05	5.55	7.50	8.00	6.54	7.29	6.54	7.29	8.90	10.22	9.39	10.75
Labourer			4.65	5.30	5.39	5.94	5.39	5.94	5.45,6.15	6.07,7.36	6.30	7.02
Marble, tile and terrazzo setter	5.72	6.47	5.72	6.47	6.49	7.07	6.49	7.07	6.66	7.06	7.37	7.84
Painter (brush)	5.25	5.75	5.40	5.95	6.18	6.73	6.18	6.73	7.30	8.15,7.65	7.20	8.20
Plasterer	5.63	6.13			6.52	7.07	6.52	7.07		8.30,8.40		8.78
Plumber	6.50	7.05	7.70	8.75	6.54	7.29	6.54	7.29	8.44		8.69	10.19
Sheet metal worker	6.50	7.05	6.90	7.65	6.51	7.06	6.51	7.06	8.45	8.87	8.63	9.97
MAINTENANCE TRADES												
Carpenter	4.80	5.52	4.68	5.14	4.24	4.58	4.76	5.43	5.12	5.91	5.34	6.27
Electrician	5.33	6.01	5.75	6.40	4.92	5.32	5.27	5.99	5.66	6.47	6.08	7.33
Machinist	5.14	6.01	4.93	5.81	4.56	5.25	5.14	5.86	5.37	6.21	5.87	6.76
Millwright	5.25	5.55	6.12	6.46	4.59	5.24	5.08	5.79	5.47	6.27	5.95	7.12
Pipefitter	5.57	6.40	5.83	6.46	5.00	5.85	5.53	6.15	5.67	6.59	5.80	6.66
Tool and die maker	5.03	5.51	4.76	5.39	4.51	5.23	5.16	5.80	5.77	6.40	5.67	6.46
Welder	5.08	5.85	5.89	6.46	4.88	5.51	4.95	5.86	5.25	6.00	5.77	6.78
SERVICE OCCUPATIONS												
Truck driver, light and heavy	3.73	4.37	4.02	4.72	3.95	4.20	4.28	5.03	4.60	5.31	4.66	5.34
Trucker, power	4.06	5.49	4.49	4.84	3.61	4.22	4.42	5.18	4.51	5.16	4.91	5.62
OFFICE OCCUPATIONS, MALE	$ a wk	$ a wk	$ a wk	$ a wk	$ a wk	$ a wk	$ a wk	$ a wk	$ a wk	$ a wk	$ a wk	$ a wk
Bookkeeper, senior	185	204	169	223	177	194	219	224	203	233	195	229
Clerk, general office, intermediate	144	156	158	181	140	151	149	165	152	171	170	192
Clerk, general office, senior	178	196	191	216	180	206	189	212	195	216	209	242
Clerk, order	140	158	158	193	155	164	138	186	172	196	193	208
Draughtsman, intermediate	188	216	247	254	174	190	195	215	209	231	193	219
Draughtsman, senior	223	251	275	292	210	243	246	268	262	289	242	277
OFFICE OCCUPATIONS, FEMALE												
Clerk, general office, intermediate	131	144	123	142	128	145	132	147	138	156	134	153
Bookkeeping, billing and calculating machine operator	111	144	108	128	113	132	116	130	131	148	123	137
Secretary, senior	146	166	137	171	136	151	159	176	166	186	161	188
Stenographer, junior	122	132	114	128	107	122	121	133	132	146	129	151
Stenographer, senior	137	149	125	140	127	132	137	150	146	163	149	174
Telephone operator	108	120	104	127	114	122	122	130	127	144	120	146
Typist, junior	102	116	96	118	104	116	106	118	115	132	114	136
Typist, senior	122	132	103	123	111	127	125	133	131	147	129	150

8.34 Average wage and salary rates for selected occupations in certain cities across Canada, Oct. 1, 1974 and 1975 (concluded)

Industry and occupation	Winnipeg, Man. 1974	1975	Regina, Sask. 1974	1975	Saskatoon, Sask. 1974	1975	Calgary, Alta. 1974	1975	Edmonton, Alta. 1974	1975	Vancouver, BC 1974	1975
	$ an hr	$ an hr	$ an hr	$ an hr	$ an hr	$ an hr	$ an hr	$ an hr	$ an hr	$ an hr	$ an hr	$ an hr
ALL INDUSTRIES¹												
General labourer, male	3.90	4.53	3.65	3.77	3.96	4.47	3.80	4.90	4.25	5.23	4.48	5.67
CONSTRUCTION (building and structures only)												
Bricklayer and mason	6.55	..	7.30	8.95	7.30	8.95	7.20	8.95	7.20	8.95	7.87	8.93
Bulldozer engineer			6.50	7.67	6.50	7.67	7.20	8.15	7.20	8.15	8.15	9.46
Carpenter	6.40	8.10	6.81	8.21	6.81	8.21		8.80		8.80	7.97	9.22
Cement finisher			6.50	8.00	6.50	8.00	6.85		6.85		7.51	8.75
Crane engineer	5.60	6.75,7.60	7.45	9.01	7.45	9.01	7.85,7.60	9.25,9.45	7.85,7.60	9.25,9.45	7.90,8.15	8.78,9.46
Electrician	7.05	8.10	7.66	9.17			8.05	9.55	8.05		8.62	10.00
Labourer	5.00	..	5.73	7.00	5.73	7.00	5.95	7.10	6.00	7.15	6.71	7.98
Marble, tile and terrazzo setter	6.05	..					7.05,7.20	8.95	7.05,7.20	8.95	7.92,7.66	9.16,8.72
Painter (brush)	5.80	..	6.15	8.00	6.15	8.00	6.20	8.50	6.20	7.90	7.59	8.97
Plasterer	6.20	..	5.62	6.67	5.62	6.67	7.20	8.75	7.95	8.52	8.02	9.40
Plumber	7.20	8.20	7.56	9.01	7.56	9.01	7.95	9.35	8.00	8.75	8.34	9.55
Sheet metal worker	6.40	7.50	6.97	8.27	6.57	8.14				9.35	8.07	9.33
MAINTENANCE TRADES												
Carpenter	4.81	5.47	4.84	5.58	4.97	5.28	5.91	6.66	5.17	6.38	6.17	7.44
Electrician	5.43	6.22	6.03	6.64	5.49	6.50	6.28	7.11	5.67	7.42	6.54	7.67
Machinist	4.93	5.99	5.94	6.70	5.24	6.03	5.39	6.36	5.63	6.55	6.29	7.47
Millwright	4.88	6.10	5.96	6.44	5.03	6.48	6.07	6.67	5.66	7.13	6.74	7.52
Pipefitter	5.28	6.12	5.90	6.31	5.37	6.25	5.47	7.10	5.35	7.32	6.54	7.53
Tool and die maker	4.93	5.93					5.57	6.44	6.01	6.60	6.55	7.66
Welder	5.00	5.97	5.78	6.00	5.24	6.41	5.70	6.58	5.65	6.85	6.57	7.37
SERVICE OCCUPATIONS												
Truck driver, light and heavy	4.25	4.94	4.17	4.85	4.17	5.12	4.60	5.63	4.55	5.33	5.44	6.53
Trucker, power	4.00	4.75	4.72	4.55	4.33	5.27	4.59	5.19	4.49	5.18	5.82	6.73
	$ a wk	$ a wk	$ a wk	$ a wk	$ a wk	$ a wk	$ a wk	$ a wk	$ a wk	$ a wk	$ a wk	$ a wk
OFFICE OCCUPATIONS, MALE												
Bookkeeper, senior	168	208	198	215	194	..	217	257	202	244	219	255
Clerk, general office, intermediate	148	167	139	158	151	193	168	185	139	189	164	185
Clerk, general office, senior	189	204	167	203	170	210	196	234	177	215	213	241
Clerk, order	136	172	160	191	139	178	159	189	162	192	190	222
Draughtsman, intermediate	190	217	188	215	198	228	199	233	197	245	215	246
Draughtsman, senior	245	277	225	260	217	251	246	279	233	282	261	297
OFFICE OCCUPATIONS, FEMALE												
Clerk, general office, intermediate	127	145	129	143	134	158	133	155	125	161	148	167
Bookkeeping, billing and calculating machine operator	112	129	120	139	110	139	123	143	125	144	139	163
Secretary, senior	152	171	160	177	153	179	163	188	150	189	172	200
Stenographer, junior	117	136	118	131	119	132	128	148	126	149	136	155
Stenographer, senior	140	158	131	147	135	155	140	163	142	181	152	177
Telephone operator	112	128	115	127	115	145	118	139	117	145	133	157
Typist, junior	103	122	104	113	102	120	108	138	108	141	131	142
Typist, senior	121	143	125	138	117	134	119	152	110	166	138	157

¹"All industries" consists of manufacturing, logging, mining, transportation (including storage, communication and utilities), trade, finance, public administration and services.

Sources

8.1 - 8.5 Labour Force Survey Division, Census and Household Surveys Field, Statistics Canada.
8.6 - 8.11 Census Characteristics Division, Census and Household Surveys Field, Statistics Canada.
8.12 - 8.20 Labour Division, General Statistics Branch, Statistics Canada.
8.21 Public Relations Branch, Canada Department of Labour.
8.22 - 8.23 Labour Division, General Statistics Branch, Statistics Canada.
8.24 - 8.30 Public Relations Branch, Canada Department of Labour.
8.31 - 8.32 Census Characteristics Division, Census and Household Surveys Field, Statistics Canada.
8.33 Labour Division, General Statistics Branch, Statistics Canada.
8.34 Public Relations Branch, Canada Department of Labour.

Scientific research and development

Chapter 9

Scientific research and development

Chapter 9

Science in Canada

The development of Canada's natural resources and industry has involved the federal government in scientific activities since the establishment of Canada in 1867. These activities have concerned themselves with two principal areas of investigation: the natural sciences and the human sciences.

Natural sciences 1976-77

The natural sciences include such disciplines as biology, chemistry, physics, astronomy, geology and oceanography. Data are collected on the expenditures on, and manpower devoted to, research and development (R&D) and related scientific activities (RSA) in these sciences. Although research and development is the central element, related scientific activities precede, complement and extend research and development work. Included in related scientific activities are scientific data collection, scientific information testing and standardization, feasibility studies and educational support.

Federal government expenditures on activities in the natural sciences were expected to reach $1,290.6 million in 1976-77, an increase of 10% over 1975-76, and representing 3.4% of the total 1976-77 budget. R&D accounted for 72% of this of which 56% was for intramural work (i.e. work done in federal establishments and laboratories). RSA expenditures for the same year were estimated at $340.4 million. Of this sum, scientific data collection represented 55%, scientific information 20%, testing and standardization 12%, feasibility studies 9% and education support 4%.

Three sectors of the federal government were expected to account for approximately half of the natural sciences expenditures for 1976-77: Fisheries and the Environment, $304.1 million; National Research Council, $235.6 million; and Agriculture, $121.1 million.

Federal support of human sciences

The term human sciences encompasses the disciplines generally referred to as the social sciences and humanities (excluding the performing arts). The human sciences include all disciplines involving the study of human actions and conditions and the social, economic and institutional mechanisms affecting them as well as the applied social science fields (e.g. anthropology, economics, human geography, business administration, communications, criminology and industrial relations).

Federal government expenditures on activities in the human sciences were expected to reach $433.7 million in 1976-77 continuing the average increase of 21% a year since 1970-71. R&D accounted for $122.7 million of this sum and RSA $310.9 million. It was anticipated that the federal government would perform 75% of the scientific activities. Universities and non-profit institutions would receive 12% of total expenditures, foreign performers 7%, business enterprises 4%, provincial and municipal governments 1% and other Canadian performers 1%.

Three sectors of the federal government were expected to account for approximately half of the human sciences expenditures for 1976-77: Statistics Canada, $174.7 million; Canada Council, $32.4 million; and National Health and Welfare, $24.8 million. Human sciences expenditures are 1.1% of the total federal budget (1.2% in 1975-76).

9.1.3   Government, business and university sectors

The federal government has a decisive impact on Canada's scientific progress as the major source of funds for activities carried out in other sectors, i.e. other levels of government, universities and business enterprises. It is also responsible for major programs in areas such as space, nuclear energy, natural resource identification and development, agriculture and economic and social data collection.

The business enterprise sector is primarily concerned with using science in order to produce new products or processes for industrial operations. The university sector trains manpower required by all three sectors and carries out fundamental research which has yet no obvious application in the fields of interest of the other two sectors.

The current concern with possible energy shortages, with the development of ocean and northern resources, with environmental changes, and with the productivity of Canadian industry ensures that government involvement with scientific investigation will continue into the foreseeable future.

In federal spending, the natural sciences were expected to account for 75% of the total expenditures on science in 1976-77. R&D is a relatively more important activity in the natural sciences; in 1976-77, 71% of the natural sciences expenditures was earmarked for R&D while only 28% of the human sciences expenditures was designated for this activity.

Expenditures in the human sciences are increasing at a greater rate than those in the natural sciences. The human sciences expenditures have been increasing at an average annual rate of 21% a year since 1970-71 (the first year for human sciences statistics) while the natural sciences have been increasing at 9%. Some portion of the human sciences increase is due to improved reporting as respondents gained experience. Nonetheless, there has been a significant increase in the emphasis placed on human sciences activities by the federal government.

The real growth of scientific activities is undoubtedly less than would appear, since the expenditure data do not show the effects of inflation. No completely acceptable method of deflating scientific expenditures has yet been devised. Although the support for human sciences activities is at a considerably lower level than that of the natural sciences, in constant dollar terms the human sciences expenditures have continued to increase while natural sciences expenditures are actually declining.

9.1.4   Science policy

In 1966 the federal government established the Science Council of Canada, a Crown corporation charged with assessing independently Canada's scientific and technological resources, requirements and potential and making recommendations thereon by publication of reports. The Science Council is concerned with both R&D and with the application of science and technology to Canada's social and economic problems. It draws its membership from industry, the universities and government, and its views are independent of those of the internal government structure.

The council has published several reports based on commissioned studies from consultants on different areas of science and has also published its own reports. Some of the topics include energy conservation, technology transfer in construction and a case study of offshore petroleum exploration. In addition, the council recommended that Canada focus its scientific and technological effort through the creation of "major programs" designed to help solve some of the country's social and economic problems. These programs include a space program for Canada, water resources management and development, transportation, urban development, computer applications and scientific and technological aid to developing areas of the world.

In 1967, the Special Senate Committee on Science Policy was formed to consider a report on the scientific policy of the federal government with the object of appraising its priorities, organization, budget and efficiency. The first report,

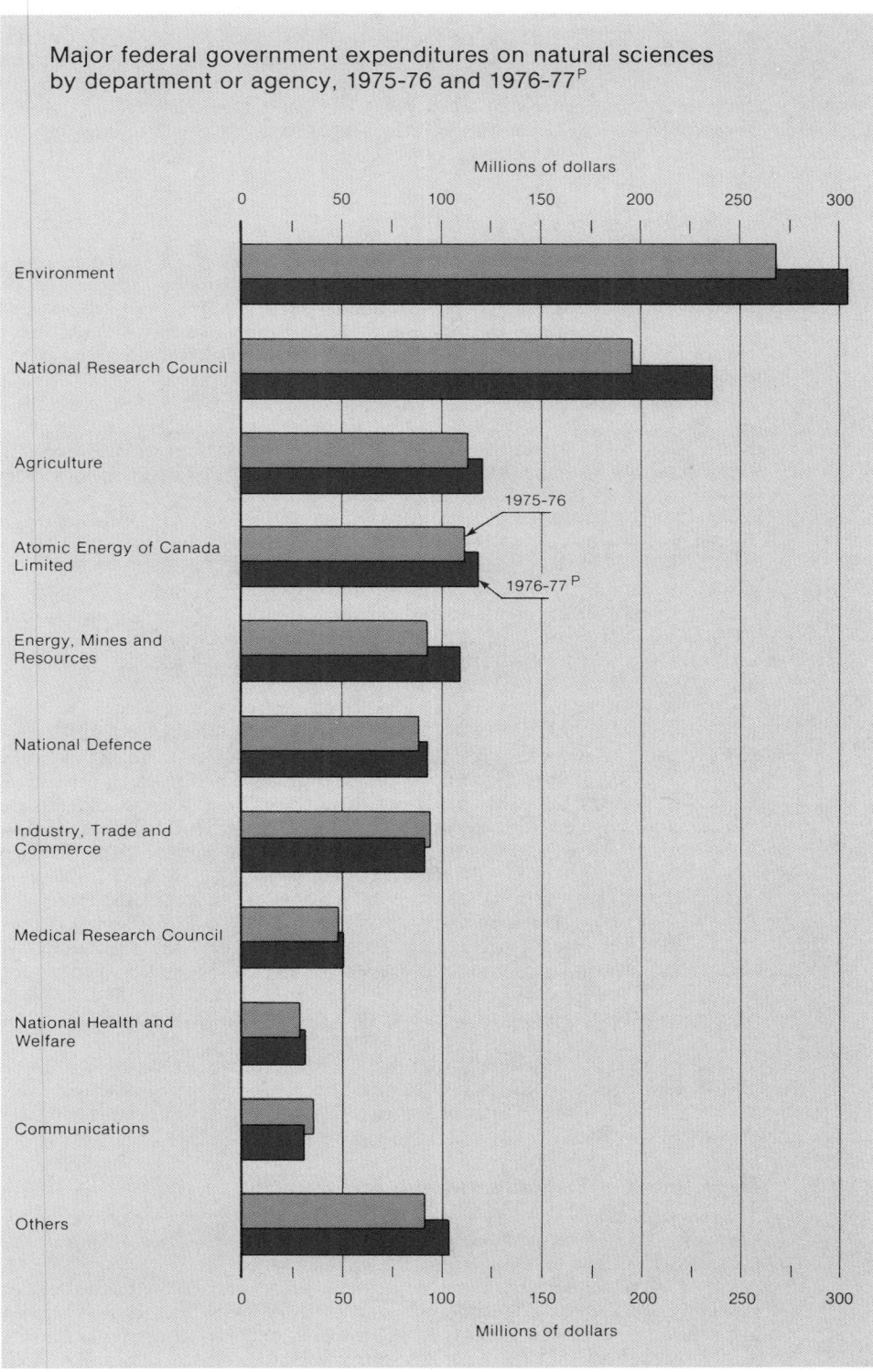

Major federal government expenditures on natural sciences
by department or agency, 1975-76 and 1976-77[P]

published in December 1970, describes what the committee considered to be major deficiencies in the policy. The second, published in January 1972, contains specific recommendations on targets and strategies for the 1970s. The third volume of the report recommended specific changes in the federal structures concerned with science and technology. The committee planned to publish a fourth report in 1977 concerning the changes in science policy since the first report and Canadian activities in future research.

9.2   Federal agencies

Federal government agencies support scientific activities in both the natural and human sciences. Information on the expenditures of the federal government on scientific activities is secured by two annual surveys carried out by Statistics Canada, one for natural sciences, the other for human sciences. Each survey covers the actual costs of scientific programs for the preceding fiscal year and estimated expenditures for the following two years. (*Federal government activities in the natural sciences 1975-77*, Catalogue No. 13-202 and *Federal government activities in the human sciences 1975-77*, Catalogue No. 13-205.)

Twenty-seven departments and agencies reported natural sciences expenditures with eight planning to spend over $50 million in 1976-77. The major funder of natural sciences R&D was the National Research Council with 23% of expenditures. The Department of Fisheries and the Environment was the major funder of RSA with 47%.

Table 9.5 shows the expenditures for natural sciences activities by department and performer. In 1976-77 approximately 66%, or $854.1 million of federal government expenditures in the natural sciences was for work done within its own establishments. An estimated full-time equivalent of 25,211 persons employed by the federal government was engaged in natural sciences activities in 1975-76 with 16,224 in R&D work.

Most of the payments to extramural performers for natural sciences activities go to Canadian industry (45% of 1976-77 current extramural expenditures) and to Canadian universities (37%). Support of industrial R&D is provided principally through a group of special programs designed to develop a research capacity in Canadian industry by assisting current R&D work. Expenditures under these programs were expected to reach $99.4 million in 1976-77. Support of R&D in Canadian universities and related institutions is also provided primarily through grants programs, with planned expenditures for grants totalling $138.2 million in 1976-77. Expenditures for natural sciences activities are shown in Tables 9.3, 9.5 and 9.6, and for human sciences activities in Tables 9.7, 9.8, 9.10 and 9.11.

Most of the human sciences activities (75%) are performed intramurally. Data collection is the major human science activity ($187.6 million planned for 1976-77) followed by R&D ($122.7 million). Fifty departments and agencies devote resources to human sciences activities, 16 of them having expenditures of over $5 million.

Three areas of the federal government account for approximately half of the human sciences expenditures in each year. For 1976-77, Statistics Canada was allocated $174.7 million, Canada Council $32.4 million and National Health and Welfare $24.8 million.

9.2.1   Department of Fisheries and the Environment

The Department of Fisheries and the Environment is the major funder of scientific activities. Expenditures for 1976-77 were set at $304.1 million in the natural sciences and $9.4 million in the human sciences.

The diverse interests of the department are expressed in the variety of research carried out in its laboratories. A major performer of R&D is the Fisheries and Marine Service which operates nine research establishments across Canada with headquarters in Ottawa and research vessels on both coasts. Research activities are concerned with the use and conservation of freshwater and marine resources. Along with its research program the service conducts development activities in support of industries that depend on fishery resources. The Ocean and Aquatic Affairs Directorate, a component of the Fisheries and Marine Service, conducts oceanographic research and surveys and charts coastal and inland navigable waters. The service was expected to spend a total of $94.1 million on intramural scientific activities in 1976-77.

The Atmospheric Environment Service performs basic atmospheric research, such as studies of atmospheric electricity, and applied research to support forecasting and data collection activities. Work is done on the climates of Canada and the application of meteorological information to other scientific activities such as pollution research. In addition, the service collects large quantities of meteorological data. Other related activities include the development and testing of meteorological instruments and the operation of the National Library of Meteorology at Toronto. Total intramural expenditures in 1976-77 were planned at $106.6 million.

The Environmental Management Service consists of four main elements: the Lands Directorate, the Inland Waters Directorate, the Canadian Forestry Service and the Canadian Wildlife Service. Allocations for the 1976-77 intramural scientific expenditures totalled $85.9 million. The Lands Directorate is concerned with land classification, land inventory and land-use planning. Its scientific activities consist of data collection and information services. The Inland Waters Directorate conducts research on the scientific aspects of the behaviour of water, on improved methods of water and waste water treatment and on the development of water treatment technology. Total intramural expenditures in 1976-77 were set at $30.4 million. Much of the scientific activity of the directorate is conducted at the Canada Centre for Inland Waters in Burlington, Ont. The Candian Forestry Service conducts most of Canada's research into the protection and utilization of forest resources and the improvement of tree growth. It operates regional laboratories, field stations and experimental areas across Canada. In 1976-77 the service planned a $34.6 million expenditure on intramural scientific activities. Research on the protection and preservation of wildlife is the responsibility of the Canadian Wildlife Service, which expected to spend $9.5 million on intramural scientific activities in this area in 1976-77.

The Environmental Protection Service has the principal responsibility for dealing with environmental problems, particularly the development and enforcement of environmental protection regulations and controls. It also serves as an information source for other federal departments administering legislation under which environmental regulations are developed. Its intramural scientific expenditures for 1976-77 were expected to be $5.9 million.

National Research Council   9.2.2

The National Research Council (NRC) is the principal agency of the federal government with responsibility for scientific activities. Created in 1917 to provide Canada with qualified scientists and to promote research, the council has profoundly influenced the development of science in Canada. Its operations cover all aspects of the scientific effort through three programs: Engineering and Natural Sciences Research, Scientific and Technical Information, and Grants and Scholarships in Aid of Research.

The National Research Council's intramural research activities account for most of the Engineering and Natural Sciences Research program. This program consists of six activities: basic and exploratory engineering and scientific research; research on long-term problems of national concern; research in direct support of industrial innovation and development; research to provide technological support of social objectives; national facilities; and research and services related to standards.

These research activities are carried out within three laboratory groups. The Engineering Laboratories consist of the Divisions of Building Research,

Mechanical Engineering, Radio and Electrical Engineering and the National Aeronautical Establishment; the Physical/Chemical Sciences Laboratories include the Divisions of Physics and Chemistry and the Herzberg Institute of Astrophysics; the Biological Sciences Laboratories include the Division of Biological Sciences, the Prairie Regional Laboratory in Saskatoon and the Atlantic Regional Laboratory in Halifax.

The 1976-77 intramural research budget was expected to be $71.4 million, with approximately $22.1 million of this for basic research which is largely concentrated in the Herzberg Institute of Astrophysics. The remainder was divided among the Divisions of Biological Sciences, Chemistry and Physics.

Research on long-term problems of national concern includes work on problems relating to energy, transportation, food, building and construction. The study of energy-related problems is the subject of an interdivisional effort in which seven divisions are involved in a wide range of projects, including energy conservation, vertical-axis wind turbine, laser fusion research, isotope fractionation and cryogenic power handling.

Examples of other research on long-term problems are: legume seed research in the Prairie Regional Laboratory, which is expected to lead to commercial production in Canada of high protein foods derived from legume crops (e.g. field peas and flavobeans); research in the Division of Mechanical Engineering to establish the design, installation, and operation of ship hulls, oil platforms and terminal structures in an arctic environment; and field and laboratory investigations by the Division of Building Research into problems relating to northern construction and technology.

Research in direct support of industrial innovation and development includes intramural research performed for industrial companies on request, contract or collaboration basis. The Industrial Research Assistance Program is also included in this activity.

Research to provide technological support of social objectives such as public safety, environment, health, and education, is also conducted in many of the divisions. The Division of Biological Sciences is studying the anaerobic bacterial digestion of organic wastes (e.g. from food processing and sewage) for production of methane and reduction of pollutant content. The Divisions of Physics, Biological Sciences, Mechanical Engineering, Building Research and the National Aeronautical Establishment are cooperating in a joint study of environmental and physiological noise problems.

One of the several ways in which the National Research Council supports the research effort in industry, universities and other government departments is through the provision of national facilities. Examples of major facilities provided by NRC's laboratories are the large-scale towing tank operated by the Marine Dynamics and Ship Laboratory of the Division of Mechanical Engineering, the wind-tunnel complex of the National Aeronautical Establishment and Algonquin Radio Observatory maintained by the Herzberg Institute of Astrophysics.

Research and services related to standards include all work in support of standards, codes and specifications that are in the national or international public domain. These activities are also conducted on an interdivisional basis. The Division of Physics is responsible for the maintenance of physical standards. The recently formed Environmental Secretariat in the Division of Biological Sciences assembles criteria for use by the authorities responsible for setting environmental standards. The Division of Building Research provides technical and secretarial support to the NRC associate committees responsible for the National Building and Fire Codes of Canada.

The National Research Council is also active in the field of scientific and technical information. It is responsible for the operation of the Canada Institute for Scientific and Technical Information, the publication of journals of research and the development of a Canadian network of scientific and technical information services.

The National Research Council's Industrial Research Assistance Program (IRAP) was originally developed to assist industry to become more competitive and innovative by promoting the formation of R&D teams in industry.

An IRAP grant provides financial assistance for an applied research project conceived by a company with an end product or process in view. To be eligible, companies must be incorporated in Canada, undertake to do the major part of the proposed research in Canada, exploit results through Canadian operations, and have access to export markets for the product. Under this program the NRC pays the direct salaries of scientists, engineers and technicians. The company is expected to provide laboratory space, equipment and consumable supplies and to pay overhead costs. Estimated grants were $16.9 million for 1976-77.

Federal scientific establishments are located across Canada, although most expenditures and personnel are concentrated in the National Capital Region.

The Scholarships and Grants in Aid of Research Program will continue to be administered by the NRC until the proposed Natural Sciences Research Council is established. The program promotes and supports the development and maintenance of research in Canadian universities and the provision of highly qualified manpower in the natural sciences and engineering. The program has three principal sub-objectives: to support excellence in research for the creation of new knowledge in the natural sciences and engineering, to promote and support the development of research in selected fields of regional and national importance, and to assist in the provision and development of highly qualified manpower. The program includes peer-adjudicated grants, developmental grants, highly qualified manpower training and development, and national and international activities. Expenditures for this program were planned at $93.0 million in 1976-77.

Statistics Canada   9.2.3

Statistics Canada is the major performer of activities in the human sciences with expenditures estimated at $174.7 million in 1976-77, $160.7 million for data collection. This included expenditures for the 1976 quinquennial census.

Statistics Canada provides the statistical information required for understanding the Canadian economy and society. The information is needed to develop and monitor the economic and social policies and programs of virtually all levels of government, as well as to support research work and decision-making throughout the nation. For example, the Labour Force Survey's unemployment statistics and the consumer price index are key indicators of the economic health of the nation. The agency's program consists almost totally of related scientific activities in the human sciences and represents nearly half of total federal spending on human science RSA.

One of Statistics Canada's key jobs is conducting the Census of Canada at five- and 10-year intervals on population and housing; the latest 10-year census was in 1971 and the five-year census in 1976. The bureau also undertakes a comprehensive Census of Agriculture at the same time and regularly surveys social and economic changes under more than 20 broad subject-matter headings.

The growth of Statistics Canada, both in personnel and in the complexity of statistical activity, has paralleled Canada's development as a modern industrial state. The agency's staff includes the largest single body of social scientists in one organization in Canada. Several hundred additional persons are employed part-time on special surveys and censuses.

Statistical collection covers every area of Canada. Most Statistics Canada information is available to the public through publications but for users requiring information in a more sophisticated form there is an increasing output on micro-film, computer tapes and special tabulations.

Department of Agriculture   9.2.4

The Department of Agriculture's research program is the largest single budgetary program devoted entirely to research with expected intramural expenditures of

$108.4 million in 1976-77. Research, conducted at the Central Experimental Farm in Ottawa and at regional laboratories across Canada, involves all elements of the food chain, soils, crops, animals, plant and animal products and diseases, in addition to problems of food processing and storage. Other programs engaged in scientific activities include the Administration Program (scientific information services), the Canadian Grain Commission (grain research at the Winnipeg laboratory), the Health of Animals Program (animal and poultry diseases) and the Production and Marketing Program.

The agriculture industry accounts for some 3.4% of Canada's gross domestic product. Moreover, agriculture is a major export industry; wheat accounted for over 6% of Canada's merchandise exports in 1975, and in 1976 food, feeds, beverages and tobacco contributed a surplus of $1.3 billion to the international balance of payments.

Rising labour and energy costs have made agriculture increasingly dependent on technology. This, combined with Canada's size, wide range of climatic and soil conditions and correspondingly wide range of agricultural crops and animals, makes it essential to coordinate research effectively.

The Research Branch performs most of the department's research studies and supports a number of expanded research programs. One is aimed at the economical conversion of cellulose and carbohydrate waste materials to feedstock for ruminants and other animal species; others are concerned with the extraction and processing of proteins derived from plants, models for predicting crop production on the basis of soil and weather information and remotely sensed light reflectance from crop canopies, and a combined cultural and chemical control system for wild oats.

The branch is pursuing a central core of food-related research programs intended to improve the genetic characteristics of crops and livestock. One byproduct of such studies is that branch scientists have developed techniques for sexing and for the successful transfer of cattle embryos. These techniques will increase the international exchange of superior gene pools. Continued research into the causes of early pregnancy failure, the mechanisms of transmission of diseases which reduce reproductive efficiency, and the artificial control of the female estrus cycle may lead to further improvements in the productivity of the Canadian breeding stock.

A modest increase is planned in the resources devoted to research programs that tackle energy and environmental problems. The emphasis of energy research will be on the energy efficiency of agricultural production systems and the conversion of animal wastes to usable energy forms. The environmental program will continue to emphasize research into the use of biotic agents for controlling agricultural pests and studies of the nature and effect of toxicants arising from infestations, additives, chemical control agents or inadvertant contamination.

The federal government, in cooperation with the various provincial governments, supports an active soil survey program. Surveys have shown that the land available for agriculture and food production is limited. Only about 5% of Canada's total land area, or about 120 million acres (49 million ha) is improved farm land and it is estimated that no more than 40 million acres (16 million ha) of land, most of it marginal, remains to be brought into use. This has given added impetus to land use research. It is expected that the Research Branch will give priority to improved evaluation methods and criteria concerning land productivity, and to the collection, collation, and manipulation of field data relating to crop yield, soil properties, economic inputs, climatic factors and other aspects.

The Economic Branch is expanding its activities in production economics, new technologies and management systems for farm use, appraisal of agricultural research resources, and energy modelling and monitoring of the agricultural system. The Production and Marketing Branch contributes to producer and industry groups, universities and provincial agencies for the development and adaptation of new agricultural crops and varieties for commercial production. The Health of Animals Branch is intensifying its research efforts on diagnostic procedures for animal diseases, the development of wildlife rabies vaccine and studies of the prevention of diseases in high density cow-calf operations.

Agricultural research in Canada is conducted through a network of federal, provincial, university and industrial organizations. About 50% of the work is performed in federal laboratories. The Department of Agriculture, as the focus of this federal involvement, has played an active role in developing the research infrastructure and in establishing cooperative research programs. Through its research agreement program, the department awards about $1.3 million a year to scientists at Canadian universities. It contributes to the provinces for the expansion of veterinary science teaching facilities at the Universities of Guelph, Montreal and Saskatchewan.

Atomic Energy of Canada Limited   9.2.5

Atomic Energy of Canada Limited (AECL), with an intramural R&D budget of $79.3 million in 1976-77, is a Crown corporation responsible for nuclear research and utilization. The main research and development centres are Chalk River Nuclear Laboratories, Chalk River, Ont., and Whiteshell Nuclear Research Establishment at Pinawa, Man. These laboratories carry out a full range of activities: underlying research in physics, chemistry, materials science and radiation biology; research and development on advanced nuclear reactors and other nuclear power systems; and research and development to improve current models of nuclear power plants. Three other groups are responsible for utilization: Power Projects, Heavy Water Projects and Commercial Products. They also carry out some development work related to commercial objectives.

The corporation's prime responsibility is to develop nuclear energy technology to meet Canadian requirements. Its objective is to make available by the year 2000 about 80 000 MW of nuclear-electric capacity (one and one half times Canada's present total electric capacity). It also produces radio-isotopes and develops associated products such as radiation processing equipment and radio-therapy instruments for use in medicine and industry.

Applied research and development activities are carried out on power reactor systems, nuclear fuel, environmental protection and radioactive waste management, heavy water production, radiation equipment and radioactive isotopes. The applied work is supported by basic research in physics, chemistry and materials science. In addition, the corporation contracts out over $6 million of research and development annually to industry. There is close collaboration with utilities and industry since this program provides the technological base for the largest industrial program ever initiated, developed and put into industrial practice by Canadians.

R&D ranges from work at the laboratory bench to experiments using multi-million dollar research reactors and associated facilities. Much of the nuclear power activity involves the CANDU pressurized heavy water system; as well, work is conducted in support of heavy water plants. Particular attention is paid to developing reliability through sound design and good maintenance procedures, so that high capacity factors already achieved (87% for the Pickering generating station in 1976) will continue in the future. A slowly increasing percentage of the work is devoted to the development of new fuel cycles to ensure nuclear fuel supplies adequate for centuries.

AECL activities have led to the development of the unique CANDU system of nuclear power. Its success was marked in 1973 by the completion of the Pickering Nuclear Generating Station, the world's largest operating nuclear station and by the choice of Canadian designs for nuclear power plants planned by Argentina and the Republic of Korea. CANDU reactors are operating in India and Pakistan; Argentina and Korea have placed orders for 600 MW units; other countries, including Denmark, Iran and Romania, have indicated interest. Britain selected the SGHWR concept, which is similar to CANDU, for its next generation nuclear stations and is considering technology exchange with Canada.

The entire research program is mission-oriented and there is close interaction between basic and applied researchers. This gives access to expert consultants in relevant disciplines and to international research results through personal contacts. Thus AECL keeps abreast of developments in all methods of nuclear power generation.

The corporation is mindful of its responsibilities to protect people and the natural environment from the undesirable effects of radiation. About 10% of its research effort is devoted to radioactive waste management, health physics, environmental research and biology research.

9.2.6   Department of Energy, Mines and Resources

The Department of Energy, Mines and Resources (EMR) promotes the discovery, development, use and conservation of the country's mineral and energy resources. The Earth Sciences Program, with scientific expenditures of $47.8 million slated for intramural activities in 1976-77, provides the basic geodetic survey and topographical mapping of Canada. It conducts geological research and surveys to provide data on earth materials and terrain, to assess geological and terrain factors affecting the use of these materials, and to develop techniques for monitoring the characteristics of earth materials and terrain features. The Earth Sciences Program also conducts geophysical, seismic, gravity and magnetic studies of the earth's crust and interior, as well as research and field surveys in the area of the Arctic continental shelf. Through the Canada Centre for Remote Sensing the department is involved in the development of facilities and techniques for the production and use of remotely-sensed data from satellites and high flying aircraft.

The Mineral and Energy Resources Program of EMR is another major performer of scientific activities with total intramural allocations of $48.1 million for 1976-77, $34.0 million for R&D. This includes research on the technology of mining, extraction, metallurgy, processing and use of metals and alloys, processing and use of fossil fuels, minerals and mineral processing as well as studies of pollution from thermal, metallurgical and mining processes and the development of prevention and abatement techniques. Geological research and surveys are an important part of this program's activities, including research on the geological history of the earth, development of geological instruments and methods and surveys to describe and interpret the bedrock geology of Canada and to provide information to facilitate the discovery of mineral deposits.

The department encourages the effective use of Canadian mineral and energy resources (mainly fossil and nuclear fuel) and administers these resources on federal lands in the provinces and in the newly declared offshore areas. New knowledge in geology, resource technology and earth physics is gathered and catalogued; this information base for resource development is then made available to the private sector.

The research activities in geoscience, minerals and energy technology provide the base needed for minerals and energy policy development. Thus research programs of the Geological Survey are directed in part to developing new exploration techniques and resource analysis techniques for land and offshore areas. Other research improves methods of understanding mineral and hydrocarbon occurrences, encouraging exploration and resource assessment.

At the Earth Physics Branch a research program is directed toward a better understanding of Canadian earthquakes, seismicity, and seismic risk and hazard. Investigations of the gravity and magnetic fields and the geothermal regime of the earth are carried out in aid of navigation, transportation, communications, surveying and geophysical prospecting.

Some of the R&D activities bear directly on issues of environmental protection. For example, the studies of permafrost not only provide information that will help in planning northern development but also provide the necessary data for assessing the environmental impact.

The geodetic framework, which is the responsibility of the Surveys and Mapping Branch, consists of tens of thousands of precisely located points and is essential to all other surveys and studies of the earth, as well as for most large engineering projects. Multi-purpose topographic mapping is the foundation of a host of federal and national activities such as resource development, transportation, communications, urban and rural administration, education, defence and recreation.

The growing technology of remote sensing from satellites and aircraft is used by the Canadian Centre for Remote Sensing to provide data for such activities as ice reconnaissance, crop forecasting and forest fire prevention.

Department of National Defence   9.2.7

R&D projects for the Department of National Defence are varied and often have important applications in areas other than defence. Many projects relate to the defence of Canada's frontiers, especially the North, involving such problems as human and machine adaptation to extreme cold. Testing and standardization activities for the department are conducted primarily by the test and evaluation establishments of the Canadian Armed Forces.

The main responsibility for science and technology rests with the Research and Development Branch. The branch is establishing a broad technology base which will be maintained in the six Defence Research Establishments across Canada, in industry and in other departments and agencies. In line with the contracting-out policy, external resources are used whenever practical, but in many areas vital to defence the technology base is maintained in-house. Outside contractors are used, where possible, to provide advice on military training or operations and on human performance in the military environment. They are also used for equipment-related activities, ranging from demonstrations of feasibility, through development, to performance evaluation and engineering tests.

One program conducted by the Defence Research Establishments (DRE) is the Technical Program on the Acoustic Detection of Submarines. This program is carried out jointly by the DRE Atlantic and the DRE Pacific in the three oceans bordering Canada, using research ships and scientific equipment developed mainly by the DRE . The program aims to improve the military ability for reconnaissance, location and surveillance of submarines in waters of Canadian interest. It is concerned with all aspects of underwater acoustic propagation: natural and man-made interfering noise, signal processing and analysis, and transducer technology. International cooperation and information exchange are important parts of the program.

One important role of the technology base is to provide the background for development. The Penetrating Rocket System is an example. This improved air-to-ground rocket uses a high-performance composite propellant in which DRE Valcartier had developed expertise. Canadian industry had the necessary technical background and the production facilities, having produced earlier rockets for the Valcartier program. When the Canadian Forces saw the need for an improved rocket in 1972, Canada had the capability to design, develop and manufacture it. DRE Valcartier designed the rocket motor and produced initial models. Industry then produced a prototype lot of 60 which was successfully test fired, indicating that the technology had been satisfactorily transferred from government laboratory to industry. Then followed pre-production models, performance testing at the Aerorspace Engineering Test Establishment and the development of operating procedures. The rocket was cleared for use on the CF-104 aircraft and clearance trails for other aircraft were initiated. In January 1976 the department let a production contract for rocket motors to meet the CF-104 requirement, and some NATO countries expressed an interest in the weapon.

Department of Industry, Trade and Commerce   9.2.8

A major function of the Department of Industry, Trade and Commerce is to assist product and process development and to increase productivity in Canadian industry through the greater use of research and the application of advanced technology. The department achieves these objectives mainly through the use of financial assistance programs. The total scientific expenditures of the department were estimated at $92.5 million for 1976-77, $91.4 million for natural sciences activities. Canadian industry was allocated 90% ($83.5 million) of the total.

The Industrial Research and Development Incentives Act (IRDIA), which has provided support for industrial R&D since 1966, was discontinued as of December 31, 1975. Since IRDIA grants were for past R&D, the department accepts applications for expenditures made by industry before the end of 1975. Total expenditures for this program reached $229.5 million as of March 1976. Payments for 1976-77 were estimated at $24.0 million.

The department administers the Program for the Advancement of Industrial Technology (PAIT) initiated in 1965. Its basic purpose is to improve the technological capacity and expand the innovation activity of Canadian industry by supporting development projects involving genuine technical advances with good prospects for commercial exploitation. The grants cover up to 50% of the cost of development and innovation; some non-capital pre-production costs were also covered. Expenditures in 1976-77 were estimated to be $24.9 million.

Projects initiated under the Defence Industry Productivity Program (DIP) have played a major role in helping industry to develop its skills on a specialized basis in fields of technology which have defence and civil applications and which Canada is favourably situated to exploit. Costs of a project are shared by the department and the Canadian firm concerned and, in some instances, by the governments of other NATO countries. Among projects assisted have been communications and aircraft navigation systems, gas turbine engines for aircraft, flight safety and simulation equipment, and information display facilities. Export of the products of these developments continue to increase, including significant orders for such diverse applications as commercial airlines, public communication networks and television distribution systems.

Industry, Trade and Commerce is assisting in the establishment and maintenance of industrial research institutes at universities. Institutes which have been supported under the program are located in Nova Scotia Technical College, École Polytechnique de Montréal, Ryerson Polytechnical Institute, and the universities of McGill, British Columbia, Quebec, Western Ontario, Alberta, Sherbrooke, Guelph, Dalhousie and Carleton.

9.2.9   Department of National Health and Welfare

The Department of National Health and Welfare provides substantial support for R&D and other activities in the health sciences. The Health Resources Fund was established in 1966 to assist in the construction of teaching and research facilities at universities, hospitals and other institutions engaged in health research and training. Through this program NHW provides capital grants covering up to 50% of the cost of approved projects.

The department provides funds for R&D in welfare related subjects, drug abuse, and fitness and sports participation, as well as R&D related to health needs, health planning and the utilization of health services and health care facilities. R&D projects are supported primarily in Canadian universities and non-profit institutions, and grants are provided to provincial governments through the department's Income Security and Social Assistance Program.

Departmental expenditures are detailed in Tables 9.3, 9.5, 9.8, 9.9 and 9.10.

9.2.10   Medical Research Council

The Medical Research Council (MRC) supports research and development in the health sciences (excluding public health) in Canadian universities and affiliated institutions. Research is supported primarily in the faculties of medicine, dentistry and pharmacy; however, projects in other areas which are relevant to health problems are considered. Research funds are distributed through three main programs: grants-in-aid of research, direct personnel support and special programs. The estimated 1976-77 payments of the MRC to Canadian universities was $46.3 million.

The major portion of MRC expenditures are for grants-in-aid of research, of which there are two main types: operating grants and major equipment grants. These are intended to cover the normal direct costs of research. Grant expenditures were forecast at $43.1 million for 1976-77. To encourage maximum utilization of facilities major equipment grants are normally made to the head of the department or division where the equipment will be located. Wherever possible, highly specialized equipment is provided for regional or national use, an example being the high resolution mass spectrograph facility at McMaster University. Operating grants represent the bulk of the grants program expenditures. Normally made to a principal investigator to support his own research, such grants are not intended to cover the entire costs of a project; space and basic facilities must be provided by the institution. The scientific merit of applications is assessed by the council's Grants Committees, comprised of working scientists assisted by external reviewers.

The special programs of the MRC are designed to promote the development of medical research in Canada. This includes the financing of MRC groups for research in especially productive areas; for example, the Group for Transplantation Research at the University of Alberta. Development grants assist universities in recruiting highly qualified investigators for full-time positions in areas (geographic or subject) needing development. In order to encourage collaboration and exchange of information the council offers visiting professorships, awards to visiting scientists and support for scientific symposia. General research grants are made to deans of medicine, dentistry and pharmacy for use at their discretion in support of research in their schools.

Canadian International Development Agency (CIDA)   9.2.11

The main objective of CIDA is to support the efforts of developing countries in fostering their economic growth and the evolution of their social systems in ways that will produce a wide distribution of the benefits of development among the populations of these countries, enhance the quality of life and improve the capacity of all sectors of their population to participate in national development efforts.

Expenditures by CIDA include grants to international research organizations, scholarships to foreign students for study in Canada and assistance to Canadian scholars for studies related to international development.

Total expenditures for scientific activities in 1976-77 were expected to be $45.7 million, $30.6 million for natural sciences activities. Funds to the foreign sector were estimated at $40.4 million.

A principal activity is the participation in the Consultative Group on International Agricultural Research, which coordinates support for agencies such as the International Maize and Wheat Improvement Centre (Mexico) and the International Rice Research Institute (the Philippines). CIDA contributes over $7 million — about 9% of the international total — in grants to such institutions. These agencies study a wide range of crops with the object of doubling current yields through genetic improvement and by selectively breeding a crop for pest and disease resistance. Success with wheat doubled India's production over a six-year period. At least one of the improved varieties is grown in Canada. Similarly, rice production has been increased by more than 30 million tons (27 million t) per annum. These increases are enough to provide a subsistence ration of a pound (0.454 kg) of grain a day each for 300 million people.

In addition to the crop-oriented institutes, CIDA supports the International Laboratory for Research on Animal Diseases in Kenya, which is searching for immunological solutions to trypanosomiasis (spread by tse-tse flies) and East Coast fever (spread by ticks). Control of these diseases in Africa will increase pasture-land available for cattle ranching and other animal agriculture.

In 1976 the agency began to support a new research effort on malaria, sleeping sickness, schistosomiasis and other parasitic diseases which are extremely widespread in tropical countries. This will be administered through an organization similar to the Consultative Group, with the World Health Organization as the executive agency. In addition, the agency planned to contribute $1.3 million to the World Health Organization program of research and training in human reproduction.

9.2.12   International Development Research Centre

The International Development Research Centre (IDRC) helps developing regions to build up research capabilities, innovative skills and institutions required to solve their problems. It is a public corporation funded by the federal government through a grant from CIDA. The main approach to this goal is through support of specific projects in developing countries.

Research to improve food production and nutrition has been a foremost concern. Other projects have studied modernization and its consequences, especially in rural communities in developing countries. Environmental health, disease prevention and care in these communities, and the many variables that influence the size of families, have also been focal points of research. The centre also collects and disseminates information about development.

The Agricultural, Food and Nutrition Sciences Division supports research into plant, animal, marine and forest resources, such as research on crops, farming systems and reforestation in arid and semi-arid lands, multiple and inter-cropping, the use of agricultural wastes and by-products in animal feed, fish farming and shellfish culture, fish preservation and processing, post-harvest technology and the needs of the rural family.

An important example of the division's work is research on cassava, a tropical root crop and staple food in many developing countries. It has serious nutritional drawbacks such as low protein content and high toxicity; it is highly perishable after harvesting. The centre has provided, often in conjunction with the CIDA, over $4 million in support of a network of cassava research projects in recent years. The aim of these projects is to improve production by the use of new varieties and thus increase the use of cassava in Asia and Latin America, as well as to make sure that farmers in each region can get the results of applied research.

Social Sciences and Human Resources Division's research focuses on the effect of modernization and change, especially on rural peoples, on strategies for harmonious development of urban and rural areas, on the formation of appropriate science and technology policies, on delivery systems for mass primary education, and on the determinants of population change and the formulation of population policies. The division also administers a scholarship program to increase the number of scholars trained in the problems of development.

The main research interests of the Population and Health Sciences Division are environmental health and disease prevention, fertility regulation, and rural health care delivery in developing countries. An example is the support for research into biological control of vector-borne diseases. The centre has approved a one-year grant of $500,000 to a special program, coordinated through the World Health Organization, to develop new tools for prevention, diagnosis and treatment of tropical parasitic diseases. This will help countries where the diseases are endemic by providing training in biomedical sciences and various forms of institutional support. The focus initially will be on the major human parasitic infections encountered in tropical zones.

9.2.13   Department of Communications

The Department of Communications expected to spend $31.1 million for natural sciences activities in 1976-77. A total of $30.7 million was allocated to R&D of which $21.7 million was for intramural expenditure.

The department undertakes scientific and technical research both directly, at its Communications Research Centre (CRC) near Ottawa, and indirectly, through a program of industry and university contracts for specific research projects.

The CRC has had wide experience in the fields of defence communications, high frequency transmission, the ionosphere and radar. The department is re-orienting research efforts to relate them more closely to the public telecommunications sector — to telephone, telegraph, broadcasting, cable distribution, data networks and mobile communications.

The department is also re-examining its existing radio research programs with a view to ensuring that research in this area is carried out in line with the department's responsibility to manage the radio frequency spectrum.

A working paper in 1975-76 highlighted the major foreseeable public telecommunications developments in Canada over the next decade. Among key problem areas identified were: under-developed rural communication; over-wiring in the urban sector; critical congestion and spectrum scarcity in radio communication; and technological advancement that could radically revise the economics of wide-band transmission.

Preliminary consultations began with industry researchers and planners to identify priorities for research into urban communications. A long-range program to look at the possible effects on communications of such factors as energy shortages, conservation, employment and inflation was identified.

During 1975-76 the department continued its program of general research for the Department of National Defence in radar and high frequency communications and the two departments assessed new cooperative ventures in defence telecommunications.

A $700,000 university research program continued with 50 projects, designed to provide the department with the benefit of academic research and to provide university researchers with opportunities to work in telecommunications. Ten were in the field of space communications, 14 in conventional communications, seven in radio wave propagation and 19 in socio-economic aspects of communications.

Communication using fibre optics — thin glass threads through which communication is transmitted by light — is a subject of continuing research. During the next decade, the use of this new technology is expected to spread, particularly since the cost and scarcity of the copper used in conventional wire and cable systems is becoming an increasingly important factor. Fibre optics also hold the promise of greater transmission capacity with less interference than wired systems. More than 80 scientists gathered at the Communications Research Centre in May 1975 to attend a symposium on fibre optics, and in Halifax an experimental fibre optics system developed by the CRC went into operation, replacing a Department of National Defence coaxial cable installation.

A joint project of the department and the RCMP to develop a computer terminal for use in police cars continued. The terminal, including a video screen and typewriter keyboard mounted near the patrol car dashboard, would put mobile police officers in instant communication with a nation-wide computerized information system.

In the far North, hunters, trappers and others in small remote communities often need reliable, portable communications systems. The department is conducting research on the practicability of a combined short-range relay system and a longer range, high-frequency radio system for providing reliable low-cost trail communications. Another project is aimed at developing techniques for integrating high-frequency radio transmissions in the North with existing communications and satellite networks.

Microwaves are used extensively in both terrestrial and satellite communications, and a research program is under way to study the effects of rain, turbulence, weather systems and other atmospheric conditions on microwave propagation.

The location of satellite earth stations is an important part of satellite communications planning; through a contract with Teleglobe Canada, the department has been studying site diversity.

The departmental radar research laboratory investigates new uses of radar such as in remote sensing of the environment; studies the application of new technology to radar systems; helps users specify and select new radar equipment; and investigates problems encountered in operating radar systems.

In its efforts to improve radio communication, the departmental radio communications laboratory continued experiments in the use of the ionosphere, which deflects radio waves, to communicate over long distances.

From March 1973 to September 1975 the department conducted an educational technology program in response to the need of educators for assistance and advice in the application of communications media to education.

9.2.14   The Canada Council

The Canada Council expected to spend $32.4 million in 1976-77 in support of activities in the human sciences, $25.5 million in the university sector. Funds for R&D amounted to $16.4 million.

The Canada Council, created by an Act of Parliament in 1957 to promote the arts, the humanities and the social sciences, carries out its work mainly through a broad program of fellowships and grants. The council also shares responsibility for Canada's cultural relations with other countries, and administers the Canadian Commission for UNESCO and special programs financed by private donations.

Research funds of the council are channelled through five programs: grants to university faculty and other scholars for free research in the human sciences; the Killam grants (senior research scholarships and special postdoctoral research scholarships to support scholars of exceptional ability in significant research); leave fellowships for university faculty who wish to engage in some form of creative scholarship, research or study; research fellowships to permit younger scholars to undertake full-time research; and, as part of the Cultural Exchange Program administered for the Department of External Affairs, grants to Canadian scholars for research in France.

Canada Council support for scientific information activities includes publication grants to specialized journals and block grants to the Humanities Research Council of Canada and the Social Science Research Council of Canada for the publication of scholarly manuscripts and for support of attendance at the annual meetings of the Canadian Learned Societies.

In 1976-77 Canada Council expenditures for education support was planned at $11.7 million. This included doctoral fellowships for students in the human sciences who have completed at least one year of graduate study beyond the honours BA or its equivalent; grants to Canadian universities and organizations to support prominent visiting scholars from other countries; and grants to foreign students for advanced study in Canada.

9.2.15   Ministry of State for Science and Technology

The Ministry of State for Science and Technology is responsible for the development and formulation of policies for the optimum development and application of science and technology in Canada. It reviews and assesses scientific and technological activities and programs in many different departments of the federal government and encourages cooperation among the federal government and the provinces, public and private organizations and with other nations. The ministry consists of four branches: Government, Industry, University and Corporate Services.

The Government Branch has overall responsibility for projects which have a direct impact upon government policy and activities in science and technology and is divided into three areas of activity: the Government Projects Division, the Program Review and Assessment Division, and the International Division.

The Government Projects Division operates on a project basis. In close consultation with concerned departments it furthers policy development in the oceans, space and northern science technology areas and undertakes a review of research and development in forestry.

The growing importance of Canada's offshore natural resources, underlined by the government's declared policy on oceans in November 1973, has caused MOSST to become increasingly involved in policy development and implementation on ocean matters. In particular, the division has devoted attention to the government's goal of achieving world recognized excellence in operating on and below ice-covered waters.

The Program Review and Assessment Division interacts with departments on program planning, and provides advice to the Treasury Board Secretariat on requests by departments and agencies for financial and manpower resources. Criteria have been developed and advice provided on the decentralization of S&T facilities, transportation R&D, the impact of the Make-or-Buy policy on intramural scientific activities and the effect of cost increases on the budgets of the granting councils. An important part of the development of assessment methodology is the work under way to devise management tools such as price deflators for analysis of the differential impact of inflation among science based programs. The usefulness of "science indicators" to measure the condition of scientific activity in Canada is also being examined as a further aid to the management of science and technology resources.

The Industry Branch identifies the scientific and technological implications of policies and programs affecting the industrial sector and maintains an overview of various policies and programs in order to create a coordinated approach to R&D assistance and promotion. It examines and makes proposals for areas involving industrial R&D as well as science and technology which cut across departmental responsibility lines, or which are not within the particular province of other departments and agencies. The branch is also concerned with forecasting and assessing potential impact of scientific and technological advances upon Canadian society and environment.

The University Branch is responsible for advising the government on matters of general policy affecting federal support of university research and for continuing liaison between the government and the university community.

During 1975-76 there was extensive debate on the funding of university research. The branch participated in round-table discussions and at meetings sponsored by various organizations such as the Association of Universities and Colleges of Canada, the Royal Society and the Learned Societies. The debate served to clarify for the ministry the concerns of scientists and others associated with university research.

To inform the government a study of federal funding of university research was initiated. It was to consist of an analysis of federal contributions through the granting councils, federal contributions through other federal departments and agencies, and a comparison of federal and other sources of funds for sponsored research in universities.

R&D in industry   9.3

Industry performs about 37% of all Canadian R&D which makes it the largest performing sector. This is 3% more than the combined total of provincial and federal governments and 8% more than the university and private non-profit sectors.

The Canadian industrial R&D effort, however, falls well behind most other industrialized countries when R&D expenditures are compared to an indicator of economic activity such as gross domestic product (GDP). In fact, the ratio of Canada's industrial R&D/GDP is only 25% to 40% of the ratios for the Federal Republic of Germany, Sweden, the US, France, Japan and the Netherlands.

Most industrial R&D is performed by a small number of firms. In recent years, the 25 leading performers have accounted for more than 50% of current intramural R&D expenditures; the first 200 performers spent approximately 88% of such expenditures.

Not only are R&D expenditures concentrated in a few companies but they are also concentrated regionally. Ontario and Quebec account for 90% of current intramural R&D expenditures. Another 8% of the expenditures are spent in British Columbia and Alberta, leaving 2% of the work performed in the other provinces.

Industry's total R&D expenditures increased from $132 million in 1959 to $643 million in 1974, an average annual increase of 10%. In terms of constant dollars, current R&D expenditures increased rapidly during the early 1960s but have since slowed to an almost static level.

Canadian industrial R&D is largely financed by industry itself. In 1974 the reporting company provided 69% of its R&D funds; 15% came from the federal government; 9% from other Canadian sources; and 7% from foreign sources. The foreign sources are mainly parent or affiliated companies. The proportion of funds coming from each of these sources has not changed much over the past several years. Most of the federal government's financial support goes to the aircraft and electrical products industries.

All industries do not have the same need for R&D. Some, like electrical products, compete largely through new products based on R&D. Others, such as food and beverages, rely more on advertising and style than on R&D. Furthermore, subsidiary companies may rely on their foreign parents for most of their R&D requirements. For example, Chrysler, Ford and General Motors in the US together spent $2,059.5 million on R&D in 1975, three times as much as all Canadian industry. The different R&D intensity of industries is illustrated by the following percentages of non-government financed R&D to manufacturing value-added for 1974: electrical products, 4.6%; petroleum and coal products, 2.8%; machinery, 2.5%; chemical and chemical products, 2.1%; primary metals, 1.4%; transportation equipment, 0.8%; paper and allied products, 0.6%; food and beverages, 0.3%; and metal fabricated products, 0.1%.

9.4   Provincial agencies

9.4.1   Economic planning

Nova Scotia's Voluntary Planning, an organization representing non-government elements of the Nova Scotia community, was established in 1963 with the objective of involving the private sector in a continuing program of economic and social development.

The organization comprises the following main components: sector committees representing "grass roots" elements of producers, private business, labour and government in agriculture, construction, fisheries, forestry, mining, tourism, transportation and secondary manufacturing; advisory councils in consumer affairs, education, energy and labour-management affairs; the Provincial Planning Board, which is made up of the sector and council chairmen, together with other representatives of business, labour and government; and a small professional staff which provides administrative and technical support to the volunteer groups.

Voluntary Planning provides for the involvement of the private sector in development planning; facilitates the identification of problems by the private sector and relates appropriate private and public resources in an attempt to resolve these problems; and involves the private sector in the analysis of government planning proposals prior to final approval.

Through this planning agency government has a single contact with major elements of the private sector and the private sector has both a forum for discussing mutual problems and a direct channel to government for submitting coordinated views on any aspect of development planning.

A major activity of the fiscal year 1975-76 was a review of the Royal Commission on Education, Public Services and Provincial-Municipal Relations.

Another consisted of assistance to the provincial government in the preparation of a position paper on the General Agreement on Tariffs and Trade.

Current activities include an ongoing review of manpower needs and training programs in all sectors (in consultation with provincial departments and with the federal Department of Manpower and Immigration); the development of a proposal for a manpower skills inventory in the construction industry; in conjunction with the provincial government's changes in residential and non-residential tax system, the development of new tax proposals for forest land and for agricultural land; assistance in the formation of the Christmas Tree Council of Nova Scotia and through that body an Atlantic Provinces' Christmas Tree Grading System; an assessment of the implications of the current spruce budworm infestation in Nova Scotia; and the completion of a background paper on energy and a review of alternative energy sources for the province.

Quebec Planning and Development Board. Under the terms of its constituent act (16-17 Elizabeth II, c.14 and QS 1969, c.16), the Quebec Planning and Development Board has a mandate to devise plans, programs and projects to develop its territory and to coordinate the implementation of such programs and development activities.

The board usually acts as a liaison office between various government departments when programs and development projects are to get under way. In such cases, the board must inform the Interdepartmental Planning and Development Committee of the way in which it intends to carry out its responsibilities and seek guidance from it. Two organizations, one government-administered and one made up of other interested parties have been set up under the act to advise the board. One is the Interdepartmental Planning and Development Committee; the other, the Quebec Planning and Development Council, is made up of representatives of the major socio-economic groups of Quebec and regional representatives nominated by regional development councils.

The board is a corporation in the meaning of the Civil Code and its personnel are under the jurisdiction of the Quebec Public Service Commission. In planning matters, the board stresses studies and research aimed at developing medium-term development of Quebec. The Regional Development Branch draws up various development plans for each region of Quebec. One other aspect of its work is coordination of the activities of all departments at the regional level through regional administrative conferences.

The Ontario Economic Council, established by legislation in 1968, was conceived as an organization in which representatives of a broad cross-section of informed people could pool their knowledge and experience regarding social and economic questions, commission research and formulate policy recommendations to the public and private sectors. Twenty-one Ontario citizens serve on the council representing business, industry, finance, labour, agriculture and universities. Each member serves without compensation for a term of one, two or three years.

Essentially, the council operates as an independent advisory body reporting some of its findings directly to the Ontario government and publishing others for wider distribution. Earlier reports cover the fields of immigration, government reform, poverty, urban development, social change, municipal reform and municipal waste disposal.

Until recently the council's research activities have concentrated on six areas. Four are directly concerned with major areas of public expenditure in Ontario: health, urban development, education and social security. The other two are concerned with national independence and northern Ontario development. A new area of major interest is intergovernmental relations, with shared-cost programs in health, education, urban development, and social security.

The council is preparing a study on Ontario's economic prospects over the next decade. The purpose of this paper is not primarily to provide an economic forecast, but to attempt to identify some of the main economic problems which may require policy attention.

9.4.2   Provincial research councils

Eight provinces have established research councils or foundations, with responsibility for assisting firms with technical problems and of aiding the development of provincial natural resources. Their total expenditures on scientific activities in 1974 were $29.9 million. Scientific R&D is the main activity of the institutes (49% of their total expenditures). They are also actively involved in other scientific activities such as resource surveys (10%); analysis and testing (9%); industrial engineering (7%); and library and technical information (5%).

Nova Scotia Research Foundation Corporation is a Crown corporation of Nova Scotia. Control is vested in a board of directors appointed by the province. Established in 1975 by an act of the legislature to replace the Nova Scotia Research Foundation, its objective is "to assist in the economic development of Nova Scotia by promoting, stimulating and encouraging the effective utilization of science and technology by industry and government and for this purpose to undertake, either singly or in conjunction with others, such research, development, surveys, investigations and operations as may, in the opinion of the board, be appropriate".

The corporation's laboratories in Dartmouth were built with funds from the Atlantic Development Board on a site donated by the province. The buildings, first occupied in 1969, now house a staff of 93 which includes 41 engineers and scientists and 36 technicians. The corporation's six scientific and technical divisions provide a strong multidisciplinary capability.

The Geophysics Division carries out gravity, seismic, magnetic, well-logging and electromagnetic surveys on land, and seismic bottom profiling and magnetic surveys at sea for industry and government. The Chemistry Division stresses research and development related to minerals and other natural resources. Services are available to industry and government in inorganic and food chemistry, pollution control and chemical engineering.

The Operational Research Division provides a service using the mathematical techniques of systems analysis. The Engineering Physics Division and the Centre for Ocean Technology emphasize ocean-oriented electronic and mechanical engineering. The Industrial and Information Services Division provides technical information on materials, equipment and processes and provides engineering assistance to manufacturing industries. The Biology Division carries out research on the distribution, growth, conservation and utilization of commercial seaweed. The division is involved in microbiological research related to water pollution and the treatment of industrial waste waters.

The New Brunswick Research and Productivity Council is a body corporate set up in 1962 by legislation. It is governed by an independent group of prominent citizens from management, labour and the professions who are appointed for three-year terms. The capital investment was provided by the federal government. The majority of the council's operations are carried out on a cost-recovery basis under contract with industry, trade associations and national and international agencies. The council maintains a well-equipped centre for engineering and problem-solving, industrial research and development for projects in the province, and conducts research on a cost-recovery basis for other clients in Canada and abroad.

The Quebec Industrial Research Centre (CRIQ) plays an important role in the industrial strategy of the Quebec government. The function of the CRIQ is to permit promising ideas to pass from the planning stage to industry and to commercial operation through various forms of assistance. The centre is responsible for carrying out applied research and for developing new products and processes, and has concentrated its work particularly on applications for small and medium-size businesses. Hence it attempts to ease the problems encountered by businesses which are unable to set up research facilities essential to their economic and technological development.

The Ontario Research Foundation (ORF), established in 1928, is an independent corporation. It derives its powers from a special act of the Ontario legislature. Its board of governors consists of leading members of the industrial, commercial and scientific communities. The organization was financed initially by an endowment fund provided by industrial and commercial corporations through the Canadian Manufacturers' Association, and a matching grant from the provincial government. Most of its income is derived from contract research undertaken mainly for industry. Since 1967 the Ontario government has provided an annual grant to ORF, the amount of which is directly proportional to ORF's income from Canadian industry. The foundation is concerned primarily with the development of Canadian industry through the application of science and technology. At the request of the various levels of government, it undertakes work relative to federal and provincial needs. Foundation activities are not restricted to Ontario; work is undertaken for any organization in Canada on an equal basis.

The foundation undertakes industrial research, development and testing for companies and government agencies, and maintains an effective applied research and development facility for the use of industry and government agencies. Ontario government funds support the back-up research necessary, and help bring to the attention of industry and government agencies the research opportunities that promise economic or social benefits. Situated in the Sheridan Park Research Community near Toronto, ORF has a staff of approximately 300 scientists, engineers, technicians and service personnel.

Since its establishment, ORF has provided both large and small companies with a variety of scientific and technical services. These have ranged from short-term investigations, market research and feasibility studies, through product and process development to long-range fundamental scientific investigations. All projects are conducted confidentially; this includes all business, technical or proprietary information revealed to ORF by clients or prospective clients. Patents resulting from research and development studies are assigned to the client.

The Manitoba Research Council consists of seven members, as well as four advisory committees whose members represent natural-resource-based industry, manufacturing, labour, the universities and government. The main reason for the establishment of the council is to assist Manitoba industry to improve its market position by developing a more scientifically based production capability. The council maintains an office in Winnipeg. Permanent staff members are provided by the provincial government. Its work is financed by provincial government appropriations, although fees and service charges may be levied for its services. The council promotes or carries out research and development investigations related to the natural resources and industrial operations of the province. Research sponsored by the council is performed in existing research laboratories of the province. Much of the research is aimed at establishing Manitoba as a centre of excellence in food products, electronics, materials research and building systems.

In addition, through a Technical Assistance Centre, industries are encouraged to incorporate new technological developments in their operations. The centre is staffed by engineers and scientists, all of whom have had extensive industrial experience. The centre received more than 120 inquiries for assistance during 1975-76 and a substantial amount of technical data on material selection and properties was conveyed to entrepreneurs.

The Saskatchewan Research Council was set up in 1947 under an act of the Saskatchewan legislature. The council carries out research in the natural and management sciences with the aim of improving the provincial economy. At first the council carried out its research programs at the University of Saskatchewan by means of grants to members of the staff and scholarships to graduate students. The 1947 act was amended in 1954 to empower the council to acquire property, employ staff and conduct its own financial affairs. Laboratory buildings were erected on the University of Saskatchewan campus in 1958 and extended in 1963. The present program places emphasis on consulting and technical assistance to industry and provincial government departments, research in the areas of metallic and industrial minerals, water, the environment, slurry pipeline transportation and selected aspects of agriculture. A large part of the program is carried out by a full-time staff of about 125 but some of the council's research is still promoted by grants to university staff. The members of the council consist of representatives of the Saskatchewan government, the university and industry.

Research Council of Alberta. The government of Alberta set up a scientific and industrial Research Council in cooperation with the University of Alberta in 1921 to promote mineral development. Considerable effort is still directed toward the development of natural resources, but increasing emphasis is being given to research related to the establishment of new industries within the province, to transportation and to environmental problems. The principal areas of activity are fossil fuels development and utilization, geological surveys and research, groundwater, soils, industrial minerals, chemical product and process development, technical and economic evaluations, microbiology, technical assistance to industry, gasoline and oil testing, pipeline transportation, highway research, river engineering, environmental studies and hail research.

The organization is controlled by a council of 15, representative of the Alberta government, the universities and industry. Research fields are reviewed by advisory committees of specialists drawn from industry, the universities and provincial government. The council is financed by provincial government appropriations and by contract research for private industry and government agencies. The main council laboratories and offices are on the University of Alberta campus in Edmonton, with pilot plant and laboratory facility east of the city. The full-time staff comprises approximately 325 scientists, engineers, technologists and supporting personnel.

BC Research performs a technical function for the British Columbia Research Council, a non-profit industrial research society with offices and laboratories at Vancouver, BC. This function enables even the smallest firms to improve their competitive position in Canadian and world markets by the use of the most up-to-date scientific knowledge. BC Research carries out contract research for clients on a confidential basis, initiates in-house research programs designed to promote and utilize the resources of the province, and provides a free technical information service in collaboration with the National Research Council. BC Research is active in applied biology, chemistry, engineering, physics, ocean engineering, operations research, industrial engineering, social impact and economic studies.

Sources
9.1 - 9.3 Science Statistics Centre, Education, Science and Culture Division, Statistics Canada.
9.4 Supplied by respective provincial departments and agencies.

Tables

Tables

..	not available	e	estimate
...	not appropriate or not applicable	p	preliminary
—	nil or zero	r	revised
--	too small to be expressed		certain tables may not add due to rounding

9.1 Total expenditure on natural science R&D, by source of funds, 1965-74, with current expenditure in parentheses (million dollars)

Year	General government[1]	Industry	University	Private non-profit	Foreign	Total
1965[r]	326 (266)	213 (163)	54 (54)	8 (8)	33 (33)	634 (524)
1966[r]	359 (288)	251 (200)	71 (71)	9 (9)	29 (29)	719 (597)
1967[r]	428 (348)	274 (231)	96 (96)	10 (10)	25 (25)	833 (710)
1968[r]	480 (399)	277 (241)	120 (120)	12 (12)	25 (25)	914 (797)
1969[r]	509 (438)	321 (272)	139 (139)	13 (13)	26 (26)	1,008 (888)
1970[r]	528 (458)	333 (283)	157 (157)	14 (13)	31 (31)	1,063 (942)
1971[r]	584 (512)	354 (298)	181 (181)	19 (18)	29 (29)	1,167 (1,038)
1972[r]	621 (551)	342 (299)	190 (190)	22 (21)	40 (40)	1,215 (1,101)
1973	690 (617)	381 (339)	199 (199)	24 (23)	37 (37)	1,331 (1,215)
1974	761 (688)	446 (373)	241 (241)	27 (26)	40 (40)	1,515 (1,368)

[1]Federal and provincial governments and provincial research councils.

9.2 Total expenditure on natural science R&D, by sector of performance, 1965-74, with current expenditure in parentheses (million dollars)

Year	General government[1]	Industry	University and private non-profit	Canada total	Foreign
1965	236 (182)	287 (237)	111 (105)	634 (524)	28 (28)
1966	258 (207)	317 (266)	144 (124)	719 (597)	32 (32)
1967	303 (243)	334 (291)	196 (176)	833 (710)	36 (36)
1968	331 (269)	341 (305)	242 (223)	914 (797)	40 (40)
1969	338 (289)	392 (343)	278 (256)	1,008 (888)	41 (41)
1970	354 (309)	407 (357)	302 (276)	1,063 (942)	48 (48)
1971	384 (335)	444 (388)	339 (315)	1,167 (1,038)	57 (57)
1972	418 (370)	441 (398)	356 (333)	1,215 (1,101)	68 (68)
1973	464 (414)	490 (448)	377 (353)	1,331 (1,215)	81 (81)
1974	521 (466)	564 (491)	430 (411)	1,515 (1,368)	94 (94)

[1]Federal and provincial governments and provincial research councils.

9.3 Federal government expenditure on the natural sciences, by department or agency and scientific activity, 1975-76 and 1976-77 (million dollars)

Department or agency	Current R&D	Data collection	Scientific information	Testing and standardization	Feasibility studies	Education support	Administration of extramural programs	Capital	Total
1975-76									
Environment	89.5	117.9	12.6	2.5	1.4	1.7	0.1	42.4	268.2
National Research Council	160.1	0.3	11.2	6.4	0.6	8.5	4.6	4.4	196.1
Agriculture	92.2	0.8	—	0.1	- -	—	—	16.8	113.4
Atomic Energy of Canada Limited	100.0	1.3	3.4	—	—	—	—	6.9	110.9
Energy, Mines and Resources	41.1	28.4	14.3	0.8	1.5	—	0.1	6.1	92.5
National Defence	57.5	—	2.1	18.2	2.1	—	2.5	6.9	89.3
Industry, Trade and Commerce	90.7	—	—	—	—	1.0	2.9	—	94.7
Medical Research Council	45.9	0.2	0.2	—	—	1.2	1.1	—	48.6
National Health and Welfare	20.4	1.8	0.4	4.4	- -	—	0.4	1.1	28.6
Communications	26.7	—	0.2	—	0.3	—	—	8.9	36.1
Others	44.6	5.0	12.6	3.1	19.1	1.3	5.5	3.0	90.9
Total	768.7	155.7	57.0	35.5	25.0	13.7	17.2	96.5	1,169.3

9.3   Federal government expenditure on the natural sciences, by department or agency and scientific activity, 1975-76 and 1976-77 (million dollars) (concluded)

Department or agency	Current R&D	Current related scientific activities					Adminis-tration of extra-mural programs	Capital	Total
		Data collec-tion	Scien-tific infor-mation	Testing and stan-dardiz-ation	Feasi-bility studies	Educa-tion support			
1976-77P									
Environment	100.8	138.9	15.2	2.5	1.3	1.9	0.2	43.2	304.1
National Research Council	191.9	0.4	13.4	7.5	0.7	9.4	5.2	7.2	235.6
Agriculture	104.3	0.9	3.6	0.1	- -	—	—	12.2	121.1
Atomic Energy of Canada Limited	107.1	1.6	3.2	—	—	—	—	7.1	118.9
Energy, Mines and Resources	49.2	35.0	16.0	0.9	1.7	—	0.2	6.8	109.8
National Defence	60.7	—	2.1	20.4	2.4	—	2.7	5.4	93.6
Industry, Trade and Commerce	87.6	—	—	—	—	0.9	3.0	—	91.4
Medical Research Council	47.4	0.2	0.2	—	—	1.0	1.3	—	50.2
National Health and Welfare	21.8	2.5	0.6	5.3	0.1	—	0.5	0.9	31.6
Communications	24.3	—	0.2	—	0.2	—	—	6.3	31.1
Others	45.4	5.4	11.3	3.4	24.5	1.4	9.1	2.6	103.2
Total	840.5	184.9	65.8	40.1	30.9	14.6	22.2	91.7	1,290.6

9.4   Federal government employees engaged in activities in the natural sciences, by department or agency and category, 1974-75 and 1975-76 (full-time equivalent)

Department or agency	Intramural R&D			Intramural related scientific activities			Adminis-tration of extra-mural programs	Total
	Scien-tific and profes-sional	Tech-nical	Other	Scien-tific and profes-sional	Tech-nical	Other		
1974-75								
Environment	1,182.5	1,215.5	1,001.4	979.5	2,017.0	892.4	7.7	7,296.0
Agriculture	963.2	1,033.7	2,006.4	48.0	63.3	69.4	—	4,184.0
National Research Council	717.0	874.0	653.0	202.0	159.0	331.0	83.0	3,019.0
Energy, Mines and Resources	680.5	333.4	218.0	261.4	691.6	632.9	5.6	2,823.4
National Defence	517.0	881.0	842.0	81.0	6.5	72.0	—	2,399.5
Atomic Energy of Canada Limited	639.0	846.0	868.0	36.0	46.0	69.0	—	2,504.0
National Health and Welfare	170.3	209.7	72.8	49.2	34.2	76.0	2.5	614.7
Communications	206.0	171.0	249.0	6.0	—	9.0	—	641.0
Consumer and Corporate Affairs	—	—	—	164.0	31.0	232.0	—	427.0
Others	149.1	79.8	78.7	88.1	44.0	62.3	368.1	870.1
Total	5,224.6	5,644.1	5,989.3	1,915.2	3,092.6	2,446.0	466.9	24,778.7
1975-76								
Environment	1,209.5	1,122.0	945.5	922.5	2,082.0	932.0	12.8	7,226.3
Agriculture	948.0	1,026.5	1,887.7	37.0	72.3	81.0	—	4,052.5
National Research Council	760.0	903.0	664.0	204.0	127.0	348.0	100.0	3,106.0
Energy, Mines and Resources	666.0	400.0	220.0	258.0	751.0	619.0	9.0	2,923.0
National Defence	477.0	731.0	593.0	223.0	375.0	445.0	15.0	2,859.0
Atomic Energy of Canada Limited	648.0	828.0	852.0	31.0	33.0	63.0	—	2,455.0
National Health and Welfare	197.4	220.5	67.3	66.7	43.8	83.9	10.7	690.3
Communications	160.0	188.0	261.0	15.0	—	10.0	—	634.0
Consumer and Corporate Affairs	—	—	—	194.0	37.0	197.0	—	428.0
Others	109.6	85.7	53.3	71.1	48.8	49.8	418.3	836.6
Total	5,175.5	5,504.7	5,543.8	2,022.3	3,569.9	2,828.7	565.8	25,210.7

9.5   Federal government expenditure on the natural sciences, by department or agency and performer, 1975-76 and 1976-77 (million dollars)

Department or agency	Federal government	Canadian industry	Canadian universities	Canadian non-profit institutions	Other Canadian performers	Foreign	Total
1975-76							
Environment	259.1	2.9	3.3	1.0	1.7	0.2	268.2
National Research Council	87.4	23.5	75.7	1.5	0.6	7.4	196.1
Agriculture	111.2	0.3	1.6	—	0.3	—	113.4
Atomic Energy of Canada Limited	86.1	23.5	0.8	0.1	0.4	0.1	111.0
Energy, Mines and Resources	81.3	7.6	1.4	- -	2.1	0.1	92.5
National Defence	71.5	13.0	2.6	- -	0.2	2.0	89.3
Industry, Trade and Commerce	3.0	88.3	0.6	1.6	1.2	—	94.7
Medical Research Council	1.1	—	45.1	0.1	- -	2.2	48.5
National Health and Welfare	16.0	- -	11.0	1.3	0.3	—	28.6
Communications	23.5	9.9	0.7	—	—	2.0	36.1
Canadian International Development Agency	0.4	—	1.2	—	—	22.5	24.1
Transport	5.8	4.5	1.4	0.1	0.3	- -	12.1
Consumer and Corporate Affairs	8.7	—	—	—	—	—	8.7
Regional Economic Expansion	—	—	—	—	0.2	—	0.2
Atomic Energy Control Board	—	0.1	9.0	—	—	—	9.1
Others	13.6	9.8	2.0	0.1	0.9	10.3	36.7
Total	768.7	183.4	156.4	5.8	8.2	46.8	1,169.3
1976-77P							
Environment	292.5	4.5	3.9	1.5	1.5	0.2	304.1
National Research Council	101.9	37.1	88.5	1.2	0.7	6.3	235.7
Agriculture	117.3	0.5	2.7	—	0.5	0.1	121.1
Atomic Energy of Canada Limited	91.1	26.9	0.5	- -	0.3	—	118.9
Energy, Mines and Resources	95.9	9.9	1.6	- -	2.3	- -	109.8
National Defence	76.7	13.3	0.9	0.3	- -	2.4	93.6
Industry, Trade and Commerce	3.0	83.4	0.4	3.6	0.9	—	91.4
Medical Research Council	1.3	—	46.3	- -	- -	2.4	50.2
National Health and Welfare	18.4	—	11.1	1.6	0.5	—	31.6
Communications	22.2	2.7	0.7	—	—	5.5	31.1
Canadian International Development Agency	0.4	—	1.4	—	—	28.8	30.6
Transport	6.9	9.8	1.6	0.1	0.5	- -	18.9
Consumer and Corporate Affairs	9.2	—	—	—	—	—	9.2
Regional Economic Expansion	—	- -	—	—	1.1	—	1.1
Atomic Energy Control Board	—	0.2	0.5	- -	—	—	0.6
Others	17.2	9.6	2.8	- -	0.8	12.0	42.6
Total	854.1	198.0	162.9	8.6	9.2	57.9	1,290.6

9.6   Federal government expenditure on the natural sciences, by activity and performer, 1975-76 and 1976-77 (million dollars)

Scientific activity	Federal government	Canadian industry	Canadian universities	Canadian non-profit institutions	Other Canadian performers	Foreign	Total
1975-76							
R&D	*498.5*	*173.0*	*143.8*	*4.4*	*6.4*	*26.3*	*852.5*
Current expenditure	428.8	173.0	143.8	4.4	6.4	26.3	782.8
Administration of extramural programs	14.0	—	—	—	—	—	14.0
Capital expenditure	69.7	—	—	—	—	—	69.7
Related scientific activities	*270.1*	*10.4*	*12.6*	*1.3*	*1.8*	*20.4*	*316.8*
Current expenditure	243.3	10.4	12.6	1.3	1.8	20.4	290.0
Scientific data collection	145.6	7.3	1.4	0.3	0.4	0.7	155.7
Scientific information	53.9	0.4	0.1	0.7	1.0	0.8	56.9
Testing and standardization	33.1	1.9	0.1	—	0.2	0.2	35.5
Feasibility studies	5.9	0.6	0.1	- -	- -	18.3	25.0
Education support	1.6	0.2	10.9	0.2	0.2	0.4	13.7
Administration of extramural programs	3.2	—	—	—	—	—	3.2
Capital expenditure	26.8	—	—	—	—	—	26.8
Total	768.6	183.4	156.4	5.7	8.2	46.7	1,169.3

9.6   Federal government expenditure on the natural sciences, by activity and performer, 1975-76 and 1976-77 (million dollars) (concluded)

Scientific activity	Federal government	Canadian industry	Canadian universities	Canadian non-profit institutions	Other Canadian performers	Foreign	Total
1976-77P							
R&D	*541.5*	*186.0*	*149.2*	*7.2*	*7.2*	*31.3*	*922.4*
Current expenditure	477.6	186.0	149.2	7.2	7.2	31.3	858.5
Administration of extramural programs	18.0	—	—	—	—	—	18.0
Capital expenditure	63.9	—	—	—	—	—	63.9
Related scientific activities	*312.6*	*11.9*	*13.6*	*1.3*	*2.1*	*26.6*	*368.1*
Current expenditure	284.9	11.9	13.6	1.3	2.1	26.6	340.4
Scientific data collection	173.4	8.6	1.6	0.4	0.4	0.4	184.9
Scientific information	62.0	0.4	0.1	0.5	1.2	1.4	65.8
Testing and standard-ization	37.2	2.2	0.2	—	0.1	0.4	40.1
Feasibility studies	6.3	0.6	0.1	- -	- -	23.7	30.9
Education support	1.8	0.1	11.6	0.3	0.2	0.5	14.6
Administration of extra-mural programs	4.2	—	—	—	—	—	4.2
Capital expenditure	27.7	—	—	—	—	—	27.7
Total	854.1	198.0	162.9	8.5	9.2	57.9	1,290.6

9.7   Expenditure on natural and human sciences R&D, by source of funds, 1970-74, with current expenditure in parentheses (million dollars)

Year	General government	Business enterprises[1]	Universities	Private non-profit institutions	Foreign	Total
1970	579 (529)	333 (283)	185 (185)	16 (15)	31 (31)	1,144 (1,043)
1971	646 (586)	354 (298)	209 (209)	21 (20)	29 (29)	1,259 (1,142)
1972	692 (638)	342 (299)	221 (221)	24 (23)	40 (40)	1,319 (1,221)
1973	776 (719)	381 (339)	234 (234)	27 (26)	37 (37)	1,455 (1,355)
1974	856 (792)	446 (373)	284 (284)	30 (29)	40 (40)	1,656 (1,518)

[1]Excludes human science activities.

9.8   Federal government expenditure on the human sciences, by department or agency and scientific activity, 1975-76 and 1976-77 (million dollars)

Department or agency	Current R&D	Current related scientific activities					Adminis-tration of extra-mural programs	Capital	Total
		Data collec-tion	Infor-mation services	Economic and feasi-bility studies	Operations and policy studies	Educa-tion support			
1975-76									
Statistics Canada	3.9	107.4	4.5	—	1.1	- -	—	0.8	117.7
Canada Council	13.3	—	3.0	—	0.2	10.5	1.7	—	28.7
National Health and Welfare	11.6	1.3	0.9	1.1	4.5	1.1	1.2	- -	21.8
International Develop-ment Research Centre	11.1	1.4	—	0.3	—	1.7	6.0	—	20.5
Canadian International Development Agency	10.7	—	—	—	0.5	2.1	0.4	—	13.7
National Library	—	—	10.4	—	—	—	—	- -	10.4
Manpower and Immigration	2.8	2.2	0.2	0.6	4.3	0.1	- -	- -	10.3
Treasury Board	- -	1.8	0.3	—	9.9	—	—	—	12.0
Indian Affairs and Northern Development	4.1	0.3	0.3	0.4	0.8	- -	0.3	1.9	8.2
Urban Affairs	3.8	0.2	—	—	2.7	0.2	0.1	- -	7.1
Others	45.2	17.7	15.1	3.5	18.9	2.7	3.0	0.7	106.5
Total	106.5	132.3	34.7	5.9	42.9	18.4	12.7	3.4	356.9
1976-77P									
Statistics Canada	3.6	160.7	7.2	1.1	1.5	- -	—	0.6	174.7[1]
Canada Council	15.4	—	3.1	—	0.3	11.7	1.9	—	32.4
National Health and Welfare	13.5	1.7	0.7	1.3	4.8	1.3	1.4	- -	24.8
International Develop-ment Research Centre	7.7	1.2	—	1.2	—	4.1	6.1	—	20.3
Canadian International Development Agency	11.8	—	—	—	0.5	2.3	0.5	—	15.1
National Library	—	—	13.3	—	—	—	—	- -	13.3
Manpower and Immigration	3.4	2.6	0.2	0.7	4.9	0.1	0.1	- -	12.1
Treasury Board	0.1	1.2	0.3	—	9.7	—	—	—	11.3
Indian Affairs and Northern Development	5.0	0.4	0.2	0.5	1.1	0.1	0.4	2.5	10.2
Urban Affairs	4.2	- -	0.1	—	4.9	0.8	0.1	—	10.2
Others	46.4	19.7	14.6	2.7	19.6	2.4	3.4	0.6	109.3
Total	111.1	187.5	39.7	7.5	47.3	22.8	13.9	3.7	433.7

[1]Includes additional expenditures for the 1976 Census.

9.9   Federal government employees engaged in activities in the human sciences, by department or agency and category, 1974-75 and 1975-76 (full-time equivalent)

Department or agency	Intramural R&D			Intramural related scientific activities			Adminis-tration of extramural programs	Total
	Scientific and profes-sional	Technical	Other	Scientific and profes-sional	Technical	Other		
1974-75								
Statistics Canada	59.3	13.3	29.7	692.5	566.0	3,975.3	—	5,336.1
National Library	—	—	—	149.0	24.0	266.0	—	439.0
Manpower and Immigration	44.0	4.0	50.0	139.0	10.0	142.0	2.0	391.0
National Health and Welfare	59.5	13.9	43.6	37.3	19.8	27.7	27.9	229.7
Treasury Board	—	—	—	29.0	9.0	172.0	—	210.0
International Development Research Centre	—	—	—	13.0	—	47.0	78.0	138.0
Indian Affairs and Northern Development	43.5	11.0	54.0	27.2	9.0	21.3	0.4	166.4
Canada Council	—	—	—	—	—	7.5	83.5	91.0
Urban Affairs	17.5	7.0	17.0	49.5	2.0	26.0	5.0	124.0
Canadian International Development Agency	—	—	—	5.0	3.0	7.0	16.0	31.0
Others	682.7	116.4	362.9	580.0	229.4	859.4	56.8	2,887.6
Total	906.5	165.6	557.2	1,721.5	872.2	5,551.2	269.6	10,043.8
1975-76								
Statistics Canada	90.0	36.3	79.0	744.5	638.2	3,651.0	—	5,239.0
National Library	—	—	—	157.0	30.0	267.0	—	454.0
Manpower and Immigration	38.0	5.0	47.0	113.0	20.0	124.0	2.0	349.0
National Health and Welfare	54.1	15.0	19.7	55.2	26.6	61.6	36.1	268.3
Treasury Board	—	—	—	28.0	8.0	223.0	—	259.0
International Development Research Centre	—	—	—	—	—	—	208.0	208.0
Indian Affairs and Northern Development	46.0	11.0	54.8	30.5	8.5	32.5	0.2	183.5
Canada Council	—	—	—	—	—	8.0	91.5	99.5
Urban Affairs	29.0	3.5	27.0	5.5	—	4.5	7.0	76.5
Canadian International Development Agency	—	—	—	9.0	1.0	5.0	19.0	34.0
Others	619.3	101.9	390.3	541.9	257.2	865.6	89.3	2,865.5
Total	876.4	172.7	617.8	1,684.6	989.5	5,242.2	453.1	10,036.3

9.10   Federal government expenditure on the human sciences, by department or agency and performer, 1975-76 and 1976-77 (million dollars)

Department or agency	Federal government	Canadian business enterprises	Canadian universities	Canadian non-profit institutions	Other Canadian performers	Foreign	Total
1975-76							
Statistics Canada	117.7	—	—	—	—	—	117.7
Canada Council	1.9	—	22.5	1.0	—	3.3	28.7
National Health and Welfare	8.5	0.2	5.6	3.3	3.8	0.4	21.8
International Development Research Centre	6.0	0.4	—	0.1	0.9	13.1	20.5
Canadian International Development Agency	0.9	—	2.3	—	—	10.5	13.7
National Library	10.4	—	—	—	—	—	10.4
Manpower and Immigration	9.2	0.8	0.1	—	0.2	- -	10.3
Treasury Board	12.0	—	—	0.1	—	—	12.1
Indian Affairs and Northern Development	6.6	0.3	0.3	0.3	0.7	—	8.2
Urban Affairs	2.7	1.5	0.8	1.2	0.9	- -	7.1
Environment	7.2	0.6	0.1	—	0.7	—	8.6
Transport	1.7	2.5	1.1	- -	0.5	—	5.8
Public Archives	6.4	—	—	—	—	—	6.4
Finance	5.4	—	—	—	—	—	5.4
Central Mortgage and Housing Corporation	1.9	0.5	1.0	0.1	0.3	—	3.9
Others	56.9	6.4	4.3	5.0	3.2	0.5	76.3
Total	255.4	13.2	38.1	11.1	11.2	27.8	356.9

9.10   Federal government expenditure on the human sciences, by department or agency and performer, 1975-76 and 1976-77 (million dollars) (concluded)

Department or agency	Federal government	Canadian business enterprises	Canadian universities	Canadian non-profit institutions	Other Canadian performers	Foreign	Total
1976-77P							
Statistics Canada	174.7	—	—	—	—	—	174.7
Canada Council	2.3	—	25.5	1.1	—	3.6	32.4
National Health and							
Welfare	9.3	0.5	6.7	3.6	4.2	0.5	24.8
International Develop-							
ment Research Centre	6.1	0.1	—	0.4	0.9	12.8	20.4
Canadian International							
Development Agency	0.9	—	2.6	—	—	11.5	15.1
National Library	13.4	—	—	—	—	—	13.4
Manpower and Immigration	10.7	1.0	0.1	—	0.2	- -	12.1
Treasury Board	11.2	—	—	0.1	—	—	11.3
Indian Affairs and							
Northern Development	8.2	0.4	0.4	0.4	0.8	—	10.2
Urban Affairs	6.0	1.0	1.3	1.2	0.7	—	10.2
Environment	7.7	1.0	0.2	—	0.5	—	9.4
Transport	2.1	3.9	0.9	0.1	0.7	—	7.6
Public Archives	7.1	—	—	—	—	—	7.1
Finance	6.5	—	—	—	—	—	6.5
Central Mortgage and							
Housing Corporation	2.7	0.7	1.3	0.2	0.5	—	5.4
Others	57.6	6.6	4.6	1.3	2.6	0.5	73.1
Total	326.5	15.2	43.6	8.4	11.0	29.0	433.7

9.11   Federal government expenditure on the human sciences, by activity and performer, 1975-76 and 1976-77 (million dollars)

Scientific activity	Federal government	Canadian business enterprises	Canadian universities	Canadian non-profit institutions	Other Canadian performers	Foreign	Total
1975-76							
R&D	*51.7*	*7.5*	*21.2*	*7.9*	*8.9*	*20.8*	*118.0*
Current expenditures	49.5	7.5	21.2	7.9	8.9	20.8	115.8
Administration of							
extramural programs	9.2	—	—	—	—	—	9.2
Capital expenditures	2.2	—	—	—	—	—	2.2
Related scientific activities	*203.8*	*5.7*	*16.9*	*3.2*	*2.2*	*7.0*	*238.9*
Current expenditures	202.5	5.7	16.9	3.2	2.2	7.0	237.7
Education support	0.2	- -	12.6	0.4	0.1	5.0	18.4
Data collection	126.5	2.6	0.7	0.3	0.9	1.4	132.3
Information services	30.0	0.8	2.1	1.5	0.3	- -	34.7
Economic and feasibility							
studies	3.6	0.7	0.6	0.2	0.3	0.4	5.9
Operation and policy studies	38.8	1.6	0.9	0.8	0.6	0.2	42.9
Administration of extramural							
programs	3.4	—	—	—	—	—	3.4
Capital expenditures	1.2	—	—	—	—	—	1.2
Total	255.5	13.2	38.1	11.1	11.1	27.8	356.9
1976-77P							
R&D	*55.7*	*9.4*	*25.0*	*5.2*	*8.9*	*18.5*	*122.7*
Current expenditures	52.9	9.4	25.0	5.2	8.9	18.5	119.9
Administration of							
extramural programs	8.8	—	—	—	—	—	8.8
Capital expenditures	2.8	—	—	—	—	—	2.8
Related scientific activities	*270.8*	*5.8*	*18.6*	*3.2*	*2.1*	*10.5*	*310.9*
Current expenditures	269.9	5.8	18.6	3.2	2.1	10.5	310.0
Education support	0.2	- -	13.9	0.7	0.1	7.8	22.8
Data collection	182.0	3.1	0.8	0.3	0.2	1.2	187.6
Information services	34.4	0.6	2.1	1.6	0.8	- -	39.7
Economic and feasibility							
studies	4.0	0.8	0.8	0.2	0.3	1.3	7.5
Operation and policy studies	44.1	1.1	0.9	0.2	0.6	0.2	47.3
Administration of extramural							
programs	5.1	—	—	—	—	—	5.1
Capital expenditures	0.9	—	—	—	—	—	0.9
Total	326.5	15.2	43.6	8.4	11.0	29.0	433.7

9.12   R&D expenditure of Canadian industrial firms, years ended Mar. 31, 1967-76 (million dollars)

Year	In Canada					Payments outside Canada	Total
	Intramural			Extramural	Total[1]		
	Current	Capital	Total				
1967r	290.6	43.8	334.4	15.1	337.7	34.5	372.2
1968r	305.1	35.9	341.0	16.0	344.7	36.3	381.0
1969r	342.9	49.3	392.2	22.8	396.1	37.4	433.5
1970r	357.2	49.3	406.5	29.9	410.0	44.2	454.2
1971r	387.6	56.0	443.6	30.4	446.6	51.2	497.8
1972r	397.5	43.7	441.2	31.1	444.4	59.3	503.7
1973	447.6	42.4	490.0	39.7	493.3	70.3	563.6
1974	491.1	73.6	564.7	44.8	568.2	74.9	643.1
1975P	552.9	67.5	620.4	41.4	623.7	82.5	706.2
1976P	605.1	70.6	675.7	41.6	679.0	80.0	759.0

[1]To avoid double counting, certain transfers from one respondent to another have been subtracted from the sum of all Canadian intramural and extramural expenditures. Such transfers would be entered once as intramural and once as extramural.

9.13   Industrial R&D expenditure, 1973 and 1974

Industry group	Intramural R&D expenditure			Source of funds			
	Current $'000,000	Capital $'000,000	Total $'000,000	Reporting company		Federal government	
				$'000,000	% of total	$'000,000	% of total
1973							
Mines and wells	23.9	1.8	25.7	19.6	76	1.0	4
Chemical based	93.0	7.3	100.4	82.2	82	7.3	7
Wood-based	19.7	1.1	20.8	12.1	58	2.6	12
Metals	41.6	2.2	43.8	40.0	91	2.1	5
Machinery transportation equipment	110.7	5.0	115.7	58.4	50	41.3	35
Electrical	113.3	12.4	125.7	82.7	66	19.0	15
Other manufacturing	7.5	0.9	8.4	6.3	75	0.9	11
Other industries	37.9	11.7	49.6	31.0	63	5.4	11
Total	447.6	42.4	490.1	332.3	68	79.6	16
1974							
Mines and wells	23.4	5.2	28.6	22.6	79	1.8	6
Chemical-based	104.9	22.9	127.8	109.7	86	7.3	6
Wood-based	25.3	1.8	27.1	15.2	56	2.6	10
Metals	48.0	7.6	55.6	48.6	87	2.7	5
Machinery and transportation equipment	105.8	4.6	110.4	54.8	50	39.5	36
Electrical	134.5	19.6	154.1	102.1	66	19.6	13
Other manufacturing	7.4	1.5	8.9	6.5	73	1.0	11
Other industries	41.8	10.4	52.2	32.9	63	9.7	19
Total	491.1	73.6	564.7	392.4	69	84.2	15

Sources

9.1 - 9.13 Education, Science and Culture Division, Institutional and Public Finance Statistics Branch, Statistics Canada.

Renewable resources   Chapter 10

Renewable resources   Chapter 10

Forestry   10.1

The forests of Canada are largely coniferous and make up 35% of the total land area; of this forest, less than 5% is reserved, i.e. parks and reserves where, by legislation, wood production is not primary. In 1974, 4,871 million cu ft (138 000 000 m³) of roundwood was cut. The harvesting and processing of this timber generated work for 297,000 persons with $3,281 million in salaries and wages. The "value added" by processing beyond the raw materials stage amounted to $6,934 million which was 10.5% of the value added of all goods-producing industries.

Canada is a major exporter of forest products. Exports of wood, wood products and paper in 1974 amounted to $5,652 million which was 18% of the value of all commodity exports. Paper and paperboard constituted 38% of all forest products exports; newsprint alone accounted for 30%.

British Columbia, Ontario and Quebec are the most important timber-producing provinces. In 1974 British Columbia sawmills produced 64% of all lumber in Canada and most of the sulphate pulp and softwood plywood while Ontario and Quebec produced most of the groundwood pulp and hardwood plywood.

There is a growing awareness of the importance of the forest in such areas as recreation, wildlife habitat and streamflow regulation. The recognition of these values is fostering a broader and more realistic concept of forestry.

Forest resources   10.1.1

Forest regions   10.1.1.1

The forests of Canada cover a vast area in the north temperate climatic zone but wide variations in physiographic, soil and climatic conditions cause marked differences in their character; hence, eight fairly well-defined forest regions can be recognized. By far the largest of these is the Boreal Region which represents 82% of the total forested area. The Great Lakes–St. Lawrence Region covers 6.5% and the Subalpine Region 3.7%. The Montane, Coast, and Acadian regions each account for approximately 2% while the remaining Columbia and Deciduous regions each represent less than 1%.

Boreal Forest Region. This region comprises the greater part of the forested area of Canada. It forms a continuous belt from Newfoundland and the coast of Labrador westward to the Rocky Mountains and northwestward to Alaska. White spruce and black spruce are characteristic species; other prominent conifers are tamarack which ranges generally throughout, balsam fir and jack pine in the eastern and central portions, and alpine fir and lodgepole pine in the western and northwestern parts. Although the Boreal forests are primarily coniferous there is a general admixture of deciduous trees such as white birch and poplar; these are important in the central and south-central portions, particularly along the edge of the prairie. In turn, the proportion of spruce and larch increases to the north and, with the more rigorous climate, the close forest gives way to an open lichen-woodland which finally changes into tundra. In the eastern section, along the southern border of the region, there is a considerable intermixture of species from the Great Lakes–St. Lawrence forest, such as eastern white pine, red pine, yellow birch, sugar maple, black ash and eastern white cedar.

Great Lakes–St. Lawrence Forest Region. Extending inland from the edges of the Great Lakes and the St. Lawrence River lies a forest of a very mixed nature which is characterized by eastern white pine, red pine, eastern hemlock and

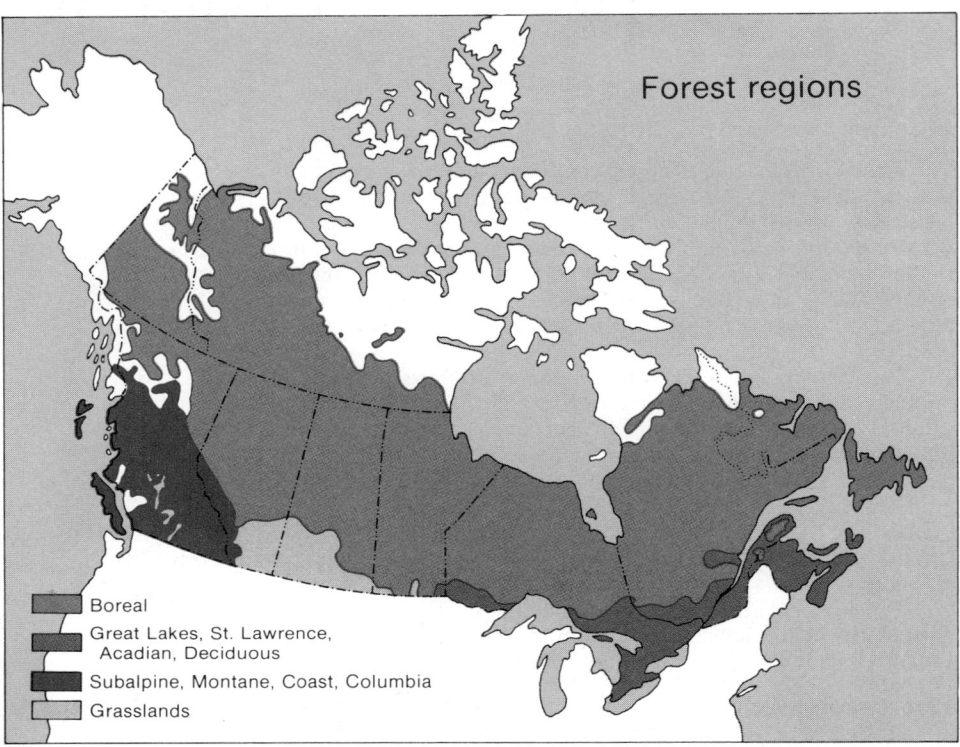

Forest regions

Boreal
Great Lakes, St. Lawrence,
  Acadian, Deciduous
Subalpine, Montane, Coast, Columbia
Grasslands

yellow birch. With these are associated certain dominant broadleaved species common to the Deciduous Forest Region, including sugar maple, red maple, red oak, basswood and white elm. Other species with wide ranges are the eastern white cedar and largetooth aspen and, to a lesser extent, beech, white oak, butternut and white ash. Boreal species such as white spruce, black spruce, balsam fir, jack pine, poplars, and white birch are intermixed, and red spruce is abundant in certain central and eastern portions. This region extends in a westward direction into southeastern Manitoba but does not include the area north of Lake Superior.

Subalpine Forest Region. This is a coniferous forest located on the mountain uplands of Alberta and British Columbia, from the Rocky Mountain range through the interior of British Columbia to the Pacific Coast inlets. The characteristic species are Engelmann spruce, alpine fir and lodgepole pine. There is a close relationship between the Subalpine Forest Region and the Boreal Forest Region, which also shares black spruce, white spruce and trembling aspen. There is also some penetration of interior Douglas-fir from the Montane forest, and western hemlock, western red cedar and amabilis fir from the coastal forests. Other species are western larch, whitebark pine, limber pine and, on the Coast Mountains, yellow cypress and mountain hemlock.

Montane Forest Region. The region occupies a large part of the interior uplands of British Columbia, as well as a part of the Kootenay Valley and a small area on the east side of the Rocky Mountains. It is a northern extension of the typical forest of much of the western mountain system in the United States, and comes in contact with the Coast, Columbia, and Subalpine Forest regions. Ponderosa pine is a characteristic species of the southern portions. Interior Douglas-fir is found throughout, but more particularly in the central and southern parts; lodgepole pine and trembling aspen are generally present, the latter being particularly well represented in the north-central portions. Engelmann spruce and alpine fir from the Subalpine Forest Region, together with white birch, are important constituents in the northern parts. White spruce, although primarily Boreal in affinity, also grows here. Extensive prairie communities of bunch-grasses and herbs are found in many of the river valleys.

Coast Forest Region. This region is part of the Pacific Coast forest of North America. Essentially coniferous, it consists principally of western red cedar and western hemlock, with Sitka spruce abundant in the north and Douglas-fir in the south. Amabilis fir and yellow cypress are represented throughout the region and, together with mountain hemlock and alpine fir, are common at the higher altitudes. Western white pine is found in the southern parts, while western yew is in widely scattered groups. Deciduous trees, such as black cottonwood, red alder and bigleaf maple, have a limited distribution. Arbutus and Garry oak grow only on the southeast coast of Vancouver Island, the adjacent islands and mainland. The arbutus is a broadleaved evergreen. Both are species whose centres of population lie southward in the United States.

Acadian Forest Region. Over the greater part of the Maritime provinces there is a forest closely related to the Great Lakes–St. Lawrence forest and, to a lesser extent, to the Boreal forest. Red spruce is a characteristic though not exclusive species, and associated with it are balsam fir, yellow birch and sugar maple, with some red pine, eastern white pine, jack pine and eastern hemlock. Beech was formerly a more important forest constituent than at present, but beech bark disease has drastically reduced its representation in Nova Scotia, Prince Edward Island and southern New Brunswick. Other species of wide distribution are white spruce, black spruce, red oak, white elm, black ash, red maple, white birch, grey birch and poplars. Eastern white cedar, although present in New Brunswick, is extremely rare elsewhere and jack pine is apparently absent from the upper St. John Valley and the western half of Nova Scotia.

Columbia Forest Region. A large part of the Kootenay Valley, the upper valleys of the Thompson and Fraser rivers and the Quesnel Lake area of British Columbia contain a coniferous forest, called the Columbia Forest Region, which closely resembles the Coast Forest Region. Western red cedar and western hemlock are the characteristic species in this interior "wet belt". Associated trees are the interior Douglas-fir which has general distribution and, in the southern parts, western white pine, western larch, grand fir and western yew. Engelmann spruce from the Subalpine Forest Region is important in the upper Fraser Valley and is found to some extent at the upper levels of the forest in the remainder of the region. At lower elevations in the west and in parts of the Kootenay Valley, the forest merges with the Montane Forest Region and in a few places borders directly on grassland.

Deciduous Forest Region. A small portion of the deciduous forest, which is widespread in the United States, extends into southwestern Ontario between Lakes Huron, Erie and Ontario. Here, with the deciduous trees common to the Great Lakes–St. Lawrence Forest Region, such as sugar maple, beech, white elm, basswood, red ash, white oak and butternut, are scattered a number of other deciduous species which have their northern limits in this locality. Among these are the tulip-tree, cucumber-tree, pawpaw, red mulberry, Kentucky coffee-tree, redbud, black gum, blue ash, sassafras, mockernut hickory, pignut hickory, black oak and pin oak. In addition, black walnut, sycamore and swamp white oak are confined largely to this region. Conifers are few but there is scattered distribution of eastern white pine, tamarack, eastern red cedar and eastern hemlock.

The Grasslands. Although not a forest region, the prairies of Manitoba, Saskatchewan and Alberta support several species of trees in great numbers.

Trembling aspen forms groves or "bluffs" around wet depressions, and continuous dense stands along the northern boundary. Several other species of poplar are usually found along rivers and in moist locations, along with willows and some white spruce. There are sporadic stands of white birch, Manitoba maple, bur oak and ash. In British Columbia, where the grasslands are confined to deep valleys and low areas of the interior, there are scattered representations of ponderosa pine, birches, poplars, spruce and mountain alder.

10.1.1.2   Forest land

Inventories of the forest resources of Canada are made periodically by provincial forest authorities and, with their cooperation, the Canadian Forestry Service of the Department of Fisheries and the Environment compiles national statistics.

The 1973 National Forest Inventory reported an area of 1,259,192 sq miles (3 261 292 km²) of forest land (Table 10.1). Of this total, 59,742 sq miles (154 731 km²) are reserved by legislation for primary uses other than timber production. Of the remainder of non-reserved forest land, 632,448 sq miles (1 638 033 km²) are allocated to wood production and are held under licence, lease and/or under sustained yield management. The balance of 567,000 sq miles (1 468 500 km²) whether for reasons of suitability or economic accessibility is capable of producing crops of merchantable size and as inventories are extended and refined, its area can be expected to increase. Currently, about 75% of the non-reserved forest land of Canada has been inventoried in the sense of gathering statistically reliable information on area and forest cover.

Provincial Crown forest land constituted 69% of the non-reserved forest land of Canada, leaving 23% under federal jurisdiction and 8% in private ownership. Of the provincial forest land 69% is allocated to timber production and of the federal forest land less than 2% is so allocated. Although precise use of private forest land is a matter of speculation, individual studies and limited statistics suggest that timber production still predominates despite a tendency to convert some of this land to recreational use. At the time of the 1973 inventory 8% of the non-reserved forest land was considered inadequately stocked for timber production.

The estimates of volumes of timber, which are given by province in Table 10.1, are also subject to constant revision as more accurate and complete inventories are compiled. The volumes reported in the 1973 National Forest Inventory are somewhat larger than those reported previously due to updating of inventories in some provinces. The estimates, however, are low because timber volumes for Labrador, the Yukon Territory and Northwest Territories are not available and because British Columbia has adopted procedures whereby data on volume of mature timber only were compiled.

10.1.1.3   Canada's forest trees

There are approximately 140 recognized tree species in Canada, excluding the various subspecies and varieties. Of this number, 31 species are conifers or "softwood", about two thirds of which are of commercial value; less than one fifth of the native broadleaved trees or "hardwoods" can be considered as commercially significant.

The most abundant forest trees in Canada, in terms of standing timber, are the spruces, pines, true firs, poplars, hemlocks, birches, cedars, Douglas-fir, maples and larches. However, the economic importance of these species, except for the spruces, does not necessarily correspond to their abundance.

About one third of Canada's timber volume is spruce. White spruce and black spruce range from the Atlantic Coast almost to the Pacific and northward into Alaska. Sitka spruce, the largest of the native spruces, is found in the Pacific Coast area; Engelmann spruce is established farther inland, extending to the foothills of the Rockies in southwestern Alberta; and red spruce is found only in eastern Canada. Spruce is used extensively for pulpwood, lumber and plywood.

Among the pines, two species — jack pine and lodgepole pine — make up 11% of Canada's standing timber. Jack pine grows from Nova Scotia to northern

Alberta and the Northwest Territories and lodgepole pine is found in western Alberta, British Columbia and the Yukon Territory. Eastern white pine, which grows from the Atlantic to the eastern edge of the prairies, and western white pine produce valuable softwood lumber. Ponderosa pine, found in the drier areas of southern British Columbia, and red pine, found in eastern Canada, are important commercial species.

The four native firs are all commercial species, although balsam fir far outranks the other species in this regard. It is the only fir found in eastern Canada and ranges from Newfoundland through all the provinces except British Columbia. Alpine fir, essentially a high altitude tree, is found over a wide area in British Columbia and its range extends well into the western half of central Alberta and the Yukon Territory. Amabilis fir is a west coast species, while grand fir is found in both the Pacific coastal areas and the interior of British Columbia. Fir is commonly cut as pulpwood and, to a lesser extent, as sawlogs.

Douglas-fir, one of Canada's best known commercial trees, is not a true fir. The tree responsible more than any other for British Columbia's world-wide reputation for timber is the coastal form of Douglas-fir which is dominant in the forests of the province's lower coastal areas. An interior form, known as blue Douglas-fir, is used on a large scale for lumber, plywood, construction timbers, piling and kraft pulp.

The poplars are the most abundant of the native broadleaved trees. They include trembling and largetooth aspen, balsam poplar, and the three cotton-woods. The most widely distributed is trembling aspen, followed by balsam poplar; both species occur from Newfoundland to Alaska. The largest of the native poplars is black cottonwood; its range covers the lower two thirds of British Columbia and extends well into Alberta to the east in a pattern that follows the natural drainage basins. It also reaches as far north as the Yukon Territory along the coast. This species is in demand for veneer stock. Other cottonwoods — eastern cottonwood and its western form known as plains cottonwood, and narrowleaf cottonwood — have a much more limited distribution.

Hemlocks, ranking fifth in volume of standing timber, have considerable commercial importance. Western hemlock grows plentifully along the Pacific Coast and west of the Rockies in the interior wet belt of British Columbia. It is one of the principal timber-producing species in western Canada and is also an important source of pulpwood. Eastern hemlock is found from the Atlantic to western Ontario, although not in a wide or continuous pattern. It is used to produce a number of products including pulpwood, plywood and lumber. Mountain hemlock is found in British Columbia in parts of the coastal forest and in the heavier rainfall areas of the interior.

Of the six native birches, only two are of commercial importance — yellow birch and white birch. Most abundant is white birch which grows over a vast part of Canada from the Atlantic to the Pacific and extends up to the northern tree limit. One variety, western paper birch, reaches heights of 100 ft (30 m) and diameters of three feet (one metre) or more. Yellow birch is a valuable hardwood species used extensively for flooring, veneer and plywood. Its range extends from the Atlantic to Lake Superior.

The native trees commonly known as "cedars" include the arbor-vitae (eastern white cedar and western red cedar), yellow cypress (yellow cedar) and a juniper (eastern red cedar). Together they make up an important group of commercial species. Eastern white cedar is found from Nova Scotia to Manitoba and as far north as James Bay in Quebec and Ontario. Its wood, which is light and resistant to decay, is used for posts, poles, boats and other purposes where timber is exposed to situations favourable to decay. Western red cedar is of major importance in British Columbia where it ranges from the Pacific Coast to the Rocky Mountains. It is used for lumber, exterior siding, shingles, poles and posts, doors, window sashes and other purposes where resistance to decay is required. Yellow cypress — commonly called yellow cedar or Alaska cedar — is found mainly in the Pacific Coast region where it grows down to sea level in the more northerly sections. As it extends farther south, it seeks higher elevations. Its wood, like that of the other cedars, is valued where resistance to decay is needed.

There are 10 native species of maple, six of which are of commercial value. Only two species are known as hard maples, producing wood that is both hard and strong — sugar maple and the closely related black maple. Sugar maple ranges from the Atlantic to Lake Superior, while black maple is found mainly in southern Ontario. Hard maple constitutes one of the most valuable commercial hardwoods in Canada. It is used for furniture, flooring, veneer, quality plywood, turnery and other specialized purposes where strength and hardness are needed. Sugar maple and, to a lesser degree, black maple are tapped for the maple sugar industry. Bigleaf maple is found on the lower Pacific Coast mainland and on Vancouver Island. The wood is only moderately hard and lacks strength but, owing to the limited local supply of hardwoods, this tree is of some importance for furniture and other specialized uses in the immediate area. Red maple and silver maple are eastern species. Red maple ranges from Newfoundland to western Ontario, while silver maple is concentrated mainly in southern Ontario and southwestern Quebec. Their wood is weaker and softer than that of the hard maples and these trees are not important timber producers. The Manitoba maple, ranging from Ontario across the southern parts of Manitoba, Saskatchewan and southeastern Alberta, produces a soft, moderately light wood that is low in strength. It is better known as a shelterbelt tree.

There are three species of larch in Canada. Two of them — eastern larch, better known as tamarack, and western larch — have commercial value. Tamarack is widely distributed from Newfoundland to the British Columbia–Yukon border and reaches far into the Northwest Territories. The wood is used for poles, posts, piling, boxes, crates and pulp. Western larch, found mainly in southeastern British Columbia, is one of the important timber-producing trees of western Canada. The wood, hard and strong, is used mainly in construction but is also made into flooring, interior and exterior furnishings, and pulp.

Other trees of less commercial significance include oak, ash, beech, elm and basswood. Valuable as the wood of these species may be, it is usually obtainable in limited quantities only. However, the species may have considerable local importance and they also contribute greatly to the forest landscape.

Canada's better known species are the commercially exploited trees, but in the forest all species have a role to play in maintaining the ecological balance, controlling water run-off and preventing soil erosion, and in providing a habitat for native fauna and recreational facilities.

10.1.1.4   Land use

The Lands Directorate of the Department of Fisheries and the Environment is responsible for investigating national aspects of land use in terms of management, research, planning and environmental concerns.

In support of resource management, the directorate operates a number of mapping programs. The largest is the Canada Land Inventory (CLI). Under federal-provincial agreement, all settled lands of Canada have been classified according to their capabilities for agriculture, forestry, recreation and wildlife. These data, widely used for land-use planning at the regional level, have been placed in a computer system known as the Canada Geographic Information System (CGIS), enabling the production of statistics on land capability at the national level. In response to the need for other mapping techniques for those areas not covered by the CLI program, a biophysical land classification system has been developed and applied in the James Bay area. Further development of ecological (biophysical) land classification methodologies through the application of satellite imagery and high-altitude aerial photography is a major concern.

National research programs have focused on the land resource aspects of outdoor recreation and on an examination of the trends and factors of land-use change, particularly in urban-rural fringe areas. Several thematic mapping projects have illustrated land-use issues in key regions such as along the Windsor–Quebec axis and in the Vancouver–Victoria area. A computerized bibliographic reference system which currently houses outdoor recreation references exclusively is being expanded to cover a wide range of literature on land-use matters.

Another role of the directorate has been to assess the land-use impact of major development projects. Advice and guidelines have been provided for such proposals as the Vancouver Airport expansion.

Forest depletion   10.1.2

The average annual forest depletion by cutting and fire is shown in Table 10.2 for the 10-year period 1964-73. The primary sources of Canada's current wood production are the areas of Crown forest land allocated to wood production and private forest land. These two ownerships constitute 404.8 million acres (163.8 million hectares). On a volume basis, it was estimated in 1968 that the annual permissible allowable cut to maintain productive forests was 8,481 million cu ft (240 million m³). In the 10-year period 1964-73, average annual utilization of wood harvested amounted to about 4,100 million cu ft (116 million m³) or about half the allowable cut. In addition to cutting and fire, extensive forest depletion is caused by insects, diseases and natural mortality but no reliable estimates of these losses, either physical or economic, are available.

A large surplus of timber exists in Canada although there are shortages in some regions and species which could be overcome by increased silvicultural and management techniques. In addition, greater utilization of individual trees and of certain species could further extend the resource.

A total of 7,777 forest fires occurred across Canada in 1974, destroying 2.3 million acres (one million hectares) of valuable forest land (Table 10.3). Through carelessness and incendiarism, man has been blamed for 73% of all forest fires reported in 1974 (Table 10.4). Lightning caused 2,141 fires or 27% of the total.

Forest administration   10.1.3

Federal forestry programs   10.1.3.1

The federal government is directly responsible through several departments and agencies for the protection and administration of forest resources in the Yukon Territory and Northwest Territories and on other federal lands such as the national parks, Indian reserves, military areas, and forest experiment stations. In addition, there are important federal responsibilities with respect to the nation's forest resources as a whole. These responsibilities, which relate to forestry research and development and the provision of information and technical services, are defined and established by the Forestry Development and Research Act (1966) and the Department of the Environment Act (1970).

The primary federal organization concerned with forestry is the Canadian Forestry Service of Fisheries and Environment Canada. Its program covers seven categories: forest policy and program planning; production forestry; environmental and amenity forestry; background research; operations; extension services; and international forestry.

To promote improved management of forest resources and better forest products, the Canadian Forestry Service, through publications, workshops, and seminars disseminates technical information to forest resource and wood processing managers. Forest advisory services are provided for federal departments and international agencies, and assessments are also made of operational trials and treatments conducted by resource organizations and industry. In the forest products field, special testing services (unavailable commercially) are provided both for government and industry. The service also participates in the development of codes and specifications for forest products.

Through its publications, press releases, films, displays, visitor centres and demonstration areas, the service seeks to increase public awareness and understanding of forest values and to enlist support in the protection and wise use of the forest resource.

10.1.3.2   Provincial forestry programs

All forest land in provincial territory, with the exception of the minor portions in national parks, federal forest experiment stations, military areas and Indian reserves, is administered by the respective provincial governments. The forestry program of each is outlined below.

Newfoundland. The forest resources of this province are geographically separated by the Strait of Belle Isle into two distinct regions — the island of Newfoundland and Labrador on the mainland. A forest inventory of Labrador, completed in 1975, was conducted on lands south of 56°N. The inventoried area disclosed a total of 99,619 sq miles (258 012 km²) of which 21,380 sq miles (55 374 km²) were productive forest area. The total volume of black spruce and balsam fir in Labrador as indicated by the inventory is 113,260,100 cunits (320 716 350 m³). A forest inventory of the island of Newfoundland shows that of a total area of 43,029 sq miles (111 445 km²), over 14,619 sq miles (37 863 km²) are classified as productive forest. This area supports a total gross volume of 99.5 million cunits (281.8 million m³) of softwoods and hardwoods. The principal commercial species of trees are black spruce and balsam fir. White pine, white spruce, and white and yellow birch are of lesser commercial importance.

Sixty percent of the productive forest lands on the island has been licensed, leased, or is owned in fee simple by the pulp and paper industry while 37% remains under the direct jurisdiction of the province. Tenure of the remaining 3% is varied and includes federal and provincial parks.

Responsibility and authority over Crown forests in the province are vested in the Forestry Branch of the Department of Forestry and Agriculture. The branch employs more than 200 professional, technical and support staff. Nineteen management units in four regions of the province undertake the operational field work of forest protection, timber surveys, permits, enforcement, scaling, silviculture and forest management. Headquarters at St. John's is responsible for planning and program development. A new forest policy of increased utilization on a sustained yield basis, backed by legislation and intensified forest management, is being implemented following an exhaustive study of all aspects of forests in the province.

A forest management inventory of the province is currently being conducted. It is estimated that this new inventory will be completed within five years. The legislation requires every owner of 300 acres (121 ha) or more of forest land either to submit a plan for certification utilizing the annual sustainable yield of such land or to pay a high tax on the basis of unmanaged land. Limit holders are also being assessed an annual tax for managed land on the basis of area held.

The province's forest resource is primarily used for the production of newsprint, linerboard and lumber. Two newsprint mills, one at Grand Falls and the other at Corner Brook, have a combined production capacity of approximately 2,050 tons (1 860 t) a day. A linerboard mill in Stephenville began production in 1973 and has a daily capacity of 1,000 tons (907 t). There is also a growing sawmill industry producing about half of the province's lumber requirements. This proportion is increasing and it is estimated that about 70% of provincial needs can be produced from the mix and extent of timber resources available. The total forest industry contributes approximately $173 million annually to the gross provincial product.

Forest research is principally carried out by the Canadian Forestry Service of the federal Department of Fisheries and the Environment. Post high school education in forestry is available at Memorial University of Newfoundland and at the College of Trades and Technology (CTT). Memorial University offers a two-year diploma course in forestry and is affiliated with the forestry faculty of the University of New Brunswick. At the CTT students may obtain a diploma after successfully completing a two-year forest technology course.

Prince Edward Island. Roughly 45% of Prince Edward Island's 2,184 sq miles (5 657 km²) of land area is tree-covered. The wooded areas consist of scattered patches throughout the province with the greatest concentration being in the eastern section. All woodland is privately owned except some 50 sq miles (129 km²) of provincially owned forest land.

The Forestry Branch of the Department of Agriculture and Forestry administers all forestry matters in the province — reforestation, protection, extension and woodlot improvement. The reforestation program has been expanding yearly, in particular with greater emphasis on the genetic improvement of the white spruce. Greater attention is being paid to the province's endangered species — yellow birch, black and white ash, red oak and red spruce — that have practically disappeared due to shipbuilding and overcutting of the higher grades.

Nova Scotia. Of Nova Scotia's land area of 20,402 sq miles (52 841 km²), 17,159 sq miles (44 442 km²) are classed as forest and 75% of the forest land is considered suitable for regular harvesting. Although 91% of the forest land in Canada is held by the Crown in the right of the federal and provincial governments, only 24% is so held in Nova Scotia. Of the private woodlands, 71% are in parcels of up to 1,000 acres (405 ha).

Provincial Crown lands are administered by the Department of Lands and Forests through a staff of foresters and rangers. Extension personnel assist owners of small private woodlands. The department administers the Lands and Forests Act as it pertains to all lands and is responsible for forest fire suppression. Forest fire detection is facilitated through 35 observation towers and an aerial patrol service with two helicopters and six fixed-wing aircraft. In 1975, 731 fires burned 6,989 acres (2 828 ha) of forest. The largest fire covered 2,447 acres (990 ha). Fire suppression crews and rangers with equipment are stationed throughout the province.

The forest industry is important to the economy of Nova Scotia, contributing directly or indirectly about $150 million to the gross provincial product annually. In 1975 there were in operation some 441 sawmills of various types and sizes, one hardboard mill, two newsprint mills, one groundwood pulp mill and one chemical pulp mill. Roundwood production was 88.5 million cu ft (2 506 000 m³), of which 85 million cu ft (2 407 000 m³) was domestic pulpwood, 3 million cu ft (85 000 m³) was peeled pulpwood for export, and 500,000 cu ft (14 000 m³) was poles and piling. Sawn products accounted for 13.9 million cu ft (394 000 m³) (volume-in-product), of which 13.3 million cu ft (379 000 m³) was lumber. Chip production totalled 8.5 million cu ft (240 000 m³), of which 8.1 million cu ft (229 000 m³) derived from sawmill residues and 400,000 cu ft (11 000 m³) came from whole-tree chipping, the latter a recent development in Nova Scotia.

A small reforestation program, active since the 1930s, has been greatly expanded in the 1970s. Experimental work on container planting, direct seeding, soil capability and site preparation continues, and efforts are being made to improve seed sources. Total softwood inventory as of September 1975 was 10 million seedlings and transplants, and 2.5 million trees were planted.

Timber, pulpwood and Christmas trees are sold through public tender, and cutting on Crown lands is done on recommendation of resource managers of the Department of Lands and Forests. Management cruises, regeneration studies and experimental cuttings are conducted on Crown lands and a program of operating these lands under long-term, integrated-use management plans is under way. During 1974-75, 5,232 acres (2 117 ha) of Crown forest were thinned and improved, bringing the total area of Crown silvicultural treatments to 45,727 acres (18 505 ha) since 1965. Twenty-four miles (39 km) of new Crown land access road were added to the existing 337 miles (542 km) and 29 miles (47 km) were under construction.

The provincial forest inventory, a continuous system designed to operate on a 10-year cycle, commenced its second cycle in 1971. Aerial colour photography, begun on Cape Breton Island in 1969, is being extended to the rest of the province. Remeasurement of a system of 1,765 randomly located sample plots every five years provides continuing data on growth, harvest rates and mortality.

Forest research is carried on by federal government agencies and by the Nova Scotia Research Foundation. Investigations cover stand improvement, tree nutrition, cutting methods, and insect and disease activities. Extension projects include fire prevention, a province-wide motion picture program, distribution of information on forest and wildlife conservation, promotion of the Christmas tree industry, a hunter safety program, woodlot improvement, preparation of material for the mass media, and technical assistance to sawmill operators.

New Brunswick. Of New Brunswick's 27,835 sq miles (72 092 km²), approximately 87% is classed as forest land suitable for regular harvest. About 46% of the forest land is owned by the Crown, administered and managed by the Department of Natural Resources through its five forest districts and four support branches. The Department of Natural Resources recently took over administration of forest extension programs for privately owned woodlots.

The forest industry is of prime importance to the economy of New Brunswick, directly contributing over $220 million in value-added from primary forestry and forest-related industries and directly employing nearly 14,000 people. The total volume of standing timber is estimated at 205 million cunits (580 million m³); coniferous species make up 70% and deciduous species the remainder. Approximately 3 million cunits (8.5 million m³) of timber are currently harvested annually with 70% of the harvest being cut as pulpwood.

A comprehensive examination of the province's forest resources and related industry was completed in 1974. The study's conclusions and the subsequent signing of a five-year federal-provincial forestry development agreement resulted in increased emphasis on more intensive forest management. A large-scale silvicultural program has been initiated by the Department of Natural Resources and funded under the agreement. In 1976, approximately 12 million seedlings would be planted on Crown lands with a planned increase to 25 million seedlings by 1978.

New Brunswick is initiating changes in allocating the timber from Crown land. The traditional system depends on issuing forest management licences to companies or individuals for certain areas. The licences authorize the cutting and removal of forest products in accordance with plans and permits approved by the Department of Natural Resources. Royalties are paid for the timber cut.

To evaluate new methods of timber allocation a pilot area has been selected in northeast New Brunswick. A forest management licence for approximately one million acres (404,686 ha) has been cancelled and replaced by a long-term guarantee to provide annually, to the former licensee, a specified volume of standing timber for harvesting. A Crown corporation has been established to coordinate the harvesting and allocation of timber from this reserve. The wood is allocated to industries in the area on the basis of "optimum use". The remainder of the province is still on a forest management licence system.

New Brunswick carries out an aerial spraying program to protect balsam fir and spruce from the spruce budworm which has been carried out since 1952 by a Crown corporation originally sponsored by the federal and provincial governments and by several of the major forest products companies.

New Brunswick does not maintain a forest research organization but cooperates with the Canadian Forestry Service in its research program. The University of New Brunswick has undertaken a small number of forest research projects in cooperation with the National Research Council, the provincial government and other organizations. The University of New Brunswick offers undergraduate and graduate courses in forestry leading to BSF and MScF degrees. It is also responsible for the administration of the Maritime Forest Ranger School in conjunction with the governments of New Brunswick and Nova Scotia and with private industry.

Quebec. Forests with economic potential cover 264,000 sq miles (684 000 km²), about 45% of the total area of the province. This forest cover stretches northward to an irregular line near 52°N in the east and west and 53°N in the centre of the province. The forests may be divided into two separate tenure groups, private and public. Private forests cover an area of 27,000 sq miles (70 000 km²). Public forests cover 237,300 sq miles (614 600 km²) of which 190,000 sq miles (492 000 km²) are productive and under management plans. Public forests carry a volume of almost 134,335 million cu ft (3 804 million m³) of standing timber of various species; private forests contain 16,600 million cu ft (470 million m³). Coniferous species make up 75% of the total volume. Public forests under management and private forests supply the pulp and paper mills and the sawmills of Quebec. Private forests account for about 20% of the annual cut, about two million cunits (5.7 million m³). Forests account for about 25% of the gross provincial product.

Management of public forests and assistance to private forestry is carried out by the Forestry Branch of the Department of Lands and Forests which controls development and the use of woodlands, and undertakes conservation measures. Principal management controls are: the annual inventory of some 30,000 sq miles (78 000 km²) of forest land; study and regulation of silvicultural practices for this area and the zoning of the land for its best use; and restoration of lands destined for forestation by replanting or by proper treatment. To achieve this Quebec maintains some 100 million plants in nursery stock. Regulations governing the use of the forests cover operational control, the issuance of permits for establishment of mills and cutting permits, measurement of wood harvested on Crown land, aid to development of private forests, and building and maintenance of forest roads. Through regional conservation groups this branch is responsible for forest protection against insects, fire and fungus attack.

Ontario. Forested land in Ontario amounts to 310,369 sq miles (803 852 km²), of which 164,472 sq miles (425 981 km²) are classified as forest land bearing or capable of bearing timber of a commercial character suitable for regular harvest and not withdrawn from such use. About 90% of the productive forested land is owned by the Crown, administered and managed by the Ontario Ministry of Natural Resources through three main programs: Land Management, Outdoor Recreation and Resource Products.

The Forest Management Branch is responsible for the regeneration, tending and improvement of the forests under The Woodlands Improvement Act. It also has the task of promoting forestry on privately owned lands through its extension program. The branch operates 10 forest tree nurseries with a current production target of about 74.3 million trees. Complementing this are up-to-date tree improvement and nursery soil management programs. The branch, directly or indirectly, supervises all planting projects on Crown lands but regeneration agreements have been signed with all major licensees under which the latter assume responsibility for planting projects.

During 1974, 41.7 million nursery-produced trees were planted on about 57,300 acres (23 200 ha) of Crown and Agreement lands, and 5.4 million tubed seedlings were planted on about 5,350 acres (2 165 ha). Other silvicultural treatments included the direct seeding of 59,870 acres (24 230 ha), treatment for natural regeneration on 42,740 acres (17 300 ha) and stand improvement (cleaning, spraying, thinning and pruning) on 75,000 acres (30 350 ha). In all, 240,400 acres (97 300 ha) of Crown and Agreement lands were silviculturally treated in 1974 to promote regeneration or to improve the forests. Owners of private lands may purchase planting stock for forestry purposes from government nurseries at nominal prices and may also receive free professional advice on any forestry matter, including silviculture, harvesting and marketing. In 1974 (spring and fall), planting stock furnished for private lands totalled 17.8 million units.

Under The Woodlands Improvement Act it is possible to have planting and improvement work carried out completely under government direction and mainly at public expense. Since its inception in 1966, the program provided assistance for 190,850 acres (77 230 ha) of privately owned land.

Ontario has enabling legislation to permit municipalities and conservation authorities to place abandoned and submarginal agricultural lands to which they have acquired title under agreement with the Ministry, which undertakes to plant and manage the properties for a specified period. Over 255,900 acres (103 560 ha) under such agreements are managed intensively and the older plantations are receiving regular thinnings. The trees removed are in demand for pulpwood, posts, poles and sawlogs, making the undertakings financially attractive. In addition, properties close to centres of population have acquired value as recreational areas. Forest pest problems in 1974 were dominated by the spruce budworm which infested almost 24 million acres (9.7 million ha), but spraying operations to control this insect were limited to 48,000 acres (19 400 ha) in three separate high-value local areas. Smaller acreages on Crown lands and lands managed under agreement totalling 10,000 acres (4 050 ha) were also treated for white pine weevil, pine and spruce sawflies, white grubs, white pine blister rust, annosus root rot, and mice.

The Forest Research Branch provides scientific and technical knowledge for the management of forest lands and is more specifically oriented toward attaining production targets. Various disciplines including tree ecology and physiology, site and fertilization, tree genetics and breeding, mensuration, silviculture, equipment design and development are used to solve problems in tree improvement, stock production, regeneration and forest tending. Research is carried out throughout Ontario and results are published in journals and reports. Headquarters is at Maple and there are four field stations at Thunder Bay, Sault Ste Marie, Dorset and Midhurst.

The Timber Sales Branch coordinates and supervises preparation of management plans for Crown management units and approves the plans prepared for company management units. Forest inventory requirements and priorities for such plans are determined by the branch. As at March 31, 1975, 179 plans (88 Crown units, 31 company units and 60 Agreement Forests) were completed or in process of completion for about 190,000 sq miles (492 000 km²). Forest access is most important in the implementation of management plans and the planning of access roads is part of the branch's responsibilities. The branch arranges for the allocation, disposition and measurement of Crown timber through Crown land licensing, timber sales and wood scaling. During 1974, some 480 Crown timber licences covering an area of 97,256 sq miles (251 900 km²) were effected. The harvest of timber from Crown land amounted to 512.8 million cu ft (14.5 million m³). Primary wood-using industries operating in the province are licensed and their performance is monitored. In 1974, there were 824 primary wood-using plants in Ontario. The branch is also responsible for the promotion of new industrial development and growth of the forest industry. Information is collected and analyzed on the production, transportation and utilization of timber.

The Forest Fire Control Branch is responsible for the area under organized forest protection in Ontario totalling 200,000 sq miles (518 000 km²) and including the main central band of accessible forests. This area is organized into eight regions and 38 districts. In 11 additional administrative districts, south of this area in the highly developed agricultural counties, municipalities are responsible for fire control. The vast inaccessible areas to the north of the fire districts, totalling over 114,000 sq miles (295 000 km²), do not support significant stands of merchantable timber and, except for the protection of private property and human life, are not normally protected. Within the fire regions, agreements were in effect in 1974 with 209 municipalities for the prevention and control of forest fires. An agreement was also in effect with the federal government for fire protection of 968,968 acres (392 127 ha) of Indian lands.

Organized forest fire detection is accomplished primarily by aerial patrols with a limited amount of backup detection provided by two or three lookout towers in areas of high value (e.g. Algonquin Park). Public reporting of forest fires (unorganized detection) is an important part of the program. The basic fire-fighting strike force comprises 135 trained five-man fire crews and 39 fire-bombing aircraft. The Ministry of Natural Resources owns 43 aircraft, most of which can drop either long- or short-term retardant on fires. Rented helicopters are also used. The communications system includes a network of ground stations, radiotelephones, fireline radios, aircraft radios, portable aircraft radiotelephones, Telex and facsimile.

Manitoba. The administration of provincial Crown forest lands in Manitoba is the responsibility of the Renewable Resources Division of the Department of Renewable Resources and Transportation Services. The Renewable Resources Division consists of three sub-divisions which have specific responsibilities pertinent to administration and management of forests and forest lands.

The Planning Division is responsible for developing short- and long-term forest resource utilization and land use plans and programs. The Forest Inventory Section provides basic information and data needed. The Forest Research Section undertakes practical research for development of programs, particularly in silvicultural research. The Timber Sales Office is responsible for licensing, allocation of permits, statistics data and collection of royalties on the timber harvest. The Operations Division implements forestry programs and projects. It also helps to develop plans for specific areas in the four regions of the province.

In the Lands and Forests Branch, the Forestry Programs Section is charged with administering the various forestry acts and regulations. Policy guidelines, programs and procedures are established by the Forest Protection, Timber Management and Silvicultural sections of the division.

These sections coordinate fire, insect and disease control activities, control measures for the propagation, improvement, management and harvest of forests. A provincial forest nursery is maintained to supply stock for reforestation of denuded Crown land and several natural tree seed orchards have been established to improve nursery stock. Seedlings are supplied to farmers for woodlots and to commercial Christmas tree producers; an average of more than 4 million are planted each year in reforestation projects on Crown lands. Conventional planting programs are being reduced in some areas and reforestation of cut-over lands is being achieved by scarification and seeding. Forest stand improvement consists of thinning, cleaning and chemical spraying to remove undesirable species and encourage growth of preferred trees. Forest inventories cover about 10,350 sq miles (26 806 km²) and, on the basis of these inventories, working plans with annual allowable cuts on a management unit basis are made.

Forest management licences may be granted for periods of up to 20 years and are renewable; timber sales may be from one year upward and timber permits for periods of up to one year. Two pulp and paper mills and one large sawmill provide the backbone for Manitoba's primary forest industry. A dozen intermediate-size sawmills and operations augment the production of these mills. Numerous small sawmills and timber harvesting operations provide the balance of production.

The province's new thrust in northern Manitoba has resulted in a number of remote timber harvesting and forest product operations. This thrust will continue as a means of resolving socio-economic problems in isolated communities and as a way of further utilizing the forest resource.

There are 128,370 sq miles (332 477 km²) under forest protection with zones of priority in less accessible areas. Fires are detected through a comprehensive network of lookout towers and a highly efficient aircraft detection system and supporting ground patrols. Approximately 90,000 sq miles (233 000 km²) are covered by aerial patrols.

Public education in fire prevention and forest conservation is carried out through radio, television, newspapers, pamphlets, signs, films, and tours.

Saskatchewan. The forests of Saskatchewan cover 136,000 sq miles (352000 km²) of which 44,500 sq miles (115000 km²) are productive and suitable for regular harvest. Provincial forests constitute approximately 96% of all forest land.

The Forestry Branch of the Department of Tourism and Renewable Resources consists of four sections — forest management, wood products and operations, inventory and silviculture — and develops and evaluates forest policies and management programs which are carried out by regional authorities. For purposes of resource administration, the province is divided into seven regions. These are subdivided into conservation officer districts which vary in size according to resource base and population to be served. The Department of Northern Saskatchewan administers the northern forested area. The Fire Control Division of this department is responsible for development of techniques in prevention, detection and suppression of forest fires.

A network of 75 lookout towers equipped with two-way radios is maintained throughout the province and is supplemented by aircraft on regular patrol duty during high-hazard periods. The Department of Northern Saskatchewan communication system is being converted to VHF. Two-way radio sets, operated in towers, vehicles, aircraft and bush camps, are used for the detection and suppression of forest fires; helicopters and fixed-wing aircraft capable of water-dropping provide aerial support. In order to increase provincial forest protection capabilities, six land-based Tracker aircraft have been acquired and are being converted to deliver and discharge long-term fire retardants.

Alberta. The 148,167 sq miles (383751 km²) of forest lands in Alberta include 106,755 sq miles (276494 km²) which are capable of producing forest crops. The Alberta Forest Service of the Department of Energy and Natural Resources through its five branches (Administration, Timber Management, Forest Protection, Land Use and Training) is responsible for their administration. Jurisdiction is decentralized into 10 forests, each responsible for the forest area within its boundaries. Each forest is under the control of a superintendent supported by specialists in timber management, fire, land use, construction and communications. These forests are further subdivided into ranger districts under a district forest officer responsible to the superintendent.

The Timber Management Branch is responsible for the timber quota system, management and annual operating plans for leased and licensed Crown lands, forest management plans and disposal of Crown timber. The branch carries on silvicultural programs, processes applications, takes inventories of forest resources, inspects cutting areas to ensure proper logging practices and collects dues and fees.

The Forest Protection Branch is in charge of all phases of protection including prevention, detection and suppression of wild fires. This branch includes specialists such as a meteorologist, a telecommunications officer and an Aircraft Dispatch Section to assist in the overall protection program.

The Forest Land Use Branch is responsible for planning and supervising land-use practices in the forested area including grazing, recreation and watershed management, particularly on the east slopes of the Rocky Mountains containing the headwaters of the North and South Saskatchewan rivers. The Forestry Training Branch provides facilities and instruction for the second year of a two-year forest technology course given by the Northern Alberta Institute of Technology. It also conducts in-service training for all the branches in the Forest Service and other divisions of the department.

Basic research in the forestry program is generally carried out by the Canadian Forestry Service. A federal research laboratory in Edmonton provides much of this research service.

British Columbia. Over 210,394 sq miles (544918 km²) or 60% of British Columbia's area, is inventoried as forest land. This includes over 276 million cu ft (7.82 million m³) of mature merchantable timber, most of it coniferous species. Of the provincial forest land 95% is publicly owned and managed by the British

Columbia Forest Service, the forest administrative agency for the province. For administration and management purposes, the province is divided into six forest districts with headquarters at Vancouver, Kamloops, Nelson, Williams Lake, Prince Rupert and Prince George. Further decentralization of authority is effected by subdivision into 99 ranger districts. Each district is supervised by a forest ranger who supervises the harvesting of trees by logging companies and plays a vital role in environmental protection. Fourteen directional, servicing or policy-forming divisions constitute the head office of the Forest Service at Victoria: Timber, Training School, Reforestation, Protection, Valuation, Inventory, Research, Administration, Engineering, Personnel, Resource Planning, Information, Accounts, Range, and Special Studies.

Efforts continue to bring BC's forest resources under sustained-yield management even though with an annual scale (1975) of approximately 17,684,686 cunits (50 077 460 m³) the total inventory would appear sufficient to support current needs in perpetuity. One of the results of sustained-yield administration has been the swinging of a greater proportion of the annual forest harvest to the interior of the province; in 1975 the wet belt forests on the coast accounted for about 42.7% of the total forest cut and the interior for 57.3%. For all practical purposes, the entire interior forest is publicly owned; a large proportion of the privately owned, leased or licensed forests is on the coast. Several systems of timber disposal are in effect. The Tree Farm Licence is a contract between the government and a company or individual whereby the latter agrees to manage, protect and harvest an area of forest land, including any privately held forest land, on a sustained-yield basis. Tree Farm Licences are subject to re-examination for renewal every 21 years. Public Sustained-Yield Units are areas within which the Forest Service manages the Crown timber on a sustained-yield basis. Within the Public Sustained-Yield Units, recognized established logging operators can apply for Timber Sale Licences or Timber Sale Harvesting Licences which entitle them to log at a given rate per year, based on a number of factors including the operator's average rate of production at the time the unit was established.

Forest fire prevention techniques and organization for effective forest fire suppression are vital aspects of planned sustained-yield management. Extensive use is made of aircraft under various terms of contract. Air tankers and fire-spotter aircraft are employed during the fire season and helicopters and other aircraft are employed under contract for patrol duties and for the transport of fire suppression crews. Rugged topography and many remote and sparsely populated areas demand the availability of a variety of transportation methods to achieve early discovery of and attack on forest fires.

Close liaison with the Canadian Forestry Service of the federal Department of Fisheries and the Environment provides detailed information on insect and fungal enemies of the forest and on fire research.

To achieve an efficient administration of multiple use of Crown forest lands, the Forest Service, in conjunction with other government departments, has developed the "Integrated Use" concept. The Forest Service recognizes that inevitably some forest lands will be withdrawn from timber production to accommodate other users. These losses must be offset by increased production on remaining areas.

Statistics of the forest industries   10.1.4

The extensive forests of Canada provide raw materials for several large primary industries: sawmills and planing mills, shingle mills, veneer and plywood mills, particleboard plants and pulp and paper mills, which in turn provide raw materials for a wide range of secondary industries that convert wood products into manufactured goods such as sash, doors, millwork, wooden boxes, furniture, converted papers and paper goods. Much of the output of the primary forest industries is exported; the sawmill industry and the pulp and paper industry, especially, contribute substantially to the value of the export trade of Canada and thereby provide an important part of the foreign exchange necessary to pay for imports. Statistics of manufacturing activity and total activity of the wood industries and the paper and allied industries will be found in Chapter 17.

10.1.4.1   Logging industry

The forests of Canada provide raw materials for sawmills and planing mills, shingle mills, veneer and plywood mills, particleboard plants and pulp and paper mills as well as roundwood for export in the unmanufactured state and other products such as fuelwood, poles and piling, fence posts, mining timber and Christmas trees. Tables 10.5 and 10.6 give the estimated quantities of wood cut in Canada, by province and by type of product, for 1971-74. The total volume of wood cut decreased slightly from 5,078 million cu ft (144 million m³) in 1973 to 4,871 million cu ft (138 million m³) in 1974.

10.1.4.2   Wood industries

The standard industrial classification subdivides the wood industries group as follows: sawmills and planing mills, shingle mills, veneer and plywood mills, sash, door and other millwork plants, hardwood flooring mills, manufacturers of prefabricated buildings, manufacturers of kitchen cabinets, wooden box factories, the coffin and casket industry, the wood preservation industry, the wood handles and turning industry, particleboard, and miscellaneous wood industries.

The sawmills and planing mills, the shingle mills, the veneer and plywood mills and the particleboard plants (the latter are included in the miscellaneous wood industries group) use mainly roundwood as a raw material and sometimes are called primary wood industries; they are dealt with separately below. The secondary wood industries further manufacture part of the production of the primary wood industries into a great variety of products. However, most of the production of the primary wood industries is not further processed.

Sawmill and planing mill industry. Lumber is by far the most important single commodity in this industry and British Columbia is the most important province in this field. The total value of shipments of establishments classified to this industry in 1974 amounted to $2,329.8 million of which lumber accounted for $1,877.7 million; shipments of lumber from British Columbia amounted to $1,278.2 million (Tables 10.7 - 10.8).

In addition to this lumber, a small amount is produced by establishments classified to other industries bringing total lumber production in Canada in 1974 to 13,612 million fbm (32 121 million m³) compared with 15,529 million fbm (36 644 million m³) in 1973, a decrease of 12.3%.

Shingle mill industry. Most of the shingles and shakes produced in Canada are from British Columbia mills. All establishments in this classification reported shipments of 1,759,597 squares (16 347 000 m²) of shingles and shakes valued at $47.0 million in 1974. British Columbia alone accounted for 1,542,971 squares (14 335 000 m²) valued at $43.4 million. However, considerable quantities are produced by establishments classified to other industries and by individuals intermittently operating one or two shingle machines or producing shingles by hand; although no adequate measure of this production is available it is known to contribute significantly to the total. Of the total production in 1974, 2,083,609 squares (19 357 000 m²) were exported, of which 2,028,609 squares (18 846 000 m²) went to the United States.

Veneer and plywood industry. The production of hardwood veneer and plywood in Canada is confined largely to the eastern provinces and the production of softwood veneer and plywood almost entirely to British Columbia. For the latter, Douglas-fir is most commonly used because of the availability of large-diameter logs of this species from which large sheets of clear veneer can be obtained. Of the hardwoods, birch is by far the most important species. Although most of the raw materials are of Canadian origin, some decorative woods are imported, particularly walnut.

Most of the production of softwood veneers is further manufactured into softwood plywood by Canadian mills. Some hardwood veneers are also shipped to other veneer and plywood mills in Canada for further manufacture or to other industries such as the furniture industry for veneering purposes but a significant portion is exported. Total exports in 1974 amounted to 779,665,000 sq ft (72 433 000 m²) valued at $38.0 million, of which 704,341,000 sq ft (65 435 000 m²) valued at $33.0 million went to the United States.

Most of the plywood is consumed in Canada although exports are important. In 1974 these amounted to 54,132,000 sq ft (5 029 000 m²) of hardwood plywood valued at $9.7 million and 364,762,000 sq ft (33 887 000 m²) of softwood plywood valued at $51.7 million. The greater part of the exports of hardwood plywood went to the United States: 45,962,000 sq ft (4 270 010 m²) valued at $7.8 million, but most of the softwood plywood exports went to Britain: 248,735,000 sq ft (23 108 000 m²) valued at $34.8 million. Quantity and value of veneer and plywood shipments for 1972-74 are given in Table 10.9.

Paper and allied industries   10.1.4.3

The Standard Industrial Classification subdivides the paper and allied industries group into the following industries: the pulp and paper industry, the asphalt roofing manufacturers, the paper box and bag manufacturers, and other paper converters. Statistics of manufacturing activity and total activity of the paper and allied industries group are given in Chapter 17.

Pulp and paper industry. This industry is by far the most important of the group. For many years it has been the leading industry in Canada contributing about 2% of the total gross national product and 12.8% of the total value of the country's exports in 1974. In that year there were 147 pulp and paper mills in operation.

These mills consume enormous quantities of roundwood: 17,960,304 cunits (50 857 923 m³) with a cost value of $837.6 million was used in 1974. In that year, 229,905 cunits (651 019 m³) of pulpwood were imported and 424,368 cunits (1 201 677 m³) were exported. In addition, pulp and paper mills use wood residues of the sawmill and other industries for pulping such as cores of peeler logs, slabs and edgings or wood chips, shavings, and recently, sawdust. The total of such wood residues used by the industry in 1974 amounted to the equivalent of 10,700,541 cunits (30 300 561 m³) of pulpwood valued at $386.4 million. The industry also consumes large amounts of electric power, chemicals and other goods and services and requires large quantities of clean water.

Some of the production of the pulp and paper industry is consumed in Canada or serves as a raw material for the paper-using or secondary paper and allied industries and certain other industries but a great part of it is exported, particularly newsprint and various types of pulp, most of it to the United States. Some plants included in the pulp and paper industry classification also convert basic paper and paperboard into more highly manufactured papers, paper goods and boards but their output represents only a small part of Canada's total production of converted papers and boards. Table 10.10 gives shipment and production figures for pulp and Table 10.11 gives shipments of basic paper and paperboard for 1972-74. Table 10.12 shows exports of pulp and newsprint for 1971-75.

Asphalt roofing manufacturers. These establishments produce composition roofing and sheathing, consisting of paper felt saturated with asphalt or tar and, in some cases, coated with a mineral surfacing. Their total shipments in 1974 were valued at $101.8 million.

Paper box and bag industries. These industries include manufacturers of folding cartons and set-up boxes, of corrugated boxes and of paper bags. Their total shipments in 1974 amounted, respectively, to $280.4 million, $527.8 million and $373.8 million, compared with $231.1 million, $416.8 million and $233.3 million in 1973.

Other paper converters. This group produces a host of paper products, among them envelopes, waxed paper, clay-coated and enamelled paper and board, aluminum foil laminated with paper or board, paper cups and food trays, facial tissues, sanitary napkins, paper towelling and napkins and toilet tissue. The total value of manufacturing shipments of this industry in 1974 amounted to $690.4 million compared with $521.7 million in 1973.

10.2   Fisheries

In addition to cooperating with other nations to conserve high-seas fisheries resources through joint research projects and international agreements, Canada has taken further action to protect and manage the fisheries in its coastal areas by announcing the extension effective January 1, 1977, of its coastal fisheries jurisdiction to 200 nautical miles (370 km). Other countries which fish off Canada's coasts have been notified that conservation and management measures will be introduced by Canada to provide for protection and rebuilding of the fish stocks, many of which have been seriously depleted. Several bilateral agreements have been concluded with foreign countries to allow them to continue to fish within Canada's extended jurisdiction for stocks surplus to Canada's harvesting capacity and to provide a smooth transition to the new regime of fisheries management off the coasts of Canada.

The federal government has full legislative jurisdiction over the coastal and inland fisheries of Canada and all laws for the protection, conservation and development of these fisheries resources are enacted by Parliament. The management of fisheries is, however, shared with provincial governments to which certain administrative responsibilities have been delegated.

The federal Department of Fisheries and the Environment exercises responsibility for the management of all fisheries, both marine and freshwater, in Nova Scotia, New Brunswick, Newfoundland, Prince Edward Island, the Yukon Territory and Northwest Territories. In Ontario, Manitoba, Saskatchewan and Alberta the management of all fisheries is conducted by the provincial governments. In Quebec, the provincial government manages both marine and freshwater fisheries but the inspection of fish and fishery products produced for sale outside the province is carried out by the federal Department of Fisheries and the Environment, as it is in all other provinces. In British Columbia, the fisheries for marine and anadromous (fish that migrate to the sea from fresh water) species are managed by the Department of Fisheries and the Environment but the provincial government manages its freshwater fisheries. In the national parks the fisheries are managed by the Canadian Wildlife Service.

In most instances, licences for sport fishing are distributed by the respective provincial or territorial governments which retain all revenues so collected.

Close contact with provincial authorities is maintained through Fisheries and Marine Service regional offices in line with the departmental policy of decentralization. Coordination and discussion between federal and provincial fisheries managers on policies, programs and matters of mutual concern are facilitated through several federal-provincial committees: the Federal-Provincial Atlantic Fisheries Committee (consisting of representatives from the federal government and from New Brunswick, Newfoundland, Nova Scotia, Prince Edward Island and Quebec); the Federal-Provincial Freshwater Fisheries Committee (representatives from the federal government and Ontario, Alberta, Manitoba and Saskatchewan); the Federal-Provincial Ontario Fisheries Committee; and the Federal-Provincial British Columbia Fisheries Committee.

10.2.1   Federal government activities

The work of the federal government in the conservation, development and general regulation of the nation's coastal and freshwater fisheries is performed by the Fisheries and Marine Service.

The Fisheries and Marine Service, a major component of the Department of Fisheries and the Environment, undertakes a broad range of responsibilities. These include: management of Canada's ocean and inland fisheries; hydrographic surveying and charting of navigable coastal and inland waters; administration of small craft harbours; fisheries and oceanographic research contributing to the understanding, management and optimum use of renewable aquatic resources and marine waters; environmental impact studies affecting coastal and inland waters; and research in support of international agreements relating to fisheries management and marine environmental quality.

Functions of the Fisheries and Marine Service are grouped under two major units: Fisheries Management, and Ocean and Aquatic Sciences. The service carries on most of its programs at regional and field locations. Regional headquarters for Fisheries Management are located at Vancouver, BC; Winnipeg, Man.; Quebec, Que.; Halifax, NS; and St. John's, Nfld.; and for Ocean and Aquatic Sciences at Victoria, BC; Burlington, Ont.; and Dartmouth, NS. Research institutes and laboratories are located at a number of centres across Canada.

Several appointed public corporations and boards are involved in activities closely aligned with those of the Fisheries and Marine Service, including the Fisheries Prices Support Board, the Canadian Saltfish Corporation and the Freshwater Fish Marketing Corporation.

International fisheries. Many injurious effects on aquatic resources are results of historical practice, insufficient knowledge, multiple uses of water, social and economic conditions, and national and international competition. Problems under national control are corrected as conditions warrant but many resources are shared with other nations and must be managed jointly.

Canada cooperates with many nations in obtaining scientific data and formulating policies for development and conservation of fisheries through membership in 10 international fisheries commissions and one international council. These international organizations are established under the terms of formal conventions. Canadian representatives are appointed by Order in Council and include officials of the Department of Fisheries and the Environment and members of the fishing industry. Canada is a party to the following: the Convention between Canada and the US for the Preservation of the Halibut Fishery of the Northern Pacific Ocean and Bering Sea; the Convention between Canada and the US for the Protection, Preservation and Extension of the Sockeye Salmon Fisheries in the Fraser River System (pink salmon added subsequently by protocol); the International Convention for the High Seas Fisheries of the North Pacific Ocean; the Interim Convention on Conservation of North Pacific Fur Seals; the International Convention for the Northwest Atlantic Fisheries; the Convention on Great Lakes Fisheries between Canada and the United States of America; the International Convention for the Regulation of Whaling; the Convention between the United States of America and the Republic of Costa Rica for the Establishment of an Inter-America Tropical Tuna Commission; the International Council for the Exploration of the Sea; the International Convention for the Conservation of Atlantic Tunas, and the Canada-Norway Sealing Commission.

Canada maintains membership in the Committee of Fisheries of the Food and Agriculture Organization of the United Nations and in the Codex Alimentarius Commission which is concerned with world food quality standards.

Provincial government activities   10.2.2

Newfoundland. The provincial Department of Fisheries is primarily concerned with promoting development in all sectors of the province's fishing industry. Experiments and demonstrations are conducted on new designs of fishing gear and the modification of existing types, the construction of multi-purpose fishing

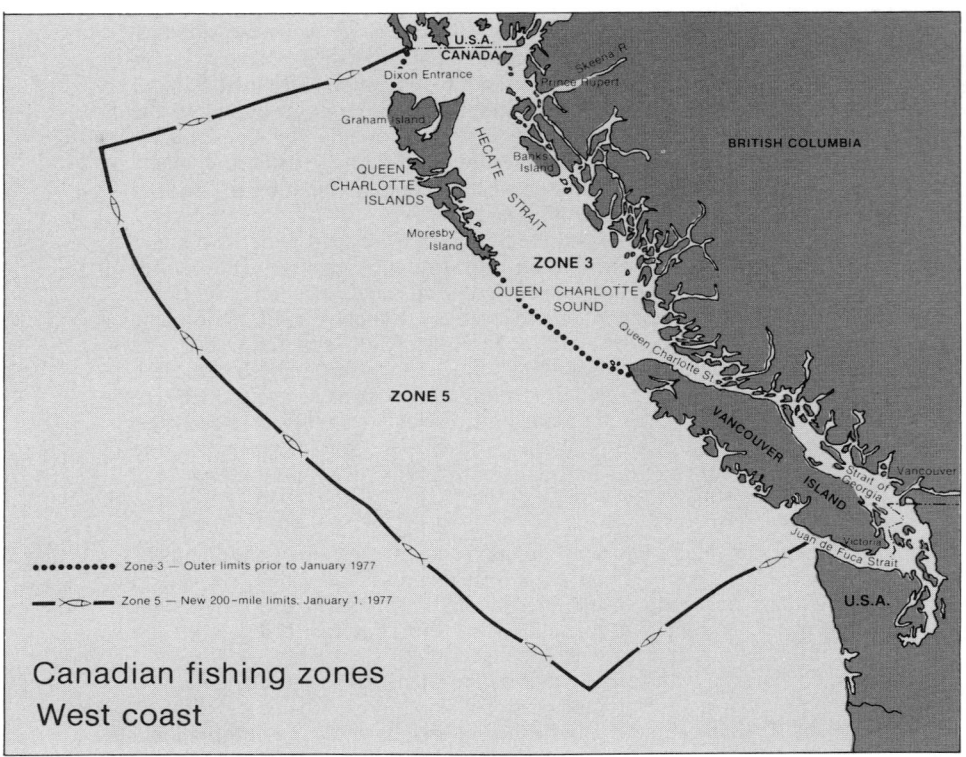

Canadian fishing zones
West coast

Zone 3 — Outer limits prior to January 1977

Zone 5 — New 200-mile limits. January 1, 1977

craft and the exploration of potential fishing grounds with a view to increasing catching efficiency and landings. Subsidies are also paid to fishermen on certain types of inshore fishing gear.

Loans are made to processors for the establishment and expansion of fish processing plants and for deep sea draggers. Aid to fishermen for the construction of modern vessels capable of a greater variety of fishing operations and larger production is provided by loans from the Newfoundland Fisheries Loan Board. The Fishing and Coasting Vessels Rebuilding and Repairs (Bounties) Act, 1958 authorizes financial assistance in maintaining and prolonging the life of the existing fleet. The Coasting Vessels (Bounties) Act, 1959 authorizes the granting, for locally built ships, of a maximum bounty of $150 a gross registered ton for vessels between 100 and 400 gross registered tons (283 m³ and 1 133 m³). The Fishing Ships (Bounties) Act, 1970 authorizes the payment of a bounty of $200 per registered gross tonnage on boats 10 registered tons (28 m³) under deck up to 150 registered tons (425 m³) which are built under permit. A small Boat Bounty Program provides a bounty of 35% on the approved cost of fishing boats measuring in length from 20 to 35 ft (6 to 11 m) or over, providing that they do not exceed 10 tons gross (28 m³). Loans are made available to fishermen to build new boats, purchase used boats, acquire new engines, buy certain approved types of mechanical and electronic fishing equipment and convert boats from one type of fishing operation to another.

In terms of direct employment generated, fisheries continue to outrank all other resource sectors. In 1975 approximately 15,000 fishermen and 7,000 plant workers were engaged in the industry. Total landings of all fish species amounted to 570 million lb. (259 million kg), with a landed value of $44 million and a market value of approximately $130 million.

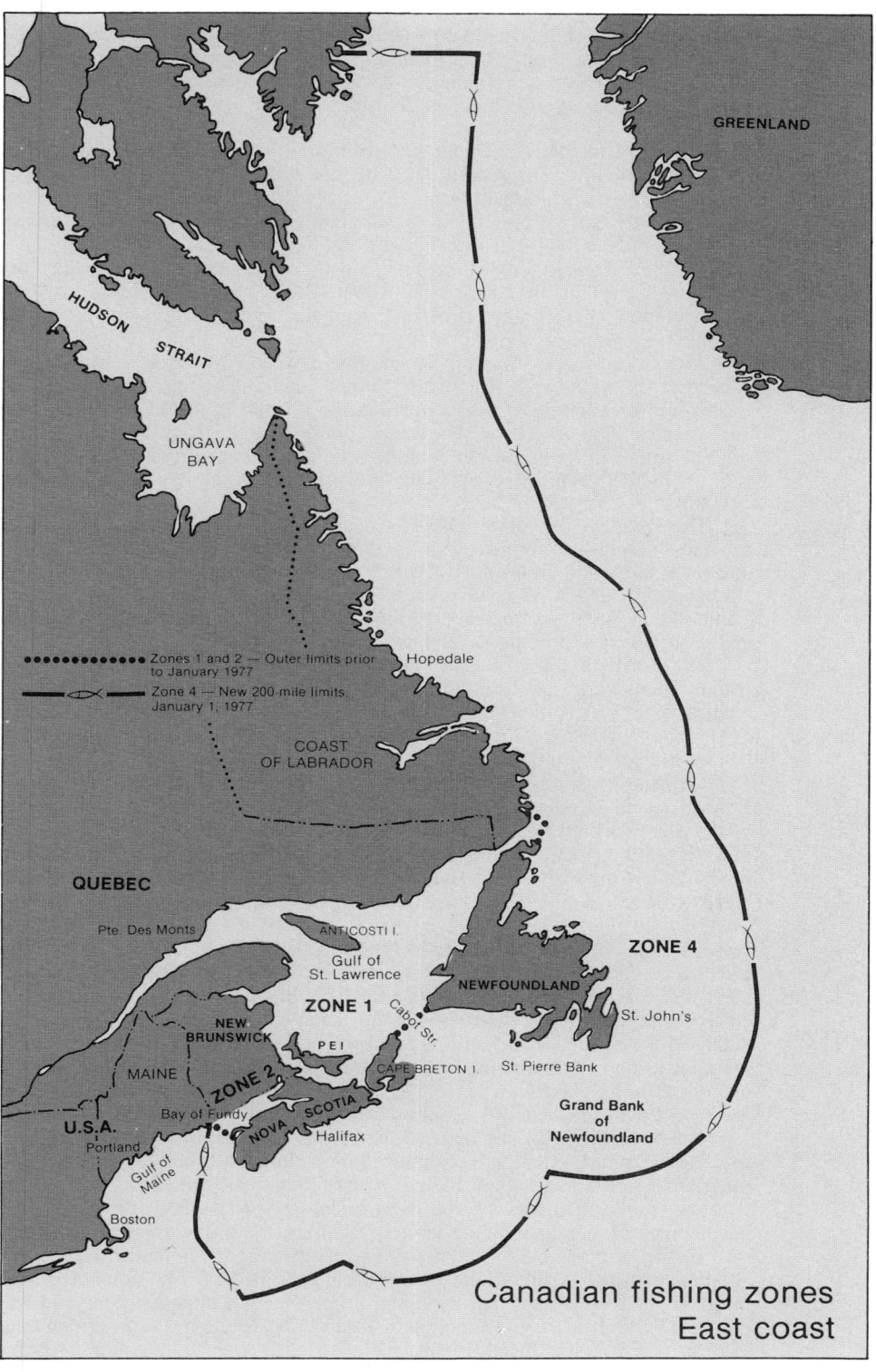

GREENLAND

HUDSON
STRAIT

UNGAVA
BAY

●●●●●●●●●●●● Zones 1 and 2 — Outer limits prior
                to January 1977

━━━━━━━━⊲∘⊳━ Zone 4 — New 200-mile limits
                January 1, 1977

Hopedale

COAST
OF LABRADOR

QUEBEC

Pte. Des Monts

ANTICOSTI I.

Gulf of
St. Lawrence

ZONE 1

NEWFOUNDLAND

ZONE 4

St. John's

NEW
BRUNSWICK

P E I

Cabot Str.

MAINE

ZONE 2

CAPE BRETON I.

St. Pierre Bank

Bay of Fundy

SCOTIA

U.S.A.

NOVA

Halifax

Grand Bank
of
Newfoundland

Portland

Gulf of
Maine

Boston

Canadian fishing zones
East coast

The inland waters of Newfoundland, although they provide excellent sport fishing, are not commercially exploited. The lakes and ponds actually remain under the authority of the Department of Tourism but, under federal-provincial agreement, these waters, including rivers and streams, are under federal control in matters of conservation and guardianship.

Prince Edward Island. The Prince Edward Island fishing industry ranks third in the island economy. The landed value of the 1975 catch was in excess of $12 million and after processing, its value exceeded $20 million. The industry involves 3,200 fishermen and helpers and between 700 and 800 people in the fish processing industry at 24 processing facilities.

The PEI Department of Fisheries, with six divisions, supplements the activities of the federal Fisheries and Marine Service and is responsible for the administration of programs aimed at upgrading the industry and increasing returns to those engaged in it.

An active program in the Aquaculture Division is aimed at diversifying opportunities in the fisheries sector through increased production, improved quality and broadening of the resource base in shellfish, salmonoids, seaplants and lobsters. The Resource Harvesting Division conducts exploratory fishing projects and resource assessment studies to locate and quantify new and existing species, and conducts gear technology studies relating to harvesting methods and equipment.

The Product Handling Division is responsible for port development programs designed to improve fish handling, processing and holding techniques and to ensure better fish quality. The Processing and Quality Control Division administers the PEI Fish Inspection Act and Regulations, enforces quality standards, assists the processing industry to improve methods and productivity and promotes new product development.

The Economics and Statistics Division provides technical assistance to the fishing industry in financial management, feasibility analysis and statistical studies. The Extension Division administers information programs, conducts field demonstrations, prepares fishermen's training programs and conducts technical upgrading projects.

Loans are made to fishermen and the fishing industry through the Prince Edward Island Lending Authority, a Crown corporation established in 1969, which is empowered to grant credit in the sectors of fisheries, industry, tourism and agriculture. Provincial responsibilities concerning freshwater fisheries are discharged by the Fish and Wildlife Division of the Department of Environment and Tourism.

Nova Scotia. The fishing industry in Nova Scotia is of major importance to the province's economy. Landed value of fish in 1975 was approximately $92 million while the market value was in the order of $225 million. Annual household income generated by the fisheries is in the vicinity of $240 million including such "spin-off" industrial effect as derives from boat building and repair and gear manufacturing. Fish products account for more than 20% of Nova Scotia's exports. Over 11,500 fishermen and 4,500 plant workers are directly employed in the industry and 191 fish processing plants are in operation.

The Nova Scotia Department of Fisheries is engaged in almost all aspects of the fishing industry and has significant input into some of the policies and programs legislated and administered by the federal government.

The primary thrusts of the department are in industrial and resource development, training, and field service. The Industrial Development Division is responsible for programs related to fishing vessels, gear and equipment, harbours and wharves, port facilities and processing plants. It deals with equipment and facilities involved in catching, handling, processing and marketing fish and fish products, and provides technical assistance and direction to fishermen and processors, as well as incentive financial assistance to encourage improvement and new technology aimed at greater productivity. Loans are available to fishermen and processors through the Nova Scotia Resources Development Board, a branch of the Department of Development.

The Resource Utilization Division is involved in a broad range of projects directed toward making the greatest use of all fishery resources, processing these to the highest level, and marketing the products at a good price. It includes efforts in aquaculture aimed at producing fishery resources in a controlled environment. Activity is also directed to development of underutilized and unexploited species, recovery and use of fish presently discarded, and encouragement of production of more food fish and less fish meal.

The Training and Field Services Division is responsible for extensive training programs for commercial fishermen. It operates the Fisheries Training Centre located in Pictou as well as courses held in fishing communities throughout the province. The division also provides a Field Service consisting of seven fisheries representatives who act in liaison with fishermen and all segments of the fishing industry.

New Brunswick. Commercial fishing is one of the most important industries of New Brunswick employing about 5,000 fishermen with annual earnings of $25.5 million and 7,000 plant workers. The annual marketed value of all fish and shellfish products is about $105 million of which some 80% is exported to the US. New Brunswick's commercial fisheries, both tidal and inland, are under the jurisdiction of the federal government, while angling in Crown waters is the responsibility of the provincial Department of Natural Resources. However, the New Brunswick government plays a major role in resource assessment and development, fisheries training, financial assistance to the industry and long-term planning. The Department of Fisheries and Environment has a highly qualified staff of biologists, engineers and naval architects, grouped into six branches. Close liaison is maintained with other federal and provincial departments and agencies concerned with the fishing industry.

The Fish Inspection and Marketing Branch administers the New Brunswick Fish Inspection Act and Regulations although for greater effectiveness and to avoid duplication of personnel, arrangements have been made with the federal Department of Fisheries and the Environment to cover this activity. The branch promotes the expansion and modernization of existing fish processing plants and the establishment of new plants and is carrying out a program of product development to increase the added value of its catch. Another program is aimed at promoting the consumption of fish within the province. Efforts include studying existing markets and developing new ones in collaboration with other government agencies.

The Research and Development Branch carries out programs in cooperation with the federal Department of Fisheries and the Environment. Technical and financial assistance is given the provincial department for projects undertaken toward modernizing fishing and processing methods, experimenting with new types of fish-catching equipment and demonstrating its operation to fishermen, and exploring and developing unexploited or under-exploited species of molluscs, crustaceans, fishes and seaweeds. This work has resulted in the establishment of snow crab, shrimp, Irish moss,.tuna, sea urchin and eel fisheries.

The Fisheries Training Branch provides technical training to fishermen and plant personnel. Training is also provided for managers and supervisors. The branch operates a School of Fisheries at Caraquet in northeastern New Brunswick where, in the 1974-75 academic year, 279 fishermen received training. Recently, construction work began on a Marine Emergency Duty Centre. This facility will include a two-storey mock-up of a fishing vessel to be used for fire fighting and a separate building with classroom facilities.

The newly-created Planning and Coordination Branch, although still in an embryonic stage, strives to formalize planning of government efforts in fisheries, acquatic resources, and fisheries development. To improve programming, the branch has taken over the setting up of a mechanism for industry-government consultation.

The Fishermen's Loan Board of New Brunswick, a provincial corporation established in 1946, now operates under the Fishermen's Loan Act of 1952 and the Regulations of November 1, 1963. The board consists of two major branches, the Loans Administration Branch and the Boat Building Branch. Each has three sections. The former includes the credit, accounting and field staff sections (which covers all the coastal regions of the province) and the latter consists of the vessel inspection, evaluation and contracts section. The board's main function is to make loans to the fishing industry for modernizing and developing the fishing fleet. It provides financial assistance at moderate interest to fishermen and processing firms and corporations to build modern fishing vessels, finance major repairs, and purchase engines and equipment.

The Loans Administration Branch investigates loan applications, secures loans with insurance, maintains accounts, and collects repayment. The Boat Building and Repairing Branch studies, inspects, modifies and approves plans and specifications of fishing vessels financed by the board.

Since the board's inception, it has granted 3,169 loans to New Brunswick fishermen for a total of over $49.5 million. Outstanding loans amounted to $23.2 million at the end of March 1975. Loans are repayable within five to eight years on most small inshore fishing vessels. Repayment schedules on large trawlers may extend to 15 years based on the gross proceeds of the catch. Others are on a 15-year annual instalment contract. Most of the new fishing vessels being built for fishermen and processing firms in the province are financed by the board.

Sport fishing contributes substantially to the economy of the province. Great Atlantic salmon rivers like the Miramichi, the Restigouche and the Saint John are known around the world for their prolific production of this majestic game fish and attract many thousands of tourists each year. Anglers catch as many as 50,000 salmon a year in the Miramichi system alone. Many other species are sought by both residents and non-residents in hundreds of streams, rivers and lakes.

Quebec. In 1975 Quebec fishermen landed 116 million lb. (53 million kg) of fish and shellfish in the vast reservoir formed by the St. Lawrence River, gulf and estuary. The landed value to the fishermen was $14.5 million and the market value of the produce reached $29 million.

The industry is of prime importance on a regional basis. It is the backbone of the economy of the Magdalen Islands and the lower North Shore and is a major activity in the Gaspé peninsula. Overall there are 5,700 commercial fishermen, including about 600 full-time coastal fishermen, 800 sea-going helpers and 600 officers and crew operating the seiners, long-liners and draggers. Some 30 processing plants employ about 1,400 workers (seasonally adjusted). In this sector, commercial fishing has a multiplier effect on employment and incomes. Fishermen and shipowners build and repair their fishing vessels within the region, thus giving employment to shipyards. Local labour is also used for building and maintaining the various marine installations necessary for docking, safety and discharge of cargo, for operating ice-making plants, and in freezer and storage operations.

In 1975 redfish (33.1%), cod (25.8%) and herring (17.7%) made up 76.6% of the total catch. In terms of value, the proportions were: cod 29.3%, lobster 20.9%, redfish 13.9% and shrimp 10.3%.

The Quebec sea-going fishing fleet includes 150 wooden or steel-hulled vessels of between 15 and 450 net registered tons (42 m³ and 1 274 m³); 3,487 craft of all types are engaged in the coastal fishery. The government has tried to modernize the ocean-going fleet through grants and construction loans for the building of a 132-ft (40 m) steel seiner and prototype 65-ft (20 m) container-seiner also steel-hulled, as well as seven wooden long-liners and draggers.

Government aid to the commercial fishery consists of loans for building or refitting of vessels, grants toward acquisition of coastal craft and fishing gear, and a wide range of technical assistance. The Commercial Fisheries Branch allocated $1.1 million during the year in grants for boat-building, the purchase of fishing gear, collection of catch from coastal fishermen, land-based teams, marketing assistance and marine insurance. Interest-free loans amounting to $700,000 were approved for construction and repair of fishing vessels.

The main objectives of the Commercial Fisheries Branch under the Canada–Quebec Agreement of 1968 (renegotiated in 1971) were a more efficient use of funds from the private as well as government sectors and concentration of fisheries in centres with well-equipped port facilities. Under the terms of the initial agreement, $4.8 million was budgeted for infrastructure related to ocean-going fisheries, and this amount was increased to $10 million in the agreement as renewed. The program had been expected to reach its peak in 1975 but due to increased costs of infrastructure it became necessary to make a supplementary agreement in the amount of $14 million to be spread over the 1974-78 period to continue work already begun. These facilities will eventually be completed under a new agreement, and talks are already under way.

In the Gaspé region, five production centres have been set aside, three of which will be developed as industrial fisheries complexes at Rivière-au-Renard, Paspébiac and Grande-Rivière for specialized production, with secondary production centres at Newport and Sandy Beach. In the Magdalen Islands, two centres have been set aside — an industrial complex at Cap-aux-Meules and a secondary production centre at Havre-Aubert. Landing points will supplement these centres, providing coastal fishermen with unloading and storage facilities. They will not have processing plants on site but will be linked by a fish transportation system to the nearest production centres. The Commercial Fisheries Branch hopes to have landing points completed at Gascons, Cloridorme and Les Méchins in the Gaspé region and Millerand and Étang-du-Nord in the Magdalen Islands before the present agreement expires.

Sport fishing in the inland waters of Quebec is under the jurisdiction of the Department of Tourism, Fish and Game, which employs 523 full-time conservation officers and issues the required sport-fishing licences. Six hatcheries are maintained by the department, where speckled trout, brown trout, rainbow trout, grey trout, ouananiche, maskinonge and salmon are reared for the restocking of lakes and streams.

Excellent fishing may be found in all provincial parks and reserves. Gaspé and Laurentide parks are renowned for trout fishing and the waters of Chibougamau Reserve and La Vérendrye Park, situated on the height of land, abound in pickerel, pike and grey trout. Nineteen salmon rivers are open to anglers — the Petit Saguenay, Laval, Moisie, Matane, Cap Chat, Ste-Anne, St. Jean, Matapédia, Dartmouth, Port Daniel, Petite Cascapédia, Restigouche, Loutre, Jupiter, McDonald, Patate, Boreal, Chaloupe and Saumon.

A Quebec wildlife committee made up of area representatives makes recommendations to the provincial government concerning legislation required for the maintenance of satisfactory fishing conditions and other problems arising out of the ever-changing conditions of modern life and their effect on the wildlife of the province.

Ontario. The fishery resources of Ontario are administered by the Fisheries Branch of the Ministry of Natural Resources under the authority of the federal Fisheries Act, the Ontario Fishery Regulations and the Ontario Game and Fish Act.

The commercial freshwater fishing industry in Ontario has a capital value of over $18 million and produces an annual yield of from 53 million lb. (24 million kg) to 72 million lb. (33 million kg) of fish including nearly 10 million lb. (5 million kg) of bait fish. Fishermen receive $12 million from the sale of this catch. Subsequent handling and processing of fish result in a contribution of about $25 million to the provincial economy. The industry, although widely scattered, is centred chiefly on the Great Lakes, particularly Lake Erie. Direct employment is provided for about 2,200 commercial food-fish fishermen and 2,500 bait-fish fishermen; many more are employed indirectly. Approximately 900 are engaged in fish handling and processing. The species harvested commercially include yellow perch, smelt, whitefish, pickerel, pike, lake trout, herring, chub, carp, white perch, sturgeon, white bass, bullhead, catfish, eel, goldeye, sunfish, burbot, freshwater drum, rock bass, crappie, sauger and suckers. Over 90% of all fish landed in Ontario are harvested from the Great Lakes. More than 500 smaller inland lakes are commercially fished, mainly those in the northwestern portion of the province.

Fishing methods and equipment have been modernized extensively during the past few years and include the use of diesel-driven steel-hull tugs with depth sounding devices, radar and ship-to-ship and ship-to-shore communications. Modern icing facilities and transportation methods are in use as well as new types of fishing gear. Programs to develop more efficient and economical fishing and processing techniques have resulted in efficient bulk-handling techniques for smelt and a viable fish-meal plant which produces a marketable product from fish-processing wastes and fish unsuitable for food. Trawling on Lake Erie has proved efficient in harvesting smelt year-round. Most Ontario fishermen are organized into local associations and many of these are represented by the Ontario Council of Commercial Fisheries.

Ontario has an estimated freshwater area of approximately 68,490 sq miles (177 388 km²). Excellent angling opportunities are available for such prized fish as brook, rainbow and lake trout, yellow pickerel (walleye), smallmouth and largemouth bass, northern pike, and maskinonge. A wide selection of ice-angling equipment including snowmobile rentals is available and seasons have been extended in many parts of the province for certain species of fish. The Ontario Recreation Survey indicated that 2.4 million Ontario residents 12 years of age or older fished in 1973.

Revenue from the sale of angling licences in 1975 was $5.6 million. Prices and numbers sold vary greatly according to licence type. Canadian residents bought 22,637 licences at $4.00. Non-residents bought 467,776 seasonal licences at $10.75 and 165,527 at $6.00. Total expenditures in Ontario related to resident and non-resident angling were estimated to be over $400 million in 1975. The management of this resource is administered by a field staff of conservation officers, biologists and technicians.

Ontario operates 14 fish hatcheries and rearing stations; notably for brook, rainbow and lake trout, splake, smallmouth and largemouth bass and maskinonge. The basic aim of the hatcheries is the economic production of high-quality species to sustain and rehabilitate recreational and commercial fishing. Studies are conducted on the improvement of transportation and planting techniques, including the use of aircraft and trucks, to improve survival and returns to the angler. The marking of hatchery fish by removal of a single fin is providing valuable information on survival of fish stocks and angler success; 150 fish sanctuaries provide protection during spawning. Research programs are directed toward specific fisheries management problems in the Great Lakes and in the smaller inland waters.

Manitoba. Manitoba's interior location belies the importance of its fisheries resources which stem from an abundance of fresh water in about 40,000 sq miles (104 000 km²) of lakes and streams covering 16% of the province.

In the year ended March 31, 1976, the commercial fishery produced 20.6 million lb. (9.3 million kg) of fish, a 4.3% increase from the 19.7 million lb. (8.9 million kg) of the previous year. The value to the fishermen increased from $5.4 million to $5.9 million. Lake Winnipeg contributed 8.3 million lb. (3.8 million kg; 41%), followed by the northern waters with 5.2 million lb. (2.4 million kg; 25%), Lake Winnipegosis with 3.0 million lb. (1.4 million kg; 14%), Lake Manitoba with 2.4 million lb. (1.1 million kg; 8%), and other southern lakes with 1.7 million lb. (0.8 million kg; 8%). Sixteen species or groups of species normally enter into the commercial catch but only a few species predominate. In 1975-76, whitefish contributed 5.2 million lb. (2.4 million kg), pike 3.4 million lb. (1.5 million kg), walleye (pickerel) 4.5 million lb. (2.0 million kg) and sauger 3.3 million lb. (1.5 million kg). A miscellany of species, primarily suckers and carp, contributed 4.2 million lb. (1.9 million kg). All of the commercial catch is marketed by the Freshwater Fish Marketing Corporation, a federal Crown agency, and is exported mainly to the United States. Gill-nets are the main fishing gear. About 1,980 fishermen were employed during open-water fishing and 1,384 in winter fishing.

Fisheries administration is under the control of the minister responsible for Renewable Resources and Transportation Services and is divided into research, program development and field operations sectors. Field operations are divided among four regional units. Conservation officers enforce both the commercial and the angling regulations and carry out other duties in connection with fisheries management. Professional biologists carry out studies which monitor the resource and extend the knowledge of it. Fish culture plays an important role in fisheries management. Pickerel hatcheries are located on Lakes Winnipegosis and Manitoba. A hatchery is located at Grand Rapids on Lake Winnipeg and a trout hatchery is located in Whiteshell Provincial Park. Two temporary facilities for collection of spawn are also used.

The sport fishery is an important use of the fishery resource, with walleye, pike, perch and several kinds of trout the principal sport species. A total of 177,081 angling licences were sold in 1975-76 of which 142,226 were purchased by Canadian residents.

Saskatchewan. Fisheries resources of the province are administered by the Fisheries and Wildlife Branch of the Department of Tourism and Renewable Resources and by the Resource Development Branch of the Department of Northern Saskatchewan. The latter, with headquarters in La Ronge, administers the northern Saskatchewan commercial fishery and the former, with head office in Prince Albert, administers the southern Saskatchewan commercial fishery and the provincial sport fishery.

During 1974, 2,222 commercial fishing licences were issued to fish 198 lakes, while in 1975, 2,253 licences were issued on 195 lakes. The harvest of 12 million lb. (5.44 million kg) was worth $2.1 million to the fishermen; in 1975 the harvest of 10.4 million lb. (4.72 million kg) was worth $2.2 million. The industry, although widely scattered, is centred chiefly in the northern half of the province; about 70% of the production came from northern waters in recent years. In order of market value, the species composition of the catch in 1974 was whitefish, walleye, pike, lake trout and tullibee; while in 1975 the order was whitefish, walleye, lake trout, pike and tullibee.

One shallow saline lake in southern Saskatchewan produced 61,000 lb. (28 000 kg) of brine shrimp and brine shrimp eggs in 1974, and 72,000 lb. (33 000 kg) of brine shrimp in 1975. These are processed for sale to fish hobbyists. In 1974, 1.1 million lb. (500 000 kg) of buffalofish and carp was harvested from the Qu'Appelle drainage; in 1975, 900,000 lb. (410 000 kg) of these species was taken. During 1974, 22,000 lb. (10 000 kg) of bait fish was harvested by 21 commercial bait fishermen; in 1975, 26 fishermen harvested 27,000 lb. (12 000 kg) bait fish.

Interest in aquaculture grew greatly in 1974 but stabilized in 1975. In 1974 and 1975 respectively, 2,412 and 2,538 aquaculture enterprises were licensed to raise rainbow trout. The majority of operations were intended for the private use of the owner. About 907,000 rainbow fingerlings stocked in the spring of 1974 resulted in an estimated 154,000 lb. (70 000 kg) harvest, while in 1975, 1,043,000 fingerlings were stocked with a yield in the fall of about 194,000 lb. (88 000 kg).

In 1974 and 1975, 170,037 and 177,322 angling licences respectively were sold. Northern pike, walleye, lake trout, perch, arctic grayling, rainbow trout and goldeye continued to be the principal species taken. A continuous program of inventory of sport fishing stocks is maintained to provide up-to-date information for management purposes. During 1974, 201 waters were examined and in 1975, 299. Expansion of the exotic-species program continued with about 100 lakes and streams having established populations of trout and salmon to date.

The provincial hatchery at Fort Qu'Appelle reared 16.5 million fish of eight species for distribution in 147 waters in 1974. Walleye and rainbow trout were the species most widely distributed, each being stocked in 42 waters. Brook trout was stocked in 36 waters, arctic grayling in seven, brown trout in four, and whitefish in four. In 1975, 17.7 million fish of seven species were reared in the provincial hatchery for distribution in 155 waters. Walleye was the species most widely distributed, being stocked in 52 waters. Rainbow trout was stocked in 45 waters, brook trout in 35, and lake trout and splake in 10.

The limnological and fisheries research program is designed to provide basic information on the productivity of water bodies, to secure information on the abundance and relationship of fish species, and to investigate and assess factors affecting fish populations. This information is subsequently used to develop fishery management policies and programs. Angler and commercial catch data are collected primarily in northern Saskatchewan to improve management of the fishery resource.

The Fisheries Management Program was designed to develop fishing opportunities for more than 200,000 anglers and 1,000 commercial fishermen. Almost one in every seven residents participates in the sport fishery. New waters and sport fishing opportunities are being developed. The introduction of non-indigenous trout and salmon species has proved popular.

The commercial fishery is regulated to utilize the fish species not available to sport fishermen. In excess of 3.1 million lb. (1.4 million kg) of fish were harvested from southern Saskatchewan lakes in 1975.

Alberta. Commercial and sport fishing are administered by the Fish and Wildlife Division of the Department of Recreation, Parks and Wildlife, under the authority of the Fisheries Act (Canada) and the Fish Marketing Act (Alberta).

Production of commercial fish from Alberta's 6,485 sq miles (16 796 km²) of fresh water for the fiscal year ended March 31, 1976 was 4.3 million lb. (1.9 million kg), a decrease from the 1974-75 total of 5.2 million lb. (2.4 million kg). The landed value of the catch was $976,180 compared with $934,457 in 1974-75 and the market value was $1.7 million compared with $1.8 million in 1974-75. Lake whitefish is the most valuable species caught commercially and accounted for 53% of the total value but only 47% of the total landings. Tullibee had the second highest landings followed by pike, ling, suckers, walleye, perch and lake trout. A major part of the quantity of fish taken is marketed outside the province, mainly in the United States, by the Freshwater Fish Marketing Corporation except for tullibee which are primarily used as animal food.

There were 218,460 angling licences sold in Alberta in 1975-76 of which 214,283 were to resident and non-resident Canadians and 4,177 to non-resident non-Canadians. The comparable figures for 1974-75 were 211,591; 206,331; and 5,260 licences respectively. There were 1,963 trophy lake licences and 574 spear fishing licences sold during 1975-76 as compared with 1,219 and 519 respectively in 1974-75. In 1975-76 a total of 214 lakes was stocked with nearly 7.4 million fish and fish eggs: 70.1% rainbow trout, 16.3% lake whitefish (green eggs), 5.3% brook trout, 3.4% walleye fry, 2.4% perch, 1.4% lake trout, 1.1% brown trout and 0.004% adult lake whitefish. There were 1,179 private, 41 commercial, and six restricted game fish farm licences issued in 1975-76 as compared with 1,108 private, 34 commercial, and nine restricted licences for the previous year. The fish farming operations handled 458,000 fish in 1975-76 as compared with 457,000 in 1974-75.

Fisheries are administered regionally with nine fisheries biologists located in various centres, each responsible for a geographical area. There is also a research group in Edmonton (two biologists and a technician) and an Aquatic Habitat Protection and Development Group (four biologists and one technician).

British Columbia. The Department of Fisheries, formed in 1947, was replaced in 1957 by the Department of Recreation and Conservation, with the Marine Resources Branch the provincial organization concerned with all marine commercial and recreational fisheries. Jurisdiction over the fisheries of British Columbia rests with the federal authority; the ownership of the fisheries in non-tidal waters is vested in the Crown in the right of the province, as are shell fisheries and marine plant management in tidal waters. The province administers non-tidal fisheries although the regulations covering them are made under federal Order in Council on the advice of the province.

The provincial Fisheries Act provides for taxation of fisheries and, under civil and property rights, for the regulation and control of the various fish processing plants under a system of licensing. The commercial harvesting of oysters and marine aquatic plants is regulated by provincial permits and licences. Provision is made for arbitration of disputes regarding fish prices that may arise between fishermen and operators of licensed plants. Administration of the act involves collection of revenue and supervision of plant operations.

Regulation of net fishing in non-tidal waters, including commercial fishing and authority for regulation of the game fisheries in non-tidal waters, is vested in the Fish and Wildlife Branch which operates a number of trout hatcheries and egg-taking stations for restocking purposes.

The branch cooperates closely with the Fisheries and Marine Service of Canada. The biological research into those species of shellfish over which the province has control, principally oysters and clams as well as marine plants, is conducted by the Fisheries and Marine Service of Canada at the Pacific Biological Station, Nanaimo, BC, under agreement with the federal and provincial authorities.

Statistics of the fishing industry   10.2.3

The waters off the Pacific and Atlantic coasts of Canada rank among the most productive fishing grounds in the world and provide a livelihood to some 50,000 sea fishermen (Table 10.13). Inland waters support another 5,100 fishermen, while an additional 16,000 persons are employed in fish processing plants.

Fish landings   10.2.3.1

The declining trend in fish landings continued in 1974 as landings fell 15% to slightly less than 2 billion lb. (slightly less than 1 billion kg). In contrast to previous years, the demand for fishery products was not large enough to generate sufficiently higher prices to offset the declining catch. The result was a 10% reduction in the gross earnings of fishermen which fell to $285 million in 1974 and a 13% decline in the marketed value of this catch at $685 million (Tables 10.14 and 10.15).

Atlantic Coast landings were down 14% to 1,538 million lb. (698 million kg) in 1974 while the landed value declined less sharply to $164 million, a drop of about 2%. The year 1974 was the sixth consecutive year of a declining catch and many of the factors which were at play in 1973 were equally valid for 1974. Overtaxing of the offshore resources, particularly by foreign fleets, is thought to be the primary factor for the decline in the catch, but others contributing to it were weather and ice conditions, water temperature and labour problems which idled a considerable portion of the Newfoundland and Nova Scotia fishing fleets.

Groundfish account for the most important portion, contributing about 45% of the total value of the landings. Although the quantity of groundfish landed declined 24%, the two other major groups, pelagic and estuarial and molluscs and crustaceans, remained about the same. Landings of scallops (the second most valuable shellfish species) increased in quantity to 14 million lb. (6 million kg) from 11 million lb. (5 million kg) in 1973, and increased 14% in value to $18.6 million. (Table 10.16)

Pacific Coast landings dropped from 389 million lb. (176 million kg) in 1973 to 298 million lb. (135 million kg) in 1974. This decline of 24% represents a reduction in Pacific Coast fishermen's incomes by about $29 million. Most of this decline occurred in the salmon fishery.

Halibut, the mainstay of the Pacific groundfish fishery was again a disappointment in 1974 declining almost 50% to 7.5 million lb. (3.4 million kg). Depletion of resources in the Bering Sea and Gulf of Alaska is thought to be the main reason.

The landings of salmon, the most important species to the Pacific fishery, dropped sharply to 134 million lb. (61 million kg) in 1974, a decline of 27% from 1973. This decline represented a $26 million loss to Pacific Coast salmon fishermen. A shift in the 1974 salmon catch breakdown saw sockeye become the principal species at 35% of the catch in volume terms followed by chum and pink at 21% and 18% respectively.

10.2.3.2   Products and marketing

Declining export prices and weak US demand for fish products combined to weaken the demand for and prices of frozen groundfish products.

The marketed value of processed product on the Atlantic Coast was $425 million and on the Pacific Coast $220 million. These figures represent decreases of 8% and 23% respectively compared with 1973. Atlantic Coast production of frozen fillets and blocks fell 26% to $121 million in 1974 (see Table 10.19) and in absolute terms, the $42 million decline would appear to be the largest single element in the overall drop in this region. Only pelagic and estuarial fish products were able to show an increase in product value on the Atlantic Coast, rising 21% to almost $94 million. (Table 10.17)

On the Pacific Coast, salmon, as a group, were the most valuable species in Canada in 1974 with all types of products having a marketed value of $166 million. Canned salmon pack was valued at $114 million in 1974. (Table 10.18)

10.3   The fur industry

The value of the 1974-75 Canadian production of raw furs amounted to $41.5 million made up of $24.9 million (60%) from wildlife pelts and $16.6 million (40%) from farm pelts. The world market for furs was active in 1974-75 but prices were mainly below the previous season's high levels; in addition, production of many of the important species was lower than in 1973-74. These factors combined to produce a decline of 20.2% in value compared with the record 1973-74 production of raw furs with $52.1 million. (Tables 10.20 and 10.21)

Fur trapping. In recent seasons prices for almost all kinds of Canadian wild furs have been on the increase, and although in 1974-75 there was a price decline, pelt values were still substantially above historic levels. Over the past three seasons the higher returns encouraged trappers to work their traplines to full advantage, resulting in increased production of many species, especially the long-haired types such as fox, raccoon and coyote. Lynx is also high on the list of popular furs; however, in 1974-75 this cyclic species was approaching the lower end of its period of abundance and the numbers taken reflected this decline.

With the encouragement provided by recent strong price levels the production of many of the fur-bearer species is approaching optimum levels. This has not been the case for many years. Throughout the 1950s and 1960s raw fur prices failed to keep pace with the general price rise and there was little incentive for trappers to work their traplines to maximum potential. As a result a good percentage of fur bearers went unharvested. Since nature does not stockpile its creatures the incomplete trapline coverage resulted in wastage.

With the incentive provided by higher returns many resource-based undertakings have contributed materially to the northern economy. A thriving fur industry can distribute revenue to even the most remote hamlets of the North.

Fur farming. Mink are raised in all provinces except Newfoundland. In 1974 the principal producers, in order of importance, were Ontario, British Columbia, Nova Scotia, Quebec and Alberta (Table 10.22).

The 1974 production of ranched mink totalling 1,113,061 pelts was slightly above the total of 1,065,808 pelts produced in 1973. After several seasons when mink pelt prices increased, returns for the 1974 production declined by approximately 18% from an average of $18.00 a pelt in 1973 to $14.76 in 1974. Difficulties experienced by producers through the lower returns were compounded by the continuing rise in production costs.

Due to the unfavourable cost-return situation and other factors, the number of Canadian mink farms continued to decline and the total at the end of 1975 was 393 (Table 10.22). It would probably not be entirely correct to use the shrinking tally of farms as a strict measure of the prosperity of the industry. The number of mink farms has declined, through good years and bad, since 1939 when there were 3,333 farms which produced 170,296 pelts (an average of 51 pelts per farm). In earlier years beginners in the mink business got started through the acquisition of a small number of breeding animals and built up from that point. Now entry into the business on a scale that would hold the promise of some return on investment within a reasonable time involves a high outlay of capital. This is a limiting factor in attracting newcomers to the industry while mink farming is experiencing attrition in numbers due to retirements.

In 1974, 1,548 fox pelts were produced on 55 farms across the country; this is 11% above the 1973 output of 1,395 pelts from 42 farms. The increase in production is attributed to the improved economic climate in the market for the long-haired furs. Values for silver and mutation fox pelts have risen sharply in the past decade, and the 1974 average price of $104.87 a pelt was the highest recorded in over 50 years. Encouraged by the upturn, producers are expanding their operations and the demand for breeding animals is stronger than for many years.

Fur marketing. The bulk of Canada's fur production is sold at public auction through five fur auction firms in Montreal, North Bay, Winnipeg, Regina and Vancouver. At the auctions, furs are purchased through competitive bidding by buyers who may be purchasing for their own account or for firms in Canada or abroad. Canadian raw furs are usually sold in the raw or undressed state, facilitating entry into many countries which maintain tariffs on imports of dressed furs.

In 1974-75 exports of raw furs amounted to $41 million, slightly below the 1973-74 exports valued at $41.7 million. Imports for 1974-75 totalled $55.9 million, a slight increase over the 1973-74 value of $55.7 million and substantially above the earlier high of $39.6 million in 1972-73. The increase in imports is due not only to a healthy fur retail business in Canada, but also to requirements occasioned through growing exports of fur garments. In 1975 exports of fur pieces amounted to $36.5 million, the highest value on record for this class of export.

The export of fur fashion garments on an important scale is a fairly new development on the Canadian fur scene. Historically, Canadian exports of furs have consisted mainly of undressed pelts from fur farms and the trapline. There are fairly definite limits to which this last type of export can be developed. The production of wildlife pelts is relatively limited and not likely to be increased to any meaningful extent. In addition, in view of the highly competitive world fur farming situation, it is not practicable to visualize an open-end type increase in the production and export of ranch-raised furs.

In the fur manufacturing industry no such limits apply. Other factors, however, are present, principally import tariffs and competition from fur manufacturers in the importing countries. A high degree of efficiency in design and manufacture is required by Canada to compete and there is a growing "export group" among Canadian fur manufacturers which is extending the horizons of this formerly largely domestic industry.

10.4   Wildlife

Wildlife is an important renewable natural resource. The original inhabitants of what is now Canada depended on it for food and clothing and still do in some remote areas. The coming of the Europeans brought development of the fur trade which guided the course of exploration and settlement. When the country was being opened up, a number of mammals and birds became seriously depleted or extinct. As settlement progressed, wildlife habitat was reduced by cutting and burning of forests, pollution of streams, industrial and urban development, drainage of wetlands, building of dams, and other changes in the land.

Today, the arctic and alpine tundra, a major vegetational region, has begun to show serious man-made changes. The adjacent sub-arctic and sub-alpine non-commercial forests have been affected principally by increased human travel which has brought an increase in the number of forest fires, although the great forests farther south retain much of their original character despite exploitation. Arable lands, originally forest or grassland, have completely changed but they have, in some cases, become more suitable than the original wilderness for some forms of wildlife. The surplus of game and fur species available for harvest across Canada is seldom fully utilized and wildlife will remain generally abundant where habitat is preserved and management enlightened.

Canada is known for its varied and abundant wildlife. It maintains most of the world's stock of woodland caribou, mountain sheep, wolves, grizzly bears and wolverines. These animals exist because of the vast habitat and because of the efforts that have been made to preserve them.

In 1885, the Rocky Mountain Park (now Banff National Park) was established in Alberta, preserving an area of over 2,500 sq miles (6 475 km²) in its natural state; in 1887, the continent's first bird sanctuary was established at Last Mountain Lake in Saskatchewan; in 1893 when wood bison faced extinction, laws were passed to protect them and a nucleus herd of plains bison was established at Wainwright, Alta. in 1907. These were among the early attempts at wildlife conservation in Canada.

For a long time, certain species were protected from man and predator. Now, because of better understanding of how nature works, it has been recognized that many factors cause fluctuations in wildlife numbers, and hunting seasons and bag limits are based to a greater extent on environment. Given a fully stocked environment, the annual increase need only replace the losses. Surplus production can therefore be taken by predatory animals or, in the case of game species, by man, without endangering the species.

As a natural resource, wildlife within each province comes under the jurisdiction of the provincial government. However, the federal government does have responsibility for wildlife on federal land and for research and management of migratory birds.

10.4.1   The Canadian Wildlife Service

The Canadian Wildlife Service (CWS) began as an agency to administer the Migratory Birds Convention Act passed in 1917. It was expanded in 1947 to meet the need for scientific research in wildlife management and is now a part of the Environmental Management Service of the Department of Fisheries and the Environment.

The CWS conducts scientific research into wildlife problems in the Northwest Territories, the Yukon Territory and the national parks. Under the Cooperative Research Section, the service represents federal interests in the International Polar Bear Agreement and the Border Grizzly Administrative and Technical Committees. Research projects in various areas of western and northern Canada continue on both polar and grizzly bear populations. Caribou and muskoxen in northern Canada are species of concern and the CWS is conducting long-term studies of both species in cooperative programs with the Northwest Territories Fish and Wildlife Service.

The CWS also carries out research in the national parks. Studies in limnology, ornithology, mammalogy and general ecosystem relationships are in progress. Long-term studies on wolf and grizzly bear ecology have just begun and a biophysical inventory of the mountain parks is continuing in Jasper and Banff. A bison-livestock interaction study is proceeding in and around Wood Buffalo National Park. Shorter duration projects are defined each year and undertaken for Parks Canada according to its priorities.

The Convention on International Trade in Endangered Species of Wild Fauna and Flora was signed by Canada in July 1974. The CWS was designated the scientific authority and the management authority for the convention in Canada. The Canada Wildlife Act, passed by Parliament in 1973, provides the federal government and the CWS with a legislative basis for undertaking joint federal-provincial wildlife management programs. Under the act, the CWS has initiated a rare and endangered species program. Continuing studies on the wood bison, whooping crane and peregrine falcon are to be augmented with new projects on other species. The International Agreement on the Conservation of Polar Bears came into effect on May 26, 1976. Canada was the first of the five signatories to ratify this agreement. As administrator of the Migratory Birds Convention Act the CWS, in consultation with provincial wildlife agencies, is responsible for recommending the annual revisions of the Migratory Birds Regulations which govern open seasons, bag limits and hunting practices. Enforcement of the act and regulations is carried out by the Royal Canadian Mounted Police with CWS and provincial cooperation.

The loss of wetlands to drainage and filling for agricultural and other purposes poses a serious threat to waterfowl. To counteract this the CWS in cooperation with provincial agencies began a major program in 1967 to preserve wetlands by purchase or long-term lease. Since then, 46,000 acres (19 000 ha) have been bought for $9 million. The CWS also has charge of 80 bird sanctuaries covering 44,400 sq miles (115 000 km²).

The CWS conducts two annual surveys of waterfowl hunters, selected from the 471,500 holders of the Canada migratory game bird hunting permits, to obtain estimates of the species and age of the major waterfowl species taken by hunters. Other continuing projects related to migratory game birds include a national goose harvest survey, annual surveys of crop damage in the Prairie provinces and of waterfowl populations and habitat conditions in western Canada, a program to reduce hazards caused by birds flying near airports, and a search for a substitute for lead shot which each year causes lead poisoning and subsequent death of a large number of waterfowl. Bird-banding provides valuable information on the migration and the biology of birds, and is especially useful in waterfowl management. The CWS headquarters in Ottawa keeps sets of continental banding records and controls the activities of banders operating in Canada.

Special attention is being given to species greatly reduced in number or in danger of extinction. The program in which 21 young were raised from whooping crane eggs taken from the breeding grounds and incubated at the Patuxent Wildlife Research Center in Maryland is continuing. Eventually, the progeny from these chicks will be released into the wild but only after a sufficiently large supply of breeding birds has been developed. In 1976, 13 chicks were produced and by July the total population was estimated to be some 80 birds.

Research continues on the effects of toxic chemicals on wildlife at various sites across the country. In Alberta, a study continues on the way in which herbicides alter the habitat on which wildlife depends. The results of field work on the relation between chemical contamination of the lower Great Lakes and the breeding success of fish-eating birds were published. Research began on the effects of differing habitat quality and chemical contamination on the reproductive success of common loons in eastern and northeastern Ontario.

Studies continued into the health of game and fur-bearing animals and rodents in northern Canada and into parasitism in these mammals as well as in birds. Measures were taken to control anthrax among bison in Wood Buffalo National Park and in the Northwest Territories; no outbreaks occurred in 1976.

Under the interpretation program, the CWS operates four wildlife centres across Canada. Wye Marsh Wildlife Centre at Midland, Ont. interprets the Northern Hardwood Biotic Region; Cap Tourmente and Percé Wildlife Centres, both in Quebec, focus on the habitat of the greater snow geese and the natural and human history of the Atlantic gulf coast, respectively; and Creston Valley Wildlife Centre highlights the Columbia Biotic Region. Planning is under way for a centre, situated in Saskatchewan, which would focus on the Prairie Grassland Biotic Region.

Research on both the consumptive and non-consumptive use of the wildlife resource is a growing concern. The CWS has participated in several projects which will shed light on the role of wildlife in the social and economic spheres in Canada.

The CWS has been participating in the Canada Land Inventory which is a federal-provincial program to gather information on how land in the settled parts of Canada is being used, and how best it could be used for agriculture, forestry, recreation and wildlife.

10.4.2   Provincial wildlife management

Newfoundland. The functions of the Wildlife Division are: to preserve all indigenous species from extinction; to provide other species where suitable unused habitat exists, bearing in mind the real and aesthetic values of wildlife that are important to man; to maintain all species in the greatest number possible, consistent with the habitat needs of the species and without serious conflict with the other resource needs; and to provide and regulate the harvest surplus of wildlife populations.

The Wildlife Division manages the game populations through changes in the hunting regulations. Research is conducted mainly on caribou and moose, but ptarmigan, arctic hare, martens, otter, mink, muskrat, ospreys and bald eagles are also being studied. Management surveys are conducted on all game species and some fur bearers. Transplant programs are carried out on the two rare animals — arctic hare and pine marten — to try and re-establish them throughout the island portion of the province.

The wild fur industry in Newfoundland, as elsewhere, has been characterized by short-term instability and a long-term decline. However, recent fur sales have set record prices and this suggests that the decline of the past decade may be temporarily halted. The number of trappers in the province is the same as 10 years ago and as a result of continued interest by trappers, research and management studies are being conducted on all fur bearers. Previously, beaver was the only fur bearer benefiting from a management program. It is hoped that these studies will provide the information necessary to produce the management program required to ensure survival of the species.

Prince Edward Island. The Fish and Wildlife Division of the Department of the Environment has full or partial responsibility for research and management of all the wildlife on Prince Edward Island. All non-migratory wildlife is the full responsibility of the province while the management responsibilities for fish and migratory birds are shared with the federal government. A prime responsibility is the continual monitoring of game populations to assist in setting seasons and bag limits. Attempts are being made to establish a viable population of pheasants by the introduction of new species. A research project on ruffed grouse populations was concluded early in 1976. Sharptail grouse habitat was investigated in Manitoba and Ontario to evaluate the possibility of a successful introduction to Prince Edward Island.

Habitat improvement is of prime importance for all forms of wildlife. Fishery management consists largely of the building of fish ladders to facilitate fish passage and other stream improvement measures such as stream bed stabilization. Silting has long been a problem in some Island streams. A pilot project to monitor silt, and to identify and correct its source is being carried out on the Dunk River, one of the largest systems on the Island. A pilot program attempting to establish an early run salmon stock on the Morell River has been initiated; stock was obtained from New Brunswick rivers through the cooperation of the federal Department of Fisheries and the Environment.

Nova Scotia. The Wildlife Division, Department of Lands and Forests, is primarily concerned with the maintenance of a stable and healthy environment to ensure optimum populations of vertebrate wildlife.

Programs are conducted annually to assess the status of important game and fur bearer species in the province. In addition to the fact-finding phase of the program, staff of the Wildlife Division is actively involved with public relations, marsh development program in cooperation with Ducks Unlimited (Canada), environmental impact studies, wildlife depredation problems, development of integrated resource management plans for Crown lands, and specific research on the snowshoe hare and American dog tick. Among other concerns are cooperative programs with the Trappers Association of Nova Scotia and NS Wildlife Federation, providing technical information to various federal and provincial agencies involved with projects affecting land use and water quality, acquisition of wetlands, designation of unique areas for long-term management and protection, inventory of non-game species particularly in the coastal zone, maintenance of a modest "put and take" trout fishery, assessment of lakes and streams to determine potential for management, cooperative programs with Acadia and Dalhousie universities, and updating legislation for wildlife management.

New Brunswick. The wildlife resources of New Brunswick are the responsibility of the Fish and Wildlife Branch of the Department of Natural Resources. Orders in Council issued under the New Brunswick Game Act provide a means of controlling bag limits and hunting pressure in the utilization of surpluses of wildlife species.

Biological surveys of game animals are carried out to determine the condition of population. Principal areas of concern are the management of the following animals and their habitat: moose, white-tailed deer, black bear, beaver, muskrat and woodcock. Some factors limiting the numbers of big-game animals in New Brunswick are the condition and extent of the winter habitat. Research and active management programs to integrate forestry practices with deer winter habitat requirements will continue to be the main thrust of deer management. A study area consisting of 1 million acres (404 686 ha) of Crown land was established in 1974 in the Bathurst area to evaluate the "multiple-use" concept. Game, fish, recreation and forest management will be integrated to optimize exploitation of renewable resources.

A New Brunswick Trappers Association endorsed by the Fish and Wildlife Branch was established in 1974 in an attempt to improve the quality of raw furs. Its primary objectives include the personal involvement of resident trappers in the wise use and management of the fur resource in the province. The current demand for long-haired furs such as bobcat, fox and fisher has diverted trapping pressure from beaver, otter, mink and muskrat.

Sport fishing contributes substantially to the economy. Atlantic salmon anglers fished an average of 82,358 days to catch an average of 33,303 salmon and grilse each year during 1969-72. The Miramichi River system accounted for 82% (27,509) of the average salmon and grilse angler catch during this period. However, more angler-days are spent and fish caught in NB by anglers fishing for brook trout. In 1970, 1,017,000 angler-days were spent participating in the inland sport fishery including trout and Atlantic salmon angling. Atlantic salmon angling comprised only 8.5% of this total.

Quebec. The management and protection of wildlife within Quebec is the responsibility of the Fish and Game Branch of the Department of Tourism, Fish and Game. The branch, operating under the Wildlife Conservation Act which is the legal basis for protecting fish and wildlife animal species, consists of five services. The Wildlife Management Service is responsible for the management of all wildlife and particularly of species of interest to hunters and fishermen. Biologists are assigned to nine districts and their work includes the collection of data on animal populations and habitats. The Wildlife Research Service conducts projects to improve the basic knowledge of fish and wildlife in order to help wildlife managers. The Fish Hatchery Service operates seven hatcheries, inspects commercial hatcheries and controls imports of eggs and salmonoids. The Conservation Service is responsible for enforcing fishing and hunting regulations and for informing the public of the scope and importance of such regulations. The Leasing Service of fishing and hunting rights deals with outfitters and private clubs.

Ontario. Wildlife management in Ontario is administered by the Division of Fish and Wildlife of the Ministry of Natural Resources. Objectives for this division are to provide and encourage a continuous supply of recreational and economic opportunities and to develop public awareness of relevant ecological principles. Within the division, the Wildlife Branch is responsible for wildlife management. Management functions are distributed between main office and eight regional and 49 district offices.

The deer herd in Ontario has experienced a decline during the past few decades, manifested by a southward retraction of about 200 miles (320 km) in the northern limit of the range of white-tailed deer and reduced deer populations throughout the remaining range. The primary cause of the decline has been the maturation of the forest following the reduction of logging and fires since the 1930s. Several severe winters were instrumental in reducing the deer herd to a size compatible with the reduced range quality. The management program has been aimed at increasing the amount of browse available in winter yards and maintaining suitable winter cover. Moose management is concentrated on production and harvest inventory and evaluation of the effects of various forest practices and conditions on moose range. The number of moose hunters has been increasing and more intensive management measures for moose are being formulated.

In upland game and waterfowl management, effort is directed to the maintenance and improvement of habitat since habitat determines the potential wildlife numbers. Management is carried out on areas under agreement between landowners and the province and on provincial wildlife areas. These areas have helped to increase opportunities for nature study and hunting in southern Ontario and some of them ensure preservation of the wetland habitats important to a great variety of wildlife, especially waterfowl. Waterfowl banding, production surveys and harvest inventory assist in developing waterfowl management programs.

The major effort in fur management is directed toward beaver, with aerial censuses of beaver colonies and specimen collections by trappers. Monthly summaries of all fur bearers taken by each trapper are prepared. The harvest of beaver, marten and fisher is controlled by quota. About three quarters of the fur harvested is auctioned through the Ontario Trappers' Association Fur Sales Service in North Bay. A concerted effort to develop more humane traps was started in 1973 in cooperation with the Ontario Trappers' Association. Workshops on humane trapping, pelt preparation, animal biology and management practices have continued to upgrade trappers' skills and knowledge.

Manitoba. The Manitoba Department of Renewable Resources and Transportation Services is responsible for programs designed to maximize the recreational and economic benefits of wildlife resources while preserving the ecological diversity of native species. Authority provided by provincial legislation (The Wildlife Act, the Predator Control Act and Regulations) allows for legal protection and management of the 26 mammal, 160 bird, five reptile and three amphibian species. The federal Migratory Birds Convention Act deals with the protection of migratory game birds, migratory insectivorous birds and migratory non-game birds.

Wildlife authorities manage wildlife, game bird, goose and fur-bearing animal refuges and 41 wildlife management areas. The distribution of hunting and trapping pressure by setting definite seasons and bag limits is one management tool utilized. A quota system is used for moose, elk and caribou. Wildlife habitat development projects were undertaken successfully in 1975. The department plans to establish additional wildlife management areas particularly in southwestern Manitoba.

A five-year Federal-Provincial Program designed to revitalize Manitoba's primary wild fur industry became effective in April 1975. Grant's Lake managed hunting area continued for the second year in 1975. With the cooperation of landowners a managed waterfowl hunt was held on private land surrounding Oak Hammock Marsh. The wildlife management area and an adjacent buffer zone were closed to hunting. Both Grant's Lake and Oak Hammock Marsh Managed Hunting Areas were open during the 1976 season.

Saskatchewan. The Fisheries and Wildlife Branch of the Department of Tourism and Renewable Resources is responsible for administering and managing the province's wildlife resources. The legislative authority is provided through the Game and Fur Acts.

Wildlife Management Programs are oriented toward maintaining and enhancing wildlife populations for 100,000 hunters and an even greater number of non-consumptive users. Because consumptive demands exceed the supply of most big game species, hunting is regulated by restricted bag limits, shortened seasons and allocation of hunting licences on a priority basis.

Habitat loss continues to be a major problem and new initiatives are proposed to arrest this loss. Funds from a surtax on hunting licences have permitted acquisition of more than 40,000 acres (16 000 ha) of prime wildlife habitat. Attempts are under way to improve hunter-landowner relations with season manipulation and good hunting habits. A federal-provincial agreement exists to reduce grain crop losses caused by waterfowl. A livestock compensation program provides assistance to farmers for loss of animals shot by hunters.

Fur management stresses conservation, utilization and development of the fur resources. Training sessions update trappers on new, more humane trapping techniques and quality pelt preparation.

Current fisheries studies evaluate the coarse fish production potential of Saskatchewan waters, to determine reasons for population fluctuations of certain species and to investigate the basic productivity of selected waters. A study to develop aquatic habitat protection guidelines is also in progress. Projects are currently under way on white-tailed deer, moose, elk and game birds from the point of view of basic ecological requirements.

Special studies in fisheries and wildlife are under way in connection with a comprehensive Qu'Appelle Valley land use evaluation and development plan.

Alberta. The management of fish and wildlife resources of Alberta is under the jurisdiction of the Fish and Wildlife Division of the Department of Recreation, Parks and Wildlife.

The Sam Livingston Fish Hatchery and Rearing Station in Calgary supplied over 5.75 million fish for the province's stocking program in 1975. An Aquaculture Specialist coordinated and provided technical expertise to the developing fish-farming industry of the private sector. Nine new projects aimed at improving various aquatic habitat characteristics through such techniques as water level stabilization, flow regulation, and erection of fish barriers, were approved for sites throughout the province. These will be undertaken by the Habitat Development Section. Fisheries research in 1975 continued attempts to establish a homing, self-sustaining population of rainbow trout in the Chain Lakes Reservoir, and to develop a rainbow trout stocking formula for the pot-hole fisheries. The Habitat Protection Section continued to review applications associated with development projects affecting terrestrial and aquatic resources. The harvest of commercial species in Alberta in 1975-76 totalled almost 4.3 million lb. (2.0 million kg), which was a decrease from the previous year's total of 5.2 million lb. (2.4 million kg).

Wildlife populations are managed for aesthetic, recreational and economic purposes. To ensure sustained optimum yields and harvests, the following methods are utilized: determination of population inventories and production, delineation and modification of limiting factors through habitat protection and development, intensive enforcement and public education.

During 1975, species management plans were completed for pheasants and moose. Research and management efforts continued on ungulates, waterfowl and upland birds. Key habitat areas for ungulates were identified and mapped, and land capabilities for fur bearers and upland birds were classified as part of the Alberta Land Inventory program. Through participation in the Alberta Oil Sands Environmental Program, research projects were begun in the Athabasca oil sands area on moose, fur bearers, rare and endangered species, and recreational use of the wildlife resource. A review of biocide effects on wildlife populations was initiated, and continued into 1976. The ground work was completed for a program to intensify ungulate production in the boreal forest area, with future efforts to continue over the next several years. In early 1975, the first annual big game harvest survey questionnaire was mailed to a random selection of Alberta hunters to determine harvest and recreational opportunity provided by the hunting of four major game species. Results indicated approximately 465,000 hunter-days in the 1974 harvest, with a further 5% increase (to 490,000 hunter-days) recorded for the 1975 season.

British Columbia. The Fish and Wildlife Branch of the Department of Recreation and Conservation is responsible for the protection, enhancement and use of wildlife and freshwater fish resources of British Columbia. Administrative and technical headquarters are in Victoria, with seven regional headquarters in the main centres of population, 59 district offices, three fish hatcheries and a number of permanent field stations throughout the province. The branch licenses hunters and anglers and enforces closed seasons, bag limits and other regulatory measures. It licenses and regulates trapping of fur-bearing animals, commercial propagation of game birds and fish, and activities of big-game guides.

Through liaison with other government agencies and with private concerns involved in mining, forestry, agriculture, water use and transportation, the branch fosters the preservation of a suitable land and water environment for wildlife and recreation. The branch enhances the abundance and health of desirable species of animals by the acquisition of key areas of range for big game and waterfowl and by the operation of fish hatcheries and the stocking of lakes.

The branch's objective is to contribute to the economy of British Columbia through wise management of game resources and of non-tidal fisheries, paying attention to such matters as pollution and integrated use of lands for forestry, agriculture and wildlife. The branch conducts programs of education and information to make the public aware of the value of wildlife resources and of the principles of wise management.

10.4.3   Territorial wildlife management

Yukon Territory. The Yukon Game Branch of the Department of Tourism, Conservation and Information is responsible for management of the Yukon's wildlife resource. It administers and enforces the Game Ordinance and Fur Export Ordinance, and assists federal agencies with the enforcement of the Migratory Birds Convention Act, Canada Wildlife Act, International Agreement on the Conservation of Polar Bears, International Agreement of Trade in Endangered Species, the Game Export Act and the Freshwater Fishery Regulations. It also administers the Brands Ordinance and Pounds Ordinance.

With headquarters in Whitehorse, it has five regional offices in Dawson City, Mayo, Ross River, Watson Lake and Haines Junction.

The branch promotes the judicious use of big game species, upland game birds, and sport fish for Yukoners and non-residents, licensing hunters and anglers and enforcing closed seasons, bag limits and other regulatory measures. It licenses and regulates trapping of fur-bearing animals, commercial propagation of wildlife, and activities of outfitters and guides.

To increase knowledge about wildlife species and provide the basis for proper management, it conducts and supports biological research and public educational programs.

Northwest Territories. The Fish and Wildlife Service manages the wildlife resources of the Northwest Territories, and provides opportunities for native peoples to follow their traditional pursuits of hunting, trapping, and fishing. It has headquarters in Yellowknife, three regional offices at Fort Smith, Inuvik, and Frobisher Bay, one district office at Rankin Inlet, and 25 area offices throughout the territories.

Wildlife management is carried out mainly by harvest monitoring and control. Harvest quotas are allocated by management zones. Management studies are conducted primarily to establish the quantity and seasonal distribution of large mammals, including polar bear.

Trapping is encouraged through a series of programs to assist native peoples to return to the land. Included are Trappers' Incentive Grants (a fur subsidy program based on a percentage of the season's harvest), Fur Marketing Service, and the Outpost Camp Program which provides financial assistance to groups who wish to move back to the land and live off the natural resources available through hunting and trapping.

On July 1, 1976, the service assumed responsibility for the administration of sports fishing licences in the territories. Fish and wildlife officers are appointed fishery officers for enforcement purposes. Under permit from the federal Fisheries and Marine Service, they also carry out monitoring of commercial fisheries and the testing of lakes and rivers to determine the viability of commercial operations to supply local domestic markets.

Continued hydrocarbon and mineral exploration and development, as well as the question of construction of natural gas pipelines, have resulted in greater involvement of the Fish and Wildlife Service in environmental management through participation in various federal-territorial regulatory committees. Close liaison is maintained with hunters' and trappers' associations as a link between the resource-dependent residents and the companies involved in exploration and development of non-renewable resources. Guidance has been provided to industry in conducting impact assessment studies, particularly relating to pipeline construction, and joint industry-government funding has been arranged to launch field studies of wildlife populations.

The Northwest Territories Game Advisory Council has been established to advise the Commissioner of the Northwest Territories on matters pertaining to wildlife policy and legislation. All members of the council are northern residents and represent the Inuit Tapirisat of Canada, the Northwest Territories Métis Association, the Indian Brotherhood of the Northwest Territories, and the outdoor recreation industry.

Sources

10.1 - 10.1.2 Information Services Directorate, Department of Fisheries and the Environment.

10.1.3 Information Services Directorate, Department of Fisheries and the Environment; provincial returns from respective provincial government departments.

10.1.4 Manufacturing and Primary Industries Division, Industry Statistics Branch, Statistics Canada.

10.2 - 10.2.1 Information Services Directorate, Department of Fisheries and the Environment.

10.2.2 Supplied by the respective provincial government departments.

10.2.3 Manufacturing and Primary Industries Division, Industry Statistics Branch, Statistics Canada.

10.3 Agriculture Division, Industry Statistics Branch, Statistics Canada.

10.4.1 Information Services Directorate, Department of Fisheries and the Environment.

10.4.2 Supplied by the respective provincial government departments.

10.4.3 Supplied by the respective territorial government departments.

Tables

Tables

..	not available	e	estimate
...	not appropriate or not applicable	p	preliminary
—	nil or zero	r	revised
--	too small to be expressed		certain tables may not add due to rounding

10.1 1973 National Forest Inventory

Province or territory	Forest land sq miles		Non-reserved forest land tenure sq miles			Volume[3] MM cu ft		
	Total[1]	Non-reserved[2]	Crown provincial	Crown federal	Privately owned	Soft-woods	Hard-woods	Total
Newfoundland	49,225	48,181	46,259	- -	1,922	7,775	1,241	9,016
Prince Edward Island	967	961	47	2	912	136	64	200
Nova Scotia	17,159	16,416	4,002	33	12,381	6,283	2,672	8,955
New Brunswick	24,366	23,877	10,802	83	12,992	14,655	5,793	20,448
Quebec	268,747	268,371	240,161	291	27,919	96,965	33,466	130,431
Ontario	166,884	166,075	148,281	1,603	16,191	91,390	58,269	149,659
Manitoba	52,306	50,923	49,495	397	1,031	12,174	3,584	15,758
Saskatchewan	49,497	47,220	45,078	590	1,552	10,343	7,011	17,354
Alberta	118,692	97,976	94,381	692	2,903	33,638	20,102	53,740
British Columbia	210,394	203,650	193,147	619	9,884	260,375	7,224	267,599[4]
Yukon Territory	89,714	81,200	- -	81,200	- -	..	..	..
Northwest Territories	211,241	194,600	- -	194,600	- -	..	..	..
Canada	1,259,192	1,199,450	831,653	280,110	87,687	533,734	139,426	673,160

[1]Land capable of producing stands of trees 4" dbh and larger on 10% or more of the area.
[2]Excludes land in parks, game refuges, water conservation areas and nature preserves, where, by legislation, wood production is not primary.
[3]Non-reserved inventoried areas only; excludes Labrador, the Yukon Territory and Northwest Territories for which no data are available.
[4]Mature timber only.

10.2 Forest utilization and depletion by fire, 10-year average 1964-73

Item	Usable wood MM cu ft	Percentage of total depletion
Products utilized		
Logs and bolts[1]	2,557	56.4
Domestic use	2,529	55.8
Exported	28	0.6
Pulpwood	1,355	29.9
Domestic use	1,268	28.0
Exported	87	1.9
Fuelwood (incl. wood for charcoal)	157	3.5
Other products	50	1.1
Total utilization	4,119	90.9
Wastage by forest fires	412	9.1
Total depletion[2]	4,531	100.0

[1]Includes some wood used in pulp manufacture.
[2]Excludes losses caused by insects, disease or natural mortality for which no reliable estimates are available.

10.3 Forest fire losses, 1974[1], compared with 10-year average 1964-73

Item		Average 1964-73	1974
Fires	No.	7,846	7,777
Under 10 acres	..	6,777	6,844
10 acres or over	..	1,069	933
Area burned	acres	2,307,228	1,963,259
Merchantable timber	..	420,689	353,179
Young growth	..	783,629	1,032,304
Cut-over lands	..	69,663	168,422
Non-forested lands	..	1,033,247	409,354
Estimated values destroyed[2]	$	15,151,239	26,329,375
Merchantable timber	$	8,921,550	16,662,821
Young growth	$	4,420,635	7,071,761
Cut-over lands	$	209,528	6,928
Other property burned	$	1,599,526	2,587,865
Actual cost of fire fighting	$	15,426,872	12,122,431
Total damage and fire-fighting cost	$	30,578,111	38,451,806
Area under protection	sq miles	1,579,718	962,655

[1]Excludes losses for Newfoundland and national parks for which figures are not currently available.
[2]Excludes such values as damage to soil, stream-flow, wildlife, recreation and tourist facilities.

10.1   1973 National Forest Inventory   M

Province or territory	Forest land km²		Non-reserved forest land tenure km²			Volume³ Million cubic metres		
	Total[1]	Non-reserved[2]	Crown provincial	Crown federal	Privately owned	Soft-woods	Hard-woods	Total
Newfoundland	127 492	124 788	119 810	- -	4 978	220	35	255
Prince Edward Island	2 505	2 489	122	5	2 362	4	2	6
Nova Scotia	44 442	42 517	10 365	85	32 067	178	76	254
New Brunswick	63 108	61 841	27 977	215	33 649	415	164	579
Quebec	696 052	695 078	622 014	754	72 310	2 746	948	3 694
Ontario	432 228	430 132	384 046	4 152	41 934	2 588	1 650	4 238
Manitoba	135 472	131 889	128 191	1 028	2 670	345	101	446
Saskatchewan	128 197	122 299	116 751	1 528	4 020	293	199	492
Alberta	307 411	253 757	244 446	1 792	7 519	953	569	1 522
British Columbia	544 918	527 450	500 248	1 603	25 599	7 373	205	7 578[4]
Yukon Territory	232 358	210 307	- -	210 307	- -	. .	. .	. .
Northwest Territories	547 112	504 012	- -	504 012	- -	. .	. .	. .
Canada	3 261 295	3 106 559	2 153 970	725 481	227 108	15 115	3 949	19 064

[1]Land capable of producing stands of trees 10 cm dbh and larger on 10% or more of the area.
[2]Excludes land in parks, game refuges, water conservation areas and nature preserves, where, by legislation, wood production is not primary.
[3]Non-reserved inventoried areas only; excludes Labrador, the Yukon Territory and Northwest Territories for which no data are available.
[4]Mature timber only.

10.2   Forest utilization and depletion by fire, 10-year average 1964-73   M

Item	Usable wood '000,000 m³	Percentage of total depletion
Products utilized		
Logs and bolts[1]	72.4	56.4
Domestic use	71.6	55.8
Exported	0.8	0.6
Pulpwood	38.4	29.9
Domestic use	35.9	28.0
Exported	2.5	1.9
Fuelwood (incl. wood for charcoal)	4.4	3.5
Other products	1.4	1.1
Total utilization	116.6	90.9
Wastage by forest fires	11.7	9.1
Total depletion[2]	128.3	100.0

[1]Includes some wood used in pulp manufacture.
[2]Excludes losses caused by insects, disease or natural mortality for which no reliable estimates are available.

10.3   Forest fire losses, 1974[1], compared with 10-year average 1964-73   M

Item		Average 1964-73	1974
Fires	No.	7,846	7,777
Under 4 hectares	''	6,777	6,844
4 hectares or over	''	1,069	933
Area burned	ha	933 702	794 503
Merchantable timber	''	170 247	142 926
Young growth	''	317 123	417 759
Cut-over lands	''	28 192	68 158
Non-forested lands	''	418 140	165 660
Estimated values destroyed[2]	$	15,151,239	26,329,375
Merchantable timber	$	8,921,550	16,662,821
Young growth	$	4,420,635	7,071,761
Cut-over lands	$	209,528	6,928
Other property burned	$	1,599,526	2,587,865
Actual cost of fire fighting	$	15,426,872	12,122,431
Total damage and fire-fighting cost	$	30,578,111	38,451,806
Area under protection	km²	4 091 451	2 493 265

[1]Excludes losses for Newfoundland and national parks for which figures are not currently available.
[2]Excludes such values as damage to soil, stream-flow, wildlife, recreation and tourist facilities.

10.4   Forest fires, by cause, 1974[1], compared with 10-year average 1964-73

Cause	Average 1964-73		1974	
	No.	%	No.	%
Recreation	1,679	21.4	1,600	20.6
Settlement	899	11.5	732	9.4
Woods operations	363	4.6	591	7.6
Railways	472	6.0	494	6.4
Other industries	304	3.9	312	4.0
Incendiary	345	4.4	405	5.2
Miscellaneous known	1,247	15.9	1,133	14.6
Unknown	399	5.1	369	4.7
Total, man-caused	5,708	72.8	5,636	72.5
Lightning	2,138	27.2	2,141	27.5
Total, all fires	7,846	100.0	7,777	100.0

[1]Excludes Newfoundland and national parks for which figures are not currently available.

10.5   Volume of wood cut, by province, 1971-74 (thousand cubic feet)

Province or territory	1971	1972	1973	1974
Newfoundland	82,080	83,170	104,250	113,400
Prince Edward Island	7,470	6,640	6,070	6,700
Nova Scotia	114,282	115,011	127,000	141,180
New Brunswick	243,846	255,161	313,160	310,100
Quebec	938,690	982,710	1,036,500	1,155,200
Ontario	559,340	613,100	651,400	666,300
Manitoba	54,937	64,800	64,570	74,200
Saskatchewan	80,930	93,270	96,000	98,100
Alberta	146,129	172,800	197,720	178,600
British Columbia	1,997,082	1,993,558	2,476,858	2,121,910
Yukon Territory and Northwest Territories	2,417	3,420	4,930	5,200
Canada	4,227,203	4,383,640	5,078,458	4,870,890

10.6   Volume of wood cut, by type of product, 1971-74 (thousand cubic feet)

Type of product	1971	1972	1973	1974
Logs and bolts	2,752,727	2,867,942	3,421,502	3,012,170
Pulpwood	1,303,197	1,357,066	1,496,570	1,696,300
Fuelwood	131,835	119,484	122,277	124,020
Poles and piling	5,239	4,276	3,740	2,530
Round mining timber	3,044	2,685	1,959	1,950
Fence posts	12,009	14,327	15,068	16,310
Miscellaneous roundwood	19,152	17,860	17,342	17,610
Total	4,227,203	4,383,640	5,078,458	4,870,890

10.7   Lumber production and shipments and value of all shipments of the sawmill and planing mill industry, by province, 1973 and 1974

Year and province or territory	Lumber		Value of shipments[1] $'000	Value of shipments[1] of goods of own manufacture $'000
	Production M/bm	Quantity shipped[1] M/bm		
1973				
Newfoundland	19,440	18,899	3,203	3,657
Prince Edward Island	966	966	120	270
Nova Scotia	159,352	159,435	24,059	28,339
New Brunswick	279,296	292,095	48,117	69,085
Quebec	2,330,415	2,369,777	323,735	392,460
Ontario	1,036,524	1,001,067	163,532	196,598
Manitoba	78,364	74,799	9,742	11,366
Saskatchewan	167,121	193,066	23,599	25,372
Alberta	577,905	616,747	83,808	93,114
British Columbia	10,099,101	9,971,405	1,546,890	1,737,938
Yukon Territory and Northwest Territories	3,080	3,080	351	346
Canada	14,751,564	14,701,336	2,227,156	2,558,545

10.5   Volume of wood cut, by province, 1971-74 (thousand cubic metres) M

Province or territory	1971	1972	1973	1974
Newfoundland	2 324	2 355	2 952	3 211
Prince Edward Island	212	188	172	190
Nova Scotia	3 236	3 257	3 596	3 998
New Brunswick	6 905	7 225	8 868	8 781
Quebec	26 580	27 828	29 350	32 712
Ontario	15 839	17 361	18 446	18 868
Manitoba	1 556	1 835	1 828	2 101
Saskatchewan	2 292	2 641	2 718	2 778
Alberta	4 138	4 893	5 599	5 057
British Columbia	56 551	56 451	70 137	60 086
Yukon Territory and Northwest Territories	68	97	140	147
Canada	119 701	124 131	143 806	137 929

10.6   Volume of wood cut, by type of product, 1971-74 (thousand cubic metres) M

Type of product	1971	1972	1973	1974
Logs and bolts	77 949	81 211	96 887	85 295
Pulpwood	36 903	38 428	42 378	48 034
Fuelwood	3 733	3 383	3 462	3 512
Poles and piling	148	121	106	72
Round mining timber	86	76	55	55
Fence posts	340	406	427	462
Miscellaneous roundwood	542	506	491	499
Total	119 701	124 131	143 806	137 929

10.7   Lumber production and shipments and value of all shipments of the sawmill and planing mill industry, by province, 1973 and 1974 M

Year and province or territory	Lumber		Value of shipments[1] $'000	Value of shipments[1] of goods of own manufacture $'000
	Production m³	Quantity shipped[1] m³		
1973				
Newfoundland	45 873	44 597	3,203	3,657
Prince Edward Island	2 280	2 280	120	270
Nova Scotia	376 029	376 225	24,059	28,339
New Brunswick	659 065	689 267	48,117	69,085
Quebec	5 499 167	5 592 050	323,735	392,460
Ontario	2 445 924	2 362 255	163,532	196,598
Manitoba	184 918	176 506	9,742	11,366
Saskatchewan	394 362	455 585	23,599	25,372
Alberta	1 363 704	1 455 361	83,808	93,114
British Columbia	23 831 222	23 529 893	1,546,890	1,737,938
Yukon Territory and Northwest Territories	7 268	7 268	351	346
Canada	34 809 812	34 691 287	2,227,156	2,558,545

10.7 Lumber production and shipments and value of all shipments of the sawmill and planing mill industry, by province, 1973 and 1974 (concluded)

Year and province or territory	Lumber Production Mfbm	Quantity shipped[1] Mfbm	Value of shipments[1] $'000	Value of shipments[1] of goods of own manufacture $'000
1974				
Newfoundland	10,751	[2]	[2]	3,557
Prince Edward Island	—	—	—	[2]
Nova Scotia	146,907	130,964	22,640	29,076
New Brunswick	293,326	280,243	46,433	78,795
Quebec	2,114,528	2,130,793	292,155	380,876
Ontario	1,095,687	972,123	152,841	198,957
Manitoba	101,241	96,278	11,565	17,418
Saskatchewan	119,047	135,978	14,635	16,368
Alberta	490,349	508,061	57,197	67,612
British Columbia	8,600,173	8,869,619	1,278,239	1,536,297
Yukon Territory and Northwest Territories	1,293	[2]	..	..
Canada	12,973,302	13,136,632	1,877,695	2,329,835

[1]Shipment figures contain some duplication because sales of lumber from one sawmill to another are reported as shipments by both establishments.
[2]Confidential.

10.8 Lumber shipments[1] of the sawmill and planing mill industry, by species, 1972-74

Kind of wood	1972 Quantity Mfbm	1972 Value $'000	1973 Quantity Mfbm	1973 Value $'000	1974 Quantity Mfbm	1974 Value $'000
Spruce	6,677,840	734,549	6,999,973	985,036	6,576,563	822,771
Douglas-fir	1,709,643	205,403	1,570,784	247,481	1,316,860	202,576
Hemlock	2,352,498	259,060	2,573,190	402,424	2,176,176	335,491
Cedar (red and white)	987,784	141,905	1,006,770	207,474	903,115	191,313
White pine	264,594	37,638	262,929	48,754	234,578	47,976
Jack pine	429,270	50,144	562,521	73,512	496,236	62,951
Maple	215,250	38,791	219,748	43,186	213,917	42,500
Yellow birch	129,213	21,838	133,459	26,186	104,204	22,267
Lodgepole pine	660,189	69,799	720,661	93,619	673,748	71,479
Balsam fir	238,031	26,396	176,408	27,051	133,857	19,898
Other	391,401	46,145	474,893	72,433	307,378	58,473
Total	14,055,713	1,631,668	14,701,336	2,227,156	13,136,632	1,877,695

[1]See footnote 1, Table 10.7.

10.9 Veneer and plywood shipments, by type, 1972-74

Type	1972 Quantity M sq ft	1972 Value $'000	1973 Quantity M sq ft	1973 Value $'000	1974 Quantity M sq ft	1974 Value $'000
Veneer						
Softwoods	2,020,196[1],[r]	31,221[r]	2,059,295[1]	37,063	1,656,846[1]	32,439
Hardwoods	1,302,649[2],[r]	38,951[r]	1,237,907[2]	45,419	1,021,223[2]	44,006
Softwood plywood	2,255,371[3]	240,903	2,428,138[3]	289,666	2,081,448[3]	262,244
Hardwood plywood	382,710[4]	43,719	422,967[4]	59,334	369,789[4]	57,610

[1] Basis 1/8".
[2]Surface measure.
[3]Basis 3/8" unsanded.
[4]Basis 1/4" sanded two sides.

10.7   Lumber production and shipments and value of all shipments of the sawmill and planing mill industry, by province, 1973 and 1974 (concluded)   M

Year and province or territory	Lumber Production m^3	Quantity shipped[1] m^3	Value of shipments[1] $\$'000$	Value of shipments[1] of goods of own manufacture $\$'000$
1974				
Newfoundland	25 370	[2]	[2]	3,557
Prince Edward Island	—	—	—	[2]
Nova Scotia	346 662	309 041	22,640	29,076
New Brunswick	692 172	661 300	46,433	78,795
Quebec	4 989 730	5 028 111	292,155	380,876
Ontario	2 585 533	2 293 955	152,841	198,957
Manitoba	238 902	227 191	11,565	17,418
Saskatchewan	280 920	320 872	14,635	16,368
Alberta	1 157 095	1 198 890	57,197	67,612
British Columbia	20 294 146	20 929 968	1,278,239	1,536,297
Yukon Territory and Northwest Territories	3 061	[2]	..	..
Canada	30 613 591	30 998 997	1,877,695	2,329,835

[1]Shipment figures contain some duplication because sales of lumber from one sawmill to another are reported as shipments by both establishments.
[2]Confidential.

10.8   Lumber shipments[1] of the sawmill and planing mill industry, by species, 1972-74   M

Kind of wood	1972 Quantity m^3	1972 Value $\$'000$	1973 Quantity m^3	1973 Value $\$'000$	1974 Quantity m^3	1974 Value $\$'000$
Spruce	15 757 946	734,549	16 518 095	985,036	15 518 959	822,771
Douglas-fir	4 034 308	205,403	3 706 637	247,481	3 107 443	202,576
Hemlock	5 551 277	259,060	6 072 052	402,424	5 135 203	335,491
Cedar (red and white)	2 330 910	141,905	2 375 712	207,474	2 131 114	191,313
White pine	624 372	37,638	620 443	48,754	553 542	47,976
Jack pine	1 012 964	50,144	1 327 402	73,512	1 170 986	62,951
Maple	507 933	38,791	518 547	43,186	504 788	42,500
Yellow birch	304 909	21,838	314 928	26,186	245 894	22,267
Lodgepole pine	1 557 872	69,799	1 700 570	93,619	1 589 868	71,479
Balsam fir	561 691	26,396	416 276	27,051	315 867	19,898
Other	923 603	46,145	1 120 623	72,433	725 331	58,473
Total	33 167 785	1,631,668	34 691 285	2,227,156	30 998 995	1,877,695

[1]See footnote 1, Table 10.7.

10.9   Veneer and plywood shipments, by type, 1972-74   M

Type	1972 Quantity m^3	1972 Value $\$'000$	1973 Quantity m^3	1973 Value $\$'000$	1974 Quantity m^3	1974 Value $\$'000$
Veneer						
Softwoods	595 958[1]	31,221[r]	607 492[1]	37,063	488 770[1]	32,439
Hardwoods	151 107[2]	38,951[r]	143 597[2]	45,419	118 462[2]	44,006
Softwood plywood	1 996 003[3]	240,903	2 148 902[3]	289,666	1 842 081[3]	262,244
Hardwood plywood	225 799[4]	43,719	249 551[4]	59,334	218 176[4]	57,610

[1]Basis 3.175 mm.
[2]Surface measure.
[3]Basis 9.525 mm unsanded.
[4]Basis 6.35 mm sanded two sides.

10.10   Pulp shipments and production, 1972-74

Item		1972	1973	1974
Mill shipments of pulp[1]	'000 tons	7,383	7,936	8,381
	$'000	976,146	1,301,486	2,205,290
Groundwood pulp	'000 tons	266	303	300
	$'000	17,339	23,369	49,714
Chemical pulps	'000 tons	7,117	7,633	8,081
	$'000	958,807	1,278,117	2,155,576
Pulp production[2]	'000 tons	19,239	20,461	21,691
Quebec	"	6,496	6,163	7,002
Ontario	"	3,938	4,044	4,274
British Columbia	"	5,044	5,882	5,806
Other provinces[3]	"	3,761	4,372	4,609

[1]Includes screenings.
[2]The differences between these figures and the quantities of mill shipments represent the amounts of pulp further manufactured by the reporting companies.
[3]Prince Edward Island is the only province in which there is no production.

10.11   Shipments of basic paper and paperboard, by type and by province, 1972-74

Type and province		1972	1973	1974
TYPE				
Newsprint paper	'000 tons	8,962	9,230	9,657
	$'000	1,177,177	1,339,412	1,854,917
Book and writing paper	'000 tons	951	982	1,138
	$'000	261,657	321,394	495,976
Wrapping paper	'000 tons	574	662	679
	$'000	113,638	148,210	224,601
Paperboard	'000 tons	2,042	2,273	2,361
	$'000	313,095	378,355	550,271
All other papers	'000 tons	319	316	333
	$'000	59,627	64,909	100,197
Total	'000 tons	12,848	13,463	14,168
	$'000	1,925,194	2,252,280	3,225,962
PROVINCE				
Quebec	'000 tons	5,707	5,573	6,100
	$'000	864,192	938,560	1,381,144
Ontario	'000 tons	3,160	3,433	3,608
	$'000	547,112	665,202	916,770
British Columbia	'000 tons	2,025	2,194	2,128
	$'000	270,569	326,324	446,792
Other provinces[1]	'000 tons	1,956	2,263	2,332
	$'000	243,321	322,194	481,256

[1]Prince Edward Island is the only province in which there is no production.

10.12   Exports of pulp and newsprint to Britain, United States and all countries, 1972-75

Commodity and year	Britain		United States		All countries	
	Quantity tons	Value $'000	Quantity tons	Value $'000	Quantity tons	Value $'000
Pulp						
1972	445,122	60,816	3,497,820	472,861	6,102,175	817,335
1973	383,724	61,506	3,715,188	609,227	6,517,206	1,054,166
1974	438,721	108,812	3,925,471	1,060,380	7,081,673	1,861,235
1975	445,099	145,412	2,925,715	991,879	5,471,377	1,817,998
Newsprint						
1972	560,615	80,127	6,390,256	933,761	8,101,676	1,157,509
1973	495,140	76,604	6,905,217	1,067,833	8,396,064	1,285,928
1974	494,043	107,443	7,056,763	1,352,758	8,699,311	1,721,768
1975	375,079	102,416	5,626,109	1,357,892	6,998,193	1,741,990

10.10   Pulp shipments and production, 1972-74   M

Item		1972	1973	1974
Mill shipments of pulp[1]	'000 t	6 697	7 200	7 603
	$'000	976,146	1,301,486	2,205,290
Groundwood pulp	'000 t	241	275	272
	$'000	17,339	23,369	49,714
Chemical pulps	'000 t	6 456	6 925	7 331
	$'000	958,807	1,278,117	2,155,576
Pulp production[2]	'000 t	17 453	18 562	19 677
Quebec	,,	5 893	5 591	6 352
Ontario	,,	3 572	3 669	3 877
British Columbia	,,	4 576	5 336	5 267
Other provinces[3]	,,	3 412	3 966	4 181

[1]Includes screenings.
[2]The differences between these figures and the quantities of mill shipments represent the amounts of pulp further manufactured by the reporting companies.
[3]Prince Edward Island is the only province in which there is no production.

10.11   Shipments of basic paper and paperboard, by type and by province, 1972-74   M

Type and province		1972	1973	1974
TYPE				
Newsprint paper	'000 t	8 130	8 373	8 761
	$'000	1,177,177	1,339,412	1,854,917
Book and writing paper	'000 t	863	891	1 032
	$'000	261,657	321,394	495,976
Wrapping paper	'000 t	521	601	616
	$'000	113,638	148,210	224,601
Paperboard	'000 t	1 852	2 062	2 142
	$'000	313,095	378,355	550,271
All other papers	'000 t	289	287	302
	$'000	59,627	64,909	100,197
Total	'000 t	11 655	12 214	12 853
	$'000	1,925,194	2,252,280	3,225,962
PROVINCE				
Quebec	'000 t	5 177	5 056	5 534
	$'000	864,192	938,560	1,381,144
Ontario	'000 t	2 867	3 114	3 273
	$'000	547,112	665,202	916,770
British Columbia	'000 t	1 837	1 990	1 930
	$'000	270,569	326,324	446,792
Other provinces[1]	'000 t	1 774	2 053	2 116
	$'000	243,321	322,194	481,256

[1]Prince Edward Island is the only province in which there is no production.

10.12   Exports of pulp and newsprint to Britain, United States and all countries, 1972-75   M

Commodity and year	Britain		United States		All countries	
	Quantity t	Value $'000	Quantity t	Value $'000	Quantity t	Value $'000
Pulp						
1972	403 808	60,816	3 173 169	472,861	5 535 800	817,335
1973	348 109	61,506	3 370 362	609,227	5 912 310	1,054,166
1974	398 001	108,812	3 561 127	1,060,380	6 424 386	1,861,235
1975	403 787	145,412	2 654 164	991,879	4 963 550	1,817,998
Newsprint						
1972	508 581	80,127	5 797 143	933,761	7 349 717	1,157,509
1973	449 183	76,604	6 264 307	1,067,833	7 616 781	1,285,928
1974	448 188	107,443	6 401 788	1,352,758	7 891 882	1,721,768
1975	340 266	102,416	5 103 920	1,357,892	6 348 654	1,741,990

10.13 Persons employed in the primary fishing industry, by province, 1973 and 1974

Province or territory	Sea fisheries		Inland fisheries	
	1973	1974	1973	1974
Newfoundland	15,313	..	...	...
Prince Edward Island	2,636	..	...	...
Nova Scotia	10,600	..	...	...
New Brunswick	4,997	..	...	...
Quebec	5,450	5,703	...	...
Ontario	...	...	2,215	2,208
Manitoba	...	...	1,827	1,685[1]
Saskatchewan	...	...	992	785[1]
Alberta	...	...	370	304[1]
British Columbia	11,717	11,906	...	...
Yukon Territory	...	...	155	55
Northwest Territories	...	...	114	112
Total	50,713	..	..	..

[1]Fishermen who sold fish to the Freshwater Fish Marketing Corporation.

10.14 Value of all fishery products, by province, 1973 and 1974 (thousand dollars)

Province or territory	1973	1974
Newfoundland	144,780	114,612
Prince Edward Island	23,721[r]	20,402
Nova Scotia	177,655[r]	183,644
New Brunswick	101,357[r]	100,581
Quebec	35,478	29,836
Ontario	20,752	19,310
Manitoba		
Saskatchewan	16,590	19,217
Alberta		
Northwest Territories		
British Columbia and Yukon Territory[1]	285,052	220,559
Total[2]	786,480[r]	685,416

[1]Includes landings by Canadian fishermen in United States ports.
[2]The sum of provincial totals differs from Canada total as intershipments between provinces have been removed from the Atlantic Coast.

10.15 Landings of sea and inland fish and other sea products, by province, 1973 and 1974

Province or territory	1973		1974	
	Quantity '000 lb.	Value $'000	Quantity '000 lb.	Value $'000
Newfoundland	675,349	47,297	516,943	42,098
Prince Edward Island	62,847	11,243	35,664	8,921
Nova Scotia	615,336	74,956	624,519	78,480
New Brunswick	286,433	22,112	250,502	21,525
Quebec	157,320	13,137	118,747	14,051
Ontario	54,311	10,684	54,984	10,023
Manitoba	22,603	5,041	25,027	5,147
Saskatchewan	8,419	1,625	13,059	1,971
Alberta	4,611	802	5,212	931
British Columbia[1]	388,773	130,409	297,753	100,976
Yukon Territory	54	37	8	..
Northwest Territories	3,241	809	2,938	738
Total	2,279,297	318,152	1,945,356	284,861
Sea fish	2,179,036	298,472	1,835,816	265,218
Inland fish	100,261	19,680	109,540	19,643

[1]Includes halibut landed in United States ports.

10.15   Landings of sea and inland fish and other sea products, by province, 1973 and 1974   **M**

Province or territory	1973		1974	
	Quantity *t*	Value *$'000*	Quantity *t*	Value *$'000*
Newfoundland	306 333	47,297	234 481	42,098
Prince Edward Island	28 507	11,243	16 177	8,921
Nova Scotia	279 112	74,956	283 277	78,480
New Brunswick	129 924	22,112	113 626	21,525
Quebec	71 359	13,137	53 863	14,051
Ontario	24 635	10,684	24 940	10,023
Manitoba	10 253	5,041	11 352	5,147
Saskatchewan	3 819	1,625	5 923	1,971
Alberta	2 092	802	2 364	931
British Columbia[1]	176 344	130,409	135 058	100,976
Yukon Territory	24	37	4	. .
Northwest Territories	1 470	809	1 333	738
Total	1 033 872	318,152	882 398	284,861
Sea fish	988 394	298,472	832 711	265,218
Inland fish	45 478	19,680	49 687	19,643

[1]Includes halibut landed in United States ports.

10.16   Landings of the chief commercial fish, 1973 and 1974

Area and species	1973 Quantity '000 lb.	1973 Value $'000	1974 Quantity '000 lb.	1974 Value $'000
ATLANTIC COAST				
Groundfish	*1,098,382*	*80,727*	*838,726*	*73,848*
Catfish	6,595	360	6,756	427
Cod	324,533	29,670	287,878	32,126
Flounder and sole	286,171	19,189	232,876	17,792
Haddock	33,452	6,427	27,151	5,736
Hake	28,674	1,812	24,916	1,883
Halibut	2,720	2,058	2,457	1,911
Pollock	50,022	2,893	46,215	3,251
Redfish	349,300	17,306	193,331	9,480
Other	16,915	1,012	17,146	1,242
Pelagic and estuarial	*599,477*	*23,597*	*607,430*	*25,723*
Alewives	13,103	336	12,549	460
Herring[1]	498,953	12,232	497,360	13,445
Mackerel	47,655	2,253	36,679	1,804
Salmon	4,796	3,471	4,883	3,657
Smelts	3,346	581	4,192	664
Swordfish	23	2	3	--
Other	31,601	4,722	51,764	5,693
Molluscs and crustaceans	*87,108*	*63,233*	*86,112*	*64,035*
Clams	8,633	1,039	5,663	747
Lobsters	35,599	40,568	31,388	37,963
Oysters	2,251	427	2,753	508
Scallops	11,143	16,231	14,044	18,572
Other	29,482	4,968	32,264	6,245
Other[2]	5,296	506	5,781	650
Total, Atlantic Coast	1,790,263	168,063	1,538,049	164,256
PACIFIC COAST				
Groundfish	*42,317*	*14,073*	*36,204*	*9,876*
Cod (gray)	13,269	1,304	15,592	1,921
Flounder and sole	6,902	706	7,315	1,048
Halibut[3]	14,472	10,698	7,460	5,440
Lingcod	3,277	701	3,884	1,117
Sablefish	1,435	474	747	231
Other	2,962	190	1,206	119
Pelagic and estuarial	*330,476*	*113,485*	*245,709*	*87,831*
Herring	122,630	10,951	98,479	12,043
Salmon	185,204	99,998	134,246	73,998
Chum	72,190	32,670	27,487	10,680
Coho	22,370	18,910	20,545	13,834
Pink	28,462	7,882	24,385	5,791
Sockeye	47,303	26,497	46,906	29,841
Spring	14,755	13,986	14,816	13,803
Other	124	53	107	49
Other	22,642	2,536	12,984	1,790
Molluscs and crustaceans	*15,980*	*2,851*	*15,840*	*3,269*
Clams	1,575	196	2,448	383
Crabs	2,580	1,159	2,503	1,317
Oysters	9,874	875	8,105	880
Shrimps and prawns	1,729	508	2,650	624
Other	222	113	134	65
Total, Pacific Coast	388,773	130,409	297,753	100,976
INLAND				
Freshwater fish	*96,004*	*19,476*	*102,238*	*19,232*
Bass	1,512	303	2,360	407
Catfish	1,022	253	1,021	276
Herring, lake (cisco) and tullibee	3,391	704	3,355	873
Perch	19,578	5,916	13,900	4,350
Pickerel (yellow)	8,064	3,406	8,144	3,421
Pike	7,388	782	7,754	913
Saugers	4,175	1,372	3,968	1,252
Smelts	17,556	1,004	16,903	963
Sturgeon	182	149	156	124
Trout	1,292	338	1,416	403
Whitefish	16,956	4,262	17,880	4,680
Other	14,888	987	25,381	1,570
Other[4]	5,934	285	7,358	454
Total, Inland	101,938	19,761	109,596	19,686
Total	2,280,974	318,233	1,945,398	284,918

[1]Includes sardines.
[2]Includes livers and scales; excludes seaweeds and "Other" (seals, whales, oils, etc.)
[3]Includes landings by Canadian fishermen at United States ports.
[4]Sea fish caught inland.

10.16   Landings of the chief commercial fish, 1973 and 1974   **M**

Area and species	1973 Quantity *t*	1973 Value $'000	1974 Quantity *t*	1974 Value $'000
ATLANTIC COAST				
Groundfish	*498 219*	*80,727*	*380 438*	*73,848*
Catfish	2 991	360	3 064	427
Cod	147 206	29,670	130 579	32,126
Flounder and sole	129 805	19,189	105 631	17,792
Haddock	15 174	6,427	12 315	5,736
Hake	13 006	1,812	11 302	1,883
Halibut	1 234	2,058	1 114	1,911
Pollock	22 690	2,893	20 963	3,251
Redfish	158 440	17,306	87 693	9,480
Other	7 673	1,012	7 777	1,242
Pelagic and estuarial	*271 917*	*23,597*	*275 525*	*25,723*
Alewives	5 943	336	5 692	460
Herring[1]	226 321	12,232	225 599	13,445
Mackerel	21 616	2,253	16 637	1,804
Salmon	2 175	3,471	2 215	3,657
Smelts	1 518	581	1 901	664
Swordfish	10	2	1	- -
Other	14 334	4,722	23 480	5,693
Molluscs and crustaceans	*39 511*	*63,233*	*39 060*	*64,035*
Clams	3 916	1,039	2 569	747
Lobsters	16 147	40,568	14 237	37,963
Oysters	1 021	427	1 249	508
Scallops	5 054	16,231	6 370	18,572
Other	13 373	4,968	14 635	6,245
Other[2]	2 402	506	2 622	650
Total, Atlantic Coast	812 049	168,063	697 645	164,256
PACIFIC COAST				
Groundfish	*19 195*	*14,073*	*16 422*	*9,876*
Cod (gray)	6 019	1,304	7 072	1,921
Flounder and sole	3 131	706	3 318	1,048
Halibut[3]	6 564	10,698	3 384	5,440
Lingcod	1 486	701	1 762	1,117
Sablefish	651	474	339	231
Other	1 344	190	547	119
Pelagic and estuarial	*149 901*	*113,485*	*111 451*	*87,831*
Herring	55 624	10,951	44 669	12,043
Salmon	84 007	99,998	60 893	73,998
Chum	32 745	32,670	12 468	10,680
Coho	10 147	18,910	9 319	13,834
Pink	12 910	7,882	11 061	5,791
Sockeye	21 456	26,497	21 276	29,841
Spring	6 693	13,986	6 720	13,803
Other	56	53	49	49
Other	10 270	2,536	5 889	1,790
Molluscs and crustaceans	*7 248*	*2,851*	*7 184*	*3,269*
Clams	714	196	1 110	383
Crabs	1 170	1,159	1 135	1,317
Oysters	4 479	875	3 676	880
Shrimps and prawns	784	508	1 202	624
Other	101	113	61	65
Total, Pacific Coast	176 344	130,409	135 057	100,976
INLAND				
Freshwater fish	*43 547*	*19,476*	*46 374*	*19,232*
Bass	686	303	1 070	407
Catfish	464	253	463	276
Herring, lake (cisco) and tullibee	1 538	704	1 522	873
Perch	8 880	5,916	6 305	4,350
Pickerel (yellow)	3 658	3,406	3 694	3,421
Pike	3 351	782	3 517	913
Saugers	1 894	1,372	1 800	1,252
Smelts	7 963	1,004	7 667	963
Sturgeon	83	149	71	124
Trout	586	338	642	403
Whitefish	7 691	4,262	8 110	4,680
Other	6 753	987	11 513	1,570
Other[4]	2 692	285	3 338	454
Total, Inland	46 239	19,761	49 712	19,686
Total	1 034 632	318,233	882 414	284,918

[1]Includes sardines.
[2]Includes livers and scales; excludes seaweeds and "Other" (seals, whales, oils, etc.).
[3]Includes landings by Canadian fishermen at United States ports.
[4]Sea fish caught inland.

10.17   Market value of all fishery products, by area and species, 1973 and 1974 (thousand dollars)

Area and species	1973	1974	Area and species	1973	1974
ATLANTIC COAST			PACIFIC COAST		
Groundfish	244,306	197,119	Groundfish	20,848	16,306
Catfish	1,262	1,476	Cod (gray)	3,128	4,531
Cod	82,550	70,115	Flounder and sole	1,796	2,192
Flounder and sole	52,796	41,358	Halibut²	12,963	6,996
Haddock	12,071	10,832	Lingcod	1,266	1,766
Hake	3,522	3,939	Sablefish	896	492
Halibut	3,440	3,029	Other	799	329
Pollock	8,292	8,586			
Redfish	55,087	29,732	Pelagic and estuarial	259,119	198,110
Other	25,286	28,052	Herring	34,641	29,815
			Salmon	221,642	165,841
Pelagic and estuarial	77,308	93,572	Chum	56,554	22,350
Alewives	695	1,197	Coho	27,863	24,375
Herring (includes sardines)	54,477	63,386	Pink	27,220	22,215
Mackerel	4,234	4,972	Sockeye	69,008	65,221
Salmon	6,841	5,547	Spring	20,533	18,864
Smelts	1,225	1,385	Other	20,464	12,816
Tuna	7,530	14,409	Other	2,836	2,454
Other	2,306	2,676			
			Molluscs and crustaceans	4,600	5,585
Molluscs and crustaceans	122,660	114,812	Clams	393	795
Clams	2,626	1,957	Crabs	2,057	2,255
Crabs	18,324	15,658	Oysters	1,141	1,064
Lobsters	75,868	59,053	Shrimps and prawns	863	1,217
Oysters	788	833	Other	146	254
Scallops	21,894	32,775	Other sea products	430	451
Other	3,160	4,536			
			Total, Pacific Coast	284,997	220,452
Other sea products	18,448	19,193	Total, Inland	38,761	40,268
Total, Atlantic Coast¹	462,722	424,696	Total	786,480	685,416

¹Excludes duplication.
²Includes halibut landed by Canadian fishermen in United States ports.

10.18   Pacific Coast production of canned salmon, 1973 and 1974

Kind	1973		1974	
	Quantity 48-lb. cases	Value $'000	Quantity 48-lb. cases	Value $'000
Chum	423,363	27,561	230,634	14,227
Coho	116,198	9,556	160,051	12,962
Pink	355,695	25,218	307,192	21,720
Sockeye	642,600	63,881	709,181	64,009
Spring	11,259	776	20,279	1,293
Steelhead	999	71	1,546	101
Total	1,550,114	127,063	1,428,883	114,312

10.19   Atlantic Coast production of frozen fillets and fish blocks, 1973 and 1974

Area and species	1973		1974	
	Quantity '000 lb.	Value $'000	Quantity '000 lb.	Value $'000
NEWFOUNDLAND	133,546	91,294	101,236	65,479
Cod	43,944	32,077	33,565	22,776
Haddock	323	241	214	145
Redfish	29,855	17,041	14,891	7,173
Flatfish	54,044	40,151	41,939	32,143
Other	5,380	1,784	10,627	3,242
MARITIMES¹	97,596	56,497	93,697	46,132
Cod	19,204	13,272	19,067	11,960
Haddock	6,037	5,827	5,261	4,361
Redfish	41,746	21,367	24,920	11,378
Flatfish	11,109	8,389	10,093	7,262
Other	19,500	7,642	34,356	11,171
QUEBEC	27,750	15,849	18,298	9,557
Cod	5,850	4,201	3,364	2,738
Redfish	19,300	10,193	12,692	5,310
Flatfish	1,545	1,154	1,870	1,388
Other	1,055	301	372	121
TOTAL, ATLANTIC COAST¹	258,892	163,640	213,231	121,168
Cod	68,998	49,550	55,996	37,474
Haddock	6,360	6,068	5,475	4,506
Redfish	90,901	48,601	52,503	23,861
Flatfish	66,698	49,694	53,902	40,793
Other	25,935	9,727	45,355	14,534

¹Data slightly overstated due to interprovincial shipments included in the Maritimes.

10.18   Pacific Coast production of canned salmon, 1973 and 1974   M

Kind	1973		1974	
	Quantity 21.8-kg cases	Value $'000	Quantity 21.8-kg cases	Value $'000
Chum	423,363	27,561	230,634	14,227
Coho	116,198	9,556	160,051	12,962
Pink	355,695	25,218	307,192	21,720
Sockeye	642,600	63,881	709,181	64,009
Spring	11,259	776	20,279	1,293
Steelhead	999	71	1,546	101
Total	1,550,114	127,063	1,428,883	114,312

10.19   Atlantic Coast production of frozen fillets and fish blocks, 1973 and 1974   M

Area and species	1973		1974	
	Quantity t	Value $'000	Quantity t	Value $'000
NEWFOUNDLAND	60 575	91,294	45 919	65,479
Cod	19 932	32,077	15 225	22,776
Haddock	147	241	97	145
Redfish	13 542	17,041	6 754	7,173
Flatfish	24 514	40,151	19 023	32,143
Other	2 440	1,784	4 820	3,242
MARITIMES[1]	44 269	56,497	42 500	46,132
Cod	8 711	13,272	8 649	11,960
Haddock	2 738	5,827	2 386	4,361
Redfish	18 936	21,367	11 304	11,378
Flatfish	5 039	8,389	4 578	7,262
Other	8 845	7,642	15 583	11,171
QUEBEC	12 588	15,849	8 300	9,557
Cod	2 654	4,201	1 526	2,738
Redfish	8 754	10,193	5 757	5,310
Flatfish	701	1,154	848	1,388
Other	479	301	169	121
TOTAL, ATLANTIC COAST[1]	117 432	163,640	96 719	121,168
Cod	31 297	49,550	25 400	37,474
Haddock	2 885	6,068	2 483	4,506
Redfish	41 232	48,601	23 815	23,861
Flatfish	30 254	49,694	24 449	40,793
Other	11 764	9,727	20 572	14,534

[1]Data slightly overstated due to interprovincial shipments included in the Maritimes.

10.20   Pelts of fur-bearing animals produced, by province, years ended June 30, 1973-74 and 1974-75

Province or territory	1973-74 fur season			1974-75 fur season		
	Pelts No.	Value $	% of total value	Pelts No.	Value $	% of total value
Newfoundland	58,093	845,331	1.6	85,728	1,741,204	4.2
Prince Edward Island	14,697	259,666	0.5	15,447	192,221	0.5
Nova Scotia	158,568	2,416,776ʳ	4.6	173,627	2,148,586	5.2
New Brunswick	51,410	923,837	1.8	44,388	594,432	1.4
Quebec	524,785	7,242,988	13.9	486,594	5,448,153	13.1
Ontario	1,248,408	16,012,573	30.8	1,189,387	13,159,151	31.7
Manitoba	347,561	4,283,238	8.2	512,319	3,530,728	8.5
Saskatchewan	308,196ʳ	3,735,898ʳ	7.2	456,756	2,386,264	5.7
Alberta	532,255	6,628,344	12.7	794,200	4,284,712	10.3
British Columbia	292,944	5,289,747	10.2	293,377	4,429,081	10.7
Yukon Territory	34,684	499,001	1.0	30,905	403,543	1.0
Northwest Territories	232,334	3,067,904	5.9	230,629	2,081,640	5.0
Canada[1]	3,841,196ʳ	52,069,417ʳ	100.0	4,355,757	41,541,366	100.0

[1]Totals include pelts and values not allocated to a province or territory, mainly Alaska fur seal and Atlantic Coast hair seal.

10.21   Pelts of wildlife fur-bearing animals taken, by kind, years ended June 30, 1973-74 and 1974-75

Kind	1973-74 fur season			1974-75 fur season		
	Pelts No.	Total value $	Average value $	Pelts No.	Total value $	Average value $
Badger	5,134	110,507	21.52	3,626	56,990	15.72
Bear						
White	546	618,024	1,131.91	548	347,706	634.50
Black or brown	4,261	221,134	51.90	3,585	114,635	31.98
Grizzly	27	7,550	279.63	20	5,249	262.45
Beaver	431,071	9,072,632	21.05	357,732	5,990,920	16.75
Cougar	40	3,233	80.82	33	3,404	103.15
Coyote	87,139	3,169,119	36.37	44,366	1,416,512	31.93
Ermine (weasel)	55,968	57,463	1.03	88,098	81,011	0.92
Fisher	12,566	613,347	48.81	10,163	463,739	45.63
Fox						
Blue	208	4,909	23.60	207	4,226	20.42
Cross and red	63,321	2,650,470	41.86	43,103	1,450,227	33.65
Silver	533	24,406	45.79	429	13,827	32.23
White	53,415	1,727,350	32.34	31,913	593,249	18.59
Not specified	17,674	859,465	48.63	13,563	429,575	31.67
Lynx	35,372	3,071,387	86.83	20,648	2,331,933	112.94
Marten	62,356	907,428	14.55	47,598	538,250	11.31
Mink	68,425	1,143,721	16.71	63,083	688,792	10.92
Muskrat	1,434,871	3,728,490	2.60	1,762,589	4,519,164	2.56
Otter	18,016	739,146	41.03	15,258	629,655	41.27
Rabbit	15,308	5,719	0.37	8,353	3,595	0.43
Raccoon	73,442	1,075,603	14.65	81,504	1,015,354	12.46
Seals						
Fur, North Pacific[1]	9,169	432,860	47.21	7,543	344,312	45.62
Hair	130,496	1,789,748	13.71	157,472	3,074,246	19.52
Skunk	867	1,283	1.48	596	862	1.45
Squirrel	183,309	151,700	0.83	469,093	336,755	0.72
Wildcat	4,193	225,095	54.52	3,425	133,235	38.90
Wolf	5,088	230,090	45.22	5,510	246,957	44.82
Wolverine	1,242	105,646	85.06	1,090	115,328	105.81
Total	2,773,993	32,747,525	. . .	3,241,148	24,949,708	. . .

[1]Commonly known as Alaska fur seal; value figures are the net returns to the Canadian Government for pelts sold.

10.22 Mink farms and value of pelts produced thereon, by province, 1973-75

Province	Mink farms at year-end			Value of mink pelts produced on fur farms ($'000)		
	1973	1974	1975	1973	1974	1975
Newfoundland	—	—	—	—	—	—
Prince Edward Island	6	6	5	115	123	161
Nova Scotia	72	61	51	1,946	1,808	2,294
New Brunswick	4	3	3	119	129	229
Quebec	44	40	40	1,974	1,462	2,001
Ontario	201	168	165	7,738	7,017	8,593
Manitoba	55	44	37	1,200	976	989
Saskatchewan	29r	20	16	498r	380	258
Alberta	36	26	19	2,189	1,455	1,620
British Columbia	82	65	57	3,406	3,079	3,280
Total	529r	433	393	19,185r	16,429	19,425

10.23 Exports and imports of furs, by kind, years ended June 30, 1973-74 and 1974-75 (thousand dollars)

Kind of fur	1973-74 fur season			1974-75 fur season		
	Britain	United States	All countries	Britain	United States	All countries
EXPORTS						
Undressed						
Beaver	1,300	1,477	7,787	1,231	1,199	6,356
Chinchilla	—	140	186	1	204	246
Ermine (weasel)	57	2	102	91	8	112
Fisher	68	360	663	33	424	665
Fox, all types	1,096r	1,820r	5,636r	944	2,110	5,021
Lynx	308	1,687	2,734	81	2,127	2,537
Marten	118	458	760	60	296	509
Mink	870	7,461	12,854	357	6,811	11,439
Muskrat	2,600	61	3,092	2,624	287	3,603
Otter	13	39	446	16	45	164
Rabbit	—	33	33	—	22	22
Seal	832	—	1,252	826	5	4,464
Squirrel	179	—	179	331	4	337
Wolf	568	466	2,234	299	330	1,569
Other	1,015	541	3,721	1,002	727	3,922
Dressed						
Mink	—	38	331	33	60	540
Raccoon	—	1	215	24	20	209
Fur plates, mats, etc.	3	40	143	—	88	429
Other	29	605	1,537	91	848	1,697
Fur goods apparel	3,134	4,257	28,046	2,235	3,336	20,338
Total	12,190r	19,486r	71,951r	10,279	18,951	64,179
IMPORTS						
Undressed						
China and Jap mink	160	14	750	77	—	402
Fox	1,277	3,253	8,119	1,103	2,811	7,397
Kolinsky	115	19	335	51	—	88
Mink	2,010	6,783	19,940	2,350	5,508	20,316
Muskrat	—	6,531	6,531	—	8,623	8,627
Persian lamb	28	14	207	22	19	135
Rabbit	—	156	213	—	83	223
Raccoon	5	10,636	10,641	—	11,730	11,752
Other	719	5,257	8,979	234	4,620	6,963
Dressed						
Hatters' furs	—	136	398	—	59	535
Mink	2	2,553	2,610	9	2,608	2,766
Seal	—	1,538	1,681	1	919	1,131
Sheep and lamb	671	675	2,362	664	1,278	2,633
Fur plates, mats, etc.	103	881	2,585	60	535	1,734
Other	240	1,255	2,330	183	1,601	2,534
Fur goods apparel	309	358	1,908	259	708	2,443
Total	5,639	40,059	69,589	5,013	41,102	69,679

Sources
10.1 - 10.4 Information Services Directorate, Department of Fisheries and the Environment.
10.5 - 10.19 Manufacturing and Primary Industries Division, Industry Statistics Branch, Statistics Canada.
10.20 - 10.23 Agriculture Division, Institutions and Agriculture Statistics Field, Statistics Canada.

Agriculture

Chapter 11

Tables

Agriculture   Chapter 11

Agriculture in Canada   11.1

Trends and highlights   11.1.1

Farmers in Canada, as in other countries, felt the impact of inflation in 1975. Gross farm income and production costs were higher than they had ever been. Net farm income, at $4.3 billion, was up $900 million from 1974, but was expected to be down to about $3 billion in 1976.

The Canada Department of Agriculture continued to develop policies and programs to stabilize farm income and to relate production to national and export demands. A long-range dairy policy tying producer returns to a formula based on the consumer price index and the cost of production was announced. New developments in the domestic feed grain policy were outlined including availability of domestic feed grains at corn-competitive prices, relocation of reserve stocks, modifications in feed freight assistance, and funding for programs to assist the feed and livestock industries. The changes were made to encourage increased livestock and feed grain production according to the natural potential of each region.

The Agricultural Stabilization Act was amended to increase price support levels for cattle, sheep and hogs; industrial milk and cream; corn and soybeans; and oats and barley marketed outside the jurisdiction of the Canadian Wheat Board. Prices of these commodities would be supported at not less than 90% of their average market prices of the past five years, adjusted for changes in production costs. In June and July 1976, new support prices were announced for corn, soybeans, carrots, pears, prune plums and lambs.

Purchase programs, deficiency payments or subsidies were provided during 1975 to support potato producers in the Maritimes, Quebec and Ontario; cherry growers in Ontario and British Columbia; apple growers in Nova Scotia; and processing-pear producers in Ontario.

Early in April 1976, under the federal Fresh Fruit and Vegetable Storage Construction Financial Assistance Program, agreements were signed with four producer groups for construction or renovation of fruit and vegetable storage facilities.

New crop varieties, better methods of detecting and controlling diseases and pests, new farming techniques, and a breakthrough in predetermining the sex of cattle embryos were among federal government research accomplishments of economic importance.

Studies by the Animal Pathology Division, Health of Animals Branch, led to development of a technique for collecting a 12- to 14-day embryo from a pedigreed cow, determining the sex of the embryo, and then transferring it into the uterus of a less valuable cow. The first calf to be presexed and transferred in this manner was born at Ottawa late in 1975. Veterinary scientists devised a new management system to reduce the incidence and severity of scours in beef herds in western Canada. An antigen was also developed to detect Aleutian disease which causes high losses in mink.

Four wheat, two barley, two oats and six new forage crop varieties were released by the Research Branch for commercial production, along with one variety each of rapeseed, sunflowers, soybeans, flax, potatoes and tomatoes. Early high-yielding corn hybrids, also developed by branch scientists, were released to the seed industry. Two varieties of strawberries, Totem in British Columbia and Bounty in Nova Scotia, were important new cultivars. A new ash tree, Fall Gold, selected for its superior autumn colour, was introduced in Manitoba.

Among innovations or discoveries in diagnosis or control of diseases and pests were: a fast, simple method of detecting little cherry disease throughout the growing season; the use of new computer technology to give early warning of grasshopper attacks on the prairies; and a reduction in the time required for diagnosis of rabies from 12 days to about five. Other highlights during 1975-76 included a method for estimating prairie wheat yields based on weather and climatic information; development of new techniques to improve nitrogen fixation by plants and reduce demands for nitrogen fertilizer; advances in remote sensing and aerial photography to gather agricultural data; development of a biological method of finding the energy value of feeds; and production of lambs on schedule every eight months using artificial insemination and synchronization of estrus.

The DREAM program — Development, Research and Evaluation in Agricultural Mechanization — moved into its second year, with the Engineering Research Service awarding nearly $1 million in contracts to provincial governments, universities, and private agencies for the evaluation and design of machinery to improve farm output. One of the most successful projects was the production of a small tomato harvester designed by a tomato farmer in southern Ontario.

The New Crop Development Fund with an annual budget of $1 million provided funds to assist the development of peanuts, vinifera grapes and disease-free geraniums in Ontario; baby carrots in Quebec; sunflowers in Saskatchewan; new barley varieties in Manitoba; forage oats in Alberta; and better rapeseed varieties on the prairies. Funds were also provided to carry out an evaluation of machinery and cropping systems for larger-scale grain crop production in Nova Scotia. In addition to continuation of most of these programs, new projects announced for funding in 1976 aimed at expanding the production of flax and winter rye in Saskatchewan, and establishing mustard crops and expanding mustard seed production in eastern Canada.

The Feeds Act was amended to cover changes in the livestock and feed manufacturing industries since the last revision of the act in 1960. The main change affecting farmers concerned on-farm feed mixing; federal inspectors now have the authority to check feeds manufactured on the farm to ensure that the ingredients do not leave residues harmful to health.

The Animal Contagious Diseases Act, renamed the Animal Disease and Protection Act, was amended in 1975 to strengthen Canada's animal health programs, already recognized as among the best in the world. Changes included improved compensation for farmers whose animals are slaughtered and farm supplies ordered destroyed in disease eradication programs; regulations covering zoos and game farms, and for humane care of animals in transportation; a requirement that foreign ships keep their meat lockers sealed while in Canada; and a broader definition of animals, to give the Health of Animals Branch authority over birds, bees and animal semen.

11.1.2   Agricultural regions

Climate, soil conditions and geography have combined to form several distinct farming regions in Canada. A harsh northern climate restricts most agriculture to the southern portion of the country and nearly all farms in Canada lie within 300 miles (483 km) of the southern border. In the Atlantic provinces and central Canada farming is limited to coastal regions and river valleys, and soils vary in depth and fertility. In the Prairie region soil is fertile but rain is light. Farming is limited to high plateaus and river valleys in the western mountainous region.

Farming is nonetheless an important business in Canada. About 169.6 million acres (69 million hectares) in 10 provinces are cultivated; 108.2 million acres (43.8 million ha) are improved land. Farm income exceeds $5 billion annually and in 1973 agricultural exports exceeded $3 billion for the first time.

Mechanization and education are increasing the efficiency of farms constantly; a trend toward fewer and larger farms has become evident in the 1961 and 1971 censuses of agriculture.

Farms in Canada can be divided into four main types. Livestock farms include those specializing in feedlot finishing of cattle, large-scale feeding of hogs bought as weanlings, dairying, poultry production for meat and eggs and other aspects of breeding and raising livestock. Grain farms produce crops like wheat, oats, flax and rapeseed. Special crop farms produce vegetables, fruits, potatoes or other root crops, tobacco or forest products. Other farms combine livestock and grain production. Although each of the regions has its specialties none is limited to one type of farming.

Crops and livestock   11.1.3

The Atlantic region. This area includes Newfoundland, Prince Edward Island, Nova Scotia, New Brunswick and the Gaspé district of Quebec. It is a hilly region, with a general covering of relatively fertile soil developed under forest cover. The climate is modified by the sea but it is also affected by cold currents from the coast of Labrador and winds from the north. Precipitation averages 30 to 55 inches (760 to 1 400 millimetres) annually. Mixed farming is general and forage crops support a healthy livestock industry. It is not unusual to find the small farmers combining fishing or lumbering with farming.

In Nova Scotia the main agricultural areas surround the Bay of Fundy and Northumberland Strait where they are protected from the Atlantic gales. Dairying and poultry production are common and beef farming is increasing. The Annapolis Valley is famous for its fruit, particularly apples. New Brunswick produces potatoes and livestock in the Saint John River valley and there is mixed farming in the northwest. More than a third of the commercial farms in the province are classed as dairy farms.

Farming is the principal occupation on Prince Edward Island. Potatoes are the leading crop but the fertile land also supports mixed grains, dairying and other livestock enterprises. Small fruits and vegetables are also produced.

In Newfoundland agriculture is of only local importance because of rough terrain. Bogland offers some potential for reclaiming and vegetable farming.

The central region. This lowland area bordering the St. Lawrence River includes the farms of the Ottawa Valley and extends through southern Ontario to Lake Huron. Fertile soils, mostly formed by glacial drift and lake sediment developed under deciduous forest cover, and a mild climate modified by the Great Lakes and the St. Lawrence River account for varied farming. Precipitation averages 30 to 45 inches (760 to 1 140 mm) a year. It is the most densely populated part of the country, providing large markets for farm produce.

Well over half the commercial farms of Quebec are now classified as dairy farms, a change from the traditional small mixed farming operations of old Quebec. Sizable butter and cheese industries rely on these farms. Livestock farms, specializing in beef cattle, hogs or sheep, and mixed farms are also common and poultry and egg production is increasing. Forage crops account for the largest cultivation in the province. Oats and corn for feed are also produced. Fruits and vegetables, particularly apples, are becoming prime crops. Sugar beets and flue-cured tobacco are grown and processed in the province.

Ontario has specialized crops in its more southerly regions, but it also has by far the largest number of commercial livestock farms and is second to Quebec in the number of dairy farms. Again forage crops are the largest cultivated crops; others are corn, mixed grains, winter wheat, oats and barley.

Dairy farms are concentrated in Middlesex, Oxford and Perth counties in southwestern Ontario, in the Bruce Peninsula and in the eastern counties. Beef is a specialty in Lake Huron and Georgian Bay areas where pasture is ample. Sheep, poultry and hog production are widespread. Ontario is a major producer of apples and the Niagara Peninsula accounts for most of Canada's tender tree fruits and grapes. Vegetables are grown near most large centres. Maple syrup is a major sideline for farmers in Ontario and Quebec.

The Prairie region. Manitoba, Saskatchewan and Alberta contain 75% of the farm land in Canada. Precipitation that averages only 13 to 20 inches (330 to 510 mm) a year and a climate of bitter winters and short hot summers favour the production of high quality hard red spring wheat, by far the largest single crop in all three provinces. Rangeland and pasture also support a large cattle population and the rearing of livestock in general is a major industry.

Manitoba has the highest rainfall of the three provinces and an average of 100 frost-free days, resulting in more varied farming. Wheat and other grains predominate but rapeseed is also grown, and mixed farming with an emphasis on livestock is common. Vegetables, sugar beets and sunflowers are grown south of Winnipeg and processed locally. Dairy farms are common around Winnipeg; hog production and sheep farms are widespread and beef cattle are found in the southwest. There are also some poultry farms of local importance.

Saskatchewan grows about two thirds of all Canada's wheat and large quantities of other grains, aided by light spring rainfall and long sunny days. Rapeseed is a popular crop and irrigation assists vegetable and forage crops. Mixed farming is common in the north where rainfall is higher, and turkey farming as well as egg and broiler chicken production are increasing. Hogs and beef cattle are gaining in importance. Some commercial flocks of sheep exist.

Alberta is second to Saskatchewan in grain production but has more beef cattle than any other province. These are concentrated in large ranches in the south and in the foothills of the Rocky Mountains. Cattle-feeding operations are expanding and Alberta is a leading producer of hogs and sheep. Irrigation in the south aids in producing canning crops, sugar beets and forage crops. Dairy and poultry products are prominent in the mixed-farm economy of the province. In the northwest the Peace River district produces significant quantities of grain and livestock.

The Pacific region. The most westerly region of the country, British Columbia, is occupied largely by mountains and forests. Only 2% of the area is agricultural. There is no single regional climate: the Pacific Coast has mild temperatures and high rainfall, the interior has moderate temperatures with parts of it as dry as the prairies, and the central interior, although a little cooler, has fairly high precipitation. Farms tend to be small and highly productive and are concentrated in the south-central mainland and southern Vancouver Island.

Livestock and dairying account for the greatest part of BC's agricultural production. Hogs and beef cattle are raised on many farms, beef particularly in the central and southern interior areas. Dairying and poultry meat and egg production are concentrated in the lower Fraser Valley where the population is large. Mixed farming is scattered throughout the province.

British Columbia is Canada's largest producer of apples. The Okanagan Valley is also noted for tree fruits such as peaches, plums and cherries. Raspberries and strawberries are grown largely in the Fraser Valley and on Vancouver Island along with other horticultural crops — apricots, grapes, tomatoes, sweet corn and potatoes. The processing industry is well developed. Vancouver Island's mild climate also produces flowering bulbs.

The northern region. The agricultural region north of latitude 55° consists of parts of northern British Columbia, the Yukon Territory and the Mackenzie River valley in the Northwest Territories. Agricultural settlement in the area is not encouraged by the harsh climate and small population. Precipitation varies from light in the northern Yukon to heavy on the mountainous coast of BC. Frosts can occur in any month of the year, but crops grown on northern slopes escape some damage. The North is estimated to have 3 million acres (1.2 million ha) of potentially arable land and large expanses of grazing land, but at present there are probably fewer than 30 commercial farms in the region. Dairy products, beef cattle, forage crops, feed grains and vegetables are produced for the small local market.

Farm ownership and labour   11.1.4

Most farms in Canada are owned by the farmers who operate them, but as individual farms increase in size more land is being rented. By 1971, 26% of Canadian farmers rented some of the land they farmed; 5% rented all their land. Payment is usually cash or a share of crops or receipts.

Farm families provide most of the labour required on farms, although experienced workers are often employed on dairy farms and seasonal workers are required for harvests. In the west, operators of combine harvesters often move their machinery with the harvest, starting in the US and moving into Canada later in the season. Potato harvesters follow the same pattern in the east. Farmers often assist each other when necessary and the Department of Manpower and Immigration operates farm labour pools in areas of high demand.

Transportation   11.1.5

Railways have been the traditional method of transporting agricultural products to large markets and ports. The Prairie provinces in particular rely on trains to move wheat and livestock to Canadian markets and to elevators in Vancouver, Churchill and Thunder Bay for shipment to foreign ports. Bulky products like sugar beets are usually shipped by rail.

Many products are now being shipped by road. Although the railways have retained their importance on the Prairies many branch lines have been abandoned in other areas and most farmers now ship their produce at least part way in their own trucks. Eggs, poultry, cream, fruits and vegetables go to local markets by road and milk is generally collected at farms by tank trucks. Commercial farms and cooperatives use trucks for marketing and distributing agricultural products and in delivering supplies to farms.

Water routes supplement these means. The Great Lakes have long been used to ship grain from Thunder Bay to eastern Canada during the shipping season and since the opening of the St. Lawrence Seaway in 1959 the lakes have been open to ocean-going vessels. Churchill is another seasonal port for Prairie grains, and Vancouver and Halifax are year-round ports.

Marketing and supplies   11.1.6

The marketing of Canada's farm products is a blend of private trading, public sales and auctions, and sales under contract and through cooperatives or marketing boards. Methods vary with the type of product, the region and the preference of producers. Most products, except western grains and a few special crops, are marketed in more than one way.

Canada's principal livestock markets are at Montreal, Toronto, Winnipeg, Calgary and Edmonton, but there are many other outlets that vary from large stockyards to country collection points. Most cattle and calves are marketed by auction at public stockyards; the remainder go directly to packing plants or are exported. Most hogs, sheep and lambs are sold directly to packing houses; sales of hogs are usually handled by marketing boards.

Egg sales in Canada are regulated by the Canadian Egg Marketing Agency and the Canadian Turkey Marketing Agency performs similar services for turkey producers. Chickens raised for meat are marketed through provincial marketing boards which have the authority to allocate producer quotas, set producer prices and collect levies.

The marketing of fluid milk is a provincial responsibility and quality, prices, and deliveries are regulated by provincial marketing agencies which estimate market requirements and assign producers a share of the market. A marketing plan under which individual producers are allocated a share of the Canadian market for milk used for manufacturing is in effect in all provinces except Newfoundland. Market shares under this plan are administered by the provincial marketing agencies under the direction of the Canadian Dairy Commission.

Most of the grain marketed in Canada is grown in the Prairie provinces. The Canadian Wheat Board is responsible for various aspects of marketing wheat, oats, barley, rye, flax and rapeseed in western Canada and in Ontario all wheat grown is sold through the Ontario Wheat Producers' Marketing Board.

Fruit and vegetables are distributed through fresh and frozen food markets, canneries and other processors. Most produce is grown under a contract or a pre-arranged marketing scheme; marketing boards, producers' associations and cooperatives are common. Tobacco is controlled by marketing boards in Ontario and Quebec, soybeans by a board in Ontario and sugar beets by contracts with refineries in Quebec, Manitoba and Alberta.

Farmers' cooperatives are usually organized to handle or market producers' crops or livestock, or to supply the goods and services needed in farming, or both. Cooperative pooling arrangements for farm products guarantee farmers cash advances on their deliveries whether the products are sold immediately or not.

The marketing of seed in Canada is carried on by private seed companies, farmer-owned cooperatives and seed growers. Seed grades established by federal government regulation provide the user with information on the relative utility of different lots of seed. Pedigree seed is produced by members of the Canadian Seed Growers' Association under conditions that ensure the purity of the variety.

Farm machinery, building materials, fertilizers, agricultural chemicals and other supplies are obtained through commercial and cooperative outlets.

11.2 Federal government services

11.2.1 Canada Department of Agriculture

Responsibilities of the Canada Department of Agriculture cover three broad areas: research, promotional and regulatory services and assistance programs. Research aims at solving practical farm problems by applying fundamental scientific research to all aspects of soil management, agricultural engineering, and crop and animal production. Promotional and regulatory services attempt to control and eradicate crop and livestock pests and register chemicals and other materials used for these purposes. Also included are inspection and grading of agricultural products and the establishment of crop and livestock improvement policies. Assistance programs cover some of the sphere of price stability, emergency relief, crop insurance, compensation, and income security in the event of crop failure.

11.2.2 Farm assistance programs

Basic to the concept of Canada's national agricultural policy is the premise that a stable agriculture is in the interest of the national economy and that farmers as a group are entitled to a fair share of the national income. Consequently the Canada Department of Agriculture has conducted long-term programs designed to aid agriculture through the application of scientific research and the encouragement of improved methods of production and marketing. Over the years, as conditions have warranted, programs have been initiated to deal with special situations. Mitigating the effects of crop failure, assisting the movement of Prairie feed grains to eastern Canada and British Columbia, reclaiming soil in the Maritime provinces and combating drought in the agricultural areas of Manitoba, Saskatchewan and Alberta are examples.

Changes in the past two decades have dictated the need for a different approach to some problems. Large-scale mechanization and, in some segments of the industry, automation have reduced manpower requirements significantly; the number of farms has declined but the size of farms has increased; marketing and income problems have taken different forms; and a decline in some rural communities has occurred together with problems of regional disparity. Legislation enacted to meet these situations includes price support (Agricultural Stabilization Act), dairy market and producer income stabilization (Canadian Dairy Commission Act), crop insurance (Crop Insurance Act), feed grain assistance (Livestock Feed Assistance Act), credit facilities (Farm Credit Act, Farm Syndicates Credit Act, Farm Improvement Loans Act), marketing assistance (Canada Grain Act, Agricultural Products Board Act, Farm Products Marketing Agencies Act) and other forms of assistance to meet emergency or long-term conditions (Prairie Grain Advance Payments Act, Agricultural and Rural Development Act and Prairie Farm Rehabilitation Act). All these measures are administered by the Canada Department of Agriculture or by organizations responsible to the minister except the Farm Improvement Loans Act (administered by the Department of Finance), Prairie Grain Advance Payments Act (Department of Industry, Trade and Commerce) and the ARDA and PFRA programs (Department of Regional Economic Expansion) and the Small Farm Development Program.

The Canadian Grain Commission was established in 1971 under the Canada Grain Act replacing the former Board of Grain Commissioners for Canada. For more detailed information see Section 11.7.1.2.

The Agricultural Stabilization Board, established in 1958 by the Agricultural Stabilization Act and as amended in July 1975, is empowered to stabilize the prices of agricultural products to assist the agricultural industry in realizing fair returns for labour and investment, and to maintain a fair relationship between prices received by farmers and the costs of goods and services that they buy.

The amended act provides that the board shall take action to stabilize the prices of named agricultural commodities at prescribed prices. These commodities are slaughter cattle, hogs, sheep, industrial milk, industrial cream, corn, soybeans, and oats and barley produced outside the designated areas as defined in the Canadian Wheat Board Act. The prescribed price of a named commodity is calculated at 90% of the five-year average of market price, or at such higher percentage as the Governor in Council may determine, indexed to reflect the cash cost of production of that commodity in that year as compared to the five years immediately preceding. The Governor in Council may also designate other commodities for support under the act on a similar basis. The board has supported at one time or another, in addition to the nine named commodities, apples, asparagus, blueberries, carrots, cherries, eggs, flowers, fowl, honey, peaches, pears, plums, potatoes, raspberries, rutabagas, sugar beets, sunflower seeds, tomatoes and wool. The board may stabilize the price of any product by offer to purchase, by making deficiency payments or such other payments for the benefit of producers as may be authorized.

In stabilizing prices of certain commodities by means of assistance payments, the Stabilization Act has assisted the agricultural industry in balancing production and demand. The act guarantees minimum returns to producers for their product based on national average market prices and production costs.

Since the inception of the act the cost of stabilization programs has totalled over $2 billion. The board maintains a revolving fund of $250 million; losses incurred are made up by Parliamentary appropriations and any surplus is paid back to the Consolidated Revenue Fund. An advisory committee, named by the Minister of Agriculture and composed of farmers or representatives of farm organizations, advises the board and the minister on matters relating to stabilization.

The Agricultural Products Board was established in 1951 to administer contracts with other countries for the purchase or sale of agricultural products and to perform other commodity operations as Canadian needs may dictate. The board's recent activities have included the purchasing of surplus Canadian commodities with resulting improvement in producer prices. Some of these commodities have been processed, packaged and delivered to the World Food Program as part of Canada's commitment to the Food and Agriculture Organization of the United Nations.

The Crop Insurance Act was passed in 1959 (RSC 1970, c.C-36) to permit the federal government to assist the provinces in making all-risk crop insurance available to farmers across Canada on a shared-cost basis under the terms and conditions of federal-provincial agreements. Crop insurance is intended to protect the farmer against unforeseen losses by spreading their impact over a number of years. The initiative for establishing crop insurance rests with the provinces and schemes may be organized to meet provincial requirements for insurable crops and areas.

Under the act, the federal government contributes a portion of premium costs and/or administration costs and shares the risk by providing loans or re-insurance when indemnities greatly exceed premiums and reserves. Commencing with the 1973 crop year the farmers pay 50% of the total premiums required to make the schemes self-sustaining. The remainder is contributed by the federal government where the province elects to pay all administrative costs, or the province may elect to share the remaining premium and all the administrative costs equally with the federal government.

In the 1975-76 crop year 94,000 farmers purchased some $990 million in crop insurance coverage. Premiums totalled $98 million (including government contributions). The number of farmers participating increased by 12% over 1974-75 while coverage increased by 47%. Saskatchewan and Alberta both showed substantial increases in participation and coverage.

Yields of most crops in 1975 were average or above average all across the country and still some $66 million was paid out in indemnities. Losses in all provinces were, for the most part, of a localized nature. Hail damage in both Saskatchewan and Manitoba was somewhat heavier than normal resulting in some substantial losses. Parts of northern and western Manitoba experienced excessive rainfall in late summer and early fall. Ontario and Quebec also had areas where excessive moisture resulted in crop losses.

The crop insurance program continued to expand in 1976 with 98,000 farmers carrying over $1 billion of insurance protection. The total premium income, including government contributions, was expected to reach $115 million.

Throughout the growing season weather conditions were generally good. Average to above average yields were forecast for all provinces, with losses confined to localized pockets of hail, drought and excessive moisture.

The Canadian Dairy Commission was established by the Canadian Dairy Commission Act in 1966 and became operative on April 1, 1967. The commission is directed by three commissioners, and its objectives are "to provide efficient producers of milk and cream with the opportunity of obtaining a fair return for their labour and investment and to provide consumers of dairy products with a continuous and adequate supply of dairy products of high quality".

The commission is authorized to stabilize prices of major dairy products through offers to purchase these products at fixed prices. This establishes stable prices in the interests of both producers and consumers. The commission may borrow from the Minister of Finance the funds required for such purchases to a maximum of $300 million.

The commission administers the payment of funds provided by the government for subsidies to producers of manufacturing milk and cream. These payments supplement returns to producers from the market and permit market prices to be kept at reasonable levels. Each producer is eligible for subsidy on shipments covered by his market share quota. The commission, indirectly, pools returns to producers from products sold on the domestic and export markets through an export equalization fund. Money for this is collected by levies from producers in all provinces (except Newfoundland) under the Market Sharing

Quota Program and remitted to the commission. The funds are used to equalize export prices with domestic prices for any products exported below domestic prices over a multiple-year period. More details on activities of the commission with regard to marketing may be found in Section 11.7.2.2.

The Canadian Livestock Feed Board, established by the Livestock Feed Assistance Act, is a Crown agency reporting to Parliament through the Minister of Agriculture. It has four main objectives: to ensure that feed grain is available to meet the needs of livestock feeders; that adequate storage space in eastern Canada is available for feed grain to meet the needs of livestock feeders; that the price of feed grain in eastern Canada and in British Columbia remains reasonably stable; and that there be fair equalization of feed grain prices in eastern Canada and in British Columbia.

To these ends, the board may make payments related to the cost of feed grain storage and transportation, the latter payments having been made since 1941. Under the Feed Grain Assistance Regulations of the Appropriations Act, the original program was initiated in October 1941 to provide a market for western feed grains and to enable livestock feeders in eastern Canada and British Columbia to obtain supplies at a cost that would maintain livestock and poultry production at a high level. Since April 1967, the freight subsidy has been administered by the Canadian Livestock Feed Board under the authority of the Livestock Feed Assistance Act. This program has been modified over the years to encourage better utilization of both transport and storage facilities. Initially, it was applied only to feed grains produced in the Prairie provinces and designated for domestic livestock consumption in eastern Canada and British Columbia. Subsequently it was extended to the movement of Ontario corn and wheat into the Atlantic provinces and Quebec.

The Feed Freight Assistance Program, as it has come to be known, underwent substantial changes as part of the domestic feed grain policy announced by the federal government on May 31, 1976. These changes, which became effective August 1, 1976, included reductions of $4 a ton ($4.41/t) in rates of assistance to British Columbia, $6 a ton ($6.61/t) in rates of assistance to Ontario and western Quebec (as far east as Montreal), with lesser reductions in central Quebec. Rates of assistance to eastern Quebec and the Atlantic provinces remain unchanged. In total, expenditures under the program will be reduced from recent levels of about $20 million a year to an estimated $11 million. The volume of eligible feed grain moved under the program has amounted to approximately 2.8 million tons (2.54 million t) a year.

The Livestock Feed Assistance Act also provides for the board to buy, transport, store and sell feed grains when authorized by the Governor in Council.

The Farm Credit Corporation. The Farm Credit Corporation (FCC) was established by the Farm Credit Act as successor to the Canadian Farm Loan Board. It is responsible for the administration of the Farm Credit Act and the Farm Syndicates Credit Act and acts as an agent of Agriculture Canada in administering the Land Transfer Plan of the Small Farm Development Program.

An advisory committee of farmers and other qualified persons, appointed by the Minister of Agriculture, advises the corporation with respect to policy. Responsibility for lending decisions and operations is decentralized into seven branch offices, one for the Atlantic region and one for each of the other provinces. Field officers work out of 112 offices across Canada.

The Farm Credit Act is designed to meet the long-term mortgage credit needs of Canadian farmers, and provides three types of mortgage loans. Borrowers must be of legal age to enter into a mortgage agreement, and loans may be made only to Canadian citizens or those with landed immigrant status. All loans are repayable on an amortized basis within a period not exceeding 30 years. Funds for lending under the Farm Credit Act are borrowed from the Minister of Finance. In the fiscal year ending March 31, 1976 the FCC approved 9,945 loans for a total of $641 million, a record year.

The Farm Syndicates Credit Act authorizes the Farm Credit Corporation to make loans to syndicates of three or more farmers with respect to joint purchase and use of machinery, equipment or buildings. Amounts owing by the corporation on this account may not exceed $25 million, and loans are repayable over a period not exceeding 15 years for building and permanently installed equipment and seven years for mobile machinery. In 1975-76, the FCC lent $4,542,422 to syndicates, representing 231 loans.

The Small Farm Development Program came into effect in September 1972. Under the Land Transfer Plan of this program the FCC makes assistance available in the form of a grant to owners of small farms who wish to sell for retirement or any other reason. During 1975-76 the FCC approved $4,568,474 in vendor assistance grants to 1,475 farmers, and a total of $1,783,000 was approved under the special credit provisions to help 104 farmers expand their operations.

The National Farm Products Marketing Council (NFPMC) was established by the Farm Products Marketing Agencies Act in 1972 to advise the Minister of Agriculture on all matters pertaining to the establishment of marketing agencies. It reviews their operations, assists them in promoting more effective marketing of farm products, and coordinates related activities of provincial governments as well as the efforts of producers to establish marketing plans. The first application for the establishment of a national agency was submitted by egg producers. The Canadian Egg Marketing Agency was created in December 1972 and was followed by the Canadian Turkey Marketing Agency, proclaimed in December 1973.

Membership of the NFPMC was expanded in July 1975 to include representatives of consumer, labour and business interests. In July 1976 the need for supplemental and temporary agreements was eliminated by a permanent egg marketing agreement between the provinces and the federal government.

The operation of the national turkey and egg marketing agencies has led to a great deal of interest on the part of producers of other commodities to establish such organizations. The NFPMC has been approached by representatives of producers of corn, tobacco, pregnant mares' urine and various fruits and vegetables. Proposals to establish a national marketing agency were received from the Canadian Broiler Council, representing broiler chicken producers. These various groups have indicated support for the concept of supply management being applied at the national level.

The Farm Improvement Loans Act, administered by the Department of Finance, is designed to facilitate credit by way of loans made by the chartered banks and other lenders toward the improvement or development of a farm. It includes the purchase of implements and livestock; the purchase and installation of agricultural equipment or a farm electrical system; major repairs or overhaul of agricultural implements and equipment; fencing or works for drainage on a farm; construction, repair or alteration of farm buildings including the family dwelling; and the purchase of additional farm land. Credit is provided on security related to the purchase or project and on terms suited to the individual borrower.

The legislation has been continued through extensions since 1945, usually for three-year periods, the latest from July 1, 1974 to June 30, 1977. The maximum repayment period for land purchase is 15 years, for vehicles three years, and for all other purposes 10 years. The maximum loan or amount that may be outstanding to a borrower at any one time is $50,000. From inception of the program to December 31, 1975, loans amounting to about $3,362 million were made. During the same period, payments were made to the banks under a guarantee provision in respect of 5,715 claims amounting to $6.6 million, representing a loss ratio of one fifth of one percent. In the first six months of 1976, a total of 11,275 loans amounting to some $58.7 million were made and 42 claims under the guarantee were made for a value of $97,000.

The Prairie Grain Advance Payments Act which came into force on November 25, 1957 and was subsequently amended, provides for interest-free advance payments to producers in western Canada for farm-stored threshed wheat, oats and barley. The rate of advance payment is prescribed by regulation annually, and the rate of repayment is the same as the rate of advance. The maximum total advance is governed by quota levels, also prescribed by regulation, and may not exceed $15,000 for any individual producer for the crop year.

The act also contains provisions for special advance payments covering unharvested grain and the drying of grain. The maximum total advances receivable for these special advances are $3,500 and $1,500 respectively.

Provincial government services   11.3

Departments of agriculture   11.3.1

Newfoundland. Government agricultural services in Newfoundland are provided by the Department of Forestry and Agriculture. Under the general direction of the minister, the deputy minister is responsible for administration of the department and three assistant deputy ministers are responsible for program evaluation and development for the principal branches of the organization: Agriculture, Lands and Forestry. Programs are carried to the public by the Regional Services Branch. Three regional supervisors, with agricultural representatives, each serve the public in a specified area known as an agriculture management unit.

Departmental policies in support of the agriculture industry include: a land clearing grant for private farmers; a capital assistance grant for purchase of buildings and equipment; subsidized provision of agricultural limestone; bonus payments for retention of quality breeding stock; grants-in-aid for construction of vegetable storage facilities; a subsidized regional pasture program; grants to agricultural societies; and technical information and farm management services.

Departmental assistance is also given under the provincial Farm Development Loan Board, the Newfoundland Marketing Board and the Newfoundland Farm Products Corporation.

Prince Edward Island. The Prince Edward Island Department of Agriculture and Forestry is composed of the following branches and divisions: the Field Services Branch which consists of the Farm Management Section, the District Offices Section, the Farm Development Section, the Livestock Section and the Crops and Engineering Section; the Forestry Branch, which consists of the Forest Nursery Division and the Bunbury Nursery Division; the Management Services Group which contains the Economics, Marketing and Statistics Division, the Information Division, Administration, and Grain Elevators; the Technical Services Branch; and the Veterinary and Dairy Branch.

The work of the department is aimed at serving the needs of farm families in PEI, especially in efforts to stabilize farm incomes and improve farm management ability. Programs and policies range from 4-H soil-testing competitions and developing individual plans for the family farm development program to crop insurance promotion, working with commodity groups and providing up-to-date production recommendations.

Nova Scotia. The Nova Scotia Department of Agriculture and Marketing directs the government's agricultural program by implementing provincial agricultural policies. The department is administered by a minister, deputy minister and branch directors concerned primarily with extension and economics, horticulture and biology, livestock services, market development, soils and crops, and formal agricultural education through the Nova Scotia Agricultural College located in Truro. The department is particularly interested in encouraging rural people to help themselves through such organizations as the Nova Scotia Federation of Agriculture, the Nova Scotia Fruit Growers' Association and other commodity-oriented groups.

New Brunswick. Provincial government agricultural policy and programs in New Brunswick are administered and directed by the Department of Agriculture and Rural Development. Under the minister, the department is administered by a deputy minister, an assistant deputy minister and the directors of branches concerned with administration, extension, livestock and poultry, veterinary services, communications and marketing, plant industry, agricultural engineering, home economics, credit unions and cooperatives, and planning and development. It also has a Farm Adjustment Board, a Natural Products Control Board, a Dairy Products Commission, and a Forest Products Commission.

Quebec. The aim of the Quebec Department of Agriculture is to promote agricultural development through the best possible use of the province's resources by providing up-to-date advice and technical assistance to farmers. Modernization of agriculture and raising the standard of living in rural areas are of particular concern.

The minister responsible for agriculture directs the department and the Quebec Sugar Refinery, the Farm Credit Bureau, the Agricultural Marketing Authority and the Crop Insurance Administration, the Société québécoise d'initiatives agro-alimentaires and the Commission administrative des régimes d'assurance-stabilisation des revenues agricoles, each operated by an autonomous board of directors. Under the general direction of the minister, the deputy minister is responsible for administration of the department, information, special projects, agricultural organizations, policy coordination and the planning and execution of programs established under these policies. Three assistant deputy ministers are responsible for the principal branches of the organization: Production; Research, Education and Administration; and Marketing.

The Production Branch makes its principal services and divisions directly available to the farmer: veterinary services, animal husbandry, artificial insemination, regional offices and laboratories, engineering and plant products. Veterinary services include work in the health of animals field, the contributory animal health insurance plan and the provincial laboratories at Quebec and St-Hyacinthe as well as the veterinary medicines distribution centre at St-Hyacinthe. The animal husbandry section deals with dairy and butcher cattle, pork, fowl, sheep and horses, fur-bearing animals and domestic rabbits. The artificial insemination service works closely with breeders' groups. Twelve regional offices and five laboratories, an information section and a young farmers section are responsible for adult education, technical training, regional development and soils, and plant and animal development. The engineering section is concerned with mechanized operations, farm buildings and agricultural water services. The plant production section advises and assists farmers on field crops, horticulture, maple products and apiculture. The section assesses damage to uninsured crops, and operates two laboratories conducting soil and plant tissue analysis, the Manicouagan potato breeding centre, and the pilot blueberry processing plant at Normandin. It is also responsible for financial and administrative management of the St-Bruno blueberry freezing plant.

In the Research, Education and Administration Branch, the Research and Education Division is responsible for various organizations and services, the La Pocatière and St-Hyacinthe institutes of agricultural technology and a research section dealing with crop protection, soils and research stations. The assistant deputy minister in charge of the branch is the president of the Quebec Research Council, the coordination and promotion centre for most of the agricultural research carried out in Quebec directing research into specific fields to meet the special needs of Quebec agriculture. Its work is coordinated with the Quebec Plant Products Board, the Quebec Animal Husbandry Board, and the Quebec Products Board and priorities are determined in cooperation with those organizations. In addition it maintains close liaison with federal government researchers. Administrative and financial services are also attached to this branch, as is the personnel section, which includes civil defence.

The Marketing Sector serves both agriculture and the consumer and includes a Marketing Branch and its three divisions: economic studies, marketing and technical assistance to the food industry. The Inspection Branch groups the following divisions: crop products, dairy products and meat products. The assistant deputy minister in charge of marketing is responsible for quality control, the chemical foods laboratory and fraud prevention and suppression.

Ontario. The Ontario Ministry of Agriculture and Food conducts a variety of programs to develop a sound agricultural industry. Most assistance is given through self-help programs which benefit the individual farmer. The ministry administers 48 separate legislative acts, some of which are regulatory, on an industry-wide basis. The ministry has 54 county and district offices.

Under the Federal-Provincial Rural Development Agreement, 1975-77, the province shares equally with the Government of Canada the cost of certain rural development programs. In Ontario, ARDA is committed to programs of farm enlargement and adjustment, rural resource development and assistance to rural industries to increase employment opportunities for rural people.

Agricultural Manpower Services Branch, in cooperation with the Ministry of Colleges and Universities and the federal Department of Manpower and Immigration, assists in the identification, development and implementation of Agricultural Manpower Training programs.

Under the Federal-Provincial Agricultural Manpower Agreement, financial assistance is provided to Ontario fruit, field grown vegetable and tobacco growers for the construction and renovation of accommodation for seasonal farm workers.

The branch assists in the recruitment and placement of full-time agricultural workers for Ontario farmers. Also, in conjunction with this, the branch cooperates with other countries in providing international programs for young agriculturists.

The Soils and Crops Branch conducts programs of applied research to provide farmers with specific recommendations for their areas. Soil and crop specialists work with local branches of the Ontario Soil and Crop Improvement Association and supervise county inspectors who enforce the Weed Control Act. Extension horticulturists provide specialized advice to producers of fruit, vegetables, mushrooms, greenhouse crops and flowers.

The programs of the Veterinary Services Branch are administered by three sections. The laboratory section, through six veterinary services laboratories, provides diagnostic, investigational, consultation and extension services and administers the Fur Farms Act. The meat inspection section administers the Meat Inspection Act. The regulatory and communicable diseases section administers acts, policies and programs concerned with disease control, animal care and sale of livestock medicines.

The Live Stock Branch supervises numerous livestock improvement programs and administers a number of laws adopted by the provincial legislature relating to livestock in general. Livestock improvement programs include dairy herd improvement; beef cattle, sheep and swine performance testing; ram premium policy; the federal-provincial sheep transportation assistance policy; the testing of feed samples, a computerized ration formulation program; and northern Ontario livestock assistance. The branch makes grants to regional livestock clubs that hold sales and livestock shows, and sponsors exhibits of livestock outside the province. A staff of specialists provides feeding and management advice to livestock producers.

The Ontario Stock Yards Board, which operates under the federal Livestock and Livestock Products Act, was established to provide a marketing service for Ontario livestock producers and to protect their bargaining power.

The Crop Insurance Commission of Ontario, a branch of the ministry, offers contributory insurance against weather, insect and disease damage to winter wheat, spring grain, hay, corn (both silage and grain); soybeans, white beans; tomatoes, green peas, green and wax beans, lima beans and sweet corn for processing; red beets, apples, peaches, grapes, sweet and sour cherries, pears, set onions, seed onions, coloured beans, new seeding and flue-cured tobacco, a burley tobacco, seed corn and flax. The total cost of administration is paid by the Ontario government and 50% of the premium is paid by the federal government.

The Milk Commission of Ontario is an administrative tribunal to which dairy producers, processors and others may appeal. The commission cooperates with the Ontario Milk Marketing Board and the Ontario Dairy Council in dairy policy planning and development.

The Milk Industry Branch was established in 1973 to assume responsibility for all regulative and administrative work required under the Milk Act, the Oleomargarine Act, and the Edible Oil Products Act which was previously done by the Milk Commission of Ontario. The branch administers the milk quality, fluid milk, milk products, plant record audit and central milk testing programs which also includes the operation of infra-red analyzing of milk for butterfat, protein and lactose.

The Farm Products Inspection Branch inspects fruit and vegetables for grade, and promotes improved methods of disease control, grading, packaging, marketing, handling, storing and transportation. Under the Ontario Farm Products Marketing Board, a branch of the Ministry of Agriculture and Food, 21 producer boards market some 40 commodities with a total market value of approximately $1 billion annually.

The Ontario Food Council Branch has the broad responsibility of finding methods to coordinate better the marketing of Ontario agricultural and food products in Ontario, other Canadian provinces and abroad, and comprises representatives of producers, processors, wholesalers, distributors and consumers. The Ontario Food Terminal, operating under the Ontario Food Terminal Act, offers farmers the services of one of the largest volume wholesale fruit and vegetable markets in Canada.

Research and education are administered by the Education and Research and Special Services Division. An advisory body, the Agricultural Research Institute of Ontario, reviews current programs of research and recommends priorities.

The provincial entomologist reports on insect control programs, and the provincial apiarist is responsible for reporting on the bee and honey industry.

The Extension Branch is represented in each of the 54 county and district offices. Research developments and advice on farm management are relayed directly to farmers by agricultural representatives. Agricultural engineers are located throughout the province. The northern Ontario assistance policies are also administered by the branch, which assists the 4-H clubs and the Junior Farmers' Association of Ontario.

The Home Economics Branch conducts an extension program for rural adult groups and for young people's 4-H homemaking clubs. Programs deal with the study of foods, nutrition, clothing, textiles, home furnishings, home crafts and family and community life.

The Information Branch publishes and distributes several hundred publications on agriculture and food, home gardening and homemaking. News releases, radio tapes and television film clips are used to convey information to farmers. The film library distributes more than 2,000 films annually. The Market Information Service provides up-to-date commodity quotations and farm weather reports to the media and individual producers on a daily basis using radio and audio-tape facilities.

The Agricultural and Horticultural Societies Branch offers advice and financial aid to agricultural and horticultural societies and ploughmen's associations and manages the International Ploughing Match and Farm Machinery Show. The Economics Branch does research into marketing, policy, production, land use and dairying, and works with Statistics Canada to collect and publish statistics on farm production and marketing.

The Food Land Development Branch provides an agricultural perspective to land use planning activities. Staff contribute to and comment on official plans, amendments to plans and subdivision applications as well as project plans for hydro, highways, pipelines and other facilities. Interim management of government-owned agricultural lands is accomplished through a land lease program. The branch administers the Drainage Act and the Tile Drainage Act to provide loans for draining agricultural lands. Staff also provide policy recommendations on alternative land use programs.

Manitoba. The Department of Agriculture serves Manitoba through four divisions: Marketing and Production; Rural Development; Regional; and Management and Operations. Within these divisions are the following branches.

The Animal Industry Branch develops and administers programs that encourage the improvement and efficient production of all classes of livestock, including poultry. It is also involved in helping to improve the quality of dairy products at the producer and processor level by means of inspection, consultation, education and laboratory quality control. In cooperation with federal departments the branch administers several acts that provide consumer protection and ensure a supply of high quality livestock products.

The Soils and Crops Branch encourages the development, production and improvement of cereal, forage and special crops and horticulture, and promotes proper land use through policies that encourage good field crop husbandry, soil conservation, land development and weed control. The Economics Branch deals with educational and development programs in farm management and agricultural economics, carries out special studies and supervises the farm diversification program. The Marketing Branch performs a market development, research and analysis function aimed at establishing long-term markets for agricultural products. Market intelligence is provided to the various branches of the department, to producers and to agribusiness. The Veterinary Services Branch operates a diagnostic laboratory for animal diseases, administers the Veterinary Services District Act and the Veterinary Scholarship Fund Act, and works in cooperation with practising veterinarians and the federal Health of Animals Branch in the control of livestock and poultry diseases.

The Technical Services Branch provides programs in agricultural engineering, entomology and beekeeping and offers technical assistance to rural residents installing modern farm water systems. The Community and Family Programs Branch carries out educational and developmental programs in 4-H and youth, agricultural manpower, community affairs, rural counselling and resource analysis. It also administers the Agricultural Extension Centre at Brandon for adult education programs. The Communications Services provides press, radio and television services to all mass media outlets and produces and distributes over 570,000 booklets, leaflets and circulars each year. The Regional Division includes five regions with 38 district offices, each staffed with agricultural representatives. The major role of this division is extension of educational programs and advisory information in agriculture and rural development.

Separate from the divisions and reporting directly to the minister is the Manitoba Marketing Board which supervises the operation of producer marketing boards responsible for the orderly marketing of hogs, milk, vegetables, eggs, broiler chickens, root crops, turkeys and honey. Also reporting to the minister is the Manitoba Agricultural Products' Marketing Commission established in May 1975. The commission assists in marketing regulated agricultural products outside the control of producer boards. In addition, bi-weekly reports on feed grain prices are prepared.

Saskatchewan. Saskatchewan Agriculture is composed of three main divisions: the Production and Marketing Division, the Farm Resources Development Division and the Extension and Rural Development Division. In addition, the department includes Support Services and a Planning and Research Secretariat.

The Production and Marketing Division administers 27 acts and regulations designed to improve production, handling, processing and marketing of specific agricultural commodities. It includes the following branches: Plant Industry, Animal Industry, Veterinary Services, Agricultural Engineering Services, and Marketing and Economics; and the following agencies: the Milk Control Board, Saskatchewan Crop Insurance Corporation, Saskatchewan Hog Marketing Commission and the Saskatchewan Sheep and Wool Marketing Commission.

The Extension and Rural Development Division is responsible for development and performance of farm units. It coordinates the activities of all department personnel who deal regularly with the public. The division consists of the Regional Extension Services Branch and the Family Farm Improvement Branch. The Regional Extension Services Branch, organized into six regions, offers guidance in agricultural adjustment programs. Its work is carried out by 43 agricultural representatives stationed throughout the province and a supporting staff of regional specialists. The Family Farm Improvement Branch gives farmers technical and professional advice on farm buildings, farmstead planning, water supplies, waste disposal, mechanization and materials handling.

The Extension and Rural Development Division coordinates activities of the FarmStart Corporation. The corporation administers a credit and grant program for persons establishing or expanding livestock production as a means of developing profitable farming operations.

The Farm Resources Development Division is primarily responsible for the development of land and water resources for agricultural use. It consists of the Lands Branch and the Conservation and Land Improvement Branch. The division is also responsible for construction work for the Saskatchewan River Irrigation Project and for development work in community pastures. The Lands Branch administers over 7,000,000 acres (2 832 799 ha) of provincial lands for agricultural use. More than 12,000 farmers and ranchers lease land from the Lands Branch as full units or as additions to their private holdings. The remaining 1,500,000 acres (607 028 ha) are in provincial and cooperative pastures providing grazing for over 150,000 head of cattle belonging to more than 5,500 farmers.

The Saskatchewan Land Bank Commission and the Agricultural Implements Board are included in the Farm Resource Development Division. The Saskatchewan Land Bank Commission provides an alternative for farmers not wishing to commit themselves immediately to a heavy investment in land. It also provides Saskatchewan land-owners with a continuing sales opportunity for their land, enables new farmers to commence farming independent of substantial family assistance and permits farmers with insufficient land to add to their holding without raising large sums of money for capital investment. Major activities of the Agricultural Implements Board include registration of implement distributors, licensing and inspection of retail vendors, and investigating complaints regarding warranties and repair parts availability.

Alberta. Activities of the Department of Agriculture are coordinated by an executive committee made up of the directors of its 11 divisions, the deputy minister, three assistant deputy ministers and the director of administration. In addition, the Planning and Research Secretariat, in consultation with agribusiness, farm organizations and researchers, advises the department with regard to planning and policy.

The office of the Farmers' Advocate ensures protection of the rights of individual farmers. The office investigates problems and complaints of farmers not relating to the provincial government and its agencies.

The Marketing Sector develops programs and policies that support all parts of the marketing chain. Within this sector there are four "action oriented" sections: the Market Development Division emphasizes both export and domestic market expansion, and provides market information; the Agricultural Processing Branch encourages and supports the development of new foods manufactured from Alberta farm products; the Commodity Development Branch works with producer commodity groups concerned with marketing; and the Nutrition and Food Marketing Branch provides consumer education programs primarily in urban areas. The Market Intelligence Division supports the other divisions by providing statistical and analytical data on all segments of the Alberta food industry so that improved decision making may lead to increased income.

Two developmental divisions of Alberta Agriculture are responsible for policies and programs designed to ensure the survival of the family farm and promote the interests of rural communities. The Extension Division coordinates the extension programs of the department. In association with other extension agencies, it operates mainly through 64 district extension offices coordinated by six regional directors, complemented by an expanding staff of regional specialists in livestock, plant industry, engineering and home economics. Within the Farm Development Division are several branches dealing with engineering, home design and agricultural services. Programs in the 4-H and Home Economics Division include home management, nutrition, family living, and 4-H leadership development. The Alberta Agricultural Development Corporation guarantees or makes loans for the development of agricultural enterprises.

The Plant Industry Division administers programs and policies relating to crop improvement and protection; pest control, weeds, soils and fertilizers; horticulture, apiculture and special projects. It operates a horticultural research centre at Brooks and an extensive tree nursery at Oliver which supplies millions of trees yearly for farm planting and reforestation.

The Animal Industry Division administers legislation, policies and programs in the broad areas of livestock and poultry production and in processing and marketing. Included are: setting standards for and approving public sales of sires; record of performance programs for standards and qualifications for the artificial insemination (AI) industry; supervising feeder associations; brand registration and inspection; licensing of butchers, livestock dealers, stockyard and AI technicians; pound districts and sale of horned cattle. The testing, grading and purchasing of raw produce by all dairy plants are under regulation, as are standards of construction, manufacture, processing, sanitation and temperature control for dairy and frozen-food plants. A regular cow-testing service to provide the basis for breeding, feeding and culling dairy cattle is available to dairy producers, and chemical and bacteriological analyses are conducted for industrial directives. Licences are issued to poultry hatcheries, wholesalers, first receivers and truckers, and programs are conducted for control of pullorum-typhoid diseases of chicken- and turkey-hatching egg supply flocks. Extension programs, cost studies, disease tests and surveys, and research projects with respect to poultry, are also carried out.

The Veterinary Services Division provides diagnoses of livestock and poultry diseases and conducts investigations of disease conditions. It provides lecture service for the University of Alberta and for other groups and promotes policies aimed at reducing losses by means of disease control, stockyard inspection and swine health programs.

The Irrigation Division assists farmers in ensuring the economic viability of irrigated farm units by better conservation and management of the land, water, labour and capital resources available; its functions include recommending policies and implementation of programs related to overall irrigation system improvement.

British Columbia. The Department of Agriculture comprises five divisions: Administration, General Services, Policy Development and Planning, Production and Marketing, and Special Services. Administration includes Accounts and Personnel. General Services embraces Agricultural and Rural Development (ARDA), Farm Financial Services, Farm Products Finance, Information and Property Management. Policy Development and Planning is responsible for statistics. The Production and Marketing Division is responsible for the following branches: Agricultural Development and Extension, Apiary, Farm Economics,

Field Crops, Horticulture, Livestock and Dairy Herd Improvement, Marketing and Poultry branches. Special Services includes the Engineering, Soils, Entomology, Plant Pathology, Veterinary, Dairy and Youth Development branches. The British Columbia Marketing and Milk Board report directly to the minister.

In addition to the headquarters staff at Victoria, the department maintains 19 district offices in various parts of the province, a veterinary laboratory and poultry-testing station at Abbotsford, a beef-testing station at Kamloops and dairy and entomology laboratories at Vancouver and Cloverdale respectively; soil-testing facilities are installed at Kelowna.

11.3.2   Agricultural education

All of the provinces of central and western Canada have agricultural colleges associated with universities giving undergraduate and postgraduate courses in agricultural science and home economics. Ontario, Quebec and Saskatchewan have degree-granting veterinary colleges. In addition, all of these provinces have agricultural colleges, schools of agriculture or diploma courses offering basic training to young people intending to return to farms or interested in employment in businesses allied with agriculture.

In Alberta the three agricultural colleges — Fairview, Olds and Vermilion (now Lakeland College) — have broadened their curricula in agriculture, maintained their applied research interests, and met the diversified interests of rural communities by offering programs in business education and trades training. During 1975 the 62-year-old Vermilion Agricultural College lost its identity as an agricultural college through its incorporation into the newly established inter-provincial Lakeland College. Although the college administrative office is located in Lloydminster, Vermilion campus facilities serve the agricultural education needs of Alberta and Saskatchewan residents in the Lakeland region.

In Quebec agricultural science is taught at McGill and Laval universities. The Department of Education offers a course in farm management and operation at two CEGEPs, and 15 school boards offer vocational training in agriculture in secondary schools. The Quebec Department of Agriculture also operates two institutes of agricultural technology. The Education, Research and Special Services Division of the Ontario Ministry of Agriculture and Food offers five diploma-course programs at the Ontario Agricultural College, University of Guelph, as well as at the colleges of agricultural technology at Centralia, Kemptville, New Liskeard and Ridgetown. In the Atlantic provinces, agricultural education is centred in the Nova Scotia Agricultural College at Truro, NS. This college provides the first two years of a BSc program in Agricultural Science (three years in Agricultural Engineering) with the final two years provided by other faculties in eastern Canada. In addition, the college offers several technical programs associated with farming and agribusiness and a variety of vocational courses designed to update farmers and other industry personnel.

11.4   Yearly statistics of agriculture

The collection, compilation and publication of statistics relating to agriculture is the responsibility of Statistics Canada. Valuable information is obtained through the censuses, through partial-coverage mailed questionnaire surveys, through probability surveys, and from the administrative records of government operations.

Statistics Canada collects and publishes primary and secondary statistics of agriculture on an annual and monthly basis. Primary statistics relate mainly to reporting crop conditions, crop and livestock estimates, wages of farm labour and prices received by farmers for their products. Secondary statistics relate to farm income and expenditure, per capita food consumption, marketing of grain and livestock, dairying, milling and sugar industries and cold storage holdings. In the collection of annual and monthly statistics, the Canada Department of

Agriculture and various provincial departments, as well as such agencies as the Canadian Grain Commission and the Canadian Wheat Board, contribute statistical data and aid directly in Statistics Canada survey work. Thousands of farmers throughout Canada send in reports voluntarily and dealers and processors also provide much valuable data. The figures in this section do not include estimates for Newfoundland; agriculture plays a minor part in Newfoundland's economy and commercial production of most agricultural products is small. Subsection details are given for the most recent year available with earlier comparisons; figures for the latest year are subject to revision and it should be noted that many of those given for earlier years have been revised since the publication of the *Canada Year Book 1975.*

Farm income   11.4.1

Cash receipts from farming operations. Estimates of cash receipts from farming operations include cash revenue from the sale of farm products, Canadian Wheat Board participation payments on previous years' grain crops, cash advances on farm-stored grains and deferred income from the sale of grain in western Canada, deficiency payments made by the Agricultural Stabilization Board and supplementary payments. Cash receipts from the sale of farm products include the returns from all sales of agricultural products except those associated with direct inter-farm transfers. The prices used to value all products sold are prices to farmers at the farm level; they include any subsidies, bonuses and premiums that can be attributed to specific products but do not include storage, transportation, processing and handling charges which are not actually received by farmers.

Total cash receipts from farming operations for 1975, excluding supplementary payments, are estimated at $9,877 million for Canada, 12.0% above the revised value of $8,821 million in 1974 (Table 11.1). This gain can be attributed to expansion in cash receipts from the sale of both crop and livestock products. Notable increases occurred in sales of western grains but other crop products showed declines in 1975. Cash receipts from the sale of livestock products showed gains for all items except poultry and eggs (Table 11.2).

Farmers also received supplementary payments amounting to $30 million during 1975, down considerably from the $57 million received during 1974. These payments in 1974 and 1975 included those made by federal and provincial governments under the provisions of various crop assistance programs for farmers affected by adverse weather conditions, payments made under the Prairie Farm Assistance Act, and payments made by the province of Quebec to beef, hog, dairy, poultry and potato producers due to poor economic conditions. Total cash receipts from farming operations and supplementary payments in 1975 amounted to $9,907 million, 11.6% above the estimate of $8,879 million in 1974.

Farm net income. Two different estimates of farm net income from farming operations are prepared by Statistics Canada. *Realized net income* is obtained by adding together farm cash receipts from farming operations, supplementary payments and the value of income in kind, and deducting farm operating expenses and depreciation charges. This estimate of farm net income therefore represents the amount of income from farming that operators have left for family living, personal taxes and investment. The second estimate is referred to as *total net income,* and is obtained by adjusting realized net income to take into account changes occurring in inventories of livestock and stocks of field crops on farms between the beginning and end of the year. This estimate is used in calculating the contribution of agriculture to the "income" component of the system of national accounts and for making comparisons with net income of non-farm business enterprises (Table 11.3).

It is estimated that in Canada (excluding Newfoundland), realized net income of farm operators from farming operations amounted to $4,176.5 million in 1975, an 8.1% increase over the revised 1974 amount of $3,864.4 million.

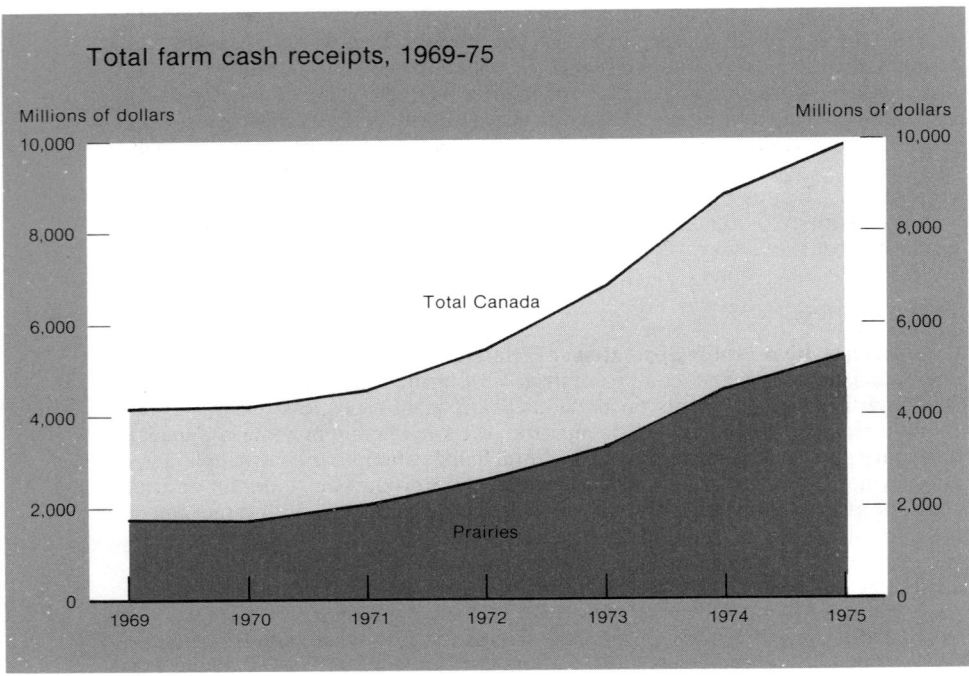

Total farm cash receipts, 1969-75

Millions of dollars

Total Canada

Prairies

Contributing to this increase in realized net income was an estimated 11.6% expansion in realized gross income to $10,829.4 million in 1975 from the 1974 figure of $9,706.0 million. All components of gross income except supplementary payments contributed to the increase with the largest, cash receipts from the sale of agricultural products, rising by 12.0% in 1975.

Farm operators incurred operating expenses and depreciation charges totalling an estimated $6,652.9 million, 13.9% above the 1974 value of $5,841.6 million. Although expenditures on most farm input items were substantially above the 1974 levels, some leading contributors to the increase in expenses were fertilizers, pesticides, wages for hired labour and interest on farm business debt.

Total farm net income from farming operations (realized net income adjusted for inventory changes) is estimated at $4,327.9 million for 1975. In 1975 a $151.4 million increase in inventories was recorded, in contrast to a negative change in 1974 of $91.3 million. This expansion in inventories was due partly to an increase in farm-held stocks of products.

11.4.2   Field crops

Canada's 1975 wheat crop, estimated at 627.5 million bu, (17.08 million t) was 28.5% above the 1974 crop of 488.5 million bu (13.29 million t) and 5.7% above the 1973 crop of 593.7 million bu (16.16 million t). The average yield per acre at 26.8 bu (1.802 tonnes per hectare) was 21.3% more than the 1974 yield of 22.1 bu (1.486 t/ha) and 6.8% more than the 1973 yield of 25.1 bu (1.688 t/ha). The average protein content of the 1975 crop of hard spring wheat was 13.0%, lower than the 1974 level of 13.5% and the 1973 level of 13.3%.

Areas of cultivation, yields and prices of the principal field crops for the years 1971-75, with averages for 1966-70 are shown in Table 11.4; areas and production of field crops by province for 1974 and 1975 in Table 11.5 and areas and production of grain in the Prairie provinces for the years 1971-75 in Table 11.6.

Table 11.7 shows the stocks of Canadian grain on hand in Canada and in the United States on July 31 for the years 1972-74 with averages for the 10-year period 1962-71.

Livestock and poultry

The total number of cattle and calves in Canada, excluding Newfoundland, at July 1, 1976 was estimated at 14.7 million head, compared to 15.3 million head at July 1, 1975. (Total cattle and calves in Newfoundland at July 1, 1975 was estimated to be 5,990 head.) Milk cows (two years and over) were estimated at 2.0 million head, down from 2.1 million head at July 1, 1975. Beef cows (two years and over) were estimated at 4.0 million head, down from 4.4 million head at July 1, 1975.

Exports of cattle and calves in 1975 totalled 223,603, up from 153,395 in 1974. Imports, at 129,501 head were down by 11.6%. Beef exports (cold dressed carcass weight equivalent) declined from 108 million lb. (49 million kg) in 1974 to 80 million lb. (36.3 million kg) in 1975. Beef imports increased from 179.5 million lb. (81.4 million kg) in 1974 to 191.0 million lb. (86.6 million kg) in 1975.

Agriculture Canada reported that the weighted average price of A1 and A2 steers at Toronto for 1975 was $46.99 compared to $49.37 in 1974 and $39.94 for the 1970-74 average.

The July 1, 1976 estimate for the total number of pigs in Canada excluding Newfoundland was 5.5 million, up from 5.3 million in 1975. Pigs slaughtered in federally inspected and approved plants in 1975 numbered 7.7 million, down significantly from 9.0 million in 1974 as reported by Agriculture Canada. The weighted average price at Toronto (dollars per cwt for index 100 hogs, dressed) in 1975 was $67.22 ($1,482/t) compared to $50.29 ($1,109/t) in 1974 and $40.07 ($883/t) for the 1970-74 average.

The number of sheep and lambs on farms at July 1, 1976 was estimated at 641,300, down from 702,600 at July 1, 1975. (The Newfoundland estimate at July 1, 1975 was 6,335 sheep.) Sheep and lambs slaughtered in federally inspected packing plants in 1975 totalled 186,566 compared to 185,077 in 1974 and 234,206 in 1973. Imports of live animals increased from 32,375 in 1974 to 57,601 in 1975. Imports of mutton and lamb increased from 38.6 million lb. (17.5 million kg) in 1974 to 44.9 million lb. (20.4 million kg).

The estimated number of laying hens on farms at July 1, 1975 was 22.8 million compared to 24.6 million at June 1, 1974. Production and consumption of poultry meat are shown in Table 11.9.

Dairying

Although there would be a further decrease in 1976, the number of dairy cows in Canada in July 1975 was the lowest in recent times. In spite of this decline, milk production continued to increase. In 1975 production stood at 17,674.9 million lb. (8 017.2 million kg) the highest since 1972. Production is concentrated in central Canada with Quebec and Ontario together accounting for 74.5% of Canadian production in 1975.

Table 11.11 shows that the farm value of milk production in Canada for 1975 was $1,461.9 million, an increase of 25.0% over 1974. The value of milk used in factories in 1975 was $808.5 million (55.3% of total production) and sales for fluid purpose amounted to $618.7 million (42.3% of total milk production).

Production of creamery butter in 1975 was 282.8 million lb. (128.3 million kg), the highest since 1972, and required 37.4% of the total national milk output. Quebec accounted for 51.0% of butter production and Ontario 31.0%.

The total production of factory cheese for 1974 was 265.3 million lb. (120.3 million kg), some 9.0% below production in 1974; Quebec accounted for 44.0% of the output and Ontario 43.0%.

Total production of concentrated whole milk products, which includes condensed milk, evaporated milk, whole milk powder, partly skimmed evaporated milk and others, decreased 7.0% from 1974 while production of concentrated milk by-products, which includes condensed skim milk, evaporated skim milk, skim milk powder, buttermilk powder, whey powder, casein and others, increased by 26.0%.

11.4.5   Horticultural crops

Fruits and vegetables. The fruit and vegetable industry is an important part of the agricultural and food distribution sectors of the economy. Fresh and processed fruits and vegetables account for more than one third of the quantity of all food consumed in Canada. There are over 30 fruit and vegetable crops grown commercially in Canada with an annual farm value of almost $500 million.

The most important fruit grown in Canada is still the apple. Commercial apple orchards are found in Nova Scotia, New Brunswick, southern Quebec, much of Ontario, and the interior of British Columbia, particularly in the Okanagan Valley. Tender tree fruits — pears, peaches, cherries, plums — are also grown in Ontario, with the most important concentrations in the Niagara Peninsula and in Essex County. These fruits, as well as apricots, are also grown on a large scale in the southern part of the Okanagan Valley in British Columbia.

Strawberries and raspberries are cultivated commercially in the Maritimes, Quebec, Ontario and British Columbia. British Columbia fruit growers also produce loganberries commercially in the lower mainland and on Vancouver Island. Grapes are grown in the Niagara district of Ontario and on a smaller scale in British Columbia. The native blueberry is found wild over large areas in Canada and is harvested in commercial quantities in the Atlantic provinces, Quebec and Ontario. A cultivated crop is grown in British Columbia. Table 11.14 shows the estimated commercial production and farm value of fruit grown in 1973-75.

The production of field-grown vegetables in Canada is seasonal. During the winter when no domestic vegetables are being harvested except in greenhouses, supplies of most fresh vegetables are imported from the United States. During the growing season a large percentage of the domestic requirements are met from Canadian crops. Some vegetables are exported from Canada, particularly to a few large centres of population in the United States close to the border. Potatoes are the most important vegetable produced in Canada. Production slightly exceeds consumption and normally about 6% is exported. Table 11.15 presents the estimated commercial cultivated area and production of vegetables in 1973-75 with average for 1968-72.

The processing industry plays an important part in the marketing of Canadian-grown fruits and vegetables. Over the years factories have been built in most of the important growing regions and considerable proportions of fruit and vegetable crops are canned, frozen or otherwise processed each season, especially peas, corn, beans and tomatoes. In recent years the importance of freezing has been increasing. Most vegetables for processing are grown under a system whereby the processor contracts annually with each grower for certain areas.

Over the past 25 years the weight and value of exported vegetables have varied considerably but there is a slight downward trend. In the same period vegetable and fruit imports increased considerably. However, processing of canned tender tree fruits has declined somewhat in recent years.

In the past few years the supply of fruits available for consumption in Canada has remained relatively unchanged, 1974 showing only a slight decrease from that in 1973. Vegetables, on the other hand, show a slight upward trend. The per capita domestic disappearance of all fruits for 1974 of 258.5 lb. (117.3 kg) fresh equivalent weight, was slightly lower than the 1973 figure of 268.2 lb. (121.7 kg). Of this total, 124.2 lb. (56.3 kg) per capita were fresh, 56.9 lb. (25.8 kg) were canned, 2.6 lb. (1.2 kg) were frozen, 62.8 lb. (28.5 kg) were made into juice and 10.3 lb. (4.7 kg) were dried. Per capita disappearance of vegetables, excluding potatoes, was 124.8 lb. (56.6 kg) for the same period, only slightly higher than the 1973 figure of 119.2 lb. (54.1 kg). Per capita disappearance of vegetables averaged 82.9 lb. (37.6 kg) of fresh vegetables, 28.1 lb. (12.7 kg) of canned vegetables and

10.4 lb. (4.7 kg) of frozen vegetables in 1974 (fresh equivalent weight). There were 540.2 lb. (245.0 kg) of fruits and vegetables, including potatoes, tomatoes and mushrooms, available per capita for consumption in Canada in 1974.

Honey. As shown in Table 11.16, honey production in 1975 was above that of 1974. Honey is produced commercially in all provinces except Newfoundland and yields vary to some extent from year to year. Alberta is consistently the largest producer, accounting for almost 30% of the total output in 1975. Honey bees are used in some fruit-growing districts for pollination and are also used for pollination of certain seed crops. To facilitate storage, shipment and uniformity of quality, large quantities of Canadian honey are pasteurized. Beekeepers' marketing cooperatives are active in several provinces. In 1975 Canada exported 10.4 million lb. (4.7 million kg) of honey valued at $4.8 million, 3.5 million lb. (1.6 million kg) more than the quantity exported in 1974. Exports went mainly to the United Kingdom, the United States, France, the Federal Republic of Germany, Japan and the Netherlands.

Sugar beets and beet sugar. Sugar beets are grown commercially in Quebec, Manitoba and Alberta and beet sugar factories are located in these provinces. In Quebec, commercial production is centred in the St-Hilaire area of the Eastern Townships; Alberta, where sugar beets are grown under irrigation, produces the largest crop. Harvested area, yield and total production of sugar beets for the years 1971-75 are shown in Table 11.17, together with available quantity and value of shipments of beet sugar.

Maple sugar and maple syrup. Maple syrup is produced commercially in Nova Scotia, New Brunswick, Quebec and Ontario. The bulk of the crop comes from the Eastern Townships of Quebec, a district famous in both Canada and the United States as the centre of the maple products industry. Virtually all of the maple products exported go to the United States with the larger proportion moving as syrup, although substantial quantities of sugar are also shipped. Much of the syrup sold in Canada has been marketed in 1-gallon cans direct to the consumer from the producer, but a considerable amount of both sugar and syrup is sold each year to processing firms. Production and value of maple sugar and maple syrup, by province, are shown in Table 11.18.

Greenhouse operations. The total area operated under glass and plastic in 1973 and 1974 amounted to 35.3 million sq ft (3.28 million m²) and 36.1 million sq ft (3.35 million m²), respectively, while the total value of growers' sales stood at $85.2 million in 1973 and $103.8 million in 1974.

Nursery industry. In 1974 the nursery trades industry had a total revenue of $88 million. Approximately 39% of this represented grower sales of traditional nursery stock and 35% was earned by supplying the demand for contracted services.

Eggs. Table 11.19 shows production and value of farm eggs by province. Egg production totalled 448.1 million dozen in 1975, compared to 459.5 million dozen in 1974. The rate of lay per 100 layers rose to 22,343 from 21,811 in 1974 and the farm selling price of eggs averaged 61.3 cents a dozen compared with 61.8 cents a dozen in 1974. The Atlantic provinces produced 8.0% of all eggs in 1975, Quebec 15.2%, Ontario 39.5%, the Prairie provinces 25.3% and British Columbia 12.0%.

Wool. Estimates of production of shorn wool in 1975 at 3.1 million lb. (1.4 million kg) were 4.0% lower than in 1974. Average farm price per lb. was 27.5 cents (60.6 cents a kg) in 1975 as compared to 34.2 cents a lb. (75.4 cents a kg) in 1974.

Tobacco. The total area planted in 1975 as compared to 1974 increased in Quebec and in the Maritime provinces and declined in Ontario, although yields were lower in Quebec, Ontario and the Maritime provinces. Total production decreased from 256.8 million lb. (116.5 million kg) in 1974 to 233.8 million lb. (106.0 million kg) in 1975. The average value per lb. advanced from 89.8 cents ($1.98 a kg) in 1974 to 93.5 cents ($2.06 a kg) in 1975 (Tables 11.20 and 11.21).

No information is available on the production of cigarettes for domestic consumption but, on the basis of domestic sales reported to Statistics Canada by manufacturers, the number of cigarettes sold rose from 50,864.4 million in 1971 to 57,122.8 million in 1974.

11.4.6   Prices of agricultural products

The index of farm prices of agricultural products (Table 11.22) was designed to measure changes occurring in the average prices farmers receive at the farm from the sale of farm products. In comparing current index numbers with those prior to August 1975, the following points should be considered. Prices of all western grains used in the construction of the index prior to that date are final prices; all later figures are adjusted initial prices only for wheat, oats and barley. Any subsequent participation payments will be added to the prices currently used and the index revised upward accordingly. Average cash prices of major Canadian grains are given in Table 11.23 and yearly average prices of Canadian livestock in Table 11.24.

11.4.7   Food consumption

The food disappearance data represent available domestic supplies of food. Production, stocks on hand at the beginning of the year, imports less exports, and stocks on hand at close of the period, as well as marketing losses and industrial uses are factors in the calculation for each commodity. All calculations are made at the retail level of distribution, except for meats for which the figures are worked out at the wholesale stage. The amount of food actually eaten would be somewhat lower than indicated because of losses and waste occurring after the products reach the consumer.

All basic foods are classified under 14 main commodity groups. The total for each group is computed using a common denominator, for example: milk solids (dry weight) for the dairy products group; fat content for fats and oils; and fresh equivalent for fruits. Most foods are included in their basic form, such as flour, fat, sugar, rather than in more highly manufactured forms.

The series in Table 11.25 represents the official estimates of yearly supplies of food moving into consumption for the years 1968-72 as an average for comparison with the years 1973 and 1974. Production of meats from slaughter in Canada, total supply, distribution and per capita disappearance of meats are shown in Table 11.26. All estimates are on a cold carcass-weight basis except canned meats, which are in terms of product.

11.5   1971 Census of Agriculture

This section presents a limited amount of information from the 1971 Census of Agriculture; details are contained in Volume IV — Parts 1, 2 and 3 of the 1971 Census of Canada. Volume IV, Parts 4 and 5 include some unique data resulting from the computer linkage of documents from the 1971 censuses of population and agriculture. The socio-economic characteristics of farm operators and their households have been cross-classified with the agricultural characteristics of farming operations for all 1971 census-farms.

Number of census-farms. For both census years, 1971 and 1966, a census-farm was defined as a holding of 1 acre (0.4 ha) or more with sales of agricultural products valued at $50 or more during the 12 months prior to the census. The number of census-farms in Canada declined 15% to 366,128 in 1971 from 430,522 in 1966, indicating an acceleration of the trend since 1941 toward an ever-decreasing number of census-farms (Table 11.27).

Farm areas. The total area of census-farms in 1971 was 169,668,614 acres (68 662 444 ha), a 2.6% decrease from the 174,124,828 acres (70 465 809 ha) recorded in 1966 (Table 11.28). The Maritime provinces, Quebec and Ontario all reported significant decreases in farm areas. Only Newfoundland, Alberta and British Columbia showed an increase, the increase in Newfoundland due to the establishment of new community pastures. For Canada as a whole, the 108,148,877 acres (43 766 293 ha) of improved land for 1971 was virtually unchanged from the area recorded in 1966. The area of unimproved land decreased 6.8% to 61,519,737 acres (24 896 152 ha) in 1971 from 65,970,451 acres (26 697 291 ha) in 1966. Woodland, decreasing by 18.8%, accounted for the majority of this loss, while other improved land decreased 3.4%.

Economic classification of census-farms. Census-farms were divided into 12 economic classes according to the total value of products sold during the past calendar year (Table 11.29). Such a classification serves as a measure of the productive size of census-farms in Canada. The former division of census-farms into "commercial" and "small-scale" farms has been dropped, since what may be felt to be a commercial farm in one region might be considered small-scale in another. The group classified as "institutional farms, etc." includes experimental farms, community pastures and institutional-type farms regardless of the amount of sales of agricultural products.

Type of farm. Table 11.30 shows that, with the exception of farms classified as "institutional farms, etc.", all census-farms with sales of $2,500 or more were classified as one of 10 major product types. A criterion of 51% or more of total sales was used for this classification. For example, a census-farm was typed as a poultry farm if 51% or more of the total agricultural sales for the farm was obtained from the sale of poultry products. However, it was classed as a dairy-type farm if 40% to 50% of total sales was obtained from dairy products, provided the sale of dairy products together with the sale of cattle and calves amounted to 51% or more of the total sales. Under these criteria, it was possible for a farm to qualify for more than one product type. To prevent this possibility, the 10 product types were given a priority rating in the order listed.

Agricultural products for marketing   11.6

The Prairie grain trade   11.6.1
The bulk of the Canadian grains and oilseeds (excluding corn) is grown in the three Prairie provinces and the Peace River Block of British Columbia. Wheat is the most important product and is produced largely for human consumption. Oats and barley are grown primarily for use as livestock feed. Of the oilseeds, rapeseed yields edible oil and flaxseed is crushed to produce linseed oil for industry; both these crops also produce meal for livestock feed.

Prairie production of wheat usually amounts to about three times domestic consumption so this is an export-oriented industry. The same may be said of rapeseed and flaxseed. The coarse grains on the other hand do not enter into international trade to the same extent but large quantities do leave the Prairie provinces to be used as feed in central and eastern Canada and British Columbia.

Production varies from year to year due both to the decisions by individual farmers on what to plant and to variations in weather conditions which affect yields. Market demand is also variable largely as a result of changes in crop production throughout the world so that sales prospects and price, for wheat and oilseeds particularly, are functions of world supplies and demand. However, Canadian producers are in the position to supply high quality wheat which enjoys certain market preferences over the production of some competitors.

The grain trade encompasses the functions of assembling, storing, transporting and marketing these crops. The trade and government institutions involved are described in more detail in Section 11.7.

There are approximately 160,000 grain producers in western Canada (Canadian Wheat Board permit holders, 1976) and the crop is sold on world

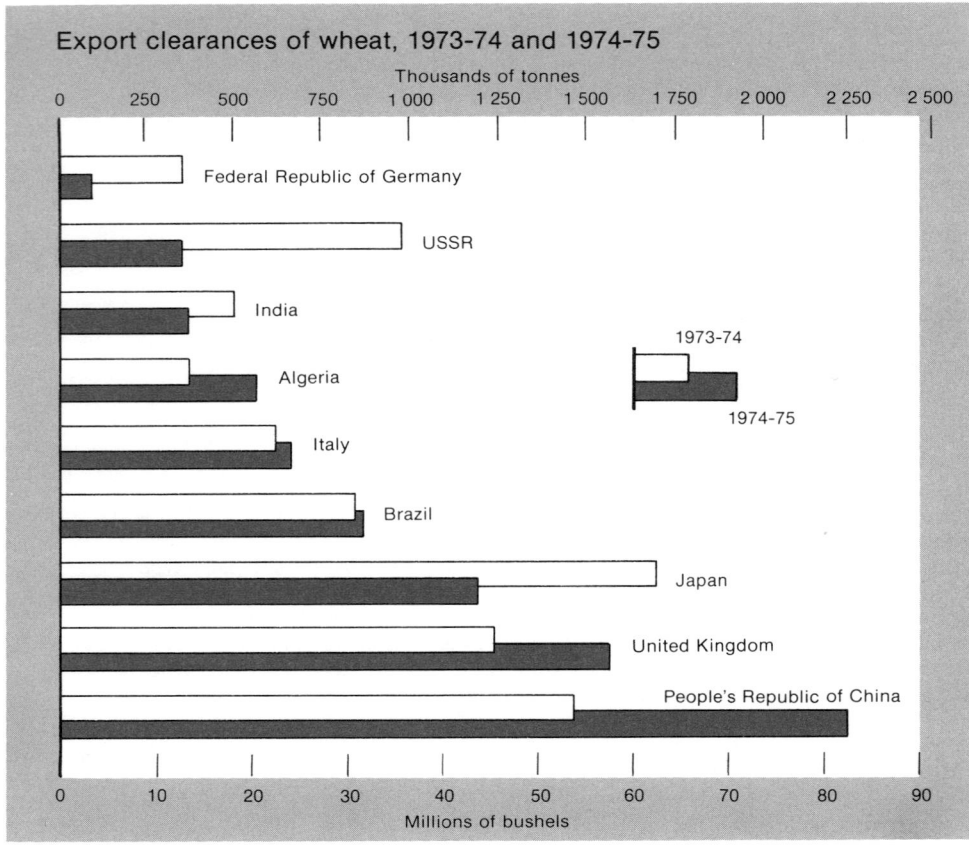

Export clearances of wheat, 1973-74 and 1974-75

markets. A high quality information system covering annual production, stocks on hand and details on movement and location of supplies is essential to the smooth functioning of the trade. It is, for instance, customary to commit supplies for delivery before harvesting the crop from which such supplies will be drawn. Statistics Canada, in cooperation with the Canadian Grain Commission, the grain trade, the provincial departments of agriculture and the Canadian farmers, plays a leading role in providing this service.

A statistical picture of the Canadian grain industry is provided in Section 11.4.2, with summary statistics on the wheat crop for 1975, compared with 1974 and 1973. Further details are given in Tables 11.4 - 11.7 and 11.31 - 11.34.

11.6.2   Livestock slaughter

Cattle slaughtered at federally inspected packing plants amounted to 3,337,687 head in 1975, up 12.2% from 2,975,833 head in 1974. All provinces showed increases with the exception of Saskatchewan.

Calves slaughtered at federally inspected packing plants amounted to 682,094 head in 1975, up 73.6% from 392,811 head in 1974. Increases occurred in all provinces except British Columbia which showed a slight decline.

Statistics on pigs, sheep and lambs slaughtered in 1975, with comparisons for 1974 and 1973, are given in Section 11.4.3.

Government aid and controls   11.7

The role of government in the grains industry   11.7.1

Government's interest and involvement in the grains industry predates Confederation and is a record of policies relating to land use and settlement; transportation; grain elevators, storage, handling and forwarding; marketing methods and opportunities; income security; and the many ramifications of international competition and the search for international cooperation in the sale of grain. The federal government's role in the grains industry is carried out by the Department of Agriculture, the Department of Industry, Trade and Commerce and two semi-autonomous bodies which report to Parliament through Ministers of the Crown: the Canadian Grain Commission and the Canadian Wheat Board.

Three other agencies also play integral roles in the Canadian grains industry: the Canadian International Grains Institute, the Canada Grains Council and the Special Advisory Group on Grains (Grains Group). The Canadian International Grains Institute contributes to the maintenance and expansion of markets for Canadian grains and oilseeds and their products in Canada and abroad. The Canada Grains Council provides a forum for coordination, consultation and consensus on industry recommendations to government. The Special Advisory Committee on Grains (Grains Group) is charged with coordinating, reviewing and recommending federal policies on grains.

Grains Group   11.7.1.1

In 1970 the minister responsible for the Canadian Wheat Board organized the Special Advisory Group on Grains (known as the Grains Group) made up of policy advisers representing the Department of Agriculture, the Department of Industry, Trade and Commerce and the Ministry of Transport. Under the minister's direction the Grains Group examines the problems of the grains industry in the areas of production, transportation and handling, and marketing. It coordinates, reviews and recommends federal policies for these areas. Implementation of recommended policies subsequently adopted by the government is through government departments or other agencies concerned with the grains industry.

Production. The Canada Department of Agriculture conducts a research program in plant breeding and production methods to improve varieties, yields and quality of grains for which there is a domestic and export demand. A recent innovation has been the provision, well in advance of spring planting, of information on initial prices to be guaranteed to farmers for the new crop of wheat, oats and barley, and on minimum deliveries to be accepted by the Canadian Wheat Board during the crop year. These are announced by the minister responsible for the Canadian Wheat Board in March of each year.

Transportation and handling. A freeze on the abandonment of railway track in the Prairie network was declared by the federal government in 1967. Modifications were made effective in 1975, following expiry of the freeze at the end of 1974. There are 19,221 miles (30 933 km) of rail lines on the Prairies. Under new Orders in Council 12,413 route miles (19 977 km) were declared basic railway network and applications for abandonment are prohibited until the year 2000. The railways are now free to apply to abandon 525 route miles (845 km) which are no longer used. The balance of the network, about 6,300 miles (10 139 km), will be the subject of regional inquiries to determine their status and future. The Hall Commission on grain handling and transportation and the Snavely Commission on grain transportation costs were expected to present reports in 1977.

Additional studies are scheduled to consider the action required to modernize the grain handling and transportation system.

Marketing. To broaden the assistance provided for sales and market development of grains, oilseeds and products, the pertinent services of the Department of Industry, Trade and Commerce are consolidated in the Grain Marketing Office. Regular contact is maintained with the Canadian Wheat Board, other agencies and organizations concerned with grain marketing, trade commissioners abroad and the private trade sector. A program of trade promotion that includes participation in missions and trade fairs abroad is also maintained.

The Grains and Oilseeds Marketing Incentives Program provides assistance in the form of cost or risk sharing to a variety of projects designed to increase the sales of grains, oilseeds and their derivatives. Assistance is normally provided to worthwhile projects which would not be realized without incentives. Canadian companies, agencies, industry associations, universities, institutes and similar bodies are qualified applicants. Projects implemented or under consideration cover various fields, including grain handling, storage, processing, market testing of products, developing new products or processes, feeding trials and demonstrations and feasibility studies related to expansion of exports of grains, oilseeds and their products.

With the cooperation of the processing industry, provincial governments and universities, a $5 million pilot plant in Saskatoon was scheduled for completion in 1977. The POS Pilot Plant Corporation (Protein, Oil and Starch) is a non-profit corporation (directed by subscribing members) which provides unique pilot-plant facilities to the Canadian grains and oilseeds processing industry.

Credit. Canada has been selling grain on credit since 1952. The original program provided for grain sales on terms of up to three years at commercial rates of interest. In 1968 the government approved a broadened and improved program for the sale of Canadian grain on credit to improve its competitive position in export markets. The new program allowed exporters to respond quickly to export opportunities in developing countries on more favourable credit terms in some circumstances.

Most credit sales of western grains are on terms of three years or less, financed under Section 12 of the Canadian Wheat Board Act with a government guarantee. Credit sales of other than the western wheat, oats and barley which are marketed by the Wheat Board, or any sales on terms of more than three years, are insured under Section 27 of the Export Development Act.

Food aid. The Canadian Food Aid Program has expanded from $2 million in 1962-63 to more than $225 million in 1975-76. Since 1963 food aid under bilateral and multilateral aid programs has been administered by the Canadian International Development Agency. Most of the food consists of wheat and wheat products, but rapeseed and rapeseed oil are also included. In the past about 80% of Canada's food aid was extended to foreign governments under bilateral programs with the remaining 20% going through multilateral channels, mainly the World Food Program. Over the last 10 years more than 72 different countries have received food aid from Canada. Regular contributions of flour are also made to the United Nations Relief and Works Agency.

At the World Food Conference in Rome in November 1974, Canada pledged the allocation of 1 million metric tons of grain annually for three years, with 400 000 t of this amount to be channelled through the World Food Program. A commitment to increase substantially other types of food aid was also made. The estimated total value of food aid in 1976-77 was approximately $230 million.

11.7.1.2   The Canadian Grain Commission

The Canadian Grain Commission was established by the Canada Grain Act in April 1971, replacing the Board of Grain Commissioners for Canada, established in 1912. It is composed of a chief commissioner and two commissioners and is under the jurisdiction of the Canada Department of Agriculture, with headquarters at Winnipeg and other offices across Canada, the largest in Vancouver, Thunder Bay and Montreal.

The commission is responsible for administration of the Canada Grain Act, including inspection, weighing and storage of grain; for fixing maximum tariffs for charges by licensed elevators; for establishing grain grading standards; and for operation of the Canadian government elevators at Moose Jaw, Saskatoon, Calgary, Edmonton, Lethbridge and Prince Rupert. All operators of elevators in western Canada and elevators in eastern Canada handling western-grown grain for export, as well as grain dealers in western Canada, must be licensed by the commission and must file security by bond or otherwise as a guarantee for the performance of all obligations imposed upon them by the Canada Grain Act or by the Canada Grain Act Regulations. On a fee basis, the commission provides mandatory official inspection, grading and weighing of grain, as well as registration of terminal elevator and eastern elevator receipts. The Economics and Statistics Division of the commission is the basic source of information on grain handled through the Canadian licensed elevator system. The commission is also responsible for administration of the Grain Futures Act. Under provisions of that statute, a supervisor of grain futures trading was appointed on August 1, 1975.

The commission's Grain Research Laboratory conducts surveys of the quality of each year's grain crops and of grain moving through the Canadian elevator system. It provides information on the quality of varieties and grades of grain to the Inspection Division, collaborates with plant breeders in studies on new grain varieties and undertakes basic research in relation to quality characteristics of cereal grains and oilseeds. With the introduction of the protein factor in segregating wheat grades, the commission has extended and decentralized its protein-testing facilities and is now able to test samples drawn from carlots of wheat and make the results known to terminal elevator operators prior to unloading cars at the terminals. The laboratory monitors this protein testing to ensure uniformity among testing units, and also assists in testing the quality of cereals developed by plant breeders to determine the licensing potential of the variety.

The commission's five assistant commissioners — one in Alberta, two in Saskatchewan, one in Manitoba and one in Ontario — investigate complaints of producers and inspect licensed elevators in their respective provinces. All grain elevators with their equipment and stocks of grain may be inspected at any time by commission officials.

The commission sets up western and eastern grain standards committees which participate in establishing grain grades and grade specifications and recommend standard and export standard samples for various grades of grain. It also appoints grain appeal tribunals to hear appeals against the grading of grain by the commission's inspectors; decisions of these tribunals are final.

The Canadian Wheat Board   11.7.1.3

The Canadian Wheat Board was established under the Canadian Wheat Board Act of 1935 for the purpose of "marketing in an orderly manner, in interprovincial and export trade, grain grown in Canada". The legislation established the Wheat Board as the sole marketing agency for Prairie wheat, oats and barley sold interprovincially or internationally. With the introduction of a new domestic feed grains policy in August 1974, marketing of feed grains for domestic use was removed from exclusive Canadian Wheat Board jurisdiction and this grain is now traded on the open market. The Canadian Wheat Board remains the sole purchaser and seller of feed grains for export. Other crops, such as rye, rapeseed, flaxseed, buckwheat and mustard are marketed by the private grain trade.

The sale of Prairie-grown wheat, oats and barley is carried out through sales negotiated directly by the Wheat Board, or through grain exporting companies acting as its agents.

Delivery of the kinds, grades and quantities of grain needed by customers is essential to the board's marketing program. This is accomplished in two stages. The first involves the delivery of grain by the producer from his farm to the local country elevator under a quota system for the kind and grade of grain required to meet market commitments, and to allocate delivery opportunities equitably among all grain producers. The second stage involves the movement of grain from country elevators to large terminals in eastern Canada, at Thunder Bay, Churchill, and the west coast by the railways under maximum tariffs established under the terms of the National Transportation Act. Shipping of grain from Thunder Bay to eastern positions is done largely by lake vessels under freight rates negotiated by the Wheat Board and by private shippers with lake vessel operators. Extensive planning and a high degree of coordination within the grain handling and transportation industry are required. The Wheat Board, which coordinates the entire movement, programs rail shipments from country elevators to terminals on a weekly basis in accordance with sales requirements.

The producer selling to the Canadian Wheat Board receives payment in two stages. An initial payment price is established by Order in Council before the start of a crop year; this price, less handling costs at the local elevator and transportation costs to Thunder Bay or Vancouver, is the initial price received by the producer and is, in effect, a guaranteed floor price. If the Wheat Board, in selling the grain, does not realize this price and the necessary marketing costs, the deficit is borne by the federal treasury; after the end of the crop year when the board has sold all the grain or otherwise disposed of it in accordance with the Canadian Wheat Board Act, the board, if authorized by Order in Council, makes a final payment to producers.

Since the implementation of the new domestic feed grains policy, a producer delivering feed grains to a country elevator has the option of selling the grain to the Canadian Wheat Board or on the open market. In the latter case he will, on delivery, receive a payment representing the final price in contrast to the Canadian Wheat Board system of initial and final payments. As a result of a modification effective in August 1976 in the feed grain policy, the Canadian Wheat Board stands ready to offer feed grains to the domestic market at prices based on a formula which reflects the value of corn and soybean meal.

The Prairie Grain Advance Payments Act, administered by the Wheat Board, provides that producers may receive through their elevator agents interest-free cash advances on farm-stored grain in accordance with a prescribed formula. The purpose of this legislation is to make cash available to producers pending delivery of their grain under the quotas established. An advance of up to $45,000 (depending on the number of producers involved in the operation) may be issued to multi-farm farms, such as partnerships, cooperative and corporate farms. Other details of this legislation are given in Section 11.2.2.

11.7.1.4   Two-Price Wheat Act

To mitigate the effects of sharp price fluctuations on domestic wheat consumers, the federal government implemented a two-price system for wheat in September 1973. The system provides a guaranteed price to the domestic miller of $3.25 a bushel (36.4 dm³) for bread wheat used for domestic consumption. Under the Two-Price Wheat Act, given Royal Assent on June 19, 1975, the government makes up the difference to farmers between the pegged domestic price and the export price on all sales into the domestic market, to a maximum payment of $1.75 a bushel (36.4 dm³). A similar system is in place for durum wheats.

The Grains and Special Crops Division of Agriculture Canada's Production and Marketing Branch is responsible for administering this program and has supervised the distribution of about $300 million since the program began. Payments are distributed directly to farmers in Quebec and the Maritimes, while in Ontario and the Prairies, monthly payments are made to the Ontario Wheat Producers' Marketing Board and the Canadian Wheat Board, for distribution among farmers through the price pooling scheme operated by each organization.

The program will remain in effect until 1980, thus providing farmers with long-range price assurance and market stability.

The Canadian International Grains Institute   11.7.1.5

The Canadian International Grains Institute was incorporated in July 1972. It
operates in affiliation with the Canadian Wheat Board and the Canadian Grain
Commission and financial responsibility is shared by the federal government and
the Canadian Wheat Board. It is designed to help maintain and enlarge markets at
home and abroad for Canadian grains, oilseeds and their products, and offers
instructional programs to foreign participants selected from countries purchasing
these commodities and to Canadians associated with the grain industry. Courses
are offered in grain handling, transportation, marketing, flour milling, bread
baking and macaroni manufacturing, and lectures and practical training are given
in analytical methods used in processing and utilization of grains and oilseeds.
Located in the Canadian Grain Commission Building in Winnipeg the institute
includes classrooms, conference rooms, offices, library, laboratories, a 9-ton
(8.16 t), 24-hour-capacity flour mill and a pilot bakery.

The Canada Grains Council   11.7.1.6

The Canada Grains Council was established in 1969 to improve coordination and
to assist in reaching agreement within the industry on recommendations to
government. Its principal aim is to coordinate supportive activities directed at
increasing Canada's share of world markets for all grains and grain products and
effecting their efficient use in Canada. Membership in the council is open to all
non-governmental organizations and associations whose members are directly
engaged in grain production, processing, handling, transportation or marketing.

The administrative costs of the council are shared by the federal government
and the industry members. The council currently has 28 member organizations
representing thousands of individuals. At least two general meetings are held each
year; the Board of Directors meets about 10 times a year. The council is served by
a small secretariat.

Western Grain Stabilization Act   11.7.1.7

The Western Grain Stabilization Act, given Royal Assent on February 25, 1976,
became effective April 1, 1976. It provides for the stabilization of the net cash
flow to the prairie grains sector. The support given will prevent the net cash flow,
that is the difference between total receipts from the production and sale of wheat,
oats, barley, rye, flaxseed and rapeseed and the cash costs of production, in each
calendar year, from falling below the average of net cash flow in the previous five
calendar years.

Under this voluntary program, participating grain producers contribute a levy
of 2% of their grain sales up to a maximum of $25,000 a year to the Western
Grain Stabilization Fund. The federal government will contribute an equal
amount to double the participating farmers' contributions. Whenever a
stabilization payment is required to prevent net cash flow from falling below the
support level, the participating producers will share in that payment in proportion
to their relative levy contributions.

The Western Grain Stabilization Act is administered by the Western Grain
Stabilization Administration in the Canadian Grain Commission Building in
Winnipeg.

The objective of the Western Grain Stabilization program is to provide
producers protection against a large unexpected decline in either world grain
prices or in sales of Canadian grain, increases in the cash costs of producing that
grain or in any combination of those factors, thereby ensuring that a strong and
viable grains sector will be maintained in Canada.

Government involvement in other farm products   11.7.2

Governments in Canada at both the federal and provincial levels have from the
beginning enacted measures to improve and expand the performance of the
agricultural sector. Originally, the emphasis was on production increases and the

control and eradication of pests and diseases. Gradually, however, with rising production and increasing specialization on the part of farmers, problems in marketing began to emerge.

To ensure quality, inspection and grading procedures and standards were established, but the periodic collapse of prices caused by bumper crops and intensified by the general inability of large numbers of producers to bargain on an equitable basis with far fewer buyers has been a much more difficult part of the marketing problem.

The first attempt to provide bargaining power to producers was the organization of voluntary marketing cooperatives. All provinces eventually passed legislation for incorporation of these cooperatives, and most of them also provided additional assistance in various forms. Federally, the introduction of the Agricultural Products Cooperative Marketing Act provided for financial guarantees to producers willing to market their crops on a pooling-of-returns basis. More information on cooperative organizations is given in Chapter 18.

Although much cooperative marketing was initially successful, it was found that the voluntary aspect represented a serious weakness. Many members dropped out in good times to make their own deals. A type of marketing organization was needed with the legal power to control the output of all producers of a certain product in a certain area, and as a result marketing control legislation was adopted providing for various types of boards, agencies and commissions.

11.7.2.1   Product controls

The federal and provincial departments of agriculture cooperate in establishing and enforcing quality standards for various foods. Some control over size and types of containers used for distribution of agricultural products is exercised by the Canada Department of Agriculture, and the Department of Consumer and Corporate Affairs enforces regulations pertaining to weights and measures.

Standards related to health and sanitation in food handling are developed and enforced at all three levels of government. Examples of provincial and municipal action include laws pertaining to pasteurization of milk, inspection of slaughter-houses and sanitary standards in restaurants. At the federal level, inspection by the Health of Animals Branch of the Canada Department of Agriculture of all meat carcasses that enter into interprovincial trade is required; the Foods and Drugs Directorates of the Department of National Health and Welfare have wide responsibility for food composition standards; and the Department of Consumer and Corporate Affairs has jurisdiction over advertising.

11.7.2.2   Marketing controls

The Agricultural Products Cooperative Marketing Act (RSC 1970, c.A-6) was passed in 1939 as a result of a federal government decision to assist orderly marketing by encouraging the establishment of pools that would give the producer the maximum sales return for his product, less a maximum margin for handling expenses agreed upon in advance. The Agricultural Products Cooperative Marketing Act now covers the marketing of all agricultural products except wheat produced in the Canadian Wheat Board area.

The purpose of this act is to aid farmers in pooling the returns from sale of their products by guaranteeing initial payments and thus assisting in the orderly marketing of the product. The government may undertake to guarantee a certain minimum initial payment to the producer at the time of delivery of the product, including a margin for handling; sales returns are made to the producer on a cooperative plan. Under an amendment to the act in 1975, the guaranteed initial payment may be set at a percentage of the estimated market price to producers for the production year. Previously the initial price was limited to a maximum 80% of the average producer price over the preceding three years. For 1975 crops, agreements were made for marketing winter wheat and beans in Ontario, apples for processing in Quebec, and rutabagas in Prince Edward Island.

The Canadian Dairy Commission, established in 1966, was the first national marketing agency to be established since creation of the Canadian Wheat Board in 1935. The commission has the power to stabilize the market by offering to purchase any dairy product and to package, process, store, ship, insure, import, export or sell or otherwise dispose of any dairy product purchased by it. The commission may also make payments to producers of milk and cream to stabilize prices of these products and may levy for export equalization.

A comprehensive milk marketing plan, with the purpose of balancing demand and supply and equalizing export assistance, was agreed to by the Canadian Dairy Commission and the milk marketing agencies of Ontario and Quebec in January 1971, establishing a market-sharing quota system for industrial milk and cream and that portion of milk, shipped by fluid producers, which is used for manufacturing purposes. Cream shippers in Quebec, Ontario and Prince Edward Island entered the plan in 1971. Producers in Alberta, Manitoba and Saskatchewan came under the program in 1972, British Columbia in 1973, and Nova Scotia and New Brunswick in 1974. All manufacturing milk and cream sold in Canada now comes under the market-sharing program. The market-sharing arrangement provides that each producer receives returns related to the target support price for manufacturing shipments up to his market share. The target support price is achieved through the offer-to-purchase program which stabilizes markets, plus the direct payments to producers. Producer returns for deliveries over market share are related to world prices for surplus dairy products.

Additional information on the role of the commission with regard to dairy production and income stabilization is given in Section 11.2.2.

Producer marketing boards were introduced during the 1930s to give agricultural producers legal authority under certain conditions to control the marketing of their produce. The Natural Products Marketing Act of 1934 attempted to provide this power at the federal level but the courts ruled that the subject was outside federal jurisdiction. The subsequently introduced Natural Products Marketing (British Columbia) Act, 1936 was found to be within the powers of provincial governments and it has since been used as a model for marketing board legislation as it evolved in all provinces.

The basic feature which enables marketing boards to control the marketing of a product is the compulsory aspect. A new board usually has to be first approved by a majority vote of the producers of the affected product. If approved, all producers of the product in the designated area, other than those who may be exempted as below a specified minimum production level, are required by law to market their produce under the authority of the board. Depending on a board's objectives and the type of product, its powers and duties may only involve negotiating a minimum price or may include production or marketing quotas, designated times and places for marketing, or such other powers which may be considered necessary to ensure an orderly and equitable market.

The powers of a producer marketing board provided by provincial legislation are necessarily limited to trade within the province. Under the Agricultural Products Marketing Act (RSC 1970, c.A-7), the federal government may delegate to a marketing board powers with respect to interprovincial and export trade similar to those it holds under provincial authority with respect to intraprovincial trade. This act also gives the Governor in Council the right to authorize a provincial marketing board to impose and collect levies from persons engaged in the production and marketing of commodities controlled by it for the purposes of the board including the creation of reserves and the equalization of returns.

The federal Farm Products Marketing Agencies Act passed in January 1972 is the enabling legislation for the creation of national marketing agencies or boards. National agencies may be set up, when producers and provincial authorities desire it, for any agricultural commodities which, due to widespread production in Canada or for other reasons, cannot be effectively marketed in an orderly manner under the jurisdiction of individual provincial boards. The act establishes a National Farm Products Marketing Council to advise the Minister of Agriculture on all matters relating to the establishment and operation of national agencies, to review the performance of and assist in promoting effective marketing by these agencies and to consult with interested provinces on a continuing basis concerning the establishment of national marketing agencies.

The first national agency formed under the act, the Canadian Egg Marketing Agency, commenced operation in June 1973 and the second, the Canadian Turkey Marketing Agency, in March 1974. These federal agencies operate in conjunction with provincial egg and turkey boards; they do not deal directly with producers.

During 1974-75 there were 108 provincially authorized marketing boards operating in Canada, including the milk control boards which have a lesser degree of producer control than the others, as well as the earlier mentioned federal boards. Boards are established in all provinces, led by Quebec with 26 and Ontario with 22. An estimated 57% of 1974 farm cash income was received from sales made under the jurisdiction of marketing boards. A variety of agricultural commodities were sold under marketing boards, including grains, hogs, milk, fruit, potatoes and other vegetables, tobacco, poultry, eggs, wood, soybeans, honey, maple products and pulpwood. At year end 1975, the federal government had delegated authority to 79 provincial boards to control the marketing of their products in interprovincial and export trade.

Sources

11.1 Information Division, Canada Department of Agriculture.
11.2 Information Division, Canada Department of Agriculture; Agriculture Stabilization Board; Grains Group, Department of Industry, Trade and Commerce; Crop Insurance Division, Canada Department of Agriculture; Canadian Dairy Commission; Canadian Livestock Feed Board; Farm Credit Corporation; Guaranteed Loans Administration, Department of Finance; Grain Marketing Office, Department of Industry, Trade and Commerce.
11.3 Supplied by respective provincial government departments.
11.4 Agriculture Division, Institutions and Agriculture Statistics Field, Statistics Canada; except tobacco: Food, Beverages and Textiles Section, Manufacturing and Primary Industries Division, Statistics Canada.
11.5 Census of Agriculture Division, Institutions and Agriculture Statistics Field, Statistics Canada.
11.6 Agriculture Division, Institutions and Agriculture Statistics Field, Statistics Canada.
11.7 Grains Group, Department of Industry, Trade and Commerce; Marketing and Trade Division, Canada Department of Agriculture.

Tables

..	not available
...	not appropriate or not applicable
—	nil or zero
--	too small to be expressed
e	estimate
p	preliminary
r	revised

Equivalent values of metric units:
1 hectare (ha) = 2.47 acres
1 metric tonne (t) wheat = 36.744 bu
                oats   = 64.842 bu
                barley = 45.930 bu
certain tables may not add due to rounding

It should be noted that figures shown for the latest year are subject to revision, and that some figures for earlier years have been revised. Figures for Newfoundland are not included, as agricultural activity there is of minor importance and production small.

11.1 Cash receipts from farming operations (excluding supplementary payments), by province, 1971-75 (thousand dollars)

Province	1971	1972	1973	1974	1975
Prince Edward Island	38,868	44,840	71,887	83,076	81,166
Nova Scotia	65,618	73,572	96,650	102,777	112,644
New Brunswick	52,801	64,955	95,537	103,089	96,321
Quebec	691,515	776,355	978,827	1,145,359	1,322,874
Ontario	1,427,965	1,622,681	1,971,576	2,460,426	2,581,835
Manitoba	367,841	487,812	618,238	823,491	934,508
Saskatchewan	901,408	1,202,828	1,466,292	2,039,168	2,468,996
Alberta	775,443	917,353	1,199,084	1,682,547	1,873,143
British Columbia	224,448	246,750	330,620	381,292	405,554
Total	4,545,907	5,437,146	6,828,711	8,821,225	9,877,041

11.2 Cash receipts from farming operations, by commodity or other source, 1972-75 (thousand dollars)

Item	1972	1973	1974	1975
Wheat	829,064	870,069	1,548,421	1,711,115
Wheat, Canadian Wheat Board payments	118,426	331,182	506,112	826,920
Oats	26,321	30,652	55,307	60,667
Oats, Canadian Wheat Board payments	5,314	12,861	—	27,809
Barley	217,332	229,475	468,566	471,317
Barley, Canadian Wheat Board payments	2,966	100,800	96,069	149,479
Canadian Wheat Board cash advances	23,249	29,947	48,105	19,866
Canadian Wheat Board cash advance repayments	-50,698	-23,476	-36,684	-33,765
Deferred grain receipts	—	-305,246	-625,816	-695,450
Liquidation of deferred grain receipts	—	—	305,246	625,816
Rye	12,082	20,476	24,923	26,675
Flaxseed	53,760	119,062	135,435	80,217
Rapeseed	156,876	247,008	337,896	259,485
Soybeans	35,784	50,348	78,511	44,925
Corn	61,762	99,155	164,156	152,979
Sugar beets	20,902	22,293	43,799	39,919
Potatoes	78,999	159,969	211,475	164,805
Fruits	99,278	140,849	140,232	126,856
Vegetables	140,650	161,490	191,677	183,473
Tobacco	150,053	142,807	207,681	198,188
Other crops	153,923	232,956	225,868	247,324
Total, cash receipts from crops	2,136,043	2,672,677	4,126,979	4,688,620
Cattle and calves	1,204,978	1,479,511	1,677,340	1,817,975
Pigs	570,472	825,494	778,092	886,471
Sheep and lambs	8,991	10,673	12,867	13,467
Dairy products	778,590	849,455	1,095,903	1,348,411
Poultry	295,853	437,939	472,150	412,532
Eggs	163,777	243,785	269,095	258,358
Other livestock and products	55,082	73,290	74,887	76,687
Total, cash receipts from livestock and products	3,077,743	3,920,147	4,380,334	4,813,901
Forest and maple products	35,879	44,368	41,229	42,360
Dairy supplementary payments	101,410	131,022	221,059	259,770
Deficiency payments	86,071	60,497	36,041	22,596
Provincial Income Stabilization program	—	—	15,583	49,794
Total, cash receipts excl. supplementary payments	5,437,146	6,828,711	8,821,225	9,877,041
Supplementary payments	14,039	11,508	57,475	30,290
Total, cash receipts	5,451,185	6,840,219	8,878,700	9,907,331

11.3 Net income of farm operators from farming operations¹, by item and by province, 1972-75 (thousand dollars)

Item and province	1972	1973	1974	1975
ITEM				
1. Cash receipts from farming operations	5,437,146	6,828,711	8,821,225	9,877,041
2. Income in kind	559,141	677,525	827,265	922,070
3. Supplementary payments	14,039	11,508	57,475	30,290
4. Realized gross income (items 1+2+3)	6,010,326	7,517,744	9,705,965	10,829,401
5. Operating and depreciation charges	3,887,716	4,781,050	5,841,586	6,652,915
6. Realized net income (items 4-5)	2,122,610	2,736,694	3,864,379	4,176,486
7. Value of inventory changes	-248,521	515,406	-91,307	151,389
8. Total gross income (items 4+7)	5,761,805	8,033,150	9,614,658	10,980,790
Total, net income (8-5)	1,874,089	3,252,100	3,773,072	4,327,875
PROVINCE				
Prince Edward Island	12,424	28,702	44,778	18,662
Nova Scotia	21,722	31,268	24,531	23,270
New Brunswick	18,575	42,159	56,036	17,584
Quebec	265,796	365,727	392,538	449,112
Ontario	495,441	694,880	848,528	921,268
Manitoba	187,738	373,576	337,266	417,789
Saskatchewan	415,487	901,915	1,136,442	1,518,733
Alberta	366,081	669,524	782,493	814,786
British Columbia	90,825	144,349	150,460	146,671

¹Includes estimated value of farm homes, supplementary payments made under the provisions of the Prairie Farm Assistance Act and payments under the Western Grain Producers' Acreage Payment Regulations.

11.4 Acreages, yields and prices of principal field crops, 1971-75, with average for 1966-70

Crop and year	Area '000 acres	Yield per acre	Production	Average price	Total value¹ $'000
Wheat		*bu*	*'000 bu*	*$ per bu*	
Av. 1966-70	25,337	24.3	614,605	1.50	924,576
1971	19,407	27.3	529,552	1.35	717,345
1972	21,350	25.0	533,288	1.86	993,349
1973	23,661	25.1	593,738	4.47	2,654,826
1974	22,077	22.1	488,513	..	..
1975	23,423	26.8	627,515	..	..
Oats					
Av. 1966-70	7,377	47.1	347,424	0.65	224,929
1971	6,831	53.2	363,479	0.57	206,739
1972	6,104	49.2	300,208	0.89	266,733
1973	6,698	48.8	326,880	1.58	515,076
1974	6,106	41.7	254,745	..	..
1975	5,958	48.6	289,619	..	..
Barley					
Av. 1966-70	8,738	37.9	330,944	0.82	270,302
1971	13,980	43.0	601,628	0.69	412,660
1972	12,509	41.4	518,316	1.25	646,184
1973	11,958	39.3	469,570	2.50	1,171,970
1974	11,800	34.3	404,286	..	..
1975	11,041	39.6	437,251	..	..
Rye					
Av. 1966-70	754	20.2	15,254	0.99	15,109
1971	957	22.9	21,915	0.81	17,711
1972	634	21.3	13,524	1.44	19,521
1973	634	22.5	14,282	2.55	36,423
1974	843	22.4	18,914	..	..
1975	790	26.1	20,585	..	..
Mixed grains					
Av. 1966-70	1,769	48.9	86,442	0.87	75,509
1971	2,055	52.1	107,078	0.81	86,446
1972	2,065	50.5	104,285	1.03	107,437
1973	2,002	48.5	97,013	1.94	187,735
1974	1,811	44.6	80,754	..	..
1975	1,835	48.9	89,807	..	..
Flaxseed					
Av. 1966-70	2,024	12.6	25,516	2.55	64,939
1971	1,768	12.7	22,387	2.20	49,282
1972	1,321	13.3	17,617	4.02	70,863
1973	1,450	13.4	19,400	9.31	180,697
1974	1,450	9.5	13,800	..	..
1975	1,400	12.5	17,500	..	..
Rapeseed					
Av. 1966-70	2,052	17.1	35,100	2.23	78,282
1971	5,306	17.9	95,000	2.16	205,530
1972	3,270	17.5	57,300	3.16	181,086
1973	3,150	16.9	53,200	5.72	304,078
1974	3,160	16.2	51,300	..	..
1975	4,320	17.8	77,100	..	..

11.4   Harvested area, yields and prices of principal field crops, 1971-75, with average for 1966-70   M

Crop and year	Area '000 ha	Yield kg per ha	Production '000 t	Average price $ per t	Total value[1] $'000
Wheat					
Av. 1966-70	10 254	1 631	16 727	55.27	924,576
1971	7 854	1 835	14 412	49.77	717,345
1972	8 640	1 680	14 514	68.44	993,349
1973	9 575	1 688	16 159	164.29	2,654,826
1974	8 934	1 488	13 295	..	..
1975	9 479	1 802	17 078	..	..
Oats					
Av. 1966-70	2 985	1 795	5 358	41.98	224,929
1971	2 764	2 028	5 606	36.88	206,739
1972	2 470	1 874	4 630	57.61	266,733
1973	2 711	1 859	5 041	102.18	515,076
1974	2 471	1 590	3 929	..	
1975	2 411	1 853	4 467	..	..
Barley					
Av. 1966-70	3 536	2 038	7 205	37.52	270,302
1971	5 658	2 315	13 099	31.50	412,660
1972	5 062	2 229	11 285	57.26	646,184
1973	4 839	2 113	10 224	114.63	1,171,970
1974	4 775	1 843	8 802	..	
1975	4 468	2 131	9 520	..	..
Rye					
Av. 1966-70	305	1 269	387	39.04	15,109
1971	387	1 439	557	31.80	17,711
1972	257	1 339	344	56.75	19,521
1973	257	1 412	363	100.34	36,423
1974	341	1 408	480	..	
1975	320	1 634	523	..	..
Mixed grains					
Av. 1966-70	716	2 464	1 764	42.81	75,509
1971	832	2 627	2 186	39.55	86,446
1972	836	2 547	2 129	50.46	107,437
1973	810	2 444	1 980	94.82	187,735
1974	733	2 248	1 648	..	
1975	743	2 467	1 833	..	..
Flaxseed					
Av. 1966-70	819	791	648	100.21	64,939
1971	715	796	569	86.61	49,282
1972	535	836	447	158.53	70,863
1973	587	840	493	366.53	180,697
1974	587	598	351	..	
1975	567	785	445	..	..
Rapeseed					
Av. 1966-70	830	959	796	98.34	78,282
1971	2 147	1 004	2 155	95.37	205,530
1972	1 323	983	1 300	139.30	181,086
1973	1 275	947	1 207	251.93	304,078
1974	1 279	909	1 163	..	
1975	1 748	1 001	1 749	..	..

11.4   Acreages, yields and prices of principal field crops, 1971-75, with average for 1966-70 (concluded)

Crop and year	Area '000 acres	Yield per acre	Production	Average price	Total value[1] $'000
Corn for grain		*bu*	*'000bu*	*$ per bu*	
Av. 1966-70	974	82.3	80,094	1.33	106,389
1971	1,410	82.2	115,977	1.18	136,990
1972	1,327	75.0	99,538	1.65	164,100
1973	1,310	84.2	110,365	2.66	293,751
1974	1,460	69.5	101,440	..	..
1975	1,569	91.5	143,493	..	..
Potatoes		*cwt*	*'000 cwt*	*$ per cwt*	
Av. 1966-70	309	168.9	52,249	1.76	92,164
1971	268	181.8	48,810	1.84	83,318
1972	244	179.8	43,886	3.65	149,443
1973	261	182.6	47,586	5.47	246,636
1974	283	195.1	55,146	..	..
1975	260	185.9	43,390	..	..
Tame hay		*ton*	*'000 tons*	*$ per ton*	
Av. 1966-70	12,626	1.98	25,010	18.36	459,258
1971	12,053	2.01	24,182	20.01	483,811
1972	12,459	1.86	23,229	23.14	537,446
1973	12,850	2.00	25,748	29.04	747,838
1974	13,033	1.95	25,402	..	..
1975	13,014	1.99	25,933	..	..

[1]Gross value of farm production; does not represent cash income from sales.

11.5   Harvested area and production of field crops, by province, 1974 and 1975

Field crop and province	Area ('000 acres) 1974	1975	Total production 1974	1975
			'000 bu	*'000 bu*
WHEAT	*22,077*	*23,423*	*488,513*	*627,515*
Prince Edward Island	10	9	444	341
Nova Scotia	3	4	120	112
New Brunswick	4	4	144	146
Quebec	60	85	1,535	2,626
Ontario				
Winter	420	455	19,070	22,405
Spring	10	11	300	385
Manitoba	2,800	3,100	59,000	78,000
Saskatchewan	14,500	15,200	304,000	387,000
Alberta	4,200	4,500	102,000	135,000
British Columbia	70	55	1,900	1,500
OATS	*6,106*	*5,958*	*254,745*	*289,619*
Prince Edward Island	51	50	2,805	2,350
Nova Scotia	19	18	920	747
New Brunswick	51	55	2,295	2,310
Quebec	625	625	23,810	25,062
Ontario	495	500	23,415	25,950
Manitoba	1,200	1,100	43,000	50,000
Saskatchewan	1,900	1,850	75,000	86,000
Alberta	1,700	1,700	80,000	94,000
British Columbia	65	60	3,500	3,200
BARLEY	*11,799*	*11,041*	*404,286*	*437,251*
Prince Edward Island	20	21	1,048	840
Nova Scotia	6	6	271	232
New Brunswick	10	10	447	354
Quebec	53	54	1,650	2,063
Ontario	340	360	15,470	18,062
Manitoba	1,800	1,500	53,000	51,000
Saskatchewan	4,200	3,500	134,000	130,000
Alberta	5,200	5,400	192,000	228,000
British Columbia	170	190	6,400	6,700
FALL RYE	*801*	*748*	*18,164*	*19,695*
Quebec	2	2	44	45
Ontario	47	57	1,385	1,910
Manitoba	90	100	2,160	2,460
Saskatchewan	335	310	6,700	7,200
Alberta	325	275	7,800	7,950
British Columbia	2	4	75	130
SPRING RYE	*42*	*42*	*750*	*890*
Manitoba	2	2	40	40
Saskatchewan	15	15	230	300
Alberta	25	25	480	550
ALL RYE	*843*	*790*	*18,914*	*20,585*
Quebec	2	2	44	45
Ontario	47	57	1,385	1,910
Manitoba	92	102	2,200	2,500
Saskatchewan	350	325	6,930	7,500
Alberta	350	300	8,280	8,500
British Columbia	2	4	75	130

11.4 Harvested area, yields and prices of principal field crops, 1971-75, with average for 1966-70 (concluded) M

Crop and year	Area '000 ha	Yield kg per ha	Production '000 t	Average price $ per t	Total value[1] $'000
Corn for grain					
Av. 1966-70	394	5 162	2 034	52.31	106,389
1971	571	5 159	2 946	46.50	136,990
1972	537	4 708	2 528	64.91	164,100
1973	530	5 289	2 803	104.80	293,751
1974	591	4 360	2 577	..	..
1975	635	5 740	3 645	..	..
Potatoes					
Av. 1966-70	125	18 960	2 370	38.89	92,164
1971	108	20 500	2 214	37.63	83,318
1972	99	20 111	1 991	75.06	149,443
1973	106	20 358	2 158	114.29	246,636
1974	115	21 748	2 501	..	..
1975	105	20 905	2 195	..	..
Tame hay					
Av. 1966-70	5 110	4 440	22 689	20.24	459,258
1971	4 878	4 497	21 938	22.05	483,811
1972	5 042	4 179	21 073	25.50	537,446
1973	5 200	4 492	23 358	32.02	747,838
1974	5 274	4 369	23 044	..	..
1975	5 267	4 467	23 526	..	..

[1]Gross value of farm production; does not represent cash income from sales.

11.5 Harvested area and production of field crops, by province, 1974 and 1975 M

Field crop and province	Area ('000 hectares) 1974	Area ('000 hectares) 1975	Total production ('000 tonnes) 1974	Total production ('000 tonnes) 1975
WHEAT	8 934	9 479	13 295.3	17 078.3
Prince Edward Island	4	4	12.1	9.3
Nova Scotia	1	2	3.3	3.0
New Brunswick	2	2	3.9	4.0
Quebec	24	34	41.8	71.5
Ontario				
Winter	170	184	519.0	609.8
Spring	4	4	8.2	10.5
Manitoba	1 133	1 255	1 605.7	2 122.8
Saskatchewan	5 868	6 151	8 273.6	10 532.5
Alberta	1 700	1 821	2 776.0	3 674.1
British Columbia	28	22	51.7	40.8
OATS	2 472	2 410	3 928.9	4 466.5
Prince Edward Island	21	20	43.3	36.2
Nova Scotia	8	7	14.2	11.5
New Brunswick	21	22	35.4	35.6
Quebec	253	253	367.2	386.5
Ontario	200	202	361.1	400.2
Manitoba	486	445	663.2	771.1
Saskatchewan	769	749	1 156.7	1 326.3
Alberta	688	688	1 233.8	1 449.7
British Columbia	26	24	54.0	49.4
BARLEY	4 774	4 467	8 802.3	9 520.3
Prince Edward Island	8	8	22.8	18.3
Nova Scotia	2	2	5.9	5.1
New Brunswick	4	4	9.7	7.7
Quebec	21	22	35.9	44.9
Ontario	138	146	336.8	393.3
Manitoba	728	607	1 154.0	1 110.4
Saskatchewan	1 700	1 416	2 917.5	2 830.5
Alberta	2 104	2 185	4 180.4	4 964.2
British Columbia	69	77	139.3	145.9
FALL RYE	325	302	461.4	500.2
Quebec	1	1	1.1	1.1
Ontario	19	23	35.2	48.5
Manitoba	36	40	54.9	62.5
Saskatchewan	136	125	170.2	182.9
Alberta	132	111	198.1	201.9
British Columbia	1	2	1.9	3.3
SPRING RYE	17	17	19.0	22.6
Manitoba	1	1	1.0	1.0
Saskatchewan	6	6	5.8	7.6
Alberta	10	10	12.2	14.0
ALL RYE	342	319	480.4	522.8
Quebec	1	1	1.1	1.1
Ontario	19	23	35.2	48.5
Manitoba	37	41	55.9	63.5
Saskatchewan	142	131	176.0	190.5
Alberta	142	121	210.3	215.9
British Columbia	1	2	1.9	3.3

11.5   Harvested area and production of field crops, by province, 1974 and 1975 (continued)

Field crop and province	Area ('000 acres)		Total production	
	1974	1975	1974	1975
			'000 bu	'000 bu
PEAS	79	75	1,680	1,793
Quebec	1	1	8	9
Ontario	2	—	22	—
Manitoba	40	35	830	750
Saskatchewan	6	14	140	360
Alberta	29	24	650	650
British Columbia	1	1	30	24
BEANS	171	147	3,548	3,352
Quebec	1	1	19	22
Ontario	170	146	3,529	3,330
SOYBEANS	415	390	10,290	13,478
Ontario	415	390	10,290	13,478
BUCKWHEAT	64	47	1,216	901
New Brunswick	2	1	57	36
Quebec	10	10	195	215
Ontario	12	11	264	220
Manitoba	40	25	700	430
MIXED GRAINS	1,811	1,835	80,754	89,807
Prince Edward Island	77	90	4,358	4,050
Nova Scotia	8	7	369	318
New Brunswick	5	5	252	212
Quebec	125	125	4,675	5,325
Ontario	820	825	43,800	46,102
Manitoba	200	200	6,000	7,500
Saskatchewan	200	175	6,400	6,900
Alberta	370	400	14,600	19,000
British Columbia	6	8	300	400
FLAXSEED	1,450	1,400	13,800	17,500
Manitoba	700	750	6,600	8,400
Saskatchewan	550	450	4,700	5,900
Alberta	200	200	2,500	3,200
RAPESEED	3,160	4,320	51,300	77,100
Manitoba	500	750	8,500	12,500
Saskatchewan	1,450	1,800	23,200	33,000
Alberta	1,150	1,700	18,700	30,500
British Columbia	60	70	900	1,100
			'000 lb.	'000 lb.
SUNFLOWER SEED	21	62	18,200	66,000
Manitoba	21	62	18,200	66,000
MUSTARD SEED	350	163	260,000	110,500
Manitoba	40	23	30,000	14,500
Saskatchewan	200	76	150,000	50,000
Alberta	110	64	80,000	46,000
			'000 bu	'000 bu
SHELLED CORN	1,460	1,563	101,440	142,648
Quebec	165	131	11,520	11,266
Ontario	1,290	1,420	89,730	130,632
Manitoba	5	12	190	750
POTATOES	282	260	55,146	46,432
Prince Edward Island	52	46	12,400	8,878
Nova Scotia	4	4	638	636
New Brunswick	58	54	13,761	9,952
Quebec	53	50	8,425	7,128
Ontario	46	44	8,592	8,913
Manitoba	35	32	4,900	4,500
Saskatchewan	2	2	380	525
Alberta	23	18	4,000	3,400
British Columbia	9	10	2,050	2,500
			'000 tons	'000 tons
FIELD ROOTS	11	5	141	63
Prince Edward Island	1	- -	9	6
Nova Scotia	1	1	8	4
New Brunswick	1	- -	8	3
Quebec	4	4	48	50
Ontario	4	—	68	—
TAME HAY	13,033	13,014	25,402	25,933
Prince Edward Island	128	127	225	238
Nova Scotia	145	152	300	281
New Brunswick	160	160	277	304
Quebec	2,675	2,700	4,980	5,238
Ontario	2,700	2,700	6,320	6,472
Manitoba	1,250	1,250	2,400	2,500
Saskatchewan	2,000	2,000	3,200	3,400
Alberta	3,350	3,300	6,100	5,800
British Columbia	625	625	1,600	1,700
FODDER CORN	1,048	971	11,070	13,202
Quebec	162	190	2,045	2,688
Ontario	840	730	8,485	9,864
Manitoba	28	33	210	290
British Columbia	18	18	330	360

11.5   Harvested area and production of field crops, by province, 1974 and 1975 (continued)   M

Field crop and province	Area ('000 hectares)		Total production ('000 tonnes)	
	1974	1975	1974	1975
PEAS	*31*	*30*	*45.7*	*48.8*
Quebec	- -	- -	0.2	0.2
Ontario	1	—	0.6	—
Manitoba	16	14	22.6	20.4
Saskatchewan	2	6	3.8	9.8
Alberta	12	10	17.7	17.7
British Columbia	- -	- -	0.8	0.7
BEANS	*69*	*59*	*96.5*	*91.2*
Quebec	- -	- -	0.5	0.6
Ontario	69	59	96.0	90.6
SOYBEANS	*168*	*158*	*280.1*	*366.8*
Ontario	168	158	280.1	366.8
BUCKWHEAT	*26*	*18*	*26.3*	*19.7*
New Brunswick	1	- -	1.2	0.8
Quebec	4	4	4.2	4.7
Ontario	5	4	5.7	4.8
Manitoba	16	10	15.2	9.4
MIXED GRAINS	*733*	*743*	*1 648.2*	*1 833.1*
Prince Edward Island	31	36	89.0	82.7
Nova Scotia	3	3	7.5	6.5
New Brunswick	2	2	5.1	4.3
Quebec	51	51	95.4	108.7
Ontario	332	334	894.0	941.0
Manitoba	81	81	122.5	153.1
Saskatchewan	81	71	130.6	140.8
Alberta	150	162	298.0	387.8
British Columbia	2	3	6.1	8.2
FLAXSEED	*587*	*567*	*350.5*	*444.6*
Manitoba	283	304	167.6	213.4
Saskatchewan	223	182	119.4	149.9
Alberta	81	81	63.5	81.3
RAPESEED	*1 278*	*1 748*	*1 163.5*	*1 748.5*
Manitoba	202	304	192.8	283.5
Saskatchewan	587	728	526.2	748.4
Alberta	465	688	424.1	691.7
British Columbia	24	28	20.4	24.9
SUNFLOWER SEED	*8*	*25*	*8.3*	*29.9*
Manitoba	8	25	8.3	29.9
MUSTARD SEED	*142*	*66*	*117.9*	*50.2*
Manitoba	16	9	13.6	6.6
Saskatchewan	81	31	68.0	22.7
Alberta	45	26	36.3	20.9
SHELLED CORN	*591*	*633*	*2 576.7*	*3 623.5*
Quebec	67	53	292.6	286.2
Ontario	522	575	2 279.3	3 318.2
Manitoba	2	5	4.8	19.1
POTATOES	*114*	*106*	*2 501.4*	*2 106.0*
Prince Edward Island	21	19	562.5	402.7
Nova Scotia	2	2	28.9	28.8
New Brunswick	23	22	624.2	451.4
Quebec	21	20	382.2	323.3
Ontario	19	18	389.7	404.3
Manitoba	14	13	222.3	204.1
Saskatchewan	1	1	17.2	23.8
Alberta	9	7	181.4	154.2
British Columbia	4	4	93.0	113.4
FIELD ROOTS	*4*	*2*	*128.0*	*57.1*
Prince Edward Island	- -	- -	8.2	5.4
Nova Scotia	- -	- -	7.3	3.6
New Brunswick	- -	- -	7.3	2.7
Quebec	2	2	43.5	45.4
Ontario	2	—	61.7	—
TAME HAY	*5 276*	*5 267*	*23 044.3*	*23 526.0*
Prince Edward Island	52	51	204.1	215.9
Nova Scotia	59	62	272.2	254.9
New Brunswick	65	65	251.3	275.8
Quebec	1 083	1 093	4 517.8	4 751.8
Ontario	1 093	1 093	5 733.4	5 871.3
Manitoba	506	506	2 177.2	2 268.0
Saskatchewan	809	809	2 903.0	3 084.4
Alberta	1 356	1 335	5 533.8	5 261.7
British Columbia	253	253	1 451.5	1 542.2
FODDER CORN	*424*	*392*	*10 042.6*	*11 976.7*
Quebec	66	77	1 855.2	2 438.5
Ontario	340	295	7 697.5	8 948.5
Manitoba	11	13	190.5	263.1
British Columbia	7	7	299.4	326.6

11.5   Harvested area and production of field crops, by province, 1974 and 1975 (concluded)

Field crop and province	Area ('000 acres)		Total production	
	1974	1975	1974	1975
			'000 tons	'000 tons
SUGAR BEETS	68	80	828	1,039
Quebec	6	8	82	155
Manitoba	27	32	221	396
Alberta	35	40	525	488

11.6   Harvested area and production of grain in the Prairie provinces, 1971-75

Grain	1971	1972	1973	1974	1975
ACREAGES ('000 acres)					
Wheat	18,885	20,800	23,100	21,500	22,800
Oats	5,315	4,660	5,300	4,800	4,650
Barley	13,312	11,900	11,350	11,200	10,400
Rye	906	582	582	792	727
Flaxseed	1,762	1,320	1,450	1,450	1,400
Rapeseed	5,306	3,270	3,150	3,100	4,250
PRODUCTION ('000 bu)					
Wheat	510,000	513,000	574,000	465,000	600,000
Oats	288,000	238,000	273,000	198,000	230,000
Barley	570,000	492,000	444,000	379,000	409,000
Rye	20,520	11,940	12,865	17,410	18,500
Flaxseed	22,300	17,600	19,400	13,800	17,500
Rapeseed	95,000	57,300	53,200	50,400	76,000

11.7   Carryover of Canadian grain, 10-year average 1966-75 and crop years ended July 31, 1971-75 (thousand bushels)

Grain and year	Total in Canada and United States	Total in Canada	In commercial storage in Canada	On farms in Canada	Prairie provinces	
					On farms	In primary elevators
Wheat						
Av. 1966-75	587,425	587,425	345,403	242,022	238,500	194,051
1971	734,154	734,154	339,334	394,820	392,000	212,181
1972	583,757	583,757	272,257	311,500	308,000	130,257
1973	365,401	365,401	250,401	115,000	110,000	140,751
1974	370,704	370,704	289,704	81,000	75,000	147,933
1975	295,329	295,329	235,329	60,000	55,000	99,477
Oats						
Av. 1966-75	107,499	107,499	25,534	81,965	66,200	15,143
1971	125,373	125,373	34,223	91,150	75,000	23,568
1972	118,257	118,257	22,257	96,000	78,000	13,857
1973	79,679	79,679	14,679	65,000	52,000	8,272
1974	77,379	77,379	19,379	58,000	45,000	10,980
1975	73,402	73,402	25,402	48,000	35,000	16,881
Barley						
Av. 1966-75	167,294	167,294	88,049	79,245	73,700	52,420
1971	144,269	144,269	82,619	61,650	55,000	53,138
1972	175,843	175,843	89,843	86,000	76,000	42,075
1973	193,024	193,024	105,024	88,000	82,000	64,972
1974	208,410	208,410	142,410	66,000	60,000	84,951
1975	188,509	188,509	137,509	51,000	45,000	70,104
Rye						
Av. 1966-75	10,916	10,916	7,386	3,530	3,500	3,726
1971	12,943	12,943	7,543	5,400	5,400	3,705
1972	15,796	15,796	10,296	5,500	5,500	7,216
1973	10,304	10,304	8,704	1,600	1,600	4,744
1974	10,510	10,510	8,010	2,500	2,500	4,249
1975	13,365	13,365	9,865	3,500	3,500	5,914
Flaxseed						
Av. 1966-75	10,446	10,446	7,856	2,590	2,590	3,441
1971	25,306	25,306	16,106	9,200	9,200	6,951
1972	16,032	16,032	10,032	6,000	6,000	5,342
1973	7,673	7,673	7,073	600	600	2,815
1974	7,911	7,911	6,411	1,500	1,500	3,739
1975	8,605	8,605	6,105	2,500	2,500	3,487
Rapeseed						
Av. 1966-75	13,275	13,275	10,565	2,710	2,710	5,614
1971	11,029	11,029	10,829	200	200	4,392
1972	43,139	43,139	26,839	16,300	16,300	17,542
1973	20,678	20,678	20,278	400	400	8,759
1974	12,386	12,386	10,886	1,500	1,500	5,933
1975	17,633	17,633	13,633	4,000	4,000	7,653

11.5   Harvested area and production of field crops, by province, 1974 and 1975 (concluded)   M

Field crop and province	Area ('000 hectares)		Total production ('000 tonnes)	
	1974	1975	1974	1975
SUGAR BEETS	27	32	751.2	942.5
Quebec	2	3	74.4	140.6
Manitoba	11	13	200.5	359.2
Alberta	14	16	476.3	442.7

11.6   Harvested area and production of grain in the Prairie provinces, 1971-75   M

Grain	1971	1972	1973	1974	1975
HARVESTED AREA ('000 ha)					
Wheat	7 642	8 417	9 348	8 701	9 227
Oats	2 151	1 886	2 145	1 942	1 882
Barley	5 387	4 816	4 593	4 532	4 209
Rye	367	236	236	321	294
Flaxseed	713	534	587	587	567
Rapeseed	2 147	1 323	1 275	1 255	1 720
PRODUCTION ('000 t)					
Wheat	13 880	13 962	15 622	12 655	16 329
Oats	4 442	3 670	4 210	3 054	3 547
Barley	12 410	10 712	9 667	8 252	8 905
Rye	521	303	327	442	470
Flaxseed	566	447	493	351	445
Rapeseed	2 155	1 300	1 207	1 143	1 724

11.7   Carryover of Canadian grain, 10-year average 1966-75 and crop years ended July 31, 1971-75 (thousand metric tonnes)   M

Grain and year	Total in Canada and United States	Total in Canada	In commercial storage in Canada	On farms in Canada	Prairie provinces	
					On farms	In primary elevators
Wheat						
Av. 1966-75	15 987.1	15 987.1	9 400.3	6 586.8	6 490.9	5 281.2
1971	19 980.4	19 980.4	9 235.2	10 745.2	10 668.5	5 774.6
1972	15 887.2	15 887.2	7 409.6	8 477.6	8 382.4	3 545.0
1973	9 944.6	9 944.6	6 814.8	3 129.8	2 993.7	3 830.6
1974	10 089.0	10 089.0	7 884.5	2 204.5	2 041.2	4 026.1
1975	8 037.5	8 037.5	6 404.6	1 632.9	1 496.9	2 707.3
Oats						
Av. 1966-75	1 657.9	1 657.9	393.8	1 264.1	1 020.9	233.5
1971	1 933.5	1 933.5	527.8	1 405.7	1 156.7	363.5
1972	1 823.8	1 823.8	343.3	1 480.5	1 202.9	213.7
1973	1 228.8	1 228.8	226.4	1 002.4	802.0	127.6
1974	1 193.4	1 193.4	298.9	894.5	694.0	169.3
1975	1 132.1	1 132.1	391.8	740.3	539.8	260.3
Barley						
Av. 1966-75	3 642.4	3 642.4	1 917.0	1 725.4	1 604.6	1 141.3
1971	3 141.1	3 141.1	1 798.8	1 342.3	1 197.5	1 156.9
1972	3 828.5	3 828.5	1 956.1	1 872.4	1 654.7	916.1
1973	4 202.6	4 202.6	2 286.6	1 916.0	1 785.3	1 414.6
1974	4 537.6	4 537.6	3 100.6	1 437.0	1 306.3	1 849.6
1975	4 104.3	4 104.3	2 993.9	1 110.4	979.8	1 526.3
Rye						
Av. 1966-75	277.3	277.3	187.6	89.7	88.9	94.6
1971	328.8	328.8	191.6	137.2	137.2	94.1
1972	401.2	401.2	261.5	139.7	139.7	183.3
1973	261.7	261.7	221.1	40.6	40.6	120.5
1974	267.0	267.0	203.5	63.5	63.5	107.9
1975	339.5	339.5	250.6	88.9	88.9	150.2
Flaxseed						
Av. 1966-75	265.4	265.4	199.6	65.8	65.8	87.4
1971	642.8	642.8	409.1	233.7	233.7	176.6
1972	407.2	407.2	254.8	152.4	152.4	135.7
1973	194.9	194.9	179.7	15.2	15.2	71.5
1974	200.9	200.9	162.8	38.1	38.1	95.0
1975	218.6	218.6	155.1	63.5	63.5	88.6
Rapeseed						
Av. 1966-75	301.1	301.1	239.6	61.5	61.5	127.3
1971	250.1	250.1	245.6	4.5	4.5	99.6
1972	978.4	978.4	608.7	369.7	369.7	397.8
1973	469.0	469.0	459.9	9.1	9.1	198.7
1974	280.9	280.9	246.9	34.0	34.0	134.6
1975	399.9	399.9	309.2	90.7	90.7	173.6

11.8   Livestock slaughtered at federally inspected establishments, 1970-75

Year	Cattle	Calves	Sheep	Pigs
1970	2,700,833	499,162	181,332	8,280,481
1971	2,786,908	464,240	205,082	9,742,759
1972	2,878,591	402,370	214,769	9,357,143
1973	2,878,016	291,524	234,206	8,721,921
1974	2,975,833	392,811	185,077	8,939,335
1975	3,337,687	682,094	186,566	7,656,334

11.9   Production and domestic disappearance of poultry meat[1], 1974 and 1975

Year and item	Net production '000 lb.	Total supply '000 lb.	Domestic disappearance '000 lb.	Per capita consumption lb.
1974				
Fowl and chickens	781,377	834,097	773,601	34.40
Turkeys	241,942	285,699	236,115	10.50
Geese	3,705	4,040	3,373	0.15
Ducks	7,745	9,201	8,256	0.37
Total	1,034,769	1,133,037	1,021,345	45.42
1975				
Fowl and chickens	696,304	757,938	731,770	32.10
Turkeys	189,572	243,746	215,869	9.50
Geese	2,105	2,300	1,430	0.06
Ducks	8,282	10,772	10,206	0.45
Total	896,263	1,014,756	959,275	42.11

[1] Eviscerated weight.

11.10   Production and utilization of milk, by province, 1972-75 (thousand pounds)

Province and year		Milk used in manufacture		Milk otherwise used			Total milk production
		On farms[1]	In factories	Fluid sales[2]	Farm-home consumed	Fed on farms	
Prince Edward Island	1972	562	151,085	22,135	9,546	6,836	190,164
	1973	234	138,262	23,934	8,633	6,128	177,191
	1974	—	132,711	24,567	7,378	7,249	171,905
	1975	—	155,213	24,972	6,384	8,351	194,920
Nova Scotia	1972	1,591	112,959	215,940	9,283	8,001	347,774
	1973	1,100	99,448	216,512	8,547	7,014	332,621
	1974	—	91,615	222,630	7,763	7,307	329,315
	1975	—	97,803	224,221	7,459	8,875	338,358
New Brunswick	1972	2,434	91,275	137,827	8,501	6,856	246,893
	1973	1,849	79,406	138,284	7,541	6,558	233,638
	1974	—	71,441	140,531	7,224	6,808	226,004
	1975	—	80,520	140,133	6,233	7,973	234,859
Quebec	1972	5,429	4,971,116	1,352,872	101,440	182,370	6,613,227
	1973	4,095	4,615,217	1,387,515	93,598	193,614	6,294,039
	1974	—	4,714,159	1,415,002	86,762	195,554	6,411,477
	1975	—	5,149,795	1,366,528	83,346	225,819	6,825,488
Ontario	1972	4,821	3,821,967	2,208,652	93,872	249,900	6,379,212
	1973	3,603	3,404,808	2,240,428	88,580	271,597	6,009,016
	1974	—	3,431,726	2,261,135	83,553	269,295	6,045,709
	1975	—	3,749,688	2,216,154	83,453	299,011	6,348,306
Manitoba	1972	3,931	469,159	248,558	42,266	48,650	812,564
	1973	2,902	458,962	261,575	38,695	42,837	804,971
	1974	—	420,625	260,413	37,088	44,464	762,590
	1975	—	444,676	255,892	29,694	44,264	774,526
Saskatchewan	1972	16,918	346,027	196,254	85,035	47,250	691,484
	1973	12,636	310,846	195,290	77,934	53,827	650,533
	1974	—	252,005	194,846	64,273	49,828	560,952
	1975	—	258,651	188,917	43,815	44,572	535,955
Alberta	1972	15,818	824,403	409,044	80,843	87,840	1,417,948
	1973	11,887	798,001	420,426	73,890	92,620	1,396,824
	1974	—	694,265	434,920	64,889	89,426	1,283,500
	1975	—	754,604	437,519	50,741	90,392	1,333,256
British Columbia	1972	1,310	330,205	603,137	17,335	24,950	976,937
	1973	1,123	314,195	626,092	16,353	28,383	986,146
	1974	—	312,380	657,543	15,830	34,382	1,020,135
	1975	—	366,852	660,938	15,961	45,530	1,089,281
Total	1972	52,814	11,118,196	5,394,419	448,121	662,653	17,676,203
	1973	39,429	10,219,145	5,510,056	413,771	702,578	16,884,979
	1974	—	10,120,927	5,611,587	374,760	704,313	16,811,587
	1975	—	11,057,802	5,515,274	327,086	774,787	17,674,949

[1] Used in farm butter only.
[2] Represents milk and cream, in milk equivalent, sold off farms for fluid purposes.

11.9   Production and domestic disappearance of poultry meat[1], 1974 and 1975   M

Year and item	Net production t	Total supply t	Domestic disappearance t	Per capita consumption kg
1974				
Fowl and chickens	354 427	378 340	350 900	15.60
Turkeys	109 743	129 591	107 100	4.76
Geese	1 681	1 833	1 530	0.07
Ducks	3 513	4 174	3 745	0.17
Total	469 364	513 938	463 275	20.60
1975				
Fowl and chickens	315 838	343 795	331 925	14.56
Turkeys	85 988	110 561	97 917	4.31
Geese	955	1 043	649	0.03
Ducks	3 757	4 886	4 629	0.20
Total	406 538	460 285	435 120	19.10

[1]Eviscerated weight.

11.10   Production and utilization of milk, by province, 1972-75 (metric tonnes)   M

Province and year		Milk used in manufacture		Milk otherwise used			Total milk production
		On farms[1]	In factories	Fluid sales[2]	Farm-home consumed	Fed on farms	
Prince Edward Island	1972	255	68 531	10 040	4 330	3 101	86 257
	1973	106	62 715	10 856	3 916	2 780	80 373
	1974	—	60 197	11 143	3 347	3 288	77 975
	1975	—	70 403	11 327	2 896	3 788	88 414
Nova Scotia	1972	722	51 237	97 949	4 211	3 629	157 748
	1973	499	45 109	98 208	3 877	3 181	150 874
	1974	—	41 556	100 983	3 521	3 314	149 374
	1975	—	44 363	101 705	3 383	4 026	153 477
New Brunswick	1972	1 104	41 402	62 517	3 856	3 110	111 989
	1973	839	36 018	62 725	3 421	2 975	105 978
	1974	—	32 405	63 744	3 277	3 088	102 514
	1975	—	36 523	63 563	2 827	3 616	106 529
Quebec	1972	2 463	2 254 860	613 652	46 012	82 722	2 999 709
	1973	1 857	2 093 427	629 366	42 455	87 822	2 854 927
	1974	—	2 138 307	641 834	39 355	88 702	2 908 198
	1975	—	2 335 908	619 847	37 805	102 430	3 095 990
Ontario	1972	2 187	1 733 615	1 001 828	42 580	113 353	2 893 563
	1973	1 634	1 544 395	1 016 241	40 179	123 194	2 725 643
	1974	—	1 556 605	1 025 634	37 899	122 150	2 742 288
	1975	—	1 700 830	1 005 231	37 854	135 629	2 879 544
Manitoba	1972	1 783	212 807	112 744	19 172	22 067	368 573
	1973	1 316	208 182	118 648	17 552	19 431	365 129
	1974	—	190 792	118 121	16 823	20 169	345 905
	1975	—	201 702	116 071	13 469	20 078	351 320
Saskatchewan	1972	7 674	156 955	89 019	38 571	21 432	313 651
	1973	5 732	140 997	88 582	35 350	24 416	295 077
	1974	—	114 308	88 381	29 154	22 602	254 445
	1975	—	117 322	85 691	19 874	20 218	243 105
Alberta	1972	7 175	373 943	185 539	36 670	39 844	643 171
	1973	5 392	361 967	190 702	33 516	42 012	633 589
	1974	—	314 913	197 276	29 433	40 563	582 185
	1975	—	342 283	198 455	23 016	41 001	604 755
British Columbia	1972	594	149 778	273 578	7 863	11 317	443 130
	1973	509	142 516	283 991	7 418	12 874	447 308
	1974	—	141 693	298 256	7 180	15 595	462 724
	1975	—	166 401	299 796	7 240	20 652	494 089
Total	1972	23 957	5 043 128	2 446 866	203 265	300 575	8 017 791
	1973	17 884	4 635 326	2 499 319	187 684	318 685	7 658 898
	1974	—	4 590 776	2 545 372	169 989	319 471	7 625 608
	1975	—	5 015 735	2 501 686	148 364	351 438	8 017 223

[1]Used in farm butter only.
[2]Represents milk and cream, in milk equivalent, sold off farms for fluid purposes.

11.11 Farm values of milk production, by province, 1973-75 (thousand dollars)

Province and year		Value of milk used in manufacture		Value of milk otherwise used			Value of total milk production
		On farms[1]	In factories	Fluid sales [2]	Farm-home consumed	Fed on farms[3]	
Prince Edward Island	1973	7	5,001	1,771	312	690	7,705[4]
	1974	—	5,973	2,341	313	845	9,348[4]
	1975	—	10,091	2,728	319	755	13,304[4]
Nova Scotia	1973	30	3,630	18,549	305	343	22,857
	1974	—	4,451	23,693	304	328	28,689[4]
	1975	—	6,920	27,065	380	512	34,466[4]
New Brunswick	1973	53	2,350	10,751	266	539	13,959
	1974	—	2,526	13,494	300	641	16,920[4]
	1975	—	4,508	15,376	329	794	20,805[4]
Quebec	1973	126	217,199	98,539	4,418	10,893	326,689[4]
	1974	—	283,555	130,032	5,206	12,803	425,033[4]
	1975	—	399,532	152,969	6,468	17,874	549,578[4]
Ontario	1973	108	153,796	165,797	4,022	15,452	336,671[4]
	1974	—	197,145	210,170	4,729	17,747	426,013[4]
	1975	—	272,530	241,153	5,984	23,707	527,094[4]
Manitoba	1973	82	14,616	17,116	1,277	3,259	36,119[4]
	1974	—	19,499	23,794	1,721	3,283	47,955[4]
	1975	—	26,900	28,093	1,672	3,748	59,019[4]
Saskatchewan	1973	340	8,203	13,141	2,533	3,591	27,758[4]
	1974	—	8,310	18,197	2,378	3,391	32,165[4]
	1975	—	13,223	19,943	1,915	3,141	37,723[4]
Alberta	1973	330	29,220	28,717	3,295	7,375	68,601[4]
	1974	—	32,269	39,830	3,361	7,202	82,178[4]
	1975	—	45,617	46,392	3,349	8,558	101,729[4]
British Columbia	1973	31	13,124	55,598	760	1,404	70,875[4]
	1974	—	19,052	73,440	1,073	2,424	95,651[4]
	1975	—	29,180	85,004	1,421	4,214	118,228[4]
Total	1973	1,107	447,139	409,979	17,188	43,546	911,234[4]
	1974	—	572,780	534,991	19,385	48,664	1,163,952[4]
	1975	—	808,501	618,723	21,837	63,303	1,461,946[4]

[1]Used in farm butter only.
[2]Represents the value of milk and cream sold off farms for fluid purposes.
[3]Includes values of skim milk and buttermilk retained on farms.
[4]Represents the market price less levies on manufacturing milk collected under provincial authority. Levies by category of milk are not available, therefore cash receipts do not add.

11.12 Production of butter and cheese, by province, 1973-75 (thousand pounds)

Province and year		Butter				Cheese Factory[1]
		Creamery	Farm	Whey	Total	
Prince Edward Island	1973	2,799	10	55	2,864	2,293
	1974	2,628	—	83	2,711	3,065
	1975	3,116	—	113	3,229	3,882
Nova Scotia	1973	1,660	47	—	1,707	1,808
	1974	1,029	—	—	1,029	2,235
	1975	1,174	—	—	1,174	2,243
New Brunswick	1973	2,475	79	—	2,554	554
	1974	2,102	—	—	2,102	411
	1975	2,364	—	—	2,364	132
Quebec	1973	120,821	175	2,209	123,205	119,816
	1974	110,425	—	2,909	113,334	149,909
	1975	144,685	—	4,196	148,881	117,446
Ontario	1973	73,677	154	4,764	78,595	103,033
	1974	74,118	—	5,112	79,230	107,089
	1975	85,480	—	4,776	90,256	114,519
Manitoba	1973	12,006	124	—	12,130	9,753
	1974	10,165	—	—	10,165	9,366
	1975	10,462	—	—	10,462	10,201
Saskatchewan	1973	11,859	540	—	12,399	463
	1974	9,070	—	—	9,070	1,059
	1975	8,902	—	—	8,902	1,216
Alberta	1973	23,282	508	—	23,790	6,236
	1974	18,695	—	—	18,695	7,042
	1975	20,587	—	—	20,587	8,714
British Columbia	1973	3,652	48	—	3,700	2,533
	1974	3,880	—	—	3,880	2,886
	1975	6,010	—	—	6,010	3,480
Total	1973	252,231	1,685	7,028	260,944	259,972
	1974	232,112	—	8,104	240,216	286,585
	1975	282,780	—	9,085	291,865	265,312

[1]Factory-made cheese includes cheddar and other cheese made from whole milk and cream. Amounts for other cheese are included in Quebec, Ontario and Alberta figures, but, as fewer than three firms reported in the other provinces, data cannot be included except in the Canada total.

11.12   Production of butter and cheese, by province, 1973-75 (metric tonnes)   M

Province and year		Butter				Cheese Factory[1]
		Creamery	Farm	Whey	Total	
Prince Edward Island	1973	1 270	5	25	1 300	1 040
	1974	1 192	—	38	1 230	1 390
	1975	1 413	—	51	1 464	1 761
Nova Scotia	1973	753	21	—	774	820
	1974	467	—	—	467	1 014
	1975	533	—	—	533	1 017
New Brunswick	1973	1 123	36	—	1 159	251
	1974	953	—	—	953	186
	1975	1 072	—	—	1 072	60
Quebec	1973	54 803	79	1 002	55 884	54 348
	1974	50 088	—	1 320	51 408	67 998
	1975	65 628	—	1 903	67 531	53 273
Ontario	1973	33 419	70	2 161	35 650	46 735
	1974	33 619	—	2 319	35 938	48 575
	1975	38 773	—	2 166	40 939	51 945
Manitoba	1973	5 446	56	—	5 502	4 424
	1974	4 611	—	—	4 611	4 248
	1975	4 745	—	—	4 745	4 627
Saskatchewan	1973	5 379	245	—	5 624	210
	1974	4 114	—	—	4 114	480
	1975	4 038	—	—	4 038	552
Alberta	1973	10 561	230	—	10 791	2 829
	1974	8 480	—	—	8 480	3 194
	1975	9 338	—	—	9 338	3 953
British Columbia	1973	1 657	22	—	1 679	1 149
	1974	1 760	—	—	1 760	1 309
	1975	2 726	—	—	2 726	1 579
Total	1973	114 411	764	3 188	118 363	117 921
	1974	105 284	—	3 677	108 961	129 993
	1975	128 266	—	4 120	132 386	120 343

[1]Factory-made cheese includes cheddar and other cheese made from whole milk and cream. Amounts for other cheese are included in Quebec, Ontario and Alberta figures, but, as fewer than three firms reported in the other provinces, data cannot be included except in the Canada total.

11.13   Domestic disappearance of dairy products, 1973-75

Product	1973		1974		1975	
	Total '000 lb.	Per capita[1] lb.	Total '000 lb.	Per capita[1] lb.	Total '000 lb.	Per capita[1] lb.
Milk and cream	5,510,056	249.04	5,611,587	249.64	5,515,274	241.57
Milk	4,728,868	213.73	4,811,585	214.05	4,743,071	207.75
Cream as milk	781,188	35.31	800,002	35.59	772,203	33.82
Butter	301,810	13.64	298,682	13.29	272,260	11.92
Creamery	293,277	13.25	290,647	12.93	263,266	11.53
Farm	1,685	0.08	—	—	—	—
Whey	6,848	0.31	8,035	0.36	8,994	0.39
Cheese	319,214	14.43	357,166	15.89	356,925	15.63
Cheddar	108,935	4.92	101,736	4.52	101,482	4.44
Process	121,886	5.51	128,055	5.70	128,057	5.61
Other	88,393	4.00	127,375	5.67	127,386	5.58
Concentrated whole milk products[2]	275,304	12.44	258,477	11.50	243,314	10.65
Evaporated	231,768	10.48	217,364	9.67	200,991	8.80
Condensed	20,186	0.91	18,923	0.84	16,694	0.73
Powdered	2,854	0.13	1,461	0.06	1,845	0.08
Concentrated milk by-products[3]	222,907	10.07	238,863	10.63	249,679	10.94
Evaporated	20,251	0.92	20,018	0.89	22,171	0.97
Condensed	2,472	0.11	2,599	0.12	1,932	0.09
Powdered	114,584	5.18	127,474	5.67	138,496	6.07
All dairy products in terms of milk						
Butter	6,862,682	310.18	6,801,140	302.56	6,160,424	269.83
Cheese	3,154,575	142.78	3,548,135	157.84	3,545,264	155.28
Concentrated	625,132	28.27	577,959	25.71	539,951	23.65
Total[4]	17,509,401	798.09	17,815,728	799.14	17,025,056	752.71

[1]Includes Newfoundland for all manufactured dairy products.
[2]Includes, in addition to the items listed, partly skimmed evaporated milk, whole milk powder of less than 26% fat, formula milks, evaporated milk of 2% fat, and concentrated liquid milk.
[3]Includes, in addition to the items listed, powdered buttermilk, sugar of milk, casein, powdered whey, special formula skim milk products and concentrated liquid skim milk. Since the quantities used for human consumption and livestock feeding cannot be separated, per capita figures include both.
[4]Includes ice cream mix in terms of milk.

11.14   Estimated commercial production and farm value of fruit, 1973-75

Kind of fruit and year	Quantity	Weight tons	Farm value $'000	Kind of fruit and year	Quantity	Weight tons	Farm value $'000
Apples	'000 bu			Peaches	'000 bu		
1973	19,668	413,026	65,741	1973	1,964	49,089	11,699
1974	21,328	447,909	53,973	1974	2,252	56,305	14,553
1975	24,158	507,310	46,888	1975	2,610	65,257	15,556
Apricots				Pears			
1973	148	3,712	756	1973	1,385	34,657	4,860
1974	127	3,180	937	1974	1,669	41,715	6,798
1975	..	..	..	1975	1,685	42,128	6,459
Cherries (sour)				Plums and prunes			
1973	222	5,556	2,456	1973	416	10,391	2,256
1974	338	8,456	3,756	1974	283	7,084	1,699
1975	337	8,436	..	1975	465	11,603	2,519
Cherries (sweet)				Raspberries	'000 qt		
1973	460	11,502	4,864	1973	9,799	7,189	6,725
1974	374	9,344	4,347	1974	10,283	7,533	5,318
1975	564	14,114	5,802	1975	10,308	7,577	4,158
Strawberries	'000 qt			Grapes	'000 lb.		
1973	23,659	15,379	9,494	1973	132,016	66,009	12,898
1974	24,758	16,232	11,045	1974	159,682	79,840	18,563
1975	27,883	18,287	13,649	1975	169,258	84,629	20,689
Loganberries	'000 lb.			Blueberries			
1973	403	202	110	1973	36,013	18,006	10,365
1974	347	174	117	1974	19,496	9,748	3,946
1975	..	..	..	1975	31,531	15,766	8,131

11.13   Domestic disappearance of dairy products, 1973-75   M

Product	1973 Total *t*	1973 Per capita[1] *kg*	1974 Total *t*	1974 Per capita[1] *kg*	1975 Total *t*	1975 Per capita[1] *kg*
Milk and cream	*2 499 319*	*112.97*	*2 545 373*	*113.23*	*2 501 686*	*109.57*
Milk	2 144 978	96.95	2 182 498	97.09	2 151 421	94.23
Cream as milk	354 341	16.02	362 875	16.14	350 265	15.34
Butter	*136 898*	*6.19*	*135 480*	*6.02*	*123 495*	*5.41*
Creamery	133 028	6.01	131 835	5.86	119 415	5.23
Farm	764	0.04	—	—	—	—
Whey	3 106	0.14	3 645	0.16	4 080	0.18
Cheese	*144 793*	*6.54*	*162 008*	*7.21*	*161 898*	*7.08*
Cheddar	49 412	2.23	46 147	2.05	46 031	2.01
Process	55 287	2.50	58 085	2.59	58 086	2.54
Other	40 094	1.81	57 776	2.57	57 781	2.53
Concentrated whole milk products[2]	*124 876*	*5.64*	*117 243*	*5.22*	*110 365*	*4.83*
Evaporated	105 128	4.75	98 595	4.39	91 168	3.99
Condensed	9 156	0.41	8 583	0.38	7 572	0.33
Powdered	1 295	0.06	663	0.03	837	0.04
Concentrated milk by-products[3]	*101 109*	*4.57*	*108 346*	*4.82*	*113 252*	*4.96*
Evaporated	9 186	0.42	9 080	0.40	10 057	0.44
Condensed	1 121	0.05	1 179	0.05	876	0.04
Powdered	51 974	2.35	57 821	2.57	62 821	2.75
All dairy products in terms of milk						
Butter	3 112 860	140.70	3 084 945	137.24	2 794 321	122.39
Cheese	1 430 891	64.76	1 609 407	71.60	1 608 105	70.43
Concentrated	283 555	12.82	262 158	11.66	244 918	10.73
Total[4]	7 942 131	362.01	8 081 078	362.48	7 722 436	341.42

[1]Includes Newfoundland for all manufactured dairy products.
[2]Includes, in addition to the items listed, partly skimmed evaporated milk, whole milk powder of less than 26% fat, formula milks, evaporated milk of 2% fat, and concentrated liquid milk.
[3]Includes, in addition to the items listed, powdered buttermilk, sugar of milk, casein, powdered whey, special formula skim milk products and concentrated liquid skim milk. Since the quantities used for human consumption and livestock feeding cannot be separated, per capita figures include both.
[4]Includes ice cream mix in terms of milk.

11.14   Estimated commercial production and farm value of fruit, 1973-75   M

Kind of fruit and year	Quantity/Weight *t*	Farm value *$'000*	Kind of fruit and year	Quantity/Weight *t*	Farm value *$'000*
Apples			Peaches		
1973	374 691	65,741	1973	44 533	11,699
1974	406 336	53,973	1974	51 079	14,553
1975	460 224	46,888	1975	59 200	15,556
Apricots			Pears		
1973	3 367	756	1973	31 440	4,860
1974	2 885	937	1974	37 843	6,798
1975	..	..	1975	38 218	6,459
Cherries (sour)			Plums and prunes		
1973	5 040	2,456	1973	9 427	2,256
1974	7 671	3,756	1974	6 426	1,699
1975	7 653	..	1975	10 526	2,519
Cherries (sweet)			Raspberries		
1973	10 434	4,864	1973	6 522	6,725
1974	8 477	4,347	1974	6 834	5,318
1975	12 804	5,802	1975	6 874	4,158
Strawberries			Grapes		
1973	13 952	9,494	1973	59 882	12,898
1974	14 725	11,045	1974	72 430	18,563
1975	16 590	13,649	1975	76 774	20,689
Loganberries			Blueberries		
1973	183	110	1973	16 335	10,365
1974	158	117	1974	8 843	3,946
1975	..	..	1975	14 303	8,131

11.15   Estimated commercial acreage and production of vegetables, 1973-75, with average for 1968-72

Vegetable	Average 1968-72		1973		1974		1975	
	Area acres	Production '000 lb.	Area acres	Production '000 lb.	Area acres	Production '000 lb.	Area acres	Production '000 lb.
Asparagus	3,152	5,494	3,690	6,981	3,789	6,242	3,860	6,174
Beans	23,342	94,485	25,700	100,946	24,264	98,138	22,348	94,634
Beets	2,276	40,698	2,230	38,388	2,540	41,054	2,591	43,778
Cabbage	7,960	158,997	9,270	177,610	9,582	179,068	9,728	199,598
Carrots	14,272	344,328	15,230	349,236	15,970	417,020	16,114	489,592
Cauliflower	3,468	36,729	3,540	34,521	3,338	35,814	3,551	40,494
Celery	1,126	43,954	1,190	51,539	1,105	47,042	1,125	56,120
Corn	63,170	499,273	70,230	495,400	72,259	497,684	77,425	604,986
Cucumbers	9,744	122,529	9,640	136,350	9,358	127,966	9,393	139,108
Lettuce	5,144	60,798	5,140	69,977	5,181	72,542	4,866	70,730
Onions	9,142	220,372	9,320	215,357	8,603	223,264	8,556	226,572
Parsnips	558	9,795	520	7,383	425	5,598	430	5,930
Peas	50,750	133,185	58,690	145,988	64,059	168,844	66,747	172,494
Rutabagas	8,650	213,921	9,070	205,356	9,413	218,982	8,607	200,272
Spinach	852	6,519	770	4,540	869	5,564	884	5,426
Tomatoes	28,260	750,615	27,930	871,326	28,187	758,228	28,981	842,820

11.16   Honey production, by province, and total value, 1972-75, with 10-year average for 1964-73

Province		Average 1964-73	1972	1973	1974	1975
Prince Edward Island	'000 lb.	45	56	63	24	69
Nova Scotia	"	246	342	347	285	384
New Brunswick	"	132	148	196	122	193
Quebec	"	2,872	1,590	4,836	3,073	5,130
Ontario	"	8,577	6,708	9,203	5,395	8,632
Manitoba	"	7,802	9,476	8,372	8,580	8,056
Saskatchewan	"	6,957	8,554	6,605	7,128	6,496
Alberta	"	17,546	20,150	21,605	17,940	13,904
British Columbia	"	2,920	3,575	3,402	3,239	3,555
Total production	'000 lb.	47,097	50,599	54,629	45,786	46,419
Total value	$'000	10,606	15,623	25,185	21,135	23,191

11.17   Harvested area, yield, production and value of sugar beets and quantity and value of beet sugar shipments, 1971-75

Year	Sugar beets					Beet sugar (all types)	
	Harvested area acres	Yield per acre tons	Total production tons	Average price per ton $	Total farm value $'000	Shipments '000 lb.	Value $'000
1971	81,096	14.99	1,215,917	18.27	22,215	244,371	24,902
1972	77,610	13.78	1,069,744	19.81	21,193	274,151	30,859
1973	68,640	14.48	994,162	39.15	38,917	..	..
1974	67,548	12.27	828,493	..	..	..	..
1975	79,485	13.07	1,039,018	..	..	..	..

11.18   Production and value of maple sugar and maple syrup, by province, 1973-75, with 5-year average for 1968-72

Province and year	Maple sugar		Maple syrup			Total value, sugar and syrup $
	Quantity lb.	Value $	Quantity gal	Average price per gal $	Value $	
Nova Scotia						
Av. 1968-72	13,000	12,000	5,000	7.40	37,000	49,000
1973	10,000	11,000	3,000	10.67	32,000	43,000
1974	9,000	12,000	4,000	11.25	45,000	57,000
1975	8,000	14,000	3,000	13.33	40,000	54,000
New Brunswick						
Av. 1968-72	23,000	23,000	9,000	7.89	71,000	94,000
1973	11,000	15,000	6,000	9.83	59,000	74,000
1974	19,000	29,000	6,000	11.67	70,000	99,000
1975	20,000	35,000	9,000	12.89	116,000	151,000
Quebec						
Av. 1968-72	307,000	217,000	1,687,000	5.05	8,514,000	8,731,000
1973	275,000	283,000	2,287,000	6.92	15,826,000	16,109,000
1974	258,000	299,000	1,599,000	6.90	11,028,000	11,327,000
1975	300,000	366,000	1,229,000	7.78	9,562,000	9,928,000

11.15   Estimated commercial area and production of vegetables, 1973-75, with average for 1968-72   M

Vegetable	Average 1968-72		1973		1974		1975	
	Area ha	Production t	Area ha	Production t	Area ha	Production t	Area ha	Production t
Asparagus	1 276	2 492	1 493	3 167	1 533	2 831	1 562	2 800
Beans	9 446	42 858	10 400	45 788	9 819	44 515	9 044	42 925
Beets	921	18 460	902	17 413	1 028	18 622	1 049	19 857
Cabbage	3 221	72 120	3 751	80 563	3 878	81 224	3 937	90 536
Carrots	5 776	156 185	6 163	158 411	6 463	189 157	6 521	222 075
Cauliflower	1 403	16 660	1 433	15 658	1 351	16 245	1 437	18 368
Celery	456	19 937	482	23 378	447	21 338	455	25 456
Corn	25 564	226 466	28 421	224 710	29 242	225 746	31 333	274 417
Cucumbers	3 943	55 578	3 901	61 847	3 787	58 044	3 801	63 098
Lettuce	2 082	27 578	2 080	31 741	2 097	32 904	1 969	32 083
Onions	3 700	99 959	3 772	97 684	3 482	101 271	3 462	102 771
Parsnips	226	4 443	210	3 349	172	2 539	174	2 690
Peas	20 538	60 412	23 751	66 219	25 924	76 586	27 012	78 242
Rutabagas	3 501	97 033	3 670	93 148	3 809	99 329	3 483	90 842
Spinach	345	2 957	312	2 059	352	2 524	358	2 461
Tomatoes	11 436	340 473	11 303	395 227	11 407	343 926	11 728	382 297

11.16   Honey production, by province, and total value, 1972-75, with 10-year average for 1964-73   M

Province		Average 1964-73	1972	1973	1974	1975
Prince Edward Island	t	20	25	29	11	31
Nova Scotia	"	112	155	157	129	174
New Brunswick	"	60	67	89	55	88
Quebec	"	1 303	721	2 194	1 394	2 327
Ontario	"	3 890	3 043	4 174	2 447	3 915
Manitoba	"	3 539	4 298	3 797	3 892	3 654
Saskatchewan	"	3 156	3 880	2 996	3 233	2 947
Alberta	"	7 959	9 140	9 800	8 137	6 307
British Columbia	"	1 324	1 622	1 543	1 469	1 613
Total production	t	21 363	22 951	24 779	20 767	21 056
Total value	$'000	10,606	15,623	25,185	21,135	23,191

11.17   Harvested area, yield, production and value of sugar beets and quantity and value of beet sugar shipments, 1971-75   M

Year	Sugar beets					Beet sugar (all types)	
	Harvested area ha	Yield per ha kg	Total production t	Average price per t $	Total farm value $'000	Shipments '000 kg	Value $'000
1971	32 818	33 611	1 103 061	20.14	22,215	110 845	24,902
1972	31 408	30 898	970 455	21.84	21,193	124 353	30,859
1973	27 778	32 468	901 889	43.15	38,917	..	..
1974	27 336	27 495	751 596	..	..	..	..
1975	32 166	29 304	942 581	..	..	..	..

11.18   Production and value of maple sugar and maple syrup, by province, 1973-75, with 5-year average for 1968-72   M

Province and year	Maple sugar		Maple syrup			Total value, sugar and syrup $
	Quantity kg	Value $	Quantity dm³	Average price per dm³ $	Value $	
Nova Scotia						
Av. 1968-72	6 000	12,000	23 000	1.61	37,000	49,000
1973	5 000	11,000	14 000	2.29	32,000	43,000
1974	4 000	12,000	18 000	2.50	45,000	57,000
1975	4 000	14,000	14 000	2.86	40,000	54,000
New Brunswick						
Av. 1968-72	10 000	23,000	41 000	1.73	71,000	94,000
1973	5 000	15,000	27 000	2.19	59,000	74,000
1974	9 000	29,000	27 000	2.59	70,000	99,000
1975	9 000	35,000	41 000	2.83	116,000	151,000
Quebec						
Av. 1968-72	139 000	217,000	7 669 000	1.11	8,514,000	8,731,000
1973	125 000	283,000	10 397 000	1.52	15,826,000	16,109,000
1974	117 000	299,000	7 269 000	1.52	11,028,000	11,327,000
1975	136 000	366,000	5 587 000	1.71	9,562,000	9,928,000

11.18   Production and value of maple sugar and maple syrup, by province, 1973-75, with 5-year average for 1968-72 (concluded)

Province and year	Maple sugar		Maple syrup			Total value, sugar and syrup $
	Quantity lb.	Value $	Quantity gal	Average price per gal $	Value $	
Ontario						
Av. 1968-72	13,000	16,000	186,000	6.89	1,281,000	1,297,000
1973	12,000	21,000	124,000	8.90	1,103,000	1,124,000
1974	16,000	28,000	142,000	10.46	1,486,000	1,514,000
1975	9,000	20,000	120,000	11.98	1,437,000	1,457,000
Total						
Av. 1968-72	356,000	268,000	1,887,000	5.25	9,903,000	10,171,000
1973	308,000	330,000	2,420,000	7.03	17,020,000	17,350,000
1974	302,000	368,000	1,751,000	7.21	12,629,000	12,997,000
1975	337,000	435,000	1,361,000	8.20	11,155,000	11,590,000

11.19   Production, and value of farm eggs, by province, 1974 and 1975

Province	1974				1975			
	Average number of layers '000	Average production per 100 layers No.	Net eggs laid[1] '000 doz	Total value (sold and used) $'000	Average number of layers '000	Average production per 100 layers No.	Net eggs laid[1] '000 doz	Total value (sold and used) $'000
Newfoundland	445	21,153	7,857	6,387	377	21,450	6,740	5,445
Prince Edward Island	141	20,161	2,363	1,604	143	19,943	2,373	1,683
Nova Scotia	1,088	21,286	19,299	13,226	943	22,598	17,756	13,265
New Brunswick	477	22,044	8,770	6,087	478	22,249	8,852	6,719
Quebec	3,656	21,170	64,613	42,134	3,822	22,148	70,563	45,951
Ontario	10,040	22,638	189,323	109,883	9,140	23,115	175,966	100,239
Manitoba	2,802	21,630	50,498	27,541	2,708	22,054	49,757	25,593
Saskatchewan	1,258	20,095	21,019	12,618	1,260	19,764	20,722	12,981
Alberta	2,362	20,728	40,769	26,717	2,394	21,093	42,039	27,592
British Columbia	3,014	21,874	54,942	37,674	2,812	22,749	53,301	34,999
Total	25,283	21,811	459,451	283,871	24,077	22,343	448,069	274,467

[1]Total laid less loss.

11.20   Harvested area, production and value of the commercial crop of leaf tobacco, by province, 1973-75

Year	Quebec			Ontario			Other provinces		
	Harvested area acres	Production '000 lb.	Value $'000	Harvested area acres	Production '000 lb.	Value $'000	Harvested area acres	Production '000 lb.	Value $'000
1973	9,393	14,387	10,538	106,314	236,240	186,789	5,160	6,686	5,312
1974	8,889	11,006	9,432	110,186	240,924	216,786	3,771	4,857	4,376
1975	9,265	14,783	13,072	89,408	212,862	199,724	4,149	6,162	5,701

11.21   Harvested area, production and value of the commercial crop of leaf tobacco, by main type, 1973-75

Type of tobacco and year		Harvested area acres	Average yield per acre lb.	Total production '000 lb.	Average farm price per lb. ¢	Gross farm value $'000
Flue-cured	1973	117,295	2,142	251,204	79.3	199,317
	1974	121,048	2,084	252,294	90.1	227,384
	1975	99,490	2,294	228,230	93.8	214,182
Burley	1973	1,220	2,187	2,668	57.0	1,520
	1974	937	2,142	2,007	73.6	1,477
	1975	1,145	2,015	2,307	81.1	1,872
Cigar leaf	1973	1,727	1,405	2,427	51.1	1,239
	1974	1,220	1,187	1,448	65.7	951
	1975	1,375	1,466	2,016	69.4	1,399
Total[1]	1973	120,867	2,129	257,313	78.8	202,639
	1974	123,846	2,073	256,787	89.8	230,594
	1975	102,822	2,274	233,807	93.5	218,497

[1]Includes other types not specified.

11.18   Production and value of maple sugar and maple syrup, by province, 1973-75, with 5-year average for 1968-72 (concluded) M

Province and year	Maple sugar		Maple syrup			Total value, sugar and syrup $
	Quantity kg	Value $	Quantity dm³	Average price per dm³ $	Value $	
Ontario						
Av. 1968-72	6 000	16,000	846 000	1.51	1,281,000	1,297,000
1973	5 000	21,000	564 000	1.96	1,103,000	1,124,000
1974	7 000	28,000	646 000	2.30	1,486,000	1,514,000
1975	4 000	20,000	546 000	2.63	1,437,000	1,457,000
Total						
Av. 1968-72	161 000	268,000	8 579 000	1.15	9,903,000	10,171,000
1973	140 000	330,000	11 002 000	1.55	17,020,000	17,350,000
1974	137 000	368,000	7 960 000	1.59	12,629,000	12,997,000
1975	153 000	435,000	6 188 000	1.80	11,155,000	11,590,000

11.20   Harvested area, production and value of the commercial crop of leaf tobacco, by province, 1973-75 M

Year	Quebec			Ontario			Other provinces		
	Harvested area ha	Production t	Value $'000	Harvested area ha	Production t	Value $'000	Harvested area ha	Production t	Value $'000
1973	3 801	6 526	10,538	43 024	107 157	186,789	2 088	3 033	5,312
1974	3 597	4 992	9,432	44 591	109 281	216,786	1 526	2 203	4,376
1975	3 749	6 705	13,072	36 182	96 553	199,724	1 679	2 795	5,701

11.21   Harvested area, production and value of the commercial crop of leaf tobacco, by main type, 1973-75 M

Type of tobacco and year		Harvested area ha	Average yield per ha kg	Total production t	Average farm price per kg $	Gross farm value $'000
Flue-cured	1973	47 468	2 400	113 944	1.749	199,317
	1974	48 986	2 336	114 439	1.987	227,384
	1975	40 262	2 571	103 523	2.069	214,182
Burley	1973	494	2 449	1 210	1.256	1,520
	1974	379	2 401	910	1.623	1,477
	1975	463	2 259	1 046	1.790	1,872
Cigar leaf	1973	699	1 575	1 101	1.125	1,239
	1974	494	1 330	657	1.447	951
	1975	556	1 644	914	1.531	1,399
Total[1]	1973	48 913	2 386	116 715	1.736	202,639
	1974	50 119	2 324	116 477	1.980	230,594
	1975	41 611	2 549	106 053	2.060	218,497

[1]Includes other types not specified.

11.22   Average index[1] numbers of farm prices of agricultural products, by province, 1971-75 (1961 = 100)

Province	1971	1972	1973	1974	1975
Prince Edward Island	133.0	153.3	266.7	299.0	265.0
Nova Scotia	120.6	132.9	177.5	210.0	215.9
New Brunswick	123.3	140.5	228.1	262.3	234.4
Quebec	138.7	154.7	198.5	228.3	257.0
Ontario	129.4	143.4	187.8	206.4	223.7
Manitoba	102.1	119.7	189.3	226.8	222.9
Saskatchewan	96.4	112.0	189.5	234.2	224.9
Alberta	110.8	129.6	196.6	226.6	222.9
British Columbia	124.2	134.9	167.8	196.6	207.7
Total	117.2	132.9	191.5	222.2	228.1

[1]A description of this index, its coverage and the methods used will be found in Statistics Canada *Quarterly bulletin of agricultural statistics* (Cat. No. 21-003) for July-September 1969.

11.23   Average cash prices a bushel of major Canadian grains, crop years ended July 31, 1971-75 (basis, in store Thunder Bay)

Year	Averages in cents and eighths a bushel						
	Wheat		Oats[1] 2 C.W.	Barley[1] 3 C.W. −Six-Row	Rye[2] 2 C.W.	Flaxseed[2] 1 C.W.	Rapeseed[2] 1 Canada
	No. 1 N.	1 C.W. Red Spring 14%[1]					
1971	179/2	. . .	83/2	130/7	109/3	253/5	278/1
1972	. . .	168/4	67/2	113/7	98/6	257/2	247/1
1973	. . .	262/5	109/2	176/5	158/5	482/6	364
1974	. . .	549/3[3]	174/4	307/4[4]	294/7	1,014/2	635/5
1975	. . .	526/3	188	354/7[4]	262	954/2	723/2

[1]Canadian Wheat Board daily fixed prices.
[2]Winnipeg Commodity Exchange daily closing cash quotations.
[3]1 C.W. Red Spring 13.5%.
[4]2 C.W. Six-Row.

11.24   Weighted average prices per 100 lb. of Canadian livestock at public stockyards, 1964-75 (dollars)

Item	Average prices									
	1964-73	1969-73	1973	1974	1975	1964-73	1969-73	1973	1974	1975
	Toronto					Calgary				
A1,2 steers	31.50	36.28	46.56	49.37	46.99	29.51	34.17	45.11	47.92	43.56
D1,2 cows	22.15	25.94	34.53	28.69	23.03	20.94	25.17	33.91	26.06	21.30
Feeder steers over 750 lb.	31.39	37.20	46.54	44.45	39.51	30.22	36.37	46.54	43.55	38.45
Choice and good veal calves	38.71	43.96	56.37	51.51	38.61	34.26	43.06	49.54	30.09	27.12
Index 100 hogs, dressed	34.59	37.15	54.66	50.29	67.22	30.39	32.74	48.69	45.52	65.41
Good lambs	30.85	34.94	42.87	48.64	58.54	23.93	26.92	33.24	36.90	39.95
	Winnipeg					Edmonton				
A1,2 steers	30.31	34.98	45.14	48.76	43.80	29.06	33.70	44.36	45.70	41.31
D1,2 cows	22.06	26.40	35.06	27.12	21.27	20.11	24.13	32.50	23.60	18.95
Feeder steers over 750 lb.	30.62	36.86	46.76	40.62	35.37	30.26	36.59	46.12	41.33	36.80
Choice and good veal calves	42.72	51.12	66.44	70.30	44.24	36.14	45.18	51.72	33.24	28.89
Index 100 hogs, dressed	32.11	34.56	51.31	46.12	62.55	30.44	32.97	49.92	44.86	64.96
Good lambs	26.37	30.61	36.29	44.94	56.77	23.69	26.83	33.03	36.71	40.40

11.25   Per capita supplies of food moving into consumption 1973 and 1974, with average for 1968-72

Kind of food and weight base		Pounds per capita per annum			Percentages of 1968-72 average	
		Average 1968-72	1973	1974	1973	1974
CEREALS	*retail wt*	150.6	151.3	153.6	100.5	102.0
Wheat flour	"	130.0	129.8	132.1	99.8	101.6
Rye flour	"	0.8	0.8	0.9	100.0	112.5
Oatmeal and rolled oats	"	3.7	2.7	3.1	73.0	83.8
Pot and pearl barley	"	0.1	0.1	0.1	100.0	100.0
Corn flour and meal	"	4.2	5.5	5.5	131.0	131.0
Buckwheat flour	"	- -	- -	- -	. .	. .
Rice	"	5.4	6.2	5.1	114.8	94.4
Breakfast food	"	6.4	6.2	6.8	96.9	106.3
SUGARS AND SYRUPS	*sugar content*	112.7	119.8	95.4	106.3	84.6
Sugar	*retail wt*	100.7	107.7	91.8	107.0	91.2
Maple sugar	"	0.3	0.7	0.5	233.3	166.7
Honey	"	1.8	1.7	1.7	94.4	94.4
Other	"	9.8	9.6	1.4	98.0	14.3

11.23   Average cash prices a metric tonne of major Canadian grains, crop years ended July 31, 1971-75 (basis, in store Thunder Bay)   M

Year	Averages in dollars per tonne		Oats[1] 2 C.W.	Barley[1] 3 C.W. — Six-Row	Rye[2] 2 C.W.	Flaxseed[2] 1 C.W.	Rapeseed[2] 1 Canada
	Wheat						
	No. 1 N.	1 C.W. Red Spring 14%[1]					
1971	65.86	. . .	53.98	60.11	43.06	99.85	122.63
1972	. . .	61.91	43.61	52.30	38.88	101.27	108.96
1973	. . .	96.50	70.84	81.12	62.45	190.05	160.50
1974	. . .	201.86[3]	113.15	141.23[4]	116.09	399.29	280.26
1975	. . .	193.41	121.90	162.99[4]	103.14	375.67	318.90

[1]Canadian Wheat Board daily fixed prices.
[2]Winnipeg Commodity Exchange daily closing cash quotations.
[3]1 C.W. Red Spring 13.5%.
[4]2 C.W. Six-Row.

11.24   Weighted average prices per 100 kg of Canadian livestock at public stockyards, 1964-75 (dollars)   M

Item	Average prices									
	1964-73	1969-73	1973	1974	1975	1964-73	1969-73	1973	1974	1975
	Toronto					Calgary				
A1,2 steers	69.45	79.98	102.65	108.84	103.60	65.06	75.33	99.45	105.65	96.03
D1,2 cows	48.83	57.19	76.13	63.25	50.77	46.16	55.49	74.76	57.45	46.96
Feeder steers over 340 kg	69.20	82.01	102.60	98.00	87.10	66.62	80.18	102.60	96.01	84.77
Choice and good veal calves	85.34	96.92	124.27	113.56	85.12	75.53	94.93	109.22	100.35	59.79
Index 100 hogs, dressed	76.26	81.90	120.50	110.87	148.19	67.00	72.18	107.34	100.35	144.20
Good lambs	68.01	77.03	94.51	107.23	129.06	52.76	59.35	73.28	81.35	88.07
	Winnipeg					Edmonton				
A1,2 steers	66.82	77.12	99.52	107.50	96.56	64.07	74.30	97.80	100.75	91.07
D1,2 cows	48.63	58.20	77.29	59.79	46.89	44.33	53.20	71.65	52.03	41.78
Feeder steers over 340 kg	67.51	81.26	103.09	89.55	77.98	66.71	80.67	101.68	91.12	81.13
Choice and good veal calves	94.18	112.70	146.48	154.98	97.53	79.68	99.60	114.02	73.28	63.69
Index 100 hogs, dressed	70.79	76.19	113.12	101.68	137.90	67.11	72.69	110.05	98.90	143.21
Good lambs	58.14	67.48	80.01	99.08	125.16	52.23	59.15	72.82	80.93	89.07

11.25   Per capita supplies of food moving into consumption 1973 and 1974, with average for 1968-72   M

Kind of food and weight base		kg per capita per annum			Percentages of 1968-72 average	
		Average 1968-72	1973	1974	1973	1974
CEREALS	retail wt	68.3	68.6	69.7	100.5	102.0
Wheat flour	''	59.0	58.9	59.9	99.8	101.6
Rye flour	''	0.4	0.4	0.4	100.0	112.5
Oatmeal and rolled oats	''	1.7	1.2	1.4	73.0	83.8
Pot and pearl barley	''	- -	- -	- -	100.0	100.0
Corn flour and meal	''	1.9	2.5	2.5	131.0	131.0
Buckwheat flour	''	- -	- -	- -		
Rice	''	2.4	2.8	2.3	114.8	94.4
Breakfast food	''	2.9	2.8	3.1	96.9	106.3
SUGARS AND SYRUPS	sugar content	51.1	54.3	43.3	106.3	84.6
Sugar	retail wt	45.7	48.9	41.6	107.0	91.2
Maple sugar	''	0.1	0.3	0.2	233.3	166.7
Honey	''	0.8	0.8	0.8	94.4	94.4
Other	''	4.4	4.4	0.6	98.0	14.3

11.25   Per capita supplies of food moving into consumption 1973 and 1974, with average for 1968-72 (continued)

Kind of food and weight base		Pounds per capita per annum			Percentages of 1968-72 average	
		Average 1968-72	1973	1974	1973	1974
PULSES AND NUTS	retail wt	11.0	10.2	15.8	92.7	136.4
Dry beans	"	2.4	1.3	4.8	54.2	200.0
Baked canned beans	"	5.5	5.6	5.5	101.8	94.5
Dry peas	"	1.7	0.9	2.7	52.9	158.8
Peanuts	"	5.2	6.0	5.8	115.4	111.5
Tree nuts	"	1.5	2.1	2.0	140.0	133.3
OILS AND FATS	fat content	46.1	47.9	48.7	103.9	105.6
Margarine	retail wt	9.5	9.8	10.7	103.2	112.6
Shortening and shortening oils	"	15.2	17.5	17.0	115.1	111.8
Salad oils	"	6.1	7.0	7.6	114.8	124.6
Butter	"	15.3	13.6	13.3	88.9	86.9
FRUIT	fresh equiv.	..	268.2	258.5	..	..
Fresh	retail wt	..	122.5	124.2	..	..
Canned	net wt canned	..	30.8	31.1	..	..
Frozen	retail wt	..	3.0	2.7	..	..
Juice	net wt canned	..	39.3	37.0	..	..
Tomatoes, fresh	retail wt	13.3	12.0	10.8	90.2	81.2
canned	net wt canned	5.9	7.1	7.4	120.3	125.4
Tomato juice	"	8.3	8.5	8.9	102.4	107.2
pulp, paste and purée	"	2.2	3.8	3.0	172.7	136.4
ketchup	"	4.2	4.4	5.1	104.8	121.4
Citrus fruit, fresh	retail wt	26.9	30.5	30.3	113.4	112.6
juice	net wt canned	14.8	17.4	18.2	117.6	123.0
Apples, fresh	retail wt	25.2	23.3	26.9	92.5	106.7
canned	net wt canned	0.4	0.2	0.2	50.0	50.0
juice	"	6.2	5.1	4.1	82.3	66.1
frozen	retail wt	..	0.4	--	..	..
sauce	net wt canned	1.2	1.4	1.6	116.7	133.3
pie filling	"	0.5	0.4	0.5	80.0	100.0
Apricots, fresh	retail wt	0.2	0.3	0.2	150.0	100.0
canned	net wt canned	0.5	0.4	0.2	80.0	40.0
Bananas, fresh	retail wt	20.7	21.4	21.6	103.4	104.3
Blueberries, fresh	"	0.5	0.4	0.3	80.0	60.0
canned	net wt canned	--	--	--	..	..
frozen	retail wt	..	--	0.1	..	..
Cherries, fresh	"	0.9	1.4	1.3	155.6	144.4
canned	net wt canned	0.3	0.2	0.2	66.7	66.7
frozen	retail wt	0.6	0.6	0.5	100.0	83.3
Cranberries, fresh	"	0.4	0.7	0.6	175.0	150.0
Melons, fresh	"	8.1	8.3	7.2	102.5	88.9
Peaches, fresh	"	5.3	4.4	4.8	83.0	90.6
canned	net wt canned	3.5	3.8	3.5	108.6	100.0
frozen	retail wt	..	--	--	..	..
Pears, fresh	"	3.2	4.2	3.7	131.3	115.6
canned	net wt canned	1.8	2.2	2.0	122.2	111.1
Pineapples, fresh	retail wt	0.3	0.5	0.5	166.7	166.7
canned	net wt canned	2.4	2.6	2.1	108.3	87.5
juice	"	1.0	1.1	1.0	110.0	100.0
Plums fresh	retail wt	1.8	1.9	2.3	105.6	127.8
canned	net wt canned	0.3	0.3	0.3	100.0	100.0
Raspberries, fresh	retail wt	..	..	..	..	..
canned	net wt canned	0.1	0.1	0.1	100.0	100.0
frozen	retail wt	0.5	0.4	0.5	80.0	100.0
Strawberries, fresh	"	1.8	1.9	2.2	105.6	122.2
canned	net wt canned	0.1	0.1	0.1	100.0	100.0
frozen	retail wt	1.4	1.4	1.4	100.0	100.0
Grapes, fresh	"	10.6	11.3	11.2	106.6	105.7
Unspecified, fresh	"	..	..	0.3	..	..
canned	net wt canned	4.6	4.0	5.0	87.0	108.7
frozen	retail wt	..	0.2	0.2	..	..
juice	net wt canned	4.3	5.6	3.9	130.2	90.7
jams, jellies, marmalade	processed wt	5.0	4.5	4.5	90.0	90.0
VEGETABLES[1]	fresh equiv.	114.4	119.2	124.8	104.2	109.1
Fresh	retail wt	72.8	78.7	82.9	108.1	113.9
Canned	net wt canned	18.7	19.4	19.6	103.7	104.8
Frozen	retail wt	5.6	6.1	7.0	108.9	125.0
Cabbage, fresh	"	9.9	10.8	11.4	109.1	115.2
Lettuce	"	14.4	16.1	17.2	111.8	119.4
Spinach, fresh	"	0.6	0.5	0.7	83.3	116.7
Carrots, fresh	"	13.4	12.0	13.4	89.6	100.0
canned	net wt canned	0.9	1.3	1.1	144.4	122.2
frozen	retail wt	0.5	0.8	1.1	160.0	220.0
Beans, fresh	"	0.9	1.3	1.2	144.4	133.3
canned	net wt canned	3.7	3.7	3.7	100.0	100.0
frozen	retail wt	0.8	0.7	0.9	87.5	112.5
Peas, fresh	"	0.1	0.1	0.2	100.0	200.0
canned	net wt canned	5.2	4.5	4.5	86.5	86.5
frozen	retail wt	2.4	2.5	2.5	104.2	104.2
Beets, fresh	"	0.6	0.3	0.3	50.0	50.0
canned	net wt canned	0.7	0.8	0.8	114.3	114.3
Cauliflower, fresh	retail wt	1.9	1.8	1.9	94.7	100.0
Celery, fresh	"	7.1	7.5	7.4	105.6	104.2
Corn, fresh	"	4.2	3.9	3.9	92.9	92.9
canned	net wt canned	4.9	5.4	5.5	110.2	112.2
frozen	retail wt	0.8	0.8	0.6	100.0	75.0

11.25 Per capita supplies of food moving into consumption 1973 and 1974, with average for 1968-72 (continued) M

Kind of food and weight base		kg per capita per annum			Percentages of 1968-72 average	
		Average 1968-72	1973	1974	1973	1974
PULSES AND NUTS	retail wt	5.0	4.6	6.8	92.7	136.4
Dry beans	''	1.1	0.6	2.2	54.2	200.0
Baked canned beans	''	2.5	2.5	2.4	101.8	94.5
Dry peas	''	0.8	0.4	1.2	52.9	158.8
Peanuts	''	2.4	2.7	2.6	115.4	111.5
Tree nuts	''	0.7	1.0	0.9	140.0	133.3
OILS AND FATS	fat content	20.9	21.7	22.1	103.9	105.6
Margarine	retail wt	4.3	4.4	4.9	103.2	112.6
Shortening and shortening oils	''	6.9	7.9	7.7	115.1	111.8
Salad oils	''	2.8	3.2	3.4	114.8	124.6
Butter	''	6.9	6.2	6.0	88.9	86.9
FRUIT	fresh equiv.	..	121.7	117.3	..	..
Fresh	retail wt	..	55.6	56.3	..	..
Canned	net wt canned	..	14.0	14.1	..	..
Frozen	retail wt	..	1.4	1.2	..	..
Juice	net wt canned	..	17.8	16.8	..	..
Tomatoes, fresh	retail wt	6.0	5.4	4.9	90.2	81.2
canned	net wt canned	2.7	3.2	3.4	120.3	125.4
Tomato juice	''	3.8	3.9	4.0	102.4	107.2
pulp, paste and purée	''	1.0	1.7	1.4	172.7	136.4
ketchup	''	1.9	2.0	2.3	104.8	121.4
Citrus fruit, fresh	retail wt	12.2	13.8	13.7	113.4	112.6
juice	net wt canned	6.7	7.9	8.3	117.6	123.0
Apples, fresh	retail wt	11.4	10.6	12.2	92.5	106.7
canned	net wt canned	0.2	0.1	0.1	50.0	50.0
juice	''	2.8	2.3	1.9	82.3	66.1
frozen	retail wt	..	0.2	- -	..	..
sauce	net wt canned	0.5	0.6	0.7	116.7	133.3
pie filling	''	0.2	0.2	0.2	80.0	100.0
Apricots, fresh	retail wt	0.1	0.1	0.1	150.0	100.0
canned	net wt canned	0.2	0.2	0.1	80.0	40.0
Bananas, fresh	retail wt	9.4	9.7	9.8	103.4	104.3
Blueberries, fresh	''	0.2	0.2	0.1	80.0	60.0
canned	net wt canned	..	- -	- -	..	..
frozen	retail wt	..	- -	- -	..	..
Cherries, fresh	''	0.4	0.6	0.6	155.6	144.4
canned	net wt canned	0.1	0.1	0.1	66.7	66.7
frozen	retail wt	0.3	0.3	0.2	100.0	83.3
Cranberries, fresh	''	0.2	0.3	0.3	175.0	150.0
Melons, fresh	''	3.7	3.8	3.3	102.5	88.9
Peaches, fresh	''	2.4	2.0	2.2	83.0	90.6
canned	net wt canned	1.6	1.7	1.6	108.6	100.0
frozen	retail wt	..	- -	- -	..	..
Pears, fresh	''	1.5	1.9	1.7	131.3	115.6
canned	net wt canned	0.8	1.0	0.9	122.2	111.1
Pineapples, fresh	retail wt	0.1	0.2	0.2	166.7	166.7
canned	net wt canned	1.1	1.2	1.0	108.3	87.5
juice	''	0.5	0.5	0.5	110.0	100.0
Plums, fresh	retail wt	0.8	0.9	1.0	105.6	127.8
canned	net wt canned	0.1	0.1	0.1	100.0	100.0
Raspberries, fresh	retail wt	..	..	..	..	..
canned	net wt canned	- -	- -	- -	100.0	100.0
frozen	retail wt	0.2	0.2	0.2	80.0	100.0
Strawberries, fresh	''	0.8	0.9	1.0	105.6	122.2
canned	net wt canned	- -	- -	- -	100.0	100.0
frozen	retail wt	0.6	0.6	0.6	100.0	100.0
Grapes, fresh	''	4.8	5.1	5.1	106.6	105.7
Unspecified, fresh	''	..	..	0.1	..	..
canned	net wt canned	2.1	1.8	2.3	87.0	108.7
frozen	retail wt	..	0.1	0.1	..	..
juice	net wt canned	2.0	2.5	1.8	130.2	90.7
jams, jellies, marmalade	processed wt	2.3	2.0	2.0	90.0	90.0
VEGETABLES[1]	fresh equiv.	51.9	54.1	56.6	104.2	109.1
Fresh	retail wt	33.0	35.7	37.6	108.1	113.9
Canned	net wt canned	8.5	8.8	8.9	103.7	104.8
Frozen	retail wt	2.5	2.8	3.2	108.9	125.0
Cabbage, fresh	''	4.5	4.9	5.2	109.1	115.2
Lettuce	''	6.5	7.3	7.8	111.8	119.4
Spinach, fresh	''	0.3	0.2	0.3	83.3	116.7
Carrots, fresh	''	6.1	5.4	6.1	89.6	100.0
canned	net wt canned	0.4	0.6	0.5	144.4	122.2
frozen	retail wt	0.2	0.4	0.5	160.0	220.0
Beans, fresh	''	0.4	0.6	0.5	144.4	133.3
canned	net wt canned	1.7	1.7	1.7	100.0	100.0
frozen	retail wt	0.4	0.3	0.4	87.5	112.5
Peas, fresh	''	- -	- -	0.1	100.0	200.0
canned	net wt canned	2.4	2.0	2.0	86.5	86.5
frozen	retail wt	1.1	1.1	1.1	104.2	104.2
Beets, fresh	''	0.3	0.1	0.1	50.0	50.0
canned	net wt canned	0.3	0.4	0.4	114.3	114.3
Cauliflower, fresh	retail wt	0.9	0.8	0.9	94.7	100.0
Celery, fresh	''	3.2	3.4	3.4	105.6	104.2
Corn, fresh	''	1.9	1.8	1.8	92.9	92.9
canned	net wt canned	2.2	2.4	2.5	110.2	112.2
frozen	retail wt	0.4	0.4	0.3	100.0	75.0

11.25   Per capita supplies of food moving into consumption 1973 and 1974, with average for 1968-72 (concluded)

Kind of food and weight base		Pounds per capita per annum			Percentages of 1968-72 average	
		Average 1968-72	1973	1974	1973	1974
Cucumbers, fresh	''	2.6	3.0	3.4	115.4	130.8
Onions, not processed	''	12.0	11.8	11.2	98.3	93.3
Asparagus, fresh	''	0.3	0.3	0.3	100.0	100.0
canned	net wt canned	0.4	0.5	0.5	125.0	125.0
frozen	retail wt	..	- -	- -	..	..
Rutabagas, fresh	''	4.3	4.8	5.4	111.6	125.6
Broccoli, fresh	''	0.7	1.0	1.2	142.9	171.4
frozen		0.2	0.3	0.3	150.0	150.0
Brussels sprouts, fresh	''	0.2	0.2	0.2	100.0	100.0
frozen	''	0.2	0.2	0.2	100.0	100.0
Unspecified, fresh	''	1.7	0.6	0.9	35.3	52.9
canned	net wt canned	2.8	2.9	3.3	103.6	117.9
frozen	retail wt	1.0	0.5	1.2	50.0	120.0
MUSHROOMS	fresh equiv.	2.5	3.9	4.5	156.0	180.0
Fresh	retail wt	0.7	1.0	1.2	142.9	171.4
Canned	net wt canned	1.2	2.0	2.2	166.7	183.3
POTATOES	fresh equiv.	159.8	154.5	152.4	96.7	95.4
White	''	159.6	153.9	151.6	96.4	95.0
Sweet	''	0.4	0.6	0.7	150.0	175.0
MEAT	carcass wt	159.5	159.9	164.3	100.3	103.0
Pork	''	58.6	57.6	59.8	98.3	102.1
Beef	''	87.6	91.8	94.7	104.8	108.1
Veal	''	4.9	3.2	3.5	65.3	71.4
Mutton and lamb	''	4.5	3.7	2.5	82.2	55.6
Offal	''	3.9	3.6	3.7	92.3	94.9
Canned meat[2]	net wt canned	..	0.9	..	..	..
EGGS	fresh equiv.	31.8	29.2	28.5	91.8	89.6
POULTRY[3]	eviscerated wt	43.6	46.8	45.5	107.3	104.4
Chicken	''	29.5	32.8	31.0	111.2	105.1
Fowl	''	3.5	3.3	3.2	94.3	91.4
Turkey	''	10.1	10.2	10.5	101.0	104.0
Duck	''	0.3	0.4	0.6	133.3	200.0
Goose	''	0.2	0.2	0.2	100.0	100.0
FISH	edible wt	12.3	12.2	11.8	99.2	95.9
Fish and shellfish, fresh and frozen[4]	''	7.6	7.4	7.4	97.4	97.4
Fish, cured (smoked, salted, pickled)	''	0.9	0.6	0.4	66.7	44.4
Fish and shellfish, canned	''	3.9	4.2	4.0	107.7	102.6
MILK AND CHEESE	milk solids	58.9	59.5	60.2	101.0	102.2
Cheddar cheese	retail wt	3.9	4.9	5.2	125.6	133.3
Process cheese	''	4.7	5.5	5.7	117.0	121.3
Other cheese	''	3.3	4.0	4.3	121.2	130.3
Cottage cheese	''	2.0	2.4	2.3	120.0	115.0
Evaporated whole milk	''	12.3	10.5	9.7	85.4	78.9
Condensed whole milk	''	0.9	0.9	0.8	100.0	88.9
Powdered whole milk and cream	''	0.3	0.1	0.1	33.3	33.3
Miscellaneous milk products[5]	''	0.2	0.1	0.1	50.0	50.0
Powdered skim milk[6]	''	6.8	5.2	5.6	76.5	82.4
buttermilk	''	0.5	0.4	0.3	80.0	60.0
whey	''	2.2	2.3	2.6	104.5	118.2
Miscellaneous by-products[7]	''	1.8	2.0	1.9	111.1	105.6
Fluid whole milk[8]	''	273.8	267.7	267.1	97.8	97.6
Milk in ice cream	''	38.6	40.8	40.2	105.7	104.1
BEVERAGES	tea leaf equiv.	2.4	2.5	2.5	104.2	104.2
Coffee	green beans	9.3	9.3	9.4	100.0	101.1
Cocoa	''	..	3.8	3.2	..	..

[1]Includes pickles, relishes, vegetables used in soups, etc.
[2]Per capita consumption not comparable with previous years.
[3]Excludes Newfoundland.
[4]Excludes herring, fresh and frozen, and all fish used for bait.
[5]Includes formula milk, concentrated liquid milk and malted milk.
[6]Part of this product is used for animal feeds.
[7]Includes evaporated and condensed skim milk, condensed buttermilk, sugar of milk, formula skim milk products and concentrated liquid skim milk.
[8]Includes cream expressed as milk.

11.25   Per capita supplies of food moving into consumption 1973 and 1974, with average for 1968-72 (concluded)   M

Kind of food and weight base		kg per capita per annum			Percentages of 1968-72 average	
		Average 1968-72	1973	1974	1973	1974
Cucumbers, fresh	``	1.2	1.4	1.5	115.4	130.8
Onions, not processed		5.4	5.4	5.1	98.3	93.3
Asparagus, fresh	``	0.1	0.1	0.1	100.0	100.0
canned	net wt canned	0.2	0.2	0.2	125.0	125.0
frozen	retail wt	..	--	--	..	..
Rutabagas, fresh	``	2.0	2.2	2.4	111.6	125.6
Broccoli, fresh	``	0.3	0.5	0.5	142.9	171.4
frozen	``	0.1	0.1	0.1	150.0	150.0
Brussels sprouts, fresh	``	0.1	0.1	0.1	100.0	100.0
frozen	``	0.1	0.1	0.1	100.0	100.0
Unspecified, fresh	``	0.8	0.3	0.4	35.3	52.9
canned	net wt canned	1.3	1.3	1.5	103.6	117.9
frozen	retail wt	0.5	0.2	0.5	50.0	120.0
MUSHROOMS	fresh equiv.	1.1	1.8	2.0	156.0	180.0
Fresh	retail wt	0.3	0.5	0.5	142.9	171.4
Canned	net wt canned	0.5	0.9	1.0	166.7	183.3
POTATOES	fresh equiv.	72.5	70.1	69.1	96.7	95.4
White	``	72.4	69.8	68.8	96.4	95.0
Sweet	``	0.2	0.3	0.3	150.0	175.0
MEAT	carcass wt	72.3	72.5	74.5	100.3	103.0
Pork	``	26.6	26.1	27.1	98.3	102.1
Beef	``	39.7	41.6	43.0	104.8	108.1
Veal	``	2.2	1.5	1.6	65.3	71.4
Mutton and lamb	``	2.0	1.7	1.1	82.2	55.6
Offal	``	1.8	1.6	1.7	92.3	94.9
Canned meat[2]	net wt canned	..	0.4	..	..	..
EGGS	fresh equiv.	14.4	13.2	12.9	91.8	89.6
POULTRY[3]	eviscerated wt	19.8	21.2	20.6	107.3	104.4
Chicken	``	13.4	14.9	14.1	111.2	105.1
Fowl	``	1.6	1.5	1.5	94.3	91.4
Turkey	``	4.6	4.6	4.8	101.0	104.0
Duck	``	0.1	0.2	0.3	133.3	200.0
Goose	``	0.1	0.1	0.1	100.0	100.0
FISH	edible wt	5.6	5.5	5.4	99.2	95.9
Fish and shellfish fresh and frozen[4]	``	3.4	3.4	3.4	97.4	97.4
Fish, cured (smoked, salted, pickled)	``	0.4	0.3	0.2	66.7	44.4
Fish and shellfish, canned	``	1.8	1.9	1.8	107.7	102.6
MILK AND CHEESE	milk solids	26.7	27.0	27.3	101.0	102.2
Cheddar cheese	retail wt	1.8	2.2	2.4	125.6	133.3
Process cheese	``	2.1	2.5	2.6	117.0	121.3
Other cheese	``	1.5	1.8	2.0	121.2	130.3
Cottage cheese	``	0.9	1.1	1.0	120.0	115.0
Evaporated whole milk	``	5.6	4.8	4.4	85.4	78.9
Condensed whole milk	``	0.4	0.4	0.4	100.0	88.9
Powdered whole milk and cream	``	0.1	--	--	33.3	33.3
Miscellaneous milk products[5]	``	0.1	--	--	50.0	50.0
Powdered skim milk[6]	``	3.1	2.4	2.5	76.5	82.4
buttermilk	``	0.2	0.2	0.1	80.0	60.0
whey	``	1.0	1.0	1.2	104.5	118.2
Miscellaneous by-products[7]	``	0.8	0.9	0.9	111.1	105.6
Fluid whole milk[8]	``	124.2	121.4	121.2	97.8	97.6
Milk in ice cream	``	17.5	18.5	18.2	105.7	104.1
BEVERAGES						
Tea	tea leaf equiv.	1.1	1.1	1.1	104.2	104.2
Coffee	green beans	4.2	4.2	4.3	100.0	101.1
Cocoa	``	..	1.7	1.5	..	..

[1]Includes pickles, relishes, vegetables used in soups, etc.
[2]Per capita consumption not comparable with previous years.
[3]Excludes Newfoundland.
[4]Excludes herring, fresh and frozen, and all fish used for bait.
[5]Includes formula milk, concentrated liquid milk and malted milk.
[6]Part of this product is used for animal feeds.
[7]Includes evaporated and condensed skim milk, condensed buttermilk, sugar of milk, formula skim milk products and concentrated liquid skim milk.
[8]Includes cream expressed as milk.

11.26   Supply, distribution and disappearance of meats, 1971-75

Item		1971[1]	1972	1973	1974	1975
BEEF						
Animals slaughtered	'000	3,372.9	3,392.7	3,411.7	3,629.3	4,069.9
Estimated dressed weight	'000 lb.	1,877,575	1,898,328	1,910,575	1,999,106	2,190,873
On hand, Jan. 1	"	43,473	35,366	41,776	52,296	44,180
Imports for consumption	"	153,158	213,661	218,957	179,486	190,967
Total supply	"	2,074,206	2,147,355	2,171,308	2,230,888	2,426,020
Exports	"	113,635	83,829	88,241	57,461	44,808
Used for canning	"	...	...	...	...	...
On hand, Dec. 31	"	35,366	41,776	52,296	44,180	46,556
Domestic disappearance	"	1,925,205	2,021,750	2,030,771	2,129,247	2,334,656
Per capita disappearance	lb.	89.2	92.5	91.8	94.7	102.3
VEAL						
Animals slaughtered	'000	838.2	644.6	482.2	615.8	1,008.8
Estimated dressed weight	'000 lb.	98,516	80,525	65,857	77,415	122,273
On hand, Jan. 1	"	5,316	3,367	8,230	4,433	3,451
Imports for consumption	"	[2]	[2]	[2]	[2]	[2]
Total supply	"	103,832	83,892	74,087	81,848	125,724
Exports	"	[2]	[2]	[2]	[2]	[2]
Used for canning	"	...	...	...	...	...
On hand, Dec. 31	"	3,367	8,230	4,433	3,451	3,339
Domestic disappearance	"	100,465	75,662	69,654	78,397	122,385
Per capita disappearance	lb.	4.7	3.5	3.1	3.5	5.4
MUTTON AND LAMB						
Animals slaughtered	'000	422.8	446.3	501.1	424.3	423.5
Estimated dressed weight	'000 lb.	18,189	19,850	21,893	18,167	18,090
On hand, Jan. 1	"	11,260	11,068	9,103	7,233	6,814
Imports for consumption	"	52,765	80,548	58,410	38,397	44,643
Total supply	"	82,214	111,466	89,406	63,797	69,547
Exports	"	93	676	156	126	187
Used for canning	"	...	...	...	...	...
On hand, Dec. 31	"	11,068	9,103	7,233	6,814	4,123
Domestic disappearance	"	71,053	101,687	82,017	56,857	65,237
Per capita disappearance	lb.	3.3	4.7	3.7	2.5	2.9
PORK						
Animals slaughtered	'000	11,904.0	10,654.7	10,398.8	10,289.3	8,358.3
Estimated dressed weight[3]	'000 lb.	1,557,254	1,392,607	1,360,418	1,347,230	1,090,424
On hand, Jan. 1	"	26,878	28,969	18,803	33,114	22,892
Imports for consumption	"	16,954	44,983	54,131	80,190	98,679
Total supply	"	1,601,086	1,466,559	1,433,352	1,460,534	1,211,995
Exports	"	97,166	115,517	125,614	92,174	89,687
Used for canning	"	...	...	...	...	...
On hand, Dec. 31	"	28,969	18,803	33,114	22,892	16,592
Domestic disappearance	"	1,474,951	1,332,239	1,274,624	1,345,468	1,105,716
Per capita disappearance	lb.	68.3	61.0	57.6	59.9	48.4
OFFAL						
Estimated production	'000 lb.	133,398	127,023	125,461	129,683	130,873
On hand, Jan. 1	"	8,061	9,036	7,390	10,223	9,333
Imports for consumption	"	8,934	10,948	8,934	8,899	6,555
Total supply	"	150,393	147,007	141,785	148,805	146,761
Exports	"	45,460	50,876	51,820	56,224	59,465
Used for canning	"	...	...	...	...	...
On hand, Dec. 31	"	9,036	7,390	10,223	9,333	9,212
Domestic disappearance	"	95,897	88,741	79,742	83,248	78,084
Per capita disappearance	lb.	4.4	4.1	3.6	3.7	3.4

[1]Intercensal revisions.
[2]Included with beef.
[3]Trimmed of larding fat.

11.27   Number of census-farms, by province, censuses 1966 and 1971

Province or territory	1966	1971
Newfoundland	1,709	1,042
Prince Edward Island	6,357	4,543
Nova Scotia	9,621	6,008
New Brunswick	8,706	5,485
Quebec	80,294	61,257
Ontario	109,887	94,722
Manitoba	39,747	34,981
Saskatchewan	85,686	76,970
Alberta	69,411	62,702
British Columbia	19,085	18,400
Yukon Territory and Northwest Territories	19	18
Canada	430,522	366,128

11.26   Supply, distribution and disappearance of meats, 1971-75   M

Item		1971[1]	1972	1973	1974	1975
BEEF						
Animals slaughtered	'000	3,372.9	3,392.7	3,411.7	3,629.3	4,069.9
Estimated dressed weight	t	851 654	861 067	866 622	906 779	993 763
On hand, Jan. 1	"	19 719	16 042	18 949	23 721	20 040
Imports for consumption	"	69 471	96 915	99 317	81 413	86 621
Total supply	"	940 844	974 024	984 888	1 011 913	1 100 424
Exports	"	51 544	38 024	40 025	26 064	20 325
Used for canning	"					
On hand, Dec. 31	"	16 042	18 949	23 721	20 040	21 117
Domestic disappearance	"	873 258	917 051	921 142	965 809	1 058 982
Per capita disappearance	kg	40.5	42.0	41.6	43.0	46.4
VEAL						
Animals slaughtered	'000	838.2	644.6	482.2	615.8	1,008.8
Estimated dressed weight	t	44 686	36 526	29 872	35 115	55 462
On hand, Jan. 1	"	2 411	1 527	3 733	2 011	1 565
Imports for consumption	"	[2]	[2]	[2]	[2]	[2]
Total supply	"	47 097	38 053	33 605	37 126	57 027
Exports	"	[2]	[2]	[2]	[2]	[2]
Used for canning	"					
On hand, Dec. 31	"	1 527	3 733	2 011	1 565	1 515
Domestic disappearance	"	45 570	34 320	31 594	35 561	55 512
Per capita disappearance	kg	2.1	1.6	1.4	1.6	2.4
MUTTON AND LAMB						
Animals slaughtered	'000	422.8	446.3	501.1	424.3	423.5
Estimated dressed weight	t	8 250	9 004	9 930	8 240	8 205
On hand, Jan. 1	"	5 107	5 020	4 129	3 281	3 091
Imports for consumption	"	23 934	36 536	26 494	17 417	20 250
Total supply	"	37 291	50 560	40 553	28 938	31 546
Exports	"	42	307	71	57	85
Used for canning	"					
On hand, Dec. 31	"	5 020	4 129	3 281	3 091	1 870
Domestic disappearance	"	32 229	46 124	37 201	25 790	29 591
Per capita disappearance	kg	1.5	2.1	1.7	1.1	1.3
PORK						
Animals slaughtered	'000	11,904.0	10,654.7	10,398.8	10,289.3	8,358.3
Estimated dressed weight[3]	t	706 359	631 676	617 075	611 093	494 608
On hand, Jan. 1	"	12 192	13 140	8 529	15 020	10 384
Imports for consumption	"	7 690	20 404	24 553	36 374	44 760
Total supply	"	726 241	665 220	650 157	662 487	549 752
Exports	"	44 074	52 398	56 978	41 809	40 681
Used for canning	"					
On hand, Dec. 31	"	13 140	8 529	15 020	10 384	7 526
Domestic disappearance	"	669 027	604 293	578 159	610 294	501 545
Per capita disappearance	kg	31.0	27.7	26.1	27.2	22.0
OFFAL						
Estimated production	t	60 508	57 617	56 908	58 823	59 363
On hand, Jan. 1	"	3 656	4 099	3 352	4 637	4 233
Imports for consumption	"	4 052	4 966	4 052	4 037	2 973
Total supply	"	68 216	66 682	64 312	67 497	66 569
Exports	"	20 620	23 077	23 505	25 503	26 973
Used for canning	"					
On hand, Dec. 31	"	4 099	3 352	4 637	4 233	4 178
Domestic disappearance	"	43 497	40 253	36 170	37 761	35 418
Per capita disappearance	kg	2.0	1.9	1.6	1.7	1.5

[1] Intercensal revisions.
[2] Included with beef.
[3] Trimmed of larding fat.

11.28   Use of agricultural land, by province, censuses 1966 and 1971 (acres)

Land use	Province or territory					
	Newfoundland		Prince Edward Island		Nova Scotia	
	1966	1971	1966	1971	1966	1971
Improved land	*20,566*	*19,148*	*569,799*	*494,131*	*485,859*	*386,021*
Under crops[1]	12,409	8,736	398,373	351,384	314,143	242,959
Pasture (improved)	5,320	7,881	152,191	114,271	132,355	107,390
Summerfallow	258	499	2,896	9,186	2,587	6,272
Other	2,579	2,032	16,339	19,290	36,774	29,400
Unimproved land	*28,947*	*43,556*	*357,179*	*280,499*	*1,366,036*	*942,854*
Woodland	13,750	11,338	279,681	210,911	1,084,273	740,338
Other	15,197	32,218	77,498	69,588	281,763	202,516
Total	49,513	62,704	926,978	774,630	1,851,895	1,328,875
	New Brunswick		Quebec		Ontario	
	1966	1971	1966	1971	1966	1971
Improved land	*638,649*	*487,380*	*7,629,346*	*6,449,992*	*12,004,305*	*10,864,601*
Under crops[1]	427,832	322,310	5,166,421	4,337,236	8,358,741	7,855,890
Pasture (improved)	166,835	114,836	2,121,141	1,712,106	2,935,693	2,336,446
Summerfallow	5,822	8,594	48,779	81,672	229,852	237,916
Other	38,160	41,640	293,005	318,978	480,019	434,349
Unimproved land	*1,173,046*	*851,753*	*5,256,723*	*4,351,124*	*5,821,740*	*5,098,455*
Woodland	973,888	682,237	3,777,489	3,098,920	2,834,417	2,300,621
Other	199,158	169,516	1,479,234	1,252,204	2,987,323	2,797,834
Total	1,811,695	1,339,133	12,886,069	10,801,116	17,826,045	15,963,056
	Manitoba		Saskatchewan		Alberta	
	1966	1971	1966	1971	1966	1971
Improved land	*12,446,065*	*12,803,988*	*45,468,776*	*46,426,487*	*27,276,251*	*28,460,328*
Under crops[1]	8,693,682	9,122,474	27,018,238	27,339,147	17,707,659	18,092,544
Pasture (improved)	770,519	730,499	1,909,653	1,958,192	2,310,945	2,744,940
Summerfallow	2,668,830	2,655,197	15,895,825	16,559,825	6,659,125	7,008,714
Other	313,034	295,818	645,060	569,323	598,522	614,130
Unimproved land	*6,637,752*	*6,204,271*	*19,940,587*	*18,630,388*	*21,706,624*	*21,045,959*
Woodland	1,212,959	960,183	1,347,741	999,180	1,859,257	1,666,085
Other	5,424,793	5,244,088	18,592,846	17,631,208	19,847,367	19,379,874
Total	19,083,817	19,008,259	65,409,363	65,056,875	48,982,875	49,506,287
	British Columbia		Yukon Territory and Northwest Territories		Canada	
	1966	1971	1966	1971	1966	1971
Improved land	*1,614,141*	*1,755,247*	*620*	*1,554*	*108,154,377*	*108,148,877*
Under crops[1]	955,287	1,092,593	219	405	69,053,004	68,765,678
Pasture (improved)	436,920	397,864	168	1,039	10,941,740	10,225,464
Summerfallow	117,684	172,816	25	36	25,631,683	26,740,727
Other	104,250	91,974	208	74	2,527,950	2,417,008
Unimproved land	*3,678,169*	*4,067,984*	*3,648*	*2,894*	*65,970,451*	*61,519,737*
Woodland	799,935	844,257	534	101	14,183,924	11,514,171
Other	2,878,234	3,223,727	3,114	2,793	51,786,527	50,005,566
Total	5,292,310	5,823,231	4,268	4,448	174,124,828	169,668,614

[1]Includes field, vegetable, fruit and nursery crop land.

11.28   Use of agricultural land, by province, censuses 1966 and 1971 (hectares)   M

Land use	Province or territory					
	Newfoundland		Prince Edward Island		Nova Scotia	
	1966	1971	1966	1971	1966	1971
Improved land	8 323	7 748	230 590	199 967	196 620	156 217
Under crops[1]	5 022	3 535	161 216	142 200	127 129	98 322
Pasture (improved)	2 153	3 189	61 590	46 244	53 562	43 459
Summerfallow	104	202	1 172	3 717	1 047	2 538
Other	1 044	822	6 612	7 806	14 882	11 898
Unimproved land	11 714	17 626	144 545	113 514	552 815	381 559
Woodland	5 564	4 588	113 183	85 353	438 790	299 604
Other	6 150	13 038	31 362	28 161	114 025	81 955
Total	20 037	25 374	375 135	313 481	749 435	537 776
	New Brunswick		Quebec		Ontario	
	1966	1971	1966	1971	1966	1971
Improved land	258 452	197 235	3 087 486	2 610 219	4 857 970	4 396 748
Under crops[1]	173 137	130 434	2 090 776	1 755 217	3 382 662	3 179 166
Pasture (improved)	67 516	46 472	858 395	692 865	1 188 033	945 526
Summerfallow	2 356	3 478	19 740	33 051	93 018	96 281
Other	15 443	16 851	118 575	129 086	194 257	175 775
Unimproved land	474 714	344 692	2 127 320	1 760 837	2 355 975	2 063 271
Woodland	394 118	276 091	1 528 695	1 254 088	1 147 048	931 028
Other	80 596	68 601	598 625	506 749	1 208 927	1 132 243
Total	733 166	541 927	5 214 806	4 371 056	7 213 945	6 460 019
	Manitoba		Saskatchewan		Alberta	
	1966	1971	1966	1971	1966	1971
Improved land	5 036 743	5 181 589	18 400 558	18 788 131	11 038 306	11 517 486
Under crops[1]	3 518 208	3 691 734	10 933 892	11 063 759	7 166 035	7 321 792
Pasture (improved)	311 818	295 622	772 809	792 452	935 206	1 110 838
Summerfallow	1 080 037	1 074 520	6 432 811	6 701 523	2 694 852	2 836 326
Other	126 680	119 713	261 046	230 397	242 213	248 530
Unimproved land	2 686 203	2 510 779	8 069 668	7 539 450	8 784 359	8 516 997
Woodland	490 867	388 572	545 411	404 354	752 415	674 241
Other	2 195 336	2 122 207	7 524 257	7 135 096	8 031 944	7 842 756
Total	7 722 946	7 692 368	26 470 226	26 327 581	19 822 665	20 034 483
	British Columbia		Yukon Territory and Northwest Territories		Canada	
	1966	1971	1966	1971	1966	1971
Improved land	653 219	710 324	251	629	43 768 518	43 766 293
Under crops[1]	386 591	442 157	89	164	27 944 757	27 828 480
Pasture (improved)	176 815	161 010	68	420	4 427 965	4 138 097
Summerfallow	47 625	69 936	10	15	10 372 772	10 821 587
Other	42 188	37 221	84	30	1 023 024	978 129
Unimproved land	1 488 502	1 646 255	1 476	1 171	26 697 291	24 896 151
Woodland	323 722	341 659	216	41	5 740 029	4 659 619
Other	1 164 780	1 304 596	1 260	1 130	20 957 262	20 236 532
Total	2 141 721	2 356 579	1 727	1 800	70 465 809	68 662 444

[1]Includes field. vegetable, fruit and nursery crop land.

11.29   Economic classification of census-farms, by province, censuses 1966 and 1971 (number)

Economic class	Newfoundland 1966	1971	Prince Edward Island 1966	1971	Nova Scotia 1966	1971
Value of products sold of						
$50,000 or over	} 33	{ 24	} 97	{ 115	} 159	{ 213
35,000-$49,999		11		88		122
25,000- 34,999	19	33	74	133	91	161
15,000- 24,999	38	38	225	288	262	383
10,000- 14,999	31	38	385	385	399	321
7,500- 9,999	30	20	407	347	322	242
5,000- 7,499	47	37	744	562	525	379
3,750- 4,999	38	28	600	359	445	297
2,500- 3,749	65	53	796	503	664	450
1,200- 2,499	131	95	1,127	674	1,410	946
250- 1,199	541	301	1,274	721	3,149	1,619
50- 249	731	339	619	360	2,167	855
Institutional farms, etc.	5	25	9	8	28	20
Total	1,709	1,042	6,357	4,543	9,621	6,008

Economic class	New Brunswick 1966	1971	Quebec 1966	1971	Ontario 1966	1971
Value of products sold of						
$50,000 or over	} 167	{ 138	} 799	{ 902	} 4,385	{ 4,603
35,000-$49,999		132		837		4,041
25,000- 34,999	118	180	643	1,625	3,733	5,698
15,000- 24,999	315	344	2,345	5,094	9,692	11,532
10,000- 14,999	334	366	4,156	6,898	11,522	9,950
7,500- 9,999	346	258	4,761	5,681	9,210	7,111
5,000- 7,499	532	399	9,644	8,576	13,173	9,416
3,750- 4,999	424	293	8,105	5,175	8,489	5,898
2,500- 3,749	702	493	11,508	6,144	10,520	7,418
1,200- 2,499	1,464	865	15,651	7,172	14,377	9,894
250- 1,199	2,588	1,251	14,120	7,597	14,410	10,874
50- 249	1,699	748	8,414	5,453	10,294	8,203
Institutional farms, etc.	17	18	148	103	82	84
Total	8,706	5,485	80,294	61,257	109,887	94,722

Economic class	Manitoba 1966	1971	Saskatchewan 1966	1971	Alberta 1966	1971
Value of products sold of						
$50,000 or over	} 630	{ 606	} 1,093	{ 737	} 2,195	{ 2,236
35,000-$49,999		531		895		1,797
25,000- 34,999	585	926	1,789	1,919	1,876	2,657
15,000- 24,999	2,556	3,138	8,571	7,556	5,909	7,292
10,000- 14,999	4,452	4,263	13,610	11,496	8,012	8,007
7,500- 9,999	4,238	3,751	11,496	10,061	6,987	6,167
5,000- 7,499	6,409	5,233	15,570	13,779	10,130	8,079
3,750- 4,999	3,933	3,285	8,614	7,965	6,328	4,821
2,500- 3,749	4,569	3,603	9,219	8,522	7,534	5,477
1,200- 2,499	5,760	4,212	9,149	8,122	9,362	6,494
250- 1,199	4,235	3,341	4,278	4,009	6,599	5,674
50- 249	2,341	2,055	2,042	1,642	4,318	3,823
Institutional farms, etc.	39	37	255	267	161	178
Total	39,747	34,981	85,686	76,970	69,411	62,702

Economic class	British Columbia 1966	1971	Yukon Territory and Northwest Territories 1966	1971	Canada 1966	1971
Value of products sold of						
$50,000 or over	} 724	{ 869	} —	—	10,282	{ 10,443
35,000-$49,999		572				9,026
25,000- 34,999	456	728	—	—	9,384	14,060
15,000- 24,999	1,236	1,204	—	—	31,149	36,869
10,000- 14,999	1,314	1,070	2	—	44,217	42,794
7,500- 9,999	956	814	—	—	38,753	34,452
5,000- 7,499	1,329	1,201	—	—	58,103	47,661
3,750- 4,999	947	824	—	1	37,923	28,946
2,500- 3,749	1,445	1,343	2	2	47,024	34,008
1,200- 2,499	2,513	2,353	3	6	60,947	40,833
250- 1,199	4,071	4,407	6	5	55,271	39,799
50- 249	4,066	2,979	1	4	36,692	26,461
Institutional farms, etc.	28	36	5	—	777	776
Total	19,085	18,400	19	18	430,522	366,128

11.30   Census-farms with sales of $2,500 or more, classified by type of farm and by province, Census 1971 (number)

Type of farm	Province or territory					
	Nfld.	PEI	NS	NB	Que.	Ont.
Dairy	70	629	1,019	821	28,646	17,718
Cattle, hogs, sheep (excl. dairy farms)	40	980	655	535	5,183	28,129
Poultry	54	21	169	111	1,561	1,912
Wheat	—	—	—	—	20	313
Small grains (excl. wheat farms)	—	11	9	4	342	5,189
Field crops, other than small grains	30	616	76	670	1,124	4,593
Fruits and vegetables	58	26	250	98	1,472	3,856
Forestry	5	6	114	119	331	165
Miscellaneous specialty	5	8	109	26	423	1,606
Mixed	20	483	167	219	1,830	2,186
Livestock combination	3	400	77	132	1,169	902
Field crops combination	—	16	8	15	137	567
Other combination	17	67	82	72	524	717
Total	282	2,780	2,568	2,603	40,932	65,667
	Man.	Sask.	Alta.	BC	YT and NWT	Canada
Dairy	1,614	701	2,490	1,633	—	55,341
Cattle, hogs, sheep (excl. dairy farms)	9,829	15,913	25,843	2,501	2	89,610
Poultry	519	210	413	644	1	5,615
Wheat	2,738	26,516	3,893	166	—	33,646
Small grains (excl. wheat farms)	7,249	13,900	9,105	390	—	36,199
Field crops, other than small grains	376	112	814	387	—	8,798
Fruits and vegetables	65	14	40	1,948	—	7,827
Forestry	16	3	28	162	—	949
Miscellaneous specialty	209	128	320	571	—	3,405
Mixed	2,721	5,433	3,587	223	—	16,869
Livestock combination	1,418	2,269	1,612	37	—	8,019
Field crops combination	767	1,808	1,301	86	—	4,705
Other combination	536	1,356	674	100	—	4,145
Total	25,336	62,930	46,533	8,625	3	258,259

11.31   Lake shipments of Canadian grain from Thunder Bay, navigation seasons 1974 and 1975 (bushels)

Year and item	To Canadian ports	To US ports	To overseas ports	Total shipments
1974				
Wheat	260,233,840	2,319,468	19,691,030	282,244,338
Oats	10,228,084	—	427,412	10,655,496
Barley	67,363,513	11,257,745	2,301,465	80,922,723
Rye	1,324,020	—	1,095,352	2,419,372
Flaxseed	1,093,456	—	6,359,823	7,453,279
Rapeseed	—	—	2,049,560	2,049,560
Mustard seed	—	—	—	—
Total	340,242,913	13,577,213	31,924,642	385,744,768
1975				
Wheat	321,459,314	—	4,140,074	325,599,388
Oats	17,633,660	—	7,274,972	24,908,632
Barley	101,651,079	5,909,191	4,237,966	111,798,236
Rye	5,388,863	549,640	3,246,145	9,184,648
Flaxseed	762,903	—	4,706,785	5,469,688
Rapeseed	836,256	—	1,567,913	2,404,169
Mustard seed	—	—	—	—
Total	447,732,075	6,458,831	25,173,855	479,364,761

11.32   Supply and disposition of Canadian grain, crop years ended July 31, 1974 and 1975 (million bushels)

Item	Wheat	Oats	Barley	Rye	Flaxseed	Rapeseed
CROP YEAR 1973-74						
Carryover, Aug. 1, 1973	365.4	79.7	193.0	10.3	7.7	20.7
Production in 1973	593.7	326.9	469.6	14.3	19.4	53.2
Imports	—	7.3	—	—	- -	—
Total, supply	959.1	413.9	662.6	24.6	27.1	73.9
Exports[1]	419.4	0.8	127.5	4.6	15.5	39.2
Domestic use[2]	169.0	335.7	326.7	9.5	3.7	22.3
Total, disposition	959.1	413.9	662.6	24.6	27.1	73.9
Carryover, July 31, 1974	370.7	77.4	208.4	10.5	7.9	12.4
CROP YEAR 1974-75						
Carryover, Aug. 1, 1974	370.7	77.4	208.4	10.5	7.9	12.4
Production in 1974	488.5	254.7	404.3	18.9	13.8	51.3
Imports	—	1.9	—	—	- -	—
Total, supply	859.2	334.0	612.7	29.4	21.7	63.7
Exports[1]	394.6	1.4	138.4	4.8	10.5	26.1
Domestic use[2]	169.3	259.2	285.8	11.2	2.6	19.9
Total, disposition	859.2	334.0	612.7	29.4	21.7	63.7
Carryover, July 31, 1975	295.3	73.4	188.5	13.4	8.6	17.7

[1]Includes seed wheat, wheat flour in terms of wheat; seed oats, rolled oats and oatmeal in terms of oats; and malt in terms of barley.
[2]Includes human food, seed requirements, industrial use, loss in handling and animal feed.

11.31   Lake shipments of Canadian grain from Thunder Bay, navigation seasons 1974 and 1975 (metric tonnes)   M

Year and item	To Canadian ports	To US ports	To overseas ports	Total shipments
1974				
Wheat	7 082 405	63 126	535 902	7 681 433
Oats	157 739	—	6 592	164 331
Barley	1 466 668	245 109	50 108	1 761 885
Rye	33 632	—	27 823	61 455
Flaxseed	27 775	—	161 547	189 322
Rapeseed	—	—	46 483	46 483
Mustard seed	—	—	—	—
Total	8 768 219	308 235	828 455	9 904 909
1975				
Wheat	8 748 689	—	112 674	8 861 363
Oats	271 949	—	112 196	384 145
Barley	2 213 191	128 657	92 271	2 434 119
Rye	136 883	13 962	82 456	233 301
Flaxseed	19 379	—	119 558	138 937
Rapeseed	18 966	—	35 560	54 526
Mustard seed	—	—	—	—
Total	11 409 057	142 619	554 715	12 106 391

11.32   Supply and disposition of Canadian grain, crop years ended July 31, 1974 and 1975 (thousand metric tonnes)   M

Item	Wheat	Oats	Barley	Rye	Flaxseed	Rapeseed
CROP YEAR 1973-74						
Carryover, Aug. 1, 1973	9 944.6	1 229.1	4 202.1	261.6	195.6	469.5
Production in 1973	16 157.9	5 041.5	10 224.3	363.2	492.8	1 206.6
Imports	—	112.6	—	—	. .	—
Total, supply	26 102.5	6 383.2	14 426.4	624.8	688.4	1 676.1
Exports[1]	11 414.2	12.3	2 776.0	116.8	393.7	889.0
Domestic use[2]	4 599.4	5 177.2	7 113.1	241.3	94.0	505.8
Total, disposition	26 102.5	6 383.2	14 426.4	624.8	688.4	1 676.1
Carryover, July 31, 1974	10 088.9	1 193.7	4 537.3	266.7	200.7	281.3
CROP YEAR 1974-75						
Carryover, Aug. 1, 1974	10 088.9	1 193.7	4 537.3	266.7	200.7	281.3
Production in 1974	13 294.8	3 928.0	8 802.6	480.1	350.5	1 163.5
Imports	—	29.3	—	—	. .	—
Total, supply	23 383.7	5 151.0	13 339.9	746.8	551.2	1 444.8
Exports[1]	10 739.3	21.6	3 013.3	121.9	266.7	591.9
Domestic use[2]	4 607.6	3 997.4	6 222.6	284.5	66.0	451.3
Total, disposition	23 383.7	5 151.0	13 339.9	746.8	551.2	1 444.8
Carryover, July 31, 1975	8 036.8	1 132.0	4 104.0	340.4	218.5	401.6

[1]Includes seed wheat, wheat flour in terms of wheat; seed oats, rolled oats and oatmeal in terms of oats; and malt in terms of barley.
[2]Includes human food, seed requirements, industrial use, loss in handling and animal feed.

11.33   Licensed grain storage capacity and grain in store, crop years 1972-73 and 1974-75

Crop year and storage position	Licensed storage capacity	Canadian grain[1] in licensed storage			Proportion of licensed storage capacity occupied		
	Dec. 1, 1972 '000 bu	Nov. 29, 1972 '000 bu	Mar. 28, 1973 '000 bu	July 31, 1973 '000 bu	Dec. 1, 1972 %	Mar. 30, 1973 %	July 31, 1973 %
1972-73							
Primary elevators	374,493	250,235	234,003	230,313	66.8	62.5	61.5
Process elevators	13,357	7,569	7,490	7,438	56.7	56.1	55.7
Interior terminals	17,100	7,699	10,039	5,271	45.0	58.7	30.8
Pacific Coast	28,319	17,107	13,756	13,677	60.4	48.6	48.3
Churchill	5,000	2,050	2,050	3,479	41.0	41.0	69.6
Thunder Bay	103,986	60,234	73,750	56,943	57.9	70.9	54.8
Georgian Bay and upper Lake ports	34,050	25,064	7,617	10,445	73.6	22.4	30.7
Lower Lake and upper St. Lawrence ports	17,100	9,263	7,677	3,988	54.2	44.9	23.3
Lower St. Lawrence ports	65,807	33,041	18,247	17,177	50.2	27.7	26.1
Maritime ports (excl. Newfoundland)	8,229	5,032	2,780	2,025	61.1	33.8	24.6
Total, 1972-73	667,441	417,294	377,409	350,756	62.5	56.5	52.6
	Aug. 1, 1974 '000 bu	July 31, 1974 '000 bu	Jan. 1, 1975 '000 bu	Apr. 2, 1975 '000 bu	July 31, 1974 %	Jan. 1, 1975 %	Apr. 2, 1975 %
1974-75							
Primary elevators	362,273	257,785	225,803	207,397	71.2	62.3	57.2
Process elevators	17,573	8,965	7,214	6,880	51.0	41.1	39.2
Interior terminals	142,816	64,476	61,458	75,510	45.1	43.0	52.9
Transfer	124,991	64,793	52,097	28,911	51.8	41.7	23.1
Total, 1974-75	647,653	396,019	346,572	318,698	61.1	53.5	49.2

[1]Wheat, oats, barley, rye, flaxseed and rapeseed.

11.34   Wheat milled for flour, and production and exports of wheat flour, 10-year average 1966-75 and crop years ended July 31, 1972-75

Crop year	Wheat milled for flour '000 bu	Wheat flour production cwt	Wheat flour exports Amount cwt	Production %
Av. 1965-66 — 1974-75	88,392	39,058,224	11,161,218	28.6
1971-72	88,124	39,071,806	10,745,908	27.5
1972-73	86,390	38,049,127	10,154,053	26.7
1973-74	84,660	37,377,341	8,173,422	21.9
1974-75	88,893	39,021,816	8,148,145	20.9

11.34   Wheat milled for flour, and production and exports of wheat flour, 10-year average 1966-75 and crop years ended July 31, 1972-75   M

Crop year	Wheat milled for flour t	Wheat flour production '000 t	Wheat flour exports Amount '000 t	Production %
Av. 1965-66—1974-75	2 406	1 772	506	28.6
1971-72	2 398	1 772	487	27.5
1972-73	2 351	1 726	461	26.7
1973-74	2 304	1 695	371	21.9
1974-75	2 419	1 770	370	20.9

Sources
11.1-11.19 Agriculture Division, Institutions and Agriculture Statistics Field, Statistics Canada.
11.20-11.21 Food, Beverages and Textiles Section, Manufacturing and Primary Industries Division, Statistics Canada.
11.22-11.26 Agriculture Division, Institutions and Agriculture Statistics Field, Statistics Canada.
11.27-11.30 Census of Agriculture Division, Institutions and Agriculture Statistics Field, Statistics Canada.
11.31-11.34 Agriculture Division, Institutions and Agriculture Statistics Field, Statistics Canada.

Mines and minerals   Chapter   12

Mines and minerals — Chapter 12

Canada's mineral industry — 12.1

Review of the industry — 12.1.1

The Canadian mineral industry experienced the pressures of strong demand in 1974, followed by recessionary conditions in the major industrialized countries that extended into 1975. The value of mineral production in 1975 increased 14% compared with an increase of 40% the previous year.

Canada's mineral production in 1975 was valued at $13,403 million compared with $11,711 million in 1974 and $8,369 million in 1973. Metal mines output and mineral fuels production showed a decrease of $8.2 million and an increase of $1,652 million, respectively, in 1975; non-metal mines showed a moderate increase of about $33.7 million.

Canada produces about 60 different minerals from domestic deposits. The 10 leading minerals comprised 82% of the total output by value in 1975 compared with 83% in 1974 and 83% in 1973. The 1975 value for the 10 leading minerals totalled $11,015 million. Individual values were: petroleum $3,781 million, copper $1,017 million, nickel $1,109 million, zinc $895 million, iron ore $923 million, natural gas $1,730 million, natural gas by-products $768 million, cement $265 million, asbestos $267 million and sand and gravel $260 million. The first four accounted for 57% of the total value of mineral production in 1975 compared to 58% the previous year (Tables 12.1 - 12.5).

Canada produces many of the minerals needed for modern economies although a few, such as manganese, chromium, bauxite and tin, are imported.

The strength of Canada's mineral industry is based on export sales. About 82.0% of the total mineral production was exported with crude minerals comprising 67.2% of the total mineral exports. Apparent consumption of minerals in Canada ranged from 25.6% for copper to 13.8% for zinc.

Exports of minerals and fabricated mineral products have led to several periods of sustained expansion in the Canadian economy in the past and they have been a major factor in the recent increase in Canada's export trade. In 1975 these exports were valued at $10,987 million or 34.2% of the $32,096 million total of merchandise exports. This proportion is typical of the past decade and has been maintained despite the sharp increase in Canada's automobile trade with the US in the late 1960s. Increased demand in the US was the main factor in the increase in Canada's exports. The major consumers of Canada's exports of mineral products were: the United States 68.0%, Japan 9.1%, the European Economic Community (EEC) 8.0%, and Britain 6.5%. Comparable percentages for 1974 were: United States 67.8%, Japan 9.7%, EEC 6.5% and Britain 6.4%. Exports to Japan increased markedly although the United States remained Canada's most important export customer.

Mineral production is divided into four sectors: metallics, non-metallics, mineral fuels and structural materials. The contribution of each of these groups to the total value of production in 1975 was as follows (1974 figures in parentheses): mineral fuels 51.1% (44.4%), metallics 36% (41%), non-metallics 6.9% (7.7%) and structural materials 6.0% (6.8%). The value of mineral fuels production increased with the continued rise in export sales. Structural materials are sold mainly in the domestic market where the demand is more stable.

Canada leads the world in mineral exports and ranks third in mineral production behind the United States and the Soviet Union. The mineral industry has always been a major factor in Canada's economic development and is still the main force in the northward advance of Canada's frontiers of population and economic activity.

The prices of most minerals, especially the non-ferrous metals, showed great strength in part of 1974, but in general declined in 1975. This is partly due to inflation and partly a result of a greater than anticipated economic expansion in the United States, Japan and Europe, followed by recessionary conditions in 1974 and 1975. The price index for ferrous metals, iron ore, ferro-alloys and additives showed an increase of 15.0% over 1974. Non-ferrous metals reached their peak value in 1970 and declined less than 1% in 1975. Non-metallic mineral prices continued to rise rapidly, with their value showing an increase of 18.3%.

Petroleum, natural gas, copper, nickel, zinc and iron ore together contribute three quarters of the total Canadian mineral output value and some discussion of production locations and markets is warranted.

Petroleum and natural gas production and refining is Canada's largest mineral industry. Domestic production and exports are small in the context of the world's industry but are of great significance to Canada. The industry's growth in the past two decades has been of particular importance because of its effect on the balance of payments, as a source of revenue to the several levels of government, and for its impact on engineering and construction.

In 1975 total production of crude oil, gas and gas by-products was valued at $6,279 million, an increase of 28.1% over the 1974 value of $4,900 million. Crude oil production is concentrated in Alberta, with Saskatchewan in second place and minor production elsewhere. The pattern of crude oil distribution in Canada reflects the National Oil Policy, which traditionally allocated markets west of the Ottawa Valley to Canada's mid-continent producers, while Quebec and Maritime markets were supplied by oil from overseas. Canada has produced oil almost equivalent to its total domestic needs and has tended to import oil in eastern Canada from overseas and export oil to US markets in the mid-west. The possibility of depletion has been of concern and has affected the amount made available for export. Alberta oilfields are producing at close to capacity and the region's economic reserves of oil will last 12 years at current depletion rates. Canada's North is the focus of much optimism for large-scale oil finds.

Natural gas is an important domestic product and an increasingly important export product. Generally gas and oil are found together. In Canada, the western provinces have the major proven reserves of gas. The value of gas and gas by-products produced in Canada in 1975 was $2,497.4 million, compared with that of oil at $3,781.1 million.

Canada's gas reserves are sufficient for 17 years but the known reserves of commercial gas declined for the first time in 1972. This does not include the discoveries of gas in the Arctic because there is as yet no economical method of transporting it to markets in the south. Sales of natural gas and gas by-products totalled $2,498.0 million, an increase of 81.3% over the previous year. Existing proven reserves of gas in Canada are sufficient to meet normal domestic market growth and to continue meeting present export commitments only in the short term. However, if long-term domestic market growth and current exports to the United States are to be maintained, additional reserves of natural gas must be found in the next decade.

Nickel ranked third among Canadian minerals produced in 1975. World over-supply, which led to the accumulation of large stockpiles by Canadian producers during 1971 and 1972, eased in 1973 as demand increased and the market stabilized. Canada is the world's leading producer of nickel.

Copper was fourth by output value in 1975. Production of recoverable copper from Canadian mines dropped to 798,132 tons (724 053 tonnes), a decrease of 11.8% from the previous year. Copper remained in over-supply in the world but a better balance between supply and demand had been achieved. Copper is produced in all provinces except Prince Edward Island and Alberta. British Columbia, Ontario and Quebec accounted for 39.7%, 39.2% and 19.9% of copper production in 1975, respectively.

Iron ore production rose in 1975 to 49.4 million long tons (50.2 million t). Production was valued at $923 million, an increase of 27.5% compared to the

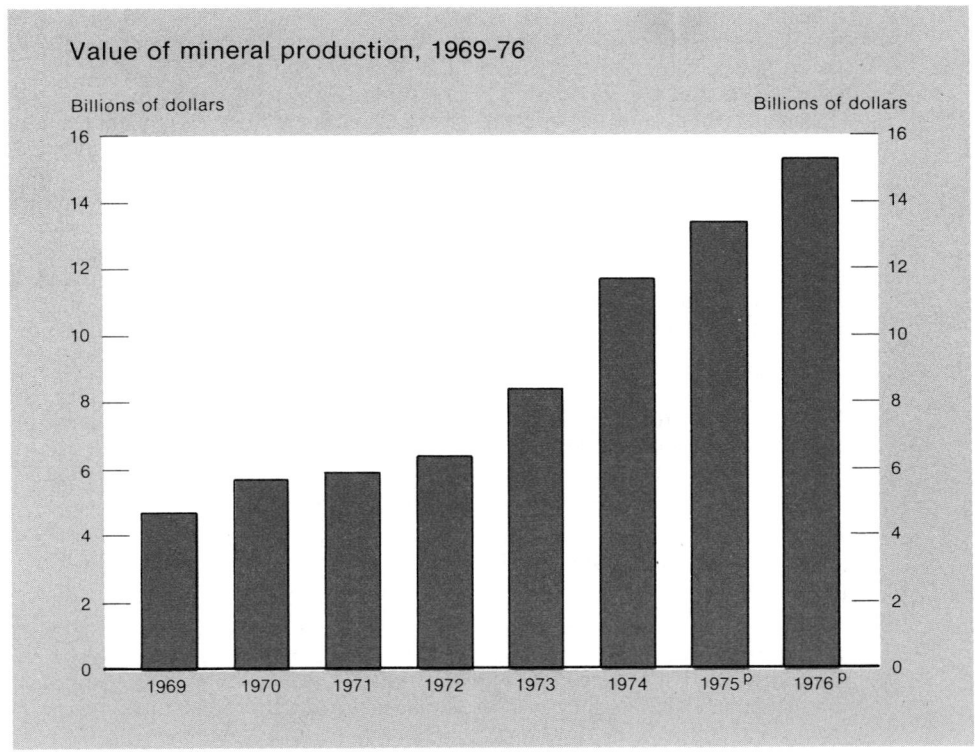

Value of mineral production, 1969-76

Billions of dollars

previous year. Of the 39.7 million tons (40.3 million t) exported in 1975, the United States received 21.3 million (21.6 million t), Britain 3.4 million (3.5 million t), Western Europe 10.4 million (10.6 million t) and Japan 4.6 million (4.7 million t). Projects currently under way in the Quebec–Labrador area will increase both production and pelletizing capacities. Production capacity is expected to increase from 46 million tons (47 million t) of iron ore products in 1970 to approximately 78 million tons (79 million t) by 1978. Newfoundland, Quebec, Ontario and British Columbia are the only producers of iron ore.

Zinc production in 1975 attained a record value of $895.4 million, an increase of 3.3% over 1974; production decreased by 3.9%. Canada remained the world's leading mine producer.

In 1975 mineral investment (including both capital and repair expenditures) in mineral fuels was $1.9 billion, 30% higher than 1974, compared with non-metal mines at $479.1 million that rose 1.4% and metal mines at $1,157.1 million that increased 1.5%. Similarly, in mineral manufacturing, investment in non-metallics at $335.9 million was 6.2% higher than 1974, compared with petroleum and coal products at $582.6 million that rose 7.8% and primary metals at $1,445.0 million that rose 15.0%.

Overall capital expenditures increased in the minerals sector and the mineral fuels sector (excluding coal). Investment in iron mines increased slightly to $485.6 million from $393.1 million in 1974. Capital expenditures in the mineral fuels sector (excluding coal) increased to $1,622.5 million, an increase of 32.3% over the previous year, with more emphasis being placed on exploration in areas where new finds of gas and oil have been reported.

The volume index of mineral production, which measures the mining industry's absolute growth, based on the revised index of 1971 = 100, increased to 118.2 from 109.5 in 1974. In comparison the volume index of total industrial production increased to 117.6 from 117.3 in 1974.

Alberta and Ontario accounted for 44.8% and 17.5%, respectively, of the Canadian output value of minerals in 1975. Alberta produced 38.6% and Ontario produced 20.7% of the output value of minerals in 1974. In 1975 British Columbia accounted for 9.1%, Quebec 8.5%, Saskatchewan 6.2%, Manitoba 4.0%, Newfoundland and Labrador 4.2%, Yukon Territory 1.7%, Northwest Territories 1.4%, New Brunswick 1.9%, Nova Scotia 0.7% and Prince Edward Island for a minimal amount. Alberta produced 85.0% of the mineral fuels, Ontario produced 40.8% of the metals and 37.6% of the structural materials, and Quebec produced 27.0% of the non-metals. Tables 12.6 - 12.8 show the mineral production and value of production by province.

Newfoundland and Labrador. Mineral production in Newfoundland and Labrador was valued at $568.2 million compared to $448.5 million in 1974, an increase of 26.7%. Iron ore production increased 30.8% to 25.6 million tons (26.0 million t) in Labrador. Production of lead dropped 29.1% in 1975, and zinc production rose 41.6%. Asbestos production increased 12.6%. Fluorspar production, valued at $7.0 million, decreased $120,000 in value from 1974.

Prince Edward Island. Sand and gravel is the only mining product of this province. Production, valued at $1.54 million, increased 5.9% in value over the previous year.

Nova Scotia. Total mining production increased 20.5% in value to $96.7 million in 1975. The quantity of coal produced in 1975 was 1.85 million tons (1.68 million t), up from 1.41 million tons (1.28 million t) in 1974. A new mine at Lingan began production in 1974. Production of non-metallics dropped to $25.8 million in 1975 from $27.6 million in 1974, with gypsum accounting for $12.5 million, 48.4%.

New Brunswick. Mineral production increased to $251.4 million from $213.5 million in 1974. Metal products, which are produced mainly around Bathurst, represented 88.3% of the total mineral output. Zinc, lead and copper were the principal minerals produced. Coal production rose to 450,000 tons (408 000 t) in 1975 from 415,000 tons (376 000 t) in 1974.

Quebec. Total mineral output was $1,142.5 million, a decrease of 4.2% over 1974. Metallics accounted for 57.5% of production, non-metallics 22.0%, and structural materials 20.5%. Mineral fuels production was insignificant. Copper, iron ore and zinc were the major metallics produced, accounting for 14.5%, 18.2% and 8.6%, respectively, of Quebec's total mineral output. Asbestos was the major non-metallic, accounting for 15.5% of the total. Titanium dioxide, a non-metallic, is produced only in Quebec and has firm world markets; production was valued at $55.1 million in 1975 compared to $51.9 million in 1974.

Ontario produced minerals valued at more than $2,339 million in 1975, mostly metallics. The value of metallics decreased by 4.2% from the previous year. Nickel, copper, zinc, precious metals and iron ore contributed 34.9%, 15.9%, 11.9%, 10.9% and 9.2%, respectively, to the provincial output. The range of minerals is more diverse in Ontario than in any other province. Output of fuels in Ontario is relatively small. The principal non-metals — salt, nepheline syenite, asbestos, gypsum, quartz and sulphur — are produced in relatively small quantities. Structural materials produced in 1975 decreased in value to $303 million from $308 million in 1974.

Manitoba. Mineral production in 1975 was valued at $533.2 million, an increase of 9.7% from the previous year. Metallic minerals accounted for 85.8% of the total, with nickel, copper and zinc representing 55.0%, 16.9% and 10.3%, respectively. Crude petroleum contributed 5.9% of the provincial total. Manitoba produced 26.4% of Canada's nickel, an increase of 3.6% over the total value for the previous year. The value of zinc production increased 14.0% over 1974.

Saskatchewan produces mainly mineral fuels and non-metals because the metal-rich geological formations of eastern Canada and the Rockies do not dominate the geology in Saskatchewan. Crude petroleum and potash represented 47.2% and 42.0% of the 1975 mineral production. Metallics constituted only 2.2% of the total. Renewed interest in uranium may result in increased production in the metals sector.

Alberta. Mineral production was valued at $6,000.8 million in 1975 with crude petroleum, natural gas and natural gas by-products representing 94.0% of the total. Sulphur, produced as a by-product in the processing of natural gas, represented 1.5% of the mineral production. Alberta produced 86.1% of Canada's petroleum and 94.8% of Canada's natural gas in 1975. Coal production accounted for 3.1% of provincial mineral production. Structural materials made up most of the remainder.

British Columbia. Mineral output increased 5.9% to $1,223.9 million in 1975. Metallics comprised 48.1% and mineral fuels 41.4% of all mineral production with copper, zinc, molybdenum and lead accounting for 27.7%, 6.7%, 5.5% and 2.5%, respectively, of the total. Coal, crude petroleum and natural gas represented 26.7%, 7.7% and 5.7% of the total production, respectively. Production of copper in all forms was down sharply with mine production value decreasing 31.0% from the previous year. Coal production increased to 10.5 million tons (9.5 million t) in 1975. Asbestos was the leading non-metallic mineral produced.

Northwest Territories. The value of mineral production in 1975 decreased to $189.5 million from $223.1 million in 1974. Metallic minerals accounted for almost all of the total. Zinc, lead, gold and silver comprised 58.1%, 16.3%, 16.2% and 5.2%, respectively, of the total mineral output. Crude oil and natural gas are of considerable potential value.

Yukon Territory. The value of production increased to $228.9 million compared to $171.5 million in 1974. Zinc, lead, silver, copper and asbestos made up 41.6%, 24.6%, 12.9%, 5.1% and 14.0%, respectively. Output is not large by national standards but is increasing rapidly.

Metals

12.1.2

Nickel. Canadian production of nickel in 1975 amounted to 269,826 tons (244 782 t) valued at $1.11 billion. World production of nickel decreased 3.9%; Canadian production decreased 9.1% because of labour strikes and cutbacks in production. Consumption of nickel in the non-communist world was about 410,000 tons (372 000 t) compared with about 552,000 tons (501 000 t) in 1974, one of the sharpest declines in the history of the industry. Producers' stocks had risen to about three times normal at the end of the year.

At Sudbury, Ont., The International Nickel Company of Canada, Limited (INCO) began work on the development of a new mine, Levack East, where production is expected to begin in 1984. In Manitoba, work continued on deepening the Birchtree mine and on underground exploration at the Pipe mine. INCO announced plans to build a plant in the Sudbury district for the direct rolling of metal powders to manufacture coinage strip. The plant was scheduled to be in operation in the second half of 1977.

Six companies mined nickel ores in Canada during 1975. Falconbridge, the second largest producer, continued development work at the Lockerby mine which is scheduled to be producing at capacity in 1978. The Thierry deposit, near Pickle Crow, Ont., of Union Minière Explorations and Mining Company Limited, was being prepared for production. This new mine was scheduled to start production in 1976.

Copper. Canadian mine production of recoverable copper amounted to 798,132 tons (724 052 t) valued at $1,016.8 million in 1975 (Table 12.9). Canada produced 9.7% of the world's copper and ranks as the fourth largest producer. World mine production of copper decreased 5% from the previous year. Canadian exports of copper concentrates decreased 9% while exports of refined copper increased by 12%. Domestic consumption of copper fell by 25% to the lowest level since 1964.

Copper and nickel-copper ores were smelted at five locations in Canada at the end of 1975. The International Nickel Company of Canada, Limited (INCO) continued to operate an oxygen flash smelter at Copper Cliff, Ont. Falconbridge Nickel Mines Limited operated a smelter at Falconbridge, Ont., treating nickel-copper concentrates. Ores and concentrates from most mines in the Atlantic provinces, Quebec and Ontario were processed at the Noranda smelter of Noranda Mines, Limited or at the Murdochville smelter of Gaspé Copper Mines, Limited, both in Quebec. Major expansion programs have been completed at both the Noranda and Murdochville smelters. At Murdochville, smelter capacity has been raised by 27,000 tons (24 000 t) of anode copper a year. A 300,000 tons-a-year (270 000 t/yr) sulphuric acid plant has been constructed and some of the acid produced will be used to leach copper from low-grade oxide ores from the Copper Mountain mine. The expanded facilities encountered serious and lengthy start-up problems in 1974 and 1975. At Noranda the smelter was expanded by the construction of a Noranda continuous smelting process reactor capable of producing 55,000 tons (50 000 t) a year of blister copper in one furnace directly from concentrates. Operation of the reactor began early in 1973. A shortage of concentrates was experienced in 1975 and production fell by 38,000 tons (34 000 t) relative to 1974. Hudson Bay Mining and Smelting Co., Limited operates a smelter at Flin Flon, Man. and produces anode copper which is refined at the Montreal refinery of Canadian Copper Refiners Limited. A new flue system was completed in 1975, including the erection of an 825-ft (251 m) smokestack to improve the dispersion of sulphur gases.

Electrolytic copper refineries were operated by INCO at Copper Cliff and by Canadian Copper Refiners Limited, (CCR) a subsidiary of Noranda Mines, Limited, at Montreal East, Que. INCO's copper refining capacity at Copper Cliff was 212,000 tons (192 000 t) a year. Copper is recovered in part as a by-product from the refining of nickel. Canadian Copper Refiners Limited has a capacity of 480,000 tons (435 000 t) of refined copper a year, making CCR the world's largest copper refinery.

As a result of the need to cut shipments to Japan, and the higher treatment charges sought by Japanese smelters, a significant shift of Canadian concentrate sales away from Japan took place in 1975. The displaced concentrates were processed at smelters in North America.

In 1975 a significant erosion of mine production capacity occurred, particularly in eastern Canada, with the closure of a number of small mines — six in Quebec, one in Ontario and two in British Columbia — due to depletion of ore reserves. These mines had produced a total of 28,000 tons (25 000 t) of copper in their last full year of operation.

In 1975, production increased 14% in the Atlantic provinces, declined 18% in Quebec and 7% in Ontario. Production also declined substantially in western Canada, with British Columbia down 16%, Manitoba down 10% and Saskatchewan down 3%.

No new mines began production in 1975, because of low copper prices of 1974-75, excess production capacity in the world, temporary saturation of the Japanese market for copper concentrates, and a slowdown in exploration in Canada.

Copper production in Newfoundland in 1975 totalled 8,190 tons (7 430 t) valued at $10.4 million from two mines. In New Brunswick copper production was 13,139 tons (11 920 t) valued at $16.7 million from four mines; two of these recommenced production late in the year. In Quebec production declined to 129,858 tons (117 805 t) valued at $165.4 million from 158,991 tons (144 234 t) valued at $246.5 million in 1974. About 25 mines were operated during 1975, the main centres of production being Rouyn–Noranda, Val d'Or, Matagami, Chibougamau, Murdochville and Stratford Centre.

Copper was produced at about 35 mines in Ontario in 1975, the main operations being the nickel-copper mines of the Sudbury district copper-zinc and copper mines near Timmins, and copper-zinc mines near Manitouwadge. Producers' shipments amounted to 292,296 tons (265 166 t) valued at $372.4 million compared to 312,943 tons (283 897 t) valued at $483.9 million in 1974.

Production in Manitoba and Saskatchewan was 79,284 tons (71 925 t) valued at $101.0 million. The major producer was Hudson Bay Mining and Smelting Co., Limited, which produced copper in the Flin Flon and Snow Lake areas. Sherritt Gordon Mines, Limited at Lynn Lake, Fox Lake and Ruttan, and INCO at Thompson were the other main producers.

Production of copper in British Columbia in 1975 amounted to 265,999 tons (241 310 t) valued at $338.9 million compared to 316,968 tons (287 549 t) valued at $491.4 million in 1974. Most of the production in British Columbia comes from large open-pit mines. Production in the Yukon Territory decreased substantially in 1975 due to a reduction in shipments of concentrates from Whitehorse Copper Mines Ltd.

Iron ore. *All iron ore figures quoted in this text refer to long ton units of 2,240 lb. (1 016 kg).* Iron ore shipments in 1975 were 44,640,000 tons (45 360 000 t) compared with the previous year's 46,643,611 tons (47 392 097 t). These figures include about half a million tons (510 000 t) of by-product iron ore. The value of the shipments excluding by-product ore was $923 million compared with $724 million for the previous year.

Iron ore was produced by 16 mining companies at 18 locations, with nine operations in Ontario, four in Quebec, two in Labrador, two in British Columbia and one in Quebec–Labrador.

Shipments by province in 1975 were as follows: Newfoundland 22,836,000 tons (23 202 000 t); Quebec 10,893,000 tons (11 068 000 t); Ontario 9,683,000 tons (9 838 000 t) and British Columbia 1,228,000 tons (1 248 000 t). The Iron Ore Company of Canada (IOC) is the largest Canadian producer with 22,404,000 tons (22 764 000 t) followed by Quebec Cartier Mining at 8,136,000 tons (8 267 000 t) and Wabush Mines at 3,207,000 tons (3 258 000 t).

IOC's expansion of the Carol Lake concentrator from 10 million tons (10 200 000 t) to 22 million tons (22 400 000 t) a year and construction of a 6 million tons-a-year (6 100 000 t/yr) concentrator and pellet plant at Sept-Îles was completed in 1975. The concentrator ranks among the world's largest iron ore beneficiation plants. Its production capacity was expected to be reached in 1977. Unexpected mechanical and metallurgical problems associated with the complex treatment ore of Schefferville precluded the efficient operation of the new facilities at Sept-Îles and at the end of 1975 pellet plant production capacity had reached only 3 million tons (3 050 000 t) a year.

Quebec Cartier Mining Company (QCM) continued to develop the Mount Wright iron ore project in Quebec, despite construction slowdowns due to labour strikes in 1974. Production in 1975 was 406,000 tons (413 000 t). Included in the Mount Wright development is the construction of a concentrator with a minimum production capacity of 18 million tons (18 300 000 t) of iron ore concentrate (66% Fe) with provision for an ultimate annual capacity of 24 million tons (24 400 000 t) of concentrate. Minimum capacity is expected to be reached in 1978. Two thirds of the production will be exported to Europe and one third will go to US Steel. QCM is also involved in the Fire Lake development in Quebec. The participants in this project include Sidbec-Dosco Limited with 50.1% of the ownership, British Steel Corporation 41.67% and QCM 8.23%. The new company formed to develop the Fire Lake iron deposit is called Sidbec-Normines Ltd.

Crude ore from Fire Lake is transported by rail to the Lac Jeannine concentrator where 6 million tons (6 100 000 t) a year of concentrate are produced from both the Fire Lake mine and the Lac Jeannine mine where ore reserves were expected to be depleted by 1976. At Port Cartier a pellet plant is under construction to use the concentrate from the Lac Jeannine concentrator. When completed the plant is expected to produce 3.0 million tons (3 050 000 t) a year of pellets with an iron content of 65% and a silica content greater than 6% and 3.0 million tons (3 050 000 t) a year of pellets grading 68% iron and less than 2% silica. The former product will be used in standard blast furnaces while the latter will be used as direct reduction feed mainly for Sidbec-Dosco's operations at Contrecoeur.

Shipments from Wabush Mines decreased considerably from 5.4 million tons (5 500 000 t) in 1974 to 3.2 million tons (3 300 000 t) in 1975. This was because of a six-month strike.

In Ontario, labour problems also took their toll of production at several iron ore mines such as at Steep Rock Iron Mine Limited, Caland Ore Company Limited, the Griffith mine and The International Nickel Company of Canada, Limited. During the year, Canadian Pacific Investments Limited (CPI) acquired 60% of the issued shares of Steep Rock Iron Mines Limited (SRIM) which in turn owns the Lake St. Joseph property. CPI also controls Algoma Steel Corporation which purchased iron ore from SRIM's existing mine at Atikokan, Ont. Also, Dominion Foundries and Steel Limited (DOFASCO) purchased the property of Anaconda Iron Ore Limited at Nakina, Ont.

Iron ore deposits investigated in Canada during 1975 included the Lac Albanel owned partly by the province of Quebec; Star O'Keefe Iron Ore owned by Canadian Javelin with a deposit near Mount Wright, Que.; and the Clear Hills deposit near Peace River, Alta.

In Newfoundland in 1975 a significant event in iron ore development was the unexpected reversion to the province of certain mineral lands embracing 1.29 sq miles (3.34 km²) of the Julian Lake iron ore deposit near Wabush in Labrador. In exercising this expropriation the Newfoundland government claimed that Canadian Javelin had not proceeded "with due diligence" to develop mining operations at the site.

Canadian imports of iron ore increased from 2.3 million tons (2 300 000 t) in 1974 to 4.7 million tons (4 800 000 t) in 1975. Imports are likely to increase in the medium term as Canadian steelmakers continue to invest in US taconite operations. The Tilden mine in Michigan, in which both the Algoma Steel Corporation Limited and The Steel Company of Canada (STELCO) have equity, came into production in December 1974 with the resultant increase of iron ore shipments to Canada throughout the year. Additional iron ore imports were expected to flow in 1976 when the Eveleth Taconite Company of Minnesota, in which DOFASCO holds equity and the Hibbing Taconite Company in Minnesota, in which STELCO has an equity, came into production.

Exports of iron ore declined in 1975 to 36.0 million tons (36 600 000 t) from 36.9 million tons (37 500 000 t) in 1974. Consumption was an estimated 12.5 million tons (12 700 000 t) in 1975 as compared to 12.9 million tons (13 107 000 t) in 1974.

Lead and zinc. Canadian production of lead in 1975 was 373,065 tons (338 439 t) valued at $152 million, an increase of 15.0% in volume and 13.0% in value compared to the previous year (Table 12.12). Output of refined lead was 189,064 tons (171 516 t), a 36% increase from 1974.

Production of zinc in 1975 was 1.2 million tons (1.1 million t) valued at $895 million. Production increased 3.2% in value with volume unchanged from the previous year (Table 12.13). Output of refined zinc was 470,622 tons (426 941 t) in 1975, almost unchanged from 1974.

Exports of refined lead in 1975 increased to 121,195 tons (109 946 t) up 49.8% from 1974. Exports of refined zinc in 1975 declined to 272,525 tons (247 231 t) down 16.5% from 1974 reflecting the commercial recession in major export markets. Exports of zinc and lead in ores and concentrates also declined due to the recession.

In the Atlantic provinces lead production increased 7.3% to 73,440 tons (66 624 t) and zinc production increased 24% to 230,868 tons (209 440 t) in 1975. Brunswick Mining and Smelting Corporation Limited in New Brunswick was the Maritimes' largest producer. Newfoundland Zinc Mines Ltd. commenced production June 29, 1975 at its zinc property near Daniels Harbour, Nfld. and is expected to produce about 40,000 tons (36 000 t) of zinc annually.

In Quebec zinc production decreased 5.5% to 131,015 tons (118 855 t). Mining companies associated with Noranda Mines, Limited produced most of the zinc in Quebec. Mattagami Lake Mines Limited, the largest producer, mined 87,118 tons (79 032 t) in 1975. Normetal Mines Ltd. and Joutel Copper Mines Limited closed in 1975 due to ore exhaustion. However, La Société minière Louvem Inc. commenced zinc production at its former copper property near Val d'Or producing 33,963 tons (30 811 t) during the year. Lemoine Mines Ltd. near Chibougamau completed construction at its zinc-copper mine late in 1975 and began production early in 1976. Only 1,597 tons (1 449 t) of lead was produced in Quebec in 1975.

In Ontario zinc production decreased 22.7% to 371,339 tons (336 873 t). Texasgulf Canada Ltd., a wholly-owned subsidiary of Texas Gulf, Inc., which operates Canada's largest zinc mine at Timmins produced 276,814 tons (251 121 t) of zinc in 1975 compared to 302,702 tons (274 607 t) in 1974. The other major mines, Mattabi Mines Limited and Geco Mines Limited also recorded a substantial drop in production because of lesser volumes of lower grade ore being mined. The Sturgeon Lake joint venture operated by Falconbridge Copper Limited commenced production in February 1975 producing 24,753 tons (22 456 t) of zinc during the year. Lead production in Ontario declined 26.7% to 7,426 tons (6 737 t).

In Manitoba and Saskatchewan zinc production increased 2.9% to 77,641 tons (70 435 t). Mine production at Hudson Bay Mining and Smelting Co., Limited declined to 33,697 tons (30 569 t) as the company continued a program of new mine development to offset mines being phased out of production. Sherritt Gordon Mines, Limited increased production at the Ruttan Lake and Fox Lake mines with a total of 67,023 tons (60 802 t) in 1975.

In British Columbia zinc production increased 27.6% to 109,372 tons (99 221 t) and lead production increased 25.5% to 76,447 tons (69 352 t). Production at Cominco Ltd.'s Sullivan and H.B. mines returned to normal levels following a four-month strike in 1974. Elsewhere in the province, the Annex mine of Reeves MacDonald Mines, Limited was closed due to ore exhaustion and Western Mines Limited slightly decreased lead and zinc production in 1975.

In the Yukon Territory lead production increased 39.0% to 138,234 tons (125 404 t) and zinc production increased 45.5% to 126,878 tons (115 102 t). Anvil Mining Corp. Limited, Canada's largest lead producer, returned to normal production levels in 1975 following a one-month strike in 1974. Kerr Addison Mines Limited and Aex Minerals Corporation Limited which jointly own the Grum lead-zinc-silver deposit near Faro undertook a major feasibility study in 1975 of this deposit which contains over 30 million tons (27.2 million t) of ore.

In the Northwest Territories lead production decreased 10.5% to 75,777 tons (68 744 t) and zinc production decreased 22.6% to 146,696 tons (133 080 t). Pine Point Mines Limited, which was the sole producer of lead and zinc, produced a lesser tonnage of lower grade ore. Discussions continued with the Government of Canada concerning development of the Polaris property of Arvik Mines Ltd. on Little Cornwallis Island. The Polaris orebody contains an estimated 25 million tons (22.7 million t) of ore grading 18% zinc-lead. Mineral Resources International continued construction at its Strathcona Sound zinc-lead-silver deposit on Baffin Island to be put into production in 1976. The ore reserves are estimated at 6.9 million tons (6.3 million t) grading 15.5% combined lead-zinc.

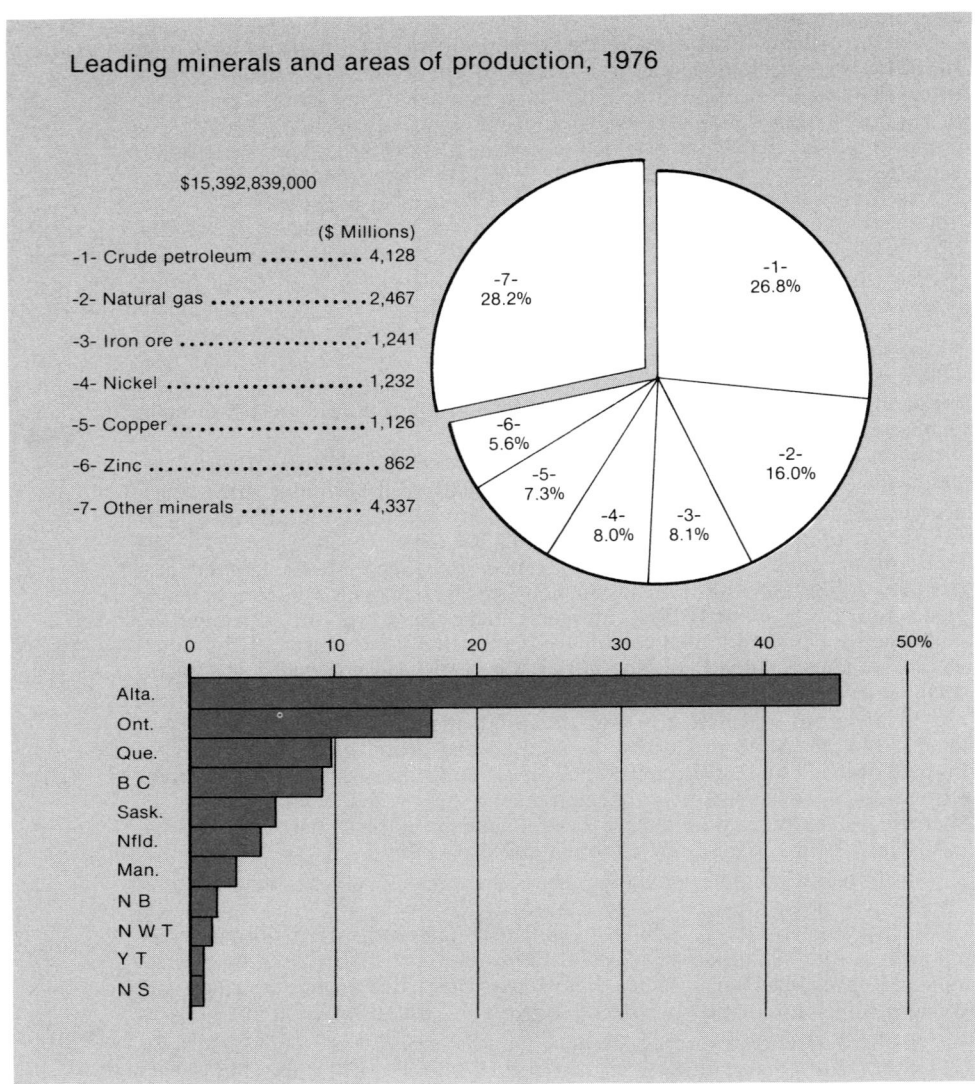

Leading minerals and areas of production, 1976

$15,392,839,000

($ Millions)
-1- Crude petroleum 4,128

-2- Natural gas 2,467

-3- Iron ore 1,241

-4- Nickel 1,232

-5- Copper.....................1,126

-6- Zinc 862

-7- Other minerals 4,337

-7-
28.2%

-1-
26.8%

-6-
5.6%

-5-
7.3%

-4-
8.0%

-3-
8.1%

-2-
16.0%

There were four zinc refineries in operation at the end of 1975 — Canadian Electrolytic Zinc Limited in Quebec, Hudson Bay Mining and Smelting Co., Limited in Manitoba, Texasgulf Canada Ltd. in Ontario and Cominco Ltd. in British Columbia. Canadian Electrolytic Zinc expanded capacity at year-end 1975 to 225,000 tons (204 000 t) a year.

The lead refinery of Cominco Ltd. at Trail, BC, with a capacity of 170,000 tons (154 000 t) annually, and that of Brunswick Mining and Smelting Corporation Limited at Belledune, NB, with an annual capacity of 79,400 tons (72 000 t), were Canada's only producers of primary lead metal.

Gold. The price of gold declined sharply in 1975 following a marked increase in 1974 from a low of US$114.75 an ounce troy (US$3.6893 a gram) on the London Gold Market at the beginning of the year to a high of US$197.50 an oz t

(US$6.3498/g) on December 30, 1974. Many factors were responsible for this reversal. Among these were the lack of interest in the purchase of gold by US citizens following legalization of gold ownership in that country on and after December 31, 1974, the decision by the US government to offer for sale by auction 2 million oz t (62 million g) of gold from its official reserves, an improvement in the US trade balance with a resulting strengthening of the US dollar relative to other currencies, an announcement at the end of August by the International Monetary Fund (IMF) that a tentative agreement had been reached on the sale of 25 million oz t (778 million g) of gold from its official reserves over a four-year period, and the restitution of the same quantity to member countries of the IMF.

The metal opened the year on the London market at US$185.00 an oz t (US$5.9479/g). The US Treasury sold a total of 1,203,500 oz t (37 433 034 g) at auctions in January and June at average prices of US$167.50 and $165.05 an oz t (US$5.3853/g and US$5.3065/g), respectively. Following these auctions the price of gold stabilized near the auction prices and the monthly averages for the period April to August varied from a high of US$169.84 an oz t (US$5.4605/g) in April to a low of $162.99 an oz t (US$5.2403/g) in August. Following the IMF announcement of gold sales the price dropped sharply and for the period September to December the monthly average prices varied from US$144.09 to $139.30 an oz t (US$4.6321/g to US$4.4786/g). Any further decline in the price of gold would create problems for many gold mines.

Gold production in Canada in 1975 was 1,674,000 oz t (52 067 221 g) valued at $276,125,000 compared with 1,698,392 oz t (52 825 896 g) in 1974 valued at $263,794,000. One lode gold mine closed in 1975. At the end of the year, 21 lode gold mines were in operation. The gold produced was sold on the open market and therefore no mines were eligible for assistance payments under the terms of the Emergency Gold Mining Assistance Act. The act expired on June 30, 1976.

Lode gold mines accounted for 74.1% of the total gold produced in Canada in 1975 compared with 71.4% in 1974. Gold recovered as a by-product from base-metal mining accounted for 25.7% and placer mining 0.2%. Ontario continued to be the largest gold-producing province, accounting for 46.3% of the total, followed by Quebec with 27.8%, Northwest Territories with 11.1% and British Columbia with 8.6%. Canada ranked third in world gold production, well behind South Africa and the Soviet Union.

All gold produced in the Atlantic provinces in 1975 was recovered as a by-product of base-metal mining. Gold production totalled 18,000 oz t (560 000 g) compared with 15,901 oz t (494 577 g) in 1974.

Gold production in Quebec in 1975 amounted to 465,000 oz t (14 463 000 g) compared with 440,559 oz t (13 702 917 g) in 1974. The lode gold mines recorded an increase in production mainly because Agnico-Eagle Mines Limited increased its output substantially. By-product base-metal mines recorded a decrease in production. Chibex Limited began production in November 1974 at its property near Chibougamau but closed in mid-1975 because of poor operating results.

Gold production in Ontario was 775,000 oz t (24 105 195 g) compared with 801,105 oz t (24 917 151 g) in 1974. Gold produced from lode gold mines accounted for 91.7% of the provincial total. In December 1975 Rengold Mines Ltd. began tune-up operations at its leased property near Misanabi, the former Renabie mine.

Virtually all gold produced in the Prairie provinces was recovered as a by-product from base-metal ores. Production in 1975 was 60,000 oz t (1 866 209 g) compared with 67,807 oz t (2 109 033 g) in 1974.

In British Columbia, with the exception of a small amount of gold recovered from the placer deposits in the central part of the province and in the Atlin district, all gold produced in 1975 was recovered as a by-product of base-metal mines, mainly from the treatment of copper ores. Total gold production was 144,000 oz t (4 478 901 g) compared with 162,081 oz t (5 041 283 g) in 1974.

Northair Mines Ltd. was constructing a 300 tons-a-day (272 t/d) mill at its gold-silver property about 70 miles (113 km) north of Vancouver and expected to start milling early in 1976.

Gold production in the Yukon Territory was 26,000 oz t (808 690 g) compared with 26,472 oz t (823 371 g) in 1974. Gold was recovered from base-metal operations and placer mines.

Gold produced in the Northwest Territories was recovered from lode gold mines near Yellowknife. Production in 1975 was 186,000 oz t (5 785 247 g) compared with 184,467 oz t (5 737 565 g) in 1974. Cominco Ltd. was sinking a new surface shaft to a depth of 5,800 ft (1 768 m) at its Con mine and increasing mill capacity from 450 to 650 tons (408 t to 590 t) a day.

Silver. Canada's mine production of silver in 1975, 39,101,000 oz t (1 216 178 kg), was 3.71 million oz t (115 353 kg) less than in 1974. Canada in 1975 lost its position as the world's largest mine producer of silver, a rank it held from 1968 to 1974 with the exception of 1970. In 1975, the USSR and Peru outranked Canada.

Mine production of silver in the Atlantic provinces increased 5.4% in 1975 from the previous year. Greater output by New Brunswick Mining and Smelting Corporation Limited at its zinc-lead-copper-silver mine near Bathurst, NB accounted for most of the increase. Silver output in Quebec, recovered mainly from base-metal ores, was slightly higher in 1975 than in 1974.

Ontario was the leading silver-producing province with its output in 1975 accounting for 37% of Canadian mine production. The largest producer in Canada, and probably the world, was Texasgulf Canada Ltd., which recovered over 9 million oz t (280 000 kg) of silver in copper, lead and zinc concentrates at its Kidd Creek mine near Timmins.

In the Prairie region much of the silver came from nine base-metal mines operated by Hudson Bay Mining and Smelting Co., Limited near Flin Flon and Snow Lake, Man. Most of the remainder was derived from the Fox and Ruttan copper-zinc mines operated by Sherritt Gordon Mines Limited at Lynn Lake and Ruttan, Man., respectively.

Base-metal ores continued to be the main source of British Columbia's mine production of silver. Cominco Ltd., the province's major silver producer, recovered silver from the lead-zinc-silver ores of its Sullivan mine in southeastern British Columbia and from purchased ores and concentrates. By-product silver output from the Sullivan mine was considerably higher in 1975 than in 1974 because of a four-month suspension of operations caused by a labour strike in 1974. Because of depressed copper prices some of BC's copper producers curtailed operations in 1975 and thereby reduced their by-product silver output.

Silver production in 1975 in the Northwest Territories was substantially lower than in 1974 because of reduced output by Echo Bay Mines Ltd. Echo Bay and Terra Mining and Exploration Limited, which operate silver-copper properties near Port Radium on the east shore of Great Bear Lake, were the principal silver producers in the Northwest Territories.

An increase of 12.5% in silver production in 1975 over 1974 in the Yukon Territory resulted mainly from greater by-product output at the lead-zinc-silver mine of Cyprus Anvil Mining Corporation at Faro.

Base-metal ores continued to be the main source of Canadian silver output, accounting for over 98% of total mine production in 1975. Most of the remaining 2% came from silver-cobalt ores mined in the Cobalt district of northern Ontario and the balance was by-product recovery from lode and placer gold ores.

Canadian silver production was valued at $176.6 million in 1975 (Table 12.4). The $21.5 million decrease from 1974 resulted from reduced output and slightly lower prices. The price of silver in Canada fluctuated in 1975 between a low of $3.925 an oz t ($126.192/kg) and a high of $5.413 ($174.032/kg). Reported consumption of silver in 1975 was 10.62 million oz t (330 000 kg) compared with 10.67 million oz t (332 000 kg) in 1974.

In 1975 refined silver was produced at five Canadian primary silver refineries, the largest being Canadian Copper Refiners Limited at Montreal East, Que. It recovered 19.8 million oz t (616 000 kg) from the treatment of anode and blister copper. The silver refinery of Cominco Ltd. at Trail, BC, was the second-largest producer, recovering some 8.8 million oz t (274 000 kg) of by-product silver in the processing of lead and zinc ores and concentrates. Other producers of refined silver were The International Nickel Company of Canada, Limited (INCO) at Copper Cliff, Ont. (from nickel-copper concentrates) and the Royal Canadian Mint at Ottawa, Ont. (from gold bullion). At Belledune, NB, Brunswick Mining and Smelting Corporation Limited, Smelting Division, recovered by-product silver bullion from lead concentrates treated in a blast furnace.

Molybdenum. Canadian shipments of molybdenum in 1975 were 27.4 million lb. (12.4 million kg) valued at $68.9 million. Over 95% of Canadian molybdenum is produced in British Columbia; Quebec is the only other producing province. Canada is the second largest producer in the world, accounting for some 16% of world production.

Prior to 1969, most molybdenum in Canada was produced from primary sources. Since 1969, molybdenum produced as a by-product or as a co-product with copper from large low-grade copper-molybdenum deposits in British Columbia has become an increasingly important source of production. In 1975, by-product and co-product molybdenum accounted for approximately 45% of Canadian production.

There are two primary producers of molybdenum in Canada — Endako Mines Division of Canex Placer Limited and Brynnor Mines Limited — both in British Columbia. Endako is the largest molybdenum producer accounting for approximately one half of Canada's production. Molybdenum is recovered as a by-product or co-product of copper at four mines in British Columbia (Brenda Mines Limited, Lornex Mining Corporation Limited, Utah Mines Limited and Gibraltar Mines Limited), and from one mine in Quebec (Gaspé Copper Mines, Limited). Brenda is the second largest producer in Canada accounting for approximately 25% of the country's molybdenum production.

During 1975 there was little exploration undertaken. The only property under active consideration was the 'extension' of the Boss Mountain deposit of Brynnor Mines Limited. A high-grade portion of the deposit is being mined by Brynnor; however, this high-grade area will be depleted within five years. The 'extension' is of a much lower grade and further drilling was undertaken in 1976 to determine if production would be warranted.

Platinum group metals. Production of platinum group metals in 1975 was 430,000 oz t (13 374 000 g) valued at $61,231,000 compared with 384,618 oz t (11 962 957 g) in 1974 valued at $60,794,030. Canada produces platinum metals as a by-product of nickel refining. When nickel matte is electrolytically refined, the platinum group metals — platinum, palladium, rhodium, ruthenium, iridium and osmium concentrate in the residue. The residue or sludge is upgraded and sent to refineries in Britain and the US for recovery of the platinum metals. Canada ranked third in world platinum metals production in 1975 behind South Africa and the USSR.

The world-wide decline in business activity in 1975 was reflected in a lower price for most of the platinum metals. The two largest South African producers initiated a 25% reduction in output in 1975 to better align supply and demand.

Cobalt. Canadian shipments of cobalt amounted to 2.95 million lb. (1.34 million kg) valued at $11.6 million in 1975 compared with 3.45 million lb. (1.56 million kg) valued at $10.1 million in 1974. Cobalt is recovered principally as a by-product of nickel-copper ores; there is also some cobalt recovered from silver-cobalt ores.

Canada's leading producer, The International Nickel Company of Canada, Limited (INCO), recovers cobalt in the form of crude oxide at its nickel refineries at Port Colborne, Ont. and Thompson, Man. Cobalt oxide and salts are also recovered at INCO's nickel refinery at Clydach, Wales. Falconbridge Nickel Mines Limited ships nickel-copper matte from its mine at Falconbridge, Ont. to Kristiansand, Norway for refining. The refinery which was damaged by fire during 1972 was completely rebuilt in 1973. In 1975, Falconbridge indefinitely deferred construction of its proposed refinery complex at Bécancour, Que. The refinery was to have produced 500,000 lb. (230 000 kg) of cobalt a year in high purity cobalt salts.

Sherritt Gordon Mines, Limited recovers cobalt metal powder from nickel refinery end-solutions at its hydrometallurgical refinery at Fort Saskatchewan, Alta. The refinery treats nickel-copper concentrates from its Lynn Lake mine operation in Manitoba and also treats, on a toll basis, concentrates from Western Mining Corporation Limited's nickel operations in Western Australia. Sherritt Gordon closed its Lynn Lake operation in 1976. Any future cobalt production from the refinery at Fort Saskatchewan will be from purchased concentrates or from toll refined concentrates.

Columbium (niobium) and tantalum. Canadian shipments of columbium as columbium pentoxide (Cb_2O_5) were 3.71 million lb. (1.68 million kg) valued at $6.43 million in 1975 compared with 4.23 million lb. (1.92 million kg) valued at $6.68 million in 1974.

St. Lawrence Columbium and Metals Corporation, with a mine, mill and concentrator near Oka, Que. is Canada's only producer of columbium and has one of only two mines in the world that produce columbium in pyrochlore concentrates as a primary product; the other larger operation is near Araxa, Brazil.

Niobec Inc., a joint venture of Teck Corporation, Copperfields Mining Corporation and Quebec Mining Exploration Company (SOQUEM), continued development of its St-Honoré pyrochlore deposit, some eight miles (about 13 km) north of Chicoutimi, Que. The mill has been designed for an initial capacity of 1,500 tons (1 361 t) of ore a day with provision for rapid expansion to 2,000 tons (1 814 t) a day if future demand warrants it. Niobec began production early in 1976.

Shipments of tantalum pentoxide (Ta_2O_5) in 1975 were 395,000 lb. (179 000 kg) valued at $3.26 million compared with 438,442 lb. (199 000 kg) valued at $3.58 million in 1974. Tantalum Mining Corporation of Canada Limited (Tanco) at Bernic Lake, Man. is Canada's only producer of tantalum. Tanco accounts for approximately 22% of world production. Ore reserves as of December 31, 1975 were sufficient for only seven years at the current level of production. Since Tanco's production is committed for five years, there is concern over the long-term availability of tantalum in Canada. Tanco planned an extensive exploration program in 1976 in an effort to extend its reserves.

Tungsten. Canadian shipments of tungsten trioxide (WO_3) were 3.0 million lb. (1.4 million kg) in 1975, a decrease of 16% from the previous year. Canada Tungsten Mining Corporation Limited at Tungsten in the Northwest Territories is Canada's only producer. Canada Tungsten began production from a new zone in 1974 where reserves are sufficient to sustain production for at least 20 years. Some separation problems have, however, been encountered with a talc-like material in the new ore and tungsten trioxide recovery rate dropped to about 64% in the first quarter of 1975 from over 80% in 1973. As a result of improvements made by the company, tungsten trioxide recovery was expected to rise to 75% in 1976. Amax Exploration, Inc. completed a preliminary feasibility study in 1975 on its MacTung deposit, the largest known deposit in the world, estimated to contain 30 million tons (27 million t) of ore averaging 0.9% WO_3. Brunswick Tin Mines Limited continued the investigation of a complex orebody near Fredericton, NB, containing several recoverable minerals, the most important being tungsten. An adit into the orebody was completed in 1975 and samples were sent to the Department of Energy, Mines and Resources for testing. Results were better than anticipated and a production decision was expected in 1976.

Cadmium. Cadmium production in 1975 was 2.7 million lb. (1 200 000 kg) valued at $7.2 million compared to 2.7 million lb. (1 200 000 kg) valued at $10.9 million in 1974. Most of the zinc ores in Canada contain recoverable cadmium in quantities varying from 0.001% to 0.067%, and zinc concentrates contain up to 0.7% cadmium. The largest mine production comes from Kidd Creek mine of Texasgulf Canada Limited near Timmins, Ont., followed by the Geco mine of Noranda Mines Limited at Manitouwadge, Ont. Other important producers are Cominco Ltd. in British Columbia, Hudson Bay Mining and Smelting Co., Limited in Saskatchewan and Manitoba, the Noranda group of companies in Ontario, Quebec and New Brunswick, Pine Point Mines Limited in the Northwest Territories and Anvil Mining Corp. in the Yukon Territory.

Cadmium is recovered as a by-product from the smelting and refining of zinc ores and concentrates. Metallic cadmium is recovered as a by-product at the electrolytic zinc plants of Cominco Ltd. at Trail, BC, Hudson Bay Mining and Smelting Co., Limited at Flin Flon, Man., Canadian Electrolytic Zinc Limited at Valleyfield, Que., and Texasgulf Canada Limited near Timmins, Ont. In 1975 metallic cadmium produced in Canada totalled 2.5 million lb. (1 241 000 kg) unchanged from 1974.

Selenium and tellurium. Production of selenium in 1975 increased to 670,000 lb. (304 000 kg) valued at $10.6 million from 599,950 lb. (272 133 kg) valued at $9.4 million in 1974. Production of tellurium decreased to 80,000 lb. (36 000 kg) valued at $763,000 from 124,313 lb. (56 387 kg) valued at $1,009,422 in 1974. Selenium and tellurium are recovered from the anode muds resulting from the electrolytic refining of copper at the plants of Canadian Copper Refiners Limited at Montreal East, Que. and The International Nickel Company of Canada, Limited at Copper Cliff, Ont.

Magnesium. Canadian production of magnesium was 4,961 tons (4 501 t) valued at $8.3 million. Production was down from 6,556 tons (5 948 t) in 1974 and well below the 10,637-ton (9 650 t) output reached in 1969. Exports of Canadian magnesium metal have entered the US duty-free under the Canada–US Defense Production Sharing Program but this program has recently operated on a reduced scale. The US duty on magnesium ingots and further-processed products has been reduced progressively in accordance with the Kennedy Round of trade negotiations under the General Agreement on Tariffs and Trade. However, only in certain high purity items can the Canadian product find a market in the US. Exports of Canadian magnesium ingots face a 20% tariff when entering the US domestic market whereas the comparable Canadian tariff is 5%. Releases from the General Services Administration stockpile in the US totalled 140 tons (127 t) of magnesium metal in 1975, down substantially from the 20,981 tons (19 034 t) released in 1974. At the end of 1975 there remained 1,621 tons (1 471 t) in the stockpile authorized for disposal.

The only Canadian producer of primary magnesium, Chromasco Corporation Limited, has operated a mine and smelter at Haley, Ont., 50 miles (80.5 km) west of Ottawa, since 1942.

Industrial minerals   12.1.3

Asbestos. Canadian shipments of asbestos fibre were 1.14 million tons (1.03 million t) valued at $266.9 million in 1975, compared with 1.81 million tons (1.64 million t) valued at $302.0 million in 1974. All of the Canadian production consists of chrysotile and approximately 85% of it comes from Quebec, almost 5% from British Columbia, 5% from the Yukon Territory, 4% from Newfoundland and about 1% from Ontario.

Canada is the world's largest exporter of asbestos, shipping approximately 95% of its production to more than 70 countries. The United States is the largest market, accounting for about 40% of Canadian exports followed by Japan, the Federal Republic of Germany, Britain and France. These five countries consumed about 70% of Canadian exports, which totalled over 1.18 million tons (1.07 million t) in 1975 compared with almost 1.79 million tons (1.62 million t) in 1974. The decrease in 1975 exports, as well as the reduced production, resulted from a seven-month labour strike affecting nearly all Quebec producers. Also in Quebec decreased production resulted from a fire in late 1974 that destroyed the King-Beaver mill, owned by Asbestos Corporation Limited, and a pit slide at the Jeffrey mine, owned by Canadian Johns-Manville Company, Limited.

World demand for asbestos fibre is expected to remain strong and may continue to outpace supply for several years. Most mining companies and asbestos products manufacturers are satisfactorily adapting to stricter environmental regulations.

Canadian Johns-Manville began operations in 1974 at its Bolduc mine near Barraute, Quebec. Ore is transported to the Jeffrey mine for processing where an expected 60,000 short tons (54 000 t) of product a year for a two-to-three year period will supplement output.

At Putuniq (Asbestos Hill) Ungava, a new mine owned by Asbestos Corporation Limited reached full capacity operation in 1975. Approximately 300,000 tons (272 000 t) of concentrates a year are produced and shipped to the Federal Republic of Germany, where about 100,000 tons (91 000 t) of salable fibre results after final milling.

United Asbestos Inc. near Matachewan, Ont. commenced production in mid-1975. Annual fibre production is expected to be 100,000 tons (91 000 t) when full capacity operation is attained.

At Cassiar, BC, Cassiar Asbestos Corporation Limited placed a new tramline and concentrator in operation. Fibre production was approximately 97,000 tons (88 000 t) in 1975.

In Quebec, two prospective producers continued evaluation of their properties. Abitibi Asbestos Mining Company Limited, a subsidiary of Brinco Ltd., situated 52 miles (84 km) north of Amos, is potentially a large producer. Feasibility studies are well advanced and ore reserves are estimated at 100 million tons (91 million t) averaging 3.5% asbestos fibre. Production could take place in 1978 or 1979. Rio Algom Mines, Limited continued the investigation of a deposit owned by McAdam Mining Corporation Limited about 20 miles (32 km) east of Chibougamau.

In the Yukon Territory 112,000 tons (102 000 t) of fibre was shipped from Cassiar's Clinton Creek mine. Drilling results failed to confirm additional ore reserves and as a result production is expected to cease in mid-1978.

Advocate Mines Limited, Newfoundland's only asbestos producer, maintained an average annual production of 70,000 tons (64 000 t) in 1974 and 1975.

The Reeves mine near Timmins, Ont., owned by Canadian Johns-Manville Company, Limited closed in February 1975, reportedly because of difficulties related to compliance with new provincial regulations governing fibre emissions in the working atmosphere. Total asbestos production in Ontario, including that of Hedman Mines Limited, was approximately 16,000 tons (15 000 t) in 1974 and again in 1975.

Potash. Canadian shipments, all from Saskatchewan, amounted to 6.4 million tons (5.8 million t) of potassium dioxide equivalent in 1974 and 5.3 million tons (4.8 million t) in 1975 (Table 12.18). The installed annual capacity is 8.33 million tons (7.55 million t) of potassium dioxide equivalent. Production allowables set by the Saskatchewan government under the prorationing plan were raised to 100% of capacity in August 1974 because of strong demand and they were not reduced in 1975. Saskatchewan imposed a new tax called a "reserves tax" which will greatly increase returns to the province. Saskatchewan also introduced plans to participate in new projects, and adopted legislation allowing it to purchase or expropriate existing potash mines.

In New Brunswick, International Minerals and Chemical Corporation (Canada) Limited has been given rights to explore for potash and salt in a 77 sq mile (199 km²) area near Salt Springs where salt and potash were discovered in 1973; by the end of 1975 the company had drilled five holes in the Sussex area.

Salt. Canadian shipments of salt amounted to 6.00 million tons (5.45 million t) valued at $60.6 million in 1974 and 5.68 million tons (5.16 million t) valued at $60.6 million in 1975 (Table 12.19). About 70% of the total was rock salt used for snow and ice control on streets and highways and for chemical manufacturing. The remainder is fine vacuum salt and salt as brine used for producing caustic soda and chlorine.

There are three rock salt mines, one in Nova Scotia and two in Ontario. Salt is also produced as a by-product of potash mining in Saskatchewan. Fine salt evaporator plants and brining operations are located in Nova Scotia, Ontario, Manitoba, Saskatchewan and Alberta.

A joint federal-provincial exploration program discovered a potash-salt deposit in Kings County, NB, in 1971. In 1973 a second federal-provincial program resulted in a similar discovery at Salt Springs in the same county. International Minerals and Chemical Corporation (Canada) Limited has been granted exploration rights, as already noted.

Sulphur. Canadian sulphur shipments in all forms in 1975 amounted to 4.7 million long tons (4.8 million t) valued at $99.7 million (Table 12.20). Shipments decreased 16% in volume but increased 27% in value compared to 1974. Reduced volume reflects the world economic downturn which began in late 1974.

Canadian sulphur is obtained from three sources: sour natural gas and petroleum including the tar sands, which produce elemental sulphur; smelter gases which produce sulphuric acid; and pyrite concentrates which are used in the manufacture of sulphuric acid. Small amounts of elemental sulphur are recovered as a by-product of electrolytic refining of nickel sulphide matte and a small quantity of liquid sulphur dioxide is produced from pyrites and smelter gases. In Canada 85% of sulphur shipments in 1975 were in elemental form, nearly all from sour natural gas.

The dramatic growth in the Canadian sulphur industry during the 10 years from 1963 to 1973 culminated in the peaking of output from sour natural gas, principally in Alberta. Canadian production of sulphur in all forms in 1973 was 7.97 million long tons (8.1 million t), 7.3 million long tons (7.4 million t) in elemental form. In 1975, total output was estimated at 7.4 million long tons (7.5 million t), the 9% decline resulting almost entirely from reduced output from sour natural gas in western Canada. Since 1968 Canada has been the world's largest supplier of elemental sulphur.

Gypsum. In 1975 Canadian production of crude gypsum fell to 6.3 million tons (5.7 million t) from 7.9 million tons (7.2 million t) in 1974, most of it exported to the US. Exports were mainly from Nova Scotia and Newfoundland quarries operated by Canadian subsidiaries of US gypsum products manufacturers.

Nine companies produced crude gypsum in Canada in 1975 at 15 locations, while five companies manufactured gypsum products at 17 locations. Production of gypsum in Canada is closely related to the building construction industry, particularly the residential building sector, in both Canada and the eastern United States; the decline in housing activity is reflected in the sharp drop in production.

Nepheline syenite. Nepheline syenite was produced from two operations on Blue Mountain, 25 miles (40 km) northeast of Peterborough, Ont. In 1975 production was estimated at 520,000 tons (472 000 t), a decrease of 16% from 1974 (Table 12.22) reflecting the world economic slump. The value of shipments in 1975 was $8.7 million, down 6% from that of 1974. Exports accounted for 75% of total shipments. Sales to the US representing 96% of Canada's total exports, decreased 19%. Nepheline syenite is preferred to feldspar as a source of essential alumina and alkalis in glass manufacture. Other uses include the manufacture of ceramics, enamels and as a filler in paints, papers, plastics and foam rubber. Canada is the world's largest producer of nepheline syenite.

Structural materials. The value in current dollars of all construction undertaken in Canada in 1975 was roughly $28.1 billion, an increase of 14% over 1974. Production of structural materials, including cement, sand and gravel, stone, clay and clay products and lime, was valued at $806.7 million in 1975, representing 6% of the total value of mineral production in Canada.

Canadian production of cement in 1975 was 11 million tons (10 million t), a reduction reflecting less construction in place and fewer concrete-intensive projects. Cement was produced in all provinces except Prince Edward Island with Ontario and Quebec accounting for 70% of the Canadian total. Current cement producing capacity is 16.6 million tons (15.1 million t) a year. During 1975 the following additions boosted the industry's capability: a new 500,000 tons-a-year (450 000 t/yr) kiln was brought on stream at the St. Constant, Que. plant of Canada Cement Lafarge Ltd.; an expansion program begun in 1973 at Lake Ontario Cement Limited's Picton, Ont. plant culminated in the start-up of a new 850,000 tons-a-year (770 000 t/yr) suspension preheater kiln system; and at Enshaw, Alta., Canada Cement netted an additional 200,000 tons a year (180 000 t/yr) on completion of a major modernization program.

Production of sand and gravel in 1975 was 225 million tons (204 million t) valued at $260 million (Table 12.24). Sand and gravel must be quarried, screened, washed, stockpiled and transported in large volume to compensate for the low unit value received. Transportation and handling often double the plant cost, making it economically desirable to establish plants close to major consuming centres. Urban expansion has greatly accelerated the demand for sand and gravel, and as land use conflicts have intensified many pits and quarries have been overrun by growing communities. Sand and gravel are used as fill, as granular base course and finish course in highway construction and as aggregate in concrete and asphalt.

Production of stone in 1975 was 97 million tons (88 million t) valued at $171 million (Table 12.25). Dimension stone, for use as building and ornamental stone, accounts for about 1% of total stone production. Crushed stone for use as aggregate in concrete and asphalt, as railroad ballast and road metal accounts for about 80% and the remainder is used in the metallurgical, chemical and allied industries.

Shipments of clay and clay products in 1975 were valued at $70 million, about the same as the previous year (Table 12.26). Deposits of clay for use in the manufacture of papers, refractories, high quality whitewares and stoneware products are scarce in Canada. Consequently china clay (kaolin), fire clay, ball clay and stoneware clay are mostly imported. In Canada common clays and shales, higher in alkalis and lower in alumina than the other clays, are used to manufacture brick and tile products.

12.1.4   Mineral fuels

Coal. For production figures see Tables 12.4 and 12.8. For an outline of the industry see Chapter 13 Energy, Section 13.4.

In the following paragraphs certain symbols are used when recording SI units to express metric equivalents: M = mega (million) or 10^6, G = giga (billion) or 10^9, and T = tera (trillion) or 10^{12}. For example 96.6 million cubic metres will appear as 96.6 Mm³, and volumes such as 10.7 trillion cubic decimetres a day will be expressed as 10.7 Tdm³/d.

Oil and natural gas. Canadian production of crude oil and natural gas liquids in 1975 declined for the second consecutive year to 620 million barrels (98.6 Mm³). Crude oil output, including synthetic crude oil from the Athabasca tar sands amounted to 525 million barrels (83.5 Mm³) or 1.4 million barrels a day (b/d) (220 000 m³/d) (Table 12.27). Gas plant production of natural gas liquids totalled 113 million bbl (18 Mm³) or 310,000 b/d (49 000 m³/d). Natural gas production rose slightly in 1975 to 3,086,792 million cubic feet (87 408 689 Mdm³) or 8,456 million cubic feet a day (239 447 Mdm³/d) (Table 12.28).

At the end of 1975 Canada's proven liquid hydrocarbon reserves, which include conventional crude oil and natural gas liquids (propane, butane and pentanes plus), amounted to 8.2 billion bbl (1.3 Gm³). This is comprised of 6.6 billion bbl (1.0 Gm³) of crude oil and 1.6 billion bbl (254 Mm³) of natural gas liquids. At the 1975 annual production level of 618 million bbl (98.3 Mm³), the life index (reserves to production ratio) for conventional crude oil and natural gas liquids increased for the first time in five years to 13.2 years as production slowed down due to reduced exports. Reserves added in 1975 totalled 56.6 million bbl (9.0 Mm³), and of this amount, 20.4 million bbl (3.24 Mm³) were attributable to revisions, 31.5 million bbl (5.01 Mm³) to extensions of established fields and only 4.6 million bbl (731 000 m³) to new discoveries. According to the Canadian Petroleum Association (CPA), proved remaining marketable reserves of natural gas increased by about 226,360 million cubic feet (6 410 Mm³) to a total of 57.0 trillion cubic feet (1 614 Tm³) in 1975. Using the 1975 level of production, the life index for natural gas increased to 21.3 years. In compiling its reserve estimates, the CPA assumed that delta gas would be brought to market via the same pipeline system as the Prudhoe Bay gas, and therefore delta gas could be categorized as proven. This is not the case for the Arctic islands; a minimum reserve base is required before this gas could be considered within economic reach. Therefore gas reserves that have been found in the Arctic islands and offshore areas are classified as probable rather than proven. Alberta with 45.32 trillion cubic feet (1.28 Tm³) of marketable gas reserves accounted for 80% of Canadian reserves at the end of 1975.

Canadian refinery capacity increased by 60,000 b/d (10 000 m³/d) in 1975 due primarily to the addition of Imperial Oil Enterprises Ltd.'s large new refinery at Edmonton, Alta. At the end of 1975, crude oil refining capacity of Canada's 38 operating refineries totalled 2,083,000 b/d (331 000 m³/d).

Alberta. During 1975 crude oil production in Alberta decreased by 203,000 b/d (32 000 m³/d) to 1,208,000 b/d (192 000 m³/d) and accounted for 85% of total Canadian crude oil production. Of this amount, synthetic crude oil production from the Athabasca tar sands contributed 43,189 b/d (6 867 m³/d) in 1975.

Both exploratory and development drilling footages increased slightly in Alberta in 1975, partly due to provincial incentive programs but primarily because of substantial increases in field prices for both oil and gas. Drilling statistics show that development drilling increased 5% to 7.19 million ft (2.19 million m) and exploratory drilling increased 12% to 4.78 million ft (1.46 Mm). Despite increased efforts, no large oil discoveries were made in 1975.

The shallow gas-bearing formations of southern Alberta continued to be the principal target for explorers in the province and several discoveries were recorded. The drilling program to evaluate the British Block, which got under way late in 1973, resulted in the discovery of additional reserves of 2 trillion cubic feet (.057 Tm³). Drilling for gas increased by 239 wells to 1,958 in 1975.

According to an appraisal of Alberta's oil sands completed in 1973 by the Alberta Energy Resources Conservation Board (AERCB), there is an ultimate in-place reserve of crude bitumen of 1,000 billion bbl (159 Gm³) of which 250 billion bbl (39.7 Gm³) are recoverable by known methods of technology. The bulk of the recoverable reserves are located in the Athabasca deposit with the remainder distributed between the Cold Lake, Peace River, Wabasca and Buffalo Head Hills deposits. Of the 250 billion bbl (39.7 Gm³) of recoverable synthetic crude oil, only 26.5 billion bbl (4.2 Gm³) are amenable to open-cast mining methods and all of this is located in the Athabasca deposit. The remaining 223.5 billion bbl (35.5 Gm³) are expected to be eventually recovered by in situ recovery techniques which are still in the experimental stage of development. At the present time Great Canadian Oil Sands Limited's 50,000 b/d (8 000 m³/d) is the only production from the oil sands; they have been in operation since 1967. Construction of Syncrude Canada Ltd.'s project was expected to be about 30% complete by the end of 1975. Predicted 125,000 b/d (20 000 m³/d) operation is scheduled to start production in 1978. Proposals which were put forward by two major oil companies were withdrawn because of large capital outlays required for construction and the risk of not receiving a satisfactory return on investment over the life of the project.

Saskatchewan. Saskatchewan's crude oil production declined by 40,507 b/d (6 440 m³/d) to 162,088 b/d (25 770 m³/d) in 1975, accounting for 11% of the Canadian total. Marketable natural gas production, at 69.0 billion cu ft (1 954 Gdm³) accounted for 2.1% of total Canadian production. Total drilling in Saskatchewan amounted to 649,000 ft (198 000 m) compared with 706,000 ft (215 000 m) in 1974. There were no significant oil or gas discoveries made in Saskatchewan during 1975.

British Columbia. In 1975 production of crude oil in British Columbia declined by 12,500 b/d (1 987 m³/d) to 39,393 b/d (6 263 m³/d) and represented 3% of total national production. Net withdrawals of natural gas in the province totalled 426 billion cu ft (12 063 Gdm³), down 3% from 1974.

In 1975 exploratory drilling at 292,700 ft (89 200 m) declined by 63,470 ft (19 300 m) from the previous year and development drilling increased by 7,500 ft (2 300 m) to 356,500 ft (108 700 m). There were no significant oil discoveries made in 1975 but several significant gas discoveries were recorded, four of which may eventually prove to be major fields. These discoveries were made in the Grizzly Valley area, the Cecil Lake area, the Kotcho Lake area and Nelson Forks area, all in northeastern British Columbia.

Manitoba. Production of crude oil in Manitoba amounted to 12,093 b/d (1 923 m³/d) in 1975, down slightly from 1974. All fields in Manitoba are producing at maximum capability. There is no natural gas production in Manitoba. Drilling in the province during 1975 declined by 70% to 21,938 ft (6 687 m). There were no oil discoveries made in Manitoba during 1975.

Yukon Territory, Northwest Territories and Arctic islands. Crude oil production north of the 60th parallel is confined to the Norman Wells field in the Northwest Territories. Oil from this field is processed in a small local refinery which serves local markets. Natural gas production declined substantially to 276 million cu ft (7.82 million m³) in 1973, because of a substantial reduction in production from the Pointed Mountain field, the principal producing gas field in the Northwest Territories.

There were 44 wells drilled in northern Canada in 1975 for a total of 371,450 ft (113 218 m) compared with 60 wells and 503,227 ft (153 384 m) in 1974. All but five of these wells were classed as exploratory. Of these wells one was classed as an oil discovery and three as gas discoveries and all were located in the Mackenzie Delta. Results of a step-out well drilled by Shell Canada Limited indicate 1 trillion cu ft (28 Tdm³) of gas and 80 million bbl (12.7 Mm³) of oil. Offshore drilling from man-made islands continued in 1975, while specially-designed drill ships are expected to take exploration even further offshore. In the Arctic islands, no new significant finds of oil or gas were made in 1975; however, three successful step-out wells enlarged the boundaries of three established fields. Also a successful step-out well was drilled eight miles (15 km) from shore in 400 ft (122 m) of water from a floating ice platform. This well substantially enlarged previous estimates of the size of the Hecla field on the east coast of Melville Island. The well is important from a technological as well as a commercial point of view as it marked another major breakthrough in Arctic exploratory drilling technology.

Eastern Canada. Aggregate drilling in Ontario declined in 1975 by 10% to 215,553 ft (65 701 m). Exploratory drilling accounted for 46% of the total, down 17% from the previous year. No noteworthy discoveries were made. In Lake Erie, one Devonian gas discovery was recorded by the Consumers Gas Company.

Offshore from the east coast 10 wells were drilled for a total of 104,680 ft (31 906 m) in 1975, compared to 19 wells and 185,352 ft (56 495 m) in 1974. Drilling commenced in this region in 1966. A total of 68 wells have since been drilled, four of them significant discoveries of oil and gas. All of these were drilled in the vicinity of Sable Island. Seven offset wells were drilled around the first discovery well on Sable Island and six of these were successful, but with pay sections considerably reduced from the initial discovery. The results of this drilling suggest that it would be most difficult to develop this field on a commercial basis. Elsewhere off the east coast, the Bjarni H-81 well drilled on the Labrador shelf penetrated a thick gas-bearing sandstone formation and the results of preliminary tests indicate that this might be the first major discovery in the offshore east region. During the drilling seasons of 1974 and 1975 a number of significant discoveries were made on the Labrador shelf. Due to extremely difficult operating conditions it will be a long and difficult task to discover the full hydrocarbon potential of this area. It will also be difficult to develop any of the fields discovered.

Uranium. Canadian uranium shipments in 1975 totalled 6,126 tons of uranium oxide (4 714 tonnes uranium) while production increased only slightly higher than the previous year to 4,565 tons U_3O_8 (3 512 t U) (Table 12.16). Over 80% of production came from the Elliot Lake area of Ontario where Denison Mines Limited and Rio Algom Mines Limited recover uranium from quartz-pebble conglomerates. The remainder came from two operations in northern Saskatchewan, that of Eldorado Nuclear Limited near Uranium City, and Gulf Minerals Canada Limited at Rabbit Lake. The latter, Canada's first new uranium producer since the late 1950s, began production late in the year. Canadian production was lower than expected in 1975, due mainly to the lack of experienced miners, and to the mining of lower-grade ores made possible by the recent rapid rise in uranium prices. Eldorado, Denison and Rio Algom continued with major programs to expand their mining and milling operations. In addition, during 1974 and 1975 there were three separate development programs under way; Madawaska Mines Limited was in the process of reopening the Faraday Mine near Bancroft, Ont., Agnew Lake Mines Limited continued its experimental in situ mining-leaching program at its property near Espanola, Ont., and Amok Limited completed a feasibility study of its Cluff Lake deposits in the Carswell Dome area of Saskatchewan.

In response to the rise in uranium prices, increased uranium exploration was evident in virtually all of the provinces and the territories. A significant discovery was made in mid-1975 at Key Lake, Sask. as the result of a drilling program carried out by Uranerz Exploration and Mining Limited, jointly with Inexco Mining Company and the Saskatchewan Mining Development Corporation. The joint federal-provincial uranium reconnaissance program launched in 1975 by the Geological Survey of Canada was also important. The program is expected to take 10 years and cost some $30 million.

In September 1974, the federal government announced new uranium export guidelines, which provide for sufficient uranium to be reserved for domestic use, to enable all nuclear power reactors operating, under construction or planned for operation 10 years into the future, to operate at a capacity factor of 80%, for 30 years from their in-service dates. In line with this policy, a Uranium Resource Appraised Group (URAG) was established in the Department of Energy, Mines and Resources to assess annually Canada's uranium resources. The first assessment was published in August 1975.

During 1975 the Atomic Energy Control Board (AECB) announced that it had approved export contracts for the delivery of some 74,000 tons of U_3O_8 (56 900 t U) more than 90% destined for export to the US, Japan, Britain, the Federal Republic of Germany and Spain. Smaller quantities were approved for export to Finland, Italy, Belgium and Switzerland. Approved contract and export commitments totalled some 110,000 tons U_3O_8 (85 000 t U).

12.2   Government aid to the mineral industry

12.2.1   Federal government aid

Federal assistance to the mining industry takes the form of provision of detailed geological, geophysical, topographical, geodetic, geographical and marine data; the provision of technical information concerning the processing of ores, industrial minerals and fuels on a commercial scale; certain tax incentives; and financial and technical assistance to the gold-mining industry under the Emergency Gold Mining Assistance Act.

The Department of Energy, Mines and Resources. The federal Department of Energy, Mines and Resources was created by the Government Organization Act on October 1, 1966 (RSC 1970, c.E-6). In addition to its administrative establishment, the department is made up of three sectors — Science and Technology, Mineral Development and Energy Policy.

The Science and Technology Sector contains the Canada Centre for Mineral and Energy Technology (the former Mines Branch), the Geological Survey of Canada, the Surveys and Mapping Branch, the Earth Physics Branch, the Polar Continental Shelf Project, the Canada Centre for Remote Sensing, and the Explosives Branch.

The Canada Centre for Mineral and Energy Technology, a large laboratory and pilot-plant complex, conducts research into methods of extracting and processing minerals and fuels. Emphasis is placed on recovery techniques for ores and minerals with low-grade impurities or complex mineral composition. Fuels research includes evaluation of Canada's fossil fuels and the development of refining methods for the low-grade, high-sulphur petroleum of the Athabasca oil sands. A five-year project will greatly lower waste rock production and costs by improving the wall design of open-pit mines. Research is also being conducted on coal beneficiation and carbonization. In the related area of pyrometallurgy, the extraction of metal by heat, applied research is concentrated on the development of a shaft electric furnace for smelting iron ore. In the mineral sciences, the centre carries out physical, chemical, crystallographic and magnetic studies to determine the characteristics important to extraction and processing methods. The centre also produces standard reference ores and metals needed by mining and metallurgical companies. In metals research, in addition to improving techniques for metal forming, attention is focused on ensuring the structural soundness of metal pipelines for the Arctic. Other programs are directed toward the reduction of pollution and the conversion of mineral waste into useful materials such as fillers and ceramics.

The Canada Centre for Mineral and Energy Technology is assisted by the National Advisory Committee on Mining and Metallurgical Research, comprising representatives from industry, government and universities.

The Geological Survey of Canada (GSC) maps and studies the geology of Canada. As the major organization engaged in this work, its activities support two programs of the Department of Energy, Mines and Resources: the Mineral and Energy Resources Program and the Earth Sciences Program. A principal aim of the former is to ascertain available mineral and energy resource potential and thus the survey is active in estimating the abundance and distribution of mineral and fuel resources. This is done by providing a systematic geological framework, by defining the settings favourable to mineral and fuel occurrences and by appraising foreign resources. The Earth Sciences Program is concerned with use and conservation of resources and the preservation of the environment. To this end, the Geological Survey provides geologically based information on land resources and terrain performance derived from geological, geomorphic, geophysical, geotechnical and related studies of earth and rock materials, land forms and associated dynamic processes.

Each year the GSC sends about 100 parties into various parts of Canada. The results of its studies are published in memoirs, bulletins, papers, maps and scientific technical journals. Its headquarters is in Ottawa and of several regional offices the largest are the Institute of Sedimentary and Petroleum Geology in Calgary and the Atlantic Geoscience Centre in Dartmouth. The former studies the geology of Canada's western and northern sedimentary basins and the latter investigates the bottom morphology and structure of the continental shelves and the floors of the open ocean. A smaller group of geologists on the west coast is developing similar marine-geology studies there.

The Earth Physics Branch carries out geophysical work of interest to the mineral industry. It collects and publishes maps and charts on the geomagnetic field in Canada. Most of this information is obtained from airborne geomagnetic surveys which have ranged over all of Canada and as far as Scandinavia. The branch maintains a network of 11 permanent magnetic observatories, including the Automatic Magnetic Observatory System at Yellowknife which began operating in 1974. It also operates a network of 33 seismic stations for the study of the earth's interior and to assess seismic risk. In gravity research, another means of studying the composition of the earth's crust, the branch maps variations in the earth's gravity on a regional basis including the Arctic and the continental shelves. The results of all gravity measurements are available in a new gravity map of Canada on a scale of 1:5,000,000 or about 80 miles to the inch (50.7 km to the cm), for easy comparison with the new geological and tectonic maps of Canada on a similar scale. Geothermal studies in mines and deep boreholes provide information to the mineral industry on the underground thermal regime, including permafrost.

No mineral development is possible without accurate, large-scale topographical maps. The Surveys and Mapping Branch has completed the topographical mapping of the country at the medium scale of 1:250,000, or about four miles to the inch (2.5 km to the cm). About 40% of the larger-scale mapping at 1:50,000 has been completed of more settled areas and those of greater economic importance. Also available for selected areas are maps at other scales. Another branch function is the establishment of a basic network of survey control points across Canada that provide precise figures of latitude, longitude and elevation above sea level. In addition to its topographic maps, the branch produces various multicoloured maps for other government agencies, aeronautical charts and the National Atlas of Canada, which describes Canada's physical, economic and social geography. The branch's National Air Photo Library has on file over 4 million aerial photographs of Canada, in black and white, and colour, taken over the last half-century from aircraft and more recently from the Earth Resources Technology Satellite (ERTS) and Skylab.

The Explosives Branch is responsible for the administration of the Canada Explosives Act, which controls the manufacture, authorization, storage, sale, importation and transportation by road of explosives.

The Mineral Development Sector is responsible for research programs and policies in the field of non-renewable resources. It conducts fundamental and applied resource-engineering-economic research and field investigation into non-renewable resource problems on a total industry basis, in a regional, national and international context. The work covers all aspects of the mineral industry from resource to consumption. The sector publishes resource-engineering-economic reports and advises government departments and agencies on non-renewable resource policy. Current activities include regional studies of the mineral economy in Canada; assessment of mineral projects for which federal support has been requested; resource and reserve studies in a number of mineral commodities; and the safeguarding of Canadian mineral interests through participation in the work of international agencies. The sector administered the Emergency Gold Mining Assistance Act to aid mining communities largely dependent upon the gold mines. In collaboration with the Canadian International

Development Agency and with the support of industry, the sector sets up training courses for mineral scientists, technologists and economists brought to Canada under various aid programs, and advises on mineral projects undertaken by Canada as an aid to developing countries. The sector publishes extensively and maintains the National Mineral Inventory, a listing of about 16,000 mineral showings and deposits in Canada that may be consulted by the public.

The Energy Policy Sector is primarily a policy-making group with a direct impact on the mining industry. It assesses individual projects and developments relative to each energy source and in terms of their interrelationships. It appraises trends in oil and gas exploration and production, transportation, processing and marketing in Canada and abroad, and provides information to federal government agencies, industry and the public on oil and gas developments. In the field of uranium, the sector continues to coordinate uranium matters in the areas of stockpiling, establishment of uranium-enrichment facilities and export. With respect to coal, it provides research and development grants and advises on production expansion rates in the light of profitability and projected demand. The sector also administers federal interests in offshore mineral resources as well as in federally owned mineral rights in the provinces.

Tax incentives to the mining industry. Although mineral industry enterprises are subject to federal income tax, certain benefits granted to them under the Income Tax Act serve as incentives to exploration and development. An outline of tax amendments and regulations affecting mining in general appears in previous editions of the *Canada Year Book*. The most up-to-date information on income tax allowances which apply to the mining industry may be obtained from the Department of National Revenue (Taxation) and the appropriate provincial taxation offices.

Under the provisions of the amended Income Tax Act (effective January 1, 1972) the exemption from income tax for the first three years of operation of new mining ventures terminated at the end of 1973. However initial capital expenditures in a new mining operation on buildings, machinery and equipment and certain community and transportation facilities may be deducted as rapidly as income will permit. However, new mining ventures will not be liable for federal income tax until initial capital expenditures have been recovered. In the case of a major expansion of an existing mine, capital expenditures on buildings and on machinery and equipment also may be deducted immediately.

The tax reform effected on January 1, 1972 was further modified by the federal budgets of November 18, 1974, and June 23, 1975. To offset the new or greater royalties and increased mining taxes imposed by various provinces, the Government of Canada eliminated royalties, rentals, fees and mining taxes as deductions for income tax purposes. At the same time, the federal income tax rate for the mining industry was reduced to 25% to partially compensate for the non-deductibility of royalties and mining taxes. This decrease of about 15 percentage points from the normal federal rate of taxation was known as the "mining tax abatement". The budget proposals of June 23, 1975 replaced the mining tax abatement with a "resource allowance". This deduction in computing income is 25% of net production income before deductions for interest, exploration and development expenses and depletion are made.

Prior to May 6, 1974 individuals and corporations whose principal business was not related to the oil, gas or mining industry were permitted to deduct their exploration and development expenses incurred in searching for oil, gas or minerals in Canada by an amount each year equal to their total income from oil, gas and mineral resources for the year or 20% of the previously undeducted exploration and development expenses, whichever was the greater amount. After May 6, 1974 these taxpayers became entitled to deduct, in computing their annual income, 30% of the previously undeducted exploration and development expenses incurred in searching for oil and gas properties, computed in the same manner as for petroleum and mining companies.

Provincial government aid   12.2.2

Newfoundland. The Mineral Development Division of the Department of Mines and Energy provides the following services in support of exploration and mining activities: a program of mineral assessment to encourage development of mineral resources; inspection of exploration work and mining operations; control of removal of beach sand and gravel as a conservation measure; identification of mineral rock specimens; technical advice to those who seek it; cooperation with the Geological Survey of Canada and other federal government agencies; and publication of data for educational and informational purposes. Geological, geochemical and geophysical reports and maps, and compilations of general data pertaining to specific areas are procurable at nominal cost. Other information from unclassified files is available to interested parties. Prospectors' or miners' permits are issued by the division and mining claims are recorded.

Nova Scotia. The Engineering and Inspection Division of the Department of Mines carries out safety inspection of mines, quarries and allied processing plants, development sites and storage facilities for explosives. Diamond drills are available to exploration and producing companies on a contract basis and industry is assisted in surface and subsurface development and construction projects. The division also carries out mine rescue and first aid training and administers all matters relating to mineral rights.

The Mineral Resources and Geological Services Division carries out geological, geochemical and geophysical surveys and studies of occurrences of specific minerals. It publishes the results in annual and specific reports, including maps. The Analytical and Ore Dressing Section, which is affiliated with Nova Scotia Technical College, provides an important service to both the department and industry.

New Brunswick. The Department of Natural Resources has two branches providing services to the mining industry, the Mines Branch and the Mineral Resources Branch.

The Mines Branch administers safety regulations. Mines and associated plants are inspected regularly, and mine rescue training is conducted. Mineral statistics reports and reviews of mining operations are prepared.

The Mineral Resources Branch provides the mineral, petroleum and construction industries with basic geological, geochemical and geophysical inspection, as well as maps and data to assist in the discovery and optimum utilization of the province's mineral resources. The administration of Crown owned mineral, petroleum-gas and bituminous shale rights is also the responsibility of this branch, including issuing prospecting licences, recording mining claims and issuing mining licences and leases. Regional offices and core storage facilities are maintained at Sussex and Bathurst. All work filed for assessment credit is filed at these offices and in Fredericton.

Quebec. The Mines Branch of the Department of Natural Resources is responsible for implementing the Mining Act (SQ 1965, c.34) and the Mining Duties Act (SQ 1965, c.35). The branch incorporates the following three directorates: Geology, Mining Domain and Mineral Economics and Development. The Geology Directorate consists of six services: Geological Exploration, Mineral Deposits, Geotechnics, Technical Documentation, Cartography and Technical Revision. The directorate undertakes the geological study of the province and produces detailed area reports and geoscientific maps. The Geotechnics Service deals with developmental problems of particular environments and their geological setting.

The Mining Domain Directorate includes the Mining Titles Service, the Mines Inspection Service, and the Engineering Service. The directorate controls the mining rights granted on Crown lands, registers mining claims and issues development permits or special permits governing the sale or rental of lands for mining purposes. It ensures that holders of mining rights carry out development work prescribed. Mine inspectors verify that working conditions in mines, quarries and mills conform to legal safety standards. The Mining Domain Directorate is also responsible for carrying out whatever engineering work is required to open up new mining areas or operations, including the building of access roads, and constructing mining townsites.

The Mineral Economics and Development Directorate is concerned with the optimum use of Quebec's mineral resources in line with both development and conservation. Three services are now being organized: Projects, Economic Evaluation and Promotion. The directorate's aim is to identify and promote projects that lend themselves to quick and tangible results in the development of Quebec's mineral resources. It arranges studies on marketing, financing, transportation, development and exploitation techniques, profitability and any other essential criteria affecting the development of mineral resources. Also included in the Mines Branch is the Mineral Research Centre responsible for metallurgical research and development.

Ontario. The Mines Division of the Ontario Ministry of Natural Resources contributes to the economy of Ontario by promoting and regulating the utilization of available supplies of minerals by resource products industries. The Mines Division has four branches.

The Mineral Resources Branch, essentially a strategic planning group, ensures the orderly development and utilization of non-renewable resources.

The Geological Branch encourages optimum exploration through geological, geophysical and geochemical surveys of the province, the publication of maps and reports on mineral occurrences and the education of prospectors and others involved in mineral exploration. It is also responsible for a program designed to stimulate exploration in the Red Lake, Geraldton–Beardmore, Kirkland Lake and Cobalt areas. Atikokan and eastern Ontario areas were included in 1974 and 1975. One third of the cost of exploration to a maximum of $33,333 is provided to small- and medium-sized companies to explore in these areas.

The Mineral Research Branch is composed of the Assay Laboratory in Toronto and the Temiskaming Testing Laboratory in Cobalt. The Assay Laboratory provides assay and analytical services and conducts investigations to aid in discovery and development of mineral deposits. It serves the mining industry and the public at large. The Temiskaming Testing Laboratory at Cobalt operates a bulk sampling and assay laboratory to assist the producers of the area in marketing their silver-cobalt ores.

The Mines Engineering Branch administers Part IX of The Mining Act which calls for regular examination of all operating mines, quarries, sand and gravel pits and certain metallurgical works to ensure the health and safety of employees and the general public. Regional geologists and mines engineers provide advice or support to the line organization of the ministry. The Lands Administration and Surveys and Mapping Branches of the Lands Division handle the recording of mining claims, assessment work and the preparation of title to mining lands.

Manitoba. The Mineral Resources Division of the Manitoba Department of Mines, Resources and Environmental Management offers the following services: recording the staking and acquisition of Crown mineral rights; compiling assessment information and inspecting mineral rights dispositions; compiling geological data on mineral occurrences; issuing reports and maps covering geological, geophysical and geochemical surveys; operating an analytical and assay laboratory to assist prospectors and geologists in evaluating mineral occurrences and in classifying rocks and minerals; giving engineering approval of mining works and inspecting mining operations with regard to the health and safety of employees; controlling in-plant environmental and safety regulations; training mine rescue crews and inspecting mine rescue facilities; inspecting oil well drilling sites. Manitoba's Mineral Disposition Regulation provides for provincial participation in mineral exploration and development. The Exploration Operations Branch of the division explores for, investigates and assesses mineral occurrences in the province from the grass-roots level to a highly sophisticated operational base.

Saskatchewan. The Mineral Lands Branch of the Department of Mineral Resources disposes of Crown minerals, administers incentive programs to attract the mineral industry, and maintains records respecting areas let out by lease, permit, drilling reservation, claim or claim block. Recording offices, located at Regina, La Ronge, Uranium City and Creighton, assist the public in determining lands available.

Officers of the Mines Safety Branch of the Department of Labour make regular examinations of all mines to ensure proper conditions for health and safety. Safety education, particularly in first aid and mine rescue instruction, is also part of the work of this branch.

The Precambrian Geology Division of the Geological Sciences Branch conducts geological surveys in the Canadian Shield areas of the province and publishes maps and reports for the information and guidance of the industry. Resident geologists are stationed at Uranium City and La Ronge, which have core storage and examination facilities.

A new policy for northern Saskatchewan, announced in March 1975, provides for participation with industry in mineral development through the Saskatchewan Mineral Development Corporation.

Alberta. The Energy Resources Conservation Board is responsible for administering all aspects of the energy resources of Alberta, including their conservation, regulation and transmission. The board regulates coal mines and quarries and maintains standards of safety. The oil and gas industries are served similarly, but regulatory measures also prevent the waste of oil and gas resources. The board compiles periodic reports and annual records. The Workmen's Compensation Board maintains safety standards and pays the cost of training mine rescue crews.

The mining industry is served also by the Research Council of Alberta which has made bedrock and surficial geological surveys over many parts of the province. Groundwater and soil surveys and projects concerned with the uses and development of minerals are included in its responsibilities. The council has studied the occurrence of Alberta coals and their particular chemical and physical properties, the use of coals in the generation of power, and their upgrading and cleaning. Studies have also been made of glass sands, salt, fertilizers, cement manufacture and brick and tile manufacture.

The province, together with the Canadian Association of Oil Well Drilling Contractors and the Canadian Petroleum Association, maintains a supervisory and safety training program concerned with the drilling of oil and gas wells. Of assistance also to mining and oil companies are the special reductions provided for in the Alberta Income Tax Act.

British Columbia. The British Columbia Department of Mines and Petroleum Resources assists the mining industry through two established branches and two new divisions, Economics and Planning, and Mineral Taxation.

Inspectors of the Mineral Resources Branch are stationed throughout the province. They inspect coal mines, metal mines and quarries, examine prospects, mining properties, roads and trails, and carry out special investigations under the Mineral Act. Environmental Control inspectors conduct dust, ventilation and noise surveys and recommend improvements in environmental conditions. Other inspectors administer the Roads and Trails and Prospectors Grub-stake programs, and the reclamation sections of provincial mining statutes.

The Geological Division carries out a variety of geological studies and publishes data. It makes assessments of the mineral potential of land; collects, stores and disseminates geological statistical data; and records the exploration and mining activities of the industry. An inventory of mineral deposits is under way with a view to establishing a quantitative appraisal. The division offers a restricted number of free assays for prospectors, identifies rocks and minerals, and conducts lectures in prospecting. The Mining Titles Division administers laws concerning the acquisition of rights to minerals and coal. It provides information, including approximate-site maps, on mineral claims and placer leases and their ownership and also data on the ownership, location and status of coal licences and leases.

The Petroleum Resources Branch administers the Petroleum and Natural Gas Act and related regulations. Every well location must be approved by the branch before drilling begins. All drilling and production operations are inspected frequently to ensure full compliance with regulations governing facilities and practices, plugging of abandoned wells, surface restoration of well sites, procedures for well-testing and measurement, disposal of produced water, fire protection and general conservation. Complaints of property damage are investigated. Comprehensive records of all drilling and producing operations are published or made available for study. Samples of bit cuttings as well as all core from every well drilled are retained for study, and detailed reservoir engineering and geological studies are carried out. Estimates of reserves of oil and natural gas are made annually. Crown owned oil and natural gas rights are evaluated prior to disposition by public tender.

British Columbia has made provision for Crown participation in future mineral development and was the first Canadian province to adopt the use of the metric system for staking, effective March 1, 1975. A committee to study all aspects of mining regulations and taxation in the province was established in 1975. The committee includes representatives of industry and labour.

12.3   Mining legislation

12.3.1   Federal and departmental jurisdictions

Mineral rights vested in the Crown in right of Canada include those situated in the Yukon and Northwest Territories and offshore within the limits of Canada's continental margins, as well as those underlying certain federally owned lands within the provinces.

The Supreme Court of Canada in its Opinion of November 1967 stated that, as between Canada and the province of British Columbia, Canada has proprietary rights in and legislative jurisdiction over "lands, including the mineral and other natural resources, of the seabed and subsoil seaward from the ordinary low-water mark on the coast of the mainland and the several islands of British Columbia, outside the harbours, bays, estuaries and other similar inland waters, to the outer limit of the territorial sea of Canada, as defined in the Territorial Sea and Fishing Zones Act...". The court also stated that the federal government has legislative jurisdiction "in respect of the mineral and other natural resources of the seabed and subsoil beyond that part of the territorial sea of Canada... to a depth of 200 metres or, beyond that limit, to where the depth of the superjacent waters admits of the exploitation of the mineral and other natural resources of the said areas...".

The Department of Energy, Mines and Resources, through its Resource Management and Conservation Branch, is responsible for administration and enforcement of legislation and regulations relating to mineral resources off Canada's east and west coasts and in the Hudson Bay and Hudson Strait regions, as well as with respect to federally owned mineral rights that become available for development in the provinces. The Department of Indian Affairs and Northern Development, through the Northern Natural Resources and Environment Branch, is similarly responsible for mineral rights in the Yukon Territory and Northwest Territories and in Canada's high-Arctic offshore regions.

Mineral rights of Indian reserves in the provinces are also vested in the Crown in right of Canada and are administered by the Indian-Eskimo Economic

Development Branch of the Department of Indian Affairs and Northern Development in consultation with the Indian band councils. The rights to a reserve may be taken up only after the Indian band has given approval for development through a referendum vote. The minerals are then administered under the Indian Oil and Gas Regulations or the Indian Mining Regulations, except in British Columbia where mining rights must be acquired under provincial statutes and the BC Indian Reserves Mineral Resources Agreement of 1943. The Indian Oil and Gas Regulations provide for disposal of rights by public tender in the form of permit or lease parcels. The Indian Mining Regulations, on the other hand, provide for disposal based on terms negotiated with the Indian band council. The Indian councils are thus assuming a greater share of responsibility in the management of their mineral resources. Officers of the Department of Indian Affairs and Northern Development are advisers to the Indian councils on mineral matters and are responsible for the administration and enforcement of relevant regulations.

Federal mining laws and regulations   12.3.2

Mining exploration and development is carried out in the Yukon Territory in accordance with the provisions of the Yukon Quartz Mining Act and the Yukon Placer Mining Act. In the Northwest Territories, including Arctic coastal waters, operations are governed by the Canada Mining Regulations 1961, as amended. The Territorial Dredging Regulations, Territorial Coal Regulations and Territorial Quarrying Regulations are common to both territories. In the Yukon Territory, mining rights may be acquired by staking claims. A one-year lease may be obtained to prospect for the purposes of placer mining, renewable for two additional one-year periods; a 21-year lease, renewable for a like period, may be obtained under the Yukon Quartz Mining Act.

Under the Canada Mining Regulations, a prospector must be licensed. Staked claims must be converted to lease or relinquished within 10 years. In certain areas, a system of exploration over large areas is allowed by permit. Any individual over 18 years of age or any joint-stock company incorporated or licensed to do business in Canada may hold a prospector's licence. No lease is granted to an individual unless the minister of the department involved is satisfied that the applicant is a Canadian citizen and will be the beneficial owner of the interest acquired under such lease. No lease is granted to a corporation unless it is incorporated in Canada and unless the minister is satisfied that at least 50% of the issued shares are owned by Canadian citizens or that the shares are listed on a recognized Canadian stock exchange. Any new mine beginning production after the Canada Mining Regulations came into force in 1961 is not required to pay royalties for 36 months.

An exploration assistance fund for petroleum and other minerals in the Yukon and Northwest Territories was established by the federal government in 1966. Assistance to a single applicant is limited in aggregate to $50,000, but not exceeding 40% of the approved cost of an exploration program. Assistance is available only to Canadian citizens or companies incorporated in Canada. Named the Northern Mineral Exploration Program, it is designed to encourage investment from Canadian sources not previously attracted to investment in northern exploration operations.

Provincial mining laws and regulations   12.3.3

In general, all Crown mineral lands lying within provincial boundaries (with the exception of those within Indian reserves, national parks and other lands which are under federal jurisdiction) are administered by the provincial governments. The exception is Quebec where mining rights on federal lands are administered by the province.

The granting of land in any province except Ontario no longer automatically carries with it mining rights upon or under such land. In Ontario, mineral rights are expressly reserved if they are not to be included. In Nova Scotia, no mineral rights belong to the owner of the land except those pertaining to gypsum, agricultural limestone and building materials, and deposits of either limestone or building materials may be declared to be minerals. Such declaration is based on economic value or the public interest. In such case, the initial privilege of acquiring the declared minerals lies with the owner of the surface rights who must then conform with the requirements of the Mines Act. In Newfoundland, mineral and quarry rights are expressly reserved. Some early grants in British Columbia, Alberta, Saskatchewan, Manitoba, New Brunswick, Quebec and Newfoundland also included certain mineral rights. Otherwise, mining rights must be obtained separately by lease or grant from the provincial authority. Mining activities may be classified as placer, general minerals (or veined minerals and bedded minerals), fuels (coal, petroleum and gas) and quarrying. Provincial mining regulations under these divisions are summarized in the following paragraphs.

In most provinces where placer deposits occur, regulations define the size of placer holdings, the terms under which they may be acquired and held, and the royalties to be paid.

General minerals are sometimes described as quartz, lode, or minerals in place. The most elaborate laws and regulations apply in this division. In all provinces except Alberta, Saskatchewan and Manitoba, a prospector's or miner's licence, valid for one year, must be obtained to search for mineral deposits, the licence being general in some areas but limited in others; a claim of promising ground of a specified size may then be staked. In British Columbia a licence is required only for staking and any number of dispositions may be staked under one licence. A claim must be recorded within a time limit and payment of recording fees made, except in Quebec where no fees are required. Work to a specified value per annum must be performed upon the claim for a period of up to 10 years except in Quebec where a development licence may be renewed on a yearly basis; in Manitoba and Saskatchewan no work commitment in the first year of the claim is required. The maximum life of a prospecting licence in Nova Scotia is six years continuous from the original date of issue, after which the operator is expected to go to lease with a productive deposit. In Quebec and Nova Scotia a specified cost of work must be performed and any excess amount expended may be applied to subsequent renewals of the development licence. The taxation applied most frequently is a percentage of net profits of producing mines or royalties. In Saskatchewan, subsurface mineral regulations covering non-metallics stipulate the size and type of dispositions that may be made in order to maintain the disposition in good standing, provide for fees, rentals and royalties, and set out generally the rights and obligations of the disposition holder.

Coal, petroleum and natural gas. In provinces where coal occurs, the size of holdings is laid down together with the conditions of work and rental under which they may be held. In Quebec, the search for petroleum and natural gas may be carried out under an exploration licence followed by an operating lease; the exploration licence covers a period of five years and an area of not over 60,000 acres (24 281 ha), whereas the operating lease extends over a 20-year period and an area not less than 500 (202 ha) or more than 5,000 acres (2 023 ha). In Nova Scotia, mining rights to certain minerals, including petroleum, occurring under differing conditions may be held by different licensees. Provision is sometimes made for royalties. Acts or regulations govern methods of production. In the search for petroleum and natural gas, an exploration permit or reservation is usually required; however, in Saskatchewan, Alberta and British Columbia leases usually follow the exploration reservation whether or not any discovery of oil or gas is made. In Alberta, exploration costs are applicable in part on the first year's lease rental, in Manitoba they may be applied to the lease rental for a period of up to three years, in British Columbia credit is given for up to 24 months' rental, and in Saskatchewan, credit is given for up to three years' rental, having regard to the amount of excess credit established. In other provinces, the discovery of oil or gas is usually prerequisite to obtaining a lease or grant of a limited area, subject to carrying out drilling obligations and paying a rental, a fee, or a royalty on production.

Quarrying regulations define the size of holdings and the terms of lease or grant. In Nova Scotia, sand deposits of a quality suitable for uses other than building purposes and limestone deposits of metallurgical grade belong to the Crown; gypsum deposits belong to the owner of the property. Under the New Brunswick Quarriable Substances Act, 1968, quarriable substances (ordinary stone, building and construction stone, sand, gravel, peat and peat moss) are vested in the owner of the land in or on which they lie; the minister with the approval of the Lieutenant Governor in Council may designate a shore area lying outside Crown land to be subject to the act; and no person shall take or remove or cause to be taken or removed more than one half cubic yard (0.383 m³) of a quarriable substance from Crown land or a designated shore area without obtaining a permit or lease. On Quebec public lands and on those granted to individuals after January 1, 1966, the stone, sand and gravel, like other building materials, belong to the Crown; quarries located on land granted to individuals prior to 1966 remain in the possession of the owners of the surface; the right to exploit all building materials except sand and gravel may be acquired by ordinary staking-out and the right to work sand and gravel beds is set by regulation. In Saskatchewan, sand and gravel on the surface and all sand and gravel obtainable by stripping off the overburden or other surface operation belong to the owner of the surface of the land. In Alberta, sand, gravel, clay and marl recovered by excavating from the surface belong to the owner of the surface of the land. British Columbia, Manitoba and Saskatchewan have made provision for participation by the Crown, at the option of the Crown, in all future mineral development. Such participation may be by way of association, joint venture or otherwise, usually through a Crown corporation. Copies of mining legislation including regulations and other details may be obtained from the provincial authorities concerned.

Sources
12.1 - 12.2.1 Minerals and Metals Division, Mineral Development Sector, Department of Energy, Mines and Resources.
12.2.2 Resources and Development Division, Mineral Development Sector, Department of Energy, Mines and Resources.
12.3 - 12.3.3 Mining Industry Financial and Corporate Analysis Division, Mineral Development Sector, Department of Energy, Mines and Resources.

Tables

Tables

..	not available	bbl	barrels
...	not appropriate or not applicable	b/d	barrels a day
—	nil or zero	Mcf	thousand cubic feet
--	too small to be expressed	MMcf	million cubic feet
e	estimate	MMMcf	billion cubic feet
p	preliminary	MMMMcf	trillion cubic feet
r	revised	million = 10⁶, billion = 10⁹, trillion = 10¹²

million $= 10^6$, billion $= 10^9$, trillion $= 10^{12}$

certain tables may not add due to rounding

12.1 Value of mineral production, 1886-1975

Year	Total value $'000	Value per capita $	Year	Total value $'000	Value per capita $	Year	Total value $'000	Value per capita $
1886	10,221	2.23	1925	226,583	24.38	1965	3,714,861	189.11
1890	16,763	3.51	1930	279,874	27.42	1969	4,734,284	225.43
1895	20,506	4.08	1935	312,344	28.84	1970	5,722,059	268.68
1900	64,421	12.15	1940	529,825	46.55	1971	5,962,692	276.45
1905	69,079	11.51	1945	498,755	41.31	1972r	6,408,026	293.66
1910	106,824	15.29	1950¹	1,045,450	76.24	1973r	8,369,515	378.80
1915	137,109	17.18	1955	1,795,311	114.37	1974	11,711,004	521.74
1920	227,860	26.63	1960	2,492,510	139.48	1975p	13,402,603	587.83

¹Value of Newfoundland production included from 1950.

12.2 Value of mineral production by class, 1966-75 (thousand dollars)

Year	Metallics	Non-metallics	Fuels	Structural materials	Total
1966	1,984,673	363,388	1,151,836	480,650	3,980,546
1967	2,285,279	406,269	1,234,596	454,660	4,380,805
1968	2,492,600	446,922	1,343,163	439,563	4,722,249
1969	2,377,523	450,189	1,465,400	441,172	4,734,284
1970	3,073,344	480,538	1,717,731	450,446	5,722,059
1971	2,940,287	500,827	2,014,410	507,168	5,962,692
1972	2,955,655r	513,488	2,367,554	571,329	6,408,026r
1973r	3,850,072	614,523	3,227,142	677,778	8,369,515
1974	4,820,675	895,436	5,201,723	793,170	11,711,004
1975p	4,812,449	929,172	6,854,264	806,718	13,402,603

12.3 Quantity indexes of production of the principal mining industries, 1966-75 (1971=100)

Mining industry	1966	1967	1968	1969	1970	1971	1972	1973	1974	1975
Metal mines	79.0	84.3	88.5	83.1	99.2	100.0	96.5	106.2	105.7	99.7
Placer gold and gold quartz	148.1	132.6	120.4	116.9	104.0	100.0	90.9	81.1	69.9	71.2
Iron	71.3	77.0	92.6	81.1	102.5	100.0	82.4	106.7	106.9	106.2
Miscellaneous	77.3	83.9	84.8	81.6	97.7	100.0	100.3	107.3	107.2	99.5
Non-metal mines (except coal)	74.8	79.1	87.4	92.1	96.1	100.0	98.4	107.6	120.2	100.3
Asbestos	87.3	85.9	92.9	90.9	100.1	100.0	96.7	102.6	101.0	64.7
Mineral fuels	61.2	66.7	72.7	79.9	92.2	100.0	119.1	129.8	123.7	114.5
Coal	69.6	69.2	67.2	66.8	86.0	100.0	148.3	160.6	158.4	201.7
Crude oil and natural gas	60.4	66.5	73.3	81.2	92.8	100.0	116.7	127.2	120.9	107.3
Total, mines (incl. milling) quarries and oil wells	73.4	77.7	83.3	83.9	95.8	100.0	106.0	115.4	114.3	106.2

12.4   Quantity and value of mineral production, 1974 and 1975

Mineral		1974		1975P	
		Quantity	Value $	Quantity	Value $
METALLICS		...	*4,820,674,603*	...	*4,812,449,000*
Antimony	lb.		5,618,994		5,516,000
Bismuth	"	244,726	2,006,263	81,000	643,000
Cadmium	"	2,735,870	10,880,554	2,682,000	7,162,000
Calcium	"	1,049,587	915,487	826,000	1,108,000
Cobalt	"	3,447,078	10,113,909	2,949,000	11,578,000
Columbium (Cb₂O₅)	"	4,233,055	6,680,316	3,714,000	6,430,000
Copper	"	1,810,833,758	1,402,570,829	1,596,263,000	1,016,819,000
Gold	oz t	1,698,392	263,794,245	1,674,000	276,125,000
Indium	"	259,000			
Iron ore	ton	51,571,084	724,150,257	49,415,000	923,184,000
Iron, remelt	"		71,286,396		75,595,000
Lead	lb.	648,749,678	134,330,107	746,130,000	151,837,000
Magnesium	"	13,132,868	9,260,172	9,922,000	8,324,000
Mercury	"	1,064,000			
Molybdenum	"	30,736,353	61,778,008	27,414,000	68,893,000
Nickel	"	593,199,351	974,594,029	539,652,000	1,109,230,000
Platinum group	oz t	384,618	60,794,030	430,000	61,231,000
Selenium	lb.	599,950	9,449,212	670,000	10,575,000
Silver	oz t	42,809,721	198,166,197	39,101,000	176,627,000
Tantalum (Ta₂O₅)	lb.	438,442	3,576,026	395,000	3,260,000
Tellurium	"	124,313	1,009,422	80,000	763,000
Tin	"	714,005	2,565,155	623,000	2,192,000
Tungsten (WO₃)	"	3,557,600		2,987,000	
Uranium (U₃O₈)	"	9,590,511	..	12,251,000	..
Yttrium (Y₂O₃)	"				
Zinc	"	2,484,627,508	867,134,995	2,387,617,000	895,357,000
NON-METALLICS		...	*895,436,510*	...	*929,172,000*
Asbestos	ton	1,811,938	302,013,081	1,143,000	266,943,000
Barite	"	..	978,444	..	1,083,000
Diatomite	"	..		..	..
Feldspar	"		—		—
Fluorspar	"		7,119,090	..	7,000,000
Gemstones	lb.	7,738	18,613		18,000
Gypsum	ton	7,964,423	22,437,366	6,255,000	19,720,000
Helium	Mcf	..			
Magnesitic dolomite and brucite	ton		4,357,551		4,000,000
Nepheline syenite	"	617,279	9,179,453	520,000	8,663,000
Nitrogen	Mcf				
Peat moss	ton	407,201	20,852,642	383,000	20,630,000
Potash (K₂O)	"	6,366,971	308,925,159	5,346,000	346,806,000
Pyrite, pyrrhotite	"	53,959	347,043	21,000	90,000
Quartz	"	2,762,028	12,184,497	2,561,000	13,499,000
Salt	"	6,003,981	60,619,437	5,683,000	60,593,000
Soapstone, talc, pyrophyllite	"	94,746	1,912,855	74,000	1,683,000
Sodium sulphate	"	703,472	14,192,225	546,000	23,762,000
Sulphur, in smelter gas	"	731,186	9,812,515	776,000	10,417,000
Sulphur, elemental	"	5,547,996	68,555,657	4,476,000	89,190,000
Titanium dioxide, etc.	"	..	51,930,882	..	55,075,000
FUELS		...	*5,201,723,000*	...	*6,854,264,000*
Coal	ton	23,536,000	302,826,000	27,000,000	575,800,000
Natural gas	Mcf	3,045,506,000	723,766,000	3,074,659,000	1,729,631,000
Natural gas by-products	bbl	113,304,000	653,562,000	110,468,000	767,766,000
Oil, crude	"	614,777,000	3,521,569,000	525,342,000	3,781,067,000
STRUCTURAL MATERIALS		...	*793,170,185*	...	*806,718,000*
Clay products		..	70,621,375	..	69,956,000
Cement	ton	11,436,398	274,648,551	10,763,000	265,283,000
Lime	"	2,009,284	41,811,920	1,889,000	40,439,000
Sand and gravel	"	236,587,541	238,620,332	224,960,000	260,340,000
Stone	"	97,485,477	167,468,007	97,100,000	170,700,000
Total		...	*11,711,004,298*	...	*13,402,603,000*

12.4   Quantity and value of mineral production, 1974 and 1975   **M**

Mineral		1974		1975P	
		Quantity	Value $	Quantity	Value $
METALLICS		...	*4,820,674,603*	...	*4,812,449,000*
Antimony	kg	...	5,618,994	...	5,516,000
Bismuth	''	111 006	2,006,263	36 741	643,000
Cadmium	''	1 240 970	10,880,554	1 216 535	7,162,000
Calcium	''	476 085	915,487	374 667	1,108,000
Cobalt	''	1 563 568	10,113,909	1 337 644	11,578,000
Columbium (Cb₂O₅)	''	1 920 081	6,680,316	1 684 642	6,430,000
Copper	''	821 380 376	1,402,570,829	724 053 000	1,016,819,000
Gold	g	52 825 896	263,794,245	52 067 220	276,125,000
Indium	''	8 055 800	...	...	...
Iron ore	t	46 784 500	724,150,257	44 828 534	923,184,000
Iron, remelt	''		71,286,396		75,595,000
Lead	kg	294 267 904	134,330,107	338 438 875	151,837,000
Magnesium	''	5 956 969	9,260,172	4 500 543	8,324,000
Mercury	''	482 622	...	...	...
Molybdenum	''	13 941 775	61,778,008	12 434 781	68,893,000
Nickel	''	269 070 700	974,594,029	244 782 030	1,109,230,000
Platinum group	g	11 962 957	60,794,030	13 374 495	61,231,000
Selenium	kg	272 133	9,449,212	303 907	10,575,000
Silver	''	1 331 531	198,166,197	1 216 177	176,627,000
Tantalum (Ta₂O₅)	''	198 874	3,576,026	179 169	3,260,000
Tellurium	''	56 387	1,009,422	36 287	763,000
Tin	''	323 867	2,565,155	282 588	2,192,000
Tungsten (WO₃)	''	1 613 700	...	1 354 880	...
Uranium (U₃O₈)	''	4 350 183	...	5 556 960	...
Yttrium (Y₂O₃)	''	...	...	...	...
Zinc	''	1 127 008 080	867,134,995	1 083 004 854	895,357,000
NON-METALLICS		...	*895,436,510*	...	*929,172,000*
Asbestos	t	1 643 763	302,013,081	1 036 912	266,943,000
Barite	''	...	978,444	...	1,083,000
Diatomite	''	...	...	...	...
Feldspar	''	—	—	—	—
Fluorspar	''	...	7,119,090	...	7,000,000
Gemstones	kg	3 510	18,613	...	18,000
Gypsum	t	7 225 203	22,437,366	5 674 441	19,720,000
Helium	'000m³	...	...	...	...
Magnesitic dolomite and brucite	t	...	4,357,551	...	4,000,000
Nepheline syenite	''	559 986	9,179,453	471 736	8,663,000
Nitrogen	'000m³	...	...	...	...
Peat moss	t	369 407	20,852,642	347 452	20,630,000
Potash (K₂O)	''	5 776 019	308,925,159	4 849 810	346,806,000
Pyrite, pyrrhotite	''	48 951	347,043	19 051	90,000
Quartz	''	2 505 670	12,184,497	2 323 300	13,499,000
Salt	''	5 446 720	60,619,437	5 155 531	60,593,000
Soapstone, talc, pyrophyllite	''	85 952	1,912,855	67 132	1,683,000
Sodium sulphate	''	638 179	14,192,225	495 323	23,762,000
Sulphur, in smelter gas	''	663 321	9,812,515	703 975	10,417,000
Sulphur, elemental	''	5 033 057	68,555,657	4 060 559	89,190,000
Titanium dioxide, etc.	''	...	51,930,882	...	55,075,000
FUELS		...	*5,201,723,000*	...	*6,854,264,000*
Coal	t	21 351 500	302,826,000	24 493 988	575,800,000
Natural gas	'000m³	86 272 610	723,766,000	87 098 452	1,729,631,000
Natural gas by-products	m³	18 013 897	653,562,000	17 563 009	767,766,000
Oil, crude	''	97 741 735	3,521,569,000	83 522 706	3,781,067,000
STRUCTURAL MATERIALS		...	*793,170,185*	...	*806,718,000*
Clay products		...	70,621,375	...	69,956,000
Cement	t	10 374 926	274,648,551	9 764 029	265,283,000
Lime	''	1 822 792	41,811,920	1 713 672	40,439,000
Sand and gravel	''	214 628 607	238,620,332	204 080 279	260,340,000
Stone	''	88 437 337	167,468,007	88 087 638	170,700,000
Total		...	*11,711,004,298*	...	*13,402,603,000*

12.5 Percentage of the total value contributed by principal minerals, 1966-75

Mineral	1966	1967	1968	1969	1970	1971	1972	1973	1974	1975P
METALLICS[1]	49.9	52.2	52.8	50.2	53.7	49.3	46.1	46.0	41.2	35.9
Copper	11.4	13.3	12.9	12.4	13.6	12.7	12.5	13.8	12.0	7.6
Gold	3.1	2.6	2.2	2.0	1.5	1.3	1.9	2.3	2.3	2.0
Iron ore	10.8	10.7	11.3	9.6	10.3	9.3	7.6	7.2	6.2	6.9
Lead	2.3	2.0	1.9	2.0	2.2	1.8	1.8	1.5	1.1	1.1
Molybdenum	0.9	0.9	0.8	1.1	1.0	0.6	0.7	0.6	0.5	0.5
Nickel	9.5	10.6	11.2	10.2	14.5	13.4	11.2	9.7	8.3	8.3
Platinum group	0.8	0.8	1.0	0.7	0.8	0.7	0.5	0.5	0.6	0.5
Silver	1.2	1.4	2.2	1.8	1.4	1.2	1.2	1.4	1.7	1.3
Uranium	1.4	1.2	1.1	1.1	..	..	..	..	..	..
Zinc	7.3	7.3	6.9	7.8	7.0	7.0	7.5	7.8	7.4	6.7
NON-METALLICS[1]	9.1	9.3	9.5	9.5	8.4	8.4	8.0	7.3	7.7	6.9
Asbestos	4.1	3.7	3.9	4.1	3.6	3.4	3.2	2.8	2.6	2.0
Gypsum	0.3	0.3	0.3	0.3	0.2	0.3	0.3	0.3	0.2	0.1
Nepheline syenite	0.1	0.1	0.1	0.1	0.1	0.1	0.1	0.1	0.1	0.1
Potash	1.6	1.5	1.4	1.5	1.9	2.3	2.1	2.1	2.6	2.6
Quartz	0.1	0.1	0.1	0.1	0.1	0.1	0.2	0.1	0.1	0.1
Salt	0.6	0.6	0.7	0.6	0.6	0.7	0.6	0.6	0.5	0.5
Sodium sulphate	0.2	0.2	0.2	0.2	0.1	0.1	0.1	0.1	0.1	0.2
Sulphur, in smelter gas	0.2	0.2	0.2	0.2	0.1	0.1	0.1	0.1	0.1	0.1
Sulphur, elemental	1.0	1.6	1.7	1.3	0.5	0.4	0.3	0.3	0.6	0.7
Titanium dioxide, etc.	0.5	0.5	0.6	0.6	0.6	0.7	0.6	0.6	0.4	0.4
FUELS[1]	28.9	28.2	28.4	31.0	30.0	33.8	37.0	38.6	44.4	51.2
Coal	2.0	1.3	1.1	1.1	1.5	2.0	2.4	2.1	2.6	4.3
Natural gas	4.5	4.5	4.8	5.5	5.5	5.7	6.2	5.4	6.2	12.9
Oil, crude	19.8	19.8	19.8	21.4	20.2	22.7	24.5	26.8	30.1	28.2
STRUCTURAL MATERIALS	12.1	10.3	9.3	9.3	7.9	8.5	8.9	8.1	6.7	6.0
Clay products	1.1	1.0	1.0	1.0	0.9	0.8	0.8	0.7	0.6	0.5
Cement	3.9	3.3	3.1	3.4	2.7	3.1	3.3	2.9	2.3	2.0
Lime	0.5	0.4	0.4	0.4	0.4	0.4	0.4	0.4	0.4	0.3
Sand and gravel	3.8	3.3	2.8	2.6	2.3	2.6	2.8	2.6	2.0	1.9
Stone	2.8	2.3	2.0	1.9	1.5	1.6	1.6	1.5	1.4	1.3
Total	100.0	100.0	100.0	100.0	100.0	100.0	100.0	100.0	100.0	100.0

[1]Includes minor items not specified.

12.6   Value of mineral production, by province, 1966-75 (thousand dollars)

Year	Province or territory						
	Newfound-land (incl. Labrador)	Prince Edward Island	Nova Scotia	New Brunswick	Quebec	Ontario	Manitoba
1966	244,020	1,063	85,596	90,208	771,180	957,852	179,342
1967	266,365	1,775	52,544	90,440	741,436	1,194,549	184,679
1968	309,712	977	56,940	88,452	725,078	1,355,629	209,626
1969	256,936	452	58,562	94,593	717,156	1,222,172	246,275
1970	353,261	640	58,159	104,791	803,286	1,593,039	332,214
1971	343,431	978	60,083	107,233	766,473	1,554,777	330,060
1972	290,659	1,097	57,522	120,171	785,962	1,535,683r	323,292
1973r	374,418	1,680	60,808	164,178	935,530	1,854,695	414,013
1974	448,473	1,454	80,251	213,519	1,192,440	2,429,530	486,249
1975P	568,212	1,540	96,688	251,393	1,142,457	2,339,449	533,189

Year	Saskat-chewan	Alberta	British Columbia	Yukon Territory	Northwest Territories	Canada
1966	348,505	848,667	330,898	11,976	111,239	3,980,546
1967	361,824	974,366	379,555	14,991	118,283	4,380,805
1968	357,082	1,092,444	389,307	21,366	115,636	4,722,249
1969	344,625	1,205,308	433,633	35,403	119,171	4,734,284
1970	379,190	1,395,994	490,158	77,512	133,814	5,722,059
1971	409,956	1,640,508	540,527	93,111	115,555	5,962,692
1972	409,889	1,978,750	677,883	106,781	120,337	6,408,026r
1973r	509,773	2,760,227	978,037	150,667	165,489	8,369,515
1974	790,330	4,518,383	1,155,787	171,538	223,050	11,711,004
1975P	826,536	6,000,849	1,223,915	228,898	189,477	13,402,603

12.7   Value of metallics, non-metallics, fuels and structural materials produced, by province, 1974 and 1975 (thousand dollars)

Year and province or territory	Metallics	Non-metallics	Fuels	Structural materials	Total
1974					
Newfoundland (incl. Labrador)	407,354	25,972	—	15,147	448,473
Prince Edward Island	—	—	—	1,454	1,454
Nova Scotia	214	27,621	24,524	27,892	80,251
New Brunswick	184,143	5,639	5,442	18,295	213,519
Quebec	671,324	307,266	27	213,823	1,192,440
Ontario	2,049,707	64,184	7,590	308,049	2,429,530
Manitoba	413,530	3,599	27,164	41,956	486,249
Saskatchewan	22,268	327,666	421,354	19,042	790,330
Alberta	15	73,922	4,376,520	67,926	4,518,383
British Columbia	709,178	36,814	330,208	79,587	1,155,787
Yukon Territory	148,596	22,752	190	—	171,538
Northwest Territories	214,346	—	8,704	—	223,050
Canada, 1974	4,820,675	895,437	5,201,723	793,171	11,711,004
1975P					
Newfoundland (incl. Labrador)	526,875	27,869	—	13,468	568,212
Prince Edward Island	—	—	—	1,540	1,540
Nova Scotia	—	25,785	47,600	23,303	96,688
New Brunswick	221,882	5,667	7,156	16,688	251,393
Quebec	656,624	251,188	8	234,637	1,142,457
Ontario	1,963,694	61,104	11,604	303,047	2,339,449
Manitoba	457,664	3,740	31,657	40,128	533,189
Saskatchewan	18,542	375,294	413,979	18,721	826,536
Alberta	—	96,249	5,827,932	76,668	6,000,849
British Columbia	588,692	50,306	506,399	78,518	1,223,915
Yukon Territory	196,689	31,970	239	—	228,898
Northwest Territories	181,787	—	7,690	—	189,477
Canada, 1975P	4,812,449	929,172	6,854,264	806,718	13,402,603

12.8   Detailed mineral production, by province, 1974 and 1975ᵖ (thousands)

Mineral		Province or territory					
		Newfound-land (incl. Labrador)		Nova Scotia		New Brunswick	
		1974	1975	1974	1975	1974	1975
METALLICS	$	407,354	526,875	213	—	184,143	221,882
Antimony	lb.	—	—	—	—	..	..
	$	—	—	—	—	4,739	4,681
Bismuth	lb.	—	—	—	—	154	23
	$	—	—	—	—	1,259	182
Cadmium	lb.	6	5	—	—	72	70
	$	23	12	—	—	285	187
Calcium	lb.	—	—	—	—	—	—
	$	—	—	—	—	—	—
Cobalt	lb.	—	—	—	—	—	—
	$	—	—	—	—	—	—
Columbium (Cb₂O₅)	lb.	—	—	—	—	—	—
	$	—	—	9	—	—	—
Copper	lb.	12,467	16,380	9	—	25,063	26,277
	$	9,665	10,434	7	—	19,429	16,739
Gold	oz t	12	13	—	—	4	5
	$	1,802	2,066	—	—	667	757
Indium	oz t	—	—	—	—	—	—
	$	—	—	—	—	—	—
Iron ore	ton	24,280	25,576	—	—	—	—
	$	372,188	486,636	—	—	—	—
Iron, remelt	ton	—	—	—	—	—	—
	$	—	—	—	—	—	—
Lead	lb.	30,980	22,352	433	—	105,444	124,527
	$	6,415	4,549	90	—	21,833	25,341
Magnesium	lb.	—	—	—	—	—	—
	$	—	—	—	—	—	—
Mercury	lb.	—	—	—	—	—	—
	$	—	—	—	—	—	—
Molybdenum	lb.	—	—	—	—	—	—
	$	—	—	—	—	—	—
Nickel	lb.	—	—	—	—	—	—
	$	—	—	—	—	—	—
Platinum group	oz t	—	—	—	—	—	—
	$	—	—	—	—	—	—
Selenium	lb.	—	—	—	—	—	—
	$	—	—	—	—	—	—
Silver	oz t	556	528	25	—	4,464	4,790
	$	2,572	2,384	117	—	20,666	21,638
Tantalum (Ta₂O₅)	lb.	—	—	—	—	—	—
	$	—	—	—	—	—	—
Tellurium	lb.	—	—	—	—	—	—
	$	—	—	—	—	—	—
Tin	lb.	—	—	—	—	—	—
	$	—	—	—	—	—	—
Tungsten (WO₃)	lb.	—	—	—	—	—	—
	$	—	—	—	—	—	—
Uranium (U₃O₈)	lb.	—	—	—	—	—	—
	$	—	—	—	—	—	—
Yttrium (Y₂O₃)	lb.	—	—	—	—	—	—
	$	—	—	—	—	—	—
Zinc	lb.	42,090	55,450	—	—	330,271	406,286
	$	14,690	20,794	—	—	115,265	152,357
NON-METALLICS	$	25,972	27,869	27,621	25,785	5,639	5,667
Asbestos	ton	76	64	—	—	—	—
	$	16,111	18,135	—	—	—	—
Barite	ton	—	—	..	..	—	—
	$	—	—	465	450	—	—
Diatomite	ton	—	—	—	—	—	—
	$	—	—	—	—	—	—
Feldspar	ton	.—	—	—	—	—	—
	$	—	—	—	—	—	—
Fluorspar	ton	..	..	—	—	—	—
	$	7,119	7,000	—	—	—	—
Gemstones	lb.	—	—	—	—	—	—
	$	—	—	—	—	—	—
Gypsum	ton	556	508	5,899	4,406	87	59
	$	1,859	1,964	15,496	12,490	305	230
Helium	Mcf	—	—	—	—	—	—
	$	—	—	—	—	—	—
Magnesitic dolomite and brucite	ton	—	—	—	—	—	—
	$	—	—	—	—	—	—
Nepheline syenite	ton	—	—	—	—	—	—
	$	—	—	—	—	—	—
Nitrogen	Mcf	—	—	—	—	—	—
	$	—	—	6	6	95	89
Peat moss	ton	—	—	6	6	95	89
	$	—	—	354	340	4,808	4,900
Potash (K₂O)	ton	—	—	—	—	—	—
	$	—	—	—	—	—	—
Pyrite, pyrrhotite	ton	—	—	—	—	—	—
	$	—	—	—	—	—	—
Quartz	ton	..	..	..	..	—	—
	$	375	350	128	150	—	—
Salt	ton	—	—	863	795	—	—
	$	—	—	11,179	12,355	—	—

12.8   Detailed mineral production, by province, 1974 and 1975ᴾ (thousands)   M

Mineral		Province or territory					
		Newfound-land (incl. Labrador)		Nova Scotia		New Brunswick	
		1974	1975	1974	1975	1974	1975
METALLICS	$	407,354	526,875	213	—	184,143	221,882
Antimony	kg	—	—	—	—	..	..
	$	—	—	—	—	4,739	4,681
Bismuth	kg	—	—	—	—	70	10
	$	—	—	—	—	1,259	182
Cadmium	kg	3	2	—	—	32	32
	$	23	12	—	—	285	187
Calcium	kg	—	—	—	—	—	—
	$	—	—	—	—	—	—
Cobalt	kg	—	—	—	—	—	—
	$	—	—	—	—	—	—
Columbium (Cb₂O₅)	kg	—	—	—	—	—	—
	$	—	—	—	—	—	—
Copper	kg	5 655	7 430	4	—	11 368	11 919
	$	9,665	10,434	7	—	19,429	16,739
Gold	g	361	404	—	—	134	156
	$	1,802	2,066	—	—	667	757
Indium	g	—	—	—	—	—	—
	$	—	—	—	—	—	—
Iron ore	t	22 027	23 202	—	—	—	—
	$	372,188	486,636	—	—	—	—
Iron, remelt	t	—	—	—	—	—	—
	$	—	—	—	—	—	—
Lead	kg	14 053	10 139	196	—	47 829	56 484
	$	6,415	4,549	90	—	21,833	25,341
Magnesium	kg	—	—	—	—	—	—
	$	—	—	—	—	—	—
Mercury	kg	—	—	—	—	—	—
	$	—	—	—	—	—	—
Molybdenum	kg	—	—	—	—	—	—
	$	—	—	—	—	—	—
Nickel	kg	—	—	—	—	—	—
	$	—	—	—	—	—	—
Platinum group	g	—	—	—	—	—	—
	$	—	—	—	—	—	—
Selenium	kg	—	—	—	—	—	—
	$	—	—	—	—	—	—
Silver	kg	17	16	1	—	139	149
	$	2,572	2,384	117	—	20,666	21,638
Tantalum (Ta₂O₅)	kg	—	—	—	—	—	—
	$	—	—	—	—	—	—
Tellurium	kg	—	—	—	—	—	—
	$	—	—	—	—	—	—
Tin	kg	—	—	—	—	—	—
	$	—	—	—	—	—	—
Tungsten (WO₃)	kg	—	—	—	—	—	—
	$	—	—	—	—	—	—
Uranium (U₃O₈)	kg	—	—	—	—	—	—
	$	—	—	—	—	—	—
Yttrium (Y₂O₃)	kg	—	—	—	—	—	—
	$	—	—	—	—	—	—
Zinc	kg	19 092	25 152	—	—	149 808	184 288
	$	14,690	20,794	—	—	115,265	152,357
NON-METALLICS	$	25,972	27,869	27,621	25,785	5,640	5,667
Asbestos	t	69	58	—	—	—	—
	$	16,111	18,135	—	—	—	—
Barite	t	—	—	..	..	—	—
	$	—	—	465	450	—	—
Diatomite	t	—	—	—	—	—	—
	$	—	—	—	—	—	—
Feldspar	t	—	—	—	—	—	—
	$	—	—	—	—	—	—
Fluorspar	t	..	..	—	—	—	—
	$	7,119	7,000	—	—	—	—
Gemstones	kg	—	—	—	—	—	—
	$	—	—	—	—	—	—
Gypsum	t	504	461	5 352	3 997	79	54
	$	1,859	1,964	15,496	12,490	305	230
Helium	m³	—	—	—	—	—	—
	$	—	—	—	—	—	—
Magnesitic dolomite and brucite	t	—	—	—	—	—	—
	$	—	—	—	—	—	—
Nepheline syenite	t	—	—	—	—	—	—
	$	—	—	—	—	—	—
Nitrogen	m³	—	—	—	—	—	—
	$	—	—	—	—	86	81
Peat moss	t	—	—	5	5	86	81
	$	—	—	354	340	4,808	4,900
Potash (K₂O)	t	—	—	—	—	—	—
	$	—	—	—	—	—	—
Pyrite, pyrrhotite	t	—	—	—	—	—	—
	$	—	—	—	—	—	—
Quartz	t	..	..	..	..	—	—
	$	375	350	128	150	—	—
Salt	t	—	—	783	721	—	—
	$	—	—	11,179	12,355	—	—

12.8   Detailed mineral production, by province, 1974 and 1975ᵖ (thousands) (continued)

Mineral		Province or territory					
		Newfoundland (incl. Labrador)		Nova Scotia		New Brunswick	
		1974	1975	1974	1975	1974	1975
NON-METALLICS (concluded)							
Soapstone, talc, pyrophyllite	ton	..	..	—	—	—	—
	$	508	420	—	—	—	—
Sodium sulphate	ton	—	—	—	—	—	—
	$	—	—	—	—	—	—
Sulphur, in smelter gas	ton	—	—	—	—	39	40
	$	—	—	—	—	526	537
Sulphur, elemental	ton	—	—	—	—	—	—
	$	—	—	—	—	—	—
Titanium dioxide, etc.	ton	—	—	—	—	—	—
	$	—	—	—	—	—	—
FUELS	$	—	—	24,524	47,600	5,442	7,156
Coal	ton	—	—	1,410	1,850	415	450
	$	—	—	24,524	47,600	5,387	7,100
Natural gas	Mcf	—	—	—	—	88	90
	$	—	—	—	—	44	45
Natural gas by-products	bbl	—	—	—	—	—	—
	$	—	—	—	—	—	—
Oil, crude	bbl	—	—	—	—	8	8
	$	—	—	—	—	11	11
STRUCTURAL MATERIALS	$	15,146	13,468	27,892	23,303	18,295	16,688
Clay products	$	350	300	2,763	3,155	1,048	1,310
Cement	ton	..	..	..	..	..	..
	$	4,025	3,468	4,375	3,348	4,587	4,403
Lime	ton	..	..	..	..	..	..
	$	—	—	—	—	1,357	1,275
Sand and gravel	ton	6,772	5,900	11,578	8,900	8,251	6,500
	$	8,728	7,800	16,169	12,500	5,558	4,500
Stone	ton	680	600	1,666	1,300	2,899	2,600
	$	2,044	1,900	4,586	4,300	5,744	5,200
Total 1974	$	448,473	..	80,251	..	213,519	..
Total 1975	$	..	568,212	..	96,688	..	251,393

Mineral		Quebec		Ontario		Manitoba	
		1974	1975	1974	1975	1974	1975
METALLICS	$	671,324	656,624	2,049,707	1,963,694	413,530	457,664
Antimony	lb.	—	—	—	—	—	—
	$	—	—	—	—	—	—
Bismuth	lb.	1	1	16	7	—	—
	$	6	11	133	57	—	—
Cadmium	lb.	335	267	1,680	1,519	174	56
	$	1,333	712	6,681	4,056	694	151
Calcium	lb.	—	—	1,050	826	—	—
	$	—	—	915	1,108	—	—
Cobalt	lb.	—	—	2,775	2,406	672	543
	$	—	—	8,142	9,439	1,972	2,139
Columbium (Cb₂O₅)	lb.	4,233	3,714	—	—	—	—
	$	6,680	6,430	—	—	—	—
Copper	lb.	317,981	259,717	625,886	584,592	156,711	141,564
	$	246,502	165,440	483,995	372,385	121,484	90,176
Gold	oz t	441	465	801	775	53	46
	$	68,428	76,771	124,428	127,833	8,163	7,528
Indium	oz t	—	—	—	—	—	—
	$	—	—	—	—	—	—
Iron ore	ton	13,829	12,200	12,022	10,264	—	—
	$	159,116	207,942	180,090	214,007	—	—
Iron, remelt	ton	..	..	—	—	—	—
	$	71,286	75,595	—	—	—	—
Lead	lb.	2,112	3,195	20,222	14,853	87	288
	$	437	650	4,187	3,023	18	59
Magnesium	lb.	—	—	13,133	9,922	—	—
	$	—	—	9,260	8,324	—	—
Mercury	lb.	—	—	—	—	—	—
	$	—	—	—	—	—	—
Molybdenum	lb.	335	627	—	—	—	—
	$	986	1,590	—	—	—	—
Nickel	lb.	—	—	460,879	398,880	130,802	140,772
	$	—	—	749,782	815,934	222,232	293,296
Platinum group	oz t	—	—	385	430	—	—
	$	—	—	60,794	61,231	—	—
Selenium	lb.	353	440	129	106	86	89
	$	5,564	8,096	2,024	195	1,348	1,644
Silver	oz t	2,970	3,245	17,852	14,506	1,267	994
	$	13,750	14,656	82,639	65,525	5,867	4,492
Tantalum (Ta₂O₅)	lb.	—	—	—	—	438	395
	$	—	—	—	—	3,576	3,260
Tellurium	lb.	88	49	19	15	12	12
	$	714	470	158	141	99	114
Tin	lb.	—	—	399	549	—	—
	$	—	—	1,398	1,932	—	—

12.8   Detailed mineral production, by province, 1974 and 1975ᵖ (thousands) (continued)   M

Mineral		Province or territory					
		Newfoundland (incl. Labrador)		Nova Scotia		New Brunswick	
		1974	1975	1974	1975	1974	1975
NON-METALLICS (concluded)							
Soapstone, talc, pyrophyllite	t	..	..	—	—	—	—
	$	508	420	—	—	—	—
Sodium sulphate	t	—	—	—	—	—	—
	$	—	—	—	—	—	—
Sulphur, in smelter gas	t	—	—	—	—	36	36
	$	—	—	—	—	526	537
Sulphur, elemental	t	—	—	—	—	—	—
	$	—	—	—	—	—	—
Titanium dioxide, etc.	t	—	—	—	—	—	—
	$	—	—	—	—	—	—
FUELS	$	—	—	24,524	47,600	5,442	7,156
Coal	t	—	—	1 279	1 678	376	408
	$	—	—	24,524	47,600	5,387	7,100
Natural gas	m³	—	—	—	—	2 493	2 550
	$	—	—	—	—	44	45
Natural gas by-products	m³	—	—	—	—	—	—
	$	—	—	—	—	—	—
Oil, crude	m³	—	—	—	—	1	1
	$	—	—	—	—	11	11
STRUCTURAL MATERIALS	$	15,146	13,468	27,892	23,303	18,295	16,688
Clay products	$	350	300	2,763	3,155	1,048	1,310
Cement	t	..	..	..	..	..	..
	$	4,025	3,468	4,375	3,348	4,587	4,403
Lime	t	—	—	—	—	..	..
	$	—	—	—	—	1,357	1,275
Sand and gravel	t	6 144	5 352	10 504	8 074	7 485	5 897
	$	8,728	7,800	16,169	12,500	5,558	4,500
Stone	t	617	544	1 511	1 179	2 630	2 359
	$	2,044	1,900	4,586	4,300	5,744	5,200
Total 1974	$	448,473	...	80,251	...	213,519	...
Total 1975	$	...	568,212	...	96,688	...	251,393

		Quebec		Ontario		Manitoba	
		1974	1975	1974	1975	1974	1975
METALLICS	$	671,324	656,624	2,049,707	1,963,694	413,530	457,664
Antimony	kg	—	—	—	—	—	—
	$	—	—	—	—	—	—
Bismuth	kg	- -	- -	7	3	—	—
	$	6	11	133	57	—	—
Cadmium	kg	152	121	762	689	79	25
	$	1,333	712	6,681	4,056	694	151
Calcium	kg	—	—	476	375	—	—
	$	—	—	915	1,108	—	—
Cobalt	kg	—	—	1 259	1 091	305	246
	$	—	—	8,142	9,439	1,972	2,139
Columbium (Cb₂O₅)	kg	1 920	1 685	—	—	—	—
	$	6,680	6,430	—	—	—	—
Copper	kg	144 234	117 806	283 897	265 166	71 083	64 212
	$	246,502	165,440	483,995	372,385	121,484	90,176
Gold	g	13 703	14 463	24 917	24 105	1 635	1 431
	$	68,428	76,771	124,428	127,833	8,163	7,528
Indium	g	—	—	—	—	—	—
	$	—	—	—	—	—	—
Iron ore	t	12 545	11 068	10 906	9 311	—	—
	$	159,116	207,942	180,090	214,007	—	—
Iron, remelt	t	..	..	—	—	—	—
	$	71,286	75,595	—	—	—	—
Lead	kg	958	1 449	9 172	6 737	40	131
	$	437	650	4,187	3,023	18	59
Magnesium	kg	—	—	5 957	4 501	—	—
	$	—	—	9,260	8,324	—	—
Mercury	kg	—	—	—	—	—	—
	$	—	—	—	—	—	—
Molybdenum	kg	152	284	—	—	—	—
	$	986	1,590	—	—	—	—
Nickel	kg	—	—	209 051	180 929	59 331	63 853
	$	—	—	749,782	815,934	222,232	293,296
Platinum group	g	—	—	11 963	13 374	—	—
	$	—	—	60,794	61,231	—	—
Selenium	kg	160	200	58	48	39	40
	$	5,564	8,096	2,024	195	1,348	1,644
Silver	kg	92	101	555	451	39	31
	$	13,750	14,656	82,639	65,525	5,867	4,492
Tantalum (Ta₂O₅)	kg	—	—	—	—	199	179
	$	—	—	—	—	3,576	3,260
Tellurium	kg	40	22	9	7	6	5
	$	714	470	158	141	99	114
Tin	kg	—	—	181	249	—	—
	$	—	—	1,398	1,932	—	—

12.8 Detailed mineral production, by province, 1974 and 1975ᵖ (thousands) (continued)

Mineral		Province or territory					
		Quebec		Ontario		Manitoba	
		1974	1975	1974	1975	1974	1975
METALLICS (concluded)							
Tungsten (WO₃)	lb.	—	—	—	—	—	—
	$	—	—	—	—	—	—
Uranium (U₃O₈)	lb.	—	—	8,443	10,569	—	—
	$	—	—	..	..	—	—
Yttrium (Y₂O₃)	lb.	—	—	..	..	—	—
	$	—	—	..	..	—	—
Zinc	lb.	276,565	262,030	960,117	742,677	137,755	146,146
	$	96,521	98,261	335,081	278,504	48,076	54,805
NON-METALLICS	$	307,266	251,188	64,184	61,104	3,599	3,740
Asbestos	ton	1,537	854	16	16	—	—
	$	234,416	176,634	1,335	1,395	—	—
Barite	ton	—	—	—	—	—	—
	$	—	—	—	—	—	—
Diatomite	ton	—	—	—	—	—	—
	$	—	—	—	—	—	—
Feldspar	ton	—	—	—	—	—	—
	$	—	—	—	—	—	—
Fluorspar	ton	—	—	—	—	—	—
	$	—	—	—	—	—	—
Gemstones	lb.	—	—	—	—	—	—
	$	—	—	—	—	—	—
Gypsum	ton	—	—	774	742	207	90
	$	—	—	2,784	2,620	581	202
Helium	Mcf	—	—	—	—	—	—
	$	—	—	—	—	—	—
Magnesitic dolomite and brucite	ton	..	..	—	—	—	—
	$	4,358	4,000	—	—	—	—
Nepheline syenite	ton	—	—	617	520	—	—
	$	—	—	9,179	8,663	—	—
Nitrogen	Mcf	—	—	—	—	—	—
	$	—	—	—	—	—	—
Peat moss	ton	192	160	10	11	20	28
	$	8,761	7,920	482	560	1,176	1,780
Potash (K₂O)	ton	—	—	—	—	—	—
	$	—	—	—	—	—	—
Pyrite, pyrrhotite	ton	54	21	—	—	—	—
	$	347	90	—	—	—	—
Quartz	ton	771	493	1,237	1,360	435	387
	$	5,388	5,338	3,850	4,977	1,684	1,575
Salt	ton	—	—	4,456	4,253	32	30
	$	—	—	40,170	37,018	150	170
Soapstone, talc, pyrophyllite	ton	..	..	..	..	—	—
	$	682	628	723	635	—	—
Sodium sulphate	ton	—	—	—	—	—	—
	$	—	—	—	—	—	—
Sulphur, in smelter gas	ton	103	112	422	388	—	—
	$	1,384	1,503	5,662	5,207	—	—
Sulphur, elemental	ton	—	—	—	1	2	1
	$	—	—	—	29	7	13
Titanium dioxide, etc.	ton	..	..	—	—	—	—
	$	51,931	55,075	—	—	—	—
FUELS	$	27	8	7,590	11,604	27,164	31,657
Coal	ton	—	—	—	—	—	—
	$	—	—	—	—	—	—
Natural gas	Mcf	183	50	7,537	12,671	—	—
	$	27	8	3,248	6,413	—	—
Natural gas by-products	bbl	—	—	—	—	—	—
	$	—	—	—	—	—	—
Oil, crude	bbl	—	—	734	721	4,749	4,441
	$	—	—	4,342	5,191	27,164	31,657
STRUCTURAL MATERIALS	$	213,822	234,637	308,049	303,047	41,957	40,128
Clay products	$	12,214	12,507	39,074	38,363	778	676
Cement	ton	3,248	3,489	4,606	4,021	702	523
	$	83,518	90,715	103,580	92,491	13,795	10,468
Lime	ton	633	641	1,054	958	..	..
	$	15,364	15,715	19,374	18,193	1,831	1,584
Sand and gravel	ton	39,493	43,000	79,713	76,200	19,039	18,400
	$	23,396	31,500	85,105	92,000	22,168	24,800
Stone	ton	50,509	53,100	34,460	33,700	2,451	1,700
	$	79,330	84,200	60,916	62,000	3,384	2,600
Total 1974	$	1,192,440	..	2,429,530	..	486,249	..
Total 1975	$	..	1,142,457	..	2,339,449	..	533,189

12.8   Detailed mineral production, by province, 1974 and 1975ᴾ (thousands) (continued)   M

Mineral		Province or territory					
		Quebec		Ontario		Manitoba	
		1974	1975	1974	1975	1974	1975
METALLICS (concluded)							
Tungsten (WO₃)	kg	—	—	—	—	—	—
	$	—	—	—	—	—	—
Uranium (U₃O₈)	kg	—	—	3 830	4 794	—	—
	$	—	—	...	...	—	—
Yttrium (Y₂O₃)	kg	—	—	...	...	—	—
	$	—	—	...	...	—	—
Zinc	kg	125 448	118 855	435 502	336 873	62 484	66 291
	$	96,521	98,261	335,081	278,504	48,076	54,805
NON-METALLICS	$	307,266	251,188	64,184	61,104	3,599	3,740
Asbestos	t	1 394	775	15	15	—	—
	$	234,416	176,634	1,335	1,395	—	—
Barite	t	—	—	—	—	—	—
	$	—	—	—	—	—	—
Diatomite	t	—	—	—	—	—	—
	$	—	—	—	—	—	—
Feldspar	t	—	—	—	—	—	—
	$	—	—	—	—	—	—
Fluorspar	t	—	—	—	—	—	—
	$	—	—	—	—	—	—
Gemstones	kg	—	—	—	—	—	—
	$	—	—	—	—	—	—
Gypsum	t	—	—	703	673	188	82
	$	—	—	2,784	2,620	581	202
Helium	m³	—	—	—	—	—	—
	$	—	—	—	—	—	—
Magnesitic dolomite and brucite	t	...	...	—	—	—	—
	$	4,358	4,000	—	—	—	—
Nepheline syenite	t	—	—	560	472	—	—
	$	—	—	9,179	8,663	—	—
Nitrogen	m³	—	—	—	—	—	—
	$	—	—	—	—	—	—
Peat moss	t	174	145	9	10	19	25
	$	8,761	7,920	482	560	1,176	1,780
Potash (K₂O)	t	—	—	—	—	—	—
	$	—	—	—	—	—	—
Pyrite, pyrrhotite	t	49	19	—	—	—	—
	$	347	90	—	—	—	—
Quartz	t	699	447	1 122	1 234	395	351
	$	5,388	5,338	3,850	4,977	1,684	1,575
Salt	t	—	—	4 043	3 858	29	27
	$	—	—	40,170	37,018	150	170
Soapstone, talc, pyrophyllite	t	...	...	...	...	—	—
	$	682	628	723	635	—	—
Sodium sulphate	t	—	—	—	—	—	—
	$	—	—	—	—	—	—
Sulphur, in smelter gas	t	94	102	383	352	—	—
	$	1,384	1,503	5,662	5,207	—	—
Sulphur, elemental	t	—	—	—	1	1	1
	$	—	—	—	29	7	13
Titanium dioxide, etc.	t	...	...	—	—	—	—
	$	51,931	55,075	—	—	—	—
FUELS	$	27	8	7,590	11,604	27,164	31,657
Coal	t	—	—	—	—	—	—
	$	—	—	—	—	—	—
Natural gas	m³	5 184	1 416	213 507	358 942	—	—
	$	27	8	3,248	6,413	—	—
Natural gas by-products	m³	—	—	—	—	—	—
	$	—	—	—	—	—	—
Oil, crude	m³	—	—	117	115	755	706
	$	—	—	4,342	5,191	27,164	31,657
STRUCTURAL MATERIALS	$	213,822	234,637	308,049	303,047	41,957	40,128
Clay products	$	12,214	12,507	39,074	38,363	778	676
Cement	t	2 947	3 165	4 179	3 648	637	474
	$	83,518	90,715	103,580	92,491	13,795	10,468
Lime	t	574	582	956	869	...	...
	$	15,364	15,715	19,374	18,193	1,831	1,584
Sand and gravel	t	35 827	39 009	72 314	69 128	17 271	16 692
	$	23,396	31,500	85,105	92,000	22,168	24,800
Stone	t	45 821	48 172	31 261	30 572	2 223	1 542
	$	79,330	84,200	60,916	62,000	3,384	2,600
Total 1974	$	1,192,440	...	2,429,530	...	486,249	...
Total 1975	$	...	1,142,457	...	2,339,449	...	533,189

12.8   Detailed mineral production, by province, 1974 and 1975ᴾ (thousands) (continued)

Mineral		Province or territory					
		Saskatchewan		Alberta		British Columbia	
		1974	1975	1974	1975	1974	1975
METALLICS	$	22,268	18,542	15	—	709,178	588,692
Antimony	lb.	—	—	—	—	488	430
	$	—	—	—	—	880	835
Bismuth	lb.	—	—	—	—	74	50
	$	—	—	—	—	609	393
Cadmium	lb.	32	9	—	—	432	752
	$	129	25	—	—	1,718	2,008
Calcium	lb.	—	—	—	—	—	—
	$	—	—	—	—	—	—
Cobalt	lb.	—	—	—	—	—	—
	$	—	—	—	—	—	—
Columbium (Cb₂O₅)	lb.	—	—	—	—	—	—
	$	—	—	—	—	—	—
Copper	lb.	17,608	17,004	—	—	633,936	531,998
	$	13,650	10,831	—	—	491,426	338,883
Gold	oz t	15	14	..	—	162	144
	$	2,354	2,352	15	—	25,174	23,821
Indium	oz t	—	—	—	—	259	..
	$	—	—	—	—	..	..
Iron ore	ton	—	—	—	—	1,441	1,375
	$	—	—	—	—	12,757	14,599
Iron, remelt	ton	—	—	—	—	—	—
	$	—	—	—	—	—	—
Lead	lb.	—	—	—	—	121,812	152,894
	$	—	—	—	—	25,222	31,114
Magnesium	lb.	—	—	—	—	—	—
	$	—	—	—	—	—	—
Mercury	lb.	—	—	—	—	1,064	..
	$	—	—	—	—	..	..
Molybdenum	lb.	—	—	—	—	30,402	26,787
	$	—	—	—	—	60,792	67,303
Nickel	lb.	—	—	—	—	1,518	—
	$	—	—	—	—	2,579	—
Plantinum group	oz t	—	—	—	—	—	—
	$	—	—	—	—	—	—
Selenium	lb.	33	35	—	—	—	—
	$	513	640	—	—	—	—
Silver	oz t	225	272	..	—	5,842	6,076
	$	1,042	1,230	..	—	27,043	27,447
Tantalum (Ta₂O₅)	lb.	—	—	—	—	—	—
	$	—	—	—	—	—	—
Tellurium	lb.	5	4	—	—	—	—
	$	38	38	—	—	—	—
Tin	lb.	—	—	—	—	315	74
	$	—	—	—	—	1,167	260
Tungsten (WO₃)	lb.	—	—	—	—	—	—
	$	—	—	—	—	—	—
Uranium (U₃O₈)	lb.	1,148	1,682	—	—	—	—
	$	..	..	—	—	—	—
Yttrium (Y₂O₃)	lb.	—	—	—	—	—	—
	$	—	—	—	—	—	—
Zinc	lb.	13,012	9,135	—	—	171,374	218,744
	$	4,541	3,426	—	—	59,810	82,029
NON-METALLICS	$	327,666	375,294	73,922	96,249	36,814	50,306
Asbestos	ton	—	—	—	—	92	97
	$	—	—	—	—	27,399	38,809
Barite	ton	—	—	—	—	..	..
	$	—	—	—	—	514	633
Diatomite	ton	—	—	—	—	..	..
	$	—	—	—	—	..	..
Feldspar	ton	—	—	—	—	—	—
	$	—	—	—	—	—	—
Fluorspar	ton	—	—	—	—	—	—
	$	—	—	—	—	—	—
Gemstones	lb.	—	—	—	—	8	..
	$	—	—	—	—	19	18
Gypsum	ton	—	—	—	—	441	450
	$	—	—	—	—	1,412	2,214
Helium	Mcf	..	..	—	—	—	—
	$	..	..	—	—	—	—
Magnesitic dolomite and brucite	ton	—	—	—	—	—	—
	$	—	—	—	—	—	—
Nepheline syenite	ton	—	—	—	—	—	—
	$	—	—	—	—	—	—
Nitrogen	Mcf	..	..	—	—	—	—
	$	..	..	—	—	—	—
Peat moss	ton	7	7	7	18	71	64
	$	436	300	444	730	4,392	4,100
Potash (K₂O)	ton	6,367	5,346	—	—	—	—
	$	308,925	346,806	—	—	—	—
Pyrite, pyrrhotite	ton	—	—	—	—	—	—
	$	—	—	—	—	—	—
Quartz	ton	151	122	..	..	20	35
	$	189	152	437	762	134	195
Salt	ton	296	292	356	313	—	—
	$	5,281	6,891	3,840	4,159	—	—
Soapstone, talc, pyrophyllite	ton	—	—	—	—	—	—
	$	—	—	—	—	—	—

12.8   Detailed mineral production, by province, 1974 and 1975ᴾ (thousands) (continued)   M

Mineral		Province or territory					
		Saskatchewan		Alberta		British Columbia	
		1974	1975	1974	1975	1974	1975
METALLICS	$	*22,268*	*18,542*	*15*	—	*709,178*	*588,692*
Antimony	kg	—	—	—	—	221	195
	$					880	835
Bismuth	kg	—	—	—	—	34	23
	$					609	393
Cadmium	kg	15	4	—	—	196	341
	$	129	25	—	—	1,718	2,008
Calcium	kg	—	—	—	—	—	—
	$						
Cobalt	kg	—	—	—	—	—	—
	$						
Columbium (Cb₂O₅)	kg	—	—	—	—	—	—
	$						
Copper	kg	7 987	7 713	—	—	287 549	241 310
	$	13,650	10,831	—	—	491,426	338,883
Gold	g	471	435	3	—	5 041	4 479
	$	2,354	2,352	15	—	25,174	23,821
Indium	g	—	—	—	—	8 056	..
	$						
Iron ore	t	—	—	—	—	1 307	1 247
	$	—	—	—	—	12,757	14,599
Iron, remelt	t	—	—	—	—	—	—
	$						
Lead	kg	—	—	—	—	55 253	69 352
	$					25,222	31,114
Magnesium	kg	—	—	—	—	—	—
	$						
Mercury	kg	—	—	—	—	483	..
	$						
Molybdenum	kg	—	—	—	—	13 790	12 150
	$					60,792	67,303
Nickel	kg	—	—	—	—	689	—
	$					2,579	
Platinum group	g	—	—	—	—	—	—
	$						
Selenium	kg	15	16	—	—	—	—
	$	513	640	—	—		
Silver	kg	7	8	..	—	182	189
	$	1,042	1,230	..	—	27,043	27,447
Tantalum (Ta₂O₅)	kg	—	—	—	—	—	—
	$						
Tellurium	kg	2	2	—	—	—	—
	$	38	38	—	—		
Tin	kg	—	—	—	—	143	34
	$					1,167	260
Tungsten (WO₃)	kg	—	—	—	—	—	—
	$						
Uranium (U₃O₈)	kg	521	763	—	—	—	—
	$	..	..	—	—	—	—
Yttrium (Y₂O₃)	kg	—	—	—	—	—	—
	$						
Zinc	kg	5 902	4 144	—	—	77 734	99 221
	$	4,541	3,426	—	—	59,810	82,029
NON-METALLICS	$	*327,666*	*375,294*	*73,922*	*96,249*	*36,814*	*50,306*
Asbestos	t	—	—	—	—	83	88
	$	—	—	—	—	27,399	38,809
Barite	t	—	—	—	—	..	..
	$	—	—	—	—	514	633
Diatomite	t	—	—	—	—	..	..
	$	—	—	—	—	..	..
Feldspar	t	—	—	—	—	..	..
	$						
Fluorspar	t	—	—	—	—	—	—
	$						
Gemstones	kg	—	—	—	—	4	..
	$					19	18
Gypsum	t	—	—	—	—	400	408
	$	—	—	—	—	1,412	2,214
Helium	m³	..	..	—	—	—	—
	$	..	..	—	—	—	—
Magnesitic dolomite and brucite	t	—	—	—	—	—	—
	$						
Nepheline syenite	t	—	—	—	—	—	—
	$						
Nitrogen	m³	..	..	—	—	—	—
	$	..	..	—	—	—	—
Peat moss	t	6	6	6	16	64	58
	$	436	300	444	730	4,392	4,100
Potash (K₂O)	t	5 776	4 850	—	—	—	—
	$	308,925	346,806	—	—	—	—
Pyrite, pyrrhotite	t	—	—	—	—	—	—
	$						
Quartz	t	137	111	..	..	18	32
	$	189	152	437	762	134	195
Salt	t	269	265	323	284	—	—
	$	5,281	6,891	3,840	4,159	—	—
Soapstone, talc, pyrophyllite	t	—	—	—	—	—	—
	$	—	—	—	—	—	—

12.8   Detailed mineral production, by province, 1974 and 1975ᵖ (thousands) (continued)

Mineral		Saskatchewan 1974	Saskatchewan 1975	Alberta 1974	Alberta 1975	British Columbia 1974	British Columbia 1975
NON-METALLICS (concluded)							
Sodium sulphate	ton	...	...	...	...	—	—
	$	12,629	20,913	1,563	2,849	—	—
Sulphur, in smelter gas	ton	—	—	—	—	167	236
	$	—	—	—	—	2,241	3,170
Sulphur, elemental	ton	17	15	5,470	4,404	59	55
	$	206	232	67,638	87,749	704	1,167
Titanium dioxide, etc.	ton	—	—	—	—	—	—
	$	—	—	—	—	—	—
FUELS	$	421,354	413,979	4,376,520	5,827,932	330,208	506,399
Coal	ton	3,842	3,750	9,337	10,500	8,532	10,450
	$	8,317	8,900	111,031	185,000	153,567	327,200
Natural gas	Mcf	61,636	61,000	2,537,515	2,580,006	405,809	389,570
	$	9,001	9,455	645,138	1,639,898	60,581	70,123
Natural gas by-products	bbl	1,085	1,015	109,871	107,114	2,348	2,339
	$	6,201	5,878	634,802	748,063	12,559	13,825
Oil, crude	bbl	73,947	58,171	515,437	446,359	18,948	14,432
	$	397,835	389,746	2,985,549	3,254,971	103,501	95,251
STRUCTURAL MATERIALS	$	19,042	18,721	67,926	76,668	79,587	78,518
Clay products	$	2,406	2,672	6,177	7,299	5,811	3,674
Cement	ton	266	240	1,052	977	981	1,026
	$	6,901	6,249	26,780	25,410	27,088	28,731
Lime	ton	—	—	156	133	34	40
	$	—	—	3,035	2,659	851	1,013
Sand and gravel	ton	11,840	11,500	24,703	23,400	34,225	30,200
	$	9,736	9,800	31,042	40,300	35,265	35,600
Stone	ton	—	—	180	200	4,642	3,900
	$	—	—	892	1,000	10,571	9,500
Total 1974	$	790,330	...	4,518,383	...	1,155,787	...
Total 1975	$	...	826,536	...	6,000,849	...	1,223,915

Mineral		Yukon Territory 1974	Yukon Territory 1975	Northwest Territories 1974	Northwest Territories 1975	Canada 1974	Canada 1975
METALLICS	$	148,596	196,689	214,346	181,787	4,820,675	4,812,449
Antimony	lb.	—	—	—	—	...	...
	$	—	—	—	—	5,619	5,516
Bismuth	lb.	—	—	—	—	245	81
	$	—	—	—	—	2,006	643
Cadmium	lb.	4	4	—	—	2,736	2,682
	$	17	11	—	—	10,881	7,162
Calcium	lb.	—	—	—	—	1,050	826
	$	—	—	—	—	915	1,108
Cobalt	lb.	—	—	—	—	3,447	2,949
	$	—	—	—	—	10,114	11,578
Columbium (Cb₂O₅)	lb.	—	—	—	—	4,233	3,714
	$	—	—	—	—	6,680	6,430
Copper	lb.	20,087	18,180	1,085	551	1,810,834	1,596,263
	$	15,571	11,580	841	351	1,402,571	1,016,819
Gold	oz t	26	26	184	186	1,698	1,674
	$	4,112	4,245	28,651	30,752	263,794	276,125
Indium	oz t	—	—	—	—	259	...
	$	—	—	—	—	...	...
Iron ore	ton	—	—	—	—	51,571	49,415
	$	—	—	—	—	724,150	923,184
Iron, remelt	ton	—	—	—	—	...	...
	$	—	—	—	—	71,286	75,595
Lead	lb.	198,950	276,466	168,708	151,555	648,750	746,130
	$	41,195	56,260	34,933	30,841	134,330	151,837
Magnesium	lb.	—	—	—	—	13,133	9,922
	$	—	—	—	—	9,260	8,324
Mercury	lb.	—	—	—	—	1,064	...
	$	—	—	—	—	...	...
Molybdenum	lb.	—	—	—	—	30,736	27,414
	$	—	—	—	—	61,778	68,893
Nickel	lb.	—	—	—	—	593,199	539,652
	$	—	—	—	—	974,594	1,109,230
Platinum group	oz t	—	—	—	—	385	430
	$	—	—	—	—	60,794	61,231
Selenium	lb.	—	—	—	—	600	670
	$	—	—	—	—	9,449	10,575
Silver	oz t	5,790	6,516	3,817	2,174	42,810	39,101
	$	26,801	29,434	17,670	9,821	198,166	176,627
Tantalum (Ta₂O₅)	lb.	—	—	—	—	438	395
	$	—	—	—	—	3,576	3,260
Tellurium	lb.	—	—	—	—	124	80
	$	—	—	—	—	1,009	763
Tin	lb.	—	—	—	—	714	623
	$	—	—	—	—	2,565	2,192
Tungsten (WO₃)	lb.	—	—	3,558	2,987	3,558	2,987
	$	—	—	...	...	...	...
Uranium (U₃O₈)	lb.	—	—	—	—	9,591	12,251

12.8   Detailed mineral production, by province, 1974 and 1975ᴾ (thousands) (continued)   M

Mineral		Province or territory					
		Saskatchewan		Alberta		British Columbia	
		1974	1975	1974	1975	1974	1975
NON-METALLICS (concluded)							
Sodium sulphate	t	..	..				
	$	12,629	20,913	1,563	2,849	—	—
Sulphur, in smelter gas	t	—	—	—	—	151	214
	$	—	—	—	—	2,241	3,170
Sulphur, elemental	t	16	14	4 962	3 995	54	50
	$	206	232	67,638	87,749	704	1,167
Titanium dioxide, etc.	t	—	—	—	—	—	—
	$	—	—	—	—	—	—
FUELS	$	421,354	413,979	4,376,520	5,827,932	330,208	506,399
Coal	t	3 485	3 402	8 470	9 525	7 740	9 480
	$	8,317	8,900	111,031	185,000	153,567	327,200
Natural gas	m³	1 746 015	1 727 998	71 882 321	73 086 000	11 495 693	11 035 677
	$	9,001	9,455	645,138	1,639,898	60,581	70,123
Natural gas by-products	m³	173	161	17 468	17 030	373	372
	$	6,201	5,878	634,802	748,063	12,559	13,825
Oil, crude	m³	11 757	9 248	81 948	70 965	3 012	2 295
	$	397,835	389,746	2,985,549	3,254,971	103,501	95,251
STRUCTURAL MATERIALS	$	19,042	18,721	67,926	76,668	79,587	78,518
Clay products	$	2,406	2,672	6,177	7,299	5,811	3,674
Cement	t	242	218	955	886	890	931
	$	6,901	6,249	26,780	25,410	27,088	28,731
Lime	t	—	—	141	121	31	36
	$	—	—	3,035	2,659	851	1,013
Sand and gravel	t	10 741	10 433	22 410	21 228	31 048	27 397
	$	9,736	9,800	31,042	40,300	35,265	35,600
Stone	t	—	—	163	181	4 211	3 538
	$	—	—	892	1,000	10,571	9,500
Total 1974	$	790,330	...	4,518,383	...	1,155,787	...
Total 1975	$	...	826,536	...	6,000,849	...	1,223,915

		Yukon Territory		Northwest Territories		Canada	
		1974	1975	1974	1975	1974	1975
METALLICS	$	148,596	196,689	214,346	181,787	4,820,675	4,812,449
Antimony	kg	—	—	—	—	..	..
	$	—	—	—	—	5,619	5,516
Bismuth	kg	—	—	—	—	111	37
	$	—	—	—	—	2,006	643
Cadmium	kg	2	2	—	—	1 241	1 217
	$	17	11	—	—	10,881	7,162
Calcium	kg	—	—	—	—	476	375
	$	—	—	—	—	915	1,108
Cobalt	kg	—	—	—	—	1 564	1 338
	$	—	—	—	—	10,114	11,578
Columbium (Cb_2O_5)	kg	—	—	—	—	1 920	1 685
	$	—	—	—	—	6,680	6,430
Copper	kg	9 111	8 246	492	250	821 380	724 053
	$	15,571	11,580	841	351	1,402,571	1,016,819
Gold	g	823	809	5 738	5 785	52 826	52 067
	$	4,112	4,245	28,651	30,752	263,794	276,125
Indium	g	—	—	—	—	8 056	..
	$						
Iron ore	t	—	—	—	—	46 785	44 829
	$	—	—	—	—	724,150	923,184
Iron, remelt	t	—	—	—	—	..	..
	$	—	—	—	—	71,286	75,595
Lead	kg	90 242	125 403	76 525	68 744	294 268	338 439
	$	41,195	56,260	34,933	30,841	134,330	151,837
Magnesium	kg	—	—	—	—	5 957	4 501
	$	—	—	—	—	9,260	8,324
Mercury	kg	—	—	—	—	483	..
	$						
Molybdenum	kg	—	—	—	—	13 942	12 435
	$	—	—	—	—	61,778	68,893
Nickel	kg	—	—	—	—	269 071	244 782
	$	—	—	—	—	974,594	1,109,230
Platinum group	g	—	—	—	—	11 963	13 374
	$	—	—	—	—	60,794	61,231
Selenium	kg	—	—	—	—	272	304
	$	—	—	—	—	9,449	10,575
Silver	kg	180	202	119	68	1 332	1 216
	$	26,801	29,434	17,670	9,821	198,166	176,627
Tantalum (Ta_2O_5)	kg	—	—	—	—	199	179
	$	—	—	—	—	3,576	3,260
Tellurium	kg	—	—	—	—	56	36
	$	—	—	—	—	1,009	763
Tin	kg	—	—	—	—	324	283
	$	—	—	—	—	2,565	2,192
Tungsten (WO_3)	kg	—	—	1 614	1 355	1 614	1 355
	$	—	—	..	..	..	..
Uranium (U_3O_8)	kg	—	—	—	—	4 350	5 557
	$	—	—	—	—	..	..

12.8   Detailed mineral production, by province, 1974 and 1975ᴾ (thousands) (concluded)

Mineral		Province or territory					
		Yukon Territory		Northwest Territories		Canada	
		1974	1975	1974	1975	1974	1975
METALLICS (concluded)							
Yttrium (Y₂O₃)	lb.	—	—	—	—	..	..
	$	—	—	—	—	..	..
Zinc	lb.	174,499	253,757	378,944	293,392	2,484,628	2,387,617
	$	60,900	95,159	132,251	110,022	867,135	895,357
NON-METALLICS	$	22,752	31,970	—	—	895,437	929,172
Asbestos	ton	91	112	—	—	1,812	1,143
	$	22,752	31,970	—	—	302,013	266,943
Barite	ton					..	..
	$	—	—	—	—	978	1,083
Diatomite	ton	—	—	—	—	..	..
	$	—	—	—	—	..	..
Feldspar	ton	—	—	—	—	—	—
	$	—	—	—	—	—	—
Fluorspar	ton	—	—	—	—	..	..
	$	—	—	—	—	7,119	7,000
Gemstones	lb.	—	—	—	—	8	..
	$	—	—	—	—	19	18
Gypsum	ton	—	—	—	—	7,964	6,255
	$	—	—	—	—	22,437	19,720
Helium	Mcf	—	—	—	—	..	..
	$	—	—	—	—	..	..
Magnesitic dolomite and brucite	ton	—	—	—	—	..	..
	$	—	—	—	—	4,358	4,000
Nepheline syenite	ton	—	—	—	—	617	520
	$	—	—	—	—	9,179	8,663
Nitrogen	Mcf	—	—	—	—	..	..
	$	—	—	—	—	..	..
Peat moss	ton	—	—	—	—	407	383
	$	—	—	—	—	20,853	20,630
Potash (K₂O)	ton	—	—	—	—	6,367	5,346
	$	—	—	—	—	308,925	346,806
Pyrite, pyrrhotite	ton	—	—	—	—	54	21
	$	—	—	—	—	347	90
Quartz	ton	—	—	—	—	2,762	2,561
	$	—	—	—	—	12,184	13,499
Salt	ton	—	—	—	—	6,004	5,683
	$	—	—	—	—	60,619	60,593
Soapstone, talc, pyrophyllite	ton	—	—	—	—	95	74
	$	—	—	—	—	1,913	1,683
Sodium sulphate	ton	—	—	—	—	703	546
	$	—	—	—	—	14,192	23,762
Sulphur, in smelter gas	ton	—	—	—	—	731	776
	$	—	—	—	—	9,813	10,417
Sulphur, elemental	ton	—	—	—	—	5,548	4,476
	$	—	—	—	—	68,556	89,190
Titanium dioxide, etc.	ton	—	—	—	—	..	..
	$	—	—	—	—	51,931	55,075
FUELS	$	190	239	8,704	7,690	5,201,723	6,854,264
Coal	ton	—	—	—	—	23,536	27,000
	$	—	—	—	—	302,826	575,800
Natural gas	Mcf	1,138	2,076	31,600	29,196	3,045,506	3,074,659
	$	190	239	5,537	3,450	723,766	1,729,631
Natural gas by-products	bbl	—	—	—	—	113,304	110,468
	$	—	—	—	—	653,562	767,766
Oil, crude	bbl	—	—	954	1,210	614,777	525,342
	$	—	—	3,167	4,240	3,521,569	3,781,067
STRUCTURAL MATERIALS	$	—	—	—	—	793,170[1]	806,718[2]
Clay products	$	—	—	—	—	70,621	69,956
Cement	ton	—	—	—	—	11,436	10,763
	$	—	—	—	—	274,649	265,283
Lime	ton	—	—	—	—	2,009	1,889
	$	—	—	—	—	41,812	40,439
Sand and gravel	ton	—	—	—	—	236,588[1]	224,960[2]
	$	—	—	—	—	238,620[1]	260,340[2]
Stone	ton	—	—	—	—	97,485	97,100
	$	—	—	—	—	167,468	170,700
Total 1974	$	171,538	..	223,050	..	11,711,004[1]	..
Total 1975	$	..	228,898	..	189,477	..	13,402,603[2]

[1] Includes 974,398 tons of sand and gravel valued at $1,453,966 produced in Prince Edward Island.
[2] Includes 960,000 tons of sand and gravel valued at $1,540,000 produced in Prince Edward Island.

12.8   Detailed mineral production, by province, 1974 and 1975ᵖ (thousands) (concluded)   M

Mineral		Province or territory					
		Yukon Territory		Northwest Territories		Canada	
		1974	1975	1974	1975	1974	1975
METALLICS (concluded)							
Yttrium (Y₂O₃)	kg	—	—	—	—	..	..
	$	—	—	—	—	..	..
Zinc	kg	79 151	115 102	171 886	133 080	1 127 008	1 083 005
	$	60,900	95,159	132,251	110,022	867,135	895,357
NON-METALLICS	$	*22,752*	*31,970*	—	—	*895,437*	*929,172*
Asbestos	t	82	102	—	—	1 644	1 037
	$	22,752	31,970	—	—	302,013	266,943
Barite	t	—	—	—	—	..	..
	$	—	—	—	—	978	1,083
Diatomite	t	—	—	—	—	..	..
	$	—	—	—	—	..	..
Feldspar	t	—	—	—	—	..	..
	$	—	—	—	—	—	—
Fluorspar	t	—	—	—	—	..	..
	$	—	—	—	—	7,119	7,000
Gemstones	kg	—	—	—	—	4	..
	$	—	—	—	—	19	18
Gypsum	t	—	—	—	—	7 225	5 674
	$	—	—	—	—	22,437	19,720
Helium	m³	—	—	—	—	..	..
	$	—	—	—	—	..	..
Magnesitic dolomite and brucite	t	—	—	—	—	..	..
	$	—	—	—	—	4,358	4,000
Nepheline syenite	t	—	—	—	—	560	472
	$	—	—	—	—	9,179	8,663
Nitrogen	m³	—	—	—	—	..	..
	$	—	—	—	—	..	..
Peat moss	t	—	—	—	—	369	347
	$	—	—	—	—	20,853	20,630
Potash (K₂O)	t	—	—	—	—	5 776	4 850
	$	—	—	—	—	308,925	346,806
Pyrite, pyrrhotite	t	—	—	—	—	49	19
	$	—	—	—	—	347	90
Quartz	t	—	—	—	—	2 506	2 323
	$	—	—	—	—	12,184	13,499
Salt	t	—	—	—	—	5 447	5 156
	$	—	—	—	—	60,619	60,593
Soapstone, talc, pyrophyllite	t	—	—	—	—	86	67
	$	—	—	—	—	1,913	1,683
Sodium sulphate	t	—	—	—	—	638	495
	$	—	—	—	—	14,192	23,762
Sulphur, in smelter gas	t	—	—	—	—	663	704
	$	—	—	—	—	9,813	10,417
Sulphur, elemental	t	—	—	—	—	5 033	4 061
	$	—	—	—	—	68,556	89,190
Titanium dioxide, etc.	t	—	—	—	—	..	..
	$	—	—	—	—	51,931	55,075
FUELS	$	*190*	*239*	*8,704*	*7,690*	*5,201,723*	*6,854,264*
Coal	t	—	—	—	—	21 352	24 494
	$	—	—	—	—	302,826	575,800
Natural gas	m³	32 237	58 809	895 160	827 060	86 272 610	87 098 452
	$	190	239	5,537	3,450	723,766	1,729,631
Natural gas by-products	m³	—	—	—	—	18 014	17 563
	$	—	—	—	—	653,562	767,766
Oil, crude	m³	—	—	152	192	97 742	83 523
	$	—	—	3,167	4,240	3,521,569	3,781,067
STRUCTURAL MATERIALS	$	—	—	—	—	*793,170*[1]	*806,718*[2]
Clay products	$	—	—	—	—	70,621	69,956
Cement	t	—	—	—	—	10 375	9 764
	$	—	—	—	—	274,649	265,283
Lime	t	—	—	—	—	1 823	1 714
	$	—	—	—	—	41,812	40,439
Sand and gravel	t	—	—	—	—	214 629[1]	204 081[2]
	$	—	—	—	—	238,620[1]	260,340[2]
Stone	t	—	—	—	—	88 437	88 088
	$	—	—	—	—	167,468	170,700
Total 1974	$	171,538	..	223,050	..	11,711,004[1]	..
Total 1975	$	..	228,898	..	189,477	..	13,402,603[2]

[1]Includes 883 959 t of sand and gravel valued at $1,453,966 produced in Prince Edward Island.
[2]Includes 870 898 t of sand and gravel valued at $1,540,000 produced in Prince Edward Island.

12.9 Producers' shipments of copper, by province, and total value, 1969-75

Year	Newfoundland tons	Nova Scotia tons	New Brunswick tons	Quebec tons	Ontario tons	Manitoba tons
1969	20,464	19	6,791	160,068	238,810	37,097
1970	15,193	27	8,022	172,642	295,092	47,906
1971	13,980	16	10,266	184,823	302,370	55,264
1972	9,513	—	10,310	176,432	289,723	59,832
1973	8,647	3	10,310	157,841	287,324	71,333
1974	6,233	5	12,532	158,991	312,943	78,356
1975p	8,190	—	13,139	129,858	292,296	70,782

Year	Saskatchewan tons	British Columbia tons	Yukon Territory tons	Northwest Territories tons	Canada Shipments tons	Canada Value $'000
1969	18,230	83,708	7,433	626	573,246	588,281
1970	19,473	105,822	7,880	660	672,717	779,242
1971	11,146	140,310	2,566	689	721,430	760,016
1972	12,546	233,506	874	567	793,303	806,427
1973	10,224	350,099	11,593	867	908,241	1,157,507
1974	8,804	316,968	10,043	542	905,417	1,402,571
1975p	8,502	265,999	9,090	276	798,132	1,016,819

12.10 Producers' shipments of nickel, by province, and total value, 1969-75

Year	Quebec tons	Ontario tons	Manitoba tons	Saskatchewan tons	British Columbia tons	Yukon Territory tons	Canada Quantity tons	Canada Value $'000
1969	155	146,781	64,920	266	1,490	—	213,612	481,055
1970	801	224,255	79,121	—	1,704	—	305,881	830,167
1971	748	215,754	76,568	—	1,272	—	294,342	800,064
1972	305	189,428	66,227	—	1,620	1,407	258,987	717,485
1973	362	196,647	74,582	—	1,234	1,702	274,527	813,101
1974	—	230,440	65,401	—	759	—	296,600	974,594
1975p	—	199,440	70,386	—	—	—	269,826	1,109,230

12.11 Iron ore shipments and production of pig iron and steel ingots and castings, 1969-75

Year	Iron ore shipments: Newfoundland (incl. Labrador) '000 tons	Quebec '000 tons	Ontario '000 tons	British Columbia '000 tons	Canada Quantity '000 tons	Canada Value $'000	Production of pig iron '000 tons	Production of steel ingots and castings '000 tons
1969	14,716	12,779	10,517	2,042	40,054	454,076	7,431	10,048
1970	23,559	15,048	11,828	1,879	52,314	588,631	9,069	12,250
1971	21,877	12,367	11,178	1,930	47,352	555,136	8,635	12,177
1972	18,072	11,615	11,755	1,256	42,698	489,023	9,356r	13,067r
1973	24,398	13,971	12,424	1,565	52,358	606,106	10,524r	14,665r
1974	24,280	13,829	12,021	1,441	51,571	724,150	10,386	15,017
1975p	25,576	12,200	10,264	1,375	49,415	923,184	10,086	14,357

12.12 Producers' shipments of lead from Canadian ores, by province, and total value, 1969-75

Year	Newfoundland tons	Nova Scotia tons	New Brunswick tons	Quebec tons	Ontario tons
1969	22,207	2,735	51,092	1,558	12,097
1970	17,730	1,299	62,675	2,159	11,960
1971	13,481	415	65,405	647	8,915
1972	12,202	—	45,490	1,676	10,605
1973	8,444	291	44,011	1,351	11,496
1974	15,490	217	52,722	1,056	10,111
1975p	11,176	—	62,264	1,597	7,426

Year	Manitoba tons	British Columbia tons	Yukon Territory tons	Northwest Territories tons	Canada Quantity tons	Canada Value $'000
1969	560	105,036	14,028	106,457	318,632[1]	96,673
1970	505	107,419	65,835	119,603	389,185	123,138
1971	201	123,964	108,668	83,814	405,510	109,488
1972	196	97,575	111,461	90,220	369,425	113,990
1973	64	93,577	117,761	99,944	376,939	121,676
1974	44	60,906	99,475	84,354	324,375	134,330
1975p	144	76,447	138,234	75,777	373,065	151,837

[1]Includes 2,862 tons of producers' shipments from Saskatchewan in 1969.

12.9   Producers' shipments of copper, by province, and total value, 1969-75   M

Year	Province or territory					
	New-foundland t	Nova Scotia t	New Brunswick t	Quebec t	Ontario t	Manitoba t
1969	18 565	17	6 161	145 211	216 645	33 654
1970	13 783	24	7 277	156 618	267 703	43 460
1971	12 682	15	9 313	167 669	274 305	50 135
1972	8 630	—	9 353	160 056	262 832	54 279
1973	7 844	3	9 353	143 191	260 656	64 712
1974	5 654	5	11 369	144 234	283 897	71 083
1975P	7 430	—	11 920	117 805	265 166	64 212

Year	Saskat-chewan t	British Columbia t	Yukon Territory t	Northwest Territories t	Canada Shipments t	Value $\$'000$
1969	16 538	75 939	6 743	568	520 041	588,281
1970	17 666	96 000	7 149	599	610 279	779,242
1971	10 111	127 287	2 328	625	654 470	760,016
1972	11 382	211 833	793	514	719 672	806,427
1973	9 275	317 604	10 517	787	823 942	1,157,507
1974	7 987	287 549	9 111	492	821 381	1,402,571
1975P	7 713	241 310	8 246	250	724 052	1,016,819

12.10   Producers' shipments of nickel, by province, and total value, 1969-75   M

Year	Quebec t	Ontario t	Manitoba t	Saskat-chewan t	British Columbia t	Yukon Territory t	Canada Quantity t	Value $\$'000$
1969	141	133 157	58 894	241	1 352	—	193 785	481,055
1970	727	203 441	71 777	—	1 546	—	277 491	830,167
1971	679	195 729	69 461	—	1 154	—	267 023	800,064
1972	277	171 846	60 080	—	1 470	1276	234 949	717,485
1973	328	178 395	67 660	—	1 119	1544	249 046	813,101
1974	—	209 052	59 331	—	689	—	269 072	974,594
1975P	—	180 929	63 853	—	—	—	244 782	1,109,230

12.11   Iron ore shipments and production of pig iron and steel ingots and castings, 1969-75   M

Year	Iron ore shipments						Production of pig iron $'000\ t$	Production of steel ingots and castings $'000\ t$
	Newfound-land (incl. Labrador) $'000\ t$	Quebec $'000\ t$	Ontario $'000\ t$	British Columbia $'000\ t$	Canada Quantity $'000\ t$	Value $\$'000$		
1969	13 350	11 593	9 541	1 852	36 336	454,076	6 741	9 115
1970	21 372	13 651	10 730	1 705	47 458	588,631	8 227	11 113
1971	19 846	11 219	10 141	1 751	42 957	555,136	7 834	11 047
1972	16 395	10 537	10 664	1 139	38 735	489,023	8 488	11 854
1973	22 133	12 674	11 271	1 420	47 498	606,106	9 547	13 304
1974	22 026	12 545	10 905	1 307	46 784	724,150	9 422	13 623
1975P	23 202	11 068	9 311	1 247	44 828	923,184	9 150	13 024

12.12   Producers' shipments of lead from Canadian ores, by province, and total value, 1969-75   M

Year	Province or territory				
	Newfoundland t	Nova Scotia t	New Brunswick t	Quebec t	Ontario t
1969	20 146	2 481	46 350	1 413	10 974
1970	16 084	1 178	56 858	1 959	10 850
1971	12 230	376	59 334	587	8 088
1972	11 069	—	41 268	1 520	9 621
1973	7 660	264	39 926	1 226	10 429
1974	14 052	197	47 829	958	9 173
1975P	10 139	—	56 485	1 449	6 737

Year	Manitoba t	British Columbia t	Yukon Territory t	Northwest Territories t	Canada Quantity t	Value $\$'000$
1969	508	95 287	12 726	96 576	289 057[1]	96,673
1970	458	97 449	59 725	108 502	353 063	123,138
1971	182	112 458	98 582	76 035	367 872	109,488
1972	178	88 519	101 116	81 846	335 137	113,990
1973	58	84 892	106 831	90 668	341 954	121,676
1974	40	55 253	90 242	76 525	294 269	134,330
1975P	131	69 352	125 404	68 744	338 439	151,837

[1]Includes 2 596 t of producers' shipments from Saskatchewan in 1969.

12.13 Producers' shipments of zinc, by province, and total value, 1969-75

Year	Province or territory					
	Newfoundland _tons_	Nova Scotia _tons_	New Brunswick _tons_	Quebec _tons_	Ontario _tons_	Manitoba _tons_
1969	32,903	132	152,728	198,531	360,286	48,889
1970	29,913	—	161,094	205,030	340,242	39,463
1971	20,833	—	161,514	174,419	365,725	24,986
1972	26,582	—	174,536	163,244	403,391r	45,607
1973	8,695	—	192,563	155,259	456,364	66,396
1974	21,045	—	165,136	138,282	480,059	68,877
1975P	27,725	—	203,143	131,015	371,339	73,073

Year	Saskatchewan _tons_	British Columbia _tons_	Yukon Territory _tons_	Northwest Territories _tons_	Canada Quantity _tons_	Value _$'000_
1969	25,143	148,333	16,531	224,148	1,207,624	367,842
1970	21,833	137,795	77,983	238,558	1,251,911	398,859
1971	8,647	152,726	116,567	224,317	1,249,734	418,161
1972	16,625	134,174	118,613	169,870	1,252,642r	477,783r
1973	13,424	151,437	126,661	181,275	1,352,074	652,944
1974	6,506	85,687	87,249	189,472	1,242,313	867,135
1975P	4,568	109,372	126,878	146,696	1,193,809	895,357

12.14 Producers' shipments of gold, by province, and total value, 1969-75

Year	Province or territory						
	New-foundland _oz t_	Nova Scotia _oz t_	New Brunswick _oz t_	Quebec _oz t_	Ontario _oz t_	Manitoba _oz t_	Saskat-chewan _oz t_
1969	8,982	13	1,396	761,370	1,229,666	28,011	39,562
1970	6,811	—	5,120	703,015	1,162,042	34,642	44,889
1971	7,341	—	4,236	646,839	1,133,987	30,063	25,960
1972	14,069	42	3,205	539,669	1,019,303	38,032	30,527
1973	14,345	—	5,202	478,680	922,303	48,023	26,527
1974	11,605	—	4,296	440,559	801,105	52,554	15,156
1975P	13,000	—	5,000	465,000	775,000	46,000	14,000

Year	Alberta _oz t_	British Columbia _oz t_	Yukon Territory _oz t_	Northwest Territories _oz t_	Canada Quantity _oz t_	Value _$'000_
1969	133	117,792	29,682	328,502	2,545,109	95,925
1970	152	101,197	17,862	332,844	2,408,574	88,057
1971	79	89,413	14,473	308,339	2,260,730	79,903
1972	3	122,159	4,079	307,479	2,078,567	119,742
1973	175	189,145	20,865	249,075	1,954,340	190,376
1974	97	162,081	26,472	184,467	1,698,392	263,794
1975P	—	144,000	26,000	186,000	1,674,000	276,125

12.15 Producers' shipments of silver, by province, and total value, 1969-75

Year	Average price per oz t (Canadian funds) $	Province or territory					
		New-foundland _oz t_	Nova Scotia _oz t_	New Brunswick _oz t_	Quebec _oz t_	Ontario _oz t_	Manitoba _oz t_
1969	1.93	1,024,639	267,585	4,058,976	4,334,867	22,260,439	462,763
1970	1.85	793,402	71,668	4,577,956	4,261,959	19,876,430	660,755
1971	1.56	563,604	55,292	5,057,627	4,378,011	18,681,633	694,298
1972	1.67	572,928	7	3,906,470	3,558,027	19,587,694	808,376
1973	2.53	572,918	22,838	3,568,678	3,050,999	19,617,406	1,082,763
1974	4.63	555,689	25,190	4,464,463	2,970,356	17,852,419	1,267,403
1975P	4.52	528,000	—	4,790,000	3,245,000	14,506,000	994,000

Year		Saskat-chewan _oz t_	British Columbia _oz t_	Yukon Territory _oz t_	Northwest Territories _oz t_	Canada Quantity _oz t_	Value _$'000_
1969	1.93	649,699	5,760,534	2,685,060	2,026,367	43,530,941[1]	84,015
1970	1.85	491,953	6,511,316	4,240,709	2,764,642	44,250,804[1]	81,864
1971	1.56	238,763	7,674,186	5,747,703	2,932,446	46,023,570[1]	71,797
1972	1.67	384,443	6,926,036	4,988,967	4,059,261	44,792,209	74,803
1973	2.53	458,241	7,619,413	6,073,973	5,420,344	47,487,589[1]	119,954
1974	4.63	225,203	5,841,995	5,789,783	3,817,207	42,809,721[1]	198,166
1975P	4.52	272,000	6,076,000	6,516,000	2,174,000	39,101,000	176,627

[1]Includes relatively small quantities produced in Alberta.

12.13   Producers' shipments of zinc, by province, and total value, 1969-75   M

Year	Newfoundland	Nova Scotia	New Brunswick	Quebec	Ontario	Manitoba
	t	t	t	t	t	t
1969	29 849	120	138 553	180 104	326 846	44 351
1970	27 137	—	146 142	186 000	308 662	35 800
1971	18 899	—	146 523	158 230	331 780	22 667
1972	24 115	—	158 336	148 092	365 950	41 374
1973	7 888	—	174 690	140 849	414 006	60 233
1974	19 092	—	149 809	125 447	435 502	62 484
1975P	25 152	—	184 288	118 855	336 873	66 291

Year	Saskatchewan	British Columbia	Yukon Territory	Northwest Territories	Canada Quantity	Value
	t	t	t	t	t	$'000
1969	22 809	134 565	14 997	203 344	1 095 538	367,842
1970	19 807	125 006	70 745	216 416	1 135 715	398,859
1971	7 844	138 551	105 748	203 497	1 133 739	418,161
1972	15 082	121 721	107 604	154 103	1 136 377	477,783r
1973	12 178	137 381	114 905	164 450	1 226 580	652,944
1974	5 902	77 734	79 151	171 886	1 127 007	867,135
1975P	4 144	99 221	115 102	133 080	1 083 006	895,357

12.14   Producers' shipments of gold, by province, and total value, 1969-75   M

Year	Newfoundland	Nova Scotia	New Brunswick	Quebec	Ontario	Manitoba	Saskatchewan
	g	g	g	g	g	g	g
1969	279 371	404	43 420	23 681 254	38 246 888	871 239	1 230 516
1970	211 846	—	159 250	21 866 211	36 143 546	1 077 487	1 396 204
1971	228 331	—	131 754	20 118 942	35 270 938	935 064	807 446
1972	437 595	1 306	99 687	16 785 582	31 703 867	1 182 927	949 496
1973	446 179	—	161 800	14 888 612	28 686 830	1 493 682	825 082
1974	360 956	—	133 621	13 702 917	24 917 151	1 634 612	471 404
1975P	404 345	—	155 517	14 463 117	24 105 195	1 430 760	435 449

Year	Alberta	British Columbia	Yukon Territory	Northwest Territories	Canada Quantity	Value
	g	g	g	g	g	$'000
1969	4 137	3 663 741	923 213	10 217 554	79 161 737	95,925
1970	4 728	3 147 579	555 570	10 352 606	74 915 027	88,057
1971	2 457	2 781 055	450 161	9 590 415	70 316 563	79,903
1972	93	3 799 570	126 871	9 563 666	64 650 660	119,742
1973	5 443	5 883 067	648 974	7 747 098	60 786 767	190,376
1974	3 017	5 041 283	823 371	5 737 565	52 825 897	263,794
1975P	—	4 478 901	808 690	5 785 247	52 067 221	276,125

12.15   Producers' shipments of silver, by province, and total value, 1969-75   M

Year	Average price per kg (Canadian funds) $	Newfoundland	Nova Scotia	New Brunswick	Quebec	Ontario	Manitoba
		kg	kg	kg	kg	kg	kg
1969	62.05	31 870	8 323	126 248	134 829	692 377	14 394
1970	59.48	24 678	2 229	142 390	132 562	618 226	20 552
1971	50.16	17 530	1 720	157 310	136 171	581 064	21 595
1972	53.69	17 820	- -	121 505	110 667	609 245	25 143
1973	81.21	17 820	710	110 998	94 897	610 170	33 678
1974	148.83	17 284	783	138 860	92 388	555 272	39 421
1975P	145.23	16 423	—	148 986	100 931	451 187	30 917

Year	Average price per kg (Canadian funds) $	Saskatchewan	British Columbia	Yukon Territory	Northwest Territories	Canada Quantity	Value
		kg	kg	kg	kg	kg	$'000
1969	62.05	20 208	179 173	83 515	63 027	1 353 964[1]	84,015
1970	59.48	15 301	202 525	131 901	85 990	1 376 354[1]	81,864
1971	50.16	7 426	238 694	178 774	91 209	1 431 493[1]	71,797
1972	53.69	11 958	215 424	155 174	126 257	1 393 193	74,803
1973	81.21	14 253	236 990	188 922	168 592	1 477 030[1]	119,954
1974	148.83	7 005	181 706	180 082	118 728	1 331 531[1]	198,166
1975P	145.23	8 460	188 985	202 670	67 619	1 216 178	176,627

[1]Includes relatively small quantities produced in Alberta.

12.16   Quantity and value of producers' shipments of uranium (U₃O₈), by province, 1969-75

Year	Ontario Quantity '000 lb.	Value $'000	Saskatchewan Quantity '000 lb.	Value $'000	Canada Quantity '000 lb.	Value $'000
1969	..	40,308	..	12,843	7,708	53,151
1970	6,677	..	1,532	..	8,209	..
1971	7,010	..	1,204	..	8,214	..
1972	8,428	..	1,335	..	9,763	..
1973	8,115	..	1,402	..	9,517	..
1974	8,443	..	1,148	..	9,591	..
1975P	10,569	..	1,682	..	12,251	..

12.17   Quantity and value of producers' shipments of asbestos, 1969-75

Year	Quantity '000 tons	Value $'000
1969	1,611	195,211
1970	1,662	208,147
1971	1,635	203,999
1972	1,687	206,089
1973	1,863	234,323
1974	1,812	302,013
1975P	1,143	266,943

12.18   Producers' shipments of potash, 1969-75

Year	K₂O eq. '000 tons	Value $'000
1969	3,492	69,383
1970	3,420	108,695
1971	4,000	134,955
1972	3,852	135,513
1973	4,909	176,876
1974	6,367	308,925
1975P	5,346	346,806

12.19   Producers' shipments of salt, by province, and total value, 1969-75

Year	Nova Scotia '000 tons	Ontario '000 tons	Manitoba '000 tons	Saskat-chewan '000 tons	Alberta '000 tons	Canada Quantity '000 tons	Value $'000
1969	501	3,760	43	107	247	4,658	30,406
1970	685	4,158	29	203	284	5,359	36,098
1971	889	4,172	27	209	245	5,542	40,111
1972	813	4,038	31	251	284	5,417	40,144
1973	752	4,162	36	285	330	5,565	49,631
1974	863	4,457	32	296	356	6,004	60,619
1975P	795	4,253	30	292	313	5,683	60,593

12.20   Quantity and value of sulphur produced from smelter gases and in pyrite and pyrrhotite shipments, and of elemental sulphur sales, 1969-75

Year	Sulphur in smelter gases Quantity[2] '000 tons	Value $'000	Producers' shipments pyrite and pyrrhotite Gross weight[3] '000 tons	Sulphur content '000 tons	Value $'000	Sales of elemental sulphur[1] Quantity '000 tons	Value $'000
1969	676	7,953	376	171	2,219	2,973	60,726
1970	706	7,433	363	176	1,699	3,548	28,354
1971	618	4,632	318	155	1,162	3,149	21,300
1972	679	5,118	126	60	456	3,636	19,588
1973	757	10,070	26[r]	13[e]	173	4,594	23,816
1974	731	9,813	54	27[e]	347	5,548	68,556
1975P	776	10,417	21	10[e]	90	4,476	89,190

[1]Recovered from sour natural gas and nickel sulphide ores.
[2]Includes sulphur in acid made from roasting zinc sulphide concentrates at Arvida and Port Maitland.
[3]Excludes pyrite and pyrrhotite used to produce iron residues or sinter.

12.21   Producers' shipments of gypsum, by province, and total value, 1969-75

Year	New-foundland '000 tons	Nova Scotia '000 tons	New Brunswick '000 tons	Ontario '000 tons	Manitoba '000 tons	British Columbia '000 tons	Canada Quantity '000 tons	Value $'000
1969	469	4,755	82	622	165	281	6,374	14,995
1970	492	4,775	73	537	172	270	6,319	14,199
1971	561	4,890	77	699	130	345	6,702	15,083
1972	735	5,999	75	726	176	388	8,099	19,336
1973	809	6,178	92	755	190	365	8,389	21,067
1974	556	5,899	87	774	207	441	7,964	22,437
1975P	508	4,406	59	742	90	450	6,255	19,720

12.16 Quantity and value of producers' shipments of uranium (U₃O₈), by province, 1969-75   M

Year	Ontario Quantity t	Value $'000	Saskatchewan Quantity t	Value $'000	Canada Quantity t	Value $'000
1969	..	40,308	..	12,843	3 496	53,151
1970	3 029	..	695	..	3 724	..
1971	3 180	..	546	..	3 726	..
1972	3 823	..	606	..	4 429	..
1973	3 681	..	636	..	4 317	..
1974	3 830	..	521	..	4 351	..
1975P	4 794	..	763	..	5 557	..

12.17 Quantity and value of producers' shipments of asbestos, 1969-75   M

Year	Quantity '000 t	Value $'000
1969	1 461	195,211
1970	1 508	208,147
1971	1 483	203,999
1972	1 530	206,089
1973	1 690	234,323
1974	1 644	302,013
1975P	1 037	266,943

12.18 Producers' shipments of potash, 1969-75   M

Year	K₂O eq. '000 t	Value $'000
1969	3 168	69,383
1970	3 103	108,695
1971	3 629	134,955
1972	3 494	135,513
1973	4 453	176,876
1974	5 776	308,925
1975P	4 850	346,806

12.19 Producers' shipments of salt, by province, and total value, 1969-75   M

Year	Nova Scotia '000 t	Ontario '000 t	Manitoba '000 t	Saskatchewan '000 t	Alberta '000 t	Canada Quantity '000 t	Value $'000
1969	454	3 411	39	97	224	4 225	30,406
1970	621	3 772	26	184	258	4 861	36,098
1971	806	3 785	24	190	222	5 027	40,111
1972	738	3 663	28	228	258	4 915	40,144
1973	682	3 776	33	259	299	5 049	49,631
1974	783	4 043	29	269	323	5 447	60,619
1975P	721	3 858	27	265	284	5 155	60,593

12.20 Quantity and value of sulphur produced from smelter gases and in pyrite and pyrrhotite shipments, and of elemental sulphur sales, 1969-75   M

Year	Sulphur in smelter gases Quantity[2] '000 t	Value $'000	Producers' shipments pyrite and pyrrhotite Gross weight[3] '000 t	Sulphur content '000 t	Value $'000	Sales of elemental sulphur[1] Quantity '000 t	Value $'000
1969	613	7,953	341	155	2,219	2 697	60,726
1970	640	7,433	329	160	1,699	3 219	28,354
1971	561	4,632	288	141	1,162	2 857	21,300
1972	616	5,118	114	54	456	3 299	19,588
1973	687	10,070	24	12e	173	4 168	23,816
1974	663	9,813	49	24e	347	5 033	68,556
1975P	704	10,417	19	9e	90	4 061	89,190

[1] Recovered from sour natural gas and nickel sulphide ores.
[2] Includes sulphur in acid made from roasting zinc sulphide concentrates at Arvida and Port Maitland.
[3] Excludes pyrite and pyrrhotite used to produce iron residues or sinter.

12.21 Producers' shipments of gypsum, by province, and total value, 1969-75   M

Year	New-foundland '000 t	Nova Scotia '000 t	New Brunswick '000 t	Ontario '000 t	Manitoba '000 t	British Columbia '000 t	Canada Quantity '000 t	Value $'000
1969	425	4 314	74	564	150	255	5 782	14,995
1970	446	4 332	66	487	156	245	5 732	14,199
1971	509	4 436	70	634	118	313	6 080	15,083
1972	667	5 442	68	659	160	352	7 348	19,336
1973	734	5 605	83	685	172	331	7 610	21,067
1974	504	5 351	79	702	188	400	7 224	22,437
1975P	461	3 997	54	673	82	408	5 675	19,720

12.22　Production and exports of nepheline syenite, 1969-75

| Year | Production | | Exports | |
	Quantity '000 tons	Value $'000	Quantity '000 tons	Value $'000
1969	501	5,935	396	5,120
1970	487	5,801	383	5,063
1971	517	6,206	410	5,333
1972	559	5,902	442	5,789
1973	569	7,860	449	6,101
1974	617	9,179	493	7,846
1975P	520	8,663	392	7,103

12.23　Producers' shipments and value, imports, exports and apparent consumption of cement, 1969-75

| Year | Shipments (sold or used) | | Imports '000 tons | Exports[1] '000 tons | Apparent consumption[2] '000 tons |
	'000 tons	$'000			
1969	8,250	162,091	53	634	7,669
1970	7,946	155,740	97	567	7,477
1971r	9,076	183,374	56	888	8,244
1972	10,039	210,685	43	1,299	8,783
1973r	11,271	241,945	129	1,410	9,990
1974	11,436	274,649	277	1,265	10,448
1975P	10,763	265,283	464	1,099	10,129

[1]Standard portland cement.
[2]Shipments plus imports less exports.

12.24　Producers' shipments of sand and gravel, by province, and total value, 1969-75

| Year | Province or territory | | | | | |
	New-foundland '000 tons	Prince Edward Island '000 tons	Nova Scotia '000 tons	New Brunswick '000 tons	Quebec '000 tons	Ontario '000 tons
1969	3,957	902	9,167	3,994	41,500	82,657
1970	4,335	827	7,187	6,883	36,795	82,877
1971	5,564	1,554	6,004	4,985	41,605	77,631
1972	5,433	1,578	9,896	7,561	44,993	76,380
1973	6,466	1,632	11,348	9,553	51,543	80,568
1974	6,772	974	11,578	8,251	39,493	79,713
1975P	5,900	960	8,900	6,500	43,000	76,200

| Year | Manitoba '000 tons | Saskatchewan '000 tons | Alberta '000 tons | British Columbia '000 tons | Canada | |
					Quantity '000 tons	Value $'000
1969	8,142	7,673	14,904	28,685	201,581	122,159
1970	14,930	8,963	16,042	23,817	202,656	133,558
1971	16,695	11,321	18,679	29,253	213,291	152,628
1972	14,763	8,512	20,556	35,522	225,194	178,100
1973	12,782	6,836	18,607	34,126	233,461	213,437
1974	19,039	11,840	24,703	34,225	236,588	238,620
1975P	18,400	11,500	23,400	30,200	224,960	260,340

12.25　Producers' shipments of stone[1], by province, and total value, 1969-75

| Year | Province or territory | | | | |
	New-foundland '000 tons	Nova Scotia '000 tons	New Brunswick '000 tons	Quebec '000 tons	Ontario '000 tons
1969	190	1,016	1,208	32,009	27,034
1970	182	1,192	1,322	30,144	27,673
1971	204	1,643	1,431	37,515	28,239
1972	204	1,047	1,901	41,384	31,092
1973	394	813	2,756r	48,156	35,539
1974	680	1,666	2,899	50,509	34,459
1975P	600	1,300	2,600	53,100	33,700

| Year | Manitoba '000 tons | Alberta '000 tons | British Columbia '000 tons | Canada | |
				Quantity '000 tons	Value $'000
1969	699	315	5,006	67,477	88,186
1970	1,273	166	3,371	65,323	87,976
1971	1,012	184	3,287	73,515	96,537
1972	610	196	3,769	80,203	103,326
1973	625	161	3,830	92,274r	128,693r
1974	2,450	180	4,642	97,485	167,468
1975P	1,700	200	3,900	97,100	170,700

[1]Excludes limestone used in Canadian lime and cement industries.

12.22   Production and exports of nepheline syenite, 1969-75   M

Year	Production		Exports	
	Quantity '000 t	Value $'000	Quantity '000 t	Value $'000
1969	454	5,935	359	5,120
1970	442	5,801	347	5,063
1971	469	6,206	372	5,333
1972	507	5,902	401	5,789
1973	516	7,860	407	6,101
1974	560	9,179	447	7,846
1975P	472	8,663	356	7,103

12.23   Producers' shipments and value, imports, exports and apparent consumption of cement, 1969-75   M

Year	Shipments (sold or used)		Imports '000 t	Exports[1] '000 t	Apparent consumption[2] '000 t
	'000 t	$'000			
1969	7 484	162,091	48	575	6 957
1970	7 208	155,740	88	514	6 783
1971	8 234	183,374r	51	806	7 479
1972	9 107	210,685	39	1 178	7 968
1973	10 225	241,945r	117	1 279	9 063
1974	10 375	274,649	251	1 148	9 478
1975P	9 764	265,283	421	997	9 189

[1]Standard portland cement.
[2]Shipments plus imports less exports.

12.24   Producers' shipments of sand and gravel, by province, and total value, 1969-75   M

Year	Province or territory					
	New-foundland '000 t	Prince Edward Island '000 t	Nova Scotia '000 t	New Brunswick '000 t	Quebec '000 t	Ontario '000 t
1969	3 590	818	8 316	3 623	37 648	74 985
1970	3 933	750	6 520	6 244	33 380	75 185
1971	5 048	1 410	5 447	4 522	37 743	70 426
1972	4 929	1 432	8 978	6 859	40 817	69 291
1973	5 866	1 481	10 295	8 666	46 759	73 090
1974	6 143	884	10 503	7 485	35 827	72 314
1975P	5 352	871	8 074	5 897	39 009	69 127

Year	Manitoba '000 t	Saskatchewan '000 t	Alberta '000 t	British Columbia '000 t	Canada	
					Quantity '000 t	Value $'000
1969	7 386	6 961	13 521	26 023	182 871	122,159
1970	13 544	8 131	14 553	21 606	183 846	133,558
1971	15 145	10 270	16 945	26 538	193 494	152,628
1972	13 393	7 722	18 648	32 225	204 294	178,100
1973	11 596	6 202	16 880	30 959	211 794	213,437
1974	17 272	10 741	22 410	31 048	214 629	238,620
1975P	16 692	10 433	21 228	27 397	204 080	260,340

12.25   Producers' shipments of stone[1], by province, and total value, 1969-75   M

Year	Province or territory				
	New-foundland '000 t	Nova Scotia '000 t	New Brunswick '000 t	Quebec '000 t	Ontario '000 t
1969	172	922	1 096	29 038	24 525
1970	165	1 081	1 199	27 346	25 105
1971	185	1 491	1 298	34 033	25 618
1972	185	950	1 725	37 543	28 206
1973	357	738	2 500	43 686	32 240
1974	617	1 511	2 630	45 821	31 261
1975P	544	1 179	2 359	48 172	30 572

Year	Manitoba '000 t	Alberta '000 t	British Columbia '000 t	Canada	
				Quantity '000 t	Value $'000
1969	634	286	4 541	61 214	88,186
1970	1 155	151	3 058	59 260	87,976
1971	918	167	2 982	66 692	96,537
1972	553	178	3 419	72 759	103,326
1973	567	146	3 475	83 709	128,693r
1974	2 223	163	4 211	88 437	167,468
1975P	1 542	181	3 538	88 087	170,700

[1]Excludes limestone used in Canadian lime and cement industries.

12.26   Value (total sales) of producers' shipments of clay products made from domestic clays, by province, 1969-75 (thousand dollars)

Year	Province or territory				
	New-foundland	Nova Scotia	New Brunswick	Quebec	Ontario
1969r	120	1,555	585	6,412	30,465
1970	37	2,816	940	8,160	28,649
1971	80	1,844	627	6,565	30,538
1972	257	1,684	668	8,300	30,484
1973	260	2,101	840	9,725	34,601
1974	350	2,763	1,048	12,214	39,074
1975P	300	3,155	1,310	12,507	38,363
	Manitoba	Saskat-chewan	Alberta	British Columbia	Canada
1969r	280	1,714	4,640	3,725	49,496
1970	346	1,819	4,657	4,367	51,791
1971	469	1,140	4,031	4,900	50,194
1972	667	1,758	4,438	4,301	52,557
1973	1,257	2,014	4,782	5,590	61,170
1974	778	2,406	6,177	5,811	70,621
1975P	676	2,672	7,299	3,674	69,956

12.27   Quantity and value of production[1] of crude oil, by province, 1969-75

Year	New Brunswick		Ontario		Manitoba		Saskatchewan	
	Quantity '000 bbl	Value $'000	Quantity '000 bbl	Value $'000	Quantity '000 bbl	Value $'000	Quantity '000 bbl	Value $'000
1969	9	13	1,162	3,117	6,205	15,615	87,414	196,067
1970	10	14	1,048	2,840	5,908	14,858	89,487	199,770
1971	10	13	958	2,727	5,604	15,413	88,459	217,829
1972	9	12	878	2,499	5,257	14,588	86,787	214,057
1973	10	14	809	2,866	5,084	17,148	85,935	264,057
1974	8	11	734	4,342	4,749	27,164	73,947	397,835
1975P	8	11	721	5,191	4,441	31,657	58,171	389,746
	Alberta		British Columbia		Northwest Territories		Canada	
	Quantity '000 bbl	Value $'000	Quantity '000 bbl	Value $'000	Quantity '000 bbl	Value $'000	Quantity '000 bbl	Value $'000
1969	290,012	740,435	25,387	58,357	801	967	410,990	1,014,571
1970	338,403	876,887	25,478	60,943	846	1,142	461,180	1,156,454
1971	371,501	1,055,769	25,263	63,984	944	1,208	492,739	1,356,943
1972	444,220	1,272,903	23,936	63,710	890	1,059	561,977	1,568,828
1973	541,736	1,894,724	21,316	65,643	963	2,240	655,853	2,246,692
1974	515,437	2,985,549	18,948	103,501	954	3,167	614,777	3,521,569
1975P	446,359	3,254,971	14,432	95,251	1,210	4,240	525,342	3,781,067

[1]Gross production of crude oil and condensate, less returned to formation.

12.28   Natural gas production[1], by province and total value, 1969-75

Year	New Brunswick		Quebec		Ontario		Saskatchewan		Alberta	
	Quantity MMcf	Value $'000	Quantity MMcf	Value $'000	Quantity MMcf	Value $'000	Quantity MMcf	Value $'000	Quantity MMcf	Value $'000
1969	106	95	138	21	11,332	4,275	58,656	7,244	1,605,658	218,106
1970	131	108	166	25	17,064	6,488	62,594	7,332	1,870,507	265,912
1971	105	91	170	25	16,260	6,333	71,166	8,952	2,067,247	290,672
1972	97	57	187	26	12,375	4,768	68,912	8,932	2,385,440	338,709
1973	81	31	198	28	9,528	3,678	65,887	9,044	2,537,641	388,696
1974	88	44	183	27	7,537	3,248	61,636	9,001	2,537,515	645,138
1975P	90	45	50	8	12,671	6,413	61,000	9,455	2,580,006	1,639,898
	British Columbia		Yukon Territory		Northwest Territories		Canada	
	Quantity MMcf	Value $'000	Quantity MMcf	Value $'000	Quantity MMcf	Value $'000	Quantity MMcf	Value $'000
1969	301,998	32,573	—	—	44	18	1,977,932	262,332
1970	326,565	35,200	—	—	82	35	2,277,109	315,100
1971	342,909	36,269	869	90	298	117	2,499,024	342,549
1972	432,132	43,043	2,599	279	11,795	1,372	2,913,537	397,186
1973	469,253	46,052	—	—	36,873	4,324	3,119,461	451,853
1974	405,809	60,581	1,138	190	31,600	5,537	3,045,506	723,766
1975P	389,570	70,123	2,076	239	29,196	3,450	3,074,659	1,729,631

[1]Gross production, less field-flared and waste and re-injected.

12.27   Quantity and value of production[1] of crude oil, by province, 1969-75   M

Year	New Brunswick Quantity '000 m³	Value $'000	Ontario Quantity '000 m³	Value $'000	Manitoba Quantity '000 m³	Value $'000	Saskatchewan Quantity '000 m³	Value $'000
1969	1	13	185	3,117	987	15,615	13 898	196,067
1970	2	14	167	2,840	939	14,858	14 227	199,770
1971	2	13	152	2,727	891	15,413	14 064	217,829
1972	1	12	140	2,499	836	14,588	13 798	214,057
1973	2	14	129	2,866	808	17,148	13 663	264,057
1974	1	11	117	4,342	755	27,164	11 757	397,835
1975P	1	11	115	5,191	706	31,657	9 248	389,746

Year	Alberta Quantity '000 m³	Value $'000	British Columbia Quantity '000 m³	Value $'000	Northwest Territories Quantity '000 m³	Value $'000	Canada Quantity '000 m³	Value $'000
1969	46 108	740,435	4 036	58,357	127	967	65 342	1,014,571
1970	53 802	876,887	4 051	60,943	135	1,142	73 323	1,156,454
1971	59 064	1,055,769	4 016	63,984	150	1,208	78 339	1,356,943
1972	70 625	1,272,903	3 806	63,710	141	1,059	89 347	1,568,828
1973	86 129	1,894,724	3 389	65,643	153	2,240	104 273	2,246,692
1974	81 948	2,985,549	3 012	103,501	152	3,167	97 742	3,521,569
1975P	70 965	3,254,971	2 295	95,251	192	4,240	83 522	3,781,067

[1]Gross production of crude oil and condensate, less returned to formation.

12.28   Natural gas production[1], by province and total value, 1969-75   M

Year	New Brunswick Quantity '000 m³	Value $'000	Quebec Quantity '000 m³	Value $'000	Ontario Quantity '000 m³	Value $'000	Saskatchewan Quantity '000 m³	Value $'000	Alberta Quantity '000 m³	Value $'000
1969	3 003	95	3 909	21	321 011	4,275	1 661 598	7,244	45 484 825	218,106
1970	3 711	108	4 702	25	483 386	6,488	1 773 153	7,332	52 987 425	265,912
1971	2 974	91	4 816	25	460 611	6,333	2 015 979	8,952	58 560 644	290,672
1972	2 748	57	5 297	26	350 557	4,768	1 952 128	8,932	67 574 365	338,709
1973	2 295	31	5 609	28	269 908	3,678	1 866 436	9,044	71 885 891	388,696
1974	2 493	44	5 184	27	213 507	3,248	1 746 015	9,001	71 882 321	645,138
1975P	2 550	45	1 416	8	358 942	6,413	1 727 998	9,455	73 086 000	1,639,898

Year	British Columbia Quantity '000 m³	Value $'000	Yukon Territory Quantity '000 m³	Value $'000	Northwest Territories Quantity '000 m³	Value $'000	Canada Quantity '000 m³	Value $'000
1969	8 554 951	32 573	—	—	1 246	18	56 030 543	262,332
1970	9 250 881	35 200	—	—	2 323	35	64 505 581	315,100
1971	9 713 872	36 269	24 617	90	8 442	117	70 791 955	342,549
1972	12 241 367	43 043	73 624	279	334 127	1,372	82 534 213	397,186
1973	13 292 924	46 052	—	—	1 044 532	4,324	88 367 595	451,853
1974	11 495 693	60 581	32 237	190	895 160	5,537	86 272 610	723,766
1975P	11 035 677	70 123	58 809	239	827 060	3,450	87 098 452	1,729,631

[1]Gross production, less field-flared and waste and re-injected.

Sources
12.1 - 12.28 Minerals and Metals Division, Mineral Development Sector, Department of Energy, Mines and Resources.

Energy   Chapter 13

Tables

Energy   Chapter 13

In April 1976 the government set out a broad blueprint to manage Canada's energy future. The document, "An Energy Strategy for Canada — Policies for Self-Reliance" outlined nine policy elements and five major related targets to deal with energy problems over the next 10 to 15 years. Aimed at achieving energy self-reliance within 10 years, the strategy is designed to reduce Canada's vulnerability to arbitrary changes in the price or supply of imported energy, by using domestic resources to the greatest extent possible, and protecting against interruptions in the supply of energy that must be imported.

The policy areas included in the strategy objectives are: appropriate energy pricing, energy conservation, increased exploration and development, increased resource information, substituting domestic energy for expensive imported energy, new or improved transportation and transmission systems, emergency preparedness, increased research and development, and greater Canadian content and participation.

The five major energy-related targets include: moving domestic oil prices toward international levels and moving domestic prices for natural gas to an appropriate competitive relationship with oil over the next two to four years; reducing the average rate of growth of energy use in Canada, over the next 10 years, to less than 3.5% a year; reducing Canadian net dependence on imported oil in 1985 to one third of total oil demand; maintaining self-reliance in natural gas until such time as northern resources can be brought to market under acceptable conditions; and at least doubling exploration and development in the frontier areas of Canada over the next three years, under acceptable social and environmental conditions.

The next 10 to 15 years are crucial for energy in both the short and long term. In the next decade the focus will be on self-reliance in energy, particularly oil and natural gas. It will also be the time to plan beyond 1990, when oil and gas will no longer supply most of Canada's energy needs. The government is planning a subsequent examination of Canada's longer-term energy future.

Energy supply and demand   13.1

Canada's energy needs are met by oil, natural gas, coal, uranium and electricity. In terms of primary energy consumption, the share of oil as an energy source is 45% while natural gas and coal account for 18% and 8%, respectively, with 7% of this total used to produce electricity. About 27% of energy consumption is supplied in the form of electricity which, in turn, is produced from hydro, coal, oil, natural gas and nuclear energy sources. Although nuclear power accounts for little more than 1% of total supply, it will become increasingly important as a source of electric power. Hydro-electricity and thermal generation of electricity from coal, while remaining significant, will decline in importance as nuclear power development increases and the use of natural gas and oil is gradually phased out. However, oil and natural gas are still likely to account for over 60% of total primary energy consumption at the end of the century.

The relative importance of energy sources, in terms of Canada's trade is shown in Table 13.1. There was a marked change in the export-import balance in the 10-year period 1965-75, from a deficit of $194.0 million in the value of energy in 1965, on a trade balance basis, to a surplus of $1,185.1 million in 1975. In 1974 a reversal of this trend became apparent as the decline in crude oil exports signalled that the energy trade surplus prevailing since 1969 would diminish rapidly. In 1975 with the further reduction of crude oil exports, oil imports rose and the energy trade surplus continued to decline.

Canada's primary energy demand increased at an average annual rate of 5.3% over the 15-year period 1960-75, while energy use per capita grew annually by 3.6%. Higher energy prices and increasing attention to energy conservation measures are expected to lower per capita growth to an annual average of less than 3.5% during the remainder of this decade. Trends in energy supply and demand for each of the principal energy sources are expected to continue.

Growth in oil usage and the related supply trends since 1964 are illustrated in Table 13.2. Production of crude oil and gas liquids more than doubled in the 10-year period to 1974; declines in production and exports, evident in 1974, continued in 1975. The growth rate in domestic demand began to moderate toward the end of the year. The most notable trend in 1974-75 was the decline in the export-import surplus from 297,800 to 40,100 barrels a day (b/d) or 47 300 to 6 400 cubic metres a day (m³/d). This surplus was expected to disappear in 1976.

The natural gas supply and demand situation is illustrated in Table 13.3. In the 10-year period to 1974, production of marketable pipeline gas and domestic demand almost tripled. In 1975 exports declined while domestic demand continued the growth rate of previous years. With no new export approvals since 1970, and none planned, domestic demand growth will relate directly to the ability of the industry to increase supply from present producing areas pending the opening of new sources in frontier areas.

The coal supply and demand picture has changed considerably (Table 13.4). In the 10-year period to 1974, production more than doubled, but most of the increase occurred in the years 1970-74. Domestic demand grew, reaching a peak in 1970. Despite a slight decline since, there are indications of renewed growth in the near future. Imports increased steadily until 1970 and remained within a narrow range of the 1973 level followed by a decline in 1974 due to a tightening in US supply. In 1975 imports increased again. The most pronounced change in the coal supply and demand balance was the export increase in the years 1970-74 which accompanied the production increase. Present trends point to a stabilization of imports, and demand increases in the domestic market. Exports are expected to grow but only to the extent that expanded production exceeds domestic needs.

Electric energy supply and demand (Table 13.5) shows a doubling in domestic demand over the period 1964-74 and indicates a continuation of this growth. Until 1968 exports remained close to the 1963 level and have since quadrupled while imports have not changed significantly since 1963. However, exports have remained less than 6% of total electrical generation. In 1964 thermal power based on coal, and to a lesser extent on oil and natural gas, accounted for 16% of total production with hydro-electric sources providing the remainder. By 1974 thermal power had risen to 25%. With increasing use of nuclear energy in thermal power plants, this upward trend will continue.

Total sales of secondary energy, i.e. for uses other than producing energy for sale, were apportioned as follows: residences and farms 22%, commercial and institutional use 16%, industry 33% and transportation 29%. Each energy source component has its specialized markets. In the residential market oil and gas supply 80% of requirements, and electricity the rest. The commercial sector is supplied by oil and gas (75%) and the remainder by electricity. The energy used in transportation is essentially oil. In industry, oil and gas meet 63% of the energy demand, electricity 24% and coal 13%. The composition of the energy mix changes over time, with changing price and supply conditions, but no dramatic changes from this pattern are foreseen for the remainder of the decade.

Quadrupling oil prices, declining reserves and the increasing costs of exploration and development had made 1974 an eventful period in the management of the energy economy. The changed circumstances involved export controls, export charges, import compensation, voluntary product price restraint, a single price for domestic production, the intervention of provincial marketing agencies, and the existence of an international energy agreement.

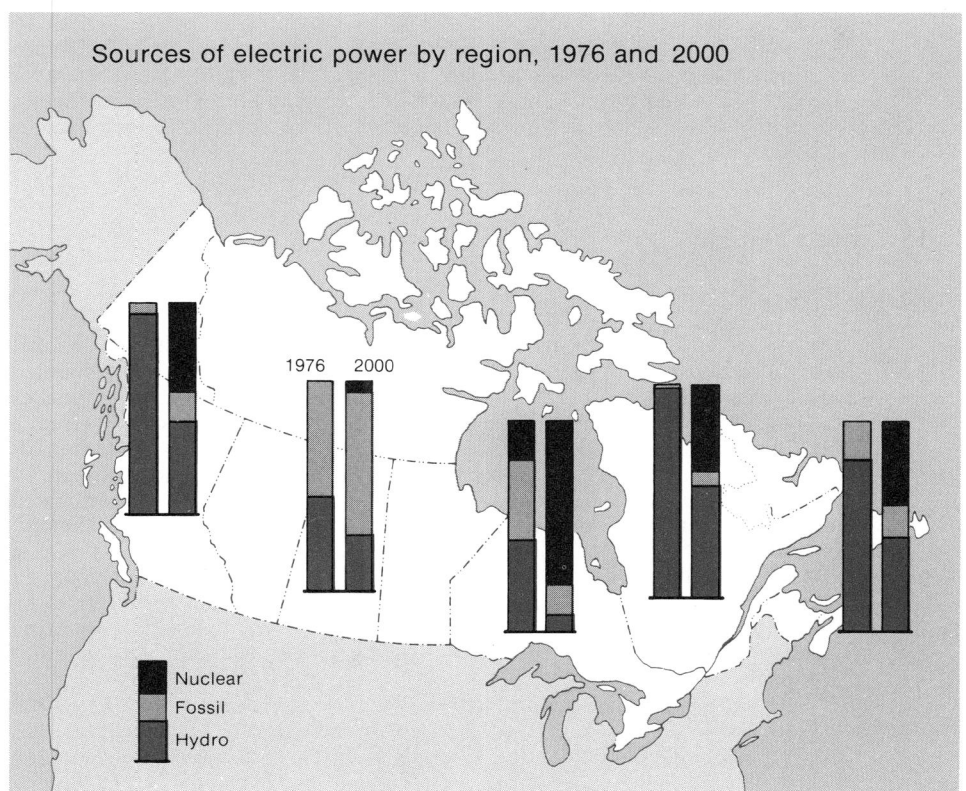

Sources of electric power by region, 1976 and 2000

1976   2000

Nuclear
Fossil
Hydro

Against this background, the government introduced several steps in 1975 to adapt its energy policy to altered circumstances. To achieve greater self-reliance in oil the interprovincial pipeline system was extended to Montreal. Following publication of the National Energy Board (NEB) report on Canada's oil supply and requirements, the Department of Energy, Mines and Resources announced its decision to reduce exports to the US by almost one third.

The government also continued its single price policy for crude oil for all Canadians. The price of domestic oil was raised to $8.00 in July 1975 and $9.05 in July 1976, and a fiscal structure was maintained to ensure an equitable distribution of revenues among producers, consumers and governments and to leave the industry sufficient incentive to continue exploration and development. The Energy Supply Allocation Board, created in 1974 with the authority to allocate crude oil and petroleum products in an emergency, had its responsibilities broadened in 1975 to include administration of the Oil Import Compensation Program. In June 1976, the board's mandate, under the Emergency Supplies Emergency Act, expired but it retained responsibility for the compensation program. The board's functions were reconstituted within the Department of Energy, Mines and Resources. Petro-Canada, the national petroleum company, was set up to ensure, as far as possible, that the rate of development of Canadian petroleum resources would be in the national interest, and to negotiate abroad to secure imported oil on the best terms possible. Federal government assistance was proposed to expand the production of electricity based on nuclear sources and to facilitate a comprehensive interconnection of provincial utilities to ensure greater efficiency and security of supplies. An Office of Energy Research and

Development, established in January 1974, continued to assess and coordinate research activities. Assistance was offered to provinces to help complete an inventory of Canadian resources in uranium, coal, oil and natural gas. The Office of Energy Conservation, also set up in January 1974 in the Department of Energy, Mines and Resources, continued to develop and recommend a program of energy conservation and to coordinate efforts of agencies responsible for conservation.

13.2   Oil and gas

13.2.1   Reserves

Oil. At the end of 1975 Canada's proven reserves of recoverable conventional crude oil and natural gas liquids (propane, butanes and pentanes plus) amounted to 8.2 billion barrels (bbl) (1.3 billion m³), most of them in Alberta. The estimates do not include reserves attributed to the Athabasca tar sands or recently discovered reserves in frontier areas. Proven oil reserves showed a net decline for the sixth consecutive year and represent a reserves-to-production ratio of 14 years. Canada's remaining ultimate potentially recoverable reserves, as estimated in 1975 by the Geological Survey of Canada (GSC), were placed at 40 billion bbl (6.4 billion m³) of oil and 301 trillion cu ft (MMMMcf) (8 523 billion m³) of gas. These potential reserves include, in addition to amounts already proven, about 23 billion bbl (3.7 billion m³) and 201 MMMMcf (5 692 billion m³) "yet to be discovered on the basis of geological predictions". These figures represent the mean GSC estimates of the amount of ore and gas which will ultimately be found in Canada.

According to an appraisal of Alberta's oil sands completed in 1973 by the Alberta Energy Resources Conservation Board, the ultimate recoverable reserves of synthetic crude oil from all of Alberta's bituminous deposits amount to 250 billion bbl (39.7 billion m³). Of this, approximately 26.5 billion bbl (4.2 billion m³) is considered recoverable by open cast mining methods similar to those now in use at the Great Canadian Oil Sands Limited's plant near Fort McMurray. The bulk of the oil located in deeper formations will only be recovered by in situ thermal or other techniques still being developed.

Natural gas. Raw natural gas may vary widely in composition. In addition to the usually predominant methane, varying proportions of ethane, propane, butanes and pentanes plus may be present. Hydrogen sulphide may be so abundant as to be an important source of sulphur. After processing has removed the water content, hydrogen sulphide, pentanes plus and other petroleum gases, the marketable gas consists mainly of methane, some ethane and small amounts of propane and butanes. The heating value of the marketed gas averages about 1,000 Btu per cu ft (37 259 kilojoules per cubic metre) of gas.

The most important use of natural gas is as a fuel for space and water heating. Domestically it is used as fuel in larger home appliances and industrially in the automobile, steel, metal-working, glass and food-processing fields. In metallurgical processing, its clean, easily controlled flow makes it possible to attain precise temperatures for rolling, shaping, drawing and tempering steel.

The constituents of natural gas have become major sources of feedstock for the petrochemical industry. Natural gas supplies the basic raw material for ammonia, plastics, synthetic rubber, insecticides, detergents, dyes and synthetic fibres such as nylon, orlon and terylene.

Canada's ultimately recoverable reserves of natural gas have been estimated at 82.7 MMMMcf (2 342 billion m³) of gas in place, most of it in the western provinces of Alberta and British Columbia. Cumulative production to the end of 1975 was 25.8 MMMMcf (731 billion m³), leaving 56.9 MMMMcf (1 611 billion m³) available to meet future demand. On the basis of 1975 production of marketable gas, the reserves-to-production ratio is 23.7 years. Gas reserves rose 2.6 MMMMcf (74 billion m³) in 1975 compared to a year earlier but included gas formerly considered uneconomic and was not attributable to new discoveries. These new reserves, all in Alberta, have been added to the proven and recoverable category as a direct result of increases in Alberta wellhead and plant-gate gas prices.

Exploration and development   13.2.2

Oil   13.2.2.1

The level of exploratory drilling activity in the conventional producing areas of western Canada in 1975 was down slightly from that of 1974 but a marked increase was evident in 1976. Preliminary estimates indicate that some 1,600 exploratory wells were drilled in 1975 compared with 1,650 in 1974, a decline of 3%. Exploratory drilling in the frontier regions continued to decline in 1975, following peak activity in 1973. In the North, 44 wells were drilled including 12 delineation wells, down from a total of 60 in 1974. By the end of September 1976, an additional 25 wells had been drilled.

Off the east coast, nine wells were drilled compared with 21 in 1974, with only five area wells finalized in the first three quarters of 1976. There was no drilling activity off the west coast or in Hudson Bay in 1975, nor were any such operations planned for 1976. Details of drilling activity appear in Table 13.6.

Western provinces. In spite of the Alberta incentive programs, exploratory drilling in 1975 did not increase significantly. Development drilling increased 7.4% reflecting increased interest in the shallow gas fields of southeastern Alberta and the net increase in drilling activities in that province was 5.3%. In Saskatchewan, 262 wells were drilled in 1975. Exploratory drilling decreased by 15% and development drilling increased slightly. British Columbia registered a sharp decline of 44.5%. Activity in Manitoba was nominal and no significant developments were indicated. It was not until the early months of 1976 that renewed drilling activity in western Canada became apparent, with the emphasis being on gas exploration and development in Alberta and British Columbia.

Northern regions. Drilling and onshore geophysical activity in the North declined in 1975 compared with 1974, while marine seismic activity showed a slight increase; this trend continued into 1976. Footage drilled in 1975 decreased by 28% and exploration expenditures by 14%, with an estimated $215 million spent.

In the Mackenzie Delta region, one new oil and gas discovery, the Sun et al Garry P-04, was recorded late in 1975. Early in 1976 a gas find was made at the Imperial Netserk F-40 site and an oil and gas find at the Gulf-Mobil Kamik D-48 site. Further drilling will be needed to determine the commercial significance of these three discoveries. The Garry and Netserk wells were drilled from artificial islands in shallow waters of the Beaufort Sea off the Delta; 15 such islands have been constructed of dredged silt, sand and/or gravel, and significant hydrocarbons have been encountered in drilling from four of them. A new phase of exploratory activity began in 1976 with the first drilling in the deeper waters of the Beaufort Sea north of the Delta, using ice-strengthened but conventional floating drilling equipment.

Single successful delineation wells were drilled during 1975 in the Parsons Lake, Adgo, Kumak and Niglintgak fields, the first of gas and the latter three of both oil and gas. To the end of September 1976, one additional oil and gas success had been put down at Niglintgak, while the Gulf-Mobil group had drilled four new delineation gas wells in the Parsons Lake field.

In the Arctic islands, one oil discovery in 1975 in the Panarctic Bent Horn F-72 A well on Cameron Island, a one-mile (1.6 km) southwest stepout to the N-72 well produced an encouraging show of oil in 1974. The F-72 A well flowed 10,000 bbl (1 600 m³) of 43° API oil a day on production tests of the same Middle

Devonian carbonate reservoir. In 1976 a third well, A-02 drilled one mile (1.6 km) southwest of the F-72 A discovery, encountered the same reservoir horizon some 1,200 ft (360 m) structurally higher and tested 5,400 bbl (900 m³) of oil a day. Although further drilling is required to determine the commercial significance of the Bent Horn accumulation, this was the first important discovery of oil in the Arctic islands in what has been essentially a gas-prone region.

There were no new wildcat gas discoveries in the Arctic islands in 1975; however, two successful gas delineation wells were drilled in the large Drake Point gas field on Melville Island. One, sited from a reinforced ice platform, confirmed production six miles (9.7 km) offshore to the east. An outpost gas well onshore also extended reserves in the Hecla gas field. In the first months of 1976, two additional gas wells in the latter field were both drilled from reinforced ice platforms; one well produced hydrocarbons in a sandstone horizon deeper than the main productive unit, while the second extended the field six miles (9.7 km) to the northwest in the offshore. Panarctic has indicated that potential reserves in these two gas fields may be in the order of 10.6 MMMMcf (300 billion m³), making them the two largest gas accumulations in all of Canada.

Also early in 1976, a new gas discovery was made in the Jackson Bay G-16 well, drilled from shore-fast ice off Ellef Ringnes Island in 200 ft (60 m) of water. This find adds to the potential already indicated in this sector by the King Christian and other previous gas discoveries.

Eastern offshore region. There were 11 wells drilled off the east coast in 1975 compared with 19 completions in 1974; five new holes were put down in the first nine months of 1976. The most active area was the Labrador Sea where, despite icebergs, deep water and a very brief season for exploration, six wells were drilled in 1975. Three significant gas discoveries by the Eastcan group resulted from drilling only six prospective structures on the Labrador shelf, including Bjarni in 1973 (confirmed by testing in 1974), Gudrid in 1974 and Snorri recently. The latter well indicated hydrocarbons in 1975 on mechanical logs, but was not tested until 1976, when gas flows of 9.8 MMcf (280 000 m³) a day were recorded along with condensate at 235 bbl (37 m³) a day.

Drilling south of the Labrador Sea declined significantly in 1975 with only two wells put down on the Grand Banks, two on the Scotian shelf, and the first well to be drilled in the Bay of Fundy, compared with eight Grand Banks and nine Scotian shelf wells for 1974. No discoveries resulted. The decline in activity was due to the poor results encountered. Exploration on the Scotian shelf was given a boost in early 1976 when Petro-Canada, the national oil company, became a participant in exploration and planned to spend more than $24 million in drilling six wells there in 1976. Of the five 1976 wells drilled off the east coast in the first three quarters of the year (all on the Scotian shelf), four were financed in whole or in part by Petro-Canada; however, all were dry. No drilling on the Grand Banks or in the Gulf of St. Lawrence was anticipated for 1976.

At the end of the third quarter of 1976, among four drilling units at work off Labrador were three for the Eastcan group and one for BP and partners, which included Petro-Canada. Wells at two of the sites were suspended short of projected depth during 1975 due to the lateness of the season.

Other offshore regions. There was no drilling activity in Hudson Bay in 1975, and none anticipated for 1976. The last two offshore wells in this region were drilled in 1974 by the Aquitaine group. The last wells off the west coast were put down in 1969, and although some interest has been shown in further drilling, activity has been temporarily suspended.

13.2.2.2   Gas

Exploration and development drilling for gas continued the upward trend in 1975 in the western provinces. Completions rose by 9.3% over 1974 to 2,080 wells. Of these, 1,958 were in southeastern Alberta, indicating the industry's continued interest in the shallow gas zones where the gas is a dry sweet commodity not requiring processing. Of the 548 exploratory wells drilled in the western provinces, 504 were in Alberta and 68% of these were shallow zone exploratory wells.

Three gas discoveries were made in the Willson Creek–Limestone Mountain area of west central Alberta, and a number of gas discoveries and successful extensions to existing fields occurred, particularly in the Peace River area. In Saskatchewan both exploratory and development drilling declined, with most of the activity consisting of development wells in the expanding shallow gas fields in the southwestern corner of the province. In British Columbia some significant discoveries were made in the northeastern and southern areas. Most development drilling was aimed at the Devonian Slave Point producing trend which includes the Sierre, East Kotcho Lake and Helmet fields.

Oil and gas legislation   13.2.3

Oil and gas exploration and development in the Yukon and Northwest Territories and Canadian offshore areas are governed by the Territorial Lands Act, the Public Lands Grants Act, the Oil and Gas Production and Conservation Act, and pertinent regulations under the existing Canada Oil and Gas Land Regulations.

Oil and gas exploration permits have been granted for three, four or six years, depending on latitude and region, either on application or, in the case of land previously held under permit, by sale through public tender. A permit is renewable for up to six one-year periods, with provision for additional renewals under special terms and conditions. The permit holder must undertake exploratory work of specified value, ranging from five to 20 cents an acre (two to eight cents a hectare) for periods of the primary term. Work obligations for each one-year renewal period increase up to 50 cents an acre (20 cents a hectare). The permit holder must post a guarantee deposit in the form of cash, bonds or promissory notes prior to each work period. These deposits are returned on receipt of satisfactory evidence that exploratory work has been performed, and are forfeited to the Crown if work obligations are not fulfilled. Oil and gas leases from such permits may be selected in accordance with prescribed guidelines for up to 50% of a permit area, with the portion not converted to lease reverting to the Crown.

An oil and gas exploration permit may be issued to any individual over 21 years of age or to any joint stock company incorporated or licensed to do business in Canada, or incorporated in any province of Canada. Extraterritorial companies applying for permits in the Northwest Territories must be registered under the Companies Ordinance of the Northwest Territories. Certain Canadian participation provisions apply to the lease stage. An oil and gas lease may be granted where the minister of the department involved is satisfied that the applicant is a Canadian citizen over 21 years of age and will be the beneficial owner of the interest granted, or to a corporation incorporated in Canada, and at least 50% of the issued shares of the corporation are beneficially owned by Canadian citizens or the shares are listed on a recognized Canadian stock exchange and that Canadians will have an opportunity of participating in the financing and ownership of the corporation, or the operation is wholly owned by a corporation that meets either of these two corporate requirements, or a combination of individual and corporate requirements.

On May 19, 1976 the ministers of Energy, Mines and Resources and Indian Affairs and Northern Development jointly issued a "Statement of Policy regarding a Proposed Petroleum and Natural Gas Act and New Canada Oil and Gas Land Regulations", preparatory to tabling new legislation in Parliament. It was proposed that the new act would authorize regulations affecting existing contractual obligations, including provisions designed to accelerate oil and gas activity. Among the stipulations are: marked increases in work obligations for existing permits in most areas; issuance of production rights only upon the commencement of production, and for shorter periods of time; an option for Petro-Canada to acquire a 25% working interest in any existing grant for which a special-renewal permit is granted or in any provisional lease issued before a discovery has been made; a guideline of 25% as the minimum level of Canadian participation in production licences and for provisional leases when a discovery has been made; authorizing the administering authority to order the commencement and continuation of production; authorizing the minister to stipulate the posted price of oil and gas production, on the basis of fair market value at fieldgate or extraction plant; authorizing the government to take its royalty in production or in cash; requiring permit holders, lessees and licensees to submit to the administering authority copies of contracts and agreements that transfer any interests or create oil and gas supply arrangements, and make provision for possible ministerial approval of farmouts.

Other proposals include: providing for shorter confidential periods for proprietary information, i.e. geophysical, geological, feasibility, environmental; authorizing the minister to order exploration drilling on a specified prospect within a reasonable time; broadening the minister's authority in ordering development drilling of discovered reserves; making administrative and operational conditions subject to amendment of the regulations from time to time; providing for the issuance of Crown reserves (areas not covered at present by permit or lease, or which revert to the Crown on surrender of existing permits and leases) in the form of exploration agreements and production licences upon terms and conditions stipulated.

It is intended that those sections of the existing Canada Oil and Gas Land Regulations that are not involved in or are not inconsistent with the Statement of Policy nor with operational and conservation measures covered under other legislation, will be retained in their intent in the new regulations.

The phase-in of new levels of work obligations will commence one year from the date of the announcement or on promulgation, whichever comes last. The phasing in and implementation of those other elements of the proposed new regulations affecting existing permits and leases will be made effective as of the date of their promulgation.

The Oil and Gas Production and Conservation Act provides for comprehensive control over all oil and gas operations in the Yukon and Northwest Territories and offshore regions including such matters as safety, prevention of waste and pollution, production, conservation, storage, transmission, and unitization of oil and gas fields. An Oil and Gas Committee of five members appointed by the Governor in Council may hold inquiries, hear appeals, and issue any necessary orders to carry out its mandate.

Federally owned mineral rights within the provinces that are available for development (except those in Indian lands) are administered by the Department of Energy, Mines and Resources in accordance with regulations made under the Public Lands Grants Act.

13.2.4   Production

Oil. Production of Canadian crude oil and equivalent in 1975 declined by 14.5% or an average of 267,200 b/d (42 500 m³/d) from the 1974 production of 1,843,300 b/d (293 100 m³/d). Exports of crude oil and equivalent to the United States dropped by 199,600 b/d (31 700 m³/d) while domestic demand decreased by 67,600 b/d (10 700 m³/d).

In Alberta production of conventional crude oil was down by 200,000 b/d (31 800 m³/d), synthetic crude oil by 3,000 b/d (500 m³/d) and pentanes plus by 10,000 b/d (1 600 m³/d) for a total decline of 213,000 b/d (33 900 m³/d) or 13.6%. Saskatchewan crude oil production decreased by 18.1% or 40,000 b/d (6 400 m³/d). The severe cutback first experienced in 1974 in heavy and sour crude production continued. The US District II refineries, traditional consumers of these Saskatchewan crude types, considered them uncompetitive after the export tax was added to the posted price. British Columbia crude oil and equivalent production was reduced by 13,000 b/d (2 100 m³/d) to 42,000 b/d (6 700 m³/d) while Manitoba showed a decrease of 1,000 b/d (160 m³/d) to 12,000 b/d (1 900 m³/d) (Table 13.7).

Natural gas. Marketable gas production was 2.4 MMMMcf (68 billion m³) in 1975, about the same level as 1974. Alberta produced 85.5% of the supply and British Columbia and the territories 12.4%. Production in British Columbia and the Northwest Territories was adversely affected in 1974 by reservoir-water breakthrough. Damage caused by this development is expected to curtail production from these fields for the foreseeable future.

Transportation   13.2.5

Oil. Canadian oil moves to market through an intricate network of oil pipelines extending from the producing fields west to Sumas, BC, near Vancouver, and east to the Niagara area of Ontario. This network serves Canadian refineries in British Columbia, Alberta, Saskatchewan, Manitoba and Ontario, and US markets in the Puget Sound, mid-west, Chicago and upper New York state areas. In 1974 the length of the entire pipeline system was 19,323 miles (31 097 km).

Prime components of this system are the trunk lines of the Interprovincial Pipe Line Company and the Trans Mountain Oil Pipe Line Company. Both pipelines start in Edmonton and are fed by a network of gathering lines which transport oil to the main trunk lines at that point. Interprovincial also receives oil from the Hardisty fields, 100 miles (161 km) southeast of Edmonton; from the Lloydminster heavy asphaltic crude field which provides a blend of pentanes plus and crude; and through the Bow River Pipe Line Ltd., oil from the most southerly fields in the province. At Edson, approximately 100 miles (161 km) west of Edmonton on the Trans Mountain pipeline, an interconnection with the Peace River pipeline brings oil from fields in northwestern Alberta.

The other prime mover of oil from Alberta, the Aurora pipeline, with a length of only one mile (1.6 km) within Canada, receives crude oil and equivalent from the Rangeland gathering system and moves it to Billings, Montana, both for refining and further shipment to points in the US mid-west.

Outside Alberta, the Interprovincial pipeline receives and transports Saskatchewan and Manitoba crude oil. The main gathering systems deliver a blend of crude oil and pentanes plus from the Lloydminster area to Kerrobert. Southwest Saskatchewan crude oil joins the line at Regina and southeast Saskatchewan crude at Cromer, Man., the junction for delivery of southwestern Manitoba crude oil.

In British Columbia a gathering pipeline system carries crude over a distance of 500 miles (805 km) from fields near Fort St. John to connect with the Trans Mountain system at Kamloops.

Interprovincial Pipe Line Company's system is Canada's largest oil pipeline. It incorporates a wholly-owned subsidiary in the US, Lakehead Pipe Line Company Incorporated, and in 1975 had a right-of-way of 3,263 miles (5 251 km) accommodating 6,101 miles (9 819 km) of main pipeline, of which 3,608 miles (5 807 km) are in Canada. In 1975 the system received 1,162,408 b/d (184 808 m³/d) and delivered 1,160,198 b/d (184 457 m³/d), most of it in the form of crude oil. Domestic refiners received 647,646 b/d (102 967 m³/d) of this throughput; the remainder was delivered in the US.

Trans Mountain Oil Pipe Line Company operates a pipeline system for transporting crude and natural gas liquid from Edmonton and other points in Alberta and British Columbia to Burnaby, BC, and a subsidiary operates branch lines to refineries in the state of Washington. The 24-inch (61 cm) main line is 723 miles (1 164 km) long including a spur line to the US boundary near Sumas, BC. The company operates 20 pumping stations, 18 of them in Canada. The present main line's sustainable capacity is over 410,000 b/d (65 000 m³/d). Nine refineries are now connected to Trans Mountain, five in British Columbia and four in the state of Washington. In 1974 Trans Mountain built additional crude oil loading facilities in Vancouver to load tankers delivering oil to eastern Canada via the Panama Canal.

The Montreal refining centre is served by a pipeline from tidewater at Portland, Maine, the nearest port on the Atlantic seaboard from which tanker-borne crude oil from Venezuela, the Middle East and Africa may be trans-shipped by pipeline to Montreal. This joint system of the Montreal Pipe Line Company and its wholly-owned subsidiary in the US, Portland Pipe Line Corporation, shortens tanker voyages as it bypasses the seaboard of the Maritime provinces, the Gulf of St. Lawrence and the St. Lawrence River segments. However, there are deepwater port sites in the Atlantic region and on the St. Lawrence which have been considered for development as tanker terminals to provide pipeline routes within Canadian territory to Montreal. The Portland–Montreal system consists of 236 miles (380 km) of right-of-way and 708 miles (1 139 km) of main pipeline. In 1974, 467,746 b/d (74 366 m³/d) of crude oil went through the system.

The oil embargo of the winter of 1973, coupled with frequent price increases of offshore oil, led the federal government to decide on a policy of an all-Canadian coast-to-coast pipeline network for security of supply, self-reliance in oil and oil products and to further economic development throughout the country. As phase one of this network, in May 1975, the government approved the company's application to extend the Interprovincial pipeline system from Sarnia to Montreal to provide consumers in eastern Ontario and western Quebec with access to more secure domestic supplies of western Canadian crude oil. The system went into operation in June 1976. The 30-inch (76 cm) line has an initial capacity of 250,000 b/d (40 000 m³/d).

Natural gas. The authorization of large-volume gas removal from British Columbia and Alberta, beginning in the mid-1950s, led to the construction of the first major gas transmission lines in Canada. Today, the complete system serves major Canadian centres from Vancouver to Montreal and transports gas to the international border for US markets from California to New England. The next expansion will be directed to opening up Arctic gas resources. The initial economic, engineering and environmental studies for a Mackenzie Valley gas pipeline were completed in 1973 and an application was filed before Canadian and US regulatory authorities in 1974 for authorization and approvals to own and operate the pipeline. Research is also being carried out into the feasibility of transporting natural gas from the Arctic islands.

Most Canadian natural gas now produced must be processed before it can be marketed. Gathering lines take raw gas from the producing wells to a collection point on a transmission system or to the inlet of a gas processing plant. Main transmission systems receive marketable gas from field gathering lines or plants and transport it through trunk lines to Canadian distribution companies or to interconnected US transmission pipelines at the international border. Distribution systems serve the ultimate customers in the centres of population. With the introduction of PVC (polyvinylchloride) small-diameter pipe, distribution companies — especially in the western provinces — have been rapidly extending their service to rural customers by means of this easily laid durable pipe. At the end of 1974, a total of 73,012 miles (117 501 km) of pipeline were in operation, of which 8,613 miles (13 861 km) were gathering, 25,107 miles (40 406 km) were transmission and 39,292 (63 234 km) were distribution.

Unlike an oil pipeline company, which is a common carrier transporting oil for a fixed charge, a gas transmission pipeline company either owns the gas it transports or is a subsidiary of the company purchasing the gas at source. The principal exception is the Alberta Gas Trunk Line Company Limited which delivers virtually all of the gas removed from Alberta to the main transmission companies at the provincial boundary.

The system of TransCanada Pipelines Limited begins at the Alberta border near Burstall, Sask., where it receives from Alberta Gas Trunk Line the gas it has purchased in Alberta. It receives gas from four Saskatchewan locations, then passes south of Regina to a point south of Winnipeg where it branches into two lines. The original line goes eastward to Thunder Bay, North Bay and south to Toronto. At Toronto this line again divides with the westward branch serving the Hamilton area as well as delivering gas to the US at the Niagara Falls border crossing; the eastward branch follows the Lake Ontario shore and the St. Lawrence River to Montreal before terminating at Philipsburg, Que., on the international border. A number of lateral lines extending from the main transmission line serve communities along this route. The second line from Winnipeg goes south to the border at Emerson where it connects with the Great Lakes Transmission Company system, a company jointly owned by TransCanada and an American company. This pipeline follows a route south of Lake Superior, crosses the Straits of Mackinac to the lower Michigan peninsula where it swings south, then east to reconnect with the TransCanada system at Sarnia, Ont. The TransCanada system is Canada's longest pipeline, operating 5,678 miles (9 138 km) of line in 1975 through which it delivered 1,101 MMMcf (31 billion m³) of gas. The US market took 23.8%, the balance being sold in Saskatchewan, Manitoba, Ontario and Quebec. Ontario accounted for the greatest volume of sales. In 1975, TransCanada commenced construction of a 24-inch (61 cm) diameter pipeline which consists of a 48-mile (77 km) loop line from Toronto to Montreal with a 17-mile (27 km) extension to Ottawa. TransCanada is a member of the Canadian Arctic Gas Study Limited and manager of the Polar Gas Project.

The Westcoast Transmission Company Limited's large-diameter transmission line extends from Fort Nelson in the northeastern corner of British Columbia to Sumas on the BC–US border, near Vancouver. The system includes a number of lateral lines gathering gas from producing areas in BC, western Alberta and the Pointed Mountain field in the Northwest Territories. In addition to serving Vancouver and communities along its route, Westcoast delivers gas to Pacific Northern Gas Ltd., a distribution company serving communities and industries along a 500-mile (805 km) route between the Westcoast mainline at Summit Lake and the Pacific Coast communities of Prince Rupert and Kitimat. It also supplies Inland Natural Gas Co. which operates an extensive distribution system serving communities in southern and central British Columbia. Westcoast's export sales are made to the El Paso Natural Gas Company for distribution in the Pacific Northwest region of the US. Westcoast operated 2,243 miles (3 610 km) of pipeline with total sales in 1975 of 353.2 MMMcf (10 billion m³). During 1974, the BC government acquired a 13.3% interest in Westcoast Transmission and the company was guaranteed a rate of return as a carrier but the British Columbia Power Corporation took over all the gas purchasing functions of the company.

The Alberta Gas Trunk Line Company Limited transports most of Alberta's export gas from the producing fields to the provincial boundaries where it is delivered to a large interprovincial transmission pipeline. Its two main segments are the Foothills Division and the Plains Division. The former transports gas for the Alberta Natural Gas, Alberta and Southern, and Westcoast Transmission systems; the latter for TransCanada and Consolidated pipelines. In the northwest of the province a smaller system, the Northern Division, delivers gas to the main Westcoast Transmission trunk line. The system operated 4,473 miles (7 199 km) of pipeline in 1975 with daily average receipts of 4.9 MMMcf (138.8 million m³).

Usually, natural gas pipeline systems confine their activities to gathering in the field, transmission, or distributing to ultimate customers. However several large systems combine elements of all three. In Alberta integrated companies like Canadian Western Natural Gas Company Limited and Northwestern Utilities Limited serve their customers from field to ultimate user with a combined total of more than 10,276 miles (16 538 km) of pipeline. Saskatchewan Power

Corporation delivers all gas sold in that province through a 7,739-mile (12 455 km) distribution and transmission system serving most of the populated areas. Norcen Energy Resources Limited operates probably the most widespread distribution system in Canada by serving industries and communities close to the TransCanada pipeline between Winnipeg and Montreal. Two large utility companies serve the industrialized areas of southern Ontario: Consumers' Gas Company operating in the Toronto area, the Niagara Peninsula and eastern Ontario, and Union Gas Limited serving southwestern Ontario.

New oil and gas pipeline regulations were issued in 1975 by the National Energy Board (NEB) after consultation with the industry and other authorities. The board's Rules of Practice and Procedure were amended to include additional requirements respecting Canadian content and environmental assessments.

Northern pipelines. Extensive exploration for oil and gas has been going on in the Canadian North and in frontier regions for many years. Transportation and use of gas from the North, however, began to receive active consideration only after the major discoveries in Prudhoe Bay, Alaska in 1968. Recognizing that similar discoveries might well be made in the Canadian Arctic, the Canadian government set up a Task Force on Northern Oil Development to advise on all regional and national matters relating to northern oil and gas development, transportation, marketing and research.

In August 1970 and June 1972 the federal government issued guidelines for construction and operation of northern pipelines which included preservation of the environment, prevention of pollution and thermal erosion, freedom of navigation, protection of the rights of northern residents, and their training and employment.

On March 21, 1974, Canadian Arctic Gas Pipeline Ltd. (CAGPL) filed applications to construct and operate a natural gas pipeline from Alaska and the Mackenzie Delta to southern markets via a Mackenzie Valley route. Mr. Justice Thomas R. Berger, of the Supreme Court of British Columbia, was appointed by the Government of Canada to conduct an inquiry into the regional social, environmental and economic impact of the construction, operation and subsequent abandonment of the proposed Mackenzie Valley natural gas pipeline in the Yukon Territory and Northwest Territories. Preliminary hearings were held in the summer of 1974 and the formal inquiry opened in Yellowknife on March 3, 1975.

An application was completed by Foothills Pipe Lines Ltd. in the summer of 1975 to construct a pipeline to deliver Canadian gas from the Mackenzie Delta to southern markets along a route similar to that proposed by Canadian Arctic Gas Pipeline, but without crossing the Yukon to take delivery of Arctic gas.

The Polar Gas Project was initiated in 1973 to organize the research and engineering of a pipeline to bring Arctic islands gas to southern markets. The founding participants of the group are Panarctic Oils, TransCanada Pipelines, Canadian Pacific Investments, Tenneco Texas Eastern and Pacific Lighting. Polar Gas intended to file an application in 1977, for the construction of a pipeline.

The Alcan pipeline was sponsored by Northwest Pipeline Corporation of Salt Lake City, Utah and the two Canadian sponsors of Foothills Pipe Lines Ltd., Westcoast Transmission Company of Vancouver and Alberta Gas Trunk Line Company, of Calgary. The Alcan pipeline would transport only US gas from the North Slope of Alaska along the Alaska Pipeline right-of-way to Fairbanks, where it would follow the Alcan right-of-way southeast through Alaska across the Yukon Territory and northeastern BC and into northwestern Alberta, joining the existing pipeline in BC and Alberta for distribution in US markets. The route will generally parallel the Alaska–Canada Highway. Applications were filed with the US Federal Power Commission and the Canadian government in 1976.

The Berger hearings were divided into four phases:
Engineering and construction of the proposed pipeline. This phase included such matters as the size of the pipeline; its location; the timing of construction; the

composition and deployment of construction crews; and the construction of facilities.

Impact of a pipeline and Mackenzie corridor development on the physical environment. This phase of the hearings studied the impact on the land, the air and the water; and covered such matters as permafrost; river crossings; slope stability; gravel and other borrow locations.

Impact of a pipeline and Mackenzie corridor development on the living environment. This phase of the hearings included studies of the impact on plant and animal life, including wildlife, mammals and fish.

Impact of a pipeline and Mackenzie corridor development on the human environment. This phase of the hearings was concerned with social and economic impacts.

The NEB commenced hearings in October 1975, for a thorough examination of the Mackenzie Valley Pipeline in terms of the following areas of interest:

Facilities: Alternate systems of transportation, design and capacity of facilities, construction plan and pipeline operations and maintenance; right-of-way, interconnection pipeline facilities, and alternate routes; cost of facilities; and agreements between Trunk Line and Trunk Line (Canada).

Contracts and financial matters: Contracts, including the examination of supply, transportation sales contracts; and financial matters, including proforma financial statements, cost of service and tariffs and financing plans.

Socio-economic environmental and other public interest matters: Impact on the Canadian economy; Canadian content; social-economic factors; environmental matters; and other matters of public interest.

Supply and requirements: Supply of gas which might be available to the pipeline from Canadian and Alaskan sources; supply of Canadian gas from all other sources; requirements for gas to satisfy the Canadian market.

Processing   13.2.6

Oil. Recent changes in energy prices and the reduction in exports have led to a significant change in the outlook for new refinery construction. Canada has a surplus of capacity and the prospect of a slower growth of demand. Table 13.8 gives details of oil refinery capacity in Canada in 1975, with scheduled completion dates for new facilities. Some expansion of existing refineries is already in progress. In 1975 Canada had 38 operating refineries with a total refining capacity at year-end of more than 2 million b/d (300 000 m³/d). Refinery runs were about 1.8 million b/d (290 000 m³/d); net sales of products averaged 1.6 million b/d (250 000 m³/d), representing a decline of 2% over 1974. Production of Canadian refineries is closely in balance with total market demand, although there is some interchange of individual products to and from the US. Both exports and imports were down from 1974.

In the past, the location and size of Canada's refineries were determined by the tendency to install them close to centres of consumption. Thus approximately 57% of the total capacity is in the populous regions of southern Ontario and Quebec. Ontario has two main refining centres, in Sarnia and south of Toronto; Quebec has the largest refining centre, in Montreal, as well as a refinery in Quebec City. British Columbia has seven refineries, most of them close to Vancouver.

A more recent trend has been to increase the size of individual refineries to effect economies of scale. Although the average size of individual refineries is increasing all over Canada, this is particularly evident in Alberta, Saskatchewan and Manitoba. Many small refineries close to individual cities are now being phased out and replaced by two large refineries in Edmonton, close to the main sources of crude in Alberta. They will be of optimum size and will confine any possible environmental problems to one area. Saskatchewan will lose one small refinery, but one of those remaining will be expanded.

A third factor influencing refinery location has been proximity to deepwater ports where crude input is received by tanker. The economies obtained with huge tankers have stimulated the construction of large refineries in the Atlantic provinces, specifically at Saint John, NB, and Point Tupper, NS. These are located in areas of relatively low population density so that a major proportion of their output is either shipped inland or re-exported. Changes in international markets had a major impact on the "export" refineries in 1975, resulting in a marked decrease in product exports.

In 1975 Canadian refineries yielded an average 35% of motor gasoline, 33% of middle distillates including light heating oil, diesel oil and jet fuel and about 20% of heavy fuel oil. Other products included liquefied petroleum gas, petrochemical feedstocks, aviation gasoline, asphalt, coke and lubricating oil. To meet the high yields of light products most refineries are equipped with a catalytic cracker and total installed cracking capacity in 1975 was equivalent to about 21% of the crude distillation capacity. Catalytic reforming amounted to about 18% of crude capacity. This process upgrades gasoline quality and also delivers aromatic petroleum chemical feedstocks. To meet the need for high quality low-sulphur distillates, hydrogen-treating plants have been installed totalling 36% of crude feed and it is common practice to hydrosulphurize most or all of the gas, oil and light distillates. Six hydrocracking units have been installed in Canada capable of treating 4% of crude feed. This new process is of value in upgrading heavy fuels to motor gasoline and middle distillates.

Canada's petrochemical complex will be significantly enlarged by the construction of the country's first "petrochemical refinery" at Sarnia, Ont. Scheduled to start production in 1978, the refinery will manufacture both fuel products and petrochemicals. New petrochemical plants will be built in the area for further processing of the chemical products.

At Sarnia, three refineries are integrated with nine petrochemical companies. The oil refineries supply petroleum gases, naphtha and aromatics. The chemical companies convert them to a large number of intermediate and final products. Western Canadian natural gas is also piped into this complex. The intermediate products include ethylene, propylene, butadiene, aromatics and ethylene oxide. Final products include carbon black, synthetic rubbers, detergent alkylates, polyethylene, polystyrene, polyvinylchloride, ammonia, fertilizers, petroleum additives and many others. Many products are sold back to the refineries for blending into fuel products. Fuels are piped directly to the petrochemical plants for process heat and power requirements. Montreal and Edmonton are major petrochemical centres but plants are distributed widely across Canada.

Canadian refineries are investing in environmental control and conservation equipment to meet new standards. Process cooling water has been minimized or abandoned entirely in favour of air cooling. Water effluent undergoes gravity separation and secondary processes such as air flotation, biological oxidation or filtration. Low sulphur fuels and dispersion from tall smoke stacks minimize the discharge of sulphur dioxide from process heaters. Increased emphasis on products designed to reduce pollution by the consumer has resulted in sulphur-free fuels and motor gasolines with reduced harmful emission levels.

The pioneer Athabasca oil sands plant of Great Canadian Oil Sands Ltd. at Fort McMurray includes refining equipment to process the recovered bitumen to a synthetic crude oil. A second oil sands plant is now under construction by Syncrude Canada Ltd., whose participants include the federal, Alberta and Ontario governments. Research programs are being staffed to develop improved techniques for the extraction and processing of this resource.

Natural gas. Processing capacity at the end of 1975 was 16.5 MMMcf (467.2 million m³) a day, an increase of only 0.3 MMMcf (8.5 million m³) over 1974. This small increase reflects the fact that no new fields were discovered during 1975. No major plant has been commissioned since 1972. Plant output includes pipeline gas, propane, butanes, pentanes plus and sulphur.

Research and development   13.2.7

Technical advances to assure adequate sources of energy depend on research and development. In April 1975 the federal government announced the establishment of the Canadian Energy Research Institute. Funded by the Department of Energy, Mines and Resources, the Alberta Department of Mining, Energy and Natural Resources and the private Energy Research Association, the institute will be located at the University of Calgary. It will conduct research and analysis on alternative solutions to medium- and long-range energy problems, develop independent source data, and provide economic research. Creation of the institute is a response to a growing demand for information on energy matters from both the private and the public sectors.

Marketing of petroleum products   13.3

Higher prices for petroleum products in domestic and export markets continued to reduce sales in 1975. Net sales of petroleum products were 582 million bbl (93 million m³) in 1975, down 1.3% from 590 million bbl (94 million m³) a year earlier, a reversal of the 5.4% historical growth pattern over the past decade. Net sales of natural gas in Canada climbed a marginal 0.8% and exports were down slightly.

Oil   13.3.1

The NEB report in October 1974 on exports of oil analyzed established reserves and the likelihood of new oil field discoveries, and reviewed the long-term demand for Canadian oil. The report forecast a decline in production from established oil fields starting in 1975 and continuing into the 1980s, when oil from frontier areas in the north and from the oil sands in Alberta should become available in significant amounts.

Faced with a demand for oil in 1982 that, on the basis of supply and demand trends, will result in an overall national deficit of 200,000 b/d (32 000 m³/d), the board recommended that exports of crude oil and petroleum products be progressively reduced with minimum injury to areas of the US now dependent on Canadian supplies. Subsequent action by the government set a limit on exports of 800,000 b/d (127 000 m³/d) and 750,000 b/d (119 000 m³/d) for the first and second halves of 1975 respectively.

In the September 1975 NEB report, *Canadian oil supply and requirements,* it was recommended that, in view of the increased domestic demand in 1976 due to the extension of the Interprovincial Pipeline to Montreal, the export allocation during 1976 be further reduced. Accordingly, the government set the 1976 export allocation at an average of 460,000 b/d (73 000 m³/d). To achieve this average, progressive reductions were to be made from 510,000 b/d (81 000 m³/d) in January 1976 to 385,000 b/d (61 000 m³/d) by December 1976 in line with increases in the Sarnia to Montreal crude oil movement to an anticipated 250,000 b/d (40 000 m³/d) by year-end.

The amount of oil that can be exported is computed annually, with a system of monthly licences in force to ensure that Canadian requirements are met. The NEB formula fixes the annual amount of crude oil available for export in relation to the amount of oil that can be produced, Canadian demand, and a conservation factor estimated for that year. This has the effect of reducing oil exports progressively as the estimated period of self sufficiency decreases in the area of Canada served by oil of Canadian origin.

In the early 1970s export demand for Canadian refined products increased substantially, largely because the demand for heavy fuel oil in the US northeast grew beyond the refinery capacity of the region. The increased demand was primarily met by the two large new refineries at St-Romuald, Que. and Point Tupper, NS. The refinery at Come By Chance, Nfld., built in 1972, was also designed to meet this market but went into receivership in February 1976 and ceased operations.

As a result of concern about future supplies, the NEB imposed controls on the export of petroleum products in June 1973. Marketers are required to obtain annual export licences to which export ceilings are attached. The licensed amounts for 1975 were 7,035,000 bbl (1 118 000 m³) of motor gasoline, 22,622,000 bbl (3 597 000 m³) of middle distillates, 37,247,000 bbl (5 922 000 m³) of heavy fuel oil for a total licensed export of 66,944,000 bbl (10 643 000 m³). Actual product exports in 1975 were 35,945,000 bbl (5 715 000 m³) or approximately 54% of the authorized amount.

Since late 1973, the price of crude oil in international markets has quadrupled as a result of actions by the Organization of Petroleum Exporting Countries (OPEC). In September 1973, the Canadian government announced a price freeze on crude oil at $3.80/bbl ($23.90/m³) and instituted voluntary price constraints on petroleum products. In January 1974, a First Ministers' Conference extended the price freeze on crude oil and the federal government announced incentives to support half the capital cost of electrical interconnections and the first nuclear plant for each province in an effort to reduce eastern Canadian dependence on imported oil. The provincial governments agreed to a single-price oil policy in Canada. This policy allows Canadians to purchase oil at prices below international prices, while offsetting increases in the price of imported oil with increases in the price of Canadian oil exports.

In April 1974, the price of domestic oil was set at $6.50/bbl ($40.88/m³) and it was increased to $8.00/bbl ($50.32/m³) in July 1975. Subsequently, in July 1976, the price of domestic oil was set at $9.05/bbl ($56.92/m³) and rose to $9.75/bbl ($61.33/m³) in January 1977. In April 1974, the federal government established the Oil Import Compensation Program, retroactive to January 1, to insulate the Canadian economy from the rapid increase in the price of foreign crude. The program enabled the government to maintain a single price policy by subsidizing the imports of crude oil and petroleum products consumed in Canada. Compensation paid between the inception of the program and the end of April 1976 totalled $2,901 million, of which $157 million was paid in 1973-74, $1,162 million in 1974-75 and $1,582 million in 1975-76.

During 1975 total imports of crude oil were 298.6 million bbl (47.5 million m³) as compared to 299.5 million bbl (47.6 million m³) in 1974. Venezuela has traditionally been the main supplier of oil imported into eastern Canada, but historical patterns were altered in 1974 and 1975 when a larger share of import demand was met by crude oil from the Middle East. The crude supply during 1975 was composed of 526,000 b/d (84 000 m³/d) from the Middle East, 255,000 b/d (41 000 m³/d) from Venezuela and 37,000 b/d (6 000 m³/d) from other countries. Total imports of crude oil have decreased with the completion of the Sarnia–Montreal pipeline in June 1976. It is expected that the Canadian crude oil delivered to Montreal via the pipeline will displace more crude oil from the Middle East than from Venezuela.

In 1975 and 1976, the federal government completed two major programs to enhance Canada's energy self-reliance. First, it established a Canadian national oil company, Petro-Canada in July 1975. Petro-Canada has taken over the government's existing interest in the petroleum industry. It holds a 45% interest in Panarctic Oils Ltd. and a 15% interest in the Syncrude project. Second, it completed the domestic pipeline system to Montreal in July 1976. It was anticipated during the last half of 1976, that the new Sarnia–Montreal pipeline would keep imports down by delivering crude oil from western Canada to Montreal refiners. By October 1976 it was contributing an estimated 148,000 b/d (24 000 m³/d) of western Canadian crude to Montreal. As of November 1976, the pumping capacity was scheduled to allow 250,000 b/d (40 000 m³/d) of crude oil to reach Montreal refineries.

There have been important changes in other aspects of the Canadian energy situation. Royalty and tax laws affecting the production of oil and gas and other mineral fuels have changed substantially. The prices of other fuels and electricity have risen as a result of both the increase in oil prices and the high rates of inflation in all industrialized countries. The success rate in finding additional resources of oil and gas in Canada and its territorial waters has been less than was hoped and forecast capital and operating costs associated with the exploration, development, production and transport of oil and gas from the oil sands and the Arctic areas have increased so substantially that serious questions have been raised about the pace and price at which these resources can be commercially developed.

Government innovation   13.3.1.1

The price of crude oil was raised in mid-1975 from \$6.50/bbl (\$40.88/m³) to \$8.00/bbl (\$50.32/m³). Alberta and Saskatchewan introduced changes in their royalty formulas in response to this, while British Columbia introduced a new oil royalty system. The price of gas in interprovincial trade was raised substantially, being fixed at \$1.25/Mcf (\$44.14/thousand m³) at the Toronto city-gate effective November 1, 1975. Alberta announced that the Provincial Petroleum Marketing Commission would equalize wellhead prices for all producers by uniformly 'flowing back' any surplus in the export over the domestic price. All three provinces introduced or improved incentive schemes to encourage exploration and development of hydrocarbons within their borders.

In December 1974 Alberta announced an increase in the select price for oil from \$4.41 to \$4.71 and in July 1975 the royalty rate was reduced from 65% to 50% on the portion of the price between \$6.50 and \$8.00. This brought the average royalty on oil to 36% from 42%. A refund of the corporation tax arising because of the non-deductibility of royalties was also announced. In the summer of 1975 Saskatchewan and British Columbia introduced similar schemes of tax indemnification and lowered the royalty on oil, and BC created an exploration incentive scheme. With this same purpose of promoting exploration, the Government of Canada also introduced two modifications to the taxation system for petroleum to take effect in 1976. The special tax abatement of November 1974 was to be replaced by a resource allowance of 25% of adjusted production income thus recognizing, to a degree, the special position of the provinces in respect of resources and increasing the incentive impact of the exploration and development allowances. At the same time, the rate of tax was reduced to the general corporate income tax rate of 46% from 50%. These changes reduced slightly the anticipated federal share of resource revenues.

Legislation   13.3.1.2

Adoption of the Petroleum Administration Act in June 1975 authorized the federal government to set the price of oil and gas domestically as well as in the export market and to continue the oil import compensation program.

Marketing innovations. Crude oil produced in western Canada is purchased by refining and marketing companies, transported to refineries by pipeline and processed into petroleum products for market distribution, usually through the marketing outlets of the major refining companies. With increasing product availability in the late 1960s and early 1970s, refineries found it profitable to market increasing volumes through independent outlets in competition with their brand name dealers. Independent discount gas bars offered lower prices, less service and fewer promotional extras. Major oil companies have opened their own discount and self-service outlets to capture a share of this market. The "self-service" market is one manifestation of the changes probably yet to occur because of sharply increased prices.

Other influences for change are the government's long-term program of energy conservation announced in 1974, the establishment of a national petroleum company, and government participation in the Syncrude project on terms granting that consortium an "internationally oriented" price for its product. Other concessions were granted when the federal government joined Alberta and

Ontario as participants with private industry in this development, which is seen as a commercial and technical venture on which future oil sands development will be based.

13.3.1.3   Multilateral cooperation in energy matters

International Energy Agency. In response to the selective Arab oil embargo of 1973-74 and the rapid rise in oil prices imposed by OPEC, Canada joined with other industrialized countries in establishing the International Energy Agency (IEA) in November 1974. The basic objective of this 19-member organization is to reduce the vulnerability of participating countries to changes in the price and availability of imported oil through multilateral cooperation. It is hoped that the IEA will contribute to the development of a stable world energy order that will take due account of the concerns of producing and consuming countries, both industrialized and developing.

To meet this objective IEA member countries agreed to an emergency sharing plan providing for the equitable allocation of international oil supplies in the event of future curtailments. The IEA has established a data information system on the international oil market, and member countries in 1976 adopted a program of long-term cooperation directed at reducing the dependence of the group on imported oil and promoting stability and equity in the international oil market. Canada was one of the countries originally involved in the formation of the agency and has played an active part in its development.

International initiatives were also taken after the developments of 1973-74 to ease the adjustments necessary to finance the balance-of-payments deficits of oil-importing countries. In 1974 the International Monetary Fund (IMF) established the IMF oil facility, a special fund of almost $4 billion. This amount was borrowed mainly from the oil-exporting countries and loaned to importing countries, mostly in the developing world, for an average term of five years and in amounts related to the increase in their oil-import bills. In 1975 the facility was renewed for more than $6 billion and provision for an interest subsidy on loans made to the most seriously affected oil-importing developing countries. The second major initiative was the agreement in 1975 by OECD countries to establish a "safety net" for industrialized countries in the form of a mutual aid fund, in the amount of $25 billion, to provide credit or credit guarantees as a last resort to the financially weaker members of the organization. These two innovative concepts, together with substantial aid transfers by both the industrialized countries and the oil exporters and a greater demand than expected for imports on the part of OPEC, have substantially eased the recycling problems that had been anticipated.

On a broader scale, a new approach to international cooperation was successfully launched at the Conference on International Economic Cooperation in December 1975. Ministers representing eight industrialized and 19 developing countries, including seven OPEC members, agreed to establish four commissions to examine problems related to energy, raw materials (including food), development, and finance. These commissions, restricted to 15 members each, were to report at the end of 1976. Canada was one of two co-chairmen of the conference, and has had a continuing coordinating role in its work. In addition, Canadian representatives participate directly in the two commissions dealing with energy and development.

13.3.2   Natural gas

Demand for natural gas in 1975 increased slightly from 1974. Net sales in Canada of 1,325 MMMcf (38 billion m³) were only 0.8% more than the 1974 total of 1,314 MMMcf (37 billion m³), while exports of 946.9 MMMcf (26.8 billion m³) showed a decrease of 1.3%.

Ontario, the largest provincial market, consuming 48% of all natural gas used in Canada, had a 2.1% reduction in sales between 1974 and 1975. Quebec's low increase of 2.7% during 1975, in sharp contrast to the 25% increase in 1974, is a result of no additional natural gas being available from Alberta for the Quebec market. Alberta, the second largest consuming province, with 23% of all Canadian gas sales, accounted for most of the increase in Canadian consumption in 1975. Commercial sales were the major factor in the Alberta increase. Saskatchewan and Manitoba had net sales decreases. The largest increase in domestic demand occurred in British Columbia where net sales of 145 MMMcf (4.1 billion m³) showed a 12.5% increase. However, BC sales were still less than consumption in 1973 when decline in production set in at the Beaver River and Pointed Mountain fields, two of the principal natural gas supplying fields.

Local and provincial natural gas utility companies purchase gas from major gas pipeline companies and operate their own pipeline systems to supply the public. Primarily active in the final distribution of gas, they currently spend increasing amounts on exploration and production in western Canada because of rising wellhead prices and projected shortfalls relative to expanding demand.

Commercial users recorded the highest rate of growth at 3.8%, compared with an increase of 2.1% for residential users. This was offset by a 0.8% decline in sales to industrial users and electric utilities.

Net exports of natural gas to the US totalled 947 MMMcf (26.8 billion m³) for the year, a 2.2% decrease from the 959 MMMcf (27.2 billion m³) exported the previous year. This decrease was attributable to delivery problems in the Beaver River field in northern British Columbia. While there may be sufficient gas reserves in a field to satisfy customer demand for a period of time, declining pressures and other production factors may limit the rate at which the gas can be extracted and delivered to market. Such problems in the Beaver River field caused a shortfall in meeting contractual obligations of Westcoast Transmission Company Limited to customers in the Pacific Northwest region of the US.

The government decided future exports would be within the recommendations of the NEB report of April 1975, *Canadian natural gas — supply and requirements.* In the event of gas shortages, timing and amounts of cutbacks would be determined only after consultation between the federal and provincial governments and the US government.

New export price   13.3.2.1

A hearing in 1974 into the pricing of Canadian natural gas being exported led to establishment of a uniform border price substantially above the prices prevailing. Long-term licences to export gas cover about 1 MMMMcf (28.3 billion m³) a year (about 40% of Canadian production). At the 1974 hearing, export prices were found to be unrealistically low when compared with the greatly increased cost of fuel oil, the principal alternative to gas for residential, commercial and most industrial uses. The NEB recommended that natural gas exported to the US should be priced on the basis of a scarce, non-renewable natural resource; that initially a new export price of $1 per thousand cubic feet (Mcf) ($35.31/thousand m³) be established; and that the price be increased progressively toward the commodity value. In supporting this recommendation, the government also endorsed the principle of further price increases. In approving the new export price of $1/Mcf ($35.31/thousand m³), the government stipulated that additional export revenues thus generated should be paid to gas producers to encourage additional exploration and production. In British Columbia most of the additional revenue was paid to the British Columbia Petroleum Corporation.

In May 1975 the Minister of Energy, Mines and Resources announced increased export prices of natural gas to $1.40/Mcf ($49.44/thousand m³) in August and $1.60/Mcf ($56.50/thousand m³) in November 1975. These were followed by increases to $1.80/Mcf ($63.57/thousand m³) in September 1976 and $1.94/Mcf ($68.51/thousand m³) in January 1977.

For the domestic market, the federal government raised the price of natural gas, after consultation with the provinces, from approximately $0.82/Mcf

($28.96/thousand m³) to $1.25/Mcf ($44.14/thousand m³) at the Toronto city-gate, November 1, 1975. This was increased to $1.405/Mcf ($49.62/thousand m³) in July 1976 and $1.505/Mcf ($53.15/thousand m³) in January 1977.

Inquiry into natural gas supplies. Hearings on the supply, demand and delivery of Canadian natural gas were held in a number of gas producing and consuming areas of Canada starting in November 1974, and completed in March 1975. The NEB released its report in July 1975.

Over the longer term it may be assumed that there will be a growing demand for natural gas in Canada at prices competitive with oil. Exploration in the Arctic areas and off the Labrador Coast has been more successful in finding large natural gas reserves than oil. The ability to use these resources to meet demands in the settled areas of Canada depends on building pipelines. A proposal to build a 48-inch (122 cm) gas pipeline from Prudhoe Bay in Alaska and the Mackenzie Delta in Canada to carry Alaskan gas to the US and to move Delta and Beaufort Sea gas to Canadian markets was placed before the NEB in March 1974. An alternative proposal to build a 42-inch (107 cm) line from the Delta to carry only Canadian gas to the existing pipeline systems of Alberta and British Columbia was filed in the summer of 1975.

Construction of northern pipelines would make substantial supplies of gas available, but estimates indicate that costs of frontier gas would be higher than the current Canadian price or the "commodity value" of gas in terms of the present price of oil in Canada.

The Government of Canada has expressed the view that the price of natural gas in Canada should rise over a period of years to reflect a more competitive valuation with respect to oil, on a delivered energy equivalent basis. Phased increases in gas prices, to reflect such a "commodity value" with crude oil, were discussed by provincial and federal representatives for more than a year prior to the Energy Conference of April 1975. No price changes were announced but the federal government reiterated its stand and discussions were to continue.

13.4   Uranium and nuclear energy

To meet the fuel requirements for the growing number of nuclear power generating stations around the world, the demand for uranium has increased markedly since 1974 and is expected to continue growing dramatically over the next two decades at least. This strong demand is in sharp contrast to that over the previous decade when the demand was small, prices were depressed, and many mines that had opened in response to the military demand from the US and UK in the late 1950s were forced to close.

In the early 1970s the over-supply of uranium throughout the world had driven prices to below $5/lb. ($11/kg) of uranium oxide (U_3O_8). The increased demand which began in 1974 resulted in prices climbing to about $40/lb. ($88/kg) U_3O_8 in 1976.

Export demand and the need to meet domestic requirements resulted in the announcement of a new uranium policy in September 1974. Sufficient uranium will be reserved for domestic use to enable each nuclear power reactor which is operating, committed for construction or planned for operation in the next 10 years to operate at an average annual capacity factor of 80% for 30 years from the start of the period, or in the case of reactors which are not yet in operation, for 30 years from their in-service dates. Current projections indicate an operational nuclear capacity approaching 15 000 MW by 1986, requiring an immediate allocation of about 81,000 tons (73 000 t) of uranium oxide for these reactors. This reserve requirement is apportioned among mining companies according to their uranium resources relative to the total Canadian recoverable resources as determined by a Uranium Resource Appraisal Group established in the Department of Energy, Mines and Resources.

This group has estimated, based on information up to the end of 1975, that Canada has 462,000 tons (419 000 t) of U_3O_8 mineable for up to $40/lb. ($88/kg). This is a 7.8% increase over the estimate of the previous year, after taking account of production of 4,600 tons (4 200 t) during 1975, and indicates the results of increased exploration since the recovery of prices that began in 1974.

The largest reserves and mines at present are in the Elliot Lake area of Ontario. In other areas, Madawaska Mines Ltd. has re-opened a mine near Bancroft, Ont., the Crown company Eldorado Nuclear Ltd. continues to operate its mine near Uranium City, Sask., and Gulf Minerals Canada Ltd. has begun production from its Rabbit Lake deposit in Saskatchewan. Exploration is active in many parts of Canada and some significant deposits have been identified in northeastern Saskatchewan. This exploration is expected to lead to a considerable increase in Canada's known uranium resources which will permit continuation of other major export programs while ensuring ample fuel supply for the growing number of domestic nuclear power generating stations.

The decision to build nuclear power generating stations rests with the provincial electrical utilities. Ontario Hydro has decided that the majority of new generation will be nuclear, New Brunswick Power is building its first unit and Hydro-Québec is building a commercial unit near the demonstration unit built by the federal Crown corporation, Atomic Energy of Canada Ltd., at Gentilly, Que. Hydro-Québec announced in 1976 its expectation of going to a large nuclear power program beginning in the late 1980s.

As of the summer of 1976 there were seven nuclear power units operating in Canada.

Station	Owner	Output (MWe)
NPD	OH/AECL	25
Douglas Point	AECL[1]	208
Gentilly 1	AECL[2]	250
Pickering 1 to 4	OH	2 056

[1]Operated by Ontario Hydro.
[2]Operated by Hydro-Québec.

Units under construction or committed are:

Station	Owner	Output (MWe)	In-service date
Bruce 1-4[1]	OH	2 984	1977-79
Pickering 5-8	OH	2 064	1981-83
Gentilly 2	HQ	638	1979
LePreau	NBEPC	635	1981
Bruce 5-8	OH	3 076	1983-86

[1]The first unit of the Bruce station was started in the summer of 1976 and was still under commissioning tests at time of publication.

The total output of operating and committed stations is 11 936 MWe. A further 2 900 MWe is expected to be in service by 1986, with projections of 50 000 to 75 000 MWe by the year 2000. It is predicted that nuclear energy will provide about 40% of the electricity generated by the turn of the century.

Coal   13.5

Canadian production of coal in 1975 was 27.9 million short tons (25 300 000 t) valued at $575 million (Table 13.9). Production increased by almost 20% while the dollar value of output rose by 90% over that of the previous year. Production increased in all provinces with British Columbia posting the largest gain in terms of value. Extraction of coal in western Canada totalled 25.6 million short tons (23 200 000 t) while the output of Nova Scotia and New Brunswick mines totalled 2.3 million short tons (2 100 000 t). Imports from the US reached 17.4 million short tons (15 800 000 t) up from the unusually low figure of 13.6 million short tons (12 300 000 t) in 1974.

About 30% of production, or 12.6 million short tons (11 400 000 t), was exported in 1975 with British Columbia and Alberta contributing approximately 97% of the export tonnage. Japan received 11.6 million short tons (10 500 000 t) or 92% of all exports. Spot shipments of coal were made to a growing list of countries including the US, France, Federal Republic of Germany, Denmark, Holland and the UK.

Canada's coal industry serves two principal types of markets: the production of thermal power and the manufacture of coke for the steel industry. The use of coal for thermal power generation has a promising potential particularly in Alberta, Saskatchewan, Ontario and British Columbia. Virtually all of Canada's coking coal is exported and competes in the international market.

In 1975 approximately 8.0 million short tons (7 300 000 t) of coking coal was converted to coke. Imports from the US provided roughly 90% of the coking coal used, with Canadian steel companies importing approximately 55% from captive mines in that country.

Coal used for thermal-electric power generation increased by 7% to 18.2 million short tons (16 500 000 t) in 1975. Domestic coal, mainly subbituminous coal in Alberta and lignite in Saskatchewan, supplied over 9 million short tons (8 200 000 t) to local power stations. Bituminous coal is used in small quantities for thermal power generation in New Brunswick and Nova Scotia. Ontario Hydro imported the remainder used in the thermal power industry.

Demand for coal by other Canadian industries reached 1.5 million short tons (1 400 000 t), while the demand for coal for space heating was approximately 300,000 short tons (272 000 t) in 1975.

British Columbia. Within British Columbia, coal mining is being conducted in the Crowsnest Pass region in the southeastern portion of the province.

Kaiser Resources Ltd., with two operating mines in the Crowsnest coal field, produced about 6.2 million short tons (5 600 000 t) of coking coal and 800,000 short tons (726 000 t) of oxidized coal in 1975. An expansion program that altered the capacity of its surface mining operation and a new contract allowed Kaiser to increase its commitments to Japan during 1975. A joint feasibility study between Kaiser and two Japanese companies on the development of a new hydraulic mine south of Kaiser's operations continued during the 1975 field season, and was expected to be completed in 1976.

The Fording Coal Limited mine near Elkford, about 40 miles (64 km) north of Sparwood, BC, produced approximately 3.2 million short tons (2 900 000 t) of coal in 1975. Fording ships almost all its production to Japan. In an effort to improve its clean coal yield Fording began work on modification of its preparation plant during 1975.

Byron Creek Collieries produced 350,000 short tons (318 000 t) of coal in 1975, 200,000 (181 000 t) of this going to Ontario Hydro, with other destinations being Manitoba and Japan.

Through 1976 studies were conducted in three areas of British Columbia on potential metallurgical and thermal coal developments. In northeastern British Columbia, these included marketing, transportation, socio-economic and feasibility studies at several locations with the prospects of metallurgical exports dependent on world demand conditions as well as production, transportation and other costs. Decisions on this development were expected in 1977. In southeastern British Columbia, European, Japanese and Canadian interests have been looking at the prospects of developing more capacity at four locations. BC Hydro and Power Authority was conducting studies into the feasibility of using the Hat Creek lignite deposits near Ashcroft for future power generation.

Alberta. In tonnage terms Alberta is Canada's leading coal-producing province, producing both subbituminous and bituminous coals. Subbituminous coal is primarily used for electricity generation, although its use in a newly developed direct-reduction iron-making process opens the possibility of new markets. Most bituminous coal is exported to Japan. Bituminous production reached 4.5 million short tons (4 100 000 t) while subbituminous production rose to 6.5 million short tons (5 900 000 t). These levels represented increases of 25% and 16% respectively, over 1974 outputs.

Alberta continued to expand its subbituminous industry in 1975 and 1976 to meet its demand for energy. Alberta subbituminous coal was also used to produce power in Saskatchewan. Thermal electric plants are generally located close to coal mines to facilitate low cost power generation. At Wabamun Lake, 40 miles (64 km) west of Edmonton, Calgary Power Ltd. operates two power plants on coal from two mines. Other coal-fired power plants include the Drumheller, Battle River and Grande Cache stations. While coal will continue to play an important role in Alberta's electric utility planning for some time, the decision in 1976 not to approve the Dodds–Round Hill development, 40 miles (64 km) southeast of Edmonton, demonstrated the government's concern with projects that produce conflicting demands on certain agricultural land.

Alberta's new coal policy released in 1976 stressed increased royalties, more comprehensive regulations and a new land classification system. Royalties were increased from 10 cents a ton (11 cents a tonne) to a sliding percentage scale based on profits and capital investments. Environmental, social, economic and reclamation studies will now be required prior to any new development, and all proposed developments must go through several evaluations by different government agencies and departments. The policy divides Alberta into four zones varying from one in which no exploration or development will be permitted to one in which the restrictions are less severe.

In mid-1976, the Alberta cabinet gave its conditional approval to two coal developments. The Luscar Sterco Ltd. project 100 miles (161 km) west of Edmonton and Gregg River Resources Ltd. 10 miles (16 km) south of Hinton were allowed to proceed on condition that they conform with the regulations contained in the new coal policy. The Luscar Sterco Ltd. project is to supply thermal coal to Ontario Hydro for a period of 15 years.

Four mines produce coking coal in Alberta. In 1975 the largest operator, McIntyre Mines Limited near Grande Cache, produced about 1.9 million short tons (1 700 000 t) of mainly coking coal for markets in Japan, the US and Canada. In 1975 McIntyre shipped 350,000 short tons (318 000 t) of coal to Ontario and Nova Scotia steel producers and was continuing test shipments in 1976.

After a five month miners' strike curtailed production to 800,000 short tons (726 000 t) in 1974, Cardinal River Coals Ltd. produced approximately 1.5 million short tons (1 400 000 t) in 1975. Cardinal River diversified its markets in 1975 by making a shipment to Ontario in addition to its Japanese shipments.

The Canmore Mines Ltd. produced 185,000 short tons (168 000 t) of semi-anthracite coal in 1975. Coleman Collieries Limited produced 850,000 short tons (771 000 t) of coal in 1975 from underground and open-pit mines. The underground operations are being phased out, and in the future production will come from the Tent Mountain open-pit site. Deliveries to Japan are scheduled to reach 900,000 short tons (816 000 t) by 1977.

Saskatchewan. In 1975, four lignite mines in the Estevan–Bienfait region of southern Saskatchewan produced about 3.9 million short tons (3 500 000 t) of lignite. The Manitoba and Saskatchewan Coal Company (Limited) and Utility Coals Limited produced nearly 2.8 million short tons (2 500 000 t) for the Saskatchewan Power Corporation Boundary Dam power station. Other production in Saskatchewan came from the Bienfait M & S Mine and Manalta's Klimax Mine, both of which served power generation and industrial markets.

Lignite production is expanding to meet the growing requirements of the Saskatchewan Power Corporation. The Boundary Dam station at Estevan is the largest user of lignite. When the generating capacity of this station is increased by 300 MW in 1977, its coal consumption will increase to 4.5 million short tons (4 100 000 t) annually. Recent contracts with Ontario Hydro and the planned East Poplar River power station will further expand the markets for Saskatchewan lignite, which for several years have included two thermal power stations in Manitoba.

New Brunswick. In 1974 N.B. Coal Limited, a provincial Crown company, produced a total of 461,000 short tons (418 000 t) of coal from six surface mines within the Minto coal field. Approximately 156,000 short tons (142 000 t) went to pulp and paper mills in Quebec and the remainder was delivered to the NB Electric Power Commission's Grand Lake and Chatham power stations.

Nova Scotia. Production of coal in Nova Scotia reached 1.8 million short tons (1 600 000 t) in 1975, up almost 30% over 1974. Production was limited in 1975 by a fire in No. 26 mine at Glace Bay that resulted in its closure for several weeks. Another increase was expected in 1976 with expanded production at the Lingan and No. 26 mines, and the opening of the Prince Mine at Point Aconi. Approximately two thirds of the Nova Scotia production is thermal coal, with about one third consumed in Nova Scotia and the other one third exported to Europe and Canadian destinations. Approximately 600,000 short tons (544 000 t) was used by the Nova Scotia steel industry. In the latter part of 1976, Stelco Ltd. (Hamilton) was to begin receiving its first shipments of Nova Scotia coal, the result of a new five-year, 2.5 million short tons (2 300 000 t) contract. The expansion of production and the completion of a new wash plant indicate the resiliency of the Nova Scotia coal industry. While the new Prince Mine is projected to have a life of only 10 years, a jointly funded federal-provincial inventory program is under way to evaluate potential new deposits of coal in several areas of Nova Scotia.

Outlook. Strong demand for Canadian coking and thermal coal reflects expanding foreign requirements and projected growth of the domestic electric utility industry. Japanese steel companies could double imports from Canada in the next 10 years to approximately 25 million tons (23 000 000 t) annually. Other countries are also interested in this resource, including Britain, South Korea, Mexico and the Federal Republic of Germany. Contracts of Ontario Hydro for thermal coal and the delivery system to be developed for this, mark a new phase in Canada's coal industry. In a time of rising coal prices and potential reduced availability, development of a delivery system to provide a potential alternate source of supply will benefit coal consumers in central Canada. Increasing prices and decreasing availability of alternate fuels, together with the advances in coal gasification technology could put major demands on western Canadian thermal resources in the 1980s. Some of the major problems facing Canada's coal industry include longer lead times for mine development, introduction of new and more stringent regulations, shortages and longer delivery times for mining and processing equipment, the costs of and the need to upgrade transportation and terminal handling capacities, higher construction, development and operating costs, and anticipated shortages of skilled labour.

13.6   Electric power

13.6.1   Electric power development

Additions to generating capacity during 1975 raised the total installed capacity at year-end by 2.2% to 58 738 MW (megawatt = 1 000 kilowatts). The 1 258 MW added during the year included 311 MW of hydro-electric generation and 947

MW of conventional thermal generation together with some minor changes in gas turbine and internal combustion installations.

Conventional thermal installations provided 75.3% of new capacity added in 1975, compared with 20.3% in 1974, largely as a result of the completion of the fifth 500-MW unit at the coal-fired Nanticoke station in Ontario. Other thermal additions included a 150-MW unit at Battle River in Alberta and the sixth 152-MW unit at the Burrard Station in British Columbia. There were no new nuclear additions in 1975.

Hydro-electric generation additions took place in British Columbia where the first two of four 125-MW units were added at the Kootenay Canal Station. Other additions included a 31.05-MW unit at Première Chute in Quebec and a 30-MW unit at Aishihik in the Yukon Territory.

Load growth in terms of energy in 1975 declined by 0.3%, a situation only approached in recent years by the 1.5% growth recorded in 1961. The slower growth in total electricity used in Canada combined with reduced exports resulted in a reduction of 2.3% in total net generation to 272.62 TWh (1 Terrawatthour = 10^9 kWh). On a national basis, electrical energy consumption totalled 265.23 TWh which is distributed across the country in the ratio of approximately 34% in each of Quebec and Ontario, 12% in BC, 5% to 6% in each of Alberta and Manitoba and 2% to 3% in each of Newfoundland, New Brunswick, Nova Scotia and Saskatchewan, with Prince Edward Island, the Yukon and Northwest Territories each accounting for less than two tenths of 1% of the total. However, growth rates varied considerably across the country from a decrease of 6.0% in Newfoundland to an increase of 17.7% in the Yukon. The "growth" pattern is quite consistently linked to significant reduction in industrial electricity demand in all provinces (excluding the territories) and ranged from decreases of 27.5% in Saskatchewan to 3.3% in Alberta. The average decline for Canada as a whole was 11.4%, reflecting the performance of the economy which exhibited GNP growth of only 2.2%; it also reflected a reduction of 2.3% in the index of real domestic product. In contrast, domestic and commercial electrical energy consumption grew by 8.8% and 6% respectively, largely balancing the reduction in industrial demand. Since utility generation planning decisions are predicated on meeting longer-term average growth expectations the low growth in total electrical energy utilization presents special problems for utility revenues, especially when these are already under pressure from rising costs.

Net export of electrical energy continued the downward trend of the previous year falling to 7.4 TWh or 2.7% of net generation compared with 13.0 TWh and 4.6% in 1974. It is interesting to note that electrical energy generated in Canada (i.e. by Ontario Hydro) from coal imported from the US exceeded 20 TWh or nearly three times the net electrical energy export from Canada to the US.

A joint study is under way by the eastern provinces, including Quebec and the Atlantic provinces, to determine the opportunities for sharing generating capability and reinforcing transmission capacity. The Interprovincial Advisory Committee on Energy has been looking into opportunities for better regional ties and cooperation between provinces at the planning and operational levels.

Generating capacity   13.6.2

Power generating capability is the measurement of the available generating resources of all hydro and thermal facilities at the time of the one-hour firm peak load for each reporting company and is not equal to the installed capacity of such generating facilities. Electric power generated in Canada during 1975 was equivalent to 53.0% of the amount which in theory could be generated if the total installed capacity at the end of the year were operating continuously. The balance reflects fluctuations in load below peak demand during daily and seasonal cycles together with reserves of generating capacity.

Total generating capability has grown at a rapid rate especially in the past few decades. The annual rate of increase was 7.9% in the period 1963-73 and 7.1% in the period 1971-75. In comparison, the forecast rate of growth for the years 1976-80 is 6.5%; thermal generating capability is expected to grow at an average rate of nearly 11% a year in the forecast period compared with 12.6% in the period 1963-73, and hydro-electric capability is expected to increase at 4.2% a year compared with 6.1% in the 1963-74 period. This rate of growth in hydro generating capability in the forecast period is attributable to the large power projects under construction in relatively remote areas that will be completed within the next few years.

Among the provinces, Ontario has the largest generating capability in all forms, followed by Quebec, British Columbia and Newfoundland. Quebec has the largest hydro generation capability, followed by Ontario, Newfoundland and British Columbia. Ontario has the largest thermal generation capability, followed by Alberta and British Columbia.

The largest absolute growth in generating capability for the forecast years 1976-80 is indicated for Ontario at 7 295 MW, followed by Quebec at 4 626 MW, British Columbia at 3 166 MW and New Brunswick at 2 000 MW. Ontario will meet most of its increased generating capability by adding 4 145 MW in fossil-fuelled capability and 2 984 MW nuclear. British Columbia will add 3 098 MW hydro and 68 MW thermal, and Quebec 3 377 MW hydro and 1 249 MW thermal.

13.6.3   Hydro-electric power generation

Hydro-electric generation forms a significant though decreasing part in Canada's electrical development. By the end of 1975, the hydro portion of the country's total generating capacity had fallen to 63.1% from over 90%, 20 years earlier.

In view of the vast water resources existing throughout Canada, it would appear that many undeveloped sites could be potential sources of hydro-electric power. However, not all these possibilities represent economically viable sources. Only a fraction of the sites with a theoretical power potential can actually be developed competitively. Before a site can be termed a source of potential power, a detailed analysis of such factors as cost, geography, geology and ecology must be performed. Until such a study is completed on a national scale, estimates of Canada's undeveloped water-power resources (recently estimated to be in excess of 60 000 MW), may be misleading.

Figures of water-power resources already developed are given in Table 13.10 and are based on the manufacturer's rating in kilowatts as shown on the generator name-plate, or derived from the electrical rating. The maximum economic installation at a power site can be determined only by careful consideration of all the conditions and circumstances pertinent to its individual development. It is normal practice to install units having a combined capacity in excess of the available continuous power at Q50 (flow available 50% of the time), and frequently in excess of the power available at Qm (arithmetical mean flow). There are a number of reasons for this. Excess capacity may be installed for use at peak-load periods, to take advantage of periods of high flow, or to facilitate plant or system maintenance. In some instances, storage dams have been built after initial development to smooth out fluctuations in river flows. In other cases, deficiencies in power output during periods of low flow have been offset by auxiliary power supplied from thermal plants, or by interconnection with other plants operating under different load conditions or located on rivers with different flow characteristics. The extent to which installed capacity exceeds the available continuous power at various rates of flow depends on factors that govern the system or plant operation, and varies widely from one area to another.

The distribution of installed hydro-electric generating capacity given in Table 13.10 reveals that substantial amounts of water power have been developed in all provinces and territories except Prince Edward Island. As natural-resource development proceeds, the fortunate incidence of water power near mineral, forest and other resources becomes increasingly apparent. The vast hydro potential of northern rivers may well prove to be a prime factor in the eventual realization of the natural wealth of the Canadian North.

The water-power resources of Nova Scotia and New Brunswick, although small in comparison with those of other provinces, are a valuable source of energy and make a substantial contribution to the economies of the two provinces. Numerous rivers provide moderate-sized power sites either within economic transmission distance of the principal cities and towns or advantageously situated for use in development of the timber and mineral resources. These provinces have, however, turned to thermal generation, initially coal-fired with a subsequent shift to oil. Plans are now well advanced for development of nuclear generation in New Brunswick and there have been recent indications of a possible return to coal as a fuel source for new installations.

Thermal power generation   13.6.4

The immense water-power resources and the brisk pace of their development have tended to overshadow the considerable contribution being made by thermal energy to Canada's power economy. From a modest 133 MW of generating capacity installed at the end of 1900, Canada's installed hydro capacity rose to 37 090 MW by the end of 1975 and thermal capacity to 21 648 MW (Table 13.10).

The same table shows that thermal generation is predominant in Prince Edward Island and Nova Scotia. By the end of 1971, the Yukon Territory had joined the Northwest Territories, Alberta, Saskatchewan and Ontario in having more than half their total capacity thermal-electric. Thermal generation is expected to become increasingly predominant in Ontario. Although coal is still the most important fossil fuel for thermal plants in Nova Scotia, oil is the preferred choice for new thermal power generation in the other Atlantic provinces.

Over 90% of all thermal power generating equipment in Canada is driven by steam turbines fired by coal, oil, gas or, in the case of nuclear equipment, uranium. The magnitude of loads carried by steam plants combined with the economies of scale has led to the installation of steam units with capacities as high as 540 MW, and units in the 800-MW size range were committed for as early as 1976. Additions of these larger units are only possible where systems are large enough to accommodate them. Additional types of thermal generation are provided by gas turbine and internal combustion equipment; their flexibility makes them particularly suitable for meeting power loads in smaller centres, especially in the more isolated areas. Gas turbines are frequently used for peak loads; their rapid start-up ability and minimal capital cost are manifest advantages.

After World War II, industrial expansion and rapidly growing residential and agricultural development placed extremely heavy demands on power generating facilities, impossible to satisfy by hydro sources alone. An extensive program of thermal plant construction began in the early 1950s; by 1956 thermal capacity represented 15% of the total. Since then, the annual installed capacity has averaged 56% hydro-electric with the remainder in thermal generation. At the end of 1975 thermal capacity accounted for 36.9% of Canada's installed capacity.

Thermal plants accounted for only 25.8% of total generation in 1975 because much of the capacity installed is operated for peak-load duty only, with hydro-electric capacity providing base-load generation. This pattern will change with the introduction of additional nuclear-fuelled thermal generation plants which can operate economically at high capacity for base-load purposes.

Nuclear thermal power. Commercial electric power generated from the heat of nuclear reaction became a reality in Canada in 1962 when the 20-MW Nuclear Power Demonstration (NPD) station at Rolphton, Ont., the forerunner of a series of large nuclear stations, fed power for the first time into a distribution system in Ontario.

Atomic Energy of Canada Limited (AECL), a federal Crown company incorporated in 1952, has concentrated on development of the CANDU power reactor using heavy water (deuterium oxide) as a moderator for slowing or "moderating" the neutrons released by nuclear fission. The high neutron economy obtained by using this moderator with neutron-transparent core materials (zirconium alloys) means that Canada's abundant resources of natural uranium may be used as fuel. The CANDU system is however, sufficiently flexible that enriched uranium, plutonium recovered from spent fuel, or thorium may be incorporated into its fuel system.

The production of heavy water has been a critical item in the Canadian nuclear power program. The first 800-ton-a-year (726 t) heavy water production plant at Ontario Hydro's Bruce nuclear power development on Lake Huron went into operation in 1973 and is producing at over 80% of its design capacity. Ontario Hydro is now building the first of two additional plants at the Bruce site and completion is scheduled for 1978. In Nova Scotia rehabilitation of the Glace Bay plant continued with start-up scheduled for 1976, and operation of the Port Hawkesbury plant was considerably improved after modifications. Ownership of this plant was transferred from Canadian General Electric to AECL in May 1975. There will be a two-year delay in the construction of the new 800-ton-a-year (726 t) La Prade plant owned by AECL at the Gentilly site in Quebec. The first 400-ton unit (363 t) is expected to be operating by 1981.

At Douglas Point, on the shore of Lake Huron, the country's first full-scale nuclear power station went into operation in 1966. The station, built with the cooperation of Ontario Hydro, houses a 220-MW CANDU reactor. Experience gained in the design and operation of the NPD and Douglas Point reactors encouraged and contributed to the development of larger units. Construction of the 2 160-MW Pickering nuclear station near Toronto is now complete; two of the station's four units came on line in 1971 and units 3 and 4 produced their first electricity ahead of schedule in 1972 and 1973. Work on the Bruce nuclear station for Ontario Hydro is proceeding with four 800-MW units planned for installation from 1976 to 1979. In addition, a duplicate of the Pickering station, at the Bruce site, has been committed and Hydro-Québec and New Brunswick Electric Power Commission have started construction of 600-MW CANDU stations at Gentilly and at Point LePreau.

A further step in the development of the CANDU reactor is the use of boiling light water instead of pressurized heavy water as the coolant. The initial Gentilly nuclear power station (Gentilly 1) utilizes boiling light water in its CANDU reactor; this station came into service in 1971 with 266 MW of nuclear-electric capacity.

13.6.5   Load demand and electrical energy use

Firm power peak load is the measure of the maximum average net kilowatt demand of one-hour duration from all loads, including commercial, residential, farm and industrial consumers as well as the line losses. Such load demand increased at the rate of 7.5% a year from 1963 to 1973 and 7.4% a year from 1969 to 1973; peak-load demand is forecast to increase at the average rate of 7.4% a year in the period 1976-80. As a result of the rapid increase in generating capability and the somewhat slower but steady increase in the peak loads, together with the slight reduction in deliveries of firm power to the US, the indicated reserve on net capability in the 1961-75 period increased each year except 1961, 1963, 1964, 1966 and 1972. The reserve ratio as a percentage of firm power peak load reached a high of 28.2% in 1960 and fell to 13.7% in 1968 but is expected to increase to 20.0% in 1980. Absolute figures are given in Table 13.11.

As indicated in Table 13.12, total electrical energy consumed in Canada during 1974, showed industrial loads at 42% down sharply from 67% in 1950; domestic and farm consumption at 22%, up from 13% in 1950; and commercial consumption at 27% in 1974, the latest year for which detailed statistics were available, up from 11% in 1950.

While availability of electric energy at reasonable cost is an important element in Canada's industrial growth, in only a few industries is the cost of electric power a key element in economic competitiveness. Energy distribution for industry can be subdivided approximately as follows: one third to the mineral industry (including smelting and refining), one quarter to the pulp and paper industry, one tenth to chemical manufacturing and the remaining portion to all other industrial categories.

The growth among non-industrial customers results from a greater reliance by Canada's population on facilities powered by electricity. Tremendous quantities of electric energy are required, for example, to meet rapidly escalating demands for heating, cooling, lighting, transportation, elevators, electrical appliances and farm machinery. The shift of population from rural areas to cities and towns, where electrical demand is greatest, contributed to this growth.

Details of the regional pattern of electric energy use can be seen in Table 13.13. Of total energy made available in Canada during 1974 more than two thirds was consumed in Ontario and Quebec with all other regions accounting for the remaining one third. The share of total consumption by these other regions has, however, been rising (combined total of 26% in 1960 as against 33% in 1974) and dropped from 34% in Ontario to 33%. The actual portion of total energy consumed by industry in 1974 ranged from a high of 51% in British Columbia and Quebec, to a low of 28% in the Prairie region. Domestic and farm consumption remains greatest in the Prairie provinces and Ontario but for different reasons. In Ontario, where the majority of people are urban dwellers, high demand from the large cities accounts for the higher level, while in the Prairies it results from a substantial farming load combined with a normal level of domestic usage.

Part of Canada's growing need for electric power reflects a growth in population but per capita consumption increased 5.3% to 11 900 kWh in 1974, up more than 95% since 1960. The Atlantic provinces experienced the largest increase, 242% to 8 900 kWh per capita, followed closely by the Prairie provinces with 197% to 9 200 kWh. The lowest over the period was in BC with only a 70% increase to 14 100 kWh per capita. Quebec recorded the highest per capita consumption in 1974, 14 900 kWh. Table 13.14 sets out details of this per capita consumption by region.

Electric power transmission   13.6.6

Loads handled by small, widely scattered generating systems in the early days of the electric power industry did not warrant the expense of interconnecting power systems. However, as demand for dependable electric power increased and as improved techniques reduced power transmission costs, the benefits of integrating power systems to achieve reliability of service and flexibility of operation were reappraised. Today, most of Canada's generating stations are components of large, integrated, and often interconnected, power systems operated by power utilities.

Research in power transmission has developed techniques enabling power producers to utilize hydro-electric sites previously considered beyond economic transmission distances. Most noticeable, perhaps, is the progressive stepping-up of transmission-line voltages. A number of transmission lines are designed for operation at 500 kilovolts (kV) and 735 kV. A 574-mile (924 km), 500-kV line is in service to carry power from the Peace River to the lower mainland of British Columbia. In Ontario, a 435-mile (700 km), 500-kV line carries power from hydro-electric plants in the James Bay watershed to Toronto. In 1965 Hydro-Québec achieved world leadership when power was carried for the first time at 735 kV over the 375-mile (604 km) transmission line linking Quebec's Manicouagan–Outardes hydro complex with the urban demand centres of Quebec and Montreal. By the end of 1971, the initial program for 1,228 miles (1 976 km) of the 735-kV line had been completed, and three 735-kV circuits connecting the Churchill Falls generation station to the Hydro-Québec grid are now in service.

Most power is transmitted as alternating current but there are three applications of high-voltage direct-current (HVDC). In service in British Columbia is a 260-kV HVDC link from the mainland to Vancouver Island. This facility has a capacity of 312 MW and includes 21 miles (34 km) of undersea cable; it is a monopolar system using the ground as a return path for current. It was being expanded to 624 MW for an in-service date of 1976. A 450-kV HVDC system was placed in service in 1973 linking the Kettle generation station on the Nelson River to Winnipeg where two 555-mile (893 km) lines have been completed and converter equipment with an initial capacity of 810 MW is in service. The planned ultimate rating of this system is 3 200 MW. Another application designed to provide a non-synchronous tie between the power systems of New Brunswick and Quebec is a 320-MW back-to-back HVDC system located at Eel River, NB. This facility was placed in service in 1972 employing solid state thyristor valves in place of the mercury arc valves used for the earlier-committed HVDC systems in British Columbia and Manitoba.

Interconnections of 66 kV and 138 kV already exist between British Columbia and Alberta and a 230-kV tie is being planned. Saskatchewan, Manitoba, Ontario and portions of the Quebec system are interconnected and, through the Ontario Hydro system, are linked with northeastern United States systems. Quebec, New Brunswick and Nova Scotia systems are interconnected. The first major international tie connecting regions of the Maritimes in Canada with the United States became a reality during 1970 on completion of a 345-kV link between the New Brunswick and Maine systems. British Columbia has an international tie with the Pacific Northwest (500 kV) and a 230-kV link between Manitoba and the United States was completed in 1970.

The search for economies in transmission systems has led to changes not only in materials used but also in tower erection and cable-stringing methods. Guyed V-shaped and Y-shaped transmission towers are being used increasingly in place of self-supporting towers where the terrain is suitable, and erection costs are being reduced by the use of helicopters to transport tower sections to the site.

13.6.7   Electric utilities

Federal government regulation of electric utilities with respect to the export of electric power and the construction of lines over which such power is exported falls within the jurisdiction of the NEB.

Power is generated in Canada by publicly and privately operated utilities and by industrial establishments. Of the total electric power generated in 1974, 70.5% was produced by publicly operated utilities, 15.6% by privately operated utilities and 13.9% by industrial establishments. However, ownership varies greatly in different areas of the country. Although Quebec power installations were at one time privately owned, almost all were transferred to public ownership in 1963. In Ontario almost all electric power has been produced by a publicly owned utility for over 60 years.

Because the determination of market prices and regulation of services is limited to inter-fuel competition with oil, gas and coal, there is some regulation of electric utilities in all provinces. In all but two provinces major generation and main transmission of power is the responsibility of a provincial Crown corporation. Investor-owned electric utilities are prominent in Alberta, New-foundland and Prince Edward Island and continue to play a significant role in Ontario and British Columbia; they contributed about 15.6% of the total power generated in Canada in 1974. Non-utility generating facilities in industrial establishments represented 10.2% of installed capacity at the end of 1974 and generated 13.9% of the total electric energy produced in Canada in that year; however, on a percentage basis, there is a continuing decline in industrial generation as it becomes increasingly attractive to purchase power from utilities which can take advantage of larger unit sizes and operational flexibility. Even when process steam is required for industry, there are instances when it is advantageous to purchase both steam and power from the electric utility.

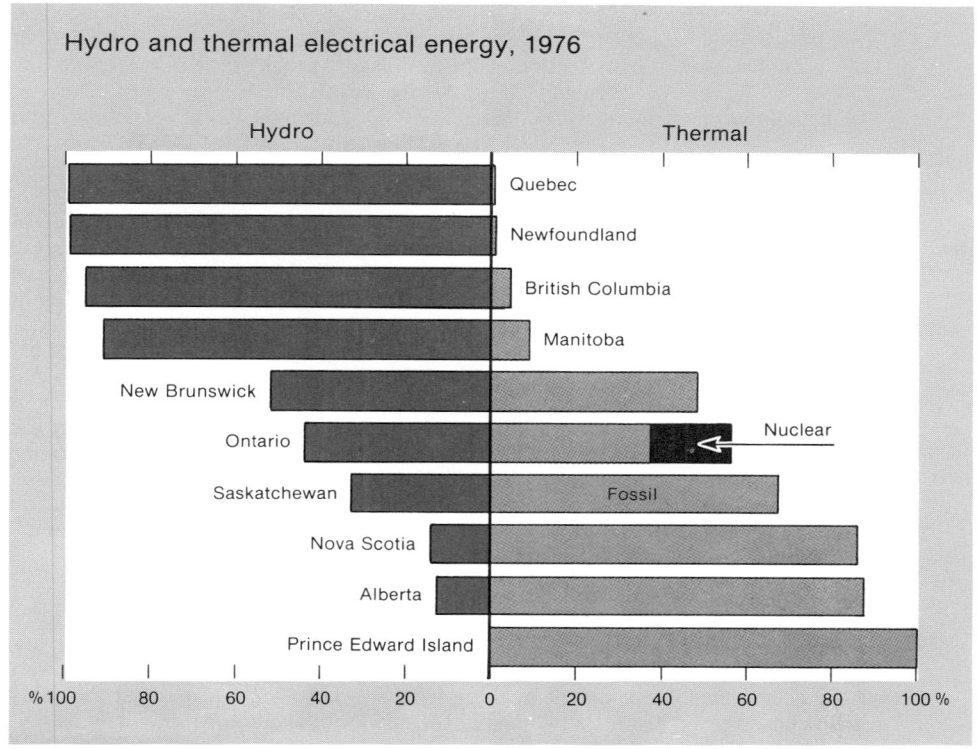

Hydro and thermal electrical energy, 1976

Hydro   Thermal

Quebec
Newfoundland
British Columbia
Manitoba
New Brunswick
Ontario — Nuclear
Saskatchewan — Fossil
Nova Scotia
Alberta
Prince Edward Island

% 100   80   60   40   20   0   20   40   60   80   100 %

Provincial developments in 1975   13.6.8

Newfoundland. The water-power resources of Newfoundland and Labrador are substantial. On the island, although the rivers are generally not long, topography and run-off favour hydro-electric power development and there are several potential hydro sites in Labrador in addition to sites on the Churchill River (Labrador), downstream of the Churchill Falls development.

The Newfoundland and Labrador Power Commission was established in 1954 to supply power wherever needed throughout the province. The commission began large-scale production of electric energy in 1967 when the Baie d'Espoir plant began operating and the provincial transmission grid was established. Power is supplied from this grid directly to several industries and to investor-owned electrical distribution companies for urban distribution. The Newfoundland Light and Power Company is the principal distributor. Bowater Power Company Limited supplies the Bowater Newfoundland Pulp and Paper Mills Limited and several mining operations. Electricity is provided to isolated areas by the Newfoundland and Labrador Power Commission through a Rural Electricity Authority and through Power Distribution Districts, principally by means of diesel generating facilities.

During 1975, the province established a new power entity, the Newfoundland and Labrador Hydro Electric Corporation (Newfoundland Hydro) with three constituents: the Churchill Falls (Labrador) Corporation, Gull Island Power Company Limited and the Newfoundland and Labrador Power Commission. The objective of the new corporation is to develop the hydro-electric resources of Newfoundland and Labrador.

While the corporation continued planning activity throughout the year on development of the proposed lower Churchill River at Gull Island and transmission via HVDC to the island of Newfoundland, it was decided in December to defer construction of the Gull Hydro project for a minimum of one year. However, the concept of Gull Hydro as a future energy source was not abandoned. Depending on updated load growth projections, Newfoundland Hydro may have to commit a 150-MW addition to the existing 300-MW Holyrood oil-fired thermal station, to meet energy demands that will arise before hydro energy from Labrador can become available under the revised scheduling.

In the near-term, generation additions were to include gas turbines at Stephenville (50 MW, 1976), Burin Peninsula (25 MW, 1976), St. John's (50 MW, 1976; 70 MW, 1978), Flowers Cove (15 MW, 1978) and an additional 154 MW hydro unit at Baie d'Espoir was scheduled for 1977 to increase the capacity of that station to 613 MW.

Energy demands from the Newfoundland and Labrador system declined 6% over 1974 due to a major reduction in industrial sales, influenced by strikes and market conditions. However, total load growth for the next several years is expected to exceed 8% per annum. About 94% of the electricity used in the province was produced by hydro, the remainder from oil-fired thermal plants. Power generation from Churchill Falls brought the province's hydro generation close to that of Ontario and exceeded British Columbia (35.3 TWh, 38.4 TWh and 31.1 TWh respectively) but approximately 84% of hydro production represented Churchill Falls power supplied to Quebec.

Prince Edward Island. The absence of large streams in the province has led to an almost total dependence on oil-fuelled thermal-power generation except for a few minor hydro plants. The Maritime Electric Company, Limited provides direct service to customers except in Summerside, where a municipal electric utility purchases power from that company for distribution; the town maintains a 6.9-MW diesel plant on stand-by.

The rapid increase in oil prices has escalated power costs for all classes of consumers. A submarine power cable to connect Prince Edward Island to the mainland via New Brunswick was expected to be installed by the end of 1977 to provide access to other power sources, including larger and more efficient fossil-fuelled plants and in due time nuclear generation. The federal government has announced a grant and long-term loan of $27 million for the project, which has been estimated to cost a total of $36 million.

Electricity used showed the highest growth rate for any province, 9.3% in 1975, exceeded only by the Yukon Territory. This reflects the predominance of residential and commercial loads in Prince Edward Island which as in other regions have shown considerable growth.

Nova Scotia. In 1973 the operations of the Nova Scotia Light and Power Company Limited and the Nova Scotia Power Commission were integrated into a single utility, the Nova Scotia Power Corporation, following provincial government purchase of shares held by private investors.

One of two 30-MW gas turbine units was added in 1975 in Cape Breton and the second was being installed in 1976. Progress was made on the addition of a 150-MW unit at Tufts Cove scheduled for service in 1976. Four 30-MW gas turbines were on order for service at Dartmouth.

About 89% of the province's electrical energy production was from thermal generation, and the fuel sources for this generation were 24% coal, 75% heavy oil, and 1% light oil. Increases in the costs of oil have given rise to consideration of several alternative generation additions.

Nova Scotia Power Corporation is considering installing a new thermal station in Cape Breton to use coal from a new mine in that area; the concept is a four-unit 600-MW station with the first unit targeted for service in 1979. The last substantial hydro site in the province, at Wreck Cove in Cape Breton, is being developed to provide 200 MW of peaking capacity, with a 100-MW unit to be added in 1977 and another in 1978.

Coal is expected to continue to be a major fuel for power generation in the Atlantic region, especially in Nova Scotia where the principal source of supply is the Sydney coal field of Cape Breton. The extent of expansion of capacity based on coal in the Atlantic region will depend on the amount of coal that can be economically developed. Exploration programs in New Brunswick and Nova Scotia were under way in 1975 to hasten an assessment of the overall local coal resource for thermal generation.

A major re-evaluation of tidal power as a further solution to the electrical energy supply problem has been launched and sites in both Nova Scotia and New Brunswick are being investigated in this $3 million study that is being funded jointly by Canada and the two provinces concerned.

Construction began in 1976 on an additional 138-kV transmission line between Truro, NS and Moncton, NB over a distance of approximately 130 miles (209 km) and capable of operation at 345 kV, to reinforce the Nova Scotia/New Brunswick interconnection.

New Brunswick. The New Brunswick Electric Power Commission was incorporated under the Electric Power Act of 1920. Power supply to meet present local demands was partly secured by a purchase agreement with Hydro-Québec covering the period 1971-76 which provided for supply of over 11 000 GWh of surplus energy a year made available as a result of completion of the Churchill Falls development in Labrador.

Although no new additions to generation were made during 1975, the province was actively proceeding on a generation expansion program which will raise the installed capacity in 1980 by 2 010 MW, an increase of 151%. These additions include hydro, oil-fired thermal, and nuclear generation.

The first 320-MW unit of the 960-MW oil-fired thermal station at Coleson Cove was in service in early 1976 with two additional units scheduled for installation later in the year. The Mactaquac hydro station on the Saint John River is being increased to 638 MW capacity with the installation of the fifth and sixth units in 1978 and in 1979 a 200-MW dual-fuelled (oil or coal) unit will be added to the Dalhousie thermal station.

Planning for reinforcement of the provincial transmission system is under way. The existing system will eventually have an overlay at 345 kV to connect the nuclear station in southern New Brunswick with load centres. Reinforcement of the Nova Scotia interconnection at 345 kV was scheduled for completion before the end of 1976.

Construction began in 1975 on the first nuclear power station in the Maritime region at Point LePreau, on the Bay of Fundy. Initial operation of the first 630-MW CANDU unit is expected by 1980. Provision is being made for a second 630-MW unit to be added later. Expansion of nuclear generation will allow the province to reduce its dependence on high-cost fossil fuels for power production.

Quebec. The richest of all provinces in water-power resources, Quebec possesses about 40% of the total for Canada and led in developed water power with installations of 13 831 MW in 1975, representing about 37.3% of the national total. Power production is facilitated by the regulation of stream flow through storage dams owned and operated by the Department of Natural Resources, and some responsibility for regulation rests with the Quebec Hydro-Electric Commission.

The abundance of Quebec's water power wealth, much of it in reasonable proximity to existing demand areas, has limited the application of thermal power to specific local use. With new developments in transmission technology allowing economic long-distance transportation of large blocks of power, it seems likely that Quebec will continue to concentrate on hydro-electric power and to develop more remote rivers. Nevertheless, Hydro-Québec is beginning to look toward thermal generation since it will serve not only to help guarantee an adequate power supply in the face of increasingly heavy demands but also to render the almost exclusively hydro-electric base more flexible through integrated operation. Quebec's largest conventional thermal plant, the Tracy station near Sorel, has an installed capacity of 600 MW.

Work on the Outardes-2 site in the Manicouagan region began again in 1974, after six years of inactivity following the 1968 decision to purchase energy from Churchill Falls. The project is the final part of the 5 500-MW, $1.5 billion Manicouagan–Outardes complex. The three 151.3-MW units were expected to be in service in 1978.

The first of six 197.5-MW hydraulic units at Manicougan 3 was connected to the Hydro-Québec system in December 1975. Five additional units were added during 1976, for a total of 1 185 MW. The only other generating unit added during 1975 was a 31-MW unit at the Première Chute hydro-electric station.

Construction by Hydro-Québec of a 600-MW nuclear generating station, Gentilly 2, was proceeding satisfactorily and was expected to be in service in 1979. The demonstration nuclear unit, Gentilly 1, owned by Atomic Energy of Canada but connected to the Hydro-Québec system, was put back into operation late in 1974 but was not expected to operate at full load until 1976. The plant had been shut down primarily because of the shortage of heavy water; in the interim improvements and modifications to ensure greater stability and better protection for the reactor system were incorporated. Gentilly 1 is a boiling light water version of the CANDU family, while Gentilly 2 is a standard pressurized heavy water design similar to the Pickering units in Ontario.

A 36-MW gas turbine generating station at Les Boules was removed from service in 1974.

Major long-range expansion plans are centred on the James Bay development. A work stoppage in 1974 forced a delay of about six months in the projected date for first power deliveries from the LG-2 station to autumn 1980. During the period 1980-85 an estimated 10 190 MW will be installed at four sites on La Grande River. LG-2, about 73 miles (117 km) from the James Bay coast and the first site to be developed, will be completed to a total of 5 328 MW by the end of 1982; the remaining sites will be LG-1 (910 MW) about 19 miles (31 km) below LG-2; LG-3 (1 920 MW) approximately 75 miles (121 km) upstream of LG-2, and LG-4 (2 032 MW) some 140 miles (225 km) further upstream.

An agreement in principle between the Quebec government and the Inuit and Cree peoples of northern Quebec was signed during 1974, and negotiations continued in 1975, culminating on November 11 when a final agreement was signed between the government of Quebec (also the James Bay Energy Corporation, James Bay Development Corporation and Hydro-Québec), the Grand Council of the Crees of Quebec, the Northern Quebec Inuit Association and the Government of Canada. The final agreement includes provisions granting to the native peoples 5,345 sq miles (13 843 km²) of land as well as exclusive hunting, fishing and trapping rights on an additional 60,130 sq miles (155 736 km²); the native people will participate in administering and controlling a hunting, fishing and trapping region throughout the area. Provision is also made for local government, native economic development and environmental protection. In addition, the Inuit and Indian people will receive a tax-free grant totalling $225 million over 20 years, of which $75 million must be paid in the initial 10 years, with the balance to come from royalties on the hydro development. The final $75 million will be in the form of Quebec debentures to compensate for foregone mining benefits.

The Abitibi region of the province is electrically isolated from the rest of the Hydro-Québec system but will be linked through the James Bay transmission facilities by the 1980s. To provide additional generation for rapidly increasing short-term needs, three 60-MW gas turbines were added at Cadillac in 1976. The region is interconnected with the northern Ontario system and plans were being made to purchase energy from Ontario by 1977.

Projects under consideration include hydro sites on the Saint-Maurice River and a pumped storage site at Lac Saint-Joachim, 30 miles (48 km) below Quebec. Preliminary studies have been made of other pumped storage sites and of undeveloped hydro sites along the north shore of the St. Lawrence River (Magpie, Sainte-Marguerite, Moisie rivers) and in the Lac Saint-Jean area.

Hydro-Québec estimates that the demand for electric energy will increase by 7.8% a year during the 1974-85 period. Financing for over 12 000 MW of new capacity to meet this demand will require large capital investment and to ensure adequate internal generation of funds, a three-year plan of rate increases was submitted to the Quebec government. Subject to export licensing an agreement has been developed involving supply of surplus energy to the Power Authority of the State of New York (PASNY) up to 14.4 billion kWh during the period 1977-81 via a proposed 765-kV interconnecting transmission system. Construction began in 1976. The agreement provides the right to recall any energy needed for Quebec's own use. From 1982-97, according to the agreement, PASNY may make annual purchases of 3 billion kWh with provision for purchase of an equal amount during the winter by Hydro-Québec. This exchange recognizes the seasonal differences in demand between Canadian and US utility systems.

Ontario. Most of the electric power produced in the province is generated by The Hydro-Electric Power Commission of Ontario. The province's largest hydro-electric generating station is located on the Niagara River at Queenston, where the Sir Adam Beck–Niagara generating stations Nos. 1 and 2 and the associated pumped storage-generating station have a combined capacity of 1 815 MW.

Ontario has more thermal capacity than any other province in Canada; total installed capacity in 1975 was 11 537 MW, about 53% of the national total. Ontario Hydro's Lakeview station at Toronto is Canada's largest thermal generating station with an installed capacity of 2 400 MW. The Lambton station near Sarnia reached its designed capacity of 2 000 MW in 1970. Except for the oil-fired Lennox (near Kingston) and Wesleyville stations, Ontario's fossil-fuelled thermal plants were all built for coal-firing. The R.L. Hearn plant in Toronto was subsequently converted to burn natural gas.

The East and West Systems, formerly separate operating entities, were fully integrated in 1970 and, although the capacity of the interconnection is a limiting factor in the exchange of power, the combined facilities form a unified provincial network. For general day-to-day operations the province is divided into seven regions, with regional offices in major municipalities.

The primary concern of Ontario Hydro is the provision of electric power by generation or purchase to more than 350 electric utilities for resale in municipalities having "at cost" contracts with the commission. The commission also supplies power in bulk to direct customers, mostly industrial consumers whose requirements are so large or so unusual as to make service by local municipal utilities impracticable; these include mines, industries in unorganized areas, and certain interconnected systems. These operations represent about 90% of its energy sales. The commission also delivers electric power to retail customers in rural areas and in a small group of 15 municipalities served by commission-owned local distribution facilities. However, retail service is generally provided by municipal electric utilities, owned and operated by local commissions which supply consumers in most cities and towns, many villages and certain populous township areas. In addition to administering the enterprise over which it has direct control, the commission, under the Power Commission Act and the Public Utilities Act, exercises certain regulatory functions, particularly with respect to the group of municipal electric utilities it serves.

Expansion of Ontario Hydro's capacity in 1975 was limited to installation of the fifth 500-MW unit at Nanticoke. One 573.75-MW unit at the new Lennox oil-fuelled station became operational late in 1975 and was scheduled for commercial service early in 1976. Following repair of extensive damage resulting from a fire in 1974, the No. 2 unit at Nanticoke was restored to service in December 1975. Peak demand in that month was 15 742 MW, an increase of 15.3% from the previous year, a growth partially attributable to increased demands in the residential and commercial categories, both of which are weather-sensitive. Total electrical energy made available in the province was 0.6% above 1974 with indications that reduced industrial demand or economic constraints were the main cause of the unusually low growth.

Plans for future additions to the Ontario Hydro system are somewhat uncertain. The only hydro additions currently scheduled are two 39-MW units at Arnprior and one 24-MW unit at Andrew's Falls. Fossil-fuelled additions include sixth and seventh 500-MW units at the Nanticoke coal-fired station in 1976 followed by the eighth unit in 1977. Two of the remaining three oil-fuelled 573.75-MW units at Lennox were planned for service in 1976 and the final unit in 1977. An oil-fired station at Wesleyville, near Port Hope, of similar design to Lennox, is scheduled to come into service in 1981-82.

In northwest Ontario, extensions to the coal-fired Thunder Bay plant are expected to add a 150-MW unit in 1980 and a second unit in 1981. A new coal-fuelled generating station in Atikokan is being planned for 1983-85 when four 200-MW units will be installed. Both the Thunder Bay and Atikokan units will be designed to use coal from western Canada.

Preliminary planning has been undertaken for a third thermal power plant in northwestern Ontario to be located along the north channel of Lake Huron. This is tentatively scheduled for initial service in 1987 and would consist of four 750-MW fossil-fuelled units.

An extensive program of nuclear generation is expected to add 11 760 MW of new capacity in the period 1976-88. This program consists of four unit stations, three employing 800-MW units and one, Pickering B, with 540-MW units. Bruce A was scheduled to have one 800-MW unit added each year (1976 to 1979). Other nuclear additions are scheduled from 1981 through 1988: Pickering B (1981-83); Bruce B (1983-86); and Darlington (1986-88).

Future electricity plans and rates for electrical energy in Ontario are being reviewed by several groups. The Ontario Energy Board completed a review of bulk power rates for 1976 after a series of hearings completed in September 1975. A committee of the Ontario Legislature established to review electricity rates recommended a 22% increase for 1976. During 1975 the Ontario government established a Royal Commission on Electric Power Planning with a mandate to explore long-term aspects of electric power development.

Gas is burned to a limited extent (less than 6% of generation), primarily to meet environmental constraints. Lennox oil-fired capacity will give an added flexibility in fuel sources and help ensure an adequate supply of electrical energy. However, coal imported from the US is still the most significant fuel, producing about 25% of the electricity in Ontario and serving the needs of the steel industry there. In 1974-75 the cost of this coal more than doubled and difficulties arose in getting full deliveries or in making contracts for future requirements. Canadian stockpiles have been adequate to meet the situation but have been severely depleted partly because of strikes in the transportation and US mining industries. Alternate Canadian sources of both thermal and metallurgical coal to supplement US supplies may be available after some years but in the immediate future Ontario must remain dependent on US supplies. There is increasing and urgent interest in securing future supplies of both metallurgical and thermal coal from western Canada. Meeting these requirements will require an expansion in production and, particularly, in transportation facilities. The present transport system could probably handle up to 1 million tons (900 000 t) a year by rail to the Lakehead and by ship to the plants. Construction of a 12 million-ton-capacity (11 million t) coal terminal is projected for Thunder Bay. Rail facilities from BC and

Alberta will need upgrading to move coal by unit trains to Thunder Bay, and either the railways or the Ontario purchasers of coal will have to acquire trainsets of locomotives and hopper cars. Over the longer term, transportation of most of the coal by pipeline in the form of a slurry is a possibility.

Manitoba. Manitoba Hydro is the primary agency responsible for the generation and distribution of electric power in the province. The corporation was formed April 1, 1961, merging the Manitoba Power Commission, the provincial distributing agency created in 1919 to serve rural Manitoba, and the Manitoba Hydro-Electric Board, the power generating and development authority established in 1951.

With immense hydro-electric capabilities on the Winnipeg, Churchill, Nelson and Saskatchewan rivers, Manitoba has more water-power resources than the other Prairie provinces. Until recently, hydro-electric generating stations on the Winnipeg River supplied most of the power requirements of southern Manitoba. Manitoba Hydro's high-voltage, long-distance transmission lines, however, will bring increasing amounts of power south from hydro-electric stations on northern rivers.

Manitoba Hydro supplies over 250,000 consumers in 700 communities throughout rural Manitoba and suburban Winnipeg and operates nine hydro-electric stations, two thermal-electric stations and a number of isolated diesel plants with installed capacity totalling 2 966 MW at the end of 1975. These stations join the City of Winnipeg Hydro Electric System's Pointe du Bois and Slave Falls stations to form the Manitoba Integrated System.

Pine Falls, McArthur, Seven Sisters and Great Falls hydro stations are on the Winnipeg River approximately 70 miles (113 km) northeast of Winnipeg; Grand Rapids hydro station is on the Saskatchewan River 285 miles (459 km) northwest of Winnipeg; and Kelsey and Kettle Rapids hydro stations are 400 and 450 miles (644 and 724 km) northeast of Winnipeg on the Nelson River. Responsibility for operation of the Sherritt Gordon Mines, Limited's Laurie River hydro stations 1 and 2 was assumed by Manitoba Hydro in May 1970.

The development of the Nelson River hydro-electric potential is continuing. The final three of 12 units at the Kettle generating station were added in 1974 bringing the total to 1 224 MW. At Long Spruce, the first two units were planned for operation late in 1977 and completion to a total of 980 MW by 1979; by the end of 1974 the powerhouse and spillway were more than 50% completed. Installation of the second stage diversion was finished in 1975 and was followed by construction of the earth-fill section of the main dam. Tenders on the first stage of construction for a third site on the Nelson River at Limestone Rapids were opened in March 1976. Access roads and site clearing began in 1975.

Important regulation and channel improvement work progressed through 1976 on structures and channels forming the waterway from Lake Winnipeg into the Nelson River. As part of this project, the Jenpeg generating station located in the diversion channel was expected to begin operation in mid-1976, when three of six 28-MW low head bulb type units were scheduled to come into service. Other work on the diversion route through the Rat–Burntwood river systems between the Churchill and Nelson rivers was almost complete, notably at the Missi Falls and Notigi Lake sites. The Missi Falls structure would regulate flow from Southern Indian Lake to the Churchill River. The Notigi control structure at the outlet of Notigi Lake to the Rat River would initially regulate flow but provided for future generator installation.

Plans for expansion of the HVDC transmission system connecting the Nelson River generating sites to southern Manitoba involved the addition of converter capacity at the sending and receiving stations. Transmission developments in 1975 included the commitment of converter equipment for the second bipole of the Nelson River HVDC system. This will be a thyristor design with a voltage rating ±500 kV and a capacity of 1 800 MW, adequate to handle the combined capacity of Kettle, Long Spruce and Limestone. HVDC transmission additions are to be phased in over 1978-83 as required by the timing of generation additions.

Manitoba Hydro planned to extend its interconnections with the United States to augment the current 230-kV connection with the Northern States Power Company in Minnesota. An application to the NEB for licensing of a second international 230-kV circuit to interconnect with Minnesota Power and Light was approved in March 1976. Advantages to Manitoba of these interconnections include electricity sales from seasonal variations in water flow, and from use of temporary water storage, which utilize the flexibility of hydro system operation; interconnected US utilities depend mainly on thermal generation and have peak demand during summer unlike the Manitoba utilities which, in the same way as all Canadian utilities, encounter peak demand during winter. Manitoba also has significant interchanges with Saskatchewan and northwestern Ontario.

Saskatchewan. The Saskatchewan Power Corporation was established in 1949 by the Power Corporation Act (RSS 1965, c.40, as amended) as a successor to the Saskatchewan Power Commission which had been in operation since 1929. The corporation's original functions included the generation, transmission and distribution, sale and supply of electric energy to make electric power available throughout the province at reasonable rates. Since 1952, the corporation has also been authorized to produce or purchase and to transmit, distribute, sell and supply natural or manufactured gas.

A 70-MW gas turbine unit came into service in November 1975 at Landis, 75 miles (121 km) northwest of Saskatoon. Provision is being made for an underground gas storage cavern to provide for winter peak operation without placing excessive demands on the gas system.

In 1977 an additional 300-MW unit at the Boundary Dam lignite-fuelled thermal station would raise the total installed capacity to 882 MW. The next proposed addition is a new lignite-fuelled station to be known as Poplar River near Coronach in south central Saskatchewan with a tentative commissioning date of 1979 for the first 300-MW unit. Further development under consideration includes hydro sites at Wintego on the Churchill River and at Nipawin on the Saskatchewan River.

In 1975 some 68.8% of electric power was generated by thermal stations and the balance by hydro-electric stations.

Alberta. Electric power generation in Alberta is provided by two major investor-owned companies and three municipal utilities. In addition, a number of municipal systems handle local distribution of power purchased from the investor-owned utilities. Electrical utility companies previously known as Canadian Utilities Limited and Northland Utilities Limited were merged in 1972 to form Alberta Power Limited.

The Alberta Energy Resources Conservation Board regulates the construction and operation of electric utilities under the Hydro and Electric Energy Act of the province of Alberta, and the Public Utilities Board regulates the rates.

Addition to capacity in 1975 was limited to the second 150-MW unit in Alberta Power's Battle River coal-fired thermal station. However, work is actively proceeding on several generation projects. Calgary Power expected to commission two 375-MW units in 1976 at its Sundance coal-fired thermal station on Lake Wabamun, west of Edmonton. A further 375-MW unit is to be completed in 1978 and the fourth in 1980 raising the total capacity of the Sundance station at that time to 2 100 MW (6 units).

Environmental effects were being reduced to a minimum through the construction of a 1,200-acre (486 hectares) cooling pond at Sundance and through the provision of electrostatic precipitators on all Sundance units. Results from precipitators in use on the two 300-MW operating units at this station show 99.5% removal of particulates. Precipitators were also being added to the older

Wabamun station. Expenditures for all environmental protection devices at the two stations will probably exceed $80 million.

Late in 1975, Calgary Power applied to the Energy Resources Conservation Board of Alberta for approval to construct a 2 250-MW coal-fired generating station in the Camrose–Ryley area. The plant is to consist of six 375-MW units to be brought into service between 1982 and 1986.

Edmonton Power is continuing the construction of additions to its Clover Bar gas-fired thermal station, adding a 165-MW unit in 1976 and another in 1978, thus doubling the total station capacity to 660 MW. Environmental studies continued on the effect of warm water discharge on the biota of the North Saskatchewan River which is used for cooling and on the reduction of nitrogen oxides in the stack discharge.

Alberta, with large resources of mineable subbituminous coal, has opted to develop this low-cost resource as a fuel for thermal power stations; hence most new thermal capacity in the province to the year 2000 will probably be based on this fuel. Toward the end of the century, however, underground mining may be required to provide additional production of subbituminous coals in Alberta.

Major transmission developments in Alberta in 1975 were additions to 240-kV and 138-kV lines. Calgary Power completed a 240-kV line from Sundance to Red Deer. Alberta Power and Calgary Power completed a 138/240-kV line between Alberta Power's Battle River plant and Calgary Power's Matiskow substation to the east of Battle River.

British Columbia, with substantial water resources, meets over 90% of its electricity needs through hydro generation. Only a small portion is thermal, involving oil and some gas. Current planning indicates that hydro development will continue through the year 2000 with thermal generation becoming important by the mid-1980s. Initially, thermal generation will be mainly from coal since nuclear generation is not likely to be undertaken prior to 1990.

The foremost producer and distributor of electric power in British Columbia is the British Columbia Hydro and Power Authority, a provincial Crown corporation. BC Hydro operates a diversified system of public utilities including transportation services and gas distribution. Electric power is generated, transmitted and distributed throughout areas of the province containing more than 90% of the population. Natural gas is purchased and distributed in Greater Vancouver and the Fraser Valley, and liquefied petroleum gas in Greater Victoria.

New generating capacity in 1975 totalled 181-MW thermal and 250 MW of hydro. The sixth 150-MW unit at the Burrard station came in service in 1975 and a 28.6-MW gas turbine unit was commissioned at Prince Rupert. The only hydro addition in 1975 was at the new Kootenay Canal plant where the first two of four 125-MW units were put into service; the remaining two were scheduled for completion in 1976. A 53.9-MW unit was added in 1976 at the Keogh station near Port Hardy, and a 40.5-MW unit was scheduled for completion.

Major additions to hydro generation are under construction and during the period 1976-80, 3 215 MW of new hydro capacity will be added to the system. Work is progressing on the Mica project where two 435-MW units were scheduled for completion in 1976 and two more in 1977. On the Peace River 14 miles (23 km) downstream of the G.M. Shrum generating station, construction of the Site 1 project is under way. First power from this four-unit 700-MW station is expected in 1979 with completion in 1980. A fourth major hydro-electric development will be the Seven Mile site on the Pend-d'Oreille River 6 miles (10 km) upstream of the existing Waneta Station, where preliminary work on the construction camp started in 1975. Three of the four 175-MW units planned for this development are being scheduled for service in 1980. Planning related to a major hydro development on the Columbia River near Revelstoke is also actively under way.

While no major new transmission lines were brought into service in 1975, work continued on the 500-kV lines to connect the Mica project to the BC grid.

Coal is an abundant resource in British Columbia, with large quantities of bituminous coal located in the province.

For the longer term, detailed studies are being made of lignite coal deposits at Hat Creek, 13 miles (21 km) west of Cache Creek, as a possible source of fuel for a large thermal electric generating station. This deposit is now estimated at 500 million tons (454 million tonnes) which could support a 2 000-MW generating station, and more coal may well be located in areas surrounding the proven body.

Yukon Territory and Northwest Territories. The Northern Canada Power Commission, a Crown corporation established in 1948, is empowered to survey utility requirements, construct and operate public utility plants in the Northwest Territories, the Yukon Territory and, subject to the approval of the Governor in Council, elsewhere in Canada. Projects undertaken by the commission must be financially self-sustaining.

A preliminary evaluation of hydro-electric potential has been made for most of the major rivers in the Yukon Territory and in the central portion of the Mackenzie district of the Northwest Territories confirming the existence of substantial waterpower potential. The Yukon River and its tributaries contain some of the larger undeveloped hydro-electric resources in North America.

The Northern Canada Power Commission has hydro-electric power developments on the Yukon River near Whitehorse and on the Mayo River near Mayo in the Yukon Territory; in the Northwest Territories on the Snare River northwest of Yellowknife and on the Taltson River northeast of Fort Smith.

In the Yukon Territory the Northern Canada Power Commission commissioned its 30-MW Aishihik hydro development in September 1975. Plans were well advanced for a 20-MW addition to the Whitehorse Rapids hydro development and studies were carried on to select the best site for a major hydro development to meet future load growth on a long-term basis.

In the Northwest Territories, major additions in generating capacity between 1974-75 were confined to diesel installations which exceeded 10 MW in units ranging up to 2 500 kW. Work continued on the 10-MW Snare Forks hydro development and a 4-MW addition to the 18-MW Taltson station, both scheduled for service in 1976, and planning was completed in respect to the 4-MW Snare Cascades development on the Snare River.

13.6.9   Electric power statistics

Electric power statistics in this section are based on reports of all electric utilities and all industrial establishments that generate energy, regardless of whether or not any is sold, and therefore show the total production and distribution of electric energy in Canada. Utilities are defined as companies, commissions, municipalities or individuals whose primary function is to sell most of the electric energy that they have either generated or purchased. Industrial establishments are defined as companies or individuals generating electricity mainly for use in their own plants.

Power generated in 1975 totalled 272 624 GWh (1 gigawatthour = 10^6 kWh) a decrease of 2.3% from 1974 compared with an increase of 6.4% from 1973 to 1974. Approximately 74% of the total generation is by hydro, but the proportions of hydro and thermal differ markedly from province to province as indicated by 1974 ratios ranging from 99.7% hydro and 0.3% thermal in Quebec to 100% thermal in Prince Edward Island. Other predominantly hydro provinces are Newfoundland 98.9%, Manitoba 96.8% and British Columbia 90.5%. Hydro (49.0%) and thermal (51.0%) generation were virtually in balance in Ontario where nuclear generation contributed 29.6% of the thermal component and 15.1% of the province's total electrical energy production. In the remaining provinces hydro has been overtaken by thermal, e.g. Saskatchewan 38.3%/61.7%, Nova Scotia 11.4%/88.6% and Alberta 9.5%/90.5%. Hydro generation was predominant in the northern territories at 74% in the Yukon Territory and 76% in the Northwest Territories. Detailed figures are shown in Table 13.15.

Table 13.16 gives summary figures of power production and distribution classified by province or territory and Tables 13.17 and 13.18 give figures classified by type of production establishment. Installed capacity in Canada at the end of 1975 totalled 58 738 MW compared to 57 480 MW in 1974, and 54 327 MW in 1973. Of the 1974 total, 51 609 MW were accounted for by utilities and the remainder by industrial establishments. Exports to the United States in 1974 amounted to approximately 15 400 GWh, a decrease of 5.4% over 1973, and declined to 11 376 GWh in 1975; net exports totalled 12 959 GWh in 1974 and declined by 42% to 7 390 GWh in 1975.

Average domestic and farm consumption rose from 8 170 kWh in 1973 to 8 723 kWh in 1974. For domestic and farm customers across Canada the average annual bill was $153.78 in 1974 as against $137.01 in 1973. Table 13.19 provides more detailed information including the total number of customers served.

In 1974 natural gas accounted for 15.7% of thermal generation by utilities, coal for 52.2%, petroleum fuels for 10.2% and nuclear fuel for 21.9%; corresponding proportions in 1973 were 19.4%, 48.9%, 9.5% and 22.2%, respectively. Details of the type of fuel used, by province, appear in Table 13.20.

Sources
13.1 - 13.6 Energy Policy Sector, Department of Energy, Mines and Resources.

Tables

..	not available	bbl	barrels
...	not appropriate or not applicable	b/d	barrels a day
—	nil or zero	Mcf	thousand cubic feet
- -	too small to be expressed	MMcf	million cubic feet
e	estimate	MMMcf	billion cubic feet
p	preliminary	MMMMcf	trillion cubic feet
r	revised	kW	kilowatt (1 000 watts)
certain tables may not add due to rounding		MW	megawatt (1 000 000 watts)
		GW	gigawatt (1 000 000 000 watts)
		million = 10^6, billion = 10^9, trillion = 10^{12}	

13.1   Trade in energy, 1965 and 1975 (million dollars)

Item	1965	1975
Petroleum		
Exports	300.8	3,673.7
Imports	473.3	3,583.1
Balance	-172.5	90.6
Natural gas		
Exports	104.2	1,092.2
Imports	7.5	7.5
Balance	96.7	1,084.7
Petroleum and natural gas		
Exports	405.0	4,765.9
Imports	480.8	3,590.6
Balance	-75.8	1,175.3
Coal and coke		
Exports	14.0	493.6
Imports	134.8	576.3[1]
Balance	-120.8	-82.7
Electric energy		
Exports	16.9	104.3
Imports	14.3	11.8
Balance	2.6	92.5
Total		
Exports	435.9	5,363.8
Imports	629.9	4,178.7
Balance	-194.0	1,185.1

[1]Includes rail freight charge from the mine to the US border.

13.2   Petroleum, supply and demand, 1964, 1974 and 1975 (thousand barrels a day)

Item	1964	1974	1975P
Supply			
Production	*847.7*	*1,994.6*	*1,734.2*
Crude oil	819.3	1,843.3	1,576.1
Gas plant, liquefied petroleum gas	28.4	151.3	158.1
Imports	*504.2*	*884.1*	*859.2*
Crude oil	392.3	797.7	817.1
Products	111.9	86.4	42.1
Total, supply	1,351.9	2,878.7	2,593.4
Demand			
Domestic demand	*1,056.5*	*1,738.7*	*1,720.4*
Motor gasoline	332.6	566.1	590.6
Diesel fuel	91.2	186.4	187.9
Light fuel oil	201.1	295.1	278.2
Heavy fuel oil	182.7	292.9	265.7
Other (including refinery use and loss)	248.9	398.2	398.0
Exports	*303.4*	*1,141.9*	*899.3*
Crude oil	277.9	907.0	707.4
Products	25.5	234.9	191.9
Total, demand	1,359.9	2,880.6	2,619.7
Inventory change	-8.0	-1.9	-26.3

13.2   Petroleum, supply and demand, 1964, 1974 and 1975 (thousand cubic metres a day)   M

Item	1964	1974	1975P
Supply			
Production	*134.8*	*317.2*	*275.7*
Crude oil	130.3	293.1	250.6
Gas plant, liquefied petroleum gas	4.5	24.1	25.1
Imports	*80.2*	*140.5*	*136.5*
Crude oil	62.4	126.8	129.9
Products	17.8	13.7	6.7
Total, supply	215.0	457.7	412.3
Demand			
Domestic demand	*168.0*	*276.4*	*273.5*
Motor gasoline	52.9	90.0	93.9
Diesel fuel	14.5	29.6	29.9
Light fuel oil	32.0	46.9	44.2
Heavy fuel oil	29.0	46.6	42.2
Other (including refinery use and loss)	39.6	63.3	63.3
Exports	*48.3*	*181.5*	*143.0*
Crude oil	44.2	144.2	112.5
Products	4.1	37.3	30.5
Total, demand	216.3	457.9	416.5
Inventory change	-1.3	-0.2	-4.2

13.3   Natural gas, supply and demand, 1964, 1974 and 1975 (billion cubic feet)

Item	1964	1974	1975P
Supply			
Net production	1,135.0	3,037.5	3,079.1
Marketable pipeline gas[1]	947.3	2,420.8	2,447.0
Imports	9.6	13.3	10.2
Total, supply	956.9	2,434.1	2,457.2
Demand			
Domestic demand	*555.7*	*1,439.3*	*1,453.2*
Residential	163.6	293.0	299.2
Commercial	83.5	275.4	285.2
Industrial	257.4	745.9	739.6
Other (including pipeline losses, etc.)	51.2	125.0	129.2
Exports	392.2	959.2	946.9
Total, demand	947.9	2,398.5	2,400.1
Storage and line pack increase	9.0	35.6	57.1

[1]After deduction of field and plant use/loss, processing shrinkage.

13.4   Coal, supply and demand, 1964, 1974 and 1975 (thousand tons)

Item	1964	1974	1975
Supply			
Net production	11,219	23,446	27,881
Imports	14,738	13,627	17,438
Total, supply	25,957	37,073	45,319
Demand			
Consumption	*24,730*	*27,387*	*28,123*
Electrical utilities	6,265	17,002	18,230
Metallurgical use	6,023	8,297	8,040
General industry	12,442	2,088	1,853
Exports	1,292	11,876	12,600
Total, demand	26,022	39,263	40,723
Inventory change	-65	-2,190	+4,596

13.5   Electric energy, supply and demand, 1964 and 1974 (gigawatt hours)

Item	1964	1974
Net generation		
Utilities	*102 889*	*241 417*
Hydro	84 871	178 207
Thermal	18 018	49 345
Nuclear	- -	13 865
Industries	*32 098*	*38 839*
Hydro	28 472	32 730
Thermal	3 625	6 109
Utilities and industries	*134 987*	*280 256*
Hydro	113 344	210 936
Thermal	21 643	55 454
Nuclear	- -	13 865
Imports	3 121	2 441
Total, supply	138 108	282 698
Demand		
Residential and farm	27 278	59 295
Commercial and other	13 136	72 572
Industrial	81 505	111 447
Losses, unallocated	12 030	23 983
Total, domestic demand	133 949	267 298
Exports	4 159	15 400
Total, demand	138 108	282 698

13.3   Natural gas, supply and demand, 1964, 1974 and 1975 (million cubic metres)   M

Item	1964	1974	1975P
Supply			
Net production	32 139.6	86 012.4	87 190.4
Marketable pipeline gas¹	26 824.6	68 549.4	69 291.3
Imports	271.8	376.6	288.8
Total, supply	27 096.4	68 926.0	60 580.1
Demand			
Domestic demand	*15 735.7*	*40 756.4*	*41 150.0*
Residential	4 632.6	8 296.8	8 472.4
Commercial	2 364.5	7 798.5	8 076.0
Industrial	7 288.8	21 121.5	20 943.1
Other (including pipeline losses, etc.)	1 449.8	3 539.6	3 658.5
Exports	11 105.9	27 161.5	26 813.2
Total, demand	26 841.6	67 917.9	67 963.2
Storage and line pack increase	254.8	1 008.1	1 616.9

¹After deduction of field and plant use/loss, processing shrinkage.

13.4   Coal, supply and demand, 1964, 1974 and 1975 (thousand metric tonnes)   M

Item	1964	1974	1975
Supply			
Net production	10 178	21 270	25 293
Imports	13 370	12 362	15 819
Total, supply	23 548	33 632	41 112
Demand			
Consumption	*22 435*	*24 845*	*25 513*
Electrical utilities	5 684	15 424	16 538
Metallurgical use	5 464	7 527	7 294
General industry	11 287	1 894	1 681
Exports	1 172	10 774	11 431
Total, demand	23 607	35 619	36 944
Inventory change	-59	-1 987	+4 168

13.6   Wells drilled, by type and region, 1974 and 1975

Region	Oil 1974	1975	Gas 1974	1975	Dry 1974	1975	Total 1974	1975
Western Canada	*778*	*782*	*1,927*	*2,080*	*1,342*	*1,257*	*4,047*	*4,119*
Alberta	681	670	1,747	1,958	1,106	1,100	3,534	3,728
Saskatchewan	85	105	122	85	77	72	284	262
British Columbia	6	2	52	31	90	45	148	78
Manitoba	3	2	—	—	18	5	21	7
Yukon Territory and Northwest Territories	3	3	6	6	51	35	60	44
Eastern Canada	*4*	*4*	*62*	*68*	*115*	*82*	*181*	*154*
Ontario	4	4	60	68	90	63	154	135
Quebec	—	—	—	—	6	3	6	3
Atlantic provinces	—	—	—	—	—	7	—	7
East coast offshore	—	—	2	—	19	9	21	9
Total	782	786	1,989	2,148	1,457	1,339	4,228	4,273

13.7   Crude oil and equivalent production, by province, 1972-75 (thousand barrels a day)

Item and province	1972	1973	1974[r]	1975	Percentage change 1974-75
Crude oil	*1,481*	*1,743*	*1,635*	*1,381*	*-15.5*
Alberta	1,160	1,431	1,363	1,163	-14.7
Saskatchewan	237	235	202	162	-19.8
British Columbia	65	58	52	39	-25.0
Manitoba	14	14	13	12	-7.7
Other	5	5	5	5	—
Pentanes plus/condensate	*166*	*169*	*162*	*152*	*-6.2*
Alberta	162	165	158	148	-6.3
Saskatchewan	1	1	1	1	—
British Columbia	3	3	3	3	—
Synthetic crude oil Canada — Alberta	51	51	46	43	-6.5
Total	1,698	1,963	1,843	1,576	-14.5
Alberta	1,373	1,647	1,567	1,354	-13.6
Saskatchewan	238	236	203	163	-19.7
British Columbia	68	61	55	42	-23.6
Manitoba	14	14	13	12	-7.7
Other	5	5	5	5	—

13.8   Oil refining, by province, 1975

Province or territory	Existing refineries[1] No.	Capacity '000 b/d	% of total	New refineries planned or under construction Capacity '000 b/d	Scheduled for completion
Newfoundland	2	114	5.5	—	...
Nova Scotia	3	182	8.7	—	...
New Brunswick	1	120	5.8	130[2]	1976
Quebec	7	644	30.9	—	...
Ontario	7	540	25.9	246	1977
Manitoba	1	30	1.4	—	...
Saskatchewan	3	38	1.8	—	...
Alberta	6	262	12.6	30	1978
British Columbia	7	150	7.2	—	...
Northwest Territories	1	3	0.2	—	...
Total	38	2,083	100.0	406	...

[1]Expansion of some existing refineries is in progress.
[2]A significant expansion which should be noted.

13.9   Coal production[1], by type and province, 1974 and 1975

Type and province	1974[r] '000 tons	$'000	1975p '000 tons	$'000
Bituminous	*14,009*	*273,634*	*17,401*	*543,400*
Nova Scotia	1,410	24,524	1,826	47,600
New Brunswick	415	5,387	461	7,100
Alberta	3,651	90,156	4,524	161,500
British Columbia	8,533	153,567	10,590	327,200
Subbituminous Alberta	5,595	20,875	6,568	23,500
Lignite Saskatchewan	3,842	8,317	3,912	8,900
Total	23,446	302,826	27,881	575,800

[1]Includes production of clean coal and shipments of raw coal from the mine.

13.7   Crude oil and equivalent production, by province, 1972-75 (thousand cubic metres a day)   M

Item and province	1972	1973	1974	1975	Percentage change 1974-75
Crude oil	*235.4*	*277.1*	*260.0*	*219.6*	*-15.5*
Alberta	184.4	227.5	216.7	184.9	-14.7
Saskatchewan	37.7	37.4	32.1	25.8	-19.8
British Columbia	10.3	9.2	8.3	6.2	-25.0
Manitoba	2.2	2.2	2.1	1.9	-7.7
Other	0.8	0.8	0.8	0.8	—
Pentanes plus/condensate	*26.5*	*26.9*	*25.8*	*24.2*	*-6.2*
Alberta	25.8	26.2	25.1	23.5	-6.3
Saskatchewan	0.2	0.2	0.2	0.2	—
British Columbia	0.5	0.5	0.5	0.5	—
Synthetic crude oil					
Canada — Alberta	8.1	8.1	7.3	6.8	-6.5
Total	270.0	312.1	293.1	250.6	-14.5
Alberta	218.3	261.8	249.1	215.2	-13.6
Saskatchewan	37.9	37.6	32.3	26.0	-19.7
British Columbia	10.8	9.7	8.8	6.7	-23.6
Manitoba	2.2	2.2	2.1	1.9	-7.7
Other	0.8	0.8	0.8	0.8	—

13.8   Oil refining, by province, 1975   M

Province or territory	Existing refineries[1]			New refineries planned or under construction	
	No.	Capacity '000 m³/d	% of total	Capacity '000 m³/d	Scheduled for completion
Newfoundland	2	18.1	5.5	—	...
Nova Scotia	3	28.9	8.7	—	...
New Brunswick	1	19.1	5.8	20.7[2]	1976
Quebec	7	102.4	30.9	—	...
Ontario	7	85.9	25.9	39.1	1977
Manitoba	1	4.8	1.4	—	...
Saskatchewan	3	6.0	1.8	—	...
Alberta	6	41.7	12.6	4.8	1978
British Columbia	7	23.8	7.2	—	...
Northwest Territories	1	0.5	0.2	—	...
Total	38	331.2	100.0	64.6	...

[1]Expansion of some existing refineries is in progress.
[2]A significant expansion which should be noted.

13.9   Coal production[1], by type and province, 1974 and 1975   M

Type and province	1974		1975P	
	'000 t	$'000	'000 t	$'000
Bituminous	*12 708*	*273,634*	*15 786*	*543,400*
Nova Scotia	1 279	24,524	1 657	47,600
New Brunswick	376	5,387	418	7,100
Alberta	3 312	90,156	4 104	161,500
British Columbia	7 741	153,567	9 607	327,200
Subbituminous				
Alberta	5 076	20,875	5 958	23,500
Lignite				
Saskatchewan	3 485	8,317	3 549	8,900
Total	21 269	302,826	25 293	575,800

[1]Includes production of clean coal and shipments of raw coal from the mine.

13.10   Installed generating capacity, as at Dec. 31, 1974 and 1975 (megawatts)

Year and province or territory	Steam Conventional	Nuclear	Internal combustion	Gas turbine	Total thermal	Hydro	Total
1974							
Newfoundland (incl. Labrador)	355	—	66	36	456	6 206	6 662
Prince Edward Island	70	—	7	41	118	—	118
Nova Scotia	1 012	—	6	25	1 043	160	1 203
New Brunswick	621	—	9	23	653	680	1 333
Quebec	675	266	74	—	1 014	13 800	14 814
Ontario	8 417	2 400	26	509	11 353	7 008	18 361
Manitoba	447	—	23	28	498	2 475	2 973
Saskatchewan	1 085	—	33	89	1 207	567	1 774
Alberta	2 491	—	37	189	2 718	718	3 436
British Columbia	1 122	—	135	264	1 522	5 103	6 625
Yukon Territory	—	—	40	—	40	26	66
Northwest Territories	1	—	76	2	79	35	114
Canada, 1974	16 296	2 666	534	1 206	20 701	36 779	57 480
Net additions, 1974	590	—	10	40	640	2 513	3 153
Percentage increase, 1973-74	3.8	—	1.9	3.4	3.2	7.3	5.8
1975P							
Newfoundland (incl. Labrador)	355	—	66	36	456	6 206	6 662
Prince Edward Island	70	—	7	41	118	—	118
Nova Scotia	1 012	—	6	55	1 073	160	1 233
New Brunswick	621	—	9	23	653	680	1 333
Quebec	675	266	74	—	1 014	13 831	14 845
Ontario	8 917	2 400	26	509	11 853	7 008	18 861
Manitoba	447	—	23	28	498	2 475	2 973
Saskatchewan	1 085	—	33	159	1 277	567	1 844
Alberta	2 641	—	37	195	2 874	718	3 592
British Columbia	1 274	—	135	293	1 703	5 353	7 056
Yukon Territory	—	—	40	—	40	56	96
Northwest Territories	1	—	86	2	89	35	124
Canada, 1975	17 098	2 666	544	1 340	21 648	37 090	58 738
Net additions, 1975	802	—	10	134	947	311	1 258
Percentage increase, 1974-75	4.9	—	1.9	11.1	4.6	0.8	2.2

13.11   Capability and firm power peak-load requirements, actual 1965 and 1972-75, and forecast 1976-80 (megawatts)

Item	Actual 1965	1972	1973	1974	1975	Forecast 1976	1977	1978	1979	1980
NET GENERATING CAPABILITY										
Hydro-electric	20 779	31 455	34 807	36 624	37 318	39 427	40 683	42 095	42 855	45 748
Steam, conventional	6 354	12 725	15 161	13 694	16 484	19 782	22 167	23 243	24 030	24 382
nuclear	—	1 753	2 284	1 775	2 284	2 284	3 776	4 522	5 905	6 535
Internal combustion	243	376	375	393	410	403	425	447	441	436
Gas turbine	460	1 098	1 180	1 156	1 437	1 988	2 040	2 146	2 580	2 650
Total, net generating capability	27 836	47 407	53 807	53 642	57 933	63 884	69 091	72 453	75 811	79 751
Receipts of firm power from United States	—	5	1	2	1	52	2	2	2	2
Deliveries of firm power to United States	89	427	416	394	228	623	634	538	541	545
Total, net capability	27 747	46 985	53 392	53 250	57 706	63 313	68 459	71 917	75 272	79 208
PEAK LOADS										
Firm power peak loads within Canada	24 167	38 823	42 699	42 528	45 995	49 708	53 564	57 553	61 579	66 025
Indicated shortages	—	98	—	—	192	—	—	—	—	—
Total, indicated peak loads within Canada	24 167	38 921	42 699	42 528	46 187	49 708	53 564	57 553	61 579	66 025
Indicated reserve	3 580	8 064	10 693	10 722	11 519	13 605	14 895	14 364	13 693	13 183

13.12   Electric energy consumption in Canada, selected years 1950-74

Year	Total consumption GWh	Percentage consumption			
		Commercial[1]	Domestic and farm	Industrial	Losses and unaccounted
1950	53 459	11	13	67	9
1955	77 946	12	16	63	9
1960	109 302	12	19	60	9
1965	144 165	16	21	55	8
1970	202 337	14	21	57	8
1972[r]	231 557	15	22	54	9
1973[r]	249 298	27	22	42	9
1974	267 298	27	22	42	9

[1]Includes street lighting.

13.13   Electric energy consumption, by region, 1960, 1965, 1973 and 1974

Region and year		Total consumption GWh	% of total consumption	Percentage consumption			
				Commercial[1]	Domestic and farm	Industrial	Losses and unaccounted
Atlantic provinces	1960	4 924	5	13	20	58	9
	1965	8 228	6	15	18	60	7
	1973	17 031	7	17	21	54	8
	1974	18 997	7	20	22	46	12
Quebec	1960	44 002	40	7	11	74	8
	1965	52 229	36	12	16	66	6
	1973	82 205	33	15	20	57	8
	1974	91 499	34	20	20	51	9
Ontario	1960	37 157	34	15	25	48	12
	1965	49 276	34	20	26	45	9
	1973	84 283	34	17	24	51	8
	1974	88 802	33	35	25	32	8
Prairie provinces	1960	9 617	9	22	31	34	13
	1965	14 994	10	26	30	34	10
	1973	31 534	12	17	24	47	12
	1974	33 311	13	37	26	28	9
British Columbia[2]	1960	13 602	12	9	16	68	7
	1965	19 438	14	12	15	66	7
	1973	34 245	14	14	18	60	8
	1974	34 688	13	22	18	51	9
Canada	1960	109 302	100	12	19	60	9
	1965	144 165	100	16	21	55	8
	1973	249 298	100	16	21	54	9
	1974	267 298	100	27	22	42	9

[1]Includes street lighting.
[2]Includes the Yukon Territory and Northwest Territories.

13.14   Electric energy consumption per capita, by region, 1960, 1965, 1973 and 1974

Region and year		Total consumption GWh	Population '000	Consumption per capita kWh
Atlantic provinces	1960	4 924	1,867	2 600
	1965	8 228	1,968	4 200
	1973	17 031	2,113	8 100
	1974	18 997	2,134	8 900
Quebec	1960	44 002	5,142	8 600
	1965	52 229	5,685	9 200
	1973	82 205	6,081	13 500
	1974	91 499	6,134	14 900
Ontario	1960	37 157	6,111	6 100
	1965	49 276	6,788	7 300
	1973	84 283	7,939	10 600
	1974	88 802	8,094	11 000
Prairie provinces	1960	9 617	3,112	3 100
	1965	14 994	3,365	4 500
	1973	31 534	3,589	8 800
	1974	33 311	3,632	9 200
British Columbia[1]	1960	13 602	1,638	8 300
	1965	19 438	1,838	10 600
	1973	34 245	2,373	14 400
	1974	34 688	2,452	14 100
Canada	1960	109 302	17,870	6 100
	1965	144 165	19,644	7 300
	1973	249 298	22,095	11 300
	1974	267 298	22,446	11 900

[1]Includes the Yukon Territory and Northwest Territories.

13.15   Electric energy generated, by type of station, 1965 and 1971-75, and by province 1974 and 1975 (megawatt hours)

Year and province or territory	Generated by Water power	Thermal power	Total	Year and province or territory	Generated by Water power	Thermal power	Total
1965	117 063 328	27 210 502	144 273 830	1973	192 842 504	70 492 397	263 334 901
1971	160 984 485	55 487 718	216 472 203	1974	210 936 420	69 319 855	280 256 275
1972	179 998 571	60 214 177	240 212 748	1975P	202 403 904	70 220 094	272 623 998
1974				1975P			
Newfoundland	28 331 582	476 511	28 808 093	Newfoundland	35 342 407	385 276	35 727 683
Prince Edward Island	—	383 049	383 049	Prince Edward Island	—	418 644	418 644
Nova Scotia	728 930	4 704 048	5 432 978	Nova Scotia	623 605	4 837 900	5 461 505
New Brunswick	2 592 575	2 978 245	5 570 820	New Brunswick	2 163 217	2 449 523	4 612 740
Quebec	83 895 051	283 921	84 178 972	Quebec	75 745 680	235 278	75 980 958
Ontario	41 473 669	41 171 537	82 645 206	Ontario	38 420 558	40 066 796	78 487 354
Manitoba	14 240 963	280 826	14 521 789	Manitoba	14 332 904	479 279	14 812 183
Saskatchewan	3 127 224	4 260 851	7 388 075	Saskatchewan	2 703 101	4 356 446	7 059 547
Alberta	1 721 560	12 650 295	14 371 855	Alberta	1 422 073	13 538 343	14 960 416
British Columbia	34 366 734	1 889 248	36 255 982	British Columbia	31 126 311	3 279 374	34 405 685
Yukon Territory	196 418	111 763	308 181	Yukon Territory	253 126	88 071	341 197
Northwest Territories	261 714	129 561	391 275	Northwest Territories	270 922	85 164	356 086
Canada, 1974	210 936 420	69 319 855	280 256 275	Canada, 1975	202 403 904	70 220 094	272 623 998

13.16   Summary electric power statistics, by province, 1974

Province or territory	Installed generating capacity MW	Energy made available in Canada MWh	Exported to United States MWh	Ultimate customers[1]	Total revenue from ultimate customers[2] $'000	Electrical utilities Employees	Salaries and wages $'000
Newfoundland	6 662	6 580 360	—	139,040	58,809	1,784	20,814
Prince Edward Island	118	383 049	—	37,394	12,749	216	2,183
Nova Scotia	1 203	5 589 225	—	278,093	88,009	2,318	24,862
New Brunswick	1 333	6 444 489	2 496 567	238,823	77,981	1,707	19,687
Quebec	14 814	91 499 333	881 047	2,169,146	706,182	15,128	199,949
Ontario	18 361	88 802 236	7 872 354	2,639,733	1,006,369	21,910	309,082
Manitoba	2 973	11 623 052	1 352 389	344,871	116,479	2,662	34,467
Saskatchewan	1 774	7 298 283	—	337,247	98,597	1,688	24,150
Alberta	3 436	14 389 977	—	583,055	201,678	2,726	31,688
British Columbia	6 625	33 988 092	2 797 372	914,662	291,681	4,187	56,040
Yukon Territory	66	308 181	—	6,533	6,618	106	1,131
Northwest Territories	114	391 275	—	10,510	11,666	168	2,639
Canada	57 480	267 297 552	15 399 729	7,699,107	2,676,818	54,600	726,692

[1]Excludes industrial establishments that purchase power and have generating facilities.
[2]Excludes revenue from sales to industrial establishments that purchase power and have generating facilities.

13.17   Summary electric power statistics, by type of establishment, 1974

Item		Electrical utilities Publicly operated	Privately operated	Total	Industrial establishments	Total
Installed generating capacity	MW	42 114	9 495	51 609	5 870	57 480
Energy generated	MWh	197 680 028	43 737 409	241 417 437	38 838 838	280 256 275
Hydro	"	143 605 889	34 600 991	178 206 880	32 729 540	210 936 420
Thermal	"	54 074 139	9 136 418	63 210 557	6 109 298	69 319 855
Energy made available in Canada	"	..	..	..	..	267 297 552
Disposal of energy in Canada[1]	"	199 441 093	16 959 420	216 400 513	50 897 039	267 297 552
Energy exported to United States	"	13 099 314	453 550	13 552 864	1 846 865	15 399 729
Ultimate customers in Canada	No.	7,186,601	509,450	7,696,051	3,056	7,699,107
Domestic and farm	"	6,360,153	435,453	6,795,606	2,846	6,798,452
General: loads under 5 000 kW	"	825,618	73,526	899,144	179	899,323
loads over 5 000 kW	"	830	471	1,301	31	1,332
Street lighting	"	..	..	..	..	..
Revenue from ultimate customers[2]	$'000	2,461,967	209,634	2,671,601	5,217	2,676,818
Revenue from exports to United States	"	154,730	3,233	157,963	10,921	168,884
Employees	No.	50,634	3,966	54,600	..	..
Salaries and wages	$'000	680,915	45,777	726,692	..	..

[1]Excludes sales by electrical utilities to industrial establishments with generating facilities, sales by industrial establishments with generating facilities to electrical utilities, and inter-industrial sales.
[2]Excludes revenue from sales by electrical utilities to industrial establishments with generating facilities, and inter-industrial sales.

13.18   Electric power generated classified by type of establishment, by province, 1974 (megawatt hours)

Province or territory	Electrical utilities		Industrial establishments	Total
	Publicly operated	Privately operated		
Newfoundland	2 777 882	25 619 684	410 527	28 808 093
Prince Edward Island	1 458	381 591	—	383 049
Nova Scotia	4 931 514	—	501 464	5 432 978
New Brunswick	4 824 402	132 746	613 672	5 570 820
Quebec	60 037 209	4 321 236	19 820 527	84 178 972
Ontario	76 890 516	1 867 870	3 886 820	82 645 206
Manitoba	14 421 794	—	99 995	14 521 789
Saskatchewan	6 547 927	636 090	204 058	7 388 075
Alberta	3 236 147	10 402 427	733 281	14 371 855
British Columbia	23 420 877	329 389	12 505 716	36 255 982
Yukon Territory	258 016	23 236	26 929	308 181
Northwest Territories	332 286	23 140	35 849	391 275
Canada	197 680 028	43 737 409	38 838 838	280 256 275

13.19   Domestic and farm service by electrical utilities and industrial establishments, 1971-74

Item		1971	1972	1973	1974
Customers	No.	6,215,140	6,425,017	6,612,142	6,798,452
Megawatt hours sold	,,	46 541 538	50 205 464	54 019 542	54 295 419
Revenue received	$'000	748,779	811,014	906,280ʳ	1,045,289
Kilowatt hours per customer	No.	7 488	7 814	8 170	8 723
Average annual bill	$	120.48	126.23	137.01ʳ	153.78
Revenue per MWh	¢	1.61	1.62	1.68	1.76

13.20   Fuel used by electrical utilities to generate power, by province, 1974

Province or territory	Coal		Petroleum fuels		Gas	
	Quantity tons	Value $	Quantity gal	Value $	Quantity Mcf	Value $
Newfoundland	—	—	32,528,399	8,898,324	—	—
Prince Edward Island	—	—	32,395,556	6,416,995	—	—
Nova Scotia	668,040	11,279,298	232,815,279	21,907,163	—	—
New Brunswick	321,823	4,253,425	114,972,254	19,696,454	—	—
Quebec	—	—	9,310,067	3,077,142	—	—
Ontario	7,409,398	101,634,253	9,071,736	2,612,550	54,816,027	35,302,801
Manitoba	145,318	822,089	4,022,273	961,106	36,400	22,143
Saskatchewan	3,198,639	7,058,863	2,386,832	406,416	10,408,003	3,896,521
Alberta	5,259,223	9,357,038	3,196,626	597,137	54,493,117	11,447,059
British Columbia	—	—	13,341,168	3,562,770	967,862	746,388
Yukon Territory	—	—	5,383,194	2,181,548	—	—
Northwest Territories	—	—	8,394,884	2,928,218	—	—
Canada	17,002,441	134,404,966	467,818,268	73,245,823	120,721,409	51,414,912

13.20   Fuel used by electrical utilities to generate power, by province, 1974   M

Province or territory	Coal		Petroleum fuels		Gas	
	Quantity t	Value $	Quantity l	Value $	Quantity m³	Value $
Newfoundland	—	—	147 877 029	8,898,324	—	—
Prince Edward Island	—	—	147 273 113	6,416,995	—	—
Nova Scotia	606 036	11,279,298	1 058 399 212	21,907,163	—	—
New Brunswick	291 953	4,253,425	522 674 214	19,696,454	—	—
Quebec	—	—	42 324 402	3,077,142	—	—
Ontario	6 721 693	101,634,253	41 240 928	2,612,550	1 552 217 214	35,302,801
Manitoba	131 830	822,089	18 285 615	961,106	1 030 733	22,143
Saskatchewan	2 901 756	7,058,863	10 850 753	406,416	294 721 860	3,896,521
Alberta	4 771 087	9,357,038	14 532 149	597,137	1 543 073 420	11,447,059
British Columbia	—	—	60 650 150	3,562,770	27 406 803	746,388
Yukon Territory	—	—	24 472 484	2,181,548	—	—
Northwest Territories	—	—	38 163 898	2,928,218	—	—
Canada	15 424 355	134,404,966	2 126 743 947	73,245,823	3 418 450 030	51,414,912

Sources
13.1 - 13.20 Manufacturing and Primary Industries Division, Industry Statistics Branch, Statistics Canada; and Energy Development Sector, Department of Energy, Mines and Resources.

Housing and construction

Chapter 14

Tables

Housing
and construction

Housing activity

The year 1975 was notable for housing in two ways. Production, slowed in 1974 and early 1975, recovered and by year end more than 230,000 housing starts exceeded by a substantial margin the government's minimum target of 210,000. The largest increases were in semi-detached, duplex and row housing which taken together increased from 25,955 starts in 1974 to 37,166 in 1975. Single-family housing starts increased slightly from 122,143 to 123,929 but apartment starts moderated from 74,025 to 70,361.

The other notable trend was a shift from more expensive housing production toward the medium and lower price ranges. This trend was reinforced by new and modified federal assistance programs and by limitations observed by lenders on high-ratio loans. It also had a significant effect on residential construction, bringing it more closely in line with the most urgent housing needs of Canadians.

During 1975 a continued effort was made by all levels of government to increase the supply of serviced land and to stabilize land prices. Progress was made to speed up approval processes and get serviced land on the market more quickly. Amendments to the National Housing Act provided for a contribution of $1,000 to municipalities for each unit of moderate-cost medium-density housing completed, an incentive to stimulate desirable residential development.

Progress was made also in the implementation of the Rural and Native Housing Program, Residential Rehabilitation and Neighbourhood Improvement. As anticipated, these programs which depend for their success on the direct involvement of client groups grew at a steadily accelerating pace. During 1975, Parliament enacted two bills amending the National Housing Act. The first, given Royal Assent on March 26, broadened the Assisted Home-Ownership Program and the Assisted Rental Program by making interest-reducing federal grants available to qualified home buyers or rental-housing entrepreneurs who obtained their financing through private mortgage loans.

Previously these grants were available only with direct CMHC mortgages. These changes helped to draw almost $750 million of private mortgage loan commitments into new modest housing. At the same time, the amendments allowed CMHC to acquire and lease land at favourable rates to non-rofit and cooperative housing projects. They offered more generous assi,tance to municipalities for sewerage treatment projects and extended the program to trunk storm sewer systems for new residential development.

In December the NHA was amended again in support of the Federal Housing Action Program. By this program, the federal government committed itself to a target of a million new housing starts by the end of 1979, with a significantly greater proportion in the lower and medium price ranges. This would meet the forecast minimum needs of Canadians over the next four years, taking into account family formation, vacancies and other factors. The target for 1976 was set at 235,000 housing starts. A million new starts would mean more than a million jobs in the construction industry and associated businesses.

The December amendments made further modifications in the Assisted Home-Ownership and Assisted Rental programs. Outright grants were continued and increased under AHOP for families needing them. In addition for the first time, loans which would be interest-free during the first five years were made available to anyone, with or without children, who wished to buy a moderately-priced home within the local AHOP price limits. The loans would have the effect of reducing monthly mortgage and tax payments to the level that would apply if the interest rate were 8%. Similar arrangements could be made with builders or owners of rental housing who were prepared to enter an agreement with CMHC regarding rents and other matters. The effect of providing assistance in this way through repayable loans rather than subsidies, with the bulk of the mortgage financing being provided by the approved lenders, was to conserve public capital, and to ease the financial burden on the home buyer in the early years of ownership.

In addition to providing grants of $1,000 a unit to municipalities for low-cost medium-density housing, the bill also extended the benefits of the Sewage Treatment Assistance Program to water treatment projects required to open land for residential development.

14.2   Government assistance

Although the federal government entered the housing field in 1918 when it made money available to the provinces for re-lending to municipalities, the first general piece of federal housing legislation was the Dominion Housing Act passed in 1935. This was followed by the National Housing Acts of 1938 and 1944. The present National Housing Act, defined as "an Act to promote the construction of new houses, the repair and modernization of existing houses and the improvement of housing and living conditions", was passed in 1954.

In general the federal government, through successive Housing Acts, has attempted to stimulate and supplement the market for housing rather than assume direct responsibilities that belong to other levels of government or that could be borne more effectively by private enterprise. The aim has been to increase the flow of mortgage money and to encourage lenders to make loans on more favourable terms to prospective home-owners. Almost half of the country's present stock of approximately 6.5 million dwelling units have been built since the first covering legislation was enacted. About one third of these were financed in one way or another under the Housing Acts.

The Farm Credit Act, providing for federal long-term loan assistance for housing and other farm purposes, and the Farm Improvement Loans Act, providing for guarantees for intermediate- and short-term loans made by approved lending agencies to farmers for housing and other purposes, are described in greater detail in Chapter 11. The Veterans' Land Act provides a form of loan and grant assistance to veterans for housing and other purposes; it is dealt with in Chapter 6. These three statutes are concerned only incidentally with housing.

All provinces have complementary legislation providing for joint federal-provincial housing and land assembly projects, and most have enacted separate legislation on housing. Details are available from the respective provincial government departments.

Central Mortgage and Housing Corporation. This federal Crown corporation, created by Act of Parliament in 1945 (RSC 1970, c.C-16), makes loans and contributions to individuals and organizations for housing. The funds may be used for construction of new housing or rehabilitation of existing units, neighbourhood improvement, planning and servicing new communities, land assembly, construction of student housing, and the construction and expansion of sewerage and water supply projects. These "start-up funds" enable individuals or private non-profit organizations to undertake housing projects for low-income groups and for housing on Indian reserves, among other purposes.

The corporation may also construct and administer housing and certain other buildings on its own account and for other government departments and agencies. Its responsibilities include providing architectural and engineering designs, calling public tenders, administering construction contracts, including on-site surveying and engineering and carrying out full architectural and engineering inspections.

CMHC is concerned with building technology in formulating standards for housing construction, the use of suitable materials and the development of new building techniques. The corporation has no laboratory facilities but has experience of performance in the field and seeks the advice of specialists in various agencies and departments of the federal government. Research is conducted into such factors as the demand for new housing, the volume of new housing being built and the supply of mortgage money available. CMHC also coordinates and publishes statistical information on housing. Funds provided under the NHA support the Canadian Housing Design Council, the Community Planning Association of Canada and the Canadian Council on Urban and Regional Research.

The average family income of purchasers of NHA-financed houses in 1975 was $15,192. These incomes were 12% higher than the corresponding averages for purchasers in 1974, in line with the general increase in incomes in 1975. As in previous years the majority of purchasers of NHA homes were drawn from the middle third of the range of family income. The average age of purchasers of NHA houses was 31.0 years in 1975 compared to 31.4 in 1974. In 1975, 47.4% of the purchasers had two or more children and 20.3% had previously been home-owners.

The average cost of NHA-financed single-family dwellings purchased in 1975, including many started in the previous year, was $36,999. On these houses purchasers provided down payments averaging $8,175. Compared with 1974 these payments represented an increase of 20.0% in cost and 13.0% in down payment. As in other years most of the NHA-financed single-family houses purchased in 1975 were bungalows, representing 68.7% of the total compared with 72.7% in 1974. The proportion of split-level dwellings increased from 23.7% to 25.6%. Two-storey dwellings rose from 2.4% in 1974 to 5.0% in 1975. Of these dwellings about 95.1% had one to three bedrooms and the remainder had four or more. Types of dwelling units started in selected metropolitan areas in 1974 and 1975 are shown in Table 14.2.

Direct and insured lending   14.2.1

Direct loans. CMHC may make direct loans in the open market for both home-ownership and rental housing if, in the opinion of CMHC, loans are not available through approved lenders. Loans are made to any eligible home-owner applicant but direct loans to builders are normally subject to a requirement that the houses be pre-sold to suitable buyers.

A total of $13.6 million in direct corporation loans to the private sector was approved during 1975. This represented 1.2% of the total NHA loans for home-ownership and rental loans during the year. In the private sector, the corporation's lending continued to be directed mainly to families with moderate incomes in smaller centres and resource areas in which mortgage financing is difficult to obtain. The corporation made loans for 604 new family housing units in 1975, compared to 542 units in 1974 and 898 units in 1973.

Direct loans and grants were also provided under the Assisted Home-Ownership Program to help low- and moderate-income families to purchase a home without spending more than 25% of their gross income on shelter. Assistance was provided in accordance with a graduated scale of adjusted family incomes. As family income decreases assistance increases. Following interest rate adjustments down to CMHC's lowest rate a maximum grant of $600 a year was available to further reduce monthly charges. Generally the program served families in the income range of $6,000 to $11,000 per annum, although this figure could range up to $16,000 in high-cost areas. In December 1975 the form of assistance was changed as a result of amendment to the NHA. Outright grants were replaced by loans, interest free for five years, designed to reduce the effective interest rate during the first years to a basic 8%.

Housing starts,[1] 1966-75

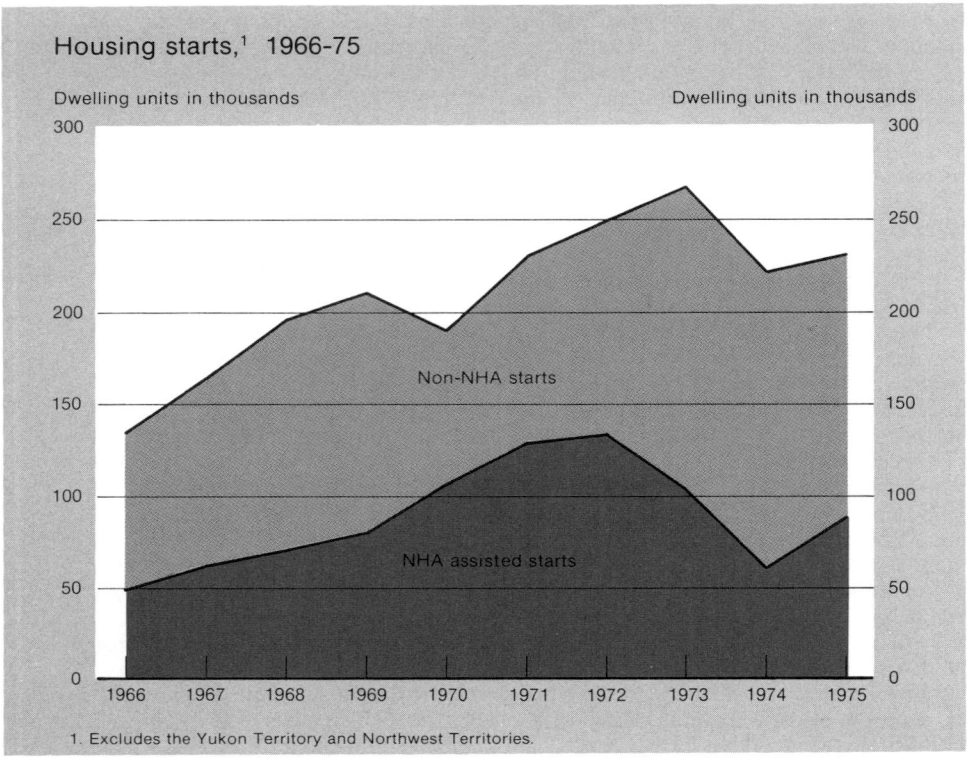

Dwelling units in thousands   Dwelling units in thousands

Non-NHA starts

NHA assisted starts

1. Excludes the Yukon Territory and Northwest Territories.

Since the inception of the program in mid-June 1973, homes have been purchased by 41,368 families with help from the Assisted Home Ownership Plan, involving $1,025 million in loans and contributions. Overall activity has supported the purchase of 9,129 existing housing units and 32,239 new homes. In the fall of 1974 the program was directed exclusively to new construction to encourage housing starts and to increase employment opportunities in house-building.

CMHC may make loans to any organization, corporation or individual to assist in financing the construction of low-rental housing projects. In addition to self-contained units, development may include hostel or dormitory accommodation for elderly and low-income individuals. Loans may be made for a maximum of 95% of the lending value established by CMHC. The repayment period may not exceed the useful life of the project or a maximum of 50 years. Interest rates are established by the Governor in Council and specifications as well as financing and operating arrangements must be approved by the corporation. In 1975, NHA loans were approved to entrepreneurs and other private borrowers for a total of $254 million. This provided 11,268 housing units for individuals and families of low and moderate income.

Long-term loans are available to a province, a municipality or their agencies, a hospital, school board, university or college, cooperative association or charitable corporation for construction of student housing projects, or to acquire existing buildings and convert them into student residences. In all cases the government of the province concerned must approve the loan. CMHC may lend up to 90% of the project cost subject to maximum amounts set regionally by CMHC. For each student housed in dormitory or hostel accommodation the maximum is $15,000. The term of the loan may not exceed 50 years or the existing life of the building, whichever is less. The interest rate is prescribed by the Governor in Council. During 1975, one loan amounting to $250,000 was approved to provide accommodation for 53 students. This brought to 349 the number of student housing loans approved during the 14 years since this legislation came into effect, and a total of $441.25 million loaned. Altogether 68,833 single and 7,114 married students and their families have been accommodated under this program.

Insured loans. Insured mortgage loans may be made for both home-ownership and for rental housing. They are normally available from approved lenders to individual home-owner applicants, to builders constructing houses for sale or rent and for some special groups such as cooperative housing associations and farmers. Insured loans are also available for the purchase, improvement, re-financing or sale of existing dwellings. The conditions governing NHA loans are contained in National Housing Loan Regulations.

Upon application the borrower pays CMHC a fee of $35 a unit to help defray the costs of examining plans and specifications, determining lending values and conducting compliance inspections during construction. An approved lender requires evidence that a home-owner or home-purchaser is providing at least 5% of the value of the house from his own resources. For the home-owner this equity may be in the form of cash or a combination of cash, land and labour; for the home-purchaser it may be in cash or labour. The regulations require that gross debt service — the ratio of repayments of principal and interest plus municipal taxes to the income of the borrower — should not exceed 30%, but higher ratios may be considered on their merits. The borrower pays an insurance fee which is added to the amount of the loan and is repaid over the term of the mortgage. The fee ranges from seven eighths of 1% to 1.25% of the loan, according to type of unit and timing of mortgage advances. The NHA interest rate is free to find its own level in relation to the open market.

In June 1974, loan maximums for home-ownership of new and existing single-family units to be held under freehold, leasehold or condominium tenure and condominium types in apartment form were set by CMHC on a national, regional or local basis. They vary from $44,650 to $55,000 and cover 95% of the first $47,000 of lending value plus 75% of the balance up to the applicable maximum. For rental accommodation maximum loan levels are the same as for ownership but are based on 90% of the first $44,444 and 75% of the balance up to the prescribed maximum. The maximum loan for hostel beds is $15,000 per bed. Maximum loan levels are reviewed quarterly by CMHC. The period of repayment may be up to 40 years for new homes and rental housing. For existing housing this period is the lesser of 40 years or the remaining life of the building.

The investment of $2.3 billion by the approved lenders for new construction in 1975 was three times the $776 million invested in 1974. Loans made in 1975 involved 123,025 units, an increase of 124% from the 54,963 units financed a year earlier.

Home improvement loans. CMHC is authorized to give a limited guarantee to chartered banks or approved instalment credit agencies in return for an insurance fee paid by the borrower on loans made for additions, repairs and alterations to existing houses and apartments. A home improvement loan and the balance owing on any existing NHA home improvement loan on the property may not exceed $4,000 for a one-family dwelling or $4,000 for the first unit of a duplex, semi-detached or multiple-family dwelling, plus $1,500 for each additional unit. Loans are repayable in monthly instalments over a period not exceeding 10 years. The maximum rate of interest is restricted to 2.25% above the long-term government bond rate adjusted quarterly to the nearest one eighth of 1%. In 1975 chartered banks and approved instalment credit agencies granted 5,124 loans for home improvement totalling $15.8 million, compared to 6,346 loans amounting to $18.6 million in 1974. These lenders reported $25 million as the outstanding debt on these loans at the end of 1975.

Non-NHA mortgage financing. Conventional and other forms of financing in 1975 grossed $5.43 billion for 212,668 units as compared to $4.58 billion for 194,688 units in 1974.

14.2.2   Neighbourhood improvement, residential rehabilitation and site clearance

Neighbourhood improvement. The Neighbourhood Improvement Program (NIP) authorizes CMHC to make contributions and loans to municipalities or their agencies to improve the amenities of older run-down neighbourhoods and the housing and living conditions of the residents. It is intended that rehabilitation of the existing housing stock, for which assistance is available under the Residential Rehabilitation Assistance Program, should be an integral part of any project undertaken through NIP.

The program is operated on the basis of annual agreements with the provinces which set out the criteria whereby municipalities and neighbourhoods may participate. In general, however, it is expected that participating neighbourhoods will have the following characteristics: they will be predominantly residential although they may contain local stores, schools, banks, churches, small businesses and perhaps some non-conforming uses of land; a significant proportion of the existing housing stock will be in need of improvement and repair to comply with minimum standards of health and safety; most of the housing in the neighbourhood will be occupied by people of low to moderate income and the existing social and recreational amenities will be considered inadequate.

The agreements also prescribe the allocation of funds to the provinces for re-allocation to municipalities selected by the province and accepted by CMHC. Municipalities will, in turn, select neighbourhoods for participation in the program. NIP agreements were signed with all provinces in 1974. By the end of 1975 these agreements provided for a total of $93.8 million in federal contributions and $12.9 million in federal loans; 82 municipalities had been selected by the provinces to participate and 73 projects had begun by year end.

Site clearance. The Site Clearance Program allows the corporation to help municipalities acquire and demolish properties outside Neighbourhood Improvement areas where such properties either do not meet minimum housing standards or are being used for a purpose inconsistent with the character of the area. It is designed to assist the efforts of municipalities to enforce uniform minimum standards for existing residential buildings. Land, after acquisition and clearance, is to be used for housing, recreational or social facilities. The Site Clearance Program is also operated through annual agreements with the provinces. The agreements made in 1974 for the Neighbourhood Improvement Program include provision for the Site Clearance Program.

Assistance is also available for the clearance of small pockets of substandard residential and/or non-residential buildings in a community that does not require the assistance procedure of NIP. The assistance involves both federal loans and grants. To qualify, the sum of acquisition and demolition costs of contiguous properties must not exceed $500,000. During 1975 federal contributions totalling $1.6 million were allocated for 19 site clearance projects.

Residential rehabilitation. Loans of up to $10,000, with a forgiveness provision of up to $3,750, are available from CMHC to assist in the improvement and repair of substandard dwellings. This assistance is available to home-owners earning $11,000 a year or less, landlords who agree to rent controls, and non-profit corporations and cooperatives. The program applies in areas participating in NIP, other areas through special agreements with provinces and to non-profit corporations and non-profit cooperatives in any area. Priority is given to repair of the housing structure and upgrading of the plumbing, electrical and heating systems. The nature and quality of repair work should extend the useful life of the property for about 15 years. Non-profit corporations are eligible for the same assistance as landlords for the repair of family housing units. In addition these corporations may use the assistance for the conversion of existing residential buildings into a greater number of family housing units or into accommodation of the hostel or dormitory type. The funds may also be used to increase the accommodation available in an existing hostel or dormitory. Loans under this program are conditional on the province or municipality adopting and enforcing appropriate occupancy and maintenance standards to ensure that the property will not fall into disrepair again.

The Residential Rehabilitation Assistance Program (RRAP) was active in some 80 municipalities with an additional 80 to become involved in 1976. In addition RRAP is operative in six specially designated areas in Newfoundland, Quebec and Ontario. During 1975 more than $13 million was committed to the program allowing 4,812 units to be rehabilitated.

Community housing   14.2.3

Cooperatives. Cooperatives are considered to be associations of people, usually incorporated, who group together for a mutual undertaking and agree to take on certain responsibilities and follow certain rules. Cooperative associations for housing are incorporated under provincial legislation. The number of members required to obtain a charter to start a cooperative varies from one province to another, usually between five and seven. Some provinces have special regulations for housing groups. A group of people must be incorporated to obtain a loan under the NHA but incorporation is not necessary to apply to CMHC for start-up funds for a cooperative project. Generally the terms and assistance available to individuals under the act are also available to groups which are organized in cooperatives. Loans may be obtained for the purchase of existing housing and for the rehabilitation of such housing if necessary. Previously loans for cooperative projects were limited to new buildings.

Cooperative housing is a general term applying to various forms of housing constructed or purchased by groups of people organized to secure housing to be owned by those who occupy it. In Canada two forms of cooperative housing are now generally known and provided for in the NHA: building cooperatives and continuing cooperatives. The former is made up of a group of people, usually numbering about five to 15, organized to construct houses which they will own individually. The form of ownership is the main difference in the continuing cooperative: the housing continues to be owned indefinitely by all members jointly. A cooperative of this type is usually organized to provide some form of multiple housing and the number of members is ordinarily 25, 50 or more.

A building cooperative organized to construct houses to be owned individually by the members on completion may qualify for loan and grant assistance under the Assisted Home-Ownership Program if the incomes of the members meet the requirements of the program. A continuing housing cooperative providing accommodation for low-income members may be eligible, under various provisions of the NHA, for start-up funds, for a 100% loan and a 10% contribution if it is a non-profit cooperative, for a loan under the terms and conditions of the Assisted Home-Ownership Program or for loans and grants under the Residential Rehabilitation Assistance Program.

During the year 1,469 units were approved under cooperative housing arrangements, almost double the 1974 total. CMHC support for 1975 activities, provided under the non-profit housing provisions of the NHA, amounted to $43.6 million. Financial assistance included $38.8 million in direct CMHC loans and $4.8 million in grants to continuing non-profit cooperative associations.

Non-profit. A section of the National Housing Act is designed to make it easier for non-profit housing organizations to develop housing projects for people of limited means, particularly the elderly and the handicapped. A non-profit organization is one in which no part of the income is payable or otherwise available for the personal benefit of any proprietor, member or shareholder. Non-profit organizations may be provincially-municipally owned or constituted exclusively for charitable purposes. The latter group is eligible for start-up funds not exceeding $10,000 to ensure that the group is able to prepare properly a loan application to CMHC and to cover expenditures for research and organization, incorporation, site selection, options, professional fees and the technical skills required to put the project in place, selection of tenants and other costs.

Both categories of non-profit borrowers may apply to CMHC for a contribution not exceeding 10% of the cost of the project as estimated by CMHC at the time of application, less any forgivable federal residential rehabilitation loan or federal grants such as those made under the Local Initiatives Program or by the Department of National Revenue in the form of tax refunds. The cost may include both real estate and hard furnishings of the sort used in community buildings for social and recreational purposes. In the case of hostels, hard furnishings would include built-in and non-movable furniture and equipment.

Non-profit organizations formed exclusively for charitable purposes and those which are municipally owned may obtain loans to cover 100% of lending value. In the case of the provincial non-profit organizations, loans to the value of 95% of the lending value are available, with the borrower providing the other 5%. In all cases the 10% contribution from CMHC must be applied against the reduction of the loan.

In 1975 loans were made to non-profit organizations for 4,948 dwelling units and 4,506 hostel beds for a total of $160 million. The corresponding total for the previous year was $125 million. Loans committed to non-profit organizations during the year supported the provision of low-rent accommodation for the elderly, low-income families and special groups. Included in the special groups category is housing for the mentally retarded, physically handicapped, halfway houses for persons recovering from alcohol addiction, and receiving homes for children who are wards of the courts.

Start-up funds. "Start-up" funds not exceeding $10,000 a project were introduced in 1973 to assist potential sponsors to develop proposals for low-rental housing to be financed under the non-profit provisions of the NHA. In 1975 grants totalling $631,000 were approved enabling 63 non-profit and cooperative groups to complete their plans and receive loan approvals for their projects. Costs covered by the grants include expenditures for incorporation as a non-profit society, professional fees, site selection, land options and administration expenses.

In addition to the "start-up" funds, grants were made available for formal management training in social housing activities and to assist non-profit resource groups offering professional and technical services to community organizations sponsoring NHA-financed housing developments. A total of $698,476 was approved for these purposes during 1975.

14.2.4   Municipal infrastructure

Since December 1960 the NHA has made funds available to assist in the elimination or prevention of water and soil pollution. CMHC is authorized to make a loan to a province, municipality or municipal sewerage corporation to construct or expand sewage treatment and trunk collector facilities. The loan may not exceed two thirds of the cost of the project and the maximum repayment term is 50 years from date of completion. Interest is set by the Governor in Council. Agreements covering such projects contain a "forgiveness" clause applicable to both the principal of the loan and accrued interest conditional on satisfactory completion. There was a record demand in 1975, and 322 loans totalling $217.7 million were made. In late 1975 the Municipal Infrastructure Program was expanded to include assistance for the provision of storm trunk sewers and water supply projects required to open up raw land for new residential construction purposes.

Public housing   14.2.5

Under the NHA and complementary provincial legislation the federal and provincial governments may enter into partnership agreements to build rental housing for families and individuals with low incomes or to purchase and rehabilitate existing housing for this purpose. Hostel or dormitory accommodation may be included. The federal government pays up to 75% of the capital costs and the provincial government the remainder, although the latter may call upon the municipality concerned to bear a portion of the provincial share. Rents for units in federal-provincial projects are related to the tenant's family income and size of family. Operating deficits are shared on the same contractual basis as the capital costs.

As an alternative CMHC may make long-term loans to a province, or to a municipality or public housing agency with the approval of the province, to provide public housing. Projects may consist of new construction or the renovation of existing buildings and include dormitory and hostel accommodation as well as self-contained family units. Loans may be up to 90% of the total cost as determined by CMHC and for a term as long as 50 years, but not in excess of the useful life of the development. In addition the loan may be increased by 15% to cover the cost of added amenities which go beyond strictly residential use. The interest rate is set by the Governor in Council. If this alternative is selected federal grants may be made covering up to 50% of losses incurred in the operation of public housing projects for a period not exceeding the term of the loan. Annual subsidies are shared by CMHC and the province concerned.

During 1975 loans totalling $237.4 million were approved to provide 10,401 public housing units. This covered 90% of the cost of construction or acquisition of the units. Comparable figures for 1974 are $177.4 million and 9,239 units. Under the federal-provincial cost-sharing arrangements a further $25.8 million was approved for 886 housing units as compared to 2,501 units and $53.5 million for 1974. The federal government may share in the operating deficits of public housing projects equally under the loan arrangement and accept 75% of the costs under the partnership arrangement. The federal share of subsidy payments for the 135,700 units occupied at the end of 1975 is estimated to be $85.0 million.

Provinces, municipalities or their agencies may enter into agreements with the owners of private accommodation under which the latter agree to rent to low-income families at rentals based on income. The federal government provides 50% of the difference between the subsidized rent paid by the tenant and the full market rent normally charged by the owner.

Included in the federal-provincial cost-sharing arrangements is a program of housing for sale. Subsidy assistance for home-ownership has been provided under a variety of arrangements in Newfoundland, Prince Edward Island, Nova Scotia, New Brunswick, Manitoba, Saskatchewan and British Columbia. Under these arrangements mortgage payments are related to the incomes of the purchasers, with the federal government providing 75% of the difference between the mortgage payment made by the purchaser and the actual amount required to retire the loan and interest. During the year 2,258 units were provided under these arrangements, for a total of 9,697.

Land assembly and new communities   14.2.6

The federal and provincial governments may enter into an agreement to provide for a land assembly project which involves the development of land for housing. The federal government pays up to 75% of the cost and the provincial government the remainder. The latter may call upon the municipality concerned to bear a portion of the provincial share. As an alternative, loans up to 90% of the cost of assembling and servicing land for public housing are available at a preferential interest rate to provinces, municipalities and their agencies.

Under federal-provincial partnerships seven projects for 1,077 residential building lots and one land bank project with a total area of 1,770 acres (716 ha) were approved in 1975. Since the inception of the program in 1948, 34,526 lots have been authorized for development. Of these, 25,369 have been offered for sale and 23,440 have been sold. A total of 33,631 acres (13 610 ha) have been authorized for acquisition in land banks. Of lands actually acquired, 22,181 acres (8 976 ha) remain to be developed. Section 42 of the National Housing Act authorizes the corporation to make loans to provinces and their agencies up to 90% of the cost of assembling and developing land for housing. During 1975, 92 loans amounting to $57.2 million were approved under this section.

The NHA also provides assistance through CMHC for new communities either through cost-sharing arrangements between federal and provincial governments or through loans with certain forgiveness elements to the provinces or their designated agencies. CMHC may participate in the acquisition of land for the new communities, including land for transportation corridors and open space in or around the communities, planning the communities and designing and installing services. Both the federal commitment to the loan arrangement and the federal-provincial cost-sharing agreement are dependent upon the province satisfying several points: the agency or corporation responsible for the planning and development of the new community must be designated, and CMHC must be satisfied that measures will be taken to allow the public to receive any economic benefits that may accrue from selling the lands and services to the private sector in the new community, and that acceptable plans for urban growth, including the location, size and order of development of other new communities, have been established. A federal-provincial agreement between CMHC and the government of any province will determine which new community will receive assistance.

The amount of capital costs, profits and losses to be shared by CMHC shall not exceed 75% of the total capital costs, profits and losses of the project. A loan to a province or its designated agency may be made in an amount of 90% of the cost as determined by CMHC for the acquisition of land for the new communities, including land for transportation corridors and open spaces in or around the communities, for planning the communities, and for the design and installation of the services. The term of the loan will be 25 years. This term may be extended to 50 years for that part to be used for land and services leased on a long-term leasehold basis for private use.

To encourage the rapid development of recreational and social facilities CMHC may forgive up to 50% of that portion of the loan covering acquisition of land for these purposes. A forgiveness of an amount not exceeding 50% of the part of the loan used for initial planning costs may also be approved. This would include salaries, accommodation and expenses of the new community development corporation or agency and necessary consultants to provide overall administration, site investigations, surveys, background research, concept plans, overall development plans as may be required by the province and detailed phasing elements of layout and urban design.

14.2.7   Mortgage administration

The NHA mortgage debt outstanding at the end of 1975 amounted to $17.7 billion, representing 28.9% of the mortgage debt in Canada. With a portfolio of over $6.8 billion, CMHC continued to hold the largest single share of the NHA mortgage debt. The chartered banks held $4.0 billion, life insurance companies held $2.0 billion and other approved lenders held $2.5 billion. The remainder was held by pension funds and purchasers in the secondary mortgage market. In 1975 sales of insured mortgages by approved lenders totalled $402 million. Of this amount $127 million was purchased by various pension funds. The number of NHA loans in arrears increased in 1975. As at December 31, 1975 there were

2,429 loans (0.32% of mortgages outstanding) in arrears for three months or more compared with 2,206 loans (0.29%) a year earlier.

The Mortgage Insurance Fund paid $17.0 million on 119 claims during 1975, a small decrease from 1974 when $19.8 million was paid on 588 claims. Claims paid in 1975 represented 0.09% of the $17.7 billion insured mortgages outstanding. Arrears on all CMHC-owned property as at December 31, 1975 totalled 468 accounts, 2.6% of the total number of rental units. The vacancy rate at December 31, 1975 was 7.6% of rental units under CMHC management.

Census data on housing   14.3

Dwellings and housing growth rates   14.3.1

Since 1941 decennial censuses of Canada have provided a comprehensive inventory of the nation's dwelling stock in a complete housing census taken in conjunction with the censuses of population and agriculture. Detailed information covering the 1941-71 period may be found in the relevant census volumes and reports. Summary data from the 1971 Census included here relate to a selection of the housing characteristics for which data were collected. More detailed information, including cross-classifications of the data, may be obtained from the User Inquiry Service of Census Field, Statistics Canada.

The 1971 Census recorded a total of 6 million occupied dwellings in Canada. (A dwelling, for census purposes, is a structurally separate set of living quarters with a private entrance either from outside the building or from a common hall or stairway inside.) This total represented a 32.5% increase in dwellings since the 1961 Census compared to an increase in population of 18.2%. It is apparent that, despite slower population growth resulting from declining birth rates and lower immigration, the need for dwellings has continued to increase at a rate comparable to the record growth rates of the 1950s. This is attributable largely to the increased rate of family formation as children of the postwar "baby boom" reached working and marriageable age, and to the establishment of increasing numbers of one- and two-person households in both younger and older age groups. These trends in housing growth rates, including comparisons from 1951 to 1971 for such characteristics as type of dwelling, tenure, and number of rooms are summarized in Table 14.3.

Dwelling types, tenure and size   14.3.2

Dwelling types. Single detached homes continued to be the predominant type of housing accommodation in Canada in 1971, although their relative numbers have gradually declined in favour of multiple-type dwellings. Twenty years earlier, at the 1951 Census, two thirds of all dwellings were single detached but this ratio gradually dropped to 59.5% by 1971. In the 1961-71 period single detached homes increased by 20.6%, whereas multiple-type units — single attached (double and row houses), apartments, flats — grew at the significantly higher rate of 52.9%.

Table 14.4 shows the distribution of the two broad dwelling-type classes in 1971 by province and by metropolitan area. Saskatchewan had the largest proportion of single detached homes, 81.5% of its occupied dwellings being in this category. Almost 60% of Quebec's dwellings were multiple-type units and only 40% were single detached, by far the lowest proportion among the provinces. The distribution within the major metropolitan centres reflected these provincial ratios in general terms, except that in most cases the proportion of multiple-unit dwelling types was considerably higher than for the province as a whole. This was particularly evident in Montreal and Toronto, where only 23.7% and 45.9%, respectively, of all occupied dwellings were single detached homes.

Tenure. The recent trend toward apartment living and higher density accommodation has resulted in a significant increase in the number of rented dwellings (from 34.0% of all dwellings in 1961 to 39.7% in 1971), reversing an earlier trend which had seen the rate of home-ownership increase steadily from 56.7% of all homes in 1941 to 66.0% in 1961.

As in the case of dwelling types, there was considerable variation among provinces in the proportions of owned dwellings in 1971, ranging from a low of 47.4% in Quebec to a high of 80.0% in Newfoundland. Table 14.5 shows that the swing toward tenant occupancy in the 1961-71 period was characteristic of all provinces, and at a fairly uniform rate. However, the trend was less marked in New Brunswick and Quebec, where the decline in the percentage of home-owners between 1961 and 1971 was not as sharp as in the other provinces.

Home-ownership is a characteristic which varies greatly between rural and urban areas and is generally in inverse ratio to the size of the community. For example, in large urban agglomerations of 500,000 population and over, only 46.1% of all dwellings were owner-occupied in 1971, compared with 63.2% for the urban size-groups under 100,000 population and 82.0% in rural areas. Among the various census metropolitan areas, the eastern centres of Halifax, Saint John, Montreal, Quebec and Ottawa-Hull showed the lowest percentages of home-ownership and the highest tenancy rates.

Dwelling size. Despite the high increase in apartment rental accommodation during the 1961-71 decade as compared to owner-occupied single homes, the average size of Canadian dwellings showed a slight increase from 5.3 to 5.4 rooms. Not all provinces followed this pattern, however. As Table 14.6 shows, the average number of rooms per dwelling declined in all provinces east of Ontario, with increases in Ontario and throughout the West. In the nation as a whole, Prince Edward Island had the highest average in 1971 at 6.1 rooms per dwelling, and the Yukon Territory and Northwest Territories the lowest at 4.3. A "crowded" dwelling, for census purposes, is considered to be one in which the number of persons exceeds the number of rooms. Using this rough measure, the number of crowded dwellings decreased by 24.2% in the decade between 1961 and 1971. Perhaps even more significant, the number of crowded dwellings fell from 16.5% of the total housing stock in 1961 to 9.4% in 1971. This dramatic improvement, only slightly apparent in the 1951-61 period, appears to result from both a decline in the average number of persons in a household and an increase in the average number of rooms in a dwelling.

Provincially, the smallest proportions of crowded dwellings in relation to total housing stock were in Ontario and British Columbia, where only 6.8% of all dwellings had less than one room per person in 1971. Proportions were highest in Quebec and Nova Scotia (12.4%), Newfoundland (23.6%) and the Northwest Territories and the Yukon Territory (30.7%).

14.3.3   Period of construction and length of occupancy

Period of construction. Figures from the 1971 Census indicate that 28.8% of the occupied housing stock was built after 1960. Consistent with the increase in rented dwellings 34.0% of rented dwellings were built after 1960, compared to 25.4% for owned dwellings. The proportion of dwellings built after 1960 was particularly low in rural farm areas, at 11.6%.

Table 14.7 shows the percentage distribution in 1971 of period of construction by province and by census metropolitan area. There were significant variations from province to province in the proportion of new dwellings. The lowest percentages of dwellings built after 1960 were found in the Atlantic provinces, Prince Edward Island having the lowest at 19.0%. Newfoundland was an exception, however, its 28.6% being close to the national average. Figures above the national average were found only in Alberta, British Columbia, and the Yukon Territory and Northwest Territories, which reported, respectively, 34.5%, 35.3%, and 58.4% of dwellings built after 1960. Values for census metropolitan areas ranged from 19.3% for Windsor to 40.9% for Edmonton.

Length of occupancy. The 1971 Census data on length of occupancy of household heads, displayed in Table 14.7, provide an indication of the mobility of Canadians. Of all household heads in 1971, 66.8% had lived for 10 years or less in the dwelling in which they were enumerated, and 17.8% for less than one year — little changed from the 68.6% and 15.3% respectively recorded in 1961. Length of occupancy was greatest in rural farm areas, where 65.6% of household heads had occupied the same dwelling for more than 10 years.

The pattern of provincial variation for length of occupancy was similar to that for period of construction. The proportion of household heads occupying their present dwelling for 10 years or less was lowest in the Maritimes, ranging from 50.3% in Prince Edward Island to 55.0% in New Brunswick. The highest percentages were 70.6% in Alberta, 74.1% in British Columbia, and 90.7% in the Yukon Territory and Northwest Territories. For census metropolitan areas the range extended from 59.5% for Windsor to 76.1% for Calgary and 76.2% for Edmonton. Fully 25.7% of household heads in Calgary had occupied their dwellings for less than one year.

Values, rents and mortgages   14.3.4

Values. The 1971 Census required householders in owner-occupied non-farm dwellings to estimate the market value of their homes. Table 14.8 presents median values of single detached dwellings by province and by metropolitan area. The 1971 median value of $19,020 represented a 72.6% increase over the $11,021 in 1961. The median value in rural areas was $10,310, compared to $26,902 for urban centres with populations of 500,000 and over.

Median values in the provinces ranged from $7,828 in Newfoundland to $23,768 in Ontario. The Maritime provinces also showed extremely low values, as did the Yukon Territory and Northwest Territories. Only Alberta and British Columbia joined Ontario in having median dwelling values above the national figure. Among the census metropolitan areas, Chicoutimi–Jonquière's median value of $15,489 was the lowest. Toronto's at $32,408 was highest followed by Vancouver where the median value was $26,702.

Rents. The monthly cash rent paid was reported for tenant-occupied non-farm dwellings in the 1971 Census, and the national average at that time was situated at $110. This was 69.2% higher than the $65 average in 1961. The average rent recorded in rural areas, $71, was much lower than the $122 in urban agglomerations of 500,000 population and over.

Table 14.8 shows average cash rent by province and by metropolitan area. Among the provinces, Prince Edward Island had the lowest rents, averaging $86, while Ontario's average of $129 was the highest. As was the case for median dwelling values, only Alberta and British Columbia along with Ontario were above the national average. Again, like dwelling values, Toronto had the highest average cash rent among the census metropolitan areas, $151, while Chicoutimi–Jonquière shared last place with Saint John, each with an average cash rent of $83.

Mortgages. Householders in owner-occupied non-farm dwellings in the 1971 Census were asked if there were one or more mortgages on their dwelling, and the type of holder of the first mortgage. These data, like those on dwelling values, were tabulated for single detached dwellings. Table 14.8 shows the percentage of mortgaged dwellings by province and by metropolitan area.

In 1971, 52.8% of single detached owner-occupied non-farm dwellings were mortgaged, compared to 45.5% in 1961. The proportion was only 32.4% in rural areas, compared to 66.4% in the largest urban centres. For the mortgaged dwellings, the holder of the first mortgage was a bank or an insurance, loan, trust or mortgage company in 62.6% of the cases. The first mortgage was held by a private individual 19.4% of the time and by government only 9.8% of the time. There was considerable variation from province to province in the proportion of mortgaged dwellings. Newfoundland had by far the lowest proportion, 17.4%, while Alberta led with 59.1%. Among census metropolitan areas the extremes were registered by St. John's (45.5%) and Montreal (75.5%).

14.3.5   Heating fuel

In view of world energy shortages, census data on home heating fuels are of particular interest. The 1971 Census data show that 57.1% of occupied Canadian dwellings were heated principally by oil or other liquid fuels, while 32.1% used gas as the main heating fuel. The major change since 1961 was a strong increase in the proportion of dwellings heated by gas, from 18.8% to 32.1%. This was offset by a correspondingly large decrease, from 10.6% to just 1.1%, in the proportion of dwellings using coal or coke as the main heating fuel. The category "other fuels" declined from 14.3% to 9.8% as a result of an increase from 0.7% to 5.8% in the proportion of dwellings which were electrically heated and a decrease from 13.0% to 3.5% in the proportion of dwellings heated by wood. The use of gas as a heating fuel was less predominant in rural areas, 13.4% compared to 37.2% in urban areas.

Table 14.9 gives the percentage distribution of dwellings by principal heating fuel, by province and by metropolitan area. There was a sharp difference between Quebec and Ontario in the proportions of dwellings heated principally by oil and by gas. In Quebec and the Atlantic provinces the proportion using gas as fuel was never higher than 8.0% (Quebec), while the proportion using oil was 79.3% or higher in all cases. In Ontario and the western provinces the proportion using gas was never lower than 37.1% (Ontario) and went as high as 83.6% for Alberta, while the proportion using oil was never above 54.0% and was as low as 9.4% in Alberta. Among census metropolitan areas, Victoria was an exception to this east-west rule, its 2.4% of dwellings heated principally by gas being one of the lowest proportions in the country.

14.3.6   Household facilities and equipment

Census data. Decennial censuses provide an inventory of a variety of household facilities and equipment to measure advances in living standards and to provide data for market research. The 1971 Census covered items such as plumbing and sanitary facilities, heating equipment, and accessories such as refrigerators, freezers, dishwashers, clothes dryers and television sets. Only the data on the first of these subjects, i.e. the incidence of homes with running water, bath and toilet facilities, are shown by province in Table 14.10. More recent information on other items is available from annual sample surveys (see below).

Continuing the rising trend in recent decades, there was again a marked improvement in the number of dwellings equipped with plumbing and sanitary facilities during the 1961-71 period. Dwellings with running water increased from 89.1% of all dwellings in 1961 to 96.1% in 1971. Similarly, households reporting a bath or shower for their exclusive use advanced from 77.1% to 90.8%, and households with exclusive use of a flush toilet from 79.0% to 93.1%.

Although nine of every 10 Canadian dwellings were supplied with these amenities in 1971, in rural localities the ratios were considerably lower than the national percentages. In rural areas of the Prairie provinces, for example, one of every three dwellings still lacked running water and installed bath or shower facilities, and closer to one of every two lacked a flush toilet. Rural Newfoundland showed similar ratios, but in the Yukon Territory and Northwest Territories only about one rural dwelling in three was so equipped. (Table 14.10)

Annual estimates. Table 14.11 presents some summary statistics derived from a sample survey conducted by Statistics Canada in conjunction with the April 1975 labour force survey. About 30,000 households, chosen by area sampling methods, were included. Unlike decennial censuses, the sample survey cannot produce data for the smaller localities and areas, but much of the information shown in Table 14.11 for Canada is available also for individual provinces and selected metropolitan areas. Moreover, a much wider range of household facilities and equipment items is covered in the annual survey than can be accommodated in a general census.

Table 14.11 shows that colour television sets in Canadian households increased more than other household facilities. Between April 1974 and April 1975, households with colour TV sets increased to 53.4% of the total from 44.5%, while possession of black and white TV sets decreased to 67.8% compared to 73.3% a year earlier. More than 40% of households were equipped with cable television service. Ownership of dishwashers increased 2.3% to reach a level of 15.2% while possession of two or more cars increased to 23.0% from 21.6%.

In April 1975, more than one household in 10 reported air conditioning facilities: 620,000 households owned window-type air conditioners and 212,000 households were equipped with central unit air conditioners.

Construction   14.4

Value of construction work   14.4.1

The data on the construction industry represent the estimated total value of all new and repair construction performed by contractors and by the labour forces of utility, manufacturing, mining and logging firms, government departments, home-owner builders and other persons or firms not primarily engaged in the construction industry. Table 14.12 shows the value of new and repair construction work and Table 14.13 the value of such work performed by contractors and others during the period 1971-75, preliminary expenditures for 1974 and intentions for 1975. Table 14.22 gives estimates of total expenditures in Canada on each type of construction for which information is available.

Principal statistics of the construction industry for 1973-75 are shown by province and for contractors, utilities, governments and others in Table 14.14. The statistics given for Canada as a whole may be considered as relatively accurate but those for individual provinces and by class of builder are approximations only. All estimates given for cost of materials used are based on ratios of this item to total value of work performed, derived from annual surveys of construction work performed by contractors and others and applied to the total value-of-work figures. Estimates of labour content are similarly based but, in addition, are adjusted to include working owners and partners and their withdrawals. Although the ratios were calculated in some detail by type of industry, still further refinements are required. There are also some difficulties in obtaining the precise location of projects undertaken or to be undertaken by large companies operating in a number of provinces. However, if used with these qualifications in mind, the table provides useful estimates.

Chapter 21 includes detailed price index numbers of construction and capital goods, which measure price changes in residential and non-residential building materials and changes in construction wage rates; price indexes of highway construction which show annual costs to provincial governments in contracts awarded for highway construction as a percentage of prices paid in 1961; and price indexes of electrical utility construction (distribution systems, transmission lines, transformer stations) which provide an estimate of the impact of price change on the cost of materials, labour and equipment used in constructing and equipping such utilities.

Building permits issued   14.4.2

The estimated value of proposed construction is indicated by the value of building permits issued. Figures of building permits are collected from approximately 1,700 municipalities across the country and are available for individual municipalities, for metropolitan areas, for provinces and for economic areas in Quebec, Ontario and Manitoba.

The total value of permits issued for building construction in 1975 was $10,598.0 million, a figure 14.2% higher than in 1974. Residential construction value increased by 33.9% and overall non-residential construction value decreased by 5.0%, reflecting a decrease of 33.4% in the industrial, 1.8% in the commercial, and a 22.4% increase in the institutional and government construction sectors.

Permit values rose in all provinces except Newfoundland which showed a slight decrease. The value of building permits issued in each province in 1974 and 1975 is given in Table 14.15, in 50 municipalities in Table 14.16 and in 22 metropolitan areas in Table 14.17. These metropolitan areas made up 70.0% of the 1975 total for Canada.

14.5   Capital expenditures

Capital spending in Canada by all sectors of the economy during 1976 was expected to reach $41,954 million, an increase of 10.4% over the 1975 level of $37,997 million. These estimates were in current dollars without any adjustment for price increase and reflected the intended outlays by respondents between December 1975 and February 1976. The survey covered business establishments, educational and other institutions and governments at all levels.

Intended capital expenditures on new construction in 1976 were estimated at $26,810 million, an increase of 12.2% over the 1975 total of $23,894 million. The two main elements of construction are shown at $8,614 million ($7,085 million in 1975) for residential and $18,196 million ($16,810 million) for non-residential. The increase for housing was 21.6% and for non-residential construction, 8.2%. Although starts in housing were projected to increase to only 235,000 in 1976, up from the 231,000 begun in 1975, the increasing value of residential construction was influenced by a large carryover of unfinished projects, started late in 1975, and by some expected price increase.

Acquisition of new machinery and equipment during 1976 was expected to amount to $15,144 million, 7.4% above the 1975 total of $14,103 million. Rates of increase were 16.4% for 1975, 25.3% in 1974 and 24.7% in 1973.

Table 14.18 shows the trend in capital spending over the years 1967-76 in both current and constant (1971) dollars. Table 14.19 summarizes capital and repair expenditures by economic sector and Table 14.20 contains details of the manufacturing, mining and utilities sectors for 1974-76. A summary of capital expenditures in Table 14.21, representing gross additions to the capital stock of each province and territory, reflects economic activity in the area and employment and income-giving effects in other regions. For example, spending millions of dollars on plant and equipment in western Canada may generate considerable activity in machinery industries in Ontario and Quebec as well as construction activity in the western provinces.

Sources

14.1 - 14.2 Central Mortgage and Housing Corporation.

14.3 Census Characteristics Division, Census and Household Surveys Field, Statistics Canada.

14.4 - 14.5 Construction Division, Industry Statistics Branch, Statistics Canada.

Tables

..	not available	e	estimate
...	not appropriate or not applicable	p	preliminary
—	nil or zero	r	revised
--	too small to be expressed		certain tables may not add due to rounding

14.1 Dwelling units[1] started and completed, by type of financing, 1973-75, and by region, 1974 and 1975

Year and region	Dwelling units started					Dwelling units completed
	National Housing Act		Conven-tional institu-tional loans	All other financing	Total	
	CMHC	Approved lenders loans				
1973	29,027	75,469	93,641	70,392	268,529	246,581
1974	30,363r	31,046r	75,000	85,714	222,123	257,243
1975	41,800	47,132	66,905	75,619	231,456	216,964
1974						
Atlantic provinces	3,927r	582r	7,249	6,356	18,114	19,526
Quebec	8,343	7,798	14,272	21,229	51,642	58,596
Ontario	10,079	14,453	30,723	30,248	85,503	104,360
Prairie provinces	4,635	5,879	12,082	12,848	35,444	40,221
British Columbia	3,379	2,334	10,674	15,033	31,420	34,540
1975						
Atlantic provinces	6,040	1,217	5,870	6,411	19,538	18,014
Quebec	10,952	11,842	15,497	16,450	54,741	51,540
Ontario	12,754	22,068	24,498	20,648	79,968	81,865
Prairie provinces	7,467	7,947	10,988	16,655	43,057	34,015
British Columbia	4,587	4,058	10,052	15,455	34,152	31,530

[1]Excludes the Yukon Territory and Northwest Territories.

14.2 Dwelling units started in metropolitan areas, large urban centres and urban agglomerations, 1974 and 1975

Area (1971 Census)	Dwelling units started					
	1974	1975				
	Total	Total	Single de-tached	Semi-de-tached and duplex	Row	Apart-ment; other
METROPOLITAN AREAS	133,413	138,740	61,503	10,527	16,724	49,986
Calgary	6,487	7,872	4,877	874	896	1,225
Chicoutimi — Jonquière	1,463	1,261	958	28	—	275
Edmonton	5,362	8,647	4,974	576	1,687	1,410
Halifax	3,095	2,708	1,163	294	79	1,172
Hamilton	5,968	6,720	1,890	447	1,695	2,688
Kitchener	4,085	3,380	1,764	343	624	649
London	3,311	3,783	1,574	375	710	1,124
Montreal	24,758	26,702	12,109	903	794	12,896
Ottawa — Hull	9,709	7,156	2,110	655	1,625	2,766
Quebec	3,209	4,884	3,298	122	43	1,421
Regina	2,271	2,982	1,995	6	406	575
Saint John	1,139	2,283	861	180	109	1,133
St. Catharines — Niagara	3,233	3,195	1,777	742	422	254
St. John's	1,876	2,151	943	6	762	440
Saskatoon	1,232	2,486	1,512	20	—	954
Sudbury	449	922	687	90	—	145
Thunder Bay	874	919	491	20	73	335
Toronto	29,580	26,457	7,338	3,598	4,744	10,777
Vancouver	14,452	13,315	6,433	618	1,395	4,869
Victoria	2,630	3,980	1,481	92	334	2,073
Windsor	2,602	1,643	887	28	62	666
Winnipeg	5,628	5,294	2,381	510	264	2,139
LARGE URBAN CENTRES AND URBAN AGGLOMERATIONS	16,565	18,622	8,988	2,148	1,775	5,711
Brantford	821	1,816	537	82	206	991
Cornwall	367	351	129	70	18	134
Drummondville	316	290	114	2	—	174
Guelph	1,776	778	318	86	194	180
Kamloops	939	756	323	157	149	127
Kingston	636	766	441	106	20	199
Lethbridge	781	960	513	102	—	345
Moncton	1,377	972	790	20	—	162
North Bay	429	528	198	40	34	256
Oshawa	1,589	2,376	568	503	761	544
Peterborough	850	1,091	354	28	55	654
Prince George	1,254	1,547	1,211	160	74	102

14.2   Dwelling units started in metropolitan areas, large urban centres and urban agglomerations, 1974 and 1975 (concluded)

Area (1971 Census)	Dwelling units started					
	1974	1975				
	Total	Total	Single de-tached	Semi-de-tached and duplex	Row	Apart-ment; other
LARGE URBAN CENTRES AND URBAN AGGLOMERATIONS (concluded)						
St-Jean	747	658	295	—	9	354
St-Jérôme	...	...	...	...	...	...
Sarnia	811	1,572	741	280	255	296
Sault Ste Marie	776	891	535	132	—	224
Shawinigan	235	268	214	—	—	54
Sherbrooke	347	470	209	4	—	257
Sydney/Sydney Mines	817	1,030	641	200	—	189
Timmins	342	432	258	170	—	4
Trois-Rivières	1,355	1,070	599	6	—	465
Valleyfield	...	...	...	...	...	...
Other areas	72,145	74,094	53,438	2,728	3,264	14,664
Canada[1]	222,123	231,456	123,929	15,403	21,763	70,361

[1]Excludes the Yukon Territory and Northwest Territories.

14.3   Summary of housing characteristics, censuses of 1951, 1961 and 1971

Item		1951[1]	1961	1971	Percentage increase	
					1951-61	1961-71
Total occupied dwellings	No.	3,409,295	4,554,493	6,034,510	33.6	32.5
	%	100.0	100.0	100.0	...	...
TYPE OF DWELLING[2]						
Single detached	No.	2,275,615	2,978,501	3,591,770	30.9	20.6
	%	66.7	65.4	59.5	...	...
Single attached	No.	237,655	404,933	679,590	70.4	67.8
	%	7.0	8.9	11.3	...	...
Apartments and flats	No.	885,565	1,151,098	1,699,045	30.0	47.6
	%	26.0	25.3	28.2	...	...
TENURE						
Owned	No.	2,236,955	3,005,587	3,636,925	34.4	21.0
	%	65.6	66.0	60.3	...	...
Rented	No.	1,172,340	1,548,906	2,397,585	32.1	54.8
	%	34.4	34.0	39.7	...	...
SIZE OF DWELLING						
Average rooms per dwelling	No.	5.3	5.3	5.4	...	...
Crowded dwellings[3]	No.	641,820	750,942	569,495	17.0	-24.2
	%	18.8	16.5	9.4	...	...

[1]Excludes the Yukon Territory and Northwest Territories.
[2]Excludes mobile dwellings.
[3]Dwellings in which the number of persons exceeds the number of rooms.

14.4   Type of dwelling, by province and by census metropolitan area, 1971

Province and census metropolitan area	Total dwellings[1]	Single detached	Multiple-unit types[2]	Single detached %	Multiple-unit types[2] %
PROVINCE					
Newfoundland	110,440	85,970	23,765	77.8	21.5
Prince Edward Island	27,880	21,010	6,235	75.4	22.4
Nova Scotia	207,505	148,050	54,265	71.3	26.2
New Brunswick	157,635	110,630	43,535	70.2	27.6
Quebec	1,604,785	641,665	956,560	40.0	59.6
Ontario	2,225,490	1,365,580	851,200	61.4	38.2
Manitoba	288,370	208,455	76,170	72.3	26.4
Saskatchewan	267,565	218,050	45,405	81.5	17.0
Alberta	464,615	329,600	124,205	70.9	26.7
British Columbia	667,545	454,335	193,975	68.1	29.1
Yukon Territory and Northwest Territories	12,675	8,430	3,325	66.5	26.2
Canada	6,034,505	3,591,770	2,378,635	59.5	39.4
METROPOLITAN AREA					
Calgary, Alta.	121,155	73,055	47,140	60.3	38.9
Chicoutimi—Jonquière, Que.	29,655	13,620	15,830	45.9	53.4
Edmonton, Alta.	144,730	90,205	53,520	62.3	37.0
Halifax, NS	59,690	28,570	29,925	47.9	50.1
Hamilton, Ont.	146,280	92,920	53,275	63.5	36.4
Kitchener, Ont.	66,555	38,675	27,840	58.1	41.8
London, Ont.	87,140	53,030	33,775	60.9	38.8
Montreal, Que.	805,775	190,780	614,010	23.7	76.2
Ottawa—Hull, Ont., Que.	170,025	78,815	90,510	46.4	53.2

14.4   Type of dwelling, by province and by census metropolitan area, 1971 (concluded)

Province and census metropolitan area	Total dwellings[1]	Single detached	Multiple-unit types[2]	Single detached %	Multiple-unit types[2] %
METROPOLITAN AREA (concluded)					
Quebec, Que.	127,375	45,085	81,925	35.4	64.3
Regina, Sask.	42,525	29,050	13,245	68.3	31.1
Saint John, NB	28,690	12,880	15,335	44.9	53.5
St. Catharines—Niagara, Ont.	88,940	65,350	23,405	73.5	26.3
St. John's, Nfld.	29,740	15,965	13,700	53.7	46.1
Saskatoon, Sask.	38,590	25,520	12,760	66.1	33.1
Sudbury, Ont.	39,390	23,725	15,360	60.2	39.0
Thunder Bay, Ont.	32,195	24,525	7,595	76.2	23.6
Toronto, Ont.	773,985	354,965	418,755	45.9	54.1
Vancouver, BC	345,870	216,455	127,205	62.6	36.8
Victoria, BC	66,365	42,875	22,855	64.6	34.4
Windsor, Ont.	74,170	52,910	21,135	71.3	28.5
Winnipeg, Man.	166,480	105,570	60,570	63.4	36.4

[1]Includes mobile homes.
[2]Includes double and row houses, apartments, flats, duplexes, etc.

14.5   Owned and rented dwellings, by province and type of locality, censuses of 1961 and 1971

Province or territory and type of locality	1961 Owned	Rented	Owned/rented ratio	1971 Owned	Rented	Owned/rented ratio
PROVINCE						
Newfoundland	76,691	11,249	87.2/12.8	88,335	22,110	80.0/20.0
Prince Edward Island	18,958	4,984	79.2/20.8	20,725	7,155	74.3/25.7
Nova Scotia	131,405	43,935	74.9/25.1	147,705	59,800	71.2/28.8
New Brunswick	94,022	38,692	70.8/29.1	109,450	48,185	69.4/30.6
Quebec	583,981	607,387	49.0/51.0	761,340	843,450	47.4/52.6
Ontario	1,157,229	483,521	70.5/29.5	1,400,340	825,145	62.9/37.1
Manitoba	176,156	63,598	73.5/26.5	190,585	97,790	66.1/33.9
Saskatchewan	188,226	57,198	76.7/23.3	194,535	73,035	72.7/27.3
Alberta	248,537	101,272	71.0/29.0	296,705	167,910	63.9/36.1
British Columbia	326,090	133,442	71.0/29.0	422,785	244,765	63.3/36.7
Yukon Territory and Northwest Territories	4,292	3,628	54.2/45.8	4,425	8,240	35.0/65.0
Canada	3,005,587	1,548,906	66.0/34.0	3,636,925	2,397,585	60.3/39.7
TYPE OF LOCALITY						
Urban	1,946,559	1,333,909	59.3/40.7	2,572,885	2,164,535	54.3/45.7
500,000 and over	1,178,136[1]	910,934[1]	56.4/43.6[1]	956,765	1,118,550	46.1/53.9
100,000-499,999				556,375	428,770	56.5/43.5
30,000- 99,999	261,603	166,644	61.1/38.9	304,450	230,365	56.9/43.1
5,000- 29,999	261,955	149,879	63.6/36.4	449,685	248,740	64.4/35.6
Under 5,000	244,865	106,452	69.7/30.3	305,610	138,105	68.9/31.1
Rural	1,059,028	214,997	83.1/16.9	1,064,045	233,050	82.0/18.0
Non-farm	641,038	183,434	77.8/22.2	758,830	210,830	78.3/21.7
Farm	417,990	31,563	93.0/ 7.0	305,210	22,215	93.2/ 6.8

[1]1961 figures available for urban group "100,000 and over" only.

14.6   Average number of rooms per dwelling and percentage of crowded dwellings[1], by province, censuses of 1961 and 1971

Province	Average number of rooms per dwelling 1961	1971	Percentage of crowded dwellings[1] 1961	1971
Newfoundland	5.9	5.8	29.9	23.6
Prince Edward Island	6.4	6.1	17.0	12.8
Nova Scotia	5.8	5.7	18.2	12.4
New Brunswick	5.9	5.7	21.0	15.2
Quebec	5.3	5.2	21.8	12.4
Ontario	5.5	5.6	11.8	6.8
Manitoba	4.9	5.2	16.8	9.2
Saskatchewan	4.9	5.3	18.7	9.8
Alberta	4.9	5.4	17.5	8.3
British Columbia	4.9	5.2	12.1	6.8
Yukon Territory and Northwest Territories	3.4	4.3	45.4	30.7
Canada	5.3	5.4	16.5	9.4

[1]Dwellings in which the number of persons exceeds the number of rooms.

14.7   Period of construction and length of occupancy, by province and by census metropolitan area, 1971 (percentage)

Province and census metropolitan area	Period of construction				Length of occupancy					
	Before 1946	1946-60	1961-71[1]	Total	Less than 1 year	1-2 years	3-5 years	6-10 years	More than 10 years	Total
PROVINCE										
Newfoundland	35.0	36.4	28.6	100.0	11.1	11.7	13.5	16.1	47.6	100.0
Prince Edward Island	62.2	18.7	19.0	100.0	11.7	11.4	12.3	14.8	49.7	100.0
Nova Scotia	53.2	25.6	21.1	100.0	14.4	13.1	12.7	14.1	45.7	100.0
New Brunswick	50.4	27.9	21.7	100.0	14.1	13.0	13.3	14.6	45.0	100.0
Quebec	37.5	33.9	28.6	100.0	17.2	17.5	15.5	17.9	32.0	100.0
Ontario	39.8	32.2	28.0	100.0	17.5	17.0	16.2	16.3	32.9	100.0
Manitoba	42.6	32.2	25.3	100.0	17.8	14.6	14.6	16.2	36.8	100.0
Saskatchewan	42.3	32.6	25.1	100.0	14.7	12.6	14.2	18.1	40.4	100.0
Alberta	26.8	38.7	34.5	100.0	20.6	16.7	16.5	16.8	29.4	100.0
British Columbia	29.6	35.1	35.3	100.0	22.5	18.3	17.6	15.7	25.9	100.0
Yukon Territory and Northwest Territories	9.5	32.2	58.4	100.0	34.9	26.4	17.9	11.5	9.2	100.0
Canada	38.0	33.2	28.8	100.0	17.8	16.6	15.8	16.6	33.2	100.0
METROPOLITAN AREA										
Calgary, Alta.	19.7	40.6	39.7	100.0	25.7	18.1	17.3	15.0	23.9	100.0
Chicoutimi—Jonquière, Que.	36.8	40.4	22.8	100.0	15.8	15.5	14.0	15.4	39.2	100.0
Edmonton, Alta.	18.0	41.2	40.9	100.0	23.6	18.6	17.3	16.6	23.8	100.0
Halifax, NS	34.8	32.8	32.4	100.0	22.7	17.5	16.1	15.4	28.2	100.0
Hamilton, Ont.	37.5	34.1	28.4	100.0	16.7	17.0	16.9	16.6	32.8	100.0
Kitchener, Ont.	32.9	29.9	37.2	100.0	21.7	18.4	15.4	15.2	29.2	100.0
London, Ont.	39.4	29.7	30.9	100.0	21.2	17.2	16.5	14.6	30.5	100.0
Montreal, Que.	31.1	36.4	32.4	100.0	19.5	19.9	16.5	19.0	25.1	100.0
Ottawa—Hull, Ont., Que.	28.7	33.9	37.4	100.0	21.5	19.1	17.4	17.2	24.9	100.0
Quebec, Que.	35.2	29.6	35.2	100.0	18.9	17.3	15.9	17.4	30.5	100.0
Regina, Sask.	30.5	35.9	33.7	100.0	21.5	16.9	15.7	18.6	27.3	100.0
Saint John, NB	53.7	23.9	22.4	100.0	16.1	16.0	16.7	17.4	33.8	100.0
St. Catharines—Niagara, Ont.	41.8	35.8	22.4	100.0	14.9	14.3	14.8	15.9	40.1	100.0
St. John's, Nfld.	36.2	32.2	31.6	100.0	14.6	14.6	15.6	17.7	37.5	100.0
Saskatoon, Sask.	27.6	35.0	37.3	100.0	24.3	17.5	15.7	16.7	25.8	100.0
Sudbury, Ont.	30.6	41.4	28.1	100.0	19.6	18.1	15.7	15.3	31.2	100.0
Thunder Bay, Ont.	44.4	35.3	20.2	100.0	14.6	14.1	15.2	16.9	39.2	100.0
Toronto, Ont.	30.7	35.3	34.0	100.0	19.1	19.4	17.5	17.2	26.8	100.0
Vancouver, BC	30.8	35.5	33.7	100.0	22.1	17.9	17.3	15.6	27.1	100.0
Victoria, BC	36.2	32.9	30.9	100.0	22.0	18.1	17.3	16.6	26.0	100.0
Windsor, Ont.	49.1	31.6	19.3	100.0	16.9	14.0	13.5	15.1	40.5	100.0
Winnipeg, Man.	41.5	33.4	25.1	100.0	20.2	16.1	15.1	15.5	33.1	100.0

[1]Includes the first five months only of 1971.

14.8   Median value and proportion with mortgages for single detached owner-occupied non-farm dwellings and average cash rent for tenant-occupied non-farm dwellings, by province and by census metropolitan area, 1971

Province and census metropolitan area	Non-farm dwellings				
	Single detached owner-occupied			Tenant-occupied	
	No.	Median value $	Dwellings with mortgage %	No.	Average monthly cash rent $
PROVINCE					
Newfoundland	77,080	7,828	17.4	21,980	93
Prince Edward Island	14,325	9,454	36.0	6,975	86
Nova Scotia	124,705	10,829	32.9	59,410	104
New Brunswick	91,420	9,153	33.5	47,890	87
Quebec	499,640	14,667	58.4	836,935	92
Ontario	1,117,965	23,768	56.4	815,190	129
Manitoba	148,015	14,904	47.6	95,585	104
Saskatchewan	129,870	11,467	40.0	68,620	89
Alberta	219,110	19,933	59.1	162,460	116
British Columbia	366,085	23,502	56.8	242,620	120
Yukon Territory and Northwest Territories	3,510	8,639	36.0	8,245	95
Canada	2,791,730	19,020	52.8	2,365,905	110
METROPOLITAN AREA					
Calgary, Alta.	62,045	22,461	74.7	52,135	127
Chicoutimi—Jonquière, Que.	11,410	15,489	69.9	13,505	83
Edmonton, Alta.	71,555	23,665	69.9	64,205	124
Halifax, NS	24,275	22,820	64.2	29,915	129
Hamilton, Ont.	82,280	25,172	62.7	52,775	123
Kitchener, Ont.	35,215	23,968	63.9	26,415	120
London, Ont.	45,370	20,916	63.1	34,725	121
Montreal, Que.	165,350	18,603	75.5	519,165	99
Ottawa—Hull, Ont., Que.	69,075	25,758	72.3	83,880	135
Quebec, Que.	39,080	19,422	73.9	73,365	99
Regina, Sask.	24,070	16,443	62.4	16,865	102
Saint John, NB	11,060	15,528	54.8	14,155	83
St. Catharines—Niagara, Ont.	57,170	19,966	52.6	24,890	106
St. John's, Nfld.	13,810	19,945	45.5	9,995	104

14.8   Median value and proportion with mortgages for single detached owner-occupied non-farm dwellings and average cash rent for tenant-occupied non-farm dwellings, by province and by census metropolitan area, 1971 (concluded)

Province and census metropolitan area	Non-farm dwellings				
	Single detached owner-occupied			Tenant-occupied	
	No.	Median value $	Dwellings with mortgage %	No.	Average monthly cash rent $
METROPOLITAN AREA (concluded)					
Saskatoon, Sask.	21,065	17,230	62.0	15,635	101
Sudbury, Ont.	18,990	22,306	61.2	16,485	121
Thunder Bay, Ont.	21,620	16,212	50.4	8,565	98
Toronto, Ont.	316,790	32,408	66.1	347,420	151
Vancouver, BC	186,025	26,702	61.9	141,715	130
Victoria, BC	37,250	25,007	58.2	25,545	119
Windsor, Ont.	46,550	22,327	51.3	21,790	123
Winnipeg, Man.	91,115	17,780	58.3	67,905	108

14.9   Percentage distribution of principal fuels used for home heating, by province and by census metropolitan area, 1971

Province and census metropolitan area	Total	Oil or other liquid fuel	Gas	Coal or coke	Other
PROVINCE					
Newfoundland	100.0	82.3	0.1	2.6	15.0
Prince Edward Island	100.0	87.2	0.5	1.5	10.8
Nova Scotia	100.0	83.6	0.8	5.5	10.1
New Brunswick	100.0	84.5	0.8	0.7	14.0
Quebec	100.0	79.3	8.0	0.1	12.6
Ontario	100.0	54.0	37.1	0.8	8.1
Manitoba	100.0	32.3	54.4	2.1	11.2
Saskatchewan	100.0	32.7	60.4	1.6	5.2
Alberta	100.0	9.4	83.6	3.2	3.8
British Columbia	100.0	47.0	40.8	0.5	11.6
Yukon Territory and Northwest Territories	100.0	79.5	3.7	0.1	16.6
Canada	100.0	57.1	32.1	1.1	9.8
METROPOLITAN AREA					
Calgary, Alta.	100.0	2.3	94.9	- -	2.8
Chicoutimi—Jonquière, Que.	100.0	87.5	0.7	0.1	11.7
Edmonton, Alta.	100.0	2.7	94.0	0.4	3.0
Halifax, NS	100.0	93.9	0.5	0.6	4.9
Hamilton, Ont.	100.0	53.5	40.9	1.5	4.0
Kitchener, Ont.	100.0	55.1	36.1	0.6	8.2
London, Ont.	100.0	30.7	63.0	0.5	5.8
Montreal, Que.	100.0	76.8	14.1	0.2	8.9
Ottawa—Hull, Ont., Que.	100.0	78.7	13.5	0.1	7.7
Quebec, Que.	100.0	86.5	0.3	0.1	13.1
Regina, Sask.	100.0	8.6	88.9	0.1	2.3
Saint John, NB	100.0	95.5	1.2	0.4	2.9
St. Catharines—Niagara, Ont.	100.0	31.6	64.8	0.2	3.3
St. John's, Nfld.	100.0	88.1	0.1	1.6	10.3
Saskatoon, Sask.	100.0	3.4	94.3	- -	2.2
Sudbury, Ont.	100.0	68.5	22.7	0.2	8.6
Thunder Bay, Ont.	100.0	34.4	60.3	0.3	5.0
Toronto, Ont.	100.0	53.8	39.7	0.9	5.6
Vancouver, BC	100.0	38.1	55.6	0.4	5.8
Victoria, BC	100.0	83.4	2.4	0.7	13.5
Windsor, Ont.	100.0	12.8	77.8	0.6	8.8
Winnipeg, Man.	100.0	17.6	76.2	0.4	5.8

14.10   Percentage of dwellings with specified facilities, by province and type of locality, Census 1971

Province or territory and type of locality	Percentage of dwellings with		
	Running water	Bath or shower (exclusive use)	Flush toilet (exclusive use)
Newfoundland	83.7	66.3	73.6
Rural	70.4	45.3	54.0
Urban	93.0	81.0	87.4
Prince Edward Island	86.1	75.0	78.0
Rural	78.1	63.6	65.9
Urban	98.3	92.3	96.2
Nova Scotia	92.2	80.3	84.7
Rural	83.4	65.6	70.3
Urban	98.7	91.2	95.4

14.10   Percentage of dwellings with specified facilities, by province and type of locality, Census 1971 (concluded)

Province or territory and type of locality	Percentage of dwellings with		
	Running water	Bath or shower (exclusive use)	Flush toilet (exclusive use)
New Brunswick	92.1	80.5	86.2
Rural	83.4	65.1	72.5
Urban	98.0	90.9	95.4
Quebec	98.9	92.2	97.4
Rural	95.3	77.1	92.3
Urban	99.6	95.1	98.3
Ontario	98.0	94.5	95.7
Rural	89.9	82.4	84.3
Urban	99.5	96.8	98.0
Manitoba	90.2	85.4	85.1
Rural	66.9	59.9	55.3
Urban	98.9	95.0	96.3
Saskatchewan	83.8	78.7	77.5
Rural	66.5	60.3	55.9
Urban	97.6	93.4	94.6
Alberta	92.6	88.5	88.9
Rural	72.6	66.2	64.7
Urban	99.0	95.6	96.5
British Columbia	98.0	95.0	95.6
Rural	92.5	88.1	88.5
Urban	99.6	96.9	97.6
Yukon Territory and Northwest Territories	66.0	64.1	62.3
Rural	35.1	33.5	30.0
Urban	87.5	85.2	84.6
Canada	96.1	90.8	93.1
Rural	84.4	73.5	77.3
Urban	99.3	95.6	97.5

14.11   Annual estimates of household facilities and equipment, 1975

Item	Estimated households 1975 (April) '000	Percentage of households	
		1975 (April)	1974 (April)
Total households	6,703	100.0	100.0
Principal heating facilities			
Furnaces	5,331	79.5	80.8
Oil	3,026	45.1	46.9
Gas	2,249	33.6	33.1
Wood or coal	42	0.6	0.7
Other equipment	1,372	20.5	19.2
Oil	429	6.4	6.6
Gas	141	2.1	2.4
Wood or coal	74	1.1	1.3
Electricity	703	10.5	8.6
Cooking fuel			
Electricity	5,701	85.1	83.6
Piped gas	620	9.2	10.0
Bottled gas	119	1.8	1.8
Wood or coal	99	1.5	1.8
Kerosene, oil or other	158	2.4	2.5
Fuel used for piped hot water supply			
Electricity	3,311	49.4	49.2
Gas	2,267	33.8	32.6
Oil	876	13.1	13.4
Coal or wood	23	0.3	0.5
No hot water supply	219	3.3	4.3
Refrigerators and home freezers			
Electric refrigerators	6,653	99.3	98.9
Home freezers	2,804	41.8	39.8
Washing machines			
Automatic	3,492	52.1	49.0
Other electric	1,660	24.8	28.6
Clothes dryers	3,460	51.6	48.3
Telephones	6,464	96.4	95.8
Radios			
All types, except car	6,589	98.3	98.2
FM receivers	5,074	75.7	71.7

14.11   Annual estimates of household facilities and equipment, 1975 (concluded)

Item	Estimated households 1975 (April) '000	Percentage of households	
		1975 (April)	1974 (April)
TV sets			
All types	6,489	96.8	96.4
Black and white	4,544	67.8	73.3
Colour	3,581	53.4	44.5
Record players	5,073	75.7	74.5
Automobiles	5,286	78.9	78.0
One automobile	3,745	55.9	56.4
Two or more automobiles	1,541	23.0	21.6
Miscellaneous			
Window-type air conditioners	620	9.2	7.6
Central-unit air conditioners	212	3.2	2.6
Automatic dishwashers	1,019	15.2	12.9
Adult-sized bicycles	2,266	33.8	30.4
Snowmobiles	671	10.0	9.3
Motorcycles	337	5.0	[1]
Vacuum cleaners	5,801	86.5	83.9[2]
Electric sewing machines	4,386	65.4	67.9[2]
Portable humidifiers	1,341	20.0	13.4[3]
Microwave ovens	52	0.8	[1]
Cable television	2,710	40.4	[1]
Tape recorders	2,325	34.7	31.6[2]

[1]New items in 1975.
[2]1973 figures, data not collected in 1974.
[3]1972 figure, data not collected in 1973 and 1974.

14.12   Value of new and repair construction work performed, 1971-75[1]

Year	New $'000,000	Repair $'000,000	Total $'000,000	Total construction as percentage of gross national expenditure
1971	13,276	2,589	15,865	17.0
1972	14,469	2,820	17,289	16.7
1973[r]	16,954	3,220	20,174	17.0
1974[r]	20,499	3,716	24,215	17.4
1975	23,079	4,170	27,249	—

[1]Actual expenditures 1971-73; preliminary actual 1974, intentions 1975.

14.13   Value of construction work performed, by contractors and others, 1971-75[1] (million dollars)

Item	1971	1972	1973[r]	1974[r]	1975
Contract construction	12,703	13,744	15,904	19,194	21,153
New	11,108	11,984	13,883	16,901	18,574
Repair	1,595	1,760	2,021	2,293	2,579
Other construction[2]	3,162	3,545	4,270	5,021	6,096
New	2,168	2,485	3,071	3,598	4,505
Repair	994	1,060	1,199	1,423	1,591
Total, construction	15,865	17,289	20,174	24,215	27,249
New	13,276	14,469	16,954	20,499	23,079
Repair	2,589	2,820	3,220	3,716	4,170

[1]Actual expenditures 1971-73; preliminary actual 1974; intentions 1975.
[2]Work done by the labour forces of utilities, government departments and other employers not primarily engaged in the construction industry.

14.14   Labour content, cost of materials and value of work performed in construction, by province and by employer, 1973-75[1]

Province and employer	Year	Labour content		Cost of materials used $'000	Value of work performed $'000
		No.	Value $'000		
PROVINCE					
Newfoundland	1973	17,077	181,307	170,829	497,998
	1974	20,324	220,342	215,142	595,184
	1975	19,019	227,449	219,111	605,704
Prince Edward Island	1973	4,837	41,036	48,672	115,649
	1974	4,284	38,793	46,734	109,811
	1975	3,904	38,657	46,279	108,807
Nova Scotia	1973	21,912	214,323	256,349	621,037
	1974	22,970	245,009	286,056	694,629
	1975	22,359	263,293	310,923	745,480

14.14   Labour content, cost of materials and value of work performed in construction, by province and by employer, 1973-75¹ (concluded)

Province and employer	Year	Labour content		Cost of materials used $'000	Value of work performed $'000
		No.	Value $'000		
PROVINCE (concluded)					
New Brunswick	1973	21,840	191,054	212,333	517,861
	1974	28,221	267,840	289,869	728,569
	1975	29,733	314,245	335,718	835,509
Quebec	1973	139,682	1,583,427	1,673,044	4,373,282
	1974	158,683	2,009,794	2,116,908	5,518,622
	1975	162,764	2,300,725	2,386,531	6,338,707
Ontario	1973	237,103	2,681,124	2,844,763	7,135,957
	1974	240,492	3,169,990	3,329,493	8,402,512
	1975	242,525	3,547,003	3,663,569	9,369,473
Manitoba	1973	29,114	314,098	349,516	888,887
	1974	27,263	350,592	391,064	984,986
	1975	25,471	364,556	401,128	1,021,448
Saskatchewan	1973	25,237	251,849	282,947	699,919
	1974	28,493	333,259	373,168	918,409
	1975	30,022	390,310	437,889	1,075,759
Alberta	1973	72,627	843,139	895,300	2,334,347
	1974	77,202	988,041	1,058,201	2,749,746
	1975	82,782	1,179,214	1,237,681	3,265,634
British Columbia, the Yukon Territory and Northwest Territories	1973	85,457	1,044,791	1,207,251	2,988,827
	1974	87,873	1,231,729	1,420,159	3,512,886
	1975	87,833	1,365,240	1,568,532	3,882,665
Canada	1973	654,886	7,346,148	7,941,004	20,173,764
	1974	695,805	8,855,389	9,526,794	24,215,354
	1975	706,412	9,990,692	10,607,361	27,249,186
EMPLOYER					
Contractors	1973	514,587	5,846,961	6,208,532	15,903,586
	1974	546,381	7,077,686	7,478,731	19,194,100
	1975	543,271	7,828,129	8,125,835	21,153,222
Utilities	1973	50,664	605,781	831,578	1,991,825
	1974	52,320	697,919	962,681	2,281,796
	1975	60,043	889,231	1,223,879	2,900,513
Governments	1973	47,404	460,551	346,132	1,066,643
	1974	51,588	560,722	426,431	1,298,630
	1975	55,770	674,561	506,540	1,550,333
Miscellaneous	1973	42,231	432,855	554,762	1,211,710
	1974	45,516	519,062	658,951	1,440,828
	1975	47,328	598,771	751,107	1,645,118

¹Actual expenditures 1973; preliminary actual 1974; intentions 1975.

14.15   Value of building permits issued, by province, 1974 and 1975 with totals for 1971-75 (thousand dollars)

Province or territory and year		Residential construction			Non-residential construction			Total
		New	Improvements	Total	Industrial	Commercial	Institutional and government	
Newfoundland	1974	33,189	3,573	36,762	8,899	9,632	13,278	68,571
	1975	26,474	3,027	29,501	4,864	17,565	12,838	64,768
Prince Edward Island	1974	15,974	1,880	17,854	3,526	4,485	14,605	40,470
	1975	33,529	2,444	35,973	4,508	7,726	22,249	70,456
Nova Scotia	1974	141,254	9,086	150,340	29,346	61,131	61,014	301,831
	1975	183,179	15,934	199,113	16,458	75,798	49,547	340,916
New Brunswick	1974	72,152	5,435	77,587	16,587	32,454	41,002	167,630
	1975	102,948	9,217	112,165	15,094	50,931	53,607	231,797
Quebec	1974	754,841	49,816	804,657	396,154	531,797	288,059	2,020,667
	1975	1,044,023	85,282	1,129,305	208,180	432,078	261,889	2,031,452
Ontario	1974	1,869,685	132,518	2,002,203	533,896	905,229	385,367	3,826,695
	1975	2,227,173	235,226	2,462,399	434,829	918,508	493,205	4,308,941
Manitoba	1974	137,019	5,851	142,870	19,104	71,840	39,671	273,485
	1975	157,033	12,238	169,271	15,164	70,395	36,322	291,152
Saskatchewan	1974	122,761	4,201	126,962	21,451	53,321	36,548	238,282
	1975	227,692	12,085	239,777	13,128	85,700	91,580	430,185
Alberta	1974	437,080	12,935	450,015	198,434	323,335	98,143	1,069,927
	1975	729,517	41,385	770,902	85,905	280,130	134,460	1,271,397
British Columbia	1974	711,747	50,883	762,630	87,782	297,926	111,495	1,259,833
	1975	902,120	69,314	971,434	76,868	307,290	184,255	1,539,847
Yukon Territory	1974	—	—	—	—	—	—	—
	1975	—	—	—	—	—	—	—

14.15   Value of building permits issued, by province, 1974 and 1975 with totals for 1971-75 (thousand dollars) (concluded)

Province or territory and year		Residential construction			Non-residential construction			Total
		New	Improve-ments	Total	Indus-trial	Commer-cial	Institutional and government	
Northwest Territories	1974	3,332	498	3,830	719	1,515	6,620	12,684
	1975	8,828	272	9,100	828	5,362	1,834	17,124
Total	1971	3,121,347	81,716	3,203,063	470,924	1,069,785	967,809	5,711,581
	1972	3,480,725	157,686	3,638,411	520,479	1,411,599	893,119	6,463,608
	1973	4,552,220	210,862	4,763,082	853,754	1,970,340	971,762	8,558,938
	1974	4,299,034	276,676	4,575,710	1,315,898	2,292,665	1,095,802	9,280,075
	1975	5,642,516	486,424	6,128,940	875,826	2,251,483	1,341,786	10,598,035

14.16   Estimated value of proposed construction as indicated by building permits issued in 50 municipalities, 1974 and 1975 (thousand dollars)

Province and municipality	1974	1975	Province and municipality	1974	1975
NEWFOUNDLAND			Oshawa	40,826	48,936
St. John's	40,172	39,272	Ottawa	222,787	190,315
			Scarborough (borough)	392,936	282,352
PRINCE EDWARD ISLAND			Thunder Bay	49,904	46,679
Charlottetown	3,065	2,742	Toronto	392,936	538,134
			Windsor	85,884	56,509
NOVA SCOTIA			York (borough)	12,819	15,490
Halifax	54,666	79,723	York North (borough)	283,304	212,009
NEW BRUNSWICK			MANITOBA		
Fredericton	22,625	34,443	Fort Garry ⎫		
Moncton	29,638	25,478	St. Boniface ⎬ [2]	211,200	220,639
Saint John	44,649	74,013	St. James ⎪		
			Winnipeg ⎭		
QUEBEC			SASKATCHEWAN		
La Salle	13,284	17,933	Moose Jaw	19,672	19,360
Montreal	313,019	287,534	Prince Albert	10,929	17,354
Quebec	62,197	48,325	Regina	90,873	150,939
Ste. Foy	36,673	40,476	Saskatoon	50,933	127,839
St. Laurent	54,382	43,275			
Sept-Îles	20,305	21,439	ALBERTA		
Sherbrooke	29,093	27,000	Calgary	273,373	391,313
Trois-Rivières	22,205	25,723	Edmonton ⎫ [3]	240,044	303,076
			Jasper Place ⎭		
ONTARIO			Lethbridge	42,552	43,874
Brampton	107,846[1]	85,185[1]	Medicine Hat	127,225	33,834
Burlington	65,414	63,520	Red Deer	22,541	25,858
Etobicoke (borough)	131,098	100,573			
Hamilton	123,637	148,186	BRITISH COLUMBIA		
Kitchener	56,647	72,855	Burnaby District	92,742	105,549
London	99,580	105,287	Richmond Township	82,646	103,648
London Township	2,548	2,980	Surrey District	61,980	90,128
Mississauga	170,430	229,317	Vancouver	139,813	152,282
Nepean Township	41,054	31,330	Victoria	75,620	56,392

[1]Includes townships of Chinguacousy and Toronto Gore and part of Mississauga.
[2]Metropolitan Corporation of Greater Winnipeg.
[3]Jasper Place included with Edmonton following annexation.

14.17   Estimated value of building permits issued in metropolitan areas, 1974 and 1975 (thousand dollars)

Metropolitan area	1974	1975	Metropolitan area	1974	1975
Calgary	273,373	391,313	Saint John	47,082	74,789
Chicoutimi-Jonquière	56,556	56,264	St. Catharines-Niagara	120,110	142,934
Edmonton	316,024	394,968	St. John's[1]	40,172	39,279
Halifax	138,183	170,593	Saskatoon	50,933	127,839
Hamilton	228,300	277,126	Sudbury	32,261	57,477
Kitchener	119,185	148,196	Thunder Bay	52,334	49,590
London	120,193	129,102	Toronto	1,618,794	1,835,372
Montreal	986,751	1,109,303	Vancouver	582,082	702,950
Ottawa-Hull	465,095	436,385	Victoria	162,111	177,476
Quebec	176,478	195,075	Windsor	116,591	82,446
Regina	90,873	150,939	Winnipeg	211,200	220,639

[1]Although this is a metropolitan area, only St. John's proper is included in the building permits survey.

14.18   Capital expenditures[1] on construction and on machinery and equipment, in current and constant (1971) dollars, 1967-76

| Year | Capital expenditures ($'000,000) | | | | | | | | Capital expenditures as percentage of gross national expenditure[2] | |
| | Construction | | Machinery and equipment | | Total | | | | | |
	Current dollars	Constant 1971 dollars	Current dollars	Constant 1971 dollars	Current dollars	Constant 1971 dollars			Current dollars	Constant 1971 dollars
1967	9,474	11,072	5,874	6,499	15,348	17,571			23.5	23.2
1968	9,909	11,486	5,546	6,142	15,455	17,628			21.7	21.9
1969	10,824	11,918	6,103	6,580	16,927	18,498			21.6	21.9
1970	11,319	11,962	6,479	6,673	17,798	18,635			21.0	21.4
1971	13,274	13,274	6,910	6,910	20,184	20,184			21.8	21.8
1972	14,470	13,794	7,748	7,559	22,218	21,353			21.7	21.8
1973	16,953	14,577	9,665	8,999	26,618	23,576			22.4	22.5
1974	20,498	15,318	11,953	9,870	32,451	25,188			23.4	23.1
1975	23,894	15,876	14,103	10,168	37,997	26,044			24.1	23.5
1976	26,810	—	15,144	—	41,954	—			—	—

[1]Actual expenditures 1967-73; preliminary actual 1974 and 1975; intentions 1976.
[2]The percentage is calculated by dividing "Gross Fixed Capital Formation", as defined by the National Income and Expenditure Accounts, by the total "Gross National Expenditure".

14.19   Summary of capital and repair expenditures, by economic sector, 1974-76[1] (million dollars)

| Type of enterprise and year | | Capital | | | Repair | | | Capital and repair | | |
		Construction	Machinery and equipment	Total	Construction	Machinery and equipment	Total	Construction	Machinery and equipment	Total
Agriculture and fishing	1974	433	1,533	1,966	172	366	538	605	1,899	2,504
	1975	519	1,998	2,517	205	384	589	724	2,382	3,106
	1976	554	2,299	2,853	217	431	648	771	2,730	3,501
Forestry	1974	98	145	244	35	113	148	133	258	391
	1975	89	98	187	32	106	138	121	204	325
	1976	93	92	185	39	123	162	132	215	347
Mining, quarrying and oil wells	1974	1,587	449	2,035	231	613	844	1,817	1,062	2,879
	1975	2,000	622	2,622	235	641	876	2,236	1,263	3,498
	1976	2,753	700	3,453	285	708	993	3,038	1,408	4,446
Construction industry	1974	66	401	467	16	354	370	82	756	837
	1975	75	457	532	18	403	421	93	860	953
	1976	83	504	587	20	444	464	103	948	1,051
Manufacturing	1974	1,425	3,525	4,950	344	1,966	2,310	1,770	5,490	7,260
	1975	1,537	3,888	5,425	347	1,946	2,293	1,884	5,834	7,718
	1976	1,597	4,133	5,730	383	2,164	2,547	1,980	6,297	8,277
Utilities	1974	3,154	3,087	6,241	617	1,385	2,002	3,771	4,472	8,243
	1975	4,147	3,771	7,918	671	1,478	2,148	4,817	5,249	10,066
	1976	4,705	3,871	8,577	739	1,629	2,368	5,444	5,500	10,945
Trade (wholesale and retail)	1974	392	589	980	91	113	204	483	702	1,185
	1975	336	608	943	86	115	200	422	722	1,144
	1976	334	685	1,019	90	119	209	423	804	1,227
Finance, insurance and real estate	1974	1,337	208	1,545	89	29	118	1,426	237	1,663
	1975	1,475	187	1,663	92	34	127	1,568	221	1,789
	1976	1,486	217	1,704	93	36	129	1,580	253	1,833
Commercial services	1974	455	1,349	1,804	37	150	187	493	1,499	1,991
	1975	847	1,548	2,394	34	180	214	881	1,728	2,608
	1976	537	1,641	2,178	34	208	242	570	1,849	2,419
Institutions	1974	1,064	275	1,338	155	44	199	1,218	318	1,537
	1975	1,163	280	1,444	164	53	217	1,327	333	1,661
	1976	1,229	288	1,518	170	55	225	1,399	343	1,742
Government departments	1974	3,751	551	4,302	681	138	819	4,432	689	5,121
	1975	4,622	646	5,268	720	172	892	5,342	818	6,160
	1976	4,826	714	5,539	757	189	946	5,583	902	6,485
Housing	1974	7,010	—	7,010	1,451	—	1,451	8,461	—	8,461
	1975	7,085	—	7,085	1,634	—	1,634	8,718	—	8,718
	1976	8,614	—	8,614	1,812	—	1,812	10,425	—	10,425
Total	1974	20,771	12,111	32,882	3,919	5,270	9,189	24,691	17,381	42,072
	1975	23,894	14,103	37,997	4,237	5,511	9,749	28,132	19,614	47,746
	1976	26,810	15,144	41,954	4,639	6,104	10,743	31,449	21,249	52,697

[1]Actual expenditures 1974; preliminary actual 1975; intentions 1976.

14.20   Capital and repair expenditures for certain economic sectors, 1974-76[1] (million dollars)

Type of enterprise and year		Capital			Repair			Capital and repair		
		Con-struc-tion	Ma-chinery and equip-ment	Total	Con-struc-tion	Ma-chinery and equip-ment	Total	Con-struc-tion	Ma-chinery and equip-ment	Total
MANUFACTURING										
Food and beverages	1974	139.3	278.8	418.1	30.7	160.0	190.7	170.0	438.8	608.8
	1975	117.1	274.6	391.7	28.2	146.2	174.4	145.3	420.8	566.1
	1976	122.6	276.4	399.0	28.8	149.7	178.5	151.4	426.1	577.5
Tobacco products	1974	7.1	18.6	25.7	3.0	9.5	12.5	10.1	28.1	38.2
	1975	6.0	18.2	24.2	1.7	7.7	9.4	7.7	25.9	33.6
	1976	4.1	17.7	21.8	2.2	7.3	9.5	6.3	25.0	31.3
Rubber	1974	36.1	100.3	136.4	5.0	46.7	51.7	41.1	147.0	188.1
	1975	25.2	81.2	106.4	4.8	47.5	52.3	30.0	128.7	158.7
	1976	19.5	73.4	92.9	4.3	50.0	54.3	23.8	123.4	147.2
Leather	1974	3.3	9.0	12.3	1.4	7.1	8.5	4.7	16.1	20.8
	1975	3.7	9.5	13.2	1.3	7.5	8.8	5.0	17.0	22.0
	1976	3.5	9.2	12.7	1.3	7.1	8.4	4.8	16.3	21.1
Textile	1974	38.6	102.6	141.2	7.6	51.3	58.9	46.2	153.9	200.1
	1975	34.1	124.8	158.9	7.8	43.4	51.2	41.9	168.2	210.1
	1976	27.5	112.6	140.1	7.7	46.5	54.2	35.2	159.1	194.3
Knitting mills	1974	1.2	15.6	16.8	0.8	4.5	5.3	2.0	20.1	22.1
	1975	0.8	9.4	10.2	0.7	3.4	4.1	1.5	12.8	14.3
	1976	0.7	9.1	9.8	0.7	3.3	4.0	1.4	12.4	13.8
Clothing	1974	5.5	14.8	20.3	1.6	5.4	7.0	7.1	20.2	27.3
	1975	4.7	10.9	15.6	1.3	4.5	5.8	6.0	15.4	21.4
	1976	3.1	12.3	15.4	1.2	4.6	5.8	4.3	16.9	21.2
Wood	1974	85.5	202.0	287.5	18.5	138.1	156.6	104.0	340.1	444.1
	1975	69.4	188.5	257.9	14.6	117.3	131.9	84.0	305.8	389.8
	1976	51.3	185.7	237.0	17.0	139.8	156.8	68.3	325.5	393.8
Furniture and fixtures	1974	17.1	25.5	42.6	3.4	8.3	11.7	20.5	33.8	54.3
	1975	8.0	18.2	26.2	3.1	8.3	11.4	11.1	26.5	37.6
	1976	7.3	16.5	23.8	2.9	8.5	11.4	10.2	25.0	35.2
Paper and allied industries	1974	120.5	433.8	554.3	33.5	380.1	413.6	154.0	813.9	967.9
	1975	112.9	494.8	607.7	28.8	345.6	374.4	141.7	840.4	982.1
	1976	128.5	646.6	775.1	37.0	435.7	472.7	165.5	1,082.3	1,247.8
Printing, publishing and allied industries	1974	16.7	68.9	85.6	5.9	19.2	25.1	22.6	88.1	110.7
	1975	19.7	74.0	93.7	5.4	18.6	24.0	25.1	92.6	117.7
	1976	11.8	74.2	86.0	5.3	18.3	23.6	17.1	92.5	109.6
Primary metals	1974	148.0	549.7	697.7	51.6	507.3	558.9	199.6	1,057.0	1,256.6
	1975	170.6	635.3	805.9	59.6	579.5	639.1	230.2	1,214.8	1,445.0
	1976	163.3	604.4	767.7	66.2	624.4	690.6	229.5	1,228.8	1,458.3
Metal fabricating	1974	59.7	147.9	207.6	15.3	87.6	102.9	75.0	235.5	310.5
	1975	44.7	153.9	198.6	12.8	77.8	90.6	57.5	231.7	289.2
	1976	46.1	142.0	188.1	14.3	88.7	103.0	60.4	230.7	291.1
Machinery	1974	42.8	82.5	125.3	11.2	31.5	42.7	54.0	114.0	168.0
	1975	37.2	85.8	123.0	13.1	32.1	45.2	50.3	117.9	168.2
	1976	40.9	99.0	139.9	13.2	35.6	48.8	54.1	134.6	188.7
Transportation equipment	1974	102.4	199.9	302.3	18.0	120.8	138.8	120.4	320.7	441.1
	1975	69.2	194.0	263.2	17.2	103.7	120.9	86.4	297.7	384.1
	1976	50.0	158.9	208.9	20.2	113.4	133.6	70.2	272.3	342.5
Electrical products	1974	31.0	108.2	139.2	11.5	49.0	60.5	42.5	157.2	199.7
	1975	34.0	102.7	136.7	10.0	43.8	53.8	44.0	146.5	190.5
	1976	32.4	129.0	161.4	11.1	45.7	56.8	43.5	174.7	218.2
Non-metallic mineral products	1974	29.5	144.7	174.2	11.3	130.9	142.2	40.8	275.6	316.4
	1975	38.4	154.9	193.3	11.6	131.0	142.6	50.0	285.9	335.9
	1976	55.7	180.9	236.6	12.3	139.6	151.9	68.0	320.5	388.5
Petroleum and coal products	1974	321.7	107.8	429.5	83.8	27.0	110.8	405.5	134.8	540.3
	1975	350.1	105.8	455.9	94.0	32.7	126.7	444.1	138.5	582.6
	1976	325.4	114.1	439.5	104.2	35.5	139.7	429.6	149.6	579.2
Chemical and chemical products[2]	1974	198.7	381.1	579.8	25.7	163.6	189.3	224.4	544.7	769.1
	1975	382.9	593.4	976.3	27.3	178.0	205.3	410.2	771.4	1,181.6
	1976	491.5	671.1	1,162.6	29.2	193.0	222.2	520.7	864.1	1,384.8
Miscellaneous	1974	20.6	33.8	54.4	4.6	17.9	22.5	25.2	51.7	76.9
	1975	8.2	27.8	36.0	3.5	17.1	20.6	11.7	44.9	56.6
	1976	11.5	27.4	38.9	3.7	17.6	21.3	15.2	45.0	60.2
Capital items charged to operating expenses	1974	—	499.1	499.1	—	—	—	—	499.1	499.1
	1975	—	530.4	530.4	—	—	—	—	530.4	530.4
	1976	—	572.4	572.4	—	—	—	—	572.4	572.4
Total, manufacturing	1974	1,425.3	3,524.6	4,949.9	344.4	1,965.8	2,310.2	1,769.7	5,490.4	7,260.1
	1975	1,536.9	3,888.1	5,425.0	346.8	1,945.7	2,292.5	1,883.7	5,833.8	7,717.5
	1976	1,596.7	4,132.9	5,729.6	382.8	2,164.3	2,547.1	1,979.5	6,297.2	8,276.7
MINING[3]										
Gold	1974	24.5	5.9	30.4	1.2	8.5	9.7	25.7	14.4	40.1
	1975	23.5	6.1	29.6	1.0	11.7	12.7	24.5	17.8	42.3
	1976	20.0	4.3	24.3	1.0	12.9	13.9	21.0	17.2	38.2
Iron	1974	159.0	40.7	199.7	21.5	171.9	193.4	180.5	212.6	393.1
	1975	195.8	95.0	290.8	13.9	180.9	194.8	209.7	275.9	485.6
	1976	339.8	99.3	439.1	16.3	189.4	205.7	356.1	288.7	644.8

14.20   Capital and repair expenditures for certain economic sectors, 1974-76[1] (million dollars) (continued)

Type of enterprise and year		Capital			Repair			Capital and repair		
		Construction	Machinery and equipment	Total	Construction	Machinery and equipment	Total	Construction	Machinery and equipment	Total
MINING[3] (concluded)										
Copper-gold-silver	1974	97.7	66.7	164.4	14.7	108.7	123.4	112.4	175.4	287.8
	1975	113.2	52.7	165.9	9.9	98.0	107.9	123.1	150.7	273.8
	1976	136.0	67.0	203.0	8.2	96.1	104.3	144.2	163.1	307.3
Silver-lead-zinc	1974	38.9	13.8	52.7	5.6	19.3	24.9	44.5	33.1	77.6
	1975	54.4	27.4	81.8	6.7	24.2	30.9	61.1	51.6	112.7
	1976	49.3	37.0	86.3	8.7	25.8	34.5	58.0	62.8	120.8
Other metal mines[4]	1974	89.5	30.8	120.3	15.7	75.0	90.7	105.2	105.8	211.0
	1975	91.5	41.3	132.8	22.4	87.5	109.9	113.9	128.8	242.7
	1976	114.1	93.4	207.5	26.7	105.3	132.0	140.8	198.7	339.5
Asbestos	1974	45.4	28.9	74.3	2.4	50.7	53.1	47.8	79.6	127.4
	1975	45.7	18.4	64.1	4.3	44.9	49.2	50.0	63.3	113.3
	1976	68.2	25.8	94.0	6.0	62.7	68.7	74.2	88.5	162.7
Other non-metal mines[5]	1974	70.6	96.8	167.4	10.7	116.3	127.0	81.3	213.1	294.4
	1975	64.8	169.9	234.7	8.0	123.1	131.1	72.8	293.0	365.8
	1976	72.0	179.1	251.1	17.2	133.9	151.1	89.2	313.0	402.2
Petroleum and gas[6]	1974	1,060.9	165.3	1,226.2	159.0	62.3	221.3	1,219.9	227.6	1,447.5
	1975	1,411.3	211.2	1,622.5	169.2	70.4	239.6	1,580.5	281.6	1,862.1
	1976	1,953.6	194.5	2,148.1	200.9	81.6	282.5	2,154.5	276.1	2,430.6
Total, mining	1974	1,586.5	448.9	2,035.4	230.8	612.7	843.5	1,817.3	1,061.6	2,878.9
	1975	2,000.2	622.0	2,622.2	235.4	640.7	876.1	2,235.6	1,262.7	3,498.3
	1976	2,753.0	700.4	3,453.4	285.0	707.7	992.7	3,038.0	1,408.1	4,446.1
UTILITIES										
Transportation										
Air transport	1974	20.7	352.2	372.9	5.0	190.1	195.1	25.7	542.3	568.0
	1975	31.1	226.3	257.4	4.8	180.9	185.7	35.9	407.2	443.1
	1976	40.8	84.7	125.5	4.9	189.3	194.2	45.7	274.0	319.7
Railway transport	1974	284.6	163.1	447.7	287.9	401.2	689.1	572.5	564.3	1,136.8
	1975	356.3	393.3	749.6	335.5	447.3	782.8	691.8	840.6	1,532.4
	1976	425.7	220.9	646.6	356.7	458.3	815.0	782.4	679.2	1,461.6
Water transport and services	1974	67.7	95.5	163.2	13.7	52.0	65.7	81.4	147.5	228.9
	1975	52.2	81.5	133.7	15.2	48.4	63.6	67.4	129.9	197.3
	1976	44.9	92.5	137.4	16.0	46.8	62.8	60.9	139.3	200.2
Motor transport	1974	31.6	164.0	195.6	7.3	148.7	156.0	38.9	312.7	351.6
	1975	20.4	115.3	135.7	6.9	128.8	135.7	27.3	244.1	271.4
	1976	39.4	113.8	153.2	7.4	143.4	150.8	46.8	257.2	304.0
Urban transit systems	1974	73.2	54.1	127.3	16.6	43.8	60.4	89.8	97.9	187.7
	1975	165.3	100.4	265.7	17.8	52.3	70.1	183.1	152.7	335.8
	1976	253.7	157.3	411.0	21.3	64.4	85.7	275.0	221.7	496.7
Pipelines	1974	236.4	25.1	261.5	21.6	7.6	29.2	258.0	32.7	290.7
	1975	314.6	40.7	355.3	19.5	9.7	29.2	334.1	50.4	384.5
	1976	296.3	63.7	360.0	21.5	8.2	29.7	317.8	71.9	389.7
Capital items charged to operating expenses	1974	—	22.1	22.1	—	—	—	—	22.1	22.1
	1975	—	23.7	23.7	—	—	—	—	23.7	23.7
	1976	—	21.4	21.4	—	—	—	—	21.4	21.4
Total, transportation	1974	714.2	876.1	1,590.3	352.1	843.4	1,195.5	1,066.3	1,719.5	2,785.8
	1975	939.9	981.2	1,921.1	399.7	867.4	1,267.1	1,339.6	1,848.6	3,188.2
	1976	1,100.8	754.3	1,855.1	427.8	910.4	1,338.2	1,528.6	1,664.7	3,193.3
Communication										
Broadcasting[7]	1974	51.7	77.5	129.2	7.0	8.8	15.8	58.7	86.3	145.0
	1975	52.7	89.7	142.4	6.0	9.2	15.2	58.7	98.9	157.6
	1976	56.8	102.7	159.5	4.4	9.6	14.0	61.2	112.3	173.5
Telephone and telegraph	1974	508.7	981.4	1,490.1	89.8	373.1	462.9	598.5	1,354.5	1,953.0
	1975	508.8	1,157.2	1,666.0	95.5	423.5	519.0	604.3	1,580.7	2,185.0
	1976	570.2	1,297.3	1,867.5	112.4	510.1	622.5	682.6	1,807.4	2,490.0
Capital items charged to operating expenses	1974	—	18.7	18.7	—	—	—	—	18.7	18.7
	1975	—	21.8	21.8	—	—	—	—	21.8	21.8
	1976	—	25.0	25.0	—	—	—	—	25.0	25.0
Total, communication	1974	560.4	1,077.6	1,638.0	96.8	381.9	478.7	657.2	1,459.5	2,116.7
	1975	561.5	1,268.7	1,830.2	101.5	432.7	534.2	663.0	1,701.4	2,364.4
	1976	627.0	1,425.0	2,052.0	116.8	519.7	636.5	743.8	1,944.7	2,688.5
Miscellaneous utilities										
Grain elevators	1974	10.4	8.0	18.4	5.8	6.0	11.8	16.2	14.0	30.2
	1975	15.4	16.8	32.2	6.0	7.0	13.0	21.4	23.8	45.2
	1976	18.9	28.0	46.9	6.1	7.2	13.3	25.0	35.2	60.2
Electric power	1974	1,699.5	1,053.7	2,753.2	140.0	137.0	277.0	1,839.5	1,190.7	3,030.2
	1975	2,464.8	1,435.8	3,900.6	142.3	154.8	297.1	2,607.1	1,590.6	4,197.7
	1976	2,777.7	1,592.0	4,369.7	162.7	174.6	337.3	2,940.4	1,766.6	4,707.0
Gas distribution	1974	147.9	43.8	191.7	17.6	10.0	27.6	165.5	53.8	219.3
	1975	145.9	37.4	183.3	16.9	8.5	25.4	162.8	45.9	208.7
	1976	152.3	40.6	192.9	18.4	9.8	28.2	170.7	50.4	221.1
Other utilities[8]	1974	21.4	11.0	32.4	5.1	6.5	11.6	26.5	17.5	44.0
	1975	19.1	9.4	28.5	4.3	7.1	11.4	23.4	16.5	39.9
	1976	28.4	7.3	35.7	7.3	7.2	14.5	35.7	14.5	50.2

14.20   Capital and repair expenditures for certain economic sectors, 1974-76[1] (million dollars) (concluded)

Type of enterprise and year		Capital			Repair			Capital and repair		
		Con-struc-tion	Ma-chinery and equip-ment	Total	Con-struc-tion	Ma-chinery and equip-ment	Total	Con-struc-tion	Ma-chinery and equip-ment	Total
UTILITIES (concluded)										
Capital items charged to operating expenses	1974	—	16.6	16.6	—	—	—	—	16.6	16.6
	1975	—	21.8	21.8	—	—	—	—	21.8	21.8
	1976	—	24.2	24.2	—	—	—	—	24.2	24.2
Total, miscellaneous utilities	1974	1,879.2	1,133.1	3,012.3	168.5	159.5	328.0	2,047.7	1,292.6	3,340.3
	1975	2,645.2	1,521.2	4,166.4	169.5	177.4	346.9	2,814.7	1,698.6	4,513.3
	1976	2,977.3	1,692.1	4,669.4	194.5	198.8	393.3	3,171.8	1,890.9	5,062.7
Total, utilities	1974	3,153.8	3,086.8	6,240.6	617.4	1,384.8	2,002.2	3,771.2	4,471.6	8,242.8
	1975	4,146.6	3,771.1	7,917.7	670.7	1,477.5	2,148.2	4,817.3	5,248.6	10,065.9
	1976	4,705.1	3,871.4	8,576.5	739.1	1,628.9	2,368.0	5,444.2	5,500.3	10,944.5

[1]Actual expenditures 1974; preliminary actual 1975; intentions 1976.
[2]Includes expenditures for heavy water plants.
[3]Capital construction expenditures include on-property exploration and development but exclude outside or general exploration.
[4]Includes capital and repair expenditures for metal and non-metal exploration companies.
[5]Includes coal mines, gypsum, salt, potash and miscellaneous non-metal mines, and quarrying.
[6]Includes expenditures on facilities related to petroleum and gas wells and extraction of petroleum from shales or sands, natural gas processing plants and contract drilling for petroleum and gas.
[7]Includes community antenna television and satellite communication systems.
[8]Includes toll highways and bridges, warehousing, water systems of private and provincial enterprises and other utilities.

14.21   Capital and repair expenditures, by province, 1974-76[1],[2] (million dollars)

Province or territory and year		Capital			Repair			Capital and repair		
		Con-struc-tion	Ma-chinery and equip-ment	Total	Con-struc-tion	Ma-chinery and equip-ment	Total	Con-struc-tion	Ma-chinery and equip-ment	Total
Newfoundland	1974	520	178	698	87	153	240	607	332	938
	1975	549	179	728	77	160	237	626	339	965
	1976	652	187	839	88	175	263	740	362	1,103
Prince Edward Island	1974	84	34	118	19	11	30	104	45	148
	1975	82	34	116	17	12	29	100	45	145
	1976	72	36	108	18	12	29	90	48	138
Nova Scotia	1974	587	306	893	124	138	262	711	444	1,155
	1975	630	277	907	130	130	260	760	407	1,167
	1976	758	293	1,051	137	141	278	896	433	1,329
New Brunswick	1974	650	326	976	105	117	222	755	443	1,198
	1975	742	406	1,148	112	136	249	854	543	1,397
	1976	737	453	1,190	123	146	269	860	599	1,458
Quebec	1974	4,747	2,651	7,398	851	1,172	2,023	5,598	3,823	9,422
	1975	5,967	2,983	8,949	951	1,187	2,139	6,918	4,170	11,088
	1976	6,445	3,179	9,624	1,033	1,283	2,316	7,478	4,462	11,940
Ontario	1974	7,088	4,728	11,816	1,413	1,958	3,371	8,501	6,686	15,187
	1975	7,481	5,551	13,032	1,523	2,053	3,576	9,004	7,604	16,608
	1976	8,157	5,984	14,140	1,639	2,297	3,937	9,796	8,281	18,077
Manitoba	1974	808	572	1,379	174	206	380	982	777	1,759
	1975	859	678	1,536	186	208	394	1,045	885	1,930
	1976	974	709	1,684	195	220	415	1,170	929	2,098
Saskatchewan	1974	681	580	1,262	176	249	425	858	829	1,687
	1975	884	858	1,742	195	251	447	1,079	1,110	2,189
	1976	1,101	942	2,043	218	286	504	1,319	1,228	2,547
Alberta	1974	2,506	1,324	3,831	455	421	876	2,961	1,745	4,706
	1975	3,332	1,576	4,908	503	461	964	3,835	2,037	5,872
	1976	4,262	1,776	6,039	565	533	1,097	4,827	2,309	7,136
British Columbia	1974	2,736	1,360	4,096	490	815	1,305	3,226	2,175	5,401
	1975	3,007	1,408	4,416	518	873	1,391	3,525	2,281	5,806
	1976	3,298	1,479	4,777	594	971	1,566	3,892	2,450	6,343
Yukon Territory and Northwest Territories	1974	364	51	416	25	31	55	389	82	471
	1975	362	153	515	25	40	65	387	194	580
	1976	354	106	460	28	42	70	382	148	529
Canada	1974	20,771	12,111	32,882	3,919	5,270	9,189	24,691	17,381	42,072
	1975	23,894	14,103	37,997	4,238	5,511	9,749	28,132	19,614	47,746
	1976	26,810	15,144	41,954	4,639	6,104	10,743	31,449	21,249	52,697

[1]Actual expenditures 1974; preliminary actual 1975; intentions 1976.
[2]Capital expenditures on machinery and equipment include an estimate for "capital items charged to operating expenses", in the manufacturing, utilities and trade totals.

14.22   Value of construction work performed, by type of structure, 1973-75[1] (thousand dollars)

Type of structure	1973[r] New	Repair	Total	1974[r] New	Repair	Total	1975 New	Repair	Total
BUILDING CONSTRUCTION									
Residential	5,977,448	1,187,832	7,165,280	6,975,228	1,354,677	8,329,905	6,715,000	1,547,021	8,262,021
Industrial	887,999	260,574	1,148,573	1,136,848	283,814	1,420,662	1,224,147	312,278	1,536,425
Factories, plants, workshops, food canneries	725,019	204,420	929,439	959,078	230,278	1,189,356	1,036,333	246,358	1,282,691
Mine and mine mill buildings	143,974	32,508	176,482	155,552	31,286	186,838	149,068	38,707	187,775
Railway stations, offices, roadway buildings	11,822	13,656	25,478	11,616	14,240	25,856	23,086	17,413	40,499
Railway shops, engine houses, water and fuel stations	7,184	9,990	17,174	10,602	8,010	18,612	15,660	9,800	25,460
Commercial	1,947,375	264,161	2,211,536	2,543,063	300,787	2,843,850	2,912,661	315,869	3,228,530
Warehouses, storehouses, refrigerated storage, etc.	166,115	25,788	191,903	226,285	29,825	256,110	253,266	31,012	284,278
Grain elevators	10,560	4,937	15,497	8,446	2,905	11,351	9,216	3,063	12,279
Hotels, clubs, restaurants, cafeterias, tourist cabins	199,341	22,366	221,707	253,103	23,975	277,078	205,874	23,078	228,952
Office buildings	776,114	103,603	879,717	1,025,974	126,475	1,152,449	1,297,198	130,364	1,427,562
Stores, retail and wholesale	531,430	52,779	584,209	577,284	62,599	639,883	523,436	68,007	591,443
Garages and service stations	99,974	38,705	138,679	128,902	40,470	169,372	179,389	44,156	223,545
Theatres, arenas, amusement and recreational buildings	162,239	14,391	176,630	319,893	13,640	333,533	443,139	15,293	458,432
Laundries and dry-cleaning establishments	1,602	1,592	3,194	3,176	898	4,074	1,143	896	2,039
Institutional	1,034,656	165,348	1,200,004	1,215,262	158,316	1,373,578	1,480,707	174,102	1,654,809
Schools and other educational buildings	631,256	84,225	715,481	716,716	78,656	795,372	825,928	86,751	912,679
Churches and other religious buildings	15,220	8,085	23,305	17,305	5,956	23,261	24,053	5,609	29,662
Hospitals, sanatoria, clinics, first-aid stations, etc.	268,432	45,468	313,900	335,460	56,471	391,931	400,851	62,690	463,541
Other	119,748	27,570	147,318	145,781	17,233	163,014	229,875	19,052	248,927
Other building	521,157	158,575	679,732	707,819	213,317	921,136	879,865	249,676	1,129,541
Farm buildings (excl. dwellings)	230,302	88,371	318,673	303,587	120,200	423,787	356,731	138,348	495,079
Broadcasting, radio and television, relay and booster stations, telephone exchanges	64,057	14,156	78,213	105,026	16,596	121,622	130,725	19,838	150,563
Aeroplane hangars	7,424	6,350	13,774	10,266	10,389	20,655	17,788	10,675	28,463
Passenger terminals, bus, boat or air	41,349	1,384	42,733	53,376	6,366	59,742	72,885	6,684	79,569
Armouries, barracks, drill halls, etc.	4,101	10,833	14,934	5,160	10,287	15,447	6,186	9,929	16,115
Bunkhouses, dormitories, camp cookeries, bush depots and camps	21,127	6,558	27,685	26,380	6,787	33,167	20,845	6,337	27,182
Laboratories	34,314	4,018	38,332	35,828	4,413	40,241	45,886	4,404	50,290
Other	118,483	26,905	145,388	168,196	38,279	206,475	228,819	53,461	282,280
Total, building construction	10,368,635	2,036,490	12,405,125	12,578,220	2,310,911	14,889,131	13,212,380	2,598,946	15,811,326
ENGINEERING CONSTRUCTION									
Marine	120,293	27,400	147,693	168,310	29,982	198,292	179,721	31,641	211,362
Docks, wharves, piers, breakwaters	59,971	15,238	75,209	97,093	17,163	114,256	84,329	15,959	100,288
Retaining walls, embankments, riprapping	7,434	989	8,423	10,069	1,153	11,222	12,733	2,491	15,224
Canals and waterways	23,664	2,384	26,048	17,667	3,132	20,799	19,766	3,998	23,764
Dredging and pile driving	13,556	3,861	17,417	19,713	3,747	23,460	26,463	4,512	30,975
Dyke construction	6,361	670	7,031	12,671	507	13,178	22,590	843	23,433
Logging booms	454	623	1,077	1,070	553	1,623	384	549	933
Other	8,853	3,635	12,488	10,027	3,727	13,754	13,456	3,289	16,745
Road, highway and aerodrome	1,520,777	305,046	1,825,823	1,747,894	360,303	2,108,197	1,985,955	396,962	2,382,917
Highway, road and street construction, (incl. grading, scraping, oiling, filling)	1,432,464	294,569	1,727,033	1,638,133	347,519	1,985,652	1,859,124	383,646	2,242,770
Parking lots	14,563	3,597	18,160	15,673	6,154	21,827	10,733	6,173	16,906
Sidewalks, paths	20,486	5,089	25,575	25,352	4,435	29,787	29,502	4,838	34,340
Aerodromes, landing fields, runways, tarmac	53,264	1,791	55,055	68,736	2,195	70,931	86,596	2,305	88,901

14.22 Value of construction work performed, by type of structure, 1973-75¹ (thousand dollars) (concluded)

Type of structure	1973ʳ			1974ʳ			1975		
	New	Repair	Total	New	Repair	Total	New	Repair	Total
ENGINEERING CONSTRUCTION (concluded)									
Waterworks and sewerage systems	699,859	91,249	791,108	931,064	100,407	1,031,471	1,111,200	110,234	1,221,434
Tile drains, drainage ditches, storm sewers	137,299	19,053	156,352	159,952	20,894	180,846	186,209	25,239	211,448
Water mains, hydrants and services	163,136	36,030	199,166	248,971	41,509	290,480	282,815	44,858	327,673
Sewerage systems and connections	363,167	26,925	390,092	466,880	27,577	494,457	568,046	28,072	596,118
Pumping stations, water	29,357	7,526	36,883	44,554	8,166	52,720	56,261	9,514	65,775
Water storage tanks	6,900	1,715	8,615	10,707	2,261	12,968	17,869	2,551	20,420
Dams and irrigation	66,826	18,815	85,641	85,935	21,266	107,201	108,703	24,500	133,203
Dams and reservoirs	27,567	5,997	33,564	40,602	5,611	46,213	47,188	6,554	53,742
Irrigation and land reclamation projects	39,259	12,818	52,077	45,333	15,655	60,988	61,515	17,946	79,461
Electric power	1,384,920	135,467	1,520,387	1,677,688	163,433	1,841,121	2,279,898	183,623	2,463,521
Electric power generating plants, including water conveying and controlling structures	815,446	43,326	858,772	985,672	47,476	1,033,148	1,346,642	56,350	1,402,992
Electric transformer stations	4,246	938	5,184	5,701	1,269	6,970	3,590	1,242	4,832
Power transmission and distribution lines, trolley wires	549,104	88,270	637,374	663,063	108,754	771,817	893,783	120,686	1,014,469
Street lighting	16,124	2,933	19,057	23,252	5,934	29,186	35,883	5,345	41,228
Railway, telephone and telegraph	555,364	250,601	805,965	687,941	337,270	1,025,211	897,406	404,098	1,301,504
Railway tracks and roadbeds	201,742	153,944	355,686	258,024	231,253	489,277	386,413	282,316	668,729
Signals and interlockers	12,031	21,977	34,008	13,793	17,984	31,777	23,570	23,014	46,584
Telegraph and telephone lines, underground and marine cables	341,591	74,680	416,271	416,124	88,033	504,157	487,423	98,768	586,191
Gas and oil facilities	1,274,686	224,765	1,499,451	1,453,269	232,098	1,685,367	1,639,515	258,042	1,897,557
Gas mains and services	92,814	12,803	105,617	112,286	13,498	125,784	129,642	14,785	144,427
Pumping stations, oil	25,740	6,220	31,960	13,675	7,414	21,089	12,410	5,388	17,798
Pumping stations, gas	13,924	2,039	15,963	16,868	2,122	18,990	23,192	1,414	24,606
Oil storage tanks	21,942	5,200	27,142	23,453	5,340	28,793	36,572	4,892	41,464
Gas storage tanks	405	217	622	6,849	80	6,929	12,150	114	12,264
Oil pipelines	75,820	9,119	84,939	53,831	8,081	61,912	51,196	9,091	60,287
Gas pipelines	95,722	1,518	97,240	71,681	2,110	73,791	107,317	2,362	109,679
Oil and gas wells	777,517	102,691	880,208	904,094	70,862	974,956	880,835	81,520	962,355
Oil refinery — processing units	115,203	63,170	178,373	144,376	79,849	224,225	274,290	90,848	365,138
Natural gas processing plants	55,599	21,788	77,387	106,156	42,742	148,898	111,911	47,628	159,539
Other engineering	962,710	129,861	1,092,571	1,169,239	160,124	1,329,363	1,664,250	162,112	1,826,362
Bridges, trestles, culverts, overpasses, viaducts	151,306	31,137	182,443	169,563	35,498	205,061	184,379	43,165	227,544
Tunnels and subways	57,327	1,236	58,563	66,249	427	66,676	128,315	491	128,806
Incinerators	6,415	914	7,329	4,418	941	5,359	5,635	1,054	6,689
Park systems, landscaping, sodding, etc.	46,350	13,787	60,137	67,592	10,450	78,042	69,094	10,624	79,718
Swimming pools, tennis courts, outdoor recreation facilities	10,921	1,995	12,916	25,625	1,532	27,157	34,137	1,339	35,476
Mine shafts and other below surface workings	221,975	4,040	226,015	256,477	4,588	261,065	277,777	4,835	282,612
Fences, snowsheds, signs, guard rails	48,248	20,732	68,980	65,575	27,211	92,786	76,311	29,814	106,125
Other engineering	420,168	56,020	476,188	513,740	79,477	593,217	888,602	70,790	959,392
Total, engineering construction	6,585,435	1,183,204	7,768,639	7,921,340	1,404,883	9,326,223	9,866,648	1,571,212	11,437,860
Total, all construction	16,954,070	3,219,694	20,173,764	20,499,560	3,715,794	24,215,354	23,079,028	4,170,158	27,249,186

¹Actual expenditures 1973; preliminary actual 1974; intentions 1975.

Sources

14.1 - 14.3 Central Mortgage and Housing Corporation.
14.4 - 14.9 Housing and Families Section, Census and Household Surveys Field, Statistics Canada.
14.10 Construction Division, Industry Statistics Branch, Statistics Canada.
14.11 Consumer and Income Expenditure Division, Census and Household Surveys Field, Statistics Canada.
14.12 - 14.22 Construction Division, Industry Statistics Branch, Statistics Canada.

Transportation

Chapter 15

Tables

Transportation   Chapter 15

Trends in transportation services   15.1

Because of Canada's size, geography and dependence on trade, freight
transportation has always occupied a dominant role within the overall economic
system and during the last decade has shown dramatic growth. This marked
acceleration followed steady increases over the previous 30 years.

Total freight transportation measured by operating revenues of for-hire
carriers increased from an estimated $400 million in 1930 to an estimated $7.4
billion in 1974. In freight transport the fastest growing segment was the for-hire
trucking industry which increased its revenue from an estimated $8 million in
1930 to an estimated $3.1 billion in 1974.

The two traditional modes of transport, rail and water, increased their
combined annual revenues from an estimated $400 million in 1930 to an
estimated $3.3 billion in 1974. The new modes of transportation such as pipelines
and air freight have been growing at a high annual rate during the last 20 to 25
years. They have not, however, reached the same degree of importance as the
older conventional modes.

Notwithstanding the importance of the overall increase in revenues from all
means of transport, an even more drastic change took place in the distribution of
market shares held by the different modes of freight transport. The two traditional
ones, rail and water, which enjoyed almost complete dominance in 1930, steadily
decreased their combined share of the total transportation market from 98% in
1930 to 44% by 1974. Pipelines, which accounted for only one half of 1% of the
market in 1950, increased their share of the total to 10% by 1974.

The Canadian for-hire trucking industry, which in 1930 represented only 2%
of the market, increased its market share to 42% by 1974 and thus became the
largest mode of freight transport, as measured by operating revenues. Summary
statistics on the for-hire trucking industry are presented in Table 15.18.

Government promotion and regulation   15.1.1

The federal government plays a twofold role in developing transportation
services. One is promotional, to ensure the growth and development of the kind
of transportation appropriate to need; the other is regulatory and includes
economic regulation of rates and services and the application of technical
regulations to meet safety requirements. The building of canals from the time of
Confederation to the construction of the St. Lawrence Seaway, underwriting
railway development and branch-line extension, establishing Air Canada,
investing in airports and aeronautical installations and building the Trans-Canada
Highway fall within the first category.

The Department of Transport and the various Crown agencies reporting to
Parliament through the Minister of Transport have jurisdiction over canals,
harbours, shipping, civil aviation and interprovincial and international railways.
Jurisdiction over for-hire extraprovincial and international highway transport also
rests with the federal government but these powers are at present exercised by the
provincial highway transport boards (with one exception) as provided for in the
federal Motor Vehicle Transport Act of 1954 (RSC 1970, c.M-14).

On July 16, 1976 the Governor in Council exempted from the application of
the Motor Vehicle Transport Act the Roadcruiser service operated by Canadian
National Railways in Newfoundland. This bus service is now under the
jurisdiction of the Motor Vehicle Transport Committee of the Canadian
Transport Commission, and is subject to the provisions of Part III of the National
Transportation Act (RSC 1970, c.N-17).

Railway regulation was developed in a period when railways enjoyed a virtual transportation monopoly. Measures to protect the public against excessive charges, unjust discrimination and other objectionable monopoly practices, together with measures to ensure safe operation, have subjected railways to the most comprehensive regulation of any Canadian industry. However, the rapid growth of road, air and pipeline services has ended the near-monopoly and forced the railways into a highly competitive situation.

The National Transportation Act (RSC 1970, c.N-17) defines a national transportation policy for Canada with a view to achieving maximum efficiency in all available modes of transportation at the lowest cost. The act established the Canadian Transport Commission (CTC) to carry out the functions formerly performed by the Board of Transport Commissioners for Canada, the Air Transport Board and the Canadian Maritime Commission. In addition, it created a framework within which the CTC might regulate interprovincial and international motor transport as well as the transportation by pipeline of commodities other than oil and gas.

In general, the purpose of the act is to develop the transportation industry while protecting the public against excessive or discriminatory charges. The railways are relieved of some of the more onerous and outdated restrictions on their freedom to meet competition. On the other hand, a shipper who has no practical alternative to rail shipment can apply to the commission to have a maximum rate fixed. The act also provides, subject to explicit safeguards in the public interest, for the abandonment of rail lines and the withdrawal of passenger services where they are no longer needed.

The Canadian Transport Commission has established several committees, five of which are Railway Transport, Air Transport, Water Transport, Commodity Pipeline Transport and Motor Vehicle Transport. The commission is a court of record. Its decisions are binding within its jurisdiction and may be reviewed only by appeal to the Supreme Court of Canada on a question of law or jurisdiction with leave of that court, or by the Governor in Council. However, a party to a licence application under the Aeronautics Act or the Transport Act may appeal to the Minister of Transport.

The commission has jurisdiction under several acts, including the Railway Act, the Aeronautics Act and the Transport Act, over transportation by rail, air and inland water.

Under the Railway Act the commission has jurisdiction over construction, maintenance and operation of railways that are subject to the legislative authority of the Parliament of Canada, including matters of engineering, location of lines, crossings and crossing protection, safety of train operation, operating rules, investigation of accidents, accommodation for traffic and facilities for service, abandonment of operation and uniformity of railway accounting. The commission regulates tolls for the use of international bridges and tunnels.

Except for certain statutory rates, and subject to certain powers to deal with rates that the commission finds to be contrary to the public interest, the railways are free to charge rates as they wish. However, rates must be compensatory, as defined in the Railway Act, and the commission may prescribe tolls for captive shippers if existing tolls unduly favour the railways.

The commission is responsible for the economic regulation of commercial air services in Canada and is required to advise the Minister of Transport on matters relating to civil aviation. The regulatory function relates to Canadian air services within Canada and abroad and to foreign air services operating in and out of Canada. It involves licensing all such services and regulating the licensees. The commission issues regulations dealing with, among other things, the classification of air-carriers and commercial air services, accounts, records and reports, and traffic tolls and tariffs.

The CTC takes an active part in the work of the International Civil Aviation Organization and may undertake bilateral negotiations for the exchange of traffic rights. In 1974 Air Canada, CP Air, Nordair and Pacific Western Airlines were Canada's designated international scheduled carriers.

Pursuant to the provisions of the Transport Act, the commission processes applications for licences for ships to transport goods and/or passengers, for hire or reward, between ports or places in Canada on the Great Lakes and on the Mackenzie and Yukon rivers. Provisions of the act do not apply to the transport of goods in bulk on waters other than the Mackenzie River. Before granting a licence, the commission must determine that the proposed service is and will be required by the present and future public convenience and necessity and, in so doing, may take into consideration any objection provided for in the statute. Tariffs of tolls must be filed and the commission has regulatory powers over tolls for such transport.

The commission, under the terms of the Pilotage Act, is empowered to investigate objections to proposed tariffs of pilotage charges, including the holding of public hearings, and to make recommendations thereon to the appropriate pilotage authority. Under the Shipping Conferences Exemption Act, ocean carriers which are members of a shipping conference are required to file with the commission copies of their agreements, arrangements, contracts, patronage contracts and tariffs. These documents are made available for inspection by any person during regular business hours of the commission.

The commission is also authorized, under the provisions of the St. Lawrence Seaway Authority Act, to consider any complaint filed with respect to unjust discrimination in existing tariffs and to make a finding thereon to be reported to the said authority.

In Canada the coasting laws restrict the operation of ships from one point to another to Canadian or British ships, depending upon the area. In order to enable a ship of any foreign country to engage in such operations, application has to be made to the Minister of National Revenue to obtain a waiver of the coasting laws. The commission is then called upon to advise the minister as to the availability of a suitable Canadian ship.

The CTC also administers subsidies paid by the federal government for maintaining certain coastal and inland shipping services. Table 15.1 shows the net amount of these subsidies paid in 1974-75 as well as the contract subsidies in 1975-76.

Rail transport   15.2

Canadian railway transport is dominated by two transcontinental systems, supplemented by a number of regional railways. The government owned Canadian National Railway System is the country's largest public utility and operates the longest trackage in Canada. It serves all 10 provinces as well as the Great Slave Lake area of the Northwest Territories. In addition it operates a highway transport service, a fleet of coastal steamships, a chain of large hotels and resorts, a telecommunications service, and, as an autonomous subsidiary (Air Canada), a scheduled Canadian and international air service. Canadian Pacific Limited is a joint-stock corporation operating a railway service in eight provinces. Similar to and competitive with the Canadian National Railway System, it is a multi-transport organization with a fleet of inland and ocean-going vessels as well as coastal vessels, a fleet of trucks, a chain of year-round and resort hotels, a telecommunications service, and a domestic and foreign airline service. Through a major subsidiary, Canadian Pacific Investments Limited, important interests are held in mining (e.g. Cominco Ltd.), oil and gas, forest products, real estate and related operations, hotel and food services, and steel production and associated services. The British Columbia Railway operates over a 1,000-mile (1 600 km) route from North Vancouver to Fort Nelson in northeastern British Columbia. The Northern Alberta Railway, jointly owned by CP and CN, serves the area north of Edmonton with a 900-mile (1 400 km) system. Northern Ontario is served by the provincially owned Ontario Northland Railways with a 600-mile (1 000 km) system stretching from North Bay to Moosonee, and by the privately owned Algoma Central Railway operating over 300 miles (500 km) of line between Sault Ste Marie and Hearst.

In addition, a US–Canada passenger service, inaugurated by the National Railroad Passenger Corporation (AMTRAK), is operated between Seattle, Wash. and Vancouver, BC and between Montreal, Que. and Washington, DC via New York City, Springfield, Mass. and resort areas in Vermont.

The largest contributors to Canada's total 1975 railway revenue were Canadian National (53.5%) and Canadian Pacific (36.8%). The Quebec North Shore and Labrador Railway, built to transport ore and concentrates from the iron mines of the Schefferville and Wabush areas of Quebec and Labrador to water transportation facilities on the St. Lawrence River, accounted for 2.0% of the revenues. Others contributing 1.0% or more of the total revenue were the British Columbia Railway (1.8%) and the Ontario Northland Railways (1.0%).

In recent years the railways have faced strong competition from highway and air transport for the movement of people and goods. Still indispensable for carrying bulk commodities, railways are necessary to the development of natural resources in isolated areas of Canada. Only pipelines have competed with railways in this respect by providing an alternate economical means of transporting the products of oil and gas fields for long distances overland.

The rapid growth of containerization in recent years has made the integration of the services of railway, highway, shipping and other modes of transport of growing importance. However, because Canada's two major railways are already involved in several forms of transportation, they are in an excellent position to meet the challenge of this and other trends appearing in the transportation industry. Canadian railways have evolved over the past century from a position of virtual monopoly in the movement of goods and people, through a highly competitive stage to the present system of cooperation and coordination with other modes of transport. This permits each type of transport to perform the particular function it can do best.

15.2.1   Government aid

In the 19th century governments promoted the building of railways. Private developers received assistance in the form of land grants, cash payments, loans or purchase of shares. Debenture issues of the Canadian National Railway System, except those for rolling-stock, are guaranteed by the federal government. Provincial governments had guaranteed the bonds of some lines that were later incorporated in the CNR system. As these mature or are called, they are paid off by the CNR in large measure through funds raised by issuing new bonds guaranteed by the federal government. At December 31, 1975 railway bonds guaranteed by the Government of Canada amounted to $583 million.

The National Transportation Act provided for normal railway subsidy payments of $110 million for 1967, declining by $14 million a year, the last payment being $12 million for 1974, and allows railways to file claims and receive specific payments for losses incurred on branch lines and passenger-train services. Total payments of $217.7 million for 1974 represented specific payments to the two major railways, exceeding and replacing their shares of the normal subsidy. Claims for 1975 had to be filed by June 30, 1976.

Truckers receive federal assistance through freight rate subsidies similar to the subsidies to railways provided under the Maritime Freight Rate Act. Since 1969 the Atlantic Region Freight Assistance Act has allowed subsidies on goods moved from Nova Scotia, Prince Edward Island, New Brunswick, the island of Newfoundland, and Quebec south of the St. Lawrence River and east of Highway 23 to points in Canada outside that territory. In October 1970 assistance was authorized for goods moved by highway transport within that area as well. In April 1974 selective assistance for specified commodities moving by railway or highway transport to points in Canada outside the territories was authorized at a level of 50% of that portion of the freight rate earned within the territory.

Rail transport statistics

Trackage and rolling-stock. Table 15.2 illustrates the historical development of first main track from 17,657 miles (28 416 km) in 1900 to 43,941 miles (70 716 km) in 1975. It also presents statistics on main and other types of track by province and territory and that operated by Canadian carriers in the US for the years 1971-75.

Table 15.3 gives freight and passenger equipment in operation in 1974 and 1975. The freight carrying capabilities of the railways are steadily being improved with larger, more efficient cars and locomotives and modernized handling and terminal services. Each year hundreds of units, particularly freight cars, are converted and modified to make them suitable for specific types of traffic or are replaced by special-purpose equipment designed for particular hauling jobs. Because of the fuel consumption efficiency of the railways and higher fuel costs, there is a trend to greater freight movement by rail. Container and piggyback traffic has also increased in the past few years.

Revenue freight. Total freight carried by all common carrier railways (including national loadings and receipts from US connections) in 1974 and 1975 is shown in Table 15.4 under the commodity structure adopted in 1970 based on Statistics Canada's Standard Commodity Classification. Despite some loss of continuity with previous data, the new commodity breakdown permits improved comparisons with other series (such as water transport, imports and exports) which are also based on this classification.

Capital structure and finance. Tables 15.5 - 15.8 give information on capital investment in road and equipment, and on operating revenues, expenses and net income of all common carrier railways operating in Canada, except those of the Cartier Railway which are not available. In transportation statistics a distinction is made between expenditures and expenses. In the following data, the term "expenses" refers to the expenses of furnishing rail transportation service and of operations incident thereto, including maintenance and depreciation of the plant used in such service.

The capital structure of the Canadian National Railway System is presented in Table 15.6 and financial details of operations in both Canada and the United States in Table 15.7. Revenues and expenses include those of express and commercial communications and highway transport (rail) operations. Tax accruals and rents are charged to operating expenses.

Total operating revenues and expenses of common carrier railways operating in Canada (except the Cartier Railway) continued to rise, both reaching peak levels in 1975; increases over 1974 amounted to 6.4% and 11.5% respectively (as calculated from Table 15.8). A net operating deficit of $68.2 million was recorded in 1975.

Road transport

The federal government establishes motor vehicle safety standards, while registration of motor vehicles and regulation of motor vehicle traffic lie within the jurisdiction of the provincial and territorial governments. An outline of legislation, as well as summaries of motor vehicle and traffic regulations common to all provinces and territories, are presented in the following sections.

Federal safety regulations

The Motor Vehicle Safety Act, in effect since January 1, 1971, permits the promulgation of the Motor Vehicle Safety Regulations. The act establishes mandatory safety standards for new motor vehicles to ensure minimum standards of vehicle safety and environment protection. The standards mandated by the act are addressed to the safe design, construction and functioning of new motor vehicles in order to save lives and prevent injuries. The legislation, administered by the Department of Transport, applies to all new motor vehicles manufactured in or imported into Canada. It requires that all such vehicles and their components meet motor vehicle safety regulations at the point of manufacture or importation and obliges manufacturers to issue notices of safety defects. The safety of vehicles in use continues to be a provincial responsibility.

The safety regulations currently include 41 standards relating to the design and performance of passenger cars, trucks, buses, motorcycles, competition motorcycles, minibikes and trailers; six standards limiting motor vehicle exhaust, evaporative and noise emissions; and 12 standards applying to snowmobiles. These standards are reviewed regularly and additions or revisions incorporated to keep pace with engineering or technical advances. The regulations require all Canadian motor vehicle manufacturers or distributors to apply the national safety mark, accompanied by a label certifying compliance with all applicable federal motor vehicle safety standards, to every classified vehicle produced after January 1, 1971. Vehicles imported for sale or private use must also be certified to comply with the act and regulations.

The Motor Vehicle Tire Safety Act, adopted by Parliament in April 1976, provides authority for the enforcement of minimum safety standards for certain motor vehicle tires manufactured in or imported into Canada.

The Road and Motor Vehicle Safety Branch of the Department of Transport is responsible for the administration of the Motor Vehicle Safety Act and the Motor Vehicle Tire Safety Act, and the enforcement of regulations pertaining to them. In conjunction with this responsibility it has joined with the provinces in a five-year cooperative program aimed at reducing by 15% the fatality rate on Canadian roads by 1979. The Department of Transport is also constructing a Motor Vehicle Test Centre at Blainville, Que., and conducting research into cost-effective measures to improve traffic safety. The branch works closely with other federal government departments, the provinces and such international organizations as NATO, OECD and OAS on various specific road safety projects.

15.3.2   Motor vehicle and traffic regulations

Operators' licences. The operator of a motor vehicle must be over a specified age, usually 16 (17 in Newfoundland and generally 16 in Alberta and New Brunswick but 18 for certain classes of motor vehicle), and must carry a licence, obtainable in most provinces only after qualification tests. In New Brunswick the holder of an out-of-province licence must be 18. A licence is renewable annually in Saskatchewan and the Northwest Territories and annually at the end of the licensee's birth month in Manitoba; in Alberta it is renewable every five years but annually where a medical report is required; in British Columbia it is renewable every five years expiring on the licensee's birth date and classified according to the qualifications of the licensee; in Quebec drivers' permits expire on the holder's birthday in odd-numbered years for those born in odd-numbered years and vice versa for those born in even-numbered years; in New Brunswick a licence is renewable every two years and expires at the end of the licensee's birth month; in Newfoundland, Ontario and the Yukon Territory a licence is issued on a three-year basis and expires on the licensee's birth date; in Nova Scotia and Prince Edward Island a licence is issued on a three-year basis and expires at the end of the licensee's birth month.

Special licences are required for chauffeurs in all provinces except Newfoundland, British Columbia, New Brunswick and the Yukon Territory. In British Columbia, New Brunswick, Manitoba and the Yukon Territory, although no special chauffeur's licence is issued, all drivers' licences are classified according to demonstrated skills at the time of licensing. There are six classes of licence, one for motorcycles and five for other vehicles. Special tests are given to taxi drivers (in British Columbia only), bus drivers and drivers of single vehicles over 24,000 lb. (11 000 kg) GVW and tractor-trailer combinations. In the Northwest Territories persons 16 to 18 years old may obtain a chauffeur's licence at the discretion of the Registrar, on receipt of a letter of approval from the RCMP and a letter from the employer verifying that the licence is necessary for employment. In some provinces a motorcycle operator is required to pass a special examination and have his driver's licence endorsed authorizing him to operate this class of vehicle; if he has no driver's licence, he may be issued a licence to operate only a motorcycle. In Alberta a person 14 years of age or over is permitted to operate a moped, but must be 16 years of age to operate a motorcycle. In Quebec all snowmobile operators must hold permits issued for that purpose. Drivers' licences issued under the Highway Code are considered valid for snowmobiles. Special restrictions apply to minors; 10 is the minimum age for obtaining a permit and operating conditions and locations are controlled.

Motor vehicle regulations. Motor vehicles and trailers are usually registered annually with the payment of specified fees. Most motor vehicles carry a registration plate on the front and one on the rear; trailers carry one on the rear. In Alberta passenger cars, vehicles licensed for Drive-ur-self service and trucks display two plates. Vehicles operated by dealers, motorcycles and off-highway vehicles have one rear licence plate.

In some provinces registration plates stay with the vehicle when it is sold, but in Quebec, Manitoba, Saskatchewan, Alberta, British Columbia and the Yukon, the owner retains them. In the Northwest Territories the registration expires when a vehicle changes hands. The owner notifies the registrar, returns the number plates and the new owner registers the transferred vehicle in his name. In Nova Scotia vehicles change hands by due process of law and title must be secured before plates and permits are issued. A change of ownership must be recorded with the registration authority.

Exemption from registration is granted for a specified period, usually at least 90 days, although the maximum in Quebec is three months for non-residents. In Nova Scotia, a non-resident full-time student residing temporarily in the province may receive, without fee, a driver's licence, plates and permit in exchange for the same valid out-of-province documents; the latter are returned to his home province, state or territory. In Ontario the exemption period is six consecutive months for non-residents from other provinces and three for those with vehicles registered outside Canada. The regulations in Manitoba allow residents to use registration plates from other jurisdictions for 90 days; visitors are exempt from registration if the vehicle is not used for business; an out-of-province student is exempt if his vehicle is properly registered in his home jurisdiction and he obtains a student sticker for the vehicle's windshield. In Saskatchewan an out-of-province student is exempt for the school year provided the vehicle is properly registered in his home jurisdiction and, if necessary, he can prove financial responsibility. The Alberta regulations permit non-residents to operate vehicles currently registered in their home province or in the United States for six months; the period is extended to a school year for out-of-province students whose vehicles carry non-resident student stickers. In British Columbia the exemption period is one month; tourists are allowed six months and out-of-province students, attending a university recognized by statute, are allowed a school year, if the vehicles are properly registered in their home jurisdictions. The Yukon Territory grants a 90-day exemption to tourists.

Safety regulations require vehicles to meet certain mechanical standards. All motor vehicles and trailers registered in Nova Scotia must pass an annual safety inspection. A vehicle which has been sold may not be registered to the new owner unless it passed an inspection during the past year. Newfoundland requires a certificate of mechanical fitness before renewing registration of vehicles two years old or more. In Ontario, Manitoba and Newfoundland a certificate of mechanical fitness is required before a vehicle sold second-hand can be issued a permit for

Mileage Guide	Calgary	Charlottetown	Edmonton	Fredericton	Halifax	Montreal	Ottawa	Quebec	Regina	St. John's	Saskatoon	Thunder Bay	Toronto	Vancouver	Victoria	Whitehorse	Winnipeg	Yellowknife
Calgary	●	3055	186	2832	3133	2326	2208	2494	475	3842	385	1274	2134	657	698	1482	830	1125
Charlottetown	3055	●	3075	223	144	736	854	587	2587	804	2747	1788	1071	3719	3760	4371	2232	4014
Edmonton	186	3075	●	2857	3158	2339	2221	2507	488	3860	328	1287	2147	773	814	1296	843	939
Fredericton	2832	223	2857	●	215	518	636	364	2369	1008	2529	1570	853	3501	3542	4153	2014	3796
Halifax	3133	144	3158	215	●	819	937	567	2670	838	2830	1871	1154	3802	3843	4454	2315	4097
Montreal	2326	736	2339	518	819	●	118	168	1851	1521	2011	1052	335	2983	3024	3635	1496	3278
Ottawa	2208	854	2221	636	937	118	●	286	1733	1639	1893	934	248	2865	2906	3517	1378	3160
Quebec	2494	587	2507	364	567	168	286	●	2019	1372	2179	1220	503	3151	3192	3803	1664	3446
Regina	475	2587	488	2369	2670	1851	1733	2019	●	3372	160	799	1659	1132	1173	1784	355	1427
St. John's	3842	804	3860	1008	838	1521	1639	1372	3372	●	3532	2573	1856	4504	4545	5156	3017	4799
Saskatoon	385	2747	328	2529	2830	2011	1893	2179	160	3532	●	959	1819	1042	1083	1624	515	1267
Thunder Bay	1274	1788	1287	1570	1871	1052	934	1220	799	2573	959	●	860	1931	1972	2583	444	2226
Toronto	2134	1071	2147	853	1154	335	248	503	1659	1856	1819	860	●	2791	2832	3435	1304	3086
Vancouver	657	3719	773	3501	3802	2983	2865	3151	1132	4504	1042	1931	2791	●	41	1676	1387	1498
Victoria	698	3760	814	3542	3843	3024	2906	3192	1173	4545	1083	1972	2832	41	●	1717	1428	1539
Whitehorse	1482	4371	1296	4153	4454	3635	3517	3803	1784	5156	1624	2583	3435	1676	1717	●	2190	1680
Winnipeg	830	2232	843	2014	2315	1496	1378	1664	355	3017	515	444	1304	1387	1428	2190	●	1782
Yellowknife	1125	4014	939	3796	4097	3278	3160	3446	1427	4799	1267	2226	3086	1498	1539	1680	1782	●

Official highway distances

operation. Used car dealers must certify that vehicles comply with provincial equipment requirements.

Traffic regulations. In Canada, vehicles keep to the right-hand side of the road and motorists are required to observe traffic signs and lights. In Newfoundland, Quebec, New Brunswick, Ontario, Manitoba and Alberta the speed limits are 60 mph (97 km/h) and 50 mph (80.5 km/h) at night. In Nova Scotia, Saskatchewan and British Columbia the limit is 50 mph (80.5 km/h), although the latter two provinces may raise it in certain places. In Prince Edward Island it is 55 mph (88.5 km/h) and 50 mph (80.5 km/h) at night. In the Yukon and Northwest Territories for all vehicles the limit is 60 mph (97 km/h) unless otherwise posted.

Slower speeds are required in cities, towns and villages, at road intersections, railway crossings or at other places or times where the view of the highway for a safe distance ahead is in any way obscured. In Nova Scotia, British Columbia and the Northwest Territories slower speeds are also required in school zones and when passing public playgrounds. Most provinces require vehicles to stop when a school bus is stopped to load or discharge children. Truck speed limits are sometimes 5 mph (8 km/h) below automobile speed limits, but usually they are the same as for passenger vehicles. In most provinces accidents resulting in personal injury or property damage in excess of $200 ($100 in Quebec, $350 in Alberta) must be reported to a police officer (in Nova Scotia to the Registrar of Motor Vehicles or to a police officer, in Quebec to a police officer or to the Motor

Kilometre Guide	Calgary	Charlottetown	Edmonton	Fredericton	Halifax	Montreal	Ottawa	Quebec	Regina	St. John's	Saskatoon	Thunder Bay	Toronto	Vancouver	Victoria	Whitehorse	Winnipeg	Yellowknife
Calgary	•	4917	299	4558	5042	3743	3553	4014	764	6183	620	2050	3434	1057	1123	2385	1336	1811
Charlottetown	4917	•	4949	359	232	1184	1374	945	4163	1294	4421	2878	1724	5985	6051	7034	3592	6460
Edmonton	299	4949	•	4598	5082	3764	3574	4035	785	6212	528	2071	3455	1244	1310	2086	1357	1511
Fredericton	4558	359	4598	•	346	834	1024	586	3813	1622	4070	2527	1373	5634	5700	6684	3241	6109
Halifax	5042	232	5082	346	•	1318	1508	912	4297	1349	4554	3011	1857	6119	6185	7168	3726	6593
Montreal	3743	1184	3764	834	1318	•	190	270	2979	2448	3236	1693	539	4801	4867	5850	2408	5275
Ottawa	3553	1374	3574	1024	1508	190	•	460	2789	2638	3046	1503	399	4611	4677	5660	2218	5086
Quebec	4014	945	4035	586	912	270	460	•	3249	2208	3507	1963	810	5071	5137	6120	2678	5546
Regina	764	4163	785	3813	4297	2979	2789	3249	•	5427	257	1286	2670	1822	1888	2871	571	2297
St. John's	6183	1294	6212	1622	1349	2448	2638	2208	5427	•	5684	4141	2987	7248	7314	8298	4855	7723
Saskatoon	620	4421	528	4070	4554	3236	3046	3507	257	5684	•	1543	2927	1677	1743	2614	829	2039
Thunder Bay	2050	2878	2071	2527	3011	1693	1503	1963	1286	4141	1543	•	1384	3108	3174	4157	715	3582
Toronto	3434	1724	3455	1373	1857	539	399	810	2670	2987	2927	1384	•	4492	4558	5528	2099	4966
Vancouver	1057	5985	1244	5634	6119	4801	4611	5071	1822	7248	1677	3108	4492	•	66	2697	2232	2411
Victoria	1123	6051	1310	5700	6185	4867	4677	5137	1888	7314	1743	3174	4558	66	•	2763	2298	2477
Whitehorse	2385	7034	2086	6684	7168	5850	5660	6120	2871	8298	2614	4157	5528	2697	2763	•	3524	2704
Winnipeg	1336	3592	1357	3241	3726	2408	2218	2678	571	4855	829	715	2099	2232	2298	3524	•	2868
Yellowknife	1811	6460	1511	6109	6593	5275	5086	5546	2297	7723	2039	3582	4966	2411	2477	2704	2868	•

Official highway distances

Vehicle Bureau) and a driver involved must not leave the scene of an accident until he has rendered all possible aid and disclosed his name to the injured party. A similar regulation applies to snow vehicle drivers in Ontario, Quebec, New Brunswick and Saskatchewan and to any off-highway vehicle driver in Alberta.

Driver licensing controls. All provinces and territories impose penalties for infractions of driving regulations, ranging from fines to suspension of driving permits, impounding of vehicle or imprisonment. In most provinces penalties have been linked to a driver-improvement program; the aim is to correct faulty driving habits, not to take drivers off the road.

Safety responsibility legislation. Each province has enacted safety responsibility legislation. In general, laws provide for the automatic suspension of the driver's licence and/or motor vehicle registration of a person convicted of a serious offence (impaired driving, driving under suspension, dangerous driving) or a person whose uninsured vehicle is involved directly or indirectly in an accident resulting in damage in excess of $200 or injury or death to any person (in Manitoba the amount is $100 and in Nova Scotia, $50). In Saskatchewan, Quebec, New Brunswick and Nova Scotia, if a judgment is rendered for damages against the driver or owner, the driver's licence and registration remain suspended until the judgment is satisfied and proof of financial responsibility for the future is filed. In Saskatchewan and the Northwest Territories uninsured motor vehicles may be impounded following an accident of any consequence, i.e. an accident resulting in personal injury or death, or property damage in excess of $200. Under the Quebec Code of Civil Procedure, the plaintiff may seize, before judgment, the motor vehicle which has caused him damage, whatever the amount of property damage, whether covered for third-party insurance or not. In British Columbia, if a judgment is rendered against a driver and not satisfied, the driver's licence may be suspended until reinstated at the discretion of the Superintendent of Motor Vehicles. In the Yukon Territory an inadequately insured vehicle may be impounded if it is involved in an accident, regardless of the property damage. In Ontario, a driver's licence may be suspended for failure to satisfy judgments for damages occasioned by a motor vehicle where such damages are not paid by the province's Motor Vehicle Accident Claims Fund.

Newfoundland, the Northwest Territories and Prince Edward Island require proof of insurance before vehicle registration, and on its termination the vehicle permit and licence plates must be surrendered. In Ontario, Manitoba and Alberta a non-resident motorist need not carry proof of insurance. Registered owners in Nova Scotia must prove financial responsibility on police request; failure may result in suspension of driver's licence and registration. In Saskatchewan, British Columbia, Manitoba and Alberta a compulsory insurance plan is in effect. In the Manitoba plan, a driver's insurance certificate must be held as well as a licence. In the Northwest Territories and Newfoundland public liability and property damage insurance is compulsory regardless of location of vehicle registration. In Quebec and Ontario snowmobiles must carry insurance in the amounts of $35,000 and $50,000 respectively to cover possible liability.

Unsatisfied judgment fund. All provinces and territories, except Manitoba, Saskatchewan, British Columbia, the Northwest Territories and Yukon Territory, have enacted legislation providing for the establishment of a fund, frequently called an unsatisfied judgment fund (in Ontario and Alberta, the Motor Vehicle Accident Claims Fund). Judgments awarded for damages arising out of motor vehicle accidents which cannot be collected by the ordinary process of law are paid out of this fund. In Newfoundland, Prince Edward Island, Nova Scotia and Quebec the fund is maintained by insurance companies. In all the other provinces, except Saskatchewan, Manitoba and British Columbia where insurance is compulsory, the funds are obtained by collecting an annual fee from the registered owner of every motor vehicle or from every person to whom a driver's licence is issued. (In Manitoba, a person having a claim against an uninsured motorist may have it paid by MPIC upon obtaining a judgment.) The fee usually does not exceed $1 a year; in New Brunswick the fee is $3 a year; in Ontario a fee of $100 is paid by the uninsured motorist (in the absence of the fee being paid, the uninsured, if apprehended, is liable to a fine) and, in addition, the fund is subsidized by a $1 annual charge from each licensed driver.

Some provincial legislation covers payment of judgments in hit-and-run accidents. When these occur, if neither the owner nor the driver can be identified, action may be taken against the Registrar of Motor Vehicles (the Minister of Finance in Newfoundland, the Superintendent of Insurance in Ontario and the Administrator of the Motor Vehicle Accident Claims Fund in Alberta); any judgment secured against the responsible authority is paid out of the fund. The amount that can be so paid is limited. In Newfoundland and Nova Scotia the limits are $10,000 for one person, $20,000 for two or more persons injured in one accident and $5,000 for property damage. In Nova Scotia the limit is $35,000 in respect of any one accident and in New Brunswick, $50,000. In Prince Edward Island and Quebec the limit is $35,000 for all damages in the same accident, subject to a deduction of $200 from all damage to the property of others; damages resulting in bodily injury or death are, up to $30,000, payable by priority over damages to property and the latter are, up to $5,000, payable by priority over the former out of the amount of any insurance or other guarantee of indemnity. In Alberta the limit is $50,000 for death or personal injury to one or more persons and $5,000 for damage to property, subject to a limit of $50,000 in any one accident; if, in one accident, claims result from bodily injury to or death of one or more persons and loss of or damage to property, claims arising out of bodily injury or death have priority over claims resulting from loss of or damage to property to the amount of $45,000, and claims arising out of loss of or damage to property have priority over claims resulting from bodily injury or death to the amount of $5,000. In Ontario the limits are $50,000, inclusive of $5,000 for any property damage claim. Many small claims are handled by the Motor Vehicle Accident Claims Branch (under the Ministry of Consumer and Commercial Relations), subject to a $50 franchise clause in respect of property damage, but the procedure is such that claims can be settled without resort to litigation.

Road transport statistics   15.3.3

Roads and streets. At the end of 1972 Canada had 251,352 miles (404 512 km) of highways and roads under federal or provincial jurisdictions and 277,198 miles (446 105 km) of roads and streets under local government jurisdiction (Table 15.9). Most is in the more populated sections. Roads built by logging, pulp and paper, and mining companies provide some access to remote communities but large areas of most provinces and the territories are still sparsely settled and are virtually without roads.

Table 15.10 presents expenditure data for all roads and streets in 1971-72 and 1972-73. In 1972-73 total expenditures equalled $2,696 million, an increase of 7.4% over the previous year. Construction expenditures increased 8.4% and maintenance and administration costs rose by 5.8%.

Motor vehicles. Registrations continue to increase yearly, a record of 11.0 million being reached in 1974. Of that total, 8.5 million were passenger cars. Registration by province is given in Table 15.11 and types of vehicles registered by province in Table 15.12.

The taxation of motive fuels, motor vehicles, garages, drivers and chauffeurs is an important source of provincial revenue. In every province licences or permits are required for motor vehicles, trailers, operators or drivers, paid chauffeurs, dealers, garages and gasoline and service stations. The more important sources from which revenue from motor vehicles is derived are shown in Table 15.13.

Motive fuels for motor vehicle use are taxable at the point of sale. To estimate the amount of fuel sold for motor vehicles, tax-exempt sales to the federal government and other consumers, exports and sales on which tax refunds are paid are eliminated from gross sales. As shown in Table 15.14, consumption of taxable gasoline, which is used almost entirely for automotive purposes, rose 3.9% in 1974 and net sales of diesel oil 16.2%.

Statistics of intercity and rural passenger bus companies for 1974 are shown in Table 15.15. Table 15.16 presents summary statistics of the Canadian urban transit industry, and Table 15.17 of the motor carriers (freight).

Water transport   15.4

The Canada Shipping Act (RSC 1970, c.S-9) is the most significant statute dealing with shipping. Other important legislative measures include the Pilotage Act, the Arctic Waters Pollution Prevention Act and the Navigable Waters Protection Act. Under the Canada Shipping Act, the Arctic Waters Pollution Prevention Act and their amendments, the Parliament of Canada has complete jurisdiction over the regulation of shipping in Canadian-controlled waters.

Shipping   15.4.1

Except in the case of the coastal trade, all Canadian waterways, including canals, lakes and rivers, are open on equal terms to the shipping of all countries of the world so that Canadian shipping must compete with foreign flag shipping.

The carriage of goods and persons from one Canadian port to another, commonly referred to as the coastal trade, is restricted to ships registered in Canada within the region from Havre-Saint-Pierre on the St. Lawrence River upstream to the head of the Great Lakes. Elsewhere in Canada, the coastal trade is restricted to ships registered and owned in a Commonwealth country.

Canadian registry. Under Part I of the Canada Shipping Act ships exceeding 15 net registered tons (42 m³) and pleasure yachts over 20 net registered tons (56 m³) must be registered; vessels of lower capacity, if not registered, must be licensed if powered by a motor of 10 hp or more. Section 6 of the act restricts ownership: an owner must be a British subject, or a body corporate incorporated under the law of a Commonwealth country with its principal place of business in that country. A ship registrable in Canada may be recorded, pending registration, by a Registrar of Shipping while still under construction.

Vessels on the Canadian shipping registry. As at December 31, 1975, there were 31,288 ships constituting 4,135,367 gross tons (11 710 057 m³) registered in Canada. This represents an increase over the previous calendar year of 797 ships.

Shipping traffic. Table 15.21 shows the number and tonnage of all vessels (except those of less than 15 registered net tons (equivalent to 42 m³), naval vessels and fishing vessels) entering Canadian customs and non-customs ports.

Freight movement through large ports take different forms, including cargoes for or from foreign countries and cargoes loaded and unloaded in coastwise shipping, i.e. domestic freight moving between Canadian points. Table 15.22 presents data by province on cargoes loaded and unloaded from vessels in international and coastwise shipping. In 1975 a total of 303.0 million tons (274.9 million t) were loaded and unloaded at the principal Canadian ports, compared with 302.1 million tons (274.1 million t) in 1974. In-transit movement in vessels that pass through harbours without loading or unloading and movements from one point to another within harbours are also numerous in many ports.

Shipping statistics, which cover traffic in and out of both customs and non-customs ports, do not include freight in transit or freight moved from one point to another within the harbour. Table 15.23 shows the principal commodities loaded and unloaded in international and coastwise shipping at the 19 ports handling the largest cargo volumes in 1975. These ports handled 80.9% of all Canada's international shipping and 61.8% of the coastwise trade. The specific commodities shown are those transported in volume and often in bulk form.

15.4.2   Ports and harbours

The ports and harbours of Canada comprise 25 large deep-water ports and about 650 smaller ports and multi-purpose government wharves on the east and west coasts, along the St. Lawrence Seaway and Great Lakes, in the Arctic, and on interior lakes and rivers.

The administration of Canadian ports is generally under the Ministry of Transport's Canadian Marine Transportation Administration. Canada's harbours are subdivided into National Harbours Board ports, harbour commission ports, public harbours and government wharves. About 2,000 fishing harbours and facilities for recreational boating are administered by the Department of Fisheries and the Environment.

The National Harbours Board, a Crown corporation, is responsible for administering the Jacques Cartier and Champlain bridges at Montreal, the grain elevators at Prescott and Port Colborne, Ont. and port facilities such as wharves and piers, transit sheds and grain elevators, at the harbours of St. John's, Nfld.; Halifax, NS; Saint John and Belledune, NB; Sept-Îles, Chicoutimi, Baie-des-Ha! Ha!, Quebec, Trois-Rivières and Montreal, Que.; Churchill, Man.; and Vancouver and Prince Rupert, BC. The number of vessels and the amount of tonnage handled at these ports in 1974 and 1975 are reported in Table 15.21.

The capital value of fixed assets administered by the board amounted to $436.0 million at December 31, 1973, $471.6 million in 1974 and $505.4 million in 1975. These figures include expenditures on all buildings, machinery and durable plant improvements less deductions for depreciation, and represent a fair approximation of the properties' present value. During 1975 the federal government advanced $27.0 million to the National Harbours Board for capital expenditures of $15.1 million at Prince Rupert, $9.5 million at Vancouver, $1.6 million at Churchill, $131,000 at Sept-Îles, and $646,571 at Halifax.

Harbour commissions. Eleven of Canada's major multi-purpose harbours are administered by harbour commissions, federal bodies corporate operating semi-autonomously under the general supervision of the Ministry of Transport. These ports include The Lakehead (Thunder Bay), Windsor, Hamilton, Toronto, Oshawa and Belleville, Ont. on the Great Lakes; Winnipeg–St. Boniface, Man. on the Red River–Lake Winnipeg System; Fraser River (New Westminster), North Fraser, Nanaimo and Port Alberni, BC. The harbour commissions include municipal as well as federal appointees, and are responsible for general administration, operation and maintenance as well as for close liaison with the Ministry of Transport and with the provincial, regional and local interests they serve.

Public harbours. More than 300 public harbours are directly administered by the Canadian Marine Transportation Administration. Harbour masters and wharf-ingers at these ports are mostly fees-of-office employees appointed by the Minister of Transport. Some of the larger public harbours are Baie-Comeau, Que.; Corner Brook and Come By Chance, Nfld.; Sydney and Port Hawkesbury, NS; Sault Ste Marie and Goderich, Ont.; and Victoria, Kitimat and Tasu, BC.

Government wharves. Many of the government wharves for which the Marine Transportation Administration is responsible are located within public harbours and are used for commercial traffic including auto/truck ferries. Some major interprovincial federal ferry terminals are administered by the Canadian Surface Transportation Administration. Provincial governments administer ferry wharves which are part of an intraprovincial service.

The Ministry of Transport is responsible for planning and providing adequate public port facilities to serve commercial interests and to improve or phase out facilities in response to economic growth or changes in traffic patterns resulting from new industries, trends to new types of ships and new developments in cargo handling. Specialized deep-water terminals for bulk commodities, particularly coal and oil, are also provided when needed under long-term full cost recovery agreements with individual shippers. These often complement related development programs sponsored by the Department of Regional Economic Expansion.

Rates and charges. The ministry establishes and collects fees from users of port facilities, and all rates assessed by ports under federal jurisdiction are subject to ministry approval. Harbour dues, cargo rates, wharfage, berthage and other charges on goods and vessels are subject to some regional and local variation and are designed to recover a reasonable share of the annual federal investment in Canada's harbours through the Department of Public Works as well as the Ministry of Transport and its component agencies.

Private facilities. In addition to public facilities, there are extensive wharf and associated cargo handling facilities owned by private companies, particularly specialized facilities for handling coal, iron ore, petroleum, grain and pulpwood. At Sept-Îles, Que. the Iron Ore Company of Canada owns and operates extensive facilities to load pelletized iron ore onto ocean-going and Seaway vessels. Port-Cartier harbour was constructed by mining interests in the early 1960s and through large diversified investments of private capital has also become one of Canada's leading export grain terminals. At Port Hawkesbury, NS, Gulf Oil Canada Limited operates a terminal to unload large supertankers; in Quebec City

Canadian Pacific operates a container terminal at Wolfe's Cove; and at Port Alfred, Que. and Kitimat, BC the Aluminum Company of Canada Limited operates multi-purpose terminals to service their smelter operations. There are also many industry owned and operated marine facilities on the Great Lakes and other interior waterways required for Canadian and international movements of ores, coal, petroleum products, limestone and other bulk materials.

Shipping. The continuing trend to the use of larger ships has resulted in increased investment in ports to provide for facilities farther from shore, channel dredging, larger turning basins and more complex systems of aids to navigation and traffic control. Also, environmental considerations often require expensive terminal construction.

Increasing use of containers brings significant changes in cargo routing and handling. Saint John, Halifax, Quebec, Montreal, Toronto, Vancouver and New Westminster have major container terminals. Both CP Rail and Canadian National operate fast container trains between these ports and inland centres in Canada and the United States.

Container ships travel at high speeds and port turnaround time is critical to the economics of operating them. Port facilities have to be more efficient and specialized; they include special ramps for roll-on roll-off vessels; large container cranes which can handle 20 or more 15-ton (14 t) containers in an hour; special container packing facilities; large open storage areas for containers, automobiles, lumber and bulk products like coal; and rail and truck loading and unloading facilities. Increasing container storage space rather than handling or ship movement has become the critical factor.

15.4.3   The St. Lawrence Seaway

The St. Lawrence Seaway Authority, constituted as a corporation by Act of Parliament in 1951, undertook the construction (and subsequent maintenance and operation) of Canadian facilities between Montreal and Lake Erie to allow navigation by vessels of 27-ft (8.23 m) draft. At the same time, construction of similar facilities in the International Rapids Section of the St. Lawrence River was undertaken by the Saint Lawrence Seaway Development Corporation of the United States. The seaway was opened to commercial traffic on April 1, 1959 and officially inaugurated on June 26, 1959. With its opening, certain ancillary canals were transferred to the Seaway Authority's jurisdiction for operation and maintenance purposes. These include Lachine (closed in 1971), a section of the Cornwall Canal (closed in 1968), a portion of the third Welland Canal and the Canadian lock at Sault Ste Marie. Major construction undertaken in 1967 on the channel to bypass the city of Welland was completed for the 1973 season.

Seaway traffic. Tables 15.25 and 15.26 give combined traffic statistics for the St. Lawrence and Welland canals in 1974 and 1975. Duplicate transits are eliminated so that the figures show actual shipments through the St. Lawrence Seaway.

In 1975, 3,559 ships carrying about 24.3 million tons (22 million t) of cargo moved upbound through the seaway and 3,540 vessels carrying 42.6 million tons (38.6 million t) moved downbound. Ocean-going ships carried 18.9% of the total cargoes and lakers 81.1%. Of the total tonnage carried upbound in 1975, 20.0 million tons (18.1 million t) were domestic cargo, 4.3 million tons (3.9 million t) were foreign traffic; downbound, 34.2 million tons (31.0 million t) were domestic freight and 8.4 million tons (7.6 million t) were carried to and from foreign ports.

On the Montreal–Lake Ontario section, upbound traffic amounted to 21.9 million tons (19.9 million t) in 1975 and downbound traffic to 26.1 million tons (23.7 million t), an increase of 8.8% over 1974. Almost 75.1% of the former was accounted for by iron ore shipped from St. Lawrence ports to Hamilton and Lake Erie and the downbound traffic consisted largely of overseas shipments of grain. There were 213 more upbound transits and 231 more downbound transits in 1975 than in 1974, indicating a slight increase in the number of vessels using this portion of the seaway. Bulk commodities made up 92.5% of the total traffic through the section in 1975, the principal commodities through the St. Lawrence canals being iron ore, wheat, corn, barley, fuel oil, and manufactured iron and steel. Traffic patterns show that 34.7% of the total movement was between Canadian ports, 38.8% between Canadian and United States ports, and 26.3% consisted of foreign trade to and from Canada and the United States. The small remainder was traffic between ports in the United States.

There were 6,041 transits through the Welland Canal in 1975, with a cargo volume of 18.9 million tons (17.1 million t) upbound and 41.0 million tons (37.2 million t) downbound; bulk cargo accounted for 94.9% of the traffic. Although many vessels pass through both the St. Lawrence and Welland canals on "through" trips, there is a substantial amount of local traffic between Great Lakes ports which involves only the Welland Canal. These movements are largely of iron ore, grain and coal. The Welland Canal traffic was 11.8 million tons (10.7 million t) greater than that reported for the Montreal–Lake Ontario section.

Income of the St. Lawrence Seaway Authority for the 15-month period ended March 31, 1976 amounted to $25.1 million, made up of toll revenue of $20.3 million assessed for transits through the seaway locks between Montreal and Lake Erie and sundry revenues (rentals, wharfage, bridge revenue) of $4.8 million. Total expenses (excluding depreciation and interest) for the 15-month period ended March 31, 1976 amounted to $38.8 million of which operation and maintenance expenses amounted to $27.4 million and regional and headquarters administration expenses to $11.4 million (Table 15.27).

Canadian Coast Guard   15.4.4

The Canadian Coast Guard, formerly known as the Marine Services component of the Canadian Marine Transportation Administration was renamed on August 14, 1975. Headed by a commissioner and deputy commissioner, the duties, powers and responsibilities of the Canadian Coast Guard are the same as before the change of name. There are eight headquarters branches and five regional officers pursuing the following objectives: the support of waterborne commerce by providing way facilities and services which promote the safe and efficient movement of marine traffic; the provision of the necessary framework that will permit the marine industry to conduct its affairs in an orderly and efficient manner; the support of the objectives of other departments and agencies of government as they apply to the marine field; the promotion of continuous improvement, innovation, growth or phase-out of various types of marine transportation and the associated ancillary services; and the recovery of financial costs from the users or other beneficiaries of facilities and services provided by Marine Services.

The field organization consists of five Canadian Coast Guard regions, each with a number of field offices. The Commissioner of the Coast Guard also has a functional responsibility for the Pacific, Great Lakes, Laurentian and Atlantic Pilotage Authorities. Each authority is a Crown corporation established under the Pilotage Act.

The Aids and Waterways Branch consists of a Marine Aids Division and a Waterways Development Division. The Marine Aids Division is responsible for policies and standards for visual, oral and electronic shore-based and floating aids to navigation. It provides policies and standards for Marine Traffic Control systems and routing schemes and administers the Navigable Waters Protection Act. The Waterways Development Division is responsible for planning, research and development on navigable waterways, hydraulic model activities, hydraulic engineering expertise and water resources management.

The Ship Safety Branch is concerned with the safety of life and property at sea and the protection of the environment insofar as ships are concerned. The branch has three divisions: the Board of Steamship Inspection, Nautical Services and Air Cushion Vehicles.

The Board of Steamship Inspection is composed of all certified steamship inspectors employed by the ministry. The headquarters component develops socially and economically feasible standards for the design and construction of ships, their machinery, fittings and equipment, and translates these standards into statutes and regulations to be followed by builders and operators of vessels. The board establishes procedures to ensure that these standards are met.

The Nautical Services Division develops standards for the following: methods of loading, unloading and stowing of cargo; quantities of cargo; work practices; number and qualification of personnel, and discipline aboard ship; and navigating and operating procedures including traffic routing. The division operates the registry of ships and administers the licensing of small vessels. It is responsible for reviewing measurement of ships and protecting the interests of the owners of wrecked ships and their cargo and the interest of the Crown in unclaimed wreck. The division provides a service for the engagement of seamen and assistance in disputes over wages and discharge.

The Air Cushion Vehicles Division prepares domestic regulations for the design, construction, maintenance and operation of air cushion vehicles. It ensures that domestic regulations concerning air cushion vehicles crews and maintenance engineers are implemented.

The Fleet Systems Branch has responsibility for approximately 160 vessels of various sizes designed to perform various functions. These vessels are all attached to Coast Guard regions in accordance with the type of work and workload in each region. The headquarters component provides policies, standards and guidelines for the operation of the fleet. It also has operating responsibility for the portion of the fleet which operates in the Arctic in the summer months. The Canadian Coast Guard College at Point Edward, NS is responsible for developing ships' officers for the Canadian Coast Guard Fleet.

The Telecommunications and Electronics Branch provides expert knowledge in communications and computers, quality assurance, guidance systems and ship electronics and avionics to Canadian Coast Guard line operations.

The Pilotage Branch establishes national technical standards and conducts research to ensure that standards are maintained. It prescribes standards for health, uniform financial reporting procedures, procedures for hearings held by the four regional pilotage authorities and recommends the establishment of compulsory pilotage areas.

The Legislation Branch is responsible for certain activities of a legal and legislative nature and for participation in Law of the Sea matters. It is also involved in amendments to the Maritime Pollution Claims Fund and in the development of the Maritime Code which will eventually replace the existing Canada Shipping Act.

The Office of the Senior Marine Officer, Planning, provides the secretariat for the Plans Development Review Committee (PDRC), the senior Coast Guard committee in the Comprehensive Planning System, and is responsible for the coordination of Coast Guard planning. The PDRC sets Coast Guard objectives, strategies and priorities, develops policies and takes decisions on the program forecast, estimates and budgets.

The Senior Marine Officer, Emergencies, is responsible for the development of contingency plans; the development, testing, acquisition and allocation of certain pollution clean-up equipment; advice and assistance at the time of a pollution incident; and certain wartime activities.

The Senior Marine Officer, Casualty Investigations, is responsible for developing accident investigation procedures and carrying out fact finding and preliminary inquiries according to the provisions of the Canada Shipping Act.

The Harbours and Ports Division administers semi-commercial Canadian ports and provides advice on the development of new port facilities.

The Coast Guard Fleet provides icebreaking and cable-laying services, weather-ships for meteorological observation, vessels and helicopters for aids to navigation work and search and rescue equipment. Icebreakers are allocated on the basis of severity of weather conditions. During the winter on the east coast, day-to-day operations are conducted by an ice operations office in Sydney, NS. During summer Arctic operations the fleet is deployed jointly by Ottawa headquarters and an ice operations office at Frobisher Bay. The Coast Guard Fleet has one cable vessel which is under contract on a year-round basis and is stationed at St. John's, Nfld. The Coast Guard operates two weather-ships on the west coast which provide meteorological data from a position 900 miles (1 700 km) off the BC coast. These vessels operate rotationally. Buoy vessels and helicopters are provided to carry out aids to navigation work while smaller craft are also used for this purpose where possible.

The Department of National Defence coordinates Marine Search and Rescue Services with the cooperation of all government departments which operate ships. The Ministry of Transport operates a number of specialized vessels for search and rescue work which, during distress situations, are controlled by the coordinating authority. These vessels consist of cutters, lifeboats and one hovercraft. The cutters are normally deployed in patrol areas when not involved with an accident. Their operation is controlled from Halifax, Vancouver and Trenton.

The Pilotage Act, in effect since June 1971, decentralized the pilotage function by establishing four regional pilotage authorities as Crown corporations with wide powers to establish, operate and maintain, in the interest of safety, an efficient pilotage service within their region.

The four, created February 1, 1972 are: the Atlantic Pilotage Authority, the Laurentian Pilotage Authority, the Great Lakes Pilotage Authority and the Pacific Pilotage Authority. Each operates independently of the Canadian Coast Guard regional office in the same area because of their Crown corporation status. Each authority is responsible for adopting its own by-laws and regulations. Under the act, pilots may elect to be employees of the authority or their services may be provided to an authority on a contract basis. Each of the pilotage authorities is responsible for establishing its own tariffs.

Regional Marine Emergency Officers are responsible for invoking appropriate contingency plans at the time of an incident and have the responsibility of ensuring that the plans are followed. They develop regional contingency plans and are members of provincial and municipal committees dealing with oil pollution matters.

In addition, the Laurentian Coast Guard Region has certain specific responsibilities for channel maintenance in the St. Lawrence River downstream from Montreal and in the Saguenay River. It includes sweeping and the administration of dredging contracts as required.

Civil aviation   15.5

Administration and policy   15.5.1

Administration. Civil aviation in Canada is under the jurisdiction of the federal government and is administered under the authority of the Aeronautics Act and the National Transportation Act as amended. The Aeronautics Act is in three parts. Part I deals with the technical side of civil aviation including matters of aircraft registration, licensing of personnel, establishing and maintaining airports and facilities for air navigation, air traffic control, accident investigation and the safe operation of aircraft. It is administered by the Canadian Air Transportation Administration (CATA) through the administrator and six regional administrators across Canada. Part II deals with the economic aspects of commercial air services and assigns to the Canadian Transport Commission certain regulatory functions respecting commercial air services. Part III deals with matters of internal administration in connection with the act.

Federal civil aviation policy. The federal government announced some revisions to its air policy in 1973. On November 23, the Minister of Transport tabled in the House of Commons a "Statement on Air Policy" which listed the following objectives: to ensure safe, efficient and convenient air services; to contribute to the economic and social well-being of the country; and to ensure that air services are so balanced as to permit the industry to develop efficiently and profitably.

Domestically, the role of the regional carriers and their relationship with the mainline carriers (Air Canada and Canadian Pacific Air Lines) remained basically unchanged from that described in the "Statement of Principles for Regional Air Carriers" tabled by the Minister of Transport on October 20, 1966. Regional carriers would provide regular route operations into the North and operate local or regional routes to supplement the domestic mainline operations of Air Canada and CP Air. Greater scope would be allowed regional carriers in developing routes and services. Greater cooperation between the mainline and regional carriers would be developed in a variety of fields, ranging from technical and servicing arrangements to joint-fare arrangements. A limited policy of temporary subsidies for regional routes would be introduced, based on a "use it or lose it" formula. Firmer control would be exercised over the financial structure of regional carriers in connection with new licensing arrangements. Regional carriers would be assisted in acquiring aircraft through a scheme for consultation between government and the carriers and among the individual carriers.

In a statement of August 15, 1969 the Minister of Transport defined more precisely the regions in which each of the five regional carriers would be permitted to supplement, or authorized to replace, mainline operations. The CTC's Air Transport Committee issued decisions authorizing new services by regional air-carriers in accordance with the regional air policy, which the committee is continuing to apply.

The relative roles of Air Canada and CP Air in the domestic sphere were defined in the transcontinental policy of 1967. These were based on a formula that would maintain Air Canada's pre-eminence on transcontinental services, on the assumption that the carrier might from time to time be called on to perform special services which would not necessarily be in its commercial best interests.

The development of air policy continues, with a new focus on the question of third level or local air-carriers whose scope of operation is increasing rapidly.

With respect to the international operations of the two major airlines, the policy statement of November 1973 outlined a number of principles which stressed that the economic viability of proposed routes was to remain a major consideration so that international services would generally not be established solely for national prestige. The government reaffirmed that it would refrain from granting or seeking temporary authorizations for international scheduled services, and authorized a series of bilateral negotiations with a number of foreign countries. Cooperation between the two major carriers was also encouraged. The policy assigned specific areas and countries to Air Canada and CP Air which they would serve once bilateral agreements had been satisfactorily concluded. This division was aimed at assisting the airlines in long-range planning for both passenger and cargo services.

Canada's position in the field of aviation as well as its geographical location makes imperative its cooperation with other nations engaged in international civil aviation. Canada therefore took a major part in the original discussions that led to the establishment of the International Civil Aviation Organization which has its headquarters in Montreal. By the end of 1973, Canada had bilateral agreements with 26 other countries. New air agreements were signed with the Federal Republic of Germany and with the People's Republic of China.

Air traffic control. The primary functions of air traffic control in the Department of Transport are to prevent collisions between aircraft operating within controlled airspace and between aircraft and obstructions on the manoeuvring area of controlled airports, and to expedite and maintain a safe, orderly flow of air traffic. These functions are carried out by air traffic controllers in airport control towers, terminal control units and area control centres.

Airport control service is provided to aircraft operating on the manoeuvring area or in the close vicinity, five to 10 nautical-mile radius (9 to 19 km), of civil airports where the volume and complexity of air traffic indicate its need in the interest of flight safety. Service is also provided to other traffic, such as vehicles and maintenance equipment, on the manoeuvring area of an airport. Radio is the prime means of communication although light signals may be used where radio is not available. Airport control towers are in operation at: Gander International and St. John's, Nfld.; Halifax International and Sydney, NS; Charlottetown, PEI; Moncton and Saint John, NB; Baie-Comeau, Dorval International, Mirabel International, Quebec, Saint-Honoré, Saint-Hubert, Saint-Jean, Sept-Îles and Val d'Or, Que.; Buttonville, Hamilton, London, North Bay, Oshawa, Ottawa International, Sault Ste Marie, St. Catharines, Sudbury, Thunder Bay, Toronto International, Toronto Island and Windsor, Ont.; Brandon, St. Andrew's, Thompson and Winnipeg International, Man.; Regina and Saskatoon, Sask.; Calgary International, Edmonton International, Edmonton Municipal, Grande Prairie, Lethbridge and Springbank, Alta.; Abbotsford, Castlegar, Fort St. John, Kamloops, Kelowna, Langley, Penticton, Pitt Meadows, Prince George, Vancouver International and Victoria International, BC; Whitehorse, YT; Inuvik and Yellowknife, NWT. Temporary control service is provided at Vancouver Harbour. Site preparation and construction has been started at Goose Bay for a new tower and operations building. A transportable tower has been purchased for use where required in the North, and is in storage in Edmonton. Each region has a mobile control tower for use with air shows.

Terminal control service is provided to aircraft which are "climbing out", after departure from, or "letting down" for a landing at an airport. It is a service provided to flights operating in accordance with the instrument flight rules in order to separate them from one another and from en route aircraft operating through the terminal area which normally is an airspace within 30-50 nautical miles (56-93 km) of an airport and which, in some cases, may encompass more than one airport. Radar is normally used, in conjunction with direct controller-pilot radio communication. Procedural means are used at some remote locations where radar is not yet available. The service is provided from all area control centres but separate terminal control units are installed at high-traffic-density airports at Halifax, Quebec City, North Bay, Ottawa, Thunder Bay, Regina, Saskatoon and Calgary, where no area control centre is located.

Area control service is essentially an aircraft separation and flight-following service provided to aircraft operating en route between airports. All flights that elect to file flight plans are given flight-following service and separation is provided to all aircraft operating according to the rules for instrument flight or controlled visual flight within designated controlled airspace. Designated controlled airspace consists of (1) high level airspace, i.e. the Southern Control Area, at and above 18,000 ft (5 486 m) above sea level (asl); the Northern Control Area, at and above flight level 230; and the Arctic Control Area, at and above flight level 290; and (2) low level airspace, i.e. all airways, terminal control areas and control area extensions in airspace below the high level airspace. In addition, separation is provided to aircraft operating above 5,500 ft (1 676 m) asl over almost all of the western half of the North Atlantic Ocean. Separation is provided using both radar and procedural means, with direct and indirect communication between controller and pilot. An extensive land line communication system links an area control centre with all affiliated airport control towers, terminal control units and communication stations and with adjacent area control centres in Canada and adjoining states, as well as with other agencies providing supporting and auxiliary services or having a need to deal directly with the centre, such as air-carrier operations agencies and military operations agencies. Area control centres provide several additional services. The Aircraft Movement Information Service assists the Department of National Defence in identifying all aircraft operating in specified areas. The Customs Notification Service facilitates the notification of appropriate customs agencies by pilots planning to cross the Canada–United States border. When necessary, appropriate search and rescue organizations are notified by the Alerting Service. Pilots en route may receive current information such as weather reports and field condition reports from the Flight Information Service. Area control centres are located at Gander, Nfld.; Moncton, NB; Montreal, Que.; Toronto, Ont.; Winnipeg, Man.; Edmonton, Alta.; and Vancouver, BC. A new area control centre has been constructed at Montreal, and design and construction are in progress for new centres at Moncton, Gander, Toronto and Edmonton.

The Airspace Reservation Coordination Office provides reserved airspace for specified operations within controlled airspace and information to other pilots concerning these reservations and military activity areas in controlled and uncontrolled airspace. The office, located in Ottawa, is responsible for providing the service in all Canadian airspace and in the Gander Oceanic Control Area.

Telecommunications Electronics. The Canadian Air Transportation Administration also provides telecommunications electronics and flight service to other components of the department, to other departments and agencies and to civil aviation users in Canada. This activity involves approximately 200 electronic engineers who are responsible for preparing specifications, design of telecommunications and electronics systems, and procurement of electronic equipment and systems employed in civil aviation in Canada. In concert with this the department employs about 1,500 Technician Electronics, who are responsible for the maintenance of highly complex electronic equipment and systems such as instrument landing systems, non-directional beacons, distance measuring equipment, communications equipment and consoles, and radar.

Finally, there are approximately 1,100 radio operators employed at 116 air radio stations in Canada. This highly trained and skilled group is involved and responsible for pre-flight weather briefings, flight planning, monitoring of sophisticated aids to navigation, broadcast services, and airport advisory service to aircraft. Over a year, this activity involves approximately 900,000 flight plans, 1,500,000 air-ground communications and over 1,300,000 landing and take-off of aircraft at airports throughout Canada having no control towers.

Airworthiness. To comply with a 1970 CATA policy decision, the Airworthiness Division of Civil Aeronautics is responsible for validating the airworthiness certification of all foreign and domestic manufactured aircraft and components prior to the issuance of a type approval or a certificate of airworthiness; and the supervision of manufacturers and repair organizations for compliance to Canadian airworthiness standards.

Airports. The Department of Transport owns 145 airports in Canada including such major international airports as Vancouver, Calgary, Edmonton, Winnipeg, Toronto, Montreal (2), Halifax and Gander. Of these, 87 are operated by the Department of Transport, 48 by municipalities and 10 by others. Municipal airports, served by scheduled air service, are eligible to receive an operating subsidy from the Department of Transport. The department also assists the construction of smaller community airports through capital grants.

15.5.2   Commercial air services

The Canadian flag carriers operating international and domestic air routes are Air Canada and CP Air, which together earn 68% of the total operating revenues of Canadian commercial air-carriers. The five regional carriers (Eastern Provincial

Airways, Nordair, Quebecair, Pacific Western Airlines and Transair) earn 13% of the total operating revenues. The remaining 19% is earned by some 600 smaller airlines, many of them operating in areas of Canada which are relatively inaccessible by surface transport. On international routes, the Canadian flag carriers provide scheduled services to Europe, the Soviet Union, Asia Minor, Japan and Hong Kong, Mexico and South America, Morocco, the Caribbean, Australia and the United States (including Hawaii). Thirty-three foreign airlines have scheduled services between Canada and other countries.

The Canadian Transport Commission (Air Transport Committee), in its Directory of Canadian Commercial Air Services, classifies commercial air-carriers into two major groups, domestic and international.

Domestic air-carriers, which operate wholly within Canada, are divided into seven classes: scheduled carriers which provide public transportation of persons, goods or mail to designated points according to a service schedule, at a toll per unit; regular specific point carriers, to the extent that facilities are available, which provide public transportation to points according to a service pattern, at a toll per unit; specific point carriers which provide public transportation, serving points consistent with traffic requirements and operating conditions, at a toll per unit; charter carriers which offer public transportation from a base specified in the licence, at a toll per mile (1.61 km) or per hour for the charter of the entire aircraft, or at such other tolls as may be permitted by the Air Transport Committee; contract carriers which do not offer public transportation but carry persons or goods solely under contract; flying clubs which are incorporated as non-profit organizations and provide flying training and recreational flying; and specialty carriers operating for purposes not provided by other classes such as aerial photography and survey, aerial distribution (crop dusting, seeding), aerial inspection, reconnaissance and advertising, aerial control (fire control, fire-fighting, fog dispersal), aerial construction and air ambulance and mercy services.

International air-carriers, which operate between points in Canada and points in any other country, constitute two more classes of carrier: international scheduled carriers which provide public transportation serving points according to a service schedule at a toll per unit; and international carriers which are domestic and foreign air-carriers operating specific point or contract commercial service.

Canada's international flag carriers   15.5.2.1

Air Canada, a Crown corporation incorporated in 1937 as Trans-Canada Air Lines, maintains passenger, mail and commodity services over a network extending to 64 destinations in Canada, the United States, Ireland, the British Isles, Europe, Bermuda and the Caribbean. After earning net profits in all but two of the last 10 years, the company has been adversely affected by world economic pressures especially in the area of fuel, and as a result a loss of $12 million was recorded in 1975. Air Canada carried 10.7 million revenue passengers in 1975, approximately the same number that were carried in 1974.

Passenger revenues amounted to $786.4 million in 1975, up from $708.3 million in 1974. Total revenues were $957.1 million, compared with $848.5 million in 1974. Operating expenses in 1975 climbed to $917.8 million, compared with $814.7 million the previous year.

At December 31, 1975 the airline's fleet consisted of 120 aircraft: six Boeing 747s, 10 Lockheed L-1011s, 37 DC-8s, 14 Boeing 727s and 53 DC-9s. Two L-1011s were leased for the peak summer traffic periods only.

Canadian Pacific Air Lines Limited (CP Air), a private airline, was established in 1942 by integrating 10 air-carrier bushline companies and has since developed into a major international flag carrier. In 1975 CP Air carried 2.5 million revenue passengers. Operating revenues for the year reached $332 million.

CP Air's network radiates from the company's headquarters in Vancouver to Japan, Hong Kong, the Netherlands, Hawaii, Fiji, Australia, Portugal, Spain,

Italy, Greece, Israel, Mexico, Peru, Chile and Argentina. There are regular west coast flights between Vancouver, San Francisco and Los Angeles. In November 1973, the Minister of Transport announced certain revisions to the government's international aviation policy and, at the same time, designated CP Air to serve Milan, Italy. The policy statement confirmed CP Air's rights on the routes it now serves and provided possibilities of serving North Africa, Iran, Brazil, and new destinations in the Pacific and the Far East where the airline's operations are important to Canada's relations with the developing nations. Within Canada CP Air's transcontinental services link Vancouver, Edmonton, Calgary, Winnipeg, Toronto, Ottawa and Montreal; the company also operates interior services in British Columbia and the Yukon Territory. CP Air operates 29 aircraft: four Boeing 747s, 12 Douglas DC-8s, seven Boeing 737s and six Boeing 727s.

15.5.2.2   Regional airlines

Eastern Provincial Airways (1963) Limited is the regional carrier for the Atlantic provinces. In 1975 it carried 603,944 revenue passengers and 5,540 tons (5 026 t) of freight. Operating revenues were $34.6 million, 22% higher than 1974 revenues of $28.4 million. Scheduled services were operated to Charlottetown, PEI; Moncton–Chatham–Charlo–Fredericton and Saint John, NB; Sydney and Halifax, NS; Deer Lake–Stephenville–Gander and St. John's, Nfld.; Goose Bay–Wabush (Labrador City) and Churchill Falls in Labrador; and Montreal and the Magdalen Islands in Quebec.

The company's fleet at the end of 1975 consisted of seven Boeing 737s, one Hawker-Siddeley 748 and two DC-3s.

Nordair Ltée-Ltd.,with its head office at Dorval, Que., was established in 1957 by the merger of Mont Laurier Aviation and Boreal Airways. Since its formation Nordair has expanded steadily; it operates scheduled services in Quebec, Ontario and the Northwest Territories, as well as extensive domestic and international charter flights throughout Canada and from eastern Canada to the southern United States and the Caribbean.

Scheduled services operate between Montreal, Ottawa, Hamilton, Windsor and Pittsburgh. In 1975, 148,842 passengers were carried on these routes. Scheduled services are also operated between Montreal, Val-d'Or, Fort George, Matagami, La Grande, Chibougamau, Great Whale River and Fort Chimo, Que. and Frobisher Bay and Resolute Bay, NWT; 104,044 passengers and 7,606 tons (6 900 t) of cargo were moved between these points in 1975. An application is before the Danish civil aviation authorities for permission to inaugurate regular air service between Frobisher Bay and Sondrestrom-Fjord in Greenland. This application already has the approval of the Canadian government.

Nordair's charter flights accommodate inclusive tour travels and group travel. Under contract Nordair also provides lateral air services between the DEW-line sites along the Arctic Coast and two specially equipped Electra aircraft operate extensive ice reconnaissance services for the federal Department of Fisheries and the Environment. Nordair's fleet is composed of one Douglas DC-8-61F, six Boeing 737-200Cs, three Lockheed L-188 turbo-props, three F-227s and one Grumman Turbo Mallard.

Pacific Western Airlines Limited, with head office at Vancouver International Airport, operates scheduled passenger and cargo services over 14,000 undupli-cated route-miles (22 531 km) in western and northwestern Canada. Mainline scheduled services operate from Vancouver to Victoria, Comox, Powell River, Campbell River, Port Hardy and Sandspit on the Pacific Coast. Service is also provided between Vancouver and Seattle. In the interior and northern region of BC, flights are scheduled from Vancouver to Penticton, Kelowna, Cranbrook, Castlegar and Kamloops through to Calgary and Edmonton, Alta.; in the northern interior service is provided from Vancouver to Smithers, Dawson Creek, Williams Lake, Quesnel and Prince George. From Edmonton, scheduled flights operate to Cambridge Bay, Fort Simpson, Fort Smith, Hay River, Inuvik, Norman Wells, Resolute and Yellowknife in the Northwest Territories and to Fort Chipewyan, Fort McMurray, High Level and Peace River, Alberta and Uranium City, Saskatchewan. The only no-reservations AirBus service in Canada operates between Calgary and Edmonton. Pacific Western also operates extensive international passenger and cargo charters.

In 1975 passengers carried totalled 2.14 million. The company's fleet of 24 aircraft includes two Boeing 727s, 13 Boeing 737s, two Boeing 707s, three Convair 640s and four Lockheed Hercules (cargo only).

Quebecair, with its head office at Montreal International Airport, Dorval, offers scheduled services in Quebec and Labrador. The company was founded in 1946 under the name Le Syndicat d'Aviation de Rimouski. The name was changed to Rimouski Airlines in 1947 and to Quebecair in 1953 when it was amalgamated with Gulf Aviation. During 1965 Quebecair acquired Northern Wings Limited and Northern Wings Helicopters, in 1967 A. Fecteau Transport Ltée and in 1974 Air Gaspé Inc.

Quebecair is responsible for operating scheduled services and the subsidiaries handle flights by light aircraft, charter and contract services. Scheduled services are operated over 6,000 miles (9 656 km) serving some 46 localities in nine economic regions of Quebec and Labrador. Points linked are Montreal, Quebec City, Murray Bay (Charlevoix), Baie-Comeau (Hauterive), Churchill Falls (Twin Falls), Gagnon, Wabush (Labrador City), Mingan, Mont-Joli–Rimouski, Rivière-au-Tonnerre, Saguenay (Bagotville), Schefferville, Sept-Îles, La Grande 2 (James Bay), Gaspé, Îles-de-la-Madeleine, Rouyn–Noranda, Bonaventure, Charlo, Roberval, Port Meunier, Ste-Anne-des-Monts, Senneterre, Mistassini, Témiscaming, Lac Caché, Lac Mistassini, Rupert River, Fort George, Val-d'Or, Amos, Rupert House, Chibougamau, Matagami, Blanc Sablon, Saint-Paul, Old Fort Bay, Saint-Augustin, La Tabatière, Tête à la Baleine, Harrington Harbour, Gethsemani, Kégaska, Natashquan, Aguanish, Baie Johan Beetz and Havre-Saint-Pierre. Quebecair also operates group charters within Canada and to the United States, the Caribbean, Bermuda, Mexico and South America, using jet aircraft.

Revenue passengers transported by Quebecair in 1976 numbered 576,600 on scheduled services and 317,000 passengers on charter services; goods were hauled on a total of close to 5 million ton-miles (7 million t/km).

Quebecair's large and varied fleet of aircraft enables it to meet the diverse requirements of today's charter market. The combined fleet of Quebecair and its subsidiaries totals 67 units: two Boeing 707s, one Boeing 727, three BAC 111 jets, four F-27 turbo-props, six Douglas DC-3s, 11 DHC-3 Otters, three Cessna 180s, three Beechcraft Queen Air 80s, 14 DHC-6 Beavers, three Cessna 185s, two Beechcraft 99s, one Hawker-Siddeley and 14 helicopters.

Transair Limited. This company was formed in November 1969 through the merger of Transair Limited and Midwest Airlines Ltd., both of Winnipeg. With headquarters at the Winnipeg International Airport, the company operates scheduled services in Manitoba, the NWT, the Yukon and northwestern Ontario as far east as Toronto. Points linked are Gillam, The Pas, Flin Flon, Lynn Lake, Thompson, Churchill, Yellowknife, Whitehorse, Dryden, Thunder Bay, Sault Ste Marie and Toronto. Several other points in the NWT are also served by flights from Churchill. Midwest Airlines Ltd., a wholly-owned subsidiary of Transair, operates in Manitoba's inland region. Charter flights operate from Canada to Florida, Hawaii, Mexico and the Carribbean.

The Transair fleet consists of 23 aircraft: one Boeing 707, three Boeing 737s, two Fokker F-28s, two YS-11s, three Twin Otters and 12 Bell Jet Ranger helicopters. In 1975 Transair carried 409,000 passengers, compared with 484,000 passengers in 1974.

15.5.2.3   Commonwealth and foreign scheduled commercial air services

At the end of 1975 there were 33 foreign air-carriers holding valid Canadian operating certificates and licences issued for international scheduled commercial air services into Canada: Aeroflot (USSR), Aeronaves dé Mexico, S.A., Air France, Air Jamaica (1968) Ltd., Alitalia-Linee Aeree Italiane, Allegheny Airlines Inc., American Airlines Inc., British Airways, British West Indian Airways, Czechoslovak Airlines, Delta Airlines Inc., Eastern Air Lines, El Al Israel Airlines Ltd., Frontier Airlines Inc., Hughes Air West (a division of Hughes Air Corporation), Iberia Air Lines of Spain, Irish International Airlines, Japan Air Lines Company Ltd., KLM Royal Dutch Airlines, Lufthansa German Airlines, North Central Airlines Inc., Northwest Airlines Inc., Olympic Airways S.A., Qantas Airways Limited, Royal Air Maroc, Sabena Belgian World Airlines, Scandinavian Airlines System, Seaboard World Airlines Inc., Swissair, Transportes Aeroes Portugueses S.A.R.L., United Air Lines Inc., Western Air Lines Inc. and Wien Air Alaska, Inc.

15.5.3   Civil aviation statistics

Airport activity. In 1975, the 60 major airports with air traffic control towers operated by the Department of Transport handled 6,398,181 aircraft landings and take-offs. At the three Department of National Defence airports where civilian passenger traffic is allowed, 77,502 aircraft movements were recorded. The 126 smaller airports without control tower facilities, which report daily traffic counts, registered 1,683,042 movements.

In the Canadian air traffic control system, continued growth was experienced in 1975. Airport activity increased some 28.1% since 1971 when 5,056,559 aircraft landings and take-offs were registered. The upward trend which prevailed in 1975 was fairly general; nearly four fifths of all major stations experienced gains in total traffic.

Toronto International airport continued to be the leader in itinerant activity with 228,688 movements, followed by Vancouver International with 198,416 and Montreal International (Dorval) with 187,860.

Light aircraft weighing under 4,000 lb. (1 814 kg) accounted for slightly more than half of all itinerant traffic. Heavy airline aircraft such as the B707, B747, DC8, DC10 and the Tristar accounted for 152,086 movements. Piston engine aircraft contributed the major share (61.1%) of overall itinerant traffic. Jet aircraft accounted for 26.1% and other aircraft such as turbo-props, helicopters and gliders for the remainder.

There were 262,479 international movements recorded in 1975, an increase of 11,356 or a 4.5% gain over 1974. The international airports at Toronto, Montreal and Vancouver, in that order, were responsible for nearly 60% of the international total.

In 1975 Canada's busiest airport in terms of overall traffic was Saint-Hubert, Que. with a total of 292,929 movements, followed closely by Pitt Meadows, BC with 275,691. Both these satellite airports reported high "local" counts, characterized by light aircraft traffic largely of a training or recreational nature.

Commercial air services. Tables 15.29 and 15.30 provide statistics on commercial air services performed by Canadian airlines with gross annual flying revenues exceeding $150,000 and by scheduled foreign airlines. The data for Canadian airlines refer to both domestic and international operations. Figures for the scheduled foreign airlines pertain only to the hours and distance flown over Canadian territory, excluding passengers and goods in transit through Canada. Table 15.30 contains comparative data for domestic and international traffic in 1974 and 1975.

Personnel licences. At December 31, 1975 the total number of personnel licences in force in Canada was 52,496 compared with 51,034 on the same date in

1974. The 1975 licences were constituted as follows with 1974 figures in parentheses: glider pilots 2,054 (1,821), private pilots 33,015 (31,656), commercial pilots 6,705 (6,522), senior commercial pilots 826 (876), airline transport pilots 3,593 (3,999), flight navigators 150 (186), air traffic controllers 1,696 (1,818), flight engineers 133 (141), aircraft maintenance engineers 4,318 (4,009) and gyrocopter pilots 6 (6).

Urban transportation   15.6

Almost 60% of all transportation activity in Canada takes place in urban areas, where approximately 75% of the population lives. Of 8.5 million cars registered in 1974, there were 5.3 million in cities, accounting for 80% of all urban travel. Municipal transit companies operate buses, subways and streetcars, but in spite of a substantial capital investment in facilities and vehicles, have had limited success in competing with the flexibility, comfort and privacy afforded by the automobile. However, a growing adverse public reaction to further road building and increasing concern over energy conservation, air pollution and congestion generated by private cars has led to a new emphasis on public transit.

Although provincial and municipal governments have greater responsibility for urban transportation, the federal government is reviewing its transportation policies with particular regard to their effect on urban areas. Airports, ports and rail services are the most important federal concerns but there have been initiatives in the urban transit field. Means of supplying more direct assistance to urban transit are being actively examined and the excise duty on large cars has been increased as an energy conservation measure. The Department of Transport has established an urban transportation research branch to develop and demonstrate improvements to traffic management and public transport.

The demand for adequate transport facilities in urban areas has placed a heavy financial burden on municipalities. Provincial cost-sharing programs which have assisted in meeting the capital and operating costs of transportation systems in urban areas have until recently been strongly oriented to freeways and roads. Several provinces are now shifting the emphasis from highway construction toward transit planning and construction.

Newfoundland does not have a current program related to urban transportation problems although considerable work and planning are under way toward improving access to, from and across St. John's. The city is served by a bus system subsidized by the provincial government at $4.00 per capita of the city population. No federal financial assistance is received but discussions are to be undertaken at the federal level related to future urban transportation requirements.

New Brunswick. The NB Six Cities Public Transit Study, completed in July 1976 at a cost of $150,000, reviewed existing systems of transit and recommended future plans for each of the six cities: St. John, Moncton, Fredericton, Bathurst, Edmundston and Campbellton. Funding was by the federal Department of Regional Economic Expansion and the province.

Quebec is developing an integrated multi-mode urban transportation policy. A program of aid for public transit announced in December 1975 attests to the government's interest in providing an alternative to individual transportation. The Quebec government, through its Department of Transport, pays the full cost of studies on setting up or improving public transit systems and subsidizes 30% of acquisition or improvement costs to transit corporations or inter-municipal groups, for vehicles manufactured in Quebec. It subsidizes operating deficits of public transit systems at rates of 45% to 55% depending on the utilization rate of each system. In medium-density areas where the quality of service must be upgraded, municipal corporations may be set up. Where such a transit corporation takes over a system, the Quebec Transport Department may pay up to 33% of takeover costs.

On this basis government subsidies, which totalled $50 million in 1975, exceeded $70 million in 1976. To increase the viability of urban transit, the government has promoted the integration of school buses into the public transit system of more than 40 municipalities. Five transit commissions in Quebec have received most of the government assistance. They include the Montreal Urban Community Transit Commission, the Quebec Urban Community Transit Commission, the Laval Transit Commission, the Outaouais Regional Transportation Commission and the Montreal South Shore Transit Commission. Together they serve more than 3 million people. The Montreal transit authority received $32.5 million in government grants in 1975, $2.5 million of it earmarked for the purchase of buses.

All transit commissions have revised their routes and effected various improvements such as reserved bus lanes (Quebec) off-road loading bays and express services (Outaouais) and métrobuses (Montreal). They have begun or continued a program of installing bus-passenger shelters and inaugurating reduced rates for senior citizens.

In addition to studies carried out by the Department of Transport regarding the servicing of Mirabel and inter-modal transit on the Montreal South Shore, two studies on the points of origin and destination have been carried out in the Montreal area by the Montreal Urban Community and Laval transit authorities. The South Shore authority took part in a pilot study with the federal and provincial governments on sharing operating costs and deficits with the various municipalities served by a transit organization.

These studies are the basis for development of a transportation policy for the entire Montreal metropolitan region. This policy is aimed at coordinating all transit systems and grappling with the integration of plans for the Montreal region: the projected express system to serve Mirabel and other parts of the metropolis (TRAMM), continuing suburban commuter train service now provided by both CN and CP, future extensions of the subway, and the transportation situation on the South Shore.

Ontario has an Urban Transportation Subsidy Program that encourages the upgrading and use of public transit in cities and towns. Its aim is to make public transit more attractive and convenient to provide a balanced means of population movement. Under the program, the province pays 50% of a municipality's operating deficit, 75% subsidy on capital expenditures and 75% for transit studies. Capital expenditures include the purchase of buses, streetcars, trolley buses, passenger shelters and service trucks, as well as construction of new terminals and maintenance garages. In 1975, operating subsidies totalled approximately $46 million and capital subsidies $34 million. Additional capital funds are given to Metropolitan Toronto for subway construction.

Ontario, through the Ministry of Transportation and Communications, also subsidizes and administers demonstration projects such as Dial-a-Bus and Trans-Cab. Usually it provides 100% funding for these projects over a period of time. Then the municipality has the option of taking the project over under a normal subsidy (50% of the operating deficit).

The province also backs new concepts that make public transit more attractive and efficient. These include a Kingston Marketing Demonstration and a variable working hours project.

GO Transit is the only transit project which began as a demonstration and continues to be totally subsidized and administered by the province although day-to-day service is provided by operators under contract to the government. GO Transit's inter-regional nature makes it unsuitable as a municipal operation. GO Transit began operating in 1967 as an east-west train-commuter service between Pickering and Oakville, a 42-mile (68 km) stretch along the Lake Ontario shoreline, with the government paying all the capital costs and covering any operational deficits incurred. The Lakeshore GO Train service has since been extended by a bus feeder service serving Oshawa and Hamilton and a separate GO

Bus service is in operation along the east-west Lakeshore corridor. Other GO Bus lines are operating between Toronto and Barrie, 60 miles (97 km) to the north, and in the regions to the west, northwest and northeast of Metropolitan Toronto.

A second GO Train system extending 30 miles (48 km) northwest from Toronto to Georgetown was inaugurated in 1974. GO expects to open a new rail route to Milton–Streetsville in 1978 and to inaugurate rail service between Toronto and Richmond Hill. Union Station is the main hub of GO Transit activity in Toronto, providing passengers immediate access to the metropolitan transportation grid.

To accommodate an ever-increasing passenger volume, GO Transit ordered 80 new double-decker rail coaches, expected to be in service early in 1978. The new double-decker equipment with 75% more capacity per coach will relieve overcrowding at rush hours on the Lakeshore line and will permit more commuters to take advantage of public transit.

GO Transit is operated by Canadian National Railways, Gray Coach and Travelways for the Toronto Area Transit Operating Authority (TATOA). This Crown agency was established by the government of Ontario in 1974 to integrate commuter services for more than 100,000 people who commute daily into Metro Toronto. TATOA is responsible for advising, coordinating and providing information related to the operation of transit systems in the regional municipalities of Metro Toronto, Peel and York.

Manitoba. A feasibility study was undertaken at a cost of $300,000 on development of a seven-mile (11.3 km) transportation corridor, along an existing railway right-of-way, from the Winnipeg city centre to the University of Manitoba. Phase One of the study was to be released in the fall of 1976, dealing with the feasibility of the route, while Phase Two was expected in the spring of 1977, dealing with implementation and development.

The province is providing about $540,000 for innovative transit programs in Winnipeg including a dial-a-bus system in the southern part of the city, a downtown free shuttle service (DASH) operating during business hours, suburban feeder services in four areas of the city where roads are not adequate for regular buses, a bus shelter design program, and a preferential signing and control system for buses at a number of major intersections.

The province also provided direct grants of $6.5 million to Winnipeg, $121,000 to Brandon, and $12,300 to Flin Flon to help cover operating deficits.

The Manitoba Transportation Economics Council was set up to improve the quality and efficiency of transportation in Manitoba, and to enhance economic and social development for the benefit of transportation users and carriers.

Saskatchewan. The provincial government was involved in the introduction of Telebus in Regina in 1971. Telebus offers door-to-door service within individual zones of the city and door-to-connection with scheduled line service for trips between zones. Most of the vehicles are small, carrying 16-24 passengers, but during peak hours standard 42-passenger buses are added. About one third of Regina now receives full service and the entire area receives at least part-time service. Initial feasibility studies were sponsored and financed by the federal, provincial and municipal governments.

The Transit Assistance for Cities Program began April 1, 1974. The program provided cities 50% of the cost of approved rolling stock, 75% of the cost of demonstration projects and studies, 75% of transit facility construction costs, and a three-cents-per-passenger-carried subsidy. Nine cities participated in the 1975-76 fiscal year with expenditures of $1,673,910 and seven cities in 1976-77 with expenditures of $1,434,840.

Urban Assistance for Transportation of the Handicapped program began April 1, 1975 to assist urban municipalities in providing transportation systems for the handicapped. Assistance provided was as follows: 75% of cost of approved rolling stock; 50% of incurred operating deficit; 75% of transit system facility construction costs; 75% of costs for transit studies and demonstration projects. Three cities participated in the 1975-76 and 1976-77 fiscal years. Expenditures were $336,291 in 1975-76 and $203,250 in 1976-77.

Alberta has committed approximately $400 million in urban transportation assistance to its cities between 1974 and 1984. The Alberta Department of Transportation initiated a number of six-year programs in 1974, providing assistance to Alberta cities. Included are: research assistance totalling $9.6 million for studies on public transportation, inter-urban transportation and demonstration projects, among others; public transit capital assistance totalling nearly $96.8 million; deficit subsidies for operating public transit systems, which will total approximately $21 million over six years; and railway relocation study assistance funds, added in 1975, equal to 50% of the federal government's contributions to approved railway relocation study projects.

On July 6, 1976 the Minister of Transportation announced a new program of assistance to be initiated in 1977, continuing until 1984. This will provide, as the initial input of funds, a minimum of $160 million to assist Alberta cities in planning and constructing one major continuous roadway through each city. Edmonton and Calgary were the first cities eligible.

Studies assisted by the research program include a major Surface Transportation Noise Attenuation Study at a cost of over $400,000 involving evaluations of social, psychological and technological effects and ways to reduce roadway noise. The research program is providing $300,000 toward Edmonton's study of transportation for physically disabled adults. The cost of this project is being shared by Alberta Transportation, Transport Canada's Transportation Development Agency, and the city of Edmonton. A third project being assisted deals with urban transportation signs. Undertaken jointly by Alberta Transportation and the cities of Calgary and Edmonton, it is designed to develop uniform guide and information signs and route identification in Alberta cities.

British Columbia. In 1975, the expansion of bus services in Greater Vancouver continued. A network of Fastbus and Localbus routes was inaugurated throughout Surrey, Delta and White Rock, and a new crosstown service along 49th Avenue launched in Vancouver. In the Capital Region, a new Fastbus route was started in Victoria and suburban services previously provided by commercial operators assumed and expanded southeast of Victoria and along the Saanich Peninsula. Modifications were made to other services including Town and Country Buses serving the lower Fraser Valley. Five small city systems joined the provincial program: Kamloops, Kelowna, Port Alberni, Prince George and Prince Rupert. Three other cities, Maple Ridge, Penticton and Trail, voted to join.

Delivery of new buses and trolley-buses ordered in 1974 continued; 68 used buses were purchased, and 105 new buses were ordered for delivery in 1976. A temporary bus storage and servicing facility was opened in Surrey. Construction began on two 400-passenger vessels and terminals of the Burrard Inlet Rapid Transit Ferry. Planning of light rapid transit lines in Vancouver and Victoria continued and a light rail vehicle was purchased for demonstration in 1976. A study of commuter rail service between Vancouver and Port Coquitlam was undertaken and four used diesel powered passenger cars were purchased.

Sources
15.1 Transportation and Communications Division, Industry Statistics Branch, Statistics Canada.
15.1.1 Canadian Transport Commission.
15.2 Transportation and Communications Division, Industry Statistics Branch, Statistics Canada.
15.2.1 Canadian Transport Commission.

15.2.2 Transportation and Communications Division, Industry Statistics Branch, Statistics Canada.

15.3.1 Public Affairs, Ministry of Transport.

15.3.2 Supplied by respective provincial and territorial governments.

15.3.3 Transportation and Communications Division, Industry Statistics Branch, Statistics Canada.

15.4 - 15.4.1 Public Affairs, Department of Transport; Transportation and Communications Division, Industry Statistics Branch, Statistics Canada.

15.4.2 Public Affairs, Department of Transport; National Harbours Board.

15.4.3 The St. Lawrence Seaway Authority.

15.4.4 - 15.5.1 Public Affairs, Department of Transport.

15.5.2 Canadian Transport Commission and the respective airlines.

15.5.3 Transportation and Communications Division, Industry Statistics Branch, Statistics Canada.

15.6 Public Affairs, Department of Transport and the respective provincial governments.

Tables

..	not available	e	estimate
...	not appropriate or not applicable	p	preliminary
—	nil or zero	r	revised
--	too small to be expressed	certain tables may not add due to rounding

15.1 Net subsidies paid for maintenance of coastal and inland shipping services, 1974-75 and contract subsidies 1975-76 (dollars)

Service	Net subsidy[1] 1974-75	Contract subsidy[2] 1975-76
WEST COAST		
Gold River—Zeballos, BC	55,000	107,315
Vancouver—northern BC ports	2,545,158	3,748,500
Vancouver Island—Ahousat freight service	60,000	67,100
Vancouver Island—Kyuquot freight service	65,000	75,500
EAST COAST		
St. Barbe, Nfld.—Blanc-Sablon, Que.	219,971	225,000
Burnside—St. Brendan's, Nfld.	46,896	69,307
Carmanville—Fogo Island, Nfld.	144,500	155,251
Cobb's Arm—Change Islands, Nfld.	26,500	58,000
Dalhousie, NB—Miguasha, Que.	46,000	5,036
Grand Manan and the mainland, NB	259,000	259,000
Greenspond—Badger's Quay, Nfld.	40,000	53,522
Montreal—Quebec—Rimouski—north shore ports, Que.	732,000	1,748,000
Grindstone (Îles-de-la-Madeleine), Que.—Souris, PEI	701,216	1,141,396
Pelee Island and the mainland, Ont.	120,237	142,265
Pictou, NS—Charlottetown, PEI—Grindstone, Que.	120,000	159,240
Portugal Cove—Bell Island, Nfld.	701,432	993,425
Prince Edward Island—Newfoundland	174,843	231,588
Wood Islands, PEI—Caribou, NS	2,364,830	2,600,000
Montreal, Que.—Corner Brook—St. John's, Nfld.	2,223,497	3,810,073
Little Bay Islands—St. Patrick, Nfld.	113,000	205,950
Total	10,759,081	15,855,468

[1]Net amount paid after recapture.
[2]Negotiated amount subject to recapture.

15.2 Railway track mileage operated, 1900-75

First main[1] track mileage		Area and type of track	1971	1972	1973	1974	1975
1900	17,657	First main					
1905	20,487	Newfoundland	944	944	944	944	944
1910	24,731	Prince Edward Island	254	254	254	254	254
1915	34,882	Nova Scotia	1,291	1,247	1,247	1,247	1,249
1920	38,805	New Brunswick	1,665	1,665	1,665	1,665	1,665
1925	40,350	Quebec	5,329	5,324	5,409	5,409	5,398
1930	42,047	Ontario	9,935	9,876	9,876	9,847	9,811
1935	42,916	Manitoba	4,746	4,743	4,743	4,743	4,597
1940	42,565	Saskatchewan	8,565	8,565	8,565	8,561	8,493
1945	42,352	Alberta	6,245	6,228	6,227	6,227	6,161
1950[2]	42,979	British Columbia	4,653	4,653	4,776	4,786	4,786
1955	43,444	Yukon Territory	58	58	58	58	58
1960	44,029	Northwest Territories	129	129	129	129	129
1965	43,157	United States	339	339	339	396	396
1970	43,983						
1971	44,153	Total, first main	44,153	44,025	44,232	44,266	43,941
1972	44,025						
1973	44,232						
1974	44,266	All other	15,557	16,012	16,014	15,981	16,104
1975	43,941						
		Total	59,710	60,037	60,246	60,247	60,045

[1]Defined as a single track extending the entire distance between terminals, upon which the length of the road is based.
[2]Newfoundland included from 1950.

15.2   Railway track kilometres operated, 1900-75   M

First main[1] track km		Area and type of track	1971	1972	1973	1974	1975
1900	28 416	First main					
1905	32 971	Newfoundland	1 519	1 519	1 519	1 519	1 519
1910	39 801	Prince Edward Island	409	409	409	409	409
1915	56 137	Nova Scotia	2 078	2 007	2 007	2 007	2 010
1920	62 451	New Brunswick	2 680	2 680	2 680	2 680	2 680
1925	64 937	Quebec	8 576	8 568	8 705	8 705	8 687
1930	67 668	Ontario	15 989	15 894	15 894	15 847	15 789
1935	69 067	Manitoba	7 638	7 633	7 633	7 633	7 398
1940	68 502	Saskatchewan	13 784	13 784	13 784	13 778	13 668
1945	68 159	Alberta	10 050	10 023	10 021	10 021	9 915
1950[2]	69 168	British Columbia	7 488	7 488	7 686	7 702	7 702
1955	69 916	Yukon Territory	93	93	93	93	93
1960	70 858	Northwest Territories	208	208	208	208	208
1965	69 454	United States	546	546	546	637	637
1970	70 784						
1971	71 057	Total, first main	71 058	70 852	71 185	71 239	70 715
1972	70 851						
1973	71 185	All other	25 037	25 769	25 772	25 719	25 917
1974	71 239						
1975	70 716						
		Total	96 095	96 621	96 957	96 958	96 632

[1]Defined as a single track extending the entire distance between terminals, upon which the length of the road is based.
[2]Newfoundland included from 1950.

15.3   Railway rolling-stock in service as at Dec. 31, 1974 and 1975

Type	1974	1975	Type	1974	1975
Locomotives	3,884	3,977	Freight cars	190,892	193,197
Steam	–	–	Automobile	2,617	2,776
Diesel-electric	3,870	3,963	Ballast	2,296	2,199
Electric	14	14	Box	95,538	92,669
			Flat	24,898	25,722
Passenger cars	2,056	1,936	Gondola	20,414	21,370
Turbo train			Hopper	27,398	29,287
Power unit cars	6	6	Ore	7,151	7,731
Coach	15	15	Refrigerator	4,772	5,016
Parlour	6	6	Stock	2,463	2,359
Self-propelled cars	116	117	Tank	494	379
Coach	728	713	Other	2,851	3,689
Combination	35	32			
Dining	90	87	Privately owned cars	18,930	22,000
Parlour	124	116	Tank	14,426	14,699
Sleeping	369	344	Other	4,504	7,301
Baggage, postal and express	557	495			
Other	10	5			

15.4   Commodities[1] hauled as revenue freight by railways, 1974 and 1975 (thousand tons)

Commodity	1974	1975	Commodity	1974	1975
LIVE ANIMALS	219	240	Gypsum	4,446	4,011
			Limestone	4,972	4,130
Cattle	199	227	Other crude non-metallic minerals	18,493	14,682
Other live animals	20	13	Waste materials	1,076	982
FOOD, FEED, BEVERAGES AND TOBACCO	34,999	34,309	FABRICATED MATERIALS, INEDIBLE	75,899	64,269
Meat, fresh or frozen	723	316	Lumber	7,387	6,490
Other animal products	240	222	Other wood fabricated materials	2,304	2,217
Barley	5,216	6,104	Wood pulp and other pulp	6,055	4,921
Wheat	16,760	16,784	Newsprint	6,053	4,767
Other grains	2,397	2,485	Other paper and paperboard	3,743	3,075
Milled cereals and cereal products	1,934	1,988	Chemicals	6,501	5,429
Fruits and fruit preparations	748	591	Potash	10,010	8,047
Vegetables and vegetable preparations	1,458	1,317	Other fertilizers	2,566	2,316
Sugar	459	452	Petroleum and coal products	14,841	13,844
Other food and food preparations	1,257	1,043	Metals and primary metal products	9,230	6,963
Animal feed	2,810	2,496	Cement	1,970	1,908
Beverages	942	458	Other fabricated materials	5,239	4,292
Tobacco and tobacco products	55	53			
CRUDE MATERIALS, INEDIBLE	137,590	129,354	END PRODUCTS, INEDIBLE	10,864	10,714
Crude animal and vegetable materials	2,204	1,810	Road motor vehicles and parts	5,846	2,756
Pulpwood	12,198	8,409	Other end products	5,018	7,958
Other crude wood materials	3,195	2,552			
Textile fibres	131	94	SPECIAL TYPES OF TRAFFIC	9,522	8,734
Iron ore	56,016	54,018	Piggyback (trailer and container)[2]	5,431	4,332
Nickel-copper ore	3,816	4,505	Freight forwarder	1,889	1,989
Bauxite ore and alumina	3,055	2,623	Other special traffic	2,202	2,413
Other metallic ores	8,360	7,940			
Scrap metal, slags and drosses	2,874	2,359	NON-CARLOAD SHIPMENTS[3]	2,422	1,482
Coal	16,365	20,806			
Crude oil and bituminous substances	389	433	Total	271,515	249,102

[1]In this table duplications are eliminated, i.e. freight that is interlined between two or more Canadian railways is counted only once. The statistics do not cover United States operations of Canadian railways except for the Canadian Pacific Railway line through Maine, US, and certain other short mileages which are deemed to be an integral part of the Canadian railway system. Sections of United States railways operating into Canada are regarded as Canadian railways and are included. Freight carried by the Cartier Railway is included in this table; however, financial data for this railway are not available for inclusion in the financial tables.
[2]Excludes traffic moved in railway-operated containers and trailers.
[3]Includes express-rated traffic.

15.5   Capital invested in railway road and equipment property, 1971-75 (thousand dollars)

Investment	1971	1972	1973	1974	1975
Road	172,002	176,137	203,405	284,628	359,926
Equipment	11,654	Cr. 53,720	30,571	77,321	174,650
General	2,227	4,405	8,426	5,789	Cr. 6,983
Undistributed[1]	16,600	Cr. 2,637	49,250	Cr. 13,755	29,890
CNR non-rail property	5,312	5,379	14,989	20,363	18,595
CPR " "	Cr. 231	Cr. 16,189	27,003	Cr. 46,929	Cr. 1,459
Other " "	11,519	8,172	7,258	12,811	12,754
Total	202,483	124,185	291,652	353,983	557,483
Cumulative investment to Dec. 31	8,461,792	8,585,977	{ 8,877,629 / 8,848,751[2] }	9,202,734	9,760,217

[1]Credit entries in this table result when the annual "write-offs" are greater than the annual investment in any category.
[2]Revised to reflect restatement of data by two railways.

15.4   Commodities[1] hauled as revenue freight by railways, 1974 and 1975 (thousand metric tonnes)   M

Commodity	1974	1975	Commodity	1974	1975
LIVE ANIMALS	*199*	*218*	Gypsum	4 033	3 639
			Limestone	4 511	3 747
Cattle	181	206	Other crude non-metallic minerals	16 777	13 319
Other live animals	18	12	Waste materials	976	891
FOOD, FEED, BEVERAGES					
AND TOBACCO	*31 751*	*31 122*	FABRICATED MATERIALS,		
			INEDIBLE	*68 855*	*58 305*
Meat, fresh or frozen	656	287			
Other animal products	218	201	Lumber	6 701	5 888
Barley	4 732	5 537	Other wood fabricated materials	2 090	2 011
Wheat	15 204	15 226	Wood pulp and other pulp	5 493	4 464
Other grains	2 175	2 254	Newsprint	5 491	4 325
Milled cereals and cereal products	1 754	1 803	Other paper and paperboard	3 396	2 790
Fruits and fruit preparations	679	536	Chemicals	5 898	4 925
Vegetables and vegetable preparations	1 323	1 195	Potash	9 081	7 300
Sugar	416	410	Other fertilizers	2 328	2 101
Other food and food preparations	1 140	946	Petroleum and coal products	13 464	12 559
Animal feed	2 549	2 264	Metals and primary metal products	8 373	6 317
Beverages	855	415	Cement	1 787	1 731
Tobacco and tobacco products	50	48	Other fabricated materials	4 753	3 894
CRUDE MATERIALS, INEDIBLE	*124 819*	*117 349*	END PRODUCTS, INEDIBLE	*9 855*	*9 719*
Crude animal and vegetable materials	1 999	1 642	Road motor vehicles and parts	5 303	2 500
Pulpwood	11 066	7 629	Other end products	4 552	7 219
Other crude wood materials	2 898	2 315			
Textile fibres	119	85	SPECIAL TYPES OF TRAFFIC	*8 639*	*7 923*
Iron ore	50 817	49 004	Piggyback (trailer and container)[2]	4 927	3 930
Nickel-copper ore	3 462	4 087	Freight forwarder	1 714	1 804
Bauxite ore and alumina	2 771	2 380	Other special traffic	1 998	2 189
Other metallic ores	7 584	7 203			
Scrap metal, slags and drosses	2 607	2 140	NON-CARLOAD SHIPMENTS[3]	*2 197*	*1 344*
Coal	14 846	18 875	Total	246 315	225 980
Crude oil and bituminous substances	353	393			

[1]In this table duplications are eliminated, i.e. freight that is interlined between two or more Canadian railways is counted only once. The statistics do not cover United States operations of Canadian railways except for the Canadian Pacific Railway line through Maine, US, and certain other short mileages which are deemed to be an integral part of the Canadian railway system. Sections of United States railways operating into Canada are regarded as Canadian railways and are included. Freight carried by the Cartier Railway is included in this table; however, financial data for this railway are not available for inclusion in the financial tables.
[2]Excludes traffic moved in railway-operated containers and trailers.
[3]Includes express-rated traffic.

15.6   Capital structure of the Canadian National Railway System as at Dec. 31, 1971-75 (thousand dollars)

Year	Shareholders' capital		Funded debt held by public		Government loans and appropriations— active assets in public accounts	Total
	Government of Canada shareholders' account	Capital stock held by public	Guaranteed by federal and provincial governments	Other		
1971	2,023,540	4,345	816, 276	2,024	1,078,195	3,924,380
1972	2,023,540	4,345	809,532	2,024	1,082,453	3,921,894
1973	2,023,540	4,345	803,474	2,024	1,088,898	3,922,281
1974	2,162,550	4,345	596,229	2,024	1,292,574	4,057,722
1975	2,224,606	4,345	582,888	2,024	1,438,071	4,251,934

15.7   Total operating revenues, operating expenses, net revenue, fixed charges and deficits of the Canadian National Railway System (Canadian and United States operations), 1971-75 (thousand dollars)

Year	Total operating revenue	Total operating expenses	Income before fixed charges	Total fixed charges	Net income or deficit[1]	Cash deficit or surplus[2]
1971	1,211,551	1,175,301	70,014	91,574	Dr. 21,560	Dr. 24,268
1972	1,334,047	1,293,081	76,476	90,177	'' 13,701	'' 17,822
1973	1,482,507	1,440,001	76,168	96,240	'' 20,072	'' 21,324
1974	1,817,106	1,782,456	86,990	124,016	'' 37,025	'' 37,733
1975	1,916,778	1,986,426	Dr. 22,046	138,535	'' 160,581	'' 16,368

[1]Includes appropriations for insurance fund.
[2]Contributed by or paid to the Government of Canada.

15.8   Railway operating revenues and expenses (Canadian operations), 1970-75

Item and year	Total revenues $'000	Total expenses (before fixed charges) $'000	Ratio of expenses to revenues %	Per mile of first main track			Freight revenue per freight-train mile $
				Revenues $	Expenses $	Net revenues $	
All railways							
1970	1,679,759	1,573,579	93.68	38,357	35,932	2,425	22.91
1971	1,805,661	1,698,206	92.07	41,072	38,628	2,444	24.56
1972	1,940,594	1,842,575	93.24	44,079	41,853	2,226	25.33
1973	2,122,988	2,032,984	93.84	47,997	45,962	2,035	28.10
1974	2,568,994	2,512,922	96.24	58,036	56,769	1,267	31.10
1975	2,733,811	2,801,967	101.31	62,216	63,767	Dr. 1,551	33.14
CNR							
1970	852,178	807,986	94.81	36,317	34,434	1,883	22.06
1971	923,012	888,808	96.26	39,388	37,929	1,459	23.84
1972	1,017,510	988,813	97.13	43,614	42,384	1,230	25.71
1973	1,118,767	1,096,184	97.98	47,953	46,985	968	29.41r
1974	1,385,730	1,371,929	99.00	59,459	58,867	592	33.26
1975	1,462,646	1,555,308	106.34	63,088	67,085	Dr. 3,997	36.09
CPR							
1970	616,846	578,262	93.74r	38,230	35,839	2,391	22.33
1971	659,912	613,921	89.45	40,998	38,141	2,857	23.82
1972	711,168	653,184	87.55	44,195	40,592	3,603	25.60
1973	772,859	711,316	87.57	48,044r	44,218	3,826	26.02
1974	935,179	867,495	88.53	57,930	53,737	4,193	28.50
1975	1,007,306	940,306	90.20	63,073	58,878	4,195	35.06

15.9   Road and street mileage classified by type and by province, 1972

Province or territory and jurisdiction	Surfaced				Earth	Total
	Rigid pavement	Flexible pavement	Gravel	Other		
FEDERAL AND PROVINCIAL JURISDICTION	2,736	69,970	138,381	—	40,265	251,352
Newfoundland	—	1,939	3,744	—	130	5,813
Prince Edward Island	912	825	942	—	596	3,275
Nova Scotia	13	5,363	10,287	—	76	15,739
New Brunswick	—	5,528	6,916	—	2	12,446
Quebec	349	17,609	16,933	—	12,676	47,567
Ontario	1,103	9,497	6,262	—	220	17,082
Manitoba	316	4,488	7,355	—	—	12,159
Saskatchewan	—	8,722	4,361	—	1,395	14,478
Alberta	22	6,792	65,072	—	16,872	88,758
British Columbia	21	9,146	13,580	—	7,938	30,685
Yukon Territory and Northwest Territories	—	61	2,929	—	360	3,350

15.8   Railway operating revenues and expenses (Canadian operations), 1970-75   M

Item and year	Total revenues $'000	Total expenses (before fixed charges) $'000	Ratio of expenses to revenues %	Per km of first main track			Freight revenue per freight-train km $
				Revenues $	Expenses $	Net revenues $	
All railways							
1970	1,679,759	1,573,579	93.68	23,834	22,327	1,507	14.24
1971	1,805,661	1,698,206	92.07	25,521	24,002	1,519	15.26
1972	1,940,594	1,842,575	93.24	27,389	26,006	1,383	15.74
1973	2,122,988	2,032,984	93.84	29,823	28,559	1,264	17.46
1974	2,568,994	2,512,922	96.24	36,062	35,275	787	19.32
1975	2,733,811	2,801,967	101.31	38,659	39,623	Dr. 964	20.59
CNR							
1970	852,178	807,986	94.81	22,566	21,396	1,170	13.71
1971	923,012	888,808	96.26	24,475	23,568	907	14.81
1972	1,017,510	988,813	97.13	27,100	26,336	764	15.98
1973	1,118,767	1,096,184	97.98	29,796	29,195	601	18.27
1974	1,385,730	1,371,929	99.00	36,946	36,578	368	20.67
1975	1,462,646	1,555,308	106.34	39,201	41,685	Dr. 2,484	22.43
CPR							
1970	616,846	578,262	93.74ʳ	23,755	22,269	1,486	13.88
1971	659,912	613,921	89.45	25,475	23,700	1,775	14.80
1972	711,168	653,184	87.55	27,462	25,223	2,239	15.91
1973	772,859	711,316	87.57	29,853	27,476	2,377	16.17
1974	935,179	867,495	88.53	35,996	33,391	2,605	17.71
1975	1,007,306	940,306	90.20	39,192	36,585	2,607	21.79

15.9   Road and street kilometres classified by type and by province, 1972   M

Province or territory and jurisdiction	Surfaced				Earth	Total
	Rigid pavement	Flexible pavement	Gravel	Other		
FEDERAL AND PROVINCIAL JURISDICTION	4 404	112 607	222 702	—	64 799	404 512
Newfoundland	—	3 121	6 025	—	209	9 355
Prince Edward Island	1 468	1 328	1 516	—	959	5 271
Nova Scotia	21	8 631	16 555	—	122	25 329
New Brunswick	—	8 896	11 130	—	3	20 029
Quebec	562	28 339	27 251	—	20 400	76 552
Ontario	1 775	15 284	10 078	—	354	27 491
Manitoba	509	7 223	11 837	—	—	19 569
Saskatchewan	—	14 037	7 018	—	2 245	23 300
Alberta	35	10 931	104 723	—	27 153	142 842
British Columbia	34	14 719	21 855	—	12 775	49 383
Yukon Territory and Northwest Territories	—	98	4 714	—	579	5 391

15.9   Road and street mileage classified by type and by province, 1972 (concluded)

Province or territory and jurisdiction	Surfaced				Earth	Total
	Rigid pavement	Flexible pavement	Gravel	Other		
MUNICIPAL JURISDICTION	*5,119*	*51,072*	*146,350*	*275*	*74,382*	*277,198*
Newfoundland	14	509	606	14	34	1,177
Prince Edward Island	7	69	16	–	–	92
Nova Scotia	62	941	217	–	3	1,223
New Brunswick	58	821	160	6	12	1,057
Quebec	2,103	12,076	10,114	63	2,195	26,551
Ontario	578	25,594	48,158	64	3,412	77,806
Manitoba	1,457	666	23,724	44	13,038	38,929
Saskatchewan	196	1,456	58,027	–	54,703	114,382
Alberta	471	2,813	2,669	64	828	6,845
British Columbia	173	6,090	2,585	8	153	9,009
Yukon Territory and Northwest Territories	–	37	74	12	4	127

15.10   Construction, maintenance and administration expenditure on roads and streets, by province, years ended Mar. 31, 1972 and 1973 (thousand dollars)

Item and province or territory	Construction		Maintenance and administration		Total expenditure	
	1972	1973	1972	1973	1972	1973
EXPENDITURE ON PROVINCIAL AND FEDERAL ROADS[1,2]	*982,431*r	*1,051,781*	*461,367*r	*472,085*	*1,443,798*r	*1,523,866*
Newfoundland	38,426	37,915	17,052	19,534	55,478	57,449
Prince Edward Island	5,907	7,122	4,965	6,007	10,872	13,129
Nova Scotia	55,113	45,655	24,425	28,989	79,538	74,644
New Brunswick	38,168	44,445	28,267	29,898	66,435	74,343
Quebec	363,592	407,353	122,169	129,612	485,761	536,965
Ontario	212,137r	183,912	159,838r	153,406	371,975r	337,318
Manitoba	29,294	41,079	19,850	21,013	49,144	62,092
Saskatchewan	52,331	47,016	18,485	16,646	70,816	63,662
Alberta	68,470	74,444	19,125	14,957	87,595	89,401
British Columbia	105,658	138,825	38,132	42,497	143,790	181,322
Yukon Territory and Northwest Territories	13,335r	24,015	9,059r	9,526	22,394r	33,541
EXPENDITURE ON MUNICIPAL ROADS[2,3]	*501,797*	*556,936*	*565,500*	*614,702*	*1,067,297*	*1,171,638*
Newfoundland	3,114	3,472	5,580	4,654	8,694	8,126
Prince Edward Island	280	400	690	741	970	1,141
Nova Scotia	6,493	11,304	8,488	9,038	14,981	20,342
New Brunswick	4,491	5,128	7,745	7,759	12,236	12,887
Quebec	70,813	89,059	136,984	147,726	207,797	236,785
Ontario	256,755	286,371	258,757	290,129	515,512	576,500
Manitoba	18,747	18,243	21,796	23,284	40,543	41,527
Saskatchewan	22,893	26,212	36,496	35,555	59,389	61,767
Alberta	72,170	68,957	53,448	56,070	125,618	125,027
British Columbia	45,502	47,018	34,826	38,830	80,328	85,848
Yukon Territory and Northwest Territories	539	772	690	916	1,229	1,688

[1]Includes small amounts paid by private companies and other organizations in connection with railway grade crossings, overpasses, etc.
[2]Provincial and federal subsidies to municipalities amounted to $327 million in 1971-72 and $331 million in 1972-73 and should be added to provincial and federal expenditures and subtracted from municipal expenditures to arrive at net expenditures for the respective levels of government.
[3]Fiscal year for municipalities ends the previous Dec. 31.

15.11   Motor vehicles registered, by province, 1970-74

Province or territory	1970[1]	1971[1]	1972	1973	1974
Newfoundland	118,641	129,200	140,650	153,585	163,975
Prince Edward Island	40,233	42,691	45,430	49,141	53,332
Nova Scotia	271,573r	310,383	304,028	325,871	346,392
New Brunswick	201,274	216,710	235,108	256,042	274,173
Quebec	2,115,126	2,279,722	2,370,405r	2,556,260r	2,799,352
Ontario	3,047,599	3,209,862	3,382,497	3,583,379r	3,891,603
Manitoba	403,187	419,314	428,360	471,507	508,751
Saskatchewan	464,405	464,924	496,214	523,557r	568,918
Alberta	768,759	813,395	864,397	933,673r	1,035,562
British Columbia	1,046,697	1,115,028	1,191,953	1,281,917	1,333,277
Yukon Territory	11,371	11,796	11,232r	10,663r	13,620
Northwest Territories	8,474	9,111	11,158	12,845	13,048
Canada	8,497,339r	9,022,136	9,481,432r	10,158,440r	11,002,003

[1]Includes a small number of snowmobiles.

15.9   Road and street kilometres classified by type and by province, 1972 (concluded)   M

Province or territory and jurisdiction	Surfaced				Earth	Total
	Rigid pavement	Flexible pavement	Gravel	Other		
MUNICIPAL JURISDICTION	*8 237*	*82 192*	*235 526*	*443*	*119 707*	*446 105*
Newfoundland	23	819	975	23	55	1 895
Prince Edward Island	11	111	26	—	—	148
Nova Scotia	100	1 514	349	—	5	1 968
New Brunswick	93	1 321	257	10	19	1 700
Quebec	3 384	19 434	16 277	101	3 533	42 729
Ontario	930	41 190	77 503	103	5 491	125 217
Manitoba	2 345	1 072	38 180	71	20 983	62 651
Saskatchewan	315	2 343	93 385	—	88 036	184 079
Alberta	758	4 527	4 295	103	1 333	11 016
British Columbia	278	9 801	4 160	13	246	14 498
Yukon Territory and Northwest Territories	—	60	119	19	6	204

15.12   Types of motor vehicles registered, by province, 1974 with totals for 1970-73

Year, province or territory	Passenger cars[1]	Trucks and buses[2]	Motor-cycles	Other[3]	Total
Newfoundland	121,859	32,553	2,563	7,000	163,975
Prince Edward Island	39,430	12,064	1,442	396	53,332
Nova Scotia	253,521	65,938	6,922	20,011	346,392
New Brunswick	208,229	51,422	7,653	6,869	274,173
Quebec	2,186,808	330,131	150,572	131,841	2,799,352
Ontario	3,255,498	567,685	68,420	[5]	3,891,603
Manitoba	378,194	119,401	8,585	2,571	508,751
Saskatchewan	328,940	223,167	8,183	8,628	568,918
Alberta	687,345[4]	317,743	30,474	[5]	1,035,562
British Columbia	999,957[4]	296,783	34,982	1,555	1,333,277
Yukon Territory	6,785	5,248	572	1,015	13,620
Northwest Territories	5,658	5,430	799	1,161	13,048
Canada 1974	8,472,224	2,027,565	321,167	181,047[6]	11,002,003
1973	7,866,084	1,843,307	287,820	161,229[6]	10,158,440
1972	7,407,275	1,681,977	248,501	143,679[6]	9,481,432
1971	6,967,247	1,556,557	198,867	299,465[6,7]	9,022,136[7]
1970	6,602,176	1,481,197	157,402	256,564[6,7]	8,497,339[7]

[1]Includes taxis and rent-a-car. [2]Includes other types of motor vehicles, while certain classes of trucks and/or buses have been included under passenger cars. [3]Includes farm tractors (where registered), ambulances, etc. [4]Estimated, due to new licence program. [5]Included in trucks and buses. [6]Figures not complete. [7]Includes some licensed snowmobiles for 1970 and 1971.

15.13   Provincial revenue from the registration and operation of motor vehicles, by province, for the licence year 1974 (dollars)

Province or territory	Motor vehicle licences and fees[1]	Chauffeur and driver licences	Public service vehicle fees[2]	Motive fuel taxes	Other[3]	Total	Commission allowed gasoline agents[4]
Newfoundland	6,037,069	650,000	201,222	32,605,713	851,883	40,345,887	162,424
Prince Edward Island	1,843,634	164,863	75,707	7,892,595	285,295	10,262,094	80,100
Nova Scotia	16,225,431	1,134,018	383,024	53,474,886	1,352,410	72,569,769	369,302
New Brunswick	12,811,969	615,200	[5]	44,766,815	1,135,643	59,329,627	228,280
Quebec	127,310,943	9,429,492	5,081,597	392,243,893	8,430,650	542,496,575	2,248,926
Ontario	190,472,400	9,688,000	[5]	571,601,024	24,655,558	796,416,982	[6]
Manitoba	11,958,252	1,684,719	3,719,985	55,255,261	737,609	73,355,826	315,308
Saskatchewan	17,073,479	1,103,556	[5]	46,278,654	2,922,976	67,378,665	742,168
Alberta	31,187,177	2,066,928	387,950	79,692,088	5,034,853	118,368,996	929,714
British Columbia	44,040,475	1,786,044	722,253	146,532,907	35,399	193,117,078	1,267,241
Yukon Territory	694,769	31,637	254,864	3,275,538	393,109	4,649,917	—
Northwest Territories	605,876	[5]	..	4,546,439	..	5,152,315	—
Canada	460,261,474	28,354,457	10,826,602	1,438,165,813	45,835,385	1,983,443,731	6,343,463

[1]Includes passenger automobiles, motor trucks and buses, motorcycles, other motor vehicles, trailers and transfer of motor vehicle ownership.
[2]Includes passenger and freight.
[3]Includes gasoline or service station licences, garage licences, fines for infractions of motor vehicle act and other miscellaneous revenue.
[4]Deducted from gross tax collections to obtain motive fuel taxes.
[5]Included with motor vehicle licences and fees.
[6]Commission payments discontinued, effective May 1, 1972.

15.14   Sales of motive fuels, by province, 1970-74 (thousand gallons)

Province or territory	1970[1]	1971	1972	1973	1974
Gasoline					
Newfoundland	74,558	84,389	93,767	105,747	117,614
Prince Edward Island	25,815	27,408	30,015	33,863	35,259
Nova Scotia	176,419	185,042	198,091	216,578	229,653
New Brunswick	145,063	154,691	172,317	185,589	194,533
Quebec	1,357,824	1,417,194	1,511,596	1,637,975	1,662,141
Ontario	2,052,671	2,125,564	2,292,393	2,463,796	2,532,861
Manitoba	227,358	231,396	249,361	266,641	279,963
Saskatchewan	226,311	234,018	242,585	259,720	274,779
Alberta	456,949	474,355	509,934	556,205	602,847
British Columbia	542,068	577,612	611,593	679,086	727,297
Yukon Territory	7,589	7,888	8,002	8,986	10,331
Northwest Territories	8,535	6,843	7,626	7,223	7,381
Total, net sales	5,301,160	5,526,400	5,927,280	6,421,409	6,674,659
Sales exempt from tax or taxed at lesser rates	571,515	563,519	567,935	601,965	633,569
Total, gross sales	5,872,675	6,089,919	6,495,215	7,023,374	7,308,228
Diesel oil Total, net sales	459,433	543,062	686,450	835,286	970,815
Liquefied petroleum gases Total, net sales	..	..	..	..	12,016

[1]Includes liquefied petroleum gases.

15.14   Sales of motive fuels, by province, 1970-74 (thousand litres)   **M**

Province or territory	1970[1]	1971	1972	1973	1974
Gasoline					
Newfoundland	338 947	383 640	426 273	480 735	534 684
Prince Edward Island	117 357	124 599	136 451	153 944	160 291
Nova Scotia	802 017	841 218	900 540	984 583	1 044 023
New Brunswick	659 469	703 239	783 369	843 704	884 365
Quebec	6 172 790	6 442 691	6 871 851	7 446 382	7 556 243
Ontario	9 331 627	9 663 005	10 421 425	11 200 638	11 514 614
Manitoba	1 033 590	1 051 947	1 133 618	1 212 174	1 272 737
Saskatchewan	1 028 830	1 063 867	1 102 813	1 180 710	1 249 170
Alberta	2 077 331	2 156 461	2 318 206	2 528 558	2 740 597
British Columbia	2 464 290	2 625 876	2 780 357	3 087 186	3 306 358
Yukon Territory	34 500	35 860	36 378	40 851	46 966
Northwest Territories	38 801	31 109	34 668	32 836	33 555
Total, net sales	24 099 549	25 123 512	26 945 949	29 192 301	30 343 603
Sales exempt from tax or taxed at lesser rates	2 598 159	2 561 808	2 581 884	2 736 587	2 880 262
Total, gross sales	26 697 708	27 685 320	29 527 833	31 928 888	33 223 865
Diesel oil					
Total, net sales	2 088 624	2 468 809	3 120 663	3 797 285	4 413 412
Liquefied petroleum gases					
Total, net sales	. .	. .	. .	. .	54 626

[1] Includes liquefied petroleum gases.

15.15   Canadian intercity bus industry, 1974

Item		Class 1 and 2 ($500,000 and over)	Class 3 ($100,000-499,999)	Class 4, 5 and 0 (under $100,000)	Total, all classes
Establishments reporting	*No.*	18	11	39	68
Total operating revenue	*$'000*	133,440	2,452	2,410	138,302
Number of employees (including working owners)	*No.*	4,663	173	178	5,014
Equipment operated					
Highway buses	‥	1,235	50	63	1,348
Urban and suburban buses	‥	265	37	25	327
School buses	‥	24	32	41	97
Other equipment	‥	—	5	9	14
Total, equipment	‥	1,524	124	138	1,786
Fare passengers carried	*'000*	36,961	..	..	..
Total vehicle miles travelled	*'000*	120,305[1]	..	..	..

[1]Equivalent 193 612 000 km.

15.16   The Canadian Urban Transit Industry, 1974

Item		Class 1 and 2 ($500,000 and over)	Class 3 ($100,000-499,999)	Class 4, 5 and 0 (under $100,000)	Total, all classes
Establishments reporting	*No.*	28	29	25	82
Total operating revenues	*$'000*	332,827	12,334	1,782	346,942
Number of employees (including working owners)	*No.*	24,770	1,164	153	26,087
Equipment operated					
Highway buses	‥	12	29	9	50
Urban and suburban buses	‥	6,777	505	77	7,359
School buses	‥	310	94	31	435
Other equipment	‥	1,839	3	2	1,844
Total, equipment	‥	8,938	631	119	9,688
Fare passengers carried	*'000*	1,046,354	..	..	..
Total, vehicle miles	*'000*	280,688[1]	..	..	..

[1]Equivalent 451 724 000 km.

15.17   Commodities transported by motor carriers, by weight, 1974 (thousand tons)

Commodity	1974	Commodity	1974
LIVE ANIMALS	991	Crude oil and bituminous substances	375
		Other crude non-metallic minerals	10,969
Cattle	672	Waste materials	1,020
Other live animals	319		
		FABRICATED MATERIALS, INEDIBLE	50,759
FOOD, FEED, BEVERAGES AND TOBACCO	13,682		
		Lumber	2,465
Meat, fresh or frozen	525	Other wood fabricated materials	1,442
Other animal products	2,332	Woodpulp and other pulp	1,274
Grains	2,135	Newsprint	962
Milled cereals and cereal products	75	Other paper and paperboard	605
Fruits and fruit preparations	358	Chemicals	4,921
Vegetables and vegetable preparations	1,619	Fertilizers	1,382
Sugar	410	Petroleum and coal products	12,798
Other food and food preparations	3,200	Metals and primary metal products	10,404
Animal feed	1,111	Cement	7,735
Beverages	1,702	Other fabricated materials	6,771
Tobacco and tobacco products	215		
		END PRODUCTS, INEDIBLE	11,202
CRUDE MATERIALS, INEDIBLE	18,737	Road motor vehicles and parts	2,459
		Other end products	8,743
Crude animal and vegetable materials	887		
Pulpwood	106	CONTAINERS	1,487
Other crude wood materials	3,802		
Textile fibres	14	GENERAL FREIGHT	2,015
Iron ore	1,250		
Other metallic ores	284	Total	98,873
Coal	30		

1974 For-Hire Trucking Survey (Catalogue 53-224) — a survey of the intercity movements of commodities by motor carriers with revenue of at least $100,000 annually.

15.17   Commodities transported by motor carriers, by mass, 1974 (thousand metric tonnes)   **M**

Commodity	1974	Commodity	1974
LIVE ANIMALS	*899*	Crude oil and bituminous substances	340
		Other crude non-metallic minerals	9 951
Cattle	610	Waste materials	925
Other live animals	289		
		FABRICATED MATERIALS, INEDIBLE	*46 048*
FOOD, FEED, BEVERAGES AND TOBACCO	*12 413*	Lumber	2 236
		Other wood fabricated materials	1 308
Meat, fresh or frozen	476	Woodpulp and other pulp	1 156
Other animal products	2 116	Newsprint	873
Grains	1 937	Other paper and paperboard	549
Milled cereals and cereal products	68	Chemicals	4 464
Fruits and fruit preparations	325	Fertilizers	1 254
Vegetables and vegetable preparations	1 469	Petroleum and coal products	11 610
Sugar	372	Metals and primary metal products	9 438
Other food and food preparations	2 903	Cement	7 017
Animal feed	1 008	Other fabricated materials	6 143
Beverages	1 544		
Tobacco and tobacco products	195	END PRODUCTS, INEDIBLE	*10 163*
		Road motor vehicles and parts	2 231
CRUDE MATERIALS, INEDIBLE	*16 998*	Other end products	7 932
Crude animal and vegetable materials	805	CONTAINERS	*1 349*
Pulpwood	96		
Other crude wood materials	3 449	GENERAL FREIGHT	*1 828*
Textile fibres	13		
Iron ore	1 134		
Other metallic ores	258	Total	89 698
Coal	27		

1974 For-Hire Trucking Survey (Catalogue 53-224) — a survey of the intercity movements of commodities by motor carriers with revenue of at least $100,000 annually.

15.18   Canadian for-hire trucking industry, excluding household-goods movers, by province, 1974

Item		Province or region			
		Atlantic provinces[1]	Quebec	Ontario	Manitoba
Establishments reporting	No.	1,259	2,883	3,922	501
Total operating revenues	$'000	153,807	645,043	1,145,289	139,455
Total operating expenses	''	138,780	600,443	1,057,753	129,373
Net operating revenues	''	15,027	44,600	87,536	10,082
Average number of employees (including working owners)	No.	6,209	30,959	46,205	5,729
Equipment:					
Straight trucks	''	3,283	12,490	13,460	1,765
Truck tractors	''	1,686	7,719	15,593	1,807
Semi-trailers	''	2,391	11,212	25,488	3,433
Full-trailers	''	347	3,277	3,879	254
Other equipment	''	200	1,295	1,599	606
Total, equipment	''	7,907	35,993	60,019	7,865
		Saskatchewan	Alberta and Northwest Territories[2]	British Columbia and Yukon Territory[3]	Canada
Establishments reporting	No.	458	2,152	2,011	13,186
Total operating revenues	$'000	42,152	387,402	453,012	2,966,160
Total operating expenses	''	37,423	352,323	423,237	2,739,332
Net operating revenues	''	4,729	35,079	29,775	226,828
Average number of employees (including working owners)	No.	2,120	13,799	20,460	125,481
Equipment:					
Straight trucks	''	854	4,713	6,784	43,349
Truck tractors	''	699	4,888	2,820	35,212
Semi-trailers	''	689	6,951	5,552	55,716
Full-trailers	''	92	588	426	8,863
Other equipment	''	103	440	1,293	5,536
Total, equipment	''	2,437	17,580	16,875	148,676

[1]Carriers based in Newfoundland, Prince Edward Island, Nova Scotia and New Brunswick grouped to meet confidentiality requirements.
[2]Northwest Territories and Alberta grouped for confidentiality.
[3]Carriers based in Yukon Territory grouped with carriers in British Columbia for confidentiality.

15.19   Canadian for-hire trucking industry, excluding household-goods movers by revenue class, 1974

Item		Class 1 ($2,000,000 and over)	Class 2 ($500,000- 1,999,999)	Class 3 ($100,000- 499,999)	Class 4 ($25,000- 99,999)	Class 5 (under $25,000)	Total, all classes
Establishments reporting	No.	192	607	2,394	5,506	4,487	13,186
Total operating revenue	$'000,000	1,545	572	509	272	68	2,966
Equipment operated							
Straight trucks	No.	10,323	6,452	11,228	10,196	5,150	43,349
Truck tractors	"	18,818	7,780	5,915	2,424	275	35,212
Trailers (semi- and full-)	"	41,186	12,803	7,978	2,346	266	64,579
Other equipment	"	2,562	1,013	1,033	708	220	5,536
Total, equipment	"	72,889	28,048	26,154	15,674	5,911	148,676

15.20   Canadian for-hire trucking industry excluding household-goods movers, by major type of service, 1974

Item		General freight	Bulk liquids	Dump (sand gravel, snow)	Forest products	Other commodities	Total
Establishments operating	No.	3,595	857	4,441	1,539	2,754	13,186
Total operating revenues	$'000	1,696,296	155,464	266,924	165,701	681,775	2,966,160
Total operating expenses	"	1,609,033	137,778	218,929	146,411	627,181	2,739,332
Net operating revenues	"	87,263	17,686	47,995	19,290	54,594	226,828
Average number of employees (including working owners)	No.	71,408	5,635	12,974	6,419	29,045	125,481
Equipment operated							
Straight trucks	"	22,293	2,109	8,804	2,325	7,818	43,349
Truck tractors	"	20,493	1,981	1,606	1,781	9,351	35,212
Semi-trailers	"	38,531	2,279	983	1,635	12,288	55,716
Full-trailers	"	5,939	292	624	683	1,325	8,863
Other equipment	"	2,711	169	628	371	1,657	5,536
Total, equipment	"	89,967	6,830	12,645	6,795	32,439	148,676

15.21   Vessels entered at Canadian ports, 1971-75

Year	In international seaborne shipping		In coastwise shipping		Total	
	Vessels	Net registered tons[1]	Vessels	Net registered tons[1]	Vessels	Net registered tons[1]
1971	24,970	114,252,881	68,083	96,274,780	93,053	210,527,661
1972	24,771	121,535,914	63,438	92,675,867	88,209	214,211,781
1973r	23,436	121,466,828	58,456	90,480,407	81,892	211,947,235
1974	20,992	112,832,551	53,368	86,095,620	74,360	198,928,171
1975	20,225	115,591,697	46,867	83,731,925	67,092	199,323,622

[1]The capacity of the spaces within the hull, and the enclosed spaces above the deck, available for cargo and passengers; excluding spaces used for the accommodation of officers and crew, navigation, propelling machinery and fuel. A registered ton is equivalent to 100 cu ft (2.831 685 m³) and it is expected that this internationally recognized measure, like the nautical mile and the knot, will continue in use for some considerable time.

15.22 Cargoes loaded and unloaded at principal Canadian ports from vessels in international seaborne and coastwise shipping, by province, 1975 with total for 1974 (tons)

Province and port	International Loaded	International Unloaded	Coastwise Loaded	Coastwise Unloaded	Total 1975	Total 1974
NEWFOUNDLAND	2,714,374	4,067,476	2,427,212	3,279,129	12,488,191	13,423,206
St. John's	19,577	7,319	123,293	850,922	1,001,111	1,017,773
Stephenville	542,167	—	191,497	409,930	1,143,594	1,037,062
Holyrood	25,683	345,385	207,859	124,934	703,861	1,051,913
Corner Brook	213,254	26,799	11,947	364,742	616,742	716,347
Botwood	266,283	60,449	—	145,797	472,529	545,168
Port aux Basques	817	200	85,088	544,114	630,219	638,350
PRINCE EDWARD ISLAND	54,057	12,048	96,419	718,472	880,996	733,477
Charlottetown	957	10,800	95,974	701,258	808,989	665,358
NOVA SCOTIA	6,938,393	9,869,153	5,526,884	2,777,249	25,111,679	27,264,572
Halifax	3,284,274	5,495,901	2,109,176	853,381	11,742,732	13,289,670
Port Hawkesbury	1,492,406	4,057,152	2,098,553	70,316	7,718,427	8,078,301
Hantsport	1,038,308	—	—	—	1,038,308	1,675,505
Sydney	529,316	287,474	212,496	1,515,164	2,544,450	1,711,219
Little Narrows	357,710	—	392,918	—	750,628	1,081,779
North Sydney	8,156	328	515,431	99,506	623,421	633,940
NEW BRUNSWICK	2,937,593	7,287,927	1,923,138	950,090	13,098,748	12,595,300
Saint John	2,101,253	6,765,621	1,911,288	72,514	10,850,676	9,997,900
Dalhousie	534,331	—	—	178,171	712,502	802,858
Newcastle	198,299	—	—	248,929	447,228	629,778
QUEBEC	55,353,997	17,389,027	13,389,752	23,934,441	110,067,217	105,549,131
Sept-Îles — Pointe-Noire	25,336,976	456,829	3,473,896	927,458	30,195,159	30,327,452
Montreal	4,803,774	3,754,654	4,731,822	5,342,688	18,632,938	19,654,305
Port-Cartier	13,153,841	1,810,240	5,552	2,658,256	17,627,889	15,430,379
Quebec	3,064,385	4,011,456	1,176,293	4,243,875	12,496,009	12,942,745
Baie-Comeau	3,477,322	1,188,476	78,343	2,589,878	7,334,019	4,093,624
Sorel	2,399,541	795,589	13,926	3,499,530	6,708,586	5,208,718
Port-Alfred	354,141	3,186,454	10,966	452,641	4,004,202	4,640,426
Trois-Rivières	883,679	256,006	23,389	1,678,350	2,841,424	3,404,758
Havre-Saint-Pierre	362,585	—	2,577,452	27,356	2,967,393	3,064,612
Contrecoeur	955,805	1,770,207	305,997	468,006	3,500,015	3,596,953
Chicoutimi	—	—	—	676,619	676,619	655,936
Forestville	—	—	564,483	35,776	600,259	35,637
ONTARIO	9,844,564	27,206,824	25,848,283	17,662,673	80,562,344	74,042,080
Thunder Bay	3,100,271	146,929	15,791,920	988,700	20,027,820	18,151,823
Hamilton	187,789	8,849,665	373,426	4,859,487	14,270,367	11,869,371
Sarnia	1,514,405	4,243,110	2,875,372	457,538	9,090,425	8,553,312
Sault Ste Marie	90,077	4,150,074	209,572	1,480,992	5,930,715	5,177,798
Toronto	291,335	1,157,611	220,304	1,317,914	2,987,164	2,790,681
Clarkson	310,220	54,653	184,131	2,616,392	3,165,396	3,638,511
Windsor — Walkerville	382,765	700,441	238,601	620,153	1,941,960	3,193,882
Port Colborne	1,083,409	250,761	222,763	630,937	2,187,870	2,308,267
Colborne	—	—	2,556,267	—	2,556,267	2,404,873
Picton	604,967	102,416	288,672	59,179	1,055,234	1,446,475
Goderich	650,214	384	1,004,658	172,766	1,828,022	1,463,628
Lakeview (Port Credit)	—	1,795,896	—	107,619	1,903,515	2,152,780
Depot Harbour	734,808	—	—	—	734,808	723,024
Little Current	454,551	33,668	35,087	31,702	555,008	854,262
Midland	—	16,482	84,451	955,945	1,056,878	820,082
Prescott	7,664	58,211	120,361	354,835	541,071	427,669
Michipicoten Harbour	—	177,869	31,898	41,742	251,509	673,165
Kingston	—	5,910	56,868	423,266	486,044	442,887
Parry Sound	—	44,696	4,149	507,500	556,345	611,121
MANITOBA	659,564	30,137	14,153	—	703,854	664,430
Churchill	659,564	30,137	14,153	—	703,854	664,430
BRITISH COLUMBIA	34,422,703	4,438,239	10,709,462	10,506,625	60,077,029	67,741,488
Vancouver[1]	26,522,605	3,106,227	2,701,806	3,190,681	35,521,319	36,761,096
New Westminster	559,274	419,567	780,988	721,338	2,481,167	3,772,755
Nanaimo	646,307	21,769	48,104	553,637	1,269,817	1,757,122
Duncan Bay — Campbell River	263,913	32,097	106,222	751,412	1,153,644	1,700,907
Britannia Beach	10,066	—	785,203	115,349	910,618	2,145,290
Victoria	568,775	195,460	760,817	451,538	1,976,590	1,796,477
Powell River	213,614	56,206	362,109	581,039	1,212,968	1,537,288
Crofton	593,306	2,923	16,084	352,193	964,506	1,495,004
Kitimat	262,902	484,534	161,436	22,218	931,090	1,298,715
Prince Rupert	799,621	16,279	68,751	176,053	1,060,704	1,439,018
Port Alberni	539,764	35,594	80,696	328,467	984,521	1,135,075
Tasu	1,055,324	—	—	5,948	1,061,272	1,062,709
Ladysmith	25,980	14,089	403,643	56,094	499,806	463,101
Chemainus	156,820	13,171	120,455	53,548	343,994	555,694
Vanguard	—	—	240,748	280,365	521,113	656,282
Quatsino	22,371	15,957	96,570	61,265	196,163	392,921
Marble Bay	93,844	—	18,200	34,239	146,283	106,525
Blubber Bay	197,290	—	66,099	2,890	266,279	254,990
NORTHWEST TERRITORIES	453	204	297	106,921	107,875	124,164
Total	112,925,698	70,301,035	59,935,600	59,935,600	303,097,933	302,137,848

[1]Includes Roberts Bank.

15.22 Cargoes loaded and unloaded at principal Canadian ports from vessels in international seaborne and coastwise shipping, by province, 1975 with total for 1974 (metric tonnes) M

Province and port	International Loaded	International Unloaded	Coastwise Loaded	Coastwise Unloaded	Total 1975	Total 1974
NEWFOUNDLAND	2 462 439	3 689 952	2 201 930	2 974 776	11 329 097	12 177 328
St. John's	17 760	6 640	111 850	771 943	908 193	923 308
Stephenville	491 846	—	173 723	371 882	1 037 451	940 807
Holyrood	23 299	313 328	188 567	113 338	638 532	954 279
Corner Brook	193 461	24 312	10 838	330 888	559 499	649 859
Botwood	241 568	54 838	—	132 265	428 671	494 568
Port aux Basques	741	181	77 191	493 612	571 725	579 101
PRINCE EDWARD ISLAND	49 040	10 930	87 470	651 787	799 227	665 399
Charlottetown	868	9 798	87 066	636 171	733 903	603 603
NOVA SCOTIA	6 294 404	8 953 145	5 013 905	2 519 478	22 780 932	24 734 004
Halifax	2 979 443	4 985 798	1 913 412	774 174	10 652 827	12 056 186
Port Hawkesbury	1 353 888	3 680 586	1 903 775	63 790	7 002 039	7 328 511
Hantsport	941 937	—	—	—	941 937	1 519 993
Sydney	480 187	260 792	192 773	1 374 534	2 308 286	1 552 392
Little Narrows	324 509	—	356 449	—	680 958	981 373
North Sydney	7 399	298	467 591	90 270	565 558	575 101
NEW BRUNSWICK	2 664 940	6 611 496	1 744 641	861 907	11 882 984	11 426 264
Saint John	1 906 225	6 137 668	1 733 891	65 784	9 843 568	9 069 942
Dalhousie	484 737	—	—	161 634	646 371	728 341
Newcastle	179 894	—	—	225 825	405 719	571 325
QUEBEC	50 216 301	15 775 060	12 146 979	21 712 960	99 851 300	95 752 561
Sept-Îles — Point-Noire	22 985 318	414 428	3 151 465	841 376	27 392 587	27 512 602
Montreal	4 357 910	3 406 165	4 292 637	4 846 805	16 903 517	17 830 086
Port-Cartier	11 932 964	1 642 222	5 037	2 411 529	15 991 752	13 998 204
Quebec	2 779 963	3 639 132	1 067 115	3 849 979	11 336 189	11 741 461
Baie-Comeau	3 154 573	1 078 167	71 072	2 349 498	6 653 310	3 713 673
Sorel	2 176 827	721 746	12 633	3 174 720	6 085 926	4 725 269
Port-Alfred	321 271	2 890 702	9 948	410 629	3 632 550	4 209 724
Trois-Rivières	801 660	232 245	21 218	1 522 574	2 577 697	3 088 745
Havre-Saint-Pierre	328 932	—	2 338 225	24 817	2 691 974	2 780 169
Contrecoeur	867 092	1 605 905	277 596	424 568	3 175 161	3 263 101
Chicoutimi	—	—	—	613 818	613 818	595 055
Forestville	—	—	512 090	32 455	544 545	32 329
ONTARIO	8 930 838	24 681 616	23 449 168	16 023 307	73 084 929	67 169 845
Thunder Bay	2 812 519	133 292	14 326 189	896 934	18 168 934	16 467 057
Hamilton	170 359	8 028 281	338 766	4 408 452	12 945 858	10 767 712
Sarnia	1 373 845	3 849 285	2 608 494	415 071	8 246 695	7 759 434
Sault Ste Marie	81 716	3 764 884	190 121	1 343 533	5 380 254	4 697 219
Toronto	264 295	1 050 167	199 856	1 195 591	2 709 909	2 531 663
Clarkson	281 427	49 580	167 041	2 373 551	2 871 599	3 300 802
Windsor—Walkerville	347 239	635 429	216 455	562 593	1 761 716	2 897 441
Port Colborne	982 852	227 487	202 087	572 376	1 984 802	2 094 025
Colborne	—	—	2 319 006	—	2 319 006	2 181 664
Picton	548 817	92 910	261 879	53 686	957 292	1 312 220
Goderich	589 864	348	911 410	156 731	1 658 353	1 327 781
Lakeview (Port Credit)	—	1 629 209	—	97 630	1 726 839	1 952 969
Depot Harbour	666 607	—	—	—	666 607	655 916
Little Current	412 362	30 543	31 830	28 760	503 495	774 973
Midland	—	14 952	76 613	867 219	958 784	743 966
Prescott	6 953	52 808	109 190	321 901	490 852	387 975
Michipicoten Harbour	—	161 360	28 937	37 868	228 165	610 685
Kingston	—	5 361	51 590	383 980	440 931	401 780
Parry Sound	—	40 548	3 764	460 396	504 708	554 400
MANITOBA	598 346	27 340	12 839	—	638 525	602 761
Churchill	598 346	27 340	12 839	—	638 525	602 761
BRITISH COLUMBIA	31 227 751	4 026 303	9 715 461	9 531 450	54 500 965	61 454 044
Vancouver[1]	24 060 903	2 817 922	2 451 037	2 894 537	32 224 399	33 349 105
New Westminster	507 365	380 625	708 500	654 387	2 250 877	3 422 586
Nanaimo	586 320	19 749	43 639	502 251	1 151 959	1 594 034
Duncan Bay — Campbell River	239 418	29 118	96 363	681 669	1 046 568	1 543 037
Britannia Beach	9 132	—	712 324	104 643	826 099	1 946 174
Victoria	515 984	177 318	690 202	409 628	1 793 132	1 629 737
Powell River	193 787	50 989	328 500	527 110	1 100 386	1 394 604
Crofton	538 238	2 652	14 591	319 504	874 985	1 356 245
Kitimat	238 501	439 562	146 452	20 156	844 671	1 178 174
Prince Rupert	725 404	14 768	62 370	159 713	962 255	1 305 455
Port Alberni	489 666	32 290	73 206	297 980	893 142	1 029 723
Tasu	957 374	—	—	5 396	962 770	964 073
Ladysmith	23 569	12 781	366 179	50 888	453 417	420 118
Chemainus	142 265	11 949	109 275	48 578	312 067	504 117
Vanguard	—	—	218 403	254 343	472 746	595 369
Quatsino	20 295	14 476	87 607	55 579	177 957	356 452
Marble Bay	85 134	—	16 511	31 061	132 706	96 638
Blubber Bay	178 978	—	59 964	2 622	241 564	231 323
NORTHWEST TERRITORIES	411	185	269	96 997	97 862	112 640
Total	102 444 470	63 776 027	54 372 662	54 372 662	274 965 821	274 094 846

[1] Includes Roberts Bank.

15.23   Principal commodities in water-borne cargo loaded and unloaded at ports handling the largest tonnages in 1975 (tons)

Port and commodity	International Loaded	Unloaded	Coastwise Loaded	Unloaded	Total
VANCOUVER[1]	26,522,605	3,106,227	2,701,806	3,190,681	35,521,319
Coal, bituminous	11,324,982	—	182,677	—	11,507,659
Wheat	4,099,680	—	—	—	4,099,680
Sand and gravel	14,700	908,045	7,300	1,694,704	2,624,749
Sulphur in ores	1,739,487	—	7,937	—	1,747,424
Lumber and timber	1,440,100	7,386	62,407	118,490	1,628,383
Potash	1,877,688	—	—	—	1,877,688
Logs	94,428	30,556	13,280	700,572	838,836
Barley	1,254,746	—	—	—	1,254,746
Fuel oil	219,268	47,360	1,136,573	—	1,403,201
Pulpwood	86,252	1,785	436,137	44,114	568,288
Rapeseed	692,322	—	—	—	692,322
Containerized freight	358,635	401,902	—	—	760,537
Salt	—	347,840	34,684	—	382,524
Gasoline	65,835	—	390,031	—	455,866
Pulp	742,992	5,486	8,870	79,053	836,401
Cement	93,717	21,100	3,728	138,641	257,186
Newsprint	25,441	—	2,170	186,613	214,224
Inorganic chemicals	17,064	28,808	152,946	4,600	203,418
Limestone	118,985	—	5,850	195,687	320,522
Flaxseed	90,604	—	—	—	90,604
Asbestos	56,686	—	—	—	56,686
Waste and scrap, n.e.s.	—	—	29,348	4,700	34,048
Building paper and board	74	37	25,598	128	25,837
Passenger autos and chassis	37	6,510	166	38	6,751
Fertilizers, n.e.s.	68,221	16,817	1,595	—	86,633
Other commodities not listed	2,040,661	1,282,595	200,509	23,341	3,547,106
SEPT-ÎLES — POINTE-NOIRE	25,336,976	456,829	3,473,896	927,458	30,195,159
Iron ore and concentrates	25,321,250	—	3,456,857	—	28,778,107
Fuel oil	—	246,250	64	632,967	879,281
Bentonite	—	150,281	—	16,970	167,251
Other commodities not listed	15,726	60,298	16,975	277,521	370,520
THUNDER BAY	3,100,271	146,929	15,791,920	988,700	20,027,820
Wheat	124,223	—	9,465,387	—	9,589,610
Iron ore and concentrates	1,735,906	—	2,584,953	—	4,320,859
Barley	301,833	—	2,499,861	—	2,801,694
Oats	134,899	—	310,498	—	445,397
Rapeseed	40,316	—	20,906	—	61,222
Flaxseed	131,787	—	23,827	—	155,614
Fuel oil	—	—	—	290,397	290,397
Gasoline	—	—	—	195,673	195,673
Hulls, screenings and chaff	18,960	—	58,822	—	77,782
Newsprint	85,196	—	—	83	85,279
Rye	108,744	—	131,022	—	239,766
Concentrated and complete feeds	205,057	—	2,639	—	207,696
Other commodities not listed	213,350	146,929	694,005	502,547	1,556,831
MONTREAL	4,803,774	3,754,654	4,731,822	5,342,688	18,632,938
Fuel oil	800,122	525,107	2,955,583	695,795	4,976,607
Wheat	1,511,404	242,320	28,851	2,179,456	3,962,031
Containerized freight	780,800	607,204	—	—	1,388,004
Gasoline	59,064	—	1,068,375	336,687	1,464,126
Crude petroleum	—	19,786	14,969	157,466	192,221
Salt	6,886	316,815	8,758	299,000	631,459
Cement	230,510	—	53,862	—	284,372
Gypsum	—	—	—	570,824	570,824
Raw sugar	—	421,895	—	—	421,895
Barley	248,041	—	1,922	497,877	747,840
Corn	110,322	255,898	—	16,478	382,698
Organic chemicals, n.e.s.	68,982	30,662	23,381	3,193	126,218
Coal, bituminous	—	199,535	—	—	199,535
Petroleum and coal products, n.e.s.	9,111	—	23,192	271,729	304,032
Structural shapes	13,996	41,206	35,847	355	91,404
Lubricating oil and grease	68	27,158	144,041	—	171,267
Machinery, n.e.s.	34,503	27,664	33,459	5,382	101,008
Manganese ore	—	103,499	3,538	—	107,037
Plate and sheet steel	15,136	99,803	5,004	36	119,979
Molasses, crude	—	108,258	—	—	108,258
Bars and rods, steel	4,646	86,857	3,169	—	94,672
Other commodities not listed	910,183	640,987	327,871	308,410	2,187,451
PORT-CARTIER	13,153,841	1,810,240	5,552	2,658,256	17,627,889
Iron ore and concentrates	9,098,568	—	3,572	—	9,102,140
Wheat	2,855,524	915,721	—	2,064,329	5,835,574
Corn	591,633	638,627	—	—	1,230,260
Barley	308,256	19,201	—	273,299	600,756
Fuel oil	—	—	—	213,731	213,731
Other commodities not listed	299,860	236,691	1,980	106,897	645,428
HAMILTON	187,789	8,849,665	373,426	4,859,487	14,270,367
Iron ore and concentrates	—	2,651,711	—	4,002,691	6,654,402
Coal, bituminous	—	5,573,043	—	462,331	6,035,374
Fuel oil	—	—	39,563	247,268	286,831
Plate and sheet steel	81,762	17,434	188,328	—	287,524
Sand and gravel	—	168,806	14	25	168,845
Soybeans	—	135,785	—	11,281	147,066
Gasoline	—	—	—	—	—
Other commodities not listed	106,027	302,886	145,521	135,891	690,325

15.23   Principal commodities in water-borne cargo loaded and unloaded at ports handling the largest tonnages in 1975 (metric tonnes)   M

Port and commodity	International Loaded	International Unloaded	Coastwise Loaded	Coastwise Unloaded	Total
VANCOUVER[1]	24 060 903	2 817 922	2 451 037	2 894 537	32 224 399
Coal, bituminous	10 273 851	—	165 722	—	10 439 573
Wheat	3 719 167	—	—	—	3 719 167
Sand and gravel	13 336	823 765	6 622	1 537 410	2 381 133
Sulphur in ores	1 578 036	—	7 200	—	1 585 236
Lumber and timber	1 306 437	6 700	56 615	107 492	1 477 244
Potash	1 703 410	—	—	—	1 703 410
Logs	85 664	27 720	12 047	635 548	760 979
Barley	1 138 286	—	—	—	1 138 286
Fuel oil	198 917	42 964	1 031 082	—	1 272 963
Pulpwood	78 246	1 619	395 657	40 020	515 542
Rapeseed	628 064	—	—	—	628 064
Containerized freight	325 348	364 599	—	—	689 947
Salt	—	315 555	31 465	—	347 020
Gasoline	59 725	—	353 830	—	413 555
Pulp	674 031	4 977	8 047	71 716	758 771
Cement	85 019	19 142	3 382	125 773	233 316
Newsprint	23 080	—	1 969	169 292	194 341
Inorganic chemicals	15 480	26 134	138 750	4 173	184 537
Limestone	107 941	—	5 307	177 524	290 772
Flaxseed	82 195	—	—	—	82 195
Asbestos	51 425	—	—	—	51 425
Waste and scrap, n.e.s.	—	—	26 624	4 264	30 888
Building paper and board	67	34	23 222	116	23 439
Passenger autos and chassis	34	5 906	151	34	6 125
Fertilizers, n.e.s.	61 889	15 256	1 447	—	78 592
Other commodities not listed	1 851 257	1 163 551	181 899	21 175	3 217 882
SEPT-ÎLES — POINTE-NOIRE	22 985 318	414 428	3 151 465	841 376	27 392 587
Iron ore and concentrates	22 971 052	—	3 136 008	—	26 107 060
Fuel oil	—	223 394	58	574 218	797 670
Bentonite	—	136 333	—	15 395	151 728
Other commodities not listed	14 266	54 701	15 399	251 763	336 129
THUNDER BAY	2 812 519	133 292	14 326 189	896 934	18 168 934
Wheat	112 693	—	8 586 855	—	8 699 548
Iron ore and concentrates	1 574 787	—	2 345 030	—	3 919 817
Barley	273 818	—	2 267 836	—	2 541 654
Oats	122 378	—	281 679	—	404 057
Rapeseed	36 574	—	18 966	—	55 540
Flaxseed	119 555	—	21 615	—	141 170
Fuel oil	—	—	—	263 444	263 444
Gasoline	—	—	—	177 512	177 512
Hulls, screenings and chaff	17 200	—	53 362	—	70 562
Newsprint	77 289	—	—	75	77 364
Rye	98 651	—	118 861	—	217 512
Concentrated and complete feeds	186 025	—	2 394	—	188 419
Other commodities not listed	193 548	133 292	629 591	455 903	1 412 334
MONTREAL	4 357 910	3 406 165	4 292 637	4 846 805	16 903 517
Fuel oil	725 858	476 369	2 681 260	631 215	4 514 702
Wheat	1 371 123	219 829	26 173	1 977 169	3 594 294
Containerized freight	708 330	550 846	—	—	1 259 176
Gasoline	53 582	—	969 213	305 437	1 328 232
Crude petroleum	—	17 950	13 580	142 851	174 381
Salt	6 247	287 410	7 945	271 248	572 850
Cement	209 115	—	48 863	—	257 978
Gypsum	—	—	—	517 843	517 843
Raw sugar	—	382 737	—	—	382 737
Barley	225 019	—	1 744	451 666	678 429
Corn	100 082	232 147	—	14 949	347 178
Organic chemicals, n.e.s.	62 579	27 816	21 211	2 897	114 503
Coal, bituminous	—	181 015	—	—	181 015
Petroleum and coal products, n.e.s.	8 265	—	21 039	246 508	275 812
Structural shapes	12 697	37 381	32 520	322	82 920
Lubricating oil and grease	62	24 637	130 672	—	155 371
Machinery, n.e.s.	31 301	25 096	30 353	4 882	91 632
Manganese ore	—	93 893	3 210	—	97 103
Plate and sheet steel	13 731	90 540	4 540	33	108 844
Molasses, crude	—	98 210	—	—	98 210
Bars and rods, steel	4 215	78 795	2 875	—	85 885
Other commodities not listed	825 704	581 494	297 440	279 785	1 984 423
PORT-CARTIER	11 932 964	1 642 222	5 037	2 411 529	15 991 752
Iron ore and concentrates	8 254 082	—	3 240	—	8 257 322
Wheat	2 590 488	830 728	—	1 872 728	5 293 944
Corn	536 720	579 353	—	—	1 116 073
Barley	279 645	17 419	—	247 933	544 997
Fuel oil	—	—	—	193 894	193 894
Other commodities not listed	272 028	214 722	1 796	96 975	585 521
HAMILTON	170 359	8 028 281	338 766	4 408 452	12 945 858
Iron ore and concentrates	—	2 405 592	—	3 631 180	6 036 772
Coal, bituminous	—	5 055 780	—	419 420	5 475 200
Fuel oil	—	—	35 891	224 318	260 209
Plate and sheet steel	74 173	15 816	170 848	—	260 837
Sand and gravel	—	153 138	13	23	153 174
Soybeans	—	123 182	—	10 234	133 416
Gasoline	—	—	—	—	—
Other commodities not listed	96 186	274 774	132 014	123 278	626 252

15.23   Principal commodities in water-borne cargo loaded and unloaded at ports handling the largest tonnages in 1975 (tons) (continued)

Port and commodity	International Loaded	International Unloaded	Coastwise Loaded	Coastwise Unloaded	Total
QUEBEC	3,064,385	4,011,456	1,176,293	4,243,875	12,496,009
Crude petroleum	–	3,380,830	29,309	287,763	3,697,902
Fuel oil	228,890	8,320	944,116	949,224	2,130,550
Wheat	1,194,108	50,916	–	1,130,352	2,375,376
Barley	337,447	9,099	–	493,154	839,700
Containerized freight	265,885	228,437	–	–	494,322
Gasoline	–	21,244	166,423	574,338	762,005
Zinc ore and concentrates	472,960	–	–	–	472,960
Pulpwood	–	–	–	564,480	564,480
Corn	75,905	194,333	–	16,451	286,689
Cement	17,390	–	855	–	18,245
Newsprint	94,557	–	–	–	94,557
Salt	–	23,675	–	74,925	98,600
Asbestos	4,994	–	–	–	4,994
Other commodities not listed	372,249	94,602	35,590	153,188	655,629
HALIFAX	3,284,274	5,495,901	2,109,176	853,381	11,742,732
Crude petroleum	–	4,565,684	45,157	14,969	4,625,810
Gypsum	1,762,393	–	165,836	–	1,928,229
Fuel oil	33,327	42,440	1,317,875	441,066	1,834,708
Containerized freight	668,951	721,156	–	–	1,390,107
Gasoline	77,966	–	556,359	203,024	837,349
Wheat	351,512	–	–	146,795	498,307
Other commodities not listed	390,125	166,621	23,949	47,527	628,222
SAINT JOHN	2,101,253	6,765,621	1,911,288	72,514	10,850,676
Crude petroleum	146,896	6,085,367	–	–	6,232,263
Fuel oil	165,718	7,555	1,453,990	38,135	1,665,398
Gasoline	36,043	–	437,671	34,319	508,033
Wheat	446,523	–	–	–	446,523
Containerized freight	220,559	230,341	–	–	450,900
Raw sugar	–	238,107	–	–	238,107
Pulp	321,057	2,232	–	–	323,289
Wheat flour	164,118	6	–	–	164,124
Newsprint	190,008	–	–	–	190,008
Other commodities not listed	410,331	202,013	19,627	60	632,031
SARNIA	1,514,405	4,243,110	2,875,372	457,538	9,090,425
Coal, bituminous	–	2,662,465	–	–	2,662,465
Fuel oil	1,232,209	–	1,316,441	107,442	2,656,092
Gasoline	191,402	–	1,045,621	–	1,237,023
Limestone	–	1,438,161	–	–	1,438,161
Wheat	–	–	174,624	128,516	303,140
Petroleum coal products	21,128	15,300	45,235	20,026	101,689
Inorganic chemicals, n.e.s.	2,425	–	174,230	5,163	181,818
Lubricating oil and grease	–	–	13,488	125,745	139,233
Organic chemicals, n.e.s.	28,461	–	–	18,386	46,847
Other commodities not listed	38,780	127,184	105,733	52,260	323,957
PORT HAWKESBURY	1,492,406	4,057,152	2,098,553	70,316	7,718,427
Crude petroleum	884,064	4,040,310	242,606	–	5,166,980
Fuel oil	1,904	–	1,507,382	70,241	1,579,527
Gypsum	533,262	–	–	–	533,262
Petroleum and coal products, n.e.s.	–	–	72,763	75	72,838
Gasoline	–	–	275,802	–	275,802
Other commodities not listed	73,176	16,842	–	–	90,018
BAIE-COMEAU	3,477,322	1,188,476	78,343	2,589,878	7,334,019
Wheat	1,696,696	342,591	–	1,248,205	3,287,492
Barley	875,212	83,221	–	809,330	1,767,763
Newsprint	290,631	–	17,805	–	308,436
Alumina and bauxite ores	–	220,608	–	–	220,608
Fuel oil	–	–	–	190,249	190,249
Corn	318,692	173,491	–	164,627	656,810
Soybeans	257,862	269,986	–	–	527,848
Pulpwood	–	–	–	–	–
Other commodities not listed	38,229	98,579	60,538	177,467	374,813
SOREL	2,399,541	795,589	13,926	3,499,530	6,708,586
Titanium ore	–	–	–	2,576,481	2,576,481
Wheat	1,081,329	207,192	–	853,619	2,142,140
Slag, drosses, by-products	735,720	–	–	–	735,720
Pig iron	348,498	–	13,196	–	361,694
Coal, n.e.s.	–	342,677	–	–	342,677
Barley	20,400	20,571	–	38,031	79,002
Phosphate rock	–	–	–	–	–
Fuel oil	–	–	–	20,279	20,279
Other commodities not listed	213,594	225,149	730	11,120	450,593
SAULT STE MARIE	90,077	4,150,074	209,572	1,480,992	5,930,715
Coal, bituminous	–	1,981,997	–	–	1,981,997
Iron ore and concentrates	–	1,373,510	–	1,035,022	2,408,532
Limestone	–	672,069	300	–	672,369
Fuel oil	–	–	–	284,125	284,125
Plate and sheet steel	43,467	–	131,074	188	174,729
Gasoline	–	–	–	157,965	157,965
Other commodities not listed	46,610	122,498	78,198	3,692	250,998

15.23   Principal commodities in water-borne cargo loaded and unloaded at ports handling the largest tonnages in 1975 (metric tonnes) (continued)   M

Port and commodity	International Loaded	International Unloaded	Coastwise Loaded	Coastwise Unloaded	Total
QUEBEC	*2 779 963*	*3 639 132*	*1 067 115*	*3 849 979*	*11 336 189*
Crude petroleum	—	3 067 037	26 589	261 054	3 354 680
Fuel oil	207 646	7 548	856 488	861 122	1 932 804
Wheat	1 083 277	46 190	—	1 025 438	2 154 905
Barley	306 127	8 254	—	447 382	761 763
Containerized freight	241 207	207 235	—	—	448 442
Gasoline	—	19 272	150 976	521 031	691 279
Zinc ore and concentrates	429 062	—	—	—	429 062
Pulpwood	—	—	—	512 088	512 088
Corn	68 860	176 296	—	14 924	260 080
Cement	15 776	—	776	—	16 552
Newsprint	85 781	—	—	—	85 781
Salt	—	21 478	—	67 971	89 449
Asbestos	4 530	—	—	—	4 530
Other commodities not listed	337 699	85 821	32 287	138 970	594 777
HALIFAX	*2 979 443*	*4 985 798*	*1 913 412*	*774 174*	*10 652 827*
Crude petroleum	—	4 141 919	40 966	13 580	4 196 465
Gypsum	1 598 816	—	150 444	—	1 749 260
Fuel oil	30 234	38 501	1 195 556	400 128	1 664 419
Containerized freight	606 862	654 222	—	—	1 261 084
Gasoline	70 730	—	504 720	184 180	759 630
Wheat	318 886	—	—	133 170	452 056
Other commodities not listed	353 915	151 156	21 726	43 116	569 913
SAINT JOHN	*1 906 225*	*6 137 668*	*1 733 891*	*65 784*	*9 843 568*
Crude petroleum	133 262	5 520 552	—	—	5 653 814
Fuel oil	150 337	6 854	1 319 038	34 595	1 510 824
Gasoline	32 698	—	397 048	31 134	460 880
Wheat	405 079	—	—	—	405 079
Containerized freight	200 088	208 962	—	—	409 050
Raw sugar	—	216 007	—	—	216 007
Pulp	291 258	2 025	—	—	293 283
Wheat flour	148 885	5	—	—	148 890
Newsprint	172 372	—	—	—	172 372
Other commodities not listed	372 246	183 263	17 805	54	573 368
SARNIA	*1 373 845*	*3 849 285*	*2 608 494*	*415 071*	*8 246 695*
Coal, bituminous	—	2 415 348	—	—	2 415 348
Fuel oil	1 117 841	—	1 194 255	97 470	2 409 566
Gasoline	173 637	—	948 571	—	1 122 208
Limestone	—	1 304 678	—	—	1 304 678
Wheat	—	—	158 416	116 588	275 004
Petroleum coal products	19 167	13 880	41 037	18 167	92 251
Inorganic chemicals, n.e.s.	2 200	—	158 059	4 684	164 943
Lubricating oil and grease	—	—	12 236	114 074	126 310
Organic chemicals, n.e.s.	25 819	—	—	16 679	42 498
Other commodities not listed	35 181	115 379	95 919	47 409	293 888
PORT HAWKESBURY	*1 353 888*	*3 680 586*	*1 903 775*	*63 790*	*7 002 039*
Crude petroleum	802 009	3 665 308	220 088	—	4 687 405
Fuel oil	1 727	—	1 367 474	63 722	1 432 923
Gypsum	483 767	—	—	—	483 767
Petroleum and coal products, n.e.s.	—	—	66 009	68	66 077
Gasoline	—	—	250 203	—	250 203
Other commodities not listed	66 384	15 279	—	—	81 663
BAIE-COMEAU	*3 154 573*	*1 078 167*	*71 072*	*2 349 498*	*6 653 310*
Wheat	1 539 217	310 793	—	1 132 353	2 982 363
Barley	793 979	75 497	—	734 212	1 603 688
Newsprint	263 656	—	16 152	—	279 808
Alumina and bauxite ores	—	200 132	—	—	200 132
Fuel oil	—	—	—	172 591	172 591
Corn	289 113	157 388	—	149 347	595 848
Soybeans	233 928	244 927	—	—	478 855
Pulpwood	—	—	—	—	—
Other commodities not listed	34 681	89 429	54 919	160 995	340 024
SOREL	*2 176 827*	*721 746*	*12 633*	*3 174 720*	*6 085 926*
Titanium ore	—	—	—	2 337 344	2 337 344
Wheat	980 965	187 961	—	774 390	1 943 316
Slag, drosses, by-products	667 434	—	—	—	667 434
Pig iron	316 152	—	11 971	—	328 123
Coal, n.e.s.	—	310 871	—	—	310 871
Barley	18 507	18 662	—	34 501	71 670
Phosphate rock	—	—	—	—	—
Fuel oil	—	—	—	18 397	18 397
Other commodities not listed	193 769	204 252	662	10 088	408 771
SAULT STE MARIE	*81 716*	*3 764 884*	*190 121*	*1 343 533*	*5 380 254*
Coal, bituminous	—	1 798 037	—	—	1 798 037
Iron ore and concentrates	—	1 246 027	—	938 956	2 184 983
Limestone	—	609 691	272	—	609 963
Fuel oil	—	—	—	257 754	257 754
Plate and sheet steel	39 433	—	118 908	171	158 512
Gasoline	—	—	—	143 303	143 303
Other commodities not listed	42 284	111 128	70 940	3 349	227 701

15.23   Principal commodities in water-borne cargo loaded and unloaded at ports handling the largest tonnages in 1975 (tons) (concluded)

Port and commodity	International		Coastwise		Total
	Loaded	Unloaded	Loaded	Unloaded	
PORT-ALFRED	*354,141*	*3,186,454*	*10,966*	*452,641*	*4,004,202*
Alumina and bauxite ores	—	2,625,868	—	—	2,625,868
Fuel oil	—	35,452	—	371,494	406,946
Coke	5,923	298,272	—	—	304,195
Newsprint	198,906	—	—	—	198,906
Fluorspar	—	53,736	—	—	53,736
Inorganic chemicals, n.e.s.	—	163,168	—	—	163,168
Pulpwood	—	—	—	27,705	27,705
Aluminum	97,153	557	—	—	97,710
Other commodities not listed	52,159	9,401	10,966	53,442	125,968
TORONTO	*291,335*	*1,157,611*	*220,304*	*1,317,914*	*2,987,164*
Fuel oil	56,297	14,718	147,942	217,264	436,221
Coal, bituminous	—	179,587	—	22,344	201,931
Cement	—	—	—	480,875	480,875
Wheat	—	—	7,650	185,272	192,922
Salt	—	85,742	—	144,759	230,501
Raw sugar	—	187,758	—	—	187,758
Soybeans	—	288,573	—	30,760	319,333
Barley	—	—	—	114,954	114,954
Other commodities not listed	235,038	401,233	64,712	121,686	822,669
TROIS-RIVIÈRES	*883,679*	*256,006*	*23,389*	*1,678,350*	*2,841,424*
Wheat	688,583	99,470	6,097	640,607	1,434,757
Fuel oil	—	29,676	—	587,064	616,740
Barley	—	—	4,118	47,326	51,444
Pulpwood	—	—	—	243,527	243,527
Newsprint	157,813	—	—	—	157,813
Salt	—	—	—	38,692	38,692
Other commodities not listed	37,283	126,860	13,174	121,134	298,451
NEW WESTMINSTER	*559,274*	*419,567*	*780,988*	*721,338*	*2,481,167*
Sand and gravel	—	109,900	632,113	265,767	1,007,780
Logs	6,865	—	7,650	174,374	188,889
Pulpwood	95,194	—	85,565	1,000	181,759
Lumber and timber	42,068	106	7,825	1,350	51,349
Cement	30	1,000	9,800	147,320	158,150
Waste and scrap, n.e.s.	1,000	—	3,100	—	4,100
Other commodities not listed	414,117	308,561	34,935	131,527	889,140
LAKEVIEW (PORT CREDIT)	—	*1,795,896*	—	*107,619*	*1,903,515*
Coal, bituminous	—	1,795,896	—	107,619	1,903,515
Other commodities not listed	—	—	—	—	—

[1]Includes Roberts Bank.

15.24   Vessels and tonnage handled by harbours administered by the National Harbours Board[1], 1974 and 1975

Port or elevator	Year	Vessel arrivals		Cargo handled *tons*	Grain elevator shipments *bu*
		No.	Gross registered tons[2]		
St. John's, Nfld.	1974	1,834	3,941,000	1,125,160	...
	1975	1,450	3,280,000	1,035,279	...
Halifax	1974	2,250	16,724,613	13,875,240	17,390,822
	1975	2,086	16,295,974	12,490,801	17,917,173
Saint John	1974	1,840	14,039,081	5,899,426	10,115,286
	1975	1,747	15,214,644	5,394,293	15,965,968
Belledune, NB	1974	68	572,758	714,422	...
	1975	47	447,125	532,472	...
Sept-Îles	1974	1,391	18,873,000	30,539,196	...
	1975	1,343	18,858,000	30,109,129	...
Chicoutimi	1974	143	467,863	665,303	...
	1975	157	503,203	705,420	...
Baie-des-Ha! Ha!	1974	507	3,582,619	4,664,336	...
	1975	442	3,126,522	4,031,193	...
Quebec	1974	1,740	11,864,000	13,929,997	81,108,845
	1975	1,382	11,138,000	12,695,398	78,798,703
Trois-Rivières	1974	948	3,863,000	3,639,778	35,535,397
	1975	733	3,465,000	3,007,631	28,765,938
Montreal	1974	3,931	31,917,543	23,842,036	145,194,693
	1975	4,027	32,554,109	22,664,086	129,577,877
Prescott	1974	59	457,000	401,471	11,941,078
	1975	97	777,000	638,558	13,531,909
Port Colborne	1974	16	107,165	113,404	5,185,207
	1975	34	198,227	259,622	9,014,621

15.23 Principal commodities in water-borne cargo loaded and unloaded at ports handling the largest tonnages in 1975 (metric tonnes) (concluded) M

Port and commodity	International Loaded	International Unloaded	Coastwise Loaded	Coastwise Unloaded	Total
PORT-ALFRED	*321 271*	*2 890 702*	*9 948*	*410 629*	*3 632 550*
Alumina and bauxite ores	—	2 382 147	—	—	2 382 147
Fuel oil	—	32 162	—	337 014	369 176
Coke	5 373	270 588	—	—	275 961
Newsprint	180 444	—	—	—	180 444
Fluorspar	—	48 748	—	—	48 748
Inorganic chemicals, n.e.s.	—	148 024	—	—	148 024
Pulpwood	—	—	—	25 134	25 134
Aluminum	88 136	505	—	—	88 641
Other commodities not listed	47 318	8 528	9 948	48 482	114 276
TORONTO	*264 295*	*1 050 167*	*199 856*	*1 195 591*	*2 709 909*
Fuel oil	51 072	13 352	134 211	197 099	395 734
Coal, bituminous	—	162 919	—	20 270	183 189
Cement	—	—	—	436 242	436 242
Wheat	—	—	6 940	168 076	175 016
Salt	—	77 784	—	131 323	209 107
Raw sugar	—	170 331	—	—	170 331
Soybeans	—	261 789	—	27 905	289 694
Barley	—	—	—	104 285	104 285
Other commodities not listed	213 223	363 992	58 706	110 392	746 313
TROIS-RIVIÈRES	*801 660*	*232 245*	*21 218*	*1 522 574*	*2 577 697*
Wheat	624 672	90 238	5 531	581 149	1 301 590
Fuel oil	—	26 922	—	532 576	559 498
Barley	—	—	3 736	42 933	46 669
Pulpwood	—	—	—	220 924	220 924
Newsprint	143 166	—	—	—	143 166
Salt	—	—	—	35 101	35 101
Other commodities not listed	33 823	115 085	11 951	109 891	270 750
NEW WESTMINSTER	*507 365*	*380 625*	*708 500*	*654 387*	*2 250 877*
Sand and gravel	—	99 700	573 443	241 100	914 243
Logs	6 228	—	6 940	158 189	171 357
Pulpwood	86 359	—	77 623	907	164 889
Lumber and timber	38 163	96	7 099	1 225	46 583
Cement	27	907	8 890	133 646	143 470
Waste and scrap, n.e.s.	907	—	2 812	—	3 719
Other commodities not listed	375 681	279 922	31 692	119 319	806 614
LAKEVIEW (PORT CREDIT)	—	*1 629 209*	—	*97 630*	*1 726 839*
Coal, bituminous	—	1 629 209	—	97 630	1 726 839
Other commodities not listed	—	—	—	—	—

[1] Includes Roberts Bank.

15.24 Vessels and tonnage handled by harbours administered by the National Harbours Board[1], 1974 and 1975 M

Port or elevator	Year	Vessel arrivals No.	Vessel arrivals Gross registered tons[2]	Cargo handled *t*	Grain elevator shipments *bu*[3]
St. John's, Nfld.	1974	1,834	3,941,000	1 020 728	...
	1975	1,450	3,280,000	939 189	...
Halifax	1974	2,250	16,724,613	12 587 406	17,390,822
	1975	2,086	16,295,974	11 331 464	17,917,173
Saint John	1974	1,840	14,039,081	5 351 869	10,115,286
	1975	1,747	15,214,644	4 893 620	15,965,968
Belledune, NB	1974	68	572,758	648 113	...
	1975	47	447,125	483 050	...
Sept-Îles	1974	1,391	18,873,000	27 704 693	...
	1975	1,343	18,858,000	27 314 542	...
Chicoutimi	1974	143	467,863	603 553	...
	1975	157	503,203	639 946	...
Baie-des-Ha! Ha!	1974	507	3,582,619	4 231 414	...
	1975	442	3,126,522	3 657 037	...
Quebec	1974	1,740	11,864,000	12 637 081	81,108,845
	1975	1,382	11,138,000	11 517 071	78,798,703
Trois-Rivières	1974	948	3,863,000	3 301 951	35,535,397
	1975	733	3,465,000	2 728 477	28,765,938
Montreal	1974	3,931	31,917,543	21 629 131	145,194,693
	1975	4,027	32,554,109	20 560 513	129,577,877
Prescott	1974	59	457,000	364 208	11,941,078
	1975	97	777,000	579 290	13,531,909
Port Colborne	1974	16	107,165	102 878	5,185,207
	1975	34	198,227	235 525	9,014,621

15.24   Vessels and tonnage handled by harbours administered by the National Harbours Board[1], 1974 and 1975 (concluded)

Port or elevator	Year	Vessel arrivals		Cargo handled tons	Grain elevator shipments bu
		No.	Gross registered tons[2]		
Churchill	1974	83	535,478	669,818	23,277,345
	1975	49	505,846	704,083	23,620,744
Vancouver	1974	22,813r	78,900,582r	41,899,851	195,532,194
	1975	21,153	80,318,220	38,456,511	219,322,569
Prince Rupert	1974	1,641	3,317,000	1,712,603	26,324,741
	1975	1,484	3,303,000	1,606,803	17,211,038
Total	1974	39,264r	189,162,702r	143,692,041	551,605,608
	1975	36,231	189,984,870	134,331,279	553,726,540

[1]National Harbours Board data may differ in some instances from data in Tables 15.22 and 15.23, due to some differences in physical definitions of the ports, and to the use in some cases of different source documents.
[2]See footnote 2, Table 15.24 (metric).

15.25   Summary statistics of St. Lawrence Seaway traffic[1], 1974 and 1975

Item	Upbound				Downbound			
	1974		1975		1974		1975	
	No. of transits	Cargo tons	No. of transits	Cargo tons	No. of transits	Cargo tons	No. of transits	Cargo tons
Type of vessel								
Ocean								
Cargo	644	5,029,689	805	4,047,953	640	6,143,421	820	8,139,175
Tanker	45	307,735	31	240,374	44	295,082	34	236,957
Inland								
Cargo	1,630	17,733,997	1,947	17,350,558	1,615	25,372,979	1,932	32,432,220
Tug and barge	75	603,953	80	568,729	86	189,614	77	187,997
Tanker	452	1,736,747	343	1,458,207	451	1,860,136	330	1,092,783
Coastal								
Cargo	46	291,273	62	439,776	54	220,595	44	330,538
Tug and barge	27	75,277	25	82,173	33	58,245	31	56,827
Tanker	17	125,564	19	101,789	19	92,260	22	129,933
Non-cargo								
Tug and barge	154	—	141	—	114	—	130	—
All other[2]	92	—	106	—	111	—	120	—
Total	3,182	25,904,235	3,559	24,289,559	3,167	34,232,332	3,540	42,606,430
Type of cargo								
Bulk	1,529	22,077,770	1,439	21,232,379	2,082	33,154,274	2,511	41,404,524
General	402	3,469,572	379	2,665,318	109	504,586	138	345,209
Mixed	73	356,893	94	391,862	133	573,472	180	856,697
Passengers	12	—	9	—	12	—	9	—
In ballast								
Ocean	83	—	274	—	59	—	42	—
Laker	817	—	1,084	—	525	—	388	—
Coastal	22	—	34	—	26	—	23	—
Other	244	—	246	—	221	—	249	—
Type of traffic								
Domestic								
Canada to Canada	1,146	6,585,862	1,275	6,451,992	1,353	14,130,357	1,531	16,899,020
Canada to United States	1,240	13,730,485	1,301	13,285,617	25	105,130	33	263,649
United States to Canada	18	46,789	51	108,239	995	13,259,575	1,022	16,796,656
United States to United States	89	203,675	97	155,384	110	298,767	100	270,973
Foreign								
Canada								
Import	129	590,283	180	560,543	—	—	—	—
Export	—	—	—	—	185	1,418,471	196	1,327,679
United States								
Import	560	4,747,141	655	3,727,784	—	—	—	—
Export	—	—	—	—	499	5,020,032	658	7,048,453

[1]Combined traffic of the Montreal–Lake Ontario section and the Welland Canal, with duplications eliminated.
[2]Includes naval vessels.

15.24   Vessels and tonnage handled by harbours administered by the National Harbours Board[1], 1974 and 1975 (concluded)   M

Port or elevator	Year	Vessel arrivals No.	Gross registered tons[2]	Cargo handled t	Grain elevator shipments bu[3]
Churchill	1974	83	535,478	607 649	23,277,345
	1975	49	505,846	638 733	23,620,744
Vancouver	1974	22,813ʳ	78,900,582ʳ	38 010 905	195,532,194
	1975	21,153	80,318,220	34 887 160	219,322,569
Prince Rupert	1974	1,641	3,317,000	1 553 647	26,324,741
	1975	1,484	3,303,000	1 457 667	17,211,038
Total	1974	39,264ʳ	189,162,702ʳ	130 355 226	551,605,608
	1975	36,231	189,984,870	121 863 284	553,726,540

[1]National Harbours Board data may differ in some instances from data in Tables 15.22 and 15.23, due to some differences in physical definitions of the ports, and to the use in some cases of different source documents.
[2]The capacity of the spaces within the hull, and the enclosed spaces above the deck, available for cargo and passengers; including spaces used for the accommodation of officers and crew, navigation, propelling machinery and fuel. A registered ton is equivalent to 100 cu ft (2.831 685 m³) and it is expected that this internationally recognized measure, like the nautical mile and the knot, will continue in use for some considerable time.
[3]Metric conversion for grain shipments not possible at this time.

15.25   Summary statistics of St. Lawrence Seaway traffic[1], 1974 and 1975   M

Item	Upbound 1974 No. of transits	Cargo t	1975 No. of transits	Cargo t	Downbound 1974 No. of transits	Cargo t	1975 No. of transits	Cargo t
Type of vessel								
Ocean								
Cargo	644	4 562 857	805	3 672 241	640	5 573 218	820	7 383 735
Tanker	45	279 172	31	218 064	44	267 694	34	214 964
Inland								
Cargo	1,630	16 088 011	1,947	15 740 161	1,615	23 017 979	1,932	29 422 015
Tug and barge	75	547 897	80	515 942	86	172 015	77	170 548
Tanker	452	1 575 550	343	1 322 863	451	1 687 487	330	991 356
Coastal								
Cargo	46	264 238	62	398 958	54	200 120	44	299 859
Tug and barge	27	68 290	25	74 546	33	52 839	31	51 553
Tanker	17	113 910	19	92 341	19	83 697	22	117 873
Non-cargo								
Tug and barge	154	—	141	—	114	—	130	—
All other[2]	92	—	106	—	111	—	120	—
Total	3,182	23 499 925	3,559	22 035 116	3,167	31 055 049	3,540	38 651 903
Type of cargo								
Bulk	1,529	20 028 616	1,439	19 261 690	2,082	30 077 051	2,511	37 561 552
General	402	3 147 543	379	2 417 936	109	457 753	138	313 168
Mixed	73	323 768	94	355 491	133	520 245	180	777 182
Passengers	12	—	9	—	12	—	9	—
In ballast								
Ocean	83	—	274	—	59	—	42	—
Laker	817	—	1,084	—	525	—	388	—
Coastal	22	—	34	—	26	—	23	—
Other	244	—	246	—	221	—	249	—
Type of traffic								
Domestic								
Canada to Canada	1,146	5 974 594	1,275	5 853 149	1,353	12 818 844	1,531	15 330 533
Canada to United States	1,240	12 456 086	1,301	12 052 509	25	95 372	33	239 178
United States to Canada	18	42 446	51	98 193	995	12 028 884	1,022	15 237 670
United States to United States	89	184 771	97	140 962	110	271 037	100	245 823
Foreign								
Canada								
Import	129	535 496	180	508 516	—	—	—	—
Export	—	—	—	—	185	1 286 815	196	1 204 450
United States								
Import	560	4 306 534	655	3 381 789	—	—	—	—
Export	—	—	—	—	499	4 554 096	658	6 394 249

[1]Combined traffic of the Montreal–Lake Ontario section and the Welland Canal, with duplications eliminated.
[2]Includes naval vessels.

15.26   St. Lawrence Seaway traffic[1] classified by type of cargo, 1974 and 1975

Commodity	1974 Cargo tons	% of total	1975 Cargo tons	% of total
AGRICULTURAL PRODUCTS	*18,136,200*	*30.1*	*23,642,158*	*35.3*
Wheat	9,508,375	15.8	13,580,747	20.3
Corn	3,091,690	5.1	3,444,515	5.1
Rye	355,382	0.6	262,032	0.4
Oats	502,149	0.8	509,002	0.8
Barley	1,919,609	3.2	2,711,451	4.1
Flour, wheat	37,268	0.1	14,771	- -
Flour, edible, other	15,180	- -	23,717	- -
Soybeans	1,423,723	2.4	1,718,283	2.6
Soybean oil, cake and meal	248,144	0.4	123,130	0.2
Beans and peas	94,208	0.2	136,966	0.2
Malt	88,550	0.1	79,065	0.1
Flaxseed	222,051	0.4	152,631	0.2
Other agricultural products	629,871	1.0	885,848	1.3
ANIMAL PRODUCTS	*254,385*	*0.4*	*154,334*	*0.2*
Packing house products, edible	77,768	0.1	7,403	- -
Hides, skins and pelts	60,319	0.1	45,814	0.1
Other animal products	116,298	0.2	101,117	0.1
MINERAL PRODUCTS	*31,366,785*	*52.2*	*33,082,803*	*49.5*
Bituminous coal	6,486,199	10.8	8,708,245	13.0
Coke	1,349,390	2.2	951,314	1.4
Iron ore	17,839,226	29.7	19,002,064	28.5
Aluminum ore and concentrates	16,570	- -	29,094	- -
Clay and bentonite	290,850	0.5	190,583	0.3
Gravel and sand	113,201	0.2	297,819	0.4
Stone, ground or crushed	1,457,026	2.4	1,250,427	1.9
Stone, rough	5,674	- -	4,380	- -
Petroleum, crude	1,239,629	2.1	182,343	0.3
Salt	1,549,689	2.6	1,494,853	2.2
Phosphate rock	—	—	69,163	0.1
Sulphur	84,571	0.1	34,807	0.1
Other mineral products	934,760	1.6	867,711	1.3
FOREST PRODUCTS	*103,255*	*0.2*	*121,032*	*0.2*
MANUFACTURES AND MISCELLANEOUS	*10,080,198*	*16.8*	*9,582,380*	*14.3*
Gasoline	279,137	0.5	348,897	0.5
Fuel oil	2,656,394	4.4	2,570,389	3.9
Lubricating oils and greases	208,855	0.3	162,038	0.2
Petroleum products, other	155,375	0.3	144,948	0.2
Rubber, crude, natural and synthetic	19,540	- -	26,319	- -
Chemicals	401,938	0.7	422,226	0.6
Sodium products	126,773	0.2	148,546	0.2
Tar, pitch and creosote	87,674	0.1	67,121	0.1
Pig iron	135,223	0.2	136,290	0.2
Iron and steel, bars, rods, slabs	545,736	0.9	615,812	0.9
Iron and steel, nails, wire	67,682	0.1	27,699	- -
Iron and steel, manufactured	2,993,365	5.0	1,838,976	2.8
Machinery and machines	66,515	0.1	91,299	0.1
Cement	280,532	0.5	226,433	0.3
Wood pulp	15,389	- -	57,731	0.1
Newsprint	56,719	0.1	69,469	0.1
Syrup and molasses	51,399	0.1	19,754	- -
Sugar	224,351	0.4	317,103	0.5
Food products	63,221	0.1	145,604	0.2
Scrap iron and steel	136,749	0.2	660,582	1.1
Other manufactures and miscellaneous	1,507,631	2.6	1,485,144	2.3
PACKAGE FREIGHT	*195,744*	*0.3*	*313,282*	*0.5*
Domestic	195,744	0.3	313,282	0.5
Foreign	—		—	
Total	60,136,567	100.0	66,895,989	100.0

[1]Combined traffic of the Montreal — Lake Ontario section and the Welland Canal, with duplications eliminated.

15.26   St. Lawrence Seaway traffic[1] classified by type of cargo, 1974 and 1975   M

Commodity	1974		1975	
	Cargo *t*	% of total	Cargo *t*	% of total
AGRICULTURAL PRODUCTS	*16 452 883*	*30.1*	*21 447 805*	*35.3*
Wheat	8 625 853	15.8	12 320 246	20.3
Corn	2 804 734	5.1	3 124 811	5.1
Rye	322 397	0.6	237 711	0.4
Oats	455 542	0.8	461 759	0.8
Barley	1 741 440	3.2	2 459 787	4.1
Flour, wheat	33 809	0.1	13 400	- -
Flour, edible, other	13 771	- -	21 516	- -
Soybeans	1 291 580	2.4	1 558 800	2.6
Soybean oil, cake and meal	225 112	0.4	111 702	0.2
Beans and peas	85 464	0.2	124 253	0.2
Malt	80 331	0.1	71 727	0.1
Flaxseed	201 441	0.4	138 465	0.2
Other agricultural products	571 409	1.0	803 628	1.3
ANIMAL PRODUCTS	*230 774*	*0.4*	*140 010*	*0.2*
Packing house products, edible	70 550	0.1	6 716	- -
Hides, skins and pelts	54 720	0.1	41 562	0.1
Other animal products	105 504	0.2	91 732	0.1
MINERAL PRODUCTS	*28 455 470*	*52.2*	*30 012 214*	*49.5*
Bituminous coal	5 884 181	10.8	7 899 987	13.0
Coke	1 224 146	2.2	863 018	1.4
Iron ore	16 183 474	29.7	17 238 382	28.5
Aluminum ore and concentrates	15 032	- -	26 394	- -
Clay and bentonite	263 855	0.5	172 894	0.3
Gravel and sand	102 694	0.2	270 177	0.4
Stone, ground or crushed	1 321 792	2.4	1 134 368	1.9
Stone, rough	5 147	- -	3 973	- -
Petroleum, crude	1 124 573	2.1	165 419	0.3
Salt	1 405 854	2.6	1 356 108	2.2
Phosphate rock	—	—	62 744	0.1
Sulphur	76 722	0.1	31 576	0.1
Other mineral products	848 000	1.6	787 174	1.3
FOREST PRODUCTS	*93 671*	*0.2*	*109 798*	*0.2*
MANUFACTURES AND MISCELLANEOUS	*9 144 602*	*16.8*	*8 692 990*	*14.3*
Gasoline	253 229	0.5	316 514	0.5
Fuel oil	2 409 840	4.4	2 331 818	3.9
Lubricating oils and greases	189 470	0.3	146 998	0.2
Petroleum products, other	140 954	0.3	131 495	0.2
Rubber, crude, natural and synthetic	17 726	- -	23 876	- -
Chemicals	364 632	0.7	383 037	0.6
Sodium products	115 007	0.2	134 759	0.2
Tar, pitch and creosote	79 537	0.1	60 891	0.1
Pig iron	122 672	0.2	123 640	0.2
Iron and steel, bars, rods, slabs	495 083	0.9	558 655	0.9
Iron and steel, nails, wire	61 400	0.1	25 128	- -
Iron and steel, manufactured	2 715 535	5.0	1 668 291	2.8
Machinery and machines	60 341	0.1	82 825	0.1
Cement	254 494	0.5	205 417	0.3
Wood pulp	13 961	- -	52 373	0.1
Newsprint	51 455	0.1	63 021	0.1
Syrup and molasses	46 628	0.1	17 921	- -
Sugar	203 528	0.4	287 671	0.5
Food products	57 353	0.1	132 090	0.2
Scrap iron and steel	124 057	0.2	599 270	1.1
Other manufactures and miscellaneous	1 367 700	2.6	1 347 300	2.3
PACKAGE FREIGHT	*177 576*	*0.3*	*284 205*	*0.5*
Domestic	177 576	0.3	284 205	0.5
Foreign	—	—	—	—
Total	54 554 976	100.0	60 687 022	100.0

[1]Combined traffic of the Montreal–Lake Ontario section and the Welland Canal, with duplications eliminated.

15.27   St. Lawrence Seaway Authority expenditure, 1973-75 (dollars)

Item	1973	1974	1975[1]
Administration			
Headquarters	5,907,909	6,071,519	6,421,843
Regional	3,183,531	3,458,176	4,966,314
Operation and maintenance			
Salaries and benefits	11,826,974	13,375,174	19,380,609
Maintenance materials and services	5,588,528	7,041,428	5,951,156
Other operation and maintenance expenses	1,068,812	1,414,820	2,071,025
Total	27,575,754	31,361,117	38,790,947

[1]15-month period ended Mar. 31, 1976.

15.28   Aircraft movements by class of operation at airports with Ministry of Transport air traffic control towers, 1971-75

Operation	1971	1972	1973	1974	1975
Local operations[1]	2,736,404	2,710,601	2,667,345	3,153,170	3,404,782
Itinerant operations[2]	1,999,938	2,234,754	2,586,625	2,539,541	2,993,399
Simulated approaches[3]	159,034	—	—	—	—
Total, movements	4,895,376	4,945,355	5,253,970	5,692,711	6,398,181
Number of towers	53	55	56	57	60

[1]Landing or take-off by aircraft that remain at all times within the tower control zone.
[2]Landing or take-off by aircraft that enter or leave the tower control zone.
[3]Missed instrument or practice instrument approaches without landing. Prior to June 1, 1971 simulated approaches were counted at source as only one movement. A further modification effective May 1, 1972 grouped simulated approaches under "local movements" and no longer under "type of operation".

15.29   Summary statistics[1] of commercial air services, 1971-75

Item		1971	1972	1973	1974	1975
Canadian carriers, revenue traffic only						
Unit toll transportation[2]						
Departures	'000	428	469	524	562	578
Hours flown	"	506	531	590	629	641
Miles flown	"	157,962	163,191	182,796	199,071	206,147
Passengers carried	"	11,082	12,557	15,316	17,225	17,697
Passenger-miles	"	9,561,454	11,488,011	13,596,692	15,392,287	15,651,753
Cargo and excess baggage ton-miles	"	285,254	314,249	337,935	360,424	371,082
Mail ton-miles	"	48,701	53,438	59,642	64,539	64,591
Cargo and excess baggage	'000 tons	170	186	197	210	219
Mail carried	"	39	41	48	53	50
Bulk transportation[3]						
Departures	'000	439	428	445	494	472
Hours flown	"	545	550	634	678	705
Miles flown	"	58,698	63,800	70,757	74,692	79,034
Passengers carried	"	1,402	1,523	1,790	2,011	2,414
Passenger-miles	"	1,941,115	2,010,413	2,482,981	2,716,723	3,928,819
Goods ton-miles	"	48,113	69,478	81,501	81,725	94,384
Freight carried	'000 tons	123	133	162	156	169
Other flying services[4]						
Hours flown	'000	182	202	233	252	268
Canadian carriers, all services						
Revenue traffic						
Departures	'000	867	897	969	1,056	1,050
Hours flown	"	1,233	1,283	1,457	1,559	1,614
Miles flown	"	216,660	226,991	253,553	273,763	285,181
Passengers carried	"	12,484	14,080	17,106	19,237	20,111
Passenger-miles	"	11,502,569	13,498,424	16,079,673	18,109,010	19,580,572
Goods ton-miles	"	382,068	437,165	479,078	506,689	530,057
Goods carried	'000 tons	332	360	407	420	438
Non-revenue traffic						
Hours flown	'000	40	47	55	55	53
Passenger-miles	"	..	..	..	..	..
Goods ton-miles	"	..	..	..	..	..

15.29   Summary statistics[1] of commercial air services, 1971-75   M

Item		1971	1972	1973	1974	1975
Canadian carriers, revenue traffic only						
Unit toll transportation[2]						
Departures	'000	428	469	524	562	578
Hours flown	''	506	531	590	629	641
Kilometres flown	''	254 215	262 630	294 182	320 374	331 761
Passengers carried	''	11,082	12,557	15,316	17,225	17,697
Passenger-kilometres	''	15 387 669	18 488 162	21 881 755	24 771 485	25 189 055
Cargo and excess baggage						
tonne-kilometres	''	416 463	458 795	493 376	526 209	541 769
Mail tonne-kilometres	''	71 102	78 018	87 076	94 225	94 301
Cargo and excess baggage	'000 t	154	169	179	191	199
Mail carried	''	35	37	44	48	45
Bulk transportation[3]						
Departures	'000	439	428	445	494	472
Hours flown	''	545	550	634	678	705
Kilometres flown	''	94 465	102 676	113 872	120 205	127 193
Passengers carried	''	1,402	1,523	1,790	2,011	2,414
Passenger-kilometres	''	3 123 922	3 235 446	3 995 971	4 372 142	6 322 821
Goods tonne-kilometres	''	70 244	101 436	118 989	119 316	137 798
Freight carried	'000 t	112	121	147	142	153
Other flying services[4]						
Hours flown	'000	182	202	233	252	268
Canadian carriers, all services						
Revenue traffic						
Departures	'000	867	897	969	1,056	1,050
Hours flown	''	1,233	1,283	1,457	1,559	1,614
Kilometres flown	''	348 680	365 307	408 054	440 579	458 954
Passengers carried	''	12,484	14,080	17,106	19,237	20,111
Passenger-kilometres	''	18 511 590	21 723 608	25 877 725	29 143 627	31 511 876
Goods tonne-kilometres	''	557 809	638 249	699 440	739 752	773 868
Goods carried	'000 t	301	327	369	381	397
Non-revenue traffic						
Hours flown	'000	40	47	55	55	53
Passenger-kilometres	''	..	..	..	..	..
Goods tonne-kilometres	''	..	..	..	..	..

15.29   Summary statistics[1] of commercial air services, 1971-75 (concluded)

Item		1971	1972	1973	1974	1975
Fuel consumed	'000 gal	519,801	562,440	641,518	713,332	754,335
Oil consumed	"	350	408	354	375	404
Average employees	'000	30	31	34	39	40
Salaries and wages paid	$'000	304,209	345,236	413,341	511,660	603,691
Operating revenues	"	884,404	1,017,746	1,214,069	1,552,644	1,833,207
Operating expenses	"	827,794	941,434	1,133,584	1,481,678	1,766,705
Canadian and scheduled foreign carriers, all services						
Hours flown	'000	1,265	1,314	1,493	1,590	1,649
Miles flown	"	228,458	239,015	266,690	287,290	298,342
Passengers carried	"	15,723	17,737	21,707	24,257	25,245
Goods carried	'000 tons	399	438	507	521	540

This table includes data for Levels I-IV carriers only.
[1]Although most figures in this table have been taken from the audited reports of commercial air-carriers, some preliminary figures have been used.
[2]Transportation of passengers or goods at a toll per unit.
[3]Transportation of passengers or goods at a toll per mile or per hour for the entire aircraft.
[4]Comprises activities such as flying training, aerial photography, and aerial advertising.

15.30   Comparative statistics of domestic and international air traffic, 1974 and 1975

Item		Canadian airlines		Scheduled foreign airlines		Total
		Domestic services	International services	United States[1]	Other foreign[1]	
1974						
Unit toll transportation[2], revenue traffic only						
Departures	'000	505	56	..	..	..
Hours flown	"	474	155	11	19	659
Miles flown	"	134,116	64,954	4,242	8,654	211,966
Passengers carried	"	13,346	3,879	3,461	1,343	22,029
Passenger-miles	"	8,461,816	6,930,471	242,888	1,081,253	16,716,428
Goods ton-miles	"	189,936	235,028	3,301	40,065	468,330
Goods carried	'000 lb.	349,410	176,535	83,694	116,687	726,326
Bulk transportation[3], revenue traffic only						
Departures	'000	477	17	..	..	..
Hours flown	"	622	56	1	1	680
Miles flown	"	53,154	21,538	260	372	75,324
Passengers carried	"	960	1,051	48	168	2,227
Passenger-miles	"	147,641	2,569,082	8,792	56,840	2,782,355
Goods ton-miles	"	45,139	36,586	7	618	82,350
Freight carried	'000 lb.	285,249	27,617	37	2,280	315,183
1975						
Unit toll transportation[2], revenue traffic only						
Departures	'000	518	60	..	..	..
Hours flown	"	483	158	16	18	675
Miles flown	"	140,153	65,835	5,746	6,938	218,672
Passengers carried	"	13,787	3,909	3,592	1,339	22,627
Passenger-miles	"	8,763,229	6,888,524	288,227	727,640	16,667,620
Goods ton-miles	"	208,309	227,364	3,673	30,611	469,957
Goods carried	'000 lb.	366,089	171,808	83,703	118,471	740,071
Bulk transportation[3], revenue traffic only						
Departures	'000	453	19	..	..	..
Hours flown	"	639	66	—	1	706
Miles flown	"	51,154	28,039	194	283	79,670
Passengers carried	"	974	1,441	57	146	2,618
Passenger-miles	"	129,730	3,799,121	8,826	51,668	3,989,345
Goods ton-miles	"	47,590	46,801	27	323	94,741
Freight carried	'000 lb.	311,107	27,363	88	1,040	339,598

[1]Hours and miles flown are those flown only over Canada.
[2]Transportation of passengers or goods at a toll per unit.
[3]Transportation of passengers or goods at a toll per mile or per hour for the entire aircraft.

15.29   Summary statistics[1] of commercial air services, 1971-75 (concluded)   M

Item		1971	1972	1973	1974	1975
Fuel consumed	'000 l	2 363 062	2 556 903	2 916 399	3 242 871	3 429 275
Oil consumed	''	1 591	1 855	1 609	1 705	1 837
Average employees	'000	30	31	34	39	40
Salaries and wages paid	$'000	304,209	345,236	413,341	511,660	603,691
Operating revenues	''	884,404	1,017,746	1,214,069	1,552,644	1,833,207
Operating expenses	''	827,794	941,434	1,133,584	1,481,678	1,766,705
Canadian and scheduled foreign carriers, all services						
Hours flown	'000	1,265	1,314	1,493	1,590	1,649
Kilometres flown	''	367 668	384 657	429 196	462 348	480 135
Passengers carried	''	15,723	17,737	21,707	24,257	25,245
Goods carried	'000 t	362	397	460	473	490

This table includes data for Levels I-IV carriers only.
[1]Although most figures in this table have been taken from the audited reports of commercial air-carriers, some preliminary figures have been used.
[2]Transportation of passengers or goods at a toll per unit.
[3]Transportation of passengers or goods at a toll per kilometre or per hour for the entire aircraft.
[4]Comprises activities such as flying training, aerial photography, and aerial advertising.

15.30   Comparative statistics of domestic and international air traffic, 1974 and 1975   M

Item		Canadian airlines		Scheduled foreign airlines		Total
		Domestic services	International services	United States[1]	Other foreign[1]	
1974						
Unit toll transportation[2], revenue traffic only						
Departures	'000	505	56	..	..	..
Hours flown	''	474	155	11	19	659
Kilometres flown	''	215 839	104 533	6 827	13 927	341 126
Passengers carried	''	13,346	3,879	3,461	1,343	22,029
Passenger-kilometres	''	13 617 973	11 153 512	390 890	1 740 108	26 902 483
Goods tonne-kilometres	''	277 301	343 134	4 819	58 494	683 748
Goods carried	'000 kg	158 490	80 075	37 963	52 928	329 456
Bulk transportation[3], revenue traffic only						
Departures	'000	477	17	..	..	..
Hours flown	''	622	56	1	1	680
Kilometres flown	''	85 543	34 662	418	599	121 222
Passengers carried	''	960	1,051	48	168	2,227
Passenger-kilometres	''	237 605	4 134 537	14 149	91 475	4 477 766
Goods tonne-kilometres	''	65 902	53 415	10	902	120 229
Freight carried	'000 kg	129 387	12 527	17	1 034	142 965
1975						
Unit toll transportation[2], revenue traffic only						
Departures	'000	518	60	..	..	..
Hours flown	''	483	158	16	18	675
Kilometres flown	''	225 554	105 951	9 247	11 166	351 918
Passengers carried	''	13,787	3,909	3,592	1,339	22,627
Passenger-kilometres	''	14 103 050	11 086 005	463 856	1 171 023	26 823 934
Goods tonne-kilometres	''	304 125	331 945	5 362	44 691	686 123
Goods carried	'000 kg	166 055	77 931	37 967	53 738	335 691
Bulk transportation[3], revenue traffic only						
Departures	'000	453	19	..	..	..
Hours flown	''	639	66	—	1	706
Kilometres flown	''	82 324	45 124	312	455	128 215
Passengers carried	''	974	1,441	57	146	2,618
Passenger-kilometres	''	208 780	6 114 093	14 204	83 152	6 420 229
Goods tonne-kilometres	''	69 480	68 328	39	472	138 319
Freight carried	'000 kg	141 116	12 412	40	472	154 040

[1]Hours and kilometres flown are those flown only over Canada.
[2]Transportation of passengers or goods at a toll per unit.
[3]Transportation of passengers or goods at a toll per kilometre or per hour for the entire aircraft.

Sources
15.1 Canadian Transport Commission.
15.2 - 15.23 Transportation and Communications Division, Industry Statistics Branch, Statistics Canada.
15.24 National Harbours Board.
15.25 - 15.27 St. Lawrence Seaway Authority.
15.28 - 15.30 Transportation and Communications Division, Industry Statistics Branch, Statistics Canada.

Communications   Chapter   16

Tables

Communications

Chapter 16

Telecommunications

The size, topography and climate of Canada have significantly influenced the development of telecommunications in this country. Vast networks of telephone, telegraph, radio and television facilities are necessary to provide efficient communication among Canadians and between Canada and the rest of the world. Canada possesses a unique mix of telecommunications systems — federal, provincial, municipal and investor-owned — whose operations are coordinated to carry messages to all parts of the country by land lines, microwave, tropospheric scatter, high-frequency radio and satellite communications systems and to other parts of the world by undersea cable and international satellites.

The almost universal availability of telecommunications service at low cost has been a major factor in stimulating Canada's economic growth and a positive force in binding the country together. The requirement for more and better telecommunications services rises with the increase in population, and keeping costs and rates low necessitates constant innovation.

Canada's telecommunications carrier industry, with $11.8 billion invested in plant, is expanding at the rate of more than $1.5 billion a year. Investment for 1975 was $1.6 billion, a figure expected to reach $2.5 billion a year by 1980, increasing to $4 billion a year by 1985.

The Canadian Telecommunications Carriers Association (CTCA), established in 1972, provides the framework for cooperation on an industry-wide basis for the major telecommunications carriers in Canada. The association consists of 21 telecommunications carrier organizations, each represented on the board of directors. It brings together in one organization the Trans-Canada Telephone System and its nine members, the Canadian Independent Telephone Association, six other telephone companies, Canadian National and Canadian Pacific Telecommunications, Teleglobe Canada and Telesat Canada.

CTCA is active in the affairs of the Geneva-based International Telecommunication Union and attempts to secure, through the federal Department of Communications, the compatibility of the Canadian telecommunications system with those of other countries.

Telecommunications media

Voice communications

Telephony. There are more than 13 million telephones and 14 million miles (22.5 million km) of circuits in Canada. More than 12 million telephones of the national total are provided by the nine member companies of the Trans-Canada Telephone System (TCTS): Alberta Government Telephones, British Columbia Telephone Company, Bell Canada, The Island Telephone Company Limited, Manitoba Telephone System, Maritime Telegraph and Telephone Company Limited, The New Brunswick Telephone Company, Limited, Newfoundland Telephone Company Limited and Saskatchewan Telecommunications. Almost a million telephones are provided by edmonton telephones, Northern Telephone Limited, Okanagan Telephone Company, Ontario Northland Communications, Québec-Téléphone, Télébec Ltée, Thunder Bay Telephone Department and Canadian National Telecommunications. There are also about a thousand smaller telephone companies.

Canadian National Telecommunications provides telephone service for residents in the Yukon Territory and Northwest Territories, parts of Newfoundland and in northern sections of British Columbia.

Each Canadian telecommunications organization is responsible for service within its own territory and for integrating its facilities with those of all other telephone companies.

Collectively, these companies operate the world's longest microwave system and have access to Canada's domestic satellite system — a telecommunications meld which carries telephone conversations, radio and television programs and computer data coast to coast. Through the integrated North American network and Teleglobe Canada's intercontinental connections, the Canadian system can reach nearly all of the world's 400 million telephones.

Each year Canadians place some 2.5 million telephone calls to countries outside North America. On September 7, 1976 TCTS and Teleglobe Canada introduced direct dialing from Vancouver to the United Kingdom, the Federal Republic of Germany, Japan, Hong Kong, Australia, New Zealand and the Philippines. Within the next three years, the service will be expanded to include most major Canadian cities. By late 1978, it is expected that Belgium, Denmark, France, Greece, Italy, the Netherlands, Norway, Sweden and Switzerland will also join the group of countries that Canadian telephone customers may dial direct. For a basic monthly charge most telephone users can place as many calls as they wish in a defined area and talk as long as they like. Originally, flat-rate local service in Canada was restricted to the area served by the customer's own exchange. The expansion of major cities and the merging of small towns created larger communities, bringing demand for more extensive flat-rate calling areas. As a result, most telephone companies have introduced Extended Area Service which enables customers to place calls in a much wider area without paying long distance rates. For this increased service the customer pays a slightly higher monthly fee, based on the number of telephones within his extended area. Continuing increase in the use of the telephone reflects customer response.

Ownership and regulation of Canada's telecommunications carriers varies. The majority of telephones in Canada are owned and operated by investor-owned companies such as Bell Canada, British Columbia Telephone Company, Québec-Téléphone, Maritime Telegraph and Telephone Company Limited and The New Brunswick Telephone Company, Limited. The Island Telephone Company Limited, Newfoundland Telephone Company Limited, Northern Telephone Limited, Télébec Ltée and Okanagan Telephone Company are subsidiaries of investor-owned telephone companies. Two major systems, Bell Canada and British Columbia Telephones, are federally regulated by the Canadian Radio-television and Telecommunications Commission; the other investor-owned systems are regulated by provincial agencies.

Alberta Government Telephones, Manitoba Telephone System and Saskatchewan Telecommunications are provincially owned corporations. Ontario Northland Communications, a division of Ontario Northland Transportation Commission, a provincially owned corporation, provides telephone and telegraph services in the northeastern part of Ontario. Thunder Bay Telephone Department and edmonton telephones are the country's two largest municipal systems.

Many of the smaller telephone companies are grouped in the Canadian Independent Telephone Association. Canadian National and Teleglobe Canada are federal Crown corporations.

16.1.1.2   Record communications

Public message. Canada's public message-telegram-service is provided by CNCP Telecommunications. A joint venture of the telecommunications divisions of the Canadian National and Canadian Pacific railways, CNCP offers public message service in all provinces and territories. Messages can be forwarded or received from any point in Canada or throughout the world via cable and satellite facilities of Teleglobe Canada.

There has been a gradual decline in public message volumes and a correspondingly progressive growth in Telex and Teletypewriter Exchange

Service (TWX). Nevertheless, the service continues on behalf of users who are not on Telex or TWX. Telepost, introduced in 1975, is a service provided jointly by CNCP and Canada Post by which messages are transmitted electronically via CNCP facilities and delivered by Canada Post on the next scheduled delivery.

A unique characteristic of the public message service is that the majority of the users file messages at telegraph offices via telephone and Telex. Relatively few telegrams are filed in person at the counter.

Telex and TWX. Each year some 2.5 million Telex and TWX messages and some 1.5 million telegrams to overseas points are switched through the facilities of Teleglobe Canada; the total world-wide complex provides access to more than 900,000 TWX and Telex subscribers.

Telex, the first North American dial-and-type teleprinter service, was introduced in Canada in 1957. Since then, it has grown to more than 35,000 customers and 160 exchanges throughout the country. It interconnects with Telex and TWX networks in the United States and Alaska, and with networks throughout the world.

TWX has some 6,000 subscribers in Canada who have the capability to reach another 40,000 TWX users in the United States and, through an agreement between TCTS and Western Union Telegraph Company, with 55,000 US Telex users. TWX subscribers connect with overseas customers through International Telex, provided by Teleglobe Canada.

Telex and TWX are now considered universal services, available to some 200 countries and territories, almost half of which are linked to Teleglobe Canada's ELTEX, a computer-controlled exchange permitting subscriber-to-subscriber dialing without the assistance of an operator. Computerized switching integrates the Canadian domestic Telex and TWX networks with the overseas network, handling more than 4,000 messages an hour.

Private wire teletype systems. Although private wire services are still significant in the telecommunications industry, the prime communications users are replacing their private wire systems with computer-controlled store-and-forward systems, or by Telex and TWX.

Data communications   16.1.1.3

Member companies of the Trans-Canada Telephone System and CNCP Telecommunications offer a wide selection of data communications services, making available instant information that is vital to the activities of a modern industrial country.

In business, industry, government and education, information systems have become a basic tool. In most cases, the heart of the system is a computer, required to handle vast amounts of information. The telecommunications links make the computer's stored information available anywhere in Canada, or around the world. Typically a computer communications system consists of a central computer, a number of terminals to access the computer and transmission facilities to link the computer and the terminals. The telecommunications carriers provide terminals, communications processing and communications facilities. A wide range of terminals is provided by many of the carriers: teletype terminals that can be used for computer access, cathode ray tube terminals that display information on a screen and a variety of more specialized machines. Customers may also use their own terminal equipment.

To transmit the data, a number of different systems may be used. Many customers have private-line networks linking their scattered locations. Others employ pay-as-you-use data transmission services. A wide range of transmission speeds is available from less than 100 words a minute up to the equivalent of 50,000 words a minute.

A significant development in data communications was the introduction of digital transmission networks in early 1973, the first nation-wide commercial digital systems in the world. Digital transmission permits reduced costs by more efficient use of existing circuits and ensures greatly improved accuracy, vital in high-speed data transfer.

The provision of data communications in Canada is undertaken competitively by the two major national carriers, CNCP Telecommunications and the Trans-Canada Telephone System. Data communication between Canada and points outside North America is provided through the facilities of Teleglobe Canada. In cooperation with the British Post Office, Teleglobe inaugurated the Canada–UK Data Link on January 1, 1976. Work is under way to expand the service to other countries with the aim of ultimately introducing a public data network in conjunction with the domestic carriers and foreign telecommunications administrations.

16.1.1.4   The network

Three microwave routes and a satellite system form the backbone of Canada's telecommunications network. Two of the routes belong to the Trans-Canada Telephone System, the third to CNCP Telecommunications. Canada's first coast-to-coast microwave system, completed in 1958 by TCTS, and extending almost 4,000 miles (6 400 km) carries the bulk of network traffic. Telesat Canada provides additional facilities throughout Canada over satellite communications, and Teleglobe Canada uses Intelsat satellites, as well as undersea cables to provide the global connection.

Telesat Canada launched Anik I, the world's first domestic geostationary commercial communications satellite on November 9, 1972. A back-up satellite, Anik II, was launched in April 1973, and another, Anik III, in May 1975.

Initial commercial service to Telesat customers began during January 1973 through a network of earth stations strategically located across Canada. Basically, satellite communication is a long microwave link; transmission is comparable to that of existing microwave systems with the added advantage of the capability of transmitting virtually all forms of telecommunications to those areas which had not previously been well served by more conventional means.

The Anik series provides television distribution to all parts of Canada and improved telephone communications to the North, and supplements existing microwave systems. The Anik generation of satellites has a projected seven-year life cycle.

The satellites used by Telesat and Teleglobe Canada are stationed about 22,300 miles (35 900 km) above the earth. Although Anik is exclusively a Canadian domestic system, other satellites in the Intelsat international system and the vast network of undersea cables make it possible for Canadians to communicate with virtually all countries in the world.

Satellite transmission made its debut with the launching of Telstar in 1962, 10 years after the first long distance telephone and multi-purpose submarine cable in the world (TAT I) was laid across the Atlantic by Teleglobe Canada and three other carriers. CANTAT I was laid in 1961 with 80 circuits but now CANTAT II, with 1,840 circuits, meets growing demand for overseas telecommunications.

16.1.1.5   Telecommunications in the North

Anik, the Inuit word for "brother", is appropriate to the Canadian satellites series. The advent of Anik I opened a new era of telecommunications in the North providing reliability, flexibility and new services, including television broadcasting, to remote communities not served by terrestrial communications facilities. Previously, northern communication was accomplished mainly by tropospheric scatter systems and high-frequency radio. Both methods, as well as microwave and land line facilities, are still used as dictated by circumstance.

Telecommunications services in the remote North are operated by Ontario Northland Communications, British Columbia Telephone Company, CN Telecommunications and Bell Canada. BC Tel provides telecommunications services along the west coast to Alaska.

CN Telecommunications covers an area that runs north through British Columbia from Fort St. John and includes all of the Yukon Territory and Northwest Territories west of longitude 102°. Bell Canada serves points east to, and including, northwestern Ontario and from the Quebec border east. Ontario Northland Communications serves northeastern Ontario.

Within the vast expanses of the North, both CNT and Bell Canada automatic telephone exchanges are connected to the Canadian networks, through them to the North American networks and through Teleglobe Canada to overseas networks. Tropospheric scatter and the domestic satellite systems are used to penetrate the heart of the Arctic and connect to the North American continental telecommunications network. It is also possible to communicate within the coverage area through HF equipment with mining camps, oil and gas exploration sites, construction camps, outposts and other centres.

The basic network of satellite, microwave, radio and land line facilities together with the switched telephone and telegraph networks can be expanded to meet the growing needs in those areas for some time to come.

Telephone and telegraph statistics   16.1.2

Telephone statistics. In 1975 Canada had an estimated 860 telephone systems compared to 937 in 1974; of these, 850 filed returns with Statistics Canada compared to 904 in 1974 (Table 16.1). Although the number of cooperative systems declined from 815 in 1974 to 737 in 1975, growth in the telephone industry was particularly evident in the large telephone companies. The largest incorporated telephone company, Bell Canada, operates in Ontario, Quebec and the Northwest Territories. In 1975 it owned and operated 7.9 million of the approximately 13.2 million telephones in Canada. The BC Telephone Company, also owned by shareholders, operated 1.5 million of the total telephones in 1975.

Table 16.2 shows the distribution of telephones by province in 1974 and 1975. Of the 1975 total, 70.2% or 9.2 million were residential telephones and 3.9 million were business telephones. Alberta had the most telephones per 100 population with 62.4, followed by Ontario at 61.4 and British Columbia at 59.9. As Table 16.3 shows, each Canadian averaged 914 calls in 1974 and 922 in 1975.

Table 16.4 shows the capitalization, revenue and expenditure of telephone companies together with the number of employees, salaries and wages paid for the years 1970-75. Provincial figures for 1974 and 1975 are given in Table 16.5.

Telecommunications statistics. Nine telecommunications companies operated in Canada during 1974. This was the second year of commercial operations of Telesat Canada which added over $28 million in revenue to the operation of commercial telecommunications carriers. The operating revenues of telecommunications companies increased from $190.7 million in 1973 to $230.1 million in 1974 or 20.7% while expenses for the same period increased from $140.1 million to $172.6 million or 23.2% (Table 16.6). The property and equipment for these nine telecommunications companies increased by $66.7 million to $856.0 million in 1974, from $789.3 million in 1973. These figures include the investment in property and equipment by Telesat Canada, which in 1974 was reported at $108.8 million.

Federal regulations and services   16.1.3

The Department of Communications. The department, established in April 1969, is responsible for ensuring that all Canadians obtain the best possible access to a rapidly expanding range of communications services. Fulfilling this task involves not only technological research and planning, but also exploration of the complex social, human and economic issues which result from changing patterns of communications. The department protects Canadian interests in the realm of international telecommunications and manages the radio frequency spectrum to permit the development and growth of radio communications.

The duties, powers and functions of the Minister of Communications include all matters relating to telecommunications over which the Parliament of Canada has jurisdiction, not by law assigned to any other department, branch or agency of the Government of Canada. The general development and use of communication undertakings, facilities, systems and services for Canada also come under the minister's jurisdiction. The department is organized into four sectors: policy, space program, research and services.

The policy sector formulates and recommends international and national telecommunications policies and proposes legislation for the government's consideration. This sector coordinates federal-provincial relations and is the focal point for contacts with Teleglobe Canada and the Canadian Radio-television and Telecommunications Commission. It also provides technological and socio-economic forecasts, identifies areas needing new research and development, and carries out strategic planning.

The department's field organization (Atlantic, Quebec, Ontario, Central and Pacific), is primarily concerned with management of the electromagnetic spectrum.

The space sector comprises all space-related activities. These responsibilities include Canada's Communications Technology Satellite (renamed Hermes); relations with Telesat Canada and other agencies concerned with space; development of new space systems and applications; and planning and international functions in this rapidly growing area of communications technology. The Communications Technology Satellite (Hermes) was launched January 17, 1976 from the Kennedy Space Centre in Florida, to begin a two-year program of experiments in communications.

The research sector carries out research and development in the complex field of communications, both in-house and through a system of university and industrial contracts. It performs research and development concerned with new communications and computer/communications systems and services, conducts extensive research in the use of the radio frequency spectrum and provides scientific advice to aid in formulating departmental policy and developing new programs. It also seeks to ensure that an adequate level of communications research and development capability is maintained in Canada. The department's principal research facility is the Communications Research Centre, just west of Ottawa. Responsiblities here are research policy and planning, radio and radar research, and technological and systems research and development.

Within the services sector, the Telecommunications Regulatory Service establishes technical standards for broadcasting facilities and equipment, issues technical certificates and radio operating licences and manages the radio frequency spectrum. Another branch, the Government Telecommunications Agency, provides consulting and centralized telecommunications services for the government.

The Canadian Radio-television and Telecommunications Commission Act which was proclaimed for effect April 1, 1976 transferred the regulatory jurisdiction over certain telecommunications common carriers previously exercised by the Canadian Transport Commission to the Canadian Radio-television and Telecommunications Commission. Telephone and telegraph companies incorporated under federal legislation are now subject to the jurisdiction of the CRTC.

Radiocommunications in Canada, except for those matters covered by the Broadcasting Act, are regulated under the Radio Act and Regulations and the Canada Shipping Act and Ship Station Radio Regulations. The Radio Act and Regulations, in addition to providing for the licensing of radio stations performing terrestrial radio services, also provide for licensing earth and space stations engaged in space radiocommunication services. Radiocommunications in Canada are administered in accordance with the International Telecommunication Convention and Radio Regulations annexed thereto; the International Civil Aviation Convention; and the International Convention for the Safety of Life at

Sea. A number of Canada–United States conventions and agreements are also in effect: the Convention for the Promotion of Safety on the Great Lakes by means of Radio; the convention relating to the operation, by citizens of either country, of certain radio equipment or stations in the other country; the agreement relating to the coordination and use of radio frequencies above 30 Megahertz; the television and FM agreements; and the agreement relating to the operation in either country of radiotelephone stations licensed in the Citizens Radio Service of the United States and the General Radio Service of Canada. In addition, Canada is a party to the North American Regional Broadcasting Agreement.

The Canadian Radio-television and Telecommunications Commission (CRTC). Under the Canadian Radio-television and Telecommunications Commission Act the CRTC also regulates all federally regulated broadcast undertakings in Canada. The CRTC issues broadcasting licences under the Broadcasting Act of 1968. However, licences are not issued unless the Minister of Communications certifies to the commission that the applicant has satisfied the requirements of the Radio Act and Regulations, and has been or will be issued a technical construction and operating certificate under that act. Broadcasting undertakings include radio (AM and FM) and television broadcasting stations, community antenna television (CATV) systems, and network operations. The technical rules and procedures for the allocation of frequency channels and installation and technical operation of broadcasting station facilities are set forth in the department's *Broadcasting procedures and radio standards specifications.* These documents form the basis for determining the acceptability of applications for technical construction and operating certificates and for the control of the technical operation of broadcasting undertakings. The availability of the technical facilities for broadcasting is subject to the terms of the North American Regional Broadcasting Agreement, the Canada–US Television Agreement and the Canada–US FM Agreements. The CRTC also regulates the tariffs of telephone and telegraph companies incorporated under federal legislation.

International telegraph and telephone communications are subject to the International Telecommunication Convention and its regulations or regional agreements, or both. Overseas cables landed in Canada are subject to the External Submarine Cables Regulations under the Telegraphs Act.

Licensing and regulating of radiocommunications. Licensing is the federal government's method of maintaining control over radiocommunications in Canada. Under the Radio Act, radio stations (other than those used in broadcasting undertakings) employing any form of Hertzian wave transmission, including television and radar, must be licensed by the Department of Communications, unless exempted by regulation. The following general radio regulations provide for six classes of radio station licence: coast, land, mobile, ship, earth and space. Various categories of service may be authorized under each of these classes, e.g. public commercial service, private commercial service, amateur, experimental.

The number of radio station licences in force in the year ended March 31, 1976 was 515,222 compared with 395,614 for the previous year. These figures include stations operated by federal, provincial and municipal government departments and agencies, stations on ships and aircraft registered in Canada and stations in land vehicles operated for both public and private purposes, but they do not include stations in the broadcasting service. Licensing activities during the year ended March 31, 1976 include: authorizations 57,723, licence amendments 98,881, cancellations 25,620, total licences in force 515,222, and net increase in licences 119,608.

A large part of the 30% increase in radio station licences over the previous year was because of the phenomenon of Citizen's Band radio, officially known in Canada as General Radio Service (GRS). More than 200,000 Canadians hold GRS licences, and the figure is increasing rapidly.

Radio standards in general are drawn up in consultation with the electronics industry, interested organizations, associations and the general public, taking into account such technical factors as those which affect frequency spectrum utilization, reliability of apparatus, and compatibility under conditions of service. The Department of Communications maintains an engineering laboratory to develop standard specifications and to test apparatus to ensure compliance with the standards.

Licensing involves assigning specific frequencies to each station. Bands of frequencies are allocated for various types of services, often on a shared non-interference basis. Frequency selection, compatibility evaluation, domestic registration (computerized data base with a file size of more than 55 million characters), and notification with the International Frequency Registration Board (IFRB) of the International Telecommunications Union at Geneva are carried out to ensure efficient use of the spectrum. Assignments are made in keeping with international and domestic statutes and regulations, regional agreements and domestic policies. The IFRB is notified of frequency assignments for technical examination and for inclusion, with appropriate "in-service" dates, in the Master International Frequency Register so that Canadian assignments will receive international recognition and be given protection from interference by foreign stations. In-service dates are necessary when determining prior right to the use of particular frequencies.

The enforcement activities of the Department of Communications include the technical inspection of all radio stations including monitoring and measurement of their radiated signals to ensure compliance with the regulations and conditions of licensing; the location and suppression of radio interference; the technical examination of candidates for the various classes of certificates of proficiency in radio which must be held by the operators of radio stations; and the direction of prosecutions in the courts. These functions are carried out through personnel located at five regional offices, 42 district offices, 10 fixed monitoring stations (five of which have direction-finding facilities), eight mobile monitoring vehicles and 13 regional spectrum observation centres across Canada.

Radio aids to marine and aeronautical navigation. Federal services in aid of marine and aeronautical navigation are provided by the Department of Transport. Six regional offices, located at Vancouver, Edmonton, Winnipeg, Toronto, Montreal and Moncton, are responsible for the construction and operation of the facilities.

Radio aids to marine navigation are provided for radio-equipped Canadian vessels and foreign ships using Canadian waters. This safety and communications service for shipping covers the east and west coasts, the Great Lakes, the St. Lawrence River and Gulf, Hudson Bay, Hudson Strait and the Canadian Arctic and includes regularly broadcast weather reports, storm warnings and notices of danger to navigation. Ships at sea may obtain medical advice from any coast station. The stations carry out communications by radiotelegraph and/or radiotelephone and most of them provide connections to land telephone lines. Halifax and Vancouver stations provide long-range radiotelegraph and radio-telephone services to ships. Coast stations on Hudson Bay and Hudson Strait provide, in addition to their regular services, commercial communications for various prospecting and development organizations, make weather observations, handle administrative traffic and assist aircraft with information on landing conditions.

Automatic radiobeacon stations are maintained on the east and west coasts, the St. Lawrence River and Gulf, the Great Lakes and Hudson Bay and Hudson Strait, and provide navigational aid to mariners by transmitting signals on which bearings may be taken. There are five types of radiobeacons in operation: sequenced, continuously operating (marine and dual-purpose marine/air), marker, ship-calibrating and periodically operating. Sequenced radiobeacons are arranged, where possible, in groups up to a maximum of six stations transmitting in sequence on a common frequency, the sequence being repeated continually regardless of weather conditions. Continuously operating marine radiobeacons transmit a continuous carrier modulated by a tone which is keyed at fixed intervals to provide the identifying Morse characteristic. Continuously operating dual-purpose marine/air radiobeacons are provided for the use of both ships and aircraft. They transmit a continuous carrier modulated by a tone which is interrupted eight times a minute for the transmission of a one- or two-letter identifier. Marker radiobeacons, with a range of 10 nautical miles (18.5 km), do not have a characteristic Morse identifier, but can be identified only by the operating frequency. They operate continuously, transmitting half-second dashes for 13½ seconds then remaining silent for one and a half seconds. Ship-calibrating radiobeacons are available at certain locations to enable ships fitted with direction finders to calibrate their equipment. These radiobeacons operate for a six-hour period on the advertised frequency. Periodically operating radiobeacons are located in areas where there is a limited marine requirement. They normally transmit their characteristic signal continuously for one minute in every 10, using continuous carrier and tone-keyed modulation. This type of automatic radiobeacon is designed to operate unattended for long periods in areas that are isolated or inaccessible for part of the year.

Loran is a long-range radio aid to marine and air navigation providing accurate fixes at distances up to 750 miles (1 207 km) by day and 1,500 miles (2 414 km) by night. Two Loran A stations operate in Nova Scotia, three in Newfoundland and two on the west coast. These stations, in conjunction with Loran stations of the United States Coast Guard, give service to ships and aircraft plying the North Atlantic and Pacific routes. Decca is a short-range radio aid to navigation providing accurate fixes at distances up to 250 miles (401 km). Four chains of Decca stations are in operation — the Newfoundland, the Nova Scotia, the Anticosti and the Cabot Strait — giving service to ships off Newfoundland and Nova Scotia and in the St. Lawrence River and Gulf.

It has become general practice to equip merchant ships with radar and important buoys are fitted with radar reflectors to increase their radar visibility. Eleven radar responder beacons are in year-round operation on the east coast, 10 on the west coast, and six in the St. Lawrence River; 10 in the western Arctic and 10 in the Great Lakes are in operation during the navigation season. Low-power transceivers are provided for use in emergencies at lighthouses, particularly at locations that would otherwise be cut off from aid in case of illness.

Radio aids to air navigation are provided by the Department of Transport from coast to coast and from the United States border to the Arctic regions for use by Canadian aircraft and foreign air-carriers flying over Canadian territory.

Low-frequency radio aids operating on the frequency band 200-415 kHz are generally located within a distance of 50 to 100 nautical miles (92.6–185 km) of each other to form the low-frequency airways system. A few are located "off airways" in remote regions and a number of low-power radiobeacons serve major airports as terminal and landing aids. The Department of Transport operates 267 en route, low-frequency aids (four of which are the older type radio range class) and 95 low-power terminal radiobeacons. These facilities are used primarily in association with airborne direction-finding equipment. Voice channels on a number of low-frequency aids are also used for aircraft communications and weather broadcast purposes.

Operating on the higher frequency bands VHF (very high frequency) and UHF (ultra high frequency), the Department of Transport operates 27 VHF omnidirectional ranges (VOR), 77 instrument landing systems (ILS) and 30 tactical air navigation systems (TACAN). At these locations the VOR and TACAN station are co-located and the complete station is called a VORTAC, with 31 VOR plus distance measuring equipment (DME).

The VOR and VORTAC stations form the VHF airways system which closely parallels the older low-frequency airways system. Additional stations are being installed. Use of the VOR permits the pilot to select any desired course to fly to the station and, in the case of a VORTAC, additional information is provided which is a readout of the distance of the aircraft from the station.

Instrument landing systems provide radio signals which permit aircraft landings during periods of low visibility. Radio transmitters provide lateral and slope guidance to the approach end of the runway and also provide an indication of the distance to the runway threshold.

For air traffic control purposes, there are three main classes of radar in operation at Canadian airports consisting of 15 airport and airways surveillance radars with a range of 150 nautical miles (278 km), 10 airport surveillance radars with a range of 50 nautical miles (92.6 km), and eight precision approach radars, which are short-range radars used for landing at major airports.

Radiotelephone communications are provided by 117 ground stations called Aeradio Stations, from which pilots may obtain weather data, air traffic control instructions and other information concerning flight safety. These stations operate for the most part on the VHF band but in the North and on international routes HF is used to provide the necessary long-range coverage. Thirteen of the 113 stations engage in international communications services for Canadian and foreign air-carriers. All these ground stations are connected to a fixed teletype network of more than 48,000 circuit miles (77 249 km) to meet aeronautical communications needs.

16.1.4   International services

Teleglobe Canada, formerly Canadian Overseas Telecommunication Corporation, interfaces with domestic telephone companies and other telecommunications carriers and provides the link between Canada and almost every country in the world in a complex global communications system. Its mandate is to establish, maintain and operate Canada's external telecommunications services and to coordinate their use with the services of other countries.

Canadians now may telephone around the world almost as easily as they call across town. Businessmen contact overseas clients rapidly with international Telex. Over vast distances, television viewers receive live satellite coverage of major sports events such as the 1976 Olympic Games.

When Teleglobe Canada was established as a Crown corporation in 1950, it acquired existing facilities which amounted to three telephone and 13 telegraph circuits. Today the corporation has built up a vast, modern international telecommunications system mainly through interconnections with global networks of submarine cables and communications satellite circuits. A major breakthrough in recent telecommunications history came in 1956. TAT I, the first long-distance and multi-purpose submarine cable, with 36 circuits, was laid across the Atlantic between Oban, Scotland, and Clarenville, Newfoundland, by Canada (represented by Teleglobe Canada), the United Kingdom and the United States. This marked the beginning of the decline of telegraph service, which had long dominated the telecommunications world, in favour of telephone service. In addition to quality telephone service, the TAT I coaxial cable provided picture transmission, broadcast programs, and customer-to-customer teleprinter (Telex) service.

When it was decided at a Commonwealth Telecommunications Conference in 1958 to set up a round-the-world cable system, Canada was again in the forefront. The first link in the globe-circling network, the 80-circuit CANTAT I, was laid between the United Kingdom and Canada in 1961. Another 80-circuit cable, COMPAC, followed in 1963 across the Pacific between Canada and Australia. Canada was also involved in the third link, SEACOM, extending to the Far East, as well as in the 24-circuit ICECAN cable linking Canada, Greenland and Iceland; the 640-circuit CANBER cable linking Canada and Bermuda; and, most recently, the largest of all, the 1,840-circuit CANTAT II. The anticipated final Commonwealth cable link to Malaysia, India, Ceylon, Pakistan, East Africa,

South Africa, and back to the United Kingdom was never undertaken as the world embarked on the next major breakthrough in communications — the satellite.

As one of 11 founding members of the International Telecommunications Satellite Organization (INTELSAT), Teleglobe Canada was the first Canadian telecommunications carrier to work in the field of satellite communications. Established in 1964 to operate a global communications satellite system, INTELSAT has since grown to include 95 member countries and has passed through four generations of increasingly large and more powerful satellites. Teleglobe Canada is represented on the INTELSAT Board of Governors and on the board's Advisory Committees on Finance, Planning, and Technical Matters.

To keep pace with the expansion of overseas facilities from Canada, Teleglobe Canada has modernized its three international gateways in Montreal, Toronto and Vancouver, and introduced sophisticated terminal equipment, automatic telephone switching centres, computer-controlled telegraph, Telex and private wire (AUTOCOM) operations, and video and data transmission facilities. Since September 1976, telephone subscribers in the greater Vancouver area can dial direct to the United Kingdom, the Federal Republic of Germany, Japan, Hong Kong, Australia, New Zealand and the Philippines. It was expected that this service would become available to other Canadian cities over the next three years and would be extended to many more countries around the world.

With succeeding Olympic Games, international telecommunications become more important as media coverage of the events is extended to an ever-expanding world community. For Teleglobe Canada, the XXI Olympiad was a project that meant four years of studies and planning, one-year advanced provisioning of Telex and telephone facilities, expansion across the network and interfacing with thousands of foreign journalists to meet their needs for instantaneous communication with the media outlets they represented. Teleglobe Canada made use of its earth stations at Mill Village, NS and Lake Cowichan, BC and of a transportable earth station set up in Montreal exclusively for the Olympic Games to transmit 800 hours of television programming to millions of viewers in Asia, Europe, Latin America and Africa via the INTELSAT satellites over the Atlantic and the Pacific. This represented more hours of television programming than have ever before been transmitted internationally for a single event.

Teleglobe Canada participates actively in many international and national communications organizations including the Commonwealth Telecommunications Organizations, INTELSAT, the International Telecommunication Union, the Canadian Telecommunications Carriers Association, and the International Cable Protection Committee.

Radio and television   16.2

The broadcasting system in Canada has both public and private components. The earliest legislation with respect to Canadian broadcasting was passed in May 1932, creating the Canadian Radio Broadcasting Commission, but the basic principles for radio and television broadcasting have been revised over the years. Under Part II of the Broadcasting Act of 1968 the Canadian Radio-Television Commission was entrusted with the direction of the Canadian broadcasting system. The commission regulated and supervised all aspects of the system except for technical matters relating to the planning and construction of broadcasting facilities which were the responsibility of the Department of Communications. In April 1976 the commission became the Canadian Radio-television and Telecommunications Commission and was given regulatory power over all federally regulated telecommunications carriers.

The Canadian Broadcasting Corporation, a publicly owned corporation established by Act of Parliament (now Part III of the Broadcasting Act), provides the national broadcasting service in English and in French in Canada. Its radio and television facilities extend from the Atlantic Ocean to the Pacific, and north to the Arctic Circle. The CBC, created in 1936 to replace the earlier public broadcasting agency that had operated since 1932, is financed mainly by public funds voted annually by Parliament, with supplementary revenue obtained from commercial advertising. The head office is in Ottawa and the main production centres are Toronto for the English networks and Montreal for the French. Regional centres operate across the country.

An applicant for a licence to establish and operate an AM, FM or TV broadcasting station, a community antenna television system (CATV, that is, cable television) or a network files application forms with the Secretary of the CRTC. If found acceptable by the commission, a public notice of the application is issued in the *Canada Gazette* and in one or more newspapers of general circulation within the area served or to be served by such station or system prior to the holding of a public hearing. The same procedure applies to an application for renewal or amendment of an existing licence.

16.2.1   Cable television

Basically, cable television is an antenna system linked to the individual subscriber's set by cable through a series of amplifiers, making it possible to bring in signals he could not otherwise obtain. Cable systems are capable of carrying AM and FM radio as well as VHF and UHF television signals. For this service, the subscriber customarily pays an installation fee and a monthly rental of about $5. In 1975 there were 440 licensed cable television undertakings operating in Canada. The largest number, 164, was in Quebec with 132 in Ontario and 76 in British Columbia. In September 1975, 41.9% of Canadian homes subscribed to cable television, compared to 40.4% in 1974 and 34.7% in 1973.

Cable television is recognized as an integral part of the Canadian broadcasting system and policies and regulations that concern it must take into account the effect on other aspects of the national system. Cable television systems (CATV) are operated by private companies, each of which must be approved by the Department of Communications and licensed by the CRTC.

In early 1975, the CRTC published proposals for cable regulations, with position papers, which were later discussed at public hearings in Ottawa. These papers dealt with the community channel, radio services, augmented channel service (converter service), special programming channels, and pay television. In December 1975 the CRTC published *Policies respecting broadcasting receiving undertakings (cable television)*. It had released its new Cable Television Regulations in November 1975 which came into force April 1, 1976.

The policies specified that cable television licensees should: make a contribution to the quality and diversity of the Canadian broadcasting and program production industries; assume an increasing responsibility to contribute to the strength of the total broadcasting system; contribute a unique social service in the form of a community programming channel; and improve the quality of cable television service and the relations between the cable television industry and the public it serves.

The community channel. The regulations effective from April 1976 require the cable television licensee to provide a community channel on the basic service as a priority. On this channel only programming produced by the licensee, or by community members served by the licensee, with or without the assistance of the licensee, is permitted. The commission expects that a continuing effort will be made to develop the potential of the community channel. Licensees will be required, in applications for new, renewed, or amended licences, to state the amounts spent or to be spent on the community channel and to make a separate entry for this amount in their annual returns.

Radio services. The licensees of systems of 3,000 or more subscribers are required to carry the signals of certain radio stations licensed by the CRTC, among them all local FM stations. Detailed specifications concerning regional AM and FM stations and optional signals were included in the regulations. A public announcement July 19, 1976 reiterated the CRTC's policy that licensees must carry stations licensed by the CRTC. The announcement also said that stations should complement, not compete with each other.

Augmented channel service. In the 1975 policy proposals, the question of converter service and fees to be charged for it was discussed. Cable television licensees distribute a basic service — received on channels 2 to 13 on the standard VHF television set — but with a device called a converter more signals can be received. This additional service is now called the augmented channel service. In 1972 the CRTC began licensing cable television operators to provide augmented channel service. A number of fee structures evolved for provision of the service, but the commission decided that the so-called combined-tier approach was the most suitable. Here, the licensee charges a single fee to all subscribers covering the reception of all channels distributed by the licensee on its basic service and on its augmented service. The converter devices may be bought or leased and installed at the discretion of the individual subscriber. The commission's view is that "the channels of television service distributed by licensees on their cable television systems should be considered a single service whatever device is required to receive it in the subscriber's home."

Licensees are required to carry, on the augmented channel service received via a converter device, "any priority service they cannot carry on their basic service. Where this has been done, the licensees may be authorized by the commission to distribute other services on the augmented channel service."

Special programming channels. After public discussion of a proposed supplementary programming channel, the CRTC concluded that it "is not a desirable objective at this time and as a consequence ... favours the present policy of considering proposals for special programming channels on a case-by-case basis."

Pay television. The concept of pay television — payment of a fee to receive television signals, either off-air or via cable — was developed in the 1950s but did not attract much attention until recently. A CRTC paper in February 1975 said that it was questionable whether the Canadian broadcasting system can absorb the impact of pay television service. However, the commission acknowledged "that some form of pay television is highly probable in the future", and that as a result the "over-the-air broadcasters, program producers, and cable television licensees must work together to effect an integrated use of the broadcasting system to assist Canadian production".

The Minister of Communications, in a speech in June 1976, said that pay television must be an integral part of the Canadian broadcasting system. The CRTC in a public announcement June 30, 1976 asked for submissions from the public on how this might be done.

Television broadcasting   16.2.2

Television programming in Canada began in 1952 in Montreal and Toronto, and colour broadcasting in 1966. Of the estimated 6.6 million households in the country, approximately 6.4 million are equipped with one or more television sets. An estimated 61.0% of Canadian households had colour television sets in September 1975 with highest colour ownership in Alberta at approximately 71.9%, and lowest in Newfoundland at 41.2%. Two of the four Canadian television networks are operated by the CBC, one in English and one in French. The other networks are the English-language network of the CTV Television Network Limited which extends across Canada, the French-language network TVA, at present serving only Quebec, and a third private Canadian television network, Global Communications Limited, serving Ontario.

By March 31, 1975 Canada had 742 television undertakings owned and operated by the CBC, private English-language affiliates of the CBC, the CTV television network and the TVA network, (including rebroadcasting stations) independent TV stations number 48.

From the start, the development of Canadian television was complicated by geographical and language factors. About half the people of Canada live near the southern border and have access to programs broadcast by one or all of the major US networks. This fact and the need to maintain a Canadian identity and to articulate Canadian interests contributed to the rapid development of Canadian television services. Toronto and Montreal now rank among the world's principal television production centres in the English and French languages; Vancouver, Edmonton, Winnipeg, Ottawa, Quebec City, Halifax, Moncton and St. John's are CBC regional production centres. Three Canadian communications "Anik" satellites play an increasingly significant role in the effort to bring radio, television, and telephone services to the more remote parts of the country, particularly in the Canadian North.

16.2.3   Radio broadcasting

Despite the impact of television, radio remains an important means of communication for Canada's population. The CBC networks provide a wide variety of programming nationally and private local stations attract a large percentage of the listening audience. About 97% of the households in Canada are equipped with radio. In about half of them there is more than one set, and often there is a radio in the car and one or more portable transistor sets. It is estimated that there is one radio for every person in Canada.

16.2.4   Canadian Broadcasting Corporation (CBC)

Facilities and coverage. The CBC operates two national television networks, English and French; four radio networks, AM and FM in English and French; a special medium and shortwave radio service in the North including native language programs; and an international shortwave and transcription service. In 1976 the CBC owned some 380 radio outlets (full stations or rebroadcasting transmitters), and its radio network service was also carried on more than 100 privately owned outlets. CBC-owned television stations or rebroadcasters totalled about 240, and the CBC television networks also included about 225 privately owned affiliates or rebroadcasters. The corporation has production centres in Toronto (English), Montreal (French), and in several of the main cities across the country.

CBC AM radio networks are within reach of 99% of the Canadian population and CBC television networks cover 98%. Remaining unserved locations are gradually being provided with radio and TV transmitters under the Accelerated Coverage Plan (ACP), a six-year program approved by the federal government in 1974. In fiscal 1975-76, the first 28 transmitters to be installed under the ACP went into service, and more than 80 other licences were applied for and approved by the CRTC. The ACP will involve nearly 700 engineering projects by the time it is completed.

Other engineering projects in 1975-76 included the completion and opening of the CBC's new regional broadcasting centre in Vancouver, opening of the 4,500-mile (7 242 km) English FM stereo network linking eight cities from St. John's to Vancouver, and further modernization of the Radio Canada International shortwave transmitting plant at Sackville, NB.

Olympic Games. As the official host broadcaster at the 1976 Summer Olympics in Montreal, the CBC provided facilities for world-wide radio and television coverage. A special CBC unit, the Olympics Radio and Television Organization (ORTO), planned and coordinated broadcasting installations at the 27 different Olympic sites as well as studios, control rooms and office facilities in three Montreal broadcasting centres. Some 180 foreign broadcasting organizations were represented at the Olympics, and ORTO provided them with coverage which reached a total international audience of more than a billion people. The CBC's French and English domestic networks also used the ORTO service and provided Canadian listeners and viewers with day-long coverage throughout the two weeks of the games.

General programming. CBC radio and television continued to offer varied program schedules in news, current affairs, music, drama, sports, religion, science, children's programs, consumer interests and light entertainment. With the introduction of FM stereo networks, CBC radio planners looked forward to new developments in both AM and FM programming, and made a particular study of requirements in the arts. The Northern Radio Service combined network programming with local and regional broadcasts in English, French and 10 native languages and dialects. One of the important goals for CBC television was to maintain attractive Canadian programs in competition with other sources of television.

All CBC networks supported the work of Canadian artists and performers through presentation of Canadian drama, literature, music and films. CBC programs or performers won more than 60 awards in Canadian and international competitions. Selected programs from English and French CBC television networks were made available for post-broadcast distribution to educational bodies through the National Film Board.

International activities. Radio Canada International (RCI), the CBC's overseas shortwave service with headquarters in Montreal, broadcasts daily in 11 languages and distributes free recorded programs for use by broadcasters throughout the world. A new RCI development in 1976 was the rebroadcast of the CBC's popular current affairs program *As It Happens* to audiences in the southern United States and the Caribbean. A weekly digest of *As It Happens,* together with Canadian material in French, was relayed to Canadian listeners in continental Europe. A tape service of topical Canadian material was developed for about 700 Mexican radio stations, and trial tape services were started for the Caribbean and Japan.

Under agreement with the Department of National Defence, the CBC Armed Forces Service provides recorded and shortwave programs for Canadian Forces radio stations in the Federal Republic of Germany, with staff seconded to manage the stations. The Armed Forces Service reports to Radio Canada International.

CBC continued activities as a member of various international broadcasting organizations. Highlights of 1976 included hosting the second International Symposium on Radio in the 80s, held in Ottawa, and participation in major co-productions for the 20th anniversary of the Communauté radio-phonique des programmes de langue française, celebrated in Montreal. CBC experts were seconded as instructors in Barbados, Jamaica and Senegal and a number of foreign broadcasters were accepted for training attachments with the CBC. English and French CBC programs were sold to about 20 different countries, and exchanges of television programs were arranged with the USSR, Poland and Hungary. CBC also acted as official host broadcaster at the 1976 United Nations Conference on Human Habitation in Vancouver.

Finance. The CBC's total operating expenses for the fiscal year 1975-76 were $395 million, including $10.7 million for the 1976 Summer Olympics. This operating budget was provided by parliamentary appropriation of $287 million, general revenues of $74 million (including $71 million from commercials), a contribution of $10.5 million from the Olympics Organizing Committee (COJO), with the balance represented by depreciation. The expenditure for capital assets was $55 million of the $56 million parliamentary vote.

In constant dollars the increase in expenditures in 1975-76 was 6.2% over that of 1974-75. The largest part of the increase in operating expenditures went to the financing of price and wage increases. The balance was allocated to programming improvements and the operation of new facilities.

16.2.5   Statistics of the broadcasting industry

Statistics on radio and television broadcasting are obtained by Statistics Canada in cooperation with the Canadian Radio-television and Telecommunications Commission. In 1975 returns were received from 282 private radio reporting units and 65 television reporting units covering the operation of 391 private radio stations, 59 private originating television stations and the CTV network. Operating revenue of the broadcasting industry, including CBC, for the year amounted to $505.8 million, an increase of 18.6% over 1974. Of the total, radio accounted for $210.3 million or 41.6% and television for $295.5 million or 58.4%. Revenue from national and network time sales represented 54.0% of the total air time sales and local time sales were 46.0%. Operating expenses in 1975 at $665.8 million were 13.7% higher than in 1974. However, total operating revenue, plus the net cost of operating the CBC, which is financed from its parliamentary grant, exceeded these expenses, resulting in a net profit after depreciation and interest charges and other adjustment of $70.6 million for 1975 compared to $52.7 million in 1974.

In 1975 there were 23,496 employees engaged in the radio and television broadcasting industry, an increase of 1,235 or 5.5% over 1974. Salaries and wages paid by the industry totalled $346.7 million. After provision for income taxes, the final net profit of the private sector of the broadcasting industry in 1975 was $34.4 million compared with $21.4 million in 1974. The impression of an immediate upswing in television broadcasting profits in 1975 should be tempered by the substantial losses of Global Communications Limited in 1974 which depressed television broadcasting profits in that year.

Statistics of the cable television industry. Table 16.7 presents financial statistics of the Canadian cable television industry. This industry, comprising 338 operating systems, reported an increase of 21.6% in total operating revenue for the year ended August 31, 1975, rising to $162.3 million from $133.4 million for the previous year. Subscription revenue from individual subscribers and multi-outlet contracts accounted for $149.6 million. Operating expenses before deducting interest and depreciation charges rose from $66.5 million to $85.8 million in 1975, resulting in net operating revenue of $76.5 million compared with $66.9 million in the previous year. After deducting interest, depreciation and making other adjustments, the industry achieved a net profit to August 31, 1975 of $30.4 million compared with $28.4 million earned in the previous year.

16.3   Postal service

The basic function of the Canadian Postal Service is to receive, convey and deliver postal matter with speed and security. To do this it maintains thousands of post offices and uses air, rail, road and water transportation facilities. Associated functions include sales of stamps and other articles of postage, registration of letters and other mail for dispatch, parcel insurance, accounting for COD articles and transaction of money-order business. Because of its transcontinental facilities, the Post Office assists other government departments with such tasks as selling hunting permits, collecting annuity payments, distributing income tax forms and public service employment application forms, and displaying official posters.

Post offices are established wherever the population warrants. In rural areas and small urban centres they transact all the functions of a city office. In larger urban areas, postal stations have functions similar to the main post office, including general delivery service, lock-box delivery and letter-carrier delivery. Canada's larger postal installations are complex, semi- or fully-automated plants with Optical Character Reading Machines (OCRs) capable of reading printed or typed addresses; machines which automatically and at high high speed cull, face and cancel stamps; Letter Sorting Machines (LSMS) capable of handling 26,000 pieces of mail an hour; conveyors and chutes, parcel and bag sorting machines, wrapomatic parcel sealing machines, photo-electric counters and intercom systems. Outside some of the regular post office buildings there are stamp-vending machines and curbside mail boxes.

The operating service of the Post Office Department is organized into four regions which are divided into districts. The operating and support functions required to provide postal service to the public are the responsibility of local postmasters who receive technical and administrative assistance from district and regional offices at strategic points.

Postal service is provided throughout Canada. The country's airmail system utilizes most transcontinental flights, supported by many branch and connecting lines, and links up with United States domestic and other international airmail systems. First-class domestic mail is carried by air between Canadian points whenever this expedites delivery. Air stage routes provide an all-class mail service to many northern areas which can be served only by air. There are over 46,000 miles (74 030 km) of airmail and air stage routes.

The Assured Mail Program, guaranteeing next-delivery-day service of first-class letters if mailed early in the day, launched in Toronto in 1971, was extended to all major Canadian cities in 1972. By late 1973 the country was completely coded with postal coding machines operating in the main Ottawa postal station. By January 1975, coding machinery was in operation in six other Canadian centres, Winnipeg, Regina, Saskatoon, Calgary, Edmonton and Toronto.

The gradual movement of Canadians from rural to urban areas was responded to by the Post Office through expanded and improved customer service, and by the end of the fiscal year 1975-76 there were 8,506 postal facilities in operation in Canada. With the growth in urban density, letter-carrier service grew to provide more convenient service to city dwellers. By the end of March 1976, an additional 272,085 new points of call were added to the 5,236,843 already being served through 12,480 full and 469 partial letter-carrier routes from 279 post offices. Rural and suburban services were reduced slightly owing to the lessened demand. The number of rural routes decreased by 14 to 4,942 and suburban service reduced by one to 44.

Revenue and expenditure of the Post Office Department for the year ended March 31, 1976 were $568 million and $768.3 million, respectively; gross revenue receipts were received mainly from postage, either in the form of postage stamps and stamped stationery, postage meter and postage register machine impressions, or in cash. During the year 34 million money orders were issued having a value of $1,089 million.

The press   16.4

Daily newspapers published in Canada in 1976 numbered 117, counting morning and evening editions separately. Combined circulation was about 5 million — 82% in English and 18% in French (Table 16.8). Publishers' surveys show that each newspaper is read by an average of three persons.

Daily newspaper advertising net revenue in 1974 was $483.0 million and circulation revenue was $120.3 million. In 1975, there were 17 daily newspapers with a circulation in excess of 100,000, accounting for 61% of total circulation. There were 13 dailies published in the French language, 11 of them located in Quebec. Although the circulation of daily newspapers blankets the more populous areas well beyond publishing points, smaller cities and towns and rural areas are also served by 825 weekly newspapers catering to local interests and exercising important local influence. The Canadian society is also enriched by 247 newspapers and periodicals published in Canada by ethno-cultural groups.

About 30% of Canada's daily newspapers are privately owned or independent. There are three major newspaper chains in the country, Southam Press Ltd. (14 dailies), Thomson Newspapers Ltd. (34 dailies) and FP Publications Ltd. (nine dailies). Both Southam and Thomson Newspapers are publicly owned companies with shares traded on Canadian stock exchanges. Papers in the Thomson chain are concentrated in the smaller cities. Southam accounts for about 21% of total daily circulation, Thomson for 10% and FP for about 21%.

In addition to their own news-gathering staffs and facilities, Canadian newspapers subscribe to a number of syndicated agencies and wire services, the largest being The Canadian Press which is a cooperative agency owned and operated by Canadian dailies. Largely by teletype and wirephoto transmission, it provides its 109 member newspapers with world and Canadian news and also serves radio and television stations. CP has its own news-gathering staff and each member newspaper provides important local news for transmission to fellow members. Members share the cost in ratio to their circulations.

CP carries world news from Reuters (the British agency), from The Associated Press (the United States cooperative) and from Agence France-Presse (of France) and these agencies receive CP news on a reciprocal basis. CP maintains a French-language service in Quebec.

United Press International of Canada, the second major news wire service in Canada, is a private company and a part of United Press International World Service. It provides Canadian and international news and pictures to newspapers and TV and radio stations across Canada and is an outlet for Canadian news through United Press International facilities throughout the world. Certain foreign newspapers maintain bureaus in Ottawa and elsewhere in Canada to collect and interpret Canadian news.

Press statistics. Table 16.8 gives numbers and circulations of reporting English- and French-language newspapers, by province, for 1975 and 1976, estimated from *Canadian Advertising*. Circulation figures are given for daily English- and French-language newspapers only. Such circulation figures are relatively easy to obtain because, in their own interest, newspapers qualify for and subscribe to the Audit Bureau of Circulation. For these, ABC "net paid" figures have been used; "controlled" (free) distribution newspapers are not included. On the other hand, circulation data for foreign-language newspapers, weekly newspapers, weekend newspapers and magazines are incomplete. Ethno-cultural publications numbered 247 in 1976 (Table 16.9); 31 were Ukrainian, 23 Italian, 18 German, 17 Jewish, 12 Polish, 11 each published by Blacks, Dutch and Portuguese, 10 each by Chinese and Hungarian groups and smaller numbers for people of 27 additional groups or national origins, as well as four inter-ethnic publications.

Ethnic Press Analysis Service. During 1975-76 the Ethnic Press Analysis Service, Department of Secretary of State, received and analyzed over 200 ethnic newspapers and periodicals in more than 30 languages. The analysis of the ethnic publications was carried out by a staff of 15 contract analysts. The information gathered from the press was used to prepare a monthly review entitled the *Canadian Ethnic Press Review*. This publication, produced in a limited edition, is distributed to officers and libraries of various government departments and agencies. The service also carried on liaison activities with the Canada Ethnic Press Federation and its four affiliated press associations in Toronto, Montreal, Winnipeg and Vancouver.

Native Communications Program. The Native Communications Program received Cabinet and Treasury Board approval in early 1974. Grants are provided under two sub-programs: Resource Organizations and Native Association Newspapers. The first provides funds to communications societies set up to serve the communications needs of all native people in a given area. The second offers a maximum grant of $25,000 to eligible associations that are receiving core funding from the department, as well as to the National Association of Friendship Centres. In 1975-76, 19 grants were made at a total cost of $1.5 million. Of these grants, 10 were to native association newspapers.

The largest communications society funded by the Secretary of State Department under this program is the Alberta Native Communications Society, which received $300,000 in grants during the fiscal year. In the 10 years of its existence the society has grown from a weekly 15-minute radio program to include films, video tapes and radio programming on eight broadcast stations and educational programming on radio and television. It provides consultation services and theatre, as well as training for 10 native students in community colleges, on all phases of communications.

Sources
16.1 - 16.1.1 Canadian Telecommunications Carriers Association.
16.1.2 Transportation and Communications Division, Industry Statistics Branch, Statistics Canada.
16.1.3 Information Services, Department of Communications; Public Affairs, Department of Transport.
16.1.4 Teleglobe Canada.
16.2 - 16.2.3 Information Services, Canadian Radio-television and Telecommunications Commission.
16.2.4 Audience Services, Canadian Broadcasting Corporation.
16.2.5 Transportation and Communications Division, Industry Statistics Branch, Statistics Canada.
16.3 Public Affairs Branch, Post Office Department.
16.4 The Canadian Press; Canadian Daily Newspaper Publishers Association; United Press International of Canada Ltd.; Ethnic Press Analysis Service, Department of the Secretary of State; Native Citizens' Directorate, Department of the Secretary of State.

Tables

..	not available	e	estimate
...	not appropriate or not applicable	p	preliminary
—	nil or zero	r	revised
- -	too small to be expressed		certain tables may not add due to rounding

16.1 Pole-line and wire mileage and number of telephones in use, 1970-75

Year	Systems reporting	Route mileage	Length of wire *miles*	Telephones in use Business	Residential	Total	Per 100 population
1970	1,376	297,727	56,230,618	2,853,601	6,896,410	9,750,011	45.2
1971	1,171	298,235	59,199,244	2,996,276	7,272,505	10,268,781	47.3
1972	1,170	303,000	62,996,211	3,183,076	7,804,065	10,987,141	50.0
1973	985	342,000	67,940,003	3,428,292	8,249,152	11,677,444	52.3
1974	904	351,000	73,132,711	3,691,581	8,762,750	12,454,331	55.0
1975	850	334,000	77,668,111	3,928,375	9,236,635	13,165,010	57.2

16.1 Pole-line and wire length and number of telephones in use, 1970-75   M

Year	Systems reporting	Route length *km*	Length of wire *km*	Telephones in use Business	Residential	Total	Per 100 population
1970	1,376	479 145	90 494 408	2,853,601	6,896,410	9,750,011	45.2
1971	1,171	471 916	95 271 948	2,996,276	7,272,505	10,268,781	47.3
1972	1,170	487 631	101 382 574	3,183,076	7,804,065	10,987,141	50.0
1973	985	550 396	109 338 836	3,428,292	8,249,152	11,677,444	52.3
1974	904	564 880	117 695 690	3,691,581	8,762,750	12,454,331	55.0
1975	850	537 521	124 994 708	3,928,375	9,236,635	13,165,010	57.2

16.2 Telephones in use, by province, 1974 and 1975

Year and province or territory	Telephones On private lines Business	Residential	On party lines Business	Residential	Extensions Business	Residential	Coin telephones Business
1974							
Newfoundland	17,296	84,168	1,324	28,062	14,473	22,783	1,625
Prince Edward Island	2,847	16,947	389	11,281	2,235	5,575	317
Nova Scotia	19,391	173,647	1,689	46,573	12,415	58,773	3,668
New Brunswick	22,395	129,282	1,131	41,445	27,041	48,222	2,016
Quebec	262,338	1,515,126	7,676	284,704	232,181	464,574	23,681
Ontario	379,602	2,102,533	10,826	432,612	310,156	874,414	32,023
Manitoba	46,983	256,232	3,211	56,916	36,173	71,924	3,400
Saskatchewan	37,271	201,953	2,460	65,532	28,167	64,777	3,127
Alberta	90,475	464,707	3,084	67,672	77,680	171,569	7,488
British Columbia	122,382	510,908	3,115	250,186	91,623	226,101	8,217
Yukon Territory	1,686	2,653	123	1,729	1,134	759	104
Northwest Territories	3,116	5,878	116	1,179	1,771	1,151	169
Canada	1,005,782	5,464,034	35,144	1,287,891	835,049	2,010,622	85,835

	Private branch exchanges Business	Residential	WATS[1] Business	Centrex Business	Mobile Business	Total	Telephones per 100 population
Newfoundland	18,268	—	—	259	267	188,525	34.5
Prince Edward Island	6,235	12	—	—	28	45,866	38.9
Nova Scotia	55,790	75	1	9,080	143	381,245	46.6
New Brunswick	21,982	—	179	6,327	141	300,161	44.8
Quebec	335,266	47	1,772	117,890	765	3,246,020	52.6
Ontario	518,453	60	2,984	192,581	1,293	4,857,537	59.4
Manitoba	63,561	9	168	4,892	87	543,556	53.6
Saskatchewan	41,144	—	23	—	545	444,999	48.8
Alberta	129,010	—	88	7,151	7,906	1,026,830	58.8
British Columbia	153,702	—	399	24,245	3,294	1,394,172	57.1
Yukon Territory	1,821	—	—	—	—	10,009	50.0
Northwest Territories	2,024	—	—	—	7	15,411	41.6
Canada	1,347,256	203	5,614	362,425	14,476	12,454,331	55.0

16.2   Telephones in use, by province, 1974 and 1975 (concluded)

Year and province or territory	Telephones						
	On private lines		On party lines		Extensions		Coin telephones
	Business	Residential	Business	Residential	Business	Residential	Business
1975							
Newfoundland	17,233	88,985	1,673	28,905	16,540	25,179	1,716
Prince Edward Island	4,598	18,017	398	11,850	3,534	6,411	301
Nova Scotia	33,923	179,839	1,574	45,759	29,173	61,134	3,477
New Brunswick	24,098	139,699	1,082	40,557	30,657	53,019	2,084
Quebec	274,294	1,592,710	7,861	286,907	241,330	509,798	24,884
Ontario	404,290	2,207,281	9,082	424,232	327,437	932,104	33,719
Manitoba	49,217	264,352	3,294	56,912	41,356	81,557	3,504
Saskatchewan	39,061	211,748	2,517	67,252	30,972	74,437	3,017
Alberta	102,527	494,572	3,298	69,695	84,007	201,203	8,004
British Columbia	132,254	563,176	3,035	237,733	96,798	246,914	8,410
Yukon Territory	1,793	2,973	160	1,710	1,128	850	126
Northwest Territories	3,437	6,390	102	1,071	1,990	1,604	189
Canada	1,086,725	5,769,742	34,076	1,272,583	904,922	2,194,210	89,431

	Private branch exchanges		WATS[1]	Centrex	Mobile	Total	Telephones per 100 population
	Business	Residential	Business	Business	Business		
Newfoundland	19,140	—	—	181	320	199,872	36.1
Prince Edward Island	4,005	—	—	—	42	49,156	41.0
Nova Scotia	29,637	—	1	9,436	266	394,219	47.5
New Brunswick	22,137	—	—	7,201	177	320,711	46.9
Quebec	350,751	46	2,288	131,710	826	3,423,405	55.0
Ontario	532,432	54	3,734	215,821	1,523	5,091,709	61.4
Manitoba	67,521	—	181	3,519	90	571,503	55.9
Saskatchewan	42,083	—	31	4,360	729	476,207	51.3
Alberta	140,844	—	—	10,199	10,962	1,125,311	62.4
British Columbia	165,663	—	515	27,184	3,546	1,485,228	59.9
Yukon Territory	1,853	—	—	—	—	10,593	50.4
Northwest Territories	2,306	—	—	—	7	17,096	45.0
Canada	1,378,372	100	6,750	409,611	18,488	13,165,010	57.2

[1]On wide area telephone service lines.

16.3   Local and long-distance calls, calls per capita and average calls per telephone, 1970-75

Year	Local calls '000	Long-distance calls '000	Total calls '000	Calls per capita	Average calls per telephone		
					Local	Long-distance	Total
1970	15,436,847	458,397	15,895,244	737	1,583	47	1,630
1971	16,439,365	495,454	16,934,819	779	1,601	48	1,649
1972	17,776,963	571,944	18,348,907	835	1,618	52	1,670
1973	18,396,642	658,248	19,054,890	854	1,575	56	1,631
1974	19,936,758	764,248	20,701,006	914	1,601	61	1,662
1975	20,340,605	853,504	21,194,109	922	1,545	65	1,610

16.4   Financial statistics of telephone systems, 1970-75

Year	Capital stock[1] $'000	Long-term debt $'000	Cost of plant $'000	Revenue $'000	Expenditure $'000	Full-time employees	Salaries and wages[2] $'000
1970	1,827,746	2,522,040	6,571,028	1,568,726	1,366,645	68,334	540,674
1971	2,005,304	2,861,144	7,255,226	1,725,302	1,504,854	69,995	600,949
1972	2,067,681	3,065,290	7,960,368	1,924,840	1,673,433	72,671	681,187
1973	2,149,479	3,297,124	8,791,434	2,200,702	1,920,424	75,407	775,700
1974	2,308,008	3,764,305	10,039,662	2,514,907	2,234,221	81,225	921,007
1975	2,519,844	4,435,368	11,426,333	3,054,705	2,650,396	82,866	1,091,350

[1]Includes premium on capital stock.
[2]Full-time and part-time.

16.5   Financial statistics of telephone systems, by province, 1974 and 1975

Year and province or territory	Capital stock[1] $'000	Cost of plant $'000	Revenue $'000	Expenditure $'000	Full-time employees	Salaries and wages[2] $'000
1974						
Newfoundland	31,145	146,344	37,065	32,485	1,224	10,719
Prince Edward Island	8,861	35,081	7,746	7,007	292	2,382
Nova Scotia	76,681	323,573	75,024	66,703	3,400	30,747
New Brunswick	58,465	263,170	65,365	57,975	2,536	25,112
Quebec[3]	1,729,747	6,034,559	1,557,695	1,365,204	44,205	511,204
Ontario	56,590	108,336	36,173	24,382	895	8,590
Manitoba	80	414,796	91,187	88,245	4,537	45,266
Saskatchewan	61,751	389,830	84,543	66,834	3,029	30,375
Alberta	10	1,053,398	242,127	232,719	8,877	109,439
British Columbia	284,678	1,270,575	317,982	292,667	12,230	147,173
Northwest Territories	—	—	—	—	—	—
Total	2,308,008	10,039,662	2,514,907	2,234,221	81,225	921,007
1975						
Newfoundland	40,396	169,423	44,730	39,511	1,220	13,604
Prince Edward Island	8,912	39,676	10,011	8,848	312	2,910
Nova Scotia	93,957	378,969	93,032	82,448	3,522	35,299
New Brunswick	73,711	296,665	78,479	68,788	2,660	30,728
Quebec[3]	1,864,102	6,724,631	1,899,693	1,585,210	45,199	590,504
Ontario	60,522	119,235	41,309	28,946	787	8,807
Manitoba	—	472,418	107,581	106,874	4,408	55,340
Saskatchewan	64,940	457,242	102,013	86,649	3,291	41,012
Alberta	2	1,310,100	296,039	296,480	10,128	147,435
British Columbia	313,302	1,457,974	381,818	346,642	11,339	165,711
Northwest Territories	—	—	—	—	—	—
Total	2,519,844	11,426,333	3,054,705	2,650,396	82,866	1,091,350

[1]Includes premium on capital stock.
[2]Full-time and part-time.
[3]Includes data of Bell Canada which operates in Quebec, Ontario and the Northwest Territories.

16.6   Summary statistics of Canadian telecommunications, 1970-75

Year	Operating revenues $'000	Operating expenses $'000	Net operating revenue $'000	Pole-line mileage	Wire mileage	Employees[1]	Telegrams '000	Cable-grams[2] '000	Money transfers $'000
1970	136,948	100,068	36,880	49,813	553,644	7,678	6,906	4,729	57,867
1971	146,413	107,567	38,846	42,328	739,836	7,553	5,888	5,347	40,833
1972	163,190	115,308	47,882	40,267	761,545	7,323	5,052	6,457	49,594
1973	190,703	140,114	50,588	37,541	754,608	7,047	3,454	7,412	41,944
1974	230,078	172,554	57,524	35,787	748,065	7,163	3,743	7,292	55,305
1975	259,059	193,811	65,249	32,152	767,609	7,162	4,115	8,016	81,798

[1]Excludes commission operators.
[2]Includes wireless messages and transatlantic Telex messages.

16.6   Summary statistics of Canadian telecommunications, 1970-75   M

Year	Operating revenues $'000	Operating expenses $'000	Net operating revenue $'000	Pole-line length km	Wire length km	Employees[1]	Telegrams '000	Cable-grams[2] '000	Money transfers $'000
1970	136,948	100,068	36,880	80 166	891 004	7,678	6,906	4,729	57,867
1971	146,413	107,567	38,846	68 120	1 190 651	7,553	5,888	5,347	40,833
1972	163,190	115,308	47,882	64 803	1 225 588	7,323	5,052	6,457	49,594
1973	190,703	140,114	50,588	60 416	1 214 424	7,047	3,454	7,412	41,944
1974	230,078	172,554	57,524	57 594	1 203 894	7,163	3,743	7,292	55,305
1975	259,059	193,811	65,249	51 744	1 235 347	7,162	4,115	8,016	81,798

[1]Excludes commission operators.
[2]Includes wireless messages and transatlantic Telex messages.

16.7   Financial statistics of the cable television industry, years ended Aug. 31, 1973-75 (dollars)

Item	1973	1974	1975
OPERATING REVENUE			
Sales revenue			
Subscription revenue	99,572,757	123,136,969	149,573,411
Installation (or move) revenue	6,405,770	8,271,154	9,160,805
Other sales revenue	975,006r	1,967,942	3,478,525
Incidental operating revenue	19,057r	56,575	60,116
Total	106,972,590	133,432,640	162,272,857
EXPENSES			
Salaries, wages and fringe benefits	24,561,319	32,628,507	42,714,947
Less wages capitalized	(2,788,582)	(4,315,689)	(6,163,954)
Program origination	1,578,644	2,114,690	2,923,246
Technical service			
Lease payments; head-end and distribution system	5,629,883	6,333,531	7,252,801
Repairs and maintenance to property, plant and equipment	2,319,280	3,143,756	3,996,373
Vehicle expenses (including lease payments)	1,788,872	2,240,688	2,874,174
Miscellaneous technical and service expenses	6,934,909r	3,174,817	5,950,059
Advertising, sales and promotion	3,329,874	2,688,575	2,945,147
Administration and general			
Professional services (legal, accounting and consulting)	1,124,167	1,267,808	1,617,453
Office supplies and expenses	3,105,128	3,804,256	4,707,676
Miscellaneous administrative and general expenses	3,340,956	8,675,846	11,440,438
Other expenses not classified above	3,466,639	4,731,334	5,507,959
Total	54,391,089	66,488,119	85,766,319
Net operating revenue before depreciation, interest and other adjustments	52,581,501	66,944,521	76,506,538
Depreciation	21,708,609	27,120,858	33,616,896
Interest	7,825,788	11,019,993	13,831,609
Other adjustments, addition to (deduction from) income	(521,045)	(366,718)	1,370,950
Net profit before income taxes	22,526,059	28,436,952	30,428,983
Provision for income taxes	10,114,656	13,991,660	15,315,876
Net profit after income taxes	12,411,403	14,445,292	15,113,107

16.8   Estimated numbers and circulations of reporting English-language and French-language newspapers, by province, 1975 and 1976

Province or territory	1975			1976		
	Daily	Circulation[1]	Weekend	Daily	Circulation[1]	Weekend
English-language newspapers						
Newfoundland	3	47,270	1	3	48,357	1
Prince Edward Island	3	31,425	—	3	31,216	—
Nova Scotia	6	166,138	—	6	168,949	—
New Brunswick	5	121,995	—	5	123,259	—
Quebec	3	300,984	1	3	295,453	1
Ontario	46	2,029,117	1	46	2,140,889	1
Manitoba	8	237,940	—	8	254,929	—
Saskatchewan	4	131,132	—	4	130,973	—
Alberta	8	371,066	—	8	383,836	—
British Columbia	17	568,041	—	18	557,672	—
Yukon Territory	—	—	—	—	—	—
Northwest Territory	—	—	—	—	—	—
Total	103	4,005,108	3	104	4,135,533	3
French-language newspapers						
Nova Scotia	—	—	—	—	—	—
New Brunswick	1	12,890	—	1	14,296	—
Quebec	11	819,662	15	11	842,105	14
Ontario	1	42,222	—	1	45,146	—
Manitoba	—	—	—	—	—	—
Saskatchewan	—	—	—	—	—	—
Alberta	—	—	—	—	—	—
British Columbia	—	—	—	—	—	—
Total	13	874,774	15	13	901,547	14

[1]Circulation not reported for all newspapers.

16.9   Ethnic newspapers and periodicals published in Canada, by province, 1976

Ethno-cultural group	NS	Que.	Ont.	Man.	Sask.	Alta.	BC	Total
Arabic	—	4	2	—	—	1	—	7
Armenian	—	1	3	—	—	—	—	4
Black	1	1	9	—	—	—	—	11
Bulgarian	—	—	2	—	—	—	—	2
Byelorussian	—	—	1	—	—	—	—	1
Chinese	—	—	3	—	—	—	7	10
Croatian	—	1	3	1	—	—	1	6
Danish	—	—	1	—	—	—	1	2
Dutch	—	1	8	1	—	—	1	11
East Indian	—	1	5	—	—	1	2	9
Estonian	—	—	2	—	—	—	—	2
Filipino	—	—	1	—	—	—	—	1
Finnish	—	—	4	—	—	—	1	5
German	—	—	9	5	1	—	3	18
Greek	—	6	2	—	—	—	2	10
Hungarian	—	—	6	1	—	—	—	7
Icelandic	—	—	—	2	—	—	—	2
Italian	—	8	12	—	—	1	2	23
Japanese	—	—	3	—	—	—	1	4
Jewish	—	8	6	2	—	—	1	17
Korean	—	—	3	—	—	—	—	3
Latvian	—	—	3	—	—	—	—	3
Lithuanian	—	1	3	—	—	—	—	4
Malayalam	—	—	1	—	—	—	—	1
Norwegian	—	—	—	—	—	—	1	1
Pakistani	—	1	1	—	—	—	—	2
Polish	—	—	10	1	—	1	—	12
Portuguese	—	5	3	—	—	—	3	11
Russian	—	—	2	—	—	—	2	4
Serbian	—	—	3	—	—	—	—	3
Slovak	—	—	6	—	—	—	—	6
Slovenian	—	—	2	—	—	—	—	2
Spanish	—	1	3	—	—	—	—	4
Swedish	—	—	1	—	—	—	1	2
Swiss	—	—	1	—	—	—	—	1
Ukrainian	—	—	19	8	2	1	1	31
Yugoslav	—	—	1	—	—	—	—	1
Inter-ethnic[1]	—	—	2	—	—	1	1	4
Total	1	39	146	21	3	6	31	247

[1] Includes more than one ethno-cultural group.

16.10   Canadian native peoples' newspapers and periodicals, by province, 1976

Province	Newspapers	Periodicals	Total
Nova Scotia	1	—	1
New Brunswick	2	—	2
Quebec	5	—	5
Ontario	18	7	25
Manitoba	6	—	6
Saskatchewan	4	2	6
Alberta	5	—	5
British Columbia	10	—	10
Yukon Territory	1	—	1
Northwest Territories	5	—	5
Total	57	9	66

Sources

16.1 — 16.7   Transportation and Communications Division, Industry Statistics Branch, Statistics Canada.
16.8   Compiled by Canada Year Book Staff from *Canadian Advertising*.
16.9 — 16.10   Department of the Secretary of State.

Manufacturing

Chapter 17

Tables

Manufacturing   Chapter 17

Manufacturing industries   17.1

Statistics on the manufacturing industries are issued by Statistics Canada on an annual, monthly and quarterly basis, depending on the type of data. The annual Census of Manufactures provides the basic annual data. Among the monthly figures available, two important types of information lend themselves to projecting figures of the annual Census of Manufactures: the survey of manufacturers' shipments, inventories and orders, and surveys of employment and related information.

The monthly shipments, inventories and orders series is published by manufacturing industry for Canada and the provinces, with breakdowns by industry group and by selected industry in the case of the totals for Canada. The data are derived from a survey of respondents to the annual census and are projections of the census total, subject to the qualification that only significant new entries into the manufacturing industries since the latest census are added. The most comprehensive figures resulting from monthly surveys of employment have been estimates of the total number of employees in the manufacturing industries of Canada and the provinces, classified into durable and non-durable goods industries. Both the monthly shipments survey and monthly estimates of employment are based partly on statistical sampling. Both sets of monthly figures also yield totals for the calendar year; while the annual census includes some reports made on a respondent's fiscal year differing from the calendar year, the effect of this is not large.

The data obtained relate to establishments — roughly corresponding to the popular concept of a plant, factory or mill — and, for certain statistics, to non-manufacturing units known as "head offices, sales offices and auxiliary units". For some purposes companies rather than plants or factories are of interest. For example, a company owning factories, mines and merchandising outlets will normally report its profit for the whole company rather than divide it among the different industrial activities in which it is engaged. Thus, the quarterly survey of corporation profits provides figures on sales, profits and certain other statistics for whole companies classified to industries on the basis of their principal activities (for instance, factories might be included in mining or mines in the manufacturing industry). Such figures are generally not comparable with establishment statistics.

Various other monthly and quarterly surveys relate to commodities rather than to establishments or companies. That is, they account for production or shipments of products without regard to the industry in which they are produced.

In addition to providing estimates of overall employment in manufacturing (and other industries), monthly surveying of employment, hours and payrolls results in indexes of employment for larger establishments by industry and by province and sub-provincial area, and in data on average hours and earnings. Monthly indexes of industrial production provide measures of the physical volume of output of the manufacturing industries. That is, they measure output, net of the effects of price changes. These indexes afford annual averages which can be used to indicate movement in the real domestic product at factor cost originating in the manufacturing industries. In addition, many users find valuable information in the large number of monthly industry selling price indexes for various manufacturing industries.

Post-census data   17.1.1

Only preliminary data based on a monthly survey are available for 1975 for manufacturing establishments as the results of the 1975 Census of Manufactures are still being processed. Table 17.1 compares the value of shipments of goods of own manufacture, by province, for 1975 (from a monthly survey) with data for 1974 and earlier censuses, and Table 17.2 makes similar comparisons for industry groups. Table 17.3 gives company data on profitability in various industry groups for the years 1973-75. Because these latter figures relate to companies and those derived from the Census of Manufactures relate to establishments (roughly speaking, plants), the two series are of limited comparability.

17.1.2   Census of Manufactures

Results of the Census of Manufactures are published industry by industry as they become available. The Census of 1974 is the latest for which all industries have been issued. Summary statistics are given in Tables 17.4 and 17.14 - 17.19. The 1970 revision of the Standard Industrial Classification (SIC) substantially affects comparability of data for some industries compiled on the new basis with data for 1969 and earlier years. All data presented here for 1970 and later years are based on the 1970 revision of the SIC except those in Table 17.3 dealing with company profits.

Central Canada accounted for about $4 out of every $5 of all value added by manufacture in the manufacturing industries of Canada in both 1973 and 1974; Ontario's contribution in 1974 was 51.7% and Quebec's 27.2%. British Columbia was in third place, accounting for some 9.4% of value added by manufacture. Alberta, Saskatchewan and Manitoba combined were almost as large a contributor, accounting for 7.4%. The Atlantic provinces accounted for 4.3%.

An interesting measure of the intensity of manufacturing activity by region is in terms of value added per capita of their population. The 1974 Canada average was $1,563; Quebec and British Columbia were both close to this average with $1,557 and $1,378, respectively, but Ontario's average was much higher at $2,240. The average for the Prairie provinces was $715 and that for the Atlantic provinces, $705.

17.1.3   Size of manufacturing establishments

The average size of a manufacturing establishment, in terms of numbers of persons employed, is somewhat over 56 persons but more than one half of the total work force in the manufacturing industries is in establishments employing 200 or more persons. While 30.2% of the manufacturing establishments in Canada have fewer than five persons employed, including working owners, these establishments, because of their small average size, account for only about one in 90 persons of the working force of the manufacturing industries (Tables 17.5 and 17.6).

The average size of a manufacturing establishment in terms of shipments of goods of own manufacture was $2.6 million in 1974 (Table 17.7). However, this average size is greatly affected by the large number of very small establishments which in fact account for only a minor share of overall shipments. Establishments with $1 million or more shipments of goods of own manufacture in 1974 accounted for about two establishments in seven in the manufacturing industries, but they reported 93.4% of the total value of shipments of goods of own manufacture.

17.1.4   Exports of manufactured goods

Export statistics are not broken down into manufactured goods and other goods but the categories "fabricated materials" and "end products" give some indication of the degree of manufacture of such exports and the total for the two can be used as a substitute for manufactured exports. Because exports are not necessarily made by the manufacturer and because of valuation problems, the resulting series are not wholly comparable with Census of Manufactures data on manufacturer's shipments of goods of own manufacture. In the latter, for instance, work by smelters owned by mining companies is valued at an imputed charge to the mine, not at the value of the metal produced. Table 17.10 shows recent trends in exports of manufactures. As the data in the table will show, exports of manufactured goods in 1975 appear to have been at a level about 3.8 times that of 1965, but those of end products — roughly speaking, finished manufactures — were 6.9 times their 1965 level. This reflects in an important degree the impact of the Canada–United States Agreement on Aumotive Products of 1965.

Federal assistance to manufacturing 17.2

The Department of Industry, Trade and Commerce is responsible for stimulating the establishment, growth and efficiency of the manufacturing, processing and tourist industries in Canada, and also for developing export trade and external trade policies. It assists Canadian industries to initiate and take advantage of technological advances, improve products and services, increase productivity and expand domestic and foreign markets through a variety of programs and services. At each phase of the product cycle — from research, development and design through production and marketing — the department can assist with information and financial assistance.

Enterprise Development Program (EDP) 17.2.1

Effective April 1, 1977 the Enterprise Development Program replaced the following Industry, Trade and Commerce innovative and adjustment assistance programs: Program for Advancement of Industrial Technology (PAIT), Industrial Design Assistance Program (IDAP), Program to Enhance Productivity (PEP), General Adjustment Assistance Program (GAAP), Automotive Adjustment Assistance program (AAA), Footwear and Tanning Industry Adjustment Program (FTIAP), and Pharmaceutical Industry Development Assistance program (PIDA).

EDP combines the basic features of these programs and is designed to facilitate coordination among various forms of assistance, making Industry, Trade and Commerce programs more accessible, particularly to smaller and medium-sized Canadian businesses. The overall objective is to enhance growth in the manufacturing and processing sectors of the Canadian economy by providing assistance to selected firms to make them more productive and internationally competitive. The focus is on firms prepared to undertake, in relation to their resources, relatively high risk projects which are viable and promise attractive rates of return on the total investment.

The Enterprise Development Program adopts a corporate approach to analysis of applicant firms to identify present and future requirements and to tailor a financing package that combines one or more forms of EDP assistance with other government assistance and private sector financing. This "merchant banking" flexibility has been described as investing in firms, not just supporting projects. A merchant bank is defined as a financial institution which endeavours to serve its clients by identifying, structuring and providing (or arranging for) all the types of financing, financial and management services required by a firm to realize its full potential.

The corporate/merchant banking approach is similar to that of an investor. The approach is to examine the resources of a firm (human, financial, physical and technological), the market opportunities and constraints, and plans of the firm to marshall its resources to exploit its present and future market opportunities.

Decision-making is carried out at different levels. Mixed private sector/public sector boards provide pragmatic market-oriented decisions by drawing on the experience of prominent businessmen. Decentralized boards in the various regions of Canada, with delegated approval limits, make faster decisions possible, with awareness of regional business conditions a factor.

Forms of EDP assistance. Five types of grants are available. These include: grants to offset partially the cost of consultants to develop proposals for projects for assistance; grants to study market feasibility; grants to study productivity improvement projects which, while requiring no new technology, could involve some risk; grants to promote greater use of industrial design for mass-produced products; and grants for technological innovations which could lead to industrial growth and economic benefit to the firm and to the Canadian economy.

Loans or loan insurance for adjustment projects facilitate restructuring of manufacturing or processing firms by providing last resort financial assistance. The purpose is to help Canadian firms to meet international competition in both domestic and export markets. In some cases, the usual sources of financing are inadequate for smaller and medium-sized firms, and loan insurance (guarantees) can be provided. Direct loans may also be provided, but these are restricted to firms which have been injured by import competition. These loans and loan insurance may provide for plant expansion, equipment modernization or working capital. Because of risks associated with last resort financing, this type of assistance may be associated with one or more of the grants described above.

In addition, three forms of special purpose assistance are available. These include: loans and grants to encourage restructuring of firms engaged in footwear or tanning industries; insurance on surety bonds for offshore turnkey projects; and insurance on loans, leases and conditional sales agreements to air-carriers in Canada and the United States to acquire de Havilland DHC-7 aircraft. More information on the Enterprise Development Program may be obtained from the Program Office, Department of Industry, Trade and Commerce, Ottawa.

Industrial Research and Development Incentives Act. This legislation enacted in March 1967, provided cash grants or equivalent tax credits to corporations that carried out research and development which was of benefit to Canada. As a result of restrictions in government spending, the payment of grants for work carried out after December 31, 1975 has been terminated. The last date for the acceptance of applications for grants was December 31, 1976. It is expected that the act will be repealed when all administrative work has been completed.

17.2.2   Automotive Program

The Canada–United States Agreement on Automotive Products of January 1965 provides for the removal of tariffs and other impediments to trade between the two countries in motor vehicles and original equipment parts. The basic objectives are creation of a broader market to permit benefits of specialization and scale, trade liberalization to enable both countries to participate in the North American market on an equitable basis, and development of conditions in which market forces would operate to attain economic patterns of investment, production and trade.

As a result, Canadian exports of vehicles and parts and employment in this industry have increased substantially, and investment in new plants and expansion of existing facilities have been extensive.

17.2.3   The Machinery Program

This program was introduced in January 1968 to increase efficiency in Canadian industry by enabling machinery users to acquire advanced capital equipment at the lowest possible cost while affording Canadian machinery producers tariff protection on what they manufacture. Canadian machinery producers are protected by a single statutory rate of duty which applies immediately when they are in a position to supply. This is particularly significant for Canadian producers of custom-engineered machinery.

The program covers a broad range of machines including general-purpose machinery, metalworking and woodworking machinery, construction and materials-handling equipment and various types of special industry machinery, such as pulp and paper and plastics industry machinery, and service industry equipment. The statutory rate of duty is 2½% British preferential and 15% most-favoured-nation.

The duty otherwise payable on machines, accessories, attachments, control equipment, tools and components may be remitted if such remission is in the public interest and the goods imported are not available from production in Canada. A Machinery and Equipment Advisory Board advises the Minister of Industry, Trade and Commerce regarding the eligibility of machinery for remission of duty. Final authority for granting remission lies with the Governor in Council.

Machinery producers may also apply for remission of duty on production parts and components which they cannot procure in Canada. This provision is intended to stimulate Canadian machinery manufacturers to specialize their production and enable them to compete more effectively.

Since June 1971 the Machinery Program has been extended to imports covering machinery for use in sawmills and logging. The Machinery and Equipment Advisory Board examines all tariff remission applications in respect of machinery and equipment or production tooling for the manufacture of original equipment, automotive parts and accessories.

Construction industry information   17.2.4

A preliminary thesaurus of Canadian construction industry terms has been compiled in both English and French to assist in resolving the ambiguity in construction terminology. A glossary equating French and English construction industry terms has also been prepared. At present the Canadian construction thesaurus is being expanded to produce a Canadian thesaurus of building science and technology.

The pilot phase of the Construction Information System operated by the Canadian Construction Information Corporation has been completed. Results from interviews with users indicate enthusiastic acceptance by the industry. The data bank continues to expand.

The department has continued to encourage the increased use of dimensional standardization and coordination of building components and buildings. Initially, conferences were held throughout Canada to acquaint policy-makers within the industry with the technological and economic advantages of modular standardization. The present program of metric conversion has resulted in an increased emphasis by industry on the benefits of modular coordination. In addition, a directory of modular building components is published.

The promotion of universal use of the National Building Code is continuing. Manitoba has established a provincial building code based on the NBC for all larger cities and towns. Alberta, Saskatchewan, Ontario, New Brunswick, Nova Scotia and British Columbia have taken similar action and Quebec is studying its feasibility. A *Building standards index* lists all codes, standards and specifications used in the Canadian construction industry.

Export opportunities for the goods and services of the construction industry continue to be identified through the department's trade posts abroad and in cooperation with industry.

Industrial design   17.2.5

The design program, authorized by the National Design Council Act 1961 and administered by the department's Office of Design is aimed at promoting and expediting improvement in the products of Canadian secondary industry. The Office of Design, in cooperation with provincial industry departments, is supporting product design and development programs whereby field teams provide in-company design assistance to small companies.

Other design programs include: financial and technical assistance to education institutions to introduce design training at the technical and university levels; seminars on various facets of design for professionals, educators, business executives and the general public; awards programs for achievements over a broad field of design endeavour; scholarships for advanced training in industrial design in Canada and abroad; grants for design research and promotion by Canadians; and technical and financial assistance to committees and groups attempting to foster effective design on a national, regional or industrial level.

A National Design Council Chairman's Award for Design Management was introduced in 1970, to be presented to the management group which, in the council's opinion, does the most to integrate and efficiently apply good design policy.

17.2.6   Defence Industry Productivity Program

This program is designed to enhance the technological competence of the Canadian defence industry in its export activities by providing financial assistance to industrial firms for selected projects. Emphasis is placed on areas of defence technology having civil export sales potential. Assistance may cover the development of products for export purposes; the acquisition of modern machine tools and other advanced manufacturing equipment to meet exacting military standards; and assistance with pre-production expenses to establish manufacturing sources in Canada for export markets. Manufacturing equipment projects are selected for assistance on the basis that the machinery acquired will make a significant contribution to increased productivity.

17.2.7   Shipbuilding assistance program

On March 5, 1975 the domestic shipbuilding assistance program, Ship Construction Subsidy Regulations (SCSR) and the export program Shipbuilding Temporary Assistance Program (STAP) were replaced by a combined program of assistance to the shipbuilding industry. This program provided for a subsidy rate of 14% of approved costs of vessels built in Canada with the subsidy being reduced to 8% at the rate of 1% annually from January 1, 1976. The program provides for an incentive grant up to 3% of the cost of vessels entitled to subsidies or purchased by the federal government. This incentive grant is paid when matched by an equal investment by a shipyard and is for investment which will result in improved performance. The program encourages the use of Canadian materials, components and equipment when they are available at competitive prices.

17.2.8   Program for Export Market Development

This program is designed to help increase exports of Canadian goods and services. Canadian companies may obtain repayable contributions toward defraying approved expenses which would otherwise inhibit their attempts to earn a share of markets. The program is divided into four main components.

Section A, incentives for participation in capital projects abroad, is applicable anywhere outside Canada. The term "capital projects" is intended to describe facilities, systems and other projects requiring the provision of skilled services, engineering products and other capital goods. Section B, market identification and marketing adjustment, emphasizes manufactured goods but it can be more widely applied. It is applicable anywhere outside Canada and continental US. Section C, participation in trade fairs abroad, is not restricted as to markets, products or services. It is applicable anywhere outside Canada but participants in Canadian national stands at the same fair abroad are not eligible. Section D, incoming foreign buyers, also has no restrictions on markets, products or services. Buyers from anywhere outside Canada and the continental US may be invited by a company to examine products and production in Canada.

The department's contribution will normally be 50% of airfare and special and unusual costs and $70 a day toward personnel costs. If a company receiving assistance succeeds in obtaining the business sought, repayment of the department's contribution will be required, but no repayment is required if the company is unsuccessful.

Promotional Projects Program   17.2.9

The program of trade fairs and missions was set up to promote the export of Canadian products and services. Its sponsored promotions are designed to meet particular requirements and include trade fairs abroad, trade missions, in-store promotions, travelling sample shows, incoming trade delegates and buyers programs, export-oriented training programs and, under the programs for export market development, incentives for participation in trade fairs abroad and incentives for incoming foreign buyers.

Fashion Design Assistance Program   17.2.10

Fashion/Canada, an incorporated body of representatives from federal and provincial governments and major associations of the Canadian fashion industry, administers this program. The designer development part of the program provides opportunities for student and established fashion designers to acquire advanced training in their craft. Design/designer promotion publicizes good Canadian fashion design to attract domestic and foreign buyers and promotes increased recognition of talented and well-trained Canadian fashion designers.

Provincial assistance to manufacturing   17.3

Newfoundland   17.3.1

The Newfoundland government, through its Department of Industrial Develop-ment, offers advice and assistance to prospective industry in determining desirable plant locations and in preparing feasibility studies. Information can be made available on the source and availability of raw materials, transportation costs, labour costs and a variety of other economic data. The government will transport industrialists anywhere in the province to obtain a first-hand look at potential plant sites. The Department of Industrial Development also provides liaison with the public and private sectors.

Financial assistance may be provided by the Newfoundland and Labrador Development Corporation in the form of loans against the securities offered by the prospective enterprise, or the acquisition and holding of shares or other securities of any company located in the province, with the right of the enterprise to buy back these shares. The corporation also provides a complete range of management advisory services.

The government may provide direct financial assistance based on cost-benefit analyses. Buildings, where they exist, and land may be provided on attractive terms. Industrial training facilities are available throughout the province for specialized courses to meet the requirements of incoming industry.

Prince Edward Island   17.3.2

Provincial assistance to manufacturers and processors is provided through Industrial Enterprises Incorporated (IEI), an autonomous Crown corporation administered by an independent board of directors composed of businessmen. IEI provides financial assistance to new and existing manufacturing industries. It identifies specific industrial opportunities, establishes their feasibility and also provides management assistance in industrial engineering, marketing and finance.

The corporation makes loan capital, working capital and equity capital available. It constructs and rents completely serviced factory buildings, provides equipment leasing, maintains industrial property and operates industrial parks at Charlottetown and Summerside offering fully serviced lots of various sizes for sale to manufacturers and processors for warehouses and essential service businesses. Long-term financing is provided at attractive rates of interest.

IEI establishes contacts with venture capital groups throughout Canada and in other countries who show an interest in PEI projects. It maintains an internal consulting group to provide management assistance to PEI companies.

17.3.3   Nova Scotia

Industrial Estates Limited (IEL), a provincial Crown corporation formed in 1957, provides up to 100% mortgage financing on the cost of land and buildings and up to 60% of the installed cost of machinery of new or expanding Nova Scotia manufacturers or processors. Repayment schedules are negotiable and may be accelerated without penalty. Tax agreements with most municipalities limit local taxes on IEL-assisted industries. IEL's Small Business Financing Division assists manufacturing or processing industries whose gross annual sales do not exceed $1 million. Financing may include short-, medium- and long-term loans, loan guarantees and minority equity positions. A loan may not exceed $150,000.

The Nova Scotia Resources Development Board, affiliated with the Department of Development, provides term financing on the security of fixed assets for projects defined under The Industrial Loan Act, The Industrial Development Act and The Fishermen's Loan Act. It provides financing for tourism facilities, farms and primary agriculture processing, fish plants and vessels, saw and planing mills.

The Department of Development sponsors the Market Assistance Program which is designed to complement the Export Market Development Program administered by the federal Department of Industry, Trade and Commerce. The program provides varying reimbursement schedules for Nova Scotia companies participating in trade fairs and exhibits, market education and market familiarization programs and incoming buyers programs.

Special municipal tax assistance as authorized under the Nova Scotia Bonus Act may provide assistance to new or expanding firms by limiting either the assessment or the tax rate for a specified period of time.

The province cooperates closely with the Cape Breton Development Corporation, a federal Crown corporation, and contributes financially to some of the industry-development projects sponsored by it.

17.3.4   New Brunswick

The Department of Commerce and Development has the major responsibility for the development of the manufacturing and processing sectors of the provincial economy. Its aims are to support and strengthen existing industries, attract new industry, increase the quality of employment, expand the tax base, maintain or improve social or environmental quality, and alleviate regional disparities.

The Industrial Development Branch is responsible for attracting new manufacturing and processing industries to New Brunswick. The branch analyzes and makes recommendations on all applications for financial assistance to industry involving capital investment or working capital funds. This assistance, provided through the New Brunswick Industrial Development Board, is offered to industries wishing to locate in the province and to existing industries planning to expand.

The Commerce and Industry Services Branch is responsible for: provision of management, technical and product improvement services to provincial industry; development of markets for provincially manufactured or processed products; development of the maximum local processing of provincial resources; and provision of management, technical and financial services to provincial industries in danger of failure.

The Planning and Regional Development Branch is responsible for: departmental input and liaison with the federal government on all matters relating to federal-provincial development agreements; capital expenditures in provincial industrial parks; evaluating cost-effectiveness of departmental programs; and the development and modification of programs.

Agencies associated with the department and reporting to the Minister of Commerce and Development are the New Brunswick Industrial Development Board, Provincial Holdings Limited and the Research and Productivity Council.

The New Brunswick Industrial Development Board was set up to provide financial assistance to manufacturers or processors in the province. Such assistance normally takes the form of a direct loan or loan guarantee. Terms and conditions are subject to individual negotiation but specifically require the applicant to provide reasonable equity and security in the form of a first charge on assets. The board is considered a lender of last resort and the applicant must therefore have unsuccessfully approached normal conventional lenders.

Provincial Holdings Limited was established by the New Brunswick government as a Crown corporation to hold and administer the province's equity position in various companies. This agency is prepared to take an equity position in manufacturing industries wishing to locate in New Brunswick. The extent of the equity taken by Provincial Holdings is negotiable and depends on various factors in a particular proposal.

The Research and Productivity Council was established primarily to provide a source of technical support services for New Brunswick industry. The council maintains a well-equipped centre for engineering and problem-solving, industrial research and development, and management consulting. RPC carries out research and problem-solving on a cost-recovery basis for clients in Canada and abroad. An industrial engineering service is made available to New Brunswick (and Prince Edward Island) companies by RPC through a National Research Council contract. In addition, the NRC, in cooperation with RPC, provides free technical information and assistance to New Brunswick (and PEI) companies.

Quebec   17.3.5

In 1971 legislation dealing with financial aid to industry was combined under two acts: Bill 20, the Quebec Industrial Development Assistance Act, which created the Quebec Industrial Development Corporation; and Bill 21, "an Act to promote industrial development through fiscal advantages". The aim of these programs is to help transform Quebec's industrial structure through aid to high-technology industries and to encourage existing industries to consolidate their production facilities while adapting them to modern techniques to improve their competitive position. Moreover, companies unable to obtain financial assistance at reasonable rates elsewhere are eligible for aid under these programs if it would contribute to the economic development of the province or any of its regions. The amount of assistance granted depends on the area, the kind of goods manufactured and the production techniques used.

The Industrial Development Corporation may grant financial assistance to a manufacturing establishment making a capital investment for construction; purchasing or expanding a plant or factory; investing in machinery, tools or equipment; purchasing licences or patents; or improving the financial organization of the business. Depending on the nature or needs of the company, the assistance may take various forms: loans at lower-than-market interest rates; assumption of part of the costs of a loan; exemption from repayment of part of the loans which the business has contracted with the corporation subject to meeting certain criteria as to productivity and the creation of new jobs; purchase by the corporation of buildings or machinery for resale or rental to a manufacturer; and purchase of shares of any manufacturing industry up to a maximum of 50% of the paid-up capital stock of the company but not more than 30% of the total assets.

Under the act to promote industrial development through fiscal advantages (Bill 21), the government may grant a reduction in income tax on corporation profits from any investment in Quebec by manufacturers provided the amount of the investment is at least $150,000. Permissible investments are for building or expansion of plants or factories or for the purchase of new machinery, tools or equipment. In computing their profits, approved companies may deduct up to 30%, 50% or 100% of their investment depending on the region in which the investment is made.

A manufacturing or processing plant selling and delivering part of its Quebec production outside the province may receive exemption from provincial sales tax on goods purchased for its use or consumption in the proportion that its out-of-province sales bears to its total sales for the year. Under the same program, a business may be exempt from provincial sales tax on gas or electricity used directly for processing. Moreover, the manufacturer is entitled to a partial reimbursement of sales tax paid on construction materials used in his industrial buildings.

A manufacturing firm may also receive total repayment of the tax paid on gasoline or diesel fuel if the fuel is used to operate machinery or as a raw material in the manufacture of certain products. Industrial machinery used in Quebec for manufacturing or processing is also exempt from provincial sales tax.

For a number of years the provincial government has sought to find easier access to export markets for Quebec producers. The International Services Branch of the Department of Trade and Industry has economic advisers attached to its delegations and offices abroad, provides financial and technical assistance to firms wishing to participate in industrial shows, organizes trade missions and provides information on export techniques and the various aspects of external trade. Amendments to the Quebec Industrial Development Act permit the Industrial Development Corporation to grant financial assistance to manufacturing or commercial operators exporting goods manufactured in Quebec, provided they meet the criteria set out in regulations under the act. The Industrial Research Institute makes information and technical assistance available to industry throughout the province.

17.3.6   Ontario

The Ontario Development Corporation (ODC), the Northern Ontario Development Corporation (NODC) and the Eastern Ontario Development Corporation (EODC) are Crown agencies established by the Ontario government to provide financial and advisory services to business in order to stimulate industrial growth, economic development and employment opportunities. They report to the Ontario legislature through the Minister of Industry and Tourism. Their activities are governed by boards of directors composed of representatives from the business and financial communities and organized labour.

Loan programs administered by the ODC, NODC and EODC include the Ontario Business Incentive Program which provides loans to encourage industrial and economic development in Ontario. Incentive loans are repayable, although initial repayment may be deferred. The loans may be interest free or at a rate lower than ODC's prevailing rate of interest.

Term loan programs include: small business loans to Canadian-owned companies in the province to expand their operations in manufacturing or services closely allied to manufacturing; venture capital loans to Canadian-owned companies to introduce new technology; pollution control equipment loans to companies which must install approved pollution control equipment and are unable to finance it from their own resources; tourist industry loans for tourist resort operators to upgrade existing facilities and to establish new accommodation; export support loans to finance the production and warehousing of goods for export against specific orders; and industrial mortgages and lease-backs to assist with the establishment or expansion of manufacturing facilities.

The ODC administers Northam Industrial Park in Cobourg and Huron Industrial Park in Centralia where it rents industrial space and housing. It also manages the sale and leasing of property in Sheridan Park near Toronto to companies engaged in industrial research and development.

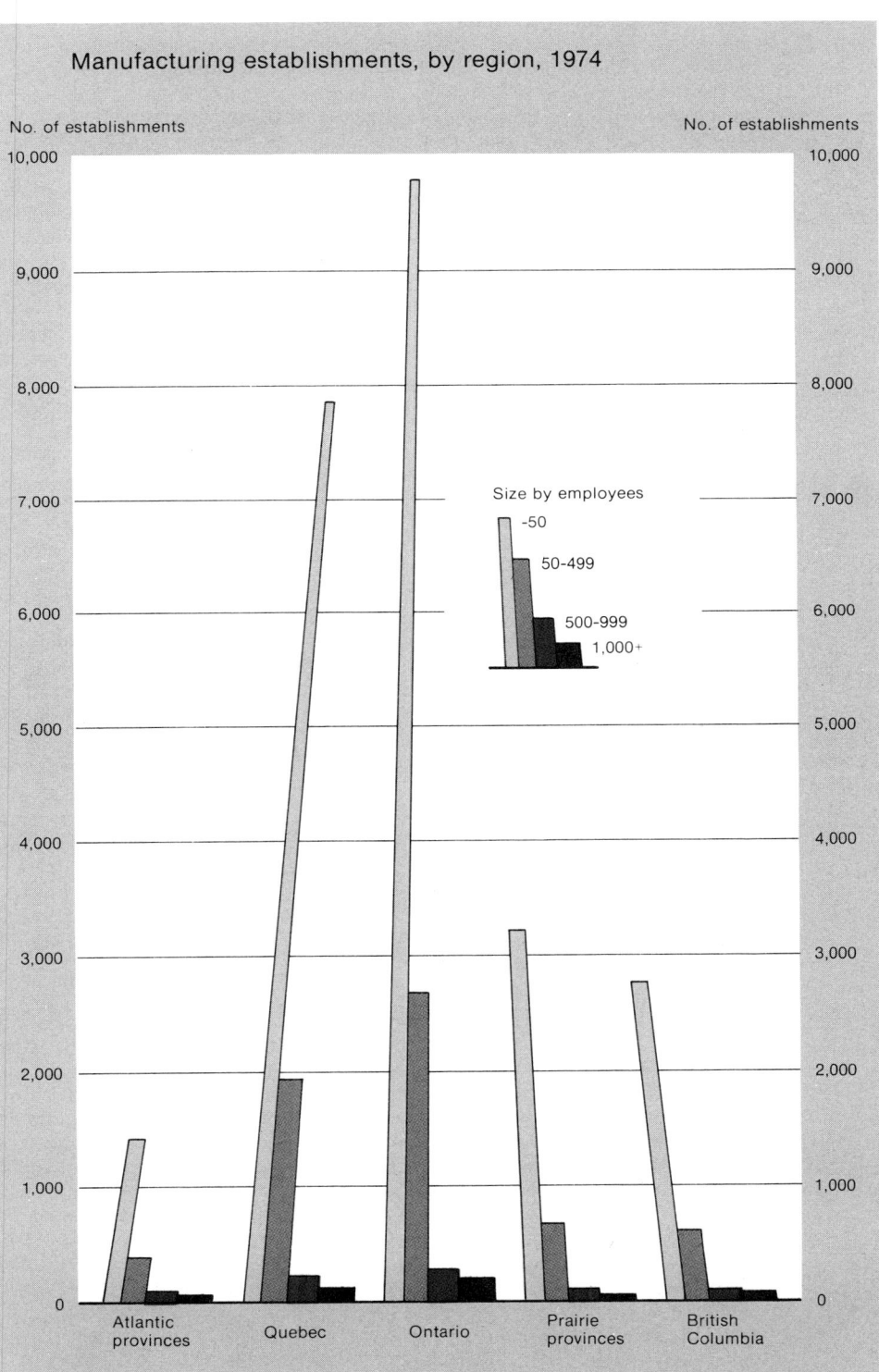

Manufacturing establishments, by region, 1974

No. of establishments

No. of establishments

Size by employees
-50
50-499
500-999
1,000+

Atlantic provinces   Quebec   Ontario   Prairie provinces   British Columbia

The Ontario Ministry of Industry and Tourism has several programs to assist business people. The Tourism Division provides information on location and expansion of tourist operations, economic studies and other pertinent material; it advises tourist and service industry operators on ways to increase and improve their operations. The Industry Division assists manufacturing companies and supporting service industries to maximize use of facilities, apply technology, establish new production facilities and find business opportunities. Technology, industrial design and development, product performance, domestic and international marketing and loan programs are discussed in seminars with independent business people, industrial commissions and municipal councils. The Manufacturing Opportunity Days program presents new products and processes, licensing opportunities, joint ventures from around the world and contracts for tendering.

Throughout the province 21 field offices meet local needs and problems and 15 international field offices cover 35 countries; six are in the United States — Boston, Chicago, Cleveland, Los Angeles, Minneapolis and New York — and others in Mexico City, São Paulo, Brussels, Frankfurt, London, Milan, Stockholm, Tokyo and Vienna. To aid the manufacturer, the international staff works in conjunction with industrial development officers in Toronto to arrange trade missions, business appointments, plant visits, incoming buyer missions, tourist incentive programs, and to provide consulting services with government and investment representatives. Some trade missions include visits to international trade fairs and exhibitions enabling executives from Ontario companies to see new products and manufacturing techniques which could increase product diversification, manufacturing volume and profits. In addition this program introduces Ontario companies to foreign concerns wishing to establish contacts for licensing or joint ventures or expansion in Canada.

In Mississauga, Ont., the Sheridan Park Corporation has established the Sheridan Park Research Community, a $42 million undertaking employing 1,600 persons in 10 resident companies and corporations. It has research laboratories and facilities that offer an exchange of ideas and techniques and help participating companies stay competitive in world markets.

17.3.7   Manitoba

The Department of Industry and Commerce encourages a planned expansion in the provincial economy through continued industrial and commercial development. In the fiscal year 1976-77 a series of changes in organization took place to facilitate new development. The activities of the department are carried out by a combination of branches and associated agencies. The branches are divided into three groups: Trade and Industry, Enterprise Development, and Economic Planning and Policy Research.

The Trade and Industry Group is composed of three branches and one corporation relating to the development of Manitoba in an industrial context with respect to trade arrangements. The Industrial Development Branch assists companies or individual entrepreneurs who are considering new manufacturing plants and expansions to existing plants. Professional service and advice are provided in such areas as feasibility studies and market research. Site location reports are prepared that respond to client requirements for information on taxation, wage rates and labour availability, financial incentive programs, supply of raw materials and other operating factors.

The Project Development Branch initiates, monitors and evaluates special projects designed to meet the needs of Manitoba's industry. The, Trade Development Branch assists manufacturers in trade promotion programs through trade fairs in Canada and the United States, trade missions, assistance to incoming buyers and advice on export tariffs, shipping and documentation.

The Manitoba Trading Corporation (Manitrade), an agency of the department, advises firms in developing and handling trade to export markets. It acts as an export department or agent for a variety of Manitoba manufacturers and assists professional firms to develop export markets for their services. It is not unusual for Manitrade to combine both Manitoba products and services by organizing consortia.

The Enterprise Development Group is the largest group in the department, consisting of 10 branches and two associated agencies. About 83% of all businesses in Manitoba are composed of small enterprises with 50 employees or less. This group is directly concerned with programs for such businesses. Its branches are: Small Enterprise Development; New Enterprise Formation; Diagnosis Management Counselling; Existing Enterprise Improvement; Expansion Assistance; Decentralized Program Delivery; Human Resource Management; Marketing, Distribution and Design, which works closely with the Manitoba Design Institute; Technology and Supply; and Regional and Community Coordination. The two agencies are the Manitoba Research Council and the Manitoba Design Institute.

The Science and Technology Branch carries out programs in cooperation with the Manitoba Research Council. The branch and the council jointly encourage the effective application of technology in Manitoba and advise the Minister of Industry and Commerce on matters relating to science and technology. Financial assistance for new product development is provided through the Research and Development Assistance Program; technical information and assistance through the Technical Assistance Centre; information and assistance to inventors; advice on product development and manufacturing techniques; and advice on technical subjects to provincial government departments, as well as to the federal government.

The Economic Planning and Policy Research Group is responsible for economic planning, evaluation, and research support. The group prepares economic reports, and conducts research and analysis leading to recommendations on economic and socio-economic issues.

The Planning Branch is directed toward improving the quality of economic research, and indicating directions for industrial development. The Policy Branch monitors the state of the national and provincial economies, and prepares reports and forecasts. The Programs Branch designs and carries out research projects directly related to the department's programs and to other government programs. The Regional Planning Branch monitors socio-economic trends in rural Manitoba. It evaluates the impact of planned, anticipated or recent developments, assists other branches in integrating statistical and local knowledge, assists in the development of regional strategies and provides a comprehensive source of data on rural Manitoba.

The Manitoba Development Corporation is a Crown corporation established in 1958. The objectives of the corporation are to assist businesses to increase productivity and to raise wage levels. The corporation encourages exports and the substitution of locally developed products for those which are imported.

The corporation provides financial assistance to businesses in the form of loans or investments or both. Technical and managerial assistance is made available in conjunction with the Manitoba Department of Industry and Commerce. The corporation also provides assistance in preparing applications for financing from banks and other sources and for federal and provincial grants.

Saskatchewan   17.3.8

The primary objectives of the Department of Industry and Commerce are to stimulate the growth of the Saskatchewan economy and to broaden and diversify the economic base of the province.

The Industry Development Branch encourages the establishment of new manufacturing, processing, distribution and warehouse facilities, resource industries and industrial service operations. It assists existing firms to expand and diversify, locates and evaluates development opportunities and provides information on Saskatchewan's economic development and potential.

The Business Assistance Branch supports existing business enterprises by providing counselling and consulting expertise in accounting, merchandising, transportation and marketing. To make these revitalizing services accessible to business firms throughout the province, branch representatives are located at seven centres outside Regina.

The Trade Development Branch promotes trade in Saskatchewan products in regional, national and international markets, particularly in the US, Europe and the Pacific Rim. Contact points for this program include the office of the Agent-General in London, England, and the Pacific Rim office in Regina.

The Research and Development Branch collects and disseminates statistical data, and prepares or contracts for economic feasibility studies to determine what imports and new products might be produced in Saskatchewan, and what primary products can be further refined or processed in the province. It also assists in intergovernmental relations with other provinces and the federal government on economic policies and programs.

Operation Recycle is a special project which administers the collection of abandoned or scrap vehicles for shredding into acceptable steel furnace feed. It is estimated that approximately 100,000 vehicles will be collected over a three-year period and other recycling projects are under active consideration.

The Industry and Commerce Development Act authorizes the department to: undertake, either for its own use or on a shared-cost basis with business enterprises, feasibility studies and research to identify new business opportunities; provide, either through department representatives or outside consultants, counselling and advice on all forms of business problems; and make financial assistance available to a community-based group to continue the operation of a business threatened by closure which would seriously disrupt the community in which it is located.

The Saskatchewan Economic Development Corporation (SEDCO), a Crown corporation, provides financial assistance to business enterprises. SEDCO was originally established in 1963 to provide loans for the establishment or expansion of manufacturing enterprises. Since August 1972, its terms of reference have been significantly broadened to permit the provision of financial assistance to virtually all types of businesses. In addition to industrial enterprises, SEDCO loans may now be made to retail, wholesale and service businesses. SEDCO assistance can take many forms, the most common being a first mortgage loan over a medium term. Security for such loans consists of specific pledges of land, buildings and/or equipment; the support of the individuals involved in the business is normally pledged as well. Repayment terms are designed to suit the income pattern of the enterprise, and may include such features as step-payments, seasonal payments or similar arrangements.

Loans can be granted for terms varying from a few months to 20 years and in amounts from a few thousand to many millions of dollars. The term is determined by the estimated life of security pledged and by the earnings of the business. Equipment-based loans would be for five to eight years, while building and equipment loans might be eight to 12 years, and real estate alone as security would warrant a loan of up to 20 years. Working capital loans would range from one month to two years.

In all cases, the corporation expects that the owners of the borrowing company will have a reasonable equity contribution in the enterprise. In certain instances, the corporation may consider taking an equity investment in its own right if required to maintain a reasonable balance between debt and equity. The corporation also has industrial sites and buildings which it is prepared to make available to eligible enterprises. Lease, lease-purchase or outright sale of such properties can be considered and, in certain circumstances, the corporation will consider constructing a facility for the subsequent sale or lease to a client.

Alberta   17.3.9

The Alberta Opportunity Company (AOC) is a Crown agency created to promote economic growth by stimulating the establishment of new businesses and aiding in the expansion of existing enterprises. AOC gives priority to Albertans and Alberta-owned enterprises, small businesses, centres of small population, job-creating projects, research and development projects, promotion of marketing and export potential, enhancement of tourist potential, provision of employment and business experience for Alberta students, encouragement of local development groups and promotion of pollution control projects.

To qualify for assistance, a business may be a proprietorship, partnership, cooperative, or corporate body, must be a business operating for gain or profit, must be located in Alberta and must provide assurance that any assistance provided will be utilized exclusively in Alberta. Eligible types of business include manufacturing, processing and assembly operations, service industries, commercial wholesale and retail trade, recreational facilities, tourist establishments, local development organizations, student business enterprises, and new industries which are unique and valuable additions to the province. The program is not designed to apply to finance companies, suppliers of residential accommodation other than tourist facilities, public utilities including power generation and distribution, or resource-based industries such as mining and oil and gas production.

Assistance may be provided for establishing new businesses, acquiring fixed assets — land, buildings and equipment — expanding existing facilities, strengthening working capital, financing raw material or finished inventories for manufacturers, and research and development projects.

Financial assistance is made available directly or by guarantee in various forms: capital loans; working capital loans; inventory financing for manufacturers for stockpiling either the raw materials used in manufacturing or finished products resulting from that process (in actual operation AOC will purchase the inventory from the manufacturer under a buy/sell agreement at established prices to a level of 80% of "laid-in" cost or wholesale price, as the case may be); research and development loans up to 50% (maximum $50,000) of the total cost of an approved project undertaken by a commercial enterprise. Such projects are restricted to applied research and development programs which contribute to improvements in one or more of the following areas: technological advances to products or development of new products, technological advances to production facilities, adoption of improved management techniques, and development of new markets.

Business management counselling services may be provided without charge by AOC professional consultants and include management advice and guidance on financial, technical and marketing matters for small- and intermediate-size Alberta businesses which are not in a financial position to obtain this type of assistance elsewhere. Services are provided through the company's head office in Ponoka and its branch offices in Calgary, Lethbridge, Grand Prairie and Edmonton.

British Columbia   17.3.10

The Department of Economic Development provides research, statistical information and support services to encourage and assist in the orderly development and growth of British Columbia's economy. The Business and Industrial Development Branch sponsors market development, promotional programs, and direct aid to British Columbia firms. It has sponsored trade missions to Asia, Europe, South America, Africa and Australia, in order to assist participating firms in securing export markets.

The Incoming Buyers Program works on the premise that one of the best showrooms for British Columbia products is British Columbia itself. Buyers from a variety of countries have inspected forest industry equipment, food products, electronic components and other products and services in their home environment. The program offers potential buyers a first-hand knowledge of technological capacity, quality control, and a company's ability to meet its sales commitments. The branch assists British Columbia companies to participate in trade shows in national and international markets. A Market Development Program sends company representatives overseas in an attempt to tap new markets, especially for firms which may not find it appropriate or possible to participate in trade missions.

A Small Business Assistance Program assists managers in studying, analyzing and diagnosing business problems and recommending solutions and in preparing financial proposals and applications for assistance through the various aid programs available. Through its Technical Assistance Program, the branch shares companies' costs in undertaking market and financial feasibility studies, as well as studies designed to improve productivity. The aim of this program is to provide incentive to companies to expand their facilities, diversify their product lines, or enter into new business.

The Department of Economic Development maintains liaison with the British Columbia Development Corporation, established as a Crown corporation to stimulate industrial growth. The corporation provides for the acquisition and servicing of land suitable for industrial use in areas where serviced industrial land was not previously available, or where high land costs prohibited the location of individual firms. It also provides direct financial assistance to large enterprises in the form of medium- and long-term capital. The aim is to complement the funding available from established lending institutions. Loans up to $150,000 are provided to smaller companies. The department maintains a trade and industry office at British Columbia House in London, England.

17.4   Government aid and controls

17.4.1   The Department of Consumer and Corporate Affairs

The functions of the department relate to consumer affairs; corporations and corporate securities; combines, mergers, monopolies and restraint of trade; bankruptcy and insolvency; patents, trade marks, copyright and industrial design.

The department has five main divisions — the Bureau of Consumer Affairs, the Bureau of Corporate Affairs, the Bureau of Intellectual Property, the Field Operations Service and the Bureau of Competition Policy. The Bureau of Consumer Affairs coordinates government activities in the field of consumer affairs; its branches include Consumer Services, Consumer Credit, Consumer Research and the Consumer Standards Directorate. The Bureau of Corporate Affairs administers legislation and regulations pertaining to corporations. Its branches include Corporations, Bankruptcy, Securities and Research. The Bureau of Intellectual Property administers laws pertaining to patents, copyright and industrial design, and trade marks, with a branch responsible for each of these three fields. Canada's participation in international intellectual property organizations is the responsibility of the Research and International Affairs Branch, and the role of informing Canadians of the services of the bureau is provided by the Technical Advisory Services Branch. The Field Operations Service supervises the department's operations across Canada, staffing regional and district offices in Vancouver, Winnipeg, Toronto, Montreal and Halifax and in several other cities. They ensure that laws and regulations administered by the department are uniformly applied and interpreted in all parts of the country. The field force includes consumer consultants and information officers in each region, complaints officers, inspectors and specialists in the fields of bankruptcy and false and misleading advertising.

The Bureau of Competition Policy has four operating branches, specializing in Resources, Manufacturing, Services and Trade Practices. There is also a

Research Branch that undertakes basic research projects. The Restrictive Trade Practices Commission is an independent administrative commission that reports directly to the minister.

Anti-combines legislation. Canadian anti-combines legislation seeks to eliminate restrictive trade practices in order to stimulate maximum production, distribution and employment through open competition. Legislative measures, including some formerly included in the Criminal Code, were amended in 1960 and consolidated into the Combines Investigation Act (RSC 1970, c.C-23). The act was amended in 1975 by Bill C-2. The amendments for the most part came into effect January 1, 1976; the remainder on July 1 of the same year.

In general terms, the Combines Investigation Act makes illegal the operation of combines that prevent, or lessen "unduly", competition in production, manufacture, purchase, barter, sale, storage, rental, transportation or supply of a product of trade or commerce, or in the price of insurance. Although the exchange of statistics or defining of product standards are not to be construed as illegal practices, this exemption is not valid if the purpose of the exchange of information is to reduce the possibility of increased competition in the fields of prices, production quantities or quality, customers, markets or distribution channels, or if it has the effect of restricting entry or expansion into that particular business, trade or industry. While combines which relate to export trade only are generally exempt from these constraints, any such arrangement that may have an adverse effect on the volume of export trade or on the businesses of Canadian competitors or domestic consumers is still subject to prosecution.

Under the act it is illegal to participate in a merger or a monopoly that has operated, or is likely to operate to the detriment of the public, whether consumers, producers or others.

Price discrimination and "predatory price cutting" are also prohibited by the act. No supplier may make a practice of discriminating among his competing trade customers by offering more advantageous prices to one over another. Under the law, if a second buyer is willing to buy on the same terms and in the same quantities, he must be given the same price. Prices established by a supplier cannot be set lower in one locality than another, or unreasonably low anywhere, if the policy is designed to eliminate or lessen competition or has that effect.

Advertising or display allowances to competing trade customers must be offered in proportion to their purchases and any expenses required to be incurred by customers must also be in proportion to their purchases. No service may be exacted in return for allowances unless all different types of customers are able to perform that service.

Other sections of the act forbid misleading or deceptive advertising, either as to normal price or as to presumably factual statements describing goods or property offered for sale. The act also provides against double ticketing, pyramid selling, referral selling, bait and switch selling, and certain types of promotional contests.

"Resale price maintenance" is another restrictive practice prohibited by the act. The suggested list price for products offered for resale at the wholesale or retail level can be only that — a suggested price. No supplier of goods for resale may prescribe the final price at which the goods must be sold, nor can he cut off supplies if a merchant refuses to abide by the suggested prices and it should be clearly indicated that the product could be sold at a lower price. Some relief to the supplier is offered by the qualifications that no one can be automatically considered to have practised resale price maintenance if the goods are withheld because there is sound reason to believe that the merchant was making a practice of using the products of the supplier as "loss-leaders" or as bait advertising, or engaging in misleading advertising or failing to provide the service that the final purchaser had a right to expect.

The Director of Investigation and Research is responsible for investigating combines and other restrictive practices, and the Restrictive Trade Practices

Commission is responsible for appraising the evidence submitted to it by the director and the parties under investigation, and for making a report to the Minister of Consumer and Corporate Affairs. When there are reasonable grounds for believing that a forbidden practice is engaged in, the director may obtain from the commission authorization to examine witnesses, search premises, or require written returns. After examining all the information available, if the director believes that it proves the existence of a forbidden practice, he submits a statement of the evidence to the commission and to the parties believed to be responsible for the practice. The commission then sets a time and place for a hearing at which both sides are represented. The commission prepares and submits a report to the Minister of Consumer and Corporate Affairs; such reports are required to be published within 30 days. At the completion of an inquiry, the director may also submit the evidence directly to the Attorney General for prosecution without going to the commission.

Effective January 1, 1976 the director may bring before the Restrictive Trade Practices Commission a broad range of business matters for review under civil procedures. The commission is empowered to issue appropriate remedial orders where serious anti-competitive effects are found. The matters include refusal to sell, tied selling, exclusive dealing, market restrictions and consignment selling. Foreign judgments, laws and directives under specific circumstances are also reviewable matters. The act also provides for civil suits by private individuals for recovery of loss or damage resulting from conduct contrary to the act.

Under the provisions of the act, general inquiries may be made into restraints of trade which, although not forbidden or punishable, may affect the public interest. In addition to imposing punishment for a contravention of the legislation, the courts, which in this instance includes the Federal Court of Canada, may issue interim injunctions restraining persons from contravening the act. Prosecutions for offences against the substantive provisions of the legislation may be taken in a superior court as defined in the Criminal Code.

Patents. Patents for inventions are issued under the provisions of the Patent Act (RSC 1970, c.P-4) and Patent Regulations have been proclaimed to carry into effect the objectives of the act. Applications for patents for inventions and requests for information about such patents should be addressed to the Commissioner of Patents, Bureau of Intellectual Property, Department of Consumer and Corporate Affairs.

In the year ended December 31, 1975, 20,544 patents were granted. Of these, 6.2% resulted from inventions made by residents of Canada, 5.6% by residents of Britain and 60% by residents of the United States.

Printed copies of Canadian patents issued from January 1, 1948 to date are available at $1 each. The *Patent Office Record*, issued weekly, contains a list of patents issued during the week covered, information about services in the Patent Office and information of concern to the patent profession.

Canadian and foreign patents may be consulted at the Patent Office Library. British patents and abridged specifications thereof from 1617 to date and United States patents from 1845 to date are available, as well as many patents, indexes, journals and reports from Australia, India, Ireland, New Zealand, Pakistan, South Africa, Austria, Belgium, Colombia, Czechoslovakia, Egypt, France, Federal Republic of Germany, Italy, Japan, Mexico, the Netherlands, Norway, Sweden, Switzerland and Yugoslavia. A list of the foreign patents available is published in the *Patent Office Record*.

Copyright, industrial design and timber marks. Copyright protection is governed by the Copyright Act (RSC 1970, c.C-30) in force since 1924. Protection is automatic without any formality, although a system of voluntary registration is provided. Copyright exists in Canada in every original literary, dramatic, musical and artistic work and in contrivances by means of which sounds may be mechanically reproduced, if the author was, at the date of making of the work, a British subject, a citizen or subject of a foreign country which has adhered to the Berne Convention and the additional protocol, or resident within Her Majesty's Dominions and if, in the case of a published work, the work was first published within Her Majesty's Realms and Territories or in such foreign country. The term for which the copyright exists is, except as otherwise expressly provided by this act, the life of the author and a period of 50 years after his death. Canada belongs to both the International (Berne) Copyright Convention and the Universal Copyright Convention. Under the terms of the Universal Copyright Convention unpublished works of Canadian authors are protected in all convention countries without formalities such as compulsory registration or special manufacturing and printing provisions. The only requirement is with respect to published works. In such cases every copy of the published work must bear, in a prominent place, the copyright symbol ©, followed by the name of the proprietor and the year of publication.

The Industrial Design Act provides a maximum 10-year period of protection for shape, pattern, ornamentation and/or configuration applied to an article of manufacture, provided that the design is registered within one year of publication in Canada. Protection is granted if an examination does not reveal any other design already registered to be identical with or closely resembling the proposed design. The name of the proprietor, the letters Rd. and the year of registration must appear upon the article to which the design applies.

People or companies who float timber on the inland waters of Ontario, Quebec and New Brunswick must, based on the Timber Marking Act, select a mark or marks and apply for registration thereof within one month after engaging in this business.

Trade marks. The Trade Marks Office, a branch within the Bureau of Intellectual Property, administers the Trade Marks Act (RSC 1970, c.T-10) which covers all legislation concerning the registration and use of trade marks and supersedes from July 1, 1954, former legislation enacted under the Unfair Competition Act, the Union Label Act and the Shop Cards Registration Act. Correspondence relating to an application for registration of a trade mark should be addressed to the Registrar of Trade Marks, Ottawa.

Applications are advertised for opposition purposes in the *Trade Marks Journal,* a weekly publication that also gives particulars of every registration of a trade mark. The required fee payable on application for registration of a trade mark is $35 and for advertisement of an application, $25.

Trade marks registered during the year ended December 31, 1975 numbered 6,898; renewals totalled 3,111.

Consumer credit. A new branch established in the Bureau of Consumer Affairs in 1976 was the Consumer Credit Branch. Its main goal was to prepare a comprehensive legislative recommendation in the field of consumer credit. The Borrowers' and Depositors' Protection Bill was tabled in the House of Commons in October 1976. Its objectives are: to reduce substantially the occurrence of excessive interest rate charges, to improve the quality and increase the quantity of information about interest that is made available to borrowers, and to eliminate unnecessary complexities in consumer credit. It involves the repeal of such existing legislation as the Interest Act and the Small Loans Act.

Trade standards   17.4.2

The Standards Council of Canada   17.4.2.1

The Standards Council of Canada with headquarters in Ottawa is the national coordinating agency through which organizations concerned with voluntary standardization may cooperate in recognizing, establishing and improving standards in Canada. It enables organizations to play a larger and more effective role in formulating and promoting the use of standards to meet the needs of the economy through the National Standards System. The system includes organizations involved in standards-writing and in testing and certification. It encourages the development of a broader and more energetic Canadian standards program to meet both national and international responsibilities.

The objects of the council are to foster and promote voluntary standardization in fields relating to the construction, manufacture, production, quality performance and safety of buildings, structures, manufactured articles and products and other goods, including components, not expressly provided for elsewhere by law, to advance the national economy, benefit the health, safety and welfare of the public, assist and protect consumers, facilitate domestic and international trade and further international cooperation in the field of standards.

At the end of 1974 the National Standards System had accredited five standards-writing organizations which are authorized to write National Standards of Canada — the Canadian Gas Association, the Canadian Government Specifications Board, the Canadian Standards Association, the Underwriters' Laboratories of Canada and Bureau de normalisation du Québec. Certification organizations and testing laboratories will also be accredited to the system. An Advisory Committee on Standards for Consumers identifies consumers needs in the standards field and makes the necessary recommendations to the council.

The council, advised by a Committee on Conversion to Metric (SI) Standards, supports Metric Commission Canada by providing the technical basis for Canadian conversion and guidance and assistance in planning for, and carrying out, a program to provide standards expressed in the International System of Units (SI) to all organizations participating in metric conversion. Representatives of the National Standards System actively participate in the conversion activities of each of the 10 steering committees and each of the approximately 115 sector committees formed under the auspices of the Metric Commission. The council is also in close touch with the interdepartmental committees for conversion of the federal, provincial and territorial governments and with the American National Metric Council in the United States.

In the international field, the council appoints the members and directs the activities of the Canadian National Committee of the International Electro-Technical Commission and is the member body for Canada in the International Organization for Standardization. The council coordinates and integrates the national and international standards and oversees the accreditation of some 350 delegates to represent Canada at over 360 international technical committee meetings each year. The council's International Standardization Branch is located at Mississauga, Ont.

In January 1977 the council, in cooperation with the accredited standards writing organizations, established a Standards Information Service, with a central information and referral service at its offices in Ottawa.

17.4.2.2   Trade standards and regulations

In its consumer program, Consumer and Corporate Affairs Canada is responsible for the administration of broad legislation which affects the business community. Policies and programming are determined by the Consumer Standards Directorate, and the necessary field supervision by the Field Operations Service.

Hazardous products. The Product Safety Branch administers the Hazardous Products Act which deals with consumer goods. The act makes specific mention of products designed for household, garden, or personal use, for use in sports or recreational activities or for use by children. It also mentions without reference to end use, poisonous, toxic, flammable, explosive and corrosive products.

Under the act, the minister is empowered to establish mandatory standards for application in Canada. Compliance orders now being enforced include the use of shatterproof glass in patio and shower doors, flammability standards for children's sleepwear and protective standards for hockey helmets. Regulations governing toys, cribs and portable car seats are designed to protect children. Other products required to meet rigid specifications include matches, charcoal, ceramics and electrical appliances.

General commodity field. The Consumer Packaging and Labelling Act and Regulations administered by the Consumer Fraud Protection Branch is designed to give uniformity to packaging and labelling practices in Canada, reduce the possibilities of fraud and deception in packaging and control the proliferation of packaged sizes. The legislation applies to most pre-packaged consumer products and came into effect on September 1, 1975 for non-food items and on March 1, 1976 for foods.

Regulations under the Textile Labelling Act, in effect since December 1, 1972, require labels on all consumer textile articles. The label must include fibre names and percentages and the identification of the dealer. The regulations also deal with misrepresentation in both labelling and advertising. The Textile Care Labelling System of coloured symbols recommending proper care for textile products is a voluntary program at this time. The Canadian Standard Size (CSS) system for children's garments, developed by the Canadian Government Specifications Board in conjunction with Consumer and Corporate Affairs Canada, is administered under the National Trade Mark and True Labelling Act. This system is also voluntary, although dealers must register for a licence before claiming that the garment does, in fact, conform to the CSS and before affixing such a label to the product.

Control of marking of precious metal articles is maintained under the Precious Metals Marking Act. The new regulations came into force in July 1973.

Food. In areas of health, grading, standards and composition, the Food and Drug Act, the Canadian Agricultural Products Standards Act and the Fish Inspection Act are generally applicable. Consumer and Corporate Affairs Canada is charged with administration of the economic fraud aspects in distribution. This responsibility relates mainly to labelling and advertising in any segment of the news media.

Advertising. Most legislation has particular requirements to ensure against misleading advertising, but the Deceptive Marketing Provisions of the Combines Investigation Act are especially noteworthy as they include general provisions against misleading advertising practices.

Measurement. The Weights and Measures Act prescribes the legal standards of weight and measure for use in Canada; it also ensures control of the types of all weighing and measuring devices used for commercial purposes, and provides for in-use surveillance directed toward the elimination of device-tampering and short-weight sales. A replacing act was passed by Parliament and new regulations were proclaimed in August 1974. The fundamental objectives of existing legislation remain unchanged. The new act is complementary to the new consumer packaging and labelling legislation.

The Electricity Inspection Act and the Gas Inspection Act control the approval before sale and use of instruments used for billing of electricity and gas whether by meter or other type of device; they also provide for continual in-use inspection.

Corporations. The Bureau of Corporate Affairs is concerned with much of the general legal framework that governs the orderly conduct of business under federal jurisdiction. The bureau is subdivided into the following branches: Bankruptcy, Corporations, and Corporate Research.

The Corporations Branch is responsible for administration of the Canada Business Corporations Act, the Canada Corporations Act, the Canada Cooperatives Association Act and the Board of Trade Act. In addition, the branch has a statutory duty to issue formal documents in connection with corporations created under other federal acts such as the Loan Companies Act, Trust Companies Act, the Canadian and British Insurance Companies Act, and the Railway Act.

Although all federal corporations other than those carrying on business as financial intermediaries must now be incorporated under the recently proclaimed (December 15, 1975) Canada Business Corporations Act, because that act does not repeal the old Canada Corporations Act until December 15, 1980, the branch is required to administer corporations subject to either act until that date. This policy of gradual implementation of the Canada Business Corporations Act was adopted to enable corporations to effect transition from the old to the new act with a minimum of pressure and inconvenience following a relatively simple continuance procedure.

Part II of the Canada Corporations Act continues to apply to all federal charitable and membership corporations. In 1977 the department planned to introduce a proposed new Not-for-Profit Corporations Act. This would abrogate Part II of the Canada Corporations Act after a five-year transition period.

Ancillary to its formal activities, the branch furnished to the public copies of corporate documents and information about registered corporate names and trade marks. In 1975-76 the branch issued 23,000 documents to the public compared to 10,500 in 1974-75, indicating the growing importance of information about specific corporations. There were also 20,321 registered corporate name and trade mark searches made; this is an increase of 4,920 from the year before.

In addition to maintaining its file on approximately 400,000 corporations that now exist in Canada (20,000 of which are federal corporations) as well as its list of some 140,000 registered trade marks, the branch undertook to automate its search services of information about registered corporate names and trade marks. Besides obtaining and furnishing information about federal and provincial corporations to the public, the branch processes applications for exemption from the statutory disclosure requirements, investigates complaints involving federal corporations and ascertains whether federal corporations are making the required statutory filings in the form prescribed by the regulations.

17.5   Bankruptcies and commercial failures

Two series of figures are included here which, although closely related in subject matter, cover different aspects of the field of bankruptcies and commercial failures. The first (Table 17.13) is limited to the supervision, by the Superintendent of Bankruptcy, of the administration of bankrupt estates under the Bankruptcy Act (RSC 1970, c.B-3); it gives information on the amounts realized from the assets as established by debtors and indicates that values actually paid to creditors are invariably very much lower than such estimates alone would imply. It can therefore be assumed that this applies in even greater degree to the more extended fields covered in the second section (Tables 17.11 and 17.12) compiled by Statistics Canada, which is limited to bankruptcies and insolvencies made under federal legislation and includes business failures only.

Administration of bankrupt estates. The Bankruptcy Act was last revised in 1949 and amended in 1966. The amendments were instigated by exposures and suggestions of illegal and improper practices in connection with bankruptcy proceedings or administration. They do not constitute a complete revision of the Bankruptcy Act but were designed to provide, as an interim measure, remedies to the most urgent areas of complaints. They provide the Superintendent of Bankruptcy with direct and immediate authority in the field of investigation and inquiry, and tighten the procedures and requirements in a number of areas, such as that of proposals which an insolvent person may make to his creditors. These amendments were intended to provide remedies in situations where it had been shown by experience that abuses of the bankruptcy process are most likely to occur. The amendments also contain a new Part X entitled ''The Orderly Payment of Debts'' which may be brought into force in any province at the request of the provincial authorities concerned. Six areas have taken advantage of this part of the legislation: Alberta in April 1967, Manitoba in June 1967, Saskatchewan in

April 1969, British Columbia in June 1970, Nova Scotia in July 1970, Prince Edward Island in April 1971 and the Northwest Territories in November 1972.

A new program called the Small Debtor Program was instituted in June 1972. While it is not an amendment to the Bankruptcy Act, it authorizes federal employees who have been appointed as trustees to handle the estates of certain wage-earners who cannot obtain the services of a private trustee.

A report issued annually by the Superintendent of Bankruptcy gives statistics and comments on various activities in the field of bankruptcy, such as prosecution for offences, issue of licences for trustees in bankruptcy, number of estates reported and closed during the year, and costs of bankruptcy administration in Canada. These data are summarized in Table 17.13.

Returns under the Bankruptcy and Winding-up Acts. Statistics Canada data on bankruptcies and insolvencies cover only failures coming under the federal Bankruptcy Act and the Winding-up Act. Figures cover business failures only. Table 17.11 gives yearly comparisons of liabilities — as estimated by debtors — for the main regions of the country. Table 17.12 shows the number of bankruptcies and insolvencies by industry and economic area for 1973.

Sources

17.1 Manufacturing and Primary Industries Division, Industry Statistics Branch, Statistics Canada.
17.2 Information Services Branch, Department of Industry, Trade and Commerce.
17.3 Supplied by the respective provincial government departments.
17.4.1 Information and Public Relations, Department of Consumer and Corporate Affairs.
17.4.2 The Standards Council of Canada; Information and Public Relations, Department of Consumer and Corporate Affairs.
17.5 Superintendent of Bankruptcy, Department of Consumer and Corporate Affairs; Business Finance Division, General Statistics Branch, Statistics Canada.

Tables

..	not available	e	estimate
...	not appropriate or not applicable	p	preliminary
—	nil or zero	r	revised
- -	too small to be expressed		certain tables may not add due to rounding

17.1 Value of shipments of goods of own manufacture, by province, 1961 and 1972-75 (million dollars)

Province or territory	1961	1972	1973	1974	1975P
Newfoundland	135.9	284.1	382.6	711.7	700.2
Prince Edward Island	30.6	..	..	..	..
Nova Scotia	381.4	993.6	1,250.7	1,696.1	1,907.2
New Brunswick	390.6	965.0	1,175.5	1,585.7	1,647.0
Quebec	7,022.2	15,091.6	17,464.9	22,396.8	23,822.1
Ontario	11,563.7	29,225.0	34,300.7	41,404.4	44,082.9
Manitoba	716.7	1,509.3	1,840.2	2,279.7	2,544.2
Saskatchewan	331.9	646.5	809.6	1,045.2	1,084.5
Alberta	935.5	2,425.3	2,973.3	3,821.3	4,453.7
British Columbia	1,927.0	5,020.3	6,387.1	7,411.1	7,236.1
Yukon Territory and Northwest Territories	3.4	..	..	..	..
Canada	23,439.0	56,234.7[1]	66,674.4[1]	82,455.1[1]	87,597.7[1]

[1]Includes Prince Edward Island, the Yukon Territory and Northwest Territories.

17.2 Value of shipments of goods of own manufacture, by industry group, 1972-75 (million dollars)

Industry group	1972	1973	1974	1975P
Food and beverage industries	10,251.2	12,375.3	14,737.7	16,261.0
Tobacco products industries	596.2	618.0	704.9	755.1
Rubber and plastics products industries	1,317.3	1,577.3	1,833.5	1,910.2
Leather industries	447.1	508.8	570.1	610.0
Textile industries	1,919.4	2,183.2	2,477.8	2,406.4
Knitting mills	470.1	530.1	600.6	584.7
Clothing industries	1,645.1	1,837.6	2,076.6	2,167.0
Wood industries	3,084.9	4,056.0	3,991.1	3,694.4
Furniture and fixture industries	958.3	1,118.5	1,338.2	1,290.3
Paper and allied industries	4,414.0	5,271.0	7,677.4	7,116.8
Printing, publishing and allied industries	1,853.5	2,160.3	2,550.5	2,843.4
Primary metal industries	4,193.4	4,918.0	6,535.4	6,553.7
Metal fabricating industries (except machinery and transportation equipment industries)	3,822.0	4,539.4	5,834.0	6,075.7
Machinery industries (except electrical machinery)	2,134.6	2,431.9	3,137.8	3,695.2
Transportation equipment industries	7,747.3	9,056.7	10,173.9	11,484.8
Electrical products industries	3,062.5	3,537.9	4,344.9	4,545.4
Non-metallic mineral products industries	1,665.5	1,923.0	2,282.5	2,484.4
Petroleum and coal products industries	2,441.1	3,073.2	5,185.3	6,294.4
Chemical and chemical products industries	2,943.1	3,503.8	4,607.7	4,999.2
Miscellaneous manufacturing industries	1,267.8	1,454.2	1,794.9	1,825.7
All manufacturing industries	56,234.7	66,674.4	82,455.1	87,597.7

17.3 Net profit before taxes and extraordinary items, as a percentage of total revenue of corporations classified to the manufacturing industries, 1973-75

Industry group[1]	1973r	1974r	1975
Food and beverage industries	5.7	4.5	4.7
Rubber industries	7.7	4.7	4.3
Textile industries[2]	4.7	5.4	2.7
Wood industries[3]	11.4	6.8	4.4
Paper and allied industries	9.5	14.9	7.9
Printing, publishing and allied industries	10.6	10.5	9.0
Primary metal industries	9.5	12.3	8.2
Metal fabricating industries	7.7	8.2	7.8
Machinery industries	7.7	9.0	9.1
Transportation equipment industries	5.7	4.9	3.9
Electrical products industries	7.3	7.5	8.9
Non-metallic mineral products industries	10.0	10.5	10.6
Petroleum and coal products industries	14.0	15.5	13.7
Chemical and chemical products industries	9.8	12.6	11.8
Miscellaneous manufacturing industries	9.4	8.6	8.3
All manufacturing industries	8.1	8.8	7.4

[1]Adaptation of 1960 revision of the Standard Industrial Classification.
[2]Includes knitting mills and clothing industries.
[3]Includes furniture and fixture industries.

17.4   Summary statistics of manufactures, 1965-74

Year	Estab-lish-ments No.	Activity						
		Manufacturing activity						
		Production and related workers			Cost of fuel and electri-city[1] $'000	Cost of materials and supplies used $'000	Value of shipments of goods of own manu-facture $'000	Value added $'000
		Number	Man-hours paid '000	Wages $'000				
1965	33,310	1,115,892	2,384,002	5,012,345	675,641	18,622,213	33,889,425	14,927,764
1966	33,377	1,172,943	2,498,012	5,575,206	731,726	20,642,695	37,303,455	16,351,740
1967	33,267	1,168,651	2,478,916	5,869,085	759,780	21,371,785	38,955,389	17,005,696
1968	32,643	1,160,226	2,458,791	6,278,429	808,764	23,090,970	42,061,555	18,332,204
1969	32,669	1,189,887	2,515,183	6,921,525	860,525	25,383,484	45,930,438	20,133,593
1970	31,928	1,167,063	2,450,058	7,232,256	903,264	25,699,999	46,380,935	20,047,801
1971	31,908	1,167,810	2,448,419	7,819,050	1,000,243	27,661,379	50,275,917	21,737,514
1972	31,553	1,213,106	2,547,609	8,763,104	1,078,916	31,137,946	56,234,663	24,314,751
1973	31,145	1,275,985	2,665,681	10,060,062	1,221,885	37,600,538	66,674,393	28,716,119
1974	31,535	1,300,792	2,713,436	11,637,073	1,623,617	47,499,791	82,455,109	35,084,752
		Total activity						
		Working owners and partners		Total employees[2]		Cost of materials and supplies used and goods purchased for resale[3] $'000	Value of shipments and other revenue[4] $'000	Value added[5] $'000
		Number	With-drawals $'000	Number	Salaries and wages $'000			
1965	33,310	14,620	59,457	1,570,299	7,822,925	21,563,010	37,638,412	15,785,311
1966	33,377	13,894	60,076	1,646,024	8,695,890	24,195,610	41,722,527	17,260,256
1967	33,267	13,377	59,187	1,652,827	9,254,190	25,546,764	44,143,808	18,049,639
1968	32,643	12,084	58,798	1,642,352	9,905,504	27,546,942	47,646,657	19,483,614
1969	32,669	11,583	59,128	1,675,332	10,848,341	30,347,637	52,130,615	21,456,276
1970	31,928	10,760	58,605	1,637,001	11,363,712	30,805,904	52,886,022	21,417,748
1971	31,908	10,286	60,939	1,628,404	12,129,897	33,462,590	57,479,421	23,187,881
1972	31,553	9,793	62,330	1,676,130	13,414,609	37,663,105	64,404,224	26,031,664
1973	31,145	8,981	..	1,751,066	15,220,033	45,697,053	76,689,795	30,766,506
1974	31,535	7,075	..	1,785,977	17,556,982	57,794,605	95,030,218	37,654,465

[1]Cannot be reported separately for manufacturing and non-manufacturing activities but related substantially to manufacturing activity.
[2]Includes production and related workers, administrative and office employees, sales, distribution and other employees; excludes working owners and partners.
[3]Includes supplies used in both manufacturing and non-manufacturing activity.
[4]Includes shipments of goods of own manufacture, value of shipments of goods purchased for resale and other operational revenue.
[5]Value of total operational revenue less total cost of materials, supplies, fuel and electricity used and goods purchased for resale in the same condition; all adjusted for inventory changes where required.

17.5   Establishments in the manufacturing industries, by number employed and by province, 1973 and 1974

Year and province or territory	Number employed									Total
	Under 5	5 to 9	10 to 19	20 to 49	50 to 99	100 to 199	200 to 499	500 to 999	1,000 or over	
1973										
Newfoundland	89	26	34	33	26	21	12	2	2	245
Prince Edward Island	54	23	22	17	9	5	1	—	—	131
Nova Scotia	237	141	122	115	59	35	28	5	4	746
New Brunswick	181	92	93	93	47	45	26	5	3	585
Quebec	2,864	1,629	1,544	1,790	981	612	376	111	40	9,947
Ontario	3,261	1,919	2,054	2,237	1,178	884	611	174	79	12,397
Manitoba	430	208	193	224	104	81	44	8	3	1,295
Saskatchewan	275	135	100	91	43	18	11	1	1	675
Alberta	607	372	311	275	118	78	46	9	—	1,816
British Columbia	1,209	583	486	470	235	144	120	28	13	3,288
Yukon Territory and Northwest Territories	7	3	8	2	—	—	—	—	—	20
Canada	9,214	5,131	4,967	5,347	2,800	1,923	1,275	343	145	31,145

17.5   Establishments in the manufacturing industries, by number employed and by province, 1973 and 1974 (concluded)

Year and province or territory	Number employed									Total
	Under 5	5 to 9	10 to 19	20 to 49	50 to 99	100 to 199	200 to 499	500 to 999	1,000 or over	
1974										
Newfoundland	103	37	24	38	29	17	11	3	2	264
Prince Edward Island	63	21	23	22	3	5	1	—	—	138
Nova Scotia	253	131	112	116	62	30	24	8	4	740
New Brunswick	193	80	83	114	39	52	22	6	3	592
Quebec	2,898	1,516	1,607	1,854	950	613	380	105	51	9,974
Ontario	3,374	1,964	2,066	2,297	1,180	883	632	182	84	12,662
Manitoba	455	184	180	221	112	85	42	10	2	1,291
Saskatchewan	281	121	103	91	46	20	14	1	1	678
Alberta	635	352	319	285	128	85	48	12	—	1,864
British Columbia	1,252	555	482	481	230	150	123	22	14	3,309
Yukon Territory and Northwest Territories	8	2	10	3	—	—	—	—	—	23
Canada	9,515	4,963	5,009	5,522	2,779	1,940	1,297	349	161	31,535

17.6   Number of establishments in manufacturing industries, by industry group and employment size group, 1973 and 1974

Year and industry group	Establishments with total employment of									Total
	Under 5	5 to 9	10 to 19	20 to 49	50 to 99	100 to 199	200 to 499	500 to 999	1,000 or over	
1973										
Food and beverage industries	1,505	1,009	905	814	387	283	176	38	12	5,129
Tobacco products industries	2	1	—	3	3	3	8	3	2	25
Rubber and plastics products industries	135	100	150	166	76	60	33	14	6	740
Leather industries	79	36	47	105	57	67	24	2	—	417
Textile industries	179	142	164	160	88	75	79	19	8	914
Knitting mills	24	29	36	78	54	58	27	4	—	310
Clothing industries	373	245	334	567	331	183	76	10	1	2,120
Wood industries	1,112	458	455	491	275	144	112	13	3	3,063
Furniture and fixture industries	1,103	289	225	256	127	99	36	2	—	2,137
Paper and allied industries	46	48	68	130	91	99	102	44	21	649
Printing, publishing and allied industries	1,640	753	602	434	188	85	48	17	6	3,773
Primary metal industries	37	39	43	86	63	49	45	22	19	403
Metal fabricating industries (except machinery and transportation equipment industries)	1,012	793	720	755	323	190	111	25	3	3,932
Machinery industries (except electrical machinery)	149	133	169	247	121	95	63	21	7	1,005
Transportation equipment industries	203	127	137	180	105	92	79	35	29	987
Electrical products industries	85	67	104	126	117	90	93	36	20	738
Non-metallic mineral products industries	295	211	258	244	107	74	41	9	2	1,241
Petroleum and coal products industries	16	18	9	22	8	18	11	2	1	105
Chemical and chemical products industries	226	184	183	202	136	90	69	19	2	1,111
Miscellaneous manufacturing industries	993	449	358	281	143	69	42	8	3	2,346
1974										
Food and beverage industries	1,629	854	851	791	381	282	170	39	13	5,010
Tobacco products industries	2	1	1	3	2	1	9	3	2	24
Rubber and plastics products industries	163	97	134	188	83	61	37	15	5	783
Leather industries	80	48	52	108	62	53	25	4	—	432
Textile industries	221	133	164	155	88	68	80	17	10	936
Knitting mills	26	32	43	79	55	52	29	4	—	320
Clothing industries	407	265	343	582	301	191	74	8	1	2,172
Wood industries	1,165	460	454	499	267	156	97	10	3	3,111
Furniture and fixture industries	1,139	292	259	277	130	97	34	5	—	2,233
Paper and allied industries	44	45	61	142	92	90	104	46	26	650
Printing, publishing and allied industries	1,607	807	606	444	189	86	48	18	7	3,812
Primary metal industries	31			322				21	23	397
Metal fabricating industries (except machinery and transportation equipment industries)	1,042	740	760	807	318	207	121	21	5	4,021

17.6 Number of establishments in manufacturing industries, by industry group and employment size group, 1973 and 1974 (concluded)

Year and industry group	Establishments with total employment of									Total
	Under 5	5 to 9	10 to 19	20 to 49	50 to 99	100 to 199	200 to 499	500 to 999	1,000 or over	
1974 (concluded)										
Machinery industries (except electrical machinery)	173	154	176	240	136	97	70	18	10	1,074
Transportation equipment industries	222	118	132	189	99	98	82	34	29	1,003
Electrical products industries	95	78	101	146	111	101	86	46	20	784
Non-metallic mineral products industries	261	183	280	244	107	73	48	8	2	1,206
Petroleum and coal products industries	16	19	5	20	11	18	11	4	1	105
Chemical and chemical products industries	188	165	184	214	137	83	75	20	2	1,068
Miscellaneous manufacturing industries	1,004	437	367	301	154	70	51	8	2	2,394

17.7 Establishments and shipments in the manufacturing industries, by shipments per establishment, 1961, 1973 and 1974

Value group	Year			
	1961			
	Establishments No.	Value of shipments of goods of own manufacture $'000	Average per establishment $'000	Proportion of total shipments %
Up to $24,999	9,245	106,779	12	0.5
$ 25,000 - $ 49,999	4,677	168,079	36	0.7
50,000 - 99,999	4,562	328,307	72	1.4
100,000 - 199,999	4,260	610,675	143	2.6
200,000 - 499,999	4,555	1,462,027	321	6.2
500,000 - 999,999	2,400	1,689,457	704	7.2
1,000,000 - 4,999,999	2,875	6,123,965	2,130	26.1
5,000,000 and over	783	12,949,667	16,539	55.3
Total and average	33,357	23,438,956	703	100.0
	1973			
	Establishments No.	Value of shipments of goods of own manufacture $'000	Average per establishment $'000	Proportion of total shipments %
Up to $24,999	3,164	44,472	14	0.1
$ 25,000 - $ 49,999	3,263	119,971	37	0.2
50,000 - 99,999	3,913	284,298	73	0.4
100,000 - 199,999	3,992	576,031	144	0.9
200,000 - 499,999	5,215	1,701,530	326	2.6
500,000 - 999,999	3,566	2,558,678	718	3.8
1,000,000 - 4,999,999	5,552	12,598,266	2,269	18.9
5,000,000 and over	2,480	48,791,148	19,674	73.2
Total and average	31,145	66,674,393	2,140	100.0
	1974			
	Establishments No.	Value of shipments of goods of own manufacture $'000	Average per establishment $'000	Proportion of total shipments %
Up to $24,999	2,519	36,211	14	- -
$ 25,000 - $ 49,999	3,033	112,690	37	0.1
50,000 - 99,999	3,915	286,467	73	0.3
100,000 - 199,999	4,079	587,546	144	0.7
200,000 - 499,999	5,270	1,720,675	327	2.1
500,000 - 999,999	3,790	2,719,231	717	3.3
1,000,000 - 4,999,999	5,965	13,573,590	2,276	16.5
5,000,000 and over	2,964	63,418,699	21,396	76.9
Total and average	31,535	82,455,109	2,615	100.0

17.8   Establishments in the manufacturing industries, by value of shipments of goods of own manufacture and by province, 1973 and 1974

Province or territory	Up to $9,999	$10,000 to $24,999	$25,000 to $49,999	$50,000 to $99,999	$100,000 to $199,999	$200,000 to $499,999	$500,000 to $999,999	$1,000,000 to $4,999,999	$5,000,000 and over	Total
1973										
Nfld.	27	27	25	20	27	26	27	66 ———		245
PEI	12	42 ———			13	64 ———				131
NS	41	72	95	89	101	120	82	97	49	746
NB	35	49	67	62	66	89	67	106	44	585
Que.	325	731	1,019	1,226	1,300	1,671	1,209	1,781	685	9,947
Ont.	264	707	1,141	1,484	1,511	2,183	1,462	2,463	1,182	12,397
Man.	61	107	154	166	161	204	135	228	79	1,295
Sask.	39	62	108	101	87	99	68	86	25	675
Alta.	47	137	221	267	265	300	203	257	119	1,816
BC	114	292	414	483	456	492	288	467	282	3,288
YT and NWT	—		7 ———		5	8 ———			—	20
Canada	965	2,199	3,263	3,913	3,992	5,215	3,566	5,552	2,480	31,145
1974										
Nfld.	26	34	29	21	30	23	35	66 ———		264
PEI	12	46 ———			9	71 ———				138
NS	33	50	91	99	96	131	77	105	58	740
NB	32	48	62	60	65	89	72	112	52	592
Que.	253	581	938	1,204	1,288	1,707	1,237	1,944	822	9,974
Ont.	196	579	1,046	1,469	1,595	2,155	1,612	2,598	1,412	12,662
Man.	40	94	146	177	156	202	142	226	108	1,291
Sask.	29	49	91	116	95	97	60	106	35	678
Alta.	30	107	194	278	278	328	205	287	157	1,864
BC	64	249	412	473	462	505	327	514	303	3,309
YT and NWT	—		9 ———		5	9 ———			—	23
Canada	715	1,804	3,033	3,915	4,079	5,270	3,790	5,965	2,964	31,535

17.9   Establishments and employment in the manufacturing industries, by number employed per establishment, 1961, 1973 and 1974

Size group		Establishments No.	Employees No.	Working owners and partners No.	Proportion of total employment[1] %
1961					
Under 5	employed	12,352	16,846	10,675	2.0
5 - 9	"	} 15,963	255,757	6,205	19.2
10 - 19	"				
20 - 49	"				
50 - 99	"	2,445	169,319	88	12.4
100 - 199	"	1,377	190,540	17	13.9
200 - 499	"	869	261,628	4	19.1
500 - 999	"	243	169,392	—	12.3
1,000 or more	"	108	234,320	—	17.1
Head offices		—	54,733	—	4.0
Total		33,357	1,352,535	16,989	100.0
1973					
Under 5	employed	9,214	13,779	6,459	1.2
5 - 9	"	5,131	32,840	1,665	2.0
10 - 19	"	4,967	68,442	582	3.9
20 - 49	"	5,346	168,254	208	9.6
50 - 99	"	2,800	196,521	42	11.2
100 - 199	"	1,923	270,842	15	15.4
200 - 499	"	1,275	386,014	10	21.9
500 - 999	"	343	234,654	—	13.3
1,000 or more	"	146	304,295	—	17.3
Head offices		—	75,425	—	4.3
Total		31,145	1,751,066	8,981	100.0
1974					
Under 5	employed	9,515	14,924	5,005	1.1
5 - 9	"	4,963	32,138	1,291	1.9
10 - 19	"	5,009	68,942	475	3.9
20 - 49	"	5,522	173,055	252	9.7
50 - 99	"	2,779	196,004	28	10.9
100 - 199	"	1,940	272,196	16	15.2
200 - 499	"	1,297	393,739	8	22.0
500 - 999	"	349	238,443	—	13.3
1,000 or more	"	161	320,276	—	17.9
Head offices		—	76,260	—	4.3
Total		31,535	1,785,977	7,075	100.0

[1]Includes working owners and partners.

17.10   Trends in domestic exports of manufactures, 1965-75 (million dollars)

Year	Fabricated materials	End products	Total manufactured goods[1]
1965	3,923.5	1,606.3	5,529.8
1966	4,217.0	2,455.1	6,672.1
1967	4,417.3	3,476.5	7,893.7
1968	5,027.9	4,702.4	9,730.4
1969	5,344.9	5,792.5	11,137.4
1970	6,083.4	6,010.1	12,093.5
1971	6,035.2	6,641.4	12,676.6
1972r	6,806.7	7,648.6	14,455.3
1973r	8,562.8	9,029.7	17,592.5
1974r	11,019.1	9,878.4	20,897.5
1975	10,180.1	11,044.7	21,224.8

[1]These categories of exports are only approximately equivalent to exports of manufactured goods.

17.11   Estimated liabilities[1] of bankruptcies and insolvencies, 1971-75 (thousand dollars)

Year	Atlantic provinces	Quebec	Ontario	Prairie provinces	British Columbia	Total
1971	10,591	121,451	97,533	72,223	20,256	322,054
1972	4,292	101,327	94,096	82,941	24,587	307,243
1973	37,578	131,062	86,734	17,396	23,931	296,701
1974	3,748	148,865	126,720	21,897	24,390	325,620
1975	2,496	167,524	102,076	21,037	38,768	331,901

[1]Estimated by debtors and therefore to be accepted with reservations.

17.12   Bankruptcies and insolvencies, by industry and economic area, 1974 and 1975

Industry	Atlantic provinces	Quebec	Ontario	Prairie provinces	British Columbia	Total	Estimated liabilities $'000
1974							
Primary industries	2	15	27	22	20	86	4,880
Manufacturing	—	107	66	11	13	197	63,047
Foods and beverages	—	5	5	2	—	12	3,094
Textiles	—	4	1	1	—	6	1,832
Clothing	—	29	4	—	—	33	5,467
Wood	—	14	5	1	3	23	1,638
Paper and allied industries	—	15	15	4	2	36	9,132
Primary and fabricated metal, machinery, transportation equipment, electrical products and non-metallic mineral products	—	21	23	2	5	51	31,740
Chemical	—	4	2	—	—	6	752
Other industries	—	15	11	1	3	30	9,392
Construction	9	224	229	47	59	568	73,606
General contractors	8	134	132	30	35	339	52,941
Special trade contractors	1	90	97	17	24	229	20,665
Transportation, communications and other utilities	3	100	149	58	42	352	36,920
Trade	26	564	496	84	69	1,239	93,112
Food	4	91	67	19	8	189	14,282
General merchandise	2	13	26	4	—	45	4,867
Automotive products	2	109	102	16	15	244	9,192
Apparel and shoes	6	108	72	6	6	198	9,512
Hardware	1	6	11	4	3	25	1,300
Household furniture and appliances	9	79	84	19	13	204	14,361
Drugs	—	7	2	—	—	9	429
Other trades	2	151	132	16	24	325	39,169
Finance, insurance and real estate	—	20	26	7	7	60	20,988
Service	2	142	162	22	24	352	33,067
Education, health and welfare	—	14	13	1	2	30	1,672
Recreational	—	7	7	1	1	16	1,137
Business	1	14	23	3	3	44	9,378
Personal	1	90	82	14	14	201	14,222
Other	—	17	37	3	4	61	6,658
Total, all industries	42	1,172	1,155	251	234	2,854	325,620

17.12 Bankruptcies and insolvencies, by industry and economic area, 1974 and 1975 (concluded)

Industry	Atlantic provinces	Quebec	Ontario	Prairie provinces	British Columbia	Total	Esti- mated liabilities $'000
1975							
Primary industries	—	16	18	5	7	46	12,802
Manufacturing	2	110	100	13	16	241	76,173
Foods and beverages	1	11	4	2	1	19	4,593
Textiles	—	5	3	—	—	8	8,042
Clothing	—	13	1	—	1	15	3,019
Wood	—	21	13	2	5	41	13,047
Paper and allied industries	—	13	20	1	3	37	4,348
Primary and fabricated metal, machinery, transportation equipment, electrical products and non-metallic mineral products	1	25	34	7	3	70	34,511
Chemical	—	3	4	—	1	8	1,317
Other industries	—	19	21	1	2	43	7,296
Construction	4	124	189	19	28	364	53,444
General contractors	4	50	74	6	12	146	25,756
Special trade contractors	—	74	115	13	16	218	27,688
Transportation, communications and other utilities	—	53	119	22	15	209	22,225
Trade	8	334	350	37	55	784	90,907
Food	3	34	32	1	11	81	7,378
General merchandise	1	7	19	1	1	29	10,281
Automotive products	1	60	78	14	10	163	6,790
Apparel and shoes	2	68	44	3	5	122	16,354
Hardware	—	17	5	2	2	26	1,921
Household furniture and appliances	1	35	49	7	5	97	8,466
Drugs	—	4	2	—	1	7	785
Other trades	—	109	121	9	20	259	38,932
Finance, insurance and real estate	4	10	28	2	5	49	23,542
Service	3	146	206	18	25	398	52,808
Education, health and welfare	—	7	8	2	1	18	8,655
Recreational	—	11	20	1	4	36	3,922
Business	—	23	39	3	4	69	11,714
Personal	1	11	26	—	4	42	1,712
Other	2	94	113	12	12	233	26,805
Total, all industries	21	793	1,010	116	151	2,091	331,901

17.13 Summary statistics' of estates closed during 1973-75, under the Bankruptcy Act

Item		Province										Total
		Nfld.	PEI	NS	NB	Que.	Ont.	Man.	Sask.	Alta.	BC	
1973												
Bankrupt estates												
Estates closed	No.	—	1	11	30	2,289	2,565	103	91	203	359	5,652
Assets as estimated by debtors	$'000	—	—	61	272	20,218	12,077	731	185	1,269	2,970	37,783
Unsecured liabilities as estimated by debtors	::	—	3	482	1,282	85,643	63,364	3,316	1,780	6,492	12,603	174,965
Realization by trustee	::	—	—	37	275	9,735	7,560	611	146	1,119	1,452	20,935
Costs of administration	::	—	—	21	107	5,421	3,758	184	77	457	718	10,743
Costs as percentage of realization	%	—	—	57	39	56	56	30	53	41	49	51
Paid to unsecured creditors	$'000	—	—	16	168	4,314	3,802	427	69	662	734	10,192
Retained by secured creditors	::	—	—	174	265	28,263	18,860	761	472	4,143	5,295	58,233
Average percentage recovered by unsecured creditors	%	—	—	3	13	5	6	13	4	10	6	6
Proposals												
Proposals closed	No.	—	—	1	—	173	36	2	2	—	6	220
Unsecured liabilities as estimated by debtors	$'000	—	—	191	—	25,147	18,095	452	12	—	2,614	46,511
Paid to unsecured creditors	::	—	—	142	—	2,624	6,975	37	3	—	62	9,843
1974												
Bankrupt estates												
Estates closed	No.	—	1	19	6	1,969	3,344	90	59	127	720	6,335
Assets as estimated by debtors	$'000	—	500	692	347	23,953	12,375	1,369	312	1,256	3,106	43,910
Unsecured liabilities as estimated by debtors	::	—	737	11,913	346	87,577	85,164	4,438	2,297	3,730	21,255	217,457
Realization by trustee	::	—	234	406	24	11,268	9,988	717	253	394	2,550	25,834
Costs of administration	::	—	35	347	11	6,081	5,006	226	89	188	1,236	13,219
Costs as percentage of realization	%	—	15	85	46	54	50	32	35	48	48	51
Paid to unsecured creditors	$'000	—	199	59	13	5,187	4,982	491	164	206	1,314	12,615
Retained by secured creditors	::	—	397	541	553	22,961	20,719	818	523	808	5,694	53,014
Average percentage recovered by unsecured creditors	%	—	27	3	4	5	5	11	7	6	6	6
Proposals												
Proposals closed	No.	—	—	—	1	105	54	2	1	1	10	174
Unsecured liabilities as estimated by debtors	$'000	—	—	—	87	13,057	9,749	18	—	100	1,304	24,315
Paid to unsecured creditors	::	—	—	—	33	3,792	2,202	1	81	43	400	6,552
1975												
Bankrupt estates												
Estates closed	No.	5	—	12	15	1,781	2,434	232	49	652	667	5,847
Assets as estimated by debtors	$'000	1,340	—	1,851	50	19,519	13,815	1,916	1,860	5,895	4,915	51,161
Unsecured liabilities as estimated by debtors	::	1,721	—	3,648	347	553,157	91,599	7,024	16,798	16,860	22,085	713,239
Realization by trustee	::	1,048	—	864	35	10,859	8,873	660	350	2,650	2,527	27,866
Costs of administration	::	545	—	283	23	5,739	3,905	437	163	1,230	1,532	13,857
Costs as percentage of realization	%	52	—	33	66	53	44	66	47	46	61	50
Paid to unsecured creditors	$'000	503	—	581	12	5,120	4,968	223	187	1,420	995	14,009
Retained by secured creditors	::	1,547	—	245	61	36,649	754,501	2,478	1,223	12,049	7,422	816,175
Average percentage recovered by unsecured creditors	%	29	—	16	3	1	1	3	1	8	5	2
Proposals												
Proposals closed	No.	—	—	—	—	110	15	—	3	6	18	152
Unsecured liabilities as estimated by debtors	$'000	—	—	—	—	8,725	7,207	—	7,072	3,177	8,106	34,287
Paid to unsecured creditors	::	—	—	—	—	1,773	1,786	—	18	229	1,014	4,820

'Excludes Small Debtor Program.

17.14 Summary statistics of manufactures, by industry group, 1973 and 1974

Industry group and year		Estab-lish-ments No.	Manufacturing activity							Total activity		
			Production and related workers			Cost of fuel and elec-tricity $'000	Cost of materials and supplies used $'000	Value of shipments of goods of own manu-facture $'000	Value added $'000	Total employees		Total value added $'000
			Number	Man-hours paid '000	Wages $'000					Number	Salaries and wages $'000	
Food and beverage industries	1973	5,129	146,676	303,399	1,033,417	127,739	8,417,406	12,375,344	3,970,271	222,512	1,756,091	4,222,899
	1974	5,010	144,160	298,658	1,181,779	162,623	10,372,159	14,737,733	4,456,942	220,932	1,998,817	4,766,030
Tobacco products industries	1973	25	6,709	12,461	56,434	2,374	341,805	618,022	263,071	9,403	89,027	265,868
	1974	24	6,974	12,748	64,200	2,936	417,455	704,948	302,697	9,596	98,528	306,559
Rubber and plastics products industries	1973	740	40,135	83,308	295,314	23,998	733,269	1,577,303	825,752	54,377	442,123	885,409
	1974	783	39,700	80,757	315,139	29,548	918,966	1,833,546	936,844	54,173	484,949	1,029,848
Leather industries	1973	417	23,561	47,807	122,444	3,456	271,578	508,813	239,627	27,251	158,581	248,174
	1974	432	22,831	47,575	139,457	4,060	294,271	570,139	281,244	26,444	177,296	291,625
Textile industries	1973	914	61,255	128,957	381,971	33,641	1,188,967	2,183,210	970,068	76,863	537,423	1,001,922
	1974	936	59,789	125,983	415,307	43,920	1,357,879	2,477,765	1,133,547	75,647	589,296	1,173,826
Knitting mills	1973	310	22,849	47,719	111,067	4,551	288,705	530,127	246,197	25,879	143,058	245,545
	1974	320	22,421	46,899	126,855	5,668	330,581	600,631	277,215	25,540	163,883	277,340
Clothing industries	1973	2,120	92,673	180,428	448,593	6,112	981,813	1,837,587	882,331	104,300	569,612	903,143
	1974	2,172	90,003	177,260	500,573	7,059	1,101,594	2,076,645	994,723	101,704	634,746	1,024,534
Wood industries	1973	3,063	94,818	197,824	755,805	64,497	2,181,369	4,055,996	1,946,872	111,600	938,843	1,976,683
	1974	3,111	89,297	186,506	822,983	74,869	2,242,475	3,991,121	1,708,093	106,620	1,038,109	1,747,416
Furniture and fixture industries	1973	2,137	40,507	86,506	255,891	8,848	545,423	1,118,534	581,552	49,051	340,706	595,718
	1974	2,233	42,633	91,414	303,332	10,847	666,842	1,338,179	686,970	51,441	402,267	700,318
Paper and allied industries	1973	649	93,123	197,883	885,584	284,067	2,535,690	5,271,027	2,438,652	123,138	1,248,340	2,476,434
	1974	650	99,696	210,962	1,086,609	426,636	3,455,927	7,677,438	3,888,434	131,275	1,525,816	3,945,031
Printing, publishing and allied industries	1973	3,773	51,479	102,965	439,258	12,235	700,262	2,160,309	1,459,296	90,593	811,834	1,484,626
	1974	3,812	52,764	105,322	505,481	14,785	882,885	2,550,516	1,675,208	92,425	929,939	1,700,326
Primary metal industries	1973	403	89,853	190,725	897,352	211,895	2,464,532	4,917,993	2,250,911	116,462	1,237,900	2,308,876
	1974	397	94,538	201,559	1,052,519	276,034	3,535,568	6,535,413	2,846,389	122,219	1,455,671	2,911,812
Metal fabricating industries (except machinery and transportation equipment industries)	1973	3,932	111,043	235,046	940,437	44,188	2,239,851	4,539,418	2,321,560	144,921	1,313,501	2,437,659
	1974	4,021	117,605	247,938	1,119,803	55,475	2,897,111	5,833,972	3,033,153	153,745	1,568,346	3,190,913
Machinery industries (except electrical machinery)	1973	1,005	54,216	114,077	481,318	19,104	1,324,196	2,431,899	1,165,625	81,640	772,468	1,337,275
	1974	1,074	59,708	125,058	594,785	23,404	1,663,113	3,137,820	1,561,801	89,155	943,565	1,785,522
Transportation equipment industries	1973	987	131,715	285,411	1,278,429	58,151	6,056,058	9,056,704	3,071,648	173,358	1,800,378	3,663,988
	1974	1,003	130,407	278,401	1,397,988	68,994	6,693,771	10,173,886	3,521,288	171,970	1,975,402	4,275,971
Electrical products industries	1973	738	82,023	169,555	592,838	25,052	1,813,445	3,537,898	1,793,396	127,928	1,087,096	2,086,408
	1974	784	88,311	182,805	728,866	29,787	2,296,434	4,344,902	2,216,045	133,204	1,273,787	2,520,030
Non-metallic mineral products industries	1973	1,241	41,502	89,202	366,030	109,769	707,009	1,922,982	1,109,376	55,949	522,112	1,149,843
	1974	1,206	42,884	90,876	424,096	151,200	869,855	2,282,508	1,296,066	57,566	604,898	1,346,563
Petroleum and coal products industries	1973	105	6,822	15,288	84,538	27,856	2,563,984	3,073,197	573,928	16,087	210,443	580,695
	1974	105	7,787	17,047	105,398	36,160	4,404,161	5,185,318	967,662	17,435	254,539	978,252
Chemical and chemical products industries	1973	1,111	39,447	83,587	344,508	142,295	1,575,079	3,503,823	1,802,054	77,328	775,242	1,975,645
	1974	1,068	40,924	85,782	401,850	185,409	2,233,126	4,607,691	2,334,358	79,795	893,309	2,578,974
Miscellaneous manufacturing industries	1973	2,346	45,579	93,533	288,835	12,058	670,093	1,454,206	803,932	62,426	465,254	919,694
	1974	2,394	48,360	99,885	350,052	14,201	865,618	1,794,937	966,076	65,091	543,820	1,103,575
Total	1973	31,145	1,275,985	2,665,681	10,060,062	1,221,885	37,600,538	66,674,393	28,716,119	1,751,066	15,220,033	30,766,506
	1974	31,535	1,300,792	2,713,436	11,637,073	1,623,617	47,499,791	82,455,109	35,084,752	1,785,977	17,556,982	37,654,465

17.15 Summary statistics¹ of the 40 leading industries, ranked according to value of shipments of goods of own manufacture, 1973 and 1974

Industry	Establishments No.	Manufacturing activity — Production and related workers — Number	Man-hours paid '000	Wages $'000	Cost of fuel and electricity $'000	Cost of materials and supplies used $'000	Value of shipments of goods of own manufacture $'000	Value added $'000	Total activity — Total employees — Number	Salaries and wages $'000	Total value added $'000
1973											
1 Motor vehicle manufacturers	21	32,770	74,709	390,680	16,673	3,701,864	4,715,829	1,033,835	46,831	591,800	1,551,760
2 Pulp and paper mills	146	61,783	131,688	645,084	270,637	1,700,933	3,790,939	1,803,889	80,085	884,242	1,812,569
3 Slaughtering and meat processors	473	22,714	48,057	193,904	15,441	2,775,570	3,288,521	530,028	30,937	281,466	555,154
4 Petroleum refining	42	5,947	13,408	76,940	25,960	2,505,051	2,975,852	537,380	14,843	198,766	539,560
5 Sawmills and planing mills	1,519	43,643	111,951	454,797	43,326	1,359,528	2,558,546	1,274,620	62,476	553,569	1,279,634
6 Iron and steel mills	45	41,202	86,245	438,622	86,745	1,082,758	2,317,520	1,154,569	53,008	595,382	1,169,567
7 Motor vehicle parts and accessories manufacturers	229	44,135	96,232	434,386	23,772	1,272,132	2,304,562	1,031,855	52,831	547,836	1,043,613
8 Dairy products industry	646	13,117	27,959	100,004	24,332	1,281,124	1,715,904	417,053	27,819	230,781	467,409
9 Miscellaneous machinery and equipment manufacturers	794	35,907	75,943	315,329	12,447	825,849	1,602,915	809,781	53,444	498,389	899,894
10 Smelting and refining	28	23,696	50,591	235,013	99,507	409,079	1,059,648	551,062	32,396	347,573	590,724
11 Miscellaneous food processors, n.e.s.	262	11,237	23,323	85,067	11,065	598,189	1,045,610	457,391	19,178	164,587	490,672
12 Metal stamping and pressing industry	520	19,465	41,790	162,130	8,170	586,045	1,034,865	452,258	25,099	230,352	468,027
13 Commercial printing	2,183	31,055	62,401	247,788	6,329	392,750	987,157	596,864	42,894	376,995	608,327
14 Feed industry	719	5,564	12,005	37,953	9,492	802,108	974,116	164,811	9,132	68,672	192,721
15 Communications equipment manufacturers	226	25,324	52,613	177,603	4,454	359,485	888,984	577,641	43,719	380,619	679,841
16 Rubber products industries	106	18,391	38,535	156,676	12,964	375,921	835,884	450,746	28,014	253,817	503,283
17 Publishing and printing	618	15,406	30,396	145,272	5,076	170,928	766,766	591,627	32,707	300,763	589,587
18 Plastics fabricating industry, n.e.s.	634	21,741	44,773	138,638	11,034	357,348	741,419	375,006	26,363	188,306	382,126
19 Men's clothing factories	469	33,362	65,735	165,846	2,360	386,156	704,599	333,348	38,193	216,458	340,778
20 Wire and wire products manufacturers	273	14,515	30,436	124,416	7,811	368,434	691,071	320,522	18,877	172,591	332,913
21 Miscellaneous metal fabricating industries	497	17,253	36,386	138,044	8,403	328,872	675,001	348,364	22,494	194,196	363,506
22 Women's clothing factories	574	26,847	51,693	132,969	1,554	379,938	661,858	287,769	30,208	170,871	293,217
23 Fish products industry	330	18,925	36,984	93,891	7,568	371,325	621,410	254,048	21,424	115,453	280,400
24 Manufacturers of electrical industrial equipment	179	15,858	32,800	122,520	5,024	273,058	604,336	338,771	27,579	247,189	408,269
25 Bakeries	1,690	17,789	36,410	114,204	11,889	259,549	598,381	327,302	27,982	197,249	342,187
26 Household furniture manufacturers, n.e.s.	655	22,728	48,728	137,668	4,659	290,682	590,980	303,833	26,818	177,825	305,538
27 Manufacturers of industrial chemicals (organic), n.e.s.	34	5,230	11,448	58,742	46,031	279,135	587,519	261,367	9,713	124,081	280,235
28 Fabricated structural metal industry	153	13,135	28,116	138,941	4,386	261,233	581,968[a]	326,723	18,164	194,106	370,637
29 Fruit and vegetable canners and preservers	205	11,073	22,588	67,438	5,870	355,787	581,863	228,556	14,885	105,632	249,971
30 Aircraft and aircraft parts manufacturers	94	15,936	32,349	142,716	5,071	228,640	538,130[a]	364,100	25,963	257,053	378,960
31 Miscellaneous chemical industries, n.e.s.	344	7,855	16,875	61,905	9,140	277,176	532,729	252,193	14,373	135,086	292,518
32 Breweries	42	6,126	12,950	65,260	6,849	146,131	532,090	383,300	10,507	117,594	391,031
33 Manufacturers of electric wire and cable	35	7,017	14,965	60,449	4,435	347,160	527,366	190,694	9,830	91,970	192,840
34 Miscellaneous paper converters	223	11,172	23,409	82,337	5,047	275,857	521,716	243,326	16,396	136,762	260,837
35 Manufacturers of pharmaceuticals and medicines	143	6,269	12,651	45,357	3,795	172,447	518,811	350,000	14,649	139,093	374,412
36 Manufacturers of industrial chemicals (inorganic), n.e.s.	95	5,882	12,363	61,176	63,315	187,953	513,222	259,452	9,678	105,378	277,496
37 Poultry processors	100	8,103	16,218	45,520	3,729	395,116	487,717	101,388	9,281	56,393	105,345
38 Veneer and plywood mills	86	13,082	26,599	110,104	8,035	255,378	486,704	226,425	14,478	127,210	232,162
39 Soft drink manufacturers	337	5,730	12,193	42,532	7,454	239,096	484,062	241,352	13,448	115,184	264,485
40 Manufacturers of major appliances	33	9,884	20,398	75,376	3,695	265,026	463,294	192,376	13,455	111,736	223,441

17.15 Summary statistics¹ of the 40 leading industries, ranked according to value of shipments of goods of own manufacture, 1973 and 1974 (concluded)

Industry	Establishments No.	Production and related workers — Number	Man-hours paid '000	Wages $'000	Cost of fuel and electricity $'000	Cost of materials and supplies used $'000	Value of shipments of goods of own manufacture $'000	Value added $'000	Total employees Number	Salaries and wages $'000	Total value added $'000
1974											
1 Pulp and paper mills	147	66,584	142,883	802,836	409,152	2,306,718	5,703,192	3,033,697	86,203	1,097,108	3,048,776
2 Motor vehicle manufacturers	22	35,099	75,866	447,433	20,759	4,132,841	5,381,924	1,338,900	49,402	678,920	1,999,500
3 Petroleum refining	43	6,782	14,934	95,683	33,471	4,317,929	5,057,234	922,454	15,967	238,439	925,246
4 Slaughtering and meat processors	487	24,097	50,609	231,702	20,006	2,919,992	3,578,951	634,505	32,836	337,118	668,034
5 Iron and steel mills	47	42,091	91,870	513,882	124,842	1,593,651	3,036,163	1,385,329	54,253	701,909	1,398,735
6 Sawmills and planing mills	1,530	49,194	103,535	489,521	49,075	1,314,925	2,329,835	976,108	58,346	605,422	982,571
7 Motor vehicle parts and accessories manufacturers	227	41,249	88,000	434,372	25,384	1,256,568	2,281,103	1,026,730	49,642	551,948	1,042,950
8 Dairy products industry	556	12,933	27,520	112,657	31,295	1,590,415	2,083,009	482,434	27,316	256,774	545,872
9 Miscellaneous machinery and equipment manufacturers	849	39,619	82,875	388,783	15,373	1,058,979	2,065,405	1,066,607	58,610	611,869	1,181,934
10 Smelting and refining	28	25,792	53,868	282,998	118,404	537,981	1,409,857	753,472	35,249	418,967	794,193
11 Miscellaneous food processors, n.e.s.	256	11,371	23,173	94,601	14,361	861,740	1,381,660	531,966	19,508	186,590	566,845
12 Metal stamping and pressing industry	550	20,112	42,679	191,534	9,932	694,244	1,246,256	580,155	26,307	273,395	604,184
13 Communications equipment manufacturers	260	27,583	57,905	233,389	5,610	529,182	1,225,422	742,370	44,281	443,960	827,027
14 Feed industry	698	5,553	11,842	46,169	11,679	1,011,966	1,221,640	210,742	9,198	81,793	233,321
15 Commercial printing	2,208	32,289	64,628	288,584	7,767	514,568	1,214,666	710,137	44,116	434,396	724,033
16 Wire and wire products manufacturers	282	15,043	31,730	144,149	10,064	524,711	960,342	445,576	19,535	200,100	464,125
17 Plastics fabricating industry, n.e.s.	674	21,629	44,213	155,449	13,617	488,762	958,376	477,045	26,506	214,975	488,342
18 Publishing and printing	614	15,311	30,451	164,757	6,041	211,120	878,842	663,128	32,786	343,900	660,084
19 Rubber products industries	109	18,071	36,544	159,690	15,931	430,204	875,170	459,800	27,667	269,974	541,506
20 Manufacturers of industrial chemicals (organic), n.e.s.	34	5,432	11,793	69,941	61,568	444,986	859,843	387,039	10,201	148,802	437,358
21 Miscellaneous metal fabricating industries	501	18,010	37,461	158,228	10,624	434,512	858,146	443,575	23,663	225,436	466,469
22 Fabricated structural metal industry	163	14,813	31,106	168,756	5,782	372,594	832,799²	461,409	20,020	237,127	513,913
23 Men's clothing factories	482	32,254	64,700	183,849	2,733	428,930	790,465	375,389	36,996	239,050	382,712
24 Manufacturers of electrical industrial equipment	184	17,636	36,420	150,207	6,445	360,543	764,509	431,142	30,076	302,000	513,118
25 Women's clothing factories	586	25,752	49,456	147,081	1,739	424,192	745,710	327,349	29,124	188,723	337,618
26 Bakeries	1,680	16,486	33,997	125,461	13,766	337,584	726,591	376,319	26,578	216,866	394,960
27 Miscellaneous chemical industries, n.e.s.	328	8,290	17,263	73,065	12,336	401,360	724,181	331,623	15,270	160,454	373,795
28 Household furniture manufacturers, n.e.s.	721	23,771	51,638	166,257	5,962	358,928	711,455	360,292	28,103	214,212	361,899
29 Fruit and vegetable canners and preservers	209	11,479	23,581	78,847	7,756	449,156	694,549	270,788	15,348	120,171	295,491
30 Miscellaneous paper converters	219	12,009	24,733	97,765	6,675	376,978	690,448	325,994	17,422	161,674	346,789
31 Manufacturers of electric wire and cable	38	7,662	16,342	74,633	5,377	455,719	674,187	243,467	10,539	111,147	247,848
32 Manufacturers of industrial chemicals (inorganic), n.e.s.	90	5,792	12,270	68,787	80,924	256,300	668,950	349,686	9,633	116,913	372,465
33 Cane and beet sugar processors	15	2,125	4,527	21,422	5,612	616,728	650,920	69,417	2,832	30,767	71,984
34 Aircraft and aircraft parts manufacturers	95	14,442	30,106	143,430	6,315	225,092	620,160²	381,156	24,143	264,292	393,501
35 Breweries	44	6,709	13,711	80,706	9,135	196,079	612,870	414,965	11,421	143,219	423,722
36 Manufacturers of pharmaceuticals and medicines	136	6,458	12,768	50,769	4,937	203,530	579,840	390,775	15,046	156,899	422,276
37 Soft drink manufacturers	322	5,611	11,787	47,565	8,959	318,703	578,589	254,759	13,607	128,826	286,099
38 Fish products industry	348	16,216	32,614	101,431	10,571	353,506	576,427	225,045	18,774	125,904	247,451
39 Agricultural implement industry	143	11,873	24,931	123,519	5,002	323,258	571,912	270,032	15,194	164,219	287,605
40 Corrugated box manufacturers	84	8,675	17,550	80,213	4,656	317,496	527,788	208,181	11,533	113,990	207,855

¹Data compiled according to the 1970 revision of the Standard Industrial Classification.
²Value of production.

17.16 Summary statistics of manufactures, by province, 1973 and 1974

Province or territory and year		Establishments No.	Manufacturing activity — Production and related workers			Cost of fuel and electricity $'000	Cost of materials and supplies used $'000	Value of shipments of goods of own manufacture $'000	Value added $'000	Total activity — Total employees		Total value added $'000
			Number	Man-hours paid '000	Wages $'000					Number	Salaries and wages $'000	
Newfoundland	1973	245	11,492	24,995	78,190	17,075	186,843	382,610	182,754	13,924	101,270	196,779
	1974	264	11,280	24,557	95,165	27,478	442,565	711,731	270,874	14,168	126,198	280,281
Prince Edward Island	1973	131	1,898	3,849	9,365	1,118	54,646	81,619	26,662	2,400	12,844	29,090
	1974	138	1,741	3,699	11,276	1,627	65,363	94,142	29,776	2,263	15,490	33,524
Nova Scotia	1973	746	27,557	55,860	180,184	31,527	772,840	1,250,695	466,475	36,788	267,868	492,461
	1974	740	27,150	56,805	212,008	52,108	1,078,629	1,696,092	601,734	36,583	311,633	625,098
New Brunswick	1973	585	23,400	49,507	155,057	46,795	698,436	1,175,511	434,820	29,940	213,995	457,239
	1974	592	23,674	50,278	187,823	78,202	943,831	1,585,655	603,086	30,475	258,210	628,891
Quebec	1973	9,947	391,518	819,445	2,684,885	348,090	9,772,414	17,464,942	7,595,970	533,759	4,166,825	8,025,855
	1974	9,974	398,857	834,115	3,157,287	488,276	12,790,307	22,396,844	9,549,110	541,500	4,831,383	10,044,846
Ontario	1973	12,397	616,935	1,298,651	5,186,725	554,598	19,085,501	34,300,652	15,030,331	861,767	7,947,955	16,416,698
	1974	12,662	632,850	1,325,495	5,914,093	692,739	23,577,721	41,404,361	18,128,835	883,730	9,074,122	19,920,508
Manitoba	1973	1,295	39,371	80,447	269,839	31,452	1,117,979	1,840,195	714,835	52,716	396,276	755,050
	1974	1,291	40,642	83,747	325,581	38,216	1,386,579	2,279,697	906,434	54,309	471,038	962,611
Saskatchewan	1973	675	12,246	25,375	95,376	15,201	494,861	809,648	319,973	16,753	136,307	330,995
	1974	678	13,117	26,881	114,752	18,145	669,466	1,045,160	373,245	17,917	164,165	391,123
Alberta	1973	1,816	40,061	82,998	324,780	38,934	1,945,670	2,973,328	1,013,963	56,863	496,145	1,056,035
	1974	1,864	43,030	89,257	400,522	47,978	2,525,293	3,821,306	1,318,276	60,827	603,881	1,371,080
British Columbia	1973	3,288	111,345	224,200	1,074,252	136,936	3,466,642	6,387,094	2,927,288	145,946	1,478,671	3,002,569
	1974	3,309	108,257	218,194	1,216,812	178,661	4,013,277	7,411,103	3,300,302	143,964	1,698,586	3,392,543
Yukon Territory	1973	7	28	58	251	43	616	1,411	749	54	449	823
	1974[1]	—	—	—	—	—	—	—	—	—	—	—
Northwest Territories	1973	13	134	296	1,158	116	4,090	6,689	2,299	156	1,427	2,912
	1974	23	194	408	1,753	186	6,759	9,020	3,079	241	2,277	3,959
Canada	1973	31,145	1,275,985	2,665,681	10,060,062	1,221,885	37,600,538	66,674,393	28,716,119	1,751,066	15,220,033	30,766,506
	1974	31,535	1,300,792	2,713,436	11,637,073	1,623,617	47,499,791	82,455,109	35,084,752	1,785,977	17,556,982	37,654,465

[1] Included with Northwest Territories for 1974.
[2] Includes Yukon Territory for 1974.

17.17 Summary statistics of manufactures, by census metropolitan area, 1973 and 1974

Census metropolitan area and year	Establishments No.	Manufacturing activity Production and related workers Number	Man-hours paid '000	Wages $'000	Cost of fuel and electricity $'000	Cost of materials and supplies used $'000	Value of shipments of goods of own manufacture $'000	Value added $'000	Total activity Total employees Number	Salaries and wages $'000	Total value added $'000
Calgary, Alta.	527	11,925	24,413	97,254	8,097	521,733	819,082	296,773	16,747	145,363	309,051
	553	13,068	26,893	121,969	9,337	729,651	1,129,755	408,534	18,117	179,071	425,916
Chicoutimi–Jonquière, Que.	93	7,491	16,791	73,627	10,810	189,022	405,148	205,958	10,160	104,609	230,197
	100	8,766	18,394	98,700	21,215	295,354	519,241	206,071	12,022	140,039	227,991
Edmonton, Alta.	617	16,278	33,859	139,005	16,853	770,403	1,200,831	423,888	22,852	206,226	446,172
	642	17,494	36,099	168,416	19,694	1,013,253	1,330,316	534,256	24,507	249,962	560,499
Halifax, NS	142	4,806	10,136	37,264	3,246	260,210	377,589	120,948	6,734	56,453	122,509
	142	4,846	10,098	41,653	4,749	386,990	530,157	150,177	6,955	64,403	152,097
Hamilton, Ont.	657	53,129	109,817	489,369	61,946	1,549,686	2,971,027	1,398,436	67,959	662,462	1,435,544
	678	54,062	113,140	560,608	77,787	2,053,775	3,670,888	1,612,109	69,149	760,041	1,663,378
Kitchener, Ont.	510	37,578	77,804	280,921	16,533	850,214	1,581,831	740,596	48,036	387,671	761,135
	519	39,514	80,949	327,758	19,237	991,071	1,793,667	848,000	50,152	448,983	882,388
London, Ont.	381	23,546	49,233	197,425	10,215	990,338	1,510,856	524,324	31,498	284,528	566,297
	387	24,023	49,315	226,640	11,813	1,153,349	1,771,481	639,821	32,270	326,024	699,551
Montreal, Que.	5,329	208,340	433,372	1,438,106	108,862	5,471,477	9,698,965	4,291,828	279,104	2,190,909	4,500,861
	5,414	212,534	440,234	1,676,235	147,702	7,346,190	12,503,789	5,301,556	283,650	2,520,600	5,551,924
Ottawa–Hull, Ont., Que.	361	13,638	28,260	109,196	18,056	303,281	618,690	309,622	20,293	180,452	327,271
	362	14,340	30,382	133,645	27,645	403,712	845,396	421,766	21,173	217,662	442,695
Quebec, Que.	516	17,438	36,060	121,298	15,045	463,590	824,062	352,051	22,489	169,367	362,730
	514	16,209	33,634	132,439	19,407	561,987	1,013,077	448,015	20,900	183,024	462,400
Regina, Sask.	137	3,937	8,349	34,773	4,903	160,825	273,379	119,963	5,428	48,833	123,286
	139	4,293	8,656	39,692	5,798	240,852	369,270	122,972	5,918	56,463	132,035
Saint John, NB	85	5,395	11,865	44,812	11,780	304,005	460,198	147,344	6,908	59,707	151,597
	82	5,612	12,150	54,795	20,030	474,039	657,051	184,635	7,079	72,281	190,571
St. Catharines – Niagara, Ont.	419	32,104	68,841	320,032	46,866	765,689	1,589,331	782,735	40,806	423,868	795,303
	427	32,585	69,691	353,472	55,116	986,472	1,974,455	981,003	41,238	467,507	999,657
St. John's, Nfld.	72	2,179	4,606	14,577	1,500	38,980	82,043	42,320	2,878	20,382	45,271
	72	2,061	4,419	16,718	1,897	47,803	97,346	47,896	2,838	24,452	52,625
Saskatoon, Sask.	136	3,275	6,699	23,614	2,664	141,871	208,254	68,550	4,442	33,745	71,575
	142	3,565	7,435	29,357	3,079	195,309	280,169	85,487	4,871	42,365	88,655
Sudbury, Ont.	70	5,643	11,986	56,264	25,627	42,309	180,213	112,103	7,026	73,344	116,674
	70	7,144	15,418	75,215	32,231	52,570	228,883	144,186	8,474	93,350	149,112
Thunder Bay, Ont.	99	5,880	11,834	54,253	18,074	146,878	319,540	155,931	7,176	68,034	155,731
	103	6,057	12,510	62,865	18,909	188,301	397,798	198,952	7,488	80,239	201,503
Toronto, Ont.	5,896	235,820	494,232	1,888,623	117,125	7,219,896	12,918,111	5,760,213	332,265	2,947,218	6,219,978
	6,058	241,408	503,828	2,167,048	140,967	8,840,961	15,526,776	6,885,253	338,980	3,364,043	7,377,053
Vancouver, BC	1,957	54,945	110,115	506,844	32,623	1,727,795	3,042,302	1,340,768	71,838	692,651	1,392,346
	1,946	54,254	109,015	577,991	39,259	2,086,420	3,584,519	1,524,496	71,787	796,735	1,592,875
Victoria, BC	208	3,918	8,056	37,915	1,548	92,518	185,997	96,160	5,257	51,587	99,894
	211	3,743	7,863	42,308	1,670	97,378	188,671	92,613	4,814	55,490	95,262
Windsor, Ont.	388	29,649	66,672	332,344	18,670	1,398,562	2,318,885	909,069	37,256	439,918	1,051,796
	391	28,089	61,013	329,549	21,689	1,407,465	2,405,861	1,044,805	35,432	447,834	1,216,046
Winnipeg, Man.	911	31,648	64,681	215,000	12,996	902,602	1,467,786	567,491	41,609	308,242	596,850
	904	32,828	67,395	256,085	17,076	1,111,011	1,798,546	714,002	43,003	362,907	753,032

17.18   Percentages of value of shipments of goods of own manufacture accounted for by the four leading enterprises in the 40 leading industries of Canada, ranked by 1972 shipments

Industry	Estab-lish-ments No.	Enter-prises No.	Value of shipments of goods of own manufacture $'000,000	Percentage of shipments accounted for by four leading enterprises			
				1965	1968	1970	1972
Motor vehicle manufacturers	22	17	4,033.6	93.3	94.6	93.3	¹
Pulp and paper mills	141	65	3,127.8	36.9	35.9	36.1	34.5
Slaughtering and meat processors	468	415	2,551.4	58.0	55.4	53.4	54.0
Petroleum refining	41	14	2,361.7	84.8	78.1	79.0	73.7
Motor vehicle parts and accessories manufacturers	211	171	1,903.2	54.2	49.7	46.1	48.9
Iron and steel mills	48	35	1,900.8	78.8	76.9	75.2	77.8
Sawmills and planing mills	1,567	1,463	1,893.6	16.8	22.1	20.8	18.2
Dairy products industry	731	498	1,573.7	..	..	29.2	33.0
Miscellaneous machinery and equipment manufacturers	759	710	1,454.4	15.0	16.6	16.1	12.5
Smelting and refining	26	14	978.0	80.6	79.8	79.0	78.7
Miscellaneous food processors, n.e.s.	281	231	905.9	¹	33.8	33.6	35.2
Metal stamping and pressing industry	528	479	878.5	..	..	39.0	39.5
Commercial printing	2,150	2,072	859.7	13.5	15.9	17.1	19.5
Communications equipment manufacturers	228	191	755.8	..	..	55.8	56.5
Rubber products industries	104	86	722.6	..	..	61.6	60.7
Publishing and printing	644	565	680.2	28.7	35.3	37.5	42.5
Feed industry	731	601	667.0	28.8	29.4	29.4	29.1
Men's clothing factories	462	428	621.1	11.1	11.7	12.0	11.7
Women's clothing factories	598	573	607.1	6.4	7.1	8.0	8.2
Plastics fabricating industry, n.e.s.	590	542	594.7	22.6	20.8	16.2	13.3
Wire and wire products manufacturers	265	233	560.5	48.3	44.1	43.0	43.3
Miscellaneous metal fabricating industries	488	458	558.0	20.0	18.9	14.6	15.1
Bakeries	1,768	1,705	540.4	32.2	31.0	31.6	33.5
Manufacturers of electrical industrial equipment	176	134	525.9	64.3	57.9	55.5	51.1
Fruit and vegetable canners and preservers	215	170	523.4	..	..	41.6	39.8
Household furniture manufacturers, n.e.s.	667	638	492.5	..	..	13.0	13.4
Aircraft and aircraft parts manufacturers	96	91	486.9	76.8	76.8	72.0	¹
Breweries	42	7	484.8	94.5	94.8	94.0	96.6
Manufacturers of industrial chemicals (organic), n.e.s.	35	25	483.3	..	..	60.5	59.9
Manufacturers of pharmaceuticals and medicines	141	126	462.7	26.1	28.0	29.5	27.8
Miscellaneous paper converters	231	187	453.0	29.4	32.9	33.3	33.5
Fabricated structural metal industry	156	134	450.4	46.9	45.1	43.9	38.0
Fish products industry	350	258	444.5	35.6	40.0	39.1	42.5
Distilleries	29	14	443.4	84.2	87.5	86.4	80.9
Miscellaneous chemical industries, n.e.s.	348	280	433.7	..	..	36.4	32.3
Manufacturers of electric wire and cable	35	17	432.6	74.9	77.4	83.0	79.2
Tobacco products manufacturers	17	11	421.4	91.3	95.8	96.8	97.2
Soft drink manufacturers	363	301	412.9	40.8	43.5	45.9	46.2
Manufacturers of industrial chemicals (inorganic), n.e.s.	90	37	401.1	..	..	52.4	52.4
Manufacturers of major appliances	33	27	396.5	46.1	50.2	62.8	60.2

¹Confidential.

17.19   Selected statistics for the 100 largest manufacturing enterprises, by manufacturing value added, 1972

Enterprise group¹	Establishments²		Value of manufacturing shipments		Value added				Total employees		Production workers	
					Manufacturing activity		Total activity					
	No.	%	$'000,000	%	$'000,000	%	$'000,000	No.	%	No.	%
4 largest enterprises	125	0.4	5,445	9.7	1,725	7.1	2,086	87,751	5.2	64,204	5.3
8 "	207	0.7	8,094	14.4	2,822	11.6	3,323	146,854	8.8	109,091	9.0
12 "	291	0.9	9,874	17.6	3,758	15.5	4,403	211,515	12.6	149,995	12.4
16 "	492	1.6	12,436	22.1	4,499	18.5	5,183	254,443	15.2	177,662	14.6
20 "	638	2.0	13,668	24.3	5,115	21.0	5,818	285,417	17.0	198,185	16.3
25 "	803	2.5	14,996	26.7	5,783	23.8	6,495	326,178	19.5	227,575	18.8
50 "	1,194	3.8	19,885	35.4	8,173	33.6	8,988	459,167	27.4	317,491	26.2
100 "	1,822	5.8	26,413	47.0	10,912	44.9	11,811	609,804	36.4	417,311	34.4
All manufacturing enterprises	31,553	100.0	56,235	100.0	24,315	100.0	26,032	1,676,130	100.0	1,213,106	100.0

¹An enterprise consists of one company or a group of companies under a common control.
²Companies own one or more establishments or plants. The above table does not include non-manufacturing establishments of enterprises.

Sources

17.1 - 17.10 Manufacturing and Primary Industries Division, Industry Statistics Branch, Statistics Canada.
17.11 - 17.12 Business Finance Division, General Statistics Branch, Statistics Canada.
17.13 Superintendent of Bankruptcy, Department of Consumer and Corporate Affairs.
17.14 - 17.19 Manufacturing and Primary Industries Division, Industry Statistics Branch, Statistics Canada.

Merchandising and trade

Chapter 18

Tables

Merchandising and trade

Chapter 18

Merchandising and service industries

18.1

This section deals with the distribution of goods and services which flow from producer to consumer — principally through wholesale and retail channels and through service businesses — in what is generally known as the marketing process.

Merchandising industries include wholesaling and warehousing, which exist in a variety of forms: wholesale merchants, agents and brokers, primary products dealers, manufacturers' sales branches, petroleum bulk tank plants and truck distributors. Retailing encompasses all sales activities related to the transmittal of goods to consumers for household or personal use, both through traditional store locations and such "non-store" facilities as direct selling and machine vending.

Data on merchandising and service industries are gathered in the course of periodic business censuses as well as by means of monthly, annual and occasional surveys. In recent years, a considerable degree of interest has been focused on the service trades, including those of a non-profit-oriented nature, resulting in an expanded statistical coverage of that area of activity.

Retail trade

18.1.1

Data for retail trade are collected by Statistics Canada from monthly surveys of all retail chains (four or more stores in the same kind of business under one owner), and of a sample of independent retailers.

Table 18.1 shows retail trade data from 1972 to 1975 and indicates the percentage changes which occurred during this period. Between 1972 and 1975, retail sales rose from $34.1 billion to $51.2 billion, an increase of 50.1%. Above-average sales increases were recorded by jewellery stores (63.4%), motor vehicle dealers (63.2%), and family clothing (57.9%). Among the smallest sales increases recorded were those in variety stores (21.6%), garages (24.6%) and all other food stores (24.7%). All provinces showed retail sales increases of over 46.0%, with Alberta (67.0%) recording the highest increase, followed by Saskatchewan (64.5%) and Prince Edward Island (54.6%). Manitoba, with an increase of 46.5%, recorded the smallest increase of all the provinces.

Chain and independent stores. A retail chain is defined as an organization operating four or more retail stores in the same kind of business under the same legal ownership. All department stores are classified as "chains" even if they do not meet the foregoing definition. An independent retailer is one who operates one to three stores, even if he is a member of a voluntary group organization.

Table 18.2 provides information on the sales trends of chains and independent stores by kind of business in 1972 and 1975 and the percentage change during that period. From 1972 to 1975, retail sales through chain stores rose by 57.7% and those through independent stores by 44.9%. As in the past, combination store (groceries and meat) chains continued their sales increases (61.6%) at the expense of independent stores (47.1%). Although general store chains were less important (in terms of total dollar volume) than independents, from 1972 to 1975 they continued to make more headway (120.5%) than independents (31.7%). In the chain-dominated variety store category, however, independents recorded a larger sales increase (27.7%) than their chain store competitors (19.8%).

Sales by service stations and garage chains are far lower than the total sales of independents in this category but a trend to chains seems to be continuing; sales increases of chains compared to those of independents were 137.3% to 33.6% from 1972-75. Men's clothing store chains account for appreciably fewer sales than independent merchants, but from 1972 to 1975 chains in this category recorded sales increases of 71.9% compared with 17.7% for independents. Similar increases in the strength of chains can be observed in shoe stores, women's clothing stores, family clothing stores, book and stationery stores, and sporting goods and accessories stores. In each case, the sales increases of chains compared to those of independents were much higher in the 1972-75 period.

Table 18.3 illustrates the relative importance of chains by kind of business and the trends from 1972 to 1975. The percentages shown in this table represent the chains' share of the market, the balance being accounted for by the independents. In 1975, chain stores accounted for 42.5% of the total market (and independent stores for 57.5%) compared to 40.4% in 1972. The largest change occurred in book and stationery stores where chain stores increased their market share from 26.1% in 1972 to 45.9% in 1975. Family clothing store chains increased their market share from 31.7% in 1972 to 43.3% in 1975. The largest declines in the market share of chains occurred in specialty shoe stores, where they dropped from 53.9% in 1972 to 46.0% in 1975, and in hardware stores where the chains' share of the market fell from 20.2% in 1972 to 15.6% in 1975. Although chain stores have been steadily increasing their market share, independent stores still account for nearly 60% of all retail sales in Canada.

Department stores. Department stores (Table 18.4) have shown one of the most consistent and substantial growth rates of all categories of retail trade. Their sales were exceeded only by combination stores (groceries and meats) and motor vehicle dealers. In 1975, department store volumes reached $5,786 million, excluding catalogue sales, an increase of 55.8% from 1972. The market share of department stores for 1975 was 11.3%.

The largest increases for departments within such stores in 1975 were recorded by jewellery (101.6%), hardware, paints and wallpaper (85.3%), photographic equipment and supplies (75.4%) and food and kindred products (73.7%). Nine departments recorded sales of over $200 million, the highest of which was food and kindred products, $330.9 million; followed by major appliances, $313.3 million; furniture, $289.8 million; men's clothing, $279.3 million; women's and misses' sportswear, $278.1 million; toiletries, cosmetics and drugs $271.3 million; television, radio and music, $245.5 million; men's furnishings, $245.0 million; and housewares and small electrical appliances, $210.4 million. The lowest increase in sales was recorded in piece goods (12.5%), while the department with lowest sales was millinery, $16.1 million.

New motor vehicle sales. The largest homogeneous group of commodities sold through retail trade outlets is "new motor vehicles". In 1975, the $7,261.0 million sales of new motor vehicles accounted for 70.0% of the retail business carried out by motor vehicle dealers and 14.2% of total retail sales.

Statistics Canada obtains new motor vehicle sales data monthly from both Canadian manufacturers and importers. These respondents supply data on both unit sales and dollar sales. The new motor vehicles referred to in this context are the passenger cars, trucks and buses sold by motor vehicle dealers to the public. Excluded are all export sales and domestic sales of motorcycles, snowmobiles and other all-terrain vehicles. Passenger cars include not only private cars but taxis and car rental fleets, and other passenger cars used for business and commercial purposes. "Commercial vehicles" refers solely to trucks and buses. Overseas manufactured vehicles include only those imported (some by Canadian and US manufacturers) in a fully assembled state from countries other than the United States.

Sales of new motor vehicles increased during 1975 to record levels (Table 18.5) for the fifth successive year, in terms of both number and retail value. The number of new passenger cars and commercial vehicles sold advanced 5.4% over the 1974 total of 1,249,304 units to 1,316,629 units, while the value of sales rose to $7,261.0 million, 22.7% higher than the $5,917.0 million reported during the preceding 12 months. These growth rates are in sharp contrast to year-over-year changes between 1973 and 1974, when the number of units sold increased only 1.8% and dollar values rose 10.2%.

The 1975 experience was not uniform throughout Canada. Total unit sales rose in only four of the 10 provinces, led by Ontario and Alberta. However, at least partially as a result of price increases which occurred during the year, the dollar value of sales of all Canadian- and US-manufactured vehicles and overseas-produced passenger cars forged ahead of 1974 levels in every province and region. During 1975, dollar sales of new passenger cars in Canada expanded at a somewhat faster rate than those of new commercial vehicles. New car values rose 24.9% (on an increase of 4.9% in number of units sold) over 1974. At the national level, passenger car values of $5,018.4 million for 989,280 units represented 69.1% of new motor vehicle sales during 1975, slightly higher than the 67.9% reported in 1974.

This dollar improvement in new passenger car sales was bolstered by strong growth in the Canadian and US sector which recorded a 25.9% rise over 1974 (compared to 18.9% for overseas vehicles). In number of units sold, however, overseas products fared slightly better, with a 5.2% increase over 1974 (reaching 153,601 units as against 145,957 for the previous year), than Canadian and US models (sales of which rose 4.9% during the same period, from 796,840 to 835,679 units). As a result, the market share of Canadian and US passenger cars, following three years of steady advances, remained constant during 1975 at 84.5% of total passenger car units sold in Canada (Table 18.6).

The 5.2% increase in number and 18.9% rise in the retail value of imported passenger cars represented a complete recovery from the depressed sales levels experienced during the preceding year. Of the 153,601 overseas-produced passenger cars sold in Canada during 1975 at a total retail value of $668.2 million, 95,772 units valued at $356.8 million were manufactured in Japan. Sales of European-built passenger cars accounted for 57,829 units at a value of $311.3 million.

Sales of new Canadian- and US-manufactured commercial vehicles, which increased 8.0% in number to 310,590 units and 18.7% in value to $2,174.9 million, provided the major impetus to overall growth in this sector during 1975. For the second consecutive year, however, the imported commercial vehicles sector declined in both number and value of units sold. The number of foreign-built trucks sold throughout the country declined 11.0% to 16,759 units, following a 7.8% drop the previous year. In terms of dollar value, sales of such vehicles fell 1.2% during 1975 to $67.8 million; in 1974, the decline in value was 0.3%.

Campus book stores. Retail trade statistics are collected annually from more than 200 book stores located on the campuses of universities and other post-secondary educational institutions. Owing to their location and the highly seasonal nature of their business, campus book stores are not included in the census of merchandising and services, nor are they included in the monthly estimates of retail trade. Since they are not considered retail outlets a separate survey is conducted to provide data. In the 1974-75 academic year, as shown in Table 18.7, 210 campus book stores registered net sales of $61 million, a 22.7% increase over the previous academic year. Of the total dollar sales, 65.0% was accounted for by textbooks, 10.2% by trade books, 15.6% by stationery and supplies and 9.2% by sales of miscellaneous items.

Non-store retailing. Consumer goods, in addition to being sold in retail stores, often reach the household consumer through other, more direct, channels of distribution. These channels are characterized by the fact that the commodities handled bypass the retail outlet completely in moving from primary producer, manufacturer, importer, as wholesaler or specialized direct seller, to the household consumer. The Merchandising and Services Division of Statistics Canada conducts annual surveys of two distinct forms of non-store retailing: merchandise sales through vending machines and sales by manufacturers and distributors specializing in direct-sales methods such as catalogue and mail-order sales, door-to-door canvassing, and house-parties.

Vending machine sales. This survey is designed to measure the value of merchandise sales made through automatic vending machines owned and operated by independent operators and subsidiaries or divisions of manufacturers and wholesalers of vended products. Excluded from coverage are the sales through many thousands of vending machines (carrying such commodities as cigarettes, beverages, confectionery) which are owned and operated by retail stores, restaurants and service stations; these sales statistics are usually inextricable from data collected in the course of other surveys.

During 1975, the 627 operators of 110,287 vending machines covered by this survey reported sales of $250 million, including $2.4 million from "bulk confectionery" machines (Table 18.8). These sales exceeded by 9.9% the sales of $227.4 million reported in 1974. As Table 18.9 indicates, increased sales through the following principal types of machines were chiefly responsible for the overall advance in receipts between 1974 and 1975: cigarette machine sales which expanded 6.4% to gross $112.2 million; coffee machine sales which rose 15.2% to a total of $41.7 million and soft drink machine sales which increased 10.8% to account for $38.4 million. Notable gains were also recorded for packaged confectionery, pastry and snack food machines, in which receipts rose 14.9% to $24.3 million; fresh food dispensing machines, which recorded a 10.3% increase in sales to $15.4 million; packaged milk (and juice) machines, with receipts up 13.6% to $8.6 million; and hot canned food and soup machines which increased sales by 3.2% to reach $4.2 million in 1975.

Of the 84,132 full-size vending machines (excluding the small "bulk confectionery" machines) on location at year-end 1975, 36.8% were placed in industrial plants, 22.6% were placed in hotels, motels, taverns, restaurants, etc., while 13.8% were placed in institutions, such as hospitals, schools and colleges.

Direct selling. During 1975, Canadian householders spent $1,333.6 million on a wide variety of goods purchased directly through channels of distribution which bypass traditional retailing outlets (Table 18.10). Major product lines handled by direct-selling businesses include dairy products ($221.8 million), newspapers ($176.8 million), cosmetics and costume jewellery ($124.9 million), household electrical appliances, including vacuum cleaners ($120.9 million), and dinner-ware, kitchenware and utensils ($68.0 million).

"Door-to-door" selling is the best known of the various channels of "direct selling" and accounted for 63.2%, or $842.6 million, of the $1,333.6 million (Tables 18.10 and 18.11) spent on direct sales in 1975. Sales made by "mail-order" are another mode of direct selling by which specialized retailers contact the household consumer. In 1975, mail-order business accounted for 14.7%, or $195.8 million, of direct sales. Commodities which rely heavily on this channel of distribution include magazines and phonograph records (100% in each case), books (67.7%), clothing (34.1%), pharmaceuticals and medicines (22.2%). It should be noted that these figures of mail-order purchases do not include data on foreign mail-order sales made to Canadians or the mail-order sales of Canadian department stores.

Other methods of direct selling which bypass the regular retail outlet and which are included in the approximate $1.3 billion total sales figure mentioned above are the sales made from showrooms and premises of manufacturing companies and primary producers (which accounted for 18.0%) and the miscellaneous sales made from temporary roadside stands and market stalls, at exhibitions and shows, and purchases of meals and alcoholic beverages on airlines, ferries and railways (4.1%).

Sales financing and consumer credit   18.1.2

Sales financing. Ancillary to the retailing industry are the financial institutions which facilitate consumer instalment purchases, particularly of the more expensive variety of consumer durables such as automobiles and household appliances. Separate statistics have for many years been maintained by Statistics Canada on the retail instalment financing undertaken by the sales finance industry, especially their participation in the financing of automobile purchases. The firms classified to this industry include independent sales finance companies, the sales finance company subsidiaries of car, truck and farm implement manufacturers, and the sales financing business of consumer loan companies.

Not reported in these statistics are the instalment sales financing done by acceptance companies which are the subsidiaries of, or which are associated exclusively with, large retailing organizations. The sales financing activity of these companies is regarded as an extension of the merchandising function, and their statistics are included with the accounts receivable reported by department stores and other retail merchandising establishments. At year-end 1975 about a dozen such acceptance companies reported accounts receivable of $1,263.5 million for purchases of consumer goods through their associated retail outlets.

By year-end 1975 the sales finance industry, as delineated above, held outstanding balances of $3,236 million covering the retail instalment financing of both consumer goods ($1,156 million) and commercial and industrial goods ($2,080 million) (Table 18.12). During the course of the year, the industry augmented its purchases of new finance paper by $2,602 million, $1,041 of consumer goods' paper and $1,560 million of commercial and industrial finance paper.

Since 1970 the composition of the portfolios of sales finance companies has shifted from a preponderance of consumer goods paper to a marked emphasis on commercial and industrial goods financing (from 46% of the total in 1970 to 60% in 1975). The sales finance companies are still active in the financing of passenger car sales with balances of $1,276 million at year-end 1975. This figure includes balances outstanding on new passenger cars acquired for business use such as taxis and commercial fleets. In Table 18.12, these are shown as "commercial vehicles". The banks, however, which have increased their share over the years, now hold balances of $3,705 million.

Consumer credit. Consumer credit arises through an advance of cash, or value received as goods or services, or through use of credit cards, by firms extending such credit to individuals for non-commercial purposes in exchange for a promise to pay at a later date — generally by instalments which include interest and other finance charges. These statistics on consumer indebtedness exclude fully secured loans, home-improvement loans and long-term indebtedness such as residential mortgages. Statistics are not available on certain other forms of consumer credit such as interpersonal loans, bills owed to dentists and other professional practitioners, to clubs or other personal service establishments. In March 1970 a Statistics Canada survey showed that consumer credit accounted for 24% of all personal indebtedness, residential mortgages for 68% and other miscellaneous debt accounted for the remaining 8% (Catalogue No. 13-547).

The Merchandising and Services Division of Statistics Canada maintains a consolidated statistical series on consumer credit extended to Canadians by selected financial institutions and other holders of these balances. The component statistics of these national estimates are supplied by the Bank of Canada, the Superintendent of Insurance, as well as by this and other divisions of Statistics Canada. Data are available only at the national level for most series except the chartered banks, for which provincial data are published in the Bank of Canada's *Monthly Review.*

At the end of 1975, the total amount of consumer credit outstanding in Canada reached $23,769 million, a net increase during the year, after repayments on previous balances, of $3,203 million, or 15.6% (Table 18.13). The personal disposable income of consumers in 1975 was $107,945 million, a rise of 22.5% over the previous year. The consumers spent $95,018 million, an increase of 19.3% over 1974, saving the remainder. A decade earlier, total consumer credit outstanding amounted to 19.7% of the $36,263 million disposable income available to consumers in that year. Since then, this has gradually increased to 22.1% by year-end 1975.

Since 1955 there have been some significant shifts in "market share" among the institutions serving the needs of consumers for credit. At that time slightly less than a third or 29.9% of all consumers' credit requirements was furnished by retail vendors (department stores, furniture stores and other retail outlets), historically the earliest providers of consumer credit. Other major groups of suppliers of credit two decades ago were the sales finance and consumer loan companies which extended a further third of the total credit, mostly to finance automobile purchases, with the banks and credit unions and caisses populaires contributing almost an additional quarter, 24.5% of the amount. By 1965, retail trade outlets had lost nearly 12 percentage points in "market share", falling to 18.4%, while the chartered banks had expanded their share by 10 percentage points to reach a 31.5% share. The share of sales finance and consumer loan companies had by then shrunk slightly to 30.4% but that of the credit unions and caisses populaires had increased to 11.4%. At the present time the chartered banks have gained pre-eminence in this field, holding over half, 55.5%, of all outstanding balances; the share of credit unions and caisses populaires has also increased to 13.6%, but sharp declines in share have been experienced by the retail trade sector, which has shrunk to 10.1% and by sales finance and consumer loan companies whose share has decreased greatly since 1965 to 12.2%.

18.1.3   Service trades

Service trades generally encompass those businesses, both commercial and non-commercial, which perform a service and in which the sale of goods constitutes only a minor function. Commercial service trades are classified generally into six principal groups: amusement and recreational services (such as movie theatres, bowling alleys, billiard parlours and health clubs); personal services (barber shops, beauty parlours, laundry and dry cleaning, laundromats and shoe repair shops); restaurant services (restaurants, take-out food shops, and other eating and drinking places); miscellaneous services including photographers, automobile and truck rentals and driving schools; services to business such as lawyers, accountants, computer services, consultants, advertising agencies, and media representatives; and accommodation services which include hotels, motels and tourist camps. Non-commercial services encompass religious institutions, trade and professional associations, fraternal organizations and service clubs. Services related to education, health and finance are not included in this section. Automotive services, such as garages and other repair shops, are covered under retailing.

Traveller accommodation. Table 18.14 summarizes the major types of accommodation services in 1974. Total accommodation receipts that year amounted to $2,271.0 million, of which hotels accounted for the major share, 81.6%, with total receipts of $1,852.8 million. Receipts reported by motels totalled $271.0 million (11.9%) and the remaining $147.2 million (6.5%) was accounted for by tourist homes, tourist courts and cabins, outfitters and tent and trailer campgrounds. Total receipts include such source items as sales of rooms, food, alcoholic beverages, merchandise and other services provided by traveller accommodation business, i.e. telephone, valet, laundry and parking. A further breakdown of traveller accommodation data by province is provided in Table 18.15.

Restaurants. Data for restaurants are collected from a sample of independent restaurant operators and from a full coverage survey of chain restaurants.

Independent restaurants which hold a franchise are classed as independents. Restaurants in hotels are generally excluded from restaurant statistics and included with hotels.

Receipts in the 1971-75 period rose 54.0% nationally to $1,980.5 million; increases ranged from a low of 31.2% in Nova Scotia to a high of 69.9% in Manitoba (see Table 18.16 for the provincial breakdown). Independent restaurant operations accounted for 85.5% of the total restaurant receipts in Canada.

Power laundries, dry-cleaning and dyeing plants. In 1974 a total of 2,643 power laundries, dry-cleaning and dyeing plants operated in Canada with a revenue of $321.8 million, an increase of 13.9% from $282.4 million in 1973. Of these plants, 348 were laundries, with a revenue of $151.0 million, and 2,295 were dry-cleaning and dyeing plants with receipts totalling $170.8 million. In 1974 power laundries showed a 13.8% increase in revenue over the previous year while the revenue of dry-cleaning and dyeing plants increased by 14%.

Motion picture distribution and production. This industry consists of exhibitors who operate regular movie theatres and drive-in theatres, film distributors, and private firms and government agencies engaged in the production of motion picture films.

In 1975 receipts from admissions were $211.4 million, of which $182.1 million were obtained by regular theatres and $29.3 million by drive-in theatres. Revenues obtained from other sources, such as snack bars, brought total receipts to $220.3 million (Table 18.17). There were 1,173 regular theatres and 315 drive-in theatres in operation in Canada.

The average admission price was $2.32 (including taxes) in regular theatres (ranging from a low of $1.22 in the Yukon and Northwest Territories to $2.50 in Quebec) and in drive-in theatres it was $2.43. The per capita annual expenditure in motion picture and drive-in theatres reached a high of $8.30 in 1953, then gradually declined to a low of $3.91 in 1962, increasing gradually since then to reach a level of $10.04.

The number of paid admissions in regular motion picture theatres reached a high in 1952, then declined gradually until 1963; after an increase in 1964, admissions continued to decline again until 1970. In 1975, however, admissions rose slightly more than 6%, from 79 million to 84 million (see Table 18.17). The trend of paid admissions in drive-in theatres was somewhat different. These reached a high in 1954, after which they declined quite rapidly for a couple of years. From 1957 to 1965 the number of admissions fluctuated around the 10 million mark. Ticket sales increased after that, reaching 12.3 million in 1968. After 1968, the number of admissions declined again. The number of admissions to both kinds of theatre has not kept pace with the rising population, and seems to have stabilized at around 90 million a year. In 1975 the average utilized seating capacity was computed to have been only 16% in Canada as a whole. Smaller centres have higher capacity utilization than larger centres.

In 1975, 85 firms distributed films through 144 offices in Canada. Total receipts increased by 30.2% to $114 million in 1975 from $87.5 million in 1974. Revenue from the rental of films for theatrical use amounted to $79.8 million, representing 69.9% of total receipts. Revenue from the rental of films for television accounted for 23.3% and the remaining 6.8% came from the rental of film for other uses. In 1975, 864 new films were distributed, compared with 1,006 in 1974. New feature films numbered 739 and included 439 English, 194 French, and 106 films in other languages. Of the 739 new feature films, 315 came from the US, 124 from France, 79 from Italy, 52 from Britain, 24 from Canada and 145 from other countries.

Motion picture production in 1975 was undertaken by 280 private firms reporting a gross revenue of $44.3 million. A total of 8,844 original motion picture films were reported, 8,609 by private firms and 235 by government agencies; of these, 2,957 were motion picture and television commercials. In total, 956

television and theatrical motion pictures other than commercials were produced — 117 for theatre showing and 839 for television. The remaining 4,931
films were for non-theatrical (also non-television) motion picture productions
(818), silent motion pictures (19), filmstrips (2,267) and other types of
productions (1,827).

Advertising agencies. In 1975, 242 advertising agencies reported gross billings of
$721.1 million (Table 18.18). This does not represent the total expenditure on
advertising in the country since much advertising is not produced or placed by and
through advertising agencies. Among the expenditures not generally channelled
through advertising agencies are classified advertisements in newspapers, and a
certain amount of catalogue and direct mail advertising. Of the total gross billings,
$228.6 million was in print media (including newspapers, weekend roto
magazines, consumer magazines, trade papers, yellow pages and farm publications), $248.2 million in television, $77.4 million in radio, $16.2 million for
outdoor and transportation, $20.1 million for direct mail and $6.4 million for
other media.

Total media billings amounted to $570.3 million, production charges
accounted for another $126.3 million and $24.1 million was for market research
surveys and other services. From 1972 to 1975 gross billings increased by 34.8%.
Total advertising billings, which comprise the expenditure on time and space as
well as production costs, increased by 33.2%; total media billings, i.e. expenditure
on space and time alone, increased by 37.4%; production costs by 17.4%; and
expenditures on market research surveys and other expenditures increased by
103%. During this time, the share of total media billings accounted for by print
media dropped from 41.4% to 40.1%, while that of television increased from
41.3% to 43.5%; radio's share dropped from 14.1% to 13.6% and outdoor media
showed a decline from 3.2% to 2.8%.

Computer service industry. In 1974 a survey of the computer service industry
revealed that 345 companies in Canada provided computer services involving 206
computers of various capacities, 1,150 terminals and 1,847 access ports. Total
operating revenue amounted to almost $211 million of which "hardware" sales
and rentals accounted for $6.7 million, processing for $141 million, "software"
for $51 million and equipment maintenance, education and other services for $13
million.

Of the total operating revenue, $33 million or 15.5% was generated from
computer services provided to financial institutions, $43 million or 20.3% from
manufacturing firms, and $20 million or 9.3% for primary industries such as
mining, logging and fishing. A variety of other businesses and institutions
accounted for the remainder.

Non-commercial services. Statistics Canada has embarked on a program of
coverage for the non-commercial services sector of the economy. This area is
defined as encompassing various religious organizations; non-profit amusement
and recreation services; non-profit lodging houses and residential clubs;
industrial, trade and professional associations; fraternal organizations and service
clubs; political, community and civic organizations; and other membership
organizations engaged in non-commercial activity.

In 1973 there were 21,695 religious organizations with charitable status
having revenue in excess of $688 million and expenditures of nearly $590 million,
compared to 21,635 religious organizations having revenue in excess of $621
million and expenditures of more than $530 million for 1972 (see Table 18.19).

Another recently-completed study indicated that, in 1973, professional and
trade associations had total revenues of $231.6 million and expenditures of $224.5
million. In 1974 this survey also covered Chambers of Commerce, Boards of
Trade, Jaycees and Better Business Bureaus. In the latter year, there were 2,796
establishments reporting total revenues of $277.0 million and expenditures of
$267.8 million. (Table 18.20).

Wholesale trade

In the field of wholesale statistics a program of upgrading has been implemented which includes biennial coverage of the operations of wholesale merchants, beginning in 1973 and of agents and brokers, commencing in 1974. As well as producing more up-to-date statistics on these two types of operation, the results, in the case of wholesale merchants, will be used as the base for a new sample of monthly sales and inventory estimates.

Wholesalers are primarily engaged in buying merchandise for resale to retailers; to industrial, commercial, institutional and professional users; to farmers for farm use; to other wholesalers; or acting as agents in connection with such transactions. Businesses engaged in more than one activity, e.g. wholesaling and retailing or wholesaling and manufacturing, are considered to be primarily in wholesale trade if the greater part of their gross margin (the difference between the total sales and the cost of goods sold) is due to their wholesaling activity.

Wholesale trade statistics give a measure of the total volume of Canadian wholesale trade, i.e. the total volume of trade (domestic and export sales) conducted by all wholesalers operating in Canada, whether they are Canadian-owned or subsidiaries of foreign companies. The total volume of trade measured by Statistics Canada cannot be equated with the value of goods passing through the wholesale sector of the economy because at times wholesale businesses sell to each other and thus the value of the same merchandise may be recorded more than once.

According to certain common characteristics, each wholesale establishment and location (wholesale outlet) is assigned to one of the following types of operation: primary product dealers (grain, livestock, raw furs, fish, leaf tobacco, pulpwood, etc., including cooperative marketing associations); wholesale merchants (buying and selling goods on own account); agents and brokers (buying and selling goods for others on a commission basis); manufacturers' sales branches (wholesale businesses owned by manufacturing firms for marketing their own products); or petroleum bulk tank plants and truck distributors (wholesale distribution of petroleum products).

Wholesale merchandising, one of the main types of operation (accounting for about 60% of the total wholesale volume of trade) had estimated sales in 1975 of $45,379 million, up by 5.0% from the 1974 volume of $43,210 million. Industrial goods trades accounted for $24,390 million of the 1975 total volume of trade while the remaining $20,989 million was in consumer goods trades, which showed an accelerated growth for the year of 11.2% as compared with the industrial goods increase of 0.2%. Data for 1973-75 are given in Table 18.21.

Farm implement and equipment sales. Data are collected annually from manufacturers and importers active in the farm implement and equipment field. Dollar sales are reported at dealers' buying price before the deduction of dealers' cash discounts, value of trade-ins, volume or performance bonuses and export sales are excluded. The value of repair parts is excluded from Table 18.22 but their dollar value in 1975 of $144.0 million was 9.0% greater than the $132.2 million reported for 1974.

Farm equipment sales reached a low point in 1970 but in subsequent years have shown a steady recovery, attaining a record level of $966.3 million in 1975. The two most important products were farm use tractors with a sales volume of $373.3 million, representing 38.6% of total sales volume and harvesting machinery with sales of $181.8 million or 18.8% of all farm implement and equipment sales in 1975.

Construction machinery and equipment sales include sales by Canadian distributors, direct sales by manufacturers to end-users (at actual final selling price) and revenue derived from the renting of equipment to users. In 1974 new machinery entering the market (by outright sale, first lease or rental) was valued at $1,316.0 million, 23.2% above 1973 (Table 18.23). The sale of used machinery rose by 18.7% from $178.5 million in 1973 to $211.9 million in 1974. Rental income increased 7.9% from $106.9 million to $115.3 million. Of the $1,316.0 million, $420.5 million was accounted for by repair and consumable parts. The largest single item in terms of dollar sales was crawler-type tractors: 2,956 units entered the market for a value totalling $162.0 million. Sales of new equipment by distributors totalled $969.7 million, while sales by manufacturers amounted to $120.5 million.

Diesel and natural gas engine sales. In 1975, 19,328 diesel engine units were sold in Canada, a decrease of 21.2% from the 24,515 sold in 1974 (Table 18.24). In addition, 18,891 engine units were exported or re-exported as compared to 13,985 in 1974. In 1975, 1,115 natural gas engines were sold in Canada, including 19 units which were exported.

18.1.5   Cooperatives

In 1974 the gross business volume of Canadian cooperatives boomed and reached $4,930 million, $1,366 million or 38% over the previous year. Grain marketing volume led the way with an unprecedented jump of $846 million, or 76%, powered by runaway world wheat prices. Other farm product marketings were also up but at a less spectacular rate. Supply sales climbed at a very high rate of 31%. Service revenue and other income recorded a combined gain of 28% for the period. Dollar totals for the four broad categories of cooperative business volume were: farm product marketings, $3,229 million; supply sales, $1,558 million; service revenue $103 million; and other income, $40 million.

Cooperatives covered here exclude recreational (such as community halls and rinks), financial (credit unions) and those run by native peoples. Those included are classified by their primary function into four main groups: marketing and purchasing (the largest), service, fishermen's and wholesales. The service group is frequently subdivided into service and production. Production cooperatives provide services directly related to agricultural production such as artificial breeding, or are directly involved in production such as cooperative farming. The first three groups are known as "local" cooperatives since they deal directly with individual members; the wholesale cooperatives perform wholesaling functions for the locals.

Assets of the locals appreciated at an almost unheard of rate of 52%. The tremendous upsurge in the value of grain inventory accounted for more than half the $786 million gain. The number of reporting associations rose slightly during the year with the incorporation of some new cooperatives in Quebec outweighing the downward trend in most of the other provinces. Membership totals rose almost 100,000 or about 5%. The largest increases occurred in British Columbia, in the area of health insurance, followed by Quebec which experienced an increase generally and Alberta, in the area of gas utilities and livestock marketing.

For 1974, business volume of marketing and purchasing cooperatives climbed at a slightly higher rate, 40%, than overall cooperative volume and at a substantially greater rate than the previous year's 28%. All provinces shared in the huge gain which brought total revenues to $4,770 million (Table 18.25). Marketing of farm products by this group of cooperatives crossed the $3 billion mark for the first time at $3,143 million, a jump of 44% in the year. Grains and seeds, as mentioned above, was the outstanding commodity group in this banner year, providing $845 million of the $967 million increase. Dairy revenues rose across the country with ever-rising production costs pushing up prices. Fruit and vegetable cooperatives prospered, most notably in British Columbia, which produced a bumper crop at a time of low world production and consequent higher prices. Livestock volume declined about 9% on lower marketings and lower prices in the West for both hogs and feeder cattle. Poultry and egg volume was slightly ahead. An increased cooperative share of the market in Quebec was offset by the sale of a large cooperative poultry processing operation in British Columbia to private interests. Marketing results of other commodities were mixed and in total almost unchanged from the preceding year. On the downtrend were fur, maple products and other miscellaneous commodities, while honey, tobacco, wool and lumber registered increases (Table 18.26).

Merchandising of farm supplies and consumer goods by marketing and purchasing cooperatives rose $371 million, or 31%, in 1974. Food dollar volume expanded 18%, slightly more than the 16% increase in the food component of the consumer price index. Sales of fertilizer and agricultural chemicals boomed for a second straight year on record physical volumes and prices. Feed sales jumped 44% mostly due to record grain prices. Farm machinery sales climbed 17% but would have been much higher had all orders been filled. As it was, machinery manufacturers could not keep up with surging demand brought on by greatly expanded farm cash receipts. All other sales categories rose at rates above 25% in a combination of higher unit sales and rising prices.

Gross business volume of the production cooperatives fell $9 million, or 18.9%, to $46.5 million. Moderate increases in the central and Maritime provinces were outweighed by western declines. Alberta and Saskatchewan revenues were severely depressed by a cutback in livestock feeding owing to the high level of grain prices. Assets expanded to $42 million, a gain of $2 million, with expansion in Quebec overcoming declines in Alberta and Saskatchewan.

Revenues of the other service cooperatives, including many new ones, expanded at an accelerated rate in 1974. Gross revenues came to $62 million with most provinces contributing to a gain of $15 million or 32%. Quebec, with many new incorporations, had gains in transportation, housing and miscellaneous services, while in British Columbia there was greater participation in dental insurance plans. Alberta volume rose on the strength of rural electric and new gas utilities business. Saskatchewan and Ontario revenue totals were boosted by the inclusion of some cooperatives not reported in the previous year. Service cooperatives' assets amounted to $183 million for 1974 as compared to $134 million a year earlier. Ontario with expanded activity in the housing sector and Alberta with rural electrification expansion and new development of gas utilities accounted for the bulk of the asset increase.

Total business volume of fishing cooperatives for 1974 rose almost $6 million, or 12%, with most of the gain occurring in British Columbia. Assets of the fishing cooperatives increased about $6 million, most of it going into British Columbia inventories and accounts receivable and financed by accounts payable to members.

Wholesale cooperative revenues rose 33% or $346 million in 1974 to a level of $1,389 million. Supply sales contributed three quarters of the increase, gaining $272 million, or 37%, and exceeding $1 billion for the first time. The jump in supply volume was broadly based with all sales categories moving upward in a year of record farm receipts and generally high spending levels throughout the economy. However, it was also a year of widespread shortages and delayed deliveries for many items, and wholesalers accordingly were hard-pressed to meet member demands. Marketing volume of the wholesalers rose about 23% or $73 million to a total of $386 million. About two thirds of the gain came from Quebec dairy sales which benefitted from the acquisition of a private dairy company by cooperative interests in that province. Assets of the wholesalers grew $98 million, or 33%, to $398 million in the year.

Control and sale of alcoholic beverages   18.1.6

The retail sale of alcoholic beverages in Canada is controlled by provincial and territorial government liquor control authorities. Alcoholic beverages are sold directly by most of these authorities to the consumer or to licensees for resale. However, in some provinces beer and wine are sold directly by breweries and wineries to consumers or to licensees for resale. During the year ended March 31, 1975, provincial government liquor authorities operated 1,496 retail stores and had 349 agencies in smaller centres.

Table 18.27 shows the value and volume of sales of alcoholic beverages in the years ended March 31, 1974 and 1975. The value does not always represent the final retail selling price of alcoholic beverages to the consumer because in some cases only the selling price to licensees is known. Volume of sales is a more realistic indicator of trends in consumption, but as a measure of personal consumption by Canadians it is subject to the same limitations as value sales and includes, in addition, purchases by non-residents.

Government revenue specifically related to alcoholic beverages and details of sales by value and volume for each province are given in Table 18.28. A Statistics Canada publication, *The control and sale of alcoholic beverages in Canada* (Catalogue No. 63-202) shows further detail as well as volume figures of production and warehousing transactions, the value and volume of imports and exports and the assets and liabilities of provincial liquor commissions.

18.2   International trade

18.2.1   Summary

Canadian imports totalled $34.6 billion in 1975 and exceeded total exports of $33.1 billion by $1.5 billion giving the first deficit in 15 years (Table 18.29). Trade balances are given on a "Customs" basis, based on data tabulated from Customs documents according to procedures and concepts explained in 18.2.4 Sources of Statistics. Trade balances are also available on a "balance-of-payments" basis, reflecting a number of adjustments applied to the Customs total to make them consistent with the concepts and definitions used in the system of national accounts.

The recession which started in 1974 had a more immediate and severe effect on Canadian exports of raw and fabricated materials than on imports to Canada of manufactured goods. This was a major factor in the decline of the Canadian merchandise trade balance in 1974 and in the deficit in 1975. The value of trade more than doubled for imports and almost doubled for exports between 1971 and 1975. The period of most rapid growth in value was 1973 and 1974 when price inflation, particularly for crude petroleum and related energy products, was at its highest.

Of 1975 import value, 60% was accounted for by end products (Table 18.30). Crude materials accounted for 15%, fabricated materials for 17%, and food, feed, beverages and tobacco for 8%. Largest commodity import groups were automobiles, trucks and parts 23.5%, crude petroleum 9.5%, industrial machinery 9.3%, chemicals 4.3% and agricultural machinery 3.6%. Principal sources of 1975 imports were the United States, 68%, the United Kingdom, 3.5%, other European Economic Community (EEC) countries, 6.0% and Japan, 3.5% (Table 18.34).

Import value more than doubled in the period 1971 to 1975. Much of this growth was due to a nearly 60% increase in prices, yielding a 41% growth in volume, measured in terms of 1971 prices (Table 18.36). Import volume slackened in 1974 to a rate of 10% from a rate of 16% in 1972 and 1973 and declined 5.4% in 1975.

The largest increase in import prices since 1971 took place in 1974 when a 23.4% rise was experienced. The main contributors to the 1974 price increase were crude materials which jumped 121.3% (crude petroleum being a major factor) and fabricated materials which increased 33.7%. End product prices also started to accelerate in 1974. They increased 10% in 1974 and 17% in 1975.

End products, although much less important for exports than for imports, formed the largest export section, accounting for 32% of total value in 1975 followed closely by fabricated materials with 30% and crude materials with 25%. Food, feed, beverages and tobacco accounted for 12% (Table 18.31). Largest commodity export groups were automobiles, trucks and parts 19.6%, lumber, wood pulp and newsprint 15.5%, crude and fabricated metals including ores and

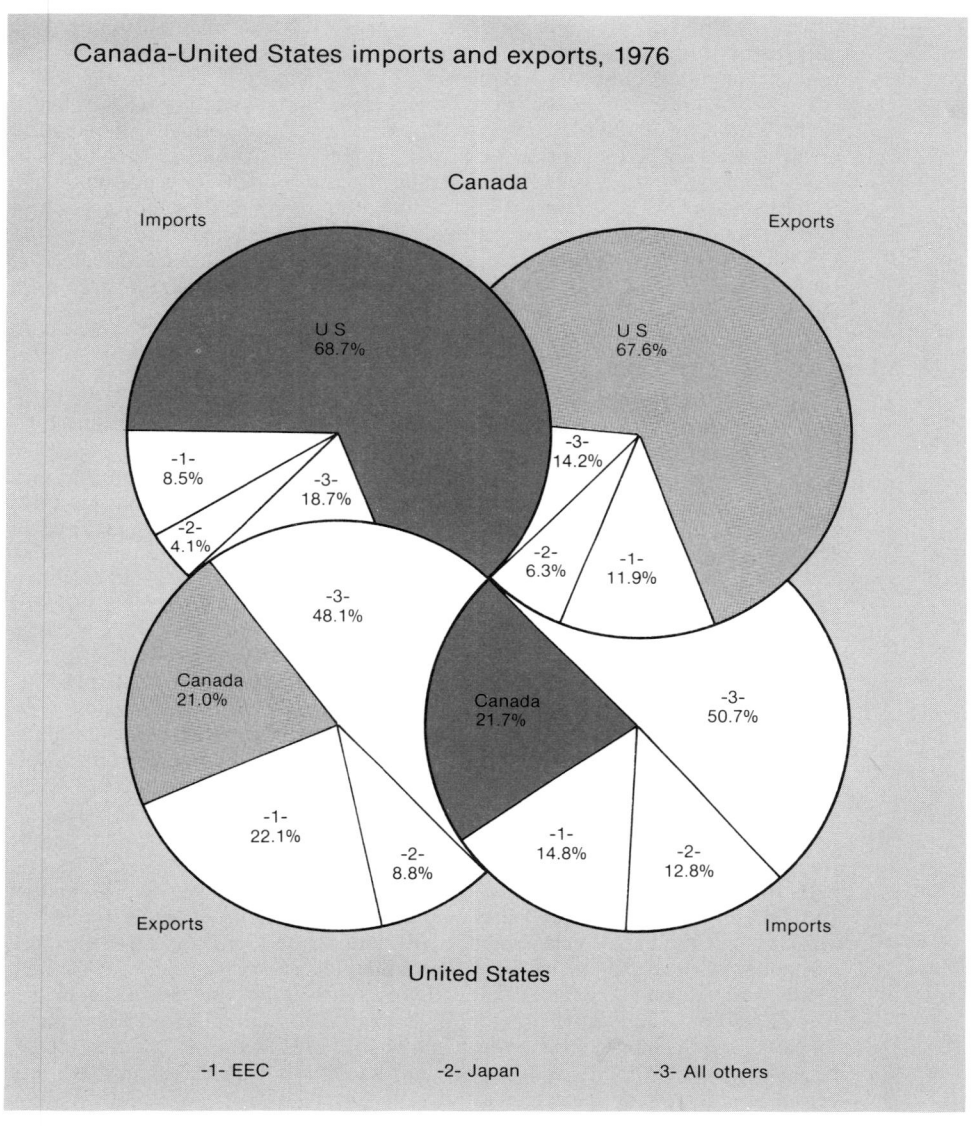

Canada-United States imports and exports, 1976

Canada

Imports

Exports

US
68.7%

US
67.6%

-1-
8.5%

-3-
18.7%

-2-
4.1%

-3-
14.2%

-3-
48.1%

-2-
6.3%

-1-
11.9%

Canada
21.0%

Canada
21.7%

-3-
50.7%

-1-
22.1%

-2-
8.8%

-1-
14.8%

-2-
12.8%

Exports

Imports

United States

-1- EEC   -2- Japan   -3- All others

concentrates 14.5%, crude petroleum 9.4% and cereals and preparations 8.4%. Among total exports, 65% went to the United States, 5.4% to the United Kingdom, 7.1% to other EEC countries and 6.4% to Japan (Table 18.34).

In the case of exports, nearly all the increase in value of 86% between 1971 and 1975 was accounted for by price increases, export volume in 1975 being only 7% above the level in 1971. Export volume increased about 10% in 1972 and 1973, declined 4% in 1974 and 8% in 1975. Export volume thus started to decline a year earlier than import volume. In 1974 the main decline in export volume took place in food, feed, beverages and tobacco, down 17%, and crude materials, down 10%. In 1975 the main decline in export volume was in fabricated materials, down 20%, and again in crude materials, down 12.5%. Crude material volume was affected by controls on crude petroleum and natural gas exports. Growth in end products export volume was less than 1% in 1974 and in 1975 (Table 18.36).

The rapid rise in prices has been greater for exports than imports and started sooner. As a result, the terms of trade have moved substantially in Canada's favour since 1971. Export prices increased 14% in 1973, 33% in 1974 and 11% in 1975. The large spurt in 1974 was caused by increases of 73% for crude materials, crude petroleum being again a major factor, 50% for food, feed, beverages and tobacco and 31% for fabricated materials. In 1975 the main contributors to the 11% increase in export prices were crude materials, up 17%, fabricated materials, up 14%, and end products, up 11%. The food, feed, beverages and tobacco price index increased only 1% (Table 18.36).

18.2.2   Trade with the United States

About two thirds of Canada's external trade is with the United States. In 1975, imports totalled $23.6 billion, up 10.3% from 1974, while exports rose only 1.2% to $21.7 billion (compared to increases of 29.4% and 24.9% respectively for 1974 over 1973) (Table 18.34). After adjusting for conceptual differences which normally add to the balance calculated from Canadian data, the reconciled trade deficit with the United States measured US$1.3 billion compared to a surplus of US$0.9 billion in 1974 (Table 18.35).

Much of the decline in exports in 1975 occurred in the fabricated materials section, particularly exports of lumber ($740 million, down 18% in 1975 and 30% in 1974), copper ($128 million, down 49%), and wood pulp ($996 million, down 6%). Exports to the United States of newsprint ($1,358 million) and petroleum and coal products ($499 million) increased only slightly from 1974 (Table 18.33).

Imports of industrial machinery rose 14.5% in 1975 to $2,457 million while imports of chemicals and related products dropped marginally to $1,162 million (after an increase of 45% in 1974). Rolling mill products and non-ferrous metals dropped to $208 million and $279 million respectively, returning to 1973 levels after reaching $436 million and $425 million respectively in 1974 (Table 18.32).

A unique and important part of Canada's trade with the United States is the free passage of automotive products. In 1975 the value of motor vehicles and parts imported was $7,475 million (up 16.8%) and exported was $5,781 million (up 7.6%). In this instance "parts" refers to components designed for motor vehicles or motor vehicle engines. Excluded are some general purpose components which may be used elsewhere than in a motor vehicle, such as tires, radios, batteries and generators. The ratio of exports to imports has fallen steadily from a high of 112.5% in 1970 to 77.3% in 1975. The ratio of completed vehicles to parts is much higher for exports (1.94 in 1975) than for imports (0.75), because a high volume of parts are imported into Canada, assembled into complete vehicles and exported.

Lower supply quotas to the United States of crude petroleum (volume declined 21% in 1975) offset increases in price (up 13%) for a net reduction of export value by 10.8% to $3,052 million. However, price adjustments to natural gas more than doubled the value of exports to $1,092 million despite a marginal decline in volume.

18.2.3   Trade with other countries

In 1975 imports to Canada from the United Kingdom increased by 8.5% to $1,222 million (Table 18.32). The United Kingdom thus regained its position as the second largest source of imports, Japan having held this position in 1973 and 1974. Imports from the United Kingdom consisted of a wide variety of manufactured goods including industrial and agricultural machinery ($266 million, up 35%), passenger automobiles ($39 million, up 25%), distilled alcoholic beverages ($35 million, up 16%) and various personal and household goods ($124 million).

Canadian exports to the United Kingdom dropped 7.2% to $1,789 million, the loss being due in part to copper exports which dropped 31% to $119 million and to lumber which fell 59% to $55 million. Other major exports in 1975 were wheat ($203 million in 1975, down 2%), nickel in ores ($227 million, up 65%), wood pulp ($145 million, up 24%) and newsprint ($102 million, down 6%).

Trade with EEC countries other than the United Kingdom continued to grow in 1975 reaching $2,074 million (up 8%) for imports and $2,347 million (also up 8%) for exports. Imports have grown at an average of nearly 20% a year since 1970 and comprised mainly end products (61% of total in 1975) and fabricated materials (27%). Major imports include industrial machinery ($293 million, up 36% in 1975), chemicals ($145 million, down 18%) and passenger automobiles ($161 million, up 17%). Exports, apart from a peak and dip in 1970-72, have kept pace with imports. Exports in 1975 were dominated by wood pulp ($401 million, up 7%) and wheat ($235 million, down 22%) followed by iron ore ($144 million, up 56%) and copper and alloys ($160 million, up 48%). End products made up 12.8% ($296 million, up 24%) of exports.

Trade with Japan, which increased nearly sevenfold in the decade prior to 1974, declined in 1975. Imports in 1975 were down 16% to $1,205 million following a 41% increase in 1974. Passenger automobiles and trucks, which made up 22% of imports in 1974, fell 26% to $231 million (19% of total) in 1975. Imports of communications equipment dropped 21% to $166 million and rolling mill products, which tripled in value to $211 million in 1974, fell back to $92 million in 1975.

Exports to Japan were down 5% to $2,122 million in 1975 after a 23% increase in 1974. Two thirds of Canadian exports to Japan are of crude materials (wheat included). In 1975, sales of wheat amounted to $251 million, down 19% and of rapeseed to $194 million, an increase of 21%. Exports of lumber, after doubling in value to $117 million in 1973, declined to $89 million in 1975. The value of exports of copper in ores was halved to $222 million (from $490 million in 1974) as volume dropped 21% and prices dropped 43%. On the other hand, coal exports doubled to $455 million (from $230 million) as volume rose 8% and prices jumped 83%.

Imports of crude petroleum totalled $3,304 million in 1975, up 25% from 1974 and more than triple the 1973 value. Primary sources were Venezuela, $1,059 million (down 11%), Iran, $756 million (up 23%), and Saudi Arabia, $746 million (up 134%). The ratio of exports of crude petroleum and natural gas to imports of crude petroleum has fallen from 192% in 1971 to 125% in 1975.

Raw sugar imports increased 14% to $459 million in 1975 after increasing 148% in 1974. Since the price of raw sugar nearly tripled in 1974, this represented a net decline in 1974 volume. Major suppliers in 1975 were Australia, 35%, South Africa, 29%, Cuba, 15% and Mauritius, 14%.

Exports of wheat fell 3% to $2,001 million and prices fell about 6% after more than doubling in 1974. Principal buyers in 1975 were China with 15% of the total, the USSR with 14% and India with 6%.

Sources of statistics   18.2.4

Canada's external trade statistics are tabulated from copies of administrative documents collected by Revenue Canada, Customs at its ports across Canada. The Customs Act requires that each time goods are imported into or exported from Canada a document be filed with Customs giving such descriptions of the goods and details of the transaction as are required for Customs administration. It follows that the method of compilation of external trade statistics is determined and limited to some extent by Customs regulations and procedures.

Statistics on trade in electricity and on exports of crude petroleum and natural gas cannot, for administrative reasons, be obtained from Customs documents. They are instead collected by the Manufacturing and Primary Industries Division of Statistics Canada.

Concepts and definitions used in the compilation of external trade statistics are published in *Summary of external trade*, Statistics Canada Catalogue No. 65-001. Among them are the following:

System of trade. Canadian statistics are tabulated according to the "general" system of trade. Thus imports include all goods which have crossed Canada's geographical boundary, whether they are entered through Customs for immediate consumption in Canada or stored in bonded Customs warehouses. Domestic exports include goods grown, extracted or manufactured in Canada (including goods of foreign origin which have been materially transformed in Canada). Re-exports are exports of goods of foreign origin which have not been materially transformed in Canada (including goods withdrawn for export from bonded Customs warehouses).

Coverage. Merchandise trade includes only goods which add to or subtract from the stock of material resources in Canada as a result of their movement across the Canadian border.

Valuation. Exports are recorded at values which usually reflect the actual selling price. Most exports are valued at the place in Canada where they are laden aboard a carrier for export (e.g. mine, farm or factory) but a significant proportion of exports by water or air reflect values which include transportation charges to the port of export. Some overland shipments to the United States are recorded at a value which includes transportation charges to the ultimate destination.

Imports are generally recorded at the values established for Customs duty purposes. Customs values are identical to selling prices for most arms-length transactions. However, Customs values exceed company transfer prices for most transactions between affiliated firms. Import documents are required to show values which exclude all transportation charges. Some imports from the United States are, however, purchased on a "delivered" basis and their prices therefore reflect an allowance for transportation costs.

Trading partner attribution. Imports are attributed to the country from which the goods were first consigned directly to Canada, whether or not this is the country of origin. An exception is made in the case of goods of Central or South American origin consigned to Canada from the United States; such imports are credited to the country of origin.

Exports are attributed to the country which is the last known destination of the goods at the time of export. (Many primary products are shipped to entrepôt points, particularly in Europe, for re-export to the ultimate destination which is unknown when the goods leave Canada.) The country classification employed by the External Trade Division of Statistics Canada is designed for purposes of economic geography and therefore does not reflect the views or intentions of the Government of Canada on international issues of recognition, sovereignty or jurisdiction.

Reconciliation. Canadian trade statistics are rarely in agreement with the counterpart trade statistics of its trading partners. The major factors contributing to the discrepancies are the differences in concepts and collection procedures for trade statistics. Conceptual differences are most common in the statistical treatment of special categories of trade such as military supplies, government financed gifts of commodities, postal and express shipments, tourist purchases, bunker and warehouse trade, in the definition of territorial areas, and in the system of crediting trade by countries. Differences in collection procedures lead to discrepancies in valuation, since the value of trade can be based on Customs value, transaction value, or fair market value with or without the inclusion of transportation charges; to discrepancies in timing, since the definition of a statistical month or year can differ; and to discrepancies in the capture of trade data, since the documentation of export trade tends to be less closely monitored than import trade. The United States and Canada have agreed on a set of concepts and definitions describing a framework within which it has been possible to reconcile differences in trade statistics published by the two countries.

Indexes of price and volume. With the publication of indexes for April 1975, the weighting system used for the trade price and volume indexes was changed to correspond with the system used to estimate gross national product (GNP) at constant prices. The reference period for the indexes was also changed from 1968 = 100 to 1971 = 100. The purpose of these changes was to reduce discrepancies between the trade and GNP indexes caused by differences in weighting systems and to align the time references of the various index numbers published by Statistics Canada.

The 1971 trade indexes are based on an expanded set of price indicators selected to represent 1971 trading patterns. Individual price indicators are either commodity unit values calculated directly from the trade statistics or, particularly in the case of end products, price indexes obtained from other Canadian or foreign statistics.

An explanation of the methodology used to construct the new indexes and an analysis of the impact of the changes were published in the December 1976 supplement to the *Summary of external trade,* Catalogue No. 65-001. The title of the supplement is *The 1971 — based price and volume indexes of Canada's external trade.*

Principal trading areas. Effective January 1976 the "principal trading areas" shown in some tables include new groupings which are defined as follows: other EEC — Belgium, Denmark, France, Federal Republic of Germany, Ireland, Italy, Luxembourg and the Netherlands (the UK is also a member of the EEC but is shown separately because of the importance of its trade with Canada); other OECD — Austria, Finland, Greece, Iceland, Norway, Portugal, Spain, Sweden, Switzerland, Turkey, Australia and New Zealand (the EEC countries, United States, Japan and Canada are also members of OECD); other America — this group includes all countries and territories of North and South America (other than the US and Canada) including Greenland, Bermuda and Puerto Rico.

Federal trade services   18.3

Canada's economy continues to be vitally dependent on international trade. Competition among industrial nations is intense and increased exports are not easy to achieve. A successful export trade can only be assured by combining good products, efficient production and aggressive, intelligent marketing with government support.

Federal government support is provided through the Department of Industry, Trade and Commerce and the Export Development Corporation. The department assists Canadian industry throughout the complete cycle — from research, design and development through production to marketing of the finished product. The Export Development Corporation, a Crown agency which reports to Parliament through the Minister of Industry, Trade and Commerce, provides insurance, guarantees, loans and other financial facilities to help Canadian exporters.

Department of Industry, Trade and Commerce   18.3.1

Departmental units involved in international trade are: Office of General Relations, Office of Special Import Policy, Export and Import Permits Division, the International Bureaux, Trade Commissioner Service, Office of International Projects, International Financing Branch, Grains Marketing Office, Office of Transportation Policy Adviser, and Office of Export Programs and Services.

The Office of General Relations includes a General Trade Policy Branch and a Commodity Trade Policy Branch, responsible, within the department, for formulating and implementing Canadian trade policy with particular reference to the activities of the General Agreement on Tariffs and Trade (GATT), the Organization for Economic Cooperation and Development (OECD), the United Nations Conference on Trade and Development (UNCTAD) and the trade policy aspects of domestic industrial and agricultural policies. It is also responsible for commodity trade policy questions generally and in particular the preparation and conduct of negotiations of intergovernmental commodity agreements such as those for wheat, coffee and sugar.

The Office of Special Import Policy implements government policies relating to low-cost imports. It proposes action to be taken by government in the light of recommendations of the Textile and Clothing Board (with respect to imports of textiles and clothing) and of the Anti-dumping Tribunal (with respect to other low-cost products), as well as in other instances where low-cost imports have caused or are threatening serious injury to domestic production. It conducts bilateral restraint negotiations with other governments and implements special measures of protection by means of import controls when required. It is also responsible for the conduct of international textile negotiations within the GATT and participates in the work of the Textiles Surveillance body established under the Arrangement regarding International Trade and Textiles.

The Export and Import Permits Division is responsible for all matters relating directly or indirectly to commodity control measures under the authority of the Export and Import Permits Act and the United Nations Rhodesia Regulations. The purpose of the act is to ensure, by means of export controls, that there is an adequate supply and distribution in Canada of goods necessary for defence or other purposes; that no specified goods having a strategic nature will be made available to any destination wherein their use might be detrimental to the security of Canada; that an intergovernmental arrangement or commitment is implemented; that any action taken to promote the further processing in Canada of a natural resource that is produced in Canada is not rendered ineffective by reason of the unrestricted exportation of that natural resource; and that the export of any raw or processed material that is produced in Canada in circumstances of surplus supply and depressed prices is limited or kept under surveillance.

By means of import controls, the act is also intended to ensure an adequate supply in Canada of goods that are scarce in world markets, or subject to governmental controls in the countries of origin or to allocation by intergovernmental arrangement; to implement action taken under certain other specified federal acts; and to implement an intergovernmental arrangement or commitment. Other functions of this division are to advise exporters and importers on interpretation and requirements of the export control, area control and import control lists and regulations; to study the economic implications of the act; and to review control lists and practices.

The International Bureaux (European Bureau, Pacific, Asia and Africa Bureau, and Western Hemisphere Bureau) provide the central departmental points of contact on matters affecting Canada's trade and economic relations with other countries and areas. The bureaux are centralized sources of information on Canada's trade with specific countries or regions and they provide a regional perspective for matters of both international trade relations and export trade development. Their responsibilities include: developing Canada's international trade strategy and programs for individual countries and areas; maintaining and improving access for Canadian products to export markets through negotiation of trade agreements with other countries; and consulting on trade relations and trade problems at the official level with foreign governments. They also provide information, advice and guidelines to government agencies and to the business community on foreign governments' trade and economic regulations and practices; maintain contact, normally through Canadian posts abroad, with foreign markets and foreign governments on matters pertaining to markets for Canadian exports; and provide advice to the department, to other Canadian government agencies and to the Canadian business community on export market problems and opportunities.

The Trade Commissioner Service has 89 trade offices in 65 countries. Its primary role is to promote Canada's export trade and to represent and protect its commercial interests abroad. Accordingly, a trade commissioner performs a variety of tasks: to act as an export marketing consultant; to bring foreign buyers into contact with Canadian sellers; to help organize trade fairs and trade missions; to recommend modes of distribution and suitable agents; and to report on changes in tariffs, exchange controls and other matters affecting Canada's trade with the countries to which he is accredited. He initiates programs to develop new markets for Canadian products, responds to inquiries from Canadian firms and provides advice to the visiting Canadian exporter. In addition, he acts on behalf of the foreign programs of a number of federal government departments and undertakes agricultural reporting at specified posts. For a Canadian firm wishing to develop a market in his territory, the trade commissioner can supply information on product usage, if any, local production and import data, and prospective users or agents.

The scheduled return of trade commissioners for official tours of Canada is a means of assisting Canadian firms interested in the export trade. Trade associations are informed in advance of these visits so that appointments may be arranged by businessmen wishing to meet with trade commissioners, through the Trade Commissioner Service, trade associations, or one of the department's regional offices.

The Office of International Projects consists of three branches: the Defence Programs Branch, the Capital Projects Branch and the Centre for Joint Ventures and Turnkey Projects.

The Defence Programs Branch promotes defence export trade through marketing programs aimed at the sale of Canadian defence and defence-related high-technology equipment to friendly countries, and the establishment of arrangements with Canada's allies for cooperative industrial research, development and production in defence-related matters. A major activity is the Canada–United States defence-development and production-sharing program which entails the joint development and reciprocal procurement of defence items.

The Capital Projects Branch identifies and assists industry to pursue opportunities for capital projects including those related to resource development, tourism, education, airports, urban developments, food production and processing which involve such elements as engineering, planning, equipment procurement, construction, commissioning and training. The branch is also the focal point in the department for the professional services of architects, engineering and management consultants and aerial surveyors and for the exploitation of overseas opportunities to provide technical assistance and training on a commercial basis. The development of innovative marketing thrusts such as consortia development and the utilization of trading houses to assist small business to participate in export markets is an important element of branch activities.

The Centre for Joint Ventures and Turnkey Projects is responsible for the promotion and marketing abroad of Canadian capability to participate in multidisciplinary industrial projects either as a turnkey project or as a joint venture to establish a continuing industrial or service operation in a foreign country. This centre provides a point of contact in the department through which businessmen may obtain information and guidance.

The International Financing Branch (IFB) participates in the development of policies and procedures for external aid, export credits and other export financing arrangements. Since financing is an integral part of all transactions, IFB has been concentrating its resources on identifying specific financial needs of Canadian exporters in order that they may compete aggressively against foreign traders. IFB keeps Canadian exporters informed about the range of financing facilities provided by Canadian governments and through international financial institutions in which the Canadian government and other developed nations are equity participants.

The Grains Marketing Office is concerned with federal government activities in marketing assistance and industrial development for grain, oilseeds and their bulk derivatives. It contributes to overall grain production, transportation and marketing policy formulation through the Grains Group function and works closely with the Canadian Wheat Board on grain sales and promotion programs. Its continuing operational responsibility includes the institution and administration of programs designed to expand exports of grain, oilseeds and their products and to help provide stability in the market. Among these are the Grains and Oilseeds Marketing Incentive Program (GOMI), grain credit facilities and Prairie grain advance payments. The office participates in the activities of international organizations concerned with grain and oilseeds such as the International Wheat Council and the Food and Agriculture Organization of the United Nations.

The Office of the Transportation Policy Adviser is concerned with the transportation environment and with short- and long-term transportation problems that affect Canadian trade and industrial development. Continuing reviews are made of freight rates and services to shippers, and of regional, national and international transportation policies and measures that have an impact on Canadian trade, and assistance is provided to shippers in selecting appropriate transportation routes and modes at lowest possible freight costs. The branch participates in national and international organizations and conferences concerned with cargo movement, intermodal transport, distribution systems, simplification of documentation, facilitation of trade procedures, and international maritime development.

The Office of Export Programs and Services administers the export incentive programs under the Promotional Projects Program (PPP) and the Program for Export Market Development (PEMD).

Through the PPP, Canadian trade fairs abroad, trade missions and trade visits are initiated, organized and implemented. The range of these activities includes participation in international trade fairs, solo shows and in-store promotions; the organizing of technical seminars and trade missions abroad; and the sponsoring of foreign visits to Canada to stimulate the sale of Canadian products in various export markets. The department also provides promotional publicity and specially designed exhibit settings for the trade fair participants.

Missions and technical seminars vary depending on the objective but in general out-going missions are used for market investigation, evaluation and identification of technical market access problems, while incoming missions are designed to invite foreign government or company representatives, who can influence buying, to inspect the industrial capacity and technical capabilities of Canadian firms and the products and services they can supply. Technical seminars are used to acquaint potential buyers with Canadian expertise and technology in specific fields as a basis for joint ventures and/or sales of Canadian products and services. The Promotional Projects Program also provides financial assistance to take advantage, at short notice, of foreign market opportunities by bringing foreign government trade representatives, buyers and export-oriented trainees to Canada.

In contrast to the PPP, project initiatives under PEMD come from Canadian industry rather than the government. The objective is to develop and sustain exports of Canadian goods and services. The department is prepared to make repayable contributions toward a company's costs in developing export business which, because of costs and the risks involved, might discourage such initiatives. There are several sections in PEMD, each designed to deal effectively with a particular market in terms of regions, products or services and marketing techniques. In all sections, companies are encouraged to develop self-sustaining export markets for their products. Section "A" deals with Canadian participation in capital projects abroad; Section "B" with the export of Canadian products and services; Section "C" with participation in trade fairs outside Canada; Section "D" with the bringing of foreign buyers to Canada; and Section "E" with the formation of export consortia.

Office of Tourism   18.3.2

The Canadian Government Office of Tourism (CGOT) is an agency of the Department of Industry, Trade and Commerce. The CGOT is headed by the Assistant Deputy Minister, Tourism, who, through the Deputy Minister, advises the Minister of Industry, Trade and Commerce on policy and operational matters relating to the development and promotion of tourism in Canada. He also represents federal government interests in domestic and international tourism organizations.

A reorganization in March 1976 reflected changing conditions affecting tourism in Canada. The CGOT was organized into two branches: Marketing, and Policy Planning and Industry Relations.

The Marketing Branch undertakes functions necessary to help ensure a competitive "travel product" — market development and the actual marketing of the "travel product" which is Canada itself. This branch promotes travel to Canada from other countries, promotes travel within Canada by Canadians and coordinates its activities with those of the provinces, territories and the private sector. In a complex marketing program, the branch analyzes and identifies the market, and uses highly sophisticated electronic and print advertising campaigns, direct mail, and a publicity and promotion program involving written material, displays, photographs and films.

The branch maintains 26 market development and promotional offices in the United States and seven overseas countries: Britain, France, Federal Republic of Germany, the Netherlands, Mexico, Australia and Japan. It also has travel trade programs to promote tours to and within Canada and to stimulate growth in the convention and corporate meeting business.

The Policy Planning and Industry Relations Branch (PPIR) is responsible for policy and development planning and research to ensure that the supply and demand sides of tourism grow in a balanced way. The branch is responsible for coordinating liaison on tourism resources among other federal agencies, the provinces, territories and municipalities, and among private sector tourism-related organizations, both domestically and internationally. PPIR also gathers and disseminates information on tourism to the travel industry, the media and the public, and provides marketing operational support.

Export Development Corporation (EDC)   18.3.3

EDC is the commercially self-sustaining federal Crown corporation established to develop Canada's export trade. It offers three types of assistance to exporters: export credit insurance, insuring Canadian firms against non-payment when Canadian goods and services are sold abroad; long-term export loans to foreign buyers of Canadian capital equipment and technical services; and foreign investment guarantees, insuring Canadians against loss of investments abroad by reason of political actions. EDC may also guarantee financial institutions against loss incurred in financing either the Canadian supplier or the foreign buyer.

Export credits insurance. Export credits insurance offers Canadian exporters protection against non-payment by foreign buyers for any reason beyond the control of either the exporter or the buyer. The main risks covered are: insolvency of or default by the buyer; repudiation which has not resulted from a breach of contract by the exporter and where proceedings against the buyer would serve no purpose; blockage of funds or transfer difficulties; war or revolution in the buyer's country; cancellation or non-renewal of an export permit and the imposition of restrictions on the export of goods not previously subject to restriction; and the incurring, as a result of interruption or diversion of a voyage, of additional handling, transport or other changes in respect to goods exported.

Classes of insurable transactions are: consumer goods and miscellaneous general commodities sold on short credit terms usual for the particular trade, and which normally range from documentary sight draft to a maximum of 180 days; capital goods such as heavy machinery sold on medium credit terms which may extend to a maximum of five years; services such as the supply of design, engineering, construction, technological, and marketing services to a foreign customer; photogrammetric and geophysical surveys; and "invisible" exports such as the sale or licensing to a foreign customer of any right in a patent, trademark, or copyright, advertising fees, fees to auditors and architectural consultants.

In the case of goods or services sold on short-term credit, a whole-turnover policy is issued which covers an exporter's entire export sales for one year. For goods or services sold on medium credit terms, specific policies are issued for each transaction.

There are two types of policies, a contracts policy which protects from the time an exporter receives the order until he is paid, and a shipments policy which protects him from the time of shipment only. The contracts policy is designed for the exporter who manufactures goods to particular specifications, or goods which are so marked or stamped that they are of no value except to the original buyer.

EDC normally covers a maximum of 90% of the amount of the loss with the exporter required to retain the remaining 10%. With this protection a policy-holder's working capital remains intact. The most he stands to lose in any transaction is a portion of his profit margin.

Aid in financing. To assist him in export financing, a policy-holder may request EDC to assign the proceeds of any losses payable under a policy to a bank or other agent providing financing in respect of export sales. He may assign an individual bill or he may make a blanket assignment of all his foreign accounts receivable. As a further aid, EDC may issue unconditional guarantees to chartered banks or to any person who will agree to provide non-recourse supplier financing. Such guarantees are usually issued in respect of insured sales of capital goods. EDC may also issue unconditional guarantees to banks who will agree to finance the manufacturing period of an insurable medium-term export credit sale.

Export loans. EDC makes loans to foreign purchasers, or guarantees private loans to foreign purchasers at internationally competitive interest rates when extended credit terms are required and when commercial financing is not available.

The following are some examples of capital equipment and services, by industry, that are eligible for export financing. Power industry: conventional and nuclear power plants, electrification programs and transmission lines; transportation industry: equipment for telecommunications such as telephone systems, microwave facilities and earth satellite stations; and other capital goods industries: equipment for wood, pulp and paper, chemical, mining, construction and metallurgical projects. Under certain conditions, long-term loans and guarantees would be available for airport terminals and hotels. Financing may be provided for services even when they are not directly associated with equipment supply. They may be related to appraisal and development of natural resources, primary and secondary industry projects, and public utilities projects.

A Canadian exporter usually submits a loan application to EDC on behalf of a buyer, or the buyer may submit the application directly. The borrower need not be the importer in the transaction, as for example when a government might borrow on behalf of one of its agencies, or a bank on behalf of one of its clients. EDC may make loans to foreign national development banks for re-lending to importers in their countries to enable them to buy Canadian capital goods.

A transaction is normally one for which extended credit terms (beyond five years) are necessary and justifiable. Repayment schedules vary according to industry practice. The project must be financially and economically sound, and the foreign buyer and the country to which the goods are shipped must be credit worthy. The transaction should also have the highest possible Canadian material/labour content and meet a minimum standard in this respect.

Interest and fees levied by EDC generally reflect the need to meet competition in particular cases, and to provide for operating expenses. As a general rule the rates amount to 0.05% over the cost of money to EDC. There is normally no charge to the Canadian exporter.

EDC seeks the maximum possible involvement of Canadian banks and other financial institutions. The goal is to provide internationally competitive financing. Instead of competing with private sector financial institutions, it works with them in a variety of ways. These include direct participation, down payment financing on behalf of foreign borrowers, pre-shipment financing, local cost financing beyond that available from EDC, and as paying agents for EDC in certain transactions.

Foreign investment guarantees. EDC may provide guarantees which protect Canadian businessmen investing abroad against loss due to the political events of expropriation, war or insurrection, or the inability to repatriate funds. The program covers almost any right that the Canadian investor might acquire in a foreign enterprise, including equity, loans, management contracts, royalty and licensing agreements. Only new projects in developing countries receptive to foreign interests are accepted by EDC.

Investments may be in the form of cash, contribution in kind, or the issuance of a guarantee to another party investing in another country. The investment may be made directly in a foreign enterprise, or indirectly through a related company based in Canada, the host country, or even a third country.

Coverage under a guarantee can have a term of up to 15 years. It can be cancelled only by the investor, and not by EDC, as long as the conditions of the guarantee are maintained. The investor, however, has a wide range of flexibility in his selection of coverage, enabling him to cover only the assets actually at risk. He may insure also for one or more of the political events of expropriation, war and insurrection, or inconvertibility of funds.

The programs call for the investor to carry a percentage of the liability; the remainder is borne by EDC. This co-insurance requirement is extended to all contracts regardless of investor or country. The normal co-insurance to be carried by the investor is 15%.

Details on how to apply for export credits insurance, long-term loans or foreign investment guarantees are available from the head office of the Export Development Corporation in Ottawa or its regional offices in Montreal, Toronto or Vancouver. When arranging for a long-term loan, the exporter should make a preliminary approach to find out whether a proposed transaction is eligible for financing. With foreign investment guarantees it is essential that an application be made to EDC before proceeding with an investment since only new investments qualify for EDC support.

Maximum liabilities. To implement its objective of promoting Canadian exports through insurance, loans, and guarantees, EDC has authority to undertake maximum financial liabilities of $6,850 million on a roll-over basis.

The ceiling for liabilities under contracts of export credits, insurance and guarantees issued at EDC's risk is $750 million. In addition, insurance and guarantees may be given at government risk when, having regard to any one transaction, the amount or term is considered to be excessive for EDC. A separate fund of $750 million maximum outstanding liability is provided for this.

Financing a long-term and, in exceptional cases, medium-term credit for major export sales of capital equipment and services may total $5,100 million. Within the overall ceiling, two authorities have been established, one for lending by EDC for its own account on approval by the EDC Board of Directors to a limit on outstanding liabilities of $4,250 million, the other for lending for the account of the Canadian government to a limit of $850 million. The latter facility applies to large export transactions or to other special situations considered by the government to be in the "national interest".

A ceiling of $250 million for liabilities under the foreign investment insurance program is provided, and cover is restricted to a maximum of 15 years.

18.4   Tariffs and trade agreements

18.4.1   Canadian tariff structure

Information relating to rates of duty, value for duty and anti-dumping duty is available from the Department of National Revenue, Customs and Excise, which administers the Customs Act, the Customs Tariff and the Anti-dumping Act. Details of the organization and functions of the Tariff Board will be found in Appendix 1.

The Canadian tariff consists, in the main, of four sets of tariff rates — British preferential, most-favoured-nation, general and general preferential.

British preferential tariff rates are applied to imported commodities from British Commonwealth countries, with the exception of Hong Kong, when conveyed without trans-shipment from a port of any British country enjoying the benefits of the British Commonwealth preferential tariff into a port of Canada. Some Commonwealth countries have trade agreements with Canada that provide for rates of duty, on certain specified goods, lower than the British preferential rates.

Most-favoured-nation rates are usually higher than the British preferential rates and lower than the general tariff rates. They are applied to commodities imported from countries with which Canada has trade agreements. These rates would apply to British countries when they are lower than the British preferential tariff rates. The most important trade agreement concerning the effective rates applied to goods imported from countries entitled to most-favoured-nation rates is the General Agreement on Tariffs and Trade (GATT).

General tariff rates are applied to goods imported from the few countries with which Canada has not made trade agreements.

The General Preferential Tariff came into effect on July 1, 1974, as a result of Canada's acceding to the Generalized System of Preferences which is designed to allow lower rates of duty on goods imported from developing countries. Generally, the rates are the lesser of the British Preferential Tariff or the Most-Favoured-Nation Tariff minus one third.

Despite the numerous tariff items in the Customs Tariff and the various rates of duty applicable to each item, there are numerous goods which are duty free under all four tariffs.

Valuation. In general, the Customs Act provides that the value for duty of imported goods shall be the fair market value of like goods as established in the home market of the exporter at the time when and place from which the goods are shipped directly to Canada when sold "(a) to purchasers located at that place with whom the vendor deals at arm's length and who are at the same or substantially the same trade level as the importer, and (b) in the same or substantially the same quantities for home consumption in the ordinary course of trade under competitive conditions". In cases where like goods are not sold for home consumption but similar goods are sold, the value for duty shall be the cost of production of the goods imported plus an amount for gross profit equal in percentage to that earned on the sale of similar goods in the country of export. The value for duty ordinarily may not be less than the amount for which the goods were sold to the purchaser in Canada, exclusive of all charges thereon after their shipment from the country of export. Internal taxes in the country of export, when not incurred on exported goods, do not form part of the value for duty. There are also further provisions for determining value for duty under the act.

Anti-dumping Act. Canada's Anti-dumping Act provides, in brief, that where goods are dumped, i.e. the export price is less than the normal value, and such dumping has caused, is causing, or is likely to cause material injury to the production of like goods in Canada, or has materially retarded or is materially retarding the establishment of the production in Canada of like goods as determined by the Anti-dumping Tribunal, there shall be levied, collected and paid an anti-dumping duty. This anti-dumping duty is in an amount equal to the margin of dumping of the entered goods.

Drawback. Drawback legislation is designed to remove the customs duty and sales tax included in the manufacturers' costs so as to enable them to compete more equitably both abroad and at home with foreign manufacturers. It does this by granting a drawback, in the case of Canadian exporters, of customs duty and sales taxes paid on imported parts or materials used in Canada in the manufacture of goods subsequently exported. In the case of certain strategic industries in Canada, (i.e. aircraft, automobiles and other secondary manufacturers) their costs of plant equipment or key materials are also reduced in the same manner when the specified imported goods are used in eligible Canadian manufacturers. Other areas where drawbacks are payable include: ships stores; joint Canada–US projects; and imported goods exported or destroyed in Canada.

Tariff and trade arrangements   18.4.2

Canada's tariff arrangements with other countries fall into three main categories: trade agreements with a number of Commonwealth countries; the General Agreement on Tariffs and Trade (GATT); and other arrangements.

Canada signed the Protocol of Provisional Application of the General Agreement on Tariffs and Trade on October 30, 1947 and brought the General Agreement into force on January 1, 1948. The agreement provides for scheduled tariff concessions and the exchange of most-favoured-nation treatment among the contracting parties, and lays down rules and regulations to govern the conduct of international trade. As at July 1974 there were 83 members and two provisional members, Tunisia and the Philippines. GATT is applied on a de facto basis also to a number of newly independent states pending decision as to their future commercial policies.

Trade relations between Canada and a number of other countries are governed by trade agreements of various kinds, by exchange of most-favoured-nation treatment under Orders in Council, by continuation to newly independent states of the same treatment originally negotiated with the countries previously responsible for their commercial relations and by even less formal arrangements.

Britain and Ireland would terminate by 1977 the preferential tariffs extended to Canada. Phasing out these preferences began February 1, 1973, as a result of the accession by those countries to the European Economic Community (EEC).

Tariff and trade arrangements with Commonwealth countries as at October 1976   18.4.2.1

Australia. Trade Agreement in force June 30, 1960, modified and continued by an Exchange of Letters, October 25, 1973. GATT effective January 1, 1948. (Bindings of rates of duty and margins of preference on specified products and exchange of tariff preferences.)

Bahamas. Relations are based on the Canada — West Indies Trade Agreement and protocol thereto (see Commonwealth Caribbean). GATT de facto application. (Exchange of preferential tariff treatment.)

Bangladesh (formerly East Pakistan). GATT effective December 16, 1972. (Canada accords British preferential treatment. Bangladesh accords most-favoured-nation treatment to Canada.)

Barbados. Relations are based on Canada — West Indies Trade Agreement and protocol thereto (see Commonwealth Caribbean). GATT effective November 30, 1966. (Exchange of preferential tariff treatment.)

Botswana. GATT de facto application. (Canada accords British preferential tariff treatment.)

Britain. Trade Agreement effective September 1, 1937; modified by exchanges of letters November 16, 1938 and October 30, 1947, was terminated by Britain on January 31, 1973 as a result of Britain's accession to the EEC. The tariff preferences it extended to Canada were being phased out over a transitional period ending in 1977. GATT effective January 1, 1948.

Commonwealth Caribbean — Belize (formerly British Honduras), Bermuda, Leeward Islands, Windward Islands. Canada — British West Indies Trade Agreement was signed July 6, 1925, and came in force April 30, 1927; Canadian notice of termination of November 23, 1938, was replaced by notice of December 27, 1939 which continued the agreement. Protocol signed July 8, 1966, provides inter alia for continuation of 1925 agreement. Belize, Bermuda, the Leeward Islands and the Windward Islands participate in GATT. (Exchange of preferential tariff treatment.)

Cyprus. GATT effective August 16, 1960. (Exchange of British preferential tariff treatment.)

Fiji. Maintains de facto application of GATT. (Canada accords British preferential tariff treatment to Fiji. Fiji extends most-favoured-nation treatment to Canada.)

Gambia. GATT effective February 18, 1965. (Canada accords British preferential tariff treatment to Gambia. Gambia extends most-favoured-nation treatment to Canada.)

Ghana. GATT effective October 18, 1957. (Canada accords British preferential tariff treatment to Ghana, except on cocoa beans. Ghana extends most-favoured-nation treatment to Canada.)

Grenada. Relations are based on the Canada — West Indies Trade Agreement and protocol thereto (see Commonwealth Caribbean). Participation in GATT. (Exchange of preferential tariff treatment.)

Guyana. Relations are based on the Canada — West Indies Trade Agreement and protocol thereto (see Commonwealth Caribbean). GATT effective July 5, 1966. (Exchange of preferential tariff treatment.)

India. Since 1897 Canada has unilaterally accorded British preferential treatment without contractual obligation. GATT effective July 8, 1948. (Canada accords British preferential tariff treatment to India. India extends most-favoured-nation treatment to Canada.)

Jamaica. Relations are based on Canada — West Indies Trade Agreement and protocol thereto (see Commonwealth Caribbean). GATT effective August 6, 1962. (Exchange of preferential tariff treatment.)

Kenya. GATT effective December 12, 1963. (Canada accords British preferential tariff treatment to Kenya. Kenya extends most-favoured-nation treatment to Canada.)

Lesotho. GATT de facto application. (Canada accords British preferential tariff treatment to Lesotho.)

Malawi. Malawi and Canada observe the terms of 1958 Trade Agreement between Canada and the former Federation of Rhodesia and Nyasaland. GATT effective July 6, 1964. (Exchange of preferential tariff treatment.)

Malaysia. GATT effective September 16, 1963. (Canada accords British preferential tariff treatment to Malaysia. Malaysia extends some preferential rates to Canada.)

Maldives. Relations governed by Trade Agreement of 1937 with Britain. GATT de facto application. (Canada accords British preferential tariff treatment.)

Malta. Canada — Britain Trade Agreement of 1937 was legal basis for exchange of British preferential tariff treatment. This agreement terminated by Britain January 31, 1973 as a result of Britain's accession to the EEC. GATT effective September 16, 1964.

Mauritius. GATT effective March 12, 1968. (Exchange of British preferential tariff treatment.)

New Zealand. Trade Agreement in force May 24, 1932, modified and continued in force by an Exchange of Letters dated July 26, 1973. GATT effective July 26, 1948. (Bindings of rates of duty on specified products and the exchange of tariff preferences.)

Nigeria. Relations governed by Trade Agreement of 1937 with Britain. GATT effective October 1, 1960. (Canada accords British preferential treatment to Nigeria. Nigeria extends most-favoured-nation treatment to Canada.)

Rhodesia. Canada does not recognize the present government of Rhodesia. (Trade embargo exists between Canada and Rhodesia with certain humanitarian exceptions.)

Sierra Leone. Relations governed by Trade Agreement of 1937 with Britain. GATT effective April 27, 1961. (Canada accords British preferential tariff treatment to Sierra Leone. Sierra Leone extends most-favoured-nation tariff treatment to Canada.)

Singapore. GATT membership August 10, 1973. (Canada and Singapore exchange British preferential tariff treatment.)

Sri Lanka, Republic of (formerly Ceylon). GATT effective July 29, 1948. (Canada accords British preferential tariff treatment to Sri Lanka. Sri Lanka extends most-favoured-nation tariff treatment to Canada.)

Swaziland. GATT de facto application. (Canada accords British preferential treatment to Swaziland.)

Tanzania. GATT effective for Tanganyika December 9, 1961 and extended to Zanzibar upon formation of United Republic, April 23, 1964. (Canada accords British preferential tariff treatment to Tanzania. Tanzania extends most-favoured-nation treatment to Canada.)

Tonga. Tonga maintains de facto application of GATT. (Exchange of British preferential tariff treatment.)

Trinidad and Tobago. Relations are based on Canada — West Indies Trade Agreement and protocol thereto (see Commonwealth Caribbean). GATT effective August 31, 1962. (Exchange of preferential tariff treatment.)

Uganda. GATT effective October 9, 1962. (Canada accords British preferential tariff treatment to Uganda. Uganda extends most-favoured-nation tariff treatment to Canada.)

Western Samoa. No agreement. (Exchange of British preferential tariff treatment.)

Zambia. GATT de facto application. (Canada accords British preferential tariff treatment to Zambia. Zambia extends most-favoured-nation treatment to Canada.)

Tariff and trade arrangements with non-Commonwealth countries as at October 1976   18.4.2.2

Afghanistan. Trade Agreement entered into force November 27, 1974. (Exchange of most-favoured-nation treatment.)

Algeria. Franco — Canadian Trade Agreement of 1933 applied to Algeria. Algeria maintains de facto application of GATT. (Since the creation of Algeria as an independent state in 1962, Canada has continued to grant most-favoured-nation treatment.)

Arab Republic of Egypt. Exchange of notes in force December 3, 1952. GATT effective May 9, 1970. (Exchange of most-favoured-nation treatment.)

Argentina. GATT effective October 11, 1967. (Exchange of most-favoured-nation treatment.)

Austria. GATT effective October 19, 1951. (Exchange of most-favoured-nation treatment.)

Bahrain. Bahrain maintains de facto application of GATT. (Exchange of most-favoured-nation treatment.)

Belgium — Luxembourg. Convention of Commerce with Belgium — Luxembourg Economic Union (including Belgian colonies) entered into effect October 22, 1924. GATT effective January 1, 1948. (Exchange of most-favoured-nation treatment.)

Benelux (Belgium — Netherlands — Luxembourg Customs Union). (See Belgium — Luxembourg and Netherlands.)

Benin, People's Republic of, (formerly Dahomey). Franco — Canadian Trade Agreement of 1933 applied to Dahomey. GATT effective August 1, 1960. (Exchange of most-favoured-nation treatment.)

Bolivia. Order in Council of July 20, 1935 accepted Article 15 of UK — Bolivia Treaty of Commerce. (Exchange of most-favoured-nation treatment.)

Brazil. Trade Agreement in force April 16, 1943. GATT effective July 31, 1948. (Exchange of most-favoured-nation treatment.)

Bulgaria. Trade Agreement effective January 7, 1974, provides for most-favoured-nation treatment and exception for British preferential tariffs. To be extended for yearly periods.

Burma. GATT effective July 29, 1948. (Exchange of most-favoured-nation treatment.)

Burundi. GATT effective November 25, 1965. (Exchange of most-favoured-nation treatment.)

Cameroon. Franco — Canadian Trade Agreement of 1933 applied to Cameroon. GATT effective November 28, 1960. (Exchange of most-favoured-nation treatment.)

Central African Republic. Franco — Canadian Trade Agreement of 1933 applied to Central African Republic. GATT effective August 14, 1960. (Exchange of most-favoured-nation treatment.)

Chad. Franco — Canadian Trade Agreement of 1933 applied to Chad. GATT effective August 11, 1960. (Exchange of most-favoured-nation treatment.)

Chile. Trade Agreement in force October 29, 1943. GATT effective March 16, 1948. (Exchange of most-favoured-nation treatment.)

China, People's Republic of. Canada — China Trade Agreement of October 13, 1973. (Exchange of most-favoured-nation treatment.)

Colombia. Treaty of Commerce with Britain of February 16, 1866 applies to Canada. Modified by protocol of August 20, 1912 and exchange of notes December 30, 1938. (Exchange of most-favoured-nation treatment.)

Congo (Brazzaville). Franco — Canadian Trade Agreement of 1933 applies to Congo (Brazzaville). GATT effective August 15, 1960. (Exchange of most-favoured-nation treatment.)

Costa Rica. Modus vivendi in force January 26, 1951. (Exchange of most-favoured-nation treatment.)

Cuba. GATT effective January 1, 1948. (Exchange of most-favoured-nation treatment.)

Czechoslovakia. Convention of Commerce in force November 14, 1928. GATT effective May 21, 1948. (Exchange of most-favoured-nation treatment.)

Denmark (including Greenland). Treaties of Peace and Commerce with Britain of February 13, 1660 and July 11, 1670 apply to Canada. GATT effective May 28, 1950. (Exchange of most-favoured-nation treatment.)

Dominican Republic. Trade Agreement in force January 22, 1941. GATT effective May 19, 1950. (Exchange of most-favoured-nation treatment, including scheduled concessions.)

Ecuador. Modus vivendi in force December 1, 1950. (Exchange of most-favoured-nation treatment.)

El Salvador. Exchange of notes in force November 17, 1937. (Exchange of most-favoured-nation treatment.)

Equatorial Guinea. Since August 1, 1928, UK — Spain Treaty of Commerce of 1922. Canada — Spain Trade Agreement signed May 25, 1954. GATT de facto application. (Since the creation of Equatorial Guinea as an independent state in 1968, Canada has continued to grant most-favoured-nation treatment.)

Ethiopia. Exchange of notes effective June 3, 1955. (Exchange of most-favoured-nation treatment.)

Finland. Exchange of notes effective November 17, 1948. GATT effective May 25, 1950. (Exchange of most-favoured-nation treatment.)

France and French overseas territories. Trade Agreement in force June 10, 1933. Exchange of notes of September 29, 1934 and additional protocol of February 26, 1935. GATT effective January 1, 1948. (Exchange of most-favoured-nation treatment, including scheduled concessions.)

Gabon. Franco — Canadian Trade Agreement of 1933 applied to Gabon. GATT effective August 17, 1960. (Exchange of most-favoured-nation treatment.)

Germany, Federal Republic of. GATT effective October 1, 1951. (Exchange of most-favoured-nation treatment.)

Greece. Modus vivendi by exchange of notes of July 24-28, 1947. GATT effective March 1, 1951. (Exchange of most-favoured-nation treatment.)

Greenland. (See Denmark.)

Guatemala. Trade Agreement in force January 14, 1939. (Exchange of most-favoured-nation treatment.)

Guinea. Franco — Canadian Trade Agreement of 1933 applied to Guinea. (Since the creation of Guinea as an independent state in 1958, Canada has continued to grant most-favoured-nation treatment.)

Guinea — Bissau. Canada — Portugal Trade Agreement of April 29, 1955 applied. (Since the creation of Guinea — Bissau in 1974, Canada has continued to grant most-favoured-nation treatment.)

Haiti. Trade Agreement in force January 10, 1939. GATT effective January 1, 1950. (Exchange of most-favoured-nation treatment.)

Honduras. Exchange of notes effective July 18, 1956. Ratified in Honduras September 5, 1956. (Exchange of most-favoured-nation treatment.)

Hungary. Trade Agreement January 1, 1972 effective until January 1, 1977, included exchange of most-favoured-nation treatment and provided for annual consultations. GATT effective August 8, 1973.

Iceland. GATT effective April 21, 1968. (Exchange of most-favoured-nation treatment.)

Indonesia. GATT effective March 1, 1948. (Exchange of most-favoured-nation treatment.)

Iran. Iran accorded most-favoured-nation treatment by Order in Council from September 5, 1956. (Canada grants most-favoured-nation tariff rates as long as Iran accords reciprocal treatment.)

Iraq. Special arrangement by Order in Council effective September 15, 1951. (Exchange of most-favoured-nation treatment.)

Ireland. Trade Agreement in force January 2, 1933, modified by exchange of letters on December 21, 1967, was terminated by Ireland on January 31, 1973, as a result of Ireland's accession to the EEC. (The tariff preferences it extends to Canada are being phased out over a transitional period ending in 1977.) GATT effective December 22, 1967.

Israel. GATT effective July 5, 1962. (Exchange of most-favoured-nation treatment.)

Italy. Modus vivendi by exchange of notes effective April 28, 1948. GATT effective January 1, 1950. (Exchange of most-favoured-nation treatment.)

Ivory Coast. Franco — Canadian Trade Agreement of 1933 applied to Ivory Coast. GATT effective August 7, 1960. (Exchange of most-favoured-nation treatment.)

Japan. Agreement on Commerce effective June 7, 1954. GATT effective September 10, 1955. (Exchange of most-favoured-nation treatment.)

Khmer Republic (formerly Cambodia). Franco — Canadian Trade Agreement of 1933 applied to Cambodia. Became a de facto member of GATT in 1968. (Since the creation of Cambodia as an independent state in 1955, Canada has continued to grant most-favoured-nation treatment.)

Korea, Republic of. Trade Agreement in force December 20, 1966. GATT effective April 14, 1967. (Exchange of most-favoured-nation treatment.)

Kuwait. GATT effective June 18, 1961. (Exchange of most-favoured-nation treatment.)

Laos. Franco — Canadian Trade Agreement of 1933 applied to Laos. (Since the creation of Laos as an independent state in 1955, Canada has continued to grant most-favoured-nation treatment.)

Lebanon. Special arrangement by Order in Council of November 19, 1946. (Canada grants most-favoured-nation tariff rates as long as Lebanon accords reciprocal treatment.)

Liberia. Special arrangement by Order in Council effective March 1, 1955. (Canada grants most-favoured-nation treatment.)

Liechtenstein. (See Switzerland.)

Luxembourg. (See Belgium — Luxembourg.)

Malagasy Republic. Franco — Canadian Trade Agreement of 1933 applied to Malagasy Republic. GATT effective September 30, 1963. (Exchange of most-favoured-nation treatment.)

Mali. Franco — Canadian Trade Agreement of 1933 applied to Mali. Mali maintains a de facto application of GATT. (Since the creation of Mali as an independent state in 1960, Canada has continued to grant most-favoured-nation treatment.)

Mauritania. Franco — Canadian Trade Agreement of 1933 applied to Mauritania. GATT effective November 28, 1960. (Exchange of most-favoured-nation treatment.)

Mexico. Trade Agreement in force June 5, 1947. (Exchange of most-favoured-nation treatment.)

Morocco. Various agreements relating to former French, Spanish and International Zones of Morocco. (Since the creation of Morocco as an independent state in 1956, Canada has continued to grant most-favoured-nation treatment.)

Netherlands. Convention of Commerce of July 11, 1924 includes Netherlands Antilles and Surinam. GATT effective January 1, 1948. (Exchange of most-favoured-nation treatment.)

Nicaragua. Trade Agreement in force December 19, 1946. GATT effective May 28, 1950. (Exchange of most-favoured-nation treatment.)

Niger. Franco — Canadian Trade Agreement of 1933 applied to Niger. GATT effective August 3, 1960. (Exchange of most-favoured-nation treatment.)

Norway. Convention of Commerce and Navigation with UK of March 18, 1826 applied to Canada. GATT effective July 10, 1948. (Exchange of most-favoured-nation treatment.)

Pakistan. Canada unilaterally accords British preferential treatment without contractual obligation. GATT effective July 30, 1948. (Canada accords British preferential tariff treatment to Pakistan. Pakistan accords most-favoured-nation tariff treatment to Canada.)

Panama. Exchange of notes in force August 12, 1935. (Exchange of most-favoured-nation treatment.)

Paraguay. Exchange of notes in force June 21, 1940. (Exchange of most-favoured-nation treatment.)

Peru. GATT effective October 8, 1951. (Exchange of most-favoured-nation treatment.)

Philippines. Trade Agreement in force August 29, 1972. Granted provisional accession to GATT on August 9, 1973. (Exchange of most-favoured-nation treatment.)

Poland. Convention of Commerce in force August 15, 1936. GATT effective October 18, 1967. (Exchange of most-favoured-nation treatment.)

Portugal, Portuguese adjacent islands and Portuguese overseas provinces. Trade Agreement in force April 29, 1955. GATT effective May 6, 1962. (Exchange of most-favoured-nation treatment.)

Qatar. Qatar maintains de facto application of GATT. (Exchange of most-favoured-nation treatment.)

Romania. Trade Agreement went into effect March 22, 1971 and was renewed March 22, 1974 for a further one-year period. GATT effective November 14, 1971. (Exchange of most-favoured-nation treatment and Romania endeavours to provide improved access for Canadian exports. Provides for annual consultations.)

Rwanda. GATT effective January 1, 1966. (Canada grants most-favoured-nation treatment.)

Senegal. Franco — Canadian Trade Agreement of 1933 applied to Senegal. GATT effective June 20, 1960. (Exchange of most-favoured-nation treatment.)

South Africa. Trade Agreement in force October 13, 1932. Exchange of notes August 2-31, 1935, effective retroactively from July 1, 1935. GATT effective June 14, 1948. (Exchange of British preferential rates on scheduled items. Exchange of most-favoured-nation treatment.)

Spain and Spanish possessions. Since August 1, 1928, Canada has adhered to UK — Spain Treaty of Commerce of October 31, 1922. Trade Agreement signed

May 26, 1954. GATT effective August 29, 1963. (Exchange of most-favoured-nation treatment.)

Sweden. UK — Sweden Convention of Commerce and Navigation of March 18, 1826 applies to Canada. GATT effective May 1, 1950. (Exchange of most-favoured-nation treatment.)

Switzerland. UK — Switzerland Treaty of Friendship, Commerce and Reciprocal Establishment of September 6, 1855 applies to Canada. By exchange of notes Liechtenstein included under terms of this agreement, effective July 11, 1947. GATT effective August 1, 1966. (Exchange of most-favoured-nation treatment.)

Syrian Arab Republic. Special arrangement by Order in Council of November 19, 1946. (Canada grants most-favoured-nation treatment tariff rates as long as Syria accords reciprocal treatment.)

Thailand. Modus vivendi effective April 22, 1969. (Exchange of most-favoured-nation treatment.)

Togo. Franco — Canadian Trade Agreement of 1933 applied to Togo. GATT effective March 20, 1964. (Exchange of most-favoured-nation treatment.)

Tunisia. Trade Agreement in force August 8, 1972. Tunisia acceded to GATT provisionally in 1959. (Exchange of most-favoured-nation treatment.)

Turkey. Exchange of notes in effect March 15, 1948. GATT effective October 17, 1951. (Exchange of most-favoured-nation treatment.)

Union of Soviet Socialist Republics. Trade Agreement effective from April 1972 to April 1976. (Exchange of most-favoured-nation treatment and annual consultation.)

United States of America. Trade Agreement of November 17, 1938 suspended as long as both countries continue to be contracting parties to GATT. GATT effective January 1, 1948. (Exchange of most-favoured-nation treatment.)

Upper Volta. Franco — Canadian Trade Agreement of 1933 applied to Upper Volta. GATT effective August 5, 1960. (Exchange of most-favoured-nation treatment.)

Uruguay. Trade Agreement in force May 15, 1940. Additional protocol signed October 19, 1953. GATT effective December 16, 1953. (Exchange of most-favoured-nation treatment.)

Venezuela. Modus vivendi in force October 11, 1950. (Exchange of most-favoured-nation treatment. Made for one year and renewed annually.)

Viet-Nam. Franco — Canadian Trade Agreement of 1933 applied to Viet-Nam. (Since 1955, Canada has continued to accord most-favoured-nation rates.)

Yemen, People's Democratic Republic of. Yemen maintains de facto application of GATT. (Exchange of most-favoured-nation treatment.)

Yugoslavia. Trade Agreement signed but not ratified October 1973, provides most-favoured-nation treatment except for British preferential tariffs and exception for customs unions and free trade areas.

Zaïre (formerly Congo, Kinshasa). Belgo — Canadian Convention of Commerce of 1924 applied to Congo (Kinshasa). GATT effective September 11, 1971. (Exchange of most-favoured-nation treatment.)

18.4.2.3   Tariff preferences for specified countries

Canada implemented a system of tariff preferences for specified countries on July 1, 1974. Imports of most manufactured and semi-manufactured products from designated beneficiary countries will be subject to the lower of the British preferential tariff or the most-favoured-nation tariff, less one third. The only notable product group to which the preference system does not apply is textiles.

Beneficiary countries: Algeria, American Samoa, Antigua, Argentina, Ascension, Bahamas, Bahrain, Bangladesh, Barbados, Belize, Benin (formerly Dahomey), Bermuda, Bolivia, Botswana, Brazil, British Indian Ocean Territory, British Solomon Islands, British Virgin Islands, Brunei, Bulgaria, Burma, Burundi, Cameroon, Cayman Islands, Central African Republic, Chad, Chile, Christmas Island, Cocos Islands, Colombia, Comoro Islands, Congo, Cook Islands, Costa Rica, Cuba, Cyprus, Dominica, Dominican Republic, Ecuador, Egypt, El Salvador, Equatorial Guinea, Ethiopia, Falkland Islands, Fiji, French Polynesia, French Southern and Antarctic Territories, French Territory of the Afars and the Issas, Gabon, Gambia, Ghana, Gibraltar, Gilbert and Ellice Islands, Greece, Grenada, Guam, Guatemala, Guinea, Guyana, Haiti, Honduras, Hong Kong, India, Indonesia, Iran, Iraq, Israel, Ivory Coast, Jamaica, Kenya, Khmer Republic (formerly Cambodia), Korea (Republic of), Kuwait, Laos, Lebanon, Lesotho, Liberia, Madagascar, Malawi, Malaysia, Maldives, Mali, Malta, Mauritania, Mauritius, Mexico, Montserrat, Morocco, Nauru, Netherlands Antilles, New Caledonia and dependencies, Nicaragua, Niger, Nigeria, Norfolk Island, Pakistan, Panama, Papua New Guinea, Paraguay, Peru, Philippines, Pitcairn, Qatar, Romania, Rwanda, St. Kitts — Nevis — Anguilla, St. Helena, St. Lucia, St. Pierre and Miquelon, St. Vincent, Senegal, Seychelles, Sierra Leone, Singapore, Spanish North Africa, Sri Lanka, Surinam, Swaziland, Syrian Arab Republic, Tanzania (United Republic of), Thailand, Togo, Tonga, Trinidad and Tobago, Tristan da Cunha, Tunisia, Turkey, Turks and Caicos Islands, Uganda, United Arab Emirates, United States Virgin Islands, Upper Volta, Uruguay, Venezuela, Viet-Nam (Republic of), Western Samoa, Yemen (Democratic), Yugoslavia, Zaïre, Zambia.

Sources
18.1 - 18.1.4 Merchandising and Services Division, Industry Statistics Branch, Statistics Canada.
18.1.5 Marketing and Trade Division, Economics Branch, Canada Department of Agriculture.
18.1.6 Public Finance Division, Institutional and Public Finance Statistics Branch, Statistics Canada.
18.2 External Trade Division, General Statistics Branch, Statistics Canada.
18.3 Information Services Branch, Department of Industry, Trade and Commerce.
18.4.1 Information Services, Department of National Revenue.
18.4.2 Information Services Branch, Department of Industry, Trade and Commerce.

Tables

..	not available	e	estimate
...	not appropriate or not applicable	p	preliminary
—	nil or zero	r	revised
- -	too small to be expressed		certain tables may not add due to rounding

18.1 Retail trade, by kind of business and by province; 1972-75, percentage change 1972-75 and percentage distribution 1975

Kind of business and province	1972 $'000,000	1973 $'000,000	1974 $'000,000	1975[1] $'000,000	Percentage change 1972-75	Percentage distribution 1975
Kind of business						
Combination stores (groceries and meat)	6,201.5	6,949.1	8,342.4	9,728.4	+56.9	19.0
Grocery confectionery and sundries stores	1,519.8	1,645.8	1,920.5	2,255.4	+48.4	4.4
All other food stores	719.5	787.2	870.3	897.1	+24.7	1.8
Department stores	3,713.8	4,316.1	5,055.1	5,786.0	+55.8	11.3
General merchandise stores	1,123.4	1,221.9	1,470.7	1,598.2	+42.3	3.1
General stores	673.1	736.3	887.2	995.5	+47.9	1.9
Variety stores	673.4	710.7	772.3	818.8	+21.6	1.6
Motor vehicle dealers	6,240.4	7,422.4	8,303.3	10,183.7	+63.2	19.9
Used car dealers	118.7	130.2	142.4	182.6	+53.8	0.4
Service stations	2,241.7	2,499.3	3,041.8	3,302.1	+47.3	6.5
Garages	445.2	479.1	553.3	554.8	+24.6	1.1
Automotive parts and accessories stores	734.6	754.3	918.6	1,088.0	+48.1	2.1
Men's clothing stores	515.7	557.2	606.4	663.5	+28.7	1.3
Women's clothing stores	639.0	643.3	745.0	862.7	+35.0	1.7
Family clothing stores	468.6	562.7	642.9	739.7	+57.9	1.5
Specialty shoe stores	55.1	39.9	51.6	48.9	-11.3	0.1
Family shoe stores	312.2	354.8	373.8	425.0	+36.1	0.8
Hardware stores	433.4	452.0	528.6	580.9	+34.0	1.1
Household furniture stores	450.3	499.0	589.7	693.7	+54.1	1.4
Household appliance stores	154.5	168.8	182.8	200.0	+29.4	0.4
Furniture, TV, radio and appliance stores	348.6	404.1	437.1	477.9	+37.1	0.9
Pharmacies, patent medicine and cosmetics stores	1,026.7	1,106.7	1,304.0	1,488.1	+44.9	2.9
Book and stationery stores	127.3	150.4	178.4	191.5	+50.4	0.4
Florists	126.4	136.9	161.9	170.6	+35.0	0.3
Jewellery stores	261.2	313.5	385.0	426.8	+63.4	0.8
Sporting goods and accessories stores	339.1	373.0	423.8	517.4	+52.6	1.0
Personal accessories stores	519.0	573.9	650.2	680.4	+31.1	1.3
All other stores	3,924.8	4,346.5	5,029.9	5,641.5	+43.7	11.0
Total	34,107.0	38,335.2	44,568.9	51,199.2	+50.1	100.0
Province or territory						
Newfoundland	637.7	717.1	843.3	972.0	+52.4	1.9
Prince Edward Island	155.6	175.7	208.2	240.6	+54.6	0.5
Nova Scotia	1,102.0	1,227.3	1,444.6	1,619.4	+47.0	3.2
New Brunswick	891.9	976.8	1,141.4	1,338.3	+50.1	2.6
Quebec	8,611.9	9,696.7	11,200.6	12,812.2	+48.8	25.0
Ontario	13,058.4	14,505.2	16,564.1	19,156.2	+46.7	37.4
Manitoba	1,495.9	1,699.5	1,988.6	2,191.9	+46.5	4.3
Saskatchewan	1,363.4	1,532.7	1,903.9	2,242.5	+64.5	4.4
Alberta	2,728.3	3,069.6	3,734.3	4,557.0	+67.0	8.9
British Columbia	3,986.9	4,645.8	5,428.6	5,938.6	+49.0	11.6
Yukon and Northwest Territories	75.1	88.9	111.2	130.9	+74.3	0.2

[1] Subject to revision.

18.2 Sales of chain and independent stores, by kind of business, 1972 and 1975 and percentage change 1972-75

Kind of business	Chain stores			Independent stores		
	1972 $'000,000	1975[1] $'000,000	Percentage change 1972-75	1972 $'000,000	1975[1] $'000,000	Percentage change 1972-75
Combination stores (groceries and meat)	4,166.2	6,734.0	+61.6	2,035.3	2,994.5	+47.1
Grocery confectionery and sundries stores	243.8	375.7	+54.1	1,276.0	1,879.8	+47.3
All other food stores	59.8	86.8	+45.2	659.7	810.3	+22.8
Department stores	3,713.8	5,786.0	+55.8	—	—	—
General merchandise stores	887.3	1,249.7	+40.8	236.1	348.5	+47.6
General stores	123.1	271.4	+120.5	550.0	724.1	+31.7
Variety stores	517.9	620.4	+19.8	155.5	198.5	+27.7
Motor vehicle dealers	94.9	125.6	+32.3	6,145.5	10,058.1	+63.7
Used car dealers	—	—	—	118.7	182.6	+53.8
Service stations	296.9	704.6	+137.3	1,944.7	2,597.5	+33.6
Garages	—	—	—	445.2	554.8	+24.6
Automotive parts and accessories stores	144.5	169.0	+17.0	590.1	919.0	+55.7
Men's clothing stores	104.2	179.1	+71.9	411.5	484.4	+17.7
Women's clothing stores	293.8	450.7	+53.4	345.2	412.0	+19.4

[1] Subject to revision.

18.2   Sales of chain and independent stores, by kind of business, 1972 and 1975 and percentage change 1972-75 (concluded)

Kind of business	Chain stores			Independent stores		
	1972 $'000,000	1975[1] $'000,000	Per-centage change 1972-75	1972 $'000,000	1975[1] $'000,000	Per-centage change 1972-75
Family clothing stores	148.5	320.0	+115.5	320.1	419.8	+31.1
Specialty shoe stores	29.7	22.5	−24.2	25.4	26.4	+3.9
Family shoe stores	163.1	243.8	+49.5	149.1	181.2	+21.5
Hardware stores	87.5	90.7	+3.7	345.9	490.2	+41.7
Household furniture stores	86.7	144.4	+66.6	363.6	549.3	+51.1
Household appliance stores	34.8	39.2	+12.6	119.7	160.8	+34.3
Furniture, TV, radio and appliance stores	101.7	166.4	+63.6	246.9	311.5	+26.2
Pharmacies, patent medicine and cosmetics stores	187.0	333.5	+78.3	839.8	1,154.6	+37.5
Book and stationery stores	33.2	87.9	+164.8	94.1	103.6	+10.1
Florists	6.8	8.3	+22.1	119.6	162.3	+35.7
Jewellery stores	101.4	182.7	+80.2	159.9	244.1	+52.7
Sporting goods and accessories stores	8.3	20.6	+148.2	330.8	496.9	+50.2
Personal accessories stores	88.4	165.8	+87.6	430.6	514.6	+19.5
All other stores	2,068.1	3,173.1	+53.4	1,856.7	2,468.4	+32.9
Total, all stores	13,791.3	21,752.0	+57.7	20,315.7	29,447.6	+44.9

[1]Subject to revision.

18.3   Percentage market share of chain stores, by kind of business, 1972-75

Kind of business	1972	1973	1974	1975[1]
Combination stores (groceries and meat)	67.2	68.2	69.5	69.2
Grocery confectionery and sundries stores	16.0	15.7	17.4	16.7
All other food stores	8.3	8.6	10.2	9.7
Department stores	100.0	100.0	100.0	100.0
General merchandise stores	79.0	79.3	79.8	78.2
General stores	18.3	17.7	19.2	27.3
Variety stores	76.9	77.0	75.7	75.8
Motor vehicle dealers	1.5	1.3	1.2	1.2
Used car dealers	−	−	−	−
Service stations	13.2	16.3	19.2	21.3
Garages	−	−	−	−
Automotive parts and accessories stores	19.7	15.4	17.0	15.5
Men's clothing stores	25.3	22.7	24.4	27.0
Women's clothing stores	46.0	43.1	46.6	52.2
Family clothing stores	31.7	39.6	40.4	43.3
Specialty shoe stores	53.9	33.3	42.4	46.0
Family shoe stores	52.2	55.6	54.4	57.4
Hardware stores	20.2	15.6	15.7	15.6
Household furniture stores	19.3	20.2	23.1	20.8
Household appliance stores	22.5	22.3	21.5	19.6
Furniture, TV, radio and appliance stores	29.2	32.3	31.0	34.8
Pharmacies, patent medicine and cosmetics stores	18.2	17.8	20.1	22.4
Book and stationery stores	26.1	32.2	35.5	45.9
Florists	5.4	5.4	5.7	4.9
Jewellery stores	38.8	41.0	41.6	42.8
Sporting goods and accessories stores	2.4	3.8	5.0	4.0
Personal accessories stores	17.0	18.5	20.7	24.4
All other stores	52.7	53.7	54.0	56.2
Total, all stores	40.4	40.8	42.2	42.5

[1]Subject to revision.

18.4   Department store sales by department, 1972-75

Department	Sales				
	1972 $'000,000	1973[1] $'000,000	1974[1] $'000,000	1975[1] $'000,000	Percentage change 1972-75
Women's, misses' and children's clothing					
Women's and misses' dresses, house-dresses, aprons and uniforms	92.0	103.4	107.7	117.2	+27.4
Women's and misses' coats and suits	74.8	87.6	106.5	122.2	+63.4
Women's and misses' sportswear	176.7	210.2	251.4	278.1	+57.4
Furs	16.1	19.1	20.5	19.4	+20.5
Infants' and children's wear and nursery equipment	104.3	109.6	134.7	160.1	+53.5
Girls' and teenage girls' wear	59.4	65.0	80.0	91.1	+53.4
Lingerie and women's sleepwear	66.7	75.4	82.5	98.1	+47.1
Intimate apparel	47.8	52.8	55.5	59.7	+24.9
Millinery	11.5	13.4	15.3	16.1	+40.0
Women's and girls' hosiery	50.0	51.4	53.7	57.5	+15.0
Women's and girls' gloves, mitts and accessories	60.0	69.1	79.6	89.9	+49.8

18.4   Department store sales by department, 1972-75 (concluded)

Department	Sales 1972 $'000,000	1973[1] $'000,000	1974[1] $'000,000	1975[1] $'000,000	Percentage change 1972-75
Women's, misses' and children's footwear	108.2	117.6	131.4	149.0	+37.7
Total, women's, misses' and children's clothing	867.5	974.6	1,118.8	1,258.4	+45.1
Men's and boys' clothing					
Men's clothing	178.3	212.3	242.6	279.3	+56.6
Men's furnishings	174.7	196.6	221.3	245.0	+40.2
Boys' clothing and furnishings	69.0	73.9	90.6	93.4	+35.4
Men's and boys' footwear	61.1	71.6	83.1	96.1	+57.3
Total, men's and boys' clothing	483.1	554.4	637.6	713.8	+47.8
Food and kindred products	190.5	219.4	255.5	330.9	+73.7
Toiletries, cosmetics and drugs	185.2	204.7	232.6	271.3	+46.5
Photographic equipment and supplies	60.9	71.3	84.1	106.8	+75.4
Piece goods	53.5	54.9	58.7	60.2	+12.5
Linens and domestics	94.1	107.9	129.4	148.9	+58.2
Smallwares and notions	45.4	46.1	54.7	59.0	+30.0
China and glassware	59.9	60.0	68.8	75.9	+26.7
Floor coverings	84.1	101.0	117.9	114.5	+36.1
Draperies, curtains and furniture covers	72.0	86.5	98.5	106.4	+47.8
Lamps, pictures, mirrors and all other home furnishings	36.9	49.4	55.5	59.3	+60.7
Furniture	176.2	227.9	282.9	289.8	+64.5
Major appliances	182.1	233.0	275.0	313.3	+72.0
Television, radio and music	166.5	198.2	232.5	245.5	+47.4
Housewares and small electrical appliances	125.4	152.0	172.5	210.4	+67.8
Hardware, paints, wallpaper, etc.	105.1	128.6	160.9	194.7	+85.3
Plumbing, heating and building materials	36.3	42.3	53.5	53.8	+48.2
Jewellery	67.9	91.9	115.6	136.9	+101.6
Toys and games	82.9	94.8	109.1	132.9	+60.3
Sporting goods and luggage	116.8	138.1	164.2	195.2	+67.1
Stationery, books and magazines	101.8	125.4	154.0	172.4	+69.4
Gasoline, oil, auto accessories, repairs and supplies	81.3	93.4	112.8	128.6	+58.2
Receipts from meals and lunches	79.9	95.4	113.7	135.0	+69.0
Receipts from repairs and services } All other departments	158.5	164.6	212.6	272.1	+71.7
Total, all departments	3,713.9	4,315.8	5,071.3	5,786.0	+55.5

[1]Subject to revision.

18.5   Retail sales of new motor vehicles, 1968-75

Year	Passenger cars No.	$'000	Trucks and buses No.	$'000	Total No.	$'000
1968	741,915	2,481,141	147,538	634,648	889,453	3,115,789
1969	760,803	2,603,835	156,702	719,044	917,505	3,322,879
1970	640,360	2,158,543	133,881	653,787	774,241	2,812,330
1971	780,762	2,737,516	159,570	815,535	940,332	3,553,051
1972	858,959	3,170,305	206,662	1,142,754	1,065,621	4,313,059
1973	970,828	3,835,173	255,870	1,535,201	1,226,698	5,370,374
1974	942,797	4,016,879	306,507	1,900,106	1,249,304	5,916,985
1975	989,280	5,018,402	327,349	2,242,606	1,316,629	7,261,008

18.6   Retail sales of new motor vehicles by type and source, 1968-75

Year	Passenger cars Canadian/US	Overseas	Trucks and buses Canadian/US	Overseas	Total Canadian/US	Overseas
	Number					
1968	637,393	104,522	142,241	5,297	779,634	109,819
1969	638,270	122,533	149,597	7,105	787,867	129,638
1970	497,185	143,175	124,664	9,217	621,849	152,392
1971	592,319	188,443	147,001	12,569	739,320	201,012
1972	653,933	205,026	189,577	17,085	843,510	222,111
1973	782,914	187,914	235,449	20,421	1,018,363	208,335
1974	796,840	145,957	287,686	18,821	1,084,526	164,778
1975	835,679	153,601	310,590	16,759	1,146,269	170,360
	Thousand dollars					
1968	2,238,712	242,429	620,184	14,464	2,858,896	256,893
1969	2,308,109	295,726	699,536	19,508	3,007,645	315,234
1970	1,795,709	362,834	628,532	25,255	2,424,241	388,089
1971	2,225,121	512,395	779,544	35,991	3,004,665	548,386
1972	2,554,779	615,526	1,087,306	55,448	3,642,085	670,974
1973	3,197,173	638,000	1,466,448	68,753	4,663,621	706,753
1974	3,455,140	561,739	1,831,532	68,574	5,286,672	630,313
1975	4,350,220	668,182	2,174,855	67,751	6,525,075	735,933

18.7   Retail sales in campus book stores, academic years 1971-72 to 1974-75

Province and items sold	1971-72 $'000	1972-73 $'000	1973-74 $'000	1974-75 $'000	Percentage change 1973-74 to 1974-75
Province					
Atlantic region	3,759	3,779	4,148	4,762	+14.8
Nova Scotia	1,599	1,578	1,750	2,069	+18.2
New Brunswick	1,234	1,199	1,323	1,531	+15.7
Quebec	6,895	8,290	9,541	11,208	+17.5
Ontario	18,240	19,251	21,871	27,340	+25.0
Manitoba	2,293	2,481	2,772	3,505	+26.4
Saskatchewan	1,816	1,791	1,954	2,475	+26.7
Alberta	4,327	4,574	5,140	6,292	+22.4
British Columbia	3,584	3,978	4,542	5,711	+25.7
Canada	40,914	44,144	49,968	61,294	+22.7
Items sold					
Text books[1]	27,140	29,201	33,108	39,835	+20.3
Trade books[2]	5,383	5,103	5,338	6,259	+17.3
Stationery and supplies	5,673	6,271	7,506	9,571	+27.5
Miscellaneous[3]	2,718	3,569	4,016	5,629	+40.2

[1]Includes all professional and educational books.
[2]Includes hard covers and paperbacks.
[3]Includes newspapers, magazines, periodicals and sundries.

18.8   Vending machine operators, 1963-75

Year	Firms No.	Annual change %	Machines[1] No.	Annual change %	Sales $'000	Annual change %
1963	673	+12.2	78,477	+6.9	67,580.0	+16.9
1964	651	-3.3	75,392	-3.9	78,561.8	+16.2
1965	764	+17.4	85,091	+12.9	89,815.4	+14.3
1966	769	+0.7	84,154	-1.1	107,539.6	+19.7
1967	790	+2.8	91,289	+8.5	119,650.9	+11.3
1968	791	+0.1	95,867	+5.0	127,058.6	+6.2
1969	..	..	100,948	+5.3	142,909.6	+12.5
1970	768	..	103,751	+2.8	156,822.1	+9.7
1971	697	-9.2	97,965	-5.6	162,249.1	+3.5
1972[2]	692	-0.7	106,758	+9.0	178,909.0	+10.3
1973	648	-6.4	104,253	-2.3	207,081.4	+15.7
1974	667	+2.9	106,278	+1.9	227,445.2	+9.8
1975	627	-6.0	110,287	+3.8	249,959.6	+9.9

[1]Maximum during the year; ovens, coin and bill changers are excluded.
[2]Beginning 1972, data of small operators excluded.

18.9   Sales through vending machines, distribution and percentage change, by selected type of machine, 1974 and 1975

Type of machine	1974 $'000	1974 %	1975 $'000	1975 %	Percentage change 1974-75
Cigarettes	105,431.4	46.4	112,212.4	44.9	+6.4
Beverages					
Coffee	36,148.3	15.9	41,655.8	16.7	+15.2
Soft drinks					
Can or bottle	16,249.2	7.1	18,330.5	7.3	+12.8
Disposable cups	18,397.1	8.1	20,059.5	8.0	+9.0
Packaged milk	7,527.8	3.3	8,551.9	3.4	+13.6
Other beverages	823.5	0.4	377.1	0.1	-54.2
Confections and foods					
Bulk confectionery	2,003.8	0.9	2,430.2	1.0	+21.3
Packaged confectionery	12,345.1	5.4	13,948.5	5.6	+13.0
Pastries	7,172.3	3.2	7,906.2	3.2	+10.2
Snack food	1,665.6	0.7	2,481.7	1.0	+49.0
Hot canned foods and soups	4,077.3	1.8	4,207.5	1.7	+3.2
Ice cream	840.2	0.4	891.6	0.3	+6.1
Fresh food (casseroles, hot dogs, sandwiches, salads, etc.)	13,989.4	6.1	15,436.6	6.2	+10.3
Other vending machines for food	153.7	- -	793.3	0.3	+416.1
All other food and non-food	620.5	0.3	676.8	0.3	+9.1
Total	227,445.2	100.0	249,959.6	100.0	+9.9

18.10   Direct sales by commodity, 1972-75

Commodity	1972 $'000	1973 $'000	1974 $'000	1975 $'000	Percentage change 1974-75
Meat, fish and poultry	12,571	14,263	15,658	16,754	+7.0
Frozen food plans	23,568	29,352	30,701	27,220	-11.3
Dairy products	184,075	187,757	203,716	221,847	+8.9
Bakery products	42,082	45,533	46,763	47,044	+0.6
All other foods and beverages	34,362	35,712	42,584	43,685	+2.6
Canvas, awnings, sails, tents, etc.	5,549	6,032	6,967	8,305	+19.2
Clothing	9,244	9,878	11,362	12,123	+6.7
Fur goods	7,067	8,262	9,818	11,713	+19.3
Furniture, re-upholstery and repairs	35,980	42,204r	47,733	56,953	+19.3
Books	63,287	72,022	82,889	90,909	+9.7
Newspapers	136,670	146,237	164,800	176,830	+7.3
Magazines	18,227	20,135	20,839	22,452	+7.7
Aluminum windows, doors, screens and awnings	18,386	21,354	24,109	27,220	+12.9
Dinnerware, kitchenware and utensils	31,625	38,731	49,806	67,981	+36.5
Sailboats and pleasure craft	9,186	12,528	12,568	15,718	+25.1
Household electrical appliances	63,053	84,750	103,519	120,929	+16.8
Pharmaceuticals and medicines	5,172	3,455	2,882	2,809	-2.5
Brushes, brooms, mops and household soaps and cleaners	27,352	26,099	31,331	38,510	+22.9
Cosmetics and costume jewellery	91,386	102,972	123,758	124,925	+0.9
Phonograph records	26,421	23,190	26,352	18,845	-28.5
Greenhouse flowers and nursery seeds, stocks, etc.	25,461	36,027r	38,216	50,937	+33.3
Miscellaneous[1]	63,936	77,082	130,676	129,867	-0.6
Total, all commodities	934,660	1,043,575r	1,227,047	1,333,576	+8.7

[1]Includes leather goods, textiles, stamps, coins and personal stationery and sales of merchandise to credit-card holders of gasoline oil companies, etc.

18.11   Methods of distribution of direct sales, 1974 and 1975

Commodity	By door-to-door canvassing 1974 %	1975 %	By mail 1974 %	1975 %	From manufacturers' premises 1974 %	1975 %	Through other channels[1] 1974 %	1975 %
Meat, fish and poultry	—	—	—	—	88.7	88.5	11.3	11.5
Frozen food plans	—	—	—	—	100.0	100.0	—	—
Dairy products	100.0	100.0	—	—	—	—	—	—
Bakery products	100.0	100.0	—	—	—	—	—	—
All other foods and beverages	53.0	54.8	—	—	3.4	1.3	43.6	43.9
Canvas, awnings, sails, tents, etc.	14.4	15.8	—	—	85.6	84.2	—	—
Clothing	15.4	15.6	—	34.1	84.6	50.3	—	—
Fur goods	—	—	—	—	100.0	100.0	—	—
Furniture, re-upholstery and repairs	—	—	—	—	100.0	100.0	—	—
Books	34.4	32.3	65.6	67.7	—	—	—	—
Newspapers	88.8	89.5	6.7	6.1	0.2	0.2	4.3	4.2
Magazines	—	—	100.0	100.0	—	—	—	—
Aluminum windows, doors, screens and awnings	57.0	57.2	—	—	43.0	42.8	—	—
Dinnerware, kitchenware and utensils	100.0	100.0	—	—	—	—	—	—
Sailboats and pleasure craft	—	—	—	—	100.0	100.0	—	—
Household electrical appliances	72.6	75.5	—	—	27.4	24.5	—	—
Pharmaceuticals and medicines	55.8	77.8	44.2	22.2	—	—	—	—
Brushes, brooms, mops and household soaps and cleaners	100.0	100.0	—	—	—	—	—	—
Cosmetics and costume jewellery	99.0	92.4	—	6.5	1.0	1.1	—	—
Phonograph records	—	—	100.0	100.0	—	—	—	—
Greenhouse flowers and nursery seeds, stocks, etc.	—	—	7.4	12.1	36.2	35.9	56.4	52.0
Miscellaneous	13.5	21.5	59.2	48.6	25.9	29.9	1.4	—
Total, all commodities	62.1	63.2	15.8	14.7	17.9	18.0	4.2	4.1

[1]Includes roadside stands, market stalls, shows, exhibitions and other display and demonstration venues.

18.12   Sales finance companies' new paper purchased and balances outstanding, by class of goods, 1972-75 (million dollars)

Class of goods	Paper purchased				Balances outstanding Dec. 31			
	1972	1973	1974	1975	1972	1973	1974	1975
Consumer goods	*941*	*1,080*	*1,127*	*1,041*	*1,025*	*1,150*	*1,168*	*1,156*
New passenger cars	445	515	548	546	530	609	617	638
Used passenger cars	179	186	199	185	204	200	203	201
Radio and television sets, household appliances, furniture and other consumer goods	317	379	380	310	291	341	348	317
Commercial and industrial goods	*1,076*	*1,383*	*1,453*	*1,560*	*1,204*	*1,529*	*1,870*	*2,080*
New commercial vehicles	576	784	838	871	607	826	1,049	1,122
Used commercial vehicles	94	111	120	119	86	115	134	151
Other commercial goods	406	488	495	570	511	588	687	807
Total	2,017	2,463	2,580	2,602	2,229	2,679	3,038	3,236

18.13   Consumer credit balances outstanding, selected holders, 1955-75 (million dollars)

Item	1955	1960	1965	1970	1974ʳ	1975
Instalment financing by sales finance and consumer loan companies[1]	616	886	1,198	1,136	1,169	1,156
Cash loans						
Under $1,500	89	392	628	525	296	252
Over $1,500	173	100	348	1,190	1,501	1,504
Chartered banks	441	857	2,241	4,663	10,817	13,175
Quebec savings banks	2	6	16	22	44	58
Life insurance companies policy loans	250	344	411	759	1,066	1,149
Credit unions and caisses populaires	174	433	813	1,493	2,762	3,243
Department stores	226	368	575	720	1,126	1,232
Furniture, TV, radio and household appliance store loans	175	195	167	148	188	192
Other retail dealers	351	397	571	683	907	994
Other credit card issuers	20	43	72	186	274	338
Public utility companies	..	..	116	181	271	277
Trust and mortgage companies	..	..	..	..	145	199
Total	2,517	4,021	7.157	11,706	20,566	23,769

[1]Data for years after 1970 show principal amount outstanding only, excluding unearned interest and other finance charges.

18.14   Summary statistics of major traveller accommodation groups, 1973 and 1974

Accommodation group	Locations No.	Rooms No.	Cabins and cottages No.	Tent trailer spaces No.	Total receipts $'000
1973					
Hotels	4,984	179,294	3,660	3,121	1,566,227
Motels	4,032	71,559	3,494	5,026	235,191
Tourist homes	455	3,459	90	243	2,754
Tourist courts and cabins	2,756	1,234	22,363	8,139	33,015
Outfitters	1,884	954	13,466	7,315	41,005
Tent and trailer campgrounds	2,910	252	3,321	261,427	50,624
Total	17,021	256,752	46,394	285,271	1,928,816
1974					
Hotels	4,893	181,680	3,949	2,322	1,852,764
Motels	4,067	73,391	3,557	5,136	271,004
Tourist homes	393	2,883	33	44	2,589
Tourist courts and cabins	2,573	991	21,008	7,992	33,861
Outfitters	1,946	1,068	13,637	7,892	46,638
Tent and trailer campgrounds	3,057	395	3,581	284,029	64,123
Total	16,929	260,408	45,765	307,415	2,270,979

18.15   Locations and receipts of major traveller accommodation groups, by province, 1973 and 1974

Province or territory	Hotels		Motels		Total receipts[1]	
	Locations No.	Receipts $'000	Locations No.	Receipts $'000	$'000	% distribution
1973						
Newfoundland	68	20,376	29	4,259	26,644	1.4
Prince Edward Island	24	3,542	58	3,891	8,869	0.5
Nova Scotia	93	25,274	163	11,929	39,784	2.1
New Brunswick	65	17,590	178	13,577	33,422	1.8
Quebec	1,833	357,563	715	42,943	419,124	21.7
Ontario	1,216	472,560	1,438	75,686	608,445	31.6
Manitoba	266	108,791	115	6,898	119,883	6.2
Saskatchewan	407	85,588	146	8,705	99,832	5.2
Alberta	438	197,632	315	21,053	223,006	11.6
British Columbia	514	258,835	842	43,439	319,600	16.6
Yukon Territory	42	8,380	23	1,804	11,476	0.6
Northwest Territories	18	10,096	10	1,007	12,595	0.7
Canada	4,984	1,566,227	4,032	235,191	1,928,816[2]	100.0
1974						
Newfoundland	75	23,608	39	5,732	31,729	1.4
Prince Edward Island	26	5,238	58	3,299	10,147	0.4
Nova Scotia	102	34,178	159	12,139	49,208	2.2
New Brunswick	72	21,524	179	14,808	39,331	1.7
Quebec	1,778	407,712	738	48,669	479,828	21.1
Ontario	1,166	554,592	1,450	87,026	709,416	31.2
Manitoba	263	127,974	113	7,612	140,445	6.2
Saskatchewan	371	95,027	141	10,685	111,667	4.9
Alberta	454	240,717	317	25,785	272,084	12.0
British Columbia	525	319,398	843	51,950	390,661	17.2
Yukon Territory	41	10,756	20	[3]	14,327	0.6
Northwest Territories	20	12,040	10	[3]	15,001	0.7
Canada	4,893	1,852,764	4,067	271,004	2,270,979[2]	100.0

[1]Includes tourist homes, tourist courts and cabins, outfitters, and tent and trailer campgrounds.
[2]Components do not add to totals because there is no provincial breakdown for federal campgrounds.
[3]Confidential.

18.16   Restaurant receipts, by province, 1971-75

Province	1971 $'000	1972 $'000	1973 $'000	1974 $'000	1975 $'000	Percentage change 1971-75
Newfoundland	11,987	13,069	15,479	16,859	18,505	+54.4
Prince Edward Island	3,191	3,208	3,650	4,048	4,763	+49.3
Nova Scotia	31,267	33,981	37,072	37,871	41,027	+31.2
New Brunswick	25,756	28,005	30,935	32,544	36,549	+41.9
Quebec	439,376	481,131	536,585	574,620	635,382	+44.6
Ontario	446,697	483,234	554,188	648,947	722,196	+61.7
Manitoba	59,084	63,369	71,178	87,068	100,382	+69.9
Saskatchewan	36,198	38,486	43,651	52,253	58,547	+61.7
Alberta	105,327	107,765	114,819	134,953	159,160	+51.1
British Columbia[1]	127,358	134,359	153,833	182,342	203,989	+60.2
Canada	1,286,241	1,386,607	1,561,390	1,771,505	1,980,500	+54.0

[1]Includes the Yukon Territory and Northwest Territories.

18.17   Receipts, taxes and paid admissions of motion picture and drive-in theatres, 1968-75

Year	Motion picture theatres		Drive-in theatres	
	Receipts and taxes $'000	Paid admissions '000	Receipts and taxes $'000	Paid admissions '000
1968	106,309	84,937	15,588	12,252
1969	109,848	78,918	16,691	11,308
1970	119,802	80,826	18,164	11,489
1972[1]	131,394	81,241	19,054	10,559
1973	139,541	77,438	22,171	11,581
1974	160,904	79,020	24,563	11,372
1975	195,545	84,161	31,256	12,843

[1]No survey was conducted in 1971.

18.18   Billings of advertising agencies, 1972-75 (thousand dollars)

Type of medium or service	1972	1973	1974	1975
Media billings				
Print media	171,983	193,386	218,270	228,617
Television	171,359	192,171	229,950	248,167
Radio	58,428	63,045	73,185	77,361
Outdoor	13,480	13,923	14,450	16,204
Total, media billings	415,250	462,525	535,855	570,349
Production cost				
Print	48,485	47,380	47,924	49,901
Television	28,201	38,512	38,687	40,892
Radio	5,039	5,651	8,136	6,916
Outdoor	2,505	2,433	1,776	2,380
Direct mail	20,782	16,889	21,004	20,132
Other	2,942	3,727	3,827	6,470
Total, production cost	107,954	114,592	121,354	126,691
Total, advertising billings	523,204	577,117	657,209	697,041
Research				
Market surveys, etc.	11,862	9,045	18,591	24,096
Total, gross billings	535,066	586,162	675,800	721,137

18.19   Revenue and expenditure of religious organizations, by province, 1972 and 1973

Province	Establishments		Revenue		Expenditure		Difference	
	1972 No.	1973 No.	1972 $'000	1973 $'000	1972 $'000	1973 $'000	1972 $'000	1973 $'000
Newfoundland	446	450	11,619	12,841	9,733	10,341	+1,886	+2,500
Prince Edward Island	188	190	3,835	3,787	3,733	3,469	+102	+318
Nova Scotia	1,058	1,078	20,973	21,859	18,411	19,367	+2,562	+2,492
New Brunswick	946	958	18,189	19,527	16,006	16,679	+2,183	+2,848
Quebec	3,131	3,126	113,962	119,391	97,547	105,591	+16,415	+13,800
Ontario	8,283	8,311	286,294	318,238	243,504	272,972	+42,790	+45,266
Manitoba	1,356	1,389	32,366	37,856	28,761	32,354	+3,605	+5,502
Saskatchewan	2,086	2,090	30,051	36,095	26,063	30,263	+3,988	+5,832
Alberta	2,042	2,036	46,102	51,733	37,060	40,543	+9,042	+11,190
British Columbia	2,004	1,968	57,396	66,172	49,179	57,076	+8,217	+9,096
Yukon Territory	40	43	717	815	624	718	+93	+97
Northwest Territories	55	56	135	169	169	183	−34	−14
Canada	21,635	21,695	621,639	688,481	530,790	589,554	+90,846	+98,927

18.20   Revenue and expenditure of trade associations, by province, 1973 and 1974[1]

Province	Establishments		Revenue		Expenditure	
	1973 No.	1974 No.	1973 $'000	1974 $'000	1973 $'000	1974 $'000
Newfoundland	28	38	1,212	1,625	1,138	1,305
Prince Edward Island	44	41	394	454	389	493
Nova Scotia	82	120	2,016	3,136	1,983	2,922
New Brunswick	71	110	2,408	2,676	2,328	2,609
Quebec	259	516	48,566	49,436	48,400	47,021
Ontario	842	1,057	130,596	165,146	126,414	161,740
Manitoba	118	170	6,070	8,527	5,633	7,915
Saskatchewan	127	180	6,260	7,269	5,879	6,858
Alberta	169	254	18,794	19,024	17,357	17,794
British Columbia[2]	170	310	15,299	19,705	14,962	19,217
Canada	1,910	2,796	231,615	276,998	224,483	267,874

[1]Includes Chambers of Commerce, Boards of Trade and Jaycees which were not surveyed in 1973.
[2]Includes the Yukon Territory and Northwest Territories.

18.21   Sales of wholesale merchants, by kind of business, 1973-75

Kind of business	1973 $'000,000	1974 $'000,000	1975 $'000,000	Per-centage change 1974-75
Consumer goods trades	16,135.9	18,866.1	20,989.1	+11.2
Automotive parts and accessories	2,060.4	2,529.2	2,808.5	+11.0
Motor vehicles	841.8	917.2	972.8	+6.1
Drugs and drug sundries	754.7	892.6	982.9	+10.1
Clothing and furnishings	358.2	396.2	415.9	+5.0
Footwear	83.3	96.0	92.9	−3.3
Other textiles and clothing accessories	705.3	851.3	831.5	−2.3
Household electrical appliances	801.6	897.0	993.1	+10.7
Tobacco, confectionery and soft drinks	1,182.5	1,342.7	1,555.6	+15.9
Fresh fruits and vegetables	653.2	751.3	795.2	+5.8
Meat and dairy products	1,060.7	1,083.2	1,090.9	+0.7
Floor coverings	369.6	424.3	426.3	+0.5
Groceries and food specialties	4,799.7	5,804.0	6,693.4	+15.3
Hardware	754.7	903.8	956.1	+5.8
Other consumer goods	1,710.4	1,977.5	2,374.0	+20.1
Industrial goods trades	17,945.3	24,344.1	24,390.1	+0.2
Coal and coke	43.1	69.7	84.3	+20.9
Grain	2,098.9	4,267.3	4,278.2	+0.3
Electrical wiring supplies, construction materials, apparatus and equipment	626.3	798.2	856.8	+7.3
Other construction materials and supplies, including lumber	4,719.7	5,358.1	5,367.7	+0.2
Farm machinery	1,258.8	1,607.0	2,006.4	+24.9
Industrial and transportation equipment and supplies	3,168.7	3,888.5	4,496.9	+15.7
Commercial, institutional and service equipment and supplies	789.1	940.5	994.9	+5.8
Newsprint, paper and paper products	518.9	694.3	729.3	+5.1
Scientific and professional equipment and supplies	407.8	482.9	565.3	+17.1
Iron and steel	1,758.2	2,736.3	1,998.1	−27.0
Junk and scrap	619.5	1,024.2	614.7	−40.0
Other industrial goods	1,936.1	2,477.1	2,397.6	−3.2
Total, all trades	34,081.2	43,210.2	45,379.2	+5.0

18.22   Sales of farm implements and equipment, by province and by major group, 1972-75

Province and major group	1972 $'000	1973 $'000	1974 $'000	1975 $'000
Province				
Atlantic provinces	11,033	14,184	17,918	23,062
Quebec	56,559	67,343	84,821	108,559
Ontario	114,712	142,149	173,663	214,763
Manitoba	38,003	60,971	76,839	106,442
Saskatchewan	101,111	143,602	175,653	262,116
Alberta	86,693	130,073	163,604	226,734
British Columbia	12,134	15,544	21,199	24,623
Total	420,245	573,866	713,696	966,299
Major group				
Tractors — farm use	162,691	212,492	256,573	373,341
Ploughs	11,519	12,192	16,550	23,448
Tilling, cultivating and weeding machinery	26,094	40,769	56,414	80,530
Planting, seeding and fertilizing machinery	17,957	23,638	31,106	39,467
Haying machinery	29,663	41,489	49,444	64,987
Harvesting machinery	78,162	114,074	126,162	181,765
Machines for preparing crops for market or for use	23,682	33,436	43,166	50,399
Farm wagons, boxes and sleighs	15,848	23,901	29,101	35,629
Barn equipment	16,712	22,864	30,501	30,324
Farm dairy machinery and equipment	11,631	12,857	16,120	18,973
Spraying and dusting equipment	2,887	4,430	6,540	10,270
Pump and irrigation equipment and miscellaneous farm equipment	23,401	31,722	52,019	57,156

18.23   New construction machinery and equipment sales, by commodity group, 1972-74

Commodity group	1972 Units No.	1972 Value $'000	1973 Units No.	1973 Value $'000	1974 Units No.	1974 Value $'000
Tractors, crawler-type	2,502	127,817	3,016	148,271	2,956	161,989
Tractors, wheel-type	1,373	25,094	1,940	32,964	2,270	44,105
Front-end loaders, wheel-type	2,245	93,752	2,775	123,830	2,786	136,125
Attachments for tractors and front-end loaders	807	2,837	1,925	5,124	3,040	10,157
Scrapers	132	13,525	183	19,382	196	24,123
Off-highway haulers, heavy duty	...	...	300	43,556	354	57,027
Excavator/cranes, crawler mounted	584	45,391	711	60,011	906	87,275
Excavator/cranes, rubber tire mounted	415	30,438	535	37,122	615	48,907
Excavator/crane attachments	193	971	172	813	154	749
Tower and climbing cranes	...	...	...	...	11	496
Trenchers and ditchers	123	1,884	251	2,971	326	3,295
Graders, motor	637	24,858	745	31,566	714	32,901
Logging skidders	1,367	28,900	1,982	48,344	2,180	59,243
Compactors and rollers, vibratory, hand-guided	1,243	3,342	1,426	3,308	1,714	5,300
Compactors, vibratory	272	3,904	318	6,161	341	8,546
Compactors and rollers, static, self-propelled	204	2,763	306	3,327	317	4,860
Air compressors	920	9,305	1,143	12,620	1,212	15,313
Rock drills	588	5,354	...	...	1,104	15,357
Pumps, contractors' type	5,011	3,622	8,362	6,643	9,142	7,536
Contractors' tools, hand-held	1,768	980	1,918	1,241	1,739	1,691
Concrete machinery	1,437	9,061	1,691	11,729	2,177	16,149
Asphalt equipment	158	7,196	204	9,152	333	13,222
Aggregate processing equipment	...	24,248	...	21,719	...	31,742
All other construction type machinery and attachments	...	55,639	...	98,205	...	109,387
All repair and consumable parts	...	260,211	...	330,868	...	420,484
Total	...	811,434	...	1,067,794	...	1,315,979

18.24   Sales of diesel engines, by province, 1972-75

Province	Units[1] 1972	1973	1974	1975
Atlantic provinces	1,345	2,150	2,031	1,720
Quebec	3,924	4,337	5,456	4,243
Ontario	4,925	6,394	6,530	4,834
Manitoba	893	1,068	1,064	1,013
Saskatchewan	681	648	1,249	1,339
Alberta	1,592	2,300	3,798	2,692
British Columbia	3,469	3,890	4,387	3,487
Canada	16,829	20,787	24,515	19,328

[1]Horsepower range 0-100 to 401 and over.

18.25   Summary statistics of cooperative marketing and purchasing associations, 1970-74 and by province, 1972-74

Year and province		Associ- ations	Share- holders or members	Farm marketings $'000	Sales of merchan- dise $'000	Total business[1] $'000
1970		1,230	1,431,000	1,288,400	743,100	2,074,400
1971		1,210	1,476,000	1,403,100	819,000	2,266,400
1972		1,120	1,491,000	1,708,300	906,300	2,666,900
1973		1,116	1,527,000	2,176,100	1,178,600	3,415,700
1974		1,123	1,546,000	3,142,800	1,550,000	4,769,600
Newfoundland	1972	37	16,000	1,700	19,100	21,400
	1973	37	17,000	1,700	24,000	26,100
	1974	35	17,000	3,300	27,400	31,300
Prince Edward Island	1972	14	10,000	3,700	12,400	16,400
	1973	17	10,000	5,200	14,700	20,000
	1974	16	10,000	5,200	15,900	21,600
Nova Scotia	1972	81	34,000	52,800	37,300	92,000
	1973	84	35,000	72,700	45,300	120,000
	1974	83	34,000	89,800	58,700	151,000
New Brunswick	1972	42	18,000	10,900	24,300	36,000
	1973	39	20,000	12,300	29,600	42,700
	1974	40	20,000	16,400	36,400	54,100
Quebec	1972	340	145,000	263,400	211,500	481,400
	1973	350	172,000	271,100	283,400	564,200
	1974	381	194,000	348,000	379,500	742,000
Ontario	1972	105	107,000	101,700	136,100	242,600
	1973	105	101,000	116,400	169,300	290,300
	1974	97	95,000	164,500	219,400	390,000

18.25   Summary statistics of cooperative marketing and purchasing associations, 1970-74 and by province, 1972-74 (concluded)

Year and province		Associ-ations	Share-holders or members	Farm marketings $'000	Sales of merchan-dise $'000	Total business[1] $'000
Manitoba	1972	74	182,000	59,600	68,800	146,100
	1973	73	185,000	88,600	83,600	192,300
	1974	71	190,000	126,300	109,900	258,300
Saskatchewan	1972	236	443,000	617,300	159,900	788,700
	1973	229	437,000	865,700	187,100	1,068,200
	1974	226	400,000	1,230,400	240,900	1,487,200
Alberta	1972	112	323,000	314,900	144,300	463,400
	1973	114	326,000	397,200	187,500	588,700
	1974	105	346,000	619,800	251,200	877,400
British Columbia	1972	75	65,000	138,900	59,300	202,200
	1973	63	67,000	165,700	75,500	244,800
	1974	64	76,000	186,600	102,100	294,600
Interprovincial	1972	4	148,000	143,300	33,100	176,600
	1973	5	157,000	179,500	78,500	258,400
	1974	5	164,000	352,500	108,600	462,000

[1]Includes service revenue and other income.

18.26   Sales of products handled by marketing and purchasing cooperatives, 1971-74 (thousand dollars)

Product	1971	1972	1973	1974
Marketing	*1,403,100*	*1,708,300*	*2,176,100*	*3,142,800*
Dairy products	412,700	478,500	514,000	643,300
Fruits and vegetables	48,900	48,800	58,500	80,400
Grains and seeds	627,400	811,300	1,106,400	1,951,200
Livestock and livestock products	235,400	281,900	363,200	329,600
Eggs and poultry	61,300	66,600	98,300	102,900
Miscellaneous	17,400	21,200	35,700	35,400
Purchasing	*819,000*	*906,300*	*1,178,600*	*1,550,000*
Food products	271,500	295,500	357,400	422,400
Clothing and home furnishings	26,900	31,100	35,500	44,500
Hardware	62,600	75,100	102,400	135,800
Petroleum products	127,300	140,800	166,200	217,100
Feed	159,400	159,500	236,700	342,100
Fertilizer and spray material	49,800	62,700	88,900	132,500
Machinery and equipment	39,500	51,700	77,600	91,200
Building material	45,100	48,600	59,600	81,500
Miscellaneous	36,900	41,300	54,300	82,900
Total	2,222,100	2,614,600	3,354,700	4,692,800

18.27   Value and volume of sales of alcoholic beverages, years ended Mar. 31, 1974 and 1975

Province or territory	Spirits 1974	1975	Wines 1974	1975	Beer 1974	1975	Total 1974	1975
	Value $'000							
Nfld.	25,183	29,288	3,124	3,811	40,685	44,085	68,992	77,184
PEI	8,059	9,161	998	1,114	5,371	6,264	14,428	16,539
NS	49,944	56,790	8,485	9,591	40,015	46,212	98,444	112,593
NB	30,984	36,157	5,637	6,514	32,250	37,943	68,871	80,614
Que.	225,957	264,019	89,209	108,051	267,139	297,490	582,305	669,560
Ont.	478,605	547,220	105,714	121,366	382,573	422,232	966,892	1,090,818
Man.	65,266	76,425	10,217	10,789	45,654	50,471	121,137	137,685
Sask.	58,425	70,047	6,558	7,070	36,663	44,334	101,646	121,451
Alta.	122,171	149,842	23,719	26,683	81,246	91,689	227,136	268,214
BC	174,584	207,963	46,614	54,142	115,580	126,575	336,778	388,680
YT	2,560	3,435	891	726	2,168	2,662	5,619	6,823
NWT	4,357	4,986	813	899	3,534	3,689	8,704	9,574
Canada	1,246,095	1,455,333	301,979	350,756	1,052,878	1,173,646	2,600,952	2,979,735
	Volume '000 gal							
Nfld.	625	707	202	238	10,387	9,932	11,214	10,877
PEI	208	227	87	85	1,555	1,571	1,850	1,883
NS	1,284	1,391	754	791	12,188	12,518	14,226	14,700
NB	775	874	536	549	9,264	9,865	10,575	11,288
Que.	6,225	6,967	7,867	8,842	123,821	126,268	137,913	142,077
Ont.	13,848	15,011	9,038	9,514	154,148	156,115	177,034	180,640
Man.	1,865	2,024	1,134	1,072	16,693	17,792	19,692	20,888
Sask.	1,621	1,831	714	697	12,495	13,163	14,830	15,691
Alta.	3,114	3,677	2,258	2,372	27,088	28,875	32,460	34,924
BC	4,934	5,595	4,577	4,781	44,112	45,273	53,623	55,649
YT	64	71	40	44	579	637	683	752
NWT	93	97	66	61	711	680	870	838
Canada	34,656	38,472	27,273	29,046	413,041	422,689	474,970	490,207

18.27   Value and volume of sales of alcoholic beverages, years ended Mar. 31, 1974 and 1975   M

Province or territory	Spirits		Wines		Beer		Total	
	1974	1975	1974	1975	1974	1975	1974	1975
	Value $'000							
Nfld.	25,183	29,288	3,124	3,811	40,685	44,085	68,992	77,184
PEI	8,059	9,161	998	1,114	5,371	6,264	14,428	16,539
NS	49,944	56,790	8,485	9,591	40,015	46,212	98,444	112,593
NB	30,984	36,157	5,637	6,514	32,250	37,943	68,871	80,614
Que.	225,957	264,019	89,209	108,051	267,139	297,490	582,305	669,560
Ont.	478,605	547,220	105,714	121,366	382,573	422,232	966,892	1,090,818
Man.	65,266	76,425	10,217	10,789	45,654	50,471	121,137	137,685
Sask.	58,425	70,047	6,558	7,070	36,663	44,334	101,646	121,451
Alta.	122,171	149,842	23,719	26,683	81,246	91,689	227,136	268,214
BC	174,584	207,963	46,614	54,142	115,580	126,575	336,778	388,680
YT	2,560	3,435	891	726	2,168	2,662	5,619	6,823
NWT	4,357	4,986	813	899	3,534	3,689	8,704	9,574
Canada	1,246,095	1,455,333	301,979	350,756	1,052,878	1,173,646	2,600,952	2,979,735
	Volume litres							
Nfld.	2 841	3 214	918	1 082	47 220	45 151	50 979	49 447
PEI	946	1 032	395	386	7 069	7 142	8 410	8 560
NS	5 837	6 323	3 428	3 596	55 406	56 907	64 671	66 826
NB	3 523	3 973	2 437	2 496	42 114	44 846	48 074	51 315
Que.	28 299	31 672	35 763	40 196	562 890	574 014	626 952	645 882
Ont.	62 953	68 240	41 087	43 250	700 757	709 699	804 797	821 189
Man.	8 478	9 201	5 155	4 874	75 887	80 882	89 520	94 957
Sask.	7 369	8 324	3 246	3 168	56 802	59 839	67 417	71 331
Alta.	14 156	16 716	10 265	10 783	123 142	131 266	147 563	158 765
BC	22 430	25 435	20 807	21 734	200 533	205 811	243 770	252 980
YT	291	323	182	200	2 632	2 896	3 105	3 419
NWT	423	441	300	278	3 232	3 091	3 955	3 810
Canada	157 546	174 894	123 983	132 043	1 877 684	1 921 544	2 159 213	2 228 481

18.28   Revenue of all governments[1] specifically derived from the control, taxation and sale of alcoholic beverages, years ended Mar. 31, 1971-75 (thousand dollars)

Government	1971	1972	1973	1974	1975
Government of Canada	423,518	471,936	499,819	554,177	613,709
Provincial and territorial governments					
Newfoundland	14,450	17,142	20,740	24,461	28,428
Prince Edward Island	3,983	4,510	5,182	5,874	6,698
Nova Scotia	26,249	28,269	33,648	37,529	42,618
New Brunswick	19,279	22,117	24,487	26,373	29,604
Quebec	116,102	142,618	151,997	164,920	184,798
Ontario	195,008	221,789	255,773	282,394	309,234
Manitoba	30,760	34,347	37,745	41,236	46,379
Saskatchewan	27,606r	31,041r	36,978r	41,610	50,376
Alberta	56,209	64,493	73,799	84,204	94,750
British Columbia	66,181	85,419	97,484	108,870	120,643
Total, provincial governments	555,827r	651,745r	737,833	817,471	913,528
Yukon Territory	1,865	1,985	2,303	2,542	2,743
Northwest Territories	2,404	2,817	3,295	3,752	4,664
Total, provincial and territorial governments	560,096r	656,547r	743,431r	823,765	920,935
Total, all governments	983,614r	1,128,483r	1,243,250r	1,377,942	1,534,644

[1]Revenue of the Government of Canada comprises excise duties, excise taxes, import duties and certain fees and licences. Revenue of provinces and territories includes revenue collected directly by the provincial and territorial governments as well as revenue of liquor authorities but excludes revenue resulting from general retail sales taxation.

18.29   Total imports, exports and trade balance, Canada, 1955-75

Year	Imports $'000,000	Percentage change over previous year	Exports $'000,000	Percentage change over previous year	Trade balance $'000,000	Ratio of exports to imports %
1955	4,578	15.4	4,332	10.3	-245	94.6
1956	5,566	21.6	4,839	11.7	-727	86.9
1957	5,488	-1.4	4,890	1.0	-599	89.1
1958	5,060	-7.8	4,899	0.2	-161	96.8
1959	5,530	9.3	5,144	5.0	-386	93.0
1960	5,495	-0.6	5,390	4.8	-105	98.1
1961	5,781	5.2	5,903	9.5	121	102.1
1962	6,294	8.9	6,357	7.7	63	101.0
1963	6,578	4.5	6,990	9.9	411	106.3
1964	7,488	13.8	8,303	18.8	816	110.9
1965	8,633	15.3	8,767	5.6	134	101.5
1966	10,072	16.7	10,343	18.0	271	102.7
1967	10,873	7.9	11,420	10.4	547	105.0
1968	12,360	13.7	13,679	19.8	1,319	110.7
1969	14,130	14.3	14,871	8.7	741	105.2
1970	13,952	-1.3	16,820	13.1	2,868	120.6
1971	15,618	11.9	17,820	5.9	2,202	114.1
1972	18,669	19.5	20,150	13.1	1,481	107.9
1973	23,325	24.9	25,421	26.2	2,095	109.0
1974	31,692	35.9	32,441	27.6	749	102.4
1975	34,636	9.3	33,103	2.0	-1,532	95.6

18.30   Imports[1] into Canada from all countries, by section and commodity, 1971-75 and percentage of 1975 total (million dollars)

Section and commodity	1971	1972	1973	1974	1975	% of 1975 total
LIVE ANIMALS	39.3	44.7	137.1	111.8	75.3	0.2
FOOD, FEED, BEVERAGES AND TOBACCO	1,117.5	1,355.8	1,844.4	2,404.4	2,606.7	7.5
Meat and fish	160.5	238.0	339.4	314.0	337.7	1.0
Fruits and vegetables	423.4	481.0	609.2	693.3	773.5	2.2
Raw sugar	97.0	130.5	162.0	401.8	459.2	1.3
CRUDE MATERIALS, INEDIBLE	1,321.7	1,539.8	2,018.1	4,072.7	5,087.1	14.7
Metal ores, concentrates and scrap	242.0	238.9	330.4	397.3	468.4	1.4
Coal	151.4	178.8	167.1	302.9	576.3	1.7
Crude petroleum	541.1	680.7	942.5	2,646.2	3,303.6	9.5
FABRICATED MATERIALS, INEDIBLE	3,140.2	3,579.0	4,281.6	6,481.6	5,944.3	17.2
Wood and paper	222.9	300.6	404.2	559.3	644.6	1.9
Textiles	500.5	588.3	658.9	816.9	740.4	2.1
Chemicals	711.3	829.8	1,023.1	1,537.2	1,475.6	4.3
Iron and steel	496.5	528.5	652.8	1,259.6	936.8	2.7
Bars and rods, steel	56.1	69.3	94.8	247.5	136.1	0.4
Plate, sheet and strip, steel	176.7	187.4	222.6	472.2	276.9	0.8
Non-ferrous metals	245.0	290.8	373.5	608.1	426.6	1.2

18.30   Imports[1] into Canada from all countries, by section and commodity, 1971-75 and percentage of 1975 total (million dollars) (concluded)

Section and commodity	1971	1972	1973	1974	1975	% of 1975 total
END PRODUCTS, INEDIBLE	9,832.2	11,947.7	14,797.5	18,332.3	20,597.5	59.5
General purpose machinery	623.9	730.1	896.2	1,142.9	1,347.8	3.9
Special industry machinery	859.7	1,021.4	1,229.9	1,577.5	1,860.2	5.4
Machine tools, metal working	75.4	81.7	118.9	149.1	172.0	0.5
Agricultural machinery and tractors	384.9	490.5	636.0	901.7	1,237.4	3.6
Transportation equipment	4,599.2	5,550.2	6,990.6	8,399.9	9,474.7	27.4
Sedans, new	1,162.8	1,293.8	1,568.8	1,817.4	2,288.8	6.6
Other passenger automobiles and chassis	139.7	178.2	207.8	204.8	259.4	0.7
Trucks, truck tractors and chassis	306.2	441.8	570.2	829.5	809.5	2.3
Other motor vehicles	148.0	193.5	230.2	281.8	324.2	0.9
Motor vehicle engines	303.4	337.6	382.3	400.5	437.3	1.3
Motor vehicle engine parts	155.1	217.1	366.9	333.3	390.7	1.1
Motor vehicle parts, except engines	1,894.9	2,272.3	2,754.5	3,227.1	3,627.5	10.5
Aircraft, complete with engines	132.8	121.2	260.1	376.4	290.9	0.8
Other equipment and tools	1,879.7	2,325.9	2,805.0	3,486.5	3,530.0	10.2
Electronic computers	184.2	212.4	276.8	333.1	343.4	1.0
SPECIAL TRANSACTIONS — TRADE	167.2	202.5	246.7	289.4	324.7	0.9
Total, imports	15,618.1	18,669.4	23,325.3	31,692.1	34,635.5	100.0

[1]Includes other commodities not listed.

18.31   Domestic exports[1] from Canada to all countries, by section and commodity, 1971-75 and percentage of 1975 total (million dollars)

Section and commodity	1971	1972	1973	1974	1975	% of 1975 total
LIVE ANIMALS	67.3	86.1	144.7	89.9	83.3	0.3
FOOD, FEED, BEVERAGES AND TOBACCO	2,045.0	2,269.0	3,012.6	3,780.5	4,013.5	12.4
Meat and fish	376.4	443.9	637.9	524.8	576.7	1.8
Cereals and preparations	1,147.1	1,257.9	1,634.8	2,555.6	2,703.9	8.4
Wheat	833.2	927.1	1,220.6	2,064.9	2,001.2	6.2
CRUDE MATERIALS, INEDIBLE	3,263.7	3,559.6	5,024.8	7,793.2	7,950.5	24.6
Metal ores, concentrates and scrap	1,414.6	1,396.9	1,999.5	2,375.8	2,231.1	6.9
Crude petroleum	787.4	1,007.5	1,482.1	3,419.9	3,051.5	9.4
Natural gas	250.7	306.8	350.7	493.6	1,092.2	3.4
FABRICATED MATERIALS, INEDIBLE	5,796.8	6,578.2	8,223.9	10,695.7	9,840.3	30.4
Wood and paper	3,014.3	3,562.6	4,485.4	5,508.8	5,011.4	15.5
Lumber, softwood	798.7	1,128.2	1,558.7	1,254.5	948.6	2.9
Woodpulp and similar pulp	798.1	830.2	1,082.3	1,888.8	1,826.6	5.7
Newsprint paper	1,084.5	1,158.0	1,287.7	1,725.9	1,742.6	5.4
Textiles	84.3	95.0	116.1	136.2	99.5	0.3
Chemicals	544.5	574.9	700.0	984.8	1,020.0	3.2
Fertilizers and fertilizer materials	238.4	249.3	282.6	421.2	456.3	1.4
Petroleum and coal products	117.4	210.3	311.6	611.3	638.5	2.0
Iron and steel	389.7	395.7	480.0	755.8	747.8	2.3
Non-ferrous metals	1,307.4	1,319.9	1,604.1	2,004.9	1,715.2	5.3
Copper and alloys	384.6	408.4	521.5	653.8	475.0	1.5
Nickel and alloys	319.5	311.7	377.3	440.3	413.6	1.3
END PRODUCTS, INEDIBLE	6,193.2	7,136.2	8,386.6	9,235.5	10,358.7	32.0
Industrial machinery	427.3	451.6	554.4	762.9	918.5	2.8
Agricultural machinery and tractors	175.0	217.0	290.3	398.5	541.5	1.7
Transportation equipment	4,570.8	5,324.1	6,079.0	6,333.0	7,083.3	21.9
Passenger automobiles and chassis	2,065.1	2,191.1	2,414.4	2,731.4	3,014.3	9.3
Trucks, truck tractors and chassis	524.8	641.1	775.5	895.5	1,056.1	3.3
Other motor vehicles	160.9	145.3	117.9	114.9	144.3	0.4
Motor vehicle engines and parts	441.7	514.7	543.9	460.8	518.3	1.6
Motor vehicle parts, except engines	978.5	1,226.1	1,562.9	1,514.0	1,616.4	5.0
Other equipment and tools	418.0	489.5	582.3	662.4	742.2	2.3
SPECIAL TRANSACTIONS - TRADE	30.6	41.8	45.4	79.6	78.7	0.2
Total, domestic exports	17,396.6	19,670.8	24,837.9	31,674.5	32,325.0	100.0
Total, re-exports	423.5	479.1	582.8	766.8	778.4	. . .
Total	17,820.1	20,150.0	25,420.7	32,441.2	33,103.4	. . .

[1]Includes other commodities not listed.

18.32   Imports into Canada from all countries from the United States and from the United Kingdom, by section and commodity, 1974 and 1975 (thousand dollars)

Section and commodity	All countries		United States		United Kingdom	
	1974	1975	1974	1975	1974	1975
LIVE ANIMALS	111,777	75,257	102,314	64,490	4,454	4,956
FOOD, FEED, BEVERAGES AND TOBACCO	2,404,416	2,606,670	1,138,745	1,255,881	86,550	107,706
Meat, fresh, chilled or frozen	169,100	180,145	70,895	107,951	374	266
Other meat and meat preparations	26,011	23,951	9,069	9,542	1,182	753
Fish and marine animals	118,901	133,574	57,207	74,021	1,832	2,389
Dairy produce, eggs and honey	86,458	71,474	17,316	19,993	915	887
Indian corn, shelled	151,210	102,671	151,207	102,666	–	3
Other cereals and cereal preparations	95,465	81,964	76,528	64,884	8,814	7,968
Bananas and plantains, fresh	41,515	54,326	315	554	–	3
Grapes, fresh	41,017	47,509	37,838	43,727	–	–
Oranges, mandarins and tangerines, fresh	48,734	54,768	36,477	40,948	–	–
Other fresh fruits and berries	101,152	117,567	91,713	108,365	6	1
Fruits, dried or dehydrated	28,318	31,873	15,988	17,630	86	68
Orange juice and concentrates	36,407	46,948	28,169	34,275	1	–
Other fruit juices and concentrates	17,970	17,118	10,732	10,142	587	873
Fruits and products, canned	48,022	58,046	25,566	29,304	1,390	1,985
Other fruits and fruit preparations	24,466	20,784	8,517	8,696	191	63
Nuts, except oil nuts	44,346	39,269	19,458	19,254	259	260
Tomatoes, fresh	37,237	45,920	28,913	39,068	–	–
Other fresh vegetables	126,507	148,160	120,345	141,654	13	3
Other vegetables and vegetable preparations	97,643	91,230	42,899	42,734	3,316	2,713
Raw sugar	401,806	459,208	3	29	–	–
Refined sugar, molasses and syrups	57,353	62,145	42,547	48,014	201	164
Sugar preparations and confectionery	48,905	60,951	18,209	20,263	16,876	22,732
Cocoa and chocolate	50,476	48,951	11,908	12,780	6,753	11,837
Coffee	131,684	168,557	49,056	66,308	56	4,689
Tea	29,820	35,094	1,557	2,455	5,658	7,119
Other foods and materials for foods	104,819	116,094	70,815	80,316	3,903	3,394
Oil seed cake and meal	51,455	54,598	51,450	54,597	–	–
Other fodder and feed	28,627	34,823	27,690	33,593	136	210
Distilled alcoholic beverages	68,725	79,462	4,305	5,310	30,311	35,011
Other beverages	70,910	94,338	3,191	4,951	2,853	3,415
Tobacco	19,355	25,153	8,862	11,858	838	903
CRUDE MATERIALS, INEDIBLE	4,072,678	5,087,075	1,077,881	1,432,372	29,641	23,566
Fur skins, undressed	57,902	57,928	34,738	34,781	4,468	4,325
Other crude animal products	31,750	27,346	24,367	20,502	331	439
Soybeans	90,505	86,210	90,485	86,200	–	–
Other oil seeds, oil nuts and oil kernels	40,773	45,499	38,418	41,669	5	14
Rubber and allied gums, natural	46,337	40,005	4,684	5,606	269	38
Other crude vegetable products	60,644	67,731	45,796	53,406	1,746	856
Crude wood materials	71,895	65,091	71,618	64,549	–	–
Wool and fine animal hair	28,083	25,663	6,170	4,986	11,303	11,275
Cotton	73,077	54,063	65,425	42,367	156	33
Man-made fibres	56,076	52,137	47,653	48,162	2,699	519
Other textile fibres	4,684	3,344	1,398	1,203	53	17
Iron ore and concentrates	38,108	123,038	25,854	97,614	–	–
Scrap iron and steel	56,540	56,474	56,531	56,455	2	10
Aluminum ores, concentrates and scrap	116,799	132,982	22,961	33,296	2	2
Other metals in ores, concentrates and scrap	185,848	155,937	96,323	80,614	5,486	3,110
Coal	302,899	576,311	302,789	574,120	110	191
Crude petroleum	2,646,203	3,303,613	–	3	–	–
Other crude bituminous substances	6,370	8,515	6,279	8,469	–	–
Abrasives, natural	12,521	12,628	10,501	10,099	232	111
Phosphate rock	40,368	85,170	40,088	84,610	–	–
Other crude non-metallic minerals	67,528	84,200	49,809	61,585	2,116	2,046
Other waste and scrap materials	37,768	23,189	35,993	22,076	662	577
FABRICATED MATERIALS, INEDIBLE	6,481,627	5,944,253	4,209,404	4,044,203	332,556	298,930
Leather and leather fabricated materials	64,842	103,843	43,684	78,179	13,286	12,678
Rubber fabricated materials	73,327	72,626	60,761	57,509	2,458	2,924
Lumber	116,594	109,796	106,537	103,810	–	1
Veneer	21,056	20,420	16,024	17,741	409	248
Plywood and wood building boards	125,740	133,345	80,846	94,436	58	125
Other wood fabricated materials	70,999	81,040	53,689	68,355	895	759
Wood pulp and similar pulp	19,373	30,253	17,398	21,930	323	–
Paper and paperboard	205,586	269,782	191,678	259,041	3,749	3,862
Cotton yarn and thread	23,862	18,164	12,913	10,214	3,026	1,722
Man-made fibre yarn and thread	125,169	103,028	78,239	63,878	7,611	6,484
Other yarn and thread	22,786	26,778	12,159	12,952	3,731	4,422
Cordage, twine and rope	61,103	48,809	10,869	9,322	2,689	2,187
Broad woven fabrics, wool and hair	17,169	20,736	576	684	8,364	6,732
Broad woven fabrics, cotton	132,522	106,305	61,291	58,921	1,925	1,890
Broad woven fabrics, man-made	75,788	75,251	25,734	29,322	2,208	1,515
Broad woven fabrics, mixed fibres	106,389	92,559	55,886	57,787	7,147	4,916
Other broad woven fabrics	26,851	14,989	3,246	1,210	526	423
Coated or impregnated fabrics	96,237	95,553	73,120	70,083	5,048	4,658
Other textile fabricated materials	128,992	138,248	74,135	80,180	8,652	7,367
Vegetable oils and fats, except essential oils	97,903	78,857	54,762	37,460	6,098	1,926
Other oils, fats, waxes, extracts, derivatives	60,875	55,885	52,361	46,528	1,575	3,884

18.32   Imports into Canada from all countries from the United States and from the United Kingdom, by section and commodity, 1974 and 1975 (thousand dollars) (continued)

Section and commodity	All countries 1974	1975	United States 1974	1975	United Kingdom 1974	1975
Inorganic chemicals	159,354	170,121	106,155	125,781	12,728	10,424
Organic chemicals	358,152	365,243	239,530	245,353	23,458	20,813
Fertilizers and fertilizer materials	32,409	53,640	30,205	46,214	234	242
Synthetic and reclaimed rubber	60,628	61,035	47,957	49,862	742	1,331
Plastic materials, not shaped	347,943	245,550	277,405	214,870	11,193	5,032
Plastic film and sheet	96,933	86,083	78,623	74,181	3,758	2,398
Other plastics basic shapes and forms	79,121	75,610	71,846	69,551	1,308	1,193
Dyestuffs, except dyeing extracts	45,937	37,190	15,567	13,739	4,763	5,049
Pigments, lakes and toners	32,317	23,632	19,720	15,686	2,427	1,835
Paints and related products	37,522	50,055	34,454	43,210	2,198	2,337
Other chemical products	286,879	307,405	244,882	263,280	10,741	14,051
Fuel oil	236,242	107,141	36,478	12,862	—	—
Lubricating oils and greases	48,750	45,559	39,434	39,155	637	326
Coke of petroleum and coal	54,728	80,822	40,904	72,707	5,599	3,300
Other petroleum and coal products	33,905	42,322	28,159	31,611	949	3,099
Bars and rods, steel	247,456	136,140	103,261	39,025	6,839	8,942
Plate, sheet and strip, steel	472,196	276,870	253,394	131,348	14,543	13,705
Structural shapes, steel and sheet piling	184,385	63,555	79,450	37,187	20,091	11,297
Pipes and tubes, iron and steel	150,491	183,058	89,140	94,753	6,866	11,161
Wire and wire rope steel	68,962	65,787	14,002	11,788	12,863	13,728
Other iron and steel and alloys	136,063	211,365	95,652	139,542	5,713	9,437
Aluminum, including alloys	173,659	111,138	152,278	94,499	8,099	5,389
Copper and alloys	96,484	54,785	67,090	37,996	4,338	3,609
Nickel and alloys	92,939	96,590	28,693	30,844	3,481	1,198
Precious metals, including alloys	141,338	76,177	114,604	69,059	23,296	6,382
Tin, including alloys	43,886	33,357	27,256	9,062	1,711	805
Other non-ferrous metals and alloys	59,768	54,587	35,218	37,618	1,891	2,048
Bolts, nuts and screws	108,298	108,042	87,900	89,484	3,624	3,630
Other basic hardware	120,937	111,541	92,935	90,012	6,473	5,654
Chains	30,664	32,212	15,220	17,705	3,157	4,577
Valves	78,775	119,101	49,742	68,858	12,198	20,364
Pipe fittings	75,766	95,669	45,384	56,383	6,949	6,716
Other metal fabricated basic products	151,222	162,258	130,241	134,583	7,467	5,626
Clay bricks, clay tiles and refractories	89,678	106,623	58,023	66,850	3,529	6,938
Sheet and plate glass	36,317	31,361	22,467	24,286	1,492	510
Other glass basic products	51,836	46,917	41,653	38,487	3,136	2,486
Abrasive basic products	37,789	34,126	31,325	27,356	1,252	730
Natural and synthetic gem stones	35,876	42,763	4,086	6,375	1,372	764
Other non-metallic mineral basic products	78,450	96,087	63,998	76,285	4,881	5,266
Electricity	5,167	12,636	5,167	12,636	—	—
Other fabricated materials, inedible	129,231	133,836	103,994	104,580	6,783	7,817
END PRODUCTS, INEDIBLE	18,332,251	20,597,547	14,596,501	16,496,209	660,033	772,756
Machinery	*3,622,087*	*4,445,427*	*2,936,260*	*3,532,431*	*196,764*	*265,450*
Engines and turbines, diesel, general purpose	58,362	75,749	40,216	49,480	11,130	18,962
Engines and turbines, general purpose, n.e.s.	99,344	116,500	75,326	91,868	11,631	13,189
Electric generators and motors	140,368	175,761	100,580	108,940	19,089	34,783
Bearings	107,479	119,761	71,046	76,564	6,099	6,695
Other mechanical power transmission equipment	88,728	96,610	77,064	78,444	6,742	9,481
Compressors, blowers and vacuum pumps	80,746	101,288	64,006	86,219	5,616	8,291
Pumps, except oil well pumps	56,130	72,665	45,032	56,569	4,670	6,615
Packaging machinery	50,245	62,899	42,576	51,290	905	1,596
Other general purpose industrial machinery	132,309	177,266	112,652	134,777	7,654	9,913
Conveyors and conveying systems	23,423	30,464	18,490	19,733	2,026	2,918
Elevators and escalators	14,823	15,990	13,385	13,509	415	791
Industrial trucks, tractors, trailers, stackers	103,520	96,168	89,015	83,938	8,617	6,343
Hoisting machinery	98,516	145,323	79,975	123,559	1,797	1,702
Other materials handling equipment	88,876	61,340	81,539	53,845	900	1,489
Drilling machinery and drill bits	113,736	141,189	103,542	126,758	1,482	2,151
Power shovels	110,885	124,387	92,933	101,933	1,798	347
Bulldozing and similar equipment	18,393	24,914	16,425	21,657	226	314
Front end loaders	122,130	152,424	114,866	140,884	822	1,441
Other excavating machinery	63,197	89,177	61,560	78,706	375	1,263
Mining, oil and gas machinery	103,377	151,443	81,452	113,539	11,626	16,456
Construction and maintenance machinery	111,065	146,034	98,412	132,395	2,381	2,342
Machine tools, metalworking	149,117	172,163	100,595	107,944	11,761	14,704
Welding apparatus and equipment	38,403	35,267	33,970	32,096	1,039	900
Rolling-mill machinery	34,154	43,424	22,176	26,513	9,120	12,379
Other metalworking machinery	115,428	121,282	86,376	89,098	10,292	10,192
Pulp and paper industries machinery	63,068	87,731	45,265	57,709	2,243	7,810
Printing presses	48,207	55,640	37,576	41,140	2,527	4,692
Other printing machinery and equipment	55,481	63,244	47,808	54,923	2,724	2,418
Spinning, weaving and knitting machinery	45,542	47,882	21,362	21,971	6,439	4,748
Other textile industries machinery	63,732	55,159	43,109	34,158	3,038	4,310
Food, beverages and tobacco industries machinery	60,393	67,897	41,237	44,531	4,658	5,508
Plastics and chemical industry machinery	63,287	82,736	49,748	65,796	1,605	1,782
Other special industry machinery	197,923	198,209	136,185	136,486	6,298	5,723
Soil preparation, seeding and fertilizing machinery	60,120	97,414	53,607	88,765	1,102	1,218

18.32   Imports into Canada from all countries from the United States and from the United Kingdom, by section and commodity, 1974 and 1975 (thousand dollars) (concluded)

Section and commodity	All countries 1974	1975	United States 1974	1975	United Kingdom 1974	1975
END PRODUCTS, INEDIBLE (concluded)						
Combine reaper-threshers	55,284	85,367	53,687	79,556	435	1,099
Other haying and harvesting machinery	105,444	142,297	101,662	136,735	446	607
Other agricultural machinery and equipment	133,981	136,364	124,315	126,770	2,174	2,066
Wheel tractors, new	253,926	390,048	202,610	312,949	17,609	21,609
Track-laying tractors and used tractors	114,355	149,884	97,781	127,742	643	963
Tractor engines and tractor parts	178,590	236,066	157,102	202,945	6,610	15,641
Transportation and Communication Equipment	*9,357,369*	*10,327,289*	*8,063,580*	*9,098,954*	*141,374*	*167,277*
Railway and street railway rolling stock	82,681	109,049	74,263	96,715	4,086	5,621
Sedans, new	1,817,392	2,288,795	1,487,157	1,982,489	17,879	26,132
Other passenger automobiles and chassis	204,829	259,422	144,755	200,452	13,661	13,217
Trucks, truck tractors and chassis	829,472	809,519	780,589	772,758	710	11
Other motor vehicles	281,769	324,177	198,270	251,729	2,661	4,851
Motor vehicle engines	400,516	437,287	360,426	376,008	1,299	793
Motor vehicle engine parts	333,278	390,701	318,954	375,990	4,131	3,812
Motor vehicle parts, except engines	3,227,055	3,627,501	3,112,040	3,515,270	15,320	15,588
Marine engines and parts	91,939	104,637	68,898	72,665	4,548	9,515
Ships, boats and parts, except engines	105,797	102,665	59,554	57,129	5,945	5,998
Aircraft, complete with engines	376,388	290,921	367,193	281,454	596	6,520
Aircraft engines and parts	124,248	221,607	103,028	196,164	20,751	25,019
Aircraft parts, except engines	166,639	182,804	160,962	175,107	3,047	5,176
Other transportation equipment	357,907	325,655	244,460	202,279	9,610	11,246
Telephone and telegraph equipment	86,201	90,183	65,599	70,014	4,421	5,479
Television, radio sets and phonographs	266,000	221,424	107,926	96,432	1,090	1,279
Electronic tubes and semi-conductors	143,607	92,593	107,457	71,263	4,066	3,698
Other telecommunication and related equipment	461,652	448,347	302,051	305,035	27,553	23,321
Other Equipment and Tools	*2,529,054*	*2,677,478*	*2,052,543*	*2,158,530*	*84,514*	*100,410*
Air conditioning and refrigeration equipment	190,380	179,367	164,532	149,314	4,061	2,665
Electric lighting fixtures and portable lamps	88,537	85,727	67,721	68,036	1,209	1,892
Switchgear and protective equipment	52,225	66,451	36,486	37,733	3,257	9,615
Industrial control equipment	45,882	47,957	38,753	40,320	1,723	1,963
Other electric lighting distribution equipment	112,937	123,002	92,197	95,523	5,070	10,033
Auxiliary electric equipment for engines	104,543	120,795	95,247	112,702	2,869	1,828
Electrical property measuring instruments	54,220	57,539	43,756	47,404	5,167	4,744
Miscellaneous measuring, controlling instruments	84,708	85,658	75,121	75,161	2,904	2,556
Medical and related equipment	76,735	93,111	66,647	79,927	2,726	3,945
Navigation equipment	12,106	18,863	10,478	16,445	258	626
Other measuring, laboratory equipment, etc.	207,355	239,559	161,381	185,667	5,881	7,215
Safety and sanitation equipment	57,778	71,869	53,403	62,108	1,853	2,249
Service industry equipment	65,836	66,631	58,961	60,481	1,806	1,738
Furniture and fixtures	158,859	149,921	105,323	104,539	4,511	4,203
Hand tools and cutlery	171,848	178,022	122,751	125,352	11,904	14,859
Electronic computers	333,115	343,350	317,118	324,518	5,018	7,106
Other office machines and equipment	275,619	315,518	158,855	195,725	18,985	16,334
Miscellaneous equipment and tools	436,372	434,139	383,812	377,576	5,314	6,840
Personal and Household Goods	*1,283,494*	*1,456,464*	*436,055*	*501,241*	*123,724*	*124,057*
Outerwear, except knitted	170,480	201,937	43,997	34,488	6,678	6,836
Outerwear, knitted	151,750	188,715	10,616	13,324	10,828	11,026
Other apparel and apparel accessories	119,980	142,957	49,054	64,142	8,345	9,410
Footwear	136,685	157,502	10,438	12,166	11,197	8,182
Watches, clocks, jewellery and silverware	101,589	123,644	28,903	42,574	12,321	14,321
Sporting and recreation equipment	101,476	110,899	54,007	60,087	5,455	6,277
Games, toys and children's vehicles	78,802	75,537	37,385	39,543	6,875	6,176
House furnishings	130,512	141,075	78,495	94,552	14,350	10,766
Kitchen utensils, cutlery and tableware	132,744	139,999	46,023	52,971	31,589	34,770
Other personal and household goods	159,474	174,199	77,138	87,392	16,087	15,562
Miscellaneous End Products	*1,540,248*	*1,690,889*	*1,108,064*	*1,205,053*	*113,656*	*115,562*
Medicinal and pharmaceutical products	144,616	167,381	82,104	81,598	18,142	17,698
Medical, ophthalmic, orthopaedic supplies	118,310	144,339	86,942	109,573	4,325	4,660
Newspapers, magazines and periodicals	98,655	118,446	87,267	102,991	2,393	4,604
Books and pamphlets	172,242	205,255	131,612	156,591	14,329	16,810
Other printed matter	101,110	110,018	88,157	94,550	4,205	5,918
Stationers' and office supplies	81,879	84,537	59,268	60,602	6,551	7,482
Unexposed photographic film and plates	95,654	106,355	52,060	63,195	27,749	22,065
Other photographic goods	263,543	260,160	193,414	185,700	4,841	4,255
Containers and closures	139,447	135,572	125,435	122,336	3,410	4,019
Other end products, inedible	324,791	358,824	201,805	227,918	27,712	28,051
SPECIAL TRANSACTIONS — TRADE	289,371	324,711	231,864	266,126	13,104	14,054
Total, imports	31,692,121	34,635,513	21,356,710	23,559,280	1,126,338	1,221,969

In this table a dash indicates that either there was no trade or the amount was less than $500.

18.33   Domestic exports from Canada to all countries, to the United States and to the United Kingdom, by section and commodity, 1974 and 1975 (thousand dollars)

Section and commodity	All countries 1974	1975	United States 1974	1975	United Kingdom 1974	1975
LIVE ANIMALS	89,941	83,319	72,303	65,821	647	235
FOOD, FEED, BEVERAGES AND TOBACCO	3,780,499	4,013,451	803,519	860,816	396,614	348,847
Meat, fresh, chilled or frozen	133,658	149,416	60,604	45,359	5,078	3,783
Other meat and meat preparations	17,200	17,431	9,793	8,634	201	186
Fish, whole or dressed, fresh or frozen	82,680	98,557	45,910	48,272	3,442	2,967
Fish, fillets and blocks, fresh or frozen	111,511	134,479	108,196	125,064	93	16
Fish, preserved, except canned	44,237	43,732	20,813	20,115	7	21
Fish, canned	64,677	42,950	14,027	7,429	24,251	15,421
Shellfish	70,811	90,121	60,539	76,572	2,426	4,147
Dairy produce, eggs and honey	77,415	53,565	24,205	9,752	1,670	1,919
Barley	324,506	440,437	55,914	52,460	8,793	—
Wheat	2,064,852	2,001,152	15,263	9,001	208,225	203,302
Other cereals, unmilled	23,615	66,182	7,300	8,879	1,596	1,285
Wheat flour	60,099	103,763	2,229	811	1,985	627
Other cereals, milled	40,210	51,650	10,400	19,451	3,507	2,896
Cereal preparations	42,308	40,676	39,188	37,458	388	217
Fruits and fruit preparations	30,285	29,402	20,587	17,670	2,719	1,801
Vegetables and vegetable preparations	81,701	82,641	28,208	22,847	28,559	26,547
Sugar and sugar preparations	44,080	71,887	17,336	34,686	414	320
Other foods and materials for food	76,679	69,373	19,000	14,966	4,395	3,402
Oil seed cake and meal	20,849	11,588	2,050	330	16,349	10,311
Other feeds of vegetable origin	40,004	43,675	25,289	27,681	17	233
Other fodder and feed	47,109	36,090	14,648	14,692	18,434	12,738
Whisky	193,940	242,431	187,318	235,129	1,226	1,942
Other beverages	12,552	19,544	11,686	18,674	240	34
Tobacco	75,521	72,705	3,015	4,885	62,600	54,731
CRUDE MATERIALS, INEDIBLE	7,793,217	7,950,534	5,042,216	5,229,216	360,548	411,181
Raw hides and skins	42,718	44,782	9,698	13,407	602	141
Fur skins, undressed	44,581	40,258	14,858	14,113	9,866	7,332
Other crude animal products	26,538	21,527	20,668	17,303	452	282
Seeds for sowing	24,849	17,582	14,792	11,827	3,343	1,376
Flaxseed	148,631	83,815	5,063	969	14,406	5,079
Rapeseed	199,843	223,551	25	44	198	775
Other oil seeds, oil nuts and oil kernels	32,015	28,523	11,494	14,955	1,003	521
Other crude vegetable products	36,070	35,619	28,925	31,432	148	142
Pulpwood	12,690	11,224	9,351	7,442	—	—
Pulpwood chips	14,300	14,372	14,298	14,336	—	—
Other crude wood products	36,313	35,263	21,515	14,954	119	171
Textile and related fibres	26,053	16,689	15,493	9,512	1,965	836
Iron ores and concentrates	542,553	685,726	345,134	429,157	55,641	45,022
Scrap iron and steel	31,385	32,159	25,426	21,482	94	88
Aluminum ores, concentrates and scrap	34,171	26,385	27,665	21,067	312	344
Copper in ores, concentrates and scrap	648,121	330,103	57,365	56,424	3,712	2,752
Lead in ores, concentrates and scrap	64,652	56,046	5,967	10,078	2,825	609
Nickel in ores, concentrates and scrap	438,233	516,116	95,816	67,175	136,958	226,563
Precious metals in ores, concentrates and scrap	146,889	129,554	57,343	50,208	56,422	50,270
Zinc in ores, concentrates and scrap	318,512	297,752	58,033	39,017	9,809	2,482
Radioactive ores and concentrates	51,309	47,052	27,974	28,129	22,121	17,937
Other metals in ores, concentrates and scrap	99,949	110,226	19,172	21,143	7,620	10,988
Crude petroleum	3,419,852	3,051,511	3,419,852	3,051,511	—	—
Natural gas	493,640	1,092,168	493,640	1,092,168	—	—
Coal and other crude bituminous substances	319,128	493,579	46,114	13,388	2,554	10,162
Asbestos unmanufactured	345,202	302,136	113,808	98,679	24,847	23,174
Sulphur	91,017	113,207	20,967	22,909	1,604	654
Other crude non-metallic minerals	80,564	77,305	46,293	44,900	2,822	3,362
Other waste and scrap materials	23,440	16,302	15,468	11,487	1,103	118
FABRICATED MATERIALS, INEDIBLE	10,695,733	9,840,291	7,042,570	6,527,036	991,219	809,704
Leather and leather fabricated materials	11,137	13,206	8,231	6,657	1,021	1,306
Lumber, softwood	1,254,494	948,559	873,044	723,590	133,088	53,490
Lumber, hardwood	36,112	24,058	26,991	16,340	1,041	1,549
Shingles and shakes	54,331	65,090	52,772	64,028	217	79
Other sawmill products	10,472	9,139	9,992	7,396	375	138
Veneer	43,603	38,843	38,575	32,680	605	373
Plywood	62,366	51,278	8,077	7,439	35,701	33,486
Other wood fabricated materials	34,405	21,468	19,387	13,953	12,494	3,914
Wood pulp and similar pulp	1,888,770	1,826,617	1,060,380	996,502	117,376	145,412
Newsprint paper	1,725,856	1,742,577	1,352,758	1,357,892	108,723	102,416
Other paper for printing	93,606	80,173	68,541	60,491	12,978	8,546
Paperboard	123,902	70,456	13,823	3,654	36,501	24,439
Other paper	180,917	133,137	89,445	50,371	25,778	25,961
Yarn, thread, cordage, twine and rope	21,741	13,989	7,407	5,003	4,969	3,307
Cotton broad woven fabrics	20,482	13,825	5,664	3,946	2,678	3,360
Other broad woven fabrics	33,639	31,152	6,072	3,010	7,314	7,946
Other textile fabricated materials	60,371	40,484	31,479	18,087	3,894	2,763
Oils, fats, waxes, extracts and derivatives	75,240	63,220	12,460	10,984	14,398	5,431
Chemical elements	87,201	55,793	32,452	26,562	42,207	23,845
Other inorganic chemicals	146,678	191,917	112,212	158,283	11,129	9,230
Organic chemicals	122,799	104,879	81,395	57,091	10,045	9,115

18.33 Domestic exports from Canada to all countries, to the United States and to the United Kingdom, by section and commodity, 1974 and 1975 (thousand dollars) (continued)

Section and commodity	All countries		United States		United Kingdom	
	1974	1975	1974	1975	1974	1975
FABRICATED MATERIALS, INEDIBLE (concluded)						
Fertilizers and fertilizer materials	421,224	456,345	340,904	379,364	214	622
Synthetic rubber and plastic materials	103,919	102,988	54,216	56,308	14,755	17,053
Plastics basic shapes and forms	44,859	39,049	19,423	18,243	4,492	3,594
Other chemical products	58,119	69,008	32,474	43,883	3,507	3,242
Petroleum and coal products	611,274	638,454	492,459	499,392	16,753	11,617
Ferro-alloys	15,868	9,643	9,184	6,046	4,478	2,620
Primary iron and steel	118,012	99,469	77,687	51,560	2,984	7,628
Castings and forgings, steel	112,666	117,104	109,374	113,811	1,502	720
Bars and rods, steel	65,939	52,145	47,551	32,396	3,555	4,189
Plate, sheet and strip, steel	197,168	165,501	125,100	104,588	5,812	3,483
Railway track material	24,295	30,014	11,651	10,042	2	—
Other iron and steel and alloys	221,894	273,878	187,122	201,958	2,381	906
Aluminum, including alloys	512,830	437,985	272,576	266,059	56,281	11,965
Copper and alloys	653,843	474,956	250,346	128,360	173,010	118,899
Lead, including alloys	41,128	49,515	17,144	14,742	16,109	17,871
Nickel and alloys	440,286	413,648	279,824	310,401	54,001	69,446
Precious metals, including alloys	102,573	108,962	99,392	102,649	1,082	4,833
Zinc, including alloys	227,263	204,745	183,079	137,427	22,182	43,601
Other non-ferrous metals and alloys	26,929	25,431	18,160	15,124	5,251	5,929
Metal fabricated basic products	218,638	228,845	174,912	160,862	6,266	5,956
Abrasive basic products	65,872	59,074	55,687	49,663	3,233	3,348
Other non-metallic mineral basic products	112,010	105,509	80,948	79,013	5,243	4,041
Electricity	174,596	104,285	174,596	104,285	—	—
Other fabricated materials, inedible	36,405	33,881	17,606	16,900	5,592	2,034
END PRODUCTS, INEDIBLE	9,235,521	10,358,703	7,735,743	8,286,689	162,739	195,425
Machinery	*1,161,409*	*1,459,942*	*870,481*	*1,006,733*	*26,606*	*23,876*
Engines and turbines, general purpose	47,144	66,383	24,203	25,950	3,137	2,325
Electric generator and motors	28,460	32,398	15,803	16,710	1,281	795
Other general purpose industrial machinery	124,786	164,563	79,468	96,782	5,570	4,354
Materials handling machinery and equipment	131,558	123,514	92,840	31,018	2,740	1,177
Drilling, excavating, mining machinery	85,362	132,586	41,973	66,341	1,601	3,334
Metalworking machinery	71,367	76,124	56,661	55,501	3,117	1,905
Woodworking machinery and equipment	59,201	70,854	34,981	34,920	1,600	1,336
Construction machinery and equipment	47,752	75,551	24,973	38,192	584	687
Plastics industry machinery and equipment	57,930	52,554	52,032	47,032	1,280	636
Pulp and paper industries machinery	33,802	32,532	25,252	20,208	366	334
Other special industry machinery	75,581	91,406	47,683	50,073	2,748	3,378
Soil preparation, seeding, fertilizing machinery	66,279	91,755	64,038	84,352	276	248
Combine reaper-threshers and parts	132,786	180,098	127,873	163,453	638	1,640
Other haying and harvesting machinery	56,398	75,919	51,367	67,295	762	899
Other agricultural machinery and equipment	65,798	70,040	60,374	63,721	557	609
Tractors	77,205	123,665	70,960	95,185	349	220
Transportation and Communication Equipment	*6,759,521*	*7,526,553*	*6,072,310*	*6,502,493*	*49,894*	*86,043*
Railway and street railway rolling stock	40,188	70,452	11,026	8,225	3	46
Passenger automobiles and chassis	2,731,366	3,014,289	2,629,620	2,859,682	39	175
Trucks, truck tractors and chassis	895,541	1,056,139	811,823	865,490	6	137
Other motor vehicles	114,942	144,253	90,727	91,501	3,306	392
Motor vehicle engines and parts	460,835	518,334	456,444	508,256	241	643
Motor vehicle parts and accessories	1,513,968	1,616,368	1,386,400	1,455,967	3,637	2,873
Ships, boats and parts	142,709	241,860	82,799	125,295	4,874	48,717
Aircraft, complete with engines	55,222	29,987	8,313	5,338	2,679	635
Aircraft, engines and parts	124,772	210,217	93,624	156,814	9,056	11,745
Aircraft parts, except engines	253,443	181,401	218,830	144,287	6,639	8,077
Other transportation equipment	72,868	91,726	66,953	83,979	106	361
Television and radio sets and phonographs	34,587	28,421	32,523	26,799	427	178
Other telecommunication and related equipment	319,080	323,106	183,228	170,860	18,881	12,064
Other Equipment and Tools	*662,425*	*742,192*	*380,347*	*407,472*	*44,562*	*49,341*
Heating and refrigeration equipment	45,462	31,604	27,355	19,659	5,224	3,143
Cooking equipment for food	9,102	8,873	2,394	1,846	3,276	4,458
Electric lighting and distribution equipment	108,765	110,020	49,033	46,549	6,148	4,404
Navigation equipment and parts	57,326	68,112	35,521	41,498	956	2,376
Other measuring, controlling, laboratory, medical and optical equipment	77,944	101,601	43,640	54,528	3,950	6,906
Hand tools and miscellaneous cutlery	27,663	34,861	11,793	12,885	1,618	1,919
Office machines and equipment	217,346	271,785	117,643	146,282	19,203	21,004
Other equipment and tools	118,817	115,337	92,968	84,226	4,187	5,131
Personal and Household Goods	*261,560*	*229,716*	*162,645*	*138,214*	*19,953*	*18,415*
Apparel and apparel accessories	127,725	107,979	82,173	63,645	7,073	7,193
Footwear	17,560	19,730	15,052	17,740	1,389	716
Toys, games, sporting, recreation equipment	52,668	43,092	36,596	27,575	4,223	3,610
Other personal and household goods	63,607	58,915	28,824	29,254	7,277	6,896

18.33   Domestic exports from Canada to all countries, to the United States and to the United Kingdom, by section and commodity, 1974 and 1975 (thousand dollars) (concluded)

Section and commodity	All countries		United States		United Kingdom	
	1974	1975	1974	1975	1974	1975
END PRODUCTS, INEDIBLE (concluded)						
Miscellaneous End Products	*390,604*	*400,313*	*249,959*	*231,776*	*21,717*	*17,746*
Medicinal and pharmaceutical products	40,824	44,328	11,120	10,154	1,682	1,757
Medical, ophthalmic, orthopaedic supplies	12,807	16,731	5,315	7,584	942	596
Printed matter	64,751	66,793	56,523	57,151	1,709	2,050
Photographic goods	42,169	45,550	31,024	36,410	5,635	4,364
Firearms, ammunition and ordnance	27,009	22,786	22,117	18,002	929	362
Containers and closures	39,528	31,202	29,704	19,867	1,894	2,144
Prefabricated buildings and structures	61,729	72,224	48,636	39,206	713	201
Other end products	101,787	100,699	45,520	43,402	8,213	6,276
SPECIAL TRANSACTIONS — TRADE	79,585	78,745	66,139	60,061	176	1,064
Total, domestic exports	31,674,495	32,325,043	20,762,490	21,029,639	1,911,943	1,766,455

In this table a dash indicates that either there was no trade or the amount was less than $500.

18.34   Trade of Canada with principal trading areas, 1965-75

Item	United States		United Kingdom		Other EEC		Japan		Other countries	
	Value $'000,000	% of total	Value $'000,000	% of total	Value $'000,000	% of total	Value $'000,000	% of total	Value $'000,000	% of total
Imports										
1965	6,045	70.0	619	7.2	535	6.2	230	2.7	1,204	13.9
1966	7,204	71.5	673	6.7	613	6.1	270	2.7	1,312	13.0
1967	7,952	73.1	649	6.0	635	5.8	294	2.7	1,344	12.4
1968	9,051	73.2	696	5.6	698	5.6	360	2.9	1,556	12.6
1969	10,243	72.5	791	5.6	831	5.9	496	3.5	1,770	12.5
1970	9,917	71.1	738	5.3	849	6.1	582	4.2	1,866	13.4
1971	10,951	70.1	837	5.4	984	6.3	803	5.1	2,043	13.1
1972	12,878	69.0	950	5.1	1,214	6.5	1,071	5.7	2,556	13.7
1973	16,502	70.7	1,005	4.3	1,477	6.3	1,011	4.3	3,331	14.3
1974	21,357	67.4	1,126	3.6	1,920	6.1	1,430	4.5	5,859	18.5
1975	23,559	68.0	1,222	3.5	2,074	6.0	1,205	3.5	6,575	19.0
Exports										
1965	5,033	57.4	1,185	13.5	656	7.5	317	3.6	1,576	18.0
1966	6,253	60.5	1,132	10.9	671	6.5	395	3.8	1,893	18.3
1967	7,332	64.2	1,178	10.3	721	6.3	574	5.0	1,615	14.1
1968	9,285	67.9	1,226	9.0	789	5.8	608	4.4	1,771	12.9
1969	10,551	70.9	1,113	7.5	887	6.0	626	4.2	1,693	11.4
1970	10,900	64.8	1,501	8.9	1,242	7.4	813	4.8	2,366	14.1
1971	12,025	67.5	1,395	7.8	1,145	6.4	831	4.7	2,424	13.6
1972	13,974	69.3	1,385	6.9	1,178	5.8	965	4.8	2,648	13.1
1973	17,129	67.4	1,604	6.3	1,581	6.2	1,814	7.1	3,293	13.0
1974	21,400	66.0	1,929	5.9	2,175	6.7	2,231	6.9	4,707	14.5
1975	21,652	65.4	1,789	5.4	2,347	7.1	2,122	6.4	5,193	15.7

18.35   Measures of bilateral trade between Canada and the United States, 1970-75 (billions of US dollars)

Year	Published by Canada			Published by United States			Reconciled figures		
	Imports from US	Exports to US	Canadian surplus	Exports to Canada	Imports from Canada	Canadian surplus	From US to Canada	From Canada to US	Canadian surplus
1970	9.5	10.5	1.0	9.1	11.1	2.0	9.1	10.6	1.4
1971	10.8	11.9	1.1	10.4	12.7	2.3	10.6	12.0	1.4
1972	13.0	14.1	1.1	12.4	14.9	2.5	12.6	14.2	1.5
1973	16.5	17.1	0.6	15.1	17.7	2.6	16.1	17.3	1.2
1974	21.7	21.7	—	19.9	22.3	2.3	21.1	22.1	0.9
1975	23.1	21.1	-1.9	21.9	22.2	0.4	22.7	21.4	1.3

18.36 Price and volume indexes of trade in Canada by section, 1972-75 (1971=100)

Item and year	Food, feed, beverages and tobacco		Crude materials, inedible		Fabricated materials, inedible		End products, inedible		All sections	
	Index	Percentage change from previous year	Index	Percentage change from previous year	Index	Percentage change from previous year	Index	Percentage change from previous year	Index	Percentage change from previous year
Current weighted price indexes										
Imports										
1972	107.7	7.7	106.4	6.4	99.4	-0.6	102.1	2.1	102.3	2.3
1973	129.9	20.6	129.0	21.2	110.7	11.4	105.4	3.2	110.1	7.6
1974	162.8	25.3	285.5	121.3	148.0	33.7	115.8	9.9	135.9	23.4
1975	172.0	5.7	350.1	22.6	162.6	9.9	135.2	16.8	157.1	15.6
Domestic exports										
1972	105.7	5.7	101.9	1.9	104.6	4.6	102.1	2.1	103.4	3.4
1973	147.1	39.2	121.6	19.3	122.0	16.6	104.5	2.4	117.9	14.0
1974	221.7	50.7	209.9	72.6	160.0	31.1	114.7	9.8	156.3	32.6
1975	223.9	1.0	244.6	16.5	183.1	14.4	127.6	11.2	173.4	10.9
Fixed weighted volume indexes										
Imports										
1972	112.6	12.6	109.5	9.5	114.7	14.7	119.0	19.0	116.8	16.8
1973	127.0	12.8	118.4	8.1	123.2	7.4	142.8	20.0	135.7	16.2
1974	132.2	4.1	107.9	-8.9	139.5	13.2	161.1	12.8	149.3	10.0
1975	135.6	2.6	109.9	1.9	116.4	-16.6	155.0	-3.8	141.2	-5.4
Domestic exports										
1972	105.0	5.0	107.1	7.1	108.5	8.5	112.8	12.8	109.4	9.4
1973	100.1	-4.7	126.6	18.2	116.3	7.2	129.6	14.9	121.1	10.7
1974	83.4	-16.7	113.8	-10.1	115.3	-0.9	130.0	0.3	116.5	-3.8
1975	87.7	5.2	99.6	-12.5	92.7	-19.6	131.1	0.8	107.2	-8.0

18.37 Values of total exports and imports by geographic region and country, 1973-75 (thousand dollars)

Region and country[1]	Exports[2] 1973r	1974r	1975	Imports[2] 1973r	1974r	1975
WESTERN EUROPE						
United Kingdom	1,604,436 (3)	1,928,544 (3)	1,789,261 (3)	1,005,397 (3)	1,126,338 (4)	1,221,969 (2)
Gibraltar	12	118	12,121	6	—	1
Ireland	16,605	33,980	18,369	26,558	24,345	31,588
Malta	329	5,477	2,479	460	941	660
Austria	12,586	20,764	20,133	59,261	54,429	56,643
Belgium and Luxembourg	286,286 (9)	370,779 (9)	381,146 (8)	103,819	173,445	143,304
Denmark	24,667	25,539	27,645	57,042	80,746	78,258
Finland	17,085	18,647	20,457	21,164	31,298	28,904
France	218,863	323,944	350,116 (10)	326,827 (6)	394,625 (7)	487,414 (8)
Germany, Federal Republic of	447,612 (4)	556,558 (4)	609,132 (4)	607,214 (4)	767,468 (5)	795,154 (5)
Greece	60,907	45,647	36,413	23,387	18,895	16,976
Iceland	783	1,479	1,074	226	355	437
Italy	298,815 (5)	468,133 (5)	479,292 (6)	237,289 (8)	316,438 (10)	379,557 (9)
Netherlands	288,107 (7)	395,650 (8)	481,289 (5)	118,052	163,133	158,589
Norway	181,551	233,945	171,425	77,652	106,317	120,095
Portugal	19,718	28,965	18,131	25,802	32,332	28,570
Spain	68,273	119,527	116,357	61,591	85,172	101,921
Sweden	61,172	113,227	98,010	166,301 (9)	233,357	264,851
Switzerland	69,158	101,145	81,280	117,797	136,776	179,255
Total, Western Europe	3,676,966	4,792,069	4,714,130	3,035,844	3,746,411	4,094,146
EASTERN EUROPE						
Albania	12,330	6,305	10,487	—	15	22
Bulgaria	486	5,288	2,537	1,709	4,143	3,754
Czechoslovakia	9,979	22,972	10,072	42,793	61,823	46,445
German Democratic Republic	3,035	3,276	4,271	5,747	7,013	5,387
Hungary	7,674	7,218	6,889	13,275	15,714	15,036
Poland	45,195	85,695	117,088	29,626	43,893	40,811
Romania	13,021	5,357	62,149	14,993	25,785	19,238
Union of Soviet Socialist Republics	292,276 (6)	31,548	418,830 (7)	22,984	23,085	28,489
Yugoslavia	37,251	30,724	36,788	12,292	15,830	18,901
Total, Eastern Europe	421,247	198,383	669,112	143,419	197,301	178,084
MIDDLE EAST						
Bahrain	788	1,138	1,382	749	264	8
Cyprus	2,277	1,735	2,135	568	3,027	737
Qatar	435	3,522	1,542	—	—	6,411
United Arab Emirates	1,920	4,894	4,894	50,255	86,387	140,589
Egypt, Arab Republic of	3,069	14,029	6,672	492	689	335
Ethiopia	520	2,982	3,388	228	368	911
Iran	55,430	62,571	150,439	133,479	618,002 (6)	758,077 (6)
Iraq	1,054	119,354	67,679	20,550	36,671	133,956
Israel	37,217	52,508	65,275	22,492	24,778	28,213
Jordan	580	5,416	2,442	—	—	7
Kuwait	1,849	4,943	16,091	3,694	64,728	110,522
Lebanon	21,386	45,149	41,109	1,943	22,502	1,320
Libya	12,899	5,871	23,032	41,637	30,556	36,150
Saudi Arabia	13,349	17,972	35,254	60,380	318,907 (9)	745,961 (7)
Somalia	833	732	1,427	1	2	56
Sudan	3,235	2,809	4,407	161	533	180

18.37 Values of total exports and imports by geographic region and country, 1973-75 (thousand dollars) (continued)

Region and country[1]	Exports[2]			Imports[2]		
	1973r	1974r	1975	1973r	1974r	1975
MIDDLE EAST (concluded)						
Syria	2,055	13,838	5,083	21	91	1,208
Turkey	26,052	57,814	44,313	3,899	2,948	3,382
Yemen	851	8,078	7,008	23,865	104,262	196,655
Total, Middle East	185,798	325,355	483,572	364,416	1,314,715	2,164,676
OTHER AFRICA						
Gambia	99	161	167	—	—	5
Ghana	8,621	20,989	19,181	6,559	7,426	5,776
Kenya	6,233	5,987	9,091	10,012	11,745	12,362
Malawi	1,084	609	1,385	421	514	248
Mauritius and Dependencies	423	1,567	1,389	29,387	76,704	63,057
Nigeria	22,961	25,523	41,564	82,158	53,754	78,371
Rhodesia	3	2	3	3	7	3
Sierra Leone	178	636	419	3,804	3,255	3,769
South Africa, Republic of	67,109	96,884	134,710	81,071	117,163	193,822
Tanzania	4,839	13,297	20,689	4,615	9,112	6,904
Uganda	416	708	234	2,202	3,549	2,647
Zambia	6,933	24,465	21,229	359	18	7
Commonwealth Africa, n.e.s.	1,433	790	149	7,354	15,330	9,366
Algeria	27,607	157,678	101,173	1,428	6,767	1,704
Angola	950	2,083	1,007	53,585	94,483	479
Benin	210	1,379	2,055	2	10	52
Cameroon	979	1,582	5,864	3,496	3,338	3,861
French Africa, n.e.s.	5,281	5,379	10,485	201	85	40
Gabon	744	1,854	551	2,418	4,821	25,828
Guinea	147	242	139	2,331	10,389	15,100
Ivory Coast	2,576	2,510	2,840	820	4,064	2,556
Liberia	2,386	3,817	2,600	905	814	589
Madagascar	247	603	731	586	823	1,520
Mauritania	98	144	2,715	4,780	7,206	14
Morocco	3,291	2,597	19,075	1,801	1,058	2,113
Mozambique	1,197	2,808	2,245	4,343	4,404	4,402
Portuguese Africa, n.e.s.	430	876	1,345	18	95	10
Senegal	3,534	3,267	5,752	13	53	359
Spanish Africa	327	459	556	1	25	11
Togo	451	996	414	3	5	18
Tunisia	13,539	12,797	10,000	50	128	111
Zaire, Republic of	3,444	9,814	12,217	6,529	8,561	8,267
Total, other Africa	187,770	402,502	431,973	311,256	445,707	443,372
OTHER ASIA						
Bangladesh	54,326	60,817	85,730	4,880	6,120	5,030
Hong Kong	29,333	41,670	43,867	109,939	134,816	170,930
India	157,328	127,711	202,046	38,466	59,272	46,650
Malaysia	29,986	30,414	24,906	53,996	62,217	56,745
Pakistan	43,423	71,968	95,527	6,707	15,666	7,864
Singapore	17,434	31,327	36,739	41,114	51,970	46,624
Sri Lanka, Republic of	4,519	3,589	14,556	7,581	18,622	12,846

18.37   Values of total exports and imports by geographic region and country, 1973-75 (thousand dollars) (continued)

Region and country[1]	Exports[2] 1973ʳ	1974ʳ	1975	Imports[2] 1973ʳ	1974ʳ	1975
OTHER ASIA (concluded)						
Afghanistan	336	1,791	774	26	68	117
Burma	1,900 (8)	1,139	354	13	17	18
China, People's Republic of	287,986	438,967 (6)	377,260 (9)	52,904	61,349	56,328
Indonesia	17,766	53,993	66,776	3,128	4,610	14,266
Japan	1,813,768 (2)	2,231,264 (2)	2,122,016 (2)	1,010,852 (2)	1,429,773 (2)	1,205,316 (3)
Khmer Republic – Laos	136	278	9	8	3	10
Korea, North	11,348	42,602	4,924	114	90	108
Korea, South	65,913	71,799	82,125	90,564	135,044	166,385
Philippines	31,953	57,693	58,922	18,219	15,691	22,430
Portuguese Asia	3	10	1	331	1,012	330
Taiwan	34,423	42,694	38,554	163,763 (10)	193,758	181,904
Thailand	15,059	25,565	22,556	4,130	6,591	6,065
Viet-Nam	1,758	7,556	4,241	16	232	228
Total, other Asia	2,618,698	3,342,845	3,281,882	1,606,752	2,196,920	2,000,193
OCEANIA						
Australia	219,813 (10)	325,334 (10)	252,001	242,574 (7)	335,026 (8)	344,756 (10)
Fiji	1,002	1,067	1,237	7,764	4,507	225
New Zealand	51,047	66,064	51,970	73,119	76,384	48,591
British Oceania, n.e.s.	258	135	148	43	21	3
French Oceania	946	1,697	1,300	–	–	5
United States Oceania	977	1,420	2,080	5,414	3,214	–
Total, Oceania	274,043	395,716	308,736	328,914	419,153	393,581
SOUTH AMERICA						
Falkland Islands	3	16	7	–	–	–
Guyana	8,180	11,595	14,760	14,390	14,191	11,682
Argentina	42,744	73,500	57,517	14,459	18,091	13,160
Bolivia	5,341	6,453	5,513	1,156	4,816	5,336
Brazil	116,680	405,121 (7)	200,651	87,074	112,223	170,217
Chile	26,927	33,688	30,744	35,674	54,589	19,091
Colombia	34,422	42,809	38,863	32,639	39,078	32,239
Ecuador	6,748	13,134	22,761	15,498	39,079	21,148
French Guiana	189	128	23	43	27	–
Paraguay	401	523	405	997	1,473	1,232
Peru	52,222	67,465	81,127	18,893	13,408	11,412
Surinam	1,852	2,334	3,026	7,881	8,700	6,421
Uruguay	4,038	4,597	6,469	354	808	1,465
Venezuela	154,116	249,523	322,708	522,488 (5)	1,291,054 (3)	1,106,751 (4)
Total, South America	453,864	910,886	784,574	751,545	1,597,537	1,400,154

18.37   Values of total exports and imports by geographic region and country, 1973-75 (thousand dollars) (concluded)

Region and country[1]	Exports[2] 1973r	1974r	1975	Imports[2] 1973r	1974r	1975
CENTRAL AMERICA AND ANTILLES						
Bahamas	14,697	16,919	14,417	10,903	20,906	23,880
Barbados	16,303	15,002	14,159	3,158	4,670	7,957
Belize	1,621	2,130	2,668	4,215	1,800	1,439
Bermuda	12,145	14,528	22,349	601	561	492
Jamaica	43,480	49,718	51,392	22,040	24,559	18,078
Leeward and Windward Islands	11,065	13,533	15,584	2,334	551	862
Trinidad and Tobago	28,426	29,656	31,647	13,720	22,323	25,083
Costa Rica	7,049	14,925	11,815	12,779	9,663	18,538
Cuba	82,111	150,868	226,172	16,611	76,315	81,456
Dominican Republic	15,726	32,933	28,125	8,056	8,088	24,305
El Salvador	5,618	9,085	8,185	4,931	7,242	8,069
French West Indies	1,853	853	1,611	536	66	17
Guatemala	7,001	9,672	11,189	6,908	10,286	19,475
Haiti	10,149	11,380	12,479	2,743	4,281	3,582
Honduras	4,746	8,594	8,138	16,520	15,328	11,755
Mexico	120,504	193,091	222,364	83,282	114,265	95,362
Netherlands Antilles	3,167	5,280	3,678	47,176	67,414	24,458
Nicaragua	3,943	5,507	4,045	3,413	6,612	6,061
Panama	12,701	18,221	17,721	4,243	3,492	5,880
Puerto Rico	53,694	53,709	52,635	14,530	18,623	24,730
Virgin Islands of the United States	2,766	3,742	1,776	1,278	386	24
Total, Central America and Antilles	458,764	659,344	762,151	279,978	417,432	401,503
NORTH AMERICA						
Greenland	6,169	3,366	2,535	940	36	284
St. Pierre and Miquelon	8,360	11,311	12,359	241	199	240
United States	17,129,027 (1)	21,399,469 (1)	21,652,421 (1)	16,502,015 (1)	21,356,710 (1)	23,559,280 (1)
Total, North America	17,143,556	21,414,146	21,667,315	16,503,197	21,356,945	23,559,804
Total, all countries	25,420,706	32,441,245	33,103,445	23,325,320	31,692,121	34,635,513

In this table a dash indicates that either there was no trade or the amount was less than $500.
[1]The country classification was designed for purposes of economic geography and does not reflect the views of the Government of Canada on international issues of recognition, sovereignty or jurisdiction.
[2]Figures in parentheses indicate rank of 10 leading countries, 1973-75.

Sources

18.1 - 18.24 Merchandising and Services Division, Industry Statistics Branch, Statistics Canada.
18.25 - 18.26 Marketing and Trade Division, Economics Branch, Canada Department of Agriculture.
18.27 - 18.28 Public Finance Division, Institutional and Public Finance Statistics Branch, Statistics Canada.
18.29 - 18.37 External Trade Division, General Statistics Branch, Statistics Canada.

Banking, finance and insurance

Chapter 19

Tables

Banking, finance and insurance

Chapter 19

Banking

19.1

The Bank of Canada

19.1.1

Canada's central bank, the Bank of Canada, began operations on March 11, 1935, under the terms of the Bank of Canada Act, 1934, which charged it with the responsibility for regulating "credit and currency in the best interests of the economic life of the nation", and conferred on it specific powers for discharging this responsibility. Through the exercise of these powers, the Bank of Canada broadly determines the combined total of the most common forms of Canadian money held by the community — chartered bank deposits and currency. Revisions to the Bank of Canada Act, 1934, were made in 1936, 1938, 1954 and 1967, and are included in RSC 1970, c.B-2.

The provisions of the Bank of Canada Act enable the central bank to determine the total amount of cash reserves available to the chartered banks as a group and in that way to control the rate of expansion of the total assets and deposit liabilities of the banking system as a whole. The Bank Act, which regulates the operation of the chartered banks, requires that each chartered bank maintain a stipulated minimum average amount of cash reserves, calculated as a percentage of its Canadian dollar deposit liabilities, in the form of deposits at the Bank of Canada and holdings of Bank of Canada notes. The minimum cash reserve requirement, which came into effect under the legislation beginning February 1, 1968, is 12% of demand deposits and 4% of other deposits. The ability of the chartered banks as a group to expand their total assets and deposit liabilities is therefore limited by the total amount of cash reserves available. An increase in cash reserves will encourage the banks as a group to expand their total assets (which consist chiefly of loans and marketable securities) with a concomitant increase in their deposit liabilities; a decrease in cash reserves will bring about a decline in their total assets and deposit liabilities as they seek to restore their cash reserve ratios.

The chief method by which the Bank of Canada alters the level of cash reserves of the chartered banks over time, and through them the total of chartered bank deposits, is by purchases and sales of government securities. Payment by the central bank for the securities it purchases in the market adds to the cash reserves of the chartered banks as a group and puts them in a position to expand their assets and deposit liabilities. Conversely, payment to the central bank for securities it sells causes a reduction in the cash reserves of the chartered banks and requires them to reduce their holdings of assets and deposit liabilities.

The influence the Bank of Canada exerts on credit conditions (i.e. on interest cost and other terms of borrowing in financial markets) stems from its ability to limit the growth of bank credit and of the community's holdings of bank deposits and currency. The growth rate of the banking system is one of the factors exerting an important influence on the level of interest rates and other terms of access to credit prevailing in financial markets generally. Current credit conditions (and expectations about future trends in such conditions) in turn have an influence on business and household decisions to spend or to save. Many other factors have an important effect on spending decisions and the behaviour of the economy is subject to such influences as economic and financial developments abroad; the investment, price and wage policies of business firms in Canada; and the character of public policies at all levels of government with regard to expenditure and taxation. In using the powers at its disposal, the Bank of Canada attempts to bring about credit conditions appropriate to both domestic and external conditions. Its operations must be based, not on any simple mechanical formula, but rather on continuous observation and appraisal of the constantly changing prospects for the economy as reflected in the complex pattern of economic and financial developments.

In a technical sense, the powers that the central bank possesses allow it to exert a strong influence over economic activity but, in practice, the range through which credit conditions can be permitted to vary is necessarily limited. Changes in credit conditions in Canada affect the position of some groups in the economy much more than others, and this uneven impact is bound to inhibit the central bank's operations. Furthermore, interest rates in Canada cannot change greatly in relation to those abroad without producing large capital movements which might complicate Canada's international payments position. These considerations suggest that monetary policy must be used in appropriate combination with other public economic policies in order to help achieve national economic goals.

Although the Bank of Canada has the power to determine the rate of growth of the combined total of currency and chartered bank deposits, it has no means of determining how much of this total is held in the form of currency and how much in the form of chartered bank deposits. This depends entirely on the preferences of the public, since bank deposits can be converted freely into notes and coin and back again.

Although the cash reserve system in Canada — which is similar to that in a number of other countries — enables the central bank to determine within broad limits the total amount of chartered bank assets and deposit liabilities, the Bank of Canada leaves the allocation of bank and other forms of credit to the private sector of the economy. Each chartered bank is free to attempt to gain as large a share as possible of the total cash reserves available by competing for deposits and to decide what proportion of its funds to invest in particular kinds of securities and in loans to particular types of borrowers. The influence of the central bank — based in essence on its power to expand or contract chartered bank cash reserves through its market purchases or sales of securities — is both indirect and impersonal and is brought to bear on financial conditions generally through the chartered banks and the numerous interconnected channels of the capital market.

The Bank of Canada may buy or sell securities issued or guaranteed by Canada or any province, short-term securities issued by Britain, treasury bills or other obligations of the United States and certain types of short-term commercial paper. It may buy or sell gold, silver, nickel and bronze coin, or any other coin, and gold and silver bullion as well as foreign exchange and may accept non-interest-bearing deposits from the Government of Canada, the government of any province, any chartered bank and any bank regulated by the Quebec Savings Bank Act. The Bank of Canada may open accounts in other central banks; accept deposits from other central banks, the International Monetary Fund, the International Bank for Reconstruction and Development, and any other official international financial organization; and pay interest on such deposits. The Bank of Canada does not accept deposits from individuals nor does it compete with the chartered banks in the commercial banking field. It acts as the fiscal agent for the Government of Canada in the payment of interest and principal and generally in respect of the management of the public debt of Canada. The sole right to issue paper money for circulation in Canada is vested in the Bank of Canada.

The central bank also may require the chartered banks to maintain, in addition to the legal minimum cash reserve requirement mentioned above, a secondary reserve which the Bank of Canada may vary within certain limits. The secondary reserve, which consists of cash reserves in excess of the minimum requirement, treasury bills and day-to-day loans to investment dealers, cannot be more than 6% of total deposits when first introduced nor can it exceed 12%; effective March 1975, the required level was 5.5%. In the event the Bank of

Canada wishes to introduce or increase the secondary reserve requirement, one month's notice to the chartered banks is required; the amount of any increase in the requirement cannot exceed 1% a month. In the case of a lowering of the secondary reserve requirement, however, the percentage change in any one month is not restricted.

The Bank of Canada may make loans or advances for periods not exceeding six months to chartered banks, or to banks to which the Quebec Savings Bank Act applies, on the pledge of certain classes of securities. Loans or advances may be made under certain conditions and for limited periods to the Government of Canada or of any province. The Bank of Canada is required to make public at all times the minimum rate at which it is prepared to make loans or advances; this rate is known as the bank rate. From November 1, 1956 until June 24, 1962, the bank rate was established weekly at a fixed margin of one quarter of 1% above the latest weekly average tender rate for 91-day treasury bills. Bank rates since October 12, 1962 have been fixed from time to time and are given in Table 19.1. The rate as at March 8, 1976 was 9.50% per annum.

On May 12, 1974 the Bank of Canada announced a change in its practice with respect to the maximum rate at which it is prepared to enter into purchase and sale agreements with money market dealers. The practice had been to set the Purchase and Resale Agreement (PRA) rate at ¼ of 1% above the average 91-day treasury bill rate at the latest weekly tender, subject to a minimum of bank rate minus ¾ of 1% and a maximum at the level of bank rate. Under the new practice the maximum PRA rate is bank rate plus ½ of 1%.

Assets and liabilities of the Bank of Canada at December 31, 1973-75 are shown in Table 19.2. The bank is not required to maintain gold or foreign exchange reserves against its liabilities.

Prior to the 1967 amendment to the Bank of Canada Act, there existed some uncertainty about the exact relationship between the central bank and the government. The changes in the Bank of Canada Act in 1967 were designed to clarify this matter. They provide for regular consultation between the Governor of the Bank of Canada and the Minister of Finance as well as for a formal procedure whereby, in the event of a disagreement between the government and the central bank which cannot be resolved, the government may, after further consultation has taken place, issue a directive to the Bank of Canada as to the monetary policy that it is to follow. Any such directive must be in writing, it must be in specific terms, and it must be applicable for a specified period. It must be published immediately in the *Canada Gazette* and tabled in Parliament. The amendment makes it clear that the government must take the ultimate responsibility for monetary policy and it provides a mechanism for that purpose but the central bank is in no way relieved of its responsibility for monetary policy and its execution.

The Bank of Canada is under the management of a board of directors composed of the Governor, the Deputy Governor and twelve directors. The Governor and Deputy Governor are appointed for terms of seven years each by the directors, with the approval of the Governor in Council. The directors are appointed by the Minister of Finance, with the approval of the Governor in Council, for terms of three years each. The Deputy Minister of Finance is a member of the board but does not have the right to vote. There is an executive committee of the board composed of the Governor, the Deputy Governor, two directors and the Deputy Minister of Finance (who is without a vote); this committee has the same powers as the board except that its decisions must be submitted to the board at its next meeting. In addition to the Deputy Governor who is a member of the board, there may be one or more deputy governors appointed by the Board of Directors to perform such duties as are assigned by the board.

The head office of the Bank of Canada is in Ottawa. It has agencies in Halifax, Saint John, Montreal, Ottawa, Toronto, Winnipeg, Regina, Calgary and Vancouver and is represented in St. John's and Charlottetown.

The Federal Business Development Bank was established by an Act of Parliament in 1974 as a federal Crown corporation to succeed the Industrial Development Bank. Under the act, which came into force in October 1975, FBDB assists in the establishment and development of business enterprises in Canada by providing them with financial and management services. It supplements such services available from other sources and it gives particular attention to the needs of smaller businesses.

The Board of Directors of the bank consists of the President, four persons from the public service of Canada, and 10 persons from outside the public service of Canada. The authorized capital is $200 million and the bank may also raise funds by the issue and sale of debt obligations provided that its total direct and contingent liabilities shall not exceed 10 times its capital. Assets and liabilities of FBDB are given in Table 19.3.

FBDB extends financial assistance in various forms to new or existing businesses of almost every type in Canada which are unable to obtain required financing from other sources on reasonable terms and conditions. To qualify for FBDB financing, a business should have investment in it by other lenders which should reasonably ensure their continuing commitment to the business and the business should reasonably be expected to prove successful.

The bank's management counselling service known as Counselling Assistance to Small Enterprises (CASE) assists small businesses to improve their methods of doing business. This service, which supplements counselling services available from the private sector, makes available the experience of retired business persons.

To help improve management skills in small businesses, FBDB conducts management training seminars in smaller cities and towns across Canada. The bank also publishes booklets on a wide range of topics pertaining to the management of small business in Canada and provides information about assistance programs for small business.

The FBDB has 88 branches across Canada located in the following centres: St. John's, Grand Falls, Corner Brook, Sydney, Truro, Halifax, Bridgewater, Charlottetown, Moncton, Fredericton, Saint John, Bathurst, Sept-Îles, Rimouski, Chicoutimi, Quebec, Lévis, Sherbrooke, Granby, Trois-Rivières, Drummondville, Longueuil, St-Léonard, Montreal (2), St-Laurent, Valleyfield, St-Jérôme, Ottawa, Hull, Rouyn–Noranda, Kingston, Oshawa, Scarborough, Toronto (2), Etobicoke, Oakville, Barrie, St. Catharines, Hamilton, Kitchener–Waterloo, Owen Sound, Stratford, London, Chatham, Windsor, Woodstock, Timmins, Sudbury, Sault Ste Marie, Thunder Bay, Kenora, Winnipeg, Brandon, Regina, Saskatoon, Prince Albert, Lethbridge, Calgary (2), Red Deer, Edmonton (3), Grande Prairie, Yellowknife, Whitehorse, Cranbrook, Kelowna, Kamloops, Williams Lake, Chilliwack, Prince George, Terrace, Abbotsford, Langley, New Westminster, Burnaby, North Vancouver, Vancouver (2), Richmond, Campbell River, Nanaimo and Victoria.

19.1.2   Currency

The development by which bank notes became the chief circulating medium in Canada prior to 1935 is described in the *1938 Canada Year Book* pp 900-905. Those features of the development which then became permanent are outlined in the *1941 Canada Year Book* pp 809-810.

When the Bank of Canada commenced operations in 1935 it assumed liability for Dominion notes outstanding. These were replaced in public circulation and partly replaced in cash reserves by the central bank's legal tender notes in denominations of $1, $2, $5, $10, $20, $50 and $100. Deposits of chartered banks at the Bank of Canada completed the replacement of the old Dominion notes of $1,000 to $50,000 denomination that had previously been used as cash reserves. The chartered banks were required under the Bank Act of 1934 to reduce gradually the issue of their own bank notes during the years 1935-45 to an amount not in excess of 25% of their paid-up capital on March 11, 1935. Bank of Canada notes thus replaced chartered bank notes as the issue of the latter was reduced. Further restrictions introduced by the 1944 revision of the Bank Act cancelled the right of chartered banks to issue or reissue notes after January 1, 1945, and in January 1950 the chartered banks' liability for such of their notes issued for circulation in Canada as then remained outstanding was transferred to the Bank of Canada in return for payment of a like sum to the Bank of Canada.

Bank of Canada note liabilities for the years 1973-75 are given in Table 19.4. Note circulation in public hands as at December 31, 1975 amounted to $6,078.6 million, compared to $5,212.8 million in 1974 and $4,620.2 million in 1973. Bank of Canada statistics concerning currency and chartered bank deposits are given in Table 19.5.

Coinage   19.1.3

Under the Currency and Exchange Act (RSC 1970, c.C-39), gold coins may be issued in the denomination of $20 (nine tenths fine or millesimal fineness 900); and subsidiary coins in denominations of $1, 50 cents, 25 cents, 10 cents (five tenths fine or millesimal fineness 500, or pure nickel), 5 cents (pure nickel), and 1 cent (bronze — copper, tin and zinc). Provision is made for the temporary alteration of composition in the event of a shortage of prescribed metals. A tender of payment of money in coins is a legal tender in the case of gold coins issued under the authority of Section 4 of the Currency and Exchange Act for the payment of any amount; in the case of denomination of 10 cents or greater but not exceeding $1 for the payment of an amount up to $10; in the case of denomination of 5 cents for payment up to $5; and in the case of 1 cent for payment of up to 25 cents.

Table 19.6 gives figures for the value of Canadian coins in circulation. Receipts of gold bullion at the Royal Canadian Mint and bullion and coinage issued are given in Table 19.7.

The Ottawa Mint, established as a branch of the Royal Mint under the United Kingdom Coinage Act of 1870, was opened on January 2, 1908. On December 1, 1931, by an Act of the Canadian Parliament it became the Royal Canadian Mint and operated as a branch of the Department of Finance. The Mint was established as a Crown corporation in 1969 by the Government Organization Act of 1969 to allow for a more industrial type of organization and for flexibility in producing coins of Canada and other countries; to buy, sell, melt, assay and refine gold and precious metals; and to produce medals, plaques and other devices.

Financial and budgeting arrangements are similar to those of other Crown companies carrying on industrial or commercial operations. Loans are made from the Consolidated Revenue Fund for operating and capital expenses, with the total outstanding at any time limited to $35 million. Provision is made for loans for temporary purposes and a reserve is established against losses. Operations are conducted with the aim of making a small profit.

On December 16, 1971, a decision was made by the Cabinet to locate a new plant for the production of coin for general circulation in the Winnipeg area of Manitoba. Work on the site was begun in October 1972 and the plant was officially opened on April 30, 1976.

The Olympic (1976) Act, assented to on July 27, 1973, authorized the issue of silver coins in the denominations of $5 and $10 during the years 1973, 1974, 1975 and 1976 to commemorate the XXI Olympiad. A payment of money in Olympic coins is a legal tender for payment of an amount not exceeding $20.

Chartered banks   19.1.4

Canada's commercial banking system consists of 12 privately owned banks of which eight have been in operation for many years. Four began operation recently; one in July 1968, another in January 1973, and two more in late 1976. At the end of December 1975, these banks operated 7,035 banking offices in Canada and 267 abroad. Canadian chartered banks accept various types of deposit from the public including accounts payable on demand, both chequing and non-chequing, notice deposits and fixed-term deposits. In addition to holding a portfolio of securities, they make loans under a wide variety of conditions for commercial, industrial, agricultural and consumer purposes. They also deal in foreign exchange, receive and pay out bank notes, provide safekeeping facilities and perform various other services. For the most part, these operations are carried out in Canada by the extensive network of bank branches. The head offices of the banks confine their activities largely to general administration and policy-making functions, the management of the banks' investment portfolio and related matters. A detailed account of the branch banking system in Canada is given in the *1967 Canada Year Book,* pp 1126-1128.

All banks operating in Canada are chartered (i.e. licensed) by Parliament under the terms of the Bank Act. The act regulates certain internal aspects of bank operations such as the auditing of accounts, the issuing of stock, the setting aside of reserves and similar matters. In addition, the Bank Act regulates the banks' relationship with the public, the government and the Bank of Canada.

The Bank Act has been revised at approximately 10-year intervals; the most recent revision was enacted by Parliament early in 1967 and came into effect on May 1 of that year. Increased competition and flexibility in the Canadian banking system were reflected in various new Bank Act provisions. These imposed certain restrictions on corporate and other relationships between banks and other financial institutions, while removing certain existing restrictions on the banks' operations which had placed them at some competitive disadvantage in recent years compared with their principal financial competitors.

In the past, various forms of intercorporate financial relationships between chartered banks and other financial enterprises had developed in Canada. In some instances these involved investment by banks in the shares of these enterprises, and vice versa; in others the relationship involved interlocking directorships. These practices are severely restricted under the terms of the 1967 Bank Act, which limits bank ownership of any Canadian corporation to 10% of the voting shares and also provides that no more than one fifth of the directors of any company may become directors of a bank. In addition, after a two-year period a director of a trust or mortgage loan company which accepts deposits from the public may not be appointed or elected a director of a bank. In order to ensure that competition is not curtailed by agreements among the banks on interest rates to be paid on deposits or charged for loans, the 1967 Bank Act prohibits the making of such agreements (except with the consent of the Minister of Finance). At the same time the provision that was formerly in the Bank Act limiting to 6% the interest rate which chartered banks could charge on loans was abolished effective January 1, 1968. Under the 1967 Bank Act, the determination of interest rates on loans and deposits is left to market forces.

The 1967 Bank Act also granted the banks new mortgage-lending powers, permitting them to charge current rates of interest on mortgage loans under the National Housing Act, and also, for the first time, to make conventional residential mortgage loans. In the case of conventional residential mortgages, the amount of an individual mortgage cannot exceed 75% of the appraised value of the property. The maximum amount of a bank's assets to be held in the form of conventional residential mortgages must not be more than 10% of the bank's Canadian dollar deposit liabilities plus debentures. The banks have also been given authority to issue their own debentures with an original term to maturity of at least five years; such securities are not subject to reserve requirements and rank in priority after deposit liabilities. The amount of debentures that any bank may have outstanding is limited by restricting the increase per annum to 10% of the paid-up capital and rest fund and an upper limit of one half of the bank's paid-up capital and rest fund.

The amendments to the Bank Act in 1967 contained a number of revisions respecting the ownership of Canadian chartered banks. No individual or associated shareholders may vote more than 10% of a bank's total shares outstanding and, if more than 25% of a bank's shares are owned by non-residents, the total outstanding liabilities of the bank may not exceed 20 times its authorized capital stock.

The Bank Act also stipulates the minimum statutory cash reserve requirement that the chartered banks must observe. The minimum amount of Bank of Canada notes and deposits each bank must hold as cash reserves was changed in a series of monthly steps from 8% of all Canadian dollar deposits under the old Bank Act to 12% of demand deposits and 4% of other deposits as at February 1968. In addition, the Bank of Canada was given stand-by powers to require the banks to hold a "secondary reserve" which would consist of cash in excess of their statutory requirements, holdings of treasury bills and day-to-day loans to investment dealers. When initially introduced, this secondary reserve cannot exceed 6% of a bank's deposit liabilities. Thereafter it may be increased in monthly steps of 1% to a maximum of 12%. The Bank of Canada may reduce or remove such a secondary reserve at any time. Secondary reserve requirements since March 1968 are as follows: March 1968, 6%; April 1968, 7%; June 1969, 8%; July 1970, 9%; December 1971, 8.5%; January 1972, 8%; December 1974, 7%; January 1975, 6%; March 1975, 5.5%.

The 1967 Bank Act was due to expire in 1977. A white paper related to the government's proposals for further revision was promulgated in August 1976 to provide public discussion prior to the enactment of new legislation.

Chartered bank financial statistics for recent years are given in Tables 19.8 - 19.12; month-end data are available in the *Bank of Canada Review.*

Branches of chartered banks. Although there are fewer chartered banks now than at the beginning of the century, there has been a great increase in the number of branch banking offices. As a result of amalgamations, the number of banks declined from 34 in 1901 to 10 in 1931, and remained at that figure until the incorporation of a new bank — The Mercantile Bank of Canada — in 1953 brought the total to 11. Since then the amalgamation in 1955 of the Bank of Toronto and the Dominion Bank as the Toronto Dominion Bank, the amalgamation of Barclays Bank (Canada) with the Imperial Bank of Canada in 1956 and the amalgamation of the Canadian Bank of Commerce and the Imperial Bank of Canada as the Canadian Imperial Bank of Commerce on June 1, 1961 reduced this number to eight. The Bank of British Columbia was granted a charter by Parliament in December 1966 and commenced operations in July 1968. The Unity Bank of Canada was granted a charter in November 1972 and commenced operations in 1973. The Canadian Commercial and Industrial Bank was granted a charter in June 1976 and commenced operations in September 1976. The Northland Bank received its charter in December 1975 and began operations in November 1976. The number of branches of chartered banks in each province at various periods between 1920 and 1975 is given in Table 19.13.

Branches of individual Canadian chartered banks by province as at December 31, 1974 and 1975 and outside Canada as at December 31, 1975 are given in Tables 19.14 and 19.15.

Cheque payments. The value of cheques cashed in 50 clearing centres across Canada rose steadily during 1974 and 1975, with a smaller increase in 1976, reaching totals of $1,698,780 million, $2,138,527 million and $2,469,599 million respectively. This represented increases of 24.0%, 25.9% and 15.5% in the three years. All five geographic regions showed growth, with the largest percentage increases over the three years in the Prairie provinces, followed by Quebec, British Columbia, the Atlantic provinces and Ontario. Payments in the two leading centres also increased, with Montreal showing the greatest gain, 30.9%, in 1974 and Toronto 30.4% in 1975. In 1976 payments in these two centres reached all-time highs, Toronto advancing 10.9% and Montreal 19.8% (Table 19.33).

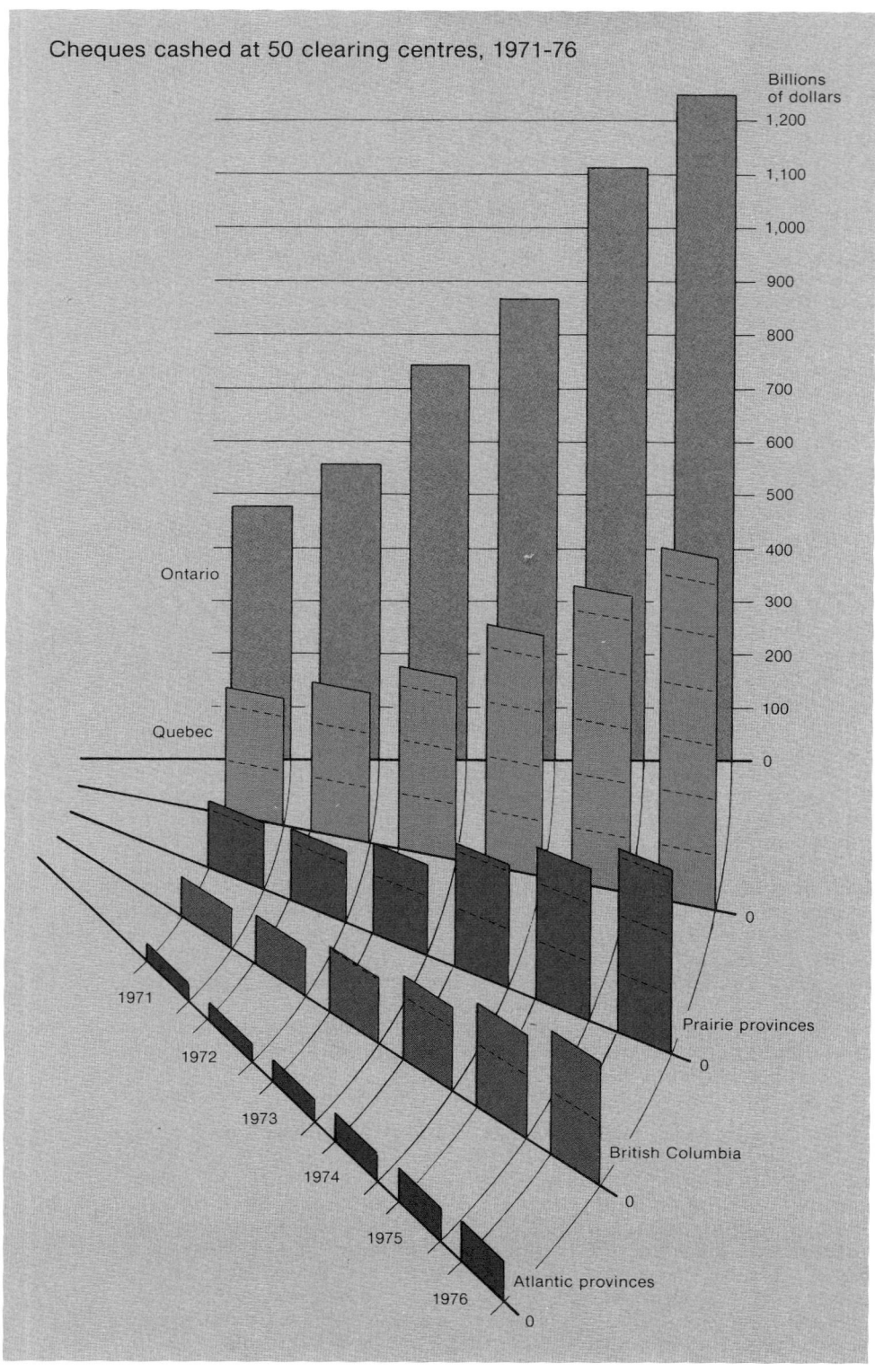

Cheques cashed at 50 clearing centres, 1971-76

Other banking institutions   19.1.5

In addition to the savings departments of the chartered banks and of trust and loan companies, there are provincial government savings banking institutions in Ontario and Alberta, and the Montreal City and District Savings Bank in Quebec, established under federal legislation and reporting monthly to the Department of Finance. Cooperative credit unions also encourage savings and extend small loans to their members.

Province of Ontario Savings Office. The establishment of the Province of Ontario Savings Office was authorized by the Ontario Legislature at the 1921 Session and the first branches were opened in March 1922. Interest at the rate of 8.5% per annum (as at September 1, 1976), compounded half-yearly, is paid on accounts; deposits are repayable on demand. Total deposits as at December 31, 1975 were $298 million and the number of depositors was approximately 76,700; 21 branches are in operation throughout the province.

Province of Alberta Treasury Branches. Established in 1938 by the Treasury Branches Act, the system operates 89 branches, two sub-branches and 82 agencies throughout the province. As at March 31, 1976, deposits from customers totalled $822.5 million while advances to individuals, merchants, corporations and municipal bodies totalled $681.5 million. Profits for the year ended March 31, 1976, before allowances for reserves, were $12.1 million. Of this amount $6 million was transferred to the general revenue of the province. Financial services include current accounts (non-interest-bearing); regular (chequing) and super (non-chequing) savings, interest-bearing accounts; term deposits for terms ranging from one day to six years bearing competitive interest rates; agricultural loans, business loans, life-insured personal loans, mobile home financing, home improvement loans, small businessmen's loans, commercial and industrial mortgage loans, and 15-year residential mortgage loans. The Treasury Branches are also authorized lending agents for Government of Canada — Farm Improvement Loans and Small Business Loans.

The Montreal City and District Savings Bank was founded in 1846 and has operated under a federal charter since 1871. At October 31, 1975, it had a paid-up capital and reserve of $27.6 million, savings deposits of $927.8 million and total liabilities of $968.6 million. Assets of a like amount included $259.9 million, consisting of federal, provincial, municipal and other securities.

Credit unions. The first credit union in Canada was founded in Lévis, Que., in 1900 to promote thrift by encouraging saving and to provide loans to members who could not get credit elsewhere or could get it only at high interest rates. For many years growth was slow; in 1911, when the first figures were available, assets amounted to $2 million and by 1940 they were only $25 million. However, since that time there has been a spectacular increase. The first credit union legislation was passed in Nova Scotia in 1932 followed by legislation in Manitoba and Saskatchewan in 1937 and in Ontario and British Columbia in 1938.

Credit unions are under provincial legislation. Almost all local offices in each province belong to central credit unions operating within the province. The number of chartered credit unions in Canada at the end of 1975 was 4,117 which reported a total membership of 7.3 million and assets of $12,331 million (Table 19.16). Quebec, with 3.9 million members and assets of $5,746 million accounted for 53% and 46%, respectively, of total membership and total assets of all credit unions in Canada (Table 19.17).

Canadian credit unions in the 1960s and 1970s have continued their rapid growth. Outstanding loans of credit unions at year-end increased by 22.7% in 1975 over the previous year to reach $8,772 million. Assets at $12,331 million increased by 23.0% and savings at $11,816 million increased by 25.2% over 1974. Membership of 7.3 million represented 31.7% of the total population. Assets, liabilities and members' equity of local credit unions are given in Table 19.18.

There were 19 central credit unions in 1975; these are organized as centralized banking entities to serve the needs of their local credit union members, mainly by accepting deposits of surplus funds from them and providing a source of funds for them to borrow when they cannot meet the demand for local loans. Most of the centrals also admit cooperatives as members. Total assets of the centrals increased by 35% to $2,601 million over the previous year. The Credit Union National Association serves as the central organization for the provincial centrals.

The centrals had combined total assets of $2,601 million at the end of 1975 as compared with $1,920 million a year earlier. Most of the funds are invested in securities and these are financed mainly by demand and term deposits from local credit union members. The combined total assets of local and central credit unions therefore exceeded $15 billion at the end of 1975.

19.2   Other financial institutions

19.2.1   Trust and mortgage companies

Trust and mortgage companies are registered with either the federal or provincial governments. They operate under the Loan Companies Act (RSC 1970, c.L-12) and the Trust Companies Act (RSC 1970, c.T-16), as amended, or under corresponding provincial legislation.

Trust companies operate as financial intermediaries in two distinct areas: banking and fiduciary. Under the banking function, trust corporations are permitted to accept funds in exchange for their own credit instruments such as trust deposits and guaranteed investment certificates. This aspect of its business is often referred to as the "guaranteed funds" portion and differs little from the savings business of chartered banks.

Trust corporations are the only corporations in Canada with power to conduct fiduciary business. In this capacity they act as executors, trustees and administrators under wills or by appointment, as trustees under marriage or other settlements, as agents in the management of estates of the living, as guardians of minor or incapable persons, as financial agents for municipalities and companies, as transfer agents and registrars for stock and bond issues, as trustees for bond issues and, where so appointed, as authorized trustees in bankruptcies.

Mortgage corporations may also accept deposits and may issue both short-term and long-term debentures. The investment of these funds is spelled out specifically in the acts under which most of the funds are invested in mortgages secured by real estate.

Trust and mortgage companies were established and grew rapidly under provincial legislation in the late 19th and early 20th centuries. Some companies were chartered by special acts of Parliament but it was not until 1914 that the federal government began to regulate trust and mortgage companies registered under its acts. In 1975 there were 65 trust companies of which 25 were federally incorporated and 69 mortgage companies of which 18 came under federal jurisdiction. The federal Superintendent of Insurance regulates the federal companies and also, by arrangement with the provinces, trust and mortgage companies incorporated in Nova Scotia and trust companies incorporated in New Brunswick and Manitoba. Companies must be licensed by each province in which they wish to operate.

Although there may be some differences among the various federal and provincial acts, the broad lines of the legislation are common. In their intermediary business the companies have the power to borrow or, in the case of trust companies, to accept funds in guaranteed accounts subject to maximum permitted ratios of these funds to shareholders' equity. The funds may be invested in specified assets which include: first mortgages secured by real property; government securities, and the bonds and equity of corporations having established earnings records; loans on the security of such bonds and stocks; and unsecured personal loans. Trust and mortgage companies are not required to hold specified cash reserves, as are the chartered and savings banks, but there are broadly defined "liquid asset" requirements in a number of the acts.

In the 1920s trust and mortgage companies held about one half of the private mortgage business in Canada but their growth rate fell off sharply because of the effect of the depression and World War II on the mortgage business. Since then the strong demand for mortgage financing has led to sustained rapid expansion.

At the end of 1975 total assets of trust companies in the Statistics Canada survey were $14,559 million compared with $12,442 million a year earlier, an increase of 17%. Trust companies have been putting a high proportion of their funds into mortgages with the result that 72% of their total assets were represented by mortgages at the end of 1975. The trust companies had $10,493 million in term deposits outstanding and $2,814 million in demand deposits at the end of 1975, accounting for 91% of total funds. About 21% of the demand or savings deposits were in chequable accounts. There is considerable variety among the trust companies and a few have developed a substantial short-term business, raising funds by issuing certificates for terms as short as 30 days and also operating as lenders in the money market. Nevertheless, the main business of the trust companies in their intermediary role is to channel savings into mortgages. In addition, trust companies, as at December 31, 1975 had $33 billion under administration in estate, trust and agency accounts. Summary statistics are given in Tables 19.19, 19.34 and 19.35.

Mortgage companies had total assets of $8,017 million at the end of 1975 compared with $6,743 million a year earlier. Their holdings of mortgages amounted to $6,560 million, or 82% of total assets. To finance their investments, these companies sold $4,975 million of term deposits and debentures and $772 million of demand deposits.

More complete and up-to-date financial information may be found in quarterly financial statements published by Statistics Canada and the Bank of Canada, the reports of the Superintendent of Insurance on loan and trust companies and the reports of provincial supervisory authorities.

Small loans companies

19.2.2

Small loans companies and money-lenders are subject to the Small Loans Act (RSC 1970, c.S-11). This act, first passed in 1939, sets maximum charges on personal cash loans not in excess of $1,500 and is administered by the Department of Insurance. Lenders not licensed under the act may not charge more than 1% a month. Those wishing to make small loans at higher rates must be licensed each year by the Minister of Finance under the Small Loans Act. The act allows maximum rates, including charges of every kind, of 2% a month on unpaid balances not exceeding $300, 1% a month on the portion of unpaid balances exceeding $300 but not exceeding $1,000 and ½ of 1% on any remainder of the balance exceeding $1,000. Loans in excess of $1,500 are not regulated and lenders operating entirely above this limit and the larger loans of licensed lenders are thus exempt from the act; nor does the act regulate charges for the instalment financing of sales. Prior to January 1, 1957 the act applied only to loans of $500 or less and the maximum interest charge allowed was 2% a month.

At the end of 1975, there were four small loans companies and 41 money-lenders licensed under the act. Small loans companies are incorporated federally; money-lenders include provincially incorporated companies. Many of the small loans companies and money-lenders are affiliated with other financial institutions, principally Canadian sales finance companies and United States finance or loan companies. The affiliations with sales finance companies reflect the close relationship between instalment financing and the consumer loan business.

Statistics Canada publishes quarterly balance sheets for sales finance and consumer loan companies as a whole and does not attempt to distinguish the two groups within the industry (see *Financial institutions*, Catalogue No. 61-006).

The subsidiary small loans companies and money-lenders obtain most of their funds through their parent companies. A few of the larger companies have supplemented their bank loans by selling short-term paper in the market but the amount has been small compared with the short-term market borrowing of the sales finance companies. The smaller independent companies rely mainly on their shareholders and on borrowing from the chartered banks.

Annual figures of assets and liabilities given in Table 19.20 for 1974 and 1975 are from the Department of Insurance report. More complete data on the business of licensed lenders are given in the report on small loans companies and money-lenders, published annually by the Superintendent of Insurance.

There was a marked decrease in 1975 compared with 1974 in the number and amount of small loans made by the combined companies. Small loans made to the public during the year numbered 533,922 as against 647,739 in 1974, a drop of about 17.6%; the amount of such loans decreased from $412.2 million to $348.7 million, a drop of about 15.4%. The average small loan made was $653 in 1975 and $636 in 1974. At the end of the year, small loans outstanding numbered 496,024 for an amount of $252.1 million, or an average of $508 per loan; comparable figures for 1974 were 592,086, $296.2 million and $500, respectively.

Gross profits of small loans companies and money-lenders before income taxes and before taking into account any increase or decrease in reserves for bad debts decreased from $61.6 million in 1974 ($8.1 million being the loss on small loans and $69.7 million the profit on business other than small loans) to $61.2 million in 1975 ($8.2 million being the loss on small loans and $69.4 million the profit on other business).

19.3   Insurance

Insurance business is transacted in Canada by about 900 companies and societies. All of them are licensed or registered by provincial insurance authorities; at the end of 1975, 425 were also registered by the federal Department of Insurance. Details of the classes of insurance each company or society is authorized to transact and statistical information may be found in the various published reports of the individual superintendents of insurance for the provinces. Financial statistics of the federally registered companies and fraternal benefit societies are published in the annual *Report of the Superintendent of Insurance for Canada.*

19.3.1   Life insurance

Total life insurance in force in Canada at the end of 1975 amounted to $222,889 million of which about 94% was written by federally registered companies and fraternal benefit societies. The remainder was written by companies and societies that were provincially licensed only.

At the end of 1975, 149 companies were registered by the federal Department of Insurance to transact life insurance (58 Canadian, 12 British and 79 foreign). There were also 41 registered fraternal benefit societies (15 Canadian and 26 foreign).

The business of federally registered companies in Canada grew from $91 million in 1880 to $208,079 million at the end of 1975. Table 19.21 gives figures since 1880 for amounts of new insurance effected during the indicated year and an analysis of amounts in force at the end of the year among Canadian, British and foreign companies. Canadian companies reported an additional $51,660 million in force out of Canada at the end of 1975.

During 1975, there were over 1,009,000 new policies effected with a value of over $32,000 million. Over 127,000 policies ceased by death or maturity with a value of over $715 million. Tables 19.22 and 19.23 compare newly effected written business and total amounts in force for 1974 and 1975.

Net insurance premiums written in 1975 totalled $2,004 million as compared with $1,808 million in 1974. Net insurance claims (death, disability and maturity) totalled $771 million in 1975 as compared with $697 million in 1974. Table 19.24 gives a provincial analysis of the premium income in 1975 on a direct written basis only.

Assets of Canadian life insurance companies on a world-wide basis totalled over $23,000 million at the end of 1975. Assets of British companies applicable to business in Canada, on deposit with the Receiver General, vested in trust or secured by policies in Canada, totalled $1,933 million. Those of foreign companies on a similar basis totalled $3,183 million. In addition, there were assets under the control of the Chief Agent in Canada: $83 million for British companies and $137 million for foreign companies. The major categories of assets and related liabilities for 1974 and 1975 are given in Table 19.25.

Total income of Canadian companies amounted to $5,161 million of which $929 million was applicable to out-of-Canada business. The income of British companies applicable to Canadian business totalled $494 million; and of foreign companies, $819 million. The major sources of income and selected expenditures are given in Table 19.26.

For registered fraternal benefit societies, the certificates in force in Canada totalled $1,959 million at the end of 1975, as compared to $1,786 million at the end of 1974. Premiums written in Canada totalled $35 million during 1975, of which $29 million was applicable to Canadian societies and $6 million to foreign societies. Canadian societies also reported $99 million in premiums written out of Canada.

Property and casualty insurance   19.3.2

Direct premiums written in Canada for property insurance, automobile insurance, personal accident and sickness insurance, liability insurance and other forms of casualty insurance totalled $4,622 million in 1975 of which about 77% was written by federally registered companies. The remainder was written by other provincially licensed companies including a large number of parish, municipal, county and farmers' mutuals, by Lloyd's and by provincial government insurance offices.

At the end of 1975, there were 355 companies (135 Canadian, 36 British and 184 foreign) registered by the federal Department of Insurance to transact other than life insurance. Of these, 101 were life companies whose non-life business was ordinarily only personal accident and sickness insurance.

For federally registered companies, the premium income on a net basis has increased from just under $4 million in 1880 to $3,552 million in 1975. An analysis of premiums and related total claims by class of insurance (including marine) is given in Table 19.27 (net premiums) and by province in Table 19.28 (direct premiums).

Property insurance net premiums written in Canada during 1975 were $908 million, an increase over 1974 of $145 million or 19%. The net premiums earned in 1975 were $888 million and the net claims incurred were $590 million indicating a claims ratio of 66%. The claims ratio for 1974 was 76%. Net premiums for automobile insurance written in Canada during 1975 were $1,448 million, an increase over 1974 of $323 million or 29%. The net premiums earned in 1975 were $1,298 million and the net claims incurred were $1,014 million, indicating a claims ratio of 78%. The claims ratio for 1974 was 83%.

Personal accident and sickness insurance net premiums written in Canada during 1975 were $831 million, an increase over 1974 of $132 million or 19%. The net premiums earned in 1975 were $805 million and the net claims incurred were $619 million indicating a claims ratio of 77%. The claims ratio for 1974 was 77%. Net premiums for liability insurance written in Canada during 1975 were $175 million, an increase over 1974 of $33 million or 24%. The net premiums earned in 1975 were $166 million and net claims incurred were $104 million indicating a claims ratio of 63%. The claims ratio for 1974 was 61%.

Assets of Canadian property and casualty companies on a world-wide basis totalled $3,191 million at the end of 1975. Assets of British companies applicable to their in-Canada business, on deposit with the Receiver General or vested in trust, totalled $412 million. Those of foreign companies on a similar basis totalled $1,562 million. In addition, there were assets under the control of the Chief Agent in Canada; $100 million for British companies and $432 million for foreign companies. The major categories of the assets and their related liabilities for 1974 and 1975 are given in Table 19.29.

Underwriting experience in Canada over the past 10 years has ranged from a loss of $54 million in 1964 to a gain of $51 million in 1967. The loss for 1975 was nearly $160 million (Table 19.30).

19.3.3   Fire losses

Fire losses in Canada reached $463.8 million in 1975, an increase of $35.0 million or 8.2% over losses reported in 1974. The total number of fires was 69,881, a decrease of 3,883 or 5.3% from 1974 (Tables 19.31 and 19.32). This represents an average daily loss of $1,270,691 from 191 fires. There were 822 deaths from fire in 1975, a decrease of 98 or 10.7%. Of this total, 203 or 24.7% were children.

19.3.4   Government insurance

19.3.4.1   Federal government insurance

In recent years, various insurance schemes have been adopted by the federal government or undertaken cooperatively by the federal and provincial governments. Information on unemployment insurance, hospital insurance, veterans insurance, and export credit insurance, will be found in the appropriate chapters on Labour, Health, Incomes and social security and Merchandising and trade.

Deposit insurance. The Canada Deposit Insurance Corporation was established in 1967 to provide, for the benefit of persons having deposits with a member of the corporation, insurance against the loss of deposits up to a maximum of $20,000 for any one depositor. Membership in the Deposit Insurance Corporation is obligatory for chartered banks, Quebec savings banks and those federally incorporated loan and trust companies that accept deposits from the public. Provincially incorporated loan and trust companies that accept deposits from the public are eligible to apply for membership if they have the consent of the province of incorporation. The definition of deposits, as set out in the general by-law of the corporation, might be summarized as money received by a member institution that is repayable on demand or notice and money that is repayable on a fixed date not more than five years after the money is received. Deposits not payable in Canada or in Canadian currency are not insured.

19.3.4.2   Provincial government insurance

Manitoba. The Manitoba Public Insurance Corporation is a Crown corporation established under the Automobile Insurance Act. The act and its regulations provided for the establishment of a universal, compulsory automobile insurance plan and of other plans of automobile insurance within the province. The corporation was created by order of the Lieutenant Governor in Council on September 29, 1970 and commenced operations on November 1, 1971. On November 18, 1974, legislation came into effect changing the former Automobile Insurance Act to the Manitoba Public Insurance Corporation Act. This act reflects a broader scope of insurance activities; as of mid-1975, the Manitoba Public Insurance Corporation began offering a wide range of non-compulsory general insurance coverages in competition with private insurance companies. General insurance offered is for fire damage to commercial and residential establishments; guarantee or surety and performance bonding on contracts and persons; public liability to protect householders and homeowners against injury to persons on their property; theft insurance against burglary, robbery and general theft. Various other forms of general insurance will be phased in gradually.

The universal, compulsory automobile insurance plan, known as Autopac, provides the following basic coverage on Manitoba-licensed motor vehicles: (1) bodily injury (including passenger hazard) and property damage liability to $50,000; no-fault all-perils coverage with $200 deductible (private passenger cars) and nil deductible for loss caused by fire, lightning, or theft of the entire vehicle; if a vehicle is stolen, the owner may be reimbursed for transportation expenses up to $8 a day for up to 30 days; and (2) no-fault personal injury benefits (paid automatically without limiting the insured's right to seek a larger settlement); death benefits to a maximum of $10,000; funeral expenses to a maximum of $500; benefits up to $6,000 for dismemberment, disfigurement, or impairment; loss-of-income payment of $75 a week for total disability and $25 a week for partial disability, beginning one week after disability; for a total disability, payments continue for the period during which the insured remains totally disabled, with no time limit, and for partial disability, payments continue up to 104 weeks. Revenue for the plan comes from two sources — premiums on drivers' licences and premiums on vehicles. Premiums on drivers' licences recognize driver responsibility; a driver is allowed to accumulate five demerit points (based on driving convictions) before being assessed an additional driver-insurance premium. Premiums are based on such factors as year, make, model, use and rating territory, based on the address of the vehicle owner.

Saskatchewan. The Saskatchewan Government Insurance Office (SGIO), a Crown corporation established by the Saskatchewan Government Insurance Act, 1944, commenced business in May 1945. It provides all types of insurance other than sickness and life. The aim of the legislation is to provide residents of the province with low-cost insurance designed for their particular needs. Rates are based on loss experience in Saskatchewan only and the surplus is invested, to the extent possible, within the province. Premium income for 1975 amounted to $39.4 million and earned deficit amounted to $729,000. The total amount made available to the Saskatchewan Government Finance Office from 1945 to December 31, 1975 was in excess of $10 million. Assets at the latter date were $97.5 million of which $41.5 million was invested in bonds and debentures issued by the province and by Saskatchewan municipalities, hospitals and schools. Independent insurance agents, numbering 532, sell insurance throughout the province on behalf of the SGIO.

The Automobile Accident Insurance Act, administered by the SGIO on behalf of the provincial government, provides a comprehensive automobile accident insurance plan. Premiums paid by motorists create a fund from which benefits are paid in the event of death, injury or damages sustained in automobile accidents. Any surplus over payments is used to increase benefits, reduce premiums or absorb deficits in periods of high accident frequency. The surplus is not transferable to the general operation of the SGIO, nor is any surplus credited to the provincial government. The plan provides protection against loss arising out of a motorist's liability to pay for bodily injury or death of others and damage to property of others, up to a limit of $35,000, regardless of the number of claims arising from any one accident. Comprehensive coverage, including collision and upset, subject to $200 deductible for private passenger cars and farm trucks is also provided. Rates vary from $6 to $135 for private passenger cars and $5 to $70 for farm trucks. There are various rates for other types of motor vehicles depending on size and usage. From the inception of the act in 1946 to December 31, 1975, more than $360 million was paid in claims.

The Saskatchewan Government Insurance Office, under contract with the Saskatchewan Department of Tourism and Renewable Resources, offers insurance to farmers covering damage to crops by certain wildlife such as ducks, geese, sandhill cranes, deer, elk, bear and antelope.

Alberta. A variety of agencies in Alberta offer forms of prepaid protection corresponding to insurance but the nature of the enabling legislation governing these plans emphasizes the fact that they do not constitute insurance. Because such exemptions are specifically provided by the insurance laws of the province, reference to these plans is necessary only to make it clear that they do not come within the scope of the Alberta Insurance Act. It should be noted that the Alberta Hail Insurance Act and the Alberta Crop Insurance Act are administered by the Alberta Hail and Crop Insurance Corporation and each contains a clause exempting its operations from the provisions of the Alberta Insurance Act.

Sources

19.1.1 - 19.1.2 Banking and Financial Analysis Department, Bank of Canada.

19.1.3 Royal Canadian Mint.

19.1.4 Banking and Financial Analysis Department, Bank of Canada; The Canadian Bankers' Association; Business Finance Division, Business Statistics Field, Statistics Canada.

19.1.5 The Province of Ontario Savings Office; Treasury Branches of Alberta; The Montreal City and District Savings Bank; Business Finance Division, Business Statistics Field, Statistics Canada.

19.2.1 Business Finance Division, Business Statistics Field, Statistics Canada.

19.2.2 - 19.3.2 Special Services Division, Department of Insurance.

19.3.3 Dominion Fire Commissioner, Department of Public Works.

19.3.4 Canada Deposit Insurance Corporation; The Manitoba Public Insurance Corporation; Saskatchewan Government Insurance Office; Department of Consumer Affairs, Government of Alberta.

Tables

..	not available	e	estimate
...	not appropriate or not applicable	p	preliminary
—	nil or zero	r	revised
- -	too small to be expressed		certain tables may not add due to rounding

19.1 Bank rates from Oct. 12, 1962 to Mar. 8, 1976

Date of change	% per annum	Date of change	% per annum	Date of change	% per annum
Oct. 12, 1962	5.00	July 2, 1968	7.00	Oct. 25, 1971	4.75
Nov. 13, 1962	4.00	July 29, 1968	6.50	Apr. 9, 1973	5.25
May 6, 1963	3.50	Sept. 3, 1968	6.00	May 14, 1973	5.75
Aug. 12, 1963	4.00	Dec. 18, 1968	6.50	June 11, 1973	6.25
Nov. 24, 1964	4.25	Mar. 3, 1969	7.00	Aug. 7, 1973	6.75
Dec. 6, 1965	4.75	June 11, 1969	7.50	Sept. 13, 1973	7.25
Nov. 14, 1966	5.25	July 16, 1969	8.00	Apr. 15, 1974	8.25
Jan. 30, 1967	5.00	May 12, 1970	7.50	May 13, 1974	8.75
Apr. 7, 1967	4.50	June 1, 1970	7.00	July 24, 1974	9.25
Sept. 27, 1967	5.00	Sept. 1, 1970	6.50	Nov. 18, 1974	8.75
Nov. 20, 1967	6.00	Nov. 12, 1970	6.00	Jan. 13, 1975	8.25
Jan. 22, 1968	7.00	Feb. 15, 1971	5.75	Sept. 3, 1975	9.00
Mar. 15, 1968	7.50	Feb. 24, 1971	5.25	Mar. 8, 1976	9.50

19.2 Assets and liabilities of the Bank of Canada, as at Dec. 31, 1973-75 (million dollars)

Item	1973	1974	1975
Assets			
Foreign exchange	32.5	8.0	14.2
Advances to chartered and savings banks	—	8.0	—
Bills bought in open market, excluding treasury bills	39.2	139.7	44.1
Investments			
Treasury bills of Canada	1,081.1	1,590.3	2,081.4
Other securities issued or guaranteed by Canada maturing within three years	2,282.3	2,528.7	2,804.1
Other securities issued or guaranteed by Canada not maturing within three years	2,612.5	2,859.6	2,923.1
Bonds and debentures issued by Industrial Development Bank	656.8	892.0	1,029.5
Other securities	778.6	572.7	1,081.7
Industrial Development Bank capital stock	64.0	73.0	—
Bank premises	29.5	44.7	55.0
All other assets	422.8	467.4	462.9
Total, assets	7,999.2	9,184.1	10,495.9
Liabilities			
Capital paid up	5.0	5.0	5.0
Rest fund	25.0	25.0	25.0
Notes in circulation			
Held by chartered banks	931.0	1,077.6	1,204.4
All other	4,620.2	5,212.8	6,078.6
Deposits			
Government of Canada	6.4	16.7	26.6
Chartered banks	2,006.5	2,361.3	2,748.5
Other	54.2	101.3	63.3
Foreign currency liabilities	25.2	1.9	7.7
All other liabilities	325.9	382.5	336.7
Total, liabilities	7,999.2	9,184.1	10,495.9

19.3 Assets and liabilities of the Federal Business Development Bank, as at Oct. 31, 1975 and 1976

Item		1975	1976
Assets			
Loans and investments[1]	$'000,000	1,179.5	1,347.4
Other assets	"	21.7	25.6
Total, assets	"	1,201.2	1,373.0
Liabilities			
Capital and reserves	"	113.3	157.3
Notes and debentures outstanding	"	1,039.6	1,176.5
Other liabilities	"	48.3	39.1
Total, liabilities	"	1,201.2	1,373.0
Accounts on books			
Amount outstanding	"	1,189.2	1,361.8
Customers on books	No.	27,856	31,154

[1] Net after allowance for doubtful accounts of $22.8 million in 1975 and $31.9 million in 1976.

19.4   Bank of Canada note liabilities, as at Dec. 31, 1973-75 (thousand dollars)

Denomination	1973	1974	1975
Bank of Canada notes			
$1	178,378	203,032	216,747
$2	129,432	143,047	161,901
$5	311,355	331,830	352,313
$10	968,676	1,057,131	1,135,514
$20	2,361,845	2,781,724	3,303,249
$25	46	46	46
$50	379,375	398,505	485,584
$100	1,104,052	1,236,165	1,451,646
$500	25	25	25
$1,000	105,145	126,084	163,141
Total	5,538,329	6,277,588	7,270,166
Note issues in process of retirement[1]	12,889	12,888	12,886
Total, Bank of Canada note liabilities	5,551,218	6,290,476	7,283,052
Held by:			
Chartered banks	931,014	1,077,645	1,204,448
Others	4,620,204	5,212,831	6,078,604

[1]Includes, in 1975, chartered banks' notes $8,134,340, Dominion of Canada notes $4,635,536, provincial notes $27,568 and defunct banks' notes $88,156; these amounts have changed little in recent years.

19.5   Canadian dollar currency and chartered bank deposits, as at Dec. 31, 1968-75 (million dollars)

Year	Currency outside banks			Chartered bank deposits				Total currency and chartered bank deposits[1]			
	Notes	Coin	Total	Personal savings deposits	Govern-ment of Canada deposits	Other deposits[1]	Total[1]	Total including govern-ment deposits	Held by general public		
									Including personal savings deposits	Excluding personal savings deposits	
1968	2,660	399	3,059	13,622	669	10,507	24,798	27,857	27,188	13,566	
1969	2,903	434	3,337	15,030	1,308	9,540	25,878	29,214	27,906	12,876	
1970	3,106	461	3,568	16,615	1,257	10,972	28,845	32,412	31,155	14,540	
1971	3,506	488	3,993	17,783	2,239	14,572	34,594	38,587	36,348	18,565	
1972	4,056	518	4,574	19,949	2,407	16,892	39,248	43,822	41,415	21,466	
1973	4,620	589	5,209	24,604	2,361	19,220	46,186	51,395	49,034	24,430	
1974	5,213	656	5,868	29,789	4,682	21,784	56,255	62,124	57,442	27,652	
1975	6,079	699	6,778	33,237	3,663	27,359	64,259	71,037	67,374	34,137	

[1]Less total float, i.e. cheques and other items in transit.

19.6   Canadian coin[1] in circulation, as at Dec. 31, 1968-75

Year	Silver $'000	Nickel $'000	Tombac[2] $'000	Steel $'000	Bronze $'000	Total $'000	Per capita $
1968	316,837	75,464	549	3,445	39,705	436,000	20.82
1969	316,715	117,199	549	3,444	43,004	480,911	22.62
1970	316,610	137,890	549	3,444	46,092	504,583	23.60
1971	317,033	159,151	549	3,443	49,297	529,473	24.42
1972	317,269	185,141	549	3,442	53,494	559,896	25.65
1973	325,981	243,246	549	3,441	58,259	631,476	28.58
1974	386,350	321,434	549	3,440	65,199	776,972	34.41
1975	444,548	382,334	549	3,440	71,490	902,361	..

[1]The figures shown are of net issues of coin.
[2]Tombac, a copper-zinc alloy, was used to conserve nickel for war purposes; no coins of this metal have been issued since 1944.

19.7   Receipts of gold bullion at the Royal Canadian Mint and bullion and coinage issued, 1968-75

Year	Gold received '000 oz t	Gold bullion issued '000 oz t	Silver coin issued $'000	Nickel coin issued $'000	Bronze coin issued $'000
1968	2,237	2,222	26,167	45,472	3,150
1969	2,147	2,089	—	41,741	3,301
1970	2,114	2,150	—	20,702	3,089
1971	2,010	2,009	556	21,277	3,207
1972	1,931	1,895	350	26,006	4,199
1973	1,476	1,483	8,804	58,128	4,768
1974	1,280	1,337	60,382	78,208	6,941
1975	1,079	1,056	58,203	60,939	6,295

19.7   Receipts of gold bullion at the Royal Canadian Mint and bullion and coinage issued, 1968-75   M

Year	Gold received '000 g	Gold bullion issued '000 g	Silver coin issued $'000	Nickel coin issued $'000	Bronze coin issued $'000
1968	69 578	69 112	26,167	45,472	3,150
1969	66 779	64 975	—	41,741	3,301
1970	65 753	66 872	—	20,702	3,089
1971	62 518	62 487	556	21,277	3,207
1972	60 061	58 941	350	26,006	4,199
1973	45 909	46 126	8,804	58,128	4,768
1974	39 812	41 585	60,382	78,208	6,941
1975	33 561	32 845	58,203	60,939	6,295

19.8   Statement of chartered bank assets and liabilities, as at Dec. 31, 1973-75 (thousand dollars)

Assets and liabilities	1973	1974	1975
Assets			
Gold coin and bullion	102,521	241,436	151,724
Other coin in Canada	34,193	53,867	69,291
Other coin outside Canada	1,213	1,305	1,954
Notes of and deposits with Bank of Canada	2,937,468	3,438,919	3,952,903
Government and bank notes other than Canadian	82,723	82,329	84,095
Deposits with banks in Canadian currency	379,834	562,260	499,081
Deposits with banks in currencies other than Canadian	14,758,530	14,885,099	15,468,113
Cheques and other items in transit (net)	2,421,955	2,639,562	2,360,024
Government of Canada treasury bills, at amortized value	3,433,442	3,702,842	3,434,189
Other Government of Canada issued or guaranteed securities maturing within three years, at amortized value	1,730,720	2,161,465	2,484,948
Government of Canada issued or guaranteed securities maturing after three years, at amortized value	2,081,334	2,199,996	1,814,666
Canadian provincial government issued or guaranteed securities, at amortized value	477,140	480,466	656,195
Canadian municipal and school corporation issued or guaranteed securities not exceeding market value	493,021	464,572	486,796
Other Canadian securities, not exceeding market value	1,487,645	2,097,336	2,236,988
Securities other than Canadian, not exceeding market value	496,181	637,089	506,899
Mortgages and hypothecs insured under the National Housing Act 1954	2,889,820	3,316,002	4,178,032
Day, call and short loans to investment dealers and brokers in Canadian currency, secured	1,046,542	1,372,160	1,373,057
Day, call and short loans to investment dealers and brokers in currencies other than Canadian, secured	536,842	525,897	427,429
Loans to Canadian provincial governments in Canadian currency	107,597	61,674	105,362
Loans to Canadian municipalities and school corporations in Canadian currency less provision for losses	1,133,189	1,455,530	1,795,280
Other loans in Canadian currency, less provision for losses	32,551,280	39,443,466	45,858,113
Other loans in currencies other than Canadian, less provision for losses	7,081,863	11,692,477	14,429,560
Bank premises at cost, less amounts written off	610,489	731,893	861,902
Securities of and loans to corporations controlled by the bank	260,121	379,207	409,109
Customers' liability under acceptances, guarantees and letters of credit, as per contra	2,526,756	4,287,685	4,645,998
Other assets	91,147	100,288	86,751
Total, assets	79,753,566	97,014,822	108,378,459

19.8   Statement of chartered bank assets and liabilities, as at Dec. 31, 1973-75 (thousand dollars) (concluded)

Assets and liabilities	1973	1974	1975
Liabilities			
Deposits by Government of Canada in Canadian currency	2,361,383	4,682,130	3,663,123
Deposits by Canadian provincial governments in Canadian currency	723,808	621,539	1,076,667
Deposits by banks in Canadian currency	492,637	924,805	1,285,360
Deposits by banks in currencies other than Canadian	13,322,655	15,196,536	16,268,270
Personal savings deposits payable after notice, in Canada, in Canadian currency	24,604,249	29,789,439	33,236,723
Other deposits payable after notice, in Canadian currency	9,282,512	11,209,857	13,357,248
Other deposits payable on demand, in Canadian currency	11,100,229	11,569,555	14,254,165
Other deposits in currencies other than Canadian	11,254,683	14,116,603	15,092,765
Advances from Bank of Canada, secured	—	8,000	—
Acceptances, guarantees and letters of credit	2,526,756	4,287,685	4,645,998
Other liabilities	403,970	554,294	682,584
Accumulated appropriations for losses	801,784	809,323	949,247
Debentures issued and outstanding	656,972	780,404	952,230
Capital paid up	343,197	354,500	379,290
Rest account	1,862,156	2,103,194	2,521,510
Undivided profits at latest financial year-end	16,575	6,958	13,279
Total, liabilities	79,753,566	97,014,822	108,378,459

19.9   Canadian cash reserves, 1968-75 (million dollars)

Year	Bank of Canada deposits	Bank of Canada notes	Total	Canadian dollar deposit liabilities	Average cash reserve ratio
1968	965	525	1,490	23,314	6.4
1969	1,090	560	1,650	25,916	6.4
1970	1,112	587	1,699	27,066	6.3
1971	1,356	610	1,966	31,329	6.3
1972	1,615	686	2,301	36,951	6.2
1973	1,902	768	2,670	42,246	6.3
1974	2,106	888	2,993	49,814	6.0
1975	2,653	985	3,638	60,225	6.0

Bank of Canada deposits are averages of the months in the year shown; the monthly levels are averages of the juridical days in that month. Bank of Canada notes and Canadian dollar deposits are also averages of the months in the year shown; the monthly levels in this case are averages of the four consecutive Wednesdays ending with the second last Wednesday in the previous month. Until June 1967 the required cash reserve ratio was 8% on both demand and notice deposits. For the next eight months the required minimum monthly average on demand deposits was increased by one half of 1% per month and that on notice deposits was decreased by one half of 1%. Since February 1968 the required ratios have been 12% for demand deposits and 4% for notice deposits as prescribed under the Bank Act.

19.10   Classification of chartered bank deposit liabilities payable to the public in Canada in Canadian currency, as at Apr.30, 1975 and 1976 (number of accounts)

Deposit accounts of the public of:	1975 Personal savings deposit accounts	Other deposit accounts of the public	Total deposit accounts of the public	1976 Personal savings deposit accounts	Other deposit accounts of the public	Total deposit accounts of the public
Less than $100	8,183,723	149,758	10,789,036	8,503,981	154,867	11,164,305
$100 or over but less than $1,000	6,499,023	184,023	9,430,950	6,768,684	193,829	9,867,222
$1,000 or over but less than $10,000	5,187,879	163,084	6,404,805	5,832,258	186,445	7,220,516
$10,000 or over but less than $100,000	661,148	103,789	919,011	759,569	114,762	1,043,968
$100,000 or over	7,614	17,928	39,142	9,471	27,307	51,332
Total deposits	20,539,387	618,582	27,582,944	21,873,963	677,210	29,347,343

19.11   Classification of chartered bank loans in Canadian currency, as at Dec. 31, 1974 and 1975 (million dollars)

Class of loan	1974	1975
General loans		
Personal	11,681.8	14,048.0
To individuals, fully secured by marketable bonds and stocks	821.5	829.6
Home improvement loans	43.0	43.8
To individuals, not elsewhere classified	10,817.3	13,174.9
Farmers		
Farm Improvement Loans Act	457.0	477.6
Other farm loans	1,838.4	2,240.0

19.11   Classification of chartered bank loans in Canadian currency, as at Dec. 31, 1974 and 1975 (million dollars) (concluded)

Class of loan	1974	1975
Industry	7,706.9	8,532.7
Chemical and rubber products	439.6	553.2
Electrical apparatus and supplies	484.3	397.0
Foods, beverages and tobacco	1,203.4	1,048.3
Forest products	946.4	987.5
Furniture	137.1	144.2
Iron and steel products	975.5	1,252.5
Mining and mine products	897.5	993.9
Petroleum and products	828.1	1,330.2
Textiles, leather and clothing	592.1	607.8
Transportation equipment	475.2	462.8
Other products	727.7	755.4
Merchandisers	3,363.4	3,607.9
Construction contractors	1,353.8	1,513.5
Public utilities, transportation and communications	1,412.1	1,661.6
Other business	6,732.0	7,917.7
Religious, educational, heath and welfare institutions	456.6	469.1
Total, general loans	35,002.0	40,468.1
Other loans		
Provincial governments	61.7	105.4
Municipal governments and school districts	1,455.5	1,795.3
Special	743.9	718.6
Other	285.2	369.0
Loans to finance the purchase of Canada Savings Bonds	490.2	495.2
Grain dealers and exporters	545.7	655.3
Instalment and other financial companies	698.7	743.4
Total, other loans	4,280.9	4,882.1
Total, loans in Canadian currency	39,282.9	45,350.3

19.12   Chartered bank revenues, expenses, shareholders' equity and accumulated appropriations for losses, as at Oct. 31, 1973-75 (million dollars)

Item	1973	1974	1975
For financial year ended Oct. 31			
Revenues			
Income from loans	4,161.4	6,807.6	7,664.4
Income from securities[1]	590.8	753.0	840.2
Other operating income	449.5	543.5	693.3
Total, revenues	5,201.7	8,104.0	9,197.9
Expenses			
Interest on deposits and bank debentures	2,861.1	5,269.8	5,519.0
Salaries, premiums, contributions and other staff benefits	918.2	1,148.7	1,430.5
Property expenses, including depreciation	258.5	314.6	377.4
Other operating expenses[2]	385.0	496.4	636.7
Total, expenses[3]	4,422.8	7,229.4	7,963.6
Balance of revenue[3]	778.9	874.6	1,234.3
Less:			
Loss experience not included in other operating expenses	27.5	137.2	62.8
Appropriations for losses, net[4]	74.7	7.5	139.9
Income taxes	355.0	425.4	570.8
Leaving for dividends and shareholders' equity	321.7	304.4	460.8
Dividends	147.2	166.8	190.8
Total additions to shareholders' equity	274.8	196.4	448.0
From above operations	174.5	137.6	270.0
From issue of new shares including premiums	100.3	58.8	178.0
As at end of financial year			
Shareholders' equity			
Undivided profits	16.6	7.0	13.3
Rest account	1,862.1	2,060.0	2,476.5
Capital paid up	343.2	351.3	376.5
Total, shareholders' equity	2,221.9	2,418.3	2,866.3
Accumulated appropriations for losses	801.8	809.3	949.2

[1]Excludes realized profits and losses on securities held in investment account which are included in the item "Loss experience not included in other operating expenses".
[2]Includes provision for losses based on five-year average loss experience and taxes other than income taxes.
[3]Before provision for income taxes and appropriations for losses other than those included in "Other operating expenses".
[4]General and tax-paid appropriations for losses: net after any transfers out of accumulated appropriatons for losses to undivided profits or rest account.

19.13　Branches¹ of chartered banks, by province, as at Dec. 31, 1920-75

Province or territory	1920	1930	1940	1950	1960	1970	1974	1975
Newfoundland	–	–	–	39	71	114	127	128
Prince Edward Island	41	28	25	23	27	30	32	32
Nova Scotia	169	138	134	144	173	202	222	226
New Brunswick	121	102	97	100	113	136	162	164
Quebec	1,150	1,183	1,083	1,164	1,427	1,524	1,521	1,547
Ontario	1,586	1,409	1,208	1,257	1,785	2,307	2,670	2,749
Manitoba	349	239	162	165	234	310	336	339
Saskatchewan	591	447	233	238	296	350	356	359
Alberta	424	304	172	246	394	521	617	633
British Columbia	242	229	192	294	514	684	803	824
Yukon Territory and Northwest Territories	3	4	5	9	17	21	32	34
Canada	4,676	4,083	3,311	3,679	5,051	6,199	6,878	7,035

¹Figures include sub-agencies and sub-branches in Canada receiving deposits for the banks employing them.

19.14　Branches¹ of individual Canadian chartered banks, by province, as at Dec. 31, 1974 and 1975

Bank	Province or territory										
	Nfld.		PEI		NS		NB		Que.		Ont.	
	1974	1975	1974	1975	1974	1975	1974	1975	1974	1975	1974	1975
Bank of Montreal	34	34	3	3	33	34	28	28	216	218	478	489
The Bank of Nova Scotia	53	54	10	10	65	67	50	50	83	88	386	395
The Toronto-Dominion Bank	2	2	2	2	4	4	6	6	92	97	480	493
La Banque Provinciale du Canada	–	–	2	2	–	–	21	22	268	270	30	30
Canadian Imperial Bank of Commerce	18	18	9	9	36	36	26	26	195	203	727	744
The Royal Bank of Canada	20	20	6	6	83	84	30	31	206	214	530	553
Banque Canadienne Nationale	–	–	–	–	–	–	–	–	459	454	19	23
The Mercantile Bank of Canada	–	–	–	–	1	1	1	1	2	2	3	4
Bank of British Columbia	–	–	–	–	–	–	–	–	–	–	–	–
Unity Bank of Canada	–	–	–	–	–	–	–	–	–	–	17	18
Total	127	128	32	32	222	226	162	164	1,521	1,547	2,670	2,749

Bank	Man.		Sask.		Alta.		BC		YT and NWT		Total	
	1974	1975	1974	1975	1974	1975	1974	1975	1974	1975	1974	1975
Bank of Montreal	74	72	62	63	128	128	166	170	6	6	1,228	1,245
The Bank of Nova Scotia	29	31	40	41	88	89	102	102	2	2	908	929
The Toronto-Dominion Bank	47	47	45	44	87	90	102	104	3	3	870	892
La Banque Provinciale du Canada	–	–	–	–	–	–	–	–	–	–	321	324
Canadian Imperial Bank of Commerce	84	86	106	107	177	185	222	229	18	20	1,618	1,663
The Royal Bank of Canada	94	95	103	104	131	134	182	188	3	3	1,388	1,432
Banque Canadienne Nationale	6	6	–	–	–	–	–	–	–	–	484	483
The Mercantile Bank of Canada	1	1	–	–	2	2	1	1	–	–	11	12
Bank of British Columbia	–	–	–	–	3	4	25	27	–	–	28	31
Unity Bank of Canada	1	1	–	–	1	1	3	3	–	–	22	24
Total	336	339	356	359	617	633	803	824	32	34	6,878	7,035

¹Figures include sub-agencies and sub-branches in Canada for receiving deposits.

19.15　Canadian chartered banks¹ outside Canada, as at Dec. 31, 1975

Region and country	Representation	Region and country	Representation
Asia/Middle East		Jamaica	102
Arab Republic of Egypt	2	Martinique	1
Bahrain	1	Montserrat	1
Hong Kong	7	Netherlands Antilles	2
India	1	Puerto Rico	11
Indonesia	3	St. Kitts	1
Japan	5		
Lebanon	4		
Malaysia	1	St. Lucia	7
Philippines	1	St. Vincent	2
Singapore	6	Tobago	3
Taiwan	1	Trinidad	48
Thailand	1	Virgin Islands	8
United Arab Emirates	3		
Australia		Europe	
Australia	4	Belgium	2
		France	7
Caribbean		Germany, Federal Republic of	7
Antigua	3	Great Britain	30
Bahamas	51	Greece	2
Barbados	27	Ireland	2
Dominica	1	Italy	2
Grand Cayman	9	Netherlands	5
Grenada	6	Norway	1
Guadeloupe	1	Spain	1
Haiti	5	Switzerland	1

19.15   Canadian chartered banks[1] outside Canada, as at Dec. 31, 1975 (concluded)

Region and country	Representation	Region and country	Representation
North America		South America	
Belize	9	Argentina	5
Dominican Republic	21	Brazil	4
Mexico	3	Colombia	10
Panama	3	Guyana	11
United States	67	Venezuela	14

[1]Chartered banks are represented by branches, agencies, representative offices, and/or branches of subsidiary companies.

19.16   Credit unions in Canada, 1968-75

Year	Credit unions chartered	Members	Assets $'000	Loans granted to members $'000
1968	4,861	4,632,382	3,699,840	1,482,003
1969	4,769	5,002,722	4,064,065	1,525,655
1970	4,593	5,203,402	4,591,953	1,781,331
1971	4,441	5,623,994	5,587,728	1,828,888
1972	4,351	5,843,820	6,761,224	2,970,397
1973	4,256	6,382,054	8,465,786	3,765,767
1974	4,194	6,805,625	10,026,257	4,111,857
1975	4,117	7,268,552	12,331,379	4,983,082

19.17   Summary statistics of credit unions, by province, 1974 and 1975

Province or territory	Credit unions chartered	Members	Assets $'000	Shares $'000	Deposits $'000	Loans granted to members $'000
1974						
Newfoundland	45	6,725	5,518	3,500	1,586	3,797
Prince Edward Island	14	17,105	14,062	5,280	4,762	8,023
Nova Scotia	133	128,438	102,654	53,253	37,592	64,807
New Brunswick	146	142,762	105,169	66,215	28,426	62,544
Quebec	1,776	3,711,616	4,852,245	478,652	4,077,278	1,638,569
Ontario	1,408	1,341,029	1,815,379	789,373	915,718	827,913
Manitoba	242	272,387	491,848	1,352	439,009	252,644
Saskatchewan	327	396,474	1,034,548	298,321	638,124	438,763
Alberta	276	246,008	393,052	101,150	249,218	223,144
British Columbia	286	542,288	1,210,802	190,356	880,730	590,917
Northwest Territories	3	793	980	58	831	736
Total	4,656	6,805,625	10,026,257	1,987,510	7,273,274	4,111,857
1975						
Newfoundland	42	7,601	7,878	4,309	2,472	5,374
Prince Edward Island	13	18,095	16,202	5,748	5,977	9,289
Nova Scotia	126	132,595	123,666	59,445	52,366	75,086
New Brunswick	145	164,005	136,475	80,456	43,055	80,842
Quebec	1,611	3,921,406	5,745,824	566,047	4,861,294	1,770,199
Ontario	1,340	1,421,847	2,220,964	900,833	1,176,706	1,123,854
Manitoba	192	295,357	638,346	1,474	591,639	317,159
Saskatchewan	249	426,279	1,341,703	343,331	856,429	569,490
Alberta	212	284,279	543,442	113,448	376,466	357,732
British Columbia	183	595,644	1,554,269	201,992	1,221,727	672,587
Northwest Territories	4	1,444	2,610	101	2,060	1,470
Total	4,117	7,268,552	12,331,379	2,277,184	9,190,191	4,983,082

19.18   Assets, liabilities and members' equity of local credit unions in Canada, 1973-75 (million dollars)

Item	1973	1974	1975P	Item	1973	1974	1975P
Assets							
				Fixed assets			
Cash and demand deposits				Land and buildings	150	180	204
On hand	265	168	192	Equipment and furniture	39	45	52
In banks	51	80	52	Stabilization fund deposits	15	19	28
In centrals	516	1,045	1,092	Other assets	91	110	152
Other	56	3	50	Total assets	8,465	10,026	12,331
Investments							
Term deposits	487	563	1,158	Liabilities			
Government of Canada	30	28	33				
Provincial governments	219	206	204	Accounts payable			
Municipal governments	489	442	411	Interest	56	83	114
Shares in centrals	80	94	127	Dividends	18	20	22
Religious institutions	16			Other	30	38	44
Hospitals	25 }	145	194	Loans payable			
Other	322			Centrals	177	236	239
Loans				Banks	14	8	9
Cash loans				Other	20	9	18
Personal	2,370	2,782	3,285	Deposits			
Farm	97	121	161	Ordinary	3,670	4,389	5,491
Co-operatives and other enterprises	43	60	95	Term	2,285	2,884	3,699
Other	31	68	49	Other liabilities	40	51	59
Mortgage loans							
Dwellings	2,769	3,520	4,234	Members' equity			
Farm	127	171	208	Share capital	1,846	1,988	2,277
Co-operatives and other enterprises	141	140	320	Reserves	265	279	302
Other	52	74	80	Undivided earnings	44	41	57
Allowance for doubtful loans	-16	38	50	Total, liabilities and members' equity	8,465	10,026	12,331

19.19   Revenues and expenses of trust and mortgage companies, 1973-75 (million dollars)

Item	Trust companies			Mortgage companies		
	1973	1974	1975	1973	1974	1975
Revenues						
Interest earned	761	1,017	1,202	435	552	670
Dividends	10	12	17	16	18	34
Fees and commissions	226	274	316	4	1	2
Other revenues	29	34	43	32	23	24
Total, revenues	1,026	1,337	1,578	487	594	730
Expenses						
Interest	598	864	1,004	317	432	511
Depreciation	6	8	9	2	2	2
Amortization	—	—	—	1	1	1
Income taxes	54	38	51	34	28	41
Other expenses	300	376	440	81	82	96
Total, expenses	958	1,286	1,504	435	545	651
Net profit	68	51	74	52	49	79

19.20   Assets and liabilities of small loans companies and money-lenders, 1974 and 1975 (thousand dollars)

Assets and liabilities	1974	1975
Assets		
Small loans balances	296,243	252,097
Balances, large loans and conditional sales agreements	1,162,713	1,160,500
Cash	16,364	15,671
Other	86,058	116,921
Total, assets	1,561,378	1,545,189
Liabilities		
Borrowed money	941,702	882,897
Unearned charges on large loans and conditional sales agreements	254,404	257,422
Reserves for losses	48,985	47,662
Paid-up capital	111,421	138,724
Surplus paid in by shareholders	21,356	21,354
Earned surplus	146,389	158,269
Other	37,121	38,861
Total, liabilities	1,561,378	1,545,189

19.21   Life insurance effected and in force in Canada by insurance companies under federal registration, 1880-1975 (million dollars)

Year	New insurance effected during year	Amounts in force Dec. 31			
		Canadian	British	Foreign	Total
1880	14	38	20	34	91
1900	68	267	39	124	431
1920	630	1,664	77	916	2,657
1940	590	4,609	146	2,221	6,975
1960	5,693	30,418	1,555	12,676	44,649
1965	8,967	47,900	3,071	18,685	69,656
1970	12,915	76,775	5,727	28,615	111,116
1972	17,566	96,293	6,944	33,168	136,405
1973	19,441	109,504	7,671	36,435	153,610
1974	25,488	128,178	8,785	40,157	177,120
1975	32,526	151,974	10,476	45,629	208,079

19.22   Summary of the number of life insurance policies and related amounts in force in Canada reported by federally registered companies, 1974 and 1975

Policies	Number of policies '000		Amounts in force $'000,000	
	1974	1975	1974	1975
New policies effected during year	782	1,009	25,488	32,526
Total policies in force Dec. 31	10,605	11,025	177,120	208,079
Policies ceased by death or maturity	132	127	654	715

19.23   Amounts of ordinary[1] and group life insurance policies effected and in force in Canada reported by federally registered companies, 1974 and 1975 (million dollars)

Policies	Canadian		British		Foreign	
	1974	1975	1974	1975	1974	1975
Effected during year						
Ordinary[1]	9,089	10,749	1,144	1,436	3,693	4,620
Group	8,591	11,970	478	657	2,492	3,094
In force Dec. 31						
Ordinary[1]	54,903	61,907	6,537	7,464	19,525	22,025
Group	73,275	90,066	2,248	3,013	20,632	23,604

[1]Includes industrial policies.

19.24   Life insurance premiums (direct written), by province, 1975 (million dollars)

Province or territory	Ordinary[1]	Group	Total
Newfoundland	15	8	23
Prince Edward Island	4	2	6
Nova Scotia	45	16	61
New Brunswick	31	12	43
Quebec	413	157	570
Ontario	572	229	801
Manitoba	55	22	77
Saskatchewan	42	17	59
Alberta	101	39	140
British Columbia	129	55	184
Yukon Territory and Northwest Territories	2	1	3
Miscellaneous	18	3	21
Total	1,427	561	1,988

[1]Includes industrial policies.

19.25   Major assets and liabilities of federally registered life insurance companies as at Dec. 31, 1974 and 1975 (million dollars)

Assets and liabilities	Canadian[1] 1974	Canadian[1] 1975	British[2] 1974	British[2] 1975	Foreign[2] 1974	Foreign[2] 1975
Assets						
Bonds	6,703	7,414	498	599	1,274	1,298
Stocks	1,693	1,820	279	280	7	7
Mortgages	7,685	8,162	476	517	1,414	1,561
Real estate	1,159	1,298	102	108	47	45
Policy loans	1,514	1,615	68	76	173	184
Other assets	824	920	108	126	150	165
Segregated	1,592	2,168	214	310	44	60
Total	21,170	23,397	1,745[3]	2,016[3]	3,109[3]	3,320[3]
Liabilities						
Actuarial reserves	15,287	16,580	1,359	1,510	2,489	2,635
Outstanding claims	224	271	11	12	47	53
Amounts on deposit	1,263	1,360	6	6	137	151
Other liabilities	1,527	1,719	58	56	165	173
Segregated	1,578	2,152	217	319	35	47
Total	19,879	22,082	1,651	1,903	2,873	3,059
Surplus or excess[4]	1,251	1,273	94	113	236	261
Capital stock	39	41	...	...	...	...

[1]Assets at book values, in and out of Canada (segregated funds at market values).
[2]Assets at market values, in Canada only.
[3]Includes assets under control of Chief Agent in Canada.
[4]Excess of assets over liabilities in Canada for British and foreign companies; for such companies, "capital stock" is not applicable in Canada.

19.26   Major items of income and expenditure of federally registered life insurance companies, 1975 (million dollars)

Income and expenditure	Canadian[1]	British[2]	Foreign[2]
Income			
Insurance premiums and annuity considerations	3,385	310	533
Investment income — regular funds	1,433	136	243
Net investment gain — segregated funds	261	36	8
Other items	82	12	35
Total income	5,161	494	819
Selected expenditure			
Claims incurred	1,604	110	276
Dividends to policyholders	353	42	91
Commissions and general expenses	814	64	137
Taxes, licences and fees	116	4	67

[1]World-wide business.
[2]Business in Canada only.

19.27   Property and casualty net premiums written and net claims incurred, by class of insurance and by incorporation of company, 1975 (million dollars)

Insurance class	Net premiums written Canadian	Net premiums written British	Net premiums written Foreign	Net premiums written Total	Net claims incurred
Property[1]	428	97	383	908	590
Automobile	853	153	442	1,448	1,013
Liability	95	19	60	174	104
Accident and sickness	521	12	298	831	619
Other casualty[2]	75	17	60	152	54
Marine	8	7	24	39	32
Total	1,980	305	1,267	3,552	2,412

[1]Includes fire, personal property, real property, windstorm, earthquake, inland transportation, livestock, theft, forgery, plate glass.
[2]Includes hail, fidelity, surety, boiler and machinery, aircraft, credit, title, mortgage.

19.28   Property and casualty direct premiums written and claims incurred, by province and by category of company, 1974 and 1975 (million dollars)

Province or territory	Premiums written				Claims incurred
	Companies federally registered	Companies provincially licensed	Lloyd's	Total	
1974					
Newfoundland	45	6	6	57	41
Prince Edward Island	13	1	¹	14	9
Nova Scotia	98	¹	1	99	74
New Brunswick	93	1	1	95	69
Quebec	836	266	56	1,158	854
Ontario	1,240	161	25	1,426	1,023
Manitoba	68	56	3	127	102
Saskatchewan	43	33	1	77	52
Alberta	238	34	12	284	207
British Columbia	212	227	14	453	393
Yukon Territory and Northwest Territories	12	¹	1	13	9
Total	2,898	785	120	3,803	2,833
1975					
Newfoundland	57	8	11	76	47
Prince Edward Island	16	1	¹	17	9
Nova Scotia	130	¹	2	132	85
New Brunswick	120	2	2	124	80
Quebec	1,006	298	87	1,391	972
Ontario	1,516	209	34	1,759	1,177
Manitoba	80	85	3	168	119
Saskatchewan	51	43	2	96	80
Alberta	319	44	15	378	226
British Columbia	248	201	16	465	459
Yukon Territory and Northwest Territories	15	¹	1	16	7
Total	3,558	891	173	4,622	3,261

¹Less than $500,000.

19.29   Major assets and liabilities of federally registered property and casualty insurance companies, 1974 and 1975 (million dollars)

Assets and liabilities	Canadian¹		British²		Foreign²	
	1974	1975	1974	1975	1974	1975
Assets						
Bonds	1,266	1,598	310	314	1,245	1,494
Stocks	489	546	90	90	70	75
Amounts due from agents and premiums receivable	213	287	46	35	120	133
Other	582	760	64	73	252	292
Total	2,550	3,191	510	512	1,687	1,994
Liabilities						
Unearned premiums	574	735	131	105	448	515
Unpaid claims	1,061	1,318	203	166	677	772
Other	355	440	23	21	155	191
Total	1,990	2,493	357	292	1,280	1,478
Surplus or excess³	360	285	153	220	407	516
Capital stock and amounts transferred	200	413	...	...	...	...

¹Business in and out of Canada, investments on book value basis. Deduction, if any, for excess of market over book value in "Other" assets.
²Business in Canada only, investments on market value basis.
³Excess of assets over liabilities in Canada for British and foreign companies; for such companies, "capital stock" is not applicable in Canada.

19.30   Property and casualty insurance, underwriting results in Canada, 1975 with totals for 1971-75 (million dollars)

Registered companies	Underwriting income earned	Claims[1] incurred	Expenses incurred	Dividends to policyholders	Underwriting gain
Canadian[2]					
Property and casualty	1,349.1	905.9	482.0	2.0	-41.0
A and S branches[3]	455.2	376.3	75.1	24.1	-20.3
British	323.8	234.0	111.4	[4]	-21.6
Foreign					
Property and casualty	934.1	691.5	305.1	2.6	-65.1
A and S branches[3]	239.8	177.8	55.8	18.5	-12.3
Total, 1975	3,302.0	2,385.5	1,029.4	47.4	-160.3
1974	2,743.2	2,118.5	874.2	40.2	-289.7
1973	2,460.1	1,804.2	772.8	31.8	-148.7
1972	2,166.1	1,509.5	695.0	23.4	-61.8
1971	1,953.6	1,326.7	645.6	15.2	-33.9

[1]Includes adjustment expenses.
[2]Excludes transactions out of Canada.
[3]Accident and sickness branches of life insurance companies.
[4]Less than $500,000.

19.31   Fire losses[1], by type of property and cause of fire, 1974 and 1975

Type of property and reported cause of fire	1974		1975	
	Fires reported	Property loss $'000	Fires reported	Property loss $'000
Type of property				
Residential	43,904	139,118	39,750	166,795
Mercantile	4,473	72,736	4,625	83,068
Farm	5,420	28,692	5,127	31,406
Manufacturing	1,694	66,816	2,016	75,303
Institutional and assembly	2,791	43,184	2,458	42,549
Miscellaneous	15,482	78,233	15,905	64,694
Total	73,764	428,779	69,881	463,815
Reported cause				
Smokers' carelessness	13,312	26,104	11,013	29,574
Stoves, furnaces, boilers and smoke pipes	5,625	27,087	5,435	36,521
Electrical wiring and appliances	15,590	78,614	11,079	76,055
Matches	2,788	9,512	2,388	9,173
Defective and overheated chimneys and flues	671	2,445	581	2,238
Hot ashes, coals and open fires	4,702	41,558	1,887	10,566
Petroleum and its products	2,805	18,243	2,865	12,463
Lights, other than electric	307	577	320	1,042
Lightning	3,326	4,548	3,007	4,454
Sparks on roofs	73	193	62	513
Exposure fires	1,635	13,415	1,713	14,751
Spontaneous ignition	579	4,975	587	9,316
Incendiarism	5,648	46,813	4,964	58,507
Miscellaneous known causes (explosions, fireworks, friction, hot grease or metal, steam or hot water pipes, etc.)	9,617	50,856	14,096	52,943
Unknown	7,086	103,838	9,884	145,699

[1]Excludes forest fires.

19.32   Fire losses[1], by province, 1972-75

Province or territory	Property loss		1974			1975		
	1972 $'000	1973 $'000	Fires reported	Property loss $'000	Loss per capita $	Fires reported	Property loss $'000	Loss per capita $
Newfoundland	4,507	7,312	796	12,774	23.57	685	15,835	28.42
Prince Edward Island	1,273	1,555	368	1,440	12.31	448	2,356	19.64
Nova Scotia	7,118	12,888	1,978	14,331	17.63	2,203	14,196	17.06
New Brunswick	4,875	9,592	1,129	15,388	23.24	1,032	19,620	28.51
Quebec	78,859	95,668	20,441	128,105	20.88	17,257	130,175	20.85
Ontario	79,237	114,772	24,367	128,899	15.93	23,913	131,552	15.79
Manitoba	14,649	15,147	5,726	21,903	21.66	5,649	22,177	21.57
Saskatchewan	6,569	6,711	2,485	7,934	8.75	2,452	21,729	23.23
Alberta	18,087	25,629	8,464	30,324	17.69	7,895	32,864	18.00
British Columbia	37,389	45,693	7,526	62,842	26.24	7,996	69,392	27.85
Yukon Territory and Northwest Territories	1,703	3,252	484	4,839	84.89	351	3,917	66.40
Canada	254,267	338,219	73,764	428,779	19.10	69,881	463,814	20.07

[1]Excludes forest fires.

19.33 Cheques cashed at 50 clearing centres, by province or region, 1974-76 (million dollars)

Clearing centre	1974	1975	1976
ATLANTIC PROVINCES	39,182	48,005	57,869
Charlottetown	1,469	1,973	2,100
Fredericton	3,305	4,650	5,788
Glace Bay	177	203	215
Halifax	14,054	15,980	20,437
Moncton	3,654	5,760	5,286
Saint John	5,212	6,296	6,524
St. John's	9,871	11,451	15,787
Sydney	1,441	1,692	1,733
QUEBEC	442,229	549,834	651,094
Chicoutimi	1,941	2,221	2,490
Drummondville	1,056	1,221	1,388
Granby	1,446	1,626	1,706
Montreal	374,599	457,879	548,487
Quebec	55,930	78,895	87,697
Saint-Hyacinthe	1,553	1,867	2,382
Shawinigan Falls	481	529	588
Sherbrooke	2,593	2,964	3,455
Trois-Rivières	1,960	1,898	2,058
Valleyfield	670	734	843
ONTARIO	868,741	1,113,864	1,248,446
Brantford	3,171	3,547	4,364
Chatham	4,741	5,944	7,541
Cornwall	1,628	1,522	1,791
Guelph	2,793	2,748	3,203
Hamilton	27,389	32,454	34,499
Kingston	2,667	3,289	3,590
Kitchener	7,876	9,083	9,893
London	21,301	24,940	27,302
Niagara Falls	1,707	1,597	2,163
Oshawa	14,689	17,164	19,007
Ottawa	27,971	32,676	39,130
Peterborough	2,073	2,363	2,783
St. Catharines	3,778	4,445	8,842
Sarnia	2,623	3,227	4,169
Sault Ste Marie	5,008	7,214	13,589
Sudbury	2,644	3,205	3,399
Thunder Bay	3,436	3,966	4,742
Timmins	930	1,229	1,447
Toronto	719,526	938,561	1,040,414
Windsor	12,791	14,691	16,578
PRAIRIE PROVINCES	215,180	262,828	317,917
Brandon	993	1,166	1,356
Calgary	62,325	77,127	102,380
Edmonton	43,930	59,242	71,066
Lethbridge	2,367	2,732	3,155
Medicine Hat	891	1,034	1,413
Moose Jaw	738	888	1,053
Prince Albert	835	954	1,146
Regina	17,748	21,491	25,442
Saskatoon	4,939	5,776	7,123
Winnipeg	80,412	92,419	103,784
BRITISH COLUMBIA	133,449	163,996	194,272
Vancouver[1]	113,259	133,137	161,426
Victoria	20,190	30,858	32,846
Total	1,698,780	2,138,527	2,469,599

[1]Includes New Westminster.

19.34 Assets, liabilities and shareholders' equity of trust companies (company and guaranteed funds), 1973-75 (million dollars)

Item	1973	1974	1975
Assets			
Demand deposits, incl. cash and foreign currency	87	155	163
Investments			
Investments in Canadian securities			
Federal	426	381	362
Provincial	329	302	358
Municipal	98	122	104
Sales finance and commercial paper	256	318	250
Term deposits with chartered banks	665	658	948
Term deposits with trust and mortgage companies	52	46	36
Corporation bonds and debentures	491	436	467
Collateral loans	222r	266	267
Mortgages			
Loans under NHA	1,468	1,582	1,717
Conventional mortgage loans	5,725r	7,264	8,824
Investments in Canadian preferred and common shares	170	227	280
Investments in foreign securities	27	24	32
Investments in subsidiary and affiliated companies	77	82	100
Interest, rents and other receivables	129	166	180
Real estate and equipment	80	106	117
Other assets	207r	307	354
Total, assets	10,509	12,442	14,559
Liabilities			
Demand and savings deposits			
Chequing	554	492	603
Non-chequing	1,494	1,712	2,211
Term deposits			
Under 1 year	1,419r	1,695	1,351
1 to 5 years	6,131r	7,421	9,037
Over 5 years	27	63	105
Bank loans	14	23	21
Short-term loans and notes payable	..	..	..
Debts owing parent and affiliated companies	22	18	19
Interest, dividends, taxes and other payables	268	365	455
Shareholders' equity			
Capital paid up	227	308	366
Investment reserves	37	35	38
Reserve fund	227	212	226
Retained earnings	89	98	127
Total, liabilities and shareholders' equity	10,509	12,442	14,559

19.35   Assets, liabilities and shareholders' equity of mortgage companies, 1973-75 (million dollars)

Item	1973	1974	1975	Item	1973	1974	1975
Assets				Liabilities			
Demand deposits, incl. cash and				Demand and savings deposits			
foreign currency	29	34	29	Chequing	179	166	191
Investments				Non-chequing	467	494	581
Investments in Canadian securities							
Federal	109	87	99	Term deposits			
Provincial	65	56	57	Under 1 year	153	188	156
Municipal	5	4	3	1 to 5 years	2,804	3,453	4,284
Sales finance and commercial paper	21	29	40	Over 5 years	496	492	535
Term deposits with chartered banks	170	212	226	Bank loans	128	65	83
Term deposits with trust and							
mortgage companies	6	3	2	Short-term loans and notes payable	260	360	383
Corporation bonds and debentures	86	68	65				
Collateral loans	41ʳ	35	42	Debts owing parent and			
				affiliated companies	211	135	215
Mortgages				Interest, dividends, taxes, and			
Loans under NHA	673	688	767	other payables	661	803	889
Conventional mortgage loans	4,080ʳ	4,821	5,793				
Investments in Canadian preferred							
and common shares	96	112	141	Shareholders' equity			
Investments in foreign securities	3	5	6	Capital paid up	272	319	387
Investments in subsidiary and				Investment reserves	26	21	26
affiliated companies	291	346	416	Reserve fund	168	113	129
Interest, rents and other receivables	61	81	88	Retained earnings	88	134	158
Real estate and equipment	56	62	60				
Other assets	121ʳ	100	183	Total liabilities and			
Total, assets	5,913	6,743	8,017	shareholders' equity	5,913	6,743	8,017

Sources
19.1 - 19.5, 19.8 - 19.12 Banking and Financial Analysis Department, Bank of Canada.
19.6 - 19.7 Royal Canadian Mint.
19.13 - 19.15 The Canadian Bankers' Association.
19.16 - 19.19, 19.33 - 19.35 Business Finance Division, Business Statistics Field, Statistics Canada.
19.20 - 19.30 Special Services Division, Department of Insurance.
19.31 - 19.32 Dominion Fire Commissioner, Department of Public Works.

Government finance   Chapter 20

Tables

Government finance   Chapter 20

Consolidated finance statistics   20.1

Data on each level of government constitute the basis of the intergovernment
consolidation which is presented for the years 1969-73 in Table 20.1. The
consolidation process integrates the separate levels of government to reveal the
fiscal framework of the public sector viewed as an economic unit. The
consolidated figures reflect the impact of government transactions on the rest of
the economy; they indicate the involvement of government in providing public
goods and services as well as showing the financial requirements necessary to
support such spending. The numerous intergovernmental transactions either as
revenue or as expenditure are eliminated in order to obtain a meaningful measure
of the collective impact of all governments upon the general public. Thus multiple
accounting for a given transaction is avoided by eliminating from the combined
total of either gross general revenue or gross general expenditure all general and
specific intergovernment transfer payments, as well as all sales and purchases of
goods and services which do not constitute an addition to collective government
financial activities. The new classification set out in *The Canadian system of
government financial management statistics* (Statistics Canada Catalogue No.
68-506) which had been applied for the first time to 1970 data has been extended
retrospectively. Consequently, data presented in Table 20.1 are comparable from
year to year.

Federal government finance   20.2

General accounts   20.2.1

Tables 20.2 - 20.5 and 20.20 present financial statistics of the federal government
prepared in accordance with the revised concepts as published in *The Canadian
system of government financial management statistics*. Financial statistics in Tables
20.7 and 20.8 are extracted directly from the *Public Accounts of Canada*.

Tables 20.2 and 20.3 give details of gross general revenue and expenditure
for the years ended March 31, 1973 to 1975. Revenue increased from $21,426
million to $32,192 million while expenditures rose from $20,912 million to
$30,891 million.

Transfers from the federal government to provincial governments, territories and local governments for the years ended March 31, 1974 and 1975 are
shown in Table 20.20. Comparable figures for the previous year are available in
the 1975 edition of the *Canada Year Book* pp 791-793.

Table 20.4 provides details of the assets and liabilities of the federal
government as at March 31, 1973 to 1975. Table 20.5 analyzes gross bonded debt
according to average interest rate, average term of issue and place of payment as
at March 31, 1973 to 1975.

In addition to direct gross bonded debt, the Government of Canada has
assumed certain contingent liabilities. The major categories of this indirect or
contingent debt are the guarantee of insured loans under the National Housing
Act and the guaranteed bonds and debentures of the Canadian National Railways.
The remainder consists chiefly of guarantees of loans made by chartered banks to
the Canadian Wheat Board, to farmers and to university students and of
guarantees under the Export Development Act. Table 20.6 provides details of the
guaranteed debt of the Government of Canada as at March 31, 1974 and 1975.

Table 20.7 summarizes the public debt position during the period 1971-75 as
to interest and amount outstanding. Details of unmatured debt and treasury bills
outstanding and information on new security issues of the federal government

may be found in the *Public Accounts of Canada.* They are summarized by standard classification in Statistics Canada publication *Federal government finance* (Catalogue No. 68-211).

20.2.2   Individual and corporation taxes

Statistics of income tax collections are gathered at the time the payments are made and are therefore up to date. Over 85% of individual taxpayers are wage- or salary-earners who have almost the whole of their tax liability deducted at the source by their employers. All other taxpayers are required to pay most of their estimated tax during the taxation year. Thus, the greater part of the tax is collected during the same year in which the related income is earned and only a limited residue remains to be collected when the returns are filed. The collections for a given fiscal year include employer remittances of tax deductions, Canada Pension Plan contributions, unemployment insurance premiums and instalments, embracing portions of two or more taxation years, and year-end payments; they cannot therefore be closely related to the statistics for a given taxation year. As little information about a taxpayer is received when the payment is made and as a single cheque from one employer may frequently cover the tax payment of hundreds of employees, the payments cannot be statistically related to taxpayers by occupation or income. Descriptive classifications of taxpayers are available only from tax returns, but collection statistics, if interpreted with the current tax structure and the above factors in mind, indicate the trend of income in advance of the final compilation of statistics. The statistics given in Table 20.8 pertain to revenue collections by the Department of National Revenue, Taxation. The collections are for fiscal years ended March 31.

Individual income tax statistics collected by the Department of National Revenue, Taxation are presented in Tables 20.9 - 20.11 on a calendar-year basis and are compiled from a sample of all returns received. Taxpayers and amounts of income and tax are shown for selected cities and by occupational class and income classes.

Statistics on the taxation of corporate income showing a reconciliation of income taxes to taxable income and book profits are published on an industry basis by Statistics Canada. Data for 1972 and 1973 are summarized for nine industrial divisions in Table 20.13. Income data are also available on a provincial basis, as shown in Table 20.12 for years 1969 to 1973.

20.2.3   Excise taxes

Excise taxes collected by Revenue Canada, Customs and Excise, are given for the years ended March 31, 1973 to 1975 in Table 20.14.

Gross excise duties collected for the year ended March 31, 1975 were: spirits $311.9 million; beer or malt liquor $178.3 million; tobacco, cigarettes and cigars $258.2 million; licences $32,514; for a total of $748.4 million. A drawback of 99% of the duty may be granted when domestic spirits, testing not less than 50% over proof, are delivered in limited quantities for medicinal or research purposes to universities, scientific or research laboratories, public hospitals or health institutions in receipt of federal and provincial government aid.

20.3   Federal-provincial fiscal relations

Fiscal relations between the federal, provincial and territorial governments take various forms and are governed either by an act of Parliament or by formal agreement. Through the equalization program the federal government enables the provinces to provide an adequate level of public services; under Tax Collection Agreements it acts as a tax collecting agent for some provinces; and under other arrangements the federal government shares in the financing of certain programs. These three types of arrangement, general purpose transfer payments, tax collection agreements and specific purpose transfer payments, are covered in this section.

General purpose transfer payments   20.3.1

General purpose transfers refer to payments from one level of government to another level which the transferee is not required to use for a specific purpose. They were formerly identified as "unconditional" transfers. The various programs under which they are paid, as well as their amounts for the fiscal years ended March 31, 1974 and 1975, are indicated in Table 20.20.

Statutory subsidies, established by the British North America Act, 1867, consist of contributions by the federal government toward the support of provincial governments. They include an allowance per head of population, allowances for interest on debt and other special amounts as agreed upon under the terms of the union and subsequently. These subsidies amounted to $33.8 million in the fiscal year ended on March 31, 1975. The share of federal estate taxes remitted to the provinces in fiscal 1974-75 ($3.6 million) is in respect of deaths which occurred prior to January 1, 1972.

Under the Public Utilities Income Tax Transfer Act, the federal government remits to the provinces 95% of the tax it collects from non-government-owned public utility companies that generate or distribute to the public electrical energy, gas and steam. The intent of this policy is to give to provinces tax revenue from companies engaged in the exploitation of provincial natural resources.

The most important payments included in general purpose transfers are made under the equalization program. This program, established in 1967 and reviewed every five years, was based on the philosophy that all Canadian citizens are entitled to a standard of public services that is fairly comparable among the various regions. In a country as vast as Canada, natural resources and economic wealth are unevenly distributed, some provinces having above-national-average wealth while others are well below that average. Through the equalization system the federal government makes available, from general revenue it collects in all provinces, part of the nation's wealth to provinces with income lower than national average capacity to raise revenues, making it possible for these provinces to provide reasonable standards of services without recourse to unduly high levels of taxation.

According to the formula set out in the Federal-Provincial Fiscal Arrangements Act, 1972 and amendments, provincial revenue subject to equalization is divided into 22 revenue sources, for each of which a revenue base is defined. The act was amended in November 1973 to include revenues from school taxes in provincial revenues subject to equalization. To determine the amount of equalization to which a provincial government is entitled, its population as a proportion of the all-provinces' population and its revenue base as a proportion of the all-provinces' revenue base for each of the 22 revenue sources are calculated. Where the former proportion is higher than the latter for any of the revenue sources, the province has a fiscal capacity deficiency for that revenue source; if the magnitude of these proportions is reversed, the province has a fiscal capacity excess. The total revenue of all provinces for each revenue source is multiplied by each province's fiscal deficiency or fiscal excess related to the appropriate revenue source and, for any province, the amount of equalization payable is the sum total of the "deficiency" products less the sum total of the "excess" products.

Total equalization payments to the seven provinces having an overall fiscal capacity deficiency have increased from $549.6 million in fiscal year 1967-68 to $2,287.0 million in the year ended March 31, 1975.

Tax collection agreements   20.3.2

Tax Collection Agreements, replacing the tax-sharing system in operation since 1951, were introduced under the Federal-Provincial Arrangements Act, 1962. Under these agreements, the federal government undertook to collect provincial personal and corporation income taxes on behalf of the provinces. All provinces, except Quebec, signed the agreements in respect of personal income tax, and all provinces except Quebec and Ontario entered into agreements covering the collection of corporation income tax.

An abatement system, introduced in 1962 and amended in 1967, facilitated the establishment by the provinces of their own tax rates. The 1967 act was amended in 1972 in order to adjust the terms of the agreements to the new federal Income Tax Act introduced in 1972 following the tax reform. In the 1972 amendment the abatement system was abandoned as was the reference to federal "basic tax". Instead, the federal rates of personal income tax were adjusted downward for the full amount of the former provincial abatement. This downward adjustment corresponded to 30.5% of "basic federal tax" and is equivalent to the former 28% abatement.

In addition, Part IV of the Federal-Provincial Fiscal Arrangements Act, 1972, provided a guarantee that for five years the provinces would not suffer a loss of income tax revenue as a result of adopting income tax acts modelled on the new federal act, meant to implement the 1971 tax reform, provided that their rates are equivalent to those levied under the previous act. Revenue is guaranteed at a yield level equal to that obtained had the 1971 tax systems still been in effect.

20.3.3   Specific purpose transfer payments

This type of transfer payment is generally referred to as a conditional grant, that is, a grant which is to be used for a specific purpose by the receiving government. Most of these grants are made under agreements governing joint federal-provincial programs. Total federal payments to provinces and municipalities of this nature have increased from $1,816.7 million in 1969-70 to $4,014.8 million in 1974-75, as shown in Table 20.20.

These programs take three forms: the federal government contributes financial assistance to a program administered by a province; the federal and provincial governments each assume the sole responsibility for the construction, administration and financing of separate aspects of a joint project; or the province contributes financially to a joint program administered by the federal government.

The first category of joint programs is by far the most common. The federal government agrees to make money available to a province on certain conditions such as specification of the field, service or project to which the money must be applied. In addition to administering the programs, the provinces may be required to make financial contributions or to provide certain facilities and to meet specified standards of operation. Various programs in the field of social policy are of this kind. For example, the federal government undertakes to contribute a specified share of the costs incurred by the provinces in respect of public hospital insurance programs, as described in Chapter 5.

Although the hospital insurance program, with its specifications of eligible hospitals, sharable costs and the amount of the federal contribution, is characteristic of many conditional grant programs, there are others in which the conditions are nominal. For example, under the Canada Assistance Plan the federal government undertakes to share one half the cost of welfare, the scale and conditions of the assistance being determined by the provinces.

Joint programs in the second category — those in which the federal and provincial governments accept sole responsibility for portions of a total project — are few, and generally of a public works nature such as the irrigation projects carried out jointly by the Prairie Farm Rehabilitation Administration and the province of Alberta on the St. Mary's and Bow rivers.

Joint programs in the third category are also few in number. The South Saskatchewan River dam was an example. Canada undertook to pay the costs of the dam in the first instance, with Saskatchewan subsequently reimbursing Canada for one quarter of the federal expenditures (up to a maximum of $25 million) on the dam and reservoir. By March 31, 1968, the full amount had been recovered from Saskatchewan.

Federal transfers to provincial, territorial and local governments for the fiscal year ended March 31, 1975 totalled $6.7 billion, compared with $5.3 billion for the previous year (Table 20.20). Table 20.21 summarizes federal and provincial shared-cost programs as at March 31, 1975, showing the provinces participating, provincial percentage share and federal contributions.

In 1965 provinces were given the option to assume full financial and administrative responsibility for certain programs in return for fiscal compensation, and in April 1965 the federal government enacted the Established Programs (Interim Arrangements) Act. The nature and number of programs were itemized in the schedules to the act. Schedule I listed the major and continuing conditional grant programs and Schedule II listed smaller and more transient ones. The Schedule I programs were: hospital insurance, old age assistance, blind persons allowances, disabled persons allowances, and the welfare portion of unemployment assistance; the technical and vocational training programs for youths who were not yet members of the labour force; and the health grant program, except those elements that involved research and demonstration. The Schedule II programs were: agricultural lime assistance; forestry programs; hospital construction grants; campgrounds and picnic areas; and the roads-to-resources program. The act was subsequently amended to include the Canada Assistance Plan.

A province wishing to avail itself of a Schedule I program was required to enter into a supplemental agreement in which it undertook to assume full responsibility for administration and financing. The federal government undertook to abate, by a specified percentage, the individual income tax on the income of residents of the province, pay associated equalization and make an operating cost adjustment. Because of their smaller size and lack of continuity, the compensation associated with Schedule II programs did not provide for federal tax abatement or associated equalization payments. Compensation of these programs was to be paid directly to the province by the federal Minister of Finance.

The Established Programs (Interim Arrangements) Act was designed to provide for an interim period during which a province might assume greater administrative and financial responsibility for the programs listed and more permanent arrangements governing joint programs might be devised. The length of the interim period was set out in the act for each program, and tax abatement for Schedule I programs varied from 1% for the health grant program to 14% for hospital insurance. Amendments to the act in 1972 extended the length of the interim period for the special welfare and hospital insurance programs to March 31, 1977 and December 31, 1977, respectively. The interim period for the health grants program was not extended beyond March 31, 1972 as this program was being phased out. Only the province of Quebec availed itself of the offer made in 1965. For 1976-77, the abatement is 16 points for hospital insurance and five points for the special welfare program.

Provincial government finance   20.4

Because of variation from province to province in administrative structure and, to a lesser extent, in accounting and reporting practices, adjustments are made to financial data reported in public accounts to produce statistics which will be comparable between different provinces and with those for the other levels of government. In 1972 the concepts and classifications of the national system of government financial statistics were redefined by Statistics Canada (see *The Canadian system of government financial management statistics,* Catalogue No. 68-506). Financial statistics for the years 1971 onward are compiled in accordance with these revisions and are not comparable with data for prior years published in earlier editions of the *Canada Year Book.*

Gross general revenue and expenditure for the year ended March 31, 1974 are given in Table 20.22, liabilities in Table 20.15, and liabilities of other governments and entities guaranteed by provincial and territorial governments in Table 20.16. More information on outstanding provincial bonds and debentures is contained in Table 20.17.

20.5   Local government finance

Local government taxation. In 1973, the latest year for which complete data are available, local government revenues from taxation rose by 1.7% to $4,245 million, and the rate of collections stood at 99.99%. Taxes receivable expressed as a proportion of taxation revenue declined to 10.4% compared to 11.2% in 1972. Rates of collection declined slightly in 1973 compared with 1972 in Newfoundland, Nova Scotia, Quebec and the territories, but improved in the other provinces. Lower percentages of taxes receivable relative to taxation revenue were recorded in all provinces except Quebec and the territories.

Local government revenue, expenditure and debt. General revenue of local government in 1973 increased by 9.6% to $10,500 million over 1972 while general expenditure at $11,248 million also showed an increase of 9.6%. Debenture and other long-term debt amounted to $10,476 million as at December 31, 1973 compared with $9,884 million at December 31, 1972. Details are given in Tables 20.23 - 20.25.

20.6   Tax rates

Taxes are imposed in Canada by the three levels of government. The Government of Canada has the right to raise money "by any mode or system of taxation" while the provincial legislatures are restricted to direct taxation within the province. Municipalities derive their incorporation with its associated powers, fiscal and otherwise, provincially and are thus also limited to direct taxation.

A direct tax is generally recognized as one "which is demanded from the very person who it is intended or desired should pay it". This concept has limited the provincial governments to the imposition of income tax, retail sales tax, succession duties and an assortment of other direct levies. In turn, municipalities acting under provincial legislation tax real estate, water consumption and places of business. The federal government levies taxes on income, excise taxes, excise and customs duties, and a sales tax.

Since 1941 a series of federal-provincial tax agreements has been concluded to promote the orderly imposition of direct taxes. The duration of each agreement was normally five years. Under earlier agreements, the participating provinces undertook — in return for compensation — not to use, or permit their municipalities to use, certain of the direct taxes. These were replaced by arrangements under which the federal personal and corporation income tax otherwise payable in all provinces and the estate tax otherwise payable in three provinces were abated by certain percentages to make room for provincial levies.

Federal tax reform amendments which became effective for the most part from 1972, included a new personal income tax rate structure which was not designed to be abated in the previous way. At the same time the federal estate tax was terminated. As a result, the arrangement under which federal taxes are abated has general application only for the corporation income tax. All provinces impose taxes on the income of individuals and corporations and four of the 10 provinces impose taxes on property passing at death. Alberta, Saskatchewan, New Brunswick, Nova Scotia, Prince Edward Island and Newfoundland do not now impose succession duties. The federal government has tax collection agreements under which it collects provincial personal income taxes for all provinces except Quebec and provincial corporation income taxes for all provinces except Ontario and Quebec. The provinces which impose succession duties also collect them.

20.6.1   Federal taxes

Individual income tax. The federal government has adopted a tax system of self-assessment in which taxpayers volunteer the facts about their incomes and calculate the taxes they must pay. Every individual who is resident in Canada is liable for the payment of income tax on all his income. A non-resident is liable for

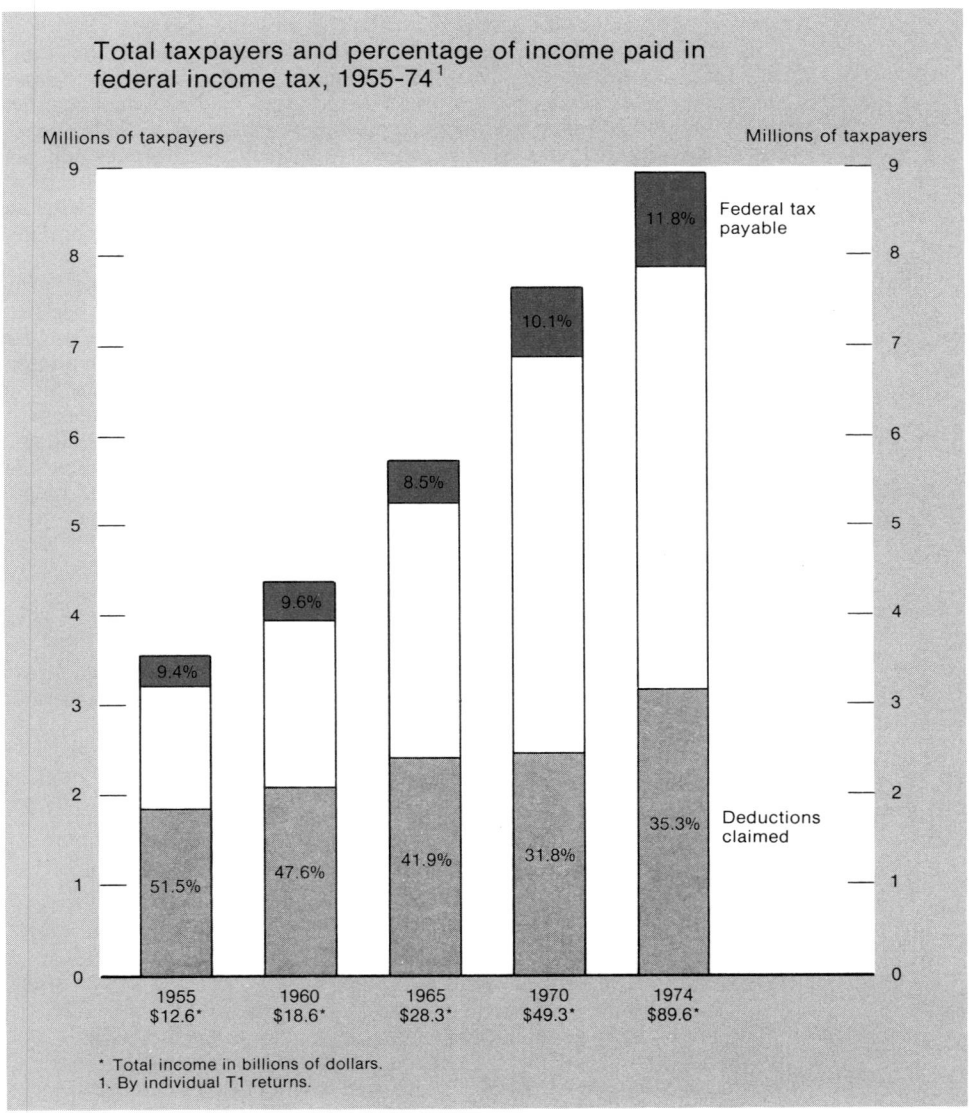

Total taxpayers and percentage of income paid in
federal income tax, 1955-74 [1]

Millions of taxpayers

Federal tax
payable

Deductions
claimed

	1955	1960	1965	1970	1974
	$12.6*	$18.6*	$28.3*	$49.3*	$89.6*

* Total income in billions of dollars.
1. By individual T1 returns.

tax only on income from sources in Canada. "Residence" is the place where a person resides or where he maintains a dwelling ready at all times for his use. There are also statutory extensions of the meaning of "resident" to include a person who has sojourned in Canada for an aggregate period of 183 days in a taxation year, a person who was during the year a member of the Armed Forces of Canada, an officer or servant of Canada or of any one of its provinces, or the spouse or dependent child of any such person. The extended meaning of resident also includes employees who go from Canada to work under certain international development assistance programs.

Canadian tax law uses the concepts "income" and "taxable income". Income means income from all sources inside or outside Canada and includes income for the year from businesses, property, offices and employments. Since January 1, 1972, it has also included one half of any capital gains.

In computing income, an individual must include benefits from employment, fees, commissions, dividends, annuities, pension benefits, interest, alimony and maintenance payments. Also included are unemployment insurance benefits, family allowance payments, scholarships in excess of $500, benefits under a disability insurance plan to which his employer contributes and other miscellaneous items of income. A number of items are expressly excluded from income, including certain war service disability pensions, social assistance payments, compensation in respect of an injury or death under a provincial Workmen's Compensation Act and family income security payments.

Certain amounts are deductible in computing income. These include contributions to a registered employees pension plan, premiums to a registered retirement savings plan, premiums under the unemployment insurance program, alimony payments and union dues. A taxpayer 18 years of age or over who does not own a house may deduct contributions up to $1,000 a year to a lifetime maximum of $10,000 to a registered home ownership savings plan. The proceeds of such plans will be taxable when they are paid to the taxpayer unless they are applied by him to the purchase of a home. An employee may deduct 3% of salary or wages (up to a maximum of $250 a year) to cover expenses of earning his income. No receipts or details of actual expenditures are necessary to claim this deduction. Expenses of meals and lodging while away from home are deductible by employees who have to travel as they perform their work, such as employees who work on trains or who drive trucks. When a mother has her children cared for in order that she may work, she may deduct this expense subject to certain limitations. Expenses of moving to a new work location are deductible from income earned in the new location. Students attending universities, colleges or certain other certified educational institutions in Canada may deduct their tuition fees.

An individual carrying on a business may deduct business expenses. These include wages, rents, depreciation (called capital cost allowances), municipal taxes, interest on borrowed money, reserves for doubtful debts, contributions to pension plans or profit-sharing plans for his employees, and bad debts.

Half of capital gains is included in income. Taxable capital gains are determined by deducting capital losses from capital gains and dividing by two. In the event that losses exceed capital gains, $2,000 of allowable capital losses may be deducted from other income. Capital gains or losses relate to disposition of property. Other gains or losses (e.g. resulting from a lottery or gambling) are not included. The sale of personal property at a price not exceeding $1,000 and the sale of a home do not give rise to a capital gain or loss.

The amount of the guaranteed income supplement, which is a payment made to individuals who have little or no income in addition to their old age pension, is also deductible. Individuals who have incurred business losses in other years may deduct these in computing taxable income. Amendments to the Income Tax Act have introduced additional deductions. For the 1975 and subsequent taxation years, a taxpayer has been able to deduct up to $1,000 of a combination of interest and dividend income in a year. In addition, a taxpayer who is 65 or over is able to deduct up to $1,000 of his pension income including amounts he receives from pension plans and from annuities under registered retirement savings plans and deferred profit sharing plans. A taxpayer under 65 may deduct up to $1,000 of "qualified pension income". This includes amounts received from a pension plan or as a consequence of the death of a spouse. The pension income deduction is transferable between spouses to the extent that the spouse of a taxpayer cannot use the deduction.

Having computed income, an individual calculates taxable income by subtracting certain exemptions and deductions. Before 1974 the levels of exemptions and deductions were fixed from time to time by Parliament. The introduction in the 1974 taxation year of a mechanism for indexing personal income tax results in automatic adjustments each year to reflect the inflation rate in the levels of exemptions and deductions. The adjusted personal exemptions and deductions for each year are based on such factors as married or single status, dependent children, other dependents, charitable donations, medical expenses, income of a spouse and/or children, age (if 65 or over) and certain disabilities. Details are provided in the annual Tax Guide which is sent to each taxpayer; copies are also available in post offices and district taxation offices.

The deadline for individual income tax is April 30 for income of the previous calendar year. Most of the income tax returns are received in March and April, and during the first week of May. Until 1975, all individual income tax returns were mailed to the Taxation Data Centre in Ottawa, where initial processing took place. With the official opening on January 20, 1976 of the Data Centre, Prairie region, residents of Manitoba, Saskatchewan, Alberta and most of the Northwest Territories sent their completed tax forms to Winnipeg for initial processing. This involved approximately 2 million returns or 16% of the total for Canada.

The Winnipeg centre is the first in a series of regional centres being established as part of the decentralization of taxation data processing facilities. The decentralization plans are the result of mounting space and staff demands on the Taxation Data Centre in Ottawa. In 1976, there were close to 12 million taxpayers in Canada and estimates show this number will increase to almost 15 million by 1980 and to 18 million by 1985.

Two provisions enacted in 1971 provided for averaging income over a period of years where income for a year is unusually high. The first is an averaging calculation that is made by Revenue Canada if an individual's income for the year is 20% more than the average of his incomes for the preceding four years and 10% more than his income for the preceding year. This calculation, which is made without application by the taxpayer, reduces the effects of the progressive schedule of rates upon an unusual increase in income in the year. The calculation was first made for 1973, using 1972 as a base. It is possible to use four preceding years in the base commencing in 1976. The second averaging device, which first became effective for 1972, is by way of purchase of a special type of annuity contract called an income-averaging annuity. The cost of this annuity is deductible from income in the year it is purchased and the annuity payments are included in income when received.

The amount of tax is determined by applying a progressive schedule of rates to taxable income. The tax bracket limits are adjusted yearly by means of the indexing mechanism. Thus taxpayers are prevented from being pushed into higher marginal tax brackets in the absence of real growth in their income. The schedule of rates for the 1976 taxation year started at 6% on the first $654 of taxable income (first unit) and increased to 47% on taxable income in excess of $78,420.

After all calculations are made, there is deducted from the tax otherwise payable an amount, called the federal tax cut. In 1976, this was equal to the greater of $200 or 8% of tax payable to a maximum of $500. In addition, a surtax of 10% of federal tax otherwise payable in excess of $8,000 was applicable for the 1976 taxation year. This surtax applied to those with taxable income in excess of $30,000.

Individuals who reside in the Yukon Territory or the Northwest Territories or who reside outside Canada but are deemed to be residents in Canada for tax purposes (such as diplomats and others posted outside the country) must pay an additional tax (30% in 1976) of their tax otherwise payable. This tax is intended to correspond in an approximate way to the income tax imposed by the provinces on their residents.

To a large extent, individual income tax is payable as income is earned. Taxpayers in receipt of salary or wages have tax deducted from pay by the employer and in this way pay nearly 100% of their tax liability during the calendar year. The balance of the tax, if any, is payable at the time of filing the tax return on or before April 30 of the following year. Individuals with more than 25% of income in a form not subject to tax deductions at source must pay tax by quarterly instalments. Returns of these individuals must be filed on or before April 30 of the following calendar year. Farmers and fishermen pay two thirds of tax on or before December 31 each year and the remainder on or before April 30 of the following year. Table 20.18 shows the amount of personal income tax payable on various levels of income in 1976.

Canadian employers are required to deduct and remit to the government income tax from the amounts paid to their employees as wages and salaries. Revenue Canada, Taxation provides employers with deduction tables to guide them in calculating the amount of federal and provincial income taxes, Canada Pension Plan contributions and Unemployment Insurance premiums to be withheld.

On December 31, 1975, the Taxation Data Centre had on record more than 643,121 employers with deductions for the 1975 year. On March 31, 1976, the end of the department's fiscal year, employers' tax deductions, CPP contributions, and UI premiums totalled approximately $18,942 million.

Corporation income tax. The Income Tax Act levies a tax upon income from anywhere in the world of corporations resident in Canada and upon the income attributable to operations in Canada of non-resident corporations carrying on business in Canada. One half of capital gains must be included in income. In computing income, corporations may deduct operating expenses including municipal real estate taxes, reserves for doubtful debts, bad debts and interest on borrowed money.

Corporations may deduct over a period of years the capital cost of all depreciable property. The normal capital cost allowances are computed each year, on the diminishing balance principle. Regulations established a number of classes of property and maximum rates. Typical rates include 5% for most buildings, 20% for machinery and 30% for automobiles. Accelerated depreciation (full write-off in two years) is allowed in respect of machinery and equipment acquired by manufacturers and processors after May 8, 1972 for use in Canada.

Current or capital expenditures on scientific research related to the business of the taxpayer may be written off for tax purposes in the year when incurred or any subsequent year.

A corporation whose principal business is mining, oil production or a related activity may deduct Canadian exploration expenses (as defined) from income from any source in the year in which the expenses are incurred and any unused balance can be carried forward indefinitely. Corporations which do not meet the principal business test may deduct Canadian exploration expenses incurred between May 25, 1976 and July 1, 1979. For such corporations Canadian exploration expenses incurred on or before May 25, 1976 must be amortized at 30% on a declining balance basis. For all corporations, the amount which may be deducted for Canadian development expenses (as defined) may not exceed 30% of the unamortized balance.

Taxpayers with resource profits (as defined) are entitled to a resource allowance equal to 25% of such resource profits before the deduction of interest expense, exploration and development expense and earned depletion. In addition to the resource allowance, a taxpayer with resource profits may deduct earned depletion in computing his income for a taxation year. The earned depletion deduction for a particular taxation year is the lesser of the earned depletion base (one third of qualifying expenditures to date less previous claims) and 25% of the resource profits. Canadian exploration and development expenses are qualifying expenditures.

Provincial royalties and mining taxes are not deductible in computing taxable income for federal purposes.

Capital equipment and facilities for a new mine may be written off immediately against income from the mine. The assets eligible for this accelerated depreciation include buildings, mining machinery, processing facilities and "social capital" such as access roads, sewage plants, housing, schools, airports and docks. The accelerated write-off provision for new mines will also apply in the case of a major expansion of an existing mine where there has been at least a 25% increase in milling capacity. The list of eligible assets is the same as for new mines except that "social capital" does not qualify.

Taxpayers operating timber limits receive an annual cost allowance with respect to the cost of the limit. The rate of the allowance is based on the amount of timber cut in the year.

In computing taxable income, corporations, with certain exceptions, may deduct dividends received from other Canadian taxable corporations and also from certain non-resident affiliates. Business losses may be carried back one year or forward five years and deducted in computing taxable income. Corporations may also deduct donations to charitable organizations up to a maximum of 20% of their income.

The standard rate of federal corporation income tax is 46%. A special deduction reduces this rate on Canadian manufacturing and processing profits to 40%. These rates are reduced by 10% on income earned in a province. This "provincial abatement" is intended to make room for provincial corporation income taxes which range from 10% to 15%.

A "small business deduction" reduces the standard federal rate of tax on certain business income to 25%. This rate is reduced to 20% on Canadian manufacturing and processing profits. Both of these rates are reduced by the 10% provincial abatement on income earned in a province. This small business deduction is restricted to private Canadian corporations which are not controlled by a non-resident or by a Canadian public corporation. It applies only to income from an active business carried on in Canada and not to investment income. The maximum amount of taxable income on which the deduction may be calculated is $150,000 in any one year. A corporation is entitled to this deduction only until it has accumulated $750,000 of taxable income since 1971.

A corporation that qualifies as an "investment corporation" pays tax at a standard federal rate of only 25%. This rate is also reduced by the provincial abatement.

The investment income (other than dividends) of a private corporation is subject to the standard rate of federal tax (i.e. 46% in 1976 less the provincial abatement) but an amount not exceeding 25% of such income is refunded when dividends are paid to shareholders. Dividends received by a private corporation from portfolio investments are subject to a special 33⅓% tax but this is refunded when dividends are paid to shareholders.

A corporation may elect to pay a special 15% tax on its 1971 undistributed income on hand. Dividends received from this tax-paid undistributed income are not included in the income of the receiving shareholder but the amount of the dividend will reduce the adjusted cost basis of the shares for capital gains tax purposes. Dividends paid from the untaxed half of a private corporation's capital gains are also excluded from the income of the recipient shareholders but with no similar reduction in the adjusted cost base of the shares for capital gains tax purposes.

Special rules are provided for the taxation of special-purpose companies such as mutual fund corporations, life insurance companies, non-resident-owned investment companies and cooperatives.

A corporation may reduce its tax otherwise payable by a credit for taxes paid to foreign governments on foreign source income. This credit may not exceed the Canadian tax related to such income. A corporation may also deduct from its tax an amount equal to two thirds of a provincial tax on income from logging operations not exceeding 6⅔% of its income from logging operations in the province. (At present only Quebec and British Columbia impose logging taxes.) Corporations are required to pay their tax by monthly instalments throughout their taxation year.

Taxation of non-residents. An individual or corporation not resident in Canada is liable for Canadian income tax on income from employment or from carrying on business in Canada and on one half of capital gains less losses on disposals of "taxable Canadian property". The taxation of capital gains may be restricted by the provisions in tax treaties between Canada and other countries. The expression "carrying on business in Canada" includes producing, growing, packaging or improving any article in Canada and also soliciting orders or offering anything for sale in Canada through an agent or servant. However, this is usually modified by tax treaties so that an enterprise of the other country is taxed by Canada on its industrial and commercial profits only if it carries on business through a permanent establishment in this country.

The taxable income of non-resident individuals derived from employment or carrying on business or from capital gains in Canada is taxed under the same schedule of rates as are Canadian resident individuals.

Income earned by non-resident corporations carrying on business or from capital gains in Canada is taxed at the regular rates of corporation income tax. The distributable business earnings of a branch of a non-resident corporation are also subject to an additional tax often referred to as a branch tax. This tax applies to the branch earnings net of taxes that are not reinvested in the business in Canada.

Certain specific items of income paid to non-residents from sources in Canada are subject to a 25% tax withheld at the source by the Canadian payer. This non-resident withholding tax applies to interest (except interest on certain bonds and interest paid to certain exempt lenders), dividends, rents, royalties (including royalties from motion pictures and television films), management fees, income from a trust or estate, alimony, pension benefits (other than the Old Age Security pension and the Canada Pension Plan or Quebec Pension Plan benefits), payments from deferred income plans and the taxable portion of annuities.

The 25% rate of non-resident withholding tax may be modified by tax treaties. The rate of tax applicable to dividends is reduced by 5% in the case of dividends paid by a corporation that has a degree of Canadian ownership. Generally, a corporation is regarded as having a degree of Canadian ownership where 25% of its equity and voting shares are owned by Canadians and/or corporations controlled in Canada, or where the voting shares of the corporation are listed on a Canadian stock exchange and no more than 75% of its issued outstanding voting shares are owned by a non-resident alone or in combination with related persons.

Non-residents who receive from sources in Canada only the kinds of income subject to the non-resident withholding tax do not file returns to Canada. However, those who receive rents on real property, timber royalties, pension benefits or proceeds from deferred income plans may elect to file returns and be taxed at either personal or corporation rates.

Estate and gift taxes. The federal government formerly imposed an estate tax and a tax on gifts. They do not apply in the case of a death occurring after 1971 or to a gift made after 1971.

Excise taxes. The Excise Tax Act levies a general sales tax and special excise taxes. These taxes are levied on goods imported into Canada as well as on goods produced in Canada. They are not levied on goods exported.

The general sales tax is 12%. It is levied on the manufacturer's sale price of goods produced or manufactured in Canada or on the duty-paid value of goods imported into Canada. "Duty-paid value" includes the amount of customs duties, if any. For alcoholic beverages and tobacco products the sale price for purposes of the sales tax includes excise duties levied under the Excise Act. The rate of sales tax on a long list of construction materials and equipment for buildings is 5%.

Some goods are exempt from sales tax. Drugs, electricity, fuels for lighting or heating, all clothing and footwear, foodstuffs and a comprehensive list of transportation and construction equipment are exempt. In addition articles and materials purchased by public hospitals and certain welfare institutions are not subject to sales tax. The products of farms, forests, mines and fisheries are, to a large extent, exempt as is most equipment used in farming and fishing. Machinery and equipment used directly in production, materials consumed or expended in production and equipment acquired by manufacturers or producers to prevent or reduce pollution to water, soil or air from their manufacturing operations are all exempt. A number of items are exempt when purchased by municipalities. These and other exemptions are set forth in the schedules to the Excise Tax Act.

The Excise Tax Act also imposes a number of special excise taxes which are in addition to the sales tax. Where these are ad valorem taxes they are levied on the same price or duty-paid value as the general sales tax. Those levied as at December 31, 1975 are given in Table 20.19.

Excise duties. The Excise Act levies taxes (referred to as excise duties) upon alcohol, alcoholic beverages (other than wines) and tobacco products. These duties are not levied on imports but the customs tariff applies special duties to these products equivalent to the excise duties levied on the products manufactured in Canada. Exported goods are not subject to excise duties.

The duties on spirits are on a proof gallon basis. They do not apply to denatured alcohol intended for use in the arts and industries, or for fuel, light or power, or any mechanical purpose. Canadian brandy (a spirit distilled exclusively from juices of native fruits without the addition of sweetening materials) is subject to an excise duty. Excise duties are imposed on tobacco, cigars and cigarettes in addition to the special excise taxes.

Customs duties. Most goods imported into Canada are subject to customs duties at various rates as provided by tariff schedules. Customs duties which once were the chief source of revenue for the country have declined in importance as a source of revenue to the point where they now provide less than 10% of the total. Quite apart from its revenue aspects, however, the tariff still occupies an important place as an instrument of economic policy.

The Canadian Tariff consists mainly of four sets of rates, namely, General Preferential, British Preferential, Most-Favoured-Nation and General. The General Preferential rates apply to goods imported from designated developing countries. The British Preferential rates are applied to imported commodities shipped directly to Canada from countries within the British Commonwealth. Rates lower than the British Preferential are applied on certain goods imported from designated Commonwealth countries.

The Most-Favoured-Nation rates apply to goods from countries that have been accorded tariff treatment more favourable than the General Tariff but which are not entitled to the British or General Preferential Tariffs. Canada has Most-Favoured-Nation arrangements with almost every country outside the Commonwealth. The most important is the General Agreement on Tariffs and Trade.

The General Tariff applies to imports from countries not entitled to the British Preferential, General Preferential, or Most-Favoured-Nation treatment. Few countries are in this category and they are not significant in terms of trade coverage.

In all cases where the tariff applies there are provisions for drawbacks of duty on imports of materials used in the manufacture of products later exported. These drawbacks assist Canadian manufacturers to compete with foreign manufacturers of similar goods. There is a second class of drawbacks known as "home consumption" drawbacks. These apply to imported articles used in the production of specified classes of goods manufactured for home consumption.

Provincial taxes   20.6.2

All of Canada's provinces levy a wide variety of taxes, fees, licences and other forms of imposition. Among such levies, a relatively small number account for about 75% of total provincial revenue from own sources. Only the more important levies are briefly described here. Complete details may be found in *Principal taxes in Canada*, Statistics Canada Catalogue No. 68-201E.

Personal income tax. All provincial governments levy a tax on the income of individuals who reside within their boundaries and on the income earned by non-residents from sources within those boundaries. Rates of provincial individual income tax are expressed as percentages of "basic federal tax", with the exception of Quebec which has its own system. The "basic federal tax" on which provinces apply their rates is the federal tax after the dividend tax credit but before any foreign tax credit and special federal tax reductions. Provincial rates in 1976 were as follows: Newfoundland, 42%; Prince Edward Island, 36%; Nova Scotia, 38.5%; New Brunswick, 40.6%; Ontario, 30.5%; Manitoba, 42.5%; Saskatchewan, 40%; Alberta, 26%; and British Columbia, 32.5%. Newfoundland and British Columbia had increased their rates from 40% and 30.5%, respectively on July 1, 1976. Their effective rates for the 1976 taxation year were 41% and 31.5%, respectively. For personal income tax the federal government acts as collection agent for the above agreeing provinces.

In Quebec, provincial individual income tax is not related to basic federal tax but is levied at graduated rates which take into account the federal income tax abatement of 24%. The rates are progressive, varying from 16% on taxable income between $2,000 to $9,000 to a maximum of 28% on income exceeding $60,000. The determination of taxable income is based on exemptions and deductions similar to those for the federal tax. The government of Quebec does not participate in the tax collection agreements and therefore collects its own.

Ontario, Manitoba, Alberta and British Columbia have introduced tax credit schemes which are administered, at a small fee, through the tax collection machinery of Revenue Canada. This is to alleviate the burden of certain other taxes or of specified categories of taxpayers by means of an income tax credit or rebate. Manitoba and Saskatchewan have introduced a surtax on provincial income tax payable in excess of a certain amount.

Corporation income tax. All provinces levy a tax on the taxable income of corporations. In provinces other than Quebec and Ontario, the provincial corporation income tax is imposed on the same basis as that established for federal corporation income tax purposes, and is collected by the federal government under tax collection agreements. In Quebec and Ontario, the determination of corporation taxable income follows closely, but not exactly, the federal rules. Each collects its own levy. Corporate taxable income earned in a province is eligible for the 10% federal abatement to compensate corporations for provincial taxes payable. This 10% abatement does not apply to income earned in the Yukon and Northwest Territories since they do not impose their own corporate income tax.

The rate that applies in Newfoundland is 14%; Nova Scotia, 12%; New Brunswick and Prince Edward Island, 10%; Quebec and Saskatchewan, 12%; and Alberta, 11%. Three provinces introduced a preferential low tax rate for small business income. The dual corporate rates for these provinces are: Ontario, 12%/9%; Manitoba, 15%/13%; and British Columbia, 15%/12%.

Business taxes. Quebec, Ontario, Manitoba and British Columbia impose a tax on paid-up or utilized capital of corporations which have a permanent establishment within their boundaries at a rate of .02%. Certain types of companies such as banks, railway, express, trust and insurance companies are subject to special rules for computing taxable paid-up capital or special taxes, licences or fees applicable in such cases. Quebec has a place of business tax of $50 for companies whose paid-up capital exceeds $25,000 and $25 when below that amount.

Gift tax. The gift tax is levied on the aggregate taxable value of gifts made by a donor resident in a province as well as on a gift of real property situated within a province made by a donor who is not a resident in the province. The rates range from 15% on the first $25,000 to 50% on gifts in excess of $200,000. There are exemptions for gifts made to a spouse or charitable organization, deductions for gifts made to other donee up to an aggregate annual amount, and credits for the tax levied by other jurisdictions on property situated outside the province. The responsibility for the assessment and collection of this tax was transferred to the provinces of Ontario, Manitoba, Saskatchewan and British Columbia effective October 31, 1975 when the federal government administration agreements ended. Quebec also collects its own gift tax.

Succession duties. Succession duty is levied on property of the deceased situated in a province regardless of where the deceased was domiciled at the time of death as well as on the dutiable value of property passing to the beneficiary who is a resident in a province. The rate depends on the net value of the whole estate wherever situated, the amount of property passing to the beneficiary, and the relationship of the beneficiary to the deceased.

The federal government withdrew from the death tax field as of December 31, 1971. Since the federal estate tax had been shared with the provinces whether or not they themselves levied succession duties, the federal withdrawal from this field of taxation meant a potential loss of revenue to provinces without succession duties. For such provinces, the federal government agreed to collect (for three years) any succession duties they wished to levy. Quebec, Ontario and British Columbia which had been imposing succession duties maintained their own system. The remaining provinces (with the exception of Alberta) enacted succession duty tax legislation with effect on January 1, 1972. Prince Edward Island, New Brunswick, Nova Scotia and Newfoundland have subsequently rescinded their legislation. Since January 1, 1975, Manitoba and Saskatchewan have been administering their own succession duties.

Provincial sales tax. All provinces except Alberta impose a retail sales tax on a wide range of consumer goods and services purchased or brought into the province. It is collected by vendors who, acting as agents, remit the tax to the provincial governments for a commission. To conform to the constitutional limitations, provincial taxation must not only be direct but also must be within the province. Consequently, under provincial acts the consumer must pay a tax on the fair market value of goods purchased for consumption and not for resale. Any purchase of goods outside the province for use inside the province is taxable, but the tax is not applicable to goods sold for delivery in other provinces or to exported commodities. Each act, however, specifies a number of items which are exempt; these relate mainly to the necessities of life and material used in the farming or fisheries industries. Provincial tax rates are as follows: Newfoundland, 10%; Prince Edward Island, Nova Scotia, New Brunswick and Quebec, 8%; Ontario and British Columbia, 7%; Manitoba and Saskatchewan, 5%.

Gasoline and diesel fuel oil taxes. Each province and both territories impose a tax on the purchase of gasoline and diesel fuel by motorists and truckers and other fuel intended to generate motive power. A number of activities are exempt or partially exempt from motive fuel taxation. Generally speaking, these pertain to gasoline and diesel fuel used by producers of primary products, commercial fishermen and municipal governments.

Tobacco taxes. A tax on consumers of tobacco products is levied in all provinces and both territories. Cigarettes are taxed on a unit basis at rates ranging from eight twenty fifths of one cent per cigarette in Alberta and the Northwest Territories to one cent each in Newfoundland. The tax on cigars is calculated as a percentage or an amount based on the final selling price. These taxes are usually collected at the wholesale level to facilitate collection and administration but may also be collected by retail dealers acting as collection agents of the province.

Amusement taxes and race track taxes. Each province with the exception of Newfoundland, Alberta and British Columbia has a tax on admission to places of entertainment. In Quebec, this tax is collected by the municipalities which retain the proceeds even though the rate is determined by an act of the provincial government. In Manitoba and Saskatchewan the province does not levy the tax but has given the right to impose an admissions tax to its municipalities. In addition, all provinces levy a tax on all legal wagering on horse races in the province. The federal government also has a Pari-Mutuel-Levy ranging from 0.5% to 1.0% on monies wagered which is for the supervision of race tracks.

Tax on premium income of insurance companies. All provinces and the Yukon Territory impose a tax on the premium income of insurance companies. Ontario imposes a tax of 3% calculated on gross premiums and an additional tax of .5% on the premium income from insurance covering property, fire, inland transport, livestock, plate glass, sprinkler leakage, theft and weather. British Columbia levies a tax of 2% on gross premiums and 5% on the premiums paid to unlicensed insurers or reciprocal exchanges. All other provinces tax premium income at the rate of 2%.

Tax on logging operations. Quebec and British Columbia levy a tax on income from logging operations of individuals, partnerships, associations or corporations. The rate of taxation is 10% in Quebec and 15% in British Columbia on net income in excess of $10,000; if the net income is greater than $10,000 the whole amount is taxable with no basic exemption. In Quebec 33.3% of the tax is allowed as a deduction from provincial income tax. In British Columbia, as a result of the dual corporation income tax rate, the tax credit allowed from provincial corporation income tax is 44.4% of logging taxes paid for the small business portion and 29.4% for any remainder. The federal income tax also allows a credit which is the lesser of two thirds of the logging taxes paid to a province or 6⅔ of the logging income earned in a province.

Hospitalization and medical care insurance premiums. While most provinces finance the provincial share of their hospitalization and medical care programs out of general revenue, some finance their share in part by premiums and the balance from general revenue. (For details see Chapter 5 Health, Section 5.2.2.) Three provinces and one territory levy premiums and one province a payroll tax and a special income tax to finance their share of the costs. Quebec finances its health programs through a payroll tax at a rate of 1.5% of gross salaries paid by employers and through a special income tax of 1.5% on the net income of individuals. In the latter case, the maximum annual amount is $235, if at least three quarters of the net income is made up of salaries; in other cases the maximum payable is $375. Since the new rates only came into force on June 1, 1976 the effective rate was 1.2% for 1976.

Ontario has a conjoint hospitalization and medical care insurance premium which is set at the monthly rate of $16.00 for single persons and $32.00 for a family. In Alberta the hospitalization and medical care premiums are also combined at a rate per month of $6.40 for single subscribers and $12.80 for families. Only the medical care program is financed through a premium in British Columbia at a monthly rate of $7.50 for single persons, $15.00 for a family of two and $18.75 for a family of more than two persons. In the Yukon Territory, medical care premiums are on a monthly basis as follows: $4.75 for single persons, $9.25 for a family of two and $11.00 for a family of more than two persons. The above rates are for persons who do not qualify for premium assistance. In many cases premiums are exempt for welfare recipients and persons 65 years of age or over or a province may subsidize a percentage of the premiums of residents with little or no taxable income.

Motor vehicle licences and fees. Each province levies a fee on the compulsory registration of a motor vehicle whereupon the vehicle is issued with licence plates. The fees vary from province to province and, in the case of passenger cars, may be assessed on the weight of the vehicle, the wheel base, the year of manufacture, the number of cylinders of the engine, or at a flat rate. The fees for commercial motor vehicles and trailers are based on the gross weight for which the vehicle is registered, i.e., the weight of the vehicle empty plus the load it is permitted to carry. Every operator or driver of a motor vehicle is required to register periodically and pay a fee for a driver's licence. The licences are valid for periods of from one to five years and the fees vary from $1 to $7 a year.

Land transfer taxes. Ontario levies a tax based on the price at which ownership of land is transferred. The tax for Canadian residents is 0.3% on the purchase up to $35,000 and 0.6% on anything in excess of that amount; for non-residents the tax is 20% of the purchase price. In addition, Ontario levies a tax of 20% on the increase in value on the sale of designated land (all real property except Canadian resource property). Quebec levies a 33% tax on the value of immovable property transferred to non-residents. Municipalities may levy duties on immovable property transferred to other than Canadian non-residents. In Alberta, a registration fee is charged proportional to the registered value of land; $5 for the first $1,000 and $1 for each additional $1,000 up to $25,000, and 50 cents per $1,000 in excess of that amount. There is also an Assurance Fund fee charged on transfers of land based on the difference between the old registered price and the new registered price at the rate of .05% on any increase in the value of land up to $5,000 and .025% on any excess over $5,000. British Columbia and Saskatchewan do not have a land transfer tax but have an equivalent in land title fee which is based on land value.

Provincial property taxes. Most provinces levy, in varying degrees, real property taxes. In Prince Edward Island and New Brunswick, where services formerly carried out by municipal authorities were taken over by provincial governments, the real property tax field is shared by both provincial and municipal governments. The provincial governments levy a flat rate real property tax on a province-wide basis and each municipality has its own separate rate as required to meet its expenditure. All collections, however, are effected by the provinces which remit the municipal share to individual municipalities. Some provinces impose property taxes of limited application on land in unorganized areas not subject to a municipal rate. Nova Scotia imposes a tax applicable to land where more than 1,000 acres (404.7 hectares) is occupied. The provincial property tax in Ontario is levied on the assessed value of real property in municipally unorganized territories where residents may enjoy provincial services. Saskatchewan levies a tax in areas not contributing toward the support of a hospital as well as in unorganized districts for support of Regional Health Offices. British Columbia's provincial property tax is levied on the assessed value of land and improvements in unorganized (non-municipal) areas at rates ranging between that of farm land and wild land. In other provinces funds collected from taxes in unorganized areas are placed in a trust account to cover administrative costs and other expenditures applicable to their respective areas.

Local taxes   20.6.3

For purposes of financial statistics local government is comprised of three principal categories — municipalities, local school authorities and special purpose authorities. Consequently, local taxes are levied by either one of these entities or by all of them depending upon the taxing powers granted to each of them by their respective provincial legislatures. For more than a century, the main source of revenue of local governments has been related to real properties within their jurisdictions. Various taxes have been gradually implemented to supplement the real property tax from which, however, they still derive the bulk of their revenue.

Local property tax. Municipalities throughout Canada levy taxes on real properties situated within their boundaries. Generally speaking, they set the rates and collect the proceeds of their own levy or, in addition, on behalf of other local governments in their area, particularly local school authorities. However, in most of Quebec outside the Montreal area and in the unorganized parts of Ontario, school boards levy and collect their own real property taxes.

The real property tax rate is generally expressed in mills (rate per $1,000 of the base) or as a rate per $100 of the base. This base is the assessed value of each property. Methods of determining assessed value vary widely not only among the provinces but also among municipalities within a province. However, for taxation purposes, it is generally referred to as "fair market value" which is considered to be a percentage of "actual market value".

Business taxes. Among other taxes that municipalities levy, business taxes rank next to the real property tax as a producer of municipal revenue. Such taxes are levied directly on the tenant or the operator of a business. The bases on which business taxes are levied are very diversified among the provinces. The most common in use are: a percentage of the assessed value of real property, value of stock-in-trade, the assessed annual rental value of immovables and the area of premises occupied for business purposes.

Water charges. In general, municipalities recoup all, or part, of the cost of supplying water through special charges for water consumption. Such charges take various forms such as, for example, a water tax based on the rental value of the property occupied, or a charge based on the actual consumption of water.

Sources

20.1 - 20.2.1 Public Finance Division, Institutional and Public Finance Statistics Branch, Statistics Canada.

20.2.2 Operations Research and Statistics Division, Systems and Planning Branch, Department of National Revenue, Taxation; Business Finance Division, General Statistics Branch, Statistics Canada.

20.2.3 - 20.2.4 Public Finance Division, Institutional and Public Finance Statistics Branch, Statistics Canada.

20.3 Information Division, Department of Finance.

20.4 - 20.5 Public Finance Division, Institutional and Public Finance Statistics Branch, Statistics Canada.

20.6 - 20.6.1 Information Division, Department of Finance; Information Services, Department of National Revenue, Taxation.

20.6.2 - 20.6.3 Public Finance Division, Institutional and Public Finance Statistics Branch, Statistics Canada.

Tables

..	not available	e	estimate
...	not appropriate or not applicable	p	preliminary
—	nil or zero	r	revised
- -	too small to be expressed		certain tables may not add due to rounding

20.1 Consolidated government revenue and expenditure, after elimination of intergovernment transfers, fiscal years ended nearest Dec. 31, 1969-73 (million dollars)

Source or function	1969[1]	1970	1971	1972	1973
Consolidated government revenue by source					
Income tax					
Individuals	7,730.6	9,147.7	10,194.5	12,007.3	13,616.1
Corporations	3,700.7	3,189.4	3,181.4	3,897.5	4,914.2
General sales tax	3,973.6	4,071.6	4,664.3	5,384.9	6,598.8
Real and personal property tax	2,828.9	3,301.0	3,424.4	3,707.8	3,909.5
Other tax revenue	6,658.9[r]	6,970.3	7,500.1	8,153.5	9,522.2
Non-tax revenue	4,895.1[r]	5,457.9	6,409.6	7,440.1	9,152.3
Total	29,787.8[r]	32,137.9	35,374.3	40,591.1	47,713.1
Consolidated government expenditure by function					
General government	1,606.9	1,972.8	2,284.0	2,506.1	2,916.4
Protection of persons and property	2,767.2	3,078.6	3,374.4	3,650.0	4,178.2
Transportation and communications	2,997.5	3,246.6	3,683.0	4,084.2	4,791.8
Health	3,440.1	4,224.0	4,842.7	5,478.0	6,069.4
Social welfare	4,738.5	5,807.6	6,967.8	8,665.6	10,539.5
Education	5,403.3	5,993.0	6,538.0	6,953.0	7,303.1
Natural resources	519.4	537.8	629.4	720.3	878.5
Recreation and culture	493.7	584.2	759.8	910.8	1,153.1
Housing	264.7	296.1	509.6	427.6	449.8
Foreign affairs	251.8	289.1	311.5	385.4	439.1
Debt charges	2,293.0	2,617.7	3,069.4	3,374.9	3,934.9
Other expenditures	3,092.6	2,792.9	3,305.9	3,852.7	4,359.2
Total	27,868.7	31,440.4	36,275.5	41,008.6	47,013.0
Consolidated government revenue less consolidated government expenditure	+1,919.1	+697.5	-901.2	-417.5	+700.1

[1] A preliminary revision of the data has been effected for 1969 to put the data on a more comparable basis with the following years.

20.2 Gross general revenue of the federal government, years ended Mar. 31, 1973-75 (million dollars)

Source	1973	1974	1975
Taxes			
Income			
Individuals	8,378	9,226	11,710
Corporations	2,919	3,710	4,836
On certain payments or credits to non-residents	292	324	428
General sales	3,052	3,590	3,866
Alcoholic beverages	426	460	502
Tobacco	565	611	625
Other commodities and services	44	20	32
Customs duties	1,182	1,385	1,809
Estate taxes	61	14	7
Social insurance levies[1]	742	1,017	1,670
Universal pension plan levies[2]	879	998	1,213
Oil export charge	—	287	1,669
Other	1	—	—
Total, taxes	18,541	21,642	28,367
Natural resources	11	14	21
Privileges, licences and permits	22	24	24
Sales of goods and services	699	965	941
Return on investments	1,329	1,568	1,904
Contributions to non-trusteed public service pension plans	221	220	253
Postal receipts	558	586	611
Bullion and coinage	24	58	48
Fines and penalties	14	16	15
Miscellaneous	7	9	8
Total, gross general revenue from own sources	21,426	25,102	32,192
Specific purpose transfers from other levels of government	—	—	—
Total, gross general revenue	21,426	25,102	32,192

[1] Unemployment insurance.
[2] Canada Pension Plan.

20.3   Gross general expenditure of the federal government, years ended Mar. 31, 1973-75 (million dollars)

Function	1973	1974	1975
General government	1,257ʳ	1,382	1,710
Protection of persons and property[1]	2,299	2,602	2,890
Transportation and communications[2]	1,370	1,765	2,194
Health	1,789	1,951	2,296
Hospital care	963	1,068	1,310
Other	826	883	986
Social welfare	6,858ʳ	8,109	10,079
Universal pension plans	207	279	399
Old age security	2,524	3,035	3,445
Veterans' benefits	477	561	639
Unemployment insurance	2,171	2,159	2,490
Family and youth allowances	610	996	1,824
Assistance to disabled, handicapped, unemployed and other needy persons	638	814	955
Other	231ʳ	265	327
Education	847	919	1,039
Natural resources	334	570	1,582
Agriculture, trade and industry, and tourism	1,015	1,145	1,490
Environment	100	246	270
Recreation and culture	215	253	274
Labour, employment and immigration	489	331	344
Housing	99	138	212
Foreign affairs and international assistance	385	439	584
Supervision and development of regions and localities	140	144	152
Research establishments	278	302	326
General purpose transfers to other levels of government	1,640	1,883	2,696
Transfers to own enterprises	294	362	481
Debt charges	1,502	1,735	2,271
Other	1	1	1
Total, gross general expenditure	20,912	24,277	30,891

[1]Includes National Defence.
[2]Includes Post Office.

20.4   Assets and liabilities of the federal government, as at Mar. 31, 1973-75 (million dollars)

Item	1973ʳ	1974	1975	Item	1973ʳ	1974	1975
Assets				Liabilities			
Cash on hand or on deposit	1,294	440	2,684	Payables	7,241	8,794	9,848
Receivables	373	399	689	Loans and advances	370	—	—
Loans and advances	21,623	23,088	23,859	Treasury bills	4,290	4,905	5,630
Investments	13,491	15,757	18,820	Canada Savings Bonds	10,989	10,406	12,915
Other assets	998	1,166	1,726	Other bonds	13,759	13,860	14,541
				Other liabilities	5,369	6,209	6,535
Total, assets	37,779	40,850	47,778	Total, liabilities	42,018	44,174	49,469

20.5   Gross bonded debt of the federal government, average interest rate, term of issue and place of payment as at Mar. 31, 1973-75

Item		1973	1974	1975
Bonded debt	$'000	24,748,493	24,266,365	27,456,159
Average interest rate	%	6.39	6.78	7.33
Average term of issue	yr	11.40	11.68	9.09
Place of payment				
Canada	$'000	24,414,834	24,008,281	27,248,560
New York	"	259,815	258,084	207,599
Federal Republic of Germany	"	73,844	—	—

20.6   Guaranteed debt of the Government of Canada, years ended Mar. 31, 1974 and 1975 (thousand dollars)

Item	1974		1975	
	Amount of guarantee	Amount outstanding as at Mar. 31, 1974	Amount of guarantee	Amount outstanding as at Mar. 31, 1975
Railway securities guaranteed as to principal and interest				
Canadian National 3¼% due Feb. 1, 1974	—	—	—	—
Canadian National 2¼% due June 15, 1975, US$6,000,000[1]	6,000	6,000	6,000	6,000
Canadian National 5% due May 15, 1977	74,438	74,438	72,710	72,710
Canadian National 4% due Feb. 1, 1981	300,000	300,000	300,000	300,000
Canadian National 5¼% due Jan. 1, 1985	86,032	86,032	84,032	84,032
Canadian National 5% due Oct. 1, 1987	137,004	137,004	133,487	133,487
Grand Trunk Western Railroad Company				
Total, railway securities	603,474	603,474	596,229[2]	596,229

20.6   Guaranteed debt of the Government of Canada, years ended Mar. 31, 1974 and 1975 (thousand dollars) (concluded)

Item	1974		1975	
	Amount of guarantee	Amount outstanding as at Mar. 31, 1974	Amount of guarantee	Amount outstanding as at Mar. 31, 1975
Other outstanding guarantees and contingent liabilities				
Loans made by lenders under Part IV of the National Housing Act, 1954 for home extension and improvements	30,000[3]	23,987[3]	30,000[4]	24,740[4]
Insured loans made by approved lenders under the National Housing Act 1954	19,000,000[3,5]	11,089,000[3,5]	19,000,000[4,6]	11,915,000[4,6]
Liability for insurance and guarantees under the Export Development Act	1,150,000	646,431	1,750,000	866,400
Loans made by chartered banks under the Farm Improvement Loans Act	381,402	296,373	457,226	311,633
Loans made by chartered banks and credit unions under the Fisheries Improvement Loans Act	5,951	3,830	12,515	4,865
Loans made by chartered banks under the Small Businesses Loans Act	55,369	28,566	67,836	31,836
Loans made by chartered banks and credit unions under the Canada Student Loans Act[7]	620,235	612,342	690,139	688,703
Loans made by chartered banks to the Canadian Wheat Board	1,210,000	443,411	1,350,000	1,055,985
Loans made by lenders under the Regional Development Incentives Act and the Regional Economic Expansion Act	12,844	9,024	21,832	18,405
Loans made by lenders under the Cape Breton Development Act	30,000	27,000	30,000	25,500
Loans made by lenders under the General Adjustment Assistance Program	250,000	56,756	250,000	73,842
Licensing agreement provisions in the sale of aircraft to Venezuela	17,000	17,000	17,600	17,600
Total, guaranteed debt	23,366,275	13,857,194	24,273,377	15,630,738
Loans made by approved lending institutions under National Housing Act prior to 1954	Unstated	Indeterminate	Unstated	Indeterminate
Guarantees to owners of returns from moderate rental housing projects	Unstated[8]	Indeterminate[8]	Unstated[9]	Indeterminate[9]

[1]Liability is subject to exchange rate in effect June 15, 1975.
[2]Balances valued as at Jan. 1, 1975.
[3]As at Dec. 31, 1973.
[4]As at Dec. 31, 1974.
[5]As reported (in accordance with Section 45, National Housing Regulations) by approved lenders as at Dec. 31, 1973.
[6]As reported (in accordance with Section 45, National Housing Regulations) by approved lenders as at Dec. 31, 1974.
[7]Includes contingent liability in respect of alternative payments to non-participating province.
[8]As at Dec. 31, 1973, funds totalling $7,583,313 were held by the Central Mortgage and Housing Corporation for the purpose of settling claims. In 1973 rental contracts totalled $1,729,000.
[9]As at Dec. 31, 1974, funds totalling $7,990,000 were held by the Central Mortgage and Housing Corporation for the purpose of settling claims. In 1974, rental contracts totalled $307,000.

20.7   Government of Canada public debt and interest payments thereon, years ended Mar. 31, 1971-75

Year ended Mar. 31	Gross debt $'000,000	Net active assets $'000,000	Net debt $'000,000	Net debt per capita[1] $	Increase or decrease in net debt during year $'000,000	Interest paid on debt $'000,000	Interest paid per capita[2] $
1971	42,976	25,653	17,322	798.97	+379	1,780	83.25
1972	47,687	29,750	17,937	831.63	+615	1,964	89.95
1973[r]	51,716	34,260	17,456	790.03	-481	2,105	96.43
1974	55,557	37,429	18,128	807.65	+672	2,549	115.36
1975	62,696	43,421	19,275	847.72	+1,147	3,164	138.78

[1]Based on the official estimates of population for June 1 of the year indicated.
[2]Based on the official estimates of population for June 1 of the year immediately preceding the one indicated.

20.8   Revenue collected (net of refunds) by the Department of National Revenue, Taxation, years ended Mar. 31, 1972-76 (thousand dollars)

Year ended Mar. 31	Income tax[1]				Estate tax and succession duties[3]	Total collections
	Individual[2]	Corporation	Special refundable tax	Total		
1972	10,372,651	2,664,602	-1,699	13,035,554	132,016	13,167,570
1973	12,421,913	3,287,807	-840	15,708,880	71,594	15,780,474
1974	13,967,315	4,087,710	-396	18,054,629	39,117	18,093,746
1975	17,880,320	5,386,385	—	23,266,705	24,701	23,291,406
1976	20,013,553	6,610,695	—	26,624,248	—	26,624,248

[1]Includes transfers to Old Age Security Fund.
[2]Includes non-resident withholding tax and Canada Pension Plan contributions by employers, employees and self-employed persons; includes social development tax 1972; includes unemployment insurance premiums 1972-76.
[3]Includes federal estate taxes as well as succession duties and gift taxes collected on behalf of certain provinces.

20.9 Number of taxpayers and amounts of income and tax, by selected cities, 1973 and 1974

City and province	1973			1974		
	Taxpayers	Total income assessed $'000,000	Federal tax payable $'000,000	Taxpayers	Total income assessed $'000,000	Federal tax payable $'000,000
Brantford, Ont.	33,089	277.8	34.9	32,696	322.9	41.3
Calgary, Alta.	188,166	1,709.6	225.9	206,215	2,137.3	281.2
Dartmouth, NS	29,819	253.5	30.5	31,240	302.0	35.8
Edmonton, Alta.	225,600	1,960.7	258.3	244,569	2,499.0	324.6
Guelph, Ont.	30,550	259.5	32.8	29,840	298.3	37.5
Halifax, NS	60,597	521.0	65.4	65,876	632.8	76.7
Hamilton, Ont.	220,727	1,995.4	269.1	219,455	2,321.3	308.8
Hull, Que.	50,271	441.5	42.2	51,433	537.7	52.4
Kingston, Ont.	40,385	360.9	47.4	41,809	412.8	52.1
Kitchener — Waterloo, Ont.	82,660	713.6	92.9	84,910	828.7	104.7
London, Ont.	116,397	1,043.4	137.9	118,305	1,200.9	154.9
Moncton, NB	27,015	203.3	22.3	28,762	253.3	27.8
Montreal, Que.	801,865	7,386.8	738.9	798,436	8,680.8	856.4
New Westminster, BC	21,965	195.5	26.3	21,095	217.3	28.7
Niagara Falls, Ont.	28,466	233.9	28.6	30,864	294.2	34.5
Oakville, Ont.	27,890	304.6	46.7	30,920	377.6	56.7
Oshawa, Ont.	43,557	427.6	60.2	48,510	506.2	67.5
Ottawa, Ont.	208,427	2,080.5	296.6	225,569	2,503.5	344.7
Peterborough, Ont.	29,143	247.6	31.1	30,734	302.7	36.7
Quebec, Que.	151,407	1,384.2	134.5	147,666	1,567.7	152.1
Regina, Sask.	60,690	499.4	60.3	64,688	639.8	78.5
Saint John, NB	34,822	265.5	30.0	37,326	331.8	37.6
St. Catharines, Ont.	58,633	518.0	65.8	60,886	636.9	81.4
St. John's, Nfld.	41,081	325.5	39.8	44,397	406.5	49.3
Sarnia, Ont.	32,541	314.6	42.3	34,907	391.1	53.7
Saskatoon, Sask.	52,972	439.4	51.5	57,706	555.4	65.2
Sault Ste Marie, Ont.	32,727	302.9	39.1	33,482	352.1	45.7
Sherbrooke, Que.	31,693	267.2	24.6	32,374	323.4	29.1
Sudbury — Copper Cliff, Ont.	54,928	502.0	65.6	60,900	617.4	76.8
Sydney — Glace Bay, NS	39,456	285.4	29.3	40,025	333.5	34.3
Thunder Bay, Ont.	47,234	411.9	52.8	50,928	516.3	66.3
Toronto, Ont.	1,115,434	10,390.7	1,483.5	1,158,990	12,147.4	1,677.5
Trois-Rivières, Que.	20,735	175.9	16.0	21,362	216.0	19.6
Vancouver, BC	477,477	4,390.3	603.3	505,354	5,371.3	726.9
Victoria, BC	98,126	863.8	107.9	102,288	1,030.7	126.5
Windsor, Ont.	106,852	1,025.5	138.3	105,908	1,140.2	146.3
Winnipeg, Man.	250,199	2,033.2	244.0	262,891	2,487.8	295.8

20.10 Number of taxpayers and amounts of income and tax, by occupational class, 1973 and 1974

Occupational class	1973			1974		
	Taxpayers	Total income assessed $'000	Federal tax payable $'000	Taxpayers	Total income assessed $'000	Federal tax payable $'000
Employees	7,145,963	61,228,163	7,229,713	7,567,679	74,435,815	8,676,177
Farmers	176,959	1,688,632	179,050	187,233	2,421,318	287,841
Fishermen	18,192	159,776	20,208	17,532	141,697	14,008
Self-employed professionals						
Accountants	6,082	164,171	33,212	6,996	215,014	45,335
Medical doctors and surgeons	23,709	1,013,079	242,705	24,495	1,092,115	258,690
Dentists	5,881	183,251	40,092	5,652	200,789	45,108
Lawyers and notaries	10,451	382,486	90,083	10,658	455,639	111,471
Consulting engineers and architects	2,693	90,890	20,845	3,123	106,523	24,236
Entertainers and artists	7,959	66,719	8,062	6,652	60,581	6,720
Other professionals	16,245	216,260	35,860	18,777	283,820	46,647
Salesmen	23,174	251,936	33,477	24,455	316,880	42,285
Business proprietors	292,978	2,734,311	337,558	303,544	3,327,047	410,159
Investors	246,893	2,518,109	315,736	240,989	3,175,306	390,290
Property owners	59,461	597,348	86,572	55,450	669,889	90,783
Pensioners	253,098	1,471,151	113,005	249,209	1,691,691	108,080
All others	204,781	834,964	47,880	207,788	1,045,531	58,169
Total	8,494,519	73,601,246	8,834,058	8,930,232	89,639,655	10,615,999

20.11 Individual income tax statistics, by income class, 1973 and 1974

Income class based on total income	Taxpayers		Total income assessed		Federal tax payable		Average federal tax	
	1973	1974	1973 $'000	1974 $'000	1973 $'000	1974 $'000	1973 $	1974 $
Under $2,000	136,951	73,164	220,514	112,020	1,221	782	9	11
$2,000 and under $3,000	570,950	427,755	1,454,416	1,080,503	13,821	1,240	24	3
$3,000 " $5,000	1,702,565	1,381,666	6,864,717	5,622,715	322,301	158,234	189	115
$5,000 " $7,000	1,661,968	1,594,449	9,912,118	9,528,604	777,565	594,369	468	373
$7,000 " $10,000	1,975,292	1,985,792	16,655,662	16,779,778	1,720,957	1,519,358	871	765
$10,000 " $15,000	1,669,022	2,155,194	20,066,526	26,221,158	2,582,226	3,089,599	1,547	1,434
$15,000 " $25,000	599,922	1,037,703	10,940,808	18,957,754	1,713,043	2,796,929	2,855	2,695
$25,000 " $50,000	142,927	224,527	4,696,213	7,303,039	937,897	1,384,222	6,562	6,165
$50,000 and over	34,922	49,982	2,790,273	4,034,080	765,028	1,071,266	21,907	21,433
Total	8,494,519	8,930,232	73,601,247	89,639,651	8,834,059	10,615,999	1,040	1,189

20.12 Allocation of taxable income, by province, 1969-73 (million dollars)

Province or territory	1969	1970	1971	1972	1973
Newfoundland	69.6	76.5	84.6	84.0	112.9
Prince Edward Island	13.3	13.4	15.0	16.0	19.5
Nova Scotia	124.2	125.0	145.0	159.2	187.8
New Brunswick	97.3	90.6	110.7	126.9	162.4
Quebec	1,477.0	1,474.8	1,629.8	1,863.2	2,289.1
Ontario	2,968.7	2,836.6	3,220.9	3,804.2	4,792.2
Manitoba	254.3	256.4	263.0	322.0	393.9
Saskatchewan	145.9	127.8	158.4	193.1	253.5
Alberta	530.9	553.1	653.6	796.3	1,125.1
British Columbia	857.9	698.3	793.4	934.7	1,420.9
Yukon Territory	5.5	4.6	5.0	6.0	8.1
Northwest Territories	14.4	15.0	10.6	17.0	41.6
Other	85.2	98.1	113.8	139.3	141.4
Canada	6,644.0	6,370.1	7,203.7	8,461.9	10,948.6

20.13 Income taxes by industrial division, 1972 and 1973 (million dollars)

Income taxes and year	Agri-culture, forestry, fishing	Mining	Manu-fac-turing	Con-struc-tion	Trans-portation, commun-ication, and other utilities	Whole-sale trade	Retail trade	Finance	Services	Total
Book profit before taxes[1]										
1972	55.2	667.1	4,002.1	358.5	1,050.5	925.3	618.8	1,282.8	345.1	9,305.3
1973	161.0	1,938.3	5,978.6	495.7	1,245.8	1,346.0	774.5	1,793.9	466.4	14,200.1
Taxable income										
1972	68.5	279.9	3,360.3	392.4	644.6	989.9	682.2	1,615.3	428.8	8,461.9
1973	119.3	597.5	4,594.6	459.4	737.1	1,302.8	785.1	1,839.8	513.0	10,948.6
Federal income taxes										
1972	14.0	101.0	1,171.5	102.4	222.2	311.2	189.3	521.7	117.5	2,750.8
1973	27.2	231.9	1,435.5	123.0	271.0	424.2	215.2	626.2	145.0	3,499.1
Provincial income taxes										
1972	6.4	30.4	388.7	41.9	70.7	111.2	73.1	165.0	45.1	932.5
1973	12.0	64.9	533.3	50.0	83.9	150.5	86.3	195.0	56.2	1,232.1
Total income taxes										
1972	20.4	131.4	1,560.2	144.2	292.9	422.5	262.4	686.7	162.5	3,683.3
1973	39.2	296.8	1,968.7	173.0	354.9	574.7	301.5	821.2	201.2	4,731.2

[1]After losses. Adjusted to exclude intercorporate dividends and net capital gains.

20.14 Excise taxes collected, by commodity, years ended Mar. 31, 1973-75 (thousand dollars)

Commodity	1973	1974	1975
Sales tax[1]	2,288,727	2,692,861	2,900,071
Other excise taxes			
Cigarettes, tobacco and cigars	343,082	375,708	367,275
Jewellery, watches, ornaments, etc.	15,015	15,513	20,829
Matches and lighters	1,259	1,635	2,349
Television sets, radios, tubes and phonographs	78	275	—
Toilet preparations	25,673	765	41
Wines	10,006	10,087	12,700
Sundry commodities	2,217	2,053	8,198
Interest and penalties	3,433	2,426	2,696
Less refunds and drawbacks	-315	-466	-647
Total	2,689,175	3,100,857	3,313,512

[1]Net after deduction of refunds and drawbacks; excludes tax credited to the Old Age Security Fund.

20.15   Liabilities of provincial and territorial governments as at Mar. 31, 1973 and 1974 (thousand dollars)

Province or territory and year		Short-term bank loans and over-drafts	Payables	Loans and advances	Treasury bills	Savings bonds	Bonds and debentures	Notes	Deposits and other liabilities	Total
Newfoundland	1973ʳ	19,490	34,063	33,007	6,003	—	880,345	36,760	38,971	1,048,639
	1974	22,301	38,357	64,873	—	—	1,007,857	32,322	38,603	1,204,313
Prince Edward Island	1973	1,896	8,646	15,259	6,500	—	101,983	—	12,073	146,357
	1974	4,868	12,528	20,077	1,000	—	103,724	—	12,893	155,090
Nova Scotia	1973	43,704	66,944	58,915	—	—	1,025,114	—	34,309	1,228,986
	1974	51,183	76,887	84,849	—	—	1,049,142	—	47,304	1,309,365
New Brunswick	1973ʳ	—	77,731	15,991	6,489	—	589,804	—	29,211	719,226
	1974	10,151	92,191	29,608	7,892	—	665,911	—	25,526	831,279
Quebec	1973ʳ	67,795	575,883	539,609	69,200	346,072	2,732,202	—	113,916	4,444,677
	1974	75,276	748,118	677,548	76,112	326,594	3,031,740	—	96,416	5,031,804
Ontario	1973	—	31,806	225,489	260,000	—	7,091,186	—	227,735	7,836,216
	1974	248	33,410	238,522	90,000	—	8,181,862	—	263,652	8,807,694
Manitoba	1973ʳ	65,609	29,287	37,836	40,901	52,870	598,463	—	46,385	871,351
	1974	92,189	32,506	43,770	39,026	49,971	681,340	—	55,969	994,771
Saskatchewan	1973	52,373	5,663	16,120	31,649	11,250	694,718	—	972	812,745
	1974	56,235	11,440	12,163	30,399	9,580	728,391	—	516	848,724
Alberta	1973ʳ	81,598	94,706	6,402	2,589	—	1,324,939	39,000	24,806	1,574,040
	1974	25,000	116,236	87,573	101,930	—	1,375,422	—	60,630	1,766,791
British Columbia	1973	13,425	85,025	—	4,614	—	607,247	—	20,536	730,847
	1974	45,779	102,839	—	3,596	—	660,629	—	35,130	847,973
Yukon Territory	1973	—	2,557	34,904	—	—	—	—	2,441	39,902
	1974	—	2,637	39,019	—	—	—	—	3,078	44,734
Northwest Territories	1973	2,280	11,737	68,724	—	—	—	—	2,443	85,184
	1974	—	9,773	86,048	—	—	—	—	2,516	98,337
Canada	1973ʳ	348,170	1,024,048	1,052,256	427,945	410,192	15,646,001	75,760	553,798	19,538,170
	1974	383,230	1,276,922	1,384,050	349,955	386,145	17,486,018	32,322	642,233	21,940,875

20.16   Liabilities guaranteed by provincial and territorial governments[1] as at Mar. 31, 1973 and 1974 (thousand dollars)

Province or territory and year		Bonds and debentures	Bank loans	Other	Total
Newfoundland	1973	148,924	29,896	109,305	288,125
	1974	164,973	37,753	103,734	306,460
Prince Edward Island	1973	9,691	6,320	366	16,377
	1974	8,911	4,494	355	13,760
Nova Scotia	1973	189,253	43,982	6,699	239,934
	1974	258,611	38,900	1,535	299,046
New Brunswick	1973	339,449	47,193	3,194	389,836
	1974	399,685	29,237	31,528	460,450
Quebec	1973	3,481,666	180,309	37,705	3,699,680
	1974	3,687,003	197,135	69,284	3,953,422
Ontario	1973	2,796,758	89,203	158,800	3,044,761
	1974	3,062,448	101,113	192,900	3,356,461
Manitoba	1973	987,057	—	3,000	990,057
	1974	1,178,091	—	1,000	1,179,091
Saskatchewan	1973	17,856	12,669	52,198	82,723
	1974	12,817	14,367	51,199	78,383
Alberta	1973	482,890	57,737	12,596	553,223
	1974	482,156	96,639	11,489	590,284
British Columbia	1973	2,683,844	13	—	2,683,857
	1974	2,958,891	9	22,443	2,981,343
Northwest Territories	1973	—	139	—	139
	1974	—	140	—	140
Canada	1973	11,137,388	467,461	383,863	11,988,712
	1974	12,213,586	519,787	485,467	13,218,840

[1] Excludes liabilities of provincial government special funds guaranteed by provincial governments but considered as provincial government liabilities.

20.17   Bonds and debentures[1], by market, of provincial governments outstanding as at Mar. 31, 1973 and 1974 (thousand dollars)

Province and year		Domestic	Foreign			International	Total
			Traditional				
			United States	Europe	Other		
Newfoundland	1973	353,069	167,496	126,932	—	125,930	773,427
	1974	391,562	206,855	141,459	—	139,373	879,249
Prince Edward Island	1973	72,300	8,418	—	—	—	80,718
	1974	69,769	8,347	—	—	—	78,116
Nova Scotia	1973	314,345	428,773	20,862	—	44,115	808,095
	1974	298,400	425,997	20,445	—	43,515	788,357
New Brunswick	1973	230,077	162,266	—	—	33,043	425,386
	1974	225,117	211,006	—	—	32,543	468,666
Quebec	1973r	1,774,293	423,150	150,845	32,682	84,494	2,465,464
	1974	1,930,240	604,325	112,293	32,682	78,332	2,757,872
Ontario	1973	1,267,859	1,216,637	134,948	—	—	2,619,444
	1974	1,255,430	1,436,240	92,308	—	—	2,783,978
Manitoba	1973	99,275	155,000	46,171	—	—	300,446
	1974	139,275	155,000	45,041	—	—	339,316
Saskatchewan	1973	229,524	137,807	25,154	—	—	392,485
	1974	247,815	119,879	9,103	—	—	376,797
Alberta	1973r	653,013	134,018	—	—	106	787,137
	1974	603,013	128,348	—	—	98	731,459
British Columbia	1973r	123,750	143,314	—	—	22,500	289,564
	1974	133,500	139,583	—	—	22,500	295,583
Total	1973r	5,117,505	2,976,879	504,912	32,682	310,188	8,942,166
	1974	5,294,121	3,435,580	420,649	32,682	316,361	9,499,393

[1]Includes savings bonds.

20.18   Personal income tax payable on various levels of income, 1976 (dollars)

Status	Income[1]	Federal income tax[2]	Provincial income tax[3]
Single taxpayer — no dependents	2,000	—	—
	3,000	—	12
	4,000	6	63
	5,000	184	117
	8,000	777	298
	10,000	1,205	428
	15,000	2,419	802
	20,000	3,771	1,250
	50,000	15,370	4,636
	100,000	39,693	11,380
Married taxpayer — no children	3,000	—	—
	4,000	—	—
	5,000	—	13
	8,000	396	182
	10,000	805	306
	20,000	3,249	1,077
	50,000	14,585	4,418
	100,000	38,747	11,118
Married taxpayer — two children under age 16	4,000	—	—
	5,000	—	8
	8,000	345	166
	10,000	751	290
	20,000	3,176	1,053
	50,000	14,476	4,388
	100,000	38,616	11,082

[1]Taxpayer is assumed to be under age 65 and to receive wage and salary income. Family allowances, at 1976 rates, are added to income where applicable. Taxpayer is assumed to take standard deduction of $100 in respect of medical expenses and charitable contributions. In addition to personal exemptions, the employment expense deduction of 3% of wage and salary income to a maximum of $150, and social security contributions, calculated at 1976 rates, are deducted from income in computing taxable income.
[2]Federal income tax includes the tax cut of 8%, minimum $200, maximum $500. In addition, federal income tax also includes the surtax of 10% of tax otherwise payable in excess of $8,000.
[3]Provincial income tax is calculated at the standard rate of 30.5% of federal basic tax. No account is taken of various provincial tax credits.

20.19   Special excise taxes levied as at Dec. 31, 1975

Item	Tax
Cigarettes	3¢ per 5 cigs.
Cigars	20½% ad valorem
Pipe tobacco, cut tobacco, snuff	90¢ per lb.
Jewellery, including articles of ivory, amber, shell, precious or semi-precious stones, clocks and watches[1], goldsmiths' and silversmiths' products, except gold-plated or silver-plated ware for the preparation or serving of food or drink	10% ad valorem
Lighters	10¢ per lighter
Playing cards	20¢ per pack
Slot machines — coin, disc or token-operated games or amusement devices	10% ad valorem
Matches	10% ad valorem
Tobacco, pipes, cigar and cigarette holders and cigarette rolling devices	10% ad valorem
Wines[2]	
Wines of all kinds containing not more than 7% absolute alcohol by volume	25¢ per gal
Non-sparkling wines containing more than 7% absolute alcohol by volume but not more than 40% proof spirit	50¢ per gal
Sparkling wines	$2.50 per gal
Wines (additional excise taxes)[3]	
Wines of all kinds containing not more than 7% absolute alcohol by volume	2½¢ per gal
Wines of all kinds containing more than 7% absolute alcohol by volume	5¢ per gal
Insurance premiums paid to British or foreign companies not authorized to transact business in Canada or to non-resident agents of authorized British or foreign companies	10% of net premium for property surety, fidelity and liability insurance. (Most other kinds of insurance are exempt.)
Air transportation tax on tickets purchased in Canada for transportation of persons	
(a) in the taxation area[4]	8% ad valorem, maximum $8
(b) beginning in the taxation area and ending outside the taxation area	$8[5]
Automobiles, station-wagons and vans designed for use as passenger vehicles[6]	$20 for the first 100 lb. in excess of the weight limit[7] $25 for the second 100 lb. in excess of the weight limit $30 for each additional 100 lb. in excess of the weight limit
Motorcycles with engines that have a displacement of greater than 250 cm³	5% ad valorem
Motors exceeding 20 hp (including drive assemblies) for boats	10% ad valorem
Aircraft but not including gliders or aircraft purchased or imported for use exclusively in the provision of such class or classes of air services as the Governor in Council may by regulation prescribe	10% ad valorem
Gasoline for personal use	10¢ per gal

All the foregoing items, except insurance premiums, are also subject to the general sales tax of 12%. Cigarettes, cigars and tobacco are subject to additional taxes under the Excise Act (referred to as excise duties).
[1]Special excise tax only applies on the amount by which the sale price or the duty-paid value of the clock or watch exceeds $50.
[2]These taxes apply only to wines manufactured in Canada. The customs tariff on wines includes a levy on imported wines to correspond to the taxes on domestic production.
[3]These taxes apply to both domestic and imported wines.
[4]Includes Canada, the islands of St. Pierre and Miquelon, and the US except Hawaii.
[5]Reduced to $4 for a child under 12 travelling at a fare 50% or more below the applicable fare; nil if the fare is 90% below the applicable fare.
[6]Excludes ambulances, hearses, vehicles for police or firefighting, or automobiles designed to carry 12 or more passengers.
[7]The weight limit is 4,500 lb. for automobiles and 5,100 lb. for station-wagons and vans.

20.20 Transfers by the federal government to provincial governments, territories and local governments, years ended Mar. 31, 1974 and 1975 (thousand dollars)

Year, payee and purpose	Nfld.	PEI	NS	NB	Que.	Ont.	Man.	Sask.	Alta.	BC	All provinces	YT	NWT	Canada
1974														
PROVINCIAL GOVERNMENTS AND TERRITORIES														
General purpose transfers														
Statutory subsidies	9,708	659	2,174	1,774	4,484	5,504	2,149	2,108	3,102	2,117	33,779	—	—	33,779
Federal estate tax	-70	-34	-1,028	101	-106	1,479	-114	166	-286	—	108	—	—	108
Federal corporation income tax on privately owned public utilities	1,922	390	202	5	2,357	12,538	451	16	6,085	1,930	25,896	389	78	26,363
Equalization	156,942	35,037	189,909	145,174	611,635	23,258	127,494	166,514	5,979	1,999	1,463,941	—	—	1,463,941
Established Programs (Interim Arrangements) Act	—	—	—	—	206,538	—	—	—	—	—	206,538	—	—	206,538
Grants in lieu of taxes	—	150	—	2,100	—	—	—	—	—	549	2,799	—	—	2,799
Other	—	—	—	200	—	—	—	—	—	—	200	14,945	69,868	85,013
Total, general purpose transfers	168,502	36,202	191,257	149,354	824,908	42,779	129,980	168,804	14,880	6,595	1,733,261	15,334	69,946	1,818,541
Specific purpose transfers														
Protection of persons and property	84	103	123	79	828	2,139	272	139	350	608	4,725	51	—	4,776
Courts of law	2	84	—	—	—	1,076	136	13	125	303	1,739	37	—	1,776
Other (civil emergency measures)	82	19	123	79	828	1,063	136	126	225	305	2,986	14	—	3,000
Transportation and communications														
Road	11,005	480	10,509	13,509	9,743	97	—	—	529	1,192	47,064	—	—	47,064
Railway Grade Crossing Fund	—	—	—	231	2,533	—	—	—	—	—	5,062	—	—	5,062
Other	11,005	480	10,509	13,278	7,210	97	—	—	529	1,192	42,002	—	—	42,002
Health														
Hospital insurance and diagnostic services	34,561	6,911	53,245	43,252	—	530,048	73,925	60,212	119,764	140,276	1,062,194	1,240	3,767	1,067,201
Hospital care	34,561	6,911	53,245	43,252	—	530,048	73,925	60,212	119,764	140,276	1,062,194	1,123	2,409	1,065,726
Indians and Inuit	—	—	—	—	—	—	—	—	—	—	—	117	1,358	1,475
Medical care	26,498	3,547	24,832	20,455	195,838	253,268	33,080	28,953	55,999	70,697	713,167	764	1,365	715,296
Health Resources Fund	9,788	—	—	391	10,453	9,927	1,895	1,241	3,299	—	36,994	—	6	37,000
Medical Care Act	16,710	3,547	24,832	20,064	185,385	243,341	31,185	27,712	52,700	70,697	676,173	638	1,136	677,947
Medicare – Indians and Inuit	—	—	—	—	—	—	—	—	—	—	—	126	223	349
Preventive services														
Public health research	..	..	..	..	..	..	..	..	..	..	..	..	..	..
Other	..	..	..	..	..	..	..	..	..	..	..	..	..	..
Professional training	62	21	77	72	616	785	101	102	154	165	2,155	—	7	2,162
Total, health	61,121	10,479	78,154	63,779	196,454	784,101	107,106	89,267	175,917	211,138	1,777,516	2,004	5,139	1,784,659
Social welfare														
Assistance to disabled, handicapped, unemployed and other needy individuals	24,920	5,214	28,192	31,209	-40	213,944	38,917	36,202	54,416	84,427	517,401	767	1,876	520,044
Old age assistance	-11	48	-1	-1	-24	-14	-3	-1	-3	-5	-63	-1	-1	-64
Disabled persons allowances	69	32	201	878	-14	6,660	955	827	1,619	972	12,215	2	12	12,229
Blind persons allowances	193	—	274	231	-2	28	70	22	116	120	1,084	2	15	1,101
Canada Assistance Plan	24,669	5,134	27,718	30,101	—	207,270	37,895	35,354	52,684	83,340	504,165	763	1,850	506,778
Other	1,577	—	34	14	158	4,164	722	—	1,716	27	8,412	215	250	8,877
Total, social welfare	26,497	5,214	28,226	31,223	118	218,108	39,639	36,202	56,132	84,454	525,813	982	2,126	528,921
Education														
Indian and Inuit schools	—	—	—	—	—	—	—	—	—	547	547	—	—	547

20.20 Transfers by the federal government to provincial governments, territories and local governments, years ended Mar. 31, 1974 and 1975 (thousand dollars) (continued)

Year, payee and purpose	Nfld.	PEI	NS	NB	Que.	Ont.	Man.	Sask.	Alta.	BC	All provinces	YT	NWT	Canada
1974 (continued)														
PROVINCIAL GOVERNMENTS AND TERRITORIES (concluded)														
Education (concluded)														
Post-secondary	5,443	955	22,492	7,317	205,161	153,646	17,716	13,925	54,711	13,083	494,449	—	—	494,449
Capital assistance in providing training facilities (Adult Occupational Training Act)	—	39	6	—	55	9	17	105	41	—	272	—	—	272
Post-secondary education	5,443	916	22,486	7,317	196,070	153,637	17,699	13,820	54,670	13,083	485,141	—	—	485,141
Canada Student Loans Act	—	—	—	—	9,036	—	—	—	—	—	9,036	—	—	9,036
Other	194	184	801	6,561	52,607	24,094	2,079	630	943	1,029	89,122	—	—	89,122
Total, education	5,637	1,139	23,293	13,878	257,768	177,740	19,795	14,555	55,654	14,659	584,118	—	—	584,118
Natural resources														
Fish and game	4,344	1,330	2,071	1,600	340	100	32	—	—	1,100	10,917	—	8	10,925
Forests														
Inventory of forest reserves	305	—	—	—	—	—	—	—	—	—	305	—	—	305
Mines	614	—	—	952	—	—	—	—	—	—	1,566	—	—	1,566
Oil and gas (Oil Export Tax Act)	—	—	—	—	—	—	1,184	15,737	122,087	4,301	143,309	—	—	143,309
Water power	—	—	—	5,000	—	561	—	—	—	2,228	7,789	—	—	7,789
Total, natural resources	5,263	1,330	2,071	7,552	340	661	1,216	15,737	122,087	7,629	163,886	—	8	163,894
Agriculture, trade and industry, and tourism														
Agriculture	1,866	15,860	4,064	9,288	41,120	7,994	6,435	8,668	10,450	2,635	108,380	—	—	108,380
Agricultural and Rural Development Act	794	—	2,975	1,527	5,452	5,817	2,015	1,512	2,499	1,426	24,017	—	—	24,017
Land surveying and mapping	1,051	—	1,026	908	—	—	—	—	—	—	2,985	—	—	2,985
Rural area development	—	15,694	—	6,823	33,627	—	2,193	—	—	—	58,337	—	—	58,337
Canada Land Inventory	21	—	—	—	114	—	100	70	—	448	753	—	—	753
Rabies control	—	—	—	1	11	44	—	—	2	—	58	—	—	58
Crop insurance	—	134	46	—	1,473	2,133	2,019	6,525	3,864	461	16,655	—	—	16,655
Assistance re crop losses due to adverse weather	—	32	17	29	443	—	27	256	39	300	1,143	—	—	1,143
Research	—	—	—	—	—	—	—	—	5	—	5	—	—	5
Irrigation rehabilitation	—	—	—	—	—	—	—	—	3,500	—	3,500	—	—	3,500
Waterfowl crop depredation	—	—	—	—	—	—	81	305	541	—	927	—	—	927
Trade and industry	18	—	—	—	10,010	—	1	—	—	—	10,029	—	—	10,029
Tourism	—	—	—	—	106	43	45	17	31	74	316	—	—	316
Total, agriculture, trade and industry, and tourism	1,884	15,860	4,064	9,288	51,236	8,037	6,481	8,685	10,481	2,709	118,725	—	—	118,725
Environment														
Pest control operations	—	—	—	631	3,487	—	—	—	—	—	4,118	—	—	4,118
Recreation and culture	70	87	86	85	—	90	477	—	—	—	895	72	390	1,357
Recreational facilities	—	—	—	—	—	—	477	—	—	—	477	—	300	777
Other	70	87	86	85	—	90	—	—	—	—	418	72	90	580
Labour, employment and immigration	953	10	200	92	2,355	2,832	16	222	1,239	1,493	9,412	1	8	9,421
Labour and employment	945	7	189	85	2,314	2,803	3	208	1,222	1,473	9,249	—	7	9,256
Other	8	3	11	7	41	29	13	14	17	20	163	1	1	165
Housing														
General assistance	232	—	—	—	—	14	—	—	5	75	326	24	—	350
Supervision and development of regions and localities	12,475	2	3,552	13,303	55,245	—	1,445	780	2,407	35	89,244	—	—	89,244
Total, specific purpose transfers	125,221	34,704	150,278	153,419	577,574	1,193,819	176,447	165,587	424,801	323,992	3,325,842	3,083	7,722	3,336,647
Total, transfers to provincial governments and territories	293,723	70,906	341,535	302,773	1,402,482	1,236,598	306,427	334,391	439,681	330,587	5,059,103	18,417	77,668	5,155,188

20.20 Transfers by the federal government to provincial governments, territories and local governments, years ended Mar. 31, 1974 and 1975 (thousand dollars) (continued)

Year, payee and purpose	Nfld.	PEI	NS	NB	Que.	Ont.	Man.	Sask.	Alta.	BC	All provinces	YT	NWT	Canada
1974 (concluded)														
LOCAL GOVERNMENTS														
General purpose transfers														
Grants in lieu of taxes	418	156	5,145	2	14,754	28,439	4,255	1,722	3,523	5,001	63,415	251	287	63,953
Specific purpose transfers														
Transportation and communications														
Air	43	68	19	40	2,036	3,655	931	216	913	687	8,608	190	—	8,798
Road	43	68	19	40	559	851	380	89	586	687	3,322	190	—	3,512
Railway Grade Crossing Fund	—	—	—	—	1,477	2,804	551	127	327	—	5,286	—	—	5,286
Social welfare														
Assistance to disabled, handicapped, unemployed and other needy individuals	3,232	351	1,919	1,734	13,214	4,470	897	723	1,458	4,990	32,988	28	209	33,225
Education														
Primary and secondary	—	—	—	—	114	407	1,204	561	1,006	—	3,292	—	—	3,292
Environment														
Sewage collection and disposal	67	543	2,639	889	4,160	16,424	1,400	109	1,985	10,963	39,179	—	36	39,215
Housing														
General assistance	935	—	113	267	7,953	4,665	161	12	663	1,692	16,461	—	—	16,461
Total, specific purpose transfers	4,277	962	4,690	2,930	27,477	29,621	4,593	1,621	6,025	18,332	100,528	218	245	100,991
Total, transfers to local governments	4,695	1,118	9,835	2,932	42,231	58,060	8,848	3,343	9,548	23,333	163,943	469	532	164,944
Total, transfers to provincial governments, territories and local governments	298,418	72,024	351,370	305,705	1,444,713	1,294,658	315,275	337,734	449,229	353,920	5,223,046	18,886	78,200	5,320,132
1975														
PROVINCIAL GOVERNMENTS AND TERRITORIES														
General purpose transfers														
Statutory subsidies	9,708	659	2,174	1,774	4,484	5,504	2,156	2,100	3,132	2,117	33,808	—	—	33,808
Federal estate tax	26	38	32	-289	2,098	684	437	-168	797	—	3,655	—	—	3,655
Federal corporation income tax on privately owned public utilities	1,744	453	200	—	948	7,628	1,410	9	12,495	1,768	26,655	263	117	27,035
Equalization	197,457	43,007	231,448	189,531	1,085,534	214,131	151,854	103,692	44,862	25,463	2,286,979	—	—	2,286,979
Established Programs (Interim Arrangements) Act	—	—	—	—	176,406	—	—	—	—	—	176,406	—	—	176,406
Grants in lieu of taxes	—	84	—	1,912	—	—	—	—	—	1,156	3,152	489	148	3,789
Other	—	—	—	—	—	—	—	—	—	—	—	14,664	79,834	94,498
Total, general purpose transfers	208,935	44,241	233,854	192,928	1,269,470	227,947	155,857	105,633	61,286	30,504	2,530,655	15,416	80,099	2,626,170
Specific purpose transfers														
Protection of persons and property														
Courts of law	126	39	507	349	2,614	4,959	649	174	857	1,578	11,852	—	77	11,929
Other (civil emergency measures)	78	17	443	295	2,233	4,466	574	104	741	1,424	10,375	—	54	10,429
Transportation and communications														
Road	48	22	64	54	381	493	75	70	116	154	1,477	—	23	1,500
Railway Grade Crossing Fund	3,341	7	—	2,076	10,423	491	8,555	4,240	7,784	3,422	40,339	—	—	40,339
Other	—	—	—	93	3,091	491	25	—	254	922	4,883	—	—	4,883
Other	3,341	—	—	1,983	7,332	—	8,530	4,240	7,530	2,500	35,456	—	—	35,456
Health														
Hospital care	42,101	7,951	62,651	51,898	—	651,857	84,765	72,471	142,291	187,379	1,303,364	1,400	4,468	1,309,232
Hospital insurance and diagnostic services	42,101	7,951	62,651	51,898	—	651,857	84,765	72,471	142,291	187,379	1,303,364	1,349	2,928	1,307,641
Hospital care	—	—	—	—	—	—	—	—	—	—	—	51	1,540	1,591

20.20   Transfers by the federal government to provincial governments, territories and local governments, years ended Mar. 31, 1974 and 1975 (thousand dollars) (continued)

Year, payee and purpose	Nfld.	PEI	NS	NB	Que.	Ont.	Man.	Sask.	Alta.	BC	All provinces	YT	NWT	Canada
1975 (continued)														
PROVINCIAL GOVERNMENTS AND TERRITORIES (continued)														
Health (concluded)														
Medical care	26,128	3,949	27,209	22,669	220,237	281,731	35,576	31,545	61,246	81,813	792,103	773	1,522	794,398
Health Resources Fund	7,784	—	—	279	13,065	6,564	643	918	1,822	272	31,347	—	—	31,347
Medical Care Act	18,344	3,949	27,209	22,390	207,172	275,167	34,933	30,627	59,424	81,541	760,756	678	1,256	762,690
Medicare — Indians and Inuit	—	—	—	—	—	—	—	—	—	—	—	95	266	361
Preventive services														
Public health research	275	28	682	164	3,093	3,624	942	473	554	799	10,634	—	56	10,690
Other														
Professional training	60	21	83	73	621	829	109	103	164	165	2,228	—	—	2,228
Total, health	68,564	11,949	90,625	74,804	223,951	938,041	121,392	104,592	204,255	270,156	2,108,329	2,173	6,046	2,116,548
Social welfare														
Assistance to disabled, handicapped, unemployed and other needy individuals	33,511	7,138	31,986	36,729	715	307,728	50,598	35,632	70,076	139,829	713,942	741	6,117	720,800
Old age assistance	-19	—	-1	—	1	-18	-1	-1	-1	-1	-41	—	—	-41
Disabled persons allowances	165	69	546	1,266	-5	7,085	672	853	2,835	23	13,509	1	17	13,527
Blind persons allowances	144	31	252	237	-2	18	55	18	100	-14	839	—	6	845
Canada Assistance Plan	33,221	7,038	31,189	35,226	721	300,643	49,872	34,762	67,142	139,821	699,635	740	6,094	706,469
Other	—	1	—	248	—	15,763	1,875	25	116	9	18,037	650	6	18,693
Total, social welfare	33,511	7,139	31,986	36,977	715	323,491	52,473	35,657	70,192	139,838	731,979	1,391	6,123	739,493
Education														
Indian and Inuit schools	—	—	—	—	—	—	—	—	—	203	203	—	—	203
Post-secondary	4,750	1,135	19,178	6,263	243,679	142,685	15,925	13,231	52,515	14,916	514,277	—	—	514,277
Post-secondary education	4,750	1,135	19,178	6,263	232,981	142,685	15,925	13,231	52,515	14,916	503,579	—	—	503,579
Canada Student Loans Act	—	—	—	—	10,698	—	—	—	—	—	10,698	—	—	10,698
Other	494	406	1,450	6,464	51,017	26,475	1,794	992	1,352	2,058	92,502	53	4	92,559
Total, education	5,244	1,541	20,628	12,727	294,696	169,160	17,719	14,223	53,867	17,177	606,982	53	4	607,039
Natural resources														
Fish and game	1,322	—	1,651	—	915	47	162	—	—	883	4,980	—	—	4,980
Forests	116	—	—	—	—	—	—	—	—	—	116	—	—	116
Inventory of forest reserves	639	—	—	823	—	—	—	234	—	—	1,696	—	—	1,696
Mines	—	—	—	—	—	—	—	—	—	—	—	—	—	—
Oil and gas (Oil Export Tax Act)	—	—	—	—	—	—	507	12,195	95,353	3,056	111,111	—	—	111,111
Water power	30	—	—	—	—	1,872	—	—	—	4,882	6,784	—	—	6,784
Other	149	47	—	—	—	—	—	—	—	—	196	—	—	196
Total, natural resources	2,256	47	1,651	823	915	1,919	669	12,429	95,353	8,821	124,883	—	—	124,883
Agriculture, trade and industry, and tourism														
Agriculture	6,075	19,117	4,851	8,267	29,752	10,688	7,434	19,936	10,375	2,107	118,602	—	—	118,602
Agricultural and Rural Development Act	1,715	—	4,766	486	5,542	5,365	2,448	4,213	2,003	924	27,462	—	—	27,462
Land surveying and mapping	4,318	—	—	375	—	—	—	—	—	—	4,693	—	—	4,693
Rural area development	—	18,896	—	7,406	21,442	—	1,676	—	—	—	49,420	—	—	49,420
Canada Land Inventory	31	—	—	—	51	—	3	—	—	331	416	—	—	416
Rabies control	—	—	—	—	16	63	4	2	—	—	85	—	—	85
Crop insurance	—	221	85	—	1,766	3,869	2,765	14,578	7,300	652	31,236	—	—	31,236
Assistance re crop losses due to adverse weather	—	—	—	—	112	13	277	683	454	200	1,739	—	—	1,739

20.20 Transfers by the federal government to provincial governments, territories and local governments, years ended Mar. 31, 1974 and 1975 (thousand dollars) (concluded)

Year, payee and purpose	Nfld.	PEI	NS	NB	Que.	Ont.	Man.	Sask.	Alta.	BC	All provinces	YT	NWT	Canada
1975 (concluded)														
PROVINCIAL GOVERNMENTS AND TERRITORIES (concluded)														
Agriculture (concluded)														
Research	11	—	—	—	823	1,378	—	—	—	—	2,212	—	—	2,212
Waterfowl crop depredation	—	—	—	—	—	—	261	460	618	—	1,339	—	—	1,339
Trade and industry	35,644	—	4,607	26,450	18,820	4,642	8,005	468	2,887	2,500	104,023	—	—	104,023
Tourism	—	—	—	—	108	13	42	3	22	61	249	—	—	249
Total, agriculture, trade and industry, and tourism	41,719	19,117	9,458	34,717	48,680	15,343	15,481	20,407	13,284	4,668	222,874	—	—	222,874
Environment														
Pest control operations	—	—	—	565	2,035	—	—	—	—	106	2,706	—	—	2,706
Recreation and culture	93	59	111	117	—	95	237	27	—	36	775	70	80	925
Recreational facilities	—	—	—	—	—	—	217	—	—	—	217	—	—	217
Other	93	59	111	117	—	95	20	27	—	36	558	70	80	708
Labour, employment and immigration														
Labour and employment	477	574	1,733	164	5,510	3,390	97	910	2,169	2,825	17,849	—	—	17,849
Housing														
General assistance	413	—	—	—	—	—	—	—	—	—	413	68	—	481
Supervision and development of regions and localities	11,284	2	10,085	7,377	21,176	50	1,264	467	1,643	426	53,774	—	547	54,321
Total, specific purpose transfers	167,028	40,474	166,784	170,696	610,715	1,456,939	218,536	193,126	449,404	449,053	3,922,755	3,755	12,877	3,939,387
Total, transfers to provincial governments and territories	375,963	84,715	400,638	363,624	1,880,185	1,684,886	374,393	298,759	510,690	479,557	6,453,410	19,171	92,976	6,565,557
LOCAL GOVERNMENTS														
General purpose transfers														
Grants in lieu of taxes	747	78	4,319	62	14,645	33,099	5,131	1,929	3,532	5,489	69,031	214	265	69,510
Specific purpose transfers														
Transportation and communications	490	—	62	56	622	1,366	454	117	828	358	4,353	22	—	4,375
Air	490	—	62	56	484	642	327	92	821	358	3,332	22	—	3,354
Road	—	—	—	—	138	724	127	25	7	—	1,021	—	—	1,021
Social welfare														
Assistance to disabled, handicapped, unemployed and other needy individuals	1,930	231	931	866	6,073	3,554	387	341	640	2,086	17,039	34	86	17,159
Education														
Primary and secondary	—	—	233	—	—	253	547	142	591	—	1,766	—	—	1,766
Environment	92	225	1,212	860	7,374	15,344	246	101	2,116	4,702	32,272	—	17	32,289
Water purification and supply	—	—	53	—	—	—	—	—	—	—	53	—	—	53
Sewage collection and disposal	92	225	972	860	7,374	15,344	246	101	2,116	4,702	32,032	—	17	32,049
Other	—	—	187	—	—	—	—	—	—	—	187	—	—	187
Recreation and culture														
Cultural facilities	—	—	—	—	—	40	—	—	—	—	40	—	—	40
Housing														
General assistance	1,221	—	171	1,218	6,778	7,944	335	3	557	1,548	19,775	—	—	19,775
Total, specific purpose transfers	3,733	456	2,609	3,000	20,847	28,501	1,969	704	4,732	8,694	75,245	56	103	75,404
Total, transfers to local governments	4,480	534	6,928	3,062	35,492	61,600	7,100	2,633	8,264	14,183	144,276	270	368	144,914
Total, transfers to provincial governments, territories and local governments	380,443	85,249	407,566	366,686	1,915,677	1,746,486	381,493	301,392	518,954	493,740	6,597,686	19,441	93,344	6,710,471

20.21 Conditional grants and shared-cost programs as at Mar. 31, 1975

Department and project	Provinces participating[1]	Provincial share[2] %	Federal contribution 1974-75 $'000
AGRICULTURE			
Crop insurance	8 (Nfld.,NB)	50-100 of admin. costs	31,140
4-H Club assistance	10	50	166
Experimental crop insurance	Que.	50	96
Programs under $100,000	NS,NB,Que., Sask., Alta.		28
Crop loss assistance	6 (Nfld.,PEI,NS,NB)	50	1,739
Contributions for rabies	Que.,Ont.,Man.,Sask.	60	85
Aid to universities - veterinary teaching	Que.,Ont.	50	2,200
ENERGY, MINES AND RESOURCES			
Aeromagnetic surveys	PEI,Que.,BC	50	330
Electrical interconnection studies	Nfld.,PEI	terms of agreement	196
BC — Yukon — NWT boundary	BC	50	33
Mineral development programs	Nfld.,Sask.,Alta.	terms of agreement	629
ENVIRONMENT			
Canada Land Inventory	Nfld.,Que.,Sask.,BC	50	416
Metropolitan Toronto and Upper Thames	Ont.	terms of agreement	290
Lake Winnipeg, Churchill — Nelson River Agreement	Man.	50	123
Churchill — Nelson Basin studies	Man.	50	10
Migratory birds crop depredation	Man.,Sask.,Alta.	50	1,339
Shore damage to property on Great Lakes	Ont.	terms of agreement	73
Industrial development	BC	50	102
Fraser River flood control	BC	50	4,830
Preparation of a comprehensive water quality plan of the St. Lawrence	Que.	terms of agreement	298
Process technology	Nfld.	terms of agreement	600
Pest control	NB,Que.	terms of agreement	2,599
Environmental assessment	Que.,BC	50	1,576
Newfoundland Forest Inventory	Nfld.	10	116
Delta Project — Manitoba	Man.	terms of agreement	350
Various programs under $100,000	Nfld.,Que.	terms of agreement	34
INDIAN AFFAIRS AND NORTHERN DEVELOPMENT			
Community development on and off reserve	Nfld.	terms of agreement	1,396
Child Care Agreement	Man. + YT	terms of agreement	161
Maintenance of highway — Rocky Harbour to St. Pauls	Nfld.	terms of agreement	123
Forest fire protection agreements	Ont.	terms of agreement	58
Registered Trapline Fur Agreement	Man.	50	60
Roads on and to reserves	Man.,Sask.	20-50	525
Natural resources agreements	Ont.	terms of agreement	136
Vocational and technical training	Ont.	terms of agreement	384
Housing relocation — Kouchibouguac Park	NB	terms of agreement	742
Purchase of land	Nfld.,NB	terms of agreement	1,986
INDUSTRY, TRADE AND COMMERCE			
Tourism	10	50	295
JUSTICE			
All programs included	10 + NWT	terms of agreement	10,429

20.21   Conditional grants and shared-cost programs as at Mar. 31, 1975 (continued)

Department and project	Provinces participating[1]	Provincial share[2] %	Federal contribution 1974-75 $'000
MANPOWER AND IMMIGRATION			
Agricultural manpower	9 (Nfld.)	50	1,984
Federal-provincial health agreements	Ont.	terms of agreement	1
Manpower training research	PEI,NB,Que.,Ont.,Sask.	50	69
NATIONAL DEFENCE			
Contributions to provinces and municipalities for civil defence purposes	10 + NWT	25	1,500
NATIONAL HEALTH AND WELFARE			
Health care programs			
Health Resources Fund Act	8³ (PEI,NS)	50	31,347
Training of health personnel	10	—	2,228
Medical Care Act	10 + YT and NWT	50	762,690
Hospital Insurance and Diagnostic Services Act	10 + YT and NWT	50	1,868,202⁴
Income security and social assistance programs			
Old age assistance	8 (PEI,NB)	50	41 Cr.⁴,⁵
Blind Persons Allowances	10 + NWT	25	1,068⁴
Disabled Persons Allowances	10 + YT and NWT	50	1,807⁴
Guaranteed income experimental projects	Man.	25	1,763
Unemployment assistance	Que.,Sask.,Alta. + NWT	50	129⁴
Canada Assistance Plan	10 + YT and NWT	50	1,056,062⁴
Services to young offenders	NB,Ont.	50	12,500
Nursing home care	Ont.,Man.,Alta.	50	45,598
National welfare grants	PEI,NB,Ont.,Sask.,BC + NWT	50	41
Vocational rehabilitation of disabled persons	9 (Que.) + NWT	50	12,000
PUBLIC WORKS			
Interior and exterior alterations to Johnson Building, Barrington St., Halifax, NS for Information Canada	NS	terms of agreement	4
Maintenance cost of Perley Bridge — agreement that federal government pay 75%, Ontario 25%. Maintenance cost of Macdonald-Cartier Bridge — agreement that federal government pay 33 ⅓%, Ontario 66 ⅔%.	Ont.	terms of agreement	54
Project Churchill — cost-sharing agreement with Manitoba for construction services and social infrastructures at Churchill, Man.	Man.	terms of agreement	2,483
REGIONAL ECONOMIC EXPANSION			
Fund for Rural Economic Development (FRED)	PEI,NB,Que.,Man.	terms of agreement	46,274
Agricultural and Rural Development (ARDA)	9 (PEI)	50	28,513
Special areas infrastructure and highways	7 (PEI,Ont.,BC)	terms of agreement	29,267
General Development Agreements	9 (PEI)	10-50	104,024
Interim Planning Agreements	6 (PEI,Que.,Ont.,Man.)	terms of agreement	2,049
Miscellaneous agreements	8 (Ont.,BC)	terms of agreement	8,896

20.21   Conditional grants and shared-cost programs as at Mar. 31, 1975 (concluded)

Department and project	Provinces participating[1]	Provincial share[2] %	Federal contribution 1974-75 $'000
SECRETARY OF STATE			
Post-secondary education	10	50	503,579
Language texts for citizenship classes	Que.,Ont.,Sask.	—	137
Bilingualism development	10+ YT and NWT	—	91,325
Citizenship Development — Indian Participation	YT	terms of agreement	15
Citizenship and language instruction for immigrants	Que.,Ont.,Sask.,Alta.,BC	50	1,097
TRANSPORT			
Cost-sharing contract between the Ministry of Transport and the Ontario Ministry of Transportation and Communications and the Regional Municipality of Ottawa — Carleton	Ont.	60	9
Contract for an Air Cushion Vehicle cargo demonstration	Que.	44	100
Contributions to assist in highway work	Man.,Sask.,Alta.,BC	—	22,800
URBAN AFFAIRS			
National Capital Commission	Que.,Ont.	terms of agreement	13,702

[1] Provinces not participating are shown in parentheses.
[2] As here used, 50% may mean the province must contribute 50% of the cost of the project or must match the federal contribution.
[3] The estimate for Newfoundland is $7,784,000 and for New Brunswick, $279,000. This figure includes additional contributions from the $25 million Atlantic portion of the fund as follows: Newfoundland $2,714,000, New Brunswick $93,000.
[4] Includes the contribution to Quebec under the Established Programs (Interim Arrangements) Act, which may have taken the form of a tax abatement and an operating cost adjustment payment or recovery.
[5] Cr. indicates a recovery.

20.22   Gross general revenue and expenditure of provincial and territorial governments, year ended Mar. 31, 1974 (thousand dollars)

Source or function	Nfld.	PEI	NS	NB	Que.	Ont.	Man.	Sask.	Alta.	BC	YT	NWT	Canada
Gross general revenue by source													
Income Tax													
Individuals	46,569	9,115	101,368	80,001	1,778,077	1,417,495	159,859	107,045	281,747	409,041	—	—	4,390,316
Corporations	16,251	1,880	20,439	14,339	296,221	528,311	48,094	26,971	114,759	136,768	—	—	1,204,232
General sales tax	71,876	15,228	100,978	84,689	860,636	1,314,814	117,845	94,242	—	345,586	—	—	3,005,905
Motive fuel tax	30,506	7,596	51,089	42,203	383,215	547,171	56,684	60,224	102,624	132,145	2,950	2,994	1,419,400
Health insurance premiums	—	—	—	—	—	530,054	—	6,886	56,059	84,564	1,005	—	689,730
Social insurance levies	6,397	944	10,273	10,444	142,429	207,294	15,576	12,836	33,357	67,977	1,827	1,898	507,528
Other provincial taxes	13,972	9,063	13,635	50,257	815,055	377,312	34,393	22,104	29,402	88,262	153	266	1,457,180
Natural resource revenue	4,733	336	3,228	7,415	64,032	96,621	27,595	66,514	609,632	357,309	948	688	1,237,835
Privileges, licences and permits	17,836	2,310	19,053	15,315	191,496	288,387	24,838	19,449	44,191	58,633	2,166	3,776	683,143
Liquor profits	14,009	3,844	36,626	23,168	119,000	206,707	35,822	19,269	79,015	105,701	3,244	7,897	649,102
Non-tax revenue from own sources	52,378	16,809	79,533	48,175	562,332	664,079	98,356	122,641	246,906	215,953	8,872	—	2,118,305
General purpose transfers from other levels of government	168,502	36,052	191,834	153,153	783,162	20,513	130,482	181,269	79,334	8,872	11,717	62,514	1,827,405
Specific purpose transfers from other levels of government	118,352	36,288	150,921	150,154	558,061	1,195,713	193,027	156,972	311,032	342,362	17,039	21,532	3,251,454
Total	561,383	139,476	778,976	679,314	6,553,714	7,394,671	953,733	896,424	1,988,057	2,353,173	41,050	101,564	22,441,536

20.22 Gross general revenue and expenditure of provincial and territorial governments, year ended Mar. 31, 1974 (thousand dollars) (concluded)

Source or function	Province or territory												Canada
	Nfld.	PEI	NS	NB	Que.	Ont.	Man.	Sask.	Alta.	BC	YT	NWT	
Gross general expenditure by function													
General government	24,887	10,035	30,237	35,564	282,138	346,572	35,924	48,628	91,554	129,804	4,885	39,238	1,079,465
Protection of persons and property	15,377	2,576	21,231	20,186	217,098	292,394	33,552	26,259	55,288	67,190	2,836	3,057	757,043
Transportation and communications	67,245	17,836	89,693	83,708	617,921	662,309	82,857	88,896	126,671	238,757	13,306	2,829	2,092,028
Health	129,165	23,421	182,035	154,331	1,632,275	2,195,787	247,790	206,666	447,271	560,358	4,002	9,060	5,792,162
Social welfare	62,727	12,589	72,649	66,237	978,522	834,515	136,023	95,598	217,563	316,067	2,250	6,501	2,801,240
Education	156,575	37,712	188,067	181,823	1,561,999	2,061,999	234,372	175,989	452,970	406,678	9,383	29,446	5,497,013
Natural resources	17,243	3,287	17,098	14,315	103,533	84,017	24,506	13,824	54,839	89,627	295	1,260	423,842
Agriculture, trade and industry, and tourism	27,088	9,039	22,587	18,956	145,757	105,032	29,947	35,929	57,410	33,124	239	4,897	490,005
Housing	1,736	7,186	10,922	—	37,246	33,465	—	32,652	5,954	100,688	1,267	7,731	238,847
Debt charges	69,483	9,462	77,526	44,423	333,057	590,335	55,631	47,249	98,552	40,554	2,445	4,816	1,373,532
General purpose transfers to other levels of government	3,846	598	23,959	23,089	216,017	209,765	19,012	—	51,847	59,956	—	—	608,089
All other expenditures	41,979	5,285	49,157	30,429	218,422	300,029	47,412	29,418	82,701	70,779	3,404	10,706	889,719
Total	617,350	139,026	785,159	673,060	6,343,984	7,716,219	947,026	801,106	1,742,620	2,113,582	44,312	119,541	22,042,985

20.23 General revenue of local governments, fiscal years ended nearest Dec. 31, 1972 and 1973 (thousand dollars)

Year and source	Nfld.	PEI	NS	NB	Que.	Ont.	Man.	Sask.	Alta.	BC	YT	NWT	Canada
1972													
Revenue from own sources	19,967	5,473	130,190	29,271	1,292,219	2,146,620	238,011	237,935	452,031	567,779	1,678	4,074	5,125,248
Taxes	15,177	3,643	98,991	19,005	982,970	1,760,816	175,969	175,886	317,366	460,001	757	1,659	4,012,240
Real property	9,303	3,516	83,239	18,937	819,167[1]	1,510,939	156,268	152,861	279,585	425,048	692	1,516	3,461,071
Special assessments	438	82	2,464	68	79,339	40,418	6,542	11,128	16,844	20,850	65	47	178,285
Personal property	...	3	8,300				470						8,773
Corporations and business	3,232	32	4,352		60,959	209,459	11,529	10,190	20,937	14,024			334,810
Other	2,204	10	636		23,505[a]		1,160				96	96	29,301
Grants in lieu of taxes	1,821	116	10,358	111	26,653	57,375	18,555	5,617	14,434	9,037	269	742	145,088
Federal government	227	93	4,581		4,963	27,639	4,316	1,225	3,106	3,544	128	404	50,226
Federal government enterprises	152	3			3,270	4,233	865	268		401			12,341
Provincial governments	29	20	3,149	111	4,637	5,223	8,731	409	7,686	2,241	141	338	30,190
Provincial government enterprises	—		735		2,946	20,280	1,830	906		2,821			32,157
Local government enterprises	—				2,952			421	3,642				7,500
Non-government organizations	1,413		1,892		7,885		2,813			30			12,674
Sales of goods and services	1,783	1,138	13,053	7,666	186,802	212,064	24,884	32,947	60,648	59,349	415	1,224	601,973
Water	1,645	484	5,842	6,792	132,159	108,354	12,681	12,381	23,959	30,046	277	562	335,182
Other	138	654	7,211	874	54,643	103,710	12,203	20,566	36,689	29,303	138	662	266,791
Rentals	184	50	719	571	8,701	9,016	310	1,037	6,736	5,371	28	126	32,849
Concessions and franchises	4		10	15		2,639	98	69	3,859	332	1	148	7,175
Licences and permits	248	29	572	403	9,414	20,112	3,013	1,904	8,271	12,297	105	98	56,466
Remittances from own enterprises	—	210	365			6,913		4,807	14,808	1,991			29,523
Interest	76	5	2,071	202	10,991	14,564	4,280	1,358	2,321	8,527	21	7	47,872
Interest and penalties on taxes	16	32	1,043	57	12,001	14,413	1,920	1,938	4,432	2,937	33	26	38,268
Fines	15	202	740	264	15,968	7,809	1,588	7,136	5,677	5,097	34	12	39,344
Miscellaneous	643	48	2,268	977	38,719	40,899	7,394		13,479	2,840	15	32	114,450

20.23 General revenue of local governments, fiscal years ended nearest Dec. 31, 1972 and 1973 (thousand dollars) (concluded)

Year and source	Nfld.	PEI	NS	NB	Que.	Ont.	Man.	Sask.	Alta.	BC	YT	NWT	Canada
1972 (concluded)													
Transfers	17,447	22,274	132,540	21,853	1,138,729	1,976,181	174,513	181,734	394,226	390,503	751	2,082	4,452,833
General purpose	4,044	556	7,128	18,139	192,829	98,884	8,906	3,020	41,776	—	588	525	376,395
Provincial governments	4,044	556	7,128	18,139	192,829	98,884	8,906	3,020	41,776	—	588	525	376,395
Specific purpose	13,403	21,718	125,412	3,714	945,900	1,877,297	165,607	178,714	352,450	390,503	163	1,557	4,076,438
Federal government	4,437	1,021	4,069	2,870	25,764	31,476	6,865	2,642	6,341	9,389	63	88	95,025
Provincial governments	8,966	20,697	121,343	844	920,136	1,845,821	158,742	176,072	346,109	381,114	100	1,469	3,981,413
Total, general revenue	37,414	27,747	262,730	51,124	2,430,948	4,122,801	412,524	419,669	846,257	958,282	2,429	6,156	9,578,081
1973													
Revenue from own sources	22,779	5,284	142,997	33,470	1,423,723	2,279,050	256,525	241,342	520,319	676,969	2,242	5,065	5,609,765
Taxes	16,324	3,109	105,369	22,387	1,056,114	1,809,177	189,494	182,791	339,411	517,724	974	2,145	4,245,019
Real property	10,426	2,885	84,407	22,273	885,134[3]	1,538,271	168,824	159,268	301,150	477,248	974	1,981	3,652,841
Special assessments	417	78	3,279	114	82,771	39,802	6,287	9,968	16,030	24,929	—	51	183,726
Personal property	—	—	8,548	—	—	—	530	—	—	—	—	—	9,078
Corporations and business	3,594	143	7,156	—	67,687	222,023	12,342	10,981	22,231	15,452	—	113	361,722
Grants in lieu of taxes	1,090	36	13,091	—	42,912	68,912	21,684	5,688	17,695	9,969	452	762	182,004
Federal government	247	15	4,815	—	5,462	26,727	5,003	1,275	4,088	3,423	217	296	51,568
Federal government enterprises	189	—	—	—	4,434	3,823	926	279	—	965	—	—	14,204
Provincial governments	180	21	3,588	—	13,025	19,204	10,086	452	8,060	2,699	235	466	55,277
Provincial government enterprises	94	—	—	—	3,522	19,158	2,861	812	—	2,812	—	—	34,734
Local government enterprises	380	—	849	—	4,878	11,304	—	413	5,547	—	—	—	11,617
Non-government organizations	—	—	3,830	—	11,304	—	2,808	—	—	70	—	—	14,604
Sales of goods and services	3,844	1,424	16,363	8,083	206,825	257,019	25,736	32,935	95,642	81,590	538	835	730,834
Water	2,319	507	6,111	5,325	146,404	115,774	12,986	12,885	27,424	33,695	410	658	364,498
Other	1,525	917	10,252	2,758	60,421	141,245	12,750	20,050	68,218	47,895	128	177	366,336
Rentals	201	111	807	665	8,444	11,830	1,040	1,207	7,169	25,789	30	126	57,419
Concessions and franchises	4	—	74	—	—	4,858	242	70	4,873	965	—	124	11,210
Licences and permits	292	36	672	421	9,467	25,183	3,338	1,804	9,196	15,016	104	96	65,625
Remittances from own enterprises	—	212	20	—	3,269	250	—	3,221	17,007	1,705	—	—	25,684
Interest	79	8	1,724	292	15,551	19,678	5,840	5,856	2,673	12,080	27	60	63,868
Interest and penalties on taxes	21	22	1,708	28	15,104	15,090	1,851	1,185	4,782	3,085	68	36	42,980
Fines	16	232	786	322	16,218	8,413	1,837	2,457	5,811	6,226	32	10	42,360
Miscellaneous	908	94	2,383	1,272	50,106	58,640	5,463	4,128	16,060	2,820	17	871	142,762
Transfers	14,524	26,783	161,250	24,917	1,188,094	2,181,574	206,861	195,329	432,866	454,341	888	2,757	4,890,184
General purpose	3,112	556	17,917	20,947	223,205	218,599	9,477	3,188	34,533	59,437	648	595	592,214
Provincial governments	3,112	556	17,917	20,947	223,205	218,599	9,477	3,188	34,533	59,437	648	595	592,214
Specific purpose	11,412	26,227	143,333	3,970	964,889	1,962,975	197,384	192,141	398,333	394,904	240	2,162	4,297,970
Federal government	5,876	1,943	6,386	2,890	21,392	29,772	4,928	1,474	14,874	22,106	139	253	112,033
Provincial governments	5,536	24,284	136,947	1,080	943,497	1,933,203	192,456	190,667	383,459	372,798	101	1,909	4,185,937
Total, general revenue	37,303	32,067	304,247	58,387	2,611,817	4,460,624	463,386	436,671	953,185	1,131,310	3,130	7,822	10,499,949

[1] Includes $100,877,000 special taxes and $447,185,000 for school tax revenue.
[2] Includes $8,936,000 amusement tax.
[3] Includes $147,519,000 special taxes and $453,892,000 for school tax revenue.
[4] Includes $10,206,000 amusement tax.

20.24 General expenditure of local governments, fiscal years ended nearest Dec. 31, 1972 and 1973 (thousand dollars)

Year and function	Nfld.	PEI	NS	NB	Que.	Ont.	Man.	Sask.	Alta.	BC	YT	NWT	Canada
1972													
General government	3,495	621	10,672	4,658	124,715	117,947	16,745	15,744	24,792	42,357	406	882	363,034
Executive and legislative	543	25	849	440	6,598	10,554	1,670	1,372	2,185	2,303	43	30	26,612
Administrative	2,589	431	7,757	3,741	117,464	94,563	9,702	10,344	17,944	34,834	334	748	300,451
Other	363	165	2,066	477	653	12,830	5,373	4,028	4,663	5,220	29	104	35,971
Protection of persons and property	775	901	18,287	12,140	236,902	298,528	28,852	18,785	59,489	87,352	364	283	762,658
Police services	193	620	7,791	6,046	153,773	170,715	14,782	9,433	31,848	38,789	39	41	434,070
Courts of law and correctional services	—	—	3,520	—	5,054	—	15	159	24	7,622	—	—	16,394
Fire-fighting services	291	281	6,345	5,584	69,373	104,056	11,172	6,929	21,713	29,899	254	178	256,075
Emergency measures	—	—	25	85	—	4,690	143	115	159	76	—	16	10,236
Regulatory services	38	—	—	—	—	12,746	22	1,006	1,647	4,627	35	40	20,161
Other	253	—	606	425	8,702	6,321	2,778	1,143	4,181	1,329	36	8	25,722
Transportation and communications	11,689	1,076	19,471	15,522	310,266	564,814	45,692	56,410	120,703	88,410	1,247	834	1,236,134
Common services	360	14	1,085	110	—	9,245	2,108	2,048	1,380	12,404	343	194	29,291
Road	11,215	1,062	18,273	15,276	277,869	480,801	42,830	54,212	117,371	74,996	904	619	1,095,428
Administration	165	—	714	998	36,837	11,102	1,038	2,069	2,562	1,431	4	—	56,920
Engineering	35	—	821	106	—	5,792	1,864	1,692	2,412	1,864	—	—	14,586
Roads and streets	8,999	796	12,178	10,123	160,882	387,376	31,325	42,226	89,637	58,421	624	506	803,093
Snow and ice removal	1,044	63	2,178	2,144	61,999	21,962	3,390	2,236	5,952	2,731	14	38	103,751
Bridges, subways, tunnels, etc.	—	—	—	—	—	7,240	1,733	2,013	8,046	1,351	186	—	20,577
Street lighting	758	158	1,915	1,482	13,797	21,152	2,371	2,556	5,262	5,424	62	58	54,995
Traffic services	37	19	366	232	3,285	13,361	1,025	830	2,436	2,720	12	17	24,340
Parking	20	26	89	191	1,069	990	81	400	718	704	2	—	4,290
Other	157	—	4	—	—	11,826	—	190	346	350	—	—	12,876
Public transit	114	—	94	21	32,397	53,877	748	134	235	968	—	21	88,609
Other	—	—	19	115	—	20,891	3	16	1,717	42	—	—	22,806
Environment	24,236	2,671	23,529	15,576	200,719	267,803	24,243	20,583	57,503	122,622	842	2,389	762,716
Water purification and supply	14,076	336	7,266	8,600	128,027	79,595	11,234	10,435	18,392	35,292	409	1,210	314,872
Sewage collection and disposal	8,579	2,136	12,800	3,786	41,293	141,333	7,777	4,604	27,237	74,471	280	964	325,260
Garbage and waste collection and disposal	1,571	199	3,402	3,187	28,794	46,238	5,105	5,335	10,788	12,722	151	215	117,707
Other	10	—	61	3	2,605	637	127	209	1,086	137	2	—	4,877
Health	18	1	19,310	47	7,441	252,247	31,313	61,235	124,164	7,597	32	21	503,426
Preventive services	5	:	337	1	7,372	50,773	3,071	1,691	6,188	6,398	32	17	75,885
Medical care	2	—	23	—	—	—	75	33	501	360	—	—	995
Hospital care	—	1	18,942	1	—	201,474	28,167	59,484	117,378	605	—	—	426,120
Other	11	—	8	69	69	—	27	—	97	234	—	4	426
Social welfare	—	24	21,542	45	7,061	293,570	6,226	3,768	10,733	88,814	—	—	431,783
Administration	—	—	1,168	—	6,115	—	871	173	157	3,297	—	—	11,781
Assistance	—	—	11,605	—	275	137,133	5,322	2,205	5,778	81,486	—	—	243,804
Services	—	—	8,478	—	—	156,437	30	497	4,025	3,827	—	—	173,294
Other	—	24	291	45	671	—	3	893	773	204	—	—	2,904
Housing – general assistance	1,416	239	2,734	1,820	40,656	32,886	4,469	1,803	4,588	9,956	78	509	101,154
Environmental planning and zoning	—	3	363	176	5,929	10,052	2,428	302	4	4,273	18	17	23,565
Community development	1,259	226	1,928	1,476	30,972	18,254	1,726	815	3,433	4,734	57	321	65,201
Other	157	10	443	168	3,755	4,580	315	686	1,151	949	3	171	12,388
Natural resources	—	—	45	—	—	42,011	1,031	315	474	5,038	—	—	48,914
Agriculture, trade and industry, and tourism	—	3	210	274	3,427	10,943	370	86	64	333	14	3	15,727
Agriculture	—	—	—	—	—	—	—	—	—	21	14	—	35
Trade and industry	—	3	210	274	3,427	10,943	370	86	64	312	—	3	15,692
Regional development commissions	—	—	14	—	2,463	—	104	20	—	54	—	3	2,655
Industrial parks and commissions	—	3	196	274	964	10,943	266	66	64	258	—	3	13,037
Tourism	:	:	:	:	:	:	:	:	:	:	:	:	:

20.24 General expenditure of local governments, fiscal years ended nearest Dec. 31, 1972 and 1973 (thousand dollars) (continued)

Year and Function	Nfld.	PEI	NS	NB	Que.	Ont.	Man.	Sask.	Alta.	BC	YT	NWT	Canada
1972 (concluded)													
Recreation and culture													
Recreational facilities	1,591	950	6,860	8,215	126,367	220,720	18,443	16,308	42,779	68,785	203	658	511,879
Cultural facilities	1,337	924	4,388	6,840	54,355	156,137	13,826	8,808	30,329	54,862	199	603	332,608
Other	—	26	2,243	241	36,929	59,675	3,699	7,346	11,620	12,510	—	22	134,320
Education — primary and secondary	249	—	229	1,134	35,083	4,908	918	154	830	1,413	4	33	44,951
Fiscal services													
Debt charges	1,156	21,227	135,680	63	1,277,756e	1,920,183	214,309	180,872	390,123	462,131	—	1,609	4,605,109
Interest on short-term borrowing	5,468	2,720	15,679	5,614	309,908	327,825	37,438	30,619	70,972	93,374	166	436	900,219
Interest on long-term borrowing[1]	4,104	2,693	12,916	5,375	301,132	227,942	24,950	18,965	56,183	71,183	94	361	726,291
Other	463	137	24	—	73	7,704	451	266	35	2,331	—	—	11,557
Transfers to reserves and allowances	2,209	2,507	12,858	4,720	286,981[1]	220,161	23,961	15,846	53,621	66,653	94	73	689,867
Transfers to own enterprises	1,432	49	34	655	14,078	77	538	2,853	2,920	2,199	—	32	24,867
Other services	476	27	2,118	239	8,776	66,288	5,820	8,869	8,234	21,915	72	75	122,909
Other	888	—	645	—	—	33,595	6,668	—	6,162	276	—	—	51,019
Other	51	9	731	1,588	257	13,060	—	2,785	7,002	1,680	—	2	24,380
Total, general expenditure	49,895	30,442	274,750	65,562	2,645,475	4,362,537	429,131	406,528	913,386	1,078,449	3,352	7,626	10,267,133
1973													
General government	3,480	748	12,881	4,880	172,710	146,287	15,529	16,308	34,794	46,675	470	1,046	455,808
Executive and legislative	687	47	994	388	7,842	12,329	2,075	1,609	2,136	2,787	52	55	31,001
Administrative	1,658	581	9,614	3,958	163,426	119,792	11,135	12,760	26,140	37,004	379	889	387,336
Other	1,135	120	2,273	534	1,442	14,166	2,319	1,939	6,518	6,884	39	102	37,471
Protection of persons and property	1,929	1,085	11,654	13,695	302,022	335,146	32,878	21,131	71,854	99,836	511	317	902,308
Police services	509	767	2,070	6,539	212,624	192,655	16,578	11,845	39,750	42,232	24	24	535,177
Courts of law and correctional services	—	—	7,450	6,377	4,610	25	25	600	443	9,351	51	51	17,207
Fire-fighting services	1,145	316	19	341	73,908	115,618	12,708	7,749	26,605	33,964	369	173	286,382
Emergency measures	—	—	407	260	25	5,796	128	116	1,691	6,599	8	8	14,698
Regulatory services	99	2	304	178	—	17,023	191	571	1,680	6,130	48	50	26,461
Other	176	—	—	—	10,880	4,054	3,248	250	1,685	1,560	11	11	22,383
Transportation and communications	12,029	1,358	21,844	16,781	317,863	631,407	49,122	59,209	134,949	99,039	956	1,289	1,345,846
Common services	745	34	1,903	1,725	10,880	10,109	2,499	3,003	2,706	13,623	261	180	36,788
Road	11,174	1,324	19,901	14,988	300,696	545,584	46,329	56,057	132,187	83,772	695	1,076	1,213,783
Administration	123	—	815	349	33,331	11,587	1,192	2,221	2,011	2,069	14	—	53,712
Engineering	718	—	922	177	—	3,339	1,932	1,531	337	2,313	—	—	11,269
Roads and streets	7,733	1,083	14,340	10,713	185,123	440,872	33,276	45,796	101,792	66,742	511	895	908,876
Snow and ice removal	1,379	42	1,185	1,674	61,855	22,796	2,501	697	5,584	1,490	76	83	99,752
Bridges, subways, tunnels, etc.	3	—	7	2	—	4,187	2,379	2,729	12,178	1,086	8	—	20,547
Street lighting	742	166	1,971	1,537	15,370	21,970	2,719	1,740	7,283	5,808	63	66	60,424
Traffic services	37	13	565	312	4,318	17,497	974	256	2,609	3,377	19	21	31,482
Parking	20	20	96	224	699	16,279	80	—	281	708	4	4	18,671
Other	419	—	—	—	—	7,057	1,276	—	112	179	—	7	9,050
Public transit	—	—	—	—	—	43,394	273	35	—	176	—	—	43,946
Other	110	—	40	48	17,167	51,329	21	114	176	1,468	—	13	51,329
Environment	11,810	5,952	31,557	18,554	231,184	335,437	27,020	19,903	71,843	146,423	1,101	1,750	902,534
Water purification and supply	5,817	539	10,277	9,816	96,515	126,898	12,757	9,991	33,289	38,595	622	903	346,019
Sewage collection and disposal	4,250	5,088	17,443	7,134	98,469	154,214	8,142	3,833	27,429	92,050	176	629	418,857
Garbage and waste collection and disposal	1,741	202	3,789	1,604	33,295	51,736	6,049	6,073	10,970	15,518	303	218	131,498
Other	2	123	48	—	2,905	2,589	72	6	155	260	—	—	6,160
Health	21	1	28,822	2,905	2,896	258,370	34,446	65,988	130,180	16,873	35	30	537,681
Preventive services	11	—	379	19	2,823	50,741	3,273	1,945	3,434	8,389	34	19	71,052
Medical care	—	—	26	4	—	200,849	80	11	11	557	—	—	458,765
Hospital care	—	1	28,375	—	—	6,780	31,057	63,991	126,627	7,792	1	11	722
Other	10	—	42	15	73	—	36	4	108	135	—	—	7,142

20.24 General expenditure of local governments, fiscal years ended nearest Dec. 31, 1972 and 1973 (thousand dollars) (concluded)

Year and function	Nfld.	PEI	NS	NB	Que.	Ont.	Man.	Sask.	Alta.	BC	YT	NWT	Canada
1973 (concluded)													
Social welfare	—	24	24,201	—	11,293	295,145	5,467	3,594	9,647	103,158	—	—	452,529
Administration	—	—	1,635	—	11,275	—	1,487	140	878	3,698	—	—	19,113
Assistance	—	—	11,269	—	—	130,320	3,745	2,668	5,440	94,889	—	—	248,331
Services	—	24	10,379	—	18	164,825	87	644	2,640	3,081	—	—	181,698
Other	—	—	918	—	—	—	148	142	689	1,490	—	—	3,387
Housing — general assistance	2,789	177	1,946	3,119	34,379	40,082	6,201	1,509	14,392	16,156	180	374	121,304
Environmental planning and zoning	—	2	570	342	7,342	13,607	2,533	280	4	5,337	11	63	30,091
Community development	2,764	175	1,274	2,343	22,732	21,016	3,434	1,186	14,388	10,451	111	265	80,139
Other	25	—	102	434	4,305	5,459	234	43	—	368	58	46	11,074
Natural resources	—	—	52	49	—	48,321	1,015	—	55	5,319	—	—	54,811
Agriculture, trade and industry, and tourism	558	2	1,696	518	2,048	8,851	236	790	768	720	24	—	16,211
Agriculture	—	—	—	—	—	—	—	705	337	—	—	—	1,042
Trade and industry	558	—	1,552	307	1,703	8,851	156	85	210	310	24	—	13,756
Regional development commissions	—	—	26	—	194	—	93	—	26	103	—	—	442
Industrial parks and commissions	558	—	1,526	307	1,509	8,851	63	85	184	207	24	—	13,314
Tourism	—	2	144	211	345	—	80	—	221	410	—	—	1,413
Recreation and culture	4,221	869	7,811	11,242	142,112	278,400	26,132	16,086	72,508	110,401	183	919	670,884
Recreational facilities	3,951	818	5,110	10,656	83,622	194,676	15,262	11,216	61,805	96,986	176	890	485,168
Cultural facilities	267	51	2,355	469	35,097	76,272	4,924	4,827	9,563	12,744	7	14	146,590
Other	3	—	346	117	23,393	7,452	5,946	43	1,140	671	—	15	39,126
Education — primary and secondary	1,340	22,582	152,817	—	1,195,739e	1,962,678	223,012	191,838	394,203	579,518	—	1,847	4,725,574
Fiscal services	5,742	2,317	21,268	7,936	384,801	371,355	32,464	28,561	74,892	104,353	204	499	1,034,392
Debt charges	4,112	2,260	15,116	6,860	377,749	244,026	20,227	18,264	56,140	80,561	130	479	825,924
Interest on short-term borrowing	649	130	1,283	812	8,501	9,592	730	3,272	1,263	3,185	—	75	29,492
Interest on long-term borrowing[1]	3,329	2,109	13,409	5,831	363,426[1]	234,432	19,437	14,858	54,451	74,866	130	357	786,635
Other	134	21	424	217	5,822	2	60	134	426	2,510	—	47	9,797
Transfers to reserves and allowances	672	57	5,578	1,076	7,052	97,889	5,847	8,733	10,689	23,509	74	20	161,196
Transfers to own enterprises	958	—	574	—	—	29,440	6,390	1,564	8,063	283	—	—	47,272
Other services	122	12	758	561	73	10,009	—	1	5,307	11,069	17	3	27,932
Total, general expenditure	44,041	35,127	327,557	77,354	2,797,120	4,721,488	453,522	424,918	1,015,392	1,339,540	3,681	8,074	11,247,814

[1]School debenture interest in Quebec is estimated at $92 million in 1972 and at $89 million in 1973.

20.25 Direct debt of local governments, fiscal years ended nearest Dec. 31, 1972 and 1973 (thousand dollars)

Year and direct debt	Nfld.	PEI	NS	NB	Que.	Ont.	Man.	Sask.	Alta.	BC	YT	NWT	Canada
1972													
Long-term (debentured)	28,934	31,406	183,866	79,513	2,579,458[1]	4,015,235[2]	392,190	260,995	1,067,933	1,075,516	1,995	5,000	9,722,041
Less sinking funds		4,836	1,828	1,894	1,044	514,643	41,175	36,975	4,481	66,953	–	–	673,829
Net long-term (debentured)	28,934	26,570	182,038	77,619	2,578,414	3,500,592	351,015	224,020	1,063,452	1,008,563	1,995	5,000	9,048,212
Short-term borrowings	20,928	1,069	44,771	11,173	301,393	153,207	70,475	21,460	38,444	72,281	250	1,332	736,783
Accounts and other payables	36,398	8,558	33,892	16,495	224,253	260,858	32,781	22,475	84,139	68,161	455	1,156	789,621
Other liabilities	8,737	25	7,311	5,464	57,240	26,579	41,102	22,097	39,638	21,949	35	941	231,118
Total, direct debt less sinking funds	94,997	36,222	268,012	110,751	3,161,300	3,941,236	495,373	290,052	1,225,673	1,170,954	2,735	8,429	10,805,734
1973													
Long-term (debentured)	29,692	29,866	188,333	71,433	2,800,694[3]	4,173,444[4]	403,058	218,924	1,145,775	1,181,065	2,341	5,981	10,250,606
Less sinking funds		4,922	2,782	1,708	1,436	569,783	48,621	37,430	5,484	61,901	–	–	734,067
Net long-term (debentured)	29,692	24,944	185,551	69,725	2,799,258	3,603,661	354,437	181,494	1,140,291	1,119,164	2,341	5,981	9,516,539
Short-term borrowings	20,418	928	56,925	21,704	360,870	152,471	86,031	21,408	39,176	70,892	–	727	831,550
Accounts and other payables	55,385	5,414	39,367	32,143	224,667	311,745	48,154	26,186	118,868	96,570	842	1,936	961,277
Other liabilities	7,637	1,850	8,849	7,398	311,711	46,029	12,201	23,663	57,770	26,110	105	1,793	505,116
Total, direct debt less sinking funds	113,132	33,136	290,692	130,970	3,696,506	4,113,906	500,823	252,751	1,356,105	1,312,736	3,288	10,437	11,814,482

[1]Data for Quebec schools not available. Includes $18,042,000 debentures of the Montreal Transportation Commission guaranteed by the city of Montreal.
[2]Includes other long-term debt due to Ontario Water Resources Commission.
[3]Data for Quebec schools not available. Includes $30,377,000 debentures of the Montreal Transportation Commission of which $16,672,000 is guaranteed by the city of Montreal.
[4]Includes other long-term debt due to the Department of Fisheries and the Environment.

Sources
20.1 - 20.7 Public Finance Division, Institutional and Public Finance Statistics Branch, Statistics Canada.
20.8 -20.11 Statistics Section, Systems and Planning Branch, Department of National Revenue, Taxation.
20.12 - 20.13 Corporation Taxation Statistics, Business Finance Division, Statistics Canada.
20.14 - 20.17 Public Finance Division, Institutional and Public Finance Statistics Branch, Statistics Canada.
20.18 - 20.19 Tax Analysis and Commodity Tax Division, Department of Finance.
20.20 Public Finance Division, Institutional and Public Finance Statistics Branch, Statistics Canada.
20.21 Tax Analysis and Commodity Tax Division, Department of Finance.
20.22 - 20.25 Public Finance Division, Institutional and Public Finance Statistics Branch, Statistics Canada.

Selected economic indicators

Chapter 21

Tables

Selected economic indicators

Chapter 21

In this chapter various statistical statements and studies are presented, covering broad areas of Canadian economic activity. These are based on the Canadian System of National Accounts (SNA) which consists of national income and expenditure accounts, indexes of real domestic product, the balance of international payments and financial flows. Input-output tables are also part of the System of National Accounts but have not been included in this analysis. The integrated aggregative economic accounts provide an interrelated framework for analysis of the Canadian economy and its relationship with other countries. In its broad outline, the Canadian System of National Accounts bears a close relationship to the international standard as described in the United Nations publication *A system of national accounts*. Included is a section on price indexes and a review of the first year's operation of the Anti-Inflation Board.

National income and expenditure

21.1

National income and expenditure accounts provide accounting summaries for the nation as a whole and portray economic activity in terms of transactions taking place between major groups of transactors, namely, governments, corporate and government business enterprises, persons and unincorporated businesses and non-residents. By combining and summarizing these operations into their various classes, information may be obtained on the functioning of the economy which is of particular interest to governments concerned with problems of unemployment, taxation and prices, and to businessmen concerned with programs of investment and marketing.

Tables 21.1 - 21.9 are based on the revised historical series of the national income and expenditure accounts. Annual coverage since 1926 is available in Statistics Canada occasional publication *Income and expenditure accounts, 1926 to 1974*, Catalogue No. 13-531 and in the annual publication *System of national accounts — national income and expenditure accounts* Catalogue No. 13-201.

National income. Net national income at factor cost measures the current earnings of Canadian factors of production (land, labour and capital) from productive activity. It includes wages and salaries, profits, interest, net rent and net income of farm and non-farm unincorporated business.

Gross national product (GNP), by totalling all costs arising in production, measures the market value of all final goods and services produced in the current period by Canadian factors of production. It is equal to national income plus net indirect taxes (indirect taxes less subsidies) plus capital consumption allowances and miscellaneous valuation adjustments.

Personal income is the sum of current receipts of income whether or not these receipts represent earnings from production. It includes transfer payments from government (such as family allowances, unemployment insurance benefits and war service gratuities) in addition to wages and salaries, net income of farm and non-farm unincorporated business, interest, dividends and net rental income of persons. It does not include undistributed profits of corporations and other elements of the national income not paid out to persons.

Gross national expenditure (GNE) measures the same aggregate as gross national product (i.e. total production of final goods and services at market prices) by tracing the disposition of production through final sales to persons, governments and business on capital account, including changes in inventories, and to non-residents (exports). Imports of goods and services, including payments of interest and dividends to non-residents, are deducted since the purpose is to measure only Canadian production.

21.1.1 Economic growth in 1975

Gross national product in 1975 was $161.1 billion, an increase of 11.4% from the level of the previous year; however, this growth includes an increase in prices of over 10.8%. The recession that began in 1974 bottomed out early in 1975, but because the subsequent recovery proved to be relatively weak, the total level of real output in the economy increased by a mere 0.6%. The performances of individual expenditure aggregates reflected the basic recessionary character of the year. Investment in residential construction and exports of goods and services both declined in real terms. There was a dramatic swing in inventories of almost $2.6 billion, and personal expenditure on consumer goods and services recorded its smallest real growth since 1970. There was a modest increase in the current dollar value of exports, but this was outweighed by a substantial increase in imports, and the balance of trade in goods and services worsened by $3.3 billion. The slight increase in real gross national expenditure was accompanied by a significant deceleration in prices, but the overall gross national expenditure implicit price index nevertheless increased by 10.8%.

21.1.2 Consumer outlays

Current dollar expenditure on consumer goods and services grew by 15.8% in 1975, but this represents an increase of only 4.9% in real terms. For the year, the largest real increase in percentage terms was in expenditure on semi-durable goods, which grew by 7.3%; this increase was accompanied by a relatively modest price increase of 6.1%. Expenditure on durables was also fairly strong, growing by 17% in current dollars and 7.1% in real terms, as spending on new and used automobiles grew by 21.3%. Spending on services and non-durable goods increased by 16.4% and 15.3%, respectively, in current dollars, but by only 4.8% and 2.7% in real terms; there were price increases of over 11% during the year in both of these expenditure categories.

21.1.3 Investment

Total gross fixed capital formation grew to $39.2 billion, an increase of 16.8%; this is a considerable slowdown from the increases of the previous two years, and in real terms capital formation grew by only 2.5%. The weakness was concentrated in residential construction which declined by 7.4% in real terms as a result of a precipitous drop in housing starts in late 1974 and early 1975. There was a significant shift in the composition of residential construction during the year, as starts of duplexes and row housing increased by 40%, while single detached housing starts rose by only 1.5% and apartment starts declined by 4.9%. Business investment in plant and equipment grew by 5.0% in constant dollars, as non-residential construction grew by 10% and investment in machinery and equipment, by 1.1%; within non-residential construction, the increase was stronger in engineering (highways, pipelines, utilities) than in building construction.

Investment in inventories swung from an accumulation of $2.9 billion in 1974 to a decumulation of $0.3 billion in 1975, all of which took place in business non-farm inventories. There was strong liquidation in both manufacturing and wholesale trade after large accumulations in 1974. Retail trade was virtually flat for the year (close to zero value of physical change) after an accumulation of approximately $0.3 billion in 1974.

21.1.4 The external sector

The external sector was one of the major sources of weakness in 1975. Exports rose 2.9% while imports were up 10.9%, resulting in a $3.3 billion deterioration in the trade balance to a record deficit of $5.4 billion. The traditional deficit on service transactions worsened by $1.0 billion, but the swing in merchandise trade from a surplus of $1.7 billion in 1974 to a deficit of $0.6 billion accounted for about 70% of the overall swing in the trade balance. The increase in exports was due to a very large increase in natural gas exports, together with substantial increases in iron ore, coal, newsprint paper, asbestos, aluminum, industrial machinery, and motor vehicles and parts, while the rise in imports was accounted for by strong increases in energy goods, most notably petroleum, and increases in machinery and equipment and motor vehicles and parts. On the service account, the deterioration resulted from higher interest and dividend payments and investment income paid abroad.

Incomes   21.1.5

Labour income rose by 15.3% in 1975, compared with an increase of 18.1% in 1974. A major factor in the lower rate of growth was the effect of larger lay-offs and more man-days lost in industrial disputes. There were only marginal increases in employment during 1975, and most of the increase in labour income reflected higher average earnings. Wages and salaries in the goods-producing industries increased by 11.4% compared with 16.3% in 1974, as the industries in this group were particularly affected by strikes and lay-offs. Wages and salaries in the service-producing industries rose by 16.8% after an 18.7% increase the year before, with a slower rate of employment growth the major reason for the deceleration.

Corporation profits before taxes fell by 1.1% in 1975, the first decline since 1970 and only the second in 15 years. It follows four years of substantial increases. Profits in both mining and manufacturing decreased, while profits in trade and finance increased.

Accrued net income of farm operators fell 0.7% over the year, with an 8% increase in gross income being offset by higher operating costs. The value of grain production rose over 10%, due mainly to larger crop production, but the value of livestock production declined marginally. Net income of non-farm unincorporated business was up 13.4% year over year, the largest increases occurring in the finance, insurance, real estate and community business, and personal service industries.

The shares of gross national product held by labour income and profits followed their normal cyclical patterns and reflected the marginal increase in real output in 1975, as labour's share rose to 57% from 55.1% the year before, and profits' share fell to 11.5% from 13.0%. Farm income's share of gross national product fell slightly, while that of non-farm unincorporated business was unchanged.

Some price deceleration was evident in 1975, as the gross national expenditure implicit price index increased by 10.8% compared to 14.3% in 1974, and the increase in the final domestic demand index fell to 11.8% from 12.5% the year before. The indexes for personal expenditure on services and non-durable goods, and gross fixed capital formation showed larger increases than the gross national expenditure index, partly because of a 13.7% increase in import prices. The implicit price indexes for personal expenditure on services and non-durable goods both increased at relatively high rates, growing by 11.2% and 12.2%, respectively, while durables and semi-durables rose at more moderate 9.2% and 6.1% rates. Overall, the implicit price index for personal expenditure increased 10.7%. The index for total fixed capital formation grew by 11.7%; the rate of change of prices declined in both the public and private sectors for every major class of construction.

The government sector   21.1.6

Total revenue of all levels of government (excluding intergovernment transfers) rose by 8.2% in 1975, the lowest rate of increase in several years. All major tax categories showed considerably lower rates of growth than in 1974, which reflected both lower tax rates and the slowdown in business activity. On the other hand, total government expenditures continued the strong growth of the previous year, although at a slightly lower rate, and increased by 21.6%. Outlays on goods and services rose by about 17.5%, as wage and salary payments, which account for over 50% of total government expenditure on goods and services, increased by about 21%. Transfer payments to persons grew by 22.8% with higher unemployment benefits an important factor in the increase. Thus, with expenditure rising more rapidly than revenues, the government sector as a whole registered a deficit, on a national accounts basis, of $4.0 billion in 1975, the first large deficit since the early sixties.

21.2   Domestic product by industry

21.2.1   Indexes of real domestic product

Since the early 1960s Statistics Canada has published a set of production data pertaining to the entire spectrum of Canadian industries in its full industry detail (including the index of industrial production). These data, in the form of production indexes, are measures of value added for each industry revalued in the dollars of the base year. Technically, they are termed "indexes of real domestic product (RDP) at factor cost originating by industry". In constructing the index for total RDP, where the gross output of one industry flows to another industry (intermediate input) and/or to final demand (non-industrial sales), the portion double-counted is eliminated. This is accomplished by subtracting intermediate inputs (materials, fuels, advertising, etc.) valued in terms of the dollars of a common base year from gross output, valued in the same constant dollars, to yield a constant dollar value added aggregate.

RDP indexes are published on an annual, quarterly and monthly basis. The monthly and quarterly data are published both seasonally adjusted and without seasonal adjustment. The seasonally adjusted data are considered to be preferable for the analysis of emerging trends as the strong seasonal fluctuations to which sub-annual data are frequently subject have been removed, thus revealing the underlying trend as well as the cyclical and irregular factors affecting the data. In general, the annual indexes are more suitable for studies of longer-term production trends, growth rates and inter-industry comparisons, whereas monthly indexes provide a much better tool for the study of the cyclical behaviour of industries and short-term changes in production.

Spurred on by strong domestic and foreign demand for the goods and services produced by Canadian industries, total real output in the 1961-75 period achieved an average annual rate of growth of 5.4% in contrast to the average rate of growth of 4.7% in the 1946-61 period. During 1974 and 1975 there was a marked slowdown in the rate of growth of the economy.

Domestic demand has been influenced by demographic factors operating since World War II; younger age groups are displaying both their purchasing power and changing tastes. Buoyant foreign demand for Canadian commodities has been a dominant force since 1961, with sales of manufactured goods, particularly durable goods, having recorded the most dramatic gains.

Within this period a generally healthy investment climate has prevailed. Both residential and non-residential construction made good gains. In the case of non-residential construction the rapid pace of activity peaked in 1966 and various inhibiting factors contributed to weakness in the industry into the early 1970s. Since 1971 the pace again increased. For residential construction there was a decline in activity in 1974 followed by a sharper decline in 1975.

The influx of the postwar generation was reflected in the rapid increase in the labour force. Over most of the period the expanding economy generated sufficient employment opportunities to adequately absorb these increases. In the latter part of the 1960s, this influx combined with slackness in the overall economy to produce a lower rate of growth in labour force employment than in the labour force itself. By 1972, the trend had climaxed and unemployment rates fell in 1973 and 1974. With the weakness in economic activity in 1975, unemployment rates jumped to 6.9%.

Manufacturing, particularly durable goods manufacturing, is a major element in the strength of the Canadian economy. Motor vehicle and parts manufacturing has been one of the underlying reasons for this strength. The growth in motor vehicle production slowed due to a strike in 1970 but resumed its pattern of strong year-to-year growth until 1975. Many other durable goods industries also benefited from strong consumer demand. Major appliance manufacturers, small appliance manufacturers, and manufacturers of household radio and television sets all had growth rates above the rate of growth of the total economy. These industries were also weaker in 1974 and 1975 as price increases and higher levels of unemployment caused consumers to postpone purchases. A number of the other durable goods-producing industries have sustained high levels of output in the 1970s due to the increases in residential construction activity in the US and Canada. These include sawmills, veneer and plywood mills and a number of components of the non-metallic mineral products manufacturing industries.

The performance of the construction industry has been a conspicuous feature of the economy. Heavy injections of industrial capital took place in the mid-1960s to develop additional facilities or expand capacity. Pace setters were such industries as petroleum and coal products, chemicals, pulp and paper, and electric power. Outlays for social capital such as hospitals and educational institutions also increased. Construction projects for Canada's Centennial and Expo 67 provided an extra stimulus. However, since 1967 tightened monetary conditions, rising costs, a mid-1969 decision to defer capital cost allowances on commercial projects in some areas and strikes in 1969, 1970, 1972 and 1974 all restrained output in this sector. Residential construction tends to be one of the more volatile sectors of the economy. The relevant demographic factors have indicated that a solid demand for housing exists. Despite this, less favourable supply conditions such as scarcity of mortgage funds and rising interest rates and construction costs have from time to time adversely affected residential construction, particularly in 1966, the latter half of 1969 and the first half of 1970. Strikes in 1970 and, to a lesser extent in 1972, exacerbated the situation. However, both private and public mortgage funds had become increasingly available from the latter part of 1970 until mid-1974. This impetus contributed to the continuing growth in construction and other sectors of the economy. Construction (especially in the residential sector) declined in 1974 and 1975 adding to the weakness in aggregate real domestic product.

The community, business and personal services group has grown at a fairly steady pace in the past decade tending to be relatively insensitive to short-term fluctuations and has thus been one of the sustaining forces in the economy. Health and welfare services, services to business management and miscellaneous services have been prime contributors since 1968. In 1970, 1974 and 1975 the rate of increase in output of this industry group outstripped that of the aggregate output of the economy.

In summary, since the end of 1970, total production increased strongly until the end of 1973 and then remained substantially unchanged during 1974 and 1975. At the aggregate level there was renewed strength in domestic demand. External demand was also very strong in the 1971 to 1973 period and resulted in a rapid advance in the volume of merchandise exports. During this 1971 to 1973 period, the goods-producing industries were the dominant force in the economy. However, in 1974 and 1975, the volume of merchandise exports declined and the service-producing industries provided most of the economy's sustaining strength.

Value added for goods-producing industries   21.2.2

The data contained in this section are published in Statistics Canada's report *Survey of production* (Catalogue No. 61-202). The scope of this report is limited to current dollar values for goods-producing industries. This is in contrast to the real domestic product series which includes all industries and revalues current production in terms of the prices (dollars) of the base year.

Tables 21.12 and 21.13 show census value added data by province and by industry. Census value added is derived by deducting the cost of intermediate material inputs from the gross value of production (excluding excise and other sales taxes) or revenue. The census value added in current prices increased 10.8% in 1972, 24.0% in 1973 and 23.2% in 1974.

21.2.3 Aggregate productivity trends

The level of, and changes in, productivity have a vital influence on economic growth, overall cost structure, international competitiveness and, in the final analysis, on the quality of life. In the measurement of productivity, output is related to one or more kinds of inputs utilized in the production process.

The measures of productivity presented here relate output to a single input only, namely labour time. It must be emphasized that changes in output per unit of labour input cannot be attributed directly and solely to labour; such measures reflect not only changes in the skills and effort of the labour force but also the contribution of other productive resources with which labour works as well as the effectiveness with which all are combined and organized for the purpose of production. In other words, changes in technology, capital investment, capacity utilization, work flow, managerial skills and labour-management relations each has a bearing on movements in what is termed "labour productivity". The measures of unit labour cost are the ratios of labour compensation to output. Unit labour cost can also be obtained as the ratio of average compensation to productivity; thus unit labour cost will increase when average compensation grows more rapidly than productivity.

Sources of data. The output components of the various indexes of output per unit of labour input and unit labour cost referred to here are the indexes of "real domestic product (RDP) by industry". Developed within the conceptual framework of the Canadian System of National Accounts, they measure in constant dollar terms the contribution of each component industry to total output.

The major sources for the employment and man-hour indexes were the monthly labour force and employment surveys and these were supplemented by data from such sources as the annual censuses of manufactures and mining and the decennial census of population. Since the data from these diverse sources varied considerably in their coverage, concepts and methods of compilation, care had to be exercised in selection, adaptation and combination of the data into aggregate measures of labour input which would be conceptually and statistically consistent, both internally and in relation to the output data. Labour force survey data were used for the paid worker estimates of agriculture and of fishing and trapping while those for manufacturing and mining were based on adjusted annual census data. Estimates for most of the remaining industry divisions were derived from employment survey data. Estimates of other than paid workers (own-account workers, employers and unpaid family workers) were derived mainly from the labour force survey. Estimates of average hours worked, which were needed for the indexes of output per man-hour, were also based on labour force survey data except in the case of manufacturing where man-hours data reported in the census of manufactures were also utilized. Labour compensation is the sum of wages, salaries, supplementary labour income and an imputed labour income for self-employed workers. For imputed labour income the average hourly income of paid workers is attributed to self-employed persons in the same industry division. Indexes of output per person employed, output per man-hour and unit labour cost for commercial industries and the major components are presented in Table 21.14.

Growth rates. Between 1961 and 1975, output per person employed in the commercial industries increased at an annual average rate of 3.2%. Output per man-hour increased more rapidly, 3.9% a year, reflecting reductions in the average work week (Table 21.14). On reviewing the years since 1961 a decline in the rate of productivity growth can be observed. Output per man-hour increased at an average annual rate of 4.5% for the years 1961-66, 4.4% for the years 1966-71 and 1.8% for the years 1971-75.

Productivity growth in the commercial service-producing industries continued to lag behind the comparable rate of increase in the commercial goods-producing industries. From 1961 to 1975, the average annual rate of increase in output per man-hour was 3.0% in the commercial service sector and 4.8% in the commercial goods sector. In manufacturing, from 1961-75, output per man-hour rose 4.0% per annum.

Unit labour cost for commercial industries increased at an average annual rate of 1.0% for the period 1961-66, 3.6% for the years 1966-71 and 10.0% between 1971-75.

Price indexes   21.3

The price indexes provided here are classified into price indexes of goods and services paid by consumers at the retail level; industry and commodity price indexes at levels other than retail; purchase price indexes of selected capital goods; farm input price indexes; and securities price indexes.

Retail price indexes   21.3.1

This section describes price indexes currently available for commodities purchased by consumers at the retail level.

Consumer price index. The consumer price index measures the movement from month to month in retail prices of goods and services bought by a representative cross-section of the Canadian urban population living in centres with a population in excess of 30,000. Since April 1973, the index has been based on the 1967 expenditure pattern of families ranging in size from two to six persons, with annual incomes of $4,000 to $12,000. The CPI is a base-weighted index measuring the effect of changing prices on the cost of purchasing a fixed basket containing some 300 items. In August 1975, the index was officially converted to a 1971 = 100 time reference base without altering the 1967 weighting pattern.

The movement of the CPI up to the end of 1974 is described in previous editions of the *Canada Year Book.* Between 1974 and 1975, the CPI rose 10.8% as measured by the percentage difference in the annual average indexes of the two years, an increase almost identical to the 10.9% rise registered between 1973 and 1974. Between 1975 and 1976, however, the rise in the CPI was 7.5%, characterizing 1976 as a year of moderating price movements compared to the price advances experienced in the period from 1974 to 1975. Based on these movements of the CPI, the purchasing power of the 1971 dollar declined from an average of 80 cents in 1974 to 72 cents in 1975 and down to 67 cents in 1976.

Between December 1974 and December 1975, all seven of the major index components experienced increases. Food registered an increase of 12.9% and accounted for approximately 27% of the change in the all-items index. This was followed by a 9.9% increase in the housing component which contributed 36% to the overall change. Transportation, which advanced 11.7%, accounted for an additional 18%, while the other major components contributed an average 5% each to the change in the all-items CPI.

By contrast, during the period December 1975 to December 1976, food prices declined 0.7% and were largely responsible for the moderate movement in the all-items index. Housing charges, which increased by 10.0%, contributed to a little over one half of the total change, followed by transportation prices which advanced 8.6% and accounted for a little over one fifth of the total CPI movement. The contribution of higher clothing prices to the all-items rise more than doubled during 1974-75 and 1975-76 (December to December).

Consumer price movements viewed in terms of goods and services offer another perspective of the incidence of price change (see Table 21.16). Between December 1974 and December 1975, the price of goods rose by 10.9% compared to a 4.9% increase between December 1975 and December 1976. On the other hand, the price of services advanced 10.7% in the former period and rose by 12.1% in the latter. Increases in the price of goods accounted for well over one half of the total change between December 1974 and December 1975 while contributing to only one third of the all-items rise between December 1975 and December 1976. The contribution of durable and semi-durable goods to the all-items rise doubled in the more recent period, from 8% to 16%, while the contribution of non-durable goods, including food, decreased from 48% in the former period to 15% in the period December 1975–December 1976. In contrast, price advances for services accounted for approximately 44% of the total CPI change between December 1974 and December 1975 while contributing to over two thirds of the advance in the latest year.

For detail on movements in the CPI, see *Consumer price index,* Statistics Canada Catalogue No. 62-001, monthly or *Consumer prices and price indexes,* Statistics Canada Catalogue No. 62-010, quarterly. For additional information on methodology and weighting patterns, see *The consumer price index for Canada (1961 = 100) (revision based on 1967 expenditures),* Statistics Canada Catalogue No. 62-539.

Regional city consumer price indexes are presented in Table 21.17 for 14 selected cities. These indexes measure percentage changes in retail prices over time within the specified cities and should not be used to make comparisons in price levels between cities. Price increases in the period 1975-76 ranged from 6.7% in Ottawa to 9.7% in Vancouver; 12 cities exhibited price changes in the 6% to 10% range in that year. For more detailed information on the movements of consumer price indexes for regional cities, see *Consumer price indexes for regional cities,* Statistics Canada, Catalogue No. 62-009, monthly.

Table 21.18 provides a comparison of Canada's CPI experience with those of a selected group of countries. Consumer prices in Canada advanced faster than those of the United States in 1974-75 but somewhat less than a number of industrialized countries in Europe. Price movements in Canada for the year 1974-75 may be compared with price movements in other countries for the same period in Table 21.18. For this comparison, countries are listed alphabetically by region.

Intercity consumer price indexes. Table 21.37 provides indexes that compare levels of prices among 11 major Canadian cities. These indexes express prices in each city as a percentage of the combined cities average which equals 100. The comparisons shown are those in effect as of October 1975 and June 1976 for six components of the consumer price index. The selected components in the table make up more than 60% of the average urban consumer's budget. For technical reasons, shelter costs (for both rented and owned facilities) and restaurant meals are not included in the comparisons.

The retail prices used for the intercity comparisons are largely those routinely collected in each city for the production of the consumer price index. The exception is the "food at home" component which is derived from data collected in a special survey undertaken in October 1975 and October 1976. Comparability between cities is ensured as far as possible by matching quotations for goods and services characterized by similar qualities and types of retail outlets. Since comparisons relate to prices that include sales and excise taxes, variations in the proportion of sales tax applied between provinces on a wide range of largely non-food commodities may account for a large part of intercity price differentials.

21.3.2   Industry and commodity price indexes

These relate to sales and purchases, at levels other than retail, of raw materials, semi-processed goods and manufactured products. They are constructed in two ways: on an industry basis, in which the indexes are prepared for individual industries and aggregated for groups of industries; and on a commodity basis, in which indexes are prepared for individual commodities and aggregated for groups of commodities. "Industry selling price indexes" for manufacturing industries are the principal industry-classified indexes available in Canada. The "general wholesale index" is a commodity-classified index.

Industry selling price indexes: manufacturing. Indexes of the selling prices of some 120 individual industries classified to manufacturing in the Standard Industrial Classification are produced and published monthly. In addition, indexes are available for major groups of manufacturing industries and for all manufacturing.

The indexes measure the change through time of prices received by manufacturers for their products. Prices reflected in the index are f.o.b. manufacturing establishment, excluding taxes levied on manufacturers' sales. The items and weights in the current indexes are based on manufacturers' shipments in 1971. The composite index for manufacturing is presented in Table 21.19, for the years 1957-76.

The general wholesale index includes mainly manufacturers' prices but also incorporates prices of wholesalers, assemblers of primary products, and agents and operators of other types of commercial enterprise which trade in commodities of a type, or in quantities, characteristic of primary marketing functions. Prices are grouped according to a commodity classification scheme based on chief component material similarities. Indexes classified according to degree of manufacture are also available. In Table 21.20, the general wholesale index is presented for the period 1953-76. This index is used as a conventional summary figure against which to observe the behaviour of particular price groups such as farm products, industrial materials and building materials, for which separate price indexes have been constructed.

World wholesale price indexes. Comparisons of Canadian wholesale price indexes with those of other countries for the years 1973-75 are given in Table 21.21.

Price indexes of selected capital goods   21.3.3

This section covers price indexes currently available for inputs into residential and non-residential building construction, completed new houses, highway construction, engineering construction, and machinery and equipment purchased by the construction and forestry industries.

Residential and non-residential building construction indexes. Price indexes of residential and non-residential building construction are base-weighted input indexes of materials and labour. They are presented in Table 21.22 for the years 1966-75 on the 1971 base. The indexes for residential construction are published in more detail in Table 21.23. Indexes are available for the total inputs of material and labour for five regions within Canada, and are also calculated for the inputs into individual trades in residential construction.

Since the building material prices in these indexes reflect price movements on purchasers' markets they contain sales tax changes. The wage rate component, from 1971 forward, is derived mainly from surveys of agreements conducted by the Canadian Construction Association for construction trades in various centres; these are base rates which reflect union scale or collective agreements. The combined indexes of materials and wage rates do not necessarily reflect changes in the price of construction output since they do not take account of changes in profit margins or in productivity but instead concentrate only on the prices of the inputs.

New housing price indexes. These are base-weighted Laspeyres type indexes of builders' selling prices, measuring pure price change for work put-in-place and land for new residential construction. Monthly market selling prices agreed between builder and buyer in purchase contracts are reported monthly. In the price sample are major builders who construct 100 or more housing units a year (or possibly fewer units if comparable models can be priced through time). Prices cover dwelling structure, land and services to land if these are not provided separately by municipality; they exclude legal fees, provincial land transfer tax and similar costs to buyer for property acquisition. Prices are for single unit houses except in Toronto and Ottawa where single, semi-detached and row condominium units are priced.

The index uses a fixed-weighted formula. Weights reflect the relative importance of individual models in a firm's total output, and the relative importance of individual companies in the single family housing market. New firms brought into the sample are assigned weights reflecting their importance at time of entry. Quality changes not reflected in the index include model substitutions, changes in size and location of building lots, design and construction techniques and provision of such extra features as appliances. When actual cost data are not available quality changes are assumed to be proportional to differences in selling prices at a selected point in time. Indexes for the periods covered are shown in Table 21.24. Indexes for six other cities are also available, beginning in January 1975.

Highway construction indexes. These relate to prices paid by provincial governments in contracts awarded for highway construction. They are base-weighted indexes and measure the effect of price change on the cost of specified new highway construction projects represented by contracts of approximately $50,000 or more awarded by provincial governments. Indexes for the period 1956-75 are given in Table 21.39.

Prices contained in the index are for units of construction work put in place, such as a cubic yard (0.76 m³) of earth excavation or a ton (0.907 t) of bituminous hot-mix paving. Also included are prices of some materials, such as culvert pipe, usually supplied to the contractor by the highways department. *Prices and price indexes* (Statistics Canada Catalogue No. 62-002) for December 1967 contains details of the problems of estimating price change for highway construction.

Electrical utility construction indexes. The price indexes of electrical utility construction, which include those of distribution systems, transmission lines, transformer stations and hydro-electric generating stations, give an estimate of the impact of price change on the cost of materials, labour and equipment used in constructing and equipping electrical utilities. The index provides an estimate of how much more, or less, it would cost to reproduce the base-period program of construction in another period using the same construction technology and assuming similar rates of profit and productivity. Price indexes for the years 1971-75 are presented in Table 21.25.

Price indexes of machinery and equipment. Table 21.26 shows base-weighted price indexes of machinery and equipment purchased by the construction and by the forestry industries. Prices used for the indexes are, for the most part, selling prices reported monthly by manufacturers, although in some cases distributors' prices are used. Prices of imported machinery and equipment are included in the index, represented either by commodity price indexes of the US Bureau of Labor Statistics or by prices collected directly from foreign manufacturers. All prices have been adjusted as relevant to include duty, exchange and federal sales tax.

21.3.4 Farm input price indexes

Farm input price indexes measure, through time, changes in prices of commodities and services used as inputs into the agriculture industry. The weights for the indexes are based on the 1958 Farm Income and Expenditure Survey. The time base is 1961 = 100. Indexes for 41 series are published quarterly for eastern, western and total Canada. Annual averages for the total index are provided from 1967 to 1976 in Table 21.27.

Major economic indicators
Seasonally adjusted

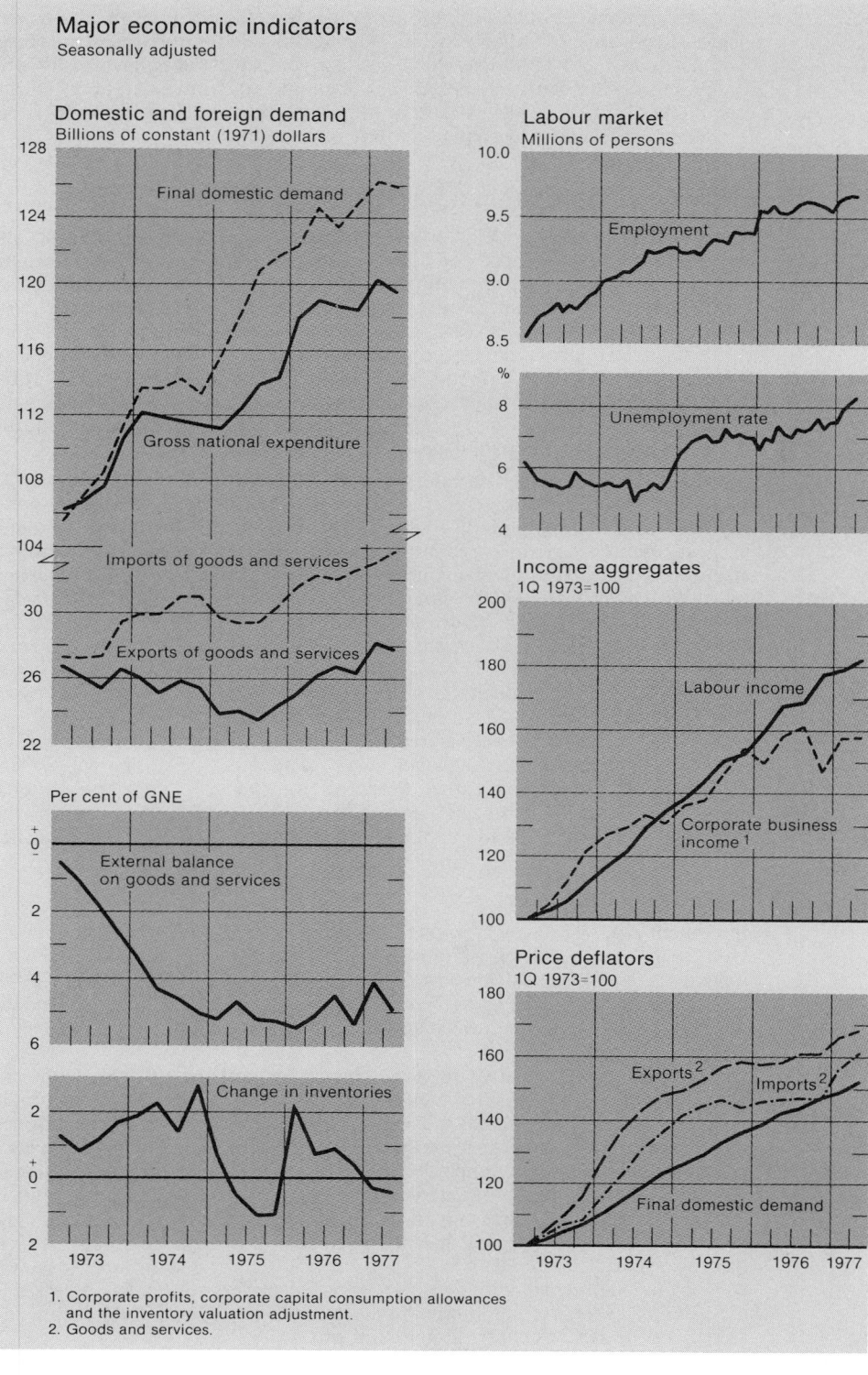

Domestic and foreign demand
Billions of constant (1971) dollars

Final domestic demand

Gross national expenditure

Imports of goods and services

Exports of goods and services

Per cent of GNE

External balance
on goods and services

Change in inventories

Labour market
Millions of persons

Employment

%

Unemployment rate

Income aggregates
1Q 1973=100

Labour income

Corporate business
income [1]

Price deflators
1Q 1973=100

Exports [2]

Imports [2]

Final domestic demand

1. Corporate profits, corporate capital consumption allowances
   and the inventory valuation adjustment.
2. Goods and services.

21.3.5   Security price indexes

Security price indexes measure, through time, the effect of price change on the value of a portfolio of Canadian stocks bought and held for investment purposes. The portfolio represents stocks of Canadian companies listed on at least one Canadian stock exchange. In the case of the mining, uranium and primary oil and gas indexes, only issues of producing mines are eligible. The indexes in Table 21.28 express current prices as a percentage of prices in 1971.

21.4   Balance of international payments

The Canadian balance of international payments summarizes transactions between residents of Canada and those of the rest of the world. Current account transactions, which measure the flow of goods and services between Canada and other countries, are included, with minor adjustments, as a component of gross national expenditure. Capital account transactions between residents and non-residents are included in the financial flow accounts. A summary of the Canadian balance of international payments is provided in Table 21.29 for 1969-75. Table 21.30 contains some additional information on current account transactions during that period and Table 21.31 contains a detailed presentation of the Canadian balance of international payments for 1974-75.

International conditions. The international recession which developed in 1974 continued into 1975 but there were signs of recovery from mid-year. There was a reduction in real output in industrialized countries of about 2% during 1975 and, in most countries, unemployment rose to high levels. As a result of the drop in aggregate demand, the volume of international trade fell for the first time in many years. With much larger volume declines in their imports than in their exports and stronger increases in their export prices than in their import prices, the current account balance of the industrialized countries taken together moved from a deficit to a surplus in 1975. This was accompanied by a marked reduction in the combined current account surplus of the major oil exporting countries and by an increase in the deficit of the non-oil developing countries.

Exchange rates between major world currencies were unsettled during 1975. However, the rate for the Canadian dollar, after declining during early 1975, showed a rising trend thereafter. Proposals for changes to the international monetary system that had been prepared during 1975 were agreed upon by the Interim Committee of the International Monetary Fund at a meeting in Jamaica in January 1976.

21.4.1   Current account

International transactions in goods, services and unilateral transfers between Canada and the rest of the world resulted in a current account deficit of $4,965 million in 1975, up considerably from the $1,492 million deficit recorded in 1974. This development was largely attributable to a sharp contraction in the merchandise trade balance, which swung from a surplus of $1,698 to a deficit of $639 million.

During 1975 the total value of merchandise exports rose marginally by just over 2% to $33.3 billion. Merchandise imports, however, advanced at a more rapid pace, rising by 10% to $34.0 billion. The rise in the value of exports reflected significant increases in export prices which were, however, largely offset by a decline in physical volume. Import prices, on the other hand increased at a greater rate while physical volume registered only a slight decline. A substantial shift in the balance occurred in trade in crude petroleum as exports dropped by 16% while imports increased by 25%. The balance on trade in this major commodity swung from a surplus of $936 million in 1974 to a deficit of $289 million which was over 40% of the total merchandise deficit in 1975. There were substantial increases in the value of exports of automotive products, natural gas, coal and iron ore and reductions in sales of copper, lumber and wheat.

Apart from crude petroleum, major contributions to the advance in imports were made by higher purchases of automotive products, coal and wheel tractors. Imports of automotive products increased by more than $1.0 billion and the deficit in automotive trade increased by over one third to $1.7 billion.

The non-merchandise deficit of $4.3 billion was $1.1 billion higher than in 1974. Net payments in respect of service transactions rose by $979 million to $4,732 million. The surplus on transfers declined by $157 million to $406 million. The expansion in the services deficit was largely due to increased deficits recorded on the travel and interest and dividends accounts. The deficit on international travel transactions widened by more than $400 million to $727 million. Net payments in respect of interest and dividends rose by 29% to $1,970 million. The decline in the surplus in unilateral transfers was more than accounted for by a 55% increase to over $500 million in official contributions to developing countries. The International Food Aid Program represented a substantial element of this assistance. Other important elements were economic and social assistance by way of exports, training and grants, and contributions to international organizations and to non-governmental groups in Canada engaged in foreign aid programs.

Capital movements   21.4.2
Capital movements between Canada and other countries during 1975 produced a record net inflow of $4,561 million, substantially higher than the net inflow of $1,516 million recorded in 1974. Long-term capital inflows amounted to $4,106 million and short-term capital inflows to $455 million. These massive inflows were less than the current account deficit of $4,965 million, and were accompanied by a reduction in Canada's net official monetary assets of $404 million.

Direct investment. Net inflows for foreign direct investment in Canada, constituting the investment of parent companies in their subsidiaries and affiliates in Canada, amounted to $630 million in 1975, compared with $725 million in 1974. Net outflows occurred in the petroleum and natural gas sector, mainly due to the acquisition of foreign-owned assets by the Canada Development Corporation. The manufacturing and mining sectors, on the other hand, experienced net inflows of funds.

Canadian direct investment abroad declined by $125 million to $650 million. This was still relatively high by historical standards. Investments abroad by companies in the mining and manufacturing sectors, each constituting about one quarter of total Canadian direct investment abroad, were the most important elements in the annual outflow, followed by the financial and petroleum sectors. Geographically, the United States, the European Economic Community (including the United Kingdom), and all other countries accounted for about 50%, 12% and 38% respectively of the direct investment outflow.

Security transactions. International transactions in Canadian and foreign long-term portfolio securities gave rise to a record net inflow of $4,727 million, surpassing by a wide margin the previous record inflow of $1,772 million in 1974. At $5,150 million, sales of new Canadian issues abroad were of unprecedented magnitude. The value and number of new Canadian issues floated on the Eurodollar market reached record levels in 1975. Traditionally, most foreign funds acquired by Canadian borrowers originate in the United States. In the latter part of 1975, however, Canadian dollar issues on the Eurobond market totalled more than $500 million, compared with a total of $63 million raised from this type of issue during 1974. During 1975, Canadian currency issues on the Eurobond market exceeded issues in all other currencies except United States dollars and Deutschmarks. The removal of the 15% Canadian withholding tax on interest payments to non-residents on certain types of new corporate issues in July 1975, the high credit rating of the borrowers, and high coupon rates offered, combined to make such issues highly attractive to non-residents. Moreover, the combination of generally lower interest rates in the Eurobond market than in

Canada, and less costly registration requirements there than in North America, provided additional incentives drawing Canadian borrowers to offshore markets.

Trading in outstanding Canadian bonds and debentures also reached a record high during 1975 with net sales of $302 million, $26 million higher than in 1974 but only marginally above the previous record of $292 million which occurred in 1972.

Retirements of Canadian securities during the year resulted in a net outflow of $691 million, $65 million more than in 1974 but $50 million below the 1973 figure. Sales in Canada of new foreign securities amounted to $69 million. Retirements of foreign securities held by Canadians were estimated at $12 million and transactions in outstanding foreign securities resulted in a net inflow of $18 million.

Other capital flows in long-term forms are, for the most part, composed of advances in respect of Canada's aid program, long-term loans, mortgage investments, movements of insurance funds and certain migrants' capital. Development assistance outflows in the form of soft loans and subscriptions from the Canadian government to developing countries and international development agencies totalled $378 million of which 70% was in the form of bilateral loans.

Repayments on outstanding postwar loans led to a net capital inflow of $40 million, up $2 million from the previous year's inflow.

The financing of medium- and long-term export credits extended directly or indirectly at the risk of the Canadian government resulted in a net capital outflow of $397 million, down substantially from the record outflow of $588 million in 1974.

Other capital movements in long-term forms consisted of bank and other long-term loans, mortgage investments, movements of insurance funds, and deferred migrants' capital, representing funds left abroad by migrants at the time of their migration. Transactions in these forms led to a net capital inflow of $134 million, down $85 million from the 1974 figure.

Capital movements in short-term forms resulted in a net inflow of $455 million, down $200 million from the net inflow recorded in 1974. In the first quarter alone, the net inward movement of short-term capital amounted to $1.3 billion, followed by a net outflow in the rest of the year. Taken together, the operations of the chartered banks in both Canadian and foreign currencies and trading in the Canadian money market gave rise to heavy inflows of short-term capital. These inflows were reduced somewhat by other short-term capital transactions which gave rise to a net outflow of funds.

Net foreign currency claims of the Canadian chartered banks on non-residents decreased, leading to a net capital inflow of $88 million, a substantial swing from the net outflow of $1,354 million reported in 1974.

Increased holdings of Canadian dollar deposits by non-residents led to a net capital inflow of $557 million, down slightly from the record inflow of $592 million in 1974.

Trading in money market paper (consisting of Government of Canada treasury bills, commercial paper, finance company paper and other short-term paper) produced a net inflow of $442 million, up substantially from the net inflow of $154 million recorded in 1974. There were net inflows of $217 million in finance company paper, of $147 million in other short-term paper, of $41 million in commercial paper and of $37 million in Government of Canada treasury bills.

An increase in foreign currency assets held abroad by the Canadian non-bank sector led to a net capital outflow of $236 million, a substantial shift from the net inflow of $1,590 million recorded in 1974 when residents made a significant reduction in their foreign assets.

Government of Canada demand notes held by international investment agencies produced a net capital outflow of $4 million as international agencies decreased their holdings of these non-interest bearing non-negotiable notes received as part of Government of Canada loans and subscriptions.

Other finance company obligations, consisting of borrowing from non-resident banks, and parent companies abroad, resulted in a net capital outflow of $92 million, a swing from the net inflow of $158 million recorded in 1974.

All other short-term capital transactions (including the balancing item of about $600 million, representing unidentified transactions in both the current and capital accounts) led to a net capital outflow of $700 million, up $155 million from the 1974 net outflow.

Official international monetary assets and liabilities   21.4.3

Canada's international reserves decreased by US$500 million during 1975 to stand at US$5,325 million at the end of the year. This change represented a net decrease of US$400 million from transactions passing through the reserve accounts and a decrease of US$100 million due to the depreciation in the United States dollar value of the Special Drawing Right (SDR). Expressed in Canadian currency, the decrease in reserves due to transactions amounted to $404 million, and was accounted for by a decrease of $569 million in holdings of United States dollars, an increase of $154 million in Canada's reserve position at the International Monetary Fund (IMF) and increases of $7 million in holdings of SDRs and of $4 million in holdings of other convertible currencies. The increase in Canada's reserve position at the IMF was partly due to the Canadian contribution to the IMF's oil facility, which was established in August 1974 and used by the IMF to assist members with balance of payments problems caused by increases in petroleum prices. Canada's commitment totalling C$300 million over a two-year period became fully drawn during the third quarter of 1975.

Since July 1, 1974, the SDR has been valued by the IMF in terms of a basket of currencies of 16 countries, including Canada. Relative weights for each currency are broadly proportionate to the country's exports, but are modified to recognize that the share in trade does not necessarily give an adequate measure of a currency's weight in the world economy. The Canadian dollar accounts for 6% of the total weight.

Foreign exchange   21.4.4

The dollar was established as the official currency of the united provinces of Canada on January 1, 1858, and extended to cover the new Dominion by the Uniform Currency Act of 1870. The gold sovereign remained the standard for the Canadian dollar until 1910 when the currency was defined in terms of fine gold, making it the exact gold equivalent of the United States dollar. Both British and US gold coins, however, were legal tender in Canada during this period.

The 1870 Act defined the Canadian dollar as 15/73 of the British gold sovereign, that is, the par rate of exchange between the dollar and the pound sterling was fixed at $4.866, making the Canadian currency the equivalent of the US dollar at parity. With minor variations the value of the pound sterling in Canada remained at this level until 1914.

For a complete description of the fluctuations between the Canadian and US dollars up to 1950 see the *1972 Canada Year Book* pp 1252-1254.

On September 30, 1950, the Minister of Finance announced that official fixed foreign exchange rates which had been in effect at varying levels since 1939 would be withdrawn effective October 2, and that the rate would henceforth be determined in the market for foreign exchange. This policy was carried out within the framework of exchange control until December 14, 1951, at which time the Foreign Exchange Control regulations were revoked by the Governor in Council, terminating the period of exchange control that had prevailed in Canada since 1939. The Foreign Exchange Control Act was repealed in 1952. On May 2, 1962, the Minister of Finance announced that the Canadian dollar was being stabilized at a fixed par value of 92½ cents in terms of United States currency. This action was taken with the concurrence of the International Monetary Fund (IMF) and, in accordance with the Articles of Agreement of that organization, the Government of Canada undertook to maintain the Canadian exchange rate within a margin of 1% on either side of the established par value.

On May 31, 1970, the Government of Canada announced a decision not to maintain the exchange rate of the Canadian dollar within the 1% parity band prescribed by the IMF for the time being. The movements of the US dollar in Canadian funds from January 1968 to December 1975 are shown in Table 21.35. Details of Canada's official international reserves and of undelivered contracts in US dollars are presented in Table 21.36.

21.5   Canada's international investment position

Canada has been among the world's largest importers of capital as the demand for real resources from abroad has been associated with a pattern of consistent current account deficits and net inflows of capital. This pattern was interrupted by sizeable current account surpluses in 1970 and 1971 and then a much smaller one in 1973. In 1974 a current account deficit of $1.5 billion was registered followed by a record deficit of $5.0 billion in 1975. In addition to capital inflows, which are a counterpart to net deficits on the current account, undistributed earnings accruing to non-residents have also been a significant factor. These two sources of funds have helped capital formation in Canada and thereby stimulated production, earnings and employment.

Preliminary estimates produced on the basis of available data indicate that Canada's balance of international indebtedness reached a book value of about $43 billion by the end of 1975. Long-term foreign investment at $68 billion had increased by over $7.5 billion reflecting predominantly an inflow of long-term portfolio capital and an increase in earnings accruing to non-residents. Other long-term liabilities including non-resident equity in Canada's assets abroad brought the total of long-term liabilities to about $72 billion. Various short-term claims on Canadians increased the total of Canada's external liabilities to over $81 billion.

Canadian long-term investment abroad increased by some $2.5 billion to about $21 billion at the end of 1975. The major elements in this increase were outflows of long-term direct investment capital, reinvested earnings accruing to Canadians from their investments abroad, export credits, and loans and subscriptions of the Government of Canada to foreign countries and international financial agencies. Short-term claims on non-residents including resident holdings of foreign currencies and net official monetary assets brought the total of Canada's external assets to about $38 billion.

Canada's balance of international indebtedness rose by $2.3 billion to $32.3 billion in 1973 (Table 21.32), the last year for which complete data are available. The net indebtedness of Canada to investors in other countries has shown an almost uninterrupted growth from its postwar low of $4.0 billion in 1949. In 1973 not only net indebtedness but also gross assets and liabilities registered record absolute annual increases. There was a growth of $5.9 billion in gross liabilities, well above the previous highest increase of $4.4 billion recorded in 1969, while gross assets rose by an unprecedented $3.6 billion, compared with the previous record increase of $2.9 billion, which occurred in 1970.

The term balance of international indebtedness is used here, in a balance of payments context, to include equity investment and contractual borrowing. It is determined by offsetting Canada's outstanding claims against other countries with the outstanding obligations of Canadians to other countries. The totals of international claims and obligations which have been acquired over the years, arising from capital transactions and other factors, constitute the international assets and liabilities determining a country's international investment position.

During the period for which regular official estimates have been published, from 1926 to 1973, Canada's gross external liabilities rose on average at an annual compound rate of 5% compared with a corresponding growth rate of over 7% in gross external assets. The overall increase in net international indebtedness from $5.1 billion to $32.3 billion is equivalent to an average annual rate of 4%.

Canadian assets abroad

There has been considerable growth in foreign investment in Canada and in the balance of Canadian indebtedness to non-residents, but Canadian assets abroad, rising at a faster rate than Canada's external liabilities, at the end of 1973 were equal to about one half of liabilities abroad compared with 45% at the end of 1970 and 26% at the end of 1939. This development was accompanied by a change in the structure of Canada's assets abroad (Table 21.33). The share of private long-term investment (including direct, portfolio, and miscellaneous investment) in Canada's foreign assets fell from almost 75% of the total in 1939 to 42% in 1973. Canadian long-term investment abroad has grown since 1970 at an average annual rate of 11% to 15.9 billion at 1973 year-end. The bulk of Canadian long-term investment abroad is in the form of private capital, especially in the direct investment sector. The remainder consists mostly of government loans and advances and subscriptions to international investment agencies.

At the end of 1973 the total book value of Canadian long-term direct investment abroad in subsidiaries, controlled companies, affiliates and branches totalled $7,810 million, an increase of $1,104 million over 1972. This was the largest increase ever recorded for Canadian direct investment. Direct investment for 1972, which grew only marginally to $6.7 billion, was affected by the exclusion of the foreign assets of IU International Corporation (formerly International Utilities Corporation) which had ceased to be a Canadian resident by the end of 1971. Since the move of IU International to the United States, the Canadian participation in this enterprise has been measured as Canadian portfolio investment abroad.

Direct investment in United States firms increased 14% to $3,924 million at the end of 1973 to account for just over one half of Canadian investment abroad. Direct investment in the United Kingdom, which had remained relatively static from 1968 to 1971, rose by 7% in 1972 and then by about 27% to $797 million in 1973. Despite the large gain in 1973, the United Kingdom remained in third place after Brazil, the second largest recipient country. In other Commonwealth countries, direct investment has also been the predominant form of Canada's assets. Although at the end of 1973 direct investment accounted for about two thirds of Canada's long-term investment in these countries, its share was somewhat lower than in most of the previous years due to the expansion of Government of Canada credits made under the new international development assistance or "soft" loan program. Direct investment, rising by 15% to $1,929 million, at 1973 year-end, continued to represent the largest part, at 40%, of Canada's assets in all other countries. However, export credits made directly or indirectly at the risk of the Government of Canada have grown significantly to represent an important element in Canada's assets in this group of countries. Miscellaneous investment, of which export credits is the largest component, rose by 19% to $1,559 million.

Net official monetary assets, other Canadian short-term holdings of exchange and short-term receivables taken together have expanded to $16.4 billion, to represent one half of gross assets at the end of 1973 (Table 21.32).

External liabilities

At the end of 1971 Canadian gross external liabilities amounted to $64.6 billion. Non-resident owned long-term investment comprised 90% or $58.1 billion of this total. Direct investment (investment in Canadian enterprises from the foreign country of control) totalled $32.8 billion accounting for 57% of all non-resident owned long-term investment in Canada. There was a sharp increase of 11% in 1973 in foreign direct investment compared to rises of only 6% recorded in each of the two previous years. The figures for 1971 and 1972 were affected significantly by the reclassification of large enterprises. These enterprises, previously treated as United States-controlled, were reclassified to Canadian control following shifts in share ownership. Non-resident holdings of government bonds increased by 5% to $9.9 billion while portfolio holdings of other Canadian securities rose by $0.8 billion to $8.6 billion.

Historically Canada has drawn heavily on external sources of capital for its economic development. During the exceptional growth period that occurred before World War I, non-resident investment was very high and the main source of that investment was the United Kingdom. However, during the first part of the interwar period, the United States became the principal source of external capital and thereafter the international debt owned in the United States exceeded that in the United Kingdom. The increase in United States investment in Canada was particularly strong during the resource boom following World War II. At the end of 1973, United States long-term investment in Canada at $42.1 billion comprised about 77% of all non-resident long-term investment in Canada (Table 21.34). This was down, however, from the high of approximately 81% recorded in 1967. About 62% of the stock of US investment at 1973 year-end was direct while 18% or $7.5 billion was invested in government bonds. United Kingdom long-term investments in Canada totalled $5.0 billion at the end of 1973. As a proportion of total non-resident investments in Canada, the United Kingdom's share was 9%, well below their 36% share at the end of 1939 before wartime repatriations. After reaching a low point in 1948, the value of United Kingdom investments in Canada increased each year until 1962. In 1963 repatriation of investments in railways (in Canada) and further provincial takeovers of other utilities caused a slight decline. Since then, UK investment in Canada has grown slightly.

Long-term investment by residents of countries other than the United States and the United Kingdom amounted to $7.5 billion at the end of 1973. The growth rate of long-term investment from this source was above the rates for the United States and the United Kingdom. They comprised just under 10% of total foreign long-term investment in 1968, 11.6% in 1970 and approximately 13.7% in 1973. About 47% of total long-term investment owned by residents of this group of countries was direct investment while government bonds comprised 27%.

21.5.3   Foreign investment in Canadian industry

Foreign investment in Canadian industry is measured in terms of both the proportion of foreign-owned capital to long-term capital employed in selected industry groups and the proportion of total capital employed in non-resident controlled enterprises. The estimated book value of total long-term capital employed in non-financial enterprises rose to $115.9 billion at the end of 1973, a 10% increase over 1972. Although foreign-owned investment in Canadian non-financial industries has remained unchanged at 34% there was a shift of one percentage point between ownership by United States investors, which decreased to 27%, and ownership by investors in countries other than the United States, which increased to 7%.

In the manufacturing sector, the degree of foreign ownership remained relatively stable at 53%. The proportion of foreign control in 1973 also remained unchanged at 59% of the total. The share of foreign ownership of total investment in petroleum and natural gas was 58%, up one percentage point from 1972. In other mining and smelting the proportion of foreign ownership remained at 56%. The percentages of foreign-controlled capital in the preceding two extractive industries were 76% and 57% respectively. In the utilities categories where foreign control is low, some 15% of total capital in railways was foreign-owned but only 2% was employed in foreign-controlled enterprises, while in the "other utilities" sector non-residents owned 18% of the long-term capital (mainly in the form of funded debt) but controlled enterprises employing only 7% of the total capital.

21.6   Financial activity, 1975 and 1976

During 1976 the domestic non-financial sectors of the Canadian economy raised over $37.9 billion on financial markets, an increase of $5.6 billion over the previous year. At 17.3% the rate of growth of total borrowing by the domestic non-financial sectors was more rapid than that of nominal GNP which grew by 14.5%. Placed in perspective to the flow of final goods and services produced by the Canadian economy, the flow of credit raised by these sectors was 20.6% of GNP. This ratio was not unlike those of the previous two years, although relatively high by historical standards. The heavy credit demands contributed to the maintenance of interest rates in Canada which were high by international norms and a large volume of borrowing overflowed into foreign capital markets.

Summary of trends. In broad terms financial activity in Canada was characterized by: an increase in the proportion of total funds raised going to the private non-financial corporate sector, reduced borrowing by the government sector proper but heavy borrowing by the associated enterprises of governments, some downward movement in interest rates but the continued existence of large international interest rate differentials, increased emphasis on the foreign sector as a source of long-term funds for Canadian borrowers, and a gradual reduction in the rate of growth of the narrowly defined money supply. There was increased emphasis on intermediated credit flows in 1976 compared to the preceding year. In 1975, approximately 72% of the increase in financial assets of the domestic non-financial sectors was represented by claims on financial institutions; in 1976 this percentage increased to over 91%.

Following a recession that was milder than in many of the western industrialized countries, the Canadian economy entered a recovery phase in mid-1975. Gross national product increased at rates of 14.5% and 4.6% in nominal and real terms respectively during 1976. While these rates of expansion were higher than in 1975 (with 9.8% and 0.2% respectively), there was a perceptible slowing in the expansion of economic activity as the year progressed. Much of the growth in 1976 was concentrated in the first quarter of the year when seasonally adjusted real GNP increased at an annual rate of 13.0%; during the fourth quarter seasonally adjusted real GNP declined at an annual rate of 2.5%. A spasmodic recovery was also characteristic of economic conditions in a number of Canada's trading partners including the United States. As a consequence, while the growth in Canada's exports was reasonably strong, the foreign sector did not provide as much stimulus to final demand in Canada as had been previously generally anticipated.

During 1976, macroeconomic policy in Canada was directed toward facilitating a return to reasonable price stability. The approach adopted was that of gradualism. In Canada this policy involved a reduction in the rate of growth of the money supply, a somewhat more restrictive fiscal stance and wage-profit-margin guidelines designed to speed up adjustments to progressively lower rates of inflation. Broadly similar policies were pursued in several OECD countries.

An increase in expenditures on fixed capital formation typically follows and reinforces other expenditures which initiate a revival in economic activity. In several industrialized countries, including Canada, investment expenditures in 1976 failed to turn up decisively several quarters after what appears to have been the beginning of a recovery. Over the year real capital formation in Canada increased by less than 1%. The flow of investment expenditures by business was particularly insipid. In real terms, investment by business (including government enterprises) in plant and equipment was essentially flat and expenditures by business on non-residential construction declined by close to 7%. Observers suggested a number of reasons for the malingering aspect of investment expenditures including the following: the existence of substantial amounts of excess capacity, low anticipated rates of return on new investment, the increase in energy costs, high unit labour costs in Canada relative to the United States, some misgivings by entrepreneurs about the strength and duration of the recovery which began in mid-1975 and political uncertainties.

The corporate sector. Despite the weakness of capital expenditures, the demands placed on capital markets by the private corporate sector were higher in 1976 than in 1975. Private non-financial corporations raised $8.3 billion in net funds using conventional market channels, 40% higher than in 1975. Several factors contributed to the rise in the amount of external funds raised by this sector. These include: slow growth in internally generated funds in a number of industries, a large build-up in inventories early in the year, a continued need for balance sheet restructuring and building up of corporate liquidity and the removal of the withholding tax on certain funds raised abroad. Non-financial corporations in Canada tended to rely more heavily on external finance than had been the case in the United States over the previous three years. As a result the balance sheet positions of corporations in the United States would appear to be stronger than those of Canadian non-financial corporations in the sense that portfolio restructuring appears to have been both more intensive and extensive in the United States. The trend toward longer-term forms of financing, which began in Canada late in 1974, was accentuated in 1975 and continued in 1976. Borrowing by the non-financial private corporate sector was less heavily slanted toward longer-term forms of financing in 1976 than it was in 1975. The increase in shorter-term debt incurred by this sector, however, was in part associated with a heavy build-up of inventories in the first quarter, and appears to have been but a temporary relapse in the general trend toward longer-term forms of borrowing.

Government borrowing. The government sector reduced its demands for funds in both absolute and relative terms from the amount raised in 1975. Excluding funds raised through the social security system the government sector raised $8.0 billion in 1976, down from $8.9 billion in the previous year. Borrowing by the associated enterprises of government, however, increased from $4.0 billion in 1975 to $6.3 billion in 1976. Much of this borrowing was done by provincial utilities in foreign capital markets.

Mortgages and consumer credit. Other major centres of borrowing activity were the mortgage market and the market for consumer credit. Borrowing in the form of mortgages by the non-financial sectors of the economy increased by 11.7% to $9.5 billion from $8.5 billion in 1975. Consumer credit accounted for slightly over 10% of total borrowing by the domestic non-financial sectors and amounted to $3.8 billion. The ratio of personal sector debt to personal disposable income has drifted upward in recent years, reflecting higher housing prices and associated larger mortgages.

Supply of funds. In 1976 the most noticeable shift in the roles played by suppliers of funds was the large increase in the volume of long-term funds provided by the rest-of-the-world sector. Funds supplied by the foreign sector in the form of conventional financial instruments increased by more than 93% between 1975 and 1976 when a flow of $10.5 billion was recorded. The proportion of total funds provided by the rest of the world increased from 7% in 1974 to 15% in 1975 and to 25% in 1976. Domestic private financial intermediaries assumed increased importance as conduits for credit flows from the previous year. During 1976 approximately $30 billion representing over 63% of total funds supplied was channelled through the domestic financial intermediary system with the deposit accepting institutions accounting for the bulk of the increased flow. The volume of funds supplied by public sector financial institutions remained essentially unchanged from 1975 at $2.3 billion. The role of direct finance declined in 1976 relative to 1975 and financial asset accumulation by the private domestic non-financial sectors of the economy was highly concentrated in claims on financial institutions.

Foreign exchange markets. During the second half of 1975 a number of observers expected downward pressure on the Canadian dollar early in 1976. As it turned out the downward pressure originating in the current account of the balance of payments was more than offset by large capital flows. As a result there was upward pressure on the spot value of the Canadian dollar over much of the year. There was, however, an abrupt downward adjustment in the fourth quarter.

Interest rates. High interest rates in Canada compared to the United States and Europe encouraged borrowers to raise capital outside the country. The elevated short-term rates in Canada were in large measure a direct consequence of the efforts of monetary authorities to reduce the rate of expansion of the money supply. While the general movement in short-term interest rates was downward over the year, the decline in short-term rates at the outset of the year was reversed by Bank of Canada operations and short-term interest rates peaked in March. In the autumn when the rate of growth of the narrowly defined money supply was below the target range of the Bank of Canada, its policies were designed to accommodate a downward adjustment in interest rates. Over the year as a whole, short-term rates fell by about 100 basis points; the 90-day finance paper rate, for example, fell from 9.34% in December 1975 to 8.16% by the close of 1976. Long-term interest rates also moved downward over the year, with the rate on long-term federal government securities falling by 102 basis points.

A summary of the financial market for 1975 and 1976 is presented in Table 21.38. More detailed data for individual sectors and summary matrices are available in the quarterly Statistics Canada publication *Financial flow accounts* (Catalogue No. 13-002).

The anti-inflation program   21.7

In the fall of 1975, despite a 7% unemployment rate, Canada was in the grip of inflation. The consumer price index was 10.6% above its level a year earlier, but wage and salary increases were even higher than was consistent with the rate of price increases, with average base wage rate increases over 20% for the first year of new collective agreements. In the early 1970s, almost all industrial countries including Canada had followed policies that led to an economic boom. The resulting demand pressures, coupled with poor harvests in many countries and with the sharp increase in oil prices, stimulated the greatest commodity price explosion since the early 1950s.

By 1974 the world economic cycle was turning, and major industrial economies were sliding into a recession. In Canada, policies were directed toward maintaining output and employment in the face of this recession. With real income and employment falling sharply in many countries, output and incomes held up well in Canada and employment continued to rise. Rates of price and income increase, falling elsewhere by mid-1975, were not doing so in Canada, where costs were increasing faster than in other countries competing for international markets. Through the first half of 1975, labour costs per unit of output in Canada were up 17.5% compared to 11% in the United States.

The prices of some goods had begun to recede in late 1974, but by the middle of 1975 overall rates of increase in consumer prices were again rising. Large increases in municipal taxes, and in the prices of items such as insurance, housing and energy were anticipated. Some Canadian workers were asking for unprecedented wage increases to make up for erosion of their purchasing power and to protect themselves against anticipated escalation in the rate of inflation. Businessmen, unsure about future cost increases, were raising prices in anticipation of further increases in wages and material costs.

Inflation was a major threat. Anti-inflation policies were designed to bring the rate of inflation down without introducing restrictive monetary and fiscal policies that could cause a sharp decline in output and a further increase in the unemployment rate. These policies were set out in the white paper "Attack on inflation", released October 14, 1975.

The program to reduce inflation   21.7.1

The essential element of the program was gradual monetary and fiscal restraint. To ensure restraint by both business and labour, guidelines to restrict price and wage increases were enacted. Administrative machinery including the Anti-

Inflation Board (AIB) was established to ensure compliance by the largest and most powerful economic groups. The price and income controls were meant to complement the monetary and fiscal policies, not substitute for them.

It was planned that the various elements of the anti-inflation program should work together in this manner: monetary and fiscal policies were designed to achieve a sustained economic recovery consistent with price increase targets of 8% in the first program year, 6% in the second year, and 4% in the third; controls on wages, salaries and professional fees should hold the growth in unit costs to a level consistent with the annual price target; controls on prices and profits should ensure that reduced rates of cost increase were fully reflected in reduced rates of price increase; prices should increase by less than the increase in compensation, so that workers could gain, on average, at least a 2% increase in real income. This "winding down" process should continue, as reduced rates of cost increase continued to be passed along in lower rates of price increase.

The economic recovery began about mid-1975 following a relatively mild recession. Real gross national expenditure declined during the last half of 1974 and the first half of 1975. During the second half of 1975 real growth was almost 4% at an annual rate, and during the first half of 1976 the rate of real growth was 5.6%. Throughout this recovery, employment continued to rise at an annual rate of more than 2%, a rate just sufficient to absorb the increase in the labour force. The rate of unemployment remained at about 7%.

21.7.2   Cost and wage developments

Because of the combined effect of the slowdown in the rate of wage increase and the recovery in the rate of productivity increase, unit labour costs during the first half of 1976 were held to about 10.5% above their level a year earlier. For the first half of 1975 the rate of increase had been 17.5%.

During each of the first three quarters of 1975 — prior to the initiation of the controls program — first year wage settlements contained increases of more than 20%. During the first and second quarters of 1976, first year wage settlements declined to 16.4% and 13.4% respectively. Later actual increases are somewhat lower because these Labour Canada statistics do not reflect the effect of AIB review of wage settlements above the guidelines. AIB compensation data, reported in Chapter 8, also show a trend toward deceleration in wage increases.

21.7.3   Price developments

In the third quarter of 1976 prices were not rising as fast as they had been and the rate of increase remained below that for wages and salaries. It was expected that the year-over-year increase in the consumer price index (CPI) would be about 6.5% by October 1976, compared with 10.6% in October 1975. This sharp decline in the rate of increase came in part from favourable developments in the price of imports and food prices at the farm gate, and in part from the impact of the controls program.

Certain elements of the CPI are not subject to direct control. Although they are monitored by governments, and are affected by overall economic policy, the prices of food at the farm gate, energy at source, imports, government services and taxes are not controlled by the AIB. The food at farm gate and import components of the CPI increased somewhat less than the total index from August 1975 to August 1976. CPI components which are subject to the direct influence of the control program increased by about 8% over that year, down from about 11% during the previous year.

The target was to reduce the year-over-year rate of increase in the CPI to no more than 6% by October 1977. Barring unforeseen crop failures or world-wide curtailment of supply of other basic commodities, it was the view of the board that the target was attainable.

Sources

21.1 Gross National Product Division, System of National Accounts (Current) Branch, Statistics Canada.

21.2.1 - 21.2.2 Industry Product Division, System of National Accounts (Current) Branch, Statistics Canada.

21.2.3 Input-Output Division, System of National Accounts (Structural) Branch, Statistics Canada.

21.3 Prices Division, General Statistics Branch, Statistics Canada.

21.4 - 21.5 Balance of Payments Division, System of National Accounts (Current) Branch, Statistics Canada; Department of Banking and Financial Analysis, Bank of Canada.

21.6 Financial Flows and Multinational Enterprise Division, System of National Accounts (Current) Branch, Statistics Canada.

21.7 Editing Services, Communications Division, Anti-Inflation Board.

Tables

..	not available	e	estimate
...	not appropriate or not applicable	p	preliminary
—	nil or zero	r	revised
- -	too small to be expressed		certain tables may not add due to rounding

21.1 Gross national product in current and constant (1971) dollars, and index of gross national expenditure in constant (1971) dollars, 1950-75

Year	Gross national product		Index of gross national expenditure in constant (1971) dollars[r] (1971 = 100)
	Millions of current dollars	Millions of constant (1971) dollars	
1950	18,491	33,762	35.9
1951	21,640	35,450	37.7
1952	24,588	38,617	41.0
1953	25,833	40,605	43.1
1954	25,918	40,106	42.6
1955	28,528	43,891	46.6
1956	32,058	47,599	50.6
1957	33,513	48,718	51.8
1958	34,777	49,844	53.0
1959	36,846	51,737	55.0
1960	38,359	53,231	56.6
1961	39,646	54,741	58.2
1962	42,927	58,475	62.1
1963	45,978	61,487	65.3
1964	50,280	65,610	69.7
1965	55,364	69,981	74.4
1966	61,828	74,844	79.5
1967	66,409	77,344	82.2
1968	72,586	81,864	87.0
1969	79,815	86,225	91.6
1970	85,685	88,390	93.9
1971[r]	94,115	94,115	100.0
1972[r]	104,669	99,680	105.9
1973[r]	122,582	106,845	113.5
1974[r]	144,616	110,293	117.2
1975	161,132	110,975	117.9

21.2 National income and gross national product, by component, 1972-75 (million dollars)

Item	1972[r]	1973[r]	1974[r]	1975
Wages, salaries and supplementary labour income	57,570	66,358	78,520	90,586
Military pay and allowances	979	1,092	1,203	1,326
Corporation profits before taxes[1]	10,799	15,032	18,800	18,587
Deduct: dividends paid to non-residents[2]	-1,031	-1,277	-1,619	-1,752
Interest, and miscellaneous investment income[3]	4,577	5,382	7,424	8,094
Accrued net income of farm operators from farm production[4]	1,662	3,009	3,812	3,786
Net income of non-farm unincorporated business, incl. rent[5]	6,170	6,778	7,225	8,194
Inventory valuation adjustment	-1,032	-2,362	-4,251	-2,865
Net national income at factor cost	79,694	94,012	111,114	125,956
Indirect taxes less subsidies	13,876	15,672	18,317	17,548
Capital consumption allowances and miscellaneous valuation adjustments	11,474	13,241	15,502	17,478
Residual error of estimate	-375	-343	-317	150
Gross national product at market prices	104,669	122,582	144,616	161,132

[1]Excludes profits of government business enterprises.
[2]Includes withholding tax.
[3]Includes profits (net of losses) of government business enterprises and other government investment income.
[4]Includes value of physical change in farm inventories and accrued earnings of farm operators arising out of operations of the Canadian Wheat Board.
[5]Includes net income of independent professional practitioners and imputed net rent on owner-occupied dwellings.

21.3 Gross national expenditure, 1972-75 (million dollars)

Item	1972[r]	1973[r]	1974[r]	1975
Personal expenditure on consumer goods and services	61,531	70,659	82,064	95,018
Government current expenditure on goods and services	20,291	23,045	27,838	32,712
Gross fixed capital formation	22,598	27,203	33,597	39,230
Government	3,968	4,305	5,462	6,486
Business	18,630	22,898	28,135	32,744
Residential construction	5,367	6,742	8,028	8,580
Non-residential construction	6,205	7,327	9,178	11,361
Machinery and equipment	7,058	8,829	10,929	12,803

21.3   Gross national expenditure, 1972-75 (million dollars) (concluded)

Item	1972r	1973r	1974r	1975
Value of physical change in inventories	544	1,588	2,855	-308
Government	16	-15	26	31
Business				
Non-farm	801	1,484	3,129	-486
Farm and grain in commercial channels	-273	119	-300	147
Exports of goods and services	24,580	30,725	38,904	40,033
Deduct: imports of goods and services	-25,250	-30,981	-40,959	-45,404
Residual error of estimate	375	343	317	-149
Gross national expenditure at market prices	104,669	122,582	144,616	161,132

21.4   Gross national expenditure in constant (1971) dollars, 1972-75 (million dollars)

Item	1972r	1973r	1974r	1975
Personal expenditure on consumer goods and services	59,162	63,171	66,347	69,593
Government current expenditure on goods and services	18,848	19,680	21,020	21,810
Gross fixed capital formation	21,612	23,997	25,231	25,848
Government	3,782	3,776	3,991	4,218
Business	17,830	20,221	21,240	21,630
Residential construction	5,057	5,562	5,454	5,052
Non-residential construction	5,879	6,441	6,956	7,652
Machinery and equipment	6,894	8,218	8,830	8,926
Value of physical change in inventories	515	1,346	2,281	-307
Government	15	-16	18	16
Business				
Non-farm	835	1,359	2,370	-330
Farm and grain in commercial channels	-335	3	-107	7
Exports of goods and services	23,655	26,161	25,557	23,755
Deduct: imports of goods and services	-24,489	-27,848	-30,432	-29,668
Residual error of estimate	377	338	289	-56
Gross national expenditure in constant (1971) dollars	99,680	106,845	110,293	110,975

21.5   Year-to-year percentage change in gross national expenditure, 1972-75

Item	1972r	1973r	1974r	1975
Personal expenditure on consumer goods and services				
Value	11.3	14.8	16.1	15.8
Volume	7.0	6.8	5.0	4.9
Price	4.0	7.6	10.6	10.4
Government current expenditure on goods and services				
Value	10.5	13.6	20.8	17.5
Volume	2.6	4.4	6.8	3.8
Price	7.7	8.7	13.1	13.3
Gross fixed capital formation				
Value	10.4	20.4	23.5	16.8
Volume	5.6	11.0	5.1	2.5
Price	4.6	8.4	17.5	14.0
Government				
Value	5.7	8.5	26.9	18.8
Volume	0.8	-0.2	5.7	5.7
Price	4.9	8.7	20.1	12.3
Business				
Value	11.4	22.9	22.9	16.4
Volume	6.6	13.4	5.0	1.8
Price	4.5	8.3	17.1	14.3
Residential construction				
Value	19.5	25.6	19.1	6.9
Volume	12.6	10.0	-1.9	-7.4
Price	6.1	14.2	21.5	15.4
Non-residential construction				
Value	4.3	18.1	25.3	23.8
Volume	-1.2	9.6	8.0	10.0
Price	5.5	7.9	15.9	12.6
Machinery and equipment				
Value	12.4	25.1	23.8	17.2
Volume	9.8	19.2	7.5	1.1
Price	2.4	4.9	15.3	15.8
Exports of goods and services				
Value	10.8	25.0	26.6	2.9
Volume	6.7	10.6	-2.3	-7.1
Price	3.9	13.0	29.6	10.7
Imports of goods and services				
Value	14.7	22.7	32.2	10.9
Volume	11.2	13.7	9.3	-2.5
Price	3.1	8.0	20.9	13.7
Gross national expenditure at market prices				
Value	11.5	19.5	15.0	12.2
Volume	5.9	7.2	3.2	0.6
Price	5.0	9.2	14.3	10.8

21.6   Personal income, by source and by province, 1972-75 (million dollars)

Source and province or territory	1972r	1973r	1974r	1975
Source				
Wages, salaries and supplementary labour income	57,570	66,358	78,520	90,586
Military pay and allowances	979	1,092	1,203	1,326
Net income received by farm operators from farm production	1,711	2,996	3,255	3,786
Net income of non-farm unincorporated business including rent	6,170	6,778	7,225	8,194
Interest, dividends and miscellaneous investment income	7,028	8,445	10,326	11,646
Current transfers				
From government				
Transfer payments to persons (excl. interest on public debt)	9,918	11,205	13,799	16,939
Capital assistance	46	59	61	141
From corporations (charitable and other contributions and bad debts)	172	189	213	228
From non-residents	173	210	223	268
Total, personal income	83,767	97,332	114,825	133,114
Province or territory				
Newfoundland	1,301	1,521	1,866	2,211
Prince Edward Island	286	352	386	477
Nova Scotia	2,435	2,824	3,307	3,802
New Brunswick	1,814	2,088	2,499	3,036
Quebec	20,842	23,879	28,426	32,870
Ontario	34,797	39,721	46,243	52,901
Manitoba	3,565	4,227	4,915	5,742
Saskatchewan	2,767	3,657	4,460	5,481
Alberta	6,270	7,434	8,898	10,721
British Columbia	9,421	11,305	13,431	15,411
Yukon Territory and Northwest Territories	189	232	287	335
Foreign countries[1]	80	92	107	127

[1]Income of Canadians temporarily abroad, including pay and allowances of Canadian Armed Forces abroad.

21.7   Disposition of personal income, 1972-75 (million dollars)

Item	1972r	1973r	1974r	1975
Personal expenditure on consumer goods and services	61,531	70,659	82,064	95,018
Current transfers				
To government				
Income taxes	11,385	13,285	16,159	18,029
Succession duties and estate taxes	230	205	177	147
Employer and employee contributions to social insurance and government pension funds	3,016	3,551	4,864	5,838
Other	1,036	1,072	1,126	1,155
To corporations (transfer portion of interest on the consumer debt)	699	990	1,504	1,637
To non-residents	178	225	222	228
Personal saving	5,692	7,345	8,709	11,062
Total, personal income	83,767	97,332	114,825	133,114

21.8   Personal expenditure on consumer goods and services, 1972-75 (million dollars)

Item	1972r	1973r	1974r	1975
Food and non-alcoholic beverages	9,425	11,189	13,231	15,490
Tobacco and alcoholic beverages	3,924	4,310	4,828	5,445
Clothing, footwear and accessories	4,842	5,618	6,588	7,498
Gross rent, fuel and power	11,412	12,586	14,322	16,539
Furniture, furnishing and household equipment and operation	6,047	7,183	8,556	9,744
Transportation and communication	8,784	10,142	11,572	13,531
Medical care and health services	1,858	2,121	2,477	2,796
Other	15,239	17,510	20,490	23,975
Total	61,531	70,659	82,064	95,018
Durables	9,111	10,872	12,513	14,634
Semi-durables	8,109	9,504	11,270	12,823
Non-durables	19,265	22,300	26,322	30,347
Services	25,046	27,983	31,959	37,214

21.9   Federal, provincial and local government revenue and expenditure[1], 1972-75 (million dollars)

Item	1972[r]	1973[r]	1974[r]	1975
Revenue				
Direct taxes: persons and unincorporated business				
Income taxes	11,385	13,285	16,159	18,029
Succession duties and estate taxes	230	205	177	147
Employer and employee contributions to social insurance				
and government pension funds	3,016	3,551	4,864	5,838
Direct taxes: corporate and government business enterprises	3,920	5,058	6,919	7,170
Direct taxes: non-residents (withholding taxes)	287	322	430	465
Indirect taxes	14,760	16,760	20,924	21,386
Other current transfers from persons	1,036	1,072	1,126	1,155
Investment income				
Interest and royalties	3,074	3,803	5,073	6,132
Remitted profits of government business enterprises	616	567	625	621
Total, revenue	38,324	44,623	56,297	60,943
Current expenditure				
Purchases of goods and services	20,291	23,045	27,838	32,712
Transfer payments to persons	9,918	11,205	13,799	16,939
Current transfers to non-residents	279	312	402	584
Interest on the public debt	4,137	4,754	5,386	6,335
Capital assistance	245	326	293	472
Subsidies	884	1,088	2,607	3,838
Saving	2,570	3,893	5,972	63
Total, current expenditure	38,324	44,623	56,297	60,943
Surplus or deficit (on a national accounts basis)				
Saving	2,570	3,893	5,972	63
Add: capital consumption allowances	1,495	1,723	2,081	2,415
Deduct: gross capital formation	-3,984	-4,290	-5,488	-6,517
Equals: surplus or deficit	81	1,326	2,565	-4,039

[1]Excludes current transfers from other levels of government.

21.10   Annual growth rates of real domestic product, by industry, selected periods, 1961-75

Industry	1961-66[r]	1966-75	1961-75	1970-75
Agriculture	5.5	-1.3	0.8	-2.3
Forestry	6.6	2.5	3.9	1.2
Fishing and trapping	2.6	-3.1	-0.6	-5.7
Mines (incl. milling), quarries and oil wells	5.9	5.3	6.7	3.3
Manufacturing	8.5	4.5	5.6	4.5
Non-durables	6.3	4.2	4.9	3.8
Durables	11.0	4.7	6.5	5.2
Construction	7.0	3.3	4.2	4.4
Electric power, gas and water utilities	7.3	7.7	7.7	6.7
Transportation, storage and communication	6.9	6.4	6.6	6.1
Transportation	7.4	6.0	6.5	5.2
Trade	6.8	5.6	5.7	6.7
Wholesale	8.3	5.2	5.9	6.1
Retail	5.8	5.9	5.6	7.1
Finance, insurance and real estate	4.8	5.1	5.0	5.4
Community, business and personal services	7.0	5.1	6.0	4.6
Public administration and defence	1.9	4.1	3.5	4.5
Real domestic product	6.7	4.8	5.4	4.8

**21.11   Quantity indexes of real domestic product at factor cost, by industry of origin, 1972-75
(1971 = 100)**

Industry	1972	1973	1974	1975
Agriculture	87.9	90.2	80.2	85.9
Forestry	102.4	122.1	119.6	97.5
Fishing and trapping	97.6	103.3	87.3	74.6
Mines (incl. milling), quarries and oil wells	106.5	118.5	118.2	109.5
Manufacturing	107.0	116.2	119.7	113.8
Non-durables	106.6	113.8	117.1	111.9
Durables	107.5	118.6	122.3	115.7
Construction	102.6	108.0	112.8	112.9
Electric power, gas and water utilities	107.3	117.4	125.2	126.2
Transportation, storage and communication	106.8	115.5	123.0	124.3
Trade	108.9	117.5	125.4	125.9
Wholesale	107.9	117.4	126.1	121.3
Retail	109.5	117.6	125.0	128.9
Finance, insurance and real estate	104.2	111.0	117.8	122.6
Community, business and personal services	104.5	109.4	115.0	119.1
Public administration and defence	104.2	109.8	114.1	118.8
Real domestic product	105.2	112.6	117.3	117.6

21.12   Census value added in goods-producing industries, by province, 1972-74

Province or territory	1972r		1973r		1974	
	$'000	%	$'000	%	$'000	%
Newfoundland	612,246	1.4	734,911	1.4	1,000,693	1.5
Prince Edward Island	94,565	0.2	145,983	0.3	163,703	0.2
Nova Scotia	839,288	2.0	1,021,222	1.9	1,236,762	1.9
New Brunswick	703,702	1.6	970,738	1.8	1,303,020	2.0
Quebec	10,174,148	23.4	11,767,389	22.1	14,599,262	22.1
Ontario	18,460,617	42.7	21,930,368	40.9	26,139,137	39.6
Manitoba	1,518,797	3.6	2,058,145	3.8	2,360,229	3.5
Saskatchewan	1,640,537	3.8	2,474,921	4.6	3,545,203	5.4
Alberta	4,408,091	10.2	6,019,888	11.1	8,500,646	12.9
British Columbia	4,655,270	10.8	6,295,319	11.8	6,918,798	10.5
Yukon Territory and Northwest Territories	113,410	0.3	184,511	0.3	254,348	0.4
Canada	43,220,671	100.0	53,603,395	100.0	66,021,801	100.0

21.13   Census value added in goods-producing industries, by industry and province, 1974

Industry	Newfoundland		Prince Edward Island		Nova Scotia		New Brunswick	
	$'000	%	$'000	%	$'000	%	$'000	%
Agriculture	—	—	64,821	39.6	51,938	4.2	80,407	6.2
Forestry	36,933	3.7	—	—	20,511	1.7	72,834	5.6
Fisheries	42,903	4.3	12,027	7.3	81,141	6.6	22,080	1.7
Trapping	160	—	145	0.1	471	—	805	0.1
Mining	211,052	21.1	172	0.1	85,281	6.9	80,920	6.2
Electric power	130,530	13.0	6,332	3.9	59,845	4.8	73,835	5.6
Manufacturing	270,874	27.1	29,776	18.2	601,735	48.7	603,086	46.3
Construction	308,241	30.8	50,430	30.8	335,840	27.1	369,053	28.3
Total	1,000,693	100.0	163,703	100.0	1,236,762	100.0	1,303,020	100.0

Industry	Quebec		Ontario		Manitoba		Saskatchewan	
	$'000	%	$'000	%	$'000	%	$'000	%
Agriculture	656,828	4.5	1,044,718	4.0	584,838	24.8	1,988,358	56.1
Forestry	260,870	1.8	186,730	0.7	11,821	0.5	18,058	0.5
Fisheries	13,653	0.1	9,655	—	5,147	0.2	1,971	0.1
Trapping	5,090	—	8,274	—	3,083	0.1	3,238	0.1
Mining	700,838	4.8	1,634,201	6.3	274,982	11.7	670,307	18.9
Electric power	728,326	5.0	974,173	3.7	134,554	5.7	87,296	2.5
Manufacturing	9,549,110	65.4	18,128,835	69.4	906,434	38.4	373,242	10.5
Construction	2,684,547	18.4	4,152,551	15.9	439,370	18.6	402,733	11.3
Total	14,599,262	100.0	26,139,137	100.0	2,360,229	100.0	3,545,203	100.0

Industry	Alberta		British Columbia		Yukon Territory and Northwest Territories		Canada	
	$'000	%	$'000	%	$'000	%	$'000	%
Agriculture	1,284,031	15.1	205,014	3.0	—	—	5,960,953	9.0
Forestry	26,362	0.3	586,715	8.5	—	—	1,220,834	1.9
Fisheries	931	—	100,976	1.5	738	0.3	291,222	0.4
Trapping	4,440	0.1	1,884	—	2,935	1.2	30,525	—
Mining	4,200,684	49.4	793,177	11.5	234,439	92.1	8,886,053	13.5
Electric power	181,758	2.1	307,647	4.4	13,157	5.2	2,697,453	4.1
Manufacturing	1,318,276	15.5	3,300,302	47.7	3,079	1.2	35,084,749	53.1
Construction	1,484,164	17.5	1,623,083	23.4	¹	¹	11,850,012	18.0
Total	8,500,646	100.0	6,918,798	100.0	254,348	100.0	66,021,801	100.0

¹Included with British Columbia.

21.14   Aggregate productivity measures, 1966-75 (1961=100)

Year and industry	Output	Persons employed	Man-hours	Output per person	Output per man-hour	Labour compen-sation	Unit labour cost
Commercial industries							
1966	141.4	116.7	112.9	121.1	125.3	149.1	105.5
1967	145.5	118.9	114.3	122.4	127.3	163.0	112.0
1968	154.1	119.0	113.1	129.4	136.3	173.7	112.7
1969	163.5	122.8	115.5	133.2	141.5	192.5	117.8
1970	167.2	122.7	114.3	136.3	146.3	206.0	123.2
1971	177.7	124.4	115.2	142.9	154.2	225.4	126.8
1972	187.7	127.5	117.4	147.2	159.9	250.7	133.6
1973	202.4	132.8	122.6	152.4	165.1	290.4	143.5
1974	211.3	139.3	127.8	151.7	165.3	341.8	161.8
1975	210.2	139.1	126.9	151.1	165.6	389.7	185.4
Annual rate of change							
1961-66 %	7.1	3.2	2.5	3.8	4.5	8.3	1.0
1966-75 %	5.0	2.1	1.4	2.9	3.5	11.0	5.8
1961-75 %	5.6	2.3	1.6	3.2	3.9	10.0	4.2

21.14   Aggregate productivity measures, 1966-75 (1961=100) (continued)

Year and industry		Output	Persons employed	Man-hours	Output per person	Output per man-hour	Labour compen-sation	Unit labour cost
Commercial non-agricultural industries								
1966		141.2	122.9	120.7	114.9	116.9	152.3	107.9
1967		147.0	125.0	122.3	117.6	120.2	166.4	113.2
1968		155.7	125.5	121.5	124.1	128.1	177.6	114.1
1969		165.2	130.1	124.8	127.0	132.4	197.4	119.5
1970		169.1	130.6	124.1	129.5	136.3	212.1	125.4
1971		179.1	132.6	125.2	135.1	143.0	232.6	129.9
1972		190.6	136.9	129.0	139.2	147.8	259.6	136.2
1973		206.0	143.5	135.4	143.6	152.1	299.7	145.5
1974		216.0	150.9	141.5	143.1	152.7	353.7	163.8
1975		214.4	150.6	140.1	142.4	153.0	403.4	188.2
Annual rate of change								
1961-66	%	7.2	4.2	3.9	2.9	3.2	8.7	1.4
1966-75	%	5.2	2.4	1.8	2.7	3.3	11.2	5.8
1961-75	%	5.8	2.9	2.3	2.8	3.4	10.3	4.2
Commercial goods-producing industries								
1966		145.4	110.8	108.1	131.3	134.5	149.3	102.7
1967		146.1	111.1	107.5	131.5	135.9	160.7	110.0
1968		155.4	110.1	105.7	141.2	147.0	169.6	109.2
1969		164.8	111.1	106.0	148.3	155.5	185.3	112.4
1970		166.3	108.4	102.7	153.4	161.9	194.5	116.9
1971		177.7	108.9	102.7	163.2	173.0	211.9	119.3
1972		185.7	109.6	103.0	169.4	180.3	231.5	124.7
1973		200.8	113.5	107.3	176.9	187.1	271.9	135.4
1974		204.9	117.2	110.4	174.8	185.6	317.6	155.0
1975		197.8	113.2	106.5	174.7	185.7	355.5	179.7
Annual rate of change								
1961-66	%	7.7	2.1	1.6	5.4	6.0	8.3	0.6
1966-75	%	4.2	0.4	–	3.8	4.2	10.0	5.5
1961-75	%	5.1	0.8	0.3	4.3	4.8	9.2	3.9
Commercial non-agricultural goods-producing industries								
1966		145.3	121.4	122.7	119.7	118.4	155.7	107.2
1967		149.2	121.1	121.3	123.2	123.0	167.1	112.0
1968		158.8	120.4	120.2	131.9	132.1	176.7	111.3
1969		168.4	122.4	121.1	137.6	139.1	193.8	115.1
1970		170.3	119.9	118.1	142.0	144.2	204.8	120.3
1971		180.6	120.6	118.1	149.8	153.0	224.2	124.1
1972		191.4	123.1	120.9	155.5	158.3	246.2	128.6
1973		207.9	129.1	127.2	161.0	163.4	287.6	138.3
1974		214.0	133.7	131.3	160.1	163.0	337.7	157.8
1975		205.2	128.0	124.8	160.3	164.4	377.6	184.0
Annual rate of change								
1961-66	%	7.9	4.0	4.2	3.7	3.6	9.2	1.2
1966-75	%	4.6	0.9	0.6	3.6	4.0	10.3	5.4
1961-75	%	5.5	1.7	1.5	3.7	4.0	9.7	3.9
Commercial service-producing industries								
1966		137.2	124.2	119.0	110.5	115.3	148.9	108.5
1967		144.9	128.6	123.2	112.6	117.6	165.7	114.3
1968		152.7	130.2	122.7	117.2	124.4	178.5	116.9
1969		162.1	137.2	128.0	118.1	126.6	201.1	124.1
1970		168.1	140.5	129.4	119.7	129.9	219.6	130.6
1971		177.6	143.7	131.5	123.6	135.0	241.2	135.8
1972		189.5	149.7	136.2	126.6	139.1	273.4	144.3
1973		204.1	156.9	142.6	130.1	143.1	312.2	153.0
1974		217.4	166.8	150.5	130.3	144.5	370.3	170.3
1975		222.5	171.5	153.6	129.7	144.9	430.2	193.3
Annual rate of change								
1961-66	%	6.6	4.5	3.6	2.0	2.9	8.3	1.6
1966-75	%	5.7	3.7	2.9	2.0	2.8	12.2	6.1
1961-75	%	6.0	3.9	3.0	2.1	3.0	10.9	4.6
Agriculture								
1966		145.9	79.9	77.5	182.6	188.3	104.4	71.6
1967		118.6	82.1	78.5	144.5	151.1	115.7	97.5
1968		126.0	80.2	75.2	157.2	167.5	119.6	94.9
1969		133.3	78.6	74.2	169.7	179.6	125.5	94.1
1970		131.4	75.0	70.3	175.1	187.0	121.7	92.6
1971		152.7	74.9	70.4	203.9	217.0	125.8	82.4
1972		134.2	70.6	65.3	190.1	205.5	128.1	95.5
1973		137.7	68.4	65.3	201.3	210.9	161.5	117.3
1974		122.5	69.5	66.4	176.3	184.5	176.5	144.1
1975		131.2	70.5	68.0	186.1	192.9	200.0	152.4
Annual rate of change								
1961-66	%	5.6	-4.1	-4.9	10.2	11.1	1.0	-4.4
1966-75	%	–	-2.0	-2.1	2.0	2.0	6.5	6.6
1961-75	%	1.0	-2.7	-3.1	3.8	4.2	4.6	3.6
Manufacturing								
1966		149.3	121.2	122.4	123.2	122.0	153.5	102.8
1967		153.3	121.7	122.1	126.0	125.6	164.8	107.5
1968		163.6	120.8	121.4	135.4	134.8	175.8	107.5
1969		175.4	123.2	123.3	142.4	142.3	191.9	109.4
1970		173.0	120.3	119.6	143.8	144.7	200.7	116.0
1971		183.3	119.6	118.7	153.2	154.4	213.4	116.4
1972		196.1	123.1	122.6	159.3	160.0	236.0	120.3

21.14   Aggregate productivity measures, 1966-75 (1961=100) (concluded)

Year and industry	Output	Persons employed	Man-hours	Output per person	Output per man-hour	Labour compensation	Unit labour cost
Manufacturing (concluded)							
1973	213.0	128.5	128.3	165.8	166.0	268.8	126.2
1974	219.4	132.7	132.1	165.3	166.1	310.9	141.7
1975	208.6	125.2	123.7	166.6	168.6	338.9	162.5
Annual rate of change							
1961-66 %	8.4	4.0	4.2	4.3	4.1	8.9	0.4
1966-75 %	4.5	0.7	0.5	3.7	3.9	9.1	4.4
1961-75 %	5.6	1.7	1.5	3.9	4.0	8.9	3.1
Other commercial goods-producing industries (excl. agriculture and manufacturing)							
1966	138.5	122.0	123.3	113.5	112.3	160.0	115.5
1967	142.2	120.0	119.6	118.5	118.9	171.5	120.6
1968	150.6	119.4	117.6	126.1	128.0	178.6	118.6
1969	156.4	120.7	116.4	129.6	134.3	197.4	126.2
1970	165.5	119.1	114.9	139.0	144.1	212.8	128.6
1971	176.0	122.8	116.6	143.4	150.9	244.9	139.2
1972	183.9	123.1	117.1	149.4	157.0	265.8	144.5
1973	199.4	130.3	124.9	153.0	159.6	323.8	162.4
1974	205.4	135.9	129.8	151.1	158.2	389.4	189.6
1975	199.4	134.2	127.4	148.6	156.5	452.3	226.8
Annual rate of change							
1961-66 %	7.0	4.1	4.2	2.8	2.7	9.7	2.6
1966-75 %	4.8	1.4	0.7	3.4	4.1	12.3	7.1
1961-75 %	5.4	1.9	1.4	3.5	4.0	11.0	5.3

21.15   Consumer price indexes for specific groups, 1965-76 (1971=100)

Year	Food	Housing	Clothing	Transportation	Health and personal care	Recreation, education and reading	Tobacco and alcohol	All-items index
Group weight as a percentage of total[1]	24	32	11	16	4	7	6	100
1965	83.4	77.3	83.8	80.7	79.4	77.9	81.7	80.5
1966	88.7	79.5	87.0	82.6	81.8	80.1	83.7	83.5
1967	89.9	82.9	91.4	86.1	86.0	84.1	85.8	86.5
1968	92.8	86.7	94.1	88.3	89.5	88.3	93.6	90.0
1969	96.7	91.2	96.7	92.4	93.8	93.5	97.2	94.1
1970	98.9	95.7	98.5	96.1	98.0	96.8	98.4	97.2
1971	100.0	100.0	100.0	100.0	100.0	100.0	100.0	100.0
1972	107.6	104.7	102.6	102.6	104.8	102.8	102.7	104.8
1973	123.3	111.4	107.7	105.3	109.8	107.1	106.0	112.7
1974	143.4	121.1	118.0	115.8	119.4	116.4	111.8	125.0
1975	161.9	133.2	125.1	129.4	133.0	128.5	125.3	138.5
1976	166.2	148.0	132.0	143.3	144.3	136.2	134.3	148.9

[1]These weights, indicating the components' relative importance, are based on 1967 expenditures and have been incorporated since May 1973; prior to May 1973, the weights reflected 1957 expenditures.

21.16   Consumer price index reclassified by goods and services[1], 1965-76 (1971=100)

Year	Goods Non-durable Food	Goods Non-durable Other	Semi-durable	Durable	Total	Total services	All-items
Group weight as a percentage of total[2]	25	17	12	14	67	33	100
1965	83.4	82.4	84.1	92.2	84.6	73.6	80.5
1966	88.7	84.5	87.1	92.2	87.8	76.1	83.5
1967	89.9	86.9	91.6	94.7	90.0	80.2	86.5
1968	92.8	91.5	94.5	96.2	93.4	84.4	90.0
1969	96.7	94.7	97.1	97.2	96.3	90.0	94.1
1970	98.9	97.0	98.7	98.4	98.2	95.3	97.2
1971	100.0	100.0	100.0	100.0	100.0	100.0	100.0
1972	107.6	102.9	102.4	101.2	104.6	105.2	104.8
1973	123.3	108.3	107.0	102.6	113.7	111.7	112.7
1974	143.4	120.4	117.2	110.4	128.1	120.5	125.0
1975	161.9	136.0	124.0	118.9	142.0	133.4	138.5
1976	166.2	147.6	129.9	125.3	149.0	149.6	148.9

[1]The previous supplementary classification (by type of commodity and service) has been revised. Historical series relating to the revised classification replace the previously published indexes.
[2]These weights, indicating the components' relative importance, are based on 1967 expenditures and have been incorporated since May 1973; prior to May 1973, the weights reflected 1957 expenditures.

21.17   Consumer price indexes for regional cities, 1965-76 (1971=100)

Year	St. John's, Nfld.	Hali- fax, NS	Saint John, NB	Que- bec, Que.	Mont- real, Que.	Ottawa, Ont.	Toronto, Ont.	Thunder Bay, Ont.
1965	85.4	82.8	83.9	—	84.3	81.3	82.6	—
1966	87.4	85.0	86.1	—	86.8	84.5	86.2	—
1967	89.8	87.0	88.7	—	90.2	86.5	88.8	—
1968	93.8	90.4	91.9	—	93.3	90.6	92.2	—
1969	96.6	94.6	95.7	—	96.2	94.2	95.9	—
1970	98.5	98.5	98.6	98.3	98.2	97.5	98.4	98.6
1971	100.0	100.0	100.0	100.0	100.0	100.0	100.0	100.0
1972	105.0	103.7	104.5	102.8	103.8	104.1	104.1	103.7
1973	113.7	110.9	112.2	110.1	110.7	111.9	111.3	110.8
1974	128.3	121.6	123.7	122.5	123.0	123.9	123.0	122.6
1975	143.0	133.9	138.1	135.0	136.4	135.8	136.1	136.4
1976	154.2	145.1	148.0	144.1	145.6	146.1	146.0	148.4

Year	Winni- peg, Man.	Saska- toon, Sask.	Regina, Sask.		Edmon- ton, Alta.	Calgary, Alta.	Van- couver, BC
1965	82.5		85.3		81.2		82.3
1966	85.0		87.8		83.9		84.3
1967	88.1		90.2		87.2		87.4
1968	91.9		93.8		91.0		90.6
1969	95.7		97.0		94.8		93.7
1970	98.8		99.0		97.6		96.9
1971	100.0		100.0		100.0		100.0
1972	103.8		104.0		103.9		104.0
1973	110.4		110.0		110.6		110.0
1974	122.2	120.4	120.4		122.5	120.9	123.9
1975	137.4	133.9	133.1		135.8	134.6	137.7
1976	149.3	144.9	145.0		146.7	145.8	151.0

21.18   Percentage change in consumer price indexes in Canada and other countries, 1974-75

Country	% change	Country	% change
North America		Africa	
Canada	10.8	Kenya (Nairobi)	18.4
Mexico (Mexico City)	15.0	South Africa (European population)	13.5
United States	9.1	Zaïre (Kinshasa)	28.5
South America		Asia	
Argentina (Buenos Aires)	182.8	India	5.6
Brazil (São Paulo)	30.2	Indonesia (Jakarta)	19.0
Chile (Santiago)	374.7	Korea, Republic of	25.3
		Pakistan (Karachi) — industrial	
Europe		workers	20.9
Belgium	12.7	Sri Lanka (Colombo)	6.8
Denmark	9.6		
France	11.8	Australasia	
Germany, Federal Republic of	6.0	Australia	15.1
Greece	13.4	New Zealand	14.7
Ireland	20.9		
Netherlands	10.2	Middle East	
Sweden	9.8	Iran	13.0
Switzerland	6.7	Israel	39.3
		Turkey (Ankara)	20.1
United Kingdom	24.3		

21.19   Industry selling price index (manufacturing), 1957-76 (1971=100)

Year	Index	Year	Index	Year	Index	Year	Index
1957	81.1	1962	83.3	1967	90.4	1972	104.5
1958	81.4	1963	84.4	1968	92.3	1973	116.2
1959	82.1	1964	85.1	1969	95.8	1974	138.3
1960	82.2	1965	86.2	1970	98.1	1975	153.7
1961	82.4	1966	88.7	1971	100.0	1976	161.5p

21.20   General wholesale index annual averages, 1953-76 (1935-39 = 100)

Year	Average	Year	Average	Year	Average	Year	Average
1953	220.7	1959	230.6	1965	250.4	1971	289.9
1954	217.0	1960	230.9	1966	259.5	1972	310.3
1955	218.9	1961	233.3	1967	264.1	1973	376.9
1956	225.6	1962	240.0	1968	269.9	1974	461.3r
1957	227.4	1963	244.6	1969	282.4	1975	491.6
1958	227.8	1964	245.4	1970	286.4	1976	512.3p

21.21   Index numbers of wholesale prices in Canada and other countries, 1973-75 (1970=100)

Country	1973	1974ʳ	1975	Country	1973	1974ʳ	1975
Belgium	116.3	135.7	137.4	Ireland	137.6	153.6	193.0
Brazil	166.4	214.8	273.8	Korea, Republic of	132.4	188.2	238.0
Canada	131.6ʳ	161.1	171.6	Netherlands	117.7	134.0	143.2
				New Zealand	138.3	142.6	160.0
Chile	1,226.0	13,840.0	80,534.0	Norway	116.5	137.8	151.2
Denmark	125.5	153.3	162.2	Sweden	121.0	151.0	162.0
France[1]	122.5	158.2	149.2	Switzerland	117.2	136.1	133.1
Germany, Federal Republic of	114.1	129.4	135.5	Turkey	164.8ʳ	214.0	235.9
Greece	135.8	185.7	198.4	United Kingdom[2]	144.5	215.2	235.2
India	140.7	179.0	181.6	United States	122.7	145.9	158.4

[1]Industrial products only.
[2]Basic material only.

21.22   Price indexes of residential and non-residential building materials and wage rates, 1966-75 (1971=100)

Year	Residential input indexes			Non-residential input indexes		
	Building materials	Labour	Total	Building materials	Labour	Total
1966	83.5	59.6	69.9	86.1	60.1	71.4
1967	86.7	65.5	74.6	87.8	66.1	75.6
1968	91.5	71.1	79.9	90.0	71.7	79.7
1969	96.4	76.5	85.1	94.0	77.2	84.5
1970	95.3	87.9	91.2	96.6	88.5	92.0
1971	100.0	100.0	100.0	100.0	100.0	100.0
1972	109.8	110.6	110.1	104.9	111.0	107.8
1973	124.0	121.8	123.2	113.1	122.3	117.5
1974	135.2	133.9	134.7	137.3	134.7	136.1
1975	139.8	151.6	144.0	147.0	154.1	150.4

21.23   Price indexes of inputs into residential building construction, 1971-75 (1971=100)

Province and trade	1971	1972	1973	1974	1975
Atlantic provinces	100.0	111.6	127.3	143.8	151.3
Materials	100.0	109.6	125.1	140.8	142.9
Labour	100.0	115.0	131.1	149.1	166.3
Quebec	100.0	110.0	123.3	133.6	147.1
Materials	100.0	112.1	127.1	136.5	143.3
Labour	100.0	106.2	116.2	128.3	154.4
Ontario	100.0	110.3	123.5	134.5	141.6
Materials	100.0	109.2	123.5	134.9	138.8
Labour	100.0	112.2	123.5	133.8	146.2
Prairie provinces	100.0	109.5	122.5	134.8	145.4
Materials	100.0	108.7	121.4	132.8	138.9
Labour	100.0	111.0	124.7	138.7	158.1
British Columbia	100.0	109.2	121.3	132.4	142.0
Materials	100.0	109.7	124.0	134.1	136.4
Labour	100.0	108.5	116.4	129.2	152.1
Canada	100.0	110.1	123.2	134.7	144.0
Materials	100.0	109.8	124.0	135.2	139.7
Labour	100.0	110.6	121.8	133.9	151.6
Trade					
Rough carpentry	100.0	119.4	143.0	141.7	144.1
Finished carpentry	100.0	112.4	134.3	143.3	146.7
Concrete	100.0	109.7	119.8	135.6	157.4
Masonry	100.0	107.4	116.9	130.3	145.9
Plumbing	100.0	104.1	113.0	139.8	148.1
Drywall	100.0	108.5	116.3	130.6	141.8
Windows	100.0	113.1	121.1	127.5	137.9
Cabinetry	100.0	103.7	111.3	122.8	116.4
Painting	100.0	108.6	118.0	131.6	148.6
Electrical	100.0	105.2	114.1	129.0	136.2
Forced warm air heating	100.0	104.0	109.1	119.2	130.7
Flooring, resilient	100.0	103.0	108.4	126.7	136.9
Roofing	100.0	106.8	117.6	138.7	152.1
Insulation and vapour barriers	100.0	106.9	113.6	127.9	148.1
Flooring, hardwood	100.0	108.0	136.9	150.8	149.0

21.24   New housing price indexes, for six metropolitan areas, 1971-76 (1971=100)

Year	Montreal	Toronto	Ottawa–Hull	Winnipeg	Calgary	Edmonton
1971	100.0	100.0	100.0	100.0	100.0	100.0
1972	107.6	110.2	112.7	105.2	110.0	109.1
1973	125.8	137.6	138.2	128.4	126.4	132.6
1974	177.7	171.6	171.2	163.5	162.3	172.8
1975	190.3	171.0	178.3	177.5	195.0	205.2
1976	200.9	180.7	192.5	199.8	243.1	245.8

21.25   Price indexes of electrical utility distribution systems, transmission lines, transformer stations, hydro-electric generating stations and steam electric generating stations, 1971-76 (1971 = 100)

Year	Distribution systems			Transmission lines	Transformer stations			Generating stations	
	Total direct costs	Equipment	Total		Support structures and fixtures	Equipment	Total	Hydro-electric	Steam electric
1971	100.0	100.0	100.0	100.0	100.0	100.0	100.0	100.0	100.0
1972	103.3	99.7	104.2	106.1	108.1	101.2	104.1	106.3	106.1
1973	113.4	100.7	113.8	115.3	120.5	107.3	111.2	116.1	115.9
1974	138.6	125.7	137.5	137.7	148.8	134.9	136.3	137.9	139.6
1975	153.6	136.7	153.2	161.2	165.2	162.5	159.1	157.6	158.4
1976	160.7	127.2	161.3	173.8	179.4	175.3	171.7	171.3	174.5

21.26   Price indexes of machinery and equipment, 1967-76 (1968=100)

Year	Construction	Forestry (east of the Rockies)	Year	Construction	Forestry (east of the Rockies)
1967	94.7	. . .	1972	110.8	112.3
1968	100.0	100.0	1973	114.9	117.0
1969	104.4	102.9	1974	130.0	133.4
1970	106.4	106.4	1975P	160.7	155.8
1971	108.4	109.3	1976P	167.9	162.8

21.27   Farm input price index total, 1967-76 (1961=100)

Year	East	West	Canada	Year	East	West	Canada
1967	121.4	121.6	121.5	1972	141.7	145.2	143.3
1968	124.3	125.6	124.9	1973	170.1	162.9	166.7
1969	128.1	130.2	129.1	1974r	199.1	190.7	195.2
1970	131.4	131.0	131.2	1975	214.0	217.0	215.4
1971	135.8	135.9	135.9	1976P	225.0	229.3	227.0

21.28   Index numbers of common and preferred stocks, 1971-76 (1971=100)

Year	Investors index				Mining index[1]	Uranium[1]	Primary oil and gas[1]	Preferred stocks[1]
	Total	Industrials	Utilities	Finance				
1971	100.0	100.0	100.0	100.0	100.0	100.0	100.0	100.0
1972	118.1	118.8	106.6	132.1	107.8	115.5	102.8	102.9
1973	126.6	134.1	98.5	131.8	122.1	158.8	100.9	105.6
1974	106.4	111.6	84.1	114.2	133.4	166.6	79.2	91.0
1975	102.3	104.2	83.6	120.9	110.4	179.8	80.8	85.4
1976	106.2	108.5	91.3	117.6	102.4	212.7	103.5	90.1

[1]Not included in investors index.

21.29   Summary of the Canadian balance of international payments between Canada and all non-residents, 1969-75 (million dollars)

Year	Current account balances			Capital account flows			Allocation of SDRs	Net official monetary movements
	Merchandise	Non-merchandise	Balance	Long-term	Short-term	Net		
1969	+964	-1,881	-917	+2,337	-1,355	+982	...	+65
1970r	+3,052	-1,946	+1,106	+1,007	-583	+424	+133	+1,663
1971r	+2,563	-2,132	+431	+664	-318	+346	+119	+896
1972r	+1,857	-2,243	-386	+1,588	-983	+605	+117	+336
1973r	+2,735	-2,639	+96	+385	-948	-563	—	-467
1974r	+1,698	-3,190	-1,492	+871	+645	+1,516	—	+24
1975	-639	-4,326	-4,965	+4,106	+455	+4,561	—	-404

21.30   Current account transactions between Canada and all non-residents, 1969-75 (million dollars)

Year	Current receipts			Current payments			Current account balance
	Merchandise exports	Service transactions	Transfers	Merchandise imports	Service transactions	Transfers	
1969	15,035	3,695	695	14,071	5,719	552	-917
1970	16,921	4,246	765	13,869	6,345	612	+1,106
1971r	17,877	4,304	870	15,314	6,702	604	+431
1972r	20,129	4,451	903	18,272	6,978	619	-386
1973r	25,461	5,264	1,048	22,726	8,255	696	+96
1974r	32,591	6,313	1,355	30,893	10,066	792	-1,492
1975	33,347	6,686	1,397	33,986	11,418	991	-4,965

21.31   Canadian balance of international payments, by area, 1974 and 1975 (million dollars)

Item	United States		United Kingdom		Other non-residents		All non-residents	
	1974	1975	1974	1975	1974	1975	1974	1975
CURRENT ACCOUNT								
Current receipts								
Merchandise exports (adjusted)	21,650	21,927	1,993	1,861	8,948	9,559	32,591	33,347
Service receipts								
Travel	1,328	1,337	94	129	272	349	1,694	1,815
Interest and dividends	533	488	45	35	302	303	880	826
Freight and shipping	892	845	190	174	730	748	1,812	1,767
Other service receipts	924	927	342	447	661	904	1,927	2,278
Total, service receipts	3,677	3,597	671	785	1,965	2,304	6,313	6,686
Total, exports of goods and services	25,327	25,524	2,664	2,646	10,913	11,863	38,904	40,033
Transfer receipts								
Inheritances and immigrants' funds	143	112	135	145	424	407	702	664
Personal and institutional remittances	153	191	20	24	50	53	223	268
Withholding tax	..	..	..	..	..	..	430	465
Total, current receipts	25,623	25,827	2,819	2,815	11,387	12,323	40,259	41,430
Current payments								
Merchandise imports (adjusted)	20,632	23,049	1,171	1,224	9,090	9,713	30,893	33,986
Service payments								
Travel	1,196	1,587	211	242	551	713	8,978	2,542
Interest and dividends	2,009	2,313	117	124	283	359	2,409	2,796
Freight and shipping	988	1,066	281	259	778	812	2,047	2,137
Other service payments	2,134	2,305	262	269	806	904	3,202	3,478
Withholding tax	..	..	..	..	..	..	430	465
Total, service payments	6,327	7,271	871	894	2,438	2,788	10,066	11,418
Total, imports of goods and services	26,959	30,320	2,042	2,118	11,528	12,501	40,959	45,404
Transfer payments								
Inheritances and emigrants' funds	83	85	40	44	45	50	168	179
Personal and institutional remittances	97	89	34	37	161	173	292	299
Official contributions	—	—	—	—	332	513	332	513
Total, current payments	27,139	30,494	2,116	2,199	12,066	13,237	41,751	46,395
Current account balance								
Merchandise trade	+1,018	-1,122	+822	+637	-142	-154	+1,698	-639
Service transactions	-2,650	-3,674	-200	-109	-473	-484	-3,753	-4,732
Net transfers	+116	+129	+81	+88	-64	-276	+563	+406
Total, current account balance	-1,516	-4,667	+703	+616	-679	-914	-1,492	-4,965

21.31   Canadian balance of international payments, by area, 1974 and 1975 (million dollars) (concluded)

Item	United States 1974	United States 1975	United Kingdom 1974	United Kingdom 1975	Other non-residents 1974	Other non-residents 1975	All non-residents 1974	All non-residents 1975
CAPITAL ACCOUNT								
Direct investment								
In Canada	+615	+535	-1	-56	+111	+151	+725	+630
Abroad	-482	-324	-43	-13	-250	-313	-775	-650
Portfolio transactions								
Canadian securities								
Outstanding bonds	+16	+38	+9	+142	+16	+122	+41	+302
Outstanding stocks	-68	-12	-58	-19	+14	+36	-112	+5
New issues	+1,816	+3,453	+21	+143	+586	+1,554	+2,423	+5,150
Retirements	-504	-531	-19	-34	-103	-126	-626	-691
Foreign securities								
Outstanding issues	+71	+18	-9	+7	+11	-7	+73	+18
New issues	-8	-26	-2	-19	-29	-24	-39	-69
Retirements	+8	+8	—	—	+4	+4	+12	+12
Loans and subscriptions, Government of Canada								
Advances	—	—	—	—	-350	-378	-350	-378
Repayments	—	—	+22	+22	+16	+18	+38	+40
Export credits directly or indirectly at risk of the Government of Canada	-45	-3	-18	-20	-525	-374	-588	-397
Other long-term capital transactions	+153	+223	+33	+14	-137	-103	+49	+134
Balance of capital movements in long-term forms	+1,572	+3,379	-65	+167	-636	+560	+871	+4,106
Resident holdings of foreign currencies:								
Chartered bank net foreign currency position with non-residents	+1,073	+1,484	-1,986	-504	-441	-492	-1,354	+488
Non-bank holdings of foreign currencies abroad	+172	-92	+1,386	-114	+32	-30	+1,590	-236
Non-resident holdings of Canadian:								
Dollar deposits	+165	+78	+11	+93	+421	+386	+597	+557
Government demand liabilities	—	—	—	—	+45	-4	+45	-4
Treasury bills	+9	+2	+4	+15	+64	+20	+77	+37
Commercial paper	+42	+41	—	—	+11	—	+53	+41
Finance company paper	+73	+237	+1	-1	+20	-19	+94	+217
Other short-term paper	-108	+153	+1	+9	+37	-15	-70	+147
Other finance company obligations	+148	-92	+9	+1	+1	-1	+158	-92
Other short-term capital transactions	-684	-557	+11	+4	+128	-147	-545	-700
Balance of capital movements in short-term forms	+890	+1,254	-563	-497	+318	-302	+645	+455
Total, net capital balance	+2,462	+4,633	-628	-330	-318	+258	+1,516	+4,561
Balance settled by exchange transfers	-1,111	-534	-75	-285	+1,186	+819	—	—
Allocation of Special Drawing Rights	—	—	—	—	—	—	—	—
Net official monetary movements								
Official international reserves	-165	-568	—	+1	+189	+163	+24	-404
Official monetary liabilities	—	—	—	—	—	—	—	—
Net official monetary movements	-165	-568	—	+1	+189	+163	+24	-404

21.32   Canadian balance of international indebtedness, selected years, 1939-73 (billion dollars)

Item	1939	1950	1960	1970	1971[r]	1972	1973
CANADIAN ASSETS							
Direct investment	0.7	1.0	2.5	6.2	6.5	6.7	7.8
Portfolio investment	0.7	0.6	1.3	2.7	2.9	3.2	3.6
Miscellaneous investment[1]	—	—	—	1.0	1.5	1.9	2.2
Government of Canada credits[2]	—	2.0	1.5	1.5	1.6	1.7	1.8
Government of Canada subscriptions to international financial agencies	—	0.1	0.1	0.3	0.3	0.4	0.5
Total, Canadian long-term investment abroad	1.4	3.7	5.3	11.7	12.8	13.9	15.9
Net official monetary assets	0.5	2.0	2.0	4.7	5.6	6.0	5.8
Other Canadian short-term holdings of foreign exchange	—	0.1	1.2	3.6	2.7	2.2	2.9
Gross assets[3]	1.9	5.7	8.5	20.0	21.1	22.1	24.6
Net official monetary assets	0.5	2.0	2.0	4.7	5.6	6.0	5.8
United States[3,4]	0.9	1.2	3.7	8.6	7.2	7.3	8.6
United Kingdom[3,4]	0.1	1.6	1.5	4.1	4.3	4.0	3.8
Other countries[3,4]	0.4	0.9	1.3	2.6	4.0	4.8	6.4
Short-term receivables (not included elsewhere)[5]	..	0.2	0.5	3.6	4.9	6.6	7.7
Gross assets	1.9[3]	5.9	8.9	23.6	26.0	28.7	32.3

21.32   Canadian balance of international indebtedness, selected years, 1939-73 (billion dollars) (concluded)

Item	1939	1950	1960	1970	1971r	1972	1973
CANADIAN LIABILITIES							
Direct investment	2.3	4.0	12.9	26.4	27.9	29.5	32.8
Government bonds	1.7	2.0	3.3	7.9	8.1	9.4	9.9
Other portfolio investment	2.6	2.4	4.6	6.9	7.1	7.8	8.6
Miscellaneous investment	0.3	0.3	1.4	2.9	3.1	3.2	3.3
Total, foreign long-term investment in Canada	6.9	8.7	22.2	44.0	46.2	49.9	54.6
Non-resident equity in Canadian assets abroad	0.2	0.3	1.1	2.7	3.0	2.7	3.1
Official Special Drawing Rights liabilities	. . .	. . .	. . .	0.1	0.3	0.4	0.4
Total, long-term liabilities	7.1	9.0	23.3	46.9	49.5	53.0	58.1
Non-resident holdings of Canadian dollars	0.3	0.6	0.6	0.8	0.9	1.1	1.3
Gross liabilities[3]	7.4	9.6	24.0	47.7	50.4	54.1	59.4
United States[3]	4.5	7.1	18.0	37.4	39.1	41.0	44.9
United Kingdom[3]	2.6	2.0	3.5	4.3	4.6	4.9	5.4
Other countries[3,6]	0.3	0.5	2.4	6.0	6.7	8.2	9.1
Short-term payables (not included elsewhere)[5,7]							
Finance company obligations	}	0.8	1.6	{ 1.3	1.3	1.2	1.2
Other				3.0	3.3	3.4	4.0
Gross liabilities	7.4[3]	10.4	25.6	52.1	55.0	58.7	64.6
CANADA'S INTERNATIONAL INDEBTEDNESS							
Canadian net international indebtedness	5.5[3]	4.5	16.6	28.5	29.0	30.0	32.3
Net official monetary assets	-0.5	-2.0	-2.0	-4.7	-5.6	-6.0	-5.8
United States	3.6	5.9	14.3	28.8	31.9	33.7	36.3
United Kingdom	2.5	0.4	2.0	0.2	0.3	0.9	1.6
Other countries	-0.1	-0.4	1.1	3.4	2.7	3.4	2.7
Short-term (not included elsewhere)	. .	0.6	1.1	0.8	-0.3	-2.0	-2.5

[1]Includes export credits by government and private sectors less reserve against government inactive assets.
[2]Includes medium-term non-marketable United States government securities held under the Columbia River Treaty arrangements since 1964.
[3]Excludes short-term receivables and payables.
[4]Excludes net official monetary assets.
[5]Country distribution not available.
[6]Includes international financial agencies.
[7]At the end of 1964 about $450 million previously classified as long-term investment was reclassified to short-term finance company obligations.

21.33   Canadian long-term investment abroad[1], by country and by type of investment, selected years, 1951-73 (million dollars)

Location and type of investment	1951	1960	1970r	1971r	1972	1973
United States						
Direct investment	912	1,618	3,262	3,399	3,431	3,924
Portfolio investment						
Stocks	289	827	2,110	2,182	2,379	2,674
Bonds	87	120	224	217	209	216
Miscellaneous investment	9	18	286	356	475	530
Government of Canada credits[2]	—	—	26	—	—	—
Government of Canada subscriptions to international investment agencies	—	—	—	—	—	—
Total, United States	1,297	2,583	5,908	6,154	6,494	7,344
United Kingdom						
Direct investment	74	257	586	590	630	797
Portfolio investment						
Stocks	17	26	61	64	72	82
Bonds	17	16	20	20	33	36
Miscellaneous investment	13	18	73	79	118	131
Government of Canada credits[3]	1,394	1,092	1,018	997	976	954
Government of Canada subscriptions to international investment agencies	—	—	—	—	—	—
Total, United Kingdom	1,515	1,409	1,758	1,750	1,829	2,000
Other Commonwealth countries[4]						
Direct investment	88	299	791	843	965	1,160
Portfolio investment						
Stocks	6	10	17	18	20	22
Bonds	8	18	23	27	31	36
Miscellaneous investment	. .	. .	. . .	. . .	. . .	. . .
Government of Canada credits	—	35	243	354	465	579
Government of Canada subscriptions to international investment agencies	—	—	—	—	—	—
Total, other Commonwealth countries	102	362	1,074	1,242	1,481	1,797

21.33   Canadian long-term investment abroad[1], by country and by type of investment, selected years, 1951-73 (million dollars) (concluded)

Location and type of investment	1951	1960	1970[r]	1971[r]	1972	1973
Other countries						
Direct investment	92	293	1,549[5]	1,706	1,680	1,929
Portfolio investment						
Stocks	155	187	56[5]	104	113	145
Bonds	30	111	207	256	283	366
Miscellaneous investment	-80	-54	681	1,022	1,312	1,559
Government of Canada credits	528	335	218	229	268	306
Government of Canada subscriptions to international investment agencies	66	85	268	319	403	485
Total, other countries	791	957	2,979	3,636	4,059	4,790
All countries						
Direct investment	1,166	2,467	6,188	6,538	6,706	7,810
Portfolio investment						
Stocks	467	1,050	2,244	2,368	2,584	2,923
Bonds	142	265	474	520	556	654
Miscellaneous investment	-58	-18	1,040	1,457	1,905	2,220
Government of Canada credits[6]	1,922	1,462	1,505	1,580	1,709	1,839
Government of Canada subscriptions to international investment agencies	66	85	268	319	403	485
Total, all countries	3,705	5,311	11,719	12,782	13,863	15,931

[1]Figures include the equity of non-residents in assets abroad of Canadian companies but exclude investment of insurance companies and banks (held mainly, against liabilities to non-residents).
[2]Medium-term non-marketable United States government securities acquired under the Columbia River Treaty arrangements are shown from 1964.
[3]Includes deferred interest on the United Kingdom 1946 loan agreement starting from 1956 and amounting to $101 million in 1973.
[4]Includes investment in Newfoundland prior to 1949.
[5]New series not strictly comparable with previous years.
[6]Includes United Nations bonds from 1962, which amounted to $4 million in 1973.

21.34   Foreign long-term investment in Canada, by type of investment and by country, as at Dec. 31, 1972 and 1973 (million dollars)

Year and type of investment	United States[1]	United Kingdom[1]	Other countries	Total investments of non-residents
1972				
Government securities				
Government of Canada	449	43	174	666
Provincial	5,571	256	1,407	7,234
Municipal	1,176	46	275	1,497
Total, government securities	7,196	345	1,856	9,397
Manufacturing				
Vegetable products	1,182	151	138	1,471
Animal products	256	13	19	288
Textiles	232	65	6	303
Wood and paper products	2,390	184	473	3,047
Iron and products	3,670	181	173	4,024
Non-ferrous metals	1,564	127	85	1,776
Non-metallic minerals	348	95	167	610
Chemicals and allied products	1,513	218	143	1,874
Miscellaneous manufactures	246	3	6	255
Total, manufacturing	11,401	1,037	1,210	13,648
Petroleum and natural gas	6,824	771	942	8,537
Other mining and smelting	3,552	237	489	4,278
Utilities				
Railways	414	358	127	899
Other (excl. public enterprises)	1,429	98	77	1,604
Total, public utilities	1,843	456	204	2,503
Merchandising	1,529	332	204	2,065
Financial	3,298	1,034	865	5,197
Other enterprises	860	127	116	1,103
Miscellaneous investments	2,073[2]	210	880	3,163
Total, investments, 1972	38,576	4,549	6,766	49,891
1973				
Government securities				
Government of Canada	339	77	223	639
Provincial	6,156	256	1,514	7,926
Municipal	1,024	31	293	1,348
Total, government securities	7,519	364	2,030	9,913

21.34   Foreign long-term investment in Canada, by type of investment and by country, as at Dec. 31, 1972 and 1973 (million dollars) (concluded)

Year and type of investment	United States[1]	United Kingdom[1]	Other countries	Total investments of non-residents
1973 (concluded)				
Manufacturing				
Vegetable products	1,314	159	159	1,632
Animal products	313	11	22	346
Textiles	258	65	13	336
Wood and paper products	2,544	213	515	3,272
Iron and products	4,100	208	113	4,421
Non-ferrous metals	1,727	132	108	1,967
Non-metallic minerals	376	92	253	721
Chemicals and allied products	1,685	221	158	2,064
Miscellaneous manufactures	270	3	7	280
Total, manufacturing	12,587	1,104	1,348	15,039
Petroleum and natural gas	7,596	865	1,056	9,517
Other mining and smelting	3,774	251	586	4,611
Utilities				
Railways	436	337	110	883
Other (excl. public enterprises)	1,627	119	99	1,845
Total, public utilities	2,063	456	209	2,728
Merchandising	1,777	345	238	2,360
Financial	3,746	1,231	916	5,893
Other enterprises	964	156	155	1,275
Miscellaneous investments	2,124[2]	220	930	3,274
Total, investments, 1973	42,150	4,992	7,468	54,610

Common and preferred stocks are at book values as shown in the balance sheets of the issuing companies; bonds and debentures are valued at par; and liabilities in foreign currencies are converted into Canadian dollars at par of exchange.
[1]Includes some investments held for residents of other countries.
[2]Includes Columbia River Treaty receipts.

21.35   Price of the United States dollar in Canada, by month, 1968-75 (Canadian cents per US dollar)

Month	1968	1969	1970	1971	1972	1973	1974	1975
January	108.47	107.27	107.28	101.16	100.59	99.91	99.14	99.48
February	108.73	107.44	107.31	100.75	100.46	99.55	97.67	100.05
March	108.49	107.67	107.27	100.63	99.84	99.66	97.20	100.03
April	108.01	107.62	107.28	100.76	99.56	100.06	96.73	101.11
May	107.79	107.70	107.28	100.87	98.87	100.05	96.21	102.81
June	107.68	107.95	103.84	102.12	97.94	99.83	96.64	102.64
July	107.36	108.06	103.20	102.11	98.39	99.94	97.61	103.07
August	107.26	107.81	102.14	101.33	98.22	100.38	97.98	103.53
September	107.30	107.82	101.59	101.29	98.29	100.81	98.63	102.62
October	107.27	107.79	102.14	100.44	98.26	100.09	98.30	102.50
November	107.30	107.58	102.00	100.37	98.72	99.88	98.72	101.37
December	107.31	107.42	101.74	99.92	99.67	99.94	98.81	101.38
Annual average	107.75	107.68	104.40	100.98	99.05	100.01	97.80	101.73

Rates published by Bank of Canada. Noon average market rate for business days in period.

21.36   Canada's official international reserves and undelivered contracts, 1968-75 (million US dollars)

End of:	Convertible foreign currencies[1] US dollars	Other[2]	Special Drawing Rights[3,4]	Gold[4]	Reserve position in the IMF[4]	Total[4]	Undelivered contracts in US dollars[5]
1968	1,964.9	11.6	—	863.1	206.2	3,045.8	25.2
1969	1,743.6	12.3	—	872.3	478.1	3,106.3	7.5
1970	3,022.1	14.5	182.1	790.7	669.6	4,679.0	-6.4
1971	4,060.6	13.6	371.9	791.8	332.6	5,570.4	-4.0
1972	4,355.0	12.6	505.2	834.1	342.9	6,049.9	-2.5
1973	3,927.2	12.2	563.7	926.9	338.2	5,768.2	—
1974	3,767.7	12.9	574.3	940.7	529.7	5,825.3	-8.3
1975	3,207.1	15.7	555.4	899.4	648.0	5,325.6	-4.9

[1]Convertible foreign currency holdings of the Exchange Fund Account, the Receiver General for Canada and the Bank of Canada.
[2]Valued at official rates in terms of US dollars to 1972 and at market rates beginning 1973.
[3]Holdings of Special Drawing Rights (SDRs) reflect allocations to Canada of SDRs and transactions involving Canada under the arrangements by the International Monetary Fund providing for the use of SDRs by member countries and by the IMF.
[4]Canada's gold and gold-based assets were revalued from US$35 to US$38 per oz t (US$1.13 to US$1.22 per g) of fine gold in May 1972, and to US$42.22 (US$1.36) in October 1973. Beginning July 1974, these assets are valued on the basis of the month-end value of SDRs in terms of US dollars as determined by the IMF.
[5]Includes all US dollar overnight and forward transactions of the Exchange Fund Account and the Bank of Canada that affect the total of official reserves. A positive figure indicates a net commitment to take delivery of foreign exchange in the future and a negative figure indicates a commitment to deliver foreign exchange in the future.

21.37 Intercity indexes of retail price differentials for selected commodities and services, 1975 and 1976 (combined cities average = 100)

Commodity grouping	St. John's, Nfld.	Charlotte-town, PEI	Halifax, NS	Saint John, NB	Montreal, Que.	Ottawa, Ont.	Toronto, Ont.	Winnipeg, Man.	Regina, Sask.	Edmonton, Alta.	Vancouver, BC
As at October 1975											
Food at home	110	103	99	103	98	97	98	101	101	102	110
Household operation¹	103	100	102	101	102	99	98	96	93	98	107
Transportation	111	107	102	108	107	97	99	93	93	97	96
Health and personal care	102	96	92	101	98	98	106	99	90	98	101
Recreation, education and reading	96	93	98	98	104	98	101	94	99	92	98
Tobacco and alcohol	123	114	112	110	102	101	98	101	99	96	99
As at June 1976											
Food at home	114	104	103	108	97	98	99	103	102	100	109
Household operation¹	106	101	104	101	101	99	98	97	97	99	108
Transportation	108	104	101	105	105	98	100	93	92	92	101
Health and personal care	102	90	95	97	95	104	104	99	90	99	106
Recreation, education and reading	98	92	99	98	104	98	102	94	96	91	99
Tobacco and alcohol	121	110	106	103	101	99	100	103	97	92	99

¹Excludes fuel and utilities.

21.38 Summary of the financial market, 1975 and 1976 (million dollars)

Category	1975 Jan. 1-Mar. 31	Apr. 1-June 30	July 1-Sept. 30	Oct. 1-Dec. 31	Total	1976 Jan. 1-Mar. 31	Apr. 1-June 30	July 1-Sept. 30	Oct. 1-Dec. 31	Total
Funds raised in credit markets										
Persons and unincorporated business	246	4,119	4,437	4,724	13,526	3,289	4,513	3,431	4,117	15,350
Consumer credit	148	1,107	881	1,066	3,202	227	1,604	1,004	981	3,816
Bank loans	-553	636	696	1,339	2,118	1,088	373	121	868	2,450
Other loans	-554	222	415	-24	59	289	111	-63	59	396
Short-term paper	22	4	-7	-10	9	—	11	-7	2	6
Mortgages	1,133	2,185	2,434	2,317	8,069	1,681	2,417	2,367	2,213	8,678
Bonds	50	-35	18	36	69	4	-3	9	-6	4
Non-financial private corporations	2,397	1,634	735	1,095	5,861	2,274	2,431	1,339	2,245	8,289
Bank loans	552	332	170	253	1,307	1,113	663	394	800	2,970
Other loans	452	92	3	346	893	492	90	-239	343	686
Short-term paper	360	179	-160	-277	102	-16	615	201	-207	593
Mortgages	29	29	116	171	345	121	154	207	276	758
Bonds	725	751	369	315	2,160	488	733	529	365	2,115
Stocks	279	251	237	287	1,054	76	176	247	668	1,167
Non-financial government enterprises	1,686	880	809	679	4,054	2,795	495	1,946	1,076	6,312
Bank loans	852	214	-139	-545	382	683	-35	423	-147	924
Other loans	32	-8	76	361	461	72	9	471	-40	512
Short-term paper	86	38	135	-316	-57	132	-86	-103	-40	-97
Mortgages	37	37	25	24	123	15	41	27	22	105
Bonds	674	544	707	1,140	3,065	1,879	426	1,142	1,300	4,747
Stocks	5	55	5	15	80	14	140	-14	-19	121

21.38 Summary of the financial market, 1975 and 1976 (million dollars) (concluded)

Category	1975 Jan. 1-Mar. 31	Apr. 1-June 30	July 1-Sept. 30	Oct. 1-Dec. 31	Total	1976 Jan. 1-Mar. 31	Apr. 1-June 30	July 1-Sept. 30	Oct. 1-Dec. 31	Total
General government	*1,120*	*1,179*	*1,243*	*5,364*	*8,906*	*1,678*	*1,385*	*1,233*	*3,680*	*7,976*
Bank loans	337	-232	-97	246	254	376	-291	-173	315	227
Other loans	99	83	-5	135	312	58	15	-13	94	154
Treasury bills	–	165	245	160	570	295	440	440	470	1,645
Short-term paper	388	96	101	27	612	9	-145	224	-162	-74
Mortgages	2	3	2	2	9	2	3	2	2	9
Bonds	294	1,064	997	4,794	7,149	938	1,363	753	2,961	6,015
Total borrowing by domestic non-financial sectors	5,449	7,812	7,224	11,862	32,347	10,036	8,824	7,949	11,118	37,927
Rest of the world	*268*	*513*	*218*	*496*	*1,495*	*348*	*-5*	*500*	*507*	*1,350*
Bank loans	26	253	75	290	644	164	82	263	278	787
Other loans	207	272	168	103	750	151	94	235	179	659
Mortgages	–	–	–	–	–	–	–	–	–	–
Stocks	35	-12	-25	103	101	33	-181	2	50	-96
Total borrowing, excluding domestic financial institutions	5,717	8,325	7,442	12,358	33,842	10,384	8,819	8,449	11,625	39,277
Domestic financial institutions	*525*	*369*	*-553*	*1,979*	*2,320*	*-119*	*1,526*	*364*	*1,466*	*3,237*
Bank loans	-232	177	-550	772	167	-391	502	-486	111	-264
Other loans	192	-2	-138	254	306	-397	239	241	219	302
Short-term paper	121	-109	-94	176	94	112	253	-122	460	703
Mortgages	-1	1	–	12	12	–	14	8	16	38
Bonds	254	106	179	451	990	460	445	475	410	1,790
Stocks	191	196	50	314	751	97	73	248	250	668
Total funds raised	6,242	8,694	6,889	14,337	36,162	10,265	10,345	8,813	13,091	42,514
Funds supplied directly to credit markets										
Persons and unincorporated business	403	776	158	2,685	4,022	-191	-564	-216	2,160	1,189
Non-financial private enterprises	-258	-123	304	700	623	-722	284	64	55	-319
Public sector (general government and non-financial government enterprises)	696	639	521	475	2,331	803	338	110	189	1,440
Public financial institutions	441	595	702	545	2,283	468	743	448	634	2,293
Rest of the world	972	1,014	908	2,544	5,438	3,499	1,970	2,756	2,277	10,502
Bank of Canada	22	222	551	-48	747	105	-329	382	330	488
Chartered banks	1,309	2,682	1,531	3,317	8,839	3,603	3,679	2,172	3,442	12,896
Private domestic financial institutions (excl. chartered banks)	2,657	2,889	2,214	4,119	11,879	2,700	4,224	3,097	4,004	14,025
Total funds supplied	6,242	8,694	6,889	14,337	36,162	10,265	10,345	8,813	13,091	42,514

The table above is an aggregation of financial flows data designed to provide a synopsis of Canadian credit market activity. The top portion of the table focuses on, but is not limited to, borrowing by the non-financial sectors of the economy. Only flows through what may be termed organized credit markets are included. Funds supplied by the immediate lending sector appear in the bottom portion of the table. This part of the table measures the asset increase of the same conventional credit market instruments encountered in the top portion of the table.

21.39 Highway construction price indexes, 1956-75 (1971=100)

Province and item	Year¹	0	1	2	3	4	5	6	7	8	9
Newfoundland											
Total	1950	...	...	...	...	...	...	77.3	65.0	74.0	67.5
	1960	70.8	56.8	61.9	57.4	61.5	67.8	73.6	65.4	68.6	66.1
	1970	82.6	100.0	101.1	109.6	129.0	128.0	...	...	...	...
Grading	1970	...	100.0	101.4	103.1	124.6	125.3	...	...	...	...
Granular base course	1970	...	100.0	100.9	117.6	130.5	123.3	...	...	...	...
Paving	1970	...	100.0	100.4	117.3	139.6	142.2	...	...	...	...
Total contract work	1970	...	100.0	101.1	109.3	127.9	126.5	...	...	...	...
Total supplies	1970	...	100.0	101.4	114.4	149.5	157.7	...	...	...	...
Nova Scotia											
Total	1950	...	...	...	...	...	...	77.6	70.5	69.9	74.2
	1960	79.8	67.4	66.2	64.7	65.0	78.8	78.3	82.7	80.8	83.0
	1970	90.4	100.0	107.2	118.8	164.1	185.0	...	...	...	...
Grading	1950	...	...	...	...	...	...	71.9	63.7	70.3	76.0
	1960	86.8	70.7	67.1	66.5	65.6	74.8	78.2	80.9	76.9	82.5
	1970	90.8	100.0	106.5	120.8	170.6	190.7	...	...	...	...
Granular base course	1950	...	...	...	...	...	...	68.4	64.8	60.2	66.9
	1960	67.7	61.3	59.7	55.5	58.9	82.3	78.9	85.2	83.3	83.3
	1970	88.7	100.0	107.5	117.6	162.8	175.6	...	...	...	...
Paving	1950	...	...	...	...	...	...	103.4	93.0	84.4	82.0
	1960	85.2	70.6	74.6	75.5	73.5	81.4	77.5	82.7	85.0	83.9
	1970	92.4	100.0	107.9	118.2	159.5	188.1	...	...	...	...
Total contract work	1970	...	100.0	108.3	119.4	163.3	181.6	...	...	...	...
Total supplies	1970	...	100.0	100.0	114.8	169.6	208.2	...	...	...	...
New Brunswick											
Total	1950	...	...	...	...	...	...	87.0	84.6	89.9	89.3
	1960	84.3	87.1	86.5	89.0	90.3	89.9	90.2	89.7	88.7	89.0
	1970	105.7	100.0	123.9	139.3	191.8	188.6	...	...	...	...
Grading	1950	...	...	...	...	...	...	85.7	84.5	95.2	93.8
	1960	84.0	91.2	93.4	94.2	91.3	95.2	86.1	88.2	93.3	90.5
	1970	105.9	100.0	142.9	163.1	220.6	211.7	...	...	...	...
Granular base course	1950	...	...	...	...	...	...	87.9	85.4	87.2	89.1
	1960	86.2	89.0	80.9	85.6	88.3	88.9	94.7	92.6	84.5	92.6
	1970	106.7	100.0	125.7	129.2	163.3	165.4	...	...	...	...
Paving	1950	...	...	...	...	...	...	88.7	83.1	81.7	78.2
	1960	81.4	73.0	80.2	82.7	91.9	78.5	92.1	87.9	85.1	77.9
	1970	103.7	100.0	103.4	118.6	173.7	174.3	...	...	...	...
Total contract work	1970	...	100.0	126.2	142.0	190.1	185.7	...	...	...	...
Total supplies	1970	...	100.0	104.1	115.2	206.5	214.4	...	...	...	...
Quebec											
Total	1960	...	...	...	...	79.6	76.9	82.6	80.8	80.5	85.4
	1970	87.2	100.0	106.6	120.5	154.0	180.7	...	...	...	...
Grading	1960	...	...	...	...	80.2	74.7	81.8	77.3	79.0	84.2
	1970	84.4	100.0	109.6	125.8	160.2	188.7	...	...	...	...
Granular base course	1960	...	...	...	...	78.6	76.7	82.5	83.3	79.3	85.8
	1970	89.2	100.0	101.9	116.4	147.5	173.3	...	...	...	...
Paving	1960	...	...	...	...	79.4	81.3	84.4	85.3	84.4	87.1
	1970	90.8	100.0	103.8	112.2	145.1	168.7	...	...	...	...
Total contract work	1970	...	100.0	106.6	120.4	149.8	177.7	...	...	...	...
Total supplies	1970	...	100.0	106.8	122.0	210.1	221.1	...	...	...	...
Ontario											
Total	1950	...	...	...	...	...	...	81.6	71.4	66.4	69.2
	1960	65.2	60.8	67.0	76.9	75.2	87.5	95.7	95.0	92.1	93.6
	1970	96.8	100.0	106.3	114.5	149.5	164.2	...	...	...	...
Grading	1950	...	...	...	...	...	...	76.3	63.7	58.8	58.7
	1960	58.5	53.4	60.4	71.7	71.1	81.5	93.6	93.2	90.4	90.6
	1970	95.5	100.0	108.9	117.0	155.8	171.4	...	...	...	...
Granular base course	1950	...	...	...	...	...	...	82.9	71.7	67.0	71.5
	1960	62.8	63.3	66.4	76.1	73.5	90.5	96.1	96.4	93.0	96.5
	1970	96.9	100.0	101.2	108.1	140.7	154.0	...	...	...	...
Paving	1950	...	...	...	...	...	...	89.4	86.6	80.2	85.4
	1960	83.9	70.4	82.0	89.2	87.3	93.2	98.8	95.5	93.8	93.5
	1970	99.2	100.0	108.0	117.5	150.1	165.2	...	...	...	...
Total contract work	1970	...	100.0	106.7	115.1	148.1	162.7	...	...	...	...
Total supplies	1970	...	100.0	100.2	105.3	172.1	188.7	...	...	...	...
Manitoba											
Total	1950	...	...	...	...	...	...	83.3	93.4	69.8	68.7
	1960	72.9	62.6	67.6	75.3	77.5	83.5	95.7	96.3	88.2	90.5
	1970	100.9	100.0	111.3	126.3	166.8	172.5	...	...	...	...
Grading	1950	...	...	...	...	...	...	80.9	79.3	61.2	58.4
	1960	63.0	51.4	57.6	80.7	75.6	82.6	95.3	98.4	85.6	86.2
	1970	102.1	100.0	117.8	115.6	158.9	161.1	...	...	...	...
Granular base course	1950	...	...	...	...	...	...	115.2	134.4	82.1	83.8
	1960	85.3	77.4	80.0	72.6	95.1	97.1	111.1	101.2	91.2	100.2
	1970	107.4	100.0	113.4	139.3	176.7	180.3	...	...	...	...
Paving	1950	...	...	...	...	...	...	71.3	93.2	76.0	75.9
	1960	80.6	71.2	75.7	68.9	71.4	78.1	88.9	91.0	90.3	92.0
	1970	95.9	100.0	99.9	124.7	165.2	178.2	...	...	...	...
Total contract work	1970	...	100.0	113.3	127.7	166.6	170.8	...	...	...	...
Total supplies	1970	...	100.0	99.5	118.0	167.8	182.2	...	...	...	...

21.39   Highway construction price indexes, 1956-75 (1971=100) (concluded)

Province and item	Year[1]	0	1	2	3	4	5	6	7	8	9
Saskatchewan											
Total	1950	...	...	...	...	...	...	103.7	106.5	82.6	75.5
	1960	71.6	68.0	66.9	69.8	79.4	98.2	114.3	93.5	84.9	89.8
	1970	98.5	100.0	104.4	129.6	175.8	210.4				
Grading	1950	...	...	...	...	...	...	94.9	87.7	68.2	68.7
	1960	73.1	64.2	63.5	73.1	78.5	94.7	110.5	96.3	81.3	88.5
	1970	96.0	100.0	101.8	126.6	167.3	212.8				
Granular base course	1950	...	...	...	...	...	...	117.5	135.7	101.0	81.2
	1960	65.8	63.9	65.6	60.0	76.5	103.3	121.7	86.2	85.1	88.1
	1970	98.7	100.0	103.7	126.1	167.8	201.2				
Paving	1950	...	...	...	...	...	...	98.9	97.9	83.9	81.6
	1960	78.8	85.5	77.9	80.5	87.4	96.9	109.3	100.6	93.8	96.3
	1970	104.4	100.0	107.9	135.6	191.3	214.8	...	...	...	...
Total contract work	1970	...	100.0	103.8	130.9	173.2	212.5	...	...	...	...
Total supplies	1970	...	100.0	108.3	121.5	192.2	196.9	...	...	...	...
Alberta											
Total	1970	...	100.0	99.5	128.6	184.7	209.7	...	...	...	...
Grading	1970	...	100.0	98.9	129.2	202.4	234.0	...	...	...	...
Granular base course	1970	...	100.0	99.2	136.6	178.2	217.0	...	...	...	...
Paving	1970	...	100.0	100.3	122.2	174.1	183.4	...	...	...	...
Total contract work	1970	...	100.0	98.6	128.5	184.5	210.7	...	...	...	...
Total supplies	1970	...	100.0	108.9	129.5	186.5	199.0	...	...	...	...
British Columbia											
Total	1950	...	...	...	...	...	...	102.4	95.4	80.3	82.1
	1960	81.8	71.9	68.5	69.7	76.3	91.9	93.3	85.9	91.1	103.0
	1970	96.7	100.0	95.7	101.6	170.2	183.2				
Grading	1950	...	...	...	...	...	...	102.7	93.2	76.2	79.0
	1960	76.1	64.4	68.3	71.2	72.2	92.7	91.8	80.1	90.7	103.7
	1970	96.4	100.0	95.2	102.3	171.1	175.2				
Granular base course	1950	...	...	...	...	...	...	107.1	98.8	82.4	89.4
	1960	91.0	89.1	70.0	71.0	90.5	95.7	99.6	96.3	94.6	106.4
	1970	96.8	100.0	96.1	99.2	179.4	197.8				
Paving	1950	...	...	...	...	...	...	94.1	98.2	92.0	82.3
	1960	88.8	73.6	67.2	61.8	69.7	82.8	88.7	91.8	87.0	95.4
	1970	97.6	100.0	96.4	102.9	158.2	183.7	...	...	...	...
Total contract work	1970	...	100.0	95.3	100.6	169.5	181.4	...	...	...	...
Total supplies	1970	...	100.0	103.7	122.8	185.5	220.7	...	...	...	...
Canada											
Total[2]	1950	...	...	...	...	...	...	87.1	80.9	73.0	73.2
	1960	72.1	65.0	67.6	72.2	76.2	83.0	89.4	86.0	84.8	88.7
	1970	92.7	100.0	105.1	118.3	158.7	177.5				
Grading	1950	...	...	...	...	...	...	85.5	74.8	69.8	68.7
	1960	68.4	60.4	65.7	72.6	75.7	81.1	88.6	84.8	84.1	87.7
	1970	71.4	100.0	107.3	120.1	162.2	181.7				
Contract work	1970	...	100.0	107.3	120.0	162.3	181.9	...	...	...	...
Supplies	1970	...	100.0	108.0	126.1	152.3	166.2	...	...	...	...
Granular base course	1950	...	...	...	...	...	...	88.6	84.9	72.7	74.8
	1960	71.8	68.2	66.0	68.9	76.5	85.0	91.5	87.7	84.5	90.1
	1970	93.6	100.0	102.5	118.4	154.9	173.0				
Paving	1950	...	...	...	...	...	...	92.7	92.7	83.5	82.3
	1960	83.7	72.5	76.0	77.0	79.2	83.7	88.7	88.0	87.1	88.3
	1970	94.7	100.0	104.2	117.0	156.6	174.7	...	...	...	...
Contract work	1970	...	100.0	104.3	116.9	145.9	164.8	...	...	...	...
Supplies	1970	...	100.0	103.8	117.2	190.1	205.6	...	...	...	...
Total contract work	1970	...	100.0	105.2	118.3	156.4	175.4	...	...	...	...
Total supplies	1970	...	100.0	104.1	117.9	187.2	202.6	...	...	...	...

[1]Within decade.
[2]The Canada index includes seven provinces from 1956 to 1964, when Quebec was added. Alberta was included from 1971. Prince Edward Island was excluded throughout.

Sources

21.1-21.9 Gross National Product Division, System of National Accounts (Current) Branch, Statistics Canada.
21.10-21.13 Industry Product Division, System of National Accounts (Current) Branch, Statistics Canada.
21.14 Input-Output Division, System of National Accounts (Structural) Branch, Statistics Canada.
21.15-21.28 Prices Division, General Statistics Branch, Statistics Canada.
21.29-21.34 Balance of Payments Division, System of National Accounts (Current) Branch, Statistics Canada.
21.35-21.36 Banking and Financial Analysis Department, Bank of Canada.
21.37 Prices Division, General Statistics Branch, Statistics Canada.
21.38 Financial Flows and Multinational Enterprises Division, System of National Accounts (Current) Branch, Statistics Canada.
21.39 Prices Division, General Statistics Branch, Statistics Canada.

Appendices

Government organizations and related agencies

Appendix 1

A summary organization chart of the federal government appears in Chapter 3.

Advisory Council on the Status of Women. The council received official status by Order in Council PC 1976-781 on April 1, 1976. As a federal advisory council it advises the government and at the same time informs the public on matters pertaining to the status of women. It also makes recommendations for changes in legislation and for other actions to improve the position of women.

The council consists of a chairman and two vice-chairmen who are full-time members and 27 part-time members, appointed from each province and territory by the Governor in Council for a three-year term.

The council is located in Ottawa and reports to Parliament through the minister "responsible for the status of women".

Agricultural Products Board. The Agricultural Products Board was established under authority of the Emergency Powers Act by Order in Council PC 3415 of July 31, 1951, to administer contracts with other countries to buy, or sell, agricultural products, and to carry out other commodity operations as considered necessary or desirable as determined by Canada's needs and requirements. The board was re-established under the Agricultural Products Board Act in 1952 and operates now under RSC 1970, c.A-5. Under the act the minister may require any staff of the Department of Agriculture to provide services for the board.

Agricultural Stabilization Board. Established in 1958 as a Crown corporation under the Agricultural Stabilization Act (RSC 1970, c.A-9), the board is empowered to stabilize prices of agricultural products both to assist the industry in realizing fair returns for labour and investment and to maintain a fair relationship between the prices received by farmers and the costs of goods and services that they buy. Programs under the act are administered by board staff with assistance from the Canada Department of Agriculture. The board reports to Parliament through the Minister of Agriculture.

Air Canada. Formerly Trans-Canada Air Lines, Air Canada was incorporated by an act of Parliament in 1937 (RSC 1970, c.A-11) to provide a publicly owned air transportation service, with powers to carry on its business throughout Canada and outside Canada. The corporation now maintains passenger, mail and commodity traffic services over nation-wide routes as well as services to the United States, Britain, Ireland, Belgium, France, Switzerland, the Federal Republic of Germany, Austria, Denmark, the USSR, Czechoslovakia, Bermuda, the Bahamas, Jamaica, Antigua, Barbados, the French Antilles and Trinidad. Air Canada is responsible to Parliament through the Minister of Transport.

Anti-dumping Tribunal. Under the Anti-dumping Act (RSC 1970, c.A-15, as amended by SC 1970-71, c.3), the Anti-dumping Tribunal is declared to be a court of record and makes formal inquiry into the impact of dumping on production in Canada. Within 90 days of a preliminary determination of dumping by the Deputy Minister of National Revenue for Customs and Excise, the tribunal must make an order or finding on the question of material injury, threat of material injury or retardation to production in Canada of like goods. Also, the tribunal may at any time after the date of an order or a finding made by it review, rescind, change, alter or vary the said order or finding or may rehear any matter before deciding it. In addition, the Governor in Council may request the tribunal to investigate and report on any matter relative to the importation of goods into Canada that may cause or threaten injury to the production of any goods in this country.

The tribunal consists of a chairman, four other members, a secretary, and research and support staff. Its offices are in Ottawa. The tribunal carries out its responsibilities by holding public and in camera hearings, personal interviews, in-house research, statistical and financial analysis, interviews with Canadian manufacturers and associations, and inspection of facilities. The tribunal reports to Parliament through the Minister of Finance.

Anti-Inflation Appeal Tribunal. The tribunal was established by the Anti-Inflation Act, SC 1974-75-76, c.75; amended by SC 1974-75-76, c.98 to hear appeals resulting from orders issued by the administrator under the Anti-Inflation Act. The act provides for the chairman of the Tax Review Board to be appointed chairman of the Anti-Inflation Appeal Tribunal and for members of the Tax Review Board to hold office as members of the Anti-Inflation Appeal Tribunal. The Governor in Council may appoint such numbers of members as he considers necessary to deal effectively with appeals taken to the tribunal. The principal office is at Ottawa and the tribunal sits at such times and places as are considered necessary by the chairman for the proper conduct of its business. The tribunal has all such powers, rights and privileges as are vested in a superior court of record. Its decisions or orders are subject to review and are to be set aside by the Federal Court of Appeal. The tribunal is under the jurisdiction of the Minister of Justice but is independent of the Department of Justice.

Anti-Inflation Board. An interim board was created by Order in Council 1975-2429, October 14, 1975. It was replaced December 15, 1975 by the Anti-Inflation Board which was established by the Anti-Inflation Act (SC 1974-75-76, c.75 amended by SC 1976, c.98). Under the act, the board administers the guidelines enacted to restrict price and wage increases. It is required to monitor changes in prices, profits, compensation and dividends; to consult and negotiate with the parties involved to bring such changes within the guidelines; and to inform the public about inflation and its causes. The principal office is in the National Capital Region and the board may meet at such times and places as the chairman deems advisable. The board consists of a chairman, vice-chairman and five regional members appointed by the Governor in Council. The board may also require assistance from persons having technical or specialized knowledge or from any federal department or agency. The board reports to Parliament through the Minister of Finance.

Army Benevolent Fund Board. The Army Benevolent Fund Board, established by the Army Benevolent Fund Act (SC 1947, c.49, as amended by SC 1974-75-76, c.3), administers the Army Benevolent Fund and other like funds, from special accounts in the Consolidated Revenue Fund. The board awards grants from the special account to veterans or their dependents for relief, if none is available from government sources, and for educational assistance, contingent on need and continued progress. The board has five members appointed by the Governor in Council, one of them nominated by the Royal Canadian Legion and one by the National Council of Veterans Associations in Canada. Head office is in Ottawa. The board reports to Parliament through the Minister of Veterans Affairs.

Atlantic Development Council. Created under the 1969 Government Organization Act (SC 1968-69, c.28), the Atlantic Development Council is composed of 11 members, including a chairman and vice-chairman, appointed by the Governor in Council to reflect the economic structure of the region comprised of New Brunswick, Nova Scotia, Prince Edward Island and Newfoundland. Its function is to advise the Minister of Regional Economic Expansion, in respect of the Atlantic region, on matters to which his duties, powers and functions extend, and particularly on plans, programs and proposals for fostering the economic expansion and social adjustment of the Atlantic region, and the feasibility and merits of particular programs and projects.

Atomic Energy Control Board. By act of Parliament (RSC 1970, c.A-19) proclaimed October 1946, the regulation and control of atomic energy in Canada was placed under the Atomic Energy Control Board. The board reports to Parliament through the Minister of Energy, Mines and Resources.

Atomic Energy of Canada Limited. This Crown company was incorporated in February 1952 under the Atomic Energy Control Act, 1946 (RSC 1970, c.A-19) to take over from the National Research Council on April 1, 1952 the operation of the Chalk River project. The main activities of the company include scientific research and engineering development in the atomic energy field, the development, design and marketing of nuclear power systems, and the production of radioactive isotopes and associated equipment, such as cobalt-60 beam therapy units for the treatment of cancer. AECL is responsible for the construction and operation of heavy water plants and research and development involving present and prospective heavy water production methods. The company reports to Parliament through the Minister of Energy, Mines and Resources.

Bank of Canada. Legislation of 1934 (RSC 1970, c.B-2) provided for the establishment of a central bank in Canada to regulate credit and currency, to control and protect the external value of the Canadian dollar and to stabilize the level of production, trade, prices and employment as far as may be possible within the scope of monetary action. The Bank of Canada acts as the fiscal agent of the Government of Canada, manages the public debt and has the sole right to issue notes for circulation in Canada. It is managed by a board of directors appointed by the government and composed of a governor, a deputy governor and 12 directors; the Deputy Minister of Finance is also a member of the board (ex officio). The bank reports to Parliament through the Minister of Finance.

Blue Water Bridge Authority. Created by the Blue Water Bridge Authority Act (SC 1964, c.6), this authority is responsible for the operation of the Canadian portion of the bridge spanning the St. Clair River from Point Edward, Ont. to Port Huron, Mich. Tolls set are subject to the approval of the Canadian Transport Commission. The authority is a non-profit organization and all toll moneys must be used for the operation and maintenance of the present bridge or for the building of a new one. It is not an agent of the Crown but members of the authority are appointed by the Governor in Council on the recommendation of the Minister of Transport with terms of office ranging from one to five years.

Board of Examiners for Dominion Land Surveyors. Established under the Canada Lands Survey Act (RSC 1970, c.L-5), the board examines candidates: for admission as articled pupils; for commissions as Dominion Land Surveyors; or for certificates as Dominion Topographical Surveyors. It is also responsible for the discipline of Dominion Land Surveyors. The board has three members appointed by the Governor in Council, one of whom, the chairman, is the Surveyor General of Canada Lands; it is part of the Department of Energy, Mines and Resources.

Bureau of Pensions Advocates. The bureau was established in 1971 by amendments to the Pension Act (SC 1970-71, c.31). Composed of a Chief Pensions Advocate appointed by the Governor in Council, and Pensions Advocates, officers and employees appointed under the Public Service Employment Act, it administers Part II of the Pension Act. Its function is to provide an independent professional legal aid service to applicants for awards under the Pension Act. The bureau's head office is in Ottawa; there are district offices in 18 major centres across Canada. It reports to Parliament through the Minister of Veterans Affairs.

Canada Council. The council was established by Order in Council dated April 15, 1957, under the terms of the Canada Council Act (RSC 1970, c.C-2) assented to March 28, 1957. It is composed of a chairman, a vice-chairman and 19 other members, a director and an associate director. The function of the council is to encourage the arts, humanities and social sciences in Canada, mainly through a broad program of fellowships and grants. Its principal sources of income are an annual grant from the government, which amounted to $54.7 million for the year ended March 31, 1976, ($40.9 million for the previous year) and an Endowment Fund, originally of $50 million, which has an annual yield of over $5 million. In the making, managing and disposing of investments under the act, the council has the advice of an investment committee of five, including the chairman and another member of the council. The proceedings of the council are reported each year to Parliament through the Secretary of State.

Canada Deposit Insurance Corporation. The corporation was established by legislation (RSC 1970, c.C-3), which received Royal Assent on February 17, 1967. It is empowered to insure Canadian currency deposits other than those belonging to the Government of Canada, up to $20,000 a person, in banks, federally incorporated trust and loan companies that accept deposits from the public, and in similar provincially incorporated institutions that are authorized by their provincial governments to apply for such insurance. The corporation is also empowered to act as a lender of last resort for member institutions. The corporation's board comprises a chairman, appointed by the Governor in Council, and four other directors who hold the positions of Governor of the Bank of Canada, Deputy Minister of Finance, Superintendent of Insurance and Inspector General of Banks. It reports to Parliament through the Minister of Finance.

Canada Development Corporation (CDC). CDC was established in 1971 by the Canada Development Corporation Act (SC 1970-71, c.49) to develop and maintain strong Canadian controlled and managed corporations in the private sector of the economy, to give Canadians greater opportunities to invest and participate in the economic development of Canada, and to operate profitably and in the best interests of all its shareholders. Administration of CDC is vested in a board of 21 directors and CDC is neither an agent of the Crown nor subject to the Financial Administration Act.

Authorized capital of the corporation consists of 200 million common shares without par value — 31.7 million of which have been issued, substantially all to the Government of Canada, for a consideration of $322 million — and $1,000 million in preferred shares — $245 million of which has been issued in two classes to private Canadian investors and institutions. $100 million of Class A preferred shares were placed privately in 1973 and the Class B in a public offering in 1975. The latter are convertible and voting, giving non-government shareholders 32.7% of the voting rights in CDC. The CDC Act provides that this proportion may increase up to 90%.

CDC concentrates on control-position equity investments in leading corporations in selected industries. Industries characterized by large, longer-range development projects, an upgrading of Canadian resources, a high technological base, and a good potential for building a Canadian presence in international markets are considered. Six selected thus far are: petrochemicals, mining, oil and gas, health care, pipelines, and venture capital.

Polysar Ltd. is CDC's wholly-owned operating company in petrochemicals. CDC and Polysar together own 60% of Petrosar Ltd. which is building the first world-scale crude oil topping and naphtha cracking unit in Canada at a cost of some $500 million. CDC's interest in the mining industry is represented by 30% ownership of Texasgulf Inc., one of Canada's largest mineral producers.

CDC Oil & Gas Limited, 100% owned, is CDC's operating company in oil and gas exploration and production. Through Connlab Holdings Limited, also 100% owned, CDC is developing a Canadian presence in the health care and pharmaceutical field. CDC's associated venture capital companies, Venturetek International Limited of Toronto, Innocan Investments Ltd. of Montreal, and Ventures West Capital Ltd. of Vancouver, together represent the largest pool of venture capital in Canada and have themselves invested in 26 small and medium-sized businesses.

As at December 31, 1976, CDC's consolidated assets amounted to $1,592.2 million and shareholders' equity was $713.8 million.

Canada Employment and Immigration Advisory Council. This council was established by the Employment and Immigration Reorganization Act — Part II, the Canada Employment and Immigration Advisory Council Act, proclaimed on August 15, 1977. The council replaces the Canada Manpower and Immigration Council and the Unemployment Insurance Advisory Committee. The act provided for a chairman and no fewer than 15 or more than 21 other members to be appointed by the Governor in Council, to advise the Minister of Employment and Immigration on all matters related to labour market resources, employment services, unemployment insurance and immigration.

Canada Employment and Immigration Commission. (See entries for the Department of Manpower and Immigration and the Unemployment Insurance Commission.) This commission was established by the Employment and Immigration Reorganization Act — Part I, the Employment and Immigration Department and Commission Act, in August 1977. The act merged the Department of Manpower and Immigration and the Unemployment Insurance Commission, establishing the Canada Employment and Immigration Commission and the supporting Department of Employment and Immigration.

Canada Labour Relations Board. Established under the authority of the Canada Labour Code Part V (RSC 1970, c.L-1), this board administers provisions of the code with respect to workers in industries under federal jurisdiction. It consists of a chairman, a vice-chairman, an additional vice-chairman where considered advisable by the Governor in Council and not less than four or more than eight other members.

Canada Manpower and Immigration Council. This council was replaced when the Employment and Immigration Reorganization Act was passed in August 1977. (See the entry for the Canada Employment and Immigration Advisory Council.)

Canadian Arsenals Limited. The principal function of this Crown corporation is to operate the government owned facilities for the production of certain defence materiel. It was established under the Companies Act by Letters Patent dated September 20, 1945, and is subject to the Government Companies Operation Act (RSC 1970, c.G-7) and certain provisions of the Financial Administration Act (RSC 1970, c.F-10). It reports to Parliament through the Minister of Supply and Services.

Canadian Broadcasting Corporation. The CBC is a Crown corporation established by an act of Parliament in 1936, replacing an earlier public broadcasting agency, the Canadian Radio Broadcasting Commission, created in 1932. The Broadcasting Act of 1968 (RSC 1970, c.B-11) describes the CBC as "established by Parliament for the purpose of providing the national broadcasting service".

The corporation has a president and 14 other directors appointed by the Governor in Council. The president is the chief executive officer. The executive vice-president is appointed by the corporation on the recommendation of the president and with the approval of the Governor in Council. He is responsible to the president for the management of broadcasting operations in accordance with policies prescribed by the corporation.

CBC operations are financed by public funds voted annually by Parliament, with supplementary revenue obtained from commercial advertising. The CBC's accounts are audited annually by the Auditor General of Canada and the corporation reports to Parliament through the Secretary of State of Canada.

Canadian Commercial Corporation. Established in 1946 by act of Parliament (RSC 1970, c.C-6), the Canadian Commercial Corporation is wholly owned by the Government of Canada. Initially it assumed the undertaking of the (then) Canadian Export Board covering procurement in Canada of goods and services on behalf of foreign governments and United Nations relief agencies. In 1947 responsibility for procurement of the requirements of the Department of National Defence was transferred from the Department of Reconstruction and Supply to the corporation which fulfilled these additional functions until the formation of the Department of Defence Production in 1951. In 1963 the staff of the corporation was integrated with that of the Department of Defence Production, now part of the Department of Supply and Services, which provides all the management and services required by the corporation.

The corporation continues to act primarily as the Canadian government contracting and procurement agency on behalf of foreign countries purchasing defence or other supplies and services from Canada on a government-to-government basis, with increasing emphasis on non-defence goods. It also can assist persons in Canada to obtain goods and commodities from outside Canada and to dispose of goods and commodities that are available for export from Canada. It reports to Parliament through the Minister of Supply and Services.

Canadian Consumer Council. The council was established in 1968 (RSC 1970, c.C-27) to advise the Minister of Consumer and Corporate Affairs on all facets of consumerism. It meets with the minister several times a year and consists of 23 members representing all segments of the population and all areas of Canada.

Canadian Dairy Commission. This commission, which reports to Parliament through the Minister of Agriculture, was established on December 2, 1966 (RSC 1970, c.C-7) to provide efficient producers of milk and cream with the opportunity of obtaining a fair return for their labour and investment and thus ensure that consumers of dairy products would have a continuous and adequate supply of dairy products of high quality. The commission consists of three members appointed by the Governor in Council and operates with the advice of a nine-member consultative committee appointed by the minister. Since 1970, the commission has chaired the Canadian Milk Supply Management Committee, comprised of provincial milk marketing agencies and provincial government agencies, which manages the Market Share Quota System under the terms of a federal-provincial milk marketing plan.

Canadian Film Development Corporation. This corporation, established by an act of Parliament in March 1967 (RSC 1970, c.C-8), fosters and promotes the development of a feature film industry in Canada through investment in productions, loans to producers, awards for outstanding accomplishments, and advice and assistance in distribution and administrative matters. It works in cooperation with other federal departments and agencies and with provincial departments and agencies having like interests and finances its operations from a film development advance account in the Consolidated Revenue Fund. The corporation consists of the Government Film Commissioner (ex officio) and six other members appointed by the Governor in Council for terms of five years. The corporation reports to Parliament through the Secretary of State.

Canadian Government Specifications Board (CGSB). Created in 1934 under the authority of the National Research Council Act (RSC 1970, c.N-14) as the Canadian "Government Purchasing Standards Committee", this interdepartmental agency's name was changed in 1948 to the Canadian Government Specifications Board (CGSB).

In 1965, responsibility for the CGSB's operation was transferred by Order in Council to the Department of Defence Production, now part of the Department of Supply and Services. Membership of the board was then revised to include the Secretary of the Treasury Board, the President of the National Research Council, and the deputy ministers of Consumer and Corporate Affairs, National Defence, Public Works, Supply and Services, Transport, and Industry, Trade and Commerce. The Deputy Minister of Supply and Services was designated chairman of the board.

The role of the CGSB is to provide standards for both public and private sectors for procurement, consumer requirements, legislation, technical practices, test procedures and to support international standardization in more than a hundred fields, many of which are of national interest. It has compiled more than 1,800 standards which are available in both official languages. The technical process of developing and revising standards is performed by some 300 committees and about 3,000 competent members representing the relevant interests including governments, producers, consumers, research and testing agencies, educational institutions, professional, technical and trade societies. The board works closely with the Standards Council of Canada and Metric Commission Canada in relation to national and international standardization and the metric conversion program. It is accredited by the council as a national standards writing organization.

Canadian Grain Commission. The Canada Grain Act (SC 1970-71, c.7) came into force on April 1, 1971, repealing the Canada Grain Act, 1930 (RSC 1952, c.25) and replacing the former Board of Grain Commissioners for Canada. The commission reports to Parliament through the Minister of Agriculture, as did the board, and the responsibilities are unchanged. The commission provides general supervision over the physical handling of grain in Canada by licensing elevators and elevator operators, by inspecting, grading and weighing grain received at and shipped from terminal elevators, and by other services associated with regulating the grain industry. It manages and operates the six Canadian government elevators in western Canada. The commission also administers the Grain Futures Act, which provides for grain futures trading.

The commission consists of a chief commissioner and two commissioners. Its objects are, in the interests of grain producers, to establish and maintain standards of quality for Canadian grain, to ensure a dependable commodity for domestic and export markets and to regulate grain handling in Canada. It has authority to conduct investigations and hold hearings on matters coming within its purview, and to undertake, sponsor and promote research in relation to grain and grain products. The commission is part of the Canada Department of Agriculture, but submits a separate report to the minister.

Canadian International Development Agency. The operation of Canada's international development programs are the responsibility of the Canadian International Development Agency. CIDA was originally established by Order in Council PC 1960-1476 and until 1968 was known as the External Aid Office. The agency is under the direction of a president and a governing body — the Canadian International Development Board — and reports to Parliament through the Secretary of State for External Affairs.

Canadian International Development Board. The board is the governing council responsible for directing the operations of the Canadian International Development Agency (CIDA). It is made up of the Under-Secretary of State for External Affairs, the deputy ministers of the Department of Finance and the Department of Industry, Trade and Commerce, the Governor of the Bank of Canada and the Secretary of the Treasury. It meets under the chairmanship of CIDA's president.

Canadian Livestock Feed Board. This board is a Crown corporation reporting to Parliament through the Minister of Agriculture. Established under the Livestock Feed Assistance Act in 1967, its objectives are to ensure: (a) the availability of feed grain in eastern Canada and British Columbia, (b) the availability of adequate storage space in eastern Canada, and (c) the reasonable stability and fair equalization of feed grain prices in eastern Canada and in British Columbia. The board administers the Feed Freight Equalization Program under which a portion of the costs of transportation of feed grains is paid. The act also stipulates that it is the duty of the board to make a continuing study of feed grain requirements and availability in these areas, as well as to study and make recommendations to the minister with respect to requirements for additional feed grain storage facilities in eastern Canada. It is also the duty of the board to advise the government on all matters pertaining to the stabilization and fair equalization of feed grain prices to livestock feeders and, to the greatest extent possible consistent with its objectives, to consult and cooperate with all departments, branches or other agencies of the Government of Canada or any province having duties, aims or objects related to those of the board.

In addition the board has been assigned responsibilities under the national feed grain policy which became effective on August 1, 1974. The board is called upon to examine selling practices east of Thunder Bay and to supervise the domestic market outside the designated region of the Canadian Wheat Board. The board designates the chairman of the committee supervising reserve stocks of feed grains presently held at Thunder Bay, Vancouver and various locations in eastern Canada. If the board finds bad pricing or supply practices, it will be permitted to intervene directly as buyer or seller of feed grain. This is supported by the Livestock Feed Assistance Act which stipulates that the board may buy, transport, store and sell feed grains in eastern Canada and British Columbia when authorized to do so by the Governor in Council.

The board is composed of four active members with headquarters in Montreal and a branch office in Vancouver. A seven-member advisory committee, appointed by the Governor in Council, and representing livestock feeders in eastern Canada and British Columbia, meets periodically with the board to review and discuss all aspects of feed grain supplies and prices, and policies related thereto. This committee may make recommendations to the minister and the board.

Canadian National Railways. The Canadian National Railway Company was incorporated to administer an undertaking made up mainly of railway and other service facilities and activities. It includes the assets of the former Grand Trunk Railway Company of Canada and its subsidiaries, and of the Canadian Northern System, as well as certain Crown-owned properties of which the management and operation have been entrusted to Canadian National.

The primary statutes governing its organization and operation are the Canadian National Railways Act (RSC 1970, c.C-10) and the Railway Act (RSC 1970, c.R-2). The direction and control of the company and its undertaking are vested in a board of directors; its principal officers are the chairman of the board and the president, the latter being the chief executive officer.

Canadian Patents and Development Limited (CPDL) is a Crown corporation, wholly subsidiary to the National Research Council of Canada (NRC). CPDL was originally established in 1947 to handle patentable material of NRC and other government-financed research. The passage of the Public Servants Inventions Act in 1954 made CPDL the prime patenting and licensing agency for public servant inventions which by that act, belong to the Canadian government.

CPDL may receive ideas and inventions from public servants in all federal departments and from the professional staff and employees of universities. The ideas and inventions are first assessed for patentability and commercial use. Patent applications may then be filed in various countries in respect of those which are considered commercially exploitable and patentable. Some which are not patentable may be licensed independently, or together with patents. That portion of the licence fees and royalties paid under licence agreements and retained by CPDL is used to defray CPDL commercial operating expenses.

CPDL has also entered into agreements with many universities, provincial research organizations, and other publicly financed institutions to assess, patent and license their industrial and intellectual property.

The corporation's board of directors is composed of members from industry, universities and the federal government. The head office is at 275 Slater Street, Ottawa. CPDL reports to Parliament through a designated minister.

Canadian Penitentiary Service. The penitentiary service operates under the Penitentiary Act (RSC 1970, c.P-6) and is under the jurisdiction of the Solicitor General of Canada. It is responsible for all federal penitentiaries and for the care and training of persons committed to those institutions. The Commissioner of Penitentiaries, under the direction of the Solicitor General, has control and management of the service and all matters connected therewith.

Canadian Pension Commission. This commission, established in 1933 by amendments to the Pension Act (RSC 1970, c.P-7), replaced the Board of Pension Commissioners, the first organization created to deal solely with war pensions for service in Canada's Armed Forces. The commission's main function is the administration of the Pension Act under which it adjudicates on all claims for pensions in respect of disability or death arising out of service in Canada's Armed Forces; and Parts I to X and Part XII of the Civilian War Pensions and Allowances Act, which provide for the payment of pensions in respect of death or disability arising out of civilian service directly related to the prosecution of World War II. It also adjudicates on claims for pension under various other measures, authorizes and pays monetary grants accompanying certain gallantry awards bestowed on members of the Armed Forces and administers various trust funds established by private individuals for the benefit of veterans and their dependents. The commission consists of eight to 14 commissioners and up to 10 ad hoc commissioners appointed by the Governor in Council. Its chairman has the rank of a deputy minister and it reports to Parliament through the Minister of Veterans Affairs.

Canadian Permanent Committee on Geographical Names. This committee deals with all questions of geographical nomenclature affecting Canada and undertakes research and investigation into the origin and usage of geographical names. Its membership includes representatives of federal mapping agencies and other federal offices concerned with nomenclature and a representative appointed by each province. The committee's functions were redefined in 1964 (Order in Council PC 1964-1519). The last reorganization recognized that the provinces had exclusive jurisdiction to make decisions on names within their own territory. The committee is administered by the Department of Energy, Mines and Resources.

Canadian Radio-television and Telecommunications Commission (CRTC). This commission, established under the provisions of the Broadcasting Act, 1967-68 (RSC 1970, c.B-11), regulates and supervises all aspects of the Canadian broadcasting system. The Canadian Radio-television and Telecommunications Commission Act, promulgated April 1, 1976, amended the Broadcasting Act to give the CRTC regulatory power over federally-regulated telecommunications carriers. The executive committee, after consultation with the part-time members in attendance at a commission meeting, may issue broadcasting licences or renewal licences for such terms, not exceeding five years and subject to such conditions related to the circumstances of the licensee, as the executive committee deems appropriate for the implementation of the broadcasting policy enunciated in Section 3 of the Broadcasting Act. Under the same circumstances, the executive committee may, on application by a licensee, amend any conditions of a broadcasting licence already issued. The committee also decides on applications submitted to the commission by telecommunications agencies, for instance, for rate increases. The commission usually holds public hearings in connection with issuing, suspending, etc., broadcasting licences, and concerning telecommunications matters.

The CRTC consists of nine full-time members and 10 part-time members chosen regionally and appointed by the Governor in Council. It reports to Parliament through the Minister of Communications.

Canadian Saltfish Corporation. The Canadian Saltfish Corporation was established under the Saltfish Act (SC 1969-70, c.32) and became operative on May 4, 1970. Its main purpose is to improve the earnings of fishermen and of other primary producers of salt-cured fish, through the production or purchase, processing and marketing of salt cod from participating provinces.

The corporation, with head office at St. John's, Nfld., consists of a board of directors composed of a chairman, whose office is in Ottawa, a president who is general manager, one director for each participating province and not more than five other directors, all of whom are appointed by the Governor in Council. It is assisted by an advisory committee of 15 members, also appointed by the Governor in Council, at least half of whom are fishermen or representatives of fishermen. The limit of the corporation's financial obligations is $15 million and the corporation is required to operate without grant appropriation from Parliament. The corporation reports to Parliament through the Minister of Fisheries and the Environment.

Canadian Transport Commission. The Canadian Transport Commission, a court of record created in 1967 by the National Transportation Act (RSC 1970, c.N-17), took over powers formerly vested in the Board of Transport Commissioners, the Air Transport Board and the Canadian Maritime Commission, giving it regulatory and judicial functions with respect to almost all aspects of railway, commercial air, merchant marine, and commodity pipeline services. The act also provides for the regulation of extra-provincial motor vehicle transport but applicable sections of the act were not in effect as at September 1976, except with respect to the Roadcruiser autobus service operated by the Canadian National Railways in

Newfoundland. On July 16, 1976, the CNR bus service was exempted by the Governor in Council from the provisions of the Motor Vehicle Transport Act (RSC 1970, c.M-14), and came under the jurisdiction of the Motor Vehicle Transport Committee of the Canadian Transport Commission, pursuant to Part III of the National Transportation Act. In all other cases, regulatory control over extra-provincial motor vehicle undertakings is exercised by provincial highway transport boards, acting as agents of the federal government, as provided for in the Motor Vehicle Transport Act. In addition, the commission is responsible for undertaking studies and research into the economic aspects of all modes of transport within, into or from Canada.

Five committees perform the commission's regulatory duties under the act: the Railway Transport Committee, the Air Transport Committee, the Water Transport Committee, the Motor Vehicle Transport Committee, and the Commodity Pipeline Transport Committee.

The commission consists of not more than 17 members, of whom one is president and two are vice-presidents, appointed by the Governor in Council for a maximum of 10 years; it reports to Parliament through the Minister of Transport.

Canadian Wheat Board. The board was incorporated in 1935 under the Canadian Wheat Board Act (RSC 1970, c.C-12) to market, in an orderly manner, in the interprovincial and export trade, grain grown in Canada. Its powers include authority to buy, take delivery of, store, transfer, sell, ship or otherwise dispose of grain. Except as directed by the Governor in Council, the board was not originally authorized to buy grain other than wheat but, since August 1, 1949, it may also buy oats and barley if authorized to do so by regulation approved by the Governor in Council. Only grain produced in the designated area, which includes Manitoba, Saskatchewan, Alberta and parts of British Columbia is purchased by the board, which controls the delivery of grain into elevators and railway cars in that area as well as the interprovincial movement for export of wheat, oats and barley generally. The board reports to Parliament through a designated minister, at present the Minister of Transport.

Cape Breton Development Corporation. This corporation was created by an act of Parliament, assented to on July 7, 1967 (RSC 1970, c.C-13) and came into existence by proclamation on October 1, 1967, as a proprietary Crown corporation. The corporation was established to rationalize the coal industry of Cape Breton Island and to broaden the base of the area's economy by assisting the financing and development of industry to provide employment outside the coal mines.

The Cape Breton Development Corporation acquired the former interests of the major coal producer in the Sydney coalfield and is now operating three mines, two of which are new, together with a modern coal preparation plant and other ancillaries. It is active in development of the tourist industry as well as primary products and various secondary industries.

The act provides for a board of directors, comprising a chairman, a president and five other directors. Head office is located in Sydney, NS. The corporation reports to Parliament through the Minister of Regional Economic Expansion. Its operations are financed by the Government of Canada.

Central Mortgage and Housing Corporation. This Crown agency was incorporated by an act of Parliament (RSC 1952, c.46) in December 1945 to administer the National Housing Act. Under the National Housing 1954 Act (RSC 1970, c.C-16), the corporation insures mortgage loans made by approved lenders for new and existing housing and makes direct loans in resource communities and rural areas; guarantees home improvement loans made by banks; undertakes subsidized rental housing projects and land assembly developments under federal-provincial arrangements; offers loans and subsidies for public housing projects; makes loans for land assembly projects to be used for general residential development; makes loans to individuals or organizations for low-rental housing projects; makes loans to provinces and municipalities with provincial concurrence, for sewage and water treatment projects designed to eliminate water and soil pollution; makes contributions and loans to provinces and municipalities for urban renewal operations; conducts housing research; encourages urban planning; and owns and manages rental housing units including those built for war workers and veterans. The corporation arranges for and supervises construction of housing projects on behalf of other government departments and agencies. It is responsible to Parliament through the Minister of State for Urban Affairs. The national office of the corporation is located in Ottawa with branch offices in all major urban areas.

Columbia River Treaty Permanent Engineering Board. The Permanent Engineering Board, consisting of two Canadians and two Americans, was established under Article XV of the 1964 Columbia River Treaty between Canada and the United States. The board assembles records and inspects and reports at least annually on matters within the scope of the treaty. It reports to Parliament through the Minister of Energy, Mines and Resources.

Commissioner of Official Languages. Appointed by Parliament pursuant to the Official Languages Act (RSC 1970, c.O-2), the commissioner holds office for a term of seven years, renewable until age 65. He is responsible to Parliament for ensuring recognition of the equal status of French and English as Canada's official languages and for ensuring compliance with the spirit and intent of the act in all the institutions of the Parliament and Government of Canada. The commissioner is empowered to receive and investigate complaints from the public, and, on his own initiative, to conduct investigations into possible violations of the act. The results of investigations must be communicated to the complainants and the institutions concerned and may, at the commissioner's discretion, be the subject of a special report to Parliament. The commissioner reports annually to Parliament on the conduct of his office and may make recommendations for changes in the act as he deems necessary or desirable.

Copyright Appeal Board. The board was established to provide an agency to which people using music protected by copyright could direct appeals against the fees proposed by performing rights societies for the use of the music. The Copyright Act (RSC 1970, c.C-30) empowers the board to deal only with the amount of the fees that the societies propose to collect for an ensuing calendar year. It has no authority to draft the terms and conditions of the tariffs. Hearings before the board are conducted in a quasi-judicial manner. After considering an appeal the board makes such alterations to the proposed statements of fees as it thinks appropriate and transmits the statements thus altered, revised or unchanged to the Minister of Consumer and Corporate Affairs. The decision of the board is final and binding. The Copyright Appeal Board consists of three members appointed by the Governor in Council, one of whom, as chairman, must hold or have held high judicial office.

Correctional Investigator. Appointed by Order in Council PC 1973-1431 on June 5, 1973 the Correctional Investigator has the powers of a commissioner under Part II of the Inquiries Act. This officer investigates problems of inmates on subjects for which the Solicitor General is responsible and reports to him. The office consists of the Correctional Investigator and three complaint officers. It is located in Ottawa and is independent of the Department of the Solicitor General.

Court Martial Appeal Court. This court was established as a superior court of record pursuant to Section 201 of the National Defence Act (RSC 1970, c.N-4). Accused persons found guilty by a court martial have the right to direct an appeal to the Court Martial Appeal Court in respect of the legality of any or all of the findings, or the legality of the whole or any part of the sentence. The Appeal Court is composed of not fewer than four judges of the Federal Court of Canada designated by the Governor in Council and such additional judges of a superior court of criminal jurisdiction as are appointed by the Governor in Council. One judge has been designated by the Governor in Council as the president. Appeals are heard by a minimum of three judges. The Court Martial Appeal Court may sit and hear appeals at any place under direction of the president. An appellant whose appeal has been wholly or partially dismissed by the Court Martial Appeal Court may, under certain circumstances, appeal to the Supreme Court of Canada; where the Court Martial Appeal Court has wholly or partially allowed an appeal, the Minister of National Defence may similarly enter an appeal to the Supreme Court of Canada.

Crown Assets Disposal Corporation. This agency corporation was established in 1944 as the War Assets Corporation under the Surplus Crown Assets Act (RSC 1970, c.S-20) and is subject to the Financial Administration Act (RSC 1970, c.F-10). Its name was changed to Crown Assets Disposal Corporation in 1949. The corporation is responsible for the sale of federal government surplus movable assets located in Canada and at Canadian government establishments throughout the world. It also acts as agent on behalf of foreign governments in selling their surplus property located in Canada and has an agreement with a European agency for marketing Canadian military surplus assets located abroad. While the corporation's normal method of sale is to invite written offers, on occasion it sells by public auction and through retail outlets. The act provides for a board of directors, comprising a chairman and a minimum of five other directors. Its head office is located in Ottawa. Regional offices are maintained in Halifax, Montreal, Toronto, Ottawa, Edmonton and Vancouver. The corporation is responsible to Parliament through the Minister of Supply and Services.

Defence Construction (1951) Limited. This is a Crown corporation, defined in Part VII of the Financial Administration Act and listed in Schedule "C" in the act, which contracts for major construction and maintenance projects required by the Department of National Defence. It was incorporated May 10, 1951 under the authority of the Defence Production Act. In April 1965 control and supervision of the corporation was transferred from the Minister of Defence Production to the Minister of National Defence.

The company's function is to obtain tenders, make recommendations regarding awards, to award and administer major construction and maintenance contracts which include supervision of construction work and the certification of contractors' progress claims for completed work.

The company also provides technical and administrative assistance to other government departments and agencies when so required. Head office of DCL is in Ottawa and branch offices are located in Halifax, Montreal, Toronto, Winnipeg, Vancouver and Lahr, Federal Republic of Germany.

1046   Canada Year Book 1976-77

Defence Research Board. The Defence Research Board, established in 1947 by an amendment to the National Defence Act (RSC 1970, c.N-4), advises the Minister of National Defence on scientific matters relating to defence and evaluates the contribution of science and technology to the achievement of defence objectives. The functions of the board were redefined on April 1, 1974 when its research and administrative activities and staff were absorbed within the framework of the Department of National Defence.

The board consists of a full-time chairman, a vice-chairman and 12 members appointed by the Governor in Council for three-year terms. The Deputy Minister of National Defence, the president of the National Research Council and three senior officers of the Canadian Forces are ex officio members. The board has its headquarters in Ottawa.

Department of Agriculture. This department was established in 1867 (SC 1868, c.53) and now operates under authority of RSC 1970, c.A-10. It undertakes work on all phases of agriculture. Research and experimentation are carried out by the Research, Health of Animals and Economics branches, and the Grain Research Laboratory; and the maintenance of standards and protection of products, by the Production and Marketing and Health of Animals branches. The Food Systems Branch plans and coordinates market-oriented food systems. The Canada Grain Act, as it pertains to the inspection, weighing, storage and transportation of grain, is administered by the Canadian Grain Commission, which is a part of the department. Programs concerning farm income security and price stability are provided under the Crop Insurance Act, the Canadian Dairy Commission Act, the Agricultural Stabilization Act and the Agricultural Products Board Act. The Agricultural Stabilization Board, the Agricultural Products Board, the Farm Credit Corporation, the Canadian Dairy Commission, the Canadian Livestock Feed Board and the National Farm Products Marketing Council report to Parliament through the Minister of Agriculture.

Department of Communications. The department was established under Part II of the 1969 Government Organization Act and operates under authority of the Department of Communications Act (RSC 1970, c.C-24). The Minister of Communications is responsible for fostering the orderly operation and development of communications for Canada. This includes recommending national policies and programs regarding communications services for Canada, promoting the efficiency and growth of Canadian communications systems and assisting them to adjust to changing conditions and encouraging the development and introduction of new communication facilities and resources. Its responsibilities also include managing the radio frequency spectrum to permit the orderly use of radio communications, protecting Canadian interests in international telecommunications matters, and coordinating telecommunications services for departments and agencies of the Government of Canada.

Teleglobe Canada, the Canadian Radio-television and Telecommunications Commission and Telesat Canada report to Parliament through the Minister of Communications.

Department of Consumer and Corporate Affairs. This department was established in 1967 (RSC 1970, c.C-27) replacing the Department of the Registrar General of Canada. The duties, powers and functions of the minister extend to and include all matters over which the Parliament of Canada has jurisdiction, not by law assigned to any other department, branch or agency of the Government of Canada, relating to: consumer affairs; corporations and corporate securities; combines, mergers, monopolies and restraint of trade; bankruptcies and insolvencies; and patents, copyrights, trade marks and industrial design.

The functions of the department are divided into five main areas. The Bureau of Consumer Affairs coordinates government activities in the field of consumer affairs; the Bureau of Corporate Affairs administers the government's corporate activities; the Bureau of Intellectual Property administers laws and regulations pertaining to patents, trade marks, industrial designs and copyrights; and the Field Operations Service supervises the department's operations across Canada, staffing regional and district offices in five Canadian cities from coast to coast and district offices in 30 others. Competition policy is regulated by the Bureau of Competition Policy. In addition, as Registrar General of Canada, the Minister of Consumer and Corporate Affairs is the custodian of the Great Seal of Canada, the Privy Seal of the Governor General, the Seal of the Administrator of Canada and the Seal of the Registrar General of Canada. The Restrictive Trade Practices Commission (Combines Investigation Act) is domiciled in the department and reports directly to the minister.

Department of Energy, Mines and Resources. The Department of Energy, Mines and Resources was created in 1966 by the Government Organization Act (RSC 1970, c.E-6). The department, in addition to its administrative services, the Office of Energy Conservation and the Office of Energy Research and Development, is organized into three sectors. The Energy Development Sector has responsibilities relating to the development of plans and policies for all forms of energy, the development of programs, legislation and agreements to implement those policies, the direction of studies relating to energy sources and requirements, and the coordination of policy advice. A major responsibility of the sector is research on and the formulation of a national energy policy. The Mineral Development Sector gathers economic data on non-renewable resources for use by government, industry and the public. It also develops policy proposals for the government and the Canadian mineral industry to help determine policies and decisions that will ensure an adequate, dependable and timely flow of minerals to meet the country's needs at reasonable cost. The Science and Technology Sector includes the Geological Survey of Canada, the Canada Centre for Mineral and Energy Technology (CANMET) the Surveys and Mapping Branch, the Earth Physics Branch, the Canada Centre for Remote Sensing and the Polar Continental Shelf Project, all of which are engaged in research and the provision of information, and the Explosives Division, which controls, under the provisions of the Explosives Act, the production and handling of explosives.

Atomic Energy of Canada Limited, Eldorado Nuclear Limited, Eldorado Aviation Limited, the Atomic Energy Control Board, the National Energy Board, Uranium Canada Limited and the Interprovincial Boundary Commissions report to Parliament through the Minister of Energy, Mines and Resources. Operationally the International Boundary Commission reports through the Minister of Energy, Mines and Resources; in dealing with its counterpart in the United States it is responsible to the Secretary of State for External Affairs.

Department of External Affairs. The main function of the Department of External Affairs, established in 1909 (RSC 1970, c.E-20), is the protection and advancement of Canadian interests abroad. The responsible minister is the Secretary of State for External Affairs. The senior permanent officer (deputy minister) of the department, the Under-Secretary of State for External Affairs, is assisted by the Deputy Under-Secretary and by four Assistant Under-Secretaries and is advised by officers in charge of bureaus, offices and divisions. Directors-general or directors of these units are each responsible for a part of the department's work and are assisted by foreign service officers, specialists in various occupational groups and an administrative staff. Officers serving abroad are formally designated as High Commissioner, Ambassador, Minister, Counsellor, First Secretary, Second Secretary, Third Secretary and Attaché at diplomatic posts and Consul General, Consul and Vice-Consul at consular posts. Canada maintains approximately 180 diplomatic, consular and other missions, 60 of which are non-resident.

In Ottawa the department's work is conducted by regional, functional and administrative bureaus and a number of operational units. The four regional bureaus administer 12 geographical divisions, each responsible for the countries of a region. The European Affairs Bureau includes three divisions — Western Europe, Eastern Europe and Northwestern Europe including Britain; the Bureau of Asian and Pacific Affairs includes the East Asia, Pacific and South Asia Divisions; the Bureau of African and Middle Eastern Affairs, the African Affairs I (Anglophone), African Affairs II (Francophone) and Middle Eastern Divisions; and the Bureau of Western Hemisphere Affairs, the Caribbean (Commonwealth), Latin American and United States of America Divisions. The seven functional bureaus include 20 divisions. The Bureau of Economic and Scientific Affairs comprises the Aid and Development, Commercial Policy, Scientific Relations and Environmental Problems, and Transport, Communications and Energy divisions. The Bureau of Legal Affairs includes the Legal Advisory and Legal Operations divisions; the Bureau of Consular Affairs, the Consular Operations, and Consular Policy and Research divisions; the Bureau of Defence and Arms Control Affairs, the Arms Control and Disarmament, and Defence Relations divisions; the Bureau of Public Affairs, the Academic Relations Service, Cultural Affairs, Historical, Information and World Exhibitions Program divisions; the Bureau of Coordination, the Commonwealth Institutions, Federal-Provincial Coordination and Francophone Institutions divisions; and the Bureau of United Nations Affairs, the United Nations Economic and Social Affairs and United Nations Political and Institutional Affairs divisions. The four administrative bureaus are responsible respectively for Personnel, Finance and Administration, Communications and General Services, and Security and Intelligence Liaison.

In addition, there are an Inspection Service, a Policy Analysis Group, a Protocol Division, an Operations Centre, a Central Staff, an Interdepartmental Committee on External Relations, a Coordinator of Information Systems Development, a Special Adviser on Foreign Service appointments and related policies, a Chief Air Negotiator, an Adviser on Bilingualism and a Special Adviser on Media Communications.

The International Joint Commission reports to the Secretary of State for External Affairs of Canada as well as to the Secretary of State of the United States.

Department of Finance. Created by an act of Parliament in 1869, this department now operates under the Financial Administration Act (RSC 1970, c.F-10 as amended). It is primarily responsible for advising the government on the economic and financial affairs of Canada. The department's work is carried out in five branches. The Tax Policy and Federal-Provincial Relations Branch helps to form tax policy and maintain the tax structure. It deals with personal income and commodity taxes, taxes on corporations and Canada's international tax relations. Fiscal relations with the provinces are the responsibility of a Federal-Provincial Relations Division. The branch also administers grants to municipalities in lieu of new taxes on government property and advises on the government's social development and manpower policies. The Economic Programs and Government Finance Branch is concerned with resource development, various government programs of broad economic development and the financing of Crown corporations and government agencies. The International Trade and Finance Branch is concerned with trade policy and development, the Canadian aid program and customs' tariffs. The Fiscal Policy and Economics Analysis Branch monitors the economy, analyzes the potential impact of various alternative courses for government fiscal policy and participates on Canada's behalf in a number of international organizations, including the International Monetary Fund. The Long Range Economic Planning Branch is responsible for coordinating, planning and developing medium- and long-term economic measures and policies. The Capital Markets Division is responsible for monitoring developments in capital markets and advising on the government's debt operations. The Inspector General of Banks is an office of the department. In addition, the following agencies report to Parliament through the Minister of Finance: the Anti-dumping Tribunal, the Bank of Canada, the Canada Deposit Insurance Corporation, the Industrial Development Bank, the Department of Insurance and the Tariff Board. The Minister of Finance acts as spokesman in Parliament for the Auditor General.

Department of Fisheries and the Environment. Established by an act of Parliament in June 1971 (SC 1970-71, c.42), the Department of the Environment, now known as the Department of Fisheries and the Environment, carries the main federal responsibility for leading the attack on pollution and ensuring the proper management and development of Canada's renewable resources. The department is organized into two principal components, each headed by a senior assistant deputy minister.

The Fisheries and Marine Service has under its jurisdiction Fisheries Management and Ocean and Aquatic Sciences. Fisheries Management includes resource management and conservation, enforcement of fisheries regulations, industrial development and fish inspection, marketing and promotion, biological and technical research on fish and other aquatic flora and fauna, fishing vessel insurance and vessel construction subsidy administration, management of small craft harbours across Canada, promotion and management of recreational fisheries, and administration of international and federal-provincial fisheries agreements.

Ocean and Aquatic Sciences is responsible for the consolidated physical and chemical oceanographic research, biological research related to the marine environment, environmental assessments of activities affecting freshwater and marine life, marine geophysical mapping, operating of a fleet of research and survey vessels, hydrographic surveying, tide and water levels measurement and production of navigational, bathymetric and other charts of Canadian coastal and inland waters.

Environmental Services comprises the Atmospheric Environment Service, the Environmental Protection Service and the Environmental Management Service.

The Atmospheric Environment Service acquires and processes data and provides climatological and meteorological information including weather forecasts. It carries out research on air quality and environmental matters.

The Environmental Protection Service develops and enforces regulations, standards, protocol and other instruments to implement federal environment legislation. It provides information for other federal departments administering legislation concerned with environmental regulations. The service develops national effluent and emission standards in consultation with the provinces and industry and is the public's point of contact with the department on problems relating to the protection of the environment.

The Environmental Management Service coordinates activities related to terrestrial renewable resources, their use, and the impact of their use on the environment. It is composed of five staff directorates — Forestry, Inland Waters, Wildlife, Lands, and Policy and Planning Development — all located in the National Capital Region. Line management operations are decentralized in five regional directorates covering all of Canada.

The Planning and Finance Service provides policy and planning direction, and coordinates the government's relationships in environmental and resources matters with the provinces and with other countries.

Advice to the minister is provided by a Canadian Environmental Advisory Council and separate Fisheries and Forestry Advisory Councils which include representatives from industry, the universities and the scientific community.

Department of Indian Affairs and Northern Development. This department was established in June 1966, superseding the Department of Northern Affairs and National Resources; it now operates under authority of RSC 1970, c.I-7. In 1968 the department was reorganized, creating, in addition to departmental support services and an Engineering and Architectural Branch, three distinct program areas. The Indian and Eskimo Affairs Program is responsible for the development and implementation of programs for Canada's 285,000 registered Indians, including education, economic development, local government, social assistance and lands and membership administration. The Northern Affairs Program covers the management of all natural resources north of the 60th parallel except game, the protection of the northern environment, government activities in economic development and support of the territorial governments in providing social and other local services. Parks Canada is responsible for National Parks, National Historic Parks and Sites, and joint Federal-Provincial agreements for recreation and conservation. In 1972 the Corporate Policy Group was formed to advise the deputy minister on broad policy questions, in particular those involving coordination among the programs and cooperation with other departments and agencies.

The Commissioner of the Northwest Territories and the Commissioner of the Yukon Territory report to Parliament through the Minister of Indian Affairs and Northern Development. The minister is also responsible to Parliament for the Northern Canada Power Commission, the National Battlefields Commission and the Historic Sites and Monuments Board of Canada.

Department of Industry, Trade and Commerce. In 1969, the Departments of Industry and of Trade and Commerce were merged to form the Department of Industry, Trade and Commerce (ITC), which operates under authority of RSC 1970, c.I-11. ITC promotes the establishment, growth and efficiency of manufacturing, processing and tourist industries in Canada and fosters the development of Canadian trade. The department plans and carries out programs to assist manufacturing and processing industries in adapting to new technology and changing market conditions, in developing unrealized potential and in rationalizing productive facilities and corporate structures. It promotes product and process development, increased productivity, greater use of research, modern equipment, improved industrial design, the application of advanced technology and modern management techniques, and the development and application of sound industrial standards in Canada and in world trade.

The department's functions include: improving access of Canadian goods and services into external markets through trade negotiations; contributing to the improvement of world trading conditions; providing support services for industrial and trade development, including information, import analysis and traffic services; analyzing the implications for Canadian industry, trade and commerce and for tourism of government policies related thereto in order to contribute to the formulation and review of those policies; and compiling and updating detailed information on trends and developments in Canada and abroad related to the manufacturing and processing and tourist industries.

The department is organized into seven major functional groups: Canadian Government Office of Tourism, Industry Development, Industrial Policies, Export Development, International Trade Relations, Planning, Research and Evaluation, and Administration. In addition, the department operates 11 regional offices across Canada and the Trade Commissioner Service which has 89 trade offices in 65 countries.

The minister also reports to Parliament on behalf of Statistics Canada and the Export Development Corporation. Boards and other organizations reporting to the minister are the Machinery and Equipment Advisory Board, the National Design Council, the Standards Council of Canada, the Textile and Clothing Board, Metric Commission Canada, the Foreign Investment Review Agency and the Minister's Advisory Council.

Department of Insurance. The Minister of Finance is responsible for the Department of Insurance which originated in 1875 as a branch of the Department of Finance but was constituted a separate department in 1910. It is authorized and governed by the Department of Insurance Act (RSC 1970, c.I-17). Under the Superintendent of Insurance, who is the deputy head, the department administers the statutes of Canada applicable to federally incorporated insurance, trust, loan and investment companies; provincially incorporated insurance companies registered with the department; British and foreign insurance companies operating in Canada; small loans companies and money-lenders; cooperative credit societies registered under the Cooperative Credit Associations Act; pension plans organized and administered for the benefit of persons employed in connection with certain federal works, undertakings and businesses; and life insurance issued to certain members of the public service prior to May 1954.

Under the relevant provincial statutes, the department examines trust and loan companies incorporated in Nova Scotia, trust companies incorporated in New Brunswick and insurance and trust companies incorporated in Manitoba. It reports to Parliament through the Minister of Finance.

Department of Justice. This department, established by SC 1868, c.39, now operates under authority of the Department of Justice Act (RSC 1970, c.J-2). The Minister of Justice is the official legal adviser of the Governor General and the Queen's Privy Council for Canada. It is his duty to see that the administration of public affairs is in accordance with law, to superintend all matters connected with the administration of justice in Canada that are not within the jurisdiction of the provincial governments, to advise upon the legislation and proceedings of the provincial legislatures, and generally to advise the Crown on all matters of law referred to him by the Crown. The Minister of Justice is, ex officio, Her Majesty's Attorney General of Canada. In this capacity it is his duty to advise the heads of the departments of the Government of Canada on all matters of law connected with such departments, to settle and approve all instruments issued under the Great Seal of Canada, and to regulate and conduct all litigation for or against the Crown in the right of Canada. The Minister of Justice reports to Parliament for the Tax Review Board and the Law Reform Commission of Canada.

Department of Labour. The Department of Labour was established in 1900 by an act of Parliament (SC 1900, c.24) and now operates under the authority of the Department of Labour Act (RSC 1970, c.L-2). The department administers, under the Minister of Labour, legislation dealing with: fair employment practices;

hours of work, minimum wages, annual vacations, holidays with pay, equal wages, group and individual terminations of employment, severance pay and the regulation of fair wages and hours of labour in contracts made with the Government of Canada for construction, remodelling, repair or demolition of any work; government employee compensation, merchant seamen compensation, and employment safety; and transitional assistance benefits for auto workers and adjustment assistance benefits for textile workers and for footwear and tanning workers. It promotes joint consultation with industries through labour management committees and operates a women's bureau. The department publishes the *Labour Gazette* and other publications as well as general information on labour management, employment, manpower and related subjects.

The Merchant Seamen Compensation Board reports to the Minister of Labour. The department is the official liaison agency between the Canadian government and the International Labour Organization. The Canada Labour Relations Board reports to Parliament through the Minister of Labour.

Department of Manpower and Immigration. The Department of Manpower and Immigration, created under the provisions of the Government Organization Act 1966, operated under RSC 1970, c.M-1, with responsibility for the development and utilization of manpower resources in Canada, employment services and immigration. On May 26, 1976, the Minister of Manpower and Immigration announced plans to integrate the Department of Manpower and Immigration with the Unemployment Insurance Commission.

When the Employment and Immigration Reorganization Act was proclaimed in August 1977 the Department of Manpower and Immigration and the Unemployment Insurance Commission ceased to exist. The act established the Department of Employment and Immigration, the Canada Employment and Immigration Commission and the Canada Employment and Immigration Advisory Council, and amended the Unemployment Insurance Act, 1971 and certain other statutes. The Canada Employment and Immigration Advisory Council combines the functions of the former UIC Advisory Committee and the Canada Manpower and Immigration Council. With the merger, the new commission became one of the largest government operations, numbering about 27,000 people. The title of the responsible minister was changed to Minister of Employment and Immigration.

Department of National Defence. The Department of National Defence and the Canadian Forces operate under the authority of the National Defence Act (RSC 1970, c.N-4). The Minister of National Defence is responsible for the control and management of the Canadian Forces, the Defence Research Board and all matters relating to national defence. He is also responsible for the construction and maintenance of all defence establishments and facilities required for the defence of Canada.

The deputy minister is the senior public servant in the department and the principal civilian adviser to the minister on all departmental affairs. He is responsible for ensuring that all policy direction from the government is reflected in the administration of the department and in military plans and operations. The Chief of the Defence Staff is the senior military adviser to the minister and is charged with the control and administration of the Canadian Forces. He is responsible for the effective conduct of military operations and the readiness of the Canadian Forces to meet the commitments assigned to them by the government.

A Defence Council, consisting of the Minister of National Defence as chairman, the Deputy Minister of National Defence, the Chief of Defence Staff, the Chairman of the Defence Research Board, the Vice-Chief of the Defence Staff, the Assistant Deputy Minister (Policy), and the Deputy Chief of Defence Staff, meets as required to consider and advise on major policy matters. The Crown corporation Defence Construction (1951) Limited reports to Parliament through the Minister of National Defence.

Department of National Health and Welfare. This department was established in October 1944 under the Department of National Health and Welfare Act (RSC 1970, c.N-9). An Administration Branch serves both the health and welfare branches. The Deputy Minister of National Health and Welfare administers 10 branches: Health Programs, Health Protection, Medical Services, Long Range Health Planning, Administration, Social Services Programs, Income Security Programs, Policy Research and Long Range Planning (Welfare), and Welfare Information Systems; Fitness and Amateur Sport is a branch of the department reporting to Parliament through the Minister of State for Fitness and Amateur Sport.

Departmental programs on health include hospital insurance and diagnostic services, medical care insurance, health resources, food and drug supervision, narcotics control, national health grants, federal emergency health services, environmental health, adverse drug reaction reporting, operation of a central clearing house for poison control centres, health, medical and hospital services to Indians and Inuit across Canada and all residents of the Yukon Territory and Northwest Territories, government employee health services and leprosy control as well as assistance and consultation services to the provinces on request.

Welfare programs include the Canada Pension Plan, old age security and guaranteed income supplements, family allowances, the Canada Assistance Plan and emergency welfare services. There are also developmental programs, including national welfare grants, family planning grants and information and grants to groups of retired persons under the New Horizons Program.

The National Council of Welfare reports directly to the minister who also reports to Parliament for the Medical Research Council.

Department of National Revenue. From Confederation until May 1918, customs and inland revenue acts were administered by separate departments; after that date they were amalgamated under one minister as the Department of Customs and Internal Revenue. In 1921 the name was changed to the Department of Customs and Excise. In April 1924 collection of income taxes was placed under the Minister of Customs and Excise and, under the Department of National Revenue Act, 1927, the department became known as the Department of National Revenue. It operates now under the Income Tax Act, SC 1970-71-72, c.63, as amended.

The Customs and Excise component of the department is responsible for the assessment and collection of customs and excise duties as well as of sales and excise taxes. The Taxation component is responsible for the assessment and collection of income taxes, Part I of the Canada Pension Plan, and collection of premiums and administration of the coverage provisions of the Unemployment Insurance Act through its 28 district taxation offices, head office and Taxation Data Centres in Ottawa and Winnipeg.

Department of Public Works was constituted in 1867 and operates under the legislative authority of the Public Works Act (RSC 1970, c.P-38). The department is the primary agent of the federal government in the development and management of real property, providing general purpose office accommodation for some 90 federal departments and agencies, together with a full range of architectural, engineering, construction management and realty services in support of special purpose facilities. The department operates on a decentralized basis with regional headquarters offices at Halifax, Montreal, Ottawa (National Capital Region), Toronto, Edmonton and Vancouver. There are subsidiary offices in all but the National Capital Region. The mainline functions of the department consist of Design and Construction, Realty Planning and Development and Realty Services plus Departmental Planning and Coordination (including Policy Research) and Technological Research and Development; in addition, the Dominion Fire Commissioner operates under the authority of the Minister of Public Works, with responsibility for protection of life of occupants of government property and for the minimization of property loss as a result of fire.

Department of Regional Economic Expansion. This department was established in 1969 (RSC 1970, c.R-4). It is responsible for matters relating to economic expansion and social adjustment in areas requiring special measures to improve opportunities for productive employment and access to those opportunities. It has the authority to prepare and implement, in cooperation with provincial governments and other federal agencies, development plans and programs designed to meet the special needs of areas where the growth of employment and income lags behind that of other parts of Canada.

The department has six major divisions, each under the control of an assistant deputy minister: Planning and Coordination, Administration, and the Atlantic, Quebec, Ontario and Western regional divisions. The Regional Development Incentives Act (RDIA) passed in 1969, provides development incentives to industry, in the form of cash grants, to encourage new productive employment in designated regions where such employment has been scarce. The department is also responsible for programs under the Agricultural and Rural Development Act (ARDA); the Fund for Rural Economic Development (FRED); the Prairie Farm Rehabilitation Act (PFRA) which is concerned with land-use adjustment, water development projects and the establishment of tree shelterbelts; and the Special Areas Program.

Following a comprehensive policy review in 1973, the department developed the General Development Agreement (GDA) to implement its programs. Considered essential to the success of DREE's approach to regional development, 10-year GDA's were signed with all provinces except Prince Edward Island (covered under FRED) in 1974. These agreements provide the all-important framework for encouraging coordinated federal and provincial action aimed at realizing each region's potential for socio-economic development. The GDA's are buttressed by specific subsidiary agreements that identify joint actions to be initiated. Programs are administered from regional offices at Moncton, Montreal, Toronto and Saskatoon.

The Minister of Regional Economic Expansion reports to Parliament for the Cape Breton Development Corporation. He is advised by the Atlantic Development Council on programs and policies for fostering economic development and social adjustment in the Atlantic region, and by the Canadian Council on Rural Development on programming and policy.

Department of the Secretary of State. The duties, powers and functions of the Secretary of State of Canada (RSC 1970, c.S-15) extend to and include all matters over which the Parliament of Canada has jurisdiction not by law assigned to any other department, branch or agency of the Government of Canada, relating to: citizenship; elections; State ceremonial, the conduct of State correspondence and the custody of State records and documents; the encouragement of the literary, visual and performing arts, learning and cultural activities; and libraries, archives, historical resources, museums, galleries, theatres, films and broadcasting.

The responsibilities of the Department of the Secretary of State include those pertaining to the administration of the following branches: Cultural Affairs including: Education Support, Research and Liaison, Language Programs, State Protocol and Special Events, Movable Cultural Property Export Control, Grants, Film Festivals, Translation Bureau; Citizenship Programs including: Citizenship

Registration, Multiculturalism, Native Citizens, Women, Citizenship Participation, Official Language Minority Groups and Human Rights.

The Secretary of State reports to Parliament for the Canadian Film Development Corporation, the National Arts Centre Corporation, the National Film Board, the National Library, the Public Archives, the National Museums of Canada, the Canada Council, the Canadian Broadcasting Corporation and the Public Service Commission and acts as spokesman for the Office of the Representation Commissioner.

Department of the Solicitor General. Before 1936, the Office of the Solicitor General was either a Cabinet post or a ministerial post outside the Cabinet. From 1936 to 1945 the position did not exist, the duties of the office being wholly absorbed by the Attorney General of Canada. The Solicitor General Act, 1945 re-established the Solicitor General as a Cabinet officer and provided that "the Solicitor General shall assist the Minister of Justice in the Counsel work of the Department of Justice, and shall be charged with such other duties as are at any time assigned to him by the Governor-in-Council". This legislation was repealed in 1966 when a new Department of the Solicitor General was created (RSC 1970, c.S-12); the Solicitor General of Canada became the Cabinet Minister with primary responsibility in the fields of correction and law enforcement. He is responsible for the Royal Canadian Mounted Police and the Canadian Penitentiary Service and also reports to Parliament for the National Parole Board, which is an independent agency.

Department of Supply and Services. This department was established on April 1, 1969 (RSC 1970, c.S-18) to furnish certain services previously provided by other departments, in line with the recommendations of the Royal Commission on Government Organization (Glassco Commission) which had stressed the need for the federal government to foster efficiency and effect economies wherever possible. The Minister of Supply and Services is also the Receiver General for Canada and exercises all the duties, powers and functions assigned to that office by law.

The department is organized into two major administrations, each headed by a deputy minister directly responsible to the minister. The Supply Administration administers the Supply Program, the objective to acquire and provide, at minimum cost consonant with the attainment of national goals, goods and services required by federal government departments and agencies. It also maintains federal government equipment and provides printing facilities. Since the 1973-74 fiscal year, the Supply Administration has been on a cost recovery basis with respect to the costs of services rendered to its customers. The Supply Administration has 18 regional or district supply offices across Canada and overseas supply office in London, England and Koblenz, the Federal Republic of Germany. At various locations it provides purchasing and warehousing services and other services such as field contract administration, equipment maintenance, security, emergency supply planning, assets management and printing. The Supply Administration is organized into Commercial Supply Service, Science and Engineering Procurement Service and Corporate Management Service.

The Services Administration, acting for the Receiver General, provides payment or cheque-issuing services on behalf of all federal departments, maintains the fiscal accounts of Canada and prepares the public accounts. It offers departments and agencies a broad range of management and advisory services in management consulting, auditing and computer services fields. It also provides administrative services for all departments in connection with pay, pensions and other employee benefit plans, together with financial management reports and statistical information. Service functions are carried out through regional and district offices throughout Canada and abroad.

The Minister of Supply and Services reports to Parliament for the Canadian Commercial Corporation, Canadian Arsenals Limited, Crown Assets Disposal Corporation and the Royal Canadian Mint. The minister also has the responsibilities of the Custodian of Enemy Property under the Trading with the Enemy (Transitional Powers) Act, which consists of receiving, managing, releasing and disposing of properties seized from enemy interests during wartime.

Department of Transport. The Department of Transport is a corporate structure of operating administrations and Crown corporations, having varying degrees of autonomy, together with separate agencies for development and economic regulation. A departmental headquarters staff supports the minister and deputy minister in the functions of planning, policy formulation and assessment of program achievements.

The Canadian Marine Transportation Administration coordinates the activities of the Canadian Coast Guard, National Harbours Board and the St. Lawrence Seaway Authority. Its operations include management of the St. Lawrence Seaway through the St. Lawrence Seaway Authority and direct supervision of 13 major harbours and other facilities through the National Harbours Board; 300 public harbours and 11 others are administered by the Canadian Coast Guard and commissions under the supervision of the department. It is also responsible through the Canadian Coast Guard for the provision and maintenance of aids to navigation including Vessel Traffic Management Systems, marine search and rescue, ship safety inspection services, pilotage services and the management and operation of the Coast Guard fleet.

The Canadian Air Transportation Administration controls and operates Canada's airways and 145 federal airports and provides technical safety supervision of all aeronautical activities in Canadian air space. These activities are conducted through the branches of Civil Aeronautics and Construction Services, and the support branches of Corporate Planning, Finance and Personnel. The Canadian Air Transportation Administration also provides telecommunications, electronics and flight services to other components of the ministry and to other departments and agencies.

The Canadian Surface Transportation Administration has planning, programming and coordinating responsibilities relating to federal participation in the development and, where appropriate, operation, of surface modes of transport. These include railways, highways, private and industrial motor vehicles, motor carriers, e.g. interprovincial trucking, water transportation assistance, ferry services, and urban transportation. The administration maintains an interest in and conducts research on the emerging technology of surface transportation and its potential applications in Canada.

The Arctic Transportation Agency is responsible for developing and administering policy related to department-supported transportation facilities and services in the Canadian North to further the government's national objectives there. Intermodal relationships between air, surface and marine transportation systems are a particular concern, as well as the compatibility of these systems with economic and technological growth in the North and with the needs of the residents. In this connection there is a special relationship between the agency and the Department of Indian Affairs and Northern Development.

The Transportation Development Agency is responsible for initiating, promoting and coordinating transportation research and development activities, working closely with government agencies, industry and the academic community to provide a national focus for changing technology and development opportunities in the field of transportation.

The department also includes Air Canada, Canadian National Railways, and Northern Transportation Company Limited. These three Crown corporations are autonomous, maintaining close consultation with the minister to be consistent with the government's general policies in transportation. The Minister of Transport also reports to Parliament for the Canadian Transport Commission, the National Harbours Board and the St. Lawrence Seaway Authority.

Department of Veterans Affairs. This department, established in 1944 (RSC 1970, c.V-1), is concerned exclusively with the well-being of veterans and with the dependents of veterans and of those who died during active service or as a result of disability attributable to war service. The department is empowered to provide treatment services (hospital, medical, dental and prosthetic), counselling services, education assistance, life insurance, and land settlement and home construction assistance.

The department has treatment institutions and facilities in six major urban centres and three veterans homes across Canada and it maintains administrative offices in the large cities and in London, England.

The Canadian Pension Commission, the War Veterans Allowance Board, the Bureau of Pensions Advocates, the Pension Review Board and the Army Benevolent Fund Board report to Parliament through the Minister of Veterans Affairs.

Director of Soldier Settlement and Director of the Veterans' Land Act. The Director of Soldier Settlement (SC 1919, c.71) is also the Director of the Veterans' Land Act (RSC 1970, c.V-4), and in each capacity is legally a corporation sole. For administrative purposes, however, the programs carried on under both acts constitute integral parts of the services provided by the Department of Veterans Affairs.

Economic Council of Canada. This corporation, established under legislation passed on August 2, 1963 (RSC 1970, c.E-1), consists of a full-time chairman and two full-time directors appointed for a term not to exceed seven years, and not more than 25 additional members to serve part-time and without remuneration. The council is to be as representative as possible of the private sector, labour, agriculture, primary industry, secondary industry, commerce and the general public. Its functions are to study and recommend measures that will achieve the highest possible levels of employment and efficient production so that Canada may achieve a high and consistent rate of economic growth and that all Canadians may share in rising living standards. The council reports to Parliament through the Prime Minister and publishes various reports and studies.

Eldorado Aviation Limited. This company is a wholly-owned subsidiary of Eldorado Nuclear Limited and was incorporated April 23, 1953 to carry air traffic, both passenger and freight, for Eldorado Nuclear Limited. It reports to Parliament through the Minister of Energy, Mines and Resources.

Eldorado Nuclear Limited. Set up in 1944 (RSC 1952, c.53) under the name of Eldorado Mining and Refining (1944) Limited (the date was omitted in June 1952 and the name changed in 1968), the Crown company's business is the mining and refining of uranium and the production of nuclear fuels in Canada. The company also acts as a custodian for Her Majesty of concentrates purchased under stockpiling contracts. It reports to Parliament through the Minister of Energy, Mines and Resources.

Export Development Corporation. EDC operates under authority of the Export Development Act (RSC 1970, c.E-18, as amended). It is a commercially self-sustaining federal Crown corporation established to facilitate and develop Canada's export trade. EDC reports to Parliament through the Minister of Industry, Trade and Commerce, while its affairs are administered by a 12-member board of directors. To reflect the nature of a publicly owned institution involved with the Canadian business and banking community, the board consists of senior representatives of government and the Canadian financial and private business sectors. The services of EDC are designed to assist Canadian exporters to meet international credit competition. The principal services are: export credits insurance, to insure Canadian exporters of goods and services against non-payment by foreign buyers due to credit or political events over which neither buyer nor seller has any control; long-term export loans to foreign buyers in respect of the purchase of capital goods or major services from Canada when extended terms are necessary to meet international credit competition; and foreign investment guarantees, to guarantee Canadian investments abroad against non-commercial risks such as war or revolution, expropriation or confiscation, or the inability to repatriate capital or earnings. EDC may also guarantee financial institutions against loss when they are involved in an export transaction by financing either the Canadian supplier or the foreign buyer.

Farm Credit Corporation. This corporation which was established on October 5, 1959 (RSC 1970, c.F-2) is a Crown corporation responsible to Parliament through the Minister of Agriculture. Under the Farm Credit Act it makes long-term mortgage loans to assist farmers in developing viable farm businesses. It also administers the Farm Syndicates Credit Act and acts as an agent of the Canada Department of Agriculture in administering the Land Transfer Plan of the Small Farm Development Program.

Federal Business Development Bank. The bank was established by an act of Parliament in 1974 (SC 1974-75-76, c.14) as a federal Crown corporation to succeed the Industrial Development Bank. Under the act which came into force in October 1975, FBDB assists in the establishment and development of business enterprises in Canada by providing financial and management services, and by supplementing such services available from other sources. The bank gives particular attention to the needs of small enterprises.

The board of directors consists of the president, four persons from the public service of Canada, and 10 persons from outside the public service of Canada. The bank's authorized capital is $200 million, but it may raise additional funds by the issue and sale of debt obligations, provided that the total of the bank's direct and contingent liabilities shall not exceed 10 times its capital.

Federal-Provincial Relations Office. For administrative purposes, the Federal-Provincial Relations Office is regarded as a department of government under the Prime Minister. The office came into being on January 15, 1975 under legislation passed by Parliament in December 1974. For some years prior to the creation of the new office, its functions had been the responsibility of a division of the Privy Council Office. The office is headed by the Secretary to Cabinet for Federal-Provincial Relations.

In general, the work of the office consists of assisting the Prime Minister in his overall responsibility for federal-provincial relations; assisting the Cabinet in examining federal-provincial issues of current and long-term concern, including coordination and support activities for the Cabinet Committee on Federal-Provincial Relations; assisting ministers, departments, and agencies in the conduct of their relations with provincial governments; undertaking special studies as required; monitoring provincial views on federal policies and programs, and the evolution of provincial policies as they affect federal policies; and coordinating federal participation in Conferences of First Ministers.

To carry out its responsibilities the office is divided into a Secretariat, a Policy and Program Review Section, and a Studies and Research Group.

Fisheries Prices Support Board. Under the Fisheries Prices Support Act (RSC 1970, c.F-23) the board is responsible for investigating and, where appropriate, recommending action under the act to support prices of fishery products where declines have occurred. The board, subject to approval of the Governor in Council, is empowered to purchase fishery products at prescribed prices or to make deficiency payments to producers of fishery products equal to the difference between a prescribed price and the average price at which such products were sold. The board functions under the direction of the Minister of Fisheries and the Environment.

Fisheries Research Board of Canada. The board is a research body operating under an act of Parliament (RSC 1970, c.F-24) to advise the Minister of Fisheries and the Environment on national fisheries and marine research and development policies, plans and programs. The majority of the board's 18 members are senior scientists from universities and provincial agencies; the other members are senior executives from Canada's fisheries and marine industries.

Foreign Claims Commission. By Order in Council PC 1970-2077 of December 8, 1970 the Canadian government established the Foreign Claims Commission to inquire into property claims made by Canadian citizens and the Government of Canada against foreign countries which may, from time to time, be referred to the commission by the government. The reference is made after the government has negotiated a financial agreement with the foreign country. The commissioners submit reports and recommendations regarding each claim to the Secretary of State for External Affairs and the Minister of Finance, stating whether, in the opinion of the commissioners, each claimant is eligible to receive a payment under regulations promulgated from time to time by Order in Council. Up to December 31, 1975 claims against Hungary, Romania, Poland and Czechoslovakia had been referred to the commission.

Foreign Investment Review Agency. The agency was established on December 12, 1973 by the Foreign Investment Review Act (SC 1973-74, c.46). It assesses whether there is or will be significant benefit to Canada in proposals by non-Canadians regarding acquisition of control of Canadian business enterprises or the establishment of new businesses in Canada. The agency is responsible to the Minister of Industry, Trade and Commerce.

Freshwater Fish Marketing Corporation. This corporation was established under the Freshwater Fish Marketing Act of 1969 (RSC 1970, c.F-13) and given the function of marketing and trading in fish, fish products and fish by-products in and out of Canada with the objectives of ensuring more orderly marketing for the benefit of the whole fishery and achieving higher and more stable prices for the catch. The corporation received a grant for initial operating and establishment expenses but conducts its operations on a self-sustaining basis without parliamentary appropriations; it is financed by bank loans with government guarantee of repayment, or by direct loans. The corporation consists of a board of directors composed of a chairman, a president, one director for each participating province and four other directors appointed by the Governor in Council for a term not exceeding five years. The corporation reports to Parliament through the Minister of Fisheries and the Environment.

Grains Group. In 1970 the minister responsible for the Canadian Wheat Board (the Minister of Transport at present) organized the Special Advisory Group on Grains (Grains Group) to coordinate, review and recommend federal policies for grain production, transportation and handling, and marketing. The minister responsible for the Canadian Wheat Board serves as the chairman of the Grains Group. A Group Coordinator and three advisers for the areas of production, transportation and handling, and marketing are drawn from the federal departments of Agriculture; Industry, Trade and Commerce; and Transport. The offices of the Grains Group are in Ottawa.

Heritage Canada. Established under Part II of the Canada Corporations Act (RSC 1970, c.C-32), Heritage Canada is a national trust independent of government. It is concerned with the conservation of buildings, sites and natural and scenic areas of importance to the country's heritage. Its work is financed by memberships, contributions and the interest on an endowment fund to which the federal government granted $12 million. Heritage Canada seeks to enlist the support of the general public, foundations and corporations; membership is open to anyone.

Historic Sites and Monuments Board of Canada. This board was established in 1919 and now operates under authority of RSC 1970, c.H-6. The Historic Sites and Monuments Act provides for 15 members — two representatives each from Ontario and Quebec and one from each of the eight other provinces — appointed by the Governor in Council, together with the Dominion Archivist, one representative from the National Museums of Canada and one from the Department of Indian Affairs and Northern Development, as ex officio members. The members are historians of distinction, archaeologists or restoration architects. It is their function to advise the Minister of Indian Affairs and Northern Development on matters of national historic and architectural importance with particular reference to commemoration or preservation.

Immigration Appeal Board. The Immigration Appeal Board was established in 1967 by the Immigration Appeal Board Act (RSC 1970, c.I-3) as a court of record with broad discretionary powers to permit the temporary or permanent admission of individuals, notwithstanding contrary provisions of the Immigration Act. Changes were effected by the Immigration Act, 1976 in August 1977. The acts provide for the operation of the board and in particular for the legal and administrative processes involved in appeals by individuals against deportation, detention and the refusal of admission of sponsored relatives ordered under the provisions of the Immigration Act or Regulations. A decision of the board is appealable to the Federal Court of Canada and to the Supreme Court of Canada on leave.

Indian Claims Commission. This commission, established by Order in Council PC 1969-2405, is responsible for studying Indian grievances and claims in consultation with Indian representatives and reporting on means for settlement. The one commissioner reports to the Governor in Council through the Prime Minister.

International Boundary Commission. The commission functions by virtue of the treaty of 1925 between Canada and the United States and the International Boundary Commission Act (RSC 1970, c.I-19). The commissioners, one for Canada and one for the United States, are empowered to inspect the boundary, to repair, relocate and rebuild monuments, to keep the boundary vistas open, to regulate all "work" within 10 ft (3.04 metres) of the boundary including structures of any kind or earthwork, to maintain at all times an effective boundary line and to determine the location of any point of the boundary line which may become necessary to settle any question that may arise between the two governments. Each country pays the salaries of its commissioner and his assistants and the costs of maintaining the boundary are shared equally. The Canadian section of the commission comes under the Department of Energy, Mines and Resources for administrative purposes but the Canadian commissioner reports functionally to the Secretary of State for External Affairs. The commissioners meet at least once annually, alternately in Ottawa and Washington.

International Development Research Centre. Established as a public corporation by act of Parliament (RSC 1970, c.21, 1st Supp.), the IDRC is an international organization supported financially by Canada. Its objectives are to initiate, encourage, support and conduct research into the problems of developing countries and into methods of applying and adapting scientific and technical knowledge to their socio-economic advancement. One of the centre's chief purposes is to assist these countries to develop their own research skills and facilities.

The board of governors consists of a chairman, a president and not more than 19 other members, nine of whom must be Canadian citizens. The IDRC reports to Parliament through the Secretary of State for External Affairs.

International Fisheries Commissions. The Minister of Fisheries and the Environment reports to Parliament for the Canadian sections of the several international fisheries commissions of which Canada is a member.

International Joint Commission. This commission was established under a Britain–United States treaty signed January 11, 1909 and ratified by Canada in 1911 (RSC 1970, c.I-20). The commission, composed of six members (three appointed by the President of the United States and three by the Government of Canada), is governed by five specific Articles of the Boundary Waters Treaty of 1909. The commission's approval is required for any use, obstruction or diversion of boundary waters affecting the natural level or flow of boundary waters in the other country; and for any works which, in waters flowing from boundary waters or below the boundary in rivers flowing across the boundary, raise the natural level of waters on the other side of the boundary.

Problems arising along the common frontier are also referred to the commission by either country for examination and report, such report to contain appropriate conclusions and recommendations. Provided both countries consent, questions or matters of difference between the two countries may be referred to the commission for decision.

The commission was given responsibilities under the Canada–United States Great Lakes Water Quality Agreement of April 15, 1972 to assist in the implementation of the agreement by coordinating the various programs referred to therein and monitoring their effectiveness. The commission established a Great Lakes Regional Office at Windsor, Ont., staffed by American and Canadian public servants; operating costs are shared equally by the two governments.

The commission reports to the Secretary of State for External Affairs of Canada and to the Secretary of State of the United States.

Interprovincial and Territorial Boundary Commissions. The Manitoba–Saskatchewan Interprovincial Boundary Commission and the Alberta–British Columbia Boundary Commission, each consisting of a commissioner from the respective provinces and the Surveyor General of Canada, are at present the only commissions concerned with boundaries between provinces. The latter has been established as a result of the enactment in 1974 of federal and provincial Alberta–British Columbia Boundary Acts to deal with resurveys of the sinuous boundary, the settlement of problems or disputes, and the establishment, restoration and maintenance of survey monuments. However, there are also boundary commissions responsible for the borders between the following provinces and territories: Manitoba and the Northwest Territories; Saskatchewan and the Northwest Territories; Alberta and the Northwest Territories; and British Columbia, the Yukon Territory and the Northwest Territories. All report to Parliament through the Minister of Energy, Mines and Resources.

Law Reform Commission of Canada. The Law Reform Commission of Canada was established (RSC 1970, c.23, 1st Supp.) as a permanent body to study and keep the laws of Canada under continuing and systematic review and in this way to complement the legislative and judicial processes. The work of the commission is carried out with a view to making recommendations for the improvement, modernization and reform of federal laws including, without limiting the generality of the foregoing: the removal of anachronisms and anomalies in the law; the reflection in and by the law of the distinctive concepts and institutions of the common law and civil law legal systems in Canada, and the reconciliation of differences and discrepancies in the expression and application of the law arising out of differences in those concepts and institutions; the elimination of obsolete laws; and the development of new approaches to and new concepts of the law in keeping with and responsive to the changing needs of modern Canadian society and of individual members of that society. The Law Reform Commission reports to Parliament through the Minister of Justice.

Library of Parliament. The Library of Parliament was established by an act in relation to the Library of Parliament (SC c.21) now the Library of Parliament Act (RSC 1970 c.L-7). This library had been formed initially by the amalgamation of the legislative libraries of Upper and Lower Canada following their unification as the Province of Canada in 1841. The Library of Parliament is designated as a department within the meaning and purpose of the Financial Administration Act, the Parliamentary Librarian holding the rank of deputy minister. The Parliamentary and the Associate Parliamentary Librarians are appointed by the Governor in Council. The Parliamentary Librarian under the Speaker of the Senate and the Speaker of the House of Commons, assisted by a joint committee appointed by the two Houses, is responsible for the control and management of the library including the Confederation Branch Library, the Parliamentary Reading Room and the Confederation Building Reading Room. Persons entitled to borrow books from the Library of Parliament are the Governor General, members of the Privy Council, members of the Senate and the House of Commons, officers of the two Houses, judges of the Supreme Court of Canada and the Federal Court of Canada, and members of the Parliamentary Press Gallery. The library serves the Senate and the House of Commons in both reference and research capacities, and is responsible for all books, paintings, maps, and other library effects in the joint possession of the Senate and the House of Commons. The library indexes Senate Committee Minutes of Proceedings and Reports, provides an extensive clipping service to Parliament and is also the public's information centre for parliamentary information. Its collection is accessible to other libraries through interlibrary loan.

Loto Canada. Established June 29, 1976 by Appropriation Act No. 4, 1976 (SC 1974-75-76, c.103) Loto Canada, Inc. is a Crown corporation which began operation in September 1976 on the termination of the Olympic Lottery. It manages and conducts a lottery, primarily to assist until the end of 1979 in financing the deficits of the 1976 Olympics at Montreal and the 1978 Commonwealth Games at Edmonton. A small portion of the net revenue is divided among the provinces (12.5%) and the federal government (5%). The corporation consists of a board of directors of up to seven members representing all regions of Canada. Its head office is at Ottawa. The corporation reports to Parliament through the Minister of State for Fitness and Amateur Sport.

Machinery and Equipment Advisory Board. The Machinery and Equipment Advisory Board, established in 1968, is responsible for considering applications for remission of duty on machinery and equipment classifiable under Tariff Items 42700-1 and/or 41100-1 and for advising the Minister of Industry, Trade and Commerce as to the eligibility of such machinery for remissions according to the provisions of these two tariff items. The board is composed of a chairman and the deputy ministers of Industry, Trade and Commerce, Finance and National Revenue. It is assisted by the branches of the Department of Industry, Trade and Commerce concerned with individual industries, including machinery manufacturing. The objective of the Machinery Program, which is administered by the board, is to increase efficiency throughout Canadian industry by enabling machinery users to acquire advanced equipment at the lowest possible cost while at the same time affording tariff protection on machinery available from production in Canada.

Medical Research Council. Established in 1969 and operating under authority of RSC 1970, c.M-9, the council is a departmental Crown corporation of the federal government. It is composed of a president, a vice-president, and 20 members. The primary aim of the council is the support and development of research in the health sciences in Canadian universities and affiliated institutions. It reports to Parliament through the Minister of National Health and Welfare.

Merchant Seamen Compensation Board. The board is established by authority of the Merchant Seamen Compensation Act (RSC 1970, c.M-11, as amended) and reports to the Minister of Labour. The three members are appointed by the Governor in Council. The board meets, as required, to adjudicate claims for compensation made by injured seamen employed on ships registered in Canada when they are not entitled to workmen's compensation under any provincial Workmen's Compensation Act or the Government Employees Compensation Act.

Metric Commission Canada. The commission was established by Order in Council PC 1971-1146, June 1971. It consists of a full-time chairman and up to 20 part-time commissioners, all of whom are appointed by the Governor in Council for a term of three years. An executive director acts for the commission in directing the full-time staff.

The commission advises the Minister of Industry, Trade and Commerce on plans for conversion to the metric system and assists all sectors to prepare conversion plans and disseminate information. It includes over 100 sector committees covering all areas of the Canadian economy. The staff and 11 steering committees play a coordinating role for these sector committees, with the major impetus for conversion coming from the committee members who represent industry, labour, consumer, trade, standards and service associations, governments and other concerned bodies.

Each sector committee develops a conversion plan for the sector involved: after liaison with other related sectors, the committee recommends the sector plan to a steering committee for concurrence, then the plan is reviewed and approved by the commission. Both individual sector plans and overall national guidelines are following a framework known as the Four-Phase Program of Guideline Dates for Metric Conversion (investigation, planning, scheduling and implementation) to ensure, as far as possible, that programs are phased in and coordinated so as to obtain the benefits of metric conversion with minimal costs.

The ongoing task of the steering committees and their sector committees is to monitor the progress of conversion and suggest any necessary modifications to plans in order to meet changing conditions.

Public information activities include the distribution of periodicals, pamphlets and brochures, the maintenance of an extensive film and colour transparency library, the use of a speakers' bureau to provide talks to interested organizations, exhibits for trade fairs and shows, and the production and distribution of documentary films and TV clips in both official languages. Through a mailing address for the general public (Box 4000, Ottawa, Ont.) requests are handled for information on metric conversion in Canada.

Ministry of State for Science and Technology. This ministry was established by Order in Council PC 1971-1695 on August 11, 1971, with the primary purpose of formulating and developing policies in relation to the activities of the Government of Canada that affect the development and application of science and technology. It is organized into three operational branches: Government Branch, Industry Branch and University Branch. The Minister of State for Science and Technology is also designated as the Minister for the Science Council Act, the Cabinet member to whom the Science Council of Canada reports.

Ministry of State for Urban Affairs. The ministry was created June 30, 1971 in accordance with the Government Organization Act 1970 (SC 1971, c.42). The ministry's objective is to develop the most appropriate means by which the federal government may beneficially influence the evolution of urbanization in Canada, through the integration of urban policy and objectives with other federal policies, objectives, and programs. The ministry fosters cooperative relationships in urban affairs with the provinces and, through them, their municipalities, and with private organizations and the public. Under the direction of the secretary and three assistant secretaries, the ministry is divided into three branches: Urban Analysis, responsible for initiating research on urbanization and developing federal urban policies and objectives in cooperation with other federal agencies; Intergovernmental Relations, responsible for liaison with other levels of government and the public; and Priorities and Operations, responsible for international affairs, communications, and the internal coordination and administration of ministry activities.

National Advisory Council on Fitness and Amateur Sport. The council was established in 1961 by the Fitness and Amateur Sport Act (RSC 1970, c.F-25) to advise the Minister of National Health and Welfare on all matters relating to fitness and amateur sport in Canada. The council is an autonomous organization, composed of 30 members that are appointed by the Governor in Council and who represent every Canadian province and territory. Its three committees — Fitness, Recreation and Sport — meet periodically through the year to discuss and examine matters related to their areas of concern. At least twice a year, a General Council meeting is held at which recommendations to the minister are formulated. The administrative arm for fitness and amateur sports is the Fitness and Amateur Sport Branch of the Department of National Health and Welfare. The branch, through its numerous programs and operations, is involved in improving the participation of all Canadians in physical recreation and amateur sport as well as supporting Canadian athletes in their pursuit of excellence.

National Arts Centre Corporation. The act establishing the corporation (RSC 1970, c.N-2) received assent July 15, 1966. The corporation consists of a board of trustees composed of a chairman, a vice-chairman, the mayors of Ottawa and Hull, the Director of the Canada Council, the President of the Canadian Broadcasting Corporation, the Government Film Commissioner and nine other members appointed by the Governor in Council for terms not exceeding three years, except for the first appointees whose terms range from two to four years. The objects of the corporation are to operate and maintain the National Arts Centre, to develop the performing arts in the National Capital Region and to assist the Canada Council in the development of the performing arts elsewhere in Canada. The corporation reports to Parliament through the Secretary of State.

National Battlefields Commission. This commission was established by an act of Parliament in 1908 (SC 1908, cc.57-58, as amended) to preserve the Historic Battlefields at Quebec City. Composed of nine members, seven appointed by the federal government and one each by Ontario and Quebec, the commission is supported by the federal government through annual appropriations and is responsible to Parliament through the Minister of Indian Affairs and Northern Development.

National Capital Commission. This commission, successor to the Federal District Commission, is a Crown agency created by the National Capital Act (RSC 1970, c.N-3), proclaimed February 6, 1959. Headed by a chairman, it is made up of 20 members, representing the 10 provinces and the National Capital Region.

The commission is responsible for the acquisition, development and maintenance of public land in the National Capital Region; it cooperates with municipalities by providing planning aid or financial assistance in municipal projects of benefit to the region; and it advises the Department of Public Works on the siting and appearance of all federal government buildings in the 1,800-sq mile (4662 km²) National Capital Region. The commission reports to Parliament through the Minister of State for Urban Affairs.

National Council of Welfare. The council is an advisory body of 21 private citizens, encompassing a variety of welfare-related interests. Its members include past and present welfare recipients and low-income citizens active in welfare rights, public housing tenants' and other low-income citizens' groups, social workers and others involved in social service associations, private welfare agencies and social work education. The council advises the Minister of National Health and Welfare on matters related to welfare. The Office of the National Council of Welfare carries out research and other support activities for the council and performs a liaison role with a variety of organizations across Canada involved in social welfare and social policy issues.

National Design Council. The council was established by an act of Parliament in 1961 (RSC 1970, c.N-5) to promote and expedite improvement of design in the products of Canadian industry. The council makes recommendations on design policies and the planning of programs for the furtherance of design in Canada to be implemented under the direction of the council by departments and agencies cf the federal government, regional governments and other private and institutional bodies. Programs formally carried out by the council are identified under the title of "Design Canada". The council has 17 members appointed by the Governor in Council and reports through its chairman to the Minister of Industry, Trade and Commerce.

National Energy Board. This board was established under the National Energy Board Act, 1959 (RSC 1970, c.N-6) to assure the best use of energy resources in Canada. The board, composed of nine members, is responsible for regulating the construction and operation of the oil and gas pipelines that are under the jurisdiction of the Parliament of Canada, the tolls charged for transmission by oil and gas pipelines, the export and import of gas and oil, the export of electric power, and the construction of the lines over which power is exported or imported. Under the Petroleum Administration Act, 1975, Part I, the board administers the export charge on crude oil and certain refined petroleum products, and under Part III of the act, administers on behalf of the Minister of Energy, Mines and Resources, the pricing of natural gas entering interprovincial and international trade.

The board is required to study and keep under review all matters relating to energy under the jurisdiction of the Parliament of Canada and to recommend measures it considers necessary and advisable. It reports to Parliament through the Minister of Energy, Mines and Resources.

National Farm Products Marketing Council. Established in 1972 under the National Farm Products Marketing Agencies Act (SC 1972, c.65), the council consults with producers, commodity boards, and provincial and federal governments and coordinates their views on the establishment and operation of national marketing agencies. It assists and supervises the operations of agencies and promotes more effective marketing of farm products in interprovincial and export trade. The goal is to maintain and promote an efficient, competitive and expanding agricultural industry.

The council consists of a chairman, a vice-chairman, two full-time and five part-time members appointed by the Governor in Council and is directly responsible to the Minister of Agriculture. Council headquarters is in Ottawa.

National Film Board. The National Film Board, established in 1939, operates under the National Film Act (RSC 1970, c.N-7) which provides for a board of governors of nine members — a Government Film Commissioner, appointed by the Governor in Council, who is chairman of the board, three members from the public service of Canada and five members from outside the public service. The board reports to Parliament through the Secretary of State. It is responsible for advising the Governor in Council on film activities and is authorized to produce and distribute films in the national interest and, in particular, films "designed to interpret Canada to Canadians and to other nations". The board is responsible for the production and processing of films for government departments. Its head office is in Ottawa and its operational headquarters in Montreal.

National Harbours Board. The board was established by an act of Parliament in 1936 (RSC 1970, c.N-8). It is responsible for the administration of port facilities at the harbours of St. John's, Nfld.; Halifax, NS; Saint John and Belledune, NB; Sept-Îles, Chicoutimi, Baie-des-Ha! Ha!, Quebec, Trois-Rivières and Montreal, Que.; Churchill, Man.; Vancouver and Prince Rupert, BC; the Jacques Cartier and Champlain bridges at Montreal, Que.; and the grain elevators at Prescott and Port Colborne, Ont. The board reports to Parliament through the Minister of Transport.

National Library of Canada. The National Library came formally into existence on January 1, 1953, with the proclamation of the National Library Act (RSC 1970, c.N-11). It publishes *Canadiana,* a monthly catalogue of new publications relating to Canada, with an annual cumulation. The library also publishes other bibliographies. Its Reference Branch maintains the Canadian Union Catalogue which embodies the author catalogues of the major libraries in the 10 provinces and is thus a key to the book collections of the whole country. The library's own bookstock totals more than 500,000 volumes. The National Librarian reports to Parliament through the Secretary of State.

National Museums of Canada. The National Museums of Canada is a departmental Crown corporation established April 1, 1968, by the National Museums Act (RSC 1970, c.N-12) to join under one administration the National Gallery of Canada; the National Museum of Man (including the Canadian War Museum); the National Museum of Natural Sciences; and the National Museum of Science and Technology (including the National Aeronautical Collection). The corporation reports to Parliament through the Secretary of State.

The National Museums Corporation is governed by a board of trustees, consisting of a chairman, vice-chairman and 12 members, as well as two ex officio members — the Director of the Canada Council and the President of the National Research Council. The Secretary General is responsible for directing and managing the business of the corporation except for those matters which are the responsibility of the board, or of the four museum directors. Museum directors are responsible to the board for the overall activities of their respective operations.

The purposes of the corporation, according to the act, are "to demonstrate the products of nature and the works of man, with special but not exclusive reference to Canada, so as to promote interest therein through Canada and to disseminate knowledge thereof". The corporation is empowered to collect, classify, preserve and display objects; undertake or sponsor research; arrange for and sponsor travelling exhibitions of materials in, or related to, its collections and to arrange for the publication or acquisition and the sale to the public of books, pamphlets, replicas and other relevant materials; undertake or sponsor programs for the training of persons in the professions and skills involved in the operation of museums; arrange for or provide professional and technical services to other organizations whose purposes are similar to any of those of the corporation on such terms and conditions as may be approved by the minister; and generally to do and authorize such things as are incidental or conducive to the attainment of the purposes of the corporation and the exercise of its powers.

National Parole Board. The board was established in 1959 by the Parole Act (RSC 1970, c.P-2), which gives it absolute authority for parole of inmates under sentence of imprisonment imposed under an act of Parliament or for criminal contempt of court. The board has jurisdiction over all matters of federal parole except sentences for murder. In such cases eligibility is possible after a stipulated time between 10 and 25 years has been served. The board is composed of a chairman and 18 other members appointed by Order in Council. It reports to Parliament through the Solicitor General of Canada.

National Research Council of Canada. This is an agency of the federal government established in 1916 to promote scientific and industrial research. The council operates science and engineering laboratories in Ottawa, Halifax and Saskatoon; gives direct financial support to research carried out in Canadian university and industrial laboratories; sponsors associate committees coordinating research on specific problems of national interest; and develops and maintains the nation's primary physical standards. The federal government has designated NRC as the coordinating body for the further development of a national scientific and technical information system under the general direction of the National Librarian. Other activities include the provision of free technical information to manufacturing concerns; the publication of research journals; and representation of Canada in international scientific unions. Patentable inventions developed in the council's laboratories are made available for manufacture through a subsidiary company, Canadian Patents and Development Limited. The National Research Council consists of a president, three vice-presidents and 17 members representing Canadian universities, industry and labour. NRC is incorporated under the National Research Council Act (RSC 1970, c.N-14) and reports to Parliament through a designated minister.

Northern Canada Power Commission. The commission was established by an act of Parliament in 1948 (RSC 1970, c.N-21) to provide power to points in the Northwest Territories where a need developed and where power could be supplied on a self-sustaining basis; the act was amended in 1950 to give the commission authority to provide similar services in the Yukon Territory. The name of the commission (formerly the Northwest Territories Power Commission) was changed in 1956. It is composed of a chairman and four members appointed by the Governor in Council. Of the additional members, one each is appointed on the recommendation of the Commissioner in Council of the Northwest Territories and the Commissioner in Council of the Yukon Territory.

Northern Transportation Company Limited. This company was incorporated in 1947 under the title of Northern Transportation Company (1947) Limited, the date being omitted from the name in 1952. Previously a company chartered under an Alberta statute, it had been a wholly-owned subsidiary of Eldorado Nuclear Limited until late 1975, when the company's common shares were transferred to the Minister of Transport in trust for Her Majesty in right of Canada. The company conducts the business of a common carrier in the Mackenzie River watershed, the western Arctic and Hudson Bay, and operates a wholly-owned subsidiary trucking company with operations in Alberta and the Northwest Territories. It is responsible to Parliament through the Minister of Transport.

Office of the Administrator, Anti-Inflation Act. The office was established on December 15, 1975 by the Anti-Inflation Act (SC 1974-75-76, c.75, amended by SC 1974-75-76, c.98). The administrator enforces the Anti-Inflation Board guidelines with orders that are binding when the guidelines are disputed or contravened. In price and profit matters the administrator may order excess revenues to be returned to the buyers, the market or the Crown. In compensation matters, he may order that excess payments be recovered from the employer, the employee or both. The administrator, appointed by the Governor in Council, may appoint one or more deputy administrators. He reports to Parliament through the Minister of National Revenue.

Office of the Auditor General. This office originated in 1878 and currently functions under the Financial Administration Act (RSC 1970, c.F-10). The Auditor General is responsible for examining accounts relating to the Consolidated Revenue Fund and to public property, and for reporting annually to the House of Commons the results of his examinations. He also audits the accounts of various Crown corporations and other organizations. The Minister of Finance acts as spokesman in Parliament for the Auditor General.

Office of the Chief Electoral Officer. This office was established in 1920 under the provisions of the Dominion Elections Act, now the Canada Elections Act (RSC 1970, c.14, 1st Supp.) as amended by the Election Expenses Act (SC 1973-74, c.51), and is responsible for the conduct of all federal elections as well as the elections of members of the Northwest Territories Council and of the Yukon Territory Council. In addition, it conducts any vote taken under the Canada Temperance Act. The Chief Electoral Officer is responsible directly to the House of Commons, the President of the Privy Council acting as spokesman for him in the Cabinet.

Office of the Coordinator, Status of Women. The office received official status April 1, 1976 by Order in Council PC 1976-781. The coordinator reports to and assists the minister "responsible for the Status of Women". The coordinator monitors the activities of federal departments to ensure that they are in line with the policy of promoting equality between men and women. She also coordinates new initiatives to improve the status of women within the federal government. The office, located in Ottawa, carries on the work begun in 1970 in the Privy Council Office.

Office of the Representation Commissioner. The office was established in 1963 under the provisions of the Representation Commissioner Act (RSC 1970, c.R-6). After each decennial census, the Representation Commissioner is responsible for preparing maps showing the distribution of population in each province and setting out alternative proposals respecting the boundaries of electoral districts in each province. These maps are supplied to the 11 electoral boundaries commissions (one for each province and one for the Northwest Territories) established under the provisions of the Electoral Boundaries Readjustment Act (RSC 1970, c.E-2). The Representation Commissioner is a member of each of the commissions. The Secretary of State acts as spokesman for the office in the Cabinet and the House of Commons.

Panarctic Oils Ltd. This corporation is a consortium of mining and oil and gas companies, individuals and Petro-Canada, formed in 1967 to explore for oil and gas in the Arctic. Panarctic Oils Ltd. is not a Crown corporation and does not report to Parliament.

Pension Appeals Board. This board, established under the Canada Pension Plan Act (RSC 1970, c.C-5) hears appeals under the Canada Pension Plan and under certain provincial pension plans. It also hears appeals from certain decisions of the Umpire under the Unemployment Insurance Act (SC 1971, c.48) as amended. The board consists of two judges of the Federal Court of Canada or of a superior court of a province appointed as chairman and vice-chairman, and not less than one and not more than eight other persons, each of whom must be a judge of the Federal Court or of a superior, district or county court of a province. For purposes of appeals under the Canada Pension Plan, the board reports to Parliament through the Minister of National Health and Welfare.

Pension Review Board. The board was created under the Minister of Veterans Affairs by the amendments to the Pension Act 1971 (SC 1970-71, c.31). Further amendments were made May 12, 1977 by the Act to Amend the Pension Act. Composed of a chairman, deputy chairman and three other members, the board is an independent and autonomous body that hears appeals in the National Capital Region from pension applicants dissatisfied with decisions of an Entitlement Board or two members of the Canadian Pension Commission. The board is also the responsible body when matters of interpretation of the acts are at issue.

Petro-Canada. On July 30, 1975 the Petro-Canada Act (SC 1974-75-76, c.61) established Petro-Canada as a Crown corporation to increase the supply of energy available to Canadians, to assist the government in the formulation of its national energy policy and to increase the Canadian presence in the petroleum industry. The corporation consists of a board of directors composed of a chairman, president and not more than 13 other persons appointed by the Governor in Council. Its head office is at Calgary, Alta. The corporation reports to Parliament through the Minister of Energy, Mines and Resources.

Pilotage Authorities. The Pilotage Act (SC 1971, c.52) established the Atlantic Pilotage Authority, the Laurentian Pilotage Authority, the Great Lakes Pilotage Authority and the Pacific Pilotage Authority as proprietary corporations as specified in Schedule D of the Financial Administration Act. The objects of each authority are to establish, operate, maintain and administer in the interests of safety an efficient pilotage service within the region set out in respect of the authority. Each of the four authorities has a chairman and not more than six other members appointed by the Governor in Council for a term not exceeding 10 years. The Pilotage Authorities report to Parliament through the Minister of Transport.

Post Office Department. Administration and operation of the Canada Post Office, by virtue of the Post Office Act (RSC 1970, c.P-14) and under the Postmaster General, includes all phases of postal activity, personnel, mail handling, transportation of mails by land, water, rail and air and the direction and control of financial services including the operation of the money order service.

The department's headquarters is in Ottawa, with regional headquarters in Halifax, Montreal, Toronto and Vancouver. District offices are located in St. John's, Halifax, Saint John, Quebec City, Montreal, Ottawa, North Bay, Toronto, London, Winnipeg, Saskatoon, Edmonton and Vancouver.

Prairie Farm Rehabilitation Administration (PFRA). PFRA was established in 1935 (RSC 1952, c.214) to assist in the rehabilitation of agricultural lands seriously affected by drought and soil drifting in Manitoba, Saskatchewan and Alberta. Since then it has developed 101 community pastures on 2.5 million acres of marginal and submarginal land and continues to operate 96 of them. It has also been responsible for construction of many large irrigation and water storage projects. PFRA has assisted technically and/or financially in the construction of 135,000 dugouts, dams, wells and irrigation projects for on-farm water supplies. In addition, PFRA operates a tree nursery which each year distributes several million trees free to farmers for the development of farm and field shelterbelts.

Privy Council Office. For administrative purposes, the Privy Council Office is regarded as a department of government for which the Prime Minister has responsibility as set forth in PC 1962-240. The Clerk of the Privy Council, under whose direction its functions are carried out, is considered as a deputy head and takes precedence among the chief officers of the public service. The authority of the Privy Council Office is to be found in Sections 11 and 130 of the British North America Act, 1867, which constituted a council to aid and advise in the Government of Canada, to be styled the Queen's Privy Council for Canada. In 1940, with the wartime development of Cabinet committees and the consequent need for orderly secretarial procedures such as agenda, explanatory memoranda and minutes, the Clerk of the Privy Council was designated Secretary to the Cabinet, and the Cabinet Secretariat was brought into being in the Privy Council Office. Since 1946, the Privy Council Office has been further reorganized, developed and enlarged and certain administrative functions of the Privy Council Office and the Prime Minister's Office have been closely integrated in the interests of efficiency and economy.

The organization of the Privy Council Office consists primarily of the Cabinet Secretariat with two divisions reporting to the Clerk of the Privy Council and Secretary to the Cabinet: Deputy Secretary to the Cabinet (Operations); and Deputy Secretary to the Cabinet (Plans). Each division contains a number of secretariats that support the Cabinet and its committees. The secretariats prepare and circulate agenda and necessary documents to ministers, and record and circulate decisions. They communicate with departments and agencies of the government, and provide advisory support for the Prime Minister as required. Other sections within the PCO advise the Prime Minister on senior appointments, constitutional matters, emergency and long-range planning, and the exercise of his prerogative to allocate responsibilities between ministers. Within the Privy Council Office, submissions to the Governor in Council are received, draft orders and regulations are prepared, approved orders are circulated and the duties of editing, registering and publishing the federal statutory regulations in Part II of the *Canada Gazette* are carried out.

Public Archives of Canada. The Public Archives was founded in 1872 and is administered under the Public Archives Act (RSC 1970, c.P-27) by the Dominion Archivist who has the rank of a deputy minister and reports to Parliament through the Secretary of State. Its purpose is to assemble and make available to the public a comprehensive collection of source material relating to the history of Canada. It also has broad responsibilities in regard to the promotion of efficiency and economy in the management of the federal government records. The Archives Branch in the National Library and Archives Building is a centre for research on the development of Canada. In addition to the selected records of the federal government, it possesses an extensive collection of private papers of individuals and societies, a map collection which is the most important of its kind in the country, and an extensive collection of paintings, drawings, prints, photographs, sound recordings and films relating to Canada. A specialized library is also at the disposal of searchers. The Records Management Branch operates a large records centre in Ottawa and regional centres in Toronto, Montreal, Vancouver, Winnipeg and Halifax where non-current departmental records are centralized, stored and serviced. It assists departments in their records management programs. The Administration and Technical Services Branch operates the Central Microfilm Unit for federal departments of the Government of Canada.

Under the terms of the Laurier House Act (RSC 1952, c.163), the Public Archives is responsible for the administration of Laurier House as a museum.

Public Service Commission. Arrangements were made for civil service appointments under the first Civil Service Act of 1868 but the first Civil Service Commission was not created until 1908. This established the beginnings of the merit system which is today the cornerstone of personnel administration in the public service. The Civil Service Act of 1918 gave the commission authority to control recruitment, selection, appointment, classification and organization and to recommend rates of pay. The next Civil Service Act, passed in 1961, strengthened the principles of the merit system, clarified the commission's role in other areas of personnel administration, and gave the staff associations the right to be consulted on matters about remuneration and conditions of employment.

The Public Service Employment Act (RSC 1970, c.P-32) which came into force on March 13, 1967, redefined the commission's role as the central staffing agency and extended its authority to the public service, covering certain groups of employees exempt from the previous acts. The public service is specified in Schedule A of the Public Service Staff Relations Act. It does not include Crown corporations, such as the Canadian Broadcasting Corporation, the Central Mortgage and Housing Corporation, the Canadian National Railways and Air Canada. The new act also reaffirms the merit principle, at the same time permitting delegation of the commission's authority, although not its responsibility to Parliament. Under the act, the commission is relieved of responsibility for recommending rates of pay and conditions of service to the government, for classification, and for consultation with staff associations on matters that are now the subject of collective bargaining.

On November 9, 1972, the commission was assigned the duty, by Order in Council PC 1972-2569, of investigating cases of alleged discrimination on grounds of sex, race, national origin, colour or religion with respect to the application and operation of the Public Service Employment Act, and the Anti-Discrimination Branch has been established for this purpose.

The Public Service Commission reports directly to Parliament. The Secretary of State has traditionally been the minister who presents the commission's report to the House of Commons, and answers questions in the House of Commons on the commission's behalf.

Public Service Staff Relations Board. Established in 1967 by the Public Service Staff Relations Act (RSC 1970, c.P-35, as amended by SC 1972, c.18, SC 1973-74, c.15 and SC 1974-75-76, c.67), the board is an independent body responsible for determining bargaining units, certifying bargaining agents, dealing with complaints of unfair practices and generally overseeing the administration of the legislation providing for collective bargaining in the public service of Canada. The board consists of a full-time chairman, vice-chairman and not less than three deputy chairmen who hold office for a period not exceeding 10 years and such other full-time members and part-time members as the Governor in Council considers necessary to discharge the responsibilities of the board. They hold office for a period not exceeding seven years. Information on compensation and other conditions of employment in Canada is provided to employers and bargaining agents, primarily in the public service, by the Pay Research Bureau which is under the administrative direction of the board. Under the act the Public Service Staff Relations Board reports to Parliament, through a minister of the Crown, other than a member of the Treasury Board, as designated by the Governor in Council. At present the responsible minister is the President of the Privy Council.

Queen Elizabeth II Canadian Research Fund. The Queen Elizabeth II Canadian Research Fund Act (SC 1959, c.33) established a fund of $1 million to be administered by a board of trustees to aid in research on children's diseases. The Prime Minister reports to Parliament on the operations of this fund.

Restrictive Trade Practices Commission. The commission was established by the Combines Investigation Act (RSC 1970, c.C-23 as amended by SC 1974-75-76, c.76). In respect of trade practices contained in Part IV. 1 of the act, on application of the Director of Investigation and Research and after holding a hearing at which evidence is submitted by the director and by the party against whom an order is sought, the commission may issue an order prohibiting the practice. In respect of restrictive trade practices contained in Part V of the act, the commission may hold hearings and appraise evidence submitted to it by the director and the parties under investigation in order to report to the Minister of Consumer and Corporate Affairs.

Roosevelt Campobello International Park Commission. Established by the Roosevelt Campobello International Park Commission Act (SC 1964-65, c.19), the commission consists of six members, three appointed by the Government of Canada and three by the Government of the United States, to administer the Roosevelt Campobello International Park at Campobello, NB. The Canadian section of the commission reports to Parliament through the Secretary of State for External Affairs.

Royal Canadian Mint. The Royal Canadian Mint has been in operation since 1908. It was first established as a branch of the Royal Mint under the United Kingdom Coinage Act of 1870, and opened on January 2, 1908. On December 1, 1931, by an act of the Canadian Parliament, it became the Royal Canadian Mint and operated as a branch of the Department of Finance. In 1969, by the Government Organization Act of 1969, the Mint became a Crown corporation, reporting to Parliament through the Minister of Supply and Services. It operates under authority of RSC 1970, c.R-8.

The latter change was made to provide for a more industrial type of organization and for flexibility in producing coins of Canada and other countries; buying, selling, melting, assaying and refining gold and other precious metals; and producing metals, plaques and other devices. The Mint has a seven-man board of directors appointed by the Governor in Council — the Master of the Mint who is its chief executive officer appointed to serve during pleasure, the chairman who is appointed for a four-year period, subject to re-appointment, and five other directors, two from inside and three from outside the public service, who are appointed for terms of three years. The Mint now operates basically as a manufacturing enterprise, with the object of making a profit. Financial requirements are provided through loans from the Consolidated Revenue Fund.

Royal Canadian Mounted Police. The Royal Canadian Mounted Police, a civil force organized and administered by the federal government, was established in 1873 as the North-West Mounted Police. It now operates under authority of the Royal Canadian Mounted Police Act (RSC 1970, c.R-9) and is responsible for enforcing federal laws throughout Canada. By agreement with the governments of eight provinces (all provinces except Ontario and Quebec) it is also responsible for enforcing the Criminal Code of Canada and provincial laws within those provinces under the direction of the respective Attorneys General. In these provinces the force provides police services to 166 municipalities, assuming enforcement responsibilities for criminal, provincial and municipal laws. The Yukon Territory and Northwest Territories are policed exclusively by the Royal Canadian Mounted Police. The commissioner, appointed by the Governor in Council, has control and management of the force and of all matters connected therewith, under the direction of the Solicitor General of Canada.

St. Lawrence Seaway Authority. The St. Lawrence Seaway Authority was established by an act of Parliament in 1951 (RSC 1970, c.S-1) and came into force by proclamation on July 1, 1954. The authority was incorporated for the purposes of constructing, maintaining and operating all such works as may be necessary to provide and maintain, either wholly in Canada or in conjunction with works undertaken by an appropriate authority in the United States, a deep waterway between the Port of Montreal and Lake Erie. The Crown corporation, Seaway International Bridge Corporation Limited, is subsidiary to the St. Lawrence Seaway Authority. The authority is composed of a president, a vice-president and a member, and reports to Parliament through the Minister of Transport.

Science Council of Canada. The Science Council of Canada was established in 1966 (RSC 1970, c.S-5) and became a Crown corporation on April 1, 1969. The council consists of 25 members, each having a specialized interest in science or technology. Members normally hold office for three years. All are appointed by the Governor in Council. The duties of the Science Council are to assess in a comprehensive manner Canada's scientific and technological resources, requirements and potentialities and to make recommendations thereon. The council reports to Parliament through a designated minister, at present the Minister of State for Science and Technology.

Seaway International Bridge Corporation Limited. The Seaway International Bridge Corporation Limited was established under the Companies Act, by Letters Patent, November 13, 1962. It operates the international toll bridge system between Cornwall, Ont. and Rooseveltown, NY on behalf of the owners, the St. Lawrence Seaway Authority and the Saint Lawrence Seaway Development Corporation. It reports to Parliament through the Minister of Transport.

Standards Council of Canada. The council was established by an act of Parliament (RSC 1970, c.41, 1st Supp.) which received Royal Assent on October 7, 1970. Its objectives are to foster and promote voluntary standardization in fields relating to the construction, manufacture, production, quality, performance and safety of buildings, structures, manufactured articles and products and other goods, including components thereof, not expressly provided for by law, as a means of advancing the national economy, benefiting the health, safety and welfare of the public, assisting and protecting consumers, facilitating domestic and international trade and furthering international cooperation in the field of standards. The council is responsible for coordinating the planning and execution of a program for the development of standards in the metric (SI) system. This activity is in support of the overall program which is being carried out by Metric Commission Canada.

The council consists of not more than 57 members; including six federal representatives, 10 representing the provinces and 41 other members. Membership is broadly representative of all levels of government, primary and secondary industries, distributive and service industries, trade associations, labour unions, consumer associations and the academic community. The council reports to Parliament through the Minister of Industry, Trade and Commerce.

Statistics Canada. Statistics Canada became the new name for the Dominion Bureau of Statistics with the proclamation of a new Statistics Act (SC 1971, c.15) on May 1, 1971. The bureau was initially set up by statute in 1918 as the central statistical agency for Canada (SC 1918, c.43). In 1948 this statute, which had been consolidated as the Statistics Act (RSC 1927, c.190), was repealed and replaced by the Statistics Act (RSC 1952, c.257) which was amended by SC 1952-53, c.18, assented to March 31, 1953. The 1971 act replaced that statute.

The functions of Statistics Canada are to compile, analyze and publish statistical information relative to the commercial, industrial, financial, social and general condition of the people and to conduct regularly a census of population and agriculture of Canada as required under the act.

Statistics Canada is a major publication agency of the federal government; its reports cover all aspects of the national economy and social conditions of the country. The administrative head of the bureau is the Chief Statistician of Canada who has the rank of a deputy head of a department and reports to Parliament through the Minister of Industry, Trade and Commerce.

Tariff Board. Constituted in 1931, the board derives its duties and powers from four statutes: the Tariff Board Act (RSC 1970, c.T-1); the Customs Act (RSC 1970, c.C-40); the Excise Tax Act (RSC 1970, c.E-13); and the Anti-dumping Act (RSC 1970, c.A-15).

Under the Tariff Board Act, the board makes inquiry into and reports on any matter in relation to goods that, if brought into Canada, are subject to or exempt from customs duties or excise taxes. Reports of the board are tabled in Parliament by the Minister of Finance. It is also the duty of the board to inquire into any other matter in relation to the trade and commerce of Canada that may be referred to it by the Governor in Council.

Under the provisions of the Customs Act, the Excise Tax Act and the Anti-dumping Act, the Tariff Board acts as a court to hear appeals from decisions of the Department of National Revenue, Customs and Excise, in respect of excise taxes, tariff classification, value for duty, drawback of customs duties and determination of normal value or export price in dumping matters. Declarations of the board on appeals are final and conclusive but the acts contain provisions for appeal on questions of law to the Federal Court and thence to the Supreme Court of Canada.

Tax Review Board. The Tax Review Board, formerly the Tax Appeal Board, was created and operates under the provisions of the Tax Review Board Act (SC 1970-71, c.11). The board has jurisdiction to hear appeals by taxpayers against their assessments, under the Income Tax Act and the Estate Tax Act as well as appeals under the Old Age Security Act, certain sections of the Superannuation Plan, the Unemployment Insurance Act, and in other acts of the Parliament of Canada that specify the right to appeal to the board. The board has, for the exercise of its jurisdiction, such powers, rights and privileges as are vested in a Superior Court of Canada. The board shall consist of no less than three nor more than seven members and at its full complement consists of a chairman, an assistant chairman and five members. The principal office of the board is at Ottawa; the board sits at such times and such places throughout Canada as it considers necessary for the proper conduct of its business. The board is under the jurisdiction of the Minister of Justice but is independent of the Department of Justice.

Teleglobe Canada. Created in 1950 by an act of Parliament (RSC 1970, c.C-11), under the name of the Canadian Overseas Telecommunication Corporation, this Crown agency operates all overseas communications to and from Canada — whether by undersea cable or international satellite. By means of international gateway switching-centres in Montreal, Toronto and Vancouver, Teleglobe Canada provides public telephone service to over 200 overseas territories. The corporation also provides public message telegraph service, Telex, private wire service, data and video transmissions to many points around the world. Teleglobe Canada is the designated operating entity for Canadian participation in Intelsat and represents Canada on the Commonwealth Telecommunications Council. It reports to Parliament through the Minister of Communications.

Telesat Canada. Telesat Canada was incorporated in 1969 by an act of Parliament (RSC 1970, c.T-4). Its objectives are to establish satellite telecommunication systems providing telecommunication services on a commercial basis. The recommendations of a government task force on satellite policy and the use of satellite technology for domestic communications, appointed in 1967, and a 1968 White Paper based to a large extent on those recommendations preceded the establishing legislation.

The authorized capital of the corporation consists of 10 million common shares without par value and 5 million preferred shares with a par value of $10 per share. At the end of 1972, there were 6 million common shares issued and outstanding. The corporation will ultimately be owned by three main groups of shareholders: the federal government, the telecommunications common carriers and the general public. Currently, the corporation is owned by the first two groups.

Telesat is not a Crown corporation, nor is it an agent of Her Majesty. Its annual report is tabled in the House of Commons by the Minister of Communications.

Textile and Clothing Board. This board was established (SC 1971, c.39) to receive complaints and conduct inquiries about textile and clothing goods imported into Canada under such conditions as to cause or threaten serious injury to Canadian production. After its investigative procedures are completed, the board makes written recommendations to the Minister of Industry, Trade and Commerce. The board consists of three members appointed by the Governor in Council and maintains its head office in the National Capital Region.

Treasury Board. The Treasury Board was first established as a committee of the Queen's Privy Council for Canada by Order in Council PC 3 of July 2, 1867, and was made a statutory committee in 1869. The Minister of Finance was appointed Chairman of the Board, with four other Privy Councillors to be designated as members by the Governor in Council. The Secretary of the Board and the members of his staff were employed by the Department of Finance.

By the Government Organization Act, 1966 (SC 1966, c.25) the board was established as a separate department of government with its own minister, the President of the Treasury Board. The committee constituting the Treasury Board includes, in addition to the president, the Minister of Finance and four other Privy Councillors.

The Financial Administration Act (RSC 1970, c.F-10), defines the Treasury Board's responsibilities as the central management agency of government. These responsibilities include the organization of the public service, financial management, annual and longer-term expenditure planning, and expenditure control, including allocation of resources among departments and agencies of government; management of personnel functions in the public service; and improvement in the efficiency of management and administration in the public service.

The Treasury Board Secretariat is divided into six branches. The Administrative Policy Branch is responsible for the development, interpretation, dissemination and evaluation of policies, guidelines and regulations in administrative areas, and other administrative inputs to government operations such as accommodation, travel, contracting, electronic data processing and real property management, with a view to ensuring probity and prudence in the acquisition of administrative inputs as well as their effective and efficient use in support of departmental programs. The Planning Branch is responsible for the development and application of systems and procedures for evaluating the effectiveness and efficiency of programs and projects and for providing advice and planning assistance for organizational change in government. The Personnel Policy Branch is responsible for all matters relating to personnel management in the public service including human resources requirements, human resources development and training, classification, compensation benefits, collective bargaining and staff relations in general.

The Official Languages Branch is responsible for the development, monitoring, evaluation and communication of the federal government's official languages policies and programs and for the implementation of the Official Languages Act within the public service. The Program Branch is responsible for analyzing the policy, program and project proposals of departments and recommending to the Treasury Board an optimum allocation of available financial and manpower resources to achieve program objectives, and for expenditure control and estimates preparation.

The Financial Administration Branch is responsible for the development, evaluation, and maintenance of the policies, standards, guidelines and systems which govern the financial administration and internal audit functions of the Government of Canada.

Unemployment Insurance Commission. In August 1977 the commission, which had been established under the provisions of the Unemployment Insurance Act, was merged with the Department of Manpower and Immigration into one organization, the Canada Employment and Immigration Commission. (See entries for the Department of Manpower and Immigration and the Canada Employment and Immigration Commission.)

Uranium Canada, Limited. This Crown company, incorporated in June 1971 under the Canada Corporations Act (RSC 1970, c.C-32) pursuant to Energy, Mines and Resources Vote LIIC of the Appropriation Act No. 1, 1971 and the Atomic Energy Control Act, (RSC 1970, c.A-19) is an agency corporation listed in Schedule C of the Financial Administration Act (RSC 1970, c.F-10). For all purposes it is an agent of Her Majesty and its powers may be exercised only as such. The shares of the company, with the exception of the qualifying shares of the directors, are held by the Minister of Energy, Mines and Resources in trust for Her Majesty. Registered under the trade mark UCAN, the company acts as an agent on behalf of the federal government in the acquisition and future sales of the joint stockpile of uranium concentrates established under the agreement with Denison Mines Limited, dated January 1, 1971. UCAN also holds title to the general stockpile of uranium concentrates acquired by the federal government during the years 1963-70. The corporation's head office is in Ottawa.

Via Rail Canada, Inc. Incorporated on January 12, 1977, Via Rail Canada, Inc. is a subsidiary of CN and is financed directly by the federal government. However, it operates at arm's length from CN, being neither comprised in CN nor consolidated in its accounts. Its functions are to market and manage all railway passenger services in Canada. It took over marketing June 1, 1977 and would take over management April 1, 1978. The corporation consists of a board of directors composed of a minimum of three to a maximum of 15 members including a chairman and president. The head office is located in Montreal and the company reports to the Minister of Transport.

War Veterans Allowance Board. This board, established under the authority of the War Veterans Allowance Act, is a quasi-judicial body consisting of eight members, including a chairman and a deputy chairman, appointed by the Governor in Council. The board acts as an appeal court for an applicant or recipient aggrieved by a decision of a District Authority and may, on its own motion, review and alter or reverse any adjudication of a District Authority. The board is responsible for advising the Minister of Veterans Affairs with respect to regulations concerning the War Veterans Allowance Act and Part XI of the Civilian War Pensions and Allowances Act.

Synopsis of legislation   Appendix 2

Synopsis of legislation of the first session of the 30th Parliament, September 30, 1974 to October 12, 1976, passed in the 23rd, 24th and 25th years of the reign of Her Majesty Queen Elizabeth II.

In summarizing this material it is not possible to convey the full content of the legislation. For further details the reader should refer to the *Statutes of Canada*, Chapters 1-60, 1974-75-76, Volume I, and *Statutes of Canada*, Chapters 61-118, 1974-75-76, Volume II. The chapter number is followed by the date of Royal Assent.

Chapter 1 (October 10, 1974) *West Coast Grain Handling Operations Act, 1974* provides for the resumption of grain handling at ports on the west coast of Canada.

Chapter 2 (October 30, 1974) *Appropriation Act No. 3, 1974* grants certain sums of money for the public service for the financial year ending March 31, 1975.

Chapter 3 (November 27, 1974) *An Act to amend the Army Benevolent Fund Act* gives the Army Benevolent Fund Board the authority to manage other funds of a similar nature.

Chapter 4 (November 27, 1974) *An Act to amend the Canada Pension Plan* redefines and modifies certain sections of the plan and provides, among other things, for equality of status for males and females under the act; provides for persons of certain religious sects to elect once in their lives not to make contributions under the act with respect to self-employed earnings; and removes the requirement that a person 65-70 be retired to be eligible for a pension.

Chapter 5 (November 27, 1974) *An Act to amend the Customs Act* extends Canadian customs jurisdiction to the outer limits of the territorial sea of Canada.

Chapter 6 (November 27, 1974) *An Act to amend the Customs Tariff* provides for the temporary removal of customs duties on certain petroleum products; and provides for temporary tariff reductions on consumer goods to June 30, 1974 and on sugar and related products to June 30, 1976.

Chapter 7 (November 27, 1974) *An Act to authorize federal trust companies and loan companies to increase the monetary limit of their borrowing power and to issue subordinated notes.*

Chapter 8 (November 27, 1974) *An Act to amend the War Veterans Allowance Act and the Civilian War Pensions and Allowances Act* provides for at least 12 amendments to allow veterans to meet the increased cost of living. It includes quarterly escalation of income ceilings, new benefits for children, widows and widowers, improved payments for orphans and equality of status for males and females under the act.

Chapter 9 (December 13, 1974) *An Act to amend the Immigration Act* makes it an offence for a person against whom a deportation order is made to return to Canada without the consent of the minister in the circumstances described.

Chapter 10 (December 13, 1974) *An Act to amend the Electoral Boundaries Readjustment Act* makes two additions to the definitions section of the act.

Chapter 11 (December 13, 1974) *Alberta–British Columbia Boundary Act, 1974* establishes a commission to resurvey the sinuous boundary line between these two provinces and to settle disputes respecting the boundary.

Chapter 12 (December 13, 1974) *An Act to amend the Fire Losses Replacement Account Act* extends the application of the act to property which is appropriated to the Yukon or Northwest Territories.

Chapter 13 (December 20, 1974) *Representation Act, 1974* provides for readjusted representation in the House of Commons, establishes electoral boundaries commissions and removes the temporary suspension of the Electoral Boundaries Readjustment Act.

Chapter 14 (December 20, 1974) *Federal Business Development Act* provides for incorporation of the Federal Business Development Bank as a Crown corporation.

Chapter 15 (December 20, 1974) *Indian Oil and Gas Act* provides that the Governor in Council may make regulations respecting the disposition of any interest in Indian lands necessarily incidental to the exploitation of oil and gas, and regulations prescribing the royalties obtained on the oil and gas; and provides for a special agreement, with the approval of the band council concerned, for a reduction or an increase of such royalties.

Chapter 16 (December 20, 1974) *An Act respecting the office of the Secretary to the Cabinet for Federal-Provincial Relations and respecting the Clerk of the Privy Council* provides for the appointment of the Secretary to the Cabinet for Federal-Provincial Relations and alters the designation Clerk of the Privy Council to Clerk of the Privy Council and Secretary to the Cabinet.

Chapter 17 (December 20, 1974) *An Act to amend the Export Development Act* allows for an increase in the authorized share capital, in the borrowing capacity and in the maximum potential liability of the Export Development Corporation; allows for an increase in the maximum liability of foreign customers to the corporation; permits the corporation to enter into re-insurance contracts; and provides for other related and consequential amendments.

Chapter 18 (December 20, 1974) *An Act to amend the Supreme Court Act and to make related amendments to the Federal Court Act* modifies the residence requirement for the judges, Registrar and Deputy Registrar of the Supreme Court of Canada, changing references to Ottawa to the National Capital Region; eliminates appeals to the Supreme Court from judgments; and specifies criteria to be taken into account by the Supreme Court in determining whether or not to allow appeals to that court.

Chapter 19 (December 20, 1974) *An Act to revise references to the Court of Queen's Bench of the Province of Quebec* effects the necessary changes in federal statutes to reflect the abolition of the Court of Queen's Bench in the province of Quebec.

Chapter 20 (December 20, 1974) *Statute Revision Act* provides for a continuing revision and consolidation of the statutes and regulations of Canada.

Chapter 21 (December 20, 1974) *Appropriation Act No. 4, 1974* grants certain sums of money for the public service for the financial year ending March 31, 1975.

Chapter 22 (December 20, 1974) *Appropriation Act No. 5, 1974* grants certain sums of money for the public service for the financial year ending March 31, 1975.

Chapter 23 (February 2, 1975) *An Act to amend the Customs Tariff (No. 2)* re-introduces a number of temporary tariff reductions for the period November 19, 1974 to June 30, 1976.

Chapter 24 (February 27, 1975) *An Act to amend the Excise Tax Act and the Excise Act* imposes air transportation taxes on regular and charter flights; affects taxes levied in areas such as the sale and resale of goods by licensed wholesalers operating duty-free outlets; increases the special excise tax on wines; increases the excise duties on spirits, brandy, tobacco, cigarettes and cigars; exempts from sales tax certain medical goods, bicycles, transportation and construction equipment and footwear; reduces the sales tax on construction materials and equipment for buildings; imposes a special excise tax on transportation vehicles; and re-instates the sales tax on printed matter produced by government for government use.

Chapter 25 (February 27, 1975) *An Act to amend the Electoral Boundaries Readjustment Act* modifies one of the rules regarding the make-up of electoral boundaries.

Chapter 26 (February 27, 1975) *An Act to amend the statute law relating to income tax* provides for changes in personal and corporate income tax.

Chapter 27 (March 13, 1975) *An Act to amend the Canadian Wheat Board Act* provides that final payments on deliveries of wheat in any pool period shall not be made until on or after January 1 of the calendar year following the end of the pool period.

Chapter 28 (March 13, 1975) *Northwest Territories Representation Act* increases the representation of the Northwest Territories in the House of Commons from one to two members and establishes a commission to readjust the electoral boundaries of the Northwest Territories.

Chapter 29 (March 13, 1975) *An Act respecting the Electoral Boundaries Readjustment Act* changes the name of the electoral district of Bruce in Ontario to Bruce–Grey.

Chapter 30 (March 13, 1975) *An Act respecting the Electoral Boundaries Act* changes the name of the electoral district of Lafontaine in Quebec to Lafontaine–Rosemont.

Chapter 31 (March 13, 1975) *An Act respecting the Electoral Boundaries Readjustment Act* changes the name of the electoral district of Berthier in Quebec to Berthier–Maskinonge.

Chapter 32 (March 24, 1975) *West Coast Ports Operations Act, 1975* provides for the resumption and continuation of longshoring and related operations at ports on the west coast of Canada.

Chapter 33 (March 24, 1975) *An Act respecting Canadian business corporations* revises and reforms the law applicable to business corporations and provides for uniformity of business corporation law in Canada.

Chapter 34 (March 24, 1975) *An Act to amend the Prairie Grain Advance Payments Act* increases from $6,000 to $15,000 the maximum amount that may be paid to a producer as advance payments on grain to be delivered under a permit book.

Chapter 35 (March 24, 1975) *An Act to provide for the recognition of the Beaver (Castor canadensis) as a symbol of the sovereignty of Canada.*

Chapter 36 (March 25, 1975) *Appropriation Act No. 1, 1975* grants certain sums of money for the public service for the financial year ending March 31, 1975.

Chapter 37 (March 25, 1975) *Appropriation Act No. 2, 1975* grants certain sums of money for the public service for the financial year ending March 31, 1976.

Chapter 38 (March 26, 1975) *An Act to amend the National Housing Act,* among other provisions, sets at $25 billion the aggregate amount of loans for which insurance policies have been issued under the act; authorizes the Central Mortgage and Housing Corporation to acquire land, instal services and effect improvements in order to lease land at low rental to non-profit corporations; authorizes amendments to encourage repair and improvement of family housing, hostel or dormitory accommodation, and the construction of houses and condominium units; authorizes CMHC to make loans for sewage treatment projects and grants toward preparation of comprehensive plans for sewerage facilities.

Chapter 39 (April 24, 1975) *St. Lawrence Ports Operations Act, 1975* provides for the resumption and continuation of longshoring, checking, cargo repairing and related operations at certain ports in Quebec.

Chapter 40 (April 24, 1975) *An Act to amend the Law Reform Commission Act* increases the number of full-time members of the Law Reform Commission from four to five, and phases out the positions of part-time members.

Chapter 41 (April 24, 1975) *An Act to amend the Railway Act* provides authority for the Minister of Transport to acquire from railway companies certain information relating to costs.

Chapter 42 (April 24, 1975) *An Act to amend the Civil Service Insurance Act* extends provisions relating to children, married and unmarried women, and the unmarried woman's future husband and children.

Chapter 43 (April 24, 1975) *An Act to repeal the Proprietary or Patent Medicine Act and to amend the Trade Marks Act.*

Chapter 44 (May 8, 1975) *An Act to amend the Senate and House of Commons Act, the Salaries Act and the Parliamentary Secretaries Act* provides for increases in salaries, allowances and expenses.

Chapter 45 (May 8, 1975) *An Act to amend the Farm Credit Act* provides for an increase in the capital of the Farm Credit Corporation; extends the application of the act by providing for loans to establish young farmers; and sets loan amounts.

Chapter 46 (May 8, 1975) *An Act to amend the Fort-Falls Bridge Authority Act* removes the requirement for an act or joint resolution of the Congress of the United States and permits the start of bridge construction following conclusion of an agreement with the state of Minnesota.

Chapter 47 (June 19, 1975) *Petroleum Administration Act* imposes a charge on the export of crude oil and certain petroleum products, to provide compensation for certain petroleum costs, and regulates the price of Canadian crude oil and natural gas in interprovincial and export trade.

Chapter 48 (June 19, 1975) *An Act to amend the Judges Act and certain other Acts for related purposes and in respect of the reconstitution of the Supreme Courts of Newfoundland and Prince Edward Island* provides for increases in salaries, allowances, expenses and annuities and provides for additional judges across Canada.

Chapter 49 (June 19, 1975) *The Canadian Radio-television and Telecommunications Commission Act* establishes the Canadian Radio-television and Telecommunications Commission, amends the Broadcasting Act and other acts in consequence thereof and enacts other consequential provisions.

Chapter 50 (June 19, 1975) *Cultural Property Export and Import Act* regulates the export from Canada of cultural property and deals with the import into Canada of cultural property illegally exported from foreign states.

Chapter 51 (June 19, 1975) *An Act to amend the Northern Canada Power Commission Act* increases the number of commission members from three to five, provides for their expenses, and provides for changes in the financial management and banking practices of the commission.

Chapter 52 (June 19, 1975) *An Act to amend the Territorial Lands Act* clarifies the description of territorial land or corporations in which government employees are prohibited from acquiring interests.

Chapter 53 (June 19, 1975) *British North America Act, (No. 2) 1975* amends the British North America Acts, 1867 to 1975, increases the number of senators from 102 to 104 and provides that the Yukon Territory and Northwest Territories shall each be entitled to one representative in the Senate.

Chapter 54 (June 19, 1975) *Two-Price Wheat Act* provides for payments to July 31, 1980 up to a maximum of $1.75 per bushel for wheat produced and sold in Canada for human consumption in Canada, to make up the difference between the domestic price and the average export price.

Chapter 55 (June 19, 1975) *Ocean Dumping Control Act* provides for the control of the deliberate disposal of wastes and other substances into the ocean from ships, aircraft, platforms or any other man-made structures at sea.

Chapter 56 (June 19, 1975) *An Act to amend the Salaries Act* increases the salaries of the lieutenant governors of the provinces to $35,000, from $20,000 in Ontario and Quebec and $18,000 in each of the other provinces.

Chapter 57 (June 26, 1975) *Appropriation Act No. 3, 1975* grants certain sums of money for the public service for the financial year ending March 31, 1976.

Chapter 58 (June 26, 1975) *An Act to amend the Old Age Security Act, to repeal the Old Age Assistance Act and to amend other Acts in consequence thereof.*

Chapter 59 (June 26, 1975) *An Act to amend the Department of Industry, Trade and Commerce Act* provides that copies of invoices of goods imported into Canada and other related customs documents be made available to the Minister of Industry, Trade and Commerce and designated officers of his department.

Chapter 60 (June 26, 1975) *An Act to amend the Explosives Act* provides for greater control over the purchase, possession and transportation of explosives.

Chapter 61 (July 30, 1975) *Petro-Canada Act* establishes a national petroleum company as a Crown corporation.

Chapter 62 (July 30, 1975) *An Act to amend the Excise Tax Act* imposes a special excise tax on gasoline with provision for repayment of this tax under certain circumstances, decreases the tax payable on wine and exempts from sales tax thermal insulation material.

Chapter 63 (July 30, 1975) *An Act to amend the Agricultural Stabilization Act* redefines the methods by which the Agricultural Stabilization Board establishes new price structures for certain agricultural commodities such as cattle, hogs, sheep, industrial milk and industrial cream, corn and soybeans and, in some areas, oats and barley.

Chapter 64 (July 30, 1975) *An Act to amend the Prairie Grain Advance Payments Act, No. 2* increases the maximum advance payments a producer may obtain on unthreshed grain or to finance the drying of damp or tough grain.

Chapter 65 (July 30, 1975) *An Act to amend the Federal-Provincial Fiscal Arrangements Act, 1972* provides for a change in the calculation from April 1, 1974 of provincial revenue equalization related to oil and gas revenues and provides for a change in the calculation of provincial tax revenue guarantee payments.

Chapter 66 (July 30, 1975) *An Act to amend certain statutes to provide equality of status for male and female persons* amends the Unemployment Insurance Act, the Pension Act and the National Defence Act.

Chapter 67 (July 30, 1975) *An Act to amend the Public Service Staff Relations Act* provides, among other things, for the appointment of not less than three deputy chairmen of the Public Service Staff Relations Board.

Chapter 68 (July 30, 1975) *An Act to amend the Olympic (1976) Act* authorizes the issue of gold Olympic coins and determines the selling price of the gold on the basis of the market price.

Chapter 69 (July 30, 1975) *An Act to amend the Privileges and Immunities (International Organizations) Act* provides the same privileges and immunities to the European Communities regarding its organization and officials in Canada as is provided to other international organizations.

Chapter 70 (July 30, 1975) *An Act to amend the Customs Tariff, (No. 3)* affects the rates of duty on a variety of goods such as petroleum products, hymn books, miners' safety lamps, agricultural machines, aircraft and aircraft engines.

Chapter 71 (December 2, 1975) *An Act to amend the statute law relating to income tax (No. 2)* provides for two temporary measures: a tax credit for investment in production facilities and an exemption from the withholding tax for long-term corporate borrowing; provides for a resource allowance in the areas of mining and petroleum; and provides for a reduction in the tax credit for high income individuals.

Chapter 72 (December 2, 1975) *Environmental Contaminants Act* provides that the Ministers of Environment and National Health and Welfare may appoint an Environmental Contaminants Board of Review, advisory committees, inspectors and analysts in order to protect human health and the environment from contaminating substances.

Chapter 73 (December 2, 1975) *Lieutenant Governors Superannuation Act* provides for the payment of superannuation benefits to Lieutenant Governors.

Chapter 74 (December 15, 1975) *Appropriation Act, No. 4, 1975* grants certain sums of money for the public service for the financial year ending March 31, 1976.

Chapter 75 (December 15, 1975) *Anti-Inflation Act* provides for restraint of profit margins, prices, dividends and compensation in Canada; establishes the Anti-Inflation Board and the Anti-Inflation Appeal Tribunal; and provides for the appointment of an administrator to investigate, report on and issue orders to persons reported to have contravened AIB guidelines.

Chapter 76 (December 15, 1975) *An Act to amend the Combines Investigation Act and the Bank Act and to repeal an Act to amend an Act to amend the Combines Investigation Act and the Criminal Code,* among other things, deals with the abuse of industrial or intellectual property; makes bid-rigging a "per se" offence; defines new offences relating to conspiracy, combination, agreement or arrangement outside Canada as well as in the area of amateur and professional sport; and makes new provisions for offences relating to competition such as misrepresentation, false advertisements, double-ticketing, pyramid-selling, referral-selling, bait and switch selling, selling above advertised prices and promotional contests.

Chapter 77 (December 15, 1975) *An Act to amend the Canadian Overseas Telecommunication Corporation Act* changes the name of the Canadian Overseas Telecommunication Corporation to Teleglobe Canada.

Chapter 78 (December 15, 1975) *King George V Cancer Fund Winding-up Act* provides for the liquidation of the King George V Silver Jubilee Cancer Fund for Canada and for the transfer of the net proceeds to the National Cancer Institute of Canada.

Chapter 79 (December 20, 1975) *Supplementary Borrowing Authority Act, 1975* provides that the Governor in Council may raise an amount not exceeding $2 billion for public works and general purposes.

Chapter 80 (December 20, 1975) *An Act to amend the Unemployment Insurance Act, 1971* provides for a number of amendments which include adding a new class to the existing classes of insurable employment, providing for changes in qualifying periods, benefit periods, entitlement to benefits and rates of benefits and making employers' premiums payable by statute.

Chapter 81 (December 20, 1975) *Statute Law (Superannuation) Amendment Act, 1975* amends the acts concerned with superannuation, pension continuation, retiring allowances and annuities for the public service, the Canadian Forces, the RCMP, the diplomatic service, Members of Parliament, the Governor General and judges. The act provides for amendments to the contributions, benefits, return of contributions and death benefits and includes provision for equality of status for male and female members.

Chapter 82 (December 20, 1975) *An Act to amend the National Housing Act and the Central Mortgage and Housing Corporation Act* provides for amendments which allow the Central Mortgage and Housing Corporation to make loans and grants to encourage house construction and renovation; and authorizes the Corporation to make loans and grants to municipalities and to forgive indebtedness in respect of municipal water supply projects.

Chapter 83 (December 20, 1975) *Government Annuities Improvement Act* increases the rate of return on government annuity contracts, increases their flexibility and discontinues future sales thereof.

Chapter 84 (December 20, 1975) *An Act to amend the Regional Development Incentives Act* extends to December 31, 1981 the date by which facilities must achieve commercial production or commercial operation to qualify for development incentives and/or for a loan guarantee.

Chapter 85 (December 20, 1975) *An Act to amend the Agricultural Products Cooperative Marketing Act* authorizes the Governor in Council to fix an initial payment to primary producers for products to which the act applies.

Chapter 86 (December 20, 1975) *The Animal Disease and Protection Act* amends the Animal Contagious Diseases Act. Provisions include compensation to be paid for animals, animal products or other things ordered destroyed under the act and humane care to be taken of animals in transportation.

Chapter 87 (February 25, 1976) *Western Grain Stabilization Act* provides for payments to producers to stabilize net proceeds from the production and sale of western grain.

Chapter 88 (February 25, 1976) *Halifax Relief Commission Pension Continuation Act* provides for the dissolution of the Halifax Relief Commission but authorizes the continuation of pensions, grants or allowances paid in respect of death or injury in the Halifax explosion of December 6, 1917.

Chapter 89 (March 30, 1976) *Appropriation Act No. 1, 1976* grants certain sums of money for the public service for the financial year ending March 31, 1976.

Chapter 90 (March 30, 1976) *Appropriation Act No. 2, 1976* grants certain sums of money for the public service for the financial year ending March 31, 1977.

Chapter 91 (March 30, 1976) *Temporary Immigration Security Act* provides for deportation of any person who is not a Canadian citizen and has not been lawfully admitted to Canada for permanent residence and who, in the opinion of the Minister of Manpower and Immigration, is likely to engage in violent or criminal acts that could endanger the lives or safety of persons in Canada.

Chapter 92 (March 30, 1976) *Statute Law (Veterans and Returned) Amendment Act, 1976* allows insured persons and beneficiaries to opt for payment of insurance or annuity in a lump sum or otherwise and to deam designated beneficiaries to be surviving spouses of the insured.

Chapter 93 (March 30, 1976) *Criminal Law Amendment Act, 1975* amends the Criminal Code and makes related amendments to the Crown Liability Act, the Immigration Act and the Parole Act. Among its many provisions, the act gives Canadian courts jurisdiction to try persons in respect of certain offences committed outside Canada against internationally protected persons; permits the Attorney General to act in respect of a contravention of, or conspiracy to contravene, an act of Parliament; prohibits publication of identity of complainant in cases of rape, and excludes questions concerning the sexual conduct of the complainant with persons other than the accused; permits a peace officer to require a driver whom he suspects of having alcohol in his body to take a breath analysis test; permits interprovincial lottery schemes; prohibits possession of devices designed to obtain telecommunications services without payment; makes cattle theft an indictable offence; makes it an offence to steal or forge a credit card or use a credit card knowing it to have expired or have been cancelled; provides that the right of a person to a trial by jury is terminated if he does not appear or remain in attendance at his trial; and clarifies the procedure for dealing with persons in custody who are mentally ill.

Chapter 94 (March 30, 1976) *An Act to amend the Feeds Act* broadens and clarifies the definition of "feed" and "livestock" and provides for greater control over the manufacture, sale or importation into Canada of feeds.

Chapter 95 (May 5, 1976) *Compensation for Former Prisoners of War Act* provides for compensation for former defined prisoners of war and their dependents and consequentially amends certain other statutes.

Chapter 96 (May 5, 1976) *Motor Vehicle Tire Safety Act* provides for the use of national safety marks in relation to motor vehicle tires and provides for safety standards for certain motor vehicle tires imported into or exported from Canada or sent or conveyed from one province to another.

Chapter 97 (May 5, 1976) *An Act to amend the Quarantine Act* provides legislative authority for taking prompt and appropriate action in emergency situations at Canadian ports of entry to prevent the importation into Canada of dangerous diseases not presently covered by the act.

Chapter 98 (May 20, 1976) *An Act to amend the Anti-Inflation Act* requires that the Anti-Inflation Board refer to the administrator any increase in prices, profits, compensation or dividends under certain conditions; increases the range of optional orders that the administrator could make in compensation and dividend cases; permits members of the Tax Review Board to serve as members of the Anti-Inflation Appeal Tribunal; limits the cases in which payment to the Receiver General or provision of security precedes the hearing of an appeal; and requires the concurrence of the Senate in any motion to terminate the Anti-Inflation Act.

Chapter 99 (June 15, 1976) *An Act to amend the Senate and House of Commons Act and the Supplementary Retirement Benefits Act with respect to the escalation of certain payments thereunder* prescribes a delay until 1977 in the payment of the extra salaries and allowances over and above the sessional allowances, and delays until 1977 the escalation of the sessional allowances; and temporarily limits the supplementary retirement benefits payable to members of the Senate and the House of Commons.

Chapter 100 (June 15, 1976) *An Act to amend the Aeronautics Act* permits regulations to be made requiring foreign air carriers operating into or from airports in Canada to carry out a security program with respect to passengers and goods similar to the security program required to be carried out by Canadian air carriers.

Chapter 101 (June 15, 1976) *An Act to amend an Act to Repeal the Proprietary or Patent Medicine Act and to amend the Trade Marks Act* alters the expiry date of licences to sell proprietary or patent medicine, granted in the year 1976, from December 31, 1976 to March 31, 1977.

Chapter 102 (June 29, 1976) *Appropriation Act No. 3, 1976* grants certain sums of money for the public service for the financial year ending March 31, 1977.

Chapter 103 (June 29, 1976) *Appropriation Act No. 4, 1976* grants certain sums of money for the public service for the financial year ending March 31, 1977.

Chapter 104 (June 29, 1976) *An Act to implement conventions for the avoidance of double taxation with respect to income tax between Canada and France, Canada and Belgium and Canada and Israel.*

Chapter 105 (July 16, 1976) *An Act to amend the Criminal Code in relation to the punishment for murder and certain other serious offences* removes the death penalty from the Criminal Code in Canada in relation to the punishment for murder and certain other offences such as treason and high treason.

Chapter 106 (July 16, 1976) *An Act to amend the Income Tax Act* disallows deductions for the cost of advertising space in non-Canadian newspapers or periodicals directed primarily to a market in Canada and disallows deductions for an advertisement broadcast by a broadcasting undertaking located outside Canada and directed primarily to a market in Canada.

Chapter 107 (July 16, 1976) *An Act to amend the Medical Care Act* limits the annual increase in the per capita cost of all insured services for specified years pursuant to medical care insurance plans of participating provinces.

Chapter 108 (July 16, 1976) *Citizenship Act* replaces the Canadian Citizenship Act of 1947. Among other provisions, it shortens the length of residence in Canada prior to application for citizenship from five to three years; reduces the age of majority for purposes of citizenship from 21 to 18, and gives the same status to all applicants, eliminating the preferential status formerly accorded to British subjects.

Chapter 109 (July 16, 1976) *An Act to amend the Canadian Wheat Board Act (No. 2)* provides for the election of an advisory committee to assist the Wheat Board and provides for payment of allowances and expenses to its members.

Chapter 110 (December 13, 1974) *An Act respecting British Columbia Telephone Company* provides that the total authorized capital stock of the company shall be $250 million and provides for amendments which modify certain sections of the act.

Chapter 111 (February 27, 1975) *An Act respecting International Air Transport Association* authorizes the association to admit to its membership supplemental and charter carriers operating international air charters.

Chapter 112 (July 30, 1975) *An Act respecting The Royal Canadian Legion* amends its Act of Incorporation, including provision for giving wider authority to Dominion Command with respect to the relocation or suspension of charters and the disposition of Legion property and includes provision for the voluntary winding up of a branch or command.

Chapter 113 (July 30, 1975) *An Act to provide an exception from the general law relating to marriage in the case of Richard Fritz and Marianne Strass.*

Chapter 114 (July 30, 1975) *An Act to incorporate the Canadian Commercial and Industrial Bank* provides for its authorized capital stock to be $40 million and its head office to be at Vancouver, BC.

Chapter 115 (July 30, 1975) *An Act respecting Alliance Security and Investigation, Ltd.* revives the charter of the company.

Chapter 116 (December 20, 1975) *An Act to incorporate the Northland Bank* provides for its authorized capital stock to be $20 million and for its head office to be at Winnipeg, Man.

Chapter 117 (December 20, 1975) *An Act to enable The Eastern Canada Savings and Loan Company and Central & Nova Scotia Trust Company to amalgamate.*

Chapter 118 (June 15, 1976) *An Act respecting United Grain Growers Limited* increases the authorized capital of the company from $12 million to $25 million and provides authority for the declaration of revised dividend schedules.

Canadian chronology 1975 and 1976

Appendix 3

Events in the general chronology from 1497 to 1866 were published in the *1951 Canada Year Book*, pp 46-49; from 1867 to 1953 in the *1954 Canada Year Book*, pp 1259-1264; and annually from that year in successive editions. The following listing covers the years 1975 and 1976; it should be noted that certain dates are approximate. Acknowledgement is given to the publication *Canadian News Facts*, Toronto, which has served as a reference.

1975
January
Jan. 6, The Manitoba government announced a draft bill that would force legislators and senior provincial officials to disclose financial assets and business interests. *Jan. 8,* A Manitoba government working paper stated that restrictions on ownership of land by non-residents may be necessary to preserve the quality of life in rural Manitoba. *Jan. 10,* British Columbia Premier David Barrett proposed plans for an increase in the export price of natural gas from $1 to $1.35 a thousand cubic feet ($35.30 to $47.66 a km³) with $1.93 ($68.13 a km³) anticipated by the end of 1975, revenues to be shared by the three levels of government. *Jan. 13,* The Bank of Canada lowered its rate for loans to chartered banks to 8.25% from 8.75%. Several chartered banks lowered their prime rates from 11% to 10.5%. *Jan. 14,* Statistics Canada reported unemployment increased to 6.1% in December 1974, from 5.5% a month earlier, the highest rate in almost two years. The Canadian Transport Commission allowed increases in passenger rail fares by about 10% and 15% for Canadian National Railways and CP Rail respectively. The Canadian Egg Marketing Agency reported a national surplus of 40 million eggs in storage, increasing by about 15 million a week. Food continued to be the main reason for increases in the cost of living as prices rose through 1974 at the fastest rate in 26 years. *Jan. 17,* Defence Minister James Richardson announced creation of a separate Air Command in the Canadian Armed Forces and an 11.2% increase to $2.8 billion in the defence budget. *Jan. 20,* Beryl Plumptre, chairman of the Food Prices Review Board, said that food prices in Canada would continue to increase at a 15% annual rate at least until mid-year, largely because of increased production costs and consumer preference for convenience foods. *Jan. 22,* Prime Minister Trudeau announced the declaration of International Women's Year in the House of Commons. *Jan. 23,* Secretary of State Hugh Faulkner announced a government proposal to end tax concessions to Canadian companies advertising in Canadian editions of foreign-owned periodicals. Central Mortgage and Housing Corporation reduced its mortgage lending rate to 10.75% from 11.25%. External Affairs Minister Allan MacEachen had started talks with US authorities aimed at ending US inter-ference in Canadian trade in the wake of a sale of office furniture to Cuba by the Canadian subsidiary of a California-based company. *Jan. 25,* Death of Charlotte Whitton, 78, former social worker, journalist, and four times mayor of Ottawa. *Jan. 30,* Robert Welch, Ontario minister of culture and recreation, announced an Ontario lottery which could raise between $40 and $50 million a year for physical fitness, sports, recreation and cultural activities.

February
Feb.3, A green paper on immigration was tabled in the House of Commons. *Feb. 4,* An agreement was announced by the federal, Alberta and Ontario governments to invest $600 million in Syncrude Canada Ltd. for development of the Athabasca oil sands. *Feb. 6,* A five-part energy conservation program designed to cut national energy consumption by at least 2% in 1975 was outlined by Energy Minister Donald Macdonald. Secretary of State Hugh Faulkner announced Canada Council increases in grants to the performing arts to about $17.5 million in the new fiscal year, up 38% from $12.7 million. The Alberta government's 1975-76 budget called for a record expenditure of $2.439 billion, a surplus of $51 million and a 28% tax cut in Alberta's personal income tax which would make Albertans the lowest-taxed residents of Canada. *Feb. 10,* The regional economic expansion department announced federal government grants for 50% of the cost, up to $18 million, for an underwater electrical cable from New Brunswick to Prince Edward Island, the only province solely dependent on oil-fired thermal stations for its electric power. *Feb. 11,* Statistics Canada reported a steep rise in unemployment in Ontario and a jump in the national seasonally-adjusted unemployment rate to 6.7% in January from 6.1% in December. *Feb. 19,* Federal spending estimates totalling $28.242 billion for the 1975-76 fiscal year were tabled in the House of Commons. *Feb. 24,* An agreement in principle on freight rates, described as "a major breakthrough" for western Canada against transportation inequities, was announced jointly in Calgary by federal Transport Minister Jean Marchand and transport ministers from the western provinces. Barbara Frum, host of CBC radio's current affairs program *As It Happens,*

received the 1975 National Press Club award for outstanding contribution to Canadian journalism. *Feb. 25*, A trade surplus of $472 million for 1974 was Canada's lowest since 1966 and was one quarter of the $1.9 billion surplus for 1973, Statistics Canada reported. *Feb. 26*, A basically nutritious diet for a four-person family should cost $2,000 annually, but most families were spending $3,000, according to the Food Prices Review Board. Newfoundland's Premier Frank Moores said in a speech from the throne that the federal government should declare a fishing limit of 200 nautical miles (370 km). Transport Minister Jean Marchand resigned as Quebec leader of the federal Liberal party. *Feb. 28*, The House of Commons passed a bill granting the Northwest Territories a second member of Parliament. Premier David Barrett introduced the 1975-76 British Columbia budget indicating projected expenditures of $3.2 billion, an increase of 48.3% over estimated spending for 1974-75.

March

Mar. 3, In Yellowknife, Justice Thomas Berger of the British Columbia Supreme Court opened public hearings into environmental, social and economic implications of a proposed $7 billion, 2,600-mile (4 184 km) Mackenzie Valley gas pipeline. A working paper to settle Yukon Indian land claims was outlined in Whitehorse by Minister of Indian Affairs and Northern Development Judd Buchanan. *Mar. 6*, Social and medical community services, needed by most elderly people to ensure that they did not become isolated and neglected, were lacking in Canada, according to the Canadian Council on Social Development. *Mar. 11*, The Canadian Manufacturers' Association expressed the view that 1967 legislation giving public employees the right to strike "was an experiment that didn't work", and urged the government to rescind the right. *Mar. 12*, Finance Minister John Turner told the House of Commons that high wage settlements, running at roughly more than twice the rate of settlements in the United States, were "the most disturbing feature" of the current economic situation. In Ottawa 14 individuals and 13 companies were charged with conspiring to defraud the federal and Ontario governments and the Hamilton Harbour Commission of $4,052,000 between 1969 and 1973. *Mar. 15*, Prime Minister Trudeau returned to Ottawa from a 16-day European tour with support in principle for closer ties between Canada and the European Economic Community. *Mar. 21*, Mel Hurtig, Edmonton, said that Canadian high schools failed to teach the Canadian political system; in a national survey of 3,100 high school students, 62% failed in half the answers to a 40-question questionnaire. *Mar. 24*, Royal Assent was given to a bill making the beaver the official symbol of Canada. For the fifth consecutive year Anne Murray received the Canadian recording industry's Juno award as the top female artist. *Mar. 25*, Gross spending estimates totalling $8.195 billion for the 1975-76 fiscal year, a 13.1% increase over 1974-75, were tabled in the National Assembly in Quebec. *Mar. 26*, Premier Peter Lougheed's PC government received an overwhelming mandate in the Alberta provincial election, taking all but six of the 75 seats in the legislature. Ed Broadbent, parliamentary leader of the NDP, said that he would seek the federal NDP leadership. Labour Minister John Munro announced an increase in the federal minimum wage to $2.60 an hour on July 23 from $2.20. *Mar. 27*, Potato farmers in New Brunswick and Prince Edward Island, plagued by over-production and a depressed market, would have most of their losses covered by the federal government, Agriculture Minister Eugene Whelan announced.

April

Apr. 2, The CN Tower, tallest free-standing structure in the world at 1,815 ft 5 in. (553 m), was completed in Toronto. *Apr. 3*, A record $2.119 billion in unemployment insurance benefits was paid out in 1974, an increase of about 6% over 1973, Statistics Canada reported. *Apr. 4*, The minimum wage in Quebec would be increased to $2.60 an hour from $2.30 effective June 1, Premier Bourassa announced. With one death sentence before the federal Cabinet and seven others under appeal in the courts, Solicitor General Warren Allmand said he was more convinced than ever that capital punishment was not the answer to murder. *Apr. 8*, The national seasonally-adjusted unemployment rate jumped to 7.2% in March from 6.8% in February with the unemployment rate in central Canada the worst since 1961, Statistics Canada reported. Bell Canada president Jean de Grandpré told the annual shareholders meeting that Bell Canada must have rate increases or users of its telephone and other services would face "a deterioration of services". *Apr. 10*, Prime Minister Trudeau and the 10 provincial premiers failed to reach an agreement on the future domestic price for oil at a two-day first ministers' conference on energy in Ottawa. *Apr. 11*, Canada had a record deficit of $1.33 billion in automotive trade with the United States in 1974, more than triple the 1973 deficit of $440 million, Statistics Canada reported. Canada would give $280 million in food aid to the world's starving peoples in the 1975-76 fiscal year, an increase of 41.4% from the previous year, External Affairs Minister Allan MacEachen announced. Thomas Alexander Crerar, 98, senior privy councillor in Canada, died in Victoria, BC; he had served in the governments of Robert Borden and Mackenzie King. *Apr. 14*, Premier William Davis appointed an Ontario royal commission in Toronto to study the exploitation of violence in the communications industry, with former federal Liberal Cabinet Minister Judy LaMarsh as chairman. *Apr. 15*, The House of Commons miscellaneous estimates committee approved an amended version of the government's salaries bill that would increase immediately the incomes of members of Parliament by 33.33%. *Apr. 18*, A seven-week strike by 1,600 Ottawa public high school teachers ended with ratification of a contract giving an average 34% salary increase over a 20-month period and a monthly cost-of-living allowance starting Sept. 1. Secretary of State Hugh Faulkner introduced an amendment to the Income Tax Act that would eliminate tax concessions for Canadian businesses advertising on border television stations in the United States and in Canadian editions of foreign-owned publications, most notably *Time* and *Reader's Digest. Apr. 22,* Prime Minister Trudeau appointed a royal commission to be headed by Robert Bryce to inquire into the concentration of corporate power in Canada. *Apr. 24,* Ontario Hydro chairman Robert Taylor announced plans to increase bulk power rates by about 30% in 1976. *Apr. 30,* The House of Commons approved the Petroleum Administration Act granting the federal government power to set unilaterally the domestic price of oil and natural gas in the absence of an agreement with the producing provinces.

May
May 1, Immigration Minister Robert Andras said the federal government would bring 3,000 South Vietnamese refugees to Canada. The Ontario legislature gave final reading to two key election bills: the Redistribution Act adding eight seats to the 117-member legislature and the election financing bill limiting political party spending to a maximum of 50 cents a voter. *May 2,* Environment Minister Jeanne Sauvé announced approval of construction of a $900-million nuclear generating station in New Brunswick with the federal government paying 50%; expected to be finished by 1980, the plant would supply about 30% of New Brunswick's energy requirements. *May 5,* The price of natural gas exported to the United States would increase to $1.40 a thousand cubic feet ($49.42 a km³) Aug. 1 and to $1.60 ($56.48 a km³) Nov. 1 from the current price of $1.00 ($35.30 a km³), Energy Minister Donald Macdonald announced. *May 6,* The Report of the Royal Commission on Construction Union Freedoms in Quebec recommended that the provincial government immediately impose trusteeships on four major international construction unions affiliated with the Quebec Federation of Labour. *May 7,* In a policy statement approved by leaders of 60 unions, the Canadian Labour Congress rejected as inequitable the federal government's "working-paper" proposals for voluntary wage-and-price restraints to combat inflation. *May 12,* In the Ontario legislature Attorney General John Clement introduced the Family Law Reform Act, designed to "create a co-equal status for married men and women" and "to preserve individual legal rights within a marriage." *May 14,* The Quebec National Assembly gave second reading to two bills aimed at restoring order to the province's construction industry and based on the recommendations of the Cliche commission. *May 20,* The federal Cabinet ratified a National Energy Board decision to grant approval to Interprovincial Pipeline Ltd. for construction of a 520-mile (837 km) pipeline extension to Montreal from Sarnia, Ont. The right of a private citizen to challenge the movie censorship laws of a provincial government was upheld in a unanimous ruling of the Supreme Court of Canada. *May 21,* Federal Health Minister Marc Lalonde said charges would be laid against merchants selling tainted meat for human consumption after a Quebec police commission inquiry into organized crime had completed its investigation. *May 22,* A statement by the European Economic Community Commission in Brussels recommended that member governments open negotiations with Canada. Arthur Maloney, former PC member of Parliament and prominent Canadian criminal lawyer, was named Ontario's first ombudsman. *May 23,* A Quebec film directed by Michel Brault, *Les Ordres* was named co-winner of the award for best direction at the Cannes Film Festival. *May 27,* Unemployment insurance premiums for the first four months of 1975 were up almost 50% over the same period in 1974. *May 29,* The external affairs committee unanimously passed a resolution proposed by MPs from three parties authorizing an in-depth study of Canadian development aid to and economic and social relations with other countries. *May 30,* The House of Commons gave final approval to a bill that would increase the 102-seat Senate by two seats — one each for the Yukon Territory and Northwest Territories.

June
June 4, The New Brunswick Supreme Court overturned newspaper monopoly convictions of K.C. Irving Ltd. and three associated publishing companies. Escalating salary demands in the food industry, such as the 51% to 87% raise demanded by British Columbia retail food industry unions, would continue to push up food prices, said Beryl Plumptre, chairman of the Food Prices Review Board. *June 5,* Quebec Agriculture Minister Normand Toupin announced strict new meat inspection regulations. *June 10,* Federal Fisheries Minister Roméo LeBlanc announced stronger government action against countries violating fishing quotas in the North Atlantic. Dr. Marian Sherman, 84, a Victoria, BC gynaecologist and one of the first women fellows of the Royal College of Surgeons received the Humanist Association of Canada award. *June 11,* The NDP government of Premier Allan Blakeney was re-elected with a reduced majority in Saskatchewan; the PCs captured their first seats since 1964. Higher food prices and increased housing costs helped push the consumer price index up 0.8% in May, Statistics Canada reported. *June 13,* The governments of British Columbia and France would establish a joint committee to study common needs and production areas, Norbert Segard, France's external trade minister announced. The Alberta Energy Resources Conservation Board announced that the province's conventional crude oil reserves, making up the bulk of proven domestic oil supplies, declined by 255-million barrels (40.5 Mm³) in 1974 leaving less than 13 years' supply in the ground at

current rates of consumption. Total production of the economy dropped by 1.4% during the first three months of 1975, the worst quarterly decline in the GNP since it fell 1.5% in the first quarter of 1961, Statistics Canada reported. *June 16,* Transport Minister Jean Marchand unveiled a new federal transportation policy with proposed expenditures up to $45 billion over 15 years; the aim of making advanced transport systems pay their own way would mean rapidly rising travel and shipping costs to consumers. *June 17,* A Paris court ordered the French government to compensate Canadian David McTaggart for the deliberate ramming of his protest ship *Greenpeace III* by a French naval vessel in the South Pacific in June 1972. *June 18,* The Anglican Church of Canada accepted the ordination of women into the priesthood. *June 19,* The Petroleum Administration Act, giving the federal government the power to set oil and natural gas prices, was given Royal Assent. The World Conference on International Women's Year opened in Mexico City, with Canada's delegation chaired by Coline Campbell, MP, parliamentary secretary to the minister responsible for the Status of Women, Marc Lalonde. *June 20,* The United States Air Force would close its base at Goose Bay, Labrador, when the current three-year lease expired June 30, 1976, the federal ministry of transport announced. *June 24,* The general council of the Canadian Medical Association reaffirmed its position that the decision to perform a therapeutic abortion be left up to a woman's individual doctor. *June 25,* The Ontario Association of Police Chiefs recommended stricter federal gun controls including a mandatory three-year jail term for anyone using a gun in a crime. Beryl Plumptre, chairman of the Food Prices Review Board, urged the formulation of a long-term national food policy that would coordinate dozens of policies operating at provincial and federal government levels. *June 26,* A Prince Edward Island law forbidding non-residents from owning more than 10 acres (4 ha) of land was upheld unanimously by the Supreme Court of Canada.

July

July 3, The Canadian editions of *Time* and *Reader's Digest* would lose their special tax status Jan. 1, 1976, although legislation affecting them would be delayed, Secretary of State Hugh Faulkner said. (See Appendix 2, Chapter 106.) *July 5,* Joey Smallwood, former premier of Newfoundland, was elected in St. John's as leader of the newly formed Liberal Reform Party of Newfoundland and Labrador. *July 7,* Ed Broadbent, MP for Oshawa–Whitby and NDP parliamentary leader, was elected national leader of the NDP at the party's leadership convention in Winnipeg. Ontario Treasurer Darcy McKeough brought down a $178 million mini-budget aimed at stimulating the province's sagging automobile and housing industries. *July 9,* Canada and Iran signed agreements covering a record $1.3 billion-worth of business; Industry, Trade and Commerce Minister Alastair Gillespie said that figure could go to $2 billion or

higher. *July 10,* The Economic Council of Canada recommended that Canada vigorously pursue a free trade arrangement covering all countries. *July 16,* Rapidly dwindling natural gas supplies would require the government to reduce exports to United States markets and to restrain domestic consumption until new frontier supplies were available, Energy Minister Donald Macdonald said in the House of Commons. *July 17,* Manitoba's minimum wage for workers over 18 would rise to $2.60 an hour from $2.30 effective Oct. 1, Labour Minister A.R. Paulley announced. Prime Minister Trudeau sent congratulations to the leaders of the United States and the Soviet Union on the historic linkup of the Apollo and Soyuz spaceships. *July 18,* Government screening of new investment by foreign-owned businesses would begin Oct. 15 when the second part of the Foreign Investment Review Act became effective, Alastair Gillespie announced. *July 21,* A bill to create a federal human rights commission with powers to investigate and prevent discriminatory practices by businesses under federal jurisdiction was introduced by Justice Minister Otto Lang. *July 23,* Federal Fisheries Minister Roméo LeBlanc announced in the House of Commons that the Soviet Union's Atlantic fishing fleet would be barred from Canadian ports because the "Soviet fleet has consistently overfished certain quotas." Sophia Rayburn, 108, the oldest known native-born Canadian, died in Orangeville, Ont.; she was born only four days after Confederation.

August

Aug. 5, Secretary of State Hugh Faulkner announced that Famous Players Ltd. and Odeon Theatres Ltd. would invest $1.7 million in Canadian feature film production and show at least four weeks of Canadian-made movies in all their theatres. *Aug. 7,* At a news conference Prime Minister Trudeau said Canada would continue to press for an economic coastal zone of 200 nautical miles (370 km) through international agreement rather than unilateral declaration which could only be enforced by going to war. *Aug. 8,* Higher prices for food and fuel pushed the consumer price index up sharply by 1.4% during July, Statistics Canada reported. *Aug. 11,* United States Secretary of State Henry Kissinger said in Montreal that the US supported Canada's reluctance to declare unilaterally an offshore economic zone of 200 nautical miles (370 km). *Aug. 12,* The Food Prices Review Board recommended government study of health hazards due to levels of sugar consumption, averaging 100 pounds (45 kg) a person per annum, with a view to curbing sugar use if dangers were found. *Aug. 19,* Provincial health ministers urged a national conference on health and finance before the end of September to discuss the federal government's decision to cut back on medical care plan financing. In its fourth annual report, the Law Reform Commission of Canada called for an overhaul in the way Canadians handle their criminal justice system; it noted that Canadian criminal law was tougher than that of most other Western countries and that few countries made such extensive use of prison. *Aug. 22,* Canada's premiers declared their readiness to discuss wage and price controls and called for an immediate federal-provincial conference to consider cost-shared programs. *Aug. 24,* Premier Robert Bourassa said that any new Canadian constitution would have to give Quebec final say over culture, language, communications and immigration before his government would accept it. *Aug. 25,* Canada assured the UN it would stand by its commitment to hold the Habitat conference on housing and urban life in Vancouver in the summer of 1976 and that the PLO, with UN observer status, would be permitted to attend. *Aug. 26,* Industry, Trade and Commerce Minister Alastair Gillespie said that high wage demands could kill Canada's competitiveness on world markets and urged Canadian unions to display the kind of responsibility shown by unions in the US, the Federal Republic of Germany and Japan. *Aug. 28,* Although the number of students starting classes in the new school year would be down slightly, the cost of educating them would jump 15.5% to $12.2 billion, Statistics Canada reported.

September

Sept. 2, The Bank of Canada raised its lending rate to 9%, signalling a period of tight credit; this rate was the highest since a record 9.25% in 1974. *Sept. 3,* The Quebec Association of Protestant School Boards announced it would start legal action against Quebec's Official Languages Act in Quebec Superior Court, since the federal government had refused to act against the law at the association's request Feb. 17. *Sept. 9,* Statistics Canada reported the national seasonally-adjusted unemployment rate increased to 7.3% in August, the highest since it reached 7.4% in June 1961. *Sept. 10,* Indian Affairs Minister Judd Buchanan rejected the concept of a separate native government within the Northwest Territories. *Sept. 11,* The resignation from Cabinet of Finance Minister John Turner was announced in Ottawa. A working paper of the Law Reform Commission of Canada stated that divorce should be simplified by making marriage breakdown the sole grounds, and criticized the required three-to-five year separation period. *Sept. 12,* John M. Shaheen, president of Shaheen Natural Resources Inc., announced completion of financial arrangements for a major expansion of the oil refinery at Come-By-Chance, Nfld. A government study *Internal Migration and Immigrant Settlement* indicated a reversal of Maritimers' pattern of leaving their home provinces to seek work in other parts of the country. *Sept. 16,* The PC government of Premier Frank Moores returned to power in Newfoundland with a comfortable but reduced majority; former Premier Joey Smallwood was returned to the legislature after a four-year absence. *Sept. 18,* Ontario voters elected their first minority government in 30 years; the PC government won 51 of 125 seats, and the NDP narrowly replaced the Liberals as the official opposition. Former Prime Minister

John Diefenbaker turned 80, with celebrations in Ottawa and Saskatoon. *Sept. 22,* Federal energy officials warned that a developing coal shortage would likely last at least a decade before new mines could produce enough to meet growing demands. *Sept. 24,* The federal government was considering tough new measures to control illegal immigration, Immigration Minister Robert Andras said. *Sept. 25,* Transport Minister Jean Marchand announced that the federal government had halted development of the new Toronto international airport at Pickering, Ont. *Sept. 26,* Prime Minister Trudeau shuffled six senior ministers and added two backbenchers to the federal Cabinet, Jack (Bud) Cullen and Marcel Lessard. A controversy over the application of Quebec's Official Languages Act led to the sudden resignation of Quebec Education Minister Jérôme Choquette. *Sept. 30,* Ontario Health Minister Frank Miller said the Ontario government would send neurologists to Japan to consult with experts on mercury poisoning of people who ate contaminated fish.

October

Oct. 7, President Donald MacNeill of the Ontario Medical Association urged provincial doctors to withdraw from the Ontario Health Insurance Plan to strengthen the association's bargaining for fee increases of between 35% and 50%. Special legislation to force striking forest, railway, propane and food industry workers back on the job was passed in a seven-hour emergency session of the British Columbia legislature. *Oct. 9,* The rise in the cost of living slowed sharply during September after three successive months of strong increases totalling 4%. *Oct. 10,* The 22,000-member Canadian Union of Postal Workers voted on a request by its leaders for authority to call a strike; the union was seeking a 71% increase in a one-year contract. The Canadian Wheat Board announced a sale to the Soviet Union of wheat, oats and barley valued at between $80 million and $100 million. *Oct. 13,* Prime Minister Trudeau on national television announced an immediate three-year program of penalty-backed wage and price controls for a "powerful" segment of the economy and warned the controls could last until inflation was tempered. *Oct. 14,* Former Cabinet Minister Jean-Luc Pepin was appointed chairman of the new Anti-Inflation Board, and Beryl Plumptre, Food Prices Review Board chairman, was named his assistant. Statistics Canada reported that 7.2% of the labour force was unemployed in September, a drop of .01% from August. *Oct. 15,* Action 75+: National Conference of Decision-Makers organized by the International Women's Year Secretariat of the Privy Council Office considered such questions as equal opportunity for women employees in industry and how advertising and the media depicted women. *Oct. 21,* Canada's 22,000 inside postal workers went on strike. *Oct. 24,* A study of 78 major food processors and distributors, released by the Food Prices Review Board, concluded that food company profits did not make a significant contribution to increased food prices in 1974 and the first half of 1975. *Oct. 26,* The Commons gave second reading to legislation authorizing the government to move ahead with its anti-inflation program; the bill would allow the government to impose selective wage and price controls on about 4.3 million workers and 1,500 largest companies. *Oct. 28,* The new Anti-Inflation Board held its first meeting in Ottawa. The speech from the throne opening the Ontario legislature promised early legislation retroactive to July 30 to protect tenants against unjustified rent increases.

November

Nov. 1, Federal Social Credit Leader Réal Caouette told the party's national council that he had decided to resign the leadership although he would retain his seat. *Nov. 3,* Urban Affairs Minister Barney Danson announced a federal program to make low-and medium-cost housing available to more Canadians. *Nov. 5,* The government's plan to overhaul the unemployment insurance system was approved in principle by Parliament; higher premiums for both workers and employees and new restrictions to reduce benefits paid were proposed. Agriculture Minister Eugene Whelan announced that federal subsidies for the dairy industry would be reduced as part of a program to cut production. *Nov. 6,* A bill limiting rent increases to 8% and establishing rent review boards was introduced in the Ontario legislature. A report of the Senate-Commons committee on immigration suggested that Canada set an immigration quota and attempt to steer immigrants away from large urban areas. *Nov. 7,* Higher prices for housing and food pushed the consumer price index up 0.9% in October, Statistics Canada reported. *Nov. 9,* The national Liberal party policy convention ended in Ottawa with renewed endorsement of the leadership of Prime Minister Trudeau. *Nov. 12,* Saskatchewan Premier Allan Blakeney's NDP government announced it would move to acquire ownership of at least half, and possibly all, of the provincial potash industry. Metropolitan Toronto's 8,800 secondary school teachers went on strike, disrupting classes at 135 high schools. *Nov. 14,* Quebec's Solicitor General Fernand Lalonde announced the provincial government would take over complete control of financing and construction of the main stadium for the 1976 Olympic Games. *Nov. 18,* The Anti-Inflation Board, in its first official statement, said that salary increases would be exempt from the anti-inflation program if there was evidence they were set prior to Oct. 14. To conserve energy and reduce traffic accidents, the Ontario government introduced legislation for lower highway speed limits and mandatory seat-belt use. The Canadian Bankers' Association stated that Canada's 10 chartered banks welcomed competition from non-banking financial institutions, provided they were subject to the same costly regulations. *Nov. 23,* In the first Grey Cup game without a touchdown in 38 years, the Edmonton Eskimos edged the Montreal Alouettes 9-8 for the Canadian Football League

championship. *Nov. 26,* The CRTC ordered cable television companies to black out US television programs available simultaneously on local channels, following complaints by domestic broadcasters that they were losing audiences and advertising revenues. *Nov. 27,* Defence Minister James Richardson announced that Canada would spend almost $1 billion on a fleet of new patrol aircraft and between $80 million and $200 million on modern tanks for land forces in Europe. *Nov. 28,* Toronto's striking high school teachers were told that a contract offer by the Metropolitan Toronto School Board, which they had rejected, was too high and would have to be lowered to meet federal wage guidelines. By the purchase of Canadair Limited of Montreal, the federal government became owner of the bulk of the Canadian air industry.

December

Dec. 3, The federal government's anti-inflation bill received final approval in the Commons. *Dec. 4,* Death of Graham Ford Towers, 78, chief designer and builder of the Canadian central banking system. *Dec. 11,* An Anti-Inflation Board ruling that threatened the settlement of Canada's longest postal strike was overturned by the federal Cabinet on the basis that it was in the greater public interest to let the agreement stand. In British Columbia the Social Credit party led by William Bennett upset David Barrett's NDP government and Mr. Barrett was personally defeated. *Dec. 12,* The Department of External Affairs announced that Canada's participation in Middle East peacekeeping would be extended into 1976. *Dec. 13,* Fully bilingual air communications at Quebec airports would be phased progressively into use, Transport Minister Otto Lang announced in Montreal. *Dec. 14,* A new Quebec political party, the Parti National Populaire, headed by former Liberal Cabinet Minister Jérôme Choquette was formally launched. *Dec. 15,* At an annual agricultural outlook conference in Ottawa, Thomas Bolton, president of Dominion Stores Ltd., said that a 10% to 15% rise in food prices during 1976 seemed "a pretty good guess"; Statistics Canada forecast a sharp drop in farm incomes. *Dec. 18,* The federal government announced cuts in government spending plans by about $1.5 billion in the new fiscal year, trimming current program budgets by about $466 million, and the end of Information Canada, Company of Young Canadians and Opportunities for Youth. A proposed 23.8% wage increase for Canada's pulp and paper industry was rejected by the Anti-Inflation Board in favour of 14%. *Dec. 19,* Labour Minister John Munro announced an increase in the federal minimum wage to $2.90 an hour April 1, affecting about 20,300 workers in industries under federal jurisdiction. *Dec. 28,* Prime Minister Trudeau, in a CTV interview, said Canadian values, habits and institutions would be transformed by the government's anti-inflation program; he contended that the free market system did not work, necessitating government intervention into the decision-making power of economic groups. *Dec. 31,* Donald S. Tansley, senior vice-president of CIDA, was named administrator of the federal anti-inflation program. Transport Minister Otto Lang announced that a freeze protecting 6,283 miles (10 112 km) of Prairie rail lines from abandonment had been extended at least until the end of 1976.

1976
January
Jan. 1, Queen Elizabeth appointed former Prime Minister John Diefenbaker a Companion of Honour, an order limited to the sovereign and 65 members. *Jan. 7,* Death of Nathan Phillips, 83, mayor of Toronto from 1955 to 1962. *Jan. 8,* Federal Health Minister Marc Lalonde announced that six countries had agreed to participate in a Canadian invitational hockey tournament in September, with $455,000 in prize money. *Jan. 9,* Manitoba Health Minister Larry Desjardins said that there would be no more negotiations with provincial doctors; they could accept the government's latest fee increase offer or opt out of the medical insurance plan. *Jan. 13,* Statistics Canada reported the national seasonally-adjusted unemployment rate declined slightly in December; at 7.1% it marked the 10th consecutive month unemployment had stayed above the 7% level. Provincial Treasurer Darcy McKeough announced that Ontario had become the first province to sign an agreement with Ottawa placing its 400,000 public sector employees under the federal Anti-Inflation Board. *Jan. 14,* The 125 members of the Ontario legislature would receive more than $1.5 million to establish constituency offices, the speaker's office announced. The T. Eaton Co. announced closing of its catalogue sales operation after the catalogue branch lost $17 million in 1974 and at least as much in 1975. Eaton's catalogue had been a household institution in Canada since the first one was issued in 1884. *Jan. 15,* The rise in the cost of living slowed sharply during December, mainly as a result of lower food prices. Lieutenant Governor Pauline McGibbon opened a special session of the Ontario legislature called to end the two-month strike by 8,800 Metro Toronto secondary school teachers. *Jan. 16,* Paul Martin, high commissioner to Great Britain, and Gordon Robertson, secretary to the Cabinet for federal-provincial affairs, headed the list of 60 appointments to the Order of Canada. *Jan. 17,* Canada's $60-million communications technology satellite was launched at Cape Kennedy, marking the nation's most important advance in communications technology since the launching of Anik I in 1972. Toller Cranston of Toronto won his sixth straight senior men's title at the Canadian figure skating championships in London, Ont.; Lynn Nightingale of Ottawa won her third senior women's championship. *Jan. 23,* Under new rates announced by the Insurance Corp. of British Columbia, BC motorists would pay an average of 140% more for car insurance in 1976 than in 1975. *Jan. 25,* Dr. Stuart Smith, freshman member of the

Ontario legislature, was elected leader of the Ontario Liberal party, replacing Robert Nixon. *Jan. 26,* Julien Major, executive vice-president of the Canadian Labour Congress, said the congress had launched a three-point program requiring the cooperation of employers in a bid to topple the federal anti-inflation program. John Herbert received the 1975 Chalmers Canadian Play Award for *Fortune and Men's Eyes,* performed in more than 30 countries. *Jan. 28,* The Anti-Inflation Board announced about 6,500 companies had until Feb. 27 to file reports on prices, profits, dividends and pay scales as part of the check on cooperation with selective wage and price controls. The first session of Saskatchewan's 18th legislature ended with final approval of legislation authorizing the takeover of potash companies. *Jan. 29,* Transport Minister Otto Lang announced plans for a revitalized passenger train system by 1980, improving operations in the heavily-populated region between Quebec City and Windsor, Ont.

February
Feb. 2, Newfoundland and Prince Edward Island signed 18-month anti-inflation agreements with Ottawa, placing the provinces' public sector employees under control of the federal Anti-Inflation Board. The Ontario Economic Council said Canadians would have to sacrifice an increased standard of living to obtain more economic and cultural independence. *Feb. 3,* Prime Minister Trudeau returned to the Commons following an 11-day tour of Mexico, Cuba and Venezuela. The premiers of the three Maritime provinces ended two days of talks in Bridgewater, NS, concerning new federal transportation policies. *Feb. 4,* The appeals division of the Supreme Court of Nova Scotia ruled that the province does not have the right to censor motion pictures. This supported a challenge by Canadian Press reporter Gerard McNeill, who had filed a lawsuit in 1974 against banning *Last Tango in Paris* in Nova Scotia. *Feb. 6,* In an interim report, the Ontario Royal Commission on Violence in the Communications Industry said the majority of people who participated in public hearings demanded "that the communications industry clean up its act". *Feb. 10,* Statistics Canada reported that the national seasonally-adjusted unemployment rate dropped to 6.6% in January from 7.0% the previous month. *Feb. 11,* The Ontario Medical Association voted to accept an increase of 8.1% in Ontario Hospital Insurance Plan payments, effective May 1. *Feb. 12,* Former Finance Minister John Turner resigned his seat in the House of Commons, five months after his departure from the Cabinet. Manitoba's NDP government emphasized commitment to anti-inflation measures in the speech from the throne opening the 1976 session of the legislature. *Feb. 16,* Defence Minister James Richardson said there was a possibility that negotiations for 18 Lockheed Orion aircraft would collapse unless the US corporation overcame serious financial problems. *Feb. 17,* The Nova Scotia government said in its speech from the throne that it

would concentrate on low- or no-cost changes in existing social legislation. *Feb. 20,* Premier William Bennett asked the people of British Columbia for sacrifice and service in the face of an estimated $541-million budget deficit for the fiscal year. *Feb. 22,* Among 11 candidates at the Progressive Conservative leadership convention, Joe Clark, 36, won the national leadership in a close fourth-ballot victory. *Feb. 24,* The federal government introduced legislative measures dealing with alternatives to capital punishment, and the "peace and security" package aimed at curbing a sharp rise in violent and drug-related crimes in the past 10 years. *Feb. 25,* Manitoba's NDP government unveiled spending estimates for 1976-77 of $1.158 billion, an increase of 12.7% over the current year. *Feb. 27,* The Canadian Wheat Board announced an agreement with China for purchase of 35.4 million bushels (963 449 t) of Canadian wheat, reducing stocks on hand to the lowest level in 10 years.

March
Mar. 1, The Canadian Wheat Board announced higher initial grain payments for the new crop year and urged farmers to raise production. *Mar. 4,* The economy turned in its worst performance in 21 years during 1975, according to Statistics Canada. *Mar. 5,* The Bank of Canada announced an increase in its lending rate to 9.5% from 9%. Prime Minister Trudeau warned that the federal government might take unilateral action to patriate the British North America Act if the provinces could not agree. *Mar. 7,* Justice Minister Ron Basford told the Canadian Institute of Public Affairs that he would introduce legislation to give police, prosecutors and courts more discretion in handling cases that must go to trial, in a move aimed at unclogging the courts. *Mar. 8,* Finance Minister Donald Macdonald announced that 41,000 more companies, up from the original 10,000, had been placed under the federal wage and price controls program. *Mar. 9,* The throne speech opening the Ontario legislature promised efforts to provide able-bodied welfare recipients with jobs, aid to farmers, and an attack on the backlog of court cases. *Mar. 11,* The federal government asked the Supreme Court of Canada to rule on the constitutional validity of the anti-inflation legislation. *Mar. 12,* The oil refinery at Come-By-Chance, Nfld., built in 1973 was declared bankrupt in Newfoundland Supreme Court. *Mar. 16,* The speech from the throne in the Quebec legislature voiced Quebec's opposition to unilateral action by the federal government in bringing Canada's constitution from Great Britain; the government reiterated that it would press for federal help in covering the Olympic deficit. The New Brunswick budget limited the growth of spending, halted expansion of the civil service and offered no new programs. *Mar. 18,* Dr. John J. Deutsch, internationally-known economist, educationist and government advisor, died in Kingston. *Mar. 19,* The Alberta government called for spending restraints while stressing social improvements in a $2.961-billion budget. *Mar. 24,*

Saskatchewan's budget of "responsible restraint", totalling $1.328 billion, increased taxes on high incomes, gasoline and cigarettes. Slowing the annual increase in government spending was the main theme of the $9.745-billion budget tabled in the Quebec National Assembly. The Conference Board in Canada predicted that the increase in production would be slow and the jobless rate would continue to rise. *Mar. 25,* The Law Reform Commission of Canada recommended that Parliament carefully reconsider whether abortion, indecency, bigamy, incest, obscenity and gambling should remain under the Criminal Code. The commission noted that besides the 700 Criminal Code sections there were 20,000 federal offences and 20,000 under provincial law, making it impossible at times for a citizen to know he was breaking the law. *Mar. 26,* British Columbia's Social Credit government brought down a $3.6 billion budget with increased sales, income, corporation and cigarette taxes. Newfoundland's austere $1.25-billion budget called for increased taxes on gasoline, diesel fuel and corporations. *Mar. 29,* Crawley Films Ltd., Ottawa, won an Academy Award for *The man who skied down Everest,* a first for Canada for a feature-length film. *Mar. 30,* The federal government announced that selective immunization against swine influenza would be made available to about 12 million Canadians in the fall. *Mar. 31,* Keith Spicer, the Commissioner of Official Languages, recommended that the federal government phase out basic language teaching for public servants and concentrate instead on encouraging bilingualism in schools.

April
Apr. 1-2, With an expanded budget and a permanent board increased to nine members from five, the new Canadian Radio-television and Telecommunications Commission would have regulatory authority over all forms of broadcasting and telecommunications. At a federal-provincial conference in Ottawa, Finance Minister Donald Macdonald served notice that the federal government wanted to end its revenue guarantee program with the provinces and establish limits on equalization payments to seven have-not provinces. *Apr. 5,* Death of Dr. Wilder Penfield, internationally recognized neurosurgeon who pioneered explorations of the human brain. *Apr. 6,* In a $12.576 billion budget, the Ontario government reaffirmed its spending-restraint policy and raised taxes by $330 million. Chief Justice Jules Deschenes of the Quebec Superior Court ruled against a contention by 10 Protestant school boards that Quebec's Official Language Act was unconstitutional. *Apr. 8,* Nova Scotia became the eighth province to sign an anti-inflation agreement with Ottawa. *Apr. 9,* Prime Minister Trudeau tabled copies of a letter to provincial premiers setting out three possible ways of patriating the British North America Act. Senator Gratton O'Leary, former editor of *The Ottawa Journal,* died in Ottawa. Pauline Jewett, president of Simon Fraser University, was elected

president of the Canadian Research Institute for the Advancement of Women. *Apr. 12*, Two Quebec-based writers, Brian Moore and Anne Hébert, were winners of the Governor General's literary awards; both were also winners in 1960. *Apr. 13*, The March unemployment rate was 6.9%, down from 7% in February. *Apr. 14*, In Quebec summonses were served on 100 teachers' union locals after a 24-hour walkout by 90,000 teachers; 8,500 Hydro-Québec employees and 7,000 hospital workers also staged walkouts. *Apr. 15*, Cabinet gave final approval to Dome Petroleum Ltd. of Calgary to drill the first offshore wells in the Beaufort Sea. *Apr. 20*, The Commons approved legislation granting unions the right to appeal rulings of the Anti-Inflation Board. *Apr. 22*, Canadian National Railways announced expanded passenger service in the Ontario–Quebec corridor between Windsor and Quebec City. *Apr. 27*, Anti-inflation administrator Donald Tansley warned unions that his role as enforcer of the government's controls program might require him to set tougher limits on wage increases than those allowed by the Anti-Inflation Board. *Apr. 29*, Premier Frank Moores said that Newfoundland would not consider trading the headwaters of five rivers in Labrador to Quebec for extra energy from the Churchill Falls power station.

May
May 3, Parliament opened its fourth debate in 10 years on capital punishment with Solicitor General Warren Allmand defending his abolition bill. *May 4*, Ontario's minister of colleges and universities announced that fees for foreign students enrolling in a provincial university would be increased to $1,500 from $585 for a two-term academic year. *May 10*, Treasury Board President Jean Chrétien announced that the Olympic Lottery would be continued until 1979 to help reduce the deficit for the 1976 Olympic Games in Montreal. High schools in Windsor, Ont., were reopened for the first time since the end of March, following passage of a bill by the Ontario legislature May 7 ordering an end to the strike-lockout situation. *May 11*, Statistics Canada reported national unemployment jumped to 7.4% in April, its highest level in 15 years. Quebec's 1976-77 budget indicated sharp increases in taxes on tobacco and health insurance premiums, aimed at bringing in an additional $400 million. *May 13*, In a precedent-setting judgment the Alberta Supreme Court Appellate Division ruled that divorced women may claim financial support from their former husbands any time after the divorce. *May 14*, Six provincial government employees' associations merged to form the National Union of Provincial Government Employees, Canada's fifth largest union. Air traffic controllers were asked by their union leaders to reject a conciliation board report and authorize the union to call a nation-wide walkout; at issue was the use of French in air-ground communications in Quebec. *May 17*, Delegates to the Canadian Labour Congress national convention in Quebec City gave CLC executives authority "to organize and conduct

a general work stoppage" in their campaign against the federal anti-inflation program. *May 19*, Canada and the Soviet Union signed a treaty in Moscow ensuring Soviet recognition of a 200 nautical mile (370 km) fishing zone planned by the Canadian government. Jean Sutherland Boggs, director of the National Gallery of Canada resigned May 19, claiming the gallery had lost its autonomy since its incorporation into the National Museums in 1968. *May 21*, Postmaster General Bryce Mackasey announced a two-stage increase in first class letter rates commencing September 1, 1976 and March 1, 1977. *May 24*, Denise Pelletier, one of Quebec's leading actresses, died in Montreal. *May 25*, Federal Finance Minister Donald Macdonald presented budget measures to change eligibility rules for unemployment insurance benefit payments. *May 28*, William Ross Macdonald, former speaker of both the Commons and Senate and former lieutenant governor of Ontario, died in Brantford. *May 31*, A national strike by 2,200 air traffic controllers was averted, but a split remained in the controllers' union over the use of French in air-ground communications.

June
June 3, Quebec dairy farmers demonstrated on Parliament Hill against federal regulations cutting down subsidies and production quotas for industrial milk. David Barrett, British Columbia's former NDP premier, made a strong political comeback in a Vancouver East by-election. President Ford announced that Canada would join the United States and five other major industrialized nations in an economic summit conference June 27-28 in Puerto Rico. *June 4*, Canada would declare a 200 nautical mile (370 km) offshore fisheries jurisdiction later in 1976 to take effect Jan. 1, 1977, External Affairs Minister Allan MacEachen announced. *June 8*, The Berger inquiry into social and environmental effects of a Mackenzie Valley pipeline ended a month of informal hearings in 10 cities from Vancouver to Halifax. *June 9*, The Department of Manpower and Immigration indicated that immigration to Canada dropped by 14% in 1975 to 187,881. *June 10*, Energy Minister Alastair Gillespie announced an increase of 21% in the price of natural gas to the US. *June 11*, The National Energy Board announced a cut of 12% in oil exports to the US. A sudden rise in food prices in May including a 12.4% increase in the cost of beef led to the sharpest one-month jump in the cost of living in six months. The United Nations Habitat conference on human settlements ended in Vancouver with bitter expressions of regret over divisive political disagreements. Beryl Plumptre announced her resignation as vice-chairman of the Anti-Inflation Board. *June 15*, A federal-provincial economic conference ended in disagreement after the federal government announced it would abolish a multi-million dollar program of transfer payments to the provinces when it expired March 31, 1977. *June 16*, Prime Minister Trudeau in a brief visit to Washington assured President Ford that Canada

remained committed to its anti-submarine program and presented the president with *Between Friends — Entre Amis*, a book commissioned by Canada to mark the US Bicentennial. *Woodland Waterfall* by Tom Thomson was acquired for the McMichael Canadian Collection for $85,000, reportedly the highest price ever paid for a Canadian painting. *June 21*, Alberta announced changes in coal royalties replacing 10 cents a ton (11 cents a tonne) by a formula that could increase royalties on high-grade coal to as much as $9 a ton ($9.92 a tonne). *June 22*, A team of doctors recommended that the Ontario government prohibit the eating of fish from the mercury-polluted Wabigoon–English River system in northwestern Ontario. *June 24*, In a unanimous decision overturning a 1974 ruling that had denied Helen Marie Rathwell any interest in the farm she and her husband worked for 21 years, the Saskatchewan Court of Appeal awarded the appellant a half interest in the farm land and ordered her former husband to pay trial and appeal costs. *June 29*, After a nine days' work stoppage, air traffic returned to normal following an agreement between the federal government, airline pilots and air traffic controllers. *June 30*, Environment Minister Jean Marchand resigned from the Cabinet. In a 3-2 decision, the British Columbia Court of Appeal ruled that the province owns the lands, including mineral and other resources, on the bottom of the sea between Vancouver Island and the BC mainland, rejecting federal claims. In Regina, death of W.J. Patterson, 90, former premier and lieutenant governor of Saskatchewan.

July

July 7, Canada signed an agreement with the European Economic Community pledging both sides to commercial and economic cooperation. *July 12*, In a 7-2 vote, the Supreme Court of Canada ruled that the Anti-Inflation Act was constitutional. Federal Energy Minister Alastair Gillespie warned that Ottawa would use legislation if necessary to get power to markets from the proposed Lower Churchill River development in Labrador. *July 13*, Unemployment eased during June to 7.0%, from 7.1% in May, Statistics Canada reported. *July 14*, The longest session in Canadian parliamentary history recessed with passage of a bill to abolish capital punishment. Statistics Canada reported the lowest 12-month increase in the consumer price index in nearly three years. *July 16*, The bill stripping foreign publishers and broadcasters of preferential advertising tax status became law. *July 17*, Queen Elizabeth officially opened the 1976 Summer Olympic Games in Montreal. Angelina Berthiaume-Du Tremblay, philanthropist and former president of *La Presse*, died in Montreal. *July 20*, The Law Reform Commission recommended that the Immigration Appeal Board should be changed from a court-like agency to an informal tribunal concerned with common-sense solutions to immigration problems. *July 21*, Canada's Armed Forces would receive new long-range patrol aircraft under a $1-billion contract signed with Lockheed

Aircraft Corp. *July 26*, A National Revenue department survey reported the highest average incomes in Canada in 1974 in the northern Quebec iron-ore town of Sept-Îles, at $12,592; Sydney–Glace Bay, NS, was lowest at $8,331. Dr. Henrietta Banting, widow of the discoverer of insulin, died in Toronto; Lady Banting was director of the cancer detection centre at Women's College Hospital in Toronto from 1959 to 1971. *July 31*, The 1976 Summer Olympic Games ended, at $1.5 billion the most expensive Olympic Games in history. Canada's Olympic team won five silver and six bronze medals.

August

Aug. 2, The OECD predicted that Canada's GNP would increase by at least 5% in 1976 and possibly 5.5% during the 12 months between mid-1976 and mid-1977. *Aug. 4*, Lord Thomson of Fleet, 82, publisher of more than 200 daily newspapers, died in London. *Aug. 5*, Federal Agriculture Minister Eugene Whelan announced an easing of monthly quotas on industrial milk production and a reduction in penalties levied on farmers who overproduce. *Aug. 9*, Air Canada announced a record loss of $47.5 million in the first six months of 1976. *Aug. 12*, The CLC announced that Oct. 14 would be a "national day of protest" against Ottawa's anti-inflation program. The Saskatchewan government announced it had purchased the potash mining operation of the Duval Corp. near Saskatoon for US$128.5 million. R. Howard Webster, chairman of Toronto's fledgling American League baseball team said that the team would be known as the Blue Jays. An exhibition of 42 internationally-acclaimed paintings from the Hermitage and the State Russian Museum in Leningrad opened at the Winnipeg Art Gallery. *Aug. 19*, In its final report the Ontario Royal Commission on Petroleum Products Pricing called on Ontario, as a major user of energy in Canada, to use its influence to achieve a national oil policy. The Science Council of Canada recommended that Canada stop its cities from using up valuable farm land and begin closing its doors to immigrants if Canadians wanted to maintain their standard of living. *Aug. 20*, The 17th annual premiers' conference ended without agreement on patriating Canada's constitution; opposition was reinforced to Ottawa's plan to end its system of revenue guarantees. Ontario Agriculture Minister William Newman announced that the Ontario government intended to make agricultural land tax-exempt by 1978. *Aug. 24*, Bank of Canada Governor Gerald Bouey announced that targets for the growth of money supply had been lowered to between 8% and 12% annually in a move aimed at gradually reducing inflation. *Aug. 30*, In the first case in which a provincial agency was asked to pay for violating wage and price controls, Donald Tansley, administrator of the Anti-Inflation Act, ordered the Manitoba Liquor Commission to pay $300,000 to the federal government. A delegation of 17 Chinese government officials and doctors attended the official opening of the restored birthplace of Dr. Norman Bethune in Gravenhurst, Ont. *Aug. 31*, Statistics Canada reported that Canada had 295.2 million bushels (8 034 183 t) of wheat in storage when the crop year ended July 31, far below the average stockpile of about 587.4 million bushels (15 986 719 t).

September

Sept. 7, Finance Minister Donald Macdonald announced changes in the federal anti-inflation program aimed at lightening the burden on business; he warned that it would take time to bring inflation under control, and that pay controls would be tightened in 1977. Statistics Canada reported that education expenditures increased by 305% between 1962 and 1973, and that education costs would continue to rise despite falling enrolments. *Sept. 8*, Winnipeg economist June Menzies took up her new appointment as vice-chairman of the federal Anti-Inflation Board. *Sept. 9*, New Canada Savings Bonds would have a nine-year term with an average yield of 9.13%, Finance Minister Donald Macdonald announced. *Sept. 14*, Prime Minister Trudeau brought seven new ministers into his Cabinet and rearranged the responsibilities of nine others; three long-time ministers resigned: Mitchell Sharp, C.M. Drury and Bryce Mackasey. *Sept. 15*, Team Canada, a lineup of North American professionals, won the first Canada Cup international hockey tournament in Montreal with a 5-4 overtime victory over Czechoslovakia. *Sept. 16*, The Economic Council of Canada urged the federal government to introduce flexible rules that would promote increased competition and efficiency in the banking system. The third annual report of the BC Police Commission showed that the province had the worst crime rate in Canada despite increases in RCMP and municipal police forces. *Sept. 18*, Dr. Henry Morgentaler was acquitted by a jury for the third time on a charge of performing an illegal abortion. *Sept. 21*, In its annual report the federal Advisory Council on the Status of Women estimated that 60% of the recommendations made by the Royal Commission on the Status of Women in 1973 had still not been implemented. *Sept. 23*, A resolution was passed at the 22nd annual convention of the National Pensioners and Senior Citizens Federation to ask the federal government to set up a department of pensioners affairs. The International Energy Agency, a 19-country organization of non-communist industrialized countries, accused Canadians and Americans of wasting valuable energy resources because of relatively cheap fuel prices. *Sept. 24*, John Angus MacLean, a 25-year veteran of the House of Commons and one-time federal fisheries minister, was elected leader of the PC party of PEI. *Sept. 27*, The Anti-Inflation Board announced new regulations that more than doubled the number of firms required to notify the board of price changes before they take effect. External Affairs Minister Don Jamieson said that Canada finds repugnant and totally unacceptable Arab-boycott-of-Israel measures that can affect Canadian business.

October

Oct. 2, Canada's 10 provincial premiers again failed to reach a consensus on the question of an amending formula for the BNA Act. Prime Minister Trudeau told a partisan audience in Toronto that Canada is in danger of breaking up over bilingualism unless the Liberals make major new efforts to rebuild the party outside Quebec. *Oct. 5*, The Supreme Court of Canada ruled that the death penalty is not a cruel and unusual penalty within the meaning of the Canadian Bill of Rights. *Oct. 6*, The Ontario government announced a new high school curriculum policy in response to growing public demand for more rigid standards in the province's schools. *Oct. 7*, The inflation rate rose by 0.5% to 6.5% in September as consumers began to feel the impact of higher prices for fuel oil and gasoline, Statistics Canada reported. *Oct. 8*, The Alberta Supreme Court awarded Irene Murdoch, symbol to the cause of women's rights, a $65,000 divorce payment as half-interest in her estranged husband's ranch. *Oct. 13*, Defence Minister James Richardson became the fourth member of the federal cabinet to resign within a month. *Oct. 14*, The Canadian Labour Congress estimated that over 1 million workers participated in its day of protest against federal wage and price controls. *Oct. 15*, Ottawa announced the signing of a $184-million contract for 128 West German tanks with deliveries beginning in July 1978. *Oct. 21*, Manpower Minister Bud Cullen announced government plans for $350 million worth of job-creation programs, described as the first stage of a five-year plan. *Oct. 22*, The Anti-Inflation Board claimed victory in holding the rate of inflation to 8% during the first year of wage and price controls. *Oct. 25*, The Indian Brotherhood of the Northwest Territories proposed an Indian government with status similar to that of a province for the west side of the Northwest Territories. *Oct. 26*, Prime Minister Trudeau returned to Ottawa following a six-day official visit to Japan. The federal government appointed 13 MPs to an all-party Commons sub-committee authorized to conduct a country-wide investigation of prisons and their problems. *Oct. 27*, The federal government introduced legislation that would give consumers more protection against unfair interest rates and give police new mechanisms to curtail loansharking. *Oct. 29*, Industry Minister Jean Chrétien announced that federally-owned Canadair Ltd. has been authorized to go ahead with a jet-building program that will create 3,000 new jobs and result in $1 billion in exports.

November

Nov. 1, The Canadian Wheat Board announced that the Japanese government food agency had agreed to purchase 1.4 million metric tons of wheat and 900 000 t of barley from Canada during 1977. *Nov. 2*, Pierre Juneau, former chairman of the CRTC and former Minister of Communications, was appointed chairman of the National Capital Commission. *Nov. 9*, The unemployment rate for

October reached 7.6%, the highest seasonally-adjusted rate since May 1961, Statistics Canada reported. *Nov. 12,* Sandy Hawley, 27-year-old jockey from Mississauga, Ont., broke thoroughbred racing's all-time money-winning record for one year with total purse winnings of $4,255,912. *Nov. 13,* Former Newfoundland Premier Joey Smallwood and two other members of the Liberal Reform Party accepted an invitation to join the provincial Liberal party. *Nov. 15,* The Parti Québécois, committed to the concept of Quebec independence, was victorious by a wide margin in Quebec's election. *Nov. 19,* The Berger Commission completed 20 months of hearings on a northern natural gas pipeline, still no closer to a consensus on the future of the North. Federal money managers moved to stimulate economic activity by lowering the Bank of Canada lending rate to 9% from a record 9.5%. *Nov. 24,* Prime Minister Trudeau appealed to Canadians on television to face the question of whether the country can remain united after the electoral victory of the Parti Québécois. Immigration Minister Bud Cullen introduced a new immigration act which would allow the setting of immigration levels and the directing of immigrants away from crowded cities. The Canadian Wheat Board announced a proposed sale to Poland of between 750 000 and 1.2 million metric tons of wheat, barley and oats over the next three years. *Nov. 25,* Dr. Harry Parrott, Ontario Minister of Colleges and Universities, announced that Ontario university tuition fees would be increased by $100 during the 1977-78 academic year. *Nov. 26,* Premier René Lévesque announced the formation of five super ministries to form the core of a 24-member cabinet. *Nov. 28,* The Ottawa Rough Riders scored a 23-20 victory over the Saskatchewan Roughriders in the annual Grey Cup football classic. *Nov. 30,* The Commons public accounts committee began examination of how Crown corporations handle their overseas business.

December

Dec. 5, Four Canadian women were selected as Rhodes scholars, the first female students among the 11 Canadians annually named for the awards.

Dec. 9, Government House announced that Prince Andrew, second in succession to the British throne, would attend Lakefield College School near Peterborough, Ont., for two terms commencing Jan. 6. *Dec. 10,* The Parti Québécois government dropped all remaining charges against Dr. Henry Morgentaler, ending almost seven years of legal battles for the Montreal doctor. *Dec. 13,* Fisheries Minister Roméo LeBlanc said the International Commission for the Northwest Atlantic Fisheries agreed to accept Canada's 200-mile (370 km) limit that would go into effect Jan. 1. *Dec. 14,* Canada's 10 provincial premiers left Ottawa following a two-day federal-provincial conference on tax and revenue-sharing with $680 million in additional taxing power and grants; they expressed general dissatisfaction with the new five-year formula on financial arrangements. *Dec. 16,* Following a proposal by his special adviser on communications, Prime Minister Trudeau decided to hold weekly formal press conferences to be free from impromptu daily contacts with parliamentary reporters. Health and Welfare Minister Marc Lalonde advised the provinces to suspend swine flu immunization for the time being. Death in Ottawa of Réal Caouette, 59, former leader of the national Social Credit party. *Dec. 17,* David Lewis, former leader of the New Democratic Party, and Dr. David Suzuki, professor of zoology at the University of British Columbia, were among 64 appointed companions of the Order of Canada. *Dec. 20,* Northwest Territories Indians lost an appeal for the right to file a caveat to land in the Mackenzie River Valley. Dr. Hsio-Yen Shih, an official of the Royal Ontario Museum, was appointed director of the National Gallery of Canada. *Dec. 21,* A reduction to 8.5% in the Bank of Canada lending rate indicated an easing of mortgage and bank loan interest rates. *Dec. 22,* External Affairs Minister Don Jamieson announced tightening of nuclear export safeguards policy by requiring future buyers to accept controls on their entire nuclear program. Death in Ottawa of Olive Evangeline Diefenbaker, wife of John Diefenbaker, former prime minister. *Dec. 23,* Prime Minister Trudeau said that most of the initiative to keep Quebec in Confederation must come from Canadians in other provinces.

Canadian honours   Appendix 4

An exclusively Canadian honours system was introduced in 1967 with the establishment of the Order of Canada. The honours system was enlarged in 1972 with the addition of the Order of Military Merit and three decorations to be awarded in recognition of acts of bravery.

The Order of Canada, instituted on July 1, 1967, the 100th anniversary of Confederation, is designed to honour Canadians for outstanding achievement and service to their country or to humanity at large. Originally, two levels of membership were provided: Companions of the Order and recipients of the Medal of Service. The Order was revised in 1972 and now comprises three categories of membership: Companions, Officers — which includes all those who received the Medal of Service — and Members. The last category is intended especially to recognize service in a locality or in a particular field of activity. Not more than 15 persons may be appointed in any one year as Companions and the total number of Companions is not to exceed 150. Officers of the Order may be appointed to the number of 40 persons a year and up to 80 persons may be appointed yearly as Members of the Order.

All Members of the Order are entitled to have letters placed after their names as follows: for the Companion CC, for the Officer OC and for the Member CM.

Her Majesty The Queen is Sovereign of the Order and the Governor General holds office as Chancellor and Principal Companion. Appointments to the Order are made, with the approval of the Sovereign, by the Governor General assisted by an Advisory Council which meets twice a year under the chairmanship of the Chief Justice of Canada. Members of the Advisory Council include the Clerk of the Privy Council, the Under-Secretary of State, the Chairman of the Canada Council, the President of the Royal Society of Canada, the President of the Association of Universities and Colleges of Canada and not more than two other members who may be appointed by the Governor General from among members of the Order.

While Canadians are the primary recipients of the Order, the constitution provides that persons who are not Canadian citizens and whom Canada desires to honour may be appointed as honorary members at any of the three levels of membership.

The Order of Military Merit has been established to provide a means of recognizing conspicuous merit and exceptional service by members of the Canadian Armed Forces, both Regular and Reserve. The Order has three levels of membership: Commander (CMM), Officer (OMM) and Member (MMM).

The Queen is the Sovereign of the Order and the Governor General is the Chancellor as well as a Commander of the Order. The Chief of the Defence Staff is the Principal Commander of the Order. Appointments to the Order are made by the Governor General on the recommendation of the Minister of National Defence; nominations are made by the Chief of the Defence Staff who is assisted by an advisory committee for the Order.

The number of appointments made annually will vary, depending on the number of nominations submitted and approved. The Order's constitution stipulates, however, that the total number of appointments made annually will not exceed one tenth of one per cent of the Forces' average strength. Members of foreign armed forces who render particularly meritorious service to Canada or the Canadian Armed Forces in the course of their military duties may be made honorary members of the Order at any of the three levels.

Canadian bravery decorations. A Medal of Courage was included in the Order of Canada in 1967 but it was found that a single medal would not serve to recognize in an equitable manner acts of bravery which entail varying degrees of risk. Consequently, no awards were made and the medal has now been superseded by a series of three decorations: the Cross of Valour (CV), the Star of Courage (SC) and the Medal of Bravery (MB). Instances of extraordinary heroism in circumstances of extreme peril will be marked with the award of the Cross of Valour; other outstandingly courageous actions may qualify for the award of the Star of Courage or the Medal of Bravery. The bravery decorations are awarded with the approval of the Sovereign by the Governor General on the advice of the Canadian Decorations Advisory Committee. They may be awarded to civilians, members of the Canadian Armed Forces and of the protective services, and may be awarded posthumously.

Honours and decorations announced in 1975 and 1976 and the dates of appointment of their recipients are as follows.

ORDER OF CANADA
Appointed June 25, 1975
Companions

M. Jean Gascon, CC (Appointed OC July 6, 1967, elevated to CC)

M. William Henry Gauvin, CC
Dr. A. Edgar Ritchie, CC

Officers

M. Lionel Boulet, OC
Mlle Edith Butler, OC
M. Jochem Carton, OC
Mme Solange Chaput-Rolland, OC
Dr. W.A.C.H. Dobson, OC
Mr. Robert H. Fowler, OC
Miss Sylva Gelber, OC
Dr. John Morgan Gray, OC, MBE
Dr. J. Russell Harper, OC
Dr. Elmer Iseler, OC
M. Pierre Juneau, OC
Miss Anne Murray, OC
Mr. Eric McLean, OC
M. le docteur Louis Poirier, OC, MD
Mr. Carl A. Pollock, OC
Miss Veronica Tennant, OC
M. Yves Thériault, OC
Mr. Maxwell William Ward, OC
Dr. Karel Wiesner, OC
Mrs. Mozah Zemans, OC

Members

Dr. Nancy Adams, CM
M. Guy Beaulne, CM
M. Maurice J. Bourgault, CM
Mrs. Maryon Brechin, CM
Mrs. Juliette Cavazzi, CM
M. Roger Champoux, CM
Dr. Rae Chittick, CM
Mrs. Martha Cohen, CM
Mr. William Davies, CM
Dr. Hugh A. Dempsey, CM
Mlle Hayda Denault, CM
Mr. Edmund J. Desjardins, CM
Mr. Clyde Gilmour, CM
Mrs. Agnes C. Higgins, CM
Mrs. Alma Houston, CM
M. Fred P. Hudon, CM
Mr. Ronald A. Irwin, CM
Mrs. Lori Johnson, CM
Dr. Percival Johnson, CM, MD
Dr. Wilfred Johnston, CM, DDS
Miss Jane Mallett, CM
Dr. Harding P. Moffatt, CM
Mr. Eric W. Morse, CM
Dr. Frederick G. McCrimmon, CM, MD
Lieutenant-Colonel Frank F. McEachern, CM,
    ED, CD
M. Rodolphe Pagé, CM
M. Phrixos B. Papachristidis, CM
Dr. Vera Peters, CM, MD
Mrs. Eallien L. Robinson, CM
M. Charles Roy, CM (deceased: July 2, 1975)
Mrs. Susan Rubes, CM
Mr. Ignatius A. Rumboldt, CM
Mr. Gus Ryder, CM
Mr. John C. Turnbull, DFC, CM
Mr. Alexander Walton, CM
Mr. J. Kenneth Watson, CM
Dr. Ronald Way, CM
Mr. Ben Weider, CM
Mrs. Pearl B. Whitehead, CM

Appointed January 14, 1976

Companions

The Honourable Paul Martin, PC, CC
Mr. R. Gordon Robertson, CC

Officers

Mr. R.W. Begg, OC, ED, CD
Dr. Helen R. Belyea, OC
The Honourable William A.C. Bennett, PC, OC
Mr. Jack Bush, OC
M. Pierre Camu, OC
Brigadier-général Jean-Paul Carrière, OC, ED,
    CD
M. Jean-Charles Falardeau, OC
The Honourable Muriel McQueen Fergusson,
    PC, OC, QC
Dr. Jacob Finkelman, OC, QC
Dr. Rudolph R. Haering, OC
M. Louis Hébert, OC
M. N. Matessco Matte, OC, QC
Dr. William T. Mustard, OC, MBE
Mr. Jack McClelland, OC
Dr. James C. Reaney, OC
Monsignor Hugh J. Somers, OC
M. Claude Tousignant, OC
M. Arthur Tremblay, OC
Dr. Herbert W. Whittaker, OC

Members

Mr. Alfred Billes, CM
M. Pierre Côté, CM
Dr. Helen Creighton, CM
Mlle Sylvia Daoust, CM
Mrs. Catherine Doherty, CM
Colonel F. Gérard Dufresne, CM, ED, CD
Dr. J. Alexander Edmison, CM, QC
M. Gérard Forest, CM
M. Roland Galarneau, CM
Dr. George W. Govier, CM
Brigadier-General Keith R. Greenaway, CM, CD
Miss Donna Marie Gurr, CM
Mr. Desmond Sandford Hawley, CM
Dr. Donald G. Hodd, CM
Mr. A. Bernie Hodgetts, CM
Mr. William Kurelek, CM
Mrs. Jean B. Lumb, CM
Mrs. Elaine R. May, CM
M. François Mercier, CM, QC
Le Révérend Père Auguste-M. Morisset, CM
Dr. John A. MacDonell, CM
Dr. Joseph B. MacInnis, CM
Mr. Kenneth McLean, CM
Mr. Brian N. Orvis, CM
Mr. Charles D. Ovans, CM
Mr. Alton C. Parker, CM
Mr. Arthur P. Pascal, CM
Mr. Welland W. Phipps, CM
Dr. Otto Schaefer, CM
Mr. Elijah E. Smith, CM
Dr. Isabella Stevens, CM
Frère Côme St-Germain, CM
Mlle Juliette St-Pierre, CM
Mrs. Judith Tethong, CM
Dr. Mabel Timlin, CM

Captain Gordon H. Warren, CM
Mrs. Lucille Wheeler-Vaughan, CM
Mr. Peter Wing, CM
Dr. Milton Wittick, CM

Appointed June 23, 1976

Companions
The Honourable Walter L. Gordon, CC, PC
Dr. Helen S. Hogg, CC "elevated"
M. Laurent Picard, CC

Officers
M. Michel F. Bélanger, OC
Mr. John J. Bladen, OC
Mr. John J. Carson, OC
Dr. R. Keith Downey, OC
Dr. Henry E. Duckworth, OC
Mr. Claude Edwards, OC
M. Jean-Paul Gignac, OC
Miss Karen Kain, OC
Mr. James Stuart Keate, OC
Dr. Allen T. Lambert, OC
Dr. Irving Layton, OC
M. Napoléon M. Leblanc, OC
Dr. Heinz E. Lehmann, OC, MD
M. Séraphin Marion, OC
The Very Reverend A.B.B. Moore, OC
Dr. Malcolm Ross, OC
Mme Mariette Rousseau-Vermette, OC
M. Adélard M. Savoie, OC
Commissioner James Smith, OC
Dr. Erich W. Vogt, OC
General Clarence Dexter Wiseman, OC

Members
Dr. John B. Angel, CM
M. A. Emile Beauvais, CM
Dr. Clarence M. Bethune, MBE, CM, MD
M. Solomon Marcien Bonneau, CM, QC
Mrs. Mary Bradley, CM
M. Louis Charbonneau, CM
Mrs. Irene Clarke, CM
Le Révérend Père Wilfrid Corbeil, CM
Mrs. Mabel Margaret Crosland, CM
Mr. Richard MacDowell Dumbrille, CM
Dr. Ferdinand Eckhardt, CM
Mlle Suzanne Eon, CM
Miss Edith A. Ferguson, CM
Miss Violet Amy Gillett, CM
Mr. Myer Murray Goldstein, CM
M. le docteur Valère Emile Groleau, CM, MD
Mme Georgette D. Guay, CM
Mrs. Anne Heggtveit-Hamilton, CM
Dr. Godfrey Hewitt, CM
Mr. William MacDougall Hogg, CM
Lieutenant-Colonel Alan Innes-Taylor, CM
M. le docteur Albert Jutras, CM, MD
Dr. James Roby Kidd, CM
Brother Frederick Leach, CM
Dr. Salvatore Mancuso, CM, MD
Mr. Rufus Ezra Moody, CM
Dr. Sean Murphy, CM, MD
Mrs. Emily Ostapchuk, CM
Mr. Hugh Edward Pearson, CM, MC

Mr. Isidore Constantine Pollack, CM
Mr. John Brabant Ridley, CM
Frère Ernest Rocheleau, CM
Mr. Samuel Sniderman, CM
Dr. Allan Van Cleave, CM
Mr. John J. Verigin, CM
Mr. A. Leslie Vipond, CM
Captain Richard P. White, OBE, CM, VRD
Mr. Moncrieff Williamson, CM
Mr. Lars Willumsen, CM
Mrs. Marjorie Wood, CM
Mr. John Yesno, CM

Appointed December 15, 1976

Companions
Mr. David Lewis, CC, QC
M. C.O. Roger Rousseau, CC

Officers
The Honourable John Black Aird, OC, QC
Mr. Louis Applebaum, OC
Dr. G. Malcolm Brown, OC, CD, MD
Dr. Maxwell Cohen, OC, QC
Miss Isobel Moira Dunbar, OC
M. le professeur Pierre Grenier, OC
Dr. Harry Gordon Johnson, OC
Mr. J. Fenwick Lansdowne, OC
Dr. C. Brough Macpherson, OC
Mlle Antonine Maillet, OC
Me François Mercier, OC "elevated"
Dr. J.G. Prentice, OC
Dr. William George Schneider, OC
Dr. Léonard H. Shebeski, OC
Dr. George F.G. Stanley, OC
Dr. Maurice F. Strong, OC
Dr. David T. Suzuki, OC
Dr. Thomas H.B. Symons, OC
Mr. James Worrall, OC, QC

Members
Mrs. Frances M. Adaskin, CM
Miss Estelle Marguerite Amaron, CM
Mr. Albert Batten, CM
M. Wilbrod Bherer, CM
Lieutenant-Colonel LeSueur Brodie, CM
Mrs. D.M. Anne Campbell, CM
Chanoine Louis Joseph Chamberland, CM
Dr. Robert William Chambers, CM
Le Révérend Père Anselme Chiasson, CM
Mrs. Frances Anna Clarke, CM
Dr. Edgar Andrew Collard, CM
Mr. Toller Cranston, CM
Colonel Charles P. de Volpi, CM
Dr. Mary Dover, OBE, CM
M. Yvan Dubois, CM
Mr. Christian Einfeld, CM
Dr. Douglas Firth, CM
Mr. Winston Graham Gordon, CM
Mr. Cecil Hogarth Hewitt, CM
Dr. Paul G. Hiebert, CM
Mme Mary Lamontagne, CM
Dr. Sam Landa, CM, MD
M. Jean-Louis Levesque, CM
Mr. George Edward Mara, CM

Mr. Thomas R. Melville-Ness, CM (deceased: December 18, 1976)
Dr. Masajiro Miyazaki, CM, MD
Mr. Ron Northcott, CM
Mr. Abe Okpik, CM
M. J.-Z. Léon Patenaude, CM
Mr. Watson Peck, CM
Lieutenant-Colonel Stanley Preece, CM, CD
M. Louis Pronovost, CM
Dr. John Rekai, CM, MD
M. le docteur Paul L. Rivard, CM, MD
Dr. Elizabeth Chant Robertson, CM, MD
The Reverend Robert L. Rumball, CM
Mr. Andy Russell, CM
Mrs. Margaret Sinn, CM
Mr. Deryk Snelling, CM
Mme Madeleine Thivierge, CM
Mme Michelle Tisseyre, CM
The Honourable George Joseph Tweedy, CM, QC
Dr. Arthur Wishart, CM, QC

ORDER OF MILITARY MERIT
Appointed June 16, 1975
Commanders
Brigadier-General Clayton Ernest Beattie, CMM, CD
Commodore Douglas Rainsford Learoyd, CMM, CD
Brigadier-General Joseph Roman Romanow, CMM, CD

Officers
Lieutenant-colonel Francis Anthony Bussieres, OMM, CD
Lieutenant-Colonel Russell Frederick Choat, OMM, CD
Colonel Mary Joan Fitzgerald, OMM, CD
Lieutenant-Colonel Ian Simon Fraser, OMM, CD
Major Herbert Guenther Harzan, OMM, CD
Lieutenant-Colonel George Lionel Hopkins, OMM, CD
Lieutenant-Colonel Charles Vincent Lilley, MC, OMM, CD
Colonel Allan MacPherson Ogilvie, DFC, OMM, CD
Commander Pierre Edouard Géraud Simard, OMM, CD

Members
Captain Lillian Elsie Barraud, MMM, CD
Master Corporal Ronald Clark Benson, MMM, CD
Sergeant Daryl Murray Boyd, MMM, CD
Chief Warrant Officer Daniel Clarke Cox, MMM, CD
Captain Ronald Daigle, MMM, CD
Sergent Joseph Jacques Dicaire, MMM, CD
Chief Warrant Officer Laurie Ramon Dirks, MMM, CD
Sergeant Brian Angus Donaher, MMM, CD
Warrant Officer Phyllis Keziah Duncan, MMM, CD

Captain Thomas Walter Gardner, MMM, CD
Captain John Armand Scott Haley, MMM, CD
Captain Austin Harris, MMM, CD
Chief Warrant Officer Donald George Howard, MMM, CD
Captain William Bentley Irwin, MMM, CD
Chief Warrant Officer Arthur Roy Keeble, MMM, CD
Chief Warrant Officer Robert Alexander Lyon, MMM, CD
Captain George Edward MacManus, MMM, CD
Sergeant James Gordon McConnell, MMM, CD
Master Warrant Officer John Barry McGillivray, MMM, CD
Captain James Francis Miller, MMM, CD
Adjudant-maître Laurent Montour, MMM, CD
Warrant Officer Norman Stanley Nash, MMM, CD
Captain Robert Nicholson, MMM, CD
Chief Warrant Officer Ronald Borden Page, MMM, CD
Master Corporal Frank Neville Palmer-Stone, MMM, CD
Sergeant Phyllis Rita Patry, MMM, CD
Master Warrant Officer George Patrick Poole, MMM, CD
Chief Warrant Officer James Arthur Puddifant, MMM, CD
Chief Warrant Officer Donald Bruce Reekie, MMM, CD
Adjudant Joseph Augustin Roger Roy, MMM, CD
Sergent Joseph Colomb Georges Talbot, MMM, CD
Master Warrant Officer James Melville Watt, MMM, CD
Master Corporal John Albert Yonkman, MMM, CD

Appointed January 26, 1976
Commanders
Major-général Joseph François Pierre Charbonneau, CMM, CD
Vice-Admiral Robert Hilborn Falls, CMM, CD

Officers
Colonel Stephen Frederick Andrunyk, OMM, CD
Lieutenant-Commander James Graham Clinton Atwood, OMM, CD
Colonel John James Collins, OMM, CD
Lieutenant-Colonel Ronald Allen Holden, OMM, CD
Captain (N) Derek John Kidd, DSC, OMM, CD
Captain (N) Edmund Kwong Lee, OMM, CD
Lieutenant-Colonel Robert Lewis Sylvester Joseph Martin, OMM, CD
Major Fred Robert McCall, OMM, CD
Major Ian Duncan McLennan, OMM, CD
Major Ian Aspinall Sturgess, OMM, CD
Major Jerome Paul Thompson, OMM, CD

Members
Captain Ronald Aubrey Aumonier, MMM, CD
Caporal Maurice Bélanger, MMM, CD

Master Warrant Officer Robert Edwin Clark,
MMM, CD
Master Corporal Winston Dominie, MMM, CD
Chief Warrant Officer Robert Arthur Douglas,
MMM, CD
Adjudant-chef Joseph Charles Louis Hector
Dozois, MMM, CD
Corporal Frederick Richard Edward Dunk,
MMM, CD
Captain William Webb Dyke, MMM, CD
Petty Officer First Class David Charles Folger,
MMM
Sergent Joseph Albert Gallant, MMM, CD
Chief Warrant Officer Harold Morris
Greenwood, MMM, CD
Adjudant-chef Roger Gougeon, MMM, CD
Lieutenant Robert Henry Halpin, MMM, CD
Chief Warrant Officer Frederick Ronald Hooper,
MMM, CD
Warrant Officer Bernard Joseph Hurley, MMM,
CD
Caporal-chef Joseph Robert Larry Knowlton,
MMM, CD
Adjudant-maître Jean Yves Lauzier, MMM, CD
Chief Warrant Officer Royden Glenwood
Messer, MMM, CD
Chief Warrant Officer Ernest Harry Mierau,
MMM, CD
Sergeant Kenneth John Mitchell, MMM, CD
Sergeant James Leonard Morgan, MMM, CD
Captain Kenrod Harris McLeod, MMM, CD
Master Warrant Officer Jerome Allen McSherry,
MMM, CD
Capitaine Joseph François Lucien Simard,
MMM, CD
Chief Warrant Officer Robert Graham
Sutherland, MMM, CD
Adjudant Hector Horace Lucien Carol Tremblay,
MMM, CD
Warrant Officer Alan Richard Turner, MMM,
CD
Captain Jack Kenneth Usher, MMM, CD
Chief Warrant Officer John Philip Wakefield,
MMM, CD
Warrant Officer Arthur Henry Woodruff, MMM,
CD
Warrant Officer James Henry Woodward,
MMM, CD

Appointed June 14, 1976

Commanders
Vice-Admiral Douglas Seaman Boyle, CD
Lieutenant-General William Keir Carr, DFC, CD
Lieutenant-général Jacques Chouinard, CD

Officers
Major Raymond Sinclair Crabbe, CD
Chief Petty Officer First Class William Arden
Doncaster, MMM, CD
Lieutenant-colonel Fernand Forcier, CD
Captain (N) James Brant Fotheringham, CD
Major Joseph Laurier Denis Gauthier, CD
Lieutenant-Colonel Nancy Joan Gollmer, CD
Commander John Alfred Gruber, CD

Colonel Malcolm Ira Walton, MBE, CD
Colonel John Anthony White, DFC, CD

Members
Adjudant-chef Robert Wilfrid Blais, CD
Captain Roger Patrick Bonner, CD
Captain John Bossons, CD
Master Warrant Officer Wesley Edward Byrnell,
CD
Master Warrant Officer Albert Gordon Carter,
CD
Chief Warrant Officer Joseph Albert James Cecil,
CD
Capitaine Joseph Clarence Comeau, CD
Adjudant-chef Joseph Pierre Ghislain Côté, CD
Master Warrant Officer Albert Arthur
Cunningham, CD
Adjudant Roland Maurice Desmarais, CD
Adjudant-maître Francis Joseph Deveau, CD
Sergeant Lawrence Vernon Dunlop, CD
Sergent Michel Thomas Girard Duplain, CD
Chief Warrant Officer Geoffrey George Ellwood,
CD
Master Warrant Officer Einar Elverum, CD
Adjudant-chef Georges Ferris, CD
Chief Warrant Officer Douglas Joseph Gillies,
CD
Captain Robert Kirkpatrick Northey
Glendinning, CD
Sergeant Earl Francis Gray, CD
Chief Warrant Officer George Howard, CD
Warrant Officer Ronald Carr Hutton, CD
Major Dennis Kelly Johnson, CD
Chief Warrant Officer Alfred Jones, CD
Chief Petty Officer First Class Raymond Cecil
Lawrence, CD
Captain Harry Leask, CD
Capitaine Charles Lévesque, CD
Chief Warrant Officer Frederick John MacLean,
CD
Chief Warrant Officer Donald John Matthews,
CD
Chief Petty Officer Second Class Kenneth
Richard Maybury, CD
Adjudant-maître Télesphore Emmanuel
Mousseau, CD
Caporal-chef Joseph Alfred Robert Nadeau, CD
Chief Warrant Officer Graham MacLaren
Olmstead, CD
Sergent Laurent Joseph Prévost, CD
Chief Warrant Officer John Joseph Reilly, CD
Adjudant-maître Julien Roberge, CD
Adjudant-maître Joseph Maurice Paul Sabourin,
CD
Captain Charles Judson Skinner, CD
Master Corporal George Spalding Smith, CD
Chief Warrant Officer Walter Sonnenberg, CD
Sergeant James Henry Thomson, CD
Master Corporal Richard William Travalia, CD
Lieutenant (N) David Thomas Tudor, CD
Master Warrant Officer Leslie James Turk, CD
Chief Petty Officer Second Class George Charles
Walsh, CD
Sergeant Patrick Warburton, CD

Appointed December 6, 1976

Commanders

Commodore Ross Taylor Bennett, CMM, CD
Brigadier-General Hugh Comack, CMM, CD
Lieutenant-General Hugh McLachlan, CMM, DFC, CD

Officers

Lieutenant-Colonel Allan Cairn Brown, OMM, CD
Colonel Peter Alfred Gordon Cameron, OMM, CD
Colonel Joseph Jean Alyre Doucet, OMM, CD
Major Barry Campbell Glover, OMM, CD
Colonel William Brian Hotsenpiller, OMM, CD
Lieutenant-Commander Peter Bruce Hunter, OMM, CD
Major Barry Alexander McFadyen, OMM, CD
Major Paul André Renault, OMM, CD
Lieutenant-Colonel Norman Robert Anton Smyth, OMM, CD
Colonel Brian Wooding, OMM, CD

Members

Chief Warrant Officer John Louis Ariano, MMM, CD
Adjudant-chef Joseph Jean-Charles Bienvenu, MMM, CD
Chief Warrant Officer Thomas Frederick Brush, MMM, CD
Warrant Officer John Thomas Joseph Caron, MMM, CD
Sergeant Albert Palmer Cooke, MMM, CD
Warrant Officer John Raymond Debolt, MMM, CD
Captain John Ralph Decoste, MMM, CD
Chief Warrant Officer Reginald Harding Drew, MMM, CD
Chief Warrant Officer Wendell Baxter Erb, MMM, CD
Sergeant Richard Stanley Feltham, MMM, CD
Caporal Jean-Pierre Gaudreau, MMM
Adjudant-chef Raymond Joseph Goulard, MMM, CD
Master Corporal Robert Edward Grundy, MMM, CD
Chief Warrant Officer William George Jardine, MMM, CD
Chief Warrant Officer Richard Louis Kuntz, MMM, CD
Adjudant-chef Joseph Albert Raymond Benoit Lajoie, MMM, CD
Caporal-chef Joseph Maurice Robert Laplante, MMM, CD
Master Warrant Officer Andrew Joseph Lavigne, MMM, CD
Sergeant Lawrence Vincent Leblanc, MMM, CD
Chief Warrant Officer John Murray Lochrie, MMM, CD
Adjudant-maître Joseph Pierre Jean Guy Lussier, MMM, CD
Adjudant-maître Réginald Massé, MMM, CD
Chief Warrant Officer Bruce David Meikle, MMM, CD

Captain James Anthony Murray, MMM, CD
Captain William Raymond McKay, MMM, CD
Chief Warrant Officer Joseph Michael James O'Doherty, MMM, CD
Master Warrant Officer Matthew Vincent Paschal, MMM, CD
Master Warrant Officer Sheridan Lester Patterson, MMM, CD
Chief Warrant Officer Edwin Lee Peters, MMM, CD
Chief Warrant Officer Philip John Raven, MMM, CD
Master Warrant Officer Paul Emile Joseph Rochon, MMM, CD
Master Warrant Officer William Ronald Rockey, MMM, CD
Master Warrant Officer Gerald Vernon Rogers, MMM, CD
Master Warrant Officer Frederick Parlee Smith, MMM, CD
Sergeant William Edwin Toews, MMM, CD
Chief Warrant Officer Ronald Norman Wardle, MMM, CD
Sergeant Donald Stanley Warrilow, MMM, CD
Warrant Officer Raymond Wells, MMM
Warrant Officer Terrance Herbert Wyss, MMM, CD

BRAVERY DECORATIONS
Appointed January 3, 1975

Star of Courage

Mr. Kari Joronen, SC (posthumous)
Mr. Aron Katz, SC (posthumous)
Mlle Claire Larose, EC
Mr. Victor Solomatenko, SC

Medal of Bravery

Corporal Herbert James Bond, MB, CD
Mr. Pasquale Burgio, MB
Mr. John Robert Davie, MB
Constable Roy Fraser Inman, MB
Mr. John Frank Kurulock, MB
Miss Wendy Lynn Roy, MB
Mr. James William Stephen, MB
Captain Gene Paul Storey, MB
Corporal Joseph George White, MB

Appointed August 11, 1975

Star of Courage

Mr. Byron John Campbell, SC (posthumous)
Mr. William Metcalf, SC
Mr. Lester Laverne Palmer, SC
Mr. Ludwig Raepple, SC

Medal of Bravery

Mr. Roger James Burnett, MB
Mr. James Alan Easson, MB
Mr. Robert Norman Haywood, MB
Mr. Daryl Henderson, MB
Corporal Wendell Arthur Mercer, MB
Mr. Cecil Sleep, MB
Mr. Gary Wishart, MB

Appointed August 18, 1975

Star of Courage
Captain Kenneth Arnison, SC
Capitaine Joseph Michel André Coutu, EC, CD
Captain Howard Keast, SC
Mr. Ronald George Neel Lowe, SC
Mr. Raymond Douglas Smart, SC

Medal of Bravery
RCMP Constable James Adam Bell, MB
Mr. Stephen Campbell, MB
RCMP Sergeant Thomas Charlton, MB
Mr. Ronald R. King, MB
M. Charles Leboeuf, MB
RCMP Constable Brian Leicht, MB

Appointed December 1, 1975

Cross of Valour
Miss Mary Dohey, CV

Star of Courage
Mr. John Joseph Arpin, SC
Mr. Reginald L. Bennett, SC
Mr. Montgomery Penney, SC (posthumous)
Mr. Abraham Bernard Starr, SC
Mr. Thomas Patrick Sylvester, SC

Medal of Bravery
Mr. Maxwell Brown, MB
M. Adrice Joseph Cormier, MB
Captain Vernon Ehman, MB
Mr. Christopher V. Monks, MB
Mr. Robert Anthony MacLellan, MB
Mr. Fred Robillard, MB

Appointed January 19, 1976

Star of Courage
Mr. Gerald Doherty, SC
Constable Harry Alexander Reid, SC
Lieutenant-commandeur Lucien Lauriet Voyer,
  EC (posthumous)

Medal of Bravery
M. Phillippe Raoul Bonny, MB
Mr. Graham Frederick Butt, MB
Constable Howard William Geldart, MB
Mr. Ronald Donald Groves, MB
Mr. Bryan D. Maillet, MB
Constable Barry John Mellish, MB
Constable Joseph Adrien Bernard Pilotte, MB
Mr. Larry Schlegel, MB
Mr. Francis Joseph Sheppard, MB
Mr. Russell Harry Stewart, MB

Appointed April 5, 1976

Cross of Valour
Mr. Kenneth Wilfred Bishop, CV

Star of Courage
Warrant Officer David Theodore Monteith, SC,
  CD
M. Joseph Pelletier, EC (posthumous)
Sergeant Dennis Michael Weber, SC
Corporal Gerry Ramon Zylich, SC

Medal of Bravery
Mr. Terrance Gordon Budreo, MB
Mr. James Gosen, MB
Mr. Hugh Greene, MB
Mr. Herman Frederick Irwin, MB
Mr. George Marshall Mink, MB
Mr. Bernard Nestor Stephaniuk, MB
Mr. Frederic Alvin Wiess, MB

Appointed May 15, 1976

Cross of Valour
Mrs. Jean Swedberg, CV (posthumous)

Star of Courage
Mr. Gordon Sherman Gillespie, SC
Mlle Louise Poulin, EC (posthumous)
Master Corporal William Robert Wacey, SC, CD
Lieutenant-Commander Alan Randall Welton,
  SC

Medal of Bravery
Captain Paul Malcolm Bow, MB (deceased:
  February 1, 1976)
Warrant Officer Douglas Murray Bullerwell, MB,
  CD
Sergeant Donald Calvin Duplisea, MB
Private Erroll Joseph Gapp, MB
Mr. Donald Terry Gillespie, MB
Captain Robert Raymond Henderson, MB
Constable Harry William Leonard Urwin, MB

Appointed August 23, 1976

Star of Courage
Mrs. Margaret Lucretia Pitkethly, SC
  (posthumous)

Medal of Bravery
Constable Glenn Brian Calder, MB
Mr. David Herrett, MB
Caporal Joseph Bernard Gilles Michel Lemay,
  MB
Mr. Wilbert Menacho, MB
Constable Ronald David Noye, MB
M. Claude Poirier, MB
Mr. Frank Preis, MB
Mr. Brian William Webb, MB
Mr. Osmond Yorke, MB

Appointed October 18, 1976

Star of Courage
John Albert Mahon, SC

Medal of Bravery
Mr. James Alfred Coe, MB
Captain John Joseph Goodall Connors, MB
Constable André Dubuc, MB
Master Corporal Paul Wayne Graham, MB, CD
Private Gregory Brent Lewis, MB
James David Dean Piecowye, MB
Mr. Dean Sarell, MB
Master Corporal Alexander John Sheppard, MB
Mrs. Pamela Anne Switzer, MB

Diplomatic and consular representation

Appendix 5

The following is a list of countries and organizations with which Canada maintains diplomatic, consular and/or trade representation, the status of the representatives and the postal addresses of their offices in Canada and Canadian offices abroad. This list was updated to May 1977 by the Information Services Division, Department of External Affairs.

Canadian representatives abroad

Afghanistan
Ambassador: c/o Canadian Embassy, Diplomatic Enclave No. 5, Islamabad, Pakistan.

Algeria
Ambassador: PO Box 225, Alger Gare, Alger.

Argentina
Ambassador: Casilla de Correo 1598, Buenos Aires.

Australia
High Commissioner: Commonwealth Ave., Canberra ACT 2600.

Austria
Ambassador: Luegerring 10, A-1010 Vienna.
Head of Delegation, Ambassador: The Canadian Delegation to the Mutual and Balanced Force Reduction Talks, Vienna.

Bahamas
High Commissioner: c/o Canadian High Commission, PO Box 1500, Kingston 10, Jamaica.

Bahrain
Ambassador: c/o Canadian Embassy, PO Box 1610, Tehran, Iran.

Bangladesh
High Commissioner: PO Box 569, General Post Office, Dacca-2.

Barbados
High Commissioner: PO Box 404, Bridgetown.

Belgium
Ambassador: rue de Loxum 6, 1000 Brussels.

Belize
Commissioner: c/o Canadian High Commission, PO Box 1500, Kingston 10, Jamaica.

Benin, People's Republic of
Ambassador: c/o Canadian High Commission, PO Box 1639, Accra, Ghana.

Bolivia
Ambassador: c/o Canadian Embassy, 132 Calle Libertad, Miraflores, Lima, Peru.

Botswana
High Commissioner: c/o Canadian Embassy, PO Box 26005, Arcadia, Pretoria, South Africa.

Brazil
Ambassador: Caixa Postal 07-0961, 70000, Brasilia DF.

Britain
High Commissioner: Canada House, Trafalgar Square, Cockspur Street SW, 1Y 5BJ London.

Bulgaria
Ambassador: c/o Canadian Embassy, Proleterskih Brigada 69, Belgrade, Yugoslavia.

Burma
Ambassador: c/o Canadian Embassy, PO Box 2090, Bangkok, Thailand.

Burundi
Ambassador: c/o Canadian Embassy, Édifice Shell, coin av. Wangata et boul. du 30-juin, Kinshasa, Republic of Zaïre.

Cameroon
Ambassador: PO Box 572, Yaoundé.

Cape Verde Islands
Ambassador: c/o Canadian Embassy, PO Box 3373, Dakar, Senegal.

Central African Republic
Ambassador: c/o Canadian Embassy, PO Box 572, Yaoundé, Cameroon.

Chad
Ambassador: c/o Canadian Embassy, PO Box 572, Yaoundé, Cameroon.

Chile
Ambassador: Casilla 427, Santiago.

China, People's Republic of
Ambassador: No. 10, San Li Tun Road, Chao Yang District, Peking.

Colombia
Ambassador: Apartado Aéreo 53531-Bogota 2.

Conference on Security and Cooperation in Europe
Ambassador: 10A, avenue de Budé, 1202 Geneva, Switzerland.

Congo, People's Republic of the
Ambassador: c/o Canadian Embassy, Édifice Shell, coin av. Wangata et boul. du 30-juin, Kinshasa, Republic of Zaïre.

Costa Rica
Ambassador: Apartado Postal 10303, San José.

Cuba
Ambassador: c/o PO Box 499 (HVA), Ottawa, K1N 8T7.

Cyprus
High Commissioner: c/o Canadian Embassy, 220 Hayarkon Street, Tel Aviv, Israel.

Czechoslovakia
Ambassador: Mickiewiczova 6, Prague 6.

Denmark
Ambassador: Prinsesse Maries Allé 2, 1908 Copenhagen V.

Dominican Republic
Ambassador: c/o Canadian Embassy, Avenida La Estancia No. 10, 16o piso, Ciudad Comercial Tamanaco, Caracas, Venezuela.

Ecuador
Ambassador: c/o Canadian Embassy, Calle 58, No. 10-42, Bogota, Colombia.

Egypt, Arab Republic of
Ambassador: Kasr el Doubara Post Office, Cairo.

El Salvador
Ambassador: c/o Canadian Embassy, 6th floor, Cronos Building, Calle 3 y Avenida Central, San José, Costa Rica.

Ethiopia
Ambassador: PO Box 1130, Addis Ababa.

European Communities
The European Economic Community
The European Atomic Energy Community
The European Coal and Steel Community
Head of Mission: The Mission of Canada to the European Communities, 5th floor, rue de Loxum 6, 1000 Brussels, Belgium.

Fiji
High Commissioner: c/o Canadian High Commission, PO Box 12-049, Wellington North, New Zealand.

Finland
Ambassador: P Esplanadi 25B, 00100 Helsinki 10.

France
Ambassador: 35, avenue Montaigne, 75008 Paris.

Gabon
Ambassador: c/o Canadian Embassy, PO Box 572, Yaoundé, Cameroon.

Gambia
High Commissioner: c/o Canadian Embassy, PO Box 3373, Dakar, Senegal.

Germany, Federal Republic of
Ambassador: Friedrich-Wilhelm-Strasse 18, 53 Bonn.

Ghana
High Commissioner: PO Box 1639, Accra.

Greece
Ambassador: 4 Ioannou Ghennadiou St. and Ypsilantou, Athens 140.

Grenada
High Commissioner: c/o Canadian High Commission, PO Box 404, Bridgetown, Barbados.

Guatemala
Ambassador: PO Box 400, Guatemala, CA.

Guinea
Ambassador: c/o Canadian Embassy, PO Box 3373, Dakar, Senegal.

Guinea–Bissau
Ambassador: c/o Canadian Embassy, PO Box 3373, Dakar, Senegal.

Guyana
High Commissioner: PO Box 660, Georgetown.

Haiti
Ambassador: CP 826, Port-au-Prince.

Holy See
Ambassador: Via della Conciliazione 4/D, 00193 Rome.

Honduras
Ambassador: c/o Canadian Embassy, 6th floor, Cronos Building, Calle 3 y Avenida Central, San José, Costa Rica.

Hong Kong
Commissioner: PO Box 20264, Hennessy Road Post Office.

Hungary
Ambassador: Budakeszi, u. 55/d P 8, Budapest 1021.

Iceland
Ambassador: Postuttak Oslo 1, Norway.

India
High Commissioner: PO Box 5207, New Delhi.

Indonesia
Ambassador: Djalan Budi Kemuliaan No. 6, Jakarta.

Iran
Ambassador: c/o Canadian Embassy, PO Box 1610, Tehran.

Iraq
Ambassador: c/o Canadian Embassy, PO Box 6112, Baghdad.

Ireland
Ambassador: 65 St. Stephens Green, Dublin 2.

Israel
Ambassador: PO Box 6410, Tel Aviv.

Italy
Ambassador: Via GB de Rossi 27, 00161 Rome.

Ivory Coast
Ambassador: BP 21194, Abidjan.

Jamaica
High Commissioner: PO Box 1500, Kingston 10.

Japan
Ambassador: 3-38 Akasaka 7-chome, Minato-ku, Tokyo.

Jordan
Chargé d'Affaires: c/o Canadian Embassy to Beirut, Lebanon (temporarily resident in Amman), PO Box 35014 and 35015, Amman.

Kenya
High Commissioner: PO Box 30481, Nairobi.

Korea
Ambassador: CPO Box 6299, Seoul 100.

Kuwait
Ambassador: c/o Canadian Embassy, PO Box 1610, Tehran, Iran.

Laos, People's Democratic Republic of
Ambassador: c/o Canadian Embassy, PO Box 2090, Bangkok, Thailand.

Lebanon
Chargé d'Affaires: c/o Canadian Embassy, (temporarily resident in Amman, Jordan), PO Box 35014 and 35015, Amman, Jordan.

Lesotho
High Commissioner: c/o Canadian Embassy, PO Box 26006, Arcadia, Pretoria, South Africa.

Liberia
Ambassador: c/o Canadian High Commission, PO Box 1639, Accra, Ghana.

Libyan Arab Republic
Ambassador: c/o Canadian Embassy, Kasr el Doubara Post Office, Cairo, Arab Republic of Egypt.

Luxembourg
Ambassador: c/o Canadian Embassy, rue de Loxum 6, 1000 Brussels, Belgium.

Macao
Consul: c/o Commission for Canada, PO Box 20264, Hennessy Road Post Office, Hong Kong.

Madagascar, Democratic Republic of
Ambassador: c/o Canadian Embassy, African Solidarity Bldg., Hailé Sélassie 1 Square, Addis Ababa, Ethiopia.

Malawi
High Commissioner: c/o Canadian High Commission, PO Box 1313, Lusaka, Zambia.

Malaysia
High Commissioner: PO Box 990, Kuala Lumpur.

Mali
Ambassador: c/o Canadian Embassy, PO Box 21194, Abidjan, Ivory Coast.

Malta
High Commissioner: c/o Canadian Embassy, Via GB de Rossi 27, 00161 Rome, Italy.

Mauritania
Ambassador: c/o Canadian Embassy, PO Box 3373, Dakar, Senegal.

Mauritius
High Commissioner: c/o Canadian High Commission, PO Box 1022, Dar-es-Salaam, United Republic of Tanzania.

Mexico
Ambassador: Melchor Ocampo 463-7, Mexico 5, DF.

Monaco
Consul General: c/o Canadian Consulate General, 24, av. du Prado, 13006 Marseille, France.

Mongolia
Ambassador: c/o Canadian Embassy, 23 Starokonyushenny Pereulok, Moscow, USSR.

Morocco
Ambassador: BP 709, Rabat-Agdal, Maroc.

Nepal
Ambassador: c/o Canadian High Commission, Shanti Path, Chanakyapuri, New Delhi 21, India.

Netherlands
Ambassador: Sophialaan 7, The Hague.

New Zealand
High Commissioner: PO Box 12-049, Wellington North.

Nicaragua
Ambassador: c/o Canadian Embassy, 6th floor, Cronos Building, Calle 3 y Avenida Central, San José, Costa Rica.

Niger
Ambassador: c/o Canadian Embassy, Immeuble "Le Général", avenue Botreau-Roussel, Abidjan, Ivory Coast.

Nigeria
High Commissioner: PO Box 851, Lagos.

North Atlantic Council
Permanent Representative and Ambassador: 1110 Brussels, Belgium.

Norway
Ambassador: Postuttak, Oslo 1.

Oman
Ambassador: c/o Canadian Embassy, PO Box 1610, Tehran, Iran.

Organization of American States
Ambassador and Permanent Observer: 1746 Massachusetts Ave. NW, Washington, DC, 20036, USA.

Organization for Economic Cooperation and Development
Ambassador and Permanent Representative: 19, rue de Franqueville, Paris 16°.

Pakistan
Ambassador: PO Box 1042, GPO, Islamabad.

Panama
Ambassador: c/o Canadian Embassy, 6th floor, Cronos Building, Calle 3 y Avenida Central, San José, Costa Rica.

Papua New Guinea
High Commissioner: c/o Canadian High
Commission, Commonwealth Avenue,
Canberra, ACT, Australia.

Paraguay
Ambassador: c/o Canadian Embassy, Brunetta
Bldg., Suipacha and Santa Fé, Buenos Aires,
Argentina.

Peru
Ambassador: Casilla 1212, Lima.

Philippines
Ambassador: PO Box 971, Commercial Centre,
Makati, Rizal, Manila.

Poland
Ambassador: Ulica Matejki 1/5, Warsaw, 00-481.

Portugal
Ambassador: Rua Rosa Araujo 2, 6th floor,
Lisbon 2.

Qatar
Ambassador: c/o Canadian Embassy, PO Box
1610, Tehran, Iran.

Romania
Ambassador: PO Box 2966, Post Office No. 22,
Bucharest.

Rwanda
Ambassador: c/o Canadian Embassy, Édifice Shell,
coin av. Wangata et boul. du 30-juin, Kinshasa,
Republic of Zaïre.

San Marino
Consul: c/o Canadian Embassy, Via GB de Rossi
27, 00161 Rome, Italy.

Saudi Arabia
Ambassador: PO Box 5050, Jeddah.

Senegal
Ambassador: PO Box 3373, Dakar.

Seychelles
High Commissioner: c/o Canadian High
Commission, PO Box 1022, Dar-es-Salaam,
United Republic of Tanzania.

Sierra Leone
High Commissioner: c/o Canadian High
Commission, Niger House, Tinubu Street,
Lagos, Nigeria.

Singapore
High Commissioner: PO Box 845, Singapore 1.

Somali Democratic Republic
Ambassador: c/o Canadian High Commission, PO
Box 1022, Dar-es-Salaam, United Republic of
Tanzania.

South Africa
Ambassador: PO Box 26006, Arcadia, Pretoria.

Spain
Ambassador: Apartado 587, Madrid.

Sri Lanka
High Commissioner: PO Box 1006, Colombo.

Sudan
Ambassador: c/o Canadian Embassy, 6 Sharia
Mohamed Fahmi el Sayed, Garden City,
Cairo, Arab Republic of Egypt.

Surinam, Republic of
Ambassador: c/o Canadian High Commission, PO
Box 660, Georgetown, Guyana.

Swaziland
High Commissioner: c/o Canadian Embassy, PO
Box 26006, Arcadia, Pretoria, South Africa.

Sweden
Ambassador: PO Box 16129, S-10323
Stockholm 16.

Switzerland
Ambassador: 88 Kirchenfeldstrasse, 3000 Berne.

Syrian Arab Republic
Chargé d'Affaires: c/o Canadian Embassy to
Beirut, Lebanon (temporarily resident in
Amman, Jordan), PO Box 35014 and 35015,
Amman, Jordan.

Tanzania, United Republic of
High Commissioner: PO Box 1022, Dar-es-Salaam.

Thailand
Ambassador: PO Box 2090, Bangkok.

Togo
Ambassador: c/o Canadian High Commission, E
115/3 Independence Ave., Accra, Ghana.

Tonga
High Commissioner: c/o Canadian High
Commission, ICI Bldg., Molesworth St. N1,
Wellington, New Zealand.

Trinidad and Tobago
High Commissioner: PO Box 1246, Port of Spain.

Tunisia
Ambassador: Boîte Postale 31, Belvedere, Tunis.

Turkey
Ambassador: Nenehatun Caddesi No. 75,
Gaziosmanpasa, Ankara.

Uganda
High Commissioner: c/o Canadian High
Commission, Industrial Promotion Services
Bldg., Kimathi St., Nairobi, Kenya.

Union of Soviet Socialist Republics
Ambassador: 23 Starokonyushenny Pereulok,
Moscow.

United Arab Emirates
Ambassador: c/o Canadian Embassy, PO Box
1610, Tehran, Iran.

United Nations
Ambassador and Permanent Representative: The
Permanent Mission of Canada to the United
Nations, 866 United Nations Plaza, Suite 250,
New York, NY, 10017.

Ambassador and Permanent Representative:
  Permanent Mission of Canada to the Office of
  the United Nations at Geneva and to the
  Conference of the Committee on
  Disarmament, 10A, avenue de Budé, 1202
  Geneva.
Ambassador and Permanent Representative:
  Delegation of Canada to the Multilateral Trade
  Negotiations, 17-19 Champ d'Anier, 1209
  Geneva.
Note: The Permanent Mission in Geneva is
  accredited to the UN Specialized Agencies
  having their headquarters in Geneva:
  International Labour Organization (ILO);
  International Telecommunications Union
  (ITU); World Health Organization (WHO);
  World Meteorological Organization (WMO);
  World Intellectual Property Organization
  (WIPO) and the Secretariat of the General
  Agreement on Tariffs and Trade (GATT).
Permanent Representative: Permanent Mission of
  Canada to the United Nations Environment
  Program, Comcraft House, Haïlé Sélassie
  Avenue, PO Box 30481, Nairobi.
Ambassador and Permanent Delegate: Permanent
  Delegation of Canada to the United Nations
  Educational, Scientific and Cultural
  Organization, 1, rue Miollis, Paris XVᵉ.
Permanent Representative: Permanent Mission of
  Canada to the Food and Agriculture
  Organization, Via GB de Rossi 27, 00161
  Rome.
Permanent Representative: Permanent Mission of
  Canada to the United Nations Industrial
  Development Organization, Luegerring 10,
  A-1010 Vienna.
Permanent Representative: Permanent Mission of
  Canada to the International Atomic Energy
  Agency, Luegerring 10, A-1010 Vienna.
Note: Canada is also a member of the following
  United Nations Specialized Agencies to which
  there are no accredited permanent
  representatives: Universal Postal Union
  (UPU), Berne; Inter-governmental Maritime
  Consultative Organization (IMCO), London;
  International Bank for Reconstruction and
  Development (IBRD), Washington;
  International Finance Corporation (IFC),
  Washington; International Development
  Agency (IDA), Washington; International
  Monetary Fund (IMF), Washington.

United States of America
Ambassador: 1746 Massachusetts Ave. NW,
  Washington, DC, 20036.

Upper Volta
Ambassador: c/o Canadian Embassy, Immeuble
  "Le Général", 4ième et 5ième étages, avenue
  Botreau-Roussel, Abidjan, Ivory Coast.

Uruguay
Ambassador: c/o Canadian Embassy, Brunetta
  Bldg., Suipacha and Santa Fé, Buenos Aires,
  Argentina.

Venezuela
Ambassador: Apartado del Este No. 62302,
  Caracas.

Viet-Nam, Socialist Republic of
Ambassador: c/o Canadian Embassy, San Li Tun
  No. 16, Peking, People's Republic of China.

West Indies Associated States and Montserrat
Commissioner: c/o Canadian High Commission,
  Commonwealth Development Corporation
  Building, Culloden Road, St. Michael,
  Bridgetown, Barbados.

Western Samoa
High Commissioner: c/o Canadian High
  Commission, ICI Bldg., Molesworth St. N1,
  Wellington, New Zealand.

Yemen Arab Republic
Ambassador: c/o Canadian Embassy, PO Box
  5050, Jeddah, Saudi Arabia.

Yemen, People's Democratic Republic of
Ambassador: c/o Canadian Embassy, PO Box
  5050, Jeddah, Saudi Arabia.

Yugoslavia
Ambassador: Proleterskih Brigada 69, Belgrade.

Zaïre, Republic of
Ambassador: PO Box 8341, Kinshasa.

Zambia
High Commissioner: PO Box 1313, Lusaka.

Representatives of foreign countries in Canada

Afghanistan
Ambassador: 2341 Wyoming Ave. NW,
  Washington, DC, 20008, USA.

Algeria
Ambassador: 435 Daly Ave., Ottawa, K1N 6H3.

Argentina
Ambassador: 10 Driveway, Ottawa, K2P 1C7.

Australia
High Commissioner: 90 Sparks St., Suite 600,
  Ottawa, K1P 5B4.

Austria
Ambassador: 445 Wilbrod St., Ottawa, K1N 6M7.

Bahamas
High Commissioner: c/o Embassy of the Bahamas,
  600 New Hampshire Ave. NW, Suite 865,
  Washington, DC, 20037, USA.

Bangladesh
High Commissioner: 85 Range Rd., Suite 402,
  Ottawa, K1N 8J6.

Barbados
High Commissioner: Suite 200, 151 Slater St.,
  Ottawa, K1P 5H3.

Belgium
Ambassador: 85 Range Rd., Suites 601-604,
  Ottawa, K1N 8J6.

Benin, People's Republic of
Ambassador: 58 Glebe Ave., Ottawa, K1S 2C3.

Bolivia
Counsellor and Chargé d'Affaires a.i.: 539 Prospect
    Ave., Rockcliffe Park, Ottawa, K1M 9X6.

Botswana
High Commissioner: c/o Embassy of the Republic
    of Botswana, Van Ness Centre, 4301
    Connecticut Ave. NW, Suite 404,
    Washington, DC, 20008, USA.

Brazil
Ambassador: 255 Albert St., Suite 900, Ottawa,
    K1P 6A9.

Britain
High Commissioner: 80 Elgin St., Ottawa,
    K1P 5K7.

Bulgaria
Ambassador: 325 Stewart St., Ottawa, K1N 6K5.

Burma
Ambassador: 116 Albert St., Royal Trust Bldg., 2nd
    floor, Ottawa, K1P 5G3.

Burundi
Ambassador: 2717 Connecticut Ave. NW,
    Washington, DC, 20008, USA.

Cameroon
Ambassador: 170 Clemow Ave., Ottawa, K1S 2B4.

Central African Republic
Ambassador: 381 Wilbrod Ave., Ottawa,
    K1N 6M6.

Chad
Ambassador: 2600 Virginia Ave., Suite 410,
    Washington, DC, 20037, USA.

Chile
Ambassador: 56 Sparks St., Suite 816, Ottawa,
    K1P 5A9.

China, People's Republic of
Ambassador: 411-415 St. Andrew St., Ottawa,
    K1N 5H3.

Colombia
Ambassador: Suite 112, 140 Wellington St.,
    Ottawa, K1P 5A2.

Congo
Ambassador: c/o Permanent Mission of the Congo
    to the United Nations, 14th East 65th St., New
    York, NY, 10021, USA.

Costa Rica
Ambassador: 2112 S Street NW, Washington, DC,
    20008, USA.

Cuba
Ambassador: 388 Main St., Ottawa, K1S 1E3.

Cyprus
High Commissioner: c/o Embassy of Cyprus, 2211
    R Street NW, Washington, DC, 20008, USA.

Czechoslovakia
Ambassador: 171 Clemow Ave., Ottawa, K1S 2B3.

Denmark
Ambassador: Suite 702, 85 Range Rd., Ottawa,
    K1N 8J6.

Ecuador
Ambassador: 2535-15th St. NW, Washington, DC,
    20009, USA.

Egypt, Arab Republic of
Ambassador: 454 Laurier Ave. E, Ottawa,
    K1N 6R3.

El Salvador
Ambassador: The Driveway Place, 350 Driveway,
    Suite 101, Ottawa, K1S 3N1.

Fiji
High Commissioner: c/o Fiji Mission to the United
    Nations, One United Nations Plaza, 26th floor,
    New York, NY, 10017, USA.

Finland
Ambassador: 222 Somerset St. W, 4th floor,
    Ottawa, K2P 2G3.

France
Ambassador: 42 Sussex Dr., Ottawa, K1M 2C9.

Gabon
Ambassador: 4 Range Rd., Ottawa, K1N 8J5.

Germany, Federal Republic of
Ambassador: 1 Waverley St., Ottawa, K2P 0T8.

Ghana
High Commissioner: 85 Range Rd., Suite 810,
    Ottawa, K1N 8J6.

Greece
Ambassador: Château Laurier Hotel, Suite 110,
    Ottawa, K1N 8S7.

Grenada
High Commissioner: The Driveway Place, 350
    Driveway, Suite 605, Ottawa, K1S 3N1.

Guatemala
Ambassador: The Driveway Place, 350 Driveway,
    Suite 105, Ottawa, K1S 3N1.

Guinea
Ambassador: c/o Embassy of the Republic of
    Guinea, 2112 Leroy Place NW, Washington,
    DC, 20008, USA.

Guyana
High Commissioner: Burnside Bldg., 151 Slater St.,
    Suite 309, Ottawa, K1P 5H3.

Haiti
Ambassador: 150 Driveway, Suite 111, Ottawa,
    K2P 1C7.

Holy See
Pro-Nuncio: Apostolic Nunciature, 724 Manor
    Ave., Rockcliffe Park, K1M 0E3.

Honduras
Ambassador: c/o Embassy of Honduras, 401
    Connecticut Ave. NW, Washington, DC,
    20008, USA.

Hungary
Ambassador: 7 Delaware Ave., Ottawa, K2P 0Z2.

Iceland
Ambassador: c/o Embassy of Iceland, 2022
    Connecticut Ave. NW, Washington, DC,
    20008, USA.

India
High Commissioner: 200 MacLaren St., Ottawa,
    K2P 0L6.

Indonesia
Ambassador: 255 Albert St., Suite 1010, Kent
    Square Building "C", Ottawa, K1P 6A9.

Iran
Ambassador: 85 Range Rd., Suites 307-308,
    Ottawa, K1N 8J6.

Iraq
Ambassador: 377 Stewart St., Ottawa, K1N 6K9.

Ireland
Ambassador: 170 Metcalfe St., Ottawa, K2P 1P3.

Israel
Ambassador: 45 Powell Ave., Ottawa, K1S 1Z9.

Italy
Ambassador: 170 Laurier Ave. W, Ottawa,
    K1P 5V5.

Ivory Coast
Ambassador: 9 Marlborough Ave., Ottawa,
    K1N 8E6.

Jamaica
High Commissioner: 85 Range Rd., Suites 203-204,
    Ottawa, K1N 8J6.

Japan
Ambassador: 75 Albert St., Suite 1005, Ottawa,
    K1P 5E7.

Jordan
Ambassador: 100 Bronson Ave., Suite 701, Ottawa,
    K1R 6G8.

Kenya
High Commissioner: c/o The Permanent Mission
    of Kenya to the United Nations, 866 United
    Nations Plaza, Room 486, New York, NY,
    10017, USA.

Korea
Ambassador: 151 Slater St., Suite 608, Ottawa,
    K1P 5H3.

Kuwait
Ambassador: c/o Embassy of Kuwait, 2940 Tilden
    St. NW, Washington, DC, 20008, USA.

Laos, People's Democratic Republic of
Ambassador: c/o Embassy of People's Democratic
    Republic of Laos, 2222 S Street NW,
    Washington, DC, 20008, USA.

Lebanon
Ambassador: 640 Lyon St., Ottawa, K1S 3Z5.

Lesotho
High Commissioner: 350 Sparks St., Suite 503,
    Ottawa, K1R 5A1.

Liberia
Ambassador: c/o Embassy of Liberia, 5201-16th St.
    NW, Washington, DC, 20011, USA.

Libya
Ambassador: c/o Permanent Mission of the Libyan
    Arab Republic to the United Nations, 866
    United Nations Plaza, New York, NY, 10017,
    USA.

Luxembourg
Ambassador: c/o Embassy of Luxembourg, 2210
    Massachusetts Ave. NW, Washington, DC,
    20008, USA.

Madagascar, Democratic Republic of
Ambassador: c/o Permanent Mission of the
    Malagasy Republic to the United Nations, 801
    Second Ave., Suite 404, New York, NY,
    10017, USA.

Malawi
High Commissioner: c/o Permanent Mission of the
    Republic of Malawi to the United Nations, 777
    Third Ave., New York, NY, 10017, USA.

Malaysia
High Commissioner: 60 Boteler St., Ottawa,
    K1N 8Y7.

Mali
Ambassador: c/o Embassy of Mali, 2130 R Street
    NW, Washington, DC, 20008, USA.

Malta
High Commissioner: c/o Embassy of Malta, rue
    Jules Lejaune, 44-1060 Brussels, Belgium.

Mauritania
Ambassador: c/o The Permanent Mission of the
    Islamic Republic of Mauritania to the United
    Nations, 600 Third Ave., 37th floor, New
    York, NY, 10016, USA.

Mauritius
High Commissioner: c/o Embassy of Mauritius,
    Suite 134, Van Ness Centre, 4301 Connecticut
    Ave. NW, Washington, DC, 20008, USA.

Mexico
Ambassador: 130 Albert St., Suite 206, Ottawa,
    K1P 5G4.

Mongolia
Ambassador: 7 Kensington Court, London, W8
    5DL, England.

Morocco
Ambassador: 38 Range Rd., Ottawa, K1N 8J4.

Nepal
Ambassador: c/o Embassy of Nepal, 2131 Leroy
    Place NW, Washington, DC, 20008, USA.

Netherlands
Ambassador: 275 Slater St., Ottawa, K1P 5H9.

New Zealand
High Commissioner: 77 Metcalfe St., Suite 804,
    Ottawa, K1P 5L6.

Nicaragua
Ambassador: c/o Embassy of Nicaragua, 1627 New
    Hampshire Ave. NW, Washington, DC,
    20009, USA.

Niger
Ambassador: 190 Lisgar St., Ottawa, K2P 0C4.

Nigeria
High Commissioner: Place de Ville, Tower A, 320
Queen St., Suite 2000, Ottawa, K1R 5A3.

Norway
Ambassador: 140 Wellington St., Suite 700,
Victoria Bldg., Ottawa, K1P 5A2.

Oman
Ambassador: c/o Embassy of Oman, 2342
Massachusetts Ave. NW, Washington, DC,
20008, USA.

Pakistan
Ambassador: 170 Metcalfe St., Ottawa, K2P 1P3.

Panama
Ambassador: c/o Embassy of Panama, 2862 McGill
Terrace NW, Washington, DC, 20008, USA.

Peru
Ambassador: 539 Island Park Dr., Ottawa,
K1Y 0B6.

Philippines
Ambassador: 130 Albert St., Suite 607, Ottawa,
K1P 5G4.

Poland
Ambassador: 443 Daly Ave., Ottawa, K1N 6H3.

Portugal
Ambassador: 645 Island Park Dr., Ottawa,
K1Y 0C2.

Qatar
Ambassador: c/o The Permanent Mission of Qatar
to the United Nations, 747 Third Ave., 22nd
floor, New York, NY, 10017, USA.

Romania
Ambassador: 473-475 Wilbrod St., Ottawa,
K1N 6N1.

Rwanda
Ambassador: 130 Albert St., Suite 1203, Ottawa,
K1P 5G4.

Saudi Arabia
Ambassador: 99 Bank St., Suite 901, Ottawa,
K1P 6B9.

Senegal
Ambassador: 57 Marlborough Ave., Ottawa,
K1N 8E8.

Sierra Leone
High Commissioner: 1701-19th Street NW,
Washington, DC, 20009, USA.

Singapore
High Commissioner: c/o The Permanent Mission
of Singapore to the United Nations, One
United Nations Plaza, 26th floor, New York,
NY, 10017, USA.

Somali Democratic Republic
Ambassador: c/o Embassy of the Somali
Democratic Republic, Suite 710, 600 New
Hampshire Ave. NW, Washington, DC, USA.

South Africa
Ambassador: 15 Sussex Dr., Ottawa, K1M 1M8.

Spain
Ambassador: 350 Sparks St., Suite 802, Ottawa,
K1R 5A1.

Sri Lanka
High Commissioner: 85 Range Rd., Suites 102-104,
Ottawa, K1N 8J6.

Sudan
Ambassador: c/o Embassy of the Democratic
Republic of the Sudan, 600 New Hampshire
Ave. NW, Suite 400, Washington, DC, 20037,
USA.

Swaziland
High Commissioner: c/o Embassy of the Kingdom
of Swaziland, Suite 441, Van Ness Centre,
4301 Connecticut Ave. NW, Washington, DC,
20008, USA.

Sweden
Ambassador: 140 Wellington St., Suite 604,
Ottawa, K1P 5A2.

Switzerland
Ambassador: 5 Marlborough Ave., Ottawa,
K1N 8E6.

Syria
Ambassador: c/o Permanent Mission of the Syrian
Arab Republic to the United Nations, 150 E
58th Street, Suite 1500, New York, NY,
10022, USA.

Tanzania, United Republic of
High Commissioner: 50 Range Rd., Ottawa,
K1N 8J4.

Thailand
Ambassador: 85 Range Rd., Suite 704, Ottawa,
K1N 8J6.

Togo
Ambassador: 220 Laurier Ave. W, Ottawa,
K1N 6P2.

Trinidad and Tobago
High Commissioner: 75 Albert St., Suite 508,
Ottawa, K1P 5R5.

Tunisia
Ambassador: 515 O'Connor St., Ottawa, K1S 3P8.

Turkey
Ambassador: 197 Wurtemburg St., Ottawa,
K1N 8L9.

Uganda
High Commissioner: 170 Laurier Ave. W, Suite
601, Ottawa, K1P 5V5.

Union of Soviet Socialist Republics
Ambassador: 285 Charlotte St., Ottawa, K1N 8L5.

United States of America
Ambassador: 100 Wellington St., Ottawa, K1P 5T1.

Upper Volta
Ambassador: 48 Range Rd., Ottawa, K1N 8J4.

Uruguay
Ambassador: c/o Embassy of Uruguay, 1918 F
  Street NW, Washington, DC, 20006, USA.

Venezuela
Ambassador: 320 Queen St., Suite 2220, Place de
  Ville, Tower A, Ottawa, K1P 5A3.

Yemen Arab Republic
Ambassador: Watergate Six Hundred, Suite 860,
  600 New Hampshire Ave. NW, Washington,
  DC, 20037, USA.

Yemen, People's Democratic Republic of
Ambassador: c/o Permanent Mission of the
  People's Democratic Republic of Yemen, 413
  E 51st Street, New York, NY, 10022, USA.

Yugoslavia
Ambassador: 17 Blackburn Ave., Ottawa,
  K1N 8A2.

Zaïre, Republic of
Ambassador: 18 Range Rd., Ottawa, K1N 8J3.

Zambia
High Commissioner: 130 Albert St., Suite 1610,
  Ottawa, K1P 5Y4.

*Delegation of the Commission of the European
Communities*
Head of Delegation: 350 Sparks St., Suite 1110,
  Ottawa, K1R 7S8.

Books about Canada

Appendix 6

This basic list of books about Canada, contributed by the National Library of Canada, includes a selection of publications grouped alphabetically by author and arranged under the subject classifications of The arts and the performing arts, Biography, Country and people, Economics, Government and politics, History, Literature, General reference works and Science. Titles are listed in the language in which they are published. The selection includes only books published in 1975. For additional titles, the reader should consult the lists of books in previous editions of the *Canada Year Book* or the monthly or annual editions of *Canadiana,* the national bibliography published by the National Library.

The arts and the performing arts

Amtmann, Willy. *Music in Canada, 1600-1800.* Montreal: Habitex Books; Cambridge, Ont.: Collier-Macmillan Canada, 1975. 320 p.

Art Gallery of Ontario. *Exposure: Canadian contemporary photographers/Exposure: photographes canadiens contemporains.* Toronto: Art Gallery of Ontario, 1975. 192 p.

Berton, Pierre. *Hollywood's Canada: the Americanization of our national image.* Toronto: McClelland and Stewart, 1975. 303 p.

Canada Council. Touring Office. *Touring directory of the performing arts in Canada/Tournée des spectacles: guide pour l'organisation de tournées de spectacles au Canada.* Ottawa: Touring Office, Canada Council, 1975- .

Le cinéma au Québec: bilan d'une industrie 1975- . Compilé par Jean-Pierre Tadros. Montréal: Éditions Cinéma Québec, 1975- .

Dassylva, Martial. *Un théâtre en effervescence: critiques et chroniques, 1965-1972.* Montréal: La Presse, 1975. 283 p. (Collection Échanges)

Dewdney, Selwyn. *The sacred scrolls of the southern Ojibway.* Toronto: Published for the Glenbow-Alberta Institute, Calgary, Alta. by University of Toronto Press, 1975. viii, 199 p.

Duff, Wilson. *Images stone, B.C.: thirty centuries of Northwest Coast Indian sculpture: an exhibition originating at the Art Gallery of Greater Victoria.* Saanichton, BC: Hancock House, 1975. 191 p.

Erickson, Arthur. *The architecture of Arthur Erickson.* Montreal: Tundra Books, 1975. 228 p.

Hill, Beth. *Guide to Indian rock carvings of the Pacific Northwest coast.* Saanichton, BC: Hancock House, 1975. 49 p.

Hines, Sherman. *Nova Scotia: photographs.* Halifax, NS: West House Pub., 1975. 116 p.

Hofsess, John. *Inner views: ten Canadian film-makers.* Toronto: McGraw-Hill Ryerson, 1975. 171 p.

Ingolfsrud, Elizabeth. *All about Ontario beds.* Toronto: House of Grant (Canada), 1975. 63 p. (All about antique Ontario furniture)

Karel, David, Claude Thibault et Luc Noppen. *François Baillairgé et son œuvre, 1759-1830.* Québec: Université Laval, 1975. 85 p.

Kozar, Andrew J. *R. Tait MacKenzie: the sculptor of athletes.* Knoxville, Tenn.: University of Tennessee Press, 1975. xxii, 118 p.

Laframboise, Yves. *L'architecture traditionnelle au Québec: glossaire illustré de la maison au 17e et 18e siècles.* Montréal: Éditions de l'Homme, 1975. 319 p.

Lessard, Michel et Huguette Marquis. *L'art traditionnel au Québec.* Montréal: Éditions de l'Homme, 1975. 463 p.

McLaren, Norman. *The drawings of Norman McLaren/Les dessins de Norman McLaren.* Edited from taped interviews by Michael White. Montreal: Tundra Books/Les livres Toundra, 1975. 192 p.

MacRae, Marion and Anthony Adamson. *Hallowed walls: church architecture of Upper Canada.* Toronto: Clarke, Irwin, 1975. 304 p.

Moogk, Edward B. *En remontant les années: l'histoire et l'héritage de l'enregistrement sonore au Canada: des débuts à 1930.* Ottawa: Bibliothèque nationale du Canada, 1975. 447 p.

Moogk, Edward B. *Roll back the years: history of Canadian recorded sound and its legacy: genesis to 1930.* Ottawa: National Library of Canada, 1975. 443 p.

National Film Board of Canada. Still Photography Division. *The female eye/Coup d'œil féminin.* Toronto: Clarke, Irwin, 1975. 192 p.

Porter, John H. *L'art de la dorure au Québec du 17e siècle à nos jours.* Québec: Éditions Garneau, 1975. 211 p.

Rinfret, Edouard G. *Le théâtre canadien d'expression française: répertoire analytique des origines à nos jours.* v.1- . Montréal: Éditions Leméac, 1975- . (Collection Documents)

Robert, Guy. *Jordi Bonet.* Sainte-Adèle, Qué.: Éditions du Songe, 1975. 132 p. (Texte français et traduction anglaise en regard)

Robert, Guy. *Lemieux.* Montréal: Éditions A. Stanké, 1975. 303 p.

Simard, Cyril. *Artisanat québécois.* v.1- . Montréal: Éditions de l'Homme, 1975- .

Vézina, Raymond. *Théophile Hamel, peintre national, 1817-1870.* v.1- . Montréal: Éditions Elysée, 1975- .

Wilson, P. Roy. *The beautiful old houses of Quebec.* Toronto: University of Toronto Press, 1975. 125 p.

Woodall, Ronald. *Magnificent derelicts: a celebration of older buildings.* Vancouver: J.J. Douglas, 1975. 143 p.

Biography

Brotman, Ruth C. *Pauline Donalda: the life and career of a Canadian prima donna.* s.l.: s.n., 1975. xvii, 125 p.

Brown, Robert Craig. *Robert Laird Borden: a biography.* v.1- . Toronto: Macmillan of Canada, 1975- .

Charlebois, Peter. *The life of Louis Riel.* Toronto: NC Press, 1975. 254 p.

Cherney, Brian. *Harry Somers.* Toronto: University of Toronto Press, 1975. 185 p.

Creighton, Helen. *Helen Creighton: a life in folklore.* Toronto: McGraw-Hill Ryerson, 1975. 244 p.

Diefenbaker, John G. *One Canada: memoirs of the Right Honourable John G. Diefenbaker.* v.1- . Toronto: Macmillan of Canada, 1975- .

Farrow, Moira. *Nobody here but us: pioneers of the North.* Vancouver: J.J. Douglas, 1975. x, 219 p.

Gillen, Mollie. *The wheel of things: a biography of L.M. Montgomery.* Don Mills, Ont.: Fitzhenry and Whiteside, 1975. 200 p.

Gould, Jan. *Women of British Columbia.* Saanichton, BC: Hancock House, 1975. 221 p.

Her own woman: profiles of ten Canadian women. By Myrna Kostash, et al. Toronto: Macmillan of Canada, 1975. 212 p.

Joubert, Rodolphe. *Essai sur la vie et l'œuvre d'Edouard Montpetit.* Montréal: Éditions Elysée, 1975. xi, 449 p.

Lombardo, Guy. *Auld acquaintance: the autobiography of Guy Lombardo.* Garden City, NY: Doubleday, 1975. xii, 295 p.

MacEwan, John W. Grant. *. . . and mighty women too: stories of notable Western Canadian women.* Saskatoon, Sask.: Western Producer Prairie Books, 1975. 275 p.

MacGregor, James G. *Father Lacombe.* Edmonton, Alta.: Hurtig, 1975. 350 p.

Michel, Robert. *Vivre dans l'esprit: Marie de l'Incarnation.* Montréal: Éditions Bellarmin, 1975. 337 p.

Nicholson, Gerald W.L. *Canada nursing sisters.* Toronto: Samuel Stevens, Hakkert, 1975. 272 p. (Canadian War Museum. Historical publication; no. 13)

Pearson, Lester B. *Mike: the memoirs of the Right Honourable Lester B. Pearson: volume 3, 1957-1968.* Edited by John A. Munro and Alex I. Inglis. Toronto; Buffalo: University of Toronto Press, 1975. xii, 338 p.

Pethick, Derek. *Men of British Columbia.* Saanichton, BC: Hancock House, 1975. 223 p.

Pickersgill, J.W., ed. *My years with Louis St. Laurent: a political memoir.* Toronto: University of Toronto Press, 1975. 334 p.

Prang, Margaret. *N.W. Rowell: Ontario nationalist.* Toronto: University of Toronto Press, 1975. x, 553 p.

Schull, Joseph. *Edward Blake.* Toronto: Macmillan of Canada, 1975. 257 p.

Shackleton, Doris French. *Tommy Douglas.* Toronto: McClelland and Stewart, 1975. 333 p.

Sinclair, Gordon. *Will Gordon Sinclair please sit down.* Toronto: McClelland and Stewart, 1975. 221 p.

Thomas, Lewis H. *The renaissance of Canadian history: a biography of A.L. Burt.* Toronto: University of Toronto Press, 1975. xiv, 189 p.

Waite, Peter B. *Macdonald: his life and world.* Toronto: McGraw-Hill Ryerson, 1975. 224 p.

Woodcock, George. *Amor de Cosmos: journalist and reformer.* Toronto: Oxford University Press, 1975. 177 p. (Canadian lives)

Woodcock, George. *Gabriel Dumont: the Métis chief and his lost world.* Edmonton, Alta.: Hurtig, 1975. 256 p.

Country and people

Adams, Howard. *Prison of grass: Canada from the native point of view.* Toronto: New Press, 1975. xi, 238 p. (Trent native series; no. 1)

Arès, Richard. *Les positions ethniques, linguistiques et religieuses des Canadiens français à la suite du recensement de 1971.* Montréal: Éditions Bellarmin, 1975. 210 p.

Armitage, Andrew. *Social welfare in Canada: ideals and realities.* Toronto: McClelland and Stewart, 1975. vi, 234 p.

Ashworth, Mary. *Immigrant children and Canadian schools.* Toronto: McClelland and Stewart, 1975. xii, 228 p.

Bailey, Thomas M. *The covenant in Canada: four hundred years history of the Presbyterian Church in Canada.* Hamilton, Ont.: Macnab Circle, 1975. 160 p.

Bassett, Isabel. *The parlour rebellion: profiles in the struggle for women's rights.* Toronto: McClelland and Stewart, 1975. 223 p.

Bettison, David, John K. Kenward and Larrie Taylor. *The politics of Canadian urban development.* Edmonton, Alta.: University of Alberta Press, 1975. x, 337 p.

Bileski, Kasimir. *Canadian postage stamps 1953-1974: the Elizabeth era.* Winnipeg, Man.: K. Bileski, 1975. 100 p.

Boudreau, Marielle. *La cuisine traditionnelle en Acadie.* Moncton, NB: Éditions d'Acadie, 1975. 181 p.

Bouma, Gary D. and Wilma J. Bouma. *Fertility control: Canada's lively social problem.* Don Mills, Ont.: Longman Canada, 1975. 144 p. (Canada social problems series)

Called to witness: profiles of Canadian Presbyterians: a supplement to "Enduring witness". v.1- . Edited by W. Stanford Reid. Don Mills, Ont.: Presbyterian Publications, 1975- .

Canada: the land and its people. By Doreen M. Tomkins, et al. Agincourt, Ont.: Gage Educational Pub., 1975. ix, 372 p.

Carisse, Colette et Joffre Dumazedier. *Les femmes innovatrices: problèmes post-industriels d'une Amérique francophone, le Québec.* Paris: Éditions du Seuil, 1975. 283 p. (Collection Sociologie)

Clark, Samuel D., J. Paul Grayson and Linda M. Grayson, eds. *Prophecy and protest: social movements in twentieth-century Canada.* Toronto: Gage Educational Pub., 1975. 437 p.

Collard, Edgar Andrew, ed. *The McGill you knew: an anthology of memories, 1920-1960.* Don Mills, Ont.: Longman Canada, 1975. 269 p.

Collier, Robert and V. Setty Pendakur. *Contemporary cathedrals: large scale developments in Canadian cities.* Montreal: Harvest House, 1975. xiv, 201 p. (Environment series)

Cosbie, W.G. *The Toronto General Hospitals, 1819-1965: a chronicle.* Toronto: Macmillan of Canada, 1975. vii, 373 p.

Cosentino, Frank and Glynn Leyshon. *Olympic gold: Canada's winners in the summer games.* Toronto: Holt, Rinehart and Winston of Canada, 1975. 146 p.

Dewdney, Selwyn. *They shared to survive: the native peoples of Canada.* Toronto: Macmillan of Canada, 1975. 210 p.

Donaldson, Gerald and Gerald Lampert. *The great Canadian beer book.* Toronto: McClelland and Stewart, 1975. 128 p.

Dupont, Jean-Claude. *Le sucre du pays.* Montréal: Leméac, 1975. 117 p. (Traditions du geste et de la parole; 2)

Faris, Ron. *The passionate educators: voluntary associations and the struggle for control of adult educational broadcasting in Canada, 1919-52.* Toronto: P. Martin, 1975. xv, 202 p.

Finlay, John L. *Canada in the North Atlantic triangle: two centuries in social change.* Toronto: Oxford University Press, 1975. 343 p.

Forcese, Dennis P. *The Canadian class structure.* Toronto: McGraw-Hill Ryerson, 1975. x, 148 p. (McGraw-Hill Ryerson series in Canadian sociology)

Gabeline, Donna, Dane Lanken and Gordon Pape. *Montreal at the crossroads.* Montreal: Harvest House, 1975. 220 p.

Gagnon, François-Marc. *La conversion par l'image: un aspect de la mission des Jésuites auprès des Indiens du Canada au 17ᵉ siècle.* Montréal: Éditions Bellarmin, 1975. 141 p.

Gingras, Raymond. *Liste annotée des patronymes d'origine allemande au Québec et notes diverses.* Québec: s.n., 1975. 133 p.

Le guide complet du camping et du caravaning au Canada. Par Allan Stone et Margo Oliver. Montréal: Éditions Optimum, 1975. 129 p.

Hautecoeur, Jean-Paul. *L'Acadie du discours: pour une sociologie de la culture acadienne.* Québec: Presses de l'Université Laval, 1975. xxv, 351 p. (Histoire et sociologie de la culture; 10)

Hearn, John. *Nostalgia: a guide to collecting in Canada.* Toronto: G. de Pencier Books, 1975. 192 p.

Iberville-Moreau, Luc d'. *Lost Montreal.* Toronto: Oxford University Press, 1975. 183 p.

Karras, Arthur L. *Face the north wind.* Don Mills, Ont.: Burns and MacEachern, 1975. viii, 191 p.

Katz, Michael B. *The people of Hamilton, Canada West: family and class in a mid-nineteenth century city.* Cambridge, Mass.: Harvard University Press, 1975. xiii, 381 p.

Kenyon, Walter A. *Tokens of possession: the northern voyages of Martin Frobisher.* Toronto: Royal Ontario Museum, 1975. 164 p.

Kurelek, William. *Kurelek's Canada.* Toronto: Pagurian Press; Scarborough, Ont.: McGraw-Hill Ryerson, 1975. 127 p. (Canadian heritage library)

Leyton, Elliott. *Dying hard.* Toronto: McClelland and Stewart, 1975. 141 p.

Litteljohn, Bruce M. and Wayland Drew. *Superior: the haunted shore.* Toronto: Gage Pub., 1975. 176 p.

Macdonald, Rusty H. *Four seasons west: a photographic Odyssey of the three prairie provinces.* Saskatoon, Sask.: Western Producer Prairie Books, 1975. 116 p.

Marchak, M. Patricia. *Ideological perspectives on Canada.* Toronto: McGraw-Hill Ryerson, 1975. ix, 146 p. (McGraw-Hill Ryerson series in Canadian sociology)

May, Zita Barbara. *Canada's international equestrians.* Toronto: Burns and MacEachern, 1975. 219 p.

Nader, George A. *Cities of Canada.* v.1- . Toronto: Macmillan of Canada, 1975- .

National Conference on the Education of Immigrant Students: Issues and Answers, Toronto, Ont., 1974. *Education of immigrant students: issues and answers.* Edited by Aaron Wolfgang. Toronto: Ontario Institute for Studies in Education, 1975. viii, 208 p. (Ontario Institute for Studies in Education: Symposium series; 5)

O'Brien, Andy. *How to watch the Olympic Games: summer 1976: the complete ABC/Montreal Star/New York Times guide.* Montreal: Optimum Pub.: ABC Sports, 1975. xxi, 295 p.

Owen, Alan R.G. *Psychic mysteries of Canada.* Toronto: Fitzhenry and Whiteside, 1975. xii, 243 p.

Petrigo, Walter. *Petrigo's Calgary.* Calgary, Alta.: City of Calgary: McClelland and Stewart West, 1975. 158 p.

Pitseolak, Peter and Dorothy Eber. *People from our side: an Inuit record of Seekooseelak, the land of the people of Cape Dorset, Baffin Island: a life story with photographs.* Edmonton, Alta.: Hurtig, 1975. 159 p.

Prentice, Alison L. and Susan F. Houston, eds. *Family, school and society in nineteenth-century Canada.* Toronto: Oxford University Press, 1975. x, 294 p.

Québec (Province) Ministère des communications. Service des éditions. La Documentation québécoise. *Guide du citoyen.* Québec: Éditeur officiel du Québec, 1975. 475 p. (L'État et le citoyen; no 1)

Le Rapport Parent, dix ans après. Par Richard Arès et al. Montréal: Éditions Bellarmin, 1975. 161 p.

Rumilly, Robert. *Histoire de la Société Saint-Jean-Baptiste de Montréal des Patriotes au fleurdelisé, 1834-1948.* Montréal: L'Aurore, 1975. 564 p. (Collection Connaissance des pays québécois; 13)

Russell, Andy. *The Rockies.* Edmonton, Alta.: Hurtig, 1975. 160 p.

Spiegel, Ted. *Western shores: Canada's Pacific coast.* Toronto: McClelland and Stewart, 1975. 126 p.

Stanbury, W.T. *Success and failure: Indians in urban society.* Vancouver: University of British Columbia Press, 1975. xxxi, 415 p.

Stewart, Sandy. *A pictorial history of radio in Canada.* Toronto: Gage Pub., 1975. v, 154 p.

Tagoona, Armand. *Shadows.* Ottawa: Oberon Press, 1975. 61 p.

Tepperman, Lorne. *Social mobility in Canada.* Toronto: McGraw-Hill Ryerson, 1975. xi, 220 p.

Thompson, Austin Seton. *Spadina: a story of old Toronto.* Toronto: Pagurian Press, 1975. 223 p.

Tulloch, Headley. *Black Canadians: a long line of fighters.* Toronto: NC Press, 1975. 186 p.

VanOene, W.W.J. *Inheritance preserved: the Canadian Reformed Churches in historical perspective.* Winnipeg, Man.: Premier Printing, 1975. 280 p.

Ward, Tom. *Cowtown: an album of early Calgary.* Calgary, Alta.: City of Calgary Electric System: McClelland and Stewart West, 1975. 496 p.

Witney, Dudley. *The lighthouse.* Toronto: McClelland and Stewart, 1975. 255 p.

Yeates, Maurice. *Main street: Windsor to Quebec city.* Toronto: Macmillan of Canada; Ottawa: Ministry of State for Urban Affairs and Information Canada, 1975. xiv, 431 p.

Zimmerly, David W. *Cain's land revisited: culture change in central Labrador, 1775-1972.* St. John's Nfld.: Institute of Social and Economic Research, Memorial University of Newfoundland, 1975. xiii, 346 p.

Economics

Archer, Maurice. *Canada's economic problems and policies.* Toronto: Macmillan of Canada, 1975. xi, 211 p.

Beattie, Christopher. *Minority men in a majority setting: middle-level francophones in the Canadian public service.* Toronto: McClelland and Stewart, 1975. xi, 224 p. (The Carleton library; no. 92)

Bonville, Jean de. *Jean-Baptiste Gagnepetit: les travailleurs montréalais à la fin du 19e siècle.* Montréal: L'Aurore, 1975. 253 p. (Collection Connaissance des pays québécois; 11)

Campeau, Lucien. *Les finances publiques de la Nouvelle-France sous les Cent-Associés, 1632-1665.* Montréal: Éditions Bellarmin, 1975. 222 p.

Canada. National Council of Welfare. *Poor kids: a report by the National Council of Welfare on children in poverty in Canada.* Ottawa: National Council of Welfare, 1975. 44, xiv p.

Charbonneau, Hubert. *Vie et mort de nos ancêtres: étude démographique.* Montréal: Presses de l'Université de Montréal, 1975. 267 p. (Collection Démographie canadienne; 26)

Clement, Wallace. *The Canadian corporate elite: an analysis of economic power.* Toronto: McClelland and Stewart, 1975. xxvii, 479 p. (The Carleton library; no. 89)

Croft, Roger. *Swindle: a decade of Canadian stock frauds.* Toronto: Gage Pub., 1975. ix, 198 p.

Dosman, Edgar J. *The national interest: the politics of northern development, 1968-1975.* Toronto: McClelland and Stewart, 1975. xviii, 224 p. (Canada in transition series)

Forester, Joseph E. and Anne D. Forester. *Fishing: British Columbia's commercial fishing history.* Saanichton, BC: Hancock House, 1975. 224 p.

Fréchette, Pierre, Roland Jouandet-Bernadat et Jean-P. Vézina. *L'économie du Québec.* Anjou, Qué.: Éditions HRW, 1975. xxxiv, 436 p.

Gonick, Cy. *Inflation or depression: the continuing crisis of the Canadian economy.* Toronto: James Lorimer, 1975. 448 p.

Gordon, Walter L. *Storm signals: new economic policies for Canada.* Toronto: McClelland and Stewart, 1975. 140 p.

Gould, Edwin. *Logging: British Columbia's logging history.* Saanichton, BC: Hancock House, 1975. 221 p.

Granger, Alix. *Investing profitably in Canada.* Vancouver: J.J. Douglas, 1975. 237 p.

Hameed, Syed M.A., comp. *Canadian industrial relations.* Toronto: Butterworth (Canada), 1975. xviii, 378 p.

Holland, John W. and Michael L. Skolnik. *Public policy and manpower development.* Toronto: Dept. of Education Planning, Ontario Institute for Studies in Education, 1975. viii, 152 p.

Jordan, Mary V. *Survival: labour's trials and tribulations in Canada.* Toronto: McClelland and Stewart, 1975. x, 292 p.

MacEwan, John W. Grant. *The battle for the Bay.* Saskatoon, Sask.: Western Producer Book Service, 1975. 258 p.

Martin, Samuel A. *Financing humanistic service.* Toronto: McClelland and Stewart, 1975. 269 p.

Mitchell, Don. *The politics of food.* Toronto: James Lorimer, 1975. 235 p.

Naylor, R.T. *The history of Canadian business, 1867-1914.* Toronto: James Lorimer, 1975. 2 v.

Peitchinis, Stephen G. *The Canadian labour market.* Toronto: Oxford University Press, 1975. xii, 367 p.

Québec (Province) Commission d'enquête sur l'exercice de la liberté syndicale dans l'industrie de la construction. *Rapport de la Commission d'enquête sur l'exercice de la liberté syndicale dans l'industrie de la construction.* Québec: Éditeur officiel du Québec, 1975. 355 p. (Comprend du texte anglais)

Rinehart, James W. *The tyranny of work.* Don Mills, Ont.: Longman Canada, 1975. 181 p. (Canadian problems series)

Roby, Yves. *Les caisses populaires Alphonse Desjardins, 1900-1920.* Lévis, Qué.: Fédération de Québec des Caisses populaires Desjardins, 1975. 113 p.

Ross, Alexander C. *The risk takers.* Toronto: Maclean-Hunter, 1975. 177 p.

Williams, Jack. *The story of unions in Canada.* Don Mills, Ont.: J.M. Dent, 1975. iv, 252 p.

Government and politics

Avakumovic, Ivan. *The Communist Party in Canada: a history.* Toronto: McClelland and Stewart, 1975. x, 309 p.

Benjamin, Jacques. *Comment on fabrique un Premier ministre québécois: de 1960 à nos jours.* Montréal: L'Aurore, 1975. 190 p. (Collection Connaissance des pays québécois; 12)

Betcherman, Lita-Rose. *The swastika and the maple leaf: fascist movements in Canada in the thirties.* Toronto: Fitzhenry and Whiteside, 1975. 167 p.

Bothwell, Robert and Normand Hillmer, eds. *The in-between time: Canadian external policy in the 1930s.* Toronto: Copp Clark Pub., 1975. 223 p. (Issues in Canadian history)

Charbonneau, Jean-Pierre. *La filière canadienne.* Montréal: Éditions de l'Homme, 1975. 597 p.

Clarence-Smith, J.A. and Jean Kerby. *Private law in Canada: a comparative study/Le droit privé au Canada: études comparatives.* v.1- . Ottawa: University of Ottawa Press, 1975- .

Colloque sur le nationalisme québécois vis-à-vis des États-Unis, Saint-Marc, Québec, 1974. *Le nationalisme québécois à la croisée des chemins.* Québec: Centre québécois de relations internationales, Université Laval, 1975. 375 p. (Choix; 7)

Les communautés urbaines de Montréal et de Québec: premier bilan: compte rendu de la journée d'étude du 27 novembre 1974. Sous la direction de Guy Lord, André Tremblay, Marie-Odile Trépanier; textes de Lawrence Hanigan et al. Montréal: Presses de l'Université de Montréal, 1975. 126 p.

Cuff, Robert D. and Jack L. Granatstein. *Canadian-American relations in wartime: from the Great War to the cold war.* Toronto: Hakkert, 1975. xiii, 205 p.

Délinquance juvénile au Québec. Montréal: Presses de l'Université de Montréal, 1975. 202 p. (Criminologie, v. 8, nos 1-2)

Dion, Léon. *Nationalisme et politique au Québec.* Montréal: Hurtubise HMH, 1975. 177 p. (Sciences de l'homme et humanisme; 7)

Fry, Michael G., comp. *Freedom and change: essays in honour of Lester B. Pearson.* Toronto: McClelland and Stewart, 1975. 258 p.

Gélinas, André. *Organismes autonomes et centraux.* Montréal: Presses de l'Université du Québec, 1975. xii, 346 p.

Government and politics of Ontario. Edited by Donald MacDonald. Toronto: Macmillan of Canada: Maclean-Hunter, 1975. x, 370 p.

Histoire d'une institution; la Commission de la Fonction publique au Canada, 1908-1967. Par J.E. Hodgetts et al. Québec: Presses de l'Université Laval, 1975. 581 p. (Canadian public administration series/Collection Administration publique canadienne)

Lemieux, Vincent et Raymond Hudon. *Patronage et politique au Québec, 1944-1972.* Québec: Éditions du Boréal express, 1975. 187 p.

Newman, Peter C. *The Canadian establishment.* v.1- . Toronto: McClelland and Stewart, 1975- .

Oliver, Peter. *Public and private persons: the Ontario political culture, 1914-1934.* Toronto; Vancouver: Clarke, Irwin, 1975. 291 p.

Pelletier, Emile. *The exploitation of Métis land.* Winnipeg, Man.: Manitoba Métis Federation Press, 1975. vii, 328 p.

Pressure group behaviour in Canadian politics. Edited by A. Paul Pross. Scarborough, Ont.: McGraw-Hill Ryerson, 1975. 196 p. (McGraw-Hill Ryerson series in Canadian politics)

Reader's Digest Association (Canada) *You and the law: the rights and responsibilities of the motorist and his family under the laws of Canada.* Montreal: Published by Reader's Digest for the Canadian Automobile Association, 1975. 911 p.

Ryan, Oscar. *Tim Buck: a conscience for Canada.* Toronto: Progress Books, 1975. xvi, 302 p.

Sealey, D. Bruce. *Statutory land rights of the Manitoba Métis.* Winnipeg, Man.: Manitoba Métis Federation Press, 1975. vi, 148 p.

Smith, David E. *Prairie liberalism: the Liberal Party in Saskatchewan, 1905-1971.* Toronto: University of Toronto Press, 1975. x, 352 p. (Canadian government series; 18)

Stursberg, Peter. *Diefenbaker: leadership gained, 1956-62.* Toronto: University of Toronto Press, 1975. xv, 278 p.

Swanson, Roger F., comp. *Canadian-American summit diplomacy, 1923-1973: selected speeches and documents.* Toronto: McClelland and Stewart, 1975. xxii, 314 p. (The Carleton library; no. 81)

Une certaine révolution tranquille: 22 juin 60-75. Par Cyrille Felteau et al. Montréal: La Presse, 1975. 337 p.

Veatch, Richard. *Canada and the League of Nations.* Toronto; Buffalo: University of Toronto Press, 1975. xi, 224 p.

Wente, Margaret, ed. *"I never say anything provocative": witticisms, anecdotes and reflections by Canada's most outspoken politician, John George Diefenbaker.* Toronto: P. Martin, 1975. 147 p.

History

Akrigg, George P.V. and Helen B. Akrigg. *British Columbia chronicle, 1778-1846: adventurers by sea and land.* Vancouver: Discovery Press, 1975. xv, 429 p.

Armour, Charles A. and Thomas Lackey. *Sailing ships of the Maritimes: an illustrated history of shipping and shipbuilding in the Maritime Provinces of Canada, 1750-1925.* Toronto: McGraw-Hill Ryerson, 1975. 224 p.

Artibise, Alan F.J. *Winnipeg: a social history of urban growth, 1874-1914.* Montreal: McGill-Queen's University Press, 1975. xiv, 382 p.

Bouchard, Russel. *Les armes traditionnelles au Canada, 1534-1890.* Chicoutimi-Nord, Qué.: Musée du Saguenay, 1975. 121 p. (Publications - Musée du Saguenay; no 1)

Canada. Musée national de l'homme. Division de l'histoire. *La ville de Québec, 1800-1850: un inventaire de cartes et plans.* Par Edward H. Dahl et al. Ottawa: Musées nationaux du Canada, 1975. ix, 413 p. (Musée national de l'homme. Division de l'histoire. Dossier; no 13) (Collection Mercure)

Chabot, Richard. *Le curé de campagne et la contestation locale au Québec de 1791 aux troubles de 1837-38.* Montréal: Hurtubise HMH, 1975. 242 p. (Les Cahiers du Québec; 20: Collection Histoire et documents d'histoire)

Choquette, Robert. *Language and religion: a history of English-French conflict in Ontario.* Ottawa: University of Ottawa Press, 1975. 264 p. (Cahiers d'histoire de l'Université d'Ottawa; no 5)

Colloque sur la situation de la recherche sur la vie française en Ontario, Université d'Ottawa, 1974. *Actes du Colloque sur la situation de la recherche sur la vie française en Ontario: tenu à l'Université d'Ottawa les 28 et 29 novembre 1974, organisé par le Centre de recherche en civilisation canadienne-française de l'Université d'Ottawa.* Ottawa: Centre de recherche en civilisation canadienne-française de l'Université d'Ottawa; Montréal: Association canadienne-française pour l'avancement des sciences, 1975. 277 p.

Dickey, John Sloan and Whitney H. Shepardson. *Canada and the American presence: the United States interest in an independent Canada.* New York, NY: New York University Press, 1975. xii, 202 p. (A Council on Foreign Relations book)

Dunn, Guillaume. *Les forts de l'Outaouais.* Montréal: Éditions du Jour, 1975. 162 p. (L'Histoire vivante; H-11)

Fumoleau, René. *As long as this land shall last: a history of Treaty 8 and Treaty 11, 1870-1939.* Toronto: McClelland and Stewart, [1975] 415 p.

Graham, Elizabeth. *Medicine man to missionary: missionaries as agents of change among the Indians of southern Ontario, 1784-1867.* Toronto: P. Martin, 1975. xi, 125 p. (Canadian experience series)

Granatstein, J.H. *Canada's war: the politics of the Mackenzie King government, 1939-1945.* Toronto: Oxford University Press, 1975. xi, 436 p.

Gray, James H. *The roar of the twenties.* Toronto: Macmillan of Canada, 1975. 358 p.

Hamelin, Louis-Edmond. *Nordicité canadienne.* Montréal: Hurtubise HMH, 1975. 458 p. (Les Cahiers du Québec; 18: Collection Géographie)

Johnson, James K., comp. *Historical essays on Upper Canada.* Toronto: McClelland and Stewart, 1975. xiii, 368 p. (The Carleton library; no. 82)

Leasor, James. *Green beach.* London: Heinemann, 1975. 249 p.

Lower, Arthur R.M. *History and myth: Arthur Lower and the making of Canadian nationalism: selected essays.* Edited by Welf H. Heick. Vancouver: University of British Columbia Press, 1975. xxii, 339 p.

McCullum, Hugh and Karmel McCullum. *This land is not for sale: Canada's original people and their land: a saga of neglect, exploitation, and conflict.* Toronto: Anglican Book Centre, 1975. 210 p.

Macpherson, Ken. *Canada's fighting ships.* Toronto: S. Stevens, Hakkert, 1975. 116 p. (Canadian War Museum. Historical publication; 12)

Mellor, John. *Forgotten heroes: the Canadians at Dieppe.* Toronto: Methuen, 1975. 163 p.

Moyles, Robert G. *Complaints is many and various, but the odd Divil likes it: nineteenth century views of Newfoundland.* Toronto: P. Martin, 1975. xii, 187 p.

Neidhardt, Wilfried S. *Fenianism in North America.* University Park, Tex.; London, Tex.: Pennsylvania State University Press, 1975. xi, 164 p.

O'Neill, Paul. *The oldest city: the story of St. John's, Newfoundland.* v.1- . Erin, Ont.: Press Porcépic, 1975- .

Parent, Étienne. *Étienne Parent, 1802-1874: biographie, textes et bibliographie.* Présentés par Jean-Charles Falardeau. Montréal: La Presse, 1975. 344 p. (Collection Échanges)

Parizeau, Gérard. *La société canadienne-française au 19ᵉ siècle: essais sur le milieu.* Montréal: Fides, 1975. 550 p.

Powley, A.E. *Broadcast from the Front: Canadian radio overseas in the Second World War.* Toronto: Hakkert, 1975. xii, 189 p. (Canadian War Museum. Historical publication; no. 11)

Revai, Elizabeth. *Alexandre Vattemare, trait d'union entre deux mondes: le Québec et les États-Unis à l'aube de leurs relations culturelles avec la France au 19ᵉ siècle.* Montréal: Éditions Bellarmin; Paris: Desclée de Brouwer, 1975. 220 p. (Essais pour notre temps: Section d'histoire; nᵒ 2)

Robert, Jean-Claude. *Du Canada français au Québec libre: histoire d'un mouvement indépendantiste.* Saint-Laurent, Qué.: Flammarion, 1975. 323 p. (l'Histoire vivante: Autonomismes-nationalités)

Trofimenkoff, Susan Mann. *Action Française: French Canadian nationalism in the twenties.* Toronto; Buffalo: University of Toronto Press, 1975. x, 157 p.

Western Canadian Studies Conference, 6th, University of Calgary, 1974. *Western Canada: past and present.* Edited by Anthony W. Rasporich. Calgary, Alta.: University of Calgary: McClelland and Stewart West, 1975. vii, 224 p.

Yon, Armand. *Le Canada français vu de France: 1830-1914.* Québec: Presses de l'Université Laval, 1975. 235 p. (Vie des lettres québécoises; 15)

Literature

La bande dessinée kébécoise. Ouvrage collectif dirigé par André Carpentier. Montréal: Éditions La Barre du Jour, 1975. 272 p. (L'édition originale de cet ouvrage est inscrite aux numéros 46, 47, 48, 49 de la revue *La Barre du Jour*)

Blais, Jacques. *De l'ordre et de l'aventure: la poésie au Québec de 1934 à 1944.* Québec: Presses de l'Université Laval, 1975. x, 410 p. (Vie des lettres québécoises; 14)

Boivin, Aurélien. *Le conte littéraire québécois au 19ᵉ siècle: essai de bibliographie critique et analytique.* Montréal: Fides, 1975. xxxviii, 385 p.

Chambers, Robert D. *Sinclair Ross and Ernest Buckler.* Montreal: McGill-Queen's University Press, 1975. 109 p. (Series in Canadian literature)

Colombo, Robert, comp. *Colombo's little book of Canadian proverbs, graffiti, limericks & other vital matters.* Edmonton, Alta.: Hurtig, 1975. 143 p.

Conference on Editorial Problems, University of Toronto, 1972. *Editing Canadian texts: papers given at the Conference on Editorial Problems, University of Toronto, November 1972.* Edited by Francess G. Halpenny. Toronto: Hakkert, 1975. 97 p.

Conron, Brandon, comp. *Morley Callaghan.* Toronto: McGraw-Hill Ryerson, 1975. v, 156 p. (Critical views on Canadian writers; 10)

Dempsey, Hugh A., ed. *The best of Bob Edwards.* Edmonton, Alta.: Hurtig, 1975. 271 p.

Gauvin, Lise. *"Parti pris" littéraire.* Montréal: Presses de l'Université de Montréal, 1975. 217 p. (Collection "Lignes québécoises" sérielles)

Geddes, Gary, ed. *Skookum wawa: writings of the Canadian Northwest.* Toronto: Oxford University Press, 1975. xv, 336 p.

Greffard, Madeleine. *Alain Grandbois.* Montréal: Fides, 1975. 191 p. (Écrivains canadiens d'aujourd'hui; 12)

Hind-Smith, Joan. *Three voices: the lives of Margaret Laurence, Gabrielle Roy, Frederick Philip Grove.* Toronto; Vancouver: Clarke, Irwin, 1975. xii, 235 p. (Canadian portraits)

Juneau, Marcel et Georges Straka. *Travaux de linguistique québécoise.* Québec: Presses de l'Université Laval, 1975. 354 p. (Langue française au Québec, 4ᵉ section; 1)

Lortie, Jeanne d'Arc. *La poésie nationaliste du Canada français, 1606-1867.* Québec: Presses de l'Université Laval, 1975. ix, 535 p. (Vie des lettres québécoises; 13)

Mayne, Seymour, ed. *The A.M. Klein symposium.* Ottawa: University of Ottawa Press, 1975. 122 p. (Reappraisals, Canadian writers)

Orkin, Mark M. and Isaac Bickerstaff. *French Canajan, hé?* Toronto: Lester and Orpen, 1975. 126 p.

Perkin, J.R.C., ed. *The undoing of Babel: Watson Kirkconnell, the man and his work.* Toronto: McClelland and Stewart, 1975. 128 p.

Ricard, François. *Gabrielle Roy.* Montréal: Fides, 1975. 191 p. (Écrivains canadiens d'aujourd'hui; 11)

Rolland, Solange Chaput-. *Les maudits journalistes.* Montréal: Cercle du livre de France, 1975. 151 p.

Saint-Pierre, Annette. *Gabrielle Roy: sous le signe du rêve.* Saint-Boniface, Man.: Éditions du Blé, 1975. 137 p.

The Search for English Canadian literature: an anthology of critical articles from the nineteenth and early twentieth centuries. Edited by Carl Ballstadt. Toronto: University of Toronto Press, 1975. 214 p.

Thério, Adrien. *Des choses à dire: journal littéraire, 1973-1974.* Montréal: Éditions Jumonville, 1975. 175 p.

Thério, Adrien, Donald Smith et Patrick Imbert. *Ignace Bourget, écrivain.* Montréal: Éditions Jumonville, 1975. 195 p.

Thomas, Clara. *The Manawaka world of Margaret Laurence.* Toronto: McClelland and Stewart, 1975. 212 p. (Canadian writers series)

Vigneault, Robert. *Claire Martin: son œuvre, les réactions de la critique.* Montréal: P. Tisseyre, 1975. 216 p.

Woodcock, George, ed. *The Canadian novel in the twentieth century: essays from Canadian literature.* Toronto: McClelland and Stewart, 1975. xi, 337 p. (New Canadian library; no. 115)

General reference works

Abrahamson, Una. *The Canadian guide to home entertaining.* Toronto: Macmillan of Canada, 1975. 176 p.

Buisseret, Irène de. *Deux langues, six idiomes: manuel pratique de traduction de l'anglais au français: préceptes, procédés, exemples, glossaires, index.* Texte rev., augm.; annoté et indexé par Denys Goulet. Ottawa: Carlton-Green, 1975. 480 p.

Canada. Archives publiques. *Guide des sources d'archives sur le Canada français, au Canada.* Ottawa: Archives publiques du Canada, 1975. 195 p.

Canada. Dept. of the Secretary of State. *A directory of Canadian women's groups/Annuaire canadien des groupes de femmes.* Ottawa: Dept. of the Secretary of State, 1975. 497 p.

Canadian essay and literature index. 1973- . Compiled by Andrew D. Armitage and Nancy Tudor. Toronto: University of Toronto Press, 1975- .

The Canadian film digest yearbook, 1975. Toronto: Film Publications of Canada, 1975. 132 p.

Carey, Neil G. *A guide to the Queen Charlotte Islands.* Anchorage, Alaska: Alaska Northwest Pub., 1975. viii, 71 p.

La chanson au Québec, 1965-1975. Par Normand Cormier et al. Montréal: Bibliothèque nationale du Québec, Ministère des affaires culturelles, 1975. ix, 219 p. (Bibliographies québécoises; no 3)

Community Planning Association of Canada/L'Association canadienne d'urbanisme. *Canadian housing resource catalogue.* Ottawa: Community Planning Association, 1975. 237 p.

Contemporary Canadian composers. Edited by Keith MacMillan and John Beckwith. Toronto: Oxford University Press (Canadian Branch), 1975. xxiv, 248 p.

Edwards, Margaret H. and John C.R. Lort. *A bibliography of British Columbia: years of growth, 1900-1950.* Victoria, BC: Social Sciences Research Centre, University of Victoria, 1975. x, 446 p.

Encyclopedia Canadiana. Editor in chief: Kenneth H. Pearson. Toronto: Grolier of Canada, 1975. 10 v.

Evans, Gwynneth, comp. *Women in federal politics: a bio-bibliography/Les femmes au fédéral: une bio-bibliographie.* Ottawa: National Library of Canada, 1975. 81 p.

Foire internationale du livre de Montréal. *Montréal-contacts 1975.* Montréal: Foire internationale du livre de Montréal, 1975. 313 p. (Texte en français et en anglais)

Fortin, Benjamin et Jean-Pierre Gaboury. *Bibliographie analytique de l'Ontario français.* Ottawa: Éditions de l'Université d'Ottawa, 1975. xii, 236 p. (Cahiers du Centre de recherche en civilisation canadienne-française; 9)

Gingras, Raymond. *Liste annotée des patronymes d'origine allemande au Québec et notes diverses.* Québec: s.n., 1975. 133 f.

Houle, Ghislaine. *La femme et la société québécoise.* Montréal: Bibliothèque nationale du Québec, Ministère des affaires culturelles, 1975. 228 p. (Bibliographies québécoises; no 1)

Houle, Ghislaine et Jacques Lafontaine. *Écrivains québécois de nouvelle culture.* Montréal: Bibliothèque nationale du Québec, Ministère des affaires culturelles, 1975. L, 137 p. (Bibliographies québécoises; no 2)

Kantautas, Adam and Filomena Kantautas. *A Lithuanian bibliography: a checklist of books and articles held by the major libraries of Canada and the United States.* Edmonton, Alta.: University of Alberta Press, 1975. xxxix, 720 p.

Lovell and Gibson. *Specimen of printing types and ornaments, in use at the printing office of Lovell and Gibson, St. Nicholas Street, Montreal.* Toronto: Bibliographical Society of Canada/La Société bibliographique du Canada, 1975. unpaged

MacTaggart, Hazel I., comp. *Publications of the Government of Ontario, 1956-1971: a checklist.* Toronto: Ministry of Government Services, 1975. 410 p.

National Film Board of Canada. *A catalogue of films projecting women.* Toronto: National Film Board of Canada, 1975. 57 p.

National Library of Canada. *Symbols of Canadian libraries/Sigles des bibliothèques canadiennes.* 6th ed. Ottawa: National Library of Canada, 1975. 74 p.

Notices en langue française du Canadian catalogue of books, 1921-1949. Avec index établi par Henri Boivin. Montréal: Bibliothèque nationale du Québec, Ministère des affaires culturelles, 1975. ix, 263, 199 p.

Out from the shadows: a bibliography of the history of women in Manitoba. Compiled by Pam Atnikov, et al. Ottawa: Manitoba Human Rights Commission, 1975. 64 p.

Pagé, Pierre, comp. *Répertoire des ouvrages de la littérature radiophonique québécoise, 1930-1970.* Montréal: Fides, 1975. 826 p. (Archives québécoises de la radio et de la télévision; v.1)

Proctor, George A. *Sources in Canadian music: a bibliography of bibliographies/Les sources de la musique canadienne: une bibliographie des bibliographies.* Sackville, NB: Ralph Pickard Bell Library, Mount Allison University, 1975. ii, 38 p. (Publication in music; no. 2)

Ryder, Dorothy E., ed. *Canadian reference sources: supplement.* Ottawa: Canadian Library Association, 1975. xi, 121 p.

Southam, Peter et Francine Barry, comps. *Caractéristiques de la pauvreté au Québec, 1940-73: bibliographie.* Québec: Institut supérieur des sciences humaines, Université Laval, 1975. v, 228 p. (Cahiers de l'ISSH. Collection Instruments de travail; no 16)

Thibault, Marie Thérèse. *Bibliographie pour la conservation et la restauration de lieux et de bâtiments historiques.* Québec: Ministère des affaires culturelles, Direction générale du patrimoine, Service de l'inventaire des biens culturels, Centre de documentation, 1975. 43 p. (Dossier; 1)

Toronto. Public Library. Osborne Collection. *The Osborne Collection of early children's books, 1476-1910: a catalogue.* Prepared at Boys and Girls House by Judith St. John. Toronto: Public Library, 1975. xii, 563-1138 p.

Université de Moncton. Centre d'études acadiennes. *Inventaire général des sources documentaires sur les Acadiens.* v.1- . Moncton, NB: Éditions d'Acadie, 1975- .

Université de Montréal. Service des collections particulières des bibliothèques. *Collection canadiana de Louis Melzack, exposition: anciens imprimés du Québec.* Montréal: Service des collections particulières, Université de Montréal, 1975. 8 f.

Science

Canada. Environmental Protection Service. *An Annotated bibliography of Canadian air pollution literature.* Compiled by Christopher J. Sparrow and Leslie T. Foster. Ottawa: Environmental Protection Service, 1975. xiv, 270 p.

Clark, Lewis J. *Lewis Clark's field guide to wild flowers of the arid flatlands in the Pacific Northwest.* Sidney, BC: Gray's Pub., 1975. 80 p. (Field guide; 5)

Clark, Lewis J. *Lewis Clark's field guide to wild flowers of the mountains in the Pacific Northwest.* Sidney, BC: Gray's Pub., 1975. 80 p. (Field guide; 6)

Environmental management: perspectives in Alberta: proceedings: a symposium organized by the Bio-sciences Society of the University of Calgary, presented March 16, 1974. Calgary: University of Calgary, Bio-sciences Society, 1975. iv, 185 p.

Foster, John and Janet Foster. *To the wild country.* Toronto: Van Nostrand Reinhold, 1975. 155 p.

Mackenzie, Chalmers J. *The Mackenzie-McNaughton wartime letters.* Edited by Mel Thistle. Toronto: University of Toronto Press, 1975. xxiv, 178 p.

Nova Scotia. Dept. of Mines. *Bibliography of the geology of Nova Scotia.* Compiled by Diane J. Gregory. Halifax: Nova Scotia Dept. of Mines, 1975. vii, 237 p.

Piérard, Jean. *Découvrir les mammifères.* Montréal: Presses de l'Université de Montréal, 1975. xiv, 452 p.

Stirling, David and Jim Woodford. *Where to go birdwatching in Canada.* Saanichton, BC: Hancock House, 1975. 127 p.

Index

Page

Page

Page

Page

Page

Page

Page

Page

Page

Page

Page

Page

Page

Page

Page

Page

Page

Page

Page

Page

Page

Page

Page